A
CONCORDANCE

to the
Apocrypha/Deuterocanonical Books
of the
Revised Standard Version

A
CONCORDANCE

to the
Apocrypha/Deuterocanonical Books
of the
Revised Standard Version

Derived from the
Bible Data Bank
of the
Centre Informatique et Bible
(Abbey of Maredsous)

Foreword by
Bruce M. Metzger

WILLIAM B. EERDMANS PUBLISHING COMPANY
COLLINS
1983

© 1983 Centre Informatique et Bible — Bible Data Bank
Abbaye de Maredsous, 5642 Denée, Belgium
All rights reserved
Printed in the United States of America

Published through special arrangement with Promotion Biblique
et Informatique, ASBL, by:

William B. Eerdmans Publishing Company
255 Jefferson Avenue, S.E.
Grand Rapids, Michigan 49503

Collins Liturgical Publications
187 Piccadilly, London W1V 9DA

Collins Liturgical Australia
Box 3023 GPO, Sydney 2001

ISBN (Collins) 00 599714 3

Library of Congress Cataloging in Publication Data
Main entry under title:

A Concordance to the Apocrypha/Deuterocanonical books
of the Revised Standard Version

"An entry for every word that appears in the 1977
edition of the RSV Apocrypha/Deuterocanonicals" — Introd.
1. Bible   O.T.   Apocrypha — Concordances.
I. Metzger, Bruce Manning.   II. Abbaye de Maredsous.
Centre Informatique et Bible.   III. Bible.   O.T.
Apocrypha.   English.   Revised Standard.   1977   (New
Oxford annotated Bible with the Apocrypha)
BS1700.C66   1983   229′.0520423   82-16310
ISBN 0-8028-2312-2

FOREWORD

It is with considerable satisfaction that one greets the publication of this concordance to the Revised Standard Version of the Apocrypha, otherwise known as the Deuterocanonical Books. These books were part of the original King James Bible of 1611 and of the Revised Version of 1881-1894. Although they were not included in the American Standard Version of 1901, it was decided, after the publication in 1952 of both Old and New Testaments of the Revised Standard Version, to proceed with a revision of these books as well. The work of revision was finished in 1957, the same year in which John W. Ellison published a computerized concordance to the RSV Old and New Testaments. Finally, in 1977 the RSV Committee made a translation of three other texts, 3 Maccabees, 4 Maccabees, and Psalm 151.

Now, for the first time, and again through the assistance of the computer, a concordance to the RSV Apocrypha/Deuterocanonical Books has become available. As it is generally known, three of these books (1 Esdras, 2 Esdras, and the Prayer of Manasseh) are considered Apocryphal by both Protestants and Roman Catholics, whereas a difference of opinion prevails regarding the others, Protestants ranking them as Apocryphal, and Catholics accepting them as authoritative, or Deuterocanonical (that is, added later to the canon). Current printings of the Old Testament used by the Greek Orthodox Church include all the Deuterocanonical Books mentioned above (except 2 Esdras), along with 3 Maccabees and Psalm 151, while 4 Maccabees stands in an appendix.

It is certain that all who make use of the present volume will be grateful to the Abbey of Maredsous and its computer team for their labors in producing a most valuable supplement to all previously published concordances to the Revised Standard Version.

Bruce M. Metzger
Chairman, RSV Bible Committee

Princeton Theological Seminary
Princeton, New Jersey.

INTRODUCTION

In this concordance the *Centre Informatique et Bible* of Maredsous, Belgium, is happy to offer to the public, in collaboration with Eerdmans Publishing Company and Collins Publishers, some of the information stored in its *Bible Data Bank*, which has been developed during the last few years.

The literature that arose between the Hebrew Scriptures and the New Testament has recently received increasing attention. Until now no concordance to the Revised Standard Version of these books has been available. We hope that this new tool will fill a need and prove to be valuable to the users of the Revised Standard Version (RSV) who are interested in the Apocrypha/Deuterocanonical Books.

Because the aim of the Centre Informatique et Bible has been to provide information that is as complete as possible within the bounds of practicality, this concordance has an entry for every word that appears in the 1977 edition of the RSV Apocrypha/Deuterocanonicals. Words that occur very frequently, however, have little value for most users of this concordance, so the biblical references and contexts of these words (listed on p. ix) have been omitted in order to avoid making the concordance unnecessarily long.

Two numbers in each entry indicate the frequency with which a word occurs in the RSV Apocrypha/Deuterocanonical Books: the first number tells how many times the word occurs in the books and the second number translates the first number into a percentage of the total number of words in those books. For example, " garden " appears seventeen times in these books and these seventeen occurrences equal 0.011 % of the total number of words (155,875).

The reader should be aware that, unlike some other concordances, this concordance lists all forms of a word under one entry. For example, " feet " will be found under " foot ", " sang " and " sung " will be found under " sing ". This arrangement eliminates the need to look in several places for different forms of the same word.

This concordance does not distinguish between two or more persons or things that have the same name. For example, it is uncertain whether four or five different persons called " Apollonius " are represented in this literature. All twenty references to an Apollonius are listed under one heading, leaving the distinctions to scholarly interpretation.

Words that have more than one meaning have been left under a single heading whenever either the difference in meaning is too small to warrant a separate heading or semiological interest clearly suggests keeping all uses of the word under a single heading. Otherwise, differences in meaning are indicated either by the creation of separate headings or the use of *italics*.

Numbers (whether ordinal or cardinal) are not found spelled out and in alphabetical order but are quoted as numerals and treated in numerical order at the end of the alphabetical listing of words. For example, the " eight " in 1 Macc. 4:56 will be found not under " eight " but under " Number: 8 ".

British forms of spelling have been used for the main entries. American forms of spelling (e.g. " defense " for " defence ", " gray " for " grey ", " labor " for " labour ", " mold " for " mould ", " vigor " for " vigour ") are given next to the British forms.

Of the many phrasal verbs, only those that include " away ", " back ", " by ", " down ", " forth ", " forward ", " in ", " off ", " on ", " out ", " over ", and " up " have been selected for special treatment.

The *Centre Informatique et Bible (Bible Data Bank)* wishes to thank all who have made this concordance possible, principally the Abbot and monks of the Abbey of Maredsous. Special thanks are due also to our friends of the Centre de Traitement Informatique of the A.S.L.K.-C.G.E.R. (Brussels) and of the Composition Programmée at the Imprimerie Nationale in Paris.

Centre Informatique et Bible
Maredsous, Belgium
July, 1982.

ABBREVIATIONS

Apocrypha/Deuterocanonical Books

Tob	Tobit	Sus	Susanna
Jud	Judith	Bel	Bel and the Dragon
Ad E	Additions to Esther	1 Ma	1 Maccabees
Wis	Wisdom	2 Ma	2 Maccabees
Sir	Sirach	1 Es	1 Esdras
Bar	Baruch	P Ma	Prayer of Manasseh
L Jr	Letter of Jeremiah	Ps 151	Psalm 151
	(= Baruch 6)	3 Ma	3 Maccabees
P Az	Prayer of Azariah and the	2 Es	2 Esdras
	Song of the Three Young Men	4 Ma	4 Maccabees

Other Abbreviations

adj.	adjective	pers. pr.	personal pronoun
adv.	adverb	prep.	preposition
conj.	conjunction	prop. n.	proper name
dem. pr.	demonstrative pronoun	rel. pr.	relative pronoun
indef. pr.	indefinite pronoun	s.	see (other heading)
interj.	interjection	subst.	substantive
interr. pr.	interrogative pronoun	*	semantically ambiguous

References and contexts of the following words are omitted*

	Occurrences		Occurrences		Occurrences
A	2,135	MAY	290	THEMSELVES	89
AN	276	ME	435	THEN	470
AND	9,095	MINE (pr.)	6	THERE	339
AS	812	MY	604	THEY	1,617
AS FOR	32	MYSELF	28	THIS	840
AT	434	NO	271	THOU	294
BE	5,385	NOR	123	THY	323
BUT	877	NOT	1,357	THYSELF	14
BY	723	O	211	TO	4,356
CAN	232	OF	5,410	UPON	327
DO	1,122	ON	559	US	471
FOR	2,161	ONE (pr.)	197	WE	439
FROM	931	OR	391	WHAT	360
HAVE	2,269	OUR	485	WHEN	703
HE	2,191	OURSELVES	16	WHICH	477
HER	598	OUT OF	92	WHO	1,413
HERSELF	19	OVER	204	WHOM	104
HIM	1,190	SHALL	562	WHOSE	58
HIMSELF	96	SHE	288	WILL (aux.)	1,503
HIS	1,702	SO	492	WITH	1,441
I	1,052	SO THAT	152	YOU	1,550
IF	323	THAN	205	YOUR	761
IN	2,491	THAT	1,873	YOURSELF	87
INTO	253	THE	10,758		
IT	1,012	THEE	108		
ITS	185	THEIR	1,185		
ITSELF	20	THEM	1,282		

Total occurrences: 83,236 = 53.40 % of 155,875 words.

* Scholars interested in further information about these words are encouraged to apply to:
Centre Informatique et Bible
Abbaye de Maredsous
B-5642 Denée, Belgium
Telephone : 82-69.93.97

A
CONCORDANCE

to the
Apocrypha/Deuterocanonical Books
of the
Revised Standard Version

A

A   2135 = 1.391 %

AARON   16 = 0.010 %
Tob 1:6   I would give these to the priests, the sons of Aaron, at the altar
Sir 36:17   according to the blessing of Aaron for thy people
    45:6   He exalted Aaron, the brother of Moses
  45:20   He added glory to Aaron and gave him a heritage
  45:25   so the heritage of Aaron is for his descendants
  50:13   all the sons of Aaron in their splendour
  50:16   Then the sons of Aaron shouted
1 Ma 7:14   A priest of the line of Aaron has come with the army
1 Es 1:13   and for their brethren the priests, the sons of Aaron
    1:14   and for their brethren the priests, the sons of Aaron
    5:5   the priests, the sons of Phinehas, son of Aaron
    8:2   son of Eleazar, son of Aaron the chief priest
2 Es 1:3   son of Aaron, of the tribe of Levi
    1:13   I gave you Moses as leader and Aaron as priest
4 Ma 7:11   For just as our father Aaron, armed with the censer
    7:12   so the descendant of Aaron, Eleazar

ABANDON   12 = 0.008 %
Sir 17:21   has neither left nor abandoned them, but spared them
  23:1   do not abandon me to their counsel
  29:17   and one who does not feel grateful will abandon his rescuer
L Jr 6:42   Yet they themselves cannot perceive this and abandon them
1 Ma 1:15   and abandoned the holy covenant
2 Ma 10:13   because he had abandoned Cyprus
3 Ma 1:19   abandoned the bridal chambers prepared for wedded union
    1:20   Mothers and nurses abandoned even new-born children here and there
4 Ma 2:10   so that virtue is not abandoned for their sakes
    7:9   and you did not abandon the holiness which you praised
  10:7   they abandoned the instruments
  18:5   to become pagans and to abandon their ancestral customs

ABASE   1
Sir 7:11   for there is One who abases and exalts

ABATE   1
2 Ma 9:18   But when his sufferings did not in any way abate

ABBREVIATE   1
2 Ma 2:26   For us who have undertaken the toil of abbreviating

ABDI   1
1 Es 9:27   Jehiel and Abdi, and Jeremoth and Elijah

ABEL   1
4 Ma 18:11   He read to you about Abel slain by Cain

ABET   1
3 Ma 2:25   abetted by the previously mentioned drinking companions and comrades

ABHOR   9 = 0.006 %
Jud 9:4   and abhorred the pollution of their blood
Ad E 14:15   and abhor the bed of the uncircumcised and of any alien
  14:16   that I abhor the sign of my proud position
  14:16   I abhor it like a menstruous rag
2 Ma 5:8   and abhorred as the executioner of his country
3 Ma 2:33   and they abhorred those who separated themselves from them
2 Es 16:49   Just as a respectable and virtuous woman abhors a harlot
  16:50   so righteousness shall abhor iniquity
4 Ma 5:8   Why, when nature has granted it to us, should you abhor eating

ABHORRENCE   1
3 Ma 2:31   Now some, however, with an obvious abhorrence of the price

ABIDE   3 = 0.002 %
Wis 3:9   and the faithful will abide with him in love
Sir 1:21   and where it abides, it will turn away all anger
2 Es 7:112   the full glory does not abide in it

ABILITY   2
Sir 29:20   Assist your neighbour according to your ability
1 Es 5:44   to the best of their ability

ABIRAM   2
Sir 45:18   Dathan and Abiram and their men and the company of Korah
4 Ma 2:17   When Moses was angry with Dathan and Abiram

ABISHUA   2
1 Es 8:2   son of Bukki, son of Abishua, son of Phinehas
2 Es 1:2   son of Abishua, son of Phinehas, son of Eleazar

ABLAZE   1
1 Ma 6:39   the hills were ablaze with them

ABOMINATION

ABLE   45 = 0.029 %
Jud 10:19   they will be able to ensnare the whole world !
Wis 17:5   And no power of fire was able to give light
Sir pr.   should be able to help the outsiders
  8:17   for he will not be able to keep a secret
L Jr 6:34   they will not be able to repay it
  6:35   Likewise they are not able to give either wealth or money
  6:41   as though Bel were able to understand
  6:57   are not able to save themselves from thieves and robbers
  6:58   and they will not be able to help themselves
  6:64   for they are not able either to decide a case
1 Ma 3:53   How will we be able to withstand them
  5:40   we will not be able to resist him
  6:27   and you will not be able to stop them
  9:8   We may be able to fight them
  9:9   But they tried to dissuade him, saying, We are not able
  10:73   And now you will not be able to withstand my cavalry
2 Ma 8:18   who is able with a single nod
  9:10   no one was able to carry the man who a little while before
1 Es 9:11   and we are not able to stand in the open air
3 Ma 4:16   praising speechless things that are not able
  4:17   that they were no longer able to take the census of the Jews
2 Es 2:28   but they shall not be able to do anything against you
  4:27   For it will not be able to bring the things
  5:38   who is able to know these things
  5:45   it might even now be able to support
  7:102   the righteous will be able to intercede for the ungodly
  7:115   Therefore no one will then be able to have mercy on him
  8:6   may be able to live
  8:47   For you come far short of being able to love my creation
  9:7   and will be able to escape
  12:38   whose hearts you know are able to comprehend
  13:47   so that they may be able to pass over
  14:22   that men may be able to find the path
  15:17   For a man will desire to go into a city, and shall not be able
4 Ma 1:33   Is it not because reason is able to rule over appetites ?
  2:6   that reason is able to control desires
  2:18   the temperate mind is able to get the better of the emotions
  4:24   he had not been able in any way
  7:18   these alone are able to control the passions of the flesh
  7:22   would no be able to overcome the emotions through godliness ?
  8:6   Just as I am able to punish those who disobey my orders
  10:7   Since they were not able in any way to break his spirit
  11:25   Since you have not been able to persuade us
  14:17   If they are not able to keep him away
  18:5   Since in no way whatever was he able to compel the Israelites

ABODE   1
Tob 3:6   to go to the eternal abode

ABOLISH   7 = 0.005 %
Ad E 14:9   to abolish what thy mouth has ordained
1 Ma 3:29   which he had caused in the land by abolishing the laws
  6:59   for it was on account of their laws which we abolished
2 Ma 2:22   and restored the laws that were about to be abolished
2 Es 15:60   and abolish a portion of your glory
  15:63   and abolish the glory of your countenance
4 Ma 4:20   but also the temple service was abolished

ABOMINABLE   12 = 0.008 %
Sir 19:23   There is a cleverness which is abominable
  41:5   The children of sinners are abominable children
1 Ma 1:48   They were to make themselves abominable
2 Ma 6:5   The altar was covered with abominable offerings
  9:13   Then the abominable fellow made a vow to the Lord
  15:5   in carrying out his abominable design
3 Ma 6:9   by the abominable and lawless Gentiles
4 Ma 9:15   Most abominable tyrant, enemy of heavenly justice, savage of mind
  9:17   he replied, You abominable lackeys
  9:32   You will not escape, most abominable tyrant
  10:10   We, most abominable tyrant
  10:17   the bloodthirsty, murderous, and utterly abominable Antiochus

ABOMINATE   1
3 Ma 3:23   they abominate those few among them

ABOMINATION   13 = 0.008 %
Wis 12:23   thou didst torment through their own abominations
  14:11   they became an abomination
Sir 1:25   but godliness is an abomination to a sinner
  10:13   and the man who clings to it pours out abominations
  13:20   Humility is an abomination to a proud man
  13:20   likewise a poor man is an abomination to a rich one
  15:13   The Lord hates all abominations
  17:26   to the light of health and hate abominations intensely
  27:30   Anger and wrath, these also are abominations
  49:2   and took away the abominations of iniquity
1 Ma 6:7   that they had torn down the abomination

1 Es	7 :13	from the abominations of the peoples of the land
P Ma	10	setting up abominations and multiplying offences

ABOUND
6 = 0.004 %

Sir	11 :12	who lacks strength and abounds in poverty
	23 :3	and my sins may not abound
2 Es	3 :33	and have seen that they abound in wealth
	7 :51	while the ungodly abound
	7 :136	because he makes his compassions abound more and more
	7 :137	for if he did not make them abound

ABOUT*
180 = 0.117 %

Tob	1 :19	and informed the king about me, that I was burying them
	4 :2	so that I may explain to him about the money before I die ?
	4 :20	And now let me explain to you about the 10 talents of silver
	6 :15	and do not worry about the demon
	7 :8	speak of those things which you talked about on the journey
	8 :12	let us bury him without any one knowing about it
	14 :3	behold, I have grown old and am about to depart this life
	14 :4	about Nineveh, that it will be overthrown
Jud	1 :2	he is the king who built walls about Ecbatana
	2 :1	about carrying out his revenge on the whole region
	2 :13	and do not delay about it
	5 :5	and I will tell you the truth about this people
	7 :14	they will be strewn about in the streets where they live
	7 :23	gathered about Uzziah and the rulers of the city
	8 :1	At that time Judith heard about these things :
	8 :5	and girded sackcloth about her loins
	8 :32	I am about to do a thing
	8 :34	until I have finished what I am about to do
	10 :9	and accomplish the things about which you spoke with me
	10 :12	for they are about to be handed over to you to be devoured
	10 :18	while they told him about her
	11 :11	by which they are about to provoke their God to anger
	11 :16	as many as shall hear about them
Ad E	13 :4	cannot be brought about
Wis	6 :16	because she goes about seeking those worthy of her
	8 :18	I went about seeking how to get her for myself
	12 :14	about those whom thou hast punished
	13 :17	When he prays about possessions
	14 :1	and about to voyage over raging waves
	14 :22	to err about the knowledge of God
Sir	9 :7	nor wander about in its deserted sections
	9 :13	and that you are going about on the city battlements
	9 :15	and let all your discussion be about the law of the Most High
	10 :27	than one who goes about boasting, but lacks bread
	11 :4	Do not boast about wearing fine clothes
	11 :9	Do not argue about a matter which does not concern you
	12 :11	Even if he humbles himself and goes about cringing
	13 :13	for you are walking about with your own downfall
	21 :1	Do so no more, but pray about your former sins
	29 :28	scolding about lodging and the reproach of the moneylender
	31 :1	and anxiety about it removes sleep
	33 :2	but he who is hypocritical about it
	36 :25	and where there is no wife, a man will wander about and sigh
	37 :11	Do not consult with a woman about her rival
	37 :11	or with a coward about war
	37 :11	with a merchant about barter or with a buyer about selling
	37 :11	with a grudging man about gratitude
	37 :11	or with a merciless man about kindness
	37 :11	with an idler about any work
	37 :11	or with a man hired for a year about completing his work
	37 :11	with a lazy servant about a big task
	38 :25	and whose talk is about bulls ?
	38 :26	and he is careful about fodder for the heifers
	41 :4	there is no inquiry about it in Hades
	41 :11	The mourning of men is about their bodies
	51 :3	from the gnashings of teeth about to devour me
Bar	2 :18	that goes about bent over and feeble
	2 :23	and from the region about Jerusalem
	3 :31	or is concerned about the path to her
L Jr	6 :43	And the women, with cords about them, sit along the passageways
P Az	1	And they walked about in the midst of the flames
	25	whom it caught about the furnace
Sus	13 :8	going in and walking about, and they began to desire her
	13 :27	for nothing like this had ever been said about Susanna
Bel	14 :12	or else Daniel will, who is telling lies about us
	14 :35	and I know nothing about the den
1 Ma	2 :45	And Mattathias and his friends went about
	2 :67	You shall rally about you all who observe the law
	3 :34	and gave him orders about all that he wanted done
	3 :48	to inquire into those matters about which the Gentiles
	4 :44	about the altar of burnt offering, which had been profaned
	5 :13	and have destroyed about a 1,000 men there
	7 :32	About 500 men of the army of Nicanor fell
	9 :49	And about 1,000 of Bacchides' men fell that day
	9 :61	And Jonathan's men seized about 50 of the men of the country
	10 :19	We have heard about you
	10 :35	or annoy any of them about any matter

	10 :63	about any matter
	11 :4	and the corpses lying about
	11 :29	and wrote a letter to Jonathan about all these things
	11 :47	and they all rallied about him
	11 :53	But he broke his word about all that he had promised
	13 :14	and that he was about to join battle with him
	13 :29	erecting about them great columns
	14 :21	have told us about your glory and honour
	16 :10	and John burned it with fire, and about 2,000 of them fell
	16 :18	Then Ptolemy wrote a report about these things
2 Ma	2 :13	and collected the books about the kings and prophets
	2 :13	and letters of kings about votive offerings
	2 :16	Since, therefore, we are about to celebrate the purification
	2 :22	and restored the laws that were about to be abolished
	3 :2	it came about that the kings themselves honoured the place
	3 :4	about the administration of the city market
	3 :7	he told about of the money about which he had been informed
	3 :9	he told about the disclosure that had been made
	3 :15	upon him who had given the law about deposits
	3 :18	because the holy place was about to be brought into contempt
	3 :38	for there certainly is about the place some power of God
	4 :1	who had informed about the money against his own country
	4 :38	and led him about the whole city to that very place
	4 :40	Lysimachus armed about 3,000 men
	4 :41	and others took handfuls of the ashes that were lying about
	4 :43	Charges were brought against Menelaus about this incident
	5 :1	About this time Antiochus made his 2nd invasion of Egypt
	5 :27	But Judas Maccabeus, with about 9 others
	6 :10	These women they publicly paraded about the city
	6 :30	When he was about to die under the blows
	7 :18	And when he was about to die, he said
	7 :42	Let this be enough, then, about the eating of sacrifices
	8 :1	and so they gathered about 6,000 men
	8 :3	and about to be levelled to the ground
	8 :11	that was about to overtake him
	9 :1	About that time, as it happened
	9 :7	And so it came about that he fell out of his chariot
	11 :2	gathered about 80,000 men and all his cavalry
	11 :5	about 5 leagues from Jerusalem
	11 :17	and have asked about the matters indicated therein
	12 :1	and the Jews went about their farming
	13 :7	By such a fate it came about
	14 :4	and went to King Demetrius in about the 151st year
	14 :5	and was asked about the disposition
	14 :41	When the troops were about to capture the tower
1 Es	1 :42	But the things that are reported about Jehoiakim
	2 :22	You will find in the chronicles what has been written about them
	3 :6	and a turban of fine linen, and a necklace about his neck
	4 :33	and he began to speak about truth
	8 :53	And again we prayed to our Lord about these things
	8 :86	And all that has happened to us has come about
	8 :91	there gathered about him a very great throng from Jerusalem
	8 :93	Let us take an oath to the Lord about this
3 Ma	1 :5	And so it came about that the enemy was routed in the action
	3 :7	instead they gossiped about the differences in worship and foods
	4 :19	he was clearly convinced about the matter
	5 :10	to report to the king about these preparations
	5 :37	must I give you orders about these things ?
	5 :42	which had come about within him for the protection of the Jews
	5 :46	the elephant keeper entered at about dawn into the courtyard
2 Es	4 :9	But now I have asked you only about fire and wind and the day
	4 :9	and you have given me no answer about them !
	4 :23	For I did not wish to inquire about the ways above
	4 :23	but about those things which we daily experience :
	4 :25	It is about these things that I have asked
	4 :28	For the evil about which you ask me has been sown
	4 :35	ask about these matters, saying
	4 :52	Concerning the signs about which you ask me
	6 :20	which is about to pass away
	6 :46	who was about to be formed
	7 :43	For it will last for about a week of years
	7 :80	but shall immediately wander about in torments
	8 :15	About all mankind thou knowest best
	8 :15	but I will speak about thy people
	8 :16	and about thy inheritance, for whom I lament
	8 :16	and about Israel, for whom I am sad
	8 :16	and about the seed of Jacob, for whom I am troubled
	8 :38	about the fashioning of those who have sinned
	8 :38	or about their death, their judgment, or their destruction
	8 :55	about the multitude of those who perish
	9 :2	when the Most High is about to visit the world
	10 :38	and tell you about the things which you fear
	10 :43	and as for her telling you about the misfortune of her son
	11 :2	and the clouds were gathered about him
	13 :22	As for what you said about those who are left
	13 :46	and now, when they are about to come again
	13 :53	And you alone have been enlightened about this
	14 :25	until what you are about to write is finished
	15 :44	and all who are about her shall wail over her

15 : 53	and talking about their death when you were drunk ?
16 : 38	has great pains about her womb for 2 or 3 hours beforehand
4 Ma **1** : 1	The subject that I am about to discuss is most philosophical
4 : 13	although otherwise he had scruples about doing so
5 : 1	and with his armed soldiers standing about him
6 : 26	When he was now burned to his very bones and about to expire
8 : 4	grouped about their mother as if in a chorus
8 : 27	But the youths, though about to be tortured
10 : 9	When he was about to die, he said
12 : 15	Then because he too was about to die, he said
17 : 1	when she also was about to be seized and put to death
18 : 11	He read to you about Abel slain by Cain
18 : 12	and he taught you about Hananiah, Azariah, and Mishael in the fire

ABOVE, prep., adv. 19 = 0.012 %

Tob **1** : 2	in Galilee above Asher
Jud **13** : 6	above Holofernes' head
13 : 18	above all women on earth
Ad E **13** : 14	that I might not set the glory of man above the glory of God
Sir **3** : 2	For the Lord honoured the father above the children
15 : 5	She will exalt him above his neighbours
30 : 16	and there is no gladness above joy of heart
49 : 8	which God showed him above the chariot of the cherubim
49 : 16	and Adam above every living being in the creation
L Jr **6** : 63	And the fire sent from above to consume mountains and woods does what it is ordered
P Az **24**	And the flame streamed out above the furnace 49 cubits
38	Bless the Lord, all waters above the heaven
2 Ma **15** : 2	and hallowed above other days
3 Ma **3** : 30	The letter was written in the above form
2 Es **4** : 7	or how many streams are above the firmament
4 : 21	and he who is above the heavens
4 : 21	can understand what is above the height of the heavens
4 : 23	For I did not wish to inquire about the ways above
15 : 59	Unhappy above all others

ABRAHAM 31 = 0.020 %

Tob **4** : 12	that Noah, Abraham, Isaac, and Jacob, our fathers of old
Jud **8** : 26	Remember what he did with Abraham, and how he tested Isaac
Ad E **13** : 15	God of Abraham, spare thy people
14 : 18	except in thee, O Lord God of Abraham
Sir **44** : 19	Abraham was the great father of a multitude of nations
44 : 22	for the sake of Abraham his father
Bar **2** : 34	to Abraham and to Isaac and to Jacob
P Az **12**	for the sake of Abraham thy beloved
1 Ma **2** : 52	Was not Abraham found faithful when tested
12 : 21	that they are brethren and are of the family of Abraham
2 Ma **1** : 2	and may he remember his covenant with Abraham
P Ma **1**	of Abraham and Isaac and Jacob
8	for Abraham and Isaac and Jacob
3 Ma **6** : 3	look upon the descendants of Abraham, O Father
2 Es **1** : 39	to them I will give as leaders Abraham, Isaac
3 : 13	whose name was Abraham
6 : 8	He said to me, From Abraham to Isaac
7 : 106	How then do we find that first Abraham prayed
4 Ma **6** : 17	May we, the children of Abraham
6 : 22	Therefore, O children of Abraham
7 : 19	like our patriarchs Abraham and Isaac and Jacob
9 : 21	the courageous youth, worthy of Abraham, did not groan
13 : 17	For if we so die, Abraham and Isaac and Jacob will welcome us
14 : 20	she was of the same mind as Abraham
15 : 28	but as the daughter of God-fearing Abraham
16 : 20	our father Abraham was zealous to sacrifice his son Isaac
16 : 25	as do Abraham and Isaac and Jacob and all the patriarchs
17 : 6	For your children were true descendants of father Abraham
18 : 1	O Israelite children, offspring of the seed of Abraham
18 : 20	brought those 7 sons of the daughter of Abraham to the catapult
18 : 23	But the sons of Abraham with their victorious mother

ABROAD 4 = 0.003 %

Wis **18** : 10	was spread abroad
Sir pr.	for those living abroad who wished to gain learning
2 Ma **4** : 39	and when report of them had spread abroad
3 Ma **5** : 26	The rays of the sun were not yet shed abroad

ABRON 1

Jud **2** : 24	and destroyed all the hilltop cities along the brook Abron

ABSALOM 3 = 0.002 %

1 Ma **11** : 70	except Mattathias the son of Absalom and Judas the son of Chalphi
13 : 11	He sent Jonathan the son of Absalom to Joppa
2 Ma **11** : 17	John and Absalom, who were sent by you

ABSENT 3 = 0.002 %

Wis **11** : 11	Whether absent or present, they were equally distressed
14 : 17	they might flatter the absent one as though present
1 Ma **4** : 4	while the division was still absent from the camp

ABSTAIN 2

4 Ma **1** : 33	we abstain from the pleasure to be had from them ?
1 : 34	we abstain because of domination by reason

ABUBUS 2

1 Ma **16** : 11	Now Ptolemy the son of Abubus had been appointed governor
16 : 15	The son of Abubus received them treacherously

ABUNDANCE 16 = 0.010 %

Tob **2** : 2	Upon seeing the abundance of food I said to my son
Sir **10** : 27	and has an abundance of everything
13 : 11	nor trust his abundance of words
18 : 12	therefore he grants them forgiveness in abundance
45 : 20	he prepared bread of first fruits in abundance
1 Ma **10** : 21	and equipped them with arms in abundance
1 Es **8** : 20	a 100 baths of wine, and salt in abundance
3 Ma **5** : 2	maddened by the lavish abundance of liquor
5 : 10	until they had been filled with a great abundance of wine
6 : 4	Pharaoh with his abundance of chariots
2 Es **1** : 20	did I not cleave the rock so that waters flowed in abundance ?
2 : 27	but you shall rejoice and have abundance
6 : 44	For immediately fruit came forth in endless abundance
6 : 56	and thou hast compared their abundance to a drop from a bucket
7 : 123	and in which are abundance and healing
15 : 41	may be filled with the abundance of those waters

ABUNDANT 11 = 0.007 %

Ad E **10** : 6	and there was light and the sun and abundant water
11 : 10	there came a great river, with abundant water
Wis **11** : 7	thou gavest them abundant water unexpectedly
Sir **1** : 7	And her abundant experience – who has understood it ?
24 : 17	and my blossoms became glorious and abundant fruit
24 : 29	for her thought is more abundant than the sea
P Az **19**	but deal with us in thy forbearance and in thy abundant mercy
1 Ma **6** : 6	and abundant spoils which they had taken
2 Es **7** : 56	but silver is more abundant than gold, and brass than silver
7 : 57	those that are abundant or those that are rare ?
7 : 136	and abundant in compassion

ABUSE, subst. 4 = 0.003 %

Sir **27** : 15	and their abuse is grievous to hear
27 : 21	and there is reconciliation after abuse
27 : 28	Mockery and abuse issue from the proud man
2 Es **10** : 22	our free men have suffered abuse

ABUSE, verb 2

Sir **7** : 20	Do not abuse a servant who performs his work faithfully
2 Es **9** : 9	Then those who have now abused my ways shall be amazed

ABUSIVE 2

Sir **18** : 18	A fool is ungracious and abusive
41 : 22	of abusive words, before friends

ABYSS 5 = 0.003 %

Sir **1** : 3	the abyss, and wisdom – who can search them out ?
16 : 18	the abyss and the earth, will tremble at his visitation
24 : 5	and have walked in the depths of the abyss
24 : 29	and her counsel deeper than the great abyss
42 : 18	He searches out the abyss, and the hearts of men

ACCEPT 26 = 0.017 %

Tob **13** : 6	who knows if he will accept you and have mercy on you ?
Jud **11** : 5	Judith replied to him, Accept the words of your servant
Wis **3** : 6	and like a sacrificial burnt offering he accepted them
12 : 24	For they went far astray on the paths of error, accepting as gods
Sir **2** : 4	Accept whatever is brought upon you
3 : 17	then you will be loved by those whom God accepts
6 : 23	Listen, my son, and accept my judgment
7 : 9	he will accept it
18 : 14	He has compassion on those who accept his discipline
32 : 14	He who fears the Lord will accept his discipline
35 : 12	Do not offer him a bribe, for he will not accept it
35 : 16	He whose service is pleasing to the Lord will be accepted
36 : 21	A woman will accept any man
P Az **16**	Yet with a contrite heart and a humble spirit may we be accepted
1 Ma **1** : 43	All the Gentiles accepted the command of the king
6 : 60	and they accepted it
9 : 31	And Jonathan at that time accepted the leadership
10 : 46	they did not believe or accept them
14 : 47	So Simon accepted and agreed to be high priest
15 : 20	And it has seemed good to us to accept the shield from them
2 Ma **1** : 26	accept this sacrifice on behalf of all thy people Israel
7 : 29	Accept death, so that in God's mercy
12 : 4	And when they accepted
3 Ma **3** : 17	They accepted our presence by word, but insincerely by deed
6 : 26	and often have accepted willingly the worst of human dangers ?
4 Ma **8** : 17	and exhorted us to accept kind treatment if we obey him

ACCEPTABLE

			4 = 0.003 %
Wis	9 : 12	Then my works will be acceptable	
Sir	2 : 5	and acceptable men in the furnace of humiliation	
	34 : 18	the gifts of the lawless are not acceptable	
	35 : 7	The sacrifice of a righteous man is acceptable	

ACCEPTANCE

			2
Sir	10 : 21	The fear of the Lord is the beginning of acceptance	
	19 : 18	The fear of the Lord is the beginning of acceptance	

ACCESS

			3 = 0.002 %
2 Ma	12 : 21	for that place was hard to besiege and difficult of access	
	14 : 3	to be safe or to have access again to the holy altar	
1 Es	2 : 24	you will no longer have access to Coelesyria and Phoenicia	

ACCOMODATE

			1
3 Ma	3 : 20	accommodated ourselves to their folly and did as was proper	

ACCOMPANIMENT

			1
3 Ma	6 : 35	to the accompaniment of joyous thanksgiving and psalms	

ACCOMPANY

			5 = 0.003 %
Tob	12 : 8	Prayer is good when accompanied by fasting, almsgiving, and righteousness	
Jud	10 : 17	to accompany her and her maid	
1 Ma	12 : 47	while a 1,000 accompanied him	
2 Ma	3 : 24	that all who had been so bold as to accompany him	
4 Ma	4 : 5	accompanied by the accursed Simon	

ACCOMPLISH

			16 = 0.010 %
Tob	14 : 11	So now, my children, consider what almsgiving accomplishes	
Jud	10 : 9	and accomplish the things about which you spoke with me	
	11 : 6	God will accomplish something through you	
	11 : 16	and God has sent me to accomplish with you	
Ad E	13 : 13	When I asked my counsellors how this might be accomplished	
	16 : 7	What has been wickedly accomplished	
2 Ma	10 : 38	When they had accomplished these things	
	12 : 18	without accomplishing anything	
	14 : 29	to accomplish this by a stratagem	
1 Es	1 : 17	were accomplished that day : the passover was kept	
	2 : 1	might be accomplished	
3 Ma	6 : 15	so accomplish it, O Lord	
	7 : 4	would never be firmly established until this was accomplished	
2 Es	6 : 38	and thy word accomplished the work	
4 Ma	8 : 3	handsome, modest, noble, and accomplished in every way	
	9 : 12	without accomplishing anything, they placed him upon the wheel	

ACCORD, subst.

			13 = 0.008 %
Jud	13 : 17	and said with one accord, Blessed art thou, our God	
	15 : 5	with one accord they fell upon the enemy	
	15 : 9	And when they met her they all blessed her with one accord	
Wis	10 : 20	and praised with one accord thy defending hand	
	18 : 9	and with one accord agreed to the divine law	
Sir	37 : 12	whose soul is in accord with your soul	
1 Ma	14 : 46	the right to act in accord with these decisions	
2 Ma	6 : 19	went up to the rack of his own accord, spitting out the flesh	
1 Es	9 : 38	the whole multitude gathered with one accord	
3 Ma	5 : 21	all those present readily and joyfully with one accord gave their approval	
	5 : 50	they prostrated themselves with one accord on the ground	
	7 : 17	in accord with the common desire, for 7 days	
4 Ma	11 : 3	I have come of my own accord	

ACCORDANCE

			24 = 0.016 %
Tob	7 : 12	in accordance with the law	
Sir	16 : 14	every one will receive in accordance with his deeds	
	46 : 1	He became, in accordance with his name	
Bar	2 : 2	in accordance with what is written in the law of Moses	
P Az	20	Deliver us in accordance with thy marvellous works	
Sus	13 : 62	acting in accordance with the law of Moses	
1 Ma	7 : 16	in accordance with the word which was written	
	10 : 64	in accordance with the proclamation	
1 Es	1 : 5	in accordance with the directions of David king of Israel	
	4 : 52	in accordance with the commandment to make 17 offerings	
	5 : 49	in accordance with the directions in the book of Moses the man of God	
	7 : 9	in accordance with the book of Moses	
	8 : 10	In accordance with my gracious decision	
	8 : 12	in accordance with what is in the law of the Lord	
	8 : 16	perform it in accordance with the will of your God	
	9 : 4	in accordance with the decision of the ruling elders	
	9 : 15	acted in accordance with all this	
3 Ma	3 : 23	in every situation, in accordance with their infamous way of life	
	7 : 6	and in accordance with the clemency	
	7 : 22	in accordance with the registration	
4 Ma	2 : 8	a way of life in accordance with the law	
	6 : 18	who have lived in accordance with truth to old age	
	6 : 18	and have maintained in accordance with law	
	8 : 1	by following a philosophy in accordance with devout reason	

ACCORDINGLY

			6 = 0.004 %
Ad E	16 : 24	which does not act accordingly	
Sir	3 : 1	and act accordingly, that you may be kept in safety	
1 Ma	12 : 23	that our envoys report to you accordingly	
2 Ma	11 : 25	Accordingly, since we choose that this nation also	
3 Ma	6 : 31	Accordingly those disgracefully treated and near to death	
4 Ma	1 : 13	Our inquiry, accordingly	

ACCORDING TO

			69 = 0.045 %
Tob	3 : 6	And now deal with me according to thy pleasure	
	4 : 8	according to the little you have	
	4 : 19	and according to his will he humbles whomever he wishes	
	6 : 12	For I know that Raguel, according to the law of Moses	
	7 : 13	take her according to the law of Moses	
	8 : 16	but thou hast treated us according to thy great mercy	
Jud	7 : 28	who punishes us according to our sins	
Wis	2 : 20	for, according to what he says, he will be protected	
	6 : 4	nor keep the law, nor walk according to the purpose of God	
	9 : 9	and what is right according to thy commandments	
	16 : 25	according to the desire of those who had need	
Sir	pr.	in living according to the law	
	pr.	being prepared in character to live according to the law	
	1 : 10	She dwells with all flesh according to his gift	
	5 : 2	walking according to the desires of your heart	
	10 : 28	and ascribe to yourself honour according to your worth	
	11 : 26	according to his conduct	
	14 : 11	My son, treat yourself well, according to your means	
	16 : 12	he judges a man according to his deeds	
	29 : 11	according to the commandments of the Most High	
	29 : 20	Assist your neighbour according to your ability	
	32 : 17	and will find a decision according to his liking	
	35 : 17	till he repays man according to his deeds	
	35 : 19	and the works of men according to their devices	
	36 : 17	according to the blessing of Aaron for thy people	
	38 : 1	according to your need of him, for the Lord created him	
	38 : 17	observe the mourning according to his merit	
	45 : 11	according to the number of the tribes of Israel	
	49 : 6	according to the word of Jeremiah	
	50 : 22	and deals with us according to his mercy	
	51 : 18	For I resolved to live according to wisdom	
Sus	13 : 3	and had taught their daughter according to the law of Moses	
1 Ma	1 : 14	according to Gentile custom	
	1 : 60	According to the decree, they put to death	
	2 : 23	according to the king's command	
	3 : 56	that each should return to his home, according to the law	
	7 : 42	and judge him according to this wickedness	
	13 : 46	they said, Do not treat us according to our wicked acts	
	13 : 46	but according to your mercy	
	15 : 21	that he may punish them according to their law	
2 Ma	6 : 23	and moreover according to the holy Godgiven law	
	11 : 25	and that they live according to the customs of their ancestors	
	12 : 38	they purified themselves according to the custom	
1 Es	1 : 2	having placed the priests according to their divisions	
	1 : 5	according to the grouping of the fathers' houses of you Levites	
	1 : 6	and keep the passover according to the commandment of the Lord	
	1 : 10	stood according to kindred	
	1 : 15	were in their place according to the arrangement made by David	
	1 : 18	according to the command of King Josiah	
	3 : 9	the victory shall be given according to what is written	
	5 : 1	according to their tribes	
	5 : 4	according to their fathers' houses in the tribes	
	5 : 55	according to the decree which they had in writing	
	5 : 60	according to the directions of David king of Israel	
	7 : 6	did according to what was written in the book of Moses	
	7 : 8	according to the number of the 12 leaders	
	7 : 9	arrayed in their garments, according to kindred	
	8 : 23	And you, Ezra, according to the wisdom of God	
	8 : 28	according to their fathers' houses and their groups	
P Ma	7	Thou, O Lord, according to thy great goodness	
3 Ma	3 : 14	it was brought to conclusion, according to plan	
	5 : 29	O king, according to your eager purpose	
	7 : 2	the great God guiding our affairs according to our desire	
2 Es	2 : 18	According to their counsel	
	8 : 37	and it will come to pass according to your words	
	10 : 13	but it is with the earth according to the way of the earth	
4 Ma	5 : 11	philosophize according to the truth of what is beneficial	
	11 : 5	according to his virtuous law ?	
	15 : 3	according to God's promise	

ACCOS

			1
1 Ma	8 : 17	So Judas chose Eupolemus the son of John, son of Accos	

ACCOUNT, subst., prep.

			30 = 0.020 %
Tob	1 : 21	over all the accounts of his kingdom	
	1 : 22	and in charge of administration of the accounts	
	6 : 14	in sorrow on my account	
Ad E	12 : 4	and Mordecai wrote an account of them	
Wis	3 : 17	Even if they live long they will be held of no account	
	6 : 15	and he who is vigilant on her account	

4

Sir pr.		on account of which we should praise Israel
	10:8	on account of injustice and insolence and wealth
	16:8	whom he loathed on account of their insolence
	23:14	and be deemed a fool on account of your habits
	32:2	that you may be merry on their account
	40:10	and on their account the flood came
	42:3	of keeping accounts with a partner
1 Ma	6:59	for it was on account of their laws which we abolished
2 Ma	2:14	on account of the war which had come upon us
	3:6	and that they did not belong to the account of the sacrifices
	4:28	on account of this issue
	6:22	on account of his old friendship with them
	7:18	For we are suffering these things on our own account
	8:35	by opponents whom he regarded as of the least account
	11:4	He took no account whatever of the power of God
	12:43	taking account of the resurrection
3 Ma	5:15	and he gave him an account of the situation
	5:42	took no account of the changes of mind
	7:7	and since we have taken into account
2 Es	4:39	And it is perhaps on account of us
	4:39	on account of the sins of those who dwell on earth
	9:7	on account of the faith by which he has believed
	12:48	on account of the desolation of Zion
	12:48	on account of the humiliation of our sanctuary

ACCOUNT, verb   6 = 0.004 %

Wis	7:8	and I accounted wealth as nothing in comparison with her
	7:9	and silver will be accounted as clay before her
	15:2	because we know that we are accounted thine
Sir	40:19	but a blameless wife is accounted better than both
3 Ma	2:17	or call us to account for this profanation
2 Es	12:7	and if I have been accounted righteous before thee beyond many others

ACCUMULATE   3 = 0.002 %

Sir	14:4	Whoever accumulates by depriving himself
	14:4	accumulates for others
	31:3	The rich man toils as his wealth accumulates

ACCURACY   1

Sir	42:4	of accuracy with scales and weights

ACCURATE   2

Sir	31:24	and their testimony to his niggardliness is accurate
	32:3	but with accurate knowledge

ACCURATELY   1

Sir	16:25	and declare knowledge accurately

ACCURSED   9 = 0.006 %

Ad E	16:15	who were consigned to annihilation by this thrice accursed man
Wis	3:13	their offspring are accursed
	12:11	For they were an accursed race from the beginning
	14:8	But the idol made with hands is accursed
2 Ma	7:9	You accursed wretch, you dismiss us from this present life
	12:35	wishing to take the accursed man alive
4 Ma	4:5	accompanied by the accursed Simon
	9:24	and take vengeance on the accursed tyrant
	18:22	For these crimes divine justice pursued and will pursue the accursed tyrant

ACCUSATION   3 = 0.002 %

Sir	26:5	and false accusation
1 Ma	7:6	And they brought to the king this accusation
2 Ma	14:27	and, provoked by the false accusations of that depraved man

ACCUSE   11 = 0.007 %

Wis	2:12	and accuses us of sins against our training
	10:14	Those who accused him she showed to be false
	12:12	Who will accuse thee
Sir	46:19	And no man accused him
1 Ma	10:61	lawless men, gathered together against him to accuse him
2 Ma	4:5	not accusing his fellow citizens
	5:8	Accused before Aretas the ruler of the Arabs
	10:13	As a result he was accused before Eupator
	10:21	and accused these men
	14:38	he had been accused of Judaism
2 Es	16:50	when she decks herself out, and shall accuse her to her face

ACCUSER   2

1 Ma	10:64	And when his accusers saw the honour that was paid him
2 Es	16:65	as your accusers in that day

ACCUSTOM   7 = 0.005 %

Jud	13:10	as they were accustomed to go for prayer
Sir	23:9	Do not accustom your mouth to oaths
	23:13	Do not accustom your mouth to lewd vulgarity
	23:15	A man accustomed to use insulting words
Bel	14:15	as they were accustomed to do

	14:21	through which they were accustomed to enter
1 Ma	6:30	20,000 horsemen, and 32 elephants accustomed to war

ACHAN   1

2 Es	7:107	and Joshua after him for Israel in the days of Achan

ACHIEVE   1

Jud	11:6	and my lord will not fail to achieve his purposes

ACHIEVEMENT   1

1 Ma	16:23	and the building of the walls which he built, and his achievements

ACHIOR   13 = 0.008 %

Jud	5:5	Then Achior, the leader of all the Ammonites, said to him
	5:22	When Achior had finished saying this
	6:1	said to Achior and all the Moabites
	6:2	And who are you, Achior, and you hirelings of Ephraim
	6:5	But you, Achior, you Ammonite hireling
	6:10	to seize Achior and take him to Bethulia
	6:13	and they bound Achior
	6:16	and they set Achior in the midst of all their people
	6:20	Then they consoled Achior, and praised him greatly
	11:9	Now as for the things Achior said in your council
	14:5	But before you do all this, bring Achior the Ammonite to me
	14:6	So they summoned Achior from the house of Uzziah
	14:10	And when Achior saw all that the God of Israel had done

ACKNOWLEDGE   9 = 0.006 %

Tob	12:22	and acknowledged that the angel of the Lord
	13:3	Acknowledge him before the nations, O sons of Israel
Wis	18:13	they acknowledged thy people to be God's son
Sir	44:23	he acknowledged him with his blessings
2 Es	8:28	but remember those who have willingly acknowledged that thou art to be feared
	9:10	For as many as did not acknowledge me in their lifetime
	9:12	these must in torment acknowledge it after death
	10:16	For if you acknowledge the decree of God to be just
4 Ma	6:34	And it is right for us to acknowledge the dominance of reason

ACQUAINT   2

Tob	5:5	Are you acquainted with that region?
2 Ma	14:9	Since you are acquainted, O king

ACQUAINTANCE   3 = 0.002 %

Sir	30:2	and will boast of him among acquaintances
2 Ma	6:21	because of their long acquaintance with him
4 Ma	6:13	partly out of sympathy from their acquaintance with him

ACQUIRE   9 = 0.006 %

Jud	8:22	and a reproach in the eyes of those who acquire us
Sir pr.		should acquire understanding
pr.		and after acquiring considerable proficiency in them
	14:15	and what you acquired by toil to be divided by lot?
	15:6	and will acquire an everlasting name
	16:24	Listen to me, my son, and acquire knowledge
	34:10	but he that has travelled acquires much cleverness
	36:24	He who acquires a wife gets his best possession
	42:4	and of acquiring much or little

ACQUIT   3 = 0.002 %

Sir	42:2	and of rendering judgment to acquit the ungodly
2 Ma	4:47	he acquitted of the charges against him
3 Ma	7:7	we justly have acquitted them

ACRABA   1

Jud	7:18	toward Acraba, which is near Chusi beside the brook Mochmur

ACROSS, prep., adv.   5 = 0.003 %

Jud	15:2	by every path across the plain and through the hill country
1 Ma	5:39	and they are encamped across the stream
	9:48	and swam across to the other side
2 Ma	8:35	across the country till he reached Antioch
2 Es	13:40	he took them across the river

ACT, subst.   31 = 0.020 %

Tob	1:1	The book of the acts of Tobit the son of Tobiel
	1:3	and I performed many acts of charity to my brethren
	1:16	I performed many acts of charity to my brethren
Jud	13:16	and yet he committed no act of sin with me
Wis	19:13	for they justly suffered because of their wicked acts
Sir	10:6	and do not attempt anything by acts of insolence
	16:14	He will make room for every act of mercy
	16:22	Who will announce his acts of justice?
	31:11	and the assembly will relate his acts of charity
	32:23	Guard yourself in every act
1 Ma	7:3	But when this act became known to him
	9:22	Now the rest of the acts of Judas, and his wars
	13:46	they said, Do not treat us according to our wicked acts
	16:17	So he committed an act of great treachery

5

	16:23	The rest of the acts of John and his wars
2 Ma	**4:33**	When Onias became fully aware of these acts
	4:39	When many acts of sacrilege
	5:18	and turned back from his rash act
	8:18	For they trust to arms and acts of daring, he said
1 Es	**1:25**	After all these acts of Josiah
	1:33	and every one of the acts of Josiah, and his splendour
	1:49	committed many acts of sacrilege and lawlessness
	1:52	because of their ungodly acts he gave command
3 Ma	**4:21**	But this was an act of the invincible providence
	5:28	This was the act of God who rules over all things
	6:24	by secretly devising acts of no advantage to the kingdom
	7:6	But we very severely threatened them for these acts
	7:9	in everything and inescapably as an antagonist to avenge such acts. Farewell
4 Ma	**4:21**	The divine justice was angered by these acts
	5:33	as to break the ancestral law by my own act
	11:4	for what act of ours are you destroying us in this way ?

ACT, verb 　　　　　　　　　　　　　　36 = 0.023 %

Ad E	**13:2**	but always acting reasonably and with kindness
	16:24	which does not act accordingly
Wis	**12:18**	for thou hast power to act whenever thou dost choose
	18:21	For a blameless man was quick to act as their champion
Sir	**3:1**	and act accordingly, that you may be kept in safety
	5:15	In great or small matters do not act amiss
	8:15	for he will act as he pleases
	15:15	and to act faithfully is a matter of your own choice
	19:21	I will not act as you wish
	22:4	but one who acts shamefully brings grief to her father
	26:24	A shameless woman constantly acts disgracefully
	32:9	Among the great do not act as their equal
	32:19	and when you have acted, do not regret it
	33:29	Do not act immoderately toward anybody
Sus	**13:62**	acting in accordance with the law of Moses
1 Ma	**8:25**	shall act as their allies wholeheartedly
	8:27	the Romans shall willingly act as their allies
	10:4	for he said, Let us act first to make peace with him
	14:45	Whoever acts contrary to these decisions
	14:46	the right to act in accord with these decisions
2 Ma	**3:30**	who had acted marvellously for his own place
	4:31	leaving Andronicus, a man of high rank, to act as his deputy
	6:29	had acted toward him with good will now changed to ill will
	7:2	One of them, acting as their spokesman, said
	12:43	In doing this he acted very well and honourably
1 Es	**1:24**	concerning those who sinned and acted wickedly toward the Lord
	9:15	acted in accordance with all this
3 Ma	**2:5**	the men of Sodom who acted arrogantly
	2:32	But the majority acted firmly with a courageous spirit
2 Es	**3:30**	and hast spared those who act wickedly
	8:27	Regard not the endeavours of those who act wickedly
	8:35	who has not acted wickedly
4 Ma	**2:8**	he is forced to act contrary to his natural ways
	2:13	so that one rebukes friends when they act wickedly
	5:24	so that in all our dealings we act impartially
	9:15	not because I am a murderer, or as one who acts impiously

ACTION 　　　　　　　　　　　　　13 = 0.008 %

Wis	**2:12**	because he is inconvenient to us and opposes our actions
	9:11	and she will guide me wisely in my actions
	19:1	for God knew in advance even their future actions
Sir	**11:31**	and to worthy actions he will attach blame
1 Ma	**4:34**	they fell in action
2 Ma	**15:28**	When the action was over and they were returning with joy
1 Es	**8:95**	Arise and take action, for it is your task
3 Ma	**1:5**	And so it came about that the enemy was routed in the action
	3:19	and are unwilling to regard any action as sincere
	5:12	And by the action of the Lord
	5:26	indicating that what the king desired was ready for action
	6:27	begging pardon for your former actions !
2 Es	**12:25**	and perform his last actions

ACTIVE 　　　　　　　　　　　　　　　　　　1

Wis	**15:11**	and inspired him with an active soul

ACTIVITY 　　　　　　　　　　　　　　　　2

Wis	**7:17**	and the activity of the elements
Sir	**11:10**	if you multiply activities you will not go unpunished

ADAIAH 　　　　　　　　　　　　　　　　　　1

1 Es	**9:30**	Of the sons of Bani : Meshullam, Malluch, Adaiah

ADAM 　　　　　　　　　　　　　　　15 = 0.010 %

Tob	**8:6**	Thou madest Adam
Sir	**33:10**	and Adam was created of the dust
	40:1	and a heavy yoke is upon the sons of Adam
	49:16	and Adam above every living being in the creation
2 Es	**3:5**	and it gave thee Adam, a lifeless body ?
	3:10	as death came upon Adam, so the flood upon them

	3:21	For the first Adam, burdened with an evil heart
	3:26	in everything doing as Adam and all his descendants had done
	4:30	For a grain of evil seed was sown in Adam's heart from the beginning
	6:54	and over these thou didst place Adam
	6:56	As for the other nations which have descended from Adam
	7:11	and when Adam transgressed my statutes
	7:70	When the Most High made the world and Adam
	7:116	that it would have been better if the earth had not produced Adam
	7:118	O Adam, what have you done ?

ADAMANT 　　　　　　　　　　　　　　　　1

4 Ma	**16:13**	but, as though having a mind like adamant

ADAR 　　　　　　　　　　　　　　　7 = 0.005 %

Ad E	**10:13**	So they will observe these days in the month of Adar
	13:6	on the 14th day of the 12th month, Adar
	16:20	so that on the 13th day of the 12th month, Adar
1 Ma	**7:43**	on the 13th day of the month of Adar
	7:49	each year on the 13th day of Adar
2 Ma	**15:36**	which is called Adar in the Syrian language
1 Es	**7:5**	by the 23rd day of the month of Adar

ADASA 　　　　　　　　　　　　　　　　　2

1 Ma	**7:40**	And Judas encamped in Adasa with 3,000 men
	7:45	from Adasa as far as Gazara

ADD 　　　　　　　　　　　　　　　21 = 0.014 %

Tob	**5:15**	And besides, I will add to your wages
	5:18	Do not add money to money
Sir	**4:3**	Do not add to the troubles of an angry mind
	5:5	Do not be so confident of atonement that you add sin to sin
	13:3	A rich man does wrong, and he even adds reproaches
	13:3	a poor man suffers wrong, and he must add apologies
	21:15	he will praise it and add to it
	26:15	A modest wife adds charm to charm
	31:30	reducing his strength and adding wounds
	42:21	Nothing can be added or taken away
	45:20	He added glory to Aaron and gave him a heritage
1 Ma	**8:30**	both parties shall determine to add or delete anything
	10:30	or from the 3 districts added to it
	10:38	As for the 3 districts that have been added to Judea
	11:1	and add it to his own kingdom
	11:34	were added to Judea from Samaria
	14:15	and added to the vessels of the sanctuary
2 Ma	**2:32**	adding only so much to what has already been said
1 Es	**2:7**	besides the other things added as votive offerings
3 Ma	**5:20**	But, he added
2 Es	**7:52**	will you add to them lead and clay ?

ADDAN 　　　　　　　　　　　　　　　　　1

1 Es	**5:36**	under the leadership of Cherub, Addan, and Immer

ADDI 　　　　　　　　　　　　　　　　　　1

1 Es	**9:31**	Of the sons of Addi : Naathus and Moossias, Laccunus

ADDITION 　　　　　　　　　　　　　9 = 0.006 %

Tob	**2:14**	as a gift in addition to my wages
1 Ma	**8:30**	and any addition or deletion that they may make shall be valid
2 Ma	**4:9**	In addition to this he promised to pay 150 more
	9:17	and in addition to all this he also would become a Jew
	12:2	and in addition to these Nicanor the governor of Cyprus
3 Ma	**1:22**	In addition, the bolder of the citizens
	4:10	and in addition they were confined under a solid deck
2 Es	**2:5**	as a witness in addition to the mother of the children
4 Ma	**1:2**	and in addition it includes the praise of the highest virtue

ADDITIONAL 　　　　　　　　　　　　　　2

1 Ma	**10:41**	And all the additional funds
1 Es	**4:52**	and an additional 10 talents a year

ADDRESS 　　　　　　　　　　　　　4 = 0.003 %

Wis	**13:17**	he is not ashamed to address a lifeless thing
1 Ma	**14:40**	For he had heard that the Jews were addressed by the Romans
2 Ma	**15:15**	and as he gave it he addressed him thus :
4 Ma	**5:15**	he began to address the people as follows :

ADDUS 　　　　　　　　　　　　　　　　　1

1 Es	**5:34**	the sons of Addus, the sons of Subas, the sons of Apherra

ADHERE 　　　　　　　　　　　　　　　　1

1 Ma	**1:57**	or if any one adhered to the law

ADIDA 　　　　　　　　　　　　　　　　　2

1 Ma	**12:38**	And Simon built Adida in the Shephelah
	13:13	And Simon encamped in Adida, facing the plain

ADIN   2
  1 Es 5:14 The sons of Adin, 454
        8:32 Of the sons of Adin, Obed the son of Jonathan

ADJOIN   2
  Sus 13:4 and had a spacious garden adjoining his house
  1 Ma 10:39 Ptolemais and the land adjoining it

ADJOINING   1
  2 Ma 12:16 so that the adjoining lake, a quarter of a mile wide

ADMINISTRATION   4 = 0.003 %
  Tob 1:21 and over the entire administration
        1:22 and in charge of administration of the accounts
  Ad E 16:5 with the administration of public affairs
  2 Ma 3:4 about the administration of the city market

ADMINISTRATOR   1
  4 Ma 7:8 Such should be those who are administrators of the law

ADMIRABLE   1
  2 Ma 7:20 The mother was especially admirable

ADMIRATION   1
  4 Ma 6:13 partly out of admiration for his endurance

ADMIRE   10 = 0.007 %
  Jud 10:7 they greatly admired her beauty, and said to her
       10:19 and admired the Israelites, judging them by her
  Wis 8:11 and in the sight of rulers I shall be admired
  Sir 22:23 nor admire a rich man who is stupid
       27:23 and he admires your words
       38:3 and in the presence of great men he is admired
  2 Ma 4:16 and those whose ways of living they admired
  4 Ma 8:5 Young men, I admire each and every one of you in a kindly
              manner
       17:16 Who did not admire the athletes of the divine legislation ?
       18:3 were not only admired by men

ADMIT   4 = 0.003 %
  Jud 13:13 they opened the gate and admitted them
  L Jr 6:56 Why then must any one admit or think that they are gods ?
  3 Ma 7:12 The king then, admitting and approving the truth of what they
              said
  4 Ma 16:1 it must be admitted that devout reason

ADMITTEDLY   1
  4 Ma 6:31 Admittedly, then, devout reason is sovereign over the emotions

ADMONISH   2
  Jud 8:27 in order to admonish them
  2 Es 7:49 and I will instruct you, and will admonish you yet again

ADONIKAM   2
  1 Es 5:14 The sons of Adonikam, 667
        8:39 Of the sons of Adonikam, the last ones

ADOPT   5 = 0.003 %
  1 Ma 1:43 Many even from Israel gladly adopted his religion
  2 Ma 6:8 that they should adopt the same policy toward the Jews
  4 Ma 2:8 Thus, as soon as a man adopts
        5:11 adopt a mind appropriate to your years
        8:8 And enjoy your youth by adopting the Greek way of life

ADOPTION   1
  2 Ma 4:13 and increase in the adoption of foreign ways

ADORA   1.
  1 Ma 13:20 and he circled around by the way to Adora

ADORE   1
  2 Es 7:78 first of all it adores the glory of the Most High

ADORN   10 = 0.007 %
  Ad E 14:2 and every part that she loved to adorn
       15:2 Then, majestically adorned
  Sir 45:12 the delight of the eyes, richly adorned
       48:11 and those who have been adorned in love
       50:9 adorned with all kinds of precious stones
  2 Ma 9:16 he would adorn with the finest offerings
  3 Ma 3:5 but since they adorned their style of life
        6:1 and throughout his life had been adorned with every virtue
  2 Es 16:47 the more they adorn their cities
  4 Ma 6:2 who remained adorned with the gracefulness of his piety

ADORNMENT   3 = 0.002 %
  1 Ma 2:11 All her adornment has been taken away
  2 Ma 2:2 upon seeing the gold and silver statues and their adornment
        2:29 has to consider only what is suitable for its adornment

ADUEL   1
  Tob 1:1 son of Ananiel, son of Aduel, son of Gabael

ADULLAM   1
  2 Ma 12:38 and went to the city of Adullam

ADULTERER   1
  Wis 3:16 But children of adulterers will not come to maturity

ADULTEROUS   1
  Sir 25:2 and an adulterous old man who lacks good sense

ADULTERY   3 = 0.002 %
  Wis 14:24 or grieve one another by adultery
       14:26 disorder in marriage, adultery, and debauchery
  Sir 23:23 and third, she has committed adultery through harlotry

ADVANCE, verb   10 = 0.007 %
  Sir 20:27 He who speaks wisely will advance himself
  1 Ma 1:3 He advanced to the ends of the earth
        6:40 and they advanced steadily and in good order
        6:42 But Judas and his army advanced to the battle
        9:12 the phalanx advanced to the sound of the trumpets
       10:77 At the same time he advanced into the plain
  2 Ma 10:27 and advanced a considerable distance from the city
       11:10 They advanced in battle order, having their heavenly ally
       13:19 He advanced against Beth-zur
       15:25 Nicanor and his men advanced with trumpets and battle songs

ADVANCE, subst.   3 = 0.002 %
  Jud 2:10 You shall go and seize all their territory for me in advance
        9:6 for all thy ways are prepared in advance
  Wis 19:1 for God knew in advance even their future actions

ADVANCED   5 = 0.003 %
  2 Ma 4:40 a man advanced in years and no less advanced in folly
        6:18 a man now advanced in age and of noble presence
  4 Ma 5:4 advanced in age, and known to many in the tyrant's court
       16:1 If, then, a woman, advanced in years and mother of 7 sons

ADVANTAGE   7 = 0.005 %
  Jud 5:11 he took advantage of them and set them to making bricks
  Sir 20:30 what advantage is there in either of them ?
       37:22 A man may be wise to his own advantage
       41:14 what advantage is there in either of them ?
  Bar 4:3 or your advantages to an alien people
  3 Ma 6:24 by secretly devising acts of no advantage to the kingdom
  4 Ma 1:17 and human affairs to our advantage

ADVANTAGEOUS   1
  2 Ma 8:7 He found the nights most advantageous for such attacks

ADVERSARY   10 = 0.007 %
  Wis 2:18 and will deliver him from the hand of his adversaries
  Sir 21:27 When an ungodly man curses his adversary
       23:3 then I will not fall before my adversaries
       36:7 destroy the adversary and wipe out the enemy
       47:7 and annihilated his adversaries the Philistines
  1 Ma 1:36 an evil adversary of Israel continually
  2 Ma 10:26 and an adversary to their adversaries
       15:16 with which you will strike down your adversaries
  1 Es 8:51 to keep us safe from our adversaries

ADVERSITY   6 = 0.004 %
  Sir 11:25 In the day of prosperity, adversity is forgotten
       11:25 and in the day of adversity, prosperity is not remembered
       12:8 nor will an enemy be hidden in adversity
       12:9 and in his adversity even his friend will separate from him
       20:9 There may be good fortune for a man in adversity
  2 Es 15:56 and will hand you over to adversities

ADVICE   2
  Tob 4:18 Seek advice from every wise man
  4 Ma 5:12 by honouring my humane advice ?

ADVISE   4 = 0.003 %
  2 Ma 7:25 and urged her to advise the youth to save himself
  4 Ma 1:1 to advise you to pay earnest attention to philosophy
        5:6 I would advise you to save yourself by eating pork
        8:5 Not only do I advise you not to display the same madness

ADVISER   1
  Sir 6:6 but let your advisers be one in a 1,000

ADVOCATE, subst.   2
  Wis 12:12 to plead as an advocate for unrighteous men ?
  4 Ma 15:25 she saw mighty advocates

AESORA   1
Jud   **4** :4   and to Choba and Aesora and the valley of Salem

AFAR   6 = 0.004 %
Tob **13** :11   Many nations will come from afar to the name of the Lord God
Jud **13** :11   Judith called out from afar to the watchmen at the gates
Sir **21** :7   He who is mighty in speech is known from afar
    24 :32   and I will make it shine afar
Bar   **4** :15   For he brought against them a nation from afar
1 Es   **5** :65   so that the sound was heard afar

AFFAIR   19 = 0.012 %
Jud **12** :11   the eunuch who had charge of all his personal affairs
    14 :13   in charge of all his personal affairs
Ad E **13** :6   who is in charge of affairs and is our 2nd father
    16 :5   with the administration of public affairs
1 Ma   **3** :32   in charge of the king's affairs
    6 :57   and the affairs of the kingdom press urgently upon us
2 Ma   **3** :7   The king chose Heliodorus, who was in charge of his affairs
    4 :6   public affairs could not again reach a peaceful settlement
    4 :30   While such was the state of affairs
    7 :24   and entrust him with public affairs
    8 :20   when 8,000 in all went into the affair, with 4,000 Macedonians
    9 :20   and your affairs are as you wish
    11 :23   in caring for their own affairs
    11 :26   and go on happily in the conduct of their own affairs
    11 :29   and look after your own affairs
1 Es   **4** :11   and no one may go away to attend to his own affairs
3 Ma   **3** :21   and the myriad affairs liberally entrusted to them from the beginning
    7 :2   the great God guiding our affairs according to our desire
4 Ma   **1** :17   and human affairs to our advantage

AFFECT   1
2 Es   **8** :50   For many miseries will affect those

AFFECTION   8 = 0.005 %
Sir **11** :15   affection and the ways of good works come from him
2 Ma   **9** :21   I remember with affection your esteem and good will
3 Ma   **5** :32   were it not for an affection
4 Ma   **2** :10   For the law prevails even over affection for parents
    13 :19   You are not ignorant of the affection of brotherhood
    13 :23   Therefore, when sympathy and brotherly affection had been so established
    13 :27   had augmented the affection of the brotherhood
    15 :13   O sacred nature and affection of parental love

AFFLICT   21 = 0.014 %
Tob **11** :15   For thou hast afflicted me, but thou hast had mercy upon me
    13 :2   For he afflicts, and he shows mercy
    13 :5   He will afflict us for our iniquities
    13 :9   he will afflict you for the deeds of your sons
Jud   **5** :12   and he afflicted the whole land of Egypt
Wis   **5** :1   in the presence of those who have afflicted him
    19 :16   afflicted with terrible sufferings
Sir   **3** :26   A stubborn mind will be afflicted at the end
    30 :14   than a rich man who is severely afflicted in body
    30 :19   So is he who is afflicted by the Lord
    30 :21   and do not afflict yourself deliberately
    31 :31   and do not afflict him by making demands of him
    35 :20   Mercy is as welcome when he afflicts them
    49 :7   For they had afflicted him
    49 :7   to pluck up and afflict and destroy
Bar   **4** :31   Wretched will be those who afflicted you and rejoiced at your fall
2 Ma   **1** :28   Afflict those who oppress and are insolent with pride
    5 :22   And he left governors to afflict the people : at Jerusalem
2 Es   **9** :41   for I am greatly embittered in spirit and deeply afflicted
    11 :42   for you have afflicted the meek and injured the peaceable
4 Ma **17** :22   that previously had been afflicted

AFFLICTED   1
Sir   **4** :4   Do not reject an afflicted suppliant

AFFLICTION   23 = 0.015 %
Tob **13** :14   Blessed are those who grieved over all your afflictions
Jud   **4** :13   and looked upon their affliction
Ad E **11** :8   affliction and great tumult upon the earth !
    14 :12   make thyself known in this time of our affliction
    16 :20   against those who attack them at the time of their affliction
Wis   **3** :2   and their departure was thought to be an affliction
Sir   **2** :11   he forgives sins and saves in time of affliction
    3 :15   in the day of your affliction
    3 :28   The affliction of the proud has no healing
    10 :13   extraordinary afflictions
    22 :23   stand by him in time of affliction
    29 :12   and it will rescue you from all affliction
    40 :9   calamities, famine and affliction and plague
    51 :3   from the many afflictions that I endured
    51 :10   not to forsake me in the days of affliction

Bar   **5** :1   Take off the garment of your sorrow and affliction, O Jerusalem
1 Ma **12** :13   many afflictions and many wars have encircled us
2 Ma   **7** :37   and by afflictions and plagues
2 Es   **8** :27   but the endeavours of those who have kept thy covenants amid afflictions
    10 :7   is in deep grief and great affliction
    15 :59   you shall come and suffer fresh afflictions
4 Ma   **6** :24   in the face of the afflictions
    18 :15   Many are the afflictions of the righteous

AFFORD   2
Sir **38** :11   and pour oil on your offering, as much as you can afford
2 Es   **9** :26   and the nourishment they afforded satisfied me

AFLAME   1
2 Ma **14** :45   Still alive and aflame with anger, he rose

AFOREMENTIONED   2
3 Ma   **5** :47   the grievous and pitiful destruction of the aforementioned people
    6 :35   But the Jews, when they had arranged the aforementioned choral group

AFORESAID   5 = 0.003 %
2 Ma   **3** :7   to effect the removal of the aforesaid money
    3 :28   this man who had just entered the aforesaid treasury
3 Ma   **1** :26   determined to bring the aforesaid plan to a conclusion
    6 :36   they instituted the observance of the aforesaid days as a festival
2 Es   **7** :99   and the aforesaid are the ways of torment

AFRAID   31 = 0.020 %
Tob   **2** :8   He is no longer afraid
    4 :8   if few, do not be afraid to give
    4 :21   Do not be afraid, my son, because we have become poor
    6 :14   and I am afraid that if I go in
    6 :17   Do not be afraid, for she was destined for you from eternity
    12 :16   and they fell upon their faces, for they were afraid
    12 :17   But he said to them, Do not be afraid
Jud   **1** :11   for they were not afraid of him
    5 :23   For, they said, we will not be afraid of the Israelites
    10 :16   do not be afraid in your heart
    11 :1   Take courage, woman, and do not be afraid in your heart
Wis   **8** :15   dread monarchs will be afraid of me when they hear of me
Sir **22** :16   will not be afraid in a crisis
    26 :5   Of 3 things my heart is afraid
    29 :7   they have been afraid of being defrauded needlessly
1 Ma   **3** :22   as for you, do not be afraid of them
    4 :8   Do not fear their numbers or be afraid when they charge
    7 :30   and he was afraid of him and would not meet him again
    10 :76   and the men of the city became afraid and opened the gates
    12 :28   they were afraid and were terrified at heart
    12 :42   he was afraid to raise his hand against him
    14 :12   and there was none to make them afraid
    16 :6   And he saw that the soldiers were afraid to cross the stream
2 Es   **6** :33   Believe and do not be afraid !
    10 :27   Then I was afraid, and cried with a loud voice and said
    10 :55   Therefore do not be afraid
    13 :8   were much afraid, yet dared to fight
    15 :18   and people shall be afraid
    16 :10   He will flash lightning, and who will not be afraid ?
4 Ma   **8** :14   Be afraid, young fellows
    8 :15   not only were they not afraid

AFTER*   161 = 0.105 %
Tob   **8** :19   After this he gave a wedding feast for them
    11 :1   After this Tobias went on his way
    14 :2   and after 8 years he regained it
    14 :5   After this they will return
Jud   **4** :3   had been consecrated after their profanation
    8 :9   to surrender the city to the Assyrians after 5 days
    8 :33   and within the days after which you have promised
    13 :9   after a moment she went out
    16 :21   After this every one returned home to his own inheritance
    16 :22   after Manasseh her husband died
    16 :25   in the days of Judith, or for a long time after her death
Ad E **11** :12   and after he awoke he had it on his mind
    15 :2   after invoking the aid of the all-seeing God and Saviour
Wis   **4** :18   After this they will become dishonoured corpses
    8 :13   to those who come after me
    15 :8   and after a little while goes to the earth
    16 :3   while thy people, after suffering want a short time
    19 :8   after gazing on marvellous wonders
    19 :16   but the latter, after receiving them with festal celebrations
Sir pr.   my grandfather Jesus, after devoting himself
    pr.   and after acquiring considerable proficiency in them
    7 :22   Do you have cattle ? Look after them
    16 :29   After this the Lord looked upon the earth
    23 :20   so it was also after it was finished
    27 :17   but if you betray his secrets, do not run after him
    27 :20   Do not go after him, for he is too far off
    27 :21   and there is reconciliation after abuse

31 : 8	and who does not go after gold
33 : 16	I was like one who gleans after the grape-gatherers
34 : 25	If a man washes after touching a dead body
39 : 17	For in God's time all things will be sought after
41 : 22	do not upbraid after making a gift
44 : 9	and so have their children after them
46 : 20	Even after he had fallen asleep
47 : 1	And after him Nathan rose up
47 : 12	After him rose up a wise son who fared amply because of him
Bar **1** : 9	after Nebuchadnezzar king of Babylon had carried away from Jerusalem
L Jr **6** : 3	after that I will bring you away from there in peace
6 : 47	They have left only lies and reproach for those who come after
Sus **13** : 12	And they watched eagerly, day after day, to see her
1 Ma **1** : 1	After Alexander son of Philip, the Macedonian
1 : 5	After this he fell sick and perceived that he was dying
1 : 7	And after Alexander had reigned 12 years, he died
1 : 9	They all put on crowns after his death
1 : 9	and so did their sons after them for many years
1 : 20	After subduing Egypt, Antiochus returned in the 143rd year
1 : 58	against those found month after month in the cities
3 : 55	After this Judas appointed leaders of the people
5 : 37	After these things Timothy gathered another army
7 : 33	After these events Nicanor went up to Mount Zion
8 : 7	and decreed that he and those who should reign after him
8 : 30	If after these terms are in effect
9 : 23	After the death of Judas
9 : 37	After these things it was reported to Jonathan
10 : 34	and the 3 days before a feast and the 3 after a feast
11 : 54	After this Trypho returned
13 : 20	After this Trypho came to invade the country and destroy it
14 : 24	After this Simon sent Numenius to Rome
16 : 6	and when his men saw him, they crossed over after him
16 : 24	from the time that he became high priest after his father
2 Ma **1** : 7	after Jason and his company revolted from the holy land and the kingdom
1 : 20	But after many years had passed, when it pleased God
2 : 2	and that the prophet after giving them the law
4 : 14	in the wrestling arena after the call to the discus
4 : 23	After a period of 3 years Jason sent Menelaus
4 : 25	After receiving the king's orders he returned
4 : 26	So Jason, who after supplanting his own brother
6 : 1	Not long after this, the king sent an Athenian senator
7 : 7	After the first brother had died in this way
7 : 10	After him, the 3rd was the victim of their sport
7 : 18	After him they brought forward the 6th
7 : 26	After much urging on his part
7 : 36	For our brothers after enduring a brief suffering
7 : 41	Last of all, the mother died, after her sons
8 : 25	After pursuing them for some distance
8 : 28	After the sabbath they gave some of the spoils
10 : 3	after a lapse of 2 years
10 : 16	after making solemn supplications
11 : 1	Very soon after this
11 : 29	and look after your own affairs
12 : 11	After a hard fight Judas and his men won the victory
12 : 12	and after receiving his pledges they departed to their tents
12 : 20	and hastened after Timothy
12 : 27	After the rout and destruction of these
12 : 32	After the feast called Pentecost
13 : 13	After consulting privately with the elders
1 Es **1** : 25	After all these acts of Josiah
1 : 31	and after he was brought back to Jerusalem he died
1 : 45	So after a year Nebuchadnezzar sent
5 : 1	After this the heads of fathers' houses were chosen to go up
5 : 56	In the 2nd year after their coming to the temple of God in Jerusalem
5 : 57	in the 2nd year after they came to Judea and Jerusalem
6 : 20	Then this Shesh-Bazzar, after coming here
7 : 10	the priests and the Levites were purified together
8 : 1	After these things
8 : 68	After these things had been done
3 Ma **1** : 9	After he had arrived in Jerusalem
1 : 12	Even after the law had been read to him
2 : 24	After a while he recovered and, though he had been punished
4 : 15	and though uncompleted it stopped after 40 days
4 : 17	But after the previously mentioned interval of time
4 : 19	After he had threatened them severely
5 : 16	The king, after considering this, returned to his drinking
5 : 18	After the party had been going on for some time
5 : 37	After summoning Hermon he said in a threatening tone
6 : 33	Likewise also the king, after convening a great banquet
7 : 20	Then, after inscribing them as holy on a pillar
2 Es **3** : 1	In the 30th year after the destruction of our city
3 : 8	And every nation walked after his own will
4 : 49	And after this a cloud full of water passed before me
5 : 4	you shall see it thrown into confusion after the 3rd period
5 : 21	And after 7 days
5 : 41	or we, or those who come after us ?
5 : 46	why one after another ?

5 : 55	and those who come after you will be smaller than you
6 : 25	after all that I have foretold to you
6 : 35	Now after this I wept again and fasted 7 days as before
7 : 29	And after these years my son the Messiah shall die
7 : 31	And after 7 days the world
7 : 66	promised to them after death
7 : 69	And if we were not to come into judgment after death
7 : 75	show this also to thy servant : whether after death
7 : 100	after they have been separated from the bodies
7 : 107	and Joshua after him for Israel in the days of Achan
7 : 117	and expect punishment after death ?
7 : 126	we did not consider what we should suffer after death
7 : 130	But they did not believe him, or the prophets after him
9 : 12	these must in torment acknowledge it after death
9 : 27	And after 7 days, as I lay on the grass
9 : 45	And after 30 years God heard your handmaid
10 : 46	And after 3,000 years Solomon built the city
11 : 17	After you no one shall rule as long as you
11 : 19	they wielded power one after another
11 : 22	And after this I looked, and behold
11 : 33	And after this I looked, and behold
12 : 14	And 12 kings shall reign in it, one after another
12 : 49	and after these days I will come to you
13 : 1	After 7 days I dreamed a dream in the night
13 : 5	After this I looked, and behold
13 : 8	After this I looked, and behold
13 : 12	After this I saw the same man come down from the mountain
13 : 56	And after 3 more days I will tell you other things
14 : 30	which you also have transgressed after them
14 : 34	and after death you shall obtain mercy
14 : 35	For after death the judgment will come
15 : 38	And, after that, heavy storm clouds shall be stirred up from the south
15 : 47	who have always lusted after you
4 Ma **1** : 23	Fear precedes pain and sorrow comes after
4 : 23	and after he had plundered them he issued a decree
6 : 3	And after they had tied his arms on each side they scourged him
6 : 8	to make him get up again after he fell
6 : 30	And after he said this
8 : 2	and that any who ate defiling food should be freed after eating
9 : 26	and after fitting themselves with iron gauntlets having sharp hooks
11 : 1	When this one died also, after being cruelly tortured
11 : 13	After he too had died, the 6th, a mere boy, was led in
12 : 19	After he had uttered these imprecations
13 : 21	When they were born after an equal time of gestation
16 : 6	After bearing 7 children, I am now the mother of none !
17 : 5	who, after lighting the way of your star-like 7 sons to piety
18 : 5	and is being chastised after his death

AFTERNOON
		1
1 Ma **10** : 80	from early morning till late afternoon

AFTERWARD
		13 = 0.008 %
Wis **5** : 11	and afterward no sign of its coming is found there
14 : 22	Afterward it was not enough for them
19 : 11	Afterward they saw also a new kind of birds
Sir **17** : 23	Afterward he will arise and requite them
40 : 6	and afterward in his sleep, as though he were on watch
Bar **3** : 37	Afterward she appeared upon earth and lived among men
L Jr **6** : 50	it will afterward be known that they are false
1 Ma **4** : 18	and afterward seize the plunder boldly
2 Ma **5** : 20	and afterward participated in its benefits
6 : 15	in order that he may not take vengeance on us afterward
1 Es **1** : 13	Afterward they prepared the passover for themselves
3 Ma **2** : 5	to those who should come afterward
2 Es **10** : 56	and afterward you will hear as much as your ears can hear

AFTERWARDS
		3 = 0.002 %
Sir **13** : 7	Should he see you afterwards, he will forsake you
2 Es **7** : 101	and afterwards they shall be gathered in their habitations
8 : 11	and afterwards thou wilt guide him in thy mercy

AGAIN
		83 = 0.054 %
Tob **2** : 8	he once ran away, and here he is burying the dead again !
6 : 7	and that person will never be troubled again
6 : 17	and will never again return
10 : 7	of ever seeing me again
13 : 2	he leads down to Hades, and brings up again
13 : 5	and again he will show mercy
13 : 9	but again he will show mercy to the sons of the righteous
13 : 10	that his tent may be raised for you again with joy
14 : 5	But God will again have mercy on them
Jud **6** : 5	you shall not see my face again from this day
16 : 25	And no one ever again spread terror
Wis **10** : 4	wisdom again saved it
13 : 8	Yet again, not even they are to be excused
14 : 1	Again, one preparing to sail
16 : 13	thou dost lead men down to the gates of Hades and back again
Sir **17** : 1	and turned him back to it again

	19:14	but if he said it, so that he may not say it again
	24:32	I will again make instruction shine forth like the dawn
	24:33	I will again pour out teaching like prophecy
	27:19	and will not catch him again
	33:1	but in trial he will deliver him again and again
	34:25	and touches it again
	34:26	and goes again and does the same things
	46:12	live again in their sons !
Bar	2:34	I will bring them again into the land
	2:35	and I will never again remove my people Israel
Sus	13:14	But turning back, they met again
1 Ma	3:15	And again a strong army of ungodly men
	4:35	to invade Judea again by him with an even larger army
	7:30	and he was afraid of him and would not meet him again
	8:32	If now they appeal again for help against you
2 Ma	2:7	until God gathers his people together again
	3:33	the same young men appeared again to Heliodorus
	4:6	public affairs could not again reach a peaceful settlement
	5:7	and fled again into the country of the Ammonites
	5:20	was restored again in all its glory
	7:11	and from him I hope to get them back again
	7:14	of being raised again by him
	7:23	will in his mercy give life and breath back to you again
	7:29	I may get you back again with your brothers
	7:33	he will again be reconciled with his own servants
	10:4	that they might never again fall into such misfortunes
	12:7	he withdrew, intending to come again
	12:44	that those who had fallen would rise again
	13:19	was turned back, attacked again, and was defeated
	14:3	to be safe or to have access again to the holy altar
	14:46	to give them back to him again
	15:39	or, again, to drink water alone
1 Es	6:18	these Cyrus the king took out again
	8:53	And again we prayed to our Lord about these things
	8:87	but we turned back again to transgress thy law
3 Ma	5:13	and again begged him who is easily reconciled
	5:25	implored the supreme God to help them again at once
	5:40	and again revoking your decree in the matter ?
2 Es	2:40	Take again your full number, O Zion
	3:9	But again, in its time
	3:12	and again they began to be more ungodly than were their ancestors
	5:13	and if you pray again, and weep as you do now
	5:21	the thoughts of my heart were very grievous to me again
	5:36	and make the withered flowers bloom again for me
	6:31	If therefore you will pray again and fast again for 7 days
	6:31	I will again declare to you greater things than these
	6:35	Now after this I wept again and fasted 7 days as before
	6:36	And on the 8th night my heart was troubled within me again
	6:41	Again, on the 2nd day
	7:1	was sent to me again
	7:49	and I will instruct you, and will admonish you yet again
	7:78	as the spirit leaves the body to return again to him who gave it
	8:9	And when the womb gives up again what has been created in it
	9:15	I said before, and I say now, and will say it again :
	9:27	my heart was troubled again as it was before
	10:19	So I spoke again to her, and said
	10:24	so that the Mighty One may be merciful to you again
	11:19	and then were never seen again
	13:46	and now, when they are about to come again
	13:47	the Most High will stop the channels of the river again
	14:35	when we shall live again
	16:67	never to commit them again
4 Ma	6:8	to make him get up again after he fell
	7:13	his muscles flabby, his sinews feeble, he became young again
	18:20	and back again to more tortures

AGAINST

278 = 0.181 %

Tob	4:9	against the day of necessity
Jud	1:5	against King Arphaxad in the great plain
	1:13	In the 17th year he led his forces against King Arphaxad
	2:7	for I am coming against them in my anger
	5:17	As long as they did not sin against their God they prospered
	5:20	and they sin against their God and we find out their offence
	6:2	and tell us not to make war against the people of Israel
	6:17	against the house of Israel
	7:1	to break camp and move against Bethulia
	7:11	Therefore, my lord, do not fight against them in battle array
	7:28	We call to witness against you heaven and earth
	8:9	spoken by the people against the ruler
	9:13	for they have planned cruel things against thy covenant
	9:13	and against the top of Zion
	9:13	and against the house possessed by thy children
	11:2	I would never have lifted my spear against them
	11:10	nor can the sword prevail against them
	11:10	unless they sin against their God
	13:5	who have risen up against us
	13:11	and his strength against our enemies
	14:2	against the Assyrian outpost
	14:13	as to come down against us and to give battle

	16:17	Woe to the nations that rise up against my people !
Ad E	11:7	to fight against the nation of the righteous
	14:11	but turn their plan against themselves
	14:11	and make an example of the man who began this against us
	14:13	and turn his heart to hate the man who is fighting against us
	16:3	they even undertake to scheme against their own benefactors
	16:20	against those who attack them at the time of their affliction
	16:23	but that for those who plot against us
Wis	2:12	he reproaches us for sins against the law
	2:12	and accuses us of sins against our training
	3:10	and rebelled against the Lord
	3:14	and who has not devised wicked things against the Lord
	4:6	against their parents when God examines them
	5:20	and creation will join with him to fight against the madmen
	5:22	the water of the sea will rage against them
	5:23	a mighty wind will rise against them
	7:30	but against wisdom evil does not prevail
	16:18	sent against the ungodly
Sir	3:14	and against your sins it will be credited to you
	4:25	Never speak against the truth
	6:12	but if you are brought low he will turn against you
	7:7	Do not offend against the public
	7:12	Do not devise a lie against your brother
	8:11	lest he lie in ambush against your words
	8:14	Do not go to law against a judge
	10:29	Who will justify the man that sins against himself ?
	12:11	watch yourself, and be on your guard against him
	13:2	The pot will strike against it, and will itself be broken
	18:27	in days of sin he guards against wrongdoing
	22:18	will not stand firm against the wind
	22:18	will not stand firm against any fear
	22:21	Even if you have drawn your sword against a friend
	22:22	If you have opened your mouth against your friend
	23:23	second, she has committed an offence against her husband
	26:11	Be on guard against her impudent eye
	26:11	and do not wonder if she sins against you
	28:3	Does a man harbour anger against another
	28:23	It will be sent out against them like a lion
	29:13	it will fight on your behalf against your enemy
	30:6	he has left behind him an avenger against his enemies
	34:3	The vision of dreams is this against that
	34:16	a guard against stumbling and a defence against falling
	35:15	as she cries out against him who has caused them to fall ?
	36:3	Lift up thy hand against foreign nations
	37:4	but in time of trouble are against him
	37:8	lest he cast the lot against you
	40:29	but a man who is intelligent and well instructed guards against that
	45:18	Outsiders conspired against him
	45:19	he wrought wonders against them
	46:1	to take vengeance on the enemies that rose against them
	46:2	and stretched out his sword against the cities !
	48:18	he lifted up his hand against Zion
	51:10	at the time when there is no help against the proud
Bar	1:13	for we have sinned against the Lord our God
	2:1	which he spoke against us
	2:1	and against our judges who judged Israel
	2:1	and against our kings and against our princes
	2:1	and against the men of Israel and Judah
	2:5	because we sinned against the Lord our God
	2:12	O Lord our God, against all thy ordinances
	4:15	For he brought against them a nation from afar
Sus	13:21	If you refuse, we will testify against you
	13:24	and the 2 elders shouted against her
	13:43	thou knowest that these men have borne false witness against me
	13:43	that they have wickedly invented against me !
	13:49	For these men have borne false witness against her
	13:55	You have lied against your own head
	13:59	You also have lied against your own head
	13:61	And they rose against the 2 elders
Bel	14:9	because he blasphemed against Bel
	14:28	they were very indignant and conspired against the king
1 Ma	1:20	He went up against Israel
	1:36	It became an ambush against the sanctuary
	1:58	They kept using violence against Israel
	1:58	against those found month after month in the cities
	2:26	as Phinehas did against Zimri the son of Salu
	2:32	against them on the sabbath day
	2:41	Let us fight against every man who comes to attack us on the sabbath day
	2:66	and fight the battle against the peoples
	3:10	and a large force from Samaria to fight against Israel
	3:17	fight against so great and strong a multitude ?
	3:20	They come against us in great pride and lawlessness
	3:23	he rushed suddenly against Seron and his army
	3:35	Lysias was to send a force against them
	3:52	And behold, the Gentiles are assembled against us to destroy us
	3:52	thou knowest what they plot against us
	3:58	who have assembled against us to destroy us and our sanctuary
	4:12	and saw them coming against them

	4 : 18	But stand now against our enemies and fight them
	4 : 41	to fight against those in the citadel
	5 : 5	and he encamped against them, vowed their complete destruction
	5 : 9	against the Israelites who lived in their territory
	5 : 10	The Gentiles around us have gathered together against us
	5 : 15	they said that against them had gathered together
	5 : 21	and fought many battles against the Gentiles
	5 : 35	and fought against it and took it
	5 : 39	ready to come and fight against you
	5 : 43	Then he crossed over against them first
	5 : 50	and he fought against the city
	5 : 58	and they marched against Jamnia
	6 : 25	And not against us alone have they stretched out their hands
	6 : 25	but also against all the lands on their borders
	6 : 26	against the citadel in Jerusalem to take it
	6 : 31	They came through Idumea and encamped against Beth-zur
	6 : 48	went up to Jerusalem against them
	6 : 57	the place against which we are fighting is strong
	6 : 63	but he fought against him, and took the city by force
	7 : 6	against the people :
	7 : 25	and brought wicked charges against them
	7 : 42	against thy sanctuary
	8 : 4	They also subdued the kings who came against them
	8 : 5	and the others who rose up against them
	8 : 6	who went to fight against them with a 120 elephants
	8 : 10	and they sent a general against the Greeks and attacked them
	8 : 32	If now they appeal again for help against you
	9 : 2	and encamped against Mesaloth in Arbela
	9 : 3	they encamped against Jerusalem
	9 : 8	Let us rise and go up against our enemies
	9 : 29	to go against our enemies and Bacchides
	9 : 64	Then he came and encamped against Beth-basi
	9 : 64	he fought against it for many days and made machines of war
	10 : 4	before he makes peace with Alexander against us
	10 : 61	lawless men, gathered together against him to accuse him
	10 : 63	and proclaim that no one is to bring charges against him
	10 : 69	and he assembled a large force and encamped against Jamnia
	10 : 70	You are the only one to rise up against us
	10 : 70	Why do you assume authority against us in the hill country ?
	10 : 76	So they fought against it
	10 : 86	and encamped against Askalon
	11 : 8	and he kept devising evil designs against Alexander
	11 : 15	And Alexander heard of it and came against him in battle
	11 : 20	and he built many engines of war to use against it
	11 : 25	kept making complaints against him
	11 : 39	He saw that all the troops were murmuring against Demetrius
	11 : 41	for they kept fighting against Israel
	11 : 50	and make the Jews stop fighting against us and our city
	11 : 55	gathered around him, and they fought against Demetrius
	11 : 65	and fought against it for many days and hemmed it in
	11 : 68	they had set an ambush against him in the mountains
	11 : 72	Then he turned back to the battle against the enemy
	12 : 13	the kings round about us have waged war against us
	12 : 24	with a larger force than before, to wage war against him
	12 : 31	So Jonathan turned aside against the Arabs
	12 : 39	and to raise his hand against Antiochus the king
	12 : 42	he was afraid to raise his hand against him
	13 : 16	so that when released he will not revolt against us
	13 : 43	In those days Simon encamped against Gazara
	13 : 47	and stopped fighting against them
	14 : 1	so that he could make war against Trypho
	15 : 4	against those who have destroyed our country
	15 : 13	So Antiochus encamped against Dor
	15 : 19	or make war against them and their cities and their country
	15 : 19	or make alliance with those who war against them
	15 : 25	continually throwing his forces against it
	15 : 39	He commanded him to encamp against Judea
	16 : 4	and they marched against Cendebaeus
	16 : 6	Then he and his army lined up against them
	16 : 13	and made treacherous plans against Simon and his sons
	16 : 16	and rushed in against Simon in the banquet hall
2 Ma	**1 : 11**	we thank him greatly for taking our side against the king
	1 : 12	For he drove out those who fought against the holy city
	2 : 20	and further the wars against Antiochus Epiphanes
	3 : 38	he replied, If you have any enemy or plotter against your government
	4 : 1	who had informed about the money against his own country
	4 : 2	He dared to designate as a plotter against the government
	4 : 38	where he had committed the outrage against Onias
	4 : 39	the populace gathered against Lysimachus
	4 : 43	Charges were brought against Menelaus about this incident
	4 : 47	he acquitted of the charges against him
	4 : 50	having become the chief plotter against his fellow citizens
	5 : 8	hated as a rebel against the laws
	7 : 6	which bore witness against the people to their faces
	7 : 18	because of our sins against our own God
	7 : 19	for having tried to fight against God !
	7 : 31	against the Hebrews
	7 : 34	when you raise your hand against the children of heaven
	8 : 4	and the blasphemies committed against his name

	8 : 16	who were wickedly coming against them
	8 : 17	which the Gentiles had committed against the holy place
	8 : 18	to strike down those who are coming against us
	9 : 7	breathing fire in his rage against the Jews
	10 : 14	and at every turn kept on warring against the Jews
	10 : 21	by setting their enemies free to fight against them
	10 : 36	wheeled around against the defenders
	11 : 2	and came against the Jews
	11 : 11	They hurled themselves like lions against the enemy
	12 : 10	on their march against Timothy
	12 : 26	Then Judas marched against Carnaim
	12 : 27	he marched also against Ephron
	12 : 32	they hastened against Gorgias, the governor of Idumea
	12 : 37	then he charged against Gorgias' men
	13 : 1	with a great army against Judea
	13 : 4	against the scoundrel
	13 : 8	against the altar whose fire and ashes were holy
	13 : 19	He advanced against Beth-zur
	14 : 26	for he had appointed that conspirator against the kingdom
	15 : 24	who come against thy holy people be struck down
	15 : 32	against the holy house of the Almighty
1 Es	**1 : 24**	so that the words of the Lord rose up against Israel
	1 : 25	and Josiah went out against him
	1 : 27	I was not sent against you by the Lord God
	1 : 29	and the commanders came down against King Josiah
	1 : 40	And Nebuchadnezzar king of Babylon came up against him
	1 : 52	until in his anger against his people
	1 : 52	to bring against them the kings of the Chaldeans
	2 : 16	against those who were living in Judea and Jerusalem :
	2 : 26	that this city from of old has fought against kings
	4 : 4	and if he sends them out against the enemy, they go
	6 : 15	But when our fathers sinned against the Lord of Israel
	8 : 92	and said to Ezra, We have sinned against the Lord
P Ma	**7**	to those who have sinned against thee
	8	who did not sin against thee
3 Ma	**3 : 1**	against those Jews who lived in Alexandria
	3 : 2	a hostile rumour was circulated against the Jewish nation
	3 : 11	wrote this letter against them :
	3 : 24	if a sudden disorder should later arise against us
	4 : 16	and uttering improper words against the supreme God
	5 : 8	that he avert with vengeance the evil plot against them
	5 : 43	and would also march against Judea
	6 : 5	and was lifted up against your holy city
	6 : 6	and turning the flame against all their enemies
	7 : 9	For you should know that if we devise any evil against them
	7 : 10	against the holy people and the law of God
2 Es	**1 : 5**	which they have committed against me
	2 : 28	but they shall not be able to do anything against you
	4 : 14	and said, Come, let us go and make war against the sea
	7 : 22	and spoke against him
	8 : 5	and against your will you depart
	8 : 34	that thou art so bitter against it ?
	11 : 6	and no one spoke against him
	13 : 5	to make war against the man who came up out of the sea
	13 : 8	all who gathered together against him
	13 : 31	And they shall plan to make war against one another
	13 : 31	city against city, place against place
	13 : 31	people against people, and kingdom against kingdom
	13 : 33	and the warfare that they have against one another
	15 : 3	Do not fear the plots against you
	15 : 15	and nation shall rise up to fight against nation
	15 : 16	growing strong against one another
	15 : 26	For the Lord knows all who transgress against him
	15 : 27	because you have sinned against him
	15 : 35	They shall dash against one another
	16 : 70	against those who fear the Lord
4 Ma	**2 : 17**	he did nothing against them in anger
	3 : 21	a revolution against the public harmony
	4 : 22	For when he was warring against Ptolemy in Egypt
	4 : 22	He speedily marched against them
	8 : 24	Let us not struggle against compulsion
	11 : 12	he said, Tyrant, they are splendid favours that you grant us against your will
	14 : 19	defend themselves against intruders
	17 : 3	against the earthquake of the tortures
	18 : 5	he left Jerusalem and marched against the Persians

AGAPE   1

1 Es	**4 : 31**	At this the king would gaze at her with mouth agape

AGE, subst.   59 = 0.038 %

Tob	**3 : 10**	and I shall bring his old age down in sorrow to the grave
	13 : 6	and exalt the King of the ages
	13 : 10	and praise the King of the ages
	14 : 5	until the times of the age are completed
	14 : 14	He died in Ecbatana of Media at the age of a 127 years
Wis	**3 : 17**	and finally their old age will be without honour
	4 : 8	For old age is not honoured for length of time
	4 : 9	and a blameless life is ripe old age
	4 : 16	will condemn the prolonged old age of the unrighteous man

Sir	3 : 12	O son, help your father in his old age
	25 : 3	how then can you find anything in your old age ?
	30 : 24	and anxiety brings on old age too soon
	36 : 17	that thou art the Lord, the God of the ages
	42 : 18	and he looks into the signs of the age
	46 : 9	which remained with him to old age
2 Ma	6 : 18	a man now advanced in age and of noble presence
	6 : 23	worthy of his years and the dignity of his old age
	6 : 25	while I defile and disgrace my old age
	6 : 27	I will show myself worthy of my old age
1 Es	4 : 40	and the power and the majesty of all the ages
	5 : 41	All those of Israel, 12 or more years of age
	5 : 58	who were 20 or more years of age
3 Ma	4 : 5	sluggish and bent with age
	6 : 1	who had attained a ripe old age
2 Es	2 : 34	because he who will come at the end of the age is close at hand
	2 : 36	Flee from the shadow of this age
	2 : 39	Those who have departed from the shadow of this age
	4 : 26	because the age is hastening swiftly to its end
	4 : 27	because this age is full of sadness and infirmities
	4 : 36	for he has weighed the age in the balance
	5 : 50	Or is she now approaching old age ?
	5 : 53	are different from those born during the time of old age
	6 : 7	Or when will be the end of the first age
	6 : 7	and the beginning of the age that follows ?
	6 : 9	For Esau is the end of this age
	6 : 9	and Jacob is the beginning of the age that follows
	6 : 20	and when the seal is placed upon the age
	7 : 113	But the day of judgment will be the end of this age
	7 : 113	and the beginning of the immortal age to come
	7 : 119	if an eternal age has been promised to us
	8 : 52	the age to come is prepared, plenty is provided
	9 : 13	those to whom the age belongs
	9 : 13	and for whose sake the age was made
	9 : 18	For there was a time in this age
	11 : 44	and behold, they are ended, and his ages are completed !
	13 : 26	this is he whom the Most High has been keeping for many ages
	14 : 10	For the age has lost its youth
	14 : 11	For the age is divided into 12 parts
	14 : 17	For the weaker the world becomes through old age
4 Ma	5 : 4	advanced in age, and known to many in the tyrant's court
	5 : 7	for I respect your age and your grey hairs
	5 : 12	and have compassion on your old age
	5 : 33	I do not so pity my old age
	5 : 36	the honourable mouth of my old age
	6 : 12	At that point, partly out of pity for his old age
	6 : 18	who have lived in accordance with truth to old age
	7 : 15	O man of blessed age
	8 : 20	and have compassion on our mother's age
	11 : 14	he said, I am younger in age than my brothers

AGE, verb   2

Sir	9 : 10	when it has aged you will drink it with pleasure
2 Es	5 : 55	as born of a creation which already is aging

AGED, adj., subst.   17 = 0.011 %

Wis	2 : 10	nor regard the grey hairs of the aged
Sir	8 : 9	Do not disregard the discourse of the aged
	25 : 4	and for the aged to possess good counsel !
	25 : 5	How attractive is wisdom in the aged
	25 : 6	Rich experience is the crown of the aged
	25 : 20	A sandy ascent for the feet of the aged
	42 : 8	or the aged man who quarrels with the young
2 Ma	8 : 30	and to the orphans and widows, and also to the aged
4 Ma	7 : 10	O aged man, more powerful than tortures
	7 : 16	an aged man despised tortures even to death
	8 : 2	being unable to compel an aged man to eat defiling foods
	8 : 3	were brought before him along with their aged mother
	9 : 6	And if the aged men of the Hebrews because of their religion
	9 : 6	which our aged instructor also overcame
	16 : 17	while an aged man endures such agonies for the sake of religion
	17 : 9	Here lie buried an aged priest and an aged woman and 7 sons

AGENT   1

2 Ma	4 : 3	by one of Simon's approved agents

AGIA   1

1 Es	5 : 38	the sons of Hakkoz, the sons of Jaddus who had married Agia

AGITATE   3 = 0.002 %

Ad E	15 : 16	And the king was agitated
3 Ma	1 : 17	were agitated and hurried out
2 Es	3 : 3	My spirit was greatly agitated

AGO   4 = 0.003 %

1 Es	6 : 14	And the house was built many years ago
3 Ma	4 : 1	for the inveterate enmity which had long ago been in their minds

2 Es	10 : 41	The woman who appeared to you a little while ago
4 Ma	9 : 5	as though a short time ago you learned nothing from Eleazar

AGONY   15 = 0.010 %

1 Ma	9 : 56	And Alcimus died at that time in great agony
2 Es	5 : 34	for every hour I suffer agonies of heart
	12 : 26	one of the kings shall die in his bed, but in agonies
4 Ma	3 : 18	it can overthrow bodily agonies even when they are extreme
	6 : 7	because his body could not endure the agonies
	6 : 34	when it masters even external agonies
	6 : 35	And I have proved not only that reason has mastered agonies
	8 : 28	and sovereign over agonies
	9 : 28	But he steadfastly endured this agony and said
	13 : 5	in those who were not turned back by fiery agonies ?
	14 : 1	so that they not only despised their agonies
	14 : 9	and in agonies of fire at that
	14 : 11	since the mind of a woman despised even more diverse agonies
	15 : 19	in his tortures gazing boldly at the same agonies
	16 : 17	while an aged man endures such agonies for the sake of religion

AGREE   14 = 0.009 %

Tob	5 : 15	So they agreed to these terms
Ad E	14 : 13	and those who agree with him
Wis	18 : 9	and with one accord agreed to the divine law
1 Ma	6 : 59	and agree to let them live by their laws as they did before
	9 : 71	He agreed, and did as he said
	14 : 46	And all the people agreed to grant Simon
	14 : 47	So Simon accepted and agreed to be high priest
2 Ma	11 : 15	agreed to all that Lysias urged
	11 : 18	and he has agreed to what was possible
	12 : 12	agreed to make peace with them
	14 : 20	they agreed to the covenant
4 Ma	4 : 17	Jason agreed that if the office were conferred upon him
	9 : 16	Agree to eat so that you may be released from the tortures
	14 : 6	agreed to go to death for its sake

AGREEMENT   9 = 0.006 %

Tob	7 : 11	until you make a binding agreement with me
Wis	10 : 5	Wisdom also, when the nations in wicked agreement had been confounded
Sir	25 : 1	agreement between brothers, friendship between neighbours
1 Ma	7 : 18	for they have violated the agreement
	10 : 26	Since you have kept your agreement with us
	13 : 47	So Simon reached an agreement with them
	15 : 27	and he broke all the agreements
2 Ma	12 : 1	When this agreement had been reached
	14 : 28	and grieved that he had to annul their agreement

AHASUERUS   5 = 0.003 %

Tob	14 : 15	which Nebuchadnezzar and Ahasuerus had captured
Ad E	11 : 2	In the 2nd year of the reign of Ahasuerus the Great
	12 : 2	to lay hands upon Ahasuerus the king
	13 : 1	The Great King, Ahasuerus
	16 : 1	The Great King, Ahasuerus

AHEAD, adv., prep.   7 = 0.005 %

Tob	11 : 3	Let us run ahead of your wife and prepare the house
Jud	2 : 19	to go ahead of King Nebuchadnezzar
Sir	12 : 17	If calamity befalls you, you will find him there ahead of you
1 Ma	9 : 11	and the slingers and the archers went ahead of the army
	10 : 23	Alexander has gotten ahead of us
	16 : 21	But some one ran ahead and reported to John at Gazara
2 Ma	8 : 8	and that he was pushing ahead with more frequent successes

AHIJAH   1

2 Es	1 : 2	son of Ahijah, son of Phinehas, son of Eli

AHIKAR   8 = 0.005 %

Tob	1 : 21	and he appointed Ahikar, the son of my brother Anael
	1 : 22	Ahikar interceded for me, and I returned to Nineveh
	1 : 22	Now Ahikar was cupbearer, keeper of the signet
	2 : 10	Ahikar, however, took care of me until he went to Elymais
	11 : 18	Ahikar and his nephew Nadab came
	14 : 10	See, my son, what Nadab did to Ahikar who had reared him
	14 : 10	But Ahikar was saved, and the other received repayment
	14 : 10	Ahikar gave alms and escaped the deathtrap

AHITUB   3 = 0.002 %

Jud	8 : 1	son of Ahitub, son of Elijah, son of Hilkiah
1 Es	8 : 2	son of Zadok, son of Ahitub, son of Amariah, son of Uzzi
2 Es	1 : 1	son of Zadok, son of Ahitub

AID, subst.   9 = 0.006 %

Ad E	15 : 2	after invoking the aid of the all-seeing God and Saviour
Wis	13 : 18	for aid he entreats a thing that is utterly inexperienced
1 Ma	11 : 47	So the king called the Jews to his aid
	12 : 15	for we have the help which comes from Heaven for our aid
2 Ma	3 : 39	watches over that place himself and brings it aid
	8 : 8	for aid to the king's government
3 Ma	5 : 6	that the Jews were left without any aid

.5 : 35 since this also was his aid which they had received
4 Ma 13 : 26 because, with the aid of their religion

AID, verb   4 = 0.003 %
1 Ma 16 : 18 asking him to send troops to aid him
2 Ma 11 : 7 to aid their brethren
3 Ma 1 : 16 and entreated the supreme God to aid in the present situation
4 : 21 of him who was aiding the Jews from heaven

AIM, subst.   1
Wis 5 : 21 Shafts of lightning will fly with true aim

AIM, verb   3 = 0.002 %
Sir 9 : 14 As much as you can, aim to know your neighbours
31 : 25 Do not aim to be valiant over wine
2 Ma 2 : 25 we have aimed to please those who are inclined to memorize

AIR   16 = 0.010 %
Jud 11 : 7 and the cattle and the birds of the air
Wis 2 : 3 and the spirit will dissolve like empty air
5 : 11 or as, when a bird flies through the air
5 : 11 the light air, lashed by the beat of its pinions
5 : 12 the air, thus divided, comes together at once
7 : 3 And when I was born, I began to breathe the common air
13 : 2 but they supposed that either fire or wind or swift air
17 : 10 refusing to look even at the air
Bar 3 : 17 those who have sport with the birds of the air
P Az 58 Bless the Lord, all birds of the air
2 Ma 4 : 24 extolled him with an air of authority
5 : 2 there appeared goldenclad horsemen charging through the air
1 Es 9 : 11 and we are not able to stand in the open air
2 Es 6 : 4 before the heights of the air were lifted up
7 : 40 or water or air, or darkness or evening or morning
8 : 20 whose eyes are exalted and whose upper chambers are in the air

AKKUB   3 = 0.002 %
1 Es 5 : 28 the sons of Akkub, the sons of Hatita
5 : 30 the sons of Akkub, the sons of Uthai, the sons of Ketab
9 : 48 Jeshua and Anniuth and Sherebiah, Jamin, Akkub

AKRABATTENE   1
1 Ma 5 : 3 in Idumea, at Akrabattene

ALACRITY   1
2 Ma 4 : 12 For with alacrity he founded a gymnasium

ALARM, subst.   1
Ad E 15 : 8 and in alarm he sprang from his throne

ALARM, verb   5 = 0.003 %
Tob 12 : 16 They were both alarmed
Jud 4 : 2 and were alarmed both for Jerusalem
14 : 7 In every nation those who hear your name will be alarmed
Wis 17 : 3 they were scattered, terribly alarmed
1 Ma 10 : 8 They were greatly alarmed when they heard

ALAS   9 = 0.006 %
1 Ma 2 : 7 and said, Alas ! Why was I born to see this
2 Es 13 : 16 alas for those who will be left in those days !
13 : 16 And still more, alas for those who are not left !
13 : 19 But alas for those also who are left
15 : 14 Alas for the world and for those who live in it !
16 : 17 Alas for me ! Alas for me !
4 Ma 16 : 9 Alas for my children, some unmarried
16 : 10 Alas, I who had so many and beautiful children

ALCIMUS   15 = 0.010 %
1 Ma 7 : 5 they were led by Alcimus, who wanted to be high priest
7 : 9 And he sent him, and with him the ungodly Alcimus
7 : 12 before Alcimus and Bacchides to ask for just terms
7 : 20 He placed Alcimus in charge of the country
7 : 21 Alcimus strove for the high priesthood
7 : 23 And Judas saw all the evil that Alcimus and those with him
7 : 25 When Alcimus saw that Judas
9 : 1 he sent Bacchides and Alcimus
9 : 54 Alcimus gave orders to tear down the wall
9 : 55 for at that time Alcimus was stricken
9 : 56 And Alcimus died at that time in great agony
9 : 57 When Bacchides saw that Alcimus was dead
2 Ma 14 : 3 Now a certain Alcimus, who had formerly been high priest
14 : 13 and to set up Alcimus as high priest of the greatest temple
14 : 26 But when Alcimus noticed their good will for one another

ALEMA   2
1 Ma 5 : 26 in Alema and Chaspho, Maked and Carnaim
5 : 35 Next he turned aside to Alema

ALERT   1
1 Ma 12 : 27 So when the sun set, Jonathan commanded his men to be alert

ALEXANDER   29 = 0.019 %
1 Ma 1 : 1 After Alexander son of Philip, the Macedonian
1 : 7 And after Alexander had reigned 12 years, he died
6 : 2 left there by Alexander, the son of Philip
10 : 1 In the 160th year Alexander Epiphanes, the son of Antiochus
10 : 4 before he makes peace with Alexander against us
10 : 15 Now Alexander the king heard of all the promises
10 : 18 King Alexander to his brother Jonathan, greeting
10 : 23 Alexander has gotten ahead of us
10 : 47 They favoured Alexander
10 : 48 Now Alexander the king assembled large forces
10 : 49 and Alexander pursued him and defeated them
10 : 51 Then Alexander sent ambassadors to Ptolemy king of Egypt
10 : 58 Alexander the king met him
10 : 59 Then Alexander the king wrote to Jonathan to come to meet him
10 : 68 When Alexander the king heard of it
10 : 88 When Alexander the king heard of these things
11 : 1 and he tried to get possession of Alexander's kingdom by trickery
11 : 2 for Alexander the king had commanded them to meet him
11 : 2 since he was Alexander's father-in-law
11 : 8 and he kept devising evil designs against Alexander
11 : 9 who was Alexander's wife
11 : 11 He threw blame on Alexander because he coveted his kingdom
11 : 12 He was estranged from Alexander
11 : 14 Now Alexander the king was in Cilicia at that time
11 : 15 And Alexander heard of it and came against him in battle
11 : 16 So Alexander fled into Arabia to find protection there
11 : 17 And Zabdiel the Arab cut off the head of Alexander
11 : 39 Now Trypho had formerly been one of Alexander's supporters
11 : 39 who was bringing up Antiochus, the young son of Alexander

ALEXANDRIA   1
3 Ma 3 : 1 against those Jews who lived in Alexandria

ALEXANDRIAN   2
3 Ma 2 : 30 they shall have equal citizenship with the Alexandrians
3 : 21 by deciding both to deem them worthy of Alexandrian citizenship

ALIEN, subst.   9 = 0.006 %
Jud 4 : 10 and every resident alien and hired labourer
Ad E 14 : 15 and abhor the bed of the uncircumcised and of any alien
16 : 10 really an alien to the Persian blood
Wis 19 : 15 for their hostile reception of the aliens
1 Ma 2 : 7 the sanctuary given over to aliens ?
3 : 36 settle aliens in all their territory
3 : 45 and the sons of aliens held the citadel
1 Es 8 : 83 is a land polluted with the pollution of the aliens of the land
2 Es 14 : 29 At first our fathers dwelt as aliens in Egypt

ALIEN, adj.   5 = 0.003 %
Wis 12 : 15 deeming it alien to thy power to condemn him
Bar 4 : 3 or your advantages to an alien people
2 Ma 6 : 24 has gone over to an alien religion
1 Es 8 : 69 the alien peoples of the land and their pollutions
8 : 70 and the holy race has been mixed with the alien peoples of the land

ALIENATE   2
3 Ma 4 : 16 with a mind alienated from truth and with a profane mouth
2 Es 7 : 48 which has alienated us from God

ALIGHT, verb   1
Sir 43 : 17 and its descent is like locusts alighting

ALIKE   2
Wis 6 : 7 and he takes thought for all alike
18 : 9 that the saints would share alike the same things

ALIVE   29 = 0.019 %
Tob 7 : 5 they replied, He is alive and in good health
8 : 12 Send one of the maids to see whether he is alive
8 : 14 And she came out and told them that he was alive
Jud 10 : 19 Surely not a man of them had better be left alive
Sir 17 : 27 as do those who are alive and give thanks ?
17 : 28 he who is alive and well sings the Lord's praises
30 : 5 while alive he saw and rejoiced
33 : 20 While you are still alive and have breath in you
1 Ma 1 : 6 and divided his kingdom among them while he was still alive
8 : 7 they took him alive
10 : 85 with those burned alive
14 : 2 he sent one of his commanders to take him alive
2 Ma 5 : 27 and kept himself and his companions alive in the mountains
7 : 24 The youngest brother being still alive
10 : 36 they kindled fires and burned the blasphemers alive
12 : 35 wishing to take the accursed man alive
14 : 45 Still alive and aflame with anger, he rose
3 Ma 5 : 18 why the Jews had been allowed to remain alive
2 Es 3 : 5 and he was made alive in thy presence

	4 : 26	If you are alive, you will see
	4 : 51	Or who will be alive in those days ?
	5 : 41	thou dost have charge of those who are alive at the end
	7 : 45	Blessed are those who are alive and keep thy commandments !
	7 : 67	that we shall be preserved alive but cruelly tormented ?
	7 : 87	before whom they sinned while they were alive
	7 : 94	that while they were alive
	7 : 129	For this is the way of which Moses, while he was alive
	14 : 34	you shall be kept alive
4 Ma	**18 : 19**	I kill and I make alive :

ALL* 1041 = 0.678 %

Tob	**1 : 3**	all the days of my life
	1 : 4	from among all the tribes of Israel
	1 : 4	where all the tribes should sacrifice
	1 : 4	was consecrated and established for all generations for ever
	1 : 5	All the tribes that joined in apostasy
	1 : 6	as it is ordained for all Israel by an everlasting decree
	1 : 7	Of all my produce I would give a tenth to the sons of Levi
	1 : 10	all my brethren and my relatives ate the food of the Gentiles
	1 : 12	because I remembered God with all my heart
	1 : 20	Then all my property was confiscated
	1 : 21	over all the accounts of his kingdom
	2 : 6	and all your festivities into lamentation
	3 : 2	all thy deeds and all thy ways are mercy and truth
	3 : 4	in all the nations among which we have been dispersed
	3 : 11	May all thy works praise thee for ever
	4 : 3	honour her all the days of your life
	4 : 5	Remember the Lord our God all your days, my son
	4 : 5	Live uprightly all the days of your life
	4 : 7	Give alms from your possessions to all who live uprightly
	4 : 11	and for all who practise it charity is an excellent offering
	4 : 12	Beware, my son, of all immorality
	4 : 12	First of all take a wife
	4 : 12	all took wives from among their brethren
	4 : 14	and be disciplined in all your conduct
	4 : 16	Give all your surplus to charity
	4 : 19	and that all your paths and plans may prosper
	4 : 19	but the Lord himself gives all good things
	8 : 5	Let the heavens and all thy creatures bless thee
	8 : 15	Let thy saints and all thy creatures bless thee
	8 : 15	let all thy angels and thy chosen people bless thee for ever
	11 : 14	and blessed are all thy holy angels
	11 : 17	So there was rejoicing among all his brethren in Nineveh
	12 : 5	Take half of all that you 2 have brought back
	12 : 6	in the presence of all the living
	12 : 19	All these days I merely appeared to you
	13 : 4	and exalt him in the presence of all the living
	13 : 5	and will gather us from all the nations
	13 : 6	If you turn to him with all your heart
	13 : 6	and with all your soul
	13 : 8	Let all men speak, and give him thanks in Jerusalem
	13 : 10	to all generations for ever
	13 : 12	Cursed are all who hate you
	13 : 12	blessed for ever will be all who love you
	13 : 14	Blessed are those who grieved over all your afflictions
	13 : 14	for they will rejoice for you upon seeing all your glory
	13 : 18	all her lanes will cry Hallelujah !
	14 : 5	with a glorious building for all generations for ever
	14 : 6	Then all the Gentiles will turn
	14 : 7	All the Gentiles will praise the Lord
	14 : 7	And all who love the Lord God in truth and righteousness
Jud	**1 : 6**	He was joined by all the people of the hill country
	1 : 6	and all those who lived along the Euphrates
	1 : 7	sent to all who lived in Persia
	1 : 7	and to all who lived in the west
	1 : 7	and all who lived along the seacoast
	1 : 9	and all who were in Samaria and its surrounding towns
	1 : 10	even beyond Tanis and Memphis, and all who lived in Egypt
	1 : 11	But all who lived in the whole region
	1 : 12	all the inhabitants of the land of Moab
	1 : 12	and the people of Ammon, and all Judea
	1 : 13	and all his cavalry and all his chariots
	1 : 16	he and all his combined forces, a vast body of troops
	2 : 2	He called together all his officers and all his nobles
	2 : 2	all the wickedness of the region
	2 : 10	You shall go and seize all their territory for me in advance
	2 : 14	and called together all the commanders, generals
	2 : 23	and plundered all the people of Rassis
	2 : 24	and destroyed all the hilltop cities along the brook Abron
	2 : 26	He surrounded all the Midianites
	2 : 27	and burned all their fields
	2 : 27	and put to death all their young men
	2 : 28	So fear and terror of him fell upon all the people
	2 : 28	and all who lived in Jamnia
	3 : 3	Behold, our buildings, and all our land
	3 : 3	and all our wheat fields, and our flocks and herds
	3 : 3	and all our sheepfolds with their tents, lie before you
	3 : 5	The men came to Holofernes and told him all this
	3 : 7	And these people and all in the country round about

	3 : 8	And he demolished all their shrines
	3 : 8	to destroy all the gods of the land
	3 : 8	so that all nations should worship Nebuchadnezzar only
	3 : 8	and all their tongues and tribes should call upon him as god
	3 : 10	in order to assemble all the supplies for his army
	4 : 1	and how he had plundered and destroyed all their temples
	4 : 3	and all the people of Judea were newly gathered together
	4 : 5	and immediately seized all the high hilltops
	4 : 10	they all girded themselves with sackcloth
	4 : 11	And all the men and women of Israel, and their children
	4 : 14	And Joakim the high priest and all the priests
	4 : 15	they cried out to the Lord with all their might
	5 : 1	and had fortified all the high hilltops
	5 : 2	So he called together all the princes of Moab
	5 : 2	and all the governors of the coastland
	5 : 4	And why have they alone, of all who live in the west
	5 : 5	Then Achior, the leader of all the Ammonites, said to him
	5 : 14	and drove out all the people of the wilderness
	5 : 15	and by their might destroyed all the inhabitants of Heshbon
	5 : 15	they took possession of all the hill country
	5 : 16	and the Shechemites and all the Gergesites
	5 : 22	all the men standing around the tent began to complain
	5 : 22	Holofernes'officers and all the men from the seacoast
	6 : 1	said to Achior and all the Moabites
	6 : 1	in the presence of all the foreign contingents :
	6 : 12	and all the slingers kept them from coming up
	6 : 16	They called together all the elders of the city
	6 : 16	and all their young men and their women ran to the assembly
	6 : 16	and they set Achior in the midst of all their people
	6 : 17	and all that he had said
	6 : 17	and all that Holofernes had said so boastfully
	6 : 21	and all that night they called on the God of Israel for help
	7 : 1	and all the allies who had joined him
	7 : 2	So all their warriors moved their camp that day
	7 : 5	they remained on guard all that night
	7 : 6	On the 2nd day Holofernes led out all his cavalry
	7 : 8	Then all the chieftains of the people of Esau
	7 : 8	and all the leaders of the Moabites
	7 : 12	and keep all the men in your forces with you
	7 : 13	for this is where all the people of Bethulia get their water
	7 : 16	These words pleased Holofernes and all his servants
	7 : 19	because all their enemies had surrounded them
	7 : 20	until all the vessels of water belonging to every inhabitant of Bethulia were empty
	7 : 23	Then all the people, the young men, the women, and the children
	7 : 23	and said before all the elders
	7 : 26	to the army of Holofernes and to all his forces
	8 : 6	She fasted all the days of her widowhood
	8 : 9	and when she heard all that Uzziah said to them
	8 : 10	she sent her maid, who was in charge of all she possessed
	8 : 14	who made all these things
	8 : 21	For if we are captured all Judea will be captured
	8 : 22	all this he will bring upon our heads among the Gentiles
	8 : 28	All that you have said has been spoken out of a true heart
	8 : 29	all the people have recognized your understanding
	8 : 32	which will go down through all generations of our descendants
	9 : 4	and all their booty to be divided among thy beloved sons
	9 : 6	for all thy ways are prepared in advance
	9 : 12	King of all thy creation, hear my prayer !
	9 : 14	the God of all power and might
	10 : 1	and had ended all these words
	10 : 4	and her earrings and all her ornaments
	10 : 4	to entice the eyes of all men who might see her
	10 : 5	and she wrapped up all her vessels
	10 : 13	and capture all the hill country
	10 : 20	Then Holofernes'companions and all his servants came out
	10 : 23	they all marvelled at the beauty of her face
	11 : 1	the king of all the earth
	11 : 2	but they have brought all this on themselves
	11 : 4	No one will hurt you, but all will treat you well
	11 : 7	under Nebuchadnezzar and all his house
	11 : 9	and he told them all he had said to you
	11 : 12	to use all that God by his laws has forbidden them to eat
	11 : 16	Therefore, when I, your servant, learned all this
	11 : 20	Her words pleased Holofernes and all his servants
	12 : 11	the eunuch who had charge of all his personal affairs
	12 : 15	So she got up and arrayed herself in all her woman's finery
	12 : 18	than in all the days since I was born
	13 : 1	and they went to bed, for they all were weary
	13 : 4	O Lord God of all might
	13 : 8	And she struck his neck twice with all her might
	13 : 13	They all ran together, both small and great
	13 : 17	All the people were greatly astonished
	13 : 18	above all women on earth
	13 : 20	And all the people said, So be it, so be it !
	14 : 4	and you and all who live within the borders of Israel
	14 : 5	But before you do all this, bring Achior the Ammonite to me
	14 : 8	all that she had done, from the day she left
	14 : 10	And when Achior saw all that the God of Israel had done

14 : 12	and to all their officers
14 : 13	in charge of all his personal affairs
15 : 2	but with one impulse all rushed out and fled
15 : 4	and Choba and Kola, and to all the frontiers of Israel
15 : 4	to tell what had taken place and to urge all
15 : 5	Those in Jerusalem and all the hill country also came
15 : 9	And when they met her they all blessed her with one accord
15 : 10	You have done all this singlehanded
15 : 10	And all the people said, So be it !
15 : 11	So all the people plundered the camp for 30 days
15 : 11	and all his silver dishes
15 : 11	and his beds and his bowls and all his furniture
15 : 12	Then all the women of Israel gathered to see her
15 : 13	and she went before all the people in the dance
15 : 13	leading all the women
15 : 13	while all the men of Israel followed
16 : 1	Then Judith began this thanksgiving before all Israel
16 : 1	and all the people loudly sang this song of praise
16 : 14	Let all thy creatures serve thee
16 : 16	and all fat for burnt offerings to thee is a very little thing
16 : 19	Judith also dedicated to God all the vessels of Holofernes
16 : 22	but she remained a widow all the days of her life
16 : 24	to all those who were next of kin to her husband Manasseh

Ad E

10 : 9	the Lord has delivered us from all these evils
10 : 10	one for the people of God and one for all the nations
10 : 11	of decision before God and among all the nations
11 : 12	and sought all day to understand it in every detail
13 : 2	and open to travel throughout all its extent
13 : 2	to re-establish the peace which all men desire
13 : 4	pointed out to us that among all the nations in the world
13 : 5	stands constantly in opposition to all men
13 : 5	doing all the harm they can
13 : 6	shall all, with their wives and children
13 : 8	calling to remembrance all the works of the Lord
13 : 9	He said : O Lord, Lord, King who rulest over all things
13 : 11	and thou art Lord of all
13 : 12	Thou knowest all things
13 : 18	And all Israel cried out mightily
14 : 5	that thou, O Lord, didst take Israel out of all the nations
14 : 5	and our fathers from among all their ancestors
14 : 5	and that thou didst do for them all that thou didst promise
14 : 12	O King of the gods and Master of all dominion !
14 : 15	Thou hast knowledge of all things
14 : 19	O God, whose might is over all
15 : 6	When she had gone through all the doors
15 : 6	all covered with gold and precious stones
15 : 16	and all his servants sought to comfort her
16 : 8	quiet and peaceable for all men
16 : 11	and was continually bowed down to by all
16 : 18	has been hanged at the gate of Susa, with all his household
16 : 18	For God, who rules over all things
16 : 21	For God, who rules over all things
16 : 22	Therefore you shall observe this with all good cheer
16 : 24	but also most hateful for all time to beasts and birds

Wis

1 : 7	and that which holds all things together knows what is said
1 : 10	because a jealous ear hears all things
1 : 14	For he created all things that they might exist
4 : 2	and throughout all time it marches crowned in triumph
5 : 9	All those things have vanished like a shadow
5 : 17	and will arm all creation to repel his enemies
6 : 7	For the Lord of all will not stand in awe of any one
6 : 7	and he takes thought for all alike
7 : 1	I also am mortal, like all men
7 : 3	and my first sound was a cry, like that of all
7 : 6	there is for all mankind one entrance into life
7 : 9	because all gold is but a little sand in her sight
7 : 11	All good things came to me along with her
7 : 12	I rejoiced in them all, because wisdom leads them
7 : 16	as are all understanding and skill in crafts
7 : 22	for wisdom, the fashioner of all things, taught me
7 : 23	all powerful, overseeing all
7 : 23	and penetrating through all spirits
7 : 24	she pervades and penetrates all things
7 : 27	Though she is but one, she can do all things
7 : 27	and while remaining in herself, she renews all things
8 : 1	and she orders all things well
8 : 3	and the Lord of all loves her
8 : 5	what is richer than wisdom who effects all things ?
9 : 1	who hast made all things by thy word
9 : 11	For she knows and understands all things
10 : 2	and gave him strength to rule all things
11 : 20	But thou hast arranged all things
11 : 23	But thou art merciful to all, for thou canst do all things
11 : 24	For thou lovest all things that exist
11 : 26	Thou sparest all things, for they are thine
12 : 1	For thy immortal spirit is in all things
12 : 7	that the land most precious of all to thee
12 : 13	whose care is for all men
12 : 15	Thou art righteous and rulest all things righteously
12 : 16	and thy sovereignty over all causes thee to spare all

13 : 1	For all men who were ignorant of God were foolish by nature
13 : 11	and skilfully strip off all its bark
14 : 25	and all is a raging riot of blood and murder
15 : 1	and ruling all things in mercy
15 : 7	making all in like manner
15 : 13	For this man, more than all others, knows that he sins
15 : 14	are all the enemies who oppressed thy people
15 : 15	For they thought that all their heathen idols were gods
15 : 18	which are worse than all others
16 : 7	not by what he saw, but by thee, the Saviour of all
16 : 12	but it was thy word, O Lord, which heals all men
16 : 17	For – most incredible of all
16 : 17	in the water, which quenches all things
16 : 25	changed into all forms, it served thy all-nourishing bounty
17 : 14	they all slept the same sleep
17 : 17	for with one chain of darkness they all were bound
18 : 5	and thou didst destroy them all together by a mighty flood
18 : 12	and they all together
18 : 14	For while gentle silence enveloped all things
18 : 16	and stood and filled all things with death
19 : 22	at all times and in all places

Sir

1 : 1	All wisdom comes from the Lord and is with him for ever
1 : 4	Wisdom was created before all things
1 : 9	he poured her out upon all his works
1 : 10	She dwells with all flesh according to his gift
1 : 21	and where it abides, it will turn away all anger
3 : 13	in all your strength do not despise him
6 : 26	Come to her with all your soul
6 : 26	and keep her ways with all your might
6 : 37	and meditate at all times on his commandments
7 : 27	With all your heart honour your father
7 : 29	With all your soul fear the Lord, and honour his priests
7 : 30	With all your might love your Maker
7 : 33	Give graciously to all the living
7 : 36	In all you do, remember the end of your life
8 : 5	remember that we all deserve punishment
8 : 7	remember that we all must die
9 : 15	and let all your discussion be about the law of the Most High
10 : 2	and like the ruler of the city, so are all its inhabitants
12 : 5	for all the good which you do to him
13 : 14	During all your life love the Lord
13 : 16	all living beings associate by species
13 : 23	When the rich man speaks all are silent
14 : 17	All living beings become old like a garment
15 : 13	The Lord hates all abominations
16 : 27	and their dominion for all generations
16 : 30	with all kinds of living beings he covered its surface
17 : 4	He placed the fear of them in all living beings
17 : 14	And he said to them, Beware of all unrighteousness
17 : 19	All their works are as the sun before him
17 : 20	and all their sins are before the Lord
17 : 30	For all things cannot be in men
17 : 32	but all men are dust and ashes
18 : 3	and all things obey his will
18 : 3	for he is king of all things
18 : 13	but the compassion of the Lord is for all living beings
18 : 26	and all things move swiftly before the Lord
19 : 20	All wisdom is the fear of the Lord
19 : 20	and in all wisdom there is the fulfilment of the law
21 : 3	All lawlessness is like a two-edged sword
22 : 6	but chastising and discipline are wisdom at all times
22 : 12	but for a fool or an ungodly man it lasts all his life
23 : 12	For all these errors will be far from the godly
23 : 15	will never become disciplined all his days
23 : 17	To a fornicator all bread tastes sweet
23 : 19	they look upon all the ways of men
23 : 23	For first of all
24 : 7	Among all these I sought a resting place
24 : 8	Then the Creator of all things gave me a commandment
24 : 18	being eternal, I therefore am given to all my children
24 : 23	All this is the book of the covenant of the Most High God
24 : 33	and leave it to all future generations
24 : 34	but for all who seek instruction
25 : 24	and because of her we all die
26 : 4	and at all times his face is cheerful
26 : 5	all these are worse than death
26 : 6	and a tongue-lashing makes it known to all
26 : 26	A wife honouring her husband will seem wise to all
26 : 26	in her pride she will be known to all as ungodly
27 : 23	In your presence his mouth is all sweetness
29 : 12	and it will rescue you from all affliction
29 : 15	Do not forget all the kindness of your surety
30 : 15	Health and soundness are better than all gold
31 : 22	In all your work be industrious
33 : 7	when all the daylight in the year is from the sun ?
33 : 10	All men are from the ground
33 : 13	for all his ways are as he pleases
33 : 15	Look upon all the works of the Most High
33 : 17	but for all who seek instruction
33 : 22	Excel in all that you do

35:5	for all these things are to be done
36:1	Have mercy upon us, O Lord, the God of all
36:2	and cause the fear of thee to fall upon all the nations
36:11	Gather all the tribes of Jacob
36:17	and all who are on the earth will know
37:15	And besides all this pray to the Most High
37:20	he will be destitute of all food
37:21	since he is lacking in all wisdom
37:24	and all who see him will call him happy
38:10	and cleanse your heart from all sin
38:29	and all his output is by number
38:31	All these rely upon their hands
39:1	will seek out the wisdom of all the ancients
39:9	and his name will live through all generations
39:14	bless the Lord for all his works
39:16	All things are the works of the Lord, for they are very good
39:17	For in God's time all things will be sought after
39:19	The works of all flesh are before him
39:26	Basic to all the needs of man's life are water and fire
39:27	All these are for good to the godly
39:29	all these have been created for vengeance
39:33	The works of the Lord are all good
39:34	for all things will prove good in their season
39:35	So now sing praise with all your heart and voice
40:1	till the day they return to the mother of all
40:8	With all flesh, both man and beast
40:10	All these were created for the wicked
40:11	All things that are from the earth turn back to the earth
40:12	All bribery and injustice will be blotted out
41:3	this is the decree from the Lord for all flesh
42:7	and make a record of all that you give out or take in
42:8	and will be approved before all men
42:17	to recount all his marvellous works
42:18	For the Most High knows all that may be known
42:22	How greatly to be desired are all his works
42:23	All these things live and remain for ever for every need
42:23	and are all obedient
42:24	All things are twofold, one opposite the other
43:22	A mist quickly heals all things
43:25	all kinds of living things, and huge creatures of the sea
43:26	and by his word all things hold together
43:27	and the sum of our words is : He is the all
43:28	For he is greater than all his works
43:30	When you exalt him, put forth all your strength
43:33	For the Lord has made all things
44:7	all these were honoured in their generations
44:14	and their name lives to all generations
44:16	he was an example of repentance to all generations
44:18	that all flesh should not be blotted out by a flood
44:23	The blessing of all men and the covenant
45:1	who found favour in the sight of all flesh
45:4	he chose him out of all mankind
45:15	and for his descendants all the days of heaven
45:16	He chose him out of all the living
46:10	so that all the sons of Israel might see
46:18	and all the rulers of the Philistines
47:8	In all that he did he gave thanks to the Holy One
47:8	he sang praise with all his heart, and he loved his Maker
48:12	in all his days he did not tremble before any ruler
48:15	For all this the people did not repent
48:15	and were scattered over all the earth
49:4	Except David and Hezekiah and Josiah they all sinned greatly
50:9	adorned with all kinds of precious stones
50:13	all the sons of Aaron in their splendour
50:15	a pleasing odour to the Most High, the King of all
50:17	Then all the people together made haste
50:22	And now bless the God of all
50:29	For if he does them, he will be strong for all things
Bar 1:3	and in the hearing of all the people who came to hear the book
1:4	and in the hearing of all the people, small and great
1:4	all who dwelt in Babylon by the river Sud
1:7	and to all the people who were present with him in Jerusalem
1:21	in all the words of the prophets whom he sent to us
2:4	And he gave them into subjection to all the kingdoms around us
2:4	to be a reproach and a desolation among all the surrounding peoples
2:7	All those calamities with which the Lord threatened us have come upon us
2:9	for the Lord is righteous in all his works
2:12	O Lord our God, against all thy ordinances
2:15	that all the earth may know that thou art the Lord our God
2:27	in all thy kindness and in all thy great compassion
3:7	for we have put away from our hearts all the iniquity of our fathers
3:8	for all the iniquities of our fathers
3:32	But he who knows all things knows her
3:32	He who prepared the earth for all time filled it with four-footed creatures
4:1	All who hold her fast will live
4:20	I will cry to the Everlasting all my days

L Jr 6:51	It will be manifest to all the nations and kings
P Az 4	For thou art just in all that thou hast done to us
4	and all thy works are true and thy ways right
4	and all thy judgments are truth
5	in all that thou hast brought upon us and upon Jerusalem
5	for in truth and justice thou hast brought all this upon us
6	and have sinned in all things
8	So all that thou hast brought upon us
8	and all that thou hast done to us
9	the most wicked in all the world
14	and are brought low this day in all the world
18	And now with all our heart we follow thee
20	Let all who do harm to thy servants be put to shame
21	let them be disgraced and deprived of all power and dominion
35	Bless the Lord, all works of the Lord
38	Bless the Lord, all waters above the heaven
39	Bless the Lord, all powers
42	Bless the Lord, all rain and dew
43	Bless the Lord, all winds
54	Bless the Lord, all things that grow on the earth
57	Bless the Lord, you whales and all creatures that move in the waters
58	Bless the Lord, all birds of the air
59	Bless the Lord, all beasts and cattle
68	Bless him, all who worship the Lord, the God of gods
Sus 13:4	and the Jews used to come to him because he was the most honoured of them all
13:6	and all who had suits at law came to them
13:30	And she came, with her parents, her children, and all her kindred
13:33	But her family and friends and all who saw her wept
13:42	who art aware of all things before they come to be
13:47	All the people turned to him, and said
13:50	Then all the people returned in haste
13:60	Then all the assembly shouted loudly and blessed God
13:63	and so did Joakim her husband and all her kindred
Bel 14:5	and so has dominion over all flesh
14:12	if you do not find that Bel has eaten it all, we will die
1 Ma 1:9	They all put on crowns after his death
1:21	the lampstand for the light, and all its utensils
1:22	he stripped it all off
1:24	Taking them all, he departed to his own land
1:28	and the house of Jacob was clothed with shame
1:41	that all should be one people
1:43	All the Gentiles accepted the command of the king
1:49	and change all the ordinances
1:51	And he appointed inspectors over all the people
2:11	All her adornment has been taken away
2:18	as all the Gentiles and the men of Judah
2:19	Even if all the nations that live under the rule of the king
2:23	a Jew came forward in the sight of all
2:28	and left all that they had in the city
2:37	for they said, Let us all die in our innocence
2:40	If we all do as our brethren have done
2:41	let us not all die as our brethren died
2:43	And all who became fugitives to escape their troubles
2:46	they forcibly circumcised all the uncircumcised boys
2:67	You shall rally about you all who observe the law
2:70	And all Israel mourned for him with great lamentation
3:2	All his brothers and all who had joined his father helped him
3:6	all the evildoers were confounded
3:27	and he sent and gathered all the forces of his kingdom
3:34	and gave him orders about all that he wanted done
3:36	settle aliens in all their territory
4:11	Then all the Gentiles will know
4:15	and all those in the rear fell by the sword
4:22	they all fled into the land of the Philistines
4:26	and reported to Lysias all that had happened
4:33	and let all who know thy name praise thee with hymns
4:37	So all the army assembled and they went up to Mount Zion
4:51	Thus they finished all the work they had undertaken
4:55	All the people fell on their faces
4:59	Then Judas and his brothers and all the assembly of Israel
5:5	and burned with fire their towers and all who were in them
5:13	and all our brethren who were in the land of Tob have been killed
5:15	and all Galilee of the Gentiles, to annihilate us
5:23	with their wives and children, and all they possessed
5:25	and told them all that had happened
5:26	all these cities were strong and large
5:27	and take and destroy all these men in one day
5:28	then he seized all its spoils and burned it with fire
5:29	and they went all the way to the stronghold of Dathema
5:38	All the Gentiles around us have gathered to him
5:42	Permit no man to encamp, but make them all enter the battle
5:43	All the Gentiles were defeated before him
5:44	together with all who were in them
5:45	Then Judas gathered together all the Israelites in Gilead
5:50	all that day and all the night
5:53	and encouraging the people all the way

5 : 63	in all Israel and among all the Gentiles
6 : 10	So he called all his friends and said to them
6 : 12	I seized all her vessels of silver and gold
6 : 14	and made him ruler over all his kingdom
6 : 19	and assembled all the people to besiege them
6 : 25	but also against all the lands on their borders
6 : 28	He assembled all his friends, the commanders of his forces
6 : 41	All who heard the noise made by their multitude
6 : 43	It was taller than all the others
6 : 58	and make peace with them and with all their nation
6 : 59	that they became angry and did all these things
6 : 62	and gave orders to tear down the wall all around
7 : 5	all the lawless and ungodly men of Israel
7 : 6	Judas and his brothers have destroyed all your friends
7 : 7	let him go and see all the ruin
7 : 7	and let him punish them and all who help them
7 : 18	Then the fear and dread of them fell upon all the people
7 : 22	and all who were troubling their people joined him
7 : 23	And Judas saw all the evil that Alcimus and those with him
7 : 24	So Judas went out into all the surrounding parts of Judea
7 : 46	And men came out of all the villages of Judea round about
7 : 46	so that they all fell by the sword
8 : 1	toward all who made an alliance with them
8 : 14	Yet for all this not one of them has put on a crown
8 : 16	and to control all their land
8 : 16	they all heed the one man
8 : 23	May all go well with the Romans
8 : 24	in all their dominion
9 : 11	as did all the chief warriors
9 : 14	then all the stouthearted men went with him
9 : 20	And all Israel made great lamentation for him
9 : 23	the lawless emerged in all parts of Israel
9 : 23	all the doers of injustice appeared
9 : 28	Then all the friends of Judas assembled
9 : 33	and all who were with him heard of it
9 : 34	and he with all his army crossed the Jordan
9 : 36	and seized John and all that he had, and departed with it
9 : 40	and they took all their goods
9 : 58	Then all the lawless plotted and said, See !
9 : 58	and he will capture them all in one night
9 : 60	and secretly sent letters to all his allies in Judea
9 : 63	When Bacchides learned of this, he assembled all his forces
10 : 5	for he will remember all the wrongs which we did to him
10 : 7	and read the letter in the hearing of all the people
10 : 15	Now Alexander the king heard of all the promises
10 : 29	And now I free you and exempt all the Jews
10 : 30	from this day and for all time
10 : 33	and let all officials cancel also the taxes on their cattle
10 : 34	And all the feasts and sabbaths
10 : 34	let them all be days of immunity and release
10 : 34	for all the Jews who are in my kingdom
10 : 36	that is due to all the forces of the king
10 : 41	And all the additional funds
10 : 43	let him be released and receive back all his property in my kingdom
10 : 47	and they remained his allies all his days
10 : 64	and saw him clothed in purple, they all fled
10 : 89	He also gave him Ekron and all its environs as his possession
11 : 26	he exalted him in the presence of all his friends
11 : 29	and wrote a letter to Jonathan about all these things
11 : 34	the latter, with all the region bordering them
11 : 34	To all those who offer sacrifice in Jerusalem
11 : 35	from all these we shall grant them release
11 : 38	he dismissed all his troops, each man to his own place
11 : 38	So all the troops who had served his fathers hated him
11 : 39	He saw that all the troops were murmuring against Demetrius
11 : 43	for all my troops have revolted
11 : 47	and they all rallied about him
11 : 51	and of all the people in his kingdom
11 : 53	But he broke his word about all that he had promised
11 : 55	All the troops that Demetrius had cast off
11 : 60	and all the army of Syria gathered to him as allies
11 : 70	All the men with Jonathan fled
12 : 27	so as to be ready all night for battle
12 : 32	and marched through all that region
12 : 43	and commended him to all his friends
12 : 44	Why have you wearied all these people when we are not at war ?
12 : 45	and the remaining troops and all the officials
12 : 48	and all who had entered with him they killed with the sword
12 : 49	and the Great Plain to destroy all Jonathan's soldiers
12 : 52	So they all reached the land of Judah safely
12 : 52	and all Israel mourned deeply
12 : 53	And all the nations round about them tried to destroy them
13 : 4	By reason of this all my brothers have perished
13 : 6	for all the nations have gathered together
13 : 9	Fight our battles, and all that you say to us we will do
13 : 10	So he assembled all the warriors
13 : 22	So Trypho got all his cavalry ready to go
13 : 26	All Israel bewailed him with great lamentation
13 : 29	so that they could be seen by all who sail the sea

13 : 33	and walled them all around
13 : 34	for all that Trypho did was to plunder
13 : 38	All the grants that we have made to you remain valid
13 : 48	He cast out of it all uncleanness
13 : 53	so he made him commander of all the forces
14 : 4	The land had rest all the days of Simon
14 : 4	as was the honour shown him, all his days
14 : 5	To crown all his honours he took Joppa for a harbour
14 : 9	they all talked together of good things
14 : 14	He strengthened all the humble of his people
14 : 35	because he had done all these things
14 : 43	and that he should be obeyed by all
14 : 43	and that all contracts in the country
14 : 46	And all the people agreed to grant Simon
14 : 47	and to be protector of them all
15 : 1	and to all the nation
15 : 5	now therefore I confirm to you all the tax remissions
15 : 5	and release from all the other payments
15 : 7	All the weapons which you have prepared
15 : 8	from henceforth and for all time
15 : 9	so that your glory will become manifest in all the earth
15 : 10	All the troops rallied to him
15 : 23	and to all the countries, and to Sampsames
15 : 27	and he broke all the agreements
15 : 36	and all that he had seen

2 Ma	1 : 3	May he give you all a heart to worship him
	1 : 22	a great fire blazed up, so that all marvelled
	1 : 24	O Lord, Lord God, Creator of all things
	1 : 26	accept this sacrifice on behalf of all thy people Israel
	2 : 14	In the same way Judas also collected all the books that had been lost
	2 : 17	It is God who has saved all his people
	2 : 17	and has returned the inheritance to all
	2 : 23	all this, which has been set forth by Jason of Cyrene in 5 volumes
	2 : 25	and to profit all readers
	3 : 3	defrayed from his own revenues all the expenses
	3 : 11	and that it totalled in all 400 talents of silver and 200 of gold
	3 : 20	And holding up their hands to heaven, they all made entreaty
	3 : 24	then and there the Sovereign of spirits and of all authority
	3 : 24	that all who had been so bold as to accompany him
	3 : 28	with a great retinue and all his bodyguard
	3 : 34	report to all men the majestic power of God
	3 : 36	And he bore testimony to all men
	4 : 5	but having in view the welfare, both public and private, of all the people
	4 : 42	and put them all to flight
	4 : 47	Menelaus, the cause of all the evil
	5 : 2	And it happened that over all the city, for almost 40 days
	5 : 3	and armour of all sorts
	5 : 4	Therefore all men prayed
	5 : 8	fleeing from city to city, pursued by all men
	5 : 15	the most holy temple in all the world
	5 : 20	was restored again in all its glory
	5 : 24	and commanded him to slay all the grown men
	5 : 26	He put to the sword all those who came out to see them
	6 : 11	were betrayed to Philip and were all burned together
	7 : 23	and devised the origin of all things
	7 : 31	But you, who have contrived all sorts of evil
	7 : 34	But you, unholy wretch, you most defiled of all men
	7 : 41	Last of all, the mother died, after her sons
	8 : 2	who were oppressed by all
	8 : 9	in command of no fewer than 20,000 Gentiles of all nations
	8 : 14	Others sold all their remaining property
	8 : 20	when 8,000 in all went into the affair, with 4,000 Macedonians
	8 : 24	and forced them all to flee
	8 : 31	they stored them all carefully in strategic places
	9 : 8	making the power of God manifest to all
	9 : 15	he would make, all of them, equal to citizens of Athens
	9 : 16	all of them, many times over
	9 : 17	and in addition to all this he also would become a Jew
	9 : 18	he gave up all hope for himself
	9 : 21	for the general security of all
	10 : 17	and beat off all who fought upon the wall
	11 : 2	gathered about 80,000 men and all his cavalry
	11 : 6	they and all the people, with lamentations and tears
	11 : 9	And they all together praised the merciful God
	11 : 11	and forced all the rest to flee
	11 : 15	agreed to all that Lysias urged
	12 : 11	and to help his people in all other ways
	12 : 13	and inhabited by all sorts of Gentiles
	12 : 21	because of the narrowness of all the approaches
	12 : 22	at the manifestation to them of him who sees all things
	12 : 27	with multitudes of people of all nationalities
	12 : 40	And it became clear to all
	12 : 41	So they all blessed the ways of the Lord
	13 : 4	that this man was to blame for all the trouble
	13 : 5	which on all sides inclines precipitously into the ashes
	13 : 6	There they all push to destruction
	13 : 12	When they had all joined in the same petition

13	: 23	yielded and swore to observe all their rights
14	: 9	with the gracious kindness which you show to all
14	: 35	O Lord of all, who hast need of nothing
14	: 36	so now, O holy One, Lord of all holiness
14	: 38	and for Judaism he had with all zeal risked body and life
15	: 2	which he who sees all things has honoured
15	: 7	But Maccabeus did not cease to trust with all confidence
15	: 11	and he cheered them all by relating a dream
15	: 12	in all that belongs to excellence
15	: 17	by fighting hand to hand with all courage
15	: 20	When all were now looking forward to the coming decision
15	: 34	And they all, looking to heaven
15	: 36	And they all decreed by public vote

1 Es

1	: 13	and carried them to all the people
1	: 21	and the men of Judah and all of Israel
1	: 25	After all these acts of Josiah
1	: 32	And in all Judea they mourned for Josiah
1	: 49	beyond all the unclean deeds of all the nations
1	: 53	old man or child, for he gave them all into their hands
1	: 54	And all the holy vessels of the Lord, great and small
1	: 56	and utterly destroyed all its glorious things
1	: 58	it shall keep sabbath all the time of its desolation
2	: 2	and he made a proclamation throughout all his kingdom
2	: 8	and all whose spirit the Lord had stirred to go up
2	: 14	All the vessels were handed over, gold and silver, 5,469
3	: 1	for all that were under him
3	: 1	and all that were born in his house
3	: 1	and all the nobles of Media and Persia
3	: 2	and all the satraps and generals and governors
3	: 12	but truth is victor over all things
3	: 14	Then he sent and summoned all the nobles of Persia and Media
3	: 18	It leads astray the minds of all who drink it
3	: 20	and forgets all sorrow and debt
3	: 21	It makes all hearts feel rich, forgets kings and satraps
4	: 2	who rule over land and sea and all that is in them ?
4	: 10	All his people and his armies obey him
4	: 19	they let all those things go, and gape at her
4	: 19	and all prefer her to gold or silver
4	: 28	Do not all lands fear to touch him ?
4	: 35	But truth is great, and stronger than all things
4	: 36	All God's works quake and tremble
4	: 37	women are unrighteous, all the sons of men are unrighteous
4	: 37	all their works are unrighteous, and all such things
4	: 39	All men approve her deeds
4	: 40	and the power and the majesty of all the ages
4	: 41	then all the people shouted, and said
4	: 41	Great is truth, and strongest of all !
4	: 44	and to send back all the vessels that were taken from Jerusalem
4	: 47	and wrote letters for him to all the treasurers
4	: 47	and all who were going up with him to build Jerusalem
4	: 48	And he wrote letters to all the governors in Coelesyria
4	: 49	And he wrote for all the Jews who were going up
4	: 50	that all the country which they would occupy
4	: 53	and that all who came from Babylonia to build the city
4	: 53	and all the priests who came
4	: 56	for all who guarded the city
4	: 57	And he sent back from Babylon all the vessels
4	: 61	and went to Babylon and told this to all his brethren
5	: 3	and all their brethren were making merry
5	: 28	the sons of Shobai, in all 139
5	: 35	All the temple servants
5	: 41	All those of Israel, 12 or more years of age
5	: 46	and all Israel in their towns
5	: 50	for all the peoples of the land were hostile to them
5	: 52	and at all the consecrated feasts
5	: 53	And all who had made any vow to God
5	: 56	and all who had come to Jerusalem from the captivity
5	: 58	with their sons and brethren, all the Levites
5	: 61	because his goodness and his glory are for ever upon all Israel
5	: 62	And all the people sounded trumpets
6	: 4	and this roof and finishing all the other things ?
6	: 10	and being completed with all splendour and care
6	: 19	with the command that he should take all these vessels back
6	: 34	that it be done with all diligence as here prescribed
7	: 8	and 12 he-goats for the sin of all Israel
7	: 11	Not all of the returned captives were purified
7	: 11	but the Levites were all purified together
7	: 12	for all the returned captives
7	: 13	all those who had separated themselves
8	: 4	for he found favour before the king in all his requests
8	: 7	but taught all Israel all the ordinances and judgments
8	: 13	all the gold and silver that may be found
8	: 21	Let all things prescribed in the law of God
8	: 23	to judge all those who know the law of your God
8	: 23	throughout all Syria and Phoenicia
8	: 24	And all who transgress the law of your God
8	: 26	and his counsellors and his friends and nobles
8	: 49	the list of all their names was reported
8	: 55	and all Israel had given
8	: 65	12 bulls for all Israel, 96 rams, 72 lambs

8	: 66	all as a sacrifice to the Lord
8	: 72	And all who were ever moved
8	: 86	And all that has happened to us has come about
8	: 93	that we will put away all our foreign wives
8	: 94	as seems good to you and to all who obey the law of the Lord
8	: 96	and Levites of all Israel take oath
9	: 3	to all who had returned from the captivity
9	: 6	And all the multitude sat in the open square before the temple
9	: 10	Then all the multitude shouted and said with a loud voice
9	: 12	and let all those in our settlements who have foreign wives
9	: 15	acted in accordance with all this
9	: 16	all of them by name
9	: 36	All these had married foreign women
9	: 40	for all the multitude, men and women
9	: 40	and all the priests to hear the law
9	: 41	and all the multitude gave attention to the law
9	: 45	for he had the place of honour in the presence of all
9	: 46	And when he opened the law, they all stood erect
9	: 47	and all the multitude answered, Amen
9	: 49	and to the Levites who were teaching the multitude, and to all
9	: 50	now they were all weeping as they heard the law
9	: 53	And the Levites commanded all the people, saying
9	: 54	Then they all went their way

P Ma

	2	thou who hast made heaven and earth with all their order
	4	at whom all things shudder, and tremble before thy power
	15	all the days of my life
	15	For all the host of heaven sings thy praise

3 Ma

1	: 1	he gave orders to all his forces
1	: 4	her locks all dishevelled
1	: 8	he was all the more eager to visit them as soon as possible
1	: 11	nor even all of the priests
1	: 11	but only the high priest who was preeminent over all
1	: 16	Then the priests in all their vestments prostrated themselves
1	: 27	to call upon him who has all power
1	: 29	because indeed all at that time preferred death
2	: 2	and sovereign of all creation
2	: 3	For you, the creator of all things and the governor of all
2	: 21	Thereupon God, who oversees all things
2	: 21	the first Father of all
2	: 28	and all Jews shall be subjected
2	: 30	In order that he might not appear to be an enemy to all
3	: 1	and he ordered that all should promptly be gathered into one place
3	: 5	they were established in good repute among all men
3	: 6	which was common talk among all
3	: 12	in Egypt and all its districts
3	: 18	because of the benevolence which we have toward all
3	: 19	they become the only people among all nations
3	: 20	since we treat all nations with benevolence
3	: 21	we made known to all our amnesty towards their compatriots here
3	: 26	For when these all have been punished
3	: 29	and shall become useless for all time to any mortal creature
4	: 4	were they being sent off, all together, by the generals
4	: 6	all together raising a lament instead of a wedding song
4	: 11	to all coming back into the city
4	: 16	organizing feasts in honour of all his idols
4	: 18	the task was impossible for all the generals in Egypt
5	: 2	to drug all the elephants – 500 in number
5	: 7	they all called upon the Almighty Lord and Ruler of all power
5	: 17	by celebrating all the more
5	: 21	all those present readily and joyfully with one accord gave their approval
5	: 22	in sleep as in devising all sorts of insults
5	: 28	This was the act of God who rules over all things
5	: 29	Then Hermon and all the king's friends
6	: 2	governing all creation with mercy
6	: 6	and turning the flame against all their enemies
6	: 8	you, Father, watched over and restored unharmed to all his family
6	: 9	all-merciful and protector of all
6	: 12	But you, O Eternal One, who have all might and all power
6	: 15	Let it be shown to all the Gentiles
6	: 16	and all the arrogance of his forces
6	: 18	visible to all but the Jews
6	: 23	and saw them all fallen headlong to destruction
6	: 26	those who from the beginning differed from all nations
6	: 30	deciding that they should celebrate their rescue with all joyfulness
6	: 32	Putting an end to all mourning and wailing
6	: 39	on which the Lord of all most gloriously revealed his mercy
6	: 39	and rescued them all together and unharmed
7	: 1	and all in authority in his government
7	: 4	because of the ill-will which these people had toward all nations
7	: 6	which we have towards all men
7	: 16	crowned with all sorts of very fragrant flowers
7	: 16	in words of praise and all kinds of melodious songs
7	: 18	all things to them for their journey
7	: 22	Besides they all recovered all of their property
7	: 23	Blessed be the Deliverer of Israel through all times ! Amen

2 Es 1:8 Pull out the hair of your head and hurl all evils upon them
1:10 I struck down Pharaoh with his servants, and all his army
1:11 I have destroyed all nations before them
1:11 I have slain all their enemies
2:42 and they all were praising the Lord with songs
3:11 and all the righteous who have descended from him
3:21 as were also all who were descended from him
3:26 in everything doing as Adam and all his descendants had done
4:38 but all of us also are full of ungodliness
5:7 shall make his voice heard by night, and all shall hear his voice
5:9 and all friends shall conquer one another
5:23 from every forest of the earth and from all its trees
5:24 and from all the lands of the world
5:24 and from all the flowers of the world
5:25 and from all the depths of the sea
5:25 and from all the cities that have been built
5:26 and from all the birds that have been created
5:26 and from all the flocks that have been made
5:27 and from all the multitude of peoples
5:27 thou hast given the law which is approved by all
5:45 If therefore all creatures will live at one time
5:45 all of them present at one time
6:20 and all shall see it together
6:23 and the trumpet shall sound aloud, and when all hear it
6:25 after all that I have foretold to you
6:33 Therefore he sent me to show you all these things
6:54 as ruler over all the works which thou hadst made
6:54 and from him we have all come
6:55 All this I have spoken before thee, O Lord
7:6 and it is full of all good things
7:29 and all who draw human breath
7:42 by which all shall see what has been determined for them
7:48 but almost all who have been created !
7:65 let all who have been born lament
7:68 For all who have been born are involved in iniquities
7:70 and all who have come from him
7:78 first of all it adores the glory of the Most High
7:87 which is worse than all the ways that have been mentioned
7:91 First of all, they shall see with great joy
7:98 which is greater than all that have been mentioned
7:104 and displays to all the seal of truth
7:117 For what good is it to all that they live in sorrow now
8:15 About all mankind thou knowest best
8:41 and yet not all that have been sown will come up in due season
8:41 and not all that were planted will take root
8:41 so also those who have been sown in the world will not all be saved
8:44 and for whose sake thou hast formed all things
8:62 I have not shown this to all men
9:45 I and my husband and all my neighbours
10:2 Then we all put out the lamps
10:2 and all my neighbours attempted to console me
10:3 But when they all had stopped consoling me
10:7 For Zion, the mother of us all
10:8 because we are all mourning
10:8 and to be sorrowful, because we are all sorrowing
10:10 And from the beginning all have been born of her
10:10 and behold, almost all go to perdition
10:23 And, what is more than all, the seal of Zion
11:2 he spread his wings over all the earth
11:2 and all the winds of heaven blew upon him
11:6 And I saw how all things under heaven were subjected to him
11:8 Do not all watch at the same time
11:12 and it reigned over all the earth
11:16 Hear me, you who have ruled the earth all this time
11:19 And so it went with all the wings
11:32 than all the wings that had gone before
11:40 have conquered all the beasts that have gone before
11:40 and over all the earth with grievous oppression
12:13 than all the kingdoms that have been before it
12:24 than all who were before them
12:31 and as for all his words that you have heard
12:37 Therefore write all these things that you have seen in a book
12:40 When all the people heard that the 7 days were past
12:40 they all gathered together
12:42 For of all the prophets you alone are left to us
13:2 and behold, a wind arose from the sea and stirred up all its waves
13:4 all who heard his voice melted as wax melts
13:8 all who gathered together against him
13:11 All these were mingled together
13:11 and burned them all up, so that suddenly
13:33 And when all the nations hear his voice
13:36 And Zion will come and be made manifest to all people, prepared and built
14:27 and I gathered all the people together, and said
15:9 and will receive to myself all the innocent blood from among them
15:11 and will destroy all its land
15:20 I call together all the kings of the earth to fear me

15:26 For the Lord knows all who transgress against him
15:29 so that all who hear them fear and tremble
15:40 shall rise, to destroy all the earth and its inhabitants
15:41 that all the fields and all the streams
15:44 they shall pour out the tempest and all its wrath upon her
15:44 and all who are about her shall wail over her
15:48 You have imitated that hateful harlot in all her deeds and devices
15:57 and all your people who are in the open country
15:59 Unhappy above all others
15:62 all your forests and your fruitful trees
16:18 the beginning of calamities, when all shall tremble
16:20 Yet for all this they will not turn from their iniquities
16:26 For in all places there shall be great solitude
16:32 and its roads and all its paths shall bring forth thorns
16:54 Behold, the Lord knows all the works of men
16:62 who made all things
16:64 Because the Lord will strictly examine all their works
16:64 and will make a public spectacle of all of you
16:67 and deliver you from all tribulation
4 Ma 1:9 All of these, by despising sufferings that bring death
1:11 For all people, even their torturers
1:14 and whether reason rules over all these
1:19 Rational judgment is supreme over all of these
1:25 which is the most complex of all the emotions
1:30 Observe now first of all
1:34 and all sorts of foods that are forbidden to us by the law
1:35 and all the impulses of the body are bridled by reason
2:6 I could prove to you all the more
2:9 In all other matters
2:16 For the temperate mind repels all these malicious emotions
2:22 as a sacred governor over them all
3:7 David had been attacking the Philistines all day long
3:9 Now all the rest were at supper
3:18 and by nobility of reason spurn all domination by the emotions
4:1 When despite all manner of slander
4:7 and did all that they could to prevent it
4:11 in the temple area that was open to all
4:12 he would praise the blessedness of the holy place before all people
4:14 So Apollonius, having been preserved beyond all expectations
4:24 but saw that all his threats and punishments were being disregarded
5:23 so that we master all pleasures and desires
5:24 so that in all our dealings we act impartially
6:20 be a laughing stock to all for our cowardice
8:29 all with one voice together, as from one mind, said :
9:18 Through all these tortures I will convince you
9:26 While all were marvelling at his courageous spirit
9:28 flayed all his flesh up to his chin
10:8 he saw his own flesh torn all around
11:5 It is because we revere the Creator of all things and live
11:10 and all his members were disjointed
12:1 the 7th and youngest of all came forward
12:8 and to all his friends that are with him
12:11 he said, You profane tyrant, most impious of all the wicked
12:12 and these throughout all time will never let you go
13:13 Each of them and all of them together looking at one another
13:13 Let us with all our hearts consecrate ourselves to God
13:17 and all the fathers will praise us
13:24 they loved one another all the more
14:5 but all of them, as though running the course toward immortality
15:12 each child singly and all together
15:24 this noble mother disregarded all these
16:7 O 7 childbirths all in vain, 7 profitless pregnancies
16:25 as do Abraham and Isaac and Jacob and all the patriarchs
17:17 The tyrant himself and all his council marvelled at their endurance
17:19 For Moses says, All who are consecrated are under your hands
17:24 and he ravaged and conquered all his enemies
18:2 knowing that devout reason is master of all emotions

ALLEGE   1
3 Ma 3:7 alleging that these people were loyal

ALLIANCE   14 = 0.009 %
1 Ma 8:1 toward all who made an alliance with them
8:17 and sent them to Rome to establish friendship and alliance
8:20 have sent us to you to establish alliance and peace with you
8:22 as a memorial of peace and alliance :
12:3 to renew the former friendship and alliance with them
12:8 which contained a clear declaration of alliance and friendship
12:16 to renew our former friendship and alliance with them
14:18 to renew with him the friendship and alliance
14:24 to confirm the alliance with the Romans
15:17 to renew our ancient friendship and alliance
15:19 or make alliance with those who war against them
2 Ma 4:11 and alliance with the Romans

3 Ma	3 : 14	by the gods"deliberate alliance with us in battle
	3 : 21	both because of their alliance with us

ALL-MERCIFUL   1
3 Ma	6 : 9	all-merciful and protector of all

ALL-NOURISHING   1
Wis	16 : 25	changed into all forms, it served thy all-nourishing bounty

ALLOT   5 = 0.003 %
Sir	11 : 18	and this is the reward allotted to him :
	17 : 11	and allotted to them the law of life
	17 : 18	and allotting to him the light of his love
	45 : 20	he allotted to him the first of the first fruits
2 Ma	8 : 27	and allotted it to them as the beginning of mercy

ALLOTTED   1
Wis	2 : 5	For our allotted time is the passing of a shadow

ALLOW   8 = 0.005 %
Sir	18 : 31	If you allow your soul to take pleasure in base desire
	25 : 25	Allow no outlet to water
	27 : 19	And as you allow a bird to escape from your hand
2 Ma	2 : 31	should be allowed to strive for brevity of expression
	11 : 24	and ask that their own customs be allowed them
3 Ma	1 : 11	were allowed to enter
	5 : 18	why the Jews had been allowed to remain alive
2 Es	15 : 10	I will not allow them

ALL-POWERFUL   3 = 0.002 %
Wis	11 : 17	For thy all-powerful hand, which created the world
	18 : 15	thy all-powerful word leaped from heaven
3 Ma	5 : 13	to show the might of his all-powerful hand

ALL-SEEING   3 = 0.002 %
Ad E	15 : 2	after invoking the aid of the all-seeing God and Saviour
2 Ma	7 : 35	You have not yet escaped the judgment of the almighty, all-seeing God
	9 : 5	But the all-seeing Lord, the God of Israel

ALL-WISE   2
4 Ma	1 : 12	giving glory to the all-wise God
	13 : 19	which the divine all-wise Providence

ALLY, subst.   19 = 0.012 %
Jud	3 : 6	and took picked men from them as his allies
	7 : 1	and all the allies who had joined him
1 Ma	8 : 20	that we may be enrolled as your allies and friends
	8 : 24	If war comes first to Rome or to any of their allies
	8 : 25	shall act as their allies wholeheartedly
	8 : 27	the Romans shall willingly act as their allies
	8 : 28	And to the enemy allies shall be given no grain
	8 : 31	upon our friends and allies the Jews ?
	9 : 60	and secretly sent letters to all his allies in Judea
	10 : 6	to equip them with arms, and to become his ally
	10 : 16	Come now, we will make him our friend and ally
	10 : 47	and they remained his allies all his days
	11 : 60	and all the army of Syria gathered to him as allies
	12 : 14	and our other allies and friends
	14 : 40	as friends and allies and brethren
	15 : 17	as our friends and allies
2 Ma	8 : 24	With the Almighty as their ally
	11 : 10	They advanced in battle order, having their heavenly ally
	12 : 36	to show himself his ally and leader in the battle

ALLY, verb   1
2 Es	11 : 30	And I saw how it allied the 2 heads with itself

ALMIGHTY, adj., subst.   40 = 0.026 %
Jud	4 : 13	and in Jerusalem before the sanctuary of the Lord Almighty
	8 : 13	You are putting the Lord Almighty to the test
	15 : 10	May the Almighty Lord bless you for ever !
	16 : 6	But the Lord Almighty has foiled them
	16 : 17	The Lord Almighty will take vengeance on them
Wis	7 : 25	and a pure emanation of the glory of the Almighty
Sir	24 : 24	the Lord Almighty alone is God
	42 : 17	which the Lord the Almighty has established
	50 : 14	and arranging the offering to the Most High, the Almighty
	50 : 17	to worship their Lord, the Almighty, God Most High
Bar	3 : 1	O Lord Almighty, God of Israel
	3 : 4	O Lord Almighty, God of Israel
2 Ma	1 : 25	who alone art just and almighty and eternal
	3 : 22	While they were calling upon the Almighty Lord
	3 : 30	now that the Almighty Lord had appeared
	5 : 20	and what was forsaken in the wrath of the Almighty
	6 : 26	I shall not escape the hands of the Almighty
	7 : 35	You have not yet escaped the judgment of the almighty, all-seeing God
	7 : 38	to bring to an end the wrath of the Almighty
	8 : 11	not expecting the judgment from the Almighty

	8 : 18	but we trust in the Almighty God
	8 : 24	With the Almighty as their ally
	15 : 8	which the Almighty would give them
	15 : 32	against the holy house of the Almighty
1 Es	9 : 46	the God of hosts, the Almighty
P Ma	1	O Lord Almighty, God of our fathers
3 Ma	2 : 2	the only ruler, almighty, give attention to us
	2 : 8	they praised you, the Almighty
	5 : 7	they all called upon the Almighty Lord and Ruler of all power
	6 : 2	King of great power, Almighty God Most High
	6 : 18	Then the most glorious, almighty, and true God
	6 : 28	Release the sons of the almighty and living God of heaven
2 Es	1 : 15	Thus says the Lord Almighty :
	1 : 22	Thus says the Lord Almighty :
	1 : 28	Thus says the Lord Almighty :
	1 : 33	Thus says the Lord Almighty : Your house is desolate
	2 : 9	says the Lord Almighty
	2 : 31	for I am merciful, says the Lord Almighty
	13 : 23	who have works and have faith in the Almighty
	16 : 62	and the spirit of Almighty God

ALMOST   4 = 0.003 %
Jud	11 : 12	and their water has almost given out
2 Ma	5 : 2	And it happened that over all the city, for almost 40 days
2 Es	7 : 48	but almost all who have been created !
	10 : 10	and behold, almost all go to perdition

ALMS   8 = 0.005 %
Tob	4 : 7	Give alms from your possessions to all who live uprightly
	12 : 8	It is better to give alms than to treasure up gold
	14 : 2	He gave alms
	14 : 10	Ahikar gave alms and escaped the deathtrap
Sir	7 : 10	nor neglect to give alms
	12 : 3	or to him who does not give alms
	29 : 8	and do not make him wait for your alms
	35 : 2	and he who gives alms sacrifices a thank offering

ALMSGIVING   8 = 0.005 %
Tob	12 : 8	Prayer is good when accompanied by fasting, almsgiving, and righteousness
	12 : 9	For almsgiving delivers from death
	14 : 11	So now, my children, consider what almsgiving accomplishes
Sir	3 : 30	so almsgiving atones for sin
	17 : 22	A man's almsgiving is like a signet with the Lord
	29 : 12	Store up almsgiving in your treasury
	40 : 17	and almsgiving endures for ever
	40 : 24	but almsgiving rescues better than both

ALONE, adj., adv.   43 = 0.028 %
Tob	1 : 6	But I alone went often to Jerusalem for the feasts
	8 : 4	When the door was shut and the 2 were alone
	8 : 6	Thou didst say, It is not good that the man should be alone
Jud	5 : 4	And why have they alone, of all who live in the west
	9 : 14	who protects the people of Israel but thou alone !
	13 : 2	So Judith was left alone in the tent
Ad E	13 : 5	We understand that this people, and it alone
	14 : 3	help me, who am alone and have no helper but thee
	14 : 14	who am alone and have no helper but thee, O Lord
Wis	10 : 1	when he alone had been created
	17 : 21	while over those men alone heavy night was spread
Sir	18 : 2	The Lord alone will be declared righteous
	24 : 5	Alone I have made the circuit of the vault of heaven
	24 : 24	the Lord Almighty alone is God
	24 : 34	Observe that I have not laboured for myself alone
	33 : 17	Consider that I have not laboured for myself alone
	46 : 8	And these 2 alone were preserved
Sus	13 : 14	when they could find her alone
	13 : 36	The elders said, As we were walking in the garden alone
Bel	14 : 14	in the presence of the king alone
1 Ma	6 : 25	And not against us alone have they stretched out their hands
	13 : 4	and I alone am left
2 Ma	1 : 24	who alone art King and art kind
	1 : 25	who alone art bountiful
	1 : 25	who alone art just and almighty and eternal
	6 : 13	In fact, not to let the impious alone for long
	7 : 37	to make you confess that he alone is God
	8 : 35	and made his way alone like a runaway slave
	15 : 39	For just as it is harmful to drink wine alone
	15 : 39	or, again, to drink water alone
1 Es	5 : 71	for we alone will build it for the Lord of Israel
	8 : 25	Blessed be the Lord alone
2 Es	7 : 44	and to you alone have I shown these things
	7 : 118	the fall was not yours alone
	8 : 7	For thou alone dost exist
	9 : 41	And she said to me, Let me alone, my lord
	12 : 36	And you alone were worthy to learn this secret of the Most High
	12 : 42	For of all the prophets you alone are left to us
	13 : 53	And you alone have been enlightened about this
4 Ma	7 : 18	these alone are able to control the passions of the flesh
	9 : 18	that sons of the Hebrews alone are invincible

15 : 17 O woman, who alone gave birth to such complete devotion !
16 : 10 am a widow and alone, with many sorrows

ALONG, prep., adv.   28 = 0.018 %
Tob 11 : 4 So they went their way, and the dog went along behind them
Jud   1 : 6 and all those who lived along the Euphrates
      1 : 7 and all who lived along the seacoast
      2 : 20 Along with them went a mixed crowd like a swarm of locusts
      2 : 23 and the Ishmaelites who lived along the desert
      2 : 24 and destroyed all the hilltop cities along the brook Abron
      2 : 28 who lived along the seacoast, at Sidon and Tyre
      6 : 8 and you will not die until you perish along with them
      9 : 3 and thou didst strike down slaves along with princes
     12 : 5 Along toward the morning watch she arose
Wis   7 : 11 All good things came to me along with her
     10 : 17 she guided them along a marvellous way
Sir   2 : 12 and to the sinner who walks along 2 ways !
L Jr 6 : 43 And the women, with cords about them, sit along the passageways
1 Ma 6 : 33 along the road to Beth-zechariah
     11 : 4 for they had piled them in heaps along his route
     12 : 50 and had perished along with his men
     13 : 20 But Simon and his army kept marching along opposite him
     15 : 41 and make raids along the highways of Judea
2 Ma 9 : 7 as it was rushing along
      9 : 25 Moreover, I understand how the princes along the borders
3 Ma 4 : 7 In bonds and in public view they were violently dragged along
      5 : 23 began to move them along in the great colonnade
      5 : 47 rushed out in full force along with the beasts
2 Es   3 : 22 the law was in the people's heart along with the evil root
     16 : 32 because no sheep will go along them
4 Ma   4 : 25 were thrown headlong from heights along with their infants
      8 : 3 were brought before him along with their aged mother

ALONGSIDE   1
1 Ma 13 : 52 alongside the citadel

ALOOF   1
Sir 37 : 9 and then stand aloof to see what will happen to you

ALOUD   6 = 0.004 %
1 Ma   3 : 50 and they cried aloud to Heaven, saying
      5 : 33 who sounded their trumpets and cried aloud in prayer
2 Ma   6 : 30 he groaned aloud and said :
      8 : 23 to read aloud from the holy book
1 Es   9 : 41 And he read aloud in the open square
2 Es   6 : 23 and the trumpet shall sound aloud, and when all hear it

ALREADY   21 = 0.014 %
Tob   3 : 8 You already have had 7
      3 : 15 Already 7 husbands of mine are dead
Wis 18 : 9 and already they were singing the praises of the fathers
     18 : 23 For when the dead had already fallen on one another in heaps
     19 : 16 those who had already shared the same rights
1 Ma 12 : 7 Already in time past
2 Ma   2 : 32 adding only so much to what has already been said
      4 : 39 because many of the gold vessels had already been stolen
      4 : 45 But Menelaus, already as good as beaten
     15 : 20 and the enemy was already close at hand
3 Ma   3 : 10 And already some of their neighbours
      4 : 20 had already given out
      5 : 15 that the hour of the banquet was already slipping by
      6 : 5 who had already gained control of the whole world by the spear
2 Es   2 : 13 The kingdom is already prepared for you ; watch !
      4 : 11 And how can one who is already worn out by the corrupt world understand incorruption ?
      5 : 55 as born of a creation which already is aging
     14 : 11 and 9 of its parts have already passed
     14 : 18 is already hastening to come
4 Ma   9 : 21 Although the ligaments joining his bones were already severed
     12 : 2 when he saw that he was already in fetters

ALSO   241 = 0.157 %
Tob   2 : 12 Once when they paid her wages, they also gave her a kid
      3 : 7 it also happened that Sarah, the daughter of Raguel
      6 : 12 The girl is also beautiful and sensible
     10 : 12 He said also to his daughter
     12 : 1 and he must also be given more
     12 : 3 and he also healed you
Jud   2 : 18 also plenty of food for every man
      2 : 25 He also seized the territory of Cilicia
      3 : 4 Our cities also and their inhabitants are your slaves
      9 : 4 O God, my God, hear me also, a widow
     11 : 7 but also the beasts of the field
     15 : 3 also took to flight
     15 : 5 Those in Jerusalem and all the hill country also came
     16 : 19 Judith also dedicated to God all the vessels of Holofernes
Ad E 16 : 24 but also most hateful for all time to beasts and birds
Wis   3 : 14 Blessed also is the eunuch
      5 : 13 So we also, as soon as we were born, ceased to be

      7 : 1 I also am mortal, like all men
     10 : 5 Wisdom also, when the nations in wicked agreement had been confounded
     10 : 8 but also left for mankind a reminder of their folly
     14 : 11 also upon the heathen idols
     16 : 8 And by this also thou didst convince our enemies
     16 : 25 Therefore at that time also
     18 : 20 The experience of death touched also the righteous
     19 : 11 Afterward they saw also a new kind of birds
     19 : 17 They were stricken also with loss of sight
Sir   pr. but also that those who love learning
      pr. was himself also led to write something
      pr. in order that, by becoming conversant with this also
      2 : 18 for as his majesty is, so also is his mercy
      6 : 17 for as he is, so is his neighbour also
     12 : 6 For the Most High also hates sinners
     14 : 21 will also ponder her secrets
     14 : 23 will also listen at her doors
     14 : 24 will also fasten his tent peg to her walls
     16 : 12 As great as his mercy, so great is also his reproof
     16 : 19 The mountains also and the foundations of the earth
     23 : 10 so also the man who always swears
     23 : 20 so it was also after it was finished
     27 : 30 Anger and wrath, these also are abominations
     43 : 6 He made the moon also, to serve in its season
     44 : 12 their children also, for their sake
     44 : 22 To Isaac also he gave the same assurance
     45 : 25 A covenant was also established with David
     46 : 11 The judges also, with their respective names
     47 : 23 Also Jeroboam the son of Nebat, who caused Israel to sin
     48 : 3 and also 3 times brought down fire
     48 : 11 for we also shall surely live
     49 : 13 The memory of Nehemiah also is lasting
L Jr 6 : 59 better also a wooden pillar in a palace
      6 : 61 So also the lightning, when it flashes, is widely seen
Sus 13 : 59 You also have lied against your own head
Bel 14 : 23 There was also a great dragon
1 Ma 1 : 22 He took also the table for the bread of the Presence
      1 : 23 he took also the hidden treasures which he found
      1 : 54 They also built altars in the surrounding cities of Judah
      3 : 33 Lysias was also to take care of Antiochus his son
      3 : 42 They also learned what the king had commanded
      3 : 49 They also brought the garments of the priesthood
      4 : 21 and when they also saw the army of Judas
      4 : 38 They saw also the chambers of the priests in ruins
      4 : 48 They also rebuilt the sanctuary
      4 : 61 He also fortified Beth-zur
      5 : 4 He also remembered the wickedness of the sons of Baean
      5 : 8 He also took Jazer and its villages
      5 : 39 They also have hired Arabs to help them
      5 : 57 So they said, Let us also make a name for ourselves
      6 : 7 with high walls as before, and also Beth-zur, his city
      6 : 25 but also against all the lands on their borders
      6 : 37 and also its Indian driver
      6 : 52 The Jews also made engines of war to match theirs
      7 : 42 So also crush this army before us today
      8 : 4 They also subdued the kings who came against them
      8 : 6 They also defeated Antiochus the Great, king of Asia
      8 : 20 Judas, who is also called Maccabeus, and his brothers
      9 : 12 and the men with Judas also blew their trumpets
      9 : 18 Judas also fell, and the rest fled
      9 : 52 He also fortified the city of Beth-zur
     10 : 24 I also will write them words of encouragement
     10 : 32 I release also my control of the citadel in Jerusalem
     10 : 33 and let all officials cancel also the taxes on their cattle
     10 : 40 I also grant 15,000 shekels of silver yearly
     10 : 45 also be paid from the revenues of the king
     10 : 63 The king also seated him at his side
     10 : 89 He also gave him Ekron and all its environs as his possession
     11 : 5 They also told the king what Jonathan had done
     11 : 31 we have written to you also
     11 : 40 He also reported to Imalkue what Demetrius had done
     12 : 2 He also sent letters to the same effect to the Spartans
     12 : 17 We have commanded them to go also to you
     12 : 33 Simon also went forth and marched through the country
     13 : 3 you know also the wars
     13 : 28 He also erected 7 pyramids, opposite one another
     13 : 34 Simon also chose men and sent them to Demetrius the king
     13 : 48 He also strengthened its fortifications
     14 : 34 He also fortified Joppa, which is by the sea
     14 : 36 as were also the men in the city of David in Jerusalem
     15 : 24 They also sent a copy of these things
     16 : 10 They also fled into the towers
     16 : 21 and that he has sent men to kill you also
2 Ma   1 : 18 in order that you also may celebrate the feast of booths
      2 : 4 It was also in the writing
      2 : 9 It was also made clear
      2 : 10 so also Solomon prayed, and the fire came down
      2 : 12 Likewise Solomon also kept the 8 days
      2 : 13 and also that he founded a library

21

2 : 14	In the same way Judas also collected all the books that had been lost
3 : 11	and also some money of Hyrcanus, son of Tobias
3 : 18	People also hurried out of their houses in crowds
3 : 26	2 young men also appeared to him, remarkably strong
4 : 35	but many also of other nations
6 : 2	and also to pollute the temple in Jerusalem
7 : 1	It happened also that 7 brothers and their mother were arrested
7 : 28	Thus also mankind comes into being
8 : 1	But Judas, who was also called Maccabeus, and his companions
8 : 4	and to remember also the lawless destruction of the innocent babies
8 : 22	He appointed his brothers, also
8 : 30	and to the orphans and widows, and also to the aged
9 : 17	and in addition to all this he also would become a Jew
10 : 2	and also destroyed the sacred precincts
10 : 7	and also fronds of palm
10 : 19	and also Zacchaeus and his men
11 : 25	Accordingly, since we choose that this nation also
11 : 28	We also are in good health
11 : 32	And I have also sent Menelaus to encourage you
11 : 34	The Romans also sent them a letter which read thus :
11 : 35	we also give consent
12 : 13	He also attacked a certain city
12 : 21	and also the baggage to a place called Carnaim
12 : 27	he marched also against Ephron
12 : 31	to be well disposed to their race in the future also
12 : 43	He also took up a collection, man by man
13 : 3	Menelaus also joined them
14 : 8	and second because I have regard also for my fellow citizens
15 : 5	he replied, And I am a sovereign also, on earth
15 : 9	and reminding them also of the struggles they had won
15 : 18	and also for brethren and relatives
15 : 39	so also the style of the story

1 Es	1 : 15	and also Asaph, Zechariah, and Eddinus
	1 : 41	Nebuchadnezzar also took some of the holy vessels of the Lord
	1 : 47	He also did what was evil in the sight of the Lord
	2 : 2	and also put it in writing :
	2 : 10	Cyrus the king also brought out the holy vessels of the Lord
	4 : 45	You also vowed to build the temple
	4 : 54	He wrote also concerning their support and the priests
	4 : 57	he also commanded to be done
	8 : 22	You are also informed that no tribute
	8 : 48	also Hashabiah and Annunus and Jeshaiah his brother

3 Ma	1 : 5	and many captives also were taken
	1 : 29	but also the walls and the whole earth around echoed
	2 : 26	but he also continued with such audacity
	2 : 26	themselves also followed his will
	2 : 29	are also to be branded on their bodies by fire
	2 : 29	and they shall also be reduced to their former limited status
	3 : 16	we came on to Jerusalem
	3 : 23	but also both by speech and by silence
	3 : 28	and also 2,000 drachmas from the royal treasury
	5 : 35	since this also was his aid which they had received
	5 : 41	and also in constant danger of being plundered
	5 : 43	and would also march against Judea
	6 : 33	Likewise also the king, after convening a great banquet
	6 : 40	on which also they made the petition for their dismissal
	7 : 5	They also led them out with harsh treatment as slaves
	7 : 8	We also have ordered each and every one
	7 : 21	They also possessed greater prestige among their enemies

2 Es	1 : 25	Because you have forsaken me, I also will forsake you
	1 : 40	Zechariah and Malachi, who is also called the messenger of the Lord
	3 : 1	I, Salathiel, who am also called Ezra, was in Babylon
	3 : 21	as were also all who were descended from him
	3 : 26	for they also had the evil heart
	4 : 4	I also will show you the way you desire to see
	4 : 15	And in like manner the waves of the sea also made a plan
	4 : 15	so that there also we may gain more territory for ourselves
	4 : 17	likewise also the plan of the waves of the sea
	4 : 21	so also those who dwell upon earth
	4 : 38	but all of us also are full of ungodliness
	4 : 42	so also do these places hasten to give back those things
	4 : 45	show me this also : whether more time is to come than has passed
	5 : 8	There shall be chaos also in many places
	5 : 54	Therefore you also should consider
	6 : 32	and has also observed the purity
	7 : 10	And he said to me, So also is Israel's portion
	7 : 55	and also iron and lead and clay
	7 : 60	So also will be the judgment which I have promised
	7 : 75	show this also to thy servant : whether after death
	7 : 76	He answered me and said, I will show you that also
	7 : 104	I will show you this also
	7 : 118	but ours also who are your descendants
	8 : 39	over their pilgrimage also, and their salvation
	8 : 41	so also those who have been sown in the world will not all be saved
	8 : 44	hast thou also made him like the farmer's seed ?

	8 : 56	For they also received freedom
	9 : 6	so also are the times of the Most High :
	10 : 14	so the earth also has from the beginning
	11 : 4	but it also was at rest with them
	11 : 14	And while it was reigning its end came also
	11 : 18	and it also disappeared
	11 : 20	in due course the wings that followed also rose up on the right side
	11 : 27	a 2nd also, and this disappeared more quickly than the first
	11 : 33	the middle head also suddenly disappeared
	11 : 34	which also ruled over the earth and its inhabitants
	12 : 3	And I looked, and behold, they also disappeared
	12 : 28	but he also shall fall by the sword in the last days
	12 : 44	if we also had been consumed in the burning of Zion !
	13 : 15	now show me also the interpretation of this dream
	13 : 19	But alas for those also who are left
	13 : 21	and I will also explain to you
	14 : 30	which you also have transgressed after them
	15 : 30	Also the Carmonians, raging in wrath
	16 : 12	and its waves and the fish also shall be troubled
	16 : 43	so also him that prunes the vines

4 Ma	1 : 4	it is also clear that it masters
	1 : 10	but I would also call them blessed
	2 : 4	but also over every desire
	4 : 20	but also the temple service was abolished
	5 : 23	and it also trains us in courage
	5 : 27	but also to eat in such a way
	6 : 35	but also that it masters pleasures
	8 : 5	but I also exhort you to yield to me and enjoy my friendship
	8 : 15	but they also opposed the tyrant with their own philosophy
	8 : 22	Also, divine justice will excuse us
	9 : 6	which our aged instructor also overcame
	9 : 10	but also was enraged, as at those who are ungrateful
	10 : 12	When he also had died in a manner worthy of his brothers
	10 : 18	God hears also those who are mute
	11 : 1	When this one died also, after being cruelly tortured
	11 : 22	I also, equipped with nobility, will die with my brothers
	12 : 1	When he also, thrown into the cauldron
	12 : 11	since you have received good things and also your kingdom from God
	14 : 1	but also mastered the emotions of brotherly love
	14 : 9	but also bore the sufferings patiently
	15 : 9	Not only so, but also because of the nobility of her sons
	16 : 2	but also that a woman has despised the fiercest tortures
	16 : 5	Consider this also
	16 : 20	For his sake also
	16 : 25	They knew also that those who die for the sake of God live in God
	17 : 1	when she also was about to be seized and put to death
	17 : 20	but also by the fact that because of them
	18 : 2	but also of those from without
	18 : 3	but also were deemed worthy to share in a divine inheritance
	18 : 6	expressed also these principles to her children :

ALTAR   58 = 0.038 %

Tob	1 : 6	I would give these to the priests, the sons of Aaron, at the altar
Jud	4 : 3	and the sacred vessels and the altar and the temple
	4 : 12	They even surrounded the altar with sackcloth
	8 : 24	and the sanctuary and the temple and the altar rest upon us
	9 : 8	and to cast down the horn of thy altar with the sword
Ad E	14 : 9	and to quench thy altar and the glory of thy house
Wis	9 : 8	and an altar in the city of thy habitation
Sir	35 : 6	The offering of a righteous man anoints the altar
	47 : 9	He placed singers before the altar
	50 : 11	and went up to the holy altar
	50 : 12	as he stood by the hearth of the altar
	50 : 14	Finishing the service at the altars
	50 : 15	he poured it out at the foot of the altar
Bar	1 : 10	and offer them upon the altar of the Lord our God
1 Ma	1 : 21	and took the golden altar
	1 : 47	to build altars and sacred precincts and shrines for idols
	1 : 54	upon the altar of burnt offering
	1 : 54	They also built altars in the surrounding cities of Judah
	1 : 59	they offered sacrifice on the altar
	1 : 59	which was upon the altar of burnt offering
	2 : 23	to offer sacrifice upon the altar in Modein
	2 : 24	he ran and killed him upon the altar
	2 : 25	and he tore down the altar
	2 : 45	and tore down the altars
	4 : 38	And they saw the sanctuary desolate, the altar profaned
	4 : 44	about the altar of burnt offering, which had been profaned
	4 : 45	So they tore down the altar
	4 : 47	and built a new altar like the former one
	4 : 49	the altar of incense, and the table into the temple
	4 : 50	Then they burned incense on the altar
	4 : 53	on the new altar of burnt offering which they had built
	4 : 56	So they celebrated the dedication of the altar for 8 days
	4 : 59	the days of the dedication of the altar should be observed
	5 : 1	that the altar had been built
	5 : 68	he tore down their altars

	6:7	which he had erected upon the altar in Jerusalem
	7:36	and stood before the altar and the temple
2 Ma	**1**:18	when Nehemiah, who built the temple and the altar, offered sacrifices
	1:19	took some of the fire of the altar
	1:32	but when the light from the altar shone back, it went out
	2:5	and the altar of incense, and he sealed up the entrance
	2:19	and the dedication of the altar
	3:15	The priests prostrated themselves before the altar
	4:14	upon their service at the altar
	6:5	The altar was covered with abominable offerings
	10:2	and they tore down the altars which had been built
	10:3	and made another altar of sacrifice
	10:26	Falling upon the steps before the altar
	13:8	against the altar whose fire and ashes were holy
	14:3	to be safe or to have access again to the holy altar
	14:33	and tear down the altar
	15:31	and stationed the priests before the altar
1 Es	**1**:18	and the sacrifices were offered on the altar of the Lord
	4:52	for burnt offerings to be offered on the altar every day
	5:48	took their places and prepared the altar of the God of Israel
	5:50	And they erected the altar in its place
	8:15	so as to offer sacrifices upon the altar of their Lord
2 Es	**10**:21	our altar thrown down, our temple destroyed

ALTER   3 = 0.002 %
Jud	**10**:7	When they saw her, and noted how her face was altered
3 Ma	**3**:23	they secretly suspect that we may soon alter our policy
4 Ma	**4**:19	and altered its form of government

ALTERNATION   1
Wis	**7**:18	the alternations of the solstices

ALTHOUGH   13 = 0.008 %
Jud	**11**:13	although it is not lawful for any of the people
1 Ma	**11**:25	Although certain lawless men of his nation
1 Es	**6**:20	and although it has been in process of construction
3 Ma	**4**:18	although most of them were still in the country
2 Es	**9**:10	although they received my benefits
4 Ma	**3**:10	and although springs were plentiful there
	3:15	But David, although he was burning with thirst
	4:13	although otherwise he had scruples about doing so
	5:7	Although you have had them for so long a time
	7:4	Although his sacred life was consumed by tortures and racks
	9:21	Although the ligaments joining his bones were already severed
	13:27	But although nature and companionship and virtuous habits
	15:24	Although she witnessed the destruction of 7 children

ALTOGETHER   1
4 Ma	**3**:15	considered it an altogether fearful danger to his soul

ALWAYS   21 = 0.014 %
Ad E	**13**:2	but always acting reasonably and with kindness
	16:4	of God, who always sees everything
	16:9	and always judging what comes before our eyes
Wis	**11**:21	For it is always in thy power to show great strength
	14:31	that always pursues the transgression of the unrighteous
	17:11	it has always exaggerated the difficulties
Sir	**17**:15	Their ways are always before him
	22:23	For one should not always despise restricted circumstances
	23:10	so also the man who always swears
	27:11	The talk of the godly man is always wise
	38:29	he is always deeply concerned over his work
1 Ma	**2**:65	always listen to him
2 Ma	**14**:15	and always upholds his own heritage by manifesting himself
	14:24	And he kept Judas always in his presence
1 Es	**1**:32	it was ordained that this should always be done
3 Ma	**7**:6	always taking their part as a father does for his children
	7:9	we always shall have not man but the Ruler over every power
2 Es	**8**:30	but love those who have always put their trust in thy glory
	15:47	who have always lusted after you
	15:53	if you had not always killed my chosen people
	16:20	nor be always mindful of the scourges

AMARIAH   3 = 0.002 %
1 Es	**8**:2	son of Zadok, son of Ahitub, son of Amariah, son of Uzzi
	9:34	Shemaiah, Amariah, Joseph
2 Es	**1**:2	son of Amariah, son of Azariah, son of Meraioth

AMASS   2
Sir	**43**:15	In his majesty he amasses the clouds
	47:18	you gathered gold like tin and amassed silver like lead

AMAZE   14 = 0.009 %
Tob	**11**:16	Those who saw him as he went were amazed
Jud	**15**:1	they were amazed at what had happened
Wis	**5**:2	and they will be amazed at his unexpected salvation
	13:4	And if men were amazed at their power and working
Sir	**11**:13	and raises up his head, so that many are amazed at him
	43:18	and the mind is amazed at its falling

1 Ma	**15**:32	he was amazed
2 Es	**9**:9	Then those who have now abused my ways shall be amazed
	13:11	When I saw it, I was amazed
4 Ma	**2**:1	And why is it amazing that
	6:11	he amazed even his torturers by his courageous spirit
	7:13	Most amazing, indeed, though he was an old man
	14:11	Do not consider it amazing
	17:16	Who were not amazed ?

AMBASSADOR   2
1 Ma	**9**:70	he sent ambassadors to him to make peace with him
	10:51	Then Alexander sent ambassadors to Ptolemy king of Egypt

AMBITION   1
Wis	**14**:18	Then the ambition of the craftsman

AMBUSH, verb   1
1 Ma	**5**:4	and ambushed them on the highways

AMBUSH, subst.   8 = 0.005 %
Sir	**5**:14	and do not lie in ambush with your tongue
	8:11	lest he lie in ambush against your words
1 Ma	**1**:36	It became an ambush against the sanctuary
	9:40	Then they rushed upon them from the ambush
	10:80	Jonathan learned that there was an ambush behind him
	11:68	they had set an ambush against him in the mountains
	11:69	Then the men in ambush emerged from their places and joined battle
2 Es	**15**:33	an enemy in ambush shall beset them

AMEN   5 = 0.003 %
Tob	**8**:8	And she said with him, Amen
1 Es	**9**:47	and all the multitude answered, Amen
P Ma	15	and thine is the glory for ever. Amen
3 Ma	**7**:23	Blessed be the Deliverer of Israel through all times ! Amen
4 Ma	**18**:24	to whom be glory for ever and ever. Amen

AMI   1
1 Es	**5**:34	the sons of Barodis, the sons of Shaphat, the sons of Ami

AMID   1
2 Es	**8**:27	but the endeavours of those who have kept thy covenants amid afflictions

AMISS   2
Sir	**5**:15	In great or small matters do not act amiss
	40:23	A friend or a companion never meets one amiss

AMMIDIAN   1
1 Es	**5**:20	The Chadiasans and Ammidians, 422

AMMON   4 = 0.003 %
Jud	**1**:12	and the people of Ammon, and all Judea
	5:2	and the commanders of Ammon
	7:18	And the sons of Esau and the sons of Ammon went up
2 Ma	**4**:26	was driven as a fugitive into the land of Ammon

AMMONITE   6 = 0.004 %
Jud	**5**:5	Then Achior, the leader of all the Ammonites, said to him
	6:5	But you, Achior, you Ammonite hireling
	7:17	So the army of the Ammonites moved forward
	14:5	But before you do all this, bring Achior the Ammonite to me
1 Ma	**5**:6	Then he crossed over to attack the Ammonites
2 Ma	**5**:7	and fled again into the country of the Ammonites

AMNESTY   1
3 Ma	**3**:21	we made known to all our amnesty towards their compatriots here

AMONG   142 = 0.092 %
Tob	**1**:4	from among all the tribes of Israel
	3:4	in all the nations among which we have been dispersed
	4:12	from among the descendants of your fathers
	4:12	all took wives from among their brethren
	4:13	by refusing to take a wife for yourself from among them
	6:15	to take a wife from among your own people ?
	11:17	So there was rejoicing among all his brethren in Nineveh
	13:3	for he has scattered us among them
	13:5	among whom you have been scattered
Jud	**1**:8	and those among the nations of Carmel and Gilead
	6:2	to prophesy among us as you have done today
	6:6	and you shall fall among their wounded, when I return
	8:12	among the sons of men ?
	8:22	all this he will bring upon our heads among the Gentiles
	9:4	and all their booty to be divided among thy beloved sons
	10:19	who have women like this among them ?
	16:25	among the people of Israel
Ad E	**10**:9	which have not occurred among the nations
	10:11	of decision before God and among all the nations
	10:13	from generation to generation for ever among his people Israel

23

	13 : 3	Haman, who excels among us in sound judgment
	13 : 4	pointed out to us that among all the nations in the world
	14 : 5	and our fathers from among all their ancestors
	16 : 4	They not only take away thankfulness from among men
	16 : 22	as a notable day among your commemorative festivals
Wis	4 : 10	and while living among sinners he was taken up
	4 : 18	and an outrage among the dead for ever
	5 : 5	Why has he been numbered among the sons of God ?
	5 : 5	And why is his lot among the saints ?
	8 : 10	Because of her I shall have glory among the multitudes
	8 : 15	among the people I shall show myself capable
	9 : 4	and do not reject me from among thy servants
	9 : 6	for even if one is perfect among the sons of men
	12 : 17	and dost rebuke any insolence among those who know it
	13 : 7	For as they live among his works they keep searching
	13 : 13	But a castoff piece from among them, useful for nothing
	19 : 21	that walked among them
Sir	1 : 15	She made among men an eternal foundation
	1 : 15	and among their descendants she will be trusted
	7 : 7	and do not disgrace yourself among the people
	7 : 16	Do not count yourself among the crowd of sinners
	10 : 20	Among brothers their leader is worthy of honour
	11 : 1	and will seat him among the great
	11 : 3	The bee is small among flying creatures
	16 : 17	Among so many people I shall not be known
	18 : 3	by his power separating among them
	23 : 14	Remember your father and mother when you sit among great men
	24 : 7	Among all these I sought a resting place
	25 : 18	Her husband takes his meals among the neighbours
	26 : 3	she will be granted among the blessings
	27 : 12	Among stupid people watch for a chance to leave
	27 : 12	but among thoughtful people stay on
	28 : 9	and inject enmity among those who are at peace
	28 : 23	it will burn among them and will not be put out
	29 : 18	and they have wandered among foreign nations
	30 : 2	and will boast of him among acquaintances
	31 : 9	for he has done wonderful things among his people
	31 : 18	If you are seated among many persons
	32 : 1	be among them as one of them
	32 : 9	Among the great do not act as their equal
	33 : 18	Hear me, you who are great among the people
	37 : 26	He who is wise among his people will inherit confidence
	39 : 4	He will serve among great men and appear before rulers
	39 : 4	for he tests the good and the evil among men
	41 : 1	to one who lives at peace among his possessions
	42 : 11	a byword in the city and notorious among the people
	44 : 23	and distributed them among 12 tribes
	45 : 22	and he has no portion among the people
	49 : 16	Shem and Seth were honoured among men
	50 : 6	Like the morning star among the clouds
Bar	2 : 4	to be a reproach and a desolation among all the surrounding peoples
	2 : 13	few in number, among the nations where thou hast scattered us
	2 : 29	a small number among the nations
	3 : 11	that you are counted among those in Hades ?
	3 : 37	Afterward she appeared upon earth and lived among men
L Jr	6 : 67	they cannot show signs in the heavens and among the nations
Sus	13 : 50	sit among us and inform us
	13 : 64	Daniel had a great reputation among the people
1 Ma	1 : 6	and divided his kingdom among them while he was still alive
	2 : 18	among the friends of the king
	3 : 38	mighty men among the friends of the king
	4 : 58	There was very great gladness among the people
	5 : 2	and they determined to destroy the descendants of Jacob who lived among them
	5 : 2	So they began to kill and destroy among the people
	5 : 63	in all Israel and among all the Gentiles
	6 : 35	And they distributed the beasts among the phalanxes
	7 : 13	The Hasidaeans were the first among the sons of Israel
	7 : 23	had done among the sons of Israel
	8 : 2	and of the brave deeds which they were doing among the Gauls
	8 : 16	and there is no envy or jealousy among them
	9 : 27	since the time that prophets ceased to appear among them
	10 : 65	and enrolled him among his chief friends
	11 : 60	and travelled beyond the river and among the cities
	12 : 7	from Arius, who was king among you
	12 : 53	and blot out the memory of them from among men
	13 : 17	lest he arouse great hostility among the people
	15 : 35	they were causing great damage among the people and to our land
2 Ma	1 : 27	set free those who are slaves among the Gentiles
	7 : 16	Because you have authority among men, mortal though you are
	8 : 28	and distributed the rest among themselves and their children
	9 : 28	among the mountains in a strange land
	12 : 3	as this : they invited the Jews who lived among them
	12 : 8	who were living among them
	14 : 35	for thy habitation among us
1 Es	8 : 91	for there was great weeping among the multitude
Ps 151	1	I was small among my brothers, and youngest in my father's house
3 Ma	2 : 2	holy among the holy ones
	2 : 4	among whom were even giants
	2 : 21	holy among the holy ones
	3 : 5	they were established in good repute among all men
	3 : 6	which was common talk among all
	3 : 19	they become the only people among all nations
	3 : 21	Among other things
	3 : 23	they abominate those few among them
	3 : 25	you are to send to us those who live among you
	4 : 2	But among the Jews
	6 : 1	Then a certain Eleazar, famous among the priests of the country
	7 : 21	They also possessed greater prestige among their enemies
2 Es	1 : 14	and did great wonders among you
	1 : 21	I divided fertile lands among you :
	2 : 7	Let them be scattered among the nations
	2 : 26	for I will require them from among your number
	3 : 33	For I have travelled widely among the nations
	5 : 28	and scattered thine only one among the many ?
	7 : 46	For who among the living is there that has not sinned
	7 : 46	or who among men that has not transgressed thy covenant ?
	7 : 76	nor number yourself among those who are tormented
	8 : 35	For in truth there is no one among those who have been born
	8 : 35	and among those who have existed
	8 : 49	and have not deemed yourself to be among the righteous
	9 : 26	and there I sat among the flowers
	9 : 29	O Lord, thou didst show thyself among us
	10 : 16	and will be praised among women
	12 : 38	and you shall teach them to the wise among your people
	14 : 9	for you shall be taken up from among men
	14 : 13	comfort the lowly among them
	14 : 17	the more shall evils be multiplied among its inhabitants
	14 : 46	in order to give them to the wise among your people
	15 : 9	and will receive to myself all the innocent blood from among them
	15 : 16	For there shall be unrest among men
4 Ma	2 : 22	but at the same time he enthroned the mind among the senses
	14 : 15	For example, among birds, the ones that are tame

AMORITE   1
Jud   5 : 15   So they lived in the land of the Amorites

AMOS   2
Tob   2 : 6   Then I remembered the prophecy of Amos
2 Es   1 : 39   and Jacob and Hosea and Amos and Micah

AMOUNT   6 = 0.004 %
Jud   2 : 18   and a huge amount of gold and silver from the royal palace
    15 : 7   got a great amount of booty
1 Ma   3 : 41   they took silver and gold in immense amounts, and fetters
    9 : 35   the great amount of baggage which they had
2 Ma   3 : 6   so that the amount of the funds could not be reckoned
    12 : 43   to the amount of 2,000 drachmas of silver

AMPLE   2
Sir   31 : 19   How ample a little is for a well-disciplined man !
    47 : 23   ample in folly and lacking in understanding

AMPLY   1
Sir   47 : 12   After him rose up a wise son who fared amply because of him

AMRAM   1
1 Es   9 : 34   Of the sons of Bani : Jeremai, Maadai, Amram, Joel

AMUSE   1
Sir   32 : 12   Amuse yourself there, and do what you have in mind

AN   276 = 0.180 %

ANAEL   1
Tob   1 : 21   and he appointed Ahikar, the son of my brother Anael

ANAIAH   1
1 Es   9 : 43   and beside him stood Mattathiah, Shema, Anaiah, Azariah

ANANIAS   3 = 0.002 %
Tob   5 : 12   He replied, I am Azarias the son of the great Ananias
    5 : 13   For I used to know Ananias and Jathan
Jud   8 : 1   son of Ananias, son of Gideon, son of Raphaim

ANANIEL   1
Tob   1 : 1   son of Ananiel, son of Aduel, son of Gabael

ANARCHY   1
Sir   26 : 27   and every person like this lives in the anarchy of war

ANASIB   1
1 Es   5 : 24   of the sons of Anasib, 972

ANATHOTH   1
  1 Es **5**:18 The men of Anathoth, 158

ANCESTOR   13 = 0.008 %
  Jud **5**:8 For they had left the ways of their ancestors
  Ad E **14**:5 and our fathers from among all their ancestors
  Sir **8**:4 lest your ancestors be disgraced
  2 Ma **8**:19 when help came to their ancestors
      11:25 and that they live according to the customs of their ancestors
  3 Ma **5**:31 a full and firm loyalty to my ancestors
      6:28 who from the time of our ancestors until now
      6:28 which they had toward us and our ancestors
  2 Es **3**:12 and again they began to be more ungodly than were their ancestors
  4 Ma **3**:8 around which the whole army of our ancestors had encamped
      5:29 nor will I transgress the sacred oaths of my ancestors
      9:24 Thereby the just Providence of our ancestors
     16:20 the ancestor of our nation

ANCESTRAL   10 = 0.007 %
  2 Ma **8**:17 and besides, the overthrow of their ancestral way of life
     14:7 Therefore I have laid aside my ancestral glory
  3 Ma **1**:3 and apostatized from the ancestral traditions
     1:23 and die courageously for the ancestral law
  4 Ma **4**:23 that if any of them should be found observing the ancestral law
     5:33 as to break the ancestral law by my own act
     8:7 the ancestral tradition of your national life
     9:1 rather than transgress our ancestral commandments
    16:16 Fight zealously for our ancestral law
    18:5 to become pagans and to abandon their ancestral customs

ANCIENT, subst.   1
  Sir **39**:1 will seek out the wisdom of all the ancients

ANCIENT, adj.   5 = 0.003 %
  Ad E **16**:7 can be seen not so much from the more ancient records
  Wis **13**:10 the work of an ancient hand
  Sir **2**:10 Consider the ancient generations
    16:7 He was not propitiated for the ancient giants
  1 Ma **15**:17 to renew our ancient friendship and alliance

AND   9095 = 5.924 %

ANDRONICUS   6 = 0.004 %
  2 Ma **4**:31 leaving Andronicus, a man of high rank, to act as his deputy
     4:32 and gave them to Andronicus
     4:34 Therefore Menelaus, taking Andronicus aside
     4:34 Andronicus came to Onias, and resorting to treachery
     4:38 he immediately stripped off the purple robe from Andronicus
     5:23 and at Gerizim, Andronicus

ANEW   3 = 0.002 %
  Wis **19**:6 For the whole creation in its nature was fashioned anew
  Sir **36**:6 Show signs anew, and work further wonders
  1 Ma **15**:25 Antiochus the king besieged Dor anew

ANGEL   54 = 0.035 %
  Tob **5**:4 and he found Raphael, who was an angel
     5:6 The angel replied, I will go with you
     5:16 and may his angel attend you
     5:21 For a good angel will go with him
     6:3 and the angel said to him, Catch the fish
     6:4 Then the angel said to him
     6:5 So the young man did as the angel told him
     6:6 Then the young man said to the angel, Brother Azarias
    6:10 the angel said to the young man
    6:13 Then the young man said to the angel, Brother Azarias
    6:15 But the angel said to him, Do you not remember the words
     8:3 and the angel bound him
    8:15 let all thy angels and thy chosen people bless thee for ever
    11:14 and blessed are all thy holy angels
    12:5 So he called the angel and said to him
    12:6 Then the angel called the 2 of them privately
    12:15 I am Raphael, one of the 7 holy angels
    12:22 and acknowledged that the angel of the Lord
  Ad E **15**:13 like an angel of God
  Wis **10**:10 and gave him knowledge of angels
    16:20 thou didst give thy people the food of angels
  Sir **48**:21 and his angel wiped them out
  L Jr **6**:7 For my angel is with you, and he is watching your lives
  P Az   26 But the angel of the Lord came down into the furnace
       37 Bless the Lord, you angels of the Lord
  Sus **13**:55 for the angel of God has received the sentence from God
    13:59 for the angel of God is waiting with his sword to saw you in 2
  Bel **14**:34 But the angel of the Lord said to Habakkuk
    14:36 Then the angel of the Lord took him by the crown of his head
    14:39 And the angel of God immediately returned Habakkuk to his own place
  1 Ma **7**:41 thy angel went forth and struck down 185,000 of the Assyrians
  2 Ma **11**:6 besought the Lord to send a good angel to save Israel

    15:22 O Lord, thou didst send thy angel
    15:23 send a good angel to carry terror and trembling before us
  3 Ma **6**:18 from which 2 glorious angels of fearful aspect descended
  2 Es **1**:19 you ate the bread of angels
     2:44 Then I asked an angel, Who are these, my lord ?
     2:46 Then I said to the angel
     2:48 Then the angel said to me, Go, tell my people
     4:1 Then the angel that had been sent to me
     5:15 But the angel who had come and talked with me held me
     5:20 as Uriel the angel had commanded me
     5:31 the angel who had come to me on a previous night was sent to me
     6:3 and before the innumerable hosts of angels were gathered together
     7:1 the angel who had been sent to me on the former nights
     7:85 are guarded by angels in profound quiet
     7:95 and guarded by angels in profound quiet
     8:21 before whom the hosts of angels stand trembling
    10:28 Where is the angel Uriel, who came to me at first ?
    10:29 the angel who had come to me at first came to me
    12:51 as the angel had commanded me
    16:66 Or how will you hide your sins before God and his angels ?
  4 Ma **4**:10 angels on horseback with lightning flashing from their weapons appeared from heaven
     7:11 and conquered the fiery angel

ANGER, subst.   58 = 0.038 %
  Tob **1**:18 For in his anger he put many to death
  Jud **2**:7 for I am coming against them in my anger
     8:14 No, my brethren, do not provoke the Lord our God to anger
     9:8 and bring down their power in thy anger
    11:11 by which they are about to provoke their God to anger
  Ad E **15**:7 he looked at her in fierce anger
  Wis **10**:3 But when an unrighteous man departed from her in his anger
    18:21 he withstood the anger and put an end to the disaster
    19:1 But the ungodly were assailed to the end by pitiless anger
  Sir **1**:21 and where it abides, it will turn away all anger
     1:22 Unrighteous anger cannot be justified
     1:22 for a man's anger tips the scale to his ruin
     4:2 nor anger a man in want
     5:4 For the Lord is slow to anger
     5:6 and his anger rests on sinners
    10:18 nor fierce anger for those born of women
    26:8 There is great anger when a wife is drunken
    26:28 and because of a 3rd anger comes over me :
    27:30 Anger and wrath, these also are abominations
    28:3 Does a man harbour anger against another
    28:8 for a man given to anger will kindle strife
    28:10 in proportion to the strength of the man will be his anger
    28:19 who has not been exposed to its anger
    30:24 Jealousy and anger shorten life
    31:30 Drunkenness increases the anger of a fool to his injury
    36:7 Rouse thy anger and pour out thy wrath
    39:28 and in their anger they scourge heavily
    39:28 and calm the anger of their Maker
    40:5 there is anger and envy and trouble and unrest
    45:18 in wrath and anger
    45:19 and in the wrath of his anger they were destroyed
  Bar **1**:13 and to this day the anger of the Lord and his wrath
     2:13 Let thy anger turn away from us, for we are left
     2:20 For thou hast sent thy anger and thy wrath upon us
  1 Ma **2**:24 He gave vent to righteous anger
     2:44 and struck down sinners in their anger
     2:49 it is a time of ruin and furious anger
     7:35 and in anger he swore this oath
     7:35 And he went out in great anger
  2 Ma **4**:38 and inflamed with anger
     4:40 and filled with anger
    10:35 fired with anger because of the blasphemies
    13:4 But the King of kings aroused the anger of Antiochus
    14:45 Still alive and aflame with anger, he rose
  1 Es **1**:52 until in his anger against his people
  3 Ma **5**:1 was filled with overpowering anger and wrath
     6:22 Then the king's anger was turned to pity and tears
  2 Es **10**:5 and answered her in anger and said
  4 Ma **1**:4 namely anger, fear, and pain
     1:24 Anger, as a man will see if he reflects on this experience
     2:16 just as it repels anger
     2:17 he did nothing against them in anger
     2:17 but controlled his anger by reason
     2:19 saying, Cursed be their anger ?
     2:20 For if reason could not control anger
     3:3 No one of us can eradicate anger from the mind
     3:3 but reason can help to deal with anger
     8:9 But if by disobedience you rouse my anger

ANGER, verb   8 = 0.005 %
  Sir **3**:16 and whoever angers his mother is cursed by the Lord
    19:21 he angers the one who supports him
  Bar **4**:6 because you angered God

1 Ma	3 :27	he was greatly angered
	15 :36	And the king was greatly angered
2 Ma	5 :17	that the Lord was angered for a little while
2 Es	1 :7	But they have angered me and despised my counsels
4 Ma	4 :21	The divine justice was angered by these acts

ANGRILY   1

3 Ma	6 :23	he wept and angrily threatened his friends, saying

ANGRY   21 = 0.014 %

Tob	5 :13	Do not be angry with me
Jud	1 :12	Then Nebuchadnezzar was very angry with this whole region
	5 :2	he was very angry
Sir	4 :3	Do not add to the troubles of an angry mind
	10 :6	Do not be angry with your neighbour for any injury
	19 :17	And do not be angry
	20 :2	How much better it is to reprove than to stay angry !
	28 :7	and do not be angry with your neighbour
Bel	14 :8	Then the king was angry
1 Ma	5 :1	they became very angry
	6 :59	that they became angry and did all these things
	11 :22	When he heard this he was angry
2 Ma	7 :33	And if our living Lord is angry for a little while
	13 :25	in fact they were so angry that they wanted to annul its terms
1 Es	8 :88	Wast thou not angry enough with us
P Ma	13	Do not be angry with me for ever or lay up evil for me
2 Es	8 :30	Be not angry with those who are deemed worse than beasts
	8 :34	But what is man, that thou art angry with him
	16 :48	the more angry I will be with them for their sins
4 Ma	2 :17	When Moses was angry with Dathan and Abiram
	9 :10	When they had said these things the tyrant not only was angry

ANGUISH   12 = 0.008 %

Tob	3 :1	and I prayed in anguish, saying
Wis	4 :19	and they will suffer anguish
	5 :3	and in anguish of spirit they will groan, and say
Sir	48 :19	and they were in anguish, like women in travail
Bar	3 :1	the soul in anguish and the wearied spirit cry out to thee
2 Ma	3 :16	disclosed the anguish of his soul
	3 :21	and the anxiety of the high priest in his great anguish
	9 :9	and while he was still living in anguish and pain
2 Es	2 :27	for when the day of tribulation and anguish comes
	16 :19	tribulation and anguish are sent as scourges
4 Ma	11 :11	In this condition, gasping for breath and in anguish of body
	14 :17	by flying in circles around them in the anguish of love

ANIMAL   19 = 0.012 %

Wis	7 :20	the natures of animals and the tempers of wild beasts
	11 :15	to worship irrational serpents and worthless animals
	12 :24	those animals which even their enemies despised
	13 :10	and likeness of animals, or a useless stone
	13 :14	or makes it like some worthless animal
	15 :18	even the most hateful animals
	15 :19	and even as animals they are not so beautiful in appearance
	16 :1	and were tormented by a multitude of animals
	17 :19	or the unseen running of leaping animals
	19 :10	how instead of producing animals
	19 :19	For land animals were transformed into water creatures
1 Ma	1 :47	to sacrifice swine and unclean animals
2 Ma	5 :27	as wild animals do
	10 :6	like wild animals
3 Ma	4 :9	They were brought on board like wild animals
4 Ma	1 :34	Therefore when we crave seafood and fowl and animals
	5 :8	the very excellent meat of this animal ?
	14 :14	Even unreasoning animals, like mankind
	14 :18	by the example of unreasoning animals

ANKLET   1

Jud	10 :4	and put on her anklets and bracelets and rings

ANNA   8 = 0.005 %

Tob	1 :9	When I became a man I married Anna
	1 :20	and nothing was left to me except my wife Anna
	2 :1	and my wife Anna and my son Tobias were restored to me
	2 :11	Then my wife Anna earned money at women's work
	5 :17	But Anna, his mother, began to weep
	11 :5	Now Anna sat looking intently down the road for her son
	11 :9	Then Anna ran to meet them, and embraced her son
	14 :12	And when Anna died he buried her with his father

ANNAN   1

1 Es	9 :32	Of the sons of Annan : Elionas and Asaias and Melchias

ANNEX   1

1 Ma	10 :38	let them be so annexed to Judea

ANNIAS   1

1 Es	5 :16	The sons of Annias, 101. The sons of Arom

ANNIHILATE   3 = 0.002 %

Ad E	13 :15	for the eyes of our foes are upon us to annihilate us
Sir	47 :7	and annihilated his adversaries the Philistines
1 Ma	5 :15	and all Galilee of the Gentiles, to annihilate us

ANNIHILATION   1

Ad E	16 :15	who were consigned to annihilation by this thrice accursed man

ANNIUTH   1

1 Es	9 :48	Jeshua and Anniuth and Sherebiah, Jamin, Akkub

ANNIVERSARY   1

4 Ma	1 :10	On this anniversary it is fitting for me

ANNOUNCE   4 = 0.003 %

Jud	11 :19	it was announced to me, and I was sent to tell you
Sir	16 :22	Who will announce his acts of justice ?
2 Es	7 :99	as henceforth is announced
	11 :16	I announce this to you before you disappear

ANNOY   3 = 0.002 %

1 Ma	10 :35	or annoy any of them about any matter
	10 :63	and let no one annoy him for any reason
	12 :14	We were unwilling to annoy you

ANNOYANCE   1

1 Es	2 :29	to the annoyance of kings

ANNOYING   1

2 Ma	9 :21	I suffered an annoying illness

ANNUALLY   1

4 Ma	4 :17	he would pay the king 3,660 talents annually

ANNUL   2

2 Ma	13 :25	in fact they were so angry that they wanted to annul its terms
	14 :28	and grieved that he had to annul their agreement

ANNUNUS   1

1 Es	8 :48	also Hashabiah and Annunus and Jeshaiah his brother

ANOINT   9 = 0.006 %

Tob	6 :8	anoint with it a man who has white films in his eyes
	11 :8	You therefore must anoint his eyes with the gall
Jud	10 :3	and anointed herself with precious ointment
	16 :8	She anointed her face with ointment
Sir	35 :6	The offering of a righteous man anoints the altar
	45 :15	Moses ordained him, and anointed him with holy oil
	46 :13	established the kingdom and anointed rulers over his people
	48 :8	who anointed kings to inflict retribution
Ps 151	:4	and anointed me with his anointing oil

ANOINTED, adj., subst.   2

Sir	46 :19	and his anointed : I have not taken any one property
2 Ma	1 :10	To Aristobulus, who is of the family of the anointed priests

ANOINTING   1

Ps 151	:4	and anointed me with his anointing oil

ANOTHER, indef. pr. or adj.   52 = 0.034 %

Tob	6 :12	cannot give her to another man
Wis	16 :14	A man in his wickedness kills another
	16 :19	and at another time even in the midst of water
	18 :18	and one here and another there, hurled down half dead
	19 :3	they reached another foolish decision
Sir	pr.	when translated into another language
	9 :8	and do not look intently at beauty belonging to another
	9 :9	Never dine with another man's wife
	11 :12	There is another who is slow and needs help
	14 :15	Will you not leave the fruit of your labours to another
	14 :18	one dies and another is born
	20 :5	while another is detested for being too talkative
	20 :6	while another keeps silent because he knows when to speak
	23 :23	and brought forth children by another man
	28 :3	Does a man harbour anger against another
	29 :5	A man will kiss another's hands until he gets a loan
	29 :22	than sumptuous food in another man's house
	32 :9	and when another is speaking, do not babble
	33 :7	Why is any day better than another
	33 :19	and do not give your property to another
	34 :23	When one builds and another tears down
	34 :24	When one prays and another curses
	36 :18	yet one food is better than another
	36 :21	but one daughter is better than another
	40 :29	When a man looks to the table of another
	40 :29	He pollutes himself with another man's food
	41 :21	and of gazing at another man's wife
Bar	2 :3	and another the flesh of his daughter
	4 :3	Do not give your glory to another
1 Ma	5 :37	After these things Timothy gathered another army

	10:16	So he said, Shall we find another such man ?
2 Ma	3:37	to send on another mission to Jerusalem
	4:8	and, from another source of revenue, 80 talents
	4:19	but to expend it for another purpose
	4:26	was supplanted by another man
	10:3	and made another altar of sacrifice
2 Es	3:32	Or has another nation known thee besides Israel ?
	5:46	why one after another ?
	6:6	and they were made through me and not through another
	6:6	and not through another
	7:6	Another example : There is a city built and set on a plain
	7:105	so no one shall ever pray for another on that day
	7:105	neither shall any one lay a burden on another
	11:19	they wielded power one after another
	12:14	And 12 kings shall reign in it, one after another
	13:12	and call to him another multitude which was peaceable
	13:39	gather to himself another multitude that was peaceable
	13:40	and they were taken into another land
	15:38	and from the north, and another part from the west
	16:27	one man will long to see another
4 Ma	13:11	another said, Bear up nobly
	13:12	and another reminded them, Remember whence you came

ANSWER, subst.   4 = 0.003 %

Sir	8:9	and learn how to give an answer in time of need
	20:6	There is one who keeps silent because he has no answer
	33:4	bind together your instruction, and make your answer
2 Es	4:9	and you have given me no answer about them !

ANSWER, verb   76 = 0.050 %

Tob	5:1	Then Tobias answered him
	5:11	But he answered
	7:3	They answered him, We belong to the sons of Naphtali
	10:7	And she answered him, Be still and stop deceiving me
Jud	6:17	He answered and told them what had taken place
	14:15	But when no one answered
Sir	4:8	and answer him peaceably and gently
	5:11	Be quick to hear, and be deliberate in answering
	5:12	If you have understanding, answer your neighbour
	11:8	Do not answer before you have heard
	46:6	and the great Lord answered him
Sus	13:54	He answered, Under a mastic tree
	13:58	He answered, Under an evergreen oak
Bel	14:5	He answered, Because I do not revere man-made idols
	14:17	He answered, They are unbroken, O king
1 Ma	2:19	But Mattathias answered and said in a loud voice :
	2:36	But they did not answer them or hurl a stone at them
	13:8	and they answered in a loud voice
	15:35	Athenobius did not answer him a word
2 Ma	14:5	He answered :
1 Es	6:13	They answered us
	9:47	and all the multitude answered, Amen
2 Es	2:45	he answered and said to me
	2:47	He answered and said to me, He is the Son of God
	4:1	whose name was Uriel, answered
	4:6	I answered and said
	4:13	He answered me and said
	4:19	I answered and said, Each has made a foolish plan
	4:20	He answered me and said, You have judged rightly
	4:22	Then I answered and said, I beseech you, my lord
	4:26	He answered me and said
	4:33	Then I answered and said
	4:34	He answered me and said
	4:36	And Jeremiel the archangel answered them and said
	4:38	Then I answered and said, O sovereign Lord
	4:40	He answered me and said
	4:44	I answered and said
	4:52	He answered me and said
	5:11	passed through you ? And it will answer, No
	5:43	Then I answered and said
	5:53	And she herself will answer you
	6:7	And I answered and said
	6:11	I answered and said, O sovereign Lord
	6:13	He answered and said to me
	7:17	Then I answered and said, O sovereign Lord, behold
	7:45	I answered and said, O sovereign Lord
	7:49	He answered me and said, Listen to me, Ezra
	7:59	He answered me and said
	7:70	He answered me and said
	7:73	or how will they answer in the last times ?
	7:75	I answered and said
	7:76	He answered me and said, I will show you that also
	7:100	He answered and said
	7:102	I answered and said
	7:104	He answered me and said
	7:106	I answered and said
	7:112	He answered me and said, This present world is not the end
	7:116	I answered and said, This is my first and last word
	7:127	He answered and said
	7:132	I answered and said, I know, O Lord

	8:1	He answered me and said
	8:4	I answered and said
	8:25	and as long as I have understanding I will answer
	8:37	He answered me and said
	8:42	I answered and said
	8:46	He answered me and said
	8:62	Then I answered and said
	9:1	He answered me and said, Measure carefully in your mind
	9:14	I answered and said
	9:17	He answered me and said
	10:5	and answered her in anger and said
	10:38	He answered me and said
	12:45	Then I answered them and said
	13:20	He answered me and said
	14:19	Then I answered and said
	14:23	He answered me and said

ANTAGONIST   3 = 0.002 %

3 Ma	7:9	in everything and inescapably as an antagonist to avenge such acts. Farewell
4 Ma	3:5	For reason does not uproot the emotions but is their antagonist
	17:14	The tyrant was the antagonist

ANTILEBANON   1

Jud	1:7	and Lebanon and Antilebanon

ANTIOCH   15 = 0.010 %

1 Ma	3:37	and departed from Antioch his capital in the 147th year
	4:35	he departed to Antioch and enlisted mercenaries
	6:63	Then he departed with haste and returned to Antioch
	10:68	he was greatly grieved and returned to Antioch
	11:13	Then Ptolemy entered Antioch and put on the crown of Asia
	11:44	So Jonathan sent 3,000 stalwart men to him at Antioch
	11:56	and gained control of Antioch
2 Ma	4:9	and to enrol the men of Jerusalem as citizens of Antioch
	4:33	at Daphne near Antioch
	5:21	and hurried away to Antioch
	8:35	across the country till he reached Antioch
	11:36	For we are on our way to Antioch
	13:23	had revolted in Antioch
	13:26	and set out for Antioch
	14:27	and commanding him to send Maccabeus to Antioch

ANTIOCHIAN   1

2 Ma	4:19	chosen as being Antiochian citizens from Jerusalem

ANTIOCHIS   1

2 Ma	4:30	as a present to Antiochis, the king's concubine

ANTIOCHUS   70 = 0.046 %

1 Ma	1:10	From them came forth a sinful root, Antiochus Epiphanes
	1:10	son of Antiochus the king
	1:16	When Antiochus saw that his kingdom was established
	1:20	After subduing Egypt, Antiochus returned in the 143rd year
	3:27	When King Antiochus heard these reports
	3:33	Lysias was also to take care of Antiochus his son
	6:1	King Antiochus was going through the upper provinces
	6:15	that he might guide Antiochus his son
	6:16	Thus Antiochus the king died there in the 149th year
	6:17	he set up Antiochus the king's son to reign
	6:55	whom King Antiochus while still living
	6:55	had appointed to bring up Antiochus his son to be king
	7:2	the army seized Antiochus and Lysias to bring them to him
	8:6	They also defeated Antiochus the Great, king of Asia
	10:1	In the 160th year Alexander Epiphanes, the son of Antiochus
	11:39	who was bringing up Antiochus, the young son of Alexander
	11:40	and insistently urged him to hand Antiochus over to him
	11:54	and with him the young boy Antiochus
	11:57	Then the young Antiochus wrote to Jonathan, saying
	12:16	We therefore have chosen Numenius the son of Antiochus
	12:39	and to raise his hand against Antiochus the king
	13:31	Trypho dealt treacherously with the young king Antiochus
	14:22	Numenius the son of Antiochus and Antipater the son of Jason, envoys of the Jews
	15:1	Antiochus, the son of Demetrius the king
	15:2	King Antiochus to Simon the high priest and ethnarch
	15:10	In the 174th year Antiochus set out
	15:11	Antiochus pursued him, and he came in his flight to Dor
	15:13	So Antiochus encamped against Dor
	15:25	Antiochus the king besieged Dor anew
	15:26	And Simon sent to Antiochus 2,000 picked men, to fight for him
2 Ma	1:14	Antiochus came to the place together with his friends
	1:15	and Antiochus had come with a few men
	2:20	and further the wars against Antiochus Epiphanes
	4:7	and Antiochus who was called Epiphanes succeeded to the kingdom
	4:21	Antiochus learned that Philometor had become hostile to his government
	4:37	Therefore Antiochus was grieved at heart
	5:1	About this time Antiochus made his 2nd invasion of Egypt

	5 : 5	When a false rumour arose that Antiochus was dead
	5 : 15	Not content with this, Antiochus dared to enter
	5 : 17	Antiochus was elated in spirit, and did not perceive
	5 : 21	So Antiochus carried off 1,800 talents from the temple
	5 : 24	Antiochus sent Apollonius, the captain of the Mysians
	7 : 24	Antiochus felt that he was being treated with contempt
	7 : 24	Antiochus not only appealed to him in words
	9 : 1	Antiochus had retreated in disorder
	9 : 2	and Antiochus and his men were defeated
	9 : 2	with the result that Antiochus was put to flight by the inhabitants
	9 : 19	Antiochus their king and general sends hearty greetings
	9 : 25	So I have appointed my son Antiochus to be king
	9 : 29	then, fearing the son of Antiochus
	10 : 9	Such then was the end of Antiochus who was called Epiphanes
	10 : 10	Now we will tell what took place under Antiochus Eupator
	10 : 13	and had gone over to Antiochus Epiphanes
	11 : 22	King Antiochus to his brother Lysias, greeting
	11 : 27	King Antiochus to the senate of the Jews
	13 : 1	that Antiochus Eupator was coming
	13 : 3	and with utter hypocrisy urged Antiochus on
	13 : 4	But the King of kings aroused the anger of Antiochus
	14 : 2	having made away with Antiochus and his guardian Lysias
3 Ma	1 : 1	that the regions which he had controlled had been seized by Antiochus
	1 : 1	where Antiochus's supporters were encamped
	1 : 4	and matters were turning out in favour of Antiochus
4 Ma	4 : 15	his son Antiochus Epiphanes succeeded to the throne
	4 : 21	and caused Antiochus himself to make war on them
	5 : 1	The tyrant Antiochus, sitting in state with his counsellors
	5 : 5	When Antiochus saw him he said
	5 : 16	We, O Antiochus, who have been persuaded
	10 : 17	the bloodthirsty, murderous, and utterly abominable Antiochus
	17 : 23	For the tyrant Antiochus
	18 : 5	The tyrant Antiochus was both punished on earth

ANTIPATER 2

1 Ma	12 : 16	and Antipater the son of Jason
	14 : 22	Numenius the son of Antiochus and Antipater the son of Jason, envoys of the Jews

ANVIL 1

Sir	38 : 28	So too is the smith sitting by the anvil

ANXIETY 8 = 0.005 %

Ad E	14 : 1	And Esther the queen, seized with deathly anxiety, fled to the Lord
Wis	7 : 23	Beneficent, humane, steadfast, sure, free from anxiety
Sir	30 : 24	and anxiety brings on old age too soon
	31 : 1	and anxiety about it removes sleep
	31 : 2	Wakeful anxiety prevents slumber
2 Ma	3 : 21	and the anxiety of the high priest in his great anguish
1 Es	8 : 71	and sat down in anxiety and grief
4 Ma	16 : 8	and the more grievous anxieties of your upbringing

ANXIOUS 5 = 0.003 %

Sir	40 : 2	their anxious thought is the day of death
Bar	3 : 18	those who scheme to get silver, and are anxious
2 Ma	15 : 19	being anxious over the encounter in the open country
2 Es	2 : 27	Do not be anxious
	3 : 3	and I began to speak anxious words to the Most High, and said

ANY* 132 = 0.086 %

Tob	1 : 18	any who came fleeing from Judea
	3 : 8	and have had no benefit from any of them
	3 : 14	that I am innocent of any sin with man
	4 : 7	Do not turn your face away from any poor man
	4 : 14	the wages of any man who works for you
	4 : 18	and do not despise any useful counsel
	6 : 12	because you rather than any other man
	14 : 10	And do not live in Nineveh any longer
Jud	2 : 13	any of your sovereign's commands
	3 : 4	come and deal with them in any way that seems good to you
	4 : 7	and it was easy to stop any who tried to enter
	5 : 20	if there is any unwitting error in this people
	7 : 22	there was no strength left in them any longer
	8 : 15	he has power to protect us within any time he pleases
	8 : 18	has there been any tribe or family or people
	8 : 20	or any of our nation
	11 : 13	although it is not lawful for any of the people
	12 : 10	and did not invite any of his officers
Ad E	13 : 12	or pride or for any love of glory that I did this
	14 : 15	and abhor the bed of the uncircumcised and of any alien
Wis	7 : 9	Neither did I liken to her any priceless gem
	7 : 24	For wisdom is more mobile than any motion
	12 : 13	For neither is there any god besides thee
	12 : 14	nor can any king or monarch confront thee
	12 : 17	and dost rebuke any insolence among those who know it
Sir	7 : 13	Refuse to utter any lie
	10 : 6	Do not be angry with your neighbour for any injury

	12 : 13	or any who go near wild beasts ?
	22 : 18	will not stand firm against any fear
	22 : 22	or a treacherous blow – in these cases any friend will flee
	25 : 13	Any wound, but not a wound of the heart !
	25 : 13	Any wickedness, but not the wickedness of a wife !
	25 : 14	Any attack, but not an attack from those who hate !
	25 : 14	And any vengeance, but not the vengeance of enemies !
	25 : 19	Any iniquity is insignificant compared to a wife's iniquity
	26 : 12	and drinks from any water near him
	33 : 7	Why is any day better than another
	36 : 18	The stomach will take any food
	36 : 21	A woman will accept any man
	37 : 11	with an idler about any work
	37 : 11	pay no attention to these in any matter of counsel
	37 : 29	Do not have an insatiable appetite of any luxury
	40 : 16	The reeds by any water or river bank
	40 : 16	will be plucked up before any grass
	40 : 27	and covers a man better than any glory
	47 : 22	nor cause any of his works to perish
	48 : 12	in all his days he did not tremble before any ruler
Bar	2 : 19	For it is not because of any righteous deeds
L Jr	6 : 25	They are bought at any cost
	6 : 56	Besides, they can offer no resistance to a king or any enemies
P Az	14	For we, O Lord, have become fewer than any nation
1 Ma	2 : 13	Why should we live any longer ?
	3 : 28	and ordered them to be ready for any need
	8 : 24	If war comes first to Rome or to any of their allies
	8 : 26	without receiving any return
	8 : 30	and any addition or deletion that they may make shall be valid
	10 : 33	from the land of Judah into any part of my kingdom
	10 : 35	or annoy any of them about any matter
	10 : 43	or in any of its precincts
	10 : 43	because he owes money to the king or has any debt
	10 : 63	about any matter
	10 : 63	and let no one annoy him for any reason
	13 : 5	in any time of distress
	13 : 39	We pardon any errors and offences committed to this day
	13 : 40	And if any of you are qualified
	14 : 44	to nullify any of these decisions or to oppose what he says
	14 : 45	or nullifies any of them
	15 : 21	Therefore if any pestilent men
2 Ma	3 : 13	said that this money must in any case be confiscated
	3 : 29	and deprived of any hope of recovery
	3 : 38	he replied, If you have any enemy or plotter against your government
	4 : 27	any of the money promised to the king
	5 : 10	he had no funeral of any sort
	9 : 7	Yet he did not any way stop his insolence
	9 : 18	But when his sufferings did not in any way abate
	9 : 24	or any unwelcome news came
	11 : 31	and none of them shall be molested in any way
	13 : 6	any man guilty of sacrilege or notorious for other crimes
1 Es	1 : 24	beyond any other people or kingdom
	4 : 18	If men gather gold and silver or any other beautiful thing
	4 : 19	or any other beautiful thing
	5 : 53	And all who had made any vow to God
	6 : 32	And he commanded that if any should transgress
	6 : 32	or nullify any of the things herein written
	8 : 22	or any other tax is to be laid
	8 : 22	on any of the priests or Levites or temple singers
	8 : 22	and that no one has authority to impose any tax upon them
	9 : 4	and that if any did not meet there
3 Ma	2 : 30	But if any of them prefer to join
	3 : 19	and are unwilling to regard any action as sincere
	3 : 27	But whoever shelters any of the Jews
	3 : 29	and shall become useless for all time to any mortal creature
	4 : 11	nor in any way claim to be inside the circuit of the city
	4 : 13	not omitting any detail of their punishment
	5 : 6	that the Jews were left without any aid
	7 : 5	they tried without any inquiry or examination
	7 : 8	with no one in any place doing them harm at all
	7 : 9	For you should know that if we devise any evil against them
	7 : 9	or cause them any grief at all
	7 : 14	anywhom they met of their fellow-countrymen
	7 : 22	so that those who held any
2 Es	2 : 23	when you find any who are dead
	2 : 43	taller than any of the others
	3 : 28	Are the deeds of those who inhabit Babylon any better ?
	4 : 40	her womb can keep the child within her any longer
	5 : 49	and a woman who has become old does not bring forth any longer
	7 : 66	nor do they know of any torment or salvation
	8 : 55	Therefore do not ask any more questions
	9 : 34	or any dish food or drink
	10 : 45	before any offering was offered in it
	10 : 53	where there was no foundation of any building
	12 : 15	for a longer time than any other of the 12
	13 : 9	nor held a spear or any weapon of war
	15 : 10	to live any longer in the land of Egypt
4 Ma	4 : 23	that if any of them should be found observing the ancestral law

	4:24	he had not been able in any way
	5:3	If any were not willing to eat defiling food
	5:13	it will excuse you from any transgression
	5:17	that we should not transgress it in any respect
	5:23	so that we endure any suffering willingly
	7:22	and knows that it is blessed to endure any suffering
	8:2	and that any who ate defiling food should be freed after eating
	8:2	but if any were to refuse
	8:27	neither said any of these things
	9:29	How sweet is any kind of death for the religion of our fathers !
	10:7	Since they were not able in any way to break his spirit
	15:6	The mother of the 7 boys, more than any other mother, loved her children
	16:11	Nor when I die, shall I have any of my sons to bury me
	16:12	did not wail with such a lament for any of them
	16:12	nor did she dissuade any of them from dying
	16:19	and therefore you ought to endure any suffering for the sake of God

ANYBODY   1
Sir **33**:29   Do not act immoderately toward anybody

ANY ONE, indef. pr. or adj.   33 = 0.021 %
Tob **1**:17   and if I saw any one of my people dead
     4:15   And what you hate, do not do to any one
      6:7   if a demon or evil spirit gives trouble to any one
     8:12   let us bury him without any one knowing about it
Jud **11**:1   for I have never hurt any one
    12:20   much more than he had ever drunk in any one day
Ad E **13**:14   and I will not bow down to any one but to thee
Wis **6**:7   For the Lord of all will not stand in awe of any one
      8:7   And if any one loves righteousness, her labours are virtues
      8:8   And if any one longs for wide experience
    12:11   and it was not through fear of any one
Sir **8**:7   Do not rejoice over any one death
    15:20   He has not commanded any one to be ungodly
    15:20   and he has not given any one permission to sin
    22:2   any one that picks it up will shake it off his hand
    33:20   do not let any one take your place
    42:12   Do not look upon any one for beauty
    46:19   and his anointed : I have not taken any one property
L Jr **6**:14   though unable to destroy any one who offends it
      6:27   If any one sets one of them upright
      6:40   Why then must any one think that they are gods
      6:44   Why then must any one think that they are gods
      6:56   Why then must any one admit or think that they are gods ?
1 Ma **1**:57   in the possession of any one
      1:57   or if any one adhered to the law
2 Ma **1**:19   that the place was unknown to any one
1 Es **2**:5   If any one of you, therefore, is of his people
3 Ma **3**:28   Any one willing to give information
      7:21   to confiscation of their belongings by any one
2 Es **3**:31   and hast not shown to any one how thy way may be comprehended
      5:11   Has righteousness, or any one who does right
      7:5   If any one, then, wishes to reach the sea
      7:105 neither shall any one lay a burden on another

ANYTHING   23 = 0.015 %
Tob **2**:4   So before I tasted anything
    12:11   I will not conceal anything from you
Jud **8**:13   but you will never know anything !
Wis **10**:12   that godliness is more powerful than anything
    11:24   for thou wouldst not have made anything
    11:25   How would anything have endured if thou hadst not willed it ?
    11:25   Or how would anything not called forth by thee
Sir **8**:12   but if you do lend anything, be as one who has lost it
    10:6   and do not attempt anything by acts of insolence
    19:13   but if he did anything, so that he may do it no more
    25:3   how then can you find anything in your old age ?
    29:26   and if you have anything at hand, let me have it to eat
Bel **14**:7   and it never ate or drank anything
1 Ma **8**:30   both parties shall determine to add or delete anything
    10:35   No one shall have authority to exact anything from them
2 Ma **9**:24   so that, if anything unexpected happened
    12:18   without accomplishing anything
1 Es **4**:39   instead of anything that is unrighteous or wicked
3 Ma **2**:3   and you judge those who have done anything in insolence and arrogance
      2:9   though you have no need of anything
2 Es **2**:28   but they shall not be able to do anything against you
4 Ma **2**:5   or anything that is your neighbour's
      9:12   without accomplishing anything, they placed him upon the wheel

APAME   1
1 Es **4**:29   Yet I have seen him with Apame, the king's concubine

APART   5 = 0.003 %
Wis **11**:20   Even apart from these
1 Es **4**:44   which Cyrus set apart when he began to destroy Babylon

	4:57	which Cyrus had set apart
	8:54	Then I set apart 12 of the leaders of the priests
2 Es	3:16	And thou didst set apart Jacob for thyself

APHAIREMA   1
1 Ma **11**:34   and the 3 districts of Aphairema and Lydda and Rathamin

APHERRA   1
1 Es **5**:34   the sons of Addus, the sons of Subas, the sons of Apherra

APOLLONIUS   20 = 0.013 %
1 Ma **3**:10   But Apollonius gathered together Gentiles
      3:12   and Judas took the sword of Apollonius
    10:69   And Demetrius appointed Apollonius the governor of Coelesyria
    10:74   When Jonathan heard the words of Apollonius
    10:75   for Apollonius had a garrison in Joppa
    10:77   When Apollonius heard of it
    10:79   Now Apollonius had secretly left a 1,000 cavalry behind them
2 Ma **3**:5   he went to Apollonius of Tarsus
      3:7   When Apollonius met the king
      4:4   and that Apollonius, the son of Menestheus
      4:21   When Apollonius the son of Menestheus was sent to Egypt
      5:24   Antiochus sent Apollonius, the captain of the Mysians
    12:2   Timothy and Apollonius the son of Gennaeus
4 Ma **4**:2   So he came to Apollonius
      4:4   When Apollonius learned the details of these things
      4:8   But, uttering threats, Apollonius went on to the temple
      4:10   and while Apollonius was going up
      4:11   Then Apollonius fell down half dead
      4:13   that Apollonius had been overcome by human treachery
      4:14   So Apollonius, having been preserved beyond all expectations

APOLLOPHANES   1
2 Ma **10**:37   and his brother Chaereas, and Apollophanes

APOLOGY   1
Sir **13**:3   a poor man suffers wrong, and he must add apologies

APOSTASY   2
Tob **1**:5   All the tribes that joined in apostasy
1 Ma **2**:15   Then the king's officers who were enforcing the apostasy

APOSTATIZE   1
3 Ma **1**:3   and apostatized from the ancestral traditions

APPAL   1
Wis **17**:3   and appalled by spectres

APPAREL, subst.   2
Jud **10**:3   and arrayed herself in her gayest apparel
Ad E **14**:2   she took off her splendid apparel

APPARITION   2
Wis **18**:17   Then at once apparitions in dreadful dreams greatly troubled them
2 Ma **5**:4   that the apparition might prove to have been a good omen

APPEAL, verb   9 = 0.006 %
Wis **8**:21   so I appealed to the Lord and besought him
    13:18   For health he appeals to a thing that is weak
    18:22   appealing to the oaths and covenants given to our fathers
Sir **47**:5   For he appealed to the Lord, the Most High
    51:10   I appealed to the Lord, the Father of my Lord
1 Ma **8**:32   If now they appeal again for help against you
2 Ma **4**:36   the Jews in the city appealed to him
      7:24   Antiochus not only appealed to him in words
      7:37   appealing to God to show mercy soon to our nation

APPEAL, subst.   2
Sir **41**:21   and of rejecting the appeal of a kinsman
2 Es **6**:44   and of varied appeal to the taste

APPEAR   47 = 0.031 %
Tob **12**:19   All these days I merely appeared to you
    12:22   had appeared to them
Ad E **14**:16   which is upon my head on the days when I appear in public
Wis **6**:16   and she graciously appears to them in their paths
    17:4   and dismal phantoms with gloomy faces appeared
Sir **35**:4   Do not appear before the Lord empty-handed
    37:18   4 turns of fortune appear, good and evil, life and death
    39:4   He will serve among great men and appear before rulers
    43:2   The sun, when it appears
    43:22   when the dew appears, it refreshes from the heat
Bar **3**:37   Afterward she appeared upon earth and lived among men
1 Ma **4**:6   At daybreak Judas appeared in the plain with 3,000 men
      4:19   a detachment appeared, coming out of the hills
      7:12   Then a group of scribes appeared in a body
      9:23   all the doers of injustice appeared
      9:27   since the time that prophets ceased to appear among them
2 Ma **1**:33   the liquid had appeared with which Nehemiah and his associates

	2:8	and the glory of the Lord and the cloud will appear
	3:25	For there appeared to them
	3:26	2 young men also appeared to him, remarkably strong
	3:30	now that the Almighty Lord had appeared
	3:33	the same young men appeared again to Heliodorus
	5:2	there appeared goldenclad horsemen charging through the air
	10:29	there appeared to the enemy from heaven
	11:8	a horseman appeared at their head
	12:16	appeared to be running over with blood
	12:22	But when Judas' first division appeared
	14:20	and it appeared that they were of one mind
	15:13	Then likewise a man appeared
1 Es	5:40	until a high priest should appear wearing Urim and Thummim
3 Ma	2:30	In order that he might not appear to be an enemy to all
	3:4	For this reason they appeared hateful to some
	5:6	For to the Gentiles it appeared
2 Es	3:6	which thy right hand had planted before the earth appeared
	3:33	Yet their reward has not appeared
	6:22	Sown places shall suddenly appear unsown
	6:40	so that thy works might then appear
	7:26	that the city which now is not seen shall appear
	7:36	Then the pit of torment shall appear
	7:114	and righteousness has increased and truth has appeared
	9:3	So when there shall appear in the world earthquakes
	10:41	The woman who appeared to you a little while ago
	10:42	but an established city has appeared to you
	12:11	is the 4th kingdom which appeared in a vision
	15:28	Behold, a terrifying sight, appearing from the east !
4 Ma	4:10	angels on horseback with lightning flashing from their weapons appeared from heaven
	7:20	when some persons appear to be dominated by their emotions

APPEARANCE   19 = 0.012 %

Tob	1:13	and good appearance in the sight of Shalmaneser
Jud	8:7	She was beautiful in appearance, and had a very lovely face
	11:23	You are not only beautiful in appearance, but wise in speech
Wis	14:17	they imagined their appearance far away
	15:5	whose appearance arouses yearning in fools
	15:19	and even as animals they are not so beautiful in appearance
	17:6	to be worse than that unseen appearance
Sir	11:2	nor loathe a man because of his appearance
	19:29	A man is known by his appearance
	25:17	The wickedness of a wife changes her appearance
	43:1	the appearance of heaven in a spectacle of glory
L Jr	6:63	But these idols are not to be compared with them in appearance of power
Sus	13:31	and beautiful in appearance
2 Ma	2:21	and the appearances which came from heaven
	3:16	To see the appearance of the high priest
1 Es	4:18	and then see a woman lovely in appearance and beauty
2 Es	15:34	and their appearance is very threatening
4 Ma	8:4	And struck by their appearance and nobility
	8:10	for your youth and handsome appearance

APPEARING   1

Sir	43:16	At his appearing the mountains are shaken

APPEASE   1

2 Ma	13:26	convinced them, appeased them, gained their good will

APPENDED   1

1 Ma	12:7	as the appended copy shows

APPETITE   6 = 0.004 %

Wis	16:2	a delicacy to satisfy the desire of appetite
	16:3	might lose the least remnant of appetite
Sir	18:30	Do not follow your base desires, but restrain your appetites
	37:29	Do not have an insatiable appetite of any luxury
4 Ma	1:33	Is it not because reason is able to rule over appetites ?
	1:35	For the emotions of the appetites are restrained

APPHUS   1

1 Ma	2:5	Eleazar called Avaran, and Jonathan called Apphus

APPLAUD   1

3 Ma	7:13	When they had applauded him in fitting manner

APPLE   1

Sir	17:22	and he will keep a person's kindness like the apple of his eye

APPLY   5 = 0.003 %

Ad E	15:10	you shall not die, for our law applies only to the people. Come near
Sir	6:32	and if you apply yourself you will become clever
2 Ma	4:20	it was applied to the construction of triremes
2 Es	13:54	and have applied yourself to mine
4 Ma	11:19	To his back they applied sharp spits

APPOINT   34 = 0.022 %

Tob	1:21	and he appointed Ahikar, the son of my brother Anael
	1:22	for Esarhaddon had appointed him second to himself
Jud	5:18	which he had appointed for them
Sir	17:17	he appointed a ruler for every nation
	33:8	and he appointed the different seasons and feasts
	33:11	and appointed their different ways
Sus	13:5	In that year 2 elders from the people were appointed as judges
1 Ma	1:51	And he appointed inspectors over all the people
	3:55	After this Judas appointed leaders of the people
	6:55	had appointed to bring up Antiochus his son to be king
	10:20	And so we have appointed you today
	10:69	And Demetrius appointed Apollonius the governor of Coelesyria
	14:42	and appoint men over its tasks
	16:11	Now Ptolemy the son of Abubus had been appointed governor
2 Ma	5:22	than the man who appointed him
	8:9	And Ptolemy promptly appointed Nicanor the son of Patroclus
	8:22	He appointed his brothers, also
	8:23	Besides, he appointed Eleazar
	9:23	appointed his successor
	9:25	So I have appointed my son Antiochus to be king
	10:11	appointed one Lysias to have charge of the government
	14:12	appointed him governor of Judea, and sent him off
	14:26	for he had appointed that conspirator against the kingdom
1 Es	5:58	And they appointed the Levites
	6:27	and those who were appointed as local rulers
	8:23	appoint judges and justices
	9:12	come at the time appointed
P Ma	7	thou hast appointed repentance for sinners
	8	hast not appointed repentance for the righteous
	8	but thou hast appointed repentance for me, who am a sinner
2 Es	3:7	and immediately thou didst appoint death
	8:52	a city is built, rest is appointed, goodness is established
4 Ma	4:16	and appointed Onias's brother Jason as high priest
	4:18	So the king appointed him high priest and ruler of the nation

APPOINTED   7 = 0.005 %

Sir	36:8	Hasten the day, and remember the appointed time
	48:10	you who are ready at the appointed time, it is written
	51:30	Do your work before the appointed time
Bar	1:14	on the days of the feasts and at appointed seasons
1 Ma	10:34	and new moons and appointed days
3 Ma	5:13	Then the Jews, since they had escaped the appointed hour
2 Es	4:27	in their appointed times

APPORTION   4 = 0.003 %

Sir	1:9	he saw her and apportioned her
	1:19	He saw her and apportioned her
	44:2	The Lord apportioned to them great glory
3 Ma	6:31	and full of joy they apportioned to celebrate the place

APPRECIATE   1

Sir	31:22	and in the end you will appreciate my words

APPROACH, verb   20 = 0.013 %

Tob	6:9	When they approached Ecbatana
	6:14	and he harms no one except those who approach her
	6:17	And when you approach her, rise up, both of you
Jud	12:13	and approached her and said
Sir	1:28	do not approach him with a divided mind
	9:13	But if you approach him, make no misstep
	21:2	for if you approach sin, it will bite you
	41:22	and do not approach her bed
1 Ma	3:16	When he approached the ascent of Beth-horon
	5:42	When Judas approached the stream of water
	11:4	When he approached Azotus
	13:23	When he approached Baskama, he killed Jonathan
2 Ma	11:5	Invading Judea, he approached Beth-zur
1 Es	5:68	So they approached Zerubbabel and Jeshua
3 Ma	1:26	and began now to approach
	5:14	approached the king and nudged him
2 Es	5:50	Or is she now approaching old age ?
	10:25	so that I was too frightened to approach her
	12:21	when its end approaches
4 Ma	14:19	and as though with an iron dart sting those who approach their hive

APPROACH, subst.   7 = 0.005 %

Jud	4:2	they were therefore very greatly terrified at his approach
	4:7	for the approach was narrow
	7:7	and examined the approaches to the city
Wis	1:5	and will be ashamed at the approach of unrighteousness
2 Ma	12:21	When Timothy learned of the approach of Judas
	12:21	because of the narrowness of all the approaches
4 Ma	15:19	and saw in their nostrils signs of the approach of death

APPROACHING   1

2 Es	13:9	And behold, when he saw the onrush of the approaching multitude

APPROPRIATE, adj.   6 = 0.004 %
1 Ma 10:40 out of the king's revenues from appropriate places
      12:11 both in our feasts and on other appropriate days
2 Ma 11:36 so that we may make proposals appropriate for you
3 Ma 7:19 And when they had landed in peace with appropriate
             thanksgiving
2 Es 10:8   It is most appropriate to mourn now
4 Ma 5:11 adopt a mind appropriate to your years

APPROPRIATE, verb   1
4 Ma 3:20 had both appropriated money to them for the temple service

APPROVAL   3 = 0.002 %
Sir 2:16   Those who fear the Lord will seek his approval
     32:10 and approval precedes a modest man
3 Ma 5:21 all those present readily and joyfully with one accord gave their
             approval

APPROVE   7 = 0.005 %
Sir 11:17   and what he approves will have lasting success
     42:8   and will be approved before all men
1 Es 4:39 All men approve her deeds
      6:22 and if it is approved by our lord the king
3 Ma 7:12 The king then, admitting and approving the truth of what they
             said
2 Es 5:27 thou hast given the law which is approved by all
4 Ma 15:27 She did not approve the deliverance

APPROVED   1
2 Ma 4:3   by one of Simon's approved agents

APT   1
Sir 18:29   and pour forth apt proverbs

ARAB   6 = 0.004 %
1 Ma 5:39 They also have hired Arabs to help them
     11:17 And Zabdiel the Arab cut off the head of Alexander
     11:39 So he went to Imalkue the Arab
     12:31 So Jonathan turned aside against the Arabs
2 Ma 5:8   Accused before Aretas the ruler of the Arabs
     12:10 not less than 5,000 Arabs with 500 horsemen attacked them

ARABIA   3 = 0.002 %
Jud 2:25   fronting toward Arabia
1 Ma 11:16 So Alexander fled into Arabia to find protection there
2 Es 15:29 The nations of the dragons of Arabia shall come out with many
             chariots

ARADUS   1
1 Ma 15:23 and to Side, and to Aradus and Gortyna

ARAH   1
1 Es 5:10 The sons of Arah, 756

ARARAT   1
Tob 1:21   and they fled to the mountains of Ararat

ARBATTA   1
1 Ma 5:23 Then he took the Jews of Galilee and Arbatta

ARBELA   1
1 Ma 9:2   and encamped against Mesaloth in Arbela

ARBITRARILY   1
4 Ma 8:25 Not even the law itself would arbitrarily slay us

ARC   1
Sir 43:12   It encircles the heaven with its glorious arc

ARCH   1
2 Es 16:59 who has spread out the heaven like an arch

ARCHANGEL   1
2 Es 4:36 And Jeremiel the archangel answered them and said

ARCHER   4 = 0.003 %
Jud 2:15   120,000 of them, together with 12,000 archers on horseback
1 Ma 9:11 and the slingers and the archers went ahead of the army
2 Es 16:7   Can one turn back an arrow shot by a strong archer ?
     16:16 Just as an arrow shot by a mighty archer does not return

ARCHIVE   3 = 0.002 %
1 Ma 14:23 and to put a copy of their words in the public archives
1 Es 6:21 let search be made in the royal archives
      6:23 in the royal archives that were deposited in Babylon

ARDAT   1
2 Es 9:26 into the field which is called Ardat

ARDUOUS   1
Wis 10:12   in his arduous contest she gave him the victory

AREA   1
4 Ma 4:11 in the temple area that was open to all

ARENA   2
2 Ma 4:14 in the wrestling arena after the call to the discus
4 Ma 11:20 have been summoned to an arena of sufferings for religion

ARETAS   1
2 Ma 5:8   Accused before Aretas the ruler of the Arabs

ARGUE   2
Sir 8:3   Do not argue with a chatterer, nor heap wood on his fire
     11:9   Do not argue about a matter which does not concern you

ARGUMENT   2
4 Ma 1:5   Their attempt at argument is ridiculous !
      8:16 what arguments might have been used

ARIARATHES   1
1 Ma 15:22 and to Attalus and Ariarathes and Arsaces

ARIGHT   5 = 0.003 %
Sir 6:17   Whoever fears the Lord directs his friendship aright
     38:10 Give up your faults and direct your hands aright
     39:7   He will direct his counsel and knowledge aright
     49:2   He was led aright in converting the people
     49:9   and did good to those who directed their ways aright

ARIOCH   1
Jud 1:6   and in the plain where Arioch ruled the Elymaeans

ARISE   33 = 0.021 %
Tob 8:9   But Raguel arose and went and dug a grave
     10:10 So Raguel arose and gave his wife Sarah
Jud 7:29   Then great and general lamentation arose
     12:5   Along toward the morning watch she arose
     14:19 and their loud cries and shouts arose
Sir 17:23   Afterward he will arise and requite them
     47:21 and a disobedient kingdom arose out of Ephraim
     48:1   Then the prophet Elijah arose like a fire
Bar 3:19   and others have arisen in their place
      5:5   Arise, O Jerusalem, stand upon the height
Bel 14:39   So Daniel arose and ate
1 Ma 13:44 and a great tumult arose in the city
     14:41 until a trustworthy prophet should arise
     16:5   Early in the morning they arose and marched into the plain
2 Ma 5:5   When a false rumour arose that Antiochus was dead
1 Es 2:8   Then arose the heads of families
      5:58 And Jeshua arose, and his sons and brethren
      6:2   and Jeshua the son of Jozadak arose
      8:95 Arise and take action, for it is your task
      8:96 Then Ezra arose and had the leaders of the priests
3 Ma 3:24 if a sudden disorder should later arise against us
      5:32 arising from our nurture in common and your usefulness
2 Es 11:12 on the right side one wing arose
     11:13 Then the next wing arose and reigned
     12:2   And the 2 wings that had gone over to it arose
     12:13 when a kingdom shall arise on earth
     12:18 great struggles shall arise
     12:20 8 kings shall arise in it
     12:32 who will arise from the posterity of David
     13:2   and behold, a wind arose from the sea and stirred up all its
              waves
     13:57 Then I arose and walked in the field
4 Ma 5:13 that arises out of compulsion
      7:20 No contradiction therefore arises

ARISTOBULUS   1
2 Ma 1:10 To Aristobulus, who is of the family of the anointed priests

ARIUS   2
1 Ma 12:7   from Arius, who was king among you
     12:20 Arius, king of the Spartans

ARK   5 = 0.003 %
2 Ma 2:4   ordered that the tent and the ark should follow with him
      2:5   and he brought there the tent and the ark
1 Es 1:3   and put the holy ark of the Lord
2 Es 10:22 the ark of our covenant has been plundered
4 Ma 15:31 *Just as Noah's ark, carrying the world in the universal flood*

ARM, verb   9 = 0.006 %
Wis 5:17   and will arm all creation to repel his enemies
1 Ma 6:35 armed with coats of mail
     14:32 he armed the men of his nation's forces and paid them wages
2 Ma 4:40 Lysimachus armed about 3,000 men
      5:2   in companies fully armed with lances and drawn swords

	13:2	and 300 chariots armed with scythes
	15:11	He armed each of them
4 Ma	3:12	armed themselves fully
	7:11	For just as our father Aaron, armed with the censer

ARM, subst., weapon   28 = 0.018 %

Jud	14:3	Then they will seize their arms and go into the camp
	15:13	bearing their arms and wearing garlands
Wis	18:22	and not by force of arms
1 Ma	1:35	they stored up arms and food
	5:43	and they threw away their arms
	6:6	that the Jews had grown strong from the arms, supplies
	6:41	and the clanking of their arms
	7:44	they threw down their arms and fled
	8:26	arms, money, or ships, as Rome has decided
	8:28	arms, money, or ships, as Rome has decided
	10:6	to equip them with arms, and to become his ally
	10:21	and equipped them with arms in abundance
	11:51	And they threw down their arms and made peace
	12:27	and to keep their arms at hand
	14:33	where formerly the arms of the enemy had been stored
2 Ma	5:25	he ordered his men to parade under arms
	8:18	For they trust to arms and acts of daring, he said
	8:27	And when they had collected the arms of the enemy
	8:31	Collecting the arms of the enemy
	9:2	Therefore the people rushed to the rescue with arms
	10:23	Having success at arms in everything he undertook
	10:27	And rising from their prayer they took up their arms
	11:7	Maccabeus himself was the first to take up arms
	15:5	and I command you to take up arms
	15:21	and the varied supply of arms
	15:21	for he knew that it is not by arms
3 Ma	1:2	took with him the best of the Ptolemaic arms
	1:23	They shouted to their fellows to take arms

ARM, subst., limb   17 = 0.011 %

Ad E	15:8	and took her in his arms until she came to herself
Wis	5:16	and with his arm he will shield them
	11:21	and who can withstand the might of thy arm ?
	16:16	were scourged by the strength of thy arm
Sir	21:21	and like a bracelet on the right arm
	36:6	make thy hand and thy right arm glorious
	38:30	He moulds the clay with his arm
Bar	2:11	and with great power and outstretched arm
2 Ma	12:35	and cut off his arm
	15:24	By the might of thy arm may these blasphemers
	15:30	ordered them to cut off Nicanor's head and arm
	15:32	and that profane man's arm
3 Ma	5:49	embracing relatives and falling into one another's arms
2 Es	15:11	and with an uplifted arm
4 Ma	6:3	And after they had tied his arms on each side they scourged him
	9:11	they bound his hands and arms with thongs on each side
	10:6	and breaking his fingers and arms and legs and elbows

ARMAMENT   1

Sir	46:6	so that the nations might know his armament

ARMED   9 = 0.006 %

1 Ma	6:37	and upon each were 4 armed men who fought from there
2 Ma	5:26	then rushed into the city with his armed men
	14:22	Judas posted armed men in readiness at key places
3 Ma	5:29	pointed out that the beasts and the armed forces were ready
	5:44	and they confidently posted the armed forces
	5:48	at the gate by the following armed forces
	6:21	The beasts turned back upon the armed forces following them
4 Ma	4:10	with his armed forces to seize the money
	5:1	and with his armed soldiers standing about him

ARMOUR, ARMOR   12 = 0.008 %

Wis	5:17	The Lord will take his zeal as his whole armour
1 Ma	3:3	he girded on his armour of war and waged battles
	4:6	but they did not have armour and swords such as they desired
	4:30	and of the man who carried his armour
	6:43	that one of the beasts was equipped with royal armour
	13:29	and upon the columns he put suits of armour
	13:29	and beside the suits of armour carved ships
2 Ma	3:25	Its rider was seen to have armour and weapons of gold
	5:3	and armour of all sorts
	10:30	with their own armour and weapons
	15:28	they recognized Nicanor, lying dead, in full armour
4 Ma	13:16	Therefore let us put on the full armour of self-control

ARMY   130 = 0.085 %

Jud	1:4	so that his armies could march out in force
	1:13	and overthrew the whole army of Arphaxad
	2:4	the chief general of his army, second only to himself
	2:7	with the feet of my armies
	2:14	and officers of the Assyrian army
	2:16	as a great army is marshalled for a campaign
	2:19	So he set out with his whole army

	2:22	From there Holofernes took his whole army
	3:6	Then he went down to the seacoast with his army
	3:10	in order to assemble all the supplies for his army
	5:1	When Holofernes, the general of the Assyrian army
	5:3	How large is their army
	5:3	Who rules over them as king, leading their army ?
	5:24	and they will be devoured by your vast army
	6:1	Holofernes, the commander of the Assyrian army
	6:6	Then the sword of my army
	7:1	The next day Holofernes ordered his whole army
	7:7	and then returned to his army
	7:9	Let our lord hear a word, lest his army be defeated
	7:11	and not a man of your army will fall
	7:17	So the army of the Ammonites moved forward
	7:18	The rest of the Assyrian army encamped in the plain
	7:20	The whole Assyrian army
	7:26	to the army of Holofernes and to all his forces
	10:13	the commander of your army
	11:18	and then you shall go out with your whole army
	13:15	the commander of the Assyrian army
	14:3	and rouse the officers of the Assyrian army
	14:19	When the leaders of the Assyrian army heard this
	16:12	they perished before the army of my Lord
Wis	12:8	and didst send wasps as forerunners of thy army
1 Ma	1:4	He gathered a very strong army
	2:44	They organized an army
	2:66	he shall command the army for you
	3:13	Now when Seron, the commander of the Syrian army
	3:15	And again a strong army of ungodly men
	3:17	But when they saw the army coming to meet them
	3:19	It is not on the size of the army
	3:23	he rushed suddenly against Seron and his army
	3:27	a very strong army
	3:57	Then the army marched out
	4:10	and crush this army before us today
	4:20	They saw that their army had been put to flight
	4:21	and when they also saw the army of Judas
	4:30	When he saw that the army was strong, he prayed, saying
	4:31	So do thou hem in this army by the hand of thy people Israel
	4:34	and there fell of the army of Lysias 5,000 men
	4:35	to invade Judea again with an even larger army
	4:37	So all the army assembled and they went up to Mount Zion
	5:28	Then Judas and his army quickly turned back
	5:34	And when the army of Timothy realized that it was Maccabeus
	5:37	After these things Timothy gathered another army
	5:40	Now as Judas and his army drew near to the stream of water
	5:43	and the whole army followed him
	5:49	Then Judas ordered proclamation to be made to the army
	6:5	that the armies which had gone into the land of Judah had been routed
	6:6	from the armies they had cut down
	6:33	and took his army by a forced march
	6:38	on the 2 flanks of the army, to harass the enemy
	6:40	Now a part of the king's army
	6:41	trembled, for the army was very large and strong
	6:42	But Judas and his army advanced to the battle
	6:42	and 600 men of the king's army fell
	6:48	The soldiers of the king's army
	7:2	the army seized Antiochus and Lysias to bring them to him
	7:4	So the army killed them
	7:14	A priest of the line of Aaron has come with the army
	7:32	About 500 men of the army of Nicanor fell
	7:35	Unless Judas and his army
	7:38	Take vengeance on this man and on his army
	7:39	and the Syrian army joined him
	7:42	So also crush this army before us today
	7:43	So the armies met in battle
	7:43	The army of Nicanor was crushed
	7:44	When his army saw that Nicanor had fallen
	8:6	and with cavalry and chariots and a very large army
	9:1	that Nicanor and his army had fallen in battle
	9:1	and with them the right wing of the army
	9:7	When Judas saw that his army had slipped away
	9:11	Then the army of Bacchides marched out from the camp
	9:11	and the slingers and the archers went ahead of the army
	9:13	The earth was shaken by the noise of the armies
	9:14	Judas saw that Bacchides and the strength of his army were on the right
	9:34	and he with all his army crossed the Jordan
	10:2	he assembled a very large army
	10:49	and the army of Demetrius fled
	10:53	and he and his army were crushed by us
	10:73	and such an army in the plain
	10:77	he mustered 3,000 cavalry and a large army
	10:78	and the armies engaged in battle
	10:80	for they surrounded his army and shot arrows at his men
	11:60	and all the army of Syria gathered to him as allies
	11:63	had come to Kadesh in Galilee with a large army
	11:67	Jonathan and his army encamped by the waters of Gennesaret
	11:68	and behold, the army of the foreigners met him in the plain

	11:70	commanders of the forces of the army
	12:42	When Trypho saw that he had come with a large army
	13:1	Simon heard that Trypho had assembled a large army
	13:11	and with him a considerable army
	13:12	Then Trypho departed from Ptolemais with a large army
	13:20	But Simon and his army kept marching along opposite him
	14:3	And he went and defeated the army of Demetrius
	16:6	Then he and his army lined up against them
	16:7	Then he divided the army
	16:8	and Cendebaeus and his army were put to flight
2 Ma	5:24	with an army of 22,000
	8:5	As soon as Maccabeus got his army organized
	8:8	and when he told his companions of the arrival of the army
	8:21	then he divided his army into 4 parts
	8:24	and wounded and disabled most of Nicanor's army
	8:35	having succeeded chiefly in the destruction of his own army !
	9:9	the whole army felt revulsion at his decay
	10:28	Just as dawn was breaking, the 2 armies joined battle
	10:35	20 young men in the army of Maccabeus
	12:20	But Maccabeus arranged his army in divisions
	12:38	Then Judas assembled his army
	13:1	with a great army against Judea
	13:13	before the king's army could enter Judea
	14:1	with a strong army and a fleet
	14:21	A chariot came forward from each army
	15:20	with their army drawn up for battle
1 Es	4:6	Likewise those who do not serve in the army or make war
	4:10	All his people and his armies obey him
3 Ma	5:3	together with those of his friends and of the army
	6:4	you destroyed together with his arrogant army
	6:17	and brought an uncontrollable terror upon the army
2 Es	1:10	I struck down Pharaoh with his servants, and all his army
	15:33	and fear and trembling shall come upon their army
4 Ma	3:8	around which the whole army of our ancestors had encamped
	4:11	to pray for him and propitiate the wrath of the heavenly army

ARNA
			1
2 Es	1:2	son of Arna, son of Uzzi, son of Borith	

AROM
			1
1 Es	5:16	The sons of Annias, 101. The sons of Arom	

AROMA
			1
Sir	24:15	I gave forth the aroma of spices	

AROUND, adv., prep.
			32 = 0.021 %
Jud	5:22	all the men standing around the tent began to complain	
	10:18	and they came and stood around her	
	13:10	and circled around the valley	
	13:13	and they kindled a fire for light, and gathered around them	
	15:3	Those who had camped in the hills around Bethulia	
Wis	17:4	but terrifying sounds rang out around them	
Sir	9:7	Do not look around in the streets of a city	
	50:12	with a garland of brethren around him	
Bar	2:4	And he gave them into subjection to all the kingdoms around us	
1 Ma	5:10	The Gentiles around us have gathered together against us	
	5:38	All the Gentiles around us have gathered to him	
	5:57	on the Gentiles around us	
	6:18	around the sanctuary	
	6:62	and gave orders to tear down the wall all around	
	11:55	gathered around him, and they fought against Demetrius	
	12:27	and he stationed outposts around the camp	
	13:20	and he circled around by the way to Adora	
	13:33	and walled them all around	
2 Ma	10:36	wheeled around against the defenders	
	13:5	and it has a rim running around it	
1 Es	1:53	These slew their young men with the sword around their holy temple	
	4:11	but they keep watch around him	
3 Ma	1:27	When those who were around him observed this	
	1:29	but also the walls and the whole earth around echoed	
	3:8	when they saw an unexpected tumult around these people	
	6:1	directed the elders around him	
4 Ma	3:8	around which the whole army of our ancestors had encamped	
	9:13	When the noble youth was stretched out around this	
	10:8	he saw his own flesh torn all around	
	11:10	they twisted his back around the wedge on the wheel	
	14:7	move in choral dance around religion	
	14:17	by flying in circles around them in the anguish of love	

AROUSE
			12 = 0.008 %
Wis	15:5	whose appearance arouses yearning in fools	
Sus	13:45	God aroused the holy spirit of a young lad named Daniel	
1 Ma	6:34	to arouse them for battle	
	10:74	his spirit was aroused	
	13:17	lest he arouse great hostility among the people	
2 Ma	4:40	And since the crowds were becoming aroused	
	13:4	But the King of kings aroused the anger of Antiochus	
	15:10	And when he had aroused their courage, he gave his orders	
	15:17	so noble and so effective in arousing valour	

2 Es	4:37	and he will not move or arouse them
	6:37	For my spirit was greatly aroused
	11:37	a creature like a lion was aroused out of the forest, roaring

ARPHAXAD
			5 = 0.003 %
Jud	1:1	in the days of Arphaxad	
	1:5	against King Arphaxad in the great plain	
	1:13	In the 17th year he led his forces against King Arphaxad	
	1:13	and overthrew the whole army of Arphaxad	
	1:15	He captured Arphaxad in the mountains of Ragae	

ARRANGE
			12 = 0.008 %
Wis	11:20	But thou hast arranged all things	
Sir	16:27	He arranged his works in an eternal order	
	47:10	and arranged their times throughout the year	
	50:14	and arranging the offering to the Most High, the Almighty	
Sus	13:14	And then together they arranged for a time	
2 Ma	12:20	But Maccabeus arranged his army in divisions	
3 Ma	1:3	had led the king away and arranged	
	3:2	While these matters were being arranged	
	4:1	a feast at public expense was arranged for the Gentiles	
	5:5	and arranged for their continued custody through the night	
	6:31	arranged for a banquet of deliverance	
	6:35	But the Jews, when they had arranged the aforementioned choral group	

ARRANGEMENT
			2
1 Es	1:15	were in their place according to the arrangement made by David	
2 Es	6:45	and the arrangement of the stars to come into being	

ARRAY, verb
			8 = 0.005 %
Jud	10:3	and arrayed herself in her gayest apparel	
	12:15	So she got up and arrayed herself in all her woman's finery	
Ad E	15:1	and arrayed herself in splendid attire	
1 Es	1:2	arrayed in their garments, in the temple of the Lord	
	1:10	properly arrayed and having the unleavened bread	
	5:59	And the priests stood arrayed in their garments	
	7:9	arrayed in their garments, according to kindred	
3 Ma	1:19	Those women who had recently been arrayed for marriage	

ARRAY, subst.
			4 = 0.003 %
Jud	7:11	Therefore, my lord, do not fight against them in battle array	
Ad E	15:6	clothed in the full array of his majesty	
Sir	43:9	a gleaming array in the heights of the Lord	
1 Es	2:30	with horsemen and a multitude in battle array	

ARREST
			4 = 0.003 %
2 Ma	7:1	It happened also that 7 brothers and their mother were arrested	
	14:39	sent more than 500 soldiers to arrest him	
	14:40	for he thought that by arresting him	
4 Ma	16:15	For when you and your sons were arrested together	

ARRIVAL
			3 = 0.002 %
Jud	10:18	for her arrival was reported from tent to tent	
1 Ma	11:44	the king rejoiced at their arrival	
2 Ma	8:12	and when he told his companions of the arrival of the army	

ARRIVE
			23 = 0.015 %
Tob	2:1	When I arrived home	
	7:1	and arrived at the house of Raguel	
	10:1	and they did not arrive	
Jud	16:18	When they arrived at Jerusalem they worshipped God	
1 Ma	3:40	and when they arrived they encamped near Emmaus in the plain	
	15:15	Then Numenius and his companions arrived from Rome	
2 Ma	2:28	to arriving at the outlines of the condensation	
	3:9	When he had arrived at Jerusalem	
	3:24	But when he arrived at the treasury with his bodyguard	
	4:21	Therefore upon arriving at Joppa he proceeded to Jerusalem	
	5:25	When this man arrived in Jerusalem	
	15:31	And when he arrived there	
1 Es	8:6	and arrived in Jerusalem	
	8:61	and we arrived in Jerusalem	
3 Ma	1:9	After he had arrived in Jerusalem	
	2:25	When he arrived in Egypt	
	3:20	But we, when we arrived in Egypt victorious	
	3:25	as soon as this letter shall arrive	
	4:1	In every place, then, where this decree arrived	
	5:26	Hermon arrived and invited him to come out	
	6:16	the king arrived at the hippodrome with the beasts	
	7:17	When they had arrived at Ptolemais, called rose-bearing	
4 Ma	2:8	and to cancel the debt when the 7th year arrives	

ARROGANCE
			23 = 0.015 %
Jud	6:19	O Lord God of heaven, behold their arrogance	
	9:10	crush their arrogance by the hand of a woman	
Ad E	16:12	But, unable to restrain his arrogance	
Wis	5:8	What has our arrogance profited us ?	
Sir	10:7	Arrogance is hateful before the Lord and before men	
	22:22	but as for reviling, arrogance, disclosure of secrets	
	48:18	and made great boasts in his arrogance	

1 Ma	1:24	He committed deeds of murder, and spoke with great arrogance
	2:49	Arrogance and reproach have now become strong
2 Ma	5:21	thinking in his arrogance
	7:36	will receive just punishment for your arrogance
	9:4	For in his arrogance he said, When I get there
	9:7	but was even more filled with arrogance
	9:8	in his superhuman arrogance
	9:11	he began to lose much of his arrogance
	13:9	The king with barbarous arrogance
	15:6	This Nicanor in his utter boastfulness and arrogance
3 Ma	1:26	But he, in his arrogance, took heed of nothing
	2:3	and you judge those who have done anything in insolence and arrogance
	2:17	or exult in the arrogance of their tongue, saying
	6:16	and all the arrogance of his forces
4 Ma	2:15	lust for power, vainglory, boasting, arrogance, and malice
	8:19	and this arrogance that threatens to destroy us ?

ARROGANT, adj., subst.   8 = 0.005 %

Wis	14:6	when arrogant giants were perishing
Sir	23:8	the reviler and the arrogant are tripped by them
1 Ma	2:47	They hunted down the arrogant men
3 Ma	1:25	to change his arrogant mind
	5:13	to the arrogant Gentiles
	6:4	you destroyed together with his arrogant army
4 Ma	4:15	an arrogant and terrible man
	9:30	as you see the arrogant design of your tyranny being defeated

ARROGANTLY   4 = 0.003 %

1 Ma	1:21	He arrogantly entered the sanctuary
	7:34	and spoke arrogantly
	7:47	and the right hand which he had so arrogantly stretched out
3 Ma	2:5	the men of Sodom who acted arrogantly

ARROW   9 = 0.006 %

Wis	5:12	or as, when an arrow is shot at a target
Sir	19:12	Like an arrow stuck in the flesh of the thigh
	26:12	and open her quiver to the arrow
1 Ma	6:51	machines to shoot arrows, and catapults
	10:80	for they surrounded his army and shot arrows at his men
2 Ma	10:30	And they showered arrows and thunderbolts upon the enemy
2 Es	16:7	Can one turn back an arrow shot by a strong archer ?
	16:13	and his arrows that he shoots are sharp
	16:16	Just as an arrow shot by a mighty archer does not return

ARSACES   3 = 0.002 %

1 Ma	14:2	When Arsaces the king of Persia and Media heard
	14:3	and seized him and took him to Arsaces
	15:22	and to Attalus and Ariarathes and Arsaces

ARSINOE   2

3 Ma	1:1	took with him his sister Arsinoe
	1:4	Arsinoe went to the troops with wailing and tears

ART   4 = 0.003 %

Wis	15:4	For neither has the evil intent of human art misled us
	17:7	The delusions of their magic art lay humbled
	18:13	because of their magic arts
Sir	49:1	prepared by the art of the perfumer

ARTAXERXES   11 = 0.007 %

1 Es	2:16	But in the time of Artaxerxes king of the Persians
	2:17	To King Artaxerxes our lord
	2:30	Then, when the letter from King Artaxerxes was read
	7:4	So with the consent of Cyrus and Darius and Artaxerxes
	8:1	when Artaxerxes the king of the Persians was reigning
	8:6	in the 7th year of the reign of Artaxerxes
	8:8	from Artaxerxes the king
	8:9	King Artaxerxes to Ezra the priest
	8:19	And I, Artaxerxes the king
	8:28	in the reign of Artaxerxes the king :
2 Es	1:3	in the reign of Artaxerxes, king of the Persians

ARTIST   1

4 Ma	17:7	to paint the history of your piety as an artist might

ARZARETH   1

2 Es	13:45	and that country is called Arzareth

AS*   812 = 0.529 %

AS for   32 = 0.021 %

ASAHEL   1

1 Es	9:14	Jonathan the son of Asahel

ASAIAS   1

1 Es	9:32	Of the sons of Annan : Elionas and Asaias and Melchias

ASAPH   4 = 0.003 %

1 Es	1:15	And the temple singers, the sons of Asaph
	1:15	and also Asaph, Zechariah, and Eddinus
	5:27	The temple singers : the sons of Asaph, 128
	5:59	and the Levites, the sons of Asaph, with cymbals

ASARAMEL   1

1 Ma	14:28	in Asaramel, in the great assembly of the priests

ASCALON   1

Jud	2:28	Those who lived in Azotus and Ascalon feared him exceedingly

ASCEND   3 = 0.002 %

Tob	12:20	for I am ascending to him who sent me
3 Ma	5:9	So their entreaty ascended fervently to heaven
2 Es	4:8	neither did I ever ascend into heaven

ASCENT   2

Sir	25:20	A sandy ascent for the feet of the aged
1 Ma	3:16	When he approached the ascent of Beth-horon

ASCRIBE   4 = 0.003 %

Sir	10:28	and ascribe to yourself honour according to your worth
	39:15	ascribe majesty to his name and give thanks to him
Bar	2:17	will not ascribe glory or justice to the Lord
	2:18	will ascribe to thee glory and righteousness, O Lord

ASCRIPTION   1

Sir	47:8	the Most High, with ascriptions of glory

ASH   23 = 0.015 %

Tob	6:16	you shall take live ashes of incense
	8:2	and he took the live ashes of incense
Jud	4:11	and put ashes on their heads
	4:15	With ashes upon their turbans
	9:1	and put ashes on her head
Ad E	14:2	she covered her head with ashes and dung
Wis	2:3	When it is extinguished, the body will turn to ashes
	15:10	His heart is ashes, his hope is cheaper than dirt
Sir	10:9	How can he who is dust and ashes be proud ?
	17:32	but all men are dust and ashes
	40:3	to the one who is humbled in dust and ashes
Bel	14:14	Then Daniel ordered his servants to bring ashes
1 Ma	3:47	and sprinkled ashes on their heads, and rent their clothes
	4:39	and sprinkled themselves with ashes
2 Ma	4:41	and others took handfuls of the ashes that were lying about
	13:5	For there is a tower in that place, 50 cubits high, full of ashes
	13:5	which on all sides inclines precipitously into the ashes
	13:8	against the altar whose fire and ashes were holy
	13:8	he met his death in ashes
3 Ma	4:6	their myrrh-perfumed hair sprinkled with ashes
2 Es	2:9	whose land lies in lumps of pitch and heaps of ashes
	9:38	and her clothes were rent, and there were ashes on her head
	13:11	but only the dust of ashes and the smell of smoke

ASHAMED   18 = 0.012 %

Jud	9:3	and their bed, which was ashamed of the deceit they had practised
Wis	1:5	and will be ashamed at the approach of unrighteousness
	13:17	he is not ashamed to address a lifeless thing
Sir	4:26	Do not be ashamed to confess your sins
	22:25	I will not be ashamed to protect a friend
	41:17	Be ashamed of immorality, before your father or mother
	41:19	Be ashamed before the truth of God and his covenant
	41:19	Be ashamed of selfish behaviour at meals
	42:1	Of the following things do not be ashamed
	42:8	Do not be ashamed to instruct the stupid or foolish
L Jr	6:27	And those who serve them are ashamed
Sus	13:11	for they were ashamed to disclose their lustful desire to possess her
	13:27	the servants were greatly ashamed
1 Ma	4:31	and let them be ashamed of their troops and their cavalry
1 Es	8:51	For I was ashamed to ask the king
	8:74	I am ashamed and confounded before thy face
4 Ma	12:11	were you not ashamed to murder his servants
	12:13	As a man, were you not ashamed, you most savage beast

ASHER   1

Tob	1:2	in Galilee above Asher

ASHORE   1

2 Ma	5:8	he was cast ashore in Egypt

ASIA   11 = 0.007 %

1 Ma	8:6	They also defeated Antiochus the Great, king of Asia
	11:13	Then Ptolemy entered Antioch and put on the crown of Asia
	11:13	the crown of Egypt and that of Asia
	12:39	Then Trypho attempted to become king of Asia
	13:32	and became king in his place, putting on the crown of Asia
2 Ma	3:3	so that even Seleucus, the king of Asia

	10 :24	and collected the cavalry from Asia in no small number
3 Ma	3 :14	When our expedition took place in Asia
2 Es	15 :46	And you, Asia, who share in the glamour of Babylon
	16 :1	Woe to you, Babylon and Asia !
4 Ma	3 :20	and were prospering, so that even Seleucus Nicanor, king of Asia

ASIBIAS   1
1 Es   9 :26   Malchijah, Mijamin, and Eleazar, and Asibias, and Benaiah

ASIDE   19 = 0.012 %
Jud 11 :13   which they had consecrated and set aside for the priests
Sir   2 :7   and turn not aside, lest you fall
      9 :9   lest your heart turn aside to her
     16 :28   They do not crowd one another aside
Sus 13 :56   Then he put him aside, and commanded them to bring the other
1 Ma 2 :22   by turning aside from our religion
      5 :35   Next he turned aside to Alema
      5 :68   But Judas turned aside to Azotus
     12 :31   So Jonathan turned aside against the Arabs
     12 :33   He turned aside to Joppa and took it by surprise
2 Ma 4 :11   He set aside the existing royal concessions to the Jews
      4 :34   Therefore Menelaus, taking Andronicus aside
      4 :46   Therefore Ptolemy, taking the king aside into a colonnade
      6 :21   Those who were in charge of that unlawful sacrifice took the man aside
     14 :7   Therefore I have laid aside my ancestral glory
1 Es   1 :27   Stand aside, and do not oppose the Lord
3 Ma   3 :10   had taken some of them aside privately
2 Es 10 :24   and lay aside your many sorrows
4 Ma 15 :18   When the first-born breathed his last it did not turn you aside

ASIEL   2
Tob   1 :1   of the descendants of Asiel and the tribe of Naphtali
2 Es 14 :24   and take with you Sarea, Dabria, Selemja, Ethanus, and Asiel

ASK   61 = 0.040 %
Tob   4 :2   I have asked for death
      4 :19   ask him that your ways may be straight
      7 :3   And Raguel asked them, Where are you from, brethren ?
      7 :4   And he asked them, Is he in good health ?
Jud   6 :16   and Uzziah asked him what had happened
     10 :12   and took her into custody, and asked her
Ad E 13 :3   When I asked my counsellors how this might be accomplished
     16 :13   asked for the destruction of Mordecai
Wis 13 :19   he asks strength of a thing whose hands have no strength
     19 :11   when desire led them to ask for luxurious food
Sir 32 :7   but no more than twice, and only if asked
     33 :19   lest you change your mind and must ask for it
     33 :31   For it is better that your children should ask from you
     51 :14   Before the temple I asked for her
Sus 13 :40   So we seized this woman and asked her who the young man was
1 Ma 3 :44   and to pray and ask for mercy and compassion
      7 :12   before Alcimus and Bacchides to ask for just terms
     10 :72   Ask and learn who I am
     11 :28   Then Jonathan asked the king
     11 :66   Then they asked him to grant them terms of peace
     12 :4   in every place, asking them to provide for the envoys
     13 :45   asking Simon to make peace with them
     16 :18   asking him to send troops to aid him
     16 :19   he sent letters to the captains asking them to come to him
2 Ma 2 :8   and as Solomon asked
      3 :31   Quickly some of Heliodorus' friends asked Onias
      3 :37   When the king asked Heliodorus
      7 :2   What do you intend to ask and learn from us ?
      7 :7   and asked him, Will you eat
     11 :17   and have asked about the matters indicated therein
     11 :24   and ask that their own customs be allowed them
     14 :5   and was asked about the disposition
     15 :3   the thrice-accursed wretch asked
1 Es   4 :42   Then the king said to him, Ask what you wish
      4 :46   this is what I ask and request of you
      6 :11   Then we asked these elders
      6 :12   we questioned them and asked them for a list of the names
      8 :51   For I was ashamed to ask the king
3 Ma   6 :37   asking for dismissal to their homes
2 Es   2 :4   Go, my children, and ask for mercy from the Lord
      2 :13   Ask and you will receive
      2 :44   Then I asked an angel, Who are these, my lord ?
      4 :6   that you ask me concerning these things ?
      4 :7   And he said to me, If I had asked you
      4 :9   But now I have asked you only about fire and wind and the day
      4 :25   It is about these things that I have asked
      4 :28   For the evil about which you ask me has been sown
      4 :35   ask about these matters, saying
      4 :40   Go and ask a woman who is with child if
      4 :52   Concerning the signs about which you ask me
      5 :11   And one country shall ask its neighbour
      5 :37   that you ask to understand
      5 :39   which thou hast asked me ?
      5 :46   He said to me, Ask a woman's womb

	5 :51	He replied to me, Ask a woman who bears children
	7 :54	Not only that, but ask the earth and she will tell you
	8 :2	Just as, when you ask the earth
	8 :55	Therefore do not ask any more questions
	10 :9	Now ask the earth
4 Ma	1 :5	Some might perhaps ask, If reason rules the emotions
	5 :14	Eleazar asked to have a word

ASK back   1
Sir 20 :15   today he lends and tomorrow he asks it back

ASKALON   3 = 0.002 %
1 Ma 10 :86   and encamped against Askalon
     11 :60   When he came to Askalon, the people of the city met him
     12 :33   as far as Askalon and the neighbouring strongholds

ASLEEP   4 = 0.003 %
Tob   8 :13   and found them both asleep
Sir 46 :20   Even after he had fallen asleep
2 Ma 12 :45   that is laid up for those who fall asleep in godliness
2 Es   7 :32   And the earth shall give up those who are asleep in it

ASMODEUS   2
Tob   3 :8   and the evil demon Asmodeus had slain each of them
      3 :17   and to bind Asmodeus the evil demon

ASNAH   1
1 Es   5 :31   the sons of Asnah, the sons of the Meunites

ASPECT   1
3 Ma   6 :18   from which 2 glorious angels of fearful aspect descended

ASPHAR   1
1 Ma   9 :33   and camped by the water of the pool of Asphar

ASS   4 = 0.003 %
Jud   2 :17   and asses and mules for transport
Sir 13 :19   Wild asses in the wilderness are the prey of lions
     33 :24   Fodder and a stick and burdens for an ass
1 Es   5 :43   and 7,036 horses, 245 mules, and 5,525 asses

ASSAIL   4 = 0.003 %
Wis 18 :17   and unexpected fears assailed them
     19 :1   But the ungodly were assailed to the end by pitiless anger
2 Ma 11 :9   ready to assail not only men but the wildest beasts or walls of iron
4 Ma 15 :32   that assail religion

ASSAULT, subst.   2
2 Ma   5 :5   and suddenly made an assault upon the city
2 Es 15 :19   but shall make an assault upon their houses with the sword

ASSEMBLE   28 = 0.018 %
Jud   3 :10   in order to assemble all the supplies for his army
Sir 16 :10   who rebelliously assembled in their stubbornness
1 Ma 2 :16   and Mattathias and his sons were assembled
      3 :44   And the congregation assembled to be ready for battle
      3 :46   So they assembled and went to Mizpah, opposite Jerusalem
      3 :52   And behold, the Gentiles assembled against us to destroy us
      3 :58   who have assembled against us to destroy us and our sanctuary
      4 :37   So all the army assembled and they went up to Mount Zion
      6 :19   and assembled all the people to besiege them
      6 :28   He assembled all his friends, the commanders of his forces
      9 :7   for he had no time to assemble them
      9 :28   Then all the friends of Judas assembled
      9 :63   When Bacchides learned of this, he assembled all his forces
     10 :2   he assembled a very large army
     10 :48   Now Alexander the king assembled large forces
     10 :69   and he assembled a large force and encamped against Jamnia
     11 :20   In those days Jonathan assembled the men of Judea
     11 :45   Then the men of the city assembled within the city
     13 :1   Simon heard that Trypho had assembled a large army
     13 :10   So he assembled all the warriors
     14 :1   In the 172nd year Demetrius the king assembled his forces
2 Ma   6 :11   Others who had assembled in the caves near by
     12 :38   Then Judas assembled his army
1 Es   8 :41   I assembled them at the river called Theras
      9 :3   that they should assemble at Jerusalem
      9 :5   assembled at Jerusalem within 3 days
3 Ma   5 :14   seeing that the guests were assembled
      5 :24   The crowds of the city had been assembled

ASSEMBLED   3 = 0.002 %
3 Ma   5 :34   and dismissed the assembled people
2 Es   6 :1   and before the assembled winds blew
     13 :37   And he, my Son, will reprove the assembled nations for their ungodliness

ASSEMBLY   22 = 0.014 %
Jud   6:16   and all their young men and their women ran to the assembly
       6:21   And Uzziah took him from the assembly to his own house
       7:29   throughout the assembly
Ad E 10:13   with an assembly and joy and gladness before God
Sir   6:34   Stand in the assembly of the elders
       7:14   Do not prattle in the assembly of the elders
      15:5   and will open his mouth in the midst of the assembly
      16:6   In an assembly of sinners a fire will be kindled
      21:9   An assembly of the wicked is like tow gathered together
      21:17   will be sought in the assembly
      23:24   She herself will be brought before the assembly
      24:2   In the assembly of the Most High she will open her mouth
      31:11   and the assembly will relate his acts of charity
      38:33   nor do they attain eminence in the public assembly
Sus 13:41   The assembly believed them
      13:60   Then all the assembly shouted loudly and blessed God
1 Ma 2:56   Caleb, because he testified in the assembly
       4:59   Then Judas and his brothers and all the assembly of Israel
       5:16   a great assembly was called
      14:19   And these were read before the assembly in Jerusalem
      14:28   in Asaramel, in the great assembly of the priests
      14:44   or to convene an assembly in the country

ASSENT   1
2 Ma   4:10   When the king assented and Jason came to office

ASSERT   1
Sir   7:5   Do not assert your righteousness before the Lord

ASSIGN   7 = 0.005 %
Sir   3:22   Reflect upon what has been assigned to you
      24:8   and the one who created me assigned a place for my tent
1 Ma 5:20   Then 3,000 men were assigned to Simon to go to Galilee
       6:35   and 500 picked horsemen were assigned to each beast
2 Es   4:19   for the land is assigned to the forest
       4:19   and to the sea is assigned a place to carry its waves
       4:21   For as the land is assigned to the forest

ASSIST   2
Sir 29:20   Assist your neighbour according to your ability
1 Es   7:2   assisting the elders of the Jews

ASSISTANCE   2
Sir 51:7   I looked for the assistance of men, and there was none
3 Ma   3:10   and to exert more earnest efforts for their assistance

ASSOCIATE, subst.   10 = 0.007 %
Wis   8:4   and an associate in his works
2 Ma   1:33   the liquid had appeared with which Nehemiah and his associates
       1:36   Nehemiah and his associates called this nephthar
1 Es   2:16   Shimshai the scribe, and the rest of their associates
       2:30   Rehum and Shimshai the scribe and their associates
       6:3   and Sathra-buzanes, and their associates came to them and said
       6:7   and Sathra-buzanes, and their associates
       6:27   and Sathra-buzanes, and their associates
       7:1   and Sathra-buzanes, and their associates
3 Ma   3:10   and friends and business associates

ASSOCIATE, verb   10 = 0.007 %
Wis   6:23   for envy does not associate with wisdom
Sir   9:4   Do not associate with a woman singer
      12:14   So no one will pity a man who associates with a sinner
      13:1   and whoever associates with a proud man will become like him
      13:2   nor associate with a man mightier and richer than you
      13:2   How can the clay pot associate with the iron kettle ?
      13:16   all living beings associate by species
2 Ma   8:9   He associated with him Gorgias
1 Es   2:25   and the others associated with them and living in Samaria
2 Es   7:76   but do not be associated with those who have shown scorn

ASSOCIATION   1
3 Ma   2:31   by their future association with the king

ASSUAGE   1
Sir 18:16   Does not the dew assuage the scorching heat ?

ASSUME   4 = 0.003 %
Wis 13:3   men assumed them to be gods
1 Ma 10:70   Why do you assume authority against us in the hill country ?
1 Es   5:38   Of the priests the following had assumed the priesthood
3 Ma   3:11   but assuming that he would persevere

ASSURANCE   2
Wis   6:18   and giving heed to her laws is assurance of immortality
Sir 44:22   To Isaac also he gave the same assurance

ASSURE   3 = 0.002 %
Sir 44:21   Therefore the Lord assured him by an oath
2 Es   7:131 so much as joy over those to whom salvation is assured
      16:21   that men will imagine that peace is assured for them

ASSYRIA   2
2 Es   2:8   Woe to you, Assyria
4 Ma 13:9   let us imitate the 3 youths in Assyria

ASSYRIAN, subst., adj.   35 = 0.023 %
Tob   1:2   who in the days of Shalmaneser, king of the Assyrians
       1:3   into the land of the Assyrians, to Nineveh
Jud   1:1   who ruled over the Assyrians in the great city of Nineveh
       1:7   Then Nebuchadnezzar king of the Assyrians
       1:11   king of the Assyrians
       2:1   king of the Assyrians
       2:4   Nebuchadnezzar king of the Assyrians called Holofernes
       2:14   and officers of the Assyrian army
       4:1   the king of the Assyrians
       5:1   When Holofernes, the general of the Assyrian army
       6:1   Holofernes, the commander of the Assyrian army
       6:17   in the presence of the Assyrian leaders
       7:17   together with 5,000 Assyrians
       7:18   The rest of the Assyrian army encamped in the plain
       7:20   The whole Assyrian army
       7:24   in not making peace with the Assyrians
       8:9   to surrender the city to the Assyrians after 5 days
       9:7   Behold now, the Assyrians are increased in their might
      10:11   and an Assyrian patrol met her
      12:13   and become today like one of the daughters of the Assyrians
      13:15   the commander of the Assyrian army
      14:2   against the Assyrian outpost
      14:3   and rouse the officers of the Assyrian army
      14:12   And when the Assyrians saw them
      14:19   When the leaders of the Assyrian army heard this
      15:6   fell upon the Assyrian camp
      16:4   The Assyrian came down from the mountains of the north
Sir 48:21   The Lord smote the camp of the Assyrians
1 Ma 7:41   thy angel went forth and struck down 185,000 of the Assyrians
1 Es   5:69   ever since the days of Esarhaddon king of the Assyrians
       7:15   because he had changed the will of the king of the Assyrians
              concerning them
3 Ma   6:5   oppressive king of the Assyrians
2 Es 13:40   whom Shalmaneser the king of the Assyrians led captive
      15:30   and shall devastate a portion of the land of the Assyrians with
              their teeth
      15:33   And from the land of the Assyrians

ASTONISH   3 = 0.002 %
Jud 11:16   things that will astonish the whole world
      13:17   All the people were greatly astonished
2 Ma   7:12   were astonished at the young man's spirit

ASTOUND   2
1 Ma   6:8   he was astounded and badly shaken
2 Ma   3:24   were astounded by the power of God

ASTOUNDING   1
2 Ma   7:18   Therefore astounding things have happened

ASTRAY   17 = 0.011 %
Tob   5:13   They did not go astray in the error of our brethren
Wis   2:21   Thus they reasoned, but they were led astray
      11:15   which led them astray
      12:24   For they went far astray on the paths of error, accepting as gods
      13:6   for perhaps they go astray while seeking God
      17:1   therefore uninstructed souls have gone astray
Sir   3:24   For their hasty judgment has led many astray
       4:19   If he goes astray she will forsake him
      13:8   Take care not to be led astray
      15:12   Do not say, It was he who led me astray
      19:2   Wine and women lead intelligent men astray
      31:5   and he who pursues money will be led astray by it
Bar   4:28   For just as you purposed to go astray from God
2 Ma   2:2   nor to be led astray in their thoughts
       6:25   they should be led astray because of me
1 Es   3:18   It leads astray the minds of all who drink it
2 Es   7:92   that it might not lead them astray from life into death

ASTYAGES   1
Bel 14:1   When King Astyages was laid with his fathers

ASUR   1
1 Es   5:31   the sons of Hakupha, the sons of Asur

AT   434 = 0.283 %

AT ALL   10 = 0.007 %
Sir 19:7   and you will lose nothing at all
L Jr   6:5   So take care not to become at all like the foreigners

P Az	27	so that the fire did not touch them at all		
Bel	14 : 18	and with you there is no deceit, none at all		
2 Ma	3 : 38	if he escapes at all		
	7 : 25	Since the young man would not listen to him at all		
3 Ma	4 : 3	What district or city, or what habitable place at all		
	7 : 8	with no one in any place doing them harm at all		
	7 : 9	or cause them any grief at all		
	7 : 21	and they were not subject at all		

ATARGATIS   1
2 Ma 12 : 26   and the temple of Atargatis

ATER   2
1 Es   5 : 15   The sons of Ater, namely of Hezekiah, 92
      5 : 28   the sons of Ater, the sons of Talmon

ATHENIAN   1
2 Ma   6 : 1   Not long after this, the king sent an Athenian senator

ATHENOBIUS   3 = 0.002 %
1 Ma 15 : 28   He sent to him Athenobius, one of his friends
     15 : 32   So Athenobius the friend of the king came to Jerusalem
     15 : 35   Athenobius did not answer him a word

ATHENS   1
2 Ma   9 : 15   he would make, all of them, equal to citizens of Athens

ATHLETE   3 = 0.002 %
4 Ma   6 : 10   And like a noble athlete the old man, while being beaten
     17 : 15   and gave the crown to its own athletes
     17 : 16   Who did not admire the athletes of the divine legislation ?

ATONE   3 = 0.002 %
Sir   3 : 3   Whoever honours his father atones for sins
     3 : 30   so almsgiving atones for sin
     20 : 28   and whoever pleases great men will atone for injustice

ATONEMENT   6 = 0.004 %
Sir   5 : 5   Do not be so confident of atonement that you add sin to sin
     35 : 3   and to forsake unrighteousness is atonement
     45 : 16   to make atonement for the people
     45 : 23   and made atonement for Israel
2 Ma   3 : 33   While the high priest was making the offering of atonement
     12 : 45   Therefore he made atonement for the dead

ATTACH   3 = 0.002 %
Sir 11 : 31   and to worthy actions he will attach blame
2 Ma 14 : 24   he was warmly attached to the man
3 Ma   3 : 7   So they attached no ordinary reproach to them

ATTACK, verb   30 = 0.020 %
Jud   2 : 6   Go and attack the whole west country
Ad E 16 : 20   against those who attack them at the time of their affliction
1 Ma   2 : 35   Then the enemy hastened to attack them
     2 : 38   So they attacked them on the sabbath
     2 : 41   Let us fight against every man who comes to attack us on the sabbath day
     4 : 2   to fall upon the camp of the Jews and attack them suddenly
     4 : 3   moved out to attack the king's force in Emmaus
     4 : 34   Then both sides attacked
     5 : 6   Then he crossed over to attack the Ammonites
     5 : 16   who were in distress and were being attacked by enemies
     5 : 27   the enemy are getting ready to attack the strongholds tomorrow
     5 : 30   and attacking the Jews within
     8 : 10   and they sent a general against the Greeks and attacked them
     9 : 48   and the enemy did not cross the Jordan to attack them
     9 : 67   Then he began to attack and went into battle with his forces
     11 : 20   to attack the citadel in Jerusalem
2 Ma 10 : 17   Attacking them vigorously
     12 : 6   attacked the murderers of his brethren
     12 : 9   he attacked the people of Jamnia by night
     12 : 10   not less than 5,000 Arabs with 500 horsemen attacked them
     12 : 13   He also attacked a certain city
     13 : 15   he attacked the king's pavilion at night
     13 : 18   tried strategy in attacking their positions
     13 : 19   was turned back, attacked again, and was defeated
     13 : 22   Judas and his men, was defeated
     15 : 1   he made plans to attack them with complete safety
     15 : 17   but to attack bravely, and to decide the matter
1 Es   4 : 8   if he tells them to attack, they attack
4 Ma   3 : 7   David had been attacking the Philistines all day long

ATTACK, subst.   10 = 0.007 %
Sir 25 : 14   Any attack, but not an attack from those who hate !
1 Ma   4 : 30   who didst crush the attack of the mighty warrior
     6 : 47   and the fierce attack of the forces
2 Ma   4 : 40   and launched an unjust attack
     4 : 41   But when the Jews became aware of Lysimachus' attack
     5 : 3   attacks and counterattacks made on this side and on that
     8 : 7   He found the nights most advantageous for such attacks

     13 : 26   This is how the king's attack and withdrawal turned out
     15 : 8   not to fear the attack of the Gentiles

ATTAIN   8 = 0.005 %
Ad E 13 : 3   and has attained the 2nd place in the kingdom
     13 : 5   so that our kingdom may not attain stability
Sir 22 : 11   weep less bitterly for the dead, for he has attained rest
     27 : 8   If you pursue justice, you will attain it
     38 : 33   nor do they attain eminence in the public assembly
2 Ma 14 : 6   and will not let the kingdom attain tranquillity
3 Ma   6 : 1   who had attained a ripe old age
2 Es 13 : 18   but cannot attain it

ATTALUS   1
1 Ma 15 : 22   and to Attalus and Ariarathes and Arsaces

ATTEMPT, subst.   2
4 Ma   1 : 5   Their attempt at argument is ridiculous !
     8 : 2   in his first attempt

ATTEMPT, verb   10 = 0.007 %
Sir 10 : 6   and do not attempt anything by acts of insolence
Bel 14 : 42   and threw into the den the men who had attempted his destruction
1 Ma 12 : 39   Then Trypho attempted to become king of Asia
2 Ma   2 : 23   we shall attempt to condense into a single book
     9 : 2   and attempted to rob the temples and control the city
     10 : 12   and attempted to maintain peaceful relations with them
3 Ma   2 : 32   in exchange for life they confidently attempted
     6 : 24   you are now attempting to deprive of dominion and life
2 Es 10 : 2   and all my neighbours attempted to console me
4 Ma   3 : 21   just at that time certain men attempted

ATTEND   6 = 0.004 %
Tob   5 : 16   and may his angel attend you
Sir 11 : 20   Stand by your covenant and attend to it
1 Ma 16 : 14   and attending to their needs
1 Es   4 : 11   and no one may go away to attend to his own affairs
2 Es   8 : 24   attend to my words
4 Ma   7 : 18   But as many as attend to religion with a whole heart

ATTENDANT   1
Jud 13 : 1   and shut out the attendants from his master's presence

ATTENTION   12 = 0.008 %
Sir pr.   with good will and attention
     13 : 22   he speaks sensibly, and receives no attention
     16 : 24   and pay close attention to my words
     37 : 11   pay no attention to these in any matter of counsel
1 Ma   7 : 11   But they paid no attention to their words
     10 : 61   but the king paid no attention to them
2 Ma   4 : 6   For he saw that without the king's attention
1 Es   9 : 41   and all the multitude gave attention to the law
3 Ma   2 : 2   the only ruler, almighty, give attention to us
2 Es   5 : 32   pay attention to me, and I will tell you more
4 Ma   1 : 1   to advise you to pay earnest attention to philosophy
     15 : 21   attract the attention of their hearers

ATTENTIVE   2
Sir   3 : 29   and an attentive ear is the wise man's desire
     25 : 9   and he who speaks to attentive listeners

ATTHARATES   1
1 Es   9 : 49   Then Attharates said to Ezra the chief priest and reader

ATTHARIAS   1
1 Es   5 : 40   And Nehemiah and Attharias told them

ATTIRE   2
Ad E 15 : 1   and arrayed herself in splendid attire
Sir 19 : 30   A man's attire and open-mouthed laughter

ATTITUDE   1
4 Ma 15 : 14   because of religion did not change her attitude

ATTRACT   3 = 0.002 %
Wis 14 : 20   and the multitude, attracted by the charm of his work
4 Ma   1 : 33   when we are attracted to forbidden foods
     15 : 21   attract the attention of their hearers

ATTRACTIVE   3 = 0.002 %
Sir 25 : 4   What an attractive thing is judgment in grey-haired men
     25 : 5   How attractive is wisdom in the aged
L Jr   6 : 43   because she was not as attractive as herself

ATTRIBUTE   1
4 Ma   6 : 33   we properly attribute to it the power to govern

AUDACIOUS		2
3 Ma 2:6	on the audacious Pharaoh who had enslaved your holy people Israel	
2:14	In our downfall this audacious and profane man	

AUDACITY		3 = 0.002 %
3 Ma 2:2	puffed up in his audacity and power	
2:21	in insolence and audacity	
2:26	but he also continued with such audacity	

AUGMENT		1
4 Ma 13:27	had augmented the affection of the brotherhood	

AUGUST		1
4 Ma 17:5	does not stand so august as you	

AURANUS		1
2 Ma 4:40	under the leadership of a certain Auranus	

AUSTERE		1
2 Ma 14:30	But Maccabeus, noticing that Nicanor was more austere	

AUSTERITY		1
2 Ma 14:30	concluded that this austerity	

AUTHENTIC		1
Wis 18:16	carrying the sharp sword of thy authentic command	

AUTHOR		1
Wis 13:3	for the author of beauty created them	

AUTHORITY		27 = 0.018 %
Ad E 13:2	not elated with presumption of authority	
16:5	And often many of those who are set in places of authority	
16:7	who exercise authority unworthily	
Wis 10:14	and authority over his masters	
14:21	because men, in bondage to misfortune or to royal authority	
Sir 17:2	but granted them authority over the things upon the earth	
30:11	Give him no authority in his youth	
45:8	and strengthened him with the symbols of authority	
45:17	In his commandments he gave him authority in statutes and judgments	
1 Ma 6:28	and those in authority	
10:6	So Demetrius gave him authority to recruit troops	
10:8	that the king had given him authority to recruit troops	
10:35	No one shall have authority to exact anything from them	
10:38	and obey no other authority but the high priest	
10:70	Why do you assume authority against us in the hill country ?	
2 Ma 3:24	then and there the Sovereign of spirits and of all authority	
4:9	if permission were given to establish by his authority	
4:24	extolled him with an air of authority	
7:16	Because you have authority among men, mortal though you are	
15:13	and of marvellous majesty and authority	
1 Es 8:22	and that no one has authority to impose any tax upon them	
3 Ma 3:7	neither to the king nor to his authorities	
7:1	and all in authority in his government	
7:12	so that freely and without royal authority or supervision	
4 Ma 4:5	On receiving authority to deal with this matter	
4:6	He said that he had come with the king's authority	
8:7	positions of authority in my government	

AUTHORIZE		1
1 Ma 1:13	He authorized them to observe the ordinances of the Gentiles	

AVAIL, verb		1
Wis 17:5	avail to illumine that hateful night	

AVARAN		2
1 Ma 2:5	Eleazar called Avaran, and Jonathan called Apphus	
6:43	And Eleazar, called Avaran, saw	

AVENGE		7 = 0.005 %
Jud 13:20	but have avenged our ruin	
1 Ma 2:67	and avenge the wrong done to your people	
6:22	and to avenge our brethren ?	
9:42	And when they had fully avenged the blood of their brother	
13:6	But I will avenge my nation and the sanctuary	
3 Ma 7:9	in everything and inescapably as an antagonist to avenge such acts. Farewell	
2 Es 15:9	I will surely avenge them, says the Lord	

AVENGER		2
Sir 30:6	he has left behind him an avenger against his enemies	
4 Ma 11:23	and I myself will bring a great avenger upon you	

AVERT		6 = 0.004 %
Sir 4:5	Do not avert your eye from the needy	
14:8	he averts his face and disregards people	
20:29	like a muzzle on the mouth they avert reproofs	
27:1	and whoever seeks to get rich will avert his eyes	

3 Ma 1:16	and to avert the violence of this evil design	
5:8	that he avert with vengeance the evil plot against them	

AVOID		7 = 0.005 %
Wis 2:16	and he avoids our ways as unclean	
17:10	though it nowhere could be avoided	
Sir 22:13	avoid him and you will find rest	
37:31	but he who is careful to avoid it prolongs his life	
38:17	for one day, or 2, to avoid criticism	
2 Ma 6:26	I should avoid the punishment of men	
2 Es 7:21	and what they should observe to avoid punishment	

AWAIT		6 = 0.004 %
Sir 16:22	Or who will await them ?	
2 Es 2:34	Await your shepherd	
7:93	and the punishment that awaits them	
7:95	and the glory which awaits them in the last days	
8:59	For just as the things which I have predicted await you	
8:59	so the thirst and torment which are prepared await them	

AWAKE, verb		9 = 0.006 %
Ad E 11:12	and after he awoke he had it on his mind	
2 Ma 15:17	and awaking manliness in the souls of the young	
1 Es 3:3	and went to sleep, and then awoke	
3:13	When the king awoke	
2 Es 5:14	Then I awoke, and my body shuddered violently	
7:35	righteous deeds shall awake	
11:29	the one which was in the middle) awoke	
12:3	Then I awoke in great perplexity of mind and great fear	
13:13	Then in great fear I awoke	

AWAKE, adj.		1
2 Es 7:31	which is not yet awake, shall be roused	

AWAKEN		1
4 Ma 5:11	Will you not awaken from your foolish philosophy	

AWARD, verb		1
3 Ma 3:28	and will be awarded his freedom	

AWARD, subst.		1
4 Ma 17:12	for on that day virtue gave the awards	

AWARE		6 = 0.004 %
Tob 11:2	Are you not aware, brother, of how you left your father ?	
Sir 21:7	but the sensible man, when he slips, is aware of it	
Sus 13:42	who art aware of all things before they come to be	
2 Ma 4:33	When Onias became fully aware of these acts	
4:41	But when the Jews became aware of Lysimachus' attack	
14:31	When the latter became aware	

AWAY		2
Wis 14:17	they imagined their appearance far away	
1 Ma 14:16	It was heard in Rome, and as far away as Sparta	

AWE		2
Wis 6:7	For the Lord of all will not stand in awe of any one	
3 Ma 7:21	being held in honour and awe	

AWE-INSPIRING		1
2 Ma 1:24	who art awe-inspiring and strong and just and merciful	

AXE		1
L Jr 6:15	It has a dagger in its right hand, and has an axe	

AXLE		2
Sir 33:5	and his thoughts like a turning axle	
4 Ma 9:20	and pieces of flesh were falling off the axles of the machine	

AZAEL		1
1 Es 9:34	Of the sons of Ezora : Shashai, Azarel, Azael	

AZAREL		1
1 Es 9:34	Of the sons of Ezora : Shashai, Azarel, Azael	

AZARIAH		15 = 0.010 %
P Az 2	Then Azariah stood and offered this prayer	
26	to be with Azariah and his companions	
66	Bless the Lord, Hananiah, Azariah, and Mishael	
1 Ma 2:59	Hananiah, Azariah and Mishael believed	
5:18	and Azariah, a leader of the people	
5:56	and Azariah, the commanders of the forces	
5:60	Then Joseph and Azariah were routed	
1 Es 8:1	Ezra came, the son of Seraiah, son of Azariah	
9:21	and Shemaiah and Jehiel and Azariah	
9:43	and beside him stood Mattathiah, Shema, Anaiah, Azariah	
9:48	Azariah and Jozabad, Hanan, Pelaiah, the Levites	
2 Es 1:1	son of Azariah, son of Hilkiah, son of Shallum	
1:2	son of Amariah, son of Azariah, son of Meraioth	

4 Ma	**16** : 21	and Hananiah, Azariah, and Mishael were hurled into the fiery furnace
	18 : 12	and he taught you about Hananiah, Azariah, and Mishael in the fire

AZARIAS   5 = 0.003 %

Tob	**5** : 12	He replied, I am Azarias the son of the great Ananias
	6 : 6	Then the young man said to the angel, Brother Azarias
	6 : 13	Then the young man said to the angel, Brother Azarias
	7 : 8	Then Tobias said to Raphael, Brother Azarias
	9 : 2	Brother Azarias, take a servant and 2 camels with you

AZARU   1

1 Es	**5** : 15	The sons of Azaru, 432

AZETAS   1

1 Es	**5** : 15	The sons of Kilan and Azetas, 67

AZGAD   2

1 Es	**5** : 13	The sons of Azgad, 1,322
	8 : 38	Of the sons of Azgad, Johanan the son of Hakkatan

AZOTUS   12 = 0.008 %

Jud	**2** : 28	Those who lived in Azotus and Ascalon feared him exceedingly
1 Ma	**4** : 15	and to the plains of Idumea, and to Azotus and Jamnia
	5 : 68	But Judas turned aside to Azotus
	9 : 15	and he pursued them as far as Mount Azotus
	10 : 77	and went to Azotus as though he were going farther
	10 : 78	Jonathan pursued him to Azotus
	10 : 83	They fled to Azotus and entered Beth-dagon
	10 : 84	But Jonathan burned Azotus and the surrounding towns
	11 : 4	When he approached Azotus
	11 : 4	and Azotus and its suburbs destroyed
	14 : 34	and Gazara, which is on the borders of Azotus
	16 : 10	that were in the fields of Azotus

B

BAAL   1

Tob	**1** : 5	used to sacrifice to the calf Baal

BAALSAMUS   1

1 Es	**9** : 43	Uriah, Hezekiah, and Baalsamus on his right hand

BAANAH   1

1 Es	**5** : 8	Bilshan, Mispar, Reeliah, Rehum, and Baanah, their leaders

BABBLE   1

Sir	**32** : 9	and when another is speaking, do not babble

BABBLER   1

Sir	**9** : 18	A babbler is feared in his city

BABE   5 = 0.003 %

Jud	**7** : 27	and we shall not witness the death of our babes before our eyes
Wis	**10** : 21	and made the tongues of babes speak clearly
	12 : 24	they were deceived like foolish babes
	18 : 5	When they had resolved to kill the babes of thy holy ones
1 Ma	**2** : 9	Her babes have been killed in her streets

BABY   4 = 0.003 %

2 Ma	**6** : 10	with their babies hung at their breasts
	8 : 4	and to remember also the lawless destruction of the innocent babies
3 Ma	**5** : 49	and others with babies at their breasts
	5 : 50	removing the babies from their breasts

BABYLON   50 = 0.033 %

Ad E	**11** : 4	whom Nebuchadnezzar king of Babylon
Bar	**1** : 1	wrote in Babylon
	1 : 4	all who dwelt in Babylon by the river Sud
	1 : 9	after Nebuchadnezzar king of Babylon had carried away from Jerusalem
	1 : 9	and brought them to Babylon
	1 : 11	and pray for the life of Nebuchadnezzar king of Babylon
	1 : 12	and we shall live under the protection of Nebuchadnezzar king of Babylon
	2 : 21	Bend your shoulders and serve the king of Babylon
	2 : 22	and will not serve the king of Babylon
	2 : 24	But we did not obey thy voice, to serve the king of Babylon
L Jr	**6** : 1	to those who were to be taken to Babylon as captives
	6 : 2	you will be taken to Babylon as captives
	6 : 3	Therefore when you have come to Babylon
	6 : 4	Now in Babylon you will see gods made of silver and gold and wood
Sus	**13** : 1	There was a man living in Babylon whose name was Joakim
	13 : 5	Iniquity came forth from Babylon
Bel	**14** : 34	Take the dinner which you have to Babylon

	14 : 35	Habakkuk said, Sir, I have never seen Babylon
	14 : 36	and lifted him by his hair and set him down in Babylon
1 Ma	**6** : 4	to return to Babylon
1 Es	**1** : 40	And Nebuchadnezzar king of Babylon came up against him
	1 : 40	and took him away to Babylon
	1 : 41	and stored them in his temple in Babylon
	1 : 45	and removed him to Babylon
	1 : 54	and the royal stores, they took and carried away to Babylon
	1 : 56	The survivors he led away to Babylon with the sword
	2 : 15	with the returning exiles from Babylon to Jerusalem
	4 : 44	which Cyrus set apart when he began to destroy Babylon
	4 : 57	And he sent back from Babylon all the vessels
	4 : 61	and went to Babylon and told this to all his brethren
	5 : 7	whom Nebuchadnezzar king of Babylon had carried away to Babylon
	6 : 15	into the hands of Nebuchadnezzar king of Babylon
	6 : 16	and carried the people away captive to Babylon
	6 : 18	from the temple in Babylon
	6 : 21	of our lord the king that are in Babylon
	6 : 23	in the royal archives that were deposited in Babylon
	6 : 26	and carried away to Babylon
	8 : 3	This Ezra came up from Babylon as a scribe
	8 : 6	for they left Babylon on the new moon of the first month
	8 : 28	who went up with me from Babylon
3 Ma	**6** : 6	The 3 companions in Babylon
2 Es	**3** : 1	I, Salathiel, who am also called Ezra, was in Babylon
	3 : 2	and the wealth of those who lived in Babylon
	3 : 28	Are the deeds of those who inhabit Babylon any better ?
	3 : 31	Are the deeds of Babylon better than those of Zion ?
	15 : 43	And they shall go on steadily to Babylon
	15 : 46	And you, Asia, who share in the glamour of Babylon
	15 : 60	as they return from devastated Babylon
	16 : 1	Woe to you, Babylon and Asia !

BABYLONIA   4 = 0.003 %

2 Ma	**8** : 20	that took place in Babylonia
1 Es	**4** : 53	and that all who came from Babylonia to build the city
	6 : 17	over the country of Babylonia
	8 : 13	in the country of Babylonia

BABYLONIAN   5 = 0.003 %

L Jr	**6** : 1	by the king of the Babylonians
	6 : 2	by Nebuchadnezzar, king of the Babylonians
Bel	**14** : 3	Now the Babylonians had an idol called Bel
	14 : 23	which the Babylonians revered
	14 : 28	When the Babylonians heard it

BACCHIDES   23 = 0.015 %

1 Ma	**7** : 8	So the king chose Bacchides, one of the king's friends
	7 : 12	before Alcimus and Bacchides to ask for just terms
	7 : 19	Then Bacchides departed from Jerusalem
	7 : 20	then Bacchides went back to the king
	9 : 1	he sent Bacchides and Alcimus
	9 : 11	Then the army of Bacchides marched out from the camp
	9 : 12	Bacchides was on the right wing
	9 : 14	Judas saw that Bacchides and the strength of his army were on the right
	9 : 25	And Bacchides chose the ungodly
	9 : 26	and brought them to Bacchides
	9 : 29	to go against our enemies and Bacchides
	9 : 32	When Bacchides learned of this, he tried to kill him
	9 : 34	Bacchides found this out on the sabbath day
	9 : 43	When Bacchides heard of this
	9 : 47	and Jonathan stretched out his hand to strike Bacchides
	9 : 49	And about 1,000 of Bacchides' men fell that day
	9 : 50	Bacchides then returned to Jerusalem
	9 : 57	When Bacchides saw that Alcimus was dead
	9 : 58	So now let us bring Bacchides back
	9 : 63	When Bacchides learned of this, he assembled all his forces
	9 : 68	They fought with Bacchides, and he was crushed by them
	10 : 12	Then the foreigners who were in the strongholds that Bacchides had built fled
2 Ma	**8** : 30	In encounters with the forces of Timothy and Bacchides

BACENOR   1

2 Ma	**12** : 35	But a certain Dositheus, one of Bacenor's men

BACK, subst.   6 = 0.004 %

Sir	**21** : 15	and casts it behind his back
1 Ma	**13** : 27	with polished stone at the front and back
3 Ma	**3** : 24	we would have these impious people behind our backs
4 Ma	**11** : 10	they twisted his back around the wedge on the wheel
	11 : 18	his back was broken, and he was roasted from underneath
	11 : 19	To his back they applied sharp spits

BACK, adv.   2

2 Ma	**9** : 21	On my way back from the region of Persia
4 Ma	**18** : 20	and back again to more tortures

BACKWARD   2
   Sir 48 : 23   In his days the sun went backward
   3 Ma 1 : 20   and without a backward look they crowded together

BAD   5 = 0.003 %
   Sir   6 : 1   for a bad name incurs shame and reproach :
     11 : 14   good things and bad, life and death, poverty and wealth
     31 : 13   Remember that a greedy eye is a bad thing
     37 : 27   see what is bad for it and do not give it that
   1 Es 9 : 6   shivering because of the bad weather that prevailed

BADLY   1
   1 Ma 6 : 8   he was astounded and badly shaken

BAEAN   1
   1 Ma 5 : 4   He also remembered the wickedness of the sons of Baean

BAFFLE   1
   Sir 10 : 10   A long illness baffles the physician

BAG   4 = 0.003 %
   Tob 9 : 5   and Gabael brought out the money bags with their seals intact
   Jud 10 : 5   and filled a bag with parched grain
     13 : 10   who placed it in her food bag
     13 : 15   Then she took the head out of the bag and showed it to them

BAGGAGE   4 = 0.003 %
   Jud 7 : 2   together with the baggage and the foot soldiers handling it
   1 Ma 9 : 35   the great amount of baggage which they had
      9 : 39   and saw a tumultuous procession with much baggage
   2 Ma 12 : 21   and also the baggage to a place called Carnaim

BAGOAS   6 = 0.004 %
   Jud 12 : 11   And he said to Bagoas
     12 : 13   So Bagoas went out from the presence of Holofernes
     12 : 15   the soft fleeces which she had received from Bagoas
     13 : 1   and Bagoas closed the tent from outside
     13 : 3   And she had said the same thing to Bagoas
     14 : 14   So Bagoas went in and knocked at the door of the tent

BAITERUS   1
   1 Es 5 : 17   The sons of Baiterus, 3,005

BAKBUK   1
   1 Es 5 : 31   the sons of Nephisim, the sons of Bakbuk

BALAMON   1
   Jud 8 : 3   in the field between Dothan and Balamon

BALANCE   6 = 0.004 %
   Sir 21 : 25   but the words of the prudent will be weighed in the balance
     26 : 15   and no balance can weigh the value of a chaste soul
     28 : 25   make balances and scales for your words
   2 Ma 9 : 8   and imagining that he could weigh the high mountains in a
        balance
   2 Es 3 : 34   Now therefore weigh in a balance our iniquities
     4 : 36   for he has weighed the age in the balance

BALBAIM   1
   Jud 7 : 3   and they spread out in breadth over Dothan as far as Balbaim

BALLOT   1
   4 Ma 15 : 26   this mother held 2 ballots

BAND, subst.   1
   1 Ma 5 : 6   where he found a strong band

BANDAGE, verb   1
   Sir 27 : 21   For a wound may be bandaged

BANI   4 = 0.003 %
   1 Es 5 : 12   The sons of Bani, 648
     8 : 36   Of the sons of Bani, Shelomith the son of Josiphiah
     9 : 30   Of the sons of Bani : Meshullam, Malluch, Adaiah
     9 : 34   Of the sons of Bani : Jeremai, Maadai, Amram, Joel

BANISH   4 = 0.003 %
   1 Ma 3 : 35   he was to banish the memory of them from the place
   2 Ma 10 : 15   they received those who were banished from Jerusalem
   2 Es 8 : 53   illness is banished from you, and death is hidden
   4 Ma 8 : 23   Why do we banish ourselves from this most pleasant life

BANK   2
   Sir 40 : 16   The reeds by any water or river bank
   1 Ma 9 : 43   to the banks of the Jordan

BANNAS   1
   1 Es 5 : 26   and Bannas and Sudias, 74

BANQUET   15 = 0.010 %
   Jud 6 : 21   and gave a banquet for the elders
     12 : 10   On the 4th day Holofernes held a banquet for his slaves only
     13 : 1   because the banquet had lasted long
   Sir 31 : 31   Do not reprove your neighbour at a banquet of wine
     32 : 5   is a concert of music at a banquet of wine
     49 : 1   and like music at a banquet of wine
   1 Ma 16 : 15   he gave them a great banquet, and hid men there
     16 : 16   and rushed in against Simon in the banquet hall
   2 Ma 2 : 27   just as it is not easy for one who prepares a banquet
   1 Es 3 : 1   Now King Darius gave a great banquet
   3 Ma 5 : 15   that the hour of the banquet was already slipping by
     5 : 16   and ordered those present for the banquet to recline opposite
        him
     5 : 17   and to make the present portion of the banquet joyful
     6 : 31   arranged for a banquet of deliverance
     6 : 33   Likewise also the king, after convening a great banquet

BAR   3 = 0.002 %
   Sir 49 : 13   and set up the gates and bars and rebuilt our ruined houses
   L Jr 6 : 18   so the priests make their temples secure with doors and locks
        and bars
   1 Ma 9 : 50   with high walls and gates and bars

BARBARIAN   1
   2 Ma 2 : 21   and pursued the barbarian hordes

BARBAROUS   5 = 0.003 %
   2 Ma 5 : 22   and in character more barbarous
     10 : 4   and not be handed over to blasphemous and barbarous nations
     13 : 9   The king with barbarous arrogance
   3 Ma 3 : 24   as traitors and barbarous enemies
     7 : 3   and to punish them with barbarous penalties as traitors

BARBAROUSLY   1
   2 Ma 15 : 2   Do not destroy so savagely and barbarously

BARELY   2
   3 Ma 1 : 23   and being barely restrained by the old men and the elders
     7 : 6   we barely spared their lives

BARK, subst.   1
   Wis 13 : 11   and skilfully strip off all its bark

BARKOS   1
   1 Es 5 : 32   the sons of Charea, the sons of Barkos

BARLEY   1
   Jud 8 : 2   had died during the barley harvest

BARODIS   1
   1 Es 5 : 34   the sons of Barodis, the sons of Shaphat, the sons of Ami

BARREN   7 = 0.005 %
   Wis 3 : 13   For blessed is the barren woman who is undefiled
     4 : 19   they will be left utterly dry and barren
   Sir 42 : 10   or, though married, lest she be barren
   2 Es 5 : 1   and the land shall be barren of faith
     9 : 43   Your servant was barren and had no child
     10 : 45   And as for her telling you that she was barren for 30 years
     10 : 46   then it was that the barren woman bore a son

BARRICADE   1
   Jud 5 : 1   and set up barricades in the plains

BARRIER   1
   1 Ma 12 : 36   and to erect a high barrier between the citadel and the city

BARTACUS   1
   1 Es 4 : 29   the daughter of the illustrious Bartacus

BARTER, subst.   1
   Sir 37 : 11   with a merchant about barter or with a buyer about selling

BARUCH   3 = 0.002 %
   Bar 1 : 1   which Baruch the son of Neraiah, son of Mahseiah
     1 : 3   And Baruch read the words of this book
     1 : 8   Baruch took the vessels of the house of the Lord

BARZILLAI   1
   1 Es 5 : 38   one of the daughters of Barzillai

BASE, subst.   1
   Sir 26 : 18   Like pillars of gold on a base of silver

BASE, adj.   4 = 0.003 %
   Wis 2 : 16   We are considered by him as something base
     15 : 12   for he says one must get money however one can, even by base
        means

Sir **18**:30 Do not follow your base desires, but restrain your appetites
18:31 If you allow your soul to take pleasure in base desire

BASELY   1
4 Ma **6**:17 never think so basely

BASENESS   2
Sir **14**:6 and this is the retribution for his baseness
14:7 and betrays his baseness in the end

BASIC   1
Sir **39**:26 Basic to all the needs of man's life are water and fire

BASIN   1
4 Ma **13**:6 and make it calm for those who sail into the inner basin

BASKAMA   1
1 Ma **13**:23 When he approached Baskama, he killed Jonathan

BAT   1
L Jr **6**:22 Bats, swallows, and birds light on their bodies and heads

BATH   1
1 Es **8**:20 a 100 baths of wine, and salt in abundance

BATHE   5 = 0.003 %
Jud **10**:3 and bathed her body with water
12:7 and bathed at the spring in the camp
Sus **13**:15 and wished to bathe in the garden, for it was very hot
13:17 and shut the garden doors so that I may bathe
4 Ma **6**:11 in fact, with his face bathed in sweat

BATTER   1
1 Ma **13**:43 and battered and captured one tower

BATTERING-RAM   1
2 Ma **12**:15 who without battering-rams or engines of war

BATTLE, subst.   85 = 0.055 %
Jud **1**:13 and defeated him in battle
5:18 they were utterly defeated in many battles
7:11 Therefore, my lord, do not fight against them in battle array
14:13 as to come down against us and to give battle
Wis **12**:9 into the hands of the righteous in battle
Sir **37**:5 and in the face of battle take up the shield
1 Ma **1**:2 He fought many battles, conquered strongholds
1:18 He engaged Ptolemy king of Egypt in battle
2:32 they encamped opposite them and prepared for battle
2:66 and fight the battle against the peoples
3:3 he girded on his armour of war and waged battles
3:12 and used it in battle the rest of his life
3:13 who stayed with him and went out to battle
3:19 that victory in battle depends
3:26 and the Gentiles talked of the battles of Judas
3:44 And the congregation assembled to be ready for battle
3:59 It is better for us to die in battle
4:13 they went forth from their camp to battle
4:14 and engaged in battle
4:17 for there is a battle before us
4:21 drawn up in the plain for battle
5:7 He engaged in many battles with them
5:19 but do not engage in battle with the Gentiles until we return
5:21 and fought many battles against the Gentiles
5:31 So Judas saw that the battle had begun
5:42 Permit no man to encamp, but make them all enter the battle
5:59 to meet them in battle
5:67 fell in battle, for they went out to battle unwisely
6:4 And they withstood him in battle
6:33 and his troops made ready for battle
6:34 to arouse them for battle
6:42 But Judas and his army advanced to the battle
7:31 he went out to meet Judas in battle near Capharsalama
7:43 So the armies met in battle
7:43 and he himself was the first to fall in the battle
7:45 kept sounding the battle call on the trumpets
8:5 they crushed in battle and conquered
9:1 that Nicanor and his army had fallen in battle
9:7 and the battle was imminent, he was crushed in spirit
9:13 and the battle raged from morning till evening
9:17 The battle became desperate
9:30 as our ruler and leader, to fight our battle
9:45 For look ! The battle is in front of us and behind us
9:47 So the battle began
9:67 Then he began to attack and went into battle with his forces
10:2 and marched out to meet him in battle
10:15 and men told him of the battles
10:49 The 2 kings met in battle
10:50 He pressed the battle strongly until the sun set
10:53 I met him in battle
10:78 and the armies engaged in battle

10:82 and engaged the phalanx in battle
11:15 And Alexander heard of it and came against him in battle
11:69 Then the men in ambush emerged from their places and joined battle
11:72 Then he turned back to the battle against the enemy
12:27 so as to be ready all night for battle
12:28 that Jonathan and his men were prepared for battle
12:50 and kept marching in close formation, ready for battle
13:9 Fight our battles, and all that you say to us we will do
13:14 and that he was about to join battle with him
15:14 and the ships joined battle from the sea
2 Ma **8**:20 and the time of the battle with the Galatians
8:23 he joined battle with Nicanor
10:28 Just as dawn was breaking, the 2 armies joined battle
10:29 When the battle became fierce
11:10 They advanced in battle order, having their heavenly ally
12:34 When they joined battle
12:36 to show himself their ally and leader in the battle
12:37 In the language of their fathers he raised the battle cry, with hymns
14:16 and engaged them in battle at a village called Dessau
14:18 and his men and their courage in battle for their country
15:20 with their army drawn up for battle
15:25 Nicanor and his men advanced with trumpets and battle songs
15:26 and Judas and his men met the enemy in battle
1 Es **1**:29 He joined battle with him in the plain of Megiddo
1:30 Take me away from the battle, for I am very weak
1:30 And immediately his servants took him out of the line of battle
2:30 with horsemen and a multitude in battle array
3 Ma **1**:4 if they won the battle
3:14 by the gods" deliberate alliance with us in battle
2 Es **15**:30 and engage them in battle
16:40 prepare for battle
4 Ma **9**:24 Fight the sacred and noble battle for religion
17:24 for infantry battle and siege

BATTLE-FRONT   1
Sir **40**:6 like one who has escaped from the battle-front

BATTLEMENT   2
Tob **13**:16 and her towers and battlements with pure gold
Sir **9**:13 and that you are going about on the city battlements

BAZLUTH   1
1 Es **5**:31 the sons of Pharakim, the sons of Bazluth

BE   5385 = 3.508 %

BEAM   5 = 0.003 %
Sir **22**:16 A wooden beam firmly bonded into a building
43:4 *and with bright beams it blinds the eyes*
L Jr **6**:20 They are just like a beam of the temple
6:55 but the gods will be burnt in 2 like beams
1 Es **6**:32 a beam should be taken out of his house

BEAR, subst.   3 = 0.002 %
Wis **11**:17 a multitude of bears, or bold lions
Sir **25**:17 and darkens her face like that of a bear
47:3 and with bears as with lambs of the flock

BEAR, verb   37 = 0.024 %
Tob **13**:11 bearing gifts in their hands, gifts for the King of heaven
Jud **7**:4 nor the valleys nor the hills will bear their weight
15:13 bearing their arms and wearing garlands
Wis **10**:7 plants bearing fruit that does not ripen
Sir **22**:15 Sand, salt, and a piece of iron are easier to bear than a stupid man
23:25 and her branches will not bear fruit
28:19 who has not borne its yoke
29:28 These things are hard to bear for a man who has feeling :
36:15 Bear witness to those whom thou didst create in the beginning
Sus **13**:43 thou knowest that these men have borne false witness against me
13:49 For these men have borne false witness against her
13:61 Daniel had convicted them of bearing false witness
2 Ma **3**:36 And he bore testimony to all men
7:6 which bore witness against the people to their faces
7:20 she bore it with good courage
10:7 Therefore bearing ivy-wreathed wands and beautiful branches
12:30 bore witness to the good will
P Ma **5** for thy glorious splendour cannot be borne
2 Es **2**:2 The mother who bore them says to them
3:33 and their labour has borne no fruit
5:46 and say to it, If you bear 10 children
5:51 He replied to me, Ask a woman who bears children
5:52 Say to her, Why are those whom you have borne recently
5:52 not like those whom you bore before
7:94 they see the witness which he who formed them bears concerning them
7:105 for then every one shall bear his own righteousness or unrighteousness

	8 : 6	by which every mortal who bears the likeness of a human being
	10 : 12	which I brought forth in pain and bore in sorrow
	10 : 15	and bear bravely the troubles that have come upon you
	10 : 46	then it was that the barren woman bore a son
	16 : 25	The trees shall bear fruit, and who will gather it ?
4 Ma	6 : 9	But he bore the pains and scorned the punishment
	10 : 2	and the same mother bore me
	14 : 9	but also bore the sufferings patiently
	15 : 26	one bearing death and the other deliverance for her children
	16 : 6	After bearing 7 children, I am now the mother of none !
	16 : 16	to bear witness for the nation

BEAR down   1
| 2 Ma | 12 : 35 | when one of the Thracian horsemen bore down upon him |

BEAR up   2
| 4 Ma | 13 : 11 | another said, Bear up nobly |
| | 14 : 12 | for the mother of the 7 young men bore up |

BEARD   2
| L Jr | 6 : 31 | their heads and beards shaved |
| 1 Es | 8 : 71 | and pulled out hair from my head and beard |

BEARING   1
| 2 Ma | 15 : 12 | of modest bearing and gentle manner |

BEAST   42 = 0.027 %
Jud	11 : 7	but also the beasts of the field
Ad E	16 : 24	but also most hateful for all time to beasts and birds
Wis	7 : 20	the natures of animals and the tempers of wild beasts
	11 : 18	or newly created unknown beasts full of rage
	12 : 9	by dread wild beasts or thy stern word
	16 : 5	For when the terrible rage of wild beasts
	17 : 9	yet, scared by the passing of beasts
	17 : 19	or the sound of the most savage roaring beasts
Sir	10 : 11	and wild beasts, and worms
	12 : 13	or any who go near wild beasts ?
	17 : 4	and granted them dominion over beasts and birds
	39 : 30	the teeth of wild beasts, and scorpions and vipers
	40 : 8	With all flesh, both man and beast
Bar	3 : 16	and those who rule over the beasts on the earth
L Jr	6 : 68	The wild beasts are better than they are
P Az	59	Bless the Lord, all beasts and cattle
1 Ma	6 : 35	And they distributed the beasts among the phalanxes
	6 : 35	and 500 picked horsemen were assigned to each beast
	6 : 36	These took their position beforehand wherever the beast was
	6 : 37	they were fastened upon each beast by special harness
	6 : 43	that one of the beasts was equipped with royal armour
2 Ma	4 : 25	and the rage of a savage wild beast
	9 : 15	to the beasts, for the birds to pick
	11 : 9	ready to assail not only men but the wildest beasts or walls of iron
3 Ma	5 : 23	Hermon, having equipped the beasts
	5 : 29	pointed out that the beasts and the armed forces were ready
	5 : 31	for the savage beasts instead of the Jews
	5 : 42	mangled by the knees and feet of the beasts
	5 : 45	Now when the beasts had been brought virtually
	5 : 47	rushed out in full force along with the beasts
	6 : 7	was cast down into the ground to lions as food for wild beasts
	6 : 16	the king arrived at the hippodrome with the beasts
	6 : 21	The beasts turned back upon the armed forces following them
2 Es	5 : 8	and the wild beasts shall roam beyond their haunts
	6 : 53	to bring forth before thee cattle, beasts, and creeping things
	7 : 65	but let the beasts of the field be glad
	7 : 65	but let the four-footed beasts and the flocks rejoice !
	8 : 30	Be not angry with those who are deemed worse than beasts
	11 : 39	Are you not the one that remains of the 4 beasts
		have conquered all the beasts that have gone before
4 Ma	9 : 28	These leopard-like beasts tore out his sinews with the iron hands
	12 : 13	As a man, were you not ashamed, you most savage beast

BEAT, subst.   1
| Wis | 5 : 11 | the light air, lashed by the beat of its pinions |

BEAT, verb   7 = 0.005 %
Tob	3 : 9	Why do you beat us ? If they are dead, go with them !
Sir	30 : 12	and beat his sides while he is young
2 Ma	4 : 45	But Menelaus, already as good as beaten
	9 : 2	and beat a shameful retreat
2 Es	15 : 51	who is beaten and wounded
4 Ma	6 : 10	And like a noble athlete the old man, while being beaten
	9 : 12	When they had worn themselves out beating with scourges

BEAT off   1
| 2 Ma | 10 : 17 | and beat off all who fought upon the wall |

BEATING   2
| Wis | 2 : 2 | and reason is a spark kindled by the beating of our hearts |
| 2 Ma | 6 : 30 | I am enduring terrible sufferings in my body under this beating |

BEAUTIFUL   27 = 0.018 %
Tob	6 : 12	The girl is also beautiful and sensible
Jud	8 : 7	She was beautiful in appearance, and had a very lovely face
	10 : 4	and made herself very beautiful
	10 : 14	she was in their eyes marvellously beautiful
	11 : 23	You are not only beautiful in appearance, but wise in speech
	12 : 13	This beautiful maidservant will please come to my lord
Wis	5 : 16	and a beautiful diadem from the hand of the Lord
	7 : 29	For she is more beautiful than the sun
	13 : 7	because the things that are seen are beautiful
	14 : 19	skilfully forced the likeness to take more beautiful form
	15 : 19	and even as animals they are not so beautiful in appearance
Sir	24 : 14	like a beautiful olive tree in the field
	24 : 18	I am the mother of beautiful love
	25 : 1	and they are beautiful in the sight of the Lord and of men :
	26 : 17	so is a beautiful face on a stately figure
	26 : 18	so are beautiful feet with a steadfast heart
	43 : 11	exceedingly beautiful in its brightness
	45 : 13	Before his time there never were such beautiful things
Sus	13 : 2	a very beautiful woman and one who feared the Lord
	13 : 31	and beautiful in appearance
2 Ma	3 : 26	gloriously beautiful and splendidly dressed
	10 : 7	Therefore bearing ivy-wreathed wands and beautiful branches
1 Es	4 : 18	If men gather gold and silver or any other beautiful thing
	4 : 19	or any other beautiful thing
3 Ma	3 : 17	with magnificent and most beautiful offerings
2 Es	6 : 3	and before the beautiful flowers were seen
4 Ma	16 : 10	Alas, I who had so many and beautiful children

BEAUTY   35 = 0.023 %
Jud	1 : 14	plundered its markets, and turned its beauty into shame
	10 : 7	they greatly admired her beauty, and said to her
	10 : 19	And they marvelled at her beauty
	10 : 23	they all marvelled at the beauty of her face
	11 : 21	either for beauty of face or wisdom of speech !
	16 : 7	with the beauty of her countenance
	16 : 9	Her sandal ravished his eyes, her beauty captivated his mind
Ad E	15 : 5	She was radiant with perfect beauty, and she looked happy
Wis	7 : 10	I loved her more than health and beauty
	8 : 2	and I became enamoured of her beauty
	13 : 3	If through delight in the beauty of these things
	13 : 3	for the author of beauty created them
	13 : 5	For from the greatness and beauty of created things
Sir	9 : 8	and do not look intently at beauty belonging to another
	9 : 8	many have been misled by a woman's beauty
	25 : 21	Do not be ensnared by a woman's beauty
	26 : 16	so is the beauty of a good wife in her well-ordered home
	36 : 22	A woman's beauty gladdens the countenance
	40 : 22	The eye desires grace and beauty
	42 : 12	Do not look upon any one for beauty
	43 : 9	The glory of the stars is the beauty of heaven
	43 : 18	The eye marvels at the beauty of its whiteness
	47 : 10	He gave beauty to the feasts
Bar	5 : 1	and put on for ever the beauty of the glory from God
L Jr	6 : 24	As for the gold which they wear for beauty
Sus	13 : 32	that they might feast upon her beauty
	13 : 56	beauty has deceived you and lust has perverted your heart
1 Ma	1 : 26	the beauty of the women faded
	2 : 12	And behold, our holy place, our beauty
1 Es	4 : 18	and then see a woman lovely in appearance and beauty
3 Ma	1 : 9	and being impressed by its excellence and its beauty
2 Es	10 : 50	and the loveliness of her beauty
	15 : 54	Trick out the beauty of your face !
4 Ma	2 : 1	the desires of the mind for the enjoyment of beauty
	8 : 5	and greatly respect the beauty and the number of such brothers

BEBAI   5 = 0.003 %
Jud	15 : 4	And Uzziah sent men to Betomasthaim and Bebai
1 Es	5 : 13	The sons of Bebai, 623
	8 : 37	Of the sons of Bebai, Zechariah the son of Bebai
	9 : 29	Of the sons of Bebai :

BECAUSE   242 = 0.158 %
Tob	1 : 12	because I remembered God with all my heart
	2 : 9	and because I was defiled
	3 : 5	because we did not keep thy commandments
	3 : 6	because I have heard false reproaches
	3 : 8	because she had been given to 7 husbands
	3 : 17	because Tobias was entitled to possess her
	4 : 13	because shiftlessness is the mother of famine
	4 : 21	Do not be afraid, my son, because we have become poor
	5 : 13	because I tried to learn your tribe and family
	6 : 11	because you are entitled to her and to her inheritance
	6 : 12	because you rather than any other man
	8 : 16	Blessed art thou, because thou hast made me glad
	8 : 17	Blessed art thou, because thou hast had compassion on 2 only children
	11 : 1	praising God because he had made his journey a success
	11 : 16	because he could see
	13 : 4	because he is our Lord and God, he is our Father for ever

	14:8	because what the prophet Jonah said will surely happen
Jud	**2:6**	because they disobeyed my orders
	5:7	because they would not follow the gods of their fathers
	5:19	because it was uninhabited
	6:2	because their God will defend them ?
	7:15	because they rebelled and did not receive you peaceably
	7:19	because all their enemies had surrounded them
	7:21	because it was measured out to them to drink
	8:9	because they were faint for lack of water
	11:14	because even the people living there have been doing this
	12:18	because my life means more to me today
	13:1	because the banquet had lasted long
	13:20	because you did not spare your own life
Ad E	**14:7**	because we glorified their gods
	16:18	because the man himself who did these things
Wis	**1:2**	because he is found by those who do not put him to the test
	1:4	because wisdom will not enter a deceitful soul
	1:6	because God is witness of his inmost feelings
	1:7	Because the Spirit of the Lord has filled the world
	1:10	because a jealous ear hears all things
	1:11	because no secret word is without result
	1:13	because God did not make death
	1:16	because they are fit to belong to his party
	2:2	Because we were born by mere chance
	2:2	because the breath in our nostrils is smoke
	2:5	because it is sealed up and no one turns back
	2:9	because this is our portion, and this is our lot
	2:12	because he is inconvenient to us and opposes our actions
	2:15	because his manner of life is unlike that of others
	3:5	because God tested them and found them worthy of himself
	3:9	because grace and mercy are upon his elect
	4:1	because it is known both by God and by men
	4:19	because he will dash them speechless to the ground
	5:14	Because the hope of the ungodly man
	5:16	because with his right hand he will cover them
	6:4	Because as servants of his kingdom you did not rule rightly
	6:5	because severe judgment falls on those in high places
	6:7	because he himself made both small and great
	6:16	because she goes about seeking those worthy of her
	7:9	because all gold is but a little sand in her sight
	7:10	because her radiance never ceases
	7:12	I rejoiced in them all, because wisdom leads them
	10:3	he perished because in rage he slew his brother
	10:8	For because they passed wisdom by
	10:21	because wisdom opened the mouth of the dumb
	11:22	Because the whole world before thee
	12:19	because thou givest repentance for sins
	13:7	because the things that are seen are beautiful
	13:16	because he knows that it cannot help itself
	14:3	because thou hast given it a path in the sea
	14:8	because he did the work
	14:11	because, though part of what God created
	14:21	because men, in bondage to misfortune or to royal authority
	14:29	for because they trust in lifeless idols
	14:30	because they thought wickedly of God
	14:30	and because in deceit they swore unrighteously
	15:2	because we know that we are accounted thine
	15:11	because he failed to know the one who formed him
	16:9	because they deserved to be punished by such things
Sir	**1:30**	because you did not come in the fear of the Lord
	7:35	because for such deeds you will be loved
	8:8	because from them you will gain instruction
	8:9	because from them you will gain understanding
	8:16	because blood is as nothing in his sight
	14:16	because in Hades one cannot look for luxury
	20:6	There is one who keeps silent because he has no answer
	20:6	while another keeps silent because he knows when to speak
	33:30	because you have bought him with blood
Bar	**1:17**	because we have sinned before the Lord
	2:5	because we sinned against the Lord our God
	3:28	so they perished because they had no wisdom
	4:6	because you angered God
	4:12	because they turned away from the law of God
L Jr	**6:27**	because through them these gods are made to stand
	6:43	because she was not as attractive as herself
Sus	**13:4**	and the Jews used to come to him because he was the most honoured of them all
	13:18	and they did not see the elders, because they were hidden
	13:41	because they were elders of the people and judges
	13:63	because nothing shameful was found in her
Bel	**14:5**	He answered, Because I do not revere man-made idols
	14:9	because he blasphemed against Bel
1 Ma	**2:30**	because evils pressed heavily upon them
	2:54	Phinehas our father, because he was deeply zealous
	2:55	Joshua, because he fulfilled the command
	2:56	Caleb, because he testified in the assembly
	2:57	David, because he was merciful
	2:63	because he has returned to the dust
	3:46	because Israel formerly had a place of prayer in Mizpah
	4:5	because he said, These men are fleeing from us
	5:3	because they kept lying in wait for Israel
	5:54	because not one of them had fallen
	5:61	because, thinking to do a brave deed
	6:3	but he could not, because his plan became known to the men of the city
	6:8	because things had not turned out for him as he had planned
	6:9	because deep grief continually gripped him
	6:49	because they had no provisions there to withstand a siege
	6:53	because it was the 7th year
	6:54	because famine had prevailed over the rest
	9:60	because their plan became known
	10:42	because it belongs to the priests who minister there
	10:43	because he owes money to the king or has any debt
	10:46	because they remembered the great wrongs
	10:47	because he had been the first to speak peaceable words to them
	11:11	He threw blame on Alexander because he coveted his kingdom
	11:14	because the people of that region were in revolt
	13:18	Because Simon did not send him the money and the sons, he perished
	13:51	because a great enemy had been crushed and removed from Israel
	14:35	because he had done all these things
2 Ma	**2:11**	because the sin offering had not been eaten
	3:18	because the holy place was about to be brought into contempt
	4:19	because that was inappropriate
	4:30	revolted because their cities had been given
	4:39	because many of the gold vessels had already been stolen
	5:21	because his mind was elated
	6:11	because their piety kept them from defending themselves
	6:29	because the words he had uttered
	6:30	because I fear him
	7:9	because we have died for his laws
	7:16	Because you have authority among men, mortal though you are
	8:15	and because he had called them by his holy and glorious name
	8:25	they were obliged to return because the hour was late
	8:36	because they followed the laws ordained by him
	10:13	because he had abandoned Cyprus
	11:13	because the mighty God fought on their side
	12:4	because they wished to live peaceably and suspected nothing
	12:7	Then, because the city's gates were closed
	12:24	because he held the parents of most of them
	13:3	but because he thought
	13:8	because he had committed many sins
	13:17	because the Lord's help protected him
	14:8	first because I am genuinely concerned
	14:8	and second because I have regard also for my fellow citizens
	15:17	because the city and the sanctuary
1 Es	**1:14**	because the priests were offering the fat until night
	1:50	because he would have spared them and his dwelling place
	4:62	because he had given them release and permission
	5:61	because his goodness and his glory are for ever upon all Israel
	7:15	because he had changed the will of the king of the Assyrians concerning them
	9:55	because they were inspired by the words which they had been taught
3 Ma	**1:11**	because not even members of their own nation
	1:29	because indeed all at that time preferred death
	2:10	And because you love the house of Israel
	2:12	And because oftentimes when our fathers were oppressed
	2:16	But because you graciously bestowed your glory
	3:4	but because he worshipped God
	3:17	because when we proposed
	5:7	because in their bonds
	5:30	because by the providence of God
2 Es	**1:25**	Because you have forsaken me, I also will forsake you
	1:34	because with you they have neglected my commandment
	2:2	Go, my children, because I am a widow and forsaken
	2:3	because you have sinned before the Lord God
	2:5	because they would not keep my covenant
	2:7	because they have despised my covenant
	2:14	because I live, says the Lord
	2:15	establish their feet, because I have chosen you, says the Lord
	2:16	because I recognize my name in them
	2:24	Pause and be quiet, my people, because your rest will come
	2:30	because I will deliver you, says the Lord
	2:31	because I will bring them out of the hiding places of the earth
	2:32	because my springs run over, and my grace will not fail
	2:34	because he who will come at the end of the age is close at hand
	2:35	because the eternal light will shine upon you for evermore
	3:2	because I saw the desolation of Zion
	4:26	because the age is hastening swiftly to its end
	4:27	because this age is full of sadness and infirmities
	6:8	because from him were born Jacob and Esau
	6:15	because the word concerns the end
	6:32	because your voice has surely been heard before the Most High
	6:55	because thou hast said that it was for us
	7:60	because it is they who have made my glory to prevail now
	7:64	because we perish and know it
	7:72	because though they had understanding they committed iniquity
	7:81	because they have scorned the law of the Most High

	7:82	because they cannot now make a good repentance
	7:87	because they shall utterly waste away in confusion
	7:92	because they have striven with great effort
	7:93	because they see the perplexity
	7:98	because they shall rejoice with boldness
	7:124	because we have lived in unseemly places ?
	7:132	because he has mercy on those who have not yet come into the world
	7:133	and gracious, because he is gracious to those
	7:134	and patient, because he shows patience
	7:135	and bountiful, because he would rather give than take away
	7:136	because he makes his compassions abound more and more
	7:138	because if he did not give out of his goodness
	7:139	and judge, because if he did not pardon those who were created by his word
	8:8	And because thou dost give life to the body
	8:43	because it has not received thy rain in due season
	8:44	and is called thy own image because he is made like thee
	8:49	because you have humbled yourself, as is becoming for you
	8:50	because they have walked in great pride
	8:52	because it is for you that paradise is opened
	9:22	because with much labour I have perfected them
	9:32	for it could not, because it was thine
	9:33	because they did not keep what had been sown in them
	10:8	because we are all mourning
	10:8	and to be sorrowful, because we are all sorrowing
	10:32	I said, Because you have forsaken me !
	10:45	it is because there were 3,000 years in the world
	12:4	because you search out the ways of the Most High
	13:18	because they understand what is reserved for the last days
	13:54	because you have forsaken your own ways
	13:58	and because he governs the times
	14:24	these 5, because they are trained to write rapidly
	14:32	And because he is a righteous judge
	15:13	because their seed shall fail and their trees shall be ruined
	15:27	because you have sinned against him
	16:32	because no sheep will go along them
	16:33	Virgins shall mourn because they have no bridegrooms
	16:33	women shall mourn because they have no husbands
	16:33	their daughters shall mourn, because they have no helpers
	16:45	Because those who labour, labour in vain
	16:64	Because the Lord will strictly examine all their works
4 Ma	1:33	Is it not because reason is able to rule over appetites ?
	2:2	because by mental effort he overcame sexual desire
	4:3	because I am loyal to the king's government
	4:25	because they had circumcised their sons
	6:7	because his body could not endure the agonies
	7:17	because not every one has prudent reason
	9:15	not because I am a murderer, or as one who acts impiously
	9:15	but because I protect the divine law
	11:5	It is because we revere the Creator of all things and live
	11:12	because through these noble sufferings you give us
	12:15	Then because he too was about to die, he said
	13:26	because, with the aid of their religion

BECAUSE OF 125 = 0.081 %

Tob	8:7	I am not taking this sister of mine because of lust, but with sincerity
Jud	11:7	not only do men serve him because of you
Ad E	12:6	because of the 2 eunuchs of the king
Wis	7:24	because of her pureness
	8:10	Because of her I shall have glory among the multitudes
	8:13	Because of her I shall have immortality
	10:4	When the earth was flooded because of him
	16:3	because of the odious creatures sent to them
	18:13	because of their magic arts
	19:13	for they justly suffered because of their wicked acts
Sir	8:14	for the decision will favour him because of his standing
	11:2	nor loathe a man because of his appearance
	15:11	Do not say, Because of the Lord I left the right way
	20:11	There are losses because of glory
	20:22	or lose it because of his foolish look
	22:26	but if some harm should happen to me because of him
	23:1	and let me not fall because of them !
	25:24	and because of her we all die
	26:28	and because of a 3rd anger comes over me :
	28:18	but not so many as have fallen because of the tongue
	29:7	Because of such wickedness, therefore
	29:9	because of his need do not send him away empty
	31:6	Many have come to ruin because of gold
	34:12	but have escaped because of these experiences
	35:5	because of the commandment
	41:7	for they suffer reproach because of him
	43:26	Because of him his messenger finds the way
	47:23	After him rose up a wise son who fared amply because of him
Bar	2:19	For it is not because of any righteous deeds
	2:26	because of the wickedness of the house of Israel
	4:12	I was left desolate because of the sins of my children
	4:22	because of the mercy which soon will come to you
L Jr	6:2	Because of the sins which you have committed before God

	6:13	their faces are wiped because of the dust from the temple
P Az	5	because of our sins
	14	because of our sins
1 Ma	1:38	Because of them the residents of Jerusalem fled
	2:58	Elijah because of great zeal for the law
	2:60	Daniel because of his innocence
	3:29	because of the dissension and disaster
	6:13	I know that it is because of this
	10:70	and I have become a laughingstock and reproach because of you
	11:33	because of the good will they show toward us
	13:22	and he did not go because of the snow
	14:35	and because of the justice and loyalty
2 Ma	2:24	because of the mass of material
	3:1	because of the piety of the high priest Onias
	3:13	But Heliodorus, because of the king's commands which he had
	3:29	speechless because of the divine intervention
	4:13	because of the surpassing wickedness of Jason
	4:37	because of the moderation and good conduct of the deceased
	4:50	But Menelaus, because of the cupidity of those in power
	5:9	in hope of finding protection because of their kinship
	5:17	because of the sins of those who dwelt in the city
	6:21	because of their long acquaintance with him
	6:25	they should be led astray because of me
	7:11	and because of his laws I disdain them
	7:18	because of our sins against our own God
	7:20	because of her hope in the Lord
	7:32	For we are suffering because of our own sins
	9:9	his flesh rotted away, and because of his stench
	9:10	Because of his intolerable stench
	10:12	because of the wrong that had been done to them
	10:35	fired with anger because of the blasphemies
	12:21	because of the narrowness of all the approaches
	12:42	what had happened because of the sin of those who had fallen
	14:17	the sudden consternation created by the enemy
1 Es	1:52	because of their ungodly acts he gave command
	3:7	and because of his wisdom he shall sit next to Darius
	4:26	Many men have lost their minds because of women
	4:26	and have become slaves because of them
	4:27	Many have perished, or stumbled, or sinned, because of women
	5:65	because of the weeping of the people
	8:77	And because of our sins and the sins of our fathers
	8:86	because of our evil deeds and our great sins
	8:90	because of these things
	9:6	shivering because of the bad weather that prevailed
P Ma	9	because of the multitude of my iniquities
	10	so that I am rejected because of my sins
3 Ma	1:21	because of what the king was profanely plotting
	2:13	that because of our many and great sins
	3:18	because of the benevolence which we have toward all
	3:21	both because of their alliance with us
	4:2	and they groaned because of the unexpected destruction
	4:17	because of their innumerable multitude
	5:41	because of its expectation
	6:22	because of the things that he had devised beforehand
	6:36	but because of the deliverance
	7:4	because of the ill-will which these people had toward all nations
	7:17	because of a characteristic of the place
2 Es	1:20	Because of the heat
	5:34	but because of my grief I have spoken
	7:74	but because of the times which he had foreordained !
	8:31	but thou, because of us sinners, art called merciful
	9:20	because of the devices of those who had come into it
	10:20	because of the troubles of Zion
	10:20	and be consoled because of the sorrow of Jerusalem
	12:5	because of the great fear with which I have been terrified this night
	13:57	because of his wonders, which he did from time to time
	15:18	For because of their pride the cities shall be in confusion
	15:19	because of hunger for bread
	15:19	and because of great tribulation
4 Ma	1:34	we abstain because of domination by reason
	3:12	because of the king's craving
	3:20	because of their observance of the law
	5:4	because of his philosophy
	7:16	If, therefore, because of piety
	7:20	because of the weakness of their reason
	9:6	And if the aged men of the Hebrews because of their religion
	9:7	and if you take our lives because of our religion
	9:9	but you, because of your bloodthirstiness toward us
	10:10	are suffering because of our godly training and virtue
	10:11	but you, because of your impiety and bloodthirstiness
	12:3	for they died in torments because of their disobedience
	12:12	Because of this, justice has laid up
	15:4	who because of their birth-pangs
	15:7	and because of the many pains she suffered with each of them
	15:8	yet because of the fear of God she disdained
	15:9	Not only so, but also because of the nobility of her sons
	15:14	because of religion did not change her attitude
	15:24	because of faith in God
	17:9	because of the violence of the tyrant

17:18 because of which they now stand before the divine throne
17:20 but also by the fact that because of them
18:4 Because of them the nation gained peace

BECOME
146 = 0.095 %

Tob 1:9 When I became a man I married Anna
1:9 and by her I became the father of Tobias
3:6 that I may depart and become dust
4:21 Do not be afraid, my son, because we have become poor
6:15 Now listen to me, brother, for she will become your wife
Jud 5:10 and there they became a great multitude
5:11 So the king of Egypt became hostile to them
12:13 and become today like one of the daughters of the Assyrians
16:23 She became more and more famous
Ad E 10:6 The tiny spring which became a river
13:2 writes thus : Having become ruler of many nations
16:2 the more proud do many men become
16:10 having become our guest
Wis 2:14 He became to us a reproof of our thoughts
4:18 After this they will become dishonoured corpses
8:2 and I became enamoured of her beauty
10:17 and became a shelter to them by day
12:27 they became incensed at those creatures
14:11 they became an abomination
14:11 and became traps for the souls of men
14:21 And this became a hidden trap for mankind
16:11 and become unresponsive to thy kindness
Sir pr. in order that, by becoming conversant with this also
5:15 and do not become an enemy instead of a friend
6:27 Search out and seek, and she will become known to you
6:29 Then her fetters will become for you a strong protection
6:32 and if you apply yourself you will become clever
6:33 and if you incline your ear you will become wise
7:6 Do not seek to become a judge
12:14 and becomes involved in his sins
13:1 and whoever associates with a proud man will become like him
14:17 All living beings become old like a garment
18:29 Those who understand sayings become skilled themselves
18:32 lest you become impoverished by its expense
18:33 Do not become a beggar by feasting with borrowed money
19:1 A workman who is a drunkard will not become rich
23:15 will never become disciplined all his days
24:17 and my blossoms became glorious and abundant fruit
24:31 and lo, my canal became a river, and my river became a sea
30:12 lest he become stubborn and disobey you
31:4 and when he rests he becomes needy
38:24 and he who has little business may become wise
38:25 How can he become wise who handles the plough
42:10 or become pregnant in her father's house
43:19 and when it freezes, it becomes pointed thorns
44:9 they have become as though they had not been born
46:1 He became, in accordance with his name
46:4 And did not one day become as long as 2 ?
46:15 and by his words he became known as a trustworthy seer
47:14 How wise you became in your youth !
47:24 Their sins became exceedingly many
50:28 and he who lays them to heart will become wise
L Jr 6:5 So take care not to become at all like the foreigners
P Az 14 For we, O Lord, have become fewer than any nation
Bel 14:28 saying, The king has become a Jew
1 Ma 1:1 He had previously become king of Greece
1:3 When the earth became quiet before him, he was exalted
1:4 and they became tributary to him
1:16 he determined to become king of the land of Egypt
1:26 maidens and young men became faint
1:33 and it became their citadel
1:35 they stored them there, and became a great snare
1:36 It became an ambush against the sanctuary
1:38 she became a dwelling of strangers
1:38 she became strange to her offspring
1:39 Her sanctuary became desolate as a desert
2:8 Her temple has become like a man without honour
2:11 no longer free, she has become a slave
2:43 And all who became fugitives to escape their troubles
2:49 Arrogance and reproach have now become strong
2:53 and became lord of Egypt
2:55 became a judge in Israel
5:1 they became very angry
6:3 but he could not, because his plan became known to the men of the city
6:8 He took to his bed and became sick from grief
6:24 and became hostile to us
6:59 that they became angry and did all these things
7:3 But when this act became known to him
7:30 It became known to Judas
8:10 but this became known to them
9:8 He became faint, but he said to those who were left
9:17 The battle became desperate
9:60 because their plan became known
10:6 to equip them with arms, and to become his ally

10:54 and I will become your son-in-law
10:56 and I will become your father-in-law, as you have said
10:70 and I have become a laughingstock and reproach because of you
10:76 and the men of the city became afraid and opened the gates
11:12 and their enmity became manifest
11:19 So Demetrius became king in the 167th year
11:40 to become king in place of his father
11:53 and he became estranged from Jonathan
12:10 so that we may not become estranged from you
12:39 Then Trypho attempted to become king of Asia
13:32 and became king in his place, putting on the crown of Asia
14:17 had become high priest in his place
14:30 Jonathan rallied the nation, and became their high priest
15:9 so that your glory will become manifest in all the earth
15:27 and became estranged from him
16:24 from the time that he became high priest after his father
2 Ma 1:33 When this matter became known
2:22 while the Lord with great kindness became gracious to them
3:24 and became faint with terror
4:16 became their enemies and punished them
4:21 Antiochus learned that Philometor had become hostile to his government
4:33 When Onias became fully aware of these acts
4:40 And since the crowds were becoming aroused
4:41 But when the Jews became aware of Lysimachus' attack
4:50 having become the chief plotter against his fellow citizens
5:15 guided by Menelaus, who had become a traitor
5:20 when the great Lord became reconciled
9:17 and in addition to all this he also would become a Jew
10:14 When Gorgias became governor of the region
10:29 When the battle became fierce
12:39 On the next day, as by that time it had become necessary
12:40 And it became clear to all
14:27 The king became excited
14:31 When the latter became aware
1 Es 1:43 Jehoiakim his son became king in his stead
4:26 and have become slaves because of them
4:43 in the day when you became king
3 Ma 3:1 he became so infuriated that not only was he enraged
3:19 they become the only people among all nations
3:29 and shall become useless for all time to any mortal creature
6:10 Even if our lives have become entangled in impieties in our exile
6:34 that the Jews would be destroyed and become food for birds
7:14 who had become defiled
2 Es 2:12 and they shall neither toil nor become weary
3:16 and Jacob became a great multitude
3:22 Thus the disease became permanent
5:35 Or why did not my mother's womb become my grave
5:49 and a woman who has become old does not bring forth any longer
9:19 have become corrupt in their ways
10:28 my end has become corruption, and my prayer a reproach
11:3 but they became little, puny wings
14:17 For the weaker the world becomes through old age
14:35 and then the names of the righteous will become manifest
15:31 shall become still stronger
4 Ma 1:11 and they became the cause of the downfall of tyranny over their nation
6:19 and ourselves become a pattern of impiety to the young
6:19 in becoming an example of the eating of defiling food
7:13 his muscles flabby, his sinews feeble, he became young again
9:24 may become merciful to our nation
17:21 they having become, as it were
18:5 to become pagans and to abandon their ancestral customs

BECOMING
1
2 Es 8:49 because you have humbled yourself, as is becoming for you

BECTILETH
2
Jud 2:21 to the plain of Bectileth
2:21 and camped opposite Bectileth

BED
22 = 0.014 %
Tob 8:4 Tobias got up from the bed and said, Sister, get up
14:11 As he said this he died in his bed
Jud 8:3 and took to his bed and died in Bethulia his city
9:3 and their bed, which was ashamed of the deceit they had practised
10:21 Holofernes was resting on his bed
13:1 and they went to bed, for they all were weary
13:2 with Holofernes stretched on his bed
13:4 Then Judith, standing beside his bed, said in her heart
13:6 She went up to the post at the end of the bed
13:7 She came close to his bed
13:9 Then she tumbled his body off the bed
15:11 and his beds and his bowls and all his furniture
Ad E 14:15 and abhor the bed of the uncircumcised and of any alien
Sir 31:19 He does not breathe heavily upon his bed
40:5 And when one rests upon his bed
41:22 and do not approach her bed

	48 : 6	and famous men from their beds
L Jr	**6** : 70	Like a scarecrow in a cucumber bed, that guards nothing
1 Ma	**6** : 8	He took to his bed and became sick from grief
1 Es	**3** : 6	and sleep on a gold bed
2 Es	**3** : 1	I was troubled as I lay on my bed
	12 : 26	one of the kings shall die in his bed, but in agonies

BEDCHAMBER   4 = 0.003 %

Jud	**13** : 3	to stand outside the bedchamber
	13 : 4	was left in the bedchamber
	14 : 15	he opened it and went into the bedchamber
	16 : 19	and the canopy which she took for herself from his bedchamber

BEDEIAH   1

1 Es	**9** : 34	Mamdai and Bedeiah and Vaniah

BEDROOM   1

1 Es	**3** : 3	and Darius the king went to his bedroom

BEE   2

Sir	**11** : 3	The bee is small among flying creatures
4 Ma	**14** : 19	since even bees at the time for making honeycombs

BEEROTH   1

1 Es	**5** : 19	The men of Chephirah and Beeroth, 743

BEFALL   10 = 0.007 %

Sir	**7** : 1	Do no evil, and evil will never befall you
	12 : 17	If calamity befalls you, you will find him there ahead of you
	25 : 19	may a sinner's lot befall her !
	33 : 1	No evil will befall the man who fears the Lord
P Az	10	shame and disgrace have befallen thy servants and worshippers
2 Ma	**5** : 20	shared in the misfortunes that befell the nation
	11 : 13	he pondered over the defeat which had befallen him
2 Es	**3** : 10	And the same fate befell them :
	10 : 48	that was the destruction which befell Jerusalem
	12 : 43	Are not the evils which have befallen us sufficient ?

BEFIT   5 = 0.003 %

Wis	**13** : 15	then he makes for it a niche that befits it
1 Es	**4** : 46	and this befits your greatness
3 Ma	**3** : 25	to suffer the sure and shameful death that befits enemies
	4 : 10	they should undergo treatment befitting traitors
4 Ma	**11** : 20	O contest befitting holiness, in which so many of us brothers

BEFORE*   326 = 0.212 %

Tob	**1** : 21	before 2 of Sennacherib's sons killed him
	2 : 4	So before I tasted anything
	3 : 3	and those which my fathers committed before thee
	3 : 5	For we did not walk in truth before thee
	3 : 8	before he had been with her as his wife
	4 : 2	so that I may explain to him about the money before I die ?
	5 : 17	as he goes in and out before us ?
	6 : 7	you make a smoke from these before the man or woman
	6 : 14	I will die as those before me did
	7 : 8	and set large servings of food before them
	8 : 20	And before the days of the feast were over
	10 : 11	The God of heaven will prosper you, my children, before I die
	10 : 12	that I may rejoice before the Lord
	11 : 17	And Tobit gave thanks before them
	12 : 12	I brought a reminder of your prayer before the Holy One
	13 : 3	Acknowledge him before the nations, O sons of Israel
	13 : 6	to do what is true before him
	13 : 6	turn back, you sinners, and do right before him
	14 : 15	But before he died he heard of the destruction of Nineveh
	14 : 15	Before his death he rejoiced over Nineveh
Jud	**3** : 2	lie prostrate before you
	3 : 3	and all our sheepfolds with their tents, lie before you
	4 : 11	prostrated themselves before the temple
	4 : 11	and spread out their sackcloth before the Lord
	4 : 13	and in Jerusalem before the sanctuary of the Lord Almighty
	4 : 14	who stood before the Lord and ministered to the Lord
	5 : 13	Then God dried up the Red Sea before them
	5 : 16	And they drove out before them the Canaanites
	5 : 21	and we shall be put to shame before the whole world
	6 : 14	and placed him before the magistrates of their city
	7 : 14	and before the sword reaches them
	7 : 23	and said before all the elders
	7 : 25	to strew us on the ground before them
	7 : 27	and we shall not witness the death of our babes before our eyes
	8 : 6	except the day before the sabbath and the sabbath itself
	8 : 6	the day before the new moon and the day of the new moon
	8 : 19	and so they suffered a great catastrophe before our enemies
	8 : 35	Go in peace, and may the Lord God go before you
	9 : 5	and those that went before and those that followed
	10 : 16	And when you stand before him
	10 : 22	with silver lamps carried before him
	11 : 22	God has done well to send you before the people
	12 : 4	before the Lord carries out by my hand

	12 : 15	and her maid went and spread on the ground for her before Holofernes
	12 : 19	Then she took and ate and drank before him
	13 : 20	walking in the straight path before our God
	14 : 3	Then fear will come over them, and they will flee before you
	14 : 5	But before you do all this, bring Achior the Ammonite to me
	14 : 7	and knelt before her, and said
	15 : 13	and she went before all the people in the dance
	16 : 1	Then Judith began this thanksgiving before all Israel
	16 : 12	they perished before the army of my Lord
	16 : 20	before the sanctuary for 3 months
	16 : 24	Before she died she distributed her property
Ad E	**10** : 11	of decision before God and among all the nations
	10 : 13	with an assembly and joy and gladness before God
	13 : 18	for their death was before their eyes
	14 : 6	And now we have sinned before thee
	14 : 13	Put eloquent speech in my mouth before the lion
	15 : 6	she stood before the king
	15 : 7	and collapsed upon the head of the maid who went before her
	16 : 9	and always judging what comes before our eyes
Wis	**2** : 8	Let us crown ourselves with rosebuds before they wither
	4 : 5	The branches will be broken off before they come to maturity
	5 : 14	it is dispersed like smoke before the wind
	7 : 9	and silver will be accounted as clay before her
	10 : 5	and preserved him blameless before God
	11 : 14	who long before had been cast out and exposed
	11 : 22	Because the whole world before thee
	12 : 12	Or who will come before thee
	12 : 27	him whom they had before refused to know
	14 : 20	the one whom shortly before they had honoured as a man
	15 : 8	this man who was made of earth a short time before
	16 : 28	to make it known that one must rise before the sun
	19 : 7	and dry land emerging where water had stood before
Sir	**1** : 4	Wisdom was created before all things
	2 : 17	and will humble themselves before him
	7 : 5	Do not assert your righteousness before the Lord
	7 : 5	nor display your wisdom before the king
	10 : 7	Arrogance is hateful before the Lord and before men
	11 : 7	Do not find fault before you investigate
	11 : 8	Do not answer before you have heard
	11 : 28	Call no one happy before his death
	14 : 13	Do good to a friend before you die
	15 : 16	He has placed before you fire and water :
	15 : 17	Before a man are life and death
	17 : 15	Their ways are always before him
	17 : 19	All their works are as the sun before him
	17 : 20	and all their sins are before the Lord
	18 : 19	Before you speak, learn
	18 : 19	and before you fall ill, take care of your health
	18 : 20	Before judgment, examine yourself
	18 : 21	Before falling ill, humble yourself
	18 : 23	Before making a vow, prepare yourself
	18 : 26	and all things move swiftly before the Lord
	19 : 17	Question your neighbour before you threaten him
	21 : 22	but a man of experience stands respectfully before it
	23 : 3	then I will not fall before my adversaries
	23 : 20	Before the universe was created, it was known to him
	23 : 24	She herself will be brought before the assembly
	24 : 10	In the holy tabernacle I ministered before him
	26 : 24	before her husband
	27 : 7	Do not praise a man before you hear him reason
	27 : 29	and pain will consume them before their death
	28 : 26	lest you fall before him who lies in wait
	31 : 16	Eat like a human being what is set before you
	31 : 18	do not reach out your hand before they do
	32 : 10	Lightning speeds before the thunder
	34 : 20	Like one who kills a son before his father's eyes
	35 : 4	Do not appear before the Lord empty-handed
	35 : 6	and its pleasing odour rises before the Most High
	36 : 4	As in us thou hast been sanctified before them
	36 : 4	so in them be thou magnified before us
	38 : 15	He who sins before his Maker
	39 : 4	He will serve among great men and appear before rulers
	39 : 5	and will make supplication before the Most High
	39 : 19	The works of all flesh are before him
	40 : 16	will be plucked up before any grass
	41 : 17	Be ashamed of immorality, before your father or mother
	41 : 17	and of a lie, before a prince or a ruler
	41 : 18	of a transgression, before a judge or magistrate
	41 : 18	and of iniquity, before a congregation or the people
	41 : 18	of unjust dealing, before your partner or friend
	41 : 19	Be ashamed before the truth of God and his covenant
	41 : 20	and of silence, before those who greet you
	41 : 22	of abusive words, before friends
	42 : 8	and will be approved before all men
	42 : 11	and put you to shame before the great multitude
	45 : 13	Before his time there never were such beautiful things
	46 : 3	Who before him ever stood so firm ?
	46 : 19	Before the time of his eternal sleep
	46 : 19	Samuel called men to witness before the Lord

	47:9	He placed singers before the altar
	48:10	to calm the wrath of God before it breaks out in fury
	48:12	in all his days he did not tremble before any ruler
	48:25	and the hidden things before they came to pass
	50:13	before the whole congregation of Israel
	50:16	for remembrance before the Most High
	50:19	before him who is merciful
	51:2	Before those who stood by thou wast my helper
	51:13	While I was still young, before I went on my travels
	51:14	Before the temple I asked for her
	51:30	Do your work before the appointed time
Bar	1:5	Then they wept, and fasted, and prayed before the Lord
	1:17	because we have sinned before the Lord
	1:18	to walk in the statutes of the Lord which he set before us
	2:10	to walk in the statutes of the Lord which he set before us
	2:19	that we bring before thee our prayer for mercy
	2:33	who sinned before the Lord
	3:2	for we have sinned before thee
	3:4	and of the sons of those who sinned before thee
	3:7	who sinned before thee
L Jr	6:2	Because of the sins which you have committed before God
	6:5	when you see the multitude before and behind them worshipping them
	6:27	but gifts are placed before them just as before the dead
	6:32	They howl and shout before their gods
P Az	15	or incense, no place to make an offering before thee
Sus	13:15	she went in as before with only 2 maids
	13:29	They said before the people
	13:42	who art aware of all things before they come to be
Bel	14:42	and they were devoured immediately before his eyes
1 Ma	1:3	When the earth became quiet before him, he was exalted
	1:18	and Ptolemy turned and fled before him
	3:22	He himself will crush them before us
	3:23	and they were crushed before him
	3:30	as he had before for his expenses and for the gifts
	4:10	and crush this army before us today
	4:17	for there is a battle before us
	4:60	and trampling them down as they had done before
	5:1	and the sanctuary dedicated as it was before
	5:7	and they were crushed before him
	5:21	and the Gentiles were crushed before him
	5:34	they fled before him, and he dealt them a heavy blow
	5:43	All the Gentiles were defeated before him
	5:44	they could stand before Judas no longer
	5:52	And they crossed the Jordan into the large plain before Beth-shan
	5:54	before they returned in safety
	5:55	and Simon his brother was in Galilee before Ptolemais
	6:6	but had turned and fled before the Jews
	6:7	with high walls as before, and also Beth-zur, his city
	6:45	and they parted before him on both sides
	6:51	Then he encamped before the sanctuary for many days
	6:59	and agree to let them live by their laws as they did before
	7:12	before Alcimus and Bacchides to ask for just terms
	7:36	and stood before the altar and the temple
	7:42	So also crush this army before us today
	9:44	for today things are not as they were before
	10:4	before he makes peace with Alexander against us
	10:34	and the 3 days before a feast and the 3 after a feast
	10:72	Men will tell you that you cannot stand before us
	10:75	He encamped before Joppa
	11:38	that the land was quiet before him
	11:52	and the land was quiet before him
	11:65	Simon encamped before Beth-zur
	12:24	with a larger force than before, to wage war against him
	14:19	And these were read before the assembly in Jerusalem
	15:5	that the kings before me have granted you
2 Ma	3:15	The priests prostrated themselves before the altar
	3:30	And the temple, which a little while before
	4:44	3 men sent by the senate presented the case before him
	4:47	if they had pleaded even before Scythians
	5:8	Accused before Aretas the ruler of the Arabs
	6:29	And those who a little before
	8:14	before he ever met them
	8:17	keeping before their eyes the lawless outrage
	8:26	For it was the day before the sabbath
	9:10	no one was able to carry the man who a little while before
	10:6	remembering how not long before, during the feast of booths
	10:13	As a result he was accused before Eupator
	10:24	Now Timothy, who had been defeated by the Jews before
	10:26	Falling upon the steps before the altar
	11:18	that needed to be brought before him
	12:27	Stalwart young men took their stand before the walls
	13:13	before the king's army could enter Judea
	14:14	who had fled before Judas, flocked to join Nicanor
	15:21	Maccabeus, perceiving the hosts that were before him
	15:23	send a good angel to carry terror and trembling before us
	15:31	and stationed the priests before the altar
	15:36	the day before Mordecai's day
1 Es	1:5	who minister before your brethren the people of Israel

	1:11	and the grouping of the fathers' houses, before the people
	1:33	and the things that he had done before and these that are now told
	3:22	and before long they draw their swords
	5:6	who spoke wise words before Darius the king of the Persians
	5:47	before the first gate toward the east
	7:14	rejoicing before the Lord
	8:4	for he found favour before the king in all his requests
	8:50	There I proclaimed a fast for the young men before our Lord
	8:74	I am ashamed and confounded before thy face
	8:90	Behold, we are now before thee in our iniquities
	8:91	weeping and lying upon the ground before the temple
	9:6	And all the multitude sat in the open square before the temple
	9:38	into the open square before the east gate of the temple
	9:41	before the gate of the temple
P Ma	4	at whom all things shudder, and tremble before thy power
3 Ma	1:24	Meanwhile the crowd, as before, was engaged in prayer
	4:4	perceiving the common object of pity before their eyes
	4:8	seeing death immediately before them
	4:14	not for the hard labour that has been briefly mentioned before
	5:50	the help which they had received before from heaven
	6:35	as we have said before
2 Es	1:11	I have destroyed all nations before them
	1:21	and the Philistines before you
	2:3	because you have sinned before the Lord God
	3:6	which thy right hand had planted before the earth appeared
	3:8	and did ungodly things before thee and scorned thee
	3:13	And when they were committing iniquity before thee
	4:3	and to put before you 3 problems
	4:14	that it may recede before it
	4:48	So I stood and looked, and behold, a flaming furnace passed by before me
	4:49	And after this a cloud full of water passed before me
	5:41	but what will those do who were before us
	5:50	let me speak before thee
	5:52	not like those whom you bore before
	5:54	than those who were before you
	6:1	before the portals of the world were in place
	6:1	and before the assembled winds blew
	6:2	and before the rumblings of thunder sounded
	6:2	and before the flashes of lightning shone
	6:2	and before the foundations of paradise were laid
	6:3	and before the beautiful flowers were seen
	6:3	and before the powers of movement were established
	6:3	and before the innumerable hosts of angels were gathered together
	6:4	and before the heights of the air were lifted up
	6:4	and before the measures of the firmaments were named
	6:4	and before the footstool of Zion was established
	6:5	and before the present years were reckoned
	6:5	and before the imaginations of those who now sin were estranged
	6:5	and before those who stored up treasures of faith were sealed
	6:20	the books shall be opened before the firmament
	6:32	because your voice has surely been heard before the Most High
	6:35	Now after this I wept again and fasted 7 days as before
	6:42	and be of service before me
	6:53	to bring forth before thee cattle, beasts, and creeping things
	6:55	All this I have spoken before thee, O Lord
	7:9	unless he passes through the danger set before him ?
	7:20	which is set before them be disregarded !
	7:87	before whom they sinned while they were alive
	7:87	and before whom they are to be judged in the last times
	8:6	that we may pray before thee
	8:17	Therefore I will pray before thee for myself and for them
	8:19	and I will speak before thee
	8:19	before he was taken up
	8:21	before whom the hosts of angels stand trembling
	8:42	If I have found favour before thee, let me speak
	8:48	before the Most High
	9:15	I said before, and I say now, and will say it again :
	9:18	before the world was made for them to dwell in
	9:27	my heart was troubled again as it was before
	9:28	and I began to speak before the Most High, and said
	10:34	only do not forsake me, lest I die before my time
	10:45	before any offering was offered in it
	10:57	and you have been called before the Most High
	11:16	I announce this to you before you disappear
	11:32	than all the wings that had gone before
	11:36	Look toward you and consider what you see
	11:40	have conquered all the beasts that have gone before
	11:43	And so your insolence has come up before the Most High
	12:7	and if I have been accounted righteous before thee beyond many others
	12:7	and if my prayer has indeed come up before thy face
	12:13	than all the kingdoms that have been before it
	12:24	than all who were before them
	12:32	and will cast up before them their contemptuous dealings
	12:33	For first he will set them living before his judgment seat
	13:32	and the signs occur which I showed you before

	14:22	If then I have found favour before thee
	15:11	and will smite Egypt with plagues, as before
	16:12	and before the glory of his power
	16:53	I have not sinned before God and his glory
	16:65	And when your sins come out before men
	16:66	Or how will you hide your sins before God and his angels ?
4 Ma	**4**:12	he would praise the blessedness of the holy place before all people
	5:4	was brought before the king
	5:6	Before I begin to torture you, old man
	6:15	We will set before you some cooked meat
	8:3	were brought before him along with their aged mother
	8:13	And when the guards had placed before them
	9:27	Before torturing him, they inquired if he were willing to eat
	12:4	will be miserably tortured and die before your time
	13:3	Instead, by reason, which is praised before God
	13:15	lying before those who transgress the commandment of God
	13:18	or betray the brothers who have died before us
	17:5	stand in honour before God
	17:18	because of which they now stand before the divine throne

BEFOREHAND 6 = 0.004 %

Wis	**18**:6	That night was made known beforehand to our fathers
1 Ma	**6**:36	These took their position beforehand wherever the beast was
3 Ma	**6**:22	because of the things that he had devised beforehand
2 Es	**8**:52	and wisdom perfected beforehand
	16:38	has great pains about her womb for 2 or 3 hours beforehand
4 Ma	**4**:25	though they had known beforehand that they would suffer this

BEG 7 = 0.005 %

Wis	**18**:2	and they begged their pardon
	19:3	those whom they had begged and compelled to depart
Sir	**40**:28	it is better to die than to beg
1 Ma	**9**:35	and begged the Nabateans, who were his friends
3 Ma	**5**:13	and again begged him who is easily reconciled
	6:27	begging pardon for your former actions !
2 Es	**1**:25	When you beg mercy of me, I will show you no mercy

BEGET 2

2 Es	**16**:46	for in captivity and famine they will beget their children
4 Ma	**10**:2	that the same father begot me and those who died

BEGGAR 4 = 0.003 %

Sir	**4**:3	nor delay your gift to a beggar
	18:33	Do not become a beggar by feasting with borrowed money
	25:2	a beggar who is proud, a rich man who is a liar
	40:28	My son, do not lead the life of a beggar

BEGGING 1

Sir	**40**:30	In the mouth of the shameless begging is sweet

BEGIN 70 = 0.046 %

Tob	**2**:13	and when she returned to me it began to bleat
	5:17	But Anna, his mother, began to weep
	7:15	Then they began to eat
	7:17	and the girl began to weep
	8:5	And Tobias began to pray
	10:4	Then she began to mourn for him, and said
	11:12	And when his eyes began to smart he rubbed them
Jud	**5**:22	all the men standing around the tent began to complain
	16:1	Then Judith began this thanksgiving before all Israel
	16:2	And Judith said, Begin a song to my God with tambourines
Ad E	**14**:11	and make an example of the man who began this against us
Wis	**7**:3	And when I was born, I began to breathe the common air
Sir	**18**:7	When a man has finished, he is just beginning
	38:16	and as one who is suffering grievously begin the lament
Sus	**13**:8	going in and walking about, and they began to desire her
1 Ma	**1**:8	Then his officers began to rule, each in his own place
	1:10	He began to reign in the 137th year
	3:25	Then Judas and his brothers began to be feared
	4:59	beginning with the 25th day of the month of Chislev
	5:2	So they began to kill and destroy among the people
	5:31	So Judas saw that the battle had begun
	7:1	and there began to reign
	9:40	and began killing them
	9:47	So the battle began
	9:55	But he only began to tear it down
	9:67	Then he began to attack and went into battle with his forces
	9:73	And Jonathan began to judge the people
	10:1	They welcomed him, and there he began to reign
	10:10	and began to rebuild and restore the city
	11:46	and began to fight
	11:54	who began to reign and put on the crown
	13:42	and the people began to write
	15:40	and began to provoke the people and invade Judea
2 Ma	**2**:32	At this point therefore let us begin our narrative
	9:11	he began to lose much of his arrogance
	13:11	and not to let the people who had just begun to revive
1 Es	**1**:39	when he began to reign in Judea and Jerusalem
	1:57	until the Persians began to reign

	2:30	and began to hinder the builders
	3:17	Then the first, who had spoken of the strength of wine, began and said :
	4:1	began to speak :
	4:13	who had spoken of women and truth, began to speak :
	4:33	and he began to speak about truth :
	4:44	which Cyrus set apart when he began to destroy Babylon
	5:53	began to offer sacrifices to God
	6:2	and began to build the house of the Lord which is in Jerusalem
	9:16	they began their sessions to investigate the matter
3 Ma	**1**:26	and began now to approach
	5:23	began to move them along in the great colonnade
	6:20	Even the king began to shudder bodily
	6:21	and began trampling and destroying them
	7:16	began their departure from the city
2 Es	**2**:47	So I began to praise those
	3:3	and I began to speak anxious words to the Most High, and said
	3:12	When those who dwelt on earth began to multiply
	3:12	and again they began to be more ungodly than were their ancestors
	5:22	and I began once more to speak words
	6:29	began to rock to and fro
	6:36	and I began to speak in the presence of the Most High
	9:28	and I began to speak before the Most High, and said
	10:41	whom you saw mourning and began to console
	10:49	and you began to console her for what had happened
	14:10	and the times begin to grow old
	14:26	tomorrow at this hour you shall begin to write
	16:6	when once it has begun to burn ?
	16:13	and will not miss when they begin to be shot
4 Ma	**1**:12	I shall begin by stating my main principle
	5:6	Before I begin to torture you, old man
	5:15	he began to address the people as follows :
	6:8	and began to kick him in the side

BEGINNING 63 = 0.041 %

Jud	**8**:29	but from the beginning of your life
Ad E	**13**:15	that has been thine from the beginning
Wis	**6**:17	The beginning of wisdom
	6:22	but I will trace her course from the beginning of creation
	7:5	For no king has had a different beginning of existence
	7:18	the beginning and end and middle of times
	9:8	which thou didst prepare from the beginning
	12:11	For they were an accursed race from the beginning
	14:6	For even in the beginning
	14:12	For the idea of making idols was the beginning of fornication
	14:13	for neither have they existed from the beginning
	14:27	is the beginning and cause and end of every evil
Sir	**1**:14	To fear the Lord is the beginning of wisdom
	10:12	The beginning of man's pride is to depart from the Lord
	10:13	For the beginning of pride is sin
	10:21	The fear of the Lord is the beginning of acceptance
	10:21	obduracy and pride are the beginning of rejection
	15:14	It was he who created man in the beginning
	16:26	from the beginning by his creation
	19:18	The fear of the Lord is the beginning of acceptance
	24:9	From eternity, in the beginning, he created me
	25:12	The fear of the Lord is the beginning of love for him
	25:12	and faith is the beginning of clinging to him
	25:24	From a woman sin had its beginning
	36:11	and give them their inheritance, as at the beginning
	36:15	Bear witness to those whom thou didst create in the beginning
	37:16	Reason is the beginning of every work
	39:25	From the beginning good things were created for good people
	39:32	Therefore from the beginning I have been convinced
	44:2	his majesty from the beginning
2 Ma	**7**:23	who shaped the beginning of man
	8:27	and allotted it to them as the beginning of mercy
1 Es	**5**:56	and Jeshua the son of Jozadak made a beginning
	8:70	and from the beginning of this matter
3 Ma	**3**:21	and the myriad affairs liberally entrusted to them from the beginning
	5:11	that beneficence which from the beginning, night and day
	6:26	those who from the beginning differed from all nations
2 Es	**2**:41	who have been called from the beginning, may be made holy
	3:4	O sovereign Lord, didst thou not speak at the beginning
	4:30	For a grain of evil seed was sown in Adam's heart from the beginning
	4:42	that were committed to them from the beginning
	6:1	At the beginning of the circle of the earth
	6:7	and the beginning of the age that follows ?
	6:8	for Jacob's hand held Esau's heel from the beginning
	6:9	and Jacob is the beginning of the age that follows
	6:10	For the beginning of a man is his hand
	6:38	thou didst speak at the beginning of creation
	7:30	as it was at the first beginnings
	7:113	and the beginning of the immortal age to come
	8:19	The beginning of the words of Ezra's prayer
	9:4	from the days that were of old, from the beginning
	9:5	the beginning is evident, and the end manifest

	9:6	the beginnings are manifest in wonders and mighty works
	9:8	which I have sanctified for myself from the beginning
	10:10	And from the beginning all have been born of her
	10:14	so the earth also has from the beginning
	12:34	the day of judgment, of which I spoke to you at the beginning
	13:14	From the beginning thou hast shown thy servant these wonders
	14:22	and I will write everything that has happened in the world from the beginning
	16:18	The beginning of sorrows
	16:18	the beginning of famine, when many shall perish
	16:18	the beginning of wars, when the powers shall be terrified
	16:18	the beginning of calamities, when all shall tremble

BEGOTTEN   1

2 Es	6:58	whom thou hast called thy first-born, only begotten

BEGRUDGE   3 = 0.002 %

Tob	4:7	and do not let your eye begrudge the gift when you make it
	4:16	and do not let your eye begrudge the gift when you make it
Sir	14:10	A stingy man's eye begrudges bread

BEGUILE   2

Ad E	16:6	beguile the sincere good will of their sovereigns
Sir	14:16	Give, and take and beguile yourself

BEHALF   8 = 0.005 %

Wis	16:24	and in kindness relaxes on behalf of those who trust in thee
Sir	29:13	it will fight on your behalf against your enemy
2 Ma	1:26	accept this sacrifice on behalf of all thy people Israel
	2:21	to those who strove zealously on behalf of Judaism
	11:15	For the king granted every request in behalf of the Jews
2 Es	4:34	but the Highest hastens on behalf of many
4 Ma	5:31	as not to be young in reason on behalf of piety
	14:3	on behalf of religion !

BEHAVE   2

2 Ma	1:17	upon those who have behaved impiously
	12:14	behaved most insolently toward Judas and his men

BEHAVIOUR, BEHAVIOR   2

Ad E	16:7	through the pestilent behaviour of those
Sir	41:19	Be ashamed of selfish behaviour at meals

BEHEAD   1

Ps 151	:7	I beheaded him, and removed reproach from the people of Israel

BEHEMOTH   2

2 Es	6:49	the name of one thou didst call Behemoth
	6:51	And thou didst give Behemoth one of the parts

BEHIND   16 = 0.010 %

Tob	1:17	and thrown out behind the wall of Nineveh
	11:4	So they went their way, and the dog went along behind them
Wis	17:3	they were unobserved behind a dark curtain of forgetfulness
Sir	21:15	and casts it behind his back
	30:4	for he has left behind him one like himself
	30:6	he has left behind him an avenger against his enemies
	47:23	and left behind him one of his sons
L Jr	6:5	when you see the multitude before and behind them worshipping them
1 Ma	5:33	Then he came up behind them in 3 companies
	9:16	they turned and followed close behind Judas and his men
	9:45	For look ! The battle is in front of us and behind us
	10:79	Now Apollonius had secretly left a 1,000 cavalry behind them
	10:80	Jonathan learned that there was an ambush behind him
3 Ma	1:17	and those who remained behind in the city
	3:24	we would have these impious people behind our backs
4 Ma	13:18	Those who were left behind said to each of the brothers

BEHOLD, interj.   107 = 0.070 %

Tob	11:6	Behold, your son is coming
	14:3	behold, I have grown old and am about to depart this life
Jud	3:2	Behold, we the servants of Nebuchadnezzar, the Great King
	3:3	Behold, our buildings, and all our land
	6:19	O Lord God of heaven, behold their arrogance
	9:7	Behold now, the Assyrians are increased in their might
	9:9	Behold their pride, and send thy wrath upon their heads
Ad E	11:5	Behold, noise and confusion
	11:6	And behold, 2 great dragons came forward
	11:8	And behold, a day of darkness and gloom
Sir	16:18	Behold, heaven and the highest heaven
Bar	2:25	and behold, they have been cast out
	3:8	Behold, we are today in our exile
	4:37	Behold, your sons are coming, whom you sent away
Bel	14:11	And the priests of Bel said, Behold, we are going outside
1 Ma	2:12	And behold, our holy place, our beauty
	2:65	Now behold, I know that Simeon your brother is wise in counsel
	3:52	And behold, the Gentiles are assembled against us to destroy us
	4:36	Behold, our enemies are crushed
	5:14	behold, other messengers, with their garments rent

	5:30	and behold, a large company, that could not be counted
	6:13	and behold, I am perishing of deep grief in a strange land
	6:26	And behold, today they have encamped
	11:68	and behold, the army of the foreigners met him in the plain
	16:5	and behold, a large force of infantry and horsemen
	16:24	behold, they are written
1 Es	8:90	Behold, we are now before thee in our iniquities
2 Es	4:48	So I stood and looked, and behold, a flaming furnace passed by before me
	4:48	and behold, the smoke remained
	5:1	Now concerning the signs : behold
	5:41	And I said, Yet behold, O Lord
	6:17	and behold, a voice was speaking
	6:18	And it said, Behold, the days are coming
	6:29	While he spoke to me, behold
	6:57	And now, O Lord, behold, these nations
	7:17	Then I answered and said, O sovereign Lord, behold
	7:26	For behold, the time will come
	7:98	for they hasten to behold the face of him
	8:63	Behold, O Lord, thou hast now shown me a multitude of the signs
	9:20	So I considered my world, and behold, it was lost
	9:20	and my earth, and behold, it was in peril
	9:31	For behold, I sow my law in you
	9:34	And behold, it is the rule that
	9:38	And behold, she was mourning and weeping with a loud voice
	10:10	and behold, almost all go to perdition
	10:25	While I was talking to her, behold
	10:26	behold, she suddenly uttered a loud and fearful cry
	10:27	And I looked, and behold
	10:29	As I was speaking these words, behold
	10:30	and behold, I lay there like a corpse
	10:32	and behold, I saw, and still see
	10:44	whom you now behold as an established city, is Zion
	10:49	And behold, you saw her likeness
	11:1	On the 2nd night I had a dream, and behold
	11:2	And I looked, and behold
	11:5	And I looked, and behold, the eagle flew with his wings
	11:7	And I looked, and behold, the eagle rose upon his talons
	11:10	And I looked, and behold
	11:11	and behold, there were 8 of them
	11:12	And I looked, and behold
	11:15	And behold, a voice sounded, saying to it
	11:20	And I looked, and behold
	11:22	And after this I looked, and behold
	11:24	And I looked, and behold
	11:25	And I looked, and behold
	11:26	And I looked, and behold
	11:28	And I looked, and behold
	11:29	and while they were planning, behold
	11:31	and behold, the head turned with those that were with it
	11:33	And after this I looked, and behold
	11:35	And I looked, and behold
	11:37	And I looked, and behold
	11:44	and behold, they are ended, and his ages are completed !
	12:2	and behold, the remaining head disappeared
	12:3	And I looked, and behold, they also disappeared
	12:4	Behold, you have brought this upon me
	12:5	Behold, I am still weary in mind
	12:13	Behold, the days are coming
	13:2	and behold, a wind arose from the sea and stirred up all its waves
	13:3	And I looked, and behold
	13:5	After this I looked, and behold
	13:6	And I looked, and behold
	13:8	After this I looked, and behold
	13:9	And behold, when he saw the onrush of the approaching multitude
	13:29	Behold, the days are coming
	14:1	behold, a voice came out of a bush opposite me
	14:20	For behold, I will go, as thou hast commanded me
	14:38	And on the next day, behold, a voice called me, saying
	14:39	Then I opened my mouth, and behold
	15:1	The Lord says, Behold
	15:5	Behold, says the Lord
	15:8	Behold, innocent and righteous blood cries out to me
	15:10	Behold, my people is led like a flock to the slaughter
	15:20	Behold, says God
	15:28	Behold, a terrifying sight, appearing from the east !
	15:34	Behold, clouds from the east
	16:14	Behold, calamities are sent forth
	16:19	Behold, famine and plague
	16:21	Behold, provisions will be so cheap upon earth
	16:36	Behold the word of the Lord, receive it
	16:37	Behold, the calamities draw near, and are not delayed
	16:52	For behold, just a little while
	16:54	Behold, the Lord knows all the works of men
	16:67	Behold, God is the judge, fear him !

	16 :68	For behold, the burning wrath of a great multitude is kindled over you
	16 :74	Behold, the days of tribulation are at hand

BEHOLD, verb   3 = 0.002 %

Sir	39 :20	From everlasting to everlasting he beholds them
	42 :25	and who can have enough of beholding his glory ?
4 Ma	17 :7	would not those who first beheld it have shuddered

BEING, subst.   11 = 0.007 %

Jud	8 :16	nor like a human being, to be won over by pleading
Ad E	14 :11	O Lord, do not surrender thy sceptre to what has no being
Wis	14 :15	what was once a dead human being
Sir	13 :16	all living beings associate by species
	14 :17	All living beings become old like a garment
	16 :30	with all kinds of living beings he covered its surface
	17 :4	He placed the fear of them in all living beings
	18 :13	but the compassion of the Lord is for all living beings
	31 :16	Eat like a human being what is set before you
	49 :16	and Adam above every living being in the creation
2 Es	8 :6	by which every mortal who bears the likeness of a human being

BEL   15 = 0.010 %

L Jr	6 :41	they bring him and pray Bel that the man may speak
	6 :41	as though Bel were able to understand
Bel	14 :3	Now the Babylonians had an idol called Bel
	14 :5	And the king said to him, Why do you not worship Bel ?
	14 :6	Do you not think that Bel is a living God ?
	14 :9	But if you prove that Bel is eating them, Daniel shall die
	14 :9	because he blasphemed against Bel
	14 :10	Now there were 70 priests of Bel
	14 :10	And the king went with Daniel into the temple of Bel
	14 :11	And the priests of Bel said, Behold, we are going outside
	14 :12	if you do not find that Bel has eaten it all, we will die
	14 :14	When they had gone out, the king set forth the food for Bel
	14 :18	You are great, O Bel
	14 :22	and gave Bel over to Daniel, who destroyed it and its temple
	14 :28	he has destroyed Bel, and slain the dragon

BELCH forth   1

Wis	11 :18	or belch forth a thick pall of smoke

BELIEF   1

2 Ma	15 :11	a sort of vision, which was worthy of belief

BELIEVE   20 = 0.013 %

Tob	2 :14	But I did not believe her
	14 :4	for I fully believe what Jonah the prophet said
Jud	14 :10	he believed firmly in God, and was circumcised
Sir	19 :15	so do not believe everything you hear
	32 :24	He who believes the law gives heed to the commandments
Sus	13 :41	The assembly believed them
1 Ma	1 :30	and they believed him
	2 :59	Hananiah, Azariah and Mishael believed
	10 :46	they did not believe or accept them
1 Es	4 :28	And now do you not believe me ?
3 Ma	6 :34	And those who had previously believed
2 Es	1 :35	who without having heard me will believe
	1 :37	yet with the spirit they will believe the things I have said
	3 :32	Or what tribes have so believed thy covenants
	5 :29	those who believed thy covenants
	6 :33	Believe and do not be afraid !
	7 :130	But they did not believe him, or the prophets after him
	9 :7	on account of the faith by which he has believed
4 Ma	5 :25	for since we believe that the law was established by God
	7 :19	since they believe that they

BELL   1

Sir	45 :9	with very many golden bells round about

BELLOW, subst.   1

4 Ma	8 :13	braziers and thumbscrews an iron claws and wedges and bellows

BELLY   4 = 0.003 %

Sir	51 :5	from the depths of the belly of Hades
3 Ma	6 :8	in the belly of a huge, sea-born monster
	7 :11	For they declared that those who for the belly's sake
2 Es	15 :35	as high as a horse's belly

BELMAIN   1

Jud	4 :4	and to Kona and Beth-horon and Belmain and Jericho

BELNUUS   1

1 Es	9 :31	and Belnuus and Manasseas

BELONG   22 = 0.014 %

Tob	5 :8	so that I may learn to what tribe he belongs
	5 :10	My brother, to what tribe and family do you belong ? Tell me
	7 :3	They answered him, We belong to the sons of Naphtali

Jud	7 :20	until all the vessels of water belonging to every inhabitant of Bethulia were empty
	8 :2	Her husband Manasseh, who belonged to her tribe and family
	10 :12	To what people do you belong
Wis	1 :16	because they are fit to belong to his party
	2 :24	and those who belong to his party experience it
Sir	9 :8	and do not look intently at beauty belonging to another
Bar	1 :15	Righteousness belongs to the Lord our God
	2 :6	Righteousness belongs to the Lord our God
1 Ma	5 :62	But they did not belong to the family of those men
	10 :42	because it belongs to the priests who minister there
	12 :23	that your cattle and your property belong to us
	12 :23	and ours belong to you
2 Ma	3 :6	and that they did not belong to the account of the sacrifices
	3 :10	belonging to widows and orphans
	15 :12	in all that belongs to excellence
1 Es	4 :40	To her belongs the strength and the kingship
	5 :37	that they belonged to Israel :
2 Es	9 :13	those to whom the age belongs
4 Ma	4 :3	but belong to King Seleucus

BELONGINGS   1

3 Ma	7 :21	to confiscation of their belongings by any one

BELOVED, subst., adj.   12 = 0.008 %

Jud	9 :4	and all their booty to be divided among thy beloved sons
Ad E	15 :5	as if beloved, but her heart was frozen with fear
Sir	4 :7	Make yourself beloved in the congregation
	20 :13	The wise man makes himself beloved through his words
	24 :11	In the beloved city likewise he gave me a resting place
	45 :1	and was beloved by God and man
	46 :13	Samuel, beloved by his Lord, prophet of the Lord
Bar	4 :16	They led away the widow's beloved sons
P Az	12	for the sake of Abraham thy beloved
1 Ma	6 :11	For I was kind and beloved in my power
3 Ma	6 :11	at the destruction of your beloved people
4 Ma	5 :34	nor will I renounce you, beloved self-control

BELOW   2

Jud	6 :11	and came to the springs below Bethulia
3 Ma	2 :30	he inscribed below :

BELSHAZZAR   2

Bar	1 :11	and for the life of Belshazzar his son
	1 :12	and under the protection of Belshazzar his son

BELTETHMUS   2

1 Es	2 :16	Bishlam, Mithridates, Tabeel, Rehum, Beltethmus
	2 :25	and Beltethmus and Shimshai the scribe

BENAIAH   2

1 Es	9 :26	Malchijah, Mijamin, and Eleazar, and Asibias, and Benaiah
	9 :35	Mattithiah, Zabad, Iddo, Joel, Benaiah

BENCH   1

3 Ma	4 :9	some were fastened by the neck to the benches of the boats

BEND   5 = 0.003 %

Bar	2 :21	Bend your shoulders and serve the king of Babylon
P Ma	11	And now I bend the knee of my heart
3 Ma	2 :1	bending his knees and extending his hands with calm dignity
	4 :5	sluggish and bent with age
2 Es	16 :13	For his right hand that bends the bow is strong

BEND down   1

2 Es	3 :18	Thou didst bend down the heavens and shake the earth

BEND over   1

Bar	2 :18	that goes about bent over and feeble

BENEATH, adv., prep.   5 = 0.003 %

Jud	13 :15	and here is the canopy beneath which he lay
Sir	51 :6	and my life was very near to Hades beneath
Bel	14 :13	for beneath the table they had made a hidden entrance
1 Ma	6 :46	stabbed it from beneath, and killed it
2 Es	6 :41	that one part might move upward and the other part remain beneath

BENEFACTOR   8 = 0.005 %

Ad E	16 :2	by the too great kindness of their benefactors
	16 :3	they even undertake to scheme against their own benefactors
	16 :13	our saviour and perpetual benefactor
Wis	19 :14	but these made slaves of guests who were their benefactors
2 Ma	4 :2	the man who was the benefactor of the city
3 Ma	3 :19	and their own benefactors
	6 :24	and even me, your benefactor
4 Ma	8 :6	so I can be a benefactor to those who obey me

BENEFICENCE   1
  3 Ma 5:11 that beneficence which from the beginning, night and day

BENEFICENT   1
  Wis 7:23 Beneficent, humane, steadfast, sure, free from anxiety

BENEFICIAL   1
  4 Ma 5:11 philosophize according to the truth of what is beneficial

BENEFIT, subst.   8 = 0.005 %
  Tob 3:8 and have had no benefit from any of them
  Wis 11:5 they themselves received benefit in their need
      11:13 the righteous had received benefit
  2 Ma 2:27 and seeks the benefit of others
      5:20 and afterward participated in its benefits
  2 Es 1:9 on whom I have bestowed such great benefits ?
      1:17 Where are the benefits which I bestowed on you ?
      9:10 although they received my benefits

BENEFIT, verb   2
  Sir 5:8 for it will not benefit you in the day of calamity
  3 Ma 5:20 said that the Jews were benefited by today's sleep

BENEVOLENCE   3 = 0.002 %
  3 Ma 3:15 but should cherish them with clemency and great benevolence
      3:18 because of the benevolence which we have toward all
      3:20 since we treat all nations with benevolence

BENJAMIN   5 = 0.003 %
  Ad E 11:2 of the tribe of Benjamin, had a dream
  2 Ma 3:4 But a man named Simon, of the tribe of Benjamin
  1 Es 2:8 of the tribes of Judah and Benjamin
      5:66 and when the enemies of the tribe of Judah and Benjamin heard it
      9:5 Then the men of the tribe of Judah and Benjamin

BEQUEATH   1
  4 Ma 13:19 has bequeathed through the fathers to their descendants

BEREA   1
  1 Ma 9:4 then they marched off and went to Berea

BEREAVE   3 = 0.002 %
  Bar 4:12 Let no one rejoice over me, a widow and bereaved of many
      4:16 and bereaved the lonely woman of her daughters
  4 Ma 12:6 who had been bereaved of so many sons

BEREAVEMENT   2
  Wis 14:15 at an untimely bereavement
  4 Ma 18:9 and did not have the grief of bereavement

BEROEA   1
  2 Ma 13:4 he ordered them to take him to Beroea

BERYL   1
  Tob 13:17 The streets of Jerusalem will be paved with beryl

BESAI   1
  1 Es 5:31 the sons of Paseah, the sons of Hasrah, the sons of Besai

BESCASPASMYS   1
  1 Es 9:31 and Naidus, and Bescaspasmys and Sesthel

BESEECH   25 = 0.016 %
  Wis 8:21 so I appealed to the Lord and besought him
  Sir 50:19 And the people besought the Most High in prayer
  2 Ma 1:8 We besought the Lord and we were heard
      7:28 I beseech you, my child
      8:2 They besought the Lord to look upon the people
      8:14 and at the same time besought the Lord
      8:29 and besought the merciful Lord
      9:26 I therefore urge and beseech you to remember
      10:4 they fell prostrate and besought the Lord
      10:16 and beseeching God to fight on their side
      10:26 they besought him to be gracious to them
      11:6 besought the Lord to send a good angel to save Israel
      12:11 The defeated nomads besought Judas
      12:24 With great guile he besought them to let him go in safety
      12:42 beseeching that the sin which had been committed
      13:12 and had besought the merciful Lord with weeping and fasting
  P Ma 11 beseeching thee for thy kindness
      13 I earnestly beseech thee, forgive me, O Lord
  2 Es 2:41 beseech the Lord's power that your people
      4:2 Then I answered and said, I beseech you, my lord
      5:56 And I said, O Lord, I beseech you,
      9:44 I besought the Most High, night and day
      12:6 Therefore I will now beseech the Most High
      13:13 and I besought the Most High, and said
  4 Ma 4:11 and with tears besought the Hebrews

BESET   2
  Wis 17:14 and which beset them from the recesses of powerless Hades
  2 Es 15:33 an enemy in ambush shall beset them

BESIDE   9 = 0.006 %
  Tob 4:4 When she dies, bury her beside me in the same grave
  Jud 6:7 and put you in one of the cities beside the passes
      7:3 They encamped in the valley near Bethulia, beside the spring
      7:18 toward Acraba, which is near Chusi beside the brook Mochmur
      13:4 Then Judith, standing beside his bed, said in her heart
  Sir 18:2 And there is no other beside him
      47:19 But laid your loins beside women
  1 Ma 13:29 and beside the suits of armour carved ships
  1 Es 9:43 and beside him stood Mattathiah, Shema, Anaiah, Azariah

BESIDES, adv., prep.   23 = 0.015 %
  Tob 5:15 And besides, I will add to your wages
  Wis 12:13 For neither is there any god besides thee
  Sir 24:24 and besides him there is no saviour
      29:25 and besides this you will hear bitter words :
      37:15 And besides all this pray to the Most High
  L Jr 6:40 Besides, even the Chaldeans themselves dishonour them
      6:56 Besides, they can offer no resistance to a king or any enemies
  Bel 14:10 besides their wives and children
      14:41 and there is no other besides thee
  2 Ma 5:23 and besides these Menelaus
      6:4 and besides brought in things for sacrifice that were unfit
      8:17 and besides, the overthrow of their ancestral way of life
      8:23 Besides, he appointed Eleazar
      10:15 Besides this, the Idumeans
      10:31 20,500 were slaughtered, besides 600 horsemen
      14:4 and besides these
  1 Es 2:7 besides the other things added as votive offerings
      5:41 besides menservants and maidservants, were 42,360
  3 Ma 2:22 besides being paralyzed in his limbs
      7:22 Besides they all recovered all of their property
  2 Es 3:32 Or has another nation known thee besides Israel ?
      7:96 and besides they see the straits and toil
      14:12 besides half of the 13th part

BESIEGE   11 = 0.007 %
  1 Ma 6:19 and assembled all the people to besiege them
      6:20 and besieged the citadel in the 150th year
      6:24 For this reason the sons of our people besieged the citadel
      11:21 that Jonathan was besieging the citadel
      11:61 So he besieged it and burned its suburbs with fire and plundered them
      15:25 Antiochus the king besieged Dor anew
  2 Ma 10:19 a force sufficient to besiege them
      10:33 and they besieged the fort 4 days
      11:6 that Lysias was besieging the strongholds
      12:21 for that place was hard to besiege and difficult of access
  4 Ma 7:4 No city besieged with many ingenious war machines

BESIEGER   1
  4 Ma 7:4 he conquered the besiegers

BEST*   15 = 0.010 %
  Tob 7:12 The merciful God will guide you both for the best
  Sir 11:3 but her product is the best of sweet things
      36:24 He who acquires a wife gets his best possession
  1 Ma 4:45 And they thought it best to tear it down
      8:7 and surrender some of their best provinces
  2 Ma 4:19 thought best not to use it for sacrifice
      13:26 made the best possible defence
      14:30 did not spring from the best motives
      15:38 that was the best I could do
  1 Es 2:20 we think it best not to neglect such a matter
      5:44 to the best of their ability
  3 Ma 1:2 took with him the best of the Ptolemaic arms
      3:26 and in the best state
  2 Es 8:15 About all mankind thou knowest best
  4 Ma 1:8 but I can demonstrate it best from the noble bravery

BESTOW   8 = 0.005 %
  Wis 14:21 bestowed on objects of stone or wood
  Sir 17:11 He bestowed knowledge upon them
      47:6 when the glorious diadem was bestowed upon him
  1 Ma 15:9 we will bestow great honour upon you and your nation and the temple
  3 Ma 2:16 But because you graciously bestowed your glory
      5:11 is bestowed by him who grants it to whomever he wishes
  2 Es 1:9 on whom I have bestowed such great benefits ?
      1:17 Where are the benefits which I bestowed on you ?

BETAKE   2
  2 Ma 4:5 So he betook himself to the king
      9:29 he betook himself to Ptolemy Philometor in Egypt

BETHANY   1
Jud 1:9   and beyond the Jordan as far as Jerusalem and Bethany

BETHASMOTH   1
1 Es 5:18   The men of Bethasmoth, 42

BETH-BASI   2
1 Ma 9:62   withdrew to Beth-basi in the wilderness
       9:64   Then he came and encamped against Beth-basi

BETH-DAGON   1
1 Ma 10:83   They fled to Azotus and entered Beth-dagon

BETHEL   2
1 Ma 9:50   and Bethel, and Timnath, and Pharathon, and Tephon
1 Es 5:21   The men of Bethel, 52

BETH-HORON   6 = 0.004 %
Jud 4:4   and to Kona and Beth-horon and Belmain and Jericho
Sir 46:6   and at the descent of Beth-horon
1 Ma 3:16   When he approached the ascent of Beth-horon
       3:24   They pursued them down the descent of Beth-horon to the plain
       7:39   and encamped in Beth-horon
       9:50   the fortress in Jericho, and Emmaus, and Beth-horon

BETHLEHEM   1
1 Es 5:17   The sons of Bethlehem, 123

BETH-SHAN   3 = 0.002 %
1 Ma 5:52   And they crossed the Jordan into the large plain before Beth-shan
      12:40   and he marched forth and came to Beth-shan
      12:41   and he came to Beth-shan

BETHULIA   20 = 0.013 %
Jud 4:6   wrote to the people of Bethulia and Betomesthaim
       6:10   to seize Achior and take him to Bethulia
       6:11   and came to the springs below Bethulia
       6:14   and they untied him and brought him into Bethulia
       7:1   to break camp and move against Bethulia
       7:3   They encamped in the valley near Bethulia, beside the spring
       7:3   and in length from Bethulia to Cyamon
       7:6   in full view of the Israelites in Bethulia
       7:13   for this is where all the people of Bethulia get their water
       7:20   until all the vessels of water belonging to every inhabitant of Bethulia were empty
       8:3   and took to his bed and died in Bethulia his city
       8:11   Listen to me, rulers of the people of Bethulia !
       10:6   Then they went out to the city gate of Bethulia
      11:9   we have heard his words, for the men of Bethulia spared him
      12:7   and went out each night to the valley of Bethulia
      13:10   and went up the mountain to Bethulia and came to its gates
      15:3   Those who had camped in the hills around Bethulia
      15:6   The rest of the people of Bethulia
      16:21   and Judith went to Bethulia, and remained on her estate
      16:23   She died in Bethulia

BETH-ZAITH   1
1 Ma 7:19   and encamped in Beth-zaith

BETH-ZECHARIAH   2
1 Ma 6:32   and encamped at Beth-zechariah
       6:33   along the road to Beth-zechariah

BETH-ZUR   15 = 0.010 %
1 Ma 4:29   They came into Idumea and encamped at Beth-zur
       4:61   He also fortified Beth-zur
       6:7   with high walls as before, and also Beth-zur, his city
       6:26   they have fortified both the sanctuary and Beth-zur
       6:31   They came through Idumea and encamped against Beth-zur
       6:49   He made peace with the men of Beth-zur
       6:50   So the king took Beth-zur
       9:52   He also fortified the city of Beth-zur
      10:14   Only in Beth-zur did some remain
      11:65   Simon encamped before Beth-zur
      14:7   he ruled over Gazara and Beth-zur and the citadel
      14:33   and Beth-zur on the borders of Judea
2 Ma 11:5   Invading Judea, he approached Beth-zur
      13:19   He advanced against Beth-zur
      13:22   with the people in Beth-zur

BETOMASTHAIM   1
Jud 15:4   And Uzziah sent men to Betomasthaim and Bebai

BETOMESTHAIM   1
Jud 4:6   wrote to the people of Bethulia and Betomesthaim

BETRAY   7 = 0.005 %
Sir 14:7   and betrays his baseness in the end
      27:16   Whoever betrays secrets destroys confidence

      27:17   but if you betray his secrets, do not run after him
      27:21   but whoever has betrayed secrets is without hope
2 Ma 6:11   were betrayed to Philip and were all burned together
4 Ma 4:1   he fled the country with the purpose of betraying it
      13:18   or betray the brothers who have died before us

BETROTH   1
1 Ma 3:56   or were betrothed, or were planting vineyards

BETTER, adj., adv.   61 = 0.040 %
Tob 3:6   For it is better for me to die than to live
      12:8   A little with righteousness is better
      12:8   It is better to give alms than to treasure up gold
Jud 7:27   For it would be better for us to be captured by them
      10:19   Surely not a man of them had better be left alive
Wis 4:1   Better than this is childlessness with virtue
      13:3   let them know how much better than these is their Lord
      15:17   for he is better than the objects he worships
Sir 10:27   Better is a man who works
      16:3   for one is better than a 1,000
      16:3   and to die childless is better than to have ungodly children
      18:16   So a word is better than a gift
      19:24   Better is the God-fearing man who lacks intelligence
      20:2   How much better it is to reprove than to stay angry !
      20:18   A slip on the pavement is better than a slip of the tongue
      20:31   Better is the man who hides his folly
      20:32   Unwearied patience in seeking the Lord is better
      23:27   that nothing is better than the fear of the Lord
      29:22   Better is the life of a poor man
      30:14   Better off is a poor man
      30:15   Health and soundness are better than all gold
      30:16   There is no wealth better than health of body
      30:17   Death is better than a miserable life
      33:7   Why is any day better than another
      33:21   For it is better that your children should ask from you
      36:18   yet one food is better than another
      36:21   but one daughter is better than another
      37:14   For a man's soul sometimes keeps him better informed
      40:18   but he who finds treasure is better off than both
      40:19   but a blameless wife is accounted better than both
      40:20   but the love of wisdom is better than both
      40:21   but a pleasant voice is better than both
      40:23   but a wife with her husband is better than both
      40:24   but almsgiving rescues better than both
      40:26   but the fear of the Lord is better than both
      40:27   and covers a man better than any glory
      40:28   it is better to die than to beg
      41:15   Better is the man who hides his folly
      42:14   Better is the wickedness of a man
L Jr 6:59   So it is better to be a king who shows his courage
      6:59   better even the door of a house that protects its contents
      6:59   better also a wooden pillar in a palace
      6:68   The wild beasts are better than they are
      6:73   Better therefore is a just man who has no idols
1 Ma 3:59   It is better for us to die in battle
      10:11   with squared stones, for better fortification
      13:5   for I am not better than my brothers
2 Es 1:18   It would have been better for us to serve the Egyptians
      3:28   Are the deeds of those who inhabit Babylon any better ?
      3:31   Are the deeds of Babylon better than those of Zion ?
      4:12   It would be better for us not to be here
      7:19   And he said to me, You are not a better judge than God
      7:63   For it would have been better if the dust itself had not been born
      7:66   For it is much better with them than with us
      7:69   perhaps it would have been better for us
      7:116   that it would have been better if the earth had not produced Adam
      12:44   how much better it would have been for us
      12:45   For we are no better than those who died there
      13:20   Yet is it better to come into these things
4 Ma 2:7   a glutton, or even a drunkard can learn a better way
      2:18   the temperate mind is able to get the better of the emotions

BETWEEN   21 = 0.014 %
Jud 3:10   here he camped between Geba and Scythopolis
      7:24   God be judge between you and us !
      8:3   in the field between Dothan and Balamon
      8:11   and pronounced this oath between God and you
Sir 13:18   What peace is there between a hyena and a dog ?
      13:18   And what peace between a rich man and a poor man ?
      25:1   agreement between brothers, friendship between neighbours
      27:2   As a stake is driven firmly into a fissure between stones
      27:2   so sin is wedged in between selling and buying
L Jr 6:54   they are like crows between heaven and earth
1 Ma 3:18   there is no difference between saving by many or by few
      7:28   Let there be no fighting between me and you
      12:36   and to erect a high barrier between the citadel and the city
      13:40   let them be enrolled, and let there be peace between us
      16:5   and a stream lay between them

2 Es	4 : 18	If now you were a judge between them
	6 : 10	between the heel and the hand seek for nothing else, Ezra !
	7 : 8	and there is only one path lying between them, that is
	7 : 8	between the fire and the water
	11 : 28	the 2 that remained were planning between themselves

BEWAIL   1
1 Ma 13 : 26 All Israel bewailed him with great lamentation

BEWARE   7 = 0.005 %
Tob	4 : 12	Beware, my son, of all immorality
Wis	1 : 11	Beware then of useless murmuring
Sir	4 : 20	Observe the right time, and beware of evil
	11 : 33	Beware of a scoundrel, for he devises evil
	17 : 14	And he said to them, Beware of all unrighteousness
	22 : 26	whoever hears of it will beware of him
	28 : 26	Beware lest you err with your tongue

BEWILDERING   1
2 Es 10 : 37 to give your servant an explanation of this bewildering vision

BEWILDERMENT   2
| 2 Es | 10 : 28 | For it was he who brought me into this overpowering bewilderment |
| | 13 : 30 | And bewilderment of mind shall come |

BEYOND   22 = 0.014 %
Jud	1 : 9	and beyond the Jordan as far as Jerusalem and Bethany
	1 : 10	even beyond Tanis and Memphis, and all who lived in Egypt
	15 : 5	even beyond Damascus and its borders
Sir	3 : 21	nor investigate what is beyond your power
	3 : 23	Do not meddle in what is beyond your tasks
	8 : 13	Do not give surety beyond your means
	13 : 2	Do not lift a weight beyond your strength
	20 : 7	but a braggart and fool goes beyond the right moment
Bar	3 : 18	whose labours are beyond measure ?
1 Ma	7 : 8	governor of the province Beyond the River
	11 : 60	and travelled beyond the river and among the cities
1 Es	1 : 24	beyond any other people or kingdom
	1 : 49	beyond all the unclean deeds of all the nations
	4 : 42	even beyond what is written, and we will give it to you
2 Es	5 : 2	beyond what you yourself see
	5 : 2	and beyond what you heard of formerly
	5 : 8	and the wild beasts shall roam beyond their haunts
	5 : 28	and dishonoured the one root beyond the others
	8 : 21	whose throne is beyond measure
	8 : 21	and whose glory is beyond comprehension
	12 : 7	and if I have been accounted righteous before thee beyond many others
4 Ma	4 : 14	So Apollonius, having been preserved beyond all expectations

BEZAI   1
1 Es 5 : 16 The sons of Bezai, 323

BID   1
2 Ma 3 : 35 and having bidden Onias farewell

BIG   1
Sir 37 : 11 with a lazy servant about a big task

BIGVAI   3 = 0.002 %
1 Es	5 : 8	Nehemiah, Seraiah, Resaiah, Bigvai, Mordecai
	5 : 14	The sons of Bigvai, 2,066
	8 : 40	Of the sons of Bigvai, Uthai the son of Istalcurus

BILLOW   1
Wis 14 : 5 and passing through the billows on a raft

BILLOWY   1
Wis 5 : 10 like a ship that sails through the billowy water

BILSHAN   1
1 Es 5 : 8 Bilshan, Mispar, Reeliah, Rehum, and Baanah, their leaders

BIND   17 = 0.011 %
Tob	3 : 17	and to bind Asmodeus the evil demon
	8 : 3	and the angel bound him
Jud	6 : 13	and they bound Achior
	8 : 3	who were binding sheaves in the field
	8 : 16	Do not try to bind the purposes of the Lord our God
Wis	17 : 17	for with one chain of darkness they all were bound
Sir	28 : 19	and has not been bound with its fetters
	33 : 4	bind together your instruction, and make your answer
1 Es	1 : 40	and bound him with a chain of brass
3 Ma	3 : 25	and bound securely with iron fetters
	5 : 5	and bound the hands of the wretched people
	6 : 19	binding them with immovable shackles
2 Es	13 : 13	some of them were bound
4 Ma	9 : 11	they bound his hands and arms with thongs on each side
	9 : 26	they bound him to the torture machine and catapult
	10 : 3	that binds me to my brothers
	11 : 9	the guards bound him and dragged him to the catapult

BIND up   1
Sir 30 : 7 He who spoils his son will bind up his wounds

BINDING   1
Tob 7 : 11 until you make a binding agreement with me

BINNUI   2
| 1 Es | 8 : 63 | and Moeth the son of Binnui, the Levites |
| | 9 : 34 | Carabasion and Eliashib and Machnadebai, Eliasis, Binnui |

BIRD   22 = 0.014 %
Jud	11 : 7	and the cattle and the birds of the air
Ad E	16 : 24	but also most hateful for all time to beasts and birds
Wis	5 : 11	or as, when a bird flies through the air
	17 : 18	or a melodious sound of birds in widespreading branches
	19 : 11	Afterward they saw also a new kind of birds
Sir	17 : 4	and granted them dominion over beasts and birds
	22 : 20	One who throws a stone at birds scares them away
	27 : 9	Birds flock with their kind
	27 : 19	And as you allow a bird to escape from your hand
	43 : 14	and the clouds fly forth like birds
	43 : 17	He scatters the snow like birds flying down
Bar	3 : 17	those who have sport with the birds of the air
L Jr	6 : 22	Bats, swallows, and birds light on their bodies and heads
	6 : 71	on which every bird sits
P Az	58	Bless the Lord, all birds of the air
2 Ma	9 : 15	to the beasts, for the birds to pick
	15 : 33	and said that he would give it piecemeal to the birds
3 Ma	6 : 34	that the Jews would be destroyed and become food for birds
2 Es	5 : 6	and the birds shall fly away together
	5 : 26	and from all the birds that have been created
	6 : 47	to bring forth living creatures, birds, and fishes
4 Ma	14 : 15	For example, among birds, the ones that are tame

BIRTH   14 = 0.009 %
Wis	8 : 3	She glorifies her noble birth by living with God
Sir	22 : 3	and the birth of a daughter is a loss
	22 : 9	conceal the lowly birth of their parents
	23 : 14	and you will curse the day of your birth
	50 : 22	who exalts our days from birth
2 Ma	5 : 22	Philip, by birth a Phrygian
	14 : 42	and suffer outrages unworthy of his noble birth
1 Es	4 : 15	Women gave birth to the king
3 Ma	1 : 3	a Jew by birth who later changed his religion
2 Es	4 : 42	makes haste to escape the pangs of birth
	6 : 21	and women with child shall give birth to premature children at 3 or 4 months
	6 : 26	who from their birth have not tasted death
4 Ma	15 : 5	Considering that mothers are the weaker sex and give birth to many
	15 : 17	O woman, who alone gave birth to such complete devotion !

BIRTHDAY   1
2 Ma 6 : 7 On the monthly celebration of the king's birthday

BIRTH PANG   4 = 0.003 %
Sir	7 : 27	and do not forget the birth pangs of your mother
4 Ma	15 : 16	who because of their birth-pangs
	15 : 16	than even the birth-pangs you suffered for them !
	16 : 8	In vain, my sons, I endured many birth-pangs for you

BISHLAM   1
1 Es 2 : 16 Bishlam, Mithridates, Tabeel, Rehum, Beltethmus

BITE, verb   3 = 0.002 %
Wis	16 : 11	To remind them of thy oracles they were bitten
Sir	12 : 13	Who will pity a snake charmer bitten by a serpent
	21 : 2	for if you approach sin, it will bite you

BITE, subst.   2
| Wis | 16 : 5 | by the bites of writhing serpents |
| | 16 : 9 | For they were killed by the bites of locusts and flies |

BITTER   17 = 0.011 %
Ad E	14 : 8	And now they are not satisfied that we are in bitter slavery
Wis	19 : 13	for they practised a more bitter hatred of strangers
Sir	7 : 11	Do not ridicule a man who is bitter in soul
	29 : 25	and besides this you will hear bitter words :
	38 : 17	Let your weeping be bitter and your wailing fervent
	41 : 1	O death, how bitter is the reminder of you
2 Ma	6 : 7	the Jews were taken, under bitter constraint
3 Ma	1 : 4	When a bitter fight resulted
	2 : 24	but went away uttering bitter threats
	4 : 15	with bitter haste and zealous intentness
	6 : 31	instead of a bitter and lamentable death
2 Es	1 : 22	When you were in the wilderness, at the bitter stream
	8 : 34	that thou art so bitter against it ?

BITTER

4 Ma	**15** : 16	O mother, tried now by more bitter pains
	18 : 20	O bitter was that day – and yet not bitter
	18 : 20	when that bitter tyrant of the Greeks

BITTERLY 7 = 0.005 %

Sir	**22** : 11	weep less bitterly for the dead, for he has attained rest
	25 : 18	and he cannot help sighing bitterly
3 Ma	**3** : 1	but was still more bitterly hostile
	4 : 12	to lament bitterly the ignoble misfortune of their brothers
4 Ma	**3** : 12	When his guards complained bitterly
	6 : 16	But Eleazar, as though more bitterly tormented by this counsel, cried out :
	12 : 14	but you will wail bitterly for having slain without cause

BITTERNESS 4 = 0.003 %

Wis	**8** : 16	for companionship with her has no bitterness
Sir	**4** : 6	for if in bitterness of soul he calls down a curse upon you
	21 : 12	but there is a cleverness which increases bitterness
	31 : 29	Wine drunk to excess is bitterness of soul

BLACK, adj. 1

2 Es	**7** : 125	but our faces shall be blacker than darkness ?

BLACKEN 1

L Jr	**6** : 21	when their faces have been blackened

BLAME, subst. 3 = 0.002 %

Sir	**11** : 31	and to worthy actions he will attach blame
1 Ma	**11** : 5	to throw blame on him
	11 : 11	He threw blame on Alexander because he coveted his kingdom

BLAME, verb 3 = 0.002 %

Wis	**13** : 6	Yet these men are little to be blamed
Sir	**41** : 7	Children will blame an ungodly father
2 Ma	**13** : 4	that this man was to blame for all the trouble

BLAMELESS 9 = 0.006 %

Ad E	**16** : 13	and of Esther, the blameless partner of our kingdom
Wis	**2** : 22	nor discern the prize for blameless souls
	4 : 9	and a blameless life is ripe old age
	10 : 5	and preserved him blameless before God
	10 : 15	'A holy people and blameless race wisdom delivered
	18 : 21	For a blameless man was quick to act as their champion
Sir	**31** : 8	Blessed is the rich man who is found blameless
	40 : 19	but a blameless wife is accounted better than both
1 Ma	**4** : 42	He chose blameless priests devoted to the law

BLASPHEME 4 = 0.003 %

Bel	**14** : 9	because he blasphemed against Bel
2 Ma	**10** : 34	blasphemed terribly and hurled out wicked words
	12 : 14	railing at them and even blaspheming and saying unholy things
2 Es	**1** : 22	thirsty and blaspheming my name

BLASPHEMER 5 = 0.003 %

Wis	**1** : 6	and will not free a blasphemer from the guilt of his words
Sir	**3** : 16	Whoever forsakes his father is like a blasphemer
2 Ma	**9** : 28	So the murderer and blasphemer
	10 : 36	they kindled fires and burned the blasphemers alive
	15 : 24	By the might of thy arm may these blasphemers

BLASPHEMOUS 2

2 Ma	**10** : 4	and not be handed over to blasphemous and barbarous nations
	13 : 11	fall into the hands of the blasphemous Gentiles

BLASPHEMY 6 = 0.004 %

1 Ma	**2** : 6	He saw the blasphemies being committed in Judah and Jerusalem
	7 : 38	remember their blasphemies, and let them live no longer
	7 : 41	When the messengers from the king spoke blasphemy
2 Ma	**8** : 4	and the blasphemies committed against his name
	10 : 35	fired with anger because of the blasphemies
2 Es	**1** : 23	I did not send fire upon you for your blasphemies

BLAZE, verb 1

Wis	**16** : 22	were being destroyed by the fire that blazed in the hail

BLAZE up 2

2 Ma	**1** : 22	a great fire blazed up, so that all marvelled
	1 : 32	When this was done, a flame blazed up

BLAZE, subst. 1

2 Ma	**4** : 22	and ushered in with a blaze of torches and with shouts

BLAZING 1

Sir	**3** : 30	Water extinguishes a blazing fire :

BLEAT 1

Tob	**2** : 13	and when she returned to me it began to bleat

BLEMISH 3 = 0.002 %

Wis	**13** : 14	and covering every blemish in it with paint
Sir	**11** : 33	lest he give you a lasting blemish
	34 : 18	the offering is blemished

BLENDING 1

Sir	**49** : 1	The memory of Josiah is like a blending of incense

BLESS 71 = 0.046 %

Tob	**4** : 19	Bless the Lord God on every occasion
	7 : 7	And he blessed him and exclaimed
	7 : 13	And he blessed them
	8 : 5	Let the heavens and all thy creatures bless thee
	8 : 15	Then Raguel blessed God and said
	8 : 15	Let thy saints and all thy creatures bless thee
	8 : 15	let all thy angels and thy chosen people bless thee for ever
	9 : 6	And Gabael blessed Tobias and his wife
	10 : 11	And when he had blessed them he sent them away, saying
	11 : 1	And he blessed Raguel and his wife Edna
	11 : 17	he blessed her, saying, Welcome, daughter !
Jud	**13** : 18	O daughter, you are blessed by the Most High God
	15 : 9	And when they met her they all blessed her with one accord
	15 : 10	May the Almighty Lord bless you for ever !
	15 : 12	and blessed her, and some of them performed a dance for her
Sir	**4** : 13	and the Lord will bless the place she enters
	32 : 13	And for these things bless him who made you
	33 : 12	some of them he blessed and exalted
	39 : 14	bless the Lord for all his works
	39 : 35	and bless the name of the Lord
	45 : 7	He blessed him with splendid vestments
	45 : 15	and bless his people in his name
	50 : 22	And now bless the God of all
	51 : 12	and I will bless the name of the Lord
L Jr	**6** : 66	For they can neither curse nor bless kings
P Az	**1**	singing hymns to God and blessing the Lord
	28	praised and glorified and blessed God in the furnace, saying :
	35	Bless the Lord, all works of the Lord
	36	Bless the Lord, you heavens
	37	Bless the Lord, you angels of the Lord
	38	Bless the Lord, all waters above the heaven
	39	Bless the Lord, all powers
	40	Bless the Lord, sun and moon
	41	Bless the Lord, stars of heaven
	42	Bless the Lord, all rain and dew
	43	Bless the Lord, all winds
	44	Bless the Lord, fire and heat
	45	Bless the Lord, winter cold and summer heat
	46	Bless the Lord, dews and snows
	47	Bless the Lord, nights and days
	48	Bless the Lord, light and darkness
	49	Bless the Lord, ice and cold
	50	Bless the Lord, frosts and snows
	51	Bless the Lord, lightnings and clouds
	52	Let the earth bless the Lord
	53	Bless the Lord, mountains and hills
	54	Bless the Lord, all things that grow on the earth
	55	Bless the Lord, you springs
	56	Bless the Lord, seas and rivers
	57	Bless the Lord, you whales and all creatures that move in the waters
	58	Bless the Lord, all birds of the air
	59	Bless the Lord, all beasts and cattle
	60	Bless the Lord, you sons of men
	61	Bless the Lord, O Israel
	62	Bless the Lord, you priests of the Lord
	63	Bless the Lord, you servants of the Lord
	64	Bless the Lord, spirits and souls of the righteous
	65	Bless the Lord, you who are holy and humble in heart
	66	Bless the Lord, Hananiah, Azariah, and Mishael
	68	Bless him, all who worship the Lord, the God of gods
Sus	**13** : 60	Then all the assembly shouted loudly and blessed God
1 Ma	**2** : 69	Then he blessed them, and was gathered to his fathers
	4 : 55	and worshipped and blessed Heaven, who had prospered them
2 Ma	**10** : 38	with hymns and thanksgivings they blessed the Lord
	12 : 41	So they all blessed the ways of the Lord
	15 : 29	and they blessed the Sovereign Lord
	15 : 34	blessed the Lord who had manifested himself, saying
1 Es	**4** : 36	The whole earth calls upon truth, and heaven blesses her
	5 : 60	praising the Lord and blessing him
	9 : 46	And Ezra blessed the Lord God Most High
4 Ma	**18** : 13	He praised Daniel in the den of the lions and blessed him

BLESSED* 61 = 0.040 %

Tob	**3** : 11	Blessed art thou, O Lord my God
	3 : 11	and blessed is thy holy and honoured name for ever
	4 : 12	They were blessed in their children
	8 : 5	Blessed art thou, O God of our fathers
	8 : 5	and blessed be thy holy and glorious name for ever
	8 : 15	Blessed art thou, O God, with every pure and holy blessing
	8 : 16	Blessed art thou, because thou hast made me glad

8 : 17	Blessed art thou, because thou hast had compassion on 2 only children	
11 : 14	Blessed art thou, O God, and blessed is thy name for ever	
11 : 14	and blessed are all thy holy angels	
11 : 17	Blessed is God who has brought you to us	
11 : 17	and blessed are your father and your mother	
13 : 1	Blessed is God who lives for ever	
13 : 1	and blessed is his kingdom	
13 : 12	blessed for ever will be all who love you	
13 : 14	How blessed are those who love you !	
13 : 14	Blessed are those who grieved over all your afflictions	
13 : 18	Blessed is God, who has exalted you for ever	
Jud **13** : 17	and said with one accord, Blessed art thou, our God	
13 : 18	and blessed be the Lord God	
14 : 7	Blessed are you in every tent of Judah !	
Wis **3** : 13	For blessed is the barren woman who is undefiled	
3 : 14	Blessed also is the eunuch	
14 : 7	For blessed is the wood by which righteousness comes	
Sir **1** : 13	on the day of his death he will be blessed	
14 : 1	Blessed is the man who does not blunder with his lips	
14 : 2	Blessed is he whose heart does not condemn him	
14 : 20	Blessed is the man who meditates on wisdom	
31 : 8	Blessed is the rich man who is found blameless	
31 : 9	Who is he ? And we will call him blessed	
34 : 15	Blessed is the soul of the man who fears the Lord !	
44 : 21	that the nations would be blessed through his posterity	
45 : 1	Moses, whose memory is blessed	
46 : 11	may their memory be blessed !	
48 : 11	Blessed are those who saw you	
50 : 28	Blessed is he who concerns himself with these things	
P Az **3**	Blessed art thou, O Lord, God of our fathers	
29	Blessed art thou, O Lord, God of our fathers	
30	And blessed is thy glorious, holy name	
31	Blessed art thou in the temple of thy holy glory	
32	Blessed art thou, who sittest upon cherubim	
33	Blessed art thou upon the throne of thy kingdom	
34	Blessed art thou in the firmament of heaven	
1 Ma **3** : 7	and his memory is blessed for ever	
4 : 30	Blessed art thou, O Saviour of Israel	
2 Ma **1** : 17	Blessed in every way be our God, who has brought judgment	
15 : 34	Blessed is he who has kept his own place undefiled	
1 Es **4** : 40	Blessed be the God of truth !	
4 : 60	Blessed art thou, who hast given me wisdom	
8 : 25	Blessed be the Lord alone	
3 Ma **7** : 23	Blessed be the Deliverer of Israel through all times ! Amen	
2 Es **7** : 45	Blessed are those who are alive and keep thy commandments !	
10 : 57	For you are more blessed than many	
13 : 24	are more blessed than those who have died	
4 Ma **1** : 10	but I would also call them blessed	
7 : 15	O man of blessed age	
7 : 22	and knows that it is blessed to endure any suffering	
10 : 15	No, by the blessed death of my brothers	
12 : 1	had died a blessed death	
17 : 18	and live through blessed eternity	

BLESSEDNESS   1
4 Ma **4** : 12   he would praise the blessedness of the holy place before all people

BLESSING   22 = 0.014 %
Tob **8** : 15	Blessed art thou, O God, with every pure and holy blessing	
Jud **13** : 20	and may he visit you with blessings	
Wis **15** : 19	both the praise of God and his blessing	
18 : 9	both blessings and dangers	
Sir **3** : 8	that a blessing from him may come upon you	
3 : 9	For a father's blessing	
7 : 32	so that your blessing may be complete	
11 : 22	The blessing of the Lord is the reward of the godly	
11 : 22	and quickly God causes his blessing to flourish	
26 : 3	A good wife is a great blessing	
26 : 3	she will be granted among the blessings	
33 : 16	by the blessing of the Lord I excelled	
34 : 17	he grants healing, life, and blessing	
36 : 17	according to the blessing of Aaron for thy people	
39 : 22	His blessing covers the dry land like a river	
40 : 17	Kindness is like a garden of blessings	
40 : 27	The fear of the Lord is like a garden of blessing	
44 : 23	The blessing of all men and the covenant	
44 : 23	he acknowledged him with his blessings	
47 : 6	and praised him for the blessings of the Lord	
50 : 20	to pronounce the blessing of the Lord with his lips	
50 : 21	to receive the blessing from the Most High	

BLIGHT, subst.   1
2 Es **15** : 13   by blight and hail and by a terrible tempest

BLIND, adj.   2
L Jr **6** : 37   They cannot restore sight to a blind man
2 Es **2** : 21   and let the blind man have a vision of my splendour

BLIND, verb   4 = 0.003 %
Wis **2** : 21   for their wickedness blinded them
Sir **20** : 29   Presents and gifts blind the eyes of the wise
     43 : 4   and with bright beams it blinds the eyes
2 Ma **10** : 30   so that, confused and blinded

BLOCK, subst.   1
2 Ma **4** : 41   some picked up stones, some blocks of wood

BLOCK up   3 = 0.002 %
Jud **16** : 4   their multitude blocked up the valleys
1 Ma **2** : 36   or block up their hiding places
      5 : 47   and blocked up the gates with stones

BLOCKADE   1
1 Es **2** : 23   and kept setting up blockades in it from of old

BLOOD   48 = 0.031 %
Jud **6** : 4	and their mountains will be drunk with their blood	
9 : 3	to be stained with blood	
9 : 4	and abhorred the pollution of their blood	
Ad E **16** : 5	for the shedding of innocent blood	
16 : 10	really an alien to the Persian blood	
Wis **7** : 2	within the period of 10 months, compacted with blood	
11 : 6	stirred up and defiled with blood	
12 : 5	and their sacrificial feasting on human flesh and blood	
14 : 25	and all is a raging riot of blood and murder	
Sir **8** : 16	because blood is as nothing in his sight	
9 : 9	and in blood you are plunged into destruction	
11 : 32	and a sinner lies in wait to shed blood	
12 : 16	his thirst for blood will be insatiable	
14 : 18	so are the generations of flesh and blood :	
17 : 31	So flesh and blood devise evil	
28 : 11	A hasty quarrel kindles fire, and urgent strife sheds blood	
33 : 30	because you have bought him with blood	
34 : 21	whoever deprives them of it is a man of blood	
34 : 22	to deprive an employee of his wages is to shed blood	
39 : 26	the blood of the grape, and oil and clothing	
50 : 15	and poured a libation of the blood of the grape	
Sus **13** : 46	I am innocent of the blood of this woman	
13 : 62	Thus innocent blood was saved that day	
1 Ma **1** : 37	On every side of the sanctuary they shed innocent blood	
7 : 17	The flesh of thy saints and their blood they poured out	
9 : 38	And they remembered the blood of John their brother	
9 : 42	And when they had fully avenged the blood of their brother	
2 Ma **1** : 8	and burned the gate and shed innocent blood	
8 : 3	and to hearken to the blood that cried out to him	
12 : 16	appeared to be running over with blood	
14 : 45	and though his blood gushed forth and his wounds were severe	
14 : 46	with his blood now completely drained from him	
2 Es **1** : 26	for you have defiled your hands with blood	
1 : 32	their blood I will require of you, says the Lord	
5 : 5	Blood shall drip from wood	
15 : 8	Behold, innocent and righteous blood cries out to me	
15 : 9	and will receive to myself all the innocent blood from among them	
15 : 22	and my sword will not cease from those who shed innocent blood on the earth	
15 : 35	and there shall be blood from the sword	
15 : 58	and drink their own blood in thirst for water	
4 Ma **3** : 15	to drink what was regarded as equivalent to blood	
6 : 6	his flesh was being torn by scourges, his blood flowing	
6 : 29	Make my blood their purification	
7 : 8	shielding it with their own blood and noble sweat	
9 : 20	The wheel was completely smeared with blood	
10 : 8	and drops of blood flowing from his entrails	
13 : 20	and growing from the same blood and through the same life	
17 : 22	And through the blood of those devout ones	

BLOODSHED   4 = 0.003 %
Sir **22** : 24   so insults precede bloodshed
     27 : 15   The strife of the proud leads to bloodshed
     40 : 9   are death and bloodshed and strife and sword
2 Ma **14** : 18   shrank from deciding the issue by bloodshed

BLOODTHIRSTINESS   2
4 Ma **9** : 9   but you, because of your bloodthirstiness toward us
     10 : 11   but you, because of your impiety and bloodthirstiness

BLOODTHIRSTY   2
2 Ma **4** : 38   and there he dispatched the bloodthirsty fellow
4 Ma **10** : 17   the bloodthirsty, murderous, and utterly abominable Antiochus

BLOOM, subst.   1
Sir **26** : 19   My son, keep sound the bloom of your youth

BLOOM, verb   1
2 Es **5** : 36   and make the withered flowers bloom again for me

BLOSSOM, subst.   3 = 0.002 %
   Sir 24:17 and my blossoms became glorious and abundant fruit
        39:14 and put forth blossoms like a lily
        51:15 From blossom to ripening grape my heart delighted in her

BLOT, subst.   2
   Sir   7:6 and thus put a blot on your integrity
        20:24 A lie is an ugly blot on a man

BLOT out   14 = 0.009 %
   Tob   4:19 and do not let them be blotted out of your mind
   Sir 23:26 and her disgrace will not be blotted out
        39:9 and it will never be blotted out
        40:12 All bribery and injustice will be blotted out
        41:11 but the evil name of sinners will be blotted out
        44:13 and their glory will not be blotted out
        44:18 that all flesh should not be blotted out by a flood
        46:20 to blot out the wickedness of the people
        47:22 he will never blot out the descendants of his chosen one
 1 Ma 12:53 and blot out the memory of them from among men
 2 Ma 12:42 might be wholly blotted out
  2 Es 2:7 let their names be blotted out from the earth
        6:27 For evil shall be blotted out
      7:139 and blot out the multitude of their sins

BLOW, verb   8 = 0.005 %
   Sir 28:12 If you blow on a spark, it will glow
        43:16 at his will the south wind blows
        43:20 The cold north wind blows, and ice freezes over the water
  L Jr 6:61 and the wind likewise blows in every land
 1 Ma 4:13 Then the men with Judas blew their trumpets
        9:12 and the men with Judas also blew their trumpets
  2 Es 6:1 and before the assembled winds blew
       11:2 and all the winds of heaven blew upon him

BLOW, subst.   10 = 0.007 %
  Wis 12:9 or to destroy them at one blow
   Sir 22:22 or a treacherous blow – in these cases any friend will flee
        27:25 and a treacherous blow opens up wounds
        28:17 The blow of a whip raises a welt
        28:17 but a blow of the tongue crushes the bones
 1 Ma 1:30 but he suddenly fell upon the city, dealt it a severe blow
        5:34 they fled before him, and he dealt them a heavy blow
 2 Ma 3:26 inflicting many blows on him
        6:30 When he was about to die under the blows
        9:5 struck him an incurable and unseen blow

BLUE   3 = 0.002 %
   Sir   6:30 and her bonds are a cord of blue
        45:10 with a holy garment, of gold and blue and purple
 1 Ma 4:23 and cloth dyed blue and sea purple, and great riches

BLUNDER   1
   Sir 14:1 Blessed is the man who does not blunder with his lips

BLUSH   1
   Tob   2:14 and I blushed for her

BOAR   1
  2 Es 15:30 shall go forth like wild boars of the forest

BOARD   1
 3 Ma 4:9 They were brought on board like wild animals

BOAST, subst.   3 = 0.002 %
 Ad E 16:4 but, carried away by the boasts of those
   Sir 25:6 and their boast is the fear of the Lord
        48:18 and made great boasts in his arrogance

BOAST, verb   12 = 0.008 %
  Jud 16:5 He boasted that he would burn up my territory
  Wis 2:16 and boasts that God is his father
        5:8 And what good has our boasted wealth brought us ?
        6:2 and boast of many nations
       17:7 and their boasted wisdom was scornfully rebuked
   Sir 10:27 than one who goes about boasting, but lacks bread
       11:4 Do not boast about wearing fine clothes
       17:9 And he gave them to boast of his marvels for ever
       30:2 and will boast of him among acquaintances
       31:10 Let it be for him a ground for boasting
       48:4 And who has the right to boast which you have ?
 3 Ma 2:17 lest the transgressors boast in their wrath

BOASTFUL   2
 3 Ma 3:11 Then the king, boastful of his present good fortune
       6:4 exalted with lawless insolence and boastful tongue

BOASTFULLY   2
  Jud 6:17 and all that Holofernes had said so boastfully
 2 Ma 15:32 which had been boastfully stretched out

BOASTFULNESS   2
 2 Ma 15:6 This Nicanor in his utter boastfulness and arrogance
 4 Ma 1:26 In the soul it is boastfulness, covetousness

BOASTING   3 = 0.002 %
   Sir 47:4 and struck down the boasting of Goliath ?
 3 Ma 6:5 speaking grievous words with boasting and insolence
 4 Ma 2:15 lust for power, vainglory, boasting, arrogance, and malice

BOAT   4 = 0.003 %
   Sir 33:2 is like a boat in a storm
 2 Ma 12:3 on boats which they had provided
      12:6 He set fire to the harbour by night, and burned the boats
 3 Ma 4:9 some were fastened by the neck to the benches of the boats

BODILY   5 = 0.003 %
 2 Ma 3:17 For terror and bodily trembling had come over the man
 3 Ma 6:20 Even the king began to shudder bodily
  2 Es 1:37 though they do not see me with bodily eyes
 4 Ma 3:18 it can overthrow bodily agonies even when they are extreme
     10:20 we let our bodily members be mutilated

BODY   69 = 0.045 %
   Tob 1:18 When the bodies were sought by the king
        2:4 I sprang up and removed the body to a place of shelter until
              sunset
        2:7 and dug a grave and buried the body
   Jud 1:16 he and all his combined forces, a vast body of troops
       10:3 and bathed her body with water
       13:8 and severed his head from his body
       13:9 Then she tumbled his body off the bed
 Ad E 14:2 and she utterly humbled her body
  Wis 1:4 nor dwell in a body enslaved to sin
        2:3 When it is extinguished, the body will turn to ashes
       8:20 or rather, being good, I entered an undefiled body
       9:15 for a perishable body weighs down the soul
      18:22 He conquered the wrath not by strength of body
   Sir 30:14 than a rich man who is severely afflicted in body
       30:15 and a robust body than countless riches
       30:16 There is no wealth better than health of body
       34:25 If a man washes after touching a dead body
       38:16 Lay out his body with the honour due him
       41:11 The mourning of men is about their bodies
       44:14 Their bodies were buried in peace
       47:19 and through your body you were brought into subjection
       48:13 and when he was dead his body prophesied
       51:2 and hast delivered my body from destruction
   Bar 2:17 whose spirit has been taken from their bodies
  L Jr 6:22 Bats, swallows, and birds light on their bodies and heads
       6:71 or like a dead body cast out in the darkness
   Bel 14:32 and every day there had been given 2 human bodies and 2 sheep
 1 Ma 3:13 including a body of faithful men
       7:12 Then a group of scribes appeared in a body
      11:4 and the charred bodies of those
 2 Ma 4:9 a gymnasium and a body of youth for it
       6:30 I am enduring terrible sufferings in my body under this beating
       6:31 not only to the young but to the great body of his nation
       7:7 rather than have your body punished limb by limb ?
       7:37 I, like my brothers, give up body and life
       9:7 and the fall was so hard as to torture every limb of his body
       9:9 And so the ungodly man's body swarmed with worms
       9:29 And Philip, one of his courtiers, took his body home
      12:39 Judas and his men went to take up the bodies of the fallen
      14:38 and for Judaism he had with all zeal risked body and life
      15:12 for the whole body of the Jews
      15:30 And the man who was ever in body and soul
 3 Ma 2:29 are also to be branded on their bodies by fire
       7:3 persuaded us to gather together the Jews of the kingdom in a
              body
  2 Es 1:32 and torn their bodies in pieces
       3:5 and it gave thee Adam, a lifeless body ?
      5:14 Then I awoke, and my body shuddered violently
      7:78 as the spirit leaves the body to return again to him who gave it
      7:88 when they shall be separated from their mortal body
     7:100 after they have been separated from the bodies
      8:8 And because thou dost give life to the body
     11:10 but from the midst of his body
     11:23 and nothing remained on the eagle's body
     11:45 and your whole worthless body
     12:3 and the whole body of the eagle was burned
     12:17 but from the midst of his body, this is the interpretation :
     16:61 who formed man, and put a heart in the midst of his body
 4 Ma 1:20 with both body and soul
       1:27 in the body, indiscriminate eating
       1:28 are 2 plants growing from the body and the soul
       1:35 and all the impulses of the body are bridled by reason

	3:1	but over those of the body
	6:7	because his body could not endure the agonies
	7:13	his body no longer tense and firm
	11:11	In this condition, gasping for breath and in anguish of body
	13:13	and let us use our bodies as a bulwark for the law
	14:10	and it consumed their bodies quickly
	17:1	so that no one might touch her body
	18:3	Therefore those who gave over their bodies in suffering

BODYGUARD   5 = 0.003 %
1 Ma 13:40   to be enrolled in our bodyguard
2 Ma 3:24   But when he arrived at the treasury with his bodyguard
      3:28   with a great retinue and all his bodyguard
1 Es 3:4   Then the 3 young men of the bodyguard
3 Ma 2:23   Then both friends and bodyguards

BOIL   3 = 0.002 %
Bel 14:27   and boiled them together and made cakes
    14:33   He had boiled pottage and had broken bread into a bowl
1 Es 1:12   and they boiled the sacrifices in brass pots and cauldrons

BOLD   5 = 0.003 %
Jud 14:13   Wake up our lord, for the slaves have been so bold
Wis 11:17   a multitude of bears, or bold lions
Sir 6:11   and be bold with your servants
2 Ma 3:24   that all who had been so bold as to accompany him
3 Ma 1:22   In addition, the bolder of the citizens

BOLDLY   3 = 0.002 %
1 Ma 4:18   and afterward seize the plunder boldly
4 Ma 3:14   and from it boldly brought the king a drink
    15:19   in his tortures gazing boldly at the same agonies

BOLDNESS   8 = 0.005 %
Jud 16:10   The Persians trembled at her boldness
Sir 25:25   and no boldness of speech in an evil wife
1 Ma 4:32   melt the boldness of their strength
     4:35   and observed the boldness which inspired those of Judas
3 Ma 2:4   who trusted in their strength and boldness
     6:34   and their firebreathing boldness was ignominiously quenched
2 Es 7:98   because they shall rejoice with boldness
4 Ma 10:5   Enraged by the man's boldness

BOLT, subst.   3 = 0.002 %
Sir 28:25   and make a door and a bolt for your mouth
1 Ma 12:38   he fortified it and installed gates with bolts
    13:33   with high towers and great walls and gates and bolts

BOND, subst.   6 = 0.004 %
Sir 6:25   and do not fret under her bonds
     6:30   and her bonds are a cord of blue
3 Ma 4:7   In bonds and in public view they were violently dragged along
     4:9   driven under the constraint of iron bonds
     5:7   because in their bonds
     6:27   Loose and untie their unjust bonds !

BOND, verb   1
Sir 22:16   A wooden beam firmly bonded into a building

BONDAGE   5 = 0.003 %
Wis 14:21   because men, in bondage to misfortune or to royal authority
1 Es 8:80   Even in our bondage we were not forsaken by our Lord
2 Es 1:7   out of the house of bondage ?
     2:1   Thus says the Lord : I brought this people out of bondage
    14:3   when my people were in bondage in Egypt

BONE   11 = 0.007 %
Sir 26:13   and her skill puts fat on his bones
    28:17   but a blow of the tongue crushes the bones
    46:12   May their bones revive from where they lie
    49:10   May the bones of the 12 prophets
    49:15   and his bones are cared for
Bar 2:24   that the bones of our kings and the bones of our fathers
1 Ma 13:25   And Simon sent and took the bones of Jonathan his brother
4 Ma 6:26   When he was now burned to his very bones and about to expire
     9:21   Although the ligaments joining his bones were already severed
    18:17   Shall these dry bones live ?

BOOK   34 = 0.022 %
Tob 1:1   The book of the acts of Tobit the son of Tobiel
    12:20   Write in a book everything that has happened
Sir pr.   and the other books of our fathers
     pr.   the prophecies, and the rest of the books
     pr.   to the translation of the following book
     pr.   in order to complete and publish the book
    24:23   All this is the book of the covenant of the Most High God
    50:27   I have written in this book
Bar 1:1   These are the words of the book
     1:3   And Baruch read the words of this book
     1:3   and in the hearing of all the people who came to hear the book

	1:14	And you shall read this book which we are sending you
	4:1	She is the book of the commandments of God
1 Ma	1:56	The books of the law which they found they tore to pieces
	1:57	Where the book of the covenant was found
	3:48	And they opened the book of the law
	12:9	since we have as encouragement the holy books
2 Ma	2:13	and collected the books about the kings and prophets
	2:14	In the same way Judas also collected all the books that had been lost
	2:23	we shall attempt to condense into a single book
	6:12	Now I urge those who read this book not to be depressed by such calamities
	8:23	to read aloud from the holy book
1 Es	1:11	as it is written in the book of Moses
	1:33	These things are written in the book of the histories
	1:33	are recorded in the book of the kings of Israel and Judah
	5:49	in accordance with the directions in the book of Moses the man of God
	7:6	did according to what was written in the book of Moses
	7:9	in accordance with the book of Moses
	9:45	Then Ezra took up the book of the law
2 Es	1:1	The 2nd book of the prophet Ezra the son of Seraiah
	6:20	the books shall be opened before the firmament
	12:37	Therefore write all these things that you have seen in a book
	14:44	So during the 40 days 94 books were written
	14:45	Make public the 24 books that you wrote first

BOOR   1
Sir 21:23   A boor peers into the house from the door

BOORISHLY   1
Sir 22:10   Children who are disdainfully and boorishly haughty

BOOTH   5 = 0.003 %
2 Ma 1:9   And now see that you keep the feast of booths
     1:18   in order that you also may celebrate the feast of booths
    10:6   in the manner of the feast of booths
    10:6   remembering how not long before, during the feast of booths
1 Es 5:51   They kept the feast of booths

BOOTY   7 = 0.005 %
Jud 4:12   and their wives as booty
     9:4   and all their booty to be divided among thy beloved sons
    15:7   got a great amount of booty
    16:5   and take my virgins as booty
L Jr 6:58   and go off with this booty
1 Ma 10:87   with much booty
2 Ma 8:20   destroyed 120,000 and took much booty

BORDER, subst.   18 = 0.012 %
Jud 1:5   which is on the borders of Ragae
     1:10   as far as the borders of Ethiopia
     2:25   and came to the southern borders of Japheth
    14:4   and you and all who live within the borders of Israel
    15:5   even beyond Damascus and its borders
1 Ma 2:46   that they found within the borders of Israel
     3:32   from the river Euphrates to the border of Egypt
     5:60   and were pursued to the borders of Judea
     6:25   but also against all the lands on their borders
    11:59   from the Ladder of Tyre to the borders of Egypt
    14:6   He extended the borders of his nation
    14:33   and Beth-zur on the borders of Judea
    14:34   and Gazara, which is on the borders of Azotus
    15:30   which you have conquered outside the borders of Judea
2 Ma 9:25   Moreover, I understand how the princes along the borders
2 Es 9:8   and will see my salvation in my land and within my borders
    12:34   those who have been saved throughout my borders
    13:48   who are found within my holy borders, shall be saved

BORDER, verb   1
1 Ma 11:34   the latter, with all the region bordering them

BORITH   1
2 Es 1:2   son of Arna, son of Uzzi, son of Borith

BORN   34 = 0.022 %
Jud 12:18   than in all the days since I was born
    12:20   since he was born
Ad E 14:5   Ever since I was born
Wis 2:2   Because we were born by mere chance
     4:6   For children born of unlawful unions are witnesses of evil
     5:13   So we also, as soon as we were born, ceased to be
     7:3   And when I was born, I began to breathe the common air
Sir 7:28   Remember that through your parents you were born
    10:18   nor fierce anger for those born of women
    10:18   one dies and another is born
    23:14   then you will wish that you had never been born
    41:9   When you are born, you are born to a curse
    44:9   they have become as though they had not been born
    49:15   And no man like Joseph has been born

Bar	**3**:26	The giants were born there, who were famous of old
1 Ma	**2**:7	and said, Alas! Why was I born to see this
1 Es	**3**:1	and all that were born in his house
2 Es	**4**:6	Who of those that have been born can do this
	5:35	Why then was I born?
	5:53	Those born in the strength of youth
	5:53	are different from those born during the time of old age
	5:55	as born of a creation which already is aging
	6:8	because from him were born Jacob and Esau
	7:63	For it would have been better if the dust itself had not been born
	7:65	let all who have been born lament
	7:68	For all who have been born are involved in iniquities
	7:127	which every man who is born on earth shall wage
	8:35	For in truth there is no one among those who have been born
	9:22	So let the multitude perish which has been born in vain
	10:10	And from the beginning all have been born of her
	14:20	but who will warn those who will be born hereafter?
4 Ma	**11**:15	Since to this end we were born and bred
	13:21	When they were born after an equal time of gestation

BORROW   2

Wis	**15**:16	For a man made them, and one whose spirit is borrowed formed them
Sir	**18**:33	Do not become a beggar by feasting with borrowed money

BORROWER   1

Sir	**29**:6	If he does not, the borrower has robbed him of his money

BOSOM, subst.   3 = 0.002 %

Sir	**9**:1	Do not be jealous of the wife of your bosom
2 Es	**15**:21	and will repay into their bosom
	15:55	The reward of a harlot is in your bosom

BOSOR   2

1 Ma	**5**:26	Many of them have been shut up in Bozrah and Bosor
	5:36	Maked, and Bosor, and the other cities of Gilead

BOTH, indef. pr. or adj.   79 = 0.051 %

Tob	**3**:16	The prayer of both was heard
	5:15	if you both return safe and sound
	5:16	and good success to you both
	5:16	So they both went out and departed
	6:5	And they both continued on their way
	6:17	And when you approach her, rise up, both of you
	7:12	The merciful God will guide you both for the best
	8:9	Then they both went to sleep for the night
	8:13	and found them both asleep
	9:6	In the morning they both got up early
	11:9	And they both wept
	12:16	They were both alarmed
Jud	**4**:2	and were alarmed both for Jerusalem
	13:13	They all ran together, both small and great
Ad E	**11**:6	both ready to fight, and they roared terribly
	16:16	who has directed the kingdom both for us
	16:23	so that both now and hereafter
Wis	**4**:1	because it is known both by God and by men
	6:7	because he himself made both small and great
	7:16	For both we and our words are in his hand
	7:21	I learned both what is secret and what is manifest
	15:7	both the vessels that serve clean uses
	15:19	both the praise of God and his blessing
	18:9	both blessings and dangers
Sir pr.		by both speaking and writing
	5:6	for both mercy and wrath are with him
	10:7	and injustice is outrageous to both
	18:17	Both are to be found in a gracious man
	20:25	but the lot of both is ruin
	22:5	and will be despised by both
	28:12	and both come out of your mouth
	40:8	With all flesh, both man and beast
	40:18	but he who finds treasure is better off than both
	40:19	but a blameless wife is accounted better than both
	40:20	but the love of wisdom is better than both
	40:21	but a pleasant voice is better than both
	40:22	but the green shoots of grain more than both
	40:23	but a wife with her husband is better than both
	40:24	but almsgiving rescues better than both
	40:25	but good counsel is esteemed more than both
	40:26	but the fear of the Lord is better than both
Sus	**13**:10	Both were overwhelmed with passion for her
	13:57	This is how you both have been dealing
	13:59	that he may destroy you both
1 Ma	**1**:16	that he might reign over both kingdoms
	4:34	Then both sides attacked
	6:26	they have fortified both the sanctuary and Beth-zur
	6:45	and they parted before him on both sides
	8:30	both parties shall determine to add or delete anything
	9:17	and many on both sides were wounded and fell
	11:34	both the territory of Judea
	12:11	both in our feasts and on other appropriate days
2 Ma	**4**:5	but having in view the welfare, both public and private, of all the people
	5:15	both to the laws and to his country
	8:19	both the time of Sennacherib, when 185,000 perished
	14:46	took them with both hands and hurled them at the crowd
1 Es	**2**:22	troubling both kings and other cities
	6:26	both of gold and of silver
	8:14	both gold and silver for bulls and rams
	9:41	in the presence of both men and women
3 Ma	**1**:1	both infantry and cavalry
	2:23	Then both friends and bodyguards
	3:21	both because of their alliance with us
	3:21	by deciding both to deem them worthy of Alexandrian citizenship
	3:23	but also both by speech and by silence
	4:20	that both the paper and the pens they used for writing
	6:30	both wines and everything else
2 Es	**6**:50	could not hold them both
	8:9	shall both be kept by thy keeping
	9:19	which is supplied both with an unfailing table
4 Ma	**1**:20	with both body and soul
	1:21	The emotions of both pleasure and pain have many consequences
	1:32	and reason obviously rules over both
	3:20	had both appropriated money to them for the temple service
	12:18	both in this present life and when you are dead
	13:4	for the brothers mastered both emotions and pains
	13:22	and from both general education and our discipline in the law of God
	15:4	a wondrous likeness both of mind and of form
	18:5	The tyrant Antiochus was both punished on earth

BOTTLE   1

Jud	**10**:5	And she gave her maid a bottle of wine and a flask of oil

BOUGAEAN   1

Ad E	**12**:6	But Haman, the son of Hammedatha, a Bougaean

BOUGH   2

Wis	**4**:4	For even if they put forth boughs for a while
Sir	**14**:26	and will camp under her boughs

BOUND, subst.   1

Bar	**3**:25	It is great and has no bounds

BOUNDLESS   3 = 0.002 %

Sir	**16**:17	for what is my soul in the boundless creation?
3 Ma	**2**:4	whom you destroyed by bringing upon them a boundless flood
	2:9	the boundless and immeasurable earth

BOUNTIFUL   2

2 Ma	**1**:25	who alone art bountiful
2 Es	**7**:135	and bountiful, because he would rather give than take away

BOUNTY   1

Wis	**16**:25	changed into all forms, it served thy all-nourishing bounty

BOW, subst.   3 = 0.002 %

Jud	**9**:7	they trust in shield and spear, in bow and sling
Wis	**5**:21	as from a well-drawn bow of clouds
2 Es	**16**:13	For his right hand that bends the bow is strong

BOW, verb   2

Sir	**4**:7	bow your head low to a great man
	33:26	Yoke and thong will bow the neck

BOW down   7 = 0.005 %

Jud	**13**:17	and bowed down and worshipped God
Ad E	**13**:12	and refused to bow down to this proud Haman
	13:14	I will not bow down to any one but to thee
	16:11	and was continually bowed down to by all
Sir	**19**:26	There is a rascal bowed down in mourning
	30:12	Bow down his neck in his youth
	50:21	and they bowed down in worship a 2nd time

BOWELS   3 = 0.002 %

Sir	**10**:9	For even in life his bowels decay
2 Ma	**9**:5	he was seized with a pain in his bowels
	9:6	for he had tortured the bowels of others

BOWL   6 = 0.004 %

Jud	**15**:11	and his beds and his bowls and all his furniture
Bel	**14**:33	He had boiled pottage and had broken bread into a bowl
1 Ma	**1**:22	the cups for drink offerings, the bowls, the golden censers
1 Es	**2**:13	29 silver censers, 30 gold bowls
	2:13	2,410 silver bowls, and a 1,000 other vessels
	8:57	and 20 golden bowls

BOY   10 = 0.007 %
 1 Ma 2 :46   they forcibly circumcised all the uncircumcised boys
       6 :17   Lysias had brought him up as a boy
      11 :54   and with him the young boy Antiochus
 2 Ma 5 :13   destruction of boys, women, and children
       5 :24   and to sell the women and boys as slaves
 4 Ma 11 :13   After he too had died, the 6th, a mere boy, was led in
      11 :24   We 6 boys have paralyzed your tyranny !
      12 :6   he sent for the boy's mother to show compassion on her
      12 :9   Extremely pleased by the boy's declaration
      15 :6   The mother of the 7 boys, more than any other mother, loved
               her children

BOZRAH   2
 1 Ma 5 :26   Many of them have been shut up in Bozrah and Bosor
       5 :28   by the wilderness road to Bozrah

BRACELET   2
 Jud 10 :4   and put on her anklets and bracelets and rings
 Sir 21 :21   and like a bracelet on the right arm

BRAGGART   1
 Sir 20 :7   but a braggart and fool goes beyond the right moment

BRAN   1
 L Jr 6 :43   burning bran of incense

BRANCH   12 = 0.008 %
 Jud 15 :12   and she took branches in her hands
 Wis 4 :5   The branches will be broken off before they come to maturity
      17 :18   or a melodious sound of birds in widespreading branches
 Sir 1 :20   and her branches are long life
      23 :25   and her branches will not bear fruit
      24 :16   Like a Terebinth I spread out my branches
      24 :16   and my branches are glorious and graceful
      40 :15   The children of the ungodly will not put forth many branches
 1 Ma 13 :37   and the palm branch which you sent
      13 :51   the Jews entered it with praise and palm branches
 2 Ma 10 :7   Therefore bearing ivy-wreathed wands and beautiful branches
      14 :4   some of the customary olive branches from the temple

BRAND   1
 3 Ma 2 :29   are also to be branded on their bodies by fire

BRANDISH   1
 2 Ma 11 :8   clothed in white and brandishing weapons of gold

BRANDISHING   1
 2 Ma 5 :3   brandishing of shields, massing of spears

BRASS   8 = 0.005 %
 Bel 14 :7   for this is but clay inside and brass outside
 1 Ma 6 :35   and with brass helmets on their heads
       6 :39   When the sun shone upon the shields of gold and brass
 1 Es 1 :12   and they boiled the sacrifices in brass pots and cauldrons
       1 :40   and bound him with a chain of brass
 2 Es 7 :55   Say to her, You produce gold and silver and brass
       7 :56   but silver is more abundant than gold, and brass than silver
       7 :56   and iron than brass, and lead than iron, and clay than lead

BRAVE   14 = 0.009 %
 Tob 7 :18   Be brave, my child
       7 :18   Be brave, my daughter
 Sir 19 :10   Be brave ! It will not make you burst !
 1 Ma 5 :56   heard of their brave deeds
       5 :61   because, thinking to do a brave deed
       5 :67   On that day some priests, who wished to do a brave deed
       8 :2   and of the brave deeds which they were doing among the Gauls
       9 :22   and the brave deeds that he did, and his greatness
      10 :15   of the brave deeds that they had done
      16 :23   and the brave deeds he did
 2 Ma 13 :15   and with a picked force of the bravest young men
      15 :11   as with the inspiration of brave words
 4 Ma 15 :10   For they were righteous and self-controlled and brave and
               magnanimous
      17 :24   and this made them brave and courageous

BRAVELY   6 = 0.004 %
 1 Ma 9 :10   If our time has come, let us die bravely for our brethren
 2 Ma 10 :35   bravely stormed the wall
      14 :43   He bravely ran up on the wall
      15 :17   but to attack bravely, and to decide the matter
 3 Ma 1 :4   to defend themselves and their children and wives bravely
 2 Es 10 :15   and bear bravely the troubles that have come upon you

BRAVERY   1
 4 Ma 1 :8   but I can demonstrate it best from the noble bravery

BRAZIER   3 = 0.002 %
 4 Ma 8 :13   braziers and thumbscrews an iron claws and wedges and bellows
      12 :10   Running to the nearest of the braziers
      12 :19   he flung himself into the braziers and so ended his life

BREAD   29 = 0.019 %
 Tob 1 :17   I would give my bread to the hungry
       4 :16   Give of your bread to the hungry
       4 :17   Place your bread on the grave of the righteous
 Jud 10 :5   and a cake of dried fruit and fine bread
 Wis 16 :20   with bread ready to eat, providing every pleasure
      16 :21   and the bread, ministering to the desire of the one who took it
 Sir 10 :27   than one who goes about boasting, but lacks bread
      12 :5   hold back his bread, and do not give it to him
      14 :10   A stingy man's eye begrudges bread
      15 :3   She will feed him with the bread of understanding
      20 :16   those who eat my bread speak unkindly
      23 :17   To a fornicator all bread tastes sweet
      29 :21   The essentials for life are water and bread and clothing
      33 :24   bread and discipline and work for a servant
      34 :21   The bread of the needy is the life of the poor
      45 :20   he prepared bread of first fruits in abundance
 Bel 14 :33   He had boiled pottage and had broken bread into a bowl
 1 Ma 1 :22   He took also the table for the bread of the Presence
       4 :51   They placed the bread on the table and hung up the curtains
 2 Ma 10 :3   and set out the bread of the Presence
 1 Es 1 :10   properly arrayed and having the unleavened bread
       1 :19   kept the passover and the feast of unleavened bread 7 days
       7 :14   And they kept the feast of unleavened bread 7 days
       9 :2   and he did not eat bread or drink water
 2 Es 1 :19   you ate the bread of angels
       5 :18   Rise therefore and eat some bread
      14 :42   and ate their bread at night
      15 :19   because of hunger for bread
      15 :58   and they shall eat their own flesh in hunger for bread

BREADTH   3 = 0.002 %
 Jud 7 :3   and they spread out in breadth over Dothan as far as Balbaim
 Sir 1 :3   The height of heaven, the breadth of the earth
 1 Es 6 :25   its height to be 60 cubits and its breadth 60 cubits

BREAK, verb   34 = 0.022 %
 Jud 7 :1   to break camp and move against Bethulia
       8 :30   and made us take an oath which we cannot break
       9 :8   Break their strength by thy might
 Sir 13 :2   The pot will strike against it, and will itself be broken
      23 :18   A man who breaks his marriage vows says to himself
      35 :18   and breaks the sceptres of the unrighteous
      43 :15   and the hailstones are broken in pieces
 L Jr 6 :17   For just as one's dish is useless when it is broken
       6 :43   and her cord was not broken
 P Az 11   and do not break thy covenant
      21   and let their strength be broken
      25   and it broke through and burned those of the Chaldeans
 Bel 14 :33   He had boiled pottage and had broken bread into a bowl
 1 Ma 6 :62   he broke the oath he had sworn
      11 :53   But he broke his word about all that he had promised
      12 :32   Then he broke camp and went to Damascus
      13 :19   but Trypho broke his word and did not release Jonathan
      15 :27   and he broke all the agreements
 2 Ma 9 :11   Then it was that, broken in spirit
      10 :28   Just as dawn was breaking, the 2 armies joined battle
      10 :36   Others broke open the gates and let in the rest of the force
 1 Es 1 :48   he broke his oath and rebelled
       9 :7   You have broken the law and married foreign women
 3 Ma 2 :20   and broken in spirit
       6 :5   you, O Lord, broke in pieces
 4 Ma 2 :11   so that one rebukes her when she breaks the law
       5 :3   they were to be broken on the wheel and killed
       5 :33   as to break the ancestral law by my own act
       7 :5   our father Eleazar broke the maddening waves of the emotions
       9 :14   and though broken in every member
       9 :25   the saintly youth broke the thread of life
      10 :6   and breaking his fingers and arms and legs and elbows
      10 :7   Since they were not able in any way to break his spirit
      11 :18   his back was broken, and he was roasted from underneath

BREAK down   2
 1 Es 1 :55   and broke down the walls of Jerusalem
 2 Es 15 :61   And you shall be broken down by them like stubble

BREAK off   3 = 0.002 %
 Wis 4 :5   The branches will be broken off before they come to maturity
 Sir 22 :20   and one who reviles a friend will break off the friendship
 2 Es 10 :5   Then I broke off the reflections with which I was still engaged

BREAK out
3 = 0.002 %

Sir **48**:10	to calm the wrath of God before it breaks out in fury
L Jr **6**:55	When fire breaks out in a temple
2 Es **5**:8	and fire shall often break out

BREAST
7 = 0.005 %

2 Ma **3**:19	Women, girded with sackcloth under their breasts
6:10	with their babies hung at their breasts
3 Ma **5**:49	and others with babies at their breasts
5:50	removing the babies from their breasts
2 Es **8**:10	that is, from the breasts
8:10	which is the fruit of the breasts
14:40	and wisdom increased in my breast

BREASTPLATE
4 = 0.003 %

Wis **5**:18	he will put on righteousness as a breastplate
Sir **43**:20	and the water puts it on like a breastplate
1 Ma **3**:3	like a giant he put on his breastplate
6:2	breastplates, and weapons

BREATH
21 = 0.014 %

Jud **7**:27	or see our wives and children draw their last breath
Wis **2**:2	because the breath in our nostrils is smoke
7:25	For she is a breath of the power of God
11:18	or such as breathe out fiery breath
11:20	men could fall at a single breath when pursued by justice
11:20	and scattered by the breath of thy power
15:11	nor nostrils with which to draw breath
Sir **33**:20	While you are still alive and have breath in you
38:28	the breath of the fire melts his flesh
L Jr **6**:25	but there is no breath in them
2 Ma **3**:31	to one who was lying quite at his last breath
7:9	And when he was at his last breath, he said
7:22	It was not I who gave you life and breath
7:23	will in his mercy give life and breath back to you again
2 Es **3**:5	and thou didst breathe into him the breath of life
7:29	and all who draw human breath
13:10	and from his lips a flaming breath
13:11	the stream of fire and the flaming breath and the great storm
16:61	and gave him breath and life and understanding
4 Ma **6**:11	and gasping heavily for breath
11:11	In this condition, gasping for breath and in anguish of body

BREATHE
7 = 0.005 %

Wis **7**:3	And when I was born, I began to breathe the common air
15:11	and breathed into him a living spirit
Sir **31**:19	He does not breathe heavily upon his bed
2 Ma **7**:5	the king ordered them to take him to the fire, still breathing
9:7	breathing fire in his rage against the Jews
2 Es **3**:5	and thou didst breathe into him the breath of life
4 Ma **15**:18	When the first-born breathed his last it did not turn you aside

BREATHE out
2

Wis **11**:18	or such as breathe out fiery breath
Sir **43**:4	it breathes out fiery vapours

BREECH
1

Sir **45**:8	the linen breeches, the long robe, and the ephod

BREED
1

4 Ma **11**:15	Since to this end we were born and bred

BREVITY
1

2 Ma **2**:31	should be allowed to strive for brevity of expression

BRIBE, subst.
2

Sir **35**:12	Do not offer him a bribe, for he will not accept it
2 Ma **4**:45	promised a substantial bribe to Ptolemy son of Dorymenes

BRIBE, verb
2

2 Ma **10**:20	were bribed by some of those who were in the towers
3 Ma **4**:19	charging that they had been bribed

BRIBERY
1

Sir **40**:12	All bribery and injustice will be blotted out

BRICK
1

Jud **5**:11	he took advantage of them and set them to making bricks

BRIDAL
5 = 0.003 %

Tob **6**:13	and that each died in the bridal chamber
6:16	When you enter the bridal chamber
1 Ma **1**:27	she who sat in the bridal chamber was mourning
3 Ma **1**:19	abandoned the bridal chambers prepared for wedded union
4:6	And young women who had just entered the bridal chamber

BRIDE
3 = 0.002 %

Wis **8**:2	and I desired to take her for my bride
Bar **2**:23	the voice of the bridegroom and the voice of the bride
1 Ma **9**:37	and are conducting the bride

BRIDEGROOM
5 = 0.003 %

Bar **2**:23	the voice of the bridegroom and the voice of the bride
1 Ma **1**:27	Every bridegroom took up the lament
9:39	and the bridegroom came out
2 Es **16**:33	Virgins shall mourn because they have no bridegrooms
16:34	Their bridegrooms shall be killed in war

BRIDLE, subst.
2

2 Ma **10**:29	5 resplendent men on horses with golden bridles
1 Es **3**:6	and have a chariot with gold bridles

BRIDLE, verb
1

4 Ma **1**:35	and all the impulses of the body are bridled by reason

BRIEF
6 = 0.004 %

Wis **15**:9	or that his life is brief
2 Ma **6**:25	for the sake of living a brief moment longer
7:36	For our brothers after enduring a brief suffering
10:10	and will give a brief summary
2 Es **12**:2	and their reign was brief and full of tumult
12:30	this was the reign which was brief and full of tumult

BRIEFLY
2

2 Ma **6**:17	we must go on briefly with the story
3 Ma **4**:14	not for the hard labour that has been briefly mentioned before

BRIER
1

2 Es **16**:32	and its fields shall be for briers

BRIGHT
3 = 0.002 %

Sir **17**:31	What is brighter than the sun ?
23:19	are 10,000 times brighter than the sun
43:4	and with bright beams it blinds the eyes

BRIGHTNESS
3 = 0.002 %

Sir **43**:11	exceedingly beautiful in its brightness
2 Es **6**:45	On the 4th day thou didst command the brightness of the sun
7:42	or noon or night, or dawn or shining or brightness or light

BRILLIANCE
1

2 Es **10**:50	has shown you the brilliance of her glory

BRILLIANT
2

Wis **17**:5	nor did the brilliant flames of the stars
17:20	For the whole world was illumined with brilliant light

BRING
157 = 0.102 %

Tob **2**:2	Go and bring whatever poor man of our brethren you may find
6:14	and bring the lives of my father and mother to the grave
7:1	and she brought them into the house
8:17	and bring their lives to fulfilment
9:2	and bring him to the wedding feast
11:17	Blessed is God who has brought you to us
12:12	I brought a reminder of your prayer before the Holy One
14:10	how he brought him from light into darkness
Jud **6**:14	and they untied him and brought him into Bethulia
8:22	all this he will bring upon our heads among the Gentiles
8:23	For our slavery will not bring us into favour
10:17	and they brought them to the tent of Holofernes
11:2	but they have brought all this on themselves
11:22	to lend strength to our hands and to bring destruction
12:2	from the things I have brought with me
12:5	Then the servants of Holofernes brought her into the tent
13:17	who hast brought into contempt this day
13:20	when our nation was brought low
14:5	But before you do all this, bring Achior the Ammonite to me
14:18	One Hebrew woman has brought disgrace
16:3	and brought me into his camp, in the midst of the people
Ad E **11**:1	and Ptolemy his son brought to Egypt the preceding Letter of Purim
11:4	had brought from Jerusalem with Jeconiah king of Judea
13:4	cannot be brought about
14:18	since the day that I was brought here until now
Wis **5**:8	And what good has our boasted wealth brought us ?
6:19	and immortality brings one near to God
10:14	until she brought him the sceptre of a kingdom
10:18	She brought them over the Red Sea
Sir **1**:30	and thus bring dishonour upon yourself
2:4	Accept whatever is brought upon you
4:17	she will bring fear and cowardice upon him
4:20	and do not bring shame on yourself
4:21	For there is a shame which brings sin
6:12	but if you are brought low he will turn against you
10:13	Therefore the Lord brought upon them
11:29	Do not bring every man into your home

	17:23	and he will bring their recompense on their heads
	20:10	and there is a gift that brings a double return
	20:26	The disposition of a liar brings disgrace
	22:4	but one who acts shamefully brings grief to her father
	23:24	She herself will be brought before the assembly
	33:12	and some of them he made holy and brought near to himself
	33:12	but some of them he cursed and brought low
	33:22	bring no stain upon your honour
	37:30	for overeating brings sickness, and gluttony leads to nausea
	42:14	and it is a woman who brings shame and disgrace
	46:8	to bring them into their inheritance, into a land flowing with milk and honey
	47:19	and through your body you were brought into subjection
	47:20	so that you brought wrath upon your children
	48:2	He brought a famine upon them
	48:12	and no one brought him into subjection
	48:17	and brought water into the midst of it
Bar	1:9	and brought them to Babylon
	1:19	From the day when the Lord brought our fathers
	1:20	when he brought our fathers out of the land of Egypt
	2:5	They were brought low and not raised up
	2:9	and the Lord has brought them upon us
	2:11	who didst bring thy people out of the land of Egypt
	2:19	that we bring before thee our prayer for mercy
	2:24	would be brought out of their graves
	2:34	I will bring them again into the land
	4:9	God has brought great sorrow upon me
	4:10	which the Everlasting brought upon them
	4:14	which the Everlasting brought upon them
	4:15	For he brought against them a nation from afar
	4:18	For he who brought these calamities upon you
	4:27	for you will be remembered by him who brought this upon you
	4:29	For he who brought these calamities upon you
	4:29	will bring you everlasting joy with your salvation
L Jr	6:41	they bring him and pray Bel that the man may speak
P Az	5	in all that thou hast brought upon us and upon Jerusalem
	5	for in truth and justice thou hast brought all this upon us
	8	So all that thou hast brought upon us
	14	and are brought low this day in all the world
Sus	13:17	Bring me oil and ointments
	13:18	to bring what they had been commanded
	13:56	Then he put him aside, and commanded them to bring the other
Bel	14:14	Then Daniel ordered his servants to bring ashes
1 Ma	3:49	They also brought the garments of the priesthood
	4:45	lest it bring reproach upon them
	4:49	They made new holy vessels, and brought the lampstand
	7:2	the army seized Antiochus and Lysias to bring them to him
	7:6	And they brought to the king this accusation
	7:7	which Judas has brought upon us and upon the land of the king
	7:25	and brought wicked charges against them
	7:47	and brought them and displayed them just outside Jerusalem
	9:26	and brought them to Bacchides
	10:63	and proclaim that no one is to bring charges against him
	13:32	and he brought great calamity upon the land
	14:29	and they brought great glory to their nation
	15:18	and have brought a gold shield weighing a 1,000 minas
2 Ma	1:4	and may he bring peace
	1:17	Blessed in every way be our God, who has brought judgment
	1:20	he ordered them to dip it out and bring it
	2:5	and he brought there the tent and the ark
	3:18	because the holy place was about to be brought into contempt
	3:39	watches over that place himself and brings it aid
	4:43	Charges were brought against Menelaus about this incident
	6:21	and privately urged him to bring meat of his own providing
	7:38	to bring to an end the wrath of the Almighty
	8:34	who had brought the 1,000 merchants to buy the Jews
	11:18	that needed to be brought before him
	14:41	they ordered that fire be brought and the doors burned
1 Es	1:52	to bring against them the kings of the Chaldeans
	4:5	if they win the victory, they bring everything to the king
	4:6	and bring some to the king
	4:17	they bring men glory
	4:22	and bring everything and give it to women ?
	4:48	to bring cedar timber from Lebanon to Jerusalem
	5:55	to bring cedar logs from Lebanon
	5:69	who brought us here
	8:47	they brought us competent men of the sons of Mahli
	8:80	but he brought us into favour
	9:17	were brought to an end
	9:39	to bring the law of Moses
	9:40	So Ezra the chief priest brought the law
3 Ma	1:8	to greet him, to bring him gifts of welcome
	1:26	determined to bring the aforesaid plan to a conclusion
	2:4	whom you destroyed by bringing upon them a boundless flood
	3:14	it was brought to conclusion, according to plan
	4:9	They were brought on board like wild animals
	4:11	When these men had been brought to the place called Schedia
	5:45	Now when the beasts had been brought virtually
	6:17	and brought an uncontrollable terror upon the army
	7:20	since at the king's command they had been brought

2 Es	1:7	Was it not I who brought them out of the land of Egypt
	1:13	Surely it was I who brought you through the sea
	2:1	Thus says the Lord : I brought this people out of bondage
	2:6	that you may bring confusion upon them
	2:6	and bring their mother to ruin
	2:31	because I will bring them out of the hiding places of the earth
	3:9	thou didst bring the flood upon the inhabitants of the world
	3:17	thou didst bring them to Mount Sinai
	4:27	For it will not be able to bring the things
	7:47	And now I see that the world to come will bring delight to few
	7:48	and has brought us into corruption and the ways of death
	7:119	but we have done deeds that bring death ?
	8:31	in ways that bring death
	10:28	For it was he who brought me into this overpowering bewilderment
	12:4	Behold, you have brought this upon me
	13:13	and some were bringing others as offerings
	13:23	He who brings the peril at that time
	15:5	I bring evils upon the world
	15:12	that the Lord will bring upon it
	15:49	and bring you to destruction and death
4 Ma	1:9	All of these, by despising sufferings that bring death
	3:14	and from it boldly brought the king a drink
	5:4	was brought before the king
	6:24	the guards brought him to the fire
	8:2	that others of the Hebrew captives be brought
	8:3	were brought before him along with their aged mother
	8:18	and venture upon a disobedience that brings death ?
	10:8	They immediately brought him to the wheel
	11:23	and I myself will bring a great avenger upon you
	13:20	they were brought to the light of day
	18:20	brought those 7 sons of the daughter of Abraham to the catapult

BRING away   1
L Jr	6:3	after that I will bring you away from there in peace

BRING back   11 = 0.007 %
Tob	10:12	The Lord of heaven bring you back safely, dear brother
	12:2	to give him half of what I have brought back
	12:5	Take half of all that you 2 have brought back
	14:5	and bring them back into their land
Jud	11:14	to bring back to them permission from the senate
Wis	16:14	but he cannot bring back the departed spirit
Bar	5:6	but God will bring them back to you
1 Ma	9:58	So now let us bring Bacchides back
2 Ma	12:39	and to bring them back to lie with their kinsmen
1 Es	1:31	and after he was brought back to Jerusalem he died
	4:24	he brings it back to the woman he loves

BRING down   6 = 0.004 %
Tob	3:10	and I shall bring his old age down in sorrow to the grave
Jud	9:8	and bring down their power in thy anger
Sir	48:3	and also 3 times brought down fire
	48:6	who brought kings down to destruction
Bar	3:29	and brought her down from the clouds ?
2 Ma	9:8	was brought down to earth and carried in a litter

BRING forth   17 = 0.011 %
Wis	19:10	the earth brought forth gnats
Sir	23:23	and bring children by another man
	45:1	From his descendants the Lord brought forth a man of mercy
2 Es	3:20	so that thy law might bring forth fruit in them
	5:8	and menstruous women shall bring forth monsters
	5:37	and bring forth for me the winds shut up in them
	5:49	For as an infant does not bring forth
	5:49	and a woman who has become old does not bring forth any longer
	6:40	that a ray of light be brought forth from thy treasuries
	6:47	to bring forth living creatures, birds, and fishes
	6:53	to bring forth before thee cattle, beasts, and creeping things
	7:62	what have you brought forth
	9:31	and it shall bring forth fruit in you
	10:12	which I brought forth in pain and bore in sorrow
	10:14	then I say to you, As you brought forth in sorrow
	11:42	you have destroyed the dwellings of those who brought forth fruit
	16:32	and its roads and all its paths shall bring forth thorns

BRING forward   7 = 0.005 %
Wis	18:21	he brought forward the shield of his ministry
1 Ma	10:82	Then Simon brought forward his force
2 Ma	7:7	they brought forward the 2nd for their sport
	7:15	Next they brought forward the 5th and maltreated him
	7:18	After him they brought forward the 6th
4 Ma	8:12	he ordered the instruments of torture to be brought forward
	9:11	Then at his command the guards brought forward the eldest

BRING in   5 = 0.003 %
Jud	12:1	Then he commanded them to bring her in
2 Ma	6:4	and besides brought in things for sacrifice that were unfit

	6:10	For example, 2 women were brought in
1 Es	9:18	Of the priests those who were brought in
4 Ma	9:26	the guards brought in the next eldest

BRING on   2

Wis	1:12	nor bring on destruction by the works of your hands
Sir	30:24	and anxiety brings on old age too soon

BRING out   5 = 0.003 %

Tob	9:5	and Gabael brought out the money bags with their seals intact
1 Es	2:10	Cyrus the king also brought out the holy vessels of the Lord
	2:11	When Cyrus king of the Persians brought these out
2 Es	2:16	and will bring them out from their tombs
	15:11	but I will bring them out with a mighty hand

BRING up   22 = 0.014 %

Tob	13:2	he leads down to Hades, and brings up again
Sir	17:18	Whom, being his first-born, he brings up with discipline
	22:9	Children who are brought up in a good life
Bar	4:8	You forgot the everlasting God, who brought you up
1 Ma	1:6	who had been brought up with him from youth
	6:15	and bring him up to be king
	6:17	Lysias had brought him up as a boy
	6:55	had appointed to bring up Antiochus his son to be king
	11:39	who was bringing up Antiochus, the young son of Alexander
	13:43	He made a siege engine, brought it up to the city
2 Ma	7:27	and have reared you and brought you up
1 Es	1:38	and brought him up out of Egypt
	4:16	and women brought up the very men who plant the vineyards
	4:20	A man leaves his own father who brought him up
3 Ma	6:7	you brought up to the light unharmed
2 Es	2:3	I brought you up with gladness
	2:15	bring them up with gladness, as does the dove
	8:12	Thou hast brought him up in thy righteousness
	9:46	And I brought him up with much care
	10:47	And as for her telling you that she brought him up with much care
4 Ma	10:2	and that I was brought up on the same teachings ?
	13:24	and brought up in right living

BROAD   3 = 0.002 %

2 Es	7:3	so that it is broad and vast
	7:5	how can he come to the broad part
	7:13	But the entrances of the greater world are broad and safe

BROKEN   1

Sir	21:14	The mind of a fool is like a broken jar

BRONZE   7 = 0.005 %

Sir	28:20	and its fetters are fetters of bronze
1 Ma	8:22	which they wrote in reply, on bronze tablets
	14:18	they wrote to him on bronze tablets
	14:27	So they made a record on bronze tablets
	14:48	to inscribe this decree upon bronze tablets
1 Es	8:57	and 12 bronze vessels of fine bronze

BROOD   2

Wis	4:3	But the prolific brood of the ungodly will be of no use
2 Es	1:30	I gathered you as a hen gathers her brood under her wings

BROOK   3 = 0.002 %

Jud	2:8	and every brook and river shall be filled with their dead, and overflow
	2:24	and destroyed all the hilltop cities along the brook Abron
	7:18	toward Acraba, which is near Chusi beside the brook Mochmur

BROTHEL   1

L Jr	6:11	and even give some of it to the harlots in the brothel

BROTHER   210 = 0.137 %

Tob	1:3	and I performed many acts of charity to my brethren
	1:10	all my brethren and my relatives ate the food of the Gentiles
	1:14	in trust with Gabael, the brother of Gabrias
	1:16	I performed many acts of charity to my brethren
	1:21	and he appointed Ahikar, the son of my brother Anael
	2:2	Go and bring whatever poor man of our brethren you may find
	4:12	all took wives from among their brethren
	4:13	So now, my son, love your brethren
	4:13	and in your heart do not disdain your brethren
	5:6	and I have stayed with our brother Gabael
	5:10	My brother, to what tribe and family do you belong ? Tell me
	5:11	I should like to know, my brother, your people and your name
	5:13	Then Tobit said to him, You are welcome, my brother
	5:13	They did not go astray in the error of our brethren
	5:13	My brother, you come of good stock
	6:6	Then the young man said to the angel, Brother Azarias
	6:10	Brother, today we shall stay with Raguel
	6:13	Then the young man said to the angel, Brother Azarias
	6:15	Now listen to me, brother, for she will become your wife
	7:3	And Raguel asked them, Where are you from, brethren ?

	7:4	So he said to them, Do you know our brother Tobit ?
	7:8	Then Tobias said to Raphael, Brother Azarias
	9:2	Brother Azarias, take a servant and 2 camels with you
	10:12	The Lord of heaven bring you back safely, dear brother
	11:2	Are you not aware, brother, of how you left your father ?
	11:17	So there was rejoicing among all his brethren in Nineveh
	14:4	Our brethren will be scattered over the earth from the good land
	14:7	will rejoice, showing mercy to our brethren
Jud	7:30	And Uzziah said to them, Have courage, my brothers !
	8:14	No, my brethren, do not provoke the Lord our God to anger
	8:22	And the slaughter of our brethren
	8:24	Now therefore, brethren
	8:24	let us set an example to our brethren
	8:26	his mother's brother
	14:1	Then Judith said to them, Listen to me, my brethren
Ad E	15:9	I am your brother. Take courage
Wis	10:3	he perished because in rage he slew his brother
	10:10	When a righteous man fled from his brother's wrath
Sir	7:12	Do not devise a lie against your brother
	7:18	or a real brother for the gold of Ophir
	10:20	Among brothers their leader is worthy of honour
	25:1	agreement between brothers, friendship between neighbours
	29:10	Lose your silver for the sake of a brother or a friend
	29:27	my brother has come to stay with me
	33:19	To son or wife, to brother or friend
	33:31	If you have a servant, treat him as a brother
	40:24	Brothers and help are for a time of trouble
	45:6	He exalted Aaron, the brother of Moses
	50:1	The leader of his brethren and the pride of his people
	50:12	with a garland of brethren around him
1 Ma	2:17	and supported by sons and brothers
	2:20	yet I and my sons and my brothers will live
	2:40	If we all do as our brethren have done
	2:41	let us not all die as our brethren died
	2:65	Now behold, I know that Simeon your brother is wise in counsel
	3:2	All his brothers and all who had joined his father helped him
	3:25	Then Judas and his brothers began to be feared
	3:42	Now Judas and his brothers saw that misfortunes had increased
	4:36	Then said Judas and his brothers
	4:59	Then Judas and his brothers and all the assembly of Israel
	5:10	and sent to Judas and his brothers a letter which said
	5:13	and all our brethren who were in the land of Tob have been killed
	5:16	to determine what they should do for their brethren
	5:17	Then Judas said to Simon his brother
	5:17	Choose your men and go and rescue your brethren in Galilee
	5:17	I and Jonathan my brother will go to Gilead
	5:24	Judas maccabeus and Jonathan his brother crossed the Jordan
	5:25	to their brethren in Gilead :
	5:32	Fight today for your brethren !
	5:55	and Simon his brother was in Galilee before Ptolemais
	5:61	they did not listen to Judas and his brothers
	5:63	The man Judas and his brothers were greatly honoured
	5:65	Then Judas and his brothers went forth
	6:22	and to avenge our brethren ?
	7:6	Judas and his brothers have destroyed all your friends
	7:10	and he sent messengers to Judas and his brothers
	7:27	and treacherously sent to Judas and his brothers
	8:20	Judas, who is also called Maccabeus, and his brothers
	9:9	and let us come back with our brethren and fight them
	9:10	If our time has come, let us die bravely for our brethren
	9:19	Then Jonathan and Simon took Judas their brother
	9:29	Since the death of your brother Judas
	9:31	and took the place of Judas his brother
	9:33	But Jonathan and Simon his brother
	9:35	And Jonathan sent his brother as leader of the multitude
	9:37	and Simon his brother
	9:38	And they remembered the blood of John their brother
	9:39	with his friends and his brothers
	9:42	And when they had fully avenged the blood of their brother
	9:65	But Jonathan left Simon his brother in the city
	9:66	He struck down Odomera and his brothers
	10:5	and to his brothers and his nation
	10:15	that Jonathan and his brothers had fought
	10:18	King Alexander to his brother Jonathan, greeting
	10:74	and Simon his brother met him to help him
	11:30	King Demetrius to Jonathan his brother
	11:59	Simon his brother he made governor
	11:64	but left his brother Simon in the country
	12:6	to their brethren the Spartans, greeting
	12:7	stating that you are our brethren
	12:11	as it is right and proper to remember brethren
	12:21	that they are brethren and are of the family of Abraham
	13:3	I and my brothers and the house of my father have done
	13:4	By reason of this all my brothers have perished
	13:5	for I am not better than my brothers
	13:8	in place of Judas and Jonathan your brother
	13:14	in place of Jonathan his brother
	13:15	that Jonathan your brother owed the royal treasury
	13:25	And Simon sent and took the bones of Jonathan his brother

	13:27	over the tomb of his father and his brothers
	13:28	for his father and mother and 4 brothers
	14:17	When they heard that Simon his brother
	14:18	and Jonathan his brothers
	14:20	and the rest of the Jewish people, our brethren, greeting
	14:26	For he and his brothers and the house of his father have stood firm
	14:29	a priest of the sons of Joarib, and his brothers
	14:40	as friends and allies and brethren
	16:2	and said to them : I and my brothers and the house of my father
	16:3	Take my place and my brother's
	16:9	At that time Judas the brother of John was wounded
	16:21	that his father and brothers had perished
2 Ma	1:1	The Jewish brethren in Jerusalem
	1:1	To their Jewish brethren in Egypt, greeting, and good peace
	2:19	The story of Judas Maccabeus and his brothers
	4:7	Jason the brother of Onias
	4:23	the brother of the previously mentioned Simon
	4:26	So Jason, who after supplanting his own brother
	4:29	Menelaus left his own brother Lysimachus
	7:1	It happened also that 7 brothers and their mother were arrested
	7:4	while the rest of the brothers and the mother looked on
	7:5	but the brothers and their mother encouraged one another to die nobly
	7:7	After the first brother had died in this way
	7:8	as the first brother had done
	7:24	The youngest brother being still alive
	7:29	Do not fear this butcher, but prove worthy of your brothers
	7:29	I may get you back again with your brothers
	7:36	For our brothers after enduring a brief suffering
	7:37	I, like my brothers, give up body and life
	7:38	and through me and my brothers
	8:22	He appointed his brothers, also
	10:21	of having sold their brethren for money
	10:37	and his brother Chaereas, and Apollophanes
	11:7	to aid their brethren
	11:22	King Antiochus to his brother Lysias, greeting
	12:6	attacked the murderers of his brethren
	12:24	and the brothers of some
	12:25	they let him go, for the sake of saving their brethren
	14:17	Simon, the brother of Judas, had encountered Nicanor
	15:14	This is a man who loves the brethren
	15:18	and also for brethren and relatives
1 Es	1:5	who minister before your brethren the people of Israel
	1:6	and prepare the sacrifices for your brethren
	1:9	And Jeconiah and Shemaiah and Nethanel his brother
	1:13	and for their brethren the priests, the sons of Aaron
	1:14	and for their brethren the priests, the sons of Aaron
	1:16	for their brethren the Levites prepared the passover for them
	1:37	And the king of Egypt made Jehoiakim his brother
	1:38	and seized his brother Zarius
	3:22	When men drink they forget to be friendly with friends and brothers
	4:61	and went to Babylon and told this to all his brethren
	5:3	and all their brethren were making merry
	5:56	together with their brethren and the Levitical priests
	5:58	And Jeshua arose, and his sons and brethren
	5:58	and Kadmiel his brother and the sons of Jeshua Emadabun
	5:58	with their sons and brethren, all the Levites
	7:12	and for their brethren the priests and for themselves
	8:16	And whatever you and your brethren are minded to do
	8:46	and ordered them to tell Iddo and his brethren
	8:48	also Hashabiah and Annunus and Jeshaiah his brother
	8:77	we with our brethren and our kings
	9:19	of the sons of Jeshua the son of Jozadak and his brethren
Ps 151	1	I was small among my brothers, and youngest in my father's house
	151:5	My brothers were handsome and tall
3 Ma	4:12	to lament bitterly the ignoble misfortune of their brothers
2 Es	7:103	brothers for brothers, relatives for their kinsmen
	12:11	to your brother Daniel
	14:33	and your brethren are farther in the interior
4 Ma	1:8	Eleazar and the 7 brothers and their mother
	4:16	and appointed Onias's brother Jason as high priest
	8:3	When the tyrant had given these orders, 7 brothers
	8:5	and greatly respect the beauty and the number of such brothers
	8:19	O men and brothers, should we not fear the instruments of torture
	9:23	Imitate me, brothers, he said
	10:3	that binds me to my brothers
	10:12	When he also had died in a manner worthy of his brothers
	10:13	to the same insanity as your brothers
	10:15	No, by the blessed death of my brothers
	10:16	that I am a brother to those who have just been tortured
	11:14	he said, I am younger in age than my brothers
	11:20	O contest befitting holiness, in which so many of us brothers
	11:22	I also, equipped with nobility, will die with my brothers
	12:2	Even though the tyrant had been fearfully reproached by the brothers
	12:3	You see the result of your brothers'stupidity
	12:16	I do not desert the excellent example of my brothers
	13:1	Since, then, the 7 brothers despised sufferings even unto death
	13:4	for the brothers mastered both emotions and pains
	13:9	Brothers, let us die like brothers for the sake of the law
	13:11	While one said, Courage, brothers
	13:18	Those who were left behind said to each of the brothers
	13:18	Do not put us to shame, brother
	13:18	or betray the brothers who have died before us
	13:20	There each of the brothers dwelt the same length of time
	13:23	the brothers were the more sympathetic to one another
	13:27	while watching their brothers being maltreated
	14:3	O sacred and harmonious concord of the 7 brothers
	14:7	O most holy 7, brothers in harmony !
	15:10	and loved their brothers and their mother
	17:13	and the brothers contended

BROTHERHOOD
		6 = 0.004 %
1 Ma	12:10	we have undertaken to send to renew our brotherhood
	12:17	concerning the renewal of our brotherhood
4 Ma	9:23	or renounce our courageous brotherhood
	10:15	I will not renounce our noble brotherhood
	13:19	You are not ignorant of the affection of brotherhood
	13:27	had augmented the affection of the brotherhood

BROTHERLY
		3 = 0.002 %
4 Ma	13:23	Therefore, when sympathy and brotherly affection had been so established
	13:26	they rendered their brotherly love more fervent
	14:1	but also mastered the emotions of brotherly love

BROTHERLY-LOVING
		1
4 Ma	13:21	From such embraces brotherly-loving souls are nourished

BRUISE
		1
Sir	23:10	will not lack bruises

BRUSH
		1
P Az	23	with naphtha, pitch, tow, and brush

BUCKET
		1
2 Es	6:56	and thou hast compared their abundance to a drop from a bucket

BUCKLE
		3 = 0.002 %
1 Ma	10:89	and he sent to him a golden buckle
	11:58	and dress in purple and wear a gold buckle
	14:44	or to be clothed in purple or put on a gold buckle

BUD, verb
		2
Sir	24:17	Like a vine I caused loveliness to bud
	39:13	and bud like a rose growing by a stream of water

BUFFET
		1
4 Ma	7:2	and though buffeted by the stormings of the tyrant

BUILD
		99 = 0.064 %
Tob	13:16	For Jerusalem will be built with sapphires and emeralds
	14:5	with a glorious building for all generations for ever
Jud	1:2	he is the king who built walls about Ecbatana
	1:3	at the gates he built towers
Wis	9:8	Thou gavest command to build a temple
	14:2	and wisdom was the craftsman who built it
Sir	21:8	A man who builds his house with other people's money
	34:23	When one builds and another tears down
	40:19	Children and the building of a city establish a man's name
	47:13	that he might build a house for his name
	48:17	and built pools for water
	49:7	and likewise to build and to plant
	49:12	in their days they built the house
1 Ma	1:14	So they built a gymnasium in Jerusalem
	1:47	to build altars and sacred precincts and shrines for idols
	1:54	They also built altars in the surrounding cities of Judah
	3:56	And he said to those who were building houses
	4:47	and built a new altar like the former one
	4:53	on the new altar of burnt offering which they had built
	5:1	that the altar had been built
	6:20	and he built siege towers and other engines of war
	6:31	and for many days they fought and built engines of war
	8:15	but they have built for themselves a senate chamber
	9:50	and built strong cities in Judea :
	10:11	to build the walls and encircle Mount Zion
	10:12	Then the foreigners who were in the strongholds that Bacchides had built fled
	11:20	and he built many engines of war to use against it
	12:35	and planned with them to build strongholds in Judea
	12:36	to build the walls of Jerusalem still higher
	12:38	And Simon built Adida in the Shephelah
	13:27	And Simon built a monument
	13:30	This is the tomb which he built in Modein
	13:38	and let the strongholds that you have built be your possession

	13:48	and built in it a house for himself
	14:36	who had built themselves a citadel
	14:37	and built the walls of Jerusalem higher
	15:7	and the strongholds which you have built and now hold
	16:9	until Cendebaeus reached Kedron, which he had built
	16:15	in the little stronghold called Dok, which he had built
	16:23	and the building of the walls which he built, and his achievements
2 Ma	1:18	when Nehemiah, who built the temple and the altar, offered sacrifices
	10:2	and they tore down the altars which had been built
	14:33	and I will build here a splendid temple to Dionysus
1 Es	1:3	in the house which Solomon the king, the son of David, had built
	2:4	and he has commanded me to build him a house at Jerusalem
	2:5	and build the house of the Lord of Israel
	2:8	to build the house in Jerusalem for the Lord
	2:18	and are building that rebellious and wicked city
	2:19	Now if this city is built and the walls finished
	2:20	And since the building of the temple is now going on
	2:24	that if this city is built and its walls finished
	2:28	to prevent these men from building the city
	2:30	And the building of the temple in Jerusalem ceased
	4:8	if he tells them to build, they build
	4:43	Remember the vow which you made to build Jerusalem
	4:45	You also vowed to build the temple
	4:47	and all who were going up with him to build Jerusalem
	4:48	and to help him build the city
	4:51	for the building of the temple until it was completed
	4:53	and that all who came from Babylonia to build the city
	4:55	until the day when the temple should be finished and Jerusalem built
	4:63	to go up and build Jerusalem and the temple
	5:53	though the temple of God was not yet built
	5:58	So the builders built the temple of the Lord
	5:63	came to the building of this one
	5:67	were building the temple for the Lord God of Israel
	5:68	We will build with you
	5:70	in building the house for the Lord our God
	5:71	for we alone will build it for the Lord of Israel
	5:72	cut off their supplies, and hindered their building
	5:73	they prevented the completion of the building
	5:73	And they were kept from building for 2 years
	6:2	and began to build the house of the Lord which is in Jerusalem
	6:4	By whose order are you building this house
	6:6	and they were not prevented from building
	6:9	building in the city of Jerusalem a great new house for the Lord
	6:11	At whose command are you building this house
	6:14	And the house was built many years ago
	6:22	and if it is found that the building
	6:24	King Cyrus ordered the building
	6:27	to build this house of the Lord on its site
	6:28	And I command that it be built completely
3 Ma	4:11	which had been built with a monstrous perimeter wall
2 Es	3:24	And thou didst command him to build a city for thy name
	5:25	and from all the cities that have been built
	7:6	Another example : There is a city built and set on a plain
	8:52	a city is built, rest is appointed, goodness is established
	9:24	but go into a field of flowers where no house has been built
	10:46	And after 3,000 years Solomon built the city
	10:51	where no house had been built
	10:53	where there was no foundation of any building
	10:54	for no work of man's building could endure in a place
	10:55	but go in and see the splendour and vastness of the building
	13:36	And Zion will come and be made manifest to all people, prepared and built
	16:42	and let him that builds a house be like one
4 Ma	14:15	protect their young by building on the housetops
	14:16	and the others, by building in precipitous chasms

BUILD up   4 = 0.003 %

1 Ma	12:37	So they gathered together to build up the city
	13:33	But Simon built up the strongholds of Judea
	15:39	and commanded him to build up Kedron and fortify its gates
	15:41	He built up Kedron and stationed there horsemen and troops

BUILDER   4 = 0.003 %

2 Ma	2:29	For as the master builder of a new house
1 Es	2:30	and began to hinder the builders
	5:58	So the builders built the temple of the Lord
	6:4	And who are the builders that are finishing these things ?

BUILDING   2

Jud	3:3	Behold, our buildings, and all our land
Sir	22:16	A wooden beam firmly bonded into a building

BUKKI   1

1 Es	8:2	son of Bukki, son of Abishua, son of Phinehas

BULL   7 = 0.005 %

Sir	6:2	lest your soul be torn in pieces like a bull
	38:25	and whose talk is about bulls ?
P Az	16	as though it were with burnt offerings of rams and bulls
1 Es	6:29	for sacrifices to the Lord, for bulls and rams and lambs
	7:7	100 bulls, 200 rams, 400 lambs
	8:14	both gold and silver for bulls and rams
	8:65	12 bulls for all Israel, 96 rams, 72 lambs

BULWARK   1

4 Ma	13:13	and let us use our bodies as a bulwark for the law

BURDEN, subst.   6 = 0.004 %

Wis	2:15	the very sight of him is a burden to us
Sir	21:16	A fool's narration is like a burden on a journey
	33:24	Fodder and a stick and burdens for an ass
1 Es	8:86	For thou, O Lord, didst lift the burden of our sins
2 Es	7:105	neither shall any one lay a burden on another
	14:14	cast away from you the burdens of man

BURDEN, verb   4 = 0.003 %

Wis	9:15	and this earthly tent burdens the thoughtful mind
Sir	3:27	A stubborn mind will be burdened by troubles
2 Es	3:21	For the first Adam, burdened with an evil heart
	7:68	and are full of sins and burdened with transgressions

BURDENSOME   1

Sir	8:15	lest he be burdensome to you

BURIAL   4 = 0.003 %

Sir	21:8	is like one who gathers stones for his burial mound
	38:16	and do not neglect his burial
2 Ma	13:7	without even burial in the earth
3 Ma	6:31	which had been prepared for their destruction and burial

BURLAP   1

Sir	40:4	to the one who is clothed in burlap

BURN, verb   66 = 0.043 %

Jud	2:26	and burned their tents and plundered their sheepfolds
	2:27	and burned all their fields
Wis	13:12	and burn the castoff pieces of his work to prepare his food
	16:19	it burned more intensely than fire
Sir	28:22	and they will not be burned in its flame
	28:23	it will burn among them and will not be put out
	43:4	but the sun burns the mountains 3 times as much
	45:14	His sacrifices shall be wholly burned
	48:1	and his word burned like a torch
Bar	1:2	and burned it with fire
L Jr	6:43	burning bran of incense
	6:55	but the gods will be burnt in 2 like beams
P Az	25	and it broke through and burned those of the Chaldeans
1 Ma	1:31	He plundered the city, burned it with fire
	1:55	and burned incense at the doors of the houses and in the streets
	1:56	and burned with fire
	2:24	When Mattathias saw it, he burned with zeal
	2:26	Thus he burned with zeal for the law
	3:5	he burned those who troubled his people
	4:20	and that the Jews were burning the camp
	4:38	and the gates burned
	4:50	Then they burned incense on the altar
	5:5	and burned with fire their towers and all who were in them
	5:28	then he seized all its spoils and burned it with fire
	5:35	and burned it with fire
	5:44	and burned the sacred precincts with fire
	5:65	and burned its towers round about
	5:68	and the graven images of their gods he burned with fire
	6:31	but the Jews sallied out and burned these with fire, and fought manfully
	10:84	But Jonathan burned Azotus and the surrounding towns
	10:84	and those who had taken refuge in it he burned with fire
	10:85	with those burned alive
	11:4	whom Jonathan had burned in the war
	11:61	So he besieged it and burned its suburbs with fire and plundered them
	12:29	for they saw the fires burning
	16:10	and John burned it with fire, and about 2,000 of them fell
2 Ma	1:8	and burned the gate and shed innocent blood
	1:33	had burned the materials of the sacrifice
	6:11	were betrayed to Philip and were all burned together
	8:33	they burned those who had set fire to the sacred gates
	10:3	and they burned incense and lighted lamps
	10:36	they kindled fires and burned the blasphemers alive
	12:6	He set fire to the harbour by night, and burned the boats
	14:41	they ordered that fire be brought and the doors burned
1 Es	1:55	And they burned the house of the Lord
	1:55	and burned their towers with fire
	4:45	which the Edomites burned
	6:16	and they pulled down the house, and burned it
3 Ma	3:29	is to be made unapproachable and burned with fire

	4:2	everywhere their hearts were burning
	5:43	and by burning to the ground the temple inaccessible to him
2 Es	7:61	they are set on fire and burn hotly, and are extinguished
	10:22	our priests have been burned to death
	12:3	and the whole body of the eagle was burned
	14:21	For thy law has been burned
	15:62	they shall burn with fire
	16:6	when once it has begun to burn ?
	16:53	for God will burn coals of fire on the head of him who says
4 Ma	3:15	But David, although he was burning with thirst
	5:30	not even if you gouge out my eyes and burn my entrails
	6:25	There they burned him with maliciously contrived instruments
	6:26	When he was now burned to his very bones and about to expire
	9:17	Cut my limbs, burn my flesh, and twist my joints
	11:19	and pierced his ribs so that his entrails were burned through
	15:14	This mother, who saw them tortured and burned one by one
	15:20	When you saw the flesh of children burned

BURN down   2

Tob	14:4	The house of God in it will be burned down
1 Ma	11:4	they showed him the temple of Dagon burned down

BURN up   6 = 0.004 %

Jud	6:4	We will burn them up
	16:5	He boasted that he would burn up my territory
Sir	23:16	will never cease until the fire burns him up
	43:21	He consumes the mountains and burns up the wilderness
1 Ma	7:35	then if I return safely I will burn up this house
2 Es	13:11	and burned them all up, so that suddenly

BURNING, subst., adj.   12 = 0.008 %

Jud	8:3	he was overcome by the burning heat
Sir	11:32	From a spark of fire come many burning coals
	23:16	The soul heated like a burning fire
	28:10	so will be the burning
	28:10	will be the burning
	43:3	and who can withstand its burning heat ?
	43:4	A man tending a furnace works in burning heat
P Az	66	and delivered us from the midst of the burning fiery furnace
2 Es	12:44	if we also had been consumed in the burning of Zion !
	16:68	For behold, the burning wrath of a great multitude is kindled over you
4 Ma	6:27	I am dying in burning torments for the sake of the law
	18:20	and in his burning rage

BURNT OFFERING   20 = 0.013 %

Jud	4:14	offered the continual burnt offerings
	16:16	and all fat for burnt offerings to thee is a very little thing
	16:18	they offered their burnt offerings
Wis	3:6	and like a sacrificial burnt offering he accepted them
Bar	1:10	so buy with the money burnt offerings and sin offerings
P Az	15	or leader, no burnt offering, or sacrifice, or oblation
	16	as though it were with burnt offerings of rams and bulls
1 Ma	1:45	to forbid burnt offerings and sacrifices
	1:54	upon the altar of burnt offering
	1:59	which was upon the altar of burnt offering
	4:44	about the altar of burnt offering, which had been profaned
	4:53	on the new altar of burnt offering which they had built
	4:56	and offered burnt offerings with gladness
	5:54	and offered burnt offerings
	7:33	to greet him peaceably and to show him the burnt offering
2 Ma	2:10	and consumed the whole burnt offerings
1 Es	4:52	for burnt offerings to be offered on the altar every day
	5:49	to offer burnt offerings upon it
	5:50	and burnt offerings to the Lord morning and evening
4 Ma	18:11	and Isaac who was offered as a burnt offering

BURST   2

Sir	19:10	Be brave ! It will not make you burst !
Bel	14:27	The dragon ate them, and burst open

BURST forth   1

Sir	1:23	and then joy will burst forth for him

BURY   27 = 0.018 %

Tob	1:17	I would bury him
	1:18	I buried them secretly
	1:19	and informed the king about me, that I was burying them
	2:7	and dug a grave and buried the body
	2:8	he once ran away, and here he is burying the dead again !
	2:9	On the same night I returned from burying him
	4:3	My son, when I die, bury me
	4:4	When she dies, bury her beside me in the same grave
	6:14	And they have no other son to bury them
	8:12	let us bury him without any one knowing about it
	12:12	and when you buried the dead
	14:6	and will bury their idols
	14:10	Bury me properly, and your mother with me
	14:12	And when Anna died he buried her with his father
Jud	8:3	So they buried him with his fathers

	16:23	and they buried her in the cave of her husband Manasseh
Wis	18:12	For the living were not sufficient even to bury them
Sir	44:14	Their bodies were buried in peace
1 Ma	2:70	and was buried in the tomb of his fathers at Modein
	7:17	and there was none to bury them
	9:19	and buried him in the tomb of their fathers at Modein
	13:23	and he was buried there
	13:25	and buried him in Modein, the city of his fathers
2 Ma	9:15	and the Jews, whom he had not considered worth burying
1 Es	1:31	and was buried in the tomb of his fathers
4 Ma	16:11	Nor when I die, shall I have any of my sons to bury me
	17:9	Here lie buried an aged priest and an aged woman and 7 sons

BUSH   4 = 0.003 %

L Jr	6:71	are like a thorn bush in a garden
1 Ma	4:38	In the courts they saw bushes sprung up as in a thicket
2 Es	14:1	behold, a voice came out of a bush opposite me
	14:3	I revealed myself in a bush and spoke to Moses

BUSHEL   1

Bel	14:3	and every day they spent on it 12 bushels of fine flour

BUSINESS   6 = 0.004 %

Sir	38:24	and he who has little business may become wise
2 Ma	4:23	and to complete the records of essential business
	15:5	and finish the king's business
3 Ma	3:10	and friends and business associates
2 Es	16:42	let him that does business be like one
	16:47	Those who conduct business, do it only to be plundered

BUSY, verb   2

Sir	8:8	but busy yourself with their maxims
	11:10	My son, do not busy yourself with many matters

BUSY, adj.   1

Wis	19:3	For while they were still busy at mourning

BUT*   877 = 0.571 %

BUTCHER   1

2 Ma	7:29	Do not fear this butcher, but prove worthy of your brothers

BUY   12 = 0.008 %

Sir	20:12	There is a man who buys much for a little
	27:2	so sin is wedged in between selling and buying
	33:30	because you have bought him with blood
Bar	1:10	so buy with the money burnt offerings and sin offerings
	3:30	and will buy her for pure gold ?
L Jr	6:25	They are bought at any cost
1 Ma	13:49	so that its garrison could neither buy nor sell
	13:49	to buy and sell
2 Ma	8:11	inviting them to buy Jewish slaves
	8:25	of those who had come to buy them as slaves
	8:34	who had brought the 1,000 merchants to buy the Jews
2 Es	16:41	let him that buys be like one who will lose

BUYER   2

Tob	1:13	and I was his buyer of provisions
Sir	37:11	with a merchant about barter or with a buyer about selling

BY, prep., adv.   723 = 0.471 %

BYWORD   3 = 0.002 %

Tob	3:4	thou madest us a byword of reproach
Wis	5:4	and made a byword of reproach – we fools !
Sir	42:11	a byword in the city and notorious among the people

C

CAGE   1

Sir	11:30	Like a decoy partridge in a cage

CAIN   1

4 Ma	18:11	He read to you about Abel slain by Cain

CAKE   2

Jud	10:5	and a cake of dried fruit and fine bread
Bel	14:27	and boiled them together and made cakes

CALAMITY   32 = 0.021 %

Ad E	16:5	and have been involved in irremediable calamities
Sir	2:2	and do not be hasty in time of calamity
	5:8	for it will not benefit you in the day of calamity
	11:24	and what calamity could happen to me in the future ?
	12:17	If calamity befalls you, you will find him there ahead of you
	23:11	for his house will be filled with calamities
	38:19	In calamity sorrow continues
	40:9	calamities, famine and affliction and plague

Bar	1:20	So to this day there have clung to us the calamities
	2:7	All those calamities with which the Lord threatened us have come upon us
	2:9	And the Lord has kept the calamities ready
	3:4	so that calamities have clung to us
	4:18	For he who brought these calamities upon you
	4:29	For he who brought these calamities upon you
L Jr	6:48	For when war or calamity comes upon them
	6:49	for they cannot save themselves from war or calamity ?
1 Ma	13:32	and he brought great calamity upon the land
2 Ma	6:12	Now I urge those who read this book not to be depressed by such calamities
	6:16	Though he disciplines us with calamities
	10:10	of the principal calamities of the wars
	14:14	thinking that the misfortunes and calamities of the Jews
2 Es	15:27	For now calamities have come upon the whole earth
	16:5	Calamities have been sent upon you
	16:8	The Lord God sends calamities, and who will drive them away ?
	16:14	Behold, calamities are sent forth
	16:16	so the calamities that are sent upon the earth shall not return
	16:18	the beginning of calamities, when all shall tremble
	16:18	when the calamities come ?
	16:21	and then the calamities shall spring up on the earth
	16:37	Behold, the calamities draw near, and are not delayed
	16:39	so the calamities will not delay in coming forth upon the earth
	16:40	and in the midst of the calamities be like strangers on the earth

CALEB 3 = 0.002 %

Sir	46:7	he and Caleb the son of Jephunneh :
	46:9	And the Lord gave Caleb strength
1 Ma	2:56	Caleb, because he testified in the assembly

CALF 4 = 0.003 %

Tob	1:5	used to sacrifice to the calf Baal
1 Es	1:7	30,000 lambs and kids, and 3,000 calves
	1:8	2,600 sheep and 300 calves
	1:9	gave the Levites for the passover 5,000 sheep and 700 calves

CALL, subst. 3 = 0.002 %

1 Ma	7:45	kept sounding the battle call on the trumpets
2 Ma	4:14	in the wrestling arena after the call to the discus
4 Ma	14:17	and warning them with their own calls

CALL*, verb 152 = 0.099 %

Tob	4:2	Why do I not call my son Tobias
	4:3	So he called him and said
	5:8	He said, Call him to me
	7:13	Then he called his daughter Sarah
	7:14	Next he called his wife Edna
	7:16	And Raguel called his wife Edna and said to her
	9:1	Then Tobias called Raphael and said to him
	12:1	Tobit then called his son Tobias and said to him
	12:5	So he called the angel and said to him
	12:6	Then the angel called the 2 of them privately
	14:3	When he had grown very old he called his son and grandsons
Jud	2:2	He called together all his officers and all his nobles
	2:4	Nebuchadnezzar king of the Assyrians called Holofernes
	2:14	and called together all the commanders, generals
	3:8	and all their tongues and tribes should call upon him as god
	5:2	So he called together all the princes of Moab
	6:16	They called together all the elders of the city
	7:28	We call to witness against you heaven and earth
	8:17	let us call upon him to help us
	10:2	and called her maid and went
	13:12	and called together the elders of the city
	16:2	exalt him, and call upon his name
Ad E	13:8	calling to remembrance all the works of the Lord
	16:11	that he was called our father
Wis	2:13	and calls himself a child of the Lord
	2:16	he calls the last end of the righteous happy
	7:7	I called upon God, and the spirit of wisdom came to me
	11:4	When they thirsted they called upon thee
	14:1	calls upon a piece of wood more fragile
	14:22	and they call such great evils peace
	18:8	thou didst call us to thyself and glorify us
Sir	2:10	Or who ever called upon him and was overlooked ?
	5:14	Do not be called a slanderer
	11:28	Call no one happy before his death
	31:9	Who is he ? And we will call him blessed
	36:12	Have mercy, O Lord, upon the people called by thy name
	37:24	and all who see him will call him happy
	42:15	I will now call to mind the works of the Lord
	46:5	He called upon the Most High, the Mighty One
	46:16	He called upon the Lord, the Mighty One
	46:19	Samuel called men to witness before the Lord
	47:18	who is called the God of Israel
	48:20	But they called upon the Lord who is merciful
Bar	2:15	for Israel and his descendants are called by thy name
	2:26	And the house which is called by thy name
	3:7	in order that we should call upon thy name

	3:33	called it, and it obeyed him in fear
	3:34	he called them, and they said, Here we are !
	5:4	For your name will for ever be called by God
L Jr	6:30	For why should they be called gods
	6:40	or call them gods ?
	6:44	or call them gods ?
	6:64	Therefore one must not think that they are gods nor call them gods
Bel	14:3	Now the Babylonians had an idol called Bel
	14:8	and he called his priests and said to them
1 Ma	2:3	Simon called Thassi
	2:4	Judas called Maccabeus
	2:5	Eleazar called Avaran, and Jonathan called Apphus
	3:1	Then Judas his son, who was called Maccabeus
	5:16	a great assembly was called
	6:10	So he called all his friends and said to them
	6:14	Then he called for Philip, one of his friends
	6:43	And Eleazar, called Avaran, saw
	7:37	Thou didst choose this house to be called by thy name
	8:20	Judas, who is also called Maccabeus, and his brothers
	10:20	you are to be called the king's friend
	11:7	as far as the river called Eleutherus
	11:47	So the king called the Jews to his aid
	12:31	who are called Zabadeans
	12:37	and he repaired the section called Chaphenatha
	16:2	And Simon called in his 2 elder sons Judas and John
	16:15	in the little stronghold called Dok, which he had built
2 Ma	1:36	Nehemiah and his associates called this nephthar
	1:36	but by most people it is called naphtha
	2:26	it is no light matter but calls for sweat and loss of sleep
	3:15	and called toward heaven
	3:22	While they were calling upon the Almighty Lord
	3:31	to call upon the Most High and to grant life
	4:7	and Antiochus who was called Epiphanes succeeded to the kingdom
	6:2	and call it the temple of Olympian Zeus
	6:2	and to call the one in Gerizim the temple of Zeus
	7:25	the king called the mother to him
	8:1	But Judas, who was also called Maccabeus, and his companions
	8:15	and because he had called them by his holy and glorious name
	9:2	For he had entered the city called Persepolis
	10:9	Such then was the end of Antiochus who was called Epiphanes
	10:12	Ptolemy, who was called Macron
	10:13	He heard himself called a traitor at every turn
	10:32	Timothy himself fled to a stronghold called Gazara
	12:6	and, calling upon God the righteous Judge
	12:15	calling upon the great Sovereign of the world
	12:17	they came to Charax, to the Jews who are called Toubiani
	12:21	and also the baggage to a place called Carnaim
	12:28	But the Jews called upon the Sovereign
	12:32	After the feast called Pentecost
	12:36	Judas called upon the Lord
	13:10	he ordered the people to call upon the Lord day and night
	13:23	he was dismayed, called in the Jews
	14:6	Those of the Jews who are called Hasidaeans
	14:16	and engaged them in battle at a village called Dessau
	14:34	and called upon the constant Defender of our nation, in these words :
	14:37	and for his good will was called father of the Jews
	14:46	calling upon the Lord of life and spirit
	15:21	and called upon the Lord who works wonders
	15:22	And he called upon him in these words :
	15:31	and had called his countrymen together
	15:36	which is called Adar in the Syrian language
1 Es	3:7	and shall be called kinsman of Darius
	3:16	And he said, Call the young men
	4:36	The whole earth calls upon truth, and heaven blesses her
	4:42	And you shall sit next to me, and be called my kinsman
	4:63	which is called by his name
	5:38	and was called by his name
	6:33	Therefore may the Lord, whose name is there called upon
	8:41	I assembled them at the river called Theras
3 Ma	1:27	to call upon him who has all power
	2:17	or call us to account for this profanation
	4:11	When these men had been brought to the place called Schedia
	5:7	they all called upon the Almighty Lord and Ruler of all power
	6:1	to cease calling upon the holy God
	7:17	When they had arrived at Ptolemais, called rose-bearing
2 Es	1:26	When you call upon me, I will not listen to you
	1:37	I call to witness the gratitude of the people that is to come
	1:40	Zechariah and Malachi, who is also called the messenger of the Lord
	2:5	I call upon you, father
	2:14	Call, O call heaven and earth to witness
	2:37	giving thanks to him who has called you to heavenly kingdoms
	2:41	who have been called from the beginning, may be made holy
	3:1	I, Salathiel, who am also called Ezra, was in Babylon
	4:25	But what will he do for his name, by which we are called ?
	6:49	the name of one thou didst call Behemoth
	6:58	whom thou hast called thy first-born, only begotten

7:132	that the Most High is now called merciful
7:138	and he is called giver
8:31	but thou, because of us sinners, art called merciful
8:32	then thou wilt be called merciful
8:44	and is called thy own image because he is made like thee
9:26	into the field which is called Ardat
10:22	and the name by which we are called has been profaned
10:57	and you have been called before the Most High
12:24	therefore they are called the heads of the eagle
13:12	and call to him another multitude which was peaceable
13:45	and that country is called Arzareth
13:55	and called understanding your mother
14:38	And on the next day, behold, a voice called me, saying
15:20	I call together all the kings of the earth to fear me
4 Ma 1:10	but I would also call them blessed
15:21	calling to their mother
16:9	or have the happiness of being called grandmother
16:16	My sons, noble is the contest to which you are called

CALL back 2
1 Es 1:50 So the God of their fathers sent by his messenger to call them back
2 Es 4:5 or call back for me the day that is past

CALL down 1
Sir 4:6 for if in bitterness of soul he calls down a curse upon you

CALL forth 1
Wis 11:25 Or how would anything not called forth by thee

CALL in 1
Jud 7:26 Now call them in and surrender the whole city

CALL on 5 = 0.003 %
Jud 6:21 and all that night they called on the God of Israel for help
9:4 and called on thee for help
Sir 13:14 and call on him for your salvation
2 Es 2:36 I publicly call on my Saviour to witness
4 Ma 12:17 and I call on the God of our fathers

CALL out 2
Jud 13:11 Judith called out from afar to the watchmen at the gates
1 Es 8:92 one of the men of Israel, called out

CALLISTHENES 1
2 Ma 8:33 Callisthenes and some others

CALM, adj. 2
3 Ma 2:1 bending his knees and extending his hands with calm dignity
4 Ma 13:6 and make it calm for those who sail into the inner basin

CALM, verb 2
Sir 39:28 and calm the anger of their Maker
48:10 to calm the wrath of God before it breaks out in fury

CAMEL 5 = 0.003 %
Tob 9:2 Brother Azarias, take a servant and 2 camels with you
Jud 2:17 He collected a vast number of camels
Sir 24:15 Like cassia and camel's thorn
1 Es 5:43 There were 435 camels
2 Es 15:36 and a man's thigh and a camel's hock

CAMP, subst. 40 = 0.026 %
Jud 6:11 and led him out of the camp into the plain
7:1 to break camp and move against Bethulia
7:2 So all their warriors moved their camp that day
7:12 Remain in your camp
10:18 There was great excitement in the whole camp
12:7 And she remained in the camp for 3 days
12:7 and bathed at the spring in the camp
13:10 and they passed through the camp
14:3 Then they will seize their arms and go into the camp
14:19 in the midst of the camp
15:5 for they were told what had happened in the camp of the enemy
15:6 fell upon the Assyrian camp
15:11 So all the people plundered the camp for 30 days
16:3 and brought me into his camp, in the midst of the people
Wis 19:7 The cloud was seen overshadowing the camp
Sir 48:21 The Lord smote the camp of the Assyrians
1 Ma 3:41 and went to the camp to get the sons of Israel for slaves
4:2 to fall upon the camp of the Jews and attack them suddenly
4:4 while the division was still absent from the camp
4:5 When Gorgias entered the camp of Judas by night
4:7 And they saw the camp of the Gentiles, strong and fortified
4:13 they went forth from their camp to battle
4:20 and that the Jews were burning the camp
4:23 Then Judas returned to plunder the camp
4:30 and didst give the camp of the Philistines
5:38 Judas sent men to spy out the camp, and they reported to him
6:32 opposite the camp of the king

9:6	and many slipped away from the camp
9:11	Then the army of Bacchides marched out from the camp
11:73	as far as Kadesh, to their camp, and there they encamped
12:26	He sent spies to their camp
12:27	and he stationed outposts around the camp
12:28	so they kindled fires in their camp and withdrew
12:32	Then he broke camp and went to Damascus
2 Ma 13:14	he pitched his camp near Modein
13:15	and slew as many as 2,000 men in the camp
13:16	In the end they filled the camp with terror and confusion
15:22	and he slew fully a 185,000 in the camp of Sennacherib
2 Es 1:15	I gave you camps for your protection
4 Ma 3:13	they went searching throughout the enemy camp

CAMP, verb 9 = 0.006 %
Tob 6:1 they came at evening to the Tigris river and camped there
Jud 2:21 and camped opposite Bectileth
3:10 here he camped between Geba and Scythopolis
7:13 and camp there to keep watch
15:3 Those who had camped in the hills around Bethulia
Sir 14:26 and will camp under her boughs
1 Ma 5:41 and camps on the other side of the river
9:33 and camped by the water of the pool of Asphar
16:4 and camped for the night in Modein

CAMPAIGN 2
Jud 2:16 as a great army is marshalled for a campaign
2 Ma 15:17 they determined not to carry on a campaign

CAN 232 = 0.151 %

CANAAN 5 = 0.003 %
Jud 5:9 and go to the land of Canaan
5:10 When a famine spread over Canaan they went down to Egypt
Bar 3:22 She has not been heard of in Canaan, nor seen in Teman
Sus 13:56 You offspring of Canaan and not of Judah
1 Ma 9:37 a daughter of one of the great nobles of Canaan

CANAANITE 4 = 0.003 %
Jud 5:3 and said to them, Tell me, you Canaanites
5:16 And they drove out before them the Canaanites
1 Es 8:69 the Canaanites, the Hittites, the Perizzites
2 Es 1:21 I drove out the Canaanites, the Perizzites

CANAL 2
Sir 24:30 I went forth like a canal from a river
24:31 and lo, my canal became a river, and my river became a sea

CANCEL 6 = 0.004 %
1 Ma 10:33 and let all officials cancel also the taxes on their cattle
10:42 this too is cancelled
11:36 And not one of these grants shall be cancelled
13:39 and cancel the crown tax which you owe
15:8 and such future debts shall be cancelled for you
4 Ma 2:8 and to cancel the debt when the 7th year arrives

CANOPY 4 = 0.003 %
Jud 10:21 under a canopy which was woven with purple and gold
13:9 and pulled down the canopy from the posts
13:15 and here is the canopy beneath which he lay
16:19 and the canopy which she took for herself from his bedchamber

CAPABLE 1
Wis 8:15 among the people I shall show myself capable

CAPARISONED 1
2 Ma 3:25 a magnificently caparisoned horse

CAPHARSALAMA 1
1 Ma 7:31 he went out to meet Judas in battle near Capharsalama

CAPITAL 1
1 Ma 3:37 and departed from Antioch his capital in the 147th year

CAPTAIN 8 = 0.005 %
Jud 14:2 and set a captain over them
14:12 and they went to the generals and the captains
1 Ma 16:1 he sent letters to the captains asking them to come to him
2 Ma 3:4 who had been made captain of the temple
4:28 When Sostratus the captain of the citadel
5:24 Antiochus sent Apollonius, the captain of the Mysians
12:19 Dositheus and Sosipater, who were captains under Maccabeus
1 Es 1:9 captains over thousands

CAPTIVATE 1
Jud 16:9 Her sandal ravished his eyes, her beauty captivated his mind

CAPTIVE 29 = 0.019 %
Tob 1:10 Now when I was carried away captive to Nineveh
7:3 who are captives in Nineveh

	13:10	May he cheer those within you who are captives
Jud	**2**:9	and I will lead them away captive
	5:18	and were led away captive to a foreign country
Ad E	**11**:4	He was one of the captives
Wis	**17**:2	they themselves lay as captives of darkness
Sir	**31**:7	and every fool will be taken captive by it
	48:15	till they were carried away captive from their land
L Jr	**6**:1	to those who were to be taken to Babylon as captives
	6:2	you will be taken to Babylon as captives
1 Ma	**1**:32	And they took captive the women and children
	8:10	and the Romans took captive their wives and children
	9:70	and obtain release of the captives
	9:72	He restored to him the captives
	10:33	And every one of the Jews taken as a captive
	14:7	He gathered a host of captives
	15:40	and take the people captive and kill them
2 Ma	**1**:19	For when our fathers were being led captive to Persia
1 Es	**6**:5	for the providence of the Lord was over the captives
	6:16	and carried the people away captive to Babylon
	7:11	Not all of the returned captives were purified
	7:12	for all the returned captives
3 Ma	**1**:5	and many captives also were taken
2 Es	**1**:3	who was a captive in the country of the Medes
	13:40	whom Shalmaneser the king of the Assyrians led captive
	15:63	They shall carry your children away captive
	16:46	and take their children captive
4 Ma	**8**:2	that others of the Hebrew captives be brought

CAPTIVITY   26 = 0.017 %

Tob	**1**:2	was taken into captivity from Thisbe
	3:4	and thou gavest us over to plunder, captivity, and death
	3:15	in the land of my captivity
	13:6	I give him thanks in the land of my captivity
	14:5	from the places of their captivity
Jud	**4**:3	For they had only recently returned from the captivity
	8:22	and the captivity of the land
	9:4	and their daughters to captivity
Bar	**4**:10	for I have seen the captivity of my sons and daughters
1 Ma	**2**:9	her glorious vessels have been carried into captivity
1 Es	**5**:7	out of their sojourn in captivity
	5:56	and all who had come to Jerusalem from the captivity
	5:67	And they learned that those who had returned from captivity
	6:8	who had been in captivity
	6:28	who have returned from the captivity of Judea
	7:6	and the rest of those from the captivity who joined them
	7:10	The people of Israel who came from the captivity
	7:13	And the people of Israel who came from the captivity ate it
	8:65	And those who had come back from captivity
	8:77	to the sword and captivity and plundering
	9:3	to all who had returned from the captivity
	9:4	those who had returned from the captivity
	9:15	And those who had returned from the captivity
2 Es	**10**:22	our Levites have gone into captivity
	13:40	which were led away from their own land into captivity
	16:46	for in captivity and famine they will beget their children

CAPTURE, verb   20 = 0.013 %

Tob	**14**:15	which Nebuchadnezzar and Ahasuerus had captured
Jud	**1**:14	and came to Ecbatana, captured its towers
	1:15	He captured Arphaxad in the mountains of Ragae
	5:18	and their cities were captured by their enemies
	7:27	For it would be better for us to be captured by them
	8:21	For if we are captured all Judea will be captured
	10:13	and capture all the hill country
	10:13	without losing one of his men, captured or slain
1 Ma	**1**:19	And they captured the fortified cities in the land of Egypt
	5:11	and capture the stronghold to which we have fled
	5:13	the enemy have captured their wives and children and goods
	5:30	carrying ladders and engines of war to capture the stronghold
	9:58	and he will capture them all in one night
	11:56	And Trypho captured the elephants
	13:43	and battered and captured one tower
2 Ma	**8**:6	He captured strategic positions
	8:25	They captured the money
	10:22	and immediately captured the 2 towers
	14:41	When the troops were about to capture the tower

CAPTURE, subst.   3 = 0.002 %

Bar	**4**:14	remember the capture of my sons and daughters
	4:24	For as the neighbours of Zion have now seen your capture
2 Ma	**8**:36	by the capture of the people of Jerusalem

CAPTURED   1

2 Ma	**8**:10	by selling the captured Jews into slavery

CARABASION   1

1 Es	**9**:34	Carabasion and Eliashib and Machnadebai, Eliasis, Binnui

CARCHEMISH   1

1 Es	**1**:25	went to make war at Carchemish on the Euphrates

CARE, subst.   25 = 0.016 %

Tob	**2**:10	Ahikar, however, took care of me until he went to Elymais
Jud	**2**:13	And you – take care not to transgress
	12:11	Go now and persuade the Hebrew woman who is in your care
Ad E	**16**:8	For the future we will take care to render our kingdom
Wis	**5**:15	the Most High takes care of them
	6:15	will soon be free from care
	7:4	I was nursed with care in swaddling cloths
	8:9	and encouragement in cares and grief
	12:13	whose care is for all men
	12:20	For if thou didst punish with such great care and indulgence
	13:13	he takes and carves with care in his leisure
Sir	**13**:8	Take care not to be led astray
	18:19	and before you fall ill, take care of your health
	32:1	take good care of them and then be seated
	38:15	may he fall into the care of a physician
L Jr	**6**:5	So take care not to become at all like the foreigners
1 Ma	**3**:33	Lysias was also to take care of Antiochus his son
	11:37	Now therefore take care to make a copy of this
2 Ma	**7**:27	and have taken care of you
1 Es	**2**:28	and to take care that nothing more be done
	6:10	and being completed with all splendour and care
	7:2	supervised the holy work with very great care
	8:19	they shall take care to give him
2 Es	**9**:46	And I brought him up with much care
	10:47	And as for her telling you that she brought him up with much care

CARE, verb   4 = 0.003 %

Sir	**13**:5	he will drain your resources and he will not care
	49:15	and his bones are cared for
2 Ma	**11**:23	in caring for their own affairs
2 Es	**2**:21	care for the injured and the weak

CAREFUL   5 = 0.003 %

Sir	**37**:31	but he who is careful to avoid it prolongs his life
	38:26	and he is careful about fodder for the heifers
	38:27	and he is careful to finish his work
	38:28	and he is careful to complete its decoration
	38:30	and he is careful to clean the furnace

CAREFULLY   4 = 0.003 %

2 Ma	**8**:31	they stored them all carefully in strategic places
2 Es	**9**:1	He answered me and said, Measure carefully in your mind
	16:30	some clusters may be left by those who search carefully
4 Ma	**11**:18	He was carefully stretched tight upon it

CARIA   1

1 Ma	**15**:23	and to Sicyon, and to Caria, and to Samos

CARMEL   1

Jud	**1**:8	and those among the nations of Carmel and Gilead

CARMONIAN   1

2 Es	**15**:30	Also the Carmonians, raging in wrath

CARNAIM   5 = 0.003 %

1 Ma	**5**:26	in Alema and Chaspho, Maked and Carnaim
	5:43	and fled into the sacred precincts at Carnaim
	5:44	Thus Carnaim was conquered
2 Ma	**12**:21	and also the baggage to a place called Carnaim
	12:26	Then Judas marched against Carnaim

CARPENTER   2

L Jr	**6**:45	They are made by carpenters and goldsmiths
1 Es	**5**:54	And they gave money to the masons and the carpenters

CARRIER   1

2 Ma	**4**:20	but by the decision of its carriers

CARRY   30 = 0.020 %

Jud	**10**:5	and gave them to her to carry
	10:22	with silver lamps carried before him
Ad E	**15**:4	while the other followed carrying her train
Wis	**5**:14	is like chaff carried by the wind
	14:1	than the ship which carries him
	18:16	carrying the sharp sword of thy authentic command
Sir	**6**:25	Put your shoulder under her and carry her
Bar	**2**:14	in the sight of those who have carried us into exile
	5:6	carried in glory, as on a royal throne
L Jr	**6**:4	which are carried on men's shoulders
	6:26	Having no feet, they are carried on men's shoulders
1 Ma	**2**:9	her glorious vessels have been carried into captivity
	4:30	and of the man who carried his armour
	5:30	carrying ladders and engines of war to capture the stronghold
2 Ma	**4**:19	to carry 300 silver drachmas for the sacrifice to Hercules
	4:19	Those who carried the money, however

	4:23	to carry the money to the king
	7:27	I carried you 9 months in my womb
	8:31	and carried the rest of the spoils to Jerusalem
	9:8	was brought down to earth and carried in a litter
	9:10	no one was able to carry the man who a little while before
	15:23	send a good angel to carry terror and trembling before us
	15:30	and carry them to Jerusalem
1 Es	1:4	and he said, You need no longer carry it upon your shoulders
	1:13	and carried them to all the people
	8:13	and to carry to Jerusalem the gifts for the Lord of Israel
	8:60	carried them to the temple of the Lord
3 Ma	2:7	but carried through safely
2 Es	4:19	and to the sea is assigned a place to carry its waves
4 Ma	15:31	Just as Noah's ark, carrying the world in the universal flood

CARRY away   16 = 0.010 %

Tob	1:10	Now when I was carried away captive to Nineveh
Ad E	16:4	but, carried away by the boasts of those
Sir	48:15	till they were carried away captive from their land
Bar	1:8	which had been carried away from the temple
	1:9	after Nebuchadnezzar king of Babylon had carried away from Jerusalem
2 Ma	3:28	his men took him up and put him on a stretcher and carried him away
1 Es	1:41	and carried them away
	1:54	and the royal stores, they took and carried away to Babylon
	2:10	which Nebuchadnezzar had carried away from Jerusalem
	5:7	whom Nebuchadnezzar king of Babylon had carried away to Babylon
	6:16	and carried the people away captive to Babylon
	6:26	and carried away to Babylon
3 Ma	3:18	they were carried away by their traditional conceit
	4:6	and were carried away unveiled
2 Es	15:63	They shall carry your children away captive
4 Ma	15:29	who carried away the prize of the contest in your heart !

CARRY back   1

1 Es	2:15	and they were carried back by Shesh-Bazzar

CARRY off   5 = 0.003 %

Sir	31:2	and a severe illness carries off sleep
Bar	4:26	they were taken away like a flock carried off by the enemy
2 Ma	5:21	So Antiochus carried off 1,800 talents from the temple
2 Es	10:22	our righteous men have been carried off
	16:68	and they shall carry off some of you

CARRY on   1

2 Ma	15:17	they determined not to carry on a campaign

CARRY out   11 = 0.007 %

Jud	2:1	about carrying out his revenge on the whole region
	2:13	but be sure to carry them out just as I have ordered you
	12:4	before the Lord carries out by my hand
	13:5	and to carry out my undertaking
L Jr	6:62	they carry out his command
2 Ma	3:8	but in fact to carry out the king's purpose
	15:5	in carrying out his abominable design
3 Ma	1:2	determined to carry out the plot he had devised
	5:4	proceeded faithfully to carry out the orders
	5:19	he had carried out completely the order given him
	6:38	So their registration was carried out

CART   3 = 0.002 %

Jud	15:11	and hitched up her carts and piled the things on them
Sir	33:5	The heart of a fool is like a cart wheel
1 Es	5:55	and carts to the Sidonians and the Tyrians

CARVE   3 = 0.002 %

Wis	13:13	he takes and carves with care in his leisure
2 Es	13:6	he carved for himself a great mountain, and flew up upon it
	13:7	from which the mountain was carved

CARVE out   1

2 Es	13:36	as you saw the mountain carved out without hands

CARVED   1

1 Ma	13:29	and beside the suits of armour carved ships

CASE   17 = 0.011 %

Sir	pr.	and to be indulgent in cases where
	4:9	and do not be fainthearted in judging a case
	11:9	nor sit with sinners when they judge a case
	22:22	or a treacherous blow – in these cases any friend will flee
	35:13	He will not show partiality in the case of a poor man
	35:19	till he judges the case of his people
L Jr	6:64	for they are not able either to decide a case
2 Ma	2:8	as they were shown in the case of Moses
	2:29	such in my judgment is the case with us
	3:13	said that this money must in any case be confiscated
	4:44	3 men sent by the senate presented the case before him

	6:14	For in the case of the other nations
1 Es	9:17	And the cases of the men who had foreign wives
2 Es	4:20	but why have you not judged so in your own case ?
	8:51	But think of your own case
4 Ma	5:21	for in either case the law is equally despised
	15:11	in the case of none of them were the various tortures

CASPIN   1

2 Ma	12:13	Its name was Caspin

CASSIA   1

Sir	24:15	Like cassia and camel's thorn

CAST   7 = 0.005 %

Jud	6:12	by casting stones at them
Sir	21:15	and casts it behind his back
	37:8	lest he cast the lot against you
L Jr	6:24	for even when they were being cast, they had no feeling
1 Ma	13:48	He cast out of it all uncleanness
2 Ma	5:8	he was cast ashore in Egypt
	5:10	He who had cast many to lie unburied

CAST away   1

2 Es	14:14	cast away from you the burdens of man

CAST down   4 = 0.003 %

Jud	9:8	and to cast down the horn of thy altar with the sword
Sir	1:30	and cast you down in the midst of the congregation
	10:14	The Lord has cast down the thrones of rulers
3 Ma	6:7	was cast down into the ground to lions as food for wild beasts

CAST off   2

Sir	6:21	and he will not be slow to cast her off
1 Ma	11:55	All the troops that Demetrius had cast off

CAST out   7 = 0.005 %

Wis	11:14	who long before had been cast out and exposed
Sir	7:26	If you have a wife who pleases you, do not cast her out
Bar	2:25	and behold, they have been cast out
L Jr	6:71	or like a dead body cast out in the darkness
2 Es	1:30	I will cast you out from my presence
	10:22	our little ones have been cast out
	16:23	And the dead shall be cast out like dung

CAST up   3 = 0.002 %

Wis	10:19	and cast them up from the depth of the sea
2 Es	5:7	and the sea of Sodom shall cast up fish
	12:32	and will cast up before them their contemptuous dealings

CASTOFF   2

Wis	13:12	and burn the castoff pieces of his work to prepare his food
	13:13	But a castoff piece from among them, useful for nothing

CAT   1

L Jr	6:22	and so do cats

CATAPULT   7 = 0.005 %

Wis	5:22	and hailstones full of wrath will be hurled as from a catapult
1 Ma	6:51	machines to shoot arrows, and catapults
4 Ma	8:13	rack and hooks and catapults and cauldrons
	9:26	they bound him to the torture machine and catapult
	11:9	the guards bound him and dragged him to the catapult
	11:26	Your fire is cold to us, and the catapults painless
	18:20	brought those 7 sons of the daughter of Abraham to the catapult

CATASTROPHE   1

Jud	8:19	and so they suffered a great catastrophe before our enemies

CATCH, verb   13 = 0.008 %

Tob	6:3	and the angel said to him, Catch the fish
	11:6	And she caught sight of him coming, and said to his father
Sir	9:4	lest you be caught in her intrigues
	23:7	the one who observes it will never be caught
	27:19	and will not catch him again
	27:26	and he who sets a snare will be caught in it
	27:29	will be caught in a snare
	34:2	As one who catches at a shadow and pursues the wind
P Az	25	whom it cast about the furnace
Sus	13:58	Under what tree did you catch them being intimate with each other ?
1 Ma	6:24	as many of us as they have caught
2 Ma	12:35	caught hold of Gorgias, and grasping his cloak
	13:21	he was sought for, caught, and put in prison

CATCH up   2

Jud	6:12	they caught up their weapons
Wis	4:11	He was caught up lest evil change his understanding

CATHUA   1
  1 Es 5:30 the sons of Cathua, the sons of Gahar

CATTLE   21 = 0.014 %
  Tob 10:10 and half of his property in slaves, cattle, and money
  Jud 4:10 They and their wives and their children and their cattle
      5:9 with much gold and silver and very many cattle
      8:7 and men and women slaves, and cattle, and fields
    11:7 and the cattle and the birds of the air
    11:12 they have planned to kill their cattle and determined
  Sir 7:22 Do you have cattle ? Look after them
  P Az 59 Bless the Lord, all beasts and cattle
  1 Ma 1:32 and seized the cattle
      2:30 they, their sons, their wives, and their cattle
      2:38 and they died, with their wives and children and cattle
    10:33 and let all officials cancel the taxes on their cattle
    12:23 that your cattle and your property belong to us
  2 Ma 12:11 promising to give him cattle
  1 Es 2:7 with gifts, and with horses and cattle
      2:9 with silver and gold, with horses and cattle
      5:1 and their menservants and maidservants, and their cattle
      8:50 and for our children and the cattle that were with us
      9:4 their cattle should be seized for sacrifice
  2 Es 6:53 to bring forth before thee cattle, beasts, and creeping things
      8:29 who have had the ways of cattle

CAULDRON   5 = 0.003 %
  2 Ma 7:3 and gave orders that pans and cauldrons be heated
  1 Es 1:12 and they boiled the sacrifices in brass pots and cauldrons
  4 Ma 8:13 rack and hooks and catapults and cauldrons
    12:1 When he also, thrown into the cauldron
    18:20 quenched fire with fire in his cruel cauldrons

CAUSE, subst.   9 = 0.006 %
  Wis 14:27 is the beginning and cause and end of every evil
  L Jr 6:54 *They cannot judge their own cause or deliver one who is wronged*
  1 Ma 9:10 and leave no cause to question our honour
  2 Ma 4:1 and had been the real cause of the misfortune
      4:47 Menelaus, the cause of all the evil
  4 Ma 1:11 and they became the cause of the downfall of tyranny over their nation
      1:16 and the causes of these
    12:14 but you will wail bitterly for having slain without cause
    16:14 *O mother, soldier of God in the cause of religion, elder and woman !*

CAUSE, verb   29 = 0.019 %
  Tob 11:8 and will cause the white films to fall away
  Jud 9:14 And cause thy whole nation and every tribe
  Wis 12:16 and thy sovereignty over all causes thee to spare all
    17:13 prefers ignorance of what causes the torment
  Sir 3:24 and wrong opinion has caused their thoughts to slip
    11:22 and quickly God causes his blessing to flourish
    18:15 nor cause grief by your words when you present a gift
    24:17 Like a vine I caused loveliness to bud
    25:3 are caused by an evil wife
    25:23 are caused by the wife who does not make her husband happy
    29:4 and cause trouble to those who help them
    35:15 as she cries out against him who has caused them to fall ?
    36:2 and cause the fear of thee to fall upon all the nations
    36:20 A perverse mind will cause grief
    44:21 and cause them to inherit from sea to sea
    45:3 By his words he caused signs to cease
    47:22 nor cause any of his works to perish
    47:23 Rehoboam, whose policy caused the people to revolt
    47:23 Also Jeroboam the son of Nebat, who caused Israel to sin
  1 Ma 1:9 and they caused many evils on the earth
      3:29 which he had caused in the land by abolishing the laws
      3:42 to do to the people to cause their final destruction
    15:31 and for the destruction that you have caused
    15:35 they were causing great damage among the people and to our land
  2 Ma 3:24 caused so great a manifestation
  3 Ma 7:9 or cause them any grief at all
  2 Es 15:2 and cause them to be written on paper
  4 Ma 3:21 and caused many and various disasters
      4:21 and caused Antiochus himself to make war on them

CAUTIOUS   1
  Sir 18:27 A wise man is cautious in everything

CAVALRY   36 = 0.023 %
  Jud 1:13 and all his cavalry and all his chariots
      2:5 to the number of 120,000 foot soldiers and 12,000 cavalry
      2:22 his infantry, cavalry, and chariots
      6:3 They cannot resist the might of our cavalry
      7:2 their force of men of war was 170,000 infantry and 12,000 cavalry
      7:6 On the 2nd day Holofernes led out all his cavalry

      7:20 their infantry, chariots, and cavalry
    16:4 their cavalry covered the hills
  1 Ma 1:17 with chariots and elephants and cavalry
      3:39 and sent with them 40,000 infantry and 7,000 cavalry
      4:1 Now Gorgias took 5,000 infantry and a 1,000 picked cavalry
      4:7 with cavalry round about it
      4:28 and 5,000 cavalry to subdue them
      4:31 and let them be ashamed of their troops and their cavalry
      8:6 and with cavalry and chariots and a very large army
      9:4 with 20,000 foot soldiers and 2,000 cavalry
      9:11 The cavalry was divided into 2 companies
    10:73 And now you will not be able to withstand my cavalry
    10:77 he mustered 3,000 cavalry and a large army
    10:77 for he had a large troop of cavalry and put confidence in it
    10:79 Now Apollonius had secretly left a 1,000 cavalry behind them
    10:82 for the cavalry was exhausted
    10:83 and the cavalry was dispersed in the plain
    12:49 Then Trypho sent troops and cavalry into Galilee
    13:22 So Trypho got all his cavalry ready to go
    15:13 and with him were a 120,000 warriors and 8,000 cavalry
    15:38 and gave him troops of infantry and cavalry
    16:7 for the cavalry of the enemy were very numerous
  2 Ma 10:24 and collected the cavalry from Asia in no small number
    11:2 gathered about 80,000 men and all his cavalry
    11:4 and his thousands of cavalry, and his 80 elephants
    12:20 who had with him a 120,000 infantry and 2,500 cavalry
    12:33 And he came out with 3,000 infantry and 400 cavalry
    13:2 5,300 cavalry, 22 elephants
    15:20 and the cavalry deployed on the flanks
  3 Ma 1:1 both infantry and cavalry

CAVE   4 = 0.003 %
  Jud 16:23 and they buried her in the cave of her husband Manasseh
  2 Ma 2:5 And Jeremiah came and found a cave
      6:11 Others who had assembled in the caves near by
    10:6 they had been wandering in the mountains and caves

CEASE   32 = 0.021 %
  Jud 10:1 When Judith had ceased crying out to the God of Israel
  Wis 5:13 So we also, as soon as we were born, ceased to be
      7:10 because her radiance never ceases
  Sir 14:19 Every product decays and ceases to exist
    16:27 and they do not cease from their labours
    17:28 thanksgiving has ceased
    23:16 will never cease until the fire burns him up
    23:17 he will never cease until he dies
    24:9 and for eternity I shall not cease to exist
    24:24 Do not cease to be strong in the Lord
    28:6 Remember the end of your life, and cease from enmity
    38:23 When the dead is at rest, let his remembrance cease
    45:3 By his words he caused signs to cease
  Bar 2:23 I will make to cease from the cities of Judah
  P Az 23 did not cease feeding the furnace fires
  1 Ma 3:45 the flute and the harp ceased to play
      9:27 since the time that prophets ceased to appear among them
      9:73 Thus the sword ceased from Israel
  2 Ma 6:1 and cease to live by the laws of God
      9:5 As soon as he ceased speaking
    13:12 and lying prostrate for 3 days without ceasing
    15:7 But Maccabeus did not cease to trust with all confidence
  1 Es 2:30 And the building of the temple in Jerusalem ceased
      4:41 He ceased speaking
  3 Ma 1:12 he did not cease to maintain that he ought to enter, saying
      3:16 who never cease from their folly
      6:1 to cease calling upon the holy God
      6:32 They ceased their chanting of dirges
  2 Es 10:4 but without ceasing mourn and fast until I die
    15:22 and my sword will not cease from those who shed innocent blood on the earth
    16:67 Cease from your sins, and forget your iniquities
  4 Ma 8:29 had ceased counselling them to eat defiling food

CEDAR   4 = 0.003 %
  Sir 24:13 I grew tall like a cedar in Lebanon
    50:12 he was like a young cedar on Lebanon
  1 Es 4:48 to bring cedar timber from Lebanon to Jerusalem
      5:55 to bring cedar logs from Lebanon

CEILING   1
  2 Ma 1:16 Opening the secret door in the ceiling

CELEBRATE   20 = 0.013 %
  Tob 6:12 we will celebrate the marriage
    11:19 and Tobias marriage was celebrated for 7 days
  Wis 14:23 or celebrate secret mysteries
  1 Ma 4:56 So they celebrated the dedication of the altar for 8 days
      7:48 and celebrated that day as a day of great gladness
      7:49 And they decreed that this day should be celebrated
      9:37 The sons of Jambri are celebrating a great wedding

10:58 and celebrated her wedding at Ptolemais with great pomp, as kings do
13:52 they should celebrate this day with rejoicing
2 Ma 1:18 we shall celebrate the purification of the temple
1:18 in order that you also may celebrate the feast of booths
2:16 Since, therefore, we are about to celebrate the purification
8:33 While they were celebrating the victory
10:6 And they celebrated it for 8 days with rejoicing
15:36 but to celebrate the 13th day of the 12th month
3 Ma 5:17 by celebrating all the more
6:30 deciding that they should celebrate their rescue with all joyfulness
6:31 and full of joy they apportioned to celebrate the place
6:33 to celebrate these events
7:18 There they celebrated their deliverance

CELEBRATING   1
3 Ma 5:36 and urged the guests to return to their celebrating

CELEBRATION   3 = 0.002 %
Wis 19:16 but the latter, after receiving them with festal celebrations
Sir 36:14 Fill Zion with the celebration of thy wondrous deeds
2 Ma 6:7 On the monthly celebration of the king's birthday

CEMETERY   2
2 Ma 9:4 I will make Jerusalem a cemetery of Jews
9:14 and to make a cemetery

CENDEBAEUS   6 = 0.004 %
1 Ma 15:38 Then the king made Cendebaeus commander-in-chief of the coastal country
15:40 So Cendebaeus came to Jamnia
16:1 and reported to Simon his father what Cendebaeus had done
16:4 and they marched against Cendebaeus
16:8 and Cendebaeus and his army were put to flight
16:9 until Cendebaeus reached Kedron, which he had built

CENSER   4 = 0.003 %
Sir 50:9 like fire and incense in the censer
1 Ma 1:22 the cups for drink offerings, the bowls, the golden censers
1 Es 2:13 29 silver censers, 30 gold bowls
4 Ma 7:11 For just as our father Aaron, armed with the censer

CENSURE, verb   1
4 Ma 2:19 censure the households of Simeon and Levi

CENSUS   1
3 Ma 4:17 that they were no longer able to take the census of the Jews

CEREAL   2
Bar 1:10 and incense, and prepare a cereal offering
2 Ma 1:8 and we offered sacrifice and cereal offering

CERTAIN   19 = 0.012 %
Ad E 13:4 there is scattered a certain hostile people
1 Ma 11:21 But certain lawless men who hated their nation
11:25 Although certain lawless men of his nation
15:3 Whereas certain pestilent men
2 Ma 4:40 under the leadership of a certain Auranus
12:13 He also attacked a certain city
12:35 But a certain Dositheus, one of Bacenor's men
14:3 Now a certain Alcimus, who had formerly been high priest
14:37 A certain Razis, one of the elders of Jerusalem
3 Ma 1:2 But a certain Theodotus
1:3 that a certain insignificant man should sleep in the tent
6:1 Then a certain Eleazar, famous among the priests of the country
7:3 Certain of our friends
2 Es 8:22 whose word is sure and whose utterances are certain
9:1 and when you see that a certain part of the predicted signs are past
4 Ma 3:11 But a certain irrational desire for the water
3:21 just at that time certain men attempted
4:1 Now there was a certain Simon
5:1 on a certain high place

CERTAINLY   8 = 0.005 %
Sir 12:2 if not by him, certainly by the Most High
31:12 and do not say, There is certainly much upon it !
L Jr 6:46 The men that make them will certainly not live very long themselves
2 Ma 3:38 for there certainly is about the place some power of God
7:31 will certainly not escape the hands of God
2 Es 5:45 that thou wilt certainly give life at one time to thy creation ?
4 Ma 2:2 It is for this reason, certainly
7:16 most certainly devout reason is governor of the emotions

CHABRIS   3 = 0.002 %
Jud 6:15 and Chabris the son of Gothoniel
8:10 to summon Chabris and Charmis, the elders of her city
10:6 with the elders of the city, Chabris and Charmis

CHADIASAN   1
1 Es 5:20 The Chadiasans and Ammidians, 422

CHAEREAS   2
2 Ma 10:32 especially well garrisoned, where Chaereas was commander
10:37 and his brother Chaereas, and Apollophanes

CHAFE   1
Sir 26:7 An evil wife is an ox yoke which chafes

CHAFF   1
Wis 5:14 is like chaff carried by the wind

CHAIN   2
Wis 17:17 for with one chain of darkness they all were bound
1 Es 1:40 and bound him with a chain of brass

CHALDEA   1
Jud 5:7 who were in Chaldea

CHALDEAN   8 = 0.005 %
Jud 1:6 Many nations joined the forces of the Chaldeans
5:6 This people is descended from the Chaldeans
Bar 1:2 at the time when the Chaldeans took Jerusalem
L Jr 6:40 Besides, even the Chaldeans themselves dishonour them
P Az 25 and it broke through and burned those of the Chaldeans
1 Es 1:52 to bring against them the kings of the Chaldeans
4:45 when Judea was laid waste by the Chaldeans
6:15 king of the Chaldeans

CHALPHI   1
1 Ma 11:70 except Mattathias the son of Absalom and Judas the son of Chalphi

CHAMBER   25 = 0.016 %
Tob 6:13 and that each died in the bridal chamber
6:16 When you enter the bridal chamber
Wis 17:4 For not even the inner chamber that held them
1 Ma 1:27 she who sat in the bridal chamber was mourning
4:38 They saw also the chambers of the priests in ruins
4:57 they restored the gates and the chambers for the priests
8:15 but they have built for themselves a senate chamber
8:19 and they entered the senate chamber and spoke as follows :
12:3 and entered the senate chamber and said
1 Es 3:15 and he took his seat in the council chamber
8:59 in Jerusalem, in the chambers of the house of our Lord
9:1 to the chamber of Jehohanan the son of Eliashib
3 Ma 1:18 The virgins who had been enclosed in their chambers
1:19 abandoned the bridal chambers prepared for wedded union
4:6 And young women who had just entered the bridal chamber
2 Es 4:35 Did not the souls of the righteous in their chambers
4:41 In Hades the chambers of the souls are like the womb
5:9 and wisdom shall withdraw into its chamber
5:37 open for me the closed chambers
7:32 and the chambers shall give up the souls
7:95 being gathered into their chambers
8:20 whose eyes are exalted and whose upper chambers are in the air
10:1 But it happened that when my son entered his wedding chamber
10:48 When my son entered his wedding chamber he died
4 Ma 15:25 For as in the council chamber of her own soul

CHAMPION   2
Wis 18:21 For a blameless man was quick to act as their champion
4 Ma 15:29 vindicator of the law and champion of religion

CHANCE, subst.   3 = 0.002 %
Wis 2:2 Because we were born by mere chance
12:10 thou gavest them a chance to repent
Sir 27:12 Among stupid people watch for a chance to leave

CHANGE, subst.   7 = 0.005 %
Wis 7:18 and the changes of the seasons
Sir 2:4 and in changes that humble you be patient
37:17 As a clue to changes of heart
2 Ma 3:16 for his face and the change in his colour
11:24 to our father's change to Greek customs
3 Ma 3:21 and we ventured to make a change
5:42 took no account of the changes of mind

CHANGE, verb   33 = 0.021 %
Jud 10:7 and her clothing changed
Ad E 15:8 Then God changed the spirit of the king to gentleness
16:9 by changing our methods
Wis 4:11 He was caught up lest evil change his understanding
12:10 and that their way of thinking would never change

	16:21	was changed to suit every one liking
	16:25	changed into all forms, it served thy all-nourishing bounty
	19:2	they would change their minds and pursue them
	19:18	For the elements changed places with one another
Sir	**6**:9	And there is a friend who changes into an enemy
	6:28	and she will be changed into joy for you
	12:18	and whisper much, and change his expression
	13:25	A man's heart changes his countenance
	18:26	From morning to evening conditions change
	25:17	The wickedness of a wife changes her appearance
	27:11	but the fool changes like the moon
	33:19	lest you change your mind and must ask for it
1 Ma	**1**:49	and change all the ordinances
2 Ma	**4**:46	induced the king to change his mind
	6:29	had acted toward him with good will now changed to ill will
1 Es	**7**:15	because he had changed the will of the king of the Assyrians concerning them
3 Ma	**1**:3	a Jew by birth who later changed his religion
	1:25	to change his arrogant mind
	3:8	and expected that matters would change
2 Es	**6**:16	for they know that their end must be changed
	6:26	and the heart of the earth's inhabitants shall be changed
	8:22	and at whose command they are changed to wind and fire
4 Ma	**4**:19	Jason changed the nation's way of life
	6:18	should now change our course
	6:24	and that he had not been changed by their compassion
	8:8	and by changing your manner of living
	11:25	to change our mind or to force us to eat defiling foods
	15:14	because of religion did not change her attitude

CHANGE over   1
2 Ma   **6**:9   to change over to Greek customs

CHANNEL   3 = 0.002 %
Sir   **24**:30   and like a water channel into a garden
2 Es   **13**:44   and stopped the channels of the river
    13:47   the Most High will stop the channels of the river again

CHANTING   1
3 Ma   **6**:32   They ceased their chanting of dirges

CHAOS   1
2 Es   **5**:8   There shall be chaos also in many places

CHAPHENATHA   1
1 Ma   **12**:37   and he repaired the section called Chaphenatha

CHARACTER   4 = 0.003 %
Sir   pr.   being prepared in character to live according to the law
2 Ma   **5**:22   and in character more barbarous
2 Es   **14**:42   *in characters which they did not know*
4 Ma   **15**:4   We impress upon the character of a small child

CHARACTERISTIC   1
3 Ma   **7**:17   because of a characteristic of the place

CHARAX   1
2 Ma   **12**:17   they came to Charax, to the Jews who are called Toubiani

CHAREA   1
1 Es   **5**:32   the sons of Charea, the sons of Barkos

CHARGE, subst.   28 = 0.018 %
Tob	**1**:22	and in charge of administration of the accounts
Jud	**8**:10	she sent her maid, who was in charge of all she possessed
	12:11	the eunuch who had charge of all his personal affairs
	14:13	in charge of all his personal affairs
Ad E	**13**:6	who is in charge of affairs and is our 2nd father
1 Ma	**3**:32	in charge of the king's affairs
	3:55	in charge of thousands and hundreds and fifties and tens
	5:19	and he gave them this command, Take charge of this people
	7:20	He placed Alcimus in charge of the country
	7:25	*and brought wicked charges against them*
	9:25	and put them in charge of the country
	10:63	*and proclaim that no one is to bring charges against him*
	14:42	and that he should take charge of the sanctuary
2 Ma	**3**:7	The king chose Heliodorus, who was in charge of his affairs
	4:43	*Charges were brought against Menelaus about this incident*
	4:47	*he acquitted of the charges against him*
	6:21	Those who were in charge of that unlawful sacrifice took the man aside
	10:11	appointed one Lysias to have charge of the government
	11:1	who was in charge of the government
	13:2	who had charge of the government
	13:23	who had been left in charge of the government
1 Es	**5**:58	to have charge of the work of the Lord
3 Ma	**5**:5	The servants in charge of the Jews went out in the evening
	5:14	the person who was in charge of the invitations
	6:30	summoned the official in charge of the revenues

	7:7	*of every charge of whatever kind*
2 Es	**5**:41	thou dost have charge of those who are alive at the end

CHARGE, verb   4 = 0.003 %
1 Ma   **4**:8   Do not fear their numbers or be afraid when they charge
2 Ma   **5**:2   there appeared goldenclad horsemen charging through the air
    12:37   then he charged against Gorgias' men
3 Ma   **4**:19   *charging that they had been bribed*

CHARIOT   17 = 0.011 %
Jud	**1**:13	and all his cavalry and all his chariots
	2:19	with their chariots and horsemen
	2:22	his infantry, cavalry, and chariots
	7:20	their infantry, chariots, and cavalry
Sir	**48**:9	in a chariot with horses of fire
	49:8	which God showed him above the chariot of the cherubim
1 Ma	**1**:17	with chariots and elephants and cavalry
	8:6	and with cavalry and chariots and a very large army
2 Ma	**9**:7	And so it came about that he fell out of his chariot
	13:2	and 300 chariots armed with scythes
	14:21	A chariot came forward from each army
1 Es	**1**:28	But Josiah did not turn back to his chariot
	1:31	And he got into his 2nd chariot
	3:6	and have a chariot with gold bridles
3 Ma	**2**:7	And when he pursued them with chariots and a mass of troops
	6:4	Pharaoh with his abundance of chariots
2 Es	**15**:29	The nations of the dragons of Arabia shall come out with many chariots

CHARIOTEER   2
Sir   **20**:32   than a masterless charioteer of one's own life
2 Ma   **9**:4   so he ordered his charioteer to drive without stopping

CHARITY   8 = 0.005 %
Tob	**1**:3	and I performed many acts of charity to my brethren
	1:16	I performed many acts of charity to my brethren
	2:14	Where are your charities and your righteous deeds ?
	4:10	For charity delivers from death
	4:11	and for all who practise it charity is an excellent offering
	4:16	Give all your surplus to charity
	12:9	Those who perform deeds of charity and of righteousness
Sir	**31**:11	and the assembly will relate his acts of charity

CHARM, subst.   5 = 0.003 %
Wis   **14**:20   and the multitude, attracted by the charm of his work
Sir   **7**:19   for her charm is worth more than gold
    26:13   A wife's charm delights her husband
    26:15   A modest wife adds charm to charm

CHARMER   1
Sir   **12**:13   Who will pity a snake charmer bitten by a serpent

CHARMIS   3 = 0.002 %
Jud   **6**:15   and Charmis the son of Melchiel
    8:10   to summon Chabris and Charmis, the elders of her city
    10:6   with the elders of the city, Chabris and Charmis

CHARRED   1
1 Ma   **11**:4   and the charred bodies of those

CHASE   1
Wis   **2**:4   and be scattered like mist that is chased

CHASM   1
4 Ma   **14**:16   and the others, by building in precipitous chasms

CHASPHO   2
1 Ma   **5**:26   in Alema and Chaspho, Maked and Carnaim
    5:36   From there he marched on and took Chaspho

CHASTE   1
Sir   **26**:15   and no balance can weigh the value of a chaste soul

CHASTEN   1
Wis   **12**:22   So while chastening us

CHASTISE   1
4 Ma   **18**:5   and is being chastised after his death

CHASTISEMENT   1
2 Es   **15**:12   for the plague of chastisement and punishment

CHASTISING   1
Sir   **22**:6   but chastising and discipline are wisdom at all times

CHASTITY   1
Sir   **7**:24   Be concerned for their chastity

CHATTERER   1
  Sir **8**:3   Do not argue with a chatterer, nor heap wood on his fire

CHEAP   2
  Wis **15**:10 His heart is ashes, his hope is cheaper than dirt
 2 Es **16**:21 Behold, provisions will be so cheap upon earth

CHECK   2
 2 Ma **14**:17 but had been temporarily checked
 4 Ma **1**:35 checked by the temperate mind

CHEEK   1
  Sir **35**:15 Do not the tears of the widow run down her cheek

CHEER, subst.   4 = 0.003 %
  Tob **11**:11 Be of good cheer, father
 Ad E **16**:22 Therefore you shall observe this with all good cheer
 2 Ma **11**:26 so that they may know our policy and be of good cheer
 3 Ma **4**:8 instead of good cheer and youthful revelry

CHEER, verb   2
  Tob **13**:10 May he cheer those within you who are captives
 2 Ma **15**:11 and he cheered them all by relating a dream

CHEERFUL   6 = 0.004 %
  Sir **13**:25 And a glad heart makes a cheerful countenance
      13:26 The mark of a happy heart is a cheerful face
      26:4 and at all times his face is cheerful
      30:25 A man of cheerful and good heart
      35:9 With every gift show a cheerful face
 4 Ma **13**:13 cheerful and undaunted, said

CHELLEAN   1
  Jud **2**:23 south of the country of the Chelleans

CHELOUS   1
  Jud **1**:9 and Chelous and Kadesh and the river of Egypt

CHEPHIRAH   1
 1 Es **5**:19 The men of Chephirah and Beeroth, 743

CHERISH   2
 2 Ma **7**:14 and to cherish the hope that God gives
 3 Ma **3**:15 but should cherish them with clemency and great benevolence

CHERUB   2
  Sir **49**:8 which God showed him above the chariot of the cherubim
  P Az   32 Blessed art thou, who sittest upon cherubim

CHERUB, prop. n.   1
 1 Es **5**:36 under the leadership of Cherub, Addan, and Immer

CHEST   1
 1 Es **1**:54 and the treasures chests of the Lord

CHEW   1
  Sir **31**:16 and do not chew greedily, lest you be hated

CHEZIB   1
 1 Es **5**:31 the sons of Chezib, the sons of Gazzam, the sons of Uzza

CHIEF, adj.   10 = 0.007 %
  Jud **2**:4 the chief general of his army, second only to himself
 1 Ma **1**:29 a chief collector of tribute
      9:11 as did all the chief warriors
    10:65 and enrolled him among his chief friends
    11:27 and made him to be regarded as one of his chief friends
 2 Ma **4**:50 having become the chief plotter against his fellow citizens
      8:9 one of the king's chief friends
    10:11 and to be chief governor of Coelesyria and Phoenicia
 1 Es **1**:8 the chief officers of the temple
      7:2 and the chief officers of the temple

CHIEF, subst.   2
 2 Es **5**:16 Now on the 2nd night Phaltiel, a chief of the people
    15:16 or the chief of their leaders

CHIEFLY   1
 2 Ma **8**:35 having succeeded chiefly in the destruction of his own army !

CHIEF PRIEST s. **HIGH PRIEST**   4 = 0.003 %
 1 Es **8**:2 son of Eleazar, son of Aaron the chief priest
     9:39 and they told Ezra the chief priest and reader
     9:40 So Ezra the chief priest brought the law
     9:49 Then Attharates said to Ezra the chief priest and reader

CHIEFTAIN   1
  Jud **7**:8 Then all the chieftains of the people of Esau

CHILD   201 = 0.131 %
  Tob **3**:10 But she said, I am the only child of my father
      3:15 I am my father's only child
      3:15 and he has no child to be his heir
      4:12 They were blessed in their children
      5:17 and said to Tobit, Why have you sent our child away ?
      5:18 but consider it rubbish as compared to our child
      6:17 and I suppose that you will have children by her
      7:10 for it is your right to take my child
      7:18 Be brave, my child
      8:17 Blessed art thou, because thou hast had compassion on 2 only children
    10:5 Am I not distressed, my child, that I let you go
    10:7 my child has perished
    10:11 The God of heaven will prosper you, my children, before I die
    10:12 and grant me to see your children by my daughter Sarah
    11:9 and said to him, I have seen you, my child
    14:11 So now, my children, consider what almsgiving accomplishes
  Jud **4**:10 They and their wives and their children and their cattle
      4:11 And all the men and women of Israel, and their children
      7:14 They and their wives and children
      7:22 Their children lost heart
      7:23 Then all the people, the young men, the women, and the children
      7:27 or see our wives and children draw their last breath
      7:32 The women and children he sent home
      9:13 and against the house possessed by thy children
    16:5 and seize my children as prey
    16:12 they were wounded like the children of fugitives
 Ad E **13**:6 shall all, with their wives and children
  Wis **2**:13 and calls himself a child of the Lord
      3:12 Their wives are foolish, and their children evil
      3:16 But children of adulterers will not come to maturity
      4:6 For children born of unlawful unions are witnesses of evil
      7:1 a descendant of the first-formed child of earth
      8:19 As a child I was by nature well endowed
    10:5 in the face of his compassion for his child
    12:5 their merciless slaughter of children
    12:25 Therefore, as to thoughtless children
    13:17 and his marriage and children
    14:15 made an image of his child
    14:23 For whether they kill children in their initiations
    16:21 For thy sustenance manifested thy sweetness toward thy children
    18:5 and one child had been exposed and rescued
    18:5 take away a multitude of their children
    18:9 For in secret the holy children of good men offered sacrifices
    18:10 and their piteous lament for their children
    18:12 their most valued children had been destroyed
    19:6 that thy children might be kept unharmed
  Sir **3**:1 Listen to me your father, O children
      3:2 For the Lord honoured the father above the children
      3:5 will be gladdened by his own children
      3:9 strengthens the houses of the children
      3:11 and it is a disgrace for children
      7:23 Do you have children ? Discipline them
    11:28 a man will be known through his children
    14:26 he will place his children under her shelter
    16:1 Do not desire a multitude of useless children
    16:3 and to die childless is better than to have ungodly children
    19:11 like a woman in labour with a child
    22:9 Children who are brought up in a good life
    22:10 Children who are disdainfully and boorishly haughty
    23:7 Listen, my children, to instruction concerning speech
    23:23 and brought forth children by another man
    23:24 and punishment will fall on her children
    23:25 Her children will not take root
    24:18 being eternal, I therefore am given to all my children
    25:7 a man rejoicing in his children
    30:9 Pamper a child, and he will frighten you
    33:21 For it is better that your children should ask from you
    40:15 The children of the ungodly will not put forth many branches
    40:19 Children and the building of a city establish a man's name
    41:5 The children of sinners are abominable children
    41:6 The inheritance of the children of sinners will perish
    41:7 Children will blame an ungodly father
    41:14 My children, observe instruction and be at peace
    42:5 and of much discipline of children
    44:9 and so have their children after them
    44:11 and their inheritance to their children's children
    44:12 their children also, for their sake
    46:9 and his children obtained it for an inheritance
    47:20 so that you brought wrath upon your children
  Bar **4**:12 I was left desolate because of the sins of my children
      4:15 and had no pity for a child
      4:19 Go, my children, go
      4:21 Take courage, my children, cry to God
      4:25 My children, endure with patience
      4:27 Take courage, my children, and cry to God
      4:32 Wretched will be the cities which your children served as slaves
      5:5 and see your children gathered from west and east

L Jr	6 : 33	to clothe their wives and children
Sus	13 : 30	And she came, with her parents, her children, and all her kindred
Bel	14 : 10	besides their wives and children
	14 : 15	In the night the priests came with their wives and children
	14 : 20	I see the footsteps of men and women and children
	14 : 21	and he seized the priests and their wives and children
1 Ma	1 : 32	And they took captive the women and children
	1 : 38	and her children forsook her
	1 : 60	the women who had their children circumcised
	2 : 38	and they died, with their wives and children and cattle
	2 : 50	Now, my children, show zeal for the law
	2 : 64	My children, be courageous and grow strong in the law
	3 : 20	to destroy us and our wives and our children
	3 : 45	not one of her children went in or out
	5 : 13	the enemy have captured their wives and children and goods
	5 : 23	with their wives and children, and all they possessed
	5 : 45	with their wives and children and goods
	8 : 10	and the Romans took captive their wives and children
	13 : 6	and your wives and children
	13 : 45	The men in the city, with their wives and children
2 Ma	5 : 13	destruction of boys, women, and children
	6 : 10	for having circumcised their children
	7 : 28	I beseech you, my child
	7 : 34	when you raise your hand against the children of heaven
	8 : 28	and distributed the rest among themselves and their children
	9 : 15	but had planned to throw out with their children
	9 : 20	If you and your children are well
	12 : 3	to embark, with their wives and children
	12 : 21	he sent off the women and the children
	14 : 25	And he urged him to marry and have children
	15 : 18	Their concern for wives and children
1 Es	1 : 53	old man or child, for he gave them all into their hands
	4 : 53	should have their freedom, they and their children
	6 : 31	for the king and his children
	8 : 50	and for our children and the cattle that were with us
	8 : 85	and leave it for an inheritance to your children for ever
	8 : 93	with their children
	9 : 36	and they put them away with their children
3 Ma	1 : 4	to defend themselves and their children and wives bravely
	1 : 20	Mothers and nurses abandoned even new-born children here and there
	3 : 25	together with their wives and children
	3 : 27	old people or children or even infants
	5 : 31	Were your parents or children present
	5 : 49	parents and children, mothers and daughters
	6 : 3	upon the children of the sainted Jacob
	7 : 2	We ourselves and our children are faring well
	7 : 6	always taking their part as a father does for his children
2 Es	1 : 5	and to their children the iniquities
	1 : 5	so that they may tell their children's children
	1 : 28	or a mother her daughters or a nurse her children
	1 : 34	and your sons will have no children
	1 : 37	whose children rejoice with gladness
	2 : 2	Go, my children, because I am a widow and forsaken
	2 : 4	Go, my children, and ask for mercy from the Lord
	2 : 5	as a witness in addition to the mother of the children
	2 : 19	by these I will fill your children with joy
	2 : 32	Embrace your children until I come
	2 : 41	The number of your children, whom you desired, is full
	3 : 12	they produced children and peoples and many nations
	4 : 40	Go and ask a woman who is with child if
	4 : 40	her womb can keep the child within her any longer
	5 : 46	and say to it, If you bear 10 children
	5 : 51	He replied to me, Ask a woman who bears children
	6 : 21	and women with child shall give birth to premature children at 3 or 4 months
	9 : 43	Your servant was barren and had no child
	15 : 25	Depart, you faithless children !
	15 : 57	Your children shall die of hunger
	15 : 63	They shall carry your children away captive
	16 : 2	and wail for your children, and lament for them
	16 : 38	Just as a woman with child, in the 9th month
	16 : 38	and when the child comes forth from the womb
	16 : 44	them that marry, like those who will have no children
	16 : 46	and take their children captive
	16 : 46	for in captivity and famine they will beget their children
4 Ma	2 : 12	It takes precedence over love for children
	4 : 9	While the priests together with women and children
	6 : 17	May we, the children of Abraham
	6 : 22	Therefore, O children of Abraham
	12 : 2	he felt strong compassion for this child
	14 : 12	under the rackings of each one of her children
	14 : 13	Observe how complex is a mother's love for her children
	14 : 18	And why is it necessary to demonstrate sympathy for children
	14 : 20	But sympathy for her children did not sway
	15 : 1	O reason of the children, tyrant over the emotions !
	15 : 1	O religion, more desirable to the mother than her children !
	15 : 4	the emotions of parents who love their children ?
	15 : 4	We impress upon the character of a small child

	15 : 5	they are the more devoted to their children
	15 : 6	The mother of the 7 boys, more than any other mother, loved her children
	15 : 8	the temporary safety of her children
	15 : 11	to suffer with them out of love for her children
	15 : 12	each child singly and all together
	15 : 15	She watched the flesh of her children consumed by fire
	15 : 20	When you saw the flesh of children burned
	15 : 20	upon the flesh of other children
	15 : 21	as did the voices of the children in torture
	15 : 23	strengthened her to disregard her temporal love for her children
	15 : 24	Although she witnessed the destruction of 7 children
	15 : 25	and the rackings of her children
	15 : 26	one bearing death and the other deliverance for her children
	16 : 1	endured seeing her children tortured to death
	16 : 6	After bearing 7 children, I am now the mother of none !
	16 : 9	Alas for my children, some unmarried
	16 : 9	I shall not see your children
	16 : 10	Alas, I who had so many and beautiful children
	17 : 6	For your children were true descendants of father Abraham
	17 : 7	as they saw the mother of the 7 children
	18 : 1	O Israelite children, offspring of the seed of Abraham
	18 : 6	expressed also these principles to her children :
	18 : 9	A happy man was he, who lived out his life with good children

CHILDBIRTH   2

L Jr	6 : 29	Sacrifices to them may be touched by women in menstruation or at childbirth
4 Ma	16 : 7	O 7 childbirths all in vain, 7 profitless pregnancies

CHILDHOOD   2

2 Ma	6 : 23	and his excellent life even from childhood
	15 : 12	and had been trained from childhood

CHILDLESS   1

Sir	16 : 3	and to die childless is better than to have ungodly children

CHILDLESSNESS   1

Wis	4 : 1	Better than this is childlessness with virtue

CHIN   2

4 Ma	9 : 28	flayed all his flesh up to his chin
	15 : 15	and the flesh of the head to the chin exposed like masks

CHISLEV   6 = 0.004 %

1 Ma	1 : 54	Now on the 15th day of Chislev, in the 145th year
	4 : 52	which is the month of Chislev
	4 : 59	beginning with the 25th day of the month of Chislev
2 Ma	1 : 9	in the month of Chislev, in the 188th year
	1 : 18	Since on the 25th day of Chislev
	10 : 5	that is, on the 25th day of the same month, which was Chislev

CHOBA   3 = 0.002 %

Jud	4 : 4	and to Choba and Aesora and the valley of Salem
	15 : 4	and Choba and Kola, and to all the frontiers of Israel
	15 : 5	and cut them down as far as Choba

CHOICE, subst.   2

Sir	15 : 15	and to act faithfully is a matter of your own choice
1 Ma	10 : 32	that he may station in it men of his own choice to guard it

CHOICE, adj.   1

Sir	24 : 15	and like choice myrrh I spread a pleasant odour

CHOKE   2

2 Es	16 : 77	Woe to those who are choked by their sins
	16 : 77	as a field is choked with underbrush

CHOKING   1

Sir	51 : 4	from choking fire on every side

CHOOSE   51 = 0.033 %

Tob	1 : 4	This was the place which had been chosen
Jud	8 : 15	For if he does not choose to help us within these 5 days
	10 : 17	They chose from their number a 100 men
	11 : 1	who chose to serve Nebuchadnezzar
Wis	7 : 10	and I chose to have her rather than light
	9 : 7	Thou hast chosen me to be king of thy people
	12 : 18	for thou hast power to act whenever thou dost choose
Sir	6 : 18	My son, from your youth up choose instruction
	15 : 17	and whichever he chooses will be given to him
	45 : 4	he chose him out of all mankind
	45 : 16	He chose him out of all the living
Bar	3 : 27	God did not choose them, nor give them the way to knowledge
Sus	13 : 23	I choose not to do it and to fall into your hands
1 Ma	1 : 63	They chose to die rather than to be defiled by food
	2 : 19	obey him, and have chosen to do his commandments
	3 : 38	Lysias chose Ptolemy the son of Dorymenes
	4 : 42	He chose blameless priests devoted to the law
	5 : 17	Choose your men and go and rescue your brethren in Galilee

7:8	So the king chose Bacchides, one of the king's friends
7:37	Thou didst choose this house to be called by thy name
8:17	So Judas chose Eupolemus the son of John, son of Accos
9:25	And Bacchides chose the ungodly
9:30	So now we have chosen you today to take his place
10:74	He chose 10,000 men and set out from Jerusalem
11:23	and he chose some of the elders of Israel
12:1	he chose men and sent them to Rome
12:16	We therefore have chosen Numenius the son of Antiochus
12:45	and choose for yourself a few men to stay with you
13:34	Simon also chose men and sent them to Demetrius the king
16:4	So John chose out of the country 20,000 warriors and horsemen
2 Ma 1:25	who didst choose the fathers and consecrate them
3:7	The king chose Heliodorus, who was in charge of his affairs
4:19	chosen as being Antiochian citizens from Jerusalem
5:19	But the Lord did not choose the nation
6:9	and should slay those who did not choose
7:14	One cannot but choose to die at the hands of men
11:25	Accordingly, since we choose that this nation also
14:12	And he immediately chose Nicanor
1 Es 5:1	After this the heads of fathers' houses were chosen to go up
8:10	who freely choose to do so
9:16	Ezra the priest chose for himself
3 Ma 2:9	chose this city and sanctified this place for your name
6:10	and destroy us, Lord, by whatever fate you choose
2 Es 2:15	establish their feet, because I have chosen you, says the Lord
2:17	for I have chosen you, says the Lord
3:13	thou didst choose for thyself one of them
5:23	thou hast chosen one vine
5:24	thou hast chosen for thyself one region
5:24	thou hast chosen for thyself one lily
6:54	the people whom thou hast chosen
7:129	Choose for yourself life, that you may live !

CHORAL 2
3 Ma 6:35	But the Jews, when they had arranged the aforementioned choral group
4 Ma 14:14	move in choral dance around religion

CHORBE 1
1 Es 5:12	The sons of Chorbe, 705

CHORUS 5 = 0.003 %
3 Ma 6:32	they formed choruses as a sign of peaceful joy
4 Ma 8:4	grouped about their mother as if in a chorus
13:8	For they constituted a holy chorus of religion and
14:8	so these youths, forming a chorus
18:23	are gathered together into the chorus of the fathers

CHOSAMAEUS 1
1 Es 9:32	and Sabbaias and Simon Chosamaeus

CHOSEN 6 = 0.004 %
Tob 8:15	let all thy angels and thy chosen people bless thee for ever
Ad E 16:21	has made this day to be a joy to his chosen people
Sir 47:22	he will never blot out the descendants of his chosen one
49:6	who set fire to the chosen city of the sanctuary
2 Es 15:53	if you had not always killed my chosen people
15:56	As you will do to my chosen people, says the Lord

CHRONIC 1
Sir 30:17	and eternal rest than chronic sickness

CHRONICLE 3 = 0.002 %
1 Ma 16:24	in the chronicles of his high priesthood
1 Es 1:42	are written in the chronicles of the kings
2:22	You will find in the chronicles what has been written about them

CHURN up 1
2 Es 16:12	the sea is churned up from the depths

CHUSI 1
Jud 7:18	toward Acraba, which is near Chusi beside the brook Mochmur

CILICIA 7 = 0.005 %
Jud 1:7	those who lived in Cilicia and Damascus
1:12	on the whole territory of Cilicia and Damascus and Syria
2:21	near the mountain which is to the north of Upper Cilicia
2:25	He also seized the territory of Cilicia
1 Ma 11:14	Now Alexander the king was in Cilicia at that time
2 Ma 4:36	When the king returned from the region of Cilicia
4 Ma 4:2	governor of Syria, Phoenicia, and Cilicia

CIRCLE, subst. 4 = 0.003 %
Wis 13:2	or the circle of the stars, or turbulent water
2 Es 5:42	He said to me, I shall liken my judgment to a circle
6:1	At the beginning of the circle of the earth
4 Ma 14:17	by flying in circles around them in the anguish of love

CIRCLE, verb 2
Jud 13:10	and circled around the valley
1 Ma 13:20	and he circled around by the way to Adora

CIRCUIT 3 = 0.002 %
Sir 24:5	Alone I have made the circuit of the vault of heaven
1 Es 4:34	for it makes the circuit of the heavens
3 Ma 4:11	nor in any way claim to be inside the circuit of the city

CIRCULATE 1
3 Ma 3:2	a hostile rumour was circulated against the Jewish nation

CIRCUMCISE 6 = 0.004 %
Jud 14:10	he believed firmly in God, and was circumcised
1 Ma 1:60	the women who had their children circumcised
1:61	and their families and those who circumcised them
2:46	they forcibly circumcised all the uncircumcised boys
2 Ma 6:10	for having circumcised their children
4 Ma 4:25	because they had circumcised their sons

CIRCUMCISION 2
1 Ma 1:15	and removed the marks of circumcision
2 Es 1:31	and circumcisions of the flesh

CIRCUMFERENCE 1
Sir 50:3	a reservoir like the sea in circumference

CIRCUMSTANCE 6 = 0.004 %
Sir 20:11	from humble circumstances
22:23	For one should not always despise restricted circumstances
29:8	Nevertheless, be patient with a man in humble circumstances
2 Es 7:18	The righteous therefore can endure difficult circumstances
7:18	have suffered the difficult circumstances
16:18	What shall they do in these circumstances

CISTERN 5 = 0.003 %
Jud 7:21	their cisterns were going dry
8:31	and the Lord will send us rain to fill our cisterns
Sir 50:3	In his days a cistern for water was quarried out
2 Ma 1:19	and secretly hid it in the hollow of a dry cistern
10:37	They killed Timothy, who was hidden in a cistern

CITADEL 32 = 0.021 %
1 Ma 1:33	and it became their citadel
3:45	and the sons of aliens held the citadel
4:2	Men from the citadel were his guides
4:41	to fight against those in the citadel
6:18	Now the men in the citadel kept hemming Israel in
6:20	and besieged the citadel in the 150th year
6:24	For this reason the sons of our people besieged the citadel
6:26	against the citadel in Jerusalem to take it
6:32	Then Judas marched away from the citadel
9:52	and Gazara, and the citadel
9:53	in the citadel at Jerusalem
10:6	and he commanded that the hostages in the citadel
10:7	and of the men in the citadel
10:9	But the men in the citadel released the hostages to Jonathan
10:32	I release also my control of the citadel in Jerusalem
11:20	to attack the citadel in Jerusalem
11:21	that Jonathan was besieging the citadel
11:41	that he remove the troops of the citadel from Jerusalem
12:36	and to erect a high barrier between the citadel and the city
13:21	Now the men in the citadel kept sending envoys to Trypho
13:49	The men in the citadel at Jerusalem
13:50	and cleansed the citadel from its pollutions
13:52	alongside the citadel
14:7	he ruled over Gazara and Beth-zur and the citadel
14:36	who had built themselves a citadel
15:28	and the citadel in Jerusalem
2 Ma 4:12	right under the citadel
4:28	When Sostratus the captain of the citadel
5:5	Menelaus took refuge in the citadel
15:31	he sent for those who were in the citadel
15:35	And he hung Nicanor's head from the citadel
4 Ma 4:20	at the very citadel of our native land

CITIZEN 14 = 0.009 %
2 Ma 4:5	not accusing his fellow citizens
4:9	and to enrol the men of Jerusalem as citizens of Antioch
4:19	chosen as being Antiochian citizens from Jerusalem
4:50	having become the chief plotter against his fellow citizens
5:6	But Jason kept relentlessly slaughtering his fellow citizens
5:8	and his fellow citizens
5:23	who lorded it over his fellow citizens
5:23	In his malice toward the Jewish citizens
9:15	he would make, all of them, equal to citizens of Athens
9:19	To his worthy Jewish citizens
14:8	and second because I have regard also for my fellow citizens
14:37	as a man who loved his fellow citizens

| | 15:30 | the defender of his fellow citizens |
| 3 Ma | 1:22 | In addition, the bolder of the citizens |

CITIZENSHIP   3 = 0.002 %

3 Ma	2:30	they shall have equal citizenship with the Alexandrians
	3:21	by deciding both to deem them worthy of Alexandrian citizenship
	3:23	they not only spurn the priceless citizenship

CITY   278 = 0.181 %

Tob	13:9	O Jerusalem, the holy city
Jud	1:1	who ruled over the Assyrians in the great city of Nineveh
	1:14	Thus he took possession of his cities
	2:24	and destroyed all the hilltop cities along the brook Abron
	2:27	and sacked their cities and ravaged their lands
	3:4	Our cities also and their inhabitants are your slaves
	3:6	and stationed garrisons in the hilltop cities
	4:12	and the cities they had inherited to be destroyed
	5:3	What cities do they inhabit ?
	5:18	and their cities were captured by their enemies
	6:7	and put you in one of the cities beside the passes
	6:12	When the men of the city saw them
	6:12	and ran out of the city to the top of the hill
	6:14	Then the men of Israel came down from their city and found him
	6:14	and placed him before the magistrates of their city
	6:16	They called together all the elders of the city
	7:7	and examined the approaches to the city
	7:13	So thirst will destroy them, and they will give up their city
	7:13	that not a man gets out of the city
	7:22	and fell down in the streets of the city
	7:23	gathered about Uzziah and the rulers of the city
	7:26	Now call them in and surrender the whole city
	7:32	and they went up on the walls and towers of their city
	7:32	And they were greatly depressed in the city
	8:3	and took to his bed and died in Bethulia his city
	8:9	to surrender the city to the Assyrians after 5 days
	8:10	to summon Chabris and Charmis, the elders of her city
	8:11	promising to surrender the city to our enemies
	8:18	or city of ours which worshipped gods made with hands
	8:33	Stand at the city gate tonight
	8:33	to surrender the city to our enemies
	10:6	Then they went out to the city gate of Bethulia
	10:6	with the elders of the city, Chabris and Charmis
	10:9	Order the gate of the city to be opened for me
	10:10	and the men of the city watched her
	13:12	When the men of her city heard her voice
	13:12	they hurried down to the city gate
	13:12	and called together the elders of the city
	14:2	let every valiant man take his weapons and go out of the city
	14:9	and made a joyful noise in their city
Ad E	11:3	He was a Jew, dwelling in the city of Susa
	16:24	Every city and country, without exception
Wis	9:8	and an altar in the city of thy habitation
	10:6	he escaped the fire that descended on the Five Cities
Sir	9:7	Do not look around in the streets of a city
	9:13	and that you are going about on the city battlements
	9:18	A babbler is feared in his city
	10:2	and like the ruler of the city, so are all its inhabitants
	10:3	but a city will grow
	16:4	a city will be filled with people
	23:21	This man will be punished in the streets of the city
	24:11	In the beloved city likewise he gave me a resting place
	26:5	The slander of a city, the gathering of a mob
	28:14	and destroyed strong cities
	31:24	The city will complain of the one who is niggardly with food
	36:13	Have pity on the city of thy sanctuary
	36:26	that skips from city to city ?
	38:32	Without them a city cannot be established
	40:19	Children and the building of a city establish a man's name
	42:11	a byword in the city and notorious among the people
	46:2	and stretched out his sword against the cities !
	48:17	Hezekiah fortified his city
	49:6	who set fire to the chosen city of the sanctuary
	50:4	and fortified the city to withstand a siege
Bar	2:23	I will make to cease from the cities of Judah
	4:32	Wretched will be the cities which your children served as slaves
	4:32	wretched will be the city which received your sons
P Az	5	the holy city of our fathers
1 Ma	1:19	And they captured the fortified cities in the land of Egypt
	1:29	2 years later the king sent to the cities of Judah
	1:30	but he suddenly fell upon the city, dealt it a severe blow
	1:31	He plundered the city, burned it with fire
	1:33	Then they fortified the city of David
	1:44	and the cities of Judah
	1:51	and commanded the cities of Judah to offer sacrifice, city by city
	1:54	They also built altars in the surrounding cities of Judah
	1:58	against those found month after month in the cities
	2:7	the ruin of my people, the ruin of the holy city
	2:15	came to the city of Modein to make them offer sacrifice

	2:17	You are a leader, honoured and great in this city
	2:27	Then Mattathias cried out in the city with a loud voice
	2:28	and left all that they had in the city
	2:31	and to troops in Jerusalem the city of David
	3:8	He went through the cities of Judah
	5:26	all these cities were strong and large
	5:27	and some have been shut up in the other cities of Gilead
	5:28	and he took the city
	5:31	and that the cry of the city went up to Heaven
	5:36	Maked, and Bosor, and the other cities of Gilead
	5:44	But he took the city
	5:46	This was a large and very strong city on the road
	5:47	But the men of the city shut them out
	5:50	and he fought against the city
	5:50	and the city was delivered into his hands
	5:51	and razed and plundered the city
	5:51	Then he passed through the city over the slain
	5:59	And Gorgias and his men came out of the city
	5:68	he plundered the cities and returned to the land of Judah
	6:1	was a city famed for its wealth in silver and gold
	6:3	So he came and tried to take the city and plunder it
	6:3	but he could not, because his plan became known to the men of the city
	6:7	with high walls as before, and also Beth-zur, his city
	6:49	and they evacuated the city
	6:63	He found Philip in control of the city
	6:63	but he fought against him, and took the city by force
	7:1	sailed with a few men to a city by the sea
	7:24	and he prevented those in the city
	7:32	and the rest fled into the city of David
	9:50	and built strong cities in Judea :
	9:52	He also fortified the city of Beth-zur
	9:65	But Jonathan left Simon his brother in the city
	9:67	and Simon and his men sallied out from the city
	10:10	and began to rebuild and restore the city
	10:63	Go forth with him into the middle of the city
	10:71	for I have with me the power of the cities
	10:75	but the men of the city closed its gates
	10:76	and the men of the city became afraid and opened the gates
	10:86	and the men of the city came out to meet him with great pomp
	11:2	and the people of the cities opened their gates to him
	11:3	But when Ptolemy entered the cities
	11:3	he stationed forces as a garrison in each city
	11:8	So King Ptolemy gained control of the coastal cities
	11:45	Then the men of the city assembled within the city
	11:46	Then the men of the city seized the main streets of the city
	11:47	and then spread out through the city
	11:48	They set fire to the city and seized much spoil on that day
	11:49	When the men of the city saw
	11:49	that the Jews had gained control of the city as they pleased
	11:50	and make the Jews stop fighting against us and our city
	11:60	and travelled beyond the river and among the cities
	11:60	When he came to Askalon, the people of the city met him
	11:66	He removed them from there, took possession of the city
	12:36	and to erect a high barrier between the citadel and the city
	12:36	to separate it from the city, in order to isolate it
	12:37	So they gathered together to build up the city
	13:25	and buried him in Modein, in the city of his fathers
	13:43	He made a siege engine, brought it up to the city
	13:44	The men in the siege engine leaped out into the city
	13:44	and a great tumult arose in the city
	13:45	The men in the city, with their wives and children
	13:47	But he expelled them from the city
	14:10	He supplied the cities with food
	14:17	and that he was ruling over the country and the cities in it
	14:20	The rulers and the city of the Spartans
	14:33	He fortified the cities of Judea
	14:34	He settled Jews there, and provided in those cities
	14:36	as were also the men in the city of David in Jerusalem
	14:37	for the safety of the country and of the city
	15:4	and those who have devastated many cities in my kingdom
	15:14	He surrounded the city
	15:14	he pressed the city hard from land and sea
	15:19	or make war against them and their cities and their country
	15:28	they are cities of my kingdom
	15:30	Now then, hand over the cities which you have seized
	15:31	and the tribute money of the cities, 500 talents more
	16:14	Now Simon was visiting the cities of the country
	16:18	and to turn over to him the cities and the country
2 Ma	1:12	For he drove out those who fought against the holy city
	2:22	and freed the city
	3:1	While the holy city was inhabited in unbroken peace
	3:4	about the administration of the city market
	3:8	of the cities of Coelesyria and Phoenicia
	3:9	and had been kindly welcomed by the high priest of the city
	3:14	There was no little distress throughout the whole city
	4:2	the man who was the benefactor of the city
	4:22	He was welcomed magnificently by Jason and the city
	4:30	revolted because their cities had been given
	4:32	he had sold to Tyre and the neighbouring cities

4:36	the Jews in the city appealed to him
4:38	and led him about the whole city to that very place
4:39	had been committed in the city by Lysimachus
4:48	for the city and the villages and the holy vessels
5:2	And it happened that over all the city, for almost 40 days
5:5	and suddenly made an assault upon the city
5:5	and at last the city was being taken
5:8	fleeing from city to city, pursued by all men
5:11	and took the city by storm
5:17	because of the sins of those who dwelt in the city
5:26	then rushed into the city with his armed men
6:8	a decree was issued to the neighbouring Greek cities
6:10	These women they publicly paraded about the city
8:3	and to have mercy on the city which was being destroyed
8:11	And he immediately sent to the cities on the sea coast
8:17	and the torture of the derided city
8:33	in the city of their fathers
9:2	For he had entered the city called Persepolis
9:2	and attempted to rob the temples and control the city
9:14	stating that the holy city
10:1	the Lord leading them on, recovered the temple and the city
10:27	and advanced a considerable distance from the city
10:36	and they occupied the city
11:2	He intended to make the city a home for Greeks
12:4	and this was done by public vote of the city
12:7	Then, because the city's gates were closed
12:13	He also attacked a certain city
12:16	They took the city by the will of God
12:27	a fortified city where Lysias dwelt
12:28	and they got the city into their hands
12:38	and went to the city of Adullam
13:13	and get possession of the city
13:14	for the laws, temple, city, country, and commonwealth
15:14	and prays much for the people and the holy city
15:17	because the city and the sanctuary
15:19	And those who had to remain in the city
15:37	And from that time the city has been in the possession of the Hebrews
1 Es 2:18	and are building that rebellious and wicked city
2:19	Now if this city is built and the walls finished
2:22	and will learn that this city was rebellious
2:22	troubling both kings and other cities
2:23	That is why this city was laid waste
2:24	that if this city is built and its walls finished
2:26	that this city from of old has fought against kings
2:28	to prevent these men from building the city
4:48	and to help him build the city
4:53	and that all who came from Babylonia to build the city
4:56	for all who guarded the city
6:8	and entered the city of Jerusalem
6:9	building in the city of Jerusalem a great new house for the Lord
3 Ma 1:6	Ptolemy decided to visit the neighbouring cities
1:17	and those who remained behind in the city
1:19	in a disorderly rush flocked together in the city
2:9	chose this city and sanctified this place for your name
2:31	to be exacted for maintaining the religion of their city
3:8	The Greeks in the city, though wronged in no way
3:16	to the temples in the cities
4:3	What district or city, or what habitable place at all
4:4	in the several cities
4:11	in front of the city
4:11	to all coming back into the city
4:11	and to those from the city going out into the country
4:11	nor in any way claim to be inside the circuit of the city
4:12	the king, hearing that the Jews' compatriots from the city
5:24	The crowds of the city had been assembled
5:41	As a result the city is in a tumult
5:44	at the places in the city most favourable for keeping guard
5:46	the city now being filled
6:5	and was lifted up against your holy city
6:30	Then the king, when he had returned to the city
6:41	to the generals in the cities
7:16	began their departure from the city
2 Es 3:1	In the 30th year after the destruction of our city
3:24	And thou didst command him to build a city for thy name
3:25	but the inhabitants of the city transgressed
3:27	So thou didst deliver the city into the hands of thy enemies
5:25	and from all the cities that have been built
7:6	Another example : There is a city built and set on a plain
7:9	If now that city is given to a man for an inheritance
7:26	that the city which now is not seen shall appear
8:52	a city is built, rest is appointed, goodness is established
10:4	And now I intend not to return to the city
10:17	Therefore go into the city to your husband
10:18	I will not go into the city, but I will die here
10:27	but there was an established city
10:42	but an established city has appeared to you
10:44	whom you now behold as an established city, is Zion
10:46	And after 3,000 years Solomon built the city
10:54	where the city of the Most High was to be revealed

12:40	and I had not returned to the city
12:50	So the people went into the city, as I told them to do
13:31	city against city, place against place
15:17	For a man will desire to go into a city, and shall not be able
15:18	For because of their pride the cities shall be in confusion
15:42	And they shall destroy cities and walls
15:57	and your cities shall be wiped out
15:60	And as they pass they shall wreck the hateful city
15:62	And they shall devour you and your cities
16:23	and its cities shall be demolished
16:28	For out of a city, 10 shall be left
16:47	the more they adorn their cities
16:70	For in many places and in neighbouring cities
4 Ma 7:4	No city besieged with many ingenious war machines

CLAIM, verb   1
3 Ma 4:11   nor in any way claim to be inside the circuit of the city

CLAIM, subst.   1
1 Ma 15:3   and I intend to lay claim to the kingdom

CLAMP   1
4 Ma 11:10   and fitting iron clamps on them

CLAN   1
2 Es 3:7   peoples and clans, without number

CLANKING   1
1 Ma 6:41   and the clanking of their arms

CLAP, subst.   1
Sir 40:13   and crash like a loud clap of thunder in a rain

CLAP, verb   2
Sir 12:18   he will shake his head, and clap his hands
2 Es 15:53   exulting and clapping yours hands

CLAW   1
4 Ma 8:13   braziers and thumbscrews an iron claws and wedges and bellows

CLAY   13 = 0.008 %
Wis 7:9   and silver will be accounted as clay before her
15:7   he fashions out of the same clay
15:7   the worker in clay decides
15:8   he forms a futile god from the same clay
15:10   and his life is of less worth than clay
Sir 33:2   How can the clay pot associate with the iron kettle ?
33:13   As clay in the hand of the potter
38:30   He moulds the clay with his arm
Bel 14:7   for this is but clay inside and brass outside
2 Es 7:52   will you add to them lead and clay ?
7:55   and also iron and lead and clay
7:56   and iron than brass, and lead than iron, and clay than lead
8:2   it will tell you that it provides very much clay

CLEAN, adj.   3 = 0.002 %
Jud 12:9   So she returned clean and stayed in the tent
Wis 15:7   both the vessels that serve clean uses
Sir 34:4   From an unclean thing what will be made clean ?

CLEAN, verb   1
Sir 38:30   and he is careful to clean the furnace

CLEANSE   7 = 0.005 %
Sir 23:10   and utters the Name will not be cleansed from sin
38:10   and cleanse your heart from all sin
1 Ma 4:36   let us go up to cleanse the sanctuary and dedicate it
4:41   until he had cleansed the sanctuary
4:43   and they cleansed the sanctuary
13:47   and cleansed the houses in which the idols were
13:50   and cleansed the citadel from its pollutions

CLEAR, adj.   9 = 0.006 %
Wis 6:22   and make the knowledge of her clear
Sir 43:1   The pride of the heavenly heights is the clear firmament
1 Ma 12:8   which contained a clear declaration of alliance and friendship
2 Ma 2:9   It was also made clear
4:17   a fact which later events will make clear
6:30   It is clear to the Lord in his holy knowledge
12:40   And it became clear to all
15:35   a clear and conspicuous sign to every one
4 Ma 1:4   it is also clear that it masters

CLEARLY   6 = 0.004 %
Wis 10:21   and made the tongues of babes speak clearly
19:18   This may be clearly inferred
2 Ma 3:28   and they recognized clearly the sovereign power of God
3 Ma 4:19   he was clearly convinced about the matter

4 Ma 2 : 7   unless reason is clearly lord of the emotions ?
     3 : 6   Now this can be explained more clearly

CLEAVE, adhere   4 = 0.003 %
  Sir 2 : 3   Cleave to him and do not depart
     6 : 34   Who is wise ? Cleave to him
   24 : 24   cleave to him so that he may strengthen you
1 Es 4 : 20   and his own country, and cleaves to his wife

CLEAVE, split   1
2 Es 1 : 20   did I not cleave the rock so that waters flowed in abundance ?

CLEFT   1
2 Es 16 : 28   in thick groves and clefts in the rocks

CLEMENCY   2
3 Ma 3 : 15   but should cherish them with clemency and great benevolence
     7 : 6   and in accordance with the clemency

CLEOPATRA   3 = 0.002 %
Ad E 11 : 1   In the 4th year of the reign of Ptolemy and Cleopatra
1 Ma 10 : 57   he and Cleopatra his daughter
   10 : 58   and Ptolemy gave him Cleopatra his daughter in marriage

CLEVER   4 = 0.003 %
  Sir 1 : 6   Her clever devices – who knows them ?
     6 : 32   and if you apply yourself you will become clever
   21 : 12   He who is not clever cannot be taught
   21 : 20   but a clever man smiles quietly

CLEVERLY   1
2 Ma 14 : 31   that he had been cleverly outwitted by the man

CLEVERNESS   5 = 0.003 %
  Sir 19 : 23   There is a cleverness which is abominable
   19 : 25   There is a cleverness which is scrupulous but unjust
   21 : 12   but there is a cleverness which increases bitterness
   32 : 4   do not display your cleverness out of season
   34 : 10   but he that has travelled acquires much cleverness

CLIFF   1
4 Ma 7 : 5   For in setting his mind firm like a jutting cliff

CLIMB   1
4 Ma 3 : 12   and taking a pitcher climbed over the enemy's ramparts

CLING   6 = 0.004 %
  Sir 10 : 13   and the man who clings to it pours out abominations
   13 : 16   and a man clings to one like himself
   25 : 12   and faith is the beginning of clinging to him
  Bar 1 : 20   So to this day there have clung to us the calamities
    3 : 4   so that calamities have clung to us
2 Es 12 : 19   As for your seeing 8 little wings clinging to his wings

CLOAK   1
2 Ma 12 : 35   caught hold of Gorgias, and grasping his cloak

CLOSE, adj., adv.   11 = 0.007 %
  Jud 13 : 7   She came close to his bed
Ad E 16 : 7   which we hand on as from investigation of matters close at hand
  Sir 16 : 24   and pay close attention to my words
   51 : 26   it is to be found close by
1 Ma 9 : 16   they turned and followed close behind Judas and his men
   12 : 50   and kept marching in close formation, ready for battle
2 Ma 4 : 42   close by the treasury
    7 : 27   But, leaning close to him
   12 : 31   as the feast of weeks was close at hand
   15 : 20   and the enemy was already close at hand
2 Es 2 : 34   because he who will come at the end of the age is close at hand

CLOSE, subst.   1
  Sir 11 : 27   and at the close of a man's life

CLOSE, verb   8 = 0.005 %
  Jud 5 : 1   and had closed the passes in the hills
   13 : 1   and Bagoas closed the tent from outside
  Sir 30 : 18   Good things poured out upon a mouth that is closed
1 Ma 10 : 75   but the men of the city closed its gates
   12 : 48   the men of Ptolemais closed the gates and seized him
2 Ma 1 : 15   they closed the temple as soon as he entered it
   12 : 7   Then, because the city's gates were closed
2 Es 14 : 41   and my mouth was opened, and was no longer closed

CLOSED   1
2 Es 5 : 37   open for me the closed chambers

CLOTH   2
  Wis 7 : 4   I was nursed with care in swaddling cloths
1 Ma 4 : 23   and cloth dyed blue and sea purple, and great riches

CLOTHE   14 = 0.009 %
Ad E 15 : 6   clothed in the full array of his majesty
  Sir 40 : 4   to the one who is clothed in burlap
   45 : 8   He clothed him with superb perfection
   50 : 11   and clothed himself with superb perfection
  L Jr 6 : 33   to clothe their wives and children
1 Ma 1 : 28   and all the house of Jacob was clothed with shame
   10 : 62   and to clothe him in purple, and they did so
   10 : 64   and saw him clothed in purple, they all fled
   14 : 43   and that he should be clothed in purple and wear gold
   14 : 44   or to be clothed in purple or put on a gold buckle
2 Ma 11 : 8   clothed in white and brandishing weapons of gold
1 Es 3 : 6   He shall be clothed in purple, and drink from gold cups
2 Es 2 : 20   defend the orphan, clothe the naked
    2 : 40   and conclude the list of your people who are clothed in white

CLOTHES   8 = 0.005 %
  Sir 11 : 4   Do not boast about wearing fine clothes
  L Jr 6 : 31   and in their temples the priests sit with their clothes rent
1 Ma 2 : 14   And Mattathias and his sons rent their clothes
    3 : 47   and sprinkled ashes on their heads, and rent their clothes
    4 : 39   Then they rent their clothes
   13 : 45   went up on the wall with their clothes rent
1 Es 4 : 17   Women make men's clothes
2 Es 9 : 38   and her clothes were rent, and there were ashes on her head

CLOTHING   9 = 0.006 %
  Tob 1 : 17   and my clothing to the naked
    4 : 16   and of your clothing to the naked
  Jud 10 : 7   and her clothing changed
  Sir 29 : 21   The essentials for life are water and bread and clothing
   39 : 26   the blood of the grape, and oil and clothing
  L Jr 6 : 33   The priests take some of the clothing of their gods
1 Ma 11 : 24   taking silver and gold and clothing and numerous other gifts
2 Ma 3 : 33   dressed in the same clothing, and they stood and said
2 Es 2 : 45   These are they who have put off mortal clothing

CLOUD   27 = 0.018 %
  Wis 2 : 4   our life will pass away like the traces of a cloud
    5 : 21   as from a well-drawn bow of clouds
   19 : 7   The cloud was seen overshadowing the camp
  Sir 13 : 23   and they extol to the clouds what he says
   24 : 4   and my throne was in a pillar of cloud
   35 : 16   and his prayer will reach to the clouds
   35 : 17   The prayer of the humble pierces the clouds
   35 : 20   as clouds of rain in the time of drought
   43 : 14   and the clouds fly forth like birds
   43 : 15   In his majesty he amasses the clouds
   50 : 6   Like the morning star among the clouds
   50 : 7   and like the rainbow gleaming in glorious clouds
   50 : 10   and like a cypress towering in the clouds
  Bar 3 : 29   and brought her down from the clouds ?
  L Jr 6 : 62   When God commands the clouds to go over the whole world
  P Az   51   Bless the Lord, lightnings and clouds
2 Ma 2 : 8   and the glory of the Lord and the cloud will appear
2 Es 4 : 49   And after this a cloud full of water passed before me
    4 : 49   drops remained in the cloud
    7 : 40   or cloud or thunder or lightning or wind
   11 : 2   and the clouds were gathered about him
   13 : 3   that man flew with the clouds of heaven
   13 : 20   than to pass from the world like a cloud
   15 : 34   Behold, clouds from the east
   15 : 38   And, after that, heavy storm clouds shall be stirred up from the south
   15 : 39   over the cloud that was raised in wrath
   15 : 40   And great and mighty clouds, full of wrath and tempest

CLOUD over   1
2 Ma 1 : 22   and the sun, which had been clouded over, shone out

CLUB   1
  Bel 14 : 26   I will slay the dragon without sword or club

CLUE   1
  Sir 37 : 17   As a clue to changes of heart

CLUSTER   3 = 0.002 %
2 Es 9 : 21   and saved for myself one grape out of a cluster
   12 : 42   like a cluster of grapes from the vintage
   16 : 30   some clusters may be left by those who search carefully

CNIDUS   1
1 Ma 15 : 23   and Cnidus and Cyprus and Cyrene

COAL   4 = 0.003 %
  Sir 8 : 10   Do not kindle the coals of a sinner
   11 : 32   From a spark of fire come many burning coals
2 Es 16 : 53   for God will burn coals of fire on the head of him who says
4 Ma 9 : 20   and the heap of coals was being quenched by drippings of gore

COAST, subst.   2
   Jud   1:12   and every one in Egypt, as far as the coasts of the 2 seas
   2 Ma   8:11   And he immediately sent to the cities on the sea coast

COASTAL   2
   1 Ma   11:8   So King Ptolemy gained control of the coastal cities
         15:38   Then the king made Cendebaeus commander-in-chief of the coastal country

COASTLAND   2
   Jud   5:2   and all the governors of the coastland
        7:8   and the commanders of the coastland came to him and said

COAT   2
   Wis   13:14   giving it a coat of red paint and colouring its surface red
   1 Ma   6:35   armed with coats of mail

COCK   1
   3 Ma   5:23   Then, as soon as the cock had crowed in the early morning

COELESYRIA   14 = 0.009 %
   1 Ma   10:69   And Demetrius appointed Apollonius the governor of Coelesyria
   2 Ma   3:5   who at that time was governor of Coelesyria and Phoenicia
        3:8   of the cities of Coelesyria and Phoenicia
        4:4   and governor of Coelesyria and Phoenicia
        8:8   the governor of Coelesyria and Phoenicia
       10:11   and to be chief governor of Coelesyria and Phoenicia
   1 Es   2:17   in Coelesyria and Phoenicia :
        2:24   you will no longer have access to Coelesyria and Phoenicia
        2:27   and exacted tribute from Coelesyria and Phoenicia
        4:48   And he wrote letters to all the governors in Coelesyria
        6:29   and that out of the tribute of Coelesyria and Phoenicia
        7:1   Then Sisinnes the governor of Coelesyria and Phoenicia
        8:67   and to the governors of Coelesyria and Phoenicia
   3 Ma   3:15   the nations inhabiting Coele-Syria and Phoenicia

COERCIVE   1
   4 Ma   9:6   that we young men should die despising your coercive tortures

COFFER   1
   1 Ma   3:28   And he opened his coffers

COINAGE   1
   1 Ma   15:6   I permit you to mint your own coinage

COLD, subst.   3 = 0.002 %
   P Az   45   Bless the Lord, winter cold and summer heat
         49   Bless the Lord, ice and cold
   2 Es   7:41   or frost or cold or hail or rain or dew

COLD, adj.   2
   Sir   43:20   The cold north wind blows, and ice freezes over the water
   4 Ma   11:26   Your fire is cold to us, and the catapults painless

COLIC   1
   Sir   31:20   and of nausea and colic are with the glutton

COLLAPSE   1
   Ad E   15:7   and collapsed upon the head of the maid who went before her

COLLAR   2
   Sir   6:24   and your neck into her collar
        6:29   and her collar a glorious robe

COLLECT   14 = 0.009 %
   Jud   2:17   He collected a vast number of camels
   Bar   1:6   and they collected money, each giving what he could
   1 Ma   1:35   and collecting the spoils of Jerusalem
        3:11   and collect the revenues from those regions
       10:30   and instead of collecting the third of the grain
       10:30   I will not collect them from the land of Judah
       13:39   and whatever other tax has been collected in Jerusalem
       13:39   shall be collected no longer
   2 Ma   2:13   and collected the books about the kings and prophets
        2:14   In the same way Judas also collected all the books that had been lost
        8:27   And when they had collected the arms of the enemy
        8:31   Collecting the arms of the enemy
       10:24   and collected the cavalry from Asia in no small number
   1 Es   8:13   and to collect for the Lord in Jerusalem

COLLECTION   2
   2 Ma   4:28   for the collection of the revenue was his responsibility
       12:43   He also took up a collection, man by man

COLLECTOR   1
   1 Ma   1:29   a chief collector of tribute

COLONNADE   3 = 0.002 %
   Sir   22:17   is like the stucco decoration on the wall of a colonnade
   2 Ma   4:46   Therefore Ptolemy, taking the king aside into a colonnade
   3 Ma   5:23   began to move them along in the great colonnade

COLONY   1
   Wis   12:7   might receive a worthy colony of the servants of God

COLOUR, COLOR, subst.   5 = 0.003 %
   Wis   15:4   a figure stained with varied colours
   2 Ma   3:16   for his face and the change in his colour
   2 Es   6:44   and flowers of inimitable colour
        9:17   and as are the flowers, so are the colours
       14:39   but its colour was like fire

COLOUR, COLOR, verb   1
   Wis   13:14   giving it a coat of red paint and colouring its surface red

COLUMN   2
   1 Ma   13:29   erecting about them great columns
       13:29   and upon the columns he put suits of armour

COMB   1
   Jud   10:3   and combed her hair and put on a tiara

COMBINE   1
   2 Es   15:31   and if they combine in great power

COMBINED   1
   Jud   1:16   he and all his combined forces, a vast body of troops

COME   423 = 0.276 %
   Tob   1:18   any who came fleeing from Judea
        5:13   My brother, you come of good stock
        6:1   they came at evening to the Tigris river and camped there
        6:5   until they came near to Ecbatana
        7:11   and when each came to her he died in the night
        9:6   and came to the wedding feast
       11:1   So he continued on his way until they came near to Nineveh
       11:6   And she caught sight of him coming, and said to his father
       11:6   Behold, your son is coming
       11:17   When Tobit came near to Sarah his daughter-in-law
       11:18   Ahikar and his nephew Nadab came
       12:18   For I did not come as a favour on my part
       13:11   Many nations will come from afar to the name of the Lord God
   Jud   1:14   and came to Ecbatana, captured its towers
        2:7   for I am coming against them in my anger
        2:25   and came to the southern borders of Japheth
        3:4   come and deal with them in any way that seems good to you
        3:5   The men came to Holofernes and told him all this
        3:9   Then he came to the edge of Esdraelon
        5:5   No falsehood shall come from your servant's mouth
        5:8   the God they had come to know
        6:5   until I take revenge on this race that came out of Egypt
       6:11   and came to the springs below Bethulia
        7:8   and the commanders of the coastland came to him and said
        7:31   But if these days pass by, and no help comes for us
        8:11   They came to her, and she said to them
        9:5   and those that are to come
        9:5   Yea, the things thou didst intend came to pass
       10:12   and where are you coming from, and where are you going ?
       10:18   and they came and stood around her
       10:23   And when Judith came into the presence of Holofernes and his servants
       11:3   since you have come to safety
       11:18   And I will come and tell you
       11:19   till you come to Jerusalem
       12:13   This beautiful maidservant will please come to my lord
       13:1   When evening came, his slaves quickly withdrew
       13:7   She came close to his bed
       13:10   and went up the mountain to Bethulia and came to its gates
       14:2   And as soon as morning comes and the sun rises
       14:3   Then fear will come over them, and they will flee before you
       14:6   And when he came and saw the head of Holofernes
       14:13   So they came to Holofernes' tent and said to the steward
       15:2   Fear and trembling came over them
       15:5   Those in Jerusalem and all the hill country also came
       15:8   came to witness the good things
       16:4   he came with myriads of his warriors
   Ad E   10:4   And Mordecai said, These things have come from God
       10:11   And these 2 lots came to the hour and moment and day
       11:10   there came a great river, with abundant water
       11:11   light came, and the sun rose
       15:8   and took her in his arms until she came to herself
       15:10   you shall not die, for our law applies only to the people. Come near
       16:9   and always judging what comes before our eyes
   Wis   1:9   and a report of his words will come to the Lord
        2:1   and there is no remedy when a man comes to his end
        2:6   Come, therefore, let us enjoy the good things that exist

3 :16	But children of adulterers will not come to maturity
4 :5	The branches will be broken off before they come to maturity
4 :20	They will come with dread when their sins are reckoned up
5 :12	the air, thus divided, comes together at once
6 :5	he will come upon you terribly and swiftly
6 :22	I will tell you what wisdom is and how she came to be
7 :7	I called upon God, and the spirit of wisdom came to me
7 :11	All good things came to me along with her
7 :14	commended for the gifts that come from instruction
8 :8	she knows the things of old, and infers the things to come
8 :13	to those who come after me
9 :6	yet without the wisdom that comes from thee
12 :12	Or who will come before me ?
12 :27	Therefore the utmost condemnation came upon them
13 :5	comes a corresponding perception of their Creator
14 :5	they come safely to land
14 :7	For blessed is the wood by which righteousness comes
16 :4	inexorable want should come
16 :5	came upon thy people
16 :10	for thy mercy came to their help and healed them
17 :12	that come from reason
17 :18	Whether there came a whistling wind
18 :20	and a plague came upon the multitude in the desert
19 :13	The punishment did not come upon the sinners
19 :14	when they came to them
19 :15	but punishment of some sort will come upon the former
Sir pr.	When I came to Egypt
1 :1	All wisdom comes from the Lord and is with him for ever
1 :30	because you did not come in the fear of the Lord
3 :8	that a blessing from him may come upon you
3 :11	For a man's glory comes from honouring his father
5 :13	Glory and dishonour come from speaking
5 :14	for shame comes to the thief
6 :19	Come to her like one who ploughs and sows
6 :26	Come to her with all your soul
11 :14	come from the Lord
11 :15	come from the Lord
11 :15	affection and the ways of good works come from him
11 :32	From a spark of fire come many burning coals
12 :3	No good will come to the man who persists in evil
15 :2	She will come to meet him like a mother
19 :9	and when the time comes he will hate you
21 :5	and his judgment comes speedily
24 :19	Come to me, you who desire me
26 :28	and because of a 3rd anger comes over me :
27 :27	and he will not know where it came from
28 :12	and both come out of your mouth
29 :26	Come here, stranger, prepare the table
29 :27	my brother has come to stay with me
31 :6	Many have come to ruin because of gold
38 :2	for healing comes from the Most High
39 :31	and when their times come, they will not transgress his word
40 :7	and wonders that his fear came to nothing
40 :10	and on their account the flood came
42 :13	for from the garments comes the moth
42 :13	and from a woman comes woman's wickedness
43 :7	From the moon comes the sign for feast days
44 :17	therefore a remnant was left to the earth when the flood came
47 :25	till vengeance came upon them
48 :25	and the hidden things before they came to pass
49 :4	the kings of Judah came to an end
50 :5	as he came out of the inner sanctuary !
Bar 1 :3	and in the hearing of all the people who came to hear the book
2 :7	All those calamities with which the Lord threatened us have come upon us
2 :30	But in the land of their exile they will come to themselves
4 :9	For she saw the wrath that came upon you from God
4 :14	Let the neighbours of Zion come
4 :22	and joy has come to me from the Holy One
4 :22	because of the mercy which soon will come to you
4 :24	which will come to you with great glory
4 :25	the wrath that has come upon you from God
4 :35	For fire will come upon her from the Everlasting for many days
4 :36	and see the joy that is coming to you from God !
4 :37	Behold, your sons are coming, whom you sent away
4 :37	they are coming, gathered from east and west
5 :9	with the mercy and righteousness that come from him
L Jr 6 :3	Therefore when you have come to Babylon
6 :47	They have left only lies and reproach for those who come after
6 :48	For when war or calamity comes upon them
Sus 13 :4	and the Jews used to come to him because he was the most honoured of them all
13 :6	and all who had suits at law came to them
13 :28	the 2 elders came
13 :30	And she came, with her parents, her children, and all her kindred
13 :37	came to her and lay with her
13 :42	who art aware of all things before they come to be
13 :50	And the elders said to him, Come
13 :52	You old relic of wicked days, your sins have now come home

Bel 14 :15	In the night the priests came with their wives and children
14 :16	Early in the morning the king rose and came
14 :40	On the 7th day the king came to mourn for Daniel
14 :40	When he came to the den he looked in, and there sat Daniel
1 Ma 1 :1	who came from the land of Kittim
1 :11	for since we separated from them many evils have come upon us
1 :20	and came to Jerusalem with a strong force
1 :29	and he came to Jerusalem with a large force
1 :64	And very great wrath came upon Israel
2 :15	came to the city of Modein to make them offer sacrifice
2 :16	Many from Israel came to them
2 :18	Now be the first to come and do what the king commands
2 :41	Let us fight against every man who comes to attack us on the sabbath day
3 :17	But when they saw the army coming to meet them
3 :19	but strength comes from Heaven
3 :20	They come against us in great pride and lawlessness
4 :12	and saw them coming against them
4 :19	a detachment appeared, coming out of the hills
4 :29	They came into Idumea and encamped at Beth-zur
4 :46	on the temple hill until there should come a prophet
4 :60	to keep the Gentiles from coming
5 :11	They are preparing to come
5 :12	Now then come and rescue us from their hands
5 :14	came from Galilee and made a similar report
5 :39	ready to come and fight against you
5 :46	So they came to Ephron
5 :53	till he came to the land of Judah
5 :59	And Gorgias and his men came out of the city
6 :3	So he came and tried to take the city and plunder it
6 :5	Then some one came to him in Persia and reported
6 :11	I said to myself, To what distress I have come !
6 :13	that these evils have come upon me
6 :29	And mercenary forces came to him from other kingdoms
6 :31	They came through Idumea and encamped against Beth-zur
6 :58	Now then let us come to terms with these men
7 :5	Then there came to him
7 :10	So they marched away and came with a large force
7 :11	for they saw that they had come with a large force
7 :14	A priest of the line of Aaron has come with the army
7 :27	So Nicanor came to Jerusalem with a large force
7 :28	I shall come with a few men to see you face to face in peace
7 :29	So he came to Judas, and they greeted one another peaceably
7 :30	that Nicanor had come to him with treacherous intent
7 :33	Some of the priests came out of the sanctuary
7 :46	And men came out of all the villages of Judea round about
8 :1	that they pledged friendship to those who came to them
8 :4	They also subdued the kings who came against them
8 :9	The Greeks planned to come and destroy them
8 :24	If war comes first to Rome or to any of their allies
8 :27	if war comes first to the nation of the Jews
9 :10	If our time has come, let us die bravely for our brethren
9 :43	he came with a large force on the sabbath day
9 :60	He started to come with a large force
9 :64	Then he came and encamped against Beth-basi
9 :69	who had counselled him to come into the country
9 :72	and came no more in their territory
10 :7	Then Jonathan came to Jerusalem
10 :16	Come now, we will make him our friend and ally
10 :57	and came to Ptolemais in the 162nd year
10 :59	Then Alexander the king wrote to Jonathan to come to meet him
10 :67	came from Crete to the land of his fathers
10 :85	*came to 8,000 men*
11 :9	Come, let us make a covenant with each other
11 :15	And Alexander heard of it and came against him in battle
11 :22	he set out and came to Ptolemais
11 :44	and when they came to the king
11 :60	When he came to Askalon, the people of the city met him
11 :63	had come to Kadesh in Galilee with a large army
12 :15	for we have the help which comes from Heaven for our aid
12 :40	and he marched forth and came to Beth-shan
12 :41	and he came to Beth-shan
12 :42	When Trypho saw that he had come with a large army
12 :45	and come with me to Ptolemais
13 :20	After this Trypho came to invade the country and destroy it
13 :21	urging him to come to them by way of the wilderness
14 :22	have come to us to renew their friendship with us
15 :11	Antiochus pursued him, and he came in his flight to Dor
15 :17	The envoys of the Jews have come to us
15 :31	Otherwise we will come and conquer you
15 :32	So Athenobius the friend of the king came to Jerusalem
15 :40	So Cendebaeus came to Jamnia
16 :3	and may the help which comes from Heaven be with you
16 :5	was coming to meet them
16 :19	he sent letters to the captains asking them to come to him
16 :22	and he seized the men who came to destroy him and killed them
2 Ma 1 :7	which came upon us in those years
1 :14	Antiochus came to the place together with his friends
1 :15	and Antiochus had come with a few men
2 :5	And Jeremiah came and found a cave

2:14	on account of the war which had come upon us
2:21	and the appearances which came from heaven
3:2	it came about that the kings themselves honoured the place
3:9	and stated why he had come
3:17	For terror and bodily trembling had come over the man
3:27	and deep darkness came over him
3:39	and he strikes and destroys those who come to do it injury
4:10	When the king assented and Jason came to office
4:34	Andronicus came to Onias, and resorting to treachery
4:44	When the king came to Tyre
6:7	and when the feast of Dionysus came
6:9	One could see, therefore, the misery that had come upon them
7:22	I do not know how you came into being in my womb
7:28	Thus also mankind comes into being
8:6	Coming without warning
8:12	Word came to Judas concerning Nicanor's invasion
8:16	who were wickedly coming against them
8:18	to strike down those who are coming against us
8:19	when help came to their ancestors
8:20	the 8,000, by the help that came to them from heaven
8:25	of those who had come to buy them as slaves
9:3	While he was in Ecbatana, news came to him
9:7	And so it came about that he fell out of his chariot
9:11	and to come to his senses under the scourge of God
9:18	for the judgment of God had justly come upon him
9:24	or any unwelcome news came
9:28	came to the end of his life by a most pitiable fate
10:21	When word of what had happened came to Maccabeus
10:27	and when they came near to the enemy they halted
11:2	and came against the Jews
12:7	he withdrew, intending to come again
12:17	they came to Charax, to the Jews who are called Toubiani
12:22	terror and fear came over the enemy
13:1	In the 149th year word came to Judas and his men
13:1	that Antiochus Eupator was coming
13:7	By such a fate it came about
13:9	was coming to show to the Jews things far worse
14:1	3 years later, word came to Judas and his men
14:7	I mean the high priesthood – and have now come here
14:28	When this message came to Nicanor, he was troubled
15:8	when help had come to them from heaven
15:24	who come against thy holy people be struck down

1 Es

4:16	From women they came
4:16	from which comes wine
4:53	and that all who came from Babylonia to build the city
4:53	and all the priests who came
5:8	They came with Zerubbabel and Jeshua
5:44	when they came to the temple of God which is in Jerusalem
5:47	When the 7th month came
5:56	and all who had come to Jerusalem from the captivity
5:57	in the 2nd year after they came to Judea and Jerusalem
5:63	came to the building of this one
5:64	while many came with trumpets and a joyful noise
5:66	they came to find out what the sound of the trumpets meant
6:3	and Sathra-buzanes, and their associates came to them and said
6:20	Then this Shesh-Bazzar, after coming here
7:10	The people of Israel who came from the captivity
7:13	And the people of Israel who came from the captivity ate it
8:1	Ezra came, the son of Seraiah, son of Azariah
8:21	so that wrath may not come
8:61	and so we came to Jerusalem
8:68	the principal men came to me and said
8:78	And now in some measure mercy has come to us from thee, O Lord
8:86	And all that has happened to us has come about
9:12	come at the time appointed
9:55	And they came together

3 Ma

1:5	And so it came about that the enemy was routed in the action
2:5	to those who should come afterward
2:10	when we come to this place and pray
4:16	even to communicate or to come to one's help
5:42	which had come about within him for the protection of the Jews
6:36	that had come to them through God
7:6	Since we have come to realize

2 Es

1:4	The word of the Lord came to me, saying
1:35	I will give your houses to a people that will come
1:37	I call to witness the gratitude of the people that is to come
1:38	look with pride and see the people coming from the east
2:24	Pause and be quiet, my people, because your rest will come
2:27	for when the day of tribulation and anguish comes
2:32	Embrace your children until I come
2:33	When I came to them they rejected me
2:34	because he who will come at the end of the age is close at hand
3:10	as death came upon Adam, so the flood upon them
3:29	For when I came here I saw ungodly deeds without number
4:12	than to come here and live in ungodliness
4:14	and said, Come, let us go and make war against the sea
4:15	and said, Come, let us go up and subdue the forest of the plain
4:16	for the fire came and consumed it
4:28	but the harvest of it has not yet come

4:29	the field where the good has been sown will not come
4:30	and will produce until the time of threshing comes !
4:35	And when will come the harvest of our reward ?
4:45	show me this also : whether more time is to come than has passed
4:46	but I do not know what is to come
5:1	the days are coming when those who dwell on earth
5:15	But the angel who had come and talked with me held me
5:16	came to me and said, Where have you been ?
5:19	Depart from me and do not come near me for 7 days
5:19	and then you may come to me
5:31	the angel who had come to me on a previous night was sent to me
5:36	He said to me, Count up for me those who have not yet come
5:41	or we, or those who come after us ?
5:55	and those who come after you will be smaller than you
6:6	just as the end shall come through me
6:18	And it said, Behold, the days are coming
6:30	I have come to show you these things this night
6:45	and the arrangement of the stars to come into being
6:54	and from him we have all come
7:2	and listen to the words that I have come to speak to you
7:5	how can he come to the broad part
7:16	And why have you not considered in your mind what is to come
7:21	For God strictly commanded those who came into the world
7:21	when they came, what they should do to live
7:26	For behold, the time will come
7:26	when the signs which I have foretold to you will come to pass
7:47	And now I see that the world to come will bring delight to few
7:69	And if we were not to come into judgment after death
7:70	and all who have come from him
7:75	we shall be kept in rest until those times come
7:96	and shall inherit what is to come
7:113	and the beginning of the immortal age to come
7:114	sinful indulgence has come to an end
7:132	because he has mercy on those who have not yet come into the world
7:136	and to those who are gone and to those yet to come
8:1	but the world to come for the sake of few
8:2	but only a little dust from which gold comes
8:5	For not of your own will did you come into the world
8:18	and I have heard of the swiftness of the judgment that is to come
8:37	and it will come to pass according to your words
8:47	For you come far short of being able to love my creation
8:52	the age to come is prepared, plenty is provided
9:20	because of the devices of those who had come into it
9:25	then I will come and talk with you
9:29	when they came into the untrodden and unfruitful wilderness
9:47	So when he grew up and I came to take a wife for him
10:3	and came to this field, as you see
10:9	over so many who have come into being upon her
10:10	and others will come
10:13	the multitude that is now in it goes as it came
10:15	and bear bravely the troubles that have come upon you
10:28	Where is the angel Uriel, who came to me at first ?
10:29	the angel who had come to me at first came to me
11:10	the voice did not come from his heads
11:13	And while it was reigning it came to its end and disappeared
11:14	And while it was reigning its end came also
11:39	so that the end of my times might come through them ?
11:40	You, the 4th that has come
12:13	Behold, the days are coming
12:17	coming not from the eagle's heads
12:32	and will come and speak to them
12:34	and he will make them joyful until the end comes
12:40	and came to me and spoke to me, saying
12:48	but I have come to this place to pray
12:49	and after these days I will come to you
13:13	Then many people came to him
13:20	Yet is it better to come into these things
13:27	and a storm coming out of his mouth
13:28	which came to conquer him
13:29	Behold, the days are coming
13:30	And bewilderment of mind shall come
13:32	And when these things come to pass
13:34	as you saw, desiring to come and conquer him
13:36	And Zion will come and be made manifest to all people, prepared and built
13:46	and now, when they are about to come again
13:58	and whatever things come to pass in their seasons
14:1	behold, a voice came out of a bush opposite me
14:18	and falsehood shall come near
14:18	is already hastening to come
14:25	and you shall come here
14:35	For after death the judgment will come
14:36	But let no one come to me now
15:27	For now calamities have come upon the whole earth
15:30	and with great power they shall come
15:33	and fear and trembling shall come upon their army

	15 : 44	They shall come to her and surround her
	15 : 59	you shall come and suffer fresh afflictions
	16 : 14	and shall not return until they come over the earth
	16 : 18	when the calamities come ?
	16 : 50	when he comes who will defend him
4 Ma	1 : 23	Fear precedes pain and sorrow comes after
	3 : 8	he came, sweating and quite exhausted, to the royal tent
	4 : 2	So he came to Apollonius
	4 : 3	and said, I have come here
	4 : 6	He said that he had come with the king's authority
	6 : 13	some of the king's retinue came to him and said
	9 : 31	I lighten my pain by the joys that come from virtue
	9 : 32	but you suffer torture by the threats that come from impiety
	11 : 3	I have come of my own accord
	12 : 2	He summoned him to come nearer
	13 : 12	and another reminded them, Remember whence you came

COME back   8 = 0.005 %

Tob	2 : 3	But he came back and said
	5 : 21	and he will come back safe and sound
Jud	5 : 19	and have come back from the places
Sir	4 : 18	Then she will come straight back to him and gladden him
	38 : 21	Do not forget, there is no coming back
1 Ma	9 : 9	and let us come back with our brethren and fight them
1 Es	8 : 65	And those who had come back from captivity
3 Ma	4 : 11	to all coming back into the city

COME down   11 = 0.007 %

Tob	3 : 17	came down from her upper room
Jud	6 : 14	Then the men of Israel came down from their city and found him
	14 : 13	as to come down against us and to give battle
	16 : 4	The Assyrian came down from the mountains of the north
Sir	50 : 20	Then Simon came down, and lifted up his hands
P Az	26	But the angel of the Lord came down into the furnace
1 Ma	10 : 71	come down to the plain to meet us
2 Ma	2 : 10	and fire came down from heaven and devoured the sacrifices
	2 : 10	so also Solomon prayed, and the fire came down
1 Es	1 : 29	and the commanders came down against King Josiah
2 Es	13 : 12	After this I saw the same man come down from the mountain

COME forth   8 = 0.005 %

Sir	24 : 3	I came forth from the mouth of the Most High
	40 : 1	from the day they come forth from their mother's womb
Sus	13 : 5	Iniquity came forth from Babylon
1 Ma	1 : 10	From them came forth a sinful root, Antiochus Epiphanes
	1 : 11	In those days lawless men came forth from Israel
2 Es	6 : 44	For immediately fruit came forth in endless abundance
	16 : 38	and when the child comes forth from the womb
	16 : 39	so the calamities will not delay in coming forth upon the earth

COME forward   7 = 0.005 %

Jud	10 : 22	he came forward to the front of the tent
Ad E	11 : 6	And behold, 2 great dragons came forward
Sir	2 : 1	My son, if you come forward to serve the Lord
1 Ma	2 : 23	a Jew came forward in the sight of all
2 Ma	5 : 18	as soon as he came forward
	14 : 21	A chariot came forward from each army
4 Ma	12 : 1	the 7th and youngest of all came forward

COME in   3 = 0.002 %

Jud	12 : 16	Then Judith came in and lay down
Sus	13 : 36	this woman came in with 2 maids
1 Es	3 : 16	So they were summoned, and came in

COME on   3 = 0.002 %

2 Ma	10 : 24	He came on, intending to take Judea by storm
	12 : 38	As the 7th day was coming on
3 Ma	3 : 16	we came on to Jerusalem also

COME out   17 = 0.011 %

Tob	8 : 14	And she came out and told them that he was alive
Jud	5 : 4	refused to come out and meet me ?
	10 : 20	Then Holofernes'companions and all his servants came out
	13 : 3	and to wait for her to come out
1 Ma	2 : 27	come out with me !
	2 : 33	Come out and do what the king commands, and you will live
	2 : 34	But they said, We will not come out
	9 : 36	But the sons of Jambri from Medeba came out
	9 : 39	and the bridegroom came out
	10 : 86	and the men of the city came out to meet him with great pomp
2 Ma	4 : 34	persuaded Onias to come out from the place of sanctuary
	5 : 26	He put to the sword all those who came out to see them
	12 : 33	And he came out with 3,000 infantry and 400 cavalry
3 Ma	5 : 26	Hermon arrived and invited him to come out
	5 : 27	and being struck by the unusual invitation to come out
2 Es	15 : 29	The nations of the dragons of Arabia shall come out with many chariots
	16 : 65	And when your sins come out before men

COME over   1

Jud	11 : 3	and have come over to us

COME up   24 = 0.016 %

Jud	6 : 12	and all the slingers kept them from coming up
	12 : 8	When she came up from the spring
Wis	19 : 12	for, to give them relief, quails came up from the sea
Sir	48 : 18	In his days Sennacherib came up, and sent the Rabshakeh
1 Ma	5 : 33	Then he came up behind them in 3 companies
2 Ma	2 : 6	Some of those who followed him came up to mark the way
	10 : 36	Others who came up in the same way
1 Es	1 : 40	And Nebuchadnezzar king of Babylon came up against him
	2 : 18	that the Jews who came up from you to us
	5 : 7	These are the men of Judea who came up
	5 : 36	The following are those who came up from Tel-melah and Tel-harsha
2 Es	8 : 41	and yet not all that have been sown will come up in due season
	8 : 43	For if the farmer's seed does not come up
	11 : 1	there came up from the sea an eagle
	11 : 43	And so your insolence has come up before the Most High
	12 : 7	and if my prayer has indeed come up before thy face
	12 : 11	The eagle which you saw coming up from the sea
	13 : 3	this wind made something like the figure of a man come up
	13 : 5	to make war against the man who came up out of the sea
	13 : 25	As for your seeing a man come up
	13 : 32	whom you saw as a man coming up from the sea
	13 : 51	Why did I see the man coming up from the heart of the sea ?

COMFORT, verb   11 = 0.007 %

Tob	7 : 17	But the mother comforted her daughter in her tears
Ad E	15 : 8	And he comforted her with soothing words, and said to her
	15 : 16	and all his servants sought to comfort her
Sir	30 : 23	Delight your soul and comfort your heart
	38 : 17	then be comforted for your sorrow
	38 : 23	and be comforted for him when his spirit has departed
	48 : 24	and comforted those who mourned in Zion
	49 : 10	for they comforted the people of Jacob
Bar	4 : 30	for he who named you will comfort you
2 Es	12 : 8	that thou mayest fully comfort my soul
	14 : 13	comfort the lowly among them

COMING   5 = 0.003 %

Wis	5 : 11	and afterward no sign of its coming is found there
1 Ma	14 : 21	and we rejoiced at their coming
2 Ma	14 : 15	When the Jews heard of Nicanor's coming
	15 : 20	When all were now looking forward to the coming decision
1 Es	5 : 56	In the 2nd year after their coming to the temple of God in Jerusalem

COMMAND*, subst.   51 = 0.033 %

Tob	4 : 19	So, my son, remember my commands
Jud	2 : 3	who had not obeyed his command should be destroyed
	2 : 13	any of your sovereign's commands
Wis	9 : 8	Thou hast given command to build a temple
	14 : 16	and at the command of monarchs graven images were worshipped
	16 : 6	to remind them of thy law's command
	18 : 16	carrying the sharp sword of thy authentic command
	19 : 6	complying with thy commands
Sir	39 : 18	At his command whatever pleases him is done
	39 : 31	they will rejoice in his commands
	43 : 5	and at his command it hastens on its course
	43 : 10	At the command of the Holy One they stand as ordered
	43 : 13	By his command he sends the driving snow
	45 : 3	He gave him commands for his people
Bar	5 : 8	The woods and every fragrant tree have shaded Israel at God's command
L Jr	6 : 62	they carry out his command
1 Ma	1 : 43	All the Gentiles accepted the command of the king
	1 : 50	And whoever does not obey the command of the king shall die
	2 : 23	according to the king's command
	2 : 31	that men who had rejected the king's command
	2 : 55	Joshua, because he fulfilled the command
	3 : 1	took command in his place
	3 : 14	who scorn the king's command
	5 : 19	and he gave them this command, Take charge of this people
	5 : 42	and gave them this command
	6 : 23	to live by what he said and to follow his commands
	9 : 55	or give commands concerning his house
2 Ma	3 : 7	and sent him with commands
	3 : 13	But Heliodorus, because of the king's commands which he had
	7 : 30	I will not obey the king's command
	7 : 30	but I obey the command of the law
	8 : 9	in command of no fewer than 20,000 Gentiles of all nations
	12 : 20	set men in command of the divisions
	14 : 12	who had been in command of the elephants
	14 : 16	At the command of the leader
1 Es	1 : 18	according to the command of King Josiah

	1:52	because of their ungodly acts he gave command
	4:5	and do not disobey the king's command
	6:11	At whose command are you building this house
	6:19	with the command that he should take all these vessels back
	7:4	and they completed it by command of the Lord God of Israel
P Ma	3	who hast shackled the sea by thy word of command
3 Ma	7:20	since at the king's command they had been brought
2 Es	2:33	I, Ezra, received a command from the Lord on Mount Horeb
	8:14	who with so great labour was fashioned by thy command
	8:22	and command whose ordinance is strong and whose command is terrible
	8:22	at whose command they are changed to wind and fire
4 Ma	6:4	Obey the king's commands !
	7:17	Not every one has full command of his emotions
	9:11	Then at his command the guards brought forward the eldest
	14:11	that reason had full command over these men in their tortures

COMMAND, verb   88 = 0.057 %

Tob	1:8	as Deborah my father's mother had commanded me
	3:6	command my spirit to be taken up
	3:6	Command that I now be released from my distress
	3:13	Command that I be released from the earth
	3:15	command that respect be shown to me
	5:1	Father, I will do everything that you have commanded me
	6:15	with which your father commanded you
Jud	5:9	Then their God commanded them to leave the place
	12:1	Then he commanded them to bring her in
	12:6	and sent to Holofernes and said, Let my lord now command
	12:7	So Holofernes commanded his guards not to hinder her
Sir	7:31	and give him his portion, as is commanded you :
	15:20	He has not commanded any one to be ungodly
	24:23	the law which Moses commanded us
	39:16	and whatever he commands will be done in his time
	48:22	which Isaiah the prophet commanded
Bar	2:9	which he has commanded us to do
	2:28	on the day when thou didst command him
L Jr	6:1	to give them the message which God had commanded him
	6:62	When God commands the clouds to go over the whole world
P Az	7	as thou hast commanded us that it might go well with us
Sus	13:18	to bring what they had been commanded
	13:56	Then he put him aside, and commanded them to bring the other
1 Ma	1:51	and commanded the cities of Judah to offer sacrifice, city by city
	2:18	Now be the first to come and do what the king commands
	2:33	Come out and do what the king commands, and you will live
	2:34	nor will we do what the king commands
	2:66	he shall command the army for you
	2:68	and heed what the law commands
	3:39	as the king had commanded
	3:42	They also learned what the king had commanded
	4:27	nor had they turned out as the king had commanded him
	7:9	and he commanded him to take vengeance on the sons of Israel
	7:26	and he commanded him to destroy the people
	10:6	and he commanded that the hostages in the citadel
	10:37	just as the king has commanded in the land of Judah
	10:81	But his men stood fast, as Jonathan commanded
	11:2	for Alexander the king had commanded them to meet him
	12:17	We have commanded them to go also to you
	12:23	We therefore command
	12:27	So when the sun set, Jonathan commanded his men to be alert
	12:43	and commanded his friends and his troops
	15:39	He commanded him to encamp against Judea
	15:39	and commanded him to build up Kedron and fortify its gates
2 Ma	5:12	And he commanded his soldiers
	5:24	and commanded him to slay all the grown men
	6:21	which had been commanded by the king
	7:4	and he commanded that the tongue of their spokesman
	8:22	each to command a division, putting 1,500 men under each
	9:8	that he could command the waves of the sea
	10:13	Unable to command the respect due his office
	14:27	and commanding him to send Maccabeus to Antioch
	14:31	and commanded them to hand the man over
	15:3	who had commanded the keeping of the sabbath day
	15:5	and I command you to take up arms
1 Es	2:4	and he has commanded me to build him a house at Jerusalem
	4:57	he also commanded to be done
	5:51	as it is commanded in the law
	5:71	as Cyrus the king of the Persians has commanded us
	6:23	Then King Darius commanded that search be made
	6:27	So Darius commanded Sisinnes
	6:28	And I command that it be built completely
	6:32	And he commanded that if any should transgress
	8:19	have commanded the treasurers of Syria and Phoenicia
	9:53	And the Levites commanded all the people, saying
3 Ma	4:11	he commanded that they should be enclosed in the hippodrome
2 Es	1:35	will do what I have commanded
	3:4	and didst command the dust
	3:24	And thou didst command him to build a city for thy name
	5:20	as Uriel the angel had commanded me
	6:40	Then thou didst command
	6:41	and didst command him to divide and separate the waters
	6:42	thou didst command the waters to be gathered together

	6:45	On the 4th day thou didst command the brightness of the sun
	6:46	and thou didst command them to serve man
	6:47	On the 5th day thou didst command the 7th part
	6:48	as it was commanded
	6:53	On the 6th day thou didst command the earth
	7:21	For God strictly commanded those who came into the world
	8:10	thou hast commanded that from the members themselves
	10:59	as he had commanded me
	12:51	as the angel had commanded me
	14:5	Then I commanded him, saying
	14:20	For behold, I will go, as thou hast commanded me
	14:27	Then I went as he commanded me
	14:31	and did not keep the ways which the Most High commanded you
	14:37	So I took the 5 men, as he commanded me
4 Ma	8:2	then in violent rage he commanded

COMMANDER   23 = 0.015 %

Jud	2:14	and called together all the commanders, generals
	5:2	and the commanders of Ammon
	6:1	Holofernes, the commander of the Assyrian army
	7:8	and the commanders of the coastland came to him and said
	10:13	the commander of your army
	13:15	the commander of the Assyrian army
	14:12	they sent word to their commanders
1 Ma	3:13	Now when Seron, the commander of the Syrian army
	5:56	and Azariah, the commanders of the forces
	6:28	He assembled all his friends, the commanders of his forces
	6:57	and said to the king, to the commanders of the forces, and to the men
	6:60	The speech pleased the king and the commanders
	6:61	So the king and the commanders gave them their oath
	11:70	commanders of the forces of the army
	12:24	Now Jonathan heard that the commanders of Demetrius had returned
	13:42	and commander and leader of the Jews
	13:53	so he made him commander of all the forces
	14:2	he sent one of his commanders to take him alive
	14:47	to be commander and ethnarch of the Jews and priests
2 Ma	4:28	of the Cyprian troops
	8:32	They killed the commander of Timothy's forces
	10:32	especially well garrisoned, where Chaereas was commander
1 Es	1:29	and the commanders came down against King Josiah

COMMANDER-IN-CHIEF   1

1 Ma	15:38	Then the king made Cendebaeus commander-in-chief of the coastal country

COMMANDMENT   56 = 0.036 %

Tob	3:4	For they disobeyed thy commandments
	3:5	because we did not keep thy commandments
	4:5	and refuse to sin or to transgress his commandments
	14:9	But keep the law and the commandments
Wis	9:9	and what is right according to thy commandments
Sir	1:5	and her ways are the eternal commandments
	1:26	If you desire wisdom, keep the commandments
	6:37	and meditate at all times on his commandments
	10:19	Those who transgress the commandments
	15:15	If you will, you can keep the commandments
	17:14	And he gave commandment to each of them
	19:19	The knowledge of the Lord's commandments
	23:27	and nothing sweeter than to heed the commandments of the Lord
	24:8	Then the Creator of all things gave me a commandment
	28:6	and be true to the commandments
	28:7	Remember the commandments
	29:1	keeps the commandments
	29:9	help a poor man for the commandment's sake
	29:11	according to the commandments of the Most High
	32:23	for this is the keeping of the commandments
	32:24	He who believes the law gives heed to the commandments
	35:1	he who heeds the commandments sacrifices a peace offering
	35:5	because of the commandment
	37:12	whom you know to be a keeper of the commandments
	45:5	and gave him the commandments face to face
	45:17	In his commandments he gave him authority in statutes and judgments
Bar	3:9	Hear the commandments of life, O Israel
	4:1	She is the book of the commandments of God
	4:13	they did not walk in the ways of God's commandments
P Az	6	and have not obeyed thy commandments
1 Ma	2:19	obey him, and have chosen to do his commandments
	2:53	Joseph in the time of his distress kept the commandment
	10:14	who had forsaken the law and the commandments
2 Ma	1:4	May he open your heart to his law and his commandments
	2:2	not to forget the commandments of the Lord
1 Es	1:6	and keep the passover according to the commandment of the Lord
	4:52	in accordance with the commandment to make 17 offerings
	8:7	or the commandments
	8:82	For we have transgressed thy commandments

3 Ma	7:11	had transgressed the divine commandments
2 Es	1:34	because with you they have neglected my commandment
	2:1	and I gave them commandments through my servants the prophets
	2:33	and refused the Lord's commandment
	3:7	And thou didst lay upon him one commandment of thine
	3:19	and thy commandment to the posterity of Israel
	3:33	though they are unmindful of thy commandments
	3:35	Or what nation has kept thy commandments so well ?
	3:36	who have kept thy commandments
	7:37	whose commandments you have despised !
	7:45	Blessed are those who are alive and keep thy commandments !
	7:72	and though they received the commandments they did not keep them
	15:24	Woe to those who sin and do not observe my commandments
	16:76	You who keep my commandments and precepts, says the Lord God
4 Ma	9:1	rather than transgress our ancestral commandments
	13:15	lying before those who transgress the commandment of God
	16:24	to die rather than violate God's commandment

COMMEMORATIVE   1
Ad E	16:22	as a notable day among your commemorative festivals

COMMEND   3 = 0.002 %
Wis	7:14	commended for the gifts that come from instruction
1 Ma	12:43	and commended him to all his friends
2 Ma	9:25	whom I have often entrusted and commended to most of you

COMMISSION, subst.   1
1 Es	8:8	The following is a copy of the written commission

COMMISSION, verb   1
2 Ma	1:20	Nehemiah, having been commissioned by the king of Persia

COMMIT   44 = 0.029 %
Tob	3:3	and those which my fathers committed before thee
	12:10	but those who commit sin are the enemies of their own lives
Jud	11:17	and he will tell me when they have committed their sins
	13:16	and yet he committed no act of sin with me
Wis	14:28	or readily commit perjury
Sir	7:8	Do not commit a sin twice
	23:16	a man who commits fornication with his near of kin
	23:23	second, she has committed an offence against her husband
	23:23	and third, she has committed adultery through harlotry
	27:1	Many have committed sin for a trifle
L Jr	6:2	Because of the sins which you have committed before God
Sus	13:52	which you have committed in the past
1 Ma	1:24	He committed deeds of murder, and spoke with great arrogance
	2:6	He saw the blasphemies being committed in Judah and Jerusalem
	13:39	We pardon any errors and offences committed to this day
	16:17	So he committed an act of great treachery
2 Ma	4:3	that even murders were committed
	4:38	where he had committed the outrage against Onias
	4:39	had been committed in the city by Lysimachus
	8:4	and the blasphemies committed against his name
	8:17	which the Gentiles had committed against the holy place
	12:42	beseeching that the sin which had been committed
	13:8	because he had committed many sins
	13:14	So, committing the decision to the Creator of the world
1 Es	1:49	committed many acts of sacrilege and lawlessness
P Ma	9	For the sins I have committed are more in number
3 Ma	2:4	You destroyed those who in the past committed injustice
	2:17	Do not punish us for the defilement committed by these men
	3:9	when it had committed no offence
	6:24	You are committing treason and surpassing tyrants in cruelty
2 Es	1:5	which they have committed against me
	1:26	and your feet are swift to commit murder
	2:23	commit them to the grave and mark it
	3:13	And when they were committing iniquity before thee
	4:42	that were committed to them from the beginning
	7:32	which have been committed to them
	7:72	because though they had understanding they committed iniquity
	7:126	For while we lived and committed iniquity
	7:138	so that those who have committed iniquities might be relieved of them
	14:31	but you and your fathers committed iniquity
	15:8	which they impiously commit
	16:67	never to commit them again
4 Ma	4:7	that those who had committed deposits to the sacred treasury
	4:12	For he said that he had committed a sin deserving of death

COMMON   13 = 0.008 %
Wis	7:3	And when I was born, I began to breathe the common air
	7:6	and a common departure
	18:11	and the common man suffered the same loss as the king
2 Ma	8:29	When they had done this, they made common supplication
	11:15	Maccabeus, having regard for the common good
	14:25	so he married, settled down, and shared the common life

3 Ma	2:33	and depriving them of common fellowship and mutual help
	3:6	which was common talk among all
	4:4	perceiving the common object of pity before their eyes
	5:32	arising from our nurture in common and your usefulness
	7:17	in accord with the common desire, for 7 days
4 Ma	13:22	from this common nurture and daily companionship
	13:25	A common zeal for nobility

COMMONWEALTH   2
2 Ma	13:14	for the laws, temple, city, country, and commonwealth
4 Ma	3:20	and recognized their commonwealth

COMMOTION   1
Sir	11:34	and he will upset you with commotion

COMMUNICATE   3 = 0.002 %
Tob	7:9	So he communicated the proposal to Raguel
3 Ma	4:11	so that they could neither communicate with the king's forces
	4:16	even to communicate or to come to ones's help

COMMUNICATION   1
2 Ma	11:17	have delivered your signed communication

COMMUNITY   5 = 0.003 %
1 Ma	1:25	Israel mourned deeply in every community
2 Ma	12:7	and root out the whole community of Joppa
3 Ma	2:27	upon the Jewish community
	3:9	for such a great community ought not be left to its fate
	6:36	in their whole community and for their descendants

COMPACT, verb   1
Wis	7:2	within the period of 10 months, compacted with blood

COMPANION   18 = 0.012 %
Jud	10:20	Then Holofernes'companions and all his servants came out
Sir	6:10	And there is a friend who is a table companion
	9:16	Let righteous men be your dinner companions
	37:2	when a companion and friend turns to enmity ?
	37:4	Some companions rejoice in the happiness of a friend
	37:5	Some companions help a friend for their stomachs' sake
	40:23	A friend or a companion never meets one amiss
	42:3	or with travelling companions
P Az	26	to be with Azariah and his companions
Bel	14:2	And Daniel was a companion of the king
1 Ma	3:14	I will make war on Judas and his companions
	12:52	and they mourned for Jonathan and his companions
	15:15	Then Numenius and his companions arrived from Rome
2 Ma	5:27	and kept himself and his companions alive in the mountains
	8:1	But Judas, who was also called Maccabeus, and his companions
	8:12	and when he told his companions of the arrival of the army
3 Ma	2:25	abetted by the previously mentioned drinking companions and comrades
	6:6	The 3 companions in Babylon

COMPANIONSHIP   3 = 0.002 %
Wis	8:16	for companionship with her has no bitterness
4 Ma	13:22	from this common nurture and daily companionship
	13:27	But although nature and companionship and virtuous habits

COMPANY   15 = 0.010 %
Jud	12:12	without enjoying her company
	14:11	and they went out in companies
Wis	6:23	neither will I travel in the company of sickly envy
	8:18	and in the experience of her company, understanding
Sir	45:18	Dathan and Abiram and their men and the company of Korah
1 Ma	2:42	Then there united with them a company of Hasidaeans
	3:13	heard that Judas had gathered a large company
	3:16	Judas went out to meet him with a small company
	5:30	and behold, a large company, that could not be counted
	5:33	Then he came up behind them in 3 companies
	5:45	a very large company
	9:11	The cavalry was divided into 2 companies
	9:12	Flanked by the 2 companies
2 Ma	1:7	after Jason and his company revolted from the holy land and the kingdom
	5:2	in companies fully armed with lances and drawn swords

COMPARABLE   1
Sir	23:12	There is an utterance which is comparable to death

COMPARE   11 = 0.007 %
Tob	5:18	but consider it rubbish as compared to our child
Wis	7:29	Compared with the light she is found to be superior
Sir	9:10	for a new one does not compare with him
	22:1	The indolent may be compared to a filthy stone
	22:2	The indolent may be compared to the filth of dunghills
	25:19	Any iniquity is insignificant compared to a wife's iniquity
	27:24	I have hated many things, but none to be compared to him
Bar	3:35	no other can be compared to him !

L Jr	6 : 63	But these idols are not to be compared with them in appearance of power
2 Es	6 : 56	and thou hast compared their abundance to a drop from a bucket
	8 : 47	But you have often compared yourself to the unrighteous

COMPARISON   1
Wis   7 : 8   and I accounted wealth as nothing in comparison with her

COMPASSION   19 = 0.012 %
Tob	8 : 17	Blessed art thou, because thou hast had compassion on 2 only children
Wis	10 : 5	in the face of his compassion for his child
Sir	18 : 13	The compassion of man is for his neighbour
	18 : 13	but the compassion of the Lord is for all living beings
	18 : 14	He has compassion on those who accept his discipline
Bar	2 : 27	in all thy kindness and in all thy great compassion
1 Ma	3 : 44	and to pray and ask for mercy and compassion
2 Ma	7 : 6	and in truth has compassion on us
	7 : 6	when he said, And he will have compassion on his servants
P Ma	7	of great compassion, long-suffering
2 Es	7 : 33	and compassion shall pass away
	7 : 136	and abundant in compassion
	7 : 136	because he makes his compassions abound more and more
4 Ma	5 : 12	and have compassion on your old age
	6 : 24	and that he had not been changed by their compassion
	8 : 10	Even I, your enemy, have compassion
	8 : 20	and have compassion on our mother's age
	12 : 2	he felt strong compassion for this child
	12 : 6	he sent for the boy's mother to show compassion on her

COMPASSIONATE   1
Sir   2 : 11   For the Lord is compassionate and merciful

COMPATRIOT   2
3 Ma	3 : 21	we made known to all our amnesty towards their compatriots here
	4 : 12	the king, hearing that the Jews' compatriots from the city

COMPEL   13 = 0.008 %
Jud	8 : 30	and they compelled us to do for them what we have promised
Wis	19 : 3	those whom they had begged and compelled to depart
2 Ma	6 : 1	to compel the Jews to forsake the laws of their fathers
	6 : 7	they were compelled to walk in the procession
	7 : 1	and were being compelled by the king
	15 : 2	And when the Jews who were compelled to follow him said
1 Es	4 : 6	and they compel one another to pay taxes to the king
4 Ma	4 : 26	he himself, through torture, tried to compel everyone in the nation
	5 : 2	and to compel them
	5 : 27	It would be tyrannical for you to compel us
	8 : 2	being unable to compel an aged man to eat defiling foods
	8 : 9	you will compel me to destroy each and every one of you
	18 : 5	Since in no way whatever was he able to compel the Israelites

COMPETE   1
Wis   15 : 9   but he competes with workers in gold and silver

COMPETENT   1
1 Es   8 : 47   they brought us competent men of the sons of Mahli

COMPETITION   1
4 Ma   17 : 13   the mother of the 7 sons entered the competition

COMPILER   1
2 Ma   2 : 28   leaving the responsibility for exact details to the compiler

COMPLAIN   5 = 0.003 %
Jud	5 : 22	all the men standing around the tent began to complain
Sir	31 : 24	The city will complain of the one who is niggardly with food
2 Es	1 : 15	and in them you complained
	1 : 16	but to this day you still complain
4 Ma	3 : 12	When his guards complained bitterly

COMPLAINT   2
1 Ma	11 : 25	kept making complaints against him
3 Ma	5 : 31	who give me no ground for complaint

COMPLETE, verb   19 = 0.012 %
Tob	14 : 5	until the times of the age are completed
Sir	pr.	in order to complete and publish the book
	26 : 2	and he will complete his years in peace
	37 : 11	or with a man hired for a year about completing his work
	38 : 28	and he is careful to complete its decoration
	50 : 19	so they completed his service
1 Ma	3 : 49	who had completed their days
	13 : 10	and hastened to complete the walls of Jerusalem
2 Ma	4 : 23	and to complete the records of essential business
	9 : 4	until he completed the journey
1 Es	4 : 51	for the building of the temple until it was completed

	6 : 10	and being completed with all splendour and care
	7 : 4	and they completed it by command of the Lord God of Israel
3 Ma	5 : 27	for which this had been so zealously completed for him
2 Es	3 : 23	So the times passed and the years were completed
	4 : 36	When the number of those like yourselves is completed
	4 : 40	when her 9 months have been completed
	6 : 35	in order to complete the 3 weeks
	11 : 44	and behold, they are ended, and his ages are completed !

COMPLETE, adj.   7 = 0.005 %
Wis	15 : 3	For to know thee is complete righteousness
Sir	7 : 32	so that your blessing may be complete
1 Ma	5 : 5	and he encamped against them, vowed their complete destruction
2 Ma	15 : 1	he made plans to attack them with complete safety
2 Es	6 : 19	and when the humiliation of Zion is complete
4 Ma	4 : 19	in complete violation of the law
	15 : 17	O woman, who alone gave birth to such complete devotion !

COMPLETELY   12 = 0.008 %
Jud	14 : 13	in order to be destroyed completely
Ad E	13 : 7	and leave our government completely secure and untroubled hereafter
1 Ma	8 : 18	was completely enslaving Israel
2 Ma	4 : 16	and wished to imitate completely
	14 : 46	with his blood now completely drained from him
1 Es	6 : 28	And I command that it be built completely
3 Ma	5 : 1	Then the king, completely inflexible
	5 : 12	and was completely frustrated in his inflexible plan
	5 : 19	he had carried out completely the order given him
	5 : 27	since he had been completely overcome by incomprehension
4 Ma	9 : 20	The wheel was completely smeared with blood
	11 : 10	so that he was completely curled back like a scorpion

COMPLETENESS   1
Wis   12 : 17   when men doubt the completeness of thy power

COMPLETION   5 = 0.003 %
2 Ma	2 : 9	for the dedication and completion of the temple
1 Es	1 : 58	until the completion of 70 years
	5 : 73	they prevented the completion of the building
	6 : 20	it has not yet reached completion
3 Ma	1 : 22	would not tolerate the completion of his plans

COMPLEX   2
4 Ma	1 : 25	which is the most complex of all the emotions
	14 : 13	Observe how complex is a mother's love for her children

COMPLY   1
Wis   19 : 6   complying with thy commands

COMPOSE   1
Sir   44 : 5   those who composed musical tunes

COMPOUND, subst.   1
Sir   38 : 8   the pharmacist makes of them a compound

COMPREHEND   6 = 0.004 %
Jud	8 : 14	and find out his mind or comprehend his thought ?
3 Ma	3 : 1	When the impious king comprehended this situation
2 Es	3 : 31	and hast not shown to any one how thy way may be comprehended
	4 : 2	and do you think you can comprehend the way of the Most High ?
	4 : 11	how then can your mind comprehend the way of the Most High ?
	12 : 38	whose hearts you know are able to comprehend

COMPREHENSION   2
Sir	1 : 19	he rained down knowledge and discerning comprehension
2 Es	8 : 21	and whose glory is beyond comprehension

COMPREHENSIVE   1
4 Ma   1 : 20   The 2 most comprehensive types of the emotions are pleasure and pain

COMPULSION   6 = 0.004 %
Bel	14 : 30	and under compulsion he handed Daniel over to them
4 Ma	5 : 13	that arises out of compulsion
	5 : 16	think that there is no compulsion more powerful
	8 : 14	when you transgress under compulsion
	8 : 22	for fearing the king when we are under compulsion
	8 : 24	Let us not struggle against compulsion

COMRADE   1
3 Ma   2 : 25   abetted by the previously mentioned drinking companions and comrades

CONCEAL 3 = 0.002 %
Tob 12:11 I will not conceal anything from you
Sir 22:9 conceal the lowly birth of their parents
2 Es 2:8 who conceal the unrighteous in your midst !

CONCEALED 2
Sir 11:4 and his works are concealed from men
16:21 so most of his works are concealed

CONCEDE 1
4 Ma 13:1 everyone must concede

CONCEIT 1
3 Ma 3:18 they were carried away by their traditional conceit

CONCEIVE 3 = 0.002 %
2 Ma 9:4 he conceived the idea of turning upon the Jews
3 Ma 1:10 and conceived a desire to enter the holy of holies
1:25 from the plan that he had conceived

CONCERN, subst. 3 = 0.002 %
Wis 6:17 and concern for instruction is love of her
2 Ma 15:18 Their concern for wives and children
3 Ma 6:41 magnanimously expressing his concern :

CONCERN, verb 15 = 0.010 %
Wis 15:9 But he is not concerned that he is destined to die
Sir 7:24 Be concerned for their chastity
8:13 but if you give surety, be concerned as one who must pay
11:9 Do not argue about a matter which does not concern you
38:29 he is always deeply concerned over his work
39:1 and will be concerned with prophecies
50:28 Blessed is he who concerns himself with these things
Bar 3:31 or is concerned about the path to her
2 Ma 2:29 must be concerned with the whole construction
14:8 first because I am genuinely concerned
2 Es 6:15 because the word concerns the end
6:16 that the speech concerns them
8:38 For indeed I will not concern myself
4 Ma 1:20 and each of these is by nature concerned
9:18 where virtue is concerned

CONCERNING 33 = 0.021 %
Ad E 10:5 For I remember the dream that I had concerning these matters
12:2 and he informed the king concerning them
Sir 17:14 concerning his neighbour
23:7 Listen, my children, to instruction concerning speech
Sus 13:5 Concerning them the Lord had said :
1 Ma 8:15 concerning the people, to govern them well
8:31 And concerning the wrongs
9:55 or give commands concerning his house
11:31 which we wrote concerning you to Lasthenes our kinsman
12:17 concerning the renewal of our brotherhood
12:21 concerning the Spartans and the Jews
12:22 please write us concerning your welfare
2 Ma 8:12 Word came to Judas concerning Nicanor's invasion
11:20 And concerning these matters and their details
1 Es 1:24 concerning those who sinned and acted wickedly toward the Lord
4:54 He wrote also concerning their support and the priests
6:6 until word could be sent to Darius concerning them
6:22 let him send us directions concerning these things
7:15 because he had changed the will of the king of the Assyrians concerning them
2 Es 4:6 that you ask me concerning these things ?
4:52 Concerning the signs about which you ask me
4:52 but I was not sent to tell you concerning your life
5:1 Now concerning the signs : behold
5:39 and how can I speak concerning the things
6:34 concerning the former times
6:34 lest you be hasty concerning the last times
7:78 Now, concerning death, the teaching is :
7:90 Therefore this is the teaching concerning them :
7:94 they see the witness which he who formed them bears concerning them
8:51 and inquire concerning the glory of those who are like yourself
15:8 I will be silent no longer concerning their ungodly deeds
4 Ma 5:10 if, by holding a vain opinion concerning the truth
5:29 'concerning the keeping of the law

CONCERT 1
Sir 32:5 is a concert of music at a banquet of wine

CONCERTED 1
3 Ma 1:28 The continuous, vehement, and concerted cry of the crowds

CONCESSION 1
2 Ma 4:11 He set aside the existing royal concessions to the Jews

CONCISELY 1
Sir 32:8 Speak concisely, say much in few words

CONCLUDE 4 = 0.003 %
1 Ma 6:9 and he concluded that he was dying
2 Ma 14:30 concluded that this austerity
3 Ma 4:11 and the voyage was concluded as the king had decreed
2 Es 2:40 and conclude the list of your people who are clothed in white

CONCLUSION 2
3 Ma 1:26 determined to bring the aforesaid plan to a conclusion
3:14 it was brought to conclusion, according to plan

CONCORD 1
4 Ma 14:3 O sacred and harmonious concord of the 7 brothers

CONCUBINE 2
2 Ma 4:30 as a present to Antiochis, the king's concubine
1 Es 4:29 Yet I have seen him with Apame, the king's concubine

CONDEMN 14 = 0.009 %
Wis 2:20 Let us condemn him to a shameful death
4:16 will condemn the ungodly who are living
4:16 will condemn the prolonged old age of the unrighteous man
12:15 deeming it alien to thy power to condemn him
17:11 condemned by its own testimony
Sir 14:2 Blessed is he whose heart does not condemn him
19:5 One who rejoices in wickedness will be condemned
Sus 13:41 and they condemned her to death
13:48 Have you condemned a daughter of Israel
13:53 condemning the innocent and letting the guilty go free
1 Ma 1:57 the decree of the king condemned him to death
P Ma 13 do not condemn me to the depths of the earth
2 Es 4:18 and which to condemn ?
7:115 who has been condemned in the judgment

CONDEMNATION 3 = 0.002 %
Wis 11:10 as a stern king does in condemnation
12:27 Therefore the utmost condemnation came upon them
Sir 5:14 and severe condemnation to the double-tongued

CONDENSATION 1
2 Ma 2:28 to arriving at the outlines of the condensation

CONDENSE 1
2 Ma 2:23 we shall attempt to condense into a single book

CONDITION 4 = 0.003 %
Sir 18:26 From morning to evening conditions change
1 Ma 6:61 On these conditions the Jews evacuated the stronghold
2 Ma 9:22 I do not despair of my condition
4 Ma 11:11 In this condition, gasping for breath and in anguish of body

CONDUCT*, subst. 7 = 0.005 %
Tob 4:14 and be disciplined in all your conduct
Sir 11:26 according to his conduct
51:19 My soul grappled with wisdom, and in my conduct I was strict
1 Ma 12:4 safe conduct to the land of Judah
2 Ma 4:37 because of the moderation and good conduct of the deceased
11:26 and go on happily in the conduct of their own affairs
2 Es 10:39 For he has seen your righteous conduct

CONDUCT, verb 4 = 0.003 %
1 Ma 9:37 and are conducting the bride
3 Ma 3:4 and conducted themselves by his law
4:15 The registration of these people was therefore conducted
2 Es 16:47 Those who conduct business, do it only to be plundered

CONFER 5 = 0.003 %
Sir 10:5 and he confers his honour upon the person of the scribe
1 Ma 11:42 but I will confer great honour on you and your nation
15:28 to confer with him, saying
2 Ma 11:20 to confer with you
4 Ma 4:17 Jason agreed that if the office were conferred upon him

CONFERENCE 2
1 Ma 11:22 but to meet him for a conference at Ptolemais
2 Ma 14:22 they held the proper conference

CONFESS 10 = 0.007 %
Tob 12:22 So they confessed the great and wonderful works of God
Ad E 12:3 and when they confessed they were led to execution
Sir 4:26 Do not be ashamed to confess your sins
20:2 And the one who confesses his fault will be kept from loss
Sus 13:14 they confessed their lust
2 Ma 6:6 nor so much as confess himself to be a Jew
7:37 to make you confess that he alone is God
2 Es 2:45 and they have confessed the name of God

2 : 47   *whom they confessed in the world*
4 Ma 13 : 5   *How then can one fail to confess*

CONFESSION
3 = 0.002 %

Bar 1 : 14   to make your confession in the house of the Lord
1 Es 8 : 91   While Ezra was praying and making his confession
9 : 8 · Now then make confession and give glory to the Lord

CONFIDENCE
10 = 0.007 %

Wis 5 : 1   Then the righteous man will stand with great confidence
Sir 26 : 21   and, having confidence in their good descent
27 : 16   Whoever betrays secrets destroys confidence
37 : 26   He who is wise among his people will inherit confidence
1 Ma 9 : 58   Jonathan and his men are living in quiet and confidence
10 : 71   If you now have confidence in your forces
10 : 77   for he had a large troop of cavalry and put confidence in it
2 Ma 15 : 7   But Maccabeus did not cease to trust with all confidence
15 : 11   not so much with confidence in shields and spears
3 Ma 2 : 7   those who had put their confidence in you

CONFIDENT
4 = 0.003 %

Jud 2 : 5   take with you men confident in their strength
Sir 5 : 5   Do not be so confident of atonement that you add sin to sin
49 : 10   and delivered them with confident hope
2 Es 7 : 98   and shall be confident without confusion

CONFIDENTLY
3 = 0.002 %

Sir 41 : 16   and not everything is confidently esteemed by every one
3 Ma 2 : 32   in exchange for life they confidently attempted
5 : 44   and they confidently posted the armed forces

CONFINE
4 = 0.003 %

Sir 23 : 19   His fear is confined to the eyes of men
P Ma 3   who hast confined the deep
3 Ma 4 : 10   and in addition they were confined under a solid deck
5 : 7   they were forcibly confined on every side

CONFIRM
14 = 0.009 %

Sir 3 : 2   and he confirmed the right of the mother over her sons
29 : 3   Confirm your word and keep faith with him
42 : 25   One confirms the good things of the other
Bar 2 : 1   So the Lord confirmed his word
2 : 24   and thou hast confirmed thy words
1 Ma 11 : 27   He confirmed him in the high priesthood
11 : 34   We have confirmed as their possession
11 : 57   I confirm you in the high priesthood
12 : 1   to confirm and renew the friendship with them
14 : 24   to confirm the alliance with the Romans
14 : 38   King Demetrius confirmed him in the high priesthood
15 : 5   now therefore I confirm to you all the tax remissions
2 Ma 12 : 25   he had confirmed his solemn promise to restore them unharmed
4 Ma 18 : 17   He confirmed the saying of Ezekiel

CONFISCATE
2

Tob 1 : 20   Then all my property was confiscated
2 Ma 3 : 13   said that this money must in any case be confiscated

CONFISCATION
1

3 Ma 7 : 21   to confiscation of their belongings by any one

CONFOUND
3 = 0.002 %

Wis 10 : 5   Wisdom also, when the nations in wicked agreement had been confounded
1 Ma 3 : 6   all the evildoers were confounded
1 Es 8 : 74   I am ashamed and confounded before thy face

CONFRONT
2

Wis 12 : 14   nor can any king or monarch confront thee
Sir 34 : 3   the likeness of a face confronting a face

CONFUSE
2

Sir 40 : 5   his sleep at night confuses his mind
2 Ma 10 : 30   so that, confused and blinded

CONFUSION
15 = 0.010 %

Tob 4 : 13   For in pride there is ruin and great confusion
Ad E 11 : 5   Behold, noise and confusion
Wis 14 : 26   confusion over what is good, forgetfulness of favours
Bar 1 : 15   but confusion of face, as at this day, to us
2 : 6   but confusion of face to us and our fathers, as at this day
2 Ma 4 : 41   and threw them in wild confusion at Lysimachus and his men
13 : 16   In the end they filled the camp with terror and confusion
3 Ma 6 : 19   and filled them with confusion and terror
2 Es 2 : 6   that you may bring confusion upon them
5 : 4   you shall see it thrown into confusion after the 3rd period
7 : 87   because they shall utterly waste away in confusion
7 : 98   and shall be confident without confusion
9 : 3   wavering of leaders, confusion of princes

15 : 18   For because of their pride the cities shall be in confusion
16 : 21   the sword, famine, and great confusion

CONGENIAL
1

Sir 27 : 16   and he will never find a congenial friend

CONGRATULATE
1

3 Ma 1 : 8   and to congratulate him on what had happened

CONGREGATION
12 = 0.008 %

Sir 1 : 30   and cast you down in the midst of the congregation
4 : 7   Make yourself beloved in the congregation
24 : 23   as an inheritance of the congregations of Jacob
33 : 18   and you leaders of the congregation, hearken
39 : 10   and the congregation will proclaim his praise
41 : 18   and of iniquity, before a congregation or the people
44 : 15   and the congregation proclaims their praise
46 : 7   they withstood the congregation
46 : 14   By the law of the Lord he judged the congregation
50 : 13   before the whole congregation of Israel
50 : 20   over the whole congregation of the sons of Israel
1 Ma 3 : 44   And the congregation assembled to be ready for battle

CONNECTED
1

2 Ma 3 : 3   connected with the service of the sacrifices

CONNECTION
1

1 Ma 13 : 15   in connection with the offices he held

CONNIVANCE
1

2 Ma 4 : 39   with the connivance of Menelaus

CONQUER
22 = 0.014 %

Wis 16 : 10   but thy sons were not conquered
18 : 22   He conquered the wrath not by strength of body
1 Ma 1 : 2   He fought many battles, conquered strongholds
5 : 44   Thus Carnaim was conquered
8 : 5   they crushed in battle and conquered
8 : 10   they plundered them, conquered the land
15 : 30   which you have conquered outside the borders of Judea
15 : 31   Otherwise we will come and conquer you
1 Es 4 : 4   and conquer mountains, walls, and towers
2 Es 5 : 9   and all friends shall conquer one another
11 : 40   have conquered all the beasts that have gone before
13 : 28   which came to conquer him
13 : 34   as you saw, desiring to come and conquer him
4 Ma 1 : 11   By their endurance they conquered the tyrant
3 : 17   For the temperate mind can conquer the drives of the emotions
6 : 33   But now that reason has conquered the emotions
7 : 4   he conquered the besiegers
7 : 11   and conquered the fiery angel
13 : 2   we would say that they had been conquered by these emotions
13 : 7   conquered the tempest of the emotions
16 : 14   By steadfastness you have conquered even a tyrant
17 : 24   and he ravaged and conquered all his enemies

CONSCIENCE
1

Wis 17 : 11   distressed by conscience

CONSECRATE
13 = 0.008 %

Tob 1 : 4   was consecrated and established for all generations for ever
Jud 4 : 3   had been consecrated after their profanation
6 : 19   upon the faces of those who are consecrated to thee
11 : 13   which they had consecrated and set aside for the priests
Sir 49 : 7   yet he had been consecrated in the womb as prophet
1 Ma 4 : 48   and consecrated the courts
2 Ma 1 : 25   who didst choose the fathers and consecrate them
2 : 8   that the place should be specially consecrated
2 Es 2 : 18   I have consecrated and prepared for you
5 : 25   thou hast consecrated Zion for thyself
4 Ma 13 : 13   Let us with all our hearts consecrate ourselves to God
17 : 19   For Moses says, All who are consecrated are under your hands
17 : 20   These, then, who have been consecrated for the sake of God

CONSECRATED
3 = 0.002 %

2 Ma 15 : 18   was for the consecrated sanctuary
1 Es 5 : 52   and at all the consecrated feasts
3 Ma 6 : 3   a people of your consecrated portion

CONSECRATION
1

2 Ma 2 : 17   and the kingship and priesthood and consecration

CONSENT, subst.
4 = 0.003 %

Sus 13 : 20   so give your consent, and lie with us
2 Ma 11 : 35   we also give consent
1 Es 6 : 22   was done with the consent of King Cyrus
7 : 4   So with the consent of Cyrus and Darius and Artaxerxes

CONSENT, verb   3 = 0.002 %

1 Ma	11 : 29	The king consented
2 Ma	11 : 24	We have heard that the Jews do not consent
2 Es	16 : 69	And those who consent to eat shall be held in derision and contempt

CONSEQUENCE   2

2 Es	8 : 33	shall receive their reward in consequence of their own deeds
4 Ma	1 : 21	The emotions of both pleasure and pain have many consequences

CONSIDER   48 = 0.031 %

Tob	5 : 18	but consider it rubbish as compared to our child
	14 : 11	So now, my children, consider what almsgiving accomplishes
Wis	1 : 16	considering him a friend, they pined away
	2 : 16	We are considered by him as something base
	8 : 17	When I considered these things inwardly
	15 : 12	But he considered our existence an idle game
Sir	2 : 10	Consider the ancient generations
	7 : 9	Do not say, He will consider the multitude of my gifts
	11 : 7	first consider, and then reprove
	33 : 17	Consider that I have not laboured for myself alone
	40 : 29	his existence cannot be considered as life
	42 : 18	and considers their crafty devices
	50 : 4	He considered how to save his people from ruin
Bar	2 : 16	O Lord, look down from thy holy habitation, and consider us
1 Ma	10 : 38	that they are considered to be under one ruler
2 Ma	2 : 29	has to consider only what is suitable for its adornment
	9 : 15	and the Jews, whom he had not considered worth burying
	11 : 36	as soon as you have considered them, send some one promptly
	14 : 20	When the terms had been fully considered
3 Ma	2 : 33	considering them to be enemies of the Jewish nation
	3 : 11	and not considering the might of the supreme God
	3 : 15	and we considered that we should not rule
	5 : 16	The king, after considering this, returned to his drinking
	5 : 50	Not only this, but when they considered
2 Es	4 : 31	Consider now for yourself
	4 : 50	And he said to me, Consider it for yourself
	5 : 54	Therefore you also should consider
	7 : 16	And why have you not considered in your mind what is to come
	7 : 84	they shall consider the torment laid up for themselves in the last days
	7 : 126	we did not consider what we should suffer after death
	9 : 20	So I considered my world, and behold, it was lost
	9 : 45	and looked upon my low estate, and considered my distress
	11 : 36	Look before you and consider what you see
	13 : 16	For as I consider it in my mind
4 Ma	2 : 14	Do not consider it paradoxical when reason
	3 : 15	considered it an altogether fearful danger to his soul
	4 : 7	considering it outrageous
	5 : 13	For consider this
	5 : 17	Therefore we consider
	8 : 11	Will you not consider this, that if you disobey
	8 : 16	Let us consider, on the other hand
	8 : 19	and consider the threats of torments
	8 : 21	and let us seriously consider that if we disobey we are dead !
	8 : 27	nor even seriously considered them
	9 : 4	For we consider this pity of yours
	14 : 11	Do not consider it amazing
	15 : 5	Considering that mothers are the weaker sex and give birth to many
	16 : 5	Consider this also

CONSIDERABLE   5 = 0.003 %

Sir	pr.	and after acquiring considerable proficiency in them
1 Ma	12 : 10	for considerable time has passed
	13 : 11	and with him a considerable army
2 Ma	10 : 27	and advanced a considerable distance from the city
3 Ma	1 : 23	and created a considerable disturbance in the holy place

CONSIDERATION   2

Ad E	16 : 9	with more equitable consideration
2 Ma	12 : 24	and no consideration would be shown them

CONSIDERING   1

2 Ma	2 : 24	For considering the flood of numbers involved

CONSIGN   1

Ad E	16 : 15	who were consigned to annihilation by this thrice accursed man

CONSIST   1

Jud	5 : 3	and in what does their power or strength consist ?

CONSISTENT   1

Sir	5 : 10	and let your speech be consistent

CONSOLATION   1

Wis	3 : 18	and no consolation in the day of decision

CONSOLE   10 = 0.007 %

Jud	6 : 20	Then they consoled Achior, and praised him greatly
Sir	35 : 17	and he will not be consoled until it reaches the Lord
3 Ma	3 : 8	They did try to console them
2 Es	10 : 2	and all my neighbours attempted to console me
	10 : 3	But when they all had stopped consoling me
	10 : 20	and be consoled because of the sorrow of Jerusalem
	10 : 41	whom you saw mourning and began to console
	10 : 49	and you began to console her for what had happened
	16 : 23	and there shall be no one to console them
4 Ma	12 : 2	and tried to console him, saying

CONSORT   1

Sir	19 : 2	and the man who consorts with harlots is very reckless

CONSPICUOUS   3 = 0.002 %

1 Ma	11 : 37	and put up in a conspicuous place on the holy mountain
	14 : 48	to put them up in a conspicuous place
2 Ma	15 : 35	a clear and conspicuous sign to every one

CONSPICUOUSLY   1

4 Ma	8 : 2	For when the tyrant was conspicuously defeated

CONSPIRACY   1

2 Ma	5 : 7	and in the end got only disgrace from his conspiracy

CONSPIRATOR   1

2 Ma	14 : 26	for he had appointed that conspirator against the kingdom

CONSPIRE   3 = 0.002 %

Sir	45 : 18	Outsiders conspired against him
Bel	14 : 28	they were very indignant and conspired against the king
3 Ma	3 : 2	by men who conspired to do them ill

CONSTANT   2

2 Ma	14 : 34	and called upon the constant Defender of our nation, in these words :
3 Ma	5 : 41	and also in constant danger of being plundered

CONSTANTLY   7 = 0.005 %

Ad E	13 : 5	stands constantly in opposition to all men
Sir	26 : 24	A shameless woman constantly acts disgracefully
	37 : 12	But stay constantly with a godly man
1 Ma	8 : 15	and every day 320 senators constantly deliberate
	12 : 11	We therefore remember you constantly on every occasion
3 Ma	3 : 11	constantly in his same purpose
	3 : 22	Since they incline constantly to evil

CONSTELLATION   2

Wis	7 : 19	the cycles of the year and the constellations of the stars
	7 : 29	and excels every constellation of the stars

CONSTERNATION   1

2 Ma	14 : 17	because of the sudden consternation created by the enemy

CONSTITUTE   1

4 Ma	13 : 8	For they constituted a holy chorus of religion and

CONSTITUTION   1

Sir	30 : 14	who is well and strong in constitution

CONSTRAIN   1

2 Ma	11 : 14	constraining him to be their friend

CONSTRAINT   2

2 Ma	6 : 7	the Jews were taken, under bitter constraint
3 Ma	4 : 9	driven under the constraint of iron bonds

CONSTRUCT   1

4 Ma	4 : 20	so that not only was a gymnasium constructed

CONSTRUCTION   3 = 0.002 %

2 Ma	2 : 29	must be concerned with the whole construction
	4 : 20	it was applied to the construction of triremes
1 Es	6 : 20	and although it has been in process of construction

CONSUL   2

1 Ma	15 : 16	Lucius, consul of the Romans, to King Ptolemy, greeting
	15 : 22	The consul wrote the same thing to Demetrius the king

CONSULT   8 = 0.005 %

Sir	8 : 17	Do not consult with a fool
	9 : 14	and consult with the wise
	37 : 10	Do not consult with one who looks at you suspiciously
	37 : 11	Do not consult with a woman about her rival
L Jr	6 : 48	the priests consult together
1 Ma	3 : 48	were consulting the images of their idols
	9 : 59	And they went and consulted with him
2 Ma	13 : 13	After consulting privately with the elders

CONSUME
| | | | 33 = 0.021 % |

Jud 11 : 13 They have decided to consume the first fruits of the grain
Ad E 11 : 11 and the lowly were exalted and consumed those held in honour
Wis 5 : 13 but were consumed in our wickedness
14 : 15 For a father, consumed with grief
16 : 16 and utterly consumed by fire
16 : 18 so that it might not consume the creatures
19 : 21 failed to consume the flesh of perishable creatures
Sir 23 : 16 will not be quenched until it is consumed
27 : 29 and pain will consume them before their death
36 : 9 Let him who survives be consumed in the fiery wrath
43 : 21 He consumes the mountains and burns up the wilderness
45 : 19 to consume them in flaming fire
L Jr 6 : 63 And the fire sent from above to consume mountains and woods does what it is ordered
6 : 72 and they will finally themselves be consumed
Bel 14 : 13 and consume the provisions
1 Ma 6 : 53 had consumed the last of the stores
2 Ma 1 : 23 And while the sacrifice was being consumed
1 : 31 And when the materials of the sacrifice were consumed
2 : 10 and consumed the whole burnt offerings
2 : 11 And Moses said, They were consumed
3 Ma 2 : 5 You consumed with fire and sulphur
2 Es 4 : 16 for the fire came and consumed it
7 : 87 and be consumed with shame
12 : 44 if we also had been consumed in the burning of Zion !
15 : 23 and will consume the foundations of the earth
16 : 15 until it consumes the foundations of the earth
16 : 78 It is shut off and given up to be consumed by fire
4 Ma 3 : 11 tormented and inflamed him, undid and consumed him
7 : 4 Although his sacred life was consumed by tortures and racks
7 : 12 though being consumed by the fire
14 : 10 and it consumed their bodies quickly
15 : 15 She watched the flesh of her children consumed by fire
18 : 14 the flame shall not consume you

CONSUMMATION
| | | | 1 |

Sir 39 : 28 in the time of consummation

CONTAIN
| | | | 2 |

1 Ma 6 : 2 Its temple was very rich, containing golden shields
12 : 8 which contained a clear declaration of alliance and friendship

CONTEMPORARY
| | | | 1 |

2 Es 5 : 54 that you and your contemporaries are smaller in stature

CONTEMPT
| | | | 8 = 0.005 % |

Jud 13 : 17 who hast brought into contempt this day
Wis 4 : 18 They will see, and will have contempt for him
14 : 30 through contempt for holiness
1 Ma 1 : 39 her sabbaths into a reproach, her honour into contempt
2 Ma 3 : 18 because the holy place was about to be brought into contempt
7 : 24 Antiochus felt that he was being treated with contempt
2 Es 9 : 9 and those who have rejected them with contempt
16 : 69 And those who consent to eat shall be held in derision and contempt

CONTEMPTUOUS
| | | | 3 = 0.002 % |

2 Es 8 : 56 and were contemptuous of his law
12 : 32 and will cast up before them their contemptuous dealings
4 Ma 8 : 28 For they were contemptuous of the emotions

CONTEMPTUOUSLY
| | | | 2 |

Sir 26 : 28 and intelligent men who are treated contemptuously
4 Ma 4 : 9 that was being treated so contemptuously

CONTEND
| | | | 2 |

Sir 8 : 1 Do not contend with a powerful man
4 Ma 17 : 13 and the brothers contended

CONTENT, subst.
| | | | 5 = 0.003 % |

L Jr 6 : 59 better even the door of a house that protects its contents
1 Ma 11 : 29 its contents were as follows :
15 : 2 its contents were as follows :
2 Ma 9 : 18 This was its content :
2 Es 16 : 57 who has measured the sea and its contents

CONTENT, adj.
| | | | 3 = 0.002 % |

Sir 29 : 23 Be content with little or much
2 Ma 5 : 15 Not content with this, Antiochus dared to enter
3 Ma 2 : 26 He was not content with his uncounted licentious deeds

CONTENTIOUSNESS
| | | | 1 |

4 Ma 8 : 26 Why does such contentiousness excite us

CONTEST
| | | | 7 = 0.005 % |

Wis 4 : 2 victor in the contest for prizes that are undefiled
10 : 12 in his arduous contest she gave him the victory
2 Es 7 : 127 This is the meaning of the contest
4 Ma 11 : 20 O contest befitting holiness, in which so many of us brothers

15 : 29 who carried away the prize of the contest in your heart !
16 : 16 My sons, noble is the contest to which you are called
17 : 11 Truly the contest in which they were engaged was divine

CONTESTANT
| | | | 2 |

4 Ma 12 : 14 the contestants for virtue
17 : 13 Eleazar was the first contestant

CONTINGENT
| | | | 1 |

Jud 6 : 1 in the presence of all the foreign contingents :

CONTINUAL
| | | | 2 |

Jud 4 : 14 offered the continual burnt offerings
1 Es 5 : 52 and thereafter the continual offerings and sacrifices

CONTINUALLY
| | | | 18 = 0.012 % |

Ad E 13 : 4 and continually disregard the ordinances of the kings
16 : 11 and was continually bowed down to by all
Wis 10 : 7 a continually smoking wasteland
Sir 17 : 19 and his eyes are continually upon their ways
20 : 19 which is continually on the lips of the ignorant
20 : 24 it is continually on the lips of the ignorant
23 : 10 for as a servant who is continually examined under torture
37 : 18 and it is the tongue that continually rules them
45 : 14 twice every day continually
51 : 11 I will praise thy name continually
1 Ma 1 : 36 an evil adversary of Israel continually
6 : 9 because deep grief continually gripped him
15 : 25 continually throwing his forces against it
P Ma 15 and I will praise thee continually
3 Ma 4 : 16 The king was greatly and continually filled with joy
2 Es 9 : 25 and pray to the Most High continually
10 : 39 that you have sorrowed continually for your people
15 : 8 and the souls of the righteous cry out continually

CONTINUE
| | | | 23 = 0.015 % |

Tob 6 : 5 And they both continued on their way
11 : 1 So he continued on his way until they came near to Nineveh
14 : 2 and he continued to fear the Lord God and to praise him
Jud 16 : 15 but to those who fear thee thou wilt continue to show mercy
16 : 20 So the people continued feasting in Jerusalem
Wis 16 : 5 thy wrath did not continue to the end
18 : 20 but the wrath did not long continue
Sir 38 : 19 In calamity sorrow continues
44 : 13 Their posterity will continue for ever
1 Ma 10 : 26 and have continued your friendship with us
10 : 27 And now continue still to keep faith with us
11 : 22 and he wrote to Jonathan not to continue the siege
11 : 23 he gave orders to continue the siege
2 Ma 5 : 27 they continued to live on what grew wild
8 : 1 and enlisted those who had continued in the Jewish faith
8 : 26 and for that reason they did not continue their pursuit
3 Ma 2 : 26 but he also continued with such audacity
3 : 3 The Jews, however, continued to maintain good will
2 Es 9 : 13 Therefore, do not continue to be curious
9 : 41 that I may weep for myself and continue to mourn
11 : 13 and it continue to reign a long time
16 : 71 who continue to fear the Lord
4 Ma 5 : 10 you continue to despise me to your own hurt

CONTINUED
| | | | 1 |

3 Ma 5 : 5 and arranged for their continued custody through the night

CONTINUOUS
| | | | 1 |

3 Ma 1 : 28 The continuous, vehement, and concerted cry of the crowds

CONTINUOUSLY
| | | | 1 |

2 Ma 3 : 26 who stood on each side of him and scourged him continuously

CONTRACT
| | | | 3 = 0.002 % |

Tob 7 : 14 and took a scroll and wrote out the contract
1 Ma 13 : 42 in their documents and contracts
14 : 43 and that all contracts in the country

CONTRADICTION
| | | | 1 |

4 Ma 7 : 20 No contradiction therefore arises

CONTRARY, adj., subst.
| | | | 9 = 0.006 % |

Ad E 13 : 4 who have laws contrary to those of every nation
Wis 15 : 7 and those for contrary uses
19 : 21 Flames, on the contrary
Sir 41 : 2 to one who is contrary, and has lost his patience !
1 Ma 14 : 45 Whoever acts contrary to these decisions
2 Ma 4 : 11 and introduced new customs contrary to the law
3 Ma 3 : 22 they took this in a contrary spirit
4 Ma 2 : 8 he is forced to act contrary to his natural ways
5 : 26 meats that would be contrary to this

CONTRITE 1
P Az 16 Yet with a contrite heart and a humble spirit may we be accepted

CONTRIVE 4 = 0.003 %
2 Ma 7:31 But you, who have contrived all sorts of evil
3 Ma 4:19 to contrive a means of escape
4 Ma 6:25 There they burned him with maliciously contrived instruments
10:16 Contrive tortures, tyrant, so that you may learn from them

CONTROL, subst. 20 = 0.013 %
1 Ma 6:56 and that he was trying to seize control of the government
6:63 He found Philip in control of the city
7:22 They gained control of the land of Judah
8:3 to get control of the silver and gold mines there
8:4 and how they had gained control of the whole region
10:32 I release also my control of the citadel in Jerusalem
10:52 for I crushed Demetrius and gained control of our country
11:8 So King Ptolemy gained control of the coastal cities
11:49 that the Jews had gained control of the city as they pleased
11:56 and gained control of Antioch
14:6 and gained full control of the country
15:3 have gained control of the kingdom of our fathers
15:9 When we gain control of our kingdom
15:28 You hold control of Joppa and Gazara
16:13 he determined to get control of the country
2 Ma 3:6 to fall under the control of the king
5:7 He did not gain control of the government, however
10:15 who had control of important strongholds
3 Ma 6:5 who had already gained control of the whole world by the spear
2 Es 11:32 Moreover this head gained control of the whole earth

CONTROL, verb 11 = 0.007 %
Sir 19:6 He who controls his tongue will live without strife
21:11 Whoever keeps the law controls his thoughts
1 Ma 8:16 and to control all their land
2 Ma 9:2 and attempted to rob the temples and control the city
3 Ma 1:1 that the regions which he had controlled had been seized by Antiochus
4 Ma 1:9 demonstrated that reason controls the emotions
2:6 that reason is able to control desires
2:17 but controlled his anger by reason
2:20 For if reason could not control anger
2:24 it does not control forgetfulness and ignorance ?
7:18 these alone are able to control the passions of the flesh

CONVENE 3 = 0.002 %
1 Ma 12:35 When Jonathan returned he convened the elders of the people
14:44 or to convene an assembly in the country
3 Ma 6:33 Likewise also the king, after convening a great banquet

CONVENIENCE 1
Sir 6:8 For there is a friend who is such at his own convenience

CONVENIENT 1
1 Ma 4:46 and stored the stones in a convenient place

CONVERGE 1
1 Ma 15:12 for he knew that troubles had converged upon him

CONVERSANT 1
Sir pr. in order that, by becoming conversant with this also

CONVERSATION 3 = 0.002 %
Ad E 12:2 He overheard their conversation and inquired into their purposes
Sir 9:15 Let your conversation be with men of understanding
19:7 Never repeat a conversation

CONVERT, verb 2
Sir 49:2 He was led aright in converting the people
2 Es 6:26 and converted to a different spirit

CONVEY 1
1 Es 5:55 and convey them in rafts to the harbour of Joppa

CONVICT 4 = 0.003 %
Wis 1:3 and when his power is tested, it convicts the foolish
1:9 to convict him of his lawless deeds
4:20 and their lawless deeds will convict them to their face
Sus 13:61 Daniel had convicted them of bearing false witness

CONVINCE 7 = 0.005 %
Wis 16:8 And by this also thou didst convince our enemies
Sir 39:32 Therefore from the beginning I have been convinced
2 Ma 13:26 convinced them, appeased them, gained their good will
3 Ma 3:24 Therefore, fully convinced by these indications
4:19 he was clearly convinced about the matter

5:5 convinced that the whole nation would experience its final destruction
4 Ma 9:18 Through all these tortures I will convince you

COOK, verb 1
4 Ma 6:15 We will set before you some cooked meat

COPPER 2
Wis 15:9 and imitates workers in copper
Sir 12:10 for like the rusting of copper, so is his wickedness

COPY, subst. 19 = 0.012 %
Ad E 13:1 This is a copy of the letter :
16:1 The following is a copy of this letter :
16:19 Therefore post a copy of this letter publicly in every place
Wis 9:8 a copy of the holy tent
L Jr 6:1 A copy of a letter which Jeremiah sent
1 Ma 8:22 and this is a copy of the letter
11:31 This copy of the letter
11:37 Now therefore take care to make a copy of this
12:5 This is a copy of the letter
12:7 as the appended copy shows
12:19 This is a copy of the letter which they sent to Onias :
14:20 This is a copy of the letter which the Spartans sent :
14:23 and to put a copy of their words in the public archives
14:23 And they have sent a copy of this to Simon the high priest
14:27 This is a copy of what they wrote :
14:49 and to deposit copies of them in the treasury
15:24 They also sent a copy of these things
1 Es 6:7 A copy of the letter
8:8 The following is a copy of the written commission

COR 1
1 Es 8:20 and likewise up to a 100 cors of wheat

CORD 4 = 0.003 %
Sir 6:30 and her bonds are a cord of blue
L Jr 6:43 And the women, with cords about them, sit along the passageways
6:43 and her cord was not broken
2 Ma 7:1 under torture with whips and cords

CORNER 2
Tob 11:13 and the white films scaled off from the corners of his eyes
Sus 13:38 We were in a corner of the garden

CORONATION 1
2 Ma 4:21 for the coronation of Philometor as king

CORPSE 7 = 0.005 %
Wis 4:18 After this they will become dishonoured corpses
18:12 by the one form of death, had corpses too many to count
Sir 48:5 You have raised a corpse from death and from Hades
1 Ma 11:4 and the corpses lying about
2 Es 10:30 and behold, I lay there like a corpse
4 Ma 15:20 and corpses fallen on other corpses

CORRECT 2
Wis 12:2 Therefore thou dost correct little by little those who trespass
4 Ma 2:18 to correct some, and to render others powerless

CORRECTION 1
2 Es 16:19 for the correction of men

CORRECTOR 1
Wis 7:15 and the corrector of the wise

CORRESPONDING 1
Wis 13:5 comes a corresponding perception of their Creator

CORROBORATION 1
3 Ma 5:19 But when he, with the corroboration of his friends

CORROSION 1
L Jr 6:12 which cannot save themselves from rust and corrosion

CORRUPT, verb 1
4 Ma 18:8 No seducer corrupted me on a desert plain

CORRUPT, adj. 2
2 Es 4:11 And how can one who is already worn out by the corrupt world understand incorruption ?
9:19 have become corrupt in their ways

CORRUPTIBLE 4 = 0.003 %
2 Es 7:31 and that which is corruptible shall perish
7:96 they rejoice that they have now escaped what is corruptible
8:34 or what is a corruptible race
14:13 And now renounce the life that is corruptible

CORRUPTION 9 = 0.006 %
Wis	14:12	and the invention of them was the corruption of life
	14:25	theft and deceit, corruption, faithlessness, tumult, perjury
2 Ma	4:7	obtained the high priesthood by corruption
2 Es	6:28	faithfulness shall flourish, and corruption shall be overcome
	7:48	and has brought us into corruption and the ways of death
	7:111	when corruption has increased and unrighteousness has multiplied
	7:113	in which corruption has passed away
	8:53	hell has fled and corruption has been forgotten
	10:28	my end has become corruption, and my prayer a reproach

COS 1
1 Ma	15:23	and to Rhodes, and to Phaselis, and to Cos

COST, subst. 6 = 0.004 %
L Jr	6:25	They are bought at any cost
1 Ma	10:44	Let the cost of rebuilding
	10:45	And let the cost of rebuilding the walls of Jerusalem
	10:45	and the cost of rebuilding the walls in Judea
2 Ma	5:6	not realizing that success at the cost of one's kindred
1 Es	6:25	the cost to be paid from the treasury of Cyrus the king

COSTLY 4 = 0.003 %
Ad E	14:2	and instead of costly perfumes
Wis	2:7	Let us take our fill of costly wine and perfumes
1 Ma	1:23	He took the silver and the gold, and the costly vessels
1 Es	6:9	of hewn stone, with costly timber laid in the walls

COUNCIL 10 = 0.007 %
Jud	6:1	When the disturbance made by the men outside the council died down
	6:17	at the council of Holofernes
	11:9	Now as for the things Achior said in your council
Sir	38:33	Yet they are not sought out for the council of the people
2 Ma	14:5	when he was invited by Demetrius to a meeting of the council
1 Es	2:17	and the other judges of their council
	3:15	and he took his seat in the council chamber
3 Ma	1:8	Since the Jews had sent some of their council and elders
4 Ma	15:25	For as in the council chamber of her own soul
	17:17	The tyrant himself and all his council marvelled at their endurance

COUNSEL¹ subst. 29 = 0.019 %
Tob	4:18	and do not despise any useful counsel
Wis	1:9	For inquiry will be made into the counsels of an ungodly man
	8:9	knowing that she would give me good counsel
	9:13	For what man can learn the counsel of God ?
	9:17	Who has learned thy counsel, unless thou hast given wisdom
Sir	6:2	Do not exalt yourself through your soul's counsel
	6:23	do not reject my counsel
	19:22	nor is there prudence where sinners take counsel
	21:13	and his counsel like a flowing spring
	22:16	so the mind firmly fixed on a reasonable counsel
	23:1	do not abandon me to their counsel
	24:29	and her counsel deeper than the great abyss
	25:4	and for the aged to possess good counsel !
	25:5	and understanding and counsel in honourable men !
	37:7	Every counsellor praises counsel
	37:7	but some give counsel in their own interest
	37:10	hide your counsel from those who are jealous of you
	37:11	pay no attention to these in any matter of counsel
	37:13	And establish the counsel of your own heart
	37:16	and counsel precedes every undertaking
	39:7	He will direct his counsel and knowledge aright
	40:25	but good counsel is esteemed more than both
	43:23	By his counsel he stilled the great deep
	44:3	giving counsel by their understanding
1 Ma	2:65	Now behold, I know that Simeon your brother is wise in counsel
2 Es	1:7	But they have angered me and despised my counsels
	2:1	and made my counsels void
	2:18	According to their counsel
4 Ma	6:16	But Eleazar, as though more bitterly tormented by this counsel, cried out :

COUNSEL, verb 2
1 Ma	9:69	who had counselled him to come into the country
4 Ma	8:29	had ceased counselling them to eat defiling food

COUNSELLOR, COUNSELOR 10 = 0.007 %
Ad E	13:3	When I asked my counsellors how this might be accomplished
Sir	37:7	Every counsellor praises counsel
	37:8	Be wary of a counsellor
	42:21	and he needs no one to be his counsellor
1 Es	8:11	who are my counsellors have decided
	8:26	and his counsellors and all his friends and nobles
	8:55	which the king himself and his counsellors and the nobles
4 Ma	5:1	The tyrant Antiochus, sitting in state with his counsellors

	9:2	to the law and to Moses our counsellor
	9:3	Tyrant and counsellor of lawlessness

COUNT, subst. 1
Wis	14:30	But just penalties will overtake them on 2 counts :

COUNT, verb 13 = 0.008 %
Tob	9:4	but my father is counting the days
	10:1	Now his father Tobit was counting each day
Jud	2:20	a multitude that could not be counted
	5:10	so great that they could not be counted
Wis	15:9	and he counts it his glory that he moulds counterfeit gods
	18:1	and counted them happy for not having suffered
	18:12	by the one form of death, had corpses too many to count
Sir	1:2	and the days of eternity – who can count them ?
	7:16	Do not count yourself among the crowd of sinners
Bar	3:11	that you are counted among those in Hades ?
1 Ma	5:30	and behold, a large company, that could not be counted
1 Es	8:64	The whole was counted and weighed
2 Es	11:11	And I counted his opposing wings

COUNT up 1
2 Es	5:36	He said to me, Count up for me those who have not yet come

COUNTENANCE 7 = 0.005 %
Jud	16:7	with the beauty of her countenance
Ad E	15:14	and your countenance is full of grace
Sir	13:25	A man's heart changes his countenance
	13:25	And a glad heart makes a cheerful countenance
	36:22	A woman's beauty gladdens the countenance
2 Es	10:25	and her countenance flashed like lightning
	15:63	and abolish the glory of your countenance

COUNTERATTACK 1
2 Ma	5:3	attacks and counterattacks made on this side and on that

COUNTERFEIT 1
Wis	15:9	and he counts it his glory that he moulds counterfeit gods

COUNTLESS 3 = 0.002 %
Sir	30:15	and a robust body than countless riches
3 Ma	5:46	with countless masses of people
	6:5	Sennacherib exulting in his countless forces

COUNTRY* 100 = 0.065 %
Tob	1:4	Now when I was in my own country, in the land of Israel
Jud	1:6	He was joined by all the people of the hill country
	2:6	Go and attack the whole west country
	2:22	and went up into the hill country
	2:23	south of the country of the Chelleans
	3:7	And these people and all in the country round about
	5:3	what people is this that lives in the hill country ?
	5:15	they took possession of all the hill country
	5:18	and were led away captive to a foreign country
	5:19	and have settled in the hill country
	6:7	into the hill country
	6:11	and from the plain they went up into the hill country
	7:1	and to seize the passes up into the hill country
	7:18	and encamped in the hill country opposite Dothan
	10:13	and capture all the hill country
	11:2	And even now, if your people who live in the hill country
	15:2	by every path across the plain and through the hill country
	15:5	Those in Jerusalem and all the hill country also came
	15:7	and the villages and towns in the hill country and in the plain
	16:21	and was honoured in her time throughout the whole country
Ad E	16:24	Every city and country, without exception
Sir	46:9	so that he went up to the hill country
	47:17	and for your interpretations, the countries marvelled at you
L Jr	6:53	For they cannot set up a king over a country or give rain to men
1 Ma	1:4	and ruled over countries, nations, and princes
	3:29	and the revenues from the country were small
	7:20	He placed Alcimus in charge of the country
	7:24	from going out into the country
	8:8	the country of Nidia and Media and Lydia
	9:24	and the country deserted with them to the enemy
	9:25	and put them in charge of the country
	9:61	And Jonathan's men seized about 50 of the men of the country
	9:65	while he went out into the country
	9:69	who had counselled him to come into the country
	10:38	from the country of Samaria
	10:52	for I crushed Demetrius and gained control of our country
	10:70	Why do you assume authority against us in the hill country ?
	11:62	And he passed through the country as far as Damascus
	11:64	but left his brother Simon in the country
	12:25	for he gave them no opportunity to invade his own country
	12:33	Simon also went forth and marched through the country
	13:20	After this Trypho came to invade the country and destroy it
	13:34	with a request to grant relief to the country
	13:49	were prevented from going out to the country and back
	14:6	and gained full control of the country

14:17	and that he was ruling over the country and the cities in it
14:28	and the elders of the country
14:29	Since wars often occurred in the country
14:31	And when their enemies decided to invade their country
14:36	so that the Gentiles were put out of the country
14:37	for the safety of the country and of the city
14:42	and over the country and the weapons and the strongholds
14:43	and that all contracts in the country
14:44	or to convene an assembly in the country
15:4	and intend to make a landing in the country
15:4	against those who have destroyed our country
15:6	as money for your country
15:15	with letters to the kings and countries
15:19	to the kings and countries
15:19	or make war against them and their cities and their country
15:21	have fled to you from their country
15:23	and to all the countries, and to Sampsames
15:38	Then the king made Cendebaeus commander-in-chief of the coastal country
16:4	So John chose out of the country 20,000 warriors and horsemen
16:13	he determined to get control of the country
16:14	Now Simon was visiting the cities of the country
16:18	and to turn over to him the cities and the country
2 Ma **4**:1	who had informed about the money against his own country
5:7	and fled again into the country of the Ammonites
5:8	and abhorred as the executioner of his country
5:9	and he who had driven many from their own country into exile died in exile
5:15	both to the laws and to his country
8:21	and made them ready to die for their laws and their country
8:35	across the country till he reached Antioch
9:23	into the upper country
13:3	not for the sake of his country's welfare
13:10	and their country and the holy temple
13:14	for the laws, temple, city, country, and commonwealth
14:2	and had taken possession of the country
14:9	deign to take thought for our country
14:18	and his men and their courage in battle for their country
15:19	being anxious over the encounter in the open country
1 Es **4**:20	and his own country, and cleaves to his wife
4:21	with no thought of his father or his mother or his country
4:50	that all the country which they would occupy
6:8	when we went to the country of Judea
6:17	over the country of Babylonia
6:23	And in Ecbatana, the fortress which is in the country of Media
8:13	in the country of Babylonia
9:37	settled in Jerusalem and in the country
3 Ma **4**:11	and to those from the city going out into the country
4:18	although most of them were still in the country
6:1	Then a certain Eleazar, famous among the priests of the country
6:25	the fortresses of our country ?
2 Es **1**:3	who was a captive in the country of the Medes
5:11	And one country shall ask its neighbour
13:45	and that country is called Arzareth
15:57	and all your people who are in the open country
4 Ma **4**:1	he fled the country with the purpose of betraying it
4:5	he proceeded quickly to our country

COUNTRYMAN

7 = 0.005 %

Tob **1**:3	and countrymen who went with me
2 Ma **4**:2	the protector of his fellow countrymen
4:10	he at once shifted his countrymen over
5:6	over enemies and not over fellow countrymen
12:5	When Judas heard of the cruelty visited on his countrymen
15:30	toward his countrymen
15:31	and had called his countrymen together

COUNTRYSIDE

1

3 Ma **3**:1	toward those in the countryside

COURAGE

32 = 0.021 %

Jud **7**:19	for their courage failed
7:30	And Uzziah said to them, Have courage, my brothers !
11:1	Take courage, woman, and do not be afraid in your heart
11:4	Have courage ; you will live, tonight and from now on
Ad E **14**:12	and give me courage
15:9	I am your brother. Take courage
Wis **8**:7	for she teaches self-control and prudence, justice and courage
Bar **4**:5	Take courage, my people, O memorial of Israel !
4:21	Take courage, my children, cry to God
4:27	Take courage, my children, and cry to God
4:30	Take courage, O Jerusalem
L Jr **6**:59	So it is better to be a king who shows his courage
1 Ma **11**:49	their courage failed
2 Ma **6**:20	as men ought to go who have the courage to refuse things
6:31	and a memorial of courage
7:20	she bore it with good courage
7:21	she fired her woman's reasoning with a man's courage
8:21	With these words he filled them with good courage
14:18	and his men and their courage in battle for their country
15:10	And when he had aroused their courage, he gave his orders
15:17	by fighting hand to hand with all courage
2 Es **12**:46	Take courage, O Israel
4 Ma **1**:4	and those that stand in the way of courage
1:6	but those that are opposed to justice, courage, and self-control
1:11	marvelled at their courage and endurance
1:18	courage, and self-control
5:23	and it also trains us in courage
13:11	While one said, Courage, brothers
15:23	But devout reason, giving her heart a man's courage
17:2	and showed the courage of your faith !
17:4	Take courage, therefore, O holy-minded mother
17:23	when he saw the courage of their virtue

COURAGEOUS

13 = 0.008 %

Wis **8**:15	and courageous in war
Sir **28**:15	Slander has driven away courageous women
1 Ma **2**:64	My children, be courageous and grow strong in the law
3 Ma **2**:32	But the majority acted firmly with a courageous spirit
4 Ma **2**:23	rule a kingdom that is temperate, just, good, and courageous
6:5	But the courageous and noble man, as a true Eleazar, was unmoved
6:11	he amazed even his torturers by his courageous spirit
6:24	When they saw that he was so courageous
7:23	For only the wise and courageous man is lord of his emotions
9:21	the courageous youth, worthy of Abraham, did not groan
9:23	or renounce our courageous brotherhood
9:26	While all were marvelling at his courageous spirit
17:24	and this made them brave and courageous

COURAGEOUSLY

3 = 0.002 %

1 Ma **6**:45	He courageously ran into the midst of the phalanx to reach it
2 Ma **7**:10	and courageously stretched forth his hands
3 Ma **1**:23	and die courageously for the ancestral law

COURSE, subst.

13 = 0.008 %

Wis **6**:22	but I will trace her course from the beginning of creation
14:3	but it is thy providence, O Father, that steers its course
18:14	and night in its swift course was now half gone
Sir **19**:17	and let the law of the Most High take its course
43:5	and at his command it hastens on its course
1 Es **4**:34	and the sun is swift in its course
6:25	with 3 courses of hewn stone
6:25	and one course of new native timber
2 Es **8**:2	so is the course of the present world
11:20	in due course the wings that followed also rose up on the right side
4 Ma **6**:18	should now change our course
14:5	but all of them, as though running the course toward immortality
15:2	2 courses were open to this mother

COURSE, adv., of course

2

2 Es **5**:47	I said, Of course it cannot
4 Ma **1**:2	I mean, of course, rational judgment

COURT

8 = 0.005 %

Ad E **11**:3	*a great man, serving in the court of the king*
12:5	*And the king ordered Mordecai to serve in the court*
Sir **50**:11	he made the court of the sanctuary glorious
1 Ma **4**:38	In the courts they saw bushes sprung up as in a thicket
4:48	and consecrated the courts
9:54	of the inner court of the sanctuary
1 Es **9**:1	Then Ezra rose and went from the court of the temple
4 Ma **5**:4	*advanced in age, and known to many in the tyrant's court*

COURTESY

2

Sir **6**:5	and a gracious tongue multiplies courtesies
20:13	but the courtesies of fools are wasted

COURTIER

1

2 Ma **9**:29	And Philip, one of his courtiers, took his body home

COURTYARD

7 = 0.005 %

Tob **2**:9	I slept by the wall of the courtyard, and my face was uncovered
Ad E **12**:1	Now Mordecai took his rest in the courtyard
12:1	the 2 eunuchs of the king who kept watch in the courtyard
2 Ma **14**:41	and were forcing the door of the courtyard
3 Ma **2**:27	and he set up a stone on the tower in the courtyard
5:10	presented himself at the courtyard early in the morning
5:46	the elephant keeper entered at about dawn into the courtyard

COUSIN

1

Tob **7**:2	How much the young man resembles my cousin Tobit !

COVENANT, subst.

52 = 0.034 %

Jud **9**:13	for they have planned cruel things against thy covenant
Wis **1**:16	and they made a covenant with him
12:21	and covenants full of good promises !
18:22	appealing to the oaths and covenants given to our fathers

Sir	11:20	Stand by your covenant and attend to it
	16:22	For the covenant is far off
	17:12	He established with them an eternal covenant
	24:23	All this is the book of the covenant of the Most High God
	28:7	remember the covenant of the Most High, and overlook ignorance
	39:8	and will glory in the law of the Lord's covenant
	41:19	Be ashamed before the truth of God and his covenant
	42:2	of the law of the Most High and his covenant
	44:12	Their descendants stand by the covenants
	44:18	Everlasting covenants were made with him
	44:20	and was taken into covenant with him
	44:20	he established the covenant in his flesh
	44:23	The blessing of all men and the covenant
	45:5	to teach Jacob the covenant, and Israel his judgments
	45:7	He made an everlasting covenant with him
	45:15	it was an everlasting covenant for him
	45:24	Therefore a covenant of peace was established with him
	45:25	A covenant was also established with David
	47:11	he gave him the covenant of kings
Bar	2:35	I will make an everlasting covenant with them
P Az	11	and do not break thy covenant
1 Ma	1:11	and misled many, saying, Let us go and make a covenant
	1:15	and abandoned the holy covenant
	1:57	Where the book of the covenant was found
	1:63	or to profane the holy covenant
	2:20	by the covenant of our fathers
	2:27	and supports the covenant
	2:50	and give your lives for the covenant of our fathers
	2:54	received the covenant of everlasting priesthood
	4:10	and remember his covenant with our fathers
	11:9	Come, let us make a covenant with each other
2 Ma	1:2	and may he remember his covenant with Abraham
	7:36	have drunk of everflowing life under God's covenant
	8:15	yet for the sake of the covenants made with their fathers
	14:20	they agreed to the covenant
	14:26	he took the covenant that had been made
	14:27	wrote to Nicanor, stating that he was displeased with the covenant
2 Es	2:5	because they would not keep my covenant
	2:7	because they have despised my covenant
	3:15	Thou didst make with him an everlasting covenant
	3:32	Or what tribes have so believed thy covenants
	4:23	and the written covenants no longer exist
	5:29	those who believed thy covenants
	7:24	They scorned his law, and denied his covenants
	7:46	or who among men that has not transgressed thy covenant ?
	7:83	for those who have trusted the covenants of the Most High
	8:27	but the endeavours of those who have kept thy covenants amid afflictions
	10:22	the ark of our covenant has been plundered

COVENANT, verb   1

Ad E	14:8	but they have covenanted with their idols

COVER, verb   21 = 0.014 %

Jud	2:7	and will cover the whole face of the earth
	2:19	and to cover the whole face of the earth to the west
	7:18	and covered the whole face of the land
	16:4	their cavalry covered the hills
Ad E	14:2	she covered her head with ashes and dung
	14:2	she covered with her tangled hair
	15:6	all covered with gold and precious stones
Wis	5:16	because with his right hand he will cover them
	13:14	and covering every blemish in it with paint
Sir	16:30	with all kinds of living beings he covered its surface
	24:3	and covered the earth like a mist
	29:21	and a house to cover one's nakedness
	37:3	O evil imagination, why were you formed to cover the land with deceit ?
	39:22	His blessing covers the dry land like a river
	40:27	and covers a man better than any glory
	47:15	Your soul covered the earth
	48:12	It was Elijah who was covered by the whirlwind
1 Ma	6:37	And upon the elephants were wooden towers, strong and covered
2 Ma	6:5	The altar was covered with abominable offerings
2 Es	1:20	I covered you with the leaves of trees
	2:29	My hands will cover you, that your sons may not see Gehenna

COVER, subst.   2

L Jr	6:68	for they can flee to cover and help themselves
1 Ma	9:38	and went up and hid under cover of the mountain

COVET   3 = 0.002 %

1 Ma	11:11	He threw blame on Alexander because he coveted his kingdom
4 Ma	2:5	Thus the law says, You shall not covet your neighbour's wife
	2:6	In fact, since the law had told us not to covet

COVETOUS   1

Wis	10:11	When his oppressors were covetous

COVETOUSNESS   1

4 Ma	1:26	In the soul it is boastfulness, covetousness

COWARD   4 = 0.003 %

Sir	34:14	nor play the coward, for he is his hope
	37:11	or with a coward about war
4 Ma	10:14	You do not have a fire hot enough to make me play the coward
	14:4	None of the 7 youths proved coward or shrank from death

COWARDICE   4 = 0.003 %

Sir	4:17	she will bring fear and cowardice upon him
1 Ma	4:32	Fill them with cowardice
4 Ma	6:17	that out of cowardice we feign a role unbecoming to us !
	6:20	be a laughing stock to all for our cowardice

COWARDLY   5 = 0.003 %

Wis	17:11	For wickedness is a cowardly thing
2 Ma	8:13	those who were cowardly and distrustful of God's justice
4 Ma	5:31	I am not so old and cowardly
	8:16	if some of them had been cowardly and unmanly
	13:10	Let us not be cowardly in the demonstration of our piety

COWER   3 = 0.002 %

Sir	32:18	and an insolent and proud man will not cower in fear
3 Ma	6:13	And let the Gentiles cower today
4 Ma	16:20	he did not cower

CRAFT   2

Ad E	16:13	and with intricate craft and deceit
Wis	7:16	as are all understanding and skill in crafts

CRAFTSMAN   8 = 0.005 %

Wis	13:1	nor did they recognize the craftsman
	14:2	and wisdom was the craftsman who built it
	14:18	Then the ambition of the craftsman
Sir	9:17	A work will be praised for the skill of the craftsmen
	38:27	So too is every craftsman and master workman
	45:11	with twisted scarlet, the work of a craftsman
L Jr	6:8	Their tongues are smoothed by the craftsman
	6:45	they can be nothing but what the craftsmen wish them to be

CRAFTY   2

Sir	11:29	for many are the wiles of the crafty
	42:18	and considers their crafty devices

CRASH   2

Wis	17:19	or the harsh crash of rocks hurled down
Sir	40:13	and crash like a loud clap of thunder in a rain

CRATES   1

2 Ma	4:29	while Sostratus left Crates

CRAVE   2

4 Ma	1:34	Therefore when we crave seafood and fowl and animals
	3:12	because of the king's craving

CREATE   57 = 0.037 %

Jud	13:18	who created the heavens and the earth
Wis	1:14	For he created all things that they might exist
	2:23	for God created man for incorruption
	10:1	when he alone had been created
	11:17	For thy all-powerful hand, which created the world
	11:18	or newly created unknown beasts full of rage
	13:3	for the author of beauty created them
	13:5	For from the greatness and beauty of created things
	14:11	because, though part of what God created
Sir	1:4	Wisdom was created before all things
	1:9	The Lord himself created wisdom
	1:14	she is created with the faithful in the womb
	7:15	which were created by the Most High
	10:18	Pride was not created for men
	11:16	Error and darkness were created with sinners
	15:14	It was he who created man in the beginning
	17:1	The Lord created man out of earth
	18:1	He who lives for ever created the whole universe
	23:20	Before the universe was created, it was known to him
	24:8	and the one who created me assigned a place for my tent
	24:9	From eternity, in the beginning, he created me
	31:13	What has been created more greedy then the eye ?
	31:27	It has been created to make men glad
	33:10	and Adam was created of the dust
	36:15	Bear witness to those whom thou didst create in the beginning
	38:1	according to your need of him, for the Lord created him
	38:4	The Lord created medicines from the earth
	38:12	And give the physician his place, for the Lord created him
	39:21	for everything has been created for its use
	39:25	From the beginning good things were created for good people

39:28	There are winds that have been created for vengeance
39:29	all these have been created for vengeance
40:1	Much labour was created for every man
40:10	All these were created for the wicked
49:14	No one like Enoch has been created on earth
Bel 14:5	but the living God, who created heaven and earth
2 Ma 14:17	because of the sudden consternation created by the enemy
1 Es 6:13	who created the heaven and the earth
3 Ma 1:23	and created a considerable disturbance in the holy place
2:9	You, O King, when you had created
2 Es 2:14	for I left out evil and created good
5:26	and from all the birds that have been created
5:43	Couldst thou not have created at one time
5:44	those who have been created in it
5:49	so have I organized the world which I created
6:41	thou didst create the spirit of the firmament
6:55	that thou didst create this world
6:59	If the world has indeed been created for us
7:48	but almost all who have been created !
7:62	like the other created things
7:139	and judge, because if he did not pardon those who were created by his word
8:3	Many have been created, but few shall be saved
8:8	what thou hast created is preserved in fire and water
8:8	endures thy creation which has been created in it
8:9	And when the womb gives up again what has been created in it
8:60	but they themselves who were created
9:19	but now those who have been created in this world

CREATION   28 = 0.018 %

Jud 9:12	King of all thy creation, hear my prayer !
Wis 2:6	and make use of the creation to the full as in youth
5:17	and will arm all creation to repel his enemies
5:20	and creation will join with him to fight against the madmen
6:22	but I will trace her course from the beginning of creation
16:24	For the creation, serving thee who has made it
19:6	For the whole creation in its nature was fashioned anew
Sir 16:16	His mercy is manifest to the whole of creation
16:17	for what is my soul in the boundless creation ?
16:26	from the beginning by his creation
49:16	and Adam above every living being in the creation
3 Ma 2:2	and sovereign of all creation
2:7	the Ruler over the whole creation
6:2	governing all creation with mercy
2 Es 5:44	The creation cannot make more haste than the Creator
5:45	that thou wilt certainly give life at one time to thy creation ?
5:45	and the creation will sustain them
5:55	as born of a creation which already is aging
5:56	show thy servant through whom thou dost visit thy creation
6:38	thou didst speak at the beginning of creation
7:75	when thou wilt renew the creation
8:8	endures thy creation which has been created in it
8:13	Thou wilt take away his life, for he is thy creation
8:39	but I will rejoice over the creation of the righteous
8:45	for thou hast mercy on thy own creation
8:47	For you come far short of being able to love my creation
13:26	who will himself deliver his creation
4 Ma 14:7	For just as the 7 days of creation

CREATOR   11 = 0.007 %

Jud 9:12	Lord of heaven and earth, Creator of the waters
Wis 13:5	comes a corresponding perception of their Creator
Sir 4:6	his Creator will hear his prayer
24:8	Then the Creator of all things gave me a commandment
2 Ma 1:24	O Lord, Lord God, Creator of all things
7:23	Therefore the Creator of the world
13:14	So, committing the decision to the Creator of the world
3 Ma 2:3	For you, the creator of all things and the governor of all
2 Es 5:44	The creation cannot make more haste than the Creator
4 Ma 5:25	the Creator of the world in giving us the law
11:5	It is because we revere the Creator of all things and live

CREATURE   26 = 0.017 %

Tob 8:5	Let the heavens and all thy creatures bless thee
8:15	Let thy saints and all thy creatures bless thee
Jud 16:14	Let all thy creatures serve thee
Wis 9:2	to have dominion over the creatures thou hast made
11:15	a multitude of irrational creatures to punish them
12:27	they became incensed at those creatures
16:1	through such creatures
16:3	because of the odious creatures sent to them
16:18	so that it might not consume the creatures
19:19	For land animals were transformed into water creatures
19:19	and creatures that swim moved over to the land
19:21	failed to consume the flesh of perishable creatures
Sir 11:3	The bee is small among flying creatures
13:15	Every creature loves its like
17:21	But the Lord, who is gracious and knows his creatures
43:25	all kinds of living things, and huge creatures of the sea

Bar 3:32	He who prepared the earth for all time filled it with four-footed creatures
P Az 57	Bless the Lord, you whales and all creatures that move in the waters
3 Ma 3:29	and shall become useless for all time to any mortal creature
2 Es 5:45	If therefore all creatures will live at one time
6:47	to bring forth living creatures, birds, and fishes
6:48	The dumb and lifeless water produced living creatures
6:49	Then thou didst keep in existence 2 living creatures
8:24	and give ear to the petition of thy creature
11:6	not even one creature that was on the earth
11:37	a creature like a lion was aroused out of the forest, roaring

CREDIBLE   1

4 Ma 7:9	but by your deeds you made your words of divine philosophy credible

CREDIT, verb   1

Sir 3:14	and against your sins it will be credited to you

CREEPING   2

Sir 10:11	For when a man is dead, he will inherit creeping things
2 Es 6:53	to bring forth before thee cattle, beasts, and creeping things

CRETE   1

1 Ma 10:67	came from Crete to the land of his fathers

CRIME   5 = 0.003 %

2 Ma 4:36	and the Greeks shared their hatred of the crime
4:49	showing their hatred of the crime
13:6	any man guilty of sacrilege or notorious for other crimes
4 Ma 11:3	from the heavenly justice for even more crimes
18:22	For these crimes divine justice pursued and will pursue the accursed tyrant

CRINGE   1

Sir 12:11	Even if he humbles himself and goes about cringing

CRISIS   2

Sir 22:16	will not be afraid in a crisis
Bar 3:5	but in this crisis remember thy power and thy name

CRITICAL   1

2 Ma 1:7	we Jews wrote to you, in the critical distress

CRITICISM   1

Sir 38:17	for one day, or 2, to avoid criticism

CROOKED   1

Wis 13:13	a stick crooked and full of knots

CROP   5 = 0.003 %

Wis 16:19	to destroy the crops of the unrighteous land
16:22	so that they might know that the crops of their enemies
16:26	might learn that it is not the production of crops that feeds man
Sir 7:3	and you will not reap a sevenfold crop
1 Ma 11:34	from the crops of the land and the fruit of the trees

CROSS, verb   8 = 0.005 %

Sir 8:16	and do not cross the wilderness with him
1 Ma 3:37	He crossed the Euphrates river
5:24	Judas maccabeus and Jonathan his brother crossed the Jordan
5:52	And they crossed the Jordan into the large plain before Beth-shan
9:34	and he with all his army crossed the Jordan
9:48	and the enemy did not cross the Jordan to attack them
12:30	for they had crossed the Eleutherus river
16:6	And he saw that the soldiers were afraid to cross the stream

CROSS over   8 = 0.005 %

Jud 5:15	and crossing over the Jordan
1 Ma 5:6	Then he crossed over to attack the Ammonites
5:40	If he crosses over to us first
5:41	we will cross over to him and defeat him
5:43	Then he crossed over against them first
16:6	so he crossed over first
16:6	and when his men saw him, they crossed over after him
3 Ma 1:2	and crossed over by night to the tent of Ptolemy

CROW, verb   1

3 Ma 5:23	Then, as soon as the cock had crowed in the early morning

CROW, subst.   1

L Jr 6:54	they are like crows between heaven and earth

CROWD, subst.   13 = 0.008 %

Jud 2:20	Along with them went a mixed crowd like a swarm of locusts
Sir 7:16	Do not count yourself among the crowd of sinners
2 Ma 3:18	People also hurried out of their houses in crowds
4:40	And since the crowds were becoming aroused

14:43	and the crowd was now rushing in through the doors
14:43	and manfully threw himself down into the crowd
14:45	he ran through the crowd
14:46	took them with both hands and hurled them at the crowd
3 Ma 1:24	Meanwhile the crowd, as before, was engaged in prayer
1:28	The continuous, vehement, and concerted cry of the crowds
3:8	and the crowds that suddenly were forming
5:24	The crowds of the city had been assembled
5:48	as well as by the trampling of the crowd

CROWD, verb   5 = 0.003 %

Sir 16:28	They do not crowd one another aside
31:14	and do not crowd your neighbour at the dish
3 Ma 1:20	and without a backward look they crowded together
5:41	it is crowded with masses of people
5:46	crowding their way into the hippodrome

CROWN, subst.   32 = 0.021 %

Wis 5:16	Therefore they will receive a glorious crown
Sir 1:11	and gladness and a crown of rejoicing
1:18	The fear of the Lord is the crown of wisdom
6:31	and put her on like a crown of gladness
11:5	but one who was never thought of has worn a crown
15:6	He will find gladness and a crown of rejoicing
25:6	Rich experience is the crown of the aged
40:4	from the man who wears purple and a crown
45:12	with a gold crown upon his turban
L Jr 6:9	People take gold and make crowns for the heads of their gods
Bel 14:36	Then the angel of the Lord took him by the crown of his head
1 Ma 1:9	They all put on crowns after his death
1:22	the curtain, the crowns
4:57	with golden crowns and small shields
6:15	He gave him the crown and his robe and the signet
8:14	Yet for all this not one of them has put on a crown
10:20	and he sent him a purple robe and a golden crown
10:29	from payment of tribute and salt tax and crown levies
11:13	Then Ptolemy entered Antioch and put on the crown of Asia
11:13	Thus he put 2 crowns upon his head
11:13	the crown of Egypt and that of Asia
11:35	and the salt pits and the crown taxes due to us
11:54	who began to reign and put on the crown
12:39	and put on the crown
13:32	and became king in his place, putting on the crown of Asia
13:37	We have received the gold crown
13:39	and cancel the crown tax which you owe
2 Ma 14:4	presenting to him a crown of gold and a palm
1 Es 4:30	and take the crown from the king's head and put it on her own
2 Es 2:43	and on the head of each of them he placed a crown
2:46	Who is that young man who places crowns on them
4 Ma 17:15	and gave the crown to its own athletes

CROWN, verb   7 = 0.005 %

Jud 15:13	and they crowned themselves with olive wreaths
Wis 2:8	Let us crown ourselves with rosebuds before they wither
4:2	and throughout all time it marches crowned in triumph
Sir 19:5	but he who withstands pleasures crowns his life
1 Ma 14:5	To crown all his honours he took Joppa for a harbour
3 Ma 7:16	crowned with all sorts of very fragrant flowers
2 Es 2:45	now they are being crowned, and receive palms

CRUCIAL   1

Sir 4:23	Do not refrain from speaking at the crucial time

CRUEL   9 = 0.006 %

Jud 9:13	for they have planned cruel things against thy covenant
Sir 13:12	Cruel is he who does not keep words to himself
2 Ma 4:25	but having the hot temper of a cruel tyrant
7:27	deriding the cruel tyrant : My son, have pity on me
1 Es 2:27	and that mighty and cruel kings ruled in Jerusalem
3 Ma 3:1	and put to death by the most cruel means
2 Es 5:18	in the power of cruel wolves
4 Ma 6:8	One of the cruel guards rushed at him
18:20	quenched fire with fire in his cruel cauldrons

CRUELLY   3 = 0.002 %

2 Es 7:67	that we shall be preserved alive but cruelly tormented ?
4 Ma 8:2	these should be tortured even more cruelly
11:1	When this one died also, after being cruelly tortured

CRUELTY   3 = 0.002 %

2 Ma 12:5	When Judas heard of the cruelty visited on his countrymen
3 Ma 6:24	You are committing treason and surpassing tyrants in cruelty
7:5	with a cruelty more savage than that of Scythian custom

CRUSH   30 = 0.020 %

Jud 9:7	and know not that thou art the Lord who crushest wars
9:10	crush their arrogance by the hand of a woman
16:3	For God is the Lord who crushes wars
Sir 28:17	but a blow of the tongue crushes the bones
35:18	till he crushes the loins of the unmerciful

36:10	Crush the heads of the rulers of the enemy
47:7	he crushed their power even to this day
1 Ma 3:22	He himself will crush them before us
3:23	and they were crushed before him
4:10	and crush this army before us today
4:14	The Gentiles were crushed and fled into the plain
4:30	who didst crush the attack of the mighty warrior
4:36	Behold, our enemies are crushed
5:7	and they were crushed before him
5:21	and the Gentiles were crushed before him
7:42	So also crush this army before us today
7:43	The army of Nicanor was crushed
8:4	until they crushed them
8:5	they crushed in battle and conquered
8:6	He was crushed by them
9:7	and the battle was imminent, he was crushed in spirit
9:15	and they crushed the right wing
9:16	that the right wing was crushed
9:68	They fought with Bacchides, and he was crushed by them
10:52	for I crushed Demetrius and gained control of our country
10:53	and he and his army were crushed by us
12:31	and he crushed them and plundered them
13:51	because a great enemy had been crushed and removed from Israel
14:13	and the kings were crushed in those days
3 Ma 2:13	we are crushed with suffering

CRY, subst.   14 = 0.009 %

Jud 14:19	and their loud cries and shouts arose
Ad E 11:10	and from their cry, as though from a tiny spring
Wis 7:3	and my first sound was a cry, like that of all
18:10	But the discordant cry of their enemies echoed back
Sir 30:7	and his feelings will be troubled at every cry
Sus 13:44	The Lord heard her cry
1 Ma 5:31	and that the cry of the city went up to Heaven
2 Ma 12:37	In the language of their fathers he raised the battle cry, with hymns
3 Ma 1:16	and they filled the temple with cries and tears
1:28	The continuous, vehement, and concerted cry of the crowds
4:2	there was incessant mourning, lamentation, and tearful cries
6:17	they raised great cries to heaven
2 Es 10:26	behold, she suddenly uttered a loud and fearful cry
11:7	and uttered a cry to his wings, saying

CRY, verb   11 = 0.007 %

Tob 13:18	all her lanes will cry Hallelujah !
Ad E 11:10	Then they cried to God
Bar 4:20	I will cry to the Everlasting all my days
4:21	Take courage, my children, cry to God
4:27	Take courage, my children, and cry to God
Sus 13:46	and he cried with a loud voice
1 Ma 3:50	and they cried aloud to Heaven, saying
4:10	And now let us cry to Heaven
5:33	who sounded their trumpets and cried aloud in prayer
13:50	Then they cried to Simon to make peace with them
2 Es 10:28	Then I was afraid, and cried with a loud voice and said

CRY out   30 = 0.020 %

Tob 6:17	and cry out to the merciful God
Jud 4:9	And every man of Israel cried out to God with great fervour
4:12	and cried out in unison
4:15	they cried out to the Lord with all their might
5:12	Then they cried out to their God
6:18	and cried out to him, and said
7:19	The people of Israel cried out to the Lord their God
7:23	and cried out with a loud voice
7:29	and they cried out to the Lord God with a loud voice
9:1	Judith cried out to the Lord with a loud voice, and said
10:1	When Judith had ceased crying out to the God of Israel
14:16	And he cried out with a loud voice
Ad E 10:9	who cried out to God and were saved
13:18	And all Israel cried out mightily
Sir 35:15	as she cries out against him who has caused them to fall ?
Bar 3:1	the soul in anguish and the wearied spirit cry out to thee
Sus 13:24	Then Susanna cried out with a loud voice
13:42	Then Susanna cried out with a loud voice, and said
1 Ma 2:27	Then Mattathias cried out in the city with a loud voice
4:40	and cried out to Heaven
9:46	Cry out now to Heaven
11:49	and they cried out to the king with this entreaty
13:45	and they cried out with a loud voice
2 Ma 8:3	and to hearken to the blood that cried out to him
3 Ma 5:51	and cried out in a very loud voice
2 Es 1:17	did you not cry out to me, saying
15:8	Behold, innocent and righteous blood cries out to me
15:8	and the souls of the righteous cry out continually
4 Ma 6:4	while a herald opposite him cried out
6:16	But Eleazar, as though more bitterly tormented by this counsel, cried out :

CRYSTALLINE   1
  Wis **19** : 21   nor did they melt the crystalline

CUB   1
  1 Ma **3** : 4   like a lion's cub roaring for prey

CUBIT   12 = 0.008 %
  Jud **1** : 2   with hewn stones 3 cubits thick and 6 cubits long
        1 : 2   he made the walls 70 cubits high and 50 cubits wide
        1 : 3   a 100 cubits high and 60 cubits wide at the foundations
        1 : 4   which were 70 cubits high and 40 cubits wide
  P Az **24**   And the flame streamed out above the furnace 49 cubits
  2 Ma **13** : 5   For there is a tower in that place, 50 cubits high, full of ashes
  1 Es **6** : 25   its height to be 60 cubits and its breadth 60 cubits

CUCUMBER   1
  L Jr **6** : 70   Like a scarecrow in a cucumber bed, that guards nothing

CULT   1
  Wis **12** : 5   These initiates from the midst of a heathen cult

CULTIVATE   3 = 0.002 %
  Sir **20** : 28   Whoever cultivates the soil will heap up his harvest
  2 Es **6** : 42   so that some of them might be planted and cultivated
      16 : 24   No one shall be left to cultivate the earth or to sow it

CULTIVATED   1
  Sir **21** : 23   but a cultivated man remains outside

CULTIVATION   3 = 0.002 %
  Sir **27** : 6   The fruit discloses the cultivation of a tree
      27 : 6   so that the expression of a thought discloses the cultivation of a man's mind
  2 Es **8** : 6   and cultivation of our understanding

CULTIVATOR   1
  4 Ma **1** : 29   each of which the master cultivator, reason, weeds and prunes

CUP   7 = 0.005 %
  Sir **50** : 15   he reached out his hand to the cup
  1 Ma **1** : 22   the cups for drink offerings, the bowls, the golden censers
      11 : 58   and granted him the right to drink from gold cups
  1 Es **2** : 13   The number of these was : a 1,000 gold cups, a 1,000 silver cups
      3 : 6   He shall be clothed in purple, and drink from gold cups
  2 Es **14** : 39   a full cup was offered to me

CUPBEARER   1
  Tob **1** : 22   Now Ahikar was cupbearer, keeper of the signet

CUPIDITY   1
  2 Ma **4** : 50   But Menelaus, because of the cupidity of those in power

CURE, verb   3 = 0.002 %
  Tob **6** : 8   and he will be cured
      12 : 3   he cured my wife, he obtained the money for me
  Wis **16** : 12   For neither herb nor poultice cured them

CURIOUS   1
  2 Es **9** : 13   Therefore, do not continue to be curious

CURL back   1
  4 Ma **11** : 10   so that he was completely curled back like a scorpion

CURRENT, subst.   1
  Sir **4** : 26   and do not try to stop the current of a river

CURSE, subst.   8 = 0.005 %
  Sir **3** : 9   but a mother's curse uproots their foundations
      4 : 6   for if in bitterness of soul he calls down a curse upon you
      23 : 26   She will leave her memory for a curse
      29 : 6   he will repay him with curses and reproaches
      41 : 9   When you are born, you are born to a curse
      41 : 9   and when you die, a curse is your lot
      41 : 10   so the ungodly go from curse to destruction
  Bar **1** : 20   and the curse which the Lord declared

CURSE, verb   13 = 0.008 %
  Tob **13** : 12   Cursed are all who hate you
  Sir **3** : 16   and whoever angers his mother is cursed by the Lord
      4 : 5   nor give a man occasion to curse you
      21 : 27   When an ungodly man curses his adversary
      21 : 27   he curses his own soul
      23 : 14   and you will curse the day of your birth
      28 : 13   Curse the whisperer and deceiver
      33 : 12   but some of them he cursed and brought low
      34 : 24   When one prays and another curses
  Bar **3** : 8   to be reproached and cursed and punished
  L Jr **6** : 66   For they can neither curse nor bless kings

  Ps **151** : 6   and he cursed me by his idols
  4 Ma **2** : 19   saying, Cursed be their anger ?

CURTAIN   3 = 0.002 %
  Wis **17** : 3   they were unobserved behind a dark curtain of forgetfulness
  1 Ma **1** : 22   the curtain, the crowns
      4 : 51   They placed the bread on the table and hung up the curtains

CUSTODY   2
  Jud **10** : 12   and took her into custody, and asked her
  3 Ma **5** : 5   and arranged for their continued custody through the night

CUSTOM   18 = 0.012 %
  Wis **14** : 16   Then the ungodly custom, grown strong with time
      14 : 23   or hold frenzied revels with strange customs
  1 Ma **1** : 14   according to Gentile custom
      1 : 42   and that each should give up his customs
      1 : 44   he directed them to follow customs strange to the land
      10 : 89   such as it is the custom to give to the kinsmen of kings
  2 Ma **4** : 11   and introduced new customs contrary to the law
      6 : 9   to change over to Greek customs
      11 : 24   to our father's change to Greek customs
      11 : 24   and ask that their own customs be allowed them
      11 : 25   and that they live according to the customs of their ancestors
      12 : 38   they purified themselves according to the custom
      13 : 4   by the method which is the custom in that place
      14 : 30   and was meeting him more rudely than had been his custom
  3 Ma **3** : 2   that they hindered others from the observance or their customs
      7 : 5   with a cruelty more savage than that of Scythian custom
  4 Ma **1** : 12   but, as my custom is
      18 : 5   to become pagans and to abandon their ancestral customs

CUSTOMARY   2
  2 Ma **14** : 4   some of the customary olive branches from the temple
      14 : 31   while the priests were offering the customary sacrifices

CUT   8 = 0.005 %
  Tob **6** : 4   Cut open the fish and take the heart and liver and gall
  Sir **38** : 27   those who cut the signets of seals
  Sus **13** : 55   and will immediately cut you in 2
  2 Ma **1** : 13   they were cut to pieces in the temple of Nanaea
      2 : 32   *while cutting short the history itself*
      10 : 30   they were thrown into disorder and cut to pieces
  4 Ma **6** : 6   and his sides were being cut to pieces
      9 : 17   Cut my limbs, burn my flesh, and twist my joints

CUT down   9 = 0.006 %
  Jud **3** : 8   and cut down their sacred groves
      14 : 4   shall pursue them and cut them down as they flee
      15 : 5   and cut them down as far as Choba
  1 Ma **6** : 6   from the armies they had cut down
  2 Ma **5** : 12   to cut down relentlessly every one they met
      10 : 35   and with savage fury cut down every one they met
  1 Es **4** : 9   if he tells them to cut down, they cut down
  4 Ma **2** : 14   The fruit trees of the enemy are not cut down

CUT off   11 = 0.007 %
  Jud **14** : 15   with his head cut off and missing
  Wis **18** : 23   and cut off its way to the living
  1 Ma **7** : 47   and they cut off Nicanor's head
      11 : 17   And Zabdiel the Arab cut off the head of Alexander
  2 Ma **1** : 16   and dismembered them and cut off their heads
      7 : 4   and cut off his hands and feet
      12 : 35   and cut off his arm
      15 : 30   ordered them to cut off Nicanor's head and arm
  1 Es **5** : 72   cut off their supplies, and hindered their building
  2 Es **7** : 114   unbelief has been cut off
  4 Ma **10** : 19   cut it off, for in spite of this

CUT out   6 = 0.004 %
  2 Ma **7** : 4   be cut out and that they scalp him
      15 : 33   and he cut out the tongue of the ungodly Nicanor
  4 Ma **10** : 17   gave orders to cut out his tongue
      10 : 21   God will visit you swiftly, for you are cutting out
      12 : 13   to cut out the tongues of men who have feelings like yours
      18 : 21   pierced the pupils of their eyes and cut out their tongues

CUTHA   1
  1 Es **5** : 32   the sons of Mehida, the sons of Cutha

CYAMON   1
  Jud **7** : 3   and in length from Bethulia to Cyamon

CYCLE   1
  Wis **7** : 19   the cycles of the year and the constellations of the stars

CYMBAL   4 = 0.003 %
  Jud **16** : 2   sing to my Lord with cymbals
  1 Ma **4** : 54   it was dedicated with songs and harps and lutes and cymbals

	13:51	and with harps and cymbals and stringed instruments
1 Es	5:59	and the Levites, the sons of Asaph, with cymbals

CYPRESS   2
Sir	24:13	and like a cypress on the heights of Hermon
	50:10	and like a cypress towering in the clouds

CYPRIAN   1
2 Ma	4:29	the commander of the Cyprian troops

CYPRUS   3 = 0.002 %
1 Ma	15:23	and Cnidus and Cyprus and Cyrene
2 Ma	10:13	because he had abandoned Cyprus
	12:2	and in addition to these Nicanor the governor of Cyprus

CYRENE   2
1 Ma	15:23	and Cnidus and Cyprus and Cyrene
2 Ma	2:23	all this, which has been set forth by Jason of Cyrene in 5 volumes

CYRUS   20 = 0.013 %
Bel	14:1	Cyrus the Persian received his kingdom
1 Es	2:1	In the first year of Cyrus as king of the Persians
	2:2	the Lord stirred up the spirit of Cyrus king of the Persians
	2:3	Thus says Cyrus king of the Persians :
	2:10	Cyrus the king also brought out the holy vessels of the Lord
	2:11	When Cyrus king of the Persians brought these out
	4:44	which Cyrus set apart when he began to destroy Babylon
	4:57	which Cyrus had set apart
	4:57	everything that Cyrus had ordered to be done
	5:55	from Cyrus king of the Persians
	5:71	as Cyrus the king of the Persians has commanded us
	5:73	as long as King Cyrus lived
	6:17	But in the first year that Cyrus reigned
	6:17	King Cyrus wrote that this house should be rebuilt
	6:18	these Cyrus the king took out again
	6:22	was done with the consent of King Cyrus
	6:24	In the first year of the reign of Cyrus
	6:24	King Cyrus ordered the building
	6:25	the cost to be paid from the treasury of Cyrus the king
	7:4	So with the consent of Cyrus and Darius and Artaxerxes

D

DABRIA   1
2 Es	14:24	and take with you Sarea, Dabria, Selemia, Ethanus, and Asiel

DAGGER   1
L Jr	6:15	It has a dagger in its right hand, and has an axe

DAGON   2
1 Ma	10:84	and the temple of Dagon
	11:4	they showed him the temple of Dagon burned down

DAILY   5 = 0.003 %
Jud	12:15	for her daily use
1 Ma	6:57	We daily grow weaker, our food supply is scant
1 Es	6:30	for daily use as the priests in Jerusalem may indicate
2 Es	4:23	but about those things which we daily experience :
4 Ma	13:22	from this common nurture and daily companionship

DAINTILY   1
Ad E	15:3	leaning daintily on one

DAINTY, subst.   1
Sir	31:3	and when he rests he fills himself with his dainties

DALLY   1
2 Ma	6:4	by the Gentiles, who dallied with harlots

DAMAGE, subst.   5 = 0.003 %
Wis	11:19	not only could their damage exterminate men
1 Ma	7:22	and did great damage in Israel
	14:36	and do great damage to its purity
	15:29	you have done great damage in the land
	15:35	they were causing great damage among the people and to our land

DAMAGE, verb   1
1 Es	6:33	to hinder or damage that house of the Lord in Jerusalem

DAMASCUS   6 = 0.004 %
Jud	1:7	those who lived in Cilicia and Damascus
	1:12	on the whole territory of Cilicia and Damascus and Syria
	2:27	Then he went down into the plain of Damascus
	15:5	even beyond Damascus and its borders

1 Ma	11:62	And he passed through the country as far as Damascus
	12:32	Then he broke camp and went to Damascus

DANCE, verb   1
2 Es	6:21	and these shall live and dance

DANCE, subst.   4 = 0.003 %
Jud	3:7	welcomed him with garlands and dances and tambourines
	15:12	and blessed her, and some of them performed a dance for her
	15:13	and she went before all the people in the dance
4 Ma	14:7	move in choral dance around religion

DANGER   21 = 0.014 %
Tob	4:4	Remember, my son, that she faced many dangers for you
Ad E	14:4	for my danger is in my hand
Wis	14:4	showing that thou canst save from every danger
	18:9	both blessings and dangers
Sir	3:26	and whoever loves danger will perish by it
	34:12	I have often been in danger of death
	43:24	Those who sail the sea tell of its dangers
1 Ma	11:23	and put himself in danger
	14:29	exposed themselves to danger
2 Ma	1:11	Having been saved by God out of grave dangers
	15:17	and the temple were in danger
3 Ma	5:41	and also in constant danger of being plundered
	6:26	and often have accepted willingly the worst of human dangers ?
2 Es	7:9	unless he passes through the danger set before him ?
	7:12	full of dangers and involved in great hardships
	7:89	and withstood danger every hour
	9:8	will survive the dangers that have been predicted
	12:18	and it shall be in danger of falling
	13:19	For they shall see great dangers and much distress
4 Ma	3:15	considered it an altogether fearful danger to his soul
	13:15	and the danger of eternal torment

DANGEROUS   1
3 Ma	5:33	So Hermon suffered an unexpected and dangerous threat

DANIEL   41 = 0.027 %
Sus	13:45	God aroused the holy spirit of a young lad named Daniel
	13:51	And Daniel said to them
	13:55	And Daniel said, Very well !
	13:59	And Daniel said to him, Very well !
	13:61	Daniel had convicted them of bearing false witness
	13:64	Daniel had a great reputation among the people
Bel	14:2	And Daniel was a companion of the king
	14:4	But Daniel worshipped his own God
	14:7	Then Daniel laughed, and said
	14:9	But if you prove that Bel is eating them, Daniel shall die
	14:9	And Daniel said to the king
	14:10	And the king went with Daniel into the temple of Bel
	14:12	or else Daniel will, who is telling lies about us
	14:14	Then Daniel ordered his servants to bring ashes
	14:16	and Daniel with him
	14:17	And the king said, Are the seals unbroken, Daniel ?
	14:19	Then Daniel laughed
	14:22	and gave Bel over to Daniel, who destroyed it and its temple
	14:24	And the king said to Daniel
	14:25	Daniel said, I will worship the Lord my God
	14:27	Then Daniel took pitch, fat, and hair
	14:27	And Daniel said, See what you have been worshipping !
	14:29	Going to the king, they said, Hand Daniel over to us
	14:30	and under compulsion he handed Daniel over to them
	14:31	They threw Daniel into the lions' den
	14:32	so that they might devour Daniel
	14:34	to Daniel, in the lions' den
	14:37	Then Habakkuk shouted, Daniel ! Daniel !
	14:38	And Daniel said, Thou hast remembered me, O God
	14:39	So Daniel arose and ate
	14:40	On the 7th day the king came to mourn for Daniel
	14:40	When he came to the den he looked in, and there sat Daniel
	14:41	Thou art great, O Lord God of Daniel
	14:42	And he pulled Daniel out
1 Ma	2:60	Daniel because of his innocence
3 Ma	6:7	Daniel, who through envious slanders
2 Es	12:11	to your brother Daniel
4 Ma	16:3	The lions surrounding Daniel were not so savage
	16:21	And Daniel the righteous was thrown to the lions
	18:13	He praised Daniel in the den of the lions and blessed him

DAPHNE   1
2 Ma	4:33	at Daphne near Antioch

DARE, verb   3 = 0.002 %
2 Ma	4:2	He dared to designate as a plotter against the government
	5:15	Not content with this, Antiochus dared to enter
2 Es	13:8	were much afraid, yet dared to fight

DARING   3 = 0.002 %
Jud	16 : 10	the Medes were daunted at her daring
2 Ma	8 : 18	For they trust to arms and acts of daring, he said
	13 : 18	The king, having had a taste of the daring of the Jews

DARIUS   22 = 0.014 %
1 Ma	1 : 1	had defeated Darius, king of the Persians and the Medes
1 Es	2 : 30	of Darius king of the Persians
	3 : 1	Now King Darius gave a great banquet
	3 : 3	and Darius the king went to his bedroom
	3 : 5	Darius the king will give rich gifts
	3 : 7	and because of his wisdom he shall sit next to Darius
	3 : 7	and shall be called kinsman of Darius
	3 : 8	and put them under the pillow of Darius the king
	4 : 47	Then Darius the king rose, and kissed him
	5 : 2	And Darius sent with them a 1,000 horsemen
	5 : 6	who spoke wise words before Darius the king of the Persians
	5 : 73	until the reign of Darius
	6 : 1	Now in the 2nd year of the reign of Darius
	6 : 6	until word could be sent to Darius concerning them
	6 : 7	wrote and sent to Darius :
	6 : 8	To King Darius, greeting
	6 : 23	Then King Darius commanded that search be made
	6 : 27	So Darius commanded Sisinnes
	6 : 34	I, King Darius, have decreed
	7 : 1	following the orders of King Darius
	7 : 4	So with the consent of Cyrus and Darius and Artaxerxes
	7 : 5	in the 6th year of King Darius

DARK, adj.   2
Wis	17 : 3	they were unobserved behind a dark curtain of forgetfulness
2 Es	12 : 42	and like a lamp in a dark place

DARKEN   1
Sir	25 : 17	and darkens her face like that of a bear

DARKNESS   24 = 0.016 %
Tob	4 : 10	and keeps you from entering the darkness
	14 : 10	how he brought him from light into darkness
	14 : 10	as he himself went down into the darkness
Ad E	11 : 8	And behold, a day of darkness and gloom
Wis	17 : 2	they themselves lay as captives of darkness
	17 : 17	for with one chain of darkness they all were bound
	17 : 21	an image of the darkness that was destined to receive them
	17 : 21	but still heavier than darkness were they to themselves
	18 : 4	and imprisoned in darkness
	19 : 17	when, surrounded by yawning darkness
Sir	11 : 16	Error and darkness were created with sinners
	16 : 16	and he divided his light and darkness with a plumb line
	17 : 26	for he will lead you out of darkness
	23 : 18	Darkness surrounds me, and the walls hide me
	45 : 5	and led him into the thick darkness
L Jr	6 : 71	or like a dead body cast out in the darkness
P Az	48	Bless the Lord, light and darkness
2 Ma	3 : 27	and deep darkness came over him
1 Es	4 : 24	he faces lions, and he walks in darkness
3 Ma	4 : 10	so that with their eyes in total darkness
2 Es	6 : 39	and darkness and silence embraced everything
	7 : 40	or water or air, or darkness or evening or morning
	7 : 125	but our faces shall be blacker than darkness ?
	14 : 20	For the world lies in darkness

DART, subst.   1
4 Ma	14 : 19	and as though with an iron dart sting those who approach their hive

DASH   3 = 0.002 %
Jud	16 : 5	and dash my infants to the ground
Wis	4 : 19	because he will dash them speechless to the ground
2 Es	15 : 35	They shall dash against one another

DASH out   1
Sus	13 : 39	and he opened the doors and dashed out

DATHAN   2
Sir	45 : 18	Dathan and Abiram and their men and the company of Korah
4 Ma	2 : 17	When Moses was angry with Dathan and Abiram

DATHEMA   2
1 Ma	5 : 9	But they fled to the stronghold of Dathema
	5 : 29	and they went all the way to the stronghold of Dathema

DAUGHTER   62 = 0.040 %
Tob	3 : 7	it also happened that Sarah, the daughter of Raguel
	3 : 9	May we never see a son or daughter of yours !
	3 : 17	to give Sarah the daughter of Raguel
	3 : 17	and Sarah the daughter of Raguel
	4 : 13	and the sons and daughters of your people
	6 : 10	He is your relative, and he has an only daughter named Sarah
	7 : 8	And his wife Edna and his daughter Sarah wept
	7 : 11	I have given my daughter to 7 husbands
	7 : 13	Then he called his daughter Sarah
	7 : 17	But the mother comforted her daughter in her tears
	7 : 18	Be brave, my daughter
	10 : 12	He said also to his daughter
	10 : 12	and grant me to see your children by my daughter Sarah
	10 : 12	See, I am entrusting my daughter to you
	11 : 17	he blessed her, saying, Welcome, daughter !
Jud	8 : 1	she was the daughter of Merari the son of Ox
	9 : 4	and their daughters to captivity
	10 : 12	She replied, I am a daughter of the Hebrews
	12 : 13	and become today like one of the daughters of the Assyrians
	13 : 18	O daughter, you are blessed by the Most High God
	16 : 7	but Judith the daughter of Merari undid him
Wis	9 : 7	and to be judge over thy sons and daughters
Sir	7 : 24	Do you have daughters ?
	7 : 25	Give a daughter in marriage
	22 : 3	and the birth of a daughter is a loss
	22 : 4	A sensible daughter obtains her husband
	22 : 5	An impudent daughter disgraces father and husband
	26 : 10	Keep strict watch over a headstrong daughter
	26 : 24	but a modest daughter will even be embarrassed
	36 : 21	but one daughter is better than another
	42 : 9	A daughter keeps her father secretly wakeful
	42 : 11	Keep strict watch over a headstrong daughter
Bar	2 : 3	and another the flesh of his daughter
	4 : 10	for I have seen the captivity of my sons and daughters
	4 : 14	remember the capture of my sons and daughters
	4 : 16	and bereaved the lonely woman of her daughters
Sus	13 : 2	And he took a wife named Susanna, the daughter of Hilkiah
	13 : 3	and had taught their daughter according to the law of Moses
	13 : 29	Send for Susanna, the daughter of Hilkiah
	13 : 48	Have you condemned a daughter of Israel
	13 : 57	with the daughters of Israel
	13 : 57	but a daughter of Judah would not endure your wickedness
	13 : 63	And Hilkiah and his wife praised God for their daughter Susanna
1 Ma	9 : 37	a daughter of one of the great nobles of Canaan
	10 : 54	give me now your daughter as my wife
	10 : 57	he and Cleopatra his daughter
	10 : 58	and Ptolemy gave him Cleopatra his daughter in marriage
	11 : 9	and I will give you in marriage my daughter
	11 : 10	For I now regret that I gave him my daughter
	11 : 12	So he took his daughter away from him
1 Es	4 : 29	the daughter of the illustrious Bartacus
	5 : 1	with their wives and sons and daughters
	5 : 38	one of the daughters of Barzillai
	8 : 70	For they and their sons have married the daughters of these people
	8 : 84	Therefore do not give your daughters in marriage to their sons
	8 : 84	and do not take their daughters for your sons
3 Ma	5 : 49	parents and children, mothers and daughters
2 Es	1 : 28	or a mother her daughters or a nurse her children
	15 : 47	you have decked out your daughters in harlotry
	16 : 33	their daughters shall mourn, because they have no helpers
4 Ma	15 : 28	but as the daughter of God-fearing Abraham
	18 : 20	brought those 7 sons of the daughter of Abraham to the catapult

DAUGHTER-IN-LAW   4 = 0.003 %
Tob	11 : 16	Then Tobit went out to meet his daughter-in-law
	11 : 17	When Tobit came near to Sarah his daughter-in-law
	12 : 12	And so, when you and your daughter-in-law Sarah prayed
	12 : 14	and your daughter-in-law Sarah

DAUNT   1
Jud	16 : 10	the Medes were daunted at her daring

DAVID   28 = 0.018 %
Sir	45 : 25	A covenant was also established with David
	47 : 1	to prophesy in the days of David
	47 : 2	so David was selected from the sons of Israel
	47 : 22	and to David a root of his stock
	48 : 15	but with rulers from the house of David
	48 : 22	and he held strongly to the ways of David his father
	49 : 4	Except David and Hezekiah and Josiah they all sinned greatly
1 Ma	1 : 33	Then they fortified the city of David
	2 : 31	and to troops in Jerusalem the city of David
	2 : 57	David, because he was merciful
	4 : 30	by the hand of thy servant David
	7 : 32	and the rest fled into the city of David
	14 : 36	as were also the men in the city of David in Jerusalem
2 Ma	2 : 13	and the writings of David
1 Es	1 : 3	in the house which Solomon the king, the son of David, had built
	1 : 5	in accordance with the directions of David king of Israel
	1 : 15	were in their place according to the arrangement made by David
	5 : 5	son of Shealtiel, of the house of David
	5 : 60	according to the directions of David king of Israel
	8 : 29	Of the sons of David, Hattush the son of Shecaniah
	8 : 49	whom David and the leaders had given

2 Es	3 : 23	and thou didst raise up for thyself a servant, named David
	7 : 108	and Samuel in the days of Saul, and David for the plague
	12 : 32	who will arise from the posterity of David
4 Ma	3 : 6	by the story of King David's thirst
	3 : 7	David had been attacking the Philistines all day long
	3 : 15	But David, although he was burning with thirst
	18 : 15	He sang to you songs of the psalmist David, who said

DAWN, subst.   7 = 0.005 %

Jud	14 : 11	As soon as it was dawn
Sir	24 : 32	I will again make instruction shine forth like the dawn
1 Ma	5 : 30	At dawn they looked up
2 Ma	10 : 28	Just as dawn was breaking, the 2 armies joined battle
	10 : 35	But at dawn on the 5th day
3 Ma	5 : 46	the elephant keeper entered at about dawn into the courtyard
2 Es	7 : 42	or noon or night, or dawn or shining or brightness or light

DAWN, verb   1

2 Ma	13 : 17	This happened, just as day was dawning

DAWNING   1

Wis	16 : 28	and must pray to thee at the dawning of the light

DAY   429 = 0.279 %

Tob	1 : 2	who in the days of Shalmaneser, king of the Assyrians
	1 : 3	all the days of my life
	1 : 16	In the days of Shalmaneser
	1 : 21	But not 50 days passed
	3 : 7	On the same day, at Ecbatana in Media
	4 : 1	On that day Tobit remembered the money
	4 : 3	honour her all the days of your life
	4 : 5	Remember the Lord our God all your days, my son
	4 : 5	Live uprightly all the days of your life
	4 : 9	against the day of necessity
	4 : 14	Do not hold over till the next day
	5 : 14	But tell me, what wages am I to pay you – a drachma a day
	8 : 19	which lasted 14 days
	8 : 20	And before the days of the feast were over
	8 : 20	until the 14 days of the wedding feast were ended
	9 : 4	but my father is counting the days
	10 : 1	Now his father Tobit was counting each day
	10 : 1	and when the days for the journey had expired
	10 : 7	And she went out every day to the road by which they had left
	10 : 7	until the 14 days of the wedding feast had expired
	11 : 19	and Tobias marriage was celebrated for 7 days
	12 : 19	All these days I merely appeared to you
Jud	1 : 1	in the days of Arphaxad
	1 : 5	it was in those days that King Nebuchadnezzar made war
	1 : 15	and he utterly destroyed him, to this day
	1 : 16	and there he and his forces rested and feasted for 120 days
	2 : 1	In the 18th year, on the 22nd day of the first month
	2 : 10	till the day of their punishment
	2 : 21	They marched for 3 days from Nineveh
	4 : 13	for the people fasted many days throughout Judea
	6 : 5	who have said these words on the day of your iniquity
	6 : 5	you shall not see my face again from this day
	6 : 15	who in those days were Uzziah the son of Micah
	6 : 19	and look this day
	7 : 1	The next day Holofernes ordered his whole army
	7 : 2	So all their warriors moved their camp that day
	7 : 6	On the 2nd day Holofernes led out all his cavalry
	7 : 20	surrounded them for 34 days
	7 : 21	to drink their fill for a single day
	7 : 28	Let him not do this day the things which we have described !
	7 : 30	Let us hold out for 5 more days
	7 : 31	But if these days pass by, and no help comes for us
	8 : 6	She fasted all the days of her widowhood
	8 : 6	except the day before the sabbath and the sabbath itself
	8 : 6	the day before the new moon and the day of the new moon
	8 : 6	and the feasts and days of rejoicing of the house of Israel
	8 : 9	to surrender the city to the Assyrians after 5 days
	8 : 11	unless the Lord turns and helps us within so many days
	8 : 12	Who are you, that have put God to the test this day
	8 : 15	For if he does not choose to help us within these 5 days
	8 : 18	For never in our generation, nor in these present days
	8 : 18	as was done in days gone by
	8 : 33	and within the days after which you have promised
	11 : 15	on that very day they will be handed over to you to be destroyed
	11 : 17	and serves the God of heaven day and night
	12 : 7	And she remained in the camp for 3 days
	12 : 10	On the 4th day Holofernes held a banquet for his slaves only
	12 : 14	and it will be a joy to me until the day of my death !
	12 : 16	ever since the day he first saw her
	12 : 18	than in all the days since I was born
	12 : 20	much more than he had ever drunk in any one day
	13 : 3	as she did every day
	13 : 7	Give me strength this day, O Lord God of Israel !
	13 : 11	even as he has done this day !
	13 : 17	who hast brought into contempt this day
	14 : 8	Now tell me what you have done during these days

	14 : 8	all that she had done, from the day she left
	14 : 10	and joined the house of Israel, remaining so to this day
	15 : 11	So all the people plundered the camp for 30 days
	16 : 17	in the day of judgment
	16 : 22	but she remained a widow all the days of her life
	16 : 24	and the house of Israel mourned for her 7 days
	16 : 25	in the days of Judith, or for a long time after her death
Ad E	10 : 11	And these 2 lots came to the hour and moment and day
	10 : 13	So they will observe these days in the month of Adar
	11 : 2	on the first day of Nisan
	11 : 8	And behold, a day of darkness and gloom
	11 : 12	and sought all day to understand it in every detail
	13 : 6	on the 14th day of the 12th month, Adar
	13 : 7	may in one day go down in violence to Hades
	14 : 16	which is upon my head on the days when I appear in public
	14 : 16	and I do not wear it on the days when I am at leisure
	14 : 18	since the day that I was brought here until now
	15 : 1	On the 3rd day, when she ended her prayer
	16 : 20	so that on the 13th day of the 12th month, Adar
	16 : 20	on that very day they may defend themselves
	16 : 21	has made this day to be a joy to his chosen people
	16 : 21	instead of a day of destruction for them
	16 : 22	as a notable day among your commemorative festivals
Wis	3 : 18	and no consolation in the day of decision
	5 : 14	and it passes like the remembrance of a guest who stays but a day
	10 : 17	and became a shelter to them by day
Sir	1 : 2	and the days of eternity – who can count them ?
	1 : 13	on the day of his death he will be blessed
	3 : 15	in the day of your affliction
	5 : 7	nor postpone it from day to day
	5 : 8	for it will not benefit you in the day of calamity
	6 : 8	but will not stand by you in your day of trouble
	6 : 10	but will not stand by you in your day of trouble
	11 : 4	nor exalt yourself in the day that you are honoured
	11 : 25	In the day of prosperity, adversity is forgotten
	11 : 25	and in the day of adversity, prosperity is not remembered
	11 : 26	to reward a man on the day of death
	12 : 6	for the mighty day of their punishment
	14 : 14	Do not deprive yourself of a happy day
	17 : 2	He gave to men few days, a limited time
	18 : 9	The number of a man's days is great
	18 : 10	so are a few years in the day of eternity
	18 : 24	Think of his wrath on the day of death
	18 : 25	in the days of wealth think of poverty and need
	18 : 27	and in days of sin he guards against wrongdoing
	22 : 12	Mourning for the dead lasts 7 days
	23 : 14	and you will curse the day of your birth
	23 : 15	will never become disciplined all his days
	26 : 1	the number of his days will be doubled
	30 : 22	and the rejoicing of a man is length of days
	33 : 7	Why is any day better than another
	33 : 9	and made some of them ordinary days
	33 : 23	At the time when you end the days of your life
	36 : 8	Hasten the day, and remember the appointed time
	37 : 25	The life of a man is numbered by days
	37 : 25	but the days of Israel are without number
	38 : 17	for one day, or 2, to avoid criticism
	38 : 27	who labours by night as well as by day
	40 : 1	from the day they come forth from their mother's womb
	40 : 1	till the day they return to the mother of all
	40 : 2	their anxious thought is the day of death
	41 : 3	remember your former days and the end of life
	41 : 13	The days of a good life are numbered
	43 : 7	From the moon comes the sign for feast days
	45 : 14	twice every day continually
	45 : 15	and for his descendants all the days of heaven
	46 : 4	And did not one day become as long as 2 ?
	46 : 7	And in the days of Moses he did a loyal deed
	47 : 1	to prophesy in the days of David
	47 : 7	he crushed their power even to this day
	47 : 13	Solomon reigned in days of peace
	48 : 12	in all his days he did not tremble before any ruler
	48 : 18	In his days Sennacherib came up, and sent the Rabshakeh
	48 : 23	In his days the sun went backward
	49 : 3	in the days of wicked men he strengthened godliness
	49 : 12	in their days they built the house
	50 : 3	In his days a cistern for water was quarried out
	50 : 8	like roses in the days of the first fruits
	50 : 8	like a green shoot on Lebanon on a summer day
	50 : 22	who exalts our days from birth
	50 : 23	and grant that peace may be in our days in Israel
	50 : 23	as in the days of old
	50 : 24	And let him deliver us in our days !
	51 : 10	not to forsake me in the days of affliction
Bar	1 : 2	in the 5th year, on the 7th day of the month
	1 : 8	At the same time, on the 10th day of Sivan
	1 : 11	that their days on earth may be like the days of heaven
	1 : 12	and we shall serve them many days and find favour in their sight

1:13	and to this day the anger of the Lord and his wrath
1:14	on the days of the feasts and at appointed seasons
1:15	but confusion of face, as at this day, to us
1:19	From the day when the Lord brought our fathers
1:20	So to this day there have clung to us the calamities
2:6	but confusion of face to us and our fathers, as at this day
2:11	and hast made thee a name, as at this day
2:25	to the heat of day and the frost of night
2:28	on the day when thou didst command him
3:14	where there is length of days, and life
3:20	Young men have seen the light of day
4:20	I will cry to the Everlasting all my days
4:35	For fire will come upon her from the Everlasting for many days

P Az

14	and are brought low this day in all the world
17	such may our sacrifice be in thy sight this day
47	Bless the Lord, nights and days

Sus

13:8	The 2 elders used to see her every day
13:12	And they watched eagerly, day after day, to see her
13:15	Once, while they were watching for an opportune day
13:28	The next day, when the people gathered at the house of her husband Joakim
13:52	You old relic of wicked days, your sins have now come home
13:62	Thus innocent blood was saved that day
13:64	And from that day onward

Bel

14:3	and every day they spent on it 12 bushels of fine flour
14:4	The king revered it and went every day to worship it
14:6	Do you not see how much he eats and drinks every day ?
14:31	and he was there for 6 days
14:32	and every day they had been given 2 human bodies and 2 sheep
14:40	On the 7th day the king came to mourn for Daniel

1 Ma

1:11	In those days lawless men came forth from Israel
1:54	Now on the 15th day of Chislev, in the 145th year
1:59	And on the 25th day of the month
2:1	In those days Mattathias the son of John, son of Simeon
2:32	against them on the sabbath day
2:34	and so profane the sabbath day
2:41	So they made this decision that day :
2:41	Let us fight against every man who comes to attack us on the sabbath day
2:49	Now the days drew near for Mattathias to die
3:29	that had existed from the earliest days
3:47	They fasted that day, put on sackcloth
3:49	who had completed their days
4:25	Thus Israel had a great deliverance that day
4:52	Early in the morning on the 25th day of the 9th month
4:54	and on the very day that the Gentiles had profaned it
4:56	So they celebrated the dedication of the altar for 8 days
4:59	the days of the dedication of the altar should be observed
4:59	with gladness and joy for 8 days
4:59	beginning with the 25th day of the month of Chislev
5:24	and went 3 days' journey into the wilderness
5:27	and take and destroy all these men in one day
5:34	As many as 8,000 of them fell that day
5:50	all that day and all the night
5:60	as many as 2,000 of the people of Israel fell that day
5:67	On that day some priests, who wished to do a brave deed
6:9	He lay there for many days
6:31	and for many days they fought and built engines of war
6:51	Then he encamped before the sanctuary for many days
6:52	and fought for many days
7:16	but he seized 60 of them and killed them in one day
7:43	on the 13th day of the month of Adar
7:45	The Jews pursued them a day's journey
7:48	and celebrated that day as a day of great gladness
7:49	And they decreed that this day should be celebrated
7:49	each year on the 13th day of Adar
7:50	So the land of Judah had rest for a few days
8:10	tore down their strongholds, and enslaved them to this day
8:15	and every day 320 senators constantly deliberate
9:20	they mourned many days and said
9:24	In those days a very great famine occurred
9:34	Bacchides found this out on the sabbath day
9:43	he came with a large force on the sabbath day
9:49	And about 1,000 of Bacchides' men fell that day
9:64	he fought against it for many days and made machines of war
10:30	I release them from this day and henceforth
10:30	from this day and for all time
10:34	and new moons and appointed days
10:34	and the 3 days before a feast and the 3 after a feast
10:34	let them all be days of immunity and release
10:47	and they remained his allies all his days
10:50	and Demetrius fell on that day
10:55	Happy was the day
11:18	But King Ptolemy died 3 days later
11:20	In those days Jonathan assembled the men of Judea
11:40	and he stayed there many days
11:47	and they killed on that day as many as a 100,000 men
11:48	They set fire to the city and seized much spoil on that day
11:65	and fought against it for many days and hemmed it in
11:74	As many as 3,000 of the foreigners fell that day

12:11	both in our feasts and on other appropriate days
13:26	and mourned for him many days
13:30	it remains to this day
13:39	We pardon any errors and offences committed to this day
13:43	In those days Simon encamped against Gazara
13:51	On the 23rd day of the 2nd month, in the 171st year
13:52	they should celebrate this day with rejoicing
14:4	The land had rest all the days of Simon
14:4	as was the honour shown him, all his days
14:13	and the kings were crushed in those days
14:27	On the 18th day of Elul, in the 172nd year
14:36	And in his days things prospered in his hands
16:2	have fought the wars of Israel from our youth until this day

2 Ma

1:18	Since on the 25th day of Chislev
2:12	Likewise Solomon also kept the 8 days
2:16	Will you therefore please keep the days ?
3:14	So he set a day and went in
5:2	And it happened that over all the city, for almost 40 days
5:14	Within the total of 3 days 80,000 were destroyed
5:25	and waited until the holy sabbath day
6:11	to observe the 7th day secretly
6:11	in view of their regard for that most holy day
7:20	Though she saw her 7 sons perish within a single day
8:26	For it was the day before the sabbath
8:27	who had preserved them for that day
10:5	It happened that on the same day
10:5	that is, on the 25th day of the same month, which was Chislev
10:6	And they celebrated it for 8 days with rejoicing
10:8	should observe these days every year
10:33	and they besieged the fort 4 days
10:35	But at dawn on the 5th day
11:30	Therefore those who go home by the 30th day of Xanthicus
12:15	overthrew Jericho in the days of Joshua
12:38	As the 7th day was coming on
12:39	On the next day, as by that time it had become necessary
13:10	he ordered the people to call upon the Lord day and night
13:12	and lying prostrate for 3 days without ceasing
13:17	This happened, just as day was dawning
14:4	During that day he kept quiet
14:21	And the leaders set a day on which to meet by themselves
15:1	on the day of rest
15:2	but show respect for the day
15:2	and hallowed above other days
15:3	who had commanded the keeping of the sabbath day
15:4	who ordered us to observe the 7th day
15:36	never to let this day go unobserved
15:36	but to celebrate the 13th day of the 12th month
15:36	the day before Mordecai's day

1 Es

1:1	he killed the passover lamb on the 14th day of the first month
1:17	were accomplished that day : the passover was kept
1:19	kept the passover and the feast of unleavened bread 7 days
1:32	have made lamentation for him to this day
1:44	and he reigned 3 months and 10 days in Jerusalem
4:21	With his wife he ends his days
4:34	and returns to its place in one day
4:43	in the day when you became king
4:52	for burnt offerings to be offered on the altar every day
4:55	until the day when the temple should be finished and Jerusalem built
4:63	and they feasted, with music and rejoicing, for 7 days
5:51	and offered the proper sacrifices every day
5:69	ever since the days of Esarhaddon king of the Assyrians
7:5	by the 23rd day of the month of Adar
7:10	kept the passover on the 14th day of the first month
7:14	And they kept the feast of unleavened bread 7 days
8:41	and we encamped there 3 days
8:61	on the 12th day of the first month
8:62	When we had been there 3 days
8:76	and we are in great sin to this day
8:77	in shame until this day
8:89	for we are left as a root this day
9:4	within 2 or 3 days
9:5	assembled at Jerusalem within 3 days
9:5	on the 20th day of the month
9:11	This is not a work we can do in one day or 2
9:50	This day is holy to the Lord
9:52	for the day is holy to the Lord
9:53	This day is holy

P Ma

15	all the days of my life

3 Ma

4:8	spent the remaining days of their marriage festival in lamentations
4:14	and at the end to be destroyed in the space of a single day
4:15	and though uncompleted it stopped after 40 days
5:2	and ordered him on the following day
5:11	that beneficence which from the beginning, night and day
5:18	through the present day
6:30	needed for a festival of 7 days
6:36	they instituted the observance of the aforesaid days as a festival
6:38	from the 25th of Pachon to the 4th of Epeiph, for 40 days
6:38	for the 5th to the 7th of Epeiph, the 3 days

	6 : 40	until the 14th day
	7 : 15	In that day they put to death more than 300 men
	7 : 15	and they kept the day as a joyful festival
	7 : 17	in accord with the common desire, for 7 days
	7 : 19	these days as a joyous festival
2 Es	1 : 16	but to this day you still complain
	1 : 31	for I have rejected your feast days, and new moons
	2 : 13	pray that your days may be few, that they may be shortened
	2 : 27	for when the day of tribulation and anguish comes
	4 : 5	or call back for me the day that is past
	4 : 9	But now I have asked you only about fire and wind and the day
	4 : 51	Do you think that I shall live until those days ?
	4 : 51	Or who will be alive in those days ?
	5 : 1	the days are coming when those who dwell on earth
	5 : 4	and the moon during the day
	5 : 13	and fast for 7 days
	5 : 19	Depart from me and do not come near me for 7 days
	5 : 20	So I fasted 7 days, mourning and weeping
	5 : 21	And after 7 days
	6 : 18	And it said, Behold, the days are coming
	6 : 31	If therefore you will pray again and fast again for 7 days
	6 : 35	Now after this I wept again and fasted 7 days as before
	6 : 38	and didst say on the first day
	6 : 41	Again, on the 2nd day
	6 : 42	On the 3rd day
	6 : 44	These were made on the 3rd day
	6 : 45	On the 4th day thou didst command the brightness of the sun
	6 : 47	On the 5th day thou didst command the 7th part
	6 : 51	which had been dried up on the 3rd day
	6 : 53	On the 6th day thou didst command the earth
	7 : 30	And the world shall be turned back to primeval silence for 7 days
	7 : 31	And after 7 days the world
	7 : 38	Thus he will speak to them on the day of judgment
	7 : 39	a day that has no sun or moon or stars
	7 : 84	they shall consider the torment laid up for themselves in the last days
	7 : 95	and the glory which awaits them in the last days
	7 : 101	They shall have freedom for 7 days
	7 : 101	so that during these 7 days
	7 : 102	whether on the day of judgment
	7 : 104	The day of judgment is decisive
	7 : 105	so no one shall ever pray for another on that day
	7 : 107	and Joshua after him for Israel in the days of Achan
	7 : 108	and Samuel in the days of Saul, and David for the plague
	7 : 110	and Hezekiah for the people in the days of Sennacherib
	7 : 113	But the day of judgment will be the end of this age
	9 : 4	from the days that were of old, from the beginning
	9 : 23	But if you will let 7 days more pass
	9 : 27	And after 7 days, as I lay on the grass
	9 : 44	And every hour and every day during those 30 years
	9 : 44	I besought the Most High, night and day
	9 : 47	I set a day for the marriage feast
	10 : 2	and I remained quiet until evening of the 2nd day
	10 : 59	who dwell on earth in the last days
	12 : 13	Behold, the days are coming
	12 : 23	In its last days the Most High will raise up 3 kings
	12 : 28	but he also shall fall by the sword in the last days
	12 : 32	until the end of days
	12 : 34	the day of judgment, of which I spoke to you at the beginning
	12 : 39	But wait here 7 days more
	12 : 40	When all the people heard that the 7 days were past
	12 : 49	and after these days I will come to you
	12 : 51	But I sat in the field 7 days
	12 : 51	and my food was of plants during those days
	13 : 1	After 7 days I dreamed a dream in the night
	13 : 16	alas for those who will be left in those days !
	13 : 18	because they understand what is reserved for the last days
	13 : 20	and not to see what shall happen in the last days
	13 : 29	Behold, the days are coming
	13 : 40	in the days of King Hoshea
	13 : 52	except in the time of his day
	13 : 56	And after 3 more days I will tell you other things
	13 : 58	And I stayed there 3 days
	14 : 1	On the 3rd day, while I was sitting under an oak
	14 : 4	where I kept him with me many days
	14 : 22	and that those who wish to live in the last days may live
	14 : 23	and tell them not to seek you for 40 days
	14 : 36	and let no one seek me for 40 days
	14 : 38	And on the next day, behold, a voice called me, saying
	14 : 42	They sat 40 days, and wrote during the daytime
	14 : 44	So during the 40 days 94 books were written
	14 : 45	And when the 40 days were ended
	15 : 21	Just as they have done to my elect until this day, so I will do
	15 : 29	and from the day that they set out
	16 : 17	Who will deliver me in those days ?
	16 : 31	so in those days 3 or 4 shall be left
	16 : 65	as your accusers in that day
	16 : 74	Behold, the days of tribulation are at hand
4 Ma	3 : 7	David had been attacking the Philistines all day long

	13 : 20	they were brought to the light of day
	14 : 7	For just as the 7 days of creation
	17 : 12	for on that day virtue gave the awards
	18 : 19	this is your life and the length of your days
	18 : 20	O bitter was that day – and yet not bitter

DAYBREAK
2
1 Ma	4 : 6	At daybreak Judas appeared in the plain with 3,000 men
3 Ma	5 : 24	and they were eagerly waiting for daybreak

DAYLIGHT
1
Sir	33 : 7	when all the daylight in the year is from the sun ?

DAYTIME
3 = 0.002 %
Tob	10 : 7	she ate nothing in the daytime
2 Es	14 : 42	They sat 40 days, and wrote during the daytime
	14 : 43	As for me, I spoke in the daytime and was not silent at night

DEAD, subst., adj.
50 = 0.033 %
Tob	1 : 17	and if I saw any one of my people dead
	2 : 8	he once ran away, and here he is burying the dead again !
	3 : 9	Why do you beat us ? If they are dead, go with them !
	3 : 15	Already 7 husbands of mine are dead
	12 : 12	and when you buried the dead
	12 : 13	in order to go and lay out the dead
Jud	2 : 8	and every brook and river shall be filled with their dead, and overflow
	6 : 4	and their fields will be full of their dead
	14 : 15	and found him thrown down on the platform dead
Wis	4 : 18	and an outrage among the dead for ever
	13 : 10	But miserable, with their hopes set on dead things
	13 : 18	for life he prays to a thing that is dead
	14 : 15	what was once a dead human being
	15 : 5	so that they desire the lifeless form of a dead image
	15 : 17	He is mortal, and what he makes with lawless hands is dead
	18 : 18	and one here and another there, hurled down half dead
	18 : 23	For when the dead had already fallen on one another in heaps
	19 : 3	and were lamenting at the graves of their dead
Sir	7 : 33	and withhold not kindness from the dead
	10 : 11	For when a man is dead, he will inherit creeping things
	17 : 28	From the dead, as from one who does not exist
	22 : 11	Weep for the dead, for he lacks the light
	22 : 11	weep less bitterly for the dead, for he has attained rest
	22 : 12	Mourning for the dead lasts 7 days
	30 : 4	The father may die, and yet he is not dead
	34 : 25	If a man washes after touching a dead body
	38 : 16	My son, let your tears fall for the dead
	38 : 21	you do the dead no good, and you injure yourself
	38 : 23	When the dead is at rest, let his remembrance cease
	48 : 13	and when he was dead his body prophesied
Bar	2 : 17	for the dead who are in Hades
	3 : 4	hear now the prayer of the dead of Israel
	3 : 10	that you are defiled with the dead
L Jr	6 : 27	but gifts are placed before them just as before the dead
	6 : 71	or like a dead body cast out in the darkness
1 Ma	6 : 17	And when Lysias learned that the king was dead
	9 : 57	When Bacchides saw that Alcimus was dead
2 Ma	5 : 5	When a false rumour arose that Antiochus was dead
	12 : 40	Then under the tunic of every one of the dead
	12 : 44	and foolish to pray for the dead
	12 : 45	Therefore he made atonement for the dead
	15 : 28	they recognized Nicanor, lying dead, in full armour
2 Es	2 : 16	And I will raise up the dead from their places
	2 : 23	when you find any who are dead
	7 : 37	that have been raised from the dead
	7 : 109	and for the one who was dead, that he might live
	16 : 23	And the dead shall be cast out like dung
4 Ma	4 : 11	Then Apollonius fell down half dead
	8 : 21	and let us seriously consider that if we disobey we are dead !
	12 : 18	both in this present life and when you are dead

DEAL*
19 = 0.012 %
Tob	3 : 6	And now deal with me according to thy pleasure
Jud	3 : 4	come and deal with them in any way that seems good to you
Sir	42 : 5	of profit from dealing with merchants
	50 : 22	and deals with us according to his mercy
Bar	2 : 27	Yet thou hast dealt with us, O Lord our God
P Az	19	but deal with us in thy forbearance and in thy abundant mercy
Sus	13 : 57	This is how you both have been dealing
1 Ma	1 : 30	but he suddenly fell upon the city, dealt it a severe blow
	5 : 3	He dealt them and despoiled them
	5 : 34	they fled before him, and he dealt them a heavy blow
	9 : 29	and to deal with those of our nation who hate us
	13 : 31	Trypho dealt treacherously with the young king Antiochus
2 Ma	6 : 14	but he does not deal in this way with us
1 Es	6 : 5	Yet the elders of the Jews were dealt with kindly
3 Ma	4 : 13	be dealt with in precisely the same fashion as the others
2 Es	7 : 72	they dealt unfaithfully with what they received
	15 : 52	Would I have dealt with you so violently, says the Lord

DEAL

4 Ma	3 :3	but reason can help to deal with anger
	4 :5	On receiving authority to deal with this matter

DEAL out   1

Sir	42 :7	Whatever you deal out, let it be by number and weight

DEALING   4 = 0.003 %

Sir	41 :18	of unjust dealing, before your partner or friend
2 Ma	14 :30	in his dealings with him
2 Es	12 :32	and will cast up before them their contemptuous dealings
4 Ma	5 :24	so that in all our dealings we act impartially

DEAR   4 = 0.003 %

Tob	10 :12	The Lord of heaven bring you back safely, dear brother
2 Es	6 :58	zealous for thee, and most dear
	7 :103	or friends for those who are most dear
	7 :104	or a friend his dearest friend

DEATH   170 = 0.111 %

Tob	1 :18	And if Sennacherib the king put to death
	1 :18	For in his anger he put many to death
	1 :19	to be put to death
	2 :8	that he will be put to death for doing this
	3 :4	and thou gavest us over to plunder, captivity, and death
	4 :2	I have asked for death
	4 :10	For charity delivers from death
	6 :12	without incurring the penalty of death
	12 :9	For almsgiving delivers from death
	14 :15	Before his death he rejoiced over Nineveh
Jud	2 :27	and put to death all their young men
	5 :22	and from Moab insisted that he must be put to death
	7 :27	and we shall not witness the death of our babes before our eyes
	11 :11	death will fall upon them, for a sin has overtaken them
	12 :14	and it will be a joy to me until the day of my death !
	14 :5	and sent him to us as if to his death
	16 :25	in the days of Judith, or for a long time after her death
Ad E	13 :18	for their death was before their eyes
Wis	1 :12	Do not invite death by the error of your life
	1 :13	because God did not make death
	1 :13	and he does not delight in the death of the living
	1 :16	But ungodly men by their words and deeds summoned death
	2 :5	and there is no return from our death
	2 :20	Let us condemn him to a shameful death
	2 :24	but through the devil's envy death entered the world
	12 :20	the enemies of thy servants and those deserving of death
	16 :13	For thou hast power over life and death
	18 :12	by the one form of death, had corpses too many to count
	18 :16	and stood and filled all things with death
	18 :20	The experience of death touched also the righteous
	19 :5	but they themselves might meet a strange death
Sir	1 :13	on the day of his death he will be blessed
	4 :28	Strive even to death for the truth
	8 :7	Do not rejoice over any one death
	9 :13	and you will not be worried by the fear of death
	11 :14	good things and bad, life and death, poverty and wealth
	11 :26	to reward a man on the day of death
	11 :28	Call no one happy before his death
	14 :12	Remember that death will not delay
	15 :17	Before a man are life and death
	18 :22	and do not wait until death to be released from it
	18 :24	Think of his wrath on the day of death
	22 :11	but the life of the fool is worse than death
	23 :12	There is an utterance which is comparable to death
	26 :5	all these are worse than death
	26 :22	and a married woman as a tower of death to her lovers
	27 :29	and pain will consume them before their death
	28 :6	remember destruction and death
	28 :21	its death is an evil death, and Hades is preferable to it
	30 :17	Death is better than a miserable life
	33 :14	Good is the opposite of evil, and life the opposite of death
	33 :23	in the hour of the death, distribute your inheritance
	34 :12	I have often been in danger of death
	37 :2	Is it not a grief to the
	37 :18	4 turns of fortune appear, good and evil, life and death
	38 :18	For sorrow results in death
	40 :2	their anxious thought is the day of death
	40 :5	and fear of death, and fury and strife
	40 :9	are death and bloodshed and strife and sword
	41 :1	O death, how bitter is the reminder of you
	41 :2	O death, how welcome is your sentence
	41 :3	Do not fear the sentence of death
	46 :20	he prophesied and revealed to the king his death
	48 :5	You have raised a corpse from death and from Hades
	48 :14	so in death his deeds were marvellous
	51 :6	My soul drew near to death
	51 :9	and prayed for deliverance from death
L Jr	6 :18	as though he were sentenced to death
	6 :36	They cannot save a man from death
P Az	66	and saved us from the hand of death
Sus	13 :22	For if I do this thing, it is death for me

	13 :28	full of their wicked plot to have Susanna put to death
	13 :41	and they condemned her to death
	13 :45	And as she was being led away to be put to death
	13 :53	Do not put to death an innocent and righteous person
	13 :62	they put them to death
Bel	14 :22	Therefore the king put them to death
1 Ma	1 :2	and put to death the kings of the earth
	1 :9	They all put on crowns after his death
	1 :57	the decree of the king condemned him to death
	1 :60	According to the decree, they put to death
	6 :24	moreover, they have put to death
	9 :23	After the death of Judas
	9 :29	Since the death of your brother Judas
2 Ma	4 :47	while he sentenced to death those unfortunate men
	6 :19	But he, welcoming death with honour
	6 :22	so that by doing this he might be saved from death
	6 :28	of how to die a good death willingly and nobly
	6 :30	that, though I might have been saved from death
	6 :31	leaving in his death an example of nobility
	7 :14	And when he was near death, he said
	7 :29	Accept death, so that in God's mercy
	13 :4	and to put him to death
	13 :8	he met his death in ashes
	13 :14	and exhorting his men to fight nobly to the death
	14 :46	This was the manner of his death
1 Es	8 :24	whether by death or some other punishment
3 Ma	1 :29	because indeed all at that time preferred death
	2 :28	Those who object to this are to be taken by force and put to death
	3 :1	and put to death by the most cruel means
	3 :25	to suffer the sure and shameful death that befits enemies
	3 :27	will be tortured to death with the most hateful torments
	4 :8	seeing death immediately before them
	5 :42	that he would send them to death without delay
	5 :51	as they stood now at the gates of death
	6 :29	since they now had escaped death
	6 :31	Accordingly those disgracefully treated and near to death
	6 :31	instead of a bitter and lamentable death
	7 :5	to put them to death
	7 :14	they punished and put to a public and shameful death
	7 :15	In that day they put to death more than 300 men
	7 :16	But those who had held fast to God even to death
2 Es	3 :7	and immediately thou didst appoint death
	3 :10	as death came upon Adam, so the flood upon them
	6 :26	who from their birth have not tasted death
	7 :48	and has brought us into corruption and the ways of death
	7 :66	promised to them after death
	7 :69	And if we were not to come into judgment after death
	7 :75	show this also to thy servant : whether after death
	7 :78	Now, concerning death, the teaching is :
	7 :92	that it might not lead them astray from life into death
	7 :117	and expect punishment after death ?
	7 :119	but we have done deeds that bring death ?
	7 :126	we did not consider what we should suffer after death
	8 :31	in ways that bring death
	8 :38	or about their death, their judgment, or their destruction
	8 :53	illness is banished from you, and death is hidden
	9 :12	these must in torment acknowledge it after death
	10 :22	our priests have been burned to death
	14 :34	and after death you shall obtain mercy
	14 :35	For after death the judgment will come
	15 :5	the sword and famine and death and destruction
	15 :26	therefore he will hand them over to death and slaughter
	15 :49	and bring you to destruction and death
	15 :53	and talking about their death when you were drunk ?
4 Ma	1 :9	All of these, by despising sufferings that bring death
	4 :12	For he said that he had committed a sin deserving of death
	4 :22	he heard that a rumour of his death had spread
	5 :37	as one who does not fear your violence even to death
	6 :21	and not protect our divine law even to death
	6 :30	and by reason he resisted even to the very tortures of death
	7 :8	in sufferings even to death
	7 :15	whom the faithful seal of death has perfected !
	7 :16	an aged man despised tortures even to death
	8 :18	and venture upon a disobedience that brings death ?
	9 :4	to be more grievous than death itself
	9 :5	by threatening us with death by torture
	9 :29	How sweet is any kind of death for the religion of our fathers !
	10 :1	When he too had endured a glorious death, the 3rd was led in
	10 :15	No, by the blessed death of my brothers
	12 :1	had died a blessed death
	13 :1	Since, then, the 7 brothers despised sufferings even unto death
	13 :27	and tortured to death
	14 :4	None of the 7 youths proved coward or shrank from death
	14 :5	hastened to death by torture
	14 :6	agreed to go to death for its sake
	14 :19	and defend it even to the death ?
	15 :10	so that they obeyed her even to death
	15 :12	to death for the sake of religion
	15 :19	and saw in their nostrils signs of the approach of death

15 : 26	one bearing death and the other deliverance for her children
16 : 1	endured seeing her children tortured to death
16 : 13	she implored them and urged them on to death
17 : 1	when she also was about to be seized and put to death
17 : 7	enduring their varied tortures to death
17 : 10	looking to God and enduring torture even to death
17 : 22	and their death as an expiation
18 : 5	and is being chastised after his death
18 : 21	and put them to death with various tortures

DEATHLY   1
Ad E 14 : 1   And Esther the queen, seized with deathly anxiety, fled to the Lord

DEATHTRAP   1
Tob 14 : 10   Ahikar gave alms and escaped the deathtrap

DEBAUCHERY   2
Wis 14 : 26   disorder in marriage, adultery, and debauchery
2 Ma   6 : 4   For the temple was filled with debauchery and revelling

DEBORAH   1
Tob   1 : 8   as Deborah my father's mother had commanded me

DEBT   5 = 0.003 %
1 Ma 10 : 43   because he owes money to the king or has any debt
15 : 8   Every debt you owe to the royal treasury
15 : 8   and such future debts shall be cancelled for you
1 Es   3 : 20   and forgets all sorrow and debt
4 Ma   2 : 8   and to cancel the debt when the 7th year arrives

DECAY, subst.   2
Sir 19 : 3   Decay and worms will inherit him
2 Ma   9 : 9   the whole army felt revulsion at his decay

DECAY, verb   2
Sir 10 : 9   For even in life his bowels decay
14 : 19   Every product decays and ceases to exist

DECEASED   1
2 Ma   4 : 37   because of the moderation and good conduct of the deceased

DECEIT   13 = 0.008 %
Jud   9 : 3   and their bed, which was ashamed of the deceit they had practised
9 : 10   By the deceit of my lips strike down the slave
Ad E 16 : 13   and with intricate craft and deceit
Wis   1 : 5   For a holy and disciplined spirit will flee from deceit
14 : 25   theft and deceit, corruption, faithlessness, tumult, perjury
14 : 30   and because in deceit they swore unrighteously
Sir   1 : 30   and your heart was full of deceit
19 : 26   but inwardly he is full of deceit
37 : 3   O evil imagination, why were you formed to cover the land with deceit ?
Bel 14 : 18   and with you there is no deceit, none at all
1 Ma   8 : 28   and do so without deceit
2 Es   6 : 27   and deceit shall be quenched
11 : 40   and for so long you have dwelt on the earth with deceit

DECEITFUL   3 = 0.002 %
Jud   9 : 13   Make my deceitful words to be their wound and stripe
Wis   1 : 4   because wisdom will not enter a deceitful soul
4 Ma 18 : 8   nor did the destroyer, the deceitful serpent

DECEITFULLY   2
1 Ma   1 : 30   Deceitfully he spoke peaceable words to them
13 : 17   Simon knew that they were speaking deceitfully to him

DECEIVE   11 = 0.007 %
Tob 10 : 7   And she answered him, Be still and stop deceiving me
Jud 12 : 16   for he had been waiting for an opportunity to deceive her
16 : 8   and put on a linen gown to deceive him
Wis   4 : 11   or guile deceive his soul
12 : 24   they were deceived like foolish babes
Sir 13 : 6   When he needs you he will deceive you
34 : 7   For dreams have deceived many
Sus 13 : 56   beauty has deceived you and lust has perverted your heart
Bel 14 : 7   Do not be deceived, O king
2 Ma   7 : 18   Do not deceive yourself in vain
2 Es 10 : 36   Or is my mind deceived, and my soul dreaming ?

DECEIVER   1
Sir 28 : 13   Curse the whisperer and deceiver

DECEPTION   2
Sir 34 : 8   Without such deceptions the law will be fulfilled
2 Ma   1 : 13   by a deception employed by the priests of Nanaea

DECIDE   24 = 0.016 %
Jud   2 : 3   and it was decided that every one
11 : 13   They have decided to consume the first fruits of the grain
Wis 15 : 7   the worker in clay decides
Sir 33 : 13   to give them as he decides
L Jr   6 : 64   for they are not able either to decide a case
1 Ma   6 : 19   So Judas decided to destroy them
8 : 26   arms, money, or ships, as Rome has decided
8 : 28   arms, money, or ships, as Rome has decided
9 : 69   Then he decided to depart to his own land
14 : 31   And when their enemies decided to invade their country
14 : 41   And the Jews and their priests decided
15 : 19   We therefore have decided to write
2 Ma   3 : 23   Heliodorus went on with what had been decided
11 : 36   But as to the matters which he decided
13 : 13   and decide the matter by the help of God
14 : 18   shrank from deciding the issue by bloodshed
15 : 17   but to attack bravely, and to decide the matter
15 : 21   but as the Lord decides
1 Es   8 : 11   who are my counsellors have decided
3 Ma   1 : 6   Ptolemy decided to visit the neighbouring cities
3 : 21   by deciding both to deem them worthy of Alexandrian citizenship
6 : 30   deciding that they should celebrate their rescue with all joyfulness
7 : 19   they decided to observe
4 Ma   1 : 14   We shall decide just what reason is and what emotion is

DECISION   17 = 0.011 %
Ad E 10 : 11   of decision before God and among all the nations
Wis   3 : 18   and no consolation in the day of decision
19 : 3   they reached another foolish decision
Sir   8 : 14   for the decision will favour him because of his standing
32 : 17   and will find a decision according to his liking
33 : 8   By the Lord's decision they were distinguished
1 Ma   2 : 41   So they made this decision that day :
14 : 44   to nullify any of these decisions or to oppose what he says
14 : 45   Whoever acts contrary to these decisions
14 : 46   the right to act in accord with these decisions
2 Ma   4 : 20   but by the decision of its carriers
11 : 25   our decision is that their temple be restored to them
13 : 14   So, committing the decision to the Creator of the world
15 : 20   When all were now looking forward to the coming decision
1 Es   8 : 10   In accordance with my gracious decision
9 : 4   in accordance with the decision of the ruling elders
4 Ma   9 : 27   and they heard his noble decision

DECISIVE   2
2 Es   7 : 78   When the decisive decree has gone forth from the Most High
7 : 104   The day of judgment is decisive

DECK, subst.   1
3 Ma   4 : 10   and in addition they were confined under a solid deck

DECK out   3 = 0.002 %
L Jr   6 : 11   They deck their gods out with garments like men
2 Es 15 : 47   you have decked out your daughters in harlotry
16 : 50   when she decks herself out, and shall accuse her to her face

DECLARATION   2
1 Ma 12 : 8   which contained a clear declaration of alliance and friendship
4 Ma 12 : 9   Extremely pleased by the boy's declaration

DECLARE   31 = 0.020 %
Tob   8 : 20   Raguel declared by oath to Tobias that he should not leave
12 : 6   worthily declaring the works of God
Sir 16 : 25   and declare knowledge accurately
18 : 2   The Lord alone will be declared righteous
26 : 29   and a tradesman will not be declared innocent of sin
39 : 10   Nations will declare his wisdom
42 : 15   and will declare what I have seen
42 : 19   He declares what has been and what is to be
44 : 8   so that men declare their praise
44 : 15   Peoples will declare their wisdom
Bar   1 : 20   and the curse which the Lord declared
2 : 20   as thou didst declare by thy servants the prophets, saying :
2 Ma   2 : 7   When Jeremiah learned of it, he rebuked them and declared :
6 : 23   he declared himself quickly
7 : 6   as Moses declared in his song
9 : 14   he was now declaring to be free
10 : 26   as the law declares
14 : 32   And when they declared on oath
15 : 4   And when they declared
Ps 151 : 3   And who will declare it to my Lord ? The Lord himself
3 Ma   4 : 17   the scribes declared to the king
7 : 4   for they declared that our government
7 : 11   For they declared that those who for the belly's sake
2 Es   1 : 5   Go and declare to my people their evil deeds
6 : 31   I will again declare to you greater things than these
6 : 48   that therefore the nations might declare thy wondrous works

7:23	they even declared that the Most High does not exist
7:54	defer to her, and she will declare it to you
8:7	and we are a work of thy hands, as thou hast declared
8:36	thy righteousness and goodness will be declared
14:5	and declared to him the end of the times

DECORATE 1
1 Ma 4:57 They decorated the front of the temple

DECORATION 4 = 0.003 %
Sir 22:17 is like the stucco decoration on the wall of a colonnade
38:28 and he is careful to complete its decoration
1 Ma 1:22 and the gold decoration on the front of the temple
2 Ma 2:29 while the one who undertakes its painting and decoration

DECOY 1
Sir 11:30 Like a decoy partridge in a cage

DECREE, verb 9 = 0.006 %
Ad E 13:6 Therefore we have decreed
1 Ma 7:49 And they decreed that this day should be celebrated
8:7 and decreed that he and those who should reign after him
13:52 And Simon decreed that every year
2 Ma 10:8 They decreed by public ordinance and vote
15:36 And they all decreed by public vote
1 Es 6:34 I, King Darius, have decreed
3 Ma 4:2 that had suddenly been decreed for them
4:11 and the voyage was concluded as the king had decreed

DECREE, subst. 18 = 0.012 %
Tob 1:6 as it is ordained for all Israel by an everlasting decree
Wis 11:7 in rebuke for the decree to slay the infants
Sir 14:12 and the decree of Hades has not been shown to you
14:17 for the decree from of old is, You must surely die !
41:3 this is the decree from the Lord for all flesh
1 Ma 1:57 the decree of the king condemned him to death
1:60 According to the decree, they put to death
14:22 we have recorded in our public decrees, as follows
14:48 to inscribe this decree upon bronze tablets
2 Ma 6:8 a decree was issued to the neighbouring Greek cities
1 Es 5:55 according to the decree which they had in writing
3 Ma 4:1 In every place, then, where this decree arrived
5:40 and again revoking your decree in the matter ?
2 Es 7:78 When the decisive decree has gone forth from the Most High
10:16 For if you acknowledge the decree of God to be just
4 Ma 4:23 and after he had plundered them he issued a decree
4:24 When, by means of his decrees
4:26 when, then, his decrees were despised by the people

DEDICATE 7 = 0.005 %
Jud 16:19 Judith also dedicated to God all the vessels of Holofernes
Sir 35:9 and dedicate your tithe with gladness
1 Ma 4:36 let us go up to cleanse the sanctuary and dedicate it
4:54 it was dedicated with songs and harps and lutes and cymbals
5:1 and the sanctuary dedicated as it was before
3 Ma 2:14 dedicated to your glorious name
7:20 and dedicating a place of prayer at the site of the festival

DEDICATION 5 = 0.003 %
1 Ma 4:56 So they celebrated the dedication of the altar for 8 days
4:59 the days of the dedication of the altar should be observed
2 Ma 2:9 for the dedication and completion of the temple
2:19 and the dedication of the altar
1 Es 7:7 They offered at the dedication of the temple of the Lord

DEED 71 = 0.046 %
Tob 2:14 Where are your charities and your righteous deeds ?
3:2 all thy deeds and all thy ways are mercy and truth
4:6 your ways will prosper through your deeds
12:9 Those who perform deeds of charity and of righteousness
12:13 your good deed was not hidden from me, but I was with you
13:9 he will afflict you for the deeds of your sons
Wis 1:9 to convict him of his lawless deeds
1:16 But ungodly men by their words and deeds summoned death
3:14 whose hands have done no lawless deed
4:20 and their lawless deeds will convict them to their face
Sir 3:8 Honour your father by word and deed
4:29 or sluggish and remiss in your deeds
7:35 because for such deeds you will be loved
11:27 his deeds will be revealed
12:1 and you will be thanked for your good deeds
15:19 and he knows every deed of man
16:12 he judges a man according to his deeds
16:14 every one will receive in accordance with his deeds
18:4 and who can search out his mighty deeds ?
18:15 My son, do not mix reproach with your good deeds
20:16 and there is no gratitude for my good deeds
27:22 Whoever winks his eye plans evil deeds
32:16 and like a light they will kindle righteous deeds
35:19 till he repays man according to his deeds

36:8	and let people recount thy mighty deeds
36:14	Fill Zion with the celebration of thy wondrous deeds
44:10	whose righteous deeds have not been forgotten
46:7	And in the days of Moses he did a loyal deed
48:4	How glorious you were, O Elijah, in your wondrous deeds !
48:14	so in death his deeds were marvellous

Bar 2:19 For it is not because of any righteous deeds
2:33 and will turn from their stubbornness and their wicked deeds
1 Ma 1:24 He committed deeds of murder, and spoke with great arrogance
2:51 Remember the deeds of the fathers
3:4 He was like a lion in his deeds
3:7 He embittered many kings, but he made Jacob glad by his deeds
5:56 heard of their brave deeds
5:61 because, thinking to do a brave deed
5:67 On that day some priests, who wished to do a brave deed
8:2 and of the brave deeds which they were doing among the Gauls
9:22 and the brave deeds that he did, and his greatness
10:15 of the brave deeds that they had done
16:23 and the brave deeds he did
2 Ma 3:36 of the deeds of the supreme God
12:3 And some men of Joppa did so ungodly a deed
1 Es 1:23 And the deeds of Josiah were upright in the sight of his Lord
1:49 beyond all the unclean deeds of all the nations
4:39 All men approve her deeds
8:86 because of our evil deeds and our great sins
3 Ma 1:27 and not to overlook this unlawful and haughty deed
2:25 he increased in his deeds of malice
2:26 He was not content with his uncounted licentious deeds
3:5 with the good deeds of upright people
3:17 They accepted our presence by word, but insincerely by deed
7:22 So the supreme God perfectly performed great deeds
2 Es 1:5 Go and declare to my people their evil deeds
3:28 Are the deeds of those who inhabit Babylon any better ?
3:29 For when I came here I saw ungodly deeds without number
3:31 Are the deeds of Babylon better than those of Zion ?
7:35 righteous deeds shall awake
7:35 and unrighteous deeds shall not sleep
7:119 but we have done deeds that bring death ?
8:33 shall receive their reward in consequence of their own deeds
14:35 and the deeds of the ungodly will be disclosed
15:6 and their harmful deeds have reached their limit
15:8 I will be silent no longer concerning their ungodly deeds
15:48 You have imitated that hateful harlot in all her deeds and devices
4 Ma 5:38 either by word or by deed
7:9 but by your deeds you made your words of divine philosophy credible
11:6 But these deeds deserve honours, not tortures
16:14 and in word and deed you have proved more powerful than a man

DEEM 9 = 0.006 %
Wis 12:15 deeming it alien to thy power to condemn him
17:6 and in terror they deemed the things which they saw
Sir 23:14 and be deemed a fool on account of your habits
2 Ma 9:21 and I have deemed it necessary to take thought
3 Ma 3:21 by deciding both to deem them worthy of Alexandrian citizenship
2 Es 8:30 Be not angry with those who are deemed worse than beasts
8:49 and have not deemed yourself to be among the righteous
13:14 and hast deemed me worthy to have my prayer heard by thee
4 Ma 18:3 but also were deemed worthy to share in a divine inheritance

DEEP, adj. 13 = 0.008 %
Wis 4:3 will strike a deep root or take a firm hold
10:18 and led them through deep waters
16:11 lest they should fall into deep forgetfulness
Sir 22:7 or who rouses a sleeper from deep slumber
24:29 and her counsel deeper than the great abyss
1 Ma 6:9 because deep grief continually gripped him
6:13 and behold, I am perishing of deep grief in a strange land
2 Ma 3:27 and deep darkness came over him
3 Ma 5:12 he was overcome by so pleasant and deep a sleep
5:47 So he, when he had filled his impious mind with a deep rage
2 Es 7:7 and deep water on the left
10:7 is in deep grief and great affliction
4 Ma 15:4 have a deeper sympathy toward their offspring than do the fathers

DEEP, subst. 6 = 0.004 %
Sir 43:23 By his counsel he stilled the great deep
P Az 32 and lookest upon the deeps
P Ma 3 who hast confined the deep
2 Es 4:7 or how many streams are at the source of the deep
4:8 I never went down into the deep, nor as yet into hell
16:57 It is he who searches the deep and its treasures

DEEPLY 12 = 0.008 %
Tob 3:10 When she heard these things she was deeply grieved
6:17 and yearned deeply for her

Sir	38:29	he is always deeply concerned over his work
Sus	13:22	Susanna sighed deeply, and said
1 Ma	1:25	Israel mourned deeply in every community
	2:39	they mourned for them deeply
	2:54	Phinehas our father, because he was deeply zealous
	12:52	and all Israel mourned deeply
	14:16	and they were deeply grieved
1 Es	1:24	and how they grieved the Lord deeply
2 Es	9:38	and was deeply grieved at heart
	9:41	for I am greatly embittered in spirit and deeply afflicted

DEFEAT, subst.   1
2 Ma	11:13	he pondered over the defeat which had befallen him

DEFEAT, verb   22 = 0.014 %
Jud	1:13	and defeated him in battle
	5:18	they were utterly defeated in many battles
	5:20	then we will go up and defeat them
	7:9	Let our lord hear a word, lest his army be defeated
	11:11	And now, in order that my lord may not be defeated
1 Ma	1:1	had defeated Darius, king of the Persians and the Medes
	3:11	and he defeated and killed him
	5:40	for he will surely defeat us
	5:41	we will cross over to him and defeat him
	5:43	All the Gentiles were defeated before him
	8:2	how they had defeated them and forced them to pay tribute
	8:6	They also defeated Antiochus the Great, king of Asia
	10:49	and Alexander pursued him and defeated them
	14:3	And he went and defeated the army of Demetrius
2 Ma	9:2	and Antiochus and his men were defeated
	10:24	Now Timothy, who had been defeated by the Jews before
	13:19	was turned back, attacked again, and was defeated
	13:22	attacked Judas and his men, was defeated
2 Es	7:128	that if he is defeated he shall suffer what you have said
4 Ma	8:2	For when the tyrant was conspicuously defeated
	9:30	as you see the arrogant design of your tyranny being defeated
	11:20	and in which we have not been defeated !

DEFEATED   1
2 Ma	12:11	The defeated nomads besought Judas

DEFENCE, DEFENSE   5 = 0.003 %
Wis	6:10	and those who have been taught them will find a defence
Sir	34:16	a guard against stumbling and a defence against falling
1 Ma	14:10	and furnished them with the means of defence
2 Ma	12:27	and made a vigorous defence
	13:26	made the best possible defence

DEFEND   15 = 0.010 %
Jud	5:21	for their Lord will defend them
	6:2	because their God will defend them ?
Ad E	16:20	on that very day they may defend themselves
Wis	16:17	for the universe defends the righteous
1 Ma	8:32	we will defend their rights and fight you on sea and on land
2 Ma	6:11	because their piety kept them from defending themselves
3 Ma	1:4	to defend themselves and their children and wives bravely
	1:27	to defend them in the present trouble
	7:6	that the God of heaven surely defends the Jews
2 Es	2:20	defend the orphan, clothe the naked
	7:122	Or that the glory of the Most High will defend those
	13:49	he will defend the people who remain
	16:50	when he comes who will defend him
4 Ma	14:19	defend themselves against intruders
	14:19	and defend it even to the death ?

DEFENDER   4 = 0.003 %
2 Ma	8:36	proclaimed that the Jews had a Defender
	10:36	wheeled around against the defenders
	14:34	and called upon the constant Defender of our nation, in these words :
	15:30	the defender of his fellow citizens

DEFENDING   1
Wis	10:20	and praised with one accord thy defending hand

DEFER   1
2 Es	7:54	defer to her, and she will declare it to you

DEFERENCE   2
Wis	6:7	nor show deference to greatness
Sir	4:22	or deference, to your downfall

DEFIANCE   1
3 Ma	3:19	who hold their heads high in defiance of kings

DEFILE   24 = 0.016 %
Tob	2:9	and because I was defiled
Jud	9:2	who had loosed the girdle of a virgin to defile her
	9:8	for they intend to defile thy sanctuary
	13:16	to defile and shame me

Wis	11:6	stirred up and defiled with blood
Sir	13:1	Whoever touches pitch will be defiled
	21:28	A whisperer defiles his own soul
	42:10	while a virgin, lest she be defiled
	47:20	You put a stain upon your honour, and defiled your posterity
Bar	3:10	that you are defiled with the dead
1 Ma	1:37	they even defiled the sanctuary
	1:46	to defile the sanctuary and the priests
	1:63	They chose to die rather than to be defiled by food
	4:45	for the Gentiles had defiled it
	7:34	But he mocked them and derided them and defiled them
	14:36	and defile the environs of the sanctuary
2 Ma	6:25	while I defile and disgrace my old age
	14:3	but had wilfully defiled himself in the times of separation
3 Ma	7:14	who had become defiled
2 Es	1:26	for you have defiled your hands with blood
	8:60	have defiled the name of him who made them
	10:22	our virgins have been defiled
4 Ma	7:6	you neither defiled your sacred teeth nor profaned your stomach
	18:8	defile the purity of my virginity

DEFILED   3 = 0.002 %
Wis	7:25	therefore nothing defiled gains entrance into her
1 Ma	4:43	and removed the defiled stones to an unclean place
2 Ma	7:34	But you, unholy wretch, you most defiled of all men

DEFILEMENT   2
2 Ma	5:27	so that they might not share in the defilement
3 Ma	2:17	Do not punish us for the defilement committed by these men

DEFILING   14 = 0.009 %
4 Ma	4:26	to eat defiling foods and to renounce Judaism
	5:3	If any were not willing to eat defiling food
	5:19	if we were to eat defiling food
	5:25	Therefore we do not eat defiling food
	5:27	that you may deride us for eating defiling food
	6:19	in becoming an example of the eating of defiling food
	7:6	by eating defiling foods
	8:2	being unable to compel an aged man to eat defiling foods
	8:2	and that any who ate defiling food should be freed after eating
	8:12	so as to persuade them out of fear to eat the defiling food
	8:29	had ceased counselling them to eat defiling food
	11:16	So if you intend to torture me for not eating defiling foods
	11:25	to change our mind or to force us to eat defiling foods
	13:2	and had eaten defiling food

DEFRAUD   1
Sir	29:7	they have been afraid of being defrauded needlessly

DEFRAY   1
2 Ma	3:3	defrayed from his own revenues all the expenses

DEGREE   2
2 Ma	4:3	When his hatred progressed to such a degree
3 Ma	5:31	and have exhibited to an extraordinary degree

DEIGN   1
2 Ma	14:9	deign to take thought for our country

DEJECTED   1
Sir	25:23	A dejected mind, a gloomy face, and a wounded heart

DELAIAH   1
1 Es	5:37	the sons of Delaiah the son of Tobiah

DELAY, subst.   5 = 0.003 %
Tob	10:4	his long delay proves it
2 Ma	14:27	as a prisoner without delay
3 Ma	5:20	Tomorrow without delay prepare the elephants in the same way
	5:42	that he would send them to death without delay
2 Es	16:38	there will not be a moment's delay

DELAY, verb   14 = 0.009 %
Tob	5:8	And he said to him, Go, and do not delay
	9:4	and if I delay long he will be greatly distressed
Jud	2:13	and do not delay about it
Sir	4:3	nor delay your gift to a beggar
	5:7	Do not delay to turn to the Lord
	7:16	remember that wrath does not delay
	14:12	Remember that death will not delay
	29:5	but at the time for repayment he will delay
	35:18	And the Lord will not delay
2 Es	4:39	that the time of threshing is delayed for the righteous
	16:37	Behold, the calamities draw near, and are not delayed
	16:39	so the calamities will not delay in coming forth upon the earth
4 Ma	6:23	And you, guards of the tyrant, why do you delay ?
	9:1	Why do you delay, O tyrant ?

DELETE 1
1 Ma 8:30 both parties shall determine to add or delete anything

DELETION 1
1 Ma 8:30 and any addition or deletion that they may make shall be valid

DELIBERATE, adj. 3 = 0.002 %
Sir 5:11 Be quick to hear, and be deliberate in answering
20:3 for so you will escape deliberate sin !
3 Ma 3:14 by the gods"deliberate alliance with us in battle

DELIBERATE, verb 2
1 Ma 4:44 They deliberated what to do
8:15 and every day 320 senators constantly deliberate

DELIBERATELY 1
Sir 30:21 and do not afflict yourself deliberately

DELIBERATION 2
Sir 32:19 Do nothing without deliberation
44:4 leaders of the people in their deliberations

DELICACY 2
Wis 16:2 a delicacy to satisfy the desire of appetite
16:3 might partake of delicacies

DELICIOUS 2
2 Ma 15:39 while wine mixed with water is sweet and delicious
4 Ma 5:9 It is senseless not to enjoy delicious things

DELIGHT, subst. 9 = 0.006 %
Wis 3:14 and a place of great delight in the temple of the Lord
8:18 and in friendship with her, pure delight
13:3 If through delight in the beauty of these things
Sir 21:16 but delight will be found in the speech of the intelligent
45:12 the delight of the eyes, richly adorned
2 Es 7:36 and opposite it the paradise of delight
7:38 here are delight and rest
7:47 And now I see that the world to come will bring delight to few
4 Ma 1:22 Thus desire precedes pleasure and delight follows it

DELIGHT, verb 9 = 0.006 %
Wis 1:13 and he does not delight in the death of the living
6:21 Therefore if you delight in thrones and sceptres
Sir 1:12 The fear of the Lord delights the heart
1:27 and he delights in fidelity and meekness
9:12 Do not delight in what pleases the ungodly
26:13 A wife's charm delights her husband
30:23 Delight your soul and comfort your heart
51:15 From blossom to ripening grape my heart delighted in her
2 Ma 15:39 delights the ears of those who read the work

DELIGHTFUL 1
4 Ma 8:23 and deprive ourselves of this delightful world ?

DELIVER 60 = 0.039 %
Tob 4:10 For charity delivers from death
12:9 For almsgiving delivers from death
14:11 and how righteousness delivers
Jud 6:3 and their God will not deliver them
8:33 the Lord will deliver Israel by my hand
16:3 for he has delivered me out of the hands of my pursuers
Ad E 10:9 the Lord has delivered us from all these evils
Wis 2:18 and will deliver him from the hand of his adversaries
10:1 she delivered him from his transgression
10:13 wisdom did not desert him, but delivered him from sin
10:15 A holy people and blameless race wisdom delivered
16:8 that it is thou who deliverest from every evil
16:11 and then were quickly delivered
19:9 praising thee, O Lord, who didst deliver them
Sir 4:9 Deliver him who is wronged from the hand of the wrongdoer
33:1 but in trial he will deliver him again and again
48:20 and delivered them by the hand of Isaiah
49:10 and delivered them with confident hope
50:24 And let him deliver us in our days !
51:2 and hast delivered my body from destruction
51:3 and didst deliver me
51:8 that thou dost deliver those who wait for thee
Bar 2:14 and for thy own sake deliver us, and grant us favour
4:18 will deliver you from the hand of your enemies
4:21 and he will deliver you
L Jr 6:54 They cannot judge their own cause or deliver one who is wronged
P Az 20 Deliver us in accordance with thy marvellous works
66 and delivered us from the midst of the burning fiery furnace
66 from the midst of the fire he has delivered us
1 Ma 2:60 was delivered from the mouth of the lions
5:50 *and the city was delivered into his hands*
7:35 *are delivered into my hands this time*
9:46 that you may be delivered from the hands of our enemies

12:15 and we were delivered from our enemies
12:17 *and greet you and deliver to you this letter from us*
16:2 so that we have delivered Israel many times
2 Ma 11:15 *which Maccabeus delivered to Lysias in writing*
11:17 *have delivered your signed communication*
12:45 that they might be delivered from their sin
1 Es 6:18 and they were delivered to Zerubbabel
8:8 *which was delivered to Ezra the priest*
8:17 and deliver the holy vessels of the Lord
8:59 Be watchful and on guard until you deliver them
8:61 he delivered us from every enemy on the way
8:62 and delivered in the house of our Lord
8:67 *And they delivered the king's orders to the royal stewards*
2 Es 2:30 because I will deliver you, says the Lord
3:27 *So thou didst deliver the city into the hands of thy enemies*
7:27 And every one who has been delivered from the evils
7:96 from which they have been delivered
12:34 But he will deliver in mercy the remnant of my people
13:26 who will himself deliver his creation
13:29 when the Most High will deliver those who are on the earth
14:26 *and some you shall deliver in secret to the wise*
14:29 and they were delivered from there
15:27 for God will not deliver you
16:17 Who will deliver me in those days ?
16:67 and deliver you from all tribulation
16:74 and I will deliver you from them
4 Ma 4:12 and that if he were delivered

DELIVERANCE 15 = 0.010 %
Jud 8:17 Therefore, while we wait for his deliverance
Wis 16:6 and received a token of deliverance
18:7 The deliverance of the righteous
Sir 51:9 and prayed for deliverance from death
1 Ma 3:6 and deliverance prospered by his hand
4:25 Thus Israel had a great deliverance that day
4:56 they offered a sacrifice of deliverance and praise
5:62 through whom deliverance was given to Israel
3 Ma 6:31 arranged for a banquet of deliverance
6:36 but because of the deliverance
7:16 and had received the full enjoyment of deliverance
7:18 There they celebrated their deliverance
7:22 for their deliverance
4 Ma 15:26 one bearing death and the other deliverance for her children
15:27 She did not approve the deliverance

DELIVERER 1
3 Ma 7:23 Blessed be the Deliverer of Israel through all times ! Amen

DELIVERY 1
2 Es 16:38 when the time of her delivery draws near

DELOS 1
1 Ma 15:23 and to the Spartans, and to Delos, and to Myndos

DELUSION 1
Wis 17:7 The delusions of their magic art lay humbled

DEMAGOGUERY 1
1 Es 5:73 and by plots and demagoguery and uprisings

DEMAND, verb 3 = 0.002 %
1 Ma 15:35 As for Joppa and Gazara, which you demand
2 Ma 7:10 When it was demanded, he quickly put out his tongue
3 Ma 5:18 and with sharp threats demanded to know

DEMAND, subst. 1
Sir 31:31 and do not afflict him by making demands of him

DEMETRIUS 50 = 0.033 %
1 Ma 7:1 In the 151st year Demetrius the son of Seleucus set forth from Rome
7:4 and Demetrius took his seat upon the throne of his kingdom
8:31 which King Demetrius is doing to them
9:1 When Demetrius heard
10:2 When Demetrius the king heard of it
10:3 And Demetrius sent Jonathan a letter
10:6 So Demetrius gave him authority to recruit troops
10:15 which Demetrius had sent to Jonathan
10:22 When Demetrius heard of these things he was grieved and said
10:25 King Demetrius to the nation of the Jews, greeting
10:46 which Demetrius had done in Israel
10:48 and encamped opposite Demetrius
10:49 and the army of Demetrius fled
10:50 and Demetrius fell on that day
10:52 for I crushed Demetrius and gained control of our country
10:67 In the 165th year Demetrius the son of Demetrius
10:69 And Demetrius appointed Apollonius the governor of Coelesyria
11:9 He sent envoys to Demetrius the king, saying
11:12 and gave her to Demetrius
11:19 So Demetrius became king in the 167th year

11 : 30	King Demetrius to Jonathan his brother
11 : 32	King Demetrius to Lasthenes his father, greeting
11 : 38	Now when Demetrius the king saw
11 : 39	He saw that all the troops were murmuring against Demetrius
11 : 40	He also reported to Imalkue what Demetrius had done
11 : 40	which the troops of Demetrius had for him
11 : 41	Now Jonathan sent to Demetrius the king the request
11 : 42	And Demetrius sent this message to Jonathan
11 : 52	So Demetrius the king sat on the throne of his kingdom
11 : 55	All the troops that Demetrius had cast off
11 : 55	gathered around him, and they fought against Demetrius
11 : 63	Then Jonathan heard that the officers of Demetrius
12 : 24	Now Jonathan heard that the commanders of Demetrius had returned
12 : 34	to the men whom Demetrius had sent
13 : 34	Simon also chose men and sent them to Demetrius the king
13 : 35	Demetrius the king sent him a favourable reply to this request
13 : 36	King Demetrius to Simon, the high priest and friend of kings
14 : 1	In the 172nd year Demetrius the king assembled his forces
14 : 2	that Demetrius had invaded his territory
14 : 3	And he went and defeated the army of Demetrius
14 : 38	King Demetrius confirmed him in the high priesthood
15 : 1	Antiochus, the son of Demetrius the king
15 : 22	The consul wrote the same thing to Demetrius the king

DEMOLISH   3 = 0.002 %

Jud	3 : 8	And he demolished all their shrines
1 Ma	9 : 62	he rebuilt the parts of it that had been demolished
2 Es	16 : 23	and its cities shall be demolished

DEMON   9 = 0.006 %

Tob	3 : 8	and the evil demon Asmodeus had slain each of them
	3 : 17	and to bind Asmodeus the evil demon
	6 : 7	if a demon or evil spirit gives trouble to any one
	6 : 14	for a demon is in love with her
	6 : 15	and do not worry about the demon
	6 : 17	Then the demon will smell it and flee away
	8 : 3	And when the demon smelled the odour
Bar	4 : 7	by sacrificing to demons and not to God
	4 : 35	and for a long time she will be inhabited by demons

DEMONSTRATE   4 = 0.003 %

4 Ma	1 : 8	but I can demonstrate it best from the noble bravery
	1 : 9	demonstrated that reason controls the emotions
	14 : 18	And why is it necessary to demonstrate sympathy for children
	16 : 2	Thus I have demonstrated not only

DEMONSTRATION   2

4 Ma	3 : 19	to a narrative demonstration of temperate reason
	13 : 10	Let us not be cowardly in the demonstration of our piety

DEMOPHON   1

2 Ma	12 : 2	as well as Hieronymus and Demophon

DEN   8 = 0.005 %

Bel	14 : 31	They threw Daniel into the lions' den
	14 : 32	There were 7 lions in the den
	14 : 34	to Daniel, in the lions' den
	14 : 35	and I know nothing about the den
	14 : 36	right over the den
	14 : 40	When he came to the den he looked in, and there sat Daniel
	14 : 42	and threw into the den the men who had attempted his destruction
4 Ma	18 : 13	He praised Daniel in the den of the lions and blessed him

DENOUNCE   3 = 0.002 %

2 Ma	14 : 37	was denounced to Nicanor
2 Es	12 : 32	he will denounce them for their ungodliness
4 Ma	9 : 14	he denounced the tyrant, saying

DENY   5 = 0.003 %

Jud	8 : 28	and there is no one who can deny your words
Bel	14 : 24	You cannot deny that this is a living god ; so worship him
2 Es	7 : 24	They scorned his law, and denied his covenants
	7 : 37	Look now, and understand whom you have denied
4 Ma	6 : 34	It would be ridiculous to deny it

DEPART   51 = 0.033 %

Tob	3 : 6	that I may depart and become dust
	5 : 16	So they both went out and departed
	14 : 3	behold, I have grown old and am about to depart this life
Jud	5 : 18	But when they departed from the way
	13 : 19	Your hope will never depart from the hearts of men
Wis	1 : 5	and will rise and depart from foolish thoughts

	10 : 3	But when an unrighteous man departed from her in his anger
	19 : 2	thy people to depart
	19 : 3	those whom they had begged and compelled to depart
Sir	2 : 3	Cleave to him and do not depart
	10 : 12	The beginning of man's pride is to depart from the Lord
	38 : 23	and be comforted for him when his spirit has departed
P Az	6	For we have sinfully and lawlessly departed from thee
Sus	13 : 7	When the people departed at noon
Bel	14 : 14	and sealed it with the king's signet, and departed
1 Ma	1 : 24	Taking them all, he departed to his own land
	2 : 19	departing each one from the religion of his fathers
	3 : 37	and departed from Antioch his capital in the 147th year
	3 : 40	So they departed with their entire force
	4 : 35	he departed to Antioch and enlisted mercenaries
	5 : 29	He departed from there at night
	6 : 4	So he fled and in great grief departed from there
	6 : 10	Sleep departs from my eyes and I am downhearted with worry
	6 : 57	So he quickly gave orders to depart
	6 : 63	Then he departed with haste and returned to Antioch
	7 : 19	Then Bacchides departed from Jerusalem
	9 : 36	and seized John and all that he had, and departed with it
	9 : 69	Then he decided to depart to his own land
	9 : 72	then he turned an departed to his own land
	10 : 13	each left his place and departed to his own land
	10 : 86	Then Jonathan departed from there
	11 : 61	From there he departed to Gaza
	13 : 12	Then Trypho departed from Ptolemais with a large army
	13 : 24	Then Trypho turned back and departed to his own land
2 Ma	2 : 3	that the law should not depart from their hearts
	12 : 12	and after receiving his pledges they departed to their tents
	12 : 18	for he had by then departed from the region
1 Es	1 : 16	no one needed to depart from his duties
	3 : 3	They ate and drank, and when they were satisfied they departed
	8 : 11	depart with you as I and the 7 friends
	8 : 61	We departed from the river Theras
3 Ma	2 : 32	and did not depart from their religion
	5 : 21	and each departed to his own home
	5 : 44	Then the friends and officers departed with great joy
	7 : 13	shouted the Hallelujah and joyfully departed
	7 : 20	they departed unharmed, free, and overjoyed
2 Es	2 : 39	Those who have departed from the shadow of this age
	3 : 22	but what was good departed, and the evil remained
	5 : 19	Depart from me and do not come near me for 7 days
	8 : 5	and against your will you depart
	15 : 25	Depart, you faithless children !

DEPARTED   1

Wis	16 : 14	but he cannot bring back the departed spirit

DEPARTURE   4 = 0.003 %

Wis	3 : 2	and their departure was thought to be an affliction
	7 : 6	and a common departure
3 Ma	7 : 10	the Jews did not immediately hurry to make their departure
	7 : 16	began their departure from the city

DEPEND   6 = 0.004 %

Jud	8 : 24	for their lives depend upon us
	9 : 11	For thy power depends not upon numbers
Sir	5 : 8	Do not depend on dishonest wealth
	31 : 20	Healthy sleep depends on moderate eating
	38 : 24	depends on the opportunity of leisure
1 Ma	3 : 19	that victory in battle depends

DEPENDABLE   1

Sir	33 : 3	for him the law is as dependable

DEPENDENT, subst.   1

Wis	14 : 15	and handed on to his dependents secret rites and initiations

DEPICT   1

Wis	18 : 24	For upon his long robe the whole world was depicted

DEPLOY   1

2 Ma	15 : 20	and the cavalry deployed on the flanks

DEPORT   2

2 Ma	2 : 1	ordered those who were being deported
	2 : 2	instructed those who were being deported

DEPOSE   3 = 0.002 %

L Jr	6 : 34	They cannot set up a king or depose one
1 Ma	8 : 13	and those whom they wish they depose
1 Es	1 : 35	Then the king of Egypt deposed him from reigning in Jerusalem

DEPOSIT, subst.   3 = 0.002 %

2 Ma	3 : 10	The high priest explained that there were some deposits
	3 : 15	upon him who had given the law about deposits
4 Ma	4 : 7	that those who had committed deposits to the sacred treasury

DEPOSIT, verb
4 = 0.003 %
- 1 Ma 14 : 49 and to deposit copies of them in the treasury
- 2 Ma 3 : 15 for those who had deposited them
- 1 Es 6 : 23 in the royal archives that were deposited in Babylon
- 4 Ma 4 : 3 there are deposited tens of thousands in private funds

DEPRAVED
1
- 2 Ma 14 : 27 and, provoked by the false accusations of that depraved man

DEPRESS
2
- Jud 7 : 32 And they were greatly depressed in the city
- 2 Ma 6 : 12 Now I urge those who read this book not to be depressed by such calamities

DEPRIVE
20 = 0.013 %
- Ad E 16 : 12 he undertook to deprive us of our kingdom and our life
- Wis 18 : 4 For their enemies deserved to be deprived of light
- Sir 4 : 1 My son, deprive not the poor of his living
-     7 : 19 Do not deprive yourself of a wise and good wife
-    14 : 4 Whoever accumulates by depriving himself
-    14 : 14 Do not deprive yourself of a happy day
-    28 : 15 and deprived them of the fruit of their toil
-    34 : 21 whoever deprives them of it is a man of blood
-    34 : 22 to deprive an employee of his wages is to shed blood
- P Az   21 let them be disgraced and deprived of all power and dominion
- 2 Ma 3 : 29 and deprived of any hope of recovery
-    13 : 10 who were on the point of being deprived of the law
- 3 Ma 1 : 12 Even if those men are deprived of this honour
-    2 : 33 and depriving them of common fellowship and mutual help
-    5 : 32 In fact you would have been deprived of life instead of these
-    6 : 12 are being deprived of life in the manner of traitors
-    6 : 24 you are now attempting to deprive of dominion and life
- 2 Es 10 : 30 and I was deprived of my understanding
- 4 Ma 4 : 7 should be deprived of them
-    8 : 23 and deprive ourselves of this delightful world ?

DEPTH
11 = 0.007 %
- Jud 8 : 14 You cannot plumb the depths of the human heart
- Wis 10 : 19 and cast them up from the depth of the sea
- Sir 24 : 5 and have walked in the depths of the abyss
-    51 : 5 from the depths of the belly of Hades
- P Ma   13 do not condemn me to the depths of the earth
- 3 Ma 2 : 7 you overwhelmed him in the depths of the sea
- 2 Es 3 : 18 and move the world, and make the depths to tremble
-    5 : 25 and from all the depths of the sea
-    8 : 23 whose look dries up the depths
-    13 : 52 what is in the depths of the sea
-    16 : 12 the sea is churned up from the depths

DEPUTY
2
- 2 Ma 4 : 29 as deputy in the high priesthood
-    4 : 31 leaving Andronicus, a man of high rank, to act as his deputy

DERANGE
1
- 3 Ma 5 : 30 his whole mind had been deranged in regard to these matters

DERIDE
6 = 0.004 %
- Sir 13 : 7 and finally he will deride you
- L Jr 6 : 43 she derides the woman next to her
- 1 Ma 7 : 34 But he mocked them and derided them and defiled them
- 2 Ma 7 : 27 deriding the cruel tyrant : My son, have pity on me
-    8 : 17 and the torture of the derided city
- 4 Ma 5 : 27 that you may deride us for eating defiling food

DERISION
2
- Wis 5 : 4 This is the man whom we once held in derision
- 2 Es 16 : 69 And those who consent to eat shall be held in derision and contempt

DESCEND
8 = 0.005 %
- Jud 5 : 6 This people is descended from the Chaldeans
- Wis 10 : 6 he escaped the fire that descended on the Five Cities
-    10 : 13 She descended with him into the dungeon
- 3 Ma 6 : 18 from which 2 glorious angels of fearful aspect descended
- 2 Es 3 : 11 and all the righteous who have descended from him
-    3 : 21 as were also all who were descended from him
-    6 : 56 As for the other nations which have descended from Adam
- 4 Ma 16 : 20 wielding a sword and descending upon him

DESCENDANT
32 = 0.021 %
- Tob 1 : 1 of the descendants of Asiel and the tribe of Naphtali
-    4 : 12 from among the descendants of your fathers
- Jud 8 : 32 which will go down through all generations of our descendants
- Wis 7 : 1 a descendant of the first-formed child of earth
- Sir 1 : 15 and among their descendants she will be trusted
-    4 : 16 and his descendants will remain in possession of her
-    44 : 11 their prosperity will remain with their descendants
-    44 : 12 Their descendants stand by the covenants
-    45 : 1 From his descendants the Lord brought forth a man of mercy
-    45 : 13 and his descendants perpetually

-    45 : 15 and for his descendants all the days of heaven
-    45 : 21 which he gave to him and his descendants
-    45 : 24 that he and his descendants
-    45 : 25 so the heritage of Aaron is for his descendants
-    47 : 22 he will never blot out the descendants of his chosen one
- Bar 2 : 15 for Israel and his descendants are called by thy name
- P Az   13 to whom thou didst promise to make their descendants
- 1 Ma 5 : 2 and they determined to destroy the descendants of Jacob who lived among them
- 2 Ma 1 : 20 sent the descendants of the priests who had hidden the fire to get it
-    7 : 17 will torture you and your descendants !
- 3 Ma 6 : 3 look upon the descendants of Abraham, O Father
-    6 : 36 in their whole community and for their descendants
- 2 Es 3 : 7 for him and for his descendants
-    3 : 15 and promise him that thou wouldst never forsake his descendants
-    3 : 17 And when thou didst lead his descendants out of Egypt
-    3 : 19 to give the law to the descendants of Jacob
-    3 : 26 in everything doing as Adam and all his descendants had done
-    7 : 118 but ours also who are your descendants
-    9 : 30 and give heed to my words, O descendants of Jacob
- 4 Ma 7 : 12 so the descendant of Aaron, Eleazar
-    13 : 19 has bequeathed through the fathers to their descendants
-    17 : 6 For your children were true descendants of father Abraham

DESCENT*
4 = 0.003 %
- Sir 26 : 21 and, having confidence in their good descent
-    43 : 17 and its descent is like locusts alighting
-    46 : 6 and at the descent of Beth-horon
- 1 Ma 3 : 24 They pursued them down the descent of Beth-horon to the plain

DESCRIBE
5 = 0.003 %
- Jud 7 : 28 Let him not do this day the things which we have described !
-    14 : 8 Then Judith described to him in the presence of the people
- Wis 7 : 1 Great are thy judgments and hard to describe
- Sir 43 : 31 Who has seen him and can describe him ?
- 2 Es 7 : 100 to see what you have described to me ?

DESECRATE
1
- Jud 4 : 12 and the sanctuary to be profaned and desecrated

DESECRATION
1
- Jud 8 : 21 and he will exact of us the penalty for its desecration

DESERT, subst., adj.
7 = 0.005 %
- Jud 2 : 23 and the Ishmaelites who lived along the desert
- Wis 5 : 7 and we journeyed through trackless deserts
-    18 : 20 and a plague came upon the multitude in the desert
- 1 Ma 1 : 39 Her sanctuary became desolate as a desert
- 2 Es 7 : 106 and Moses for our fathers who sinned in the desert
-    16 : 60 who has put springs of water in the desert
- 4 Ma 18 : 8 No seducer corrupted me on a desert plain

DESERT, verb
8 = 0.005 %
- Tob 1 : 4 deserted the house of Jerusalem
- Wis 10 : 13 wisdom did not desert him, but delivered him from sin
- 1 Ma 2 : 21 Far be it from us to desert the law and the ordinances
-    7 : 19 who had deserted to him
-    7 : 24 and took vengeance on the men who had deserted
-    9 : 24 and the country deserted with them to the enemy
-    15 : 12 and his troops had deserted him
- 4 Ma 12 : 16 I do not desert the excellent example of my brothers

DESERTED
1
- Sir 9 : 7 nor wander about in its deserted sections

DESERVE
14 = 0.009 %
- Tob 12 : 4 The old man said, He deserves it
- Ad E 16 : 18 has speedily inflicted on him the punishment he deserved
- Wis 3 : 10 But the ungodly will be punished as their reasoning deserves
-    12 : 15 who does not deserve to be punished
-    12 : 20 the enemies of thy servants and those deserving of death
-    16 : 9 because they deserved to be punished by such things
-    18 : 4 For their enemies deserved to be deprived of light
-    19 : 4 For the fate they deserved drew them on to this end
- Sir 8 : 5 remember that we all deserve punishment
- 2 Ma 4 : 38 The Lord thus repaid him with the punishment he deserved
-    15 : 21 that he gains victory for those who deserve it
- 3 Ma 7 : 10 should receive the punishment they deserved
- 4 Ma 4 : 12 For he said that he had committed a sin deserving of death
-    11 : 6 But these deeds deserve honours, not tortures

DESERVED
1
- Wis 12 : 26 will experience the deserved judgment of God

DESERVEDLY
2
- Wis 16 : 1 Therefore those men were deservedly punished
- 4 Ma 9 : 9 will deservedly undergo from the divine justice

DESIGN, subst.   6 = 0.004 %
　Wis　9 : 14　and our designs are likely to fail
1 Ma　11 : 8　and he kept devising evil designs against Alexander
2 Ma　15 : 5　in carrying out his abominable design
3 Ma　1 : 16　and to avert the violence of this evil design
4 Ma　9 : 30　as you see the arrogant design of your tyranny being defeated
　　　17 : 2　frustrated his evil designs

DESIGN, verb   2
　Jud　9 : 5　thou hast designed the things that are now
2 Ma　6 : 12　but to recognize that these punishments were designed

DESIGNATE   1
2 Ma　4 : 2　He dared to designate as a plotter against the government

DESIRABLE   4 = 0.003 %
　Wis　8 : 5　If riches are a desirable possession in life
　Sir　1 : 17　she fills their whole house with desirable goods
2 Es　7 : 57　Judge therefore which things are precious and desirable
4 Ma　15 : 1　O religion, more desirable to the mother than her children !

DESIRE, subst.   37 = 0.024 %
　Jud　12 : 16　and he was moved with great desire to possess her
　Wis　4 : 12　and roving desire perverts the innocent mind
　　　6 : 11　Therefore set your desire on my words
　　　6 : 17　is the most sincere desire for instruction
　　　6 : 20　so the desire for wisdom leads to a kingdom
　　14 : 2　For it was desire for gain that planned that vessel
　　16 : 2　a delicacy to satisfy the desire of appetite
　　16 : 21　and the bread, ministering to the desire of the one who took it
　　16 : 25　according to the desire of those who had need
　　19 : 11　when desire led them to ask for luxurious food
　Sir　3 : 29　and an attentive ear is the wise man's desire
　　5 : 2　walking according to the desires of your heart
　　6 : 37　and your desire for wisdom will be granted
　　18 : 30　Do not follow your base desires, but restrain your appetites
　　18 : 31　If you allow your soul to take pleasure in base desire
　　20 : 4　Like a eunuch's desire to violate a maiden
　　23 : 5　and remove from me evil desire
　　36 : 22　and surpasses every human desire
　Sus　13 : 11　for they were ashamed to disclose their lustful desire to possess her
3 Ma　1 : 10　and conceived a desire to enter the holy of holies
　　7 : 2　the great God guiding our affairs according to our desire
　　7 : 17　in accord with the common desire, for 7 days
4 Ma　1 : 22　Thus desire precedes pleasure and delight follows it
　　1 : 31　Self-control, then, is dominance over the desires
　　1 : 32　Some desires are mental, other are physical
　　2 : 1　the desires of the mind for the enjoyment of beauty
　　2 : 2　because by mental effort he overcame sexual desire
　　2 : 4　over the frenzied urge of sexual desire
　　2 : 4　but also over every desire
　　2 : 6　that reason is able to control desires
　　3 : 2　No one of us can eradicate that kind of desire
　　3 : 2　not to be enslaved by desire
　　3 : 11　But a certain irrational desire for the water
　　3 : 12　2 staunch young soldiers, respecting the king's desire
　　3 : 16　Therefore, opposing reason to desire
　　3 : 17　and quench the flames of frenzied desires
　　5 : 23　so that we master all pleasures and desires

DESIRE, verb   28 = 0.018 %
　Jud　16 : 22　Many desired to marry her
Ad E　13 : 2　to re-establish the peace which all men desire
　　13 : 15　and they desire to destroy the inheritance
　Wis　6 : 13　She hastens to make herself known to those who desire her
　　8 : 2　and I desired to take her for my bride
　　13 : 6　and desiring to find him
　　15 : 5　so that they desire the lifeless form of a dead image
　　15 : 6　are those who either make or desire or worship them
　　15 : 19　that one would desire them
　　16 : 3　in order that those men, when they desired food
　Sir　1 : 26　If you desire wisdom, keep the commandments
　　16 : 1　Do not desire a multitude of useless children
　　24 : 19　Come to me, you who desire me
　　25 : 21　and do not desire a woman for her possessions
　　40 : 22　The eye desires grace and beauty
　　42 : 22　How greatly to be desired are all his works
　Sus　13 : 8　going in and walking about, and they began to desire her
1 Ma　4 : 6　but they did not have armour and swords such as they desired
2 Ma　11 : 23　we desire that the subjects of the kingdom be undisturbed
　　11 : 28　If you are well, it is as we desire
　　15 : 38　that is what I myself desired
3 Ma　5 : 26　indicating that what the king desired was ready for action
2 Es　2 : 41　The number of your children, whom you desired, is full
　　4 : 4　I also will show you the way you desire to see
　　4 : 43　Then the things that you desire to see
　　8 : 32　For if thou hast desired to have pity on us

　　13 : 34　as you saw, desiring to come and conquer him
　　15 : 17　For a man will desire to go into a city, and shall not be able

DESIRED   1
　Sir　14 : 14　let not your share of desired good pass by you

DESIST   1
　Sir　35 : 17　he will not desist until the Most High visits him

DESOLATE   11 = 0.007 %
　Tob　14 : 4　and Jerusalem will be desolate
　Sir　16 : 4　but through a tribe of lawless men it will be made desolate
　　49 : 6　and made her streets desolate
　Bar　4 : 12　I was left desolate because of the sins of my children
　　4 : 19　for I have been left desolate
1 Ma　1 : 39　Her sanctuary became desolate as a desert
　　4 : 38　And they saw the sanctuary desolate, the altar profaned
2 Es　1 : 33　Thus says the Lord Almighty : Your house is desolate
　　5 : 3　and men shall see it desolate
　　16 : 23　for the earth shall be left desolate
　　16 : 32　And the earth shall be left desolate

DESOLATING   1
1 Ma　1 : 54　they erected a desolating sacrilege

DESOLATION   8 = 0.005 %
　Jud　8 : 22　and the desolation of our inheritance
　Bar　2 : 4　to be a reproach and a desolation among all the surrounding peoples
　　2 : 23　and the whole land will be a desolation without inhabitants
　　4 : 33　so she will be grieved at her own desolation
1 Es　1 : 58　it shall keep sabbath all the time of its desolation
　　8 : 81　and raised Zion from desolation
2 Es　3 : 2　because I saw the desolation of Zion
　　12 : 48　on account of the desolation of Zion

DESPAIR, verb   2
　Sir　22 : 21　do not despair, for a renewal of friendship is possible
2 Ma　9 : 22　I do not despair of my condition

DESPAIRING   1
Ad E　14 : 19　hear the voice of the despairing

DESPERATE   1
1 Ma　9 : 17　The battle became desperate

DESPISE   32 = 0.021 %
　Tob　4 : 18　and do not despise any useful counsel
　Jud　10 : 19　Who can despise these people
　　14 : 5　who despised the house of Israel
　Wis　3 : 11　for whoever despises wisdom and instruction is miserable
　　12 : 24　those animals which even their enemies despised
　Sir　3 : 13　in all your strength do not despise him
　　10 : 23　It is not right to despise an intelligent poor man
　　19 : 1　he who despises small things will fail little by little
　　22 : 5　and will be despised by both
　　22 : 23　For one should not always despise restricted circumstances
　　31 : 31　and do not despise him in his merrymaking
　　38 : 4　and a sensible man will not despise them
2 Ma　1 : 27　look upon those who are rejected and despised
　　4 : 14　Despising the sanctuary and neglecting the sacrifices
2 Es　1 : 7　But they have angered me and despised my counsels
　　2 : 7　because they have despised my covenant
　　7 : 37　whose commandments you have despised !
　　7 : 79　and who have despised his law
　　8 : 56　but they despised the Most High
　　9 : 11　and did not understand but despised it
4 Ma　1 : 9　All of these, by despising sufferings that bring death
　　4 : 26　when, then, his decrees were despised by the people
　　5 : 10　you continue to despise me to your own hurt
　　5 : 21　for in either case the law is equally despised
　　6 : 21　and if we should be despised by the tyrant as unmanly
　　7 : 16　an aged man despised tortures even to death
　　9 : 6　that we young men should die despising your coercive tortures
　　13 : 1　Since, then, the 7 brothers despised sufferings even unto death
　　13 : 9　who despised the same ordeal of the furnace
　　14 : 1　so that they not only despised their agonies
　　14 : 11　since the mind of a woman despised even more diverse agonies
　　16 : 2　but also that a woman has despised the fiercest tortures

DESPITE   2
　Sir　pr.　despite our diligent labour in translating
4 Ma　4 : 1　When despite all manner of slander

DESPOIL   3 = 0.002 %
1 Ma　3 : 20　and to despoil us
　　5 : 3　He dealt them and despoiled them
　　5 : 22　and he despoiled them

DESSAU   1
2 Ma 14:16   and engaged them in battle at a village called Dessau

DESTINE   4 = 0.003 %
Tob 6:17   Do not be afraid, for she was destined for you from eternity
Wis 15:9   But he is not concerned that he is destined to die
   17:21   an image of the darkness that was destined to receive them
2 Es 10:10   and a multitude of them are destined for destruction

DESTITUTE   1
Sir 37:20   he will be destitute of all food

DESTROY   144 = 0.094 %
Jud 1:15   and he utterly destroyed him, to this day
   2:3   who had not obeyed his command should be destroyed
   2:24   and destroyed all the hilltop cities along the brook Abron
   2:27   and destroyed their flocks and herds
   3:8   to destroy all the gods of the land
   4:1   and how he had plundered and destroyed all their temples
   4:12   and the cities they had inherited to be destroyed
   5:15   and by their might destroyed all the inhabitants of Heshbon
   6:3   He will send his forces and will destroy them
   6:3   we the king's servants will destroy them as one man
   7:13   So thirst will destroy them, and they will give up their city
   8:15   or even to destroy us in the presence of our enemies
  11:15   on that very day they will be handed over to you to be destroyed
  13:14   but has destroyed our enemies by my hand this very night !
  14:13   in order to be destroyed completely
  15:4   to rush out upon their enemies to destroy them
Ad E 10:8   The nations are those that gathered to destroy
  13:6   be utterly destroyed by the sword of their enemies
  13:15   and they desire to destroy the inheritance
  13:17   do not destroy the mouth of those who praise thee
  14:9   and to destroy thy inheritance
  16:24   shall be destroyed in wrath with spear and fire
Wis 1:11   and a lying mouth destroys the soul
  12:6   thou didst will to destroy by the hands of our fathers
  12:8   to destroy them little by little
  12:9   or to destroy them at one blow
  16:5   and they were being destroyed
  16:19   to destroy the crops of the unrighteous land
  16:22   were being destroyed by the fire that blazed in the hail
  16:27   For what was not destroyed by fire
  18:5   and thou didst destroy them all together by a mighty flood
  18:12   their most valued children had been destroyed
  18:13   yet, when their first-born were destroyed
Sir 6:3   You will devour your leaves and destroy your fruit
   6:4   An evil soul will destroy him who has it
  10:13   and destroyed them utterly
  10:16   and has destroyed them to the foundations of the earth
  10:17   He has removed some of them and destroyed them
  16:9   for those destroyed in their sins
  21:2   Its teeth are lion's teeth, and destroy the souls of men
  22:27   so that my tongue may not destroy me !
  27:16   Whoever betrays secrets destroys confidence
  27:18   For as a man destroys his enemy
  27:18   so you have destroyed the friendship of your neighbour
  28:13   for he has destroyed many who were at peace
  28:14   and destroyed strong cities
  30:23   for sorrow has destroyed many, and there is no profit in it
  31:25   for wine has destroyed many
  36:7   destroy the adversary and wipe out the enemy
  45:19   and in the wrath of his anger they were destroyed
  46:6   he destroyed those who resisted
  47:22   nor destroy the posterity of him who loved him
  49:7   to pluck up and afflict and destroy
L Jr 6:14   though unable to destroy any one who offends it
Sus 13:59   that he may destroy you both
Bel 14:22   and gave Bel over to Daniel, who destroyed it and its temple
  14:28   he has destroyed Bel, and slain the dragon
1 Ma 1:30   and destroyed many people of Israel
   2:40   they will quickly destroy us from the earth
   3:8   he destroyed the ungodly out of the land
   3:20   to destroy us and our wives and our children
   3:35   to wipe out and destroy the strength of Israel
   3:39   to go into the land of Judah and destroy it
   3:52   And behold, the Gentiles are assembled against us to destroy us
   3:58   who have assembled against us to destroy us and our sanctuary
   5:2   and they determined to destroy the descendants of Jacob who lived among them
   5:2   So they began to kill and destroy among the people
   5:9   and planned to destroy them
   5:10   to destroy us
   5:13   and have destroyed about a 1,000 men there
   5:27   and take and destroy all these men in one day
   5:51   He destroyed every male by the edge of the sword
   6:12   and I sent to destroy the inhabitants of Judah without good reason
   6:19   So Judas decided to destroy them
   7:6   Judas and his brothers have destroyed all your friends

   7:26   and he commanded him to destroy the people
   8:9   The Greeks planned to come and destroy them
   8:11   as many as ever opposed them, they destroyed and enslaved
   9:73   and he destroyed the ungodly out of Israel
  11:4   and Azotus and its suburbs destroyed
  12:49   and the Great Plain to destroy all Jonathan's soldiers
  12:53   And all the nations round about them tried to destroy them
  13:1   to invade the land of Judah and destroy it
  13:6   out of hatred to destroy us
  13:20   After this Trypho came to invade the country and destroy it
  15:4   against those who have destroyed our country
  16:22   and he seized the men who came to destroy him and killed them
  16:22   for he had found out that they were seeking to destroy him
2 Ma 3:39   and he strikes and destroys those who come to do it injury
   4:11   and he destroyed the lawful ways of living
   5:14   Within the total of 3 days 80,000 were destroyed
   6:12   not to destroy but to discipline our people
   8:3   and to have mercy on the city which was being destroyed
   8:20   destroyed 120,000 and took much booty
  10:2   and also destroyed the sacred precincts
  10:23   he destroyed more than 20,000 in the 2 strongholds
  12:19   marched out and destroyed those whom Timothy had left in the stronghold
  12:23   and destroyed as many as 30,000 men
  15:2   Do not destroy so savagely and barbarously
1 Es 1:56   and utterly destroyed all its glorious things
   4:44   which Cyrus set apart when he began to destroy Babylon
   6:33   destroy every king and nation
   8:88   to destroy us without leaving a root or seed or name ?
P Ma 13   forgive me ! Do not destroy me with my transgressions !
3 Ma 2:4   You destroyed those who in the past committed injustice
   2:4   whom you destroyed by bringing upon them a boundless flood
   4:14   and at the end to be destroyed in the space of a single day
   5:40   ordering now for a 3rd time that they be destroyed
   6:4   you destroyed together with his arrogant army
   6:10   and destroy us, Lord, by whatever fate you choose
   6:21   and began trampling and destroying them
   6:34   that the Jews would be destroyed and become food for birds
   7:12   they might destroy those everywhere in his kingdom
   7:15   since they had destroyed the profaners
2 Es 1:11   I have destroyed all nations before them
   3:9   and destroy them
   3:30   and hast destroyed thy people, and hast preserved thy enemies
   8:14   If then you wilt suddenly and quickly destroy him
   8:29   Let it not be thy will to destroy those
   8:59   For the Most High did not intend that men should be destroyed
   9:34   or what was put in is destroyed
   9:35   they are destroyed, but the things that held them remain
  10:21   our altar thrown down, our temple destroyed
  11:42   you have destroyed the dwellings of those who brought forth fruit
  12:33   then he will destroy them
  13:28   yet destroying the onrushing multitude
  13:38   and will destroy them without effort by the law
  13:49   Therefore when he destroys the multitude of the nations
  15:11   and will destroy all its land
  15:18   the houses shall be destroyed
  15:33   and destroy one of them
  15:40   shall rise, to destroy all the earth and its inhabitants
  15:42   And they shall destroy cities and walls
  15:43   and shall destroy her
  15:45   And those who survive shall serve those who have destroyed her
  15:60   and shall destroy a part of your land
  16:71   but plundering and destroying those
  16:72   For they shall destroy and plunder their goods
4 Ma 1:6   and it is not for the purpose of destroying them
   6:14   Eleazar, why are you so irrationally destroying yourself
   8:9   you will compel me to destroy each and every one of you
   8:19   and this arrogance that threatens to destroy us ?
  11:4   for what act of ours are you destroying us in this way ?
  17:9   who wished to destroy the way of life of the Hebrews

DESTROYER   3 = 0.002 %
Wis 18:25   To these the destroyer yielded, these he feared
4 Ma 2:14   but one preserves the property of enemies from the destroyers
  18:8   nor did the destroyer, the deceitful serpent

DESTRUCTION   57 = 0.037 %
Tob 14:15   But before he died he heard of the destruction of Nineveh
Jud 7:25   with thirst and utter destruction
  11:22   to lend strength to our hands and to bring destruction
  13:5   for the destruction of the enemies
  13:16   it was my face that tricked him to his destruction
Ad E 16:13   asked for the destruction of Mordecai
  16:21   instead of a day of destruction for them
  16:23   it may be a reminder of destruction
Wis 1:12   nor bring on destruction by the works of your hands
   3:3   and their going from us to be their destruction
   5:7   We took our fill of the paths of lawlessness and destruction
  12:12   for the destruction of nations which thou didst make ?

	18 : 7	and the destruction of their enemies
Sir	**9 : 9**	and in blood you be plunged into destruction
	16 : 9	He showed no pity for a nation devoted to destruction
	28 : 6	remember destruction and death
	31 : 6	and their destruction has met them face to face
	36 : 9	and may those who harm thy people meet destruction
	39 : 30	and the sword that punishes the ungodly with destruction
	41 : 10	so the ungodly go from curse to destruction
	48 : 6	who brought kings down to destruction
	51 : 2	and hast delivered my body from destruction
	51 : 12	for thou didst save me from destruction
Bar	**4 : 6**	It was not for destruction that you were sold to the nations
	4 : 25	but you will soon see their destruction
Bel	**14 : 42**	and threw into the den the men who had attempted his destruction
1 Ma	**3 : 42**	to do to the people to cause their final destruction
	3 : 43	Let us repair the destruction of our people
	4 : 32	let them tremble in their destruction
	5 : 5	and he encamped against them, vowed their complete destruction
	15 : 31	and for the destruction that you have caused
2 Ma	**5 : 13**	destruction of boys, women, and children
	8 : 4	and to remember also the lawless destruction of the innocent babies
	8 : 35	having succeeded chiefly in the destruction of his own army !
	12 : 27	After the rout and destruction of these
	13 : 6	There they all push to destruction
3 Ma	**4 : 2**	and they groaned because of the unexpected destruction
	5 : 5	convinced that the whole nation would experience its final destruction
	5 : 20	for the destruction of the lawless Jews !
	5 : 38	for the destruction of the Jews tomorrow !
	5 : 47	the grievous and pitiful destruction of the aforementioned people
	6 : 11	at the destruction of your beloved people
	6 : 23	and saw them all fallen headlong to destruction
	6 : 30	to meet their destruction
	6 : 31	which had been prepared for their destruction and burial
	6 : 38	and their destruction was set
2 Es	**1 : 16**	at the destruction of your enemies
	3 : 1	In the 30th year after the destruction of our city
	7 : 131	Therefore there shall not be grief at their destruction
	8 : 38	or about their death, their judgment, or their destruction
	10 : 10	and a multitude of them are destined for destruction
	10 : 48	that was the destruction which befell Jerusalem
	15 : 5	the sword and famine and death and destruction
	15 : 49	and bring you to destruction and death
	16 : 2	for your destruction is at hand
4 Ma	**10 : 15**	by the eternal destruction of the tyrant
	15 : 24	Although she witnessed the destruction of 7 children

DESTRUCTIVE 1

Wis	**1 : 14**	and there is no destructive poison in them

DETACHMENT 1

1 Ma	**4 : 19**	a detachment appeared, coming out of the hills

DETAIL, subst. 7 = 0.005 %

Ad E	**11 : 12**	and sought all day to understand it in every detail
2 Ma	**2 : 28**	leaving the responsibility for exact details to the compiler
	2 : 30	and to take trouble with details
	11 : 20	And concerning these matters and their details
	14 : 9	with the details of this matter
3 Ma	**4 : 13**	not omitting any detail of their punishment
4 Ma	**4 : 4**	When Apollonius learned the details of these things

DETAIL, verb 1

1 Ma	**4 : 41**	Then Judas detailed men

DETAIN 2

Tob	**10 : 2**	he said, Is it possible that he has been detained ?
1 Ma	**13 : 15**	that we are detaining him

DETECT 2

Sir	**36 : 19**	so an intelligent mind detects false words
3 Ma	**3 : 29**	Every place detected sheltering a Jew

DETERMINE 22 = 0.014 %

Jud	**11 : 12**	they have planned to kill their cattle and determined
	12 : 4	what he has determined to do
Ad E	**11 : 12**	Mordecai saw in this dream what God had determined to do
	13 : 2	I have determined to settle the lives of my subjects in lasting tranquillity
Wis	**8 : 9**	Therefore I determined to take her to live with me
Sir	**16 : 26**	and when he made them, he determined their divisions
	44 : 23	he determined his portions
1 Ma	**1 : 16**	he determined to become king of the land of Egypt
	3 : 31	and determined to go to Persia
	4 : 59	determined that every year at that season
	5 : 2	and they determined to destroy the descendants of Jacob who lived among them
	5 : 16	to determine what they should do for their brethren

	8 : 30	both parties shall determine to add or delete anything
	11 : 33	we have determined to do good
	16 : 13	he determined to get control of the country
2 Ma	**8 : 10**	Nicanor determined to make up for the king
	13 : 13	he determined to march out
	15 : 6	had determined to erect a public monument of victory
	15 : 17	they determined not to carry on a campaign
3 Ma	**1 : 2**	determined to carry out the plot he had devised
	1 : 26	determined to bring the aforesaid plan to a conclusion
2 Es	**7 : 42**	by which all shall see what has been determined for them

DETEST 3 = 0.002 %

Sir	**7 : 26**	but do not trust yourself to one whom you detest
	20 : 5	while another is detested for being too talkative
1 Ma	**7 : 26**	who hated and detested Israel

DETESTABLE 1

Wis	**12 : 4**	thou didst hate for their detestable practices

DEVASTATE 3 = 0.002 %

1 Ma	**15 : 4**	and those who have devastated many cities in my kingdom
	15 : 29	You have devastated their territory
2 Es	**15 : 30**	and shall devastate a portion of the land of the Assyrians with their teeth

DEVASTATED 1

2 Es	**15 : 60**	as they return from devastated Babylon

DEVICE 7 = 0.005 %

Sir	**1 : 6**	Her clever devices – who knows them ?
	35 : 19	and the works of men according to their devices
	42 : 18	and considers their crafty devices
3 Ma	**5 : 45**	and had been equipped with frightful devices
2 Es	**9 : 20**	because of the devices of those who had come into it
	15 : 48	You have imitated that hateful harlot in all her deeds and devices
4 Ma	**8 : 15**	and saw the dreadful devices

DEVIL 1

Wis	**2 : 24**	but through the devil's envy death entered the world

DEVISE 15 = 0.010 %

Wis	**3 : 14**	and who has not devised wicked things against the Lord
Sir	**7 : 12**	Do not devise a lie against your brother
	11 : 33	Beware of a scoundrel, for he devises evil
	13 : 26	but to devise proverbs requires painful thinking
	17 : 31	So flesh and blood devise evil
1 Ma	**11 : 8**	and he kept devising evil designs against Alexander
	13 : 29	And for the pyramids he devised an elaborate setting
2 Ma	**7 : 23**	and devised the origin of all things
3 Ma	**1 : 2**	determined to carry out the plot he had devised
	5 : 22	in sleep as in devising all sorts of insults
	5 : 28	a forgetfulness of the things he had previously devised
	6 : 22	because of the things that he had devised beforehand
	6 : 24	by secretly devising acts of no advantage to the kingdom
	7 : 9	For you should know that if we devise any evil against them
2 Es	**7 : 22**	they devised for themselves vain thoughts

DEVOID 2

Ad E	**16 : 10**	and quite devoid of our kindliness
Sir	**16 : 23**	This is what one devoid of understanding thinks

DEVOTE 11 = 0.007 %

Wis	**14 : 30**	in devoting themselves to idols
Sir	**pr.**	my grandfather Jesus, after devoting himself
	pr.	that I should myself devote some pains and labour
	7 : 20	or a hired labourer who devotes himself to you
	16 : 9	He showed no pity for a nation devoted to destruction
	31 : 7	It is a stumbling block to those who are devoted to it
	39 : 1	On the other hand he who devotes himself
1 Ma	**4 : 42**	He chose blameless priests devoted to the law
2 Ma	**2 : 28**	while devoting our effort
2 Es	**13 : 55**	for you have devoted your life to wisdom
4 Ma	**15 : 5**	they are the more devoted to their children

DEVOTION 3 = 0.002 %

Jud	**8 : 8**	for she feared God with great devotion
4 Ma	**14 : 6**	as though moved by an immortal spirit of devotion
	15 : 17	O woman, who alone gave birth to such complete devotion !

DEVOUR 15 = 0.010 %

Jud	**5 : 24**	and they will be devoured by your vast army
	10 : 12	for they are about to be handed over to you to be devoured
Sir	**6 : 3**	You will devour your leaves and destroy your fruit
	51 : 3	from the gnashings of teeth about to devour me
L Jr	**6 : 20**	when worms from the earth devour them and their robes
Bel	**14 : 21**	and devour what was on the table
	14 : 32	so that they might devour Daniel
	14 : 42	and they were devoured immediately before his eyes
2 Ma	**2 : 10**	and fire came down from heaven and devoured the sacrifices

2 Es	**6**:57	domineer over us and devour us
	11:31	and it devoured the 2 little wings which were planning to reign
	11:35	the head on the right side devoured the one on the left
	12:27	the sword shall devour them
	12:28	For the sword of one shall devour him who was with him
	15:62	And they shall devour you and your cities

DEVOUT 13 = 0.008 %

Jud	**8**:31	So pray for us, since you are a devout woman
4 Ma	**1**:1	that is, whether devout reason is sovereign over the emotions
	6:31	Admittedly, then, devout reason is sovereign over the emotions
	7:4	with the shield of his devout reason
	7:16	most certainly devout reason is governor of the emotions
	8:1	by following a philosophy in accordance with devout reason
	11:23	and enemy of those who are truly devout
	13:1	that devout reason is sovereign over the emotions
	15:23	But devout reason, giving her heart a man's courage
	16:1	it must be admitted that devout reason
	16:4	But the mother quenched so many and such great emotions by devout reason
	17:22	And through the blood of those devout ones
	18:2	knowing that devout reason is master of all emotions

DEW 7 = 0.005 %

Wis	**11**:22	and like a drop of morning dew that falls upon the ground
Sir	**18**:16	Does not the dew assuage the scorching heat ?
	43:22	when the dew appears, it refreshes from the heat
P Az	**42**	Bless the Lord, all rain and dew
	46	Bless the Lord, dews and snows
3 Ma	**6**:6	moistening the fiery furnace with dew
2 Es	**7**:41	or frost or cold or hail or rain or dew

DIADEM 4 = 0.003 %

Wis	**5**:16	and a beautiful diadem from the hand of the Lord
	18:24	and thy majesty on the diadem upon his head
Sir	**47**:6	when the glorious diadem was bestowed upon him
Bar	**5**:2	put on your head the diadem of the glory of the Everlasting

DIAGNOSIS 1

Sir	**38**:14	that he should grant them success in diagnosis

DICTATE 1

2 Es	**14**:42	and by turns they wrote what was dictated

DIE 139 = 0.091 %

Tob	**1**:15	But when Shalmaneser died
	3:6	For it is better for me to die than to live
	4:2	so that I may explain to him about the money before I die ?
	4:3	My son, when I die, bury me
	4:4	When she dies, bury her beside me in the same grave
	6:13	and that each died in the bridal chamber
	6:14	I will die as those before me did
	6:14	So now I fear that I may die
	7:11	and when each came to her he died in the night
	8:10	with the thought, Perhaps he too will die
	8:21	and that the rest would be his when my wife and I die
	10:2	Or is it possible that Gabael has died
	10:11	The God of heaven will prosper you, my children, before I die
	11:9	now I am ready to die
	14:11	As he said this he died in his bed
	14:12	And when Anna died he buried her with his father
	14:14	He died in Ecbatana of Media at the age of a 127 years
	14:15	But before he died he heard of the destruction of Nineveh
Jud	**6**:8	and you will not die until you perish along with them
	8:2	had died during the barley harvest
	8:3	and took to his bed and died in Bethulia his city
	16:22	after Manasseh her husband died
	16:23	She died in Bethulia
	16:24	Before she died she distributed her property
Ad E	**15**:10	you shall not die, for our law applies only to the people. Come near
Wis	**3**:2	In the eyes of the foolish they seemed to have died
	3:18	If they die young, they will have no hope
	4:7	But the righteous man, though he die early, will be at rest
	4:16	The righteous man who has died
	15:9	But he is not concerned that he is destined to die
	18:18	made known why they were dying
Sir	**8**:7	remember that we all must die
	10:10	the king of today will die tomorrow
	11:19	until he leaves them to others and dies
	14:13	Do good to a friend before you die
	14:17	for the decree from of old is, You must surely die !
	14:18	one dies and another is born
	16:3	and to die childless is better than to have ungodly children
	19:10	Have you heard a word ? Let it die with you
	23:17	he will never cease until he dies
	25:24	and because of her we all die
	30:4	The father may die, and yet he is not dead
	30:5	and when he died he was not grieved
	37:31	Many have died of gluttony

	40:28	it is better to die than to beg
	41:9	and when you die, a curse is your lot
Bar	**4**:1	and those who forsake her will die
L Jr	**6**:32	as some do at a funeral feast for a man who has died
Sus	**13**:43	And now I am to die !
Bel	**14**:8	If you do not tell me who is eating these provisions, you shall die
	14:9	But if you prove that Bel is eating them, Daniel shall die
	14:12	if you do not find that Bel has eaten it all, we will die
1 Ma	**1**:5	After this he fell sick and perceived that he was dying
	1:7	And after Alexander had reigned 12 years, he died
	1:50	And whoever does not obey the command of the king shall die
	1:63	They chose to die rather than to be defiled by food
	1:63	and they did die
	2:37	for they said, Let us all die in our innocence
	2:38	and they died, with their wives and children and cattle
	2:41	let us not all die as our brethren died
	2:49	Now the days drew near for Mattathias to die
	2:70	He died in the 146th year
	3:59	It is better for us to die in battle
	4:35	and how ready they were either to live or to die nobly
	6:9	and he concluded that he was dying
	6:16	Thus Antiochus the king died there in the 149th year
	6:46	but it fell to the ground upon him and there he died
	9:10	If our time has come, let us die bravely for our brethren
	9:56	And Alcimus died at that time in great agony
	11:18	But King Ptolemy died 3 days later
	14:16	that Jonathan had died
2 Ma	**4**:7	When Seleucus died
	5:9	and he who had driven many from their own country into exile died in exile
	6:26	yet whether I live or die
	6:28	of how to die a good death willingly and nobly
	6:30	When he was about to die under the blows
	6:31	So in this way he died
	7:2	For we are ready to die
	7:5	but the brothers and their mother encouraged one another to die nobly
	7:7	After the first brother had died in this way
	7:9	because we have died for his laws
	7:13	When he too had died
	7:14	One cannot but choose to die at the hands of men
	7:18	And when he was about to die, he said
	7:40	So he died in his integrity
	7:41	Last of all, the mother died, after her sons
	8:21	and made them ready to die for their laws and their country
	13:7	that Menelaus the lawbreaker died
	14:42	preferring to die nobly rather than to fall
1 Es	**1**:31	and after he was brought back to Jerusalem he died
3 Ma	**1**:23	and die courageously for the ancestral law
2 Es	**1**:18	than to die in this wilderness
	7:29	And after these years my son the Messiah shall die
	7:78	that a man shall die
	8:58	though knowing full well that they must die
	10:1	he fell down and died
	10:4	but without ceasing mourn and fast until I die
	10:18	I will not go into the city, but I will die here
	10:34	only do not forsake me, lest I die before my time
	10:48	When my son entered his wedding chamber he died
	12:26	one of the kings shall die in his bed, but in agonies
	12:45	For we are no better than those who died there
	13:24	are more blessed than those who have died
	15:4	For every unbeliever shall die in his unbelief
	15:57	Your children shall die of hunger
	16:22	and those who survive the famine shall die by the sword
4 Ma	**1**:8	of those who died for the sake of virtue
	1:10	died for the sake of nobility and goodness
	4:15	When King Seleucus died
	4:23	they should die
	6:22	die nobly for your religion !
	6:27	I am dying in burning torments for the sake of the law
	6:30	the holy man died nobly in his tortures
	7:19	do not die to God, but live in God
	8:11	nothing remains for you but to die on the rack ?
	9:1	For we are ready to die
	9:6	that we young men should die despising your coercive tortures
	10:2	that the same father begot me and those who died
	10:9	When he was about to die, he said
	10:12	When he also had died in a manner worthy of his brothers
	11:1	When this one died also, after being cruelly tortured
	11:13	After he too had died, the 6th, a mere boy, was led in
	11:15	we ought likewise to die for the same principles
	11:22	I also, equipped with nobility, will die with my brothers
	12:1	had died a blessed death
	12:3	for they died in torments because of their disobedience
	12:4	will be miserably tortured and die before your time
	12:14	Surely they by dying nobly fulfilled their service to God
	12:15	Then because he too was about to die, he said
	13:9	Brothers, let us die like brothers for the sake of the law
	13:17	For if we so die, Abraham and Isaac and Jacob will welcome us

13:18   or betray the brothers who have died before us
16:11   Nor when I die, shall I have any of my sons to bury me
16:12   nor did she dissuade any of them from dying
16:12   nor did she grieve as they were dying
16:24   to die rather than violate God's commandment
16:25   They knew also that those who die for the sake of God live in God
18:9   and when these sons had grown up their father died

DIE down   1
Jud 6:1   When the disturbance made by the men outside the council died down

DIFFER   2
Sir pr.   differ not a little as originally expressed
3 Ma 6:26   those who from the beginning differed from all nations

DIFFERENCE   2
1 Ma 3:18   there is no difference between saving by many or by few
3 Ma 3:7   instead they gossiped about the differences in worship and foods

DIFFERENT   5 = 0.003 %
Wis 7:5   For no king has had a different beginning of existence
Sir 33:8   and he appointed the different seasons and feasts
33:11   and appointed their different ways
2 Es 5:53   are different from those born during the time of old age
6:26   and converted to a different spirit

DIFFICULT   5 = 0.003 %
Sir 3:21   Seek not what is too difficult for you
2 Ma 12:21   for that place was hard to besiege and difficult of access
2 Es 7:14   pass through the difficult and vain experiences
7:18   The righteous therefore can endure difficult circumstances
7:18   have suffered the difficult circumstances

DIFFICULTY   6 = 0.004 %
Wis 6:14   He who rises early to seek her will have no difficulty
17:11   it has always exaggerated the difficulties
1 Ma 13:3   and the difficulties which we have seen
2 Ma 2:24   and the difficulty there is
3 Ma 5:15   And when he had with difficulty roused him, he pointed out
2 Es 9:21   And I saw and spared some with great difficulty

DIG   3 = 0.002 %
Tob 2:7   and dug a grave and buried the body
8:9   But Raguel arose and went and dug a grave
Sir 27:26   He who digs a pit will fall into it

DIGNITY   4 = 0.003 %
Sir 45:24   should have the dignity of the priesthood for ever
2 Ma 6:23   worthy of his years and the dignity of his old age
15:13   distinguished by his grey hair and dignity
3 Ma 2:1   bending his knees and extending his hands with calm dignity

DILIGENCE   2
Sir 11:18   There is a man who is rich through his diligence and self-denial
1 Es 6:34   that it be done with all diligence as here prescribed

DILIGENT   2
Sir pr.   despite our diligent labour in translating
38:27   each is diligent in making a great variety

DIM, adj.   1
Sir 18:18   and the gift of a grudging man makes the eyes dim

DIMINISH   3 = 0.002 %
Sir 18:6   It is not possible to diminish or increase them
31:4   The poor man toils as his livelihood diminishes
Bar 2:34   and I will increase them, and they will not be diminished

DINE   1
Sir 9:9   Never dine with another man's wife

DINNER   5 = 0.003 %
Tob 2:1   a good dinner was prepared for me and I sat down to eat
12:13   When you did not hesitate to rise and to leave your dinner
Sir 9:16   Let righteous men be your dinner companions
Bel 14:34   Take the dinner which you have to Babylon
14:37   Take the dinner which God has sent you

DIONYSUS   4 = 0.003 %
2 Ma 6:7   and when the feast of Dionysus came
6:7   in honour of Dionysus, wearing wreaths of ivy
14:33   and I will build here a splendid temple to Dionysus
3 Ma 2:29   with the ivy-leaf symbol of Dionysus

DIOSCORINTHIUS   1
2 Ma 11:21   Farewell. The 148th year, Dioscorinthius 24th

DIP out   1
2 Ma 1:20   he ordered them to dip it out and bring it

DIRECT, verb   20 = 0.013 %
Jud 11:7   who has sent you to direct every living soul
12:8   to direct her way for the raising up of her people
Ad E 16:16   who has directed the kingdom both for us
Wis 6:9   To you then, O monarchs, my words are directed
Sir 6:17   Whoever fears the Lord directs his friendship aright
25:26   If she does not go as you direct
37:15   that he may direct your way in truth
38:10   Give up your faults and direct your hands aright
39:7   He will direct his counsel and knowledge aright
49:9   and did good to those who directed their ways aright
51:20   I directed my soul to her
1 Ma 1:44   he directed them to follow customs strange to the land
4:47   Then they took unhewn stones, as the law directs
4:53   they rose and offered sacrifice, as the law directs
10:11   He directed those who were doing the work
2 Ma 3:14   to direct the inspection of these funds
3 Ma 6:1   directed the elders around him
2 Es 9:26   So I went, as he directed me
10:32   I did as you directed, and went out into the field
13:26   and he will direct those who are left

DIRECT, adj.   1
4 Ma 14:9   yes, not only heard the direct word of threat

DIRECTION   4 = 0.003 %
1 Es 1:5   in accordance with the directions of David king of Israel
5:49   in accordance with the directions in the book of Moses the man of God
5:60   according to the directions of David king of Israel
6:22   let him send us directions concerning these things

DIRGE   3 = 0.002 %
1 Ma 9:41   and the voice of their musicians into a funeral dirge
3 Ma 5:25   and with most tearful supplication and mournful dirges
6:32   They ceased their chanting of dirges

DIRT   1
Wis 15:10   His heart is ashes, his hope is cheaper than dirt

DISABLE   1
2 Ma 8:24   and wounded and disabled most of Nicanor's army

DISAGREEMENT   1
2 Ma 3:4   had a disagreement with the high priest

DISAPPEAR   14 = 0.009 %
Sir 39:9   his memory will not disappear
2 Es 11:13   And while it was reigning it came to its end and disappeared
11:14   so that it disappeared like the first
11:16   I announce this to you before you disappear
11:18   and it also disappeared
11:20   There were some of them that ruled, yet disappeared suddenly
11:22   the 12 wings and the 2 little wings disappeared
11:26   one was set up, but suddenly disappeared
11:27   a 2nd also, and this disappeared more quickly than the first
11:33   the middle head also suddenly disappeared
11:45   Therefore you will surely disappear, you eagle
12:2   and behold, the remaining head disappeared
12:3   And I looked, and behold, they also disappeared
12:26   As for your seeing that the large head disappeared

DISASTER   5 = 0.003 %
Wis 18:21   he withstood the anger and put an end to the disaster
1 Ma 3:29   because of the dissension and disaster
8:4   and inflicted great disaster upon them
2 Ma 4:16   For this reason heavy disaster overtook them
4 Ma 3:21   and caused many and various disasters

DISBELIEVE   2
Wis 18:13   For though they had disbelieved everything
2 Es 16:36   do not disbelieve what the Lord says

DISCERN   6 = 0.004 %
Wis 2:22   nor discern the prize for blameless souls
6:12   and she is easily discerned by those who love her
9:13   Or who can discern what the Lord wills ?
Sir 1:19   he rained down knowledge and discerning comprehension
Bar 3:14   that you may at the same time discern
Sus 13:42   O eternal God, who dost discern what is secret

DISCIPLINE, subst.   12 = 0.008 %
Sir 4:17   and will torment him by her discipline until she trusts him
17:15   Whom, being his first-born, he brings up with discipline
18:14   He has compassion on those who accept his discipline
19:19   is life-giving discipline
22:6   but chastising and discipline are wisdom at all times

23 : 2	and the discipline of wisdom over my mind !
32 : 14	He who fears the Lord will accept his discipline
33 : 24	bread and discipline and work for a servant
38 : 33	they cannot expound discipline or judgment
42 : 5	and of much discipline of children
Bar 4 : 13	nor tread the paths of discipline in his righteousness
4 Ma 13 : 22	and from both general education and our discipline in the law of God

DISCIPLINE, verb · · · · · · · · · · 11 = 0.007 %

Wis 3 : 5	Having been disciplined a little
11 : 9	though they were being disciplined in mercy
Sir 7 : 23	Do you have children ? Discipline them
23 : 15	will never become disciplined all his days
30 : 2	He who disciplines his son will profit by him
30 : 13	Discipline your son and take pains with him
2 Ma 6 : 12	not to destroy but to discipline our people
6 : 16	Though he disciplines us with calamities
7 : 33	to rebuke and discipline us
10 : 4	they might be disciplined by him with forbearance
2 Es 14 : 34	and discipline your hearts

DISCIPLINED · · · · · · · · · · · · · 3 = 0.002 %

Tob 4 : 14	and be disciplined in all your conduct
Wis 1 : 5	For a holy and disciplined spirit will flee from deceit
Sir 26 : 14	and there is nothing so precious as a disciplined soul

DISCLOSE · · · · · · · · · · · · · · 12 = 0.008 %

Sir 6 : 9	and will disclose a quarrel to your disgrace
19 : 8	and unless it would be a sin for you, do not disclose it
27 : 6	The fruit discloses the cultivation of a tree
27 : 6	so the expression of a thought discloses the cultivation of a man's mind
Sus 13 : 11	for they were ashamed to disclose their lustful desire to possess her
1 Ma 7 : 31	When Nicanor learned that his plan had been disclosed
2 Ma 2 : 8	And then the Lord will disclose these things
3 : 16	disclosed the anguish of his soul
2 Es 4 : 43	will be disclosed to you
7 : 26	and the land which now is hidden shall be disclosed
7 : 36	and the furnace of hell shall be disclosed
14 : 35	and the deeds of the ungodly will be disclosed

DISCLOSURE · · · · · · · · · · · · · · · · · 2

Sir 22 : 22	but as for reviling, arrogance, disclosure of secrets
2 Ma 3 : 9	he told about the disclosure that had been made

DISCORDANT · · · · · · · · · · · · · · · · · 1

Wis 18 : 10	But the discordant cry of their enemies echoed back

DISCOURAGE · · · · · · · · · · · · · · · · · 1

1 Ma 4 : 27	When he heard it, he was perplexed and discouraged

DISCOURSE · · · · · · · · · · · · · 3 = 0.002 %

Sir 8 : 8	Do not slight the discourse of the sages
8 : 9	Do not disregard the discourse of the aged
39 : 2	he will preserve the discourse of notable men

DISCOVER · · · · · · · · · · · · · · · · · 1

2 Es 5 : 40	so you cannot discover my judgment

DISCREET · · · · · · · · · · · · · · · · · 1

Sir 21 : 24	and a discreet man is grieved by the disgrace

DISCRETION · · · · · · · · · · · · · · · · · 2

Sir 33 : 29	and do nothing without discretion
1 Ma 8 : 30	they shall do so at their discretion

DISCUS · · · · · · · · · · · · · · · · · 1

2 Ma 4 : 14	in the wrestling arena after the call to the discus

DISCUSS · · · · · · · · · · · · · · · · · 2

2 Ma 2 : 30	to occupy the ground and to discuss matters from every side
4 Ma 1 : 1	The subject that I am about to discuss is most philosophical

DISCUSSION · · · · · · · · · · · · · · · · · 1

Sir 9 : 15	and let all your discussion be about the law of the Most High

DISDAIN · · · · · · · · · · · · · · 7 = 0.005 %

Tob 4 : 13	and in your heart do not disdain your brethren
Jud 8 : 20	and therefore we hope that he will not disdain us
Sir 8 : 6	Do not disdain a man when he is old
2 Ma 4 : 15	disdaining the honours prized by their fathers
7 : 11	and because of his laws I disdain them
3 Ma 3 : 22	and disdained what is good
4 Ma 15 : 8	yet because of the fear of God she disdained

DISDAINFULLY · · · · · · · · · · · · · · · · · 1

Sir 22 : 10	Children who are disdainfully and boorishly haughty

114

DISEASE · · · · · · · · · · · · · · · · · 1

2 Es 3 : 22	Thus the disease became permanent

DISGRACE, verb · · · · · · · · · · · · 7 = 0.005 %

Jud 9 : 2	and polluted her womb to disgrace her
Sir 7 : 7	and do not disgrace yourself among the people
8 : 4	lest your ancestors be disgraced
11 : 6	Many rulers have been greatly disgraced
22 : 5	An impudent daughter disgraces father and husband
P Az 21	let them be disgraced and deprived of all power and dominion
2 Ma 6 : 25	while I defile and disgrace my old age

DISGRACE, subst. · · · · · · · · · · 16 = 0.010 %

Tob 3 : 10	if I do this, it will be a disgrace to him
Jud 12 : 12	For it will be a disgrace if we let such a woman go
14 : 18	One Hebrew woman has brought disgrace
Sir 3 : 11	and it is a disgrace for children
6 : 9	and will disclose a quarrel to your disgrace
20 : 26	The disposition of a liar brings disgrace
21 : 24	and a discreet man is grieved by the disgrace
22 : 1	and every one hisses at his disgrace
22 : 3	It is a disgrace to be the father of an undisciplined son
23 : 26	and her disgrace will not be blotted out
25 : 22	There is wrath and impudence and great disgrace
42 : 14	and it is a woman who brings shame and disgrace
P Az 10	shame and disgrace have befallen thy servants and worshippers
2 Ma 5 : 7	and in the end got only disgrace from his conspiracy
3 Ma 2 : 27	He proposed to inflict public disgrace
6 : 34	groaned as they themselves were overcome by disgrace

DISGRACEFUL · · · · · · · · · · · · · · · · · 1

2 Ma 11 : 12	and Lysias himself escaped by disgraceful flight

DISGRACEFULLY · · · · · · · · · · · · · · · · · 2

Sir 26 : 24	A shameless woman constantly acts disgracefully
3 Ma 6 : 31	Accordingly those disgracefully treated and near to death

DISH · · · · · · · · · · · · · · · 5 = 0.003 %

Jud 12 : 1	where his silver dishes were kept
15 : 11	and all his silver dishes
Sir 31 : 14	and do not crowd your neighbour at the dish
L Jr 6 : 17	For just as one's dish is useless when it is broken
2 Es 9 : 34	or any dish food or drink

DISHEVELLED, DISHEVELED · · · · · · · · · · · 1

3 Ma 1 : 4	her locks all dishevelled

DISHONEST · · · · · · · · · · · · · · · · · 1

Sir 5 : 8	Do not depend on dishonest wealth

DISHONOUR, DISHONOR, verb · · · · · · 6 = 0.004 %

Sir 3 : 10	Do not glorify yourself by dishonouring your father
10 : 29	And who will honour the man that dishonours his own life ?
10 : 31	And a man dishonoured in wealth, how much more in poverty !
26 : 26	but if she dishonours him
L Jr 6 : 40	Besides, even the Chaldeans themselves dishonour them
2 Es 5 : 28	and dishonoured the one root beyond the others

DISHONOUR, DISHONOR, subst. · · · · · · 6 = 0.004 %

Jud 8 : 23	but the Lord our God will turn it to dishonour
Sir 1 : 30	and thus bring dishonour upon yourself
3 : 10	for your father's dishonour is no glory to you
5 : 13	Glory and dishonour come from speaking
29 : 6	and instead of glory will repay him with dishonour
1 Ma 1 : 40	Her dishonour now grew as great as her glory

DISHONOURED, DISHONORED · · · · · · · · · · · 1

Wis 4 : 18	After this they will become dishonoured corpses

DISJOINT · · · · · · · · · · · · · · · · · 2

4 Ma 10 : 5	they disjointed his hands and feet with their instruments
11 : 10	and all his members were disjointed

DISLIKE · · · · · · · · · · · · · · · · · 1

Sir 21 : 15	when a reveller hears it, he dislikes it

DISLOCATE · · · · · · · · · · · · · · · · · 2

4 Ma 9 : 13	his limbs were dislocated
10 : 8	and while his vertebrae were being dislocated upon it

DISLOYAL · · · · · · · · · · · · · · · · · 1

2 Ma 14 : 26	He told him that Nicanor was disloyal to the government

DISMAL · · · · · · · · · · · · · · · · · 1

Wis 17 : 4	and dismal phantoms with gloomy faces appeared

DISMAY · · · · · · · · · · · · · · · · · 2

Jud 14 : 19	they rent their tunics and were greatly dismayed
2 Ma 13 : 23	he was dismayed, called in the Jews

DISMEMBER 2
2 Ma **1**:16 and dismembered them and cut off their heads
4 Ma **10**:5 dismembering him by prying his limbs from their sockets

DISMISS 8 = 0.005 %
Jud **7**:32 Then he dismissed the people to their various posts
Sus **13**:36 shut the garden doors, and dismissed the maids
1 Ma **11**:38 he dismissed all his troops, each man to his own place
12:45 Dismiss them now to their homes
2 Ma **7**:9 You accursed wretch, you dismiss us from this present life
14:23 but dismissed the flocks of people that had gathered
3 Ma **5**:34 and dismissed the assembled people
2 Es **9**:39 Then I dismissed the thoughts with which I had been engaged

DISMISSAL 2
3 Ma **6**:37 asking for dismissal to their homes
6:40 on which also they made the petition for their dismissal

DISOBEDIENCE 3 = 0.002 %
4 Ma **8**:9 But if by disobedience you rouse my anger
8:18 and venture upon a disobedience that brings death ?
12:3 for they died in torments because of their disobedience

DISOBEDIENT 4 = 0.003 %
Sir **16**:6 and in a disobedient nation wrath was kindled
47:21 and a disobedient kingdom arose out of Ephraim
Bar **1**:19 we have been disobedient to the Lord our God
4 Ma **9**:10 as at those who are disobedient

DISOBEY 13 = 0.008 %
Tob **3**:4 For they disobeyed thy commandments
Jud **2**:6 because they disobeyed my orders
Sir **1**:28 Do not disobey the fear of the Lord
2:15 Those who fear the Lord will not disobey his words
16:28 and they will never disobey his word
23:23 she has disobeyed the law of the Most High
30:12 lest he become stubborn and disobey you
Bar **1**:18 and have disobeyed him
1 Es **4**:5 and do not disobey the king's command
4:11 nor do they disobey him
4 Ma **8**:6 Just as I am able to punish those who disobey my orders
8:11 Will you not consider this, that if you disobey
8:21 and let us seriously consider that if we disobey we are dead !

DISORDER 5 = 0.003 %
Wis **14**:26 disorder in marriage, adultery, and debauchery
17:8 and disorders of a sick soul
2 Ma **9**:1 Antiochus had retreated in disorder
10:30 they were thrown into disorder and cut to pieces
3 Ma **3**:24 if a sudden disorder should later arise against us

DISORDERLY 1
3 Ma **1**:19 in a disorderly rush flocked together in the city

DISORGANIZE 1
2 Es **15**:32 then these shall be disorganized and silenced by their power

DISPATCH 1
2 Ma **4**:38 and there he dispatched the bloodthirsty fellow

DISPEL 1
4 Ma **5**:11 dispel your futile reasonings

DISPERSE 4 = 0.003 %
Tob **3**:4 in all the nations among which we have been dispersed
Wis **5**:14 it is dispersed like smoke before the wind
1 Ma **10**:83 and the cavalry was dispersed in the plain
3 Ma **2**:19 Wipe away our sins and disperse our errors

DISPLAY, verb 5 = 0.003 %
Sir **7**:5 nor display your wisdom before the king
32:4 do not display your cleverness out of season
1 Ma **7**:47 and brought them and displayed them just outside Jerusalem
2 Es **7**:104 and displays to all the seal of truth
4 Ma **8**:5 Not only do I advise you not to display the same madness

DISPLAY, subst. 1
Sir **10**:26 Do not make a display of your wisdom when you do your work

DISPLEASE 2
2 Ma **4**:35 were grieved and displeased at the unjust murder of the man
14:27 wrote to Nicanor, stating that he was displeased with the covenant

DISPOSE 5 = 0.003 %
2 Ma **5**:25 he pretended to be peaceably disposed
12:31 to be well disposed to their race in the future also
1 Es **8**:11 Let as many as are so disposed, therefore

DISPOSE (continued)
3 Ma **3**:23 who are sincerely disposed toward us
7:11 would never be favourably disposed

DISPOSITION 3 = 0.002 %
Jud **8**:29 for your heart's disposition is right
Sir **20**:26 The disposition of a liar brings disgrace
2 Ma **14**:5 and was asked about the disposition

DISREGARD 13 = 0.008 %
Jud **1**:11 disregarded the orders of Nebuchadnezzar
11:10 do not disregard what he said
Ad E **13**:4 and continually disregard the ordinances of the kings
Wis **3**:10 who disregarded the righteous man
Sir **8**:9 Do not disregard the discourse of the aged
14:8 he averts his face and disregards people
23:11 and if he disregards it, he sins doubly
31:22 Listen to me, my son, and do not disregard me
2 Ma **5**:17 and that therefore he was disregarding the holy place
2 Es **7**:20 which is set before them be disregarded !
4 Ma **4**:24 but saw that all his threats and punishments were being disregarded
15:23 strengthened her to disregard her temporal love for her children
15:24 this noble mother disregarded all these

DISSENSION 1
1 Ma **3**:29 because of the dissension and disaster

DISSOLVE 2
Wis **2**:3 and the spirit will dissolve like empty air
4 Ma **14**:8 encircled the sevenfold fear of tortures and dissolved it

DISSUADE 2
1 Ma **9**:9 But they tried to dissuade him, saying, We are not able
4 Ma **16**:12 nor did she dissuade any of them from dying

DISTANCE 4 = 0.003 %
Wis **14**:17 since they lived at a distance
Sir **13**:10 and do not remain at a distance, lest you be forgotten
2 Ma **8**:25 After pursuing them for some distance
10:27 and advanced a considerable distance from the city

DISTANT 3 = 0.002 %
1 Ma **8**:4 even though the place was far distant from them
2 Ma **12**:9 so that the glow of the light was seen in Jerusalem, 30 miles distant
2 Es **13**:41 and go to a more distant region

DISTINCTION 2
Sir **45**:12 a distinction to be prized, the work of an expert
2 Ma **6**:23 and the grey hairs which he had reached with distinction

DISTINGUISH 4 = 0.003 %
Ad E **13**:3 and is distinguished for his unchanging good will and steadfast fidelity
Sir **33**:8 By the Lord's decision they were distinguished
33:11 In the fulness of his knowledge the Lord distinguished them
2 Ma **15**:13 distinguished by his grey hair and dignity

DISTINGUISHED 1
1 Ma **3**:32 He left Lysias, a distinguished man of royal lineage

DISTORT 1
Sir **19**:25 and there are people who distort kindness to gain a verdict

DISTRACT 1
Sir **41**:2 very old and distracted over everything

DISTRACTION 1
Sir **41**:1 to a man without distractions

DISTRESS, subst. 17 = 0.011 %
Tob **3**:6 Command that I now be released from my distress
Ad E **11**:8 tribulation and distress
14:2 and put on the garments of distress and mourning
Sir **31**:20 The distress of sleeplessness
L Jr **6**:37 they cannot rescue a man who is in distress
Sus **13**:10 but they did not tell each other of their distress
1 Ma **2**:53 Joseph in the time of his distress kept the commandment
5:16 who were in distress and were being attacked by enemies
6:11 I said to myself, To what distress I have come !
9:27 Thus there was great distress in Israel
13:5 in any time of distress
2 Ma **1**:7 we Jews wrote to you, in the critical distress
3:14 There was no little distress throughout the whole city
15:19 were in no little distress
2 Es **6**:37 and my soul was in distress
9:45 and looked upon my low estate, and considered my distress
13:19 For they shall see great dangers and much distress

DISTRESS, verb   9 = 0.006 %
Tob	9 :4	and if I delay long he will be greatly distressed
	10 :3	And he was greatly distressed
	10 :5	Am I not distressed, my child, that I let you go
	13 :10	and love those within you who are distressed
Wis	11 :11	Whether absent or present, they were equally distressed
	17 :11	distressed by conscience
Bar	2 :18	but the person that is greatly distressed
1 Ma	9 :68	They distressed him greatly
2 Es	10 :50	seeing that you are sincerely grieved and profoundly distressed for her

DISTRIBUTE   7 = 0.005 %
Jud	16 :24	Before she died she distributed her property
Sir	17 :5	as 6th he distributed to them the gift of mind
	33 :23	in the hour of the death, distribute your inheritance
	44 :23	and distributed them among 12 tribes
1 Ma	3 :36	and distribute their land
	6 :35	And they distributed the beasts among the phalanxes
2 Ma	8 :28	and distributed the rest among themselves and their children

DISTRICT   9 = 0.006 %
Jud	4 :4	So they sent to every district of Samaria
	5 :5	that dwells in the nearby mountain district
1 Ma	10 :30	or from the 3 districts added to it
	10 :38	As for the 3 districts that have been added to Judea
	11 :28	to free Judea and the 3 districts of Samaria from tribute
	11 :34	and the 3 districts of Aphairema and Lydda and Rathamin
	11 :57	and set you over the 4 districts
3 Ma	3 :12	in Egypt and all its districts
	4 :3	What district or city, or what habitable place at all

DISTRUST, verb   1
Wis	1 :2	and manifests himself to those who do not distrust him

DISTRUSTFUL   1
2 Ma	8 :13	those who were cowardly and distrustful of God's justice

DISTURB   5 = 0.003 %
Wis	17 :9	For even if nothing disturbing frightened them
	18 :19	for the dreams which disturbed them forewarned them of this
Sir	28 :9	and a sinful man will disturb friends
2 Es	5 :33	Are you greatly disturbed in mind over Israel ?
	7 :15	But now why are you disturbed, seeing that you are to perish ?

DISTURBANCE   4 = 0.003 %
Jud	6 :1	When the disturbance made by the men outside the council died down
2 Ma	3 :30	was full of fear and disturbance
	11 :25	be free from disturbance
3 Ma	1 :23	and created a considerable disturbance in the holy place

DIVERSE   1
4 Ma	14 :11	since the mind of a woman despised even more diverse agonies

DIVEST   1
2 Es	14 :14	and divest yourself now of your weak nature

DIVIDE   14 = 0.009 %
Jud	9 :4	and all their booty to be divided among thy beloved sons
Wis	5 :12	the air, thus divided, comes together at once
Sir	14 :15	and what you acquired by toil to be divided by lot ?
	16 :16	and he divided his light and darkness with a plumb line
	42 :3	and of dividing the inheritance of friends
	47 :21	so that the sovereignty was divided
1 Ma	1 :6	and divided his kingdom among them while he was still alive
	9 :11	The cavalry was divided into 2 companies
	16 :7	Then he divided the army
2 Ma	8 :21	then he divided his army into 4 parts
	8 :30	and they divided very much plunder
2 Es	1 :21	I divided fertile lands among you :
	6 :41	and didst command him to divide and separate the waters
	14 :11	For the age is divided into 12 parts

DIVIDED   1
Sir	1 :28	do not approach him with a divided mind

DIVIDING   1
2 Es	6 :7	What will be the dividing of the times ?

DIVINATION   1
Sir	34 :5	Divinations and omens and dreams are folly

DIVINE, adj.   28 = 0.018 %
Wis	18 :9	and with one accord agreed to the divine law
2 Ma	3 :29	speechless because of the divine intervention
	4 :17	to show irreverence to the divine laws
3 Ma	7 :11	had transgressed the divine commandments
4 Ma	1 :16	Wisdom, next, is the knowledge of divine and human matters
	1 :17	by which we learn divine matters reverently

	4 :13	and not by divine justice
	4 :21	The divine justice was angered by these acts
	5 :16	to govern our lives by the divine law
	5 :18	Even if, as you suppose, our law were not truly divine
	5 :18	and we had wrongly held it to be divine
	6 :21	and not protect our divine law even to death
	7 :7	O man in harmony with the law and philosopher of divine life !
	7 :9	but by your deeds you made your words of divine philosophy credible
	8 :22	Also, divine justice will excuse us
	9 :9	will deservedly undergo from the divine justice
	9 :15	but because I protect the divine law
	9 :32	the judgments of the divine wrath
	10 :21	a tongue that has been melodious with divine hymns
	11 :27	but those of the divine law that are set over us
	13 :16	which is divine reason
	13 :19	which the divine all-wise Providence
	17 :11	Truly the contest in which they were engaged was divine
	17 :16	Who did not admire the athletes of the divine legislation ?
	17 :18	because of which they now stand before the divine throne
	17 :22	divine Providence preserved Israel
	18 :3	but also were deemed worthy to share in a divine inheritance
	18 :22	For these crimes divine justice pursued and will pursue the accursed tyrant

DIVISION   11 = 0.007 %
Jud	2 :15	and mustered the picked troops by divisions
Sir	16 :26	and when he made them, he determined their divisions
	17 :17	*For in the division of the nations of the whole earth*
1 Ma	4 :1	and this division moved out by night
	4 :4	while the division was still absent from the camp
2 Ma	8 :22	each to command a division, putting 1,500 men under each
	8 :23	then, leading the first division himself
	12 :20	But Maccabeus arranged his army in divisions
	12 :20	set men in command of the divisions
	12 :22	But when Judas' first division appeared
1 Es	1 :2	having placed the priests according to their divisions

DIVULGE   1
Sir	8 :18	for you do not know what he will divulge

DO   1122 = 0.731 %

DO away   3 = 0.002 %
1 Ma	14 :14	and did away with every lawless and wicked man
	16 :13	to do away with them
	16 :19	He sent other men to Gazara to do away with John

DOCUMENT   1
1 Ma	13 :42	in their documents and contracts

DOER   2
1 Ma	9 :23	all the doers of injustice appeared
2 Es	6 :19	and when I require from the doers of iniquity

DOG, subst.   5 = 0.003 %
Tob	5 :16	and the young man's dog was with them
	11 :4	So they went their way, and the dog went along behind them
Jud	11 :19	and not a dog will so much as open its mouth to growl at you
Sir	13 :18	What peace is there between a hyena and a dog ?
	26 :25	A headstrong wife is regarded as a dog

DOING   1
Wis	11 :13	they perceived it was the Lord's doing

DOK   1
1 Ma	16 :15	in the little stronghold called Dok, which he had built

DOMINANCE   2
4 Ma	1 :31	Self-control, then, is dominance over the desires
	6 :34	And it is right for us to acknowledge the dominance of reason

DOMINANT   1
4 Ma	1 :7	that reason is dominant over the emotions

DOMINATE   3 = 0.002 %
2 Es	11 :32	and with much oppression dominated its inhabitants
4 Ma	5 :38	but you shall not dominate my religious principles
	7 :20	when some persons appear to be dominated by their emotions

DOMINATION   3 = 0.002 %
4 Ma	1 :34	we abstain because of domination by reason
	3 :18	and by nobility of reason spurn all domination by the emotions
	6 :32	we would have testified to their domination

DOMINEER   1
2 Es	6 :57	domineer over us and devour us

DOMINION 12 = 0.008 %

Ad E	14 :12	O King of the gods and Master of all dominion !
Wis	1 :14	and the dominion of Hades is not on earth
	6 :3	For your dominion was given you from the Lord
	9 :2	to have dominion over the creatures thou hast made
Sir	16 :27	and their dominion for all generations
	17 :4	and granted them dominion over beasts and birds
	24 :11	and in Jerusalem was my dominion
P Az	21	let them be disgraced and deprived of all power and dominion
Bel	14 :5	and has dominion over all flesh
1 Ma	8 :24	in all their dominion
3 Ma	6 :24	you are now attempting to deprive of dominion and life
2 Es	3 :28	Is that why she has gained dominion over Zion ?

DON 1

1 Ma	14 :9	and the youths donned the glories and garments of war

DOOM, subst. 2

Sir	38 :22	Remember my doom, for yours is like it :
3 Ma	5 :2	so that the Jews might meet their doom

DOOM, verb 2

Wis	18 :15	into the midst of the land that was doomed, a stern warrior
3 Ma	5 :22	for those they thought to be doomed

DOOR 32 = 0.021 %

Tob	8 :4	When the door was shut and the 2 were alone
	8 :13	So the maid opened the door and went in
	11 :10	Tobit started toward the door, and stumbled
Jud	14 :14	So Bagoas went in and knocked at the door of the tent
Ad E	15 :6	When she had gone through all the doors
Wis	19 :17	just as were those at the door of the righteous man
	19 :17	each tried to find the way through his own door
Sir	14 :23	will also listen at her doors
	21 :23	A boor peers into the house from the door
	21 :24	It is ill-mannered for a man to listen at a door
	28 :25	and make a door and a bolt for your mouth
L Jr	6 :18	so the priests make their temples secure with doors and locks and bars
	6 :59	better even the door of a house that protects its contents
Sus	13 :17	and shut the garden doors so that I may bathe
	13 :18	They did as she said, shut the garden doors
	13 :18	and went out by the side doors
	13 :20	Look, the garden doors are shut, no one sees us
	13 :25	And one of them ran and opened the garden doors
	13 :26	they rushed in at the side door
	13 :36	shut the garden doors, and dismissed the maids
	13 :39	and he opened the doors and dashed out
Bel	14 :11	and shut the door and seal it with your signet
	14 :14	Then they went out, shut the door
	14 :18	As soon as the doors were opened
	14 :21	and they showed him the secret doors
1 Ma	1 :55	and burned incense at the doors of the houses and in the streets
	4 :57	and furnished them with doors
2 Ma	1 :16	Opening the secret door in the ceiling
	14 :41	and were forcing the door of the courtyard
	14 :41	they ordered that fire be brought and the doors burned
	14 :43	and the crowd was now rushing in through the doors
1 Es	4 :49	should forcibly enter their doors

DOORSTEP 1

Sir	6 :36	let your foot wear out his doorstep

DOR 3 = 0.002 %

1 Ma	15 :11	Antiochus pursued him, and he came in his flight to Dor
	15 :13	So Antiochus encamped against Dor
	15 :25	Antiochus the king besieged Dor anew

DORYMENES 2

1 Ma	3 :38	Lysias chose Ptolemy the son of Dorymenes
2 Ma	4 :45	promised a substantial bribe to Ptolemy son of Dorymenes

DOSITHEUS 5 = 0.003 %

Ad E	11 :1	Dositheus, who said that he was a priest and a Levite
2 Ma	12 :19	Dositheus and Sosipater, who were captains under Maccabeus
	12 :24	Timothy himself fell into the hands of Dositheus
	12 :35	But a certain Dositheus, one of Bacenor's men
3 Ma	1 :3	But Dositheus, known as the son of Drimylus

DOTHAN 5 = 0.003 %

Jud	3 :9	near Dothan, fronting the great ridge of Judea
	4 :6	which faces Esdraelon opposite the plain near Dothan
	7 :3	and they spread out in breadth over Dothan as far as Balbaim
	7 :18	and encamped in the hill country opposite Dothan
	8 :3	in the field between Dothan and Balamon

DOUBLE, adj. 2

Sir	20 :10	and there is a gift that brings a double return
	50 :2	He laid the foundations for the high double walls

DOUBLE, verb 2

Sir	26 :1	the number of his days will be doubled
	26 :26	for the number of his years will be doubled

DOUBLE-TONGUED 3 = 0.002 %

Sir	5 :9	the double-tongued sinner does that
	5 :14	and severe condemnation to the double-tongued
	6 :1	so fares the double-tongued sinner

DOUBLY 1

Sir	23 :11	and if he disregards it, he sins doubly

DOUBT, verb 2

Wis	12 :17	when men doubt the completeness of thy power
2 Es	16 :75	Do not fear or doubt, for God is your guide

DOVE 2

2 Es	2 :15	bring them up with gladness, as does the dove
	5 :26	thou hast named for thyself one dove

DOWN, adv., prep. 5 = 0.003 %

Tob	11 :5	Now Anna sat looking intently down the road for her son
Jud	10 :10	until she had gone down the mountain
Sir	35 :15	Do not the tears of the widow run down her cheek
1 Ma	3 :24	They pursued them down the descent of Beth-horon to the plain
	4 :40	They fell face down on the ground

DOWNCAST 2

Jud	6 :9	do not look downcast !
3 Ma	2 :20	and put praises in the mouth of those who are downcast

DOWNFALL 9 = 0.006 %

Ad E	14 :11	and do not let them mock at our downfall
Sir	4 :22	or deference, to your downfall
	5 :13	and a man's tongue is his downfall
	13 :13	for you are walking about with your own downfall
	20 :18	so the downfall of the wicked will occur speedily
	25 :7	a man who lives to see the downfall of his foes
3 Ma	2 :14	In our downfall this audacious and profane man
4 Ma	1 :11	and they became the cause of the downfall of tyranny over their nation
	11 :25	is not this your downfall ?

DOWNHEARTED 1

1 Ma	6 :10	Sleep departs from my eyes and I am downhearted with worry

DOWRY 1

2 Ma	1 :14	to secure most of its treasures as a dowry

DRACHMA 5 = 0.003 %

Tob	5 :14	But tell me, what wages am I to pay you – a drachma a day
2 Ma	4 :19	to carry 300 silver drachmas for the sacrifice to Hercules
	10 :20	and on receiving 70,000 drachmas let some of them slip away
	12 :43	to the amount of 2,000 drachmas of silver
3 Ma	3 :28	and also 2,000 drachmas from the royal treasury

DRAG 3 = 0.002 %

3 Ma	4 :7	In bonds and in public view they were violently dragged along
4 Ma	6 :1	the guards who were standing by dragged him violently
	11 :9	the guards bound him and dragged him to the catapult

DRAG away 1

4 Ma	13 :18	who were being dragged away

DRAG in 1

4 Ma	10 :12	they dragged in the 4th, saying

DRAG off 1

2 Ma	12 :35	was dragging him off by main strength

DRAG out 1

3 Ma	2 :23	quickly dragged him out

DRAGON 10 = 0.007 %

Ad E	10 :7	The 2 dragons are Haman and myself
	11 :6	And behold, 2 great dragons came forward
Sir	25 :16	I would rather dwell with a lion and a dragon
Bel	14 :23	There was also a great dragon
	14 :26	I will slay the dragon without sword or club
	14 :27	which he fed to the dragon
	14 :27	The dragon ate them, and burst open
	14 :28	he has destroyed Bel, and slain the dragon
2 Es	15 :29	The nations of the dragons of Arabia shall come out with many chariots
	15 :31	And then the dragons, remembering their origin

DRAIN 3 = 0.002 %
Sir **13** : 5 he will drain your resources and he will not care
13 : 7 until he has drained you 2 or 3 times
2 Ma **14** : 46 with his blood now completely drained from him

DRAUGHT 1
3 Ma **5** : 45 by the very fragrant draughts of wine mixed with frankincense

DRAW 20 = 0.013 %
Jud **7** : 27 or see our wives and children draw their last breath
8 : 27 but the Lord scourges those who draw near to him
Wis **15** : 15 nor nostrils with which to draw breath
Sir **22** : 21 Even if you have drawn your sword against a friend
51 : 6 My soul drew near to death
51 : 23 Draw near to me, you who are untaught, and lodge in my school
1 Ma **2** : 49 Now the days drew near for Mattathias to die
5 : 40 Now as Judas and his army drew near to the stream of water
2 Ma **10** : 25 As he drew near
1 Es **3** : 22 and before long they draw their swords
Ps **151** : 7 But I drew his own sword
3 Ma **5** : 49 who were drawing their last milk
2 Es **6** : 18 and it shall be that when I draw near
7 : 29 and all who draw human breath
8 : 61 Therefore my judgment is now drawing near
12 : 21 when the middle of its time draws near
15 : 15 For the sword and misery draw near them
16 : 37 Behold, the calamities draw near, and are not delayed
16 : 38 when the time of her delivery draws near
4 Ma **14** : 13 which draws everything toward an emotion felt in her inmost parts

DRAW back 1
2 Ma **14** : 44 But as they quickly drew back

DRAW on 1
Wis **19** : 4 For the fate they deserved drew them on to this end

DRAW up 4 = 0.003 %
1 Ma **4** : 21 drawn up in the plain for battle
12 : 26 that the enemy were being drawn up in formation
2 Ma **5** : 3 troops of horsemen drawn up
15 : 20 with their army drawn up for battle

DRAWN 1
2 Ma **5** : 2 in companies fully armed with lances and drawn swords

DREAD 5 = 0.003 %
Wis **4** : 20 They will come with dread when their sins are reckoned up
8 : 15 dread monarchs will be afraid of me when they hear of me
10 : 16 and withstood dread kings with wonders and signs
12 : 9 by dread wild beasts or thy stern word
1 Ma **7** : 18 Then the fear and dread of them fell upon all the people

DREADFUL 5 = 0.003 %
Wis **5** : 2 When they see him, they will be shaken with dreadful fear
17 : 6 except a dreadful, self-kindled fire
18 : 17 Then at once apparitions in dreadful dreams greatly troubled them
4 Ma **8** : 9 with dreadful punishments through tortures
8 : 15 and saw the dreadful devices

DREAM, subst. 21 = 0.014 %
Ad E **10** : 5 For I remember the dream that I had concerning these matters
11 : 2 of the tribe of Benjamin, had a dream
11 : 4 And this was his dream :
11 : 12 Mordecai saw in this dream what God had determined to do
Wis **18** : 17 Then at once apparitions in dreadful dreams greatly troubled them
18 : 19 for the dreams which disturbed them forewarned them of this
Sir **34** : 1 and dreams give wings to fools
34 : 2 so is he who gives heed to dreams
34 : 3 The vision of dreams is this against that
34 : 5 Divinations and omens and dreams are folly
34 : 7 For dreams have deceived many
2 Ma **15** : 11 and he cheered them all by relating a dream
2 Es **10** : 59 and the Most High will show you in those dream visions
11 : 1 On the 2nd night I had a dream, and behold
12 : 35 This is the dream that you saw
13 : 1 After 7 days I dreamed a dream in the night
13 : 15 now show me also the interpretation of this dream
13 : 19 as these dreams show
13 : 53 This is the interpretation of the dream which you saw
14 : 8 the dreams that you have seen
4 Ma **6** : 5 as though being tortured in a dream

DREAM, verb 2
2 Es **10** : 36 Or is my mind deceived, and my soul dreaming ?
13 : 1 After 7 days I dreamed a dream in the night

DRENCH 2
Sir **24** : 31 I said, I will water my orchard and drench my garden plot
39 : 22 and drenches it like a flood

DRESS 4 = 0.003 %
L Jr **6** : 12 When they have been dressed in purple robes
1 Ma **11** : 58 and dress in purple and wear a gold buckle
2 Ma **3** : 26 gloriously beautiful and splendidly dressed
3 : 33 dressed in the same clothing, and they stood and said

DRIED 1
Jud **10** : 5 and a cake of dried fruit and fine bread

DRIMYLUS 1
3 Ma **1** : 3 But Dositheus, known as the son of Drimylus

DRINK, subst. 4 = 0.003 %
Sir **29** : 25 you will play the host and provide drink
2 Es **9** : 34 or any dish food or drink
4 Ma **3** : 14 and from it boldly brought the king a drink
3 : 16 he poured out the drink as an offering to God

DRINK, verb 47 = 0.031 %
Tob **4** : 15 Do not drink wine to excess
7 : 9 And Raguel said to Tobias, Eat, drink, and be merry
12 : 19 and did not eat or drink, but you were seeing a vision
Jud **7** : 21 to drink their fill for a single day
7 : 21 because it was measured out to them to drink
12 : 11 to join us and eat and drink with us
12 : 13 and drink wine and be merry with us
12 : 17 So Holofernes said to her, Drink now, and be merry with us !
12 : 18 Judith said, I will drink now, my lord
12 : 19 Then she took and ate and drank before him
12 : 20 and drank a great quantity of wine
12 : 20 much more than he had ever drunk in any one day
Ad E **14** : 17 or drunk the wine of the libations
Sir **9** : 10 when it has aged you will drink it with pleasure
15 : 3 and give him the water of wisdom to drink
24 : 21 and those who drink me will thirst for more
26 : 12 and drinks from any water near him
31 : 27 Wine is like life to men, if you drink it in moderation
31 : 28 Wine drunk in season and temperately
31 : 29 Wine drunk to excess is bitterness of soul
Bel **14** : 6 Do you not see how much he eats and drinks every day ?
14 : 7 and it never ate or drank anything
14 : 15 and ate and drank everything
1 Ma **11** : 58 and granted him the right to drink from gold cups
2 Ma **7** : 36 have drunk of everflowing life under God's covenant
15 : 39 For just as it is harmful to drink wine alone
15 : 39 or, again, to drink water alone
1 Es **3** : 3 They ate and drank, and when they were satisfied they departed
3 : 6 He shall be clothed in purple, and drink from gold cups
3 : 18 It leads astray the minds of all who drink it
3 : 22 When men drink they forget to be friendly with friends and brothers
4 : 10 Moreover, he reclines, he eats and drinks and sleeps
5 : 54 and food and drink
9 : 2 and he did not eat bread or drink water
9 : 51 so go your way, eat the fat and drink the sweet
9 : 54 to eat and drink and enjoy themselves
2 Es **8** : 4 Then drink your fill of understanding, O my soul
8 : 4 and drink wisdom, O my heart !
9 : 24 and taste no meat and drink no wine, but eat only flowers
10 : 4 but to stay here, and I will neither eat nor drink
14 : 38 Ezra, open your mouth and drink what I give you to drink
14 : 40 And I took it and drank
14 : 40 and when I had drunk it
15 : 58 and drink their own blood in thirst for water
4 Ma **3** : 15 to drink what was regarded as equivalent to blood
13 : 21 they drank milk from the same fountains

DRINKING, subst., adj. 3 = 0.002 %
3 Ma **2** : 25 abetted by the previously mentioned drinking companions and comrades
5 : 16 The king, after considering this, returned to his drinking
6 : 36 not for drinking and gluttony

DRINK OFFERING 2
1 Ma **1** : 22 the cups for drink offerings, the bowls, the golden censers
1 : 45 and drink offerings in the sanctuary

DRIP 1
2 Es **5** : 5 Blood shall drip from wood

DRIPPING 1
4 Ma **9** : 20 and the heap of coals was being quenched by drippings of gore

DRIVE, subst. 1
4 Ma **3** : 17 For the temperate mind can conquer the drives of the emotions

DRIVE, verb   16 = 0.010 %
- Jud **5**:12   and so the Egyptians drove them out of their sight
- Wis **17**:15   and now were driven by monstrous spectres
- Sir **27**:2   As a stake is driven firmly into a fissure between stones
- **29**:18   it has driven men of power into exile
- **38**:25   who drives oxen and is occupied with their work
- P Az **26**   and drove the fiery flame out of the furnace
- 1 Ma **1**:53   they drove Israel into hiding
- **7**:6   and have driven us out of our land
- 2 Ma **4**:26   was driven as a fugitive into the land of Ammon
- **5**:9   and he who had driven many from their own country into exile died in exile
- **9**:4   so he ordered his charioteer to drive without stopping
- 3 Ma **4**:5   by the violence with which they were driven
- **4**:9   driven under the constraint of iron bonds
- 2 Es **1**:33   I will drive you out as the wind drives straw
- **15**:39   and shall be driven violently toward the south and west
- **16**:72   and drive them out of their houses

DRIVE away   7 = 0.005 %
- Wis **5**:14   and like a light hoarfrost driven away by a storm
- Sir **1**:21   The fear of the Lord drives away sins :
- **8**:19   lest you drive away your good luck
- **28**:15   Slander has driven away courageous women
- **38**:20   drive it away, remembering the end of life
- 2 Es **16**:5   and who is there to drive them away ?
- **16**:8   The Lord God sends calamities, and who will drive them away ?

DRIVE back   1
- 1 Ma **7**:46   and drove them back to their pursuers

DRIVE in   1
- 3 Ma **5**:2   and to drive them in

DRIVE off   2
- Wis **17**:8   For those who promised to drive off the fears
- 2 Es **16**:6   Can one drive off a hungry lion in the forest

DRIVE out   7 = 0.005 %
- Jud **5**:8   hence they drove them out from the presence of their gods
- **5**:14   and drove out all the people of the wilderness
- **5**:16   And they drove them out before them the Canaanites
- 1 Ma **13**:11   he drove out its occupants and remained there
- 2 Ma **1**:12   For he drove out those who fought against the holy city
- 2 Es **1**:21   I drove out the Canaanites, the Perizzites
- **1**:33   I will drive you out as the wind drives straw

DRIVER   1
- 1 Ma **6**:37   and also its Indian driver

DRIVING   1
- Sir **43**:13   By his command he sends the driving snow

DROOPING   1
- Sir **25**:23   Drooping hands and weak knees

DROP, subst.   9 = 0.006 %
- Wis **11**:22   and like a drop of morning dew that falls upon the ground
- Sir **1**:2   The sand of the sea, the drops of rain
- **18**:10   Like a drop of water from the sea and a grain of sand
- 2 Es **4**:49   drops remained in the cloud
- **4**:50   for as the rain is more than the drops
- **4**:50   but drops and smoke remained
- **6**:56   and thou hast compared their abundance to a drop from a bucket
- **9**:16   as a wave is greater than a drop of water
- 4 Ma **10**:8   and drops of blood flowing from his entrails

DROPPING   1
- Tob **2**:10   and their fresh droppings fell into my open eyes

DROUGHT   1
- Sir **35**:20   as clouds of rain in the time of drought

DROWN   3 = 0.002 %
- Wis **10**:19   but she drowned their enemies
- 2 Ma **12**:4   the men of Joppa took them out to sea and drowned them
- 3 Ma **6**:4   by drowning them in the sea

DROWSY   1
- Sir **22**:8   He who tells a story to a fool tells it to a drowsy man

DRUG   2
- 3 Ma **5**:2   to drug all the elephants – 500 in number
- **5**:10   Hermon, however, when he had drugged the pitiless elephants

DRUM   1
- 1 Es **5**:2   with the music of drums and flutes

DRUNK   3 = 0.002 %
- Jud **6**:4   and their mountains will be drunk with their blood
- 1 Ma **16**:16   When Simon and his sons were drunk
- 2 Es **15**:53   and talking about their death when you were drunk ?

DRUNKARD   2
- Sir **19**:1   A workman who is a drunkard will not become rich
- 4 Ma **2**:7   a glutton, or even a drunkard can learn a better way

DRUNKEN   2
- Jud **13**:15   in his drunken stupor
- Sir **26**:8   There is great anger when a wife is drunken

DRUNKENNESS   2
- Tob **4**:15   or let drunkenness go with you on your way
- Sir **31**:30   Drunkenness increases the anger of a fool to his injury

DRY, adj.   6 = 0.004 %
- Jud **7**:21   their cisterns were going dry
- Wis **4**:19   they will be left utterly dry and barren
- **19**:7   and dry land emerging where water had stood before
- Sir **39**:22   His blessing covers the dry land like a river
- 2 Ma **1**:19   and secretly hid it in the hollow of a dry cistern
- 4 Ma **18**:17   Shall these dry bones live ?

DRY up   5 = 0.003 %
- Jud **5**:13   Then God dried up the Red Sea before them
- Sir **40**:13   The wealth of the unjust will dry up like a torrent
- 2 Es **6**:42   6 parts thou didst dry up and keep
- **6**:51   which had been dried up on the 3rd day
- **8**:23   whose look dries up the depths

DUE, adj.   14 = 0.009 %
- Wis **14**:22   but they live in great strife due to ignorance
- Sir **38**:1   Honour the physician with the honour due him
- **38**:16   Lay out his body with the honour due him
- 1 Ma **10**:36   that is due to all the forces of the king
- **11**:35   And the other payments due to us of the tithes
- **11**:35   and the taxes due to us
- **11**:35   and the salt pits and the crown taxes due to us
- 2 Ma **8**:10   the tribute due to the Romans, 2,000 talents
- **10**:13   Unable to command the respect due his office
- 2 Es **8**:41   and yet not all that have been sown will come up in due season
- **8**:43   because it has not received thy rain in due season
- **10**:16   you will receive your son back in due time
- **11**:20   in due course the wings that followed also rose up on the right side
- **14**:32   in due time he took from you what he had given

DUMB, adj., subst.   3 = 0.002 %
- Wis **10**:21   because wisdom opened the mouth of the dumb
- L Jr **6**:41   for when they see a dumb man, who cannot speak
- 2 Es **6**:48   The dumb and lifeless water produced living creatures

DUNG   3 = 0.002 %
- Ad E **14**:2   she covered her head with ashes and dung
- 1 Ma **2**:62   for his splendour will turn into dung and worms
- 2 Es **16**:23   And the dead shall be cast out like dung

DUNGEON   1
- Wis **10**:13   She descended with him into the dungeon

DUNGHILL   1
- Sir **22**:2   The indolent may be compared to the filth of dunghills

DURATION   1
- 3 Ma **5**:22   But they did not so much employ the duration of the night

DURING   20 = 0.013 %
- Jud **2**:27   during the wheat harvest
- **8**:2   had died during the barley harvest
- **14**:8   Now tell me what you have done during these days
- Sir **13**:14   During all your life love the Lord
- 2 Ma **10**:6   remembering how not long before, during the feast of booths
- **14**:4   During that day he kept quiet
- 3 Ma **4**:10   during the whole voyage
- **7**:19   during the time of their stay
- 2 Es **3**:29   and my soul has seen many sinners during these 30 years
- **5**:4   and the moon during the day
- **5**:53   are different from those born during the time of old age
- **7**:89   During the time that they lived in it
- **7**:101   so that during these 7 days
- **9**:23   do not fast during them, however
- **9**:44   And every hour and every day during those 30 years
- **12**:51   and my food was of plants during those days
- **14**:42   They sat 40 days, and wrote during the daytime
- **14**:44   So during the 40 days 94 books were written
- 4 Ma **6**:20   and during that time
- **13**:20   and was shaped during the same period of time

DUST

		24 = 0.016 %
Tob	3 : 6	that I may depart and become dust
Jud	2 : 20	like the dust of the earth
Sir	10 : 9	How can he who is dust and ashes be proud ?
	17 : 32	but all men are dust and ashes
	33 : 10	and Adam was created of the dust
	40 : 3	to the one who is humbled in dust and ashes
	41 : 10	Whatever is from the dust returns to dust
	44 : 21	that he would multiply him like the dust of the earth
L Jr	6 : 13	their faces are wiped because of the dust from the temple
	6 : 17	Their eyes are full of the dust
1 Ma	2 : 63	because he has returned to the dust
	11 : 71	and put dust on his head, and prayed
2 Ma	10 : 25	Maccabeus and his men sprinkled dust upon their heads
	14 : 15	they sprinkled dust upon their heads
3 Ma	1 : 18	rushed out with their mothers, sprinkled their hair with dust
	5 : 48	And when the Jews saw the dust raised by the elephants going out
2 Es	3 : 4	and didst command the dust
	7 : 32	and the dust those who dwell silently in it
	7 : 62	if the mind is made out of the dust
	7 : 63	For it would have been better if the dust itself had not been born
	8 : 2	but only a little dust from which gold comes
	13 : 11	but only the dust of ashes and the smell of smoke
	15 : 44	then the dust and smoke shall go up to heaven

DUTY

		4 = 0.003 %
Tob	1 : 8	the 3rd tenth I would give to those to whom it was my duty
Sir	32 : 2	when you have fulfilled your duties, take your place
2 Ma	2 : 30	It is the duty of the original historian
1 Es	1 : 16	no one needed to depart from his duties

DWELL

		44 = 0.029 %
Tob	5 : 16	God who dwells in heaven will prosper your way
Jud	5 : 5	that dwells in the nearby mountain district
Ad E	11 : 3	He was a Jew, dwelling in the city of Susa
Wis	1 : 4	nor dwell in a body enslaved to sin
	12 : 3	Those who dwelt of old in thy holy land
Sir	1 : 15	She dwells with all flesh according to his gift
	4 : 15	and whoever gives heed to her will dwell secure
	14 : 27	and will dwell in the midst of her glory
	24 : 4	I dwelt in high places
	25 : 16	I would rather dwell with a lion and a dragon
	25 : 16	than dwell with an evil wife
	50 : 26	and the foolish people that dwell in Shechem
Bar	1 : 4	all who dwelt in Babylon by the river Sud
	3 : 13	you would be dwelling in peace for ever
	3 : 20	and have dwelt upon the earth
1 Ma	2 : 7	and to dwell there when it was given over to the enemy
	2 : 29	went down to the wilderness to dwell there
	9 : 73	And Jonathan dwelt in Michmash
	10 : 10	And Jonathan dwelt in Jerusalem
	13 : 52	and he and his men dwelt there
	13 : 53	and he dwelt in Gazara
	14 : 34	where the enemy formerly dwelt
2 Ma	5 : 17	because of the sins of those who dwelt in the city
	6 : 2	as did the people who dwelt in that place
	12 : 27	a fortified city where Lysias dwelt
	12 : 30	But when the Jews who dwelt there
1 Es	1 : 21	who were dwelling in Jerusalem
	2 : 5	he is the Lord who dwells in Jerusalem
2 Es	3 : 12	When those who dwelt on earth began to multiply
	4 : 21	so also those who dwell upon earth
	4 : 39	on account of the sins of those who dwell on earth
	5 : 1	the days are coming when those who dwell on earth
	5 : 6	And one shall reign whom those who dwell on earth do not expect
	7 : 32	and the dust those who dwell silently in it
	7 : 72	those who dwell on earth shall be tormented
	8 : 17	for I see the failings of us who dwell in the land
	9 : 9	shall dwell in torments
	10 : 59	who dwell on earth in the last days
	11 : 5	to reign over the earth and over those who dwell in it
	11 : 40	and for so long you have dwelt on the earth with deceit
	13 : 30	over those who dwell on the earth
	13 : 46	Then they dwelt there until the last times
	14 : 29	At first our fathers dwelt as aliens in Egypt
4 Ma	13 : 20	There each of the brothers dwelt the same length of time

DWELL in

		1
2 Es	9 : 18	before the world was made for them to dwell in

DWELLING

		8 = 0.005 %
Tob	1 : 4	and where the temple of the dwelling of the Most High
Sir	24 : 8	And he said, Make your dwelling in Jacob
1 Ma	1 : 38	she became a dwelling of strangers
2 Ma	3 : 39	For he who has his dwelling in heaven
3 Ma	2 : 15	For your dwelling, the heaven of heavens
2 Es	4 : 7	How many dwellings are in the heart of the sea
	5 : 38	except he whose dwelling is not with men ?
	11 : 42	you have destroyed the dwellings of those who brought forth fruit

DWELLING PLACE

		1
1 Es	1 : 50	because he would have spared them and his dwelling place

DYE

		1
1 Ma	4 : 23	and cloth dyed blue and sea purple, and great riches

DYNASTY

		1
3 Ma	3 : 3	and unswerving loyalty toward the dynasty

E

EACH, indef. pr. or adj.

		91 = 0.059 %
Tob	1 : 7	each year at Jerusalem
	3 : 8	and the evil demon Asmodeus had slain each of them
	5 : 9	he entered and they greeted each other
	6 : 13	and that each died in the bridal chamber
	7 : 11	and when each came to her he died in the night
	10 : 1	Now his father Tobit was counting each day
Jud	7 : 5	Then each man took up his weapons
	12 : 7	and went out each night to the valley of Bethulia
Wis	15 : 7	and laboriously moulds each vessel for our service
	15 : 7	but which shall be the use of each of these
	19 : 17	each tried to find the way through his own door
	19 : 18	while each note remains the same
Sir	17 : 14	And he gave commandment to each of them
	38 : 27	each is diligent in making a great variety
	38 : 31	and each is skilful in his own work
Bar	1 : 6	and they collected money, each giving what he could
	1 : 21	but we followed the intent of his own wicked heart
	2 : 8	by turning away, each of us, from the thoughts of his wicked heart
Sus	13 : 10	but they did not tell each other of their distress
	13 : 13	They said to each other, Let us go home, for it is mealtime
	13 : 14	And when they went out, they parted from each other
	13 : 14	and when each pressed the other for the reason
	13 : 51	Separate them far from each other
	13 : 52	When they were separated from each other
	13 : 54	Under what tree did you see them being intimate with each other ?
	13 : 58	Under what tree did you catch them being intimate with each other ?
1 Ma	1 : 8	Then his officers began to rule, each in his own place
	1 : 42	and that each should give up his customs
	2 : 19	departing each one from the religion of his fathers
	2 : 40	And each said to his neighbour :
	3 : 56	that each should return to his home, according to the law
	5 : 49	that each should encamp where he was
	6 : 35	with each elephant they stationed a 1,000 men
	6 : 35	and 500 picked horsemen were assigned to each beast
	6 : 37	they were fastened upon each beast by special harness
	6 : 37	and upon each were 4 armed men who fought from there
	6 : 54	and they had been scattered, each to his own place
	7 : 49	each year on the 13th day of Adar
	8 : 16	They trust one man each year to rule over them
	10 : 13	each left his place and departed to his own land
	10 : 71	and let us match strength with each other there
	11 : 3	he stationed forces as a garrison in each city
	11 : 9	Come, let us make a covenant with each other
	11 : 34	which the king formerly received from them each year
	11 : 38	he dismissed all his troops, each man to his own place
	14 : 12	Each man sat under his vine and his fig tree
2 Ma	3 : 26	who stood on each side of him and scourged him continuously
	7 : 21	She encouraged each of them in the language of their fathers
	7 : 22	nor I who set in order the elements within each of you
	8 : 22	each to command a division, putting 1,500 men under each
	9 : 26	and to maintain your present good will, each of you
	13 : 2	Each of them had a Greek force of 110,000 infantry
	14 : 21	A chariot came forward from each army
	15 : 11	He armed each of them
1 Es	1 : 16	The gatekeepers were at each gate
	1 : 26	What have we to do with each other, king of Judea ?
	2 : 6	and let each man, wherever he may live
	3 : 5	Let each of us state what one thing is strongest
	3 : 8	Then each wrote his own statement
	5 : 8	each to his own town
	5 : 47	and the sons of Israel were each in his own home
	7 : 9	and the gatekeepers were at each gate
	9 : 13	with the elders and judges of each place
3 Ma	1 : 4	promising to give them each 2 minas of gold
	5 : 21	and each departed to his own home
	5 : 34	each to his own occupation
	5 : 49	and giving way to lamentation and groans they kissed each other
	6 : 25	Who is it that has taken each man from his home
	7 : 8	We also have ordered each and every one

	7:18	to each as far as his own house
	7:20	each to his own place
2 Es	2:43	and on the head of each of them he placed a crown
	4:19	I answered and said, Each has made a foolish plan
	5:47	but only each in its own time
	11:8	let each sleep in his own place, and watch in his turn
4 Ma	1:20	and each of these is by nature concerned
	1:29	each of which the master cultivator, reason, weeds and prunes
	5:2	ordered the guards to seize each and every Hebrew
	6:3	And after they had tied his arms on each side they scourged him
	8:5	Young men, I admire each and every one of you in a kindly manner
	8:9	you will compel me to destroy each and every one of you
	9:11	they bound his hands and arms with thongs on each side
	13:13	Each of them and all of them together looking at one another
	13:18	Those who were left behind said to each of the brothers
	13:20	Then each of the brothers dwelt the same length of time
	14:12	under the rackings of each one of her children
	15:7	and because of the many pains she suffered with each of them
	15:12	each child singly and all together
	15:19	nor did you weep when you looked at the eyes of each one
	16:24	encouraged and persuaded each of her sons

EAGER 4 = 0.003 %

Sir	18:14	and who are eager for his judgments
2 Ma	15:9	he made them the more eager
3 Ma	1:8	he was all the more eager to visit them as soon as possible
	5:29	O king, according to your eager purpose

EAGERLY 4 = 0.003 %

Sus	13:12	And they watched eagerly, day after day, to see her
1 Ma	1:13	and some of the people eagerly went to the king
2 Ma	11:7	Then they eagerly rushed off together
3 Ma	5:24	and they were eagerly waiting for daybreak

EAGLE 14 = 0.009 %

2 Es	11:1	there came up from the sea an eagle
	11:5	And I looked, and behold, the eagle flew with his wings
	11:7	And I looked, and behold, the eagle rose upon his talons
	11:23	and nothing remained on the eagle's body
	11:37	and I heard how he uttered a man's voice to the eagle
	11:45	Therefore you will surely disappear, you eagle
	12:1	While the lion was saying these words to the eagle, I looked
	12:3	and the whole body of the eagle was burned
	12:11	The eagle which you saw coming up from the sea
	12:17	coming not from the eagle's heads
	12:24	therefore they are called the heads of the eagle
	12:30	It is these whom the Most High has kept for the eagle's end
	12:31	and roaring and speaking to the eagle
	14:18	For the eagle which you saw in the vision

EAR 20 = 0.013 %

Wis	1:10	because a jealous ear hears all things
	6:2	Give ear, you that rule over multitudes
	15:15	nor ears with which to hear, nor fingers to feel with
Sir	3:29	and an attentive ear is the wise man's desire
	4:8	Incline your ear to the poor
	6:33	and if you incline your ear you will become wise
	16:5	and my ear has heard things more striking than these
	17:6	he gave them ears and a mind for thinking
	17:13	and their ears heard the glory of his voice
	21:5	to the ears of God
	27:14	and their quarrels make a man stop his ears
	38:28	he inclines his ear to the sound of the hammer
	51:16	I inclined my ear a little and received her
Bar	2:16	Incline thy ear, O Lord, and hear
	2:31	I will give them a heart that obeys and ears that hear
	3:9	give ear, and learn wisdom !
2 Ma	15:39	delights the ears of those who read the work
2 Es	8:24	and give ear to the petition of thy creature
	10:56	and afterward you will hear as much as your ears can hear
	15:1	speak in the ears of my people the words of the prophecy

EARLY 20 = 0.013 %

Tob	9:6	In the morning they both got up early
Wis	4:7	But the righteous man, though he die early, will be at rest
	6:14	He who rises early to seek her will have no difficulty
Sir	4:12	and those who seek her early will be filled with joy
	6:36	If you see an intelligent man, visit him early
	31:20	he rises early, and feels fit
	32:14	and those who rise early to seek him will find favour
	39:5	He will set his heart to rise early
	47:10	and the sanctuary resounded from early morning
Bel	14:16	Early in the morning the king rose and came
1 Ma	3:29	that had existed from the earliest days
	3:58	Be ready early in the morning to fight with these Gentiles
	4:52	Early in the morning on the 25th day of the 9th month
	6:33	Early in the morning the king rose
	10:80	from early morning till late afternoon
	11:67	Early in the morning they marched to the plain of Hazor

	16:5	Early in the morning they arose and marched into the plain
1 Es	9:41	from early morning until midday
3 Ma	5:10	presented himself at the courtyard early in the morning
	5:23	Then, as soon as the cock had crowed in the early morning

EARN 1

Tob	2:11	Then my wife Anna earned money at women's work

EARNEST 2

3 Ma	3:10	and to exert more earnest efforts for their assistance
4 Ma	1:1	to advise you to pay earnest attention to philosophy

EARNESTLY 2

Jud	4:12	praying earnestly to the God of Israel
P Ma	13	I earnestly beseech thee, forgive me, O Lord

EARRING 1

Jud	10:4	and her earrings and all her ornaments

EARTH 183 = 0.119 %

Tob	3:13	Command that I be released from the earth
	7:18	the Lord of heaven and earth grant you joy
	14:4	Our brethren will be scattered over the earth from the good land
Jud	2:5	Thus says the Great King, the Lord of the whole earth :
	2:7	*Tell them to prepare earth and water*
	2:7	and will cover the whole face of the earth
	2:9	to the ends of the whole earth
	2:19	and to cover the whole face of the earth to the west
	2:20	like the dust of the earth
	6:3	from the face of the earth
	6:4	So says King Nebuchadnezzar, the lord of the whole earth
	7:28	We call to witness against you heaven and earth
	9:12	Lord of heaven and earth, Creator of the waters
	11:1	the king of all the earth
	11:7	Nebuchadnezzar the king of the whole earth lives
	11:21	from one end of the earth to the other
	13:18	above all women on earth
	13:18	who created the heavens and the earth
Ad E	11:5	thunders and earthquake, tumult upon the earth !
	11:8	affliction and great tumult upon the earth !
	13:10	For thou hast made heaven and earth
Wis	1:1	Love righteousness, you rulers of the earth
	1:14	and the dominion of Hades is not on earth
	5:23	Lawlessness will lay waste the whole earth
	6:1	learn, O judges of the ends of the earth
	7:1	a descendant of the first-formed child of earth
	7:3	and fell upon the kindred earth
	8:1	She reaches mightily from one end of the earth to the other
	9:16	We can hardly guess at what is on earth
	9:18	And thus the paths of those on earth were set right
	10:4	When the earth was flooded because of him
	15:7	*For when a potter kneads the soft earth*
	15:8	*this man who was made of earth a short time before*
	15:8	*and after a little while goes to the earth*
	18:16	and touched heaven while standing on the earth
	19:10	the earth brought forth gnats
Sir	1:3	The height of heaven, the breadth of the earth
	10:4	The government of the earth is in the hands of the Lord
	10:16	and has destroyed them to the foundations of the earth
	10:17	and has extinguished the memory of them from the earth
	16:18	the abyss and the earth, will tremble at his visitation
	16:19	The mountains also and the foundations of the earth
	16:29	After this the Lord looked upon the earth
	17:1	*The Lord created man out of earth*
	17:2	but granted them authority over the things upon the earth
	17:17	For in the division of the nations of the whole earth
	24:3	and covered the earth like a mist
	24:6	In the waves of the sea, in the whole earth
	36:17	and all who are on the earth will know
	38:4	*The Lord created medicines from the earth*
	38:8	and from him health is upon the face of the earth
	39:31	and be made ready on earth for their service
	40:11	*All things that are from the earth turn back to the earth*
	43:17	The voice of his thunder rebukes the earth
	43:19	He pours the hoarfrost upon the earth like salt
	44:17	therefore a remnant was left to the earth when the flood came
	44:21	that he would multiply him like the dust of the earth
	44:21	and from the River to the ends of the earth
	46:20	and lifted up his voice out of the earth in prophecy
	47:15	Your soul covered the earth
	48:15	and were scattered over all the earth
	49:14	No one like Enoch has been created on earth
	49:14	for he was taken up from the earth
	51:9	And I sent up my supplication from the earth
Bar	1:11	that their days on earth may be like the days of heaven
	2:15	that all the earth may know that thou art the Lord our God
	3:16	and those who rule over the beasts on the earth
	3:20	and have dwelt upon the earth
	3:23	the sons of Hagar, who seek for understanding on the earth

	3:32	He who prepared the earth for all time filled it with four-footed creatures
	3:37	Afterward she appeared upon earth and lived among men
L Jr	6:20	*when worms from the earth devour them and their robes*
	6:54	they are like crows between heaven and earth
P Az	52	Let the earth bless the Lord
	54	Bless the Lord, all things that grow on the earth
Bel	14:5	but the living God, who created heaven and earth
1 Ma	1:2	and put to death the kings of the earth
	1:3	He advanced to the ends of the earth
	1:3	When the earth became quiet before him, he was exalted
	1:9	and they caused many evils on the earth
	2:37	heaven and earth testify for us
	2:40	they will quickly destroy us from the earth
	3:9	He was renowned to the ends of the earth
	8:4	from the ends of the earth
	9:13	The earth was shaken by the noise of the armies
	14:10	till his renown spread to the ends of the earth
	15:9	so that your glory will become manifest in all the earth
2 Ma	7:28	to look at the heaven and the earth
	9:8	was brought down to earth and carried in a litter
	13:7	*without even burial in the earth*
	15:5	he replied, And I am a sovereign also, on earth
1 Es	4:34	The earth is vast, and heaven is high
	4:36	The whole earth calls upon truth, and heaven blesses her
	6:13	who created the heaven and the earth
	8:77	and our priests were given over to the kings of the earth
P Ma	2	thou who hast made heaven and earth with all their order
	13	do not condemn me to the depths of the earth
3 Ma	1:29	but also the walls and the whole earth around echoed
	2:9	the boundless and immeasurable earth
	2:14	undertakes to violate the holy place on earth
2 Es	2:7	let their names be blotted out from the earth
	2:14	Call, O call heaven and earth to witness
	2:31	because I will bring them out of the hiding places of the earth
	3:4	when thou didst form the earth – and that without help
	3:6	which thy right hand had planted before the earth appeared
	3:12	When those who dwelt on earth began to multiply
	3:18	Thou didst bend down the heavens and shake the earth
	3:35	When have the inhabitants of the earth not sinned in thy sight ?
	4:21	so also those who dwell upon earth
	4:21	can understand only what is on the earth
	4:39	on account of the sins of those who dwell on earth
	5:1	the days are coming when those who dwell on earth
	5:6	And one shall reign whom those who dwell on earth do not expect
	5:10	and unrighteousness and unrestraint shall increase on earth
	5:23	from every forest of the earth and from all its trees
	5:48	Even so have I given the womb of the earth
	6:1	At the beginning of the circle of the earth
	6:15	and the foundations of the earth will understand
	6:18	to visit the inhabitants of the earth
	6:24	and the earth and those who inhabit it shall be terrified
	6:26	and the heart of the earth's inhabitants shall be changed
	6:38	Let heaven and earth be made
	6:42	in the 7th part of the earth
	6:53	On the 6th day thou didst command the earth
	7:32	And the earth shall give up those who are asleep in it
	7:54	Not only that, but ask the earth and she will tell you
	7:62	I replied and said, O earth
	7:72	those who dwell on earth shall be tormented
	7:116	that it would have been better if the earth had not produced Adam
	7:127	which every man who is born on earth shall wage
	8:2	Just as, when you ask the earth
	9:20	and my earth, and behold, it was in peril
	10:9	Now ask the earth
	10:12	My lamentation is not like the earth's
	10:13	but it is with the earth according to the way of the earth
	10:14	so the earth also has from the beginning
	10:26	so that the earth shook at the sound
	10:59	who dwell on earth in the last days
	11:2	he spread his wings over all the earth
	11:5	to reign over the earth and over those who dwell in it
	11:6	not even one creature that was on the earth
	11:12	and it reigned over all the earth
	11:16	Hear me, you who have ruled the earth all this time
	11:32	Moreover this head gained control of the whole earth
	11:34	which also ruled over the earth and its inhabitants
	11:40	and over all the earth with grievous oppression
	11:40	and for so long you have dwelt on the earth with deceit
	11:41	And you have judged the earth, but not with truth
	11:46	so that the whole earth, freed from your violence
	12:3	and the earth was exceedingly terrified
	12:13	when a kingdom shall arise on earth
	12:23	and shall rule the earth
	13:29	when the Most High will deliver those who are on the earth
	13:30	over those who dwell on the earth
	13:52	so no one on earth can see my Son
	15:20	I call together all the kings of the earth to fear me

	15:22	and my sword will not cease from those who shed innocent blood on the earth
	15:23	and will consume the foundations of the earth
	15:27	For now calamities have come upon the whole earth
	15:29	their hissing shall spread over the earth
	15:35	and shall pour out a heavy tempest upon the earth
	15:37	And there shall be fear and great trembling upon the earth
	15:40	shall rise, to destroy all the earth and its inhabitants
	16:12	The earth and its foundations quake
	16:14	and shall not return until they come over the earth
	16:15	until it consumes the foundations of the earth
	16:16	so the calamities that are sent upon the earth shall not return
	16:21	Behold, provisions will be so cheap upon earth
	16:21	and then the calamities shall spring up on the earth
	16:22	For many of those who live on the earth shall perish by famine
	16:23	for the earth shall be left desolate
	16:24	No one shall be left to cultivate the earth or to sow it
	16:32	And the earth shall be left desolate
	16:39	so the calamities will not delay in coming forth upon the earth
	16:40	and in the midst of the calamities like strangers on the earth
	16:50	who searches out every sin on earth
	16:52	and iniquity will be removed from the earth
	16:55	He said, Let the earth be made, and it was made
	16:58	and by his word has suspended the earth over the water
	16:60	to send rivers from the heights to water the earth
4 Ma	18:5	The tyrant Antiochus was both punished on earth

EARTHENWARE   1

2 Es	8:2	from which earthenware is made

EARTHLY   1

Wis	9:15	and this earthly tent burdens the thoughtful mind

EARTHQUAKE   5 = 0.003 %

Ad E	11:5	thunders and earthquake, tumult upon the earth !
Sir	22:16	will not be torn loose by an earthquake
2 Es	3:19	of fire and earthquake and wind and ice
	9:3	So when there shall appear in the world earthquakes
4 Ma	17:3	against the earthquake of the tortures

EARTHWORK   1

2 Ma	12:13	which was strongly fortified with earthworks and walls

EARTHY   1

Wis	15:13	when he makes from earthy matter fragile vessels and graven images

EASILY   3 = 0.002 %

Wis	6:12	and she is easily discerned by those who love her
	19:21	easily melted kind of heavenly food
3 Ma	5:13	and again begged him who is easily reconciled

EAST, subst., adj.   14 = 0.009 %

Jud	7:18	toward the south and the east
Bar	4:36	Look toward the east, O Jerusalem
	4:37	they are coming, gathered from east and west
	5:5	and look toward the east
	5:5	and see your children gathered from west and east
1 Ma	12:37	part of the wall on the valley to the east had fallen
1 Es	5:47	before the first gate toward the east
	9:38	into the open square before the east gate of the temple
2 Es	1:11	and scattered in the east the people of 2 provinces, Tyre and Sidon
	1:38	look with pride and see the people coming from the east
	15:20	from the east and from Lebanon
	15:28	Behold, a terrifying sight, appearing from the east !
	15:34	Behold, clouds from the east
	15:39	And the winds from the east shall prevail

EASY   10 = 0.007 %

Jud	4:7	and it was easy to stop any who tried to enter
	7:10	for it is not easy to reach the tops of their mountains
Wis	13:11	A skilled woodcutter may saw down a tree easy to handle
Sir	11:21	for it is easy in the sight of the Lord
	11:26	For it is easy in the sight of the Lord
	22:15	Sand, salt, and a piece of iron are easier to bear than a stupid man
1 Ma	3:18	Judas replied, It is easy for many to be hemmed in by few
2 Ma	2:27	just as it is not easy for one who prepares a banquet
2 Es	7:18	while hoping for easier ones
	7:18	and will not see the easier ones

EAT   96 = 0.063 %

Tob	1:10	all my brethren and my relatives ate the food of the Gentiles
	1:11	but I kept myself from eating it
	2:1	a good dinner was prepared for me and I sat down to eat
	2:5	and ate my food in sorrow
	2:13	for it is not right to eat what is stolen
	6:5	and they roasted and ate the fish
	7:9	And Raguel said to Tobias, Eat, drink, and be merry

	7:11	And Tobias said, I will eat nothing here
	7:15	Then they began to eat
	8:1	When they have finished eating
	10:7	she ate nothing in the daytime
	12:19	and did not eat or drink, but you were seeing a vision
Jud	11:12	to use all that God by his laws has forbidden them to eat
	12:2	But Judith said, I cannot eat it, lest it be an offence
	12:9	until she ate her food toward evening
	12:11	to join us and eat and drink with us
	12:15	so that she might recline on them when she ate
	12:19	Then she took and ate and drank before him
Ad E	14:17	And thy servant has not eaten at Haman's table
Wis	4:5	and their fruit will be useless, not ripe enough to eat
	13:12	and eat his fill
	16:2	and thou didst prepare quails to eat
	16:20	with bread ready to eat, providing every pleasure
Sir	6:19	and soon you will eat of her produce
	20:16	those who eat my bread speak unkindly
	24:19	and eat your fill of my produce
	24:21	Those who eat me will hunger for more
	29:26	and if you have anything at hand, let me have it to eat
	30:19	For it can neither eat nor smell
	30:25	will give heed to the food he eats
	31:16	Eat like a human being what is set before you
	31:17	Be the first to stop eating, for the sake of good manners
	31:20	Healthy sleep depends on moderate eating
	45:21	for they eat the sacrifices to the Lord
Bar	2:3	that we should eat, one the flesh of his son
Bel	14:6	Do you not see how much he eats and drinks every day ?
	14:7	and it never ate or drank anything
	14:8	If you do not tell me who is eating these provisions, you shall die
	14:9	But if you prove that Bel is eating them, Daniel shall die
	14:12	if you do not find that Bel has eaten it all, we will die
	14:15	and ate and drank everything
	14:27	The dragon ate them, and burst open
	14:39	So Daniel arose and ate
1 Ma	1:62	and were resolved in their hearts not to eat unclean food
	3:17	And we are faint, for we have eaten nothing today
2 Ma	2:11	because the sin offering had not been eaten
	6:18	was being forced to open his mouth to eat swine's flesh
	6:21	and pretend that he was eating the flesh
	7:7	and asked him, Will you eat
	7:42	Let this be enough, then, about the eating of sacrifices
1 Es	3:3	They ate and drank, and when they were satisfied they departed
	4:10	Moreover, he reclines, he eats and drinks and sleeps
	7:13	And the people of Israel who came from the captivity ate it
	8:85	and eat the good things of the land
	9:2	and he did not eat bread or drink water
	9:51	so go your way, eat the fat and drink the sweet
	9:54	to eat and drink and enjoy themselves
2 Es	1:19	you ate the bread of angels
	5:18	Rise therefore and eat some bread
	6:52	and thou hast kept them to be eaten by whom thou wilt
	7:104	to be ill or sleep or eat or be healed in his stead
	9:24	and eat only of the flowers of the field
	9:24	and taste no meat and drink no wine, but eat only flowers
	9:26	and ate of the plants of the field
	10:4	but to stay here, and I will neither eat nor drink
	12:51	and I ate only the flowers of the field
	14:42	and ate their bread at night
	15:58	and they shall eat their own flesh in hunger for bread
	16:69	And those who consent to eat shall be held in derision and contempt
4 Ma	1:27	in the body, indiscriminate eating
	4:26	to eat defiling foods and to renounce Judaism
	5:2	to eat pork and food sacrificed to idols
	5:3	If any were not willing to eat defiling food
	5:6	I would advise you to save yourself by eating pork
	5:8	Why, when nature has granted it to us, should you abhor eating
	5:14	to eat meat unlawfully
	5:19	if we were to eat defiling food
	5:25	Therefore we do not eat defiling food
	5:26	He has permitted us to eat
	5:26	but he has forbidden us to eat
	5:27	but also to eat in such a way
	5:27	that you may deride us for eating defiling food
	6:15	save yourself by pretending to eat pork
	6:19	in becoming an example of the eating of defiling food
	7:6	by eating defiling foods
	8:2	being unable to compel an aged man to eat defiling foods
	8:2	and that any who ate defiling food should be freed after eating
	8:12	so as to persuade them out of fear to eat the defiling food
	8:29	had ceased counselling them to eat defiling food
	9:16	Agree to eat so that you may be released from the tortures
	9:27	Before torturing him, they inquired if he were willing to eat
	11:13	whether he was willing to eat and be released
	11:16	So if you intend to torture me for not eating defiling foods

	11:25	to change our mind or to force us to eat defiling foods
	13:2	and had eaten defiling food

ECBATANA 11 = 0.007 %

Tob	3:7	On the same day, at Ecbatana in Media
	6:5	until they came near to Ecbatana
	6:9	When they approached Ecbatana
	7:1	When they reached Ecbatana
	14:12	Then Tobias returned with his wife and his sons to Ecbatana
	14:14	He died in Ecbatana of Media at the age of a 127 years
Jud	1:1	who ruled over the Medes in Ecbatana
	1:2	he is the king who built walls about Ecbatana
	1:14	and came to Ecbatana, captured its towers
2 Ma	9:3	While he was in Ecbatana, news came to him
1 Es	6:23	And in Ecbatana, the fortress which is in the country of Media

ECHO, subst. 1

Wis	17:19	or an echo thrown back from a hollow of the mountains

ECHO, verb 1

3 Ma	1:29	but also the walls and the whole earth around echoed

ECHO back 1

Wis	18:10	But the discordant cry of their enemies echoed back

EDDINUS 1

1 Es	1:15	and also Asaph, Zechariah, and Eddinus

EDGE 5 = 0.003 %

Jud	2:27	with the edge of the sword
	3:9	Then he came to the edge of Esdraelon
Sir	28:18	Many have fallen by the edge of the sword
1 Ma	5:28	and killed every male by the edge of the sword
	5:51	He destroyed every male by the edge of the sword

EDNA 7 = 0.005 %

Tob	7:2	Then Raguel said to his wife Edna
	7:8	And his wife Edna and his daughter Sarah wept
	7:14	Next he called his wife Edna
	7:16	And Raguel called his wife Edna and said to her
	8:12	and said to his wife Edna
	10:12	And Edna said to Tobias
	11:1	And he blessed Raguel and his wife Edna

EDOMITE 2

1 Es	4:45	which the Edomites burned
	8:69	the Jebusites, the Moabites, the Egyptians, and the Edomites

EDUCATE 2

Sir	10:1	A wise magistrate will educate his people
4 Ma	13:24	Since they had been educated by the same law

EDUCATED 1

Sir	34:9	An educated man knows many things

EDUCATION 5 = 0.003 %

Sir	4:24	and education through the words of the tongue
	21:19	To a senseless man education is fetters on his feet
	21:21	To a sensible man education is like a golden ornament
4 Ma	1:17	This, in turn, is education in the law
	13:22	and from both general education and our discipline in the law of God

EFFECT, subst. 7 = 0.005 %

Wis	14:5	should not be without effect
	16:17	the fire had still greater effect
1 Ma	8:30	If after these terms are in effect
	12:2	He also sent letters to the same effect to the Spartans
2 Ma	1:24	The prayer was to this effect :
	11:16	The letter written to the Jews by Lysias was to this effect :
2 Es	4:23	and the law of our fathers has been made of no effect

EFFECT, verb 2

Wis	8:5	what is richer than wisdom who effects all things ?
2 Ma	3:7	to effect the removal of the aforesaid money

EFFECTIVE 2

Wis	8:6	And if understanding is effective
2 Ma	15:17	so noble and so effective in arousing valour

EFFORT 6 = 0.004 %

2 Ma	2:28	while devoting our effort
1 Es	6:28	and that full effort be made to help the men
3 Ma	3:10	and to exert more earnest efforts for their assistance
2 Es	7:92	because they have striven with great effort
	13:38	and will destroy them without effort by the law
4 Ma	2:2	because by mental effort he overcame sexual desire

EGYPT 55 = 0.036 %

Tob	8 : 3	he fled to the remotest parts of Egypt
Jud	1 : 9	and Chelous and Kadesh and the river of Egypt
	1 : 10	even beyond Tanis and Memphis, and all who lived in Egypt
	1 : 12	and every one in Egypt, as far as the coasts of the 2 seas
	5 : 10	When a famine spread over Canaan they went down to Egypt
	5 : 11	So the king of Egypt became hostile to them
	5 : 12	and he afflicted the whole land of Egypt
	6 : 5	until I take revenge on this race that came out of Egypt
Ad E	11 : 1	and Ptolemy his son brought to Egypt the preceding Letter of Purim
	13 : 16	which thou didst redeem for thyself out of the land of Egypt
Sir	pr.	When I came to Egypt
Bar	1 : 19	out of the land of Egypt until today
	1 : 20	when he brought our fathers out of the land of Egypt
	2 : 11	who didst bring thy people out of the land of Egypt
1 Ma	1 : 16	he determined to become king of the land of Egypt
	1 : 17	So he invaded Egypt with a strong force
	1 : 18	He engaged Ptolemy king of Egypt in battle
	1 : 19	And they captured the fortified cities in the land of Egypt
	1 : 19	and he plundered the land of Egypt
	1 : 20	After subduing Egypt, Antiochus returned in the 143rd year
	2 : 53	and became lord of Egypt
	3 : 32	from the river Euphrates to the border of Egypt
	10 : 51	Then Alexander sent ambassadors to Ptolemy king of Egypt
	10 : 57	So Ptolemy set out from Egypt
	11 : 1	Then the king of Egypt gathered great forces
	11 : 13	the crown of Egypt and that of Asia
	11 : 59	from the Ladder of Tyre to the borders of Egypt
2 Ma	1 : 1	To their Jewish brethren in Egypt, greeting, and good peace
	1 : 10	and to the Jews in Egypt, greeting, and good health
	4 : 21	When Apollonius the son of Menestheus was sent to Egypt
	5 : 1	About this time Antiochus made his 2nd invasion of Egypt
	5 : 8	he was cast ashore in Egypt
	5 : 11	So, raging inwardly, he left Egypt
	9 : 29	he betook himself to Ptolemy Philometor in Egypt
1 Es	1 : 25	it happened that Pharaoh, king of Egypt
	1 : 26	And the king of Egypt sent word to him saying
	1 : 35	Then the king of Egypt deposed him from reigning in Jerusalem
	1 : 37	And the king of Egypt made Jehoiakim his brother
	1 : 38	and brought him up out of Egypt
3 Ma	2 : 25	When he arrived in Egypt
	3 : 12	in Egypt and all its districts
	3 : 20	But we, when we arrived in Egypt victorious
	4 : 18	the task was impossible for all the generals in Egypt
	6 : 4	the former ruler of this Egypt
	7 : 1	King Ptolemy Philopator to the generals in Egypt
2 Es	1 : 7	Was it not I who brought them out of the land of Egypt
	3 : 17	And when thou didst lead his descendants out of Egypt
	14 : 3	when my people were in bondage in Egypt
	14 : 4	and I sent him and led my people out of Egypt
	14 : 29	At first our fathers dwelt as aliens in Egypt
	15 : 10	to live any longer in the land of Egypt
	15 : 11	and will smite Egypt with plagues, as before
	15 : 12	Let Egypt mourn, and its foundations
	16 : 1	Woe to you, Egypt and Syria !
4 Ma	4 : 22	For when he was warring against Ptolemy in Egypt

EGYPTIAN 3 = 0.002 %

Jud	5 : 12	and so the Egyptians drove them out of their sight
1 Es	8 : 69	the Jebusites, the Moabites, the Egyptians, and the Edomites
2 Es	1 : 18	It would have been better for us to serve the Egyptians

EITHER* 18 = 0.012 %

Jud	11 : 21	either for beauty of face or wisdom of speech !
	13 : 4	and no one, either small or great
Wis	13 : 2	but they supposed that either fire or wind or swift air
	14 : 24	either their lives or their marriages pure
	14 : 24	but they either treacherously kill one another
	14 : 28	For their worshippers either rave in exultation
	15 : 6	are those who either make or desire or worship them
Sir	13 : 25	either for good or for evil
	20 : 30	what advantage is there in either of them ?
	41 : 14	what advantage is there in either of them ?
L Jr	6 : 35	Likewise they are not able to give either wealth or money
	6 : 64	for they are not able either to decide a case
1 Ma	4 : 35	and how ready they were either to live or to die nobly
	6 : 38	The rest of the horsemen were stationed on either side
1 Es	8 : 24	either fine or imprisonment
4 Ma	5 : 20	to transgress the law in matters either small or great
	5 : 21	for in either case the law is equally despised
	5 : 38	either by word or by deed

EKRON 1

1 Ma	10 : 89	He also gave him Ekron and all its environs as his possession

ELABORATE 1

1 Ma	13 : 29	And for the pyramids he devised an elaborate setting

ELAM 4 = 0.003 %

1 Es	5 : 12	The sons of Elam, 1,254
	5 : 22	The sons of the other Elam and Ono, 725
	8 : 33	Of the sons of Elam, Jeshaiah the son of Gotholiah
	9 : 27	Of the sons of Elam : Mattaniah and Zechariah

ELASA 1

1 Ma	9 : 5	Now Judas was encamped in Elasa

ELASAH 1

1 Es	9 : 22	and Nathanael, and Gedaliah, and Elasah

ELATE 5 = 0.003 %

Ad E	13 : 2	not elated with presumption of authority
2 Ma	5 : 17	Antiochus was elated in spirit, and did not perceive
	5 : 21	because his mind was elated
	7 : 34	do not be elated in vain and puffed up by uncertain hopes
	11 : 4	but was elated with his ten thousands of infantry

ELBOW 1

4 Ma	10 : 6	and breaking his fingers and arms and legs and elbows

ELDER, adj., subst. 47 = 0.031 %

Jud	6 : 16	They called together all the elders of the city
	6 : 21	and gave a banquet for the elders
	7 : 23	and said before all the elders
	8 : 10	to summon Chabris and Charmis, the elders of her city
	10 : 6	with the elders of the city, Chabris and Charmis
	13 : 12	and called together the elders of the city
Wis	8 : 10	and honour in the presence of the elders, though I am young
Sir	6 : 34	Stand in the assembly of the elders
	7 : 14	Do not prattle in the assembly of the elders
Bar	1 : 4	and in the hearing of the elders
Sus	13 : 5	In that year 2 elders from the people were appointed as judges
	13 : 5	from elders who were judges
	13 : 8	The 2 elders used to see her every day
	13 : 16	And no one was there except the 2 elders
	13 : 18	and they did not see the elders, because they were hidden
	13 : 19	the 2 elders rose and ran to her, and said :
	13 : 24	and the 2 elders shouted against her
	13 : 27	And when the elders told their tale
	13 : 28	the 2 elders came
	13 : 34	Then the 2 elders stood up in the midst of the people
	13 : 36	The elders said, As we were walking in the garden alone
	13 : 41	because they were elders of the people and judges
	13 : 50	And the elders said to him, Come
	13 : 61	And they rose against the 2 elders
1 Ma	1 : 26	rulers and elders groaned
	7 : 33	and some of the elders of the people
	11 : 23	and he chose some of the elders of Israel
	12 : 35	When Jonathan returned he convened the elders of the people
	13 : 36	and to the elders and nation of the Jews, greeting
	14 : 20	to Simon the high priest and to the elders and the priests
	14 : 28	and the elders of the country
	16 : 2	And Simon called in his 2 elder sons Judas and John
2 Ma	13 : 13	After consulting privately with the elders
	14 : 37	A certain Razis, one of the elders of Jerusalem
1 Es	6 : 5	Yet the elders of the Jews were dealt with kindly
	6 : 8	we found the elders of the Jews
	6 : 11	Then we asked these elders
	6 : 27	and the elders of the Jews
	7 : 2	assisting the elders of the Jews
	9 : 4	in accordance with the decision of the ruling elders
	9 : 13	with the elders and judges of each place
3 Ma	1 : 8	Since the Jews had sent some of their council and elders
	1 : 23	and being barely restrained by the old men and the elders
	1 : 25	while the elders near the king tried in various ways
	6 : 1	directed the elders around him
4 Ma	7 : 10	O elder, fiercer than fire
	16 : 14	O mother, soldier of God in the cause of religion, elder and woman !

ELDEST 2

4 Ma	9 : 11	Then at his command the guards brought forward the eldest
	9 : 26	the guards brought in the next eldest

ELEAZAR 28 = 0.018 %

Sir	45 : 23	Phinehas the son of Eleazar is the 3rd in glory
	50 : 27	Jesus the son of Sirach, son of Eleazar, of Jerusalem
1 Ma	2 : 5	Eleazar called Avaran, and Jonathan called Apphus
	6 : 43	And Eleazar, called Avaran, saw
	8 : 17	and Jason the son of Eleazar
2 Ma	6 : 18	Eleazar, one of the scribes in high position
	6 : 24	that Eleazar in his 90th year
	8 : 23	Besides, he appointed Eleazar
1 Es	8 : 2	son of Eleazar, son of Aaron the chief priest
	8 : 63	and with him was Eleazar the son of Phinehas
	9 : 26	Malchijah, Mijamin, and Eleazar, and Asibias, and Benaiah
3 Ma	6 : 1	Then a certain Eleazar, famous among the priests of the country
	6 : 16	Just as Eleazar was ending his prayer

2 Es	1:2	son of Abishua, son of Phinehas, son of Eleazar
4 Ma	1:8	Eleazar and the 7 brothers and their mother
	5:4	one man, Eleazar by name, leader of the flock
	5:14	Eleazar asked to have a word
	6:1	When Eleazar in this manner had made eloquent response
	6:5	But the courageous and noble man, as a true Eleazar, was unmoved
	6:14	Eleazar, why are you so irrationally destroying yourself
	6:16	But Eleazar, as though more bitterly tormented by this counsel, cried out :
	7:1	the reason of our father Eleazar steered the ship of religion
	7:5	our father Eleazar broke the maddening waves of the emotions
	7:10	O supreme king over the passions, Eleazar !
	7:12	so the descendant of Aaron, Eleazar
	9:5	as though a short time ago you learned nothing from Eleazar
	16:73	you stood and watched Eleazar being tortured
	17:13	Eleazar was the first contestant

ELECT   6 = 0.004 %

Wis	3:9	because grace and mercy are upon his elect
	4:15	that God's grace and mercy are with his elect
Sir	46:1	a great saviour of God's elect
2 Es	15:21	Just as they have done to my elect until this day, so I will do
	16:73	Then the tested quality of my elect shall be manifest
	16:74	Hear, my elect, says the Lord

ELEMENT   4 = 0.003 %

Wis	7:17	and the activity of the elements
	19:18	For the elements changed places with one another
2 Ma	7:22	nor I who set in order the elements within each of you
4 Ma	12:13	and are made of the same elements as you

ELEPHANT   23 = 0.015 %

1 Ma	1:17	with chariots and elephants and cavalry
	3:34	And he turned over to Lysias half of his troops and the elephants
	6:30	20,000 horsemen, and 32 elephants accustomed to war
	6:34	They showed the elephants the juice of grapes and mulberries
	6:35	with each elephant they stationed a 1,000 men
	6:37	And upon the elephants were wooden towers, strong and covered
	6:46	He got under the elephant
	8:6	who went to fight against them with a 120 elephants
	11:56	And Trypho captured the elephants
2 Ma	11:4	and his thousands of cavalry, and his 80 elephants
	13:2	5,300 cavalry, 22 elephants
	13:15	He stabbed the leading elephant and its rider
	14:12	who had been in command of the elephants
	15:20	the elephants strategically stationed
	15:21	and the savagery of the elephants
3 Ma	5:1	so he summoned Hermon, keeper of the elephants
	5:2	to drug all the elephants – 500 in number
	5:4	And Hermon, keeper of the elephants
	5:10	Hermon, however, when he had drugged the pitiless elephants
	5:20	Tomorrow without delay prepare the elephants in the same way
	5:38	Equip the elephants now once more
	5:45	the elephant keeper entered at about dawn into the courtyard
	5:48	And when the Jews saw the dust raised by the elephants going out

ELEUTHERUS   2

1 Ma	11:7	as far as the river called Eleutherus
	12:30	for they had crossed the Eleutherus river

ELI   1

2 Es	1:2	son of Ahijah, son of Phinehas, son of Eli

ELIAB   1

Jud	8:1	son of Eliab, son of Nathanael, son of Salamiel

ELIALIS   1

1 Es	9:34	Elialis, Shimei, Shelemiah, Nethaniah

ELIASHIB   4 = 0.003 %

1 Es	9:1	to the chamber of Jehohanan the son of Eliashib
	9:24	Of the temple singers : Eliashib and Zaccur
	9:28	Of the sons of Zattu : Elioenai, Eliashib
	9:34	Carabasion and Eliashib and Machnadebai, Eliasis, Binnui

ELIASIS   1

1 Es	9:34	Carabasion and Eliashib and Machnadebai, Eliasis, Binnui

ELIEHOENAI   1

1 Es	8:31	Of the sons of Pahath-moab, Eliehoenai the son of Zerahiah

ELIEZAR   2

1 Es	8:43	I sent word to Eliezar, Iduel, Maasmas
	9:19	Maaseiah, Eliezar, Jarib and Jodan

ELIGIBLE   1

Tob	6:11	for you are her only eligible kinsman

ELIJAH   7 = 0.005 %

Jud	8:1	son of Ahitub, son of Elijah, son of Hilkiah
Sir	48:1	Then the prophet Elijah arose like a fire
	48:4	How glorious you were, O Elijah, in your wondrous deeds !
	48:12	It was Elijah who was covered by the whirlwind
1 Ma	2:58	Elijah because of great zeal for the law
1 Es	9:27	Jehiel and Abdi, and Jeremoth and Elijah
2 Es	7:109	and Elijah for those who received the rain

ELIOENAI   2

1 Es	9:22	Of the sons of Pashhur : Elioenai, Maaseiah, Ishmael
	9:28	Of the sons of Zattu : Elioenai, Eliashib

ELIONAS   1

1 Es	9:32	Of the sons of Annan : Elionas and Asaias and Melchias

ELIPHELET   2

1 Es	8:39	their names being Eliphelet, Jeuel, and Shemaiah
	9:33	and Eliphelet and Manasseh and Shimei

ELISHA   1

Sir	48:12	and Elisha was filled with his spirit

ELIXIR   1

Sir	6:16	A faithful friend is an elixir of life

ELKIAH   1

Jud	8:1	son of Joseph, son of Oziel, son of Elkiah

ELNATHAN   2

1 Es	8:44	Elnathan, Shemaiah, Jarib, Nathan, Elnathan

ELOQUENT   2

Ad E	14:13	Put eloquent speech in my mouth before the lion
4 Ma	6:1	When Eleazar in this manner had made eloquent response

ELSE   9 = 0.006 %

Bel	14:12	or else Daniel will, who is telling lies about us
	14:29	or else we will kill you and your household
1 Ma	15:31	or else give me for them 500 talents of silver
1 Es	4:5	whatever spoil they take and everything else
	8:18	And whatever else occurs to you as necessary
3 Ma	6:30	both wines and everything else
2 Es	6:10	between the heel and the hand seek for nothing else, Ezra !
	7:116	or else, when it had produced him, had restrained him from sinning
4 Ma	2:19	Why else did Jacob, our most wise father

ELUDE   2

1 Ma	9:47	but he eluded him and went to the rear
4 Ma	3:13	Eluding the sentinels at the gates

ELUL   1

1 Ma	14:27	On the 18th day of Elul, in the 172nd year

ELYMAEAN   1

Jud	1:6	and in the plain where Arioch ruled the Elymaeans

ELYMAIS   2

Tob	2:10	Ahikar, however, took care of me until he went to Elymais
1 Ma	6:1	when he heard that Elymais in Persia

EMADABUN   1

1 Es	5:58	and Kadmiel his brother and the sons of Jeshua Emadabun

EMANATION   1

Wis	7:25	and a pure emanation of the glory of the Almighty

EMATHIS   1

1 Es	9:29	Jehohanan and Hananiah and Zabbai and Emathis

EMBARK   3 = 0.002 %

1 Ma	15:37	Now Trypho embarked on a ship and escaped to Orthosia
2 Ma	5:9	having embarked to go to the Lacedaemonians
	12:3	to embark, with their wives and children

EMBARKATION   1

3 Ma	4:7	as far as the place of embarkation

EMBARRASS   1

Sir	26:24	but a modest daughter will even be embarrassed

EMBITTER   2

1 Ma	3:7	He embittered many kings, but he made Jacob glad by his deeds
2 Es	9:41	for I am greatly embittered in spirit and deeply afflicted

EMBRACE, verb   12 = 0.008 %

Tob	11 :9	Then Anna ran to meet them, and embraced her son
	11 :14	Then he saw his son and embraced him, and he wept and said
Jud	12 :12	for if we do not embrace her she will laugh at us
Ad E	15 :12	and he embraced her, and said, Speak to me
Sir	30 :20	like a eunuch who embraces a maiden and groans
Sus	13 :39	We saw them embracing, but we could not hold the man
3 Ma	5 :49	embracing relatives and falling into one another's arms
2 Es	2 :15	Mother, embrace your sons
	2 :32	Embrace your children until I come
	6 :39	and darkness and silence embraced everything
4 Ma	1 :24	is an emotion embracing pleasure and pain
	13 :21	From such embraces brotherly-loving souls are nourished

EMBROIDERER   1

Sir	45 :10	the work of an embroiderer

EMERALD   3 = 0.002 %

Tob	13 :16	For Jerusalem will be built with sapphires and emeralds
Jud	10 :21	and emeralds and precious stones
Sir	32 :6	A seal of emerald in a rich setting of gold

EMERGE   3 = 0.002 %

Wis	19 :7	and dry land emerging where water had stood before
1 Ma	9 :23	the lawless emerged in all parts of Israel
	11 :69	Then the men in ambush emerged from their places and joined battle

EMINENCE   1

Sir	38 :33	nor do they attain eminence in the public assembly

EMINENT   1

Sir	10 :22	The rich, and the eminent, and the poor

EMINENTLY   1

2 Ma	13 :8	And this was eminently just

EMMAUS   4 = 0.003 %

1 Ma	3 :40	and when they arrived they encamped near Emmaus in the plain
	3 :57	and encamped to the south of Emmaus
	4 :3	moved out to attack the king's force in Emmaus
	9 :50	the fortress in Jericho, and Emmaus, and Beth-horon

EMOTION   59 = 0.038 %

4 Ma	1 :1	that is, whether devout reason is sovereign over the emotions
	1 :3	that reason rules over those emotions that hinder self-control
	1 :4	the emotions that hinder one from justice, such as malice
	1 :5	Some might perhaps ask, If reason rules the emotions
	1 :6	For reason does not rule its own emotions
	1 :7	that reason is dominant over the emotions
	1 :9	demonstrated that reason controls the emotions
	1 :13	is whether reason is sovereign over the emotions
	1 :14	We shall decide just what reason is and what emotion is
	1 :14	how many kinds of emotions there are
	1 :19	since by means of it reason rules over the emotions
	1 :20	The 2 most comprehensive types of the emotions are pleasure and pain
	1 :21	The emotions of both pleasure and pain have many consequences
	1 :24	is an emotion embracing pleasure and pain
	1 :25	which is the most complex of all the emotions
	1 :29	and so tames the jungle of habits and emotions
	1 :30	but over the emotions it is sovereign
	1 :30	that rational judgment is sovereign over the emotions
	1 :35	For the emotions of the appetites are restrained
	2 :6	Just so it is with the emotions that hinder one from justice
	2 :7	unless reason is clearly lord of the emotions ?
	2 :9	we can recognize that reason rules the emotions
	2 :15	It is evident that reason rules even the more violent emotions :
	2 :16	For the temperate mind repels all these malicious emotions
	2 :18	the temperate mind is able to get the better of the emotions
	2 :21	he planted in him emotions and inclinations
	2 :24	that if reason is master of the emotions
	3 :1	for it is evident that reason rules not over its own emotions
	3 :5	For reason does not uproot the emotions but is their antagonist
	3 :17	For the temperate mind can conquer the drives of the emotions
	3 :18	and by nobility of reason spurn all domination by the emotions
	6 :31	Admittedly, then, devout reason is sovereign over the emotions
	6 :32	For if the emotions had prevailed over reason
	6 :33	But now that reason has conquered the emotions
	7 :1	over the sea of the emotions
	7 :5	our father Eleazar broke the maddening waves of the emotions
	7 :16	most certainly devout reason is governor of the emotions
	7 :17	Not every one has full command of his emotions
	7 :20	when some persons appear to be dominated by their emotions
	7 :22	would no be able to overcome the emotions through godliness ?
	7 :23	For only the wise and courageous man is lord of his emotions
	8 :28	For they were contemptuous of the emotions
	13 :1	that devout reason is sovereign over the emotions
	13 :2	For if they had been slaves to their emotions
	13 :2	we would say that they had been conquered by these emotions
	13 :3	they prevailed over their emotions
	13 :4	for the brothers mastered both emotions and pains
	13 :5	the sovereignty of right reason over emotion
	13 :7	conquered the tempest of the emotions
	14 :1	but also mastered the emotions of brotherly love
	14 :13	which draws everything toward an emotion felt in her inmost parts
	15 :1	O reason of the children, tyrant over the emotions !
	15 :4	the emotions of parents who love their children ?
	15 :23	in the very midst of her emotions
	15 :32	by the flood of your emotions and the violent winds
	16 :1	is sovereign over the emotions
	16 :2	that men have ruled over the emotions
	16 :4	But the mother quenched so many and such great emotions by devout reason
	18 :2	knowing that devout reason is master of all emotions

EMPLOY   3 = 0.002 %

2 Ma	1 :13	by a deception employed by the priests of Nanaea
1 Es	8 :22	persons employed in this temple
3 Ma	5 :22	But they did not so much employ the duration of the night

EMPLOYEE   1

Sir	34 :22	to deprive an employee of his wages is to shed blood

EMPTY, adj.   8 = 0.005 %

Jud	7 :20	until all the vessels of water belonging to every inhabitant of Bethulia were empty
Wis	2 :3	and the spirit will dissolve like empty air
Sir	29 :9	and because of his need do not send him away empty
2 Ma	14 :44	a space opened and he fell in the middle of the empty space
3 Ma	5 :43	would quickly render it forever empty
2 Es	6 :22	and full storehouses shall suddenly be found to be empty
	7 :25	Therefore, Ezra, empty things are for the empty

EMPTY-HANDED   2

Jud	1 :11	and they sent back his messengers empty-handed and shamefaced
Sir	35 :4	Do not appear before the Lord empty-handed

ENABLE   1

Sir	42 :17	The Lord has not enabled his holy ones

ENAMOUR, ENAMOR   1

Wis	8 :2	and I became enamoured of her beauty

ENCAMP   42 = 0.027 %

Jud	7 :3	They encamped in the valley near Bethulia, beside the spring
	7 :17	and they encamped in the valley and seized the water supply
	7 :18	and encamped in the hill country opposite Dothan
	7 :18	The rest of the Assyrian army encamped in the plain
Sir	14 :24	he who encamps near her house
1 Ma	2 :32	they encamped opposite them and prepared for battle
	3 :40	and when they arrived they encamped near Emmaus in the plain
	3 :42	and that the forces were encamped in their territory
	3 :57	and encamped to the south of Emmaus
	4 :29	They came into Idumea and encamped at Beth-zur
	5 :5	and he encamped against them, vowed their complete destruction
	5 :37	and encamped opposite Raphon, on the other side of the stream
	5 :39	and they are encamped across the stream
	5 :42	Permit no man to encamp, but make them all enter the battle
	5 :49	that each should encamp where he was
	5 :50	So the men of the forces encamped
	6 :26	And behold, today they have encamped
	6 :31	They came through Idumea and encamped against Beth-zur
	6 :32	and encamped at Beth-zechariah
	6 :48	and the king encamped in Judea and at Mount Zion
	6 :51	Then he encamped before the sanctuary for many days
	7 :19	and encamped in Beth-zaith
	7 :39	and encamped in Beth-horon
	7 :40	And Judas encamped in Adasa with 3,000 men
	9 :2	and encamped against Mesaloth in Arbela
	9 :3	they encamped against Jerusalem
	9 :5	Now Judas was encamped in Elasa
	9 :64	Then he came and encamped against Beth-basi
	10 :48	and encamped opposite Demetrius
	10 :69	and he assembled a large force and encamped against Jamnia
	10 :75	He encamped before Joppa
	10 :86	and encamped against Askalon
	11 :65	Simon encamped before Beth-zur
	11 :67	Jonathan and his army encamped by the waters of Gennesaret
	11 :73	as far as Kadesh, to their camp, and there they encamped
	13 :13	And Simon encamped in Adida, facing the plain
	13 :43	In those days Simon encamped against Gazara
	15 :13	So Antiochus encamped against Dor
	15 :39	He commanded him to encamp against Judea
1 Es	8 :41	and we encamped there 3 days

3 Ma	1:1	where Antiochus's supporters were encamped
4 Ma	3:8	around which the whole army of our ancestors had encamped

ENCIRCLE
6 = 0.004 %

Sir	43:12	It encircles the heaven with its glorious arc
	45:9	And he encircled him with pomegranates
1 Ma	10:11	to build the walls and encircle Mount Zion
	12:13	many afflictions and many wars have encircled us
3 Ma	4:8	their necks encircled with ropes instead of garlands
4 Ma	14:8	encircled the sevenfold fear of tortures and dissolved it

ENCLOSE
4 = 0.003 %

2 Ma	1:34	and enclosed the place and made it sacred
3 Ma	1:18	The virgins who had been enclosed in their chambers
	4:11	he commanded that they should be enclosed in the hippodrome
2 Es	16:58	who has enclosed the sea in the midst of the waters

ENCLOSURE
2

Sir	50:2	the high retaining walls for the temple enclosure
3 Ma	1:7	By doing this, and by endowing their sacred enclosures with gifts

ENCOMPASS
1

3 Ma	6:26	Who is it that has so lawlessly encompassed with outrageous treatment

ENCOUNTER, subst.
3 = 0.002 %

1 Ma	9:11	and took its stand for the encounter
2 Ma	8:30	In encounters with the forces of Timothy and Bacchides
	15:19	being anxious over the encounter in the open country

ENCOUNTER, verb
3 = 0.002 %

1 Ma	5:25	They encountered the Nabateans, who met them peaceably
2 Ma	10:17	and slew those whom they encountered
	14:17	Simon, the brother of Judas, had encountered Nicanor

ENCOURAGE
14 = 0.009 %

Sir	17:24	and he encourages those whose endurance is failing
1 Ma	5:53	and encouraging the people all the way
	12:50	and they encouraged one another
	13:3	he encouraged them, saying to them
2 Ma	7:5	but the brothers and their mother encouraged one another to die nobly
	7:21	She encouraged each of them in the language of their fathers
	11:32	And I have also sent Menelaus to encourage you
	15:9	Encouraging them from the law and the prophets
	15:17	Encouraged by the words of Judas
1 Es	8:27	I was encouraged by the help of the Lord my God
3 Ma	1:6	and encourage them
4 Ma	13:8	encouraged one another, saying
	14:1	Furthermore, they encouraged them to face the torture
	16:24	encouraged and persuaded each of her sons

ENCOURAGEMENT
3 = 0.002 %

Wis	8:9	and encouragement in cares and grief
1 Ma	10:24	I also will write them words of encouragement
	12:9	since we have as encouragement the holy books

END, subst.
89 = 0.058 %

Jud	2:9	to the ends of the whole earth
	11:21	from one end of the earth to the other
	13:6	She went up to the post at the end of the bed
Ad E	14:13	so that there may be an end of him
Wis	2:1	and there is no remedy when a man comes to his end
	2:16	he calls the last end of the righteous happy
	2:17	and let us test what will happen at the end of his life
	3:19	For the end of an unrighteous generation is grievous
	4:17	For they will see the end of the wise man
	5:4	and that his end was without honour
	6:1	learn, O judges of the ends of the earth
	7:18	the beginning and end and middle of times
	8:1	She reaches mightily from one end of the earth to the other
	11:14	at the end of the events they marvelled at him
	14:14	and therefore their speedy end has been planned
	14:27	is the beginning and cause and end of every evil
	16:5	thy wrath did not continue to the end
	18:21	he withstood the anger and put an end to the disaster
	19:1	But the ungodly were assailed to the end by pitiless anger
	19:4	For the fate they deserved drew them on to this end
Sir	1:13	With him who fears the Lord it will go well at the end
	2:3	that you may be honoured at the end of your life
	3:26	A stubborn mind will be afflicted at the end
	7:36	In all you do, remember the end of your life
	9:11	for you do not know what his end will be
	14:7	and betrays his baseness in the end
	18:12	He sees and recognizes that their end will be evil
	21:9	and their end is a flame of fire
	21:10	but at its end is the pit of Hades
	22:8	and at the end he will say, What is it ?
	27:14	makes one's hair stand on end
	28:6	Remember the end of your life, and cease from enmity

	30:10	and in the end you will gnash your teeth
	31:22	and in the end you will appreciate my words
	38:20	drive it away, remembering the end of life
	41:3	remember your former days and the end of life
	43:27	Though we speak much we cannot reach the end
	44:21	and from the River to the ends of the earth
	48:25	He revealed what was to occur to the end of time
	49:4	the kings of Judah came to an end
Bar	3:17	in which men trust, and there is no end to their getting
1 Ma	1:3	He advanced to the ends of the earth
	3:9	He was renowned to the ends of the earth
	8:4	from the ends of the earth
	14:10	till his renown spread to the ends of the earth
2 Ma	5:7	and in the end got only disgrace from his conspiracy
	5:8	Finally he met a miserable end
	7:38	to bring to an end the wrath of the Almighty
	9:28	came to the end of his life by a most pitiable fate
	10:9	Such then was the end of Antiochus who was called Epiphanes
	13:16	In the end they filled the camp with terror and confusion
	15:39	And here will be the end
1 Es	9:17	were brought to an end
3 Ma	4:14	and at the end to be destroyed in the space of a single day
	5:49	the end of their most miserable suspense
	6:32	Putting an end to all mourning and wailing
2 Es	2:34	because he who will come at the end of the age is close at hand
	3:14	and to him only didst thou reveal the end of the times
	4:26	because the age is hastening swiftly to its end
	5:41	thou dost have charge of those who are alive at the end
	6:6	just as the end shall come through me
	6:7	Or when will be the end of the first age
	6:9	For Esau is the end of this age
	6:10	and the end of a man is his heel
	6:12	show thy servant the end of thy signs
	6:15	because the word concerns the end
	6:16	for they know that their end must be changed
	6:25	and shall see my salvation and the end of my world
	7:112	He answered me and said, This present world is not the end
	7:113	But the day of judgment will be the end of this age
	7:114	sinful indulgence has come to an end
	8:54	and in the end the treasure of immortality is made manifest
	9:5	the beginning is evident, and the end manifest
	9:6	and the end in requital and in signs
	10:28	my end has become corruption, and my prayer a reproach
	11:13	And while it was reigning it came to its end and disappeared
	11:14	And while it was reigning its end came also
	11:39	so that the end of my times might come through them ?
	12:6	that he may strengthen me to the end
	12:9	to be shown the end of the times
	12:21	when its end approaches
	12:21	but 2 shall be kept until the end
	12:30	It is these whom the Most High has kept for the eagle's end
	12:32	until the end of days
	12:34	and he will make them joyful until the end comes
	14:5	and declared to him the end of the times
	16:13	to the ends of the world
4 Ma	4:24	to put an end to the people's observance of the law
	11:15	Since to this end we were born and bred

END, verb
17 = 0.011 %

Tob	8:20	until the 14 days of the wedding feast were ended
	14:1	Here Tobit ended his words of praise
Jud	10:1	and had ended all these words
Ad E	15:1	On the 3rd day, when she ended her prayer
Sir	33:23	At the time when you end the days of your life
	50:19	till the order of worship of the Lord was ended
2 Ma	10:13	he took poison and ended his life
	15:24	With these words he ended his prayer
	15:37	So I too will here end my story
1 Es	4:21	With his wife he ends his days
3 Ma	1:2	intending single-handed to kill him and thereby end the war
	6:16	Just as Eleazar was ending his prayer
2 Es	10:22	and our rejoicing has been ended
	11:44	and behold, they are ended, and his ages are completed !
	14:9	until the times are ended
	14:45	And when the 40 days were ended
4 Ma	12:19	he flung himself into the braziers and so ended his life

ENDEAVOUR, ENDEAVOR, verb
2

2 Ma	10:15	and endeavoured to keep up the war
	11:19	I will endeavour for the future to help promote your welfare

ENDEAVOUR, ENDEAVOR, subst.
2

2 Es	8:27	Regard not the endeavours of those who act wickedly
	8:27	but the endeavours of those who have kept thy covenants amid afflictions

ENDLESS
2

2 Es	6:44	For immediately fruit came forth in endless abundance
4 Ma	17:12	The prize was immortality in endless life

ENDOW

			4 = 0.003 %

Wis 8:19 As a child I was by nature well endowed
Sir 17:3 He endowed them with strength like his own
3 Ma 1:7 By doing this, and by endowing their sacred enclosures with gifts
2 Es 4:22 why have I been endowed with the power of understanding ?

ENDURANCE   14 = 0.009 %

Sir 2:14 Woe to you who have lost your endurance !
17:24 and he encourages those whose endurance is failing
4 Ma 1:11 marvelled at their courage and endurance
1:11 By their endurance they conquered the tyrant
6:13 partly out of admiration for his endurance
7:9 through your glorious endurance
9:8 For we, through this severe suffering and endurance
9:30 by our endurance for the sake of religion ?
11:12 an opportunity to show our endurance for the law
15:30 and more manly than men in endurance !
17:12 and tested them for their endurance
17:17 The tyrant himself and all his council marvelled at their endurance
17:23 and their endurance under the tortures
17:23 as an example for their own endurance

ENDURE*   46 = 0.030 %

Jud 11:7 and as his power endures
Wis 11:25 How would anything have endured if thou hadst not willed it ?
17:17 he was seized, and endured the inescapable fate
Sir 1:23 A patient man will endure until the right moment
11:17 The gift of the Lord endures for those who are godly
40:17 and almsgiving endures for ever
41:13 but a good name endures for ever
45:26 and that their glory may endure throughout their generations
51:3 from the many afflictions that I endured
Bar 4:1 and the law that endures for ever
4:25 My children, endure with patience
P Az 67 for his mercy endures for ever
68 for his mercy endures for ever
Sus 13:57 but a daughter of Judah would not endure your wickedness
1 Ma 4:24 for he is good, for his mercy endures for ever
10:15 and of the troubles that they had endured
2 Ma 2:27 we will gladly endure the uncomfortable toil
6:30 I am enduring terrible sufferings in my body under this beating
7:36 For our brothers after enduring a brief suffering
9:12 And when he could not endure his own stench
9:28 having endured the most intense suffering
1 Es 4:38 But truth endures and is strong for ever
2 Es 1:9 How long shall I endure them
3:30 for I have seen how thou dost endure those who sin
7:18 The righteous therefore can endure difficult circumstances
8:8 endures thy creation which has been created in it
10:54 for no work of man's building could endure in a place
4 Ma 5:23 so that we endure any suffering willingly
6:7 because his body could not endure the agonies
6:9 and endured the tortures
7:22 and knows that it is blessed to endure any suffering
9:6 lived piously while enduring torture
9:22 he nobly endured the rackings
9:28 But he steadfastly endured this agony and said
10:1 When he too had endured a glorious death, the 3rd was led in
13:27 those who were left endured for the sake of religion
15:31 stoutly endured the waves
15:32 endured nobly and withstood the wintry storms
16:1 endured seeing her children tortured to death
16:8 In vain, my sons, I endured many birth-pangs for you
16:17 while an aged man endures such agonies for the sake of religion
16:19 and therefore you ought to endure any suffering for the sake of God
16:21 and endured it for the sake of God
17:4 maintaining firm an enduring hope in God
17:7 enduring their varied tortures to death
17:10 looking to God and enduring torture even to death

ENEMY   166 = 0.108 %

Tob 12:10 but those who commit sin are the enemies of their own lives
Jud 5:18 and their cities were captured by their enemies
7:19 because all their enemies had surrounded them
8:11 promising to surrender the city to our enemies
8:15 or even to destroy us in the presence of our enemies
8:19 and so they suffered a great catastrophe before our enemies
8:33 to surrender the city to our enemies
8:35 to take revenge upon our enemies
13:5 for the destruction of the enemies
13:11 and his strength against our enemies
13:14 but has destroyed our enemies by my hand this very night !
13:17 the enemies of thy people
13:18 to strike the head of the leader of our enemies
15:4 to rush out upon their enemies to destroy them
15:5 with one accord they fell upon the enemy
15:5 for they were told what had happened in the camp of the enemy
16:11 for weak people shouted and the enemy trembled

16:11 they lifted up their voices, and the enemy were turned back
Ad E 13:6 be utterly destroyed by the sword of their enemies
14:6 and thou hast given us into the hands of our enemies
Wis 5:17 and will arm all creation to repel his enemies
10:12 She protected him from his enemies
10:19 but she drowned their enemies
11:3 They withstood their enemies and fought off their foes
11:5 by which their enemies were punished
11:8 how thou didst punish their enemies
12:20 the enemies of thy servants and those deserving of death
12:22 thou scourgest our enemies 10,000 times more
12:24 those animals which even their enemies despised
15:14 are all the enemies who oppressed thy people
15:18 The enemies of thy people worship
16:4 how their enemies were being tormented
16:8 And by this also thou didst convince our enemies
16:22 so that they might know that the crops of their enemies
18:1 Their enemies heard their voices but did not see their forms
18:4 For their enemies deserved to be deprived of light
18:7 and the destruction of their enemies
18:8 For by the same means by which thou didst punish our enemies
18:10 But the discordant cry of their enemies echoed back
Sir 5:15 and do not become an enemy instead of a friend
6:4 and make him the laughingstock of his enemies
6:9 And there is a friend who changes into an enemy
6:13 Keep yourself far from your enemies
12:8 nor will an enemy be hidden in adversity
12:9 A man's enemies are grieved when he prospers
12:10 Never trust your enemy
12:16 An enemy will speak sweetly with his lips
12:16 an enemy will weep with his eyes
18:31 it will make you the laughingstock of your enemies
20:23 and needlessly make him an enemy
23:3 and my enemy will not rejoice over me
25:14 And any vengeance, but not the vengeance of enemies !
25:15 and no wrath worse than an enemy's wrath
26:27 for putting the enemy to flight
27:18 For as a man destroys his enemy
29:6 and he has needlessly made him his enemy
29:13 it will fight on your behalf against your enemy
30:3 He who teaches his son will make his enemies envious
30:6 he has left behind him an avenger against his enemies
36:7 destroy the adversary and wipe out the enemy
36:10 Crush the heads of the rulers of the enemy
42:11 lest she make you a laughingstock to your enemies
45:2 and made him great in the fears of his enemies
46:1 to take vengeance on the enemies that rose against them
46:5 when enemies pressed him on every side
46:16 when his enemies pressed him on every side
47:7 For he wiped out his enemies on every side
49:9 For God remembered his enemies with storm
51:8 and dost save them from the hand of their enemies
Bar 3:10 why is it that you are in the land of your enemies
4:6 but you were handed over to your enemies
4:18 will deliver you from the hand of your enemies
4:21 from the power and hand of the enemy
4:25 Your enemy has overtaken you
4:26 they were taken away like a flock carried off by the enemy
5:6 led away by their enemies
L Jr 6:56 Besides, they can offer no resistance to a king or any enemies
P Az 9 Thou hast given us into the hands of lawless enemies
1 Ma 2:7 and to dwell there when it was given over to the enemy
2:35 Then the enemy hastened to attack them
4:18 But stand now against our enemies and fight them
4:36 Behold, our enemies are crushed
5:13 the enemy have captured their wives and children and goods
5:16 who were in distress and were being attacked by enemies
5:27 the enemy are getting ready to attack the strongholds tomorrow
6:38 on the 2 flanks of the army, to harass the enemy
7:29 But the enemy were ready to seize Judas
7:46 and they outflanked the enemy
8:23 and may sword and enemy be far from them
8:26 And to the enemy who makes war
8:28 And to the enemy allies shall be given no grain
9:6 When they saw the huge number of the enemy forces
9:8 Let us rise and go up against our enemies
9:24 and the country deserted with them to the enemy
9:29 to go against our enemies and Bacchides
9:46 that you may be delivered from the hands of our enemies
9:48 and the enemy did not cross the Jordan to attack them
10:26 and have not sided with our enemies
10:81 and the enemy's horses grew tired
11:72 Then he turned back to the battle against the enemy
12:15 and we were delivered from our enemies
12:15 and our enemies were humbled
12:26 that the enemy were being drawn up in formation
12:28 When the enemy heard
13:51 because a great enemy had been crushed and removed from Israel
14:26 they have fought and repulsed Israel's enemies

	14:29	and resisted the enemies of their nation
	14:31	And when their enemies decided to invade their country
	14:33	where formerly the arms of the enemy had been stored
	14:34	where the enemy formerly dwelt
	15:33	which at one time had been unjustly taken by our enemies
	16:7	for the cavalry of the enemy were very numerous
2 Ma	3:38	he replied, If you have any enemy or plotter against your government
	4:16	became their enemies and punished them
	5:6	over enemies and not over fellow countrymen
	8:6	and put to flight not a few of the enemy
	8:16	and exhorted them not to be frightened by the enemy
	8:24	they slew more than 9,000 of the enemy
	8:27	And when they had collected the arms of the enemy
	8:31	Collecting the arms of the enemy
	10:21	by setting their enemies free to fight against them
	10:26	and to be an enemy to their enemies
	10:27	and when they came near to the enemy they halted
	10:29	there appeared to the enemy from heaven
	10:30	And they showered arrows and thunderbolts upon the enemy
	11:11	They hurled themselves like lions against the enemy
	12:22	terror and fear came over the enemy
	12:28	who with power shatters the might of his enemies
	13:21	gave secret information to the enemy
	14:17	because of the sudden consternation created by the enemy
	14:22	to prevent sudden treachery on the part of the enemy
	15:20	and the enemy was already close at hand
	15:26	and Judas and his men met the enemy in battle
1 Es	4:4	and if he sends them out against the enemy, they go
	5:66	and when the enemies of the tribe of Judah and Benjamin heard it
	8:61	he delivered us from every enemy on the way
3 Ma	1:5	And so it came about that the enemy was routed in the action
	2:13	subjected to our enemies, and overtaken by helplessness
	2:30	In order that he might not appear to be an enemy to all
	2:33	considering them to be enemies of the Jewish nation
	3:24	as traitors and barbarous enemies
	3:25	to suffer the sure and shameful death that befits enemies
	4:4	even some of their enemies
	6:6	and turning the flame against all their enemies
	6:10	rescue us from the hand of the enemy
	6:15	Not even when they were in the land of their enemies did I neglect them
	6:19	They opposed the forces of the enemy
	7:21	They also possessed greater prestige among their enemies
2 Es	1:11	I have slain all their enemies
	1:16	at the destruction of your enemies
	3:27	So thou didst deliver the city into the hands of thy enemies
	3:30	and hast destroyed thy people, and hast preserved thy enemies
	6:24	At that time friends shall make war on friends like enemies
	15:33	an enemy in ambush shall beset them
4 Ma	2:14	The fruit trees of the enemy are not cut down
	2:14	but one preserves the property of enemies from the destroyers
	3:11	in the enemy's territory
	3:12	and taking a pitcher climbed over the enemy's ramparts
	3:13	they went searching throughout the enemy camp
	8:10	Even I, your enemy, have compassion
	9:15	Most abominable tyrant, enemy of heavenly justice, savage of mind
	11:23	and enemy of those who are truly devout
	17:20	our enemies did not rule over our nation
	17:24	and he ravaged and conquered all his enemies
	18:4	they ravaged the enemy

ENFORCE   1
1 Ma	2:15	Then the king's officers who were enforcing the apostasy

ENGAGE   13 = 0.008 %
Wis	17:20	*and was engaged in unhindered work*
1 Ma	1:18	He engaged Ptolemy king of Egypt in battle
	4:14	and engaged in battle
	5:7	He engaged in many battles with them
	5:19	but do not engage in battle with the Gentiles until we return
	10:78	and the armies engaged in battle
	10:82	and engaged the phalanx in battle
2 Ma	14:16	and engaged them in battle at a village called Dessau
3 Ma	1:24	*Meanwhile the crowd, as before, was engaged in prayer*
2 Es	9:39	*Then I dismissed the thoughts with which I had been engaged*
	10:5	*Then I broke off the reflections with which I was still engaged*
	15:30	and engage them in battle
4 Ma	17:11	Truly the contest in which they were engaged was divine

EN-GEDI   1
Sir	24:14	I grew tall like a palm tree in En-gedi

ENGINE   11 = 0.007 %
1 Ma	5:30	carrying ladders and engines of war to capture the stronghold
	6:20	and he built siege towers and other engines of war
	6:31	and for many days they fought and built engines of war
	6:51	engines of war to throw fire and stones

	6:52	The Jews also made engines of war to match theirs
	11:20	and he built many engines of war to use against it
	13:43	He made a siege engine, brought it up to the city
	13:44	The men in the siege engine leaped out into the city
	15:25	and making engines of war
2 Ma	12:15	who without battering-rams or engines of war
	12:27	and great stores of war engines and missiles were there

ENGRAVE   2
Wis	18:24	and the glories of the fathers were engraved
Sir	45:11	with precious stones engraved like signets

ENGRAVED   1
Sir	45:11	for a reminder, in engraved letters

ENHANCE   3 = 0.002 %
2 Ma	5:16	to enhance the glory and honour of the place
	15:39	and enhances one's enjoyment
3 Ma	2:31	since they expected to enhance their reputation

ENJOY   18 = 0.012 %
Jud	12:12	without enjoying her company
Ad E	16:11	so far enjoyed the good will that we have for every nation
Wis	2:6	Come, therefore, let us enjoy the good things that exist
Sir	11:19	and now I shall enjoy my goods !
	14:5	He will not enjoy his own riches
	19:19	enjoy the fruit of the tree of immortality
	37:28	and not every person enjoys everything
	41:1	and who still has the vigour to enjoy his food !
2 Ma	11:31	to enjoy their own food and laws, just as formerly
1 Es	1:58	Until the land has enjoyed its sabbaths
	9:54	to eat and drink and enjoy themselves
2 Es	7:95	they understand the rest which they now enjoy
	7:96	which they are to receive and enjoy in immortality
4 Ma	3:20	At a time when our fathers were enjoying profound peace
	5:9	It is senseless not to enjoy delicious things
	8:5	but I also exhort you to yield to me and enjoy my friendship
	8:8	And enjoy your youth by adopting the Greek way of life
	16:18	and have enjoyed life

ENJOYMENT   4 = 0.003 %
Wis	2:9	everywhere let us leave signs of enjoyment
2 Ma	15:39	and enhances one's enjoyment
3 Ma	7:16	and had received the full enjoyment of deliverance
4 Ma	2:1	the desires of the mind for the enjoyment of beauty

ENLIGHTEN   2
Sir	45:17	and to enlighten Israel with his law
2 Es	13:53	And you alone have been enlightened about this

ENLIST   2
1 Ma	4:35	he departed to Antioch and enlisted mercenaries
2 Ma	8:1	and enlisted those who had continued in the Jewish faith

ENMITY   7 = 0.005 %
Sir	28:6	Remember the end of your life, and cease from enmity
	28:9	and inject enmity among those who are at peace
	37:2	when a companion and friend turns to enmity ?
1 Ma	11:12	and their enmity became manifest
2 Ma	14:39	Nicanor, wishing to exhibit the enmity
3 Ma	4:1	for the inveterate enmity which had long ago been in their minds
4 Ma	2:14	through the law, can prevail even over enmity

ENOCH   2
Sir	44:16	Enoch pleased the Lord, and was taken up
	49:14	No one like Enoch has been created on earth

ENOUGH, adj., adv.   17 = 0.011 %
Tob	5:19	is enough for us
Jud	4:7	only wide enough for 2 men at the most
	7:21	and they did not have enough water
Wis	4:5	and their fruit will be useless, not ripe enough to eat
	14:22	Afterward it was not enough for them
	18:25	for merely to test the wrath was enough
Sir	5:1	nor say, I have enough
	11:24	Do not say, I have enough
	39:11	and if he goes to rest, it is enough for him
	42:25	and who can have enough of beholding his glory
	43:30	and do not grow weary, for you cannot praise him enough
1 Ma	2:33	And they said to them, Enough of this !
2 Ma	7:42	Let this be enough, then, about the eating of sacrifices
1 Es	8:88	Wast thou not angry enough with us
3 Ma	3:8	were not strong enough to help them
4 Ma	10:14	You do not have a fire hot enough to make me play the coward
	15:11	strong enough to pervert her reason

ENRAGE   6 = 0.004 %
Bel	14:21	Then the king was enraged
1 Ma	6:28	The king was enraged when he heard this

ENRAGE

	9:69	So he was greatly enraged at the lawless men
3 Ma	3:1	he became so infuriated that not only was he enraged
4 Ma	9:10	but also was enraged, as at those who are ungrateful
	10:5	Enraged by the man's boldness

ENRICH   1

Sir 11:21   to enrich a poor man quickly and suddenly

ENROL   7 = 0.005 %

1 Ma	8:20	that we may be enrolled as your allies and friends
	10:36	Let Jews be enrolled in the king's forces
	10:65	and enrolled him among his chief friends
	13:40	to be enrolled in our bodyguard
	13:40	let them be enrolled, and let there be peace between us
2 Ma	4:9	and to enrol the men of Jerusalem as citizens of Antioch
1 Es	8:30	and with him a 150 men enrolled

ENSLAVE   7 = 0.005 %

Wis	1:4	nor dwell in a body enslaved to sin
1 Ma	8:10	tore down their strongholds, and enslaved them to this day
	8:11	as many as ever opposed them, they destroyed and enslaved
	8:18	was completely enslaving Israel
3 Ma	2:6	on the audacious Pharaoh who had enslaved your holy people Israel
2 Es	10:22	our young men have been enslaved and our strong men made powerless
4 Ma	3:2	not to be enslaved by desire

ENSNARE   2

Jud	10:19	they will be able to ensnare the whole world !
Sir	25:21	Do not be ensnared by a woman's beauty

ENTANGLE   1

3 Ma 6:10   Even if our lives have become entangled in impieties in our exile

ENTER   59 = 0.038 %

Tob	3:17	At that very moment Tobit returned and entered his house
	4:10	and keeps you from entering the darkness
	5:9	he entered and they greeted each other
	6:16	When you enter the bridal chamber
	12:15	and enter into the presence of the glory of the Holy One
Jud	4:7	and it was easy to stop any who tried to enter
Wis	1:4	because wisdom will not enter a deceitful soul
	2:24	but through the devil's envy death entered the world
	3:13	who has not entered into a sinful union
	8:16	When I enter my house, I shall find rest with her
	8:20	or rather, being good, I entered an undefiled body
	10:16	She entered the soul of a servant of the Lord
	14:14	For through the vanity of men they entered the world
Sir	4:13	and the Lord will bless the place she enters
	51:15	my foot entered upon the straight path
Bar	3:15	And who has entered her storehouses ?
L Jr	6:17	raised by the feet of those who enter
Bel	14:21	through which they were accustomed to enter
1 Ma	1:21	He arrogantly entered the sanctuary
	4:5	When Gorgias entered the camp of Judas by night
	5:42	Permit no man to encamp, but make them all enter the battle
	6:62	But when the king entered Mount Zion
	7:2	As he was entering the royal palace of his fathers
	8:19	and they entered the senate chamber and spoke as follows :
	10:83	They fled to Azotus and entered Beth-dagon
	11:3	But when Ptolemy entered the cities
	11:13	Then Ptolemy entered Antioch and put on the crown of Asia
	12:3	and entered the senate chamber and said
	12:48	But when Jonathan entered Ptolemais
	12:48	and all who had entered with him they killed with the sword
	13:47	and then entered it with hymns and praise
	13:51	the Jews entered it with praise and palm branches
	15:14	and permitted no one to leave or enter it
2 Ma	1:15	they closed the temple as soon as he entered it
	2:24	for those who wish to enter upon the narratives of history
	3:28	this man who had just entered the aforesaid treasury
	5:15	Not content with this, Antiochus dared to enter
	8:1	secretly entered the villages and summoned their kinsmen
	9:2	For he had entered the city called Persepolis
	13:13	before the king's army could enter Judea
1 Es	4:49	should forcibly enter their doors
	6:8	and entered the city of Jerusalem
	8:83	The land which you are entering to take possession of it
3 Ma	1:9	Then, upon entering the place
	1:10	and conceived a desire to enter the holy of holies
	1:11	were allowed to enter
	1:12	he did not cease to maintain that he ought to enter, saying
	1:13	And he inquired why, when he entered every other temple
	1:15	Why should not I at least enter
	2:28	shall enter their sanctuaries
	3:17	to enter their inner temple and honour it
	3:18	and excluded us from entering
	4:6	And young women who had just entered the bridal chamber
	5:46	the elephant keeper entered at about dawn into the courtyard

2 Es	7:80	such spirits shall not enter into habitations
	7:123	but we shall not enter it
	10:1	But it happened that when my son entered his wedding chamber
	10:48	When my son entered his wedding chamber he died
4 Ma	17:13	the mother of the 7 sons entered the competition

ENTERTAINMENT   1

Sir 32:4   Where there is entertainment, do not pour out talk

ENTHRONE   2

Bar	3:3	For thou art enthroned for ever
4 Ma	2:22	but at the same time he enthroned the mind among the senses

ENTICE   1

Jud 10:4   to entice the eyes of all men who might see her

ENTIRE   4 = 0.003 %

Tob	1:21	and over the entire administration
1 Ma	3:40	So they departed with their entire force
3 Ma	4:14	The entire race was to be registered individually
4 Ma	2:19	of the entire tribe of the Shechemites

ENTIRELY   1

4 Ma 3:1   This notion is entirely ridiculous

ENTITLE   3 = 0.002 %

Tob	3:17	because Tobias was entitled to possess her
	6:11	because you are entitled to her and to her inheritance
	6:12	are entitled to the inheritance

ENTRAILS   4 = 0.003 %

2 Ma	14:46	he tore out his entrails
4 Ma	5:30	not even if you gouge out my eyes and burn my entrails
	10:8	and drops of blood flowing from his entrails
	11:19	and pierced his ribs so that his entrails were burned through

ENTRANCE   9 = 0.006 %

Wis	7:6	there is for all mankind one entrance into life
	7:25	therefore nothing defiled gains entrance into her
Bel	14:13	for beneath the table they had made a hidden entrance
2 Ma	2:5	and the altar of incense, and he sealed up the entrance
2 Es	4:7	or which are the entrances of paradise ?
	7:4	but it has an entrance set in a narrow place
	7:7	but the entrance to it is narrow
	7:12	And so the entrances of this world were made narrow
	7:13	But the entrances of the greater world are broad and safe

ENTREAT   8 = 0.005 %

Wis	13:18	for aid he entreats a thing that is utterly inexperienced
Bar	2:8	Yet we have not entreated the favour of the Lord
3 Ma	1:16	and entreated the supreme God to aid in the present situation
	6:14	The whole throng of infants and their parents entreat you with tears
2 Es	1:28	Have I not entreated you as a father entreats his sons
	7:102	or to entreat the Most High for them
	10:37	Now therefore I entreat you

ENTREATY   3 = 0.002 %

1 Ma	11:49	and they cried out to the king with this entreaty
2 Ma	3:20	And holding up their hands to heaven, they all made entreaty
3 Ma	5:9	So their entreaty ascended fervently to heaven

ENTRUST   11 = 0.007 %

Tob	10:12	See, I am entrusting my daughter to you
Ad E	16:5	by the persuasion of friends who have been entrusted
Sir	50:24	May he entrust to us his mercy !
2 Ma	3:22	that he would keep what had been entrusted safe and secure
	3:22	for those who had entrusted it
	7:24	and entrust him with public affairs
	9:25	whom I have often entrusted and commended to most of you
	10:13	which Philometor had entrusted to him
3 Ma	3:21	and the myriad affairs liberally entrusted to them from the beginning
2 Es	2:37	Receive what the Lord has entrusted to you and be joyful
	5:17	Or do you not know that Israel has been entrusted to you

ENVELOP   1

Wis 18:14   For while gentle silence enveloped all things

ENVIABLE   1

2 Ma 7:24   that he would make him rich and enviable

ENVIOUS   4 = 0.003 %

Sir	14:3	and of what use is property to an envious man ?
	26:6	when a wife is envious of a rival
	30:3	He who teaches his son will make his enemies envious
3 Ma	6:7	Daniel, who through envious slanders

ENVIRON 3 = 0.002 %
1 Ma 10:31 And let Jerusalem and her environs
10:89 He also gave him Ekron and all its environs as his possession
14:36 and defile the environs of the sanctuary

ENVOY 12 = 0.008 %
1 Ma 11:9 He sent envoys to Demetrius the king, saying
12:4 in every place, asking them to provide for the envoys
12:8 Onias welcomed the envoy with honour
12:23 that our envoys report to you accordingly
13:14 so he sent envoys to him and said
13:21 Now the men in the citadel kept sending envoys to Trypho
14:21 The envoys who were sent to our people
14:22 Numenius the son of Antiochus and Antipater the son of Jason, envoys of the Jews
14:40 the envoys of Simon with honour
15:17 The envoys of the Jews have come to us
2 Ma 4:19 the vile Jason sent envoys
11:34 Quintus Memmius and Titus Manius, envoys of the Romans

ENVY, subst. 5 = 0.003 %
Wis 2:24 but through the devil's envy death entered the world
6:23 neither will I travel in the company of sickly envy
6:23 for envy does not associate with wisdom
Sir 40:5 there is anger and envy and trouble and unrest
1 Ma 8:16 and there is no envy or jealousy among them

ENVY, verb 3 = 0.002 %
Sir 9:11 Do not envy the honours of a sinner
45:18 and envied him in the wilderness
2 Es 2:28 The nations shall envy you

EPEIPH 2
3 Ma 6:38 from the 25th of Pachon to the 4th of Epeiph, for 40 days
6:38 for the 5th to the 7th of Epeiph, the 3 days

EPHOD 1
Sir 45:8 the linen breeches, the long robe, and the ephod

EPHRAIM 3 = 0.002 %
Jud 6:2 And who are you, Achior, and you hirelings of Ephraim
Sir 47:21 and a disobedient kingdom arose out of Ephraim
47:23 and gave to Ephraim a sinful way

EPHRON 2
1 Ma 5:46 So they came to Ephron
2 Ma 12:27 he marched also against Ephron

EPIPHANES 7 = 0.005 %
1 Ma 1:10 From them came forth a sinful root, Antiochus Epiphanes
10:1 In the 160th year Alexander Epiphanes, the son of Antiochus
2 Ma 2:20 and further the wars against Antiochus Epiphanes
4:7 and Antiochus who was called Epiphanes succeeded to the kingdom
10:9 Such then was the end of Antiochus who was called Epiphanes
10:13 and had gone over to Antiochus Epiphanes
4 Ma 4:15 his son Antiochus Epiphanes succeeded to the throne

EPISODE 1
2 Ma 3:40 This was the outcome of the episode of Heliodorus

EQUAL, adj. 8 = 0.005 %
Sir 45:2 He made him equal in glory to the holy ones
2 Ma 8:30 shares equal to their own
9:12 and no mortal should think that he is equal to God
9:15 he would make, all of them, equal to citizens of Athens
1 Es 3:12 It makes equal the mind of the king and the orphan
3 Ma 2:30 they shall have equal citizenship with the Alexandrians
4 Ma 5:20 is of equal seriousness
13:21 When they were born after an equal time of gestation

EQUAL, subst. 4 = 0.003 %
Sir 6:11 In your prosperity he will make himself your equal
13:11 Do not try to treat him as an equal
32:9 Among the great do not act as their equal
4 Ma 11:14 but I am their equal in mind

EQUAL, verb 1
Sir 7:28 that equals their gift to you ?

EQUALLY 3 = 0.002 %
Wis 11:11 Whether absent or present, they were equally distressed
14:9 For equally hateful to God
4 Ma 5:21 for in either case the law is equally despised

EQUIP 9 = 0.006 %
1 Ma 6:43 that one of the beasts was equipped with royal armour
10:6 to equip them with arms, and to become his ally
10:21 and equipped them with arms in abundance
15:3 and have equipped warships

2 Ma 10:18 well equipped to withstand a siege
3 Ma 5:23 Hermon, having equipped the beasts
5:38 Equip the elephants now once more
5:45 and had been equipped with frightful devices
4 Ma 11:22 I also, equipped with nobility, will die with my brothers

EQUIPMENT 1
1 Ma 15:26 and silver and gold, and much military equipment

EQUITABLE 1
Ad E 16:9 with more equitable consideration

EQUIVALENT 1
4 Ma 3:15 to drink what was regarded as equivalent to blood

ERADICATE 3 = 0.002 %
4 Ma 3:2 No one of us can eradicate that kind of desire
3:3 No one of us can eradicate anger from the mind
3:4 No one of us can eradicate malice

ERECT, adj. 1
1 Es 9:46 And when he opened the law, they all stood erect

ERECT, verb 8 = 0.005 %
1 Ma 1:54 they erected a desolating sacrilege
6:7 which he had erected upon the altar in Jerusalem
12:36 and to erect a high barrier between the citadel and the city
13:28 He also erected 7 pyramids, opposite one another
13:29 erecting about them great columns
2 Ma 15:6 had determined to erect a public monument of victory
1 Es 5:44 vowed that they would erect the house on its site
5:50 And they erected the altar in its place

ERECTION 1
1 Es 5:62 praising the Lord for the erection of the house of the Lord

ERR 2
Wis 14:22 to err about the knowledge of God
Sir 28:26 Beware lest you err with your tongue

ERROR 11 = 0.007 %
Tob 5:13 They did not go astray in the error of our brethren
Jud 5:20 if there is any unwitting error in this people
Wis 1:12 Do not invite death by the error of your life
12:24 For they went far astray on the paths of error, accepting as gods
Sir 11:16 Error and darkness were created with sinners
23:2 That they may not spare me in my errors
23:12 For all these errors will be far from the godly
30:11 and do not ignore his errors
1 Ma 13:39 We pardon any errors and offences committed to this day
1 Es 9:20 and to give rams in expiation of their error
3 Ma 2:19 Wipe away our sins and disperse our errors

ESARHADDON 3 = 0.002 %
Tob 1:21 Then Esarhaddon, his son, reigned in his place
1:22 for Esarhaddon had appointed him second to himself
1 Es 5:69 ever since the days of Esarhaddon king of the Assyrians

ESAU 9 = 0.006 %
Jud 7:8 Then all the chieftains of the people of Esau
7:18 And the sons of Esau and the sons of Ammon went up
1 Ma 5:3 But Judas made war on the sons of Esau
5:65 and fought the sons of Esau in the land to the south
2 Es 3:15 and to Isaac thou gavest Jacob and Esau
3:16 but Esau thou didst reject
6:8 because from him were born Jacob and Esau
6:8 for Jacob's hand held Esau's heel from the beginning
6:9 For Esau is the end of this age

ESCAPE, verb 36 = 0.023 %
Tob 13:2 and there is no one who can escape his hand
14:10 Ahikar gave alms and escaped the deathtrap
Ad E 16:4 they suppose that they will escape the evil-hating justice
Wis 1:8 therefore no one who utters unrighteous things will escape notice
10:6 he escaped the fire that descended on the Five Cities
15:19 but they have escaped
16:15 To escape from thy hand is impossible
Sir 6:35 and do not let wise proverbs escape you
11:10 and by fleeing you will not escape
16:13 The sinner will not escape with his plunder
20:3 for so you will escape deliberate sin !
22:13 guard yourself from him to escape trouble
27:19 And as you allow a bird to escape from your hand
27:20 and has escaped like a gazelle from a snare
34:12 but have escaped because of these experiences
40:6 like one who has escaped from the battle-front
42:20 No thought escapes him, and not one word is hidden from him
L Jr 6:55 their priests will flee and escape
Sus 13:22 and if I do not, I shall not escape your hands
1 Ma 2:43 And all who became fugitives to escape their troubles

4:26 Those of the foreigners who escaped went
6:21 But some of the garrison escaped from the siege
15:37 Now Trypho embarked on a ship and escaped to Orthosia
2 Ma **3**:38 if he escapes at all
6:26 I shall not escape the hands of the Almighty
7:31 will certainly not escape the hands of God
7:35 You have not yet escaped the judgment of the almighty, all-seeing God
11:12 and Lysias himself escaped by disgraceful flight
12:35 so Gorgias escaped and reached Marisa
3 Ma **5**:13 Then the Jews, since they had escaped the appointed hour
6:29 since they now had escaped death
2 Es **4**:42 makes haste to escape the pangs of birth
7:96 they rejoice that they have now escaped what is corruptible
9:7 and will be able to escape
14:15 and hasten to escape from these times
4 Ma **9**:32 You will not escape, most abominable tyrant

ESCAPE, subst.   2
Jud **7**:19 and there was no way of escape from them
3 Ma **4**:19 to contrive a means of escape

ESCORT, subst.   3 = 0.002 %
1 Ma **9**:37 from Nadabath with a large escort
1 Es **4**:47 that they should give escort to him
8:51 for foot soldiers and horsemen and an escort

ESCORT, verb   1
Jud **10**:15 some of us will escort you and hand you over to him

ESCORT in   1
Tob **8**:1 they escorted Tobias in to her

ESDRAELON   4 = 0.003 %
Jud **1**:8 and Upper Galilee and the great Plain of Esdraelon
3:9 Then he came to the edge of Esdraelon
4:6 which faces Esdraelon opposite the plain near Dothan
7:3 which faces Esdraelon

ESDRIS   1
2 Ma **12**:36 As Esdris and his men had been fighting for a long time and were weary

ESPECIALLY   5 = 0.003 %
Sir pr.   especially to the reading of the law and the prophets
2 Ma **7**:20 The mother was especially admirable
10:32 especially well garrisoned, where Chaereas was commander
3 Ma **5**:3 who were especially hostile toward the Jews
4 Ma **15**:4 Especially is this true of mothers

ESSENTIAL   2
2 Ma **4**:23 and to complete the records of essential business
4 Ma **1**:2 For the subject is essential

ESSENTIALS   1
Sir **29**:21 The essentials for life are water and bread and clothing

ESTABLISH   35 = 0.023 %
Tob **1**:4 was consecrated and established for all generations for ever
Sir **17**:12 He established with them an eternal covenant
24:10 and so I was established in Zion
28:1 and he will firmly establish his sins
31:11 His prosperity will be established
37:13 And establish the counsel of your own heart
38:32 Without them a city cannot be established
40:19 Children and the building of a city establish a man's name
42:17 which the Lord the Almighty has established
44:20 he established the covenant in his flesh
45:24 Therefore a covenant of peace was established with him
45:25 A covenant was also established with David
46:13 established the kingdom and anointed rulers over his people
1 Ma **1**:16 When Antiochus saw that his kingdom was established
8:17 and sent them to Rome to establish friendship and alliance
8:20 have sent us to you to establish alliance and peace with you
10:52 and established my rule
10:54 now therefore let us establish friendship with one another
14:11 He established peace in the land
14:18 which they had established with Judas
14:26 and established its freedom
2 Ma **4**:9 if permission were given to establish by his authority
4:11 who went on the mission to establish friendship
13:3 that he would be established in office
14:15 and prayed to him who established his own people for ever
3 Ma **3**:5 they were established in good repute among all men
3:26 the government will be established for ourselves in good order
7:4 would never be firmly established until this was accomplished
2 Es **2**:15 establish their feet, because I have chosen you, says the Lord
6:3 and before the powers of movement were established
6:4 and before the footstool of Zion was established
8:23 and whose truth is established for ever

8:52 a city is built, rest is appointed, goodness is established
4 Ma **5**:25 for since we believe that the law was established by God
13:23 Therefore, when sympathy and brotherly affection had been so established

ESTABLISHED   3 = 0.002 %
2 Es **10**:27 but there was an established city
10:42 but an established city has appeared to you
10:44 whom you now behold as an established city, is Zion

ESTATE   4 = 0.003 %
Jud **8**:7 and she maintained this estate
16:21 and Judith went to Bethulia, and remained on her estate
Sir **11**:12 he lifts him out of his low estate
2 Es **9**:45 and looked upon my low estate, and considered my distress

ESTEEM, verb   2
Sir **40**:25 but good counsel is esteemed more than both
41:16 and not everything is confidently esteemed by every one

ESTEEM, subst.   1
2 Ma **9**:21 I remember with affection your esteem and good will

ESTHER   4 = 0.003 %
Ad E **10**:6 the river is Esther, whom the king married and made queen
14:1 And Esther the queen, seized with deathly anxiety, fled to the Lord
15:9 What is it, Esther ?
16:13 and of Esther, the blameless partner of our kingdom

ESTRANGE   6 = 0.004 %
Sir **11**:34 and will estrange you from your family
1 Ma **11**:12 He was estranged from Alexander
11:53 and he became estranged from Jonathan
12:10 so that we may not become estranged from you
15:27 and became estranged from him
2 Es **6**:5 and before the imaginations of those who now sin were estranged

ETERNAL   21 = 0.014 %
Tob **3**:6 to go to the eternal abode
Wis **7**:26 For she is a reflection of eternal light
17:2 exiles from eternal providence
Sir **1**:5 and her ways are the eternal commandments
1:15 She made among men an eternal foundation
16:27 He arranged his works in an eternal order
17:12 He established with them an eternal covenant
24:18 being eternal, I therefore am given to all my children
30:17 and eternal rest than chronic sickness
46:19 Before the time of his eternal sleep
Sus **13**:42 O eternal God, who dost discern what is secret
2 Ma **1**:25 who alone art just and almighty and eternal
3 Ma **6**:12 But you, O Eternal One, who have all might and all power
7:16 to the one God of their fathers, the eternal Saviour of Israel
2 Es **2**:35 because the eternal light will shine upon you for evermore
7:119 if an eternal age has been promised to us
4 Ma **9**:9 eternal torment by fire
10:15 by the eternal destruction of the tyrant
12:12 for you intense and eternal fire and tortures
13:15 and the danger of eternal torment
15:3 religion that preserves them for eternal life

ETERNITY   9 = 0.006 %
Tob **6**:17 Do not be afraid, for she was destined for you from eternity
Wis **2**:23 and made him in the image of his own eternity
Sir **1**:2 and the days of eternity – who can count them ?
1:4 and prudent understanding from eternity
18:10 so are a few years in the day of eternity
24:9 From eternity, in the beginning, he created me
24:9 and for eternity I shall not cease to exist
2 Es **8**:20 He said : O Lord who inhabitest eternity
4 Ma **17**:18 and live through blessed eternity

ETHANUS   1
2 Es **14**:24 and take with you Sarea, Dabria, Selemia, Ethanus, and Asiel

ETHIOPIA   4 = 0.003 %
Jud **1**:10 as far as the borders of Ethiopia
Ad E **13**:1 from India to Ethiopia and to the governors under them
16:1 to the rulers of the provinces from India to Ethiopia, 127 satrapies
1 Es **3**:2 from India to Ethiopia

ETHNARCH   3 = 0.002 %
1 Ma **14**:47 to be commander and ethnarch of the Jews and priests
15:1 to Simon, the priest and ethnarch of the Jews
15:2 King Antiochus to Simon the high priest and ethnarch

EUERGETES
Sir pr. in the 38th year of the reign of Euergetes   1

EUMENES
1 Ma 8:8 These they took from him and gave to Eumenes the king   1

EUNUCH
        7 = 0.005 %
Jud 12:11 the eunuch who had charge of all his personal affairs
Ad E 12:1 the 2 eunuchs of the king who kept watch in the courtyard
  12:3 Then the king examined the 2 eunuchs
  12:6 because of the 2 eunuchs of the king
Wis 3:14 Blessed also is the eunuch
Sir 20:4 Like a eunuch's desire to violate a maiden
  30:20 like a eunuch who embraces a maiden and groans

EUPATOR
        5 = 0.003 %
1 Ma 6:17 and he named him Eupator
2 Ma 2:20 and his son Eupator
  10:10 Now we will tell what took place under Antiochus Eupator
  10:13 As a result he was accused before Eupator
  13:1 that Antiochus Eupator was coming

EUPHRATES
        8 = 0.005 %
Jud 1:6 and all those who lived along the Euphrates
  2:24 Then he followed the Euphrates
Sir 24:26 It makes them full of understanding, like the Euphrates
1 Ma 3:32 from the river Euphrates to the border of Egypt
  3:37 He crossed the Euphrates river
1 Es 1:25 went to make war at Carchemish on the Euphrates
  1:27 for my war is at the Euphrates
2 Es 13:43 And they went in by the narrow passages of the Euphrates river

EUPOLEMUS
        2
1 Ma 8:17 So Judas chose Eupolemus the son of John, son of Accos
2 Ma 4:11 secured through John the father of Eupolemus

EVACUATE
        2
1 Ma 6:49 and they evacuated the city
  6:61 On these conditions the Jews evacuated the stronghold

EVE
        1
Tob 8:6 and gavest him Eve his wife as a helper and support

EVEN, adv.
        155 = 0.101 %
Tob 3:10 even to the thought of hanging herself
Jud 1:10 even beyond Tanis and Memphis, and all who lived in Egypt
  4:12 They even surrounded the altar with sackcloth
  8:11 you have even sworn
  8:15 or even to destroy us in the presence of our enemies
  11:2 And even now, if your people who live in the hill country
  11:14 because even the people living there have been doing this
  13:11 even as he has done this day !
  15:5 even beyond Damascus and its borders
Ad E 16:3 they even undertake to scheme against their own benefactors
Wis 3:17 Even if they live long they will be held of no account
  4:4 For even if they put forth boughs for a while
  7:15 for he is the guide even of wisdom
  9:6 for even if one is perfect among the sons of men
  11:20 Even apart from these
  12:8 But even these thou didst spare, since they were but men
  12:24 those animals which even their enemies despised
  13:8 Yet again, not even they are to be excused
  14:4 so that even if a man lacks skill, he may put to sea
  14:5 even to the smallest piece of wood
  14:6 For even in the beginning
  14:18 impelled even those who did not know the king
  15:2 For even if we sin we are thine, knowing thy power
  15:12 for he says one must get money however one can, even by base means
  15:18 even the most hateful animals
  15:19 and even as animals they are not so beautiful in appearance
  16:10 even by the teeth of venomous serpents
  16:19 and at another time even in the midst of water
  16:23 even forgot its native power
  17:4 For not even the inner chamber that held them
  17:9 For even if nothing disturbing frightened them
  17:10 refusing to look even at the air
  18:12 The living were not sufficient even to bury them
  19:1 for God knew in advance even their future actions
  19:20 Fire even in water retained its normal power
Sir pr. those who love learning should make even greater progress
  pr. Not only this work, but even the law itself
  3:13 even if he is lacking in understanding, show forbearance
  4:28 Strive even to death for the truth
  7:8 even for one you will not go unpunished
  10:9 For even in life his bowels decay
  12:9 and in his adversity even his friend will separate from him
  12:11 Even if he humbles himself and goes about cringing
  13:3 A rich man does wrong, and he even adds reproaches
  13:21 but when a humble man falls, he is even pushed away by friends

13:22 If a humble man slips, they even reproach him
13:23 And should he stumble, they even push him down
14:7 even if he does good, he does it unintentionally
16:11 Even if there is only one stiff-necked person
19:21 even if later he does it
22:21 Even if you have drawn your sword against a friend
23:19 and perceive even the hidden places
26:24 but a modest daughter will even be embarrassed
27:24 even the Lord will hate him
43:30 for he will surpass even that
46:20 Even after he had fallen asleep
47:7 he crushed their power even to this day
L Jr 6:11 and even give some of it to the harlots in the brothel
  6:19 They light lamps, even more than they light for themselves
  6:24 for even when they were being cast, they had no feeling
  6:40 Besides, even the Chaldeans themselves dishonour them
  6:59 better even the door of a house that protects its contents
1 Ma 1:28 Even the land shook for its inhabitants
  1:37 they even defiled the sanctuary
  1:43 Many even from Israel gladly adopted his religion
  2:19 Even if all the nations that live under the rule of the king
  4:35 to invade Judea again with an even larger army
  7:46 not even one of them was left
  8:4 even though the place was far distant from them
2 Ma 3:3 so that even Seleucus, the king of Asia
  4:3 that even murders were committed
  4:47 if they had pleaded even before Scythians
  4:49 Therefore even the Tyrians
  6:20 even for the natural love of life
  6:23 and his excellent life even from childhood
  6:26 For even if for the present
  8:18 and even the whole world
  9:7 but was even more filled with arrogance
  12:14 railing at them and even blaspheming and saying unholy things
  13:7 without even burial in the earth
1 Es 1:49 Even the leaders of the people and of the priests
  2:19 but will even resist kings
  4:42 even beyond what is written, and we will give it to you
  8:80 Even in our bondage we were not forsaken by our Lord
  8:92 but even now there is hope for Israel
3 Ma 1:11 because not even members of their own nation
  1:11 nor even all of the priests
  1:12 Even after the law had been read to him
  1:12 Even if those men are deprived of this honour
  1:20 Mothers and nurses abandoned even new-born children here and there
  2:4 among whom were even giants
  2:22 was unable even to speak
  3:27 old people or children or even infants
  4:4 even some of their enemies
  4:16 even to communicate or to come to ones's help
  6:6 you rescued unharmed, even to a hair
  6:10 Even if our lives have become entangled in impieties in our exile
  6:11 saying, Not even their god has rescued them
  6:15 Not even when they were in the land of their enemies did I neglect them
  6:17 so that even the nearby valleys resounded with them
  6:20 Even the king began to shudder bodily
  6:24 and even me, your benefactor
  7:16 But those who had held fast to God even to death
2 Es 5:45 it might even now be able to support
  5:48 Even so have I given the womb of the earth
  7:23 they even declared that the Most High does not exist
  7:130 or even myself who have spoken to them
  8:48 But even in this respect you will be praiseworthy
  8:57 Moreover they have even trampled upon his righteous ones
  11:6 not even one creature that was on the earth
  11:17 or even half as long
  12:5 and not even a little strength is left in me
  16:27 or even to hear his voice
4 Ma 1:11 For all people, even their torturers
  1:25 In pleasure there exists even a malevolent tendency
  2:7 a glutton, or even a drunkard can learn a better way
  2:8 even though he is a lover of money
  2:10 For the law prevails even over affection for parents
  2:14 through the law, can prevail even over enmity
  2:15 It is evident that reason rules even the more violent emotions :
  2:16 for it is sovereign over even this
  3:18 it can overthrow bodily agonies even when they are extreme
  3:20 and were prospering, so that even Seleucus Nicanor, king of Asia
  4:25 even to the point that women
  5:10 It seems to me that you will do something even more senseless
  5:18 Even if, as you suppose, our law were not truly divine
  5:18 not even so would it be right for us
  5:30 not even if you gouge out my eyes and burn my entrails
  5:37 as one who does not fear your violence even to death
  6:11 he amazed even his torturers by his courageous spirit
  6:21 and not protect our divine law even to death
  6:30 and by reason he resisted even to the very tortures of death
  6:34 when it masters even external agonies

7 : 8	in sufferings even to death
7 : 16	an aged man despised tortures even to death
8 : 1	For this is why even the very young
8 : 2	these should be tortured even more cruelly
8 : 10	Even I, your enemy, have compassion
8 : 25	Not even the law itself would arbitrarily slay us
8 : 27	nor even seriously considered them
9 : 6	it would be even more fitting
10 : 18	But he said, Even if you remove my organ of speech
11 : 3	from the heavenly justice for even more crimes
12 : 2	Even though the tyrant had been fearfully reproached by the brothers
13 : 1	Since, then, the 7 brothers despised sufferings even unto death
14 : 9	Even now, we ourselves shudder
14 : 11	since the mind of a woman despised even more diverse agonies
14 : 14	Even unreasoning animals, like mankind
14 : 19	since even bees at the time for making honeycombs
14 : 19	and defend it even to the death ?
15 : 10	so that they obeyed her even to death
15 : 16	than even the birth-pangs you suffered for them !
16 : 14	By steadfastness you have conquered even a tyrant
17 : 10	looking to God and enduring torture even to death
18 : 14	Even though you go through the fire

EVENING   12 = 0.008 %

Tob	**6** : 1	they came at evening to the Tigris river and camped there
Jud	**9** : 1	when that evening's incense was being offered
	12 : 9	until she ate her food toward evening
	13 : 1	When evening came, his slaves quickly withdrew
Sir	**18** : 26	From morning to evening conditions change
1 Ma	**9** : 13	and the battle raged from morning till evening
1 Es	**5** : 50	and burnt offerings to the Lord morning and evening
	8 : 72	and I sat grief-stricken until the evening sacrifice
3 Ma	**5** : 5	The servants in charge of the Jews went out in the evening
2 Es	**7** : 40	or water or air, or darkness or evening or morning
	10 : 2	and I remained quiet until evening of the 2nd day
4 Ma	**3** : 8	Then when evening fell

EVENT   7 = 0.005 %

Wis	**11** : 14	at the end of the events they marvelled at him
	19 : 10	For they still recalled the events of their sojourn
1 Ma	**7** : 33	After these events Nicanor went up to Mount Zion
2 Ma	**4** : 17	a fact which later events will make clear
1 Es	**1** : 24	The events of his reign have been recorded in the past
3 Ma	**6** : 33	to celebrate these events
2 Es	**12** : 9	and the last events of the times

EVER*   130 = 0.085 %

Tob	**1** : 4	was consecrated and established for all generations for ever
	3 : 2	and thou dost render true and righteous judgment for ever
	3 : 11	and blessed is thy holy and honoured name for ever
	3 : 11	May all thy works praise thee for ever
	8 : 5	and blessed be thy holy and glorious name for ever
	8 : 15	let all thy angels and thy chosen people bless thee for ever
	10 : 7	of ever seeing me again
	11 : 14	Blessed art thou, O God, and blessed is thy name for ever
	12 : 17	But praise God for ever
	12 : 18	Therefore praise him for ever
	13 : 1	Blessed is God who lives for ever
	13 : 4	because he is our Lord and God, he is our Father for ever
	13 : 10	to all generations for ever
	13 : 12	blessed for ever will be all who love you
	13 : 14	and they will be made glad for ever
	13 : 18	Blessed is God, who has exalted you for ever
	14 : 5	with a glorious building for all generations for ever
Jud	**12** : 16	ever since the day he first saw her
	12 : 20	much more than he had ever drunk in any one day
	15 : 10	May the Almighty Lord bless you for ever !
	16 : 16	but who fears the Lord shall be great for ever
	16 : 17	they shall weep in pain for ever
	16 : 25	And no one ever again spread terror
Ad E	**10** : 3	from generation to generation for ever among his people Israel
	14 : 5	Ever since I was born
	14 : 10	and to magnify for ever a mortal king
Wis	**3** : 1	and no torment will ever touch them
	3 : 8	and the Lord will reign over them for ever
	4 : 18	and an outrage among the dead for ever
	5 : 15	But the righteous live for ever
	6 : 21	honour wisdom, that you may reign for ever
	14 : 13	nor will they exist for ever
Sir	**1** : 1	All wisdom comes from the Lord and is with him for ever
	2 : 10	and see : who ever trusted in the Lord and was put to shame ?
	2 : 10	Or who ever persevered in the fear of the Lord and was forsaken ?
	2 : 10	Or who ever called upon him and was overlooked ?
	17 : 9	And he gave them to boast of his marvels for ever
	18 : 1	He who lives for ever created the whole universe
	20 : 26	and his shame is ever with him
	37 : 26	and his name will live for ever
	40 : 12	but good faith will stand for ever

	40 : 17	and almsgiving endures for ever
	41 : 13	but a good name endures for ever
	42 : 23	All these things live and remain for ever for every need
	44 : 13	Their posterity will continue for ever
	45 : 13	No outsider ever put them on, but only his sons
	45 : 24	should have the dignity of the priesthood for ever
	46 : 3	Who before him ever stood so firm ?
	47 : 11	The Lord took away his sins, and exalted his power for ever
	47 : 13	and prepare a sanctuary to stand for ever
Bar	**3** : 3	For thou art enthroned for ever
	3 : 3	and we are perishing for ever
	3 : 13	you would be dwelling in peace for ever
	4 : 1	and the law that endures for ever
	4 : 23	with joy and gladness for ever
	5 : 1	and put on for ever the beauty of the glory from God
	5 : 4	For your name will for ever be called by God
P Az	**3**	and thy name is glorified for ever
	29	and to be praised and highly exalted for ever
	30	and to be highly praised and highly exalted for ever
	31	and to be extolled and highly glorified for ever
	32	and to be praised and highly exalted for ever
	33	and to be extolled and highly exalted for ever
	34	and to be sung and glorified for ever
	35	sing praise to him and highly exalt him for ever
	36	sing praise to him and highly exalt him for ever
	37	sing praise to him and highly exalt him for ever
	38	sing praise to him and highly exalt him for ever
	39	sing praise to him and highly exalt him for ever
	40	sing praise to him and highly exalt him for ever
	41	sing praise to him and highly exalt him for ever
	42	sing praise to him and highly exalt him for ever
	43	sing praise to him and highly exalt him for ever
	44	sing praise to him and highly exalt him for ever
	45	sing praise to him and highly exalt him for ever
	46	sing praise to him and highly exalt him for ever
	47	sing praise to him and highly exalt him for ever
	48	sing praise to him and highly exalt him for ever
	49	sing praise to him and highly exalt him for ever
	50	sing praise to him and highly exalt him for ever
	51	sing praise to him and highly exalt him for ever
	52	let it sing praise to him and highly exalt him for ever
	53	sing praise to him and highly exalt him for ever
	54	sing praise to him and highly exalt him for ever
	55	sing praise to him and highly exalt him for ever
	56	sing praise to him and highly exalt him for ever
	57	sing praise to him and highly exalt him for ever
	58	sing praise to him and highly exalt him for ever
	59	sing praise to him and highly exalt him for ever
	60	sing praise to him and highly exalt him for ever
	61	sing praise to him and highly exalt him for ever
	62	sing praise to him and highly exalt him for ever
	63	sing praise to him and highly exalt him for ever
	64	sing praise to him and highly exalt him for ever
	65	sing praise to him and highly exalt him for ever
	66	sing praise to him and highly exalt him for ever
	67	for his mercy endures for ever
	68	for his mercy endures for ever
Sus	**13** : 27	for nothing like this had ever been said about Susanna
1 Ma	**2** : 57	inherited the throne of the kingdom for ever
	3 : 7	and his memory is blessed for ever
	4 : 24	for he is good, for his mercy endures for ever
	8 : 11	as many as ever opposed them, they destroyed and enslaved
	8 : 23	and with the nation of the Jews at sea and on land for ever
	11 : 36	from this time forth for ever
	14 : 41	that Simon should be their leader and high priest for ever
2 Ma	**8** : 14	before he ever met them
	10 : 4	but that, if they should ever sin
	13 : 10	now if ever to help those
	14 : 15	and prayed to him who established his own people for ever
	14 : 36	keep undefiled for ever this house
	15 : 30	And the man who was ever in body and soul
1 Es	**4** : 38	But truth endures and is strong for ever
	4 : 38	and lives and prevails for ever and ever
	5 : 61	because his goodness and his glory are for ever upon all Israel
	5 : 69	ever since the days of Esarhaddon king of the Assyrians
	8 : 72	And all who were ever moved
	8 : 85	and do not seek ever to have peace with them
	8 : 85	and leave it for an inheritance to your children for ever
P Ma	**13**	Do not be angry with me for ever or lay up evil for me
	15	and thine is the glory for ever. Amen
2 Es	**4** : 8	neither did I ever ascend into heaven
	7 : 80	ever grieving and sad, in 7 ways
	7 : 105	so no one shall ever pray for another on that day
	8 : 23	and whose truth is established for ever
	9 : 31	and you shall be glorified through it for ever
4 Ma	**7** : 4	has ever held out as did that most holy man
	18 : 24	to whom be glory for ever and ever. Amen

EVERFLOWING   2

Wis   11 : 6   Instead of the fountain of an everflowing river
2 Ma   7 : 36   have drunk of everflowing life under God's covenant

EVERGREEN   1

Sus   13 : 58   He answered, Under an evergreen oak

EVERLASTING   36 = 0.023 %

Tob   1 : 6   as it is ordained for all Israel by an everlasting decree
Ad E   14 : 5   for an everlasting inheritance
Wis   8 : 13   and leave an everlasting remembrance
  10 : 14   and she gave him everlasting honour
Sir   2 : 9   for everlasting joy and mercy
  15 : 6   and will acquire an everlasting name
  39 : 20   From everlasting to everlasting he beholds them
  42 : 21   and he is from everlasting and to everlasting
  43 : 6   to mark the times and to be an everlasting sign
  44 : 18   Everlasting covenants were made with him
  45 : 7   He made an everlasting covenant with him
  45 : 15   it was an everlasting covenant for him
  49 : 12   prepared for everlasting glory
Bar   2 : 35   I will make an everlasting covenant with them
  4 : 8   You forgot the everlasting God, who brought you up
  4 : 10   which the Everlasting brought upon them
  4 : 14   which the Everlasting brought upon them
  4 : 20   I will cry to the Everlasting all my days
  4 : 22   For I have put my hope in the Everlasting to save you
  4 : 22   from your everlasting Saviour
  4 : 24   and with the splendour of the Everlasting
  4 : 29   will bring you everlasting joy with your salvation
  4 : 35   For fire will come upon her from the Everlasting for many days
  5 : 2   put on your head the diadem of the glory of the Everlasting
  5 : 7   and the everlasting hills be made low
1 Ma   2 : 51   and receive great honour and an everlasting name
  2 : 54   received the covenant of everlasting priesthood
  6 : 44   and to win for himself an everlasting name
2 Ma   7 : 9   to an everlasting renewal of life
2 Es   2 : 11   and will give to these others the everlasting habitations
  2 : 34   he will give you everlasting rest
  3 : 15   Thou didst make with him an everlasting covenant
  7 : 120   that an everlasting hope has been promised us
4 Ma   10 : 15   and by the everlasting life of the pious

EVERMORE   1

2 Es   2 : 35   because the eternal light will shine upon you for evermore

EVERY   166 = 0.108 %

Tob   4 : 18   Seek advice from every wise man
  4 : 19   Bless the Lord God on every occasion
  4 : 21   and refrain from every sin
  8 : 15   Blessed art thou, O God, with every pure and holy blessing
  10 : 7   And she went out every day to the road by which they had left
  12 : 9   and it will purge away every sin
Jud   2 : 8   and every brook and river shall be filled with their dead, and overflow
  2 : 18   also plenty of food for every man
  4 : 4   So they sent to every district of Samaria
  4 : 9   And every man of Israel cried out to God with great fervour
  4 : 10   and every resident alien and hired labourer
  7 : 20   until all the vessels of water belonging to every inhabitant of Bethulia were empty
  9 : 14   And cause thy whole nation and every tribe
  11 : 7   who has sent you to direct every living soul
  11 : 17   and every night your servant will go out into the valley
  13 : 3   as she did every day
  14 : 2   let every valiant man take his weapons and go out of the city
  14 : 7   Blessed are you in every tent of Judah !
  14 : 7   In every nation those who hear your name will be alarmed
  14 : 11   and every man took his weapons
  15 : 2   by every path across the plain and through the hill country
  16 : 16   For every sacrifice as a fragrant offering is a small thing
Ad E   11 : 7   And at their roaring every nation prepared for war
  12 : 2   and sought all day to understand it in every detail
  13 : 4   who have laws contrary to those of every nation
  13 : 10   and every wonderful thing under heaven
  14 : 2   and every part that she loved to adorn
  16 : 11   so far enjoyed the good will that we have for every nation
  16 : 19   Therefore post a copy of this letter publicly in every place
  16 : 24   Every city and country, without exception
Wis   6 : 16   and meets them in every thought
  7 : 27   in every generation she passes into holy souls
  7 : 29   and excels every constellation of the stars
  13 : 14   and covering every blemish in it with paint
  14 : 4   showing that thou canst save from every danger
  14 : 27   is the beginning and cause and end of every evil
  16 : 8   that it is thou who deliverest from every evil
  16 : 20   with bread ready to eat, providing every pleasure
  16 : 20   and suited to every taste
Sir   5 : 9   Do not winnow with every wind, nor follow every path :
  6 : 35   Be ready to listen to every narrative

  11 : 29   Do not bring every man into your home
  13 : 15   Every creature loves its like
  13 : 15   and every person his neighbour
  14 : 19   Every product decays and ceases to exist
  15 : 19   and he knows every deed of man
  16 : 14   He will make room for every act of mercy
  17 : 17   he appointed a ruler for every nation
  18 : 28   Every intelligent man knows wisdom
  24 : 6   and in every people and nation I have gotten a possession
  26 : 12   so will she sit in front of every post
  26 : 27   and every person like this lives in the anarchy of war
  29 : 3   and on every occasion you will find what you need
  30 : 7   and his feelings will be troubled at every cry
  31 : 7   and every fool will be taken captive by it
  31 : 13   Therefore it sheds tears from every face
  31 : 15   and in every matter be thoughtful
  32 : 23   Guard yourself in every act
  35 : 9   With every gift show a cheerful face
  36 : 22   and surpasses every human desire
  37 : 1   Every friend will say, I too am a friend
  37 : 7   Every counsellor praises counsel
  37 : 16   Reason is the beginning of every work
  37 : 16   and counsel precedes every undertaking
  37 : 28   and not every person enjoys everything
  38 : 27   So too is every craftsman and master workman
  39 : 33   and he will supply every need in its hour
  40 : 1   Much labour was created for every man
  41 : 16   For it is not good to retain every kind of shame
  41 : 23   and will find favour with every man
  42 : 23   All these things live and remain for ever for every need
  43 : 20   it rests upon every pool of water
  45 : 14   twice every day continually
  46 : 5   when enemies pressed him on every side
  46 : 16   when his enemies pressed him on every side
  47 : 7   For he wiped out his enemies on every side
  47 : 13   and God gave him rest on every side
  47 : 25   For they sought out every sort of wickedness
  49 : 1   it is sweet as honey to every mouth
  49 : 16   and Adam above every living being in the creation
  50 : 22   who in every way does great things
  51 : 4   from choking fire on every side
  51 : 7   They surrounded me on every side
Bar   5 : 7   For God has ordered that every high mountain
  5 : 8   The woods and every fragrant tree have shaded Israel at God's command
L Jr   6 : 18   And just as the gates are shut on every side
  6 : 61   and the wind likewise blows in every land
  6 : 71   on which every bird sits
Sus   13 : 8   The 2 elders used to see her every day
  13 : 22   I am hemmed in on every side
Bel   14 : 3   and every day they spent on it 12 bushels of fine flour
  14 : 4   The king revered it and went every day to worship it
  14 : 6   Do you not see how much he eats and drinks every day ?
  14 : 32   and every day they had been given 2 human bodies and 2 sheep
1 Ma   1 : 25   Israel mourned deeply in every community
  1 : 27   Every bridegroom took up the lament
  1 : 37   On every side of the sanctuary they shed innocent blood
  1 : 53   in every place of refuge they had
  2 : 41   Let us fight against every man who comes to attack us on the sabbath day
  4 : 59   determined that every year at that season
  5 : 28   and killed every male by the edge of the sword
  5 : 35   and he killed every male in it, plundered it
  5 : 51   He destroyed every male by the edge of the sword
  6 : 18   They were trying in every way to harm them
  8 : 4   the rest paid them tribute every year
  8 : 15   and every day 320 senators constantly deliberate
  10 : 42   which my officials have received every year
  12 : 4   in every place, asking them to provide for the envoys
  12 : 11   We therefore remember you constantly on every occasion
  13 : 10   and he fortified it on every side
  13 : 20   to every place he went
  13 : 52   And Simon decreed that every year
  14 : 14   and did away with every lawless and wicked man
  14 : 35   He sought in every way to exalt his people
  15 : 8   Every debt you owe to the royal treasury
2 Ma   1 : 17   Blessed in every way be our God, who has brought judgment
  1 : 25   who dost rescue Israel from every evil
  2 : 30   to occupy the ground and to discuss matters from every side
  9 : 7   and the fall was so hard as to torture every limb of his body
  9 : 11   for he was tortured with pain every moment
  9 : 17   and would visit every inhabited place
  10 : 8   should observe these days every year
  10 : 13   He heard himself called a traitor at every turn
  10 : 14   and at every turn kept on warring against the Jews
  11 : 3   and to put up the high priesthood for sale every year
  11 : 15   For the king granted every request in behalf of the Jews
1 Es   3 : 20   It turns every thought to feasting and mirth
  4 : 15   and to every people that rules over sea and land
  4 : 52   for burnt offerings to be offered on the altar every day

	5 : 51	and offered the proper sacrifices every day
	6 : 30	regularly every year, without quibbling
	6 : 33	destroy every king and nation
	8 : 52	and will support them in every way
	8 : 61	he delivered us from every enemy on the way
3 Ma	**1** : 13	And he inquired why, when he entered every other temple
	3 : 23	in every situation, in accordance with their infamous way of life
	3 : 24	that they are ill-disposed toward us in every way
	3 : 29	Every place detected sheltering a Jew
	4 : 1	In every place, then, where this decree arrived
	5 : 7	they were forcibly confined on every side
	5 : 51	imploring the Ruler over every power
	6 : 1	and throughout his life had been adorned with every virtue
	7 : 7	of every charge of whatever kind
	7 : 9	we always shall have not man but the Ruler over every power
2 Es	**3** : 8	And every nation walked after his own will
	5 : 23	from every forest of the earth and from all its trees
	5 : 34	for every hour I suffer agonies of heart
	7 : 89	and withstood danger every hour
	7 : 127	which every man who is born on earth shall wage
	8 : 6	by which every mortal who bears the likeness of a human being
	9 : 44	And every hour and every day during those 30 years
	13 : 33	every man shall leave his own land
	15 : 4	For every unbeliever shall die in his unbelief
	15 : 6	For iniquity has spread throughout every land
	15 : 40	and shall pour out upon every high and lofty place a terrible tempest
	16 : 29	3 or 4 olives may be left on every tree
	16 : 39	and pains will seize it on every side
	16 : 50	who searches out every sin on earth
4 Ma	**2** : 4	but also over every desire
	5 : 2	ordered the guards to seize each and every Hebrew
	8 : 3	handsome, modest, noble, and accomplished in every way
	9 : 14	and though broken in every member
	15 : 32	overwhelmed from every side
	18 : 1	obey this law and exercise pity in every way

EVERY ONE, EVERYONE   39 = 0.025 %

Jud	**1** : 12	and every one in Egypt, as far as the coasts of the 2 seas
	2 : 3	and it was decided that every one
	2 : 25	and killed every one who resisted him
	7 : 4	and every one said to his neighbour
	10 : 19	and every one said to his neighbour
	13 : 4	So every one went out
	15 : 3	Then the men of Israel, every one that was a soldier
	16 : 21	After this every one returned home to his own inheritance
Wis	**16** : 21	was changed to suit every one liking
Sir	**8** : 19	Do not reveal your thoughts to every one
	16 : 14	every one will receive in accordance with his deeds
	22 : 1	and every one hisses at his disgrace
	33 : 6	he neighs under every one who sits on him
	37 : 28	For not everything is good for every one
	41 : 16	and not everything is confidently esteemed by every one
1 Ma	**1** : 52	Many of the people, every one who forsook the law, joined them
	2 : 27	saying : Let every one who is zealous for the law
	2 : 42	every one who offered himself willingly for the law
	10 : 33	And every one of the Jews taken as a captive
2 Ma	**1** : 23	the priests offered prayer - the priests and every one
	5 : 12	to cut down relentlessly every one they met
	10 : 35	and with savage fury cut down every one they met
	12 : 40	Then under the tunic of every one of the dead
	15 : 35	a clear and conspicuous sign to every one
1 Es	**1** : 33	and every one of the acts of Josiah, and his splendour
	3 : 21	and makes every one talk in millions
3 Ma	**7** : 8	We also have ordered each and every one
2 Es	**7** : 27	And every one who has been delivered from the evils
	7 : 75	as soon as every one of us yields up his soul
	7 : 105	for then every one shall bear his own righteousness or unrighteousness
	9 : 7	And it shall be that every one who will be saved
	12 : 49	Now go, every one of you to his house
4 Ma	**1** : 2	to everyone who is seeking knowledge
	4 : 26	he himself, through torture, tried to compel everyone in the nation
	7 : 17	Not every one has full command of his emotions
	7 : 17	because not every one has prudent reason
	8 : 5	Young men, I admire each and every one of you in a kindly manner
	8 : 9	you will compel me to destroy each and every one of you
	13 : 1	everyone must concede

EVERYTHING   45 = 0.029 %

Tob	**2** : 14	You seem to know everything !
	4 : 14	Watch yourself, my son, in everything you do
	5 : 1	Father, I will do everything that you have commanded me
	12 : 20	Write in a book everything that has happened
Jud	**4** : 1	heard of everything
	8 : 25	In spite of everything
Ad E	**16** : 4	of God, who always sees everything
Wis	**18** : 13	For though they had disbelieved everything

	19 : 22	For in everything, O Lord
Sir	**10** : 27	and has an abundance of everything
	15 : 18	he is mighty in power and sees everything
	18 : 27	A wise man is cautious in everything
	19 : 15	so do not believe everything you hear
	25 : 11	The fear of the Lord surpasses everything
	31 : 14	Do not reach out your hand for everything you see
	37 : 28	For not everything is good for every one
	37 : 28	and not every person enjoys everything
	39 : 21	for everything has been created for its use
	41 : 1	who is prosperous in everything
	41 : 2	very old and distracted over everything
	41 : 16	and not everything is confidently esteemed by every one
	42 : 16	The sun looks down on everything with its light
Bel	**14** : 15	and ate and drank everything
1 Ma	**1** : 48	by everything unclean and profane
2 Ma	**7** : 28	and see everything that is in them, and recognize
	10 : 23	Having success at arms in everything he undertook
	11 : 14	and persuaded them to settle everything on just terms
	11 : 18	I have informed the king of everything
1 Es	**2** : 9	and their neighbours helped them with everything
	4 : 5	if they win the victory, they bring everything to the king
	4 : 5	whatever spoil they take and everything else
	4 : 22	and bring everything and give it to women ?
	4 : 57	everything that Cyrus had ordered to be done
	8 : 64	and the weight of everything was recorded at that very time
3 Ma	**2** : 25	who were strangers to everything just
	5 : 42	Upon this the king, a Phalaris in everything and filled with madness
	6 : 30	both wines and everything else
	6 : 40	Then they feasted, provided with everything by the king
	7 : 9	in everything and inescapably as an antagonist to avenge such acts. Farewell
2 Es	**3** : 26	in everything doing as Adam and all his descendants had done
	6 : 39	and darkness and silence embraced everything
	9 : 5	For just as with everything that has occurred in the world
	13 : 3	everything under his gaze trembled
	14 : 22	and I will write everything that has happened in the world from the beginning
4 Ma	**14** : 13	which draws everything toward an emotion felt in her inmost parts

EVERYWHERE   6 = 0.004 %

Wis	**2** : 9	everywhere let us leave signs of enjoyment
Bar	**5** : 3	For God will show your splendour everywhere under heaven
2 Ma	**2** : 18	and will gather us from everywhere under heaven
	8 : 7	And talk of his valour spread everywhere
3 Ma	**4** : 2	everywhere their hearts were burning
	7 : 12	they might destroy those everywhere in his kingdom

EVIDENCE   3 = 0.002 %

Wis	**5** : 11	no evidence of its passage is found
	10 : 7	Evidence of their wickedness still remains :
L Jr	**6** : 69	So we have no evidence whatever that they are gods

EVIDENT   5 = 0.003 %

3 Ma	**4** : 1	was now made evident and outspoken
2 Es	**9** : 5	the beginning is evident, and the end manifest
4 Ma	**1** : 3	If, then, it is evident
	2 : 15	It is evident that reason rules even the more violent emotions :
	3 : 1	for it is evident that reason rules not over its own emotions

EVIDENTLY   1

L Jr	**6** : 16	Therefore they evidently are not gods

EVIL, subst., adj.   123 = 0.080 %

Tob	**3** : 8	and the evil demon Asmodeus had slain each of them
	3 : 17	and to bind Asmodeus the evil demon
	6 : 7	if a demon or evil spirit gives trouble to any one
	12 : 7	Do good, and evil will not overtake you
Jud	**7** : 15	So you will pay them back with evil
Ad E	**10** : 9	the Lord has delivered us from all these evils
	11 : 9	they feared the evils that threatened them
	16 : 6	when these men by the false trickery of their evil natures
Wis	**3** : 12	Their wives are foolish, and their children evil
	4 : 6	For children born of unlawful unions are witnesses of evil
	4 : 11	He was caught up lest evil change his understanding
	7 : 30	but against wisdom evil does not prevail
	12 : 10	though thou wast not unaware that their origin was evil
	14 : 22	and they call such great evils peace
	14 : 27	is the beginning and cause and end of every evil
	15 : 4	For neither has the evil intent of human art misled us
	15 : 6	Lovers of evil things and fit for such objects of hope
	16 : 8	that it is thou who deliverest from every evil
Sir	**4** : 20	Observe the right time, and beware of evil
	6 : 4	An evil soul will destroy him who has it
	7 : 1	Do no evil, and evil will never befall you
	9 : 1	and do not teach her an evil lesson to your own hurt
	11 : 16	evil will grow old with those who take pride in malice
	11 : 31	for he lies in wait, turning good into evil

11:33	Beware of a scoundrel, for he devises evil
12:3	No good will come to the man who persists in evil
12:5	for you will receive twice as much evil
13:24	and poverty is evil in the opinion of the ungodly
13:25	either for good or for evil
14:8	Evil is the man with a grudging eye
17:7	and showed them good and evil
17:16	Their ways from youth tend toward evil
17:31	So flesh and blood devise evil
18:8	What is his good and what is his evil ?
18:12	He sees and recognizes that their end will be evil
19:6	and for one who hates gossip evil is lessened
19:28	he will do evil when he finds an opportunity
23:5	and remove from me evil desire
25:16	than dwell with an evil wife
25:23	are caused by an evil wife
25:25	and no boldness of speech in an evil wife
26:7	An evil wife is an ox yoke which chafes
27:22	Whoever winks his eye plans evil deeds
27:27	If a man does evil, it will roll back upon him
28:21	its death is an evil death, and Hades is preferable to it
31:10	and to do evil and did not do it ?
33:1	No evil will befall the man who fears the Lord
33:14	Good is the opposite of evil, and life the opposite of death
33:27	for idleness teaches much evil
37:3	O evil imagination, why were you formed to cover the land with deceit ?
37:18	4 turns of fortune appear, good and evil, life and death
39:4	for he tests the good and the evil among men
39:25	just as evil things for sinners
39:27	just as they turn into evils for sinners
41:11	but the evil name of sinners will be blotted out
42:6	Where there is an evil wife, a seal is a good thing
51:12	and rescue me from an evil plight
Bar **1**:21	and doing what is evil in the sight of the Lord our God
L Jr **6**:34	Whether one does evil to them or good
1 Ma **1**:9	and they caused many evils on the earth
1:11	for since we separated from them many evils have come upon us
1:15	They joined with the Gentiles and sold themselves to do evil
1:36	an evil adversary of Israel continually
1:52	and they did evil in the land
2:30	because evils pressed heavily upon them
6:12	But now I remember the evils I did in Jerusalem
6:13	that these evils have come upon me
7:23	And Judas saw all the evil that Alcimus and those with him
11:8	and he kept devising evil designs against Alexander
16:17	and returned evil for good
2 Ma **1**:5	and may he not forsake you in time of evil
1:25	who dost rescue Israel from every evil
2:18	for he has rescued us from great evils
4:47	Menelaus, the cause of all the evil
6:3	Harsh and utterly grievous was the onslaught of evil
7:31	But you, who have contrived all sorts of evil
8:4	and to show his hatred of evil
1 Es **1**:39	and he did what was evil in the sight of the Lord
1:44	He did what was evil in the sight of the Lord
1:47	He also did what was evil in the sight of the Lord
8:86	because of our evil deeds and our great sins
P Ma **7**	and repentest over the evils of men
10	and have done what is evil in thy sight
13	Do not be angry with me for ever or lay up evil for me
3 Ma **1**:16	and to avert the violence of this evil design
2:12	and rescued them from great evils
2:26	that he framed evil reports in the various localities
3:22	Since they incline constantly to evil
5:8	that he avert with vengeance the evil plot against them
7:9	For you should know that if we devise any evil against them
2 Es **1**:5	Go and declare to my people their evil deeds
1:8	Pull out the hair of your head and hurl all evils upon them
1:34	and have done what is evil in my sight
2:3	and have done what is evil in my sight
2:14	for I left out evil and created good
3:20	Yet thou didst not take away from them their evil heart
3:21	For the first Adam, burdened with an evil heart
3:22	the law was in the people's heart along with the evil root
3:22	but what was good departed, and the evil remained
3:26	for they also had the evil heart
4:4	and will teach you why the heart is evil
4:28	For the evil about which you ask me has been sown
4:29	and if the place where the evil has been sown does not pass away
4:30	For a grain of evil seed was sown in Adam's heart from the beginning
4:31	how much fruit of ungodliness a grain of evil seed has produced
4:33	Why are our years few and evil ?
6:27	For evil shall be blotted out
7:12	they are few and evil
7:27	And every one who has been delivered from the evils
7:48	For an evil heart has grown up in us
7:92	to overcome the evil thought which was formed with them
8:53	The root of evil is sealed up from you

11:45	and your most evil little wings
11:45	and your malicious heads, and your most evil talons
12:43	Are not the evils which have befallen us sufficient ?
13:38	and will reproach them to their face with their evil thoughts
14:16	For evils worse than those which you have now seen happen
14:17	the more shall evils be multiplied among its inhabitants
15:5	I bring evils upon the world
15:49	I will send evils upon you, widowhood, poverty
4 Ma **6**:14	through these evil things
17:2	frustrated his evil designs

EVILDOER 3 = 0.002 %

Ad E **14**:19	and save us from the hands of evildoers
16:15	are not evildoers but are governed by most righteous laws
1 Ma **3**:6	all the evildoers were confounded

EVIL-DOING 1

Wis **5**:23	and evil-doing will overturn the thrones of rulers

EVIL-HATING 1

Ad E **16**:4	they suppose that they will escape the evil-hating justice

EXACT, adj. 1

2 Ma **2**:28	leaving the responsibility for exact details to the compiler

EXACT, verb 5 = 0.003 %

Tob **3**:5	in exacting penalty from me for my sins
Jud **8**:21	and he will exact of us the penalty for its desecration
1 Ma **10**:35	No one shall have authority to exact anything from them
1 Es **2**:27	and exacted tribute from Coelesyria and Phoenicia
3 Ma **2**:31	to be exacted for maintaining the religion of their city

EXACTLY 2

Sir pr.	does not have exactly the same sense
2 Ma **14**:43	But in the heat of the struggle he did not hit exactly

EXAGGERATE 1

Wis **17**:11	it has always exaggerated the difficulties

EXALT 78 = 0.051 %

Tob **12**:6	exalt him and give thanks to him
12:6	It is good to praise God and to exalt his name
13:4	and exalt him in the presence of all the living
13:6	and exalt the King of the ages
13:7	I exalt my God
13:7	my soul exalts the King of heaven
13:18	Blessed is God, who has exalted you for ever
14:7	and the Lord will exalt his people
Jud **9**:7	they are exalted, with their horses and riders
10:8	and Jerusalem may be exalted
16:2	exalt him, and call upon his name
16:8	to exalt the oppressed in Israel
Ad E **11**:11	and the lowly were exalted and consumed those held in honour
Wis **19**:22	thou hast exalted and glorified thy people
Sir **1**:19	and he exalted the glory of those who held her fast
1:30	Do not exalt yourself lest you fall
4:11	Wisdom exalts her sons and gives help to those who seek her
6:2	Do not exalt yourself through your soul's counsel
7:11	for there is One who abases and exalts
11:4	nor exalt yourself in the day that you are honoured
15:5	She will exalt him above his neighbours
32:1	If they make you master of the feast, do not exalt yourself
33:9	some of them be exalted and hallowed
33:12	some of them he blessed and exalted
43:30	When you praise the Lord, exalt him as much as you can
43:30	When you exalt him, put forth all your strength
44:21	and exalt his posterity like the stars
45:6	He exalted Aaron, the brother of Moses
47:5	to exalt the power of his people
47:11	The Lord took away his sins, and exalted his power for ever
50:22	who exalts our days from birth
P Az **29**	and to be praised and highly exalted for ever
30	and to be highly praised and highly exalted for ever
32	and to be praised and highly exalted for ever
33	and to be extolled and highly exalted for ever
35	sing praise to him and highly exalt him for ever
36	sing praise to him and highly exalt him for ever
37	sing praise to him and highly exalt him for ever
38	sing praise to him and highly exalt him for ever
39	sing praise to him and highly exalt him for ever
40	sing praise to him and highly exalt him for ever
41	sing praise to him and highly exalt him for ever
42	sing praise to him and highly exalt him for ever
43	sing praise to him and highly exalt him for ever
44	sing praise to him and highly exalt him for ever
45	sing praise to him and highly exalt him for ever
46	sing praise to him and highly exalt him for ever
47	sing praise to him and highly exalt him for ever
48	sing praise to him and highly exalt him for ever
49	sing praise to him and highly exalt him for ever

	50	sing praise to him and highly exalt him for ever
	51	sing praise to him and highly exalt him for ever
	52	let it sing praise to him and highly exalt him for ever
	53	sing praise to him and highly exalt him for ever
	54	sing praise to him and highly exalt him for ever
	55	sing praise to him and highly exalt him for ever
	56	sing praise to him and highly exalt him for ever
	57	sing praise to him and highly exalt him for ever
	58	sing praise to him and highly exalt him for ever
	59	sing praise to him and highly exalt him for ever
	60	sing praise to him and highly exalt him for ever
	61	sing praise to him and highly exalt him for ever
	62	sing praise to him and highly exalt him for ever
	63	sing praise to him and highly exalt him for ever
	64	sing praise to him and highly exalt him for ever
	65	sing praise to him and highly exalt him for ever
	66	sing praise to him and highly exalt him for ever
1 Ma	1:3	When the earth became quiet before him, he was exalted
	2:63	Today he will be exalted, but tomorrow he will not be found
	8:13	and they have been greatly exalted
	11:16	and King Ptolemy was exalted
	11:26	he exalted him in the presence of all his friends
	14:35	He sought in every way to exalt his people
1 Es	9:52	and do not be sorrowful, for the Lord will exalt you
3 Ma	2:21	scourged him who had exalted himself
	6:4	exalted with lawless insolence and boastful tongue
2 Es	2:43	but he was more exalted than they
	8:20	whose eyes are exalted and whose upper chambers are in the air

EXALTATION   3 = 0.002 %

Jud	13:4	for the exaltation of Jerusalem
	15:9	and said to her, You are the exaltation of Jerusalem
1 Ma	1:40	her exaltation was turned into mourning

EXAMINATION   2

Sus	13:48	without examination and without learning the facts ?
3 Ma	7:5	they tried without any inquiry or examination

EXAMINE   10 = 0.007 %

Jud	7:7	and examined the approaches to the city
Ad E	12:3	Then the king examined the 2 eunuchs
Wis	3:13	she will have fruit when God examines souls
	4:6	against their parents when God examines them
	11:10	but thou didst examine the ungodly
Sir	13:11	and while he smiles he will be examining you
	18:20	Before judgment, examine yourself
	23:10	for as a servant who is continually examined under torture
Sus	13:51	and I will examine them
2 Es	16:64	Because the Lord will strictly examine all their works

EXAMPLE   14 = 0.009 %

Jud	8:24	let us set an example to our brethren
Ad E	14:11	and make an example of the man who began this against us
Sir	44:16	he was an example of repentance to all generations
2 Ma	6:10	For example, 2 women were brought in
	6:28	and leave to the young a noble example
	6:31	leaving in his death an example of nobility
3 Ma	2:5	and you made them an example
2 Es	7:6	Another example : There is a city built and set on a plain
4 Ma	1:7	I could prove to you from many and various examples
	6:19	in becoming an example of the eating of defiling food
	12:16	I do not desert the excellent example of my brothers
	14:15	For example, among birds, the ones that are tame
	14:18	by the example of unreasoning animals
	17:23	as an example for their own endurance

EXASPERATE   1

2 Ma	7:39	being exasperated at his scorn

EXCEEDINGLY   7 = 0.005 %

Jud	2:28	Those who lived in Azotus and Ascalon feared him exceedingly
Sir	43:11	exceedingly beautiful in its brightness
	47:24	Their sins became exceedingly many
2 Ma	8:30	and got possession of some exceedingly high strongholds
3 Ma	2:23	panic-stricken in their exceedingly great fear
2 Es	10:25	her face suddenly shone exceedingly
	12:3	and the earth was exceedingly terrified

EXCEL   4 = 0.003 %

Ad E	13:3	Haman, who excels among us in sound judgment
Wis	7:29	and excels every constellation of the stars
Sir	33:16	by the blessing of the Lord I excelled
	33:22	Excel in all that you do

EXCELLENCE   4 = 0.003 %

Sir	6:15	and no scales can measure his excellence
	31:23	and their testimony to his excellence is trustworthy
2 Ma	15:12	in all that belongs to excellence
3 Ma	1:9	and being impressed by its excellence and its beauty

EXCELLENT   8 = 0.005 %

Tob	4:11	and for all who practise it charity is an excellent offering
Ad E	16:16	and for our fathers in the most excellent order
Sir	14:25	and will lodge in an excellent lodging place
	32:2	and receive a wreath for your excellent leadership
2 Ma	1:35	he exchanged many excellent gifts
	6:23	and his excellent life even from childhood
4 Ma	5:8	the very excellent meat of this animal ?
	12:16	I do not desert the excellent example of my brothers

EXCEPT, prep.   14 = 0.009 %

Tob	1:20	and nothing was left to me except my wife Anna
	6:14	and he harms no one except those who approach her
Jud	6:2	Who is God except Nebuchadnezzar ?
	8:6	except the day before the sabbath and the sabbath itself
Ad E	14:18	except in thee, O Lord God of Abraham
Wis	17:6	except a dreadful, self-kindled fire
Sir	22:14	And what is its name except Fool ?
	49:4	Except David and Hezekiah and Josiah they all sinned greatly
Sus	13:16	And no one was there except the 2 elders
1 Ma	11:38	except the foreign troops
	11:70	except Mattathias the son of Absalom and Judas the son of Chalphi
2 Es	5:38	except he whose dwelling is not with men ?
	11:23	except the 3 heads that were at rest and 6 little wings
	13:52	except in the time of his day

EXCEPTION   1

Ad E	16:24	Every city and country, without exception

EXCESS   2

Tob	4:15	Do not drink wine to excess
Sir	31:29	Wine drunk to excess is bitterness of soul

EXCHANGE, verb   3 = 0.002 %

Sir	7:18	Do not exchange a friend for money
2 Ma	1:35	he exchanged many excellent gifts
3 Ma	4:6	exchanged joy for wailing

EXCHANGE, subst.   3 = 0.002 %

Sir	44:17	in the time of wrath he was taken in exchange
3 Ma	2:32	in exchange for life they confidently attempted
4 Ma	6:29	and take my life in exchange for theirs

EXCITE   2

2 Ma	14:27	The king became excited
4 Ma	8:26	Why does such contentiousness excite us

EXCITEMENT   1

Jud	10:18	There was great excitement in the whole camp

EXCLAIM   1

Tob	7:7	And he blessed him and exclaimed

EXCLUDE   2

1 Es	5:39	they were excluded from serving as priests
3 Ma	3:18	and excluded us from entering

EXCRUCIATINGLY   1

4 Ma	14:10	What could be more excruciatingly painful than this ?

EXCUSE, verb   3 = 0.002 %

Wis	13:8	Yet again, not even they are to be excused
4 Ma	5:13	it will excuse you from any transgression
	8:22	Also, divine justice will excuse us

EXECUTE   4 = 0.003 %

Jud	2:12	what I have spoken my hand will execute
Sir	20:4	is a man who executes judgments by violence
	35:17	and does justice for the righteous, and executes judgment
P Az	5	Thou hast executed true judgments

EXECUTION   2

Ad E	12:3	and when they confessed they were led to execution
	16:17	*You will therefore do well not to put in execution*

EXECUTIONER   1

2 Ma	5:8	and abhorred as the executioner of his country

EXEMPT, verb   1

1 Ma	10:29	And now I free you and exempt all the Jews

EXERCISE   3 = 0.002 %

Ad E	16:7	who exercise authority unworthily
3 Ma	3:18	but they were spared the exercise of our power
4 Ma	18:1	obey this law and exercise pity in every way

EXERT
                                    3 = 0.002 %
- **Wis** 16:24 exerts itself to punish the unrighteous
- **Sir** 29:6 If the lender exerts pressure, he will hardly get back half
- **3 Ma** 3:10 and to exert more earnest efforts for their assistance

EXHAUST
                                    4 = 0.003 %
- **Jud** 11:12 Since their food supply is exhausted
- **1 Ma** 3:29 Then he saw that the money in the treasury was exhausted
-     10:82 *for the cavalry was exhausted*
- **4 Ma** 3:8 *he came, sweating and quite exhausted, to the royal tent*

EXHAUSTION
                                    1
- **2 Es** 5:35 and the exhaustion of the people of Israel ?

EXHAUSTIVE
                                    1
- **2 Ma** 2:31 and to forego exhaustive treatment

EXHIBIT
                                    2
- **2 Ma** 14:39 Nicanor, wishing to exhibit the enmity
- **3 Ma** 5:31 and have exhibited to an extraordinary degree

EXHORT
                                  11 = 0.007 %
- **2 Ma** 2:3 And with other similar words he exhorted them
-     8:16 and exhorted them not to be frightened by the enemy
-     12:31 they thanked them and exhorted them
-     12:42 And the noble Judas exhorted the people
-     13:12 Judas exhorted them and ordered them to stand ready
-     13:14 and exhorting his men to fight nobly to the death
-     15:8 And he exhorted his men
- **3 Ma** 1:4 and exhorted them
- **4 Ma** 8:5 but I also exhort you to yield to me and enjoy my friendship
-     8:17 and exhorted us to accept kind treatment if we obey him
-     12:7 But when his mother had exhorted him in the Hebrew language

EXHORTATION
                                    1
- **4 Ma** 6:1 to the exhortations of the tyrant

EXILE, subst.
                                12 = 0.008 %
- **Wis** 17:2 *exiles from eternal providence*
- **Sir** 29:18 it has driven men of power into exile
- **Bar** 2:14 in the sight of those who have carried us into exile
-     2:30 But in the land of their exile they will come to themselves
-     2:32 and they will praise me in the land of their exile
-     3:7 and we will praise thee in our exile
-     3:8 Behold, we are today in our exile
- **2 Ma** 5:9 and he who had driven many from their own country into exile
-           died in exile
- **1 Es** 2:15 *with the returning exiles from Babylon to Jerusalem*
- **3 Ma** 6:10 Even if our lives have become entangled in impieties in our exile
- **2 Es** 5:17 in the land of their exile ?

EXILED
                                    1
- **2 Ma** 1:33 that, in the place where the exiled priests had hidden the fire

EXIST
                                23 = 0.015 %
- **Wis** 1:14 For he created all things that they might exist
-     2:6 Come, therefore, let us enjoy the good things that exist
-     7:17 For it is he who gave me unerring knowledge of what exists
-     8:6 who more than she is fashioner of what exists ?
-     11:24 For thou lovest all things that exist
-     13:1 to know him who exists
-     14:13 for neither have they existed from the beginning
-     14:13 nor will they exist for ever
- **Sir** 14:19 Every product decays and ceases to exist
-     16:26 The works of the Lord have existed
-     17:28 From the dead, as from one who does not exist
-     24:9 and for eternity I shall not cease to exist
- **1 Ma** 3:29 that had existed from the earliest days
- **2 Ma** 7:28 that God did not make them out of things that existed
- **1 Es** 4:17 men cannot exist without women
- **2 Es** 4:9 and without which you cannot exist
-     4:23 and the written covenants no longer exist
-     7:23 they even declared that the Most High does not exist
-     8:7 For thou alone dost exist
-     8:35 and among those who have existed
-     9:18 when I was preparing for those who now exist
-     9:18 and no one opposed me then, for no one existed
- **4 Ma** 1:25 In pleasure there exists even a malevolent tendency

EXISTENCE
                                4 = 0.003 %
- **Wis** 7:5 For no king has had a different beginning of existence
-     15:12 But he considered our existence an idle game
- **Sir** 40:29 his existence cannot be considered as life
- **2 Es** 6:49 Then thou didst keep in existence 2 living creatures

EXISTING
                                    1
- **2 Ma** 4:11 He set aside the existing royal concessions to the Jews

EXIT
                                    1
- **2 Es** 4:7 or which are the exits of hell

EXPAND
                                    1
- **4 Ma** 13:25 expanded their goodwill and harmony toward one another

EXPANSE
                                    1
- **2 Es** 7:3 There is a sea set in a wide expanse

EXPECT
                              13 = 0.008 %
- **Tob** 8:16 It has not happened to me as I expected
- **Jud** 8:14 how do you expect to search out God
- **Wis** 12:22 and when we are judged we may expect mercy
-     14:29 they swear wicked oaths and expect to suffer no harm
-     18:7 were expected by thy people
- **2 Ma** 8:11 not expecting the judgment from the Almighty
-     12:37 when they were not expecting it
-     12:44 For if he were not expecting
- **3 Ma** 2:31 since they expected to enhance their reputation
-     3:8 and expected that matters would change
-     6:30 in that same place in which they had expected
- **2 Es** 5:6 And one shall reign whom those who dwell on earth do not expect
-     7:117 and expect punishment after death ?

EXPECTATION
                              3 = 0.002 %
- **Wis** 17:13 and the inner expectation of help, being weak
- **3 Ma** 5:41 because of its expectation
- **4 Ma** 4:14 So Apollonius, having been preserved beyond all expectations

EXPEDITION
                              3 = 0.002 %
- **1 Ma** 9:68 for his plan and his expedition had been in vain
- **2 Ma** 9:23 on the occasions when he made expeditions
- **3 Ma** 3:14 When our expedition took place in Asia

EXPEL
                              3 = 0.002 %
- **1 Ma** 13:47 But he expelled them from the city
-     13:50 But he expelled them from there
- **1 Es** 9:4 and the men themselves expelled from the multitude of

EXPEND
                                  1
- **2 Ma** 4:19 but to expend it for another purpose

EXPENSE
                              7 = 0.005 %
- **Tob** 5:14 and expenses for yourself as for my son ?
- **Sir** 18:32 lest you become impoverished by its expense
- **1 Ma** 3:30 as he had before for his expenses and for the gifts
-     10:39 to meet the necessary expenses of the sanctuary
- **2 Ma** 3:3 defrayed from his own revenues all the expenses
-     9:16 and the expenses incurred for the sacrifices
- **3 Ma** 4:1 a feast at public expense was arranged for the Gentiles

EXPERIENCE, subst.
                            12 = 0.008 %
- **Wis** 8:8 And if any one longs for wide experience
-     8:18 and in the experience of her company, understanding
-     18:20 The experience of death touched also the righteous
- **Sir** 1:7 And her abundant experience – who has understood it ?
-     21:22 but a man of experience stands respectfully before it
-     25:6 Rich experience is the crown of the aged
-     34:9 and one with much experience will speak with understanding
-     34:12 but have escaped because of these experiences
-     36:20 but a man of experience will pay him back
- **2 Ma** 8:9 a general and a man of experience in military service
- **2 Es** 7:14 pass through the difficult and vain experiences
- **4 Ma** 1:24 Anger, as a man will see if he reflects on this experience

EXPERIENCE, verb
                            6 = 0.004 %
- **Wis** 2:24 and those who belong to his party experience it
-     12:26 will experience the deserved judgment of God
-     19:5 and that thy people might experience an incredible journey
- **3 Ma** 5:5 convinced that the whole nation would experience its final destruction
-     6:33 for the unexpected rescue which he had experienced
- **2 Es** 4:23 but about those things which we daily experience :

EXPERT, subst., adj.
                              2
- **Sir** 45:12 a distinction to be prized, the work of an expert
- **Bar** 3:26 great in stature, expert in war

EXPIATION
                              3 = 0.002 %
- **Sir** 28:5 who will make expiation for his sins ?
- **1 Es** 9:20 and to give rams in expiation of their error
- **4 Ma** 17:22 and their death as an expiation

EXPIRE
                              4 = 0.003 %
- **Tob** 10:1 and when the days for the journey had expired
-     10:7 until the 14 days of the wedding feast had expired
- **4 Ma** 6:26 When he was now burned to his very bones and about to expire
-     15:18 nor when the 3rd expired

EXPLAIN   16 = 0.010 %

Tob	4 : 2	so that I may explain to him about the money before I die ?
	4 : 20	And now let me explain to you about the 10 talents of silver
	7 : 10	But let me explain the true situation to you
2 Ma	3 : 10	The high priest explained that there were some deposits
1 Es	3 : 16	and they shall explain their statements
	3 : 17	Explain to us what you have written
	9 : 48	at the same time explaining what was read
2 Es	5 : 37	and then I will explain to you the travail
	10 : 32	what I am unable to explain
	12 : 12	But it was not explained to him as I now explain
	12 : 12	or have explained it to you
	13 : 21	and I will also explain to you
	13 : 51	I said, O sovereign Lord, explain this to me :
	13 : 56	and explain weighty and wondrous matters to you
4 Ma	3 : 6	Now this can be explained more clearly

EXPLANATION   2

2 Es	7 : 51	hear the explanation for this
	10 : 37	to give your servant an explanation of this bewildering vision

EXPLOIT   1

Sir	13 : 4	A rich man will exploit you if you can be of use to him

EXPLORE   1

2 Es	13 : 52	He said to me, Just as no one can explore or know

EXPOSE   6 = 0.004 %

Wis	11 : 14	who long before had been cast out and exposed
	18 : 5	and one child had been exposed and rescued
Sir	28 : 19	who has not been exposed to its anger
1 Ma	14 : 29	exposed themselves to danger
2 Ma	4 : 33	*he publicly exposed them*
4 Ma	15 : 15	and the flesh of the head to the chin exposed like masks

EXPOUND   1

Sir	38 : 33	they cannot expound discipline or judgment

EXPRESS   6 = 0.004 %

Sir	pr.	For what was originally expressed in Hebrew
	pr.	differ not a little as originally expressed
	34 : 11	and I understand more than I can express
3 Ma	6 : 41	magnanimously expressing his concern :
4 Ma	15 : 4	In what manner might I express
	18 : 6	expressed also these principles to her children :

EXPRESSION   3 = 0.002 %

Sir	12 : 18	*and whisper much, and change his expression*
	27 : 6	so the expression of a thought discloses the cultivation of a man's mind
2 Ma	2 : 31	should be allowed to strive for brevity of expression

EXPULSION   1

3 Ma	4 : 4	and shed tears at the most miserable expulsion of these people

EXTEND   4 = 0.003 %

Sir	4 : 31	Let not your hand be extended to receive
1 Ma	3 : 3	He extended the glory of his people
	14 : 6	He extended the borders of his nation
3 Ma	2 : 1	bending his knees and extending his hands with calm dignity

EXTENT   2

Ad E	13 : 2	and open to travel throughout all its extent
2 Ma	3 : 11	To such an extent the impious Simon had misrepresented the facts

EXTERMINATE   1

Wis	11 : 19	not only could their damage exterminate men

EXTERNAL   1

4 Ma	6 : 34	when it masters even external agonies

EXTINGUISH   4 = 0.003 %

Wis	2 : 3	When it is extinguished, the body will turn to ashes
Sir	3 : 30	Water extinguishes a blazing fire :
	10 : 17	and has extinguished the memory of them from the earth
2 Es	7 : 61	they are set on fire and burn hotly, and are extinguished

EXTOL   5 = 0.003 %

Sir	13 : 23	and they extol to the clouds what he says
	43 : 31	Or who can extol him as he is ?
P Az	31	and to be extolled and highly glorified for ever
	33	and to be extolled and highly exalted for ever
2 Ma	4 : 24	extolled him with an air of authority

EXTRAORDINARY   2

Sir	10 : 13	extraordinary afflictions
3 Ma	5 : 31	and have exhibited to an extraordinary degree

EXTREME, adj.   3 = 0.002 %

2 Ma	7 : 42	and the extreme tortures
3 Ma	7 : 22	restored it to them with extreme fear
4 Ma	3 : 18	it can overthrow bodily agonies even when they are extreme

EXTREME, subst.   1

2 Ma	4 : 13	There was such an extreme of Hellenization

EXTREMELY   2

4 Ma	3 : 10	but the king was extremely thirsty
	12 : 9	Extremely pleased by the boy's declaration

EXULT   4 = 0.003 %

3 Ma	2 : 17	or exult in the arrogance of their tongue, saying
	6 : 5	Sennacherib exulting in his countless forces
2 Es	1 : 16	You have not exulted in my name
	15 : 53	exulting and clapping yours hands

EXULTATION   2

Wis	14 : 28	For their worshippers either rave in exultation
Sir	1 : 11	The fear of the Lord is glory and exultation

EYE, subst.   95 = 0.062 %

Tob	2 : 10	and their fresh droppings fell into my open eyes
	2 : 10	and white films formed on my eyes
	3 : 12	And now, O Lord, I have turned my eyes and my face toward thee
	3 : 17	to scale away the white films from Tobit's eyes
	4 : 7	and do not let your eye begrudge the gift when you make it
	4 : 16	and do not let your eye begrudge the gift when you make it
	5 : 20	he will return safe and sound, and your eyes will see him
	6 : 8	anoint with it a man who has white films in his eyes
	10 : 5	you who are the light of my eyes ?
	11 : 7	that your father will open his eyes
	11 : 8	You therefore must anoint his eyes with the gall
	11 : 11	and he sprinkled the gall upon his father's eyes, saying
	11 : 12	And when his eyes began to smart he rubbed them
	11 : 13	and the white films scaled off from the corners of his eyes
Jud	2 : 11	But if they refuse, your eye shall not spare
	7 : 27	and we shall not witness the death of our babes before our eyes
	8 : 22	and a reproach in the eyes of those who acquire us
	10 : 4	to entice the eyes of all men who might see her
	10 : 14	she was in their eyes marvellously beautiful
	16 : 9	Her sandal ravished his eyes, her beauty captivated his mind
Ad E	13 : 15	for the eyes of our foes are upon us to annihilate us
	13 : 18	for their death was before their eyes
	16 : 9	and always judging what comes before our eyes
Wis	3 : 2	In the eyes of the foolish they seemed to have died
	11 : 18	or flash terrible sparks from their eyes
	15 : 15	though these have neither the use of their eyes to see with
Sir	3 : 25	If you have no eyes you will be without light
	4 : 1	and do not keep needy eyes waiting
	4 : 5	Do not avert your eye from the needy
	9 : 8	Turn away your eyes from a shapely woman
	10 : 20	are worthy of honour in his eyes
	11 : 12	but the eyes of the Lord look upon him for his good
	12 : 16	an enemy will weep with his eyes
	14 : 8	Evil is the man with a grudging eye
	14 : 9	A greedy man's eye is not satisfied with a portion
	14 : 10	A stingy man's eye begrudges bread
	15 : 19	his eyes are on those who fear him
	16 : 5	Many such things my eye has seen
	17 : 6	He made for them tongue and eyes
	17 : 8	He set his eye upon their hearts
	17 : 13	Their eyes saw his glorious majesty
	17 : 15	they will not be hid from his eyes
	17 : 19	and his eyes are continually upon their ways
	17 : 22	and he will keep a person's kindness like the apple of his eye
	18 : 18	and the gift of a grudging man makes the eyes dim
	20 : 14	for he has many eyes instead of one
	20 : 29	Presents and gifts blind the eyes of the wise
	22 : 19	A man who pricks an eye will make tears fall
	23 : 4	do not give me haughty eyes
	23 : 19	His fear is confined to the eyes of men
	23 : 19	and he does not realize that the eyes of the Lord
	26 : 9	A wife's harlotry shows in her lustful eyes
	26 : 11	Be on guard against her impudent eye
	27 : 1	and whoever seeks to get rich will avert his eyes
	27 : 22	Whoever winks his eye plans evil deeds
	30 : 20	he sees with his eyes and groans
	31 : 13	Remember that a greedy eye is a bad thing
	31 : 13	What has been created more greedy then the eye ?
	34 : 16	The eyes of the Lord are upon those who love him
	34 : 17	He lifts up the soul and gives light to the eyes
	34 : 20	Like one who kills a son before his father's eyes
	38 : 28	and his eyes are on the pattern of the object
	39 : 19	and nothing can be hid from his eyes
	40 : 22	The eye desires grace and beauty
	43 : 4	and with bright beams it blinds the eyes
	43 : 18	The eye marvels at the beauty of its whiteness

	45:12	the delight of the eyes, richly adorned
	51:27	See with your eyes that I have laboured little
Bar	1:12	and he will give light to our eyes
	2:17	open thy eyes, O Lord, and see
	2:18	and the eyes that are failing, and the person that hungers
	3:14	where there is light for the eyes, and peace
L Jr	6:17	Their eyes are full of the dust
Sus	13:9	and turned away their eyes from looking to Heaven
Bel	14:42	and they were devoured immediately before his eyes
1 Ma	6:10	Sleep departs from my eyes and I am downhearted with worry
	9:39	They raised their eyes and looked
	11:51	So the Jews gained glory in the eyes of the king
2 Ma	3:36	which he had seen with his own eyes
	8:17	keeping before their eyes the lawless outrage
	12:42	for they had seen with their own eyes
3 Ma	4:4	perceiving the common object of pity before their eyes
	4:10	so that with their eyes in total darkness
	5:33	and his eyes wavered and his face fell
	5:47	wishing to witness, with invulnerable heart and with his own eyes
2 Es	1:37	though they do not see me with bodily eyes
	8:20	whose eyes are exalted and whose upper chambers are in the air
	9:38	I lifted up my eyes and saw a woman on my right
	10:55	as far as it is possible for your eyes to see it
4 Ma	4:1	he was unable to injure Onias in the eyes of the nation
	5:30	not even if you gouge out my eyes and burn my entrails
	6:6	yet while the old man's eyes were raised to heaven
	6:26	he lifted up his eyes to God and said
	15:19	nor did you weep when you looked at the eyes of each one
	18:21	pierced the pupils of their eyes and cut out their tongues

EYELID
Sir	26:9	and she is known by her eyelids	1

EZEKIEL
Sir	49:8	It was Ezekiel who saw the vision of glory	2
4 Ma	18:17	He confirmed the saying of Ezekiel	

EZORA
1 Es	9:34	Of the sons of Ezora : Shashai, Azarel, Azael	1

EZRA
1 Es	8:1	Ezra came, the son of Seraiah, son of Azariah	33 = 0.021 %
	8:3	This Ezra came up from Babylon as a scribe	
	8:7	For Ezra possessed great knowledge	
	8:8	which was delivered to Ezra the priest	
	8:9	King Artaxerxes to Ezra the priest	
	8:19	that whatever Ezra the priest	
	8:23	And you, Ezra, according to the wisdom of God	
	8:91	While Ezra was praying and making his confession	
	8:92	and said to Ezra, We have sinned against the Lord	
	8:96	Then Ezra arose and had the leaders of the priests	
	9:1	Then Ezra rose and went from the court of the temple	
	9:7	Then Ezra rose and said to them	
	9:16	Ezra the priest chose for himself	
	9:39	and they told Ezra the chief priest and reader	
	9:40	So Ezra the chief priest brought the law	
	9:42	Ezra the priest and reader of the law	
	9:45	Then Ezra took up the book of the law	
	9:46	And Ezra blessed the Lord God Most High	
	9:49	Then Attharates said to Ezra the chief priest and reader	
2 Es	1:1	The 2nd book of the prophet Ezra the son of Seraiah	
	2:10	Thus says the Lord to Ezra :	
	2:33	I, Ezra, received a command from the Lord on Mount Horeb	
	2:42	I, Ezra, saw on Mount Zion a great multitude	
	3:1	I, Salathiel, who am also called Ezra, was in Babylon	
	6:10	between the heel and the hand seek for nothing else, Ezra !	
	7:2	and he said to me, Rise, Ezra	
	7:25	Therefore, Ezra, empty things are for the empty	
	7:49	He answered me and said, Listen to me, Ezra	
	8:1	But I will tell you a parable, Ezra	
	8:19	The beginning of the words of Ezra's prayer	
	14:1	and said, Ezra, Ezra	
	14:38	Ezra, open your mouth and drink what I give you to drink	

F

FABRIC
Sir	38:34	But they keep stable the fabric of the world	1

FACE, subst.
Tob	2:9	I slept by the wall of the courtyard, and my face was uncovered	82 = 0.053 %
	3:6	do not turn thy face away from me	
	3:12	and now, O Lord, I have turned my eyes and my face toward thee	
	4:7	Do not turn your face away from any poor man	
	4:7	and the face of God will not be turned away from you	
	12:16	and they fell upon their faces, for they were afraid	

	13:6	and will not hide his face from you
Jud	2:7	and will cover the whole face of the earth
	2:19	and to cover the whole face of the earth to the west
	6:3	from the face of the earth
	6:5	you shall not see my face again from this day
	6:19	upon the faces of those who are consecrated to thee
	7:4	These men will now lick up the face of the whole land
	7:18	and covered the whole face of the land
	8:7	She was beautiful in appearance, and had a very lovely face
	9:1	Then Judith fell upon her face
	10:7	When they saw her, and noted how her face was altered
	10:14	When the men heard her words, and observed her face
	10:23	they all marvelled at the beauty of her face
	11:21	either for beauty of face or wisdom of speech !
	13:16	it was my face that tricked him to his destruction
	14:6	he fell down on his face and his spirit failed him
	16:8	She anointed her face with ointment
Ad E	15:7	Lifting his face, flushed with splendour
Wis	4:20	and their lawless deeds will convict them to their face
	10:5	in the face of his compassion for his child
	17:4	and dismal phantoms with gloomy faces appeared
Sir	4:4	nor turn your face away from the poor
	13:26	The mark of a happy heart is a cheerful face
	14:8	he averts his face and disregards people
	18:24	and of the moment of vengeance when he turns away his face
	19:27	He hides his face and pretends not to hear
	19:29	and a sensible man is known by his face, when you meet him
	25:17	and darkens her face like that of a bear
	25:23	A dejected mind, a gloomy face, and a wounded heart
	26:4	and at all times his face is cheerful
	26:17	so is a beautiful face on a stately figure
	31:13	Therefore it sheds tears from every face
	34:3	the likeness of a face confronting a face
	35:9	With every gift show a cheerful face
	37:5	and in the face of battle take up the shield
	38:8	and from him health is upon the face of the earth
	45:5	and gave him the commandments face to face
	50:17	and fell to the ground upon their faces
Bar	1:15	but confusion of face, as at this day, to us
	2:6	but confusion of face to us and our fathers, as at this day
L Jr	6:13	their faces are wiped because of the dust from the temple
	6:21	when their faces have been blackened
P Az	18	we fear thee and seek thy face
1 Ma	4:40	They fell face down on the ground
	4:55	All the people fell on their faces
	7:3	he said, Do not let me see their faces !
	7:28	I shall come with a few men to see you face to face in peace
	11:68	but they themselves met him face to face
2 Ma	3:16	for his face and the change in his colour
	7:6	which bore witness against the people to their faces
1 Es	4:58	he lifted up his face to heaven toward Jerusalem
	8:74	I am ashamed and confounded before thy face
3 Ma	5:33	and his eyes wavered and his face fell
	6:15	and have not turned your face from us
	6:18	revealed his holy face and opened the heavenly gates
2 Es	1:31	I will turn my face from you
	4:11	When I heard this, I fell on my face
	5:16	And why is your face sad ?
	7:97	when it is shown to them how their face is to shine like the sun
	7:98	for they hasten to behold the face of him
	7:125	Or that the faces of those who practised self-control
	7:125	but our faces shall be blacker than darkness ?
	10:25	her face suddenly shone exceedingly
	12:7	and if my prayer has indeed come up before thy face
	13:3	and wherever he turned his face to look
	13:38	and will reproach them to their face with their evil thoughts
	15:54	Trick out the beauty of your face !
	16:50	when she decks herself out, and shall accuse her to her face
4 Ma	6:11	in fact, with his face bathed in sweat
	6:24	in the face of the afflictions

FACE, verb
Tob	4:4	Remember, my son, that she faced many dangers for you	8 = 0.005 %
Jud	4:6	which faces Esdraelon opposite the plain near Dothan	
	7:3	which faces Esdraelon	
1 Ma	4:61	so that the people might have a stronghold that faced Idumea	
	13:13	And Simon encamped in Adida, facing the plain	
1 Es	4:24	he faces lions, and he walks in darkness	
3 Ma	2:1	Then the high priest Simon, facing the sanctuary	
4 Ma	14:1	Furthermore, they encouraged them to face the torture	

FACT
Sus	13:48	without examination and without learning the facts ?	11 = 0.007 %
2 Ma	3:8	but in fact to carry out the king's purpose	
	3:11	To such an extent the impious Simon had misrepresented the facts	
	4:17	a fact which later events will make clear	
	6:13	In fact, not to let the impious alone for long	
	13:25	in fact they were so angry that they wanted to annul its terms	

3 Ma	5:32	In fact you would have been deprived of life instead of these
4 Ma	2:6	In fact, since the law had told us not to covet
	6:11	in fact, with his face bathed in sweat
	13:3	But in fact it was not so
	17:20	but also by the fact that because of them

FACTOR 1
4 Ma 15:11 Nevertheless, though so many factors influenced the mother

FADE 1
1 Ma 1:26 the beauty of the women faded

FAIL 34 = 0.022 %

Jud	6:9	I have spoken and none of my words shall fail
	7:19	for their courage failed
	11:6	and my lord will not fail to achieve his purposes
	14:6	he fell down on his face and his spirit failed him
Ad E	10:5	and none of them has failed to be fulfilled
Wis	2:9	Let none of us fail to share in our revelry
	3:15	and the root of understanding does not fail
	9:14	and our designs are likely to fail
	13:9	how did they fail to find sooner the Lord of these things ?
	15:11	because he failed to know the one who formed him
	19:21	failed to consume the flesh of perishable creatures
Sir	2:8	and your reward will not fail
	7:34	Do not fail those who weep, but mourn with those who mourn
	17:24	and he encourages those whose endurance is failing
	17:31	Yet its light fails
	19:1	he who despises small things will fail little by little
	29:14	but a man who has lost his sense of shame will fail him
	34:7	and those who put their hope in them have failed
	37:12	and who will sorrow with you if you fail
	40:14	likewise transgressors will utterly fail
	41:2	to one who is in need and is failing in strength
Bar	2:18	and the eyes that are failing, and the person that hungers
L Jr	6:49	How then can one fail to see that these are not gods
	6:52	Who then can fail to know that they are not gods ?
1 Ma	6:22	How long will you fail to do justice
	11:49	their courage failed
3 Ma	5:12	that he quite failed in his lawless purpose
2 Es	2:32	because my springs run over, and my grace will not fail
	3:29	And my heart failed me
	4:2	Your understanding has utterly failed regarding this world
	5:53	when the womb is failing
	7:120	but we have miserably failed ?
	15:13	because their seed shall fail and their trees shall be ruined
4 Ma	13:5	How then can one fail to confess

FAILING, subst. 1
2 Es 8:17 for I see the failings of us who dwell in the land

FAILURE 1
Wis 10:8 so that their failures could never go unnoticed

FAINT, verb 3 = 0.002 %
Jud 7:22 and the women and young men fainted from thirst
Ad E 15:15 But as she was speaking, she fell fainting
2 Es 5:14 and my soul was so troubled that it fainted

FAINT, adj. 8 = 0.005 %

Jud	8:9	because they were faint for lack of water
	8:31	and we will no longer be faint
Ad E	15:7	And the queen faltered, and turned pale and faint
Sir	2:13	Woe to the faint heart, for it has no trust !
1 Ma	1:26	maidens and young men became faint
	3:17	And we are faint, for we have eaten nothing today
	9:8	He became faint, but he said to those who were left
2 Ma	3:24	and became faint with terror

FAINTHEARTED 4 = 0.003 %
Sir 4:9 and do not be fainthearted in judging a case
    7:10 Do not be fainthearted in your prayer
1 Ma 3:56 or were faint-hearted
4 Ma 16:5 If this woman, though a mother, had been fainthearted

FAIR 1
Sir 3:15 as frost in fair weather, your sins will melt away

FAITH 14 = 0.009 %

Sir	4:16	If he has faith in her he will obtain her
	25:12	and faith is the beginning of clinging to him
	27:17	Love your friend and keep faith with him
	29:3	Confirm your word and keep faith with him
	40:12	but good faith will stand for ever
1 Ma	10:27	And now continue still to keep faith with us
2 Ma	8:1	and enlisted those who had continued in the Jewish faith
2 Es	5:1	and the land shall be barren of faith
	6:5	and before those who stored up treasures of faith were sealed
	9:7	on account of the faith by which he has believed
	13:23	who have works and have faith in the Almighty

4 Ma	15:24	because of faith in God
	16:22	You too must have the same faith in God and not be grieved
	17:2	and showed the courage of your faith !

FAITHFUL 14 = 0.009 %

Wis	3:9	and the faithful will abide with him in love
Sir	1:14	she is created with the faithful in the womb
	6:14	A faithful friend is a sturdy shelter :
	6:15	There is nothing so precious as a faithful friend
	6:16	A faithful friend is an elixir of life
	37:13	for no one is more faithful to you than it is
	44:20	and when he was tested he was found faithful
	48:22	who was great and faithful in his vision
1 Ma	2:52	Was not Abraham found faithful when tested
	3:13	including a body of faithful men
	7:8	and was faithful to the king
2 Ma	1:2	and Isaac and Jacob, his faithful servants
3 Ma	2:11	And indeed you are faithful and true
4 Ma	7:15	whom the faithful seal of death has perfected !

FAITHFULLY 4 = 0.003 %
Sir 7:20 Do not abuse a servant who performs his work faithfully
    15:15 and to act faithfully is a matter of your own choice
3 Ma 5:4 proceeded faithfully to carry out the orders
    6:25 and senselessly gathered here those who faithfully have held

FAITHFULNESS 6 = 0.004 %

Wis	3:14	for special favour will be shown him for his faithfulness
Sir	45:4	He sanctified him through faithfulness and meekness
	46:15	By his faithfulness he was proved to be a prophet
1 Ma	14:35	The people saw Simon's faithfulness
2 Es	6:28	faithfulness shall flourish, and corruption shall be overcome
	7:34	and faithfulness shall grow strong

FAITHLESS 1
2 Es 15:25 Depart, you faithless children !

FAITHLESSNESS 1
Wis 14:25 theft and deceit, corruption, faithlessness, tumult, perjury

FALL, subst. 5 = 0.003 %

Sir	27:29	Those who rejoice in the fall of the godly
Bar	4:31	Wretched will be those who afflicted you and rejoiced at your fall
	4:33	For just as she rejoiced at your fall
2 Ma	9:7	and the fall was so hard as to torture every limb of his body
2 Es	7:118	the fall was not yours alone

FALL, verb 135 = 0.088 %

Tob	2:10	and their fresh droppings fell into my open eyes
	6:17	When Tobias heard these things, he fell in love with her
	12:16	and they fell upon their faces, for they were afraid
	14:10	but Nadab fell into the trap and perished
Jud	2:28	So fear and terror of him fell upon all the people
	6:6	and you shall fall among their wounded, when I return
	7:11	and not a man of your army will fall
	9:1	Then Judith fell upon her face
	11:11	death will fall upon them, for a sin has overtaken them
	14:7	And when they raised him up he fell at Judith's feet
	15:5	with one accord they fell upon the enemy
	15:6	fell upon the Assyrian camp
	16:7	For their mighty one did not fall
Ad E	15:15	But as she was speaking, she fell fainting
Wis	6:5	because severe judgment falls on those in high places
	7:3	and fell upon the kindred earth
	8:19	and a good soul fell to my lot
	11:20	men could fall at a single breath when pursued by justice
	11:22	and like a drop of morning dew that falls upon the ground
	13:16	So he takes thought for it, that it may not fall
	16:11	lest they should fall into deep forgetfulness
	18:23	For when the dead had already fallen on one another in heaps
Sir	1:30	Do not exalt yourself lest you fall
	2:7	and turn not aside, lest you fall
	2:18	Let us fall into the hands of the Lord
	8:1	lest you fall into his hands
	9:3	lest you fall into her snares
	13:21	but when a humble man falls, he is even pushed away by friends
	15:4	He will lean on her and will not fall
	18:19	and before you fall ill, take care of your health
	18:21	Before falling ill, humble yourself
	22:19	A man who pricks an eye will make tears fall
	22:27	that it may keep me from falling
	23:1	and let me not fall because of them !
	23:3	then I will not fall before my adversaries
	23:24	and punishment will fall on her children
	27:26	He who digs a pit will fall into it
	28:18	Many have fallen by the edge of the sword
	28:18	but not so many as have fallen because of the tongue
	28:23	Those who forsake the Lord will fall into its power
	28:26	lest you fall before him who lies in wait

	29:19	The sinner who has fallen into suretyship and pursues gain
	29:19	will fall into lawsuits
	29:20	but take heed to yourself lest you fall
	34:16	a guard against stumbling and a defence against falling
	35:15	as she cries out against him who has caused them to fall ?
	36:2	and cause the fear of thee to fall upon all the nations
	38:15	may he fall into the care of a physician
	38:16	My son, let your tears fall for the dead
	46:11	those whose hearts did not fall into idolatry
	46:20	Even after he had fallen asleep
	49:13	he raised for us the walls that had fallen
	50:17	and fell to the ground upon their faces
L Jr	**6**:27	lest they fall to the ground
Sus	**13**:23	I choose not to do it and to fall into your hands
1 Ma	**1**:5	After this he fell sick and perceived that he was dying
	1:18	and many were wounded and fell
	1:30	but he suddenly fell upon the city, dealt it a severe blow
	3:11	Many were wounded and fell, and the rest fled
	3:24	800 of them fell, and the rest fled into the land of the Philistines
	3:25	and terror fell upon the Gentiles round about them
	4:2	to fall upon the camp of the Jews and attack them suddenly
	4:15	and all those in the rear fell by the sword
	4:15	and 3,000 of them fell
	4:34	and there fell of the army of Lysias 5,000 men
	4:34	they fell in action
	4:40	They fell face down on the ground
	4:55	All the people fell on their faces
	5:12	for many of us have fallen
	5:22	and as many as 3,000 of the Gentiles fell
	5:34	As many as 8,000 of them fell that day
	5:54	because not one of them had fallen
	5:60	as many as 2,000 of the people of Israel fell that day
	5:67	fell in battle, for they went out to battle unwisely
	6:42	and 600 men of the king's army fell
	6:46	but it fell to the ground upon him and there he died
	7:18	Then the fear and dread of them fell upon all the people
	7:32	About 500 men of the army of Nicanor fell
	7:38	and let them fall by the sword
	7:43	and he himself was the first to fall in the battle
	7:44	When his army saw that Nicanor had fallen
	7:46	so that they all fell by the sword
	8:10	Many of them were wounded and fell
	9:1	that Nicanor and his army had fallen in battle
	9:17	and many on both sides were wounded and fell
	9:18	Judas also fell, and the rest fled
	9:21	How is the mighty fallen, the saviour of Israel !
	9:40	Many were wounded and fell, and the rest fled to the mountain
	9:49	And about 1,000 of Bacchides' men fell that day
	10:50	and Demetrius fell on that day
	10:85	The number of those who fell by the sword
	11:74	As many as 3,000 of the foreigners fell that day
	12:26	to fall upon the Jews by night
	12:37	part of the wall on the valley to the east had fallen
	13:22	but that night a very heavy snow fell
	16:8	and many of them were wounded and fell
	16:10	and John burned it with fire, and about 2,000 of them fell
2 Ma	**3**:6	to fall under the control of the king
	3:27	When he suddenly fell to the ground
	7:3	The king fell into a rage
	7:38	which has justly fallen on our whole nation
	7:39	The king fell into a rage
	9:7	And so it came about that he fell out of his chariot
	10:4	they fell prostrate and besought the Lord
	10:4	that they might never again fall into such misfortunes
	10:26	Falling upon the steps before the altar
	12:24	Timothy himself fell into the hands of Dositheus
	12:34	it happened that a few of the Jews fell
	12:39	Judas and his men went to take up the bodies of the fallen
	12:40	that this was why these men had fallen
	12:42	what had happened because of the sin of those who had fallen
	12:44	that those who had fallen would rise again
	12:45	that is laid up for those who fall asleep in godliness
	13:11	into the hands of the blasphemous Gentiles
	14:41	Being surrounded, Razis fell upon his own sword
	14:42	preferring to die nobly rather than to fall
	14:44	a space opened and he fell in the middle of the empty space
1 Es	**9**:47	and fell to the ground and worshipped the Lord
3 Ma	**5**:33	and his eyes wavered and his face fell
	5:49	embracing relatives and falling into one another's arms
	6:23	and saw them all fallen headlong to destruction
2 Es	**4**:11	When I heard this, I fell on my face
	5:5	and the stars shall fall
	12:18	and it shall be in danger of falling
	12:18	nevertheless it shall not fall then
	12:28	but he also shall fall by the sword in the last days
	13:11	and fell on the onrushing multitude
	13:23	will himself protect those who fall into peril
	15:57	and you shall fall by the sword
	15:57	shall fall by the sword
4 Ma	**2**:14	and helps raise up what has fallen

	3:8	Then when evening fell	
	6:7	And though he fell to the ground	
	6:8	to make him get up again after he fell	
	15:20	and corpses fallen on other corpses	

FALL away   1
Tob	**11**:8	and will cause the white films to fall away

FALL down   6 = 0.004 %
Jud	**6**:18	Then the people fell down and worshipped God
	7:22	and fell down in the streets of the city
	14:6	he fell down on his face and his spirit failed him
Wis	**17**:16	And whoever was there fell down
2 Es	**10**:1	he fell down and died
4 Ma	**4**:11	Then Apollonius fell down half dead

FALL off   1
4 Ma	**9**:20	and pieces of flesh were falling off the axles of the machine

FALLING   2
Sir	**3**:31	at the moment of his falling he will find support
	43:18	and the mind is amazed at its falling

FALSE   20 = 0.013 %
Tob	**3**:6	because I have heard false reproaches
Jud	**11**:5	and I will tell nothing false to my lord this night
Ad E	**16**:6	when these men by the false trickery of their evil natures
Wis	**10**:14	Those who accused him she showed to be false
Sir	**26**:5	and false accusation
	34:1	A man of no understanding has vain and false hopes
	34:4	And from something false what will be true ?
	36:19	so an intelligent mind detects false words
L Jr	**6**:8	but they are false and cannot speak
	6:44	Whatever is done for them is false
	6:50	it will afterward be known that they are false
	6:59	than to be these false gods
	6:59	than these false gods
Sus	**13**:43	thou knowest that these men have borne false witness against me
	13:49	For these men have borne false witness against her
	13:61	Daniel had convicted them of bearing false witness
2 Ma	**5**:5	When a false rumour arose that Antiochus was dead
	14:27	and, provoked by the false accusations of that depraved man
4 Ma	**5**:34	I will not play false to you, O law that trained me

FALSEHOOD   2
Jud	**5**:5	No falsehood shall come from your servant's mouth
2 Es	**14**:18	and falsehood shall come near

FALTER   2
Ad E	**15**:7	And the queen faltered, and turned pale and faint
Sir	**12**:15	but if you falter, he will not stand by you

FAME   3 = 0.002 %
1 Ma	**3**:26	His fame reached the king
	8:1	Now Judas heard of the fame of the Romans
	8:12	and as many as have heard of their fame have feared them

FAMED   1
1 Ma	**6**:1	was a city famed for its wealth in silver and gold

FAMILIAR   1
Tob	**5**:6	I am familiar with the way

FAMILY   20 = 0.013 %
Tob	**1**:9	a member of our family
	5:10	My brother, to what tribe and family do you belong ? Tell me
	5:11	Are you looking for a tribe and a family
	5:13	because I tried to learn your tribe and family
Jud	**8**:2	Her husband Manasseh, who belonged to her tribe and family
	8:18	has there been any tribe or family or people
Ad E	**14**:5	I have heard in the tribe of my family
Sir	**11**:34	and will estrange you from your family
Sus	**13**:33	But her family and friends and all who saw her wept
1 Ma	**1**:61	and their families and those who circumcised them
	5:62	But they did not belong to the family of those men
	12:21	that they are brethren and are of the family of Abraham
2 Ma	**1**:10	To Aristobulus, who is of the family of the anointed priests
1 Es	**1**:4	and prepare yourselves by your families and kindred
	2:8	Then arose the heads of families
	5:44	Some of the heads of families
3 Ma	**3**:27	together with his family
	6:8	you, Father, watched over and restored unharmed to all his family
4 Ma	**5**:4	He was a man of priestly family, learned in the law
	15:25	nature, family, parental love

FAMINE   19 = 0.012 %
Tob	**4**:13	because shiftlessness is the mother of famine
Jud	**5**:10	When a famine spread over Canaan they went down to Egypt
	7:14	will waste away with famine

Sir	39:29	Fire and hail and famine and pestilence
	40:9	calamities, famine and affliction and plague
	48:2	He brought a famine upon them
Bar	2:25	by famine and sword and pestilence
1 Ma	6:54	because famine had prevailed over the rest
	9:24	In those days a very great famine occurred
	13:49	and many of them perished from famine
2 Es	15:5	the sword and famine and death and destruction
	15:49	famine, sword, and pestilence
	16:18	the beginning of famine, when many shall perish
	16:19	Behold, famine and plague
	16:21	the sword, famine, and great confusion
	16:22	For many of those who live on the earth shall perish by famine
	16:22	and those who survive the famine shall die by the sword
	16:34	and their husbands shall perish of famine
	16:46	for in captivity and famine they will beget their children

FAMOUS 6 = 0.004 %

Jud	16:23	She became more and more famous
Sir	44:1	Let us now praise famous men
	48:6	and famous men from their beds
Bar	3:26	The giants were born there, who were famous of old
2 Ma	2:22	and recovered the temple famous throughout the world
3 Ma	6:1	Then a certain Eleazar, famous among the priests of the country

FAN 2

4 Ma	5:32	and fan the fire more vehemently !
	9:19	and while fanning the flames they tightened the wheel further

FANCY 1

Sir	34:5	and like a woman in travail the mind has fancies

FAR 40 = 0.026 %

Jud	1:9	and beyond the Jordan as far as Jerusalem and Bethany
	1:10	as far as the borders of Ethiopia
	1:12	and every one in Egypt, as far as the coasts of the 2 seas
	2:24	as far as the sea
	7:3	and they spread out in breadth over Dothan as far as Balbaim
	15:5	and cut them down as far as Choba
Ad E	16:11	so far enjoyed the good will that we have for every nation
Wis	12:24	For they went far astray on the paths of error, accepting as gods
	14:17	they imagined their appearance far away
Sir	6:13	Keep yourself far from your enemies
	9:13	Keep far from a man who has the power to kill
	15:8	She is far from men of pride
	16:22	For the covenant is far off
	23:12	For all these errors will be far from the godly
	27:20	Do not go after him, for he is too far off
	30:23	and remove sorrow far from you
Bar	3:21	Their sons have strayed far from her way
L Jr	6:73	for he will be far from reproach
Sus	13:51	Separate them far from each other
1 Ma	2:21	Far be it from us to desert the law and the ordinances
	7:45	from Adasa as far as Gazara
	8:4	even though the place was far distant from them
	8:12	They have subdued kings far and near
	8:23	and may sword and enemy be far from them
	9:10	But Judas said, Far be it from us
	9:15	and he pursued them as far as Mount Azotus
	11:7	as far as the river called Eleutherus
	11:8	as far as Seleucia by the sea
	11:62	And he passed through the country as far as Damascus
	11:73	as far as Kadesh, to their camp, and there they encamped
	12:33	as far as Askalon and the neighbouring strongholds
	13:5	And now, far be it from me to spare my life
	14:16	It was heard in Rome, and as far away as Sparta
2 Ma	13:9	was coming to show to the Jews things far worse
3 Ma	4:7	as far as the place of embarkation
	7:18	to each as far as his own house
2 Es	4:50	so the quantity that passed was far greater
	7:48	and removed us far from life
	8:47	For you come far short of being able to love my creation
	10:55	as far as it is possible for your eyes to see it

FARE, verb 4 = 0.003 %

Sir	6:1	so fares the double-tongued sinner
	47:12	After him rose up a wise son who fared amply because of him
3 Ma	3:13	I myself and our government are faring well
	7:2	We ourselves and our children are faring well

FAREWELL 5 = 0.003 %

2 Ma	3:35	and having bidden Onias farewell
	11:21	Farewell. The 148th year, Dioscorinthius 24th
	11:33	Farewell. The 148th year, Xanthicus 15th
	11:38	Farewell. The 148th year, Xanthicus 15th
3 Ma	7:9	in everything and inescapably as an antagonist to avenge such acts. Farewell

FARM 1

Sir	7:15	Do not hate toilsome labour, or farm work

FARMER 6 = 0.004 %

Wis	17:17	for whether he was a farmer or a shepherd
2 Es	8:41	For just as the farmer sows many seeds upon the ground
	8:43	For if the farmer's seed does not come up
	8:44	hast thou also made him like the farmer's seed ?
	9:17	and as is the farmer, so is the threshing floor
	15:13	Let the farmers that till the ground mourn

FARMING 1

2 Ma	12:1	and the Jews went about their farming

FAR-OFF 1

Sir	47:16	Your name reached to far-off islands

FARTHER 3 = 0.002 %

1 Ma	10:77	and went to Azotus as though he were going farther
2 Es	14:18	For truth shall go farther away
	14:33	and your brethren are farther in the interior

FASCINATION 1

Wis	4:12	For the fascination of wickedness obscures what is good

FASHION, subst. 4 = 0.003 %

1 Es	4:12	since he is to be obeyed in this fashion ?
3 Ma	4:13	be dealt with in precisely the same fashion as the others
4 Ma	5:14	When the tyrant urged him in this fashion
	10:7	and scalped him with their fingernails in Scythian fashion

FASHION, verb 8 = 0.005 %

Wis	13:10	gold and silver fashioned with skill
	15:7	he fashions out of the same clay
	19:6	For the whole creation in its nature was fashioned anew
Ps 151	:2	My hands made a harp, my fingers fashioned a lyre
2 Es	8:8	which is now fashioned in the womb
	8:11	so that what has been fashioned may be nourished for a time
	8:14	who with so great labour was fashioned by thy command
4 Ma	2:21	Now when God fashioned man

FASHIONER 2

Wis	7:22	for wisdom, the fashioner of all things, taught me
	8:6	who more than she is fashioner of what exists ?

FASHIONING 1

2 Es	8:38	about the fashioning of those who have sinned

FAST, subst. 2

1 Es	8:50	There I proclaimed a fast for the young men before our Lord
	8:73	Then I rose from my fast

FAST, verb 11 = 0.007 %

Jud	4:13	for the people fasted many days throughout Judea
	8:6	She fasted all the days of her widowhood
Sir	34:26	So if a man fasts for his sins
Bar	1:5	Then they wept, and fasted, and prayed before the Lord
1 Ma	3:47	They fasted that day, put on sackcloth
2 Es	5:13	and fast for 7 days
	5:20	So I fasted 7 days, mourning and weeping
	6:31	If therefore you will pray again and fast again for 7 days
	6:35	Now after this I wept again and fasted 7 days as before
	9:23	do not fast during them, however
	10:4	but without ceasing mourn and fast until I die

FAST, adv. 9 = 0.006 %

Sir	1:19	and he exalted the glory of those who held her fast
	4:13	Whoever holds her fast will obtain glory
	25:11	to whom shall be likened the one who holds it fast ?
	45:23	and stood fast, when the people turned away
Bar	4:1	All who hold her fast will live
1 Ma	10:81	But his men stood fast, as Jonathan commanded
3 Ma	7:16	But those who had held fast to God even to death
2 Es	4:34	*You do not hasten faster than the Most High*
4 Ma	11:27	therefore, unconquered, we hold fast to reason

FASTEN, verb 5 = 0.003 %

Jud	16:8	and fastened her hair with a tiara
Wis	13:15	and sets it in the wall, and fastens it there with iron
Sir	14:24	will also fasten his tent peg to her walls
1 Ma	6:37	they were fastened upon each beast by special harness
3 Ma	4:9	some were fastened by the neck to the benches of the boats

FASTING 3 = 0.002 %

Tob	12:8	Prayer is good when accompanied by fasting, almsgiving, and righteousness
Jud	4:9	and they humbled themselves with much fasting
2 Ma	13:12	and had besought the merciful Lord with weeping and fasting

FAT

			7 = 0.005 %
Jud	16 : 16	and all fat for burnt offerings to thee is a very little thing
Sir	26 : 13	and her skill puts fat on his bones
	47 : 2	As the fat is selected from the peace offering
P Az		16	and with tens of thousands of fat lambs
Bel	14 : 27	Then Daniel took pitch, fat, and hair
1 Es	1 : 14	because the priests were offering the fat until night
	9 : 51	so go your way, eat the fat and drink the sweet

FATAL

			1
4 Ma	8 : 26	and such a fatal stubbornness please us

FATE

			8 = 0.005 %
Wis	17 : 17	he was seized, and endured the inescapable fate
	19 : 4	For the fate they deserved drew them on to this end
2 Ma	9 : 28	came to the end of his life by a most pitiable fate
	13 : 7	By such a fate it came about
3 Ma	3 : 9	for such a great community ought not be left to its fate
	5 : 8	from the fate now prepared for them
	6 : 10	and destroy us, Lord, by whatever fate you choose
2 Es	3 : 1	And the same fate befell them :

FATHER

			248 = 0.162 %
Tob	1 : 8	as Deborah my father's mother had commanded me
	1 : 8	for I was left an orphan by my father
	1 : 9	and by her I became the father of Tobias
	2 : 3	Father, one of our people has been strangled
	3 : 3	and those which my fathers committed before thee
	3 : 5	and those of my fathers
	3 : 7	was reproached by her father's maids
	3 : 10	But she said, I am the only child of my father
	3 : 15	and that I did not stain my name or the name of my father
	3 : 15	I am my father's only child
	4 : 12	from among the descendants of your fathers
	4 : 12	who is not of your father's tribe
	4 : 12	that Noah, Abraham, Isaac, and Jacob, our fathers of old
	5 : 1	Father, I will do everything that you have commanded me
	5 : 7	and I shall tell my father
	5 : 8	So he went in and said to his father
	5 : 16	And his father said to him, Go with this man
	6 : 12	I will speak to her father
	6 : 14	Now I am the only son my father has
	6 : 14	and bring the lives of my father and mother to the grave
	6 : 15	with which your father commanded you
	7 : 5	And Tobias said, He is my father
	7 : 13	and take her with you to your father
	8 : 5	Blessed art thou, O God of our fathers
	8 : 21	and return in safety to his father
	9 : 4	but my father is counting the days
	10 : 1	Now his father Tobit was counting each day
	10 : 7	for my father and mother have given up hope
	10 : 8	and I will send messengers to your father
	10 : 9	Tobias replied, No, send me back to my father
	11 : 2	Are you not aware, brother, of how you left your father ?
	11 : 6	And she caught sight of him coming, and said to his father
	11 : 7	that your father will open his eyes
	11 : 11	and took hold of his father
	11 : 11	and he sprinkled the gall upon his father's eyes, saying
	11 : 11	Be of good cheer, father
	11 : 15	and he reported to his father the great things
	11 : 17	and blessed are your father and your mother
	12 : 2	He replied, Father, it would do me no harm
	13 : 4	because he is our Lord and God, he is our Father for ever
	14 : 12	And when Anna died he buried her with his father
	14 : 13	He inherited their property and that of his father Tobit
Jud	5 : 7	because they would not follow the gods of their fathers
	7 : 28	and our God, the Lord of our fathers
	7 : 28	and the sins of our fathers
	8 : 3	So they buried him with his fathers
	8 : 19	and that was why our fathers were handed over to the sword
	9 : 2	O Lord God of my father Simeon
	9 : 12	Hear, O hear me, God of my father
	10 : 8	May the God of our fathers grant you favour
Ad E	13 : 6	who is in charge of affairs and is our 2nd father
	14 : 5	and our fathers from among all their ancestors
	16 : 11	that he was called our father
	16 : 16	and for our fathers in the most excellent order
Wis	2 : 16	and boasts that God is his father
	9 : 1	O God of my fathers and Lord of mercy
	9 : 12	and shall be worthy of the throne of my father
	10 : 1	Wisdom protected the first-formed father of the world
	11 : 10	For thou didst test them as a father does in warning
	12 : 6	thou didst will to destroy by the hands of our fathers
	12 : 21	to whose fathers thou gavest oaths
	14 : 3	but it is thy providence, O Father, that steers its course
	14 : 15	For a father, consumed with grief
	18 : 6	That night was made known beforehand to our fathers
	18 : 9	and already they were singing the praises of the fathers
	18 : 22	appealing to the oaths and covenants given to our fathers
	18 : 24	and the glories of the fathers were engraved

Sir	pr.	and the other books of our fathers
	3 : 1	Listen to me your father, O children
	3 : 2	For the Lord honoured the father above the children
	3 : 3	Whoever honours his father atones for sins
	3 : 5	Whoever honours his father
	3 : 6	Whoever glorifies his father will have long life
	3 : 8	Honour your father by word and deed
	3 : 9	For a father's blessing
	3 : 10	Do not glorify yourself by dishonouring your father
	3 : 10	for your father's dishonour is no glory to you
	3 : 11	For a man's glory comes from honouring his father
	3 : 12	O son, help your father in his old age
	3 : 14	For kindness to a father will not be forgotten
	3 : 16	Whoever forsakes his father is like a blasphemer
	4 : 10	Be like a father to orphans
	7 : 27	With all your heart honour your father
	8 : 9	for they themselves learned from their fathers
	22 : 3	It is a disgrace to be the father of an undisciplined son
	22 : 4	but one who acts shamefully brings grief to her father
	22 : 5	An impudent daughter disgraces father and husband
	23 : 1	O Lord, Father and Ruler of my life
	23 : 4	O Lord, Father and God of my life
	23 : 14	Remember your father and mother when you sit among great men
	30 : 4	The father may die, and yet he is not dead
	34 : 20	Like one who kills a son before his father's eyes
	41 : 7	Children will blame an ungodly father
	41 : 17	Be ashamed of immorality, before your father or mother
	42 : 9	A daughter keeps her father secretly wakeful
	42 : 10	or become pregnant in her father's house
	44 : 1	and our fathers in their generations
	44 : 19	Abraham was the great father of a multitude of nations
	44 : 22	for the sake of Abraham his father
	47 : 23	Solomon rested with his fathers
	48 : 10	to turn the heart of the father to the son
	48 : 22	and he held strongly to the ways of David his father
	51 : 10	I appealed to the Lord, the Father of my Lord
Bar	1 : 16	and our prophets and our fathers
	1 : 19	From the day when the Lord brought our fathers
	1 : 20	when he brought our fathers out of the land of Egypt
	2 : 6	but confusion of face to us and our fathers, as at this day
	2 : 19	of our fathers or our kings
	2 : 21	and you will remain in the land which I gave to your fathers
	2 : 24	that the bones of our kings and the bones of our fathers
	2 : 33	for they will remember the ways of their fathers
	2 : 34	which I swore to give to their fathers
	3 : 5	Remember not the iniquities of our fathers
	3 : 7	for we have put away from our hearts all the iniquity of our fathers
	3 : 8	for all the iniquities of our fathers
P Az	3	Blessed art thou, O Lord, God of our fathers
	5	the holy city of our fathers
	29	Blessed art thou, O Lord, God of our fathers
Bel	14 : 1	When King Astyages was laid with his fathers
1 Ma	2 : 19	departing each one from the religion of his fathers
	2 : 20	by the covenant of our fathers
	2 : 50	and give your lives for the covenant of our fathers
	2 : 51	Remember the deeds of our fathers
	2 : 54	Phinehas our father, because he was deeply zealous
	2 : 65	he shall be your father
	2 : 69	Then he blessed them, and was gathered to his fathers
	2 : 70	and was buried in the tomb of his fathers at Modein
	3 : 2	All his brothers and all who had joined his father helped him
	4 : 9	Remember how our fathers were saved at the Red Sea
	4 : 10	and remember his covenant with our fathers
	6 : 23	We were happy to serve your father
	7 : 2	As he was entering the royal palace of his fathers
	9 : 19	and buried him in the tomb of their fathers at Modein
	10 : 52	and have taken my seat on the throne of my fathers
	10 : 55	on which you returned to the land of your fathers
	10 : 67	came from Crete to the land of his fathers
	10 : 72	for your fathers were twice put to flight in their own land
	11 : 9	and you shall reign over your father's kingdom
	11 : 32	King Demetrius to Lasthenes his father, greeting
	11 : 38	So all the troops who had served his fathers hated him
	11 : 40	to become king in place of his father
	13 : 3	I and my brothers and the house of my father have done
	13 : 25	and buried him in Modein, the city of his fathers
	13 : 27	over the tomb of his father and his brothers
	13 : 28	for his father and mother and 4 brothers
	14 : 26	For he and his brothers and the house of his father have stood firm
	15 : 3	have gained control of the kingdom of our fathers
	15 : 10	and invaded the land of his fathers
	15 : 33	but only the inheritance of our fathers
	15 : 34	we are firmly holding the inheritance of our fathers
	16 : 1	and reported to Simon his father what Cendebaeus had done
	16 : 2	and said to them : I and my brothers and the house of my father
	16 : 21	that his father and brothers had perished
	16 : 24	from the time that he became high priest after his father

2 Ma	1 : 19	For when our fathers were being led captive to Persia
	1 : 25	who didst choose the fathers and consecrate them
	4 : 11	secured through John the father of Eupolemus
	4 : 15	disdaining the honours prized by their fathers
	5 : 10	and no place in the tomb of his fathers
	6 : 1	to compel the Jews to forsake the laws of their fathers
	6 : 6	nor observe the feasts of his fathers
	7 : 2	rather than transgress the laws of our fathers
	7 : 8	he replied in the language of his fathers
	7 : 21	She encouraged each of them in the language of their fathers
	7 : 24	if he would turn from the ways of his fathers
	7 : 30	that was given to our fathers through Moses
	7 : 37	for the laws of our fathers
	8 : 15	yet for the sake of the covenants made with their fathers
	8 : 33	in the city of their fathers
	9 : 23	but I observed that my father
	11 : 23	Now that our father has gone on to the gods
	11 : 24	to our father's change to Greek customs
	12 : 37	In the language of their fathers he raised the battle cry, with hymns
	12 : 39	in the sepulchres of their fathers
	13 : 9	than those that had been done in his father's time
	14 : 37	and for his good will was called father of the Jews
	15 : 29	in the language of their fathers
1 Es	1 : 5	according to the grouping of the fathers' houses of you Levites
	1 : 11	and the grouping of the fathers' houses, before the people
	1 : 31	and was buried in the tomb of his fathers
	1 : 34	and made him king in succession to Josiah his father
	1 : 50	So the God of their fathers sent by his messenger to call them back
	2 : 21	search may be made in the record of your fathers
	4 : 20	A man leaves his own father who brought him up
	4 : 21	with no thought of his father or his mother or his country
	4 : 25	A man loves his wife more than his father or his mother
	4 : 60	I give thee thanks, O Lord of our fathers
	4 : 62	And they praised the God of their fathers
	5 : 1	After this the heads of fathers' houses were chosen to go up
	5 : 4	according to their fathers' houses in the tribes
	5 : 37	though they could not prove by their fathers' houses or lineage
	5 : 63	Some of the Levitical priests and heads of fathers' houses
	5 : 68	and the heads of the fathers' houses and said to them
	5 : 70	and the heads of the fathers' houses in Israel said to them
	6 : 15	But when our fathers sinned against the Lord of Israel
	8 : 28	according to their fathers'houses and their groups
	8 : 58	the Lord of our fathers
	8 : 59	and to the heads of the fathers' houses of Israel
	8 : 76	from the times of our fathers
	8 : 77	And because of our sins and the sins of our fathers
	9 : 8	the God of our fathers
	9 : 16	the leading men of their fathers' houses
P Ma	1	O Lord Almighty, God of our fathers
Ps 151	1	I was small among my brothers, and youngest in my father's house
	151 : 1	I tended my father's sheep
	151 : 4	and took me from my father's sheep
3 Ma	2 : 12	And because oftentimes when our fathers were oppressed
	2 : 21	the first Father of all
	5 : 7	their merciful God and Father, praying
	6 : 3	look upon the descendants of Abraham, O Father
	6 : 8	you, Father, watched over and restored unharmed to all his family
	6 : 32	and took up the song of their fathers
	7 : 6	always taking their part as a father does for his children
	7 : 16	to the one God of their fathers, the eternal Saviour of Israel
2 Es	1 : 28	Have I not entreated you as a father entreats his sons
	1 : 29	and that you should be my sons and I should be your father ?
	1 : 38	And now, father
	2 : 5	I call upon you, father
	4 : 23	and the law of our fathers has been made of no effect
	7 : 103	fathers for sons or sons for parents
	7 : 104	Just as now a father does not send his son
	7 : 104	or a son his father, or a master his servant
	7 : 106	and Moses for our fathers who sinned in the desert
	8 : 31	For we and our fathers have passed our lives
	9 : 29	to our fathers in the wilderness
	9 : 32	But though our fathers received the law
	14 : 29	At first our fathers dwelt as aliens in Egypt
	14 : 31	but you and your fathers committed iniquity
4 Ma	2 : 19	Why else did Jacob, our most wise father
	3 : 20	At a time when our fathers were enjoying profound peace
	5 : 37	The fathers will receive me as pure
	7 : 1	the reason of our father Eleazar steered the ship of religion
	7 : 5	our father Eleazar broke the maddening waves of the emotions
	7 : 9	You, father, strengthened out loyalty to the law
	7 : 11	For just as our father Aaron, armed with the censer
	9 : 29	How sweet is any kind of death for the religion of our fathers !
	10 : 2	that the same father begot me and those who died
	12 : 17	and I call on the God of our fathers
	13 : 12	and the father by whose hand Isaac would have submitted
	13 : 17	and all the fathers will praise us

	13 : 19	has bequeathed through the fathers to their descendants
	15 : 4	have a deeper sympathy toward their offspring than do the fathers
	16 : 20	our father Abraham was zealous to sacrifice his son Isaac
	16 : 20	and when Isaac saw his father's hand
	17 : 6	For your children were true descendants of father Abraham
	18 : 7	I was a pure virgin and did not go outside my father's house
	18 : 9	and when these sons had grown up their father died
	18 : 23	are gathered together into the chorus of the fathers

FATHER-IN-LAW   6 = 0.004 %

Tob	10 : 8	But his father-in-law said to him, Stay with me
	10 : 12	Honour your father-in-law and your mother-in-law
	14 : 12	to Raguel his father-in-law
	14 : 13	and he gave his father-in-law and mother-in-law
1 Ma	10 : 56	and I will become your father-in-law, as you have said
	11 : 2	since he was Alexander's father-in-law

FATHERLESS   2

Sir	35 : 14	He will not ignore the supplication of the fatherless
2 Es	2 : 20	secure justice for the fatherless, give to the needy

FATHOM, verb   1

Sir	24 : 28	the last one has not fathomed her

FAULT   4 = 0.003 %

Sir	11 : 7	Do not find fault before you investigate
	20 : 2	And the one who confesses his fault will be kept from loss
	29 : 5	and will find fault with the time
	38 : 10	Give up your faults and direct your hands aright

FAULTFINDER   1

Sir	4 : 30	nor be a faultfinder with your servants

FAVOUR, FAVOR, verb   4 = 0.003 %

Sir	8 : 14	for the decision will favour him because of his standing
1 Ma	4 : 10	to see whether he will favour us
	10 : 47	They favoured Alexander
2 Ma	1 : 35	And with those persons whom the king favoured

FAVOUR, FAVOR, subst.   33 = 0.021 %

Tob	1 : 13	Then the Most High gave me favour
	12 : 18	For I did not come as a favour on my part
Jud	4 : 15	to look with favour upon the whole house of Israel
	8 : 23	For our slavery will not bring us into favour
	10 : 8	May the God of our fathers grant you favour
Wis	3 : 14	for special favour will be shown him for his faithfulness
	14 : 26	confusion over what is good, forgetfulness of favours
Sir	3 : 15	it will be remembered in your favour
	3 : 18	so you will find favour in the sight of the Lord
	3 : 31	Whoever requites favours gives thought to the future
	4 : 21	and there is a shame which is glory and favour
	32 : 14	and those who rise early to seek him will find favour
	41 : 23	and will find favour with every man
	45 : 1	who found favour in the sight of all flesh
Bar	1 : 12	and we shall serve them many days and find favour in their sight
	2 : 8	Yet we have not entreated the favour of the Lord
	2 : 14	and for thy own sake deliver us, and grant us favour
1 Ma	10 : 60	and found favour with them
	11 : 24	And he won his favour
	11 : 53	and did not repay the favours which Jonathan had done him
1 Es	8 : 4	for he found favour before the king in all his requests
	8 : 80	but he brought us into favour
3 Ma	1 : 4	and matters were turning out rather in favour of Antiochus
2 Es	4 : 44	If I have found favour in your sight
	5 : 56	if I have found favour in thy sight
	6 : 11	if I have found favour in thy sight
	7 : 75	If I have found favour in thy sight, O Lord
	7 : 102	If I have found favour in thy sight
	7 : 104	Since you have found favour in my sight
	8 : 42	If I have found favour before thee, let me speak
	12 : 7	if I have found favour in thy sight
	14 : 22	If then I have found favour before thee
4 Ma	11 : 12	he said, Tyrant, they are splendid favours that you grant us against your will

FAVOURABLE, FAVORABLE   3 = 0.002 %

1 Ma	12 : 1	Now when Jonathan saw that the time was favourable for him
	13 : 35	Demetrius the king sent him a favourable reply to this request
3 Ma	5 : 44	at the places in the city most favourable for keeping guard

FAVOURABLY, FAVORABLY   2

Tob	3 : 3	Remember me and look favourably upon me
3 Ma	7 : 11	would never be favourably disposed

FEAR, subst.   80 = 0.052 %

Tob	1 : 19	I left home in fear
Jud	2 : 28	So fear and terror of him fell upon all the people
	14 : 3	Then fear will come over them, and they will flee before you

	15 :2	Fear and trembling came over them
Ad E	**14** :19	And save me from my fear !
	15 :5	as if beloved, but her heart was frozen with fear
	15 :13	and my heart was shaken with fear at your glory
Wis	**5** :2	When they see him, they will be shaken with dreadful fear
	12 :11	and it was not through fear of any one
	17 :4	protected them from fear
	17 :8	For those who promised to drive off the fears
	17 :8	were sick themselves with ridiculous fear
	17 :10	they perished in trembling fear
	17 :12	For fear is nothing but surrender of the helps
	17 :15	for sudden and unexpected fear overwhelmed them
	18 :17	and unexpected fears assailed them
Sir	**1** :11	The fear of the Lord is glory and exultation
	1 :12	The fear of the Lord delights the heart
	1 :18	The fear of the Lord is the crown of wisdom
	1 :21	The fear of the Lord drives away sins :
	1 :27	For the fear of the Lord is wisdom and instruction
	1 :28	Do not disobey the fear of the Lord
	1 :30	because you did not come in the fear of the Lord
	2 :10	Or who ever persevered in the fear of the Lord and was forsaken ?
	4 :17	she will bring fear and cowardice upon him
	9 :13	and you will not be worried by the fear of death
	9 :16	and let your glorying be in the fear of the Lord
	10 :21	The fear of the Lord is the beginning of acceptance
	10 :22	their glory is the fear of the Lord
	16 :2	unless the fear of the Lord is in them
	17 :4	He placed the fear of them in all living beings
	19 :18	The fear of the Lord is the beginning of acceptance
	19 :20	All wisdom is the fear of the Lord
	21 :11	and wisdom is the fulfilment of the fear of the Lord
	22 :18	will not stand firm against any fear
	23 :19	His fear is confined to the eyes of men
	23 :27	that nothing is better than the fear of the Lord
	24 :18	of fear, of knowledge, and of holy hope
	25 :6	and their boast is the fear of the Lord
	25 :11	The fear of the Lord surpasses everything
	25 :12	The fear of the Lord is the beginning of love for him
	27 :3	in the fear of the Lord
	32 :18	and an insolent and proud man will not cower in fear
	36 :2	and cause the fear of thee to fall upon all the nations
	40 :2	Their perplexities and fear of heart
	40 :5	and fear of death, and fury and strife
	40 :7	and wonders that his fear came to nothing
	40 :26	but the fear of the Lord is better than both
	40 :26	There is no loss in the fear of the Lord
	40 :27	The fear of the Lord is like a garden of blessing
	45 :2	and made him great in the fears of his enemies
	45 :23	for he was zealous in the fear of the Lord
Bar	**3** :7	For thou hast put the fear of thee in our hearts
	3 :33	called it, and it obeyed him in fear
L Jr	**6** :4	and inspire fear in the heathen
	6 :7	or to let fear for these gods possess you
Sus	**13** :57	and they were intimate with you through fear
1 Ma	**3** :6	Lawless men shrank back for fear of him
	5 :41	But if he shows fear
	7 :18	Then the fear and dread of them fell upon all the people
	12 :52	and were in great fear
2 Ma	**3** :30	was full of fear and disturbance
	12 :22	terror and fear came over the enemy
	15 :18	their greatest and first fear
3 Ma	**2** :23	panic-stricken in their exceedingly great fear
	6 :13	in fear of your invincible might, O honoured One
	7 :22	restored it to them with extreme fear
2 Es	**7** :87	and shall wither with fear
	7 :98	and shall be glad without fear
	12 :3	Then I awoke in great perplexity of mind and great fear
	12 :5	because of the great fear with which I have been terrified this night
	13 :13	Then in great fear I awoke
	15 :33	and fear and trembling shall come upon their army
	15 :37	And there shall be fear and great trembling upon the earth
4 Ma	**1** :4	namely anger, fear, and pain
	1 :23	Fear precedes pain and sorrow comes after
	4 :10	instilling in them great fear and trembling
	8 :12	so as to persuade them out of fear to eat the defiling food
	14 :8	encircled the sevenfold fear of tortures and dissolved it
	15 :8	yet because of the fear of God she disdained

FEAR, verb   82 = 0.053 %

Tob	**4** :21	You have great wealth if you fear God
	6 :14	So now I fear that I may die
	14 :2	and he continued to fear the Lord God and to praise him
	14 :6	to fear the Lord God in truth
Jud	**2** :28	Those who lived in Azotus and Ascalon feared him exceedingly
	8 :8	for she feared God with great devotion
	16 :15	but to those who fear thee thou wilt continue to show mercy
	16 :16	but who fears the Lord shall be great for ever
Ad E	**11** :9	they feared the evils that threatened them

Wis	**18** :25	To these the destroyer yielded, these he feared
Sir	**1** :8	There is One who is wise, greatly to be feared
	1 :13	With him who fears the Lord it will go well at the end
	1 :14	To fear the Lord is the beginning of wisdom
	1 :16	To fear the Lord is wisdom's full measure
	1 :20	To fear the Lord is the root of wisdom
	2 :7	You who fear the Lord, wait for his mercy
	2 :8	You who fear the Lord, trust in him
	2 :9	you who fear the Lord, hope for good things
	2 :15	Those who fear the Lord will not disobey his words
	2 :16	Those who fear the Lord will seek his approval
	2 :17	Those who fear the Lord will prepare their hearts
	6 :16	and those who fear the Lord will find him
	6 :17	Whoever fears the Lord directs his friendship aright
	7 :29	With all your soul fear the Lord, and honour his priests
	7 :31	Fear the Lord and honour the priest
	9 :18	A babbler is feared in his city
	10 :19	Those who fear the Lord
	10 :20	and those who fear the Lord
	10 :24	but none of them is greater than the man who fears the Lord
	15 :1	The man who fears the Lord will do this
	15 :13	and they are not loved by those who fear him
	15 :19	his eyes are on those who fear him
	21 :6	but he that fears the Lord will repent in his heart
	23 :18	Why should I fear ?
	25 :10	But there is no one superior to him who fears the Lord
	26 :3	of the man who fears the Lord
	26 :23	but a pious wife is given to the man who fears the Lord
	26 :25	but one who has a sense of shame will fear the Lord
	32 :14	He who fears the Lord will accept his discipline
	32 :16	Those who fear the Lord will form true judgments
	33 :1	No evil will befall the man who fears the Lord
	34 :13	The spirit of those who fear the Lord will live
	34 :14	He who fears the Lord will not be timid
	34 :15	Blessed is the soul of the man who fears the Lord !
	41 :3	Do not fear the sentence of death
L Jr	**6** :16	so do not fear them
	6 :23	so do not fear them
	6 :29	do not fear them
	6 :65	Since you know then that they are not gods, do not fear them
	6 :69	therefore do no fear them
P Az	18	we fear thee and seek thy face
Sus	**13** :2	a very beautiful woman and one who feared the Lord
1 Ma	**2** :62	Do not fear the words of a sinner
	3 :25	Then Judas and his brothers began to be feared
	3 :30	He feared that he might not have such funds
	4 :8	Do not fear their numbers or be afraid when they charge
	8 :12	and as many as have heard of their fame have feared them
	12 :40	He feared that Jonathan might not permit him to do so
2 Ma	**3** :32	And the high priest, fearing that the king might get the notion
	6 :30	because I fear him
	7 :29	Do not fear this butcher, but prove worthy of your brothers
	8 :16	and not to fear the great multitude of Gentiles
	9 :29	then, fearing the son of Antiochus
	15 :8	not to fear the attack of the Gentiles
1 Es	**4** :28	Do not all lands fear to touch him ?
3 Ma	**2** :23	and fearing lest he should lose his life
2 Es	**2** :17	Do not fear, mother of the sons
	7 :79	and who have hated those who fear God
	8 :28	but remember those who have willingly acknowledged that thou art to be feared
	10 :38	and tell you about the things which you fear
	15 :3	Do not fear the plots against you
	15 :20	I call together all the kings of the earth to fear me
	15 :29	so that all who hear them fear and tremble
	16 :67	Behold, God is the judge, fear him !
	16 :70	against those who fear the Lord
	16 :71	who continue to fear the Lord
	16 :75	Do not fear or doubt, for God is your guide
4 Ma	**5** :37	as one who does not fear your violence even to death
	8 :19	O men and brothers, should we not fear the instruments of torture
	8 :22	for fearing the king when we are under compulsion
	8 :25	for fearing the instruments of torture
	13 :14	Let us not fear him who thinks he is killing us

FEARFUL   4 = 0.003 %

1 Ma	**13** :2	and he saw that the people were trembling and fearful
3 Ma	**6** :18	from which 2 glorious angels of fearful aspect descended
2 Es	**10** :26	behold, she suddenly uttered a loud and fearful cry
4 Ma	**3** :15	considered it an altogether fearful danger to his soul

FEARFULLY   1

4 Ma	**12** :2	Even though the tyrant had been fearfully reproached by the brothers

FEAST, subst.   43 = 0.028 %

Tob	**1** :6	But I alone went often to Jerusalem for the feasts
	2 :1	at the feast of Pentecost
	2 :6	how he said, Your feasts shall be turned into mourning

	8:19	After this he gave a wedding feast for them
	8:20	And before the days of the feast were over
	8:20	until the 14 days of the wedding feast were ended
	9:2	and bring him to the wedding feast
	9:6	and came to the wedding feast
	10:7	until the 14 days of the wedding feast had expired
Jud	**8**:6	and the feasts and days of rejoicing of the house of Israel
Ad E	**14**:17	and I have not honoured the king's feast
Sir	**32**:1	If they make you master of the feast, do not exalt yourself
	33:8	and he appointed the different seasons and feasts
	43:7	From the moon comes the sign for feast days
	47:10	He gave beauty to the feasts
Bar	**1**:14	on the days of the feasts and at appointed seasons
L Jr	**6**:32	as some do at a funeral feast for a man who has died
1 Ma	**1**:39	her feasts were turned into mourning
	1:45	to profane sabbaths and feasts
	10:21	at the feast of tabernacles
	10:34	And all the feasts and sabbaths
	10:34	and the 3 days before a feast and the 3 after a feast
	12:11	both in our feasts and on other appropriate days
2 Ma	**1**:9	And now see that you keep the feast of booths
	1:18	in order that you also may celebrate the feast of booths
	1:18	and the feast of the fire given
	6:6	nor observe the feasts of his fathers
	6:7	and when the feast of Dionysus came
	10:6	in the manner of the feast of booths
	10:6	remembering how not long before, during the feast of booths
	12:31	as the feast of weeks was close at hand
	12:32	After the feast called Pentecost
1 Es	**1**:19	kept the passover and the feast of unleavened bread 7 days
	5:51	They kept the feast of booths
	5:52	and at all the consecrated feasts
	7:14	And they kept the feast of unleavened bread 7 days
3 Ma	**4**:1	a feast at public expense was arranged for the Gentiles
	4:16	organizing feasts in honour of all his idols
	5:31	I would have prepared them to be a rich feast
2 Es	**1**:31	for I have rejected your feast days, and new moons
	2:38	Rise and stand, and see at the feast of the Lord
	9:47	I set a day for the marriage feast

FEAST, verb   12 = 0.008 %

Jud	**1**:16	and there he and his forces rested and feasted for 120 days
	16:20	So the people continued feasting in Jerusalem
Ad E	**13**:17	turn our mourning into feasting
Wis	**12**:5	and their sacrificial feasting on human flesh and blood
Sir	**13**:8	and not to be humiliated in your feasting
	18:33	Do not become a beggar by feasting with borrowed money
Sus	**13**:32	that they might feast upon her beauty
1 Es	**3**:20	It turns every thought to feasting and mirth
	4:63	and they feasted, with music and rejoicing, for 7 days
3 Ma	**5**:3	When he had given these orders he returned to his feasting
	6:35	passed the time in feasting
	6:40	Then they feasted, provided with everything by the king

FEATHERED   1

2 Es	**11**:1	that had 12 feathered wings and 3 heads

FEEBLE   2

Bar	**2**:18	that goes about bent over and feeble
4 Ma	**7**:13	his muscles flabby, his sinews feeble, he became young again

FEED   6 = 0.004 %

Wis	**16**:23	whereas the fire, in order that the righteous might be fed
	16:26	might learn that it is not the production of crops that feeds man
Sir	**15**:3	She will feed him with the bread of understanding
P Az	23	did not cease feeding the furnace fires
Bel	**14**:27	which he fed to the dragon
2 Es	**16**:68	and shall feed you what was sacrificed to idols

FEEL   11 = 0.007 %

Wis	**15**:15	nor ears with which to hear, nor fingers to feel with
Sir	**20**:21	so when he rests he feels no remorse
	29:17	and one who does not feel grateful will abandon his rescuer
	31:20	he rises early, and feels fit
2 Ma	**7**:24	Antiochus felt that he was being treated with contempt
	9:9	the whole army felt revulsion at his decay
1 Es	**3**:21	It makes all hearts feel rich, forgets kings and satraps
2 Es	**13**:4	when it feels the fire
4 Ma	**12**:2	he felt strong compassion for this child
	14:13	which draws everything toward an emotion felt in her inmost parts
	15:9	she felt a greater tenderness toward them

FEELING   7 = 0.005 %

Wis	**1**:6	because God is witness of his inmost feelings
Sir	**22**:19	and one who pricks the heart makes it show feeling
	29:28	These things are hard to bear for a man who has feeling :
	30:7	and his feelings will be troubled at every cry
	31:15	Judge your neighbour's feelings by your own

L Jr	**6**:24	for even when they were being cast, they had no feeling
4 Ma	**12**:13	to cut out the tongues of men who have feelings like yours

FEIGN   1

4 Ma	**6**:17	that out of cowardice we feign a role unbecoming to us !

FELLOW, subst., adj.   19 = 0.012 %

Sir	**4**:27	Do not subject yourself to a foolish fellow
	8:11	Do not get up and leave an insolent fellow
	8:15	Do not travel on the road with a foolhardy fellow
	13:23	When the poor man speaks they say, Who is this fellow ?
2 Ma	**4**:2	the protector of his fellow countrymen
	4:5	not accusing his fellow citizens
	4:38	and there he dispatched the bloodthirsty fellow
	4:50	having become the chief plotter against his fellow citizens
	5:6	But Jason kept relentlessly slaughtering his fellow citizens
	5:6	over enemies and not over fellow countrymen
	5:8	and his fellow citizens
	5:23	who lorded it over his fellow citizens
	9:13	Then the abominable fellow made a vow to the Lord
	14:8	and second because I have regard also for my fellow citizens
	14:37	as a man who loved his fellow citizens
	15:30	the defender of his fellow citizens
1 Es	**5**:48	Then Jeshua the son of Jozadak, with his fellow priests
3 Ma	**1**:23	They shouted to their fellows to take arms
4 Ma	**8**:14	Be afraid, young fellows

FELLOW-COUNTRYMEN   1

3 Ma	**7**:14	any whom they met of their fellow-countrymen

FELLOWSHIP   2

Sir	**13**:17	What fellowship has a wolf with a lamb ?
3 Ma	**2**:33	and depriving them of common fellowship and mutual help

FENCE, subst.   2

Sir	**22**:18	Fences set on a high place
	36:25	Where there is no fence, the property will be plundered

FENCE, verb   1

Sir	**28**:24	See that you fence in your property with thorns

FERTILE   2

Sir	**26**:20	Seek a fertile field within the whole plain
2 Es	**1**:21	I divided fertile lands among you :

FERVENT   2

Sir	**38**:17	Let your weeping be bitter and your wailing fervent
4 Ma	**13**:26	they rendered their brotherly love more fervent

FERVENTLY   1

3 Ma	**5**:9	So their entreaty ascended fervently to heaven

FERVOUR, FERVOR   1

Jud	**4**:9	And every man of Israel cried out to God with great fervour

FESTAL   1

Wis	**19**:16	but the latter, after receiving them with festal celebrations

FESTIVAL   9 = 0.006 %

Tob	**2**:1	which is the sacred festival of the 7 weeks
Ad E	**16**:22	as a notable day among your commemorative festivals
Wis	**15**:12	and life a festival held for profit
3 Ma	**4**:8	spent the remaining days of their marriage festival in lamentations
	6:30	needed for a festival of 7 days
	6:36	they instituted the observance of the aforesaid days as a festival
	7:15	and they kept the day as a joyful festival
	7:19	these days as a joyous festival
	7:20	and dedicating a place of prayer at the site of the festival

FESTIVITY   2

Tob	**2**:6	and all your festivities into lamentation
	11:19	with great festivity

FETTER   12 = 0.008 %

Sir	**6**:24	Put your feet into her fetters
	6:29	Then her fetters will become for you a strong protection
	21:19	To a senseless man education is fetters on his feet
	28:19	and has not been bound with its fetters
	28:20	and its fetters are fetters of bronze
	33:28	and if he does not obey, make his fetters heavy
1 Ma	**3**:41	they took silver and gold in immense amounts, and fetters
P Ma	10	I am weighted down with many an iron fetter
3 Ma	**3**:25	and bound securely with iron fetters
	4:9	others had their feet secured by unbreakable fetters
4 Ma	**12**:2	when he saw that he was already in fetters

FEW, indef. pr. or adj.   42 = 0.027 %

Tob	**4**:8	if few, do not be afraid to give
Sir	**17**:2	He gave to men few days, a limited time

	18:10	so are a few years in the day of eternity
	32:8	Speak concisely, say much in few words
	34:10	He that is inexperienced knows few things
	43:32	for we have seen but few of his works
	48:2	and by his zeal he made them few in number
	48:15	the people were left very few in number
Bar	**2**:13	few in number, among the nations where thou hast scattered us
P Az	14	For we, O Lord, have become fewer than any nation
1 Ma	**3**:17	they said to Judas, How can we, few as we are
	3:18	Judas replied, It is easy for many to be hemmed in by few
	3:18	there is no difference between saving by many or by few
	6:54	Few men were left in the sanctuary
	7:1	sailed with a few men to a city by the sea
	7:28	I shall come with a few men to see you face to face in peace
	7:50	So the land of Judah had rest for a few days
	9:9	we are too few
	9:65	and he went with only a few men
	12:45	and choose for yourself a few men to stay with you
	15:10	so that there were few with Trypho
2 Ma	**1**:15	and Antiochus had come with a few men
	2:21	so that though few in number they seized the whole land
	8:6	and put to flight not a few of the enemy
	8:9	in command of no fewer than 20,000 Gentiles of all nations
	10:17	killing no fewer than 20,000
	12:34	it happened that a few of the Jews fell
	14:30	So he gathered not a few of his men
3 Ma	**3**:23	they abominate those few among them
2 Es	**2**:13	pray that your days may be few, that they may be shortened
	4:33	Why are our years few and evil ?
	7:12	they are few and evil
	7:48	And now I see that the world to come will bring delight to few
	7:48	and that not just a few of us
	7:51	For whereas you have said that the righteous are not many but few
	7:52	If you have just a few precious stones
	7:60	for I will rejoice over the few who shall be saved
	7:140	there would probably be left only very few
	8:1	but the world to come for the sake of few
	8:3	Many have been created, but few shall be saved
	8:62	but only to you and a few like you
	10:57	as but few have been

FIDELITY   2
Ad E	**13**:3	and is distinguished for his unchanging good will and steadfast fidelity
Sir	**1**:27	and he delights in fidelity and meekness

FIELD   31 = 0.020 %
Jud	**2**:27	and burned all their fields
	3:3	and all our wheat fields, and our flocks and herds
	4:5	since their fields had recently been harvested
	6:4	and their fields will be full of their dead
	8:3	who were binding sheaves in the field
	8:3	in the field between Dothan and Balamon
	8:7	and men and women slaves, and cattle, and fields
	11:7	but also the beasts of the field
Sir	**24**:14	like a beautiful olive tree in the field
	26:20	Seek a fertile field within the whole plain
Bel	**14**:33	and was going into the field to take it to the reapers
1 Ma	**16**:10	that were in the fields of Azotus
2 Es	**4**:29	the field where the good has been sown will not come
	7:65	but let the beasts of the field be glad
	9:17	As is the field, so is the seed
	9:24	but go into a field of flowers where no house has been built
	9:24	and eat only of the flowers of the field
	9:26	into the field which is called Ardat
	9:26	and ate of the plants of the field
	10:3	and came to this field, as you see
	10:32	I did as you directed, and went out into the field
	10:51	Therefore I told you to remain in the field
	10:53	Therefore I told you to go into the field
	12:51	But I sat in the field 7 days
	12:51	and I ate only the flowers of the field
	13:57	Then I arose and walked in the field
	14:37	and we proceeded to the field
	15:41	that all the fields and all the streams
	16:28	and out of the field, 2 who have hidden themselves
	16:32	and its fields shall be for briers
	16:77	as a field is choked with underbrush

FIERCE   6 = 0.004 %
Ad E	**15**:7	he looked at her in fierce anger
Sir	**10**:18	nor fierce anger for those born of women
1 Ma	**6**:47	and the fierce attack of the forces
2 Ma	**10**:29	When the battle became fierce
4 Ma	**7**:10	O elder, fiercer than fire
	16:2	but also that a woman has despised the fiercest tortures

FIERY   10 = 0.007 %
Wis	**11**:18	or such as breathe out fiery breath
Sir	**36**:9	Let him who survives be consumed in the fiery wrath
	43:4	it breathes out fiery vapours
P Az	26	and drove the fiery flame out of the furnace
	66	and delivered us from the midst of the burning fiery furnace
3 Ma	**6**:6	moistening the fiery furnace with dew
4 Ma	**7**:11	and conquered the fiery angel
	13:5	in those who were not turned back by fiery agonies ?
	16:3	nor was the raging fiery furnace of Mishael so intensely hot
	16:21	and Hananiah, Azariah, and Mishael were hurled into the fiery furnace

FIFTY, subst., s. NUMBERS   1
1 Ma	**3**:55	in charge of thousands and hundreds and fifties and tens

FIG   1
1 Ma	**14**:12	Each man sat under his vine and his fig tree

FIGHT, verb   77 = 0.050 %
Jud	**7**:11	Therefore, my lord, do not fight against them in battle array
Ad E	**11**:6	both ready to fight, and they roared terribly
	11:7	to fight against the nation of the righteous
	14:13	and turn his heart to hate the man who is fighting against us
Wis	**5**:20	and creation will join with him to fight against the madmen
Sir	**4**:28	and the Lord God will fight for you
	8:16	Do not fight with a wrathful man
	29:13	it will fight on your behalf against your enemy
	46:6	that he was fighting in the sight of the Lord
1 Ma	**1**:2	He fought many battles, conquered strongholds
	2:40	and refuse to fight with the Gentiles
	2:41	Let us fight against every man who comes to attack us on the sabbath day
	2:66	and fight the battle against the peoples
	3:2	they gladly fought for Israel
	3:10	and a large force from Samaria to fight against Israel
	3:17	fight against so great and strong a multitude ?
	3:21	but we fight for our lives and our laws
	3:43	and fight for our people and the sanctuary
	3:58	Be ready early in the morning to fight with these Gentiles
	4:18	But stand now against our enemies and fight them
	4:41	to fight against those in the citadel
	5:21	and fought many battles against the Gentiles
	5:32	Fight today for your brethren !
	5:35	and fought against it and took it
	5:39	ready to come and fight against you
	5:50	and he fought against the city
	5:56	and of the heroic war they had fought
	5:65	and fought the sons of Esau in the land to the south
	6:31	and for many days they fought and built engines of war
	6:31	but the Jews sallied out and burned these with fire, and fought manfully
	6:37	and upon each were 4 armed men who fought from there
	6:52	and fought for many days
	6:57	the place against which we are fighting is strong
	6:63	but he fought against him, and took the city by force
	8:6	who went to fight against them with a 120 elephants
	8:32	we will defend their rights and fight you on sea and on land
	9:8	We may be able to fight them
	9:9	and let us come back with our brethren and fight them
	9:30	as our ruler and leader, to fight our battle
	9:44	Let us rise up now and fight for our lives
	9:64	he fought against it for many days and made machines of war
	9:68	They fought with Bacchides, and he was crushed by them
	10:15	that Jonathan and his brothers had fought
	10:76	So they fought against it
	11:41	for they kept fighting against Israel
	11:46	and began to fight
	11:50	and make the Jews stop fighting against us and our city
	11:55	gathered around him, and they fought against Demetrius
	11:65	and fought against it for many days and hemmed it in
	12:51	that they would fight for their lives
	13:9	Fight our battles, and all that you say to us we will do
	13:47	and stopped fighting against them
	14:13	No one was left in the land to fight them
	14:26	they have fought and repulsed Israel's enemies
	14:32	then Simon rose up and fought for his nation
	15:26	And Simon sent to Antiochus 2,000 picked men, to fight for him
	16:2	have fought the wars of Israel from our youth until this day
	16:3	and go out and fight for our nation
2 Ma	**1**:12	For he drove out those who fought against the holy city
	7:19	for having tried to fight against God !
	8:16	but to fight nobly
	10:16	and beseeching God to fight on their side
	10:17	and beat off all who fought upon the wall
	10:21	by setting their enemies free to fight against them
	11:13	because the mighty God fought on their side
	12:36	As Esdris and his men had been fighting for a long time and were weary
	13:14	and exhorting his men to fight nobly to the death

149

15:17 by fighting hand to hand with all courage
15:27 So, fighting with their hands
1 Es **1**:28 but tried to fight with him
2:26 that this city from of old has fought against kings
2 Es **13**:8 were much afraid, yet dared to fight
13:11 which was prepared to fight
15:15 and nation shall rise up to fight against nation
4 Ma **3**:4 but reason can fight at our side
9:24 Fight the sacred and noble battle for religion
16:16 Fight zealously for our ancestral law

FIGHT off 1
Wis **11**:3 They withstood their enemies and fought off their foes

FIGHT, subst. 3 = 0.002 %
2 Ma **10**:28 while the other made rage their leader in the fight
12:11 After a hard fight Judas and his men won the victory
3 Ma **1**:4 When a bitter fight resulted

FIGHTING, subst., adj. 3 = 0.002 %
1 Ma **7**:28 Let there be no fighting between me and you
12:41 with 40,000 picked fighting men
2 Ma **5**:14 40,000 in hand-to-hand fighting

FIGURE 3 = 0.002 %
Wis **15**:4 a figure stained with varied colours
Sir **26**:17 so is a beautiful face on a stately figure
2 Es **13**:3 this wind made something like the figure of a man come up

FILL, verb 51 = 0.033 %
Jud **2**:8 till their wounded shall fill their valleys
2:8 and every brook and river shall be filled with their dead, and overflow
8:31 and the Lord will send us rain to fill our cisterns
10:5 and filled a bag with parched grain
Wis **1**:7 Because the Spirit of the Lord has filled the world
12:19 and thou hast filled thy sons with good hope
18:16 and stood and filled all things with death
Sir **1**:17 she fills their whole house with desirable goods
2:16 and those who love him will be filled with the law
4:12 and those who seek her early will be filled with joy
16:4 a city will be filled with people
16:29 and filled it with his good things
17:7 He filled them with knowledge and understanding
23:11 A man who swears many oaths will be filled with iniquity
23:11 for his house will be filled with calamities
24:25 It fills men with wisdom, like the Pishon
31:3 and when he rests he fills himself with his dainties
32:15 He who seeks the law will be filled with it
33:16 and like a grape-gatherer I filled my wine press
36:14 Fill Zion with the celebration of thy wondrous deeds
39:6 he will be filled with the spirit of understanding
39:12 and I am filled, like the moon at the full
47:15 and you filled it with parables and riddles
48:12 and Elisha was filled with his spirit
Bar **3**:32 He who prepared the earth for all time filled it with four-footed creatures
1 Ma **4**:32 Fill them with cowardice
2 Ma **3**:30 was filled with joy and gladness
4:37 and filled with pity, and wept
4:40 and filled with anger
6:4 For the temple was filled with debauchery and revelling
7:21 Filled with a noble spirit
8:21 With these words he filled them with good courage
9:7 but was even more filled with arrogance
13:16 In the end they filled the camp with terror and confusion
1 Es **8**:83 and they have filled it with their uncleanness
3 Ma **1**:16 and they filled the temple with cries and tears
1:18 and filled the streets with groans and lamentations
4:3 or what streets were not filled
4:16 The king was greatly and continually filled with joy
5:1 was filled with overpowering anger and wrath
5:10 until they had been filled with a great abundance of wine
5:30 But at these words he was filled with an overpowering wrath
5:42 Upon this the king, a Phalaris in everything and filled with madness
5:46 the city now being filled
5:47 So he, when he had filled his impious mind with a deep rage
6:19 and filled them with confusion and terror
2 Es **2**:19 by these I will fill your children with joy
4:32 how great a threshing floor they will fill !
5:25 thou hast filled for thyself one river
15:41 may be filled with the abundance of those waters
4 Ma **15**:20 and when you saw the place filled

FILL in 1
Tob **8**:18 Then he ordered his servants to fill in the grave

FILL up 2
Wis **19**:4 in order that they might fill up the punishment
Bar **5**:7 and the valleys filled up, to make level ground

FILL, subst. 6 = 0.004 %
Jud **7**:21 to drink their fill for a single day
Wis **2**:7 Let us take our fill of costly wine and perfumes
5:7 We took our fill of the paths of lawlessness and destruction
13:12 and eat his fill
Sir **24**:19 and eat your fill of my produce
2 Es **8**:4 Then drink your fill of understanding, O my soul

FILM 5 = 0.003 %
Tob **2**:10 and white films formed on my eyes
3:17 to scale away the white films from Tobit's eyes
6:8 anoint with it a man who has white films in his eyes
11:8 and will cause the white films to fall away
11:13 and the white films scaled off from the corners of his eyes

FILTH 2
Sir **22**:2 The indolent may be compared to the filth of dunghills
27:4 so a man's filth remains in his thoughts

FILTHY 1
Sir **22**:1 The indolent may be compared to a filthy stone

FINAL 2
1 Ma **3**:42 to do to the people to cause their final destruction
3 Ma **5**:5 convinced that the whole nation would experience its final destruction

FINALLY 4 = 0.003 %
Wis **3**:17 and finally their old age will be without honour
Sir **13**:7 and finally he will deride you
L Jr **6**:72 and they will finally themselves be consumed
2 Ma **5**:8 Finally he met a miserable end

FIND 148 = 0.096 %
Tob **1**:18 they were not found
2:2 Go and bring whatever poor man of our brethren you may find
5:3 Find a man to go with you
5:4 and he found Raphael, who was an angel
5:8 I have found some one to go with me
8:7 Grant that I may find mercy
8:13 and found them both asleep
Jud **6**:14 Then the men of Israel came down from their city and found him
10:6 and found Uzziah standing there
14:3 and will not find him
14:15 and found him thrown down on the platform dead
14:17 and when he did not find her
Ad E **16**:14 He thought that in this way he would find us undefended
16:15 But we find that the Jews
Wis **1**:2 because he is found by those who do not put him to the test
3:5 because God tested them and found them worthy of himself
5:10 and when it has passed no trace can be found
5:11 no evidence of its passage is found
5:11 and afterward no sign of its coming is found there
6:10 and those who have been taught them will find a defence
6:12 and is found by those who seek her
6:14 for he will find her sitting at his gates
7:29 Compared with the light she is found to be superior
8:11 I shall be found keen in judgment
8:16 When I enter my house, I shall find rest with her
9:16 and what is at hand we find with labour
13:6 and desiring to find him
13:9 how did they fail to find sooner the Lord of these things ?
16:9 and no healing was found for them
19:17 each tried to find the way through his own door
Sir **pr.** I found opportunity for no little instruction
3:18 so you will find favour in the sight of the Lord
3:31 at the moment of his falling he will find support
6:14 he that has found one has found a treasure
6:16 and those who fear the Lord will find him
6:18 and until you are old you will keep finding wisdom
6:28 For at last you will find the rest she gives
11:7 Do not find fault before you investigate
11:19 when he says, I have found rest
12:16 but if he finds an opportunity
12:17 If calamity befalls you, you will find him there ahead of you
15:6 He will find gladness and a crown of rejoicing
18:17 Both are to be found in a gracious man
18:20 and in the hour of visitation you will find forgiveness
18:28 and he praises the one who finds her
19:28 he will do evil when he finds an opportunity
20:5 There is one who by keeping silent is found wise
21:16 but delight will be found in the speech of the intelligent
22:13 avoid him and you will find rest
23:12 may it never be found in the inheritance of Jacob !
25:3 how then can you find anything in your old age ?

26 : 10 lest, when she finds liberty, she use it to her hurt
27 : 16 and he will never find a congenial friend
28 : 16 Whoever pays heed to slander will not find rest
29 : 3 and on every occasion you will find what you need
29 : 5 and will find fault with the time
31 : 8 Blessed is the rich man who is found blameless
31 : 10 Who has been tested by it and been found perfect ?
32 : 14 and those who rise early to seek him will find favour
32 : 17 and will find a decision according to his liking
33 : 25 Set your slave to work, and you will find rest
35 : 10 and as generously as your hand has found
36 : 16 and let thy prophets be found trustworthy
36 : 26 and lodges wherever night finds him ?
38 : 33 and they are not found using proverbs
40 : 18 but he who finds treasure is better off than both
41 : 23 and will find favour with every man
43 : 26 Because of him his messenger finds the way
43 : 28 Where shall we find strength to praise him ?
44 : 17 Noah was found perfect and righteous
44 : 19 and no one has been found like him in glory
44 : 20 and when he was tested he was found faithful
45 : 1 who found favour in the sight of all flesh
51 : 16 and I found for myself much instruction
51 : 20 and through purification I found her
51 : 26 it is to be found close by
51 : 27 and found for myself much rest
Bar 1 : 12 and we shall serve them many days and find favour in their sight
3 : 15 Who has found her place ?
3 : 30 Who has gone over the sea, and found her
3 : 32 he found her by his understanding
3 : 36 He found the whole way to knowledge
P Az 15 or to find mercy
Sus 13 : 14 when they could find her alone
13 : 63 because nothing shameful was found in her
Bel 14 : 12 if you do not find that Bel has eaten it all, we will die
1 Ma 1 : 23 he took also the hidden treasures which he found
1 : 56 The books of the law which they found they tore to pieces
1 : 57 Where the book of the covenant was found
1 : 58 against those found month after month in the cities
2 : 46 that they found within the borders of Israel
2 : 52 Was not Abraham found faithful when tested
2 : 63 Today he will be exalted, but tomorrow he will not be found
4 : 5 he found no one there, so he looked for them in the hills
5 : 6 where he found a strong band
6 : 53 those who found safety in Judea from the Gentiles
6 : 63 He found Philip in control of the city
10 : 16 So he said, Shall we find another such man ?
10 : 60 and found favour with them
11 : 16 So Alexander fled into Arabia to find protection there
11 : 42 if I find an opportunity
12 : 21 It has been found in writing
2 Ma 1 : 20 that they had not found fire but thick liquid
2 : 1 One finds in the records that Jeremiah the prophet
2 : 5 And Jeremiah came and found a cave
2 : 6 but could not find it
5 : 9 in hope of finding protection because of their kinship
5 : 25 then, finding the Jews not at work
8 : 7 He found the nights most advantageous for such attacks
12 : 18 They did not find Timothy in that region
12 : 40 they found sacred tokens of the idols of Jamnia
14 : 5 But he found an opportunity that furthered his mad purpose
14 : 10 it is impossible for the government to find peace
1 Es 2 : 22 You will find in the chronicles what has been written about them
2 : 26 and it has been found
4 : 42 for you have been found to be the wisest
5 : 38 but were not found registered : the sons of Habaiah
5 : 39 was sought in the register and was not found
6 : 8 we found the elders of the Jews
6 : 22 and if it is found that the building
6 : 23 a scroll was found in which this was recorded :
8 : 4 for he found favour before the king in all his requests
8 : 13 all the gold and silver that may be found
8 : 42 When I found there
8 : 53 and we found him very merciful
9 : 18 and found to have foreign wives were :
2 Es 2 : 23 when you find any who are dead
3 : 34 and so it will be found which way
3 : 36 Thou mayest indeed find individual men
3 : 36 but nations thou wilt not find
4 : 44 If I have found favour in your sight
5 : 9 And salt waters shall be found in the sweet
5 : 10 and it shall be sought by many but shall not be found
5 : 56 if I have found favour in thy sight
6 : 11 if I have found favour in thy sight
6 : 22 and full storehouses shall suddenly be found to be empty
7 : 75 If I have found favour in thy sight, O Lord
7 : 102 If I have found favour in my sight
7 : 104 Since you have found favour in my sight

7 : 106 How then do we find that first Abraham prayed
8 : 42 If I have found favour before thee, let me speak
12 : 7 if I have found favour in thy sight
13 : 48 who are found within my holy borders, shall be saved
14 : 22 If then I have found favour before thee
14 : 22 that men may be able to find the path
4 Ma 3 : 14 and found the spring
4 : 23 that if any of them should be found observing the ancestral law

FIND out   8 = 0.005 %
Jud 5 : 20 and they sin against their God and we find out their offence
8 : 14 nor find out what a man is thinking
8 : 14 and find out his mind or comprehend his thought ?
8 : 34 Only, do not try to find out what I plan
Wis 2 : 19 that we may find out how gentle he is
1 Ma 9 : 34 Bacchides found this out on the sabbath day
16 : 22 for he had found out that they were seeking to destroy him
1 Es 5 : 66 they came to find out what the sound of the trumpets meant

FINE, adj.   10 = 0.007 %
Jud 10 : 5 and a cake of dried fruit and fine bread
Sir 11 : 4 Do not boast about wearing fine clothes
26 : 20 and sow it with your own seed, trusting in your fine stock
35 : 2 He who returns a kindness offers fine flour
38 : 11 and a memorial portion of fine flour
Bel 14 : 3 and every day they spent on it 12 bushels of fine flour
2 Ma 3 : 2 and glorified the temple with the finest presents
9 : 16 he would adorn with the finest offerings
1 Es 3 : 6 and a turban of fine linen, and a necklace about his neck
8 : 57 and 12 bronze vessels of fine bronze

FINE, subst.   1
1 Es 8 : 24 either fine or imprisonment

FINE, verb   1
1 Es 1 : 36 and fined the nation a 100 talents of silver

FINERY   1
Jud 12 : 15 So she got up and arrayed herself in all her woman's finery

FINGER   4 = 0.003 %
Wis 15 : 15 nor ears with which to hear, nor fingers to feel with
Ps 151 : 2 My hands made a harp, my fingers fashioned a lyre
4 Ma 10 : 6 and breaking his fingers and arms and legs and elbows
15 : 15 their toes and fingers scattered on the ground

FINGERNAIL   1
4 Ma 10 : 7 and scalped him with their fingernails in Scythian fashion

FINISH   29 = 0.019 %
Tob 8 : 1 When they have finished eating
Jud 2 : 4 When he had finished setting forth his plan
5 : 22 When Achior had finished saying this
8 : 34 until I have finished what I am about to do
14 : 9 And when she had finished, the people raised a great shout
Sir 7 : 25 you will have finished a great task
18 : 7 When a man has finished, he is just beginning
23 : 20 so it was also after it was finished
38 : 8 His works will never be finished
38 : 27 and he is careful to finish his work
38 : 28 He sets his heart on finishing his handiwork
38 : 30 he sets his heart to finish the glazing
50 : 14 Finishing the service at the altars
1 Ma 2 : 23 When he had finished speaking these words
3 : 23 When he finished speaking
4 : 19 Just as Judas was finishing this speech
4 : 51 Thus they finished all the work they had undertaken
2 Ma 15 : 5 and finish the king's business
1 Es 2 : 19 Now if this city is built and the walls finished
2 : 24 that if this city is built and its walls finished
4 : 55 until the day when the temple should be finished and Jerusalem built
6 : 4 and this roof and finishing all the other things ?
6 : 4 And who are the builders that are finishing these things ?
6 : 14 and it was finished
6 : 28 until the house of the Lord is finished
7 : 5 the holy house was finished
2 Es 7 : 1 When I had finished speaking these words
14 : 25 until what you are about to write is finished
14 : 26 And when you have finished

FIRE, subst.   149 = 0.097 %
Jud 7 : 5 and when they had kindled fires on their towers
8 : 27 For he has not tried us with fire, as he did them
13 : 13 and they kindled a fire for light, and gathered around them
16 : 17 fire and worms he will give to their flesh
Ad E 16 : 24 shall be destroyed in wrath with spear and fire
Wis 10 : 6 he escaped the fire that descended on the Five Cities
13 : 2 but they supposed that either fire or wind or swift air
16 : 16 and utterly consumed by fire

151

	16:17	the fire had still greater effect
	16:19	it burned more intensely than fire
	16:22	Snow and ice withstood fire without melting
	16:22	were being destroyed by the fire that blazed in the hail
	16:23	whereas the fire, in order that the righteous might be fed
	16:27	For what was not destroyed by fire
	17:5	And no power of fire was able to give light
	17:6	except a dreadful, self-kindled fire
	18:3	Therefore thou didst provide a flaming pillar of fire
	19:20	Fire even in water retained its normal power
Sir	2:5	For gold is tested in the fire
	3:30	Water extinguishes a blazing fire :
	7:17	for the punishment of the ungodly is fire and worms
	8:3	Do not argue with a chatterer, nor heap wood on his fire
	8:10	lest you be turned in his flaming fire
	9:8	and by it passion is kindled like a fire
	11:32	From a spark of fire come many burning coals
	15:16	He has placed before you fire and water :
	16:6	In an assembly of sinners a fire will be kindled
	21:9	and their end is a flame of fire
	22:24	The vapour and smoke of the furnace precede the fire
	23:16	The soul heated like a burning fire
	23:16	will never cease until the fire burns him up
	28:10	In proportion to the fuel for the fire
	28:11	A hasty quarrel kindles fire, and urgent strife sheds blood
	31:26	Fire and water prove the temper of steel
	38:28	the breath of the fire melts his flesh
	39:26	Basic to all the needs of man's life are water and fire
	39:29	Fire and hail and famine and pestilence
	40:30	but in his stomach a fire is kindled
	43:21	and withers the tender grass like fire
	45:19	to consume them in flaming fire
	48:1	Then the prophet Elijah arose like a fire
	48:3	and also 3 times brought down fire
	48:9	You who were taken up by a whirlwind of fire
	48:9	in a chariot with horses of fire
	49:6	who set fire to the chosen city of the sanctuary
	50:9	like fire and incense in the censer
	51:4	from choking fire on every side
	51:4	and from the midst of fire which I did not kindle
Bar	1:2	and burned it with fire
	4:35	For fire will come upon her from the Everlasting for many days
L Jr	6:55	When fire breaks out in a temple
	6:63	And the fire sent from above to consume mountains and woods does what it is ordered
P Az	2	in the midst of the fire he opened his mouth and said :
	23	did not cease feeding the furnace fires
	27	so that the fire did not touch them at all
	44	Bless the Lord, fire and heat
	66	from the midst of the fire he has delivered us
1 Ma	1:31	He plundered the city, burned it with fire
	1:56	and burned with fire
	5:5	and burned with fire their towers and all who were in them
	5:28	then he seized all its spoils and burned it with fire
	5:35	and burned it with fire
	5:44	and burned the sacred precincts with fire
	5:68	and the graven images of their gods he burned with fire
	6:31	but the Jews sallied out and burned these with fire, and fought manfully
	6:51	engines of war to throw fire and stones
	9:67	and set fire to the machines of war
	10:84	and those who had taken refuge in it he burned with fire
	11:48	They set fire to the city and seized much spoil on that day
	11:61	So he besieged it and burned its suburbs with fire and plundered them
	12:28	so they kindled fires in their camp and withdrew
	12:29	for they saw the fires burning
	16:10	and John burned it with fire, and about 2,000 of them fell
2 Ma	1:18	and the feast of the fire given
	1:19	took some of the fire of the altar
	1:20	sent the descendants of the priests who had hidden the fire to get it
	1:20	that they had not found fire but thick liquid
	1:22	a great fire blazed up, so that all marvelled
	1:33	that, in the place where the exiled priests had hidden the fire
	2:1	to take some of the fire, as has been told
	2:10	and fire came down from heaven and devoured the sacrifices
	2:10	so also Solomon prayed, and the fire came down
	7:5	the king ordered them to take him to the fire, still breathing
	8:6	he would set fire to towns and villages
	8:33	they burned those who had set fire to the sacred gates
	9:7	breathing fire in his rage against the Jews
	10:3	then, striking fire out of flint, they offered sacrifices
	10:36	and set fire to the towers
	10:36	they kindled fires and burned the blasphemers alive
	12:6	He set fire to the harbour by night, and burned the boats
	12:9	and set fire to the harbour and the fleet
	13:8	against the altar whose fire and ashes were holy
	14:41	they ordered that fire be brought and the doors burned
1 Es	1:12	They roasted the passover lamb with fire, as required

	1:55	and burned their towers with fire
	6:24	where they sacrifice with perpetual fire
3 Ma	2:5	You consumed with fire and sulphur
	2:29	are also to be branded on their bodies by fire
	3:29	is to be made unapproachable and burned with fire
	5:43	and rapidly level it to the ground with fire and spear
2 Es	1:14	I provided light for you from a pillar of fire
	1:23	I did not send fire upon you for your blasphemies
	3:19	of fire and earthquake and wind and ice
	4:5	And he said to me, Go, weigh for me the weight of fire
	4:9	But now I have asked you only about fire and wind and the day
	4:16	for the fire came and consumed it
	4:50	and the fire is greater than the smoke
	5:8	and fire shall often break out
	7:7	so that there is fire on the right hand
	7:8	between the fire and the water
	7:38	and there are fire and torments !
	7:61	they are set on fire and burn hotly, and are extinguished
	8:8	what thou hast created is preserved in fire and water
	8:22	and at whose command they are changed to wind and fire
	13:4	when it feels the fire
	13:10	he sent forth from his mouth as it were a stream of fire
	13:11	the stream of fire and the flaming breath and the great storm
	13:27	And as for your seeing wind and fire
	13:38	which was symbolized by the fire
	14:39	but its colour was like fire
	15:23	And a fire will go forth from his wrath
	15:41	fire and hail and flying swords and floods of water
	15:61	and they shall be like fire to you
	15:62	they shall burn with fire
	16:4	A fire has been sent upon you
	16:6	or quench a fire in the stubble
	16:9	Fire will go forth from his wrath
	16:15	The fire is kindled, and shall not be put out
	16:53	for God will burn coals of fire on the head of him who says
	16:73	as gold that is tested by fire
	16:78	It is shut off and given up to be consumed by fire
4 Ma	5:32	and fan the fire more vehemently !
	6:24	the guards brought him to the fire
	7:10	O elder, fiercer than fire
	7:12	though being consumed by the fire
	9:9	eternal torment by fire
	9:19	While he was saying these things they spread fire under him
	9:22	but as though transformed by fire into immortality
	10:14	You do not have a fire hot enough to make me play the coward
	11:19	that had been heated in the fire
	11:26	Your fire is cold to us, and the catapults painless
	12:12	for you intense and eternal fire and tortures
	14:9	and in agonies of fire at that
	14:10	For the power of fire is intense and swift
	15:15	She watched the flesh of her children consumed by fire
	18:12	and he taught you about Hananiah, Azariah, and Mishael in the fire
	18:14	Even though you go through the fire
	18:20	quenched fire with fire in his cruel cauldrons

FIRE, verb   2

2 Ma	7:21	she fired her woman's reasoning with a man's courage
	10:35	fired with anger because of the blasphemies

FIREBREATHING   1

3 Ma	6:34	and their firebreathing boldness was ignominiously quenched

FIRE-QUENCHING   1

Wis	19:20	and water forgot its fire-quenching nature

FIRM   15 = 0.010 %

Wis	4:3	will strike a deep root or take a firm hold
Sir	22:18	will not stand firm against the wind
	22:18	will not stand firm against any fear
	42:17	that the universe may stand firm in his glory
	46:3	Who before him ever stood so firm ?
1 Ma	1:62	But many in Israel stood firm
	14:26	For he and his brothers and the house of his father have stood firm
3 Ma	2:9	you made it a firm foundation
	5:31	a full and firm loyalty to my ancestors
	7:7	the friendly and firm goodwill
2 Es	4:17	for the sand stood firm and stopped them
4 Ma	7:5	For in setting his mind firm like a jutting cliff
	7:13	his body no longer tense and firm
	17:3	you held firm and unswerving
	17:4	maintaining firm an enduring hope in God

FIRMAMENT   7 = 0.005 %

Sir	43:1	The pride of the heavenly heights is the clear firmament
	43:8	shining forth in the firmament of heaven
P Az	34	Blessed art thou in the firmament of heaven
2 Es	4:7	or how many streams are above the firmament
	6:4	and before the measures of the firmaments were named

6:20 the books shall be opened before the firmament
6:41 thou didst create the spirit of the firmament

FIRMLY   10 = 0.007 %
Jud 14:10 he believed firmly in God, and was circumcised
Sir 22:16 A wooden beam firmly bonded into a building
      22:16 so the mind firmly fixed on a reasonable counsel
      27:2 As a stake is driven firmly into a fissure between stones
      28:1 and he will firmly establish his sins
1 Ma 15:34 we are firmly holding the inheritance of our fathers
3 Ma 2:32 But the majority acted firmly with a courageous spirit
      5:42 and he firmly swore an irrevocable oath
      7:4 would never be firmly established until this was accomplished
4 Ma 17:5 and are firmly set in heaven with them

FIRST, adv., s. **NUMBERS**   26 = 0.017 %
Tob 4:12 First of all take a wife
Jud 12:16 ever since the day he first saw her
Sir 4:17 For at first she will walk with him on tortuous paths
      11:7 first consider, and then reprove
      37:8 and learn first what is his interest
      51:20 I gained understanding with her from the first
1 Ma 5:40 If he crosses over to us first
      5:43 Then he crossed over against them first
      6:2 the Macedonian king who first reigned over the Greeks
      6:6 that Lysias had gone first with a strong force
      8:24 If war comes first to Rome or to any of their allies
      8:27 if war comes first to the nation of the Jews
      10:4 for he said, Let us act first to make peace with him
2 Ma 4:33 having first withdrawn to a place of sanctuary
      14:8 first because I am genuinely concerned
2 Es 7:70 he first prepared the judgment
      7:78 first of all it adores the glory of the Most High
      7:106 How then do we find that first Abraham prayed
      10:28 Where is the angel Uriel, who came to me at first ?
      10:29 the angel who had come to me at first came to me
      12:33 For first he will set them living before his judgment seat
      14:29 At first our fathers dwelt as aliens in Egypt
      14:45 Make public the 24 books that you wrote first
4 Ma 1:30 Observe now first of all
      6:2 First they stripped the old man
      17:7 would not those who first beheld it have shuddered

FIRST-BORN   6 = 0.004 %
Tob 5:13 to worship and offered the first-born of our flocks
Wis 18:13 yet, when their first-born were destroyed
Sir 17:18 Whom, being his first-born, he brings up with discipline
      36:12 upon Israel, whom thou hast likened to a first-born son
2 Es 6:58 whom thou hast called thy first-born, only begotten
4 Ma 15:18 When the first-born breathed his last it did not turn you aside

FIRST-FORMED   2
Wis 7:1 a descendant of the first-formed child of earth
      10:1 Wisdom protected the first-formed father of the world

FISH, subst.   13 = 0.008 %
Tob 6:2 A fish leaped up from the river
      6:3 and the angel said to him, Catch the fish
      6:3 So the young man seized the fish and threw it up on the land
      6:4 Cut open the fish and take the heart and liver and gall
      6:5 and they roasted and ate the fish
      6:6 of what use is the liver and heart and gall of the fish ?
      6:16 and lay upon them some of the heart and liver of the fish
      8:2 and put the heart and liver of the fish upon them and made a smoke
      11:4 And take the gall of the fish with you
Wis 19:10 and instead of fish
2 Es 5:7 and the sea of Sodom shall cast up fish
      6:47 to bring forth living creatures, birds, and fishes
      16:12 and its waves and the fish also shall be troubled

FISSURE   1
Sir 27:2 As a stake is driven firmly into a fissure between stones

FIT, verb   2 = 0.002 %
4 Ma 9:26 and after fitting themselves with iron gauntlets having sharp hooks
      11:10 and fitting iron clamps on them

FIT, adj.   4 = 0.003 %
Wis 1:16 because they are fit to belong to his party
      15:6 Lovers of evil things and fit for such objects of hope
Sir 31:20 he rises early, and feels fit
      36:24 a helper fit for him and a pillar of support

FITTING   7 = 0.005 %
Sir 15:9 A hymn of praise is not fitting on the lips of a sinner
      32:3 Speak, you who are older, for it is fitting that you should
      33:28 Set him to work, as is fitting for him
3 Ma 1:9 and did what was fitting for the holy place

3 Ma 7:13 When they had applauded him in fitting manner
4 Ma 1:10 On this anniversary it is fitting for me
      9:6 it would be even more fitting

FITTINGLY   1
2 Ma 15:12 one who spoke fittingly

FIVE, prop. n.   1
Wis 10:6 he escaped the fire that descended on the Five Cities

FIX   3 = 0.002 %
Wis 6:15 To fix one's thought on her is perfect understanding
Sir 22:16 so the mind firmly fixed on a reasonable counsel
2 Es 16:56 At his word the stars were fixed

FLABBY   1
4 Ma 7:13 his muscles flabby, his sinews feeble, he became young again

FLAME, subst.   20 = 0.013 %
Wis 10:17 and a starry flame through the night
      16:18 At one time the flame was restrained
      17:5 nor did the brilliant flames of the stars
      19:21 Flames, on the contrary
Sir 21:9 and their end is a flame of fire
      28:22 and they will not be burned in its flame
P Az 1 And they walked about in the midst of the flames
      24 And the flame streamed out above the furnace 49 cubits
      26 and drove the fiery flame out of the furnace
1 Ma 2:59 and were saved from the flame
2 Ma 1:32 When this was done, a flame blazed up
3 Ma 6:6 who had voluntarily surrendered their lives to the flames
      6:6 and turning the flame against all their enemies
2 Es 4:48 and when the flame had gone by I looked
      7:61 and are similar to a flame and smoke
      13:38 which were symbolized by the flames
4 Ma 3:17 and quench the flames of frenzied desires
      9:19 and while fanning the flames they tightened the wheel further
      17:1 she threw herself into the flames
      18:14 the flame shall not consume you

FLAMING   7 = 0.005 %
Wis 18:3 Therefore thou didst provide a flaming pillar of fire
Sir 8:10 lest you be turned in his flaming fire
      45:19 to consume them in flaming fire
1 Ma 6:39 and gleamed like flaming torches
2 Es 4:48 So I stood and looked, and behold, a flaming furnace passed by before me
      13:10 and from his lips a flaming breath
      13:11 the stream of fire and the flaming breath and the great storm

FLANK, subst.   2
1 Ma 6:38 on the 2 flanks of the army, to harass the enemy
2 Ma 15:20 and the cavalry deployed on the flanks

FLANK, verb   1
1 Ma 9:12 Flanked by the 2 companies

FLASH, subst.   2
2 Ma 5:3 hurling of missiles, the flash of golden trappings
2 Es 6:2 and before the flashes of lightning shone

FLASH, verb   6 = 0.004 %
Wis 11:18 or flash terrible sparks from their eyes
      16:22 and flashed in the showers of rain
L Jr 6:61 So also the lightning, when it flashes, is widely seen
2 Es 10:25 and her countenance flashed like lightning
      16:10 He will flash lightning, and who will not be afraid ?
4 Ma 4:10 angels on horseback with lightning flashing from their weapons appeared from heaven

FLASK   1
Jud 10:5 And she gave her maid a bottle of wine and a flask of oil

FLATTER   2
Wis 14:17 they might flatter the absent one as though present
1 Es 4:31 if she loses her temper with him, he flatters her

FLAY   1
4 Ma 9:28 flayed all his flesh up to his chin

FLEE   67 = 0.044 %
Tob 1:18 any who came fleeing from Judea
      1:21 and they fled to the mountains of Ararat
      8:3 he fled to the remotest parts of Egypt
Jud 5:8 and they fled to Mesopotamia, and lived there for a long time
      10:12 but I am fleeing from them
      11:3 And now tell me why you have fled from them
      11:16 I fled from them
      14:3 Then fear will come over them, and they will flee before you
      14:4 shall pursue them and cut them down as they flee

	15:2	but with one impulse all rushed out and fled
Ad E	14:1	And Esther the queen, seized with deathly anxiety, fled to the Lord
Wis	1:5	For a holy and disciplined spirit will flee from deceit
	10:10	When a righteous man fled from his brother's wrath
Sir	11:10	and by fleeing you will not escape
	21:2	Flee from sin as from a snake
	22:22	or a treacherous blow – in these cases any friend will flee
L Jr	6:55	their priests will flee and escape
	6:68	for they can flee to cover and help themselves
1 Ma	1:18	and Ptolemy turned and fled before him
	1:38	Because of them the residents of Jerusalem fled
	2:28	And he and his sons fled to the hills
	2:44	the survivors fled to the Gentiles for safety
	3:11	Many were wounded and fell, and the rest fled
	3:24	800 of them fell, and the rest fled into the land of the Philistines
	4:5	because he said, These men are fleeing from us
	4:14	The Gentiles were crushed and fled into the plain
	4:22	they all fled into the land of the Philistines
	5:9	But they fled to the stronghold of Dathema
	5:11	and capture the stronghold to which we have fled
	5:34	they fled before him, and he dealt them a heavy blow
	5:43	and fled into the sacred precincts at Carnaim
	6:4	So he fled and in great grief departed from there
	6:6	but had turned and fled before the Jews
	7:32	and the rest fled into the city of David
	7:44	they threw down their arms and fled
	9:10	to do such a thing as to flee from them
	9:18	Judas also fell, and the rest fled
	9:33	and they fled into the wilderness of Tekoa
	9:40	Many were wounded and fell, and the rest fled to the mountain
	10:2	Then the foreigners who were in the strongholds that Bacchides had built fled
	10:49	and the army of Demetrius fled
	10:64	and saw him clothed in purple, they all fled
	10:73	where there is no stone or pebble, or place to flee
	10:82	they were overwhelmed by him and fled
	10:83	They fled to Azotus and entered Beth-dagon
	11:16	So Alexander fled into Arabia to find protection there
	11:46	But the king fled into the palace
	11:55	and he fled and was routed
	11:70	All the men with Jonathan fled
	11:72	and routed them, and they fled
	11:73	When his men who were fleeing saw this
	15:21	have fled to you from their country
	16:8	the rest fled into the stronghold
	16:10	They also fled into the towers
2 Ma	5:7	and fled again into the country of the Ammonites
	5:8	fleeing from city to city, pursued by all men
	8:24	and forced them all to flee
	8:33	who had fled into one little house
	10:32	Timothy himself fled to a stronghold called Gazara
	11:11	and forced all the rest to flee
	14:14	who had fled before Judas, flocked to join Nicanor
2 Es	2:36	Flee from the shadow of this age
	8:53	hell has fled and corruption has been forgotten
	10:3	I got up in the night and fled
	15:32	and shall turn and flee
	16:41	Let him that sells be like one who will flee
4 Ma	4:1	he fled the country with the purpose of betraying it

FLEE away   1
| Tob | 6:17 | Then the demon will smell it and flee away |

FLEECE   1
| Jud | 12:15 | the soft fleeces which she had received from Bagoas |

FLEET   4 = 0.003 %
1 Ma	1:17	and with a large fleet
2 Ma	12:9	and set fire to the harbour and the fleet
	14:1	with a strong army and a fleet
3 Ma	7:17	the fleet waited for them

FLEETING   1
| Wis | 16:27 | was melted when simply warmed by a fleeting ray of the sun |

FLESH   39 = 0.025 %
Jud	16:17	fire and worms he will give to their flesh
Wis	7:1	and in the womb of a mother I was moulded into flesh
	12:5	and their sacrificial feasting on human flesh and blood
	19:21	failed to consume the flesh of perishable creatures
Sir	1:10	She dwells with all flesh according to his gift
	14:18	so are the generations of flesh and blood
	17:16	hearts of flesh in place of their stony hearts
	17:31	So flesh and blood devise evil
	19:12	Like an arrow stuck in the flesh of the thigh
	28:5	If he himself, being flesh, maintains wrath
	31:1	Wakefulness over wealth wastes away one's flesh
	38:28	the breath of the fire melts his flesh
	39:19	The works of all flesh are before him

	40:8	With all flesh, both man and beast
	41:3	this is the decree from the Lord for all flesh
	44:18	that all flesh should not be blotted out by a flood
	44:20	he established the covenant in his flesh
	45:1	who found favour in the sight of all flesh
Bar	2:3	that we should eat, one the flesh of his son
	2:3	and another the flesh of his daughter
Bel	14:5	and has dominion over all flesh
1 Ma	7:17	The flesh of thy saints and their blood they poured out
2 Ma	6:18	was being forced to open his mouth to eat swine's flesh
	6:19	went up to the rack of his own accord, spitting out the flesh
	6:21	and pretend that he was eating the flesh
	7:1	to partake of unlawful swine's flesh
	9:9	his flesh rotted away, and because of his stench
2 Es	1:31	and circumcisions of the flesh
	15:58	and they shall eat their own flesh in hunger for bread
4 Ma	6:6	his flesh was being torn by scourges, his blood flowing
	7:18	these alone are able to control the passions of the flesh
	9:17	Cut my limbs, burn my flesh, and twist my joints
	9:20	and pieces of flesh were falling off the axles of the machine
	9:28	flayed all his flesh up to his chin
	10:8	he saw his own flesh torn all around
	15:15	She watched the flesh of her children consumed by fire
	15:15	and the flesh of the head to the chin exposed like masks
	15:20	When you saw the flesh of children burned
	15:20	upon the flesh of other children

FLIGHT   16 = 0.010 %
Jud	15:3	also took to flight
Wis	5:11	and pierced by the force of its rushing flight
Sir	26:27	for putting the enemy to flight
1 Ma	4:20	They saw that their army had been put to flight
	6:47	they turned away in flight
	10:72	for your fathers were twice put to flight in their own land
	11:15	and put him to flight
	15:11	Antiochus pursued him, and he came in his flight to Dor
	16:8	and Cendebaeus and his army were put to flight
2 Ma	4:42	and put them all to flight
	8:6	and put to flight not a few of the enemy
	9:2	with the result that Antiochus was put to flight by the inhabitants
	9:4	the injury done by those who had put him to flight
	11:12	and Lysias himself escaped by disgraceful flight
	12:22	and they rushed off in flight
	12:37	and put them to flight

FLING   1
| 4 Ma | 12:19 | he flung himself into the braziers and so ended his life |

FLINT   1
| 2 Ma | 10:3 | then, striking fire out of flint, they offered sacrifices |

FLINTY   1
| Wis | 11:4 | and water was given them out of flinty rock |

FLOCK, subst.   14 = 0.009 %
Tob	5:13	to worship and offered the first-born of our flocks
	7:8	and they killed a ram from the flock
Jud	2:27	and destroyed their flocks and herds
	3:3	and all our wheat fields, and our flocks and herds
Sir	18:13	and turns them back, as a shepherd his flock
	27:9	Birds flock with their kind
	47:3	and with bears as with lambs of the flock
Bar	4:26	they were taken away like a flock carried off by the enemy
2 Ma	14:23	but dismissed the flocks of people that had gathered
2 Es	5:18	like a shepherd who leaves his flock
	5:26	and from all the flocks that have been made
	7:65	but let the four-footed beasts and the flocks rejoice !
	15:10	Behold, my people is led like a flock to the slaughter
4 Ma	5:4	one man, Eleazar by name, leader of the flock

FLOCK, verb   2
| 2 Ma | 14:14 | who had fled before Judas, flocked to join Nicanor |
| 3 Ma | 1:19 | in a disorderly rush flocked together in the city |

FLOOD, subst.   14 = 0.009 %
Wis	18:5	and thou didst destroy them all together by a mighty flood
Sir	21:13	The knowledge of a wise man will increase like a flood
	39:22	and drenches it like a flood
	40:10	and on their account the flood came
	44:17	therefore a remnant was left to the earth when the flood came
	44:18	that all flesh should not be blotted out by a flood
1 Ma	6:11	And into what a great flood I now am plunged !
2 Ma	2:24	For considering the flood of numbers involved
3 Ma	2:4	whom you destroyed by bringing upon them a boundless flood
2 Es	3:9	thou didst bring the flood upon the inhabitants of the world
	3:10	as death came upon Adam, so the flood upon them
	15:41	fire and hail and flying swords and floods of water

4 Ma 15:31	Just as Noah's ark, carrying the world in the universal flood	
15:32	by the flood of your emotions and the violent winds	

FLOOD, verb   1
Wis **10**:4   When the earth was flooded because of him

FLOOR   3 = 0.002 %
Bel **14**:19   Look at the floor, and notice whose footsteps these are
2 Es **4**:32   how great a threshing floor they will fill !
9:17   and as is the farmer, so is the threshing floor

FLOUR   4 = 0.003 %
Sir **35**:2   He who returns a kindness offers fine flour
38:11   and a memorial portion of fine flour
39:26   and iron and salt and wheat flour and milk and honey
Bel **14**:3   and every day they spent on it 12 bushels of fine flour

FLOURISH   3 = 0.002 %
Sir **1**:18   making peace and perfect health to flourish
11:22   and quickly God causes his blessing to flourish
2 Es **6**:28   faithfulness shall flourish, and corruption shall be overcome

FLOURISHING   1
Sir **14**:18   Like flourishing leaves on a spreading tree

FLOW, verb   8 = 0.005 %
Jud **7**:12   that flows from the foot of the mountain
Sir **46**:8   to bring them into their inheritance, into a land flowing with milk and honey
Bar **1**:20   to give us a land flowing with milk and honey
2 Es **1**:20   did I not cleave the rock so that waters flowed in abundance ?
2:19   and the same number of springs flowing with milk and honey
6:24   so that for 3 hours they shall not flow
4 Ma **6**:6   his flesh was being torn by scourges, his blood flowing
10:8   and drops of blood flowing from his entrails

FLOW away   1
Wis **16**:29   will melt like wintry frost, and flow away like waste water

FLOWER   13 = 0.008 %
Wis **2**:7   and let no flower of spring pass by us
3 Ma **7**:16   crowned with all sorts of very fragrant flowers
2 Es **5**:24   and from all the flowers of the world
5:36   and make the withered flowers bloom again for me
6:3   and before the beautiful flowers were seen
6:44   and flowers of inimitable colour
9:17   and as are the flowers, so are the colours
9:24   but go into a field of flowers where no house has been built
9:24   and eat only of the flowers of the field
9:24   and taste no meat and drink no wine, but eat only flowers
9:26   and there I sat among the flowers
12:51   and I ate only the flowers of the field
15:50   And the glory of your power shall wither like a flower

FLOWING   1
Sir **21**:13   and his counsel like a flowing spring

FLUSH   1
Ad E **15**:7   Lifting his face, flushed with splendour

FLUTE   3 = 0.002 %
Sir **40**:21   The flute and the harp make pleasant melody
1 Ma **3**:45   the flute and the harp ceased to play
1 Es **5**:2   with the music of drums and flutes

FLY, subst.   1
Wis **16**:9   For they were killed by the bites of locusts and flies

FLY, verb   6 = 0.004 %
Wis **5**:11   or as, when a bird flies through the air
5:21   Shafts of lightning will fly with true aim
2 Es **11**:5   And I looked, and behold, the eagle flew with his wings
13:3   that man flew with the clouds of heaven
15:41   fire and hail and flying swords and floods of water
4 Ma **14**:17   by flying in circles around them in the anguish of love

FLY away   1
2 Es **5**:6   and the birds shall fly away together

FLY down   1
Sir **43**:17   He scatters the snow like birds flying down

FLY forth   1
Sir **43**:14   and the clouds fly forth like birds

FLY up   1
2 Es **13**:6   he carved for himself a great mountain, and flew up upon it

FLYING   1
Sir **11**:3   The bee is small among flying creatures

FODDER   2
Sir **33**:24   Fodder and a stick and burdens for an ass
38:26   and he is careful about fodder for the heifers

FOE   5 = 0.003 %
Ad E **13**:15   for the eyes of our foes are upon us to annihilate us
Wis **11**:3   They withstood their enemies and fought off their foes
Sir **19**:8   With friend or foe do not report it
25:7   a man who lives to see the downfall of his foes
1 Ma **2**:9   her youths by the sword of the foe

FOIL   2
Jud **16**:6   But the Lord Almighty has foiled them
3 Ma **1**:6   Now that he had foiled the plot

FOLLOW   51 = 0.033 %
Jud **2**:24   Then he followed the Euphrates
5:7   because they would not follow the gods of their fathers
9:5   and those that went before and those that followed
15:13   while all the men of Israel followed
Ad E **13**:5   perversely following a strange manner of life and laws
15:4   while the other followed carrying her train
Sir **pr.**   and the others that followed them
5:2   Do not follow your inclination and strength
5:9   Do not winnow with every wind, nor follow every path :
18:30   Do not follow your base desires, but restrain your appetites
23:28   It is a great honour to follow God
46:6   for he wholly followed the Mighty One
46:10   that it is good to follow the Lord
51:15   from my youth I followed her steps
Bar **1**:21   but we each followed the intent of his own wicked heart
P Az **17**   and may we wholly follow thee
18   And now with all our heart we follow thee
1 Ma **1**:44   he directed them to follow customs strange to the land
2:17   Then the king's officers spoke to Mattathias as follows :
5:43   and the whole army followed him
6:23   to live by what he said and to follow his commands
7:45   and as they followed
8:19   and they entered the senate chamber and spoke as follows :
8:31   we have written to him as follows
9:16   they turned and followed close behind Judas and his men
11:29   its contents were as follows :
13:35   and wrote him a letter as follows
14:22   we have recorded in our public decrees, as follows
15:2   its contents were as follows :
2 Ma **2**:4   ordered that the tent and the ark should follow with him
2:6   Some of those who followed came up to mark the way
7:27   she spoke in their native tongue as follows
8:36   because they followed the laws ordained by him
9:27   For I am sure that he will follow my policy
11:27   To the nation the king's letter was as follows :
15:2   And when the Jews who were compelled to follow him said
1 Es **2**:25   and Syria and Phoenicia, wrote as follows :
7:1   following the orders of King Darius
3 Ma **2**:1   prayed as follows :
2:26   themselves also followed his will
5:39   remonstrated as follows :
6:1   and prayed as follows :
6:21   The beasts turned back upon the armed forces following them
2 Es **6**:7   and the beginning of the age that follows ?
6:9   and Jacob is the beginning of the age that follows
7:35   And recompense shall follow
11:20   in due course the wings that followed also rose up on the right side
4 Ma **1**:22   Thus desire precedes pleasure and delight follows it
5:15   he began to address the people as follows :
8:1   by following a philosophy in accordance with devout reason
16:5   and perhaps have spoken as follows :

FOLLOW out   1
Jud **11**:6   And if you follow out the words of your maidservant

FOLLOWER   1
2 Ma **10**:1   Now Maccabeus and his followers

FOLLOWING, adj., subst.   18 = 0.012 %
Ad E **16**:1   The following is a copy of this letter :
Sir **pr.**   to the translation of the following book
42:1   Of the following things do not be ashamed
1 Ma **10**:17   and sent it to him, in the following words :
10:25   So he sent a message to them in the following words :
10:51   with the following message :
10:69   Then he sent the following message
14:28   the following was proclaimed to us :
15:15   in which the following was written :
2 Ma **9**:18   and wrote to the Jews the following letter
1 Es **2**:16   wrote him the following letter

155

	5:36	The following are those who came up from Tel-melah and Tel-harsha
	5:38	Of the priests the following had assumed the priesthood
	8:8	The following is a copy of the written commission
3 Ma	5:2	and ordered him on the following day
	5:48	at the gate by the following armed forces
	6:41	and wrote the following letter for them
2 Es	10:59	So I slept that night and the following one

FOLLY 15 = 0.010 %

Wis	10:8	but also left for mankind a reminder of their folly
	12:23	Therefore those who in folly of life lived unrighteously
Sir	8:15	and through his folly you will perish with him
	20:31	Better is the man who hides his folly
	34:5	Divinations and omens and dreams are folly
	41:15	Better is the man who hides his folly
	47:20	and they were grieved at your folly
	47:23	ample in folly and lacking in understanding
Bar	3:28	they perished through their folly
2 Ma	4:6	and that Simon would not stop his folly
	4:40	a man advanced in years and no less advanced in folly
	14:8	For through the folly of those whom I have mentioned
	15:33	and hang up these rewards of his folly
3 Ma	3:16	who never cease from their folly
	3:20	accommodated ourselves to their folly and did as was proper

FOOD 68 = 0.044 %

Tob	1:10	all my brethren and my relatives ate the food of the Gentiles
	2:2	Upon seeing the abundance of food I said to my son
	2:5	and ate my food in sorrow
	7:8	and set large servings of food before them
Jud	2:18	also plenty of food for every man
	4:5	and stored up food in preparation for war
	5:10	and lived there as long as they had food
	11:12	Since their food supply is exhausted
	12:1	with some of his own food
	12:9	until she ate her food toward evening
	13:10	who placed it in her food bag
Wis	13:12	and burn the castoff pieces of his work to prepare his food
	16:3	in order that those men, when they desired food
	16:20	thou didst give thy people the food of angels
	19:11	when desire led them to ask for luxurious food
	19:21	easily melted kind of heavenly food
Sir	13:7	He will shame you with his foods
	29:22	than sumptuous food in another man's house
	30:18	are like offerings of food placed upon a grave
	30:25	will give heed to the food he eats
	31:21	If you are overstuffed with food
	31:23	Men will praise the one who is liberal with food
	31:24	The city will complain of the one who is niggardly with food
	36:18	The stomach will take any food
	36:18	yet one food is better than another
	37:20	he will be destitute of all food
	37:29	and do not give yourself up to food
	40:29	He pollutes himself with another man's food
	41:1	and who still has the vigour to enjoy his food !
Bel	14:11	you yourself, O king, shall set forth the food
	14:14	When they had gone out, the king set forth the food for Bel
1 Ma	1:35	they stored up arms and food
	1:62	and were resolved in their hearts not to eat unclean food
	1:63	They chose to die rather than to be defiled by food
	6:53	But they had no food in storage
	6:57	We daily grow weaker, our food supply is scant
	9:52	and in them he put troops and stores of food
	13:21	and to send them food
	13:33	and he stored food in the strongholds
	14:10	He supplied the cities with food
2 Ma	11:31	to enjoy their own food and laws, just as formerly
1 Es	5:54	and food and drink
	8:79	and to give us food in the time of our servitude
	8:80	so that they have given us food
3 Ma	3:4	they kept their separateness with respect to foods
	3:7	instead they gossiped about the differences in worship and foods
	6:7	was cast down into the ground to lions as food for wild beasts
	6:34	that the Jews would be destroyed and become food for birds
2 Es	1:19	I pitied your groaning and gave you manna for food
	9:34	or any dish food or drink
	12:51	and my food was of plants during those days
4 Ma	1:33	when we are attracted to forbidden foods
	1:34	and all sorts of foods that are forbidden to us by the law
	4:26	to eat defiling foods and to renounce Judaism
	5:2	to eat pork and food sacrificed to idols
	5:3	If any were not willing to eat defiling food
	5:19	if we were to eat defiling food
	5:25	Therefore we do not eat defiling food
	5:27	that you may deride us for eating defiling food
	6:19	in becoming an example of the eating of defiling food
	7:6	by eating defiling foods
	8:2	being unable to compel an aged man to eat defiling foods
	8:2	and that any who ate defiling food should be freed after eating

	8:12	so as to persuade them out of fear to eat the defiling food
	8:29	had ceased counselling them to eat defiling food
	11:16	So if you intend to torture me for not eating defiling foods
	11:25	to change our mind or to force us to eat defiling foods
	13:2	and had eaten defiling food

FOOL 33 = 0.021 %

Wis	5:4	and made a byword of reproach – we fools !
	15:5	whose appearance arouses yearning in fools
Sir	8:17	Do not consult with a fool
	18:18	A fool is ungracious and abusive
	19:11	With such a word a fool will suffer pangs
	19:12	so is a word inside a fool
	19:23	but there is a fool who merely lacks wisdom
	20:7	but a braggart and fool goes beyond the right moment
	20:13	but the courtesies of fools are wasted
	20:14	A fool's gift will profit you nothing
	20:16	A fool will say, I have no friend
	20:20	A proverb from a fool's lips will be rejected
	21:14	The mind of a fool is like a broken jar
	21:16	A fool's narration is like a burden on a journey
	21:18	Like a house that has vanished, so is wisdom to a fool
	21:20	A fool raises his voice when he laughs
	21:22	The foot of a fool rushes into a house
	21:26	The mind of fools is in their mouth
	22:7	He who teaches a fool
	22:8	He who tells a story to a fool tells it to a drowsy man
	22:11	and weep for the fool, for he lacks intelligence
	22:11	but the life of the fool is worse than death
	22:12	but for a fool or an ungodly man it lasts all his life
	22:14	And what is its name except Fool ?
	22:18	so a timid heart with a fool's purpose
	23:14	and be deemed a fool on account of your habits
	27:11	but the fool changes like the moon
	27:13	The talk of fool is offensive
	31:7	ʹand every fool will be taken captive by it
	31:30	Drunkenness increases the anger of a fool to his injury
	33:5	The heart of a fool is like a cart wheel
	34:1	and dreams give wings to fools
Sus	13:48	Are you such fools, you sons of Israel ?

FOOLHARDY 1

Sir	8:15	Do not travel on the road with a foolhardy fellow

FOOLISH, adj., subst. 21 = 0.014 %

Wis	1:3	and when his power is tested, it convicts the foolish
	1:5	and will rise and depart from foolish thoughts
	3:2	In the eyes of the foolish they seemed to have died
	3:12	Their wives are foolish, and their children evil
	11:15	In return for their foolish and wicked thoughts
	12:24	they were deceived like foolish babes
	13:1	For all men who were ignorant of God were foolish by nature
	14:11	and a snare to the feet of the foolish
	15:14	But most foolish, and more miserable than an infant
	19:3	they reached another foolish decision
Sir	4:27	Do not subject yourself to a foolish fellow
	15:7	Foolish men will not obtain her
	20:22	or lose it because of his foolish look
	22:13	Do not talk much with a foolish man
	42:8	Do not be ashamed to instruct the stupid or foolish
	50:26	the foolish people that dwell in Shechem
2 Ma	2:32	for it is foolish to lengthen the preface
	12:44	and foolish to pray for the dead
2 Es	4:19	I answered and said, Each has made a foolish plan
	10:6	You most foolish of women
4 Ma	5:11	Will you not awaken from your foolish philosophy

FOOLISHLY 1

Sir	16:23	a senseless and misguided man thinks foolishly

FOOT 45 = 0.029 %

Jud	2:5	to the number of 120,000 foot soldiers and 12,000 cavalry
	2:7	with the feet of my armies
	6:13	and left him lying at the foot of the hill
	7:2	together with the baggage and the foot soldiers handling it
	7:12	that flows from the foot of the mountain
	9:7	they glory in the strength of their foot soldiers
	10:4	And she put sandals on her feet
	14:7	And when they raised him up he fell at Judith's feet
Ad E	13:13	For I would have been willing to kiss the soles of his feet, to save Israel !
Wis	14:11	and a snare to the feet of the foolish
	15:15	and their feet are of no use for walking
Sir	6:24	Put your feet into her fetters
	6:36	let your foot wear out his doorstep
	16:10	nor for the 600,000 men on foot
	21:19	To a senseless man education is fetters on his feet
	21:22	The foot of a fool rushes into a house
	25:20	A sandy ascent for the feet of the aged
	26:18	so are beautiful feet with a steadfast heart

	38:29	and turning the wheel with his feet
	38:30	and makes it pliable with his feet
	40:25	Gold and silver make the foot stand sure
	46:8	out of 600,000 people on foot
	50:15	he poured it out at the foot of the altar
	51:15	my foot entered upon the straight path
Bar	**5**:6	For they went forth from you on foot
L Jr	**6**:17	raised by the feet of those who enter
	6:26	Having no feet, they are carried on men's shoulders
1 Ma	**5**:48	we will simply pass by on foot
	6:30	The number of his forces was a 100,000 foot soldiers
	9:4	with 20,000 foot soldiers and 2,000 cavalry
2 Ma	**7**:4	and cut off his hands and feet
1 Es	**8**:51	for foot soldiers and horsemen and an escort
3 Ma	**4**:9	others had their feet secured by unbreakable fetters
	5:42	mangled by the knees and feet of the beasts
2 Es	**1**:26	and your feet are swift to commit murder
	2:15	establish their feet, because I have chosen you, says the Lord
	2:25	and strengthen their feet
	5:15	and strengthened me and set me on my feet
	6:13	Rise to your feet and you will hear a full, resounding voice
	6:17	When I heard this, I rose to my feet and listened
	10:30	and set me on my feet, and said to me
	14:2	and I rose to my feet
	16:69	and be trodden under foot
4 Ma	**10**:5	they disjointed his hands and feet with their instruments
	14:6	Just as the hands and feet are moved

FOOTSTEP   2

Bel	**14**:19	Look at the floor, and notice whose footsteps these are
	14:20	I see the footsteps of men and women and children

FOOTSTOOL   1

2 Es	**6**:4	and before the footstool of Zion was established

FOR, prep., conj.   2161 = 1.408 %

FORBEARANCE   5 = 0.003 %

Wis	**2**:19	and make trial of his forbearance
	12:18	and with great forbearance thou dost govern us
Sir	**3**:13	even if he is lacking in understanding, show forbearance
P Az	19	but deal with us in thy forbearance and in thy abundant mercy
2 Ma	**10**:4	they might be disciplined by him with forbearance

FORBID   7 = 0.005 %

Jud	**11**:12	to use all that God by his laws has forbidden them to eat
1 Ma	**1**:45	to forbid burnt offerings and sacrifices
2 Ma	**6**:5	which were forbidden by the laws
	12:40	which the law forbids the Jews to wear
4 Ma	**1**:33	when we are attracted to forbidden foods
	1:34	and all sorts of foods that are forbidden to us by the law
	5:26	but he has forbidden us to eat

FORCE, subst.   91 = 0.059 %

Jud	**1**:4	so that his armies could march out in force
	1:6	Many nations joined the forces of the Chaldeans
	1:13	In the 17th year he led his forces against King Arphaxad
	1:16	he and all his combined forces, a vast body of troops
	1:16	and there he and his forces rested and feasted for 120 days
	6:3	He will send his forces and will destroy them
	7:2	their force of men of war was 170,000 infantry and 12,000 cavalry
	7:12	and keep all the men in your forces with you
	7:26	to the army of Holofernes and to all his forces
Wis	**1**:14	and the generative forces of the world are wholesome
	5:11	and pierced by the force of its rushing flight
	18:22	and not by force of arms
1 Ma	**1**:17	So he invaded Egypt with a strong force
	1:20	and came to Jerusalem with a strong force
	1:29	and he came to Jerusalem with a large force
	3:10	and a large force from Samaria to fight against Israel
	3:27	and he sent and gathered all the forces of his kingdom
	3:28	and gave a year's pay to his forces
	3:35	Lysias was to send a force against them
	3:40	So they departed with their entire force
	3:41	And forces from Syria
	3:42	and that the forces were encamped in their territory
	4:3	moved out to attack the king's force in Emmaus
	4:9	when Pharaoh with his forces pursued them
	4:16	Then Judas and his force turned back from pursuing them
	4:18	Gorgias and his force are near us in the hills
	5:11	and Timothy is leading their forces
	5:18	with the rest of the forces, in Judea to guard it
	5:32	and he said to the men of his forces
	5:38	it is a very large force
	5:40	Timothy said to the officers of his forces
	5:50	So the men of the forces encamped
	5:56	and Azariah, the commanders of the forces
	5:58	to the men of the forces that were with them
	6:6	that Lysias had gone first with a strong force

	6:28	He assembled all his friends, the commanders of his forces
	6:29	And mercenary forces came to him from other kingdoms
	6:30	The number of his forces was a 100,000 foot soldiers
	6:47	and the fierce attack of the forces
	6:56	with the forces that had gone with the king
	6:57	and said to the king, to the commanders of the forces, and to the men
	6:63	but he fought against him, and took the city by force
	7:10	So they marched away and came with a large force
	7:11	for they saw that they had come with a large force
	7:20	and left with him a force to help him
	7:27	So Nicanor came to Jerusalem with a large force
	9:6	When they saw the huge number of the enemy forces
	9:43	he came with a large force on the sabbath day
	9:60	He started to come with a large force
	9:63	When Bacchides learned of this, he assembled all his forces
	9:67	Then he began to attack and went into battle with his forces
	10:36	Let Jews be enrolled in the king's forces
	10:36	that is due to all the forces of the king
	10:48	Now Alexander the king assembled large forces
	10:69	and he assembled a large force and encamped against Jamnia
	10:71	If you now have confidence in your forces
	10:82	Then Simon brought forward his force
	11:1	Then the king of Egypt gathered great forces
	11:3	he stationed forces as a garrison in each city
	11:15	Ptolemy marched out and met him with a strong force
	11:70	commanders of the forces of the army
	12:24	with a larger force than before, to wage war against him
	13:53	so he made him commander of all the forces
	14:1	In the 172nd year Demetrius the king assembled his forces
	14:32	he armed the men of his nation's forces and paid them wages
	15:25	continually throwing his forces against it
	16:5	and behold, a large force of infantry and horsemen
2 Ma	**1**:13	with a force that seemed irresistible
	3:35	he marched off with his forces to the king
	8:30	In encounters with the forces of Timothy and Bacchides
	8:32	They killed the commander of Timothy's forces
	9:3	of what had happened to Nicanor and the forces of Timothy
	10:14	he maintained a force of mercenaries
	10:19	a force sufficient to besiege them
	10:24	gathered a tremendous force of mercenaries
	10:36	Others broke open the gates and let in the rest of the force
	13:2	Each of them had a Greek force of 110,000 infantry
	13:15	and with a picked force of the bravest young men
3 Ma	**1**:1	he gave orders to all his forces
	2:28	Those who object to this are to be taken by force and put to death
	4:11	so that they could neither communicate with the king's forces
	5:29	pointed out that the beasts and the armed forces were ready
	5:44	and they confidently posted the armed forces
	5:47	rushed out in full force along with the beasts
	5:48	at the gate by the following armed forces
	6:5	Sennacherib exulting in his countless forces
	6:16	and all the arrogance of his forces
	6:19	They opposed the forces of the enemy
	6:21	The beasts turned back upon the armed forces following them
4 Ma	**4**:5	and a very strong military force
	4:10	with his armed forces to seize the money

FORCE, verb   11 = 0.007 %

Wis	**14**:19	skilfully forced the likeness to take more beautiful form
1 Ma	**2**:25	who was forcing them to sacrifice
	8:2	how they had defeated them and forced them to pay tribute
2 Ma	**6**:18	was being forced to open his mouth to eat swine's flesh
	8:24	and forced them all to flee
	11:11	and forced all the rest to flee
	14:41	and were forcing the door of the courtyard
1 Es	**3**:24	since it forces men to do these things ?
3 Ma	**4**:5	forced to march at a swift pace
4 Ma	**2**:8	he is forced to act contrary to his natural ways
	11:25	to change our mind or to force us to eat defiling foods

FORCE back   1

2 Ma	**5**:5	When the troops upon the wall had been forced back

FORCED   1

1 Ma	**6**:33	and took his army by a forced march

FORCIBLY   3 = 0.002 %

1 Ma	**2**:46	they forcibly circumcised all the uncircumcised boys
1 Es	**4**:49	should forcibly enter their doors
3 Ma	**5**:7	they were forcibly confined on every side

FOREFATHER   4 = 0.003 %

Tob	**1**:4	the whole tribe of Naphtali my forefather
	1:5	and so did the house of Naphtali my forefather
Jud	**8**:25	who is putting us to the test as he did our forefathers
4 Ma	**9**:2	we are obviously putting our forefathers to shame

FOREGO
| | | | | 1 |
2 Ma 2 : 31 and to forego exhaustive treatment

FOREIGN
20 = 0.013 %
Tob 4 : 12 and do not marry a foreign woman
Jud 5 : 18 and were led away captive to a foreign country
6 : 1 in the presence of all the foreign contingents :
Sir 29 : 18 and they have wandered among foreign nations
36 : 3 Lift up thy hand against foreign nations
39 : 4 he will travel through the lands of foreign nations
49 : 5 and their glory to a foreign nation
1 Ma 11 : 38 except the foreign troops
15 : 33 We have neither taken foreign land
15 : 33 nor seized foreign property
2 Ma 4 : 13 and increase in the adoption of foreign ways
1 Es 8 : 92 and have married foreign women from the peoples of the land
8 : 93 that we will put away all our foreign wives
9 : 7 You have broken the law and married foreign women
9 : 9 and from your foreign wives
9 : 12 and let all those in our settlements who have foreign wives
9 : 17 And the cases of the men who had foreign wives
9 : 18 and found to have foreign wives were :
9 : 36 All these had married foreign women
3 Ma 6 : 3 who are perishing as foreigners in a foreign land

FOREIGNER
9 = 0.006 %
L Jr 6 : 5 So take care not to become at all like the foreigners
1 Ma 4 : 12 When the foreigners looked up
4 : 26 Those of the foreigners who escaped went
10 : 12 Then the foreigners who were in the strongholds that Bacchides had built fled
11 : 68 and behold, the army of the foreigners met him in the plain
11 : 74 As many as 3,000 of the foreigners fell that day
2 Ma 10 : 2 in the public square by the foreigners
10 : 5 on which the sanctuary had been profaned by the foreigners
3 Ma 6 : 3 who are perishing as foreigners in a foreign land

FOREKNOWLEDGE
3 = 0.002 %
Jud 9 : 6 and thy judgment is with foreknowledge
11 : 19 For this has been told me, by my foreknowledge
Wis 8 : 8 she has foreknowledge of signs and wonders

FOREORDAIN
1
2 Es 7 : 74 but because of the times which he had foreordained !

FORERUNNER
1
Wis 12 : 8 and didst send wasps as forerunners of thy army

FOREST
14 = 0.009 %
2 Es 4 : 13 I went into a forest of trees of the plain
4 : 14 and that we may make for ourselves more forests
4 : 15 and said, Come, let us go up and subdue the forest of the plain
4 : 16 But the plan of the forest was in vain
4 : 19 for the land is assigned to the forest
4 : 21 For as the land is assigned to the forest
5 : 23 from every forest of the earth and from all its trees
9 : 21 and one plant out of a great forest
11 : 37 a creature like a lion was aroused out of the forest, roaring
12 : 31 And as for the lion whom you saw rousing up out of the forest
15 : 30 shall go forth like wild boars of the forest
15 : 42 mountains and hills, trees of the forests
15 : 62 all your forests and your fruitful trees
16 : 6 Can one drive off a hungry lion in the forest

FORESTALL
1
Sir 19 : 27 but where no one notices, he will forestall you

FORETELL
3 = 0.002 %
2 Es 6 : 25 after all that I have foretold to you
7 : 26 when the signs which I have foretold to you will come to pass
7 : 27 that I have foretold shall see my wonders

FOREVER
1
3 Ma 5 : 43 would quickly render it forever empty

FOREWARN
1
Wis 18 : 19 for the dreams which disturbed them forewarned them of this

FORFEIT
1
1 Es 6 : 32 and his property should be forfeited to the king

FORGET
28 = 0.018 %
Wis 2 : 4 Our name will be forgotten in time
16 : 23 even forgot its native power
19 : 4 and made them forget what had happened
19 : 20 and water forgot its fire-quenching nature
Sir 3 : 14 For kindness to a father will not be forgotten
7 : 27 and do not forget the birth pangs of your mother
11 : 25 In the day of prosperity, adversity is forgotten
11 : 27 The misery of an hour makes one forget luxury

13 : 10 and do not remain at a distance, lest you be forgotten
29 : 15 Do not forget all the kindness of your surety
35 : 7 and the memory of it will not be forgotten
37 : 6 Do not forget a friend in your heart
38 : 21 Do not forget, there is no coming back
44 : 10 whose righteous deeds have not been forgotten
Bar 4 : 8 You forgot the everlasting God, who brought you up
1 Ma 1 : 49 so that they should forget the law
2 Ma 2 : 2 not to forget the commandments of the Lord
7 : 23 since you now forget yourselves for the sake of his laws
1 Es 3 : 20 and forgets all sorrow and debt
3 : 21 It makes all hearts feel rich, forgets kings and satraps
3 : 22 When men drink they forget to be friendly with friends and brothers
3 Ma 6 : 20 and he forgot his sullen insolence
2 Es 1 : 6 for they have forgotten me
1 : 14 Yet you have forgotten me, says the Lord
8 : 53 hell has fled and corruption has been forgotten
12 : 47 and the Mighty One has not forgotten you in your struggle
16 : 67 Cease from your sins, and forget your iniquities
4 Ma 18 : 18 For he did not forget to teach you

FORGETFUL
1
Sir 23 : 14 lest you be forgetful in their presence

FORGETFULNESS
6 = 0.004 %
Wis 14 : 26 confusion over what is good, forgetfulness of favours
16 : 11 lest they should fall into deep forgetfulness
17 : 3 they were unobserved behind a dark curtain of forgetfulness
3 Ma 5 : 28 a forgetfulness of the things he had previously devised
4 Ma 1 : 5 why is it not sovereign over forgetfulness and ignorance ?
2 : 24 it does not control forgetfulness and ignorance ?

FORGIVE
6 = 0.004 %
Sir 2 : 11 he forgives sins and saves in time of affliction
5 : 6 he will forgive the multitude of my sins
16 : 11 he is mighty to forgive, and he pours out wrath
28 : 2 Forgive your neighbour the wrong he has done
P Ma 13 I earnestly beseech thee, forgive me, O Lord
13 forgive me ! Do not destroy me with my transgressions !

FORGIVENESS
4 = 0.003 %
Sir 17 : 29 and his forgiveness for those who turn to him !
18 : 12 therefore he grants them forgiveness in abundance
18 : 20 and in the hour of visitation you will find forgiveness
P Ma 7 hast promised repentance and forgiveness

FORLORN
1
Jud 9 : 11 upholder of the weak, protector of the forlorn

FORM, subst.
11 = 0.007 %
Wis 14 : 19 skilfully forced the likeness to take more beautiful form
15 : 5 so that they desire the lifeless form of a dead image
16 : 25 changed into all forms, it served thy all-nourishing bounty
18 : 1 Their enemies heard their voices but did not see their forms
18 : 12 by the one form of death, had corpses too many to count
2 Ma 4 : 15 and putting the highest value upon Greek forms of prestige
9 : 18 in the form of a supplication
3 Ma 3 : 30 The letter was written in the above form
2 Es 10 : 42 but you do not now see the form of a woman
4 Ma 4 : 19 and altered its form of government
15 : 4 a wondrous likeness both of mind and of form

FORM, verb
26 = 0.017 %
Tob 2 : 10 and white films formed on my eyes
Jud 1 : 4 and his infantry form their ranks
7 : 18 and they formed a vast multitude
16 : 14 Thou didst send forth thy Spirit, and it formed them
Wis 9 : 2 and by thy wisdom hast formed man
13 : 4 how much more powerful is he who formed them
13 : 13 he forms it like the image of a man
15 : 8 he forms a futile god from the same clay
15 : 11 because he failed to know the one who formed him
15 : 16 For a man made them, and one whose spirit is borrowed formed them
15 : 16 for no man can form a god which is like himself
Sir 32 : 16 Those who fear the Lord will form true judgments
37 : 3 O evil imagination, why were you formed to cover the land with deceit ?
1 Ma 10 : 23 in forming a friendship with the Jews to strengthen himself
3 Ma 3 : 8 and the crowds that suddenly were forming
6 : 32 they formed choruses as a sign of peaceful joy
2 Es 3 : 4 when thou didst form the earth – and that without help
6 : 46 who was about to be formed
7 : 92 to overcome the evil thought which was formed with them
7 : 94 they see the witness which he who formed them bears concerning them
8 : 8 and for 9 months the womb which thou hast formed
8 : 44 But man, who has been formed by thy hands
8 : 44 and for whose sake thou hast formed all things

	13:41	But they formed this plan for themselves
	16:61	who formed man, and put a heart in the midst of his body
4 Ma	14:8	so these youths, forming a chorus

FORMATION   2
1 Ma	12:26	that the enemy were being drawn up in formation
	12:50	and kept marching in close formation, ready for battle

FORMER   18 = 0.012 %
Tob	14:5	though it will not be like the former one
Wis	19:15	but punishment of some sort will come upon the former
Sir	21:1	Do so no more, but pray about your former sins
	41:3	remember your former days and the end of life
1 Ma	4:47	and built a new altar like the former one
	12:3	to renew the former friendship and alliance with them
	12:16	to renew our former friendship and alliance with them
2 Ma	14:38	For in former times
	15:8	but to keep in mind the former times
1 Es	5:63	old men who had seen the former house
3 Ma	2:29	and they shall also be reduced to their former limited status
	6:4	the former ruler of this Egypt
	6:27	begging pardon for your former actions !
2 Es	1:36	yet will recall their former state
	6:34	concerning the former times
	7:1	the angel who had been sent to me on the former nights
	11:18	and held the rule like the former ones
	12:18	but shall regain its former power

FORMERLY   13 = 0.008 %
1 Ma	3:46	because Israel formerly had a place of prayer in Mizpah
	9:72	whom he had formerly taken from the land of Judah
	11:27	and in as many other honours as he had formerly had
	11:34	which the king formerly received from them each year
	11:39	Now Trypho had formerly been one of Alexander's supporters
	14:33	where formerly the arms of the enemy had been stored
	14:34	where the enemy formerly dwelt
	15:3	so that I may restore it as it formerly was
	15:27	he formerly had made with Simon
2 Ma	9:16	and the holy sanctuary, which he had formerly plundered
	11:31	to enjoy their own food and laws, just as formerly
	14:3	Now a certain Alcimus, who had formerly been high priest
2 Es	5:2	and beyond what you heard of formerly

FORMLESS   1
Wis	11:17	out of formless matter

FORNICATION   2
Wis	14:12	For the idea of making idols was the beginning of fornication
Sir	23:16	a man who commits fornication with his near of kin

FORNICATOR   1
Sir	23:17	To a fornicator all bread tastes sweet

FORSAKE, verb   45 = 0.029 %
Jud	7:30	for he will not forsake us utterly
Sir	2:10	Or who ever persevered in the fear of the Lord and was forsaken ?
	3:16	Whoever forsakes his father is like a blasphemer
	4:19	If he goes astray she will forsake him
	7:30	and do not forsake his ministers
	9:10	Forsake not an old friend
	10:12	his heart has forsaken his Maker
	13:4	but if you are in need he will forsake you
	13:7	Should he see you afterwards, he will forsake you
	17:25	Turn to the Lord and forsake your sins
	28:23	Those who forsake the Lord will fall into its power
	35:1	and to forsake unrighteousness is atonement
	41:8	who have forsaken the law of the Most High God !
	48:15	and they did not forsake their sins
	49:4	for they forsook the law of the Most High
	51:10	not to forsake me in the days of affliction
	51:20	therefore I will not be forsaken
Bar	3:8	who forsook the Lord our God
	3:12	You have forsaken the fountain of wisdom
	4:1	and those who forsake her will die
Bel	14:38	and hast not forsaken those who love thee
1 Ma	1:38	and her children forsook her
	1:52	Many of the people, every one who forsook the law, joined them
	10:14	who had forsaken the law and the commandments
2 Ma	1:5	and may he not forsake you in time of evil
	5:20	and what was forsaken in the wrath of the Almighty
	6:1	to compel the Jews to forsake the laws of their fathers
	6:16	he does not forsake his own people
	7:16	But do not think that God has forsaken our people
1 Es	8:80	Even in our bondage we were not forsaken by our Lord
2 Es	1:25	Because you have forsaken me, I also will forsake you
	1:27	It is not as though you had forsaken me
	1:27	you have forsaken yourselves, says the Lord
	2:2	Go, my children, because I am a widow and forsaken
	2:4	For I am a widow and forsaken

	3:15	and promise him that thou wouldst never forsake his descendants
	5:18	so that you may not forsake us
	8:56	and forsook his ways
	10:32	I said, Because you have forsaken me !
	10:34	only do not forsake me, lest I die before my time
	12:41	that you have forsaken us and sit in this place ?
	12:44	Therefore if you forsake us
	12:48	As for me, I have neither forsaken you nor withdrawn from you
	13:54	because you have forsaken your own ways

FORT   1
2 Ma	10:33	and they besieged the fort 4 days

FORTH   1
1 Ma	11:36	from this time forth for ever

FORTIFICATION   3 = 0.002 %
1 Ma	10:11	with squared stones, for better fortification
	13:48	He also strengthened its fortifications
	13:52	He strengthened the fortifications of the temple hill

FORTIFIED   3 = 0.002 %
1 Ma	1:19	And they captured the fortified cities in the land of Egypt
2 Ma	11:5	which was a fortified place
	12:27	a fortified city where Lysias dwelt

FORTIFY   21 = 0.014 %
Jud	4:5	and fortified the villages on them
	5:1	and had fortified all the high hilltops
Sir	48:17	Hezekiah fortified his city
	50:1	and in his time fortified the temple
	50:4	and fortified the city to withstand a siege
1 Ma	1:33	Then they fortified the city of David
	4:7	And they saw the camp of the Gentiles, strong and fortified
	4:60	At that time they fortified Mount Zion
	4:61	He also fortified Beth-zur
	6:26	they have fortified both the sanctuary and Beth-zur
	9:52	He also fortified the city of Beth-zur
	9:62	and they fortified it
	10:45	and fortifying it round about
	12:38	he fortified it and installed gates with bolts
	13:10	and he fortified it on every side
	14:33	He fortified the cities of Judea
	14:34	He also fortified Joppa, which is by the sea
	14:37	He settled Jews in it, and fortified it
	15:39	and commanded him to build up Kedron and fortify its gates
2 Ma	12:13	which was strongly fortified with earthworks and walls
4 Ma	13:7	by fortifying the harbour of religion

FORTITUDE   1
4 Ma	15:28	she remembered his fortitude

FORTRESS   5 = 0.003 %
1 Ma	6:62	and saw what a strong fortress the place was
	9:50	the fortress in Jericho, and Emmaus, and Beth-horon
2 Ma	13:19	a strong fortress of the Jews
1 Es	6:23	And in Ecbatana, the fortress which is in the country of Media
3 Ma	6:25	the fortresses of our country ?

FORTUNE   3 = 0.002 %
Sir	20:9	There may be good fortune for a man in adversity
	37:18	4 turns of fortune appear, good and evil, life and death
3 Ma	3:11	Then the king, boastful of his present good fortune

FOUL   1
2 Ma	3:32	that some foul play had been perpetrated by the Jews

FOUND   3 = 0.002 %
2 Ma	2:13	and also that he founded a library
	4:12	For with alacrity he founded a gymnasium
2 Es	16:59	and founded it upon the waters

FOUNDATION   21 = 0.014 %
Jud	1:3	a 100 cubits high and 60 cubits wide at the foundations
	16:15	For the mountains shall be shaken to their foundations with the waters
Wis	4:19	and shake them from their foundations
Sir	1:15	She made among men an eternal foundation
	3:9	but a mother's curse uproots their foundations
	10:16	and has destroyed them to the foundations of the earth
	16:19	The mountains also and the foundations of the earth
	50:2	He laid the foundations for the high double walls
1 Es	2:18	and laying the foundations for a temple
	5:57	and they laid the foundation of the temple of God
	6:11	and laying the foundations of this structure ?
	6:20	laid the foundations of the house of the Lord
3 Ma	2:9	you made it a firm foundation
2 Es	6:2	and before the foundations of paradise were laid
	6:15	and the foundations of the earth will understand

10 : 27	and a place of huge foundations showed itself
10 : 53	where there was no foundation of any building
15 : 12	Let Egypt mourn, and its foundations
15 : 23	and will consume the foundations of the earth
16 : 12	The earth and its foundations quake
16 : 15	until it consumes the foundations of the earth

FOUNTAIN　　　　　　　　　　5 = 0.003 %

Wis 11 : 6	Instead of the fountain of an everflowing river
Bar 3 : 12	You have forsaken the fountain of wisdom
2 Es 6 : 24	and the springs of the fountains shall stand still
14 : 47	the fountain of wisdom, and the river of knowledge
4 Ma 13 : 21	they drank milk from the same fountains

FOUR-FOOTED　　　　　　　　2

Bar 3 : 32	He who prepared the earth for all time filled it with four-footed creatures
2 Es 7 : 65	but let the four-footed beasts and the flocks rejoice !

FOWL　　　　　　　　　　　　1

4 Ma 1 : 34	Therefore when we crave seafood and fowl and animals

FRAGILE　　　　　　　　　　2

Wis 14 : 1	calls upon a piece of wood more fragile
15 : 13	when he makes from earthy matter fragile vessels and graven images

FRAGRANCE　　　　　　　　　4 = 0.003 %

Sir 24 : 15	and like the fragrance of frankincense in the tabernacle
39 : 14	send forth fragrance like frankincense
39 : 14	Scatter the fragrance, and sing a hymn of praise
2 Es 6 : 44	and odours of inexpressible fragrance

FRAGRANT　　　　　　　　　5 = 0.003 %

Jud 16 : 16	For every sacrifice as a fragrant offering is a small thing
Bar 5 : 8	The woods and every fragrant tree have shaded Israel at God's command
3 Ma 5 : 45	by the very fragrant draughts of wine mixed with frankincense
7 : 16	crowned with all sorts of very fragrant flowers
2 Es 2 : 12	The tree of life shall give them fragrant perfume

FRAME　　　　　　　　　　　1

3 Ma 2 : 26	that he framed evil reports in the various localities

FRANKINCENSE　　　　　　　5 = 0.003 %

Sir 24 : 15	and like the fragrance of frankincense in the tabernacle
39 : 14	send forth fragrance like frankincense
3 Ma 5 : 2	with large handfuls of frankincense and plenty of unmixed wine
5 : 10	and satiated with frankincense
5 : 45	by the very fragrant draughts of wine mixed with frankincense

FRAUD　　　　　　　　　　　1

2 Es 7 : 23	and proposed to themselves wicked frauds

FREE, adj.　　　　　　　　　20 = 0.013 %

Jud 16 : 23	She set her maid free
Wis 6 : 15	will soon be free from care
7 : 23	Beneficent, humane, steadfast, sure, free from anxiety
16 : 14	nor set free the imprisoned soul
Sir 10 : 25	Free men will be at the service of a wise servant
13 : 24	Riches are good if they are free from sin
Sus 13 : 53	condemning the innocent and letting the guilty go free
1 Ma 2 : 11	no longer free, she has become a slave
10 : 31	be holy and free from tax
10 : 33	I set free without payment
2 Ma 1 : 27	set free those who are slaves among the Gentiles
9 : 14	he was now declaring to be free
10 : 21	by setting their enemies free to fight against them
11 : 25	be free from disturbance
12 : 42	to keep themselves free from sin
1 Es 3 : 19	of the slave and the free, of the poor and the rich
3 Ma 7 : 20	they departed unharmed, free, and overjoyed
2 Es 10 : 22	our free men have suffered abuse
4 Ma 14 : 2	O reason, more royal than kings and freer than the free !

FREE, verb　　　　　　　　　11 = 0.007 %

Wis 1 : 6	and will not free a blasphemer from the guilt of his words
12 : 2	that they may be freed from wickedness
1 Ma 8 : 18	and to free themselves from the yoke
10 : 29	And now I free you and exempt all the Jews
11 : 28	to free Judea and the 3 districts of Samaria from tribute
2 Ma 2 : 22	and freed the city
4 : 47	who would have been freed uncondemned
1 Es 9 : 13	until we are freed from the wrath of the Lord
2 Es 11 : 46	so that the whole earth, freed from your violence
4 Ma 8 : 2	and that any who ate defiling food should be freed after eating
12 : 9	they freed him at once

FREEDOM　　　　　　　　　9 = 0.006 %

Sir 7 : 21	do not withhold from his freedom
1 Ma 14 : 26	and established its freedom
15 : 7	and I grant freedom to Jerusalem and the sanctuary
1 Es 4 : 49	from his kingdom to Judea, in the interest of their freedom
4 : 53	should have their freedom, they and their children
3 Ma 3 : 28	and will be awarded his freedom
2 Es 7 : 101	They shall have freedom for 7 days
8 : 56	For they also received freedom
9 : 11	and as many as scorned my law while they still had freedom

FREELY　　　　　　　　　　2

1 Es 4 : 10	who freely choose to do so
3 Ma 7 : 12	so that freely and without royal authority or supervision

FREEWILL　　　　　　　　　2

Jud 4 : 14	and the vows and freewill offerings of the people
16 : 18	their freewill offerings, and their gifts

FREEZE　　　　　　　　　　3 = 0.002 %

Ad E 15 : 5	as if beloved, but her heart was frozen with fear
Sir 43 : 19	and when it freezes, it becomes pointed thorns
43 : 20	The cold north wind blows, and ice freezes over the water

FRENZIED　　　　　　　　　3 = 0.002 %

Wis 14 : 23	or hold frenzied revels with strange customs
4 Ma 2 : 4	over the frenzied urge of sexual desire
3 : 17	and quench the flames of frenzied desires

FRENZY　　　　　　　　　　1

4 Ma 2 : 3	by his reason he nullified the frenzy of the passions

FREQUENT, adj.　　　　　　　1

2 Ma 8 : 8	and that he was pushing ahead with more frequent successes

FREQUENT, verb　　　　　　　1

Sir 41 : 5	and they frequent the haunts of the ungodly

FREQUENTLY　　　　　　　　3 = 0.002 %

Sus 13 : 6	These men were frequently at Joakim's house
3 Ma 4 : 12	frequently went out in secret
7 : 3	frequently urging us with malicious intent

FRESH　　　　　　　　　　　3 = 0.002 %

Tob 2 : 10	and their fresh droppings fell into my open eyes
Sir 39 : 23	just as he turns fresh water into salt
2 Es 15 : 59	you shall come and suffer fresh afflictions

FRET　　　　　　　　　　　　1

Sir 6 : 25	and do not fret under her bonds

FRIEND　　　　　　　　　　122 = 0.079 %

Ad E 16 : 5	by the persuasion of friends who have been entrusted
Wis 1 : 16	considering him a friend, they pined away
7 : 27	and makes them friends of God, and prophets
Sir 5 : 15	and do not become an enemy instead of a friend
6 : 5	A pleasant voice multiplies friends
6 : 7	When you gain a friend, gain him through testing
6 : 8	For there is a friend who is such at his own convenience
6 : 9	And there is a friend who changes into an enemy
6 : 10	And there is a friend who is a table companion
6 : 13	and be on guard toward your friends
6 : 14	A faithful friend is a sturdy shelter :
6 : 15	There is nothing so precious as a faithful friend
6 : 16	A faithful friend is an elixir of life
7 : 12	nor do the like to a friend
7 : 18	Do not exchange a friend for money
9 : 10	Forsake not an old friend
9 : 10	A new friend is like new wine
12 : 8	A friend will not be known in prosperity
12 : 9	and in his adversity even his friend will separate from him
13 : 21	When a rich man totters, he is steadied by friends
13 : 21	but when a humble man falls, he is even pushed away by friends
14 : 13	Do good to a friend before you die
19 : 8	With friend or foe do not report it
19 : 13	Question a friend, perhaps he did not do it
19 : 15	Question a friend, for often it is slander
20 : 16	A fool will say, I have no friend
20 : 23	A man may for shame make promises to a friend
22 : 20	and one who reviles a friend will break off the friendship
22 : 21	Even if you have drawn your sword against a friend
22 : 22	If you have opened your mouth against your friend
22 : 22	or a treacherous blow – in these cases any friend will flee
22 : 25	I will not be ashamed to protect a friend
27 : 16	and he will never find a congenial friend
27 : 17	Love your friend and keep faith with him
28 : 9	and a sinful man will disturb friends
29 : 10	Lose your silver for the sake of a brother or a friend
30 : 3	and will glory in him in the presence of friends
30 : 6	and one to repay the kindness of his friends

33	:6	A stallion is like a mocking friend
33	:19	To son or wife, to brother or friend
37	:1	Every friend will say, I too am a friend
37	:1	but some friends are friends only in name
37	:2	when a companion and friend turns to enmity ?
37	:4	Some companions rejoice in the happiness of a friend
37	:5	Some companions help a friend for their stomachs' sake
37	:6	Do not forget a friend in your heart
40	:23	A friend or a companion never meets one amiss
41	:18	of unjust dealing, before your partner or friend
41	:22	of abusive words, before friends
42	:3	and of dividing the inheritance of friends
Sus 13	:33	But her family and friends and all who saw her wept
Bel 14	:2	and was the most honoured of his friends
1 Ma 2	:18	among the friends of the king
2	:39	When Mattathias and his friends learned of it
2	:45	And Mattathias and his friends went about
3	:38	mighty men among the friends of the king
6	:10	So he called all his friends and said to them
6	:14	Then he called for Philip, one of his friends
6	:28	He assembled all his friends, the commanders of his forces
7	:6	Judas and his brothers have destroyed all your friends
7	:8	So the king chose Bacchides, one of the king's friends
7	:15	We will not seek to injure you or your friends
8	:12	but with their friends and those who rely on them
8	:20	that we may be enrolled as your allies and friends
8	:31	upon our friends and allies the Jews ?
9	:26	They sought and searched for the friends of Judas
9	:28	Then all the friends of Judas assembled
9	:35	and begged the Nabateans, who were his friends
9	:39	with his friends and his brothers
10	:16	Come now, we will make him our friend and ally
10	:19	that you are a mighty warrior and worthy to be our friend
10	:20	you are to be called the king's friend
10	:60	he gave them and their friends silver and gold and many gifts
10	:65	and enrolled him among his chief friends
11	:26	he exalted him in the presence of all his friends
11	:27	and made him to be regarded as one of his chief friends
11	:33	who are our friends and fulfil their obligations to us
11	:57	and make you one of the friends of the king
12	:14	and our other allies and friends
12	:43	and commended him to all his friends
12	:43	and commanded his friends and his troops
13	:36	King Demetrius to Simon, the high priest and friend of kings
14	:39	and he made him one of the king's friends
14	:40	as friends and allies and brethren
15	:17	as our friends and allies
15	:28	He sent to him Athenobius, one of his friends
15	:32	So Athenobius the friend of the king came to Jerusalem
2 Ma 1	:14	Antiochus came to the place together with his friends
3	:31	Quickly some of Heliodorus' friends asked Onias
6	:2	the Friend of Strangers
7	:24	and that he would take him for his friend
8	:9	one of the king's chief friends
10	:13	by the king's friends
11	:14	constraining him to be their friend
14	:11	the rest of the king's friends, who were hostile to Judas
1 Es 3	:22	When men drink they forget to be friendly with friends and brothers
8	:11	depart with you as I and the 7 friends
8	:13	which I and my friends have vowed
8	:26	and his counsellors and all his friends and nobles
3 Ma 2	:23	Then both friends and bodyguards
2	:26	and many of his friends
3	:10	and friends and business associates
5	:3	together with those of his friends and of the army
5	:19	But when he, with the corroboration of his friends
5	:26	and while the king was receiving his friends
5	:29	Then Hermon and all the king's friends
5	:34	The king's friends one by one sullenly slipped away
5	:44	Then the friends and officers departed with great joy
6	:23	he wept and angrily threatened his friends, saying
7	:3	Certain of our friends
2 Es 5	:9	and all friends shall conquer one another
6	:24	At that time friends shall make war on friends like enemies
7	:103	or friends for those who are most dear
7	:104	or a friend his dearest friend
4 Ma 2	:13	It is sovereign over the relationship of friends
2	:13	so that one rebukes friends when they act wickedly
12	:5	but if you yield to persuasion will be my friend
12	:8	and to all his friends that are with him

FRIENDLY 3 = 0.002 %

1 Ma 5	:48	And Judas sent them this friendly message
1 Es 3	:22	When men drink they forget to be friendly with friends and brothers
3 Ma 7	:7	the friendly and firm goodwill

FRIENDSHIP 29 = 0.019 %

Wis 7	:14	those who get it obtain friendship with God
8	:18	and in friendship with her, pure delight
Sir 6	:17	Whoever fears the Lord directs his friendship aright
22	:20	and one who reviles a friend will break off the friendship
22	:21	do not despair, for a renewal of friendship is possible
25	:1	agreement between brothers, friendship between neighbours
27	:18	so you have destroyed the friendship of your neighbour
1 Ma 8	:1	that they pledged friendship to those who came to them
8	:12	they have kept friendship
8	:17	and sent them to Rome to establish friendship and alliance
10	:20	and you are to take our side and keep friendship with us
10	:23	in forming a friendship with the Jews to strengthen himself
10	:26	and have continued your friendship with us
10	:54	now therefore let us establish friendship with one another
12	:1	to confirm and renew the friendship with them
12	:3	to renew the former friendship and alliance with them
12	:8	which contained a clear declaration of alliance and friendship
12	:10	and friendship with you
12	:16	to renew our former friendship and alliance with them
14	:18	to renew with him the friendship and alliance
14	:22	have come to us to renew their friendship with us
15	:17	to renew our ancient friendship and alliance
2 Ma 4	:11	who went on the mission to establish friendship
6	:22	on account of his old friendship with them
11	:26	and give them pledges of friendship
11	:30	will have our pledge of friendship
12	:11	to grant them pledges of friendship
14	:19	to give and receive pledges of friendship
4 Ma 8	:5	but I also exhort you to yield to me and enjoy my friendship

FRIGHT 1

Wis 11	:19	but the mere sight of them could kill by fright

FRIGHTEN 7 = 0.005 %

Wis 17	:9	For even if nothing disturbing frightened them
Sir 26	:5	and of a 4th I am frightened
30	:9	Pamper a child, and he will frighten you
1 Ma 4	:21	When they perceived this they were greatly frightened
9	:6	they were greatly frightened
2 Ma 8	:16	and exhorted them not to be frightened by the enemy
2 Es 10	:25	so that I was too frightened to approach her

FRIGHTENING 1

2 Ma 3	:25	with a rider of frightening mien

FRIGHTFUL 1

3 Ma 5	:45	and had been equipped with frightful devices

FRO 1

2 Es 6	:29	began to rock to and fro

FROG 1

Wis 19	:10	the river spewed out vast numbers of frogs

FROM 931 = 0.606 %

FROND 1

2 Ma 10	:7	and also fronds of palm

FRONT, subst. 8 = 0.005 %

Jud 10	:22	he came forward to the front of the tent
Sir 26	:12	*so will she sit in front of every post*
1 Ma 1	:22	and the gold decoration on the front of the temple
4	:57	They decorated the front of the temple
9	:45	*For look ! The battle is in front of us and behind us*
13	:27	with polished stone at the front and back
2 Ma 3	:25	and struck at him with its front hoofs
3 Ma 4	:11	*in front of the city*

FRONT, verb 2

Jud 2	:25	fronting toward Arabia
3	:9	near Dothan, fronting the great ridge of Judea

FRONTIER 1

Jud 15	:4	and Choba and Kola, and to all the frontiers of Israel

FROST 5 = 0.003 %

Wis 16	:29	will melt like wintry frost, and flow away like waste water
Sir 3	:15	as frost in fair weather, your sins will melt away
Bar 2	:25	to the heat of day and the frost of night
P Az	50	Bless the Lord, frosts and snows
2 Es 7	:41	or frost or cold or hail or rain or dew

FRUIT 49 = 0.032 %

Tob 1	:6	Taking the first fruits and the tithes of my produce
Jud 10	:5	and a cake of dried fruit and fine bread
11	:13	They have decided to consume the first fruits of the grain
Wis 3	:13	she will have fruit when God examines souls
3	:15	For the fruit of good labours is renowned

	4:5	and their fruit will be useless, not ripe enough to eat
	10:7	plants bearing fruit that does not ripen
	10:10	and increased the fruit of his toil
Sir	1:16	she satisfies men with her fruits
	6:3	You will devour your leaves and destroy your fruit
	7:31	the first fruits, the guilt offering
	7:31	and the first fruits of the holy things
	14:15	Will you not leave the fruit of your labours to another
	19:19	enjoy the fruit of the tree of immortality
	23:25	and her branches will not bear fruit
	24:17	and my blossoms became glorious and abundant fruit
	24:25	and like the Tigris at the time of the first fruits
	27:6	The fruit discloses the cultivation of a tree
	28:15	and deprived them of the fruit of their toil
	30:19	Of what use to an idol is an offering of fruit ?
	35:8	and do not stint the first fruits of your hands
	37:22	and the fruits of his understanding
	37:23	and the fruits of his understanding will be trustworthy
	45:20	he allotted to him the first of the first fruits
	45:20	he prepared bread of first fruits in abundance
	50:8	like roses in the days of the first fruits
	50:10	like an olive tree putting forth its fruit
1 Ma	3:49	and the first fruits and the tithes
	10:30	and the half of the fruit of the trees that I should receive
	11:34	from the crops of the land and the fruit of the trees
	14:8	and the trees of the plains their fruit
2 Es	2:18	12 trees loaded with various fruits
	3:20	so that thy law might bring forth fruit in them
	3:33	and their labour has borne no fruit
	4:31	how much fruit of ungodliness a grain of evil seed has produced
	6:28	and the truth, which has been so long without fruit, shall be revealed
	6:44	For immediately fruit came forth in endless abundance
	7:13	and really yield the fruit of immortality
	7:123	whose fruits remains unspoiled
	8:6	so that fruit may be produced
	8:10	which is the fruit of the breasts
	9:31	and it shall bring forth fruit in you
	9:32	yet the fruit of the law did not perish
	10:12	for I have lost the fruit of my womb
	10:14	given her fruit, that is, man, to him who made her
	11:42	you have destroyed the dwellings of those who brought forth fruit
	16:25	The trees shall bear fruit, and who will gather it ?
	16:46	for strangers shall gather their fruits
4 Ma	2:14	The fruit trees of the enemy are not cut down

FRUITFUL   1
2 Es	15:62	all your forests and your fruitful trees

FRUITLESS   2
Wis	15:4	nor the fruitless toil of painters
4 Ma	16:7	fruitless nurturings and wretched nursings !

FRUSTRATE   4 = 0.003 %
Jud	11:11	and his purpose frustrated
Sir	16:13	and the patience of the godly will not be frustrated
3 Ma	5:12	and was completely frustrated in his inflexible plan
4 Ma	17:2	frustrated his evil designs

FRY   1
2 Ma	7:5	and to fry him in a pan

FUEL   1
Sir	28:10	In proportion to the fuel for the fire

FUGITIVE   4 = 0.003 %
Jud	16:12	they were wounded like the children of fugitives
Wis	19:3	and pursued as fugitives
1 Ma	2:43	And all who became fugitives to escape their troubles
2 Ma	4:26	was driven as a fugitive into the land of Ammon

FULFIL   13 = 0.008 %
Jud	10:8	and fulfil your plans
Ad E	10:5	and none of them has failed to be fulfilled
Wis	4:13	Being perfected in a short time, he fulfilled long years
Sir	32:2	when you have fulfilled your duties, take your place
	34:8	Without such deceptions the law will be fulfilled
	36:15	and fulfil the prophecies spoken in his name
1 Ma	2:55	Joshua, because he fulfilled the command
	11:33	who are our friends and fulfil their obligations to us
1 Es	4:46	I pray therefore that you fulfil the vow
	8:21	be scrupulously fulfilled for the Most High God
2 Es	2:40	who have fulfilled the law of the Lord
	4:37	until that measure is fulfilled
4 Ma	12:14	Surely they by dying nobly fulfilled their service to God

FULFILMENT   6 = 0.004 %
Tob	8:17	and bring their lives to fulfilment
Sir	19:20	and in all wisdom there is the fulfilment of the law

	21:11	and wisdom is the fulfilment of the fear of the Lord
1 Es	1:57	in fulfilment of the word of the Lord by the mouth of Jeremiah :
	4:46	whose fulfilment you vowed to the King of heaven
3 Ma	1:22	or the fulfilment of his intended purpose

FULL, adj., subst.   59 = 0.038 %
Tob	13:6	give thanks to him with your full voice
Jud	6:4	and their fields will be full of their dead
	7:6	in full view of the Israelites in Bethulia
Ad E	15:6	clothed in the full array of his majesty
	15:14	and your countenance is full of grace
Wis	2:6	and make use of the creation to the full as in youth
	3:4	their hope is full of immortality
	5:22	and hailstones full of wrath will be hurled as from a catapult
	11:18	or newly created unknown beasts full of rage
	12:21	and covenants full of good promises !
	13:13	a stick crooked and full of knots
Sir	1:16	To fear the Lord is wisdom's full measure
	1:30	and your heart was full of deceit
	19:26	but inwardly he is full of deceit
	24:26	It makes them full of understanding, like the Euphrates
	32:20	Do not go on a path full of hazards
	39:12	and I am filled, like the moon at the full
	42:16	and the work of the Lord is full of his glory
	43:7	a light that wanes when it has reached the full
	50:6	like the moon when it is full
L Jr	6:17	Their eyes are full of the dust
Sus	13:28	full of their wicked plot to have Susanna put to death
1 Ma	2:68	Pay back the Gentiles in full
	14:6	and gained full control of the country
2 Ma	3:6	that the treasury in Jerusalem was full of untold money
	3:30	was full of fear and disturbance
	6:14	until they have reached the full measure of their sins
	11:30	and full permission for the Jews
	13:5	For there is a tower in that place, 50 cubits high, full of ashes
	15:28	they recognized Nicanor, lying dead, in full armour
1 Es	1:23	for his heart was full of godliness
	6:28	and that full effort be made to help the men
3 Ma	5:31	a full and firm loyalty to my ancestors
	5:47	rushed out in full force along with the beasts
	6:31	and full of joy they apportioned to celebrate the place
	7:16	and had received the full enjoyment of deliverance
2 Es	2:40	Take again your full number, O Zion
	2:41	The number of your children, whom you desired, is full
	4:27	because this age is full of sadness and infirmities
	4:38	but all of us also are full of ungodliness
	4:49	And after this a cloud full of water passed before me
	6:13	Rise to your feet and you will hear a full, resounding voice
	6:22	and full storehouses shall suddenly be found to be empty
	7:6	and it is full of all good things
	7:12	full of dangers and involved in great hardships
	7:25	and full things are for the full
	7:68	and are full of sins and burdened with transgressions
	7:112	the full glory does not abide in it
	8:58	that knowing full well that they must die
	12:2	and their reign was brief and full of tumult
	12:30	this was the reign which was brief and full of tumult
	14:39	a full cup was offered to me
	14:39	it was full of something like water
	15:34	full of wrath and storm
	15:40	And great and mighty clouds, full of wrath and tempest
4 Ma	7:17	Not every one has full command of his emotions
	13:16	Therefore let us put on the full armour of self-control
	14:11	that reason had full command over these men in their tortures

FULL-TONED   1
Sir	50:18	in sweet and full-toned melody

FULLY   12 = 0.008 %
Tob	14:4	for I fully believe what Jonah the prophet said
Jud	2:2	and recounted fully, with his own lips
Sir	18:5	And who can fully recount his mercies ?
1 Ma	9:42	And when they had fully avenged the blood of their brother
2 Ma	4:33	When Onias became fully aware of these acts
	5:2	in companies fully armed with lances and drawn swords
	14:20	When the terms had been fully considered
	15:22	and he slew fully a 185,000 in the camp of Sennacherib
1 Es	6:8	Let it be fully known to our lord the king that
3 Ma	3:24	Therefore, fully convinced by these indications
2 Es	12:8	that thou mayest fully comfort my soul
4 Ma	3:12	armed themselves fully

FULNESS   2
Tob	12:9	will have fulness of life
Sir	33:11	In the fulness of his knowledge the Lord distinguished them

FUND   7 = 0.005 %
1 Ma	3:30	He feared that he might not have such funds
	3:31	and raise a large fund
	10:41	And all the additional funds

2 Ma	3:6	so that the amount of the funds could not be reckoned
	3:14	to direct the inspection of these funds
4 Ma	4:3	there are deposited tens of thousands in private funds
	4:6	to seize the private funds in the treasury

FUNERAL 6 = 0.004 %

Tob	14:11	and Tobias gave him a magnificent funeral
	14:13	magnificent funerals
L Jr	6:32	as some do at a funeral feast for a man who has died
1 Ma	9:41	and the voice of their musicians into a funeral dirge
2 Ma	4:49	provided magnificently for their funeral
	5:10	he had no funeral of any sort

FURIOUS 1

1 Ma	2:49	it is a time of ruin and furious anger

FURIOUSLY 2

2 Ma	3:25	and it rushed furiously at Heliodorus
	12:15	rushed furiously upon the walls

FURNACE 20 = 0.013 %

Wis	3:6	like gold in the furnace he tried them
Sir	2:5	and acceptable men in the furnace of humiliation
	22:24	The vapour and smoke of the furnace precede the fire
	38:28	and he wastes away in the heat of the furnace
	38:30	and he is careful to clean the furnace
	43:4	A man tending a furnace works in burning heat
P Az	23	did not cease feeding the furnace fires
	24	And the flame streamed out above the furnace 49 cubits
	25	whom it caught about the furnace
	26	But the angel of the Lord came down into the furnace
	26	and drove the fiery flame out of the furnace
	27	and made the midst of the furnace like a moist whistling wind
	28	praised and glorified and blessed God in the furnace, saying :
	66	and delivered us from the midst of the burning fiery furnace
3 Ma	6:6	moistening the fiery furnace with dew
2 Es	4:48	So I stood and looked, and behold, a flaming furnace passed by before me
	7:36	and the furnace of hell shall be disclosed
4 Ma	13:9	who despised the same ordeal of the furnace
	16:3	nor was the raging fiery furnace of Mishael so intensely hot
	16:21	and Hananiah, Azariah, and Mishael were hurled into the fiery furnace

FURNISH 4 = 0.003 %

Sir	44:6	rich men furnished with resources
1 Ma	4:57	and furnished them with doors
	14:10	and furnished them with the means of defence
2 Es	8:8	and dost furnish it with members

FURNITURE 1

Jud	15:11	and his beds and his bowls and all his furniture

FURROW 2

Sir	7:3	My son, do not sow the furrows of injustice
	38:26	He sets his heart on ploughing furrows

FURTHER 6 = 0.004 %

Sir	36:6	Show signs anew, and work further wonders
2 Ma	2:20	and further the wars against Antiochus Epiphanes
	14:5	But he found an opportunity that furthered his mad purpose
1 Es	2:29	and that such wicked proceedings go no further
2 Es	7:102	show further to me, thy servant
4 Ma	9:19	and while fanning the flames they tightened the wheel further

FURTHERMORE 1

4 Ma	14:1	Furthermore, they encouraged them to face the torture

FURY 3 = 0.002 %

Sir	40:5	and fear of death, and fury and strife
	48:10	to calm the wrath of God before it breaks out in fury
2 Ma	10:35	and with savage fury cut down every one they met

FUTILE 2

Wis	15:8	he forms a futile god from the same clay
4 Ma	5:11	dispel your futile reasonings

FUTURE, subst., adj. 11 = 0.007 %

Ad E	16:8	For the future we will take care to render our kingdom
Wis	19:1	for God knew in advance even their future actions
Sir	3:31	Whoever requites favours gives thought to the future
	11:23	and what prosperity could be mine in the future ?
	11:24	and what calamity could happen to me in the future ?
	24:33	and leave it to all future generations
1 Ma	15:8	and such future debts shall be cancelled for you
2 Ma	11:19	I will endeavour for the future to help promote your welfare
	12:31	to be well disposed to their race in the future also
3 Ma	2:31	by their future association with the king

2 Es	8:46	and things that are future are for those who will live hereafter

G

GABAEL 10 = 0.007 %

Tob	1:1	son of Ananiel, son of Aduel, son of Gabael
	1:14	in trust with Gabael, the brother of Gabrias
	4:1	which he had left in trust with Gabael at Rages in Media
	4:20	which I left in trust with Gabael the son of Gabrias
	5:6	and I have stayed with our brother Gabael
	9:2	and go to Gabael at Rages in Media
	9:5	and stayed overnight with Gabael
	9:5	and Gabael brought out the money bags with their seals intact
	9:6	And Gabael blessed Tobias and his wife
	10:2	Or is it possible that Gabael has died

GABATHA 1

Ad E	12:1	with Gabatha and Tharra

GABRIAS 2

Tob	1:14	in trust with Gabael, the brother of Gabrias
	4:20	which I left in trust with Gabael the son of Gabrias

GADDI 1

1 Ma	2:2	He had 5 sons, John surnamed Gaddi

GAHAR 1

1 Es	5:30	the sons of Cathua, the sons of Gahar

GAIN, subst. 2

Wis	14:2	For it was desire for gain that planned that vessel
Sir	29:19	The sinner who has fallen into suretyship and pursues gain

GAIN, verb 42 = 0.027 %

Wis	7:25	therefore nothing defiled gains entrance into her
	13:13	and shapes it with skill gained in idleness
Sir pr.		for those living abroad who wished to gain learning
	6:7	When you gain a friend, gain him through testing
	6:33	If you love to listen you will gain knowledge
	8:8	because from them you will gain instruction
	8:9	because from them you will gain understanding
	9:2	so that she gains mastery over your strength
	19:25	and there are people who distort kindness to gain a verdict
	22:23	Gain the trust of your neighbour in his poverty
	25:9	happy is he who has gained good sense
	25:10	How great is he who has gained wisdom !
	34:23	what do they gain but toil ?
	34:25	what has he gained by his washing ?
	34:26	And what has he gained by humbling himself ?
	51:20	I gained understanding with her from the first
	51:21	therefore I have gained a good possession
	51:28	and you will gain by it much gold
1 Ma	2:48	and they never let the sinner gain the upper hand
	2:64	for by it you will gain honour
	7:22	They gained control of the land of Judah
	8:4	and how they had gained control of the whole region
	10:52	for I crushed Demetrius and gained control of our country
	10:76	and Jonathan gained possession of Joppa
	11:8	So King Ptolemy gained control of the coastal cities
	11:49	that the Jews had gained control of the city as they pleased
	11:51	So the Jews gained glory in the eyes of the king
	11:56	and gained control of Antioch
	14:6	and gained full control of the country
	15:3	have gained control of the kingdom of our fathers
	15:9	When we gain control of our kingdom
2 Ma	5:7	He did not gain control of the government, however
	8:8	When Philip saw that the man was gaining ground little by little
	10:17	they gained possession of the places
	13:26	convinced them, appeased them, gained their good will
	15:21	that he gains victory for those who deserve it
3 Ma	6:5	who had already gained control of the whole world by the spear
2 Es	3:28	Is that why she has gained dominion over Zion ?
	4:15	so that there also we may gain more territory for ourselves
	11:32	Moreover this head gained control of the whole earth
4 Ma	18:4	Because of them the nation gained peace

GALATIAN 1

2 Ma	8:20	and the time of the battle with the Galatians

GALBANUM 1

Sir	24:15	like galbanum, onycha, and stacte

GALILEE 14 = 0.009 %

Tob	1:2	in Galilee above Asher
Jud	1:8	and Upper Galilee and the great Plain of Esdraelon
	15:5	and those in Gilead and in Galilee outflanked them
1 Ma	5:14	came from Galilee and made a similar report
	5:15	and all Galilee of the Gentiles, to annihilate us

	5:17	Choose your men and go and rescue your brethren in Galilee
	5:20	Then 3,000 men were assigned to Simon to go to Galilee
	5:21	So Simon went to Galilee
	5:23	Then he took the Jews of Galilee and Arbatta
	5:55	and Simon his brother was in Galilee before Ptolemais
	10:30	from Samaria and Galilee
	11:63	had come to Kadesh in Galilee with a large army
	12:47	2,000 of whom he left in Galilee
	12:49	Then Trypho sent troops and cavalry into Galilee

GALL 6 = 0.004 %
Tob	6:4	Cut open the fish and take the heart and liver and gall
	6:6	of what use is the liver and heart and gall of the fish ?
	6:8	And as for the gall
	11:4	And take the gall of the fish with you
	11:8	You therefore must anoint his eyes with the gall
	11:11	and he sprinkled the gall upon his father's eyes, saying

GALLON 1
Bel	14:3	and 40 sheep and 50 gallons of wine

GAMAEL 1
1 Es	8:29	Of the sons of Ithamar, Gamael

GAME 3 = 0.002 %
Wis	15:12	But he considered our existence an idle game
Sir	36:19	*As the palate tastes the kinds of game*
2 Ma	4:18	When the quadrennial games were being held at Tyre

GAPE 1
1 Es	4:19	they let all those things go, and gape at her

GARDEN 17 = 0.011 %
Sir	24:30	and like a water channel into a garden
	24:31	I said, I will water my orchard and drench my garden plot
	40:17	Kindness is like a garden of blessings
	40:27	The fear of the Lord is like a garden of blessing
L Jr	6:71	are like a thorn bush in a garden
Sus	13:4	and had a spacious garden adjoining his house
	13:7	Susanna would go into her husband's garden to walk
	13:15	and wished to bathe in the garden, for it was very hot
	13:17	and shut the garden doors so that I may bathe
	13:18	They did as she said, shut the garden doors
	13:20	Look, the garden doors are shut, no one sees us
	13:25	And one of them ran and opened the garden doors
	13:26	When the household servants heard the shouting in the garden
	13:36	The elders said, As we were walking in the garden alone
	13:36	shut the garden doors, and dismissed the maids
	13:38	We were in a corner of the garden
2 Es	3:6	And thou didst lead him into the garden

GARLAND 4 = 0.003 %
Jud	3:7	welcomed him with garlands and dances and tambourines
	15:13	bearing their arms and wearing garlands
Sir	50:12	with a garland of brethren around him
3 Ma	4:8	their necks encircled with ropes instead of garlands

GARMENT 26 = 0.017 %
Jud	8:5	and wore the garments of her widowhood
	10:3	and took off her widow's garments
	14:16	and wept and groaned and shouted, and rent his garments
Ad E	14:2	and put on the garments of distress and mourning
	15:1	she took off the garments in which she had worshipped
Sir	14:17	All living beings become old like a garment
	42:13	for from the garments comes the moth
	45:10	with a holy garment, of gold and blue and purple
Bar	5:1	Take off the garment of your sorrow and affliction, O Jerusalem
L Jr	6:11	They deck their gods out with garments like men
1 Ma	3:49	They also brought the garments of the priesthood
	5:14	behold, other messengers, with their garments rent
	10:21	So Jonathan put on the holy garments
	10:62	The king gave orders to take off Jonathan's garments
	11:71	Jonathan rent his garments
	14:9	and the youths donned the glories and garments of war
2 Ma	3:15	in their priestly garments
	4:38	tore off his garments
1 Es	1:2	arrayed in their garments, in the temple of the Lord
	4:54	garments in which they were to minister
	5:45	and a 100 priests' garments
	5:59	And the priests stood arrayed in their garments
	7:9	arrayed in their garments, according to kindred
	8:71	I rent my garments and my holy mantle
	8:73	with my garments and my holy mantle rent
2 Es	2:39	have received glorious garments from the Lord

GARRISON 13 = 0.008 %
Jud	3:6	and stationed garrisons in the hilltop cities
1 Ma	4:61	And he stationed a garrison there to hold it
	6:21	But some of the garrison escaped from the siege
	9:51	And he placed garrisons in them to harass Israel
	10:75	for Apollonius had a garrison in Joppa
	11:3	he stationed forces as a garrison in each city
	11:66	and set a garrison over it
	12:34	And he stationed a garrison there to guard it
	12:36	so that its garrison could neither buy nor sell
	14:33	and he placed there a garrison of Jews
2 Ma	10:32	especially well garrisoned, where Chaereas was commander
	12:18	though in one place he had left a very strong garrison
	13:20	Judas sent in to the garrison whatever was necessary

GARRULOUS 2
Sir	25:20	such is a garrulous wife for a quiet husband
	26:27	A loud-voiced and garrulous wife

GAS 1
1 Es	5:34	the sons of Sarothie, the sons of Masiah, the sons of Gas

GASP, verb 2
4 Ma	6:11	and gasping heavily for breath
	11:11	In this condition, gasping for breath and in anguish of body

GASP, subst. 1
3 Ma	5:25	But the Jews, at their last gasp

GATE 46 = 0.030 %
Tob	11:16	at the gate of Nineveh
Jud	1:3	at the gates he built towers
	1:4	and he made its gates
	7:22	and in the passages through the gates
	8:33	Stand at the city gate tonight
	10:6	Then they went out to the city gate of Bethulia
	10:9	Order the gate of the city to be opened for me
	10:9	to open the gate for her, as she had said
	13:10	and went up the mountain to Bethulia and came to its gates
	13:11	Judith called out from afar to the watchmen at the gates
	13:11	Open, open the gate !
	13:12	they hurried down to the city gate
	13:13	they opened the gate and admitted them
Ad E	16:18	has been hanged at the gate of Susa, with all his household
Wis	6:14	for he will find her sitting at his gates
	16:13	thou dost lead men down to the gates of Hades and back again
Sir	49:13	and set up the gates and bars and rebuilt our ruined houses
L Jr	6:18	And just as the gates are shut on every side
1 Ma	4:38	and the gates burned
	4:57	they restored the gates and the chambers for the priests
	5:22	He pursued them to the gate of Ptolemais
	5:47	and blocked up the gates with stones
	9:50	with high walls and gates and bars
	10:75	but the men of the city closed its gates
	10:76	and the men of the city became afraid and opened the gates
	11:2	and the people of the cities opened their gates to him
	12:38	he fortified it and installed gates with bolts
	12:48	the men of Ptolemais closed the gates and seized him
	13:33	with high towers and great walls and gates and bolts
	15:39	and commanded him to build up Kedron and fortify its gates
2 Ma	1:8	and burned the gate and shed innocent blood
	3:19	ran together to the gates, and some to the walls
	8:33	they burned those who had set fire to the sacred gates
	10:36	Others broke open the gates and let in the rest of the force
	12:7	Then, because the city's gates were closed
1 Es	1:16	The gatekeepers were at each gate
	5:47	before the first gate toward the east
	7:9	and the gatekeepers were at each gate
	9:38	into the open square before the east gate of the temple
	9:41	before the gate of the temple
3 Ma	5:48	at the gate by the following armed forces
	5:51	as they stood now at the gates of death
	6:18	revealed his holy face and opened the heavenly gates
	6:31	or rather, who stood at its gates
2 Es	3:19	And thy glory passed through the 4 gates
4 Ma	3:13	Eluding the sentinels at the gates

GATEKEEPER 7 = 0.005 %
1 Es	1:16	The gatekeepers were at each gate
	5:28	The gatekeepers : the sons of Shallum
	5:46	and the temple singers, the gatekeepers
	7:9	and the gatekeepers were at each gate
	8:5	and gatekeepers and temple servants
	8:22	or gatekeepers or temple servants or
	9:25	Of the gatekeepers : Shallum and Telem

GATHER 86 = 0.056 %
Tob	13:5	and will gather us from all the nations
	13:13	for they will be gathered together
Jud	4:3	and all the people of Judea were newly gathered together
	7:23	gathered about Uzziah and the rulers of the city
	13:13	and they kindled a fire for light, and gathered around them
	15:12	Then all the women of Israel gathered to see her
	16:22	and was gathered to his people
Ad E	10:8	The nations are those that gathered to destroy

Sir	21:8	is like one who gathers stones for his burial mound
	21:9	An assembly of the wicked is like tow gathered together
	25:3	You have gathered nothing in your youth
	36:11	Gather all the tribes of Jacob
	47:18	you gathered gold like tin and amassed silver like lead
	50:5	How glorious he was when the people gathered round him
Bar	4:37	they are coming, gathered from east and west
	5:5	and see your children gathered from west and east
Sus	13:28	The next day, when the people gathered at the house of her husband Joakim
1 Ma	1:4	He gathered a very strong army
	2:69	Then he blessed them, and was gathered to his fathers
	3:9	he gathered in those who were perishing
	3:10	But Apollonius gathered together Gentiles
	3:13	heard that Judas had gathered a large company
	3:27	and he sent and gathered all the forces of his kingdom
	5:9	Now the Gentiles in Gilead gathered together
	5:10	The Gentiles around us have gathered together against us
	5:15	they said that against them had gathered together
	5:37	After these things Timothy gathered another army
	5:38	All the Gentiles around us have gathered to him
	5:45	Then Judas gathered together all the Israelites in Gilead
	5:64	Men gathered to them and praised them
	6:20	They gathered together
	10:61	lawless men, gathered together against him to accuse him
	11:1	Then the king of Egypt gathered great forces
	11:55	gathered around him, and they fought against Demetrius
	11:60	and all the army of Syria gathered to him as allies
	12:37	So they gathered together to build up the city
	13:2	and gathering the people together
	13:6	for all the nations have gathered together
	14:7	He gathered a host of captives
	14:30	and was gathered to his people
2 Ma	1:27	Gather together our scattered people
	2:7	until God gathers his people together again
	2:18	and will gather us from everywhere under heaven
	4:39	the populace gathered against Lysimachus
	8:1	and so they gathered about 6,000 men
	8:16	But Maccabeus gathered his men together
	10:21	he gathered the leaders of the people
	10:24	gathered a tremendous force of mercenaries
	11:2	gathered about 80,000 men and all his cavalry
	14:23	but dismissed the flocks of people that had gathered
	14:30	So he gathered not a few of his men
1 Es	4:18	If men gather gold and silver or any other beautiful thing
	5:47	they gathered as one man in the square
	8:27	and I gathered men from Israel to go up with me
	8:72	gathered round me, as I mourned over this iniquity
	8:91	there gathered about him a very great throng from Jerusalem
	9:38	the whole multitude gathered with one accord
3 Ma	1:21	Various were the supplications of those gathered there
	3:1	and he ordered that all should promptly be gathered into one place
	6:25	and senselessly gathered here those who faithfully have held
	7:3	persuaded us to gather together the Jews of the kingdom in a body
2 Es	1:30	I gathered you as a hen gathers her brood under her wings
	5:36	and gather for me the scattered raindrops
	6:3	and before the innumerable hosts of angels were gathered together
	6:42	thou didst command the waters to be gathered together
	6:47	where the water had been gathered together
	6:50	for the 7th part where the water had been gathered together
	7:95	being gathered into their chambers
	7:101	and afterwards they shall be gathered in their habitations
	11:2	and the clouds were gathered about him
	12:40	they all gathered together
	13:5	an innumerable multitude of men were gathered together
	13:8	all who gathered together against him
	13:34	and an innumerable multitude shall be gathered together
	13:39	gather to himself another multitude that was peaceable
	13:47	Therefore you saw the multitude gathered together in peace
	13:49	that are gathered together
	14:23	Go and gather the people
	14:27	and I gathered all the people together, and said
	16:25	The trees shall bear fruit, and who will gather it?
	16:30	or as when a vineyard is gathered
	16:43	like one who will not gather the grapes
	16:46	for strangers shall gather their fruits
4 Ma	2:9	nor gathers the last grapes from the vineyard
	18:23	are gathered together into the chorus of the fathers

GATHERING
			3 = 0.002 %
Jud	14:6	at the gathering of the people	
Sir	26:5	The slander of a city, the gathering of a mob	
2 Ma	14:15	and the gathering of the Gentiles	

GAUL
			1
1 Ma	8:2	and of the brave deeds which they were doing among the Gauls	

GAUNTLET
			1
4 Ma	9:26	and after fitting themselves with iron gauntlets having sharp hooks	

GAY
			1
Jud	10:3	and arrayed herself in her gayest apparel	

GAZA
			3 = 0.002 %
1 Ma	11:61	From there he departed to Gaza	
	11:61	but the men of Gaza shut him out	
	11:62	Then the people of Gaza pleaded with Jonathan	

GAZARA
			13 = 0.008 %
1 Ma	4:15	They pursued them to Gazara	
	7:45	from Adasa as far as Gazara	
	9:52	and Gazara, and the citadel	
	13:43	In those days Simon encamped against Gazara	
	13:53	and he dwelt in Gazara	
	14:7	he ruled over Gazara and Beth-zur and the citadel	
	14:34	and Gazara, which is on the borders of Azotus	
	15:28	You hold control of Joppa and Gazara	
	15:35	As for Joppa and Gazara, which you demand	
	16:1	John went up from Gazara	
	16:19	He sent other men to Gazara to do away with John	
	16:21	But some one ran ahead and reported to John at Gazara	
2 Ma	10:32	Timothy himself fled to a stronghold called Gazara	

GAZE, verb
			4 = 0.003 %
Wis	19:8	after gazing on marvellous wonders	
Sir	41:21	and of gazing at another man's wife	
1 Es	4:31	At this the king would gaze at her with mouth agape	
4 Ma	15:19	in his tortures gazing boldly at the same agonies	

GAZE, subst.
			1
2 Es	13:3	everything under his gaze trembled	

GAZELLE
			1
Sir	27:20	and has escaped like a gazelle from a snare	

GAZZAM
			1
1 Es	5:31	the sons of Chezib, the sons of Gazzam, the sons of Uzza	

GEBA
			2
Jud	3:10	here he camped between Geba and Scythopolis	
1 Es	5:20	The men of Ramah and Geba, 621	

GEDALIAH
			1
1 Es	9:22	and Nathanael, and Gedaliah, and Elasah	

GEHENNA
			1
2 Es	2:29	My hands will cover you, that your sons may not see Gehenna	

GEM
			1
Wis	7:9	Neither did I liken to her any priceless gem	

GENEALOGY
			1
1 Es	5:39	And when the genealogy of these men	

GENERAL, subst.
			17 = 0.011 %
Jud	2:4	the chief general of his army, second only to himself	
	2:14	and called together all the commanders, generals	
	4:1	that Holofernes, the general of Nebuchadnezzar	
	5:1	When Holofernes, the general of the Assyrian army	
	14:12	and they went to the generals and the captains	
1 Ma	8:10	and they sent a general against the Greeks and attacked them	
	10:65	and made him general and governor of the province	
2 Ma	8:9	a general and a man of experience in military service	
	9:19	Antiochus their king and general sends hearty greetings	
1 Es	3:2	and all the satraps and generals and governors	
	3:14	and the satraps and generals and governors and prefects	
	4:47	and governors and generals and satraps	
3 Ma	3:12	King Ptolemy Philopator to his generals and soldiers	
	4:4	were they being sent off, all together, by the generals	
	4:18	the task was impossible for all the generals in Egypt	
	6:41	to the generals in the cities	
	7:1	King Ptolemy Philopator to the generals in Egypt	

GENERAL, adj.
			6 = 0.004 %
Jud	7:29	Then great and general lamentation arose	
1 Ma	13:37	and we are ready to make a general peace with you	
2 Ma	3:18	to make a general supplication	
	9:21	for the general security of all	
3 Ma	7:12	granted them a general licence	
4 Ma	13:22	and from both general education and our discipline in the law of God	

GENERATION
			26 = 0.017 %
Tob	1:4	was consecrated and established for all generations for ever	
	13:10	to all generations for ever	
	13:11	Generations of generations will give you joyful praise	

	14:5	with a glorious building for all generations for ever
Jud	8:18	For never in our generation, nor in these present days
	8:32	which will go down through all generations of our descendants
Ad E	10:13	from generation to generation for ever among his people Israel
Wis	3:19	For the end of an unrighteous generation is grievous
	7:27	in every generation she passes into holy souls
	14:6	left to the world the seed of a new generation
Sir	2:10	Consider the ancient generations
	14:18	so are the generations of flesh and blood :
	16:27	and their dominion for all generations
	24:33	and leave it to all future generations
	39:9	and his name will live through all generations
	44:1	and our fathers in their generations
	44:7	all these were honoured in their generations
	44:14	and their name lives to all generations
	44:16	he was an example of repentance to all generations
	45:26	and that their glory may endure throughout their generations
L Jr	6:3	for a long time, up to 7 generations
1 Ma	2:51	which they did in their generations
	2:61	And so observe, from generation to generation

GENERATIVE 1
Wis 1:14 and the generative forces of the world are wholesome

GENEROSITY 1
2 Ma 13:23 and showed generosity to the holy place

GENEROUS 2
Sir 14:5 If a man is mean to himself, to whom will he be generous ?
40:14 A generous man will be made glad

GENEROUSLY 3 = 0.002 %
Sir 35:8 Glorify the Lord generously
35:10 and as generously as your hand has found
3 Ma 7:18 for the king had generously provided

GENNAEUS 1
2 Ma 12:2 Timothy and Apollonius the son of Gennaeus

GENNESARET 1
1 Ma 11:67 Jonathan and his army encamped by the waters of Gennesaret

GENTILE 68 = 0.044 %

Tob	1:10	all my brethren and my relatives ate the food of the Gentiles
	14:6	Then all the Gentiles will turn
	14:7	All the Gentiles will praise the Lord
Jud	4:12	to the malicious joy of the Gentiles
	8:22	all this he will bring upon our heads among the Gentiles
1 Ma	1:11	with the Gentiles round about us
	1:13	He authorized them to observe the ordinances of the Gentiles
	1:14	according to Gentile custom
	1:15	They joined with the Gentiles and sold themselves to do evil
	1:43	All the Gentiles accepted the command of the king
	2:12	the Gentiles have profaned it
	2:18	as all the Gentiles and the men of Judah
	2:40	and refuse to fight with the Gentiles
	2:44	the survivors fled to the Gentiles for safety
	2:48	They rescued the law out of the hands of the Gentiles and kings
	2:68	Pay back the Gentiles in full
	3:10	But Apollonius gathered together Gentiles
	3:25	and terror fell upon the Gentiles round about them
	3:26	and the Gentiles talked of the battles of Judas
	3:45	it was a lodging place for the Gentiles
	3:48	to inquire into those matters about which the Gentiles
	3:52	And behold, the Gentiles are assembled against us to destroy us
	3:58	Be ready early in the morning to fight with these Gentiles
	4:7	And they saw the camp of the Gentiles, strong and fortified
	4:11	Then all the Gentiles will know
	4:14	The Gentiles were crushed and fled into the plain
	4:45	for the Gentiles had defiled it
	4:54	and on the very day that the Gentiles had profaned it
	4:58	and the reproach of the Gentiles was removed
	4:60	to keep the Gentiles from coming
	5:1	When the Gentiles round about heard
	5:9	Now the Gentiles in Gilead gathered together
	5:10	The Gentiles around us have gathered together against us
	5:15	and all Galilee of the Gentiles, to annihilate us
	5:19	but do not engage in battle with the Gentiles until we return
	5:21	and fought many battles against the Gentiles
	5:21	and the Gentiles were crushed before him
	5:22	and as many as 3,000 of the Gentiles fell
	5:38	All the Gentiles around us have gathered to him
	5:43	All the Gentiles were defeated before him
	5:57	on the Gentiles around us
	5:63	in all Israel and among all the Gentiles
	6:18	and strengthen the Gentiles
	6:53	those who found safety in Judea from the Gentiles
	7:23	it was more than the Gentiles had done
	13:41	In the 170th year the yoke of the Gentiles was removed from Israel

	14:36	so that the Gentiles were put out of the country
2 Ma	1:27	set free those who are slaves among the Gentiles
	1:27	and let the Gentiles know that thou art our God
	6:4	by the Gentiles, who dallied with harlots
	8:5	the Gentiles could not withstand him
	8:9	in command of no fewer than 20,000 Gentiles of all nations
	8:16	and not to fear the great multitude of Gentiles
	8:17	which the Gentiles had committed against the holy place
	12:13	and inhabited by all sorts of Gentiles
	13:11	fall into the hands of the blasphemous Gentiles
	14:14	And the Gentiles throughout Judea
	14:15	and the gathering of the Gentiles
	14:38	when there was no mingling with the Gentiles
	15:8	not to fear the attack of the Gentiles
	15:10	at the same time pointing out the perfidy of the Gentiles
3 Ma	4:1	a feast at public expense was arranged for the Gentiles
	5:6	For to the Gentiles it appeared
	5:13	to the arrogant Gentiles
	6:9	by the abominable and lawless Gentiles
	6:13	And let the Gentiles cower today
	6:15	Let it be shown to all the Gentiles
2 Es	4:23	why Israel has been given over to the Gentiles as a reproach

GENTLE 3 = 0.002 %
Wis 2:19 that we may find out how gentle he is
18:14 For while gentle silence enveloped all things
2 Ma 15:12 of modest bearing and gentle manner

GENTLEMAN 7 = 0.005 %
1 Es 3:18 Gentlemen, how is wine the strongest ?
3:24 Gentlemen, is not wine the strongest
4:2 Gentlemen, are not men strongest
4:12 Gentlemen, why is not the king the strongest
4:14 Gentlemen, is not the king great, and are not men many
4:32 Gentlemen, why are not women strong
4:34 Gentlemen, are not women strong ?

GENTLENESS 1
Ad E 15:8 Then God changed the spirit of the king to gentleness

GENTLY 1
Sir 4:8 and answer him peaceably and gently

GENUINE 1
Ad E 11:1 which they said was genuine

GENUINELY 1
2 Ma 14:8 first because I am genuinely concerned

GERAR 1
2 Ma 13:24 left Hegemonides as governor from Ptolemais to Gerar

GERGESITE 1
Jud 5:16 and the Shechemites and all the Gergesites

GERIZIM 2
2 Ma 5:23 and at Gerizim, Andronicus
6:2 and to call the one in Gerizim the temple of Zeus

GERSHOM 1
1 Es 8:29 Of the sons of Phinehas, Gershom

GESTATION 1
4 Ma 13:21 When they were born after an equal time of gestation

GET 50 = 0.033 %

Tob	2:13	So I said to her, Where did you get the kid ?
	5:3	and go and get the money
	5:16	Then he said to Tobias, Get ready for the journey
	9:2	and get the money for me
Jud	6:13	However, they got under the shelter of the hill
	7:13	for this is where all the people of Bethulia get their water
	7:13	that not a man gets out of the city
	12:3	where can we get more like it for you ?
	15:7	got a great amount of booty
Wis	7:14	those who get it obtain friendship with God
	8:18	I went about seeking how to get her for myself
	15:12	for he says one must get money however one can, even by base means
Sir	6:27	and when you get hold of her, do not let her go
	24:6	and in every people and nation I have gotten a possession
	27:1	and whoever seeks to get rich will avert his eyes
	29:5	A man will kiss another's hands until he gets a loan
	36:24	He who acquires a wife gets his best possession
	40:6	He gets little or no rest
	51:25	Get these things for yourselves without money
	51:28	Get instruction with a large sum of silver
Bar	3:17	in which men trust, and there is no end to their getting
	3:18	those who scheme to get silver, and are anxious
1 Ma	3:41	and went to the camp to get the sons of Israel for slaves

	5:27	the enemy are getting ready to attack the strongholds tomorrow
	5:48	Let us pass through your land to get to our land
	6:46	He got under the elephant
	8:3	to get control of the silver and gold mines there
	10:23	Alexander has gotten ahead of us
	11:1	and he tried to get possession of Alexander's kingdom by trickery
	13:17	he sent to get the money and the sons
	13:22	So Trypho got all his cavalry ready to go
	16:13	he determined to get control of the country
2 Ma	1:20	sent the descendants of the priests who had hidden the fire to get it
	2:15	So if you have need of them, send people to get them for you
	3:32	And the high priest, fearing that the king might get the notion
	5:7	and in the end got only disgrace from his conspiracy
	7:11	and said nobly, I got these from Heaven
	8:5	As soon as Maccabeus got his army organized
	8:30	and got possession of some exceedingly high strongholds
	9:4	For in his arrogance he said, When I get there
	11:6	When Maccabeus and his men got word
	12:28	and they got the city into their hands
	13:13	and get possession of the city
	13:23	he got word that Philip
	15:7	that he would get help from the Lord
1 Es	1:31	And he got into his 2nd chariot
2 Es	5:27	thou hast gotten for thyself one people
	7:59	for he who has what is hard to get
4 Ma	2:18	the temperate mind is able to get the better of the emotions
	5:32	Therefore get your torture wheels ready

GET away   3 = 0.002 %

2 Ma	5:27	got away to the wilderness
	8:13	ran off and got away
	11:12	Most of them got away stripped and wounded

GET back   4 = 0.003 %

Sir	29:6	If the lender exerts pressure, he will hardly get back half
2 Ma	3:38	send him there, for you will get him back thoroughly scourged
	7:11	and from him I hope to get them back again
	7:29	I may get you back again with your brothers

GET up   8 = 0.005 %

Tob	8:4	Tobias got up from the bed and said, Sister, get up
	9:6	In the morning they both got up early
Jud	12:15	So she got up and arrayed herself in all her woman's finery
Sir	8:11	Do not get up and leave an insolent fellow
	31:21	get up in the middle of the meal
2 Es	10:3	I got up in the night and fled
4 Ma	6:8	to make him get up again after he fell

GIANT   7 = 0.005 %

Jud	16:7	nor did tall giants set upon him
Wis	14:6	when arrogant giants were perishing
Sir	16:7	He was not propitiated for the ancient giants
	47:4	In his youth did he not kill a giant
Bar	3:26	The giants were born there, who were famous of old
1 Ma	3:3	like a giant he put on his breastplate
3 Ma	2:4	among whom were even giants

GIDDEL   1

1 Es	5:33	the sons of Lozon, the sons of Giddel

GIDEON   1

Jud	8:1	son of Ananias, son of Gideon, son of Raphaim

GIFT   50 = 0.033 %

Tob	2:14	as a gift in addition to my wages
	4:7	and do not let your eye begrudge the gift when you make it
	4:8	make your gift from them in proportion
	4:16	and do not let your eye begrudge the gift when you make it
	13:11	bearing gifts in their hands, gifts for the King of heaven
Jud	16:18	their freewill offerings, and their gifts
Wis	7:14	commended for the gifts that come from instruction
	8:21	and it was a mark of insight to know whose gift she was
Sir	1:10	She dwells with all flesh according to his gift
	4:3	nor delay your gift to a beggar
	7:9	Do not say, He will consider the multitude of my gifts
	7:28	that equals their gift to you ?
	7:31	the gift of the shoulders, the sacrifice of sanctification
	11:17	The gift of the Lord endures for those who are godly
	17:5	as 6th he distributed to them the gift of mind
	18:15	nor cause grief by your words when you present a gift
	18:16	So a word is better than a gift
	18:17	Indeed, does not a word surpass a good gift ?
	18:18	and the gift of a grudging man makes the eyes dim
	20:10	There is a gift that profits you nothing
	20:10	and there is a gift that brings a double return
	20:14	A fool's gift will profit you nothing
	20:29	Presents and gifts blind the eyes of the wise
	26:14	A silent wife is a gift of the Lord

	32:13	and satisfies you with his good gifts
	34:18	the gifts of the lawless are not acceptable
	35:9	With every gift show a cheerful face
	38:2	and he will receive a gift from the king
	41:21	of taking away some one's portion or gift
	41:22	and do not upbraid after making a gift
L Jr	6:27	but gifts are placed before them just as before the dead
1 Ma	2:18	with silver and gold and many gifts
	3:30	as he had before for his expenses and for the gifts
	10:24	and promise them honour and gifts
	10:28	We will grant you many immunities and give you gifts
	10:39	I have given as a gift to the sanctuary in Jerusalem
	10:54	and will make gifts to you and to her
	10:60	he gave them and their friends silver and gold and many gifts
	11:24	taking silver and gold and clothing and numerous other gifts
	12:43	and he gave him gifts
	16:19	so that he might give them silver and gold and gifts
2 Ma	1:35	he exchanged many excellent gifts
	15:16	Take this holy sword, a gift from God
1 Es	2:7	with gifts, and with horses and cattle
	3:5	Darius the king will give rich gifts
	8:13	and to carry to Jerusalem the gifts for the Lord of Israel
3 Ma	1:7	By doing this, and by endowing their sacred enclosures with gifts
	1:8	to greet him, to bring him gifts of welcome
4 Ma	5:9	and wrong to spurn the gifts of nature

GIHON   1

Sir	24:27	like the Gihon at the time of vintage

GILEAD   11 = 0.007 %

Jud	1:8	and those among the nations of Carmel and Gilead
	15:5	and those in Gilead and in Galilee outflanked them
1 Ma	5:9	Now the Gentiles in Gilead gathered together
	5:17	I and Jonathan my brother will go to Gilead
	5:20	and 8,000 to Judas for Gilead
	5:25	to their brethren in Gilead :
	5:27	and some have been shut up in the other cities of Gilead
	5:36	Maked, and Bosor, and the other cities of Gilead
	5:45	Then Judas gathered together all the Israelites in Gilead
	5:55	Now while Judas and Jonathan were in Gilead
	13:22	He marched off and went into the land of Gilead

GILGAL   1

1 Ma	9:2	They went by the road which leads to Gilgal

GIRD   8 = 0.005 %

Jud	4:10	they all girded themselves with sackcloth
	4:14	with their loins girded with sackcloth
	8:5	and girded sackcloth about her loins
1 Ma	3:58	And Judas said, Gird yourselves and be valiant
2 Ma	3:19	Women, girded with sackcloth under their breasts
	10:25	and girded their loins with sackcloth
3 Ma	7:5	and, girding themselves
2 Es	16:2	Gird yourselves with sackcloth and haircloth

GIRD on   1

1 Ma	3:3	he girded on his armour of war and waged battles

GIRDLE   1

Jud	9:2	who had loosed the girdle of a virgin to defile her

GIRL   4 = 0.003 %

Tob	6:12	The girl is also beautiful and sensible
	6:13	I have heard that the girl has been given to 7 husbands
	7:17	and the girl began to weep
L Jr	6:9	as they would for a girl who loves ornaments

GIVE   450 = 0.293 %

Tob	1:6	I would give these to the priests, the sons of Aaron, at the altar
	1:7	Of all my produce I would give a tenth to the sons of Levi
	1:8	the 3rd tenth I would give to those to whom it was my duty
	1:13	Then the Most High gave me favour
	1:17	I would give my bread to the hungry
	2:12	Once when they paid her wages, they also gave her a kid
	2:14	And she said, It was given to me
	3:8	because she had been given to 7 husbands
	3:17	to give Sarah the daughter of Raguel
	4:7	Give alms from your possessions to all who live uprightly
	4:8	if few, do not be afraid to give
	4:16	Give of your bread to the hungry
	4:16	Give all your surplus to charity
	4:17	but give none to sinners
	4:19	but the Lord himself gives all good things
	5:3	Then Tobit gave him the receipt, and said to him
	5:19	For the life that is given to us by the Lord
	6:7	if a demon or evil spirit gives trouble to any one
	6:10	I will suggest that she be given to you in marriage
	6:12	cannot give her to another man
	6:13	I have heard that the girl has been given to 7 husbands
	6:15	for this very night she will be given to you in marriage

	7:11	I have given my daughter to 7 husbands
	7:13	he gave her to Tobias to be his wife, saying, Here she is
	8:6	and gavest him Eve his wife as a helper and support
	8:19	After this he gave a wedding feast for them
	9:5	He gave him the receipt
	9:5	and gave them to him
	10:2	and there is no one to give him the money ?
	10:10	So Raguel arose and gave him his wife Sarah
	11:17	And Tobit gave thanks before them
	12:1	and he must also be given more
	12:2	to give him half of what I have brought back
	12:6	and said to them : Praise God and give thanks to him
	12:6	exalt him and give thanks to him
	12:6	Do not be slow to give him thanks
	12:8	It is better to give alms than to treasure up gold
	12:20	And now give thanks to God
	13:6	give thanks to him with your full voice
	13:6	I give him thanks in the land of my captivity
	13:8	Let all men speak, and give him thanks in Jerusalem
	13:10	Give thanks worthily to the Lord
	13:11	Generations of generations will give you joyful praise
	13:18	and will give praise, saying
	14:2	He gave alms
	14:7	and his people will give thanks to God
	14:10	Ahikar gave alms and escaped the deathtrap
	14:11	and Tobias gave him a magnificent funeral
	14:13	and he gave his father-in-law and mother-in-law
Jud	**3**:8	for it had been given to him
	4:8	had given order
	6:21	and gave a banquet for the elders
	7:16	and he gave orders to do as they had said
	8:25	let us give thanks to the Lord our God
	9:2	to whom thou gavest a sword
	9:4	and thou gavest their wives for a prey
	9:9	give to me, a widow, the strength to do what I plan
	10:5	And she gave her maid a bottle of wine and a flask of oil
	10:5	and gave them to her to carry
	10:13	to give him a true report
	13:7	Give me strength this day, O Lord God of Israel !
	13:9	and gave Holofernes' head to her maid
	14:13	as to come down against us and to give battle
	15:11	They gave Judith the tent of Holofernes
	15:12	and gave them to the women who were with her
	16:17	fire and worms he will give to their flesh
	16:19	which the people had given her
	16:19	she gave as a votive offering to the Lord
Ad E	**14**:6	and thou hast given us into the hands of our enemies
	14:12	and give me courage
	16:20	And give them reinforcements
Wis	**6**:2	Give ear, you that rule over multitudes
	6:3	For your dominion was given you from the Lord
	6:18	and giving heed to her laws is assurance of immortality
	7:7	Therefore I prayed, and understanding was given me
	7:17	For it is he who gave me unerring knowledge of what exists
	8:9	knowing that she would give me good counsel
	8:12	and when I speak they will give heed
	8:21	unless God gave her to me
	9:4	give me the wisdom that sits by thy throne
	9:8	Thou hast given command to build a temple
	9:17	Who has learned thy counsel, unless thou hast given wisdom
	10:2	and gave him strength to rule all things
	10:10	and gave him knowledge of angels
	10:12	in his arduous contest she gave him the victory
	10:14	and she gave him everlasting honour
	10:17	She gave to holy men the reward of their labours
	11:4	and water was given them out of flinty rock
	11:7	thou gavest them abundant water unexpectedly
	12:9	though thou wast not unable to give the ungodly
	12:10	thou gavest them a chance to repent
	12:19	because thou givest repentance for sins
	12:21	to whose fathers thou gavest oaths
	13:10	are the men who give the name gods
	13:14	giving it a coat of red paint and colouring its surface red
	14:3	because thou hast given it a path in the sea
	16:20	thou didst give thy people the food of angels
	16:28	to give thee thanks
	17:5	And no power of fire was able to give light
	18:4	was to be given to the world
	18:22	appealing to the oaths and covenants given to our fathers
	19:12	for, to give them relief, quails came up from the sea
Sir pr.		Whereas many great teachings have been given to us
	1:12	and gives gladness and joy and long life
	3:31	Whoever requites favours gives thought to the future
	4:5	nor give a man occasion to curse you
	4:11	Wisdom exalts her sons and gives help to those who seek her
	4:15	and whoever gives heed to her will dwell secure
	6:28	For at last you will find the rest she gives
	6:37	It is he who will give insight to your mind
	7:10	nor neglect to give alms
	7:25	Give a daughter in marriage

7:25	But give her to a man of understanding
7:31	and give him his portion, as is commanded you :
7:33	Give graciously to all the living
8:9	and learn how to give an answer in time of need
8:13	Do not give surety beyond your means
8:13	but if you give surety, be concerned as one who must pay
9:2	Do not give yourself to a woman
9:6	Do not give yourself to harlots
11:33	lest he give you a lasting blemish
12:3	or to him who does not give alms
12:4	Give to the godly man, but do not help the sinner
12:5	Do good to the humble, but do not give to the ungodly
12:5	hold back his bread, and do not give it to him
12:7	Give to the good man, but do not help the sinner
13:6	he will smile at you and give you hope
14:13	and reach out and give to him as much as you can
14:16	Give, and take and beguile yourself
15:3	and give him the water of wisdom to drink
15:17	and whichever he chooses will be given to him
15:20	and he has not given any one permission to sin
17:2	He gave to men few days, a limited time
17:6	he gave them ears and a mind for thinking
17:9	And he gave them to boast of his marvels for ever
17:14	And he gave commandment to each of them
17:27	as do those who are alive and give thanks ?
18:4	To none has he given power
20:15	He gives little and upbraids much
23:4	do not give me haughty eyes
24:8	Then the Creator of all things gave me a commandment
24:11	In the beloved city likewise he gave me a resting place
24:18	being eternal, I therefore am given to all my children
26:19	and do not give your strength to strangers
26:23	A godless wife is given as a portion to a lawless man
26:23	but a pious wife is given to the man who fears the Lord
27:14	The talk of men given to swearing
27:23	and with your own words he will give offence
28:8	for a man given to anger will kindle strife
29:15	for he has given his life for you
29:27	Give place, stranger, to an honoured person
30:9	play with him, and he will give you grief
30:11	Give him no authority in his youth
30:25	will give heed to the food he eats
31:17	and do not be insatiable, lest you give offence
32:22	and give good heed to your paths
32:24	He who believes the law gives heed to the commandments
33:13	to give them as he decides
33:19	do not give power over yourself, as long as you live
33:19	and do not give your property to another
34:1	and dreams give wings to fools
34:2	so is he who gives heed to dreams
34:6	do not give your mind to them
34:17	He lifts up the soul and gives light to the eyes
35:2	and he who gives alms sacrifices a thank offering
35:10	Give to the Most High as he has given
36:11	and give them their inheritance, as at the beginning
37:7	but some give counsel in their own interest
37:21	for grace was not given him by the Lord
37:27	see what is bad for it and do not give it that
38:6	And he gave skill to men
38:12	And give the physician his place, for the Lord created him
38:20	Do not give your heart to sorrow
39:6	and give thanks to the Lord in prayer
39:15	ascribe majesty to his name and give thanks to him
41:19	of surliness in receiving and giving
44:3	giving counsel by their understanding
44:22	To Isaac also he gave the same assurance
44:23	and gave him his inheritance
45:3	He gave him commands for his people
45:5	and gave him the commandments face to face
45:7	and gave him the priesthood of the people
45:17	In his commandments he gave him authority in statutes and judgments
45:20	He added glory to Aaron and gave him a heritage
45:21	which he gave to him and his descendants
46:1	so that he might give Israel its inheritance
46:9	And the Lord gave Caleb strength
47:5	and he gave him strength in his right hand
47:8	In all that he did he gave thanks to the Holy One
47:10	He gave beauty to the feasts
47:11	he gave him the covenant of kings
47:13	and God gave him rest on every side
47:22	so he gave a remnant to Jacob
47:23	and gave to Ephraim a sinful way
49:5	for they gave their power to others
50:23	May he give us gladness of heart
51:1	I will give thanks to thee, O Lord and King
51:1	I give thanks to thy name
51:12	Therefore I will give thanks to thee and praise thee
51:17	to him who gives me wisdom I will give glory
51:22	The Lord gave me a tongue as my reward

	51:30	and in God's time he will give you your reward
Bar	1:6	and they collected money, each giving what he could
	1:12	And the Lord will give us strength
	1:12	and he will give light to our eyes
	1:20	to give us a land flowing with milk and honey
	2:4	And he gave them into subjection to all the kingdoms around us
	2:21	and you will remain in the land which I gave to your fathers
	2:31	I will give them a heart that obeys and ears that hear
	2:34	which I swore to give to their fathers
	2:35	from the land which I have given them
	3:9	give ear, and learn wisdom !
	3:23	nor given thought to her paths
	3:27	God did not choose them, nor give them the way to knowledge
	3:36	and gave her to Jacob his servant
	4:3	Do not give your glory to another
L Jr	6:1	to give them the message which God had commanded him
	6:11	and even give some of it to the harlots in the brothel
	6:28	but give none to the poor or helpless
	6:35	Likewise they are not able to give either wealth or money
	6:53	For they cannot set up a king over a country or give rain to men
	6:67	or shine like the sun or give light like the moon
P Az	9	Thou hast given us into the hands of lawless enemies
	20	and give glory to thy name, O Lord !
	67	Give thanks to the Lord, for he is good
	68	sing praise to him and give thanks to him
Sus	13:20	so give your consent, and lie with us
	13:50	for God has given you that right
Bel	14:26	But if you, O king, will give me permission
	14:26	The king said, I give you permission
	14:32	and every day they had been given 2 human bodies and 2 sheep
	14:32	but these were not given to them now
1 Ma	2:24	He gave vent to righteous anger
	2:50	and give your lives for the covenant of our fathers
	3:28	and gave a year's pay to his forces
	3:30	which he used to give more lavishly than preceding kings
	3:34	and gave him orders about all that he wanted done
	3:54	Then they sounded the trumpets and gave a loud shout
	4:30	and didst give the camp of the Philistines
	4:50	and these gave light in the temple
	5:19	and he gave them this command, Take charge of this people
	5:42	and gave them this command
	5:62	through whom deliverance was given to Israel
	6:15	He gave him the crown and his robe and the signet
	6:44	So he gave his life to save his people
	6:57	So he quickly gave orders to depart
	6:61	So the king and the commanders gave them their oath
	6:62	and gave orders to tear down the wall all around
	8:7	should pay a heavy tribute and give hostages
	8:8	These they took from him and gave to Eumenes the king
	8:26	they shall not give or supply grain
	8:28	And to the enemy allies shall be given no grain
	9:54	Alcimus gave orders to tear down the wall
	9:55	or give commands concerning his house
	10:6	So Demetrius gave him authority to recruit troops
	10:8	that the king had given him authority to recruit troops
	10:28	We will grant you many immunities and give you gifts
	10:32	and give it to the high priest
	10:36	and let the maintenance be given them
	10:39	I have given as a gift to the sanctuary in Jerusalem
	10:41	they shall give from now on for the service of the temple
	10:54	give me now your daughter as my wife
	10:58	and Ptolemy gave him Cleopatra his daughter in marriage
	10:60	he gave them and their friends silver and gold and many gifts
	10:62	The king gave orders to take off Jonathan's garments
	10:89	such as it is the custom to give to the kinsmen of kings
	10:89	He also gave him Ekron and all its environs as his possession
	11:9	and I will give you in marriage my daughter
	11:10	For I now regret that I gave him my daughter
	11:12	and gave her to Demetrius
	11:23	he gave orders to continue the siege
	11:37	and let it be given to Jonathan
	12:4	And the Romans gave them letters to the people
	12:25	for he gave them no opportunity to invade his own country
	12:43	and he gave him gifts
	14:8	the ground gave its increase
	14:48	And they gave orders
	15:31	or else give me for them 500 talents of silver
	15:33	but Simon gave him this reply :
	15:35	for them we will give a 100 talents
	15:38	and gave him troops of infantry and cavalry
	16:15	he gave them a great banquet, and hid men there
	16:19	so that he might give them silver and gold and gifts
2 Ma	1:3	May he give you all a heart to worship him
	1:18	and the feast of the fire given
	2:2	and that the prophet after giving them the law
	3:15	upon him who had given the law about deposits
	4:9	if permission were given to establish by his authority
	4:30	revolted because their cities had been given
	4:32	and gave them to Andronicus
	4:34	offered him sworn pledges and gave him his right hand
	7:3	and gave orders that pans and cauldrons be heated
	7:14	and to cherish the hope that God gives
	7:22	It was not I who gave you life and breath
	7:30	that was given to our fathers through Moses
	8:23	and gave the watchword, God's help
	8:27	giving great praise and thanks to the Lord
	8:28	After the sabbath they gave some of the spoils
	8:30	giving to those who had been tortured
	9:7	and giving orders to hasten the journey
	10:7	who had given success to the purifying of his own holy place
	10:10	and will give a brief summary
	10:38	and gives them the victory
	11:26	and give them pledges of friendship
	11:35	we also give consent
	12:5	he gave orders to his men
	12:11	promising to give him cattle
	13:15	He gave his men the watchword, God's victory
	13:21	gave secret information to the enemy
	13:22	gave pledges, received theirs, withdrew
	14:19	to give and receive pledges of friendship
	15:8	which the Almighty would give them
	15:10	And when he had aroused their courage, he gave his orders
	15:15	and gave to Judas a golden sword
	15:15	and as he gave it he addressed him thus :
	15:33	and said that he would give it piecemeal to the birds
1 Es	1:6	which was given to Moses
	1:7	And Josiah gave to the people who were present
	1:7	these were given from the king's possessions, as he promised
	1:8	to the priests for the passover
	1:9	gave the Levites for the passover 5,000 sheep and 700 calves
	1:52	because of their ungodly acts he gave command
	1:53	old man or child, for he gave them all into their hands
	2:11	he gave them to Mithridates his treasurer
	2:12	and by him they were given to Shesh-Bazzar the governor of Judea
	2:27	and that the men in it were given to rebellion and war
	3:1	Now King Darius gave a great banquet
	3:5	Darius the king will give rich gifts
	3:9	they will give him the writing
	3:9	the victory shall be given according to what is written
	3:13	they took the writing and gave it to him, and he read it
	4:15	Women gave birth to the king
	4:22	and bring everything and give it to women ?
	4:42	even beyond what is written, and we will give it to you
	4:47	that they should give escort to him
	4:51	that 20 talents a year should be given
	4:60	Blessed art thou, who hast given me wisdom
	4:60	I give thee thanks, O Lord of our fathers
	4:62	because he had given them release and permission
	5:45	and that they would give to the sacred treasury for the work
	5:54	And they gave money to the masons and the carpenters
	5:61	and they sang hymns, giving thanks to the Lord
	6:29	a portion be scrupulously given to these men
	8:3	which was given by the God of Israel
	8:6	by the prosperous journey which the Lord gave them
	8:10	I have given orders that those of the Jewish nation
	8:14	together with what is given by the nation
	8:17	which are given you for the use of the temple of your God
	8:19	they shall take care to give him
	8:49	whom David and the leaders had given
	8:55	and all Israel had given
	8:56	I weighed and gave to them 650 talents of silver
	8:79	and to give us food in the time of our servitude
	8:80	so that they have given us food
	8:81	to give us a stronghold in Judea and Jerusalem
	8:82	which thou didst give by thy servants the prophets, saying
	8:84	Therefore do not give your daughters in marriage to their sons
	8:87	and give us such a root as this
	9:8	Now then make confession and give glory to the Lord
	9:20	and to give rams in expiation of their error
	9:39	which had been given by the Lord God of Israel
	9:41	and all the multitude gave attention to the law
	9:54	and to give portions to those who had none
3 Ma	1:1	he gave orders to all his forces
	1:4	promising to give them each 2 minas of gold
	2:2	the only ruler, almighty, give attention to us
	2:20	and give us peace
	3:2	a pretext being given by a report
	3:25	Therefore we have given orders that
	3:28	Any one willing to give information
	5:3	When he had given these orders he returned to his feasting
	5:15	and he gave him an account of the situation
	5:19	he had carried out completely the order given him
	5:21	all those present readily and joyfully with one accord gave their approval
	5:31	who give me no ground for complaint
	5:37	must I give you orders about these things ?
	5:49	and giving way to lamentation and groans they kissed each other
	6:33	gave thanks to heaven unceasingly and lavishly
	7:16	joyfully and loudly giving thanks

2 Es	1 : 13	I gave you Moses as leader and Aaron as priest
	1 : 15	I gave you camps for your protection
	1 : 19	I pitied your groaning and gave you manna for food
	1 : 24	I will turn to other nations and will give them my name
	1 : 35	I will give your houses to a people that will come
	1 : 39	to them I will give as leaders Abraham, Isaac
	2 : 1	and I gave them commandments through my servants the prophets
	2 : 10	Tell my people that I will give them the kingdom of Jerusalem
	2 : 10	which I was going to give to Israel
	2 : 11	and will give to these others the everlasting habitations
	2 : 12	The tree of life shall give them fragrant perfume
	2 : 20	secure justice for the fatherless, give to the needy
	2 : 23	and I will give you the first place in my resurrection
	2 : 26	Not one of the servants whom I have given you will perish
	2 : 34	he will give you everlasting rest
	2 : 37	giving thanks to him who has called you to heavenly kingdoms
	3 : 5	and it gave thee Adam, a lifeless body ?
	3 : 15	and thou gavest to him Isaac
	3 : 15	and to Isaac thou gavest Jacob and Esau
	3 : 19	to give the law to the descendants of Jacob
	4 : 9	and you have given me no answer about them !
	5 : 27	thou hast given the law which is approved by all
	5 : 45	that thou wilt certainly give life at one time to thy creation ?
	5 : 48	Even so have I given the womb of the earth
	5 : 50	Since thou hast now given me the opportunity
	6 : 21	and women with child shall give birth to premature children at 3 or 4 months
	6 : 51	And thou didst give Behemoth one of the parts
	6 : 52	but to Leviathan thou didst give the 7th part, the watery part
	6 : 58	have been given into their hands
	7 : 9	If now that city is given to a man for an inheritance
	7 : 78	as the spirit leaves the body to return again to him who gave it
	7 : 94	they kept the law which was given them in trust
	7 : 99	which those who would not give heed shall suffer hereafter
	7 : 100	Will time therefore be given to the souls
	7 : 135	and bountiful, because he would rather give than take away
	7 : 138	because if he did not give out of his goodness
	8 : 5	for you have been given only a short time to live
	8 : 6	and give us seed for our heart
	8 : 8	And because thou dost give life to the body
	8 : 24	and give ear to the petition of thy creature
	9 : 30	and give heed to my words, O descendants of Jacob
	9 : 45	and gave me a son
	9 : 45	and we gave great glory to the Mighty One
	10 : 14	given her fruit, that is, man, to him who made her
	10 : 24	and the Most High may give you rest
	10 : 37	to give your servant an explanation of this bewildering vision
	13 : 57	giving great glory and praise to the Most High
	14 : 31	Then land was given to you
	14 : 32	in due time he took from you what he had given
	14 : 38	Ezra, open your mouth and drink what I give you to drink
	14 : 42	And the Most High gave understanding to the 5 men
	14 : 46	in order to give them to the wise among your people
	15 : 20	to turn and repay what they have given them
	16 : 61	and gave him breath and life and understanding
4 Ma	1 : 6	but so that one may not give way to them
	1 : 12	giving glory to the all-wise God
	2 : 23	To the mind he gave the law
	5 : 25	the Creator of the world in giving us the law
	8 : 3	When the tyrant had given these orders, 7 brothers
	10 : 13	As for you, do not give way
	10 : 17	gave orders to cut his tongue
	11 : 12	because through these noble sufferings you give us
	13 : 13	who gave us our lives
	15 : 5	Considering that mothers are the weaker sex and give birth to many
	15 : 17	O woman, who alone gave birth to such complete devotion !
	15 : 23	But devout reason, giving her heart a man's courage
	16 : 13	and giving rebirth for immortality
	17 : 12	for on that day virtue gave the awards
	17 : 15	and gave the crown to its own athletes

GIVE back   6 = 0.004 %

Sir	7 : 28	and what can you give back to them
Bar	4 : 23	but God will give you back to me
2 Ma	7 : 23	will in his mercy give life and breath back to you again
	9 : 16	and the holy vessels he would give back
	14 : 46	to give them back to him again
2 Es	4 : 42	so also do these places hasten to give back those things

GIVE forth   1

Sir	24 : 15	I gave forth the aroma of spices

GIVE out   3 = 0.002 %

Jud	11 : 12	and their water has almost given out
Sir	42 : 7	and make a record of all that you give out or take in
3 Ma	4 : 20	had already given out

GIVE over   13 = 0.008 %

Tob	3 : 4	and thou gavest us over to plunder, captivity, and death
Sir	30 : 21	Do not give yourself over to sorrow
Bel	14 : 22	and gave Bel over to Daniel, who destroyed it and its temple
1 Ma	2 : 7	and to dwell there when it was given over to the enemy
	2 : 7	the sanctuary given over to aliens ?
1 Es	6 : 15	he gave them over
	8 : 77	and our priests were given over to the kings of the earth
3 Ma	5 : 17	to give themselves over to revelry
2 Es	4 : 23	why Israel has been given over to the Gentiles as a reproach
	4 : 23	has been given over to godless tribes
	5 : 28	And now, O Lord, why hast thou given over the one to the many
	10 : 23	and has been given over into the hands of those that hate us
4 Ma	18 : 3	Therefore those who gave over their bodies in suffering

GIVE up   21 = 0.014 %

Tob	10 : 7	for my father and mother have given up hope
Jud	4 : 12	not to give up their infants as prey
	7 : 13	So thirst will destroy them, and they will give up their city
	9 : 3	So thou gavest up their rulers to be slain
Wis	12 : 20	to give up their wickedness
Sir	14 : 2	and who has not given up his hope
	37 : 29	and do not give yourself up to food
	38 : 10	Give up your faults and direct your hands aright
	47 : 22	But the Lord will never give up his mercy
P Az	11	For thy name's sake do not give us up utterly
1 Ma	1 : 42	and that each should give up his customs
2 Ma	6 : 27	Therefore, by manfully giving up my life now
	7 : 37	I, like my brothers, give up body and life
	9 : 18	he gave up all hope for himself
1 Es	4 : 50	that the Idumeans should give up the villages of the Jews which they held
3 Ma	2 : 31	readily gave themselves up
2 Es	7 : 32	And the earth shall give up those who are asleep in it
	7 : 32	and the chambers shall give up the souls
	8 : 9	And when the womb gives up again what has been created in it
	16 : 78	It is shut off and given up to be consumed by fire
4 Ma	8 : 19	and give up this vain opinion

GIVER   1

2 Es	7 : 138	and he is called giver

GLAD   15 = 0.010 %

Tob	8 : 16	Blessed art thou, because thou hast made me glad
	13 : 13	Rejoice and be glad for the sons of the righteous
	13 : 14	and they will be made glad for ever
Sir	13 : 25	And a glad heart makes a cheerful countenance
	26 : 4	Whether rich or poor, his heart is glad
	31 : 27	It has been created to make men glad
	40 : 14	A generous man will be made glad
Bar	3 : 34	the stars shone in their watches, and were glad
	4 : 33	and was glad for your ruin
1 Ma	3 : 7	He embittered many kings, but he made Jacob glad by his deeds
2 Ma	6 : 30	but in my soul I am glad to suffer these things
	9 : 20	I am glad. As my hope is in heaven
	10 : 33	Then Maccabeus and his men were glad
2 Es	7 : 65	but let the beasts of the field be glad
	7 : 98	and shall be glad without fear

GLADDEN   6 = 0.004 %

Sir	3 : 5	will be gladdened by his own children
	4 : 18	Then she will come straight back to him and gladden him
	25 : 7	With 9 thoughts I have gladdened my heart
	36 : 22	A woman's beauty gladdens the countenance
	40 : 20	Wine and music gladden the heart
2 Ma	15 : 27	and were greatly gladdened by God's manifestation

GLADLY   5 = 0.003 %

1 Ma	1 : 43	Many even from Israel gladly adopted his religion
	3 : 2	they gladly fought for Israel
2 Ma	2 : 27	we will gladly endure the uncomfortable toil
3 Ma	3 : 15	gladly treating them well
4 Ma	10 : 20	Gladly, for the sake of God

GLADNESS   25 = 0.016 %

Ad E	10 : 13	with an assembly and joy and gladness before God
Wis	8 : 16	and life with her has no pain, but gladness and joy
Sir	1 : 11	and gladness and a crown of rejoicing
	1 : 12	and gives gladness and joy and long life
	6 : 31	and put her on like a crown of gladness
	15 : 6	He will find gladness and a crown of rejoicing
	30 : 16	and there is no gladness above joy of heart
	30 : 22	Gladness of heart is the life of man
	31 : 28	is rejoicing of heart and gladness of soul
	35 : 9	and dedicate your tithe with gladness
	50 : 23	May he give us gladness of heart
Bar	2 : 23	the voice of mirth and the voice of gladness
	3 : 34	They shone with gladness for him who made them
	4 : 23	with joy and gladness for ever
1 Ma	4 : 56	and offered burnt offerings with gladness

	4:58	There was very great gladness among the people
	4:59	with gladness and joy for 8 days
	5:54	So they went up to Mount Zion with gladness and joy
	7:48	and celebrated that day as a day of great gladness
	10:66	And Jonathan returned to Jerusalem in peace and gladness
2 Ma	3:30	was filled with joy and gladness
3 Ma	4:1	with shouts and gladness
2 Es	1:37	whose children rejoice with gladness
	2:3	I brought you up with gladness
	2:15	bring them up with gladness, as does the dove

GLAMOUR   1
2 Es	15:46	And you, Asia, who share in the glamour of Babylon

GLAZING   1
Sir	38:30	he sets his heart to finish the glazing

GLEAM   2
Sir	50:7	and like the rainbow gleaming in glorious clouds
1 Ma	6:39	and gleamed like flaming torches

GLEAMING   1
Sir	43:9	a gleaming array in the heights of the Lord

GLEAN   2
Sir	33:16	I was like one who gleans after the grape-gatherers
4 Ma	2:9	so that he neither gleans his harvest

GLITTER   1
1 Es	8:57	that glittered like gold

GLOOM   1
Ad E	11:8	And behold, a day of darkness and gloom

GLOOMY   2
Wis	17:4	and dismal phantoms with gloomy faces appeared
Sir	25:23	A dejected mind, a gloomy face, and a wounded heart

GLORIFY   24 = 0.016 %
Ad E	14:7	because we glorified their gods
Wis	8:3	She glorifies her noble birth by living with God
	18:8	thou didst call us to thyself and glorify us
	19:22	thou hast exalted and glorified thy people
Sir	3:4	and whoever glorifies his mother
	3:6	Whoever glorifies his father will have long life
	3:10	Do not glorify yourself by dishonouring your father
	3:20	he is glorified by the humble
	10:26	nor glorify yourself at a time when you are in want
	10:28	My son, glorify yourself with humility
	35:8	Glorify the Lord generously
	38:6	that he might be glorified in his marvellous works
	45:3	the Lord glorified him in the presence of kings
	47:6	So they glorified him for his ten thousands
P Az	3	and thy name is glorified for ever
	28	praised and glorified and blessed God in the furnace, saying :
	31	and to be extolled and highly glorified for ever
	34	and to be sung and glorified for ever
2 Ma	3:2	and glorified the temple with the finest presents
1 Es	8:25	to glorify his house which is in Jerusalem
	8:81	and glorified the temple of our Lord
3 Ma	2:9	and when you had glorified it by your magnificent manifestation
2 Es	7:98	and from whom they are to receive their reward when glorified
	9:31	and you shall be glorified through it for ever

GLORIOUS   37 = 0.024 %
Tob	8:5	and blessed be thy holy and glorious name for ever
	14:5	with a glorious building for all generations for ever
Jud	9:8	and to pollute the tabernacle where thy glorious name rests
	16:13	O Lord, thou art great and glorious
Wis	5:16	Therefore they will receive a glorious crown
	18:3	and a harmless sun for their glorious wandering
Sir	6:29	and her collar a glorious robe
	6:31	You will wear her like a glorious robe
	17:13	Their eyes saw his glorious majesty
	24:16	and my branches are glorious and graceful
	24:17	and my blossoms became glorious and abundant fruit
	27:8	and wear it as a glorious robe
	36:6	make thy hand and thy right arm glorious
	43:12	It encircles the heaven with its glorious arc
	45:7	and put a glorious robe upon him
	46:2	How glorious he was when he lifted his hands
	47:6	when the glorious diadem was bestowed upon him
	48:4	How glorious you were, O Elijah, in your wondrous deeds !
	50:5	How glorious he was when the people gathered round him
	50:7	and like the rainbow gleaming in glorious clouds
	50:11	When he put on his glorious robe
	50:11	he made the court of the sanctuary glorious
P Az	22	glorious over the whole world
	30	And blessed is thy glorious, holy name
1 Ma	2:9	her glorious vessels have been carried into captivity

	14:15	He made the sanctuary glorious
2 Ma	8:15	and because he had called them by his holy and glorious name
1 Es	1:56	and utterly destroyed all its glorious things
P Ma	3	and sealed it with thy terrible and glorious name
	5	for thy glorious splendour cannot be borne
3 Ma	2:14	dedicated to your glorious name
	5:8	and in a glorious manifestation rescue them
	6:18	Then the most glorious, almighty, and true God
	6:18	from which 2 glorious angels of fearful aspect descended
2 Es	2:39	have received glorious garments from the Lord
4 Ma	7:9	through your glorious endurance
	10:1	When he too had endured a glorious death, the 3rd was led in

GLORIOUSLY   5 = 0.003 %
Tob	12:7	but gloriously to reveal the works of God
	12:11	but gloriously to reveal the works of God
2 Ma	3:26	gloriously beautiful and splendidly dressed
3 Ma	6:39	on which the Lord of all most gloriously revealed his mercy
2 Es	8:29	but regard those who have gloriously taught thy law

GLORY, subst.   111 = 0.072 %
Tob	3:16	in the presence of the glory of the great God
	12:15	and enter into the presence of the glory of the Holy One
	13:14	for they will rejoice for you upon seeing all your glory
Jud	15:9	you are the great glory of Israel
Ad E	13:12	or pride or for any love of glory that I did this
	13:14	that I might not set the glory of man above the glory of God
	14:9	and to quench thy altar and the glory of thy house
	15:13	and my heart was shaken with fear at your glory
Wis	7:25	and a pure emanation of the glory of the Almighty
	8:10	Because of her I shall have glory among the multitudes
	9:10	and from the throne of thy glory send her
	9:11	and guard me with her glory
	15:9	and he counts it his glory that he moulds counterfeit gods
	18:24	and the glories of the fathers were engraved
Sir	1:11	The fear of the Lord is glory and exultation
	1:19	and he exalted the glory of those who held her fast
	3:10	for your father's dishonour is no glory to you
	3:11	For a man's glory comes from honouring his father
	4:13	Whoever holds her fast will inherit glory
	4:21	and there is a shame which is glory and favour
	5:13	Glory and dishonour come from speaking
	10:22	their glory is the fear of the Lord
	14:27	and will dwell in the midst of her glory
	17:13	and their ears heard the glory of his voice
	20:11	There are losses because of glory
	29:6	and instead of glory will repay him with dishonour
	36:14	and thy temple with thy glory
	40:27	and covers a man better than any glory
	42:16	and the work of the Lord is full of his glory
	42:17	that the universe may stand firm in his glory
	42:25	and who can have enough of beholding his glory ?
	43:1	the appearance of heaven in a spectacle of glory
	43:9	The glory of the stars is the beauty of heaven
	44:2	The Lord apportioned to them great glory
	44:7	and were the glory of their times
	44:13	and their glory will not be blotted out
	44:19	and no one has been found like him in glory
	45:2	He made him equal in glory to the holy ones
	45:3	and showed him part of his glory
	45:20	He added glory to Aaron and gave him a heritage
	45:23	Phinehas the son of Eleazar is the 3rd in glory
	45:26	and that their glory may endure throughout their generations
	47:8	the Most High, with ascriptions of glory
	47:11	and a throne of glory in Israel
	49:5	and their glory to a foreign nation
	49:8	It was Ezekiel who saw the vision of glory
	49:12	prepared for everlasting glory
	51:17	to him who gives me wisdom I will give glory
Bar	2:17	will not ascribe glory or justice to the Lord
	2:18	will ascribe to thee glory and righteousness, O Lord
	4:3	Do not give your glory to another
	4:24	which will come to you with great glory
	4:37	at the word of the Holy One, rejoicing in the glory of God
	5:1	and put on for ever the beauty of the glory from God
	5:2	put on your head the diadem of the glory of the Everlasting
	5:4	Peace of righteousness and glory of godliness
	5:6	carried in glory, as on a royal throne
	5:7	so that Israel may walk safely in the glory of God
	5:9	in the light of his glory
P Az	20	and give glory to thy name, O Lord !
	31	Blessed art thou in the temple of thy holy glory
1 Ma	1:40	Her dishonour now grew as great as her glory
	2:12	and our glory have been laid waste
	3:3	He extended the glory of his people
	11:51	So the Jews gained glory in the eyes of the king
	12:12	And we rejoice in your glory
	14:9	and the youths donned the glories and garments of war
	14:21	have told us about your glory and honour
	14:29	and they brought great glory to their nation

	14:35	and the glory which he had resolved to win for his nation
	15:9	so that your glory will become manifest in all the earth
2 Ma	**2**:8	and the glory of the Lord and the cloud will appear
	5:16	to enhance the glory and honour of the place
	5:20	was restored again in all its glory
	14:7	Therefore I have laid aside my ancestral glory
1 Es	**4**:17	they bring men glory
	4:59	and thine is the glory
	5:61	because his goodness and his glory are for ever upon all Israel
	9:8	Now then make confession and give glory to the Lord
P Ma	**15**	and thine is the glory for ever. Amen
3 Ma	**2**:9	for the glory of your great and honoured name
	2:16	But because you graciously bestowed your glory
2 Es	**2**:11	Moreover, I will take back to myself their glory
	2:36	receive the joy of your glory
	3:19	And thy glory passed through the 4 gates
	7:42	but only the splendour of the glory of the Most High
	7:60	because it is they who have made my glory to prevail now
	7:78	first of all it adores the glory of the Most High
	7:87	at seeing the glory of the Most High
	7:91	the glory of him who receives them
	7:95	and the glory which awaits them in the last days
	7:112	the full glory does not abide in it
	7:122	Or that the glory of the Most High will defend those
	8:21	and whose glory is beyond comprehension
	8:30	but love those who have always put their trust in thy glory
	8:49	in order to receive the greatest glory
	8:51	and inquire concerning the glory of those who are like yourself
	9:37	the law, however, does not perish but remains in its glory
	9:45	and we gave great glory to the Mighty One
	10:23	for she has now lost the seal of her glory
	10:50	has shown you the brilliance of her glory
	13:57	giving great glory and praise to the Most High
	15:46	and the glory of her person
	15:50	And the glory of your power shall wither like a flower
	15:60	and abolish a portion of your glory
	15:63	and abolish the glory of your countenance
	16:12	and before the glory of his power
	16:53	I have not sinned before God and his glory
4 Ma	**1**:12	giving glory to the all-wise God
	18:24	to whom be glory for ever and ever. Amen

GLORY, verb   9 = 0.006 %

Jud	**9**:7	they glory in the strength of their foot soldiers
	10:8	that the people of Israel may glory
Sir	**24**:1	and will glory in the midst of her people
	24:2	and in the presence of his host she will glory :
	30:3	and will glory in him in the presence of friends
	38:25	and who glories in the shaft of a goad
	39:8	and will glory in the law of the Lord's covenant
	50:20	and to glory in his name
2 Es	**15**:47	to please and glory in your lovers

GLORYING   1

Sir	**9**:16	and let your glorying be in the fear of the Lord

GLOW   2

Sir	**28**:12	If you blow on a spark, it will glow
2 Ma	**12**:9	so that the glow of the light was seen in Jerusalem, 30 miles distant

GLUE   1

Sir	**22**:7	is like one who glues potsherds together

GLUTTON   2

Sir	**31**:20	and of nausea and colic are with the glutton
4 Ma	**2**:7	a glutton, or even a drunkard can learn a better way

GLUTTONY   6 = 0.004 %

Sir	**23**:6	Let neither gluttony nor lust overcome me
	37:30	for overeating brings sickness, and gluttony leads to nausea
	37:31	Many have died of gluttony
3 Ma	**6**:36	not for drinking and gluttony
4 Ma	**1**:3	namely, gluttony and lust
	1:27	gluttony, and solitary gormandizing

GNASH   1

Sir	**30**:10	and in the end you will gnash your teeth

GNASHING   1

Sir	**51**:3	from the gnashings of teeth about to devour me

GNAT   1

Wis	**19**:10	the earth brought forth gnats

GO   262 = 0.171 %

Tob	**1**:3	and countrymen who went with me
	1:6	But I alone went often to Jerusalem for the feasts
	1:7	and I would go and spend the proceeds
	1:14	So I used to go into Media

	1:15	so that I could no longer go into Media
	1:19	Then one of the men of Nineveh went
	2:2	Go and bring whatever poor man of our brethren you may find
	2:7	When the sun had set I went
	2:10	I went to physicians, but they did not help me
	2:10	Ahikar, however, took care of me until he went to Elymais
	3:6	to go to the eternal abode
	3:9	Why do you beat us ? If they are dead, go with them !
	4:15	or let drunkenness go with you on your way
	5:3	Find a man to go with you
	5:3	and go and get the money
	5:4	So he went to look for a man
	5:5	Can you go with me to Rages in Media ?
	5:6	The angel replied, I will go with you
	5:8	And he said to him, Go, and do not delay
	5:8	I have found some one to go with me
	5:8	and whether he is a reliable man to go with you
	5:11	or for a man whom you will pay to go with your son ?
	5:13	when we went together to Jerusalem
	5:13	They did not go astray in the error of our brethren
	5:16	And his father said to him, Go with this man
	5:21	For a good angel will go with him
	6:17	You will save her, and she will go with you
	8:2	As he went he remembered the words of Raphael
	8:9	Then they both went to sleep for the night
	8:9	But Raguel arose and went and dug a grave
	8:11	Then Raguel went into his house
	9:2	and go to Gabael at Rages in Media
	10:5	Am I not distressed, my child, that I let you go
	11:1	After this Tobias went on his way
	11:4	So they went their way, and the dog went along behind them
	11:6	and so is the man who went with him !
	11:16	Those who saw him as he went were amazed
	12:1	My son, see to the wages of the man who went with you
	12:13	in order to go and lay out the dead
	14:4	Go to Media, my son
Jud	**2**:6	Go and attack the whole west country
	2:10	You shall go and seize all their territory for me in advance
	2:19	to go ahead of King Nebuchadnezzar
	2:20	Along with them went a mixed crowd like a swarm of locusts
	5:9	and go to the land of Canaan
	6:7	Now my slaves are going to take you back
	7:21	their cisterns were going dry
	8:35	Go in peace, and may the Lord God go before you
	8:36	So they returned from the tent and went to their posts
	9:5	and those that went before and those that followed
	10:2	and called her maid and went
	10:10	until she had gone down the mountain
	10:11	The women went straight on through the valley
	10:12	and where are you coming from, and where are you going ?
	10:13	and I will show him a way by which he can go
	10:15	Go at once to his tent
	10:19	for if we let them go
	12:11	Go now and persuade the Hebrew woman who is in your care
	12:12	For it will be a disgrace if we let such a woman go
	12:15	and her maid went and spread on the ground for her before Holofernes
	13:1	and they went to bed, for they all were weary
	13:10	as they were accustomed to go for prayer
	13:16	As the Lord lives, who has protected me in the way I went
	14:2	let every valiant man take his weapons and go out of the city
	14:3	Then they will seize their arms and go into the camp
	14:12	and they went to the generals and the captains
	14:15	he opened it and went into the bedchamber
	14:17	Then he went to the tent where Judith had stayed
	15:13	and she went before all the people in the dance
	16:21	and Judith went to Bethulia, and remained on her estate
Ad E	**15**:6	When she had gone through all the doors
	15:7	and collapsed upon the head of the maid who went before her
Wis	**1**:10	and the sound of murmurings does not go unheard
	4:2	and they long for it when it has gone
	6:16	because she goes about seeking those worthy of her
	8:18	I went about seeking how to get her for myself
	10:8	so that her failures could never go unnoticed
	12:24	For they went far astray on the paths of error, accepting as gods
	13:6	for perhaps they go astray while seeking God
	15:8	and after a little while goes to the earth
	17:1	therefore uninstructed souls have gone astray
	18:14	and night in its swift course was now half gone
Sir	**1**:13	With him who fears the Lord it will go well at the end
	4:19	If he goes astray she will forsake him
	6:27	and when you get hold of her, do not let her go
	7:8	even for one you will not go unpunished
	8:14	Do not go to law against a judge
	9:3	Do not go to meet a loose woman
	9:13	and that you are going about on the city battlements
	10:27	than one who goes about boasting, but lacks bread
	11:10	if you multiply activities you will not go unpunished
	12:11	Even if he humbles himself and goes about cringing
	12:13	or any who go near wild beasts ?

	20 :7	but a braggart and fool goes beyond the right moment
	21 :5	The prayer of a poor man goes from his lips
	25 :26	If she does not go as you direct
	27 :19	so you have let your neighbour go
	27 :20	Do not go after him, for he is too far off
	29 :24	It is a miserable life to go from house to house
	31 :8	and who does not go after gold
	32 :11	go home quickly and do not linger
	32 :20	Do not go on a path full of hazards
	33 :31	which way will you go to seek him ?
	34 :26	and goes again and does the same things
	39 :11	and if he goes to rest, it is enough for him
	41 :10	so the ungodly go from curse to destruction
	48 :23	In his days the sun went backward
	51 :13	While I was still young, before I went on my travels
Bar	**2** :18	that goes about bent over and feeble
	3 :30	Who has gone over the sea, and found her
	3 :33	he who sends forth the light, and it goes
	4 :19	Go, my children, go
	4 :28	For just as you purposed to go astray from God
L Jr	**6** :62	When God commands the clouds to go over the whole world
P Az	7	as thou hast commanded us that it might go well with us
Sus	**13** :7	Susanna would go into her husband's garden to walk
	13 :13	They said to each other, Let us go home, for it is mealtime
	13 :53	condemning the innocent and letting the guilty go free
Bel	**14** :4	The king revered it and went every day to worship it
	14 :10	And the king went with Daniel into the temple of Bel
	14 :11	And the priests of Bel said, Behold, we are going outside
	14 :29	Going to the king, they said, Hand Daniel over to us
	14 :33	and was going into the field to take it to the reapers
1 Ma	**1** :11	and misled many, saying, Let us go and make a covenant
	1 :13	and some of the people eagerly went to the king
	2 :45	And Mattathias and his friends went about
	3 :8	He went through the cities of Judah
	3 :31	and determined to go to Persia
	3 :37	and went through the upper provinces
	3 :39	to go into the land of Judah and destroy it
	3 :41	and went to the camp to get the sons of Israel for slaves
	3 :46	So they assembled and went to Mizpah, opposite Jerusalem
	4 :26	Those of the foreigners who escaped went
	5 :17	Choose your men and go and rescue your brethren in Galilee
	5 :17	I and Jonathan my brother will go to Gilead
	5 :20	Then 3,000 men were assigned to Simon to go to Galilee
	5 :21	So Simon went to Galilee
	5 :24	and went 3 days' journey into the wilderness
	5 :29	and they went all the way to the stronghold of Dathema
	5 :39	And Judas went to meet them
	5 :45	to go to the land of Judah
	5 :46	and they could not go round it to the right or to the left
	5 :46	they had to go through it
	5 :57	let us go and make war
	5 :66	Then he marched off to go into the land of the Philistines
	6 :1	King Antiochus was going through the upper provinces
	6 :5	that the armies which had gone into the land of Judah had been routed
	6 :6	that Lysias had gone first with a strong force
	6 :22	They went to the king and said
	6 :36	wherever it went they went with it, and they never left it
	6 :56	with the forces that had gone with the king
	7 :7	let him go and see all the ruin
	8 :6	who went to fight against them with a 120 elephants
	8 :19	They went to Rome, a very long journey
	8 :23	May all go well with the Romans
	9 :2	They went by the road which leads to Gilgal
	9 :4	then they marched off and went to Berea
	9 :11	and the slingers and the archers went ahead of the army
	9 :14	then all the stouthearted men went with him
	9 :29	to go against our enemies and Bacchides
	9 :47	but he eluded him and went to the rear
	9 :59	And they went and consulted with him
	9 :65	and he went with only a few men
	9 :67	Then he began to attack and went into battle with his forces
	10 :60	So he went with pomp to Ptolemais and met the 2 kings
	10 :77	and went to Azotus as though he were going farther
	11 :2	and went to meet him
	11 :7	And Jonathan went with the king
	11 :21	went to the king and reported to him
	11 :24	for he went to the king at Ptolemais
	11 :39	So he went to Imalkue the Arab
	11 :64	He went to meet them
	12 :3	So they went to Rome
	12 :17	We have commanded them to go also to you
	12 :32	Then he broke camp and went to Damascus
	12 :45	and will turn round and go home
	13 :20	to every place he went
	13 :22	So Trypho got all his cavalry ready to go
	13 :22	and he did not go because of the snow
	13 :22	He marched off and went into the land of Gilead
	14 :3	And he went and defeated the army of Demetrius
2 Ma	**3** :5	he went to Apollonius of Tarsus

	4 :11	who went on the mission to establish friendship
	4 :31	So the king went hastily to settle the trouble
	5 :9	having embarked to go to the Lacedaemonians
	5 :12	and to slay those who went into the houses
	6 :20	as men ought to go who have the courage to refuse things
	6 :28	When he had said this, he went at once to the rack
	7 :19	But do not think that you will go unpunished
	8 :20	when 8,000 in all went into the affair, with 4,000 Macedonians
	11 :30	Therefore those who go home by the 30th day of Xanthicus
	12 :1	and the Jews went about their farming
	12 :10	When they had gone more than a mile from there
	12 :17	When they had gone 95 miles from there
	12 :24	With great guile he besought them to let him go in safety
	12 :25	they let him go, for the sake of saving their brethren
	12 :38	and went to the city of Adullam
	12 :39	Judas and his men went to take up the bodies of the fallen
	13 :25	and went to Ptolemais
	14 :4	and went to King Demetrius in about the 151st year
	14 :26	and went to Demetrius
	14 :30	and went into hiding from Nicanor
	14 :31	he went to the great and holy temple
	15 :36	never to let this day go unobserved
1 Es	**1** :25	went to make war at Carchemish on the Euphrates
	2 :18	have gone to Jerusalem
	2 :29	and that such wicked proceedings go no further
	2 :30	went in haste to Jerusalem
	3 :3	and Darius the king went to his bedroom
	3 :3	and went to sleep, and then awoke
	4 :4	and if he sends them out against the enemy, they go
	4 :19	they let all those things go, and gape at her
	4 :61	and went to Babylon and told this to all his brethren
	6 :8	when we went to the country of Judea
	8 :10	may go with you to Jerusalem
	8 :14	and lambs and what goes with them
	8 :45	and I told them to go to Iddo
	9 :1	Then Ezra rose and went from the court of the temple
	9 :51	so go your way, eat the fat and drink the sweet
	9 :54	Then they all went their way
3 Ma	**1** :4	Arsinoe went to the troops with wailing and tears
2 Es	**1** :5	Go and declare to my people their evil deeds
	2 :2	Go, my children, because I am a widow and forsaken
	2 :4	Go, my children, and ask for mercy from the Lord
	2 :10	which I was going to give to Israel
	2 :33	to go to Israel
	2 :48	Then the angel said to me, Go, tell my people
	4 :5	And he said to me, Go, weigh for me the weight of fire
	4 :13	I went into a forest of trees of the plain
	4 :14	and said, Come, let us go and make war against the sea
	4 :40	Go and ask a woman who is with child if
	7 :136	and to those who are gone and to those yet to come
	9 :24	but go into a field of flowers where no house has been built
	9 :26	So I went, as he directed me
	10 :10	and behold, almost all go to perdition
	10 :13	the multitude that is now in it goes as it came
	10 :17	Therefore go into the city to your husband
	10 :18	I will not go into the city, but I will die here
	10 :22	our Levites have gone into captivity
	10 :53	Therefore I told you to go into the field
	11 :19	And so it went with all the wings
	11 :32	than all the wings that had gone before
	11 :40	have conquered all the beasts that have gone before
	12 :49	Now go, every one of you to his house
	12 :50	So the people went into the city, as I told them to do
	13 :41	and go to a more distant region
	13 :45	Through that region there was a long way to go
	14 :20	For behold, I will go, as thou hast commanded me
	14 :23	Go and gather the people
	14 :27	Then I went as he commanded me
	15 :17	For a man will desire to go into a city, and shall not be able
	16 :32	because no sheep will go along them
4 Ma	**3** :13	they went searching throughout the enemy camp
	12 :12	and these throughout all time will never let you go
	14 :6	agreed to go to death for its sake
	18 :7	I was a pure virgin and did not go outside my father's house
	18 :14	Even though you go through the fire

GO away   5 = 0.003 %

2 Ma	**14** :34	Having said this, he went away
1 Es	**4** :11	and no one may go away to attend to his own affairs
3 Ma	**2** :24	but went away uttering bitter threats
2 Es	**14** :18	For truth shall go farther away
4 Ma	**4** :14	went away to report to the king what had happened to him

GO back   2

1 Ma	**7** :20	then Bacchides went back to the king
	13 :49	were prevented from going out to the country and back

GO by   4 = 0.003 %

Jud	**8** :18	as was done in days gone by
2 Es	**4** :45	or whether for us the greater part has gone by

	4:46	For I know what has gone by
	4:48	and when the flame had gone by I looked

GO down   14 = 0.009 %

Tob	6:2	Then the young man went down to wash himself
	14:10	as he himself went down into the darkness
Jud	2:27	Then he went down into the plain of Damascus
	3:6	Then he went down to the seacoast with his army
	5:10	When a famine spread over Canaan they went down to Egypt
	8:32	which will go down through all generations of our descendants
	14:2	as if you were going down to the plain
	14:2	only do not go down
Ad E	13:7	may in one day go down in violence to Hades
Bar	3:19	They have vanished and gone down to Hades
1 Ma	2:29	went down to the wilderness to dwell there
	2:31	had gone down to the hiding places in the wilderness
	16:14	and he went down to Jericho with Mattathias and Judas his sons
2 Es	4:8	I never went down into the deep, nor as yet into hell

GO forth   14 = 0.009 %

Sir	5:7	for suddenly the wrath of the Lord will go forth
	24:30	I went forth like a canal from a river
	43:2	making proclamation as it goes forth
Bar	5:6	For they went forth from you on foot
1 Ma	4:13	they went forth from their camp to battle
	5:65	Then Judas and his brothers went forth
	7:41	thy angel went forth and struck down 185,000 of the Assyrians
	10:63	Go forth with him into the middle of the city
	12:33	Simon also went forth and marched through the country
2 Es	6:43	For thy word went forth, and at once the work was done
	7:78	When the decisive decree has gone forth from the Most High
	15:23	And a fire will go forth from his wrath
	15:30	shall go forth like wild boars of the forest
	16:9	Fire will go forth from his wrath

GO in   16 = 0.010 %

Tob	5:8	So he went in and said to his father
	5:17	as he goes in and out before us ?
	6:14	and I am afraid that if I go in
	8:13	So the maid opened the door and went in
	11:15	And his son went in rejoicing
Jud	14:14	So Bagoas went in and knocked at the door of the tent
Sus	13:8	going in and walking about, and they began to desire her
	13:15	she went in as before with only 2 maids
Bel	14:13	through which they used to go in regularly
	14:19	and restrained the king from going in, and said
1 Ma	3:45	not one of her children went in or out
	7:36	Then the priests went in
	15:25	and he shut Trypho up and kept him from going out or in
2 Ma	3:14	So he set a day and went in
2 Es	10:55	but go in and see the splendour and vastness of the building
	13:43	And they went in by the narrow passages of the Euphrates river

GO off   1

L Jr	6:58	and go off with this booty

GO on   10 = 0.007 %

2 Ma	3:23	Heliodorus went on with what had been decided
	6:17	we must go on briefly with the story
	11:23	Now that our father has gone on to the gods
	11:26	and go on happily in the conduct of their own affairs
1 Es	2:20	And since the building of the temple is now going on
	6:10	These operations are going on rapidly
3 Ma	5:18	After the party had been going on for some time
2 Es	15:43	And they shall go on steadily to Babylon
4 Ma	4:8	But, uttering threats, Apollonius went on to the temple
	11:16	go on torturing !

GO out   50 = 0.033 %

Tob	5:16	So they both went out and departed
	5:17	as he goes in and out before us ?
	10:7	And she went out every day to the road by which they had left
	11:16	Then Tobit went out to meet his daughter-in-law
Jud	8:33	and I will go out with my maid
	10:6	Then they went out to the city gate of Bethulia
	10:9	and I will go out
	10:10	When they had done this, Judith went out
	11:17	and every night your servant will go out into the valley
	11:18	and then you shall go out with your whole army
	12:6	that your servant be permitted to go out and pray
	12:7	and went out each night to the valley of Bethulia
	12:13	So Bagoas went out from the presence of Holofernes
	13:3	for she said she would be going out for her prayers
	13:4	So every one went out
	13:9	after a moment she went out
	13:10	Then the 2 of them went out together
	14:11	and they went out in companies
Sus	13:14	And when they went out, they parted from each other
	13:18	and went out by the side doors
	13:19	When the maids had gone out

Bel	14:14	When they had gone out, the king set forth the food for Bel
	14:14	Then they went out, shut the door
1 Ma	3:11	When Judas learned of it, he went out to meet him
	3:13	who stayed with him and went out to battle
	3:16	Judas went out to meet him with a small company
	3:45	not one of her children went in or out
	5:67	fell in battle, for they went out to battle unwisely
	7:24	So Judas went out into all the surrounding parts of Judea
	7:24	from going out into the country
	7:31	he went out to meet Judas in battle near Capharsalama
	7:35	And he went out in great anger
	7:39	Now Nicanor went out from Jerusalem
	9:65	while he went out into the country
	12:41	Jonathan went out to meet him
	13:49	were prevented from going out to the country and back
	15:25	and he shut Trypho up and kept him from going out or in
	15:41	so that they might go out
	16:3	and go out and fight for our nation
2 Ma	1:32	but when the light from the altar shone back, it went out
	2:4	and that he went out to the mountain where Moses had gone up
1 Es	1:25	and Josiah went out against him
	4:23	A man takes his sword, and goes out to travel
	4:58	When the young man went out
Ps 151	6	I went out to meet the Philistine
3 Ma	4:11	and to those from the city going out into the country
	4:12	frequently went out in secret
	5:5	The servants in charge of the Jews went out in the evening
	5:48	And when the Jews saw the dust raised by the elephants going out
2 Es	10:32	I did as you directed, and went out into the field

GO over   3 = 0.002 %

2 Ma	6:24	has gone over to an alien religion
	10:13	and had gone over to Antiochus Epiphanes
2 Es	12:2	And the 2 wings that had gone over to it arose

GO up   43 = 0.028 %

Jud	2:22	and went up into the hill country
	5:20	then we will go up and defeat them
	5:24	Therefore let us go up, Lord Holofernes
	6:11	and from the plain they went up into the hill country
	7:13	We and our people go up to the tops of the nearby mountains
	7:18	And the sons of Esau and the sons of Ammon went up
	7:32	and they went up on the walls and towers of their city
	13:6	She went up to the post at the end of the bed
	13:10	and went up the mountain to Bethulia and came to its gates
Sir	46:9	so that he went up to the hill country
	50:11	and went up to the holy altar
Bar	3:29	Who has gone up into heaven, and taken her
1 Ma	1:20	He went up against Israel
	3:15	went up with him to help him
	4:36	let us go up to cleanse the sanctuary and dedicate it
	4:37	So all the army assembled and they went up to Mount Zion
	5:31	and that the cry of the city went up to Heaven
	5:54	So they went up to Mount Zion with gladness and joy
	6:48	went up to Jerusalem against them
	7:33	After these events Nicanor went up to Mount Zion
	9:8	Let us rise and go up against our enemies
	9:38	and went up and hid under cover of the mountain
	13:2	So he went up to Jerusalem
	13:45	went up on the wall with their clothes rent
	16:1	John went up from Gazara
2 Ma	2:4	and that he went out to the mountain where Moses had gone up
	6:19	went up to the rack of his own accord, spitting out the flesh
	12:31	Then they went up to Jerusalem
1 Es	2:5	may his Lord be with him, and let him go up to Jerusalem
	2:8	and all whose spirit the Lord had stirred to go up
	4:47	and all who were going up with him to build Jerusalem
	4:49	And he wrote for all the Jews who were going up
	4:63	to go up and build Jerusalem and the temple
	5:1	After this the heads of fathers' houses were chosen to go up
	5:3	And he made them go up with them
	5:4	These are the names of the men who went up
	8:27	and I gathered men from Israel to go up with me
	8:28	who went up with me from Babylon
3 Ma	3:16	and went up to honour the temple of those wicked people
2 Es	4:15	and said, Come, let us go up and subdue the forest of the plain
	15:44	then the dust and smoke shall go up to heaven
4 Ma	4:4	and went up to Seleucus to inform him of the rich treasure
	4:10	and while Apollonius was going up

GOAD   1

Sir	38:25	and who glories in the shaft of a goad

GOAL   1

2 Es	5:40	or the goal of the love that I have promised my people

GOAT
2

| Jud | 2:17 | and innumerable sheep and oxen and goats for provision |
| Sir | 47:3 | He played with lions as with young goats |

GOD, prop. n.
497 = 0.324 %

Tob	1:12	because I remembered God with all my heart
	3:11	Blessed art thou, O Lord my God
	3:16	in the presence of the glory of the great God
	4:5	Remember the Lord our God all your days, my son
	4:7	and the face of God will not be turned away from you
	4:14	and if you serve God you will receive payment
	4:19	Bless the Lord God on every occasion
	4:21	You have great wealth if you fear God
	5:16	God who dwells in heaven will prosper your way
	6:17	and cry out to the merciful God
	7:12	The merciful God will guide you both for the best
	8:5	Blessed art thou, O God of our fathers
	8:15	Then Raguel blessed God and said
	8:15	Blessed art thou, O God, with every pure and holy blessing
	10:11	The God of heaven will prosper you, my children, before I die
	11:1	praising God because he had made his journey a success
	11:14	Blessed art thou, O God, and blessed is thy name for ever
	11:16	rejoicing and praising God
	11:17	that God had been merciful to him
	11:17	Blessed is God who has brought you to us
	12:6	and said to them : Praise God and give thanks to him
	12:6	It is good to praise God and to exalt his name
	12:6	worthily declaring the works of God
	12:7	but gloriously to reveal the works of God
	12:11	but gloriously to reveal the works of God
	12:14	So now God sent me to heal you
	12:17	But praise God for ever
	12:18	but by the will of our God
	12:20	And now give thanks to God
	12:22	So they confessed the great and wonderful works of God
	13:1	Blessed is God who lives for ever
	13:4	because he is our Lord and God, he is our Father for ever
	13:7	I exalt my God
	13:11	Many nations will come from afar to the name of the Lord God
	13:15	Let my soul praise God the great King
	13:18	Blessed is God, who has exalted you for ever
	14:2	and he continued to fear the Lord God and to praise him
	14:4	The house of God in it will be burned down
	14:5	But God will again have mercy on them
	14:5	and they will rebuild the house of God
	14:5	And the house of God will be rebuilt there
	14:6	to fear the Lord God in truth
	14:7	and his people will give thanks to God
	14:7	And all who love the Lord God in truth and righteousness
Jud	4:2	and for the temple of the Lord their God
	4:9	And every man of Israel cried out to God with great fervour
	4:12	praying earnestly to the God of Israel
	5:8	and they worshipped the God of heaven
	5:8	the God they had come to know
	5:9	Then their God commanded them to leave the place
	5:12	Then they cried out to their God
	5:13	Then God dried up the Red Sea before them
	5:17	As long as they did not sin against their God they prospered
	5:17	for the God who hates iniquity is with them
	5:18	the temple of their God was razed to the ground
	5:19	But now they have returned to their God
	5:20	and they sin against their God and we find out their offence
	5:21	and their God will protect them
	6:2	because their God will defend them ?
	6:2	Who is God except Nebuchadnezzar ?
	6:3	and their God will not deliver them
	6:18	Then the people fell down and worshipped God
	6:19	O Lord God of heaven, behold their arrogance
	6:21	and all that night they called on the God of Israel for help
	7:19	The people of Israel cried out to the Lord their God
	7:24	God be judge between you and us !
	7:25	God has sold us into their hands
	7:28	and our God, the Lord of our fathers
	7:29	and they cried out to the Lord God with a loud voice
	7:30	by that time the Lord our God will restore to us his mercy
	8:8	for she feared God with great devotion
	8:11	and pronounced this oath between God and you
	8:12	Who are you, that have put God to the test this day
	8:12	and are setting yourselves up in the place of God
	8:14	how do you expect to search out God
	8:14	No, my brethren, do not provoke the Lord our God to anger
	8:16	Do not try to bind the purposes of the Lord our God
	8:16	for God is not like a man, to be threatened
	8:20	But we know no other God but him
	8:23	but the Lord our God will turn it to dishonour
	8:25	let us give thanks to the Lord our God
	8:35	Go in peace, and may the Lord God go before you
	9:1	in the house of God in Jerusalem
	9:2	O Lord God of my father Simeon
	9:4	O God, my God, hear me also, a widow

	9:11	for thou art God of the lowly, helper of the oppressed
	9:12	Hear, O hear me, God of my father
	9:12	God of the inheritance of Israel
	9:14	to know and understand that thou art God
	9:14	the God of all power and might
	10:1	When Judith had ceased crying out to the God of Israel
	10:8	May the God of our fathers grant you favour
	10:8	And she worshipped God
	11:6	God will accomplish something through you
	11:10	unless they sin against their God
	11:11	by which they are about to provoke their God to anger
	11:12	to use all that God by his laws has forbidden them to eat
	11:13	who minister in the presence of our God at Jerusalem
	11:16	and God has sent me to accomplish with you
	11:17	and serves the God of heaven day and night
	11:17	and I will pray to God
	11:22	God has done well to send you before the people
	11:23	and if you do as you have said, your God shall be my God
	12:8	she prayed the Lord God of Israel
	13:4	O Lord God of all might
	13:7	Give me strength this day, O Lord God of Israel !
	13:11	God, our God, is still with us, to show his power in Israel
	13:14	Praise God, O praise him !
	13:14	Praise God, who has not withdrawn his mercy
	13:17	and bowed down and worshipped God
	13:17	and said with one accord, Blessed art thou, our God
	13:18	O daughter, you are blessed by the Most High God
	13:18	and blessed be the Lord God
	13:19	as they remember the power of God
	13:20	May God grant this to be a perpetual honour to you
	13:20	walking in the straight path before our God
	14:10	And when Achior saw all that the God of Israel had done
	14:10	he believed firmly in God, and was circumcised
	15:10	and God is well pleased with it
	16:2	And Judith said, Begin a song to my God with tambourines
	16:3	For God is the Lord who crushes wars
	16:13	I will sing to my God a new song
	16:18	When they arrived at Jerusalem they worshipped God
	16:19	Judith also dedicated to God all the vessels of Holofernes
Ad E	10:4	And Mordecai said, These things have come from God
	10:9	who cried out to God and were saved
	10:9	God has done great signs and wonders
	10:10	one for the people of God and one for all the nations
	10:11	of decision before God and among all the nations
	10:12	And God remembered his people and vindicated his inheritance
	10:13	with an assembly and joy and gladness before God
	11:10	Then they cried to God
	11:12	Mordecai saw in this dream what God had determined to do
	13:14	that I might not set the glory of man above the glory of God
	13:15	And now, O Lord God and King
	13:15	God of Abraham, spare thy people
	14:3	And she prayed to the Lord God of Israel, and said :
	14:18	except in thee, O Lord God of Abraham
	14:19	O God, whose might is over all
	15:2	after invoking the aid of the all-seeing God and Saviour
	15:8	Then God changed the spirit of the king to gentleness
	15:13	like an angel of God
	16:4	of God, who always sees everything
	16:16	and are sons of the Most High, the most mighty living God
	16:18	For God, who rules over all things
	16:21	For God, who rules over all things
Wis	1:3	For perverse thoughts separate men from God
	1:6	because God is witness of his inmost feelings
	1:13	because God did not make death
	2:13	He professes to have knowledge of God
	2:16	and boasts that God is his father
	2:18	for if the righteous man is God's son, he will help him
	2:22	and they did not know the secret purposes of God
	2:23	for God created man for incorruption
	3:1	But the souls of the righteous are in the hand of God
	3:5	because God tested them and found them worthy of himself
	3:13	she will have fruit when God examines souls
	4:1	because it is known both by God and by men
	4:6	against their parents when God examines them
	4:10	There was one who pleased God and was loved by him
	4:15	that God's grace and mercy are with his elect
	5:5	Why has he been numbered among the sons of God ?
	6:4	nor keep the law, nor walk according to the purpose of God
	6:19	and immortality brings one near to God
	7:7	I called upon God, and the spirit of wisdom came to me
	7:14	those who get it obtain friendship with God
	7:15	May God grant that I speak with judgment
	7:25	For she is a breath of the power of God
	7:26	a spotless mirror of the working of God
	7:27	and makes friends of God, and prophets
	7:28	for God loves nothing so much
	8:3	She glorifies her noble birth by living with God
	8:4	For she is an initiate in the knowledge of God
	8:21	unless God gave her to me
	9:1	O God of my fathers and Lord of mercy

9 : 13   For what man can learn the counsel of God ?
10 : 5   and preserved him blameless before God
10 : 10   she showed him the kingdom of God
12 : 7   might receive a worthy colony of the servants of God
12 : 26   will experience the deserved judgment of God
12 : 27   they saw and recognized as the true God
13 : 1   For all men who were ignorant of God were foolish by nature
13 : 6   for perhaps they go astray while seeking God
14 : 9   For equally hateful to God
14 : 11   because, though part of what God created
14 : 22   to err about the knowledge of God
14 : 30   because they thought wickedly of God
15 : 1   But thou, our God, art kind and true, patient
15 : 19   both the praise of God and his blessing
16 : 18   that they were being pursued by the judgment of God
18 : 13   they acknowledged thy people to be God's son
19 : 1   for God knew in advance even their future actions

Sir 1 : 5   The source of wisdom is God's word in the highest heaven
3 : 17   then you will be loved by those whom God accepts
4 : 28   and the Lord God will fight for you
7 : 9   and when I make an offering to the Most High God
11 : 22   and quickly God causes his blessing to flourish
21 : 5   to the ears of God
23 : 4   O Lord, Father and God of my life
23 : 28   It is a great honour to fear God
24 : 23   All this is the book of the covenant of the Most High God
24 : 24   the Lord Almighty alone is God
36 : 1   Have mercy upon us, O Lord, the God of all
36 : 5   as we have known that there is no God but thee, O Lord
36 : 17   that thou art the Lord, the God of the ages
39 : 17   For in God's time all things will be sought after
41 : 8   who have forsaken the law of the Most High God !
41 : 19   Be ashamed before the truth of God and his covenant
45 : 1   and was beloved by God and man
46 : 1   a great saviour of God's elect
47 : 10   while they praised God's holy name
47 : 13   and God gave him rest on every side
47 : 18   In the name of the Lord God
47 : 18   who is called the God of Israel
48 : 10   to calm the wrath of God before it breaks out in fury
48 : 16   Some of them did what was pleasing to God
49 : 8   which God showed him above the chariot of the cherubim
49 : 9   For God remembered his enemies with storm
50 : 17   to worship their Lord, the Almighty, God Most High
50 : 22   And now bless the God of all
51 : 1   and will praise thee as God my Saviour
51 : 30   and in God's time he will give you your reward

Bar 1 : 10   and offer them upon the altar of the Lord our God
1 : 13   And pray for us to the Lord our God
1 : 13   for we have sinned against the Lord our God
1 : 15   Righteousness belongs to the Lord our God
1 : 18   and have not heeded the voice of the Lord our God
1 : 19   we have been disobedient to the Lord our God
1 : 21   We did not heed the voice of the Lord our God
1 : 21   and doing what is evil in the sight of the Lord our God
2 : 5   because we sinned against the Lord our God
2 : 6   Righteousness belongs to the Lord our God
2 : 11   And now, O Lord God of Israel
2 : 12   O Lord our God, against all thy ordinances
2 : 15   that all the earth may know that thou art the Lord our God
2 : 19   O Lord our God
2 : 27   Yet thou hast dealt with us, O Lord our God
2 : 31   and they will know that I am the Lord their God
2 : 35   to be their God and they shall be my people
3 : 1   O Lord Almighty, God of Israel
3 : 4   O Lord Almighty, God of Israel
3 : 4   who did not heed the voice of the Lord their God
3 : 6   For thou art the Lord our God
3 : 8   who forsook the Lord our God
3 : 13   If you had walked in the way of God
3 : 24   O Israel, how great is the house of God !
3 : 27   God did not choose them, nor give them the way to knowledge
3 : 35   This is our God
4 : 1   She is the book of the commandments of God
4 : 4   for we know what is pleasing to God
4 : 6   because you angered God
4 : 7   by sacrificing to demons and not to God
4 : 8   You forgot the everlasting God, who brought you up
4 : 9   For she saw the wrath that came upon you from God
4 : 9   God has brought great sorrow upon me
4 : 12   because they turned away from the law of God
4 : 13   they did not walk in the ways of God's commandments
4 : 21   Take courage, my children, cry to God
4 : 23   but God will give you back to me
4 : 24   so they soon will see your salvation by God
4 : 25   the wrath that has come upon you from God
4 : 27   Take courage, my children, and cry to God
4 : 28   For just as you purposed to go astray from God
4 : 36   and see the joy that is coming to you from God !
4 : 37   at the word of the Holy One, rejoicing in the glory of God

5 : 1   and put on for ever the beauty of the glory from God
5 : 2   Put on the robe of the righteousness from God
5 : 3   For God will show your splendour everywhere under heaven
5 : 4   For your name will for ever be called by God
5 : 5   rejoicing that God has remembered them
5 : 6   but God will bring them back to you
5 : 7   For God has ordered that every high mountain
5 : 7   so that Israel may walk safely in the glory of God
5 : 8   The woods and every fragrant tree have shaded Israel at God's command
5 : 9   For God will lead Israel with joy

L Jr 6 : 1   to give them the message which God had commanded him
6 : 2   Because of the sins which you have committed before God
6 : 51   and that there is no work of God in them
6 : 62   When God commands the clouds to go over the whole world

P Az 1   singing hymns to God and blessing the Lord
3   Blessed art thou, O Lord, God of our fathers
22   Let them know that thou art the Lord, the only God
28   praised and glorified and blessed God in the furnace, saying :
29   Blessed art thou, O Lord, God of our fathers
68   Bless him, all who worship the Lord, the God of gods

Sus 13 : 42   O eternal God, who dost discern what is secret
13 : 45   God aroused the holy spirit of a young lad named Daniel
13 : 50   for God has given you that right
13 : 55   for the angel of God has received the sentence from God
13 : 59   for the angel of God is waiting with his sword to saw you in 2
13 : 60   Then all the assembly shouted loudly and blessed God
13 : 63   And Hilkiah and his wife praised God for their daughter Susanna

Bel 14 : 4   But Daniel worshipped his own God
14 : 5   but the living God, who created heaven and earth
14 : 6   Do you not think that Bel is a living God ?
14 : 25   Daniel said, I will worship the Lord my God
14 : 25   for he is the living God
14 : 37   Take the dinner which God has sent you
14 : 38   And Daniel said, Thou hast remembered me, O God
14 : 39   And the angel of God immediately returned Habakkuk to his own place
14 : 41   Thou art great, O Lord God of Daniel

2 Ma 1 : 2   May God do good to you
1 : 11   Having been saved by God out of grave dangers
1 : 17   Blessed in every way be our God, who has brought judgment
1 : 20   But after many years had passed, when it pleased God
1 : 24   O Lord, Lord God, Creator of all things
1 : 27   and let the Gentiles know that thou art our God
2 : 4   and had seen the inheritance of God
2 : 7   until God gathers his people together again
2 : 17   It is God who has saved all his people
2 : 18   For we have hope in God that he will soon have mercy upon us
3 : 24   were astounded by the power of God
3 : 28   and they recognized clearly the sovereign power of God
3 : 34   report to all men the majestic power of God
3 : 36   of the deeds of the supreme God
3 : 38   for there certainly is about the place some power of God
6 : 1   and cease to live by the laws of God
7 : 6   saying, The Lord God is watching over us
7 : 14   and to cherish the hope that God gives
7 : 16   But do not think that God has forsaken our people
7 : 18   because of our sins against our own God
7 : 19   for having tried to fight against God !
7 : 28   that God did not make them out of things that existed
7 : 29   Accept death, so that in God's mercy
7 : 31   will certainly not escape the hands of God
7 : 35   You have not yet escaped the judgment of the almighty, all-seeing God
7 : 36   have drunk of everflowing life under God's covenant
7 : 36   but you, by the judgment of God
7 : 37   appealing to God to show mercy soon to our nation
7 : 37   to make you confess that he alone is God
8 : 13   those who were cowardly and distrustful of God's justice
8 : 18   but we trust in the Almighty God
8 : 23   and gave the watchword, God's help
9 : 5   But the all-seeing Lord, the God of Israel
9 : 8   making the power of God manifest to all
9 : 11   and to come to his senses under the scourge of God
9 : 12   he uttered these words : It is right to be subject to God
9 : 12   and no mortal should think that he is equal to God
9 : 17   to proclaim the power of God
9 : 18   for the judgment of God had justly come upon him
10 : 16   and beseeching God to fight on their side
10 : 25   in supplication to God
11 : 4   He took no account whatever of the power of God
11 : 9   And they all together praised the merciful God
11 : 13   because the mighty God fought on their side
12 : 6   and, calling upon God the righteous Judge
12 : 11   by the help of God
12 : 16   They took the city by the will of God
13 : 13   and decide the matter by the help of God
13 : 15   He gave his men the watchword, God's victory
14 : 33   I will level this precinct of God to the ground

	15:14	Jeremiah, the prophet of God
	15:16	Take this holy sword, a gift from God
	15:26	with invocation to God and prayers
	15:27	and praying to God in their hearts
	15:27	and were greatly gladdened by God's manifestation
1 Es	1:4	Now worship the Lord your God
	1:27	I was not sent against you by the Lord God
	1:48	and transgressed the laws of the Lord, the God of Israel
	1:50	So the God of their fathers sent by his messenger to call them back
	4:36	All God's works quake and tremble
	4:40	Blessed be the God of truth !
	4:62	And they praised the God of their fathers
	5:44	when they came to the temple of God which is in Jerusalem
	5:48	took their places and prepared the altar of the God of Israel
	5:49	in accordance with the directions in the book of Moses the man of God
	5:53	And all who had made any vow to God
	5:53	began to offer sacrifices to God
	5:53	though the temple of God was not yet built
	5:56	In the 2nd year after their coming to the temple of God in Jerusalem
	5:57	and they laid the foundation of the temple of God
	5:58	as one man pressing forward the work on the house of God
	5:67	were building the temple for the Lord God of Israel
	5:70	in building the house for the Lord our God
	6:1	they prophesied to them in the name of the Lord God of Israel
	6:31	in order that libations may be made to the Most High God
	7:4	and they completed it by command of the Lord God of Israel
	7:9	for the services of the Lord God of Israel
	7:15	for the service of the Lord God of Israel
	8:3	which was given by the God of Israel
	8:16	perform it in accordance with the will of your God
	8:17	which are given you for the use of the temple of your God
	8:18	for the temple of your God
	8:19	and reader of the law of the Most High God sends for
	8:21	Let all things prescribed in the law of God
	8:21	be scrupulously fulfilled for the Most High God
	8:23	And you, Ezra, according to the wisdom of God
	8:23	to judge all those who know the law of your God
	8:24	And all who transgress the law of your God
	8:27	I was encouraged by the help of the Lord my God
	8:65	offered sacrifices to the Lord, the God of Israel
	8:79	in the house of the Lord our God
	9:8	the God of our fathers
	9:39	which had been given by the Lord God of Israel
	9:46	And Ezra blessed the Lord God Most High
	9:46	the God of hosts, the Almighty
P Ma	1	O Lord Almighty, God of our fathers
	8	Therefore thou, O Lord, God of the righteous
	13	For thou, O Lord, art the God of those who repent
3 Ma	1:9	he offered sacrifice to the supreme God and made thank-offerings
	1:16	and entreated the supreme God to aid in the present situation
	2:21	Thereupon God, who oversees all things
	3:4	but because they worshipped God
	3:11	and not considering the might of the supreme God
	4:16	and uttering improper words against the supreme God
	5:7	their merciful God and Father, praying
	5:13	praised their holy God
	5:25	implored the supreme God to help them again at once
	5:28	This was the act of God who rules over all things
	5:30	because by the providence of God
	5:35	praised the manifest Lord God, King of kings
	6:1	to cease calling upon the holy God
	6:2	King of great power, Almighty God Most High
	6:18	Then the most glorious, almighty, and true God
	6:28	Release the sons of the almighty and living God of heaven
	6:29	praised their holy God and Saviour
	6:32	praising God, their Saviour and worker of wonders
	6:36	that had come to them through God
	7:2	the great God guiding our affairs according to our desire
	7:6	that the God of heaven surely defends the Jews
	7:9	the Most High God
	7:10	against the holy God and the law of God
	7:12	who had transgressed the law of God
	7:16	But those who had held fast to God even to death
	7:16	to the one God of their fathers, the eternal Saviour of Israel
	7:22	So the supreme God perfectly performed great deeds
2 Es	1:29	that you should be my people and I should be your God
	2:3	because you have sinned before the Lord God
	2:45	and they have confessed the name of God
	2:47	He answered and said to me, He is the Son of God
	2:48	how great and many are the wonders of the Lord God
	7:19	And he said to me, You are not a better judge than God
	7:20	rather than that the law of God
	7:21	For God strictly commanded those who came into the world
	7:48	which has alienated us from God
	7:79	and who have hated those who fear God
	8:58	and said in their hearts that there is no God

	9:45	And after 30 years God heard your handmaid
	10:16	For if you acknowledge the decree of God to be just
	15:20	Behold, says God
	15:21	Thus says the Lord God :
	15:27	for God will not deliver you
	15:48	therefore God says
	15:56	so God will do to you
	16:8	The Lord God sends calamities, and who will drive them away ?
	16:53	for God will burn coals of fire on the head of him who says
	16:53	I have not sinned before God and his glory
	16:62	and the spirit of Almighty God
	16:66	Or how will you hide your sins before God and his angels ?
	16:67	Behold, God is the judge, fear him !
	16:67	so God will lead you forth
	16:75	Do not fear or doubt, for God is your guide
	16:76	You who keep my commandments and precepts, says the Lord God
4 Ma	1:12	giving glory to the all-wise God
	2:21	Now when God fashioned man
	3:16	he poured out the drink as an offering to God
	4:9	were imploring God in the temple to shield the holy place
	5:24	so that with proper reverence we worship the only real God
	5:25	for since we believe that the law was established by God
	6:26	he lifted up his eyes to God and said
	6:27	You know, O God, that though I might have saved myself
	7:19	do not die to God, but live in God
	7:21	and trusts in God
	9:8	shall have the prize of virtue and shall be with God
	10:18	God hears also those who are mute
	10:20	Gladly, for the sake of God
	10:21	God will visit you swiftly, for you are cutting out
	12:11	since you have received good things and also your kingdom from God
	12:14	Surely they by dying nobly fulfilled their service to God
	12:17	and I call on the God of our fathers
	13:3	Instead, by reason, which is praised before God
	13:13	Let us with all our hearts consecrate ourselves to God
	13:15	lying before those who transgress the commandment of God
	13:22	and from both general education and our discipline in the law of God
	15:3	according to God's promise
	15:8	yet because of the fear of God she disdained
	15:24	because of faith in God
	16:14	O mother, soldier of God in the cause of religion, elder and woman !
	16:18	Remember that it is through God
	16:19	and therefore you ought to endure any suffering for the sake of God
	16:21	and endured it for the sake of God
	16:22	You too must have the same faith in God and not be grieved
	16:24	to die rather than violate God's commandment
	16:25	They knew also that those who die for the sake of God live in God
	17:4	maintaining firm an enduring hope in God
	17:5	stand in honour before God
	17:10	looking to God and enduring torture even to death
	17:15	Reverence for God was victor
	17:20	These, then, who have been consecrated for the sake of God
	18:23	and have received pure and immortal souls from God

GOD, idol   68 = 0.044 %

Jud	3:8	to destroy all the gods of the land
	3:8	and all their tongues and tribes should call upon him as god
	5:7	because they would not follow the gods of their fathers
	5:8	hence they drove them out from the presence of their gods
	8:18	or city of ours which worshipped gods made with hands
Ad E	14:7	because we glorified their gods
	14:12	O King of the gods and Master of all dominion !
Wis	12:13	For neither is there any god besides thee
	12:24	For they went far astray on the paths of error, accepting as gods
	12:27	which they had thought to be gods
	13:2	were the gods that rule the world
	13:3	men assumed them to be gods
	13:10	are the men who give the name gods
	14:8	and the perishable thing was named a god
	14:15	and he now honoured as a god
	15:8	he forms a futile god from the same clay
	15:9	and he counts it his glory that he moulds counterfeit gods
	15:15	For they thought that all their heathen idols were gods
	15:16	for no man can form a god which is like himself
Bar	1:21	by serving other gods
L Jr	6:4	Now in Babylon you will see gods made of silver and gold and wood
	6:5	or to let fear for these gods possess you
	6:9	People take gold and make crowns for the heads of their gods
	6:10	and sometimes the priests secretly take gold and silver from their gods
	6:11	They deck their gods out with garments like men
	6:11	these gods of silver and gold and wood
	6:14	Like a local ruler the god holds a sceptre

6 : 16	Therefore they evidently are not gods
6 : 17	so are the gods of the heathen
6 : 19	though their gods can see none of them
6 : 23	From this you will know that they are not gods
6 : 27	because through them these gods are made to stand
6 : 28	The priests sell the sacrifices that are offered to these gods
6 : 29	Since you know by these things that they are not gods
6 : 30	For why should they be called gods
6 : 30	Women serve meals for gods of silver and gold and wood
6 : 32	They howl and shout before their gods
6 : 33	The priests take some of the clothing of their gods
6 : 40	Why then must any one think that they are gods
6 : 40	or call them gods ?
6 : 44	Why then must any one think that they are gods
6 : 44	or call them gods ?
6 : 46	how then can the things that are made by them be gods ?
6 : 48	as to where they can hide themselves and their gods
6 : 49	How then can one fail to see that these are not gods
6 : 51	that they are not gods but the work of men's hands
6 : 52	Who then can fail to know that they are not gods ?
6 : 55	of wooden gods overlaid with gold or silver
6 : 55	but the gods will be burnt in 2 like beams
6 : 56	Why then must any one admit or think that they are gods ?
6 : 57	gods made of wood and overlaid with silver and gold
6 : 59	than to be these false gods
6 : 59	than these false gods
6 : 64	Therefore one must not think that they are gods nor call them gods
6 : 65	Since you know then that they are not gods, do not fear them
6 : 69	So we have no evidence whatever that they are gods
6 : 70	so are their gods of wood, overlaid with gold and silver
6 : 71	In the same way, their gods of wood
6 : 72	you will know that they are not gods
P Az 68	Bless him, all who worship the Lord, the God of gods
Bel 14 : 24	You cannot deny that this is a living god ; so worship him
1 Ma 5 : 68	and the graven images of their gods he burned with fire
2 Ma 11 : 23	Now that our father has gone on to the gods
3 Ma 3 : 14	by the gods"deliberate alliance with us in battle
6 : 11	saying, Not even their god has rescued them
2 Es 1 : 6	and have offered sacrifices to strange gods

GOD-FEARING   3 = 0.002 %

Sir 19 : 24	Better is the God-fearing man who lacks intelligence
4 Ma 15 : 28	but as the daughter of God-fearing Abraham
16 : 12	Yet the sacred and God-fearing mother

GODGIVEN   1

2 Ma 6 : 23	and moreover according to the holy Godgiven law

GODLESS   2

Sir 26 : 23	A godless wife is given as a portion to a lawless man
2 Es 4 : 23	has been given over to godless tribes

GODLINESS   7 = 0.005 %

Wis 10 : 12	that godliness is more powerful than anything
Sir 1 : 25	but godliness is an abomination to a sinner
49 : 3	in the days of wicked men he strengthened godliness
Bar 5 : 4	Peace of righteousness and glory of godliness
2 Ma 12 : 45	that is laid up for those who fall asleep in godliness
1 Es	for his heart was full of godliness
4 Ma 7 : 22	would no be able to overcome the emotions through godliness ?

GODLY, adj., subst.   15 = 0.010 %

Sir 11 : 17	The gift of the Lord endures for those who are godly
11 : 22	The blessing of the Lord is the reward of the godly
12 : 2	Do good to a godly man, and you will be repaid
12 : 4	Give to the godly man, but do not help the sinner
13 : 17	No more has a sinner with a godly man
16 : 13	and the patience of the godly will not be frustrated
23 : 12	For all these errors will be far from the godly
27 : 11	The talk of the godly man is always wise
27 : 29	Those who rejoice in the fall of the godly
28 : 22	It will not be master over the godly
33 : 14	so the sinner is the opposite of the godly
37 : 12	But stay constantly with a godly man
39 : 27	All these are for good to the godly
43 : 33	and to the godly he has granted wisdom
4 Ma 10 : 10	are suffering because of our godly training and virtue

GOING   1

Wis 3 : 3	and their going from us to be their destruction

GOLD   106 = 0.069 %

Tob 12 : 8	It is better to give alms than to treasure up gold
13 : 16	and her towers and battlements with pure gold
Jud 2 : 18	and a huge amount of gold and silver from the royal palace
5 : 9	with much gold and silver and very many cattle
8 : 7	and her husband Manasseh had left her gold and silver
10 : 21	under a canopy which was woven with purple and gold
Ad E 15 : 6	all covered with gold and precious stones

Wis 3 : 6	like gold in the furnace he tried them
7 : 9	because all gold is but a little sand in her sight
13 : 10	gold and silver fashioned with skill
15 : 9	but he competes with workers in gold and silver
Sir 2 : 5	For gold is tested in the fire
7 : 18	or a real brother for the gold of Ophir
7 : 19	for her charm is worth more than gold
8 : 2	for gold has ruined many
26 : 18	Like pillars of gold on a base of silver
28 : 24	lock up your silver and gold
29 : 11	and it will profit you more than gold
30 : 15	Health and soundness are better than all gold
31 : 5	He who loves gold will not be justified
31 : 6	Many have come to ruin because of gold
31 : 8	and who does not go after gold
32 : 5	A ruby seal in a setting of gold
32 : 6	A seal of emerald in a rich setting of gold
40 : 25	Gold and silver make the foot stand sure
41 : 12	since it will remain for you longer than a 1,000 great stores of gold
45 : 10	with a holy garment, of gold and blue and purple
45 : 11	in a setting of gold, the work of a jeweller
45 : 12	with a gold crown upon his turban
47 : 18	you gathered gold like tin and amassed silver like lead
50 : 9	like a vessel of hammered gold
51 : 28	and you will gain by it much gold
Bar 3 : 17	and who hoard up silver and gold
3 : 30	and will buy her for pure gold ?
L Jr 6 : 4	Now in Babylon you will see gods made of silver and gold and wood
6 : 8	and they themselves are overlaid with gold and silver
6 : 9	People take gold and make crowns for the heads of their gods
6 : 10	and sometimes the priests secretly take gold and silver from their gods
6 : 11	these gods of silver and gold and wood
6 : 24	As for the gold which they wear for beauty
6 : 30	Women serve meals for gods of silver and gold and wood
6 : 39	These things that are made of wood and overlaid with gold and silver
6 : 50	Since they are made of wood and overlaid with gold and silver
6 : 55	of wooden gods overlaid with gold or silver
6 : 57	gods made of wood and overlaid with silver and gold
6 : 58	Strong men will strip them of their gold and silver
6 : 70	so are their gods of wood, overlaid with gold and silver
6 : 71	overlaid with gold and silver
1 Ma 1 : 22	and the gold decoration on the front of the temple
1 : 23	He took the silver and the gold, and the costly vessels
2 : 18	with silver and gold and many gifts
3 : 41	they took silver and gold in immense amounts, and fetters
4 : 23	and they seized much gold and silver
6 : 1	was a city famed for its wealth in silver and gold
6 : 12	I seized all her vessels of silver and gold
6 : 39	When the sun shone upon the shields of gold and brass
8 : 3	to get control of the silver and gold mines there
10 : 60	he gave them and their friends silver and gold and many gifts
11 : 24	taking silver and gold and clothing and numerous other gifts
11 : 58	And he sent him gold plate and a table service
11 : 58	and granted him the right to drink from gold cups
11 : 58	and dress in purple and wear a gold buckle
13 : 37	We have received the gold crown
14 : 24	with a large gold shield weighing a 1,000 minas
14 : 43	and that he should be clothed in purple and wear gold
14 : 44	or to be clothed in purple or put on a gold buckle
15 : 18	and have brought a gold shield weighing a 1,000 minas
15 : 26	and silver and gold, and much military equipment
15 : 32	and the sideboard with its gold and silver plate
16 : 11	and he had much silver and gold
16 : 19	so that he might give them silver and gold and gifts
2 Ma 2 : 2	upon seeing the gold and silver statues and their adornment
3 : 11	and that it totalled in all 400 talents of silver and 200 of gold
3 : 25	Its rider was seen to have armour and weapons of gold
4 : 32	stole some of the gold vessels of the temple
4 : 39	because many of the gold vessels had already been stolen
11 : 8	clothed in white and brandishing weapons of gold
14 : 4	presenting to him a crown of gold and a palm
1 Es 1 : 36	and one talent of gold
2 : 6	be helped by the men of his place with gold and silver
2 : 9	with silver and gold, with horses and cattle
2 : 13	The number of these was : a 1,000 gold cups, a 1,000 silver cups
2 : 13	29 silver censers, 30 gold bowls
2 : 14	All the vessels were handed over, gold and silver, 5,469
3 : 6	He shall be clothed in purple, and drink from gold cups
3 : 6	and sleep on a gold bed
3 : 6	and have a chariot with gold bridles
4 : 18	If men gather gold and silver or any other beautiful thing
4 : 19	and all prefer her to gold or silver
5 : 45	a 1,000 minas of gold
6 : 18	And the holy vessels of gold and of silver
6 : 26	both of gold and of silver
8 : 13	all the gold and silver that may be found

	8 : 14	both gold and silver for bulls and rams
	8 : 16	with the gold and silver
	8 : 55	and I weighed out to them the silver and the gold
	8 : 56	and a 100 talents of gold
	8 : 57	that glittered like gold
	8 : 58	and the silver and the gold are vowed to the Lord
	8 : 60	who took the silver and the gold
	8 : 62	the silver and the gold were weighed
3 Ma	1 : 4	promising to give them each 2 minas of gold
2 Es	7 : 55	Say to her, You produce gold and silver and brass
	7 : 56	but silver is more abundant than gold, and brass than silver
	8 : 2	but only a little dust from which gold comes
	16 : 73	as gold that is tested by fire

GOLDEN   14 = 0.009 %

Ad E	15 : 11	Then he raised the golden sceptre and touched it to her neck
Sir	6 : 30	Her yoke is a golden ornament
	21 : 21	To a sensible man education is like a golden ornament
	45 : 9	with very many golden bells round about
1 Ma	1 : 21	and took the golden altar
	1 : 22	the cups for drink offerings, the bowls, the golden censers
	4 : 57	with golden crowns and small shields
	6 : 2	Its temple was very rich, containing golden shields
	10 : 20	and he sent him a purple robe and a golden crown
	10 : 89	and he sent to him a golden buckle
2 Ma	5 : 3	hurling of missiles, the flash of golden trappings
	10 : 29	5 resplendent men on horses with golden bridles
	15 : 15	and gave to Judas a golden sword
1 Es	8 : 57	and 20 golden bowls

GOLDENCLAD   1

2 Ma	5 : 2	there appeared goldenclad horsemen charging through the air

GOLDSMITH   1

L Jr	6 : 45	They are made by carpenters and goldsmiths

GOLIATH   1

Sir	47 : 4	and struck down the boasting of Goliath ?

GOMORRAH   1

2 Es	2 : 8	O wicked nation, remember what I did to Sodom and Gomorrah

GOOD, adj.   132 = 0.086 %

Tob	1 : 13	and good appearance in the sight of Shalmaneser
	2 : 1	a good dinner was prepared for me and I sat down to eat
	4 : 9	So you will be laying a good treasure for yourself
	4 : 19	but the Lord himself gives all good things
	5 : 13	You are a relative of mine, of a good and noble lineage
	5 : 13	My brother, you come of good stock
	5 : 16	and good success to you both
	5 : 21	For a good angel will go with him
	7 : 4	And he asked them, Is he in good health ?
	7 : 5	they replied, He is alive and in good health
	7 : 7	Son of that good and noble man !
	8 : 6	Thou didst say, It is not good that the man should be alone
	10 : 12	Let me hear a good report of you
	11 : 11	Be of good cheer, father
	12 : 6	It is good to praise God and to exalt his name
	12 : 7	It is good to guard the secret of a king
	12 : 8	Prayer is good when accompanied by fasting, almsgiving, and righteousness
	12 : 11	I have said, It is good to guard the secret of a king
	12 : 13	your good deed was not hidden from me, but I was with you
	14 : 4	Our brethren will be scattered over the earth from the good land
Jud	3 : 4	come and deal with them in any way that seems good to you
	11 : 8	that you are the one good man in the whole kingdom
	15 : 8	came to witness the good things
Ad E	16 : 22	Therefore you shall observe this with all good cheer
Wis	2 : 6	Come, therefore, let us enjoy the good things that exist
	3 : 15	For the fruit of good labours is renowned
	4 : 5	and good for nothing
	4 : 12	For the fascination of wickedness obscures what is good
	7 : 11	All good things came to me along with her
	8 : 9	knowing that she would give me good counsel
	8 : 19	and a good soul fell to my lot
	8 : 20	or rather, being good, I entered an undefiled body
	12 : 19	and thou hast filled thy sons with good hope
	12 : 21	and covenants full of good promises !
	13 : 1	and they were unable from the good things that are seen
	14 : 26	confusion over what is good, forgetfulness of favours
	18 : 9	For in secret the holy children of good men offered sacrifices
Sir	1 : 24	and the lips of many will tell of his good sense
	2 : 9	you who fear the Lord, hope for good things
	6 : 19	and wait for her good harvest
	7 : 19	Do not deprive yourself of a wise and good wife
	8 : 19	lest you drive away your good luck
	11 : 2	Do not praise a man for his good looks
	11 : 14	good things and bad, life and death, poverty and wealth
	11 : 15	affection and the ways of good works come from him
	12 : 1	and you will be thanked for your good deeds

	12 : 7	Give to the good man, but do not help the sinner
	13 : 24	Riches are good if they are free from sin
	16 : 29	and filled it with his good things
	18 : 15	My son, do not mix reproach with your good deeds
	18 : 17	Indeed, does not a word surpass a good gift ?
	20 : 3	How good it is to show repentance when you are reproved
	20 : 9	There may be good fortune for a man in adversity
	20 : 16	and there is no gratitude for my good deeds
	22 : 9	Children who are brought up in a good life
	25 : 2	and an adulterous old man who lacks good sense
	25 : 4	and for the aged to possess good counsel !
	25 : 9	happy is he who has gained good sense
	26 : 1	Happy is the husband of a good wife
	26 : 3	A good wife is a great blessing
	26 : 16	so is the beauty of a good wife in her well-ordered home
	26 : 21	and, having confidence in their good descent
	26 : 26	Happy is the husband of a good wife
	29 : 14	A good man will be surety for his neighbour
	30 : 18	Good things poured out upon a mouth that is closed
	30 : 25	A man of cheerful and good heart
	31 : 17	Be the first to stop eating, for the sake of good manners
	32 : 1	take good care of them and then be seated
	32 : 6	is the melody of music with good wine
	32 : 11	Leave in good time and do not be the last
	32 : 13	and satisfies you with his good gifts
	32 : 22	and give good heed to your paths
	37 : 9	and tell you, Your way is good
	37 : 28	For not everything is good for every one
	39 : 16	All things are the works of the Lord, for they are very good
	39 : 25	From the beginning good things were created for good people
	39 : 33	The works of the Lord are all good
	39 : 34	for all things will prove good in their season
	40 : 12	but good faith will stand for ever
	40 : 25	but good counsel is esteemed more than both
	41 : 4	and how can you reject the good pleasure of the Most High ?
	41 : 13	The days of a good life are numbered
	41 : 13	but a good name endures for ever
	41 : 16	For it is not good to retain every kind of shame
	42 : 6	Where there is an evil wife, a seal is a good thing
	42 : 25	One confirms the good things of the other
	46 : 10	that it is good to follow the Lord
	51 : 21	therefore I have gained a good possession
P Az	67	Give thanks to the Lord, for he is good
1 Ma	4 : 24	for he is good, for his mercy endures for ever
	6 : 12	and I sent to destroy the inhabitants of Judah without good reason
	6 : 40	and they advanced steadily and in good order
	14 : 9	they all talked together of good things
	15 : 20	And it has seemed good to us to accept the shield from them
2 Ma	1 : 1	To their Jewish brethren in Egypt, greeting, and good peace
	1 : 10	and to the Jews in Egypt, greeting, and good health
	4 : 37	because of the moderation and good conduct of the deceased
	4 : 45	But Menelaus, already as good as beaten
	5 : 4	that the apparition might prove to have been a good omen
	6 : 28	of how to die a good death willingly and nobly
	7 : 20	she bore it with good courage
	8 : 21	With these words he filled them with good courage
	9 : 19	and good wishes for their health and prosperity
	9 : 22	for I have good hope of recovering from my illness
	11 : 6	besought the Lord to send a good angel to save Israel
	11 : 26	so that they may know our policy and be of good cheer
	11 : 28	We also are in good health
	15 : 12	Onias, who had been high priest, a noble and good man
	15 : 23	send a good angel to carry terror and trembling before us
1 Es	2 : 21	if it seems good to you
	8 : 85	and eat the good things of the land
	8 : 94	as seems good to you and to all who obey the law of the Lord
3 Ma	1 : 10	he marvelled at the good order of the temple
	3 : 5	with the good deeds of upright people
	3 : 5	they were established in good repute among all men
	3 : 6	to their good service to their nation
	3 : 11	Then the king, boastful of his present good fortune
	3 : 12	greetings and good health
	3 : 22	and disdained what is good
	3 : 26	the government will be established for ourselves in good order
	4 : 8	instead of good cheer and youthful revelry
	7 : 1	greetings and good health
2 Es	2 : 25	Good nurse, nourish your sons
	3 : 22	but what was good departed, and the evil remained
	7 : 6	and it is full of all good things
	7 : 82	because they cannot now make a good repentance
	8 : 36	who have no store of good works
4 Ma	2 : 23	rule a kingdom that is temperate, just, good, and courageous
	4 : 1	a political opponent of the noble and good man
	12 : 11	since you have received good things and also your kingdom from God
	18 : 9	A happy man was he, who lived out his life with good children

GOOD, subst., goodness

40 = 0.026 %

Tob	12 : 7	Do good, and evil will not overtake you
Jud	15 : 10	you have done great good to Israel
Wis	3 : 5	they will receive great good
	5 : 8	And what good has our boasted wealth brought us ?
	10 : 8	they not only were hindered from recognizing the good
Sir	7 : 13	for the habit of lying serves no good
	11 : 12	but the eyes of the Lord look upon him for his good
	11 : 31	for he lies in wait, turning good into evil
	12 : 2	Do good to a godly man, and you will be repaid
	12 : 3	No good will come to the man who persists in evil
	12 : 5	Do good to the humble, but do not give to the ungodly
	12 : 5	for all the good which you do for him
	13 : 25	either for good or for evil
	14 : 7	even if he does good, he does it unintentionally
	14 : 13	Do good to a friend before you die
	14 : 14	let not your share of desired good pass by you
	17 : 7	and showed them good and evil
	18 : 8	What is his good and what is his evil ?
	33 : 14	Good is the opposite of evil, and life the opposite of death
	37 : 18	4 turns of fortune appear, good and evil, life and death
	38 : 21	you do the dead no good, and you injure yourself
	39 : 4	for he tests the good and the evil among men
	39 : 27	All these are for good to the godly
	42 : 14	than a woman who does good
	49 : 9	and did good to those who directed their ways aright
	51 : 18	and I was zealous for the good
L Jr	6 : 34	Whether one does evil to them or good
	6 : 38	or do good to an orphan
	6 : 64	or to do good to men
1 Ma	10 : 27	and we will repay you with good for what you do for us
	11 : 33	we have determined to do good
	14 : 4	He sought the good of his nation
	16 : 17	and returned evil for good
2 Ma	1 : 2	May God do good to you
	11 : 15	Maccabeus, having regard for the common good
2 Es	2 : 14	for I left out evil and created good
	4 : 29	the field where the good has been sown will not come
	7 : 117	For what good is it to all that they live in sorrow now
	7 : 119	For what good is it to us
	7 : 120	And what good is it

GOOD, subst., property

9 = 0.006 %

Sir	1 : 17	she fills their whole house with desirable goods
	11 : 19	and now I shall enjoy my goods !
	14 : 4	and others will live in luxury on his goods
1 Ma	5 : 13	the enemy have captured their wives and children and goods
	5 : 45	with their wives and children and goods
	9 : 40	and they took all their goods
2 Es	15 : 19	and plunder their goods
	16 : 46	and plunder their goods, and overthrow their houses
	16 : 72	For they shall destroy and plunder their goods

GOODNESS

11 = 0.007 %

Ad E	16 : 4	who know nothing of goodness
Wis	7 : 26	and an image of his goodness
	12 : 22	so that we may meditate upon thy goodness when we judge
Sir	45 : 23	in the ready goodness of his soul
1 Es	5 : 61	because his goodness and his glory are for ever upon all Israel
P Ma	7	Thou, O Lord, according to thy great goodness
	14	and in me thou wilt manifest thy goodness
2 Es	7 : 138	because if he did not give out of his goodness
	8 : 36	thy righteousness and goodness will be declared
	8 : 52	a city is built, rest is appointed, goodness is established
4 Ma	1 : 10	died for the sake of nobility and goodness

GOOD WILL

18 = 0.012 %

Ad E	13 : 3	and is distinguished for his unchanging good will and steadfast fidelity
	16 : 6	beguile the sincere good will of their sovereigns
	16 : 11	so far enjoyed the good will that we have for every nation
Sir	pr.	with good will and attention
1 Ma	11 : 33	because of the good will they show toward us
2 Ma	6 : 29	had acted toward him with good will now changed to ill will
	9 : 21	I remember with affection your esteem and good will
	9 : 26	and to maintain your present good will, each of you
	11 : 19	If you will maintain your good will toward the government
	12 : 30	bore witness to the good will
	13 : 26	convinced them, appeased them, gained their good will
	14 : 26	But when Alcimus noticed their good will for one another
	14 : 37	and for his good will was called father of the Jews
	15 : 30	the man who maintained his youthful good will
3 Ma	3 : 3	The Jews, however, continued to maintain good will
	6 : 26	in their goodwill toward us
	7 : 7	the friendly and firm goodwill
4 Ma	13 : 25	expanded their goodwill and harmony toward one another

GORE

1

4 Ma	9 : 20	and the heap of coals was being quenched by drippings of gore

GORGIAS

11 = 0.007 %

1 Ma	3 : 38	and Nicanor and Gorgias
	4 : 1	Now Gorgias took 5,000 infantry and a 1,000 picked cavalry
	4 : 5	When Gorgias entered the camp of Judas by night
	4 : 18	Gorgias and his force are near us in the hills
	5 : 59	And Gorgias and his men came out of the city
2 Ma	8 : 9	He associated with him Gorgias
	10 : 14	When Gorgias became governor of the region
	12 : 32	they hastened against Gorgias, the governor of Idumea
	12 : 35	caught hold of Gorgias, and grasping his cloak
	12 : 35	so Gorgias escaped and reached Marisa
	12 : 37	then he charged against Gorgias' men

GORMANDIZER

1

4 Ma	2 : 7	that someone who is habitually a solitary gormandizer

GORMANDIZING

1

4 Ma	1 : 27	gluttony, and solitary gormandizing

GORTYNA

1

1 Ma	15 : 23	and to Side, and to Aradus and Gortyna

GOSHEN

1

Jud	1 : 9	and Tahpannes and Raamses and the whole land of Goshen

GOSSIP

2

Sir	19 : 6	and for one who hates gossip evil is lessened
3 Ma	3 : 7	instead they gossiped about the differences in worship and foods

GOTHOLIAH

1

1 Es	8 : 33	Of the sons of Elam, Jeshaiah the son of Gotholiah

GOTHONIEL

1

Jud	6 : 15	and Chabris the son of Gothoniel

GOUGE out

1

4 Ma	5 : 30	not even if you gouge out my eyes and burn my entrails

GOVERN

10 = 0.007 %

Ad E	16 : 15	are not evildoers but are governed by most righteous laws
Wis	3 : 8	They will govern nations and rule over peoples
	8 : 14	I shall govern peoples, and nations will be subject to me
	12 : 18	and with great forbearance thou dost govern us
Sus	13 : 5′	who were supposed to govern the people
1 Ma	8 : 15	concerning the people, to govern them well
3 Ma	6 : 2	governing all creation with mercy
2 Es	13 : 58	and because he governs the times
4 Ma	5 : 16	to govern our lives by the divine law
	6 : 33	we properly attribute to it the power to govern

GOVERNMENT

30 = 0.020 %

Ad E	13 : 5	and is ill-disposed to our government
	13 : 7	and leave our government completely secure and untroubled hereafter
	16 : 1	and to those who are loyal to our government, greeting
Sir	10 : 4	The government of the earth is in the hands of the Lord
1 Ma	6 : 56	and that he was trying to seize control of the government
	10 : 41	which the government officials have not paid
2 Ma	3 : 38	he replied, If you have any enemy or plotter against your government
	4 : 2	He dared to designate as a plotter against the government
	4 : 21	Antiochus learned that Philometor had become hostile to his government
	5 : 7	He did not gain control of the government, however
	8 : 8	for aid to the king's government
	9 : 24	for they would know to whom the government was left
	10 : 11	appointed one Lysias to have charge of the government
	11 : 1	who was in charge of the government
	11 : 19	If you will maintain your good will toward the government
	13 : 2	who had charge of the government
	13 : 23	who had been left in charge of the government
	14 : 10	it is impossible for the government to find peace
	14 : 26	He told him that Nicanor was disloyal to the government
3 Ma	3 : 7	but were hostile and greatly opposed to his government
	3 : 13	I myself and our government are faring well
	3 : 26	the government will be established for ourselves in good order
	6 : 28	has granted an unimpeded and notable stability to our government
	7 : 1	and all in authority in his government
	7 : 4	for they declared that our government
	7 : 11	toward the king's government
4 Ma	4 : 3	because I am loyal to the king's government
	4 : 19	and altered its form of government
	8 : 7	positions of authority in my government
	12 : 5	and a leader in the government of the kingdom

GOVERNOR

37 = 0.024 %

Jud	5 : 2	and all the governors of the coastland
Ad E	13 : 1	from India to Ethiopia and to the governors under them
1 Ma	7 : 8	governor of the province Beyond the River

	10:65	and made him general and governor of the province
	10:69	And Demetrius appointed Apollonius the governor of Coelesyria
	11:59	Simon his brother he made governor
	14:42	and that he should be governor over them
	16:11	Now Ptolemy the son of Abubus had been appointed governor
2 Ma	3:5	who at that time was governor of Coelesyria and Phoenicia
	4:4	and governor of Coelesyria and Phoenicia
	5:22	And he left governors to afflict the people : at Jerusalem
	8:8	the governor of Coelesyria and Phoenicia
	10:11	and to be chief governor of Coelesyria and Phoenicia
	10:14	When Gorgias became governor of the region
	12:2	But some of the governors in various places
	12:2	and in addition to these Nicanor the governor of Cyprus
	12:32	they hastened against Gorgias, the governor of Idumea
	13:24	left Hegemonides as governor from Ptolemais to Gerar
	14:12	appointed him governor of Judea, and sent him off
1 Es	2:12	and by him they were given to Shesh-Bazzar the governor of Judea
	3:2	and all the satraps and generals and governors
	3:14	and the satraps and generals and governors and prefects
	4:47	and governors and generals and satraps
	4:48	And he wrote letters to all the governors in Coelesyria
	4:49	that no officer or satrap or governor or treasurer
	6:3	At the same time Sisinnes the governor of Syria and Phoenicia
	6:7	which Sisinnes the governor of Syria and Phoenicia
	6:18	and Shesh-Bazzar the governor
	6:27	the governor of Syria and Phoenicia
	6:27	the servant of the Lord and governor of Judea
	6:29	that is, to Zerubbabel the governor
	7:1	Then Sisinnes the governor of Coelesyria and Phoenicia
	8:67	and to the governors of Coelesyria and Phoenicia
3 Ma	2:3	For you, the creator of all things and the governor of all
4 Ma	2:22	as a sacred governor over them all
	4:2	governor of Syria, Phoenicia, and Cilicia
	7:16	most certainly devout reason is governor of the emotions

GOWN   1
Jud 16:8   and put on a linen gown to deceive him

GRACE   6 = 0.004 %
Ad E	15:14	and your countenance is full of grace
Wis	3:9	because grace and mercy are upon his elect
	4:15	that God's grace and mercy are with his elect
Sir	37:21	for grace was not given him by the Lord
	40:22	The eye desires grace and beauty
2 Es	2:32	because my springs run over, and my grace will not fail

GRACEFUL   1
Sir 24:16   and my branches are glorious and graceful

GRACEFULNESS   1
4 Ma 6:2   who remained adorned with the gracefulness of his piety

GRACIOUS   9 = 0.006 %
Sir	6:5	and a gracious tongue multiplies courtesies
	17:21	But the Lord, who is gracious and knows his creatures
	18:17	Both are to be found in a gracious man
2 Ma	2:22	while the Lord with great kindness became gracious to them
	10:26	they besought him to be gracious to them
	14:9	with the gracious kindness which you show to all
1 Es	8:10	In accordance with my gracious decision
2 Es	7:133	and gracious, because he is gracious to those

GRACIOUSLY   3 = 0.002 %
Wis	6:16	and she graciously appears to them in their paths
Sir	7:33	Give graciously to all the living
3 Ma	2:16	But because you graciously bestowed your glory

GRAIN   11 = 0.007 %
Jud	10:5	and filled a bag with parched grain
	11:13	They have decided to consume the first fruits of the grain
Sir	18:10	Like a drop of water from the sea and a grain of sand
	40:22	but the green shoots of grain more than both
1 Ma	8:26	they shall not give or supply grain
	8:28	And to the enemy allies shall be given no grain
	10:30	and instead of collecting the third of the grain
2 Es	4:30	For a grain of evil seed was sown in Adam's heart from the beginning
	4:31	how much fruit of ungodliness a grain of evil seed has produced
	4:32	When heads of grain without number are sown
	15:42	and grass of the meadows, and their grain

GRANDEUR   1
Sir 17:10   to proclaim the grandeur of his works

GRANDFATHER   1
Sir pr.   my grandfather Jesus, after devoting himself

GRANDMOTHER   1
4 Ma 16:9   or have the happiness of being called grandmother

GRANDSON   1
Tob 14:3   When he had grown very old he called his son and grandsons

GRANT, verb   45 = 0.029 %
Tob	7:18	the Lord of heaven and earth grant you joy
	8:7	Grant that I may find mercy
	10:12	and grant me to see your children by my daughter Sarah
Jud	10:8	May the God of our fathers grant you favour
	13:20	May God grant this to be a perpetual honour to you
Wis	7:15	May God grant that I speak with judgment
	12:20	granting them time and opportunity
Sir	6:37	and your desire for wisdom will be granted
	17:2	but granted them authority over the things upon the earth
	17:4	and granted them dominion over beasts and birds
	17:24	Yet to those who repent he grants a return
	18:12	therefore he grants them forgiveness in abundance
	26:3	she will be granted among the blessings
	34:17	he grants healing, life, and blessing
	38:14	that he should grant them success in diagnosis
	43:33	and to the godly he has granted wisdom
	45:26	May the Lord grant you wisdom in your heart
	50:23	and grant that peace may be in our days in Israel
Bar	2:14	and for thy own sake deliver us, and grant us favour
1 Ma	10:28	We will grant you many immunities and give you gifts
	10:40	I also grant 15,000 shekels of silver yearly
	11:34	we have granted release from the royal taxes
	11:35	from all these we shall grant them release
	11:50	Grant us peace
	11:58	and granted him the right to drink from gold cups
	11:66	Then they asked him to grant them terms of peace
	13:34	with a request to grant relief to the country
	13:37	to grant you release from tribute
	14:46	And all the people agreed to grant Simon
	15:5	that the kings before me have granted you
	15:7	and I grant freedom to Jerusalem and the sanctuary
2 Ma	3:31	to call upon the Most High and to grant life
	3:33	since for his sake the Lord has granted you your life
	11:15	For the king granted every request in behalf of the Jews
	11:35	With regard to what Lysias the kinsman of the king has granted you
	12:11	to grant them pledges of friendship
3 Ma	3:16	And when we had granted very great revenues
	5:11	is bestowed by him who grants it to whomever he wishes
	6:28	has granted an unimpeded and notable stability to our government
	6:41	The king granted their request at once
	7:12	granted them a general licence
2 Es	5:4	But if the Most High grants that you live
	8:6	O Lord who art over us, grant to thy servant
4 Ma	5:8	Why, when nature has granted it to us, should you abhor eating
	11:12	he said, Tyrant, they are splendid favours that you grant us against your will

GRANT, subst.   2
1 Ma	11:36	And not one of these grants shall be cancelled
	13:38	All the grants that we have made to you remain valid

GRAPE   10 = 0.007 %
Sir	39:26	the blood of the grape, and oil and clothing
	50:15	and poured a libation of the blood of the grape
	51:15	From blossom to ripening grape my heart delighted in her
1 Ma	6:34	They showed the elephants the juice of grapes and mulberries
2 Es	9:21	and saved for myself one grape out of a cluster
	9:22	but let my grape and my plant be saved
	12:42	like a cluster of grapes from the vintage
	16:26	The grapes shall ripen, and who will tread them ?
	16:43	like one who will not gather the grapes
4 Ma	2:9	nor gathers the last grapes from the vineyard

GRAPE-GATHERER   2
Sir	33:16	I was like one who gleans after the grape-gatherers
	33:16	and like a grape-gatherer I filled my wine press

GRAPPLE   1
Sir 51:19   My soul grappled with wisdom, and in my conduct I was strict

GRASP, verb   3 = 0.002 %
Sir	26:7	taking hold of her is like grasping a scorpion
2 Ma	12:35	caught hold of Gorgias, and grasping his cloak
2 Es	10:30	Then he grasped my right hand and strengthened me

GRASS   4 = 0.003 %
Sir	40:16	will be plucked up before any grass
	43:21	and withers the tender grass like fire
2 Es	9:27	And after 7 days, as I lay on the grass
	15:42	and grass of the meadows, and their grain

GRASSY 1
Wis **19**:7 and a grassy plain out of the raging waves

GRATEFUL 2
Sir **29**:17 and one who does not feel grateful will abandon his rescuer
2 Ma **3**:33 Be very grateful to Onias the high priest

GRATITUDE 4 = 0.003 %
Sir **20**:16 and there is no gratitude for my good deeds
37:11 with a grudging man about gratitude
2 Ma **2**:27 However, to secure the gratitude of many
2 Es **1**:37 I call to witness the gratitude of the people that is to come

GRAVE, subst. 12 = 0.008 %
Tob **2**:7 and dug a grave and buried the body
3:10 and I shall bring his old age down in sorrow to the grave
4:4 When she dies, bury her beside me in the same grave
4:17 Place your bread on the grave of the righteous
6:14 and bring the lives of my father and mother to the grave
8:9 But Raguel arose and went and dug a grave
8:18 Then he ordered his servants to fill in the grave
Wis **19**:3 and were lamenting at the graves of their dead
Sir **30**:18 are like offerings of food placed upon a grave
Bar **2**:24 would be brought out of their graves
2 Es **2**:23 commit them to the grave and mark it
5:35 Or why did not my mother's womb become my grave

GRAVE, adj. 1
2 Ma **1**:11 Having been saved by God out of grave dangers

GRAVEN 3 = 0.002 %
Wis **14**:16 and at the command of monarchs graven images were worshipped
15:13 when he makes from earthy matter fragile vessels and graven images
1 Ma **5**:68 and the graven images of their gods he burned with fire

GREAT, adj., subst. 319 = 0.208 %
Tob **3**:6 and great is the sorrow within me
3:16 in the presence of the glory of the great God
4:13 For in pride there is ruin and great confusion
4:13 and in shiftlessness there is loss and great want
4:21 You have great wealth if you fear God
5:12 He replied, I am Azarias the son of the great Ananias
5:13 the sons of the great Shemaiah
8:16 but thou hast treated us according to thy great mercy
11:15 and he reported to his father the great things
11:19 with great festivity
12:22 So they confessed the great and wonderful works of God
13:15 Let my soul praise God the great King
Jud **1**:1 who ruled over the Assyrians in the great city of Nineveh
1:5 against King Arphaxad in the great plain
1:8 and Upper Galilee and the great Plain of Esdraelon
2:5 Thus says the Great King, the Lord of the whole earth :
2:16 as a great army is marshalled for a campaign
3:2 Behold, we, the servants of Nebuchadnezzar, the Great King
3:9 near Dothan, fronting the great ridge of Judea
4:9 And every man of Israel cried out to God with great fervour
5:10 and there they became a great multitude
5:10 so great that they could not be counted
7:2 a very great multitude
7:18 and their tents and supply trains spread out in great number
7:24 For you have done us a great injury
7:29 Then great and general lamentation arose
8:8 for she feared God with great devotion
8:19 and so they suffered a great catastrophe before our enemies
10:18 There was great excitement in the whole camp
12:16 and he was moved with great desire to possess her
12:20 and drank a great quantity of wine
13:4 and no one, either small or great
13:13 They all ran together, both small and great
14:9 And when she had finished, the people raised a great shout
15:5 with great slaughter
15:7 got a great amount of booty
15:9 you are the great glory of Israel
15:9 you are the great pride of our nation !
15:10 you have done great good to Israel
16:13 O Lord, thou art great and glorious
16:16 but who fears the Lord shall be great for ever
Ad E **10**:9 God has done great signs and wonders
11:2 In the 2nd year of the reign of Ahasuerus the Great
11:3 a great man, serving in the court of the king
11:6 And behold, 2 great dragons came forward
11:8 affliction and great tumult upon the earth !
11:10 there came a great river, with abundant water
12:6 was in great honour with the king
13:1 The Great King, Ahasuerus
16:1 The Great King, Ahasuerus
16:2 by the too great kindness of their benefactors
Wis **3**:5 they will receive great good

3:14 and a place of great delight in the temple of the Lord
5:1 Then the righteous man will stand with great confidence
6:7 because he himself made both small and great
8:12 and when I speak at greater length
11:21 For it is always in thy power to show great strength
12:18 and with great forbearance thou dost govern us
12:20 For if thou didst punish with such great care and indulgence
14:22 but they live in great strife due to ignorance
14:22 and they call such great evils peace
16:17 the fire had still greater effect
17:1 Great are thy judgments and hard to describe
18:1 But for thy holy ones there was very great light
Sir pr. Whereas many great teachings have been given to us
pr. those who love learning should make even greater progress
pr. using in that period of time great watchfulness and skill
3:18 The greater you are, the more you must humble yourself
3:20 For great is the might of the Lord
3:23 for matters too great for human understanding
4:7 bow your head low to a great man
5:6 Do not say, His mercy is great
5:15 In great or small matters do not act amiss
7:25 you will have finished a great task
8:8 and learn how to serve great men
10:24 but none of them is greater than the man who fears the Lord
11:1 and will seat him among the great
15:18 For great is the wisdom of the Lord
16:12 As great as his mercy, so great is also his reproof
17:29 How great is the mercy of the Lord
18:9 The number of a man's days is great
18:32 Do not revel in great luxury
20:27 and a sensible man will please great men
20:28 and whoever pleases great men will atone for injustice
23:14 Remember your father and mother when you sit among great men
23:28 It is a great honour to follow God
24:29 and her counsel deeper than the great abyss
25:10 How great is he who has gained wisdom !
25:22 There is wrath and impudence and great disgrace
26:3 A good wife is a great blessing
26:8 There is great anger when a wife is drunken
26:21 will grow great
28:14 and overturned the houses of great men
31:12 Are you seated at the table of a great man ?
32:9 Among the great do not act as their equal
33:18 Hear me, you who are great among the people
38:3 and in the presence of great men is admired
38:27 each is diligent in making a great variety
39:4 He will serve among great men and appear before rulers
39:6 If the great Lord is willing
39:11 if he lives long, he will leave a name greater than a 1,000
41:12 since it will remain for you longer than a 1,000 great stores of gold
42:11 and put you to shame before the great multitude
43:5 Great is the Lord who made it
43:23 By his counsel he stilled the great deep
43:28 For he is greater than all his works
43:29 Terrible is the Lord and very great
43:32 Many things greater than these lie hidden
44:2 The Lord apportioned to them great glory
44:19 Abraham was the great father of a multitude of nations
45:2 and made him great in the fears of his enemies
46:1 a great saviour of God's elect
46:6 and the great Lord answered him
48:18 and made great boasts in his arrogance
48:22 who was great and faithful in his vision
50:16 they made a great noise to be heard
50:22 who in every way does great things
Bar **1**:4 and in the hearing of all the people, small and great
2:11 and with great power and outstretched arm
2:25 They perished in great misery
2:27 in all thy kindness and in all thy great compassion
2:29 this very great multitude will surely turn into
3:24 O Israel, how great is the house of God !
3:25 It is great and has no bounds
3:26 great in stature, expert in war
4:9 God has brought great sorrow upon me
4:24 which will come to you with great glory
4:34 And I will take away her pride in her great population
Sus **13**:31 Now Susanna was a woman of great refinement
13:64 Daniel had a great reputation among the people
Bel **14**:18 You are great, O Bel
14:23 There was also a great dragon
14:41 Thou art great, O Lord God of Daniel
1 Ma **1**:24 He committed deeds of murder, and spoke with great arrogance
1:33 with a great strong wall and strong towers
1:35 they stored them there, and became a great snare
1:40 Her dishonour now grew as great as her glory
1:64 And very great wrath came upon Israel
2:17 You are a leader, honoured and great in this city
2:51 and receive great honour and an everlasting name

2:58	Elijah because of great zeal for the law
2:70	And all Israel mourned for him with great lamentation
3:17	fight against so great and strong a multitude ?
3:20	They come against us in great pride and lawlessness
4:23	and cloth dyed blue and sea purple, and great riches
4:25	Thus Israel had a great deliverance that day
4:39	and mourned with great lamentation
4:58	There was very great gladness among the people
5:16	a great assembly was called
5:23	and led them to Judea with great rejoicing
5:45	the small and the great
5:61	Thus the people suffered a great rout
6:4	So he fled and in great grief departed from there
6:11	And into what a great flood I now am plunged !
6:27	they will do still greater things
7:8	he was a great man in the kingdom
7:19	and killed them and threw them into the great pit
7:22	and did great damage in Israel
7:35	And he went out in great anger
7:48	and celebrated that day as a day of great gladness
8:4	and inflicted great disaster upon them
8:6	They also defeated Antiochus the Great, king of Asia
9:20	And all Israel made great lamentation for him
9:24	In those days a very great famine occurred
9:27	Thus there was great distress in Israel
9:35	the great amount of baggage which they had
9:37	The sons of Jambri are celebrating a great wedding
9:37	a daughter of one of the great nobles of Canaan
9:56	And Alcimus died at that time in great agony
10:37	in the great strongholds of the king
10:46	because they remembered the great wrongs
10:58	and celebrated her wedding at Ptolemais with great pomp, as kings do
10:86	and the men of the city came out to meet him with great pomp
11:1	Then the king of Egypt gathered great forces
11:42	but I will confer great honour on you and your nation
12:49	and the Great Plain to destroy all Jonathan's soldiers
12:52	and were in great fear
13:3	You yourselves know what great things
13:17	lest he arouse great hostility among the people
13:26	All Israel bewailed him with great lamentation
13:29	erecting about them great columns
13:32	and brought great calamity upon the land
13:33	with high towers and great walls and gates and bolts
13:42	In the first year of Simon the great high priest
13:44	and a great tumult arose in the city
13:51	because a great enemy had been crushed and removed from Israel
14:11	and Israel rejoiced with great joy
14:27	which is the 3rd year of Simon the great high priest
14:28	in Asaramel, in the great assembly of the priests
14:29	and they brought great glory to their nation
14:32	He spent great sums of his own money
14:36	and do great damage to its purity
15:9	we will bestow great honour upon you and your nation and the temple
15:29	you have done great damage in the land
15:32	and his great magnificence
15:35	they were causing great damage among the people and to our land
16:15	he gave them a great banquet, and hid men there
16:17	So he committed an act of great treachery

2 Ma
1:22	a great fire blazed up, so that all marvelled
2:18	for he has rescued us from great evils
2:19	and the purification of the great temple
2:22	while the Lord with great kindness became gracious to them
3:21	and the anxiety of the high priest in his great anguish
3:24	caused so great a manifestation
3:28	with a great retinue and all his bodyguard
3:35	and made very great vows to the Saviour of his life
5:6	is the greatest misfortune
5:20	when the great Lord became reconciled
5:26	and killed great numbers of people
6:13	is a sign of great kindness
6:31	not only to the young but to the great body of his nation
8:16	and not to fear the great multitude of Gentiles
8:27	giving great praise and thanks to the Lord
10:38	who shows great kindness to Israel
12:15	calling upon the great Sovereign of the world
12:24	With great guile he besought them to let him go in safety
12:27	and great stores of war engines and missiles were there
13:1	with a great army against Judea
14:13	and to set up Alcimus as high priest of the greatest temple
14:31	he went to the great and holy temple
15:18	their greatest and first fear

1 Es
1:54	And all the holy vessels of the Lord, great and small
2:9	and with a very great number of votive offerings
3:1	Now King Darius gave a great banquet
3:5	and great honours of victory
4:14	Gentlemen, is not the king great, and are not men many

4:28	Is not the king great in his power ?
4:35	Is he not great who does these things ?
4:35	But truth is great, and stronger than all things
4:41	Great is truth, and strongest of all !
5:62	and shouted with a great shout
6:9	building in the city of Jerusalem a great new house for the Lord
6:14	by a king of Israel who was great and strong
7:2	supervised the holy work with very great care
8:7	For Ezra possessed great knowledge
8:76	and we are in great sin to this day
8:86	because of our evil deeds and our great sins
8:91	there gathered about him a very great throng from Jerusalem
8:91	for there was great weeping among the multitude
9:2	for he was mourning over the great iniquities of the multitude
9:11	But the multitude is great and it is winter
9:54	and to make great rejoicing

P Ma
7	of great compassion, long-suffering
7	Thou, O Lord, according to thy great goodness
14	for, unworthy as I am, thou wilt save me in thy great mercy

3 Ma
2:9	for the glory of your great and honoured name
2:12	and rescued them from great evils
2:13	that because of our many and great sins
2:23	panic-stricken in their exceedingly great fear
3:9	for such a great community ought not be left to its fate
3:15	but should cherish them with clemency and great benevolence
3:16	And when we had granted very great revenues
5:10	until they had been filled with a great abundance of wine
5:23	began to move them along in the great colonnade
5:44	Then the friends and officers departed with great joy
6:2	King of great power, Almighty God Most High
6:17	they raised great cries to heaven
6:33	Likewise also the king, after convening a great banquet
7:2	the great God guiding our affairs according to our desire
7:21	They also possessed greater prestige among their enemies
7:22	So the supreme God perfectly performed great deeds

2 Es
1:9	on whom I have bestowed such great benefits ?
1:14	and did great wonders among you
2:42	I, Ezra, saw on Mount Zion a great multitude
2:43	In their midst was a young man of great stature
2:48	how great and many are the wonders of the Lord God
3:16	and Jacob became a great multitude
4:32	how great a threshing floor they will fill !
4:45	or whether for us the greater part has gone by
4:50	and the fire is greater than the smoke
4:50	so the quantity that passed was far greater
5:1	shall be seized with great terror
5:13	you shall hear yet greater things than these
6:31	I will again declare to you greater things than these
7:12	full of dangers and involved in great hardships
7:13	But the entrances of the greater world are broad and safe
7:91	First of all, they shall see with great joy
7:92	because they have striven with great effort
7:98	which is greater than all that have been mentioned
8:14	who with so great labour was fashioned by thy command
8:49	in order to receive the greatest glory
8:50	because they have walked in great pride
9:16	as a wave is greater than a drop of water
9:21	And I saw and spared some with great difficulty
9:21	and one plant out of a great forest
9:45	and we gave great glory to the Mighty One
10:7	is in deep grief and great affliction
10:11	she who lost so great a multitude
10:24	Therefore shake off your great sadness
11:29	for it was greater than the other 2 heads
11:32	and it had greater power over the world
12:3	Then I awoke in great perplexity of mind and great fear
12:5	because of the great fear with which I have been terrified this night
12:18	great struggles shall arise
12:40	from the least to the greatest
13:6	he carved for himself a great mountain, and flew up upon it
13:11	the stream of fire and the flaming breath and the great storm
13:13	Then in great fear I awoke
13:19	For they shall see great dangers and much distress
13:57	giving great glory and praise to the Most High
15:19	and because of great tribulation
15:30	and with great power they shall come
15:31	and if they combine in great power
15:37	And there shall be fear and great trembling upon the earth
15:40	And great and mighty clouds, full of wrath and tempest
16:21	the sword, famine, and great confusion
16:26	For in all places there shall be great solitude
16:38	has great pains about her womb for 2 or 3 hours beforehand
16:68	For behold, the burning wrath of a great multitude is kindled over you
16:70	there shall be a great insurrection

4 Ma
4:10	instilling in them great fear and trembling
5:20	to transgress the law in matters either small or great
11:23	and I myself will bring a great avenger upon you
13:15	for great is the struggle of the soul

15:9   she felt a greater tenderness toward them
15:22 How great and how many torments the mother then suffered
16:4   But the mother quenched so many and such great emotions by devout reason

GREATLY   49 = 0.032 %
Tob 9:4   and if I delay long he will be greatly distressed
    10:3   And he was greatly distressed
Jud 4:2   they were therefore very greatly terrified at his approach
    6:20 Then they consoled Achior, and praised him greatly
    7:4   they were greatly terrified
    7:32 And they were greatly depressed in the city
   10:7   they greatly admired her beauty, and said to her
  12:20 And Holofernes was greatly pleased with her
  13:17 All the people were greatly astonished
  14:19 they rent their tunics and were greatly dismayed
Wis 18:17 Then at once apparitions in dreadful dreams greatly troubled them
Sir 1:8   There is One who is wise, greatly to be feared
   7:17   Humble yourself greatly
  11:6   Many rulers have been greatly disgraced
  25:2   and I am greatly offended at their life :
  42:22 How greatly to be desired are all his works
  49:4   Except David and Hezekiah and Josiah they all sinned greatly
Bar 2:18 but the person that is greatly distressed
Sus 13:27 the servants were greatly ashamed
1 Ma 2:14 put on sackcloth, and mourned greatly
   3:27 he was greatly angered
   3:31 He was greatly perplexed in mind
   4:21 When they perceived this they were greatly frightened
   5:63 The man Judas and his brothers were greatly honoured
   7:48 The people rejoiced greatly
   8:13 and they have been greatly exalted
   9:6   they were greatly frightened
   9:68 They distressed him greatly
   9:69 So he was greatly enraged at the lawless men
  10:8   They were greatly alarmed when they heard
  10:46 and how he had greatly oppressed them
  10:68 he was greatly grieved and returned to Antioch
  11:53 but oppressed him greatly
  15:36 And the king was greatly angered
  16:22 When he heard this, he was greatly shocked
2 Ma 1:11 we thank him greatly for taking our side against the king
   8:32 and one who had greatly troubled the Jews
  15:27 and were greatly gladdened by God's manifestation
3 Ma 3:7   but were hostile and greatly opposed to his government
   4:16 The king was greatly and continually filled with joy
2 Es 3:3   My spirit was greatly agitated
   5:33 Are you greatly disturbed in mind over Israel ?
   6:14 And if the place where you are standing is greatly shaken
   6:37 For my spirit was greatly aroused
   9:41 for I am greatly embittered in spirit and deeply afflicted
   9:45 And I rejoiced greatly over him
  10:39 and mourned greatly over Zion
4 Ma 4:22 and that the people of Jerusalem had rejoiced greatly
   8:5   and greatly respect the beauty and the number of such brothers

GREATNESS   6 = 0.004 %
Tob 13:4   Make his greatness known there
Wis 6:7   nor show deference to greatness
  13:5   For from the greatness and beauty of created things
Sir 51:3   in the greatness of thy mercy and of thy name
1 Ma 9:22 and the brave deeds that he did, and his greatness
1 Es 4:46 and this befits your greatness

GREECE   1
1 Ma 1:1   He had previously become king of Greece

GREEDILY   1
Sir 31:16 and do not chew greedily, lest you be hated

GREEDY   6 = 0.004 %
Sir 14:9   A greedy man's eye is not satisfied with a portion
  31:12 Do not be greedy at it
  31:13 Remember that a greedy eye is a bad thing
  31:13 What has been created more greedy than the eye ?
1 Ma 4:17 and he said to the people, Do not be greedy for plunder
4 Ma 2:9   If one is greedy, he is ruled by the law through his reason

GREEK, adj., subst.   17 = 0.011 %
1 Ma 1:10 of the kingdom of the Greeks
   6:2   the Macedonian king who first reigned over the Greeks
   8:9   The Greeks planned to come and destroy them
   8:10 and they sent a general against the Greeks and attacked them
   8:18 for they saw that the kingdom of the Greeks
2 Ma 4:10 to the Greek way of life
   4:12 to wear the Greek hat
   4:15 and putting the highest value upon Greek forms of prestige
   4:36 and the Greeks shared their hatred of the crime
   6:8   a decree was issued to the neighbouring Greek cities

   6:9   to change over to Greek customs
  11:2   He intended to make the city a home for Greeks
  11:24 to our father's change to Greek customs
  13:2   Each of them had a Greek force of 110,000 infantry
3 Ma 3:8   The Greeks in the city, though wronged in no way
4 Ma 8:8   And enjoy your youth by adopting the Greek way of life
  18:20 when that bitter tyrant of the Greeks

GREEN   2
Sir 40:22 but the green shoots of grain more than both
  50:8   like a green shoot on Lebanon on a summer day

GREET   9 = 0.006 %
Tob 5:9   he entered and they greeted each other
   7:1   Sarah met them and greeted them
Jud 15:8   and to see Judith and to greet her
Sir 41:20 and of silence, before those who greet you
1 Ma 7:29 So he came to Judas, and they greeted one another peaceably
   7:33 to greet him peaceably and to show him the burnt offering
  11:6   and they greeted one another and spent the night there
  12:17 and greet you and deliver to you this letter from us
3 Ma 1:8   to greet him, to bring him gifts of welcome

GREETING   23 = 0.015 %
Tob 7:1   They returned her greeting
Ad E 16:1   and to those who are loyal to our government, greeting
1 Ma 10:18 King Alexander to his brother Jonathan, greeting
  10:25 King Demetrius to the nation of the Jews, greeting
  11:30 and to the nation of the Jews, greeting
  11:32 King Demetrius to Lasthenes his father, greeting
  12:6   to their brethren the Spartans, greeting
  12:20 to Onias the high priest, greeting
  13:36 and to the elders and nation of the Jews, greeting
  14:20 and the rest of the Jewish people, our brethren, greeting
  15:2   and to the nation of the Jews, greeting
  15:16 Lucius, consul of the Romans, to King Ptolemy, greeting
2 Ma 1:1   To their Jewish brethren in Egypt, greeting, and good peace
   1:10   and to the Jews in Egypt, greeting, and good health
   9:19   Antiochus their king and general sends hearty greetings
  11:16 Lysias to the people of the Jews, greeting
  11:22 King Antiochus to his brother Lysias, greeting
  11:27 and to the other Jews, greeting
  11:34 to the people of the Jews, greeting
1 Es 6:8   To King Darius, greeting
   8:9   and reader of the law of the Lord, greeting
3 Ma 3:12 greetings and good health
   7:1   greetings and good health

GREY, GRAY   6 = 0.004 %
Wis 2:10 nor regard the grey hairs of the aged
   4:9   but understanding is grey hair for men
2 Ma 6:23 and the grey hairs which he had reached with distinction
  15:13 distinguished by his grey hair and dignity
4 Ma 5:7   for I respect your age and your grey hairs
   7:15 and venerable grey hair and law-abiding life

GREY-HAIRED, GRAY-HAIRED   1
Sir 25:4   What an attractive thing is judgment in grey-haired men

GREY-HEADED, GRAY-HEADED   1
3 Ma 4:5   For a multitude of grey-headed old men

GRIEF   23 = 0.015 %
Tob 3:1   Then in my grief I wept
   7:7   he was stricken with grief and wept
Wis 8:9   and encouragement in cares and grief
  11:12 for a twofold grief possessed them
  14:15 For a father, consumed with grief
Sir 14:1   and need not suffer grief for sin
  18:15 nor cause grief by your words when you present a gift
  22:4   but one who acts shamefully brings grief to her father
  26:6   There is grief of heart and sorrow
  30:9   play with him, and he will give you grief
  36:20 A perverse mind will cause grief
  37:2   Is it not a grief to the death
Bar 4:34 and her insolence will be turned to grief
1 Ma 6:4   So he fled and in great grief departed from there
   6:8   He took to his bed and became sick from grief
   6:9   because deep grief continually gripped him
   6:13 and behold, I am perishing of deep grief in a strange land
1 Es 8:71 and sat down in anxiety and grief
3 Ma 7:9   or cause them any grief at all
2 Es 5:34 but because of my grief I have spoken
   7:131 Therefore there shall be grief at their destruction
  10:7   is in deep grief and great affliction
4 Ma 18:9 and did not have the grief of bereavement

GRIEF-STRICKEN   1
1 Es 8:72 and I sat grief-stricken until the evening sacrifice

GRIEVE 31 = 0.020 %
Tob	3:10	When she heard these things she was deeply grieved
	4:3	do what is pleasing to her, and do not grieve her
	10:12	do nothing to grieve her
	13:14	Blessed are those who grieved over all your afflictions
Wis	14:24	or grieve one another by adultery
Sir	3:12	and do not grieve him as long as he lives
	4:2	Do not grieve the one who is hungry
	12:9	A man's enemies are grieved when he prospers
	21:24	and a discreet man is grieved by the disgrace
	26:28	At 2 things my heart is grieved
	30:5	and when he died he was not grieved
	47:20	and they were grieved at your folly
Bar	4:8	and you grieved Jerusalem, who reared you
	4:33	so she will be grieved at her own desolation
1 Ma	10:22	When Demetrius heard of these things he was grieved and said
	10:68	he was greatly grieved and returned to Antioch
	14:16	and they were deeply grieved
2 Ma	4:35	were grieved and displeased at the unjust murder of the man
	4:37	Therefore Antiochus was grieved at heart
	14:28	and grieved that he had to annul their agreement
1 Es	1:24	and how they grieved the Lord deeply
3 Ma	3:8	being grieved at the situation
2 Es	7:61	And I will not grieve over the multitude of those who perish
	7:80	ever grieving and sad, in 7 ways
	8:15	for whom I am grieved
	9:38	and was deeply grieved at heart
	9:40	Why are you weeping, and why are you grieved at heart ?
	10:11	or you who are grieving for one ?
	10:50	seeing that you are sincerely grieved and profoundly distressed for her
4 Ma	16:12	nor did she grieve as they were dying
	16:22	You too must have the same faith in God and not be grieved

GRIEVOUS 10 = 0.007 %
Wis	3:19	For the end of an unrighteous generation is grievous
Sir	27:15	and their abuse is grievous to hear
2 Ma	6:3	Harsh and utterly grievous was the onslaught of evil
3 Ma	5:47	the grievous and pitiful destruction of the aforementioned people
	6:5	speaking grievous words with boasting and insolence
2 Es	5:21	the thoughts of my heart were very grievous to me again
	11:40	and over all the earth with grievous oppression
	14:15	and lay to one side the thoughts that are most grievous to you
4 Ma	9:4	to be more grievous than death itself
	16:8	and the more grievous anxieties of your upbringing

GRIEVOUSLY 2
Sir	38:16	and as one who is suffering grievously begin the lament
3 Ma	2:2	who are suffering grievously from an impious and profane man

GRIP 1
1 Ma	6:9	because deep grief continually gripped him

GROAN, subst. 2
3 Ma	1:18	and filled the streets with groans and lamentations
	5:49	and giving way to lamentation and groans they kissed each other

GROAN, verb 10 = 0.007 %
Jud	14:16	and wept and groaned and shouted, and rent his garments
Wis	5:3	and in anguish of spirit they will groan, and say
Sir	30:20	he sees with his eyes and groans
	30:20	like a eunuch who embraces a maiden and groans
1 Ma	1:26	rulers and elders groaned
2 Ma	6:30	he groaned aloud and said :
3 Ma	4:2	and they groaned because of the unexpected destruction
	6:34	groaned as they themselves were overcome by disgrace
2 Es	16:39	and the world will groan
4 Ma	9:21	the courageous youth, worthy of Abraham, did not groan

GROANING 2
Wis	11:12	and a groaning at the memory of what had occurred
2 Es	1:19	I pitied your groaning and gave you manna for food

GROUND, subst. 36 = 0.023 %
Jud	5:18	the temple of their God was razed to the ground
	7:25	to strew us on the ground before them
	12:15	and her maid went and spread on the ground for her before Holofernes
	14:18	For look, here is Holofernes lying on the ground
	16:5	and dash my infants to the ground
Wis	4:19	because he will dash them speechless to the ground
	11:22	and like a drop of morning dew that falls upon the ground
Sir	11:5	Many kings have had to sit on the ground
	31:10	Let it be for him a ground for boasting
	32:20	and do not stumble over stony ground
	33:10	All men are from the ground
	50:17	and fell to the ground upon their faces
Bar	5:7	and the valleys filled up, to make level ground
L Jr	6:27	lest they fall to the ground
1 Ma	4:40	They fell face down on the ground

	6:46	but it fell to the ground upon him and there he died
	14:8	the ground gave its increase
2 Ma	2:30	to occupy the ground and to discuss matters from every side
	3:27	When he suddenly fell to the ground
	8:3	and about to be levelled to the ground
	8:8	When Philip saw that the man was gaining ground little by little
	9:14	which he was hastening to level to the ground
	14:33	I will level this precinct of God to the ground
1 Es	8:91	weeping and lying upon the ground before the temple
	9:47	and fell to the ground and worshipped the Lord
3 Ma	2:22	so that he lay helpless on the ground and
	5:31	who give me no ground for complaint
	5:43	and rapidly level it to the ground with fire and spear
	5:43	and by burning to the ground the temple inaccessible to him
	5:50	they prostrated themselves with one accord on the ground
	6:7	was cast down into the ground to lions as food for wild beasts
2 Es	8:41	For just as the farmer sows many seeds upon the ground
	9:34	when the ground has received seed, or the sea a ship
	15:13	Let the farmers that till the ground mourn
4 Ma	6:7	And though he fell to the ground
	15:15	their toes and fingers scattered on the ground

GROUP, subst. 5 = 0.003 %
1 Ma	7:12	Then a group of scribes appeared in a body
	10:61	A group of pestilent men from Israel
1 Es	5:4	over their groups :
	8:28	according to their fathers'houses and their groups
3 Ma	6:35	But the Jews, when they had arranged the aforementioned choral group

GROUP, verb 1
4 Ma	8:4	grouped about their mother as if in a chorus

GROUPING 2
1 Es	1:5	according to the grouping of the fathers' houses of you Levites
	1:11	and the grouping of the fathers' houses, before the people

GROVE 2
Jud	3:8	and cut down their sacred groves
2 Es	16:28	in thick groves and clefts in the rocks

GROW 37 = 0.024 %
Tob	8:7	and may grow old together with her
	14:3	When he had grown very old he called his son and grandsons
	14:3	behold, I have grown old and am about to depart this life
	14:13	He grew old with honour
Jud	16:23	and grew old in her husband's house
Wis	14:16	Then the ungodly custom, grown strong with time
Sir	8:6	for some of us are growing old
	10:3	but a city will grow
	11:16	evil will grow old with those who take pride in malice
	11:20	and grow old in your work
	16:27	they neither hunger nor grow weary
	24:13	I grew tall like a cedar in Lebanon
	24:14	I grew tall like a palm tree in En-gedi
	24:14	and like a plane tree I grew tall
	26:21	will grow great
	39:13	and bud like a rose growing by a stream of water
	43:30	and do not grow weary, for you cannot praise him enough
P Az	54	Bless the Lord, all things that grow on the earth
1 Ma	1:40	Her dishonour now grew as great as her glory
	2:64	My children, be courageous and grow strong in the law
	6:6	that the Jews had grown strong from the arms, supplies
	6:57	We daily grow weaker, our food supply is scant
	7:25	and those with him had grown strong
	10:81	and the enemy's horses grew tired
	16:3	But now I have grown old
2 Ma	4:50	remained in office, growing in wickedness
	5:27	they continued to live on what grew wild
2 Es	2:19	and 7 mighty mountains on which roses and lilies grow
	7:34	and faithfulness shall grow strong
	7:64	But now the mind grows with us
	7:71	for you have said that the mind grows with us
	11:3	and out of his wings there grew opposing wings
	14:10	and the times begin to grow old
	15:16	growing strong against one another
4 Ma	1:28	are 2 plants growing from the body and the soul
	13:20	and growing from the same blood and through the same life
	13:22	and they grow stronger

GROW up 4 = 0.003 %
2 Es	4:10	You cannot understand the things with which you have grown up
	7:48	For an evil heart has grown up in us
	9:47	So when he grew up and I came to take a wife for him
4 Ma	18:9	and when these sons had grown up their father died

GROWL 1
Jud	11:19	and not a dog will so much as open its mouth to growl at you

GROWN 1
2 Ma 5:24   and commanded him to slay all the grown men

GRUDGING 5 = 0.003 %
Wis 7:13   I learned without guile and I impart without grudging
Sir 14:6   No one is meaner than the man who is grudging to himself
    14:8   Evil is the man with a grudging eye
    18:18   and the gift of a grudging man makes the eyes dim
    37:11   with a grudging man about gratitude

GRUMBLE 1
Sir 10:25   and a man of understanding will not grumble

GUARD*, subst. 28 = 0.018 %
Jud 7:5   they remained on guard all that night
    7:7   and seized them and set guards of soldiers over them
    12:7   So Holofernes commanded his guards not to hinder her
Sir 6:13   and be on guard toward your friends
    12:11   watch yourself, and be on your guard against him
    22:27   O that a guard were set over my mouth
    26:11   Be on guard against her impudent eye
    34:16   a guard against stumbling and a defence against falling
1 Ma 6:50   and stationed a guard there to hold it
    9:53   as hostages and put them under guard
    13:12   and Jonathan was with him under guard
    14:3   who put him under guard
1 Es 3:4   who kept guard over the person of the king
    8:59   Be watchful and on guard until you deliver them
3 Ma 5:44   at the places in the city most favourable for keeping guard
4 Ma 3:12   When his guards complained bitterly
    5:2   ordered the guards to seize each and every Hebrew
    6:1   the guards who were standing by dragged him violently
    6:8   One of the cruel guards rushed at him
    6:23   And you, guards of the tyrant, why do you delay ?
    6:24   the guards brought him to the fire
    8:13   And when the guards had placed before them
    9:11   Then at his command the guards brought forward the eldest
    9:16   And when the guards said
    9:26   the guards brought in the next eldest
    11:9   the guards bound him and dragged him to the catapult
    11:27   For it is not the guards of the tyrant
    17:1   Some of the guards said that

GUARD, verb 16 = 0.010 %
Tob 12:7   It is good to guard the secret of a king
    12:11   I have said, It is good to guard the secret of a king
Wis 9:11   and guard me with her glory
Sir 18:27   and in days of sin he guards against wrongdoing
    22:13   guard yourself from him to escape trouble
    32:23   Guard yourself in every act
    40:29   but a man who is intelligent and well instructed guards against that
L Jr 6:70   Like a scarecrow in a cucumber bed, that guards nothing
1 Ma 5:18   with the rest of the forces, in Judea to guard it
    10:32   that he may station in it men of his own choice to guard it
    12:34   And he stationed a garrison there to guard it
1 Es 4:56   for all who guarded the city
2 Es 2:20   Guard the rights of the widow
    7:85   are guarded by angels in profound quiet
    7:95   and guarded by angels in profound quiet
4 Ma 18:7   but I guarded the rib from which woman was made

GUARDIAN 4 = 0.003 %
2 Ma 11:1   Lysias, the king's guardian and kinsman
    13:2   and with him Lysias, his guardian
    14:2   having made away with Antiochus and his guardian Lysias
4 Ma 15:32   so you, O guardian of the law

GUESS 1
Wis 9:16   We can hardly guess at what is on earth

GUEST 5 = 0.003 %
Ad E 16:10   having become our guest
Wis 5:14   and it passes like the remembrance of a guest who stays but a day
    19:14   but these made slaves of guests who were their benefactors
3 Ma 5:14   seeing that the guests were assembled
    5:36   and urged the guests to return to their celebrating

GUIDANCE 1
4 Ma 14:6   in harmony with the guidance of the mind

GUIDE, subst. 5 = 0.003 %
Wis 7:15   for he is the guide even of wisdom
    18:3   as a guide for thy people's unknown journey
1 Ma 4:2   Men from the citadel were his guides
2 Es 16:75   Do not fear or doubt, for God is your guide
4 Ma 1:30   For reason is the guide of the virtues

GUIDE, verb 10 = 0.007 %
Tob 7:12   The merciful God will guide you both for the best
Jud 13:18   who has guided you
Wis 9:11   and she will guide me wisely in my actions
    10:10   she guided him on straight paths
    10:17   she guided them along a marvellous way
    14:6   and guided by thy hand
1 Ma 6:15   that he might guide Antiochus his son
2 Ma 5:15   guided by Menelaus, who had become a traitor
3 Ma 7:2   the great God guiding our affairs according to our desire
2 Es 8:11   and afterwards thou wilt guide him in thy mercy

GUILE 3 = 0.002 %
Wis 4:11   or guile deceive his soul
    7:13   I learned without guile and I impart without grudging
2 Ma 12:24   With great guile he besought them to let him go in safety

GUILT 2
Wis 1:6   and will not free a blasphemer from the guilt of his words
Sir 7:31   the first fruits, the guilt offering

GUILTLESS 1
Sir 9:12   remember that they will not be held guiltless

GUILTY 2
Sus 13:53   condemning the innocent and letting the guilty go free
2 Ma 13:6   any man guilty of sacrilege or notorious for other crimes

GUSH forth 1
2 Ma 14:45   and though his blood gushed forth and his wounds were severe

GYMNASIUM 4 = 0.003 %
1 Ma 1:14   So they built a gymnasium in Jerusalem
2 Ma 4:9   a gymnasium and a body of youth for it
    4:12   For with alacrity he founded a gymnasium
4 Ma 4:20   so that not only was a gymnasium constructed

H

HABAIAH 1
1 Es 5:38   but were not found registered : the sons of Habaiah

HABAKKUK 6 = 0.004 %
Bel 14:33   Now the prophet Habakkuk was in Judea
    14:34   But the angel of the Lord said to Habakkuk
    14:35   Habakkuk said, Sir, I have never seen Babylon
    14:37   Then Habakkuk shouted, Daniel ! Daniel !
    14:39   And the angel of God immediately returned Habakkuk to his own place
2 Es 1:40   and Nahum and Habakkuk, Zephaniah, Haggai

HABIT 4 = 0.003 %
Sir 7:13   for the habit of lying serves no good
    23:14   and be deemed a fool on account of your habits
4 Ma 1:29   and so tames the jungle of habits and emotions
    13:27   But although nature and companionship and virtuous habits

HABITABLE 1
3 Ma 4:3   What district or city, or what habitable place at all

HABITATION 9 = 0.006 %
Wis 9:8   and an altar in the city of thy habitation
Sir 44:6   living peaceably in their habitations
Bar 2:16   O Lord, look down from thy holy habitation, and consider us
2 Ma 14:35   for thy habitation among us
2 Es 2:11   and will give to these others the everlasting habitations
    7:80   such spirits shall not enter into habitations
    7:85   they shall see how the habitations of the others
    7:101   and afterwards they shall be gathered in their habitations
    7:121   Or that safe and healthful habitations have been reserved for us

HABITUAL 1
Sir 20:25   A thief is preferable to a habitual liar

HABITUALLY 2
Sir 23:9   and do not habitually utter the name of the Holy One
4 Ma 2:7   that someone who is habitually a solitary gormandizer

HADES 21 = 0.014 %
Tob 13:2   he leads down to Hades, and brings up again
Ad E 13:7   may in one day go down in violence to Hades
Wis 1:14   and the dominion of Hades is not on earth
    2:1   and no one has been known to return from Hades
    16:13   thou dost lead men down to the gates of Hades and back again
    17:14   and which beset them from the recesses of powerless Hades
Sir 14:12   and the decree of Hades has not been shown to you
    14:16   because in Hades one cannot look for luxury
    17:27   Who will sing praises to the Most High in Hades

21:10	but at its end is the pit of Hades	
28:21	its death is an evil death, and Hades is preferable to it	
41:4	there is no inquiry about it in Hades	
48:5	You have raised a corpse from death and from Hades	
51:5	from the depths of the belly of Hades	
51:6	and my life was very near to Hades beneath	
Bar 2:17	for the dead who are in Hades	
3:11	that you are counted among those in Hades ?	
3:19	They have vanished and gone down to Hades	
P Az 66	for he has rescued us from Hades	
2 Ma 6:23	telling them to send him to Hades	
2 Es 4:41	In Hades the chambers of the souls are like the womb	

HAGAB   1
1 Es   5:30   the sons of Hagab, the sons of Shamlai, the sons of Hana

HAGABAH   1
1 Es   5:29   the sons of Hagabah

HAGAR   1
Bar   3:23   the sons of Hagar, who seek for understanding on the earth

HAGGAI   3 = 0.002 %
1 Es 6:1	the prophets Haggai and Zechariah the son of Iddo
7:3	while the prophets Haggai and Zechariah prophesied
2 Es 1:40	and Nahum and Habakkuk, Zephaniah, Haggai

HAIL, subst.   6 = 0.004 %
Wis 16:16	pursued by unusual rains and hail and relentless storms
16:22	were being destroyed by the fire that blazed in the hail
Sir 39:29	Fire and hail and famine and pestilence
2 Es 7:41	or frost or cold or hail or rain or dew
15:13	by blight and hail and by a terrible tempest
15:41	fire and hail and flying swords and floods of water

HAILSTONE   3 = 0.002 %
Wis 5:22	and hailstones full of wrath will be hurled as from a catapult
Sir 43:15	and the hailstones are broken in pieces
46:6	with hailstones of mighty power

HAIR   19 = 0.012 %
Jud 10:3	and combed her hair and put on a tiara
13:7	and took hold of the hair of his head, and said
16:8	and fastened her hair with a tiara
Ad E 14:2	she covered with her tangled hair
Wis 2:10	nor regard the grey hairs of the aged
4:9	but understanding is grey hair for men
Sir 27:14	makes one's hair stand on end
Bel 14:27	Then Daniel took pitch, fat, and hair
14:36	and lifted him by his hair and set him down in Babylon
2 Ma 6:23	and the grey hairs which he had reached with distinction
7:7	They tore off the skin of his head with the hair
15:13	distinguished by his grey hair and dignity
1 Es 8:71	and pulled out hair from my head and beard
3 Ma 1:18	rushed out with their mothers, sprinkled their hair with dust
4:6	their myrrh-perfumed hair sprinkled with ashes
6:6	you rescued unharmed, even to a hair
2 Es 1:8	Pull out the hair of your head and hurl all evils upon them
4 Ma 5:7	for I respect your age and your grey hairs
7:15	and venerable grey hair and law-abiding life

HAIRCLOTH   1
2 Es   16:2   Gird yourselves with sackcloth and haircloth

HAKKATAN   1
1 Es   8:38   Of the sons of Azgad, Johanan the son of Hakkatan

HAKKOZ   1
1 Es   5:38   the sons of Hakkoz, the sons of Jaddus who had married Agia

HAKUPHA   1
1 Es   5:31   the sons of Hakupha, the sons of Asur

HALF, subst., adj.   15 = 0.010 %
Tob 8:21	that then he should take half of Raguel's property
10:10	and half of his property in slaves, cattle, and money
12:2	to give him half of what I have brought back
12:5	Take half of all that you 2 have brought back
Wis 18:14	and night in its swift course was now half gone
18:18	and one here and another there, hurled down half dead
Sir 29:6	If the lender exerts pressure, he will hardly get back half
1 Ma 3:34	And he turned over to Lysias half of his troops and the elephants
3:37	Then the king took the remaining half of his troops
10:30	and the half of the fruit of the trees that I should receive
2 Es 11:17	or even half as long
13:45	a journey of a year and a half
14:12	as well as half of the 13th part

14:12	besides half of the 13th part
4 Ma 4:11	Then Apollonius fell down half dead

HALICARNASSUS   1
1 Ma   15:23   and to Pamphylia, to to Lycia, and to Halicarnassus

HALL   1
1 Ma   16:16   and rushed in against Simon in the banquet hall

HALLELUJAH   2
Tob 13:18	all her lanes will cry Hallelujah !
3 Ma 7:13	shouted the Hallelujah and joyfully departed

HALLOW   3 = 0.002 %
Sir 33:9	some of them be exalted and hallowed
2 Ma 15:2	and hallowed above other days
1 Es 1:49	which had been hallowed in Jerusalem

HALT, verb   1
2 Ma   10:27   and when they came near to the enemy they halted

HAMAN   8 = 0.005 %
Ad E 10:7	The 2 dragons are Haman and myself
12:6	But Haman, the son of Hammedatha, a Bougaean
13:3	Haman, who excels among us in sound judgment
13:6	that those indicated to you in the letters of Haman
13:12	and refused to bow down to this proud Haman
14:17	And thy servant has not eaten at Haman's table
16:10	For Haman, the son of Hammedatha, a Macedonian
16:17	the letters sent by Haman the son of Hammedatha

HAMATH   1
1 Ma   12:25   and met them in the region of Hamath

HAMMEDATHA   3 = 0.002 %
Ad E 12:6	But Haman, the son of Hammedatha, a Bougaean
16:10	For Haman, the son of Hammedatha, a Macedonian
16:17	the letters sent by Haman the son of Hammedatha

HAMMER, subst.   1
Sir   38:28   he inclines his ear to the sound of the hammer

HAMMERED   2
Sir 50:9	like a vessel of hammered gold
50:16	they sounded the trumpets of hammered work

HANA   1
1 Es   5:30   the sons of Hagab, the sons of Shamlai, the sons of Hana

HANAN   1
1 Es   9:48   Azariah and Jozabad, Hanan, Pelaiah, the Levites

HANANI   1
1 Es   9:21   Of the sons of Immer : Hanani and Zebadiah and Maaseiah

HANANIAH   6 = 0.004 %
P Az 66	Bless the Lord, Hananiah, Azariah, and Mishael
1 Ma 2:59	Hananiah, Azariah and Mishael believed
1 Es 8:48	Hodiah the sons of Hananiah, and their sons, 20 men
9:29	Jehohanan and Hananiah and Zabbai and Emathis
4 Ma 16:21	and Hananiah, Azariah, and Mishael were hurled into the fiery furnace
18:12	and he taught you about Hananiah, Azariah, and Mishael in the fire

HAND, subst.   208 = 0.135 %
Tob 5:17	Is he not the staff of our hands
7:13	and taking her by the hand
13:2	and there is no one who can escape his hand
13:11	bearing gifts in their hands, gifts for the King of heaven
Jud 2:12	what I have spoken my hand will execute
7:25	God has sold us into their hands
8:18	or city of ours which worshiped gods made with hands
8:33	the Lord will deliver Israel by my hand
9:10	crush their arrogance by the hand of a woman
11:13	so much as to touch these things with their hands
11:22	to lend strength to our hands and to bring destruction
12:4	before the Lord carries out by my hand
13:4	look in this hour upon the work of my hands
13:14	but has destroyed our enemies by my hand this very night !
13:15	The Lord has struck him down by the hand of a woman
14:6	in the hand of one of the men
15:12	and she took branches in her hands
16:3	for he has delivered me out of the hands of my pursuers
16:6	by the hand of a woman
16:7	by the hands of the young men
Ad E 12:2	to lay hands upon Ahasuerus the king
14:4	for my danger is in my hand
14:6	and thou hast given us into the hands of our enemies
14:14	But save us by thy hand, and help me

	14 : 19	and save us from the hands of evildoers
Wis	1 : 12	nor bring on destruction by the works of your hands
	2 : 18	and will deliver him from the hand of his adversaries
	3 : 1	But the souls of the righteous are in the hand of God
	3 : 14	whose hands have done no lawless deed
	5 : 16	and a beautiful diadem from the hand of the Lord
	5 : 16	because with his right hand he will cover them
	7 : 11	and in her hands uncounted wealth
	7 : 16	For both we and our words are in his hand
	8 : 12	they will put their hands on their mouths
	8 : 18	and in the labours of her hands, unfailing wealth
	10 : 20	and praised with one accord thy defending hand
	11 : 1	Wisdom prospered their works by the hand of a holy prophet
	11 : 17	For thy all-powerful hand, which created the world
	12 : 6	thou didst will to destroy by the hands of our fathers
	12 : 9	into the hands of the righteous in battle
	13 : 10	to the works of men's hands
	13 : 10	the work of an ancient hand
	13 : 19	for money-making and work and success with his hands
	13 : 19	he asks strength of a thing whose hands have no strength
	14 : 6	and guided by thy hand
	14 : 8	But the idol made with hands is accursed
	15 : 17	He is mortal, and what he makes with lawless hands is dead
	16 : 15	To escape from thy hand is impossible
	19 : 8	where those protected by thy hand passed through as one nation
Sir	2 : 12	Woe to timid hearts and to slack hands
	2 : 18	Let us fall into the hands of the Lord
	2 : 18	but not into the hands of men
	4 : 9	Deliver him who is wronged from the hand of the wrongdoer
	4 : 31	Let not your hand be extended to receive
	5 : 12	but if not, put your hand on your mouth
	7 : 32	Stretch forth your hand to the poor
	8 : 1	lest you fall into his hands
	10 : 4	The government of the earth is in the hands of the Lord
	10 : 5	The success of a man is in the hands of the Lord
	12 : 18	he will shake his head, and clap his hands
	15 : 16	stretch out your hand for whichever you wish
	18 : 3	he steers the world with the span of his hand
	21 : 19	and like manacles on his right hand
	22 : 2	any one that picks it up will shake it off his hand
	25 : 23	Drooping hands and weak knees
	27 : 19	And as you allow a bird to escape from your hand
	29 : 1	and he that strengthens him with his hand
	29 : 5	A man will kiss another's hands until he gets a loan
	31 : 14	Do not reach out your hand for everything you see
	31 : 18	do not reach out your hand before they do
	33 : 13	As clay in the hand of the potter
	33 : 13	so men are in the hand of him who made them
	33 : 21	than that you should look to the hand of your sons
	33 : 25	leave his hands idle, and he will seek liberty
	35 : 8	and do not stint the first fruits of your hands
	35 : 10	and as generously as your hand has found
	36 : 3	Lift up thy hand against foreign nations
	36 : 6	make thy hand and thy right arm glorious
	38 : 10	Give up your faults and direct your hands aright
	38 : 13	There is a time when success lies in the hands of physicians
	38 : 31	All these rely upon their hands
	39 : 1	On the other hand he who devotes himself
	42 : 6	and where there are many hands, lock things up
	43 : 12	the hands of the Most High have stretched it out
	46 : 2	How glorious he was when he lifted his hands
	46 : 4	Was not the sun held back by his hand ?
	47 : 4	when he lifted his hand with a stone in the sling
	47 : 5	and he gave him strength in his right hand
	48 : 18	he lifted up his hand against Zion
	48 : 19	Then their hearts were shaken and their hands trembled
	48 : 20	spreading forth their hands toward him
	48 : 20	and delivered them by the hand of Isaiah
	49 : 11	He was like a signet on the right hand
	50 : 12	from the hands of the priests
	50 : 13	with the Lord's offering in their hands
	50 : 15	he reached out his hand to the cup
	50 : 20	Then Simon came down, and lifted up his hands
	51 : 3	from the hand of those who sought my life
	51 : 8	and dost save them from the hand of their enemies
	51 : 19	I spread out my hands to the heavens
Bar	2 : 11	with a mighty hand and with signs and wonders
	4 : 18	will deliver you from the hand of your enemies
	4 : 21	from the power and hand of the enemy
L Jr	6 : 15	It has a dagger in its right hand, and has an axe
	6 : 51	that they are not gods but the work of men's hands
P Az	9	Thou hast given us into the hands of lawless enemies
	66	and saved us from the hand of death
Sus	13 : 22	and if I do not, I shall not escape your hands
	13 : 23	I choose not to do it and to fall into your hands
	13 : 34	and laid their hands upon her head
1 Ma	2 : 22	to the right hand or to the left
	2 : 47	and the work prospered in their hands
	2 : 48	They rescued the law out of the hands of the Gentiles and kings
	2 : 48	and they never let the sinner gain the upper hand

	3 : 6	and deliverance prospered by his hand
	4 : 30	by the hand of thy servant David
	4 : 30	into the hands of Jonathan, the son of Saul
	4 : 31	So do thou hem in this army by the hand of thy people Israel
	5 : 12	Now then come and rescue us from their hands
	5 : 50	and the city was delivered into his hands
	6 : 25	And not against us alone have they stretched out their hands
	7 : 35	are delivered into my hands this time
	7 : 47	and the right hand which he had so arrogantly stretched out
	9 : 46	that you may be delivered from the hands of our enemies
	9 : 47	and Jonathan stretched out his hand to strike Bacchides
	12 : 9	which are in our hands
	12 : 39	and to raise his hand against Antiochus the king
	12 : 42	he was afraid to raise his hand against him
	14 : 31	and lay hands on their sanctuary
	14 : 36	And in his days things prospered in his hands
	16 : 2	and things have prospered in our hands
2 Ma	3 : 20	And holding up their hands to heaven, they all made entreaty
	4 : 34	offered him sworn pledges and gave him his right hand
	5 : 16	He took the holy vessels with his polluted hands
	5 : 16	and swept away with profane hands
	6 : 26	I shall not escape the hands of the Almighty
	7 : 4	and cut off his hands and feet
	7 : 10	and courageously stretched forth his hands
	7 : 14	One cannot but choose to die at the hands of men
	7 : 31	will certainly not escape the hands of God
	7 : 34	when you raise your hand against the children of heaven
	12 : 24	Timothy himself fell into the hands of Dositheus
	12 : 28	and they got the city into their hands
	13 : 11	fall into the hands of the blasphemous Gentiles
	14 : 33	he stretched out his right hand toward the sanctuary
	14 : 34	Then the priests stretched forth their hands toward heaven
	14 : 42	into the hands of sinners
	14 : 46	took them with both hands and hurled them at the crowd
	15 : 12	was praying with outstretched hands
	15 : 15	Jeremiah stretched out his right hand
	15 : 17	by fighting hand to hand with all courage
	15 : 21	stretched out his hands toward heaven
	15 : 27	So, fighting with their hands
1 Es	1 : 53	old man or child, for he gave them all into their hands
	4 : 29	she would sit at the king's right hand
	4 : 30	and slap the king with her left hand
	6 : 10	and the work is prospering in their hands
	6 : 15	into the hands of Nebuchadnezzar king of Babylon
	6 : 33	that shall stretch out their hands
	7 : 15	to strengthen their hands
	8 : 47	And by the mighty hand of our Lord
	8 : 61	by the mighty hand of our Lord which was upon us
	8 : 73	and kneeling down and stretching forth my hands to the Lord
	9 : 43	Uriah, Hezekiah, and Baalsamus on his right hand
	9 : 47	And they lifted up their hands
Ps 151	2	My hands made a harp, my fingers fashioned a lyre
3 Ma	2 : 1	bending his knees and extending his hands with calm dignity
	2 : 8	And when they had seen works of your hands
	5 : 5	and bound the hands of the wretched people
	5 : 13	to show the might of his all-powerful hand
	5 : 25	stretched their hands toward heaven
	6 : 10	rescue us from the hand of the enemy
	7 : 10	but they requested the king that at their own hands
2 Es	1 : 26	for you have defiled your hands with blood
	2 : 29	My hands will cover you, that your sons may not see Gehenna
	2 : 46	and puts palms in their hands ?
	3 : 5	Yet he was the workmanship of thy hands
	3 : 6	which thy right hand had planted before the earth appeared
	3 : 27	So thou didst deliver the city into the hands of thy enemies
	5 : 30	they should be punished at thy own hands
	6 : 8	for Jacob's hand held Esau's heel from the beginning
	6 : 10	For the beginning of a man is his hand
	6 : 10	between the heel and the hand seek for nothing else, Ezra !
	6 : 58	have been given into their hands
	7 : 7	so that there is fire on the right hand
	8 : 7	and we are a work of thy hands, as thou hast declared
	8 : 44	But man, who has been formed by thy hands
	10 : 23	and has been given over into the hands of those that hate us
	10 : 30	Then he grasped my right hand and strengthened me
	13 : 9	he neither lifted his hand
	13 : 36	as you saw the mountain carved out without hands
	15 : 11	but I will bring them out with a mighty hand
	15 : 15	with swords in their hands
	15 : 22	My right hand will not spare the sinners
	15 : 53	exulting and clapping yours hands
	16 : 13	For his right hand that bends the bow is strong
4 Ma	4 : 11	stretched out his hands toward heaven
	8 : 16	Let us consider, on the other hand
	9 : 11	they bound his hands and arms with thongs on each side
	9 : 28	These leopard-like beasts tore out his sinews with the iron hands
	10 : 5	they disjointed his hands and feet with their instruments
	13 : 12	and the father by whose hand Isaac would have submitted
	14 : 6	Just as the hands and feet are moved
	15 : 20	severed hands upon hands, scalped heads upon heads

16:20 and when Isaac saw his father's hand
17:19 For Moses says, All who are consecrated are under your hands

HAND, at hand   11 = 0.007 %
Ad E **16**:7 which we hand on as from investigation of matters close at hand
Wis **9**:16 and what is at hand we find with labour
Sir **8**:16 and where no help is at hand, he will strike you down
29:26 and if you have anything at hand, let me have it to eat
1 Ma **12**:27 and to keep their arms at hand
2 Ma **12**:31 as the feast of weeks was close at hand
15:20 and the enemy was already close at hand
3 Ma **5**:46 and urged the king on to the matter at hand
2 Es **2**:34 because he who will come at the end of the age is close at hand
16:2 for your destruction is at hand
16:74 Behold, the days of tribulation are at hand

HAND on   2
Ad E **16**:7 which we hand on as from investigation of matters close at hand
Wis **14**:15 and handed on to his dependents secret rites and initiations

HAND over   24 = 0.016 %
Jud **2**:7 and will hand them over to be plundered by my troops
2:11 and you shall hand them over to slaughter and plunder
6:10 and hand him over to the men of Israel
8:19 and that was why our fathers were handed over to the sword
10:12 for they are about to be handed over to you to be devoured
10:15 some of us will escort you and hand you over to him
11:15 on that very day they will be handed over to you to be destroyed
Sir **4**:19 and hand him over to his ruin
11:6 and illustrious men have been handed over to others
Bar **4**:6 but you were handed over to your enemies
Bel **14**:29 Going to the king, they said, Hand Daniel over to us
14:30 and under compulsion he handed Daniel over to them
1 Ma **11**:40 and insistently urged him to hand Antiochus over to him
12:34 to hand over the stronghold
12:45 I will hand it over to you as well as the other strongholds
15:21 hand them over to Simon the high priest
15:30 Now then, hand over the cities which you have seized
2 Ma **8**:11 and promising to hand over 90 slaves for a talent
10:4 and not be handed over to blasphemous and barbarous nations
14:31 and commanded them to hand the man over
14:33 If you do not hand Judas over to me as a prisoner
1 Es **2**:14 All the vessels were handed over, gold and silver, 5,469
2 Es **15**:26 therefore he will hand them over to death and slaughter
15:56 and will hand you over to adversities

HANDFUL   2
2 Ma **4**:41 and others took handfuls of the ashes that were lying about
3 Ma **5**:2 with large handfuls of frankincense and plenty of unmixed wine

HANDIWORK   2
Sir **38**:28 intent upon his handiwork in iron
38:28 He sets his heart on finishing his handiwork

HANDLE, verb   4 = 0.003 %
Jud **7**:2 together with the baggage and the foot soldiers handling it
Wis **13**:11 A skilled woodcutter may saw down a tree easy to handle
Sir **38**:25 How can he become wise who handles the plough
2 Ma **7**:39 and handled him worse than the others

HANDMAID   1
2 Es **9**:45 And after 30 years God heard your handmaid

HANDSOME   3 = 0.002 %
Ps 151:5 My brothers were handsome and tall
4 Ma **8**:3 handsome, modest, noble, and accomplished in every way
8:10 for your youth and handsome appearance

HAND-TO-HAND   1
2 Ma **5**:14 40,000 in hand-to-hand fighting

HANG   9 = 0.006 %
Tob **3**:10 *even to the thought of hanging herself*
Jud **13**:6 and took down his sword that hung there
14:1 and take this head and hang it upon the parapet of your wall
14:11 they hung the head of Holofernes on the wall
Ad E **16**:18 *has been hanged at the gate of Susa, with all his household*
1 Ma **1**:61 and they hung the infants from their mothers' necks
2 Ma **6**:10 with their babies hung at their breasts
15:35 And he hung Nicanor's head from the citadel
1 Es **6**:32 *and he should be hanged upon it*

HANG up   2
1 Ma **4**:51 They placed the bread on the table and hung up the curtains
2 Ma **15**:33 and hang up these rewards of his folly

HAPPEN   53 = 0.035 %
Tob **3**:7 it also happened that Sarah, the daughter of Raguel
8:16 It has not happened to me as I expected
11:15 that had happened to him in Media

12:20 Write in a book everything that has happened
14:8 because what the prophet Jonah said will surely happen
Jud **6**:16 and Uzziah asked him what had happened
8:26 and what happened to Jacob in Mesopotamia in Syria
15:1 they were amazed at what had happened
15:5 for they were told what had happened in the camp of the enemy
Wis **2**:17 and let us test what will happen at the end of his life
19:4 and made them forget what had happened
Sir **5**:4 Do not say, I sinned, and what happened to me ?
11:24 and what calamity could happen to me in the future ?
22:26 but if some harm should happen to me because of him
37:9 and then stand aloof to see what will happen to you
Sus **13**:26 to see what had happened to her
1 Ma **4**:20 for the smoke that was seen showed what had happened
4:26 and reported to Lysias all that had happened
4:27 for things that had not happened to Israel as he had intended
5:25 and told them all that had happened
2 Ma **4**:30 it happened that the people of Tarsus and of Mallus
4:32 other vessels, as it happened
5:2 And it happened that over all the city, for almost 40 days
5:11 When news of what had happened reached the king
5:18 But if it had not happened
7:1 It happened also that 7 brothers and their mother were arrested
7:18 Therefore astounding things have happened
9:1 About that time, as it happened
9:3 of what had happened to Nicanor and the forces of Timothy
9:24 so that, if anything unexpected happened
9:25 and waiting to see what will happen
10:5 It happened that on the same day
10:21 When word of what had happened came to Maccabeus
11:1 being vexed at what had happened
12:34 it happened that a few of the Jews fell
12:42 what had happened because of the sin of those who had fallen
13:17 This happened, just as day was dawning
1 Es **1**:25 it happened that Pharaoh, king of Egypt
8:86 And all that has happened to us has come about
3 Ma **1**:8 and to congratulate him on what had happened
1:15 But since this has happened, the king said
4:12 And when this had happened
7:8 or reproaching them for the irrational things that have happened
2 Es **9**:34 and when it happens that what was sown or what was launched
9:42 And I said to her, What has happened to you ? Tell me
10:1 But it happened that when my son entered his wedding chamber
10:6 do you not see our mourning, and what has happened to us ?
10:49 and you began to console her for what had happened
13:20 and not to see what shall happen in the last days
14:16 For evils worse than those which you have now seen happen
14:22 and I will write everything that has happened in the world from the beginning
4 Ma **4**:14 went away to report to the king what had happened to him
14:9 they not only saw what was happening

HAPPILY   1
2 Ma **11**:26 and go on happily in the conduct of their own affairs

HAPPINESS   3 = 0.002 %
Tob **8**:17 in health and happiness and mercy
Sir **37**:4 Some companions rejoice in the happiness of a friend
4 Ma **16**:9 or have the happiness of being called grandmother

HAPPY   17 = 0.011 %
Ad E **15**:5 She was radiant with perfect beauty, and she looked happy
Wis **2**:16 he calls the last end of the righteous happy
18:1 and counted them happy for not having suffered
Sir **11**:28 Call no one happy before his death
13:26 The mark of a happy heart is a cheerful face
14:14 Do not deprive yourself of a happy day
25:8 happy is he who lives with an intelligent wife
25:9 happy is he who has gained good sense
25:23 are caused by the wife who does not make her husband happy
26:1 Happy is the husband of a good wife
26:26 Happy is the husband of a good wife
28:19 Happy is the man who is protected from it
37:24 and all who see him will call him happy
Bar **4**:4 Happy are we, O Israel
1 Ma **6**:23 We were happy to serve your father
10:55 Happy was the day
4 Ma **18**:9 A happy man was he, who lived out his life with good children

HARASS   3 = 0.002 %
1 Ma **6**:38 on the 2 flanks of the army, to harass the enemy
9:51 And he placed garrisons in them to harass Israel
2 Ma **10**:15 were harassing the Jews

HARBOUR, HARBOR, subst.   7 = 0.005 %
1 Ma **14**:5 To crown all his honours he took Joppa for a harbour
2 Ma **12**:6 He set fire to the harbour by night, and burned the boats
12:9 and set fire to the harbour and the fleet
14:1 had sailed into the harbour of Tripolis
1 Es **5**:55 and convey them in rafts to the harbour of Joppa

4 Ma 13 : 6   For just as towers jutting out over harbours
      13 : 7   by fortifying the harbour of religion

HARBOUR, HARBOR, verb   1
   Sir 28 : 3   Does a man harbour anger against another

HARD, adj., adv.   15 = 0.010 %
   Wis 11 : 4   and slaking of thirst from hard stone
      17 : 1   Great are thy judgments and hard to describe
   Sir 29 : 28   These things are hard to bear for a man who has feeling :
      48 : 13   Nothing was too hard for him
   Bel 14 : 30   The king saw that they were pressing him hard
 1 Ma 15 : 14   he pressed the city hard from land and sea
 2 Ma 8 : 20   and when the Macedonians were hard pressed
      9 : 7   and the fall was so hard as to torture every limb of his body
     11 : 5   and pressed it hard
    12 : 11   After a hard fight Judas and his men won the victory
    12 : 21   for that place was hard to besiege and difficult of access
 1 Es 5 : 72   But the peoples of the land pressed hard upon those in Judea
 3 Ma 4 : 14   not for the hard labour that has been briefly mentioned before
     5 : 7   But with tears and a voice hard to silence
 2 Es 7 : 59   for he who has what is hard to get

HARDEN   2
   Sir 16 : 15   The Lord hardened Pharaoh so that he did not know him
 1 Es 1 : 48   and he stiffened his neck and hardened his heart

HARDLY   3 = 0.002 %
   Wis 9 : 16   We can hardly guess at what is on earth
   Sir 26 : 29   A merchant can hardly keep from wrongdoing
      29 : 6   If the lender exerts pressure, he will hardly get back half

HARD-PRESSED   1
 2 Ma 14 : 9   and our hard-pressed nation

HARDSHIP   1
 2 Es 7 : 12   full of dangers and involved in great hardships

HARIM   1
 1 Es 5 : 25   The sons of Harim, 1,017

HARLOT   9 = 0.006 %
   Sir 9 : 6   Do not give yourself to harlots
     19 : 2   and the man who consorts with harlots is very reckless
    26 : 22   A harlot is regarded as spittle
    41 : 20   of looking at a woman who is a harlot
  L Jr 6 : 11   and even give some of it to the harlots in the brothel
 2 Ma 6 : 4   by the Gentiles, who dallied with harlots
 2 Es 15 : 48   You have imitated that hateful harlot in all her deeds and
          devices
    15 : 55   The reward of a harlot is in your bosom
    16 : 49   Just as a respectable and virtuous woman abhors a harlot

HARLOTRY   3 = 0.002 %
   Sir 23 : 23   and third, she has committed adultery through harlotry
     26 : 9   A wife's harlotry shows in her lustful eyes
 2 Es 15 : 47   you have decked out your daughters in harlotry

HARM, subst.   11 = 0.007 %
  Tob 12 : 2   He replied, Father, it would do me no harm
  Ad E 13 : 5   doing all the harm they can
  Wis 14 : 29   they swear wicked oaths and expect to suffer no harm
   Sir 4 : 22   Do not show partiality, to your own harm
     22 : 26   but if some harm should happen to me because of him
  P Az 20   Let all who do harm to thy servants be put to shame
 1 Ma 5 : 48   No one will do you harm
    15 : 19   that they should not seek their harm
 3 Ma 7 : 8   with no one in any place doing them harm at all
 2 Es 11 : 42   and have laid low the walls of those who did you no harm
    12 : 41   and what harm have we done you

HARM, verb   6 = 0.004 %
  Tob 6 : 14   and he harms no one except those who approach her
   Sir 36 : 9   and may those who harm thy people meet destruction
 1 Ma 6 : 18   They were trying in every way to harm them
    7 : 14   and he will not harm us
    9 : 71   that he would not try to harm him as long as he lived
 2 Es 7 : 115   or to harm him who is victorious

HARMFUL   2
 2 Ma 15 : 39   For just as it is harmful to drink wine alone
 2 Es 15 : 6   and their harmful deeds have reached their limit

HARMLESS   1
   Wis 18 : 3   and a harmless sun for their glorious wandering

HARMONIOUS   1
 4 Ma 14 : 3   O sacred and harmonious concord of the 7 brothers

HARMONY   6 = 0.004 %
   Sir 25 : 1   and a wife and husband who live in harmony
 4 Ma 3 : 21   a revolution against the public harmony
     7 : 7   O man in harmony with the law and philosopher of divine life !
    13 : 25   expanded their goodwill and harmony toward one another
    14 : 6   in harmony with the guidance of the mind
    14 : 7   O most holy 7, brothers in harmony !

HARNESS, subst.   1
 1 Ma 6 : 37   they were fastened upon each beast by special harness

HARP   7 = 0.005 %
   Wis 19 : 18   as on a harp the notes vary the nature of the rhythm
   Sir 40 : 21   The flute and the harp make pleasant melody
 1 Ma 3 : 45   the flute and the harp ceased to play
    4 : 54   it was dedicated with songs and harps and lutes and cymbals
    13 : 51   and with harps and cymbals and stringed instruments
  Ps 151 : 2   My hands made a harp, my fingers fashioned a lyre
 2 Es 10 : 22   our harp has been laid low, our song has been silenced

HARSH   7 = 0.005 %
   Wis 17 : 19   or the harsh crash of rocks hurled down
   Sir 6 : 20   She seems very harsh to the uninstructed
 2 Ma 6 : 3   Harsh and utterly grievous was the onslaught of evil
 3 Ma 3 : 25   with insulting and harsh treatment
    4 : 4   For with such a harsh and ruthless spirit
    4 : 6   as they were torn by the harsh treatment of the heathen
    7 : 5   They also led them out with harsh treatment as slaves

HARVEST, subst.   9 = 0.006 %
   Jud 2 : 27   during the wheat harvest
    8 : 2   had died during the barley harvest
   Sir 6 : 19   and wait for her good harvest
    20 : 28   Whoever cultivates the soil will heap up his harvest
    24 : 26   and like the Jordan at harvest time
 1 Es 4 : 6   but till the soil, whenever they sow, reap the harvest
 2 Es 4 : 28   but the harvest of it has not yet come
    4 : 35   And when will come the harvest of our reward ?
 4 Ma 2 : 9   so that he neither gleans his harvest

HARVEST, verb   1
   Jud 4 : 5   since their fields had recently been harvested

HASADIAH   1
   Bar 1 : 1   son of Zedekiah, son of Hasadiah, son of Hilkiah

HASHABIAH   3 = 0.002 %
 1 Es 1 : 9   and Hashabiah and Ochiel and Joram
    8 : 48   also Hashabiah and Annunus and Jeshaiah his brother
    8 : 54   Sherebiah and Hashabiah

HASHUM   1
 1 Es 9 : 33   Of the sons of Hashum : Mattenai and Mattattah and Zabad

HASIDAEAN   3 = 0.002 %
 1 Ma 2 : 42   Then there united with them a company of Hasidaeans
    7 : 13   The Hasidaeans were the first among the sons of Israel
 2 Ma 14 : 6   Those of the Jews who are called Hasidaeans

HASRAH   1
 1 Es 5 : 31   the sons of Paseah, the sons of Hasrah, the sons of Besai

HASSOPHERETH   1
 1 Es 5 : 33   The sons of Solomon's servants : the sons of Hassophereth

HASTE   10 = 0.007 %
   Sir 50 : 17   Then all the people together made haste
  Sus 13 : 50   Then all the people returned in haste
 1 Ma 6 : 63   Then he departed with haste and returned to Antioch
 2 Ma 11 : 37   Therefore make haste and send some men
 1 Es 2 : 30   went in haste to Jerusalem
 3 Ma 4 : 15   with bitter haste and zealous intentness
 2 Es 4 : 34   for your haste is for yourself
    4 : 42   makes haste to escape the pangs of birth
    5 : 42   so for those who are first there is no haste
    5 : 44   The creation cannot make more haste than the Creator

HASTEN   19 = 0.012 %
   Wis 6 : 13   She hastens to make herself known to those who desire her
   Sir 36 : 8   Hasten the day, and remember the appointed time
    43 : 5   and at his command it hastens on its course
 1 Ma 2 : 35   Then the enemy hastened to attack them
    13 : 10   and hastened to complete the walls of Jerusalem
 2 Ma 4 : 14   they hastened to take part in the unlawful proceedings
    9 : 7   and giving orders to hasten the journey
    9 : 14   which he was hastening to level to the ground
    12 : 20   and hastened after Timothy
    12 : 29   Setting out from there, they hastened to Scythopolis
    12 : 32   they hastened against Gorgias, the governor of Idumea
 2 Es 4 : 26   because the age is hastening swiftly to its end

	4:34	You do not hasten faster than the Most High
	4:34	but the Highest hastens on behalf of many
	4:42	so also do these places hasten to give back those things
	7:98	for they hasten to behold the face of him
	14:15	and hasten to escape from these times
	14:18	is already hastening to come
4 Ma	14:5	hastened to death by torture

HASTEN off   1
2 Ma   9:25   when I hastened off to the upper provinces

HASTILY   3 = 0.002 %
Wis   19:2   and hastily sent them forth
Sir   6:7   and do not trust him hastily
2 Ma   4:31   So the king went hastily to settle the trouble

HASTY   4 = 0.003 %
Sir   2:2   and do not be hasty in time of calamity
  3:24   For their hasty judgment has led many astray
  28:11   A hasty quarrel kindles fire, and urgent strife sheds blood
2 Es   6:34   lest you be hasty concerning the last times

HASUPHA   1
1 Es   5:29   the sons of Hasupha, the sons of Tabbaoth

HAT   1
2 Ma   4:12   to wear the Greek hat

HATCH   1
4 Ma   14:16   hatch the nestlings and ward off the intruder

HATE, verb   36 = 0.023 %
Tob   4:15   And what you hate, do not do to any one
  13:12   Cursed are all who hate you
Jud   5:17   for the God who hates iniquity is with them
Ad E   14:13   and turn his heart to hate the man who is fighting against us
  14:15   and thou knowest that I hate the splendour of the wicked
Wis   11:24   if thou hadst hated it
  12:4   thou didst hate for their detestable practices
Sir   7:15   Do not hate toilsome labour, or farm work
  9:18   and the man who is reckless in speech will be hated
  12:6   For the Most High also hates sinners
  15:11   for he will not do what he hates
  15:13   The Lord hates all abominations
  17:26   to the light of health and hate abominations intensely
  19:6   and for one who hates gossip evil is lessened
  19:9   and when the time comes he will hate you
  20:8   and whoever usurps the right to speak will be hated
  21:6   Whoever hates reproof walks in the steps of the sinner
  21:28   and is hated in his neighbourhood
  25:2   My soul hates 3 kinds of men
  25:14   Any attack, but not an attack from those who hate !
  27:24   I have hated many things, but none to be compared to him
  27:24   even the Lord will hate him
  31:16   and do not chew greedily, lest you be hated
  33:2   A wise man will not hate the law
  37:20   A man skilled in words may be hated
  42:9   or if married, lest she be hated
1 Ma   7:26   who hated and detested Israel
  9:29   and to deal with those of our nation who hate us
  11:21   But certain lawless men who hated their nation
  11:38   So all the troops who had served his fathers hated him
2 Ma   5:8   hated as a rebel against the laws
3 Ma   6:9   And now, you who hate insolence
2 Es   5:30   If thou dost really hate thy people
  7:79   and who have hated those who fear God
  10:23   and has been given over into the hands of those that hate us
  11:42   you have hated those who tell the truth

HATEFUL   12 = 0.008 %
Ad E   16:24   but also most hateful for all time to beasts and birds
Wis   14:9   For equally hateful to God
  15:18   even the most hateful animals
  17:5   avail to illumine that hateful night
Sir   10:7   Arrogance is hateful before the Lord and before men
  20:15   such a one is a hateful man
P Az   9   most hateful rebels, and to an unjust king
3 Ma   3:4   For this reason they appeared hateful to some
  3:27   will be tortured to death with the most hateful torments
2 Es   15:48   You have imitated that hateful harlot in all her deeds and devices
  15:60   And as they pass they shall wreck the hateful city
4 Ma   5:27   which are most hateful to us

HATER   2
4 Ma   11:4   Hater of virtue, hater of mankind

HATIPHA   1
1 Es   5:32   the sons of Neziah, the sons of Hatipha

HATITA   1
1 Es   5:28   the sons of Akkub, the sons of Hatita

HATRED   9 = 0.006 %
Wis   19:13   for they practised a more bitter hatred of strangers
1 Ma   11:40   and told of the hatred
  13:6   out of hatred to destroy us
2 Ma   3:1   and his hatred of wickedness
  4:3   When his hatred progressed to such a degree
  4:36   and the Greeks shared their hatred of the crime
  4:49   showing their hatred of the crime
  8:4   and to show his hatred of evil
4 Ma   9:3   in your hatred for us

HATTIL   1
1 Es   5:34   the sons of Hattil, the sons of Pochereth-hazzebaim

HATTUSH   1
1 Es   8:29   Of the sons of David, Hattush the son of Shecaniah

HAUGHTY   3 = 0.002 %
Sir   22:10   Children who are disdainfully and boorishly haughty
  23:4   do not give me haughty eyes
3 Ma   1:27   and not to overlook this unlawful and haughty deed

HAUNT   2
Sir   41:5   and they frequent the haunts of the ungodly
2 Es   5:8   and the wild beasts shall roam beyond their haunts

HAVE   2269 = 1.478 %

HAVEN   2
2 Es   12:42   and like a haven for a ship saved from a storm
4 Ma   7:3   until he sailed into the haven of immortal victory

HAZARD   1
Sir   32:20   Do not go on a path full of hazards

HAZOR   1
1 Ma   11:67   Early in the morning they marched to the plain of Hazor

HE   2191 = 1.427 %

HEAD   97 = 0.063 %
Jud   4:11   and put ashes on their heads
  8:22   all this he will bring upon our heads among the Gentiles
  9:1   and put ashes on her head
  9:9   Behold their pride, and send thy wrath upon their heads
  13:6   above Holofernes'head
  13:7   and took hold of the hair of his head, and said
  13:8   and severed his head from his body
  13:9   and gave Holofernes' head to her maid
  13:15   Then she took the head out of the bag and showed it to them
  13:15   and said, See, here is the head of Holofernes
  13:18   to strike the head of the leader of our enemies
  14:1   and take this head and hang it upon the parapet of your wall
  14:6   And when he came and saw the head of Holofernes
  14:11   they hung the head of Holofernes on the wall
  14:15   with his head cut off and missing
  14:18   and his head is not on him !
Ad E   14:2   she covered her head with ashes and dung
  14:16   which is upon my head on the days when I appear in public
  15:7   and collapsed upon the head of the maid who went before her
Wis   18:24   and thy majesty on the diadem upon his head
Sir   4:7   bow your head low to a great man
  11:1   The wisdom of a humble man will lift up his head
  11:13   and raises up his head, so that many are amazed at him
  12:18   he will shake his head, and clap his hands
  13:7   and shake his head at you
  17:23   and he will bring their recompense on their heads
  20:11   and there are men who have raised their heads
  27:25   Whoever throws a stone straight up throws it on his own head
  36:10   Crush the heads of the rulers of the enemy
  38:3   The skill of the physician lifts up his head
  44:23   he made to rest upon the head of Jacob
Bar   5:2   put on your head the diadem of the glory of the Everlasting
L Jr   6:9   People take gold and make crowns for the heads of their gods
  6:22   Bats, swallows, and birds light on their bodies and heads
  6:31   their heads and beards shaved
  6:31   and their heads uncovered
Sus   13:34   and laid their hands upon her head
  13:55   You have lied against your own head
  13:59   You also have lied against your own head
Bel   14:36   Then the angel of the Lord took him by the crown of his head
1 Ma   3:47   and sprinkled ashes on their heads, and rent their clothes
  6:35   and with brass helmets on their heads
  7:47   and they cut off Nicanor's head
  11:13   Thus he put 2 crowns upon his head
  11:17   And Zabdiel the Arab cut off the head of Alexander
  11:71   and put dust on his head, and prayed

2 Ma	1:16	and dismembered them and cut off their heads
	7:7	They tore off the skin of his head with the hair
	10:25	Maccabeus and his men sprinkled dust upon their heads
	11:8	a horseman appeared at their head
	14:15	they sprinkled dust upon their heads
	15:30	ordered them to cut off Nicanor's head and arm
	15:32	He showed them the vile Nicanor's head
	15:35	And he hung Nicanor's head from the citadel
1 Es	2:8	Then arose the heads of families
	4:30	and take the crown from the king's head and put it on her own
	5:1	After this the heads of fathers' houses were chosen to go up
	5:44	Some of the heads of families
	5:63	Some of the Levitical priests and heads of fathers' houses
	5:68	and the heads of the fathers' houses and said to them
	5:70	and the heads of the fathers' houses in Israel said to them
	6:12	of those who are at their head
	8:59	and to the heads of the fathers' houses of Israel
	8:71	and pulled out hair from my head and beard
	8:75	For our sins have risen higher than our heads
3 Ma	3:19	who hold their heads high in defiance of kings
2 Es	1:8	Pull out the hair of your head and hurl all evils upon them
	2:43	and on the head of each of them he placed a crown
	4:32	When heads of grain without number are sown
	9:38	and her clothes were rent, and there were ashes on her head
	11:1	that had 12 feathered wings and 3 heads
	11:4	But his heads were at rest
	11:4	the middle head was larger then the other heads
	11:9	but let the heads be reserved for the last
	11:10	the voice did not come from his heads
	11:23	except the 3 heads that were at rest and 6 little wings
	11:24	and remained under the head that was on the right side
	11:29	one of the heads that were at rest
	11:29	for it was greater than the other 2 heads
	11:30	And I saw how it allied the 2 heads with itself
	11:31	and behold, the head turned with those that were with it
	11:32	Moreover this head gained control of the whole earth
	11:33	the middle head also suddenly disappeared
	11:34	But the 2 heads remained
	11:35	the head on the right side devoured the one on the left
	11:45	and your malicious heads, and your most evil talons
	12:2	and behold, the remaining head disappeared
	12:17	coming not from the eagle's heads
	12:22	As for your seeing 3 heads at rest
	12:24	therefore they are called the heads of the eagle
	12:26	As for your seeing that the large head disappeared
	12:29	As for your seeing 2 little wings passing over to the head
	16:53	for God will burn coals of fire on the head of him who says
4 Ma	15:15	and the flesh of the head to the chin exposed like masks
	15:20	severed hands upon hands, scalped heads upon heads

HEADLONG   3 = 0.002 %

2 Ma	6:10	then hurled them down headlong from the wall
3 Ma	6:23	and saw them all fallen headlong to destruction
4 Ma	4:25	were thrown headlong from heights along with their infants

HEADSTRONG   3 = 0.002 %

Sir	26:10	Keep strict watch over a headstrong daughter
	26:25	A headstrong wife is regarded as a dog
	42:11	Keep strict watch over a headstrong daughter

HEAL   9 = 0.006 %

Tob	3:17	And Raphael was sent to heal the 2 of them :
	12:3	and he also healed you
	12:14	So now God sent me to heal you
Wis	16:10	for thy mercy came to their help and healed them
	16:12	but it was thy word, O Lord, which heals all men
Sir	38:7	By them he heals and takes away pain
	38:9	but pray the Lord, and he will heal you
	43:22	A mist quickly heals all things
2 Es	7:104	to be ill or sleep or eat or be healed in his stead

HEALING   8 = 0.005 %

Wis	16:9	and no healing was found for them
Sir	3:28	The affliction of the proud has no healing
	21:3	there is no healing for its wound
	28:3	and yet seek for healing from the Lord ?
	34:17	he grants healing, life, and blessing
	38:2	for healing comes from the Most High
	38:14	and in healing, for the sake of preserving life
2 Es	7:123	and in which are abundance and healing

HEALTH   16 = 0.010 %

Tob	7:4	And he asked them, Is he in good health ?
	7:5	they replied, He is alive and in good health
	8:17	in health and happiness and mercy
Wis	7:10	I loved her more than health and beauty
	13:18	For health he appeals to a thing that is weak
Sir	1:18	making peace and perfect health to flourish
	17:26	to the light of health and hate abominations intensely
	18:19	and before you fall ill, take care of your health

	30:15	Health and soundness are better than all gold
	30:16	There is no wealth better than health of body
	38:8	and from him health is upon the face of the earth
2 Ma	1:10	and to the Jews in Egypt, greeting, and good health
	9:19	and good wishes for their health and prosperity
	11:28	We also are in good health
3 Ma	3:12	greetings and good health
	7:1	greetings and good health

HEALTHFUL   1

2 Es	7:121	Or that safe and healthful habitations have been reserved for us

HEALTHY   1

Sir	31:20	Healthy sleep depends on moderate eating

HEAP, verb   3 = 0.002 %

Sir	3:27	and the sinner will heap sin upon sin
	8:3	Do not argue with a chatterer, nor heap wood on his fire
	37:24	A wise man will have praise heaped upon him

HEAP up   1

Sir	20:28	Whoever cultivates the soil will heap up his harvest

HEAP, subst.   5 = 0.003 %

Wis	18:23	For when the dead had already fallen on one another in heaps
Sir	39:17	At his word the waters stood in a heap
1 Ma	11:4	for they had piled them in heaps along his route
2 Es	2:9	whose land lies in lumps of pitch and heaps of ashes
4 Ma	9:20	and the heap of coals was being quenched by drippings of gore

HEAR   188 = 0.122 %

Tob	3:6	because I have heard false reproaches
	3:10	When she heard these things she was deeply grieved
	3:13	and that I hear reproach no more
	3:15	and pity be taken upon me, and that I hear reproach no more
	3:16	The prayer of both was heard
	6:13	I have heard that the girl has been given to 7 husbands
	6:17	When Tobias heard these things, he fell in love with her
	7:7	When he heard that Tobit had lost his sight
	10:12	Let me hear a good report of you
	14:15	But before he died he heard of the destruction of Nineveh
Jud	4:1	heard of everything
	4:13	So the Lord heard their prayers
	5:1	heard that the people of Israel had prepared for war
	5:5	Let my lord now hear a word from the mouth of your servant
	7:9	Let our lord hear a word, lest his army be defeated
	8:1	At that time Judith heard about these things :
	8:9	When Judith heard the wicked words
	8:9	and when she heard all that Uzziah said to them
	8:17	and he will hear our voice, if it pleases him
	9:4	O God, my God, hear me also, a widow
	9:12	Hear, O hear me, God of my father
	9:12	King of all thy creation, hear my prayer !
	10:14	When the men heard her words, and observed her face
	11:8	For we have heard of your wisdom and skill
	11:9	we have heard his words, for the men of Bethulia spared him
	11:16	as many as shall hear about them
	13:12	When the men of her city heard her voice
	14:7	In every nation those who hear your name will be alarmed
	14:19	When the leaders of the Assyrian army heard this
	15:1	When the men in the tents heard it
	15:5	And when the Israelites heard it
Ad E	13:17	Hear my prayer, and have mercy upon thy inheritance
	14:5	I have heard in the tribe of my family
	14:19	hear the voice of the despairing
Wis	1:10	because a jealous ear hears all things
	8:15	dread monarchs will be afraid of me when they hear of me
	11:13	For when they heard that through their own punishments
	15:15	nor ears with which to hear, nor fingers to feel with
	18:1	Their enemies heard their voices but did not see their forms
Sir	3:5	and when he prays he will be heard
	4:6	his Creator will hear his prayer
	5:11	Be quick to hear, and be deliberate in answering
	11:8	Do not answer before you have heard
	13:13	When you hear these things in your sleep, wake up !
	16:5	and my ear has heard things more striking than these
	17:13	and their ears heard the glory of his voice
	19:9	for some one has heard you and watched you
	19:10	Have you heard a word ? Let it die with you
	19:15	so do not believe everything you hear
	19:27	He hides his face and pretends not to hear
	21:15	When a man of understanding hears a wise saying
	21:15	when a reveller hears it, he dislikes it
	22:26	whoever hears of it will beware of him
	27:7	Do not praise a man before you hear him reason
	27:15	and their abuse is grievous to hear
	29:25	and besides this you will hear bitter words :
	33:4	Prepare what to say, and thus you will be heard
	33:18	Hear me, you who are great among the people
	41:23	of repeating and telling what you hear

	43 : 24	and we marvel at what we hear
	45 : 5	He made him hear his voice
	45 : 9	to make their ringing heard in the temple
	46 : 17	and made his voice heard with a mighty sound
	48 : 7	who heard rebuke at Sinai
	48 : 20	and the Holy One quickly heard them from heaven
	50 : 16	they made a great noise to be heard
	51 : 11	My prayer was heard
Bar	1 : 3	and in the hearing of all the people who came to hear the book
	2 : 14	Hear, O Lord, our prayer and our supplication
	2 : 16	Incline thy ear, O Lord, and hear
	2 : 31	I will give them a heart that obeys and ears that hear
	3 : 2	Hear, O Lord, and have mercy
	3 : 4	hear now the prayer of the dead of Israel
	3 : 9	Hear the commandments of life, O Israel
	3 : 22	She has not been heard of in Canaan, nor seen in Teman
Sus	13 : 26	When the household servants heard the shouting in the garden
	13 : 44	The Lord heard her cry
Bel	14 : 28	When the Babylonians heard it
1 Ma	3 : 13	heard that Judas had gathered a large company
	3 : 27	When King Antiochus heard these reports
	3 : 41	When the traders of the region heard what was said of them
	4 : 3	But Judas heard of it, and he and his mighty men
	4 : 27	When he heard it, he was perplexed and discouraged
	5 : 1	When the Gentiles round about heard
	5 : 16	When Judas and the people heard these messages
	5 : 56	heard of their brave deeds
	5 : 63	wherever their name was heard
	6 : 1	when he heard that Elymais in Persia
	6 : 8	When the king heard this news
	6 : 28	The king was enraged when he heard this
	6 : 41	All who heard the noise made by their multitude
	6 : 55	Then Lysias heard that Philip
	8 : 1	Now Judas heard of the fame of the Romans
	8 : 12	and as many as have heard of their fame have feared them
	9 : 1	When Demetrius heard
	9 : 33	and all who were with him heard of it
	9 : 43	When Bacchides heard of this
	10 : 2	When Demetrius the king heard of it
	10 : 8	They were greatly alarmed when they heard
	10 : 15	Now Alexander the king heard of all the promises
	10 : 19	We have heard about you
	10 : 22	When Demetrius heard of these things he was grieved and said
	10 : 26	we have heard of it and rejoiced
	10 : 46	When Jonathan and the people heard these words
	10 : 68	When Alexander the king heard of it
	10 : 74	When Jonathan heard the words of Apollonius
	10 : 77	When Apollonius heard of it
	10 : 88	When Alexander the king heard of these things
	11 : 15	And Alexander heard of it and came against him in battle
	11 : 22	When he heard this he was angry
	11 : 22	and as soon as he heard it
	11 : 23	When Jonathan heard this
	11 : 63	Then Jonathan heard that the officers of Demetrius
	12 : 24	Now Jonathan heard that the commanders of Demetrius had returned
	12 : 28	When the enemy heard
	12 : 34	for he had heard that they were ready
	13 : 1	Simon heard that Trypho had assembled a large army
	13 : 7	when they heard these words
	14 : 2	When Arsaces the king of Persia and Media heard
	14 : 16	It was heard in Rome, and as far away as Sparta
	14 : 17	When they heard that Simon his brother
	14 : 25	When the people heard these things they said
	14 : 40	For he had heard that the Jews were addressed by the Romans
	16 : 22	When he heard this, he was greatly shocked
2 Ma	1 : 5	May he hear your prayers and be reconciled to you
	1 : 8	We besought the Lord and we were heard
	10 : 13	He heard himself called a traitor at every turn
	11 : 24	We have heard that the Jews do not consent
	12 : 5	When Judas heard of the cruelty visited on his countrymen
	13 : 10	But when Judas heard of this
	14 : 15	When the Jews heard of Nicanor's coming
	14 : 18	Nevertheless Nicanor, hearing of the valour of Judas
	15 : 1	When Nicanor heard that Judas and his men
1 Es	5 : 65	so that the people could not hear the trumpets
	5 : 65	so that the sound was heard afar
	5 : 66	and when the enemies of the tribe of Judah and Benjamin heard it
	8 : 71	As soon as I heard these things
	9 : 40	and all the priests to hear the law
	9 : 50	now they were all weeping as they heard the law
Ps 151	: 3	it is he who hears
3 Ma	2 : 21	having heard the lawful supplication
	4 : 12	the king, hearing that the Jews'compatriots from the city
	5 : 35	Then the Jews, upon hearing what the king had said
	5 : 48	and heard the loud and tumultuous noise
	6 : 23	For when he heard the shouting
2 Es	1 : 35	who without having heard me will believe
	2 : 34	Therefore I say to you, O nations that hear and understand

	4 : 11	When I heard this, I fell on my face
	5 : 2	and beyond what you heard of formerly
	5 : 7	shall make his voice heard by night, and all shall hear his voice
	5 : 13	you shall hear yet greater things than these
	5 : 19	He heard what I said and left me
	6 : 13	Rise to your feet and you will hear a full, resounding voice
	6 : 17	When I heard this, I rose to my feet and listened
	6 : 23	and the trumpet shall sound aloud, and when all hear it
	6 : 32	because your voice has surely been heard before the Most High
	7 : 51	hear the explanation for this
	8 : 18	and I have heard of the swiftness of the judgment that is to come
	8 : 19	Therefore hear my voice, and understand my words
	8 : 24	hear, O Lord, the prayer of thy servant
	9 : 30	and thou didst say, Hear me, O Israel
	9 : 45	And after 30 years God heard your handmaid
	10 : 35	and I have heard what I do not understand
	10 : 56	and afterward you will hear as much as your ears can hear
	11 : 16	Hear me, you who have ruled the earth all this time
	11 : 36	Then I heard a voice saying to me
	11 : 37	and I heard how he uttered a man's voice to the eagle
	12 : 31	and as for all his words that you have heard
	12 : 40	When all the people heard that the 7 days were past
	13 : 4	all who heard his voice melted as wax melts
	13 : 14	and hast deemed me worthy to have my prayer heard by thee
	13 : 33	And when all the nations hear his voice
	14 : 8	and the interpretations that you have heard
	14 : 28	Hear these words, O Israel
	15 : 29	so that all who hear them fear and tremble
	16 : 27	or even to hear his voice
	16 : 40	Hear my words, O my people
	16 : 74	Hear, my elect, says the Lord
4 Ma	4 : 22	he heard that a rumour of his death had spread
	8 : 15	But when they had heard the inducements
	9 : 27	and they heard his noble decision
	10 : 17	When he heard this
	10 : 18	God hears also those who are mute
	14 : 9	as we hear of the tribulations of these young men
	14 : 9	yes, not only heard the direct word of threat

HEARER   2

Wis	1 : 6	and a hearer of his tongue
4 Ma	15 : 21	attract the attention of their hearers

HEARING   7 = 0.005 %

Bar	1 : 3	in the hearing of Jeconiah the son of Jehoiakim, king of Judah
	1 : 3	and in the hearing of all the people who came to hear the book
	1 : 4	and in the hearing of the mighty men and the princes
	1 : 4	and in the hearing of the elders
	1 : 4	and in the hearing of all the people, small and great
1 Ma	10 : 7	and read the letter in the hearing of all the people
2 Es	12 : 17	As for your hearing a voice that spoke

HEARKEN   4 = 0.003 %

Sir	33 : 18	and you leaders of the congregation, hearken
	36 : 17	Hearken, O Lord, to the prayer of thy servants
Bar	4 : 9	and she said : Hearken, you neighbours of Zion
2 Ma	8 : 3	and to hearken to the blood that cried out to him

HEART   166 = 0.108 %

Tob	1 : 12	because I remembered God with all my heart
	4 : 13	and in your heart do not disdain your brethren
	6 : 4	Cut open the fish and take the heart and liver and gall
	6 : 6	of what use is the liver and heart and gall of the fish ?
	6 : 7	He replied, As for the heart and the liver
	6 : 16	and lay upon them some of the heart and liver of the fish
	8 : 2	and put the heart and liver of the fish upon them and made a smoke
	13 : 6	If you turn to him with all your heart
Jud	6 : 9	If you really hope in your heart that they will not be taken
	7 : 22	Their children lost heart
	8 : 14	You cannot plumb the depths of the human heart
	8 : 27	to search their hearts
	8 : 28	All that you have said has been spoken out of a true heart
	8 : 29	for your heart's disposition is right
	10 : 16	do not be afraid in your heart
	11 : 1	Take courage, woman, and do not be afraid in your heart
	12 : 16	and Holofernes'heart was ravished with her
	13 : 4	Then Judith, standing beside his bed, said in her heart
	13 : 19	Your hope will never depart from the hearts of men
Ad E	14 : 13	and turn his heart to hate the man who is fighting against us
	15 : 5	as if beloved, but her heart was frozen with fear
	15 : 13	and my heart was shaken with fear at your glory
Wis	1 : 1	and seek him with sincerity of heart
	1 : 6	and a true observer of his heart
	2 : 2	and reason is a spark kindled by the beating of our hearts
	4 : 15	nor take such a thing to heart
	8 : 21	and with my whole heart I said :
	15 : 10	His heart is ashes, his hope is cheaper than dirt
Sir	1 : 12	The fear of the Lord delights the heart

1 : 30	and your heart was full of deceit
2 : 2	Set your heart right and be steadfast
2 : 12	Woe to timid hearts and to slack hands
2 : 13	Woe to the faint heart, for it has no trust !
2 : 17	Those who fear the Lord will prepare their hearts
5 : 1	Do not set your heart on your wealth
5 : 2	walking according to the desires of your heart
7 : 27	With all your heart honour your father
9 : 9	lest your heart turn aside to her
10 : 12	his heart has forsaken his Maker
13 : 25	A man's heart changes his countenance
13 : 25	And a glad heart makes a cheerful countenance
13 : 26	The mark of a happy heart is a cheerful face
14 : 2	Blessed is he whose heart does not condemn him
17 : 8	He set his eye upon their hearts
17 : 16	hearts of flesh in place of their stony hearts
21 : 6	but he that fears the Lord will repent in his heart
22 : 18	so a timid heart with a fool's purpose
22 : 19	and one who pricks the heart makes it show feeling
25 : 7	With 9 thoughts I have gladdened my heart
25 : 13	Any wound, but not a wound of the heart !
25 : 23	A dejected mind, a gloomy face, and a wounded heart
26 : 4	Whether rich or poor, his heart is glad
26 : 5	Of 3 things my heart is afraid
26 : 6	There is grief of heart and sorrow
26 : 18	so are beautiful feet with a steadfast heart
26 : 28	At 2 things my heart is grieved
30 : 16	and there is no gladness above joy of heart
30 : 22	Gladness of heart is the life of man
30 : 23	Delight your soul and comfort your heart
30 : 25	A man of cheerful and good heart
31 : 26	so wine tests hearts in the strife of the proud
31 : 28	is rejoicing of heart and gladness of soul
33 : 5	The heart of a fool is like a cart wheel
37 : 6	Do not forget a friend in your heart
37 : 13	And establish the counsel of your own heart
37 : 17	As a clue to changes of heart
38 : 10	and cleanse your heart from all sin
38 : 18	and sorrow of heart saps one's strength
38 : 19	and the life of the poor man weighs down his heart
38 : 20	Do not give your heart to sorrow
38 : 26	He sets his heart on ploughing furrows
38 : 27	he sets his heart on painting a lifelike image
38 : 28	He sets his heart on finishing his handiwork
38 : 30	he sets his heart to finish the glazing
39 : 5	He will set his heart to rise early
39 : 35	So now sing praise with all your heart and voice
40 : 2	Their perplexities and fear of heart
40 : 20	Wine and music gladden the heart
40 : 26	Riches and strength lift up the heart
42 : 18	He searches out the abyss, and the hearts of men
45 : 26	May the Lord grant you wisdom in your heart
46 : 11	those whose hearts did not fall into idolatry
47 : 8	he sang praise with all his heart, and he loved his Maker
48 : 10	to turn the heart of the father to the son
48 : 19	Then their hearts were shaken and their hands trembled
49 : 3	He set his heart upon the Lord
50 : 23	May he give us gladness of heart
50 : 27	who out of his heart poured forth wisdom
50 : 28	and he who lays them to heart will become wise
51 : 15	From blossom to ripening grape my heart delighted in her
51 : 21	My heart was stirred to seek her
Bar 1 : 21	but we each followed the intent of his own wicked heart
2 : 8	by turning away, each of us, from the thoughts of his wicked heart
2 : 31	I will give them a heart that obeys and ears that hear
3 : 7	For thou hast put the fear of thee in our hearts
3 : 7	for we have put away from our hearts all the iniquity of our fathers
L Jr 6 : 6	But say in your heart
6 : 20	but men say their hearts have melted
P Az 16	Yet with a contrite heart and a humble spirit may we be accepted
18	And now with all our heart we follow thee
65	Bless the Lord, you who are holy and humble in heart
Sus 13 : 35	for her heart trusted in the Lord
13 : 56	beauty has deceived you and lust has perverted your heart
1 Ma 1 : 3	and his heart was lifted up
1 : 62	and were resolved in their hearts not to eat unclean food
2 : 24	and his heart was stirred
12 : 28	they were afraid and were terrified at heart
16 : 13	His heart was lifted up
2 Ma 1 : 3	May he give you all a heart to worship him
1 : 3	and to do his will with a strong heart
1 : 4	May he open your heart to his law and his commandments
2 : 3	that the law should not depart from their hearts
3 : 16	was to be wounded at heart
3 : 17	the pain lodged in his heart
4 : 37	Therefore Antiochus was grieved at heart
11 : 9	and were strengthened in heart

15 : 27	and praying to God in their hearts
1 Es 1 : 23	for his heart was full of godliness
1 : 48	and he stiffened his neck and hardened his heart
2 : 9	from many whose hearts were stirred
3 : 21	It makes all hearts feel rich, forgets kings and satraps
8 : 25	who put this into the heart of the king
P Ma 11	And now I bend the knee of my heart
3 Ma 4 : 2	everywhere their hearts were burning
5 : 47	wishing to witness, with invulnerable heart and with his own eyes
2 Es 3 : 1	and my thoughts welled up in my heart
3 : 20	Yet thou didst not take away from them their evil heart
3 : 21	For the first Adam, burdened with an evil heart
3 : 22	the law was in the people's heart along with the evil root
3 : 26	for they also had the evil heart
3 : 28	Then I said in my heart
3 : 29	And my heart failed me
4 : 4	and will teach you why the heart is evil
4 : 7	How many dwellings are in the heart of the sea
4 : 30	For a grain of evil seed was sown in Adam's heart from the beginning
5 : 21	the thoughts of my heart were very grievous to me again
5 : 34	for every hour I suffer agonies of heart
6 : 26	and the heart of the earth's inhabitants shall be changed
6 : 36	And on the 8th night my heart was troubled within me again
7 : 48	For an evil heart has grown up in us
8 : 4	and drink wisdom, O my heart !
8 : 6	and give us seed for our heart
8 : 58	and said in their hearts that there is no God
9 : 27	my heart was troubled again as it was before
9 : 36	as well as our heart which received it
9 : 38	When I said these things in my heart
9 : 38	and was deeply grieved at heart
9 : 40	Why are you weeping, and why are you grieved at heart ?
10 : 25	and my heart was terrified
10 : 55	and do not let your heart be terrified
12 : 38	whose hearts you know are able to comprehend
13 : 3	out of the heart of the sea
13 : 25	from the heart of the sea
13 : 51	Why did I see the man coming up from the heart of the sea ?
14 : 8	Lay up in your heart the signs that I have shown you
14 : 25	and I will light in your heart the lamp of understanding
14 : 34	and discipline your hearts
14 : 40	my heart poured forth understanding
16 : 54	their imaginations and their thoughts and their hearts
16 : 61	who formed man, and put a heart in the midst of his body
16 : 63	and what you think in your hearts !
4 Ma 7 : 18	But as many as attend to religion with a whole heart
13 : 13	Let us with all our hearts consecrate ourselves to God
15 : 23	But devout reason, giving her heart a man's courage
15 : 29	who carried away the prize of the contest in your heart !

HEARTH   1
Sir 50 : 12   as he stood by the hearth of the altar

HEARTY   1
2 Ma 9 : 19   Antiochus their king and general sends hearty greetings

HEAT, subst.   15 = 0.010 %

Jud 8 : 3	he was overcome by the burning heat
Wis 2 : 4	by the rays of the sun and overcome by its heat
Sir 14 : 27	he will be sheltered by her from the heat
18 : 16	Does not the dew assuage the scorching heat ?
38 : 28	and he wastes away in the heat of the furnace
43 : 3	and who can withstand its burning heat ?
43 : 4	A man tending a furnace works in burning heat
43 : 22	when the dew appears, it refreshes from the heat
Bar 2 : 25	to the heat of day and the frost of night
P Az 44	Bless the Lord, fire and heat
45	Bless the Lord, winter cold and summer heat
2 Ma 14 : 43	But in the heat of the struggle he did not hit exactly
2 Es 1 : 20	Because of the heat
7 : 41	or summer or spring or heat or winter
15 : 50	when the heat rises that is sent upon you

HEAT, verb   4 = 0.003 %

Sir 23 : 16	The soul heated like a burning fire
2 Ma 7 : 3	and gave orders that pans and cauldrons be heated
7 : 4	These were heated immediately
4 Ma 11 : 19	that had been heated in the fire

HEATHEN   6 = 0.004 %

Wis 12 : 5	These initiates from the midst of a heathen cult
14 : 11	also upon the heathen idols
15 : 15	For they thought that all their heathen idols were gods
L Jr 6 : 4	and inspire fear in the heathen
6 : 17	so are the gods of the heathen
3 Ma 4 : 6	as they were torn by the harsh treatment of the heathen

HEAVEN
128 = 0.083 %

Tob	5:16	God who dwells in heaven will prosper your way
	7:18	the Lord of heaven and earth grant you joy
	8:5	Let the heavens and all thy creatures bless thee
	10:11	The God of heaven will prosper you, my children, before I die
	10:12	The Lord of heaven bring you back safely, dear brother
	13:7	my soul exalts the King of heaven
	13:11	bearing gifts in their hands, gifts for the King of heaven
Jud	5:8	and they worshipped the God of heaven
	6:19	O Lord God of heaven, behold their arrogance
	7:28	We call to witness against you heaven and earth
	9:12	Lord of heaven and earth, Creator of the waters
	11:17	and serves the God of heaven day and night
	13:18	who created the heavens and the earth
Ad E	13:10	For thou hast made heaven and earth
	13:10	and every wonderful thing under heaven
Wis	9:10	Send her forth from the holy heavens
	9:16	but who has traced out what is in the heavens ?
	13:2	or the luminaries of heaven
	16:20	and without their toil thou didst supply them from heaven
	18:15	thy all-powerful word leaped from heaven
	18:16	and touched heaven while standing on the earth
Sir	1:3	The height of heaven, the breadth of the earth
	1:5	The source of wisdom is God's word in the highest heaven
	16:15	in order that his works might be known under heaven
	16:18	Behold, heaven and the highest heaven
	17:32	He marshals the host of the height of heaven
	24:5	Alone I have made the circuit of the vault of heaven
	43:1	the appearance of heaven in a spectacle of glory
	43:8	shining forth in the firmament of heaven
	43:9	The glory of the stars is the beauty of heaven
	43:12	It encircles the heaven with its glorious arc
	45:15	and for his descendants all the days of heaven
	46:17	Then the Lord thundered from heaven
	48:3	By the word of the Lord he shut up the heavens
	48:20	and the Holy One quickly heard them from heaven
	51:19	I spread out my hands to the heavens
Bar	1:11	that their days on earth may be like the days of heaven
	2:2	Under the whole heaven there has not been done
	3:29	Who has gone up into heaven, and taken her
	5:3	For God will show your splendour everywhere under heaven
L Jr	6:54	they are like crows between heaven and earth
	6:67	they cannot show signs in the heavens and among the nations
P Az	13	as many as the stars of heaven
	34	Blessed art thou in the firmament of heaven
	36	Bless the Lord, you heavens
	38	Bless the Lord, all waters above the heaven
	41	Bless the Lord, stars of heaven
Sus	13:9	and turned away their eyes from looking to Heaven
	13:35	And she, weeping, looked up toward heaven
Bel	14:5	but the living God, who created heaven and earth
1 Ma	2:37	heaven and earth testify for us
	2:58	was taken up into heaven
	3:18	for in the sight of Heaven
	3:19	but strength comes from Heaven
	3:50	and they cried aloud to Heaven, saying
	3:60	But as his will in heaven may be, so he will do
	4:10	And now let us cry to Heaven
	4:24	On their return they sang hymns and praises to Heaven
	4:40	and cried out to Heaven
	4:55	and worshipped and blessed Heaven, who had prospered them
	5:31	and that the cry of the city went up to Heaven
	9:46	Cry out now to Heaven
	12:15	for we have the help which comes from Heaven for our aid
	16:3	and may the help which comes from Heaven be with you
2 Ma	2:10	and fire came down from heaven and devoured the sacrifices
	2:18	and will gather us from everywhere under heaven
	2:21	and the appearances which came from heaven
	3:15	and called toward heaven
	3:20	And holding up their hands to heaven, they all made entreaty
	3:34	And see that you, who have been scourged by heaven
	3:39	For he who has his dwelling in heaven
	7:11	and said nobly, I got these from Heaven
	7:28	to look at the heaven and the earth
	7:34	when you raise your hand against the children of heaven
	8:20	the 8,000, by the help that came to them from heaven
	9:4	But the judgment of heaven rode with him !
	9:10	had thought that he could touch the stars of heaven
	9:20	I am glad. As my hope is in heaven
	10:29	there appeared to the enemy from heaven
	14:34	Then the priests stretched forth their hands toward heaven
	15:3	if there were a sovereign in heaven
	15:4	It is the living Lord himself, the Sovereign in heaven
	15:8	when help had come to them from heaven
	15:21	stretched out his hands toward heaven
	15:23	So now, O Sovereign of the heavens
	15:34	And they all, looking to heaven
1 Es	4:34	The earth is vast, and heaven is high
	4:34	for it makes the circuit of the heavens
	4:36	The whole earth calls upon truth, and heaven blesses her
	4:46	whose fulfilment you vowed to the King of heaven
	4:58	he lifted up his face to heaven toward Jerusalem
	4:58	and praised the King of heaven, saying
	6:13	who created the heaven and the earth
	6:15	who is in heaven, and provoked him
	8:75	and our mistakes have mounted up to heaven
P Ma	2	thou who hast made heaven and earth with all their order
	9	I am unworthy to look up and see the height of heaven
	15	For all the host of heaven sings thy praise
3 Ma	2:2	Lord, Lord, king of the heavens
	2:15	For your dwelling, the heaven of heavens
	4:21	of him who was aiding the Jews from heaven
	5:9	So their entreaty ascended fervently to heaven
	5:25	stretched their hands toward heaven
	5:50	the help which they had received before from heaven
	6:17	they raised great cries to heaven
	6:28	Release the sons of the almighty and living God of heaven
	6:33	gave thanks to heaven unceasingly and lavishly
	7:6	that the God of heaven surely defends the Jews
2 Es	2:14	Call, O call heaven and earth to witness
	3:18	Thou didst bend down the heavens and shake the earth
	4:8	neither did I ever ascend into heaven
	4:21	and he who is above the heavens
	4:21	can understand what is above the height of the heavens
	6:38	Let heaven and earth be made
	11:2	and all the winds of heaven blew upon him
	11:6	And I saw how all things under heaven were subjected to him
	13:3	that man flew with the clouds of heaven
	13:5	from the 4 winds of heaven
	15:44	then the dust and smoke shall go up to heaven
	16:55	Let the heaven be made, and it was made
	16:59	who has spread out the heaven like an arch
4 Ma	4:10	angels on horseback with lightning flashing from their weapons appeared from heaven
	4:11	stretched out his hands toward heaven
	6:6	yet while the old man's eyes were raised to heaven
	17:5	The moon in heaven, with the stars
	17:5	and are firmly set in heaven with them

HEAVENLY
8 = 0.005 %

Wis	19:21	easily melted kind of heavenly food
Sir	43:1	The pride of the heavenly heights is the clear firmament
2 Ma	11:10	They advanced in battle order, having their heavenly ally
3 Ma	6:18	revealed his holy face and opened the heavenly gates
2 Es	2:37	giving thanks to him who has called you to heavenly kingdoms
4 Ma	4:11	to pray for him and propitiate the wrath of the heavenly army
	9:15	Most abominable tyrant, enemy of heavenly justice, savage of mind
	11:3	from the heavenly justice for even more crimes

HEAVILY
5 = 0.003 %

Sir	31:19	He does not breathe heavily upon his bed
	39:28	and in their anger they scourge heavily
1 Ma	2:30	because evils pressed heavily upon them
2 Ma	15:18	lay upon them less heavily
4 Ma	6:11	and gasping heavily for breath

HEAVY
15 = 0.010 %

Wis	17:21	while over those men alone heavy night was spread
	17:21	but still heavier than darkness were they to themselves
Sir	6:21	She will weigh him down like a heavy testing stone
	22:14	What is heavier than lead ?
	29:13	more than a mighty shield and more than a heavy spear
	33:28	and if he does not obey, make his fetters heavy
	40:1	and a heavy yoke is upon the sons of Adam
1 Ma	5:34	they fled before him, and he dealt them a heavy blow
	8:7	should pay a heavy tribute and give hostages
	8:31	Why have you made your yoke heavy
	13:22	but that night a very heavy snow fell
2 Ma	4:16	For this reason heavy disaster overtook them
2 Es	4:49	and poured down a heavy and violent rain
	15:35	and shall pour out a heavy tempest upon the earth
	15:38	And, after that, heavy storm clouds shall be stirred up from the south

HEBREW, subst., adj.
15 = 0.010 %

Jud	10:12	She replied, I am a daughter of the Hebrews
	12:11	Go now and persuade the Hebrew woman who is in your care
	14:18	One Hebrew woman has brought disgrace
Sir	pr.	For what was originally expressed in Hebrew
2 Ma	7:31	against the Hebrews
	11:13	and realized that the Hebrews were invincible
	15:37	And from that time the city has been in the possession of the Hebrews
4 Ma	4:11	and with tears besought the Hebrews
	5:2	ordered the guards to seize each and every Hebrew
	8:2	that others of the Hebrew captives be brought
	9:6	And if the aged men of the Hebrews because of their religion
	9:18	that sons of the Hebrews alone are invincible
	12:7	But when his mother had exhorted him in the Hebrew language

	16:15	and said to your sons in the Hebrew language
	17:9	who wished to destroy the way of life of the Hebrews

HEBRON   1
1 Ma 5:65 He struck Hebron and its villages

HEED, subst.   14 = 0.009 %
Wis   6:18 and giving heed to her laws is assurance of immortality
      8:12 and when I speak they will give heed
      13:1 while paying heed to his works
Sir   4:15 and whoever gives heed to her will dwell secure
      28:16 Whoever pays heed to slander will not find rest
      29:20 but take heed to yourself lest you fall
      30:25 will give heed to the food he eats
      32:22 and give good heed to your paths
      32:24 He who believes the law gives heed to the commandments
      34:2 so is he who gives heed to dreams
3 Ma 1:26 But he, in his arrogance, took heed of nothing
      3:6 Nevertheless those of the other races paid no heed
2 Es 7:99 which those who would not give heed shall suffer hereafter
      9:30 and give heed to my words, O descendants of Jacob

HEED, verb   12 = 0.008 %
Wis   12:26 But those who have not heeded the warning of light rebukes
Sir   23:27 and nothing sweeter than to heed the commandments of the
            Lord
      35:1 he who heeds the commandments sacrifices a peace offering
Bar   1:18 and have not heeded the voice of the Lord our God
      1:19 and we have been negligent, in not heeding his voice
      1:21 We did not heed the voice of the Lord our God
      2:5 in not heeding his voice
      3:4 who did not heed the voice of the Lord their God
1 Ma 2:68 and heed what the law commands
      8:16 they all heed the one man
1 Es 1:28 and did not heed the words of Jeremiah the prophet
      1:47 and did not heed the words

HEEDLESSLY   1
3 Ma 1:14 And someone heedlessly said that it was wrong

HEEL   4 = 0.003 %
Sir   12:17 and while pretending to help you, he will trip you by the heel
2 Es 6:8 for Jacob's hand held Esau's heel from the beginning
      6:10 and the end of a man is his heel
      6:10 between the heel and the hand seek for nothing else, Ezra !

HEGEMONIDES   1
2 Ma 13:24 left Hegemonides as governor from Ptolemais to Gerar

HE-GOAT   2
1 Es   7:8 and 12 he-goats for the sin of all Israel
      8:66 and as a thank offering 12 he-goats

HEIFER   1
Sir   38:26 and he is careful about fodder for the heifers

HEIGHT   15 = 0.010 %
Jud   7:10 but on the height of the mountains where they live
Sir   1:3 The height of heaven, the breadth of the earth
      17:32 He marshals the host of the height of heaven
      24:13 and like a cypress on the heights of Hermon
      26:16 Like the sun rising in the heights of the Lord
      43:1 The pride of the heavenly heights is the clear firmament
      43:9 a gleaming array in the heights of the Lord
Bar   5:5 Arise, O Jerusalem, stand upon the height
2 Ma 6:15 when our sins have reached their height
1 Es   6:25 its height to be 60 cubits and its breadth 60 cubits
P Ma   9 I am unworthy to look up and see the height of heaven
2 Es   4:21 can understand what is above the height of the heavens
      6:4 and before the heights of the air were lifted up
      16:60 to send rivers from the heights to water the earth
4 Ma   4:25 were thrown headlong from heights along with their infants

HEIGHTEN   1
Sir   28:10 and in proportion to his wealth he will heighten his wrath

HEIR   3 = 0.002 %
Tob   3:15 and he has no child to be his heir
Sir   23:22 and provides an heir by a stranger
2 Es   7:9 how will the heir receive his inheritance

HELIODORUS   13 = 0.008 %
2 Ma   3:7 The king chose Heliodorus, who was in charge of his affairs
      3:8 Heliodorus at once set out on his journey
      3:13 But Heliodorus, because of the king's commands which he had
      3:23 Heliodorus went on with what had been decided
      3:25 and it rushed furiously at Heliodorus
      3:31 Quickly some of Heliodorus' friends asked Onias
      3:32 with regard to Heliodorus
      3:33 the same young men appeared again to Heliodorus
      3:35 Then Heliodorus offered sacrifice to the Lord
      3:37 When the king asked Heliodorus
      3:40 This was the outcome of the episode of Heliodorus
      4:1 slandered Onias, saying that it was he who had incited
            Heliodorus
      5:18 just as Heliodorus was

HELL   4 = 0.003 %
2 Es   4:7 or which are the exits of hell
      4:8 I never went down into the deep, nor as yet into hell
      7:36 and the furnace of hell shall be disclosed
      8:53 hell has fled and corruption has been forgotten

HELLENIZATION   1
2 Ma   4:13 There was such an extreme of Hellenization

HELMET   2
Wis   5:18 and wear impartial justice as a helmet
1 Ma   6:35 and with brass helmets on their heads

HELP, subst.   37 = 0.024 %
Jud   6:21 and all that night they called on the God of Israel for help
      7:31 But if these days pass by, and no help comes for us
      9:4 and called on thee for help
Wis   13:16 for it is only an image and has need of help
      16:10 for thy mercy came to their help and healed them
      17:12 For fear is nothing but surrender of the helps
      17:13 and the inner expectation of help, being weak
Sir   4:11 Wisdom exalts her sons and gives help to those who seek her
      8:16 and where no help is at hand, he will strike you down
      11:12 There is another who is slow and needs help
      24:22 and those who work with my help will not sin
      40:24 Brothers and help are for a time of trouble
      40:26 and with it there is no need to seek for help
      51:10 at the time when there is no help against the proud
1 Ma   8:32 If now they appeal again for help against you
      10:24 that I may have their help
      12:15 for we have the help which comes from Heaven for our aid
      14:1 and marched into Media to secure help
      16:3 and may the help which comes from Heaven be with you
2 Ma   8:19 when help came to their ancestors
      8:20 the 8,000, by the help that came to them from heaven
      8:23 and gave the watchword, God's help
      8:35 having been humbled with the help of the Lord
      12:11 by the help of God
      13:13 and decide the matter by the help of God
      13:17 because the Lord's help protected him
      15:7 that he would get help from the Lord
      15:8 when help had come to them from heaven
      15:35 of the help of the Lord
1 Es   6:2 with the help of the prophets of the Lord who were with them
      8:27 I was encouraged by the help of the Lord my God
3 Ma   2:33 They remained resolutely hopeful of obtaining help
      2:33 and depriving them of common fellowship and mutual help
      4:16 even to communicate or to come to one's help
      5:50 the help which they had received before from heaven
2 Es   2:18 I will send you help, my servants Isaiah and Jeremiah
      3:4 when thou didst form the earth – and that without help

HELP, verb   49 = 0.032 %
Tob   2:10 I went to physicians, but they did not help me
Jud   7:25 For now we have no one to help us
      8:11 unless the Lord turns and helps us within so many days
      8:15 For if he does not choose to help us within these 5 days
      8:17 let us call upon him to help us
      13:5 For now is the time to help thy inheritance
Ad E   14:3 help me, who am alone and have no helper but thee
      14:14 But save us by thy hand, and help me
Wis   2:18 for if the righteous man is God's son, he will help him
      13:16 because he knows that it cannot help itself
      19:22 and thou hast not neglected to help them
Sir   pr. should be able to help the outsiders
      2:6 Trust in him, and he will help you
      3:12 O son, help your father in his old age
      12:4 Give to the godly man, but do not help the sinner
      12:7 Give to the good man, but do not help the sinner
      12:17 and while pretending to help you, he will trip you by the heel
      25:18 and he cannot help sighing bitterly
      29:4 and cause trouble to those who help them
      29:9 help a poor man for the commandment's sake
      37:5 Some companions help a friend for their stomachs' sake
      51:7 and there was no one to help me
Bar   4:17 But I, how can I help you ?
L Jr   6:58 and they will not be able to help themselves
      6:68 for they can flee to cover and help themselves
1 Ma   3:2 All his brothers and all who had joined his father helped him
      3:15 went up with him to help him
      3:53 if thou dost not help us ?
      5:39 They also have hired Arabs to help them
      7:7 and let him punish them and all who help them

	7:20	and left with him a force to help him
	8:13	Those whom they wish to help and to make kings
	10:72	and who the others are that are helping us
	10:74	and Simon his brother met him to help him
	11:43	Now then you will do well to send me men who will help me
2 Ma	3:28	but was now unable to help himself
	11:19	I will endeavour for the future to help promote your welfare
	12:11	and to help his people in all other ways
	13:10	now if ever to help those
1 Es	2:6	be helped by the men of his place with gold and silver
	2:9	and their neighbours helped them with everything
	4:48	and to help him build the city
	6:28	and that full effort be made to help the men
3 Ma	2:12	you helped them in their humiliation
	3:8	were not strong enough to help them
	5:25	implored the supreme God to help them again at once
4 Ma	2:14	and helps raise up what has fallen
	3:3	but reason can help to deal with anger
	14:17	they do what they can to help their young

HELPER 11 = 0.007 %

Tob	8:6	and gavest him Eve his wife as a helper and support
	8:6	let us make a helper for him like himself
Jud	9:11	for thou art God of the lowly, helper of the oppressed
Ad E	14:3	help me, who am alone and have no helper but thee
	14:14	who am alone and have no helper but thee, O Lord
Sir	13:22	If a rich man slips, his helpers are many
	36:24	a helper fit for him and a pillar of support
	51:2	for thou hast been my protector and helper
	51:2	Before those who stood by thou wast my helper
1 Ma	12:53	for they said, They have no leader or helper
2 Es	16:33	their daughters shall mourn, because they have no helpers

HELPLESS 4 = 0.003 %

Wis	12:6	these parents who murder helpless lives
L Jr	6:28	but give none to the poor or helpless
2 Ma	7:5	When he was utterly helpless
3 Ma	2:22	so that he lay helpless on the ground and

HELPLESSNESS 1

3 Ma	2:13	subjected to our enemies, and overtaken by helplessness

HEM in 5 = 0.003 %

Sus	13:22	I am hemmed in on every side
1 Ma	3:18	Judas replied, It is easy for many to be hemmed in by few
	4:31	So do thou hem in this army by the hand of thy people Israel
	6:18	Now the men in the citadel kept hemming Israel in
	11:65	and fought against it for many days and hemmed it in

HEN 1

2 Es	1:30	I gathered you as a hen gathers her brood under her wings

HENCE 2

Jud	5:8	hence they drove them out from the presence of their gods
1 Es	4:22	Hence you must realize that women rule over you !

HENCEFORTH 4 = 0.003 %

1 Ma	10:30	I release them from this day and henceforth
	15:8	from henceforth and for all time
2 Es	7:99	as henceforth is announced
	14:9	and henceforth you shall live with my Son

HER, adj., pers. pr. 598 = 0.390 %

HERALD 2

Sir	20:15	he opens his mouth like a herald
4 Ma	6:4	while a herald opposite him cried out

HERB 1

Wis	16:12	For neither herb nor poultice cured them

HERCULES 2

2 Ma	4:19	to carry 300 silver drachmas for the sacrifice to Hercules
	4:20	for the sacrifice to Hercules

HERD, subst. 2

Jud	2:27	and destroyed their flocks and herds
	3:3	and all our wheat fields, and our flocks and herds

HERE 43 = 0.028 %

Tob	2:8	he once ran away, and here he is burying the dead again !
	7:11	And Tobias said, I will eat nothing here
	7:13	he gave her to Tobias to be his wife, saying, Here she is
	11:15	here I see my son Tobias
	14:1	Here Tobit ended his words of praise
Jud	3:10	here he camped between Geba and Scythopolis
	9:6	Lo, we are here
	12:3	For none of your people is here with us
	13:15	and said, See, here is the head of Holofernes
	13:15	and here is the canopy beneath which he lay

	14:18	For look, here is Holofernes lying on the ground
Ad E	14:18	since the day that I was brought here until now
Wis	18:18	and one here and another there, hurled down half dead
Sir	29:26	Come here, stranger, prepare the table
Bar	3:34	he called them, and they said, Here we are !
1 Ma	12:45	For that is why I am here
2 Ma	1:6	We are now praying for you here
	9:25	and I have written to him what is written here
	14:7	I mean the high priesthood – and have now come here
	14:33	and I will build here a splendid temple to Dionysus
	15:37	So I too will here end my story
	15:39	And here will be the end
1 Es	5:69	who brought us here
	6:20	Then this Shesh-Bazzar, after coming here
	6:34	that it be done with all diligence as here prescribed
3 Ma	1:20	Mothers and nurses abandoned even new-born children here and there
	3:21	we made known to all our amnesty towards their compatriots here
	6:25	and senselessly gathered here those who faithfully have held
2 Es	3:29	For when I came here I saw ungodly deeds without number
	4:12	It would be better for us not to be here
	4:12	than to come here and live in ungodliness
	4:35	How long are we to remain here ?
	7:38	here are delight and rest
	10:4	but to stay here, and I will neither eat nor drink
	10:18	I will not go into the city, but I will die here
	10:58	But tomorrow night you shall remain here
	12:39	But wait here 7 days more
	14:2	And I said, Here I am, Lord
	14:25	and you shall come here
	14:33	And now you are here
4 Ma	4:3	and said, I have come here
	10:19	See, here is my tongue
	17:9	Here lie buried an aged priest and an aged woman and 7 sons

HEREAFTER 7 = 0.005 %

Ad E	13:7	and leave our government completely secure and untroubled hereafter
	16:23	so that both now and hereafter
Wis	2:2	and hereafter we shall be as though we had never been
2 Es	7:99	which those who would not give heed shall suffer hereafter
	8:46	and things that are future are for those who will live hereafter
	14:16	shall be done hereafter
	14:20	but who will warn those who will be born hereafter ?

HEREIN 1

1 Es	6:32	or nullify any of the things herein written

HEREWITH 1

Bar	1:10	And they said : Herewith we send you money

HERITAGE 4 = 0.003 %

Sir	45:20	He added glory to Aaron and gave him a heritage
	45:25	the heritage of the king is from son to son only
	45:25	so the heritage of Aaron is for his descendants
2 Ma	14:15	and always upholds his own heritage by manifesting himself

HERMON, mountain 1

Sir	24:13	and like a cypress on the heights of Hermon

HERMON, person 9 = 0.006 %

3 Ma	5:1	so he summoned Hermon, keeper of the elephants
	5:4	And Hermon, keeper of the elephants
	5:10	Hermon, however, when he had drugged the pitiless elephants
	5:18	the king summoned Hermon
	5:23	Hermon, having equipped the beasts
	5:26	Hermon arrived and invited him to come out
	5:29	Then Hermon and all the king's friends
	5:33	So Hermon suffered an unexpected and dangerous threat
	5:37	After summoning Hermon he said in a threatening tone

HEROIC 1

1 Ma	5:56	and of the heroic war they had fought

HERSELF 19 = 0.012 %

HESHBON 1

Jud	5:15	and by their might destroyed all the inhabitants of Heshbon

HESITATE 2

Tob	12:13	When you did not hesitate to rise and to leave your dinner
Sir	13:12	he will not hesitate to injure or to imprison

HEWN 3 = 0.002 %

Jud	1:2	with hewn stones 3 cubits thick and 6 cubits long
1 Es	6:9	of hewn stone, with costly timber laid in the walls
	6:25	with 3 courses of hewn stone

HEZEKIAH

7 = 0.005 %

Sir	48 :17	Hezekiah fortified his city
	48 :22	For Hezekiah did what was pleasing to the Lord
	49 :4	Except David and Hezekiah and Josiah they all sinned greatly
2 Ma	15 :22	in the time of Hezekiah king of Judea
1 Es	5 :15	The sons of Ater, namely of Hezekiah, 92
	9 :43	Uriah, Hezekiah, and Baalsamus on his right hand
2 Es	7 :110	and Hezekiah for the people in the days of Sennacherib

HIDDEN

10 = 0.007 %

Sir	20 :30	Hidden wisdom and unseen treasure
	39 :3	he will seek out the hidden meanings of proverbs
	41 :14	hidden wisdom and unseen treasure
	42 :19	and he reveals the tracks of hidden things
	48 :25	and the hidden things before they came to pass
Bel		for beneath the table they had made a hidden entrance
1 Ma	1 :23	he took also the hidden treasures which he found
2 Es	12 :37	and put it in a hidden place
	16 :62	and searches out hidden things in hidden places

HIDE

45 = 0.029 %

Tob	1 :19	so I hid myself
	12 :13	your good deed was not hidden from me, but I was with you
	13 :6	and will not hide his face from you
Wis	6 :22	and I will hide no secrets from you
	7 :13	I do not hide her wealth
	14 :21	And this became a hidden trap for mankind
Sir	1 :24	He will hide his words until the right moment
	3 :22	for you do not need what is hidden
	4 :23	and do not hide your wisdom
	6 :12	and will hide himself from your presence
	12 :8	nor will an enemy be hidden in adversity
	16 :17	Do not say, I shall be hidden from the Lord
	17 :15	they will not be hid from his eyes
	17 :20	Their iniquities are not hidden from him
	19 :27	He hides his face and pretends not to hear
	20 :31	Better is the man who hides his folly
	20 :31	than the man who hides his wisdom
	22 :25	and I will not hide from him
	23 :18	Darkness surrounds me, and the walls hide me
	23 :19	and perceive even the hidden places
	26 :8	she will not hide her shame
	37 :10	hide your counsel from those who are jealous of you
	39 :19	and nothing can be hid from his eyes
	41 :15	Better is the man who hides his folly
	41 :15	than the man who hides his wisdom
	42 :20	No thought escapes him, and not one word is hidden from him
	43 :32	Many things greater than these lie hidden
L Jr	6 :48	as to where they can hide themselves and their gods
Sus	13 :16	who had hid themselves and were watching her
	13 :18	and they did not see the elders, because they were hidden
	13 :37	Then a young man, who had been hidden
1 Ma	9 :38	and went up and hid under cover of the mountain
	16 :15	he gave them a great banquet, and hid men there
2 Ma	1 :19	and secretly hid it in the hollow of a dry cistern
	1 :20	sent the descendants of the priests who had hidden the fire to get it
	1 :33	that, in the place where the exiled priests had hidden the fire
	10 :37	They killed Timothy, who was hidden in a cistern
	12 :41	the righteous Judge, who reveals the things that are hidden
2 Es	5 :1	and the way of truth shall be hidden
	5 :9	then shall reason hide itself
	7 :26	and the land which now is hidden shall be disclosed
	8 :53	illness is banished from you, and death is hidden
	16 :28	and out of the field, 2 who have hidden themselves
	16 :63	Woe to those who sin and want to hide their sins !
	16 :66	Or how will you hide your sins before God and his angels ?

HIDING

2

1 Ma	1 :53	they drove Israel into hiding
2 Ma	14 :30	and went into hiding from Nicanor

HIDING PLACE

4 = 0.003 %

1 Ma	2 :31	had gone down to the hiding places in the wilderness
	2 :36	or block up their hiding places
	2 :41	in their hiding places
2 Es	2 :31	because I will bring them out of the hiding places of the earth

HIERONYMUS

1

2 Ma	12 :2	as well as Hieronymus and Demophon

HIGH, adj., adv.

42 = 0.027 %

Jud	1 :2	he made the walls 70 cubits high and 50 cubits wide
	1 :3	a 100 cubits high and 60 cubits wide at the foundations
	1 :4	which were 70 cubits high and 40 cubits wide
	4 :5	and immediately seized all the high hilltops
	5 :1	and had fortified all the high hilltops
	7 :4	neither the high mountains
Wis	6 :5	because severe judgment falls on those in high places
	9 :17	and sent thy holy Spirit from on high ?

Sir	1 :5	The source of wisdom is God's word in the highest heaven
	7 :4	Do not seek from the Lord the highest office
	16 :17	and who from on high will remember me ?
	16 :18	Behold, heaven and the highest heaven
	22 :18	Fences set on a high place
	24 :4	I dwelt in high places
	37 :14	than 7 watchmen sitting high on a watchtower
	43 :8	an instrument of the hosts on high
	50 :2	He laid the foundations for the high double walls
Bar	3 :25	it is high and immeasurable
1 Ma	4 :60	with high walls and strong towers round about
	6 :7	with high walls as before, and also Beth-zur, his city
	6 :40	was spread out on the high hills
	9 :50	with high walls and gates and bars
	12 :36	to build the walls of Jerusalem still higher
	12 :36	and to erect a high barrier between the citadel and the city
	13 :27	he made it high that it might be seen
	13 :33	with high towers and great walls and gates and bolts
	14 :37	and built the walls of Jerusalem higher
	14 :39	and paid him high honours
2 Ma	4 :15	and putting the highest value upon Greek forms of prestige
	4 :31	leaving Andronicus, a man of high rank, to act as his deputy
	6 :18	Eleazar, one of the scribes in high position
	6 :23	But making a high resolve
	8 :30	and got possession of some exceedingly high strongholds
	9 :8	and imagining that he could weigh the high mountains in a balance
	13 :5	For there is a tower in that place, 50 cubits high, full of ashes
1 Es	4 :34	The earth is vast, and heaven is high
	8 :75	For our sins have risen higher than our heads
3 Ma	3 :19	who hold their heads high in defiance of kings
2 Es	15 :35	as high as a horse's belly
	15 :40	and shall pour out upon every high and lofty place a terrible tempest
4 Ma	1 :2	and in addition it includes the praise of the highest virtue
	5 :1	on a certain high place

HIGHLAND

1

2 Es	15 :58	And those who are in the mountains and highlands

HIGHLY

40 = 0.026 %

Sir	pr.	It seemed highly necessary
	19 :24	than the highly prudent man who transgresses the law
P Az	29	and to be praised and highly exalted for ever
	30	and to be highly praised and highly exalted for ever
	31	and to be extolled and highly glorified for ever
	32	and to be praised and highly exalted for ever
	33	and to be extolled and highly exalted for ever
	35	sing praise to him and highly exalt him for ever
	36	sing praise to him and highly exalt him for ever
	37	sing praise to him and highly exalt him for ever
	38	sing praise to him and highly exalt him for ever
	39	sing praise to him and highly exalt him for ever
	40	sing praise to him and highly exalt him for ever
	41	sing praise to him and highly exalt him for ever
	42	sing praise to him and highly exalt him for ever
	43	sing praise to him and highly exalt him for ever
	44	sing praise to him and highly exalt him for ever
	45	sing praise to him and highly exalt him for ever
	46	sing praise to him and highly exalt him for ever
	47	sing praise to him and highly exalt him for ever
	48	sing praise to him and highly exalt him for ever
	49	sing praise to him and highly exalt him for ever
	50	sing praise to him and highly exalt him for ever
	51	sing praise to him and highly exalt him for ever
	52	let it sing praise to him and highly exalt him for ever
	53	sing praise to him and highly exalt him for ever
	54	sing praise to him and highly exalt him for ever
	55	sing praise to him and highly exalt him for ever
	56	sing praise to him and highly exalt him for ever
	57	sing praise to him and highly exalt him for ever
	58	sing praise to him and highly exalt him for ever
	59	sing praise to him and highly exalt him for ever
	60	sing praise to him and highly exalt him for ever
	61	sing praise to him and highly exalt him for ever
	62	sing praise to him and highly exalt him for ever
	63	sing praise to him and highly exalt him for ever
	64	sing praise to him and highly exalt him for ever
	65	sing praise to him and highly exalt him for ever
	66	sing praise to him and highly exalt him for ever

HIGH PRIEST s. CHIEF PRIEST

51 = 0.033 %

Jud	4 :6	And Joakim, the high priest
	4 :8	So the Israelites did as Joakim the high priest
	4 :14	And Joakim the high priest and all the priests
	15 :8	Then Joakim the high priest
Sir	50 :1	was Simon the high priest, son of Onias
Bar	1 :7	and they sent it to Jerusalem to Jehoiakim the high priest
1 Ma	7 :5	they were led by Alcimus, who wanted to be high priest
	7 :9	whom he made high priest

10:20	to be the high priest of your nation
10:32	and give it to the high priest
10:38	and obey no other authority but the high priest
10:69	to Jonathan the high priest :
12:3	Jonathan the high priest and the Jewish nation have sent us
12:6	Jonathan the high priest, the senate of the nation
12:7	a letter was sent to Onias the high priest
12:20	to Onias the high priest, greeting
13:36	King Demetrius to Simon, the high priest and friend of kings
13:42	In the first year of Simon the great high priest
14:17	had become high priest in his place
14:20	to Simon the high priest and to the elders and the priests
14:23	And they have sent a copy of this to Simon the high priest
14:27	which is the 3rd year of Simon the great high priest
14:30	Jonathan rallied the nation, and became their high priest
14:35	and they made him their leader and high priest
14:41	that Simon should be their leader and high priest for ever
14:47	So Simon accepted and agreed to be high priest
15:2	King Antiochus to Simon the high priest and ethnarch
15:17	They had been sent by Simon the high priest
15:21	hand them over to Simon the high priest
15:24	to Simon the high priest
16:12	for he was son-in-law of the high priest
16:24	from the time that he became high priest after his father

2 Ma
3:1	because of the piety of the high priest Onias
3:4	had a disagreement with the high priest
3:9	and had been kindly welcomed by the high priest of the city
3:10	The high priest explained that there were some deposits
3:16	To see the appearance of the high priest
3:21	and the anxiety of the high priest in his great anguish
3:32	And the high priest, fearing that the king might get the notion
3:33	While the high priest was making the offering of atonement
3:33	Be very grateful to Onias the high priest
4:13	who was ungodly and no high priest
14:3	Now a certain Alcimus, who had formerly been high priest
14:13	and to set up Alcimus as high priest of the greatest temple
15:12	Onias, who had been high priest, a noble and good man

1 Es
5:40	until a high priest should appear wearing Urim and Thummim

3 Ma
1:11	but only the high priest who was preeminent over all
2:1	Then the high priest Simon, facing the sanctuary

4 Ma
4:13	Moved by these words, Onias the high priest
4:16	and appointed Onias's brother Jason as high priest
4:18	So the king appointed him high priest and ruler of the nation

HIGH PRIESTHOOD   12 = 0.008 %

1 Ma
7:21	Alcimus strove for the high priesthood
11:27	He confirmed him in the high priesthood
11:57	I confirm you in the high priesthood
14:38	King Demetrius confirmed him in the high priesthood
16:24	in the chronicles of his high priesthood

2 Ma
4:7	obtained the high priesthood by corruption
4:24	and secured the high priesthood for himself
4:25	possessing no qualification for the high priesthood
4:29	as deputy in the high priesthood
11:3	and to put up the high priesthood for sale every year
14:7	I mean the high priesthood – and have now come here

4 Ma
4:1	Onias, who then held the high priesthood for life

HIGHWAY   4 = 0.003 %

Tob	1:15	and under him the highways were unsafe
1 Ma	5:4	and ambushed them on the highways
	15:41	and make raids along the highways of Judea
2 Es	1:13	and made safe highways for you where there was no road

HILKIAH   9 = 0.006 %

Jud	8:1	son of Ahitub, son of Elijah, son of Hilkiah
Bar	1:1	son of Zedekiah, son of Hasadiah, son of Hilkiah
	1:7	the son of Hilkiah, son of Shallum, and to the priests
Sus	13:2	And he took a wife named Susanna, the daughter of Hilkiah
	13:29	Send for Susanna, the daughter of Hilkiah
	13:63	And Hilkiah and his wife praised God for their daughter Susanna
1 Es	1:8	And Hilkiah, Zechariah, and Jehiel
	8:1	son of Hilkiah, son of Shallum
2 Es	1:1	son of Azariah, son of Hilkiah, son of Shallum

HILL   36 = 0.023 %

Jud	1:6	He was joined by all the people of the hill country
	2:22	and went up into the hill country
	4:7	ordering them to seize the passes up into the hills
	5:1	and had closed the passes in the hills
	5:3	what people is this that lives in the hill country ?
	5:15	they took possession of all the hill country
	5:19	and have settled in the hill country
	6:7	into the hill country
	6:11	and from the plain they went up into the hill country
	6:12	and ran out of the city to the top of the hill
	6:13	However, they got under the shelter of the hill
	6:13	and left him lying at the foot of the hill
	7:1	and to seize the passes up into the hill country

	7:4	nor the valleys nor the hills will bear their weight
	7:18	and encamped in the hill country opposite Dothan
	10:13	and capture all the hill country
	11:2	And even now, if your people who live in the hill country
	15:2	by every path across the plain and through the hill country
	15:3	Those who had camped in the hills around Bethulia
	15:5	Those in Jerusalem and all the hill country also came
	15:7	and the villages and towns in the hill country and in the plain
	16:4	their cavalry covered the hills
Sir	46:9	so that he went up to the hill country
Bar	5:7	and the everlasting hills be made low
P Az	53	Bless the Lord, mountains and hills
1 Ma	2:28	And he and his sons fled to the hills
	4:5	he found no one there, so he looked for them in the hills
	4:18	Gorgias and his force are near us in the hills
	4:19	a detachment appeared, coming out of the hills
	4:46	on the temple hill until there should come a prophet
	6:39	the hills were ablaze with them
	6:40	was spread out on the high hills
	10:70	Why do you assume authority against us in the hill country ?
	13:52	He strengthened the fortifications of the temple hill
	16:20	and the temple hill
2 Es	15:42	mountains and hills, trees of the forests

HILLTOP   4 = 0.003 %

Jud	2:24	and destroyed all the hilltop cities along the brook Abron
	3:6	and stationed garrisons in the hilltop cities
	4:5	and immediately seized all the high hilltops
	5:1	and had fortified all the high hilltops

HIM   1190 = 0.775 %

HIMSELF   96 = 0.063 %

HINDER, verb   12 = 0.008 %

Jud	12:7	So Holofernes commanded his guards not to hinder her
Wis	10:8	they not only were hindered from recognizing the good
Sir	18:22	Let nothing hinder you from paying a vow promptly
1 Ma	9:55	and his work was hindered
1 Es	2:30	and began to hinder the builders
	5:72	cut off their supplies, and hindered their building
	6:33	to hinder or damage that house of the Lord in Jerusalem
3 Ma	3:2	that they hindered others from the observance or their customs
2 Es	3:8	and thou didst not hinder them
4 Ma	1:3	that reason rules over those emotions that hinder self-control
	1:4	the emotions that hinder one from justice, such as malice
	2:6	Just so it is with the emotions that hinder one from justice

HIPPODROME   3 = 0.002 %

3 Ma	4:11	he commanded that they should be enclosed in the hippodrome
	5:46	crowding their way into the hippodrome
	6:16	the king arrived at the hippodrome with the beasts

HIRE, verb   2

| Sir | 37:11 | or with a man hired for a year about completing his work |
| 1 Ma | 5:39 | They also have hired Arabs to help them |

HIRED   2

| Jud | 4:10 | and every resident alien and hired labourer |
| Sir | 7:20 | or a hired labourer who devotes himself to you |

HIRELING   2

| Jud | 6:2 | And who are you, Achior, and you hirelings of Ephraim |
| | 6:5 | But you, Achior, you Ammonite hireling |

HIS   1702 = 1.109 %

HISS   1

| Sir | 22:1 | and every one hisses at his disgrace |

HISSING   2

| Wis | 17:9 | and the hissing of serpents |
| 2 Es | 15:29 | their hissing shall spread over the earth |

HISTORIAN   1

| 2 Ma | 2:30 | It is the duty of the original historian |

HISTORY   4 = 0.003 %

2 Ma	2:24	for those who wish to enter upon the narratives of history
	2:32	while cutting short the history itself
1 Es	1:33	These things are written in the book of the histories
4 Ma	17:7	to paint the history of your piety as an artist might

HIT   1

| 2 Ma | 14:43 | But in the heat of the struggle he did not hit exactly |

HITCH up   1

| Jud | 15:11 | and hitched up her carts and piled the things on them |

HITTITE   1
1 Es   8 :69   the Canaanites, the Hittites, the Perizzites

HIVE   1
4 Ma 14 :19   and as though with an iron dart sting those who approach their hive

HOARD up   1
Bar   3 :17   and who hoard up silver and gold

HOARFROST   2
Wis   5 :14   and like a light hoarfrost driven away by a storm
Sir 43 :19   He pours the hoarfrost upon the earth like salt

HOCK   1
2 Es 15 :36   and a man's thigh and a camel's hock

HODIAH   2
1 Es   8 :48   Hodiah the sons of Hananiah, and their sons, 20 men
     9 :48   Shabbethai, Hodiah, Maaseiah and Kelita

HOLD, verb   60 = 0.039 %
Jud   2 :10   and you shall hold them for me
    12 :10   On the 4th day Holofernes held a banquet for his slaves only
Ad E 11 :11   and the lowly were exalted and consumed those held in honour
Wis   1 :7   and that which holds all things together knows what is said
    3 :17   Even if they live long they will be held of no account
    5 :4   This is the man whom we once held in derision
   14 :23   or hold frenzied revels with strange customs
   15 :12   and life a festival held for profit
   17 :2   that they held the holy nation in their power
   17 :4   For not even the inner chamber that held them
Sir   1 :19   and he exalted the glory of those who held her fast
    4 :13   Whoever holds her fast will obtain glory
    9 :12   remember that they will not be held guiltless
   15 :1   and he who holds to the law will obtain wisdom
   21 :14   it will hold no knowledge
   25 :11   to whom shall be likened the one who holds it fast ?
   32 :8   be as one who knows and yet holds his tongue
   43 :26   and by his word all things hold together
   48 :22   and he held strongly to the ways of David his father
Bar   4 :1   All who hold her fast will live
L Jr   6 :14   Like a local ruler the god holds a sceptre
Sus 13 :39   We saw them embracing, but we could not hold the man
1 Ma   3 :45   and the sons of aliens held the citadel
    4 :61   And he stationed a garrison there to hold it
    6 :50   and stationed a guard there to hold it
   13 :15   in connection with the offices he held
   15 :7   and the strongholds which you have built and now hold
   15 :28   You hold control of Joppa and Gazara
   15 :34   we are firmly holding the inheritance of our fathers
2 Ma   4 :18   When the quadrennial games were being held at Tyre
    4 :27   And Menelaus held the office
   12 :24   because he held the parents of most of them
   14 :22   they held the proper conference
1 Es   4 :50   that the Idumeans should give up the villages of the Jews which they held
3 Ma   3 :19   who hold their heads high in defiance of kings
    6 :25   and senselessly gathered here those who faithfully have held
    7 :16   But those who had held fast to God even to death
    7 :21   being held in honour and awe
    7 :22   so that those who held any
2 Es   2 :43   And I was held spellbound
    5 :15   But the angel who had come and talked with me held me
    5 :44   neither can the world hold at one time
    6 :8   for Jacob's hand held Esau's heel from the beginning
    6 :50   could not hold them both
    9 :35   they are destroyed, but the things that held them remain
   11 :18   and held the rule like the former ones
   11 :21   and others of them rose up, but did not hold the rule
   11 :25   and hold the rule
   11 :40   and you have held sway over the world with much terror
   12 :15   But the 2nd that is to reign shall hold sway
   13 :9   nor held a spear or any weapon of war
   13 :28   and as for his not holding a spear or weapon of war
   16 :69   And those who consent to eat shall be held in derision and contempt
4 Ma   1 :10   for the honour in which they are held
    4 :1   Onias, who then held the high priesthood for life
    5 :10   if, by holding a vain opinion concerning the truth
    5 :18   and we had wrongly held it to be divine
   11 :27   therefore, unconquered, we hold fast to reason
   15 :26   this mother held 2 ballots
   17 :3   you held firm and unswerving

HOLD back   4 = 0.003 %
Wis 18 :23   he intervened and held back the wrath
Sir 12 :5   hold back his bread, and do not give it to him
   46 :4   Was not the sun held back by his hand ?
4 Ma 13 :6   hold back the threatening waves

HOLD out   2
Jud   7 :30   Let us hold out for 5 more days
4 Ma   7 :4   has ever held out as did that most holy man

HOLD over   1
Tob   4 :14   Do not hold over till the next day

HOLD up   1
2 Ma   3 :20   And holding up their hands to heaven, they all made entreaty

HOLD, subst.   7 = 0.005 %
Tob 11 :11   and took hold of his father
Jud 13 :7   and took hold of the hair of his head, and said
Wis   4 :3   will strike a deep root or take a firm hold
Sir   6 :27   and when you get hold of her, do not let her go
   26 :7   taking hold of her is like grasping a scorpion
Bar   3 :20   nor understood her paths, nor laid hold of her
2 Ma 12 :35   caught hold of Gorgias, and grasping his cloak

HOLE   1
4 Ma 14 :16   and in holes and tops of trees

HOLINESS   10 = 0.007 %
Wis   2 :22   nor hope for the wages of holiness
    5 :19   he will take holiness as an invincible shield
    6 :10   who observe holy things in holiness
    9 :3   and rule the world in holiness and righteousness
   14 :30   through contempt for holiness
Sir 45 :12   inscribed like a signet with Holiness
2 Ma   3 :12   who had trusted in the holiness of the place
   14 :36   so now, O holy One, Lord of all holiness
4 Ma   7 :9   and you did not abandon the holiness which you praised
   11 :20   O contest befitting holiness, in which so many of us brothers

HOLLOW, subst.   2
Wis 17 :19   or an echo thrown back from a hollow of the mountains
2 Ma   1 :19   and secretly hid it in the hollow of a dry cistern

HOLLOW, adj.   1
4 Ma   8 :24   nor take hollow pride in being put to the rack

HOLOFERNES   46 = 0.030 %
Jud   2 :4   Nebuchadnezzar king of the Assyrians called Holofernes
    2 :14   So Holofernes left the presence of his master
    2 :22   From there Holofernes took his whole army
    3 :5   The men came to Holofernes and told him all this
    4 :1   that Holofernes, the general of Nebuchadnezzar
    5 :1   When Holofernes, the general of the Assyrian army
    5 :22   Holofernes'officers and all the men from the seacoast
    5 :24   Therefore let us go up, Lord Holofernes
    6 :1   Holofernes, the commander of the Assyrian army
    6 :10   Then Holofernes ordered his slaves
    6 :17   at the council of Holofernes
    6 :17   and all that Holofernes had said so boastfully
    7 :1   The next day Holofernes ordered his whole army
    7 :6   On the 2nd day Holofernes led out all his cavalry
    7 :16   These words pleased Holofernes and all his servants
    7 :26   to the army of Holofernes and to all his forces
   10 :13   I am on my way to the presence of Holofernes
   10 :17   and they brought them to the tent of Holofernes
   10 :18   as she waited outside the tent of Holofernes
   10 :20   Then Holofernes'companions and all his servants came out
   10 :21   Holofernes was resting on his bed
   10 :23   And when Judith came into the presence of Holofernes and his servants
   11 :1   Then Holofernes said to her
   11 :20   Her words pleased Holofernes and all his servants
   11 :22   And Holofernes said to her
   12 :3   Holofernes said to her, If your supply runs out
   12 :5   Then the servants of Holofernes brought her into the tent
   12 :6   and sent to Holofernes and said, Let my lord now command
   12 :7   So Holofernes commanded his guards not to hinder her
   12 :10   On the 4th day Holofernes held a banquet for his slaves only
   12 :13   So Bagoas went out from the presence of Holofernes
   12 :15   and her maid went and spread on the ground for her before Holofernes
   12 :16   and Holofernes'heart was ravished with her
   12 :17   So Holofernes said to her, Drink now, and be merry with us !
   12 :20   And Holofernes was greatly pleased with her
   13 :2   with Holofernes stretched on his bed
   13 :6   above Holofernes'head
   13 :9   and gave Holofernes' head to her maid
   13 :15   and said, See, here is the head of Holofernes
   14 :3   and they will rush into the tent of Holofernes
   14 :6   And when he came and saw the head of Holofernes
   14 :11   they hung the head of Holofernes on the wall
   14 :13   So they came to Holofernes' tent and said to the steward

14 : 18   For look, here is Holofernes lying on the ground
15 : 11   They gave Judith the tent of Holofernes
16 : 19   Judith also dedicated to God all the vessels of Holofernes

HOLY, adj., subst.   155 = 0.101 %

Tob   3 : 11   and blessed is thy holy and honoured name for ever
      8 : 5   and blessed be thy holy and glorious name for ever
      8 : 15   Blessed art thou, O God, with every pure and holy blessing
    11 : 14   and blessed are all thy holy angels
    12 : 12   I brought a reminder of your prayer before the Holy One
    12 : 15   I am Raphael, one of the 7 holy angels
    12 : 15   and enter into the presence of the glory of the Holy One
    13 : 9   O Jerusalem, the holy city
Wis   1 : 5   For a holy and disciplined spirit will flee from deceit
    4 : 15   and he watches over his holy ones
    6 : 10   For they will be made holy
    6 : 10   who observe holy things in holiness
    7 : 27   in every generation she passes into holy souls
    9 : 8   on thy holy mountain
    9 : 8   a copy of the holy tent
    9 : 10   Send her forth from the holy heavens
    9 : 17   and sent thy holy Spirit from on high ?
   10 : 15   A holy people and blameless race wisdom delivered
   10 : 17   She gave to holy men the reward of their labours
   10 : 20   they sang hymns, O Lord, to thy holy name
   11 : 1   Wisdom prospered their works by the hand of a holy prophet
   12 : 3   Those who dwelt of old in thy holy land
   17 : 2   that they held the holy nation in their power
   18 : 1   But·for thy holy ones there was very great light
   18 : 2   and were thankful that thy holy ones
   18 : 5   When they had resolved to kill the babes of thy holy ones
   18 : 9   For in secret the holy children of good men offered sacrifices
Sir   4 : 14   Those who serve her will minister to the Holy One
    7 : 31   and the first fruits of the holy things
   17 : 10   And they will praise his holy name
   18 : 3   the holy things from the profane
   23 : 9   and do not habitually utter the name of the Holy One
   24 : 10   In the holy tabernacle I ministered before him
   24 : 18   of fear, of knowledge, and of holy hope
   26 : 17   Like the shining lamp on the holy lampstand
   33 : 12   and some of them he made holy and brought near to himself
   39 : 13   Listen to me, O you holy sons
   39 : 24   To the holy his ways are straight
   42 : 17   The Lord has not enabled his holy ones
   43 : 10   At the command of the Holy One they stand as ordered
   45 : 2   He made him equal in glory to the holy ones
   45 : 6   a holy man like him, of the tribe of Levi
   45 : 10   with a holy garment, of gold and blue and purple
   45 : 15   Moses ordained him, and anointed him with holy oil
   47 : 8   In all that he did he gave thanks to the Holy One
   47 : 10   while they praised God's holy name
   48 : 20   and the Holy One quickly heard them from heaven
   49 : 12   and raised a temple holy to the Lord
   50 : 11   and went up to the holy altar
Bar   2 : 16   O Lord, look down from thy holy habitation, and consider us
    4 : 22   and joy has come to me from the Holy One
    4 : 37   at the word of the Holy One, rejoicing in the glory of God
    5 : 5   at the word of the Holy One
P Az   5   the holy city of our fathers
    12   and for the sake of Isaac thy servant and Israel thy holy one
    30   And blessed is thy glorious, holy name
    31   Blessed art thou in the temple of thy holy glory
    65   Bless the Lord, you who are holy and humble in heart
Sus 13 : 45   God aroused the holy spirit of a young lad named Daniel
1 Ma 1 : 15   and abandoned the holy covenant
    1 : 63   or to profane the holy covenant
    2 : 7   the ruin of my people, the ruin of the holy city
    2 : 12   And behold, our holy place, our beauty
    4 : 49   They made new holy vessels, and brought the lampstand
   10 : 21   So Jonathan put on the holy garments
   10 : 31   be holy and free from tax
   11 : 37   and put up in a conspicuous place on the holy mountain
   12 : 9   since we have as encouragement the holy books
2 Ma 1 : 7   after Jason and his company revolted from the holy land and the kingdom
    1 : 12   For he drove out those who fought against the holy city
    1 : 26   and preserve thy portion and make it holy
    1 : 29   Plant thy people in thy holy place, as Moses said
    2 : 18   into his holy place
    3 : 1   While the holy city was inhabited in unbroken peace
    3 : 18   because the holy place was about to be brought into contempt
    4 : 48   for the city and the villages and the holy vessels
    5 : 15   the most holy temple in all the world
    5 : 16   He took the holy vessels with his polluted hands
    5 : 17   and that therefore he was disregarding the holy place
    5 : 19   for the sake of the holy place
    5 : 25   and waited until the holy sabbath day
    6 : 11   in view of their regard for that most holy day
    6 : 23   and moreover according to the holy Godgiven law
    6 : 28   for the revered and holy laws

    6 : 30   It is clear to the Lord in his holy knowledge
    8 : 15   and because he had called them by his holy and glorious name
    8 : 17   which the Gentiles had committed against the holy place
    8 : 23   to read aloud from the holy book
    9 : 14   stating that the holy city
    9 : 16   and the holy sanctuary, which he had formerly plundered
    9 : 16   and the holy vessels he would give back
   10 : 7   who had given success to the purifying of his own holy place
   12 : 45   it was a holy and pious thought
   13 : 8   against the altar whose fire and ashes were holy
   13 : 10   and their country and the holy temple
   13 : 23   and showed generosity to the holy place
   14 : 3   to be safe or to have access again to the holy altar
   14 : 31   he went to the great and holy temple
   14 : 36   so now, O holy One, Lord of all holiness
   15 : 14   and prays much for the people and the holy city
   15 : 16   Take this holy sword, a gift from God
   15 : 24   who come against thy holy people be struck down
   15 : 32   against the holy house of the Almighty
1 Es   1 : 3   and put the holy ark of the Lord
    1 : 41   Nebuchadnezzar also took some of the holy vessels of the Lord
    1 : 45   with the holy vessels of the Lord
    1 : 53   These slew their young men with the sword around their holy temple
    1 : 54   And all the holy vessels of the Lord, great and small
    2 : 10   Cyrus the king also brought out the holy vessels of the Lord
    5 : 40   not to share in the holy things
    6 : 18   And the holy vessels of gold and of silver
    6 : 26   and that the holy vessels of the house of the Lord
    7 : 2   supervised the holy work with very great care
    7 : 3   And the holy work prospered
    7 : 5   the holy house was finished
    8 : 17   and deliver the holy vessels of the Lord
    8 : 55   and the holy vessels of the house of our Lord
    8 : 58   And I said to them, You are holy to the Lord
    8 : 58   and the vessels are holy
    8 : 70   and the holy race has been mixed with the alien peoples of the land
    8 : 71   I rent my garments and my holy mantle
    8 : 73   with my garments and my holy mantle rent
    8 : 78   to leave to us a root and a name in thy holy place
    9 : 50   This day is holy to the Lord
    9 : 52   for the day is holy to the Lord
    9 : 53   This day is holy
3 Ma 1 : 9   and did what was fitting for the holy place
    1 : 10   and conceived a desire to enter the holy of holies
    1 : 23   and created a considerable disturbance in the holy place
    2 : 2   holy among the holy ones
    2 : 6   on the audacious Pharaoh who had enslaved your holy people Israel
    2 : 13   see now, O holy King
    2 : 14   undertakes to violate the holy place on earth
    2 : 21   holy among the holy ones
    5 : 13   praised their holy God
    6 : 1   to cease calling upon the holy God
    6 : 5   and was lifted up against your holy city
    6 : 18   revealed his holy face and opened the heavenly gates
    6 : 29   praised their holy God and Saviour
    7 : 10   against the holy God and the law of God
    7 : 20   Then, after inscribing them as holy on a pillar
2 Es   2 : 41   who have been called from the beginning, may be made holy
   10 : 22   our holy things have been polluted
   13 : 48   who are found within my holy borders, shall be saved
   14 : 22   send the Holy Spirit into me
4 Ma 4 : 9   were imploring God in the temple to shield the holy place
    4 : 12   he would praise the blessedness of the holy place before all people
    6 : 30   the holy man died nobly in his tortures
    7 : 4   has ever held out as did that most holy man
   13 : 8   For they constituted a holy chorus of religion and
   14 : 6   so those holy youths
   14 : 7   O most holy 7, brothers in harmony !

HOLY-MINDED   1
4 Ma 17 : 4   Take courage, therefore, O holy-minded mother

HOME, subst., adv.   28 = 0.018 %
Tob   1 : 19   I left home in fear
    2 : 1   When I arrived home
Jud   7 : 32   The women and children he sent home
    8 : 4   Judith had lived at home as a widow
   16 : 21   After this every one returned home to his own inheritance
Sir   4 : 30   Do not be like a lion in your home
   11 : 29   Do not bring every man into your home
   11 : 34   Receive a stranger into your home
   26 : 16   so is the beauty of a good wife in her well-ordered home
   32 : 11   go home quickly and do not linger
   36 : 26   So who will trust a man that has no home
   39 : 3   and be at home with the obscurities of parables
Sus 13 : 13   They said to each other, Let us go home, for it is mealtime

	13:52	You old relic of wicked days, your sins have now come home
1 Ma	3:56	that each should return to his home, according to the law
	12:45	Dismiss them now to their homes
	12:45	and will turn round and go home
2 Ma	9:29	And Philip, one of his courtiers, took his body home
	11:2	He intended to make the city a home for Greeks
	11:29	Menelaus has informed us that you wish to return home
	11:30	Therefore those who go home by the 30th day of Xanthicus
1 Es	5:47	and the sons of Israel were each in his own home
3 Ma	4:18	some still residing in their homes, and some at the place
	5:21	and each departed to his own home
	6:25	Who is it that has taken each man from his home
	6:27	Send them back to their homes in peace
	6:37	asking for dismissal to their homes
	7:8	to return to his own home

HOMELAND   2

4 Ma	17:21	the tyrant was punished, and the homeland purified
	18:4	and by reviving observance of the law in the homeland

HONEY   6 = 0.004 %

Sir	24:20	For the remembrance of me is sweeter than honey
	39:26	and iron and salt and wheat flour and milk and honey
	46:8	to bring them into their inheritance, into a land flowing with milk and honey
	49:1	it is sweet as honey to every mouth
Bar	1:20	to give us a land flowing with milk and honey
2 Es	2:19	and the same number of springs flowing with milk and honey

HONEYCOMB   2

Sir	24:20	and my inheritance sweeter than the honeycomb
4 Ma	14:19	since even bees at the time of making honeycombs

HONOUR, HONOR, subst.   60 = 0.039 %

Tob	14:13	He grew old with honour
Jud	13:20	May God grant this to be a perpetual honour to you
Ad E	11:11	and the lowly were exalted and consumed those held in honour
	12:6	was in great honour with the king
Wis	3:17	and finally their old age will be without honour
	5:4	and that his end was without honour
	8:10	and honour in the presence of the elders, though I am young
	10:14	and she gave him everlasting honour
Sir	7:4	nor the seat of honour from the king
	9:11	Do not envy the honours of a sinner
	10:5	and he confers his honour upon the person of the scribe
	10:19	What race is worthy of honour ? The human race
	10:19	What race is worthy of honour ?
	10:19	What race is unworthy of honour ? The human race
	10:19	What race is unworthy of honour ?
	10:20	Among brothers their leader is worthy of honour
	10:20	are worthy of honour in his eyes
	10:28	and ascribe to yourself honour according to your worth
	12:12	lest he try to take your seat of honour
	23:28	It is a great honour to follow God
	33:22	bring no stain upon your honour
	38:1	Honour the physician with the honour due him
	38:16	Lay out his body with the honour due him
	47:20	You put a stain upon your honour, and defiled your posterity
1 Ma	1:39	her sabbaths into a reproach, her honour into contempt
	2:8	Her temple has become like a man without honour
	2:51	and receive great honour and an everlasting name
	2:64	for by it you will gain honour
	3:14	and win honour in the kingdom
	9:10	and leave no cause to question our honour
	10:24	and promise them honour and gifts
	10:64	And when his accusers saw the honour that was paid him
	11:27	and in as many other honours as he had formerly had
	11:42	but I will confer great honour on you and your nation
	11:60	and paid him honour
	12:8	Onias welcomed the envoy with honour
	12:43	So he received him with honour
	14:4	as was the honour shown him, all his days
	14:5	To crown all his honours he took Joppa for a harbour
	14:21	have told us about your glory and honour
	14:23	It has pleased our people to receive these men with honour
	14:39	and paid him high honours
	14:40	the envoys of Simon with honour
	15:9	we will bestow great honour upon you and your nation and the temple
2 Ma	4:15	disdaining the honours prized by their fathers
	5:16	to enhance the glory and honour of the place
	6:7	in honour of Dionysus, wearing wreaths of ivy
	6:19	But he, welcoming death with honour
	14:21	seats of honour were set in place
1 Es	3:5	and great honours of victory
	8:4	and the king showed him honour
	9:45	for he had the place of honour in the presence of all
3 Ma	1:12	Even if those men are deprived of this honour
	4:16	organizing feasts in honour of all his idols
	7:21	being held in honour and awe

4 Ma	1:10	for the honour in which they are held
	1:26	thirst for honour, rivalry, and malice
	11:6	But these deeds deserve honours, not tortures
	17:5	stand in honour before God
	17:20	are honoured, not only with this honour

HONOUR, HONOR, verb   49 = 0.032 %

Tob	4:3	honour her all the days of your life
	10:12	Honour your father-in-law and your mother-in-law
Jud	12:13	and be honoured in his presence
	16:21	and was honoured in her time throughout the whole country
Ad E	14:17	and I have not honoured the king's feast
	16:2	The more often they are honoured
Wis	4:8	For old age is not honoured for length of time
	6:21	honour wisdom, that you may reign for ever
	14:15	and he now honoured as a god
	14:17	When men could not honour monarchs in their presence
	14:17	and made a visible image of the king whom they honoured
	14:20	the one whom shortly before they had honoured as a man
Sir	2:3	that you may be honoured at the end of your life
	3:2	For the Lord honoured the father above the children
	3:3	Whoever honours his father atones for sins
	3:5	Whoever honours his father
	3:8	Honour your father by word and deed
	3:11	For a man's glory comes from honouring his father
	7:27	With all your heart honour your father
	7:29	With all your soul fear the Lord, and honour his priests
	7:31	Fear the Lord and honour the priest
	10:23	nor is it proper to honour a sinful man
	10:24	The nobleman, and the judge, and the ruler will be honoured
	10:29	And who will honour the man that dishonours his own life ?
	10:30	A poor man is honoured for his knowledge
	10:30	while a rich man is honoured for his wealth
	10:31	A man honoured in poverty, how much more in wealth !
	11:4	nor exalt yourself in the day that you are honoured
	26:26	A wife honouring her husband will seem wise to all
	38:1	Honour the physician with the honour due him
	44:7	all these were honoured in their generations
	46:12	and may the name of those who have been honoured
	49:16	Shem and Seth were honoured among men
1 Ma	2:18	and you and your sons will be honoured
	5:63	The man Judas and his brothers were greatly honoured
	10:3	in peaceable words to honour him
	10:65	Thus the king honoured him
	10:88	he honoured Jonathan still more
2 Ma	3:2	it came about that the kings themselves honoured the place
	3:12	which is honoured throughout the whole world
	13:23	honoured the sanctuary
	15:2	which he who sees all things has honoured
1 Es	8:26	and who honoured me in the sight of the king
	8:67	and these officials honoured the people
3 Ma	3:16	and went up to honour the temple of those wicked people
	3:17	to enter their inner temple and honour it
2 Es	7:60	and through them my name has now been honoured
4 Ma	5:12	by honouring my humane advice ?
	17:20	are honoured, not only with this honour

HONOURABLE, HONORABLE   3 = 0.002 %

Sir	25:5	and understanding and counsel in honourable men !
2 Ma	7:20	and worthy of honourable memory
4 Ma	5:36	the honourable mouth of my old age

HONOURABLY, HONORABLY   2

Ad E	13:4	so that the unifying of the kingdom which we honourably intend
2 Ma	12:43	In doing this he acted very well and honourably

HONOURED, HONORED   11 = 0.007 %

Tob	3:11	and blessed is thy holy and honoured name for ever
Sir	24:12	So I took root in an honoured people
	29:27	Give place, stranger, to an honoured person
Sus	13:4	and the Jews used to come to him because he was the most honoured of them all
Bel	14:2	and was the most honoured of his friends
1 Ma	1:6	So he summoned his most honoured officers
	2:17	You are a leader, honoured and great in this city
	7:26	Then the king sent Nicanor, one of his honoured princes
3 Ma	2:9	for the glory of your great and honoured name
	6:13	in fear of your invincible might, O honoured One
4 Ma	5:35	nor will I reject you, honoured priesthood and knowledge of the law

HOOF   1

2 Ma	3:25	and struck at him with its front hoofs

HOOK   2

4 Ma	8:13	rack and hooks and catapults and cauldrons
	9:26	and after fitting themselves with iron gauntlets having sharp hooks

HOPE, subst.   35 = 0.023 %

Tob	10:7	for my father and mother have given up hope
Jud	9:11	saviour of those without hope
	13:19	Your hope will never depart from the hearts of men
Wis	3:4	their hope is full of immortality
	3:11	Their hope is vain, their labours are unprofitable
	3:18	If they die young, they will have no hope
	5:14	Because the hope of the ungodly man
	12:19	and thou hast filled thy sons with good hope
	13:10	But miserable, with their hopes set on dead things
	14:6	the hope of the world took refuge on a raft
	15:6	Lovers of evil things and fit for such objects of hope
	15:10	His heart is ashes, his hope is cheaper than dirt
	16:29	for the hope of an ungrateful man
Sir	13:6	he will smile at you and give you hope
	14:2	and who has not given up his hope
	24:18	of fear, of knowledge, and of holy hope
	27:21	but whoever has betrayed secrets is without hope
	34:1	A man of no understanding has vain and false hopes
	34:7	and those who put their hope in them have failed
	34:13	for their hope is in him who saves them
	34:14	nor play the coward, for he is his hope
	49:10	and delivered them with confident hope
Bar	4:22	For I have put my hope in the Everlasting to save you
2 Ma	2:18	For we have hope in God that he will soon have mercy upon us
	3:29	and deprived of any hope of recovery
	5:9	in hope of finding protection because of their kinship
	7:14	and to cherish the hope that God gives
	7:20	because of her hope in the Lord
	7:34	do not be elated in vain and puffed up by uncertain hopes
	9:18	he gave up all hope for himself
	9:20	I am glad. As my hope is in heaven
	9:22	for I have good hope of recovering from my illness
1 Es	8:92	but even now there is hope for Israel
2 Es	7:120	that an everlasting hope has been promised us
4 Ma	17:4	maintaining firm an enduring hope in God

HOPE, verb   10 = 0.007 %

Jud	6:9	If you really hope in your heart that they will not be taken
	8:20	and therefore we hope that he will not disdain us
Wis	2:22	nor hope for the wages of holiness
Sir	2:6	make your ways straight, and hope in him
	2:9	you who fear the Lord, hope for good things
Sus	13:60	who saves those who hope in him
2 Ma	7:11	and from him I hope to get them back again
2 Es	5:12	And at that time men shall hope but not obtain
	7:18	while hoping for easier ones
	11:46	and may hope for the judgment and mercy of him who made it

HOPEFUL   1

3 Ma	2:33	They remained resolutely hopeful of obtaining help

HOPELESSLY   1

Sir	12:11	and you will know that it was not hopelessly tarnished

HORDE   1

2 Ma	2:21	and pursued the barbarian hordes

HOREB   2

Sir	48:7	and judgments of vengeance at Horeb
2 Es	2:33	I, Ezra, received a command from the Lord on Mount Horeb

HORN   1

Jud	9:8	and to cast down the horn of thy altar with the sword

HORROR-STRICKEN   1

2 Es	15:37	and those who see that wrath shall be horror-stricken

HORSE   11 = 0.007 %

Jud	9:7	they are exalted, with their horses and riders
Wis	19:9	For they ranged like horses, and leaped like lambs
Sir	30:8	A horse that is untamed turns out to be stubborn
	48:9	in a chariot with horses of fire
1 Ma	10:81	and the enemy's horses grew tired
2 Ma	3:25	a magnificently caparisoned horse
	10:29	5 resplendent men on horses with golden bridles
1 Es	2:7	with gifts, and with horses and cattle
	2:9	with silver and gold, with horses and cattle
	5:43	and 7,036 horses, 245 mules, and 5,525 asses
2 Es	15:35	as high as a horse's belly

HORSEBACK   3 = 0.002 %

Jud	2:15	120,000 of them, together with 12,000 archers on horseback
2 Ma	12:35	who was on horseback and was a strong man
4 Ma	4:10	angels on horseback with lightning flashing from their weapons appeared from heaven

HORSEMAN   18 = 0.012 %

Jud	2:19	with their chariots and horsemen
1 Ma	6:30	20,000 horsemen, and 32 elephants accustomed to war

	6:35	and 500 picked horsemen were assigned to each beast
	6:38	The rest of the horsemen were stationed on either side
	15:41	He built up Kedron and stationed there horsemen and troops
	16:4	So John chose out of the country 20,000 warriors and horsemen
	16:5	and behold, a large force of infantry and horsemen
	16:7	and placed the horsemen in the midst of the infantry
2 Ma	5:2	there appeared goldenclad horsemen charging through the air
	5:3	troops of horsemen drawn up
	10:31	20,500 were slaughtered, besides 600 horsemen
	11:8	a horseman appeared at their head
	11:11	and slew 11,000 of them and 1,600 horsemen
	12:10	not less than 5,000 Arabs with 500 horsemen attacked them
	12:35	when one of the Thracian horsemen bore down upon him
1 Es	2:30	with horsemen and a multitude in battle array
	5:2	And Darius sent with them a 1,000 horsemen
	8:51	for foot soldiers and horsemen and an escort

HOSEA   1

2 Es	1:39	and Jacob and Hosea and Amos and Micah

HOSHEA   1

2 Es	13:40	in the days of King Hoshea

HOST, army   11 = 0.007 %

Sir	17:32	He marshals the host of the height of heaven
	24:2	and in the presence of his host she will glory :
	43:8	an instrument of the hosts on high
1 Ma	3:3	protecting the host by his sword
	14:7	He gathered a host of captives
	15:3	and have recruited a host of mercenary troops
2 Ma	15:21	Maccabeus, perceiving the hosts that were before him
1 Es	9:46	the God of hosts, the Almighty
P Ma	15	For all the host of heaven sings thy praise
2 Es	6:3	and before the innumerable hosts of angels were gathered together
	8:21	before whom the hosts of angels stand trembling

HOST, entertainer   1

Sir	29:25	you will play the host and provide drink

HOSTAGE   7 = 0.005 %

1 Ma	1:10	he had been a hostage in Rome
	8:7	should pay a heavy tribute and give hostages
	9:53	as hostages and put them under guard
	10:6	and he commanded that the hostages in the citadel
	10:9	But the men in the citadel released the hostages to Jonathan
	11:62	and took the sons of their rulers as hostages
	13:16	and 2 of his sons as hostages

HOSTILE   12 = C.008 %

Jud	5:11	So the king of Egypt became hostile to them
Ad E	13:4	there is scattered a certain hostile people
	13:7	so that those who have long been and are now hostile
Wis	19:15	for their hostile reception of the aliens
1 Ma	6:24	and became hostile to us
2 Ma	4:21	Antiochus learned that Philometor had become hostile to his government
	14:11	the rest of the king's friends, who were hostile to Judas
1 Es	5:50	for all the peoples of the land were hostile to them
3 Ma	3:1	but was still more bitterly hostile
	3:2	a hostile rumour was circulated against the Jewish nation
	3:7	but were hostile and greatly opposed to his government
	5:3	who were especially hostile toward the Jews

HOSTILITY   1

1 Ma	13:17	lest he arouse great hostility among the people

HOT   6 = 0.004 %

Sir	34:16	a shelter from the hot wind and a shade from noonday sun
Sus	13:15	and wished to bathe in the garden, for it was very hot
2 Ma	4:25	but having the hot temper of a cruel tyrant
4 Ma	10:14	You do not have a fire hot enough to make me play the coward
	15:22	as her sons were tortured on the wheel and with the hot irons !
	16:3	nor was the raging fiery furnace of Mishael so intensely hot

HOTLY   1

2 Es	7:61	they are set on fire and burn hotly, and are extinguished

HOUR   17 = 0.011 %

Jud	13:4	look in this hour upon the work of my hands
Ad E	10:11	And these 2 lots came to the hour and moment and day
Sir	11:27	The misery of an hour makes one forget luxury
	18:20	and in the hour of visitation you will find forgiveness
	33:23	in the hour of the death, distribute your inheritance
	39:33	and he will supply every need in its hour
2 Ma	8:25	they were obliged to return because the hour was late
3 Ma	2:19	and reveal your mercy at this hour
	5:13	Then the Jews, since they had escaped the appointed hour
	5:14	But now, since it was nearly the middle of the 10th hour
	5:15	that the hour of the banquet was already slipping by

2 Es	5:34	for every hour I suffer agonies of heart
	6:24	so that for 3 hours they shall not flow
	7:89	and withstood danger every hour
	9:44	And every hour and every day during those 30 years
	14:26	tomorrow at this hour you shall begin to write
	16:38	has great pains about her womb for 2 or 3 hours beforehand

HOUSE*   152 = 0.099 %

Tob	1:4	deserted the house of Jerusalem
	1:5	and so did the house of Naphtali my forefather
	3:17	At that very moment Tobit returned and entered his house
	7:1	and arrived at the house of Raguel
	7:1	and she brought them into the house
	8:11	Then Raguel went into his house
	11:3	Let us run ahead of your wife and prepare the house
	14:4	The house of God in it will be burned down
	14:5	and they will rebuild the house of God
	14:5	And the house of God will be rebuilt there
Jud	4:15	to look with favour upon the whole house of Israel
	6:17	against the house of Israel
	6:21	And Uzziah took him from the assembly to his own house
	8:5	She set up a tent for herself on the roof of her house
	8:6	and the feasts and days of rejoicing of the house of Israel
	9:1	in the house of God in Jerusalem
	9:13	and against the house possessed by thy children
	11:7	under Nebuchadnezzar and all his house
	11:23	and you shall live in the house of King Nebuchadnezzar
	12:13	who serve in the house of Nebuchadnezzar
	13:14	from the house of Israel
	14:5	who despised the house of Israel
	14:6	So they summoned Achior from the house of Uzziah
	14:10	and joined the house of Israel, remaining so to this day
	14:18	upon the house of King Nebuchadnezzar !
	16:23	and grew old in her husband's house
	16:24	and the house of Israel mourned for her 7 days
Ad E	14:9	and to quench thy altar and the glory of thy house
Wis	8:16	When I enter my house, I shall find rest with her
Sir	1:17	she fills their whole house with desirable goods
	3:9	strengthens the houses of the children
	14:24	he who encamps near her house
	21:4	thus the house of the proud will be laid waste
	21:8	A man who builds his house with other people's money
	21:18	Like a house that has vanished, so is wisdom to a fool
	21:22	The foot of a fool rushes into a house
	21:23	A boor peers into the house from the door
	23:11	and the scourge will not leave his house
	23:11	for his house will be filled with calamities
	27:3	his house will be quickly overthrown
	28:14	and overturned the houses of great men
	29:21	and a house to cover one's nakedness
	29:22	than sumptuous food in another man's house
	29:24	It is a miserable life to go from house to house
	29:27	I need my house
	42:10	or become pregnant in her father's house
	47:13	that he might build a house for his name
	48:15	but with rulers from the house of David
	49:12	in their days they built the house
	49:13	and set up the gates and bars and rebuilt our ruined houses
	50:1	who in his life repaired the house
Bar	1:8	Baruch took the vessels of the house of the Lord
	1:14	to make your confession in the house of the Lord
	2:26	And the house which is called by thy name
	2:26	because of the wickedness of the house of Israel
	2:26	and the house of Judah
	3:24	O Israel, how great is the house of God !
L Jr	6:59	better even the door of a house that protects its contents
Sus	13:4	and had a spacious garden adjoining his house
	13:6	These men were frequently at Joakim's house
	13:28	The next day, when the people gathered at the house of her husband Joakim
1 Ma	1:28	and all the house of Jacob was clothed with shame
	1:31	and tore down its houses and its surrounding walls
	1:55	and burned incense at the doors of the houses and in the streets
	3:56	And he said to those who were building houses
	7:35	then if I return safely I will burn up this house
	7:37	Thou didst choose this house to be called by thy name
	7:37	and to be for thy people a house of prayer and supplication
	9:55	or give commands concerning his house
	13:3	I and my brothers and the house of my father have done
	13:47	and cleansed the houses in which the idols were
	13:48	and built in it a house for himself
	14:26	For he and his brothers and the house of his father have stood firm
	16:2	and said to them : I and my brothers and the house of my father
2 Ma	2:29	For as the master builder of a new house
	3:18	People also hurried out of their houses in crowds
	5:12	and to slay those who went into the houses
	8:33	who had fled into one little house
	14:36	keep undefiled for ever this house
	15:32	against the holy house of the Almighty

1 Es	1:3	in the house which Solomon the king, the son of David, had built
	1:5	according to the grouping of the fathers' houses of you Levites
	1:11	and the grouping of the fathers' houses, before the people
	1:55	And they burned the house of the Lord
	2:4	and he has commanded me to build him a house at Jerusalem
	2:5	and build the house of the Lord of Israel
	2:8	to build the house in Jerusalem for the Lord
	3:1	and all that were born in his house
	5:1	After this the heads of fathers' houses were chosen to go up
	5:4	according to their fathers' houses in the tribes
	5:5	son of Shealtiel, of the house of David
	5:37	though they could not prove by their fathers' houses or lineage
	5:44	vowed that they would erect the house on its site
	5:58	as one man pressing forward the work on the house of God
	5:62	praising the Lord for the erection of the house of the Lord
	5:63	Some of the Levitical priests and heads of fathers' houses
	5:63	old men who had seen the former house
	5:68	and the heads of the fathers' houses and said to them
	5:70	and the heads of the fathers' houses in Israel said to them
	5:70	in building the house for the Lord our God
	6:2	and began to build the house of the Lord which is in Jerusalem
	6:4	By whose order are you building this house
	6:9	building in the city of Jerusalem a great new house for the Lord
	6:11	At whose command are you building this house
	6:14	And the house was built many years ago
	6:16	and they pulled down the house, and burned it
	6:17	King Cyrus wrote that this house should be rebuilt
	6:18	which Nebuchadnezzar had taken out of the house in Jerusalem
	6:20	laid the foundations of the house of the Lord
	6:22	of the house of the Lord in Jerusalem
	6:24	of the house of the Lord in Jerusalem
	6:26	and that the holy vessels of the house of the Lord
	6:26	which Nebuchadnezzar took out of the house in Jerusalem
	6:26	should be restored to the house in Jerusalem
	6:27	to build this house of the Lord on its site
	6:28	until the house of the Lord is finished
	6:32	a beam should be taken out of his house
	6:33	to hinder or damage that house of the Lord in Jerusalem
	7:5	the holy house was finished
	8:25	to glorify his house which is in Jerusalem
	8:28	according to their fathers'houses and their groups
	8:46	in the house of our Lord
	8:55	and the holy vessels of the house of our Lord
	8:59	and to the heads of the fathers' houses of Israel
	8:59	in Jerusalem, in the chambers of the house of our Lord
	8:62	and delivered in the house of our Lord
	8:79	in the house of the Lord our God
	9:16	the leading men of their fathers' houses
Ps 151	1	I was small among my brothers, and youngest in my father's house
3 Ma	1:20	some in houses and some in the streets
	2:10	And because you love the house of Israel
	2:18	We have trampled down the house of the sanctuary
	2:18	as offensive houses are trampled down
	7:18	to each as far as his own house
2 Es	1:7	out of the house of bondage ?
	1:33	Thus says the Lord Almighty : Your house is desolate
	1:35	I will give your houses to a people that will come
	9:24	but go into a field of flowers where no house has been built
	10:51	where no house had been built
	12:46	and do not be sorrowful, O house of Jacob
	12:49	Now go, every one of you to his house
	14:13	Now therefore, set your house in order
	15:18	the houses shall be destroyed
	15:19	but shall make an assault upon their houses with the sword
	15:49	to lay waste your houses
	16:31	by those who search their houses with the sword
	16:42	and let him that builds a house be like one
	16:46	and plunder their goods, and overthrow their houses
	16:47	their houses and possessions, and their persons
	16:72	and drive them out of their houses
4 Ma	18:7	I was a pure virgin and did not go outside my father's house

HOUSEHOLD   6 = 0.004 %

Ad E	16:18	has been hanged at the gate of Susa, with all his household
L Jr	6:59	or a household utensil that serves its owner's need
Sus	13:26	When the household servants heard the shouting in the garden
Bel	14:29	or else we will kill you and your household
2 Es	3:11	Noah with his household
4 Ma	2:19	censure the households of Simeon and Levi

HOUSETOP   1

4 Ma	14:15	protect their young by building on the housetops

HOVER   1

2 Es	6:39	And then the Spirit was hovering

HOW, adv., conj.   130 = 0.085 %

Tob 2:6   how he said, Your feasts shall be turned into mourning
   5:2   but how can I obtain the money when I do not know the man ?
   7:2   How much the young man resembles my cousin Tobit !
  10:8   and they will inform him how things are with you
  11:2   Are you not aware, brother, of how you left your father ?
 13:14   How blessed are those who love you !
 14:10   how he brought him from light into darkness
 14:11   and how righteousness delivers
Jud 4:1   and how he had plundered and destroyed all their temples
   5:3   How large is their army
   8:9   and how he promised them under oath
  8:14   how do you expect to search out God
  8:26   Remember what he did with Abraham, and how he tested Isaac
 10:7   When they saw her, and noted how her face was altered
Ad E 13:3   When I asked my counsellors how this might be accomplished
Wis 2:19   that we may find out how gentle he is
  6:22   I will tell you what wisdom is and how she came to be
  8:18   I went about seeking how to get her for myself
  11:8   how thou didst punish their enemies
  11:9   they learned how the ungodly
 11:25   How would anything have endured if thou hadst not willed it ?
 11:25   Or how would anything not called forth by thee
 13:3   Let them know how much better than these is their Lord
 13:4   how much more powerful is he who formed them
 13:9   how did they fail to find sooner the Lord of these things ?
 16:4   how their enemies were being tormented
 19:10   how instead of producing animals
Sir 8:8   and learn how to serve great men
  8:9   and learn how to give an answer in time of need
 10:9   How can he who is dust and ashes be proud ?
 10:31   A man honoured in poverty, how much more in wealth !
 10:31   And a man dishonoured in wealth, how much more in poverty !
 11:19   he does not know how much time will pass
 13:2   How can the clay pot associate with the iron kettle ?
 17:29   How great is the mercy of the Lord
 20:2   How much better it is to reprove than to stay angry !
 20:3   How good it is to show repentance when you are reproved
 20:17   How many will ridicule him, and how often !
 25:3   how then can you find anything in your old age ?
 25:5   How attractive is wisdom in the aged
 25:10   How great is he who has gained wisdom !
 31:19   How ample a little is for a well-disciplined man !
 38:25   How can he become wise who handles the plough
 41:1   O death, how bitter is the reminder of you
 41:2   O death, how welcome is your sentence
 41:4   and how can you reject the good pleasure of the Most High ?
 42:22   How greatly to be desired are all his works
 42:22   and how sparkling they are to see !
 46:2   How glorious he was when he lifted his hands
 47:14   How wise you became in your youth !
 48:4   How glorious you were, O Elijah, in your wondrous deeds !
 49:11   How shall we magnify Zerubbabel ?
 50:4   He considered how to save his people from ruin
 50:5   How glorious he was when the people gathered round him
Bar 3:24   O Israel, how great is the house of God !
  3:24   And how vast the territory that he possesses !
  4:17   But I, how can I help you ?
L Jr 6:46   how then can the things that are made by them be gods ?
  6:49   How then can one fail to see that these are not gods
Sus 13:57   This is how you both have been dealing
Bel 14:6   Do you not see how much he eats and drinks every day ?
1 Ma 3:17   they said to Judas, How can we, few as we are
  3:53   How will we be able to withstand them
  4:9   Remember how our fathers were saved at the Red Sea
  4:35   and how ready they were either to live or to die nobly
  6:22   How long will you fail to do justice
  8:2   how they had defeated them and forced them to pay tribute
  8:4   and how they had gained control of the whole region
  9:21   How is the mighty fallen, the saviour of Israel !
 10:46   and how he had greatly oppressed them
 14:25   How shall we thank Simon and his sons ?
2 Ma 6:28   of how to die a good death willingly and nobly
  7:17   Keep on, and see how his mighty power
  7:22   I do not know how you came into being in my womb
  9:25   Moreover, I understand how the princes along the borders
 10:6   remembering how not long before, during the feast of booths
 13:26   This is how the king's attack and withdrawal turned out
 15:37   This, then, is how matters turned out with Nicanor
1 Es 1:24   and how they grieved the Lord deeply
  3:18   Gentlemen, how is wine the strongest ?
3 Ma 5:37   How many times, you poor wretch
  5:40   O king, how long will you try us, as though we are idiots
2 Es 1:9   How long shall I endure them
  2:48   how great and many are the wonders of the Lord God
  3:30   for I have seen how thou dost endure those who sin
  3:31   and hast not shown to any one how thy way may be comprehended
  4:7   How many dwellings are in the heart of the sea
  4:7   or how many streams are at the source of the deep
  4:7   or how many streams are above the firmament
  4:11   how then can your mind comprehend the way of the Most High ?
  4:11   And how can one who is already worn out by the corrupt world understand incorruption ?
  4:30   and how much ungodliness it has produced until now
  4:31   how much fruit of ungodliness a grain of evil seed has produced
  4:32   how great a threshing floor they will fill !
  4:33   How long and when will these things be ?
  4:35   How long are we to remain here ?
  5:39   and how can I speak concerning the things
  5:45   And I said, How hast thou said to thy servant
  6:59   How long will this be so ?
  7:5   how can he come to the broad part
  7:9   how will the heir receive his inheritance
  7:53   I said, lord, how could that be ?
  7:73   or how will they answer in the last times ?
  7:74   For how long the time is that the Most High
  7:85   they shall see how the habitations of the others
  7:86   they shall see how some of them will pass over into torments
  7:97   when it is shown to them how their face is to shine like the sun
  7:97   and how they are to be made like the light of the stars
 7:106   How then do we find that first Abraham prayed
  9:13   as to how the ungodly will be punished
  9:13   but inquire how the righteous will be saved
 10:49   how she mourned for her son
 11:6   And I saw how all things under heaven were subjected to him
 11:30   And I saw how it allied the 2 heads with itself
 11:37   and I heard how he uttered a man's voice to the eagle
 12:41   How have we offended you
 12:44   how much better it would have been for us
 13:10   but I saw only how
 16:66   Or how will you hide your sins before God and his angels ?
4 Ma 1:14   how many kinds of emotions there are
  1:33   Otherwise how is it that
  2:7   Otherwise how could it be
  2:24   How is it then, one might say
  9:29   How sweet is any kind of death for the religion of our fathers !
 13:5   How then can one fail to confess
 14:13   Observe how complex is a mother's love for her children
 15:22   How great and how many torments the mother then suffered
 16:6   O how wretched am I and many times unhappy !

HOWEVER, adv., conj.   12 = 0.008 %

Tob 2:10   Ahikar, however, took care of me until he went to Elymais
Jud 6:13   However, they got under the shelter of the hill
Wis 15:12   for he says one must get money however one can, even by base means
2 Ma 2:27   However, to secure the gratitude of many
  4:19   Those who carried the money, however
  5:7   He did not gain control of the government, however
3 Ma 2:31   Now some, however, with an obvious abhorrence of the price
  3:3   The Jews, however, continued to maintain good will
  5:10   Hermon, however, when he had drugged the pitiless elephants
  5:36   The king, however, reconvened the party in the same manner
2 Es 9:23   do not fast during them, however
  9:37   the law, however, does not perish but remains in its glory

HOWL   1

L Jr 6:32   They howl and shout before their gods

HUGE   5 = 0.003 %

Jud 2:18   and a huge amount of gold and silver from the royal palace
Sir 43:25   all kinds of living things, and huge creatures of the sea
1 Ma 9:6   When they saw the huge number of the enemy forces
3 Ma 6:8   in the belly of a huge, sea-born monster
2 Es 10:27   and a place of huge foundations showed itself

HUMAN   19 = 0.012 %

Jud 8:14   You cannot plumb the depths of the human heart
  8:16   nor like a human being, to be won over by pleading
Wis 12:5   and their sacrificial feasting on human flesh and blood
 14:15   what was once a dead human being
 15:4   For neither has the evil intent of human art misled us
Sir 3:23   for matters too great for human understanding
 10:19   What race is worthy of honour ? The human race
 10:19   What race is unworthy of honour ? The human race
 31:16   Eat like a human being what is set before you
 36:22   and surpasses every human desire
Bel 14:32   and every day they had been given 2 human bodies and 2 sheep
3 Ma 6:26   and often have accepted willingly the worst of human dangers ?
2 Es 7:29   and all who draw human breath
  7:65   Let the human race lament
  8:6   by which every mortal who bears the likeness of a human being
4 Ma 1:16   Wisdom, next, is the knowledge of divine and human matters
  1:17   and human affairs to our advantage
  4:13   that Apollonius had been overcome by human treachery
 17:14   and the world and the human race were the spectators

HUMANE

HUMANE 2
Wis 7:23 Beneficent, humane, steadfast, sure, free from anxiety
4 Ma 5:12 by honouring my humane advice ?

HUMBLE, adj., subst. 12 = 0.008 %
Sir 3:20 he is glorified by the humble
10:15 and has planted the humble in their place
11:1 The wisdom of a humble man will lift up his head
12:5 Do good to the humble, but do not give to the ungodly
13:21 but when a humble man falls, he is even pushed away by friends
13:22 If a humble man slips, they even reproach him
20:11 from humble circumstances
29:8 Nevertheless, be patient with a man in humble circumstances
35:17 The prayer of the humble pierces the clouds
P Az 16 Yet with a contrite heart and a humble spirit may we be accepted
65 Bless the Lord, you who are holy and humble in heart
1 Ma 14:14 He strengthened all the humble of his people

HUMBLE, verb 16 = 0.010 %
Tob 4:19 and according to his will he humbles whomever he wishes
Jud 4:9 and they humbled themselves with much fasting
5:11 and humbled them and made slaves of them
Ad E 14:2 and she utterly humbled her body
Wis 17:7 The delusions of their magic art lay humbled
Sir 2:4 and in changes that humble you be patient
2:17 and will humble themselves before him
3:18 The greater you are, the more you must humble yourself
7:17 Humble yourself greatly
12:11 Even if he humbles himself and goes about cringing
18:21 Before falling ill, humble yourself
34:26 And what has he gained by humbling himself ?
40:3 to the one who is humbled in dust and ashes
1 Ma 12:15 and our enemies were humbled
2 Ma 8:35 having been humbled with the help of the Lord
2 Es 8:49 because you have humbled yourself, as is becoming for you

HUMILIATE 1
Sir 13:8 and not to be humiliated in your feasting

HUMILIATION 6 = 0.004 %
Jud 6:19 and have pity on the humiliation of our people
Sir 2:5 and acceptable men in the furnace of humiliation
1 Ma 3:51 and thy priests mourn in humiliation
3 Ma 2:12 you helped them in their humiliation
2 Es 6:19 and when the humiliation of Zion is complete
12:48 on account of the humiliation of our sanctuary

HUMILITY 3 = 0.002 %
Sir 10:28 My son, glorify yourself with humility
13:20 Humility is an abomination to a proud man
36:23 If kindness and humility mark her speech

HUNDRED, subst., s. NUMBERS 1
1 Ma 3:55 in charge of thousands and hundreds and fifties and tens

HUNGER, subst. 5 = 0.003 %
Sir 18:25 In the time of plenty think of the time of hunger
2 Es 15:19 because of hunger for bread
15:57 Your children shall die of hunger
15:58 shall perish of hunger
15:58 and they shall eat their own flesh in hunger for bread

HUNGER, verb 3 = 0.002 %
Sir 16:27 they neither hunger nor grow weary
24:21 Those who eat me will hunger for more
Bar 2:18 and the eyes that are failing, and the person that hungers

HUNGRY 6 = 0.004 %
Tob 1:17 I would give my bread to the hungry
4:16 Give of your bread to the hungry
Sir 4:2 Do not grieve the one who is hungry
1 Ma 13:49 So they were very hungry
2 Es 1:17 When you were hungry and thirsty in the wilderness
16:6 Can one drive off a hungry lion in the forest

HUNT down 1
1 Ma 2:47 They hunted down the arrogant men

HUNTER 1
Sir 14:22 Pursue wisdom like a hunter, and lie in wait on her paths

HUNTING 1
Jud 1:15 and struck him down with hunting spears

HURL 6 = 0.004 %
Wis 5:22 and hailstones full of wrath will be hurled as from a catapult
1 Ma 2:36 But they did not answer them or hurl a stone at them
2 Ma 11:11 They hurled themselves like lions against the enemy
14:46 took them with both hands and hurled them at the crowd

2 Es 1:8 Pull out the hair of your head and hurl all evils upon them
4 Ma 16:21 and Hananiah, Azariah, and Mishael were hurled into the fiery furnace

HURL down 4 = 0.003 %
Wis 17:19 or the harsh crash of rocks hurled down
18:18 and one here and another there, hurled down half dead
Sir 46:6 He hurled down war upon that nation
2 Ma 6:10 then hurled them down headlong from the wall

HURL out 1
2 Ma 10:34 blasphemed terribly and hurled out wicked words

HURLING 1
2 Ma 5:3 hurling of missiles, the flash of golden trappings

HURRY 2
2 Ma 3:18 People also hurried out of their houses in crowds
3 Ma 7:10 the Jews did not immediately hurry to make their departure

HURRY away 1
2 Ma 5:21 and hurried away to Antioch

HURRY down 2
Jud 10:15 by hurrying down to the presence of our lord
13:12 they hurried down to the city gate

HURRY out 1
3 Ma 1:17 were agitated and hurried out

HURT, subst. 3 = 0.002 %
Sir 9:1 and do not teach her an evil lesson to your own hurt
26:10 lest, when she finds liberty, she use it to her hurt
4 Ma 5:10 you continue to despise me to your own hurt

HURT, verb 3 = 0.002 %
Jud 11:1 for I have never hurt any one
11:4 No one will hurt you, but all will treat you well
P Az 27 or hurt or trouble them

HUSBAND 41 = 0.027 %
Tob 3:8 because she had been given to 7 husbands
3:8 Do you not know that you strangle your husbands ?
3:15 Already 7 husbands of mine are dead
6:13 I have heard that the girl has been given to 7 husbands
7:11 I have given my daughter to 7 husbands
Jud 8:2 Her husband Manasseh, who belonged to her tribe and family
8:7 and her husband Manasseh had left her gold and silver
10:3 which she used to wear while her husband Manasseh was living
16:22 after Manasseh her husband died
16:23 and grew old in her husband's house
16:23 and they buried her in the cave of her husband Manasseh
16:24 to all those who were next of kin to her husband Manasseh
Sir 4:10 and instead of a husband to their mother
22:4 A sensible daughter obtains her husband
22:5 An impudent daughter disgraces father and husband
23:22 So it is with a woman who leaves her husband
23:23 second, she has committed an offence against her husband
25:1 and a wife and husband who live in harmony
25:18 Her husband takes his meals among the neighbours
25:20 such is a garrulous wife for a quiet husband
25:22 when a wife supports her husband
25:23 are caused by the wife who does not make her husband happy
26:1 Happy is the husband of a good wife
26:2 A loyal wife rejoices her husband
26:13 A wife's charm delights her husband
26:24 before her husband
26:26 A wife honouring her husband will seem wise to all
26:26 Happy is the husband of a good wife
36:23 her husband is not like other men
40:23 but a wife with her husband is better than both
42:10 or having a husband, lest she prove unfaithful
Sus 13:7 Susanna would go into her husband's garden to walk
13:28 The next day, when the people gathered at the house of her husband Joakim
13:63 and so did Joakim her husband and all her kindred
3 Ma 4:8 Their husbands, in the prime of youth
2 Es 9:43 though I lived with my husband 30 years
9:45 I and my husband and all my neighbours
10:17 Therefore go into the city to your husband
16:33 women shall mourn because they have no husbands
16:34 and their husbands shall perish of famine
4 Ma 18:9 In the time of my maturity I remained with my husband

HYDASPES 1
Jud 1:6 and the Tigris and the Hydaspes

HYENA 1
Sir 13:18 What peace is there between a hyena and a dog ?

206

HYMN   15 = 0.010 %
Wis	10:20	they sang hymns, O Lord, to thy holy name
Sir	15:9	A hymn of praise is not fitting on the lips of a sinner
	15:10	For a hymn of praise should be uttered in wisdom
	39:14	Scatter the fragrance, and sing a hymn of praise
P Az	1	singing hymns to God and blessing the Lord
1 Ma	4:24	On their return they sang hymns and praises to Heaven
	4:33	and let all who know thy name praise thee with hymns
	13:47	and then entered it with hymns and praise
	13:51	and with hymns and songs
2 Ma	1:30	Then the priests sang the hymns
	10:7	they offered hymns of thanksgiving to him
	10:38	with hymns and thanksgivings they blessed the Lord
	12:37	In the language of their fathers he raised the battle cry, with hymns
1 Es	5:61	and they sang hymns, giving thanks to the Lord
4 Ma	10:21	a tongue that has been melodious with divine hymns

HYPOCRISY   1
2 Ma	13:3	and with utter hypocrisy urged Antiochus on

HYPOCRITE   2
Sir	1:29	Be not a hypocrite in men's sight\
	32:15	but the hypocrite will stumble at it

HYPOCRITICAL   1
Sir	33:2	but he who is hypocritical about it

HYRCANUS   1
2 Ma	3:11	and also some money of Hyrcanus, son of Tobias

I

I   1052 = 0.685 %

ICE   4 = 0.003 %
Wis	16:22	Snow and ice withstood fire without melting
Sir	43:20	The cold north wind blows, and ice freezes over the water
P Az	49	Bless the Lord, ice and cold
2 Es	3:19	of fire and earthquake and wind and ice

IDDO   4 = 0.003 %
1 Es	6:1	the prophets Haggai and Zechariah the son of Iddo
	8:45	and I told them to go to Iddo
	8:46	and ordered them to tell Iddo and his brethren
	9:35	Mattithiah, Zabad, Iddo, Joel, Benaiah

IDEA   3 = 0.002 %
Wis	14:12	For the idea of making idols was the beginning of fornication
Sir	32:18	A man of judgment will not overlook an idea
2 Ma	9:4	he conceived the idea of turning upon the Jews

IDIOT   1
3 Ma	5:40	O king, how long will you try us, as though we are idiots

IDLE   3 = 0.002 %
Wis	15:12	But he considered our existence an idle game
Sir	33:25	leave his hands idle, and he will seek liberty
	33:27	Put him to work, that he may not be idle

IDLENESS   2
Wis	13:13	and shapes it with skill gained in idleness
Sir	33:27	for idleness teaches much evil

IDLER   1
Sir	37:11	with an idler about any work

IDOL   26 = 0.017 %
Tob	14:6	and will bury their idols
Ad E	14:8	but they have covenanted with their idols
	14:10	to open the mouths of the nations for the praise of vain idols
Wis	14:8	But the idol made with hands is accursed
	14:11	also upon the heathen idols
	14:12	For the idea of making idols was the beginning of fornication
	14:27	For the worship of idols not to be named
	14:29	for because they trust in lifeless idols
	14:30	in devoting themselves to idols
	15:15	For they thought that all their heathen idols were gods
Sir	30:19	Of what use to an idol is an offering of fruit ?
L Jr	6:63	But these idols are not to be compared with them in appearance of power
	6:73	Better therefore is a just man who has no idols
Bel	14:3	Now the Babylonians had an idol called Bel
	14:5	He answered, Because I do not revere man-made idols
1 Ma	1:43	they sacrificed to idols and profaned the sabbath
	1:47	to build altars and sacred precincts and shrines for idols
	3:48	were consulting the images of their idols
	10:83	the temple of their idol, for safety
	13:47	and cleansed the houses in which the idols were
2 Ma	12:40	they found sacred tokens of the idols of Jamnia
1 Es	2:10	and stored in his temple of idols
Ps 151	:6	and he cursed me by his idols
3 Ma	4:16	organizing feasts in honour of all his idols
2 Es	16:68	and shall feed you what was sacrificed to idols
4 Ma	5:2	to eat pork and food sacrificed to idols

IDOLATRY   1
Sir	46:11	those whose hearts did not fall into idolatry

IDUEL   1
1 Es	8:43	I sent word to Eliezar, Iduel, Maasmas

IDUMEA   6 = 0.004 %
1 Ma	4:15	and to the plains of Idumea, and to Azotus and Jamnia
	4:29	They came into Idumea and encamped at Beth-zur
	4:61	so that the people might have a stronghold that faced Idumea
	5:3	in Idumea, at Akrabattene
	6:31	They came through Idumea and encamped against Beth-zur
2 Ma	12:32	they hastened against Gorgias, the governor of Idumea

IDUMEAN   3 = 0.002 %
2 Ma	10:15	Besides this, the Idumeans
	10:16	rushed to the strongholds of the Idumeans
1 Es	4:50	that the Idumeans should give up the villages of the Jews which they held

IF   323 = 0.210 %

IGNOBLE   1
3 Ma	4:12	to lament bitterly the ignoble misfortune of their brothers

IGNOMINIOUSLY   1
3 Ma	6:34	and their firebreathing boldness was ignominiously quenched

IGNORANCE   8 = 0.005 %
Wis	14:22	but they live in great strife due to ignorance
	17:13	prefers ignorance of what causes the torment
Sir	4:25	but be mindful of your ignorance
	28:7	remember the covenant of the Most High, and overlook ignorance
	51:19	and lamented my ignorance of her
2 Ma	11:31	for what he may have done in ignorance
4 Ma	1:5	why is it not sovereign over forgetfulness and ignorance ?
	2:24	it does not control forgetfulness and ignorance ?

IGNORANT, adj., subst.   5 = 0.003 %
Wis	13:1	For all men who were ignorant of God were foolish by nature
Sir	20:19	which is continually on the lips of the ignorant
	20:24	it is continually on the lips of the ignorant
	21:18	and the knowledge of the ignorant is unexamined talk
4 Ma	13:19	You are not ignorant of the affection of brotherhood

IGNORE   3 = 0.002 %
Sir	30:11	and do not ignore his errors
	35:14	He will not ignore the supplication of the fatherless
2 Es	7:23	and they ignored his ways !

ILIADUN   1
1 Es	5:58	and the sons of Joda son of Iliadun

ILL, adj., subst.   5 = 0.003 %
Jud	8:8	No one spoke ill of her
Sir	18:19	and before you fall ill, take care of your health
	18:21	Before falling ill, humble yourself
3 Ma	3:2	by men who conspired to do them ill
2 Es	7:104	to be ill or sleep or eat or be healed in his stead

ILL-BRED   1
Sir	8:4	Do not jest with an ill-bred person

ILL-DISPOSED   2
Ad E	13:5	and is ill-disposed to our government
3 Ma	3:24	that they are ill-disposed toward us in every way

ILLEGITIMATE   1
Wis	4:3	and none of their illegitimate seedlings

ILL-MANNERED   1
Sir	21:24	It is ill-mannered for a man to listen at a door

ILLNESS   5 = 0.003 %
Sir	10:10	A long illness baffles the physician
	31:2	and a severe illness carries off sleep
2 Ma	9:21	I suffered an annoying illness
	9:22	for I have good hope of recovering from my illness
2 Es	8:53	illness is banished from you, and death is hidden

ILL-TREAT 1
Sir 33:31 If you ill-treat him, and he leaves and runs away

ILLUMINE 2
Wis 17:5 avail to illumine that hateful night
17:20 For the whole world was illumined with brilliant light

ILLUSTRIOUS 2
Sir 11:6 and illustrious men have been handed over to others
1 Es 4:29 the daughter of the illustrious Bartacus

ILL WILL 4 = 0.003 %
2 Ma 6:29 had acted toward him with good will now changed to ill will
12:3 as though there were no ill will to the Jews
3 Ma 3:19 By maintaining their manifest ill-will toward us
7:4 because of the ill-will which these people had toward all nations

IMAGE 15 = 0.010 %
Wis 2:23 and made him in the image of his own eternity
7:26 and an image of his goodness
13:13 he forms it like the image of a man
13:16 for it is only an image and has need of help
14:15 made an image of his child
14:16 and at the command of monarchs graven images were worshipped
14:17 and made a visible image of the king whom they honoured
15:5 so that they desire the lifeless form of a dead image
15:13 when he makes from earthy matter fragile vessels and graven images
17:21 an image of the darkness that was destined to receive them
Sir 17:3 and made them in his own image
38:27 he sets his heart on painting a lifelike image
1 Ma 3:48 were consulting the images of their idols
5:68 and the graven images of their gods he burned with fire
2 Es 8:44 and is called thy own image because he is made like thee

IMAGINATION 4 = 0.003 %
Sir 37:3 O evil imagination, why were you formed to cover the land with deceit ?
2 Es 6:5 and before the imaginations of those who now sin were estranged
16:54 their imaginations and their thoughts and their hearts
16:63 Surely he knows your imaginations

IMAGINE 4 = 0.003 %
Wis 14:17 they imagined their appearance far away
2 Ma 5:6 but imagining that he was setting up trophies of victory
9:8 and imagining that he could weigh the high mountains in a balance
2 Es 16:21 that men will imagine that peace is assured for them

IMALKUE 2
1 Ma 11:39 So he went to Imalkue the Arab
11:40 He also reported to Imalkue what Demetrius had done

IMITATE 6 = 0.004 %
Wis 4:2 When it is present, men imitate it
15:9 and imitates workers in copper
2 Ma 4:16 and wished to imitate completely
2 Es 15:48 You have imitated that hateful harlot in all her deeds and devices
4 Ma 9:23 Imitate me, brothers, he said
13:9 let us imitate the 3 youths in Assyria

IMMEASURABLE 3 = 0.002 %
Bar 3:25 it is high and immeasurable
P Ma 6 yet immeasurable and unsearchable is thy promised mercy
3 Ma 2:9 the boundless and immeasurable earth

IMMEDIATELY 20 = 0.013 %
Jud 4:5 and immediately seized all the high hilltops
Sus 13:55 and will immediately cut you in 2
Bel 14:39 And the angel of God immediately returned Habakkuk to his own place
14:42 and they were devoured immediately before his eyes
2 Ma 4:34 he immediately put him out of the way
4:38 he immediately stripped off the purple robe from Andronicus
6:13 but to punish them immediately
7:4 These were heated immediately
8:11 And he immediately sent to the cities on the sea coast
10:22 and immediately captured the 2 towers
14:12 And he immediately chose Nicanor
14:16 they set out from there immediately
1 Es 1:30 And immediately his servants took him out of the line of battle
3 Ma 4:8 seeing death immediately before them
6:29 and the Jews, immediately released
7:10 the Jews did not immediately hurry to make their departure
2 Es 3:7 and immediately thou didst appoint death
6:44 For immediately fruit came forth in endless abundance

7:80 but shall immediately wander about in torments
4 Ma 10:8 They immediately brought him to the wheel

IMMENSE 2
1 Ma 3:41 they took silver and gold in immense amounts, and fetters
3 Ma 1:28 resulted in an immense uproar

IMMER 3 = 0.002 %
1 Es 5:24 The sons of Immer, 1,052
5:36 under the leadership of Cherub, Addan, and Immer
9:21 Of the sons of Immer : Hanani and Zebadiah and Maaseiah

IMMINENT 1
1 Ma 9:7 and the battle was imminent, he was crushed in spirit

IMMODERATELY 1
Sir 33:29 Do not act immoderately toward anybody

IMMORALITY 2
Tob 4:12 Beware, my son, of all immorality
Sir 41:17 Be ashamed of immorality, before your father or mother

IMMORTAL 8 = 0.005 %
Wis 1:15 For righteousness is immortal
12:1 For thy immortal spirit is in all things
Sir 17:30 since a son of man is not immortal
2 Es 2:45 and have put on the immortal
7:113 and the beginning of the immortal age to come
4 Ma 7:3 until he sailed into the haven of immortal victory
14:6 as though moved by an immortal spirit of devotion
18:23 and have received pure and immortal souls from God

IMMORTALITY 15 = 0.010 %
Wis 3:4 their hope is full of immortality
4:1 for in the memory of virtue is immortality
6:18 and giving heed to her laws is assurance of immortality
6:19 and immortality brings one near to God
8:13 Because of her I shall have immortality
8:17 that in kinship with wisdom there is immortality
15:3 and to know thy power is the root of immortality
Sir 19:19 enjoy the fruit of the tree of immortality
2 Es 7:13 and really yield the fruit of immortality
7:96 which they are to receive and enjoy in immortality
8:54 and in the end the treasure of immortality is made manifest
4 Ma 9:22 but as though transformed by fire into immortality
14:5 but all of them, as though running the course toward immortality
16:13 and giving rebirth for immortality
17:12 The prize was immortality in endless life

IMMOVABLE 1
3 Ma 6:19 binding them with immovable shackles

IMMUNITY 2
1 Ma 10:28 We will grant you many immunities and give you gifts
10:34 let them all be days of immunity and release

IMPART 2
Wis 7:13 I learned without guile and I impart without grudging
Sir 16:25 I will impart instruction by weight

IMPARTIAL 1
Wis 5:18 and wear impartial justice as a helmet

IMPARTIALLY 1
4 Ma 5:24 so that in all our dealings we act impartially

IMPASSABLE 1
Ad E 16:24 It shall be made not only impassable for men

IMPEL 1
Wis 14:18 impelled even those who did not know the king

IMPERFECTLY 1
Sir pr. we may seem to have rendered some phrases imperfectly

IMPERISHABLE 1
Wis 18:4 through whom the imperishable light of the law

IMPIETY 6 = 0.004 %
2 Ma 8:33 so these received the proper recompense for their impiety
1 Es 1:42 and his uncleanness and impiety
3 Ma 6:10 Even if our lives have become entangled in impieties in our exile
4 Ma 6:19 and ourselves become a pattern of impiety to the young
9:32 but you suffer torture by the threats that come from impiety
10:11 but you, because of your impiety and bloodthirstiness

IMPIOUS
7 = 0.005 %
2 Ma 3:11   To such an extent the impious Simon had misrepresented the facts
    6:13   In fact, not to let the impious alone for long
3 Ma 2:2   who are suffering grievously from an impious and profane man
    3:1   When the impious king comprehended this situation
    3:24   we would have these impious people behind our backs
    5:47   So he, when he had filled his impious mind with a deep rage
4 Ma 12:11   he said, You profane tyrant, most impious of all the wicked

IMPIOUSLY
3 = 0.002 %
2 Ma 1:17   upon those who have behaved impiously
2 Es 15:8   which they impiously commit
4 Ma 9:15   not because I am a murderer, or as one who acts impiously

IMPLANT
3 = 0.002 %
3 Ma 5:28   for he had implanted in the king's mind
4 Ma 13:19   and which was implanted in the mother's womb
    15:6   In 7 pregnancies she had implanted in herself tender love toward them

IMPLORE
4 = 0.003 %
3 Ma 5:25   implored the supreme God to help them again at once
    5:51   imploring the Ruler over every power
4 Ma 4:9   were imploring God in the temple to shield the holy place
    16:3   she implored them and urged them on to death

IMPORTANT
1
2 Ma 10:15   who had control of important strongholds

IMPOSE
1
1 Es 8:22   and that no one has authority to impose any tax upon them

IMPOSSIBLE
4 = 0.003 %
Wis 16:15   To escape from thy hand is impossible
2 Ma 3:12   And he said that it was utterly impossible
    14:10   it is impossible for the government to find peace
3 Ma 4:18   the task was impossible for all the generals in Egypt

IMPOVERISH
1
Sir 18:32   lest you become impoverished by its expense

IMPRECATION
1
4 Ma 12:19   After he had uttered these imprecations

IMPRESS
2
3 Ma 1:9   and being impressed by its excellence and its beauty
4 Ma 15:4   We impress upon the character of a small child

IMPRISON
3 = 0.002 %
Wis 18:4   and imprisoned in darkness
    18:4   those who had kept thy sons imprisoned
Sir 13:12   he will not hesitate to injure or to imprison

IMPRISONED
1
Wis 16:14   nor set free the imprisoned soul

IMPRISONMENT
1
1 Es 8:24   either fine or imprisonment

IMPROPER
1
3 Ma 4:16   and uttering improper words against the supreme God

IMPUDENCE
1
Sir 25:22   There is wrath and impudence and great disgrace

IMPUDENT
2
Sir 22:5   An impudent daughter disgraces father and husband
    26:11   Be on guard against her impudent eye

IMPULSE
2
Jud 15:2   but with one impulse all rushed out and fled
4 Ma 1:35   and all the impulses of the body are bridled by reason

IN
2491 = 1.623 %

INABILITY
1
Ad E 16:3   but in their inability to stand prosperity

INACCESSIBLE
1
3 Ma 5:43   and by burning to the ground the temple inaccessible to him

INAPPROPRIATE
1
2 Ma 4:19   because that was inappropriate

INBORN
1
Wis 12:10   and their wickedness inborn

INCENSE, subst.
15 = 0.010 %
Tob 6:16   you shall take live ashes of incense
    8:2   and he took the live ashes of incense
Jud 9:1   when that evening's incense was being offered
Wis 18:21   prayer and propitiation by incense
Sir 45:16   incense and a pleasing odour as a memorial portion
    49:1   The memory of Josiah is like a blending of incense
    50:9   like fire and incense in the censer
Bar 1:10   and incense, and prepare a cereal offering
L Jr 6:43   burning bran of incense
P Az 15   or incense, no place to make an offering before thee
1 Ma 1:55   and burned incense at the doors of the houses and in the streets
    4:49   the altar of incense, and the table into the temple
    4:50   Then they burned incense on the altar
2 Ma 2:5   and the altar of incense, and he sealed up the entrance
    10:3   and they burned incense and lighted lamps

INCENSE, verb
1
Wis 12:27   they became incensed at those creatures

INCESSANT
1
3 Ma 4:2   there was incessant mourning, lamentation, and tearful cries

INCIDENT
1
2 Ma 4:43   Charges were brought against Menelaus about this incident

INCITE
1
2 Ma 4:1   slandered Onias, saying that it was he who had incited Heliodorus

INCLINATION
3 = 0.002 %
Sir 5:2   Do not follow your inclination and strength
    15:14   and he left him in the power of his own inclination
4 Ma 2:21   he planted in him emotions and inclinations

INCLINE*
9 = 0.006 %
Sir 4:8   Incline your ear to the poor
    6:33   and if you incline your ear you will become wise
    38:28   he inclines his ear to the sound of the hammer
    51:16   I inclined my ear a little and received her
Bar 2:16   Incline thy ear, O Lord, and hear
2 Ma 2:25   we have aimed to please those who are inclined to memorize
    13:5   which on all sides inclines precipitously into the ashes
3 Ma 3:22   Since they incline constantly to evil
2 Es 3:34   the turn of the scale will incline

INCLUDE
2
1 Ma 3:13   including a body of faithful men
4 Ma 1:2   and in addition it includes the praise of the highest virtue

INCOME
1
1 Ma 10:42   from the income of the services of the temple

INCOMPLETE
1
Sir 42:24   and he has made nothing incomplete

INCOMPREHENSION
1
3 Ma 5:27   since he had been completely overcome by incomprehension

INCONVENIENT
1
Wis 2:12   because he is inconvenient to us and opposes our actions

INCORRUPTIBLE
1
2 Es 7:97   being incorruptible from then on

INCORRUPTION
2
Wis 2:23   for God created man for incorruption
2 Es 4:11   And how can one who is already worn out by the corrupt world understand incorruption ?

INCREASE, verb
18 = 0.012 %
Jud 9:7   Behold now, the Assyrians are increased in their might
Wis 10:10   and increased the fruit of his toil
Sir 18:6   It is not possible to diminish or increase them
    21:12   but there is a cleverness which increases bitterness
    21:13   The knowledge of a wise man will increase like a flood
    31:30   Drunkenness increases the anger of a fool to his injury
    43:8   increasing marvellously in its phases
Bar 2:34   and I will increase them, and they will not be diminished
1 Ma 3:42   Now Judas and his brothers saw that misfortunes had increased
2 Ma 4:13   and increase in the adoption of foreign ways
1 Es 9:7   and so have increased the sin of Israel
3 Ma 2:25   he increased in his deeds of malice
2 Es 1:6   that the sins of their parents have increased in them
    5:2   And unrighteousness shall be increased
    5:10   and unrighteousness and unrestraint shall increase on earth
    7:111   when corruption has increased and unrighteousness has multiplied

7:114 and righteousness has increased and truth has appeared
14:40 and wisdom increased in my breast

INCREASE, subst.   1
1 Ma 14:8 the ground gave its increase

INCREDIBLE   2
Wis 16:17 For – most incredible of all
19:5 and that thy people might experience an incredible journey

INCUR   10 = 0.007 %
Tob 6:12 without incurring the penalty of death
Sir 6:1 for a bad name incurs shame and reproach :
9:5 lest you stumble and incur penalties for her
23:16 and a 3rd incurs wrath
39:23 The nations will incur his wrath
2 Ma 9:16 and the expenses incurred for the sacrifices
3 Ma 1:3 that this man incurred the vengeance meant for the king
3:28 will receive the property of the one who incurs the punishment
2 Es 13:20 though incurring peril
4 Ma 11:3 so that by murdering me you will incur punishment

INCURABLE   2
Jud 5:12 with incurable plagues
2 Ma 9:5 struck him an incurable and unseen blow

INDECISION   1
2 Es 15:33 and indecision upon their kings

INDEED   9 = 0.006 %
Sir 18:17 Indeed, does not a word surpass a good gift ?
3 Ma 1:29 because indeed all at that time preferred death
2:11 And indeed you are faithful and true
2 Es 3:36 Thou mayest indeed find individual men
6:59 If the world has indeed been created for us
8:38 For indeed I will not concern myself
12:7 and if my prayer has indeed come up before thy face
4 Ma 7:13 Most amazing, indeed, though he was an old man
17:8 Indeed it would be proper

INDIA   3 = 0.002 %
Ad E 13:1 from India to Ethiopia and to the governors under them
16:1 to the rulers of the provinces from India to Ethiopia, 127 satrapies
1 Es 3:2 from India to Ethiopia

INDIAN   1
1 Ma 6:37 and also its Indian driver

INDICATE   6 = 0.004 %
Ad E 13:6 that those indicated to you in the letters of Haman
1 Ma 8:25 as the occasion may indicate to them
8:27 as the occasion may indicate to them
2 Ma 11:17 and have asked about the matters indicated therein
1 Es 6:30 for daily use as the priests in Jerusalem may indicate
3 Ma 5:26 indicating that what the king desired was ready for action

INDICATION   1
3 Ma 3:24 Therefore, fully convinced by these indications

INDIGNANT   2
Bel 14:28 they were very indignant and conspired against the king
2 Ma 13:25 The people of Ptolemais were indignant over the treaty

INDIGNANTLY   1
4 Ma 4:7 The people indignantly protested his words

INDIGNATION   1
2 Es 8:23 and whose indignation makes the mountains melt away

INDISCRIMINATE   1
4 Ma 1:27 in the body, indiscriminate eating

INDIVIDUAL   1
2 Es 3:36 Thou mayest indeed find individual men

INDIVIDUALLY   1
3 Ma 4:14 The entire race was to be registered individually

INDOLENT   2
Sir 22:1 The indolent may be compared to a filthy stone
22:2 The indolent may be compared to the filth of dunghills

INDOMITABLE   1
4 Ma 15:13 and indomitable suffering by mothers !

INDOORS   1
2 Ma 3:19 Some of the maidens who were kept indoors

INDUCE   2
2 Ma 4:12 and he induced the noblest of the young men
4:46 induced the king to change his mind

INDUCEMENT   1
4 Ma 8:15 But when they had heard the inducements

INDULGENCE   2
Wis 12:20 For if thou didst punish with such great care and indulgence
2 Es 7:114 sinful indulgence has come to an end

INDULGENT   2
Sir pr. and to be indulgent in cases where
7:24 and do not show yourself too indulgent with them

INDUSTRIOUS   1
Sir 31:22 In all your work be industrious

INEFFECTIVE   1
4 Ma 7:14 he rendered the many-headed rack ineffective

INESCAPABLE   1
Wis 17:17 he was seized, and endured the inescapable fate

INESCAPABLY   1
3 Ma 7:9 in everything and inescapably as an antagonist to avenge such acts. Farewell

INEXHAUSTIBLE   1
2 Es 9:19 and an inexhaustible pasture

INEXORABLE   1
Wis 16:4 inexorable want should come

INEXPERIENCED   2
Wis 13:18 for aid he entreats a thing that is utterly inexperienced
Sir 34:10 He that is inexperienced knows few things

INEXPRESSIBLE   1
2 Es 6:44 and odours of inexpressible fragrance

INFAMOUS   1
3 Ma 3:23 in every situation, in accordance with their infamous way of life

INFANT   11 = 0.007 %
Jud 4:12 not to give up their infants as prey
16:5 and dash my infants to the ground
Wis 11:7 in rebuke for the decree to slay the infants
15:14 But most foolish, and more miserable than an infant
1 Ma 1:61 and they hung the infants from their mothers' necks
2 Ma 5:13 and slaughter of virgins and infants
3 Ma 3:27 old people or children or even infants
6:14 The whole throng of infants and their parents entreat you with tears
2 Es 5:49 For as an infant does not bring forth
6:21 Infants a year old shall speak with their voices
4 Ma 4:25 were thrown headlong from heights along with their infants

INFANTRY   16 = 0.010 %
Jud 1:4 and his infantry form their ranks
2:19 and picked troops of infantry
2:22 his infantry, cavalry, and chariots
7:2 their force of men of war was 170,000 infantry and 12,000 cavalry
7:20 their infantry, chariots, and cavalry
1 Ma 3:39 and sent with them 40,000 infantry and 7,000 cavalry
4:1 Now Gorgias took 5,000 infantry and a 1,000 picked cavalry
15:38 and gave him troops of infantry and cavalry
16:5 and behold, a large force of infantry and horsemen
16:7 and placed the horsemen in the midst of the infantry
2 Ma 11:4 but was elated with his ten thousands of infantry
12:20 who had with him a 120,000 infantry and 2,500 cavalry
12:33 And he came out with 3,000 infantry and 400 cavalry
13:2 Each of them had a Greek force of 110,000 infantry
3 Ma 1:1 both infantry and cavalry
4 Ma 17:24 for infantry battle and siege

INFANTRYMAN   1
1 Ma 4:28 But the next year he mustered 60,000 picked infantrymen

INFER   2
Wis 8:8 she knows the things of old, and infers the things to come
19:18 This may be clearly inferred

INFERIOR   1
Sir 25:8 and he who has not served a man inferior to himself

INFIRMITY   1
2 Es 4:27 because this age is full of sadness and infirmities

INFLAME
4 = 0.003 %
2 Ma 4:38 and inflamed with anger
14:11 quickly inflamed Demetrius still more
4 Ma 3:11 tormented and inflamed him, undid and consumed him
16:3 inflamed as she saw her 7 sons tortured in such varied ways

INFLEXIBLE
2
3 Ma 5:1 Then the king, completely inflexible
5:12 and was completely frustrated in his inflexible plan

INFLICT
8 = 0.005 %
Ad E 16:18 has speedily inflicted on him the punishment he deserved
Sir 12:6 and will inflict punishment on the ungodly
48:8 who anointed kings to inflict retribution
1 Ma 8:4 and inflicted great disaster upon them
2 Ma 3:26 inflicting many blows on him
9:28 such as he had inflicted on others
3 Ma 2:6 by inflicting many and varied punishments
2:27 He proposed to inflict public disgrace

INFLICTION
1
2 Ma 9:6 with many and strange inflictions

INFLUENCE
2
4 Ma 12:6 and to influence her to persuade the surviving son
15:11 Nevertheless, though so many factors influenced the mother

INFORM
15 = 0.010 %
Tob 1:19 and informed the king about me, that I was burying them
10:8 and they will inform him how things are with you
Ad E 12:2 and he informed the king concerning them
Sir 37:14 For a man's soul sometimes keeps him better informed
Sus 13:50 sit among us and inform us
2 Ma 3:7 he told him of the money about which he had been informed
4:1 who had informed about the money against his own country
11:18 I have informed the king of everything
11:29 Menelaus has informed us that you wish to return home
13:4 and when Lysias informed him
14:20 and the leader had informed the people
1 Es 6:12 And in order that we might inform you in writing
8:22 You are also informed that no tribute
2 Es 10:38 Listen to me and I will inform you
4 Ma 4:4 and went up to Seleucus to inform him of the rich treasure

INFORMATION
2
2 Ma 13:21 gave secret information to the enemy
3 Ma 3:28 Any one willing to give information

INFORMED
1
Jud 11:8 thoroughly informed and marvellous in military strategy

INFURIATE
1
3 Ma 3:1 he became so infuriated that not only was he enraged

INGENIOUS
2
4 Ma 7:4 No city besieged with many ingenious war machines
15:24 and the ingenious and various rackings

INHABIT
11 = 0.007 %
Jud 5:3 What cities do they inhabit ?
Bar 4:35 and for a long time she will be inhabited by demons
2 Ma 3:1 While the holy city was inhabited in unbroken peace
12:13 and inhabited by all sorts of Gentiles
3 Ma 3:15 the nations inhabiting Coele-Syria and Phoenicia
2 Es 3:28 Are the deeds of those who inhabit Babylon any better ?
6:24 and the earth and those who inhabit it shall be terrified
7:74 has been patient with those who inhabit the world
7:137 the world with those who inhabit it would not have life
8:20 He said : O Lord who inhabitest eternity
8:50 who inhabit the world in the last times

INHABITANT
23 = 0.015 %
Jud 1:12 all the inhabitants of the land of Moab
3:4 Our cities also and their inhabitants are your slaves
5:15 and by their might destroyed all the inhabitants of Heshbon
7:20 until all the vessels of water belonging to every inhabitant of Bethulia were empty
Sir 10:2 and like the ruler of the city, so are all its inhabitants
Bar 1:15 to the men of Judah, to the inhabitants of Jerusalem
2:23 and the whole land will be a desolation without inhabitants
1 Ma 1:28 Even the land shook for its inhabitants
6:12 and I sent to destroy the inhabitants of Judah without good reason
11:18 by the inhabitants of the strongholds
2 Ma 9:2 with the result that Antiochus was put to flight by the inhabitants
2 Es 3:9 thou didst bring the flood upon the inhabitants of the world
3:25 but the inhabitants of the city transgressed
3:34 and those of the inhabitants of the world
3:35 When have the inhabitants of the earth not sinned in thy sight ?

6:18 to visit the inhabitants of the earth
6:26 and the heart of the earth's inhabitants shall be changed
11:32 and with much oppression dominated its inhabitants
11:34 which also ruled over the earth and its inhabitants
12:24 and its inhabitants more oppressively
14:17 the more shall evils be multiplied among its inhabitants
14:20 and its inhabitants are without light
15:40 shall rise, to destroy all the earth and its inhabitants

INHABITED
1
2 Ma 9:17 and would visit every inhabited place

INHERIT
11 = 0.007 %
Tob 4:12 and their posterity will inherit the land
14:13 He inherited their property and that of his father Tobit
Jud 4:12 and the cities they had inherited to be destroyed
Sir 10:11 For when a man is dead, he will inherit creeping things
19:3 Decay and worms will inherit him
37:26 He who is wise among his people will inherit confidence
44:21 and cause them to inherit from sea to sea
1 Ma 2:10 What nation has not inherited her palaces
2:57 inherited the throne of the kingdom for ever
2 Es 7:17 that the righteous shall inherit these things
7:96 and shall inherit what is to come

INHERITANCE
42 = 0.027 %
Tob 6:11 because you are entitled to her and to her inheritance
6:12 are entitled to the inheritance
Jud 8:22 and the desolation of our inheritance
9:12 God of the inheritance of Israel
13:5 For now is the time to help thy inheritance
16:21 After this every one returned home to his own inheritance
Ad E 10:12 And God remembered his people and vindicated his inheritance
13:15 and they desire to destroy the inheritance
13:17 Hear my prayer, and have mercy upon thy inheritance
14:5 for an everlasting inheritance
14:9 and to destroy thy inheritance
Sir 9:6 lest you lose your inheritance
22:23 that you may share with him in his inheritance
23:12 may it never be found in the inheritance of Jacob !
24:8 and in Israel receive your inheritance
24:12 in the portion of the Lord, who is their inheritance
24:20 and my inheritance sweeter than the honeycomb
24:23 as an inheritance of the congregations of Jacob
33:23 in the hour of the death, distribute your inheritance
36:11 and give them their inheritance, as at the beginning
41:6 The inheritance of the children of sinners will perish
42:3 and of dividing the inheritance of friends
44:11 and their inheritance to their children's children
44:23 and gave him his inheritance
45:22 But in the land of the people he has no inheritance
45:22 for the Lord himself is his portion and inheritance
46:1 so that he might give Israel its inheritance
46:8 to bring them into their inheritance, into a land flowing with milk and honey
46:9 and his children obtained it for an inheritance
1 Ma 2:56 received an inheritance in the land
6:24 and they have seized our inheritances
15:33 but only the inheritance of our fathers
15:34 we are firmly holding the inheritance of our fathers
2 Ma 2:4 and had seen the inheritance of God
2:17 and has returned the inheritance to all
1 Es 8:85 and leave it for an inheritance to your children for ever
2 Es 6:59 why do we not possess our world as an inheritance ?
7:9 If now that city is given to a man for an inheritance
7:9 how will the heir receive his inheritance
8:16 and about thy inheritance, for whom I lament
8:45 But spare thy people and have mercy on thy inheritance
4 Ma 18:3 but also were deemed worthy to share in a divine inheritance

INIMITABLE
1
2 Es 6:44 and flowers of inimitable colour

INIQUITY
39 = 0.025 %
Tob 13:5 He will afflict us for our iniquities
Jud 5:17 for the God who hates iniquity is with them
6:5 who have said these words on the day of your iniquity
Sir 7:6 lest you be unable to remove iniquity
17:20 Their iniquities are not hidden from him
17:26 Return to the Most High and turn away from iniquity
23:11 A man who swears many oaths will be filled with iniquity
25:19 Any iniquity is insignificant compared to a wife's iniquity
27:10 so does sin for the workers of iniquity
41:18 and of iniquity, before a congregation or the people
49:2 and took away the abominations of iniquity
Bar 3:5 Remember not the iniquities of our fathers
3:7 for we have put away from our hearts all the iniquity of our fathers
3:8 for all the iniquities of our fathers
Sus 13:5 Iniquity came forth from Babylon

1 Es	8:70	the leaders and the nobles have been sharing in this iniquity
	8:72	gathered round me, as I mourned over this iniquity
	8:90	Behold, we are now before thee in our iniquities
	9:2	for he was mourning over the great iniquities of the multitude
P Ma	9	because of the multitude of my iniquities
2 Es	1:5	and to their children the iniquities
	3:13	And when they were committing iniquity before thee
	3:34	Now therefore weigh in a balance our iniquities
	6:19	and when I require from the doers of iniquity
	6:19	the penalty of their iniquity
	7:68	For all who have been born are involved in iniquities
	7:72	because though they had understanding they committed iniquity
	7:126	For while we lived and committed iniquity
	7:138	so that those who have committed iniquities might be relieved of them
	14:31	but you and your fathers committed iniquity
	15:6	For iniquity has spread throughout every land
	16:20	Yet for all this they will not turn from their iniquities
	16:50	so righteousness shall abhor iniquity
	16:52	and iniquity will be removed from the earth
	16:65	and your own iniquities shall stand
	16:67	Cease from your sins, and forget your iniquities
	16:76	or your iniquities prevail over you
	16:77	and overwhelmed by their iniquities

INITIATE 3 = 0.002 %

Wis	8:4	For she is an initiate in the knowledge of God
	12:5	These initiates from the midst of a heathen cult
3 Ma	2:30	those who have been initiated into the mysteries

INITIATION 2

Wis	14:15	and handed on to his dependents secret rites and initiations
	14:23	For whether they kill children in their initiations

INJECT 1

Sir	28:9	and inject enmity among those who are at peace

INJURE 9 = 0.006 %

Ad E	12:6	and he sought to injure Mordecai and his people
	16:3	They not only seek to injure our subjects
Sir	13:12	he will not hesitate to injure or to imprison
	38:21	you do the dead no good, and you injure yourself
1 Ma	7:15	We will not seek to injure you or your friends
2 Ma	12:22	so that often they were injured by their own men
2 Es	11:42	for you have afflicted the meek and injured the peaceable
4 Ma	4:1	he was unable to injure Onias in the eyes of the nation
	9:7	do not suppose that you can injure us by torturing us

INJURED 1

2 Es	2:21	care for the injured and the weak

INJURY 7 = 0.005 %

Jud	7:24	For you have done us a great injury
Wis	18:2	though previously wronged, were doing them no injury
Sir	10:6	Do not be angry with your neighbour for any injury
	31:30	Drunkenness increases the anger of a fool to his injury
2 Ma	3:39	and he strikes and destroys those who come to do it injury
	9:4	the injury done by those who had put him to flight
	14:40	he would do them an injury

INJUSTICE 8 = 0.005 %

Sir	7:3	My son, do not sow the furrows of injustice
	10:7	and injustice is outrageous to both
	10:8	on account of injustice and insolence and wealth
	14:9	and mean injustice withers the soul
	20:28	and whoever pleases great men will atone for injustice
	40:12	All bribery and injustice will be blotted out
1 Ma	9:23	all the doers of injustice appeared
3 Ma	2:4	You destroyed those who in the past committed injustice

INMOST 2

Wis	1:6	because God is witness of his inmost feelings
4 Ma	14:13	which draws everything toward an emotion felt in her inmost parts

INNATE 2

3 Ma	3:22	But in their innate malice
4 Ma	16:3	as was her innate parental love

INNER 6 = 0.004 %

Wis	17:4	For not even the inner chamber that held them
	17:13	and the inner expectation of help, being weak
Sir	50:5	as he came out of the inner sanctuary !
1 Ma	9:54	of the inner court of the sanctuary
3 Ma	3:17	to enter their inner temple and honour it
4 Ma	13:6	and make it calm for those who sail into the inner basin

INNOCENCE 2

1 Ma	2:37	for they said, Let us all die in our innocence
	2:60	Daniel because of his innocence

INNOCENT, adj., subst. 14 = 0.009 %

Tob	3:14	that I am innocent of any sin with man
Ad E	16:5	for the shedding of innocent blood
Wis	4:12	and roving desire perverts the innocent mind
Sir	26:29	and a tradesman will not be declared innocent of sin
Sus	13:46	I am innocent of the blood of this woman
	13:53	condemning the innocent and letting the guilty go free
	13:53	Do not put to death an innocent and righteous person
	13:62	Thus innocent blood was saved that day
1 Ma	1:37	On every side of the sanctuary they shed innocent blood
2 Ma	1:8	and burned the gate and shed innocent blood
	8:4	and to remember also the lawless destruction of the innocent babies
2 Es	15:8	Behold, innocent and righteous blood cries out to me
	15:9	and will receive to myself all the innocent blood from among them
	15:22	and my sword will not cease from those who shed innocent blood on the earth

INNUMERABLE 7 = 0.005 %

Jud	2:17	and innumerable sheep and oxen and goats for provision
3 Ma	4:17	because of their innumerable multitude
2 Es	6:3	and before the innumerable hosts of angels were gathered together
	7:140	of the innumerable multitude
	13:5	an innumerable multitude of men were gathered together
	13:11	nothing was seen of the innumerable multitude
	13:34	and an innumerable multitude shall be gathered together

INQUIRE 12 = 0.008 %

Ad E	12:2	He overheard their conversation and inquired into their purposes
Wis	6:3	who will search out your works and inquire into your plans
1 Ma	3:48	to inquire into those matters about which the Gentiles
2 Ma	3:9	and he inquired whether this really was the situation
3 Ma	1:13	And he inquired why, when he entered every other temple
	5:27	inquired what the matter was
2 Es	4:23	For I did not wish to inquire about the ways above
	5:50	Then I inquired and said
	8:51	and inquire concerning the glory of those who are like yourself
	9:13	but inquire how the righteous will be saved
4 Ma	9:27	Before torturing him, they inquired if he were willing to eat
	11:13	When the tyrant inquired

INQUIRY 6 = 0.004 %

Wis	1:9	For inquiry will be made into the counsels of an ungodly man
	6:8	But a strict inquiry is in store for the mighty
Sir	33:3	as an inquiry by means of Urim
	41:4	there is no inquiry about it in Hades
3 Ma	7:5	they tried without any inquiry or examination
4 Ma	1:13	Our inquiry, accordingly

INSANITY 1

4 Ma	10:13	to the same insanity as your brothers

INSATIABLE 3 = 0.002 %

Sir	12:16	his thirst for blood will be insatiable
	31:17	and do not be insatiable, lest you give offence
	37:29	Do not have an insatiable appetite of any luxury

INSCRIBE 5 = 0.003 %

Sir	45:12	inscribed like a signet with Holiness
1 Ma	14:48	to inscribe this decree upon bronze tablets
3 Ma	2:30	he inscribed below :
	7:20	Then, after inscribing them as holy on a pillar
4 Ma	17:8	to inscribe upon their tomb these words

INSCRIPTION 1

3 Ma	2:27	with this inscription :

INSECURELY 1

Wis	4:4	standing insecurely they will be shaken by the wind

INSIDE, adv., prep. 4 = 0.003 %

Sir	19:12	so is a word inside a fool
Bel	14:7	for this is but clay inside and brass outside
2 Ma	1:15	inside the wall of the sacred precinct
3 Ma	4:11	nor in any way claim to be inside the circuit of the city

INSIGHT 2

Wis	8:21	and it was a mark of insight to know whose gift she was
Sir	6:37	It is he who will give insight to your mind

INSIGNIFICANT 2

Sir	25:19	Any iniquity is insignificant compared to a wife's iniquity
3 Ma	1:3	that a certain insignificant man should sleep in the tent

INSINCERELY   1
3 Ma   3 : 17   They accepted our presence by word, but insincerely by deed

INSIST   1
Jud   5 : 22   and from Moab insisted that he must be put to death

INSISTENTLY   1
1 Ma   11 : 40   and insistently urged him to hand Antiochus over to him

INSOLENCE   15 = 0.010 %
Ad E   13 : 12   thou knowest, O Lord, that it was not in insolence
Wis   12 : 17   and dost rebuke any insolence among those who know it
Sir   10 : 6   and do not attempt anything by acts of insolence
    10 : 8   on account of injustice and insolence and wealth
    16 : 8   whom he loathed on account of their insolence
Bar   4 : 34   and her insolence will be turned to grief
2 Ma   9 : 7   Yet he did not any way stop his insolence
3 Ma   2 : 3   and you judge those who have done anything in insolence and arrogance
    2 : 21   in insolence and audacity
    6 : 4   exalted with lawless insolence and boastful tongue
    6 : 5   speaking grievous words with boasting and insolence
    6 : 9   And now, you who hate insolence
    6 : 12   who by the senseless insolence of the lawless
    6 : 20   and he forgot his sullen insolence
2 Es   11 : 43   And so your insolence has come up before the Most High

INSOLENT   4 = 0.003 %
Sir   8 : 11   Do not get up and leave an insolent fellow
    32 : 18   and an insolent and proud man will not cower in fear
    35 : 18   till he takes away the multitude of the insolent
2 Ma   1 : 28   Afflict those who oppress and are insolent with pride

INSOLENTLY   1
2 Ma   12 : 14   behaved most insolently toward Judas and his men

INSPECT   2
2 Ma   5 : 18   whom Seleucus the king sent to inspect the treasury
1 Es   8 : 41   and I inspected them

INSPECTION   2
2 Ma   3 : 8   ostensibly to make a tour of inspection
    3 : 14   to direct the inspection of these funds

INSPECTOR   1
1 Ma   1 : 51   And he appointed inspectors over all the people

INSPIRATION   1
2 Ma   15 : 11   as with the inspiration of brave words

INSPIRE   4 = 0.003 %
Wis   15 : 11   and inspired him with an active soul
L Jr   6 : 4   and inspire fear in the heathen
1 Ma   4 : 35   and observed the boldness which inspired those of Judas
1 Es   9 : 55   because they were inspired by the words which they had been taught

INSTABILITY   1
3 Ma   5 : 39   wondering at his instability of mind

INSTALL   1
1 Ma   12 : 38   he fortified it and installed gates with bolts

INSTANT   1
Wis   18 : 12   since in one instant

INSTEAD   3 = 0.002 %
3 Ma   3 : 7   instead they gossiped about the differences in worship and foods
4 Ma   13 : 3   Instead, by reason, which is praised before God
    15 : 12   Instead, the mother urged them on

INSTEAD OF   19 = 0.012 %
Ad E   14 : 2   and instead of costly perfumes
    16 : 21   instead of a day of destruction for them
Wis   11 : 6   Instead of the fountain of an everflowing river
    16 : 2   Instead of this punishment
    16 : 20   Instead of these things
    19 : 10   how instead of producing animals
    19 : 10   and instead of fish
Sir   4 : 10   and instead of a husband to their mother
    5 : 15   and do not become an enemy instead of a friend
    20 : 14   for he has many eyes instead of one
    29 : 6   and instead of glory will repay him with dishonour
1 Ma   10 : 30   and instead of collecting the third of the grain
1 Es   4 : 39   instead of anything that is unrighteous or wicked
3 Ma   4 : 6   all together raising a lament instead of a wedding song
    4 : 8   their necks encircled with ropes instead of garlands
    4 : 8   instead of good cheer and youthful revelry
    5 : 31   for the savage beasts instead of the Jews

---

    5 : 32   In fact you would have been deprived of life instead of these
    6 : 31   instead of a bitter and lamentable death

INSTILL   1
4 Ma   4 : 10   instilling in them great fear and trembling

INSTITUTE   1
3 Ma   6 : 36   they instituted the observance of the aforesaid days as a festival

INSTRUCT   13 = 0.008 %
Wis   6 : 11   long for them, and you will be instructed
    6 : 25   Therefore be instructed by my words, and you will profit
Sir   37 : 23   A wise man will instruct his own people
    40 : 29   but a man who is intelligent and well instructed guards against that
    42 : 8   Do not be ashamed to instruct the stupid or foolish
    42 : 8   Then you will be truly instructed
2 Ma   2 : 2   instructed those who were being deported
2 Es   5 : 32   and I will instruct you
    7 : 49   and I will instruct you, and will admonish you yet again
    8 : 12   and instructed him in thy law
    10 : 33   Stand up like a man, and I will instruct you
    14 : 13   and instruct those that are wise
4 Ma   5 : 24   it instructs us in justice

INSTRUCTION   24 = 0.016 %
Wis   3 : 11   for whoever despises wisdom and instruction is miserable
    6 : 17   is the most sincere desire for instruction
    6 : 17   and concern for instruction is love of her
    7 : 14   commended for the gifts that come from instruction
Sir   pr.   for instruction and wisdom
    pr.   pertaining to instruction and wisdom
    pr.   I found opportunity for no little instruction
    1 : 27   For the fear of the Lord is wisdom and instruction
    6 : 18   My son, from your youth up choose instruction
    8 : 8   because from them you will gain instruction
    16 : 25   I will impart instruction by weight
    23 : 7   Listen, my children, to instruction concerning speech
    24 : 27   It makes instruction shine forth like light
    24 : 32   I will again make instruction shine forth like the dawn
    24 : 34   but for all who seek instruction
    33 : 4   bind together your instruction, and make your answer
    33 : 17   but for all who seek instruction
    39 : 8   He will reveal instruction in his teaching
    41 : 14   My children, observe instruction and be at peace
    44 : 4   wise in their words of instruction
    50 : 27   Instruction in understanding and knowledge
    51 : 16   and I found for myself much instruction
    51 : 26   and let your souls receive instruction
    51 : 28   Get instruction with a large sum of silver

INSTRUCTOR   1
4 Ma   9 : 6   which our aged instructor also overcame

INSTRUMENT   12 = 0.008 %
Sir   43 : 2   is a marvellous instrument, the work of the Most High
    43 : 8   an instrument of the hosts on high
1 Ma   13 : 51   and with harps and cymbals and stringed instruments
1 Es   5 : 59   with musical instruments and trumpets
4 Ma   6 : 1   to the instruments of torture
    6 : 25   There they burned him with maliciously contrived instruments
    8 : 1   have prevailed over the most painful instruments of torture
    8 : 12   he ordered the instruments of torture to be brought forward
    8 : 19   O men and brothers, should we not fear the instruments of torture
    8 : 25   for fearing the instruments of torture
    10 : 5   they disjointed his hands and feet with their instruments
    10 : 7   they abandoned the instruments

INSULT, subst.   3 = 0.002 %
Wis   2 : 19   Let us test him with insult and torture
Sir   22 : 24   so insults precede bloodshed
3 Ma   5 : 22   in sleep as in devising all sorts of insults

INSULTING   2
Sir   23 : 15   A man accustomed to use insulting words
3 Ma   3 : 25   with insulting and harsh treatment

INSURE   1
4 Ma   9 : 4   which insures our safety through transgression of the law

INSURRECTION   1
2 Es   16 : 70   there shall be a great insurrection

INTACT   1
Tob   9 : 5   and Gabael brought out the money bags with their seals intact

INTEGRITY 2
Sir 7:6 and thus put a blot on your integrity
2 Ma 7:40 So he died in his integrity

INTELLIGENCE 4 = 0.003 %
Wis 15:18 when judged by their lack of intelligence
Sir 19:24 Better is the God-fearing man who lacks intelligence
22:11 and weep for the fool, for he lacks intelligence
2 Ma 11:13 And as he was not without intelligence

INTELLIGENT, adj., subst. 13 = 0.008 %
Wis 7:23 that are intelligent and pure and most subtle
Sir 3:29 The mind of the intelligent man will ponder a parable
6:36 If you see an intelligent man, visit him early
7:21 Let your soul love an intelligent servant
10:23 It is not right to despise an intelligent poor man
18:28 Every intelligent man knows wisdom
19:2 Wine and women lead intelligent men astray
21:16 but delight will be found in the speech of the intelligent
22:17 A mind settled on an intelligent thought
25:8 happy is he who lives with an intelligent wife
26:28 and intelligent men who are treated contemptuously
36:19 so an intelligent mind detects false words
40:29 but a man who is intelligent and well instructed guards against that

INTELLIGENTLY 1
Sir 14:20 and who reasons intelligently

INTEND 19 = 0.012 %
Jud 9:5 Yea, the things thou didst intend came to pass
9:8 for they intend to defile thy sanctuary
Ad E 13:4 so that the unifying of the kingdom which we honourably intend
Sir 19:16 A person may make a slip without intending it
1 Ma 4:27 for things had not happened to Israel as he had intended
11:63 intending to remove him from office
15:3 and I intend to lay claim to the kingdom
15:4 and intend to make a landing in the country
2 Ma 1:14 For under pretext of intending to marry her
4:20 So this money was intended by the sender
7:2 What do you intend to ask and learn from us ?
10:24 He came on, intending to take Judea by storm
11:2 He intended to make the city a home for Greeks
12:7 he withdrew, intending to come again
3 Ma 1:2 intending single-handed to kill him and thereby end the war
1:22 or the fulfilment of his intended purpose
2 Es 8:59 For the Most High did not intend that men should be destroyed
10:4 And now I intend not to return to the city
4 Ma 11:16 So if you intend to torture me for not eating defiling foods

INTENSE 3 = 0.002 %
2 Ma 9:28 having endured the most intense suffering
4 Ma 12:12 for you intense and eternal fire and tortures
14:10 For the power of fire is intense and swift

INTENSELY 3 = 0.002 %
Wis 16:19 it burned more intensely than fire
Sir 17:26 to the light of health and hate abominations intensely
4 Ma 16:3 nor was the raging fiery furnace of Mishael so intensely hot

INTENSIFY 2
Wis 14:18 to intensify their worship
2 Ma 4:4 was intensifying the malice of Simon

INTENT, subst. 4 = 0.003 %
Wis 15:4 For neither has the evil intent of human art misled us
Bar 1:21 but we each followed the intent of his own wicked heart
1 Ma 7:30 that Nicanor had come to him with treacherous intent
3 Ma 7:3 frequently urging us with malicious intent

INTENT, adj. 2
Sir 38:28 intent upon his handiwork in iron
2 Ma 4:14 that the priests were no longer intent

INTENTION 1
2 Ma 14:5 and intentions of the Jews

INTENTLY 4 = 0.003 %
Tob 11:5 Now Anna sat looking intently down the road for her son
Sir 9:5 Do not look intently at a virgin
9:8 and do not look intently at beauty belonging to another
3 Ma 2:26 intently observing the king's purpose

INTENTNESS 1
3 Ma 4:15 with bitter haste and zealous intentness

INTERCEDE 2
Tob 1:22 Ahikar interceded for me, and I returned to Nineveh
2 Es 7:102 the righteous will be able to intercede for the ungodly

INTERCOURSE 2
2 Ma 6:4 and had intercourse with women within the sacred precincts
4 Ma 2:3 For when he was young and in his prime for intercourse

INTEREST 5 = 0.003 %
Sir 37:7 but some give counsel in their own interest
37:8 and learn first what is his interest
2 Ma 14:8 for the interests of the king
1 Es 4:49 from his kingdom to Judea, in the interest of their freedom
4 Ma 2:8 and to lend without interest to the needy

INTERIOR 2
1 Ma 4:48 and the interior of the temple
2 Es 14:33 and your brethren are farther in the interior

INTERNAL 1
2 Ma 9:5 and with sharp internal tortures

INTERPRETATION 18 = 0.012 %
Sir 47:17 and for your interpretations, the countries marvelled at you
2 Es 4:47 and I will show you the interpretation of a parable
10:43 this is the interpretation :
12:8 the interpretation and meaning of this terrifying vision
12:10 This is the interpretation of this vision which you have seen :
12:16 This is the interpretation of the 12 wings which you saw
12:17 but from the midst of his body, this is the interpretation :
12:19 this is the interpretation :
12:22 this is the interpretation :
12:30 this is the interpretation :
12:35 and this is its interpretation
13:15 now show me also the interpretation of this dream
13:21 I will tell you the interpretation of the vision
13:22 this is the interpretation :
13:25 This is the interpretation of the vision :
13:28 this is the interpretation :
13:53 This is the interpretation of the dream which you saw
14:8 and the interpretations that you have heard

INTERPRETER 1
Sir 17:5 and as 7th reason, the interpreter of his operations

INTERRUPT 2
Sir 11:8 nor interrupt a speaker in the midst of his words
32:3 and do not interrupt the music

INTERVAL 1
3 Ma 4:17 But after the previously mentioned interval of time

INTERVENE 1
Wis 18:23 he intervened and held back the wrath

INTERVENTION 1
2 Ma 3:29 speechless because of the divine intervention

INTERVIEW 1
2 Ma 4:8 promising the king at an interview 360 talents of silver

INTIMATE 3 = 0.002 %
Sus 13:54 Under what tree did you see them being intimate with each other ?
13:57 and they were intimate with you through fear
13:58 Under what tree did you catch them being intimate with each other ?

INTO 253 = 0.165 %

INTOLERABLE 1
2 Ma 9:10 Because of his intolerable stench

INTRICATE 1
Ad E 16:13 and with intricate craft and deceit

INTRIGUE 2
Sir 9:4 lest you be caught in her intrigues
2 Es 9:3 tumult of peoples, intrigues of nations

INTRODUCE 1
2 Ma 4:11 and introduced new customs contrary to the law

INTRUDER 2
4 Ma 14:16 hatch the nestlings and ward off the intruder
14:19 defend themselves against intruders

INVADE 12 = 0.008 %
Jud 4:7 since by them Judea could be invaded
1 Ma 1:17 So he invaded Egypt with a strong force
4:35 to invade Judea again with an even larger army
12:25 for he gave them no opportunity to invade his own country
13:1 to invade the land of Judah and destroy it
13:12 to invade the land of Judah

13:20 After this Trypho came to invade the country and destroy it
14:2 that Demetrius had invaded his territory
14:31 And when their enemies decided to invade their country
15:10 and invaded the land of his fathers
15:40 and began to provoke the people and invade Judea
2 Ma 11:5 Invading Judea, he approached Beth-zur

INVALIDATE 1
4 Ma 5:18 to invalidate our reputation for piety

INVASION 2
2 Ma 5:1 About this time Antiochus made his 2nd invasion of Egypt
8:12 Word came to Judas concerning Nicanor's invasion

INVENT 1
Sus 13:43 that they have wickedly invented against me !

INVENTION 1
Wis 14:12 and the invention of them was the corruption of life

INVENTOR 1
4 Ma 11:23 you inventor of tortures

INVESTIGATE 5 = 0.003 %
Wis 13:9 that they could investigate the world
Sir 3:21 nor investigate what is beyond your power
11:7 Do not find fault before you investigate
2 Ma 1:34 the king investigated the matter
1 Es 9:16 they began their sessions to investigate the matter

INVESTIGATION 1
Ad E 16:7 which we hand on as from investigation of matters close at hand

INVETERATE 1
3 Ma 4:1 for the inveterate enmity which had long ago been in their minds

INVINCIBLE 7 = 0.005 %
Jud 16:13 wonderful in strength, invincible
Wis 5:19 he will take holiness as an invincible shield
2 Ma 11:13 and realized that the Hebrews were invincible
3 Ma 4:21 But this was an act of the invincible providence
6:13 in fear of your invincible might, O honoured One
4 Ma 9:18 that sons of the Hebrews alone are invincible
11:21 For the religious knowledge, O tyrant, is invincible

INVIOLABILITY 1
2 Ma 3:12 and in the sanctity and inviolability of the temple

INVITATION 2
3 Ma 5:14 the person who was in charge of the invitations
5:27 and being struck by the unusual invitation to come out

INVITE 9 = 0.006 %
Jud 12:10 and did not invite any of his officers
Wis 1:12 Do not invite death by the error of your life
Sir 13:9 When a powerful man invites you, be reserved
13:9 and he will invite you the more often
2 Ma 8:11 inviting them to buy Jewish slaves
12:3 as this : they invited the Jews who lived among them
14:5 when he was invited by Demetrius to a meeting of the council
3 Ma 5:26 Hermon arrived and invited him to come out
4 Ma 3:19 The present occasion now invites us

INVITE in 1
Tob 5:9 So Tobias invited him in

INVOCATION 1
2 Ma 15:26 with invocation to God and prayers

INVOKE 1
Ad E 15:2 after invoking the aid of the all-seeing God and Saviour

INVOLVE 8 = 0.005 %
Ad E 16:5 and have been involved in irremediable calamities
Sir 12:14 and becomes involved in his sins
23:13 for it involves sinful speech
2 Ma 2:24 For considering the flood of numbers involved
5:18 that they were involved in many sins
3 Ma 2:28 to a registration involving poll tax
2 Es 7:12 full of dangers and involved in great hardships
7:68 For all who have been born are involved in iniquities

INVULNERABLE 2
2 Ma 8:36 and that therefore the Jews were invulnerable
3 Ma 5:47 wishing to witness, with invulnerable heart and with his own eyes

INWARDLY 3 = 0.002 %
Wis 8:17 When I considered these things inwardly
Sir 19:26 but inwardly he is full of deceit
2 Ma 5:11 So, raging inwardly, he left Egypt

IRON 21 = 0.014 %
Wis 13:15 and sets it in the wall, and fastens it there with iron
17:16 and thus was kept shut up in a prison not made of iron
Sir 13:2 How can the clay pot associate with the iron kettle ?
22:15 Sand, salt, and a piece of iron are easier to bear than a stupid man
28:20 for its yoke is a yoke of iron
38:28 intent upon his handiwork in iron
39:26 and iron and salt and wheat flour and milk and honey
48:17 he tunnelled the sheer rock with iron
2 Ma 11:9 ready to assail not only men but the wildest beasts or walls of iron
P Ma 10 I am weighted down with many an iron fetter
3 Ma 3:25 and bound securely with iron fetters
4:9 driven under the constraint of iron bonds
2 Es 7:55 and also iron and lead and clay
7:56 and iron than brass, and lead than iron, and clay than lead
4 Ma 8:13 braziers and thumbscrews an iron claws and wedges and bellows
9:26 and after fitting themselves with iron gauntlets having sharp hooks
9:28 These leopard-like beasts tore out his sinews with the iron hands
11:10 and fitting iron clamps on them
14:19 and as though with an iron dart sting those who approach their hive
15:22 as her sons were tortured on the wheel and with the hot irons !

IRRATIONAL 7 = 0.005 %
Wis 11:15 to worship irrational serpents and worthless animals
11:15 a multitude of irrational creatures to punish them
3 Ma 7:8 or reproaching them for the irrational things that have happened
4 Ma 2:19 for their irrational slaughter
3:11 But a certain irrational desire for the water
5:22 as though living by it were irrational
6:18 For it would be irrational if we

IRRATIONALLY 1
4 Ma 6:14 Eleazar, why are you so irrationally destroying yourself

IRREMEDIABLE 1
Ad E 16:5 and have been involved in irremediable calamities

IRRESISTIBLE 2
2 Ma 1:13 with a force that seemed irresistible
P Ma 5 and the wrath of thy threat to sinners is irresistible

IRREVERENCE 1
2 Ma 4:17 to show irreverence to the divine laws

IRREVOCABLE 1
3 Ma 5:42 and he firmly swore an irrevocable oath

IRRIGATE 1
4 Ma 1:29 and ties up and waters and thoroughly irrigates

ISAAC 20 = 0.013 %
Tob 4:12 that Noah, Abraham, Isaac, and Jacob, our fathers of old
Jud 8:26 Remember what he did with Abraham, and how he tested Isaac
Sir 44:22 To Isaac also he gave the same assurance
Bar 2:34 to Abraham and to Isaac and to Jacob
P Az 12 and for the sake of Isaac thy servant and Israel thy holy one
2 Ma 1:2 and Isaac and Jacob, his faithful servants
P Ma 1 of Abraham and Isaac and Jacob
8 for Abraham and Isaac and Jacob
2 Es 1:39 to them I will give as leaders Abraham, Isaac
3:15 and thou gavest to him Isaac
3:15 and to Isaac thou gavest Jacob and Esau
6:8 He said to me, From Abraham to Isaac
4 Ma 7:14 and by reason like that of Isaac
7:19 like our patriarchs Abraham and Isaac and Jacob
13:12 and the father by whose hand Isaac would have submitted
13:17 For if we so die, Abraham and Isaac and Jacob will welcome us
16:20 our father Abraham was zealous to sacrifice his son Isaac
16:20 and when Isaac saw his father's hand
16:25 as do Abraham and Isaac and Jacob and all the patriarchs
18:11 and Isaac who was offered as a burnt offering

ISAIAH 4 = 0.003 %
Sir 48:20 and delivered them by the hand of Isaiah
48:22 which Isaiah the prophet commanded
2 Es 2:18 I will send you help, my servants Isaiah and Jeremiah
4 Ma 18:14 He reminded you of the scripture of Isaiah, which says

ISHMAEL 1
1 Es 9:22 Of the sons of Pashhur : Elioenai, Maaseiah, Ishmael

ISHMAELITE   1
Jud   2:23   and the Ishmaelites who lived along the desert

ISLAND   6 = 0.004 %
Sir   43:23   and planted islands in it
     47:16   Your name reached to far-off islands
1 Ma   6:29   and from islands of the seas
     8:11   The remaining kingdoms and islands
     11:38   which he had recruited from the islands of the nations
     15:1   sent a letter from the islands of the sea

ISLE   1
1 Ma   14:5   and opened a way to the isles of the sea

ISOLATE   1
1 Ma   12:36   to separate it from the city, in order to isolate it

ISRAEL   238 = 0.155 %
Tob   1:4   Now when I was in my own country, in the land of Israel
     1:4   from among all the tribes of Israel
     1:6   as it is ordained for all Israel by an everlasting decree
     13:3   Acknowledge him before the nations, O sons of Israel
Jud   4:1   By this time the people of Israel living in Judea
     4:8   and the senate of the whole people of Israel
     4:9   And every man of Israel cried out to God with great fervour
     4:11   And all the men and women of Israel, and their children
     4:12   praying earnestly to the God of Israel
     4:15   to look with favour upon the whole house of Israel
     5:1   heard that the people of Israel had prepared for war
     6:2   and tell us not to make war against the people of Israel
     6:10   and hand him over to the men of Israel
     6:14   Then the men of Israel came down from their city and found him
     6:17   against the house of Israel
     6:21   and all that night they called on the God of Israel for help
     7:19   The people of Israel cried out to the Lord their God
     8:1   son of Sarasadai, son of Israel
     8:6   and the feasts and days of rejoicing of the house of Israel
     8:33   the Lord will deliver Israel by my hand
     9:12   God of the inheritance of Israel
     9:14   who protects the people of Israel but thou alone !
     10:1   When Judith had ceased crying out to the God of Israel
     10:8   that the people of Israel may glory
     12:8   she prayed the Lord God of Israel
     13:7   Give me strength this day, O Lord God of Israel !
     13:11   God, our God, is still with us, to show his power in Israel
     13:14   from the house of Israel
     14:4   and you and all who live within the borders of Israel
     14:5   who despised the house of Israel
     14:10   And when Achior saw all that the God of Israel had done
     14:10   and joined the house of Israel, remaining so to this day
     15:3   Then the men of Israel, every one that was a soldier
     15:4   and Choba and Kola, and to all the frontiers of Israel
     15:8   and the senate of the people of Israel
     15:8   which the Lord had done for Israel
     15:9   you are the great glory of Israel
     15:10   you have done great good to Israel
     15:12   Then all the women of Israel gathered to see her
     15:13   while all the men of Israel followed
     16:1   Then Judith began this thanksgiving before all Israel
     16:8   to exalt the oppressed in Israel
     16:24   and the house of Israel mourned for her 7 days
     16:25   among the people of Israel
Ad E   10:9   And my nation, this is Israel
     10:13   from generation to generation for ever among his people Israel
     13:9   if it is thy will to save Israel
     13:13   For I would have been willing to kiss the soles of his feet, to save Israel !
     13:18   And all Israel cried out mightily
     14:3   And she prayed to the Lord God of Israel, and said :
     14:5   that thou, O Lord, didst take Israel out of all the nations
Sir pr.   on account of which we should praise Israel
     17:17   but Israel is the Lord's own portion
     24:8   and in Israel receive your inheritance
     36:12   upon Israel, whom thou hast likened to a first-born son
     37:25   but the days of Israel are without number
     45:5   to teach Jacob the covenant, and Israel his judgments
     45:11   according to the number of the tribes of Israel
     45:17   and to enlighten Israel with his law
     45:23   and made atonement for Israel
     46:1   so that he might give Israel its inheritance
     46:10   so that all the sons of Israel might see
     47:2   so David was selected from the sons of Israel
     47:11   and a throne of glory in Israel
     47:18   who is called the God of Israel
     47:23   Also Jeroboam the son of Nebat, who caused Israel to sin
     50:13   before the whole congregation of Israel
     50:20   over the whole congregation of the sons of Israel
     50:23   and grant that peace may be in our days in Israel
Bar   2:1   and against our judges who judged Israel

     2:1   and against the men of Israel and Judah
     2:11   And now, O Lord God of Israel
     2:15   for Israel and his descendants are called by thy name
     2:26   because of the wickedness of the house of Israel
     2:28   to write thy law in the presence of the people of Israel
     2:35   and I will never again remove my people Israel
     3:1   O Lord Almighty, God of Israel
     3:4   O Lord Almighty, God of Israel
     3:4   hear now the prayer of the dead of Israel
     3:9   Hear the commandments of life, O Israel
     3:10   Why is it, O Israel
     3:24   O Israel, how great is the house of God !
     3:36   and to Israel whom he loved
     4:4   Happy are we, O Israel
     4:5   Take courage, my people, O memorial of Israel !
     5:7   so that Israel may walk safely in the glory of God
     5:8   The woods and every fragrant tree have shaded Israel at God's command
     5:9   For God will lead Israel with joy
P Az   12   and for the sake of Isaac thy servant and Israel thy holy one
     61   Bless the Lord, O Israel
Sus   13:48   Are you such fools, you sons of Israel ?
     13:48   Have you condemned a daughter of Israel
     13:57   with the daughters of Israel
1 Ma   1:11   In those days lawless men came forth from Israel
     1:20   He went up against Israel
     1:25   Israel mourned deeply in every community
     1:30   and destroyed many people of Israel
     1:36   an evil adversary of Israel continually
     1:43   Many even from Israel gladly adopted his religion
     1:53   they drove Israel into hiding
     1:58   They kept using violence against Israel
     1:62   But many in Israel stood firm
     1:64   And very great wrath came upon Israel
     2:16   Many from Israel came to them
     2:42   mighty warriors of Israel
     2:46   that they found within the borders of Israel
     2:55   became a judge in Israel
     2:70   And all Israel mourned for him with great lamentation
     3:2   they gladly fought for Israel
     3:8   thus he turned away wrath from Israel
     3:10   and a large force from Samaria to fight against Israel
     3:15   to take vengeance on the sons of Israel
     3:35   to wipe out and destroy the strength of Israel
     3:41   and went to the camp to get the sons of Israel for slaves
     3:46   because Israel formerly had a place of prayer in Mizpah
     4:11   that there is one who redeems and saves Israel
     4:25   Thus Israel had a great deliverance that day
     4:27   for things had not happened to Israel as he had intended
     4:30   Blessed art thou, O Saviour of Israel
     4:31   So do thou hem in this army by the hand of thy people Israel
     4:59   Then Judas and his brothers and all the assembly of Israel
     5:3   because they kept lying in wait for Israel
     5:60   as many as 2,000 of the people of Israel fell that day
     5:62   through whom deliverance was given to Israel
     5:63   in all Israel and among all the Gentiles
     6:18   Now the men in the citadel kept hemming Israel in
     7:5   all the lawless and ungodly men of Israel
     7:9   and he commanded him to take vengeance on the sons of Israel
     7:13   The Hasidaeans were the first among the sons of Israel
     7:22   and did great damage in Israel
     7:23   had done among the sons of Israel
     7:26   who hated and detested Israel
     8:18   was completely enslaving Israel
     9:20   And all Israel made great lamentation for him
     9:21   How is the mighty fallen, the saviour of Israel !
     9:23   the lawless emerged in all parts of Israel
     9:27   Thus there was great distress in Israel
     9:51   And he placed garrisons in them to harass Israel
     9:73   Thus the sword ceased from Israel
     9:73   and he destroyed the ungodly out of Israel
     10:46   which Demetrius had done in Israel
     10:61   A group of pestilent men from Israel
     11:23   and he chose some of the elders of Israel
     11:41   for they kept fighting against Israel
     12:52   and all Israel mourned deeply
     13:4   for the sake of Israel
     13:26   All Israel bewailed him with great lamentation
     13:41   In the 170th year the yoke of the Gentiles was removed from Israel
     13:51   because a great enemy had been crushed and removed from Israel
     14:11   and Israel rejoiced with great joy
     14:26   they have fought and repulsed Israel's enemies
     16:2   have fought the wars of Israel from our youth until this day
     16:2   so that we have delivered Israel many times
2 Ma   1:25   who dost rescue Israel from every evil
     1:26   accept this sacrifice on behalf of all thy people Israel
     9:5   But the all-seeing Lord, the God of Israel
     10:38   who shows great kindness to Israel

11 : 6   besought the Lord to send a good angel to save Israel
1 Es   1 : 3   And he told the Levites, the temple servants of Israel
1 : 4   and serve his people Israel
1 : 5   in accordance with the directions of David king of Israel
1 : 5   who minister before your brethren the people of Israel
1 : 19   And the people of Israel who were present at that time
1 : 20   No passover like it had been kept in Israel
1 : 21   none of the kings of Israel had kept such a passover
1 : 21   and the men of Judah and all of Israel
1 : 24   so that the words of the Lord rose up against Israel
1 : 32   throughout the whole nation of Israel
1 : 33   are recorded in the book of the kings of Israel and Judah
1 : 48   and transgressed the laws of the Lord, the God of Israel
2 : 3   The Lord of Israel, the Lord Most High
2 : 5   and build the house of the Lord of Israel
5 : 37   that they belonged to Israel :
5 : 41   All those of Israel, 12 or more years of age
5 : 46   and all Israel in their towns
5 : 47   and the sons of Israel were each in his own home
5 : 48   took their places and prepared the altar of the God of Israel
5 : 60   according to the directions of David king of Israel
5 : 61   because his goodness and his glory are for ever upon all Israel
5 : 67   were building the temple for the Lord God of Israel
5 : 70   and the heads of the fathers' houses in Israel said to them
5 : 71   for we alone will build it for the Lord of Israel
6 : 1   they prophesied to them in the name of the Lord God of Israel
6 : 14   by a king of Israel who was great and strong
6 : 15   But when our fathers sinned against the Lord of Israel
7 : 4   and they completed it by command of the Lord God of Israel
7 : 6   And the people of Israel, the priests, the Levites
7 : 8   and 12 he-goats for the sin of all Israel
7 : 8   of the tribes of Israel
7 : 9   for the services of the Lord God of Israel
7 : 10   The people of Israel who came from the captivity
7 : 13   And the people of Israel who came from the captivity ate it
7 : 15   for the service of the Lord God of Israel
8 : 3   which was given by the God of Israel
8 : 5   some of the people of Israel and some of the priests
8 : 7   but taught all Israel all the ordinances and judgments
8 : 13   and to carry to Jerusalem the gifts for the Lord of Israel
8 : 27   and I gathered men from Israel to go up with me
8 : 47   the son of Levi, son of Israel
8 : 55   and all Israel had given
8 : 59   and to the heads of the fathers' houses of Israel
8 : 65   offered sacrifices to the Lord, the God of Israel
8 : 65   12 bulls for all Israel, 96 rams, 72 lambs
8 : 69   The people of Israel
8 : 72   at the word of the Lord of Israel
8 : 89   O Lord of Israel, thou art true
8 : 92   one of the men of Israel, called out
8 : 92   but even now there is hope for Israel
8 : 96   and Levites of all Israel take oath
9 : 7   and so have increased the sin of Israel
9 : 26   Of Israel : of the sons of Parosh : Ramiah, Izziah
9 : 37   The priests and the Levites and the men of Israel
9 : 37   when the sons of Israel were in their settlements
9 : 39   which had been given by the Lord God of Israel
Ps 151 : 7   I beheaded him, and removed reproach from the people of Israel
3 Ma   2 : 6   on the audacious Pharaoh who had enslaved your holy people Israel
2 : 10   And because you love the house of Israel
2 : 16   upon your people Israel
6 : 4   manifesting the light of your mercy upon the nation of Israel
6 : 9   reveal yourself quickly to those of the nation of Israel
7 : 16   to the one God of their fathers, the eternal Saviour of Israel
7 : 23   Blessed be the Deliverer of Israel through all times ! Amen
2 Es   2 : 10   which I was going to give to Israel
2 : 11   which I had prepared for Israel
2 : 33   to go to Israel
3 : 19   and thy commandment to the posterity of Israel
3 : 32   Or has another nation known thee besides Israel ?
4 : 23   why Israel has been given over to the Gentiles as a reproach
5 : 17   Or do you not know that Israel has been entrusted to you
5 : 33   Are you greatly disturbed in mind over Israel ?
5 : 35   and the exhaustion of the people of Israel ?
7 : 10   And he said to me, So also is Israel's portion
7 : 107   and Joshua after him for Israel in the days of Achan
8 : 16   and about Israel, for whom I am sad
9 : 30   and thou didst say, Hear me, O Israel
12 : 46   Take courage, O Israel
14 : 28   Hear these words, O Israel
4 Ma 17 : 22   divine Providence preserved Israel

ISRAELITE
15 = 0.010 %
Jud   4 : 8   So the Israelites did as Joakim the high priest
5 : 23   For, they said, we will not be afraid of the Israelites
7 : 1   and make war on the Israelites
7 : 4   When the Israelites saw their vast number
7 : 6   in full view of the Israelites in Bethulia
7 : 10   For these people, the Israelites

7 : 17   and the springs of the Israelites
10 : 19   and admired the Israelites, judging them by her
15 : 5   And when the Israelites heard it
15 : 7   And the Israelites, when they returned from the slaughter
1 Ma   5 : 9   against the Israelites who lived in their territory
5 : 45   Then Judas gathered together all the Israelites in Gilead
6 : 21   and some of the ungodly Israelites joined them
4 Ma 18 : 1   O Israelite children, offspring of the seed of Abraham
18 : 5   Since in no way whatever was he able to compel the Israelites

ISSUE, subst.
2
2 Ma   4 : 28   on account of this issue
14 : 18   shrank from deciding the issue by bloodshed

ISSUE, verb
7 = 0.005 %
Sir 27 : 28   Mockery and abuse issue from the proud man
1 Ma   5 : 58   And they issued orders
2 Ma   6 : 8   a decree was issued to the neighbouring Greek cities
1 Es   2 : 28   Therefore I have now issued orders
3 Ma   1 : 2   that had been previously issued to him
2 Es 13 : 4   and whenever his voice issued from his mouth
4 Ma   4 : 23   and after he had plundered them he issued a decree

ISTALCURUS
1
1 Es   8 : 40   Of the sons of Bigvai, Uthai the son of Istalcurus

IT
1012 = 0.659 %

ITHAMAR
1
1 Es   8 : 29   Of the sons of Ithamar, Gamael

ITS
185 = 0.121 %

ITSELF
20 = 0.013 %

IVY
1
2 Ma   6 : 7   in honour of Dionysus, wearing wreaths of ivy

IVY-LEAF
1
3 Ma   2 : 29   with the ivy-leaf symbol of Dionysus

IVY-WREATHED
1
2 Ma 10 : 7   Therefore bearing ivy-wreathed wands and beautiful branches

IZZIAH
1
1 Es   9 : 26   Of Israel : of the sons of Parosh : Ramiah, Izziah

J

JAALAH
1
1 Es   5 : 33   the sons of Peruda, the sons of Jaalah

JACOB
43 = 0.028 %
Tob   4 : 12   that Noah, Abraham, Isaac, and Jacob, our fathers of old
Jud   8 : 26   and what happened to Jacob in Mesopotamia in Syria
Sir 23 : 12   may it never be found in the inheritance of Jacob !
24 : 8   And he said, Make your dwelling in Jacob
24 : 23   as an inheritance of the congregations of Jacob
36 : 11   Gather all the tribes of Jacob
44 : 23   he made to rest upon the head of Jacob
45 : 5   to teach Jacob the covenant, and Israel his judgments
45 : 17   to teach Jacob the testimonies
46 : 14   and the Lord watched over Jacob
47 : 22   so he gave a remnant to Jacob
48 : 10   and to restore the tribes of Jacob
49 : 10   for they comforted the people of Jacob
Bar   2 : 34   to Abraham and to Isaac and to Jacob
3 : 36   and gave her to Jacob his servant
4 : 2   Turn, O Jacob, and take her
1 Ma   1 : 28   and all the house of Jacob was clothed with shame
3 : 7   He embittered many kings, but he made Jacob glad by his deeds
3 : 45   Joy was taken from Jacob
5 : 2   and they determined to destroy the descendants of Jacob who lived among them
2 Ma   1 : 2   and Isaac and Jacob, his faithful servants
P Ma   1   of Abraham and Isaac and Jacob
8   for Abraham and Isaac and Jacob
3 Ma   6 : 3   upon the children of the sainted Jacob
6 : 13   who have power to save the nation of Jacob
2 Es   1 : 24   What shall I do to you, O Jacob ?
1 : 39   and Jacob and Hosea and Amos and Micah
3 : 15   and to Isaac thou gavest Jacob and Esau
3 : 16   And thou didst set apart Jacob for thyself
3 : 16   and Jacob became a great multitude
3 : 19   to give the law to the descendants of Jacob
3 : 32   as these tribes of Jacob ?
5 : 35   that I might not see the travail of Jacob
6 : 8   because from him were born Jacob and Esau

<table>
<tr><td>6:8</td><td>for Jacob's hand held Esau's heel from the beginning</td></tr>
<tr><td>6:9</td><td>and Jacob is the beginning of the age that follows</td></tr>
<tr><td>8:16</td><td>and about the seed of Jacob, for whom I am troubled</td></tr>
<tr><td>9:30</td><td>and give heed to my words, O descendants of Jacob</td></tr>
<tr><td>12:46</td><td>and do not be sorrowful, O house of Jacob</td></tr>
<tr><td>4 Ma 2:19</td><td>Why else did Jacob, our most wise father</td></tr>
<tr><td>7:19</td><td>like our patriarchs Abraham and Isaac and Jacob</td></tr>
<tr><td>13:17</td><td>For if we so die, Abraham and Isaac and Jacob will welcome us</td></tr>
<tr><td>16:25</td><td>as do Abraham and Isaac and Jacob and all the patriarchs</td></tr>
</table>

JADDUS 1
1 Es 5:38 the sons of Hakkoz, the sons of Jaddus who had married Agia

JAHAZIEL 1
1 Es 8:32 Of the sons of Zattu, Shecaniah the son of Jahaziel

JAHZEIAH 1
1 Es 9:14 and Jahzeiah the son of Tikvah

JAIR 1
Ad E 11:2 Mordecai the son of Jair

JAMBRI 2
1 Ma 9:36 But the sons of Jambri from Medeba came out
9:37 The sons of Jambri are celebrating a great wedding

JAMIN 1
1 Es 9:48 Jeshua and Anniuth and Sherebiah, Jamin, Akkub

JAMNIA 8 = 0.005 %
Jud 2:28 and all who lived in Jamnia
1 Ma 4:15 and to the plains of Idumea, and to Azotus and Jamnia
5:58 and they marched against Jamnia
10:69 and he assembled a large force and encamped against Jamnia
15:40 So Cendebaeus came to Jamnia
2 Ma 12:8 But learning that the men in Jamnia
12:9 he attacked the people of Jamnia by night
12:40 they found sacred tokens of the idols of Jamnia

JAPHETH 1
Jud 2:25 and came to the southern borders of Japheth

JAR 1
Sir 21:14 The mind of a fool is like a broken jar

JARIB 2
1 Es 8:44 Elnathan, Shemaiah, Jarib, Nathan, Elnathan
9:19 Maaseiah, Eliezar, Jarib and Jodan

JASHUB 1
1 Es 9:30 Jashub, and Sheal and Jeremoth

JASON 18 = 0.012 %
1 Ma 8:17 and Jason the son of Eleazar
12:16 and Antipater the son of Jason
14:22 Numenius the son of Antiochus and Antipater the son of Jason, envoys of the Jews
2 Ma 1:7 after Jason and his company revolted from the holy land and the kingdom
2:23 all this, which has been set forth by Jason of Cyrene in 5 volumes
4:7 Jason the brother of Onias
4:10 When the king assented and Jason came to office
4:13 because of the surpassing wickedness of Jason
4:19 the vile Jason sent envoys
4:22 He was welcomed magnificently by Jason and the city
4:23 After a period of 3 years Jason sent Menelaus
4:24 outbidding Jason by 300 talents of silver
4:26 So Jason, who after supplanting his own brother
5:5 Jason took no less than a 1,000 men
5:6 But Jason kept relentlessly slaughtering his fellow citizens
4 Ma 4:16 and appointed Onias's brother Jason as high priest
4:17 Jason agreed that if the office were conferred upon him
4:19 Jason changed the nation's way of life

JATHAN 1
Tob 5:13 For I used to know Ananias and Jathan

JAZER 1
1 Ma 5:8 He also took Jazer and its villages

JEALOUS 3 = 0.002 %
Wis 1:10 because a jealous ear hears all things
Sir 9:1 Do not be jealous of the wife of your bosom
37:10 hide your counsel from those who are jealous of you

JEALOUSY 2
Sir 30:24 Jealousy and anger shorten life
1 Ma 8:16 and there is no envy or jealousy among them

2

JEBUSITE
Jud 5:16 and the Perizzites and the Jebusites
1 Es 8:69 the Jebusites, the Moabites, the Egyptians, and the Edomites

JECONIAH 5 = 0.003 %
Ad E 11:4 had brought from Jerusalem with Jeconiah king of Judea
Bar 1:3 in the hearing of Jeconiah the son of Jehoiakim, king of Judah
1:9 Jeconiah and the princes and the prisoners
1 Es 1:9 And Jeconiah and Shemaiah and Nethanel his brother
1:34 And the men of the nation took Jeconiah the son of Josiah

JEDAIAH 1
1 Es 5:24 The priests: the sons of Jedaiah the son of Jeshua

JEHIEL 5 = 0.003 %
1 Es 1:8 And Hilkiah, Zechariah, and Jehiel
8:35 Of the sons of Joab, Obadiah the son of Jehiel
8:92 Then Shecaniah the son of Jehiel
9:21 and Shemaiah and Jehiel and Azariah
9:27 Jehiel and Abdi, and Jeremoth and Elijah

JEHOHANAN 2
1 Es 9:1 to the chamber of Jehohanan the son of Eliashib
9:29 Jehohanan and Hananiah and Zabbai and Emathis

JEHOIAKIM 7 = 0.005 %
Bar 1:3 in the hearing of Jeconiah the son of Jehoiakim, king of Judah
1:7 and they sent it to Jerusalem to Jehoiakim the high priest
1 Es 1:37 And the king of Egypt made Jehoiakim his brother
1:38 Jehoiakim put the nobles in prison
1:39 Jehoiakim was 25 years old
1:42 But the things that are reported about Jehoiakim
1:43 Jehoiakim his son became king in his stead

JEPHUNNEH 1
Sir 46:7 he and Caleb the son of Jephunneh:

JEREMAI 1
1 Es 9:34 Of the sons of Bani: Jeremai, Maadai, Amram, Joel

JEREMIAH 13 = 0.008 %
Sir 49:6 according to the word of Jeremiah
L Jr 6:1 A copy of a letter which Jeremiah sent
2 Ma 2:1 One finds in the records that Jeremiah the prophet
2:5 And Jeremiah came and found a cave
2:7 When Jeremiah learned of it, he rebuked them and declared:
15:14 Jeremiah, the prophet of God
15:15 Jeremiah stretched out his right hand
1 Es 1:28 and did not heed the words of Jeremiah the prophet
1:32 Jeremiah the prophet lamented for Josiah
1:47 that were spoken by Jeremiah the prophet from the mouth of the Lord
1:57 in fulfilment of the word of the Lord by the mouth of Jeremiah:
2:1 that the word of the Lord by the mouth of Jeremiah
2 Es 2:18 I will send you help, my servants Isaiah and Jeremiah

JEREMIEL 1
2 Es 4:36 And Jeremiel the archangel answered them and said

JEREMOTH 3 = 0.002 %
1 Es 9:27 Jehiel and Abdi, and Jeremoth and Elijah
9:28 Othoniah Jeremoth, and Zabad and Zerdaiah
9:30 Jashub, and Sheal and Jeremoth

JERICHO 7 = 0.005 %
Jud 4:4 and to Kona and Beth-horon and Belmain and Jericho
Sir 24:14 and like rose plants in Jericho
1 Ma 9:50 the fortress in Jericho, and Emmaus, and Beth-horon
16:11 over the plain of Jericho
16:14 and he went down to Jericho with Mattathias and Judas his sons
2 Ma 12:15 overthrew Jericho in the days of Joshua
1 Es 5:22 The sons of Jericho, 345

JEROBOAM 1
Sir 47:23 Also Jeroboam the son of Nebat, who caused Israel to sin

JERUSALEM 208 = 0.135 %
Tob 1:4 deserted the house of Jerusalem
1:6 But I alone went often to Jerusalem for the feasts
1:7 who ministered at Jerusalem
1:7 each year at Jerusalem
5:13 when we went together to Jerusalem
13:8 Let all men speak, and give him thanks in Jerusalem
13:9 O Jerusalem, the holy city
13:16 For Jerusalem will be built with sapphires and emeralds
13:17 The streets of Jerusalem will be paved with beryl
14:4 and Jerusalem will be desolate
14:5 and will rebuild Jerusalem in splendour
Jud 1:9 and beyond the Jordan as far as Jerusalem and Bethany
4:2 and were alarmed both for Jerusalem

	4:6	who was in Jerusalem at that time
	4:8	in session at Jerusalem
	4:11	living at Jerusalem
	4:13	and in Jerusalem before the sanctuary of the Lord Almighty
	5:19	and have occupied Jerusalem, where their sanctuary is
	9:1	in the house of God in Jerusalem
	10:8	and Jerusalem may be exalted
	11:13	who minister in the presence of our God at Jerusalem
	11:14	They have sent men to Jerusalem
	11:19	till you come to Jerusalem
	13:4	for the exaltation of Jerusalem
	15:5	Those in Jerusalem and all the hill country also came
	15:8	who lived at Jerusalem
	15:9	and said to her, You are the exaltation of Jerusalem
	16:18	When they arrived at Jerusalem they worshipped God
	16:20	So the people continued feasting in Jerusalem
Ad E	11:1	one of the residents of Jerusalem
	11:4	had brought from Jerusalem with Jeconiah king of Judea
Sir	24:11	and in Jerusalem was my dominion
	36:13	Jerusalem, the place of thy rest
	50:27	Jesus the son of Sirach, son of Eleazar, of Jerusalem
Bar	1:2	at the time when the Chaldeans took Jerusalem
	1:7	and they sent it to Jerusalem to Jehoiakim the high priest
	1:7	and to all the people who were present with him in Jerusalem
	1:9	after Nebuchadnezzar king of Babylon had carried away from Jerusalem
	1:15	to the men of Judah, to the inhabitants of Jerusalem
	2:2	the like of what he has done in Jerusalem
	2:23	and from the region about Jerusalem
	4:8	and you grieved Jerusalem, who reared you
	4:30	Take courage, O Jerusalem
	4:36	Look toward the east, O Jerusalem
	5:1	Take off the garment of your sorrow and affliction, O Jerusalem
	5:5	Arise, O Jerusalem, stand upon the height
P Az	5	in all that thou hast brought upon us and upon Jerusalem
1 Ma	1:14	So they built a gymnasium in Jerusalem
	1:20	and came to Jerusalem with a strong force
	1:29	and he came to Jerusalem with a large force
	1:35	and collecting the spoils of Jerusalem
	1:38	Because of them the residents of Jerusalem fled
	1:44	And the king sent letters by messengers to Jerusalem
	2:1	moved from Jerusalem and settled in Modein
	2:6	He saw the blasphemies being committed in Judah and Jerusalem
	2:18	and those that are left in Jerusalem have done
	2:31	and to troops in Jerusalem the city of David
	3:34	As for the residents of Judea and Jerusalem
	3:35	and the remnant of Jerusalem
	3:45	Jerusalem was uninhabited like a wilderness
	3:46	So they assembled and went to Mizpah, opposite Jerusalem
	6:7	which he had erected upon the altar in Jerusalem
	6:12	But now I remember the evils I did in Jerusalem
	6:26	against the citadel in Jerusalem to take it
	6:48	went up to Jerusalem against them
	7:17	round about Jerusalem
	7:19	Then Bacchides departed from Jerusalem
	7:27	So Nicanor came to Jerusalem with a large force
	7:39	Now Nicanor went out from Jerusalem
	7:47	and brought them and displayed them just outside Jerusalem
	8:22	and sent to Jerusalem to remain with them there
	9:3	they encamped against Jerusalem
	9:50	Bacchides then returned to Jerusalem
	9:53	in the citadel at Jerusalem
	10:7	Then Jonathan came to Jerusalem
	10:10	And Jonathan dwelt in Jerusalem
	10:31	And let Jerusalem and her environs
	10:32	I release also my control of the citadel in Jerusalem
	10:39	I have given as a gift to the sanctuary in Jerusalem
	10:43	And whoever takes refuge at the temple in Jerusalem
	10:45	And let the cost of rebuilding the walls of Jerusalem
	10:66	And Jonathan returned to Jerusalem in peace and gladness
	10:74	He chose 10,000 men and set out from Jerusalem
	10:87	And Jonathan and those with him returned to Jerusalem
	11:7	then he returned to Jerusalem
	11:20	to attack the citadel in Jerusalem
	11:34	To all those who offer sacrifice in Jerusalem
	11:41	that he remove the troops of the citadel from Jerusalem
	11:51	and they returned to Jerusalem with much spoil
	11:62	and sent them to Jerusalem
	11:74	And Jonathan returned to Jerusalem
	12:25	So he marched away from Jerusalem
	12:36	to build the walls of Jerusalem still higher
	13:2	So he went up to Jerusalem
	13:10	and hastened to complete the walls of Jerusalem
	13:39	and whatever other tax has been collected in Jerusalem
	13:49	The men in the citadel at Jerusalem
	14:19	And these were read before the assembly in Jerusalem
	14:36	as were also the men in the city of David in Jerusalem
	14:37	and built the walls of Jerusalem higher
	15:7	and I grant freedom to Jerusalem and the sanctuary
	15:28	and the citadel in Jerusalem
	15:32	So Athenobius the friend of the king came to Jerusalem
	16:20	and he sent other men to take possession of Jerusalem
2 Ma	1:1	The Jewish brethren in Jerusalem
	1:10	Those in Jerusalem and those in Judea
	3:6	that the treasury in Jerusalem was full of untold money
	3:9	When he had arrived in Jerusalem
	3:37	to send on another mission to Jerusalem
	4:9	and to enrol the men of Jerusalem as citizens of Antioch
	4:19	chosen as being Antiochian citizens from Jerusalem
	4:21	Therefore upon arriving at Joppa he proceeded to Jerusalem
	5:22	And he left governors to afflict the people : at Jerusalem
	5:25	When this man arrived in Jerusalem
	6:2	and also to pollute the temple in Jerusalem
	8:31	and carried the rest of the spoils to Jerusalem
	8:36	by the capture of the people of Jerusalem
	9:4	I will make Jerusalem a cemetery of Jews
	10:15	they received those who were banished from Jerusalem
	11:5	about 5 leagues from Jerusalem
	11:8	And there, while they were still near Jerusalem
	12:9	so that the glow of the light was seen in Jerusalem, 30 miles distant
	12:29	which is 75 miles from Jerusalem
	12:31	Then they went up to Jerusalem
	12:43	and sent it to Jerusalem to provide for a sin offering
	14:23	Nicanor stayed on in Jerusalem
	14:37	A certain Razis, one of the elders of Jerusalem
	15:30	and carry them to Jerusalem
1 Es	1:1	Josiah kept the passover to his Lord in Jerusalem
	1:21	who were dwelling in Jerusalem
	1:31	and after he was brought back to Jerusalem he died
	1:35	And he reigned 3 months in Judah and Jerusalem
	1:35	Then the king of Egypt deposed him from reigning in Jerusalem
	1:37	king of Judea and Jerusalem
	1:39	when he began to reign in Judea and Jerusalem
	1:44	and he reigned 3 months and 10 days in Jerusalem
	1:46	and made Zedekiah king of Judea and Jerusalem
	1:49	which had been hallowed in Jerusalem
	1:55	and broke down the walls of Jerusalem
	2:4	and he has commanded me to build him a house at Jerusalem
	2:5	may his Lord be with him, and let him go up to Jerusalem
	2:5	he is the Lord who dwells in Jerusalem
	2:7	for the temple of the Lord which is in Jerusalem
	2:8	to build the house in Jerusalem for the Lord
	2:10	which Nebuchadnezzar had carried away from Jerusalem
	2:15	with the returning exiles from Babylon to Jerusalem
	2:16	against those who were living in Judea and Jerusalem :
	2:18	have gone to Jerusalem
	2:27	and that mighty and cruel kings ruled in Jerusalem
	2:30	went in haste to Jerusalem
	2:30	And the building of the temple in Jerusalem ceased
	4:43	Remember the vow which you made to build Jerusalem
	4:44	and to send back all the vessels that were taken from Jerusalem
	4:47	and all who were going up with him to build Jerusalem
	4:48	to bring cedar timber from Lebanon to Jerusalem
	4:55	until the day when the temple should be finished and Jerusalem built
	4:57	and to be sent to Jerusalem
	4:58	he lifted up his face to heaven toward Jerusalem
	4:63	to go up and build Jerusalem and the temple
	5:2	to take them back to Jerusalem in safety
	5:8	and who returned to Jerusalem and the rest of Judea
	5:44	when they came to the temple of God which is in Jerusalem
	5:46	and some of the people settled in Jerusalem and its vicinity
	5:56	In the 2nd year after their coming to the temple of God in Jerusalem
	5:56	and all who had come to Jerusalem from the captivity
	5:57	in the 2nd year after they came to Judea and Jerusalem
	6:1	prophesied to the Jews who were in Judea and Jerusalem
	6:2	and began to build the house of the Lord which is in Jerusalem
	6:8	and entered the city of Jerusalem
	6:9	building in the city of Jerusalem a great new house for the Lord
	6:18	which Nebuchadnezzar had taken out of the house in Jerusalem
	6:19	and put them in the temple at Jerusalem
	6:20	which is in Jerusalem
	6:22	of the house of the Lord in Jerusalem
	6:24	of the house of the Lord in Jerusalem
	6:26	which Nebuchadnezzar took out of the house in Jerusalem
	6:26	should be restored to the house in Jerusalem
	6:30	for daily use as the priests in Jerusalem may indicate
	6:33	to hinder or damage that house of the Lord in Jerusalem
	8:5	There came up with him to Jerusalem
	8:6	and arrived in Jerusalem
	8:10	may go with you to Jerusalem
	8:12	in order to look into matters in Judea and Jerusalem
	8:13	and to carry to Jerusalem the gifts for the Lord of Israel
	8:13	and to collect for the Lord in Jerusalem
	8:14	for the temple of their Lord which is in Jerusalem
	8:15	which is in Jerusalem
	8:17	which is in Jerusalem

	8:25	to glorify his house which is in Jerusalem
	8:59	in Jerusalem, in the chambers of the house of our Lord
	8:60	and the vessels which had been in Jerusalem
	8:61	and we arrived in Jerusalem
	8:61	and so we came to Jerusalem
	8:81	to give us a stronghold in Judea and Jerusalem
	8:91	there gathered about him a very great throng from Jerusalem
	9:3	And a proclamation was made throughout Judea and Jerusalem
	9:3	that they should assemble at Jerusalem
	9:5	assembled at Jerusalem within 3 days
	9:37	settled in Jerusalem and in the country
3 Ma	1:9	After he had arrived in Jerusalem
	3:16	we came on to Jerusalem also
2 Es	2:10	Tell my people that I will give them the kingdom of Jerusalem
	10:20	and be consoled because of the sorrow of Jerusalem
	10:47	that was the period of residence in Jerusalem
	10:48	that was the destruction which befell Jerusalem
4 Ma	4:3	to report that in the Jerusalem treasuries
	4:22	and that the people of Jerusalem had rejoiced greatly
	18:5	he left Jerusalem and marched against the Persians

JESHAIAH 2

1 Es	8:33	Of the sons of Elam, Jeshaiah the son of Gotholiah
	8:48	also Hashabiah and Annunus and Jeshaiah his brother

JESHUA 16 = 0.010 %

Sir	49:12	and so was Jeshua the son of Jozadak
1 Es	5:5	Jeshua the son of Jozadak, son of Seraiah
	5:8	They came with Zerubbabel and Jeshua
	5:11	The sons of Pahath-moab, of the sons of Jeshua and Joab, 2,812
	5:24	The priests : the sons of Jedaiah the son of Jeshua
	5:26	The Levites : the sons of Jeshua and Kadmiel
	5:48	Then Jeshua the son of Jozadak, with his fellow priests
	5:56	and Jeshua the son of Jozadak made a beginning
	5:58	And Jeshua arose, and his sons and brethren
	5:58	and Kadmiel his brother and the sons of Jeshua Emadabun
	5:68	So they approached Zerubbabel and Jeshua
	5:70	But Zerubbabel and Jeshua
	6:2	and Jeshua the son of Jozadak arose
	8:63	and with them were Jozabad the son of Jeshua
	9:19	of the sons of Jeshua the son of Jozadak and his brethren
	9:48	Jeshua and Anniuth and Sherebiah, Jamin, Akkub

JESSE 1

Sir	45:25	the son of Jesse, of the tribe of Judah :

JEST 1

Sir	8:4	Do not jest with an ill-bred person

JESUS 2

Sir pr.		my grandfather Jesus, after devoting himself
	50:27	Jesus the son of Sirach, son of Eleazar, of Jerusalem

JEUEL 1

1 Es	8:39	their names being Eliphelet, Jeuel, and Shemaiah

JEW 157 = 0.102 %

Ad E	10:8	the name of the Jews
	11:3	He was a Jew, dwelling in the city of Susa
	16:15	But we find that the Jews
	16:19	and permit the Jews to live under their own laws
Sus	13:4	and the Jews used to come to him because he was the most honoured of them all
Bel	14:28	saying, The king has become a Jew
1 Ma	2:23	a Jew came forward in the sight of all
	4:2	to fall upon the camp of the Jews and attack them suddenly
	4:20	and that the Jews were burning the camp
	5:23	Then he took the Jews of Galilee and Arbatta
	5:30	and attacking the Jews within
	6:6	but had turned and fled before the Jews
	6:6	that the Jews had grown strong from the arms, supplies
	6:31	but the Jews sallied out and burned these with fire, and fought manfully
	6:47	And when the Jews saw the royal might
	6:52	The Jews also made engines of war to match theirs
	6:60	and he sent to the Jews an offer of peace
	6:61	On these conditions the Jews evacuated the stronghold
	7:45	The Jews pursued them a day's journey
	7:47	Then the Jews seized the spoils and the plunder
	8:20	and the people of the Jews
	8:23	and with the nation of the Jews at sea and on land for ever
	8:25	the nation of the Jews
	8:27	if war comes first to the nation of the Jews
	8:31	upon our friends and allies the Jews ?
	10:23	in forming a friendship with the Jews to strengthen himself
	10:25	King Demetrius to the nation of the Jews, greeting
	10:29	And now I free you and exempt all the Jews
	10:33	And every one of the Jews taken as a captive
	10:34	for all the Jews who are in my kingdom
	10:36	Let Jews be enrolled in the king's forces

	11:30	and to the nation of the Jews, greeting
	11:33	To the nation of the Jews
	11:47	So the king called the Jews to his aid
	11:49	that the Jews had gained control of the city as they pleased
	11:50	and make the Jews stop fighting against us and our city
	11:51	So the Jews gained glory in the eyes of the king
	12:21	concerning the Spartans and the Jews
	12:26	to fall upon the Jews by night
	13:36	and to the elders and nation of the Jews, greeting
	13:42	and commander and leader of the Jews
	13:51	the Jews entered it with praise and palm branches
	14:22	Numenius the son of Antiochus and Antipater the son of Jason, envoys of the Jews
	14:33	and he placed there a garrison of Jews
	14:34	He settled Jews there, and provided in those cities
	14:37	He settled Jews in it, and fortified it
	14:40	For he had heard that the Jews were addressed by the Romans
	14:41	And the Jews and their priests decided
	14:47	to be commander and ethnarch of the Jews and priests
	15:1	to Simon, the priest and ethnarch of the Jews
	15:2	and to the nation of the Jews, greeting
	15:17	The envoys of the Jews have come to us
	15:17	and by the people of the Jews
2 Ma	1:7	we Jews wrote to you, in the critical distress
	1:10	and to the Jews in Egypt, greeting, and good health
	3:32	that some foul play had been perpetrated by the Jews
	4:11	He set aside the existing royal concessions to the Jews
	4:35	For this reason not only Jews
	4:36	the Jews in the city appealed to him
	4:41	But when the Jews became aware of Lysimachus' attack
	5:25	then, finding the Jews not at work
	6:1	to compel the Jews to forsake the laws of their fathers
	6:6	nor so much as confess himself to be a Jew
	6:7	the Jews were taken, under bitter constraint
	6:8	that they should adopt the same policy toward the Jews
	8:10	by selling the captured Jews into slavery
	8:32	and one who had greatly troubled the Jews
	8:34	who had brought the 1,000 merchants to buy the Jews
	8:36	proclaimed that the Jews had a Defender
	8:36	and that therefore the Jews were invulnerable
	9:4	he conceived the idea of turning upon the Jews
	9:4	I will make Jerusalem a cemetery of Jews
	9:7	breathing fire in his rage against the Jews
	9:15	and the Jews, whom he had not considered worth burying
	9:17	and in addition to all this he also would become a Jew
	9:18	and wrote to the Jews the following letter
	10:8	that the whole nation of the Jews
	10:12	took the lead in showing justice to the Jews
	10:14	and at every turn kept on warring against the Jews
	10:15	were harassing the Jews
	10:24	Now Timothy, who had been defeated by the Jews before
	10:29	and they were leading the Jews
	11:2	and came against the Jews
	11:15	For the king granted every request in behalf of the Jews
	11:16	The letter written to the Jews by Lysias was to this effect :
	11:16	Lysias to the people of the Jews, greeting
	11:24	We have heard that the Jews do not consent
	11:27	King Antiochus to the senate of the Jews
	11:27	and to the other Jews, greeting
	11:31	and full permission for the Jews
	11:34	to the people of the Jews, greeting
	12:1	and the Jews went about their farming
	12:3	as this : they invited the Jews who lived among them
	12:3	as though there were no ill will to the Jews
	12:8	meant in the same way to wipe out the Jews
	12:17	they came to Charax, to the Jews who are called Toubiani
	12:28	But the Jews called upon the Sovereign
	12:30	But when the Jews who dwelt there
	12:34	it happened that a few of the Jews fell
	12:40	which the law forbids the Jews to wear
	13:9	was coming to show to the Jews things far worse
	13:18	The king, having had a taste of the daring of the Jews
	13:19	a strong fortress of the Jews
	13:21	But Rhodocus, a man from the ranks of the Jews
	13:23	he was dismayed, called in the Jews
	14:5	and intentions of the Jews
	14:6	Those of the Jews who are called Hasidaeans
	14:14	thinking that the misfortunes and calamities of the Jews
	14:15	When the Jews heard of Nicanor's coming
	14:37	and for his good will was called father of the Jews
	14:39	which he had for the Jews
	15:2	And when the Jews who were compelled to follow him said
	15:12	for the whole body of the Jews
1 Es	2:18	that the Jews who came up from you to us
	2:23	and that the Jews were rebels
	4:49	And he wrote for all the Jews who were going up
	4:50	that the Idumeans should give up the villages of the Jews which they held
	6:1	prophesied to the Jews who were in Judea and Jerusalem
	6:5	Yet the elders of the Jews were dealt with kindly

	6:8	we found the elders of the Jews
	6:27	and the elders of the Jews
	7:2	assisting the elders of the Jews
3 Ma	1:3	a Jew by birth who later changed his religion
	1:8	Since the Jews had sent some of their council and elders
	2:28	and all Jews shall be subjected
	3:1	against those Jews who lived in Alexandria
	3:3	The Jews, however, continued to maintain good will
	3:27	But whoever shelters any of the Jews
	3:29	Every place detected sheltering a Jew
	4:2	But among the Jews
	4:12	the king, hearing that the Jews'compatriots from the city
	4:17	that they were no longer able to take the census of the Jews
	4:21	of him who was aiding the Jews from heaven
	5:2	so that the Jews might meet their doom
	5:3	who were especially hostile toward the Jews
	5:5	The servants in charge of the Jews went out in the evening
	5:6	that the Jews were left without any aid
	5:13	Then the Jews, since they had escaped the appointed hour
	5:18	why the Jews had been allowed to remain alive
	5:20	said that the Jews were benefited by today's sleep
	5:20	for the destruction of the lawless Jews !
	5:25	But the Jews, at their last gasp
	5:31	for the savage beasts instead of the Jews
	5:35	Then the Jews, upon hearing what the king had said
	5:38	for the destruction of the Jews tomorrow !
	5:42	which had come about within him for the protection of the Jews
	5:48	And when the Jews saw the dust raised by the elephants going out
	6:17	And when the Jews observed this
	6:18	visible to all but the Jews
	6:29	and the Jews, immediately released
	6:30	and ordered him to provide to the Jews
	6:34	that the Jews would be destroyed and become food for birds
	6:35	But the Jews, when they had arranged the aforementioned choral group
	7:3	persuaded us to gather together the Jews of the kingdom in a body
	7:6	that the God of heaven surely defends the Jews
	7:10	the Jews did not immediately hurry to make their departure
4 Ma	5:7	when you observe the religion of the Jews

JEWELLER, JEWELER 1
Sir 45:11 in a setting of gold, the work of a jeweller

JEWISH 15 = 0.010 %
1 Ma	8:29	with the Jewish people
	12:3	Jonathan the high priest and the Jewish nation have sent us
	12:6	the priests, and the rest of the Jewish people
	14:20	and the rest of the Jewish people, our brethren, greeting
2 Ma	1:1	The Jewish brethren in Jerusalem
	1:1	To their Jewish brethren in Egypt, greeting, and good peace
	5:23	In his malice toward the Jewish citizens
	8:1	and enlisted those who had continued in the Jewish faith
	8:11	inviting them to buy Jewish slaves
	9:19	To his worthy Jewish citizens
1 Es	8:10	I have given orders that those of the Jewish nation
3 Ma	2:27	upon the Jewish community
	2:33	considering them to be enemies of the Jewish nation
	3:2	a hostile rumour was circulated against the Jewish nation
	7:10	those of the Jewish nation who had wilfully transgressed

JOAB 2
1 Es 5:11 The sons of Pahath-moab, of the sons of Jeshua and Joab, 2,812
8:35 Of the sons of Joab, Obadiah the son of Jehiel

JOAKIM 11 = 0.007 %
Jud	4:6	And Joakim, the high priest
	4:8	So the Israelites did as Joakim the high priest
	4:14	And Joakim the high priest and all the priests
	15:8	Then Joakim the high priest
Sus	13:1	There was a man living in Babylon whose name was Joakim
	13:4	Joakim was very rich
	13:6	These men were frequently at Joakim's house
	13:28	The next day, when the people gathered at the house of her husband Joakim
	13:29	who is the wife of Joakim
	13:63	and so did Joakim her husband and all her kindred
1 Es	5:5	and Joakim the son of Zerubbabel

JOARIB 2
1 Ma 2:1 a priest of the sons of Joarib
14:29 a priest of the sons of Joarib, and his brothers

JODA 1
1 Es 5:58 and the sons of Joda son of Iliadun

JODAN 1
1 Es 9:19 Maaseiah, Eliezar, Jarib and Jodan

JOEL 3 = 0.002 %
1 Es 9:34 Of the sons of Bani : Jeremai, Maadai, Amram, Joel
9:35 Mattithiah, Zabad, Iddo, Joel, Benaiah
2 Es 1:39 and Joel and Obadiah and Jonah

JOHANAN 1
1 Es 8:38 Of the sons of Azgad, Johanan the son of Hakkatan

JOHN 17 = 0.011 %
1 Ma	2:1	In those days Mattathias the son of John, son of Simeon
	2:2	He had 5 sons, John surnamed Gaddi
	8:17	So Judas chose Eupolemus the son of John, son of Accos
	9:36	and seized John and all that he had, and departed with it
	9:38	And they remembered the blood of John their brother
	13:53	And Simon saw that John his son had reached manhood
	16:1	John went up from Gazara
	16:2	And Simon called in his 2 elder sons Judas and John
	16:4	So John chose out of the country 20,000 warriors and horsemen
	16:9	At that time Judas the brother of John was wounded
	16:9	but John pursued them
	16:10	and John burned it with fire, and about 2,000 of them fell
	16:19	He sent other men to Gazara to do away with John
	16:21	But some one ran ahead and reported to John at Gazara
	16:23	The rest of the acts of John and his wars
2 Ma	4:11	secured through John the father of Eupolemus
	11:17	John and Absalom, who were sent by you

JOIN 31 = 0.020 %
Tob	1:5	All the tribes that joined in apostasy
Jud	1:6	He was joined by all the people of the hill country
	1:6	Many nations joined the forces of the Chaldeans
	1:11	and refused to join him in the war
	7:1	and all the allies who had joined him
	12:11	to join us and eat and drink with us
	14:10	and joined the house of Israel, remaining so to this day
Wis	5:20	and creation will join with him to fight against the madmen
1 Ma	1:15	They joined with the Gentiles and sold themselves to do evil
	1:52	Many of the people, every one who forsook the law, joined them
	2:43	joined them and reinforced them
	3:2	All his brothers and all who had joined his father helped him
	3:41	and the land of the Philistines joined with them
	6:21	and some of the ungodly Israelites joined them
	7:22	and all who were troubling their people joined him
	7:39	and the Syrian army joined him
	11:69	Then the men in ambush emerged from their places and joined battle
	11:73	they returned to him and joined him in the pursuit
	13:14	and that he was about to join battle with him
	15:14	and the ships joined battle from the sea
2 Ma	8:23	he joined battle with Nicanor
	10:28	Just as dawn was breaking, the 2 armies joined battle
	12:34	When they joined battle
	13:3	Menelaus also joined them
	13:12	When they had all joined in the same petition
	14:14	who had fled before Judas, flocked to join Nicanor
1 Es	1:29	He joined battle with him in the plain of Megiddo
	5:50	And some joined them from the other peoples of the land
	7:6	and the rest of those from the captivity who joined them
3 Ma	2:30	But if any of them prefer to join
4 Ma	9:21	Although the ligaments joining his bones were already severed

JOINT 1
4 Ma 9:17 Cut my limbs, burn my flesh, and twist my joints

JOINT-DISLOCATOR 1
4 Ma 8:13 wheels and joint-dislocators

JONAH 5 = 0.003 %
Tob 14:4 for I fully believe what Jonah the prophet said
14:8 because what the prophet Jonah said will surely happen
1 Es 9:23 who was Kelita, and Pethahiah and Judah and Jonah
3 Ma 6:8 And Jonah, wasting away
2 Es 1:39 and Joel and Obadiah and Jonah

JONATHAN 104 = 0.068 %
1 Ma	2:5	Eleazar called Avaran, and Jonathan called Apphus
	4:30	into the hands of Jonathan, the son of Saul
	5:17	I and Jonathan my brother will go to Gilead
	5:24	Judas maccabeus and Jonathan his brother crossed the Jordan
	5:55	Now while Judas and Jonathan were in Gilead
	9:19	Then Jonathan and Simon took Judas their brother
	9:28	and said to Jonathan
	9:31	And Jonathan at that time accepted the leadership
	9:33	But Jonathan and Simon his brother
	9:35	And Jonathan sent his brother as leader of the multitude
	9:37	After these things it was reported to Jonathan
	9:44	And Jonathan said to those with him
	9:47	and Jonathan stretched out his hand to strike Bacchides
	9:48	Then Jonathan and the men with him leaped into the Jordan
	9:58	Jonathan and his men are living in quiet and confidence

9:60	telling them to seize Jonathan and his men
9:61	And Jonathan's men seized about 50 of the men of the country
9:62	Then Jonathan with his men, and Simon
9:65	But Jonathan left Simon his brother in the city
9:70	When Jonathan learned of this
9:71	and he swore to Jonathan
9:73	And Jonathan dwelt in Michmash
9:73	And Jonathan began to judge the people
10:3	And Demetrius sent Jonathan a letter
10:7	Then Jonathan came to Jerusalem
10:9	But the men in the citadel released the hostages to Jonathan
10:10	And Jonathan dwelt in Jerusalem
10:15	which Demetrius had sent to Jonathan
10:15	that Jonathan and his brothers had fought
10:18	King Alexander to his brother Jonathan, greeting
10:21	So Jonathan put on the holy garments
10:46	When Jonathan and the people heard these words
10:59	Then Alexander the king wrote to Jonathan to come to meet him
10:62	The king gave orders to take off Jonathan's garments
10:66	And Jonathan returned to Jerusalem in peace and gladness
10:69	to Jonathan the high priest :
10:74	When Jonathan heard the words of Apollonius
10:76	and Jonathan gained possession of Joppa
10:78	Jonathan pursued him to Azotus
10:80	Jonathan learned that there was an ambush behind him
10:81	But his men stood fast, as Jonathan commanded
10:84	But Jonathan burned Azotus and the surrounding towns
10:86	Then Jonathan departed from there
10:87	And Jonathan and those with him returned to Jerusalem
10:88	he honoured Jonathan still more
11:4	whom Jonathan had burned in the war
11:5	They also told the king what Jonathan had done
11:6	Jonathan met the king at Joppa with pomp
11:7	And Jonathan went with the king
11:20	In those days Jonathan assembled the men of Judea
11:21	that Jonathan was besieging the citadel
11:22	and he wrote to Jonathan not to continue the siege
11:23	When Jonathan heard this
11:28	Then Jonathan asked the king
11:29	and wrote a letter to Jonathan about all these things
11:30	King Demetrius to Jonathan his brother
11:37	and let it be given to Jonathan
11:41	Now Jonathan sent to Demetrius the king the request
11:42	And Demetrius sent this message to Jonathan
11:44	So Jonathan sent 3,000 stalwart men to him at Antioch
11:53	and he became estranged from Jonathan
11:53	and did not repay the favours which Jonathan had done him
11:57	Then the young Antiochus wrote to Jonathan, saying
11:60	Then Jonathan set forth
11:62	Then the people of Gaza pleaded with Jonathan
11:63	Then Jonathan heard that the officers of Demetrius
11:67	Jonathan and his army encamped by the waters of Gennesaret
11:70	All the men with Jonathan fled
11:71	Jonathan rent his garments
11:74	And Jonathan returned to Jerusalem
12:1	Now when Jonathan saw that the time was favourable for him
12:3	Jonathan the high priest and the Jewish nation have sent us
12:5	which Jonathan wrote to the Spartans :
12:6	Jonathan the high priest, the senate of the nation
12:24	Now Jonathan heard that the commanders of Demetrius had returned
12:27	So when the sun set, Jonathan commanded his men to be alert
12:28	that Jonathan and his men were prepared for battle
12:29	But Jonathan and his men did not know it until morning
12:30	Then Jonathan pursued them, but he did not overtake them
12:31	So Jonathan turned aside against the Arabs
12:35	When Jonathan returned he convened the elders of the people
12:40	He feared that Jonathan might not permit him to do so
12:41	Jonathan went out to meet him
12:44	Then he said to Jonathan
12:46	Jonathan trusted him and did as he said
12:48	But when Jonathan entered Ptolemais
12:49	and the Great Plain to destroy all Jonathan's soldiers
12:50	But they realized that Jonathan had been seized
12:52	and they mourned for Jonathan and his companions
13:8	in place of Judas and Jonathan your brother
13:11	He sent Jonathan the son of Absalom to Joppa
13:12	and Jonathan was with him under guard
13:14	in place of Jonathan his brother
13:15	that Jonathan your brother owed the royal treasury
13:19	but Trypho broke his word and did not release Jonathan
13:23	When he approached Baskama, he killed Jonathan
13:25	And Simon sent and took the bones of Jonathan his brother
14:16	that Jonathan had died
14:18	and Jonathan his brothers
14:30	Jonathan rallied the nation, and became their high priest
2 Ma 1:23	Jonathan led, and the rest responded, as did Nehemiah
8:22	Simon and Joseph and Jonathan

1 Es 8:32	Of the sons of Adin, Obed the son of Jonathan
9:14	Jonathan the son of Asahel

JOPPA   15 = 0.010 %

1 Ma 10:75	He encamped before Joppa
10:75	for Apollonius had a garrison in Joppa
10:76	and Jonathan gained possession of Joppa
11:6	Jonathan met the king at Joppa with pomp
12:33	He turned aside to Joppa and took it by surprise
13:11	He sent Jonathan the son of Absalom to Joppa
14:5	To crown all his honours he took Joppa for a harbour
14:34	He also fortified Joppa, which is by the sea
15:28	You hold control of Joppa and Gazara
15:35	As for Joppa and Gazara, which you demand
2 Ma 4:21	Therefore upon arriving at Joppa he proceeded to Jerusalem
12:3	And some men of Joppa did so ungodly a deed
12:4	the men of Joppa took them out to sea and drowned them
12:7	and root out the whole community of Joppa
1 Es 5:55	and convey them in rafts to the harbour of Joppa

JORAH   1

1 Es 5:16	The sons of Jorah, 112

JORAM   1

1 Es 1:9	and Hashabiah and Ochiel and Joram

JORDAN   11 = 0.007 %

Jud 1:9	and beyond the Jordan as far as Jerusalem and Bethany
5:15	and crossing over the Jordan
Sir 24:26	and like the Jordan at harvest time
1 Ma 5:24	Judas maccabeus and Jonathan his brother crossed the Jordan
5:52	And they crossed the Jordan into the large plain before Bethshan
9:34	and he with all his army crossed the Jordan
9:42	they returned to the marshes of the Jordan
9:43	to the banks of the Jordan
9:45	the water of the Jordan is on the side and on that
9:48	Then Jonathan and the men with him leaped into the Jordan
9:48	and the enemy did not cross the Jordan to attack them

JOSEPH   11 = 0.007 %

Jud 8:1	son of Joseph, son of Oziel, son of Elkiah
Sir 49:15	And no man like Joseph has been born
1 Ma 2:53	Joseph in the time of his distress kept the commandment
5:18	But he left Joseph, the son of Zechariah
5:56	Joseph, the son of Zechariah
5:60	Then Joseph and Azariah were routed
2 Ma 8:22	Simon and Joseph and Jonathan
10:19	Maccabeus left Simon and Joseph
1 Es 9:34	Shemaiah, Amariah, Joseph
4 Ma 2:2	that the temperate Joseph is praised
18:11	and of Joseph in prison

JOSHUA   4 = 0.003 %

Sir 46:1	Joshua the son of Nun was mighty in war
1 Ma 2:55	Joshua, because he fulfilled the command
2 Ma 12:15	overthrew Jericho in the days of Joshua
2 Es 7:107	and Joshua after him for Israel in the days of Achan

JOSIAH   18 = 0.012 %

Sir 49:1	The memory of Josiah is like a blending of incense
49:4	Except David and Hezekiah and Josiah they all sinned greatly
Bar 1:8	the silver vessels which Zedekiah the son of Josiah, king of Judah, had made
1 Es 1:1	Josiah kept the passover to his Lord in Jerusalem
1:7	And Josiah gave to the people who were present
1:18	according to the command of King Josiah
1:21	as was kept by Josiah and the priests and the Levites
1:22	In the 18th year of the reign of Josiah
1:23	And the deeds of Josiah were upright in the sight of his Lord
1:25	After all these acts of Josiah
1:25	and Josiah went out against him
1:28	But Josiah did not turn back to his chariot
1:29	and the commanders came down against King Josiah
1:32	And in all Judea they mourned for Josiah
1:32	Jeremiah the prophet lamented for Josiah
1:33	and every one of the acts of Josiah, and his splendour
1:34	And the men of the nation took Jeconiah the son of Josiah
1:34	and made him king in succession to Josiah his father

JOSIPHIAH   1

1 Es 8:36	Of the sons of Bani, Shelomith the son of Josiphiah

JOURNEY, subst.   21 = 0.014 %

Tob 5:16	Then he said to Tobias, Get ready for the journey
5:16	So his son made the preparations for the journey
5:21	his journey will be successful
7:8	speak of those things which you talked about on the journey
9:5	So Raphael made the journey
10:1	and when the days for the journey had expired

	11:1	praising God because he had made his journey a success
Wis	13:18	for a prosperous journey, a thing that cannot take a step
	18:3	as a guide for thy people's unknown journey
	19:5	and that thy people might experience an incredible journey
Sir	21:16	A fool's narration is like a burden on a journey
1 Ma	5:24	and went 3 days' journey into the wilderness
	7:45	The Jews pursued them a day's journey
	8:19	They went to Rome, a very long journey
2 Ma	3:8	Heliodorus at once set out on his journey
	9:4	until he completed the journey
	9:7	and giving orders to hasten the journey
1 Es	8:6	by the prosperous journey which the Lord gave them
	8:50	to seek from him a prosperous journey for ourselves
3 Ma	7:18	all things to them for their journey
2 Es	13:45	a journey of a year and a half

JOURNEY, verb   2

Wis	5:7	and we journeyed through trackless deserts
	11:2	They journeyed through an uninhabited wilderness

JOY, subst.   37 = 0.024 %

Tob	7:18	the Lord of heaven and earth grant you joy
	13:10	that his tent may be raised for you again with joy
Jud	4:12	to the malicious joy of the Gentiles
	12:14	and it will be a joy to me until the day of my death !
	16:11	Then my oppressed people shouted for joy
Ad E	10:13	with an assembly and joy and gladness before God
	14:18	Thy servant has had no joy
	16:21	has made this day to be a joy to his chosen people
Wis	8:16	and life with her has no pain, but gladness and joy
Sir	1:12	and gives gladness and joy and long life
	1:23	and then joy will burst forth for him
	2:9	for everlasting joy and mercy
	4:12	and those who seek her early will be filled with joy
	6:28	and she will be changed into joy for you
	30:16	and there is no gladness above joy of heart
Bar	4:11	With joy I nurtured them
	4:22	and joy has come to me from the Holy One
	4:23	with joy and gladness for ever
	4:29	will bring you everlasting joy with your salvation
	4:36	and see the joy that is coming to you from God !
	5:9	For God will lead Israel with joy
1 Ma	3:45	Joy was taken from Jacob
	4:59	with gladness and joy for 8 days
	5:54	So they went up to Mount Zion with gladness and joy
	14:11	and Israel rejoiced with great joy
2 Ma	3:30	was filled with joy and gladness
	15:28	When the action was over and they were returning with joy
3 Ma	4:6	exchanged joy for wailing
	4:16	The king was greatly and continually filled with joy
	5:44	Then the friends and officers departed with great joy
	6:31	and full of joy they apportioned to celebrate the place
	6:32	they formed choruses as a sign of peaceful joy
2 Es	2:19	by these I will fill your children with joy
	2:36	receive the joy of your glory
	7:91	First of all, they shall see with great joy
	7:131	so much as joy over those to whom salvation is assured
4 Ma	9:31	I lighten my pain by the joys that come from virtue

JOYFUL   8 = 0.005 %

Tob	13:11	Generations of generations will give you joyful praise
Jud	14:9	and made a joyful noise in their city
1 Es	5:64	while many came with trumpets and a joyful noise
3 Ma	5:17	and to make the present portion of the banquet joyful
	7:15	and they kept the day as a joyful festival
2 Es	2:37	Receive what the Lord has entrusted to you and be joyful
	12:34	and he will make them joyful until the end comes
	13:13	some of whom were joyful and some sorrowful

JOYFULLY   4 = 0.003 %

3 Ma	5:21	all those present readily and joyfully with one accord gave their approval
	6:34	and had joyfully registered them
	7:13	shouted the Hallelujah and joyfully departed
	7:16	joyfully and loudly giving thanks

JOYFULNESS   1

3 Ma	6:30	deciding that they should celebrate their rescue with all joyfulness

JOYOUS   2

3 Ma	6:35	to the accompaniment of joyous thanksgiving and psalms
	7:19	these days as a joyous festival

JOZABAD   3 = 0.002 %

1 Es	8:63	and with them were Jozabad the son of Jeshua
	9:23	And of the Levites : Jozabad and Shimei and Kelaiah
	9:48	Azariah and Jozabad, Hanan, Pelaiah, the Levites

JOZADAK   6 = 0.004 %

Sir	49:12	and so was Jeshua the son of Jozadak
1 Es	5:5	Jeshua the son of Jozadak, son of Seraiah
	5:48	Then Jeshua the son of Jozadak, with his fellow priests
	5:56	and Jeshua the son of Jozadak made a beginning
	6:2	and Jeshua the son of Jozadak arose
	9:19	of the sons of Jeshua the son of Jozadak and his brethren

JUDAH   48 = 0.031 %

Jud	14:7	Blessed are you in every tent of Judah !
Sir	45:25	the son of Jesse, of the tribe of Judah :
	49:4	the kings of Judah came to an end
Bar	1:3	in the hearing of Jeconiah the son of Jehoiakim, king of Judah
	1:8	to return them to the land of Judah
	1:8	the silver vessels which Zedekiah the son of Josiah, king of Judah, had made
	1:15	to the men of Judah, to the inhabitants of Jerusalem
	2:1	and against the men of Israel and Judah
	2:23	I will make to cease from the cities of Judah
	2:26	and the house of Judah
Sus	13:56	You offspring of Canaan and not of Judah
	13:57	but a daughter of Judah would not endure your wickedness
1 Ma	1:29	2 years later the king sent to the cities of Judah
	1:44	and the cities of Judah
	1:51	and commanded the cities of Judah to offer sacrifice, city by city
	1:54	They also built altars in the surrounding cities of Judah
	2:6	He saw the blasphemies being committed in Judah and Jerusalem
	2:18	as all the Gentiles and the men of Judah
	3:8	He went through the cities of Judah
	3:39	to go into the land of Judah and destroy it
	5:45	to go to the land of Judah
	5:53	till he came to the land of Judah
	5:68	he plundered the cities and returned to the land of Judah
	6:5	that the armies which had gone into the land of Judah had been routed
	6:12	and I sent to destroy the inhabitants of Judah without good reason
	7:10	into the land of Judah
	7:22	They gained control of the land of Judah
	7:50	So the land of Judah had rest for a few days
	9:1	into the land of Judah a 2nd time
	9:57	and the land of Judah had rest for 2 years
	9:72	whom he had formerly taken from the land of Judah
	10:30	I will not collect them from the land of Judah
	10:33	from the land of Judah into any part of my kingdom
	10:37	just as the king has commanded in the land of Judah
	12:4	safe conduct to the land of Judah
	12:46	and they returned to the land of Judah
	12:52	So they all reached the land of Judah safely
	13:1	to invade the land of Judah and destroy it
	13:12	to invade the land of Judah
1 Es	1:21	and the men of Judah and all of Israel
	1:33	are recorded in the book of the kings of Israel and Judah
	1:35	And he reigned 3 months in Judah and Jerusalem
	2:8	of the tribes of Judah and Benjamin
	5:5	of the lineage of Phares, of the tribe of Judah
	5:66	and when the enemies of the tribe of Judah and Benjamin heard it
	9:5	Then the men of the tribe of Judah and Benjamin
	9:23	who was Kelita, and Pethahiah and Judah and Jonah
2 Es	1:24	You would not obey me, O Judah

JUDAISM   4 = 0.003 %

2 Ma	2:21	to those who strove zealously on behalf of Judaism
	14:38	he had been accused of Judaism
	14:38	and for Judaism he had with all zeal risked body and life
4 Ma	4:26	to eat defiling foods and to renounce Judaism

JUDAS   133 = 0.087 %

1 Ma	2:4	Judas called Maccabeus
	2:66	Judas Maccabeus has been a mighty warrior from his youth
	3:1	Then Judas his son, who was called Maccabeus
	3:11	When Judas learned of it, he went out to meet him
	3:12	and Judas took the sword of Apollonius
	3:13	heard that Judas had gathered a large company
	3:14	I will make war on Judas and his companions
	3:16	Judas went out to meet him with a small company
	3:17	they said to Judas, How can we, few as we are
	3:18	Judas replied, It is easy for many to be hemmed in by few
	3:25	Then Judas and his brothers began to be feared
	3:26	and the Gentiles talked of the battles of Judas
	3:42	Now Judas and his brothers saw that misfortunes had increased
	3:55	After this Judas appointed leaders of the people
	3:58	And Judas said, Gird yourselves and be valiant
	4:3	But Judas heard of it, and he and his mighty men
	4:5	When Gorgias entered the camp of Judas by night
	4:6	At daybreak Judas appeared in the plain with 3,000 men
	4:8	But Judas said to the men who were with him
	4:13	Then the men with Judas blew their trumpets

4 : 16	Then Judas and his force turned back from pursuing them
4 : 19	Just as Judas was finishing this speech
4 : 21	and when they also saw the army of Judas
4 : 23	Then Judas returned to plunder the camp
4 : 29	and Judas met them with 10,000 men
4 : 35	and observed the boldness which inspired those of Judas
4 : 36	Then said Judas and his brothers
4 : 41	Then Judas detailed men
4 : 59	Then Judas and his brothers and all the assembly of Israel
5 : 3	But Judas made war on the sons of Esau
5 : 10	and sent to Judas and his brothers a letter which said
5 : 16	When Judas and the people heard these messages
5 : 17	Then Judas said to Simon his brother
5 : 20	and 8,000 to Judas for Gilead
5 : 24	Judas maccabeus and Jonathan his brother crossed the Jordan
5 : 28	Then Judas and his army quickly turned back
5 : 31	So Judas saw that the battle had begun
5 : 38	Judas sent men to spy out the camp, and they reported to him
5 : 39	And Judas went to meet them
5 : 40	Now as Judas and his army drew near to the stream of water
5 : 42	When Judas approached the stream of water
5 : 44	they could stand before Judas no longer
5 : 45	Then Judas gathered together all the Israelites in Gilead
5 : 48	And Judas sent them this friendly message
5 : 49	Then Judas ordered proclamation to be made to the army
5 : 53	And Judas kept rallying the laggards
5 : 55	Now while Judas and Jonathan were in Gilead
5 : 61	they did not listen to Judas and his brothers
5 : 63	The man Judas and his brothers were greatly honoured
5 : 65	Then Judas and his brothers went forth
5 : 68	But Judas turned aside to Azotus
6 : 19	So Judas decided to destroy them
6 : 32	Then Judas marched away from the citadel
6 : 42	But Judas and his army advanced to the battle
7 : 6	Judas and his brothers have destroyed all your friends
7 : 7	which Judas has brought upon us and upon the land of the king
7 : 10	and he sent messengers to Judas and his brothers
7 : 23	And Judas saw all the evil that Alcimus and those with him
7 : 24	So Judas went out into all the surrounding parts of Judea
7 : 25	When Alcimus saw that Judas
7 : 27	and treacherously sent to Judas and his brothers
7 : 29	So he came to Judas, and they greeted one another peaceably
7 : 29	But the enemy were ready to seize Judas
7 : 30	It became known to Judas
7 : 31	he went out to meet Judas in battle near Capharsalama
7 : 35	Unless Judas and his army
7 : 40	And Judas encamped in Adasa with 3,000 men
7 : 40	Then Judas prayed and said
8 : 1	Now Judas heard of the fame of the Romans
8 : 17	So Judas chose Eupolemus the son of John, son of Accos
8 : 20	Judas, who is also called Maccabeus, and his brothers
9 : 5	Now Judas was encamped in Elasa
9 : 7	When Judas saw that his army had slipped away
9 : 10	But Judas said, Far be it from us
9 : 12	and the men with Judas also blew their trumpets
9 : 14	Judas saw that Bacchides and the strength of his army were on the right
9 : 16	they turned and followed close behind Judas and his men
9 : 18	Judas also fell, and the rest fled
9 : 19	Then Jonathan and Simon took Judas their brother
9 : 22	Now the rest of the acts of Judas, and his wars
9 : 23	After the death of Judas
9 : 26	They sought and searched for the friends of Judas
9 : 28	Then all the friends of Judas assembled
9 : 29	Since the death of your brother Judas
9 : 31	and took the place of Judas his brother
11 : 70	except Mattathias the son of Absalom and Judas the son of Chalphi
13 : 8	in place of Judas and Jonathan your brother
14 : 18	which they had established with Judas
16 : 2	And Simon called in his 2 elder sons Judas and John
16 : 9	At that time Judas the brother of John was wounded
16 : 14	and he went down to Jericho with Mattathias and Judas his sons
2 Ma 1 : 10	and the senate and Judas
2 : 14	In the same way Judas also collected all the books that had been lost
2 : 19	The story of Judas Maccabeus and his brothers
5 : 27	But Judas Maccabeus, with about 9 others
8 : 1	But Judas, who was also called Maccabeus, and his companions
8 : 12	Word came to Judas concerning Nicanor's invasion
12 : 5	When Judas heard of the cruelty visited on his countrymen
12 : 11	After a hard fight Judas and his men won the victory
12 : 11	The defeated nomads besought Judas
12 : 12	Judas, thinking that they might really be useful in many ways
12 : 14	behaved most insolently toward Judas and his men
12 : 15	But Judas and his men
12 : 21	When Timothy learned of the approach of Judas
12 : 22	But when Judas' first division appeared
12 : 23	And Judas pressed the pursuit with the utmost vigour
12 : 26	Then Judas marched against Carnaim

12 : 36	Judas called upon the Lord
12 : 38	Then Judas assembled his army
12 : 39	Judas and his men went to take up the bodies of the fallen
12 : 42	And the noble Judas exhorted the people
13 : 1	In the 149th year word came to Judas and his men
13 : 10	But when Judas heard of this
13 : 12	Judas exhorted them and ordered them to stand ready
13 : 20	Judas sent in to the garrison whatever was necessary
13 : 22	attacked Judas and his men, was defeated
14 : 1	3 years later, word came to Judas and his men
14 : 6	whose leader is Judas Maccabeus
14 : 10	For as long as Judas lives
14 : 11	the rest of the king's friends, who were hostile to Judas
14 : 13	with orders to kill Judas and scatter his men
14 : 14	who had fled before Judas, flocked to join Nicanor
14 : 17	Simon, the brother of Judas, had encountered Nicanor
14 : 18	Nevertheless Nicanor, hearing of the valour of Judas
14 : 22	Judas posted armed men in readiness at key places
14 : 24	And he kept Judas always in his presence
14 : 26	Judas, to be his successor
14 : 33	If you do not hand Judas over to me as a prisoner
15 : 1	When Nicanor heard that Judas and his men
15 : 6	over Judas and his men
15 : 15	and gave to Judas a golden sword
15 : 17	Encouraged by the words of Judas
15 : 26	and Judas and his men met the enemy in battle

JUDEA   75 = 0.049 %

Tob 1 : 18	any who came fleeing from Judea
Jud 1 : 12	and the people of Ammon, and all Judea
3 : 9	near Dothan, fronting the great ridge of Judea
4 : 1	By this time the people of Israel living in Judea
4 : 3	and all the people of Judea were newly gathered together
4 : 7	since by them Judea could be invaded
4 : 13	for the people fasted many days throughout Judea
8 : 21	For if we are captured all Judea will be captured
11 : 19	Then I will lead you through the middle of Judea
Ad E 11 : 4	had brought from Jerusalem with Jeconiah king of Judea
Bel 14 : 33	Now the prophet Habakkuk was in Judea
1 Ma 3 : 34	As for the residents of Judea and Jerusalem
4 : 35	to invade Judea again with an even larger army
5 : 8	then he returned to Judea
5 : 18	with the rest of the forces, in Judea to guard it
5 : 23	and led them to Judea with great rejoicing
5 : 60	and were pursued to the borders of Judea
6 : 48	and the king encamped in Judea and at Mount Zion
6 : 53	those who found safety in Judea from the Gentiles
7 : 24	So Judas went out into all the surrounding parts of Judea
7 : 46	And men came out of all the villages of Judea round about
9 : 50	and built strong cities in Judea :
9 : 60	and secretly sent letters to all his allies in Judea
9 : 63	and sent orders to the men of Judea
10 : 38	As for the 3 districts that have been added to Judea
10 : 38	let them be so annexed to Judea
10 : 45	and the cost of rebuilding the walls in Judea
11 : 20	In those days Jonathan assembled the men of Judea
11 : 28	to free Judea and the 3 districts of Samaria from tribute
11 : 34	both the territory of Judea
11 : 34	were added to Judea from Samaria
12 : 35	and planned with them to build strongholds in Judea
13 : 33	But Simon built up the strongholds of Judea
14 : 33	He fortified the cities of Judea
14 : 33	and Beth-zur on the borders of Judea
15 : 30	which you have conquered outside the borders of Judea
15 : 39	He commanded him to encamp against Judea
15 : 40	and began to provoke the people and invade Judea
15 : 41	and make raids along the highways of Judea
16 : 10	And he returned to Judea safely
2 Ma 1 : 1	and those in the land of Judea
1 : 10	Those in Jerusalem and those in Judea
5 : 11	he took it to mean that Judea was in revolt
8 : 9	to wipe out the whole race of Judea
10 : 24	He came on, intending to take Judea by storm
11 : 5	Invading Judea, he approached Beth-zur
13 : 1	with a great army against Judea
13 : 13	before the king's army could enter Judea
14 : 12	appointed him governor of Judea, and sent him off
14 : 14	And the Gentiles throughout Judea
15 : 22	in the time of Hezekiah king of Judea
1 Es 1 : 26	What have we to do with each other, king of Judea ?
1 : 32	And in all Judea they mourned for Josiah
1 : 33	of the kings of Judea
1 : 37	king of Judea and Jerusalem
1 : 39	when he began to reign in Judea and Jerusalem
1 : 46	and made Zedekiah king of Judea and Jerusalem
2 : 4	which is in Judea
2 : 5	which is in Judea
2 : 12	and by him they were given to Shesh-Bazzar the governor of Judea
2 : 16	against those who were living in Judea and Jerusalem :

	4:45	when Judea was laid waste by the Chaldeans
	4:49	from his kingdom to Judea, in the interest of their freedom
	5:7	These are the men of Judea who came up
	5:8	and who returned to Jerusalem and the rest of Judea
	5:57	in the 2nd year after they came to Judea and Jerusalem
	5:72	But the peoples of the land pressed hard upon those in Judea
	6:1	prophesied to the Jews who were in Judea and Jerusalem
	6:8	when we went to the country of Judea
	6:27	the servant of the Lord and governor of Judea
	6:28	who have returned from the captivity of Judea
	8:12	in order to look into matters in Judea and Jerusalem
	8:81	to give us a stronghold in Judea and Jerusalem
	9:3	And a proclamation was made throughout Judea and Jerusalem
3 Ma	**5**:43	and would also march against Judea

JUDGE, subst.   25 = 0.016 %

Jud	**7**:24	God be judge between you and us !
Wis	**6**:1	learn, O judges of the ends of the earth
	9:7	and to be judge over thy sons and daughters
Sir	**7**:6	Do not seek to become a judge
	8:14	Do not go to law against a judge
	10:24	The nobleman, and the judge, and the ruler will be honoured
	35:12	for the Lord is the judge, and with him is no partiality
	38:33	They do not sit in the judge's seat
	41:18	of a transgression, before a judge or magistrate
	46:11	The judges also, with their respective names
Bar	**2**:1	and against our judges who judged Israel
Sus	**13**:5	In that year 2 elders from the people were appointed as judges
	13:5	from elders who were judges
	13:41	because they were elders of the people and judges
1 Ma	**2**:55	became a judge in Israel
2 Ma	**12**:6	and, calling upon God the righteous Judge
	12:41	the righteous Judge, who reveals the things that are hidden
1 Es	**2**:17	and the other judges of their council
	8:23	appoint judges and justices
	9:13	with the elders and judges of each place
	9:14	served with them as judges
2 Es	**4**:18	If now you were a judge between them
	7:19	And he said to me, You are not a better judge than God
	14:32	And because he is a righteous judge
	16:67	Behold, God is the judge, fear him !

JUDGE, verb   34 = 0.022 %

Jud	**10**:19	and admired the Israelites, judging them by her
Ad E	**16**:9	and always judging what comes before our eyes
Wis	**9**:12	and I shall judge thy people justly
	11:9	were tormented when judged in wrath
	12:10	But judging them little by little
	12:13	that thou hast not judged unjustly
	12:18	Thou who art sovereign in strength dost judge with mildness
	12:21	with what strictness thou hast judged thy sons
	12:22	so that we may meditate upon thy goodness when we judge
	12:22	and when we are judged we may expect mercy
	15:18	when judged by their lack of intelligence
Sir	**4**:9	and do not be fainthearted in judging a case
	4:15	He who obeys her will judge the nations
	11:9	nor sit with sinners when they judge a case
	16:12	he judges a man according to his deeds
	31:15	Judge your neighbour's feelings by your own
	35:19	till he judges the case of his people
	45:26	to judge his people in righteousness
	46:14	By the law of the Lord he judged the congregation
Bar	**2**:1	and against our judges who judged Israel
L Jr	**6**:54	They cannot judge their own cause or deliver one who is wronged
1 Ma	**7**:42	and judge him according to this wickedness
	7:73	And Jonathan began to judge the people
1 Es	**3**:9	and the 3 nobles of Persia judge to be wisest
	8:23	to judge all those who know the law of your God
3 Ma	**2**:3	and you judge those who have done anything in insolence and arrogance
2 Es	**4**:20	He answered me and said, You have judged rightly
	4:20	but why have you not judged so in your own case ?
	7:11	what had been made was judged
	7:57	Judge therefore which things are precious and desirable
	7:87	and before whom they are to be judged in the last times
	7:139	and judge, because if he did not pardon those who were created by his word
	11:41	And you have judged the earth, but not with truth
	12:9	For thou hast judged me worthy

JUDGMENT   81 = 0.053 %

Tob	**3**:2	and thou dost render true and righteous judgment for ever
	3:5	And now thy many judgments are true
Jud	**9**:6	and thy judgment is with foreknowledge
	16:17	in the day of judgment
Ad E	**13**:3	Haman, who excels among us in sound judgment
Wis	**6**:5	because severe judgment falls on those in high places
	7:15	May God grant that I speak with judgment
	8:11	I shall be found keen in judgment

	9:3	and pronounce judgment in uprightness of soul
	9:5	with little understanding of judgment and laws
	12:12	Or who will resist thy judgment ?
	12:25	thou didst send thy judgment to mock them
	12:26	will experience the deserved judgment of God
	16:18	that they were being pursued by the judgment of God
	17:1	Great are thy judgments and hard to describe
Sir	**3**:24	For their hasty judgment has led many astray
	6:23	Listen, my son, and accept my judgment
	17:12	and showed them his judgments
	18:14	and who are eager for his judgments
	18:20	Before judgment, examine yourself
	20:4	is a man who executes judgments by violence
	21:5	and his judgment comes speedily
	25:4	What an attractive thing is judgment in grey-haired men
	32:16	Those who fear the Lord will form true judgments
	32:18	A man of judgment will not overlook an idea
	35:17	and does justice for the righteous, and executes judgment
	38:33	nor do they understand the sentence of judgment
	38:33	they cannot expound discipline or judgment
	42:2	and of rendering judgment to acquit the ungodly
	43:13	and speeds the lightnings of his judgment
	45:5	to teach Jacob the covenant, and Israel his judgments
	45:10	with the oracle of judgment, Urim and Thummim
	45:17	In his commandments he gave him authority in statutes and judgments
	48:7	and judgments of vengeance at Horeb
P Az	4	and all thy judgments are truth
	5	Thou hast executed true judgments
	8	thou hast done in true judgment
Sus	**13**:9	or remembering righteous judgments
	13:49	Return to the place of judgment
	13:53	pronouncing unjust judgments
2 Ma	**1**:17	Blessed in every way be our God, who has brought judgment
	2:29	such in my judgment is the case with us
	7:35	You have not yet escaped the judgment of the almighty, all-seeing God
	7:36	but you, by the judgment of God
	8:11	not expecting the judgment from the Almighty
	9:4	But the judgment of heaven rode with him !
	9:18	for the judgment of God had justly come upon him
	11:37	so that we may have your judgment
1 Es	**4**:40	and there is nothing unrighteous in her judgment
	8:7	but taught all Israel all the ordinances and judgments
3 Ma	**2**:22	since he was smitten by a righteous judgment
2 Es	**5**:34	and to search out part of his judgment
	5:40	so you cannot discover my judgment
	5:42	He said to me, I shall liken my judgment to a circle
	5:43	that thou mightest show thy judgment the sooner ?
	7:33	And the Most High shall be revealed upon the seat of judgment
	7:34	but only judgment shall remain, truth shall stand
	7:38	Thus he will speak to them on the day of judgment
	7:44	This is my judgment and its prescribed order
	7:60	So also will be the judgment which I have promised
	7:66	for they do not look for a judgment
	7:69	And if we were not to come into judgment after death
	7:70	he first prepared the judgment
	7:70	and the things that pertain to the judgment
	7:73	What, then, will they have to say in the judgment
	7:102	whether on the day of judgment
	7:104	The day of judgment is decisive
	7:113	But the day of judgment will be the end of this age
	7:115	who has been condemned in the judgment
	8:18	and I have heard of the swiftness of the judgment that is to come
	8:38	or about their death, their judgment, or their destruction
	8:61	Therefore my judgment is now drawing near
	11:46	and may hope for the judgment and mercy of him who made it
	12:33	For first he will set them living before his judgment seat
	12:34	the day of judgment, of which I spoke to you at the beginning
	14:35	For after death the judgment will come
4 Ma	**1**:2	I mean, of course, rational judgment
	1:18	Now the kinds of wisdom are rational judgment, justice
	1:19	Rational judgment is supreme over all of these
	1:30	that rational judgment is sovereign over the emotions
	9:32	the judgments of the divine wrath

JUDITH   33 = 0.021 %

Jud	**8**:1	At that time Judith heard about these things :
	8:4	Judith had lived at home as a widow
	8:9	When Judith heard the wicked words
	8:32	Judith said to them, Listen to me
	9:1	Then Judith fell upon her face
	9:1	Judith cried out to the Lord with a loud voice, and said
	10:1	When Judith had ceased crying out to the God of Israel
	10:10	When they had done this, Judith went out
	10:23	And when Judith came into the presence of Holofernes and his servants
	11:5	Judith replied to him, Accept the words of your servant
	12:2	But Judith said, I cannot eat it, lest it be an offence

12:4	Judith replied, As your soul lives, my lord
12:14	And Judith said, Who am I, to refuse my lord ?
12:16	Then Judith came in and lay down
12:18	Judith said, I will drink now, my lord
13:2	So Judith was left alone in the tent
13:3	Now Judith had told her maid
13:4	Then Judith, standing beside his bed, said in her heart
13:11	Judith called out from afar to the watchmen at the gates
14:1	Then Judith said to them, Listen to me, my brethren
14:7	And when they raised him up he fell at Judith's feet
14:8	Then Judith described to him in the presence of the people
14:14	for he supposed that he was sleeping with Judith
14:17	Then he went to the tent where Judith had stayed
15:8	and to see Judith and to greet her
15:11	They gave Judith the tent of Holofernes
16:1	Then Judith began this thanksgiving before all Israel
16:2	And Judith said, Begin a song to my God with tambourines
16:7	but Judith the daughter of Merari undid him
16:19	Judith also dedicated to God all the vessels of Holofernes
16:20	and Judith remained with them
16:21	and Judith went to Bethulia, and remained on her estate
16:25	in the days of Judith, or for a long time after her death

JUICE
1

1 Ma	6:34	They showed the elephants the juice of grapes and mulberries

JUNGLE
1

4 Ma	1:29	and so tames the jungle of habits and emotions

JUST, adj.
16 = 0.010 %

Tob	14:9	and be merciful and just, so that it may be well with you
Wis	14:30	But just penalties will overtake them on 2 counts :
	14:31	but the just penalty for those who sin
L Jr	6:73	Better therefore is a just man who has no idols
P Az	4	For thou art just in all that thou hast done to us
1 Ma	7:12	before Alcimus and Bacchides to ask for just terms
2 Ma	1:24	who art awe-inspiring and strong and just and merciful
	1:25	who alone art just and almighty and eternal
	7:36	will receive just punishment for your arrogance
	11:14	and persuaded them to settle everything on just terms
	13:8	And this was eminently just
3 Ma	2:3	are a just Ruler
	2:25	who were strangers to everything just
2 Es	10:16	For if you acknowledge the decree of God to be just
4 Ma	2:23	rule a kingdom that is temperate, just, good, and courageous
	9:24	Thereby the just Providence of our ancestors

JUST, adv.
65 = 0.042 %

Tob	14:5	just as the prophets said of it
Jud	2:1	just as he had said
	2:13	but be sure to carry them out just as I have ordered you
	10:16	but tell him just what you have said
Wis	19:17	just as were those at the door of the righteous man
Sir	18:7	When a man has finished, he is just beginning
	24:28	Just as the first man did not know her perfectly
	39:23	just as he turns fresh water into salt
	39:24	just as they are obstacles to the wicked
	39:25	just as evil things for sinners
	39:27	just as they turn into evils for sinners
Bar	4:28	For just as you purposed to go astray from God
	4:33	For just as she rejoiced at your fall
L Jr	6:17	For just as one's dish is useless when it is broken
	6:18	And just as the gates are shut on every side
	6:20	They are just like a beam of the temple
	6:27	but gifts are placed before them just as before the dead
1 Ma	4:19	Just as Judas was finishing this speech
	7:47	and brought them and displayed them just outside Jerusalem
	10:37	just as the king has commanded in the land of Judah
2 Ma	2:10	Just as Moses prayed to the Lord
	2:27	just as it is not easy for one who prepares a banquet
	3:28	this man who had just entered the aforesaid treasury
	5:18	just as Heliodorus was
	9:8	Thus he who had just been thinking
	10:28	Just as dawn was breaking, the 2 armies joined battle
	11:31	to enjoy their own food and laws, just as formerly
	13:11	and not to let the people who had just begun to revive
	13:17	This happened, just as day was dawning
	15:39	For just as it is harmful to drink wine alone
1 Es	5:69	For we obey your Lord just as you do
3 Ma	4:6	And young women who had just entered the bridal chamber
	6:15	but just as you have said
	6:16	Just as Eleazar was ending his prayer
2 Es	4:42	For just as a woman who is in travail
	5:40	Just as you cannot do one of the things that were mentioned
	5:42	just as for those who are last there is no slowness
	6:6	just as the end shall come through me
	7:48	and that not just a few of us
	7:52	If you have just a few precious stones

7:104	Just as now a father does not send his son
8:2	Just as, when you ask the earth
8:41	For just as the farmer sows many seeds upon the ground
8:59	For just as the things which I have predicted await you
9:5	For just as with everything that has occurred in the world
11:33	just as the wings had done
13:52	He said to me, Just as no one can explore or know
15:21	Just as they have done to my elect until this day, so I will do
16:16	Just as an arrow shot by a mighty archer does not return
16:38	Just as a woman with child, in the 9th month
16:49	Just as a respectable and virtuous woman abhors a harlot
16:52	For behold, just a little while

4 Ma	1:14	We shall decide just what reason is and what emotion is
	1:28	Just as pleasure and pain
	2:6	Just so it is with the emotions that hinder one from justice
	2:16	just as it repels anger
	3:21	just at that time certain men attempted
	7:11	For just as our father Aaron, armed with the censer
	8:5	as that of the old man who has just been tortured
	8:6	Just as I am able to punish those who disobey my orders
	10:16	that I am a brother to those who have just been tortured
	13:6	For just as towers jutting out over harbours
	14:6	Just as the hands and feet are moved
	14:7	For just as the 7 days of creation
	15:31	Just as Noah's ark, carrying the world in the universal flood

JUSTICE
33 = 0.021 %

Ad E	16:4	they suppose that they will escape the evil-hating justice
Wis	1:8	and justice, when it punishes, will not pass him by
	5:18	and wear impartial justice as a helmet
	8:7	for she teaches self-control and prudence, justice and courage
	11:20	men could fall at a single breath when pursued by justice
Sir	16:22	Who will announce his acts of justice ?
	27:8	If you pursue justice, you will attain it
	35:17	and does justice for the righteous, and executes judgment
Bar	2:17	will not ascribe glory or justice to the Lord
P Az	5	for in truth and justice thou hast brought all this upon us
1 Ma	2:29	Then many who were seeking righteousness and justice
	6:22	How long will you fail to do justice
	7:18	for they said, There is no truth or justice in them
	14:35	and because of the justice and loyalty
2 Ma	4:34	then, with no regard for justice
	8:13	those who were cowardly and distrustful of God's justice
	10:12	took the lead in showing justice to the Jews
1 Es	8:23	appoint judges and justices
2 Es	2:20	secure justice for the fatherless, give to the needy
4 Ma	1:4	the emotions that hinder one from justice, such as malice
	1:6	but those that are opposed to justice, courage, and self-control
	1:18	Now the kinds of wisdom are rational judgment, justice
	2:6	Just so it is with the emotions that hinder one from justice
	4:13	and not by divine justice
	4:21	The divine justice was angered by these acts
	5:24	it instructs us in justice
	8:14	and whatever justice you revere will be merciful to you
	8:22	Also, divine justice will excuse us
	9:9	will deservedly undergo from the divine justice
	9:15	Most abominable tyrant, enemy of heavenly justice, savage of mind
	11:3	from the heavenly justice for even more crimes
	12:12	Because of this, justice has laid up
	18:22	For these crimes divine justice pursued and will pursue the accursed tyrant

JUSTIFY
6 = 0.004 %

Sir	1:22	Unrighteous anger cannot be justified
	10:29	Who will justify the man that sins against himself ?
	13:22	he speaks unseemly words, and they justify him
	23:11	if he has sworn needlessly, he will not be justified
	31:5	He who loves gold will not be justified
2 Es	4:18	which would you undertake to justify

JUSTLY
6 = 0.004 %

Wis	9:12	and I shall judge thy people justly
	19:13	for they justly suffered because of their wicked acts
2 Ma	7:38	which has justly fallen on our whole nation
	9:6	and that very justly
	9:18	for the judgment of God had justly come upon him
3 Ma	7:7	we justly have acquitted them

JUT out
1

4 Ma	13:6	For just as towers jutting out over harbours

JUTTING
1

4 Ma	7:5	For in setting his mind firm like a jutting cliff

K

KADESH   3 = 0.002 %
Jud   1 : 9   and Chelous and Kadesh and the river of Egypt
1 Ma 11 : 63 had come to Kadesh in Galilee with a large army
      11 : 73 as far as Kadesh, to their camp, and there they encamped

KADESH-BARNEA   1
Jud   5 : 14 and he led them by the way of Sinai and Kadesh-barnea

KADMIEL   2
1 Es 5 : 26 The Levites : the sons of Jeshua and Kadmiel
      5 : 58 and Kadmiel his brother and the sons of Jeshua Emadabun

KEDESH   1
Tob   1 : 2   which is to the south of Kedesh Naphtali

KEDRON   3 = 0.002 %
1 Ma 15 : 39 and commanded him to build up Kedron and fortify its gates
      15 : 41 He built up Kedron and stationed there horsemen and troops
      16 : 9   until Cendebaeus reached Kedron, which he had built

KEEL   1
Wis   5 : 10 nor track of its keel in the waves

KEEN   1
Wis   8 : 11 I shall be found keen in judgment

KEEP   171 = 0.111 %
Tob   1 : 11 but I kept myself from eating it
      3 : 5   because we did not keep thy commandments
      3 : 15 for whom I should keep myself as wife
      4 : 10 and keeps you from entering the darkness
      14 : 9 But keep the law and the commandments
Jud   6 : 12 and all the slingers kept them from coming up
      7 : 12 and keep all the men in your forces with you
      7 : 13 and camp there to keep watch
      8 : 26 while he was keeping the sheep of Laban
      11 : 10 but keep it in your mind
      12 : 1 where his silver dishes were kept
Ad E 12 : 1 the 2 eunuchs of the king who kept watch in the courtyard
Wis   1 : 11 and keep your tongue from slander
      4 : 17 and for what he kept him safe
      6 : 4   nor keep the law, nor walk according to the purpose of God
      10 : 5 and kept him strong
      10 : 12 and kept him safe from those who lay in wait for him
      13 : 7 For as they live among his works they keep searching
      14 : 16 was kept as a law
      14 : 24 they no longer keep
      17 : 16 and thus was kept shut up in a prison not made of iron
      18 : 4 those who had kept thy sons imprisoned
      19 : 6 that thy children might be kept unharmed
Sir   1 : 26 If you desire wisdom, keep the commandments
      1 : 29 and keep watch over your lips
      2 : 15 and those who love him will keep his ways
      3 : 1   and act accordingly, that you may be kept in safety
      4 : 1   and do not keep needy eyes waiting
      6 : 13 Keep yourself far from your enemies
      6 : 18 and until you are old you will keep finding wisdom
      6 : 26 and keep her ways with all your might
      7 : 22 if they are profitable to you, keep them
      8 : 17 for he will not be able to keep a secret
      8 : 18 do nothing that is to be kept secret
      9 : 13 Keep far from a man who has the power to kill
      11 : 21 but trust in the Lord and keep at your toil
      12 : 6 And he is keeping them
      13 : 12 Cruel is he who does not keep words to himself
      13 : 13 Keep words to yourself and be very watchful
      15 : 15 If you will, you can keep the commandments
      17 : 22 and he will keep a person's kindness like the apple of his eye
      20 : 1 and there is a man who keeps silent but is wise
      20 : 2 And the one who confesses his fault will be kept from loss
      20 : 5 There is one who by keeping silent is found wise
      20 : 6 There is one who keeps silent because he has no answer
      20 : 6 while another keeps silent because he knows when to speak
      21 : 11 Whoever keeps the law controls his thoughts
      22 : 27 that it may keep me from falling
      26 : 10 Keep strict watch over a headstrong daughter
      26 : 19 My son, keep sound the bloom of your youth
      26 : 29 A merchant can hardly keep from wrongdoing
      27 : 17 Love your friend and keep faith with him
      27 : 22 and no one can keep him from them
      29 : 1 keeps the commandments
      29 : 3 Confirm your word and keep faith with him
      35 : 1 He who keeps the law makes many offerings
      35 : 3 To keep from wickedness is pleasing to the Lord
      37 : 14 For a man's soul sometimes keeps him better informed
      38 : 34 But they keep stable the fabric of the world
      42 : 3 of keeping accounts with a partner
      42 : 9 A daughter keeps her father secretly wakeful

      42 : 11 Keep strict watch over a headstrong daughter
      44 : 20 he kept the law of the Most High
Bar   2 : 9   And the Lord has kept the calamities ready
L Jr 6 : 35 if one makes a vow to them and does not keep it
1 Ma 1 : 58 They kept using violence against Israel
      2 : 53 Joseph in the time of his distress kept the commandment
      4 : 60 to keep the Gentiles from coming
      5 : 3   because they kept lying in wait for Israel
      5 : 53 And Judas kept rallying the laggards
      6 : 18 Now the men in the citadel kept hemming Israel in
      7 : 45 kept sounding the battle call on the trumpets
      8 : 12 they have kept friendship
      8 : 26 and they shall keep their obligations
      8 : 28 and they shall keep these obligations
      10 : 20 and you are to take our side and keep friendship with us
      10 : 26 Since you have kept your agreement with us
      10 : 27 And now continue still to keep faith with us
      10 : 54 in keeping with your position
      11 : 5 but the king kept silent
      11 : 8 and he kept devising evil designs against Alexander
      11 : 25 kept making complaints against him
      11 : 41 for they kept fighting against Israel
      12 : 27 and to keep their arms at hand
      12 : 40 so he kept seeking to seize and kill him
      12 : 47 He kept with himself 3,000 men
      12 : 50 and kept marching in close formation, ready for battle
      13 : 20 But Simon and his army kept marching along opposite him
      13 : 21 Now the men in the citadel kept sending envoys to Trypho
      15 : 25 and he shut Trypho up and kept him from going out or in
2 Ma 1 : 9   And now see that you keep the feast of booths
      2 : 12 Likewise Solomon also kept the 8 days
      2 : 16 Will you therefore please keep the days ?
      3 : 15 that he should keep them safe
      3 : 19 Some of the maidens who were kept indoors
      3 : 22 that he would keep what had been entrusted safe and secure
      4 : 28 kept requesting payment
      5 : 6   But Jason kept relentlessly slaughtering his fellow citizens
      5 : 27 and kept himself and his companions alive in the mountains
      6 : 6   A man could neither keep the sabbath
      6 : 11 because their piety kept them from defending themselves
      8 : 17 keeping before their eyes the lawless outrage
      8 : 27 they kept the sabbath
      9 : 25 keep watching for opportunities
      10 : 30 they kept him from being wounded
      12 : 38 and they kept the sabbath there
      12 : 42 to keep themselves free from sin
      14 : 4 During that day he kept quiet
      14 : 24 And he kept Judas always in his presence
      14 : 36 keep undefiled for ever this house
      15 : 8 but to keep in mind the former times
      15 : 34 Blessed is he who has kept his own place undefiled
1 Es 1 : 1   Josiah kept the passover to his Lord in Jerusalem
      1 : 6   and keep the passover according to the commandment of the Lord
      1 : 17 were accomplished that day : the passover was kept
      1 : 19 kept the passover and the feast of unleavened bread 7 days
      1 : 20 No passover like it had been kept in Israel
      1 : 21 none of the kings of Israel had kept such a passover
      1 : 21 as was kept by Josiah and the priests and the Levites
      1 : 22 this passover was kept
      1 : 58 it shall keep sabbath all the time of its desolation
      2 : 23 and kept setting up blockades in it from of old
      3 : 4   who kept guard over the person of the king
      4 : 11 but they keep watch around him
      5 : 51 They kept the feast of booths
      5 : 73 And they were kept from building for 2 years
      7 : 10 kept the passover on the 14th day of the first month
      7 : 14 And they kept the feast of unleavened bread 7 days
      8 : 51 kept us safe from our adversaries
3 Ma 3 : 4   they kept their separateness with respect to foods
      5 : 44 at the places in the city most favourable for keeping guard
      7 : 15 and they kept the day as a joyful festival
2 Es 1 : 24 that they may keep my statutes
      2 : 5   because they would not keep my covenant
      3 : 35 Or what nation has kept thy commandments so well ?
      3 : 36 who have kept thy commandments
      4 : 40 her womb can keep the child within her any longer
      6 : 42 6 parts thou didst dry up and keep
      6 : 49 Then thou didst keep in existence 2 living creatures
      6 : 52 and thou hast kept them to be eaten by whom thou wilt
      7 : 45 Blessed are those who are alive and keep thy commandments !
      7 : 72 and though they received the commandments they did not keep them
      7 : 75 we shall be kept in rest until those times come
      7 : 79 and have not kept the way of the Most High
      7 : 88 who have kept the ways of the Most High
      7 : 89 that they might keep the law of the Lawgiver perfectly
      7 : 94 they kept the law which was given them in trust
      8 : 9   But that which keeps and that which is kept
      8 : 9   shall both be kept by thy keeping

	8 :27	but the endeavours of those who have kept thy covenants amid afflictions
	9 :32	they did not keep it, and did not observe the statutes
	9 :33	because they did not keep what had been sown in them
	10 :15	Now, therefore, keep your sorrow to yourself
	12 :21	and 4 shall be kept for the time
	12 :21	but 2 shall be kept until the end
	12 :30	It is these whom the Most High has kept for the eagle's end
	12 :32	this is the Messiah whom the Most High has kept
	12 :38	and keep these secrets
	13 :26	this is he whom the Most High has been keeping for many ages
	13 :42	that there at least they might keep their statutes
	13 :42	which they had not kept in their own land
	14 :4	where I kept him with me many days
	14 :6	and these you shall keep secret
	14 :30	and received the law of life, which they did not keep
	14 :31	and did not keep the ways which the Most High commanded you
	14 :34	you shall be kept alive
	14 :46	but keep the 70 that were written last
	16 :76	You who keep my commandments and precepts, says the Lord God
4 Ma	6 :7	he kept his reason upright and unswerving
	15 :10	in keeping the ordinances

KEEP away   2

1 Es	6 :27	to keep away from the place, and to permit Zerubbabel
4 Ma	14 :17	If they are not able to keep him away

KEEP on   2

2 Ma	7 :17	Keep on, and see how his mighty power
	10 :14	and at every turn kept on warring against the Jews

KEEP up   2

2 Ma	10 :15	and endeavoured to keep up the war
	14 :6	are keeping up war and stirring up sedition

KEEPER   5 = 0.003 %

Tob	1 :22	Now Ahikar was cupbearer, keeper of the signet
Sir	37 :12	whom you know to be a keeper of the commandments
3 Ma	5 :1	so he summoned Hermon, keeper of the elephants
	5 :4	And Hermon, keeper of the elephants
	5 :45	the elephant keeper entered at about dawn into the courtyard

KEEPING   5 = 0.003 %

Wis	6 :18	and love of her is the keeping of her laws
Sir	32 :23	for this is the keeping of the commandments
2 Ma	15 :3	who had commanded the keeping of the sabbath day
2 Es	8 :9	shall both be kept by thy keeping
4 Ma	5 :29	concerning the keeping of the law

KELAIAH   1

1 Es	9 :23	And of the Levites : Jozabad and Shimei and Kelaiah

KELITA   2

1 Es	9 :23	who was Kelita, and Pethahiah and Judah and Jonah
	9 :48	Shabbethai, Hodiah, Maaseiah and Kelita

KEROS   1

1 Es	5 :29	the sons of Keros, the sons of Siaha, sons of Padon

KETAB   1

1 Es	5 :30	the sons of Akkub, the sons of Uthai, the sons of Ketab

KETTLE   1

Sir	13 :2	How can the clay pot associate with the iron kettle ?

KEY   1

2 Ma	14 :22	Judas posted armed men in readiness at key places

KICK   1

4 Ma	6 :8	and began to kick him in the side

KID   3 = 0.002 %

Tob	2 :12	Once when they paid her wages, they also gave her a kid
	2 :13	So I said to her, Where did you get the kid ?
1 Es	1 :7	30,000 lambs and kids, and 3,000 calves

KILAN   1

1 Es	5 :15	The sons of Kilan and Azetas, 67

KILL   70 = 0.046 %

Tob	1 :21	before 2 of Sennacherib's sons killed him
	7 :8	and they killed a ram from the flock
Jud	1 :12	that he would kill by the sword
	2 :25	and killed every one who resisted him
	11 :12	they have planned to kill their cattle and determined
	16 :5	and kill my young men with the sword
Wis	11 :19	but the mere sight of them could kill by fright
	14 :23	For whether they kill children in their initiations
	14 :24	but they either treacherously kill one another

	16 :9	For they were killed by the bites of locusts and flies
	16 :14	A man in his wickedness kills another
	18 :5	When they had resolved to kill the babes of thy holy ones
Sir	9 :13	Keep far from a man who has the power to kill
	34 :20	Like one who kills a son before his father's eyes
	47 :4	In his youth did he not kill a giant
Bel	14 :29	or else we will kill you and your household
1 Ma	2 :9	Her babes have been killed in her streets
	2 :24	he ran and killed him upon the altar
	2 :25	At the same time he killed the king's officer
	2 :37	that you are killing us unjustly
	3 :11	and he defeated and killed him
	5 :2	So they began to kill and destroy among the people
	5 :13	and all our brethren who were in the land of Tob have been killed
	5 :28	and killed every male by the edge of the sword
	5 :35	and he killed every male in it, plundered it
	6 :45	he killed men right and left
	6 :46	stabbed it from beneath, and killed it
	7 :4	So the army killed them
	7 :16	but he seized 60 of them and killed them in one day
	7 :19	and killed them and threw them into the great pit
	9 :2	and they took it and killed many people
	9 :32	When Bacchides learned of this, he tried to kill him
	9 :40	and began killing them
	9 :61	and killed them
	9 :69	and he killed many of them
	11 :10	for he has tried to kill me
	11 :18	and his troops in the strongholds were killed
	11 :45	and they wanted to kill the king
	11 :47	and they killed on that day as many as a 100,000 men
	12 :40	so he kept seeking to seize and kill him
	12 :48	and all who had entered with him they killed with the sword
	13 :23	When he approached Baskama, he killed Jonathan
	13 :31	he killed him
	15 :40	and take the people captive and kill them
	16 :16	and they killed him and his 2 sons
	16 :21	and that he has sent men to kill you also
	16 :22	and he seized the men who came to destroy him and killed them
2 Ma	4 :34	urged him to kill Onias
	4 :42	As a result, they wounded many of them, and killed some
	4 :42	and the temple robber himself they killed
	5 :26	and killed great numbers of people
	8 :30	they killed more than 20,000 of them
	8 :32	They killed the commander of Timothy's forces
	10 :17	killing no fewer than 20,000
	10 :37	They killed Timothy, who was hidden in a cistern
	12 :28	and killed as many as 25,000 of those who were within it
	14 :13	with orders to kill Judas and scatter his men
1 Es	1 :1	he killed the passover lamb on the 14th day of the first month
	1 :6	and kill the passover lamb
	4 :5	They kill and are killed
	4 :7	If he tells them to kill, they kill
3 Ma	1 :2	intending single-handed to kill him and thereby end the war
2 Es	1 :18	Why hast thou led us into the wilderness to kill us ?
	15 :53	if you had not always killed my chosen people
	16 :34	Their bridegrooms shall be killed in war
4 Ma	5 :3	they were to be broken on the wheel and killed
	13 :14	Let us not fear him who thinks he is killing us
	18 :19	I kill and I make alive :

KILLING   1

2 Ma	5 :13	Then there was killing of young and old

KILN   1

Sir	27 :5	The kiln tests the potter's vessels

KIN   2

Jud	16 :24	to all those who were next of kin to her husband Manasseh
Sir	23 :16	a man who commits fornication with his near of kin

KIND, adj.   6 = 0.004 %

Wis	12 :19	that the righteous man must be kind
	15 :1	But thou, our God, art kind and true, patient
1 Ma	6 :11	For I was kind and beloved in my power
2 Ma	1 :24	who alone art King and art kind
	12 :30	and their kind treatment of them in times of misfortune
4 Ma	8 :17	and exhorted us to accept kind treatment if we obey him

KIND, subst.   15 = 0.010 %

Wis	19 :11	Afterward they saw also a new kind of birds
	19 :21	easily melted kind of heavenly food
Sir	16 :30	with all kinds of living beings he covered its surface
	25 :2	My soul hates 3 kinds of men
	27 :9	Birds flock with their kind
	36 :19	As the palate tastes the kinds of game
	41 :16	For it is not good to retain every kind of shame
	43 :25	all kinds of living things, and huge creatures of the sea
	50 :9	adorned with all kinds of precious stones
3 Ma	7 :7	of every charge of whatever kind

	7:16	in words of praise and all kinds of melodious songs
4 Ma	1:14	how many kinds of emotions there are
	1:18	Now the kinds of wisdom are rational judgment, justice
	3:2	No one of us can eradicate that kind of desire
	9:29	How sweet is any kind of death for the religion of our fathers !

KINDLE 17 = 0.011 %

Jud	7:5	and when they had kindled fires on their towers
	13:13	and they kindled a fire for light, and gathered around them
Wis	2:2	and reason is a spark kindled by the beating of our hearts
Sir	8:10	Do not kindle the coals of a sinner
	9:8	and by it passion is kindled like a fire
	16:6	In an assembly of sinners a fire will be kindled
	16:6	and in a disobedient nation wrath was kindled
	28:8	for a man given to anger will kindle strife
	28:11	A hasty quarrel kindles fire, and urgent strife sheds blood
	32:16	and like a light they will kindle righteous deeds
	40:30	but in his stomach a fire is kindled
	51:4	and from the midst of fire which I did not kindle
1 Ma	12:28	so they kindled fires in their camp and withdrew
2 Ma	10:36	they kindled fires and burned the blasphemers alive
2 Es	15:23	and the sinners, like straw that is kindled
	16:15	The fire is kindled, and shall not be put out
	16:68	For behold, the burning wrath of a great multitude is kindled over you

KINDLINESS 1

Ad E	16:10	and quite devoid of our kindliness

KINDLY 6 = 0.004 %

Wis	1:6	For wisdom is a kindly spirit
Sir	13:6	He will speak to you kindly and say, What do you need ?
2 Ma	3:9	and had been kindly welcomed by the high priest of the city
	6:22	and be treated kindly
1 Es	6:5	Yet the elders of the Jews were dealt with kindly
4 Ma	8:5	Young men, I admire each and every one of you in a kindly manner

KINDNESS 23 = 0.015 %

Ad E	13:2	but always acting reasonably and with kindness
	16:2	by the too great kindness of their benefactors
Wis	16:2	thou didst show kindness to thy people
	16:11	and become unresponsive to thy kindness
	16:24	and in kindness relaxes on behalf of those who trust in thee
Sir	3:14	For kindness to a father will not be forgotten
	7:33	and withhold not kindness from the dead
	12:1	If you do a kindness, know to whom you do it
	17:22	and he will keep a person's kindness like the apple of his eye
	19:25	and there are people who distort kindness to gain a verdict
	29:15	Do not forget all the kindness of your surety
	30:6	and one to repay the kindness of his friends
	35:2	He who returns a kindness offers fine flour
	36:23	If kindness and humility mark her speech
	37:11	or with a merciless man about kindness
	40:17	Kindness is like a garden of blessings
Bar	2:27	in all thy kindness and in all thy great compassion
2 Ma	2:22	while the Lord with great kindness became gracious to them
	6:13	is a sign of great kindness
	9:27	and will treat you with moderation and kindness
	10:38	who shows great kindness to Israel
	14:9	with the gracious kindness which you show to all
P Ma	11	beseeching thee for thy kindness

KINDRED, subst., adj. 9 = 0.006 %

Jud	16:24	and to her own nearest kindred
Wis	7:3	and fell upon the kindred earth
Sir	22:10	stain the nobility of their kindred
Sus	13:30	And she came, with her parents, her children, and all her kindred
	13:63	and so did Joakim her husband and all her kindred
2 Ma	5:6	not realizing that success at the cost of one's kindred
1 Es	1:4	and prepare yourselves by your families and kindred
	1:10	stood according to kindred
	7:9	arrayed in their garments, according to kindred

KING 621 = 0.404 %

Tob	1:2	who in the days of Shalmaneser, king of the Assyrians
	1:18	And if Sennacherib the king put to death
	1:18	When the bodies were sought by the king
	1:19	and informed the king about me, that I was burying them
	12:7	It is good to guard the secret of a king
	12:11	I have said, It is good to guard the secret of a king
	13:6	and exalt the King of the ages
	13:7	my soul exalts the King of heaven
	13:10	and praise the King of the ages
	13:11	bearing gifts in their hands, gifts for the King of heaven
	13:15	Let my soul praise God the great King
Jud	1:2	he is the king who built walls about Ecbatana
	1:5	it was in those days that King Nebuchadnezzar made war
	1:5	against King Arphaxad in the great plain

	1:7	Then Nebuchadnezzar king of the Assyrians
	1:11	king of the Assyrians
	1:13	In the 17th year he led his forces against King Arphaxad
	2:1	king of the Assyrians
	2:4	Nebuchadnezzar king of the Assyrians called Holofernes
	2:5	Thus says the Great King, the Lord of the whole earth :
	2:19	to go ahead of King Nebuchadnezzar
	3:2	Behold, we the servants of Nebuchadnezzar, the Great King
	4:1	the king of the Assyrians
	5:3	Who rules over them as king, leading their army ?
	5:11	So the king of Egypt became hostile to them
	6:3	we the king's servants will destroy them as one man
	6:4	So says King Nebuchadnezzar, the lord of the whole earth
	9:12	King of all thy creation, hear my prayer !
	11:1	the king of all the earth
	11:4	as they do the servants of my lord King Nebuchadnezzar
	11:7	Nebuchadnezzar the king of the whole earth lives
	11:23	and you shall live in the house of King Nebuchadnezzar
	14:18	upon the house of King Nebuchadnezzar
Ad E	10:6	the river is Esther, whom the king married and made queen
	11:3	a great man, serving in the court of the king
	11:4	whom Nebuchadnezzar king of Babylon
	11:4	had brought from Jerusalem with Jeconiah king of Judea
	12:1	the 2 eunuchs of the king who kept watch in the courtyard
	12:2	to lay hands upon Ahasuerus the king
	12:2	and he informed the king concerning them
	12:3	Then the king examined the 2 eunuchs
	12:4	The king made a permanent record of these things
	12:5	And the king ordered Mordecai to serve in the court
	12:6	was in great honour with the king
	12:6	because of the 2 eunuchs of the king
	13:1	The Great King, Ahasuerus
	13:4	and continually disregard the ordinances of the kings
	13:9	He said : O Lord, Lord, King who rulest over all things
	13:15	And now, O Lord God and King
	14:3	O my Lord, thou only art our King
	14:10	and to magnify for ever a mortal king
	14:12	O King of the gods and Master of all dominion !
	14:17	and I have not honoured the king's feast
	15:6	she stood before the king
	15:8	Then God changed the spirit of the king to gentleness
	15:16	And the king was agitated
	16:1	The Great King, Ahasuerus
Wis	6:1	Listen therefore, O kings, and understand
	6:24	and a sensible king is the stability of his people
	7:5	For no king has had a different beginning of existence
	9:7	Thou hast chosen me to be king of thy people
	10:16	and withstood dread kings with wonders and signs
	11:10	as a stern king does in condemnation
	12:14	nor can any king or monarch confront thee
	14:17	and made a visible image of the king whom they honoured
	14:18	impelled even those who did not know the king
	18:11	and the common man suffered the same loss as the king
Sir	7:4	nor the seat of honour from the king
	7:5	nor display your wisdom before the king
	8:2	and has perverted the minds of kings
	10:3	An undisciplined king will ruin his people
	10:10	the king of today will die tomorrow
	11:5	Many kings have had to sit on the ground
	18:3	for he is king of all things
	38:2	and he will receive a gift from the king
	45:3	the Lord glorified him in the presence of kings
	45:25	the heritage of a king is from son to son only
	46:20	he prophesied and revealed to the king his death
	47:11	he gave him the covenant of kings
	48:6	who brought kings down to destruction
	48:8	who anointed kings to inflict retribution
	48:23	and he lengthened the life of the king
	49:4	the kings of Judah came to an end
	50:15	a pleasing odour to the Most High, the King of all
	51:1	I will give thanks to thee, O Lord and King
	51:6	the slander of an unrighteous tongue to the king
Bar	1:3	in the hearing of Jeconiah the son of Jehoiakim, king of Judah
	1:8	the silver vessels which Zedekiah the son of Josiah, king of Judah, had made
	1:9	after Nebuchadnezzar king of Babylon had carried away from Jerusalem
	1:11	and pray for the life of Nebuchadnezzar king of Babylon
	1:12	and we shall live under the protection of Nebuchadnezzar king of Babylon
	1:16	and to our kings and our princes and our priests
	2:1	and against our kings and against our princes
	2:19	of our fathers or our kings
	2:21	Bend your shoulders and serve the king of Babylon
	2:22	and will not serve the king of Babylon
	2:24	But we did not obey thy voice, to serve the king of Babylon
	2:24	that the bones of our kings and the bones of our fathers
L Jr	6:1	by the king of the Babylonians
	6:2	by Nebuchadnezzar, king of the Babylonians
	6:18	upon a man who has offended a king

	6 : 34	They cannot set up a king or depose one
	6 : 51	It will be manifest to all the nations and kings
	6 : 53	For they cannot set up a king over a country or give rain to men
	6 : 56	Besides, they can offer no resistance to a king or any enemies
	6 : 59	So it is better to be a king who shows his courage
	6 : 66	For they can neither curse nor bless kings
P Az	9	most hateful rebels, and to an unjust king
	23	Now the king's servants who threw them in
Bel	14 : 1	When King Astyages was laid with his fathers
	14 : 2	And Daniel was a companion of the king
	14 : 4	The king revered it and went every day to worship it
	14 : 5	And the king said to him, Why do you not worship Bel ?
	14 : 6	The king said to him
	14 : 7	Do not be deceived, O king
	14 : 8	Then the king was angry
	14 : 9	And Daniel said to the king
	14 : 10	And the king went with Daniel into the temple of Bel
	14 : 11	you yourself, O king, shall set forth the food
	14 : 14	When they had gone out, the king set forth the food for Bel
	14 : 14	in the presence of the king alone
	14 : 14	and sealed it with the king's signet, and departed
	14 : 16	Early in the morning the king rose and came
	14 : 17	And the king said, Are the seals unbroken, Daniel ?
	14 : 17	He answered, They are unbroken, O king
	14 : 18	the king looked at the table, and shouted in a loud voice
	14 : 19	and restrained the king from going in, and said
	14 : 20	The king said
	14 : 21	Then the king was enraged
	14 : 22	Therefore the king put them to death
	14 : 24	And the king said to Daniel
	14 : 26	But if you, O king, will give me permission
	14 : 26	The king said, I give you permission
	14 : 28	they were very indignant and conspired against the king
	14 : 28	saying, The king has become a Jew
	14 : 29	Going to the king, they said, Hand Daniel over to us
	14 : 30	The king saw that they were pressing him hard
	14 : 40	On the 7th day the king came to mourn for Daniel
	14 : 41	And the king shouted with a loud voice
1 Ma	1 : 1	had defeated Darius, king of the Persians and the Medes
	1 : 1	he succeeded him as king
	1 : 1	He had previously become king of Greece
	1 : 2	and put to death the kings of the earth
	1 : 10	son of Antiochus the king
	1 : 13	and some of the people eagerly went to the king
	1 : 16	he determined to become king of the land of Egypt
	1 : 18	He engaged Ptolemy king of Egypt in battle
	1 : 29	2 years later the king sent to the cities of Judah
	1 : 41	Then the king wrote to his whole kingdom
	1 : 43	All the Gentiles accepted the command of the king
	1 : 44	And the king sent letters by messengers to Jerusalem
	1 : 50	And whoever does not obey the command of the king shall die
	1 : 57	the decree of the king condemned him to death
	2 : 15	Then the king's officers who were enforcing the apostasy
	2 : 17	Then the king's officers spoke to Mattathias as follows :
	2 : 18	Now be the first to come and do what the king commands
	2 : 18	among the friends of the king
	2 : 19	Even if all the nations that live under the rule of the king
	2 : 22	We will not obey the king's words
	2 : 23	according to the king's command
	2 : 25	At the same time he killed the king's officer
	2 : 31	And it was reported to the king's officers
	2 : 31	that men who had rejected the king's command
	2 : 33	Come out and do what the king commands, and you will live
	2 : 34	nor will we do what the king commands
	2 : 48	They rescued the law out of the hands of the Gentiles and kings
	3 : 7	He embittered many kings, but he made Jacob glad by his deeds
	3 : 14	who scorn the king's command
	3 : 26	His fame reached the king
	3 : 27	When King Antiochus heard these reports
	3 : 30	which he used to give more lavishly than preceding kings
	3 : 32	in charge of the king's affairs
	3 : 37	Then the king took the remaining half of his troops
	3 : 38	mighty men among the friends of the king
	3 : 39	as the king had commanded
	3 : 42	They also learned what the king had commanded
	4 : 3	moved out to attack the king's force in Emmaus
	4 : 27	nor had they turned out as the king had commanded him
	6 : 1	King Antiochus was going through the upper provinces
	6 : 2	the Macedonian king who first reigned over the Greeks
	6 : 8	When the king heard this news
	6 : 15	and bring him up to be king
	6 : 16	Thus Antiochus the king died there in the 149th year
	6 : 17	And when Lysias learned that the king was dead
	6 : 17	he set up Antiochus the king's son to reign
	6 : 22	They went to the king and said
	6 : 28	The king was enraged when he heard this
	6 : 32	opposite the camp of the king
	6 : 33	Early in the morning the king rose
	6 : 40	Now a part of the king's army
	6 : 42	and 600 men of the king's army fell

	6 : 43	and he supposed that the king was upon it
	6 : 48	The soldiers of the king's army
	6 : 48	and the king encamped in Judea and at Mount Zion
	6 : 50	So the king took Beth-zur
	6 : 55	whom King Antiochus while still living
	6 : 55	had appointed to bring up Antiochus his son to be king
	6 : 56	with the forces that had gone with the king
	6 : 57	and said to the king, to the commanders of the forces, and to the men
	6 : 60	The speech pleased the king and the commanders
	6 : 61	So the king and the commanders gave them their oath
	6 : 62	But when the king entered Mount Zion
	7 : 6	And they brought to the king this accusation
	7 : 7	which Judas has brought upon us and upon the land of the king
	7 : 8	So the king chose Bacchides, one of the king's friends
	7 : 8	and was faithful to the king
	7 : 20	then Bacchides went back to the king
	7 : 25	he returned to the king
	7 : 26	Then the king sent Nicanor, one of his honoured princes
	7 : 33	that was being offered for the king
	7 : 41	When the messengers from the king spoke blasphemy
	8 : 4	They also subdued the kings who came against them
	8 : 5	Philip, and Perseus king of the Macedonians
	8 : 6	They also defeated Antiochus the Great, king of Asia
	8 : 8	These they took from him and gave to Eumenes the king
	8 : 12	They have subdued kings far and near
	8 : 13	Those whom they wish to help and to make kings
	8 : 13	they make kings
	8 : 31	which King Demetrius is doing to them
	9 : 57	he returned to the king
	10 : 2	When Demetrius the king heard of it
	10 : 8	that the king had given him authority to recruit troops
	10 : 15	Now Alexander the king heard of all the promises
	10 : 18	King Alexander to his brother Jonathan, greeting
	10 : 20	you are to be called the king's friend
	10 : 25	King Demetrius to the nation of the Jews, greeting
	10 : 36	Let Jews be enrolled in the king's forces
	10 : 36	that is due to all the forces of the king
	10 : 37	in the great strongholds of the king
	10 : 37	just as the king has commanded in the land of Judah
	10 : 40	out of the king's revenues from appropriate places
	10 : 43	because he owes money to the king or has any debt
	10 : 44	be paid from the revenues of the king
	10 : 45	also be paid from the revenues of the king
	10 : 48	Now Alexander the king assembled large forces
	10 : 49	The 2 kings met in battle
	10 : 51	Then Alexander sent ambassadors to Ptolemy king of Egypt
	10 : 55	Ptolemy the king replied and said
	10 : 58	Alexander the king met him
	10 : 58	and celebrated her wedding at Ptolemais with great pomp, as kings do
	10 : 59	Then Alexander the king wrote to Jonathan to come to meet him
	10 : 60	So he went with pomp to Ptolemais and met the 2 kings
	10 : 61	but the king paid no attention to them
	10 : 62	The king gave orders to take off Jonathan's garments
	10 : 63	The king also seated him at his side
	10 : 65	Thus the king honoured him
	10 : 68	When Alexander the king heard of it
	10 : 88	When Alexander the king heard of these things
	10 : 89	such as it is the custom to give to the kinsmen of kings
	11 : 1	Then the king of Egypt gathered great forces
	11 : 2	for Alexander the king had commanded them to meet him
	11 : 5	They also told the king what Jonathan had done
	11 : 5	but the king kept silent
	11 : 6	Jonathan met the king at Joppa with pomp
	11 : 7	And Jonathan went with the king
	11 : 8	So King Ptolemy gained control of the coastal cities
	11 : 9	He sent envoys to Demetrius the king, saying
	11 : 14	Now Alexander the king was in Cilicia at that time
	11 : 16	and King Ptolemy was exalted
	11 : 18	But King Ptolemy died 3 days later
	11 : 19	So Demetrius became king in the 167th year
	11 : 21	went to the king and reported to him
	11 : 24	for he went to the king at Ptolemais
	11 : 26	the king treated him as his predecessors had treated him
	11 : 28	Then Jonathan asked the king
	11 : 29	The king consented
	11 : 30	King Demetrius to Jonathan his brother
	11 : 32	King Demetrius to Lasthenes his father, greeting
	11 : 34	which the king formerly received from them each year
	11 : 38	Now when Demetrius the king saw
	11 : 40	to become king in place of his father
	11 : 41	Now Jonathan sent to Demetrius the king the request
	11 : 44	and when they came to the king
	11 : 44	the king rejoiced at their arrival
	11 : 45	and they wanted to kill the king
	11 : 46	But the king fled into the palace
	11 : 47	So the king called the Jews to his aid
	11 : 48	and they saved the king
	11 : 49	and they cried out to the king with this entreaty

	11 : 51	So the Jews gained glory in the eyes of the king
	11 : 52	So Demetrius the king sat on the throne of his kingdom
	11 : 57	and make you one of the friends of the king
	12 : 7	from Arius, who was king among you
	12 : 13	the kings round about us have waged war against us
	12 : 20	Arius, king of the Spartans
	12 : 39	Then Trypho attempted to become king of Asia
	12 : 39	and to raise his hand against Antiochus the king
	13 : 31	Trypho dealt treacherously with the young king Antiochus
	13 : 32	and became king in his place, putting on the crown of Asia
	13 : 34	Simon also chose men and sent them to Demetrius the king
	13 : 35	Demetrius the king sent him a favourable reply to this request
	13 : 36	King Demetrius to Simon, the high priest and friend of kings
	14 : 1	In the 172nd year Demetrius the king assembled his forces
	14 : 2	When Arsaces the king of Persia and Media heard
	14 : 13	and the kings were crushed in those days
	14 : 38	King Demetrius confirmed him in the high priesthood
	14 : 39	and he made him one of the king's friends
	15 : 1	Antiochus, the son of Demetrius the king
	15 : 2	King Antiochus to Simon the high priest and ethnarch
	15 : 5	that the kings before me have granted you
	15 : 15	with letters to the kings and countries
	15 : 16	Lucius, consul of the Romans, to King Ptolemy, greeting
	15 : 19	to the kings and countries
	15 : 22	The consul wrote the same thing to Demetrius the king
	15 : 25	Antiochus the king besieged Dor anew
	15 : 32	So Athenobius the friend of the king came to Jerusalem
	15 : 32	He reported to him the words of the king
	15 : 36	But returned in wrath to the king
	15 : 36	And the king was greatly angered
	15 : 38	Then the king made Cendebaeus commander-in-chief of the coastal country
	15 : 39	but the king pursued Trypho
	15 : 41	as the king had ordered him
	16 : 18	and sent it to the king
2 Ma	1 : 10	teacher of Ptolemy the king
	1 : 11	we thank him greatly for taking our side against the king
	1 : 20	Nehemiah, having been commissioned by the king of Persia
	1 : 24	who alone art King and art kind
	1 : 33	and it was reported to the king of the Persians
	1 : 34	the king investigated the matter
	1 : 35	And with those persons whom the king favoured
	2 : 13	and collected the books about the kings and prophets
	2 : 13	and letters of kings about votive offerings
	3 : 2	it came about that the kings themselves honoured the place
	3 : 3	so that even Seleucus, the king of Asia
	3 : 6	to fall under the control of the king
	3 : 7	When Apollonius met the king
	3 : 7	The king chose Heliodorus, who was in charge of his affairs
	3 : 8	but in fact to carry out the king's purpose
	3 : 13	But Heliodorus, because of the king's commands which he had
	3 : 13	for the king's treasury
	3 : 32	And the high priest, fearing that the king might get the notion
	3 : 35	he marched off with his forces to the king
	3 : 37	When the king asked Heliodorus
	4 : 5	So he betook himself to the king
	4 : 6	For he saw that without the king's attention
	4 : 8	promising the king at an interview 360 talents of silver
	4 : 10	When the king assented and Jason came to office
	4 : 18	and the king was present
	4 : 21	for the coronation of Philometor as king
	4 : 23	to carry the money to the king
	4 : 24	But he, when presented to the king
	4 : 25	After receiving the king's orders he returned
	4 : 27	any of the money promised to the king
	4 : 28	the 2 of them were summoned by the king
	4 : 30	as a present to Antiochis, the king's concubine
	4 : 31	So the king went hastily to settle the trouble
	4 : 36	When the king returned from the region of Cilicia
	4 : 44	When the king came to Tyre
	4 : 45	to win over the king
	4 : 46	Therefore Ptolemy, taking the king aside into a colonnade
	4 : 46	induced the king to change his mind
	5 : 11	When news of what had happened reached the king
	5 : 16	the votive offerings which other kings had made
	5 : 18	whom Seleucus the king sent to inspect the treasury
	6 : 1	Not long after this, the king sent an Athenian senator
	6 : 7	On the monthly celebration of the king's birthday
	6 : 21	which had been commanded by the king
	7 : 1	and were being compelled by the king
	7 : 3	The king fell into a rage
	7 : 5	the king ordered them to take him to the fire, still breathing
	7 : 9	but the King of the universe will raise us up
	7 : 12	As a result the king himself and those with him
	7 : 16	But he looked at the king, and said
	7 : 25	the king called the mother to him
	7 : 30	I will not obey the king's command
	7 : 39	The king fell into a rage
	8 : 8	for aid to the king's government
	8 : 9	one of the king's chief friends
	8 : 10	Nicanor determined to make up for the king
	9 : 19	Antiochus their king and general sends hearty greetings
	9 : 25	So I have appointed my son Antiochus to be king
	10 : 13	by the king's friends
	11 : 1	Lysias, the king's guardian and kinsman
	11 : 14	promising that he would persuade the king
	11 : 15	For the king granted every request in behalf of the Jews
	11 : 18	I have informed the king of everything
	11 : 22	The king's letter ran thus :
	11 : 22	King Antiochus to his brother Lysias, greeting
	11 : 27	To the nation the king's letter was as follows :
	11 : 27	King Antiochus to the senate of the Jews
	11 : 35	With regard to what Lysias the kinsman of the king has granted you
	11 : 36	are to be referred to the king
	12 : 1	Lysias returned to the king
	13 : 4	But the King of kings aroused the anger of Antiochus
	13 : 9	The king with barbarous arrogance
	13 : 13	before the king's army could enter Judea
	13 : 15	he attacked the king's pavilion at night
	13 : 18	The king, having had a taste of the daring of the Jews
	13 : 22	The king negotiated a 2nd time
	13 : 26	This is how the king's attack and withdrawal turned out
	14 : 4	and went to King Demetrius in about the 151st year
	14 : 8	for the interests of the king
	14 : 9	Since you are acquainted, O king
	14 : 11	the rest of the king's friends, who were hostile to Judas
	14 : 27	The king became excited
	14 : 29	Since it was not possible to oppose the king
	15 : 5	and finish the king's business
	15 : 22	in the time of Hezekiah king of Judea
1 Es	1 : 3	in the house which Solomon the king, the son of David, had built
	1 : 5	in accordance with the directions of David king of Israel
	1 : 7	these were given from the king's possessions, as he promised
	1 : 15	who represented the king
	1 : 18	according to the command of King Josiah
	1 : 21	none of the kings of Israel had kept such a passover
	1 : 25	it happened that Pharaoh, king of Egypt
	1 : 26	And the king of Egypt sent word to him saying
	1 : 26	What have we to do with each other, king of Judea ?
	1 : 29	and the commanders came down against King Josiah
	1 : 30	And the king said to his servants
	1 : 33	of the kings of Judea
	1 : 33	are recorded in the book of the kings of Israel and Judah
	1 : 34	and made him king in succession to Josiah his father
	1 : 35	Then the king of Egypt deposed him from reigning in Jerusalem
	1 : 37	And the king of Egypt made Jehoiakim his brother
	1 : 37	king of Judea and Jerusalem
	1 : 40	And Nebuchadnezzar king of Babylon came up against him
	1 : 42	are written in the chronicles of the kings
	1 : 43	Jehoiakim his son became king in his stead
	1 : 43	when he was made king he was 18 years old
	1 : 46	and made Zedekiah king of Judea and Jerusalem
	1 : 48	And though King Nebuchadnezzar had made him swear
	1 : 52	to bring against them the kings of the Chaldeans
	2 : 1	In the first year of Cyrus as king of the Persians
	2 : 2	the Lord stirred up the spirit of Cyrus king of the Persians
	2 : 3	Thus says Cyrus king of the Persians :
	2 : 3	has made me king of the world
	2 : 10	Cyrus the king also brought out the holy vessels of the Lord
	2 : 11	When Cyrus king of the Persians brought these out
	2 : 16	But in the time of Artaxerxes king of the Persians
	2 : 17	To King Artaxerxes our lord
	2 : 18	Now be it known to our lord the king
	2 : 19	but will even resist kings
	2 : 21	but to speak to our lord the king, in order that
	2 : 22	troubling both kings and other cities
	2 : 24	Therefore we now make known to you, O lord and king
	2 : 25	Then the king, in reply to Rehum the recorder
	2 : 26	that this city from of old has fought against kings
	2 : 27	and that mighty and cruel kings ruled in Jerusalem
	2 : 29	to the annoyance of kings
	2 : 30	Then, when the letter from King Artaxerxes was read
	2 : 30	of Darius king of the Persians
	3 : 1	Now King Darius gave a great banquet
	3 : 3	and Darius the king went to his bedroom
	3 : 4	who kept guard over the person of the king
	3 : 5	Darius the king will give rich gifts
	3 : 8	and put them under the pillow of Darius the king
	3 : 9	and said, When the king wakes
	3 : 9	and to the one whose statement the king
	3 : 11	The 2nd wrote, The king is strongest
	3 : 13	When the king awoke
	3 : 19	It makes equal the mind of the king and the orphan
	3 : 21	It makes all hearts feel rich, forgets kings and satraps
	4 : 1	Then the 2nd, who had spoken of the strength of the king
	4 : 3	But the king is stronger
	4 : 5	and do not disobey the king's command
	4 : 5	if they win the victory, they bring everything to the king

4 : 6	and bring some to the king
4 : 6	and they compel one another to pay taxes to the king
4 : 12	Gentlemen, why is not the king the strongest
4 : 14	Gentlemen, is not the king great, and are not men many
4 : 15	Women gave birth to the king
4 : 28	Is not the king great in his power ?
4 : 29	Yet I have seen him with Apame, the king's concubine
4 : 29	she would sit at the king's right hand
4 : 30	and take the crown from the king's head and put it on her own
4 : 30	and slap the king with her left hand
4 : 31	At this the king would gaze at her with mouth agape
4 : 33	Then the king and the nobles looked at one another
4 : 37	Wine is unrighteous, the king is unrighteous
4 : 42	Then the king said to him, Ask what you wish
4 : 43	Then he said to the king
4 : 43	in the day when you became king
4 : 46	And now, O lord the king
4 : 46	whose fulfilment you vowed to the King of heaven
4 : 47	Then Darius the king rose, and kissed him
4 : 58	and praised the King of heaven, saying
5 : 6	who spoke wise words before Darius the king of the Persians
5 : 7	whom Nebuchadnezzar king of Babylon had carried away to Babylon
5 : 55	from Cyrus king of the Persians
5 : 60	according to the directions of David king of Israel
5 : 69	ever since the days of Esarhaddon king of the Assyrians
5 : 71	as Cyrus the king of the Persians has commanded us
5 : 73	as long as King Cyrus lived
6 : 8	To King Darius, greeting
6 : 8	Let it be fully known to our lord the king that
6 : 14	by a king of Israel who was great and strong
6 : 15	into the hands of Nebuchadnezzar king of Babylon
6 : 15	king of the Chaldeans
6 : 17	King Cyrus wrote that this house should be rebuilt
6 : 18	these Cyrus the king took out again
6 : 21	Now therefore, if it seems wise, O king
6 : 21	of our lord the king that are in Babylon
6 : 22	was done with the consent of King Cyrus
6 : 22	and if it is approved by our lord the king
6 : 23	Then King Darius commanded that search be made
6 : 24	King Cyrus ordered the building
6 : 25	the cost to be paid from the treasury of Cyrus the king
6 : 31	for the king and his children
6 : 32	and his property should be forfeited to the king
6 : 33	destroy every king and nation
6 : 34	I, King Darius, have decreed
7 : 1	following the orders of King Darius
7 : 4	kings of the Persians
7 : 5	in the 6th year of King Darius
7 : 15	because he had changed the will of the king of the Assyrians concerning them
8 : 1	when Artaxerxes the king of the Persians was reigning
8 : 4	and the king showed him honour
8 : 4	for he found favour before the king in all his requests
8 : 6	in the 5th month (this was the king's 7th year)
8 : 8	from Artaxerxes the king
8 : 9	King Artaxerxes to Ezra the priest
8 : 19	And I, Artaxerxes the king
8 : 21	upon the kingdom of the king and his sons
8 : 25	who put this into the heart of the king
8 : 26	and who honoured me in the sight of the king
8 : 28	in the reign of Artaxerxes the king :
8 : 51	For I was ashamed to ask the king
8 : 52	for we had said to the king
8 : 55	which the king himself and his counsellors and the nobles
8 : 67	And they delivered the king's orders to the royal stewards
8 : 77	we with our brethren and our kings
8 : 77	and our priests were given over to the kings of the earth
8 : 80	with the kings of the Persians
3 Ma 1 : 3	had led the king away and arranged
1 : 3	that this man incurred the vengeance meant for the king
1 : 11	the king was by no means persuaded
1 : 15	But since this has happened, the king said
1 : 21	because of what the king was profanely plotting
1 : 25	while the elders near the king tried in various ways
2 : 2	Lord, Lord, king of the heavens
2 : 9	You, O King, when you had created
2 : 13	see now, O holy King
2 : 26	intently observing the king's purpose
2 : 31	by their future association with the king
3 : 1	When the impious king comprehended this situation
3 : 7	neither to the king nor to his authorities
3 : 11	Then the king, boastful of his present good fortune
3 : 12	King Ptolemy Philopator to his generals and soldiers
3 : 19	who hold their heads high in defiance of kings
4 : 11	and the voyage was concluded as the king had decreed
4 : 11	so that they could neither communicate with the king's forces
4 : 12	the king, hearing that the Jews'compatriots from the city
4 : 16	The king was greatly and continually filled with joy
4 : 17	the scribes declared to the king

5 : 1	Then the king, completely inflexible
5 : 10	to report to the king about these preparations
5 : 11	But the Lord sent upon the king a portion of sleep
5 : 14	approached the king and nudged him
5 : 16	The king, after considering this, returned to his drinking
5 : 18	the king summoned Hermon
5 : 20	the king, possessed by a savagery worse than that of Phalaris
5 : 21	When the king had spoken
5 : 26	and while the king was receiving his friends
5 : 26	indicating that what the king desired was ready for action
5 : 28	for he had implanted in the king's mind
5 : 29	Then Hermon and all the king's friends
5 : 29	O king, according to your eager purpose
5 : 34	The king's friends one by one sullenly slipped away
5 : 35	Then the Jews, upon hearing what the king had said
5 : 35	praised the manifest Lord God, King of kings
5 : 36	The king, however, reconvened the party in the same manner
5 : 40	O king, how long will you try us, as though we are idiots
5 : 42	Upon this the king, a Phalaris in everything and filled with madness
5 : 46	and urged the king on to the matter at hand
6 : 2	King of great power, Almighty God Most High
6 : 5	oppressive king of the Assyrians
6 : 16	the king arrived at the hippodrome with the beasts
6 : 20	Even the king began to shudder bodily
6 : 22	Then the king's anger was turned to pity and tears
6 : 30	Then the king, when he had returned to the city
6 : 33	Likewise also the king, after convening a great banquet
6 : 37	Then they petitioned the king
6 : 40	Then they feasted, provided with everything by the king
6 : 41	The king granted their request at once
7 : 1	King Ptolemy Philopator to the generals in Egypt
7 : 10	but they requested the king that at their own hands
7 : 11	toward the king's government
7 : 12	The king then, admitting and approving the truth of what they said
7 : 18	for the king had generously provided
7 : 20	since at the king's command they had been brought
2 Es 1 : 3	in the reign of Artaxerxes, king of the Persians
1 : 10	For their sake I have overthrown many kings
12 : 14	And 12 kings shall reign in it, one after another
12 : 20	8 kings shall arise in it
12 : 23	In its last days the Most High will raise up 3 kings
12 : 26	one of the kings shall die in his bed, but in agonies
13 : 40	in the days of King Hoshea
13 : 40	whom Shalmaneser the king of the Assyrians led captive
15 : 16	they shall in their might have no respect for their king
15 : 20	I call together all the kings of the earth to fear me
15 : 33	and indecision upon their kings
4 Ma 3 : 6	by the story of King David's thirst
3 : 10	but the king was extremely thirsty
3 : 12	because of the king's craving
3 : 12	2 staunch young soldiers, respecting the king's desire
3 : 14	and from it boldly brought the king a drink
3 : 20	and were prospering, so that even Seleucus Nicanor, king of Asia
4 : 3	because I am loyal to the king's government
4 : 3	but belong to King Seleucus
4 : 4	he praised Simon for his service to the king
4 : 6	He said that he had come with the king's authority
4 : 13	prayed for him lest King Seleucus suppose
4 : 14	went away to report to the king what had happened to him
4 : 15	When King Seleucus died
4 : 17	he would pay the king 3,660 talents annually
4 : 18	So the king appointed him high priest and ruler of the nation
5 : 4	was brought before the king
5 : 36	You, O king, shall not stain
6 : 4	Obey the king's commands !
6 : 13	some of the king's retinue came to him and said
7 : 10	O supreme king over the passions, Eleazar !
8 : 17	Since the king has summoned
8 : 22	for fearing the king when we are under compulsion
8 : 26	when we can live in peace if we obey the king ?
10 : 13	but obey the king and save yourself
12 : 8	he said, Let me loose, let me speak to the king
14 : 2	O reason, more royal than kings and freer than the free !

KINGDOM

Tob 1 : 21	over all the accounts of his kingdom
13 : 1	and blessed is his kingdom
Jud 1 : 12	and swore by his throne and kingdom
2 : 12	For as I live, and by the power of my kingdom
11 : 8	that you are the one good man in the whole kingdom
Ad E 13 : 2	and, in order to make my kingdom peaceable
13 : 3	and has attained the 2nd place in the kingdom
13 : 4	so that the unifying of the kingdom which we honourably intend
13 : 5	so that our kingdom may not attain stability
16 : 8	For the future we will take care to render our kingdom
16 : 12	he undertook to deprive us of our kingdom and our life
16 : 13	and of Esther, the blameless partner of our kingdom

	16:14	and would transfer the kingdom of the Persians to the Macedonians
	16:16	who has directed the kingdom both for us
Wis	6:4	Because as servants of his kingdom you did not rule rightly
	6:20	so the desire for wisdom leads to a kingdom
	10:10	she showed him the kingdom of God
	10:14	until she brought him the sceptre of a kingdom
Sir	44:3	There were those who ruled in their kingdoms
	46:13	established the kingdom and anointed rulers over his people
	47:21	and a disobedient kingdom arose out of Ephraim
Bar	2:4	And he gave them into subjection to all the kingdoms around us
P Az	33	Blessed art thou upon the throne of thy kingdom
Bel	14:1	Cyrus the Persian received his kingdom
1 Ma	1:6	and divided his kingdom among them while he was still alive
	1:10	of the kingdom of the Greeks
	1:16	When Antiochus saw that his kingdom was established
	1:16	that he might reign over both kingdoms
	1:41	Then the king wrote to his whole kingdom
	1:51	In such words he wrote to his whole kingdom
	2:57	inherited the throne of the kingdom for ever
	3:14	and win honour in the kingdom
	3:27	and he sent and gathered all the forces of his kingdom
	6:14	and made him ruler over all his kingdom
	6:29	And mercenary forces came to him from other kingdoms
	6:57	and the affairs of the kingdom press urgently upon us
	7:4	and Demetrius took his seat upon the throne of his kingdom
	7:8	he was a great man in the kingdom
	8:11	The remaining kingdoms and islands
	8:18	for they saw that the kingdom of the Greeks
	10:33	from the land of Judah into any part of my kingdom
	10:34	for all the Jews who are in my kingdom
	10:37	and let some of them be put in positions of trust in the kingdom
	10:43	let him be released and receive back all his property in my kingdom
	10:52	Since I have returned to my kingdom
	10:53	and we have taken our seat on the throne of his kingdom
	10:55	and took your seat on the throne of his kingdom
	11:1	and he tried to get possession of Alexander's kingdom by trickery
	11:1	and add it to his own kingdom
	11:9	and you shall reign over your father's kingdom
	11:11	He threw blame on Alexander because he coveted his kingdom
	11:51	and of all the people in his kingdom
	11:52	So Demetrius the king sat on the throne of his kingdom
	15:3	have gained control of the kingdom of our fathers
	15:3	and I intend to lay claim to the kingdom
	15:4	and those who have devastated many cities in my kingdom
	15:9	When we gain control of our kingdom
	15:28	they are cities of my kingdom
	15:29	and you have taken possession of many places in my kingdom
2 Ma	1:7	after Jason and his company revolted from the holy land and the kingdom
	4:7	and Antiochus who was called Epiphanes succeeded to the kingdom
	9:25	and the neighbours to my kingdom
	10:11	This man, when he succeeded to the kingdom
	11:23	we desire that the subjects of the kingdom be undisturbed
	14:6	and will not let the kingdom attain tranquillity
	14:26	for he had appointed that conspirator against the kingdom
1 Es	1:24	beyond any other people or kingdom
	2:2	and he made a proclamation throughout all his kingdom
	4:49	from his kingdom to Judea, in the interest of their freedom
	8:21	upon the kingdom of the king and his sons
	8:24	or the law of the kingdom
3 Ma	6:24	by secretly devising acts of no advantage to the kingdom
	7:3	persuaded us to gather together the Jews of the kingdom in a body
	7:12	they might destroy those everywhere in his kingdom
2 Es	2:10	Tell my people that I will give them the kingdom of Jerusalem
	2:13	The kingdom is already prepared for you ; watch !
	2:35	Be ready for the rewards of the kingdom
	2:37	giving thanks to him who has called you to heavenly kingdoms
	12:11	is the 4th kingdom which appeared in a vision
	12:13	when a kingdom shall arise on earth
	12:13	than all the kingdoms that have been before it
	12:18	In the midst of the time of that kingdom
	13:31	people against people, and kingdom against kingdom
4 Ma	2:23	rule a kingdom that is temperate, just, good, and courageous
	12:5	and a leader in the government of the kingdom
	12:11	since you have received good things and also your kingdom from God

KINGSHIP   2

2 Ma	2:17	and the kingship and priesthood and consecration
1 Es	4:40	To her belongs the strength and the kingship

KINSHIP   3 = 0.002 %

Wis	8:17	that in kinship with wisdom there is immortality
2 Ma	5:9	in hope of finding protection because of their kinship
4 Ma	10:3	I do not renounce the noble kinship

KINSMAN   16 = 0.010 %

Tob	3:15	no near kinsman or kinsman's son
	6:11	for you are her only eligible kinsman
Sir	41:21	and of rejecting the appeal of a kinsman
1 Ma	10:89	such as it is the custom to give to the kinsmen of kings
	11:31	which we wrote concerning you to Lasthenes our kinsman
2 Ma	8:1	secretly entered the villages and summoned their kinsmen
	11:1	Lysias, the king's guardian and kinsman
	11:35	With regard to what Lysias the kinsman of the king has granted you
	12:39	and to bring them back to lie with their kinsmen
1 Es	3:7	and shall be called kinsman of Darius
	4:42	And you shall sit next to me, and be called my kinsman
	5:48	and Zerubbabel the son of Shealtiel, with his kinsmen
	8:47	namely Sherebiah with his sons and kinsmen, 18
	8:54	and 10 of their kinsmen with them
2 Es	7:103	brothers for brothers, relatives for their kinsmen

KIRIATHARIM   1

1 Es	5:19	The men of Kiriatharim, 25

KISH   1

Ad E	11:2	son of Shimei, son of Kish

KISS, verb   6 = 0.004 %

Tob	7:6	Then Raguel sprang up and kissed him and wept
	10:12	And he kissed her
Ad E	13:13	For I would have been willing to kiss the soles of his feet, to save Israel !
Sir	29:5	A man will kiss another's hands until he gets a loan
1 Es	4:47	Then Darius the king rose, and kissed him
3 Ma	5:49	and giving way to lamentation and groans they kissed each other

KITTIM   1

1 Ma	1:1	who came from the land of Kittim

KNEAD   1

Wis	15:7	For when a potter kneads the soft earth

KNEE   5 = 0.003 %

Sir	25:23	Drooping hands and weak knees
P Ma	11	And now I bend the knee of my heart
3 Ma	2:1	bending his knees and extending his hands with calm dignity
	5:42	mangled by the knees and feet of the beasts
4 Ma	11:10	they tied him to it on his knees

KNEEL   1

Jud	14:7	and knelt before her, and said

KNEEL down   1

1 Es	8:73	and kneeling down and stretching forth my hands to the Lord

KNOCK   1

Jud	14:14	So Bagoas went in and knocked at the door of the tent

KNOT   1

Wis	13:13	a stick crooked and full of knots

KNOW   184 = 0.120 %

Tob	2:10	I did not know that there were sparrows on the wall
	2:14	You seem to know everything !
	3:8	Do you not know that you strangle your husbands ?
	3:14	Thou knowest, O Lord
	5:2	but how can I obtain the money when I do not know the man ?
	5:5	but Tobias did not know it
	5:11	I should like to know, my brother, your people and your name
	5:13	For I used to know Ananias and Jathan
	6:12	For I know that Raguel, according to the law of Moses
	7:4	So he said to them, Do you know our brother Tobit ?
	8:12	let us bury him without any one knowing about it
	11:7	Raphael said, I know, Tobias
	13:4	Make his greatness known there
	13:6	who knows if he will accept you and have mercy on you ?
Jud	5:8	the God they had come to know
	8:13	but you will never know anything !
	8:20	But we know no other God but him
	9:7	and know not that thou art the Lord who crushest wars
	9:14	to know and understand that thou art God
Ad E	13:12	Thou knowest all things
	13:12	thou knowest, O Lord, that it was not in insolence
	14:12	make thyself known in this time of our affliction
	14:15	and thou knowest that I hate the splendour of the wicked
	14:16	Thou knowest my necessity
	16:4	who know nothing of goodness
Wis	1:7	and that which holds all things together knows what is said

	2:1	and no one has been known to return from Hades
	2:22	and they did not know the secret purposes of God
	4:1	because it is known both by God and by men
	5:7	but the way of the Lord we have not known
	5:12	so that no one knows its pathway
	6:13	She hastens to make herself known to those who desire her
	7:12	but I did not know that she was their mother
	7:17	to know the structure of the world
	8:8	she knows the things of old, and infers the things to come
	8:9	knowing that she would give me good counsel
	8:21	and it was a mark of insight to know whose gift she was
	9:9	With thee is wisdom, who knows thy works
	9:11	For she knows and understands all things
	12:17	and dost rebuke any insolence among those who know it
	12:27	him whom they had before refused to know
	13:1	to know him who exists
	13:3	let them know how much better than these is their Lord
	13:9	for if they had the power to know so much
	13:16	because he knows that it cannot help itself
	14:18	impelled even those who did not know the king
	15:2	For even if we sin we are thine, knowing thy power
	15:2	because we know that we are accounted thine
	15:3	For to know thee is complete righteousness
	15:3	and to know thy power is the root of immortality
	15:11	because he failed to know the one who formed him
	15:13	For this man, more than all others, knows that he sins
	16:16	for the ungodly, refusing to know thee
	16:18	but that seeing this they might know
	16:22	so that they might know that the crops of their enemies
	16:28	to make it known that one must rise before the sun
	18:6	That night was made known beforehand to our fathers
	18:18	made known why they were dying
	18:19	without knowing why they suffered
	19:1	for God knew in advance even their future actions
Sir	1:6	Her clever devices – who knows them?
	4:24	For wisdom is known through speech
	6:27	Search out and seek, and she will become known to you
	8:18	for you do not know what he will divulge
	9:11	for you do not know what his end will be
	9:13	Know that you are walking in the midst of snares
	9:14	As much as you can, aim to know your neighbours
	11:19	he does not know how much time will pass
	11:28	a man will be known through his children
	12:1	If you do a kindness, know to whom you do it
	12:8	A friend will not be known in prosperity
	12:11	and you will know that it was not hopelessly tarnished
	15:19	and he knows every deed of man
	16:15	The Lord hardened Pharaoh so that he did not know him
	16:15	in order that his works might be known under heaven
	16:17	Among so many people I shall not be known
	17:21	But the Lord, who is gracious and knows his creatures
	18:28	Every intelligent man knows wisdom
	19:29	A man is known by his appearance
	19:29	and a sensible man is known by his face, when you meet him
	20:6	while another keeps silent because he knows when to speak
	21:7	He who is mighty in speech is known from afar
	23:20	Before the universe was created, it was known to him
	24:28	Just as the first man did not know her perfectly
	26:6	and a tongue-lashing makes it known to all
	26:9	and she is known by her eyelids
	26:26	in her pride she will be known to all as ungodly
	27:27	and he will not know where it came from
	32:8	be as one who knows and yet holds his tongue
	34:9	An educated man knows many things
	34:10	He that is inexperienced knows few things
	36:5	and let them know thee
	36:5	as we have known that there is no God but thee, O Lord
	36:17	and all who are on the earth will know
	37:12	whom you know to be a keeper of the commandments
	38:5	in order that his power might be known?
	42:18	For the Most High knows all that may be known
	46:6	so that the nations might know his armament
	46:15	and by his words he became known as a trustworthy seer
Bar	2:15	that all the earth may know that thou art the Lord our God
	2:30	For I know that they will not obey me
	2:31	and they will know that I am the Lord their God
	3:31	No one knows the way to her
	3:32	But he who knows all things knows her
	4:4	for we know what is pleasing to God
L Jr	6:23	From this you will know that they are not gods
	6:29	Since you know by these things that they are not gods
	6:50	it will afterward be known that they are false
	6:52	Who then can fail to know that they are not gods?
	6:65	Since you know then that they are not gods, do not fear them
	6:72	you will know that they are not gods
P Az	22	Let them know that thou art the Lord, the only God
Sus	13:43	thou knowest that these men have borne false witness against me
Bel	14:35	and I know nothing about the den
1 Ma	2:65	Now behold, I know that Simeon your brother is wise in counsel
	3:52	thou knowest what they plot against us

	4:11	Then all the Gentiles will know
	4:33	and let all who know thy name praise thee with hymns
	6:3	but he could not, because his plan became known to the men of the city
	6:13	I know that it is because of this
	7:3	But when this act became known to him
	7:30	It became known to Judas
	8:10	but this became known to them
	9:60	because their plan became known
	11:31	so that you may know what it says
	12:29	But Jonathan and his men did not know it until morning
	13:3	You yourselves know what great things
	13:3	you know also the wars
	13:17	Simon knew that they were speaking deceitfully to him
	15:12	for he knew that troubles had converged upon him
2 Ma	1:27	and let the Gentiles know that thou art our God
	1:33	When this matter became known
	7:22	I do not know how you came into being in my womb
	9:24	for they would know to whom the government was left
	11:26	so that they may know our policy and be of good cheer
	14:32	that they did not know where the man was whom he sought
	15:21	for he knew that it is not by arms
1 Es	2:18	Now be it known to our lord the king
	2:24	Therefore we now make known to you, O lord and king
	6:8	Let it be fully known to our lord the king that
	8:23	to judge all those who know the law of your God
	8:23	and those who do not know it you shall teach
P Ma	12	and I know my transgressions
3 Ma	1:3	But Dositheus, known as the son of Drimylus
	2:6	You made known your mighty power
	3:14	as you yourselves know
	3:21	we made known to all our amnesty towards their compatriots here
	5:18	and with sharp threats demanded to know
	7:9	For you should know that if we devise any evil against them
2 Es	3:32	Or has another nation known thee besides Israel?
	4:46	For I know what has gone by
	4:46	but I do not know what is to come
	4:52	for I do not know
	5:7	and one whom the many do not know
	5:17	Or do you not know that Israel has been entrusted to you
	5:38	who is able to know these things
	6:16	for they know that their end must be changed
	7:64	because we perish and know it
	7:66	nor do they know of any torment or salvation
	7:132	I answered and said, I know, O Lord
	8:15	About all mankind thou knowest best
	8:58	though knowing full well that they must die
	9:2	then you will know that it is the very time
	9:4	then you will know that it was of these that the Most High spoke
	10:35	For I have seen what I did not know
	10:52	for I knew that the Most High would reveal these things to you
	12:38	whose hearts you know are able to comprehend
	13:52	He said to me, Just as no one can explore or know
	14:21	and so no one knows the things which have been done by thee
	14:42	in characters which they did not know
	15:26	for the Lord knows all who transgress against him
	16:54	Behold, the Lord knows all the works of men
	16:56	and he knows the number of the stars
	16:63	Surely he knows your imaginations
4 Ma	4:25	though they had known beforehand that they would suffer this
	5:4	advanced in age, and known to many in the tyrant's court
	5:25	we know that in the nature of things
	6:27	You know, O God, that though I might have saved myself
	7:22	and knows that it is blessed to endure any suffering
	10:2	But he shouted, Do you not know
	16:25	They knew also that those who die for the sake of God live in God
	18:2	knowing that devout reason is master of all emotions

KNOWLEDGE 41 = 0.027 %

Ad E	14:15	Thou hast knowledge of all things
Wis	2:13	He professes to have knowledge of God
	6:22	and make the knowledge of her clear
	7:17	For it is he who gave me unerring knowledge of what exists
	8:4	For she is an initiate in the knowledge of God
	10:10	and gave him knowledge of angels
	14:22	to err about the knowledge of God
	18:6	in sure knowledge of the oaths in which they trusted
Sir	1:7	The knowledge of wisdom – to whom was it manifested?
	1:19	he rained down knowledge and discerning comprehension
	3:25	if you lack knowledge do not profess to have it
	6:33	If you love to listen you will gain knowledge
	10:30	A poor man is honoured for his knowledge
	11:15	Wisdom, understanding, and knowledge of the law
	16:24	Listen to me, my son, and acquire knowledge
	16:25	and declare knowledge accurately
	17:7	He filled them with knowledge and understanding
	17:11	He bestowed knowledge upon them
	19:19	The knowledge of the Lord's commandments

19:20	And the knowledge of his omnipotence	
19:22	But the knowledge of wickedness is not wisdom	
21:13	The knowledge of a wise man will increase like a flood	
21:14	it will hold no knowledge	
21:18	and the knowledge of the ignorant is unexamined talk	
24:18	of fear, of knowledge, and of holy hope	
32:3	but with accurate knowledge	
33:11	In the fulness of his knowledge the Lord distinguished them	
39:7	He will direct his counsel and knowledge aright	
45:5	the law of life and knowledge	
50:27	Instruction in understanding and knowledge	
Bar **3**:20	but they have not learned the way to knowledge	
3:27	God did not choose them, nor give them the way to knowledge	
3:36	He found the whole way to knowledge	
2 Ma **6**:30	It is clear to the Lord in his holy knowledge	
1 Es **8**:7	For Ezra possessed great knowledge	
2 Es **14**:47	the fountain of wisdom, and the river of knowledge	
4 Ma **1**:2	to everyone who is seeking knowledge	
1:16	Wisdom, next, is the knowledge of divine and human matters	
5:35	nor will I reject you, honoured priesthood and knowledge of the law	
11:21	For the religious knowledge, O tyrant, is invincible	
16:23	It is unreasonable for people who have religious knowledge	

KOLA 1
Jud **15**:4 and Choba and Kola, and to all the frontiers of Israel

KONA 1
Jud **4**:4 and to Kona and Beth-horon and Belmain and Jericho

KORAH 1
Sir **45**:18 Dathan and Abiram and their men and the company of Korah

L

LABAN 1
Jud **8**:26 while he was keeping the sheep of Laban

LABORIOUSLY 2
Wis **15**:7 and laboriously moulds each vessel for our service
2 Es **7**:89 they laboriously served the Most High

LABOUR, LABOR, subst. 20 = 0.013 %
Wis **3**:11 Their hope is vain, their labours are unprofitable
3:15 For the fruit of good labours is renowned
5:1 and those who make light of his labours
8:7 And if any one loves righteousness, her labours are virtues
8:18 and in the labours of her hands, unfailing wealth
9:16 and what is at hand we find with labour
10:10 she prospered him in his labours
10:17 She gave to holy men the reward of their labours
Sir pr. despite our diligent labour in translating
pr. that I should myself devote some pains and labour
7:15 Do not hate toilsome labour, or farm work
14:15 Will you not leave the fruit of your labours to another
16:27 and they do not cease from their labours
19:11 like a woman in labour with a child
40:1 Much labour was created for every man
Bar **3**:18 whose labours are beyond measure ?
3 Ma **4**:1 not for the hard labour that has been briefly mentioned before
2 Es **3**:33 and their labour has borne no fruit
8:14 who with so great labour was fashioned by thy command
9:22 because with much labour I have perfected them

LABOUR, LABOR, verb 8 = 0.005 %
Sir **24**:34 Observe that I have not laboured for myself alone
33:17 Consider that I have not laboured for myself alone
38:27 who labours by night as well as by day
51:27 See with your eyes that I have laboured little
1 Es **4**:22 Do you not labour and toil
2 Es **5**:12 they shall labour but their ways shall not prosper
16:45 Because those who labour, labour in vain

LABOURER, LABORER 2
Jud **4**:10 and every resident alien and hired labourer
Sir **7**:20 or a hired labourer who devotes himself to you

LACCUNUS 1
1 Es **9**:31 Of the sons of Addi : Naathus and Moossias, Laccunus

LACEDAEMONIAN 1
2 Ma **5**:9 having embarked to go to the Lacedaemonians

LACK, verb 18 = 0.012 %
Wis **11**:17 did not lack the means to send upon them
14:4 so that even if a man lacks skill, he may put to sea
19:4 which their torments still lacked
Sir **3**:13 even if he is lacking in understanding, show forbearance

3:25	if you lack knowledge do not profess to have it	
10:27	than one who goes about boasting, but lacks bread	
11:12	who lacks strength and abounds in poverty	
14:10	and it is lacking at his table	
19:23	but there is a fool who merely lacks wisdom	
19:24	Better is the God-fearing man who lacks intelligence	
22:11	Weep for the dead, for he lacks the light	
22:11	and weep for the fool, for he lacks intelligence	
23:10	will not lack bruises	
25:2	and an adulterous old man who lacks good sense	
37:21	since he is lacking in all wisdom	
47:23	ample in folly and lacking in understanding	
51:24	Why do you say you are lacking in these things	
1 Ma **2**:61	that none who put their trust in him will lack strength	

LACK, subst. 3 = 0.002 %
Jud **8**:9 because they were faint for lack of water
Wis **15**:18 when judged by their lack of intelligence
Sir **19**:28 And if by lack of strength he is prevented from sinning

LACKEY 1
4 Ma **9**:17 he replied, You abominable lackeys

LAD 2
Tob **10**:4 And his wife said to him, The lad has perished
Sus **13**:45 God aroused the holy spirit of a young lad named Daniel

LADDER 1
1 Ma **5**:30 carrying ladders and engines of war to capture the stronghold

LADDER, prop. n. 1
1 Ma **11**:59 from the Ladder of Tyre to the borders of Egypt

LAGGARD 1
1 Ma **5**:53 And Judas kept rallying the laggards

LAKE 1
2 Ma **12**:16 so that the adjoining lake, a quarter of a mile wide

LAMB 14 = 0.009 %
Wis **19**:9 For they ranged like horses, and leaped like lambs
Sir **13**:17 What fellowship has a wolf with a lamb ?
46:16 and he offered in sacrifice a sucking lamb
47:3 and with bears as with lambs of the flock
P Az **16** and with tens of thousands of fat lambs
1 Es **1**:1 he killed the passover lamb on the 14th day of the first month
1:6 and kill the passover lamb
1:7 30,000 lambs and kids, and 3,000 calves
1:12 They roasted the passover lamb with fire, as required
6:29 for sacrifices to the Lord, for bulls and rams and lambs
7:7 100 bulls, 200 rams, 400 lambs
7:12 and they sacrificed the passover lamb
8:14 and lambs and what goes with them
8:66 12 bulls for all Israel, 96 rams, 72 lambs

LAME 1
2 Es **2**:21 do not ridicule a lame man, protect the maimed

LAMENT, subst. 5 = 0.003 %
Wis **18**:10 and their piteous lament for their children
Sir **38**:16 and as one who is suffering grievously begin the lament
1 Ma **1**:27 Every bridegroom took up the lament
3 Ma **4**:6 all together raising a lament instead of a wedding song
4 Ma **16**:12 did not wail with such a lament for any of them

LAMENT, verb 8 = 0.005 %
Wis **19**:3 and were lamenting at the graves of their dead
Sir **51**:19 and lamented my ignorance of her
1 Es **1**:32 Jeremiah the prophet lamented for Josiah
3 Ma **4**:2 to lament bitterly the ignoble misfortune of their brothers
2 Es **7**:65 Let the human race lament
7:65 let all who have been born lament
8:16 and about thy inheritance, for whom I lament
16:2 and wail for your children, and lament for them

LAMENTABLE 1
3 Ma **6**:31 instead of a bitter and lamentable death

LAMENTATION 14 = 0.009 %
Tob **2**:6 and all your festivities into lamentation
Jud **7**:29 Then great and general lamentation arose
1 Ma **2**:70 And all Israel mourned for him with great lamentation
4:39 and mourned with great lamentation
9:20 And all Israel made great lamentation for him
13:26 All Israel bewailed him with great lamentation
2 Ma **11**:6 they and all the people, with lamentations and tears
1 Es **1**:32 have made lamentation for him to this day
3 Ma **1**:18 and filled the streets with groans and lamentations
4:2 there was incessant mourning, lamentation, and tearful cries

235

	4 : 8	spent the remaining days of their marriage festival in
		lamentations
	5 : 49	and giving way to lamentation and groans they kissed each other
2 Es	10 : 12	My lamentation is not like the earth's
	16 : 18	when there shall be much lamentation

LAMP   9 = 0.006 %

Jud	10 : 22	with silver lamps carried before him
Sir	26 : 17	Like the shining lamp on the holy lampstand
L Jr	6 : 19	They light lamps, even more than they light for themselves
1 Ma	4 : 50	and lighted the lamps on the lampstand
2 Ma	1 : 8	and we lighted the lamps and we set out the loaves
	10 : 3	and they burned incense and lighted lamps
2 Es	10 : 2	Then we all put out the lamps
	12 : 42	and like a lamp in a dark place
	14 : 25	and I will light in your heart the lamp of understanding

LAMPSTAND   5 = 0.003 %

Sir	26 : 17	Like the shining lamp on the holy lampstand
1 Ma	1 : 21	the lampstand for the light, and all its utensils
	4 : 49	They made new holy vessels, and brought the lampstand
	4 : 50	and lighted the lamps on the lampstand
2 Es	10 : 22	the light of our lampstand has been put out

LANCE   1

| 2 Ma | 5 : 2 | in companies fully armed with lances and drawn swords |

LAND*, subst.   179 = 0.117 %

Tob	1 : 3	into the land of the Assyrians, to Nineveh
	1 : 4	Now when I was in my own country, in the land of Israel
	3 : 15	in the land of my captivity
	4 : 12	and their posterity will inherit the land
	6 : 3	So the young man seized the fish and threw it up on the land
	13 : 6	I give him thanks in the land of my captivity
	14 : 4	Our brethren will be scattered over the earth from the good land
	14 : 5	and bring them back into their land
Jud	1 : 9	and Tahpannes and Raamses and the whole land of Goshen
	1 : 12	all the inhabitants of the land of Moab
	2 : 27	and sacked their cities and ravaged their lands
	3 : 3	Behold, our buildings, and all our land
	3 : 8	to destroy all the gods of the land
	5 : 9	and go to the land of Canaan
	5 : 12	and he afflicted the whole land of Egypt
	5 : 15	So they lived in the land of the Amorites
	7 : 4	These men will now lick up the face of the whole land
	7 : 18	and covered the whole face of the land
	8 : 22	and the captivity of the land
Ad E	13 : 16	which thou didst redeem for thyself out of the land of Egypt
Wis	12 : 3	Those who dwelt of old in thy holy land
	12 : 7	that the land most precious of all to thee
	14 : 5	they come safely to land
	16 : 19	to destroy the crops of the unrighteous land
	18 : 15	into the midst of the land that was doomed, a stern warrior
	19 : 7	and dry land emerging where water had stood before
	19 : 19	For land animals were transformed into water creatures
	19 : 19	and creatures that swim moved over to the land
Sir	10 : 16	The Lord has overthrown the lands of the nations
	37 : 3	O evil imagination, why were you formed to cover the land with
		deceit ?
	39 : 4	he will travel through the lands of foreign nations
	39 : 22	His blessing covers the dry land like a river
	43 : 3	At noon it parches the land
	45 : 22	But in the land of the people he has no inheritance
	46 : 8	to bring them into their inheritance, into a land flowing with
		milk and honey
	47 : 24	so as to remove them from their land
	48 : 15	till they were carried away captive from their land
Bar	1 : 8	to return them to the land of Judah
	1 : 9	and the mighty men and the people of the land
	1 : 19	out of the land of Egypt until today
	1 : 20	when he brought our fathers out of the land of Egypt
	1 : 20	to give us a land flowing with milk and honey
	2 : 11	who didst bring thy people out of the land of Egypt
	2 : 21	and you will remain in the land which I gave to your fathers
	2 : 23	and the whole land will be a desolation without inhabitants
	2 : 30	But in the land of their exile they will come to themselves
	2 : 32	and they will praise me in the land of their exile
	2 : 34	I will bring them again into the land
	2 : 35	from the land which I have given them
	3 : 10	why is it that you are in the land of your enemies
L Jr	6 : 61	and the wind likewise blows in every land
	6 : 72	and be a reproach in the land
1 Ma	1 : 1	who came from the land of Kittim
	1 : 16	he determined to become king of the land of Egypt
	1 : 19	And they captured the fortified cities in the land of Egypt
	1 : 19	and he plundered the land of Egypt
	1 : 24	Taking them all, he departed to his own land
	1 : 28	Even the land shook for its inhabitants
	1 : 44	he directed them to follow customs strange to the land
	1 : 52	and they did evil in the land

	2 : 56	received an inheritance in the land
	3 : 8	he destroyed the ungodly out of the land
	3 : 24	800 of them fell, and the rest fled into the land of the Philistines
	3 : 29	which he had caused in the land by abolishing the laws
	3 : 36	and distribute their land
	3 : 39	to go into the land of Judah and destroy it
	3 : 41	and the land of the Philistines joined with them
	4 : 22	they all fled into the land of the Philistines
	5 : 13	and all our brethren who were in the land of Tob have been
		killed
	5 : 45	to go to the land of Judah
	5 : 48	Let us pass through your land to get to our land
	5 : 53	till he came to the land of Judah
	5 : 65	and fought the sons of Esau in the land to the south
	5 : 66	Then he marched off to go into the land of the Philistines
	5 : 68	in the land of the Philistines
	5 : 68	he plundered the cities and returned to the land of Judah
	6 : 5	that the armies which had gone into the land of Judah had been
		routed
	6 : 13	and behold, I am perishing of deep grief in a strange land
	6 : 25	but also against all the lands on their borders
	6 : 49	since it was a sabbatical year for the land
	7 : 6	and have driven us out of our land
	7 : 7	which Judas has brought upon us and upon the land of the king
	7 : 10	into the land of Judah
	7 : 22	They gained control of the land of Judah
	7 : 50	So the land of Judah had rest for a few days
	8 : 3	and what they had done in the land of Spain
	8 : 10	they plundered them, conquered the land
	8 : 16	and to control all their land
	8 : 23	and with the nation of the Jews at sea and on land for ever
	8 : 32	we will defend their rights and fight you on sea and on land
	9 : 1	into the land of Judah a 2nd time
	9 : 53	And he took the sons of the leading men of the land
	9 : 57	and the land of Judah had rest for 2 years
	9 : 69	Then he decided to depart to his own land
	9 : 72	whom he had formerly taken from the land of Judah
	9 : 72	then he turned and departed to his own land
	10 : 13	each left his place and departed to his own land
	10 : 30	I will not collect them from the land of Judah
	10 : 33	from the land of Judah into any part of my kingdom
	10 : 37	just as the king has commanded in the land of Judah
	10 : 39	Ptolemais and the land adjoining it
	10 : 55	on which you returned to the land of your fathers
	10 : 67	came from Crete to the land of his fathers
	10 : 72	for your fathers were twice put to flight in their own land
	11 : 34	from the crops of the land and the fruit of the trees
	11 : 38	that the land was quiet before him
	11 : 52	and the land was quiet before him
	12 : 4	safe conduct to the land of Judah
	12 : 46	and they returned to the land of Judah
	12 : 52	So they all reached the land of Judah safely
	13 : 1	to invade the land of Judah and destroy it
	13 : 12	to invade the land of Judah
	13 : 22	He marched off and went into the land of Gilead
	13 : 24	Then Trypho turned back and departed to his own land
	13 : 32	and he brought great calamity upon the land
	14 : 4	The land had rest all the days of Simon
	14 : 8	They tilled their land in peace
	14 : 11	He established peace in the land
	14 : 13	No one was left in the land to fight them
	15 : 10	and invaded the land of his fathers
	15 : 14	he pressed the city hard from land and sea
	15 : 29	you have done great damage in the land
	15 : 33	We have neither taken foreign land
	15 : 35	they were causing great damage among the people and to our
		land
2 Ma	1 : 1	and those in the land of Judea
	1 : 7	after Jason and his company revolted from the holy land and the
		kingdom
	2 : 21	so that though few in number they seized the whole land
	4 : 26	was driven as a fugitive into the land of Ammon
	5 : 21	that he could sail on the land and walk on the sea
	9 : 28	among the mountains in a strange land
1 Es	1 : 58	Until the land has enjoyed its sabbaths
	4 : 2	who rule over land and sea and all that is in them ?
	4 : 15	and to every people that rules over sea and land
	4 : 28	Do not all lands fear to touch him ?
	4 : 56	He wrote that land and wages should be provided
	5 : 50	And some joined them from the other peoples of the land
	5 : 50	for all the peoples of the land were hostile to them
	5 : 72	But the peoples of the land pressed hard upon those in Judea
	7 : 13	from the abominations of the peoples of the land
	8 : 69	the alien peoples of the land and their pollutions
	8 : 70	and the holy race has been mixed with the alien peoples of the
		land
	8 : 83	The land which you are entering to take possession of it
	8 : 83	is a land polluted with the pollution of the aliens of the land
	8 : 85	and eat the good things of the land
	8 : 87	by mixing with the uncleanness of the peoples of the land

	8 : 92	and have married foreign women from the peoples of the land
	9 : 9	separate yourselves from the peoples of the land
3 Ma	6 : 3	who are perishing as foreigners in a foreign land
	6 : 15	Not even when they were in the land of their enemies did I neglect them
	7 : 20	safely by land and sea and river
2 Es	1 : 7	Was it not I who brought them out of the land of Egypt
	1 : 21	I divided fertile lands among you :
	2 : 9	whose land lies in lumps of pitch and heaps of ashes
	4 : 19	for the land is assigned to the forest
	4 : 21	For as the land is assigned to the forest
	5 : 1	and the land shall be barren of faith
	5 : 3	And the land which you now see ruling
	5 : 17	in the land of their exile ?
	5 : 24	and from all the lands of the world
	7 : 26	and the land which now is hidden shall be disclosed
	8 : 17	for I see the failings of us who dwell in the land
	9 : 8	and will see my salvation in my land and within my borders
	13 : 33	every man shall leave his own land
	13 : 40	which were led away from their own land into captivity
	13 : 40	and they were taken into another land
	13 : 42	which they had not kept in their own land
	14 : 31	Then land was given to you
	14 : 31	for a possession in the land of Zion
	15 : 6	For iniquity has spread throughout every land
	15 : 10	to live any longer in the land of Egypt
	15 : 11	and will destroy all its land
	15 : 30	and shall devastate a portion of the land of the Assyrians with their teeth
	15 : 33	And from the land of the Assyrians
	15 : 60	and shall destroy a part of your land
	15 : 62	your land and your mountains
4 Ma	1 : 11	and thus their native land was purified through them
	4 : 20	at the very citadel of our native land

LAND, verb   2

| 1 Ma | 10 : 1 | landed and occupied Ptolemais |
| 3 Ma | 7 : 19 | And when they had landed in peace with appropriate thanksgiving |

LANDING   1

| 1 Ma | 15 : 4 | and intend to make a landing in the country |

LANE   1

| Tob | 13 : 18 | all her lanes will cry Hallelujah ! |

LANGUAGE   9 = 0.006 %

Sir	pr.	when translated into another language
Bar	4 : 15	a shameless nation, of a strange language
2 Ma	7 : 8	he replied in the language of his fathers
	7 : 21	She encouraged each of them in the language of their fathers
	12 : 37	In the language of their fathers he raised the battle cry, with hymns
	15 : 29	in the language of their fathers
	15 : 36	which is called Adar in the Syrian language
4 Ma	12 : 7	But when his mother had exhorted him in the Hebrew language
	16 : 15	and said to your sons in the Hebrew language

LAPSE   1

| 2 Ma | 10 : 3 | after a lapse of 2 years |

LARGE   39 = 0.025 %

Tob	7 : 8	and set large servings of food before them
Jud	5 : 3	How large is their army
Sir	51 : 28	Get instruction with a large sum of silver
1 Ma	1 : 17	and with a large fleet
	1 : 29	and he came to Jerusalem with a large force
	3 : 10	and a large force from Samaria to fight against Israel
	3 : 13	heard that Judas had gathered a large company
	3 : 31	and raise a large fund
	4 : 35	to invade Judea again with an even larger army
	5 : 26	all these cities were strong and large
	5 : 30	and behold, a large company, that could not be counted
	5 : 38	it is a very large force
	5 : 45	a very large company
	5 : 46	This was a large and very strong city on the road
	5 : 52	And they crossed the Jordan into the large plain before Bethshan
	6 : 41	trembled, for the army was very large and strong
	7 : 10	So they marched away and came with a large force
	7 : 11	for they saw that they had come with a large force
	7 : 27	So Nicanor came to Jerusalem with a large force
	8 : 6	and with cavalry and chariots and a very large army
	9 : 37	from Nadabath with a large escort
	9 : 43	he came with a large force on the sabbath day
	9 : 60	He started to come with a large force
	10 : 2	he assembled a very large army
	10 : 48	Now Alexander the king assembled large forces
	10 : 69	and he assembled a large force and encamped against Jamnia
	10 : 77	he mustered 3,000 cavalry and a large army
	10 : 77	for he had a large troop of cavalry and put confidence in it
	11 : 63	had come to Kadesh in Galilee with a large army
	12 : 24	with a larger force than before, to wage war against him
	12 : 42	When Trypho saw that he had come with a large army
	13 : 1	Simon heard that Trypho had assembled a large army
	13 : 12	Then Trypho departed from Ptolemais with a large army
	14 : 24	with a large gold shield weighing a 1,000 minas
	16 : 5	and behold, a large force of infantry and horsemen
2 Ma	1 : 31	should be poured upon large stones
3 Ma	5 : 2	with large handfuls of frankincense and plenty of unmixed wine
2 Es	11 : 4	the middle head was larger then the other heads
	12 : 26	As for your seeing that the large head disappeared

LASH, verb   1

| Wis | 5 : 11 | the light air, lashed by the beat of its pinions |

LAST, adj., adv.   41 = 0.027 %

Jud	7 : 27	or see our wives and children draw their last breath
Wis	2 : 16	he calls the last end of the righteous happy
Sir	6 : 28	For at last you will find the rest she gives
	12 : 12	and at last you will realize the truth of my words
	24 : 28	the last one has not fathomed her
	32 : 11	Leave in good time and do not be the last
	33 : 16	I was the last on watch
	48 : 24	By the spirit of might he saw the last things
	51 : 14	and I will search for her to the last
1 Ma	6 : 53	had consumed the last of the stores
2 Ma	3 : 31	to one who was lying quite at his last breath
	5 : 5	and at last the city was being taken
	7 : 9	And when he was at his last breath, he said
	7 : 41	Last of all, the mother died, after her sons
1 Es	8 : 39	Of the sons of Adonikam, the last ones
3 Ma	5 : 25	But the Jews, at their last gasp
	5 : 49	they thought that this was their last moment of life
	5 : 49	who were drawing their last milk
2 Es	5 : 42	just as for those who are last there is no slowness
	6 : 34	lest you be hasty concerning the last times
	7 : 73	or how will they answer in the last times ?
	7 : 77	but it will not be shown to you until the last times
	7 : 84	they shall consider the torment laid up for themselves in the last days
	7 : 87	and before whom they are to be judged in the last times
	7 : 95	and the glory which awaits them in the last days
	7 : 116	I answered and said, This is my first and last word
	8 : 50	who inhabit the world in the last times
	8 : 63	which thou wilt do in the last times
	10 : 59	who dwell on earth in the last days
	11 : 9	but let the heads be reserved for the last
	12 : 9	and the last events of the times
	12 : 23	In its last days the Most High will raise up 3 kings
	12 : 25	and perform his last actions
	12 : 28	but he also shall fall by the sword in the last days
	13 : 18	because they understand what is reserved for the last days
	13 : 20	and not to see what shall happen in the last days
	13 : 46	Then they dwelt there until the last times
	14 : 22	and that those who wish to live in the last days may live
	14 : 46	but keep the 70 that were written last
4 Ma	2 : 9	nor gathers the last grapes from the vineyard
	15 : 18	When the first-born breathed his last it did not turn you aside

LAST, verb   5 = 0.003 %

Tob	8 : 19	which lasted 14 days
Jud	13 : 1	because the banquet had lasted long
Sir	22 : 12	Mourning for the dead lasts 7 days
	22 : 12	but for a fool or an ungodly man it lasts all his life
2 Es	7 : 43	For it will last for about a week of years

LASTHENES   2

| 1 Ma | 11 : 31 | which we wrote concerning you to Lasthenes our kinsman |
| | 11 : 32 | King Demetrius to Lasthenes his father, greeting |

LASTING   4 = 0.003 %

Ad E	13 : 2	I have determined to settle the lives of my subjects in lasting tranquillity
Sir	11 : 17	and what he approves will have lasting success
	11 : 33	lest he give you a lasting blemish
	49 : 13	The memory of Nehemiah also is lasting

LATE, adj.   3 = 0.002 %

1 Ma	10 : 80	from early morning till late afternoon
2 Ma	4 : 17	a fact which later events will make clear
	8 : 25	they were obliged to return because the hour was late

LATE, adv.   8 = 0.005 %

Sir	19 : 21	even if later he does it
	27 : 23	but later he will twist his speech
1 Ma	1 : 29	2 years later the king sent to the cities of Judah
	11 : 18	But King Ptolemy died 3 days later
2 Ma	14 : 1	3 years later, word came to Judas and his men
3 Ma	1 : 3	a Jew by birth who later changed his religion

3 : 24   if a sudden disorder should later arise against us
4 Ma 12 : 7   as we shall tell a little later

LATTER   3 = 0.002 %
Wis 19 : 16   but the latter, after receiving them with festal celebrations
1 Ma 11 : 34   the latter, with all the region bordering them
2 Ma 14 : 31   When the latter became aware

LAUGH   9 = 0.006 %
Tob   2 : 8   And my neighbours laughed at me and said
Jud 12 : 12   for if we do not embrace her she will laugh at us
Wis   4 : 18   but the Lord will laugh them to scorn
Sir 21 : 20   A fool raises his voice when he laughs
     30 : 10   Do not laugh with him, lest you have sorrow with him
Bel 14 : 7   Then Daniel laughed, and said
     14 : 19   Then Daniel laughed
1 Es   4 : 31   If she smiles at him, he laughs
4 Ma   5 : 28   But you shall have no such occasion to laugh at me

LAUGHINGSTOCK   5 = 0.003 %
Sir   6 : 4   and make him the laughingstock of his enemies
     18 : 31   it will make you the laughingstock of your enemies
     42 : 11   lest she make you a laughingstock to your enemies
1 Ma 10 : 70   and I have become a laughingstock and reproach because of you
4 Ma   6 : 20   be a laughing stock to all for our cowardice

LAUGHTER   2
Sir 19 : 30   A man's attire and open-mouthed laughter
     27 : 13   and their laughter is wantonly sinful

LAUNCH   2
2 Ma   4 : 40   and launched an unjust attack
2 Es   9 : 34   and when it happens that what was sown or what was launched

LAVISH   1
3 Ma   5 : 2   maddened by the lavish abundance of liquor

LAVISHLY   2
1 Ma   3 : 30   which he used to give more lavishly than preceding kings
3 Ma   6 : 33   gave thanks to heaven unceasingly and lavishly

LAW   233 = 0.152 %
Tob   6 : 12   For I know that Raguel, according to the law of Moses
      7 : 12   in accordance with the law
      7 : 13   take her according to the law of Moses
     14 : 9   But keep the law and the commandments
Jud 11 : 12   to use all that God by his laws has forbidden them to eat
Ad E 13 : 4   who have laws contrary to those of every nation
     13 : 5   perversely following a strange manner of life and laws
     15 : 10   you shall not die, for our law applies only to the people. Come near
     16 : 15   are not evildoers but are governed by most righteous laws
     16 : 19   and permit the Jews to live under their own laws
Wis   2 : 11   But let our might be our law of right
      2 : 12   he reproaches us for sins against the law
      6 : 4   nor keep the law, nor walk according to the purpose of God
      6 : 18   and love of her is the keeping of her laws
      6 : 18   and giving heed to her laws is assurance of immortality
      9 : 5   with little understanding of judgment and laws
     14 : 16   was kept as a law
     16 : 6   to remind them of thy law's command
     18 : 4   through whom the imperishable light of the law
     18 : 9   and with one accord agreed to the divine law
Sir pr.   through the law and the prophets
     pr.   especially to the reading of the law and the prophets
     pr.   in living according to the law
     pr.   Not only this work, but even the law itself
     pr.   being prepared in character to live according to the law
      2 : 16   and those who love him will be filled with the law
      8 : 14   Do not go to law against a judge
      9 : 15   and let all your discussion be about the law of the Most High
     11 : 15   Wisdom, understanding, and knowledge of the law
     15 : 1   and he who holds to the law will obtain wisdom
     17 : 11   and allotted to them the law of life
     19 : 17   and let the law of the Most High take its course
     19 : 20   and in all wisdom there is the fulfilment of the law
     19 : 24   than the highly prudent man who transgresses the law
     21 : 11   Whoever keeps the law controls his thoughts
     23 : 23   she has disobeyed the law of the Most High
     24 : 23   the law which Moses commanded us
     32 : 15   He who seeks the law will be filled with it
     32 : 24   He who believes the law gives heed to the commandments
     33 : 2   A wise man will not hate the law
     33 : 3   A man of understanding will trust in the law
     33 : 3   for him the law is as dependable
     34 : 8   Without such deceptions the law will be fulfilled
     35 : 1   He who keeps the law makes many offerings
     39 : 1   to the study of the law of the Most High
     39 : 8   and will glory in the law of the Lord's covenant
     41 : 8   who have forsaken the law of the Most High God !

42 : 2   of the law of the Most High and his covenant
44 : 20   he kept the law of the Most High
45 : 5   the law of life and knowledge
45 : 17   and to enlighten Israel with his law
46 : 14   By the law of the Lord he judged the congregation
49 : 4   for they forsook the law of the Most High
Bar   2 : 2   in accordance with what is written in the law of Moses
      2 : 28   to write thy law in the presence of the people of Israel
      4 : 1   and the law that endures for ever
      4 : 12   because they turned away from the law of God
Sus 13 : 3   and had taught their daughter according to the law of Moses
     13 : 6   and all who had suits at law came to them
     13 : 62   acting in accordance with the law of Moses
1 Ma   1 : 49   so that they should forget the law
      1 : 52   Many of the people, every one who forsook the law, joined them
      1 : 56   The books of the law which they found they tore to pieces
      1 : 57   or if any one adhered to the law
      2 : 21   Far be it from us to desert the law and the ordinances
      2 : 26   Thus he burned with zeal for the law
      2 : 27   saying : Let every one who is zealous for the law
      2 : 42   every one who offered himself willingly for the law
      2 : 48   They rescued the law out of the hands of the Gentiles and kings
      2 : 50   Now, my children, show zeal for the law
      2 : 58   Elijah because of great zeal for the law
      2 : 64   My children, be courageous and grow strong in the law
      2 : 67   You shall rally about you all who observe the law
      2 : 68   and heed what the law commands
      3 : 21   but we fight for our lives and our laws
      3 : 29   which he had caused in the land by abolishing the laws
      3 : 48   And they opened the book of the law
      3 : 56   that each should return to his home, according to the law
      4 : 42   He chose blameless priests devoted to the law
      4 : 47   Then they took unhewn stones, as the law directs
      4 : 53   they rose and offered sacrifice, as the law directs
      6 : 59   and agree to let them live by their laws as they did before
      6 : 59   for it was on account of their laws which we abolished
     10 : 14   who had forsaken the law and the commandments
     10 : 37   and let them live by their own laws
     13 : 3   for the laws and the sanctuary
     13 : 48   and settled in it men who observed the law
     14 : 14   he sought out the law
     14 : 29   in order that their sanctuary and the law might be preserved
     15 : 21   that he may punish them according to their law
2 Ma   1 : 4   May he open your heart to his law and his commandments
      2 : 2   and that the prophet after giving them the law
      2 : 3   that the law should not depart from their hearts
      2 : 18   as he promised through the law
      2 : 22   and restored the laws that were about to be abolished
      3 : 1   and the laws were very well observed
      3 : 15   upon him who had given the law about deposits
      4 : 2   and a zealot for the laws
      4 : 11   and introduced new customs contrary to the law
      4 : 17   to show irreverence to the divine laws
      5 : 8   hated as a rebel against the laws
      5 : 15   both to the laws and to his country
      6 : 1   to compel the Jews to forsake the laws of their fathers
      6 : 1   and cease to live by the laws of God
      6 : 5   which were forbidden by the laws
      6 : 23   and moreover according to the holy Godgiven law
      6 : 28   for the revered and holy laws
      7 : 2   rather than transgress the laws of our fathers
      7 : 9   because we have died for his laws
      7 : 11   and because of his laws I disdain them
      7 : 23   since you now forget yourselves for the sake of his laws
      7 : 30   but I obey the command of the law
      7 : 37   for the laws of our fathers
      8 : 21   and made them ready to die for their laws and their country
      8 : 36   because they followed the laws ordained by him
     10 : 26   as the law declares
     11 : 31   to enjoy their own food and laws, just as formerly
     12 : 40   which the law forbids the Jews to wear
     13 : 10   who were on the point of being deprived of the law
     13 : 14   for the laws, temple, city, country, and commonwealth
     15 : 9   Encouraging them from the law and the prophets
1 Es   1 : 33   and his understanding of the law of the Lord
      1 : 48   and transgressed the laws of the Lord, the God of Israel
      5 : 51   as it is commanded in the law
      8 : 3   skilled in the law of Moses
      8 : 7   so that he omitted nothing from the law of the Lord
      8 : 8   and reader of the law of the Lord :
      8 : 9   and reader of the law of the Lord, greeting
      8 : 12   in accordance with what is in the law of the Lord
      8 : 19   and reader of the law of the Most High God sends for
      8 : 21   Let all things prescribed in the law of God
      8 : 23   to judge all those who know the law of your God
      8 : 24   And all who transgress the law of your God
      8 : 24   or the law of the kingdom
      8 : 87   but we turned back again to transgress thy law
      8 : 94   as seems good to you and to all who obey the law of the Lord
      9 : 7   You have broken the law and married foreign women

	9:39	to bring the law of Moses
	9:40	So Ezra the chief priest brought the law
	9:40	and all the priests to hear the law
	9:41	and all the multitude gave attention to the law
	9:42	Ezra the priest and reader of the law
	9:45	Then Ezra took up the book of the law
	9:46	And when he opened the law, they all stood erect
	9:48	taught the law of the Lord
	9:50	now they were all weeping as they heard the law
3 Ma	1:12	Even after the law had been read to him
	1:23	and die courageously for the ancestral law
	3:4	and conducted themselves by his law
	7:10	against the holy God and the law of God
	7:12	who had transgressed the law of God
2 Es	1:8	for they have not obeyed my law
	2:40	who have fulfilled the law of the Lord
	3:19	to give the law to the descendants of Jacob
	3:20	so that thy law might bring forth fruit in them
	3:22	the law was in the people's heart along with the evil root
	4:23	and the law of our fathers has been made of no effect
	5:27	thou hast given the law which is approved by all
	7:17	thou hast ordained in thy law
	7:20	rather than that the law of God
	7:24	They scorned his law, and denied his covenants
	7:72	and though they obtained the law
	7:79	and who have despised his law
	7:81	because they have scorned the law of the Most High
	7:89	that they might keep the law of the Lawgiver perfectly
	7:94	they kept the law which was given them in trust
	7:133	who turn in repentance to his law
	8:12	and instructed him in thy law
	8:29	but regard those who have gloriously taught thy law
	8:56	and were contemptuous of his law
	9:11	and as many as scorned my law while they still had freedom
	9:31	For behold, I sow my law in you
	9:32	But though our fathers received the law
	9:32	yet the fruit of the law did not perish
	9:36	For we who have received the law and sinned will perish
	9:37	the law, however, does not perish but remains in its glory
	13:38	and will destroy them without effort by the law
	13:54	and have searched out my law
	14:21	For thy law has been burned
	14:22	the things which were written in thy law
	14:30	and received the law of life, which they did not keep
4 Ma	1:17	This, in turn, is education in the law
	1:34	and all sorts of foods that are forbidden to us by the law
	2:5	Thus the law says, You shall not covet your neighbour's wife
	2:6	In fact, since the law had told us not to covet
	2:8	a way of life in accordance with the law
	2:9	If one is greedy, he is ruled by the law through his reason
	2:10	For the law prevails even over affection for parents
	2:11	so that one rebukes her when she breaks the law
	2:14	through the law, can prevail even over enmity
	2:23	To the mind he gave the law
	3:20	because of their observance of the law
	4:19	in complete violation of the law
	4:23	that if any of them should be found observing the ancestral law
	4:24	to put an end to the people's observance of the law
	5:4	He was a man of priestly family, learned in the law
	5:16	to govern our lives by the divine law
	5:16	than our obedience to the law
	5:18	Even if, as you suppose, our law were not truly divine
	5:20	to transgress the law in matters either small or great
	5:21	for in either case the law is equally despised
	5:25	for since we believe that the law was established by God
	5:25	the Creator of the world in giving us the law
	5:27	not only to transgress the law
	5:29	concerning the keeping of the law
	5:33	as to break the ancestral law by my own act
	5:34	I will not play false to you, O law that trained me
	5:35	nor will I reject you, honoured priesthood and knowledge of the law
	6:18	and have maintained in accordance with law
	6:21	and not protect our divine law even to death
	6:27	I am dying in burning torments for the sake of the law
	6:30	for the sake of the law
	7:7	O man in harmony with the law and philosopher of divine life !
	7:8	Such should be those who are administrators of the law
	7:9	You, father, strengthened out loyalty to the law
	8:25	Not even the law itself would arbitrarily slay us
	9:2	to the law and to Moses our counsellor
	9:4	which insures our safety through transgression of the law
	9:15	but because I protect the divine law
	11:5	according to his virtuous law ?
	11:12	an opportunity to show our endurance for the law
	11:27	but those of the divine law that are set over us
	13:9	Brothers, let us die like brothers for the sake of the law
	13:13	and let us use our bodies as a bulwark for the law
	13:22	and from both general education and our discipline in the law of God
	13:24	Since they had been educated by the same law
	15:9	and their ready obedience to the law
	15:29	vindicator of the law and champion of religion
	15:32	so you, O guardian of the law
	16:16	Fight zealously for our ancestral law
	18:1	obey this law and exercise pity in every way
	18:4	and by reviving observance of the law in the homeland
	18:10	he taught you the law and the prophets

LAW-ABIDING   1
4 Ma 7:15 and venerable grey hair and law-abiding life

LAWBREAKER   1
2 Ma 13:7 that Menelaus the lawbreaker died

LAWFUL   3 = 0.002 %
Jud 11:13 although it is not lawful for any of the people
2 Ma 4:11 and he destroyed the lawful ways of living
3 Ma 2:21 having heard the lawful supplication

LAWFULLY   1
4 Ma 5:36 nor my long life lived lawfully

LAWGIVER   1
2 Es 7:89 that they might keep the law of the Lawgiver perfectly

LAWLESS   29 = 0.019 %
Wis	1:9	to convict him of his lawless deeds
	3:14	whose hands have done no lawless deed
	4:20	and their lawless deeds will convict them to their face
	15:17	He is mortal, and what he makes with lawless hands is dead
	17:2	For when lawless men supposed
Sir	16:4	but through a tribe of lawless men it will be made desolate
	26:23	A godless wife is given as a portion to a lawless man
	34:18	the gifts of the lawless are not acceptable
P Az	9	Thou hast given us into the hands of lawless enemies
1 Ma	1:11	In those days lawless men came forth from Israel
	1:34	And they stationed there a sinful people, lawless men
	2:44	and lawless men in his wrath
	3:5	He searched out and pursued the lawless
	3:6	Lawless men shrank back for fear of him
	7:5	all the lawless and ungodly men of Israel
	9:23	the lawless emerged in all parts of Israel
	9:58	Then all the lawless plotted and said, See !
	9:69	So he was greatly enraged at the lawless men
	10:61	lawless men, gathered together against him to accuse him
	11:21	But certain lawless men who hated their nation
	11:25	Although certain lawless men of his nation
	14:14	and did away with every lawless and wicked man
2 Ma	8:4	and to remember also the lawless destruction of the innocent babies
	8:17	keeping before their eyes the lawless outrage
3 Ma	5:12	that he quite failed in his lawless purpose
	5:20	for the destruction of the lawless Jews !
	6:4	exalted with lawless insolence and boastful tongue
	6:9	by the abominable and lawless Gentiles
	6:12	who by the senseless insolence of the lawless

LAWLESSLY   2
P Az 6 For we have sinfully and lawlessly departed from thee
3 Ma 6:26 Who is it that has so lawlessly encompassed with outrageous treatment

LAWLESSNESS   6 = 0.004 %
Wis 5:7 We took our fill of the paths of lawlessness and destruction
 5:23 Lawlessness will lay waste the whole earth
Sir 21:3 All lawlessness is like a two-edged sword
1 Ma 3:20 They come against us in great pride and lawlessness
1 Es 1:49 committed many acts of sacrilege and lawlessness
4 Ma 9:3 Tyrant and counsellor of lawlessness

LAWSUIT   1
Sir 29:19 will fall into lawsuits

LAY, verb   38 = 0.025 %
Tob	4:9	So you will be laying a good treasure for yourself
	6:16	and lay upon them some of the heart and liver of the fish
Ad E	12:2	to lay hands upon Ahasuerus the king
Wis	5:23	Lawlessness will lay waste the whole earth
Sir	21:4	Terror and violence will lay waste riches
	21:4	thus the house of the proud will be laid waste
	47:19	But laid your loins beside women
	50:2	He laid the foundations for the high double walls
	50:28	and he who lays them to heart will become wise
Bar	3:20	nor understood her paths, nor laid hold of her
Sus	13:34	and laid their hands upon her head
Bel	14:1	When King Astyages was laid with his fathers
1 Ma	2:12	and our glory have been laid waste
	14:31	and lay hands on their sanctuary
	15:3	and I intend to lay claim to the kingdom

2 Ma	1:21	to sprinkle the liquid on the wood and what was laid upon it
	14:7	Therefore I have laid aside my ancestral glory
	15:27	they laid low no less than 35,000 men
1 Es	2:18	and laying the foundations for a temple
	2:23	That is why this city was laid waste
	4:8	if he tells them to lay waste, they lay waste
	4:45	when Judea was laid waste by the Chaldeans
	5:57	and they laid the foundation of the temple of God
	6:9	of hewn stone, with costly timber laid in the walls
	6:11	and laying the foundations of this structure ?
	6:20	laid the foundations of the house of the Lord
	8:22	or any other tax is to be laid
3 Ma	2:22	so that he lay helpless on the ground and
2 Es	3:7	And thou didst lay upon him one commandment of thine
	6:2	and before the foundations of paradise were laid
	7:105	neither shall any one lay a burden on another
	10:21	For you see that our sanctuary has been laid waste
	10:22	our harp has been laid low, our song has been silenced
	10:24	and lay aside your many sorrows
	11:42	and have laid low the walls of those who did you no harm
	14:15	and lay to one side the thoughts that are most grievous to you
	15:49	to lay waste your houses

LAY out   2

Tob	12:13	in order to go and lay out the dead
Sir	38:16	Lay out his body with the honour due him

LAY up   11 = 0.007 %

Sir	3:4	is like one who lays up treasure
	29:11	Lay up your treasure
2 Ma	12:45	that is laid up for those who fall asleep in godliness
P Ma	13	Do not be angry with me for ever or lay up evil for me
2 Es	7:77	For you have a treasure of works laid up with the Most High
	7:83	The 3rd way, they shall see the reward laid up
	7:84	they shall consider the torment laid up for themselves in the last days
	8:33	For the righteous, who have many works laid up with thee
	13:56	for there is a reward laid up with the Most High
	14:8	Lay up in your heart the signs that I have shown you
4 Ma	12:12	Because of this, justice has laid up

LAZY   1

Sir	37:11	with a lazy servant about a big task

LEAD, verb   50 = 0.033 %

Jud	1:13	In the 17th year he led his forces against King Arphaxad
	5:3	Who rules over them as king, leading their army ?
	5:14	and he led them by the way of Sinai and Kadesh-barnea
	6:11	and led him out of the camp into the plain
	10:20	and led her into the tent
	11:19	Then I will lead you through the middle of Judea
	11:19	and you will lead them like sheep that have no shepherd
	15:13	leading all the women
Ad E	12:3	and when they confessed they were led to execution
Wis	2:21	Thus they reasoned, but they were led astray
	6:20	so the desire for wisdom leads to a kingdom
	7:12	I rejoiced in them all, because wisdom leads them
	10:18	and led them through deep waters
	11:15	which led them astray
	19:11	when desire led them to ask for luxurious food
Sir pr.		was himself also led to write something
	3:24	For their hasty judgment has led many astray
	13:8	Take care not to be led astray
	15:12	Do not say, It was he who led me astray
	17:26	for he will lead you out of darkness
	19:2	Wine and women lead intelligent men astray
	27:15	The strife of the proud leads to bloodshed
	31:5	and he who pursues money will be led astray by it
	37:30	for overeating brings sickness, and gluttony leads to nausea
	40:28	My son, do not lead the life of a beggar
	42:1	and do not let partiality lead you to sin :
	45:5	and led him into the thick darkness
	49:2	He was led aright in converting the people
Bar	5:9	For God will lead Israel with joy
1 Ma	5:11	and Timothy is leading their forces
	5:23	and led them to Judea with great rejoicing
	7:5	they were led by Alcimus, who wanted to be high priest
	9:2	They went by the road which leads to Gilgal
2 Ma	1:19	For when our fathers were being led captive to Persia
	1:23	Jonathan led, and the rest responded, as did Nehemiah
	2:2	nor to be led astray in their thoughts
	4:38	and led him about the whole city to that very place
	6:25	they should be led astray because of me
	8:23	then, leading the first division himself
	10:29	and they were leading the Jews
1 Es	3:18	It leads astray the minds of all who drink it
2 Es	1:18	Why hast thou led us into the wilderness to kill us ?
	3:6	And thou didst lead him into the garden
	3:17	And when thou didst lead his descendants out of Egypt
	7:92	that it might not lead them astray from life into death

	7:122	who have led a pure life
	13:40	whom Shalmaneser the king of the Assyrians led captive
	14:4	and I sent him and led my people out of Egypt
	15:10	Behold, my people is led like a flock to the slaughter
4 Ma	11:17	When he had said this, they led him to the wheel

LEAD away   9 = 0.006 %

Jud	2:9	and I will lead them away captive
	5:18	and were led away captive to a foreign country
Bar	4:16	They led away the widow's beloved sons
	5:6	led away by their enemies
Sus	13:45	And as she was being led away to be put to death
1 Es	1:56	The survivors he led away to Babylon with the sword
3 Ma	1:3	had led the king away and arranged
	4:5	was being led away
2 Es	13:40	which were led away from their own land into captivity

LEAD back   2

Tob	12:3	For he has led me back to you safely
Wis	16:13	thou dost lead men down to the gates of Hades and back again

LEAD down   2

Tob	13:2	he leads down to Hades, and brings up again
Wis	16:13	thou dost lead men down to the gates of Hades and back again

LEAD forth   1

2 Es	16:67	so God will lead you forth

LEAD in   2

4 Ma	10:1	When he too had endured a glorious death, the 3rd was led in
	11:13	After he too had died, the 6th, a mere boy, was led in

LEAD off   1

L Jr	6:43	and when one of them is led off by one of the passers-by and is lain with

LEAD on   1

2 Ma	10:1	the Lord leading them on, recovered the temple and the city

LEAD out   2

Jud	7:6	On the 2nd day Holofernes led out all his cavalry
3 Ma	7:5	They also led them out with harsh treatment as slaves

LEAD up   1

2 Es	14:4	and I led him up on Mount Sinai

LEAD, subst., initiative   1

2 Ma	10:12	took the lead in showing justice to the Jews

LEAD, subst., metal   6 = 0.004 %

Sir	22:14	What is heavier than lead ?
	47:18	you gathered gold like tin and amassed silver like lead
2 Es	7:52	will you add to them lead and clay ?
	7:55	and also iron and lead and clay
	7:56	and iron than brass, and lead than iron, and clay than lead

LEADER   54 = 0.035 %

Jud	5:5	Then Achior, the leader of all the Ammonites, said to him
	6:17	in the presence of the Assyrian leaders
	7:8	and all the leaders of the Moabites
	13:18	to strike the head of the leader of our enemies
	14:19	When the leaders of the Assyrian army heard this
Sir	9:17	so a people's leader is proved wise by his words
	10:20	Among brothers their leader is worthy of honour
	33:18	and you leaders of the congregation, hearken
	44:4	leaders of the people in their deliberations
	45:24	that he should be leader of the sanctuary and of his people
	46:18	and he wiped out the leaders of the people of Tyre
	50:1	The leader of his brethren and the pride of his people
P Az	15	or leader, no burnt offering, or sacrifice, or oblation
1 Ma	2:17	You are a leader, honoured and great in this city
	3:55	After this Judas appointed leaders of the people
	5:6	and many people with Timothy as their leader
	5:18	and Azariah, a leader of the people
	9:30	as our ruler and leader, to fight our battle
	9:35	and Jonathan sent his brother as leader of the multitude
	9:61	who were leaders in this treachery
	10:37	Let their officers and leaders be of their own number
	12:53	for they said, They have no leader or helper
	13:8	You are our leader
	13:42	and commander and leader of the Jews
	14:35	and they made him their leader and high priest
	14:41	that Simon should be their leader and high priest for ever
2 Ma	1:13	For when the leader reached Persia
	1:16	they threw stones and struck down the leader and his men
	10:21	he gathered the leaders of the people
	10:28	while the other made rage their leader in the fight
	12:36	to show himself their ally and leader in the battle
	14:6	whose leader is Judas Maccabeus
	14:16	At the command of the leader

	14 : 20	and the leader had informed the people
	14 : 21	And the leaders set a day on which to meet by themselves
1 Es	**1 : 49**	Even the leaders of the people and of the priests
	5 : 8	Bilshan, Mispar, Reeliah, Rehum, and Baanah, their leaders
	5 : 9	The number of the men of the nation and their leaders :
	6 : 12	who the leaders are
	7 : 8	according to the number of the 12 leaders
	8 : 44	who were leaders and men of understanding
	8 : 49	whom David and the leaders had given
	8 : 54	Then I set apart 12 of the leaders of the priests
	8 : 59	to the leaders of the priests and the Levites
	8 : 69	and the leaders and the priests and the Levites
	8 : 70	the leaders and the nobles have been sharing in this iniquity
	8 : 96	Then Ezra arose and had the leaders of the priests
	9 : 12	So let the leaders of the multitude stay
2 Es	**1 : 13**	I gave you Moses as leader and Aaron as priest
	1 : 39	to them I will give as leaders Abraham, Isaac
	9 : 3	wavering of leaders, confusion of princes
	15 : 16	or the chief of their leaders
4 Ma	**5 : 4**	one man, Eleazar by name, leader of the flock
	12 : 5	and a leader in the government of the kingdom

LEADERSHIP 4 = 0.003 %

Sir	**32 : 2**	and receive a wreath for your excellent leadership
1 Ma	**9 : 31**	And Jonathan at that time accepted the leadership
2 Ma	**4 : 40**	under the leadership of a certain Auranus
1 Es	**5 : 36**	under the leadership of Cherub, Addan, and Immer

LEADING 4 = 0.003 %

1 Ma	**9 : 53**	And he took the sons of the leading men of the land
2 Ma	**13 : 15**	He stabbed the leading elephant and its rider
1 Es	**8 : 45**	who was the leading man at the place of the treasury
	9 : 16	the leading men of their fathers' houses

LEAF 3 = 0.002 %

Sir	**6 : 3**	You will devour your leaves and destroy your fruit
	14 : 18	Like flourishing leaves on a spreading tree
2 Es	**1 : 20**	I covered you with the leaves of trees

LEAGUE, subst. 1

2 Ma	**11 : 5**	about 5 leagues from Jerusalem

LEAN, verb 3 = 0.002 %

Ad E	**15 : 3**	leaning daintily on one
Sir	**15 : 4**	He will lean on her and will not fall
2 Ma	**7 : 27**	But, leaning close to him

LEAP 4 = 0.003 %

Wis	**5 : 21**	and will leap to the target
	18 : 15	thy all-powerful word leaped from heaven
	19 : 9	For they ranged like horses, and leaped like lambs
1 Ma	**9 : 48**	Then Jonathan and the men with him leaped into the Jordan

LEAP out 1

1 Ma	**13 : 44**	The men in the siege engine leaped out into the city

LEAP up 2

Tob	**6 : 2**	A fish leaped up from the river
4 Ma	**11 : 1**	the 5th leaped up, saying

LEAPING 1

Wis	**17 : 19**	or the unseen running of leaping animals

LEARN 53 = 0.035 %

Tob	**1 : 9**	When I learned that I was being searched for
	5 : 8	so that I may learn to what tribe he belongs
	5 : 13	because I tried to learn your tribe and family
Jud	**11 : 16**	Therefore, when I, your servant, learned all this
Ad E	**12 : 2**	and learned that they were preparing
Wis	**6 : 1**	learn, O judges of the ends of the earth
	6 : 9	that you may learn wisdom and not transgress
	7 : 13	I learned without guile and I impart without grudging
	7 : 21	I learned both what is secret and what is manifest
	9 : 10	and that I may learn what is pleasing to thee
	9 : 13	For what man can learn the counsel of God ?
	9 : 17	Who has learned thy counsel, unless thou hast given wisdom
	10 : 12	so that he might learn
	11 : 9	they learned how the ungodly
	11 : 16	that they might learn that one is punished
	16 : 26	might learn that it is not the production of crops that feeds man
Sir	**8 : 8**	and learn how to serve great men
	8 : 9	for they themselves learned from their fathers
	8 : 9	and learn how to give an answer in time of need
	18 : 19	Before you speak, learn
	37 : 8	and learn first what is his interest
Bar	**3 : 9**	give ear, and learn wisdom !
	3 : 14	Learn where there is wisdom, where there is strength
	3 : 20	but they have not learned the way to knowledge
	3 : 23	have not learned the way to wisdom
Sus	**13 : 48**	without examination and without learning the facts ?

1 Ma	**2 : 39**	When Mattathias and his friends learned of it
	3 : 11	When Judas learned of it, he went out to meet him
	3 : 42	They also learned what the king had commanded
	6 : 17	And when Lysias learned that the king was dead
	7 : 31	When Nicanor learned that his plan had been disclosed
	7 : 42	let the rest learn that Nicanor has spoken wickedly
	9 : 32	When Bacchides learned of this, he tried to kill him
	9 : 63	When Bacchides learned of this, he assembled all his forces
	9 : 70	When Jonathan learned of this
	10 : 72	Ask and learn who I am
	10 : 80	Jonathan learned that there was an ambush behind him
	12 : 22	And now that we have learned this
	13 : 14	Trypho learned that Simon had risen up
2 Ma	**2 : 7**	When Jeremiah learned of it, he rebuked them and declared :
	4 : 21	Antiochus learned that Philometor had become hostile to his government
	7 : 2	What do you intend to ask and learn from us ?
	12 : 8	But learning that the men in Jamnia
	12 : 21	When Timothy learned of the approach of Judas
1 Es	**2 : 22**	and will learn that this city was rebellious
	5 : 67	And they learned that those who had returned from captivity
3 Ma	**1 : 1**	When Philopator learned from those who returned
2 Es	**12 : 36**	And you alone were worthy to learn this secret of the Most High
4 Ma	**1 : 17**	by which we learn divine matters reverently
	2 : 7	a glutton, or even a drunkard can learn a better way
	4 : 4	When Apollonius learned the details of these things
	9 : 5	as though a short time ago you learned nothing from Eleazar
	10 : 16	Contrive tortures, tyrant, so that you may learn from them

LEARNED 1

4 Ma	**5 : 4**	He was a man of priestly family, learned in the law

LEARNING 4 = 0.003 %

Sir	**pr.**	but also that those who love learning
	pr.	those who love learning should make even greater progress
	pr.	for those living abroad who wished to gain learning
	44 : 4	and in understanding of learning for the people

LEAST, adj., adv. 6 = 0.004 %

Wis	**16 : 3**	might lose the least remnant of appetite
Sir	**23 : 21**	and where he least suspects it, he will be seized
2 Ma	**8 : 35**	by opponents whom he regarded as of the least account
3 Ma	**1 : 15**	Why should not I at least enter
2 Es	**12 : 40**	from the least to the greatest
	13 : 42	that there at least they might keep their statutes

LEAVE, verb 134 = 0.087 %

Tob	**1 : 8**	for I was left an orphan by my father
	1 : 14	and once at Rages in Media I left 10 talents of silver
	1 : 19	I left home in fear
	1 : 20	and nothing was left to me except my wife Anna
	4 : 1	which he had left in trust with Gabael at Rages in Media
	4 : 20	which I left in trust with Gabael the son of Gabrias
	8 : 20	Raguel declared by oath to Tobias that he should not leave
	9 : 3	For Raguel has sworn that I should not leave
	10 : 7	And she went out every day to the road by which they had left
	11 : 2	Are you not aware, brother, of how you left your father ?
	12 : 13	When you did not hesitate to rise and to leave your dinner
	14 : 8	So now, my son, leave Nineveh
Jud	**2 : 5**	When you leave my presence
	2 : 14	So Holofernes left the presence of his master
	5 : 8	For they had left the ways of their ancestors
	5 : 9	Then their God commanded them to leave the place
	6 : 13	and left him lying at the foot of the hill
	7 : 22	there was no strength left in them any longer
	8 : 7	and her husband Manasseh had left her gold and silver
	10 : 19	Surely not a man of them had better be left alive
	13 : 2	So Judith was left alone in the tent
	13 : 4	was left in the bedchamber
	14 : 8	all that she had done, from the day she left
Ad E	**13 : 7**	and leave our government completely secure and untroubled hereafter
Wis	**2 : 9**	everywhere let us leave signs of enjoyment
	4 : 19	they will be left utterly dry and barren
	8 : 13	and leave an everlasting remembrance
	10 : 8	but also left for mankind a reminder of their folly
	10 : 14	and when he was in prison she did not leave him
	12 : 11	that thou didst leave them unpunished for their sins
	14 : 6	left to the world the seed of a new generation
Sir	**6 : 3**	and will be left like a withered tree
	8 : 11	Do not get up and leave an insolent fellow
	11 : 19	until he leaves them to others and dies
	14 : 15	Will you not leave the fruit of your labours to another
	15 : 11	Do not say, Because of the Lord I left the right way
	15 : 14	and he left him in the power of his own inclination
	17 : 21	has neither left nor abandoned them, but spared them
	23 : 11	and the scourge will not leave his house
	23 : 22	So it is with a woman who leaves her husband
	23 : 26	She will leave her memory for a curse
	24 : 33	and leave it to all future generations

	27:12	Among stupid people watch for a chance to leave
	30:4	for he has left behind him one like himself
	30:6	he has left behind him an avenger against his enemies
	32:11	Leave in good time and do not be the last
	33:25	leave his hands idle, and he will seek liberty
	33:31	If you ill-treat him, and he leaves and runs away
	38:12	let him not leave you, for there is need of him
	39:11	if he lives long, he will leave a name greater than a 1,000
	39:32	and have thought this out and left it in writing :
	44:8	There are some of them who have left a name
	44:17	therefore a remnant was left to the earth when the flood came
	47:23	and left behind him one of his sons
	48:15	the people were left very few in number
Bar	**2**:13	Let thy anger turn away from us, for we are left
	4:12	I was left desolate because of the sins of my children
	4:19	for I have been left desolate
L Jr	**6**:47	They have left only lies and reproach for those who come after
1 Ma	**1**:48	and to leave their sons uncircumcised
	2:18	and those that are left in Jerusalem have done
	2:28	and left all that they had in the city
	3:32	He left Lysias, a distinguished man of royal lineage
	5:18	But he left Joseph, the son of Zechariah
	6:2	left there by Alexander, the son of Philip
	6:36	wherever it went they went with it, and they never left it
	6:54	Few men were left in the sanctuary
	7:20	and left with him a force to help him
	7:46	not even one of them was left
	9:6	until no more than 800 of them were left
	9:8	He became faint, but he said to those who were left
	9:10	and leave no cause to question our honour
	9:65	But Jonathan left Simon his brother in the city
	10:13	each left his place and departed to his own land
	10:79	Now Apollonius had secretly left a 1,000 cavalry behind them
	11:64	but left his brother Simon in the country
	11:70	not one of them was left
	12:47	2,000 of whom he left in Galilee
	13:4	and I alone am left
	14:13	No one was left in the land to fight them
	15:14	and permitted no one to leave or enter it
2 Ma	**1**:31	Nehemiah ordered that the liquid that was left
	2:28	leaving the responsibility for exact details to the compiler
	4:29	Menelaus left his own brother Lysimachus
	4:29	while Sostratus left Crates
	4:31	leaving Andronicus, a man of high rank, to act as his deputy
	5:11	So, raging inwardly, he left Egypt
	5:22	And he left governors to afflict the people : at Jerusalem
	6:28	and leave to the young a noble example
	6:31	leaving in his death an example of nobility
	9:24	for they would know to whom the government was left
	10:19	Maccabeus left Simon and Joseph
	12:18	though in one place he had left a very strong garrison
	12:19	marched out and destroyed those whom Timothy had left in the stronghold
	13:23	who had been left in charge of the government
	13:24	left Hegemonides as governor from Ptolemais to Gerar
1 Es	**4**:20	A man leaves his own father who brought him up
	8:6	for they left Babylon on the new moon of the first month
	8:78	to leave to us a root and a name in thy holy place
	8:85	and leave it for an inheritance to your children for ever
	8:88	to destroy us without leaving a root or seed or name ?
	8:89	for we are left as a root this day
3 Ma	**3**:9	for such a great community ought not be left to its fate
	5:6	that the Jews were left without any aid
2 Es	**3**:11	But thou didst leave one of them
	5:18	like a shepherd who leaves his flock
	5:19	He heard what I said and left me
	7:30	so that no one shall be left
	7:78	as the spirit leaves the body to return again to him who gave it
	7:140	there would probably be left only very few
	12:5	and not even a little strength is left in me
	12:39	Then he left me
	12:42	For of all the prophets you alone are left to us
	13:16	alas for those who will be left in those days !
	13:16	And still more, alas for those who are not left !
	13:17	For those who are not left will be sad
	13:19	But alas for those also who are left
	13:22	As for what you said about those who are left
	13:24	Understand therefore that those who are left
	13:26	and he will direct those who are left
	13:33	every man shall leave his own land
	13:41	that they would leave the multitude of the nations
	13:48	But those who are left of your people
	16:23	for the earth shall be left desolate
	16:24	No one shall be left to cultivate the earth or to sow it
	16:28	For out of a city, 10 shall be left
	16:29	3 or 4 olives may be left on every tree
	16:30	some clusters may be left by those who search carefully
	16:31	so in those days 3 or 4 shall be left
	16:32	And the earth shall be left desolate
4 Ma	**9**:23	Do not leave your post in my struggle

	13:18	Those who were left behind said to each of the brothers
	13:27	those who were left endured for the sake of religion
	18:5	he left Jerusalem and marched against the Persians

LEAVE out 1
2 Es	**2**:14	for I left out evil and created good

LEBANAH 1
1 Es	**5**:29	the sons of Lebanah

LEBANON 8 = 0.005 %
Jud	**1**:7	and Lebanon and Antilebanon
Sir	**24**:13	I grew tall like a cedar in Lebanon
	50:8	like a green shoot on Lebanon on a summer day
	50:12	he was like a young cedar on Lebanon
1 Es	**4**:48	and Phoenicia and to those in Lebanon
	4:48	to bring cedar timber from Lebanon to Jerusalem
	5:55	to bring cedar logs from Lebanon
2 Es	**15**:20	from the east and from Lebanon

LEFT, adj., subst. 8 = 0.005 %
1 Ma	**2**:22	to the right hand or to the left
	5:46	and they could not go round it to the right or to the left
	6:45	he killed men right and left
	9:16	When those on the left wing saw
1 Es	**4**:30	and slap the king with her left hand
	9:44	and on his left Pedaiah, Mishael, Malchijah
2 Es	**7**:7	and deep water on the left
	11:35	the head on the right side devoured the one on the left

LEG 1
4 Ma	**10**:6	and breaking his fingers and arms and legs and elbows

LEGISLATION 1
4 Ma	**17**:16	Who did not admire the athletes of the divine legislation ?

LEISURE 3 = 0.002 %
Ad E	**14**:16	and I do not wear it on the days when I am at leisure
Wis	**13**:13	he takes and carves with care in his leisure
Sir	**38**:24	depends on the opportunity of leisure

LEND 9 = 0.006 %
Jud	**11**:22	to lend strength to our hands and to bring destruction
Wis	**15**:8	when he is required to return the soul that was lent him
Sir	**8**:12	Do not lend to a man who is stronger than you
	8:12	but if you do lend anything, be as one who has lost it
	20:15	today he lends and tomorrow he asks it back
	29:1	He that shows mercy will lend to his neighbour
	29:2	Lend to your neighbour in the time of his need
	29:7	many have refused to lend
4 Ma	**2**:8	and to lend without interest to the needy

LENDER 1
Sir	**29**:6	If the lender exerts pressure, he will hardly get back half

LENGTH 7 = 0.005 %
Jud	**7**:3	and in length from Bethulia to Cyamon
Wis	**4**:8	For old age is not honoured for length of time
	8:12	and when I speak at greater length
Sir	**30**:22	and the rejoicing of a man is length of days
Bar	**3**:14	where there is length of days, and life
4 Ma	**13**:20	There each of the brothers dwelt the same length of time
	18:19	this is your life and the length of your days

LENGTHEN 2
Sir	**48**:23	and he lengthened the life of the king
2 Ma	**2**:32	for it is foolish to lengthen the preface

LEOPARD 1
Sir	**28**:23	like a leopard it will mangle them

LEOPARD-LIKE 1
4 Ma	**9**:28	These leopard-like beasts tore out his sinews with the iron hands

LESS 10 = 0.007 %
Wis	**15**:10	and his life is of less worth than clay
Sir	**22**:11	weep less bitterly for the dead, for he has attained rest
2 Ma	**4**:40	a man advanced in years and no less advanced in folly
	5:5	Jason took no less than a 1,000 men
	10:18	When no less than 9,000
	12:4	not less than 200
	12:10	not less than 5,000 Arabs with 500 horsemen attacked them
	15:18	lay upon them less heavily
	15:27	they laid low no less than 35,000 men
2 Es	**7**:58	what is plentiful is of less worth

LESSEN
Sir	17:25	pray in his presence and lessen your offences
	19:6	and for one who hates gossip evil is lessened
	28:8	Refrain from strife, and you will lessen sins

3 = 0.002 %

LESSON
1

Sir	9:1	and do not teach her an evil lesson to your own hurt

LEST
56 = 0.036 %

Jud	7:9	Let our lord hear a word, lest his army be defeated
	12:2	But Judith said, I cannot eat it, lest it be an offence
Wis	4:11	He was caught up lest evil change his understanding
	16:11	lest they should fall into deep forgetfulness
Sir	1:30	Do not exalt yourself lest you fall
	2:7	and turn not aside, lest you fall
	6:2	lest your soul be torn in pieces like a bull
	7:6	lest you be unable to remove iniquity
	7:6	lest you be partial to a powerful man
	8:1	lest you fall into his hands
	8:2	lest his resources outweigh yours
	8:4	lest your ancestors be disgraced
	8:10	lest you be turned in his flaming fire
	8:11	lest he lie in ambush against your words
	8:15	lest he be burdensome to you
	8:19	lest you drive away your good luck
	9:3	lest you fall into her snares
	9:4	lest you be caught in her intrigues
	9:5	lest you stumble and incur penalties for her
	9:6	lest you lose your inheritance
	9:9	lest your heart turn aside to her
	9:13	lest he rob you of your life
	11:33	lest he give you a lasting blemish
	12:5	lest by means of it he subdue you
	12:12	Do not put him next to you, lest he overthrow you
	12:12	lest he try to take your seat of honour
	13:10	Do not push forward, lest you be repulsed
	13:10	and do not remain at a distance, lest you be forgotten
	18:32	lest you become impoverished by its expense
	23:14	lest you be forgetful in their presence
	26:10	lest, when she finds liberty, she use it to her hurt
	28:26	Beware lest you err with your tongue
	28:26	lest you fall before him who lies in wait
	29:20	but take heed to yourself lest you fall
	30:10	Do not laugh with him, lest you have sorrow with him
	30:12	lest he become stubborn and disobey you
	31:16	and do not chew greedily, lest you be hated
	31:17	and do not be insatiable, lest you give offence
	33:19	lest you change your mind and must ask for it
	37:8	lest he cast the lot against you
	42:9	when she is young, lest she do not marry
	42:9	or if married, lest she be hated
	42:10	while a virgin, lest she be defiled
	42:10	or having a husband, lest she prove unfaithful
	42:10	or, though married, lest she be barren
	42:11	lest she make you a laughingstock to your enemies
L Jr	6:27	lest they fall to the ground
1 Ma	4:45	lest it bring reproach upon them
	13:17	lest he arouse great hostility among the people
2 Ma	6:24	lest many of the young should suppose
3 Ma	2:17	lest the transgressors boast in their wrath
	2:23	and fearing lest he should lose his life
	3:24	we have taken Precautions lest
2 Es	6:34	lest you be hasty concerning the last times
	10:34	only do not forsake me, lest I die before my time
4 Ma	4:13	prayed for him lest King Seleucus suppose

LET
238 = 0.155 %

Tob	4:7	and do not let your eye begrudge the gift when you make it
	4:15	or let drunkenness go with you on your way
	4:16	and do not let your eye begrudge the gift when you make it
	4:19	and do not let them be blotted out of your mind
	4:20	And now let me explain to you about the 10 talents of silver
	7:8	and let the matter be settled
	7:10	But let me explain the true situation to you
	8:4	and let us pray that the Lord may have mercy upon us
	8:5	Let the heavens and all thy creatures bless thee
	8:6	let us make a helper for him like himself
	8:12	let us bury him without any one knowing about it
	8:15	Let thy saints and all thy creatures bless thee
	8:15	let all thy angels and thy chosen people bless thee for ever
	10:5	Am I not distressed, my child, that I let you go
	10:12	Let me hear a good report of you
	11:3	Let us run ahead of your wife and prepare the house
	13:8	Let all men speak, and give him thanks in Jerusalem
	13:15	Let my soul praise God the great King
Jud	5:5	Let my lord now hear a word from the mouth of your servant
	5:21	then let my lord pass them by
	5:24	Therefore let us go up, Lord Holofernes
	7:9	Let our lord hear a word, lest his army be defeated
	7:12	only let your servants take possession
	7:28	Let him not do this day the things which we have described !
	7:30	Let us hold out for 5 more days
	8:17	let us call upon him to help us
	8:24	let us set an example to our brethren
	8:25	let us give thanks to the Lord our God
	10:19	for if we let them go
	11:5	and let your maidservant speak in your presence
	12:6	and sent to Holofernes and said, Let my lord now command
	12:12	For it will be a disgrace if we let such a woman go
	14:2	let every valiant man take his weapons and go out of the city
	14:5	and let him see and recognize the man
	16:14	Let all thy creatures serve thee
Ad E	14:11	and do not let them mock at our downfall
Wis	2:6	Come, therefore, let us enjoy the good things that exist
	2:7	Let us take our fill of costly wine and perfumes
	2:7	and let no flower of spring pass by us
	2:8	Let us crown ourselves with rosebuds before they wither
	2:9	Let none of us fail to share in our revelry
	2:9	everywhere let us leave signs of enjoyment
	2:10	Let us oppress the righteous poor man
	2:10	let us not spare the widow
	2:11	But let our might be our law of right
	2:12	Let us lie in wait for the righteous man
	2:17	Let us see if his words are true
	2:17	and let us test what will happen at the end of his life
	2:19	Let us test him with insult and torture
	2:20	Let us condemn him to a shameful death
	13:3	let them know how much better than these is their Lord
	13:4	let them perceive from them
Sir	2:18	Let us fall into the hands of the Lord
	4:31	Let not your hand be extended to receive
	5:10	and let your speech be consistent
	6:6	Let those that are at peace with you be many
	6:6	but let your advisers be one in a 1,000
	6:27	and when you get hold of her, do not let her go
	6:35	and do not let wise proverbs escape you
	6:36	let your foot wear out his doorstep
	7:21	Let your soul love an intelligent servant
	9:15	Let your conversation be with men of understanding
	9:15	and let all your discussion be about the law of the Most High
	9:16	Let righteous men be your dinner companions
	9:16	and let your glorying be in the fear of the Lord
	14:14	let not your share of desired good pass by you
	18:22	Let nothing hinder you from paying a vow promptly
	19:10	Have you heard a word ? Let it die with you
	19:17	and let the law of the Most High take its course
	23:1	and let me not fall because of them !
	23:6	Let neither gluttony nor lust overcome me
	27:19	so you have let your neighbour go
	29:10	and do not let it rust under a stone and be lost
	29:26	and if you have anything at hand, let me have it to eat
	31:10	Let it be for him a ground for boasting
	33:20	do not let any one take your place
	33:30	If you have a servant, let him be as yourself
	36:3	and let them see thy might
	36:5	and let them know thee
	36:8	and let people recount thy mighty deeds
	36:9	Let him who survives be consumed in the fiery wrath
	36:16	and let thy prophets be found trustworthy
	38:12	let him not leave you, for there is need of him
	38:16	My son, let your tears fall for the dead
	38:17	Let your weeping be bitter and your wailing fervent
	38:23	When the dead is at rest, let his remembrance cease
	42:1	and do not let partiality lead you to sin :
	42:7	Whatever you deal out, let it be by number and weight
	44:1	Let us now praise famous men
	50:24	And let him deliver us in our days !
	51:26	and let your souls receive instruction
Bar	2:13	Let thy anger turn away from us, for we are left
	4:12	Let no one rejoice over me, a widow and bereaved of many
	4:14	Let the neighbours of Zion come
L Jr	6:5	or to let fear for these gods possess you
P Az	20	Let all who do harm to thy servants be put to shame
	21	let them be disgraced and deprived of all power and dominion
	21	and let their strength be broken
	22	Let them know that thou art the Lord, the only God
	52	Let the earth bless the Lord
	52	let it sing praise to him and highly exalt him for ever
Sus	13:13	They said to each other, Let us go home, for it is mealtime
	13:53	condemning the innocent and letting the guilty go free
Bel	14:9	Let it be done as you have said
1 Ma	1:11	and misled many, saying, Let us go and make a covenant
	2:27	saying : Let every one who is zealous for the law
	2:37	for they said, Let us all die in our innocence
	2:41	Let us fight against every man who comes to attack us on the sabbath day
	2:41	let us not all die as our brethren died
	2:48	and they never let the sinner gain the upper hand
	3:43	Let us repair the destruction of our people
	4:10	And now let us cry to Heaven

4 :31	and let them be ashamed of their troops and their cavalry
4 :32	let them tremble in their destruction
4 :33	and let all who know thy name praise thee with hymns
4 :36	let us go up to cleanse the sanctuary and dedicate it
5 :48	Let us pass through your land to get to our land
5 :57	So they said, Let us also make a name for ourselves
5 :57	let us go and make war
6 :58	Now then let us come to terms with these men
6 :59	and agree to let them live by their laws as they did before
7 :3	he said, Do not let me see their faces !
7 :7	let him go and see all the ruin
7 :7	and let him punish them and all who help them
7 :28	Let there be no fighting between me and you
7 :38	and let them fall by the sword
7 :38	remember their blasphemies, and let them live no longer
7 :42	let the rest learn that Nicanor has spoken wickedly
9 :8	Let us rise and go up against our enemies
9 :9	Let us rather save our own lives now
9 :9	and let us come back with our brethren and fight them
9 :10	If our time has come, let us die bravely for our brethren
9 :44	Let us rise up now and fight for our lives
9 :58	So now let us bring Bacchides back
10 :4	for he said, Let us act first to make peace with him
10 :31	And let Jerusalem and her environs
10 :33	and let all officials cancel also the taxes on their cattle
10 :34	let them all be days of immunity and release
10 :36	Let Jews be enrolled in the king's forces
10 :36	and let the maintenance be given them
10 :37	Let some of them be stationed
10 :37	and let some of them be put in positions of trust in the kingdom
10 :37	Let their officers and leaders be of their own number
10 :37	and let them live by their own laws
10 :38	let them be so annexed to Judea
10 :43	let him be released and receive back all his property in my kingdom
10 :44	Let the cost of rebuilding
10 :45	And let the cost of rebuilding the walls of Jerusalem
10 :54	now therefore let us establish friendship with one another
10 :63	and let no one annoy him for any reason
10 :71	and let us match strength with each other there
11 :9	Come, let us make a covenant with each other
11 :37	and let it be given to Jonathan
12 :53	Now therefore let us make war on them
13 :38	and let the strongholds that you have built be your possession
13 :40	let them be enrolled, and let there be peace between us
2 Ma **1** :27	and let the Gentiles know that thou art our God
2 :32	At this point therefore let us begin our narrative
6 :13	In fact, not to let the impious alone for long
6 :17	Let what we have said serve as a reminder
7 :42	Let this be enough, then, about the eating of sacrifices
10 :20	and on receiving 70,000 drachmas let some of them slip away
12 :2	would not let them live quietly and in peace
12 :24	With great guile he besought them to let him go in safety
12 :25	they let him go, for the sake of saving their brethren
13 :11	and not to let the people who had just begun to revive
14 :6	and will not let the kingdom attain tranquillity
15 :36	never to let this day go unobserved
1 Es **2** :5	may his Lord be with him, and let him go up to Jerusalem
2 :6	and let each man, wherever he may live
3 :5	Let each of us state what one thing is strongest
4 :19	they let all those things go, and gape at her
6 :8	Let it be fully known to our lord the king that
6 :21	let search be made in the royal archives
6 :22	let him send us directions concerning these things
8 :11	Let as many as are so disposed, therefore
8 :21	Let all things prescribed in the law of God
8 :93	Let us take an oath to the Lord about this
9 :12	So let the leaders of the multitude stay
9 :12	and let all those in our settlements who have foreign wives
3 Ma **2** :20	Speedily let your mercies overtake us
6 :11	Let not the vain-minded praise their vanities
6 :13	And let the Gentiles cower today
6 :15	Let it be shown to all the Gentiles
2 Es **2** :7	Let them be scattered among the nations
2 :7	let their names be blotted out from the earth
2 :21	and let the blind man have a vision of my splendour
4 :14	and said, Come, let us go and make war against the sea
4 :15	and said, Come, let us go up and subdue the forest of the plain
5 :50	let me speak before thee
6 :38	Let heaven and earth be made
7 :20	Let many perish who are now living
7 :65	Let the human race lament
7 :65	but let the beasts of the field be glad
7 :65	let all who have been born lament
7 :65	but let the four-footed beasts and the flocks rejoice !
8 :29	Let it not be thy will to destroy those
8 :42	If I have found favour before thee, let me speak
9 :22	So let the multitude perish which has been born in vain
9 :22	but let my grape and my plant be saved
9 :23	But if you will let 7 days more pass

9 :41	And she said to me, Let me alone, my lord
10 :20	Do not say that, but let yourself be persuaded
10 :55	and do not let your heart be terrified
11 :8	let each sleep in his own place, and watch in his turn
11 :9	but let the heads be reserved for the last
14 :19	Let me speak in thy presence, Lord
14 :36	But let no one come to me now
14 :36	and let no one seek me for 40 days
14 :45	and let the worthy and the unworthy read them
15 :12	Let Egypt mourn, and its foundations
15 :13	Let the farmers that till the ground mourn
16 :41	Let him that sells be like one who will flee
16 :41	let him that buys be like one who will lose
16 :42	let him that does business be like one
16 :42	and let him that builds a house be like one
16 :43	let him that sows be like one who will not reap
16 :53	Let no sinner say that he has not sinned
16 :55	He said, Let the earth be made, and it was made
16 :55	Let the heaven be made, and it was made
16 :76	do not let your sins pull you down
4 Ma **6** :28	and let our punishment suffice for them
8 :16	Let us consider, on the other hand
8 :20	Let us take pity on our youth
8 :21	and let us seriously consider that if we disobey we are dead !
8 :24	Let us not struggle against compulsion
10 :20	we let our bodily members be mutilated
12 :8	he said, Let me loose, let me speak to the king
12 :12	and these throughout all time will never let you go
13 :9	Brothers, let us die like brothers for the sake of the law
13 :9	let us imitate the 3 youths in Assyria
13 :10	Let us not be cowardly in the demonstration of our piety
13 :13	Let us with all our hearts consecrate ourselves to God
13 :13	and let us use our bodies as a bulwark for the law
13 :14	Let us not fear him who thinks he is killing us
13 :16	Therefore let us put on the full armour of self-control

LET in   1

2 Ma **10** :36	Others broke open the gates and let in the rest of the force

LETTER   49 = 0.032 %

Ad E **11** :1	and Ptolemy his son brought to Egypt the preceding Letter of Purim
13 :1	This is a copy of the letter :
13 :6	that those indicated to you in the letters of Haman
16 :1	The following is a copy of this letter :
16 :17	the letters sent by Haman the son of Hammedatha
16 :19	Therefore post a copy of this letter publicly in every place
Sir **45** :11	for a reminder, in engraved letters
L Jr **6** :1	A copy of a letter which Jeremiah sent
1 Ma **1** :44	And the king sent letters by messengers to Jerusalem
5 :10	and sent to Judas and his brothers a letter which said
5 :14	While the letter was still being read
8 :22	and this is a copy of the letter
9 :60	and secretly sent letters to all his allies in Judea
10 :3	And Demetrius sent Jonathan a letter
10 :7	and read the letter in the hearing of all the people
10 :17	And he wrote a letter
11 :29	and wrote a letter to Jonathan about all these things
11 :31	This copy of the letter
12 :2	He also sent letters to the same effect to the Spartans
12 :4	And the Romans gave them letters to the people
12 :5	This is a copy of the letter
12 :7	a letter was sent to Onias the high priest
12 :8	and received the letter
12 :10	since you sent your letter to us
12 :17	and greet you and deliver to you this letter from us
12 :19	This is a copy of the letter which they sent to Onias
13 :35	and wrote him a letter as follows
14 :20	This is a copy of the letter which the Spartans sent :
15 :1	sent a letter from the islands of the sea
15 :15	with letters to the kings and countries
16 :19	he sent letters to the captains asking them to come to him
2 Ma **2** :13	about kings of kings about votive offerings
9 :18	and wrote to the Jews the following letter
11 :16	The letter written to the Jews by Lysias was to this effect :
11 :22	The king's letter ran thus :
11 :27	To the nation the king's letter was as follows :
11 :34	The Romans also sent them a letter which read thus :
1 Es **2** :16	wrote him the following letter
2 :26	I have read the letter which you sent me
2 :30	Then, when the letter from King Artaxerxes was read
4 :47	and wrote letters for him to all the treasurers
4 :48	And he wrote letters to all the governors in Coelesyria
4 :61	So he took the letters
6 :7	A copy of the letter
3 Ma **3** :11	wrote this letter against them :
3 :25	as soon as this letter shall arrive
3 :30	The letter was written in the above form

6:41 and wrote the following letter for them
7:10 Upon receiving this letter

LEVEL, verb   4 = 0.003 %
2 Ma 8:3 and about to be levelled to the ground
   9:14 which he was hastening to level to the ground
  14:33 I will level this precinct of God to the ground
3 Ma 5:43 and rapidly level it to the ground with fire and spear

LEVEL, adj.   1
Bar 5:7 and the valleys filled up, to make level ground

LEVI   6 = 0.004 %
Tob 1:7 Of all my produce I would give a tenth to the sons of Levi
Sir 45:6 a holy man like him, of the tribe of Levi
1 Es 8:47 the son of Levi, son of Israel
   9:14 and Meshullam and Levi and Shabbethai
2 Es 1:3 son of Aaron, of the tribe of Levi
4 Ma 2:19 censure the households of Simeon and Levi

LEVIATHAN   2
2 Es 6:49 and the name of the other Leviathan
   6:52 but to Leviathan thou didst give the 7th part, the watery part

LEVITE   36 = 0.023 %
Ad E 11:1 Dositheus, who said that he was a priest and a Levite
1 Es 1:3 And he told the Levites, the temple servants of Israel
   1:5 according to the grouping of the fathers' houses of you Levites
   1:7 to the people and the priests and Levites
   1:9 gave the Levites for the passover 5,000 sheep and 700 calves
   1:10 The priests and the Levites
   1:14 so the Levites prepared it for themselves
   1:16 for their brethren the Levites prepared the passover for them
   1:21 as was kept by Josiah and the priests and the Levites
   2:8 and the priests and the Levites
   4:55 He wrote that the support for the Levites should be provided
   5:26 The Levites : the sons of Jeshua and Kadmiel
   5:46 The priests, the Levites
   5:58 And they appointed the Levites
   5:58 with their sons and brethren, all the Levites
   5:59 and the Levites, the sons of Asaph, with cymbals
   7:6 And the people of Israel, the priests, the Levites
   7:9 and the priests and the Levites stood
   7:10 after the priests and the Levites were purified together
   7:11 but the Levites were all purified together
   8:5 and Levites and temple singers
   8:10 and of the priests and Levites and others in our realm
   8:22 on any of the priests or Levites or temple singers
   8:42 none of the sons of the priests or of the Levites
   8:49 for the service of the Levites
   8:59 to the leaders of the priests and the Levites
   8:60 So the priests and the Levites
   8:63 and Moeth the son of Binnui, the Levites
   8:69 and the leaders and the priests and Levites
   8:96 and Levites of all Israel take oath
   9:23 And of the Levites : Jozabad and Shimei and Kelaiah
   9:37 The priests and the Levites and the men of Israel
   9:48 Azariah and Jozabad, Hanan, Pelaiah, the Levites
   9:49 and to the Levites who were teaching the multitude, and to all
   9:53 And the Levites commanded all the people, saying
2 Es 10:22 our Levites have gone into captivity

LEVITICAL   2
1 Es 5:56 together with their brethren and the Levitical priests
   5:63 Some of the Levitical priests and heads of fathers' houses

LEVY, subst.   1
1 Ma 10:29 from payment of tribute and salt tax and crown levies

LEVY, verb   1
2 Ma 11:3 and to levy tribute on the temple

LEWD   1
Sir 23:13 Do not accustom your mouth to lewd vulgarity

LIABLE   1
1 Ma 14:45 shall be liable to punishment

LIAR   5 = 0.003 %
Sir 15:8 and liars will never think of her
  20:25 A thief is preferable to a habitual liar
  20:26 The disposition of a liar brings disgrace
  25:2 a beggar who is proud, a rich man who is a liar
2 Es 11:42 and have loved liars

LIBATION   3 = 0.002 %
Ad E 14:17 or drunk the wine of the libations
Sir 50:15 and poured a libation of the blood of the grape
1 Es 6:31 in order that libations may be made to the Most High God

LIBERAL   1
Sir 31:23 Men will praise the one who is liberal with food

LIBERALLY   1
3 Ma 3:21 and the myriad affairs liberally entrusted to them from the beginning

LIBERTY   3 = 0.002 %
Sir 26:10 lest, when she finds liberty, she use it to her hurt
  33:25 leave his hands idle, and he will seek liberty
2 Es 7:96 and the spacious liberty

LIBRARY   1
2 Ma 2:13 and also that he founded a library

LICENCE   1
3 Ma 7:12 granted them a general licence

LICENTIOUS   1
3 Ma 2:26 He was not content with his uncounted licentious deeds

LICK up   1
Jud 7:4 These men will now lick up the face of the whole land

LIE, verb, rest   46 = 0.030 %
Jud 3:2 lie prostrate before you
   3:3 and all our sheepfolds with their tents, lie before you
   6:13 and left him lying at the foot of the hill
  10:2 she rose from where she lay prostrate
  13:15 and here is the canopy beneath which he lay
  14:18 For look, here is Holofernes lying on the ground
Wis 2:12 Let us lie in wait for the righteous man
  10:12 and kept him safe from those who lay in wait for him
  17:2 they themselves lay as captives of darkness
  17:7 The delusions of their magic art lay humbled
Sir 5:14 and do not lie in ambush with your tongue
   8:11 lest he lie in ambush against your words
  11:31 for he lies in wait, turning good into evil
  11:32 and a sinner lies in wait to shed blood
  14:22 Pursue wisdom like a hunter, and lie in wait on her paths
  27:10 A lion lies in wait for prey
  27:28 but vengeance lies in wait for him like a lion
  28:26 lest you fall before him who lies in wait
  38:13 There is a time when success lies in the hands of physicians
  43:32 Many things greater than these lie hidden
  46:12 May their bones revive from where they lie
  49:10 revive from where they lie
L Jr 6:43 and when one of them is led off by one of the passers-by and is lain with
Sus 13:20 so give your consent, and lie with us
  13:37 came to her and lay with her
1 Ma 5:3 because they kept lying in wait for Israel
   6:9 He lay there for many days
  11:4 and the corpses lying about
  16:5 and a stream lay between them
2 Ma 3:29 While he lay prostrate
   3:31 to one who was lying quite at his last breath
   4:41 and others took handfuls of the ashes that were lying about
   5:10 He who had cast many to lie unburied
  12:39 and to bring them back to lie with their kinsmen
  13:12 and lying prostrate for 3 days without ceasing
  15:18 lay upon them less heavily
  15:28 they recognized Nicanor, lying dead, in full armour
1 Es 8:91 weeping and lying upon the ground before the temple
2 Es 2:9 whose land lies in lumps of pitch and heaps of ashes
   3:1 I was troubled as I lay on my bed
   7:8 and there is only one path lying between them, that is
   9:27 And after 7 days, as I lay on the grass
  10:30 and behold, I lay there like a corpse
  14:20 For the world lies in darkness
4 Ma 13:15 lying before those who transgress the commandment of God
  17:9 Here lie buried an aged priest and an aged woman and 7 sons

LIE down   1
Jud 12:16 Then Judith came in and lay down

LIE, verb, deceive   3 = 0.002 %
Sir 7:13 for the habit of lying serves no good
Sus 13:55 You have lied against your own head
  13:59 You also have lied against your own head

LIE, subst.   8 = 0.005 %
Wis 14:28 or prophesy lies, or live unrighteously
Sir 7:12 Do not devise a lie against your brother
   7:13 Refuse to utter any lie
  20:24 A lie is an ugly blot on a man
  41:17 and of a lie, before a prince or a ruler
  51:2 from lips that utter lies

L Jr	6 :47	They have left only lies and reproach for those who come after
Bel	14 :12	or else Daniel will, who is telling lies about us

LIFE   207 = 0.135 %

Tob	1 :3	all the days of my life
	3 :15	But if it be not pleasing to thee to take my life
	4 :3	honour her all the days of your life
	4 :5	Live uprightly all the days of your life
	5 :19	For the life that is given to us by the Lord
	6 :14	and bring the lives of my father and mother to the grave
	8 :17	and bring their lives to fulfilment
	12 :9	will have fulness of life
	12 :10	but those who commit sin are the enemies of their own lives
	14 :3	behold, I have grown old and am about to depart this life
Jud	7 :27	for we will be slaves, but our lives will be spared
	8 :24	for their lives depend upon us
	8 :29	but from the beginning of your life
	10 :15	You have saved your life
	12 :18	because my life means more to me today
	13 :20	because you did not spare your own life
	16 :22	but she remained a widow all the days of her life
Ad E	13 :2	I have determined to settle the lives of my subjects in lasting tranquillity
	13 :5	perversely following a strange manner of life and laws
	16 :12	he undertook to deprive us of our kingdom and our life
Wis	1 :12	Do not invite death by the error of your life
	2 :1	Short and sorrowful is our life
	2 :4	our life will pass away like the traces of a cloud
	2 :15	because his manner of life is unlike that of others
	2 :17	and let us test what will happen at the end of his life
	4 :9	and a blameless life is ripe old age
	5 :4	We thought that his life was madness
	7 :6	there is for all mankind one entrance into life
	8 :5	If riches are a desirable possession in life
	8 :7	nothing in life is more profitable for men than these
	8 :16	and life with her has no pain, but gladness and joy
	12 :6	these parents who murder helpless lives
	12 :23	Therefore those who in folly of life lived unrighteously
	13 :11	make a useful vessel that serves life's needs
	13 :18	for life he prays to a thing that is dead
	14 :5	therefore men trust their lives
	14 :12	and the invention of them was the corruption of life
	14 :24	either their lives or their marriages pure
	15 :9	or that his life is brief
	15 :10	and his life is of less worth than clay
	15 :12	and life a festival held for profit
	15 :17	since he has life, but they never have
	16 :13	For thou hast power over life and death
Sir	1 :12	and gives gladness and joy and long life
	1 :20	and her branches are long life
	2 :3	that you may be honoured at the end of your life
	3 :6	Whoever glorifies his father will have long life
	4 :12	Whoever loves her loves life
	6 :16	A faithful friend is an elixir of life
	7 :36	In all you do, remember the end of your life
	9 :13	lest he rob you of your life
	10 :9	For even in life his bowels decay
	10 :29	And who will honour the man that dishonours his own life ?
	11 :14	good things and bad, life and death, poverty and wealth
	11 :27	and at the close of a man's life
	13 :14	During all your life love the Lord
	15 :17	Before a man are life and death
	17 :11	and allotted to them the law of life
	19 :5	but he who withstands pleasures crowns his life
	20 :22	A man may lose his life through shame
	20 :32	than a masterless charioteer of one's own life
	22 :9	Children who are brought up in a good life
	22 :11	but the life of the fool is worse than death
	22 :12	but for a fool or an ungodly man it lasts all his life
	23 :1	O Lord, Father and Ruler of my life
	23 :4	O Lord, Father and God of my life
	23 :28	and to be received by him is long life
	25 :2	and I am greatly offended at their life :
	28 :6	Remember the end of your life, and cease from enmity
	29 :15	for he has given his life for you
	29 :21	The essentials for life are water and bread and clothing
	29 :22	Better is the life of a poor man
	29 :24	It is a miserable life to go from house to house
	30 :17	Death is better than a miserable life
	30 :22	Gladness of heart is the life of man
	30 :24	Jealousy and anger shorten life
	31 :27	Wine is like life to men, if you drink it in moderation
	31 :27	What is life to a man who is without wine ?
	33 :14	Good is the opposite of evil, and life the opposite of death
	33 :23	At the time when you end the days of your life
	34 :17	he grants healing, life, and blessing
	34 :21	The bread of the needy is the life of the poor
	37 :18	4 turns of fortune appear, good and evil, life and death
	37 :25	The life of a man is numbered by days
	37 :31	but he who is careful to avoid it prolongs his life
	38 :14	and in healing, for the sake of preserving life
	38 :19	and the life of the poor man weighs down his heart
	38 :20	drive it away, remembering the end of life
	39 :26	Basic to all the needs of man's life are water and fire
	40 :18	Life is sweet for the self-reliant and the worker
	40 :28	My son, do not lead the life of a beggar
	40 :29	his existence cannot be considered as life
	41 :3	remember your former days and the end of life
	41 :4	Whether life is for 10 or a 100 or a 1,000 years
	41 :13	The days of a good life are numbered
	45 :5	the law of life and knowledge
	48 :14	As in his life he did wonders
	48 :23	and he lengthened the life of the king
	50 :1	who in his life repaired the house
	51 :3	from the hand of those who sought my life
	51 :6	and my life was very near to Hades beneath
Bar	1 :11	and pray for the life of Nebuchadnezzar king of Babylon
	1 :11	and for the life of Belshazzar his son
	3 :9	Hear the commandments of life, O Israel
	3 :14	where there is length of days, and life
L Jr	6 :7	For my angel is with you, and he is watching your lives
1 Ma	2 :40	for our lives and our ordinances
	2 :50	and give your lives for the covenant of our fathers
	3 :12	and used it in battle the rest of his life
	3 :21	but we fight for our lives and our laws
	6 :44	So he gave his life to save his people
	9 :9	Let us rather save our own lives now
	9 :44	Let us rise up now and fight for our lives
	12 :51	that they would fight for their lives
	13 :5	And now, far be it from me to spare my life
2 Ma	3 :31	to call upon the Most High and to grant life
	3 :33	since for his sake the Lord has granted you your life
	3 :35	and made very great vows to the Saviour of his life
	4 :10	to the Greek way of life
	6 :19	rather than life with pollution
	6 :20	even for the natural love of life
	6 :23	and his excellent life even from childhood
	6 :24	Such pretence is not worthy of our time of life, he said
	6 :27	Therefore, by manfully giving up my life now
	7 :9	You accursed wretch, you dismiss us from this present life
	7 :9	to an everlasting renewal of life
	7 :14	But for you there will be no resurrection to life !
	7 :22	It was not I who gave you life and breath
	7 :23	will in his mercy give life and breath back to you again
	7 :27	to this point in your life
	7 :36	have drunk of everflowing life under God's covenant
	7 :37	I, like my brothers, give up body and life
	8 :17	and besides, the overthrow of their ancestral way of life
	9 :28	came to the end of his life by a most pitiable fate
	10 :13	he took poison and ended his life
	11 :7	and he urged the others to risk their lives with him
	14 :25	so he married, settled down, and shared the common life
	14 :38	and for Judaism he had with all zeal risked body and life
	14 :46	calling upon the Lord of life and spirit
1 Es	6 :31	and prayers be offered for their life
P Ma	15	all the days of my life
3 Ma	2 :23	and fearing lest he should lose his life
	2 :32	in exchange for life they confidently attempted
	3 :5	but since they adorned their style of life
	3 :23	in every situation, in accordance with their infamous way of life
	4 :4	reflected upon the uncertainty of life
	4 :6	to share married life
	5 :32	In fact you would have been deprived of life instead of these
	5 :49	they thought that this was their last moment of life
	6 :1	and throughout his life had been adorned with every virtue
	6 :6	who had voluntarily surrendered their lives to the flames
	6 :10	Even if our lives have become entangled in impieties in our exile
	6 :12	are being deprived of life in the manner of traitors
	6 :24	you are now attempting to deprive of dominion and life
	7 :6	we barely spared their lives
2 Es	2 :12	The tree of life shall give them fragrant perfume
	3 :5	and thou didst breathe into him the breath of life
	4 :24	and our life is like a mist
	4 :52	but I was not sent to tell you concerning your life
	5 :45	that thou wilt certainly give life at one time to thy creation ?
	7 :48	and removed us far from life
	7 :92	that it might not lead them astray from life into death
	7 :98	whom they served in life
	7 :122	who have led a pure life
	7 :129	Choose for yourself life, that you may live !
	7 :137	the world with those who inhabit it would not have life
	7 :138	not one ten-thousandth of mankind could have life
	8 :8	And because thou dost give life to the body
	8 :13	Thou wilt take away his life, for he is thy creation
	8 :31	For we and our fathers have passed our lives
	8 :52	the tree of life is planted
	8 :60	and have been ungrateful to him who prepared life for them
	13 :55	for you have devoted your life to wisdom
	14 :13	And now renounce the life that is corruptible
	14 :30	and received the law of life, which they did not keep

	16:61	and gave him breath and life and understanding
4 Ma	**1**:15	Now reason is the mind that with sound logic prefers the life of wisdom
	2:8	a way of life in accordance with the law
	2:23	and one who lives subject to this will
	4:1	Onias, who then held the high priesthood for life
	4:19	Jason changed the nation's way of life
	5:16	to govern our lives by the divine law
	5:26	what will be most suitable for our lives
	5:36	nor my long life lived lawfully
	6:18	the reputation of such a life
	6:29	and take my life in exchange for theirs
	7:4	Although his sacred life was consumed by tortures and racks
	7:7	O man in harmony with the law and philosopher of divine life !
	7:15	and venerable grey hair and law-abiding life
	7:21	What person who lives as a philosopher
	8:7	the ancestral tradition of your national life
	8:8	And enjoy your youth by adopting the Greek way of life
	8:23	Why do we banish ourselves from this most pleasant life
	9:7	and if you take our lives because of our religion
	9:25	the saintly youth broke the thread of life
	10:15	and by the everlasting life of the pious
	12:18	both in this present life and when you are dead
	12:19	he flung himself into the braziers and so ended his life
	13:13	who gave us our lives
	13:20	and growing from the same blood and through the same life
	15:3	religion that preserves them for eternal life
	16:18	and have enjoyed life
	17:9	who wished to destroy the way of life of the Hebrews
	17:12	The prize was immortality in endless life
	18:9	A happy man was he, who lived out his life with good children
	18:16	There is a tree of life for those who do his will
	18:19	this is your life and the length of your days

LIFE-GIVING

Sir	**19**:19	is life-giving discipline	1

LIFELESS

Wis	**13**:17	he is not ashamed to address a lifeless thing	5 = 0.003 %
	14:29	for because they trust in lifeless idols	
	15:5	so that they desire the lifeless form of a dead image	
2 Es	**3**:5	and it gave thee Adam, a lifeless body ?	
	6:48	The dumb and lifeless water produced living creatures	

LIFELIKE

Sir	**38**:27	he sets his heart on painting a lifelike image	1

LIFETIME

2 Es	**9**:10	For as many as did not acknowledge me in their lifetime	1

LIFT

Jud	**11**:2	I would never have lifted my spear against them	9 = 0.006 %
Ad E	**15**:7	Lifting his face, flushed with splendour	
Sir	**11**:12	he lifts him out of his low estate	
	13:2	Do not lift a weight beyond your strength	
	46:2	How glorious he was when he lifted his hands	
	47:4	when he lifted his hand with a stone in the sling	
Bel	**14**:36	and lifted him by his hair and set him down in Babylon	
1 Es	**8**:86	For thou, O Lord, didst lift the burden of our sins	
2 Es	**13**:9	he neither lifted his hand	

LIFT up

Jud	**16**:11	they lifted up their voices, and the enemy were turned back	17 = 0.011 %
Sir	**11**:1	The wisdom of a humble man will lift up his head	
	34:17	He lifts up the soul and gives light to the eyes	
	36:3	Lift up thy hand against foreign nations	
	38:3	The skill of the physician lifts up his head	
	40:26	Riches and strength lift up the heart	
	46:20	and lifted up his voice out of the earth in prophecy	
	48:18	he lifted up his hand against Zion	
	50:20	Then Simon came down, and lifted up his hands	
1 Ma	**1**:3	and his heart was lifted up	
	16:13	His heart was lifted up	
1 Es	**4**:58	he lifted up his face to heaven toward Jerusalem	
	9:47	And they lifted up their hands	
3 Ma	**6**:5	and was lifted up against your holy city	
2 Es	**6**:4	and before the heights of the air were lifted up	
	9:38	I lifted up my eyes and saw a woman on my right	
4 Ma	**6**:26	he lifted up his eyes to God and said	

LIGAMENT

4 Ma	**9**:21	Although the ligaments joining his bones were already severed	1

LIGHT, adj.

Wis	**5**:1	and those who make light of his labours	6 = 0.004 %
	5:11	the light air, lashed by the beat of its pinions	
	5:14	and like a light hoarfrost driven away by a storm	
	12:26	But those who have not heeded the warning of light rebukes	

2 Ma	**2**:26	it is no light matter but calls for sweat and loss of sleep
	4:17	For it is no light thing

LIGHT, subst.

Tob	**10**:5	you who are the light of my eyes ?	51 = 0.033 %
	14:10	how he brought him from light into darkness	
Jud	**13**:13	and they kindled a fire for light, and gathered around them	
Ad E	**10**:6	and there was light and the sun and abundant water	
	11:11	light came, and the sun rose	
Wis	**5**:6	and the light of righteousness did not shine on us	
	7:10	and I chose to have her rather than light	
	7:26	For she is a reflection of eternal light	
	7:29	Compared with the light she is found to be superior	
	16:28	and must pray to thee at the dawning of the light	
	17:5	And no power of fire was able to give light	
	17:20	For the whole world was illumined with brilliant light	
	18:1	But for thy holy ones there was very great light	
	18:4	For their enemies deserved to be deprived of light	
	18:4	through whom the imperishable light of the law	
Sir	**3**:25	If you have no eyes you will be without light	
	16:16	and he divided his light and darkness with a plumb line	
	17:18	and allotting to him the light of his love	
	17:26	to the light of health and hate abominations intensely	
	17:31	Yet its light fails	
	22:11	Weep for the dead, for he lacks the light	
	24:27	It makes instruction shine forth like light	
	32:16	and like a light they will kindle righteous deeds	
	34:17	He lifts up the soul and gives light to the eyes	
	42:16	The sun looks down on everything with its light	
	43:7	a light that wanes when it has reached the full	
	50:29	for the light of the Lord is his path	
Bar	**1**:12	and he will give light to our eyes	
	3:14	where there is light for the eyes, and peace	
	3:20	Young men have seen the light of day	
	3:33	he who sends forth the light, and it goes	
	4:2	walk toward the shining of her light	
	5:9	in the light of his glory	
L Jr	**6**:67	or shine like the sun or give light like the moon	
P Az	48	Bless the Lord, light and darkness	
1 Ma	**1**:21	the lampstand for the light, and all its utensils	
	4:50	and these gave light in the temple	
2 Ma	**1**:32	but when the light from the altar shone back, it went out	
	12:9	so that the glow of the light was seen in Jerusalem, 30 miles distant	
1 Es	**8**:79	and to uncover a light for us	
3 Ma	**6**:4	manifesting the light of your mercy upon the nation of Israel	
	6:7	you brought up to the light unharmed	
2 Es	**1**:14	I provided light for you from a pillar of fire	
	2:35	because the eternal light will shine upon you for evermore	
	6:40	that a ray of light be brought forth from thy treasuries	
	6:45	the light of the moon	
	7:42	or noon or night, or dawn or shining or brightness or light	
	7:97	and how they are to be made like the light of the stars	
	10:22	the light of our lampstand has been put out	
	14:20	and its inhabitants are without light	
4 Ma	**13**:20	they were brought to the light of day	

LIGHT, verb, kindle

L Jr	**6**:19	They light lamps, even more than they light for themselves	7 = 0.005 %
1 Ma	**4**:50	and lighted the lamps on the lampstand	
2 Ma	**1**:8	and we lighted the lamps and we set out the loaves	
	10:3	and they burned incense and lighted lamps	
2 Es	**14**:25	and I will light in your heart the lamp of understanding	
4 Ma	**17**:5	who, after lighting the way of your star-like 7 sons to piety	

LIGHT, verb, settle

L Jr	**6**:22	Bats, swallows, and birds light on their bodies and heads	1

LIGHTEN, verb

4 Ma	**9**:31	I lighten my pain by the joys that come from virtue	1

LIGHTMINDED

Sir	**19**:4	One who trusts others too quickly is lightminded	1

LIGHTNING

Wis	**5**:21	Shafts of lightning will fly with true aim	10 = 0.007 %
Sir	**32**:10	Lightning speeds before the thunder	
	43:13	and speeds the lightnings of his judgment	
L Jr	**6**:61	So also the lightning, when it flashes, is widely seen	
P Az	51	Bless the Lord, lightnings and clouds	
2 Es	**6**:2	and before the flashes of lightning shone	
	7:40	or cloud or thunder or lightning or wind	
	10:25	and her countenance flashed like lightning	
	16:18	He will flash lightning, and who will not be afraid ?	
4 Ma	**4**:10	angels on horseback with lightning flashing from their weapons appeared from heaven	

LIKE*

Tob	**8**:6	let us make a helper for him like himself	299 = 0.195 %
	14:5	though it will not be like the former one	

Jud	**2**:20	Along with them went a mixed crowd like a swarm of locusts
	2:20	like the dust of the earth
	8:16	for God is not like a man, to be threatened
	8:16	nor like a human being, to be won over by pleading
	10:19	who have women like this among them ?
	11:19	and you will lead them like sheep that have no shepherd
	12:3	where can we get more like it for you ?
	12:13	and become today like one of the daughters of the Assyrians
	16:12	they were wounded like the children of fugitives
	16:15	at thy presence the rocks shall melt like wax
Ad E	**14**:16	I abhor it like a menstruous rag
	15:13	like an angel of God
Wis	**2**:3	and the spirit will dissolve like empty air
	2:4	our life will pass away like the traces of a cloud
	2:4	and be scattered like mist that is chased
	3:6	like gold in the furnace he tried them
	3:6	and like a sacrificial burnt offering he accepted them
	3:7	and will run like sparks through the stubble
	5:9	All those things have vanished like a shadow
	5:9	and like a rumour that passes by
	5:10	like a ship that sails through the billowy water
	5:14	is like chaff carried by the wind
	5:14	and like a light hoarfrost driven away by a storm
	5:14	it is dispersed like smoke before the wind
	5:14	and it passes like the remembrance of a guest who stays but a day
	5:23	and like a tempest it will winnow them away
	7:1	I also am mortal, like all men
	7:3	and my first sound was a cry, like that of all
	11:14	for their thirst was not like that of the righteous
	11:22	is like a speck that tips the scales
	11:22	and like a drop of morning dew that falls upon the ground
	12:24	they were deceived like foolish babes
	13:13	he forms it like the image of a man
	13:14	or makes it like some worthless animal
	15:7	making all in like manner
	15:16	for no man can form a god which is like himself
	16:29	will melt like wintry frost, and flow away like waste water
	19:9	For they ranged like horses, and leaped like lambs
Sir	**3**:4	is like one who lays up treasure
	3:16	Whoever forsakes his father is like a blasphemer
	4:10	Be like a father to orphans
	4:10	you will then be like a son of the Most High
	4:30	Do not be like a lion in your home
	6:2	lest your soul be torn in pieces like a bull
	6:3	and will be left like a withered tree
	6:19	Come to her like one who ploughs and sows
	6:21	She will weigh him down like a heavy testing stone
	6:22	For wisdom is like her name, and is not manifest to many
	6:31	You will wear her like a glorious robe
	6:31	and put her on like a crown of gladness
	7:12	nor do the like to a friend
	9:8	and by it passion is kindled like a fire
	9:10	A new friend is like new wine
	10:2	like the magistrate of the people, so are his officials
	10:2	and like the ruler of the city, so are all its inhabitants
	11:30	Like a decoy partridge in a cage
	11:30	and like a spy he observes your weakness
	12:10	for like the rusting of copper, so is his wickedness
	12:11	and you will be to him like one who has polished a mirror
	13:1	and whoever associates with a proud man will become like him
	13:15	Every creature loves its like
	13:16	and a man clings to one like himself
	14:17	All living beings become old like a garment
	14:18	Like flourishing leaves on a spreading tree
	14:22	Pursue wisdom like a hunter, and lie in wait on her paths
	15:2	She will come to meet him like a mother
	15:2	and like the wife of his youth she will welcome him
	16:21	Like a tempest which no man can see
	17:3	He endowed them with strength like his own
	17:22	A man's almsgiving is like a signet with the Lord
	17:22	and he will keep a person's kindness like the apple of his eye
	18:10	Like a drop of water from the sea and a grain of sand
	18:23	and do not be like a man who tempts the Lord
	19:11	like a woman in labour with a child
	19:12	Like an arrow stuck in the flesh of the thigh
	20:4	Like a eunuch's desire to violate a maiden
	20:15	he opens his mouth like a herald
	20:19	An ungracious man is like a story told at the wrong time
	20:29	like a muzzle on the mouth they avert reproofs
	21:3	All lawlessness is like a two-edged sword
	21:8	is like one who gathers stones for his burial mound
	21:9	An assembly of the wicked is like tow gathered together
	21:13	The knowledge of a wise man will increase like a flood
	21:13	and his counsel like a flowing spring
	21:14	The mind of a fool is like a broken jar
	21:16	A fool's narration is like a burden on a journey
	21:18	Like a house that has vanished, so is wisdom to a fool
	21:19	and like manacles on his right hand
	21:21	To a sensible man education is like a golden ornament
	21:21	and like a bracelet on the right arm
	22:6	Like music in mourning is a tale told at the wrong time
	22:7	is like one who glues potsherds together
	22:17	is like the stucco decoration on the wall of a colonnade
	23:16	The soul heated like a burning fire
	24:3	and covered the earth like a mist
	24:13	I grew tall like a cedar in Lebanon
	24:13	and like a cypress on the heights of Hermon
	24:14	I grew tall like a palm tree in En-gedi
	24:14	and like rose plants in Jericho
	24:14	like a beautiful olive tree in the field
	24:14	and like a plane tree I grew tall
	24:15	Like cassia and camel's thorn
	24:15	and like choice myrrh I spread a pleasant odour
	24:15	like galbanum, onycha, and stacte
	24:15	and like the fragrance of frankincense in the tabernacle
	24:16	Like a Terebinth I spread out my branches
	24:17	Like a vine I caused loveliness to bud
	24:25	It fills men with wisdom, like the Pishon
	24:25	and like the Tigris at the time of the first fruits
	24:26	It makes them full of understanding, like the Euphrates
	24:26	and like the Jordan at harvest time
	24:27	It makes instruction shine forth like light
	24:27	like the Gihon at the time of vintage
	24:30	I went forth like a canal from a river
	24:30	and like a water channel into a garden
	24:32	I will again make instruction shine forth like the dawn
	24:33	I will again pour out teaching like prophecy
	25:17	and darkens her face like that of a bear
	26:7	taking hold of her is like grasping a scorpion
	26:16	Like the sun rising in the heights of the Lord
	26:17	Like the shining lamp on the holy lampstand
	26:18	Like pillars of gold on a base of silver
	26:27	and every person like this lives in the anarchy of war
	27:11	but the fool changes like the moon
	27:20	and has escaped like a gazelle from a snare
	27:28	but vengeance lies in wait for him like a lion
	28:4	Does he have no mercy toward a man like himself
	28:23	It will be sent out against them like a lion
	28:23	like a leopard it will mangle them
	29:18	and has shaken them like a wave of the sea
	30:4	for he has left behind him one like himself
	30:18	are like offerings of food placed upon a grave
	30:20	like a eunuch who embraces a maiden and groans
	31:16	Eat like a human being what is set before you
	31:27	Wine is like life to men, if you drink it in moderation
	32:16	and like a light they will kindle righteous deeds
	33:2	is like a boat in a storm
	33:5	The heart of a fool is like a cart wheel
	33:5	and his thoughts like a turning axle
	33:6	A stallion is like a mocking friend
	33:16	I was like one who gleans after the grape-gatherers
	33:16	and like a grape-gatherer I filled my wine press
	34:5	and like a woman in travail the mind has fancies
	34:20	Like one who kills a son before his father's eyes
	36:23	her husband is not like other men
	38:22	Remember my doom, for yours is like it :
	39:12	and I am filled, like the moon at the full
	39:13	and bud like a rose growing by a stream of water
	39:14	send forth fragrance like frankincense
	39:14	and put forth blossoms like a lily
	39:22	His blessing covers the dry land like a river
	39:22	and drenches it like a flood
	40:6	like one who has escaped from the battle-front
	40:13	The wealth of the unjust will dry up like a torrent
	40:13	and crash like a loud clap of thunder in a rain
	40:17	Kindness is like a garden of blessings
	40:27	The fear of the Lord is like a garden of blessing
	43:14	and the clouds fly forth like birds
	43:17	He scatters the snow like birds flying down
	43:17	and its descent is like locusts alighting
	43:19	He pours the hoarfrost upon the earth like salt
	43:20	and the water puts it on like a breastplate
	43:21	and withers the tender grass like fire
	44:19	and no one has been found like him in glory
	44:21	that he would multiply him like the dust of the earth
	44:21	and exalt his posterity like the stars
	45:6	a holy man like him, of the tribe of Levi
	45:11	with precious stones engraved like signets
	45:12	inscribed like a signet with Holiness
	47:14	You overflowed like a river with understanding
	47:18	you gathered gold like tin and amassed silver like lead
	48:1	Then the prophet Elijah arose like a fire
	48:1	and his word burned like a torch
	48:19	and they were in anguish, like women in travail
	49:1	The memory of Josiah is like a blending of incense
	49:1	and like music at a banquet of wine
	49:11	He was like a signet on the right hand
	49:14	No one like Enoch has been created on earth
	49:15	And no man like Joseph has been born

	50:3	a reservoir like the sea in circumference
	50:6	Like the morning star among the clouds
	50:6	like the moon when it is full
	50:7	like the sun shining upon the temple of the Most High
	50:7	and like the rainbow gleaming in glorious clouds
	50:8	like roses in the days of the first fruits
	50:8	like lilies by a spring of water
	50:8	like a green shoot on Lebanon on a summer day
	50:9	like fire and incense in the censer
	50:9	like a vessel of hammered gold
	50:10	like an olive tree putting forth its fruit
	50:10	and like a cypress towering in the clouds
	50:12	he was like a young cedar on Lebanon
	50:12	and they surrounded him like the trunks of palm trees
Bar	**1**:11	that their days on earth may be like the days of heaven
	2:2	the like of what he has done in Jerusalem
	4:26	they were taken away like a flock carried off by the enemy
L Jr	**6**:5	So take care not to become at all like the foreigners
	6:11	They deck their gods out with garments like men
	6:14	Like a local ruler the god holds a sceptre
	6:20	They are just like a beam of the temple
	6:39	are like stones from the mountain
	6:54	they are like crows between heaven and earth
	6:55	but the gods will be burnt in 2 like beams
	6:67	or shine like the sun or give light like the moon
	6:70	Like a scarecrow in a cucumber bed, that guards nothing
	6:71	are like a thorn bush in a garden
	6:71	or like a dead body cast out in the darkness
P Az	27	and made the midst of the furnace like a moist whistling wind
Sus	**13**:27	for nothing like this had ever been said about Susanna
1 Ma	**2**:8	Her temple has become like a man without honour
	3:3	like a giant he put on his breastplate
	3:4	He was like a lion in his deeds
	3:4	like a lion's cub roaring for prey
	3:45	Jerusalem was uninhabited like a wilderness
	4:47	and built a new altar like the former one
	6:39	and gleamed like flaming torches
	9:29	there has been no one like him
	11:1	like the sand by the seashore
2 Ma	**7**:37	I, like my brothers, give up body and life
	8:35	and made his way alone like a runaway slave
	10:6	like wild animals
	11:11	They hurled themselves like lions against the enemy
1 Es	**1**:20	No passover like it had been kept in Israel
	8:57	that glittered like gold
3 Ma	**4**:9	They were brought on board like wild animals
	7:19	there too in like manner
2 Es	**4**:15	And in like manner the waves of the sea also made a plan
	4:24	and why we pass from the world like locusts
	4:24	and our life is like a mist
	4:36	When the number of those like yourselves is completed
	4:41	In Hades the chambers of the souls are like the womb
	5:18	like a shepherd who leaves his flock
	5:52	not like those whom you bore before
	6:17	and its sound was like the sound of many waters
	6:24	At that time friends shall make war on friends like enemies
	6:56	and that they are like spittle
	7:4	so that it is like a river
	7:61	for it is they who are now like a mist
	7:62	like the other created things !
	7:97	when it is shown to them how their face is to shine like the sun
	7:97	and how they are to be made like the light of the stars
	8:44	and is called thy own image because he is made like thee
	8:44	hast thou also made him like the farmer's seed ?
	8:51	and inquire concerning the glory of those who are like yourself
	8:62	but only to you and a few like you
	10:12	My lamentation is not like the earth's
	10:25	and her countenance flashed like lightning
	10:30	and behold, I lay there like a corpse
	10:33	Stand up like a man, and I will instruct you
	11:14	so that it disappeared like the first
	11:18	and held the rule like the former ones
	11:37	a creature like a lion was aroused out of the forest, roaring
	12:42	like a cluster of grapes from the vintage
	12:42	and like a lamp in a dark place
	12:42	and like a haven for a ship saved from a storm
	13:3	this wind made something like the figure of a man come up
	13:20	than to pass from the world like a cloud
	14:9	and with those who are like you
	14:39	it was full of something like water
	14:39	but its colour was like fire
	15:10	Behold, my people is led like a flock to the slaughter
	15:23	and the sinners, like straw that is kindled
	15:30	shall go forth like wild boars of the forest
	15:47	For you have made yourself like her
	15:50	And the glory of your power shall wither like a flower
	15:51	You shall be weakened like a wretched woman
	15:61	And you shall be broken down by them like stubble
	15:61	and they shall be like fire to you
	16:23	And the dead shall be cast out like dung

	16:40	and in the midst of the calamities be like strangers on the earth
	16:41	Let him that sells be like one who will flee
	16:41	let him that buys be like one who will lose
	16:42	let him that does business be like one
	16:42	and let him that builds a house be like one
	16:43	let him that sows be like one who will not reap
	16:43	like one who will not gather the grapes
	16:44	them that marry, like those who will have no children
	16:44	and them that do not marry, like those who are widowed
	16:51	Therefore do not be like her or her works
	16:59	who has spread out the heaven like an arch
	16:71	They shall be like mad men, sparing no one
4 Ma	**6**:10	And like a noble athlete the old man, while being beaten
	7:1	For like a most skilful pilot
	7:5	For in setting his mind firm like a jutting cliff
	7:14	and by reason like that of Isaac
	7:19	like our patriarchs Abraham and Isaac and Jacob
	11:10	so that he was completely curled back like a scorpion
	12:13	to cut out the tongues of men who have feelings like yours
	13:9	Brothers, let us die like brothers for the sake of the law
	14:14	Even unreasoning animals, like mankind
	15:15	and the flesh of the head to the chin exposed like masks
	16:13	but, as though having a mind like adamant
	17:3	Nobly set like a roof on the pillars of your sons

LIKE, verb   1
   Tob **5**:11 I should like to know, my brother, your people and your name

LIKELY   1
   Wis **9**:14 and our designs are likely to fail

LIKEN   4 = 0.003 %
   Wis **7**:9 Neither did I liken to her any priceless gem
   Sir **25**:11 to whom shall be likened the one who holds it fast ?
       36:12 upon Israel, whom thou hast likened to a first-born son
  2 Es **5**:42 He said to me, I shall liken my judgment to a circle

LIKENESS   6 = 0.004 %
   Wis **13**:10 and likeness of animals, or a useless stone
      14:19 skilfully forced the likeness to take more beautiful form
   Sir **34**:3 the likeness of a face confronting a face
  2 Es **8**:6 by which every mortal who bears the likeness of a human being
     10:49 And behold, you saw her likeness
  4 Ma **15**:4 a wondrous likeness both of mind and of form

LIKEWISE   18 = 0.012 %
   Tob **12**:12 I was likewise present with you
   Sir **13**:19 likewise the poor are pastures for the rich
      13:20 likewise a poor man is an abomination to a rich one
      24:11 In the beloved city likewise he gave me a resting place
      33:15 they likewise are in pairs, one the opposite of the other
      40:14 likewise transgressors will utterly fail
      49:7 and likewise to build and to plant
   L Jr **6**:28 and likewise their wives preserve some with salt
      6:35 Likewise they are not able to give either wealth or money
      6:61 and the wind likewise blows in every land
  2 Ma **2**:12 Likewise Solomon also kept the 8 days
     15:13 Then likewise a man appeared
  1 Es **4**:6 Likewise those who do not serve in the army or make war
      6:30 and likewise wheat and salt and wine and oil
      8:20 and likewise up to a 100 cors of wheat
  3 Ma **6**:33 Likewise the king, after convening a great banquet
  2 Es **4**:17 likewise also the plan of the waves of the sea
  4 Ma **11**:15 we ought likewise to die for the same principles

LIKING   2
   Wis **16**:21 was changed to suit every one liking
   Sir **32**:17 and will find a decision according to his liking

LILY   4 = 0.003 %
   Sir **39**:14 and put forth blossoms like a lily
     50:8 like lilies by a spring of water
  2 Es **2**:19 and 7 mighty mountains on which roses and lilies grow
      5:24 thou hast chosen for thyself one lily

LIMB   7 = 0.005 %
  2 Ma **7**:7 rather than have your body punished limb by limb ?
      9:7 and the fall was so hard as to torture every limb of his body
  3 Ma **2**:22 besides being paralyzed in his limbs
  4 Ma **9**:13 his limbs were dislocated
      9:17 Cut my limbs, burn my flesh, and twist my joints
     10:5 dismembering him by prying his limbs from their sockets

LIMIT, subst.   1
  2 Es **15**:6 and their harmful deeds have reached their limit

LIMIT, verb   1
   Sir **39**:18 and none can limit his saving power

249

LIMITED   2
Sir 17 : 2   He gave to men few days, a limited time
3 Ma 2 : 29   and they shall also be reduced to their former limited status

LINE, subst.   2
1 Ma 7 : 14   A priest of the line of Aaron has come with the army
1 Es 1 : 30   And immediately his servants took him out of the line of battle

LINE up   1
1 Ma 16 : 6   Then he and his army lined up against them

LINEAGE   4 = 0.003 %
Tob 5 : 13   You are a relative of mine, of a good and noble lineage
1 Ma 3 : 32   He left Lysias, a distinguished man of royal lineage
1 Es 5 : 5   of the lineage of Phares, of the tribe of Judah
     5 : 37   though they could not prove by their fathers' houses or lineage

LINEN, subst., adj.   4 = 0.003 %
Jud 16 : 8   and put on a linen gown to deceive him
Sir 45 : 8   the linen breeches, the long robe, and the ephod
L Jr 6 : 72   By the purple and linen that rot upon them
1 Es 3 : 6   and a turban of fine linen, and a necklace about his neck

LINGER   1
Sir 32 : 11   go home quickly and do not linger

LION   26 = 0.017 %
Ad E 14 : 13   Put eloquent speech in my mouth before the lion
Wis 11 : 17   a multitude of bears, or bold lions
Sir 4 : 30   Do not be like a lion in your home
     13 : 19   Wild asses in the wilderness are the prey of lions
     21 : 2   Its teeth are lion's teeth, and destroy the souls of men
     25 : 16   I would rather dwell with a lion and a dragon
     27 : 10   A lion lies in wait for prey
     27 : 28   but vengeance lies in wait for him like a lion
     28 : 23   It will be sent out against them like a lion
     47 : 3   He played with lions as with young goats
Bel 14 : 31   They threw Daniel into the lions' den
     14 : 32   There were 7 lions in the den
     14 : 34   to Daniel, in the lions' den
1 Ma 2 : 60   was delivered from the mouth of the lions
     3 : 4   He was like a lion in his deeds
     3 : 4   like a lion's cub roaring for prey
2 Ma 11 : 11   They hurled themselves like lions against the enemy
1 Es 4 : 24   he faces lions, and he walks in darkness
3 Ma 6 : 7   was cast down into the ground to lions as food for wild beasts
2 Es 11 : 37   a creature like a lion was aroused out of the forest, roaring
     12 : 1   While the lion was saying these words to the eagle, I looked
     12 : 31   And as for the lion whom you saw rousing up out of the forest
     16 : 6   Can one drive off a hungry lion in the forest
4 Ma 16 : 3   The lions surrounding Daniel were not so savage
     16 : 21   And Daniel the righteous was thrown to the lions
     18 : 13   He praised Daniel in the den of the lions and blessed him

LIP   22 = 0.014 %
Jud 2 : 2   and recounted fully, with his own lips
     9 : 10   By the deceit of my lips strike down the slave
     15 : 13   and with songs on their lips
Sir 1 : 24   and the lips of many will tell of his good sense
     1 : 29   and keep watch over your lips
     12 : 16   An enemy will speak sweetly with his lips
     14 : 1   Blessed is the man who does not blunder with his lips
     15 : 9   A hymn of praise is not fitting on the lips of a sinner
     20 : 19   which is continually on the lips of the ignorant
     20 : 20   A proverb from a fool's lips will be rejected
     20 : 24   it is continually on the lips of the ignorant
     21 : 5   The prayer of a poor man goes from his lips
     21 : 25   The lips of strangers will speak of these things
     22 : 27   and a seal of prudence upon my lips
     23 : 8   The sinner is overtaken through his lips
     34 : 8   and wisdom is made perfect in truthful lips
     37 : 22   may be trustworthy on his lips
     39 : 15   with praise, with songs on your lips, and with lyres
     50 : 20   to pronounce the blessing of the Lord with his lips
     51 : 2   from lips that utter lies
1 Es 4 : 46   with your own lips
2 Es 13 : 10   and from his lips a flaming breath

LIQUID   5 = 0.003 %
2 Ma 1 : 20   that they had not found fire but thick liquid
     1 : 21   to sprinkle the liquid on the wood and what was laid upon it
     1 : 31   Nehemiah ordered that the liquid that was left
     1 : 33   the liquid had appeared with which Nehemiah and his associates
4 Ma 6 : 25   threw him down, and poured stinking liquids into his nostrils

LIQUOR   1
3 Ma 5 : 2   maddened by the lavish abundance of liquor

LIST   3 = 0.002 %
1 Es 6 : 12   we questioned them and asked them for a list of the names
     8 : 49   the list of all their names was reported
2 Es 2 : 40   and conclude the list of your people who are clothed in white

LISTEN   33 = 0.021 %
Tob 6 : 12   Now listen to my plan
     6 : 15   Now listen to me, brother, for she will become your wife
Jud 8 : 11   Listen to me, rulers of the people of Bethulia !
     8 : 32   Judith said to them, Listen to me
     14 : 1   Then Judith said to them, Listen to me, my brethren
Wis 6 : 1   Listen therefore, O kings, and understand
Sir 3 : 1   Listen to me your father, O children
     6 : 23   Listen, my son, and accept my judgment
     6 : 33   If you love to listen you will gain knowledge
     6 : 35   Be ready to listen to every narrative
     14 : 23   will also listen at her doors
     16 : 24   Listen to me, my son, and acquire knowledge
     21 : 24   It is ill-mannered for a man to listen at a door
     23 : 7   Listen, my children, to instruction concerning speech
     31 : 22   Listen to me, my son, and do not disregard me
     34 : 24   to whose voice will the Lord listen ?
     34 : 26   who will listen to his prayer ?
     35 : 13   and he will listen to the prayer of one who is wronged
     39 : 13   Listen to me, O you holy sons
1 Ma 2 : 65   always listen to him
     5 : 61   they did not listen to Judas and his brothers
2 Ma 7 : 25   Since the young man would not listen to him at all
3 Ma 2 : 10   you would listen to our petition
2 Es 1 : 26   When you call upon me, I will not listen to you
     2 : 1   but they would not listen to them
     2 : 9   So will I do to those who have not listened to me
     5 : 32   and he said to me, Listen to me
     6 : 17   When I heard this, I rose to my feet and listened
     7 : 2   and listen to the words that I have come to speak to you
     7 : 49   He answered me and said, Listen to me, Ezra
     10 : 38   Listen to me and I will inform you
     11 : 38   Listen and I will speak to you
     16 : 35   Listen now to these things, and understand them

LISTENER   1
Sir 25 : 9   and he who speaks to attentive listeners

LITTER, subst.   1
2 Ma 9 : 8   was brought down to earth and carried in a litter

LITTLE*   58 = 0.038 %
Tob 4 : 8   according to the little you have
     12 : 8   A little with righteousness is better
Jud 16 : 16   and all fat for burnt offerings to thee is a very little thing
Wis 3 : 5   Having been disciplined a little
     7 : 9   because all gold is but a little sand in her sight
     9 : 5   with little understanding of judgment and laws
     12 : 2   Therefore thou dost correct little by little those who trespass
     12 : 8   to destroy them little by little
     12 : 10   But judging them little by little
     13 : 6   Yet these men are little to be blamed
     15 : 8   and after a little while goes to the earth
     16 : 6   they were troubled for a little while as a warning
Sir pr.   differ not a little as originally expressed
     pr.   I found opportunity for no little instruction
     6 : 19   For in her service you will toil a little while
     19 : 1   he who despises small things will fail little by little
     20 : 12   There is a man who buys much for a little
     20 : 15   He gives little and upbraids much
     29 : 23   Be content with little or much
     31 : 19   How ample a little is for a well-disciplined man !
     38 : 24   and he who has little business may become wise
     40 : 6   He gets little or no rest
     42 : 4   and of acquiring much or little
     51 : 16   I inclined my ear a little and received her
     51 : 27   See with your eyes that I have laboured little
1 Ma 16 : 15   in the little stronghold called Dok, which he had built
2 Ma 3 : 14   There was no little distress throughout the whole city
     3 : 30   And the temple, which a little while before
     5 : 17   that the Lord was angered for a little while
     6 : 29   And those who a little before
     7 : 33   And if our living Lord is angry for a little while
     8 : 8   When Philip saw that the man was gaining ground little by little
     8 : 33   who had fled into one little house
     9 : 10   no one was able to carry the man who a little while before
     15 : 15   were in no little distress
2 Es 6 : 29   little by little the place where I was standing
     8 : 2   but only a little dust from which gold comes
     10 : 22   our little ones have been cast out
     10 : 41   The woman who appeared to you a little while ago
     11 : 3   but they became little, puny wings
     11 : 22   the 12 wings and the 2 little wings disappeared
     11 : 23   except the 3 heads that were at rest and 6 little wings
     11 : 24   2 little wings separated from the 6

	11:25	these little wings planned to set themselves up
	11:31	and it devoured the 2 little wings which were planning to reign
	11:45	and your most evil little wings
	12:5	and not even a little strength is left in me
	12:19	As for your seeing 8 little wings clinging to his wings
	12:29	As for your seeing 2 little wings passing over to the head
	16:52	For behold, just a little while
4 Ma	6:20	It would be shameful if we should survive for a little while
	12:7	as we shall tell a little later

LIVE, verb   176 = 0.115 %

Tob	3:6	For it is better for me to die than to live
	3:15	Why should I live ?
	4:5	Live uprightly all the days of your life
	4:7	Give alms from your possessions to all who live uprightly
	5:3	and I will pay him wages as long as I live
	13:1	Blessed is God who lives for ever
	14:10	And do not live in Nineveh any longer
Jud	1:6	and all those who lived along the Euphrates
	1:7	sent to all who lived in Persia
	1:7	and to all who lived in the west
	1:7	those who lived in Cilicia and Damascus
	1:7	and all who lived along the seacoast
	1:10	even beyond Tanis and Memphis, and all who lived in Egypt
	1:11	But all who lived in the whole region
	2:12	For as I live, and by the power of my kingdom
	2:23	and the Ishmaelites who lived along the desert
	2:28	who lived along the seacoast, at Sidon and Tyre
	2:28	and those who lived in Sur and Ocina
	2:28	and all who lived in Jamnia
	2:28	Those who lived in Azotus and Ascalon feared him exceedingly
	4:1	By this time the people of Israel living in Judea
	4:11	living at Jerusalem
	5:3	what people is this that lives in the hill country ?
	5:4	And why have they alone, of all who live in the west
	5:7	At one time they lived in Mesopotamia
	5:8	and they fled to Mesopotamia, and lived there for a long time
	5:9	where they were living
	5:10	and lived there as long as they had food
	5:15	So they lived in the land of the Amorites
	5:16	and lived there a long time
	7:10	but on the height of the mountains where they live
	7:14	they will be strewn about in the streets where they live
	8:4	Judith had lived at home as a widow
	10:3	which she used to wear while her husband Manasseh was living
	11:2	And even now, if your people who live in the hill country
	11:4	Have courage ; you will live, tonight and from now on
	11:7	Nebuchadnezzar the king of the whole earth lives
	11:7	will live by your power
	11:14	because even the people living there have been doing this
	11:23	and you shall live in the house of King Nebuchadnezzar
	12:4	Judith replied, As your soul lives, my lord
	13:16	As the Lord lives, who has protected me in the way I went
	14:4	and you and all who live within the borders of Israel
	15:8	who lived at Jerusalem
Ad E	13:17	that we may live and sing praise to thy name, O Lord
	16:19	and permit the Jews to live under their own laws
Wis	3:17	Even if they live long they will be held of no account
	4:10	and while living among sinners he was taken up
	4:16	will condemn the ungodly who are living
	5:15	But the righteous live for ever
	7:28	as the man who lives with wisdom
	8:3	She glorifies her noble birth by living with God
	8:9	Therefore I determined to take her to live with me
	12:23	Therefore those who in folly of life lived unrighteously
	13:7	For as they live among his works they keep searching
	14:17	since they lived at a distance
	14:22	but they live in great strife due to ignorance
	14:28	or prophesy lies, or live unrighteously
Sir	pr.	in living according to the law
	pr.	for those living abroad who wished to gain learning
	pr.	being prepared in character to live according to the law
	3:12	and do not grieve him as long as he lives
	9:12	as long as they live
	13:5	If you own something, he will live with you
	14:4	and others will live in luxury on his goods
	18:1	He who lives for ever created the whole universe
	19:6	He who controls his tongue will live without strife
	25:1	and a wife and husband who live in harmony
	25:7	a man who lives to see the downfall of his foes
	25:8	happy is he who lives with an intelligent wife
	26:27	and every person like this lives in the anarchy of war
	33:19	do not give power over yourself, as long as you live
	34:13	The spirit of those who fear the Lord will live
	37:26	and his name will live for ever
	37:27	My son, test your soul while you live
	38:32	and men can neither sojourn nor live there
	39:9	and his name will live through all generations
	39:11	if he lives long, he will leave a name greater than a 1,000
	41:1	to one who lives at peace among his possessions

	41:19	and of theft, in the place where you live
	42:23	All these things live and remain for ever for every need
	44:6	living peaceably in their habitations
	44:9	who have perished as though they had not lived
	44:14	and their name lives to all generations
	46:12	live again in their sons !
	48:11	for we also shall surely live
	50:26	Those who live on Mount Seir, and the Philistines
	51:18	For I resolved to live according to wisdom
Bar	1:12	and we shall live under the protection of Nebuchadnezzar king of Babylon
	3:37	Afterward she appeared upon earth and lived among men
	4:1	All who hold her fast will live
L Jr	6:46	The men that make them will certainly not live very long themselves
Sus	13:1	There was a man living in Babylon whose name was Joakim
1 Ma	2:13	Why should we live any longer ?
	2:19	Even if all the nations that live under the rule of the king
	2:20	yet I and my sons and my brothers will live
	2:33	Come out and do what the king commands, and you will live
	4:35	and how ready they were either to live or to die nobly
	5:2	and they determined to destroy the descendants of Jacob who lived among them
	5:9	against the Israelites who lived in their territory
	6:55	whom King Antiochus while still living
	7:38	remember their blasphemies, and let them live no longer
	9:58	Jonathan and his men are living in quiet and confidence
	9:71	that he would not try to harm him as long as he lived
2 Ma	4:11	and he destroyed the lawful ways of living
	4:16	and those whose ways of living they admired
	5:27	they continued to live on what grew wild
	6:25	for the sake of living a brief moment longer
	6:26	yet whether I live or die
	9:9	and while he was still living in anguish and pain
	11:24	but prefer their own way of living
	11:25	and that they live according to the customs of their ancestors
	12:2	would not let them live quietly and in peace
	12:3	as this : they invited the Jews who lived among them
	12:4	because they wished to live peaceably and suspected nothing
	12:8	who were living among them
	14:10	For as long as Judas lives
1 Es	2:6	and let each man, wherever he may live
	2:16	living in Samaria and other places
	2:16	against those who were living in Judea and Jerusalem :
	2:25	and the others associated with them and living in Samaria
	4:38	and lives and prevails for ever and ever
	5:73	as long as King Cyrus lived
3 Ma	3:1	against those Jews who lived in Alexandria
	3:8	for they lived under tyranny
	3:25	you are to send to us those who live among you
2 Es	2:14	because I live, says the Lord
	3:2	and the wealth of those who lived in Babylon
	4:12	than to come here and live in ungodliness
	4:26	and if you live long, you will often marvel
	4:51	Do you think that I shall live until those days ?
	5:4	But if the Most High grants that you live
	5:45	If therefore all creatures will live at one time
	6:21	and these shall live and dance
	6:51	to live in it
	7:20	Let many perish who are now living
	7:21	when they came, what they should do to live
	7:82	that they may live
	7:89	During the time that they lived in it
	7:109	and for the one who was dead, that he might live
	7:117	For what good is it to all that they live in sorrow now
	7:121	but we have lived wickedly ?
	7:124	because we have lived in unseemly places ?
	7:126	For while we lived and committed iniquity
	7:129	Choose for yourself life, that you may live !
	7:136	to those now living
	8:5	for you have been given only a short time to live
	8:6	may be able to live
	8:13	and thou wilt make him live, for he is thy work
	8:25	For as long as I live I will speak
	8:28	Think not on those who have lived wickedly in thy sight
	8:46	Things that are present are for those who live now
	8:46	and things that are future are for those who will live hereafter
	9:43	though I lived with my husband 30 years
	12:33	For first he will set them living before his judgment seat
	13:41	where mankind had never lived
	14:9	and henceforth you shall live with my Son
	14:20	and I will reprove the people who are now living
	14:22	and that those who wish to live in the last days may live
	14:35	when we shall live again
	15:10	to live any longer in the land of Egypt
	15:14	Alas for the world and for those who live in it !
	16:22	For many of those who live on the earth shall perish by famine
	16:42	who will not live in it
4 Ma	5:36	nor my long life lived lawfully
	6:18	who have lived in accordance with truth to old age

7:19	do not die to God, but live in God
8:8	and by changing your manner of living
8:26	when we can live in peace if we obey the king ?
9:6	lived piously while enduring torture
11:5	It is because we revere the Creator of all things and live
13:24	and brought up in right living
16:25	They knew also that those who die for the sake of God live in God
17:18	and live through blessed eternity
18:17	Shall these dry bones live ?

LIVE by   5 = 0.003 %
1 Ma	6:23	to live by what he said and to follow his commands
	6:59	and agree to let them live by their laws as they did before
	10:37	and let them live by their own laws
2 Ma	6:1	and cease to live by the laws of God
4 Ma	5:22	as though living by it were irrational

LIVE out   1
| 4 Ma | 18:9 | A happy man was he, who lived out his life with good children |

LIVE, adj.   2
| Tob | 6:16 | you shall take live ashes of incense |
| | 8:2 | and he took the live ashes of incense |

LIVELIHOOD   1
| Sir | 31:4 | The poor man toils as his livelihood diminishes |

LIVER   5 = 0.003 %
Tob	6:4	Cut open the fish and take the heart and liver and gall
	6:6	of what use is the liver and heart and gall of the fish ?
	6:7	He replied, As for the heart and the liver
	6:16	and lay upon them some of the heart and liver of the fish
	8:2	and put the heart and liver of the fish upon them and made a smoke

LIVING, adj.   20 = 0.013 %
Jud	11:7	who has sent you to direct every living soul
Ad E	16:16	and are sons of the Most High, the most mighty living God
Wis	15:11	and breathed into him a living spirit
Sir	13:16	all living beings associate by species
	14:17	All living beings become old like a garment
	16:30	with all kinds of living beings he covered its surface
	17:4	He placed the fear of them in all living beings
	18:13	but the compassion of the Lord is for all living beings
	43:25	all kinds of living things, and huge creatures of the sea
	49:16	and Adam above every living being in the creation
Bel	14:5	but the living God, who created heaven and earth
	14:6	Do you not think that Bel is a living God ?
	14:24	You cannot deny that this is a living god ; so worship him
	14:25	for he is the living God
2 Ma	7:33	And if our living Lord is angry for a little while
	15:4	It is the living Lord himself, the Sovereign in heaven
3 Ma	6:28	Release the sons of the almighty living God of heaven
2 Es	6:47	to bring forth living creatures, birds, and fishes
	6:48	The dumb and lifeless water produced living creatures
	6:49	Then thou didst keep in existence 2 living creatures

LIVING, subst., person   10 = 0.007 %
Tob	12:6	in the presence of all the living
	13:4	and exalt him in the presence of all the living
Wis	1:13	and he does not delight in the death of the living
	11:26	O Lord who lovest the living
	18:12	For the living were not sufficient even to bury them
	18:23	and cut off its way to the living
Sir	7:33	Give graciously to all the living
	45:16	He chose him out of all the living
2 Es	7:14	Therefore unless the living
	7:46	For who among the living is there that has not sinned

LIVING, subst., goods   2
| Sir | 4:1 | My son, deprive not the poor of his living |
| | 34:22 | To take away a neighbour's living is to murder him |

LO   2
| Jud | 9:6 | Lo, we are here |
| Sir | 24:31 | and lo, my canal became a river, and my river became a sea |

LOAD, verb   2
| Jud | 15:11 | and she took them and loaded her mule |
| 2 Es | 2:18 | 12 trees loaded with various fruits |

LOAF   1
| 2 Ma | 1:8 | and we lighted the lamps and we set out the loaves |

LOAN   2
| Sir | 29:4 | Many persons regard a loan as a windfall |
| | 29:5 | A man will kiss another's hands until he gets a loan |

LOATHE   3 = 0.002 %
Sir	11:2	nor loathe a man because of his appearance
	16:8	whom he loathed on account of their insolence
	20:8	Whoever uses too many words will be loathed

LOATHING   1
| Wis | 11:24 | and hast loathing for none of the things |

LOCAL   3 = 0.002 %
L Jr	6:14	Like a local ruler the god holds a sceptre
1 Es	6:7	the local rulers in Syria and Phoenicia
	6:27	and those who were appointed as local rulers

LOCALITY   1
| 3 Ma | 2:26 | that he framed evil reports in the various localities |

LOCK, subst.   2
| L Jr | 6:18 | so the priests make their temples secure with doors and locks and bars |
| 3 Ma | 1:4 | *her locks all dishevelled* |

LOCK up   2
| Sir | 28:24 | lock up your silver and gold |
| | 42:6 | and where there are many hands, lock things up |

LOCUST   4 = 0.003 %
Jud	2:20	Along with them went a mixed crowd like a swarm of locusts
Wis	16:9	For they were killed by the bites of locusts and flies
Sir	43:17	and its descent is like locusts alighting
2 Es	4:24	and why we pass from the world like locusts

LODGE   5 = 0.003 %
Sir	14:25	and will lodge in an excellent lodging place
	24:7	I sought in whose territory I might lodge
	36:26	and lodges wherever night finds him ?
	51:23	Draw near to me, you who are untaught, and lodge in my school
2 Ma	3:17	the pain lodged in his heart

LODGING   3 = 0.002 %
Sir	14:25	and will lodge in an excellent lodging place
	29:28	scolding about lodging and the reproach of the moneylender
1 Ma	3:45	it was a lodging place for the Gentiles

LOFTY   2
| Sir | 3:19 | Many are lofty and renowned |
| 2 Es | 15:40 | and shall pour out upon every high and lofty place a terrible tempest |

LOG, subst.   1
| 1 Es | 5:55 | to bring cedar logs from Lebanon |

LOGIC   1
| 4 Ma | 1:15 | Now reason is the mind that with sound logic prefers the life of wisdom |

LOIN   5 = 0.003 %
Jud	4:14	with their loins girded with sackcloth
	8:5	and girded sackcloth about her loins
Sir	35:18	till he crushes the loins of the unmerciful
	47:19	But laid your loins beside women
2 Ma	10:25	and girded their loins with sackcloth

LONELY   1
| Bar | 4:16 | and bereaved the lonely woman of her daughters |

LONG, adj.   24 = 0.016 %
Tob	10:4	his long delay proves it
Jud	1:2	with hewn stones 3 cubits thick and 6 cubits long
	5:8	and they fled to Mesopotamia, and lived there for a long time
	5:16	and lived there a long time
	16:25	in the days of Judith, or for a long time after her death
Wis	4:13	Being perfected in a short time, he fulfilled long years
	17:2	and prisoners of long night, shut in under their roofs
	18:24	For upon his long robe the whole world was depicted
Sir	1:12	and gives gladness and joy and long life
	1:20	and her branches are long life
	3:6	Whoever glorifies his father will have long life
	10:10	A long illness baffles the physician
	23:28	and to be received by him is long life
	45:8	the linen breeches, the long robe, and the ephod
Bar	4:35	and for a long time she will be inhabited by demons
L Jr	6:3	for a long time, up to 7 generations
1 Ma	8:19	They went to Rome, a very long journey
2 Ma	6:21	because of their long acquaintance with him
	12:36	As Esdris and his men had been fighting for a long time and were weary
2 Es	11:13	and it continue to reign a long time
	12:15	for a longer time than any other of the 12
	13:45	Through that region there was a long way to go

4 Ma	5 : 7	Although you have had them for so long a time
	5 : 36	nor my long life lived lawfully

LONG, adv.   67 = 0.044 %

Tob	1 : 15	so that I could no longer go into Media
	2 : 8	He is no longer afraid
	5 : 3	and I will pay him wages as long as I live
	9 : 4	and if I delay long he will be greatly distressed
	14 : 10	And do not live in Nineveh any longer
Jud	5 : 10	and lived there as long as they had food
	5 : 17	As long as they did not sin against their God they prospered
	7 : 22	there was no strength left in them any longer
	8 : 31	and we will no longer be faint
	10 : 10	and they could no longer see her
	13 : 1	because the banquet had lasted long
Ad E	13 : 7	so that those who have long been and are now hostile
Wis	3 : 17	Even if they live long they will be held of no account
	11 : 14	who long before had been cast out and exposed
	14 : 24	they no longer keep
	18 : 20	but the wrath did not long continue
Sir	3 : 12	and do not grieve him as long as he lives
	9 : 12	as long as they live
	33 : 19	do not give power over yourself, as long as you live
	39 : 11	if he lives long, he will leave a name greater than a 1,000
	41 : 12	since it will remain for you longer than a 1,000 great stores of gold
	46 : 4	And did not one day become as long as 2 ?
L Jr	6 : 46	The men that make them will certainly not live very long themselves
1 Ma	2 : 11	no longer free, she has become a slave
	2 : 13	Why should we live any longer ?
	5 : 44	they could stand before Judas no longer
	6 : 22	How long will you fail to do justice
	7 : 38	remember their blasphemies, and let them live no longer
	9 : 55	so that he could no longer say a word
	9 : 71	that he would not try to harm him as long as he lived
	13 : 39	shall be collected no longer
2 Ma	4 : 14	that the priests were no longer intent
	6 : 1	Not long after this, the king sent an Athenian senator
	6 : 13	In fact, not to let the impious alone for long
	6 : 25	for the sake of living a brief moment longer
	9 : 13	who would no longer have mercy on him
	10 : 6	remembering how not long before, during the feast of booths
	14 : 10	For as long as Judas lives
1 Es	1 : 4	and he said, You need no longer carry it upon your shoulders
	2 : 24	you will no longer have access to Coelesyria and Phoenicia
	3 : 22	and before long they draw their swords
	5 : 73	as long as King Cyrus lived
	8 : 90	for we can no longer stand in thy presence
3 Ma	4 : 1	for the inveterate enmity which had long ago been in their minds
	4 : 17	that they were no longer able to take the census of the Jews
	5 : 40	O king, how long will you try us, as though we are idiots
2 Es	1 : 9	How long shall I endure them
	4 : 23	and the written covenants no longer exist
	4 : 26	and if you live long, you will often marvel
	4 : 33	How long and when will these things be ?
	4 : 35	How long are we to remain here ?
	4 : 40	her womb can keep the child within her any longer
	5 : 49	and a woman who has become old does not bring forth any longer
	6 : 28	and the truth, which has been so long without fruit, shall be revealed
	6 : 59	How long will this be so ?
	7 : 74	For how long the time is that the Most High
	8 : 25	For as long as I live I will speak
	8 : 25	and as long as I have understanding I will answer
	10 : 27	the woman was no longer visible to me
	11 : 17	After you no one shall rule as long as you
	11 : 17	or even half as long
	11 : 40	and for so long you have dwelt on the earth with deceit
	14 : 41	and my mouth was opened, and was no longer closed
	15 : 8	I will be silent no longer concerning their ungodly deeds
	15 : 10	to live any longer in the land of Egypt
4 Ma	3 : 7	David had been attacking the Philistines all day long
	7 : 13	his body no longer tense and firm

LONG, verb   4 = 0.003 %

Wis	4 : 2	and they long for it when it has gone
	6 : 11	long for them, and you will be instructed
	8 : 8	And if any one longs for wide experience
2 Es	16 : 27	one man will long to see another

LONG-SUFFERING   1

P Ma	7	of great compassion, long-suffering

LOOK, subst.   4 = 0.003 %

Sir	11 : 2	Do not praise a man for his good looks
	20 : 22	or lose it because of his foolish look

3 Ma	1 : 20	and without a backward look they crowded together
	5 : 30	and with a threatening look he said

LOOK, verb   97 = 0.063 %

Tob	3 : 3	Remember me and look favourably upon me
	5 : 4	So he went to look for a man
	5 : 11	Are you looking for a tribe and a family
	11 : 5	Now Anna sat looking intently down the road for her son
Jud	1 : 11	but looked upon him as only one man
	4 : 13	and looked upon their affliction
	4 : 15	to look with favour upon the whole house of Israel
	6 : 9	do not look downcast !
	6 : 19	and look this day
	13 : 4	look in this hour upon the work of my hands
	14 : 18	For look, here is Holofernes lying on the ground
Ad E	15 : 5	She was radiant with perfect beauty, and she looked happy
	15 : 7	he looked at her in fierce anger
Wis	17 : 10	refusing to look even at the air
Sir	7 : 22	Do you have cattle ? Look after them
	9 : 5	Do not look intently at a virgin
	9 : 7	Do not look around in the streets of a city
	9 : 8	and do not look intently at beauty belonging to another
	11 : 12	but the eyes of the Lord look upon him for his good
	14 : 16	because in Hades one cannot look for luxury
	16 : 19	shake with trembling when he looks upon them
	16 : 29	After this the Lord looked upon the earth
	23 : 19	they look upon all the ways of men
	33 : 15	Look upon all the works of the Most High
	33 : 21	than that you should look to the hand of your sons
	34 : 15	To whom does he look ? And who is his support ?
	36 : 1	and look upon us
	37 : 10	Do not consult with one who looks at you suspiciously
	40 : 29	When a man looks to the table of another
	41 : 20	of looking at a woman who is a harlot
	42 : 12	Do not look upon any one for beauty
	42 : 18	and he looks into the signs of the age
	43 : 11	Look upon the rainbow, and praise him who made it
	51 : 7	I looked for the assistance of men, and there was none
Bar	4 : 36	Look toward the east, O Jerusalem
	5 : 5	and look toward the east
P Az	32	and lookest upon the deeps
Sus	13 : 9	and turned away their eyes from looking to Heaven
	13 : 20	Look, the garden doors are shut, no one sees us
Bel	14 : 18	the king looked at the table, and shouted in a loud voice
	14 : 19	Look at the floor, and notice whose footsteps these are
1 Ma	4 : 5	he found no one there, so he looked for them in the hills
	9 : 39	They raised their eyes and looked
	9 : 45	For look ! The battle is in front of us and behind us
2 Ma	1 : 27	look upon those who are rejected and despised
	3 : 17	which plainly showed to those who looked at him
	7 : 16	But he looked at the king, and said
	7 : 28	to look at the heaven and the earth
	8 : 2	They besought the Lord to look upon the people
	11 : 29	and look after your own affairs
	12 : 45	But if he was looking to the splendid reward
	15 : 8	and now to look for the victory
	15 : 34	And they all, looking to heaven
1 Es	4 : 33	Then the king and the nobles looked at one another
	8 : 12	in order to look into matters in Judea and Jerusalem
3 Ma	6 : 3	look upon the descendants of Abraham, O Father
2 Es	1 : 38	look with pride and see the people coming from the east
	4 : 48	So I stood and looked, and behold, a flaming furnace passed by before me
	4 : 48	and when the flame had gone by I looked
	7 : 5	to look at it or to navigate it
	7 : 37	Look now, and understand whom you have denied
	7 : 38	Look on this side and on that
	7 : 66	for they do not look for a judgment
	8 : 23	whose look dries up the depths
	8 : 26	O look not upon the sins of thy people
	9 : 45	and looked upon my low estate, and considered my distress
	10 : 27	And I looked, and behold
	10 : 29	and he looked upon me
	11 : 2	And I looked, and behold
	11 : 3	And I looked
	11 : 5	And I looked, and behold, the eagle flew with his wings
	11 : 7	And I looked, and behold, the eagle rose upon his talons
	11 : 10	And I looked, and behold
	11 : 12	And I looked, and behold
	11 : 20	And I looked, and behold
	11 : 22	And after this I looked, and behold
	11 : 24	And I looked, and behold
	11 : 25	And I looked, and behold
	11 : 26	And I looked, and behold
	11 : 28	And I looked, and behold
	11 : 33	And after this I looked, and behold
	11 : 35	And I looked, and behold
	11 : 36	Look before you and consider what you see
	11 : 37	And I looked, and behold
	11 : 44	And the Most High has looked upon his times

	12:1	While the lion was saying these words to the eagle, I looked
	12:3	And I looked, and behold, they also disappeared
	13:3	And I looked, and behold
	13:3	and wherever he turned his face to look
	13:5	After this I looked, and behold
	13:6	And I looked, and behold
	13:8	After this I looked, and behold
4 Ma	13:13	Each of them and all of them together looking at one another
	15:18	nor when the 2nd in torments looked at you piteously
	15:19	nor did you weep when you looked at the eyes of each one
	17:10	looking to God and enduring torture even to death

LOOK down   2

Sir	42:16	The sun looks down on everything with its light
Bar	2:16	O Lord, look down from thy holy habitation, and consider us

LOOK forward   1

2 Ma	15:20	When all were now looking forward to the coming decision

LOOK in   1

Bel	14:40	When he came to the den he looked in, and there sat Daniel

LOOK on   1

2 Ma	7:4	while the rest of the brothers and the mother looked on

LOOK up   4 = 0.003 %

Sus	13:35	And she, weeping, looked up toward heaven
1 Ma	4:12	When the foreigners looked up
	5:30	At dawn they looked up
P Ma	9	I am unworthy to look up and see the height of heaven

LOOSE, adj.   3 = 0.002 %

Sir	9:3	Do not go to meet a loose woman
	22:16	will not be torn loose by an earthquake
4 Ma	12:8	he said, Let me loose, let me speak to the king

LOOSE, verb   2

Jud	9:2	who had loosed the girdle of a virgin to defile her
3 Ma	6:27	Loose and untie their unjust bonds !

LORD, subst., God   748 = 0.487 %

Tob	2:2	who is mindful of the Lord
	3:2	Righteous art thou, O Lord
	3:11	Blessed art thou, O Lord my God
	3:12	And now, O Lord, I have turned my eyes and my face toward thee
	3:14	Thou knowest, O Lord
	4:5	Remember the Lord our God all your days, my son
	4:19	Bless the Lord God on every occasion
	4:19	but the Lord himself gives all good things
	5:19	For the life that is given to us by the Lord
	7:18	the Lord of heaven and earth grant you joy
	8:4	and let us pray that the Lord may have mercy upon us
	8:7	And now, O Lord
	8:17	Show mercy, O Lord
	10:12	The Lord of heaven bring you back safely, dear brother
	10:12	that I may rejoice before the Lord
	12:22	and acknowledged that the angel of the Lord
	13:4	because he is our Lord and God, he is our Father for ever
	13:6	Praise the Lord of righteousness
	13:10	Give thanks worthily to the Lord
	13:11	Many nations will come from afar to the name of the Lord God
	13:13	and will praise the Lord of the righteous
	14:2	and he continued to fear the Lord God and to praise him
	14:6	to fear the Lord God in truth
	14:7	All the Gentiles will praise the Lord
	14:7	and the Lord will exalt his people
	14:7	And all who love the Lord God in truth and righteousness
Jud	2:5	Thus says the Great King, the Lord of the whole earth :
	4:2	and for the temple of the Lord their God
	4:11	and spread out their sackcloth before the Lord
	4:13	So the Lord heard their prayers
	4:13	and in Jerusalem before the sanctuary of the Lord Almighty
	4:14	who stood before the Lord and ministered to the Lord
	4:15	they cried out to the Lord with all their might
	5:21	for their Lord will defend them
	5:24	Therefore let us go up, Lord Holofernes
	6:19	O Lord God of heaven, behold their arrogance
	7:19	The people of Israel cried out to the Lord their God
	7:28	and our God, the Lord of our fathers
	7:29	and they cried out to the Lord God with a loud voice
	7:30	by that time the Lord our God will restore to us his mercy
	8:11	unless the Lord turns and helps us within so many days
	8:13	You are putting the Lord Almighty to the test
	8:14	No, my brethren, do not provoke the Lord our God to anger
	8:16	Do not try to bind the purposes of the Lord our God
	8:23	but the Lord our God will turn it to dishonour
	8:25	let us give thanks to the Lord our God
	8:27	but the Lord scourges those who draw near to him
	8:31	and the Lord will send us rain to fill our cisterns

	8:33	the Lord will deliver Israel by my hand
	8:35	Go in peace, and may the Lord God go before you
	9:1	Judith cried out to the Lord with a loud voice, and said
	9:2	O Lord God of my father Simeon
	9:7	and know not that thou art the Lord who crushest wars
	9:7	the Lord is thy name
	9:12	Lord of heaven and earth, Creator of the waters
	12:4	before the Lord carries out by my hand
	12:8	she prayed the Lord God of Israel
	13:4	O Lord God of all might
	13:7	Give me strength this day, O Lord God of Israel !
	13:15	The Lord has struck him down by the hand of a woman
	13:16	As the Lord lives, who has protected me in the way I went
	13:18	and blessed be the Lord God
	15:8	which the Lord had done for Israel
	15:10	May the Almighty Lord bless you for ever !
	16:2	sing to my Lord with cymbals
	16:3	For God is the Lord who crushes wars
	16:6	But the Lord Almighty has foiled them
	16:12	they perished before the army of my Lord
	16:13	O Lord, thou art great and glorious
	16:16	but who fears the Lord shall be great for ever
	16:17	The Lord Almighty will take vengeance on them
	16:19	she gave as a votive offering to the Lord
Ad E	10:9	The Lord has saved his people
	10:9	the Lord has delivered us from all these evils
	13:8	Then he prayed to the Lord
	13:8	calling to remembrance all the works of the Lord
	13:9	He said : O Lord, Lord, King who rulest over all things
	13:11	and thou art Lord of all
	13:11	who art the Lord
	13:12	thou knowest, O Lord, that it was not in insolence
	13:14	who art my Lord
	13:15	And now, O Lord God and King
	13:17	that we may live and sing praise to thy name, O Lord
	14:1	And Esther the queen, seized with deathly anxiety, fled to the Lord
	14:3	And she prayed to the Lord God of Israel, and said :
	14:3	O my Lord, thou only art our King
	14:5	that thou, O Lord, didst take Israel out of all the nations
	14:7	Thou art righteous, O Lord !
	14:11	O Lord, do not surrender thy sceptre to what has no being
	14:12	Remember, O Lord
	14:14	who am alone and have no helper but thee, O Lord
	14:18	except in thee, O Lord God of Abraham
Wis	1:1	think of the Lord with uprightness
	1:7	Because the Spirit of the Lord has filled the world
	1:9	and a report of his words will come to the Lord
	2:13	and calls himself a child of the Lord
	3:8	and the Lord will reign over them for ever
	3:10	and rebelled against the Lord
	3:14	and who has not devised wicked things against the Lord
	3:14	and a place of great delight in the temple of the Lord
	4:14	for his soul was pleasing to the Lord
	4:17	and will not understand what the Lord purposed for him
	4:18	but the Lord will laugh them to scorn
	5:7	but the way of the Lord we have not known
	5:15	and their reward is with the Lord
	5:16	and a beautiful diadem from the hand of the Lord
	5:17	The Lord will take his zeal as his whole armour
	6:3	For your dominion was given you from the Lord
	6:7	For the Lord of all will not stand in awe of any one
	8:3	and the Lord of all loves her
	8:21	so I appealed to the Lord and besought him
	9:1	O God of my fathers and Lord of mercy
	9:13	Or who can discern what the Lord wills ?
	10:16	She entered the soul of a servant of the Lord
	10:20	they sang hymns, O Lord, to thy holy name
	11:13	they perceived it was the Lord's doing
	11:26	O Lord who lovest the living
	12:2	and put their trust in thee, O Lord
	13:3	let them know how much better than these is their Lord
	13:9	how did they fail to find sooner the Lord of these things ?
	16:12	but it was thy word, O Lord, which heals all men
	16:26	so that thy sons, whom thou didst love, O Lord
	19:9	praising thee, O Lord, who didst deliver them
	19:22	For in everything, O Lord
Sir	1:1	All wisdom comes from the Lord and is with him for ever
	1:9	The Lord himself created wisdom
	1:11	The fear of the Lord is glory and exultation
	1:12	The fear of the Lord delights the heart
	1:13	With him who fears the Lord it will go well at the end
	1:14	To fear the Lord is the beginning of wisdom
	1:16	To fear the Lord is wisdom's full measure
	1:18	The fear of the Lord is the crown of wisdom
	1:20	To fear the Lord is the root of wisdom
	1:21	The fear of the Lord drives away sins :
	1:26	and the Lord will supply it for you
	1:27	For the fear of the Lord is wisdom and instruction
	1:28	Do not disobey the fear of the Lord

1 : 30	The Lord will reveal your secrets
1 : 30	because you did not come in the fear of the Lord
2 : 1	My son, if you come forward to serve the Lord
2 : 7	You who fear the Lord, wait for his mercy
2 : 8	You who fear the Lord, trust in him
2 : 9	you who fear the Lord, hope for good things
2 : 10	and see : who ever trusted in the Lord and was put to shame ?
2 : 10	Or who ever persevered in the fear of the Lord and was forsaken ?
2 : 11	For the Lord is compassionate and merciful
2 : 14	What will you do when the Lord punishes you ?
2 : 15	Those who fear the Lord will not disobey his words
2 : 16	Those who fear the Lord will seek his approval
2 : 17	Those who fear the Lord will prepare their hearts
2 : 18	Let us fall into the hands of the Lord
3 : 2	For the Lord honoured the father above the children
3 : 6	and whoever obeys the Lord will refresh his mother
3 : 16	and whoever angers his mother is cursed by the Lord
3 : 18	so you will find favour in the sight of the Lord
3 : 20	For great is the might of the Lord
4 : 13	and the Lord will bless the place she enters
4 : 14	the Lord loves those who love her
4 : 28	and the Lord God will fight for you
5 : 3	For the Lord will surely punish you
5 : 4	For the Lord is slow to anger
5 : 7	Do not delay to turn to the Lord
5 : 7	for suddenly the wrath of the Lord will go forth
6 : 16	and those who fear the Lord will find him
6 : 17	Whoever fears the Lord directs his friendship aright
6 : 37	Reflect on the statutes of the Lord
7 : 4	Do not seek from the Lord the highest office
7 : 5	Do not assert your righteousness before the Lord
7 : 29	With all your soul fear the Lord, and honour his priests
7 : 31	Fear the Lord and honour the priest
9 : 16	and let your glorying be in the fear of the Lord
10 : 4	The government of the earth is in the hands of the Lord
10 : 5	The success of a man is in the hands of the Lord
10 : 7	Arrogance is hateful before the Lord and before men
10 : 12	The beginning of man's pride is to depart from the Lord
10 : 13	Therefore the Lord brought upon them
10 : 14	The Lord has cast down the thrones of rulers
10 : 15	The Lord has plucked up the roots of the nations
10 : 16	The Lord has overthrown the lands of the nations
10 : 19	Those who fear the Lord
10 : 20	and those who fear the Lord
10 : 21	The fear of the Lord is the beginning of acceptance
10 : 22	their glory is the fear of the Lord
10 : 24	but none of them is greater than the man who fears the Lord
11 : 4	for the works of the Lord are wonderful
11 : 12	but the eyes of the Lord look upon him for his good
11 : 14	come from the Lord
11 : 15	come from the Lord
11 : 17	The gift of the Lord endures for those who are godly
11 : 21	but trust in the Lord and keep at your toil
11 : 21	for it is easy in the sight of the Lord
11 : 22	The blessing of the Lord is the reward of the godly
11 : 26	For it is easy in the sight of the Lord
13 : 14	During all your life love the Lord
14 : 11	and present worthy offerings to the Lord
15 : 1	The man who fears the Lord will do this
15 : 9	for it has not been sent from the Lord
15 : 10	and the Lord will prosper it
15 : 11	Do not say, Because of the Lord I left the right way
15 : 13	The Lord hates all abominations
15 : 18	For great is the wisdom of the Lord
16 : 2	unless the fear of the Lord is in them
16 : 11	For mercy and wrath are with the Lord
16 : 15	The Lord hardened Pharaoh so that he did not know him
16 : 17	Do not say, I shall be hidden from the Lord
16 : 26	The works of the Lord have existed
16 : 29	After this the Lord looked upon the earth
17 : 1	The Lord created man out of earth
17 : 5	of the 5 operations of the Lord
17 : 17	but Israel is the Lord's own portion
17 : 20	and all their sins are before the Lord
17 : 21	But the Lord, who is gracious and knows his creatures
17 : 22	A man's almsgiving is like a signet with the Lord
17 : 25	Turn to the Lord and forsake your sins
17 : 28	he who is alive and well sings the Lord's praises
17 : 29	How great is the mercy of the Lord
18 : 2	The Lord alone will be declared righteous
18 : 6	nor is it possible to trace the wonders of the Lord
18 : 11	Therefore the Lord is patient with them
18 : 13	but the compassion of the Lord is for all living beings
18 : 23	and do not be like a man who tempts the Lord
18 : 26	and all things move swiftly before the Lord
19 : 18	The fear of the Lord is the beginning of acceptance
19 : 19	The knowledge of the Lord's commandments
19 : 20	All wisdom is the fear of the Lord
20 : 32	Unwearied patience in seeking the Lord is better
21 : 6	but he that fears the Lord will repent in his heart
21 : 11	and wisdom is the fulfilment of the fear of the Lord
23 : 1	O Lord, Father and Ruler of my life
23 : 4	O Lord, Father and God of my life
23 : 19	and he does not realize that the eyes of the Lord
23 : 27	that nothing is better than the fear of the Lord
23 : 27	and nothing sweeter than to heed the commandments of the Lord
24 : 12	in the portion of the Lord, who is their inheritance
24 : 24	Do not cease to be strong in the Lord
24 : 24	the Lord Almighty alone is God
25 : 1	and they are beautiful in the sight of the Lord and of men :
25 : 6	and their boast is the fear of the Lord
25 : 10	But there is no one superior to him who fears the Lord
25 : 11	The fear of the Lord surpasses everything
25 : 12	The fear of the Lord is the beginning of love for him
26 : 3	of the man who fears the Lord
26 : 14	A silent wife is a gift of the Lord
26 : 16	Like the sun rising in the heights of the Lord
26 : 23	but a pious wife is given to the man who fears the Lord
26 : 25	but one who has a sense of shame will fear the Lord
26 : 28	the Lord will prepare him for the sword !
27 : 3	in the fear of the Lord
27 : 24	even the Lord will hate him
28 : 1	He that takes vengeance will suffer vengeance from the Lord
28 : 3	and yet seek for healing from the Lord ?
28 : 23	Those who forsake the Lord will fall into its power
30 : 19	So is he who is afflicted by the Lord
32 : 14	He who fears the Lord will accept his discipline
32 : 16	Those who fear the Lord will form true judgments
32 : 24	and he who trusts the Lord will not suffer loss
33 : 1	No evil will befall the man who fears the Lord
33 : 8	By the Lord's decision they were distinguished
33 : 11	In the fulness of his knowledge the Lord distinguished them
33 : 16	by the blessing of the Lord I excelled
34 : 13	The spirit of those who fear the Lord will live
34 : 14	He who fears the Lord will not be timid
34 : 15	Blessed is the soul of the man who fears the Lord !
34 : 16	The eyes of the Lord are upon those who love him
34 : 24	to whose voice will the Lord listen ?
35 : 3	To keep from wickedness is pleasing to the Lord
35 : 4	Do not appear before the Lord empty-handed
35 : 8	Glorify the Lord generously
35 : 11	For the Lord is the one who repays
35 : 12	for the Lord is the judge, and with him is no partiality
35 : 16	He whose service is pleasing to the Lord will be accepted
35 : 17	and he will not be consoled until it reaches the Lord
35 : 18	And the Lord will not delay
36 : 1	Have mercy upon us, O Lord, the God of all
36 : 5	as we have known that there is no God but thee, O Lord
36 : 12	Have mercy, O Lord, upon the people called by thy name
36 : 17	Hearken, O Lord, to the prayer of thy servants
36 : 17	that thou art the Lord, the God of the ages
37 : 21	for grace was not given him by the Lord
38 : 1	according to your need of him, for the Lord created him
38 : 4	The Lord created medicines from the earth
38 : 9	but pray the Lord, and he will heal you
38 : 12	And give the physician his place, for the Lord created him
38 : 14	for they too will pray to the Lord
39 : 5	to seek the Lord who made him
39 : 6	If the great Lord is willing
39 : 6	and give thanks to the Lord in prayer
39 : 8	and will glory in the law of the Lord's covenant
39 : 14	bless the Lord for all his works
39 : 16	All things are the works of the Lord, for they are very good
39 : 33	The works of the Lord are all good
39 : 35	and bless the name of the Lord
40 : 26	but the fear of the Lord is better than both
40 : 26	There is no loss in the fear of the Lord
40 : 27	The fear of the Lord is like a garden of blessing
41 : 3	this is the decree from the Lord for all flesh
42 : 15	I will now call to mind the works of the Lord
42 : 15	By the words of the Lord his works are done
42 : 16	and the work of the Lord is full of his glory
42 : 17	The Lord has not enabled his holy ones
42 : 17	which the Lord the Almighty has established
43 : 5	Great is the Lord who made it
43 : 9	a gleaming array in the heights of the Lord
43 : 29	Terrible is the Lord and very great
43 : 30	When you praise the Lord, exalt him as much as you can
43 : 33	For the Lord has made all things
44 : 2	The Lord apportioned to them great glory
44 : 16	Enoch pleased the Lord, and was taken up
44 : 21	Therefore the Lord assured him by an oath
45 : 1	From his descendants the Lord brought forth a man of mercy
45 : 3	the Lord glorified him in the presence of kings
45 : 15	to minister to the Lord and serve as priest
45 : 16	to offer sacrifice to the Lord
45 : 19	The Lord saw it and was not pleased
45 : 21	for they eat the sacrifices to the Lord

45:22	for the Lord himself is his portion and inheritance
45:23	for he was zealous in the fear of the Lord
45:26	May the Lord grant you wisdom in your heart
46:3	For he waged the wars of the Lord
46:6	and the great Lord answered him
46:6	that he was fighting in the sight of the Lord
46:9	And the Lord gave Caleb strength
46:10	that it is good to follow the Lord
46:11	and who did not turn away from the Lord
46:13	Samuel, beloved by his Lord, prophet of the Lord
46:14	By the law of the Lord he judged the congregation
46:14	and the Lord watched over Jacob
46:16	He called upon the Lord, the Mighty One
46:17	Then the Lord thundered from heaven
46:19	Samuel called men to witness before the Lord
47:5	For he appealed to the Lord, the Most High
47:6	and praised him for the blessings of the Lord
47:11	The Lord took away his sins, and exalted his power for ever
47:18	In the name of the Lord God
47:22	But the Lord will never give up his mercy
48:3	By the word of the Lord he shut up the heavens
48:20	But they called upon the Lord who is merciful
48:21	The Lord smote the camp of the Assyrians
48:22	For Hezekiah did what was pleasing to the Lord
49:3	He set his heart upon the Lord
49:12	and raised a temple holy to the Lord
50:13	with the Lord's offering in their hands
50:17	to worship their Lord, the Almighty, God Most High
50:19	And the people besought the Lord Most High in prayer
50:19	till the order of worship of the Lord was ended
50:20	to pronounce the blessing of the Lord with his lips
50:29	for the light of the Lord is his path
51:1	I will give thanks to thee, O Lord and King
51:8	Then I remembered thy mercy, O Lord
51:10	I appealed to the Lord, the Father of my Lord
51:12	and I will bless the name of the Lord
51:22	The Lord gave me a tongue as my reward
Bar 1:5	Then they wept, and fasted, and prayed before the Lord
1:8	Baruch took the vessels of the house of the Lord
1:10	and offer them upon the altar of the Lord our God
1:12	And the Lord will give us strength
1:13	And pray for us to the Lord our God
1:13	for we have sinned against the Lord our God
1:13	and to this day the anger of the Lord and his wrath
1:14	to make your confession in the house of the Lord
1:15	Righteousness belongs to the Lord our God
1:17	because we have sinned before the Lord
1:18	and have not heeded the voice of the Lord our God
1:18	to walk in the statutes of the Lord which he set before us
1:19	From the day when the Lord brought our fathers
1:19	we have been disobedient to the Lord our God
1:20	and the curse which the Lord declared
1:21	We did not heed the voice of the Lord our God
1:21	and doing what is evil in the sight of the Lord our God
2:1	So the Lord confirmed his word
2:4	where the Lord has scattered them
2:5	because we sinned against the Lord our God
2:6	Righteousness belongs to the Lord our God
2:7	All those calamities with which the Lord threatened us have come upon us
2:8	Yet we have not entreated the favour of the Lord
2:9	And the Lord has kept the calamities ready
2:9	and the Lord has brought them upon us
2:9	for the Lord is righteous in all his works
2:10	to walk in the statutes of the Lord which he set before us
2:11	And now, O Lord God of Israel
2:12	O Lord our God, against all thy ordinances
2:14	Hear, O Lord, our prayer and our supplication
2:15	that all the earth may know that thou art the Lord our God
2:16	O Lord, look down from thy holy habitation, and consider us
2:16	Incline thy ear, O Lord, and hear
2:17	open thy eyes, O Lord, and see
2:17	will not ascribe glory or justice to the Lord
2:18	will ascribe to thee glory and righteousness, O Lord
2:19	O Lord our God
2:21	Thus says the Lord :
2:22	But if you will not obey the voice of the Lord
2:27	Yet thou hast dealt with us, O Lord our God
2:31	and they will know that I am the Lord their God
2:33	who sinned before the Lord
3:1	O Lord Almighty, God of Israel
3:2	Hear, O Lord, and have mercy
3:4	O Lord Almighty, God of Israel
3:4	who did not heed the voice of the Lord their God
3:6	For thou art the Lord our God
3:6	and thee, O Lord, will we praise
3:8	who forsook the Lord our God
L Jr 6:6	It is thou, O Lord, whom we must worship
P Az 1	singing hymns to God and blessing the Lord
3	Blessed art thou, O Lord, God of our fathers
14	For we, O Lord, have become fewer than any nation
20	and give glory to thy name, O Lord !
22	Let them know that thou art the Lord, the only God
26	But the angel of the Lord came down into the furnace
29	Blessed art thou, O Lord, God of our fathers
35	Bless the Lord, all works of the Lord
36	Bless the Lord, you heavens
37	Bless the Lord, you angels of the Lord
38	Bless the Lord, all waters above the heaven
39	Bless the Lord, all powers
40	Bless the Lord, sun and moon
41	Bless the Lord, stars of heaven
42	Bless the Lord, all rain and dew
43	Bless the Lord, all winds
44	Bless the Lord, fire and heat
45	Bless the Lord, winter cold and summer heat
46	Bless the Lord, dews and snows
47	Bless the Lord, nights and days
48	Bless the Lord, light and darkness
49	Bless the Lord, ice and cold
50	Bless the Lord, frosts and snows
51	Bless the Lord, lightnings and clouds
52	Let the earth bless the Lord
53	Bless the Lord, mountains and hills
54	Bless the Lord, all things that grow on the earth
55	Bless the Lord, you springs
56	Bless the Lord, seas and rivers
57	Bless the Lord, you whales and all creatures that move in the waters
58	Bless the Lord, all birds of the air
59	Bless the Lord, all beasts and cattle
60	Bless the Lord, you sons of men
61	Bless the Lord, O Israel
62	Bless the Lord, you priests of the Lord
63	Bless the Lord, you servants of the Lord
64	Bless the Lord, spirits and souls of the righteous
65	Bless the Lord, you who are holy and humble in heart
66	Bless the Lord, Hananiah, Azariah, and Mishael
67	Give thanks to the Lord, for he is good
68	Bless him, all who worship the Lord, the God of gods
Sus 13:2	a very beautiful woman and one who feared the Lord
13:5	Concerning them the Lord had said :
13:23	rather than to sin in the sight of the Lord
13:35	for her heart trusted in the Lord
13:44	The Lord heard her cry
13:53	though the Lord said
Bel 14:25	Daniel said, I will worship the Lord my God
14:34	But the angel of the Lord said to Habakkuk
14:36	Then the angel of the Lord took him by the crown of his head
14:41	Thou art great, O Lord God of Daniel
2 Ma 1:8	We besought the Lord and we were heard
1:24	O Lord, Lord God, Creator of all things
2:2	not to forget the commandments of the Lord
2:8	And then the Lord will disclose these things
2:8	and the glory of the Lord and the cloud will appear
2:10	Just as Moses prayed to the Lord
2:22	while the Lord with great kindness became gracious to them
3:22	While they were calling upon the Almighty Lord
3:30	they praised the Lord
3:30	now that the Almighty Lord had appeared
3:33	since for his sake the Lord has granted you your life
3:35	Then Heliodorus offered sacrifice to the Lord
4:38	The Lord thus repaid him with the punishment he deserved
5:17	that the Lord was angered for a little while
5:19	But the Lord did not choose the nation
5:20	when the great Lord became reconciled
6:14	the Lord waits patiently to punish them
6:30	It is clear to the Lord in his holy knowledge
7:6	saying, The Lord God is watching over us
7:20	because of her hope in the Lord
7:33	And if our living Lord is angry for a little while
7:40	putting his whole trust in the Lord
8:2	They besought the Lord to look upon the people
8:5	for the wrath of the Lord had turned to mercy
8:14	and at the same time besought the Lord
8:27	giving great praise and thanks to the Lord
8:29	and besought the merciful Lord
8:35	having been humbled with the help of the Lord
9:5	But the all-seeing Lord, the God of Israel
9:13	Then the abominable fellow made a vow to the Lord
10:1	the Lord leading them on, recovered the temple and the city
10:4	they fell prostrate and besought the Lord
10:28	not only their valour but their reliance upon the Lord
10:38	with hymns and thanksgivings they blessed the Lord
11:6	besought the Lord to send a good angel to save Israel
11:10	for the Lord had mercy on them
12:36	Judas called upon the Lord
12:41	So they all blessed the ways of the Lord
13:10	he ordered the people to call upon the Lord day and night
13:12	and had besought the merciful Lord with weeping and fasting

	13 : 17	because the Lord's help protected him
	14 : 35	O Lord of all, who hast need of nothing
	14 : 36	so now, O holy One, Lord of all holiness
	14 : 46	calling upon the Lord of life and spirit
	15 : 4	It is the living Lord himself, the Sovereign in heaven
	15 : 7	that he would get help from the Lord
	15 : 21	and called upon the Lord who works wonders
	15 : 21	but as the Lord decides
	15 : 22	O Lord, thou didst send thy angel
	15 : 29	and they blessed the Sovereign Lord
	15 : 34	blessed the Lord who had manifested himself, saying
	15 : 35	of the help of the Lord
1 Es	1 : 1	Josiah kept the passover to his Lord in Jerusalem
	1 : 2	arrayed in their garments, in the temple of the Lord
	1 : 3	that they should sanctify themselves to the Lord
	1 : 3	and put the holy ark of the Lord
	1 : 4	Now worship the Lord your God
	1 : 6	and keep the passover according to the commandment of the Lord
	1 : 11	to make the offering to the Lord
	1 : 17	So the things that had to do with the sacrifices to the Lord
	1 : 18	and the sacrifices were offered on the altar of the Lord
	1 : 23	And the deeds of Josiah were upright in the sight of his Lord
	1 : 24	concerning those who sinned and acted wickedly toward the Lord
	1 : 24	and how they grieved the Lord deeply
	1 : 24	so that the words of the Lord rose up against Israel
	1 : 27	I was not sent against you by the Lord God
	1 : 27	And now the Lord is with me !
	1 : 27	The Lord is with me, urging me on !
	1 : 27	Stand aside, and do not oppose the Lord
	1 : 28	from the mouth of the Lord
	1 : 33	and his understanding of the law of the Lord
	1 : 39	and he did what was evil in the sight of the Lord
	1 : 41	Nebuchadnezzar also took some of the holy vessels of the Lord
	1 : 44	He did what was evil in the sight of the Lord
	1 : 45	with the holy vessels of the Lord
	1 : 47	He also did what was evil in the sight of the Lord
	1 : 47	that were spoken by Jeremiah the prophet from the mouth of the Lord
	1 : 48	by the name of the Lord
	1 : 48	and transgressed the laws of the Lord, the God of Israel
	1 : 49	and polluted the temple of the Lord
	1 : 51	and whenever the Lord spoke, they scoffed at his prophets
	1 : 54	And all the holy vessels of the Lord, great and small
	1 : 54	and the treasures chests of the Lord
	1 : 55	And they burned the house of the Lord
	1 : 57	in fulfilment of the word of the Lord by the mouth of Jeremiah :
	2 : 1	that the word of the Lord by the mouth of Jeremiah
	2 : 2	the Lord stirred up the spirit of Cyrus king of the Persians
	2 : 3	The Lord of Israel, the Lord Most High
	2 : 5	may his Lord be with him, and let him go up to Jerusalem
	2 : 5	and build the house of the Lord of Israel
	2 : 5	he is the Lord who dwells in Jerusalem
	2 : 7	for the temple of the Lord which is in Jerusalem
	2 : 8	and all whose spirit the Lord had stirred to go up
	2 : 8	to build the house in Jerusalem for the Lord
	2 : 10	Cyrus the king also brought out the holy vessels of the Lord
	4 : 60	I give thee thanks, O Lord of our fathers
	5 : 50	and burnt offerings to the Lord morning and evening
	5 : 58	to have charge of the work of the Lord
	5 : 58	So the builders built the temple of the Lord
	5 : 60	praising the Lord and blessing him
	5 : 61	and they sang hymns, giving thanks to the Lord
	5 : 62	praising the Lord for the erection of the house of the Lord
	5 : 67	were building the temple for the Lord God of Israel
	5 : 69	For we obey your Lord just as you do
	5 : 70	in building the house for the Lord our God
	5 : 71	for we alone will build it for the Lord of Israel
	6 : 1	they prophesied to them in the name of the Lord God of Israel
	6 : 2	and began to build the house of the Lord which is in Jerusalem
	6 : 2	with the help of the prophets of the Lord who were with them
	6 : 5	for the providence of the Lord was over the captives
	6 : 9	building in the city of Jerusalem a great new house for the Lord
	6 : 13	We are the servants of the Lord
	6 : 15	But when our fathers sinned against the Lord of Israel
	6 : 19	and that this temple of the Lord should be rebuilt on its site
	6 : 20	laid the foundations of the house of the Lord
	6 : 22	of the house of the Lord in Jerusalem
	6 : 24	of the house of the Lord in Jerusalem
	6 : 26	and that the holy vessels of the house of the Lord
	6 : 27	the servant of the Lord and governor of Judea
	6 : 27	to build this house of the Lord on its site
	6 : 28	until the house of the Lord is finished
	6 : 29	for sacrifices to the Lord, for bulls and rams and lambs
	6 : 33	Therefore may the Lord, whose name is there called upon
	6 : 33	to hinder or damage that house of the Lord in Jerusalem
	7 : 4	and they completed it by command of the Lord God of Israel
	7 : 7	They offered at the dedication of the temple of the Lord
	7 : 9	for the services of the Lord God of Israel

	7 : 13	and sought the Lord
	7 : 14	rejoicing before the Lord
	7 : 15	for the service of the Lord God of Israel
	8 : 6	by the prosperous journey which the Lord gave them
	8 : 7	so that he omitted nothing from the law of the Lord
	8 : 8	and reader of the law of the Lord :
	8 : 9	and reader of the law of the Lord, greeting
	8 : 12	in accordance with what is in the law of the Lord
	8 : 13	and to carry to Jerusalem the gifts for the Lord of Israel
	8 : 13	and to collect for the Lord in Jerusalem
	8 : 14	for the temple of their Lord which is in Jerusalem
	8 : 15	so as to offer sacrifices upon the altar of their Lord
	8 : 17	and deliver the holy vessels of the Lord
	8 : 25	Blessed be the Lord alone
	8 : 27	I was encouraged by the help of the Lord my God
	8 : 46	in the house of our Lord
	8 : 47	And by the mighty hand of our Lord
	8 : 50	There I proclaimed a fast for the young men before our Lord
	8 : 52	The power of our Lord will be with those who seek him
	8 : 53	And again we prayed to our Lord about these things
	8 : 55	and the holy vessels of the house of our Lord
	8 : 58	And I said to them, You are holy to the Lord
	8 : 58	and the silver and the gold are vowed to the Lord
	8 : 58	the Lord of our fathers
	8 : 59	in Jerusalem, in the chambers of the house of our Lord
	8 : 60	carried them to the temple of the Lord
	8 : 61	by the mighty hand of our Lord which was upon us
	8 : 62	and delivered in the house of our Lord
	8 : 65	offered sacrifices to the Lord, the God of Israel
	8 : 66	all as a sacrifice to the Lord
	8 : 67	and the temple of the Lord
	8 : 72	at the word of the Lord of Israel
	8 : 73	and kneeling down and stretching forth my hands to the Lord
	8 : 74	I said, O Lord
	8 : 78	And now in some measure mercy has come to us from thee, O Lord
	8 : 79	in the house of the Lord our God
	8 : 80	Even in our bondage we were not forsaken by our Lord
	8 : 81	and glorified the temple of our Lord
	8 : 82	And now, O Lord, what shall we say
	8 : 86	For thou, O Lord, didst lift the burden of our sins
	8 : 89	O Lord of Israel, thou art true
	8 : 92	and said to Ezra, We have sinned against the Lord
	8 : 93	Let us take an oath to the Lord about this
	8 : 94	as seems good to you and to all who obey the law of the Lord
	9 : 8	Now then make confession and give glory to the Lord
	9 : 13	until we are freed from the wrath of the Lord
	9 : 39	which had been given by the Lord God of Israel
	9 : 46	And Ezra blessed the Lord God Most High
	9 : 47	and fell to the ground and worshipped the Lord
	9 : 48	taught the law of the Lord
	9 : 50	This day is holy to the Lord
	9 : 52	for the day is holy to the Lord
	9 : 52	and do not be sorrowful, for the Lord will exalt you
P Ma	1	O Lord Almighty, God of our fathers
	7	for thou art the Lord Most High
	7	Thou, O Lord, according to thy great goodness
	8	Therefore thou, O Lord, God of the righteous
	9	my transgressions are multiplied, O Lord
	12	I have sinned, O Lord, I have sinned
	13	I earnestly beseech thee, forgive me, O Lord
	13	For thou, O Lord, art the God of those who repent
Ps 151 : 3		And who will declare it to my Lord ? The Lord himself
151 : 5		but the Lord was not pleased with them
3 Ma	2 : 2	Lord, Lord, king of the heavens
	5 : 7	they all called upon the Almighty Lord and Ruler of all power
	5 : 11	But the Lord sent upon the king a portion of sleep
	5 : 12	And by the action of the Lord
	5 : 35	praised the manifest Lord God, King of kings
	6 : 5	you, O Lord, broke in pieces
	6 : 10	and destroy us, Lord, by whatever fate you choose
	6 : 15	that you are with us, O Lord
	6 : 15	so accomplish it, O Lord
	6 : 39	on which the Lord of all most gloriously revealed his mercy
2 Es	1 : 4	The word of the Lord came to me, saying
	1 : 12	But speak to them and say, Thus says the Lord :
	1 : 14	Yet you have forgotten me, says the Lord
	1 : 15	Thus says the Lord Almighty :
	1 : 21	What more can I do for you ? Says the Lord
	1 : 22	Thus says the Lord Almighty :
	1 : 27	you have forsaken yourselves, says the Lord
	1 : 28	Thus says the Lord Almighty :
	1 : 32	their blood I will require of you, says the Lord
	1 : 33	Thus says the Lord Almighty : Your house is desolate
	1 : 40	Zechariah and Malachi, who is also called the messenger of the Lord
	2 : 1	Thus says the Lord : I brought this people out of bondage
	2 : 3	because you have sinned before the Lord God
	2 : 4	Go, my children, and ask for mercy from the Lord
	2 : 9	says the Lord Almighty

2 : 10 Thus says the Lord to Ezra :
2 : 14 because I live, says the Lord
2 : 15 establish their feet, because I have chosen you, says the Lord
2 : 17 for I have chosen you, says the Lord
2 : 28 says the Lord
2 : 30 because I will deliver you, says the Lord
2 : 31 for I am merciful, says the Lord Almighty
2 : 33 I, Ezra, received a command from the Lord on Mount Horeb
2 : 33 and refused the Lord's commandment
2 : 37 Receive what the Lord has entrusted to you and be joyful
2 : 38 Rise and stand, and see at the feast of the Lord
2 : 39 have received glorious garments from the Lord
2 : 40 who have fulfilled the law of the Lord
2 : 41 beseech the Lord's power that your people
2 : 42 and they all were praising the Lord with songs
2 : 47 who had stood valiantly for the name of the Lord
2 : 48 how great and many are the wonders of the Lord God
3 : 4 O sovereign Lord, didst thou not speak at the beginning
4 : 38 Then I answered and said, O sovereign Lord
5 : 23 And I said, O sovereign Lord
5 : 28 And now, O Lord, why hast thou given over the one to the many
5 : 38 And I said, O sovereign Lord
5 : 41 And I said, Yet behold, O Lord
5 : 56 And I said, O Lord, I beseech thee
6 : 11 I answered and said, O sovereign Lord
6 : 38 I said, O Lord
6 : 55 All this I have spoken before thee, O Lord
6 : 57 And now, O Lord, behold, these nations
7 : 17 Then I answered and said, O sovereign Lord, behold
7 : 45 I answered and said, O sovereign Lord
7 : 58 I said, O sovereign Lord
7 : 75 If I have found favour in thy sight, O Lord
7 : 132 I answered and said, I know, O Lord
8 : 6 O Lord who art over us, grant to thy servant
8 : 20 He said : O Lord who inhabitest eternity
8 : 24 hear, O Lord, the prayer of thy servant
8 : 36 For in this, O Lord
8 : 45 No, O Lord who art over us !
8 : 63 Behold, O Lord, thou hast now shown me a multitude of the signs
9 : 29 O Lord, thou didst show thyself among us
12 : 7 And I said, O sovereign Lord
13 : 51 I said, O sovereign Lord, explain this to me :
14 : 2 And I said, Here I am, Lord
14 : 19 Let me speak in thy presence, Lord
15 : 1 The Lord says, Behold
15 : 5 Behold, says the Lord
15 : 7 Therefore, says the Lord
15 : 9 I will surely avenge them, says the Lord
15 : 12 that the Lord will bring upon it
15 : 21 Thus says the Lord God :
15 : 24 says the Lord
15 : 26 For the Lord knows all who transgress against him
15 : 52 Would I have dealt with you so violently, says the Lord
15 : 56 As you will do to my chosen people, says the Lord
16 : 8 The Lord God sends calamities, and who will drive them away ?
16 : 11 The Lord will threaten
16 : 12 at the presence of the Lord
16 : 35 O servants of the Lord
16 : 36 Behold the word of the Lord, receive it
16 : 36 do not disbelieve what the Lord says
16 : 48 says the Lord
16 : 54 Behold, the Lord knows all the works of men
16 : 64 Because the Lord will strictly examine all their works
16 : 70 against those who fear the Lord
16 : 71 who continue to fear the Lord
16 : 74 Hear, my elect, says the Lord
16 : 76 You who keep my commandments and precepts, says the Lord God

LORD, subst., title   49 = 0.032 %
Jud 2 : 15 as his lord had ordered him to do
5 : 5 Let my lord now hear a word from the mouth of your servant
5 : 20 Now therefore, my master and lord
5 : 21 then let my lord pass them by
6 : 4 So says King Nebuchadnezzar, the lord of the whole earth
7 : 9 Let our lord hear a word, lest his army be defeated
7 : 11 Therefore, my lord, do not fight against them in battle array
10 : 15 by hurrying down to the presence of our lord
11 : 4 as they do the servants of my lord King Nebuchadnezzar
11 : 5 and I will tell nothing false to my lord this night
11 : 6 and my lord will not fail to achieve his purposes
11 : 10 Therefore, my lord and master
11 : 11 And now, in order that my lord may not be defeated
11 : 17 therefore, my lord, I will remain with you
11 : 22 upon those who have slighted my lord
12 : 4 Judith replied, As your soul lives, my lord
12 : 6 and sent to Holofernes and said, Let my lord now command
12 : 13 This beautiful maidservant will please come to my lord
12 : 14 And Judith said, Who am I, to refuse my lord ?

12 : 18 Judith said, I will drink now, my lord
14 : 13 Wake up our lord, for the slaves have been so bold
Ad E 15 : 13 And she said to him, I saw you, my lord
15 : 14 For you are wonderful, my lord
1 Ma 2 : 53 and became lord of Egypt
1 Es 2 : 17 To King Artaxerxes our lord
2 : 18 Now be it known to our lord the king
2 : 21 but to speak to our lord the king, in order that
2 : 24 Therefore we now make known to you, O lord and king
4 : 3 he is their lord and master
4 : 14 Who then is their master, or who is their lord ?
4 : 46 And now, O lord the king
6 : 8 Let it be fully known to our lord the king that
6 : 21 of our lord the king that are in Babylon
6 : 22 and if it is approved by our lord the king
2 Es 2 : 44 Then I asked an angel, Who are these, my lord ?
4 : 3 Then I said, Yes, my lord
4 : 5 I said, Speak on, my lord
4 : 22 Then I answered and said, I beseech you, my lord
4 : 41 And I said, No, lord, it cannot
5 : 33 And I said, Speak, my lord
5 : 34 And I said, No, my lord
5 : 35 And I said, Why not, my lord ?
7 : 3 I said, Speak, my lord
7 : 10 I said, He cannot, lord
7 : 53 I said, lord, how could that be ?
9 : 41 And she said to me, Let me alone, my lord
10 : 34 I said, Speak, my lord
4 Ma 2 : 7 unless reason is clearly lord of the emotions ?
7 : 23 For only the wise and courageous man is lord of his emotions

LORD, verb   1
2 Ma 5 : 23 who lorded it over his fellow citizens

LOSE   27 = 0.018 %
Tob 7 : 7 When he heard that Tobit had lost his sight
14 : 2 He was 58 years old when he lost his sight
Jud 7 : 22 Their children lost heart
10 : 13 without losing one of his men, captured or slain
Wis 16 : 3 might lose the least remnant of appetite
Sir 2 : 14 Woe to you who have lost your endurance !
8 : 12 but if you do lend anything, be as one who has lost it
9 : 6 lest you lose your inheritance
19 : 7 and you will lose nothing at all
20 : 22 A man may lose his life through shame
20 : 22 or lose it because of his foolish look
29 : 10 Lose your silver for the sake of a brother or a friend
29 : 10 and do not let it rust under a stone and be lost
29 : 14 but a man who has lost his sense of shame will fail him
41 : 2 to one who is contrary, and has lost his patience !
2 Ma 2 : 14 In the same way Judas also collected all the books that had been lost
9 : 11 he began to lose much of his arrogance
1 Es 4 : 26 Many men have lost their minds because of women
4 : 31 if she loses her temper with him, he flatters her
3 Ma 2 : 23 and fearing lest he should lose his life
2 Es 2 : 3 but with mourning and sorrow I have lost you
9 : 20 So I considered my world, and behold, it was lost
10 : 11 she who lost so great a multitude
10 : 12 for I have lost the fruit of my womb
10 : 23 for she has now lost the seal of her glory
14 : 10 For the age has lost its youth
16 : 41 let him that buys be like one who will lose

LOSS   11 = 0.007 %
Tob 4 : 13 and in shiftlessness there is loss and great want
Wis 18 : 11 and the common man suffered the same loss as the king
19 : 17 They were stricken also with loss of sight
Sir 18 : 7 and when he stops, he will be at a loss
20 : 2 And the one who confesses his fault will be kept from loss
20 : 9 and a windfall may result in a loss
20 : 11 There are losses because of glory
22 : 3 and the birth of a daughter is a loss
32 : 24 and he who trusts the Lord will not suffer loss
40 : 26 There is no loss in the fear of the Lord
2 Ma 2 : 26 it is no light matter but calls for sweat and loss of sleep

LOT, subst.   10 = 0.007 %
Ad E 10 : 10 For this purpose he made 2 lots
10 : 11 And these 2 lots came to the hour and moment and day
Wis 2 : 9 because this is our portion, and this is our lot
5 : 5 And why is his lot among the saints ?
8 : 19 and a good soul fell to my lot
Sir 14 : 15 and what you acquired by toil to be divided by lot ?
20 : 25 but the lot of both is ruin
25 : 19 may a sinner's lot befall her !
37 : 8 lest he cast the lot against you
41 : 9 and when you die, a curse is your lot

LOT, prop. n.   1
Sir **16**:8   He did not spare the neighbours of Lot

LOTHASUBUS   1
1 Es **9**:44   Lothasubus, Nabariah, and Zechariah

LOUD   26 = 0.017 %
Jud **7**:23   and cried out with a loud voice
       7:29   and they cried out to the Lord God with a loud voice
       9:1   Judith cried out to the Lord with a loud voice, and said
       13:14   Then she said to them with a loud voice
       14:16   And he cried out with a loud voice
       14:19   and their loud cries and shouts arose
Sir **40**:13   and crash like a loud clap of thunder in a rain
Sus **13**:24   Then Susanna cried out with a loud voice
       13:42   Then Susanna cried out with a loud voice, and said
       13:46   and he cried with a loud voice
Bel **14**:18   the king looked at the table, and shouted in a loud voice
       14:41   And the king shouted with a loud voice
1 Ma **2**:19   But Mattathias answered and said in a loud voice :
       2:27   Then Mattathias cried out in the city with a loud voice
       3:54   Then they sounded the trumpets and gave a loud shout
       5:31   with trumpets and loud shouts
       13:8   and they answered in a loud voice
       13:45   and they cried out with a loud voice
1 Es **5**:63   with outcries and loud weeping
       9:10   Then all the multitude shouted and said with a loud voice
3 Ma **5**:48   and heard the loud and tumultuous noise
       5:51   and cried out in a very loud voice
2 Es **9**:38   and behold, she was mourning and weeping with a loud voice
       10:26   behold, she suddenly uttered a loud and fearful cry
       10:27   Then I was afraid, and cried with a loud voice and said
       12:45   And they wept with a loud voice

LOUDLY   4 = 0.003 %
Jud **16**:1   and all the people loudly sang this song of praise
Sus **13**:60   Then all the assembly shouted loudly and blessed God
1 Es **5**:65   For the multitude sounded the trumpets loudly
3 Ma **7**:16   joyfully and loudly giving thanks

LOUD-VOICED   1
Sir **26**:27   A loud-voiced and garrulous wife

LOVE, subst.   28 = 0.018 %
Tob **6**:14   for a demon is in love with her
       6:17   When Tobias heard these things, he fell in love with her
Ad E **13**:12   or pride or for any love of glory that I did this
Wis **3**:9   and the faithful will abide with him in love
       6:17   and concern for instruction is love of her
       6:18   and love of her is the keeping of her laws
Sir **17**:18   and allotting to him the light of his love
       19:18   and wisdom obtains his love
       24:18   I am the mother of beautiful love
       25:12   The fear of the Lord is the beginning of love for him
       40:20   but the love of wisdom is better than both
       48:11   and those who have been adorned in love
Sus **13**:20   and we are in love with you
2 Ma **6**:20   even for the natural love of life
2 Es **5**:40   or the goal of the love that I have promised my people
4 Ma **2**:11   It is superior to love for one's wife
       2:12   It takes precedence over love for children
       13:26   they rendered their brotherly love more fervent
       14:1   but also mastered the emotions of brotherly love
       14:13   Observe how complex is a mother's love for her children
       14:14   have a sympathy and parental love for their offspring
       14:17   by flying in circles around them in the anguish of love
       15:6   In 7 pregnancies she had implanted in herself tender love toward them
       15:11   to suffer with them out of love for her children
       15:13   O sacred nature and affection of parental love
       15:23   strengthened her to disregard her temporal love for her children
       15:25   nature, family, parental love
       16:3   as was her innate parental love

LOVE, verb   65 = 0.042 %
Tob **4**:13   So now, my son, love your brethren
       13:10   and love those within you who are distressed
       13:12   blessed for ever will be all who love you
       13:14   How blessed are those who love you !
       14:7   And all who love the Lord God in truth and righteousness
Ad E **14**:2   and every part that she loved to adorn
Wis **1**:1   Love righteousness, you rulers of the earth
       4:10   There was one who pleased God and was loved by him
       6:12   and she is easily discerned by those who love her
       7:10   I loved her more than health and beauty
       7:28   for God loves nothing so much
       8:2   I loved her and sought her from my youth
       8:3   and the Lord of all loves her
       8:7   And if any one loves righteousness, her labours are virtues
       11:24   For thou lovest all things that exist

       11:26   O Lord who lovest the living
       16:26   so that thy sons, whom thou didst love, O Lord
Sir **pr.**   but also that those who love learning
       pr.   those who love learning should make even greater progress
       1:10   and he supplied her to those who love him
       2:15   and those who love him will keep his ways
       2:16   and those who love him will be filled with the law
       3:17   then you will be loved by those whom God accepts
       3:26   and whoever loves danger will perish by it
       4:10   and he will love you more than does your mother
       4:12   Whoever loves her loves life
       4:14   the Lord loves those who love her
       6:33   If you love to listen you will gain knowledge
       7:21   Let your soul love an intelligent servant
       7:30   With all your might love your Maker
       7:35   because for such deeds you will be loved
       13:14   During all your life love the Lord
       13:15   Every creature loves its like
       15:13   and they are not loved by those who fear him
       27:17   Love your friend and keep faith with him
       30:1   He who loves his son will whip him often
       31:5   He who loves gold will not be justified
       34:16   The eyes of the Lord are upon those who love him
       47:8   he sang praise with all his heart, and he loved his Maker
       47:16   and you were loved for your peace
       47:22   nor destroy the posterity of him who loved him
Bar **3**:36   and to Israel whom he loved
L Jr **6**:9   as they would for a girl who loves ornaments
Bel **14**:38   and hast not forsaken those who love thee
1 Ma **4**:33   Strike them down with the sword of those who love thee
2 Ma **14**:37   as a man who loved his fellow citizens
       15:14   This is a man who loves the brethren
1 Es **4**:24   he brings it back to the woman he loves
       4:25   A man loves his wife more than his father or his mother
3 Ma **2**:10   And because you love the house of Israel
2 Es **3**:14   and thou didst love him
       4:23   why the people whom you loved
       5:27   and to this people, whom thou hast loved
       5:33   Or do you love him more than his Maker does ?
       8:30   but love those who have always put their trust in thy glory
       8:47   For you come far short of being able to love my creation
       8:47   more than I love it
       11:42   and have loved liars
4 Ma **13**:24   they loved one another all the more
       15:3   She loved religion more
       15:4   the emotions of parents who love their children ?
       15:6   The mother of the 7 boys, more than any other mother, loved her children
       15:10   and loved their brothers and their mother

LOVELINESS   2
Sir **24**:17   Like a vine I caused loveliness to bud
2 Es **10**:50   and the loveliness of her beauty

LOVELY   2
Jud **8**:7   She was beautiful in appearance, and had a very lovely face
1 Es **4**:18   and then see a woman lovely in appearance and beauty

LOVER   5 = 0.003 %
Wis **15**:6   Lovers of evil things and fit for such objects of hope
Sir **26**:22   and a married woman as a tower of death to her lovers
2 Es **15**:47   to please and glory in your lovers
       15:51   so that you cannot receive your mighty lovers
4 Ma **2**:8   even though he is a lover of money

LOW, adj., adv.   12 = 0.008 %
Jud **13**:20   when our nation was brought low
Sir **4**:7   bow your head low to a great man
       6:12   but if you are brought low he will turn against you
       11:12   he lifts him out of his low estate
       33:12   but some of them he cursed and brought low
Bar **2**:5   They were brought low and not raised up
       5:7   and the everlasting hills be made low
P Az **14**   and are brought low this day in all the world
2 Ma **15**:27   they laid low no less than 35,000 men
2 Es **9**:45   and looked upon my low estate, and considered my distress
       10:22   our harp has been laid low, our song has been silenced
       11:42   and have laid low the walls of those who did you no harm

LOWER   1
Sir **29**:5   and will lower his voice

LOWLY   6 = 0.004 %
Jud **9**:11   for thou art God of the lowly, helper of the oppressed
Ad E **11**:11   and the lowly were exalted and consumed those held in honour
Wis **6**:6   For the lowliest man may be pardoned in mercy
Sir **10**:14   and has seated the lowly in their place
       22:9   conceal the lowly birth of their parents
2 Es **14**:13   comfort the lowly among them

LOYAL
		6 = 0.004 %
Ad E	16 : 1	and to those who are loyal to our government, greeting
	16 : 23	it may mean salvation for us and the loyal Persians
Sir	26 : 2	A loyal wife rejoices her husband
	46 : 7	And in the days of Moses he did a loyal deed
3 Ma	3 : 7	alleging that these people were loyal
4 Ma	4 : 3	because I am loyal to the king's government

LOYALTY
		4 = 0.003 %
1 Ma	14 : 35	and because of the justice and loyalty
3 Ma	3 : 3	and unswerving loyalty toward the dynasty
	5 : 31	a full and firm loyalty to my ancestors
4 Ma	7 : 9	You, father, strengthened out loyalty to the law

LOZON
| | | 1 |
| 1 Es | 5 : 33 | the sons of Lozon, the sons of Giddel |

LUCIUS
| | | 1 |
| 1 Ma | 15 : 16 | Lucius, consul of the Romans, to King Ptolemy, greeting |

LUCK
| | | 1 |
| Sir | 8 : 19 | lest you drive away your good luck |

LUD
| | | 1 |
| Jud | 2 : 23 | and ravaged Put and Lud |

LUMINARY
| | | 1 |
| Wis | 13 : 2 | or the luminaries of heaven |

LUMP
| | | 1 |
| 2 Es | 2 : 9 | whose land lies in lumps of pitch and heaps of ashes |

LUST, subst.
		6 = 0.004 %
Tob	8 : 7	I am not taking this sister of mine because of lust, but with sincerity
Sir	23 : 6	Let neither gluttony nor lust overcome me
Sus	13 : 14	they confessed their lust
	13 : 56	beauty has deceived you and lust has perverted your heart
4 Ma	1 : 3	namely, gluttony and lust
	2 : 15	lust for power, vainglory, boasting, arrogance, and malice

LUST, verb
| | | 1 |
| 2 Es | 15 : 47 | who have always lusted after you |

LUSTFUL
		2
Sir	26 : 9	A wife's harlotry shows in her lustful eyes
Sus	13 : 11	for they were ashamed to disclose their lustful desire to possess her

LUTE
| | | 1 |
| 1 Ma | 4 : 54 | it was dedicated with songs and harps and lutes and cymbals |

LUXURIOUS
| | | 1 |
| Wis | 19 : 11 | when desire led them to ask for luxurious food |

LUXURY
		5 = 0.003 %
Sir	11 : 27	The misery of an hour makes one forget luxury
	14 : 4	and others will live in luxury on his goods
	14 : 16	because in Hades one cannot look for luxury
	18 : 32	Do not revel in great luxury
	37 : 29	Do not have an insatiable appetite of any luxury

LYCIA
| | | 1 |
| 1 Ma | 15 : 23 | and to Pamphylia, and to Lycia, and to Halicarnassus |

LYDDA
| | | 1 |
| 1 Ma | 11 : 34 | and the 3 districts of Aphairema and Lydda and Rathamin |

LYDIA
| | | 1 |
| 1 Ma | 8 : 8 | the country of Nidia and Media and Lydia |

LYING
		2
Wis	1 : 11	and a lying mouth destroys the soul
Sir	51 : 5	from an unclean tongue and lying words

LYRE
		2
Sir	39 : 15	with praise, with songs on your lips, and with lyres
Ps 151	2	My hands made a harp, my fingers fashioned a lyre

LYSIAS
		29 = 0.019 %
1 Ma	3 : 32	He left Lysias, a distinguished man of royal lineage
	3 : 33	Lysias was also to take care of Antiochus his son
	3 : 34	And he turned over to Lysias half of his troops and the elephants
	3 : 35	Lysias was to send a force against them
	3 : 38	Lysias chose Ptolemy the son of Dorymenes
	4 : 26	and reported to Lysias all that had happened
	4 : 34	and there fell of the army of Lysias 5,000 men
	4 : 35	And when Lysias saw the rout of his troops
	6 : 6	that Lysias had gone first with a strong force

	6 : 17	And when Lysias learned that the king was dead
	6 : 17	Lysias had brought him up as a boy
	6 : 55	Then Lysias heard that Philip
	7 : 2	the army seized Antiochus and Lysias to bring them to him
2 Ma	10 : 11	appointed one Lysias to have charge of the government
	11 : 1	Lysias, the king's guardian and kinsman
	11 : 6	that Lysias was besieging the strongholds
	11 : 12	and Lysias himself escaped by disgraceful flight
	11 : 15	agreed to all that Lysias urged
	11 : 15	which Maccabeus delivered to Lysias in writing
	11 : 16	The letter written to the Jews by Lysias was to this effect :
	11 : 16	Lysias to the people of the Jews, greeting
	11 : 22	King Antiochus to his brother Lysias, greeting
	11 : 35	With regard to what Lysias the kinsman of the king has granted you
	12 : 1	Lysias returned to the king
	12 : 27	a fortified city where Lysias dwelt
	13 : 2	and with him Lysias, his guardian
	13 : 4	and when Lysias informed him
	13 : 26	Lysias took the public platform
	14 : 2	having made away with Antiochus and his guardian Lysias

LYSIMACHUS
		7 = 0.005 %
Ad E	11 : 1	and had been translated by Lysimachus the son of Ptolemy
2 Ma	4 : 29	Menelaus left his own brother Lysimachus
	4 : 39	had been committed in the city by Lysimachus
	4 : 39	the populace gathered against Lysimachus
	4 : 40	Lysimachus armed about 3,000 men
	4 : 41	But when the Jews became aware of Lysimachus' attack
	4 : 41	and threw them in wild confusion at Lysimachus and his men

M

MAADAI
| | | 1 |
| 1 Es | 9 : 34 | Of the sons of Bani : Jeremai, Maadai, Amram, Joel |

MAASEIAH
		4 = 0.003 %
1 Es	9 : 19	Maaseiah, Eliezar, Jarib and Jodan
	9 : 21	Of the sons of Immer : Hanani and Zebadiah and Maaseiah
	9 : 22	Of the sons of Pashhur : Elioenai, Maaseiah, Ishmael
	9 : 48	Shabbethai, Hodiah, Maaseiah and Kelita

MAASMAS
| | | 1 |
| 1 Es | 8 : 43 | I sent word to Eliezar, Iduel, Maasmas |

MACCABEUS
		31 = 0.020 %
1 Ma	2 : 4	Judas called Maccabeus
	2 : 66	Judas Maccabeus has been a mighty warrior from his youth
	3 : 1	Then Judas his son, who was called Maccabeus
	5 : 24	Judas maccabeus and Jonathan his brother crossed the Jordan
	5 : 34	And when the army of Timothy realized that it was Maccabeus
	8 : 20	Judas, who is also called Maccabeus, and his brothers
2 Ma	2 : 19	The story of Judas Maccabeus and his brothers
	5 : 27	But Judas Maccabeus, with about 9 others
	8 : 1	But Judas, who was also called Maccabeus, and his companions
	8 : 5	As soon as Maccabeus got his army organized
	8 : 16	But Maccabeus gathered his men together
	10 : 1	Now Maccabeus and his followers
	10 : 16	But Maccabeus and his men
	10 : 19	Maccabeus left Simon and Joseph
	10 : 21	When word of what had happened came to Maccabeus
	10 : 25	Maccabeus and his men sprinkled dust upon their heads
	10 : 30	surrounding Maccabeus and protecting him
	10 : 33	Then Maccabeus and his men were glad
	10 : 35	20 young men in the army of Maccabeus
	11 : 6	When Maccabeus and his men got word
	11 : 7	Maccabeus himself was the first to take up arms
	11 : 15	which Maccabeus delivered to Lysias in writing
	12 : 19	Dositheus and Sosipater, who were captains under Maccabeus
	12 : 20	But Maccabeus arranged his army in divisions
	13 : 24	He received Maccabeus
	14 : 6	whose leader is Judas Maccabeus
	14 : 27	and commanding him to send Maccabeus to Antioch
	14 : 30	But Maccabeus, noticing that Nicanor was more austere
	15 : 7	But Maccabeus did not cease to trust with all confidence
	15 : 21	Maccabeus, perceiving the hosts that were before him

MACEDONIAN
		7 = 0.005 %
Ad E	16 : 10	For Haman, the son of Hammedatha, a Macedonian
	16 : 14	and would transfer the kingdom of the Persians to the Macedonians
1 Ma	1 : 1	After Alexander son of Philip, the Macedonian
	6 : 2	the Macedonian king who first reigned over the Greeks
	8 : 5	Philip, and Perseus king of the Macedonians
2 Ma	8 : 20	when 8,000 in all went into the affair, with 4,000 Macedonians
	8 : 20	and when the Macedonians were hard pressed

MACHINE   6 = 0.004 %
1 Ma   6:51   machines to shoot arrows, and catapults
     9:64   he fought against it for many days and made machines of war
     9:67   and set fire to the machines of war
4 Ma   7:4   No city besieged with many ingenious war machines
     9:20   and pieces of flesh were falling off the axles of the machine
     9:26   they bound him to the torture machine and catapult

MACHNADEBAI   1
1 Es   9:34   Carabasion and Eliashib and Machnadebai, Eliasis, Binnui

MACRON   1
2 Ma   10:12   Ptolemy, who was called Macron

MAD   2
2 Ma   14:5   But he found an opportunity that furthered his mad purpose
2 Es   16:71   They shall be like mad men, sparing no one

MADDEN   1
3 Ma   5:2   maddened by the lavish abundance of liquor

MADDENING   1
4 Ma   7:5   our father Eleazar broke the maddening waves of the emotions

MADMAN   1
Wis   5:20   and creation will join with him to fight against the madmen

MADNESS   6 = 0.004 %
Wis   5:4   We thought that his life was madness
Sir   22:13   and you will never be wearied by his madness
2 Ma   6:29   were in their opinion sheer madness
3 Ma   5:42   Upon this the king, a Phalaris in everything and filled with madness
     5:45   to a state of madness
4 Ma   8:5   Not only do I advise you not to display the same madness

MAGBISH   1
1 Es   5:21   The sons of Magbish, 156

MAGIC   2
Wis   17:7   The delusions of their magic art lay humbled
     18:13   because of their magic arts

MAGISTRATE   4 = 0.003 %
Jud   6:14   and placed him before the magistrates of their city
Sir   10:1   A wise magistrate will educate his people
     10:2   like the magistrate of the people, so are his officials
     41:18   of a transgression, before a judge or magistrate

MAGNANIMOUS   1
4 Ma   15:10   For they were righteous and self-controlled and brave and magnanimous

MAGNANIMOUSLY   1
3 Ma   6:41   magnanimously expressing his concern :

MAGNIFICENCE   2
1 Ma   15:32   and his great magnificence
1 Es   1:5   and the magnificence of Solomon his son

MAGNIFICENT   4 = 0.003 %
Tob   14:11   and Tobias gave him a magnificent funeral
     14:13   magnificent funerals
3 Ma   2:9   and when you had glorified it by your magnificent manifestation
     3:17   with magnificent and most beautiful offerings

MAGNIFICENTLY   3 = 0.002 %
2 Ma   3:25   a magnificently caparisoned horse
     4:22   He was welcomed magnificently by Jason and the city
     4:49   provided magnificently for their funeral

MAGNIFY   3 = 0.002 %
Ad E   14:10   and to magnify for ever a mortal king
Sir   36:4   so in them be thou magnified before us
     49:11   How shall we magnify Zerubbabel ?

MAHLI   1
1 Es   8:47   they brought us competent men of the sons of Mahli

MAHSEIAH   1
Bar   1:1   which Baruch the son of Neraiah, son of Mahseiah

MAID   23 = 0.015 %
Tob   3:7   was reproached by her father's maids
     3:8   So the maids said to her
     8:12   Send one of the maids to see whether he is alive
     8:13   So the maid opened the door and went in
Jud   8:10   she sent her maid, who was in charge of all she possessed
     8:33   and I will go out with my maid
     10:2   and called her maid and went

     10:5   And she gave her maid a bottle of wine and a flask of oil
     10:10   she and her maid with her
     10:17   to accompany her and her maid
     12:15   and her maid went and spread on the ground for her before Holofernes
     12:19   what her maid had prepared
     13:3   Now Judith had told her maid
     13:9   and gave Holofernes' head to her maid
     16:23   She set her maid free
Ad E   15:2   she took her 2 maids with her
     15:7   and collapsed upon the head of the maid who went before her
Sus   13:15   she went in as before with only 2 maids
     13:17   She said to her maids
     13:19   When the maids had gone out
     13:21   and this was why you sent your maids away
     13:36   this woman came in with 2 maids
     13:36   shut the garden doors, and dismissed the maids

MAIDEN   4 = 0.003 %
Sir   20:4   Like a eunuch's desire to violate a maiden
     30:20   like a eunuch who embraces a maiden and groans
1 Ma   1:26   maidens and young men became faint
2 Ma   3:19   Some of the maidens who were kept indoors

MAIDSERVANT   9 = 0.006 %
Jud   11:5   and let your maidservant speak in your presence
     11:6   And if you follow out the words of your maidservant
     12:13   This beautiful maidservant will please come to my lord
     16:12   The sons of maidservants have pierced them through
Wis   9:5   For I am thy slave and the son of thy maidservant
Sir   41:22   of meddling with his maidservant
1 Es   5:1   and their menservants and maidservants, and their cattle
     5:41   besides menservants and maidservants, were 42,360
     5:42   their menservants and maidservants were 7,337

MAIL   1
1 Ma   6:35   armed with coats of mail

MAIMED   1
2 Es   2:21   do not ridicule a lame man, protect the maimed

MAIN   3 = 0.002 %
1 Ma   11:46   Then the men of the city seized the main streets of the city
2 Ma   12:35   was dragging him off by main strength
4 Ma   1:12   I shall begin by stating my main principle

MAINTAIN   15 = 0.010 %
Jud   8:7   and she maintained this estate
Sir   28:5   If he himself, being flesh, maintains wrath
1 Ma   14:35   which he had maintained toward his nation
2 Ma   9:26   and to maintain your present good will, each of you
     10:12   and attempted to maintain peaceful relations with them
     10:14   he maintained a force of mercenaries
     11:19   If you will maintain your good will toward the government
     15:30   the man who maintained his youthful good will
3 Ma   1:12   he did not cease to maintain that he ought to enter, saying
     2:31   to be exacted for maintaining the religion of their city
     3:3   The Jews, however, continued to maintain good will
     3:19   By maintaining their manifest ill-will toward us
2 Es   6:32   which you have maintained from your youth
4 Ma   6:18   and have maintained in accordance with law
     17:4   maintaining firm an enduring hope in God

MAINTENANCE   1
1 Ma   10:36   and let the maintenance be given them

MAJESTIC   2
Sir   18:5   Who can measure his majestic power ?
2 Ma   3:34   report to all men the majestic power of God

MAJESTICALLY   1
Ad E   15:2   Then, majestically adorned

MAJESTY   12 = 0.008 %
Tob   13:6   and I show his power and majesty to a nation of sinners
     13:7   and will rejoice in his majesty
Ad E   15:6   clothed in the full array of his majesty
Wis   18:24   and thy majesty on the diadem upon his head
Sir   2:18   for as his majesty is, so also is his mercy
     17:8   to show them the majesty of his works
     17:13   Their eyes saw his glorious majesty
     39:15   ascribe majesty to his name and give thanks to him
     43:15   In his majesty he amasses the clouds
     44:2   his majesty from the beginning
2 Ma   15:13   and of marvellous majesty and authority
1 Es   4:40   and the power and the majesty of all the ages

MAJORITY   1
3 Ma   2:32   But the majority acted firmly with a courageous spirit

MAKE*

455 = 0.296 %

Tob	3 : 4	thou madest us a byword of reproach
	4 : 7	and do not let your eye begrudge the gift when you make it
	4 : 8	make your gift from them in proportion
	4 : 16	and do not let your eye begrudge the gift when you make it
	5 : 16	So his son made the preparations for the journey
	6 : 7	you make a smoke from these before the man or woman
	6 : 16	so as to make a smoke
	7 : 11	until you make a binding agreement with me
	8 : 2	and put the heart and liver of the fish upon them and made a smoke
	8 : 6	Thou madest Adam
	8 : 6	let us make a helper for him like himself
	8 : 16	Blessed art thou, because thou hast made me glad
	9 : 5	So Raphael made the journey
	11 : 1	praising God because he had made his journey a success
	13 : 4	Make his greatness known there
	13 : 14	and they will be made glad for ever
Jud	1 : 2	he made the walls 70 cubits high and 50 cubits wide
	1 : 4	and he made its gates
	1 : 5	it was in those days that King Nebuchadnezzar made war
	5 : 11	he took advantage of them and set them to making bricks
	5 : 11	and humbled them and made slaves of them
	5 : 23	they are a people with no strength or power for making war
	6 : 1	When the disturbance made by the men outside the council died down
	6 : 2	and tell us not to make war against the people of Israel
	7 : 1	and make war on the Israelites
	7 : 24	in not making peace with the Assyrians
	8 : 14	who made all these things
	8 : 18	or city of ours which worshipped gods made with hands
	8 : 30	and made us take an oath which we cannot break
	9 : 13	Make my deceitful words to be their wound and stripe
	10 : 4	and made herself very beautiful
	10 : 23	and she prostrated herself and made obeisance to him
	14 : 9	and made a joyful noise in their city
	16 : 14	for thou didst speak, and they were made
Ad E	10 : 6	the river is Esther, whom the king married and made queen
	10 : 10	For this purpose he made 2 lots
	12 : 4	The king made a permanent record of these things
	13 : 2	and, in order to make my kingdom peaceable
	13 : 10	For thou hast made heaven and earth
	14 : 11	and make an example of the man who began this against us
	14 : 12	make thyself known in this time of our affliction
	16 : 5	have been made in part responsible
	16 : 21	has made this day to be a joy to his chosen people
	16 : 24	It shall be made not only impassable for men
Wis	1 : 9	For inquiry will be made into the counsels of an ungodly man
	1 : 13	because God did not make death
	1 : 16	and they made a covenant with him
	2 : 6	and make use of the creation to the full as in youth
	2 : 19	and make trial of his forbearance
	2 : 23	and made him in the image of his own eternity
	5 : 1	and those who make light of his labours
	5 : 4	and made a byword of reproach – we fools !
	6 : 7	because he himself made both small and great
	6 : 10	For they will be made holy
	6 : 13	She hastens to make herself known to those who desire her
	6 : 22	and make the knowledge of her clear
	7 : 27	and makes them friends of God, and prophets
	9 : 1	who hast made all things by thy word
	9 : 2	to have dominion over the creatures thou hast made
	9 : 9	and was present when thou didst make the world
	10 : 11	she stood by him and made him rich
	10 : 21	and made the tongues of babes speak clearly
	11 : 24	which thou hast made
	11 : 24	for thou wouldst not have made anything
	12 : 12	for the destruction of nations which thou didst make ?
	13 : 11	make a useful vessel that serves life's needs
	13 : 14	or makes it like some worthless animal
	13 : 15	then he makes for it a niche that befits it
	14 : 8	But the idol made with hands is accursed
	14 : 8	and so is he who made it
	14 : 12	For the idea of making idols was the beginning of fornication
	14 : 15	made an image of his child
	14 : 17	and made a visible image of the king whom they honoured
	15 : 6	are those who either make or desire or worship them
	15 : 7	making all in like manner
	15 : 8	this man who was made of earth a short time before
	15 : 13	when he makes from earthy matter fragile vessels and graven images
	15 : 16	For a man made them, and one whose spirit is borrowed formed them
	15 : 17	He is mortal, and what he makes with lawless hands is dead
	16 : 24	For the creation, serving thee who hast made it
	16 : 28	to make it known that one must rise before the sun
	17 : 16	and thus was kept shut up in a prison not made of iron
	18 : 6	That night was made known beforehand to our fathers
	18 : 18	made known why they were dying
	19 : 4	and made them forget what had happened

	19 : 14	but these made slaves of guests who were their benefactors
Sir pr.		those who love learning should make even greater progress
	1 : 15	She made among men an eternal foundation
	1 : 18	making peace and perfect health to flourish
	2 : 6	make your ways straight, and hope in him
	4 : 7	Make yourself beloved in the congregation
	6 : 4	and make him the laughingstock of his enemies
	6 : 11	In your prosperity he will make himself your equal
	7 : 9	and when I make an offering to the Most High God
	7 : 23	and make them obedient from their youth
	9 : 13	But if you approach him, make no misstep
	10 : 26	Do not make a display of your wisdom when you do your work
	11 : 27	The misery of an hour makes one forget luxury
	13 : 25	And a glad heart makes a cheerful countenance
	14 : 19	and the man who made it will pass away with it
	16 : 4	but through a tribe of lawless men it will be made desolate
	16 : 14	He will make room for every act of mercy
	16 : 26	and when he made them, he determined their divisions
	17 : 3	and made them in his own image
	17 : 6	He made for them tongue and eyes
	17 : 16	and they are unable to make for themselves
	18 : 18	and the gift of a grudging man makes the eyes dim
	18 : 23	Before making a vow, prepare yourself
	18 : 31	it will make you the laughingstock of your enemies
	19 : 10	Be brave ! It will not make you burst !
	19 : 16	A person may make a slip without intending it
	20 : 13	The wise man makes himself beloved through his words
	20 : 23	A man may for shame make promises to a friend
	20 : 23	and needlessly make him an enemy
	22 : 19	A man who pricks an eye will make tears fall
	22 : 19	and one who pricks the heart makes it show feeling
	24 : 5	Alone I have made the circuit of the vault of heaven
	24 : 8	And he said, Make your dwelling in Jacob
	24 : 26	It makes them full of understanding, like the Euphrates
	24 : 27	It makes instruction shine forth like light
	24 : 32	I will again make instruction shine forth like the dawn
	24 : 32	and I will make it shine afar
	25 : 8	and he who has not made a slip with his tongue
	25 : 23	are caused by the wife who does not make her husband happy
	26 : 6	and a tongue-lashing makes it known to all
	27 : 14	makes one's hair stand on end
	27 : 14	and their quarrels make a man stop his ears
	28 : 5	who will make expiation for his sins ?
	28 : 25	make balances and scales for your words
	28 : 25	make a door and a bolt for your mouth
	29 : 6	and he has needlessly made him his enemy
	29 : 8	and do not make him wait for your alms
	30 : 3	He who teaches his son will make his enemies envious
	31 : 27	It has been created to make men glad
	31 : 31	and do not afflict him by making demands of him
	32 : 1	If they make you master of the feast, do not exalt yourself
	32 : 13	And for these things bless him who made you
	33 : 4	bind together your instruction, and make your answer
	33 : 9	Some of them he made ordinary days
	33 : 12	and some of them he made holy and brought near to himself
	33 : 13	so men are in the hand of him who made them
	33 : 28	and if he does not obey, make his fetters heavy
	34 : 4	From an unclean thing what will be made clean ?
	34 : 8	and wisdom is made perfect in truthful lips
	35 : 1	He who keeps the law makes many offerings
	35 : 19	and makes them rejoice in his mercy
	36 : 6	make thy hand and thy right arm glorious
	38 : 5	Was not water made sweet with a tree
	38 : 8	the pharmacist makes of them a compound
	38 : 27	each is diligent in making a great variety
	38 : 30	makes it pliable with his feet
	39 : 5	to seek the Lord who made him
	39 : 5	and will make supplication before the Most High
	39 : 5	and make supplication for his sins
	39 : 31	and be made ready on earth for their service
	40 : 14	A generous man will be made glad
	40 : 21	The flute and the harp make pleasant melody
	40 : 25	Gold and silver make the foot stand sure
	41 : 22	and do not upbraid after making a gift
	42 : 7	make a record of all that you give out or take in
	42 : 11	lest she make you a laughingstock to your enemies
	42 : 24	and he has made nothing incomplete
	43 : 2	making proclamation as it goes forth
	43 : 5	Great is the Lord who made it
	43 : 6	He made the moon also, to serve in its season
	43 : 11	Look upon the rainbow, and praise him who made it
	43 : 33	For the Lord has made all things
	44 : 18	Everlasting covenants were made with him
	44 : 23	he made to rest upon the head of Jacob
	45 : 2	He made him equal in glory to the holy ones
	45 : 2	and made him great in the fears of his enemies
	45 : 5	He made him hear his voice
	45 : 7	He made an everlasting covenant with him
	45 : 9	to make their ringing heard in the temple
	45 : 16	to make atonement for the people

45:23	and made atonement for Israel
46:17	and made his voice heard with a mighty sound
47:9	to make sweet melody with their voices
48:2	and by his zeal he made them few in number
48:18	and made great boasts in his arrogance
49:6	and made her streets desolate
50:11	he made the court of the sanctuary glorious
50:16	they made a great noise to be heard
50:17	Then all the people together made haste
51:17	I made progress therein

Bar	**1**:8	the silver vessels which Zedekiah the son of Josiah, king of Judah, had made
	1:14	to make your confession in the house of the Lord
	2:11	and hast made thee a name, as at this day
	2:23	I will make to cease from the cities of Judah
	2:26	thou hast made as it is today
	2:35	I will make an everlasting covenant with them
	3:34	They shone with gladness for him who made them
	4:7	For you provoked him who made you
	5:7	and the everlasting hills be made low
	5:7	and the valleys filled up, to make level ground

L Jr	**6**:4	Now in Babylon you will see gods made of silver and gold and wood
	6:9	People take gold and make crowns for the heads of their gods
	6:18	so the priests make their temples secure with doors and locks and bars
	6:27	because through them these gods are made to stand
	6:35	if one makes a vow to them and does not keep it
	6:39	These things that are made of wood and overlaid with gold and silver
	6:45	They are made by carpenters and goldsmiths
	6:46	The men that make them will certainly not live very long themselves
	6:46	how then can the things that are made by them be gods ?
	6:50	Since they are made of wood and overlaid with gold and silver
	6:57	gods made of wood and overlaid with silver and gold

P Az	**13**	to whom thou didst promise to make their descendants
	15	or incense, no place to make an offering before thee
	27	and made the midst of the furnace like a moist whistling wind

Bel	**14**:13	for beneath the table they had made a hidden entrance
	14:27	and boiled them together and made cakes

1 Ma	**1**:11	and misled many, saying, Let us go and make a covenant
	1:48	They were to make themselves abominable
	2:15	came to the city of Modein to make them offer sacrifice
	2:41	So they made this decision that day :
	3:7	He embittered many kings, but he made Jacob glad by his deeds
	3:14	he said, I will make a name for myself
	3:14	I will make war on Judas and his companions
	4:49	They made new holy vessels, and brought the lampstand
	5:3	But Judas made war on the sons of Esau
	5:14	came from Galilee and made a similar report
	5:42	Permit no man to encamp, but make them all enter the battle
	5:49	Then Judas ordered proclamation to be made to the army
	5:57	So they said, Let us also make a name for ourselves
	5:57	let us go and make war
	6:14	and made him ruler over all his kingdom
	6:33	and his troops made ready for battle
	6:41	All who heard the noise made by their multitude
	6:49	He made peace with the men of Beth-zur
	6:52	The Jews also made engines of war to match theirs
	6:58	and make peace with them and with all their nation
	7:9	whom he made high priest
	8:1	toward all who made an alliance with them
	8:13	Those whom they wish to help and to make kings
	8:13	they make kings
	8:26	And to the enemy who makes war
	8:29	Thus on these terms the Romans make a treaty
	8:30	and any addition or deletion that they may make shall be valid
	8:31	Why have you made your yoke heavy
	9:20	And all Israel made great lamentation for him
	9:26	and he took vengeance on them and made sport of them
	9:64	he fought against it for many days and made machines of war
	9:70	he sent ambassadors to him to make peace with him
	10:4	for he said, Let us act first to make peace with him
	10:4	before he makes peace with Alexander against us
	10:16	Come now, we will make him our friend and ally
	10:54	and will make gifts to you and to her
	10:65	and made him general and governor of the province
	11:9	Come, let us make a covenant with each other
	11:25	kept making complaints against him
	11:27	and made him to be regarded as one of his chief friends
	11:37	Now therefore take care to make a copy of this
	11:50	and make the Jews stop fighting against us and our city
	11:51	And they threw down their arms and made peace
	11:57	and make you one of the friends of the king
	11:59	Simon his brother he made governor
	11:62	and he made peace with them
	12:40	but might make war on him
	12:53	Now therefore let us make war on them
	13:27	he made it high that it might be seen

	13:37	and we are ready to make a general peace with you
	13:38	All the grants that we have made to you remain valid
	13:43	He made a siege engine, brought it up to the city
	13:45	asking Simon to make peace with them
	13:50	Then they cried to Simon to make peace with them
	13:53	so he made him commander of all the forces
	14:1	so that he could make war against Trypho
	14:12	and there was none to make them afraid
	14:15	He made the sanctuary glorious
	14:27	So they made a record on bronze tablets
	14:35	and they made him their leader and high priest
	14:39	and he made him one of the king's friends
	15:4	and intend to make a landing in the country
	15:19	or make war against them and their cities and their country
	15:19	or make alliance with those who war against them
	15:25	and making engines of war
	15:27	he formerly had made with Simon
	15:38	Then the king made Cendebaeus commander-in-chief of the coastal country
	15:39	and to make war on the people
	15:41	and make raids along the highways of Judea
	16:13	and made treacherous plans against Simon and his sons

2 Ma	**1**:26	and preserve thy portion and make it holy
	1:34	and enclosed the place and made it sacred
	2:9	It was also made clear
	3:4	who had been made captain of the temple
	3:8	ostensibly to make a tour of inspection
	3:9	he told about the disclosure that had been made
	3:18	to make a general supplication
	3:20	And holding up their hands to heaven, they all made entreaty
	3:33	While the high priest was making the offering of atonement
	3:35	and made very great vows to the Saviour of his life
	4:17	a fact which later events will make clear
	5:1	About this time Antiochus made his 2nd invasion of Egypt
	5:3	attacks and counterattacks made on this side and on that
	5:5	and suddenly made an assault upon the city
	5:16	the votive offerings which other kings had made
	6:8	and make them partake of the sacrifices
	6:23	But making a high resolve
	7:24	that he would make him rich and enviable
	7:28	that God did not make them out of things that existed
	7:37	to make you confess that he alone is God
	8:15	yet for the sake of the covenants made with their fathers
	8:21	and made them ready to die for their laws and their country
	8:29	When they had done this, they made common supplication
	8:35	and made his way alone like a runaway slave
	9:4	I will make Jerusalem a cemetery of Jews
	9:8	making the power of God manifest to all
	9:13	Then the abominable fellow made a vow to the Lord
	9:14	and to make a cemetery
	9:15	he would make, all of them, equal to citizens of Athens
	9:23	on the occasions when he made expeditions
	10:3	and made another altar of sacrifice
	10:16	after making solemn supplications
	10:28	while the other made rage their leader in the fight
	11:2	He intended to make the city a home for Greeks
	11:36	so that we may make proposals appropriate for you
	11:37	Therefore make haste and send some men
	12:12	agreed to make peace with them
	12:27	and made a vigorous defence
	12:45	Therefore he made atonement for the dead
	13:26	made the best possible defence
	14:26	he took the covenant that had been made
	15:1	he made plans to attack them with complete safety
	15:9	he made them the more eager

1 Es	**1**:11	to make the offering to the Lord
	1:15	were in their place according to the arrangement made by David
	1:25	went to make war at Carchemish on the Euphrates
	1:32	have made lamentation for him to this day
	1:34	and made him king in succession to Josiah his father
	1:37	And the king of Egypt made Jehoiakim his brother
	1:43	when he was made king he was 18 years old
	1:46	and made Zedekiah king of Judea and Jerusalem
	1:48	And though King Nebuchadnezzar had made him swear
	2:2	made a proclamation throughout all his kingdom
	2:3	has made me king of the world
	2:21	search may be made in the record of your fathers
	2:24	Therefore we now make known to you, O lord and king
	2:26	So I ordered search to be made
	3:19	It makes equal the mind of the king and the orphan
	3:21	It makes all hearts feel rich, forgets kings and satraps
	3:21	and makes every one talk in millions
	4:4	If he tells them to make war on one another, they do it
	4:6	Likewise those who do not serve in the army or make war
	4:17	Women make men's clothes
	4:34	for it makes the circuit of the heavens
	4:43	Remember the vow which you made to build Jerusalem
	4:52	in accordance with the commandment to make 17 offerings
	5:3	and all their brethren were making merry
	5:3	And he made them go up with them

5:53	And all who had made any vow to God
5:56	and Jeshua the son of Jozadak made a beginning
6:6	and a report made
6:21	let search be made in the royal archives
6:23	Then King Darius commanded that search be made
6:28	and that full effort be made to help the men
6:31	in order that libations may be made to the Most High God
8:91	While Ezra was praying and making his confession
9:3	And a proclamation was made throughout Judea and Jerusalem
9:8	Now then make confession and give glory to the Lord
9:54	and to make great rejoicing
P Ma 2	thou who hast made heaven and earth with all their order
Ps 151 :2	My hands made a harp, my fingers fashioned a lyre
3 Ma **1**:9	he offered sacrifice to the supreme God and made thank-offerings
2:5	and you made them an example
2:6	You made known your mighty power
2:9	you made it a firm foundation
3:21	we made known to all our amnesty towards their compatriots here
3:21	and we ventured to make a change
3:21	and to make them participants in our regular religious rites
3:29	is to be made unapproachable and burned with fire
4:1	was now made evident and outspoken
4:11	and which was well suited to make them an obvious spectacle
5:17	and to make the present portion of the banquet joyful
6:40	on which also they made the petition for their dismissal
7:10	the Jews did not immediately hurry to make their departure
2 Es **1**:13	and made safe highways for you where there was no road
1:23	but threw a tree into the water and made the stream sweet
2:1	and made my counsels void
2:41	who have been called from the beginning, may be made holy
3:5	and he was made alive in thy presence
3:15	Thou didst make with him an everlasting covenant
3:18	and move the world, and make the depths to tremble
4:13	and they made a plan
4:14	and said, Come, let us go and make war against the sea
4:14	and that we may make for ourselves more forests
4:15	And in like manner the waves of the sea also made a plan
4:19	I answered and said, Each has made a foolish plan
4:23	and the law of our fathers has been made of no effect
4:42	makes haste to escape the pangs of birth
5:7	shall make his voice heard by night, and all shall hear his voice
5:26	and from all the flocks that have been made
5:36	and make the withered flowers bloom again for me
5:44	The creation cannot make more haste than the Creator
6:6	and they were made through me and not through another
6:24	At that time friends shall make war on friends like enemies
6:38	Let heaven and earth be made
6:44	These were made on the 3rd day
6:54	as ruler over all the works which thou hadst made
7:11	For I made the world for their sake
7:11	what had been made was judged
7:12	And so the entrances of this world were made narrow
7:50	For this reason the Most High has made not one world but 2
7:60	because it is they who have made my glory to prevail now
7:62	if the mind is made out of the dust
7:63	so that the mind might not have been made from it
7:70	When the Most High made the world and Adam
7:82	because they cannot now make a good repentance
7:97	and how they are to be made like the light of the stars
7:136	because he makes his compassions abound more and more
7:137	for if he did not make them abound
8:1	The Most High made this world for the sake of many
8:2	from which earthenware is made
8:13	and thou wilt make him live, for he is thy work
8:14	to what purpose was he made ?
8:23	and whose indignation makes the mountains melt away
8:44	and is called thy own image because he is made like thee
8:44	hast thou also made him like the farmer's seed ?
8:54	and in the end the treasure of immortality is made manifest
8:60	have defiled the name of him who made them
9:2	which he has made
9:13	and for whose sake the age was made
9:18	before the world was made for them to dwell in
10:14	given her fruit, that is, man, to him who made her
10:22	our young men have been enslaved and our strong men made powerless
11:39	which I had made to reign in my world
11:46	and may hope for the judgment and mercy of him who made it
12:34	and he will make them joyful until the end comes
13:3	this wind made something like the figure of a man come up
13:5	to make war against the man who came up out of the sea
13:31	And they shall plan to make war against one another
13:36	And Zion will come and be made manifest to all people, prepared and built
14:26	some things you shall make public
14:45	Make public the 24 books that you wrote first
15:19	but shall make an assault upon their houses with the sword
15:47	For you have made yourself like her

16:42	who will not make a profit
16:55	He said, Let the earth be made, and it was made
16:55	Let the heaven be made, and it was made
16:62	who made all things
16:64	and will make a public spectacle of all of you
4 Ma **4**:21	and caused Antiochus himself to make war on them
6:1	When Eleazar in this manner had made eloquent response
6:8	to make him get up again after he fell
6:29	Make my blood their purification
7:9	but by your deeds you made your words of divine philosophy credible
10:14	You do not have a fire hot enough to make me play the coward
10:19	you will not make our reason speechless
12:13	and are made of the same elements as you
13:6	and make it calm for those who sail into the inner basin
14:19	since even bees at the time for making honeycombs
17:24	and this made them brave and courageous
18:7	but I guarded the rib from which woman was made
18:19	I kill and I make alive :

MAKE away   1
2 Ma **14**:2	having made away with Antiochus and his guardian Lysias

MAKE up   2
Tob **7**:16	Sister, make up the other room, and take her into it
2 Ma **8**:10	Nicanor determined to make up for the king

MAKED, prop. n.   2
1 Ma **5**:26	in Alema and Chaspho, Maked and Carnaim
5:36	Maked, and Bosor, and the other cities of Gilead

MAKER   6 = 0.004 %
Sir **7**:30	With all your might love your Maker
10:12	his heart has forsaken his Maker
38:15	He who sins before his Maker
39:28	and calm the anger of their Maker
47:8	he sang praise with all his heart, and he loved his Maker
2 Es **5**:33	Or do you love him more than his Maker does ?

MALACHI   1
2 Es **1**:40	Zechariah and Malachi, who is also called the messenger of the Lord

MALCHIJAH   2
1 Es **9**:26	Malchijah, Mijamin, and Eleazar, and Asibias, and Benaiah
9:44	and on his left Pedaiah, Mishael, Malchijah

MALE   4 = 0.003 %
1 Ma **5**:28	and killed every male by the edge of the sword
5:35	and he killed every male in it, plundered it
5:51	He destroyed every male by the edge of the sword
4 Ma **15**:30	O more noble than males in steadfastness

MALEVOLENT   1
4 Ma **1**:25	In pleasure there exists even a malevolent tendency

MALICE   10 = 0.007 %
Sir **11**:16	evil will grow old with those who take pride in malice
2 Ma **4**:4	was intensifying the malice of Simon
5:23	In his malice toward the Jewish citizens
3 Ma **2**:25	he increased in his deeds of malice
3:22	But in their innate malice
4 Ma **1**:4	the emotions that hinder one from justice, such as malice
1:26	thirst for honour, rivalry, and malice
2:15	lust for power, vainglory, boasting, arrogance, and malice
3:4	No one of us can eradicate malice
3:4	so that we are not overcome by malice

MALICIOUS   4 = 0.003 %
Jud **4**:12	to the malicious joy of the Gentiles
3 Ma **7**:3	frequently urging us with malicious intent
2 Es **11**:45	and your malicious heads, and your most evil talons
4 Ma **2**:16	For the temperate mind repels all these malicious emotions

MALICIOUSLY   1
4 Ma **6**:25	There they burned him with maliciously contrived instruments

MALLUCH   1
1 Es **9**:30	Of the sons of Bani : Meshullam, Malluch, Adaiah

MALLUS   1
2 Ma **4**:30	it happened that the people of Tarsus and of Mallus

MALTREAT   4 = 0.003 %
2 Ma **7**:13	they maltreated and tortured the 4th in the same way
7:15	Next they brought forward the 5th and maltreated him
4 Ma **12**:13	and to maltreat and torture them in this way ?
13:27	while watching their brothers being maltreated

MAMDAI

1

1 Es 9:34 Mamdai and Bedeiah and Vaniah

MAN   1021 = 0.665 %

Tob	1:4	while I was still a young man
	1:9	When I became a man I married Anna
	1:19	Then one of the men of Nineveh went
	2:2	Go and bring whatever poor man of our brethren you may find
	3:14	that I am innocent of any sin with man
	4:7	Do not turn your face away from any poor man
	4:14	the wages of any man who works for you
	4:18	Seek advice from every wise man
	5:2	but how can I obtain the money when I do not know the man ?
	5:3	Find a man to go with you
	5:4	So he went to look for a man
	5:8	and whether he is a reliable man to go with you
	5:11	or for a man whom you will pay to go with your son ?
	5:16	And his father said to him, Go with this man
	5:16	and the young man's dog was with them
	6:2	Then the young man went down to wash himself
	6:2	and would have swallowed the young man
	6:3	So the young man seized the fish and threw it up on the land
	6:5	So the young man did as the angel told him
	6:6	Then the young man said to the angel, Brother Azarias
	6:7	you make a smoke from these before the man or woman
	6:8	anoint with it a man who has white films in his eyes
	6:10	the angel said to the young man
	6:12	cannot give her to another man
	6:12	because you rather than any other man
	6:13	Then the young man said to the angel, Brother Azarias
	7:2	How much the young man resembles my cousin Tobit !
	7:7	Son of that good and noble man !
	8:6	Thou didst say, It is not good that the man should be alone
	11:6	and so is the man who went with him !
	12:1	My son, see to the wages of the man who went with you
	12:4	The old man said, He deserves it
	13:8	Let all men speak, and give him thanks in Jerusalem
Jud	1:11	but looked upon him as only one man
	2:5	take with you men confident in their strength
	2:18	also plenty of food for every man
	2:27	and put to death all their young men
	3:5	The men came to Holofernes and told him all this
	3:6	and took picked men from them as his allies
	4:7	only wide enough for 2 men at the most
	4:9	And every man of Israel cried out to God with great fervour
	4:11	And all the men and women of Israel, and their children
	5:22	all the men standing around the tent began to complain
	5:22	Holofernes'officers and all the men from the seacoast
	6:1	When the disturbance made by the men outside the council died down
	6:3	we the king's servants will destroy them as one man
	6:10	and hand him over to the men of Israel
	6:12	When the men of the city saw them
	6:14	Then the men of Israel came down from their city and found him
	6:16	and all their young men and their women ran to the assembly
	7:2	their force of men of war was 170,000 infantry and 12,000 cavalry
	7:4	These men will now lick up the face of the whole land
	7:5	Then each man took up his weapons
	7:11	and not a man of your army will fall
	7:12	and keep all the men in your forces with you
	7:13	that not a man gets out of the city
	7:18	and they sent some of their men
	7:22	and the women and young men fainted from thirst
	7:23	Then all the people, the young men, the women, and the children
	8:3	For as he stood overseeing the men
	8:7	and men and women slaves, and cattle, and fields
	8:12	among the sons of men ?
	8:14	nor find out what a man is thinking
	8:16	for God is not like a man, to be threatened
	9:11	nor thy might upon men of strength
	10:4	to entice the eyes of all men who might see her
	10:9	So they ordered the young man
	10:10	and the men of the city watched her
	10:13	without losing one of his men, captured or slain
	10:14	When the men heard her words, and observed her face
	10:17	They chose from their number a 100 men
	10:19	Surely not a man of them had better be left alive
	11:7	not only do men serve him because of you
	11:8	that you are the one good man in the whole kingdom
	11:9	we have heard his words, for the men of Bethulia spared him
	11:14	They have sent men to Jerusalem
	13:12	When the men of her city heard her voice
	13:19	Your hope will never depart from the hearts of men
	14:2	let every valiant man take his weapons and go out of the city
	14:5	and let him see and recognize the man
	14:6	in the hand of one of the men
	14:11	and every man took his weapons

	15:1	When the men in the tents heard it
	15:3	Then the men of Israel, every one that was a soldier
	15:4	And Uzziah sent men to Betomasthaim and Bebai
	15:13	while all the men of Israel followed
	16:5	and kill my young men with the sword
	16:7	by the hands of the young men
Ad E	11:3	a great man, serving in the court of the king
	13:2	to re-establish the peace which all men desire
	13:5	stands constantly in opposition to all men
	13:14	that I might not set the glory of man above the glory of God
	14:11	and make an example of the man who began this against us
	14:13	and turn his heart to hate the man who is fighting against us
	16:2	the more proud do many men become
	16:4	They not only take away thankfulness from among men
	16:6	when these men by the false trickery of their evil natures
	16:8	quiet and peaceable for all men
	16:15	who were consigned to annihilation by this thrice accursed man
	16:18	because the man himself who did these things
	16:24	It shall be made not only impassable for men
Wis	1:3	For perverse thoughts separate men from God
	1:9	For inquiry will be made into the counsels of an ungodly man
	1:16	But ungodly men by their words and deeds summoned death
	2:1	and there is no remedy when a man comes to his end
	2:10	Let us oppress the righteous poor man
	2:12	Let us lie in wait for the righteous man
	2:18	for if the righteous man is God's son, he will help him
	2:23	for God created man for incorruption
	3:4	For though in the sight of men they were punished
	3:10	who disregarded the righteous man
	4:1	because it is known both by God and by men
	4:2	When it is present, men imitate it
	4:7	But the righteous man, though he die early, will be at rest
	4:9	but understanding is grey hair for men
	4:16	The righteous man who has died
	4:16	will condemn the prolonged old age of the unrighteous man
	4:17	For they will see the end of the wise man
	5:1	Then the righteous man will stand with great confidence
	5:4	This is the man whom we once held in derision
	5:14	Because the hope of the ungodly man
	6:6	For the lowliest man may be pardoned in mercy
	6:6	but mighty men will be mightily tested
	6:24	A multitude of wise men is the salvation of the world
	7:1	I also am mortal, like all men
	7:2	from the seed of a man and the pleasure of marriage
	7:14	for it is an unfailing treasure for men
	7:20	the powers of spirits and the reasonings of men
	7:28	as the man who lives with wisdom
	8:7	nothing in life is more profitable for men than these
	9:2	and by thy wisdom hast formed man
	9:5	a man who is weak and short-lived
	9:6	for even if one is perfect among the sons of men
	9:13	For what man can learn the counsel of God ?
	9:18	and men were taught what pleases thee
	10:3	But when an unrighteous man departed from her in his anger
	10:4	steering the righteous man by a paltry piece of wood
	10:5	recognized the righteous man
	10:6	Wisdom rescued a righteous man
	10:10	When a righteous man fled from his brother's wrath
	10:13	When a righteous man was sold
	10:17	She gave to holy men the reward of their labours
	11:19	not only could their damage exterminate men
	11:20	men could fall at a single breath when pursued by justice
	11:23	and thou dost overlook men's sins, that they may repent
	12:8	But even these thou didst spare, since they were but men
	12:12	to plead as an advocate for unrighteous men ?
	12:13	whose care is for all men
	12:17	when men doubt the completeness of thy power
	12:19	that the righteous man must be kind
	13:1	For all men who were ignorant of God were foolish by nature
	13:3	men assumed them to be gods
	13:4	And if men were amazed at their power and working
	13:6	Yet these men are little to be blamed
	13:10	are the men who give the name gods
	13:10	to the works of men's hands
	13:13	he forms it like the image of a man
	14:4	so that even if a man lacks skill, he may put to sea
	14:5	therefore men trust their lives
	14:9	are the ungodly man and his ungodliness
	14:11	and became traps for the souls of men
	14:14	For through the vanity of men they entered the world
	14:17	When men could not honour monarchs in their presence
	14:20	the one whom shortly before they had honoured as a man
	14:21	because men, in bondage to misfortune or to royal authority
	14:31	For it is not the power of the things by which men swear
	15:8	this man who was made of earth a short time before
	15:13	For this man, more than all others, knows that he sins
	15:16	For a man made them, and one whose spirit is borrowed formed them
	15:16	for no man can form a god which is like himself
	16:1	Therefore those men were deservedly punished

	16 : 3	in order that those men, when they desired food
	16 : 12	but it was thy word, O Lord, which heals all men
	16 : 13	thou dost lead men down to the gates of Hades and back again
	16 : 14	A man in his wickedness kills another
	16 : 26	might learn that it is not the production of crops that feeds man
	16 : 29	for the hope of an ungrateful man
	17 : 2	For when lawless men supposed
	17 : 21	while over those men alone heavy night was spread
	18 : 9	For in secret the holy children of good men offered sacrifices
	18 : 11	and the common man suffered the same loss as the king
	18 : 21	For a blameless man was quick to act as their champion
	19 : 17	just as were those at the door of the righteous man
Sir	1 : 15	She made among men an eternal foundation
	1 : 16	she satisfies men with her fruits
	1 : 22	for a man's anger tips the scale to his ruin
	1 : 23	A patient man will endure until the right moment
	1 : 29	Be not a hypocrite in men's sight
	2 : 5	and acceptable men in the furnace of humiliation
	2 : 18	but not into the hands of men
	3 : 11	For a man's glory comes from honouring his father
	3 : 29	The mind of the intelligent man will ponder a parable
	3 : 29	and an attentive ear is the wise man's desire
	4 : 2	nor anger a man in want
	4 : 5	nor give a man occasion to curse you
	4 : 7	bow your head low to a great man
	5 : 13	and a man's tongue is his downfall
	6 : 36	If you see an intelligent man, visit him early
	7 : 6	lest you be partial to a powerful man
	7 : 11	Do not ridicule a man who is bitter in soul
	7 : 25	But give her to a man of understanding
	7 : 35	Do not shrink from visiting a sick man
	8 : 1	Do not contend with a powerful man
	8 : 2	Do not quarrel with a rich man
	8 : 5	Do not reproach a man who is turning away from sin
	8 : 6	Do not disdain a man when he is old
	8 : 8	and learn how to serve great men
	8 : 12	Do not lend to a man who is stronger than you
	8 : 16	Do not fight with a wrathful man
	9 : 9	Never dine with another man's wife
	9 : 13	Keep far from a man who has the power to kill
	9 : 15	Let your conversation be with men of understanding
	9 : 16	Let righteous men be your dinner companions
	9 : 18	and the man who is reckless in speech will be hated
	10 : 1	and the rule of an understanding man will be well ordered
	10 : 4	and over it he will raise up the right man for the time
	10 : 5	The success of a man is in the hands of the Lord
	10 : 7	Arrogance is hateful before the Lord and before men
	10 : 11	For when a man is dead, he will inherit creeping things
	10 : 12	The beginning of man's pride is to depart from the Lord
	10 : 13	and the man who clings to it pours out abominations
	10 : 18	Pride was not created for men
	10 : 23	It is not right to despise an intelligent poor man
	10 : 23	nor is it proper to honour a sinful man
	10 : 24	but none of them is greater than the man who fears the Lord
	10 : 25	Free men will be at the service of a wise servant
	10 : 25	and a man of understanding will not grumble
	10 : 27	Better is a man who works
	10 : 29	Who will justify the man that sins against himself ?
	10 : 29	And who will honour the man that dishonours his own life ?
	10 : 30	A poor man is honoured for his knowledge
	10 : 30	while a rich man is honoured for his wealth
	10 : 31	A man honoured in poverty, how much more in wealth !
	10 : 31	And a man dishonoured in wealth, how much more in poverty !
	11 : 1	The wisdom of a humble man will lift up his head
	11 : 2	Do not praise a man for his good looks
	11 : 2	nor loathe a man because of his appearance
	11 : 4	and his works are concealed from men
	11 : 6	and illustrious men have been handed over to others
	11 : 11	There is a man who works, and toils, and presses on
	11 : 18	There is a man who is rich through his diligence and self-denial
	11 : 21	to enrich a poor man quickly and suddenly
	11 : 26	to reward a man on the day of death
	11 : 27	and at the close of a man's life
	11 : 28	a man will be known through his children
	11 : 29	Do not bring every man into your home
	11 : 30	so is the mind of a proud man
	12 : 2	Do good to a godly man, and you will be repaid
	12 : 3	No good will come to the man who persists in evil
	12 : 4	Give to the godly man, but do not help the sinner
	12 : 7	Give to the good man, but do not help the sinner
	12 : 9	A man's enemies are grieved when he prospers
	12 : 14	So no one will pity a man who associates with a sinner
	13 : 1	and whoever associates with a proud man will become like him
	13 : 2	nor associate with a man mightier and richer than you
	13 : 3	A rich man does wrong, and he even adds reproaches
	13 : 3	a poor man suffers wrong, and he must add apologies
	13 : 4	A rich man will exploit you if you can be of use to him
	13 : 9	When a powerful man invites you, be reserved
	13 : 16	and a man clings to one like himself
	13 : 17	No more has a sinner with a godly man
	13 : 18	And what peace between a rich man and a poor man ?
	13 : 20	Humility is an abomination to a proud man
	13 : 20	likewise a poor man is an abomination to a rich one
	13 : 21	When a rich man totters, he is steadied by friends
	13 : 21	but when a humble man falls, he is even pushed away by friends
	13 : 22	If a rich man slips, his helpers are many
	13 : 22	If a humble man slips, they even reproach him
	13 : 23	When the rich man speaks all are silent
	13 : 23	When the poor man speaks they say, Who is this fellow ?
	13 : 25	A man's heart changes his countenance
	14 : 1	Blessed is the man who does not blunder with his lips
	14 : 3	Riches are not seemly for a stingy man
	14 : 3	and of what use is property to an envious man ?
	14 : 5	If a man is mean to himself, to whom will he be generous ?
	14 : 6	No one is meaner than the man who is grudging to himself
	14 : 8	Evil is the man with a grudging eye
	14 : 9	A greedy man's eye is not satisfied with a portion
	14 : 10	A stingy man's eye begrudges bread
	14 : 19	and the man who made it will pass away with it
	14 : 20	Blessed is the man who meditates on wisdom
	15 : 1	The man who fears the Lord will do this
	15 : 7	Foolish men will not obtain her
	15 : 7	and sinful men will not see her
	15 : 8	She is far from men of pride
	15 : 12	for he has no need of a sinful man
	15 : 14	It was he who created man in the beginning
	15 : 17	Before a man are life and death
	15 : 19	and he knows every deed of man
	16 : 4	For through one man of understanding
	16 : 4	but through a tribe of lawless men it will be made desolate
	16 : 10	nor for the 600,000 men on foot
	16 : 12	he judges a man according to his deeds
	16 : 21	Like a tempest which no man can see
	16 : 23	a senseless and misguided man thinks foolishly
	17 : 1	The Lord created man out of earth
	17 : 2	He gave to men few days, a limited time
	17 : 22	A man's almsgiving is like a signet with the Lord
	17 : 30	For all things cannot be in men
	17 : 30	since a son of man is not immortal
	17 : 32	but all men are dust and ashes
	18 : 7	When a man has finished, he is just beginning
	18 : 8	What is man, and of what use is he ?
	18 : 9	The number of a man's days is great
	18 : 13	The compassion of man is for his neighbour
	18 : 17	Both are to be found in a gracious man
	18 : 18	and the gift of a grudging man makes the eyes dim
	18 : 23	and do not be like a man who tempts the Lord
	18 : 27	A wise man is cautious in everything
	18 : 28	Every intelligent man knows wisdom
	19 : 2	Wine and women lead intelligent men astray
	19 : 2	and the man who consorts with harlots is very reckless
	19 : 24	Better is the God-fearing man who lacks intelligence
	19 : 24	than the highly prudent man who transgresses the law
	19 : 29	A man is known by his appearance
	19 : 29	and a sensible man is known by his face, when you meet him
	19 : 30	A man's attire and open-mouthed laughter
	19 : 30	and a man's manner of walking, show what he is
	20 : 1	and there is a man who keeps silent but is wise
	20 : 4	is a man who executes judgments by violence
	20 : 7	A wise man will be silent until the right moment
	20 : 9	There may be good fortune for a man in adversity
	20 : 11	and there are men who have raised their heads
	20 : 12	There is a man who buys much for a little
	20 : 13	The wise man makes himself beloved through his words
	20 : 15	such a one is a hateful man
	20 : 19	An ungracious man is like a story told at the wrong time
	20 : 21	A man may be prevented from sinning by his poverty
	20 : 22	A man may lose his life through shame
	20 : 23	A man may for shame make promises to a friend
	20 : 24	A lie is an ugly blot on a man
	20 : 27	and a sensible man will please great men
	20 : 28	and whoever pleases great men will atone for injustice
	20 : 31	Better is the man who hides his folly
	20 : 31	than the man who hides his wisdom
	21 : 2	Its teeth are lion's teeth, and destroy the souls of men
	21 : 5	The prayer of a poor man goes from his lips
	21 : 7	but the sensible man, when he slips, is aware of it
	21 : 8	A man who builds his house with other people's money
	21 : 13	The knowledge of a wise man will increase like a flood
	21 : 15	When a man of understanding hears a wise saying
	21 : 17	The utterance of a sensible man
	21 : 19	To a senseless man education is fetters on his feet
	21 : 20	but a clever man smiles quietly
	21 : 21	To a sensible man education is like a golden ornament
	21 : 22	but a man of experience stands respectfully before it
	21 : 23	but a cultivated man remains outside
	21 : 24	It is ill-mannered for a man to listen at a door
	21 : 24	and a discreet man is grieved by the disgrace
	21 : 26	but the mouth of wise men is in their mind
	21 : 27	When an ungodly man curses his adversary

22 : 8	He who tells a story to a fool tells it to a drowsy man
22 : 12	but for a fool or an ungodly man it lasts all his life
22 : 13	Do not talk much with a foolish man
22 : 13	and do not visit an unintelligent man
22 : 15	Sand, salt, and a piece of iron are easier to bear than a stupid man
22 : 19	A man who pricks an eye will make tears fall
22 : 23	nor admire a rich man who is stupid
23 : 10	so also the man who always swears
23 : 11	A man who swears many oaths will be filled with iniquity
23 : 14	Remember your father and mother when you sit among great men
23 : 15	A man accustomed to use insulting words
23 : 16	2 sorts of men multiply sins
23 : 16	a man who commits fornication with his near of kin
23 : 18	A man who breaks his marriage vows says to himself
23 : 19	His fear is confined to the eyes of men
23 : 19	they look upon all the ways of men
23 : 21	This man will be punished in the streets of the city
23 : 23	and brought forth children by another man
24 : 25	It fills men with wisdom, like the Pishon
24 : 28	Just as the first man did not know her perfectly
25 : 1	and they are beautiful in the sight of the Lord and of men :
25 : 2	My soul hates 3 kinds of men
25 : 2	a beggar who is proud, a rich man who is a liar
25 : 2	and an adulterous old man who lacks good sense
25 : 4	What an attractive thing is judgment in grey-haired men
25 : 5	and understanding and counsel in honourable men !
25 : 7	a man rejoicing in his children
25 : 7	a man who lives to see the downfall of his foes
25 : 8	and he who has not served a man inferior to himself
26 : 3	of the man who fears the Lord
26 : 23	A godless wife is given as a portion to a lawless man
26 : 23	but a pious wife is given to the man who fears the Lord
26 : 28	and intelligent men who are treated contemptuously
26 : 28	a man who turns back from righteousness to sin
27 : 3	If a man is not steadfast and zealous
27 : 4	so a man's filth remains in his thoughts
27 : 5	so the test of a man is in his reasoning
27 : 6	so the expression of a thought discloses the cultivation of a man's mind
27 : 7	Do not praise a man before you hear him reason
27 : 7	for this is the test of men
27 : 11	The talk of the godly man is always wise
27 : 14	The talk of men given to swearing
27 : 14	and their quarrels make a man stop his ears
27 : 18	For as a man destroys his enemy
27 : 27	If a man does evil, it will roll back upon him
27 : 28	Mockery and abuse issue from the proud man
27 : 30	and the sinful man will possess them
28 : 3	Does a man harbour anger against another
28 : 4	Does he have no mercy toward a man like himself
28 : 8	for a man given to anger will kindle strife
28 : 9	and a sinful man will disturb friends
28 : 10	in proportion to the strength of the man will be his anger
28 : 14	and overturned the houses of great men
28 : 19	Happy is the man who is protected from it
29 : 5	A man will kiss another's hands until he gets a loan
29 : 8	Nevertheless, be patient with a man in humble circumstances
29 : 9	help a poor man for the commandment's sake
29 : 14	A good man will be surety for his neighbour
29 : 14	but a man who has lost his sense of shame will fail him
29 : 18	Being surety has ruined many men who were prosperous
29 : 18	it has driven men of power into exile
29 : 22	Better is the life of a poor man
29 : 22	than sumptuous food in another man's house
29 : 28	These things are hard to bear for a man who has feeling :
30 : 14	Better off is a poor man
30 : 14	than a rich man who is severely afflicted in body
30 : 22	Gladness of heart is the life of man
30 : 22	and the rejoicing of a man is length of days
30 : 25	A man of cheerful and good heart
31 : 3	The rich man toils as his wealth accumulates
31 : 4	The poor man toils as his livelihood diminishes
31 : 8	Blessed is the rich man who is found blameless
31 : 12	Are you seated at the table of a great man ?
31 : 19	How ample a little is for a well-disciplined man !
31 : 23	Men will praise the one who is liberal with food
31 : 27	Wine is like life to men, if you drink it in moderation
31 : 27	What is life to a man who is without wine ?
31 : 27	It has been created to make men glad
32 : 7	Speak, young man, if there is need of you
32 : 10	and approval precedes a modest man
32 : 17	A sinful man will shun reproof
32 : 18	A man of judgment will not overlook an idea
32 : 18	and an insolent and proud man will not cower in fear
33 : 1	No evil will befall the man who fears the Lord
33 : 2	A wise man will not hate the law
33 : 3	A man of understanding will trust in the law
33 : 10	All men are from the ground

33 : 13	so men are in the hand of him who made them
34 : 1	A man of no understanding has vain and false hopes
34 : 9	An educated man knows many things
34 : 15	Blessed is the soul of the man who fears the Lord !
34 : 20	is the man who offers a sacrifice
34 : 21	whoever deprives them of it is a man of blood
34 : 25	If a man washes after touching a dead body
34 : 26	So if a man fasts for his sins
35 : 6	The offering of a righteous man anoints the altar
35 : 7	The sacrifice of a righteous man is acceptable
35 : 13	He will not show partiality in the case of a poor man
35 : 19	till he repays man according to his deeds
35 : 19	and the works of men according to their devices
36 : 20	but a man of experience will pay him back
36 : 21	A woman will accept any man
36 : 23	her husband is not like other men
36 : 25	and where there is no wife, a man will wander about and sigh
36 : 26	So who will trust a man that has no home
37 : 11	with a grudging man about gratitude
37 : 11	or with a merciless man about kindness
37 : 11	or with a man hired for a year about completing his work
37 : 12	But stay constantly with a godly man
37 : 14	For a man's soul sometimes keeps him better informed
37 : 19	A man may be shrewd and the teacher of many
37 : 20	A man skilled in words may be hated
37 : 22	A man may be wise to his own advantage
37 : 23	A wise man will instruct his own people
37 : 24	A wise man will have praise heaped upon him
37 : 25	The life of a man is numbered by days
38 : 3	and in the presence of great men he is admired
38 : 4	and a sensible man will not despise them
38 : 6	And he gave skill to men
38 : 19	and the life of the poor man weighs down his heart
38 : 32	and men can neither sojourn nor live there
39 : 2	he will preserve the discourse of notable men
39 : 4	He will serve among great men and appear before rulers
39 : 4	for he tests the good and the evil among men
39 : 26	Basic to all the needs of man's life are water and fire
40 : 1	Much labour was created for every man
40 : 3	from the man who sits on a splendid throne
40 : 4	from the man who wears purple and a crown
40 : 8	With all flesh, both man and beast
40 : 14	A generous man will be made glad
40 : 19	Children and the building of a city establish a man's name
40 : 27	and covers a man better than any glory
40 : 29	When a man looks to the table of another
40 : 29	He pollutes himself with another man's food
40 : 29	but a man who is intelligent and well instructed guards against that
41 : 1	to a man without distractions
41 : 8	Woe to you, ungodly men
41 : 11	The mourning of men is about their bodies
41 : 15	Better is the man who hides his folly
41 : 15	than the man who hides his wisdom
41 : 21	and of gazing at another man's wife
41 : 23	and will find favour with every man
42 : 8	or the aged man who quarrels with the young
42 : 8	and will be approved before all men
42 : 14	Better is the wickedness of a man
42 : 18	He searches out the abyss, and the hearts of men
43 : 4	A man tending a furnace works in burning heat
44 : 1	Let us now praise famous men
44 : 3	and were men renowned for their power
44 : 6	rich men furnished with resources
44 : 8	so that men declare their praise
44 : 10	But these were men of mercy
44 : 23	The blessing of all men and the covenant
45 : 1	From his descendants the Lord brought forth a man of mercy
45 : 1	and was beloved by God and man
45 : 6	a holy man like him, of the tribe of Levi
45 : 18	Dathan and Abiram and their men and the company of Korah
46 : 19	Samuel called men to witness before the Lord
46 : 19	And no man accused him
47 : 5	to slay a man mighty in war
48 : 6	and famous men from their beds
49 : 3	in the days of wicked men he strengthened godliness
49 : 15	And no man like Joseph has been born
49 : 16	Shem and Seth were honoured among men
51 : 7	I looked for the assistance of men, and there was none
Bar 1 : 4	and in the hearing of the mighty men and the princes
1 : 9	and the mighty men and the people of the land
1 : 15	to the men of Judah, to the inhabitants of Jerusalem
2 : 1	and against the men of Israel and Judah
3 : 17	in which men trust, and there is no end to their getting
3 : 20	Young men have seen the light of day
3 : 37	Afterward she appeared upon earth and lived among men
4 : 15	who had no respect for an old man
L Jr 6 : 4	which are carried on men's shoulders
6 : 11	They deck their gods out with garments like men
6 : 18	upon a man who has offended a king

6 : 20 but men say their hearts have melted
6 : 26 Having no feet, they are carried on men's shoulders
6 : 32 as some do at a funeral feast for a man who has died
6 : 36 They cannot save a man from death
6 : 37 They cannot restore sight to a blind man
6 : 37 they cannot rescue a man who is in distress
6 : 41 for when they see a dumb man, who cannot speak
6 : 41 they bring him and pray Bel that the man may speak
6 : 46 The men that make them will certainly not live very long themselves
6 : 51 that they are not gods but the work of men's hands
6 : 53 For they cannot set up a king over a country or give rain to men
6 : 58 Strong men will strip them of their gold and silver
6 : 64 or to do good to men
6 : 73 Better therefore is a just man who has no idols
P Az 60 Bless the Lord, you sons of men
Sus 13 : 1 There was a man living in Babylon whose name was Joakim
13 : 6 These men were frequently at Joakim's house
13 : 21 that a young man was with you
13 : 32 As she was veiled, the wicked men ordered her to be unveiled
13 : 37 Then a young man, who had been hidden
13 : 39 We saw them embracing, but we could not hold the man
13 : 40 So we seized this woman and asked her who the young man was
13 : 43 thou knowest that these men have borne false witness against me
13 : 49 For these men have borne false witness against her
Bel 14 : 20 I see the footsteps of men and women and children
14 : 42 and threw into the den the men who had attempted his destruction
1 Ma 1 : 11 In those days lawless men came forth from Israel
1 : 26 maidens and young men became faint
1 : 34 And they stationed there a sinful people, lawless men
2 : 8 Her temple has become like a man without honour
2 : 18 as all the Gentiles and the men of Judah
2 : 31 that men who had rejected the king's command
2 : 41 Let us fight against every man who comes to attack us on the sabbath day
2 : 44 and lawless men in their wrath
2 : 47 They hunted down the arrogant men
3 : 6 Lawless men shrank back for fear of him
3 : 13 including a body of faithful men
3 : 15 And again a strong army of ungodly men
3 : 32 He left Lysias, a distinguished man of royal lineage
3 : 38 mighty men among the friends of the king
4 : 2 Men from the citadel were his guides
4 : 3 But Judas heard of it, and he and his mighty men
4 : 5 because he said, These men are fleeing from us
4 : 6 At daybreak Judas appeared in the plain with 3,000 men
4 : 7 and these men were trained in war
4 : 8 But Judas said to the men who were with him
4 : 13 Then the men with Judas blew their trumpets
4 : 29 and Judas met them with 10,000 men
4 : 30 and of the man who carried his armour
4 : 34 and there fell of the army of Lysias 5,000 men
4 : 41 Then Judas detailed men
5 : 13 and have destroyed about a 1,000 men there
5 : 15 men of Ptolemais and Tyre and Sidon
5 : 17 Choose your men and go and rescue your brethren in Galilee
5 : 20 Then 3,000 men were assigned to Simon to go to Galilee
5 : 27 and take and destroy all these men in one day
5 : 32 and he said to the men of his forces
5 : 38 Judas sent men to spy out the camp, and they reported to him
5 : 42 Permit no man to encamp, but make them all enter the battle
5 : 47 But the men of the city shut them out
5 : 50 So the men of the forces encamped
5 : 58 to the men of the forces that were with them
5 : 59 And Gorgias and his men came out of the city
5 : 62 But they did not belong to the family of those men
5 : 63 The man Judas and his brothers were greatly honoured
5 : 64 Men gathered to them and praised them
6 : 3 but he could not, because his plan became known to the men of the city
6 : 18 Now the men in the citadel kept hemming Israel in
6 : 35 with each elephant they stationed a 1,000 men
6 : 37 and upon each were 4 armed men who fought from there
6 : 42 and 600 men of the king's army fell
6 : 45 he killed men right and left
6 : 49 He made peace with the men of Beth-zur
6 : 54 Few men were left in the sanctuary
6 : 57 and said to the king, to the commanders of the forces, and to the men
6 : 58 Now then let us come to terms with these men
7 : 1 sailed with a few men to a city by the sea
7 : 5 all the lawless and ungodly men of Israel
7 : 7 Now then send a man whom you trust
7 : 8 he was a great man in the kingdom
7 : 19 And he sent and seized many of the men
7 : 24 and took vengeance on the men who had deserted
7 : 28 I shall come with a few men to see you face to face in peace
7 : 32 About 500 men of the army of Nicanor fell
7 : 38 Take vengeance on this man and on his army

7 : 40 And Judas encamped in Adasa with 3,000 men
7 : 46 And men came out of all the villages of Judea round about
8 : 2 Men told him of their wars
8 : 16 They trust one man each year to rule over them
8 : 16 they all heed the one man
9 : 5 and with him were 3,000 picked men
9 : 12 and the men with Judas also blew their trumpets
9 : 14 then all the stouthearted men went with him
9 : 16 they turned and followed close behind Judas and his men
9 : 48 Then Jonathan and the men with him leaped into the Jordan
9 : 49 And about 1,000 of Bacchides' men fell that day
9 : 53 And he took the sons of the leading men of the land
9 : 58 Jonathan and his men are living in quiet and confidence
9 : 60 telling them to seize Jonathan and his men
9 : 61 And Jonathan's men seized about 50 of the men of the country
9 : 62 Then Jonathan with his men, and Simon
9 : 63 and sent orders to the men of Judea
9 : 65 and he went with only a few men
9 : 67 and Simon and his men sallied out from the city
9 : 69 So he was greatly enraged at the lawless men
10 : 7 and of the men in the citadel
10 : 9 But the men in the citadel released the hostages to Jonathan
10 : 15 and men told him of the battles
10 : 16 So he said, Shall we find another such man ?
10 : 32 that he may station in it men of his own choice to guard it
10 : 36 to the number of 30,000 men
10 : 61 A group of pestilent men from Israel
10 : 61 lawless men, gathered together against him to accuse him
10 : 72 Men will tell you that you cannot stand before us
10 : 74 He chose 10,000 men and set out from Jerusalem
10 : 75 but the men of the city closed its gates
10 : 76 and the men of the city became afraid and opened the gates
10 : 80 for they surrounded his army and shot arrows at his men
10 : 81 But his men stood fast, as Jonathan commanded
10 : 85 came to 8,000 men
10 : 86 and the men of the city came out to meet him with great pomp
11 : 20 In those days Jonathan assembled the men of Judea
11 : 21 But certain lawless men who hated their nation
11 : 25 Although certain lawless men of his nation
11 : 38 he dismissed all his troops, each man to his own place
11 : 43 Now then you will do well to send me men who will help me
11 : 44 So Jonathan sent 3,000 stalwart men to him at Antioch
11 : 45 Then the men of the city assembled within the city
11 : 46 Then the men of the city seized the main streets of the city
11 : 47 and they killed on that day as many as a 100,000 men
11 : 49 When the men of the city saw
11 : 61 but the men of Gaza shut him out
11 : 69 Then the men in ambush emerged from their places and joined battle
11 : 70 All the men with Jonathan fled
11 : 73 When his men who were fleeing saw this
12 : 1 he chose men and sent them to Rome
12 : 27 So when the sun set, Jonathan commanded his men to be alert
12 : 28 that Jonathan and his men were prepared for battle
12 : 29 But Jonathan and his men did not know it until morning
12 : 34 to the men whom Demetrius had sent
12 : 41 with 40,000 picked fighting men
12 : 45 and choose for yourself a few men to stay with you
12 : 47 He kept with himself 3,000 men
12 : 48 the men of Ptolemais closed the gates and seized him
12 : 50 and had perished along with his men
12 : 53 and blot out the memory of them from among men
13 : 21 Now the men in the citadel kept sending envoys to Trypho
13 : 34 Simon also chose men and sent them to Demetrius the king
13 : 44 The men in the siege engine leaped out into the city
13 : 45 The men in the city, with their wives and children
13 : 48 and settled in it men who observed the law
13 : 49 The men in the citadel at Jerusalem
13 : 52 and he and his men dwelt there
14 : 9 Old men sat in the streets
14 : 12 Each man sat under his vine and his fig tree
14 : 14 and did away with every lawless and wicked man
14 : 23 It has pleased our people to receive these men with honour
14 : 32 he armed the men of his nation's forces and paid them wages
14 : 36 as were also the men in the city of David in Jerusalem
14 : 42 and appoint men over its tasks
15 : 3 Whereas certain pestilent men
15 : 21 Therefore if any pestilent men
15 : 26 And Simon sent to Antiochus 2,000 picked men, to fight for him
16 : 6 and when his men saw him, they crossed over after him
16 : 15 he gave them a great banquet, and hid men there
16 : 16 Ptolemy and his men rose up, took their weapons
16 : 19 He sent other men to Gazara to do away with John
16 : 20 and he sent other men to take possession of Jerusalem
16 : 21 and that he has sent men to kill you also
16 : 22 and he seized the men who came to destroy him and killed them
2 Ma 1 : 15 and Antiochus had come with a few men
1 : 16 they threw stones and struck down the leader and his men
3 : 4 But a man named Simon, of the tribe of Benjamin
3 : 11 a man of very prominent position

3 : 17	For terror and bodily trembling had come over the man
3 : 26	2 young men also appeared to him, remarkably strong
3 : 27	his men took him up and put him on a stretcher and carried him away
3 : 28	this man who had just entered the aforesaid treasury
3 : 32	offered sacrifice for the man's recovery
3 : 33	the same young men appeared again to Heliodorus
3 : 34	report to all men the majestic power of God
3 : 36	And he bore testimony to all men
4 : 2	the man who was the benefactor of the city
4 : 9	and to enrol the men of Jerusalem as citizens of Antioch
4 : 12	and he induced the noblest of the young men
4 : 26	was supplanted by another man
4 : 31	leaving Andronicus, a man of high rank, to act as his deputy
4 : 35	were grieved and displeased at the unjust murder of the man
4 : 40	Lysimachus armed about 3,000 men
4 : 40	a man advanced in years and no less advanced in folly
4 : 41	and threw them in wild confusion at Lysimachus and his men
4 : 44	3 men sent by the senate presented the case before him
4 : 47	while he sentenced for death those unfortunate men
5 : 4	Therefore all men prayed
5 : 5	Jason took no less than a 1,000 men
5 : 8	fleeing from city to city, pursued by all men
5 : 18	this man would have been scourged
5 : 22	than the man who appointed him
5 : 24	and commanded him to slay all the grown men
5 : 25	When this man arrived in Jerusalem
5 : 25	he ordered his men to parade under arms
5 : 26	then rushed into the city with his armed men
6 : 6	A man could neither keep the sabbath
6 : 18	a man now advanced in age and of noble presence
6 : 20	as men ought to go who have the courage to refuse things
6 : 21	Those who were in charge of that unlawful sacrifice took the man aside
6 : 26	I should avoid the punishment of men
7 : 12	were astonished at the young man's spirit
7 : 14	One cannot but choose to die at the hands of men
7 : 16	Because you have authority among men, mortal though you are
7 : 21	she fired her woman's reasoning with a man's courage
7 : 23	who shaped the beginning of man
7 : 25	Since the young man would not listen to him at all
7 : 30	While she was still speaking, the young man said
7 : 34	But you, unholy wretch, you most defiled of all men
8 : 1	and so they gathered about 6,000 men
8 : 2	which had been profaned by ungodly men
8 : 8	When Philip saw that the man was gaining ground little by little
8 : 9	a general and a man of experience in military service
8 : 16	But Maccabeus gathered his men together
8 : 22	each to command a division, putting 1,500 men under each
8 : 32	a most unholy man
9 : 2	and Antiochus and his men were defeated
9 : 9	And so the ungodly man's body swarmed with worms
9 : 10	no one was able to carry the man who a little while before
10 : 10	who was the son of that ungodly man
10 : 11	This man, when he succeeded to the kingdom
10 : 16	But Maccabeus and his men
10 : 19	and also Zacchaeus and his men
10 : 20	But the men with Simon, who were moneyhungry
10 : 21	and accused these men
10 : 22	Then he slew these men who had turned traitor
10 : 25	Maccabeus and his men sprinkled dust upon their heads
10 : 29	5 resplendent men on horses with golden bridles
10 : 33	Then Maccabeus and his men were glad
10 : 34	The men within, relying on the strength of the place
10 : 35	20 young men in the army of Maccabeus
11 : 2	gathered about 80,000 men and all his cavalry
11 : 6	When Maccabeus and his men got word
11 : 9	ready to assail not only men but the wildest beasts or walls of iron
11 : 20	I have ordered these men and my representatives
11 : 37	Therefore make haste and send some men
12 : 3	And some men of Joppa did so ungodly a deed
12 : 4	the men of Joppa took them out to sea and drowned them
12 : 5	he gave orders to his men
12 : 8	But learning that the men in Jamnia
12 : 11	After a hard fight Judas and his men won the victory
12 : 14	behaved most insolently toward Judas and his men
12 : 15	But Judas and his men
12 : 19	more than 10,000 men
12 : 20	set men in command of the divisions
12 : 22	so that often they were injured by their own men
12 : 23	and destroyed as many as 30,000 men
12 : 24	and Sosipater and their men
12 : 27	Stalwart young men took their stand before the walls
12 : 35	But a certain Dositheus, one of Bacenor's men
12 : 35	who was on horseback and was a strong man
12 : 35	wishing to take the accursed man alive
12 : 36	As Esdris and his men had been fighting for a long time and were weary
12 : 37	then he charged against Gorgias' men

12 : 39	Judas and his men went to take up the bodies of the fallen
12 : 40	that this was why these men had fallen
12 : 43	He also took up a collection, man by man
13 : 1	In the 149th year word came to Judas and his men
13 : 4	that this man was to blame for all the trouble
13 : 6	any man guilty of sacrilege or notorious for other crimes
13 : 14	and exhorting his men to fight nobly to the death
13 : 15	He gave his men the watchword, God's victory
13 : 15	and with a picked force of the bravest young men
13 : 15	and slew as many as 2,000 men in the camp
13 : 21	But Rhodocus, a man from the ranks of the Jews
13 : 22	attacked Judas and his men, was defeated
14 : 1	3 years later, word came to Judas and his men
14 : 13	with orders to kill Judas and scatter his men
14 : 18	and his men and their courage in battle for their country
14 : 22	Judas posted armed men in readiness at key places
14 : 24	he was warmly attached to the man
14 : 27	and, provoked by the false accusations of that depraved man
14 : 28	when the man had done no wrong
14 : 30	So he gathered not a few of his men
14 : 31	that he had been cleverly outwitted by the man
14 : 31	and commanded them to hand the man over
14 : 32	that they did not know where the man was whom he sought
14 : 37	as a man who loved his fellow citizens
15 : 1	When Nicanor heard that Judas and his men
15 : 6	over Judas and his men
15 : 8	And he exhorted his men
15 : 12	Onias, who had been high priest, a noble and good man
15 : 13	Then likewise a man appeared
15 : 14	This is a man who loves the brethren
15 : 25	Nicanor and his men advanced with trumpets and battle songs
15 : 26	and Judas and his men met the enemy in battle
15 : 27	they laid low no less than 35,000 men
15 : 30	And the man who was ever in body and soul
15 : 30	the man who maintained his youthful good will
15 : 32	and that profane man's arm

1 Es	1 : 21	and the men of Judah and all of Israel
	1 : 32	and the principal men, with the women
	1 : 34	And the men of the nation took Jeconiah the son of Josiah
	1 : 53	These slew their young men with the sword around their holy temple
	1 : 53	and did not spare young man or virgin
	1 : 53	old man or child, for he gave them all into their hands
	2 : 6	and let each man, wherever he may live
	2 : 6	be helped by the men of his place with gold and silver
	2 : 27	and that the men in it were given to rebellion and war
	2 : 28	to prevent these men from building the city
	3 : 4	Then the 3 young men of the bodyguard
	3 : 16	And he said, Call the young men
	3 : 22	When men drink they forget to be friendly with friends and brothers
	3 : 24	since it forces men to do these things ?
	4 : 2	Gentlemen, are not men strongest
	4 : 7	And yet he is only one man !
	4 : 14	Gentlemen, is not the king great, and are not men many
	4 : 16	and women brought up the very men who plant the vineyards
	4 : 17	Women make men's clothes
	4 : 17	they bring men glory
	4 : 17	men cannot exist without women
	4 : 18	If men gather gold and silver or any other beautiful thing
	4 : 20	A man leaves his own father who brought him up
	4 : 23	A man takes his sword, and goes out to travel
	4 : 25	A man loves his wife more than his father or his mother
	4 : 26	Many men have lost their minds because of women
	4 : 37	women are unrighteous, all the sons of men are unrighteous
	4 : 39	All men approve her deeds
	4 : 58	When the young man went out
	5 : 4	These are the names of the men who went up
	5 : 7	These are the men of Judea who came up
	5 : 9	The number of the men of the nation and their leaders :
	5 : 18	The men of Netophah, 55
	5 : 18	The men of Anathoth, 158
	5 : 18	The men of Bethasmoth, 42
	5 : 19	The men of Kiriatharim, 25
	5 : 19	The men of Chephirah and Beeroth, 743
	5 : 20	The men of Ramah and Geba, 621
	5 : 21	The men of Michmas, 122
	5 : 21	The men of Bethel, 52
	5 : 39	And when the genealogy of these men
	5 : 47	they gathered as one man in the square
	5 : 49	in accordance with the directions in the book of Moses the man of God
	5 : 58	as one man pressing forward the work on the house of God
	5 : 63	old men who had seen the former house
	6 : 28	and that full effort be made to help the men
	6 : 29	a portion be scrupulously given to these men
	8 : 27	and I gathered men from Israel to go up with me
	8 : 28	These are the principal men
	8 : 30	and with him a 150 men enrolled
	8 : 31	and with him 200 men

	8 : 32	and with him 300 men
	8 : 32	and with him 250 men
	8 : 33	and with him 70 men
	8 : 34	and with him 70 men
	8 : 35	and with him 212 men
	8 : 36	and with him a 160 men
	8 : 37	and with him 28 men
	8 : 38	and with him a 110 men
	8 : 39	and with them 70 men
	8 : 40	and with him 70 men
	8 : 44	who were leaders and men of understanding
	8 : 45	who was the leading man at the place of the treasury
	8 : 46	to send us men to serve as priests
	8 : 47	they brought us competent men of the sons of Mahli
	8 : 48	Hodiah the sons of Hananiah, and their sons, 20 men
	8 : 50	There I proclaimed a fast for the young men before our Lord
	8 : 68	the principal men came to me and said
	8 : 91	men and women and youths
	8 : 92	one of the men of Israel, called out
	9 : 4	and the men themselves expelled from the multitude of
	9 : 5	Then the men of the tribe of Judah and Benjamin
	9 : 16	the leading men of their fathers' houses
	9 : 17	And the cases of the men who had foreign wives
	9 : 37	The priests and the Levites and the men of Israel
	9 : 40	for all the multitude, men and women
	9 : 41	in the presence of both men and women
P Ma	7	and repentest over the evils of men
3 Ma	**1** : 3	that a certain insignificant man should sleep in the tent
	1 : 3	that this man incurred the vengeance meant for the king
	1 : 12	Even if those men are deprived of this honour
	1 : 23	and being barely restrained by the old men and the elders
	1 : 29	for it seemed that not only the men
	2 : 2	who are suffering grievously from an impious and profane man
	2 : 5	the men of Sodom who acted arrogantly
	2 : 14	In our downfall this audacious and profane man
	2 : 15	is unapproachable by man
	2 : 17	Do not punish us for the defilement committed by these men
	3 : 2	by men who conspired to do them ill
	3 : 5	they were established in good repute among all men
	4 : 5	For a multitude of grey-headed old men
	4 : 11	When these men had been brought to the place called Schedia
	4 : 13	ordered in his rage that these men
	6 : 25	Who is it that has taken each man from his home
	7 : 6	which we have towards all men
	7 : 9	we always shall have not man but the Ruler over every power
	7 : 15	In that day they put to death more than 300 men
2 Es	**2** : 21	do not ridicule a lame man, protect the maimed
	2 : 21	and let the blind man have a vision of my splendour
	2 : 43	In their midst was a young man of great stature
	2 : 46	Who is that young man who places crowns on them
	3 : 36	Thou mayest indeed find individual men
	5 : 3	and men shall see it desolate
	5 : 12	And at that time men shall hope but not obtain
	5 : 38	except he whose dwelling is not with men ?
	6 : 10	For the beginning of a man is his hand
	6 : 10	and the end of a man is his heel
	6 : 26	And they shall see the men who were taken up
	6 : 39	the sound of man's voice was not yet there
	6 : 46	and thou didst command them to serve man
	7 : 8	so that only one man can walk upon that path
	7 : 9	If now that city is given to a man for an inheritance
	7 : 46	or who among men that has not transgressed thy covenant ?
	7 : 78	that a man shall die
	7 : 127	which every man who is born on earth shall wage
	8 : 34	But what is man, that thou art angry with him
	8 : 44	But man, who has been formed by thy hands
	8 : 59	For the Most High did not intend that men should be destroyed
	8 : 62	I have not shown this to all men
	10 : 14	given her fruit, that is, man, to him who made her
	10 : 22	our free men have suffered abuse
	10 : 22	our righteous men have been carried off
	10 : 22	our young men have been enslaved and our strong men made powerless
	10 : 33	Stand up like a man, and I will instruct you
	10 : 54	for no work of man's building could endure in a place
	11 : 37	and I heard how he uttered a man's voice to the eagle
	13 : 3	this wind made something like the figure of a man come up
	13 : 3	that man flew with the clouds of heaven
	13 : 5	an innumerable multitude of men were gathered together
	13 : 5	to make war against the man who came up out of the sea
	13 : 12	After this I saw the same man come down from the mountain
	13 : 25	As for your seeing a man come up
	13 : 32	whom you saw as a man coming up from the sea
	13 : 33	every man shall leave his own land
	13 : 51	Why did I see the man coming up from the heart of the sea ?
	14 : 9	for you shall be taken up from among men
	14 : 14	cast away from you the burdens of man
	14 : 22	that men may be able to find the path
	14 : 37	So I took the 5 men, as he commanded me
	14 : 42	And the Most High gave understanding to the 5 men

	15 : 16	For there shall be unrest among men
	15 : 17	For a man will desire to go into a city, and shall not be able
	15 : 19	A man shall have no pity upon his neighbours
	15 : 36	and a man's thigh and a camel's hock
	16 : 19	for the correction of men
	16 : 21	that men will imagine that peace is assured for them
	16 : 27	one man will long to see another
	16 : 54	Behold, the Lord knows all the works of men
	16 : 61	who formed man, and put a heart in the midst of his body
	16 : 65	And when your sins come out before men
	16 : 71	They shall be like mad men, sparing no one
4 Ma	**1** : 24	Anger, as a man will see if he reflects on this experience
	2 : 8	Thus, as soon as a man adopts
	2 : 21	Now when God fashioned man
	3 : 21	just at that time certain men attempted
	4 : 1	a political opponent of the noble and good man
	4 : 15	an arrogant and terrible man
	5 : 4	one man, Eleazar by name, leader of the flock
	5 : 4	He was a man of priestly family, learned in the law
	5 : 6	Before I begin to torture you, old man
	6 : 2	First they stripped the old man
	6 : 5	But the courageous and noble man, as a true Eleazar, was unmoved
	6 : 6	yet while the old man's eyes were raised to heaven
	6 : 10	And like a noble athlete the old man, while being beaten
	6 : 30	the holy man died nobly in his tortures
	7 : 4	has ever held out as did that most holy man
	7 : 7	O man in harmony with the law and philosopher of divine life !
	7 : 10	O aged man, more powerful than tortures
	7 : 13	Most amazing, indeed, though he was an old man
	7 : 15	O man of blessed age
	7 : 16	an aged man despised tortures even to death
	7 : 23	For only the wise and courageous man is lord of his emotions
	8 : 2	being unable to compel an aged man to eat defiling foods
	8 : 5	Young men, I admire each and every one of you in a kindly manner
	8 : 5	as that of the old man who has just been tortured
	8 : 19	O men and brothers, should we not fear the instruments of torture
	9 : 6	And if the aged men of the Hebrews because of their religion
	9 : 6	that we young men should die despising your coercive tortures
	10 : 5	Enraged by the man's boldness
	12 : 13	As a man, were you not ashamed, you most savage beast
	12 : 13	to cut out the tongues of men who have feelings like yours
	14 : 9	as we hear of the tribulations of these young men
	14 : 11	that reason had full command over these men in their tortures
	14 : 12	for the mother of the 7 young men bore up
	14 : 20	the mother of the young men
	15 : 23	But devout reason, giving her heart a man's courage
	15 : 30	and more manly than men in endurance !
	16 : 2	that men have ruled over the emotions
	16 : 14	and in word and deed you have proved more powerful than a man
	16 : 17	while an aged man endures such agonies for the sake of religion
	16 : 17	you young men were to be terrified by tortures
	18 : 3	were not only admired by men
	18 : 9	A happy man was he, who lived out his life with good children

MANACLE   1
Sir 21 : 19   and like manacles on his right hand

MANASSEAS   1
1 Es 9 : 31   and Belnuus and Manasseas

MANASSEH   7 = 0.005 %
Jud 8 : 2   Her husband Manasseh, who belonged to her tribe and family
   8 : 7   and her husband Manasseh had left her gold and silver
   10 : 3   which she used to wear while her husband Manasseh was living
   16 : 22   after Manasseh her husband died
   16 : 23   and they buried her in the cave of her husband Manasseh
   16 : 24   to all those who were next of kin to her husband Manasseh
1 Es 9 : 33   and Eliphelet and Manasseh and Shimei

MANFULLY   3 = 0.002 %
1 Ma 6 : 31   but the Jews sallied out and burned these with fire, and fought manfully
2 Ma 6 : 27   Therefore, by manfully giving up my life now
   14 : 43   and manfully threw himself down into the crowd

MANGLE   3 = 0.002 %
Sir 28 : 23   like a leopard it will mangle them
3 Ma 5 : 42   mangled by the knees and feet of the beasts
4 Ma 9 : 15   you are mangling me in this manner

MANHOOD   1
1 Ma 13 : 53   And Simon saw that John his son had reached manhood

MANIFEST, verb   9 = 0.006 %
Wis 1 : 2   and manifests himself to those who do not distrust him
   16 : 21   For thy sustenance manifested thy sweetness toward thy children

Sir	1:7	The knowledge of wisdom – to whom was it manifested ?
2 Ma	14:15	and always upholds his own heritage by manifesting himself
	15:34	blessed the Lord who had manifested himself, saying
P Ma	14	and in me thou wilt manifest thy goodness
3 Ma	5:51	to manifest himself and be merciful to them
	6:4	manifesting the light of your mercy upon the nation of Israel
2 Es	7:35	and the reward shall be manifested

MANIFEST, adj.   15 = 0.010 %

Wis	7:21	I learned both what is secret and what is manifest
Sir	6:22	For wisdom is like her name, and is not manifest to many
	16:16	His mercy is manifest to the whole of creation
L Jr	6:51	It will be manifest to all the nations and kings
1 Ma	11:12	and their enmity became manifest
	15:9	so that your glory will become manifest in all the earth
2 Ma	9:8	making the power of God manifest to all
3 Ma	3:19	By maintaining their manifest ill-will toward us
	5:35	praised the manifest Lord God, King of kings
2 Es	8:54	and in the end the treasure of immortality is made manifest
	9:5	the beginning is evident, and the end manifest
	9:6	the beginnings are manifest in wonders and mighty works
	13:36	And Zion will come and be made manifest to all people, prepared and built
	14:35	and then the names of the righteous will become manifest
	16:73	Then the tested quality of my elect shall be manifest

MANIFESTATION   5 = 0.003 %

2 Ma	3:24	caused so great a manifestation
	12:22	at the manifestation to them of him who sees all things
	15:27	and were greatly gladdened by God's manifestation
3 Ma	2:9	and when you had glorified it by your magnificent manifestation
	5:8	and in a glorious manifestation rescue them

MANIUS   1

2 Ma	11:34	Quintus Memmius and Titus Manius, envoys of the Romans

MANKIND   12 = 0.008 %

Tob	8:6	From them the race of mankind has sprung
Wis	7:6	there is for all mankind one entrance into life
	10:8	but also left for mankind a reminder of their folly
	14:21	And this became a hidden trap for mankind
Sir	45:4	he chose him out of all mankind
L Jr	6:26	revealing to mankind their worthlessness
2 Ma	7:28	Thus also mankind comes into being
2 Es	7:138	not one ten-thousandth of mankind could have life
	8:15	About all mankind thou knowest best
	13:41	where mankind had never lived
4 Ma	11:4	Hater of virtue, hater of mankind
	14:14	Even unreasoning animals, like mankind

MANLINESS   1

2 Ma	15:17	and awaking manliness in the souls of the young

MANLY   1

4 Ma	15:30	and more manly than men in endurance !

MAN-MADE   1

Bel	14:5	He answered, Because I do not revere man-made idols

MANNA   1

2 Es	1:19	I pitied your groaning and gave you manna for food

MANNER*   21 = 0.014 %

Ad E	13:5	perversely following a strange manner of life and laws
Wis	2:15	because his manner of life is unlike that of others
	15:7	making all in like manner
Sir	19:30	and a man's manner of walking, show what he is
	31:17	Be the first to stop eating, for the sake of good manners
2 Ma	10:6	in the manner of the feast of booths
	14:46	This was the manner of his death
	15:12	of modest bearing and gentle manner
3 Ma	4:5	in such a shameful manner
	5:36	The king, however, reconvened the party in the same manner
	6:12	are being deprived of life in the manner of traitors
	7:13	When they had applauded him in fitting manner
	7:19	there too in like manner
2 Es	4:15	And in like manner the waves of the sea also made a plan
4 Ma	4:1	When despite all manner of slander
	6:1	When Eleazar in this manner had made eloquent response
	8:5	Young men, I admire each and every one of you in a kindly manner
	8:8	and by changing your manner of living
	9:15	you are mangling me in this manner
	10:12	When he also had died in a manner worthy of his brothers
	15:4	In what manner might I express

MANSERVANT   3 = 0.002 %

1 Es	5:1	and their menservants and maidservants, and their cattle
	5:41	besides menservants and maidservants, were 42,360
	5:42	their menservants and maidservants were 7,337

MANTLE   2

1 Es	8:71	I rent my garments and my holy mantle
	8:73	with my garments and my holy mantle rent

MANY, indef. pr. or adj.   236 = 0.154 %

Tob	1:3	and I performed many acts of charity to my brethren
	1:16	I performed many acts of charity to my brethren
	1:18	For in his anger he put many to death
	3:5	And now thy many judgments are true
	4:4	Remember, my son, that she faced many dangers for you
	4:8	If you have many possessions
	13:11	Many nations will come from afar to the name of the Lord God
Jud	1:6	Many nations joined the forces of the Chaldeans
	4:13	for the people fasted many days throughout Judea
	5:9	with much gold and silver and very many cattle
	5:18	they were utterly defeated in many battles
	8:11	unless the Lord turns and helps us within so many days
	11:16	as many as shall hear about them
	16:22	Many desired to marry her
Ad E	13:2	writes thus : Having become ruler of many nations
	16:2	the more proud do many men become
	16:5	And often many of those who are set in places of authority
Wis	6:2	and boast of many nations
	18:12	by the one form of death, had corpses too many to count
Sir	pr.	Whereas many great teachings have been given to us
	1:24	and the lips of many will tell of his good sense
	3:19	Many are lofty and renowned
	3:24	For their hasty judgment has led many astray
	6:6	Let those that are at peace with you be many
	6:22	For wisdom is like her name, and is not manifest to many
	8:2	for gold has ruined many
	9:8	many have been misled by a woman's beauty
	11:5	Many kings have had to sit on the ground
	11:6	Many rulers have been greatly disgraced
	11:10	My son, do not busy yourself with many matters
	11:13	and raises up his head, so that many are amazed at him
	11:29	for many are the wiles of the crafty
	11:32	From a spark of fire come many burning coals
	13:22	If a rich man slips, his helpers are many
	16:5	Many such things my eye has seen
	16:17	Among so many people I shall not be known
	20:8	Whoever uses too many words will be loathed
	20:14	for he has many eyes instead of one
	20:17	How many will ridicule him, and how often !
	23:11	A man who swears many oaths will be filled with iniquity
	27:1	Many have committed sin for a trifle
	27:24	I have hated many things, but none to be compared to him
	28:13	for he has destroyed many who were at peace
	28:14	Slander has shaken many
	28:18	Many have fallen by the edge of the sword
	28:18	but not so many as have fallen because of the tongue
	29:4	Many persons regard a loan as a windfall
	29:7	many have refused to lend
	29:18	Being surety has ruined many men who were prosperous
	30:23	for sorrow has destroyed many, and there is no profit in it
	31:6	Many have come to ruin because of gold
	31:18	If you are seated among many persons
	31:25	for wine has destroyed many
	34:7	For dreams have deceived many
	34:9	An educated man knows many things
	34:11	I have seen many things in my travels
	35:1	He who keeps the law makes many offerings
	37:19	A man may be shrewd and the teacher of many
	37:31	Many have died of gluttony
	39:9	Many will praise his understanding
	40:15	The children of the ungodly will not put forth many branches
	42:6	and where there are many hands, lock things up
	43:32	Many things greater than these lie hidden
	45:9	with very many golden bells round about
	47:24	Their sins became exceedingly many
	51:3	from the many afflictions that I endured
Bar	1:12	and we shall serve them many days and find favour in their sight
	4:12	Let no one rejoice over me, a widow and bereaved of many
	4:35	For fire will come upon her from the Everlasting for many days
L Jr	6:3	you will remain there for many years
P Az	13	as many as the stars of heaven
1 Ma	1:2	He fought many battles, conquered strongholds
	1:3	and plundered many nations
	1:9	and so did their sons after them for many years
	1:9	and they caused many evils on the earth
	1:11	and misled many, saying, Let us go and make a covenant
	1:11	for since we separated from them many evils have come upon us
	1:18	and many were wounded and fell
	1:30	and destroyed many people of Israel

	1:43	Many even from Israel gladly adopted his religion
	1:52	Many of the people, every one who forsook the law, joined them
	1:62	But many in Israel stood firm
	2:16	Many from Israel came to them
	2:18	with silver and gold and many gifts
	2:29	Then many who were seeking righteousness and justice
	2:32	Many pursued them, and overtook them
	3:7	He embittered many kings, but he made Jacob glad by his deeds
	3:11	Many were wounded and fell, and the rest fled
	3:18	Judas replied, It is easy for many to be hemmed in by few
	3:18	there is no difference between saving by many or by few
	5:6	and many people with Timothy as their leader
	5:7	He engaged in many battles with them
	5:12	for many of us have fallen
	5:21	and fought many battles against the Gentiles
	5:22	and as many as 3,000 of the Gentiles fell
	5:26	Many of them have been shut up in Bozrah and Bosor
	5:34	As many as 8,000 of them fell that day
	5:60	as many as 2,000 of the people of Israel fell that day
	6:9	He lay there for many days
	6:24	as many of us as they have caught
	6:31	and for many days they fought and built engines of war
	6:51	Then he encamped before the sanctuary for many days
	6:52	and fought for many days
	7:19	And he sent and seized many of the men
	8:10	Many of them were wounded and fell
	8:11	as many as ever opposed them, they destroyed and enslaved
	8:12	and as many as have heard of their fame have feared them
	9:2	and they took it and killed many people
	9:6	and many slipped away from the camp
	9:17	and many on both sides were wounded and fell
	9:20	they mourned many days and said
	9:22	have not been recorded, for they were very many
	9:39	to meet them with tambourines and musicians and many weapons
	9:40	Many were wounded and fell, and the rest fled to the mountain
	9:64	he fought against it for many days and made machines of war
	9:69	and he killed many of them
	10:28	We will grant you many immunities and give you gifts
	10:60	he gave them and their friends silver and gold and many gifts
	11:1	and many ships
	11:20	and he built many engines of war to use against it
	11:27	and in as many other honours as he had formerly had
	11:40	and he stayed there many days
	11:47	and they killed on that day as many as a 100,000 men
	11:65	and fought against it for many days and hemmed it in
	11:74	As many as 3,000 of the foreigners fell that day
	12:13	many afflictions and many wars have encircled us
	13:26	and mourned for him many days
	13:49	and many of them perished from famine
	15:4	and those who have devastated many cities in my kingdom
	15:29	and you have taken possession of many places in my kingdom
	16:2	so that we have delivered Israel many times
	16:8	and many of them were wounded and fell
2 Ma	1:20	But after many years had passed, when it pleased God
	1:35	he exchanged many excellent gifts
	2:27	However, to secure the gratitude of many
	3:26	inflicting many blows on him
	4:35	but many also of other nations
	4:39	When many acts of sacrilege
	4:39	because many of the gold vessels had already been stolen
	4:42	As a result, they wounded many of them, and killed some
	5:9	and he who had driven many from their own country into exile died in exile
	5:10	He who had cast many to lie unburied
	5:14	and as many were sold into slavery as were slain
	5:18	that they were involved in many sins
	6:24	lest many of the young should suppose
	9:6	with many and strange inflictions
	9:16	all of them, many times over
	12:12	Judas, thinking that they might really be useful in many ways
	12:23	and destroyed as many as 30,000 men
	12:25	And when with many words
	12:28	and killed as many as 25,000 of those who were within it
	13:8	because he had committed many sins
	13:15	and slew as many as 2,000 men in the camp
1 Es	1:49	committed many acts of sacrilege and lawlessness
	2:9	from many whose hearts were stirred
	4:14	Gentlemen, is not the king great, and are not men many
	4:26	Many men have lost their minds because of women
	4:27	Many have perished, or stumbled, or sinned, because of women
	5:64	while many came with trumpets and a joyful noise
	6:14	And the house was built many years ago
	8:11	Let as many as are so disposed, therefore
P Ma	10	I am weighted down with many an iron fetter
3 Ma	1:5	and many captives also were taken
	2:6	by inflicting many and varied punishments
	2:13	that because of our many and great sins
	2:26	and many of his friends
	5:37	How many times, you poor wretch

	6:5	showing your power to many nations
2 Es	1:10	For their sake I have overthrown many kings
	2:48	how great and many are the wonders of the Lord God
	3:12	they produced children and peoples and many nations
	3:25	This was done for many years
	3:29	and my soul has seen many sinners during these 30 years
	4:7	How many dwellings are in the heart of the sea
	4:7	or how many streams are at the source of the deep
	4:7	or how many streams are above the firmament
	4:34	but the Highest hastens on behalf of many
	5:7	and one whom the many do not know
	5:8	There shall be chaos also in many places
	5:10	and it shall be sought by many but shall not be found
	5:28	And now, O Lord, why hast thou given over the one to the many
	5:28	and scattered thine only one among the many ?
	6:17	and its sound was like the sound of many waters
	7:20	Let many perish who are now living
	7:47	but torments to many
	7:51	For whereas you have said that the righteous are not many but few
	7:110	and many others prayed for many ?
	8:1	The Most High made this world for the sake of many
	8:3	Many have been created, but few shall be saved
	8:33	For the righteous, who have many works laid up with thee
	8:41	For just as the farmer sows many seeds upon the ground
	8:50	For many miseries will affect those
	9:10	For as many as did not acknowledge me in their lifetime
	9:11	and as many as scorned my law while they still had freedom
	10:9	over so many who have come into being upon her
	10:24	and lay aside your many sorrows
	10:38	for the Most High has revealed many secrets to you
	10:57	For you are more blessed than many
	12:7	and if I have been accounted righteous before thee beyond many others
	12:23	and they shall renew many things in it
	13:13	Then many people came to him
	13:26	this is he whom the Most High has been keeping for many ages
	13:50	And then he will show them very many wonders
	14:4	where I kept him with me many days
	14:5	and I told him many wondrous things
	14:24	But prepare for yourself many writing tablets
	15:29	The nations of the dragons of Arabia shall come out with many chariots
	16:18	the beginning of famine, when many shall perish
	16:22	For many of those who live on the earth shall perish by famine
	16:70	For in many places and in neighbouring cities
4 Ma	1:7	I could prove to you from many and various examples
	1:14	how many kinds of emotions there are
	1:21	The emotions of both pleasure and pain have many consequences
	1:28	so there are many offshoots of these plants
	3:7	and together with the soldiers of his nation had slain many of them
	3:21	and caused many and various disasters
	5:4	And when many persons had been rounded up
	5:4	advanced in age, and known to many in the tyrant's court
	7:4	No city besieged with many ingenious war machines
	7:18	But as many as attend to religion with a whole heart
	10:1	and many repeatedly urged him
	11:20	O contest befitting holiness, in which so many of us brothers
	12:6	who had been bereaved of so many sons
	15:5	Considering that mothers are the weaker sex and give birth to many
	15:7	and because of the many pains she suffered with each of them
	15:11	Nevertheless, though so many factors influenced the mother
	15:20	with many spectators of the torturings
	15:22	How great and how many torments the mother then suffered
	16:4	But the mother quenched so many and such great emotions by devout reason
	16:6	O how wretched am I and many times unhappy !
	16:8	In vain, my sons, I endured many birth-pangs for you
	16:10	Alas, I who had so many and beautiful children
	16:10	am a widow and alone, with many sorrows
	18:15	Many are the afflictions of the righteous

MANY-HEADED   1

4 Ma 7:14 he rendered the many-headed rack ineffective

MARCH, subst.   2

1 Ma 6:33 and took his army by a forced march
2 Ma 12:10 on their march against Timothy

MARCH, verb   18 = 0.012 %

Jud	2:21	They marched for 3 days from Nineveh
Wis	4:2	and throughout all time it marches crowned in triumph
1 Ma	5:58	and they marched against Jamnia
	11:67	Early in the morning they marched to the plain of Hazor
	12:32	and marched through all that region
	12:33	Simon also went forth and marched through the country
	12:50	and kept marching in close formation, ready for battle

13:20	But Simon and his army kept marching along opposite him	
14:1	and marched into Media to secure help	
16:4	and they marched against Cendebaeus	
16:5	Early in the morning they arose and marched into the plain	
2 Ma 4:22	Then he marched into Phoenicia	
12:26	Then Judas marched against Carnaim	
12:27	he marched also against Ephron	
3 Ma 4:5	forced to march at a swift pace	
5:43	and would also march against Judea	
4 Ma 4:22	He speedily marched against them	
18:5	he left Jerusalem and marched against the Persians	

MARCH away 3 = 0.002 %
1 Ma 6:32	Then Judas marched away from the citadel
7:10	So they marched away and came with a large force
12:25	So he marched away from Jerusalem

MARCH forth 1
| 1 Ma 12:40 | and he marched forth and came to Beth-shan |

MARCH off 4 = 0.003 %
1 Ma 5:66	Then he marched off to go into the land of the Philistines
9:4	then they marched off and went to Berea
13:22	He marched off and went into the land of Gilead
2 Ma 3:35	he marched off with his forces to the king

MARCH on 1
| 1 Ma 5:36 | From there he marched on and took Chaspho |

MARCH out 8 = 0.005 %
Jud 1:4	so that his armies could march out in force
1 Ma 3:57	Then the army marched out
9:11	Then the army of Bacchides marched out from the camp
10:2	and marched out to meet him in battle
11:15	Ptolemy marched out and met him with a strong force
2 Ma 12:19	marched out and destroyed those whom Timothy had left in the stronghold
13:13	he determined to march out
3 Ma 1:1	and marched out to the region near Raphia

MARCHING 1
| 1 Ma 6:41 | by the marching of the multitude |

MARISA 2
| 1 Ma 5:66 | and passed through Marisa |
| 2 Ma 12:35 | so Gorgias escaped and reached Marisa |

MARK, subst. 4 = 0.003 %
Wis 8:21	and it was a mark of insight to know whose gift she was
Sir 13:26	The mark of a happy heart is a cheerful face
1 Ma 1:15	and removed the marks of circumcision
8:14	or worn purple as a mark of pride

MARK, verb 4 = 0.003 %
Sir 36:23	If kindness and humility mark her speech
43:6	to mark the times and to be an everlasting sign
2 Ma 2:6	Some of those who followed him came up to mark the way
2 Es 2:23	commit them to the grave and mark it

MARKET 4 = 0.003 %
Tob 2:3	and thrown into the market place
Jud 1:14	plundered its markets, and turned its beauty into shame
2 Ma 3:4	about the administration of the city market
1 Es 2:18	repairing its market places and walls

MARRIAGE 17 = 0.011 %
Tob 3:17	in marriage to Tobias the son of Tobit
6:10	I will suggest that she be given to you in marriage
6:12	we will celebrate the marriage
6:15	for this very night she will be given to you in marriage
11:19	and Tobias marriage was celebrated for 7 days
Wis 7:2	from the seed of a man and the pleasure of marriage
13:17	and his marriage and children
14:24	either their lives or their marriages pure
14:26	disorder in marriage, adultery, and debauchery
Sir 7:25	Give a daughter in marriage
23:18	A man who breaks his marriage vows says to himself
1 Ma 10:58	and Ptolemy gave him Cleopatra his daughter in marriage
11:9	and I will give you in marriage my daughter
1 Es 8:84	Therefore do not give your daughters in marriage to their sons
3 Ma 1:19	Those women who had recently been arrayed for marriage
4:8	spent the remaining days of their marriage festival in lamentations
2 Es 9:47	I set a day for the marriage feast

MARRIED 3 = 0.002 %
Sir 26:22	and a married woman as a tower of death to her lovers
3 Ma 4:6	to share married life
4 Ma 16:9	others married and without offspring

MARRY 17 = 0.011 %
Tob 1:9	When I became a man I married Anna
4:12	and do not marry a foreign woman
Jud 16:22	Many desired to marry her
Ad E 10:6	the river is Esther, whom the king married and made queen
Sir 42:9	when she is young, lest she do not marry
42:9	or if married, lest she be hated
42:10	or, though married, lest she be barren
2 Ma 1:14	For under pretext of intending to marry her
14:25	And he urged him to marry and have children
14:25	so he married, settled down, and shared the common life
1 Es 5:38	the sons of Hakkoz, the sons of Jaddus who had married Agia
8:70	For they and their sons have married the daughters of these people
8:92	and have married foreign women from the peoples of the land
9:7	You have broken the law and married foreign women
9:36	All these had married foreign women
2 Es 16:44	them that marry, like those who will have no children
16:44	and them that do not marry, like those who are widowed

MARSH 2
| 1 Ma 9:42 | they returned to the marshes of the Jordan |
| 9:45 | with marsh and thicket |

MARSHAL, verb 2
| Jud 2:16 | as a great army is marshalled for a campaign |
| Sir 17:32 | He marshals the host of the height of heaven |

MARVEL, subst. 1
| Sir 17:9 | And he gave them to boast of his marvels for ever |

MARVEL, verb 13 = 0.008 %
Jud 10:19	And they marvelled at her beauty
10:23	they all marvelled at the beauty of her face
11:20	and they marvelled at her wisdom and said
Wis 11:14	at the end of the events they marvelled at him
Sir 43:18	The eye marvels at the beauty of its whiteness
43:24	and we marvel at what we hear
47:17	and for your interpretations, the countries marvelled at you
2 Ma 1:22	a great fire blazed up, so that all marvelled
3 Ma 1:10	he marvelled at the good order of the temple
2 Es 4:26	and if you live long, you will often marvel
4 Ma 1:11	marvelled at their courage and endurance
9:26	While all were marvelling at his courageous spirit
17:17	The tyrant himself and all his council marvelled at their endurance

MARVELLOUS, MARVELOUS 12 = 0.008 %
Jud 11:8	thoroughly informed and marvellous in military strategy
Wis 10:17	she guided them along a marvellous way
19:8	after gazing on marvellous wonders
Sir 38:6	that he might be glorified in his marvellous works
39:20	and nothing is marvellous to him
42:17	to recount all his marvellous works
43:2	is a marvellous instrument, the work of the Most High
43:25	For in it are strange and marvellous works
43:29	and marvellous is his power
48:14	so in death his deeds were marvellous
P Az 20	Deliver us in accordance with thy marvellous works
2 Ma 15:13	and of marvellous majesty and authority

MARVELLOUSLY, MARVELOUSLY 3 = 0.002 %
Jud 10:14	she was in their eyes marvellously beautiful
Sir 43:8	increasing marvellously in its phases
2 Ma 3:30	who had acted marvellously for his own place

MASIAH 1
| 1 Es 5:34 | the sons of Sarothie, the sons of Masiah, the sons of Gas |

MASK 1
| 4 Ma 15:15 | and the flesh of the head to the chin exposed like masks |

MASON 1
| 1 Es 5:54 | And they gave money to the masons and the carpenters |

MASS, subst. 4 = 0.003 %
2 Ma 2:24	because of the mass of material
3 Ma 2:7	And when he pursued them with chariots and a mass of troops
5:41	it is crowded with masses of people
5:46	with countless masses of people

MASSACRE 1
| 2 Ma 12:6 | and massacred those who had taken refuge there |

MASSING 1
| 2 Ma 5:3 | brandishing of shields, massing of spears |

MASTER, subst., adj. 21 = 0.014 %
| Jud 2:14 | So Holofernes left the presence of his master |
| 5:20 | Now therefore, my master and lord |

	6:13	and returned to their master
	11:10	Therefore, my lord and master
	13:1	and shut out the attendants from his master's presence
Ad E	13:2	and master of the whole world
	14:12	O King of the gods and Master of all dominion !
Wis	10:14	and authority over his masters
	18:11	The slave was punished with the same penalty as the master
Sir	3:7	he will serve his parents as his masters
	19:21	When a servant says to his master
	28:22	It will not be master over the godly
	32:1	If they make you master of the feast, do not exalt yourself
	38:27	So too is every craftsman and master workman
2 Ma	2:29	For as the master builder of a new house
1 Es	4:3	he is their lord and master
	4:14	Who then is their master, or who is their lord ?
2 Es	7:104	or a son his father, or a master his servant
4 Ma	1:29	each of which the master cultivator, reason, weeds and prunes
	2:24	that if reason is master of the emotions
	18:2	knowing that devout reason is master of all emotions

MASTER, verb   7 = 0.005 %

4 Ma	1:4	it is also clear that it masters
	5:23	so that we master all pleasures and desires
	6:34	when it masters even external agonies
	6:35	And I have proved not only that reason has mastered agonies
	6:35	but also that it masters pleasures
	13:4	for the brothers mastered both emotions and pains
	14:1	but also mastered the emotions of brotherly love

MASTERLESS   1

Sir 20:32   than a masterless charioteer of one's own life

MASTERY   1

Sir 9:2   so that she gains mastery over your strength

MASTIC   1

Sus 13:54   He answered, Under a mastic tree

MATCH   2

1 Ma	6:52	The Jews also made engines of war to match theirs
	10:71	and let us match strength with each other there

MATERIAL   4 = 0.003 %

2 Ma	1:21	And when the materials for the sacrifices were presented
	1:31	And when the materials of the sacrifice were consumed
	1:33	had burned the materials of the sacrifice
	2:24	because of the mass of material

MATTANIAH   1

1 Es 9:27   Of the sons of Elam : Mattaniah and Zechariah

MATTATHIAH   1

1 Es 9:43   and beside him stood Mattathiah, Shema, Anaiah, Azariah

MATTATHIAS   14 = 0.009 %

1 Ma	2:1	In those days Mattathias the son of John, son of Simeon
	2:14	And Mattathias and his sons rent their clothes
	2:16	and Mattathias and his sons were assembled
	2:17	Then the king's officers spoke to Mattathias as follows :
	2:19	But Mattathias answered and said in a loud voice :
	2:24	When Mattathias saw it, he burned with zeal
	2:27	Then Mattathias cried out in the city with a loud voice
	2:39	When Mattathias and his friends learned of it
	2:45	And Mattathias and his friends went about
	2:49	Now the days drew near for Mattathias to die
	11:70	except Mattathias the son of Absalom and Judas the son of Chalphi
	14:29	Simon the son of Mattathias
	16:14	and he went down to Jericho with Mattathias and Judas his sons
2 Ma	14:19	Therefore he sent Posidonius and Theodotus and Mattathias

MATTATTAH   1

1 Es 9:33   Of the sons of Hashum : Mattenai and Mattattah and Zabad

MATTENAI   1

1 Es 9:33   Of the sons of Hashum : Mattenai and Mattattah and Zabad

MATTER   48 = 0.031 %

Tob	7:8	and let the matter be settled
Ad E	10:5	For I remember the dream that I had concerning these matters
	16:7	which we hand on as from investigation of matters close at hand
Wis	11:17	out of formless matter
	15:13	when he makes from earthy matter fragile vessels and graven images
Sir	3:23	for matters too great for human understanding
	5:15	In great or small matters do not act amiss
	11:9	Do not argue about a matter which does not concern you
	11:10	My son, do not busy yourself with many matters
	15:15	and to act faithfully is a matter of your own choice
	31:15	and in every matter be thoughtful

	37:11	pay no attention to these in any matter of counsel
1 Ma	3:48	to inquire into those matters about which the Gentiles
	10:35	or annoy any of them about any matter
	10:63	about any matter
2 Ma	1:33	When this matter became known
	1:34	the king investigated the matter
	2:26	it is no light matter but calls for sweat and loss of sleep
	2:30	to occupy the ground and to discuss matters from every side
	11:17	and have asked about the matters indicated therein
	11:20	And concerning these matters and their details
	11:36	But as to the matters which he decided
	13:13	and decide the matter by the help of God
	14:9	with the details of this matter
	15:17	but to attack bravely, and to decide the matter
	15:37	This, then, is how matters turned out with Nicanor
1 Es	2:20	we think it best not to neglect such a matter
	8:12	in order to look into matters in Judea and Jerusalem
	8:70	and from the beginning of this matter
	9:13	over this matter
	9:14	undertook the matter on these terms
	9:16	they began their sessions to investigate the matter
3 Ma	1:4	and matters were turning out rather in favour of Antiochus
	3:2	While these matters were being arranged
	3:8	and expected that matters would change
	4:19	he was clearly convinced about the matter
	5:27	inquired what the matter was
	5:30	his whole mind had been deranged in regard to these matters
	5:40	and again revoking your decree in the matter ?
	5:46	and urged the king on to the matter at hand
2 Es	4:35	ask about these matters, saying
	10:31	What is the matter with you ? And why are you troubled ?
	13:56	and explain weighty and wondrous matters to you
4 Ma	1:16	Wisdom, next, is the knowledge of divine and human matters
	1:17	by which we learn divine matters reverently
	2:9	In all other matters
	4:5	On receiving authority to deal with this matter
	5:20	to transgress the law in matters either small or great

MATTITHIAH   1

1 Es 9:35   Mattithiah, Zabad, Iddo, Joel, Benaiah

MATURE, adj.   1

1 Ma 16:3   and you by His mercy are mature in years

MATURITY   3 = 0.002 %

Wis	3:16	But children of adulterers will not come to maturity
	4:5	The branches will be broken off before they come to maturity
4 Ma	18:9	In the time of my maturity I remained with my husband

MAXIM   1

Sir 8:8   but busy yourself with their maxims

MAY   290 = 0.189 %

ME   435 = 0.283 %

MEADOW   1

2 Es 15:42   and grass of the meadows, and their grain

MEAL, subst.   5 = 0.003 %

Sir	25:18	Her husband takes his meals among the neighbours
	31:21	get up in the middle of the meal
	41:19	Be ashamed of selfish behaviour at meals
L Jr	6:30	Women serve meals for gods of silver and gold and wood
2 Ma	6:21	of the sacrificial meal

MEALTIME   1

Sus 13:13   They said to each other, Let us go home, for it is mealtime

MEAN, adj.   3 = 0.002 %

Sir	14:5	If a man is mean to himself, to whom will he be generous ?
	14:6	No one is meaner than the man who is grudging to himself
	14:9	and mean injustice withers the soul

MEAN, verb   11 = 0.007 %

Jud	12:18	because my life means more to me today
Ad E	16:23	it may mean salvation for us and the loyal Persians
2 Ma	1:36	which means purification
	5:11	he took it to mean that Judea was in revolt
	12:8	meant in the same way to wipe out the Jews
	14:7	I mean the high priesthood – and have now come here
	14:14	would mean prosperity for themselves
1 Es	5:66	they came to find out what the sound of the trumpets meant
3 Ma	1:3	that this man incurred the vengeance meant for the king
2 Es	10:25	While I was wondering what this meant
4 Ma	1:2	I mean, of course, rational judgment

MEAN, subst.   15 = 0.010 %

Wis	11:17	did not lack the means to send upon them
	12:27	being punished by means of them

	15:12	for he says one must get money however one can, even by base means
	18:8	For by the same means by which thou didst punish our enemies
Sir	8:13	Do not give surety beyond your means
	12:5	lest by means of it he subdue you
	14:11	My son, treat yourself well, according to your means
	33:3	as an inquiry by means of Urim
1 Ma	14:10	and furnished them with the means of defence
3 Ma	1:11	the king was by no means persuaded
	2:24	he by no means repented
	3:1	and put to death by the most cruel means
	4:19	to contrive a means of escape
4 Ma	1:19	since by means of it reason rules over the emotions
	4:24	When, by means of his decrees

MEANING   4 = 0.003 %
Sir	39:3	he will seek out the hidden meanings of proverbs
2 Es	7:127	This is the meaning of the contest
	10:40	This therefore is the meaning of the vision
	12:8	the interpretation and meaning of this terrifying vision

MEANWHILE   1
| 3 Ma | 1:24 | Meanwhile the crowd, as before, was engaged in prayer |

MEASURE*, subst.   12 = 0.008 %
Wis	11:20	by measure and number and weight
Sir	1:16	To fear the Lord is wisdom's full measure
Bar	3:18	whose labours are beyond measure ?
2 Ma	4:21	and he took measures for his own security
	6:14	until they have reached the full measure of their sins
1 Es	8:78	And now in some measure mercy has come to us from thee, O Lord
	8:95	and we are with you to take strong measures
2 Es	4:5	or measure for me a measure of wind
	4:37	and measured the times by measure
	4:37	until that measure is fulfilled
	6:4	and before the measures of the firmaments were named
	8:21	whose throne is beyond measure

MEASURE, verb   7 = 0.005 %
Wis	4:8	nor measured by number of years
Sir	6:15	and no scales can measure his excellence
	18:5	Who can measure his majestic power ?
2 Es	4:5	or measure for me a measure of wind
	4:37	and measured the times by measure
	9:1	He answered me and said, Measure carefully in your mind
	16:57	who has measured the sea and its contents

MEASURE out   1
| Jud | 7:21 | because it was measured out to them to drink |

MEAT   7 = 0.005 %
2 Ma	6:21	and privately urged him to bring meat of his own providing
2 Es	9:24	and taste no meat and drink no wine, but eat only flowers
4 Ma	5:8	the very excellent meat of this animal ?
	5:14	to eat meat unlawfully
	5:26	meats that would be contrary to this
	6:15	We will set before you some cooked meat
	10:1	to save himself by tasting the meat

MEDDLE   2
| Sir | 3:23 | Do not meddle in what is beyond your tasks |
| | 41:22 | of meddling with his maidservant |

MEDE   4 = 0.003 %
Jud	1:1	who ruled over the Medes in Ecbatana
	16:10	the Medes were daunted at her daring
1 Ma	1:1	had defeated Darius, king of the Persians and the Medes
2 Es	1:3	who was a captive in the country of the Medes

MEDEBA   1
| 1 Ma | 9:36 | But the sons of Jambri from Medeba came out |

MEDIA   19 = 0.012 %
Tob	1:14	So I used to go into Media
	1:14	and once at Rages in Media I left 10 talents of silver
	1:15	so that I could no longer go into Media
	3:7	On the same day, at Ecbatana in Media
	4:1	which he had left in trust with Gabael at Rages in Media
	4:20	at Rages in Media
	5:5	Can you go with me to Rages in Media ?
	9:2	and go to Gabael at Rages in Media
	11:15	that had happened to him in Media
	14:4	Go to Media, my son
	14:4	But in Media there will be peace for a time
	14:14	He died in Ecbatana of Media at the age of a 127 years
1 Ma	6:56	had returned from Persia and Media
	8:8	the country of Nidia and Media and Lydia
	14:1	and marched into Media to secure help
	14:2	When Arsaces the king of Persia and Media heard

1 Es	3:1	and all the nobles of Media and Persia
	3:14	Then he sent and summoned all the nobles of Persia and Media
	6:23	And in Ecbatana, the fortress which is in the country of Media

MEDICINE   1
| Sir | 38:4 | The Lord created medicines from the earth |

MEDIOCRE   1
| 2 Ma | 15:38 | if it is poorly done and mediocre |

MEDITATE   4 = 0.003 %
Wis	12:22	so that we may meditate upon thy goodness when we judge
Sir	6:37	and meditate at all times on his commandments
	14:20	Blessed is the man who meditates on wisdom
	39:7	and meditate on his secrets

MEEK   2
| Sir | 3:19 | but to the meek he reveals his secrets |
| 2 Es | 11:42 | for you have afflicted the meek and injured the peaceable |

MEEKNESS   3 = 0.002 %
Sir	1:27	and he delights in fidelity and meekness
	3:17	My son, perform your tasks in meekness
	45:4	He sanctified him through faithfulness and meekness

MEET   62 = 0.040 %
Tob	7:1	Sarah met them and greeted them
	11:9	Then Anna ran to meet them, and embraced her son
	11:16	Then Tobit went out to meet his daughter-in-law
Jud	5:4	refused to come out and meet me ?
	10:11	and an Assyrian patrol met her
	15:9	And when they met her they all blessed her with one accord
Wis	6:16	and meets them in every thought
	19:5	but they themselves might meet a strange death
Sir	9:3	Do not go to meet a loose woman
	15:2	She will come to meet him like a mother
	19:29	and a sensible man is known by his face, when you meet him
	31:6	and their destruction has met them face to face
	36:9	and may those who harm thy people meet destruction
	40:23	A friend or a companion never meets one amiss
Sus	13:14	But turning back, they met again
1 Ma	3:11	When Judas learned of it, he went out to meet him
	3:16	Judas went out to meet him with a small company
	3:17	But when they saw the army coming to meet them
	4:29	and Judas met them with 10,000 men
	5:25	They encountered the Nabateans, who met them peaceably
	5:39	And Judas went to meet them
	5:59	to meet them in battle
	7:30	and he was afraid of him and would not meet him again
	7:31	he went out to meet Judas in battle near Capharsalama
	7:43	So the armies met in battle
	9:39	to meet them with tambourines and musicians and many weapons
	10:2	and marched out to meet him in battle
	10:39	to meet the necessary expenses of the sanctuary
	10:49	The 2 kings met in battle
	10:53	I met him in battle
	10:56	but meet me at Ptolemais, so that we may see one another
	10:58	Alexander the king met him
	10:59	Then Alexander the king wrote to Jonathan to come to meet him
	10:60	So he went with pomp to Ptolemais and met the 2 kings
	10:71	come down to the plain to meet us
	10:74	and Simon his brother met him to help him
	10:86	and the men of the city came out to meet him with great pomp
	11:2	and went to meet him
	11:2	for Alexander the king had commanded them to meet him
	11:6	Jonathan met the king at Joppa with pomp
	11:15	Ptolemy marched out and met him with a strong force
	11:22	but to meet him for a conference at Ptolemais
	11:60	When he came to Askalon, the people of the city met him
	11:64	He went to meet them
	11:68	and behold, the army of the foreigners met him in the plain
	11:68	but they themselves met him face to face
	12:25	and met them in the region of Hamath
	12:41	Jonathan went out to meet him
	16:5	was coming to meet them
2 Ma	3:7	When Apollonius met the king
	5:8	Finally he met a miserable end
	5:12	to cut down relentlessly every one they met
	8:14	before he ever met them
	10:35	and with savage fury cut down every one they met
	13:8	he met his death in ashes
	14:21	And the leaders set a day on which to meet by themselves
	15:26	and Judas and his men met the enemy in battle
1 Es	9:4	and that if any did not meet there
Ps 151	6	I went out to meet the Philistine
3 Ma	5:2	so that the Jews might meet their doom
	6:30	to meet their destruction
	7:14	any whom they met of their fellow-countrymen

MEETING 2
2 Ma 14 : 5   when he was invited by Demetrius to a meeting of the council
14 : 30   and was meeting him more rudely than had been his custom

MEGIDDO 1
1 Es 1 : 29   He joined battle with him in the plain of Megiddo

MEHIDA 1
1 Es 5 : 32   the sons of Mehida, the sons of Cutha

MELCHIAS 1
1 Es 9 : 32   Of the sons of Annan : Elionas and Asaias and Melchias

MELCHIEL 1
Jud 6 : 15   and Charmis the son of Melchiel

MELODIOUS 3 = 0.002 %
Wis 17 : 18   or a melodious sound of birds in widespreading branches
3 Ma 7 : 16   in words of praise and all kinds of melodious songs
4 Ma 10 : 21   a tongue that has been melodious with divine hymns

MELODY 5 = 0.003 %
Sir 32 : 6   is the melody of music with good wine
40 : 21   The flute and the harp make pleasant melody
47 : 9   to make sweet melody with their voices
50 : 18   in sweet and full-toned melody
4 Ma 15 : 21   Neither the melodies of sirens nor the songs of swans

MELT 11 = 0.007 %
Jud 16 : 15   at thy presence the rocks shall melt like wax
Wis 16 : 22   Snow and ice withstood fire without melting
16 : 27   was melted when simply warmed by a fleeting ray of the sun
16 : 29   will melt like wintry frost, and flow away like waste water
19 : 21   nor did they melt the crystalline
19 : 21   easily melted kind of heavenly food
Sir 38 : 28   the breath of the fire melts his flesh
L Jr 6 : 20   but men say their hearts have melted
1 Ma 4 : 32   melt the boldness of their strength
2 Es 13 : 4   all who heard his voice melted as wax melts

MELT away 2
Sir 3 : 15   as frost in fair weather, your sins will melt away
2 Es 8 : 23   and whose indignation makes the mountains melt away

MEMBER 7 = 0.005 %
Tob 1 : 9   a member of our family
3 Ma 1 : 11   because not even members of their own nation
2 Es 8 : 8   and dost furnish it with members
8 : 10   thou hast commanded that from the members themselves
4 Ma 9 : 14   and though broken in every member
10 : 20   we let our bodily members be mutilated
11 : 10   and all his members were disjointed

MEMMIUS 1
2 Ma 11 : 34   Quintus Memmius and Titus Manius, envoys of the Romans

MEMOIR 1
2 Ma 2 : 13   and in the memoirs of Nehemiah

MEMORIAL 7 = 0.005 %
Sir 38 : 11   and a memorial portion of fine flour
44 : 9   And there are some who have no memorial
45 : 16   incense and a pleasing odour as a memorial portion
Bar 4 : 5   Take courage, my people, O memorial of Israel !
1 Ma 8 : 22   as a memorial of peace and alliance :
13 : 29   for a permanent memorial
2 Ma 6 : 31   and a memorial of courage

MEMORIZE 1
2 Ma 2 : 25   we have aimed to please those who are inclined to memorize

MEMORY 16 = 0.010 %
Wis 4 : 1   for in the memory of virtue is immortality
4 : 19   and the memory of them will perish
11 : 12   and a groaning at the memory of what had occurred
Sir 10 : 17   and has extinguished the memory of them from the earth
23 : 26   She will leave her memory for a curse
35 : 7   and the memory of it will not be forgotten
39 : 9   his memory will not disappear
45 : 1   Moses, whose memory is blessed
46 : 11   may their memory be blessed !
49 : 1   The memory of Josiah is like a blending of incense
49 : 13   The memory of Nehemiah also is lasting
1 Ma 3 : 7   and his memory is blessed for ever
3 : 35   he was to banish the memory of them from the place
12 : 53   and blot out the memory of them from among men
2 Ma 7 : 20   and worthy of honourable memory
2 Es 14 : 40   *for my spirit retained its memory*

MEMPHIS 1
Jud 1 : 10   even beyond Tanis and Memphis, and all who lived in Egypt

MENELAUS 17 = 0.011 %
2 Ma 4 : 23   After a period of 3 years Jason sent Menelaus
4 : 27   And Menelaus held the office
4 : 29   Menelaus left his own brother Lysimachus
4 : 32   But Menelaus, thinking he had obtained a suitable opportunity
4 : 34   Therefore Menelaus, taking Andronicus aside
4 : 39   with the connivance of Menelaus
4 : 43   Charges were brought against Menelaus about this incident
4 : 45   But Menelaus, already as good as beaten
4 : 47   Menelaus, the cause of all the evil
4 : 50   But Menelaus, because of the cupidity of those in power
5 : 5   Menelaus took refuge in the citadel
5 : 15   guided by Menelaus, who had become a traitor
5 : 23   and besides these Menelaus
11 : 29   Menelaus has informed us that you wish to return home
11 : 32   And I have also sent Menelaus to encourage you
13 : 3   Menelaus also joined them
13 : 7   that Menelaus the lawbreaker died

MENESTHEUS 2
2 Ma 4 : 4   and that Apollonius, the son of Menestheus
4 : 21   When Apollonius the son of Menestheus was sent to Egypt

MENSTRUATION 1
L Jr 6 : 29   Sacrifices to them may be touched by women in menstruation or at childbirth

MENSTRUOUS 2
Ad E 14 : 16   I abhor it like a menstruous rag
2 Es 5 : 8   and menstruous women shall bring forth monsters

MENTAL 2
4 Ma 1 : 32   Some desires are mental, other are physical
2 : 2   because by mental effort he overcame sexual desire

MENTION, verb 10 = 0.007 %
2 Ma 4 : 1   The previously mentioned Simon
4 : 23   the brother of the previously mentioned Simon
14 : 8   For through the folly of those whom I have mentioned
3 Ma 2 : 25   abetted by the previously mentioned drinking companions and comrades
4 : 14   not for the hard labour that has been briefly mentioned before
4 : 17   But after the previously mentioned interval of time
2 Es 5 : 40   Just as you cannot do one of the things that were mentioned
7 : 87   which is worse than all the ways that have been mentioned
7 : 98   which is greater than all that have been mentioned
13 : 21   the things which you have mentioned

MERAIOTH 1
2 Es 1 : 2   son of Amariah, son of Azariah, son of Meraioth

MERARI 2
Jud 8 : 1   she was the daughter of Merari the son of Ox
16 : 7   but Judith the daughter of Merari undid him

MERCENARY 5 = 0.003 %
1 Ma 4 : 35   he departed to Antioch and enlisted mercenaries
6 : 29   mercenary forces came to him from other kingdoms
15 : 3   and have recruited a host of mercenary troops
2 Ma 10 : 14   he maintained a force of mercenaries
10 : 24   gathered a tremendous force of mercenaries

MERCHANT 5 = 0.003 %
Sir 26 : 29   A merchant can hardly keep from wrongdoing
37 : 11   with a merchant about barter or with a buyer about selling
42 : 5   of profit from dealing with merchants
Bar 3 : 23   the merchants of Merran and Teman
2 Ma 8 : 34   who had brought the 1,000 merchants to buy the Jews

MERCIFUL 27 = 0.018 %
Tob 6 : 17   and cry out to the merciful God
7 : 12   The merciful God will guide you both for the best
11 : 17   that God had been merciful to him
14 : 9   and be merciful and just, so that it may be well with you
Wis 11 : 23   But thou art merciful to all, for thou canst do all things
Sir 2 : 11   For the Lord is compassionate and merciful
48 : 20   But they called upon the Lord who is merciful
50 : 19   before him who is merciful
1 Ma 2 : 57   David, because he was merciful
2 Ma 1 : 24   who art awe-inspiring and strong and just and merciful
8 : 29   and besought the merciful Lord
11 : 9   and they all together praised the merciful God
13 : 12   and had besought the merciful Lord with weeping and fasting
1 Es 8 : 53   and we found him very merciful
P Ma 7   and very merciful
3 Ma 5 : 7   their merciful God and Father, praying
5 : 51   to manifest himself and be merciful to them

2 Es	2:31	for I am merciful, says the Lord Almighty
	7:132	that the Most High is now called merciful
	8:31	but thou, because of us sinners, art called merciful
	8:32	then thou wilt be called merciful
	8:36	when thou art merciful to those
	10:24	so that the Mighty One may be merciful to you again
4 Ma	6:28	Be merciful to your people
	8:14	and whatever justice you revere will be merciful to you
	9:24	may become merciful to our nation
	12:17	to be merciful to our nation

MERCILESS
2

Wis	12:5	their merciless slaughter of children
Sir	37:11	or with a merciless man about kindness

MERCY
102 = 0.066 %

Tob	3:2	all thy deeds and all thy ways are mercy and truth
	6:17	and he will save you and have mercy on you
	8:4	and let us pray that the Lord may have mercy upon us
	8:7	Grant that I may find mercy
	8:16	but thou hast treated us according to thy great mercy
	8:17	Show them mercy, O Lord
	8:17	in health and happiness and mercy
	11:15	For thou hast afflicted me, but thou hast had mercy upon me
	13:2	For he afflicts, and he shows mercy
	13:5	and again he will show mercy
	13:6	who knows if he will accept you and have mercy on you ?
	13:9	but again he will show mercy to the sons of the righteous
	14:5	But God will again have mercy on them
	14:7	will rejoice, showing mercy to our brethren
Jud	7:30	by that time the Lord our God will restore to us his mercy
	13:14	Praise God, who has not withdrawn his mercy
	16:15	but to those who fear thee thou wilt continue to show mercy
Ad E	13:6	without pity or mercy
	13:17	Hear my prayer, and have mercy upon thy inheritance
Wis	3:9	because grace and mercy are upon his elect
	4:15	that God's grace and mercy are with his elect
	6:6	For the lowliest man may be pardoned in mercy
	9:1	O God of my fathers and Lord of mercy
	11:9	though they were being disciplined in mercy
	12:22	and when we are judged we may expect mercy
	15:1	and ruling all things in mercy
	16:10	for thy mercy came to their help and healed them
Sir	2:7	You who fear the Lord, wait for his mercy
	2:9	for everlasting joy and mercy
	2:18	for as his majesty is, so also is his mercy
	5:6	Do not say, His mercy is great
	5:6	for both mercy and wrath are with him
	16:11	For mercy and wrath are with the Lord
	16:12	As great as his mercy, so great is also his reproof
	16:14	He will make room for every act of mercy
	16:16	His mercy is manifest to the whole of creation
	17:29	How great is the mercy of the Lord
	18:5	And who can fully recount his mercies ?
	18:11	and pours out his mercy upon them
	28:4	Does he have no mercy toward a man like himself
	29:1	He that shows mercy will lend to his neighbour
	35:19	and makes them rejoice in his mercy
	35:20	Mercy is as welcome when he afflicts them
	36:1	Have mercy upon us, O Lord, the God of all
	36:12	Have mercy, O Lord, upon the people called by thy name
	44:10	But these were men of mercy
	45:1	From his descendants the Lord brought forth a man of mercy
	47:22	But the Lord will never give up his mercy
	50:22	and deals with us according to his mercy
	50:24	May he entrust to us his mercy !
	51:3	in the greatness of thy mercy and of thy name
	51:8	Then I remembered thy mercy, O Lord
	51:29	May your soul rejoice in his mercy
Bar	2:19	we bring before thee our prayer for mercy
	3:2	Hear, O Lord, and have mercy
	4:22	because of the mercy which soon will come to you
	5:9	with the mercy and righteousness that come from him
P Az	12	and do not withdraw thy mercy from us
	15	or to find mercy
	19	but deal with us in thy forbearance and in thy abundant mercy
	67	for his mercy endures for ever
	68	for his mercy endures for ever
1 Ma	3:44	and to pray and ask for mercy and compassion
	4:24	for he is good, for his mercy endures for ever
	13:46	but according to your mercy
	16:3	and you by His mercy are mature in years
2 Ma	2:7	and shows his mercy
	2:18	For we have hope in God that he will soon have mercy upon us
	6:16	Therefore he never withdraws his mercy from us
	7:23	will in his mercy give life and breath back to you again
	7:29	Accept death, so that in God's mercy
	7:37	appealing to God to show mercy soon to our nation
	8:3	and to have mercy on the city which was being destroyed
	8:5	for the wrath of the Lord had turned to mercy

	8:27	and allotted it to them as the beginning of mercy
	9:13	who would no longer have mercy on him
	11:10	for the Lord had mercy on them
1 Es	8:78	And now in some measure mercy has come to us from thee, O Lord
P Ma	6	yet immeasurable and unsearchable is thy promised mercy
	7	and in the multitude of thy mercies
	14	for, unworthy as I am, thou wilt save me in thy great mercy
3 Ma	2:19	and reveal your mercy at this hour
	2:20	Speedily let your mercies overtake us
	6:2	governing all creation with mercy
	6:4	manifesting the light of your mercy upon the nation of Israel
	6:12	watch over us now and have mercy upon us
	6:39	on which the Lord of all most gloriously revealed his mercy
2 Es	1:25	When you beg mercy of me, I will show you no mercy
	2:4	Go, my children, and ask for mercy from the Lord
	2:31	and will show mercy to them
	2:32	and proclaim mercy to them
	4:24	and we are not worthy to obtain mercy
	7:115	Therefore no one will then be able to have mercy on him
	7:132	because he has mercy on those who have not yet come into the world
	8:11	and afterwards thou wilt guide him in thy mercy
	8:45	But spare thy people and have mercy on thy inheritance
	8:45	for thou hast mercy on thy own creation
	11:46	and may hope for the judgment and mercy of him who made it
	12:34	But he will deliver in mercy the remnant of my people
	12:48	and to seek mercy
	14:34	and after death you shall obtain mercy

MERE
3 = 0.002 %

Wis	2:2	Because we were born by mere chance
	11:19	but the mere sight of them could kill by fright
4 Ma	11:13	After he too had died, the 6th, a mere boy, was led in

MERELY
4 = 0.003 %

Tob	12:19	All these days I merely appeared to you
Wis	16:4	while to these it was merely shown
	18:25	for merely to test the wrath was enough
Sir	19:23	but there is a fool who merely lacks wisdom

MEREMOTH
1

1 Es	8:62	to Meremoth the priest, son of Uriah

MERIT
1

Sir	38:17	observe the mourning according to his merit

MERRAN
1

Bar	3:23	the merchants of Merran and Teman

MERRY
6 = 0.004 %

Tob	7:9	And Raguel said to Tobias, Eat, drink, and be merry
	7:11	But for the present be merry
Jud	12:13	and drink wine and be merry with us
	12:17	So Holofernes said to her, Drink now, and be merry with us !
Sir	32:2	that you may be merry on their account
1 Es	5:3	and all their brethren were making merry

MERRYMAKING
1

Sir	31:31	and do not despise him in his merrymaking

MESALOTH
1

1 Ma	9:2	and encamped against Mesaloth in Arbela

MESHULLAM
3 = 0.002 %

1 Es	8:44	Zechariah, and Meshullam
	9:14	and Meshullam and Levi and Shabbethai
	9:30	Of the sons of Bani : Meshullam, Malluch, Adaiah

MESOPOTAMIA
4 = 0.003 %

Jud	2:24	and passed through Mesopotamia
	5:7	At one time they lived in Mesopotamia
	5:8	and they fled to Mesopotamia, and lived there for a long time
	8:26	and what happened to Jacob in Mesopotamia in Syria

MESSAGE
9 = 0.006 %

L Jr	6:1	to give them the message which God had commanded him
1 Ma	5:16	When Judas and the people heard these messages
	5:48	And Judas sent them this friendly message
	7:27	this peaceable message
	10:25	So he sent a message to them in the following words :
	10:51	with the following message :
	10:69	Then he sent the following message
	11:42	And Demetrius sent this message to Jonathan
2 Ma	14:28	When this message came to Nicanor, he was troubled

MESSENGER
12 = 0.008 %

Tob	10:8	and I will send messengers to your father
Jud	1:11	and they sent back his messengers empty-handed and shamefaced

	3 : 1	So they sent messengers to sue for peace, and said
Sir	43 : 26	Because of him his messenger finds the way
1 Ma	1 : 44	And the king sent letters by messengers to Jerusalem
	5 : 14	behold, other messengers, with their garments rent
	7 : 10	and he sent messengers to Judas and his brothers
	7 : 41	When the messengers from the king spoke blasphemy
1 Es	1 : 50	So the God of their fathers sent by his messenger to call them back
	1 : 51	But they mocked his messengers
Ps 151	4	It was he who sent his messenger
2 Es	1 : 40	Zechariah and Malachi, who is also called the messenger of the Lord

MESSIAH   3 = 0.002 %
2 Es	7 : 28	For my son the Messiah shall be revealed
	7 : 29	And after these years my son the Messiah shall die
	12 : 32	this is the Messiah whom the Most High has kept

METHOD   2
Ad E	16 : 9	by changing our methods
2 Ma	13 : 4	by the method which is the custom in that place

MEUNITE   1
1 Es	5 : 31	the sons of Asnah, the sons of the Meunites

MICAH   2
Jud	6 : 15	who in those days were Uzziah the son of Micah
2 Es	1 : 39	and Jacob and Hosea and Amos and Micah

MICHAEL   1
1 Es	8 : 34	Of the sons of Shephatiah, Zeraiah the son of Michael

MICHMAS   1
1 Es	5 : 21	The men of Michmas, 122

MICHMASH   1
1 Ma	9 : 73	And Jonathan dwelt in Michmash

MIDDAY   1
1 Es	9 : 41	from early morning until midday

MIDDLE   10 = 0.007 %
Jud	11 : 19	Then I will lead you through the middle of Judea
Wis	7 : 18	the beginning and end and middle of times
Sir	31 : 21	get up in the middle of the meal
1 Ma	10 : 63	Go forth with him into the middle of the city
2 Ma	14 : 44	a space opened and he fell in the middle of the empty space
3 Ma	5 : 14	But now, since it was nearly the middle of the 10th hour
2 Es	11 : 4	the middle head was larger then the other heads
	11 : 29	the one which was in the middle) awoke
	11 : 33	the middle head also suddenly disappeared
	12 : 21	when the middle of its time draws near

MIDIANITE   1
Jud	2 : 26	He surrounded all the Midianites

MIDNIGHT   1
Jud	12 : 5	and she slept until midnight

MIDST   35 = 0.023 %
Jud	6 : 16	and they set Achior in the midst of all their people
	11 : 19	and I will set your throne in the midst of it
	14 : 19	in the midst of the camp
	16 : 3	and brought me into his camp, in the midst of the people
Wis	4 : 10	therefore he took him quickly from the midst of wickedness
	12 : 5	These initiates from the midst of a heathen cult
	16 : 19	and at another time even in the midst of water
	18 : 15	into the midst of the land that was doomed, a stern warrior
Sir	1 : 30	and cast you down in the midst of the congregation
	9 : 13	Know that you are walking in the midst of snares
	11 : 8	nor interrupt a speaker in the midst of his words
	14 : 27	and will dwell in the midst of her glory
	15 : 5	and will open his mouth in the midst of the assembly
	24 : 1	and will glory in the midst of her people
	42 : 12	and do not sit in the midst of women
	48 : 17	and brought water into the midst of it
	51 : 4	and from the midst of fire which I did not kindle
P Az	1	And they walked about in the midst of the flames
	2	in the midst of the fire he opened his mouth and said :
	27	and made the midst of the furnace like a moist whistling wind
	66	and delivered us from the midst of the burning fiery furnace
	66	from the midst of the fire he has delivered us
Sus	13 : 34	Then the 2 elders stood up in the midst of the people
	13 : 48	Taking his stand in the midst of them, he said
1 Ma	6 : 45	He courageously ran into the midst of the phalanx to reach it
	16 : 7	and placed the horsemen in the midst of the infantry
2 Es	2 : 8	who conceal the unrighteous in your midst !
	2 : 43	In their midst was a young man of great stature
	11 : 10	but from the midst of his body
	12 : 17	but from the midst of his body, this is the interpretation :
	12 : 18	In the midst of the time of that kingdom
	16 : 40	and in the midst of the calamities be like strangers on the earth
	16 : 58	who has enclosed the sea in the midst of the waters
	16 : 61	who formed man, and put a heart in the midst of his body
4 Ma	15 : 23	in the very midst of her emotions

MIEN   1
2 Ma	3 : 25	with a rider of frightening mien

MIGHT   26 = 0.017 %
Jud	4 : 15	they cried out to the Lord with all their might
	5 : 15	and by their might destroyed all the inhabitants of Heshbon
	6 : 3	They cannot resist the might of our cavalry
	9 : 7	Behold now, the Assyrians are increased in their might
	9 : 8	Break their strength by thy might
	9 : 11	nor thy might upon men of strength
	9 : 14	the God of all power and might
	13 : 4	O Lord God of all might
	13 : 8	And she struck his neck twice with all her might
Ad E	14 : 19	O God, whose might is over all
Wis	2 : 11	But let our might be our law of right
	11 : 21	and who can withstand the might of thy arm ?
Sir	3 : 20	For great is the might of the Lord
	6 : 26	and keep her ways with all your might
	7 : 30	With all your might love your Maker
	16 : 7	who revolted in their might
	36 : 3	and let them see thy might
	48 : 24	By the spirit of might he saw the last things
1 Ma	6 : 47	And when the Jews saw the royal might
2 Ma	12 : 28	who with power shatters the might of his enemies
	15 : 24	By the might of thy arm may these blasphemers
3 Ma	3 : 11	and not considering the might of the supreme God
	5 : 13	to show the might of his all-powerful hand
	6 : 12	But you, O Eternal One, who have all might and all power
	6 : 13	in fear of your invincible might, O honoured One
2 Es	15 : 16	they shall in their might have no respect for their king

MIGHTILY   3 = 0.002 %
Ad E	13 : 18	And all Israel cried out mightily
Wis	6 : 6	but mighty men will be mightily tested
	8 : 1	She reaches mightily from one end of the earth to the other

MIGHTY   51 = 0.033 %
Jud	16 : 7	For their mighty one did not fall
Ad E	16 : 16	and are sons of the Most High, the most mighty living God
Wis	5 : 23	a mighty wind will rise against them
	6 : 6	but mighty men will be mightily tested
	6 : 8	But a strict inquiry is in store for the mighty
	18 : 5	and thou didst destroy them all together by a mighty flood
Sir	12 : 6	for the mighty day of their punishment
	13 : 2	nor associate with a man mightier and richer than you
	15 : 18	he is mighty in power and sees everything
	16 : 11	he is mighty to forgive, and he pours out wrath
	18 : 4	and who can search out his mighty deeds ?
	21 : 7	He who is mighty in speech is known from afar
	29 : 13	more than a mighty shield and more than a heavy spear
	34 : 16	a mighty protection and strong support
	36 : 8	and let people recount thy mighty deeds
	46 : 1	Joshua the son of Nun was mighty in war
	46 : 5	He called upon the Most High, the Mighty One
	46 : 6	with hailstones of mighty power
	46 : 6	for he wholly followed the Mighty One
	46 : 16	He called upon the Lord, the Mighty One
	46 : 17	and made his voice heard with a mighty sound
	47 : 5	to slay a man mighty in war
Bar	1 : 4	and in the hearing of the mighty men and the princes
	1 : 9	and the mighty men and the people of the land
	2 : 11	with a mighty hand and with signs and wonders
1 Ma	2 : 42	mighty warriors of Israel
	2 : 66	Judas Maccabeus has been a mighty warrior from his youth
	3 : 38	mighty men among the friends of the king
	4 : 3	But Judas heard of it, and he and his mighty men
	4 : 30	who didst crush the attack of the mighty warrior
	9 : 21	How is the mighty fallen, the saviour of Israel !
	10 : 19	that you are a mighty warrior and worthy to be our friend
2 Ma	7 : 17	Keep on, and see how his mighty power
	11 : 13	because the mighty God fought on their side
1 Es	2 : 27	and that mighty and cruel kings ruled in Jerusalem
	8 : 47	And by the mighty hand of our Lord
	8 : 61	by the mighty hand of our Lord which was upon us
3 Ma	2 : 6	You made known your mighty power
2 Es	2 : 19	and 7 mighty mountains on which roses and lilies grow
	6 : 32	for the Mighty One has seen your uprightness
	9 : 6	the beginnings are manifest in wonders and mighty works
	9 : 45	and we gave great glory to the Mighty One
	10 : 24	so that the Mighty One may be merciful to you again
	11 : 43	and your pride to the Mighty One
	12 : 47	and the Mighty One has not forgotten you in your struggle
	15 : 11	but I will bring them out with a mighty hand
	15 : 40	And great and mighty clouds, full of wrath and tempest

15:51 so that you cannot receive your mighty lovers
16:16 Just as an arrow shot by a mighty archer does not return
4 Ma 7:2 and overwhelmed by the mighty waves of tortures
15:25 she saw mighty advocates

MIJAMIN 1
1 Es 9:26 Malchijah, Mijamin, and Eleazar, and Asibias, and Benaiah

MILDNESS 1
Wis 12:18 Thou who art sovereign in strength dost judge with mildness

MILE 5 = 0.003 %
2 Ma 12:9 so that the glow of the light was seen in Jerusalem, 30 miles distant
12:10 When they had gone more than a mile from there
12:16 so that the adjoining lake, a quarter of a mile wide
12:17 When they had gone 95 miles from there
12:29 which is 75 miles from Jerusalem

MILITARY 4 = 0.003 %
Jud 11:8 thoroughly informed and marvellous in military strategy
1 Ma 15:26 and silver and gold, and much military equipment
2 Ma 8:9 a general and a man of experience in military service
4 Ma 4:5 and a very strong military force

MILK 7 = 0.005 %
Sir 39:26 and iron and salt and wheat flour and milk and honey
46:8 to bring them into their inheritance, into a land flowing with milk and honey
Bar 1:20 to give us a land flowing with milk and honey
3 Ma 5:49 who were drawing their last milk
2 Es 2:19 and the same number of springs flowing with milk and honey
8:10 milk should be supplied
4 Ma 13:21 they drank milk from the same fountains

MILLION 1
1 Es 3:21 and makes every one talk in millions

MINA 5 = 0.003 %
1 Ma 14:24 with a large gold shield weighing a 1,000 minas
15:18 and have brought a gold shield weighing a 1,000 minas
1 Es 5:45 a 1,000 minas of gold
5:45 5,000 minas of silver
3 Ma 1:4 promising to give them each 2 minas of gold

MIND, subst. 94 = 0.061 %
Tob 4:19 and do not let them be blotted out of your mind
Jud 8:14 and find out his mind or comprehend his thought ?
11:10 but keep it in your mind
16:9 Her sandal ravished his eyes, her beauty captivated his mind
Ad E 11:12 and after he awoke he had it on his mind
Wis 4:12 and roving desire perverts the innocent mind
8:17 and thought upon them in my mind
9:15 and this earthly tent burdens the thoughtful mind
19:2 they would change their minds and pursue them
Sir 1:28 do not approach him with a divided mind
3:26 A stubborn mind will be afflicted at the end
3:27 A stubborn mind will be burdened by troubles
3:29 The mind of the intelligent man will ponder a parable
4:3 Do not add to the troubles of an angry mind
6:37 It is he who will give insight to your mind
8:2 and has perverted the minds of kings
11:30 so is the mind of a proud man
12:16 but in his mind he will plan to throw you into a pit
14:21 He who reflects in his mind on her ways
16:20 And no mind will reflect on this
17:5 as 6th he distributed to them the gift of mind
17:6 he gave them ears and a mind for thinking
21:14 The mind of a fool is like a broken jar
21:17 and they will ponder his words in their minds
21:26 The mind of fools is in their mouth
21:26 but the mouth of wise men is in their mind
22:16 so the mind firmly fixed on a reasonable counsel
22:17 A mind settled on an intelligent thought
23:2 and the discipline of wisdom over my mind !
25:23 A dejected mind, a gloomy face, and a wounded heart
27:6 so the expression of a thought discloses the cultivation of a man's mind
32:12 Amuse yourself there, and do what you have in mind
33:19 lest you change your mind and must ask for it
34:5 and like a woman in travail the mind has fancies
34:6 do not give your mind to them
36:19 so an intelligent mind detects false words
36:20 A perverse mind will cause grief
40:5 his sleep at night confuses his mind
40:6 he is troubled by the visions of his mind
42:15 I will now call to mind the works of the Lord
43:18 and the mind is amazed at its falling
Sus 13:9 And they perverted their minds
1 Ma 3:31 He was greatly perplexed in mind

2 Ma 4:46 induced the king to change his mind
5:21 because his mind was elated
14:20 and it appeared that they were of one mind
15:8 but to keep in mind the former times
1 Es 3:18 It leads astray the minds of all who drink it
3:19 It makes equal the mind of the king and the orphan
4:26 Many men have lost their minds because of women
3 Ma 1:25 to change his arrogant mind
4:1 for the inveterate enmity which had long ago been in their minds
4:16 with a mind alienated from truth and with a profane mouth
5:28 for he had implanted in the king's mind
5:30 his whole mind had been deranged in regard to these matters
5:39 wondering at his instability of mind
5:42 took no account of the changes of mind
5:47 So he, when he had filled his impious mind with a deep rage
2 Es 4:11 how then can your mind comprehend the way of the Most High ?
5:33 Are you greatly disturbed in mind over Israel ?
7:16 And why have you not considered in your mind what is to come
7:62 if the mind is made out of the dust
7:63 so that the mind might not have been made from it
7:64 But now the mind grows with us
7:71 for you have said that the mind grows with us
9:1 He answered me and said, Measure carefully in your mind
10:31 and the thoughts of your mind troubled ?
10:36 Or is my mind deceived, and my soul dreaming ?
12:3 Then I awoke in great perplexity of mind and great fear
12:5 Behold, I am still weary in mind
13:16 For as I consider it in my mind
13:30 And bewilderment of mind shall come
14:34 If you, then, will rule over your minds
4 Ma 1:15 Now reason is the mind that with sound logic prefers the life of wisdom
1:35 checked by the temperate mind
2:1 the desires of the mind for the enjoyment of beauty
2:16 For the temperate mind repels all these malicious emotions
2:18 the temperate mind is able to get the better of the emotions
2:22 but at the same time he enthroned the mind among the senses
2:23 To the mind he gave the law
3:3 No one of us can eradicate anger from the mind
3:17 For the temperate mind can conquer the drives of the emotions
5:11 adopt a mind appropriate to your years
7:5 For in setting his mind firm like a jutting cliff
8:29 all with one voice together, as from one mind, said :
9:15 Most abominable tyrant, enemy of heavenly justice, savage of mind
11:14 but I am their equal in mind
11:25 to change our mind or to force us to eat defiling foods
13:4 The supremacy of the mind over these cannot be overlooked
14:6 in harmony with the guidance of the mind
14:11 since the mind of a woman despised even more diverse agonies
14:20 she was of the same mind as Abraham
15:4 a wondrous likeness both of mind and of form
16:13 but, as though having a mind like adamant

MIND, verb 1
1 Es 8:16 And whatever you and your brethren are minded to do

MINDFUL 3 = 0.002 %
Tob 2:2 who is mindful of the Lord
Sir 4:25 but be mindful of your ignorance
2 Es 16:20 nor be always mindful of the scourges

MINE, poss. pr. 6 = 0.004 %

MINE, subst. 1
1 Ma 8:3 to get control of the silver and gold mines there

MINGLE 1
2 Es 13:11 All these were mingled together

MINGLING 1
2 Ma 14:38 when there was no mingling with the Gentiles

MINISTER, subst. 1
Sir 7:30 and do not forsake his ministers

MINISTER, verb 10 = 0.007 %
Tob 1:7 who ministered at Jerusalem
Jud 4:14 who stood before the Lord and ministered to the Lord
11:13 who minister in the presence of our God at Jerusalem
Wis 16:21 and the bread, ministering to the desire of the one who took it
Sir 4:14 Those who serve her will minister to the Holy One
24:10 In the holy tabernacle I ministered before him
45:15 to minister to the Lord and serve as priest
1 Ma 10:42 because it belongs to the priests who minister there
1 Es 1:5 who minister before your brethren the people of Israel
4:54 garments in which they were to minister

MINISTRY
1

Wis **18** : 21   he brought forward the shield of his ministry

MINT
1

1 Ma **15** : 6   I permit you to mint your own coinage

MIRROR
2

Wis **7** : 26   a spotless mirror of the working of God
Sir **12** : 11   and you will be to him like one who has polished a mirror

MIRTH
2

Bar **2** : 23   the voice of mirth and the voice of gladness
1 Es **3** : 20   It turns every thought to feasting and mirth

MISDEED
1

4 Ma **2** : 12   so that one punishes them for misdeeds

MISERABLE
9 = 0.006 %

Wis **3** : 11   for whoever despises wisdom and instruction is miserable
      13 : 10   But miserable, with their hopes set on dead things
      15 : 14   But most foolish, and more miserable than an infant
Sir **29** : 24   It is a miserable life to go from house to house
      30 : 17   Death is better than a miserable life
2 Ma **5** : 8   Finally he met a miserable end
3 Ma **4** : 4   and shed tears at the most miserable expulsion of these people
      5 : 49   the end of their most miserable suspense
2 Es **15** : 47   woe to you, miserable wretch !

MISERABLY
2

2 Es **7** : 120   but we have miserably failed ?
4 Ma **12** : 4   will be miserably tortured and die before your time

MISERY
5 = 0.003 %

Sir **11** : 27   The misery of an hour makes one forget luxury
Bar **2** : 25   They perished in great misery
2 Ma **6** : 9   One could see, therefore, the misery that had come upon them
2 Es **8** : 50   For many miseries will affect those
      15 : 15   For the sword and misery draw near them

MISFORTUNE
13 = 0.008 %

Wis **14** : 21   because men, in bondage to misfortune or to royal authority
1 Ma **3** : 42   Now Judas and his brothers saw that misfortunes had increased
      3 : 59   than to see the misfortunes of our nation
2 Ma **4** : 1   and had been the real cause of the misfortune
      5 : 6   is the greatest misfortune
      5 : 20   shared in the misfortunes that befell the nation
      10 : 4   that they might never again fall into such misfortunes
      12 : 30   and their kind treatment of them in times of misfortune
      14 : 8   our whole nation is now in no small misfortune
      14 : 14   thinking that the misfortunes and calamities of the Jews
3 Ma **4** : 12   to lament bitterly the ignoble misfortune of their brothers
2 Es **10** : 43   and as for her telling you about the misfortune of her son
      10 : 48   and that misfortune had overtaken her

MISGUIDED
1

Sir **16** : 23   a senseless and misguided man thinks foolishly

MISHAEL
6 = 0.004 %

P Az   66   Bless the Lord, Hananiah, Azariah, and Mishael
1 Ma **2** : 59   Hananiah, Azariah and Mishael believed
1 Es **9** : 44   and on his left Pedaiah, Mishael, Malchijah
4 Ma **16** : 3   nor was the raging fiery furnace of Mishael so intensely hot
      16 : 21   and Hananiah, Azariah, and Mishael were hurled into the fiery furnace
      18 : 12   and he taught you about Hananiah, Azariah, and Mishael in the fire

MISLEAD
3 = 0.002 %

Wis **15** : 4   For neither has the evil intent of human art misled us
Sir **9** : 8   many have been misled by a woman's beauty
1 Ma **1** : 11   and misled many, saying, Let us go and make a covenant

MISPAR
1

1 Es **5** : 8   Bilshan, Mispar, Reeliah, Rehum, and Baanah, their leaders

MISREPRESENT
1

2 Ma **3** : 11   To such an extent the impious Simon had misrepresented the facts

MISS
2

Jud **14** : 15   with his head cut off and missing
2 Es **16** : 13   and will not miss when they begin to be shot

MISSILE
2

2 Ma **5** : 3   hurling of missiles, the flash of golden trappings
      12 : 27   and great stores of war engines and missiles were there

MISSION
2

2 Ma **3** : 37   to send on another mission to Jerusalem
      4 : 11   who went on the mission to establish friendship

MISSPENT
1

Wis **15** : 8   With the misspent toil

MISSTEP
1

Sir **9** : 13   But if you approach him, make no misstep

MIST
5 = 0.003 %

Wis **2** : 4   and be scattered like mist that is chased
Sir **24** : 3   and covered the earth like a mist
      43 : 22   A mist quickly heals all things
2 Es **4** : 24   and our life is like a mist
      7 : 61   for it is they who are now like a mist

MISTAKE
2

Sir **23** : 3   in order that my mistakes may not be multiplied
1 Es **8** : 75   and our mistakes have mounted up to heaven

MITHRIDATES
2

1 Es **2** : 11   he gave them to Mithridates his treasurer
      2 : 16   Bishlam, Mithridates, Tabeel, Rehum, Beltethmus

MIX
6 = 0.004 %

Sir **18** : 15   My son, do not mix reproach with your good deeds
Bel **14** : 11   and mix and place the wine
2 Ma **15** : 39   while wine mixed with water is sweet and delicious
1 Es **8** : 70   and the holy race has been mixed with the alien peoples of the land
      8 : 87   by mixing with the uncleanness of the peoples of the land
3 Ma **5** : 45   by the very fragrant draughts of wine mixed with frankincense

MIXED
1

Jud **2** : 20   Along with them went a mixed crowd like a swarm of locusts

MIZPAH
2

1 Ma **3** : 46   So they assembled and went to Mizpah, opposite Jerusalem
      3 : 46   because Israel formerly had a place of prayer in Mizpah

MOAB
3 = 0.002 %

Jud **1** : 12   all the inhabitants of the land of Moab
      5 : 2   So he called together all the princes of Moab
      5 : 22   and from Moab insisted that he must be put to death

MOABITE
3 = 0.002 %

Jud **6** : 1   said to Achior and all the Moabites
      7 : 8   and all the leaders of the Moabites
1 Es **8** : 69   the Jebusites, the Moabites, the Egyptians, and the Edomites

MOB
1

Sir **26** : 5   The slander of a city, the gathering of a mob

MOBILE
1

Wis **7** : 24   For wisdom is more mobile than any motion

MOCHMUR
1

Jud **7** : 18   toward Acraba, which is near Chusi beside the brook Mochmur

MOCK
4 = 0.003 %

Ad E **14** : 11   and do not let them mock at our downfall
Wis **12** : 25   thou didst send thy judgment to mock them
1 Ma **7** : 34   But he mocked them and derided them and defiled them
1 Es **1** : 51   But they mocked his messengers

MOCKERY
1

Sir **27** : 28   Mockery and abuse issue from the proud man

MOCKING
1

Sir **33** : 6   A stallion is like a mocking friend

MOCKINGLY
1

Wis **11** : 14   For though they had mockingly rejected him

MODEIN
9 = 0.006 %

1 Ma **2** : 1   moved from Jerusalem and settled in Modein
      2 : 15   came to the city of Modein to make them offer sacrifice
      2 : 23   to offer sacrifice upon the altar in Modein
      2 : 70   and was buried in the tomb of his fathers at Modein
      9 : 19   and buried him in the tomb of their fathers at Modein
      13 : 25   and buried him in Modein, the city of his fathers
      13 : 30   This is the tomb which he built in Modein
      16 : 4   and camped for the night in Modein
2 Ma **13** : 14   he pitched his camp near Modein

MODERATE
1

Sir **31** : 20   Healthy sleep depends on moderate eating

MODERATION
3 = 0.002 %

Sir	**31**:27	Wine is like life to men, if you drink it in moderation
2 Ma	**4**:37	because of the moderation and good conduct of the deceased
	9:27	and will treat you with moderation and kindness

MODEST
5 = 0.003 %

Sir	**26**:15	A modest wife adds charm to charm
	26:24	but a modest daughter will even be embarrassed
	32:10	and approval precedes a modest man
2 Ma	**15**:12	of modest bearing and gentle manner
4 Ma	**8**:3	handsome, modest, noble, and accomplished in every way

MODESTY
1

3 Ma	**1**:19	and, neglecting proper modesty

MOETH
1

1 Es	**8**:63	and Moeth the son of Binnui, the Levites

MOIST
1

P Az	**27**	and made the midst of the furnace like a moist whistling wind

MOISTEN
1

3 Ma	**6**:6	moistening the fiery furnace with dew

MOLEST
1

2 Ma	**11**:31	and none of them shall be molested in any way

MOMENT
15 = 0.010 %

Tob	**3**:17	At that very moment Tobit returned and entered his house
Jud	**13**:9	after a moment she went out
	14:8	until the moment of her speaking to them
Ad E	**10**:11	And these 2 lots came to the hour and moment and day
Sir	**1**:23	A patient man will endure until the right moment
	1:24	He will hide his words until the right moment
	3:31	at the moment of his falling he will find support
	18:24	and of the moment of vengeance when he turns away his face
	20:7	A wise man will be silent until the right moment
	20:7	but a braggart and fool sleep beyond the right moment
	40:7	at the moment of his rescue he wakes up
2 Ma	**6**:25	for the sake of living a brief moment longer
	9:11	for he was tortured with pain every moment
3 Ma	**5**:49	they thought that this was their last moment of life
2 Es	**16**:38	there will not be a moment's delay

MONARCH
6 = 0.004 %

Wis	**6**:9	To you then, O monarchs, my words are directed
	6:21	O monarchs over the peoples
	8:15	dread monarchs will be afraid of me when they hear of me
	12:14	nor can any king or monarch confront thee
	14:16	and at the command of monarchs graven images were worshipped
	14:17	When men could not honour monarchs in their presence

MONEY
53 = 0.035 %

Tob	**2**:11	Then my wife Anna earned money at women's work
	4:1	On that day Tobit remembered the money
	4:2	so that I may explain to him about the money before I die ?
	5:2	but how can I obtain the money when I do not know the man ?
	5:3	and go and get the money
	5:18	Do not add money to money
	9:2	and get the money for me
	9:5	and Gabael brought out the money bags with their seals intact
	10:2	and there is no one to give him the money ?
	10:10	and half of his property in slaves, cattle, and money
	10:10	he cured my wife, he obtained the money for me
Wis	**15**:12	for he says one must get money however one can, even by base means
Sir	**7**:18	Do not exchange a friend for money
	18:33	Do not become a beggar by feasting with borrowed money
	21:8	A man who builds his house with other people's money
	29:5	in speaking of his neighbour's money
	29:6	If he does not, the borrower has robbed him of his money
	31:5	and he who pursues money will be led astray by it
	51:25	Get these things for yourselves without money
Bar	**1**:6	and they collected money, each giving what he could
	1:10	And they said : Herewith we send you money
	1:10	so buy with the money burnt offerings and sin offerings
L Jr	**6**:28	and use the money
	6:35	Likewise they are not able to give either wealth or money
1 Ma	**3**:29	Then he saw that the money in the treasury was exhausted
	8:26	arms, money, or ships, as Rome has decided
	8:28	arms, money, or ships, as Rome has decided
	10:43	because he owes money to the king or has any debt
	13:15	It is for the money
	13:17	but he sent to get the money and the sons
	13:18	Because Simon did not send him the money and the sons, he perished
	14:32	He spent great sums of his own money
	15:6	as money for your country
	15:30	and the tribute money of the places
	15:31	and the tribute money of the cities, 500 talents more
2 Ma	**3**:6	that the treasury in Jerusalem was full of untold money
	3:7	he told him of the money about which he had been informed
	3:7	to effect the removal of the aforesaid money
	3:11	and also some money of Hyrcanus, son of Tobias
	3:13	said that this money must in any case be confiscated
	4:1	who had informed about the money against his own country
	4:19	Those who carried the money, however
	4:20	So this money was intended by the sender
	4:23	to carry the money to the king
	4:27	any of the money promised to the king
	8:25	They captured the money
	10:21	of having sold their brethren for money
1 Es	**5**:54	And they gave money to the masons and the carpenters
3 Ma	**2**:32	and by paying money
4 Ma	**2**:8	even though he is a lover of money
	3:20	had both appropriated money to them for the temple service
	4:10	with his armed forces to seize the money

MONEYHUNGRY
1

2 Ma	**10**:20	But the men with Simon, who were moneyhungry

MONEYLENDER
1

Sir	**29**:28	scolding about lodging and the reproach of the moneylender

MONEY-MAKING
1

Wis	**13**:19	for money-making and work and success with his hands

MONSTER
2

3 Ma	**6**:8	in the belly of a huge, sea-born monster
2 Es	**5**:8	and menstruous women shall bring forth monsters

MONSTROUS
2

Wis	**17**:15	and now were driven by monstrous spectres
3 Ma	**4**:11	which had been built with a monstrous perimeter wall

MONTH
53 = 0.035 %

Jud	**2**:1	In the 18th year, on the 22nd day of the first month
	3:10	and remained for a whole month
	8:4	for 3 years and 4 months
	16:20	before the sanctuary for 3 months
Ad E	**10**:13	So they will observe these days in the month of Adar
	10:13	on the 14th and 15th of that month
	13:6	on the 14th day of the 12th month, Adar
	16:20	so that on the 13th day of the 12th month, Adar
Wis	**7**:2	within the period of 10 months, compacted with blood
Sir	**43**:8	The month is named for the moon
Bar	**1**:2	in the 5th year, on the 7th day of the month
1 Ma	**1**:58	against those found month after month in the cities
	1:59	And on the 25th day of the month
	4:52	Early in the morning on the 25th day of the 9th month
	4:52	which is the month of Chislev
	4:59	beginning with the 25th day of the month of Chislev
	7:43	on the 13th day of the month of Adar
	9:3	In the first month of the 152nd year
	9:54	In the 153rd year, in the 2nd month
	10:21	in the 7th month of the 160th year
	13:51	On the 23rd day of the 2nd month, in the 171st year
	16:14	in the 177th year, in the 11th month, which is the month of Shebat
2 Ma	**1**:9	in the month of Chislev, in the 188th year
	7:27	I carried you 9 months in my womb
	10:5	that is, on the 25th day of the same month, which was Chislev
	15:36	but to celebrate the 13th day of the 12th month
1 Es	**1**:1	he killed the passover lamb on the 14th day of the first month
	1:35	And he reigned 3 months in Judah and Jerusalem
	1:44	and he reigned 3 months and 10 days in Jerusalem
	5:6	in the month of Nisan, the first month
	5:47	When the 7th month came
	5:53	from the new moon of the 7th month
	5:56	in the 2nd month, Zerubbabel the son of Shealtiel
	5:57	on the new moon of the 2nd month
	7:5	by the 23rd day of the month of Adar
	7:10	kept the passover on the 14th day of the first month
	8:6	in the 5th month (this was the king's 7th year)
	8:6	for they left Babylon on the new moon of the first month
	8:6	on the new moon of the 5th month
	8:61	on the 12th day of the first month
	9:5	this was the 9th month
	9:5	on the 20th day of the month
	9:16	and on the new moon of the 10th month
	9:17	by the new moon of the first month
	9:37	On the new moon of the 7th month
	9:40	on the new moon of the 7th month
2 Es	**4**:40	when her 9 months have been completed
	6:21	and women with child shall give birth to premature children at 3 or 4 months
	8:8	and for 9 months the womb which thou hast formed
	16:38	Just as a woman with child, in the 9th month

MONTHLY
1
2 Ma 6 :7   On the monthly celebration of the king's birthday

MONUMENT
3 = 0.002 %
Wis 10 :7   as a monument to an unbelieving soul
1 Ma 13 :27   And Simon built a monument
2 Ma 15 :6   had determined to erect a public monument of victory

MOON
26 = 0.017 %
Jud 8 :6   the day before the new moon and the day of the new moon
Sir 27 :11   but the fool changes like the moon
 39 :12   and I am filled, like the moon at the full
 43 :6   He made the moon also, to serve in its season
 43 :7   From the moon comes the sign for feast days
 43 :8   The month is named for the moon
 50 :6   like the moon when it is full
L Jr 6 :60   For sun and moon and stars, shining and sent forth for service, are obedient
 6 :67   or shine like the sun or give light like the moon
P Az 40   Bless the Lord, sun and moon
1 Ma 10 :34   and new moons and appointed days
1 Es 5 :52   on sabbaths and at new moons
 5 :53   from the new moon of the 7th month
 5 :57   on the new moon of the 2nd month
 8 :6   for they left Babylon on the new moon of the first month
 8 :6   on the new moon of the 5th month
 9 :16   and on the new moon of the 10th month
 9 :17   by the new moon of the first month
 9 :37   On the new moon of the 7th month
 9 :40   on the new moon of the 7th month
2 Es 1 :31   for I have rejected your feast days, and new moons
 5 :4   and the moon during the day
 6 :45   the light of the moon
 7 :39   a day that has no sun or moon or stars
4 Ma 17 :5   The moon in heaven, with the stars

MOOSSIAS
1
1 Es 9 :31   Of the sons of Addi : Naathus and Moossias, Laccunus

MORALE
1
3 Ma 1 :7   he strengthened the morale of his subjects

MORDECAI
10 = 0.007 %
Ad E 10 :4   And Mordecai said, These things have come from God
 11 :2   Mordecai the son of Jair
 11 :12   Mordecai saw in this dream what God had determined to do
 12 :1   Now Mordecai took his rest in the courtyard
 12 :4   and Mordecai wrote an account of them
 12 :5   And the king ordered Mordecai to serve in the court
 12 :6   and he sought to injure Mordecai and his people
 16 :13   asked for the destruction of Mordecai
2 Ma 15 :36   the day before Mordecai's day
1 Es 5 :8   Nehemiah, Seraiah, Resaiah, Bigvai, Mordecai

MORE, adv., adj.
153 = 0.100 %
Tob 3 :13   and that I hear reproach no more
 3 :15   and pity be taken upon me, and that I hear reproach no more
 12 :1   and he must also be given more
 12 :21   but they saw him no more
Jud 7 :30   Let us hold out for 5 more days
 12 :3   where can we get more like it for you ?
 12 :18   because my life means more to me today
 12 :20   much more than he had ever drunk in any one day
 16 :23   She became more and more famous
Ad E 16 :2   The more often they are honoured
 16 :2   the more proud do many men become
 16 :7   can be seen not so much from the more ancient records
 16 :9   with more equitable consideration
Wis 7 :10   I loved her more than health and beauty
 7 :24   For wisdom is more mobile than any motion
 7 :29   For she is more beautiful than the sun
 8 :6   who more than she is fashioner of what exists ?
 8 :7   nothing in life is more profitable for men than these
 10 :12   that godliness is more powerful than anything
 12 :22   thou scourgest our enemies 10,000 times more
 13 :4   how much more powerful is he who formed them
 14 :1   calls upon a piece of wood more fragile
 14 :19   skilfully forced the likeness to take more beautiful form
 15 :13   For this man, more than all others, knows that he sins
 15 :14   But most foolish, and more miserable than an infant
 16 :19   it burned more intensely than fire
 19 :13   for they practised a more bitter hatred of strangers
Sir 3 :18   The greater you are, the more you must humble yourself
 4 :10   and he will love you more than does your mother
 7 :19   for her charm is worth more than gold
 10 :31   A man honoured in poverty, how much more in wealth !
 10 :31   And a man dishonoured in wealth, how much more in poverty !
 11 :11   but is so much the more in want
 13 :9   and he will invite you the more often
 13 :17   No more has a sinner with a godly man

 16 :5   and my ear has heard things more striking than these
 19 :13   but if he did anything, so that he may do it no more
 21 :1   Do so no more, but pray about your former sins
 24 :21   Those who eat me will hunger for more
 24 :21   and those who drink me will thirst for more
 24 :29   for her thought is more abundant than the sea
 29 :11   and it will profit you more than gold
 29 :13   more than a mighty shield and more than a heavy spear
 31 :13   What has been created more greedy then the eye ?
 32 :7   but no more than twice, and only if asked
 34 :11   and I understand more than I can express
 37 :13   for no one is more faithful to you than it is
 39 :12   I have yet more to say, which I have thought upon
 40 :8   and upon sinners 7 times more
 40 :22   but the green shoots of grain more than both
 40 :25   but good counsel is esteemed more than both
L Jr 6 :19   They light lamps, even more than they light for themselves
1 Ma 3 :30   which he used to give more lavishly than preceding kings
 7 :23   it was more than the Gentiles had done
 9 :6   until no more than 800 of them were left
 9 :72   and came no more in their territory
 10 :88   he honoured Jonathan still more
 15 :31   and the tribute money of the cities, 500 talents more
2 Ma 4 :9   In addition to this he promised to pay 150 more
 5 :22   and in character more barbarous
 8 :8   and that he was pushing ahead with more frequent successes
 8 :24   they slew more than 9,000 of the enemy
 8 :30   they killed more than 20,000 of them
 9 :7   but was even more filled with arrogance
 10 :19   where he was more urgently needed
 10 :23   he destroyed more than 20,000 in the 2 strongholds
 12 :10   When they had gone more than a mile from there
 12 :19   more than 10,000 men
 14 :11   quickly inflamed Demetrius still more
 14 :30   But Maccabeus, noticing that Nicanor was more austere
 14 :30   and was meeting him more rudely than had been his custom
 14 :39   sent more than 500 soldiers to arrest him
 15 :9   he made them the more eager
1 Es 2 :28   and to take care that nothing more be done
 4 :25   A man loves his wife more than his father or his mother
 5 :41   All those of Israel, 12 or more years of age
 5 :58   who were 20 or more years of age
P Ma 9   For the sins I have committed are more in number
3 Ma 1 :8   he was all the more eager to visit them as soon as possible
 3 :1   but was still more bitterly hostile
 3 :10   and to exert more earnest efforts for their assistance
 5 :17   by celebrating all the more
 5 :38   Equip the elephants now once more
 7 :5   with a cruelty more savage than that of Scythian custom
 7 :15   In that day they put to death more than 300 men
2 Es 1 :21   What more can I do for you ? Says the Lord
 2 :43   but he was more exalted than they
 3 :12   and again they began to be more ungodly than were their ancestors
 4 :14   and that we may make for ourselves more forests
 4 :15   so that there also we may gain more territory for ourselves
 4 :45   show me this also : whether more time is to come than has passed
 4 :50   for as the rain is more than the drops
 5 :22   and I began once more to speak words
 5 :32   pay attention to me, and I will tell you more
 5 :33   Or do you love him more than his Maker does ?
 5 :44   The creation cannot make more haste than the Creator
 7 :56   but silver is more abundant than gold, and brass than silver
 7 :58   for what is more rare is more precious
 7 :59   rejoices more than he who has what is plentiful
 7 :125   shall shine more than the stars
 7 :136   because he makes his compassions abound more and more
 8 :47   more than I love it
 8 :55   Therefore do not ask any more questions
 9 :15   there are more who perish than those who will be saved
 9 :23   But if you will let 7 days more pass
 10 :11   Who then ought to mourn the more
 10 :23   And, what is more than all, the seal of Zion
 10 :57   For you are more blessed than many
 11 :27   a 2nd also, and this disappeared more quickly than the first
 12 :13   and it shall be more terrifying
 12 :24   and its inhabitants more oppressively
 12 :39   But wait here 7 days more
 13 :16   And still more, alas for those who are not left !
 13 :24   are more blessed than those who have died
 13 :41   and go to a more distant region
 13 :56   And after 3 more days I will tell you other things
 14 :17   the more shall evils be multiplied among its inhabitants
 16 :47   the more they adorn their cities
 16 :48   the more angry I will be with them for their sins
4 Ma 2 :6   I could prove to you all the more
 2 :15   It is evident that reason rules even the more violent emotions :
 3 :6   Now this can be explained more clearly
 5 :10   It seems to me that you will do something even more senseless

	5:16	think that there is no compulsion more powerful
	5:32	and fan the fire more vehemently !
	6:16	But Eleazar, as though more bitterly tormented by this counsel, cried out :
	7:10	O aged man, more powerful than tortures
	8:2	these should be tortured even more cruelly
	9:3	do not pity us more than we pity ourselves
	9:4	to be more grievous than death itself
	9:6	it would be even more fitting
	9:30	that you are being tortured more than I
	11:3	from the heavenly justice for even more crimes
	13:23	the brothers were the more sympathetic to one another
	13:24	they loved one another all the more
	13:26	they rendered their brotherly love more fervent
	14:2	O reason, more royal than kings and freer than the free !
	14:10	What could be more excruciatingly painful than this ?
	14:11	since the mind of a woman despised even more diverse agonies
	15:1	O religion, more desirable to the mother than her children !
	15:3	She loved religion more
	15:5	they are the more devoted to their children
	15:6	The mother of the 7 boys, more than any other mother, loved her children
	15:16	O mother, tried now by more bitter pains
	15:30	O more noble than males in steadfastness
	15:30	and more manly than men in endurance !
	16:8	and the more grievous anxieties of your upbringing
	16:14	and in word and deed you have proved more powerful than a man
	18:20	and back again to more tortures

MOREOVER
9 = 0.006 %

1 Ma	6:24	moreover, they have put to death
	10:42	Moreover, the 5,000 shekels of silver
2 Ma	6:23	and moreover according to the holy Godgiven law
	8:19	Moreover, he told them of the times
	9:25	Moreover, I understand how the princes along the borders
1 Es	4:10	Moreover, he reclines, he eats and drinks and sleeps
2 Es	2:11	Moreover, I will take back to myself their glory
	8:57	Moreover they have even trampled upon his righteous ones
	11:32	Moreover this head gained control of the whole earth

MORNING
23 = 0.015 %

Tob	9:6	In the morning they both got up early
Jud	12:5	Along toward the morning watch she arose
	14:2	And as soon as morning comes and the sun rises
Wis	11:22	and like a drop of morning dew that falls upon the ground
Sir	18:26	From morning to evening conditions change
	47:10	and the sanctuary resounded from early morning
	50:6	Like the morning star among the clouds
Bel	14:12	And when you return in the morning
	14:16	Early in the morning the king rose and came
1 Ma	3:58	Be ready early in the morning to fight with these Gentiles
	4:52	Early in the morning on the 25th day of the 9th month
	6:33	Early in the morning the king rose
	9:13	and the battle raged from morning till evening
	10:80	from early morning till late afternoon
	11:67	Early in the morning they marched to the plain of Hazor
	12:29	But Jonathan and his men did not know it until morning
	16:5	Early in the morning they arose and marched into the plain
1 Es	1:11	this they did in the morning
	5:50	and burnt offerings to the Lord morning and evening
	9:41	from early morning until midday
3 Ma	5:10	presented himself at the courtyard early in the morning
	5:23	Then, as soon as the cock had crowed in the early morning
2 Es	7:40	or water or air, or darkness or evening or morning

MORTAL
12 = 0.008 %

Ad E	14:10	and to magnify for ever a mortal king
Wis	7:1	I also am mortal, like all men
	9:14	For the reasoning of mortals is worthless
	15:17	He is mortal, and what he makes with lawless hands is dead
2 Ma	7:16	Because you have authority among men, mortal though you are
	9:12	and no mortal should think that he is equal to God
3 Ma	3:29	and shall become useless for all time to any mortal creature
2 Es	2:45	These are they who have put off mortal clothing
	7:15	And why are you moved, seeing that you are mortal ?
	7:88	when they shall be separated from their mortal body
	8:6	by which every mortal who bears the likeness of a human being
	14:14	and put away from you mortal thoughts

MOSES
35 = 0.023 %

Tob	6:12	For I know that Raguel, according to the law of Moses
	7:13	take her according to the law of Moses
Sir	24:23	the law which Moses commanded us
	45:1	Moses, whose memory is blessed
	45:6	He exalted Aaron, the brother of Moses
	45:15	Moses ordained him, and anointed him with holy oil
	46:1	and was the successor of Moses in prophesying
	46:7	And in the days of Moses he did a loyal deed
Bar	1:20	through Moses his servant at the time

	2:2	in accordance with what is written in the law of Moses
	2:28	as thou didst speak by thy servant Moses
Sus	13:3	and had taught their daughter according to the law of Moses
	13:62	acting in accordance with the law of Moses
2 Ma	1:29	Plant thy people in thy holy place, as Moses said
	2:4	and that he went out to the mountain where Moses had gone up
	2:8	as they were shown in the case of Moses
	2:10	Just as Moses prayed to the Lord
	2:11	And Moses said, They were consumed
	7:6	as Moses declared in his song
	7:30	that was given to our fathers through Moses
1 Es	1:6	which was given to Moses
	1:11	as it is written in the book of Moses
	5:49	in accordance with the directions in the book of Moses the man of God
	7:6	did according to what was written in the book of Moses
	7:9	in accordance with the book of Moses
	8:3	skilled in the law of Moses
	9:39	to bring the law of Moses
2 Es	1:13	I gave you Moses as leader and Aaron as priest
	7:106	and Moses for our fathers who sinned in the desert
	7:129	For this is the way of which Moses, while he was alive
	14:3	I revealed myself in a bush and spoke to Moses
4 Ma	2:17	When Moses was angry with Dathan and Abiram
	9:2	to the law and to Moses our counsellor
	17:19	For Moses says, All who are consecrated are under your hands
	18:18	the song that Moses taught, which says

MOST
72 = 0.047 %

Jud	4:7	only wide enough for 2 men at the most
Ad E	15:6	And he was most terrifying
	16:15	are not evildoers but are governed by most righteous laws
	16:16	and are sons of the Most High, the most mighty living God
	16:16	and for our fathers in the most excellent order
	16:24	but also most hateful for all time to beasts and birds
Wis	6:17	is the most sincere desire for instruction
	7:23	that are intelligent and pure and most subtle
	12:7	that the land most precious of all to thee
	15:14	But most foolish, and more miserable than an infant
	15:18	even the most hateful animals
	16:17	For – most incredible of all
	17:19	or the sound of the most savage roaring beasts
	18:12	their most valued children had been destroyed
Sir	16:21	so most of his works are concealed
P Az	9	most hateful rebels, and to an unjust king
	9	the most wicked in all the world
Sus	13:4	and the Jews used to come to him because he was the most honoured of them all
Bel	14:2	and was the most honoured of his friends
1 Ma	1:6	So he summoned his most honoured officers
2 Ma	1:14	to secure most of its treasures as a dowry
	1:36	but by most people it is called naphtha
	5:15	the most holy temple in all the world
	6:11	in view of their regard for that most holy day
	7:34	But you, unholy wretch, you most defiled of all men
	8:7	He found the nights most advantageous for such attacks
	8:24	and wounded and disabled most of Nicanor's army
	8:32	a most unholy man
	9:25	whom I have often entrusted and commended to most of you
	9:28	having endured the most intense suffering
	9:28	came to the end of his life by a most pitiable fate
	11:12	Most of them got away stripped and wounded
	12:14	behaved most insolently toward Judas and his men
	12:24	because he held the parents of most of them
3 Ma	3:1	and put to death by the most cruel means
	3:17	with magnificent and most beautiful offerings
	3:27	will be tortured to death with the most hateful torments
	4:4	and shed tears at the most miserable expulsion of these people
	4:18	although most of them were still in the country
	5:24	for this most pitiful spectacle
	5:25	and with most tearful supplication and mournful dirges
	5:44	at the places in the city most favourable for keeping guard
	5:49	the end of their most miserable suspense
	6:18	Then the most glorious, almighty, and true God
	6:39	on which the Lord of all most gloriously revealed his mercy
2 Es	6:58	zealous for thee, and most dear
	7:103	or friends for those who are most dear
	7:122	but we have walked in the most wicked ways ?
	10:6	You most foolish of women
	10:8	It is most appropriate to mourn now
	11:45	and your most evil little wings
	11:45	and your malicious heads, and your most evil talons
	14:15	and lay to one side the thoughts that are most grievous to you
4 Ma	1:1	The subject that I am about to discuss is most philosophical
	1:20	The 2 most comprehensive types of the emotions are pleasure and pain
	1:25	which is the most complex of all the emotions
	2:19	Why else did Jacob, our most wise father
	5:26	what will be most suitable for our lives
	5:27	which are most hateful to us

7 : 1	For like a most skilful pilot
7 : 4	has ever held out as did that most holy man
7 : 13	Most amazing, indeed, though he was an old man
7 : 16	most certainly devout reason is governor of the emotions
8 : 1	have prevailed over the most painful instruments of torture
8 : 23	Why do we banish ourselves from this most pleasant life
9 : 15	Most abominable tyrant, enemy of heavenly justice, savage of mind
9 : 30	Do you not think, you most savage tyrant
9 : 32	You will not escape, most abominable tyrant
10 : 10	We, most abominable tyrant
12 : 11	he said, You profane tyrant, most impious of all the wicked
12 : 13	As a man, were you not ashamed, you most savage beast
14 : 7	O most holy 7, brothers in harmony !

MOST HIGH, subst., adj.   130 = 0.085 %

Tob	1 : 4	and where the temple of the dwelling of the Most High
	1 : 13	Then the Most High gave me favour
	4 : 11	in the presence of the Most High
Jud	13 : 18	O daughter, you are blessed by the Most High God
Ad E	16 : 16	and are sons of the Most High, the most mighty living God
Wis	5 : 15	the Most High takes care of them
	6 : 3	and your sovereignty from the Most High
Sir	4 : 10	you will then be like a son of the Most High
	7 : 9	and when I make an offering to the Most High God
	7 : 15	which were created by the Most High
	9 : 15	and let all your discussion be about the law of the Most High
	12 : 2	if not by him, certainly by the Most High
	12 : 6	For the Most High also hates sinners
	17 : 26	Return to the Most High and turn away from iniquity
	17 : 27	Who will sing praises to the Most High in Hades
	19 : 17	and let the law of the Most High take its course
	23 : 18	The Most High will not take notice of my sins
	23 : 23	she has disobeyed the law of the Most High
	24 : 2	In the assembly of the Most High she will open her mouth
	24 : 3	I came forth from the mouth of the Most High
	24 : 23	All this is the book of the covenant of the Most High God
	28 : 7	remember the covenant of the Most High, and overlook ignorance
	29 : 11	according to the commandments of the Most High
	33 : 15	Look upon all the works of the Most High
	34 : 6	Unless they are sent from the Most High as a visitation
	34 : 19	The Most High is not pleased
	35 : 6	and its pleasing odour rises before the Most High
	35 : 10	Give to the Most High as he has given
	35 : 17	he will not desist until the Most High visits him
	37 : 15	And besides all this pray to the Most High
	38 : 2	for healing comes from the Most High
	39 : 1	to the study of the law of the Most High
	39 : 5	and will make supplication before the Most High
	41 : 4	and how can you reject the good pleasure of the Most High ?
	41 : 8	who have forsaken the law of the Most High God !
	42 : 2	of the law of the Most High and his covenant
	42 : 18	For the Most High knows all that may be known
	43 : 2	is a marvellous instrument, the work of the Most High
	43 : 12	the hands of the Most High have stretched it out
	44 : 20	he kept the law of the Most High
	46 : 5	He called upon the Most High, the Mighty One
	47 : 5	For he appealed to the Lord, the Most High
	47 : 8	the Most High, with ascriptions of glory
	48 : 5	by the word of the Most High
	49 : 4	for they forsook the law of the Most High
	50 : 7	like the sun shining upon the temple of the Most High
	50 : 14	and arranging the offering to the Most High, the Almighty
	50 : 15	a pleasing odour to the Most High, the King of all
	50 : 16	for remembrance before the Most High
	50 : 17	to worship their Lord, the Almighty, God Most High
	50 : 19	And the people besought the Lord Most High in prayer
	50 : 21	to receive the blessing from the Most High
2 Ma	3 : 31	to call upon the Most High and to grant life
1 Es	2 : 3	The Lord of Israel, the Lord Most High
	6 : 31	in order that libations may be made to the Most High God
	8 : 19	and reader of the law of the Most High God sends for
	8 : 21	be scrupulously fulfilled for the Most High God
	9 : 46	And Ezra blessed the Lord God Most High
P Ma	7	for thou art the Lord Most High
3 Ma	1 : 20	at the most high temple
	6 : 2	King of great power, Almighty God Most High
	7 : 9	the Most High God
2 Es	3 : 3	and I began to speak anxious words to the Most High, and said
	4 : 2	and do you think you can comprehend the way of the Most High ?
	4 : 11	how then can your mind comprehend the way of the Most High ?
	4 : 34	You do not hasten faster than the Most High
	5 : 4	But if the Most High grants that you live
	5 : 22	in the presence of the Most High
	5 : 34	while I strive to understand the way of the Most High
	6 : 32	because your voice has surely been heard before the Most High
	6 : 36	and I began to speak in the presence of the Most High

7 : 19	or wiser than the Most High !
7 : 23	they even declared that the Most High does not exist
7 : 33	And the Most High shall be revealed upon the seat of judgment
7 : 37	Then the Most High will say to the nations
7 : 42	but only the splendour of the glory of the Most High
7 : 50	For this reason the Most High has made not one world but 2
7 : 70	When the Most High made the world and Adam
7 : 74	For how long the time is that the Most High
7 : 77	For you have a treasure of works laid up with the Most High
7 : 78	When the decisive decree has gone forth from the Most High
7 : 78	first of all it adores the glory of the Most High
7 : 79	and have not kept the way of the Most High
7 : 81	because they have scorned the law of the Most High
7 : 83	for those who have trusted the covenants of the Most High
7 : 87	at seeing the glory of the Most High
7 : 88	who have kept the ways of the Most High
7 : 89	they laboriously served the Most High
7 : 102	or to entreat the Most High for them
7 : 122	Or that the glory of the Most High will defend those
7 : 132	that the Most High is now called merciful
8 : 1	The Most High made this world for the sake of many
8 : 48	before the Most High
8 : 56	but they despised the Most High
8 : 59	For the Most High did not intend that men should be destroyed
9 : 2	when the Most High is about to visit the world
9 : 4	then you will know that it was of these that the Most High spoke
9 : 6	so also are the times of the Most High :
9 : 25	and pray to the Most High continually
9 : 28	and I began to speak before the Most High, and said
9 : 44	I besought the Most High, night and day
10 : 24	and the Most High may give you rest
10 : 38	for the Most High has revealed many secrets to you
10 : 50	For now the Most High
10 : 52	for I knew that the Most High would reveal these things to you
10 : 54	where the city of the Most High was to be revealed
10 : 57	and you have been called before the Most High
10 : 59	and the Most High will show you in those dream visions
10 : 59	what the Most High will do to those
11 : 38	The Most High says to you
11 : 43	And so your insolence has come up before the Most High
11 : 44	And the Most High has looked upon his times
12 : 4	because you search out the ways of the Most High
12 : 6	Therefore I will now beseech the Most High
12 : 23	In its last days the Most High will raise up 3 kings
12 : 30	It is these whom the Most High has kept for the eagle's end
12 : 32	this is the Messiah whom the Most High has kept
12 : 36	And you alone were worthy to learn this secret of the Most High
12 : 39	whatever it pleases the Most High to show you
12 : 47	for the Most High has you in remembrance
13 : 13	and I besought the Most High, and said
13 : 26	this is he whom the Most High has been keeping for many ages
13 : 29	when the Most High will deliver those who are on the earth
13 : 44	For at that time the Most High performed signs for them
13 : 47	the Most High will stop the channels of the river again
13 : 56	for there is a reward laid up with the Most High
13 : 57	giving great glory and praise to the Most High
14 : 31	and did not keep the ways which the Most High commanded you
14 : 42	And the Most High gave understanding to the 5 men
14 : 45	the Most High spoke to me, saying

MOTH   1

Sir	42 : 13	for from the garments comes the moth

MOTHER   94 = 0.061 %

Tob	1 : 8	as Deborah my father's mother had commanded me
	4 : 3	and do not neglect your mother
	4 : 13	because shiftlessness is the mother of famine
	5 : 17	But Anna, his mother, began to weep
	6 : 14	and bring the lives of my father and mother to the grave
	7 : 17	But the mother comforted her daughter in her tears
	10 : 7	for my father and mother have given up hope
	11 : 17	and blessed are your father and your mother
	14 : 10	Bury me properly, and your mother with me
Jud	8 : 26	his mother's brother
Wis	7 : 1	and in the womb of a mother I was moulded into flesh
	7 : 12	but I did not know that she was their mother
Sir	3 : 2	and he confirmed the right of the mother over her sons
	3 : 4	and whoever glorifies his mother
	3 : 6	and whoever obeys the Lord will refresh his mother
	3 : 9	but a mother's curse uproots their foundations
	3 : 11	not to respect their mother
	3 : 16	and whoever angers his mother is cursed by the Lord
	4 : 10	and instead of a husband to their mother
	4 : 10	and he will love you more than does your mother
	7 : 27	and do not forget the birth pangs of your mother
	15 : 2	She will come to meet him like a mother
	23 : 14	Remember your father and mother when you sit among great men
	24 : 18	I am the mother of beautiful love
	40 : 1	from the day they come forth from their mother's womb

	40 : 1	till the day they return to the mother of all
	41 :17	Be ashamed of immorality, before your father or mother
1 Ma	**1** :61	and they hung the infants from their mothers' necks
	13 :28	for his father and mother and 4 brothers
2 Ma	**7** : 1	It happened also that 7 brothers and their mother were arrested
	7 : 4	while the rest of the brothers and the mother looked on
	7 : 5	but the brothers and their mother encouraged one another to die nobly
	7 :20	The mother was especially admirable
	7 :25	the king called the mother to him
	7 :41	Last of all, the mother died, after her sons
1 Es	**4** :21	with no thought of his father or his mother or his country
	4 :25	A man loves his wife more than his father or his mother
3 Ma	**1** :18	rushed out with their mothers, sprinkled their hair with dust
	1 :20	Mothers and nurses abandoned even new-born children here and there
	5 :49	parents and children, mothers and daughters
2 Es	**1** :28	or a mother her daughters or a nurse her children
	2 : 2	The mother who bore them says to them
	2 : 5	as a witness in addition to the mother of the children
	2 : 6	and bring their mother to ruin
	2 :15	Mother, embrace your sons
	2 :17	Do not fear, mother of the sons
	2 :30	Rejoice, O mother, with your sons
	5 :35	Or why did not my mother's womb become my grave
	5 :50	Is our mother, of whom thou hast told me, still young ?
	10 : 7	For Zion, the mother of us all
	10 : 8	you are sorrowing for one son, but we, the whole world, for our mother
	13 :55	and called understanding your mother
4 Ma	**1** : 8	Eleazar and the 7 brothers and their mother
	1 :10	to praise for their virtues those who, with their mother
	8 : 3	were brought before him along with their aged mother
	8 : 4	grouped about their mother as if in a chorus
	8 :20	and have compassion on our mother's age
	10 : 2	and the same mother bore me
	12 : 6	he sent for the boy's mother to show compassion on her
	12 : 7	But when his mother had exhorted him in the Hebrew language
	13 :19	and which was implanted in the mother's womb
	14 :12	for the mother of the 7 young men bore up
	14 :13	Observe how complex is a mother's love for her children
	14 :20	the mother of the young men
	15 : 1	O religion, more desirable to the mother than her children !
	15 : 2	2 courses were open to this mother
	15 : 4	Especially is this true of mothers
	15 : 5	Considering that mothers are the weaker sex and give birth to many
	15 : 6	The mother of the 7 boys, more than any other mother, loved her children
	15 :10	and loved their brothers and their mother
	15 :11	Nevertheless, though so many factors influenced the mother
	15 :12	Instead, the mother urged them on
	15 :13	and indomitable suffering by mothers !
	15 :14	This mother, who saw them tortured and burned one by one
	15 :16	O mother, tried now by more bitter pains
	15 :21	calling to their mother
	15 :22	How great and how many torments the mother then suffered
	15 :24	this noble mother disregarded all these
	15 :26	this mother held 2 ballots
	15 :29	O mother of the nation
	16 : 1	If, then, a woman, advanced in years and mother of 7 sons
	16 : 4	But the mother quenched so many and such great emotions by devout reason
	16 : 5	If this woman, though a mother, had been fainthearted
	16 : 6	After bearing 7 children, I am now the mother of none !
	16 :12	Yet the sacred and God-fearing mother
	16 :14	O mother, soldier of God in the cause of religion, elder and woman !
	16 :24	By these words the mother of the 7
	17 : 2	O mother, who with your 7 sons
	17 : 4	Take courage, therefore, O holy-minded mother
	17 : 7	as they saw the mother of the 7 children
	17 :13	the mother of the 7 sons entered the competition
	18 : 6	The mother of the 7 sons
	18 :23	But the sons of Abraham with their victorious mother

MOTHER-IN-LAW   2
Tob 10 :12 Honour your father-in-law and your mother-in-law
   14 :13 and he gave his father-in-law and mother-in-law

MOTION, subst.   1
Wis 7 :24 For wisdom is more mobile than any motion

MOTIVE   1
2 Ma 14 :30 did not spring from the best motives

MOULD, MOLD, verb   4 = 0.003 %
Wis 7 : 1 and in the womb of a mother I was moulded into flesh
  15 : 7 and laboriously moulds each vessel for our service

	15 : 9	and he counts it his glory that he moulds counterfeit gods
Sir	**38** :30	He moulds the clay with his arm

MOUND   1
Sir 21 : 8 is like one who gathers stones for his burial mound

MOUNT, subst.   15 = 0.010 %
Sir	**50** :26	Those who live on Mount Seir, and the Philistines
1 Ma	**4** :37	So all the army assembled and they went up to Mount Zion
	4 :60	At that time they fortified Mount Zion
	5 :54	So they went up to Mount Zion with gladness and joy
	6 :48	and the king encamped in Judea and at Mount Zion
	6 :62	But when the king entered Mount Zion
	7 :33	After these events Nicanor went up to Mount Zion
	9 :15	and he pursued them as far as Mount Azotus
	10 :11	to build the walls and encircle Mount Zion
	14 :27	and put it upon pillars on Mount Zion
2 Es	**2** :33	I, Ezra, received a command from the Lord on Mount Horeb
	2 :42	I, Ezra, saw on Mount Zion a great multitude
	3 :17	thou didst bring them to Mount Sinai
	13 :35	But he will stand on the top of Mount Zion
	14 : 4	and I led him up on Mount Sinai

MOUNT up   1
1 Es 8 :75 and our mistakes have mounted up to heaven

MOUNTAIN   47 = 0.031 %
Tob	**1** :21	and they fled to the mountains of Ararat
Jud	**1** :15	He captured Arphaxad in the mountains of Ragae
	2 :21	near the mountain which is to the north of Upper Cilicia
	5 : 5	that dwells in the nearby mountain district
	6 : 4	and their mountains will be drunk with their blood
	7 : 4	neither the high mountains
	7 :10	but on the height of the mountains where they live
	7 :10	for it is not easy to reach the tops of their mountains
	7 :12	that flows from the foot of the mountain
	7 :13	We and our people go up to the tops of the nearby mountains
	10 :10	until she had gone down the mountain
	13 :10	and went up the mountain to Bethulia and came to its gates
	14 :11	to the passes in the mountains
	16 : 4	The Assyrian came down from the mountains of the north
	16 :15	For the mountains shall be shaken to their foundations with the waters
Wis	**9** : 8	on thy holy mountain
	17 :19	or an echo thrown back from a hollow of the mountains
Sir	**16** :19	The mountains also and the foundations of the earth
	43 : 4	but the sun burns the mountains 3 times as much
	43 :16	At his appearing the mountains are shaken
	43 :21	He consumes the mountains and burns up the wilderness
Bar	**5** : 7	For God has ordered that every high mountain
L Jr	**6** :39	are like stones from the mountain
	6 :63	And the fire sent from above to consume mountains and woods does what it is ordered
P Az	53	Bless the Lord, mountains and hills
1 Ma	**4** :38	or as on one of the mountains
	9 :38	and went up and hid under cover of the mountain
	9 :40	Many were wounded and fell, and the rest fled to the mountain
	11 :37	and put up in a conspicuous place on the holy mountain
	11 :68	they had set an ambush against him in the mountains
2 Ma	**2** : 4	and that he went out to the mountain where Moses had gone up
	5 :27	and kept himself and his companions alive in the mountains
	9 : 8	and imagining that he could weigh the high mountains in a balance
	9 :28	among the mountains in a strange land
	10 : 6	they had been wandering in the mountains and caves
1 Es	**4** : 4	and conquer mountains, walls, and towers
2 Es	**2** :19	and 7 mighty mountains on which roses and lilies grow
	6 :51	where there are a 1,000 mountains
	8 :23	and whose indignation makes the mountains melt away
	13 : 6	he carved for himself a great mountain, and flew up upon it
	13 : 7	from which the mountain was carved
	13 :12	After this I saw the same man come down from the mountain
	13 :36	as you saw the mountain carved out without hands
	15 :42	mountains and hills, trees of the forests
	15 :58	And those who are in the mountains and highlands
	15 :62	your land and your mountains
	16 :60	and pools on the tops of the mountains

MOURN   39 = 0.025 %
Tob	**10** : 4	Then she began to mourn for him, and said
	10 : 7	and throughout the nights she never stopped mourning for her son Tobias
Jud	**16** :24	and the house of Israel mourned for her 7 days
Sir	**7** :34	Do not fail those who weep, but mourn with those who mourn
	48 :24	and comforted those who mourned in Zion
Bel	**14** :40	On the 7th day the king came to mourn for Daniel
1 Ma	**1** :25	Israel mourned deeply in every community
	1 :27	she who sat in the bridal chamber was mourning
	2 :14	put on sackcloth, and mourned greatly
	2 :39	they mourned for them deeply

2:70	And all Israel mourned for him with great lamentation
3:51	and thy priests mourn in humiliation
4:39	and mourned with great lamentation
9:20	they mourned many days and said
12:52	and they mourned for Jonathan and his companions
12:52	and all Israel mourned deeply
13:26	and mourned for him many days
2 Ma 5:10	had no one to mourn for him
1 Es 1:32	And in all Judea they mourned for Josiah
8:72	gathered round me, as I mourned over this iniquity
9:2	for he was mourning over the great iniquities of the multitude
2 Es 5:20	So I fasted 7 days, mourning and weeping
9:38	and behold, she was mourning and weeping with a loud voice
9:41	that I may weep for myself and continue to mourn
10:4	but without ceasing mourn and fast until I die
10:8	It is most appropriate to mourn now
10:8	because we are all mourning
10:9	and she will tell you that it is she who ought to mourn
10:11	Who then ought to mourn the more
10:39	and mourned greatly over Zion
10:41	whom you saw mourning and began to console
10:49	how she mourned for her son
15:12	Let Egypt mourn, and its foundations
15:13	Let the farmers that till the ground mourn
16:33	Virgins shall mourn because they have no bridegrooms
16:33	women shall mourn because they have no husbands
16:33	their daughters shall mourn, because they have no helpers
4 Ma 16:5	she would have mourned over them

MOURNFUL   1
3 Ma 5:25	and with most tearful supplication and mournful dirges

MOURNING   18 = 0.012 %
Tob 2:6	how he said, Your feasts shall be turned into mourning
Jud 16:8	For she took off her widow's mourning
Ad E 13:17	turn our mourning into feasting
14:2	and put on the garments of distress and mourning
Wis 19:3	For while they were still busy at mourning
Sir 19:26	There is a rascal bowed down in mourning
22:6	Like music in mourning is a tale told at the wrong time
22:12	Mourning for the dead lasts 7 days
38:17	observe the mourning according to his merit
41:11	The mourning of men is about their bodies
1 Ma 1:39	her feasts were turned into mourning
1:40	her exaltation was turned into mourning
9:41	Thus, the wedding was turned into mourning
3 Ma 4:2	there was incessant mourning, lamentation, and tearful cries
4:3	with mourning and wailing for them ?
6:32	Putting an end to all mourning and wailing
2 Es 2:3	but with mourning and sorrow I have lost you
10:6	do you not see our mourning, and what has happened to us ?

MOUTH   58 = 0.038 %
Jud 5:5	Let my lord now hear a word from the mouth of your servant
5:5	No falsehood shall come from your servant's mouth
11:19	and not a dog will so much as open its mouth to growl at you
Ad E 13:17	do not destroy the mouth of those who praise thee
14:9	to abolish what thy mouth has ordained
14:9	to stop the mouth of those who praise thee
14:10	to open the mouths of the nations for the praise of vain idols
14:13	Put eloquent speech in my mouth before the lion
Wis 1:11	and a lying mouth destroys the soul
8:12	they will put their hands on their mouths
10:21	because wisdom opened the mouth of the dumb
Sir 5:12	but if not, put your hand on your mouth
15:5	and will open his mouth in the midst of the assembly
20:15	he opens his mouth like a herald
20:29	like a muzzle on the mouth they avert reproofs
21:26	The mind of fools is in their mouth
21:26	but the mouth of wise men is in their mind
22:22	If you have opened your mouth against your friend
22:27	O that a guard were set over my mouth
23:9	Do not accustom your mouth to oaths
23:13	Do not accustom your mouth to lewd vulgarity
24:2	In the assembly of the Most High she will open her mouth
24:3	I came forth from the mouth of the Most High
26:12	As a thirsty wayfarer opens his mouth
27:23	In your presence his mouth is all sweetness
28:12	and both come out of your mouth
28:25	and make a door and a bolt for your mouth
29:24	and where you are a stranger you may not open your mouth
30:18	Good things poured out upon a mouth that is closed
39:5	he will open his mouth in prayer
39:17	and the reservoirs of water at the word of his mouth
40:30	In the mouth of the shameless begging is sweet
49:1	it is sweet as honey to every mouth
51:25	I opened my mouth and said
P Az 2	in the midst of the fire he opened his mouth and said :
10	And now we cannot open our mouths
28	Then the 3, as with one mouth

Sus 13:61	for out of their own mouths
1 Ma 2:60	was delivered from the mouth of the lions
9:55	his mouth was stopped and he was paralyzed
2 Ma 6:18	was being forced to open his mouth to eat swine's flesh
1 Es 1:28	from the mouth of the Lord
1:47	that were spoken by Jeremiah the prophet from the mouth of the Lord
1:57	in fulfilment of the word of the Lord by the mouth of Jeremiah :
2:1	that the word of the Lord by the mouth of Jeremiah
4:19	and with open mouths stare at her
4:31	At this the king would gaze at her with mouth agape
3 Ma 2:20	and put praises in the mouth of those who are downcast
4:16	with a mind alienated from truth and with a profane mouth
2 Es 9:28	And my mouth was opened
13:4	and whenever his voice issued from his mouth
13:10	he sent forth from his mouth as it were a stream of fire
13:27	and a storm coming out of his mouth
14:38	Ezra, open your mouth and drink what I give you to drink
14:39	Then I opened my mouth, and behold
14:41	and my mouth was opened, and was no longer closed
15:1	which I will put in your mouth
4 Ma 5:36	the honourable mouth of my old age

MOVE*   17 = 0.011 %
Jud 7:1	to break camp and move against Bethulia
7:2	So all their warriors moved their camp that day
12:16	and he was moved with great desire to possess her
Sir 18:26	and all things move swiftly before the Lord
L Jr 6:27	it cannot move of itself
P Az 57	Bless the Lord, you whales and all creatures that move in the waters
1 Ma 2:1	moved from Jerusalem and settled in Modein
1 Es 8:72	And all who were ever moved
3 Ma 5:23	began to move them along in the great colonnade
2 Es 3:18	and move the world, and make the depths to tremble
4:37	and he will not move or arouse them
6:41	that one part might move upward and the other part remain beneath
7:15	And why are you moved, seeing that you are mortal ?
4 Ma 4:13	Moved by these words, Onias the high priest
14:6	Just as the hands and feet are moved
14:6	as though moved by an immortal spirit of devotion
14:7	move in choral dance around religion

MOVE forward   1
Jud 7:17	So the army of the Ammonites moved forward

MOVE out   2
1 Ma 4:1	and this division moved out by night
4:3	moved out to attack the king's force in Emmaus

MOVE over   1
Wis 19:19	and creatures that swim moved over to the land

MOVEMENT   2
Wis 5:11	is traversed by the movement of its wings
2 Es 6:3	and before the powers of movement were established

MUCH, adj., adv.   76 = 0.050 %
Tob 7:2	How much the young man resembles my cousin Tobit !
12:8	than much with wrongdoing
Jud 4:9	and they humbled themselves with much fasting
5:9	with much gold and silver and very many cattle
11:13	so much as to touch these things with their hands
11:19	and not a dog will so much as open its mouth to growl at you
12:20	much more than he had ever drunk in any one day
Ad E 16:7	can be seen not so much from the more ancient records
Wis 7:28	for God loves nothing so much
13:3	let them know how much better than these is their Lord
13:4	how much more powerful is he who formed them
13:9	for if they had the power to know so much
Sir 9:14	As much as you can, aim to know your neighbours
10:31	A man honoured in poverty, how much more in wealth !
10:31	And a man dishonoured in wealth, how much more in poverty !
11:11	but is so much the more in want
11:19	he does not know how much time will pass
12:5	for you will receive twice as much evil
12:18	and whisper much, and change his expression
13:11	for he will test you through much talk
14:13	and reach out and give to him as much as you can
20:2	How much better it is to reprove than to stay angry !
20:12	There is a man who buys much for a little
20:15	He gives little and upbraids much
22:13	Do not talk much with a foolish man
29:23	Be content with little or much
31:12	and do not say, There is certainly much upon it !
32:8	Speak concisely, say much in few words
33:27	for idleness teaches much evil
34:9	and one with much experience will speak with understanding
34:10	but he that has travelled acquires much cleverness

38:11 and pour oil on your offering, as much as you can afford
40:1 Much labour was created for every man
42:4 and of acquiring much or little
42:5 and of much discipline of children
43:4 but the sun burns the mountains 3 times as much
43:27 Though we speak much we cannot reach the end
43:30 When you praise the Lord, exalt him as much as you can
46:19 not so much as a pair of shoes
51:16 and I found for myself much instruction
51:27 and found for myself much rest
51:28 and you will gain by it much gold
Bel 14:6 Do you not see how much he eats and drinks every day ?
1 Ma 4:23 and they seized much gold and silver
9:39 and saw a tumultuous procession with much baggage
10:87 with much booty
11:48 They set fire to the city and seized much spoil on that day
11:51 and they returned to Jerusalem with much spoil
15:26 and silver and gold, and much military equipment
16:11 and he had much silver and gold
2 Ma 2:32 adding only so much to what has already been said
6:6 nor so much as confess himself to be a Jew
7:26 After much urging on his part
8:20 destroyed 120,000 and took much booty
8:30 and they divided very much plunder
9:11 he began to lose much of his arrogance
15:11 not so much with confidence in shields and spears
15:14 and prays much for the people and the holy city
1 Es 9:11 for we have sinned too much in these things
3 Ma 5:22 But they did not so much employ the duration of the night
2 Es 4:30 and how much ungodliness it has produced until now
4:31 how much fruit of ungodliness a grain of evil seed has produced
7:66 For it is much better with them than with us
7:131 so much as joy over those to whom salvation is assured
8:2 it will tell you that it provides very much clay
8:43 or if it has been ruined by too much rain, it perishes
9:22 because with much labour I have perfected them
9:46 And I brought him up with much care
10:47 And as for her telling you that she brought him up with much care
10:56 and afterward you will hear as much as your ears can hear
11:32 and with much oppression dominated its inhabitants
11:40 and you have held sway over the world with much terror
12:44 how much better it would have been for us
13:8 were much afraid, yet dared to fight
13:19 For they shall see great dangers and much distress
16:18 when there shall be much lamentation

MULBERRY 1

1 Ma 6:34 They showed the elephants the juice of grapes and mulberries

MULE 3 = 0.002 %

Jud 2:17 and asses and mules for transport
15:11 and she took them and loaded her mule
1 Es 5:43 and 7,036 horses, 245 mules, and 5,525 asses

MULTIPLY 14 = 0.009 %

Sir 6:5 A pleasant voice multiplies friends
6:5 and a gracious tongue multiplies courtesies
11:10 if you multiply activities you will not go unpunished
16:2 If they multiply, do not rejoice in them
23:3 in order that my mistakes may not be multiplied
23:16 2 sorts of men multiply sins
44:21 that he would multiply him like the dust of the earth
48:16 but others multiplied sins
P Ma 9 my transgressions are multiplied, O Lord
9 they are multiplied !
10 setting up abominations and multiplying offences
2 Es 3:12 When those who dwelt on earth began to multiply
7:111 when corruption has increased and unrighteousness has multiplied
14:17 the more shall evils be multiplied among its inhabitants

MULTITUDE 76 = 0.050 %

Jud 2:20 a multitude that could not be counted
5:10 and there they became a great multitude
7:2 a very great multitude
7:18 and they formed a vast multitude
16:4 their multitude blocked up the valleys
Wis 6:2 Give ear, you that rule over multitudes
6:24 A multitude of wise men is the salvation of the world
8:10 Because of her I shall have glory among the multitudes
11:15 a multitude of irrational creatures to punish them
11:17 a multitude of bears, or bold lions
14:20 and the multitude, attracted by the charm of his work
16:1 and were tormented by a multitude of animals
18:5 take away a multitude of their children
18:20 and a plague came upon the multitude in the desert
Sir 5:6 he will forgive the multitude of my sins
7:9 Do not say, He will consider the multitude of my gifts
16:1 Do not desire a multitude of useless children
16:3 and do not rely on their multitude
34:19 by a multitude of sacrifices
35:18 till he takes away the multitude of the insolent
42:11 and put you to shame before the great multitude
44:19 Abraham was the great father of a multitude of nations
Bar 2:29 this very great multitude will surely turn into
L Jr 6:5 when you see the multitude before and behind them worshipping them
1 Ma 3:17 fight against so great and strong a multitude ?
6:41 All who heard the noise made by their multitude
6:41 by the marching of the multitude
9:35 And Jonathan sent his brother as leader of the multitude
2 Ma 8:16 and not to fear the great multitude of Gentiles
12:27 with multitudes of people of all nationalities
1 Es 2:30 with horsemen and a multitude in battle array
5:65 For the multitude sounded the trumpets loudly
8:91 for there was great weeping among the multitude
9:2 for he was mourning over the great iniquities of the multitude
9:4 and the men themselves expelled from the multitude of
9:6 And all the multitude sat in the open square before the temple
9:10 Then all the multitude shouted and said with a loud voice
9:11 But the multitude is great and it is winter
9:12 So let the leaders of the multitude stay
9:38 the whole multitude gathered with one accord
9:40 for all the multitude, men and women
9:41 and all the multitude gave attention to the law
9:45 in the sight of the multitude
9:47 and all the multitude answered, Amen
9:49 and to the Levites who were teaching the multitude, and to all
P Ma 7 and in the multitude of thy mercies
9 because of the multitude of my iniquities
3 Ma 4:5 For a multitude of grey-headed old men
4:17 because of their innumerable multitude
7:13 their priests and the whole multitude
2 Es 2:42 I, Ezra, saw on Mount Zion a great multitude
3:16 and Jacob became a great multitude
5:27 and from all the multitude of peoples
7:61 And I will not grieve over the multitude of those who perish
7:139 and blot out the multitude of their sins
7:140 of the innumerable multitude
8:41 and plants a multitude of seedlings
8:55 about the multitude of those who perish
8:63 Behold, O Lord, thou hast now shown me a multitude of the signs
9:22 So let the multitude perish which has been born in vain
10:10 and a multitude of them are destined for destruction
10:11 she who lost so great a multitude
10:13 the multitude that is now in it goes as it came
13:5 an innumerable multitude of men were gathered together
13:9 And behold, when he saw the onrush of the approaching multitude
13:11 and fell on the onrushing multitude
13:11 nothing was seen of the innumerable multitude
13:12 and call to him another multitude which was peaceable
13:28 yet destroying the onrushing multitude
13:34 and an innumerable multitude shall be gathered together
13:39 gather to himself another multitude that was peaceable
13:41 that they would leave the multitude of the nations
13:47 Therefore you saw the multitude gathered together in peace
13:49 Therefore when he destroys the multitude of the nations
16:68 For behold, the burning wrath of a great multitude is kindled over you
4 Ma 7:11 ran through the multitude of the people

MURDER, subst. 6 = 0.004 %

Wis 14:25 and all is a raging riot of blood and murder
1 Ma 1:24 He committed deeds of murder, and spoke with great arrogance
2 Ma 4:3 that even murders were committed
4:35 were grieved and displeased at the unjust murder of the man
4:36 with regard to the unreasonable murder of Onias
2 Es 1:26 and your feet are swift to commit murder

MURDER, verb 4 = 0.003 %

Wis 12:6 these parents who murder helpless lives
Sir 34:22 To take away a neighbour's living is to murder him
4 Ma 11:3 so that by murdering me you will incur punishment
12:11 were you not ashamed to murder his servants

MURDERER 3 = 0.002 %

2 Ma 9:28 So the murderer and blasphemer
12:6 attacked the murderers of his brethren
4 Ma 9:15 not because I am a murderer, or as one who acts impiously

MURDEROUS 1

4 Ma 10:17 the bloodthirsty, murderous, and utterly abominable Antiochus

MURMUR 1

1 Ma 11:39 He saw that all the troops were murmuring against Demetrius

MURMURING
			3 = 0.002 %
Wis	1:10	and the sound of murmurings does not go unheard
	1:11	Beware then of useless murmuring
Sir	46:7	and stilled their wicked murmuring

MUSCLE
| | | | 1 |
| 4 Ma | 7:13 | his muscles flabby, his sinews feeble, he became young again |

MUSIC
			8 = 0.005 %
Sir	22:6	Like music in mourning is a tale told at the wrong time
	32:3	and do not interrupt the music
	32:5	is a concert of music at a banquet of wine
	32:6	is the melody of music with good wine
	40:20	Wine and music gladden the heart
	49:1	and like music at a banquet of wine
1 Es	4:63	and they feasted, with music and rejoicing, for 7 days
	5:2	with the music of drums and flutes

MUSICAL
			2
Sir	44:5	those who composed musical tunes
1 Es	5:59	with musical instruments and trumpets

MUSICIAN
			3 = 0.002 %
1 Ma	9:39	to meet them with tambourines and musicians and many weapons
	9:41	and the voice of their musicians into a funeral dirge
1 Es	5:42	there were 245 musicians and singers

MUST
			29 = 0.019 %
Tob	11:8	You therefore must anoint his eyes with the gall
	12:1	and he must also be given more
Jud	5:22	and from Moab insisted that he must be put to death
Wis	12:19	that the righteous man must be kind
	15:12	for he says one must get money however one can, even by base means
	16:28	to make it known that one must rise before the sun
	16:28	and must pray to thee at the dawning of the light
Sir	3:18	The greater you are, the more you must humble yourself
	8:7	remember that we all must die
	8:13	but if you give surety, be concerned as one who must pay
	13:3	a poor man suffers wrong, and he must add apologies
	14:17	for the decree from of old is, You must surely die !
	33:19	lest you change your mind and must ask for it
L Jr	6:6	It is thou, O Lord, whom we must worship
	6:40	Why then must any one think that they are gods
	6:44	Why then must any one think that they are gods
	6:56	Why then must any one admit or think that they are gods ?
	6:64	Therefore one must not think that they are gods nor call them gods
2 Ma	2:29	must be concerned with the whole construction
	3:13	said that this money must in any case be confiscated
	6:17	we must go on briefly with the story
1 Es	4:22	Hence you must realize that women rule over you !
3 Ma	5:37	must I give you orders about these things ?
2 Es	6:16	for they know that their end must be changed
	8:58	though knowing full well that they must die
	9:12	these must in torment acknowledge it after death
4 Ma	13:1	everyone must concede
	16:1	it must be admitted that devout reason
	16:22	You too must have the same faith in God and not be grieved

MUSTER, verb
			3 = 0.002 %
Jud	2:15	and mustered the picked troops by divisions
1 Ma	4:28	But the next year he mustered 60,000 picked infantrymen
	10:77	he mustered 3,000 cavalry and a large army

MUTE
| | | | 1 |
| 4 Ma | 10:18 | God hears also those who are mute |

MUTILATE
| | | | 1 |
| 4 Ma | 10:20 | we let our bodily members be mutilated |

MUTUAL
| | | | 1 |
| 3 Ma | 2:33 | and depriving them of common fellowship and mutual help |

MUZZLE, subst.
| | | | 1 |
| Sir | 20:29 | like a muzzle on the mouth they avert reproofs |

MY
| | | | 604 = 0.393 % |

MYNDOS
| | | | 1 |
| 1 Ma | 15:23 | and to the Spartans, and to Delos, and to Myndos |

MYRIAD
			2
Jud	16:4	he came with myriads of his warriors
3 Ma	3:21	and the myriad affairs liberally entrusted to them from the beginning

MYRRH
| | | | 1 |
| Sir | 24:15 | and like choice myrrh I spread a pleasant odour |

MYRRH-PERFUMED
| | | | 1 |
| 3 Ma | 4:6 | their myrrh-perfumed hair sprinkled with ashes |

MYSELF
| | | | 28 = 0.018 % |

MYSIAN
| | | | 1 |
| 2 Ma | 5:24 | Antiochus sent Apollonius, the captain of the Mysians |

MYSTERIOUS
| | | | 1 |
| 3 Ma | 1:17 | supposing that something mysterious was occurring |

MYSTERY
			2
Wis	14:23	or celebrate secret mysteries
3 Ma	2:30	those who have been initiated into the mysteries

N

NAATHUS
| | | | 1 |
| 1 Es | 9:31 | Of the sons of Addi : Naathus and Moossias, Laccunus |

NABARIAH
| | | | 1 |
| 1 Es | 9:44 | Lothasubus, Nabariah, and Zechariah |

NABATEAN
			2
1 Ma	5:25	They encountered the Nabateans, who met them peaceably
	9:35	and begged the Nabateans, who were his friends

NADAB
			4 = 0.003 %
Tob	11:18	Ahikar and his nephew Nadab came
	14:10	See, my son, what Nadab did to Ahikar who had reared him
	14:10	which Nadab had set for him
	14:10	but Nadab fell into the trap and perished

NADABATH
| | | | 1 |
| 1 Ma | 9:37 | from Nadabath with a large escort |

NAHUM
| | | | 1 |
| 2 Es | 1:40 | and Nahum and Habakkuk, Zephaniah, Haggai |

NAIDUS
| | | | 1 |
| 1 Es | 9:31 | and Naidus, and Bescaspasmys and Sesthel |

NAKED
			3 = 0.002 %
Tob	1:17	and my clothing to the naked
	4:16	and of your clothing to the naked
2 Es	2:20	defend the orphan, clothe the naked

NAKEDNESS
| | | | 1 |
| Sir | 29:21 | and a house to cover one's nakedness |

NAME, subst.
			109 = 0.071 %
Tob	3:11	and blessed is thy holy and honoured name for ever
	3:15	and that I did not stain my name or the name of my father
	5:11	I should like to know, my brother, your people and your name
	8:5	and blessed be thy holy and glorious name for ever
	11:14	Blessed art thou, O God, and blessed is thy name for ever
	12:6	It is good to praise God and to exalt his name
	13:11	Many nations will come from afar to the name of the Lord God
Jud	9:7	the Lord is thy name
	9:8	and to pollute the tabernacle where thy glorious name rests
	14:7	In every nation those who hear your name will be alarmed
	16:2	exalt him, and call upon his name
Ad E	10:8	the name of the Jews
	13:17	that we may live and sing praise to thy name, O Lord
Wis	2:4	Our name will be forgotten in time
	10:20	they sang hymns, O Lord, to thy holy name
	13:10	are the men who give the name gods
	14:21	the name that ought not to be shared
Sir	6:1	for a bad name incurs shame and reproach :
	6:22	For wisdom is like her name, and is not manifest to many
	15:6	and will acquire an everlasting name
	17:10	And they will praise his holy name
	22:14	And what is its name except Fool ?
	23:9	and do not habitually utter the name of the Holy One
	23:10	and utters the Name will not be cleansed from sin
	36:12	Have mercy, O Lord, upon the people called by thy name
	36:15	and fulfil the prophecies spoken in thy name
	37:1	but some friends are friends only in name
	37:26	and his name will live for ever
	39:9	and his name will live through all generations
	39:11	if he lives long, he will leave a name greater than a 1,000
	39:15	ascribe majesty to his name and give thanks to him
	39:35	and bless the name of the Lord
	40:19	Children and the building of a city establish a man's name
	41:11	but the evil name of sinners will be blotted out

41 : 12	Have regard for your name
41 : 13	but a good name endures for ever
44 : 8	There are some of them who have left a name
44 : 14	and their name lives to all generations
45 : 15	and bless his people in his name
46 : 1	He became, in accordance with his name
46 : 11	The judges also, with their respective names
46 : 12	and may the name of those who have been honoured
47 : 10	while they praised God's holy name
47 : 13	that he might build a house for his name
47 : 16	Your name reached to far-off islands
47 : 18	In the name of the Lord God
50 : 20	and to glory in his name
51 : 1	I give thanks to thy name
51 : 3	in the greatness of thy mercy and of thy name
51 : 11	I will praise thy name continually
51 : 12	and I will bless the name of the Lord
Bar **2** : 11	and hast made thee a name, as at this day
2 : 15	for Israel and his descendants are called by thy name
2 : 26	And the house which is called by thy name
2 : 32	and will remember my name
3 : 5	but in this crisis remember thy power and thy name
3 : 7	in order that we should call upon thy name
5 : 4	For your name will for ever be called by God
P Az **3**	and thy name is glorified for ever
11	For thy name's sake do not give us up utterly
20	and give glory to thy name, O Lord !
30	And blessed is thy glorious, holy name
Sus **13** : 1	There was a man living in Babylon whose name was Joakim
1 Ma **2** : 51	and receive great honour and an everlasting name
3 : 14	he said, I will make a name for myself
4 : 33	and let all who know thy name praise thee with hymns
5 : 57	So they said, Let us also make a name for ourselves
5 : 63	wherever their name was heard
6 : 44	and to win for himself an everlasting name
7 : 37	Thou didst choose this house to be called by thy name
14 : 43	should be written in his name
2 Ma **8** : 4	and the blasphemies committed against his name
8 : 15	and because he had called them by his holy and glorious name
12 : 13	Its name was Caspin
1 Es **1** : 48	by the name of the Lord
4 : 63	which is called by his name
5 : 4	These are the names of the men who went up
5 : 38	and was called by his name
6 : 1	they prophesied to them in the name of the Lord God of Israel
6 : 12	we questioned them and asked them for a list of the names
6 : 33	Therefore may the Lord, whose name is there called upon
8 : 39	their names being Eliphelet, Jeuel, and Shemaiah
8 : 49	the list of all their names was reported
8 : 78	to leave to us a root and a name in thy holy place
8 : 88	to destroy us without leaving a root or seed or name ?
9 : 16	all of them by name
P Ma **3**	and sealed it with thy terrible and glorious name
3 Ma **2** : 9	chose this city and sanctified this place for your name
2 : 9	for the glory of your great and honoured name
2 : 14	dedicated to your glorious name
2 Es **1** : 16	You have not exulted in my name
1 : 22	thirsty and blaspheming my name
1 : 24	I will turn to other nations and will give them my name
2 : 7	let their names be blotted out from the earth
2 : 16	because I recognize my name in them
2 : 45	and they have confessed the name of God
2 : 47	who had stood valiantly for the name of the Lord
3 : 13	whose name was Abraham
3 : 24	And thou didst command him to build a city for thy name
4 : 1	whose name was Uriel, answered
4 : 25	But what will he do for his name, by which we are called ?
6 : 49	the name of one thou didst call Behemoth
6 : 49	and the name of the other Leviathan
7 : 60	and through whom my name has now been honoured
8 : 60	have defiled the name of him who made them
10 : 22	and the name by which we are called has been profaned
14 : 35	and then the names of the righteous will become manifest
4 Ma **5** : 4	one man, Eleazar by name, leader of the flock

NAME, verb   13 = 0.008 %

Tob **6** : 10	He is your relative, and he has an only daughter named Sarah
Wis **14** : 8	and the perishable thing was named a god
14 : 27	For the worship of idols not to be named
Sir **24** : 18	to those who are named by him
43 : 8	The month is named for the moon
Bar **4** : 30	for he who named you will comfort you
Sus **13** : 2	And he took a wife named Susanna, the daughter of Hilkiah
13 : 45	God aroused the holy spirit of a young lad named Daniel
1 Ma **6** : 17	and he named him Eupator
2 Ma **3** : 4	But a man named Simon, of the tribe of Benjamin
2 Es **3** : 23	and thou didst raise up for thyself a servant, named David
5 : 26	thou hast named for thyself one dove
6 : 4	and before the measures of the firmaments were named

NAMELY   4 = 0.003 %

1 Es **5** : 15	The sons of Ater, namely of Hezekiah, 92
8 : 47	namely Sherebiah with his sons and kinsmen, 18
4 Ma **1** : 3	namely, gluttony and lust
1 : 4	namely anger, fear, and pain

NANAEA   3 = 0.002 %

2 Ma **1** : 13	they were cut to pieces in the temple of Nanaea
1 : 13	by a deception employed by the priests of Nanaea
1 : 15	When the priests of the temple of Nanaea

NAPHTALI   5 = 0.003 %

Tob **1** : 1	of the descendants of Asiel and the tribe of Naphtali
1 : 2	which is to the south of Kedesh Naphtali
1 : 4	the whole tribe of Naphtali my forefather
1 : 5	and so did the house of Naphtali my forefather
7 : 3	They answered him, We belong to the sons of Naphtali

NAPHTHA   2

P Az **23**	with naphtha, pitch, tow, and brush
2 Ma **1** : 36	but by most people it is called naphtha

NARRATION   1

Sir **21** : 16	A fool's narration is like a burden on a journey

NARRATIVE   5 = 0.003 %

Sir **6** : 35	Be ready to listen to every narrative
2 Ma **2** : 24	for those who wish to enter upon the narratives of history
2 : 31	but the one who recasts the narrative
2 : 32	At this point therefore let us begin our narrative
4 Ma **3** : 19	to a narrative demonstration of temperate reason

NARROW, adj.   6 = 0.004 %

Jud **4** : 7	for the approach was narrow
2 Es **7** : 4	but it has an entrance set in a narrow place
7 : 5	unless he passes through the narrow part ?
7 : 7	but the entrance to it is narrow
7 : 12	And so the entrances of this world were made narrow
13 : 43	And they went in by the narrow passages of the Euphrates river

NARROWNESS   1

2 Ma **12** : 21	because of the narrowness of all the approaches

NATHAN   2

Sir **47** : 1	And after him Nathan rose up
1 Es **8** : 44	Elnathan, Shemaiah, Jarib, Nathan, Elnathan

NATHANAEL   2

Jud **8** : 1	son of Eliab, son of Nathanael, son of Salamiel
1 Es **9** : 22	and Nathanael, and Gedaliah, and Elasah

NATION   197 = 0.128 %

Tob **3** : 4	in all the nations among which we have been dispersed
4 : 19	For none of the nations has understanding
13 : 3	Acknowledge him before the nations, O sons of Israel
13 : 5	and will gather us from all the nations
13 : 6	and I show his power and majesty to a nation of sinners
13 : 11	Many nations will come from afar to the name of the Lord God
Jud **1** : 6	Many nations joined the forces of the Chaldeans
1 : 8	and those among the nations of Carmel and Gilead
3 : 8	so that all nations should worship Nebuchadnezzar only
4 : 1	had done to the nations
5 : 21	But if there is no transgression in their nation
8 : 20	or any of our nation
9 : 14	And cause thy whole nation and every tribe
11 : 10	for it is true : our nation cannot be punished
13 : 20	when our nation was brought low
14 : 7	In every nation those who hear your name will be alarmed
15 : 9	you are the great pride of our nation !
16 : 17	Woe to the nations that rise up against my people !
Ad E **10** : 8	The nations are those that gathered to destroy
10 : 9	And my nation, this is Israel
10 : 9	which have not occurred among the nations
10 : 10	one for the people of God and one for all the nations
10 : 11	of decision before God and among all the nations
11 : 7	And at their roaring every nation prepared for war
11 : 7	to fight against the nation of the righteous
11 : 9	And the whole righteous nation was troubled
13 : 2	writes thus : Having become ruler of many nations
13 : 4	pointed out to us that among all the nations in the world
13 : 4	who have laws contrary to those of every nation
14 : 5	that thou, O Lord, didst take Israel out of all the nations
14 : 10	to open the mouths of the nations for the praise of vain idols
16 : 11	so far enjoyed the good will that we have for every nation
16 : 13	together with their whole nation
Wis **3** : 8	They will govern nations and rule over peoples
6 : 2	and boast of many nations
8 : 14	I shall govern peoples, and nations will be subject to me
10 : 5	Wisdom also, when the nations in wicked agreement had been confounded

	10:15	from a nation of oppressors
	12:12	for the destruction of nations which thou didst make ?
	17:2	that they held the holy nation in their power
	19:8	where those protected by thy hand passed through as one nation
Sir	**4**:15	He who obeys her will judge the nations
	10:8	Sovereignty passes from nation to nation
	10:15	The Lord has plucked up the roots of the nations
	10:16	The Lord has overthrown the lands of the nations
	16:6	and in a disobedient nation wrath was kindled
	16:9	He showed no pity for a nation devoted to destruction
	17:17	For in the division of the nations of the whole earth
	17:17	he appointed a ruler for every nation
	24:6	and in every people and nation I have gotten a possession
	28:14	and scattered them from nation to nation
	29:18	and they have wandered among foreign nations
	35:18	and repays vengeance on the nations
	36:2	and cause the fear of thee to fall upon all the nations
	36:3	Lift up thy hand against foreign nations
	39:4	he will travel through the lands of foreign nations
	39:10	Nations will declare his wisdom
	39:23	The nations will incur his wrath
	44:19	Abraham was the great father of a multitude of nations
	44:21	that the nations would be blessed through his posterity
	46:6	He hurled down war upon that nation
	46:6	so that the nations might know his armament
	49:5	and their glory to a foreign nation
	50:25	With 2 nations my soul is vexed
	50:25	and the 3rd is no nation :
Bar	**2**:13	few in number, among the nations where thou hast scattered us
	2:29	a small number among the nations
	3:16	Where are the princes of the nations
	4:6	It was not for destruction that you were sold to the nations
	4:15	For he brought against them a nation from afar
	4:15	a shameless nation, of a strange language
L Jr	**6**:51	It will be manifest to all the nations and kings
	6:67	they cannot show signs in the heavens and among the nations
P Az	14	For we, O Lord, have become fewer than any nation
1 Ma	**1**:3	and plundered many nations
	1:4	and ruled over countries, nations, and princes
	2:10	What nation has not inherited her palaces
	2:19	Even if all the nations that live under the rule of the king
	3:59	than to see the misfortunes of our nation
	6:58	and make peace with them and with all their nation
	8:23	and with the nation of the Jews at sea and on land for ever
	8:25	the nation of the Jews
	8:27	if war comes first to the nation of the Jews
	9:29	and to deal with those of our nation who hate us
	10:5	and to his brothers and his nation
	10:20	to be the high priest of your nation
	10:25	King Demetrius to the nation of the Jews, greeting
	11:21	But certain lawless men who hated their nation
	11:25	Although certain lawless men of his nation
	11:30	and to the nation of the Jews, greeting
	11:33	To the nation of the Jews
	11:38	which he had recruited from the islands of the nations
	11:42	Not only will I do these things for you and your nation
	11:42	but I will confer great honour on you and your nation
	12:3	Jonathan the high priest and the Jewish nation have sent us
	12:6	Jonathan the high priest, the senate of the nation
	12:53	And all the nations round about them tried to destroy them
	13:6	But I will avenge my nation and the sanctuary
	13:6	for all the nations have gathered together
	13:36	and to the elders and nation of the Jews, greeting
	14:4	He sought the good of his nation
	14:6	He extended the borders of his nation
	14:28	and the people and the rulers of the nation
	14:29	and resisted the enemies of their nation
	14:29	and they brought great glory to their nation
	14:30	Jonathan rallied the nation, and became their high priest
	14:32	then Simon rose up and fought for his nation
	14:32	he armed the men of his nation's forces and paid them wages
	14:35	and the glory which he had resolved to win for his nation
	14:35	which he had maintained toward his nation
	15:1	and to all the nation
	15:2	and to the nation of the Jews, greeting
	15:9	we will bestow great honour upon you and your nation and the temple
	16:3	and go out and fight for our nation
2 Ma	**4**:35	but many also of other nations
	5:19	But the Lord did not choose the nation
	5:19	but the place for the sake of the nation
	5:20	shared in the misfortunes that befell the nation
	6:14	For in the case of the other nations
	6:31	not only to the young but to the great body of his nation
	7:37	appealing to God to show mercy soon to our nation
	7:38	which has justly fallen on our whole nation
	8:9	in command of no fewer than 20,000 Gentiles of all nations
	10:4	and not be handed over to blasphemous and barbarous nations
	10:8	that the whole nation of the Jews
	11:3	as he did on the sacred places of the other nations

	11:25	Accordingly, since we choose that this nation also
	11:27	To the nation the king's letter was as follows :
	14:8	our whole nation is now in no small misfortune
	14:9	and our hard-pressed nation
	14:34	and called upon the constant Defender of our nation, in these words :
1 Es	**1**:32	throughout the whole nation of Israel
	1:34	And the men of the nation took Jeconiah the son of Josiah
	1:36	and fined the nation a 100 talents of silver
	1:49	beyond all the unclean deeds of all the nations
	5:9	The number of the men of the nation and their leaders :
	6:33	destroy every king and nation
	8:10	I have given orders that those of the Jewish nation
	8:14	together with what is given by the nation
3 Ma	**1**:11	because not even members of their own nation
	2:33	considering them to be enemies of the Jewish nation
	3:2	a hostile rumour was circulated against the Jewish nation
	3:6	to their good service to their nation
	3:15	the nations inhabiting Coele-Syria and Phoenicia
	3:19	they become the only people among all nations
	3:20	since we treat all nations with benevolence
	5:5	convinced that the whole nation would experience its final destruction
	6:4	manifesting the light of your mercy upon the nation of Israel
	6:5	showing your power to many nations
	6:9	reveal yourself quickly to those of the nation of Israel
	6:13	who have power to save the nation of Jacob
	6:26	those who from the beginning differed from all nations
	7:4	because of the ill-will which these people had toward all nations
	7:10	those of the Jewish nation who had wilfully transgressed
2 Es	**1**:11	I have destroyed all nations before them
	1:24	I will turn to other nations and will give them my name
	2:7	Let them be scattered among the nations
	2:8	O wicked nation, remember what I did to Sodom and Gomorrah
	2:28	The nations shall envy you
	2:34	Therefore I say to you, O nations that hear and understand
	3:7	From him there sprang nations and tribes
	3:8	And every nation walked after his own will
	3:12	they produced children and peoples and many nations
	3:32	Or has another nation known thee besides Israel ?
	3:33	For I have travelled widely among the nations
	3:35	Or what nation has kept thy commandments so well ?
	3:36	but nations thou wilt not find
	6:48	that therefore the nations might declare thy wondrous works
	6:56	As for the other nations which have descended from Adam
	6:57	And now, O Lord, behold, these nations
	7:37	Then the Most High will say to the nations
	9:3	tumult of peoples, intrigues of nations
	13:33	And when all the nations hear his voice
	13:37	And he, my Son, will reprove the assembled nations for their ungodliness
	13:41	that they would leave the multitude of the nations
	13:49	Therefore when he destroys the multitude of the nations
	15:15	and nation shall rise up to fight against nation
	15:29	The nations of the dragons of Arabia shall come out with many chariots
4 Ma	**1**:11	and they became the cause of the downfall of tyranny over their nation
	3:7	and together with the soldiers of his nation had slain many of them
	4:1	he was unable to injure Onias in the eyes of the nation
	4:18	So the king appointed him high priest and ruler of the nation
	4:19	Jason changed the nation's way of life
	4:26	he himself, through torture, tried to compel everyone in the nation
	9:24	may become merciful to our nation
	12:17	to be merciful to our nation
	15:29	O mother of the nation
	16:16	to bear witness for the nation
	16:20	the ancestor of our nation
	17:8	as a reminder to the people of our nation :
	17:10	They vindicated their nation
	17:20	our enemies did not rule over our nation
	17:21	a ransom for the sin of our nation
	18:4	Because of them the nation gained peace

NATIONAL   1

4 Ma   **8**:7   the ancestral tradition of your national life

NATIONALITY   1

2 Ma **12**:27   with multitudes of people of all nationalities

NATIVE   5 = 0.003 %

Wis	**16**:23	even forgot its native power
2 Ma	**7**:27	she spoke in their native tongue as follows
1 Es	**6**:25	and one course of new native timber
4 Ma	**1**:11	and thus their native land was purified through them
	4:20	at the very citadel of our native land

NATURAL 2
2 Ma 6:20 even for the natural love of life
4 Ma 2:8 he is forced to act contrary to his natural ways

NATURE 15 = 0.010 %
Ad E 16:6 when these men by the false trickery of their evil natures
Wis 7:20 the natures of animals and the tempers of wild beasts
8:19 As a child I was by nature well endowed
13:1 For all men who were ignorant of God were foolish by nature
19:6 For the whole creation in its nature was fashioned anew
19:18 as on a harp the notes vary the nature of the rhythm
19:20 and water forgot its fire-quenching nature
2 Es 14:14 and divest yourself now of your weak nature
4 Ma 1:20 and each of these is by nature concerned
5:8 Why, when nature has granted it to us, should you abhor eating
5:9 and wrong to spurn the gifts of nature
5:25 we know that in the nature of things
13:27 But although nature and companionship and virtuous habits
15:13 O sacred nature and affection of parental love
15:25 nature, family, parental love

NAUSEA 2
Sir 31:20 and of nausea and colic are with the glutton
37:30 for overeating brings sickness, and gluttony leads to nausea

NAVIGATE 1
2 Es 7:5 to look at it or to navigate it

NAZIRITE 1
1 Ma 3:49 and they stirred up the Nazirites

NEAR, subst., adj. 5 = 0.003 %
Tob 3:15 no near kinsman or kinsman's son
Jud 16:24 and to her own nearest kindred
Sir 23:16 a man who commits fornication with his near of kin
3 Ma 6:31 Accordingly those disgracefully treated and near to death
4 Ma 12:10 Running to the nearest of the braziers

NEAR, prep., adv. 44 = 0.029 %
Tob 6:5 until they came near to Ecbatana
11:1 So he continued on his way until they came near to Nineveh
11:17 When Tobit came near to Sarah his daughter-in-law
Jud 2:21 near the mountain which is to the north of Upper Cilicia
3:9 near Dothan, fronting the great ridge of Judea
4:6 which faces Esdraelon opposite the plain near Dothan
7:3 They encamped in the valley near Bethulia, beside the spring
7:18 toward Acraba, which is near Chusi beside the brook Mochmur
8:27 but the Lord scourges those who draw near to him
Ad E 15:10 you shall not die, for our law applies only to the people. Come near
Wis 6:19 and immortality brings one near to God
Sir 12:13 or any who go near wild beasts ?
14:24 he who encamps near her house
14:25 he will pitch his tent near her
26:12 and drinks from any water near him
33:12 and some of them he made holy and brought near to himself
51:6 My soul drew near to death
51:6 and my life was very near to Hades beneath
51:23 Draw near to me, you who are untaught, and lodge in my school
1 Ma 2:49 Now the days drew near for Mattathias to die
3:40 and when they arrived they encamped near Emmaus in the plain
4:18 Gorgias and his force are near us in the hills
5:40 Now as Judas and his army drew near to the stream of water
7:31 he went out to meet Judas in battle near Capharsalama
8:12 They have subdued kings far and near
2 Ma 4:33 at Daphne near Antioch
6:11 Others who had assembled in the caves near by
7:14 And when he was near death, he said
10:25 As he drew near
10:27 and when they came near to the enemy they halted
11:8 And there, while they were still near Jerusalem
13:14 he pitched his camp near Modein
3 Ma 1:1 and marched out to the region near Raphia
1:25 while the elders near the king tried in various ways
2 Es 5:19 Depart from me and do not come near me for 7 days
6:18 and it shall be that when I draw near
8:61 Therefore my judgment is now drawing near
12:21 when the middle of its time draws near
14:18 and falsehood shall come near
15:15 For the sword and misery draw near them
16:37 Behold, the calamities draw near, and are not delayed
16:38 when the time of her delivery draws near
4 Ma 8:4 he smiled at them, and summoned them nearer and said
12:2 He summoned him to come nearer

NEARBY 3 = 0.002 %
Jud 5:5 that dwells in the nearby mountain district
7:13 We and our people go up to the tops of the nearby mountains
3 Ma 6:17 so that even the nearby valleys resounded with them

NEARLY 1
3 Ma 5:14 But now, since it was nearly the middle of the 10th hour

NEBAT 1
Sir 47:23 Also Jeroboam the son of Nebat, who caused Israel to sin

NEBO 1
1 Es 9:35 Of the sons of Nebo :

NEBUCHADNEZZAR 35 = 0.023 %
Tob 14:15 which Nebuchadnezzar and Ahasuerus had captured
Jud 1:1 In the 12th year of the reign of Nebuchadnezzar
1:5 it was in those days that King Nebuchadnezzar made war
1:7 Then Nebuchadnezzar king of the Assyrians
1:11 disregarded the orders of Nebuchadnezzar
1:12 Then Nebuchadnezzar was very angry with this whole region
2:1 there was talk in the palace of Nebuchadnezzar
2:4 Nebuchadnezzar king of the Assyrians called Holofernes
2:19 to go ahead of King Nebuchadnezzar
3:2 Behold, we the servants of Nebuchadnezzar, the Great King
3:8 so that all nations should worship Nebuchadnezzar only
4:1 that Holofernes, the general of Nebuchadnezzar
6:2 Who is God except Nebuchadnezzar ?
6:4 So says King Nebuchadnezzar, the lord of the whole earth
11:1 who chose to serve Nebuchadnezzar
11:4 as they do the servants of my lord King Nebuchadnezzar
11:7 Nebuchadnezzar the king of the whole earth lives
11:7 under Nebuchadnezzar and all his house
11:23 and you shall live in the house of King Nebuchadnezzar
12:13 who serve in the house of Nebuchadnezzar
14:18 upon the house of King Nebuchadnezzar !
Ad E 11:4 whom Nebuchadnezzar king of Babylon
Bar 1:9 after Nebuchadnezzar king of Babylon had carried away from Jerusalem
1:11 and pray for the life of Nebuchadnezzar king of Babylon
1:12 and we shall live under the protection of Nebuchadnezzar king of Babylon
L Jr 6:2 by Nebuchadnezzar, king of the Babylonians
1 Es 1:40 And Nebuchadnezzar king of Babylon came up against him
1:41 Nebuchadnezzar also took some of the holy vessels of the Lord
1:45 So after a year Nebuchadnezzar sent
1:48 And though King Nebuchadnezzar had made him swear
2:10 which Nebuchadnezzar had carried away from Jerusalem
5:7 whom Nebuchadnezzar king of Babylon had carried away to Babylon
6:15 into the hands of Nebuchadnezzar king of Babylon
6:18 which Nebuchadnezzar had taken out of the house in Jerusalem
6:26 which Nebuchadnezzar took out of the house in Jerusalem

NECESSARY 11 = 0.007 %
Wis 16:4 For it was necessary that upon those oppressors
Sir pr. and since it is necessary
pr. It seemed highly necessary
1 Ma 10:39 to meet the necessary expenses of the sanctuary
14:34 whatever was necessary for their restoration
2 Ma 1:18 we thought it necessary to notify you
9:21 and I have deemed it necessary to take thought
12:39 On the next day, as by that time it had become necessary
13:20 Judas sent in to the garrison whatever was necessary
1 Es 8:18 And whatever else occurs to you as necessary
4 Ma 14:18 And why is it necessary to demonstrate sympathy for children

NECESSITY 2
Tob 4:9 against the day of necessity
Ad E 14:16 Thou knowest my necessity

NECK 13 = 0.008 %
Jud 13:8 And she struck his neck twice with all her might
16:9 and the sword severed his neck
Ad E 15:11 Then he raised the golden sceptre and touched it to her neck
Sir 6:24 and your neck into her collar
30:12 Bow down his neck in his youth
33:26 Yoke and thong will bow the neck
51:26 Put your neck under the yoke
Bar 4:25 and will tread upon their necks
1 Ma 1:61 and they hung the infants from their mothers' necks
1 Es 1:48 and he stiffened his neck and hardened his heart
3:6 and a turban of fine linen, and a necklace about his neck
3 Ma 4:8 their necks encircled with ropes instead of garlands
4:9 some were fastened by the neck to the benches of the boats

NECKLACE 1
1 Es 3:6 and a turban of fine linen, and a necklace about his neck

NEED, subst. 25 = 0.016 %
Wis 11:5 they themselves received benefit in their need
13:11 make a useful vessel that serves life's needs
13:16 for it is only an image and has need of help
16:25 according to the desire of those who had need
Sir 8:9 and learn how to give an answer in time of need

13 :4	but if you are in need he will forsake you	
15 :12	for he has no need of a sinful man	
18 :25	in the days of wealth think of poverty and need	
29 :2	Lend to your neighbour in the time of his need	
29 :9	and because of his need do not send him away empty	
32 :7	Speak, young man, if there is need of you	
38 :1	according to your need of him, for the Lord created him	
38 :12	let him not leave you, for there is need of him	
39 :26	Basic to all the needs of man's life are water and fire	
39 :33	and he will supply every need in its hour	
40 :26	and with it there is no need to seek for help	
41 :2	to one who is in need and is failing in strength	
42 :23	All these things live and remain for ever for every need	
L Jr **6** :59	or a household utensil that serves its owner's need	
1 Ma **3** :28	and ordered them to be ready for any need	
12 :9	Therefore, though we have no need of these things	
16 :14	and attending to their needs	
2 Ma **2** :15	So if you have need of them, send people to get them for you	
14 :35	O Lord of all, who hast need of nothing	
3 Ma **2** :9	though you have no need of anything	

NEED, verb · 15 = 0.010 %

Sir **3** :22	for you do not need what is hidden	
11 :12	There is another who is slow and needs help	
11 :23	Do not say, What do I need	
13 :6	When he needs you he will deceive you	
13 :6	He will speak to you kindly and say, What do you need ?	
14 :1	and need not suffer grief for sin	
29 :3	and on every occasion you will find what you need	
29 :27	I need my house	
33 :31	for as your own soul you will need him	
42 :21	and he needs no one to be his counsellor	
2 Ma **10** :19	where he was more urgently needed	
11 :18	that needed to be brought before him	
1 Es **1** :4	and he said, You need no longer carry it upon your shoulders	
1 :16	no one needed to depart from his duties	
3 Ma **6** :30	needed for a festival of 7 days	

NEEDLESSLY · 4 = 0.003 %

Sir **20** :23	and needlessly make him an enemy	
23 :11	if he has sworn needlessly, he will not be justified	
29 :6	and he has needlessly made him his enemy	
29 :7	they have been afraid of being defrauded needlessly	

NEEDY, adj., subst. · 6 = 0.004 %

Sir **4** :1	and do not keep needy eyes waiting	
4 :5	Do not avert your eye from the needy	
31 :4	and when he rests he becomes needy	
34 :21	The bread of the needy is the life of the poor	
2 Es **2** :20	secure justice for the fatherless, give to the needy	
4 Ma **2** :8	and to lend without interest to the needy	

NEGLECT · 11 = 0.007 %

Tob **4** :3	and do not neglect your mother	
Ad E **13** :16	Do not neglect thy portion	
Wis **19** :22	and thou hast not neglected to help them	
Sir **7** :10	nor neglect to give alms	
17 :18	he does not neglect him	
38 :16	and do not neglect his burial	
2 Ma **4** :14	Despising the sanctuary and neglecting the sacrifices	
1 Es **2** :20	we think it best not to neglect such a matter	
3 Ma **1** :19	and, neglecting proper modesty	
6 :15	Not even when they were in the land of their enemies did I neglect them	
2 Es **1** :34	because with you they have neglected my commandment	

NEGLIGENT · 2

Sir **38** :9	My son, when you are sick do not be negligent	
Bar **1** :19	and we have been negligent, in not heeding his voice	

NEGOTIATE · 1

2 Ma **13** :22	The king negotiated a 2nd time	

NEHEMIAH · 11 = 0.007 %

Sir **49** :13	The memory of Nehemiah also is lasting	
2 Ma **1** :18	when Nehemiah, who built the temple and the altar, offered sacrifices	
1 :20	Nehemiah, having been commissioned by the king of Persia	
1 :21	Nehemiah ordered the priests	
1 :23	Jonathan led, and the rest responded, as did Nehemiah	
1 :31	Nehemiah ordered that the liquid that was left	
1 :33	the liquid had appeared with which Nehemiah and his associates	
1 :36	Nehemiah and his associates called this nephthar	
2 :13	and in the memoirs of Nehemiah	
1 Es **5** :8	Nehemiah, Seraiah, Resaiah, Bigvai, Mordecai	
5 :40	And Nehemiah and Attharias told them	

NEIGH · 1

Sir **33** :6	he neighs under every one who sits on him	

NEIGHBOUR, NEIGHBOR · 45 = 0.029 %

Tob **2** :8	And my neighbours laughed at me and said	
Jud **7** :4	and every one said to his neighbour	
10 :19	and every one said to his neighbour	
Sir **5** :12	If you have understanding, answer your neighbour	
6 :17	for as he is, so is his neighbour also	
9 :14	As much as you can, aim to know your neighbours	
10 :6	Do not be angry with your neighbour for any injury	
13 :15	and every person his neighbour	
15 :5	She will exalt him above his neighbours	
16 :8	He did not spare the neighbours of Lot	
17 :14	concerning his neighbour	
18 :13	The compassion of man is for his neighbour	
19 :14	Question a neighbour, perhaps he did not say it	
19 :17	Question your neighbour before you threaten him	
22 :23	Gain the trust of your neighbour in his poverty	
25 :1	agreement between brothers, friendship between neighbours	
25 :18	Her husband takes his meals among the neighbours	
27 :18	so you have destroyed the friendship of your neighbour	
27 :19	so you have let your neighbour go	
28 :2	Forgive your neighbour the wrong he has done	
28 :7	and do not be angry with your neighbour	
29 :1	He that shows mercy will lend to his neighbour	
29 :2	Lend to your neighbour in the time of his need	
29 :2	and in turn, repay your neighbour promptly	
29 :5	in speaking of his neighbour's money	
29 :14	A good man will be surety for his neighbour	
29 :20	Assist your neighbour according to your ability	
31 :14	and do not crowd your neighbour at the dish	
31 :15	Judge your neighbour's feelings by your own	
31 :31	Do not reprove your neighbour at a banquet of wine	
34 :22	To take away a neighbour's living is to murder him	
Bar **4** :9	and she said : Hearken, you neighbours of Zion	
4 :14	Let the neighbours of Zion come	
4 :24	For as the neighbours of Zion have now seen your capture	
Sus **13** :62	to their neighbour	
1 Ma **2** :40	and each said to his neighbour :	
2 Ma **9** :25	and the neighbours to my kingdom	
1 Es **2** :9	and their neighbours helped them with everything	
3 Ma **3** :10	And already some of their neighbours	
2 Es **5** :11	And one country shall ask its neighbour	
9 :45	I and my husband and all my neighbours	
10 :2	and all my neighbours attempted to console me	
15 :19	A man shall have no pity upon his neighbours	
4 Ma **2** :5	Thus the law says, You shall not covet your neighbour's wife	
2 :5	or anything that is your neighbour's	

NEIGHBOURHOOD, NEIGHBORHOOD · 1

Sir **21** :28	and is hated in his neighbourhood	

NEIGHBOURING, NEIGHBORING · 5 = 0.003 %

1 Ma **12** :33	as far as Askalon and the neighbouring strongholds	
2 Ma **4** :32	he had sold to Tyre and the neighbouring cities	
6 :8	a decree was issued to the neighbouring Greek cities	
3 Ma **1** :6	Ptolemy decided to visit the neighbouring cities	
2 Es **16** :70	For in many places and in neighbouring cities	

NEITHER, conj., adv. · 32 = 0.021 %

Jud **7** :4	neither the high mountains	
Wis **6** :23	neither will I travel in the company of sickly envy	
7 :9	Neither did I liken to her any priceless gem	
12 :13	For neither is there any god besides thee	
14 :13	for neither have they existed from the beginning	
15 :4	For neither has the evil intent of human art misled us	
15 :15	though these have neither the use of their eyes to see with	
16 :12	For neither herb nor poultice cured them	
Sir **16** :27	they neither hunger nor grow weary	
17 :21	has neither left nor abandoned them, but spared them	
23 :6	Let neither gluttony nor lust overcome me	
30 :19	For it can neither eat nor smell	
35 :18	neither will he be patient with them	
38 :32	and men can neither sojourn nor live there	
L Jr **6** :66	For they can neither curse nor bless kings	
1 Ma **12** :36	so that its garrison could neither buy nor sell	
15 :33	We have neither taken foreign land	
2 Ma **6** :6	A man could neither keep the sabbath	
3 Ma **3** :7	neither to the king nor to his authorities	
4 :11	so that they could neither communicate with the king's forces	
2 Es **2** :12	and they shall neither toil nor become weary	
4 :8	neither did I ever ascend into heaven	
5 :44	neither can the world hold at one time	
7 :105	neither shall any one lay a burden on another	
10 :4	but to stay here, and I will neither eat nor drink	
12 :48	As for me, I have neither forsaken you nor withdrawn from you	
13 :9	he neither lifted his hand	
15 :8	neither will I tolerate their wicked practices	
4 Ma **2** :9	so that he neither gleans his harvest	
7 :6	you neither defiled your sacred teeth nor profaned your stomach	

	8 :27	neither said any of these things
	15 :21	Neither the melodies of sirens nor the songs of swans

NEKODA 2
1 Es 5 :31 the sons of Reaiah, the sons of Rezin, the sons of Nekoda
5 :37 the sons of Nekoda, 652

NEPHEW 2
Tob 1 :22 He was my nephew
11 :18 Ahikar and his nephew Nadab came

NEPHISIM 1
1 Es 5 :31 the sons of Nephisim, the sons of Bakbuk

NEPHTHAR 1
2 Ma 1 :36 Nehemiah and his associates called this nephthar

NERAIAH 1
Bar 1 :1 which Baruch the son of Neraiah, son of Mahseiah

NESTLING 1
4 Ma 14 :16 hatch the nestlings and ward off the intruder

NETHANEL 1
1 Es 1 :9 And Jeconiah and Shemaiah and Nethanel his brother

NETHANIAH 1
1 Es 9 :34 Elialis, Shimei, Shelemiah, Nethaniah

NETOPHAH 1
1 Es 5 :18 The men of Netophah, 55

NEVER 60 = 0.039 %
Tob 3 :9 May we never see a son or daughter of yours !
6 :7 and that person will never be troubled again
6 :17 and will never again return
10 :7 and throughout the nights she never stopped mourning for her son Tobias
Jud 8 :13 but you will never know anything !
8 :18 For never in our generation, nor in these present days
11 :1 for I have never hurt any one
11 :2 I would have never lifted my spear against them
13 :19 Your hope will never depart from the hearts of men
Wis 2 :2 and hereafter we shall be as though we had never been
7 :10 because her radiance never ceases
10 :8 so that their failures could never go unnoticed
12 :10 and that their way of thinking would never change
15 :17 since he has life, but they never have
Sir 4 :25 Never speak against the truth
7 :1 Do no evil, and evil will never befall you
7 :36 and then you will never sin
9 :9 Never dine with another man's wife
11 :5 but one who was never thought of has worn a crown
12 :10 Never trust your enemy
15 :8 and liars will never think of her
16 :28 and they will never disobey his word
19 :7 Never repeat a conversation
19 :16 Who has never sinned with his tongue ?
22 :13 and you will never be wearied by his madness
23 :7 the one who observes it will never be caught
23 :12 may it never be found in the inheritance of Jacob !
23 :14 then you will wish that you had never been born
23 :15 will never become disciplined all his days
23 :16 will never cease until the fire burns him up
23 :17 he will never cease until he dies
27 :16 and he will never find a congenial friend
38 :8 His works will never be finished
39 :9 and it will never be blotted out
40 :23 A friend or a companion never meets one amiss
43 :10 they never relax in their watches
45 :13 Before his time there never were such beautiful things
47 :22 But the Lord will never give up his mercy
47 :22 he will never blot out the descendants of his chosen one
51 :18 and I shall never be put to shame
Bar 2 :35 and I will never again remove my people Israel
Bel 14 :7 and it never ate or drank anything
14 :35 Habakkuk said, Sir, I have never seen Babylon
1 Ma 2 :48 and they never let the sinner gain the upper hand
6 :36 wherever it went they went with it, and they never left it
2 Ma 6 :16 Therefore he never withdraws his mercy from us
10 :4 that they might never again fall into such misfortunes
15 :36 never to let this day go unobserved
3 Ma 3 :16 who never cease from their folly
7 :4 would never be firmly established until this was accomplished
7 :11 would never be favourably disposed
2 Es 3 :15 and promise him that thou wouldst never forsake his descendants
4 :8 I never went down into the deep, nor as yet into hell
7 :14 they can never receive those things
8 :47 Never do so !

	11 :19	and then were never seen again
	13 :41	where mankind had never lived
	16 :67	never to commit them again
4 Ma	6 :17	never think so basely
	12 :12	and these throughout all time will never let you go

NEVERTHELESS 7 = 0.005 %
Sir 29 :8 Nevertheless, be patient with a man in humble circumstances
2 Ma 14 :18 Nevertheless Nicanor, hearing of the valour of Judas
15 :5 Nevertheless, he did not succeed
3 Ma 3 :6 Nevertheless those of the other races paid no heed
2 Es 7 :22 Nevertheless they were not obedient
12 :18 nevertheless it shall not fall then
4 Ma 15 :11 Nevertheless, though so many factors influenced the mother

NEW 27 = 0.018 %
Jud 8 :6 *the day before the new moon and the day of the new moon*
16 :2 Raise to him a new psalm
16 :13 I will sing to my God a new song :
Wis 14 :6 left to the world the seed of a new generation
19 :11 Afterward they saw also a new kind of birds
Sir 9 :10 for a new one does not compare with him
9 :10 A new friend is like new wine
1 Ma 4 :47 and built a new altar like the former one
4 :49 They made new holy vessels, and brought the lampstand
4 :53 on the new altar of burnt offering which they had built
10 :34 *and new moons and appointed days*
2 Ma 2 :29 For as the master builder of a new house
4 :11 and introduced new customs contrary to the law
1 Es 5 :52 *on sabbaths and at new moons*
5 :53 *from the new moon of the 7th month*
5 :57 *on the new moon of the 2nd month*
6 :9 building in the city of Jerusalem a great new house for the Lord
6 :25 and one course of new native timber
8 :6 *for they left Babylon on the new moon of the first month*
8 :6 *on the new moon of the 5th month*
9 :16 *and on the new moon of the 10th month*
9 :17 *by the new moon of the first month*
9 :37 *On the new moon of the 7th month*
9 :40 *on the new moon of the 7th month*
2 Es 1 :31 *for I have rejected your feast days, and new moons*

NEW-BORN 1
3 Ma 1 :20 Mothers and nurses abandoned even new-born children here and there

NEWLY 2
Jud 4 :3 and all the people of Judea were newly gathered together
Wis 11 :18 or newly created unknown beasts full of rage

NEWS 4 = 0.003 %
1 Ma 6 :8 When the king heard this news
2 Ma 5 :11 When news of what had happened reached the king
9 :3 While he was in Ecbatana, news came to him
9 :24 or any unwelcome news came

NEXT* 17 = 0.011 %
Tob 4 :14 Do not hold over till the next day
7 :14 Next he called his wife Edna
Jud 7 :1 The next day Holofernes ordered his whole army
16 :24 to all those who were next of kin to her husband Manasseh
Sir 12 :12 Do not put him next to you, lest he overthrow you
L Jr 6 :43 she derides the woman next to her
Sus 13 :28 The next day, when the people gathered at the house of her husband Joakim
1 Ma 4 :28 But the next year he mustered 60,000 picked infantrymen
5 :35 Next he turned aside to Alema
2 Ma 7 :15 Next they brought forward the 5th and maltreated him
12 :39 On the next day, as by that time it had become necessary
1 Es 3 :7 and because of his wisdom he shall sit next to Darius
4 :42 And you shall sit next to me, and be called my kinsman
2 Es 11 :13 Then the next wing arose and reigned
14 :38 And on the next day, behold, a voice called me, saying
4 Ma 1 :16 Wisdom, next, is the knowledge of divine and human matters
9 :26 the guards brought in the next eldest

NEZIAH 1
1 Es 5 :32 the sons of Neziah, the sons of Hatipha

NICANOR 45 = 0.029 %
1 Ma 3 :38 and Nicanor and Gorgias
7 :26 Then the king sent Nicanor, one of his honoured princes
7 :27 So Nicanor came to Jerusalem with a large force
7 :30 that Nicanor had come to him with treacherous intent
7 :31 When Nicanor learned that his plan had been disclosed
7 :32 About 500 men of the army of Nicanor fell
7 :33 After these events Nicanor went up to Mount Zion
7 :39 Now Nicanor went out from Jerusalem
7 :42 let the rest learn that Nicanor has spoken wickedly
7 :43 The army of Nicanor was crushed

	7 : 44	When his army saw that Nicanor had fallen
	7 : 47	and they cut off Nicanor's head
	9 : 1	that Nicanor and his army had fallen in battle
2 Ma	8 : 9	And Ptolemy promptly appointed Nicanor the son of Patroclus
	8 : 10	Nicanor determined to make up for the king
	8 : 12	Word came to Judas concerning Nicanor's invasion
	8 : 14	to rescue those who had been sold by the ungodly Nicanor
	8 : 23	he joined battle with Nicanor
	8 : 24	and wounded and disabled most of Nicanor's army
	8 : 34	The thrice-accursed Nicanor
	9 : 3	of what had happened to Nicanor and the forces of Timothy
	12 : 2	and in addition to these Nicanor the governor of Cyprus
	14 : 12	And he immediately chose Nicanor
	14 : 14	who had fled before Judas, flocked to join Nicanor
	14 : 15	When the Jews heard of Nicanor's coming
	14 : 17	Simon, the brother of Judas, had encountered Nicanor
	14 : 18	Nevertheless Nicanor, hearing of the valour of Judas
	14 : 23	Nicanor stayed on in Jerusalem
	14 : 26	He told him that Nicanor was disloyal to the government
	14 : 27	wrote to Nicanor, stating that he was displeased with the covenant
	14 : 28	When this message came to Nicanor, he was troubled
	14 : 30	But Maccabeus, noticing that Nicanor was more austere
	14 : 30	and went into hiding from Nicanor
	14 : 37	was denounced to Nicanor
	14 : 39	Nicanor, wishing to exhibit the enmity
	15 : 1	When Nicanor heard that Judas and his men
	15 : 6	This Nicanor in his utter boastfulness and arrogance
	15 : 25	Nicanor and his men advanced with trumpets and battle songs
	15 : 28	they recognized Nicanor, lying dead, in full armour
	15 : 30	ordered them to cut off Nicanor's head and arm
	15 : 32	He showed them the vile Nicanor's head
	15 : 33	and he cut out the tongue of the ungodly Nicanor
	15 : 35	And he hung Nicanor's head from the citadel
	15 : 37	This, then, is how matters turned out with Nicanor
4 Ma	3 : 20	and were prospering, so that even Seleucus Nicanor, king of Asia

NICHE   1
Wis   13 : 15   then he makes for it a niche that befits it

NIDIA   1
1 Ma   8 : 8   the country of Nidia and Media and Lydia

NIGGARDLINESS   1
Sir   31 : 24   and their testimony to his niggardliness is accurate

NIGGARDLY   1
Sir   31 : 24   The city will complain of the one who is niggardly with food

NIGHT   67 = 0.044 %

Tob	2 : 9	On the same night I returned from burying him
	6 : 15	for this very night she will be given to you in marriage
	7 : 11	and when each came to her he died in the night
	8 : 9	Then they both went to sleep for the night
	10 : 7	and throughout the nights she never stopped mourning for her son Tobias
Jud	6 : 21	and all that night they called on the God of Israel for help
	7 : 5	they remained on guard all that night
	11 : 5	and I will tell nothing false to my lord this night
	11 : 17	and serves the God of heaven day and night
	11 : 17	and every night your servant will go out into the valley
	12 : 7	and went out each night to the valley of Bethulia
	13 : 14	but has destroyed our enemies by my hand this very night !
Wis	7 : 30	for it is succeeded by the night
	10 : 17	and a starry flame through the night
	17 : 2	and prisoners of long night, shut in under their roofs
	17 : 5	avail to illumine that hateful night
	17 : 14	But throughout the night, which was really powerless
	17 : 21	while over those men alone heavy night was spread
	18 : 6	That night was made known beforehand to our fathers
	18 : 14	and night in its swift course was now half gone
Sir	36 : 26	and lodges wherever night finds him ?
	38 : 27	who labours by night as well as by day
	40 : 5	his sleep at night confuses his mind
Bar	2 : 25	to the heat of day and the frost of night
P Az	47	Bless the Lord, nights and days
Bel	14 : 15	In the night the priests came with their wives and children
1 Ma	4 : 1	and this division moved out by night
	4 : 5	When Gorgias entered the camp of Judas by night
	5 : 29	He departed from there at night
	5 : 50	all that day and all the night
	9 : 58	and he will capture them all in one night
	11 : 6	and they greeted one another and spent the night there
	12 : 26	to fall upon the Jews by night
	12 : 27	so as to be ready all night for battle
	13 : 22	but that night a very heavy snow fell
	16 : 4	and camped for the night in Modein
2 Ma	8 : 7	He found the nights most advantageous for such attacks
	12 : 6	He set fire to the harbour by night, and burned the boats
	12 : 9	he attacked the people of Jamnia by night

	13 : 10	he ordered the people to call upon the Lord day and night
	13 : 15	he attacked the king's pavilion at night
1 Es	1 : 14	because the priests were offering the fat until night
	9 : 2	and spent the night there
3 Ma	1 : 2	and crossed over by night to the tent of Ptolemy
	5 : 5	and arranged for their continued custody through the night
	5 : 11	that beneficence which from the beginning, night and day
	5 : 19	pointed out that while it was still night
	5 : 22	But they did not so much employ the duration of the night
2 Es	3 : 14	secretly by night
	5 : 4	and the sun shall suddenly shine forth at night
	5 : 7	shall make his voice heard by night, and all shall hear his voice
	5 : 16	Now on the 2nd night Phaltiel, a chief of the people
	5 : 31	the angel who had come to me on a previous night was sent to me
	6 : 12	which thou didst show me in part on a previous night
	6 : 30	I have come to show you these things this night
	6 : 36	And on the 8th night my heart was troubled within me again
	7 : 1	the angel who had been sent to me on the former nights
	7 : 42	or noon or night, or dawn or shining or brightness or light
	9 : 44	I besought the Most High, night and day
	10 : 3	I got up in the night and fled
	10 : 58	But tomorrow night you shall remain here
	10 : 59	So I slept that night and the following one
	11 : 1	On the 2nd night I had a dream, and behold
	12 : 5	because of the great fear with which I have been terrified this night
	13 : 1	After 7 days I dreamed a dream in the night
	14 : 42	and ate their bread at night
	14 : 43	As for me, I spoke in the daytime and was not silent at night

NIMBLE   1
Sir   36 : 26   For who will trust a nimble robber

NINEVEH   17 = 0.011 %

Tob	1 : 3	into the land of the Assyrians, to Nineveh
	1 : 10	Now when I was carried away captive to Nineveh
	1 : 17	and thrown out behind the wall of Nineveh
	1 : 19	Then one of the men of Nineveh went
	1 : 22	Ahikar interceded for me, and I returned to Nineveh
	7 : 3	who are captives in Nineveh
	11 : 1	So he continued on his way until they came near to Nineveh
	11 : 16	at the gate of Nineveh
	11 : 17	So there was rejoicing among all his brethren in Nineveh
	14 : 4	about Nineveh, that it will be overthrown
	14 : 8	So now, my son, leave Nineveh
	14 : 10	And do not live in Nineveh any longer
	14 : 15	But before he died he heard of the destruction of Nineveh
	14 : 15	Before his death he rejoiced over Nineveh
Jud	1 : 1	who ruled over the Assyrians in the great city of Nineveh
	1 : 16	Then he returned with them to Nineveh
	2 : 21	They marched for 3 days from Nineveh

NISAN   2
Ad E   11 : 2   on the first day of Nisan
1 Es   5 : 6   in the month of Nisan, the first month

NO, adv., adj.   271 = 0.177 %

NOAH   4 = 0.003 %

Tob	4 : 12	that Noah, Abraham, Isaac, and Jacob, our fathers of old
Sir	44 : 17	Noah was found perfect and righteous
2 Es	3 : 11	Noah with his household
4 Ma	15 : 31	Just as Noah's ark, carrying the world in the universal flood

NOBILITY   8 = 0.005 %

Sir	22 : 10	stain the nobility of their kindred
2 Ma	6 : 31	leaving in his death an example of nobility
4 Ma	1 : 10	died for the sake of nobility and goodness
	3 : 18	and by nobility of reason spurn all domination by the emotions
	8 : 4	And struck by their appearance and nobility
	11 : 22	I also, equipped with nobility, will die with my brothers
	13 : 25	A common zeal for nobility
	15 : 9	Not only so, but also because of the nobility of her sons

NOBLE, adj., subst.   36 = 0.023 %

Tob	5 : 13	You are a relative of mine, of a good and noble lineage
	7 : 7	Son of that good and noble man !
Jud	2 : 2	He called together all his officers and all his nobles
Wis	8 : 3	She glorifies her noble birth by living with God
1 Ma	9 : 37	a daughter of one of the great nobles of Canaan
2 Ma	4 : 12	and he induced the noblest of the young men
	6 : 18	a man now advanced in age and of noble presence
	6 : 28	and leave to the young a noble example
	7 : 21	Filled with a noble spirit
	12 : 42	And the noble Judas exhorted the people
	14 : 42	and suffer outrages unworthy of his noble birth
	15 : 12	Onias, who had been high priest, a noble and good man
	15 : 17	so noble and so effective in arousing valour
1 Es	1 : 38	Jehoiakim put the nobles in prison

	3 : 1	and all the nobles of Media and Persia
	3 : 9	and the 3 nobles of Persia judge to be wisest
	3 : 14	Then he sent and summoned all the nobles of Persia and Media
	4 : 33	Then the king and the nobles looked at one another
	8 : 26	and his counsellors and all his friends and nobles
	8 : 55	which the king himself and his counsellors and the nobles
	8 : 70	the leaders and the nobles have been sharing in this iniquity
4 Ma	1 : 8	but I can demonstrate it best from the noble bravery
	4 : 1	a political opponent of the noble and good man
	6 : 5	But the courageous and noble man, as a true Eleazar, was unmoved
	6 : 10	And like a noble athlete the old man, while being beaten
	7 : 8	shielding it with their own blood and noble sweat
	8 : 3	handsome, modest, noble, and accomplished in every way
	9 : 13	When the noble youth was stretched out around this
	9 : 24	Fight the sacred and noble battle for religion
	9 : 27	and they heard his noble decision
	10 : 3	I do not renounce the noble kinship
	10 : 15	I will not renounce our noble brotherhood
	11 : 12	because through these noble sufferings you give us
	15 : 24	this noble mother disregarded all these
	15 : 30	O more noble than males in steadfastness
	16 : 16	My sons, noble is the contest to which you are called

NOBLEMAN   1
Sir   10 : 24   The nobleman, and the judge, and the ruler will be honoured

NOBLY   14 = 0.009 %
1 Ma	4 : 35	and how ready they were either to live or to die nobly
2 Ma	6 : 28	of how to die a good death willingly and nobly
	7 : 5	but the brothers and their mother encouraged one another to die nobly
	7 : 11	and said nobly, I got these from Heaven
	8 : 16	but to fight nobly
	13 : 14	and exhorting his men to fight nobly to the death
	14 : 42	preferring to die nobly rather than to fall
4 Ma	6 : 22	die nobly for your religion !
	6 : 30	the holy man died nobly in his tortures
	9 : 22	he nobly endured the rackings
	12 : 14	Surely they by dying nobly fulfilled their service to God
	13 : 11	another said, Bear up nobly
	15 : 32	endured nobly and withstood the wintry storms
	17 : 3	Nobly set like a roof on the pillars of your sons

NOD, subst.   1
2 Ma   8 : 18   who is able with a single nod

NOISE   7 = 0.005 %
Jud	14 : 9	and made a joyful noise in their city
Ad E	11 : 5	Behold, noise and confusion
Sir	50 : 16	they made a great noise to be heard
1 Ma	6 : 41	All who heard the noise made by their multitude
	9 : 13	The earth was shaken by the noise of the armies
1 Es	5 : 64	while many came with trumpets and a joyful noise
3 Ma	5 : 48	and heard the loud and tumultuous noise

NOMAD   1
2 Ma   12 : 11   The defeated nomads besought Judas

NONE   33 = 0.021 %
Tob	4 : 17	but give none to sinners
	4 : 19	For none of the nations has understanding
Jud	6 : 4	none of his words shall be in vain
	6 : 9	I have spoken and none of my words shall fail
	12 : 3	For none of your people is here with us
	16 : 14	there is none that can resist thy voice
Ad E	10 : 5	and none of them has failed to be fulfilled
Wis	2 : 9	Let none of us fail to share in our revelry
	4 : 3	and none of their illegitimate seedlings
	11 : 24	and hast loathing for none of the things
Sir	10 : 24	but none of them is greater than the man who fears the Lord
	18 : 4	To none has he given power
	27 : 24	I have hated many things, but none to be compared to him
	39 : 18	and none can limit his saving power
	51 : 7	I looked for the assistance of men, and there was none
L Jr	6 : 19	though their gods can see none of them
	6 : 28	but give none to the poor or helpless
Sus	13 : 43	Yet I have done none of the things
Bel	14 : 18	and with you there is no deceit, none at all
1 Ma	2 : 61	that none who put their trust in him will lack strength
	7 : 17	and there was none to bury them
	14 : 7	and there was none to oppose him
	14 : 12	and there was none to make them afraid
	14 : 44	And none of the people or priests shall be permitted
2 Ma	11 : 31	and none of them shall be molested in any way
1 Es	1 : 21	none of the kings of Israel had kept such a passover
	8 : 42	none of the sons of the priests or of the Levites
	9 : 51	and send portions to those who have none
	9 : 54	and to give portions to those who had none
3 Ma	2 : 28	None of those who do not sacrifice

4 Ma	14 : 4	None of the 7 youths proved coward or shrank from death
	15 : 11	in the case of none of them were the various tortures
	16 : 6	After bearing 7 children, I am now the mother of none !

NOON   3 = 0.002 %
Sir	43 : 3	At noon it parches the land
Sus	13 : 7	When the people departed at noon
2 Es	7 : 42	or noon or night, or dawn or shining or brightness or light

NOONDAY   1
Sir   34 : 16   a shelter from the hot wind and a shade from noonday sun

NO ONE   75 = 0.049 %
Tob	6 : 14	and he harms no one except those who approach her
	10 : 2	and there is no one to give him the money ?
	13 : 2	and there is no one who can escape his hand
Jud	7 : 25	For now we have no one to help us
	8 : 8	No one spoke ill of her
	8 : 28	and there is no one who can deny your words
	11 : 4	No one will hurt you, but all will treat you well
	13 : 4	and no one, either small or great
	14 : 15	But when no one answered
	16 : 25	And no one ever again spread terror
Ad E	13 : 9	and there is no one who can oppose thee
	13 : 11	and there is no one who can resist thee
Wis	1 : 8	therefore no one who utters unrighteous things will escape notice
	2 : 1	and no one has been known to return from Hades
	2 : 4	and no one will remember our works
	2 : 5	because it is sealed up and no one turns back
	5 : 12	so that no one knows its pathway
Sir	11 : 28	Call no one happy before his death
	12 : 14	So no one will pity a man who associates with a sinner
	14 : 6	No one is meaner than the man who is grudging to himself
	19 : 27	but where no one notices, he will forestall you
	23 : 18	and no one sees me
	25 : 10	But there is no one superior to him who fears the Lord
	27 : 22	and no one can keep him from them
	36 : 10	who say, There is no one but ourselves
	37 : 13	for no one is more faithful to you than it is
	39 : 17	No one can say, What is this ? Why is that ?
	39 : 21	No one can say, What is this ? Why is that ?
	39 : 34	And no one can say, This is worse than that
	42 : 21	and he needs no one to be his counsellor
	44 : 19	and no one has been found like him in glory
	48 : 12	and no one brought him into subjection
	49 : 14	No one like Enoch has been created on earth
	51 : 7	and there was no one to help me
Bar	3 : 31	No one knows the way to her
	4 : 12	Let no one rejoice over me, a widow and bereaved of many
Sus	13 : 16	And no one was there except the 2 elders
	13 : 20	Look, the garden doors are shut, no one sees us
1 Ma	4 : 5	he found no one there, so he looked for them in the hills
	5 : 48	No one will do you harm
	9 : 29	there has been no one like him
	10 : 35	No one shall have authority to exact anything from them
	10 : 63	and proclaim that no one is to bring charges against him
	10 : 63	and let no one annoy him for any reason
	14 : 13	No one was left in the land to fight them
	15 : 14	and permitted no one to leave or enter it
2 Ma	5 : 10	had no one to mourn for him
	9 : 10	no one was able to carry the man who a little while before
1 Es	1 : 16	no one needed to depart from his duties
	4 : 11	and no one may go away to attend to his own affairs
	8 : 22	and that no one has authority to impose any tax upon them
3 Ma	1 : 13	no one there had stopped him
	7 : 8	with no one in any place doing them harm at all
2 Es	7 : 30	so that no one shall be left
	7 : 105	so no one shall ever pray for another on that day
	7 : 115	Therefore no one will then be able to have mercy on him
	8 : 35	For in truth there is no one among those who have been born
	8 : 35	there is no one who has not transgressed
	9 : 18	and no one opposed me then, for no one existed
	11 : 6	and no one spoke against him
	11 : 17	After you no one shall rule as long as you
	13 : 52	He said to me, Just as no one can explore or know
	13 : 52	so no one on earth can see my Son
	14 : 21	and so no one knows the things which have been done by thee
	14 : 36	But let no one come to me now
	14 : 36	and let no one seek me for 40 days
	16 : 23	and there shall be no one to console them
	16 : 24	No one shall be left to cultivate the earth or to sow it
	16 : 71	They shall be like mad men, sparing no one
	16 : 77	so that no one can pass through !
4 Ma	3 : 2	No one of us can eradicate that kind of desire
	3 : 3	No one of us can eradicate anger from the mind
	3 : 4	No one of us can eradicate malice
	17 : 1	so that no one might touch her body

NOR   123 = 0.080 %

NORMAL 1
Wis **19** :20 Fire even in water retained its normal power

NORTH, subst., adj. 6 = 0.004 %
Jud **2** :21 near the mountain which is to the north of Upper Cilicia
16 :4 The Assyrian came down from the mountains of the north
Sir **43** :17 so do the tempest from the north and the whirlwind
43 :20 The cold north wind blows, and ice freezes over the water
2 Es **15** :34 and from the north to the south
15 :38 and from the north, and another part from the west

NOSTRIL 4 = 0.003 %
Wis **2** :2 because the breath in our nostrils is smoke
15 :15 nor nostrils with which to draw breath
4 Ma **6** :25 threw him down, and poured stinking liquids into his nostrils
15 :19 and saw in their nostrils signs of the approach of death

NOT 1357 = 0.884 %

NOTABLE 3 = 0.002 %
Ad E **16** :22 as a notable day among your commemorative festivals
Sir **39** :2 he will preserve the discourse of notable men
3 Ma **6** :28 has granted an unimpeded and notable stability to our government

NOTE, subst. 2
Wis **19** :18 as on a harp the notes vary the nature of the rhythm
19 :18 while each note remains the same

NOTE, verb 1
Jud **10** :7 When they saw her, and noted how her face was altered

NOTHING 60 = 0.039 %
Tob **1** :20 and nothing was left to me except my wife Anna
7 :11 And Tobias said, I will eat nothing here
10 :7 she ate nothing in the daytime
10 :12 do nothing to grieve her
Jud **11** :5 and I will tell nothing false to my lord this night
Ad E **16** :4 who know nothing of goodness
Wis **4** :5 and good for nothing
7 :8 and I accounted wealth as nothing in comparison with her
7 :25 therefore nothing defiled gains entrance into her
7 :28 for God loves nothing so much
8 :7 nothing in life is more profitable for men than these
9 :6 he will be regarded as nothing
13 :13 But a castoff piece from among them, useful for nothing
17 :6 Nothing was shining through to them
17 :9 For even if nothing disturbing frightened them
17 :12 For fear is nothing but surrender of the helps
Sir **6** :15 There is nothing so precious as a faithful friend
8 :16 because blood is as nothing in his sight
8 :18 do nothing that is to be kept secret
18 :22 Let nothing hinder you from paying a vow promptly
18 :33 when you have nothing in your purse
19 :7 and you will lose nothing at all
20 :10 There is a gift that profits you nothing
20 :14 A fool's gift will profit you nothing
23 :27 that nothing is better than the fear of the Lord
23 :27 and nothing sweeter than to heed the commandments of the Lord
25 :3 You have gathered nothing in your youth
26 :14 and there is nothing so precious as a disciplined soul
32 :19 Do nothing without deliberation
33 :29 and do nothing without discretion
39 :19 and nothing can be hid from his eyes
39 :20 and nothing is marvellous to him
40 :7 and wonders that his fear came to nothing
42 :21 Nothing can be added or taken away
42 :24 and he has made nothing incomplete
48 :13 Nothing was too hard for him
L Jr **6** :45 they can be nothing but what the craftsmen wish them to be
6 :70 Like a scarecrow in a cucumber bed, that guards nothing
Sus **13** :27 for nothing like this had ever been said about Susanna
13 :63 because nothing shameful was found in her
Bel **14** :35 and I know nothing about the den
1 Ma **3** :17 And we are faint, for we have eaten nothing today
2 Ma **7** :12 for he regarded his sufferings as nothing
12 :4 because they wished to live peaceably and suspected nothing
14 :23 and did nothing out of the way
14 :35 O Lord of all, who hast need of nothing
1 Es **2** :28 and to take care that nothing more be done
4 :36 and with him there is nothing unrighteous
4 :40 and there is nothing unrighteous in her judgment
5 :70 You have nothing to do with us
8 :7 so that he omitted nothing from the law of the Lord
3 Ma **1** :26 But he, in his arrogance, took heed of nothing
2 Es **6** :10 between the heel and the hand seek for nothing else, Ezra !
6 :56 thou hast said that they are nothing
6 :57 which are reputed as nothing
11 :23 and nothing remained on the eagle's body

13 :11 nothing was seen of the innumerable multitude
4 Ma **2** :17 he did nothing against them in anger
8 :11 nothing remains for you but to die on the rack ?
9 :5 as though a short time ago you learned nothing from Eleazar

NOTICE, subst. 2
Wis **1** :8 therefore no one who utters unrighteous things will escape notice
Sir **23** :18 The Most High will not take notice of my sins

NOTICE, verb 5 = 0.003 %
Sir **19** :27 but where no one notices, he will forestall you
L Jr **6** :20 They do not notice
Bel **14** :19 Look at the floor, and notice whose footsteps these are
2 Ma **14** :26 But when Alcimus noticed their good will for one another
14 :30 But Maccabeus, noticing that Nicanor was more austere

NOTIFY 1
2 Ma **1** :18 we thought it necessary to notify you

NOTION 2
2 Ma **3** :32 And the high priest, fearing that the king might get the notion
4 Ma **3** :1 This notion is entirely ridiculous

NOTORIOUS 3 = 0.002 %
Sir **42** :11 a byword in the city and notorious among the people
2 Ma **13** :6 any man guilty of sacrilege or notorious for other crimes
3 Ma **2** :5 who were notorious for their vices

NOURISH 3 = 0.002 %
2 Es **2** :25 Good nurse, nourish your sons
8 :11 so that what has been fashioned may be nourished for a time
4 Ma **13** :21 From such embraces brotherly-loving souls are nourished

NOURISHMENT 1
2 Es **9** :26 and the nourishment they afforded satisfied me

NOW, adv., conj. 302 = 0.197 %
Tob **1** :4 Now when I was in my own country, in the land of Israel
1 :10 Now when I was carried away captive to Nineveh
1 :22 Now Ahikar was cupbearer, keeper of the signet
3 :5 And now thy many judgments are true
3 :6 And now deal with me according to thy pleasure
3 :6 Command that I now be released from my distress
3 :12 And now, O Lord, I have turned my eyes and my face toward thee
4 :13 So now, my son, love your brethren
4 :20 And now let me explain to you about the 10 talents of silver
6 :1 Now as they proceeded on their way
6 :12 Now listen to my plan
6 :14 Now I am the only son my father has
6 :14 So now I fear that I may die
6 :15 Now listen to me, brother, for she will become your wife
7 :12 So Raguel said, Take her right now
8 :7 And now, O Lord
10 :1 Now his father Tobit was counting each day
10 :12 they are now your parents
11 :5 Now Anna sat looking intently down the road for her son
11 :9 now I am ready to die
12 :14 So now God sent me to heal you
12 :20 And now give thanks to God
14 :8 So now, my son, leave Nineveh
14 :11 So now, my children, consider what almsgiving accomplishes
Jud **5** :5 Let my lord now hear a word from the mouth of your servant
5 :19 But now they have returned to their God
5 :20 Now therefore, my master and lord
6 :7 Now my slaves are going to take you back
7 :4 These men will now lick up the face of the whole land
7 :25 For now we have no one to help us
7 :26 Now call them in and surrender the whole city
8 :24 Now therefore, brethren
9 :5 thou hast designed the things that are now
9 :7 Behold now, the Assyrians are increased in their might
11 :2 And even now, if your people who live in the hill country
11 :3 And now tell me why you have fled from them
11 :4 Have courage ; you will live, tonight and from now on
11 :9 As for the things Achior said in your council
11 :11 And now, in order that my lord may not be defeated
12 :6 and sent to Holofernes and said, Let my lord now command
12 :11 Go now and persuade the Hebrew woman who is in your care
12 :17 So Holofernes said to her, Drink now, and be merry with us !
12 :18 Judith said, I will drink now, my lord
13 :3 Now Judith had told her maid
13 :5 For now is the time to help thy inheritance
14 :8 Now tell me what you have done during these days
Ad E **12** :1 Now Mordecai took his rest in the courtyard
13 :7 so that those who have long been and are now hostile
13 :15 And now, O Lord God and King
14 :6 And now we have sinned before thee
14 :8 And now they are not satisfied that we are in bitter slavery
14 :18 since the day that I was brought here until now

	16:23	so that both now and hereafter
Wis	14:15	and he now honoured as a god
	14:20	now regarded as an object of worship
	17:15	and now were driven by monstrous spectres
	17:15	and now were paralyzed by their souls' surrender
	18:14	and night in its swift course was now half gone
Sir	11:19	and now I shall enjoy my goods !
	39:35	So now sing praise with all your heart and voice
	42:15	I will now call to mind the works of the Lord
	44:1	Let us now praise famous men
	50:22	And now bless the God of all
Bar	2:11	And now, O Lord God of Israel
	3:4	hear now the prayer of the dead of Israel
	4:24	For as the neighbours of Zion have now seen your capture
L Jr	6:4	Now in Babylon you will see gods made of silver and gold and wood
P Az	10	And now we cannot open our mouths
	18	And now with all our heart we follow thee
	23	Now the king's servants who threw them in
Sus	13:31	Now Susanna was a woman of great refinement
	13:43	And now I am to die !
	13:52	You old relic of wicked days, your sins have now come home
	13:54	Now then, if you really saw her, tell me this :
	13:58	Now then, tell me :
Bel	14:3	Now the Babylonians had an idol called Bel
	14:10	Now there were 70 priests of Bel
	14:32	but these were not given to them now
	14:33	Now the prophet Habakkuk was in Judea
1 Ma	1:40	Her dishonour now grew as great as her glory
	1:54	Now on the 15th day of Chislev, in the 145th year
	2:18	Now be the first to come and do what the king commands
	2:49	Now the days drew near for Mattathias to die
	2:49	Arrogance and reproach have now become strong
	2:50	Now, my children, show zeal for the law
	2:65	Now behold, I know that Simeon your brother is wise in counsel
	3:13	Now when Seron, the commander of the Syrian army
	3:42	Now Judas and his brothers saw that misfortunes had increased
	4:1	Now Gorgias took 5,000 infantry and a 1,000 picked cavalry
	4:10	And now let us cry to Heaven
	4:18	But stand now against our enemies and fight them
	5:9	Now the Gentiles in Gilead gathered together
	5:12	Now then come and rescue us from their hands
	5:40	Now as Judas and his army drew near to the stream of water
	5:55	Now while Judas and Jonathan were in Gilead
	6:11	And into what a great flood I now am plunged !
	6:12	But now I remember the evils I did in Jerusalem
	6:18	Now the men in the citadel kept hemming Israel in
	6:40	Now a part of the king's army
	6:58	Now then let us come to terms with these men
	7:7	Now then send a man whom you trust
	7:39	Now Nicanor went out from Jerusalem
	8:1	Now Judas heard of the fame of the Romans
	8:32	If now they appeal again for help against you
	9:5	Now Judas was encamped in Elasa
	9:9	Let us rather save our own lives now
	9:22	Now the rest of the acts of Judas, and his wars
	9:30	So now we have chosen you today to take his place
	9:44	Let us rise up now and fight for our lives
	9:46	Cry out now to Heaven
	9:58	So now let us bring Bacchides back
	10:15	Now Alexander the king heard of all the promises
	10:16	Come now, we will make him our friend and ally
	10:27	And now continue still to keep faith with us
	10:29	And now I free you and exempt all the Jews
	10:41	they shall give from now on for the service of the temple
	10:48	Now Alexander the king assembled large forces
	10:54	now therefore let us establish friendship with one another
	10:54	give me now your daughter as my wife
	10:56	And now I will do for you as you wrote
	10:71	If you now have confidence in your forces
	10:73	And now you will not be able to withstand my cavalry
	10:79	Now Apollonius had secretly left a 1,000 cavalry behind them
	11:10	For I now regret that I gave him my daughter
	11:14	Now Alexander the king was in Cilicia at that time
	11:37	Now therefore take care to make a copy of this
	11:38	Now when Demetrius the king saw
	11:39	Now Trypho had formerly been one of Alexander's supporters
	11:41	Now Jonathan sent to Demetrius the king the request
	11:43	Now then you will do well to send me men who will help me
	12:1	Now when Jonathan saw that the time was favourable for him
	12:18	And now please send us a reply to this
	12:22	And now that we have learned this
	12:24	Now Jonathan heard that the commanders of Demetrius had returned
	12:45	Dismiss them now to their homes
	12:53	Now therefore let us make war on them
	13:5	And now, far be it from me to spare my life
	13:16	Send now a 100 talents of silver
	13:21	Now the men in the citadel kept sending envoys to Trypho
	15:5	now therefore I confirm to you all the tax remissions

	15:7	and the strongholds which you have built and now hold
	15:30	Now then, hand over the cities which you have seized
	15:34	Now that we have the opportunity
	15:37	Now Trypho embarked on a ship and escaped to Orthosia
	16:3	But now I have grown old
	16:11	Now Ptolemy the son of Abubus had been appointed governor
	16:14	Now Simon was visiting the cities of the country
2 Ma	1:6	We are now praying for you here
	1:9	And now see that you keep the feast of booths
	3:28	but was now unable to help himself
	3:30	now that the Almighty Lord had appeared
	6:12	Now I urge those who read this book not to be depressed by such calamities
	6:18	a man now advanced in age and of noble presence
	6:27	Therefore, by manfully giving up my life now
	6:29	had acted toward him with good will now changed to ill will
	7:23	since you now forget yourselves for the sake of his laws
	9:14	he was now declaring to be free
	10:1	Now Maccabeus and his followers
	10:10	Now we will tell what took place under Antiochus Eupator
	10:24	Now Timothy, who had been defeated by the Jews before
	11:23	Now that our father has gone on to the gods
	13:10	now if ever to help those
	14:3	Now a certain Alcimus, who had formerly been high priest
	14:7	I mean the high priesthood – and have now come here
	14:8	our whole nation is now in no small misfortune
	14:36	so now, O holy One, Lord of all holiness
	14:43	and the crowd was now rushing in through the doors
	14:46	with his blood now completely drained from him
	15:8	and now to look for the victory
	15:20	When all were now looking forward to the coming decision
	15:23	So now, O Sovereign of the heavens
1 Es	1:4	Now worship the Lord your God
	1:27	And now the Lord is with me !
	1:33	and the things that he had done before and these that are now told
	2:18	Now be it known to our lord the king
	2:19	Now if this city is built and the walls finished
	2:20	And since the building of the temple is now going on
	2:24	Therefore we now make known to you, O lord and king
	2:28	Therefore I have now issued orders
	3:1	Now King Darius gave a great banquet
	4:28	And now do you not believe me ?
	4:46	And now, O lord the king
	6:1	Now in the 2nd year of the reign of Darius
	6:20	from that time until now
	6:21	Now therefore, if it seems wise, O king
	8:78	And now in some measure mercy has come to us from thee, O Lord
	8:82	And now, O Lord, what shall we say
	8:90	Behold, we are now before thee in our iniquities
	8:92	but even now there is hope for Israel
	9:8	Now then make confession and give glory to the Lord
	9:50	now they were all weeping as they heard the law
P Ma	11	And now I bend the knee of my heart
3 Ma	1:6	Now that he had foiled the plot
	1:26	and began now to approach
	2:13	see now, O holy King
	2:31	Now some, however, with an obvious abhorrence of the price
	4:1	was now made evident and outspoken
	5:8	from the fate now prepared for them
	5:14	But now, since it was nearly the middle of the 10th hour
	5:38	Equip the elephants now once more
	5:40	ordering now for a 3rd time that they be destroyed
	5:45	Now when the beasts had been brought virtually
	5:46	the city now being filled
	5:51	as they stood now at the gates of death
	6:9	And now, you who hate insolence
	6:12	watch over us now and have mercy upon us
	6:24	you are now attempting to deprive of dominion and life
	6:28	who from the time of our ancestors until now
	6:29	since they now had escaped death
2 Es	1:30	But now, what shall I do to you ?
	1:38	And now, father
	2:4	But now what can I do for you ?
	2:45	now they are being crowned, and receive palms
	3:34	Now therefore weigh in a balance our iniquities
	4:9	But now I have asked you only about fire and wind and the day
	4:18	If now you have a judge between them
	4:30	and how much ungodliness it has produced until now
	4:31	Consider now for yourself
	5:1	Now concerning the signs : behold
	5:3	And the land which you now see ruling
	5:13	and if you pray again, and weep as you do now
	5:16	Now on the 2nd night Phaltiel, a chief of the people
	5:28	And now, O Lord, why hast thou given over the one to the many
	5:45	it might even now be able to support
	5:50	Since thou hast now given me the opportunity
	5:50	Or is she now approaching old age ?

6 : 5	and before the imaginations of those who now sin were estranged
6 : 35	Now after this I wept again and fasted 7 days as before
6 : 57	And now, O Lord, behold, these nations
7 : 9	If now that city is given to a man for an inheritance
7 : 15	But now why are you disturbed, seeing that you are to perish ?
7 : 16	rather than what is now present ?
7 : 20	Let many perish who are now living
7 : 26	that the city which now is not seen shall appear
7 : 26	and the land which now is hidden shall be disclosed
7 : 37	Look now, and understand whom you have denied
7 : 45	I said then and I say now :
7 : 47	And now I see that the world to come will bring delight to few
7 : 60	because it is they who have made my glory to prevail now
7 : 60	and through them my name has now been honoured
7 : 61	for it is they who are now like a mist
7 : 64	But now the mind grows with us
7 : 71	And now understand from your own words
7 : 78	Now, concerning death, the teaching is :
7 : 82	because they cannot now make a good repentance
7 : 88	Now this is the order of those
7 : 95	they understand the rest which they now enjoy
7 : 96	they rejoice that they have now escaped what is corruptible
7 : 104	Just as now a father does not send his son
7 : 111	If therefore the righteous have prayed for the ungodly now
7 : 117	For what good is it to all that they live in sorrow now
7 : 132	that the Most High is now called merciful
7 : 136	to those now living
8 : 8	which is now fashioned in the womb
8 : 15	And now I will speak out :
8 : 46	Things that are present are for those who live now
8 : 61	Therefore my judgment is now drawing near
8 : 63	Behold, O Lord, thou hast now shown me a multitude of the signs
9 : 9	Then those who have now abused my ways shall be amazed
9 : 15	I said before, and I say now, and will say it again :
9 : 18	when I was preparing for those who now exist
9 : 19	but now those who have been created in this world
10 : 4	And now I intend not to return to the city
10 : 8	It is most appropriate to mourn now
10 : 9	Now ask the earth
10 : 13	the multitude that is now in it goes as it came
10 : 15	Now, therefore, keep your sorrow to yourself
10 : 23	for she has now lost the seal of her glory
10 : 37	Now therefore I entreat you
10 : 42	but you do not now see the form of a woman
10 : 44	whom you now behold as an established city, is Zion
10 : 50	For now the Most High
12 : 6	Therefore I will now beseech the Most High
12 : 12	But it was not explained to him as I now explain
12 : 49	Now go, every one of you to his house
13 : 15	now show me also the interpretation of this dream
13 : 46	and now, when they are about to come again
14 : 7	And now I say to you :
14 : 13	Now therefore, set your house in order
14 : 13	And now renounce the life that is corruptible
14 : 14	and divest yourself now of your weak nature
14 : 16	For evils worse than those which you have now seen happen
14 : 20	and I will reprove the people who are now living
14 : 33	And now you are here
14 : 36	But let no one come to me now
15 : 27	For now calamities have come upon the whole earth
16 : 35	Listen now to these things, and understand them
4 Ma 1 : 15	Now reason is the mind that with sound logic prefers the life of wisdom
1 : 18	Now the kinds of wisdom are rational judgment, justice
1 : 30	Observe now first of all
2 : 1	Now when God fashioned man
3 : 6	Now this can be explained more clearly
3 : 9	Now all the rest were at supper
3 : 19	The present occasion now invites us
4 : 1	Now there was a certain Simon
6 : 18	should now change our course
6 : 26	When he was now burned to his very bones and about to expire
6 : 33	But now that reason has conquered the emotions
14 : 9	Even now, we ourselves shudder
15 : 16	O mother, tried now by more bitter pains
16 : 6	After bearing 7 children, I am now the mother of none !
17 : 18	because of which they now stand before the divine throne

NOWHERE
		1
Wis 17 : 10	though it nowhere could be avoided

NUDGE
		1
3 Ma 5 : 14	approached the king and nudged him

NULLIFY
		6 = 0.004 %
1 Ma 14 : 44	to nullify any of these decisions or to oppose what he says
14 : 45	or nullifies any of them
1 Es 6 : 32	or nullify any of the things herein written

4 Ma 2 : 3	by his reason he nullified the frenzy of the passions
8 : 15	and by their right reasoning nullified his tyranny
17 : 2	nullified the violence of the tyrant

NUMBER, subst.
		53 = 0.035 %
Jud 2 : 5	to the number of 120,000 foot soldiers and 12,000 cavalry
2 : 17	He collected a vast number of camels
7 : 4	When the Israelites saw their vast number
7 : 18	and their tents and supply trains spread out in great number
9 : 11	For thy power depends not upon numbers
10 : 17	They chose from their number a 100 men
Wis 4 : 8	nor measured by number of years
11 : 20	by measure and number and weight
19 : 10	the river spewed out vast numbers of frogs
Sir 18 : 9	The number of a man's days is great
26 : 1	the number of his days will be doubled
26 : 26	for the number of his years will be doubled
37 : 25	but the days of Israel are without number
38 : 29	and all his output is by number
42 : 7	Whatever you deal out, let it be by number and weight
45 : 11	according to the number of the tribes of Israel
48 : 2	and by his zeal he made them few in number
48 : 15	the people were left very few in number
Bar 2 : 13	few in number, among the nations where thou hast scattered us
2 : 29	a small number among the nations
1 Ma 2 : 38	to the number of a 1,000 persons
4 : 8	Do not fear their numbers or be afraid when they charge
6 : 30	The number of his forces was a 100,000 foot soldiers
9 : 6	When they saw the huge number of the enemy forces
10 : 36	to the number of 30,000 men
10 : 37	Let their officers and leaders be of their own number
10 : 85	The number of those who had fallen by the sword
11 : 45	to the number of a 120,000
2 Ma 2 : 21	so that though few in number they seized the whole land
2 : 24	For considering the flood of numbers involved
5 : 26	and killed great numbers of people
8 : 16	to the number of 6,000
10 : 24	and collected the cavalry from Asia in no small number
12 : 16	and slaughtered untold numbers
1 Es 2 : 9	and with a very great number of votive offerings
2 : 13	The number of these was : a 1,000 gold cups, a 1,000 silver cups
5 : 9	The number of the men of the nation and their leaders :
7 : 8	according to the number of the 12 leaders
P Ma 9	For the sins I have committed are more in number
3 Ma 5 : 2	to drug all the elephants – 500 in number
2 Es 2 : 19	and the same number of springs flowing with milk and honey
2 : 26	for I will require them from among your number
2 : 38	the number of those who have been sealed
2 : 40	Take again your full number, O Zion
2 : 41	The number of your children, whom you desired, is full
3 : 7	peoples and clans, without number
3 : 29	For when I came here I saw ungodly deeds without number
4 : 32	When heads of grain without number are sown
4 : 36	When the number of those like yourselves is completed
4 : 37	and numbered the times by number
16 : 56	and he knows the number of the stars
4 Ma 8 : 5	and greatly respect the beauty and the number of such brothers
16 : 13	to the whole number of her sons

NUMBER, verb
		7 = 0.005 %
Wis 5 : 5	Why has he been numbered among the sons of God ?
Sir 37 : 25	The life of a man is numbered by days
41 : 13	The days of a good life are numbered
1 Ma 2 : 18	Then you and your sons will be numbered
2 Es 2 : 42	which I could not number
4 : 37	and numbered the times by number
7 : 76	nor number yourself among those who are tormented

NUMENIUS
		4 = 0.003 %
1 Ma 12 : 16	We therefore have chosen Numenius the son of Antiochus
14 : 22	Numenius the son of Antiochus and Antipater the son of Jason, envoys of the Jews
14 : 24	After this Simon sent Numenius to Rome
15 : 15	Then Numenius and his companions arrived from Rome

NUMEROUS
		2
1 Ma 11 : 24	taking silver and gold and clothing and numerous other gifts
16 : 7	for the cavalry of the enemy were very numerous

NUN
		1
Sir 46 : 1	Joshua the son of Nun was mighty in war

NURSE, subst.
		3 = 0.002 %
3 Ma 1 : 20	Mothers and nurses abandoned even new-born children here and there
2 Es 1 : 28	or a mother her daughters or a nurse her children
2 : 25	Good nurse, nourish your sons

NURSE, verb 2
Wis 7:4 I was nursed with care in swaddling cloths
2 Ma 7:27 and nursed you for 3 years

NURSING 1
4 Ma 16:7 fruitless nurturings and wretched nursings !

NURTURE, subst. 3 = 0.002 %
3 Ma 5:32 arising from our nurture in common and your usefulness
4 Ma 13:22 from this common nurture and daily companionship
15:13 yearning of parents toward offspring, nurture

NURTURE, verb 1
Bar 4:11 With joy I nurtured them

NURTURING 1
4 Ma 16:7 fruitless nurturings and wretched nursings !

O

O 211 = 0.137 %

OAK 2
Sus 13:58 He answered, Under an evergreen oak
2 Es 14:1 On the 3rd day, while I was sitting under an oak

OATH 26 = 0.017 %
Tob 8:20 Raguel declared by oath to Tobias that he should not leave
Jud 8:9 and how he promised them under oath
8:11 and pronounced this oath between God and you
8:30 and made us take an oath which we cannot break
Wis 12:21 to whose fathers thou gavest oaths
14:29 they swear wicked oaths and expect to suffer no harm
18:6 in sure knowledge of the oaths in which they trusted
18:22 appealing to the oaths and covenants given to our fathers
Sir 23:9 Do not accustom your mouth to oaths
23:11 A man who swears many oaths will be filled with iniquity
44:21 Therefore the Lord assured him by an oath
1 Ma 6:61 So the king and the commanders gave them their oath
6:62 he broke the oath he had sworn
7:15 and swore this oath to them
7:18 and the oath which they swore
7:35 and in anger he swore this oath
2 Ma 7:24 but promised with oaths
14:32 And when they declared on oath
14:33 and swore this oath :
15:10 and their violation of oaths
1 Es 1:48 he broke his oath and rebelled
8:93 Let us take an oath to the Lord about this
8:96 and Levites of all Israel take oath
8:96 And they took the oath
3 Ma 5:42 and he firmly swore an irrevocable oath
4 Ma 5:29 nor will I transgress the sacred oaths of my ancestors

OBADIAH 2
1 Es 8:35 Of the sons of Joab, Obadiah the son of Jehiel
2 Es 1:39 and Joel and Obadiah and Jonah

OBDURACY 1
Sir 10:21 obduracy and pride are the beginning of rejection

OBED 1
1 Es 8:32 Of the sons of Adin, Obed the son of Jonathan

OBEDIENCE 3 = 0.002 %
4 Ma 5:16 than our obedience to the law
9:2 unless we should practice ready obedience
15:9 and their ready obedience to the law

OBEDIENT 4 = 0.003 %
Sir 7:23 and make them obedient from their youth
42:23 and are all obedient
L Jr 6:60 For sun and moon and stars, shining and sent forth for service, are obedient
2 Es 7:22 Nevertheless they were not obedient

OBEISANCE 1
Jud 10:23 and she prostrated herself and made obeisance to him

OBEY 38 = 0.025 %
Jud 2:3 who had not obeyed his command should be destroyed
Sir 3:6 and whoever obeys the Lord will refresh his mother
4:15 He who obeys her will judge the nations
18:3 and all things obey his will
24:22 Whoever obeys me will not be put to shame
33:28 and if he does not obey, make his fetters heavy
Bar 2:10 Yet we have not obeyed his voice
2:22 But if you will not obey the voice of the Lord

2:24 But we did not obey thy voice, to serve the king of Babylon
2:29 saying, If you will not obey my voice
2:30 For I know that they will not obey me
2:31 I will give them a heart that obeys and ears that hear
3:33 called it, and it obeyed him in fear
P Az 6 and have not obeyed thy commandments
1 Ma 1:50 And whoever does not obey the command of the king shall die
2:19 obey him, and have chosen to do his commands
2:22 We will not obey the king's words
10:38 and obey no other authority but the high priest
12:43 to obey him as they would himself
14:43 and that he should be obeyed by all
2 Ma 7:30 I will not obey the king's command
7:30 but I obey the command of the law
1 Es 4:3 and whatever he says to them they obey
4:10 All his people and his armies obey him
4:12 since he is to be obeyed in this fashion ?
5:69 For we obey your Lord just as you do
8:94 as seems good to you and to all who obey the law of the Lord
2 Es 1:8 for they have not obeyed my law
1:24 You would not obey me, O Judah
4 Ma 6:4 Obey the king's commands !
8:6 so I can be a benefactor to those who obey me
8:17 and exhorted us to accept kind treatment if we obey him
8:26 when we can live in peace if we obey the king ?
10:13 but obey the king and save yourself
12:4 You too, if you do not obey
12:6 to obey and save himself
15:10 so that they obeyed her even to death
18:1 obey this law and exercise pity in every way

OBJECT, subst. 6 = 0.004 %
Wis 14:20 now regarded as an object of worship
14:21 bestowed on objects of stone or wood
15:6 Lovers of evil things and fit for such objects of hope
15:17 for he is better than the objects he worships
Sir 38:28 and his eyes are on the pattern of the object
3 Ma 4:4 perceiving the common object of pity before their eyes

OBJECT, verb 1
3 Ma 2:28 Those who object to this are to be taken by force and put to death

OBLATION 3 = 0.002 %
P Az 15 or leader, no burnt offering, or sacrifice, or oblation
2 Es 1:31 When you offer oblations to me
3:24 and in it to offer thee oblations from what is thine

OBLIGATION 3 = 0.002 %
1 Ma 8:26 and they shall keep their obligations
8:28 and they shall keep these obligations
11:33 who are our friends and fulfil their obligations to us

OBLIGE 1
2 Ma 8:25 they were obliged to return because the hour was late

OBSCURE, verb 1
Wis 4:12 For the fascination of wickedness obscures what is good

OBSCURITY 1
Sir 39:3 and be at home with the obscurities of parables

OBSERVANCE 5 = 0.003 %
3 Ma 3:2 that they hindered others from the observance or their customs
6:36 they instituted the observance of the aforesaid days as a festival
4 Ma 3:20 because of their observance of the law
4:24 to put an end to the people's observance of the law
18:4 and by reviving observance of the law in the homeland

OBSERVE* 36 = 0.023 %
Jud 10:14 When the men heard her words, and observed her face
Ad E 10:13 So they will observe these days in the month of Adar
16:22 Therefore you shall observe this with all good cheer
Wis 6:10 who observe holy things in holiness
Sir 4:20 Observe the right time, and beware of evil
11:30 and like a spy he observes your weakness
23:7 the one who observes it will never be caught
24:34 Observe that I have not laboured for myself alone
38:17 observe the mourning according to his merit
41:14 My children, observe instruction and be at peace
P Az 7 we have not observed them or done them
1 Ma 1:13 He authorized them to observe the ordinances of the Gentiles
2:61 And so observe, from generation to generation
2:67 You shall rally about you all who observe the law
4:35 and observed the boldness which inspired those of Judas
4:59 the days of the dedication of the altar should be observed
13:48 and settled in it men who observed the law
2 Ma 3:1 and the laws were very well observed
6:6 nor observe the feasts of his fathers
6:11 to observe the 7th day secretly

	9:23	but I observed that my father
	10:8	should observe these days every year
	13:23	yielded and swore to observe all their rights
	15:4	who ordered us to observe the 7th day
3 Ma	1:27	When those who were around him observed this
	2:26	intently observing the king's purpose
	6:17	And when the Jews observed this
	7:19	they decided to observe
2 Es	6:32	and has also observed the purity
	7:21	and what they should observe to avoid punishment
	9:32	they did not keep it, and did not observe the statutes
	15:24	Woe to those who sin and do not observe my commandments
4 Ma	1:30	Observe now first of all
	4:23	that if any of them should be found observing the ancestral law
	5:7	when you observe the religion of the Jews
	14:13	Observe how complex is a mother's love for her children

OBSERVER   1
Wis 1:6   and a true observer of his heart

OBSTACLE   1
Sir 39:24   just as they are obstacles to the wicked

OBSTINACY   1
Sir 28:10   and in proportion to the obstinacy of strife

OBTAIN   20 = 0.013 %
Tob	5:2	but how can I obtain the money when I do not know the man ?
	12:3	he cured my wife, he obtained the money for me
Wis	7:14	those who get it obtain friendship with God
Sir	4:13	Whoever holds her fast will obtain glory
	4:16	If he has faith in her he will obtain her
	15:1	and he who holds to the law will obtain wisdom
	15:7	Foolish men will not obtain her
	17:5	They obtained the use
	19:18	and wisdom obtains his love
	22:4	A sensible daughter obtains her husband
	34:18	If one sacrifices from what has been wrongfully obtained
	46:9	and his children obtained it for an inheritance
1 Ma	9:70	and obtain release of the captives
2 Ma	4:7	obtained the high priesthood by corruption
	4:32	But Menelaus, thinking he had obtained a suitable opportunity
3 Ma	2:33	They remained resolutely hopeful of obtaining help
2 Es	4:24	and we are not worthy to obtain mercy
	5:12	And at that time men shall hope but not obtain
	7:72	and though they obtained the law
	14:34	and after death you shall obtain mercy

OBVIOUS   2
3 Ma 2:31   Now some, however, with an obvious abhorrence of the price
      4:11   and which was well suited to make them an obvious spectacle

OBVIOUSLY   2
4 Ma 1:32   and reason obviously rules over both
      9:2   we are obviously putting our forefathers to shame

OCCASION, subst.   9 = 0.006 %
Tob	4:19	Bless the Lord God on every occasion
Sir	4:5	nor give a man occasion to curse you
	29:3	and on every occasion you will find what you need
1 Ma	8:25	as the occasion may indicate to them
	8:27	as the occasion may indicate to them
	12:11	We therefore remember you constantly on every occasion
2 Ma	9:23	on the occasions when he made expeditions
4 Ma	3:19	The present occasion now invites us
	5:28	But you shall have no such occasion to laugh at me

OCCUPANT   1
1 Ma 13:11   he drove out its occupants and remained there

OCCUPATION   1
3 Ma 5:34   each to his own occupation

OCCUPY   6 = 0.004 %
Jud	5:19	and have occupied Jerusalem, where their sanctuary is
Sir	38:25	who drives oxen and is occupied with their work
1 Ma	10:1	landed and occupied Ptolemais
2 Ma	2:30	to occupy the ground and to discuss matters from every side
	10:36	and they occupied the city
1 Es	4:50	that all the country which they would occupy

OCCUR   10 = 0.007 %
Ad E	10:9	which have not occurred among the nations
Wis	11:12	and a groaning at the memory of what had occurred
Sir	20:18	so the downfall of the wicked will occur speedily
	48:25	He revealed what was to occur to the end of time
1 Ma	9:24	In those days a very great famine occurred
	14:29	Since wars often occurred in the country
1 Es	8:18	And whatever else occurs to you as necessary
3 Ma	1:17	supposing that something mysterious was occurring

2 Es	9:5	For just as with everything that has occurred in the world
	13:32	and the signs occur which I showed you before

OCHIEL   1
1 Es 1:9   and Hashabiah and Ochiel and Joram

OCINA   1
Jud 2:28   and those who lived in Sur and Ocina

ODIOUS   1
Wis 16:3   because of the odious creatures sent to them

ODOMERA   1
1 Ma 9:66   He struck down Odomera and his brothers

ODOUR, ODOR   7 = 0.005 %
Tob	8:3	And when the demon smelled the odour
Sir	24:15	and like choice myrrh I spread a pleasant odour
	35:6	and its pleasing odour rises before the Most High
	45:16	incense and a pleasing odour as a memorial portion
	50:15	a pleasing odour to the Most High, the King of all
1 Es	1:12	with a pleasing odour
2 Es	6:44	and odours of inexpressible fragrance

OF   5410 = 3.524 %

OFF, adv., prep.   6 = 0.004 %
Jud	13:9	Then she tumbled his body off the bed
Sir	16:22	For the covenant is far off
	22:1	any one that picks it up will shake it off his hand
	27:20	Do not go after him, for he is too far off
	30:14	Better off is a poor man
	40:18	but he who finds treasure is better off than both

OFFENCE, OFFENSE   11 = 0.007 %
Tob	3:3	do not punish me for my sins and for my unwitting offences
Jud	5:20	and they sin against their God and we find out their offence
	8:22	and we shall be an offence
	12:2	But Judith said, I cannot eat it, lest it be an offence
Sir	17:25	pray in his presence and lessen your offences
	23:23	second, she has committed an offence against her husband
	27:23	and with your own words he will give offence
	31:17	and do not be insatiable, lest you give offence
1 Ma	13:39	We pardon any errors and offences committed to this day
P Ma	10	setting up abominations and multiplying offences
3 Ma	3:9	when it had committed no offence

OFFEND   7 = 0.005 %
Sir	7:7	Do not offend against the public
	23:11	if he offends, his sin remains on him
	25:2	and I am greatly offended at their life :
	30:13	that you may not be offended by his shamelessness
L Jr	6:14	though unable to destroy any one who offends it
	6:18	upon a man who has offended a king
2 Es	12:41	How have we offended you

OFFENSIVE   2
Sir 27:13   The talk of fool is offensive
3 Ma 2:18   as offensive houses are trampled down

OFFER, verb   59 = 0.038 %
Tob	5:13	to worship and offered the first-born of our flocks
Jud	4:14	offered the continual burnt offerings
	9:1	when that evening's incense was being offered
	16:18	they offered their burnt offerings
Wis	18:9	For in secret the holy children of good men offered sacrifices
Sir	34:20	is the man who offers a sacrifice
	35:2	He who returns a kindness offers fine flour
	35:12	Do not offer him a bribe, for he will not accept it
	38:11	Offer a sweet-smelling sacrifice
	45:16	to offer sacrifice to the Lord
	46:16	and he offered in sacrifice a sucking lamb
Bar	1:10	and offer them upon the altar of the Lord our God
L Jr	6:28	The priests sell the sacrifices that are offered to these gods
	6:56	Besides, they can offer no resistance to a king or any enemies
P Az	2	Then Azariah stood and offered this prayer
1 Ma	1:51	and commanded the cities of Judah to offer sacrifice, city by city
	1:59	they offered sacrifice on the altar
	2:15	came to the city of Modein to make them offer sacrifice
	2:23	to offer sacrifice upon the altar in Modein
	2:42	every one who offered himself willingly for the law
	4:53	they rose and offered sacrifice, as the law directs
	4:56	and offered burnt offerings with gladness
	4:56	they offered a sacrifice of deliverance and praise
	5:54	and offered burnt offerings
	7:33	that was being offered for the king
	11:34	To all those who offer sacrifice in Jerusalem
	12:11	at the sacrifices which we offer and in our prayers
2 Ma	1:8	and we offered sacrifice and cereal offering

	1:18	when Nehemiah, who built the temple and the altar, offered sacrifices
	1:23	the priests offered prayer – the priests and every one
	2:9	that being possessed of wisdom Solomon offered sacrifice
	3:32	offered sacrifice for the man's recovery
	3:35	Then Heliodorus offered sacrifice to the Lord
	4:34	offered him sworn pledges and gave him his right hand
	10:3	then, striking fire out of flint, they offered sacrifices
	10:7	they offered hymns of thanksgiving to him
	13:23	settled with them and offered sacrifice
	14:31	while the priests were offering the customary sacrifices
1 Es	1:14	because the priests were offering the fat until night
	1:18	and the sacrifices were offered on the altar of the Lord
	4:52	for burnt offerings to be offered on the altar every day
	5:49	to offer burnt offerings upon it
	5:50	and they offered sacrifices at the proper times
	5:51	and offered the proper sacrifices every day
	5:53	began to offer sacrifices to God
	6:31	and prayers be offered for their life
	7:7	They offered at the dedication of the temple of the Lord
	8:15	so as to offer sacrifices upon the altar of their Lord
	8:65	offered sacrifices to the Lord, the God of Israel
3 Ma	1:9	he offered sacrifice to the supreme God and made thank-offerings
	5:43	of those who offered sacrifices there
2 Es	1:6	and have offered sacrifices to strange gods
	1:31	When you offer oblations to me
	3:24	and in it to offer thee oblations from what is thine
	10:45	before any offering was offered in it
	10:46	and offered offerings
	14:39	a full cup was offered to me
4 Ma	3:16	he poured out the drink as an offering to God
	18:11	and Isaac who was offered as a burnt offering

OFFER, subst.   1
1 Ma	6:60	and he sent to the Jews an offer of peace

OFFERING s. **BURNT, DRINK, THANK OFF.**   39 = 0.025 %
Tob	4:11	and for all who practise it charity is an excellent offering
Jud	4:14	and the vows and freewill offerings of the people
	16:16	For every sacrifice as a fragrant offering is a small thing
	16:18	their freewill offerings, and their gifts
	16:19	she gave as a votive offering to the Lord
Sir	7:9	and when I make an offering to the Most High God
	7:31	the first fruits, the guilt offering
	14:11	and present worthy offerings to the Lord
	30:18	are like offerings of food placed upon a grave
	30:19	Of what use to an idol is an offering of fruit ?
	34:18	the offering is blemished
	34:19	with the offerings of the ungodly
	35:1	He who keeps the law makes many offerings
	35:1	he who heeds the commandments sacrifices a peace offering
	35:6	The offering of a righteous man anoints the altar
	38:11	and pour oil on your offering, as much as you can afford
	47:2	As the fat is selected from the peace offering
	50:13	with the Lord's offering in their hands
	50:14	and arranging the offering to the Most High, the Almighty
Bar	1:10	so buy with the money burnt offerings and sin offerings
	1:10	and incense, and prepare a cereal offering
P Az	15	or incense, no place to make an offering before thee
2 Ma	1:8	and we offered sacrifice and cereal offering
	2:11	because the sin offering had not been eaten
	2:13	and letters of kings about votive offerings
	3:33	While the high priest was making the offering of atonement
	5:16	the votive offerings which other kings had made
	6:5	The altar was covered with abominable offerings
	9:16	he would adorn with the finest offerings
	12:43	and sent it to Jerusalem to provide for a sin offering
1 Es	1:11	to make the offering to the Lord
	2:7	besides the other things added as votive offerings
	2:9	and with a very great number of votive offerings
	4:52	in accordance with the commandment to make 17 offerings
	5:52	and thereafter the continual offerings and sacrifices
3 Ma	3:17	with magnificent and most beautiful offerings
2 Es	10:45	before any offering was offered in it
	10:46	and offered offerings
	13:13	and some were bringing others as offerings

OFFICE   9 = 0.006 %
Sir	7:4	Do not seek from the Lord the highest office
1 Ma	11:63	intending to remove him from office
	13:15	in connection with the offices he held
2 Ma	4:10	When the king assented and Jason came to office
	4:27	And Menelaus held the office
	4:50	remained in office, growing in wickedness
	10:13	Unable to command the respect due his office
	13:3	that he would be established in office
4 Ma	4:17	Jason agreed that if the office were conferred upon him

OFFICER   20 = 0.013 %
Jud	2:2	He called together all his officers and all his nobles
	2:14	and officers of the Assyrian army
	5:22	Holofernes'officers and all the men from the seacoast
	12:10	and did not invite any of his officers
	14:3	and rouse the officers of the Assyrian army
	14:12	and to all their officers
1 Ma	1:6	So he summoned his most honoured officers
	1:8	Then his officers began to rule, each in his own place
	2:15	Then the king's officers who were enforcing the apostasy
	2:17	Then the king's officers spoke to Mattathias as follows :
	2:25	At the same time he killed the king's officer
	2:31	And it was reported to the king's officers
	5:40	Timothy said to the officers of his forces
	10:37	Let their officers and leaders be of their own number
	10:63	and he said to his officers
	11:63	Then Jonathan heard that the officers of Demetrius
1 Es	1:8	the chief officers of the temple
	4:49	that no officer or satrap or governor or treasurer
	7:2	and the chief officers of the temple
3 Ma	5:44	Then the friends and officers departed with great joy

OFFICIAL   9 = 0.006 %
Sir	10:2	like the magistrate of the people, so are his officials
1 Ma	10:33	and let all officials cancel also the taxes on their cattle
	10:41	which the government officials have not paid
	10:42	which my officials have received every year
	12:45	and the remaining troops and all the officials
	13:37	and to write to our officials
1 Es	8:67	and these officials honoured the people
3 Ma	5:39	But the officials who were at table with him
	6:30	summoned the official in charge of the revenues

OFFSHOOT   1
4 Ma	1:28	so there are many offshoots of these plants

OFFSPRING   11 = 0.007 %
Wis	3:13	their offspring are accursed
	3:16	and the offspring of an unlawful union will perish
Sir	26:21	So your offspring will survive
Sus	13:56	You offspring of Canaan and not of Judah
1 Ma	1:38	she became strange to her offspring
2 Es	2:6	so that they may have no offspring
4 Ma	14:14	have a sympathy and parental love for their offspring
	15:4	have a deeper sympathy toward their offspring than do the fathers
	15:13	yearning of parents toward offspring, nurture
	16:9	others married and without offspring
	18:1	O Israelite children, offspring of the seed of Abraham

OFTEN   15 = 0.010 %
Tob	1:6	But I alone went often to Jerusalem for the feasts
Ad E	16:2	The more often they are honoured
	16:5	And often many of those who are set in places of authority
Sir	13:9	and he will invite you the more often
	19:15	Question a friend, for often it is slander
	20:17	How many will ridicule him, and how often !
	30:1	He who loves his son will whip him often
	34:12	I have often been in danger of death
1 Ma	14:29	Since wars often occurred in the country
2 Ma	9:25	whom I have often entrusted and commended to most of you
	12:22	so that often they were injured by their own men
3 Ma	6:26	and often have accepted willingly the worst of human dangers ?
2 Es	4:26	and if you live long, you will often marvel
	5:8	and fire shall often break out
	8:47	But you have often compared yourself to the unrighteous

OFTENTIMES   1
3 Ma	2:12	And because oftentimes when our fathers were oppressed

OIL   8 = 0.005 %
Jud	10:5	And she gave her maid a bottle of wine and a flask of oil
	11:13	and the tithes of the wine and oil
Sir	38:11	and pour oil on your offering, as much as you can afford
	39:26	the blood of the grape, and oil and clothing
	45:15	Moses ordained him, and anointed him with holy oil
Sus	13:17	Bring me oil and ointments
1 Es	6:30	and likewise wheat and salt and wine and oil
Ps 151	:4	and anointed me with his anointing oil

OINTMENT   3 = 0.002 %
Jud	10:3	and anointed herself with precious ointment
	16:8	She anointed her face with ointment
Sus	13:17	Bring me oil and ointments

OLD, adj., subst.   76 = 0.050 %
Tob	3:10	and I shall bring his old age down in sorrow to the grave
	4:12	that Noah, Abraham, Isaac, and Jacob, our fathers of old
	8:7	and may grow together with her
	12:4	The old man said, He deserves it

	14:2	He was 58 years old when he lost his sight
	14:3	When he had grown very old he called his son and grandsons
	14:3	behold, I have grown old and am about to depart this life
	14:11	He was a 158 years old
	14:13	He grew old with honour
Jud	16:23	and grew old in her husband's house
	16:23	until she was 105 years old
Wis	3:17	and finally their old age will be without honour
	4:8	For old age is not honoured for length of time
	4:9	and a blameless life is ripe old age
	4:16	will condemn the prolonged old age of the unrighteous man
	8:8	she knows the things of old, and infers the things to come
	12:3	Those who dwelt of old in thy holy land
Sir	3:12	O son, help your father in his old age
	6:18	and until you are old you will keep finding wisdom
	8:6	Do not disdain a man when he is old
	8:6	for some of us are growing old
	9:10	Forsake not an old friend
	11:16	evil will grow old with those who take pride in malice
	11:20	and grow old in your work
	14:17	All living beings become old like a garment
	14:17	for the decree from of old is, You must surely die !
	25:2	and an adulterous old man who lacks good sense
	25:3	how then can you find anything in your old age ?
	30:24	and anxiety brings on old age too soon
	32:3	Speak, you who are older, for it is fitting that you should
	41:2	very old and distracted over everything
	46:9	which remained with him to old age
	50:23	as in the days of old
	51:8	and thy work from of old
Bar	3:26	The giants were born there, who were famous of old
	4:15	who had no respect for an old man
Sus	13:52	You old relic of wicked days, your sins have now come home
1 Ma	14:9	Old men sat in the streets
	16:3	But now I have grown old
2 Ma	5:13	Then there was killing of young and old
	6:22	on account of his old friendship with them
	6:23	worthy of his years and the dignity of his old age
	6:25	while I defile and disgrace my old age
	6:27	I will show myself worthy of my old age
1 Es	1:34	who was 23 years old
	1:39	Jehoiakim was 25 years old
	1:43	when he was made king he was 18 years old
	1:46	Zedekiah was 21 years old, and he reigned 11 years
	1:53	old man or child, for he gave them all into their hands
	2:23	and kept setting up blockades in it from of old
	2:26	that this city from of old has fought against kings
	5:63	old men who had seen the former house
3 Ma	1:23	and being barely restrained by the old men and the elders
	3:27	old people or children or even infants
	4:5	For a multitude of grey-headed old men
	6:1	who had attained a ripe old age
2 Es	2:22	Protect the old and the young within your walls
	5:49	and a woman who has become old does not bring forth any longer
	5:50	Or is she now approaching old age ?
	5:53	are different from those born during the time of old age
	6:21	Infants a year old shall speak with their voices
	9:4	from the days that were of old, from the beginning
	14:10	and the times begin to grow old
	14:17	For the weaker the world becomes through old age
4 Ma	5:6	Before I begin to torture you, old man
	5:12	and have compassion on your old age
	5:31	I am not so old and cowardly
	5:33	I do not so pity my old age
	5:36	the honourable mouth of my old age
	6:2	First they stripped the old man
	6:6	yet while the old man's eyes were raised to heaven
	6:10	And like a noble athlete the old man, while being beaten
	6:12	At that point, partly out of pity for his old age
	6:18	who have lived in accordance with truth to old age
	7:13	Most amazing, indeed, though he was an old man
	8:5	as that of the old man who has just been tortured

OLIVE
6 = 0.004 %

Jud	15:13	and they crowned themselves with olive wreaths
Sir	24:14	like a beautiful olive tree in the field
	50:10	like an olive tree putting forth its fruit
2 Ma	14:4	some of the customary olive branches from the temple
2 Es	16:29	As in an olive orchard
	16:29	3 or 4 olives may be left on every tree

OLYMPIAN
1

2 Ma	6:2	and call it the temple of Olympian Zeus

OMEN
2

Sir	34:5	Divinations and omens and dreams are folly
2 Ma	5:4	that the apparition might prove to have been a good omen

OMIT
2

1 Es	8:7	so that he omitted nothing from the law of the Lord
3 Ma	4:13	not omitting any detail of their punishment

OMNIPOTENCE
1

Sir	19:20	And the knowledge of his omnipotence

ON, adv., prep.
559 = 0.364 %

ONCE
10 = 0.007 %

Tob	1:14	and once at Rages in Media I left 10 talents of silver
	2:8	he once ran away, and here he is burying the dead again !
	2:12	Once when they paid her wages, they also gave her a kid
Wis	5:4	This is the man whom we once held in derision
	14:15	what was once a dead human being
Sus	13:15	Once, while they were watching for an opportune day
3 Ma	1:11	and he only once a year
	5:38	Equip the elephants now once more
2 Es	5:22	and I began once more to speak words
	16:6	when once it has begun to burn ?

ONCE, at once
13 = 0.008 %

Tob	4:14	but pay him at once
Jud	10:15	Go at once to his tent
	12:14	Surely whatever pleases him I will do at once
Wis	5:12	the air, thus divided, comes together at once
	18:17	Then at once apparitions in dreadful dreams greatly troubled them
2 Ma	3:8	Heliodorus at once set out on his journey
	4:10	he at once shifted his countrymen over
	6:28	When he had said this, he went at once to the rack
3 Ma	5:25	implored the supreme God to help them again at once
	6:41	The king granted their request at once
2 Es	6:43	For thy word went forth, and at once the work was done
	7:75	or whether we shall be tormented at once ?
4 Ma	12:9	they freed him at once

ONE, indef. pr., s. NUMBERS
197 = 0.128 %

ONE ANOTHER
31 = 0.020 %

Jud	15:2	so that they did not wait for one another
Wis	5:3	They will speak to one another in repentance
	14:24	but they either treacherously kill one another
	14:24	or grieve one another by adultery
	18:23	For when the dead had already fallen on one another in heaps
	19:18	For the elements changed places with one another
Sir	16:28	They do not crowd one another aside
1 Ma	3:43	But they said to one another
	7:29	So he came to Judas, and they greeted one another peaceably
	10:54	now therefore let us establish friendship with one another
	10:56	but meet me at Ptolemais, so that we may see one another
	11:6	and they greeted one another and spent the night there
	12:50	and they encouraged one another
	13:28	He also erected 7 pyramids, opposite one another
2 Ma	7:5	but the brothers and their mother encouraged one another to die nobly
	14:26	But when Alcimus noticed their good will for one another
1 Es	3:4	said to one another
	4:4	If he tells them to make war on one another, they do it
	4:6	and they compel one another to pay taxes to the king
	4:33	Then the king and the nobles looked at one another
3 Ma	5:49	embracing relatives and falling into one another's arms
2 Es	5:9	and all friends shall conquer one another
	13:31	And they shall plan to make war against one another
	13:33	and the warfare that they have against one another
	15:16	growing strong against one another
	15:35	They shall dash against one another
4 Ma	13:8	encouraged one another, saying
	13:13	Each of them and all of them together looking at one another
	13:23	the brothers were the more sympathetic to one another
	13:24	they loved one another all the more
	13:25	expanded their goodwill and harmony toward one another

ONIAS
26 = 0.017 %

Sir	50:1	was Simon the high priest, son of Onias
1 Ma	12:7	a letter was sent to Onias the high priest
	12:8	Onias welcomed the envoy with honour
	12:19	This is a copy of the letter which they sent to Onias :
	12:20	to Onias the high priest, greeting
2 Ma	3:1	because of the piety of the high priest Onias
	3:5	and when he could not prevail over Onias
	3:31	Quickly some of Heliodorus' friends asked Onias
	3:33	Be very grateful to Onias the high priest
	3:35	and having bidden Onias farewell
	4:1	slandered Onias, saying that it was he who had incited Heliodorus
	4:4	Onias recognized that the rivalry was serious
	4:7	Jason the brother of Onias
	4:33	When Onias became fully aware of these acts
	4:34	urged him to kill Onias

	4:34	Andronicus came to Onias, and resorting to treachery
	4:34	persuaded Onias to come out from the place of sanctuary
	4:36	with regard to the unreasonable murder of Onias
	4:38	where he had committed the outrage against Onias
	15:12	Onias, who had been high priest, a noble and good man
	15:14	And Onias spoke, saying
4 Ma	4:1	Onias, who then held the high priesthood for life
	4:1	he was unable to injure Onias in the eyes of the nation
	4:13	Moved by these words, Onias the high priest
	4:16	who removed Onias from the priesthood
	4:16	and appointed Onias's brother Jason as high priest

ONLY, adj., adv.   101 = 0.066 %

Tob	3:10	But she said, I am the only child of my father
	3:15	I am my father's only child
	6:10	He is your relative, and he has an only daughter named Sarah
	6:11	for you are her only eligible kinsman
	6:14	Now I am the only son my father has
	8:17	Blessed art thou, because thou hast had compassion on 2 only children
Jud	1:11	but looked upon him as only one man
	2:4	the chief general of his army, second only to himself
	3:8	so that all nations should worship Nebuchadnezzar only
	4:3	For they had only recently returned from the captivity
	4:7	only wide enough for 2 men at the most
	7:12	only let your servants take possession
	8:34	Only, do not try to find out what I plan
	11:7	not only do men serve him because of you
	11:23	You are not only beautiful in appearance, but wise in speech
	12:10	On the 4th day Holofernes held a banquet for his slaves only
	14:2	only do not go down
Ad E	14:3	O my Lord, thou only art our King
	15:10	you shall not die, for our law applies only to the people. Come near
	16:3	They not only seek to injure our subjects
	16:4	They not only take away thankfulness from among men
	16:24	It shall be made not only impassable for men
Wis	3:9	and he watches over his only ones
	10:8	they not only were hindered from recognizing the good
	11:19	not only could their damage exterminate men
	13:16	for it is only an image and has need of help
	19:15	And not only so
Sir	pr.	not only that the readers themselves
	pr.	Not only this work, but even the law itself
	16:11	Even if there is only one stiff-necked person
	32:7	but no more than twice, and only if asked
	37:1	but some friends are friends only in name
	45:13	No outsider ever put them on, but only his sons
	45:25	the heritage of the king is from son to son only
L Jr	6:47	They have left only lies and reproach for those who come after
P Az	22	Let them know that thou art the Lord, the only God
Sus	13:15	she went in as before with only 2 maids
1 Ma	9:55	But he only began to tear it down
	9:65	and he went with only a few men
	10:14	Only in Beth-zur did some remain
	10:70	You are the only one to rise up against us
	11:42	Not only will I do these things for you and your nation
	15:33	but only the inheritance of our fathers
2 Ma	2:29	has to consider only what is suitable for its adornment
	2:32	adding only so much to what has already been said
	4:35	For this reason not only Jews
	5:7	and in the end got only disgrace from his conspiracy
	6:31	not only to the young but to the great body of his nation
	7:24	Antiochus not only appealed to him in words
	10:28	not only their valour but their reliance upon the Lord
	11:9	ready to assail not only men but the wildest beasts or walls of iron
1 Es	2:19	they will not only refuse to pay tribute
	4:7	And yet he is only one man !
3 Ma	1:11	but only the high priest who was preeminent over all
	1:11	and he only once a year
	1:29	for it seemed that not only the men
	2:2	the only ruler, almighty, give attention to us
	3:1	he became so infuriated that not only was he enraged
	3:19	they become the only people among all nations
	3:23	they not only spurn the priceless citizenship
	5:50	Not only this, but when they considered
2 Es	3:14	and to him only didst thou reveal the end of the times
	4:9	But now I have asked you only about fire and wind and the day
	4:21	can understand only what is on the earth
	5:28	and scattered thine only one among the many ?
	5:47	but only each in its own time
	6:58	whom thou hast called thy first-born, only begotten
	7:8	and there is only one path lying between them, that is
	7:8	so that only one man can walk upon that path
	7:34	but only judgment shall remain, truth shall stand
	7:42	but only the splendour of the glory of the Most High
	7:54	Not only that, but ask the earth and she will tell you
	7:140	there would probably be left only very few
	8:2	but only a little dust from which gold comes

	8:5	for you have been given only a short time to live
	8:62	but only to you and a few like you
	9:24	and eat only of the flowers of the field
	9:24	and taste no meat and drink no wine, but eat only flowers
	10:34	only do not forsake me, lest I die before my time
	12:51	and I ate only the flowers of the field
	13:10	but I saw only how
	13:11	but only the dust of ashes and the smell of smoke
	16:47	Those who conduct business, do it only to be plundered
4 Ma	2:4	Not only is reason proved to rule
	4:20	so that not only was a gymnasium constructed
	5:24	so that with proper reverence we worship the only real God
	5:27	not only to transgress the law
	6:35	And I have proved not only that reason has mastered agonies
	7:6	which had room only for reverence and purity
	7:23	For only the wise and courageous man is lord of his emotions
	8:5	Not only do I advise you not to display the same madness
	8:15	not only were they not afraid
	9:10	When they had said these things the tyrant not only was angry
	14:1	so that they not only despised their agonies
	14:9	they not only saw what was happening
	14:9	yes, not only heard the direct word of threat
	15:9	Not only so, but also because of the nobility of her sons
	16:2	Thus I have demonstrated not only
	17:20	are honoured, not only with this honour
	18:2	not only of sufferings from within
	18:3	were not only admired by men

ONO   1

1 Es	5:22	The sons of the other Elam and Ono, 725

ONRUSH   1

2 Es	13:9	And behold, when he saw the onrush of the approaching multitude

ONRUSHING   2

2 Es	13:11	and fell on the onrushing multitude
	13:28	yet destroying the onrushing multitude

ONSLAUGHT   1

2 Ma	6:3	Harsh and utterly grievous was the onslaught of evil

ONWARD   1

Sus	13:64	And from that day onward

ONYCHA   1

Sir	24:15	like galbanum, onycha, and stacte

OPEN, adj.   15 = 0.010 %

Tob	2:10	and their fresh droppings fell into my open eyes
	6:4	Cut open the fish and take the heart and liver and gall
Ad E	13:2	and open to travel throughout all its extent
Bel	14:27	The dragon ate them, and burst open
2 Ma	10:36	Others broke open the gates and let in the rest of the force
	15:19	being anxious over the encounter in the open country
1 Es	4:19	and with open mouths stare at her
	9:6	And all the multitude sat in the open square before the temple
	9:11	and we are not able to stand in the open air
	9:38	into the open square before the east gate of the temple
	9:41	And he read aloud in the open square
2 Es	9:11	while an opportunity of repentance was still open to them
	15:57	and all your people who are in the open country
4 Ma	4:11	in the temple area that was open to all
	15:2	2 courses were open to this mother

OPEN, verb   46 = 0.030 %

Tob	8:13	So the maid opened the door and went in
	11:7	that your father will open his eyes
Jud	10:9	Order the gate of the city to be opened for me
	10:9	to open the gate for her, as she had said
	11:19	and not a dog will so much as open its mouth to growl at you
	13:11	Open, open the gate !
	13:13	they opened the gate and admitted them
	14:15	he opened it and went into the bedchamber
Ad E	14:10	to open the mouths of the nations for the praise of vain idols
Wis	10:21	because wisdom opened the mouth of the dumb
Sir	15:5	and will open his mouth in the midst of the assembly
	20:15	he opens his mouth like a herald
	22:22	If you have opened your mouth against your friend
	24:2	In the assembly of the Most High she will open her mouth
	26:12	As a thirsty wayfarer opens his mouth
	26:12	and open her quiver to the arrow
	29:24	and where you are a stranger you may not open your mouth
	39:5	he will open his mouth in prayer
	43:14	Therefore the storehouses are opened
	51:25	I opened my mouth and said
Bar	2:17	open thy eyes, O Lord, and see
P Az	2	in the midst of the fire he opened his mouth and said :
	10	And now we cannot open our mouths
Sus	13:25	And one of them ran and opened the garden doors

	13:39	and he opened the doors and dashed out
Bel	14:18	As soon as the doors were opened
1 Ma	3:28	And he opened his coffers
	3:48	And they opened the book of the law
	5:48	But they refused to open to him
	10:76	and the men of the city became afraid and opened the gates
	11:2	and the people of the cities opened their gates to him
	14:5	and opened a way to the isles of the sea
2 Ma	1:4	May he open your heart to his law and his commandments
	1:16	Opening the secret door in the ceiling
	6:18	was being forced to open his mouth to eat swine's flesh
	14:44	a space opened and he fell in the middle of the empty space
1 Es	9:46	And when he opened the law, they all stood erect
3 Ma	6:18	revealed his holy face and opened the heavenly gates
2 Es	5:37	open for me the closed chambers
	6:20	the books shall be opened before the firmament
	8:52	because it is for you that paradise is opened
	9:28	And my mouth was opened
	14:38	Ezra, open your mouth and drink what I give you to drink
	14:39	Then I opened my mouth, and behold
	14:41	and my mouth was opened, and was no longer closed

OPEN up   1
Sir 27:25   and a treacherous blow opens up wounds

OPENLY   2
Sir 51:13   I sought wisdom openly in my prayer
2 Es 14:6   These words you shall publish openly

OPEN-MOUTHED   1
Sir 19:30   A man's attire and open-mouthed laughter

OPERATION   3 = 0.002 %
Sir 17:5   of the 5 operations of the Lord
    17:5   and as 7th reason, the interpreter of his operations
1 Es 6:10   These operations are going on rapidly

OPHIR   2
Tob 13:17   and ruby and stones of Ophir
Sir 7:18   or a real brother for the gold of Ophir

OPINION   5 = 0.003 %
Sir 3:24   and wrong opinion has caused their thoughts to slip
    13:24   and poverty is evil in the opinion of the ungodly
2 Ma 6:29   were in their opinion sheer madness
4 Ma 5:10   if, by holding a vain opinion concerning the truth
    8:19   and give up this vain opinion

OPPONENT   2
2 Ma 8:35   by opponents whom he regarded as of the least account
4 Ma 4:1   a political opponent of the noble and good man

OPPORTUNE   1
Sus 13:15   Once, while they were watching for an opportune day

OPPORTUNITY   17 = 0.011 %
Jud 12:16   for he had been waiting for an opportunity to deceive her
Wis 12:20   granting them time and opportunity
Sir pr.   I found opportunity for no little instruction
    12:16   but if he finds an opportunity
    19:28   he will do evil when he finds an opportunity
    38:24   depends on the opportunity of leisure
1 Ma 11:42   if I find an opportunity
    12:25   for he gave them no opportunity to invade his own country
    15:34   Now that we have the opportunity
2 Ma 4:32   But Menelaus, thinking he had obtained a suitable opportunity
    9:25   keep watching for opportunities
    14:5   But he found an opportunity that furthered his mad purpose
    14:29   he watched for an opportunity
2 Es 5:50   Since thou hast now given me the opportunity
    9:11   while an opportunity of repentance was still open to them
4 Ma 1:12   I shall shortly have an opportunity to speak of this
    11:12   an opportunity to show our endurance for the law

OPPOSE   15 = 0.010 %
Ad E 13:9   and there is no one who can oppose thee
Wis 2:12   because he is inconvenient to us and opposes our actions
1 Ma 8:11   as many as ever opposed them, they destroyed and enslaved
    14:7   and there was none to oppose him
    14:44   to nullify any of these decisions or to oppose what he says
2 Ma 14:29   Since it was not possible to oppose the king
1 Es 1:27   Stand aside, and do not oppose the Lord
3 Ma 3:7   but were hostile and greatly opposed to his government
    6:19   They opposed the forces of the enemy
2 Es 5:29   And those who opposed thy promises have trodden down
    9:18   and no one opposed me then, for no one existed
    15:3   by the unbelief of those who oppose you
4 Ma 1:6   but those that are opposed to justice, courage, and self-control

---

	3:16	Therefore, opposing reason to desire
	8:15	but they also opposed the tyrant with their own philosophy

OPPOSING   2
2 Es 11:3   and out of his wings there grew opposing wings
    11:11   And I counted his opposing wings

OPPOSITE   21 = 0.014 %
Jud 2:21   and camped opposite Bectileth
    4:6   which faces Esdraelon opposite the plain near Dothan
    7:18   and encamped in the hill country opposite Dothan
Sir 33:14   Good is the opposite of evil, and life the opposite of death
    33:14   so the sinner is the opposite of the godly
    33:15   they likewise are in pairs, one the opposite of the other
    42:24   All things are twofold, one opposite the other
1 Ma 2:32   they encamped opposite them and prepared for battle
    3:46   So they assembled and went to Mizpah, opposite Jerusalem
    5:37   and encamped opposite Raphon, on the other side of the stream
    6:32   opposite the camp of the king
    10:48   and encamped opposite Demetrius
    13:20   But Simon and his army kept marching along opposite him
    13:28   He also erected 7 pyramids, opposite one another
2 Ma 15:33   opposite the sanctuary
3 Ma 5:16   and ordered those present for the banquet to recline opposite him
2 Es 7:36   and opposite it shall be the place of rest
    7:36   and opposite it the paradise of delight
    14:1   behold, a voice came out of a bush opposite me
4 Ma 6:4   while a herald opposite him cried out

OPPOSITION   2
Ad E 13:5   stands constantly in opposition to all men
1 Ma 11:38   and that there was no opposition to him

OPPRESS   7 = 0.005 %
Wis 2:10   Let us oppress the righteous poor man
    15:14   are all the enemies who oppressed thy people
1 Ma 10:46   and how he had greatly oppressed them
    11:53   but oppressed him greatly
2 Ma 1:28   Afflict those who oppress and are insolent with pride
    8:2   who were oppressed by all
3 Ma 2:12   And because oftentimes when our fathers were oppressed

OPPRESSED, subst., adj.   3 = 0.002 %
Jud 9:11   for thou art God of the lowly, helper of the oppressed
    16:8   to exalt the oppressed in Israel
    16:11   Then my oppressed people shouted for joy

OPPRESSION   2
2 Es 11:32   and with much oppression dominated its inhabitants
    11:40   and over all the earth with grievous oppression

OPPRESSIVE   1
3 Ma 6:5   oppressive king of the Assyrians

OPPRESSIVELY   1
2 Es 12:24   and its inhabitants more oppressively

OPPRESSOR   3 = 0.002 %
Wis 10:11   When his oppressors were covetous
    10:15   from a nation of oppressors
    16:4   For it was necessary that upon those oppressors

OR   391 = 0.255 %

ORACLE   3 = 0.002 %
Wis 16:11   To remind them of thy oracles they were bitten
Sir 45:10   with the oracle of judgment, Urim and Thummim
2 Ma 2:4   that the prophet, having received an oracle

ORCHARD   2
Sir 24:31   I said, I will water my orchard and drench my garden plot
2 Es 16:29   As in an olive orchard

ORDAIN   8 = 0.005 %
Tob 1:6   as it is ordained for all Israel by an everlasting decree
Ad E 14:9   to abolish what thy mouth has ordained
Sir 42:21   He has ordained the splendours of his wisdom
    45:15   Moses ordained him, and anointed him with holy oil
2 Ma 8:36   because they followed the laws ordained by him
1 Es 1:32   it was ordained that this should always be done
3 Ma 6:36   And when they had ordained a public rite for these things
2 Es 7:17   thou hast ordained in thy law

ORDEAL   1
4 Ma 13:9   who despised the same ordeal of the furnace

ORDER*, subst.   55 = 0.036 %
Jud 1:11   disregarded the orders of Nebuchadnezzar
    2:6   because they disobeyed my orders

	4:8	had given order
	7:16	and he gave orders to do as they had said
Ad E	16:16	and for our fathers in the most excellent order
Sir	16:27	He arranged his works in an eternal order
	50:19	till the order of worship of the Lord was ended
1 Ma	3:34	and gave him orders about all that he wanted done
	5:58	And they issued orders
	6:40	and they advanced steadily and in good order
	6:57	So he quickly gave orders to depart
	6:62	and gave orders to tear down the wall all around
	9:54	Alcimus gave orders to tear down the wall
	9:63	and sent orders to the men of Judea
	10:62	The king gave orders to take off Jonathan's garments
	11:23	he gave orders to continue the siege
	14:48	And they gave orders
2 Ma	4:25	After receiving the king's orders he returned
	7:3	and gave orders that pans and cauldrons be heated
	7:22	nor I who set in order the elements within each of you
	9:7	and giving orders to hasten the journey
	11:10	They advanced in battle order, having their heavenly ally
	12:5	he gave orders to his men
	14:13	with orders to kill Judas and scatter his men
	15:10	And when he had aroused their courage, he gave his orders
1 Es	1:5	Stand in order in the temple
	2:28	Therefore I have now issued orders
	6:4	By whose order are you building this house
	7:1	following the orders of King Darius
	8:10	I have given orders that those of the Jewish nation
	8:67	And they delivered the king's orders to the royal stewards
P Ma	2	thou who hast made heaven and earth with all their order
3 Ma	1:1	he gave orders to all his forces
	1:10	he marvelled at the good order of the temple
	3:25	Therefore we have given orders that
	3:26	the government will be established for ourselves in good order
	5:3	When he had given these orders he returned to his feasting
	5:4	proceeded faithfully to carry out the orders
	5:19	he had carried out completely the order given him
	5:37	must I give you orders about these things ?
2 Es	7:44	This is my judgment and its prescribed order
	7:88	Now this is the order of those
	7:91	for they shall have rest in 7 orders
	7:92	The first order
	7:93	The 2nd order
	7:94	The 3rd order
	7:95	The 4th order
	7:96	The 5th order
	7:97	The 6th order
	7:98	The 7th order
	7:99	This is the order of the souls of the righteous
	14:13	Now therefore, set your house in order
4 Ma	8:3	When the tyrant had given these orders, 7 brothers
	8:6	Just as I am able to punish those who disobey my orders
	10:17	gave orders to cut out his tongue

ORDER, conj., in order that   19 = 0.012 %

Jud	11:11	And now, in order that my lord may not be defeated
Wis	16:3	in order that those men, when they desired food
	16:23	whereas the fire, in order that the righteous might be fed
	19:4	in order that they might fill up the punishment
Sir	pr.	in order that, by becoming conversant with this also
	16:15	in order that his works might be known under heaven
	23:3	in order that my mistakes may not be multiplied
	30:1	in order that he may rejoice at the way he turns out
	38:5	in order that his power might be known ?
Bar	3:7	in order that we should call upon thy name
L Jr	6:18	in order that they may not be plundered by robbers
1 Ma	14:29	in order that their sanctuary and the law might be preserved
2 Ma	1:18	in order that you also may celebrate the feast of booths
	6:15	in order that he may not take vengeance on us afterward
1 Es	2:21	but to speak to our lord the king, in order that
	6:12	And in order that we might inform you in writing
	6:31	in order that libations may be made to the Most High God
	8:85	in order that you may be strong
3 Ma	2:30	In order that he might not appear to be an enemy to all

ORDER, conj., in order to   12 = 0.008 %

Tob	12:13	in order to go and lay out the dead
Jud	3:10	in order to assemble all the supplies for his army
	8:27	in order to admonish them
	14:13	in order to be destroyed completely
Ad E	13:2	and, in order to make my kingdom peaceable
Sir	pr.	in order to complete and publish the book
1 Ma	12:36	to separate it from the city, in order to isolate it
1 Es	8:12	in order to look into matters in Judea and Jerusalem
2 Es	6:35	in order to complete the 3 weeks
	8:49	in order to receive the greatest glory
	11:20	in order to rule
	14:46	in order to give them to the wise among your people

ORDER*, verb   49 = 0.032 %

Tob	8:18	Then he ordered his servants to fill in the grave
Jud	2:13	but be sure to carry them out just as I have ordered you
	2:15	as his lord had ordered him to do
	4:7	ordering them to seize the passes up into the hills
	6:10	Then Holofernes ordered his slaves
	7:1	The next day Holofernes ordered his whole army
	10:9	Order the gate of the city to be opened for me
	10:9	So they ordered the young men
	12:1	and ordered them to set a table for her
Ad E	12:5	And the king ordered Mordecai to serve in the court
Wis	8:1	and she orders all things well
Sir	10:1	and the rule of an understanding man will be well ordered
	43:10	At the command of the Holy One they stand as ordered
Bar	5:7	For God has ordered that every high mountain
L Jr	6:63	And the fire sent from above to consume mountains and woods does what it is ordered
Sus	13:32	As she was veiled, the wicked men ordered her to be unveiled
Bel	14:14	Then Daniel ordered his servants to bring ashes
1 Ma	3:28	and ordered them to be ready for any need
	5:49	Then Judas ordered proclamation to be made to the army
	15:41	as the king had ordered him
2 Ma	1:20	he ordered them to dip it out and bring it
	1:21	Nehemiah ordered the priests
	1:31	Nehemiah ordered that the liquid that was left
	2:1	ordered those who were being deported
	2:4	ordered that the tent and the ark should follow with him
	5:25	he ordered his men to parade under arms
	7:5	the king ordered them to take him to the fire, still breathing
	9:4	so he ordered his charioteer to drive without stopping
	11:20	I have ordered these men and my representatives
	13:4	he ordered them to take him to Beroea
	13:10	he ordered the people to call upon the Lord day and night
	13:12	Judas exhorted them and ordered them to stand ready
	14:41	they ordered that fire be brought and the doors burned
	15:4	who ordered us to observe the 7th day
	15:30	ordered them to cut off Nicanor's head and arm
1 Es	2:26	So I ordered search to be made
	4:57	everything that Cyrus had ordered to be done
	6:24	King Cyrus ordered the building
	8:46	and ordered them to tell Iddo and his brethren
3 Ma	3:1	and he ordered that all should promptly be gathered into one place
	4:13	ordered in his rage that these men
	4:14	but to be tortured with the outrages that he had ordered
	5:2	and ordered him on the following day
	5:16	and ordered those present for the banquet to recline opposite him
	5:40	ordering now for a 3rd time that they be destroyed
	6:30	and ordered him to provide to the Jews
	7:8	We also have ordered each and every one
4 Ma	5:2	ordered the guards to seize each and every Hebrew
	8:12	he ordered the instruments of torture to be brought forward

ORDINANCE   11 = 0.007 %

Ad E	13:4	and continually disregard the ordinances of the kings
Sir	4:17	and she will test him with her ordinances
Bar	2:12	O Lord our God, against all thy ordinances
1 Ma	1:13	He authorized them to observe the ordinances of the Gentiles
	1:49	and change all the ordinances
	2:21	Far be it from us to desert the law and the ordinances
	2:40	for our lives and our ordinances
2 Ma	10:8	They decreed by public ordinance and vote
1 Es	8:7	but taught all Israel all the ordinances and judgments
2 Es	8:22	whose ordinance is strong and whose command is terrible
4 Ma	15:10	in keeping the ordinances

ORDINARY   2

Sir	33:9	and some of them he made ordinary days
3 Ma	3:7	So they attached no ordinary reproach to them

ORGAN   1

4 Ma	10:18	But he said, Even if you remove my organ of speech

ORGANIZE   4 = 0.003 %

Jud	2:16	and he organized them
1 Ma	2:44	They organized an army
3 Ma	4:16	organizing feasts in honour of all his idols
2 Es	5:49	so have I organized the world which I created

ORGANIZED   1

2 Ma	8:5	As soon as Maccabeus got his army organized

ORIGIN   3 = 0.002 %

Wis	12:10	though thou wast not unaware that their origin was evil
2 Ma	7:23	and devised the origin of all things
2 Es	15:31	And then the dragons, remembering their origin

ORIGINAL   1
  2 Ma 2:30 It is the duty of the original historian

ORIGINALLY   2
  Sir pr. For what was originally expressed in Hebrew
       pr. differ not a little as originally expressed

ORNAMENT   4 = 0.003 %
  Jud 10:4 and her earrings and all her ornaments
  Sir 6:30 Her yoke is a golden ornament
      21:21 To a sensible man education is like a golden ornament
  L Jr 6:9 as they would for a girl who loves ornaments

ORPHAN   8 = 0.005 %
  Tob 1:8 for I was left an orphan by my father
  Sir 4:10 Be like a father to orphans
  L Jr 6:38 or do good to an orphan
  2 Ma 3:10 belonging to widows and orphans
      8:28 and to the widows and orphans
      8:30 and to the orphans and widows, and also to the aged
  1 Es 3:19 It makes equal the mind of the king and the orphan
  2 Es 2:20 defend the orphan, clothe the naked

ORTHOSIA   1
  1 Ma 15:37 Now Trypho embarked on a ship and escaped to Orthosia

OSTENSIBLY   1
  2 Ma 3:8 ostensibly to make a tour of inspection

OTHER*   151 = 0.098 %
  Tob 5:9 he entered and they greeted each other
      6:12 because you rather than any other man
      6:14 And they have no other son to bury them
      7:16 Sister, make up the other room, and take her into it
      14:10 But Ahikar was saved, and the other received repayment
  Jud 8:20 But we know no other God but him
      9:14 and that there is no other
      11:21 from one end of the earth to the other
  Ad E 15:4 while the other followed carrying her train
  Wis 2:15 because his manner of life is unlike that of others
      8:1 She reaches mightily from one end of the earth to the other
      15:13 For this man, more than all others, knows that he sins
      15:18 which are worse than all others
      19:14 Others had refused to receive strangers
  Sir pr. and the others that followed them
      pr. and the other books of our fathers
      11:6 and illustrious men have been handed over to others
      11:19 until he leaves them to others and dies
      14:4 accumulates for others
      14:4 and others will live in luxury on his goods
      14:18 which sheds some and puts forth others
      18:2 And there is no other beside him
      19:4 One who trusts others too quickly is lightminded
      21:8 A man who builds his house with other people's money
      33:15 they likewise are in pairs, one the opposite of the other
      36:23 her husband is not like other men
      39:1 On the other hand he who devotes himself
      42:24 All things are twofold, one opposite the other
      42:25 One confirms the good things of the other
      48:16 but others multiplied sins
      49:5 for they gave their power to others
  Bar 1:21 by serving other gods
      3:19 and others have arisen in their place
      3:35 no other can be compared to him !
  Sus 13:10 but they did not tell each other of their distress
      13:13 They said to each other, Let us go home, for it is mealtime
      13:14 And when they went out, they parted from each other
      13:14 and when each pressed the other for the reason
      13:51 Separate them far from each other
      13:52 When they were separated from each other
      13:54 Under what tree did you see them being intimate with each other ?
      13:56 Then he put him aside, and commanded them to bring the other
      13:58 Under what tree did you catch them being intimate with each other ?
  Bel 14:41 and there is no other besides thee
  1 Ma 5:14 behold, other messengers, with their garments rent
      5:27 and some have been shut up in the other cities of Gilead
      5:36 Maked, and Bosor, and the other cities of Gilead
      5:37 and encamped opposite Raphon, on the other side of the stream
      5:41 and camps on the other side of the river
      6:20 and he built siege towers and other engines of war
      6:29 And mercenary forces came to him from other kingdoms
      6:43 It was taller than all the others
      8:5 and the others who rose up against them
      9:48 and swam across to the other side
      10:38 and obey no other authority but the high priest
      10:71 and let us match strength with each other there
      10:72 and who the others are that are helping us
      11:9 Come, let us make a covenant with each other

      11:24 taking silver and gold and clothing and numerous other gifts
      11:27 and in as many other honours as he had formerly had
      11:35 And the other payments due to us of the tithes
      12:2 and to other places
      12:11 both in our feasts and on other appropriate days
      12:14 and our other allies and friends
      12:45 I will hand it over to you as well as the other strongholds
      13:39 and whatever other tax has been collected in Jerusalem
      15:5 and release from all the other payments
      16:19 He sent other men to Gazara to do away with John
      16:20 and he sent other men to take possession of Jerusalem
  2 Ma 2:3 And with other similar words he exhorted them
      2:27 and seeks the benefit of others
      3:19 while others peered out of the windows
      4:32 other vessels, as it happened
      4:35 but many also of other nations
      4:41 and others took handfuls of the ashes that were lying about
      5:16 the votive offerings which other kings had made
      5:23 worse than the others did
      5:27 But Judas Maccabeus, with about 9 others
      6:11 Others who had assembled in the caves near by
      6:14 For in the case of the other nations
      7:39 and handled him worse than the others
      8:14 Others sold all their remaining property
      8:33 Callisthenes and some others
      9:6 for he had tortured the bowels of others
      9:28 such as he had inflicted on others
      10:28 while the other made rage their leader in the fight
      10:36 Others who came up in the same way
      10:36 Others broke open the gates and let in the rest of the force
      11:3 as he did on the sacred places of the other nations
      11:7 and he urged the others to risk their lives with him
      11:27 and to the other Jews, greeting
      12:11 and to help his people in all other ways
      13:6 any man guilty of sacrilege or notorious for other crimes
      15:2 and hallowed above other days
  1 Es 1:24 beyond any other people or kingdom
      1:26 What have we to do with each other, king of Judea ?
      2:7 besides the other things added as votive offerings
      2:13 2,410 silver bowls, and a 1,000 other vessels
      2:16 living in Samaria and other places
      2:17 and the other judges of their council
      2:22 troubling both kings and other cities
      2:25 and the others associated with them and living in Samaria
      4:18 If men gather gold and silver or any other beautiful thing
      4:19 or any other beautiful thing
      5:22 The sons of the other Elam and Ono, 725
      5:50 And some joined them from the other peoples of the land
      6:4 and this roof and finishing all the other things ?
      8:10 and of the priests and Levites and others in our realm
      8:22 or any other tax is to be laid
      8:24 whether by death or some other punishment
  3 Ma 1:13 And he inquired why, when he entered every other temple
      1:23 they resorted to the same posture of supplication as the others
      3:2 that they hindered others from the observance or their customs
      3:6 Nevertheless those of the other races paid no heed
      3:21 Among other things
      4:9 others had their feet secured by unbreakable fetters
      4:13 be dealt with in precisely the same fashion as the others
      5:49 and giving way to lamentation and groans they kissed each other
      5:49 and others with babies at their breasts
  2 Es 1:24 I will to other nations and will give them my name
      2:11 and will give to these others the everlasting habitations
      2:27 others shall weep and be sorrowful
      2:43 taller than any of the others
      5:28 and dishonoured the one root beyond the others
      6:41 that one part might move upward and the other part remain beneath
      6:49 and the name of the other Leviathan
      6:50 And thou didst separate one from the other
      6:56 As for the other nations which have descended from Adam
      7:62 like the other created things !
      7:85 they shall see how the habitations of the others
      7:110 and many others prayed for many ?
      10:10 and others will come
      11:4 the middle head was larger then the other heads
      11:21 and others of them rose up, but did not hold the rule
      11:29 for it was greater than the other 2 heads
      12:7 and if I have been accounted righteous before thee beyond many others
      12:15 for a longer time than any other of the 12
      13:13 and some were bringing others as offerings
      13:56 And after 3 more days I will tell you other things
      15:59 Unhappy above all others
  4 Ma 1:32 Some desires are mental, other are physical
      2:9 In all other matters
      2:18 to correct some, and to render others powerless
      8:2 that others of the Hebrew captives be brought
      8:16 Let us consider, on the other hand
      14:16 and the others, by building in precipitous chasms

15 : 6 The mother of the 7 boys, more than any other mother, loved her children
15 : 20 upon the flesh of other children
15 : 20 and corpses fallen on other corpses
15 : 26 one bearing death and the other deliverance for her children
16 : 9 others married and without offspring

OTHERWISE   4 = 0.003 %
1 Ma 15 : 31 Otherwise we will come and conquer you
4 Ma 1 : 33 Otherwise how is it that
    2 : 7 Otherwise how could it be
    4 : 13 although otherwise he had scruples about doing so

OTHONIAH   1
1 Es 9 : 28 Othoniah Jeremoth, and Zabad and Zerdaiah

OUGHT   9 = 0.006 %
Wis 14 : 21 the name that ought not to be shared
2 Ma 6 : 20 as men ought to go who have the courage to refuse things
3 Ma 1 : 12 he did not cease to maintain that he ought to enter, saying
    1 : 12 I ought not to be
    3 : 9 for such a great community ought not be left to its fate
2 Es 10 : 9 and she will tell you that it is she who ought to mourn
    10 : 11 Who then ought to mourn the more
4 Ma 11 : 15 we ought likewise to die for the same principles
    16 : 19 and therefore you ought to endure any suffering for the sake of God

OUR   485 = 0.316 %

OURSELVES   16 = 0.010 %

OUT of   92 = 0.060 %

OUTBID   1
2 Ma 4 : 24 outbidding Jason by 300 talents of silver

OUTCOME   2
Wis 8 : 8 and of the outcome of seasons and times
2 Ma 3 : 40 This was the outcome of the episode of Heliodorus

OUTCRY   1
1 Es 5 : 63 with outcries and loud weeping

OUTFLANK   2
Jud 15 : 5 and those in Gilead and in Galilee outflanked them
1 Ma 7 : 46 and they outflanked the enemy

OUTLET   1
Sir 25 : 25 Allow no outlet to water

OUTLINE   1
2 Ma 2 : 28 to arriving at the outlines of the condensation

OUTPOST   2
Jud 14 : 2 against the Assyrian outpost
1 Ma 12 : 27 and he stationed outposts around the camp

OUTPUT   1
Sir 38 : 29 and all his output is by number

OUTRAGE, subst.   5 = 0.003 %
Wis 4 : 18 and an outrage among the dead for ever
2 Ma 4 : 38 where he had committed the outrage against Onias
    8 : 17 keeping before their eyes the lawless outrage
   14 : 42 and suffer outrages unworthy of his noble birth
3 Ma 4 : 14 but to be tortured with the outrages that he had ordered

OUTRAGEOUS   3 = 0.002 %
Sir 10 : 7 and injustice is outrageous to both
3 Ma 6 : 26 Who is it that has so lawlessly encompassed with outrageous treatment
4 Ma 4 : 7 considering it outrageous

OUTRAGEOUSLY   1
3 Ma 6 : 9 who are being outrageously treated

OUTSIDE, prep., adv.   11 = 0.007 %
Jud 6 : 1 When the disturbance made by the men outside the council died down
   10 : 18 as she waited outside the tent of Holofernes
   13 : 1 and Bagoas closed the tent from outside
   13 : 3 to stand outside the bedchamber
Sir 21 : 23 but a cultivated man remains outside
Bel 14 : 7 for this is but clay inside and brass outside
   14 : 11 And the priests of Bel said, Behold, we are going outside
1 Ma 7 : 47 and brought them and displayed them just outside Jerusalem
   15 : 30 which you have conquered outside the borders of Judea

2 Ma 1 : 16 and threw them to the people outside
4 Ma 18 : 7 I was a pure virgin and did not go outside my father's house

OUTSIDER   3 = 0.002 %
Sir pr. should be able to help the outsiders
   45 : 13 No outsider ever put them on, but only his sons
   45 : 18 Outsiders conspired against him

OUTSPOKEN   1
3 Ma 4 : 1 was now made evident and outspoken

OUTSTRETCHED   2
Bar 2 : 11 and with great power and outstretched arm
2 Ma 15 : 12 was praying with outstretched hands

OUTWEIGH   1
Sir 8 : 2 lest his resources outweigh yours

OUTWIT   1
2 Ma 14 : 31 that he had been cleverly outwitted by the man

OVER, prep., adv.   204 = 0.133 %

OVERCOME   15 = 0.010 %
Jud 8 : 3 he was overcome by the burning heat
   13 : 2 for he was overcome with wine
Wis 2 : 4 by the rays of the sun and overcome by its heat
Sir 23 : 6 Let neither gluttony nor lust overcome me
3 Ma 5 : 12 he was overcome by so pleasant and deep a sleep
   5 : 27 since he had been completely overcome by incomprehension
   6 : 34 groaned as they themselves were overcome by disgrace
2 Es 3 : 21 transgressed and was overcome
   6 : 28 faithfulness shall flourish, and corruption shall be overcome
   7 : 92 to overcome the evil thought which was formed with them
4 Ma 2 : 2 because by mental effort he overcame sexual desire
   3 : 4 so that we are not overcome by malice
   4 : 13 that Apollonius had been overcome by human treachery
   7 : 22 would no be able to overcome the emotions through godliness ?
   9 : 6 which our aged instructor also overcame

OVERCONFIDENT   1
Sir 32 : 21 Do not be overconfident on a smooth way

OVEREATING   1
Sir 37 : 30 for overeating brings sickness, and gluttony leads to nausea

OVERFLOW   2
Jud 2 : 8 and every brook and river shall be filled with their dead, and overflow
Sir 47 : 14 You overflowed like a river with understanding

OVERHEAR   1
Ad E 12 : 2 He overheard their conversation and inquired into their purposes

OVERJOYED   1
3 Ma 7 : 20 they departed unharmed, free, and overjoyed

OVERLAY   7 = 0.005 %
L Jr 6 : 8 and they themselves are overlaid with gold and silver
   6 : 39 These things that are made of wood and overlaid with gold and silver
   6 : 50 Since they are made of wood and overlaid with gold and silver
   6 : 55 of wooden gods overlaid with gold or silver
   6 : 57 gods made of wood and overlaid with silver and gold
   6 : 70 so are their gods of wood, overlaid with gold and silver
   6 : 71 overlaid with gold and silver

OVERLOOK   6 = 0.004 %
Wis 11 : 23 and thou dost overlook men's sins, that they may repent
Sir 2 : 10 Or who ever called upon him and was overlooked ?
   28 : 7 remember the covenant of the Most High, and overlook ignorance
   32 : 18 A man of judgment will not overlook an idea
3 Ma 1 : 27 and not to overlook this unlawful and haughty deed
4 Ma 13 : 4 The supremacy of the mind over these cannot be overlooked

OVERNIGHT   1
Tob 9 : 5 and stayed overnight with Gabael

OVERPOWERING   3 = 0.002 %
3 Ma 5 : 1 was filled with overpowering anger and wrath
   5 : 30 But at these words he was filled with an overpowering wrath
2 Es 10 : 28 For it was he who brought me into this overpowering bewilderment

OVERSEE   3 = 0.002 %
Jud 8 : 3 For as he stood overseeing the men
Wis 7 : 23 all powerful, overseeing all
3 Ma 2 : 21 Thereupon God, who oversees all things

OVERSHADOW 1
Wis **19**:7   The cloud was seen overshadowing the camp

OVERSTUFF 1
Sir **31**:21   If you are overstuffed with food

OVERTAKE 16 = 0.010 %
Tob **12**:7   Do good, and evil will not overtake you
Jud **11**:11   death will fall upon them, for a sin has overtaken them
Wis **14**:30   But just penalties will overtake them on 2 counts :
Sir **11**:10   and if you pursue you will not overtake
   23:8   The sinner is overtaken through his lips
   31:22   and no sickness will overtake you
Bar **4**:25   Your enemy has overtaken you
1 Ma **2**:32   Many pursued them, and overtook them
   12:30   Then Jonathan pursued them, but he did not overtake them
2 Ma **4**:16   For this reason heavy disaster overtook them
   8:11   that was about to overtake him
3 Ma **2**:10   and tribulation should overtake us
   2:13   subjected to our enemies, and overtaken by helplessness
   2:20   Speedily let your mercies overtake us
   2:23   seeing the severe punishment that had overtaken him
2 Es **10**:48   and that misfortune had overtaken her

OVERTHROW, verb 10 = 0.007 %
Tob **14**:4   about Nineveh, that it will be overthrown
Jud **1**:13   and overthrew the whole army of Arphaxad
Sir **10**:14   The Lord has overthrown the lands of the nations
   12:12   Do not put him next to you, lest he overthrow you
   27:3   his house will be quickly overthrown
   29:16   A sinner will overthrow the prosperity of his surety
2 Ma **12**:15   overthrew Jericho in the days of Joshua
2 Es **1**:10   For their sake I have overthrown many kings
   16:46   and plunder their goods, and overthrow their houses
4 Ma **3**:18   it can overthrow bodily agonies even when they are extreme

OVERTHROW, subst. 1
2 Ma **8**:17   and besides, the overthrow of their ancestral way of life

OVERTURN 2
Wis **5**:23   and evil-doing will overturn the thrones of rulers
Sir **28**:14   and overturned the houses of great men

OVERWHELM 9 = 0.006 %
Wis **5**:22   and rivers will relentlessly overwhelm them
   17:15   for sudden and unexpected fear overwhelmed them
Sus **13**:10   Both were overwhelmed with passion for her
1 Ma **10**:82   they were overwhelmed by him and fled
3 Ma **2**:7   you overwhelmed him in the depths of the sea
2 Es **16**:77   and overwhelmed by their iniquities
   16:77   and its path overwhelmed with thorns
4 Ma **7**:2   and overwhelmed by the mighty waves of tortures
   15:32   overwhelmed from every side

OWE 4 = 0.003 %
1 Ma **10**:43   because he owes money to the king or has any debt
   13:15   that Jonathan your brother owed the royal treasury
   13:39   and cancel the crown tax which you owe
   15:8   Every debt you owe to the royal treasury

OWN, adj. 155 = 0.101 %
Tob **1**:4   Now when I was in my own country, in the land of Israel
   6:15   to take a wife from among your own people ?
   12:10   but those who commit sin are the enemies of their own lives
Jud **2**:2   and recounted fully, with his own lips
   6:21   And Uzziah took him from the assembly to his own house
   12:1   with some of his own food
   12:1   and to serve her with his own wine
   13:20   because you did not spare your own life
   16:21   After this every one returned home to his own inheritance
   16:24   and to her own nearest kindred
Ad E **16**:3   they even undertake to scheme against their own benefactors
   16:19   and permit the Jews to live under their own laws
Wis **2**:23   and made him in the image of his own eternity
   11:13   For when they heard that through their own punishments
   12:23   thou didst torment through their own abominations
   17:11   condemned by its own testimony
   19:17   each tried to find the way through his own door
Sir **3**:5   will be gladdened by his own children
   4:22   Do not show partiality, to your own harm
   6:8   For there is a friend who is such at his own convenience
   9:1   and do not teach her an evil lesson to your own hurt
   10:29   And who will honour the man that dishonours his own life ?
   13:13   for you are walking about with your own downfall
   14:5   He will not enjoy his own riches
   15:14   and he left him in the power of his own inclination
   15:15   and to act faithfully is a matter of your own choice
   17:3   He endowed them with strength like his own
   17:3   and made them in his own image
   17:17   but Israel is the Lord's own portion

   20:32   than a masterless charioteer of one's own life
   21:27   he curses his own soul
   21:28   A whisperer defiles his own soul
   26:20   and sow it with your own seed, trusting in your fine stock
   27:23   and with your own words he will give offence
   27:25   Whoever throws a stone straight up throws it on his own head
   28:4   and yet pray for his own sins ?
   31:15   Judge your neighbour's feelings by your own
   33:31   for as your own soul you will need him
   37:7   but some give counsel in their own interest
   37:13   And establish the counsel of your own heart
   37:22   A man may be wise to his own advantage
   37:23   A wise man will instruct his own people
   38:31   and each is skilful in his own work
Bar **1**:21   but we each followed the intent of his own wicked heart
   2:14   and for thy own sake deliver us, and grant us favour
   4:33   so she will be grieved at her own desolation
L Jr **6**:54   They cannot judge their own cause or deliver one who is wronged
Sus **13**:55   You have lied against your own head
   13:59   You also have lied against your own head
   13:61   for out of their own mouths
Bel **14**:4   But Daniel worshipped his own God
   14:39   And the angel of God immediately returned Habakkuk to his own place
1 Ma **1**:8   Then his officers began to rule, each in his own place
   1:24   Taking them all, he departed to his own land
   6:54   and they had been scattered, each to his own place
   9:9   Let us rather save our own lives now
   9:69   Then he decided to depart to his own land
   9:72   then he turned an departed to his own land
   10:13   each left his place and departed to his own land
   10:32   that he may station in it men of his own choice to guard it
   10:37   Let their officers and leaders be of their own number
   10:37   and let them live by their own laws
   10:72   for your fathers were twice put to flight in their own land
   11:1   and add it to his own kingdom
   11:38   he dismissed all his troops, each man to his own place
   12:25   for he gave them no opportunity to invade his own country
   13:24   Then Trypho turned back and departed to his own land
   14:32   He spent great sums of his own money
   15:6   I permit you to mint your own coinage
2 Ma **3**:3   defrayed from his own revenues all the expenses
   3:30   who had acted marvellously for his own place
   3:36   which he had seen with his own eyes
   4:1   who had informed about the money against his own country
   4:21   and he took measures for his own security
   4:26   So Jason, who after supplanting his own brother
   4:29   Menelaus left his own brother Lysimachus
   5:9   and he who had driven many from their own country into exile died in exile
   6:16   he does not forsake his own people
   6:19   went up to the rack of his own accord, spitting out the flesh
   6:21   and privately urged him to bring meat of his own providing
   7:18   For we are suffering these things on our own account
   7:18   because of our sins against our own God
   7:32   For we are suffering because of our own sins
   7:33   he will again be reconciled with his own servants
   8:15   if not for their own sake
   8:30   shares equal to their own
   8:35   having succeeded chiefly in the destruction of his own army !
   9:12   And when he could not endure his own stench
   9:16   he would provide from his own revenues
   10:7   who had given success to the purifying of his own holy place
   10:30   with their own armour and weapons
   11:23   in caring for their own affairs
   11:24   but prefer their own way of living
   11:24   and ask that their own customs be allowed them
   11:26   and go on happily in the conduct of their own affairs
   11:29   and look after your own affairs
   11:31   to enjoy their own food and laws, just as formerly
   12:22   so that often they were injured by their own men
   12:42   for they had seen with their own eyes
   14:15   and prayed to him who established his own people for ever
   14:15   and always upholds his own heritage by manifesting himself
   14:41   Being surrounded, Razis fell upon his own sword
   15:34   Blessed is he who has kept his own place undefiled
1 Es **3**:8   Then each wrote his own statement
   4:11   and no one may go away to attend to his own affairs
   4:20   A man leaves his own father who brought him up
   4:20   and his own country, and cleaves to his wife
   4:30   and take the crown from the king's head and put it on her own
   4:46   with your own lips
   5:8   each to his own town
   5:47   and the sons of Israel were each in his own home
   6:18   and stored in his own temple
Ps 151:7   But I drew his own sword
3 Ma **1**:11   because not even members of their own nation
   3:19   and their own benefactors
   5:21   and each departed to his own home

5:34	each to his own occupation	
5:47	wishing to witness, with invulnerable heart and with his own eyes	
7:8	to return to his own home	
7:10	but they requested the king that at their own hands	
7:18	to each as far as his own house	
7:20	each to his own place	

2 Es 3:8 And every nation walked after his own will
4:20 but why have you not judged so in your own case?
5:30 they should be punished at thy own hands
5:47 but only each in its own time
7:71 And now understand from your own words
7:105 for then every one shall bear his own righteousness or unrighteousness
7:134 since they are his own works
8:5 For not of your own will did you come into the world
8:33 shall receive their reward in consequence of their own deeds
8:44 and is called thy own image because he is made like thee
8:45 for thou hast mercy on thy own creation
8:51 But think of your own case
11:8 let each sleep in his own place, and watch in his turn
13:33 every man shall leave his own land
13:40 which were led away from their own land into captivity
13:42 which they had not kept in their own land
13:54 because you have forsaken your own ways
15:35 and their own tempest
15:58 and they shall eat their own flesh in hunger for bread
15:58 and drink their own blood in thirst for water
16:65 and your own iniquities shall stand

4 Ma 1:6 For reason does not rule its own emotions
3:1 for it is evident that reason rules not over its own emotions
5:10 you continue to despise me to your own hurt
5:33 as to break the ancestral law by my own act
7:8 shielding it with their own blood and noble sweat
8:15 but they also opposed the tyrant with their own philosophy
10:8 he saw his own flesh torn all around
11:3 I have come of my own accord
14:17 and warning them with their own calls
15:25 For as in the council chamber of her own soul
17:15 and gave the crown to its own athletes
17:23 as an example for their own endurance

OWN, verb   1
Sir 13:5 If you own something, he will live with you

OWNER   4 = 0.003 %
Tob 2:12 She used to send the product to the owners
2:13 It is not stolen, is it? Return it to the owners
2:14 and told her to return it to the owners
L Jr 6:59 or a household utensil that serves its owner's need

OX   3 = 0.002 %
Jud 2:17 and innumerable sheep and oxen and goats for provision
Sir 26:7 An evil wife is an ox yoke which chafes
38:25 who drives oxen and is occupied with their work

OX, prop. n.   1
Jud 8:1 she was the daughter of Merari the son of Ox

OZIEL   1
Jud 8:1 son of Joseph, son of Oziel, son of Elkiah

P

PACE   1
3 Ma 4:5 forced to march at a swift pace

PACHON   1
3 Ma 6:38 from the 25th of Pachon to the 4th of Epeiph, for 40 days

PADON   1
1 Es 5:29 the sons of Keros, the sons of Siaha, sons of Padon

PAGAN   1
4 Ma 18:5 to become pagans and to abandon their ancestral customs

PAHATH-MOAB   2
1 Es 5:11 The sons of Pahath-moab, of the sons of Jeshua and Joab, 2,812
8:31 Of the sons of Pahath-moab, Eliehoenai the son of Zerahiah

PAIN, subst.   25 = 0.016 %
Jud 16:17 they shall weep in pain for ever
Wis 8:16 and life with her has no pain, but gladness and joy
Sir pr. that I should myself devote some pains and labour
27:29 and pain will consume them before their death
30:13 Discipline your son and take pains with him
38:7 By them he heals and takes away pain
2 Ma 3:17 the pain lodged in his heart

9:5	he was seized with a pain in his bowels	
9:9	and while he was still living in anguish and pain	
9:11	for he was tortured with pain every moment	

2 Es 10:12 which I brought forth in pain and bore in sorrow
16:38 has great pains about her womb for 2 or 3 hours beforehand
16:39 and pains will seize it on every side
4 Ma 1:4 namely anger, fear, and pain
1:20 The 2 most comprehensive types of the emotions are pleasure and pain
1:21 The emotions of both pleasure and pain have many consequences
1:23 Fear precedes pain and sorrow comes after
1:24 is an emotion embracing pleasure and pain
1:28 Just as pleasure and pain
6:9 But he bore the pains and scorned the punishment
9:31 I lighten my pain by the joys that come from virtue
13:4 for the brothers mastered both emotions and pains
15:7 and because of the many pains she suffered with each of them
15:16 O mother, tried now by more bitter pains
16:23 not to withstand pain

PAINFUL   3 = 0.002 %
Sir 13:26 but to devise proverbs requires painful thinking
4 Ma 8:1 have prevailed over the most painful instruments of torture
14:10 What could be more excruciatingly painful than this?

PAINLESS   1
4 Ma 11:26 Your fire is cold to us, and the catapults painless

PAINT, subst.   2
Wis 13:14 giving it a coat of red paint and colouring its surface red
13:14 and covering every blemish in it with paint

PAINT, verb   2
Sir 38:27 he sets his heart on painting a lifelike image
4 Ma 17:7 to paint the history of your piety as an artist might

PAINTER   1
Wis 15:4 nor the fruitless toil of painters

PAINTING   1
2 Ma 2:29 while the one who undertakes its painting and decoration

PAIR   2
Sir 33:15 they likewise are in pairs, one the opposite of the other
46:19 not so much as a pair of shoes

PALACE   6 = 0.004 %
Jud 2:1 there was talk in the palace of Nebuchadnezzar
2:18 and a huge amount of gold and silver from the royal palace
L Jr 6:59 better also a wooden pillar in a palace
1 Ma 2:10 What nation has not inherited her palaces
7:2 As he was entering the royal palace of his fathers
11:46 But the king fled into the palace

PALATE   1
Sir 36:19 As the palate tastes the kinds of game

PALE   1
Ad E 15:7 And the queen faltered, and turned pale and faint

PALL   1
Wis 11:18 or belch forth a thick pall of smoke

PALM   8 = 0.005 %
Sir 24:14 *I grew tall like a palm tree in En-gedi*
50:12 *and they surrounded him like the trunks of palm trees*
1 Ma 13:37 *and the palm branch which you sent*
13:51 *the Jews entered it with praise and palm branches*
2 Ma 10:7 and also fronds of palm
14:4 presenting to him a crown of gold and a palm
2 Es 2:45 now they are being crowned, and receive palms
2:46 and puts palms in their hands?

PALTRY   1
Wis 10:4 steering the righteous man by a paltry piece of wood

PAMPER   1
Sir 30:9 Pamper a child, and he will frighten you

PAMPHYLIA   1
1 Ma 15:23 and to Pamphylia, and to Lycia, and to Halicarnassus

PAN   3 = 0.002 %
2 Ma 7:3 and gave orders that pans and cauldrons be heated
7:5 and to fry him in a pan
7:5 The smoke from the pan spread widely

PANG   2
  Sir 19:11   With such a word a fool will suffer pangs
  2 Es 4:42   makes haste to escape the pangs of birth

PANIC-STRICKEN   1
  3 Ma 2:23   panic-stricken in their exceedingly great fear

PAPER   2
  3 Ma 4:20   that both the paper and the pens they used for writing
  2 Es 15:2   and cause them to be written on paper

PARABLE   7 = 0.005 %
  Sir 3:29   The mind of the intelligent man will ponder a parable
      39:2   and penetrate the subtleties of parables
      39:3   and be at home with the obscurities of parables
      47:15   and you filled it with parables and riddles
      47:17   For your songs and proverbs and parables
  2 Es 4:47   and I will show you the interpretation of a parable
      8:2   But I will tell you a parable, Ezra

PARADE   2
  2 Ma 5:25   he ordered his men to parade under arms
      6:10   These women they publicly paraded about the city

PARADISE   5 = 0.003 %
  2 Es 4:7   or which are the entrances of paradise ?
      6:2   and before the foundations of paradise were laid
      7:36   and opposite it the paradise of delight
      7:123   Or that a paradise shall be revealed
      8:52   because it is for you that paradise is opened

PARADOXICAL   1
  4 Ma 2:14   Do not consider it paradoxical when reason

PARALYZE   5 = 0.003 %
  Wis 17:15   and now were paralyzed by their souls' surrender
      17:19   it paralyzed them with terror
  1 Ma 9:55   his mouth was stopped and he was paralyzed
  3 Ma 2:22   besides being paralyzed in his limbs
  4 Ma 11:24   We 6 boys have paralyzed your tyranny !

PARAPET   1
  Jud 14:1   and take this head and hang it upon the parapet of your wall

PARCH   1
  Sir 43:3   At noon it parches the land

PARCHED   1
  Jud 10:5   and filled a bag with parched grain

PARDON, subst.   2
  Wis 18:2   and they begged their pardon
  3 Ma 6:27   begging pardon for your former actions !

PARDON, verb   4 = 0.003 %
  Wis 6:6   For the lowliest man may be pardoned in mercy
  Sir 28:2   and then your sins will be pardoned when you pray
  1 Ma 13:39   We pardon any errors and offences committed to this day
  2 Es 7:139   and judge, because if he did not pardon those who were created
           by his word

PARENT   18 = 0.012 %
  Tob 10:12   they are now your parents
  Wis 4:6   against their parents when God examines them
      12:6   these parents who murder helpless lives
  Sir 3:7   he will serve his parents as his masters
      7:28   Remember that through your parents you were born
      22:9   conceal the lowly birth of their parents
  Sus 13:3   Her parents were righteous
      13:30   And she came, with her parents, her children, and all her
           kindred
  1 Ma 10:9   and he returned them to their parents
  2 Ma 12:24   because he held the parents of most of them
  3 Ma 5:31   Were your parents or children present
      5:49   parents and children, mothers and daughters
      6:14   The whole throng of infants and their parents entreat you with
           tears
  2 Es 1:6   that the sins of their parents have increased in them
      7:103   fathers for sons or sons for parents
  4 Ma 2:10   For the law prevails even over affection for parents
      15:4   the emotions of parents who love their children ?
      15:13   yearning of parents toward offspring, nurture

PARENTAL   4 = 0.003 %
  4 Ma 14:14   have a sympathy and parental love for their offspring
      15:13   O sacred nature and affection of parental love
      15:25   nature, family, parental love
      16:3   as was her innate parental love

PAROSH   3 = 0.002 %
  1 Es 5:9   the sons of Parosh, 2,172
      8:30   Of the sons of Parosh, Zechariah
      9:26   Of Israel : of the sons of Parosh : Ramiah, Izziah

PART*, subst.   42 = 0.027 %
  Tob 8:3   he fled to the remotest parts of Egypt
      12:18   For I did not come as a favour on my part
  Ad E 14:2   and every part that she loved to adorn
      16:5   have been made in part responsible
  Wis 14:11   because, though part of what God created
  Sir 45:3   and showed him part of his glory
  1 Ma 6:40   Now a part of the king's army
      7:24   So Judas went out into all the surrounding parts of Judea
      9:23   the lawless emerged in all parts of Israel
      9:62   he rebuilt the parts of it that had been demolished
      10:33   from the land of Judah into any part of my kingdom
      12:23   we on our part write to you
      12:37   part of the wall on the valley to the east had fallen
  2 Ma 4:14   they hastened to take part in the unlawful proceedings
      7:26   After much urging on his part
      8:21   then he divided his army into 4 parts
      14:22   to prevent sudden treachery on the part of the enemy
  3 Ma 7:6   always taking their part as a father does for his children
  2 Es 4:45   or whether for us the greater part has gone by
      4:52   I can tell you in part
      5:34   and to search out part of his judgment
      6:12   which thou didst show me in part on a previous night
      6:41   that one part might move upward and the other part remain
           beneath
      6:42   in the 7th part of the earth
      6:42   6 parts thou didst dry up and keep
      6:47   On the 5th day thou didst command the 7th part
      6:50   for the 7th part where the water had been gathered together
      6:51   And thou didst give Behemoth one of the parts
      6:52   but to Leviathan thou didst give the 7th part, the watery part
      7:5   how can he come to the broad part
      7:5   unless he passes through the narrow part ?
      9:1   and when you see that a certain part of the predicted signs are
           past
      14:11   For the age is divided into 12 parts
      14:11   and 9 of its parts have already passed
      14:12   as well as half of the 13th part
      14:12   so 2 of its parts remain
      14:12   besides half of the 13th part
      15:38   and from the north, and another part from the west
      15:60   and shall destroy a part of your land
  4 Ma 14:13   which draws everything toward an emotion felt in her inmost
           parts

PART, verb   2
  Sus 13:14   And when they went out, they parted from each other
  1 Ma 6:45   and they parted before him on both sides

PARTAKE   4 = 0.003 %
  Wis 16:3   might partake of delicacies
  2 Ma 6:7   to partake of the sacrifices
      6:8   and make them partake of the sacrifices
      7:1   to partake of unlawful swine's flesh

PARTIAL   1
  Sir 7:6   lest you be partial to a powerful man

PARTIALITY   6 = 0.004 %
  Sir 4:22   Do not show partiality, to your own harm
      4:27   nor show partiality to a ruler
      35:12   for the Lord is the judge, and with him is no partiality
      35:13   He will not show partiality in the case of a poor man
      42:1   and do not let partiality lead you to sin :
  1 Es 4:39   With her there is no partiality or preference

PARTICIPANT   1
  3 Ma 3:21   and to make them participants in our regular religious rites

PARTICIPATE   1
  2 Ma 5:20   and afterward participated in its benefits

PARTLY   3 = 0.002 %
  4 Ma 6:12   At that point, partly out of pity for his old age
      6:13   partly out of sympathy from their acquaintance with him
      6:13   partly out of admiration for his endurance

PARTNER   3 = 0.002 %
  Ad E 16:13   and of Esther, the blameless partner of our kingdom
  Sir 41:18   of unjust dealing, before your partner or friend
      42:3   of keeping accounts with a partner

PARTRIDGE   1
  Sir 11:30   Like a decoy partridge in a cage

PARTY

			5 = 0.003 %
Wis	1:16	because they are fit to belong to his party	
	2:24	and those who belong to his party experience it	
1 Ma	8:30	both parties shall determine to add or delete anything	
3 Ma	5:18	After the party had been going on for some time	
	5:36	The king, however, reconvened the party in the same manner	

PASEAH

			1
1 Es	5:31	the sons of Paseah, the sons of Hasrah, the sons of Besai	

PASHHUR

			2
1 Es	5:25	The sons of Pashhur, 1,247	
	9:22	Of the sons of Pashhur : Elioenai, Maaseiah, Ishmael	

PASS, verb

			44 = 0.029 %
Tob	1:21	But not 50 days passed	
Jud	2:24	and passed through Mesopotamia	
	9:5	Yea, the things thou didst intend came to pass	
	10:10	and passed through the valley	
	13:10	and they passed through the camp	
Wis	5:10	and when it has passed no trace can be found	
	5:14	and it passes like the remembrance of a guest who stays but a day	
	7:27	in every generation she passes into holy souls	
	14:5	and passing through the billows on a raft	
	19:8	where those protected by thy hand passed through as one nation	
Sir	10:8	Sovereignty passes from nation to nation	
	11:19	he does not know how much time will pass	
	48:25	and the hidden things before they came to pass	
1 Ma	5:48	Let us pass through your land to get to our land	
	5:51	Then he passed through the city over the slain	
	5:66	and passed through Marisa	
	11:62	And he passed through the country as far as Damascus	
	12:10	for considerable time has passed	
2 Ma	1:20	But after many years had passed, when it pleased God	
	1:22	When this was done and some time had passed	
3 Ma	6:35	passed the time in feasting	
2 Es	3:19	And thy glory passed through the 4 gates	
	3:23	So the times passed and the years were completed	
	4:9	things through which you have passed	
	4:24	and why we pass from the world like locusts	
	4:45	show me this also : whether more time is to come than has passed	
	4:49	And after this a cloud full of water passed before me	
	4:49	and when the rainstorm had passed	
	4:50	so the quantity that passed was far greater	
	5:11	passed through you ? And it will answer, No	
	5:55	and passing the strength of youth	
	7:5	unless he passes through the narrow part ?	
	7:9	unless he passes through the danger set before him ?	
	7:14	pass through the difficult and vain experiences	
	7:26	when the signs which I have foretold to you will come to pass	
	8:31	For we and our fathers have passed our lives	
	8:37	and it will come to pass according to your words	
	9:23	But if you will let 7 days more pass	
	13:20	than to pass from the world like a cloud	
	13:32	And when these things come to pass	
	13:58	and whatever things come to pass in their seasons	
	14:11	and 9 of its parts have already passed	
	15:60	And as they pass they shall wreck the hateful city	
	16:77	so that no one can pass through !	

PASS away

			7 = 0.005 %
Wis	2:4	our life will pass away like the traces of a cloud	
Sir	14:19	and the man who made it will pass away with it	
2 Es	4:29	and if the place where the evil has been sown does not pass away	
	6:20	which is about to pass away	
	7:33	and compassion shall pass away	
	7:113	in which corruption has passed away	
	8:54	sorrows have passed away	

PASS by

			11 = 0.007 %
Jud	5:21	then let my lord pass them by	
	7:31	But if these days pass by, and no help comes for us	
Wis	1:8	and justice, when it punishes, will not pass him by	
	2:7	and let no flower of spring pass by us	
	5:9	and like a rumour that passes by	
	6:22	and I will not pass by the truth	
	10:8	For because they passed wisdom by	
Sir	14:14	let not your share of desired good pass by you	
	23:2	and that it may not pass by my sins	
1 Ma	5:48	we will simply pass by on foot	
2 Es	4:48	So I stood and looked, and behold, a flaming furnace passed by before me	

PASS over

			4 = 0.003 %
2 Es	7:86	they shall see how some of them will pass over into torments	
	12:29	As for your seeing 2 little wings passing over to the head	
	13:44	until they had passed over	
	13:47	so that they may be able to pass over	

PASS, subst.

			5 = 0.003 %
Jud	4:7	ordering them to seize the passes up into the hills	
	5:1	and had closed the passes in the hills	
	6:7	and put you in one of the cities beside the passes	
	7:1	and to seize the passes up into the hill country	
	14:11	to the passes in the mountains	

PASSAGE

			3 = 0.002 %
Jud	7:22	and in the passages through the gates	
Wis	5:11	no evidence of its passage is found	
2 Es	13:43	And they went in by the narrow passages of the Euphrates river	

PASSAGEWAY

			1
L Jr	6:43	And the women, with cords about them, sit along the passageways	

PASSER-BY

			1
L Jr	6:43	and when one of them is led off by one of the passers-by and is lain with	

PASSING

			2
Wis	2:5	For our allotted time is the passing of a shadow	
	17:9	yet, scared by the passing of beasts	

PASSION

			5 = 0.003 %
Sir	9:8	and by it passion is kindled like a fire	
Sus	13:10	Both were overwhelmed with passion for her	
4 Ma	2:3	by his reason he nullified the frenzy of the passions	
	7:10	O supreme king over the passions, Eleazar !	
	7:18	these alone are able to control the passions of the flesh	

PASSOVER

			16 = 0.010 %
1 Es	1:1	Josiah kept the passover to his Lord in Jerusalem	
	1:1	he killed the passover lamb on the 14th day of the first month	
	1:6	and kill the passover lamb	
	1:6	and keep the passover according to the commandment of the Lord	
	1:8	gave to the priests for the passover	
	1:9	gave the Levites for the passover 5,000 sheep and 700 calves	
	1:12	They roasted the passover lamb with fire, as required	
	1:13	Afterward they prepared the passover for themselves	
	1:16	for their brethren the Levites prepared the passover for them	
	1:17	were accomplished that day : the passover was kept	
	1:19	kept the passover and the feast of unleavened bread 7 days	
	1:20	No passover like it had been kept in Israel	
	1:21	none of the kings of Israel had kept such a passover	
	1:22	this passover was kept	
	7:10	kept the passover on the 14th day of the first month	
	7:12	and they sacrificed the passover lamb	

PAST, adj., subst.

			7 = 0.005 %
Sus	13:52	which you have committed in the past	
1 Ma	12:7	Already in time past	
1 Es	1:24	The events of his reign have been recorded in the past	
3 Ma	2:4	You destroyed those who in the past committed injustice	
2 Es	4:5	or call back for me the day that is past	
	9:1	and when you see that a certain part of the predicted signs are past	
	12:40	When all the people heard that the 7 days were past	

PASTURE, subst.

			2
Sir	13:19	likewise the poor are pastures for the rich	
2 Es	9:19	and an inexhaustible pasture	

PATH

			26 = 0.017 %
Tob	4:19	and that all your paths and plans may prosper	
Jud	13:20	walking in the straight path before our God	
	15:2	by every path across the plain and through the hill country	
Wis	5:7	We took our fill of the paths of lawlessness and destruction	
	6:16	and she graciously appears to them in their paths	
	9:18	And thus the paths of those on earth were set right	
	10:10	she guided him on straight paths	
	12:24	For they went far astray in the paths of error, accepting as gods	
	14:3	because thou hast given it a path in the sea	
Sir	4:17	For at first she will walk with him on tortuous paths	
	5:9	Do not winnow with every wind, nor follow every path :	
	14:22	Pursue wisdom like a hunter, and lie in wait on her paths	
	32:20	Do not go on a path full of hazards	
	32:22	and give good heed to your paths	
	50:29	for the light of the Lord is his path	
	51:15	my foot entered upon the straight path	
Bar	3:20	nor understood her paths, nor laid hold of her	
	3:23	nor given thought to her paths	
	3:31	or is concerned about the path to her	
	4:13	nor tread the paths of discipline in his righteousness	
2 Es	7:8	and there is only one path lying between them, that is	
	7:8	so that only one man can walk upon that path	

7:48	and has shown us the paths of perdition
14:22	that men may be able to find the path
16:32	and its roads and all its paths shall bring forth thorns
16:77	and its path overwhelmed with thorns

PATHWAY   1
Wis 5:12   so that no one knows its pathway

PATIENCE   7 = 0.005 %
Sir 16:13   and the patience of the godly will not be frustrated
   20:32   Unwearied patience in seeking the Lord is better
    41:2   to one who is contrary, and has lost his patience !
Bar 4:25   My children, endure with patience
1 Ma 8:4   by their planning and patience
2 Es 7:33   and patience shall be withdrawn
   7:134   and patient, because he shows patience

PATIENT   8 = 0.005 %
Wis 15:1   But thou, our God, art kind and true, patient
Sir 1:23   A patient man will endure until the right moment
   2:4   and in changes that humble you be patient
   18:11   Therefore the Lord is patient with them
   29:8   Nevertheless, be patient with a man in humble circumstances
   35:18   neither will he be patient with them
2 Es 7:74   has been patient with those who inhabit the world
   7:134   and patient, because he shows patience

PATIENTLY   2
2 Ma 6:14   the Lord waits patiently to punish them
4 Ma 14:9   but also bore the sufferings patiently

PATRIARCH   2
4 Ma 7:19   like our patriarchs Abraham and Isaac and Jacob
   16:25   as do Abraham and Isaac and Jacob and all the patriarchs

PATROCLUS   1
2 Ma 8:9   And Ptolemy promptly appointed Nicanor the son of Patroclus

PATROL, subst.   1
Jud 10:11   and an Assyrian patrol met her

PATTERN   2
Sir 38:28   and his eyes are on the pattern of the object
4 Ma 6:19   and ourselves become a pattern of impiety to the young

PAUSE   1
2 Es 2:24   Pause and be quiet, my people, because your rest will come

PAVE   2
Tob 13:17   The streets of Jerusalem will be paved with beryl
Sir 21:10   The way of sinners is smoothly paved with stones

PAVEMENT   1
Sir 20:18   A slip on the pavement is better than a slip of the tongue

PAVILLION   1
2 Ma 13:15   he attacked the king's pavilion at night

PAY, subst.   1
1 Ma 3:28   and gave a year's pay to his forces

PAY, verb   35 = 0.023 %
Tob 2:12   Once when they paid her wages, they also gave her a kid
   4:14   but pay him at once
   5:3   and I will pay him wages as long as I live
   5:11   or for a man whom you will pay to go with your son ?
   5:14   But tell me, what wages am I to pay you – a drachma a day
Wis 13:1   while paying heed to his works
Sir 8:13   but if you give surety, be concerned as one who must pay
   16:24   and pay close attention to my words
   18:22   Let nothing hinder you from paying a vow promptly
   20:12   but pays for it 7 times over
   28:16   Whoever pays heed to slander will not find rest
   29:5   and will pay in words of unconcern
   37:11   pay no attention to these in any matter of counsel
1 Ma 7:11   But they paid no attention to their words
   8:2   how they had defeated them and forced them to pay tribute
   8:4   the rest paid them tribute every year
   8:7   should pay a heavy tribute and give hostages
   10:41   which the government officials have not paid
   10:44   be paid from the revenues of the king
   10:45   also be paid from the revenues of the king
   10:61   but the king paid no attention to them
   10:64   And when his accusers saw the honour that was paid him
   11:60   and paid him honour
   14:32   he armed the men of his nation's forces and paid them wages
   14:39   and paid him high honours
2 Ma 4:9   In addition to this he promised to pay 150 more
   4:27   but he did not pay regularly
1 Es 2:19   they will not only refuse to pay tribute

4:6	and they compel one another to pay taxes to the king
6:25	the cost to be paid from the treasury of Cyrus the king
3 Ma 2:32	and by paying money
3:6	Nevertheless those of the other races paid no heed
2 Es 5:32	pay attention to me, and I will tell you more
4 Ma 1:1	to advise you to pay earnest attention to philosophy
4:17	he would pay the king 3,660 talents annually

PAY back   3 = 0.002 %
Jud 7:15   So you will pay them back with evil
Sir 36:20   but a man of experience will pay him back
1 Ma 2:68   Pay back the Gentiles in full

PAYMENT   6 = 0.004 %
Tob 4:14   and if you serve God you will receive payment
1 Ma 10:29   from payment of tribute and salt tax and crown levies
   10:33   I set free without payment
   11:35   And the other payments due to us of the tithes
   15:5   and release from all the other payments
2 Ma 4:28   kept requesting payment

PEACE   66 = 0.043 %
Tob 13:14   They will rejoice in your peace
   14:4   But in Media there will be peace for a time
Jud 3:1   So they sent messengers to sue for peace, and said
   7:24   in not making peace with the Assyrians
   8:35   Go in peace, and may the Lord God go before you
Ad E 13:2   to re-establish the peace which all men desire
Wis 3:3   but they are at peace
   14:22   and they call such great evils peace
Sir 1:18   making peace and perfect health to flourish
   6:6   Let those that are at peace with you be many
   13:18   What peace is there between a hyena and a dog ?
   13:18   And what peace between a rich man and a poor man ?
   26:2   and he will complete his years in peace
   28:9   and inject enmity among those who are at peace
   28:13   for he has destroyed many who were at peace
   28:16   nor will he settle down in peace
   35:1   he who heeds the commandments sacrifices a peace offering
   41:1   to one who lives at peace among his possessions
   41:14   My children, observe instruction and be at peace
   44:14   Their bodies were buried in peace
   45:24   Therefore a covenant of peace was established with him
   47:2   As the fat is selected from the peace offering
   47:13   Solomon reigned in days of peace
   47:16   and you were loved for your peace
   50:23   and grant that peace may be in our days in Israel
Bar 3:13   you would be dwelling in peace for ever
   3:14   where there is light for the eyes, and peace
   4:20   I have taken off the robe of peace
   5:4   Peace of righteousness and glory of godliness
L Jr 6:3   after that I will bring you away from there in peace
1 Ma 6:49   He made peace with the men of Beth-zur
   6:58   and make peace with them and with all their nation
   6:60   and he sent to the Jews an offer of peace
   7:13   to seek peace from them
   7:28   I shall come with a few men to see you face to face in peace
   8:20   have sent us to you to establish alliance and peace with you
   8:22   as a memorial of peace and alliance :
   9:70   he sent ambassadors to him to make peace with him
   10:4   for he said, Let us act first to make peace with him
   10:4   before he makes peace with Alexander against us
   10:66   And Jonathan returned to Jerusalem in peace and gladness
   11:50   Grant us peace
   11:51   And they threw down their arms and made peace
   11:62   and he made peace with them
   11:66   Then they asked him to grant them terms of peace
   13:37   and we are ready to make a general peace with you
   13:40   let them be enrolled, and let there be peace between us
   13:45   asking Simon to make peace with them
   13:50   Then they cried to Simon to make peace with them
   14:8   They tilled their land in peace
   14:11   He established peace in the land
2 Ma 1:1   To their Jewish brethren in Egypt, greeting, and good peace
   1:4   and may he bring peace
   3:1   While the holy city was inhabited in unbroken peace
   12:2   would not let them live quietly and in peace
   12:12   agreed to make peace with them
   14:10   it is impossible for the government to find peace
1 Es 8:85   and do not seek ever to have peace with them
3 Ma 2:20   and give us peace
   6:27   Send them back to their homes in peace
   7:19   And when they had landed in peace with appropriate thanksgiving
2 Es 13:47   Therefore you saw the multitude gathered together in peace
   16:21   that men will imagine that peace is assured for them
4 Ma 3:20   At a time when our fathers were enjoying profound peace
   8:26   when we can live in peace if we obey the king ?
   18:4   Because of them the nation gained peace

PEACEABLE
| | | | 12 = 0.008 % |

Ad E 13 : 2   and, in order to make my kingdom peaceable
      16 : 8   quiet and peaceable for all men
1 Ma   1 : 30   Deceitfully he spoke peaceable words to them
      7 : 10   with peaceable but treacherous words
      7 : 15   And he spoke peaceable words to them
      7 : 27   this peaceable message
    10 : 3   in peaceable words to honour him
    10 : 47   because he had been the first to speak peaceable words to them
    11 : 2   He set out for Syria with peaceable words
2 Es 11 : 42   for you have afflicted the meek and injured the peaceable
    13 : 12   and call to him another multitude which was peaceable
    13 : 39   gather to himself another multitude that was peaceable

PEACEABLY
| | | | 8 = 0.005 % |

Jud   7 : 15   because they rebelled and did not receive you peaceably
Sir   4 : 8   and answer him peaceably and gently
    44 : 6   living peaceably in their habitations
1 Ma   5 : 25   They encountered the Nabateans, who met them peaceably
    7 : 29   So he came to Judas, and they greeted one another peaceably
    7 : 33   to greet him peaceably and to show him the burnt offering
2 Ma   5 : 25   he pretended to be peaceably disposed
    12 : 4   because they wished to live peaceably and suspected nothing

PEACEFUL
| | | | 3 = 0.002 % |

2 Ma   4 : 6   public affairs could not again reach a peaceful settlement
    10 : 12   and attempted to maintain peaceful relations with them
3 Ma   6 : 32   they formed choruses as a sign of peaceful joy

PEBBLE
| | | | 1 |

1 Ma 10 : 73   where there is no stone or pebble, or place to flee

PEDAIAH
| | | | 1 |

1 Es   9 : 44   and on his left Pedaiah, Mishael, Malchijah

PEER
| | | | 3 = 0.002 % |

Sir 14 : 23   He who peers through her windows
    21 : 23   A boor peers into the house from the door
2 Ma   3 : 19   while others peered out of the windows

PEG
| | | | 1 |

Sir 14 : 24   will also fasten his tent peg to her walls

PELAIAH
| | | | 1 |

1 Es   9 : 48   Azariah and Jozabad, Hanan, Pelaiah, the Levites

PEN
| | | | 1 |

3 Ma   4 : 20   that both the paper and the pens they used for writing

PENALTY
| | | | 10 = 0.007 % |

Tob   3 : 5   in exacting penalty from me for my sins
    6 : 12   without incurring the penalty of death
Jud   8 : 21   and he will exact of us the penalty for its desecration
Wis 14 : 30   But just penalties will overtake them on 2 counts :
    14 : 31   but the just penalty for those who sin
    18 : 11   The slave was punished with the same penalty as the master
Sir   9 : 5   lest you stumble and incur penalties for her
2 Ma   4 : 48   quickly suffered the unjust penalty
3 Ma   7 : 3   and to punish them with barbarous penalties as traitors
2 Es   6 : 19   the penalty of their iniquity

PENETRATE
| | | | 3 = 0.002 % |

Wis   7 : 23   and penetrating through all spirits
    7 : 24   she pervades and penetrates all things
Sir 39 : 2   and penetrate the subtleties of parables

PENTECOST
| | | | 2 |

Tob   2 : 1   at the feast of Pentecost
2 Ma 12 : 32   After the feast called Pentecost

PEOPLE*
| | | | 438 = 0.285 % |

Tob   1 : 17   and if I saw any one of my people dead
    2 : 3   Father, one of our people has been strangled
    4 : 13   and the sons and daughters of your people
    5 : 11   I should like to know, my brother, your people and your name
    6 : 15   to take a wife from among your own people ?
    8 : 15   let all thy angels and thy chosen people bless thee for ever
    14 : 7   and his people will give thanks to God
    14 : 7   and the Lord will exalt his people
Jud   1 : 6   He was joined by all the people of the hill country
    1 : 12   and the people of Ammon, and all Judea
    2 : 23   and plundered all the people of Rassis
    2 : 28   So fear and terror of him fell upon all the people
    3 : 7   And these people and all in the country round about
    4 : 1   By this time the people of Israel living in Judea
    4 : 3   and all the people of Judea were newly gathered together
    4 : 6   wrote to the people of Bethulia and Betomesthaim
    4 : 8   and the senate of the whole people of Israel
    4 : 13   for the people fasted many days throughout Judea
    4 : 14   and the vows and freewill offerings of the people

    5 : 1   heard that the people of Israel had prepared for war
    5 : 3   what people is this that lives in the hill country ?
    5 : 5   and I will tell you the truth about this people
    5 : 6   This people is descended from the Chaldeans
    5 : 14   and drove out all the people of the wilderness
    5 : 20   if there is any unwitting error in this people
    5 : 23   they are a people with no strength or power for making war
    6 : 2   and tell us not to make war against the people of Israel
    6 : 16   and they set Achior in the midst of all their people
    6 : 18   Then the people fell down and worshipped God
    6 : 19   and have pity on the humiliation of our people
    7 : 8   Then all the chieftains of the people of Esau
    7 : 10   For these people, the Israelites
    7 : 13   for this is where all the people of Bethulia get their water
    7 : 13   We and our people go up to the tops of the nearby mountains
    7 : 19   The people of Israel cried out to the Lord their God
    7 : 23   Then all the people, the young men, the women, and the children
    7 : 32   Then he dismissed the people to their various posts
    8 : 9   spoken by the people against the ruler
    8 : 11   Listen to me, rulers of the people of Bethulia !
    8 : 11   What you have said to the people today is not right
    8 : 18   has there been any tribe or family or people
    8 : 29   all the people have recognized your understanding
    8 : 30   But the people were very thirsty
    9 : 14   who protects the people of Israel but thou alone !
    10 : 8   that the people of Israel may glory
    10 : 12   To what people do you belong
    10 : 19   Who can despise these people
    11 : 2   And even now, if your people who live in the hill country
    11 : 13   although it is not lawful for any of the people
    11 : 14   because even the people living there have been doing this
    11 : 22   God has done well to send you before the people
    12 : 3   For none of your people is here with us
    12 : 8   to direct her way for the raising up of her people
    13 : 17   All the people were greatly astonished
    13 : 17   the enemies of thy people
    13 : 20   And all the people said, So be it, so be it !
    14 : 6   at the gathering of the people
    14 : 8   Then Judith described to him in the presence of the people
    14 : 9   And when she had finished, the people raised a great shout
    14 : 17   he rushed out to the people and shouted
    15 : 6   The rest of the people of Bethulia
    15 : 8   and the senate of the people of Israel
    15 : 10   And all the people said, So be it !
    15 : 11   So all the people plundered the camp for 30 days
    15 : 13   and she went before all the people in the dance
    16 : 1   and all the people loudly sang this song of praise
    16 : 3   and brought me into his camp, in the midst of the people
    16 : 11   Then my oppressed people shouted for joy
    16 : 11   for weak people shouted and the enemy trembled
    16 : 17   Woe to the nations that rise up against my people !
    16 : 18   As soon as the people were purified
    16 : 19   which the people had given her
    16 : 20   So the people continued feasting in Jerusalem
    16 : 22   and was gathered to his people
    16 : 25   among the people of Israel
Ad E 10 : 9   The Lord has saved his people
    10 : 10   one for the people of God and one for all the nations
    10 : 12   And God remembered his people and vindicated his inheritance
    10 : 13   from generation to generation for ever among his people Israel
    12 : 6   and he sought to injure Mordecai and his people
    13 : 4   there is scattered a certain hostile people
    13 : 5   We understand that this people, and it alone
    13 : 15   God of Abraham, spare thy people
    15 : 10   you shall not die, for our law applies only to the people. Come near
    16 : 21   has made this day to be a joy to his chosen people
Wis   3 : 8   They will govern nations and rule over peoples
    4 : 15   Yet the peoples saw and did not understand
    6 : 21   O monarchs over the peoples
    6 : 24   and a sensible king is the stability of his people
    8 : 14   I shall govern peoples, and nations will be subject to me
    8 : 15   among the people I shall show myself capable
    9 : 7   Thou hast chosen me to be king of thy people
    9 : 12   and I shall judge thy people justly
    10 : 15   A holy people and blameless race wisdom delivered
    12 : 19   Through such works thou hast taught thy people
    15 : 14   are all the enemies who oppressed thy people
    15 : 18   The enemies of thy people worship
    16 : 2   thou didst show kindness to thy people
    16 : 3   while thy people, after suffering want a short time
    16 : 5   came upon thy people
    16 : 20   thou didst give thy people the food of angels
    18 : 3   as a guide for thy people's unknown journey
    18 : 7   were expected by thy people
    18 : 13   they acknowledged thy people to be God's son
    19 : 2   thy people to depart
    19 : 5   and that thy people might experience an incredible journey
    19 : 22   thou hast exalted and glorified thy people

Sir	7:7	and do not disgrace yourself among the people	
	9:17	so a people's leader is proved wise by his words	
	10:1	A wise magistrate will educate his people	
	10:2	like the magistrate of the people, so are his officials	
	10:3	An undisciplined king will ruin his people	
	14:8	he averts his face and disregards people	
	16:4	a city will be filled with people	
	16:17	Among so many people I shall not be known	
	19:25	and there are people who distort kindness to gain a verdict	
	21:8	A man who builds his house with other people's money	
	24:1	and will glory in the midst of her people	
	24:6	and in every people and nation I have gotten a possession	
	24:12	So I took root in an honoured people	
	27:12	Among stupid people watch for a chance to leave	
	27:12	but among thoughtful people stay on	
	31:9	for he has done wonderful things among his people	
	33:18	Hear me, you who are great among the people	
	35:19	till he judges the case of his people	
	36:8	and let people recount thy mighty deeds	
	36:9	and may those who harm thy people meet destruction	
	36:12	Have mercy, O Lord, upon the people called by thy name	
	36:17	according to the blessing of Aaron for thy people	
	37:23	A wise man will instruct his own people	
	37:26	He who is wise among his people will inherit confidence	
	38:33	Yet they are not sought out for the council of the people	
	39:25	From the beginning good things were created for good people	
	41:18	and of iniquity, before a congregation or the people	
	42:11	a byword in the city and notorious among the people	
	44:4	leaders of the people in their deliberations	
	44:4	and in understanding of learning for the people	
	44:15	Peoples will declare their wisdom	
	45:3	He gave him commands for his people	
	45:7	and gave him the priesthood of the people	
	45:9	as a reminder to the sons of his people	
	45:15	and bless his people in his name	
	45:16	to make atonement for the people	
	45:22	But in the land of the people he has no inheritance	
	45:22	and he has no portion among the people	
	45:23	and stood fast, when the people turned away	
	45:24	that he should be leader of the sanctuary and of his people	
	45:26	to judge his people in righteousness	
	46:7	restrained the people from sin	
	46:8	out of 600,000 people on foot	
	46:13	established the kingdom and anointed rulers over his people	
	46:18	and he wiped out the leaders of the people of Tyre	
	46:20	to blot out the wickedness of the people	
	47:4	and take away reproach from the people	
	47:5	to exalt the power of his people	
	47:23	Rehoboam, whose policy caused the people to revolt	
	48:15	For all this the people did not repent	
	48:15	the people were left very few in number	
	49:2	He was led aright in converting the people	
	49:10	for they comforted the people of Jacob	
	50:1	The leader of his brethren and the pride of his people	
	50:4	He considered how to save his people from ruin	
	50:5	How glorious he was when the people gathered round him	
	50:17	Then all the people together made haste	
	50:19	And the people besought the Lord Most High in prayer	
	50:26	and the foolish people that dwell in Shechem	
Bar	1:3	and in the hearing of all the people who came to hear the book	
	1:4	and in the hearing of all the people, small and great	
	1:7	and to all the people who were present with him in Jerusalem	
	1:9	and the mighty men and the people of the land	
	2:4	to be a reproach and a desolation among all the surrounding peoples	
	2:11	who didst bring thy people out of the land of Egypt	
	2:28	to write thy law in the presence of the people of Israel	
	2:30	for they are a stiff-necked people	
	2:35	to be their God and they shall be my people	
	2:35	and I will never again remove my people Israel	
	4:3	or your advantages to an alien people	
	4:5	Take courage, my people, O memorial of Israel !	
L Jr	6:9	People take gold and make crowns for the heads of their gods	
Sus	13:5	In that year 2 elders from the people were appointed as judges	
	13:5	who were supposed to govern the people	
	13:7	When the people departed at noon	
	13:28	The next day, when the people gathered at the house of her husband Joakim	
	13:29	They said before the people	
	13:34	Then the 2 elders stood up in the midst of the people	
	13:41	because they were elders of the people and judges	
	13:47	All the people turned to him, and said	
	13:50	Then all the people returned in haste	
	13:64	Daniel had a great reputation among the people	
1 Ma	1:13	and some of the people eagerly went to the king	
	1:30	and destroyed many people of Israel	
	1:34	And they stationed there a sinful people, lawless men	
	1:41	that all should be one people	
	1:51	And he appointed inspectors over all the people	
	1:52	Many of the people, every one who forsook the law, joined them	

	2:7	the ruin of my people, the ruin of the holy city	
	2:66	and fight the battle against the peoples	
	2:67	and avenge the wrong done to your people	
	3:3	He extended the glory of his people	
	3:5	he burned those who troubled his people	
	3:42	to do to the people to cause their final destruction	
	3:43	Let us repair the destruction of our people	
	3:43	and fight for our people and the sanctuary	
	3:55	After this Judas appointed leaders of the people	
	4:17	and he said to the people, Do not be greedy for plunder	
	4:31	So do thou hem in this army by the hand of thy people Israel	
	4:55	All the people fell on their faces	
	4:58	There was very great gladness among the people	
	4:61	so that the people might have a stronghold that faced Idumea	
	5:2	So they began to kill and destroy among the people	
	5:4	who were a trap and a snare to the people	
	5:6	and many people with Timothy as their leader	
	5:16	When Judas and the people heard these messages	
	5:18	and Azariah, a leader of the people	
	5:19	and he gave them this command, Take charge of this people	
	5:42	he stationed the scribes of the people at the stream	
	5:53	and encouraging the people all the way	
	5:60	as many as 2,000 of the people of Israel fell that day	
	5:61	Thus the people suffered a great rout	
	6:19	and assembled all the people to besiege them	
	6:24	For this reason the sons of our people besieged the citadel	
	6:44	So he gave his life to save his people	
	7:6	against the people :	
	7:18	Then the fear and dread of them fell upon all the people	
	7:19	and some of the people	
	7:22	and all who were troubling their people joined him	
	7:26	and he commanded him to destroy the people	
	7:33	and some of the elders of the people	
	7:37	and to be for thy people a house of prayer and supplication	
	7:48	The people rejoiced greatly	
	8:15	concerning the people, to govern them well	
	8:20	and the people of the Jews	
	8:29	with the Jewish people	
	9:2	and they took it and killed many people	
	9:73	And Jonathan began to judge the people	
	10:7	and read the letter in the hearing of all the people	
	10:46	When Jonathan and the people heard these words	
	11:2	and the people of the cities opened their gates to him	
	11:14	because the people of that region were in revolt	
	11:51	and of all the people in his kingdom	
	11:60	When he came to Askalon, the people of the city met him	
	11:62	Then the people of Gaza pleaded with Jonathan	
	12:4	And the Romans gave them letters to the people	
	12:6	the priests, and the rest of the Jewish people	
	12:35	When Jonathan returned he convened the elders of the people	
	12:44	Why have you wearied all these people when we are not at war ?	
	13:2	and he saw that the people were trembling and fearful	
	13:2	and gathering the people together	
	13:7	The spirit of the people was rekindled	
	13:17	lest he arouse great hostility among the people	
	13:42	and the people began to write	
	14:14	He strengthened all the humble of his people	
	14:20	and the rest of the Jewish people, our brethren, greeting	
	14:21	The envoys who were sent to our people	
	14:23	It has pleased our people to receive these men with honour	
	14:23	so that the people of the Spartans	
	14:25	When the people heard these things they said	
	14:28	and the people and the rulers of the nation	
	14:30	and was gathered to his people	
	14:35	The people saw Simon's faithfulness	
	14:35	He sought in every way to exalt his people	
	14:44	And none of the people or priests shall be permitted	
	14:46	And all the people agreed to grant Simon	
	15:17	and by the people of the Jews	
	15:35	they were causing great damage among the people and to our land	
	15:39	and to make war on the people	
	15:40	and began to provoke the people and invade Judea	
	15:40	and take the people captive and kill them	
2 Ma	1:16	and threw them to the people outside	
	1:26	accept this sacrifice on behalf of all thy people Israel	
	1:27	Gather together our scattered people	
	1:29	Plant thy people in thy holy place, as Moses said	
	1:36	but by most people it is called naphtha	
	2:7	until God gathers his people together again	
	2:15	So if you have need of them, send people to get them for you	
	2:17	It is God who has saved all his people	
	3:12	that wrong should be done to those people	
	3:18	People also hurried out of their houses in crowds	
	4:5	but having in view the welfare, both public and private, of all the people	
	4:30	it happened that the people of Tarsus and of Mallus	
	5:22	And he left governors to afflict the people : at Jerusalem	
	5:26	and killed great numbers of people	
	6:2	as did the people who dwelt in that place	

	6:12	not to destroy but to discipline our people
	6:16	he does not forsake his own people
	7:6	which bore witness against the people to their faces
	7:16	But do not think that God has forsaken our people
	8:2	They besought the Lord to look upon the people
	8:36	by the capture of the people of Jerusalem
	9:2	Therefore the people rushed to the rescue with arms
	9:24	the people throughout the realm would not be troubled
	10:21	he gathered the leaders of the people
	11:6	they and all the people, with lamentations and tears
	11:16	Lysias to the people of the Jews, greeting
	11:34	to the people of the Jews, greeting
	12:9	he attacked the people of Jamnia by night
	12:11	and to help his people in all other ways
	12:26	and slaughtered 25,000 people
	12:27	with multitudes of people of all nationalities
	12:30	which the people of Scythopolis had shown them
	12:42	And the noble Judas exhorted the people
	13:10	he ordered the people to call upon the Lord day and night
	13:11	and not to let the people who had just begun to revive
	13:22	with the people in Beth-zur
	13:25	The people of Ptolemais were indignant over the treaty
	14:15	and prayed to him who established his own people for ever
	14:20	and the leader had informed the people
	14:23	but dismissed the flocks of people that had gathered
	15:14	and prays much for the people and the holy city
	15:24	who come against thy holy people be struck down
1 Es	1:4	and serve his people Israel
	1:5	who minister before your brethren the people of Israel
	1:7	And Josiah gave to the people who were present
	1:7	to the people and the priests and Levites
	1:11	and the grouping of the fathers' houses, before the people
	1:13	and carried them to all the people
	1:19	And the people of Israel who were present at that time
	1:24	beyond any other people or kingdom
	1:49	Even the leaders of the people and of the priests
	1:52	until in his anger against his people
	2:5	If any one of you, therefore, is of his people
	4:10	All his people and his armies obey him
	4:15	and to every people that rules over sea and land
	4:41	then all the people shouted, and said
	5:46	and some of the people settled in Jerusalem and its vicinity
	5:50	And some joined them from the other peoples of the land
	5:50	for all the peoples of the land were hostile to them
	5:62	And all the people sounded trumpets
	5:65	so that the people could not hear the trumpets
	5:65	because of the weeping of the people
	5:72	But the peoples of the land pressed hard upon those in Judea
	6:16	and carried the people away captive to Babylon
	7:6	And the people of Israel, the priests, the Levites
	7:10	The people of Israel who came from the captivity
	7:13	And the people of Israel who came from the captivity ate it
	7:13	from the abominations of the peoples of the land
	8:5	some of the people of Israel and some of the priests
	8:67	and these officials honoured the people
	8:69	The people of Israel
	8:69	the alien peoples of the land and their pollutions
	8:70	For they and their sons have married the daughters of these people
	8:70	and the holy race has been mixed with the alien peoples of the land
	8:87	by mixing with the uncleanness of the peoples of the land
	8:92	and have married foreign women from the peoples of the land
	9:9	separate yourselves from the peoples of the land
	9:53	And the Levites commanded all the people, saying
Ps 151	7	I beheaded him, and removed reproach from the people of Israel
3 Ma	1:27	they turned, together with our people
	2:6	on the audacious Pharaoh who had enslaved your holy people Israel
	2:6	upon your people Israel
	3:5	with the good deeds of upright people
	3:7	alleging that these people were loyal
	3:8	when they saw an unexpected tumult around these people
	3:16	and went up to honour the temple of those wicked people
	3:19	they become the only people among all nations
	3:24	we would have these impious people behind our backs
	3:27	old people or children or even infants
	4:4	and shed tears at the most miserable expulsion of these people
	4:15	The registration of these people was therefore conducted
	5:5	and bound the hands of the wretched people
	5:34	and dismissed the assembled people
	5:41	it is crowded with masses of people
	5:46	with countless masses of people
	5:47	the grievous and pitiful destruction of the aforementioned people
	6:3	a people of your consecrated portion
	6:11	at the destruction of your beloved people
	7:4	because of the ill-will which these people had toward all nations
2 Es	1:5	Go and declare to my people their evil deeds
	1:8	they are a rebellious people

	1:11	and scattered in the east the people of 2 provinces, Tyre and Sidon
	1:29	that you should be my people and I should be your God
	1:35	I will give your houses to a people that will come
	1:37	I call to witness the gratitude of the people that is to come
	1:38	look with pride and see the people coming from the east
	2:1	Thus says the Lord : I brought this people out of bondage
	2:10	Tell my people that I will give them the kingdom of Jerusalem
	2:24	Pause and be quiet, my people, because your rest will come
	2:40	and conclude the list of your people who are clothed in white
	2:41	beseech the Lord's power that your people
	2:48	Then the angel said to me, Go, tell my people
	3:7	peoples and clans, without number
	3:12	they produced children and peoples and many nations
	3:22	the law was in the people's heart along with the evil root
	3:30	and hast destroyed thy people, and hast preserved thy enemies
	4:23	why the people whom you loved
	5:5	the peoples shall be troubled
	5:16	Now on the 2nd night Phaltiel, a chief of the people
	5:27	and from all the multitude of peoples
	5:27	thou hast gotten for thyself one people
	5:27	and to this people, whom thou hast loved
	5:30	If thou dost really hate thy people
	5:35	and the exhaustion of the people of Israel ?
	5:40	or the goal of the love that I have promised my people
	6:54	the people whom thou hast chosen
	6:58	But we thy people
	7:106	for the people of Sodom
	7:110	and Hezekiah for the people in the days of Sennacherib
	7:129	spoke to the people, saying
	8:15	but I will speak about thy people
	8:26	O look not upon the sins of thy people
	8:45	But spare thy people and have mercy on thy inheritance
	9:3	tumult of peoples, intrigues of nations
	10:39	that you have sorrowed continually for your people
	12:34	But he will deliver in mercy the remnant of my people
	12:38	and you shall teach them to the wise among your people
	12:40	When all the people heard that the 7 days were past
	12:50	So the people went into the city, as I told them to do
	13:13	Then many people came to him
	13:31	people against people, and kingdom against kingdom
	13:36	And Zion will come and be made manifest to all people, prepared and built
	13:48	But those who are left of your people
	13:49	he will defend the people who remain
	14:3	when my people were in bondage in Egypt
	14:4	and I sent him and led my people out of Egypt
	14:13	and reprove your people
	14:20	and I will reprove the people who are now living
	14:23	Go and gather the people
	14:27	and I gathered all the people together, and said
	14:46	in order to give them to the wise among your people
	15:1	speak in the ears of my people the words of the prophecy
	15:10	Behold, my people is led like a flock to the slaughter
	15:18	and people shall be afraid
	15:53	if you had not always killed my chosen people
	15:56	As you will do to my chosen people, says the Lord
	15:57	and all your people who are in the open country
	16:40	Hear my words, O my people
4 Ma	1:11	For all people, even their torturers
	4:7	The people indignantly protested his words
	4:12	he would praise the blessedness of the holy place before all people
	4:22	and that the people of Jerusalem had rejoiced greatly
	4:24	to put an end to the people's observance of the law
	4:26	when, then, his decrees were despised by the people
	5:15	he began to address the people as follows :
	6:28	Be merciful to your people
	7:11	ran through the multitude of the people
	16:23	It is unreasonable for people who have religious knowledge
	17:8	as a reminder to the people of our nation :

PERCEIVE
10 = 0.007 %

Wis	8:21	But I perceived that I would not possess wisdom
	11:13	they perceived it was the Lord's doing
	13:4	let them perceive from them
Sir	23:19	and perceive even the hidden places
L Jr	6:42	Yet they themselves cannot perceive this and abandon them
1 Ma	1:5	After this he fell sick and perceived that he was dying
	4:21	When they perceived this they were greatly frightened
2 Ma	5:17	Antiochus was elated in spirit, and did not perceive
	15:17	Maccabeus, perceiving the hosts that were before him
3 Ma	4:4	perceiving the common object of pity before their eyes

PERCEPTION
1

Wis	13:5	comes a corresponding perception of their Creator

PERDITION 2
2 Es 7:48 and has shown us the paths of perdition
10:10 and behold, almost all go to perdition

PERFECT, verb 5 = 0.003 %
Wis 4:13 Being perfected in a short time, he fulfilled long years
4:16 and youth that is quickly perfected
2 Es 8:52 and wisdom perfected beforehand
9:22 because with much labour I have perfected them
4 Ma 7:15 whom the faithful seal of death has perfected !

PERFECT, adj. 7 = 0.005 %
Ad E 15:5 She was radiant with perfect beauty, and she looked happy
Wis 6:15 To fix one's thought on her is perfect understanding
9:6 for even if one is perfect among the sons of men
Sir 1:18 making peace and perfect health to flourish
31:10 Who has been tested by it and been found perfect ?
34:8 and wisdom is made perfect in truthful lips
44:17 Noah was found perfect and righteous

PERFECTION 2
Sir 45:8 He clothed him with superb perfection
50:11 and clothed himself with superb perfection

PERFECTLY 3 = 0.002 %
Sir 24:28 Just as the first man did not know her perfectly
3 Ma 7:22 So the supreme God perfectly performed great deeds
2 Es 7:89 that they might keep the law of the Lawgiver perfectly

PERFIDY 1
2 Ma 15:10 at the same time pointing out the perfidy of the Gentiles

PERFORM 11 = 0.007 %
Tob 1:3 and I performed many acts of charity to my brethren
1:16 I performed many acts of charity to my brethren
12:9 Those who perform deeds of charity and of righteousness
Jud 15:12 and blessed her, and some of them performed a dance for her
Sir 3:17 My son, perform your tasks in meekness
7:20 Do not abuse a servant who performs his work faithfully
1 Es 8:16 perform it in accordance with the will of your God
3 Ma 7:22 So the supreme God perfectly performed great deeds
2 Es 7:24 and have not performed his works
12:25 and perform his last actions
13:44 For at that time the Most High performed signs for them

PERFUME, subst. 3 = 0.002 %
Ad E 14:2 and instead of costly perfumes
Wis 2:7 Let us take our fill of costly wine and perfumes
2 Es 2:12 The tree of life shall give them fragrant perfume

PERFUMER 1
Sir 49:1 prepared by the art of the perfumer

PERHAPS 11 = 0.007 %
Tob 8:10 with the thought, Perhaps he too will die
Wis 13:6 for perhaps they go astray while seeking God
14:19 For he, perhaps wishing to please his ruler
Sir 19:13 Question a friend, perhaps he did not do it
19:14 Question a neighbour, perhaps he did not say it
2 Es 4:8 perhaps you would have said to me
4:39 And it is perhaps on account of us
7:69 perhaps it would have been better for us
4 Ma 1:5 Some might perhaps ask, If reason rules the emotions
7:17 Some perhaps might say
16:5 and perhaps have spoken as follows :

PERIL 4 = 0.003 %
2 Es 9:20 and my earth, and behold, it was in peril
13:20 though incurring peril
13:23 He who brings the peril at that time
13:23 will himself protect those who fall into peril

PERIMETER 1
3 Ma 4:11 which had been built with a monstrous perimeter wall

PERIOD 6 = 0.004 %
Wis 7:2 within the period of 10 months, compacted with blood
Sir pr. using in that period of time great watchfulness and skill
2 Ma 4:23 After a period of 3 years Jason sent Menelaus
2 Es 5:4 you shall see it thrown into confusion after the 3rd period
10:47 that was the period of residence in Jerusalem
4 Ma 13:20 and was shaped during the same period of time

PERISH 57 = 0.037 %
Tob 10:4 And his wife said to him, The lad has perished
10:7 my child has perished
14:10 but Nadab fell into the trap and perished
Jud 6:4 They cannot withstand us, but will utterly perish
6:8 and you will not die until you perish along with them
16:12 they perished before the army of my Lord

Ad E 11:9 and were ready to perish
Wis 3:16 and the offspring of an unlawful union will perish
4:19 and the memory of them will perish
10:3 he perished because in rage he slew his brother
10:6 when the ungodly were perishing
14:6 when arrogant giants were perishing
17:10 they perished in trembling fear
18:19 so that they might not perish
Sir 3:26 and whoever loves danger will perish by it
5:7 and at the time of punishment you will perish
8:15 and through his folly you will perish with him
41:6 The inheritance of the children of sinners will perish
44:9 who have perished as though they had not lived
47:22 nor cause any of his works to perish
Bar 2:25 They perished in great misery
3:3 and we are perishing for ever
3:28 so they perished because they had no wisdom
3:28 they perished through their folly
1 Ma 2:63 and his plans will perish
3:9 he gathered in those who were perishing
6:13 and behold, I am perishing of deep grief in a strange land
12:50 and had perished along with his men
13:4 By reason of this all my brothers have perished
13:18 Because Simon did not send him the money and the sons, he perished
13:49 and many of them perished from famine
16:21 that his father and brothers had perished
2 Ma 7:20 Though she saw her 7 sons perish within a single day
8:19 both the time of Sennacherib, when 185,000 perished
1 Es 4:27 Many have perished, or stumbled, or sinned, because of women
4:37 and in their unrighteousness they will perish
3 Ma 6:3 who are perishing as foreigners in a foreign land
2 Es 2:26 Not one of the servants whom I have given you will perish
7:15 But now why are you disturbed, seeing that you are to perish ?
7:17 but that the ungodly shall perish
7:20 Let many perish who are now living
7:31 and that which is corruptible shall perish
7:61 And I will not grieve over the multitude of those who perish
7:64 because we perish and know it
8:43 or if it has been ruined by too much rain, it perishes
8:55 about the multitude of those who perish
9:15 there are more who perish than those who will be saved
9:22 So let the multitude perish which has been born in vain
9:32 yet the fruit of the law did not perish
9:33 Yet those who received it perished
9:36 For we who have received the law and sinned will perish
9:37 the law, however, does not perish but remains in its glory
12:21 and 2 of them shall perish
15:58 shall perish of hunger
16:18 the beginning of famine, when many shall perish
16:22 For many of those who live on the earth shall perish by famine
16:34 and their husbands shall perish of famine

PERISHABLE 3 = 0.002 %
Wis 9:15 for a perishable body weighs down the soul
14:8 and the perishable thing was named a god
19:21 failed to consume the flesh of perishable creatures

PERIZZITE 3 = 0.002 %
Jud 5:16 and the Perizzites and the Jebusites
1 Es 8:69 the Canaanites, the Hittites, the Perizzites
2 Es 1:21 I drove out the Canaanites, the Perizzites

PERJURY 2
Wis 14:25 theft and deceit, corruption, faithlessness, tumult, perjury
14:28 or readily commit perjury

PERMANENT 3 = 0.002 %
Ad E 12:4 The king made a permanent record of these things
1 Ma 13:29 for a permanent memorial
2 Es 3:22 Thus the disease became permanent

PERMISSION 10 = 0.007 %
Jud 11:14 to bring back to them permission from the senate
Sir 15:20 and he has not given any one permission to sin
Bel 14:26 But if you, O king, will give me permission
14:26 The king said, I give you permission
1 Ma 9:35 for permission to store with them
14:44 without his permission
2 Ma 4:9 if permission were given to establish by his authority
11:30 and full permission for the Jews
1 Es 4:62 because he had given them release and permission
4 Ma 5:15 When he had received permission to speak

PERMIT 12 = 0.008 %
Jud 12:6 that your servant be permitted to go out and pray
Ad E 16:19 and permit the Jews to live under their own laws
Wis 19:2 that, though they themselves had permitted
1 Ma 5:42 Permit no man to encamp, but make them all enter the battle
12:40 He feared that Jonathan might not permit him to do so

	14:44	And none of the people or priests shall be permitted
	15:6	I permit you to mint your own coinage
	15:14	and permitted no one to leave or enter it
1 Es	6:27	to keep away from the place, and to permit Zerubbabel
3 Ma	1:11	When they said that this was not permitted
2 Es	5:13	These are the signs which I am permitted to tell you
4 Ma	5:26	He has permitted us to eat

PERPETRATE　　　　　　　　　　　　　　　　1
2 Ma　3:32　that some foul play had been perpetrated by the Jews

PERPETUAL　　　　　　　　　　　　　4 = 0.003 %
Jud　13:20　May God grant this to be a perpetual honour to you
Ad E　16:13　our saviour and perpetual benefactor
Sir　41:6　and on their posterity will be a perpetual reproach
1 Es　6:24　where they sacrifice with perpetual fire

PERPETUALLY　　　　　　　　　　　　　　1
Sir　45:13　and his descendants perpetually

PERPLEXED　　　　　　　　　　　　　　　2
1 Ma　3:31　He was greatly perplexed in mind
　　　4:27　When he heard it, he was perplexed and discouraged

PERPLEXITY　　　　　　　　　　　　3 = 0.002 %
Sir　40:2　Their perplexities and fear of heart
2 Es　7:93　because they see the perplexity
　　　12:3　Then I awoke in great perplexity of mind and great fear

PERSEPOLIS　　　　　　　　　　　　　　　1
2 Ma　9:2　For he had entered the city called Persepolis

PERSEUS　　　　　　　　　　　　　　　　1
1 Ma　8:5　Philip, and Perseus king of the Macedonians

PERSEVERE　　　　　　　　　　　　　　　2
Sir　2:10　Or who ever persevered in the fear of the Lord and was forsaken ?
3 Ma　3:11　but assuming that he would persevere

PERSIA　　　　　　　　　　　　　14 = 0.009 %
Jud　1:7　sent to all who lived in Persia
1 Ma　3:31　and determined to go to Persia
　　　6:1　when he heard that Elymais in Persia
　　　6:5　Then some one came to him in Persia and reported
　　　6:56　had returned from Persia and Media
　　　14:2　When Arsaces the king of Persia and Media heard
2 Ma　1:13　For when the leader reached Persia
　　　1:19　For when our fathers were being led captive to Persia
　　　1:20　Nehemiah, having been commissioned by the king of Persia
　　　9:1　from the region of Persia
　　　9:21　On my way back from the region of Persia
1 Es　3:1　and all the nobles of Media and Persia
　　　3:9　and the 3 nobles of Persia judge to be wisest
　　　3:14　Then he sent and summoned all the nobles of Persia and Media

PERSIAN, subst., adj.　　　　　　　22 = 0.014 %
Jud　16:10　The Persians trembled at her boldness
Ad E　16:10　really an alien to the Persian blood
　　　16:14　and would transfer the kingdom of the Persians to the Macedonians
　　　16:23　it may mean salvation for us and the loyal Persians
Bel　14:1　Cyrus the Persian received his kingdom
1 Ma　1:1　had defeated Darius, king of the Persians and the Medes
2 Ma　1:33　and it was reported to the king of the Persians
1 Es　1:57　until the Persians began to reign
　　　2:1　In the first year of Cyrus as king of the Persians
　　　2:2　the Lord stirred up the spirit of Cyrus king of the Persians
　　　2:3　Thus says Cyrus king of the Persians :
　　　2:11　When Cyrus king of the Persians brought these out
　　　2:16　But in the time of Artaxerxes king of the Persians
　　　2:30　of Darius king of the Persians
　　　5:6　who spoke wise words before Darius the king of the Persians
　　　5:55　from Cyrus king of the Persians
　　　5:71　as Cyrus the king of the Persians has commanded us
　　　7:4　kings of the Persians
　　　8:1　when Artaxerxes king of the Persians was reigning
　　　8:80　with the kings of the Persians
2 Es　1:3　in the reign of Artaxerxes, king of the Persians
4 Ma　18:5　he left Jerusalem and marched against the Persians

PERSIST　　　　　　　　　　　　　　　　1
Sir　12:3　No good will come to the man who persists in evil

PERSON　　　　　　　　　　　　　27 = 0.018 %
Tob　6:7　and that person will never be troubled again
Ad E　16:11　as the person second to the royal throne
Sir　8:4　Do not jest with an ill-bred person
　　　10:5　and he confers his honour upon the person of the scribe
　　　13:15　and every person his neighbour

	16:11	Even if there is only one stiff-necked person
	17:22	and he will keep a person's kindness like the apple of his eye
	19:16	A person may make a slip without intending it
	26:27	and every person like this lives in the anarchy of war
	29:4	Many persons regard a loan as a windfall
	29:27	Give place, stranger, to an honoured person
	31:18	If you are seated among many persons
	37:28	and not every person enjoys everything
Bar	2:18	but the person that is greatly distressed
	2:18	and the eyes that are failing, and the person that hungers
Sus	13:53	Do not put to death an innocent and righteous person
1 Ma	2:38	to the number of a 1,000 persons
2 Ma	1:35	And with those persons whom the king favoured
	3:37	what sort of person would be suitable
1 Es	3:4	who kept guard over the person of the king
	8:22	persons employed in this temple
3 Ma	5:14	the person who was in charge of the invitations
2 Es	15:46	and the glory of her person
	16:47	their houses and possessions, and their persons
4 Ma	5:4	And when many persons had been rounded up
	7:20	when some persons appear to be dominated by their emotions
	7:21	What person who lives as a philosopher

PERSONAL　　　　　　　　　　　　　　　2
Jud　12:11　the eunuch who had charge of all his personal affairs
　　　14:13　in charge of all his personal affairs

PERSUADE　　　　　　　　　　　　13 = 0.008 %
Jud　12:11　Go now and persuade the Hebrew woman who is in your care
2 Ma　4:34　persuaded Onias to come out from the place of sanctuary
　　　7:26　she undertook to persuade her son
　　　11:14　and persuaded them to settle everything on just terms
　　　11:14　promising that he would persuade the king
3 Ma　1:11　the king was by no means persuaded
　　　7:3　persuaded us to gather together the Jews of the kingdom in a body
2 Es　10:20　Do not say that, but let yourself be persuaded
4 Ma　5:16　We, O Antiochus, who have been persuaded
　　　8:12　so as to persuade them out of fear to eat the defiling food
　　　11:25　Since you have not been able to persuade us
　　　12:6　and to influence her to persuade the surviving son
　　　16:24　encouraged and persuaded each of her sons

PERSUASION　　　　　　　　　　　　　　2
Ad E　16:5　by the persuasion of friends who have been entrusted
4 Ma　12:5　but if you yield to persuasion you will be my friend

PERTAIN　　　　　　　　　　　　　　　2
Sir　pr.　pertaining to instruction and wisdom
2 Es　7:70　and the things that pertain to the judgment

PERUDA　　　　　　　　　　　　　　　　1
1 Es　5:33　the sons of Peruda, the sons of Jaalah

PERVADE　　　　　　　　　　　　　　　1
Wis　7:24　she pervades and penetrates all things

PERVERSE　　　　　　　　　　　　　　　2
Wis　1:3　For perverse thoughts separate men from God
Sir　36:20　A perverse mind will cause grief

PERVERSELY　　　　　　　　　　　　　　1
Ad E　13:5　perversely following a strange manner of life and laws

PERVERSION　　　　　　　　　　　　　　1
Wis　14:26　pollution of souls, sex perversion

PERVERT, verb　　　　　　　　　　　5 = 0.003 %
Wis　4:12　and roving desire perverts the innocent mind
Sir　8:2　and has perverted the minds of kings
Sus　13:9　And they perverted their minds
　　　13:56　beauty has deceived you and lust has perverted your heart
4 Ma　15:11　strong enough to pervert her reason

PESTILENCE　　　　　　　　　　　　3 = 0.002 %
Sir　39:29　Fire and hail and famine and pestilence
Bar　2:25　by famine and sword and pestilence
2 Es　15:49　famine, sword, and pestilence

PESTILENT　　　　　　　　　　　　4 = 0.003 %
Ad E　16:7　through the pestilent behaviour of those
1 Ma　10:61　A group of pestilent men from Israel
　　　15:3　Whereas certain pestilent men
　　　15:21　Therefore if any pestilent men

PETHAHIAH　　　　　　　　　　　　　　1
1 Es　9:23　who was Kelita, and Pethahiah and Judah and Jonah

PETITION, subst.   4 = 0.003 %
2 Ma 13 : 12 When they had all joined in the same petition
3 Ma   2 : 10 you would listen to our petition
       6 : 40 on which also they made the petition for their dismissal
2 Es   8 : 24 and give ear to the petition of thy creature

PETITION, verb   1
3 Ma   6 : 37 Then they petitioned the king

PETTY   1
4 Ma   5 : 19 Therefore do not suppose that it would be a petty sin

PHALANX   5 = 0.003 %
1 Ma   6 : 35 And they distributed the beasts among the phalanxes
       6 : 38 while being themselves protected by the phalanxes
       6 : 45 He courageously ran into the midst of the phalanx to reach it
       9 : 12 the phalanx advanced to the sound of the trumpets
      10 : 82 and engaged the phalanx in battle

PHALARIS   2
3 Ma   5 : 20 the king, possessed by a savagery worse than that of Phalaris
       5 : 42 Upon this the king, a Phalaris in everything and filled with
               madness

PHALTIEL   1
2 Es   5 : 16 Now on the 2nd night Phaltiel, a chief of the people

PHANTOM   1
Wis   17 : 4   and dismal phantoms with gloomy faces appeared

PHARAKIM   1
1 Es   5 : 31 the sons of Pharakim, the sons of Bazluth

PHARAOH   6 = 0.004 %
Sir   16 : 15 The Lord hardened Pharaoh so that he did not know him
1 Ma   4 : 9   when Pharaoh with his forces pursued them
1 Es   1 : 25 it happened that Pharaoh, king of Egypt
3 Ma   2 : 6   on the audacious Pharaoh who had enslaved your holy people
               Israel
       6 : 4   Pharaoh with his abundance of chariots
2 Es   1 : 10 I struck down Pharaoh with his servants, and all his army

PHARATHON   1
1 Ma   9 : 50 and Bethel, and Timnath, and Pharathon, and Tephon

PHARES   1
1 Es   5 : 5   of the lineage of Phares, of the tribe of Judah

PHARMACIST   1
Sir   38 : 8   the pharmacist makes of them a compound

PHASE   1
Sir   43 : 8   increasing marvellously in its phases

PHASELIS   1
1 Ma 15 : 23 and to Rhodes, and to Phaselis, and to Cos

PHASIRON   1
1 Ma   9 : 66 and the sons of Phasiron in their tents

PHILIP   11 = 0.007 %
1 Ma   1 : 1   After Alexander son of Philip, the Macedonian
       6 : 2   left there by Alexander, the son of Philip
       6 : 14 Then he called for Philip, one of his friends
       6 : 55 Then Lysias heard that Philip
       6 : 63 He found Philip in control of the city
       8 : 5   Philip, and Perseus king of the Macedonians
2 Ma   5 : 22 Philip, by birth a Phrygian
       6 : 11 were betrayed to Philip and were all burned together
       8 : 8   When Philip saw that the man was gaining ground little by little
       9 : 29 And Philip, one of his courtiers, took his body home
      13 : 23 he got word that Philip

PHILISTINE   12 = 0.008 %
Sir   46 : 18 and all the rulers of the Philistines
      47 : 7   and annihilated his adversaries the Philistines
      50 : 26 Those who live on Mount Seir, and the Philistines
1 Ma   3 : 24 800 of them fell, and the rest fled into the land of the Philistines
       3 : 41 and the land of the Philistines joined with them
       4 : 22 they all fled into the land of the Philistines
       4 : 30 and didst give the camp of the Philistines
       5 : 66 Then he marched off to go into the land of the Philistines
       5 : 68 in the land of the Philistines
Ps 151 6   I went out to meet the Philistine
2 Es   1 : 21 and the Philistines before you
4 Ma   3 : 7   David had been attacking the Philistines all day long

PHILOMETOR   4 = 0.003 %
2 Ma   4 : 21 for the coronation of Philometor as king
       4 : 21 Antiochus learned that Philometor had become hostile to his
               government
       9 : 29 he betook himself to Ptolemy Philometor in Egypt
      10 : 13 which Philometor had entrusted to him

PHILOPATOR   3 = 0.002 %
3 Ma   1 : 1   When Philopator learned from those who returned
       3 : 12 King Ptolemy Philopator to his generals and soldiers
       7 : 1   King Ptolemy Philopator to the generals in Egypt

PHILOSOPHER   3 = 0.002 %
4 Ma   5 : 7   it does not seem to me that you are a philosopher
       7 : 7   O man in harmony with the law and philosopher of divine life !
       7 : 21 What person who lives as a philosopher

PHILOSOPHICAL   2
4 Ma   1 : 1   The subject that I am about to discuss is most philosophical
       5 : 35 I will not put you to shame, philosophical reason

PHILOSOPHIZE   1
4 Ma   5 : 11 philosophize according to the truth of what is beneficial

PHILOSOPHY   8 = 0.005 %
4 Ma   1 : 1   to advise you to pay earnest attention to philosophy
       5 : 4   because of his philosophy
       5 : 11 Will you not awaken from your foolish philosophy
       5 : 22 You scoff at our philosophy
       7 : 9   but by your deeds you made your words of divine philosophy
               credible
       7 : 21 by the whole rule of philosophy
       8 : 1   by following a philosophy in accordance with devout reason
       8 : 15 but they also opposed the tyrant with their own philosophy

PHINEAS   1
4 Ma 18 : 12 He told you of the zeal of Phineas

PHINEHAS   9 = 0.006 %
Sir   45 : 23 Phinehas the son of Eleazar is the 3rd in glory
1 Ma   2 : 26 as Phinehas did against Zimri the son of Salu
       2 : 54 Phinehas our father, because he was deeply zealous
1 Es   5 : 5   the priests, the sons of Phinehas, son of Aaron
       8 : 2   son of Bukki, son of Abishua, son of Phinehas
       8 : 29 Of the sons of Phinehas, Gershom
       8 : 63 and with him was Eleazar the son of Phinehas
2 Es   1 : 2   son of Ahijah, son of Phinehas, son of Eli
       1 : 2   son of Abishua, son of Phinehas, son of Eleazar

PHOENICIA   23 = 0.015 %
2 Ma   3 : 5   who at that time was governor of Coelesyria and Phoenicia
       3 : 8   of the cities of Coelesyria and Phoenicia
       4 : 4   and governor of Coelesyria and Phoenicia
       4 : 22 Then he marched into Phoenicia
       8 : 8   the governor of Coelesyria and Phoenicia
      10 : 11 and to be chief governor of Coelesyria and Phoenicia
1 Es   2 : 17 in Coelesyria and Phoenicia :
       2 : 24 you will no longer have access to Coelesyria and Phoenicia
       2 : 25 and Syria and Phoenicia, wrote as follows :
       2 : 27 and exacted tribute from Coelesyria and Phoenicia
       4 : 48 and Phoenicia and to those in Lebanon
       6 : 3   At the same time Sisinnes the governor of Syria and Phoenicia
       6 : 7   which Sisinnes the governor of Syria and Phoenicia
       6 : 7   the local rulers in Syria and Phoenicia
       6 : 27 the governor of Syria and Phoenicia
       6 : 27 in Syria and Phoenicia
       6 : 29 and that out of the tribute of Coelesyria and Phoenicia
       7 : 1   Then Sisinnes the governor of Coelesyria and Phoenicia
       8 : 19 have commanded the treasurers of Syria and Phoenicia
       8 : 23 throughout all Syria and Phoenicia
       8 : 67 and to the governors of Coelesyria and Phoenicia
3 Ma   3 : 15 the nations inhabiting Coele-Syria and Phoenicia
4 Ma   4 : 2   governor of Syria, Phoenicia, and Cilicia

PHRASE   1
Sir   pr.   we may seem to have rendered some phrases imperfectly

PHRYGIAN   1
2 Ma   5 : 22 Philip, by birth a Phrygian

PHYSICAL   1
4 Ma   1 : 32 Some desires are mental, other are physical

PHYSICIAN   7 = 0.005 %
Tob   2 : 10 I went to physicians, but they did not help me
Sir   10 : 10 A long illness baffles the physician
      38 : 1   Honour the physician with the honour due him
      38 : 3   The skill of the physician lifts up his head
      38 : 12 And give the physician his place, for the Lord created him

38:13　There is a time when success lies in the hands of physicians
38:15　may he fall into the care of a physician

PICK, verb　　　　　　　　　　　　　　　　1
2 Ma　9:15　to the beasts, for the birds to pick

PICK up　　　　　　　　　　　　　　　　2
Sir　22:2　any one that picks it up will shake it off his hand
2 Ma　4:41　some picked up stones, some blocks of wood

PICKED　　　　　　　　　　　　10 = 0.007 %
Jud　2:15　and mustered the picked troops by divisions
　　2:19　and picked troops of infantry
　　3:6　and took picked men from them as his allies
1 Ma　4:1　Now Gorgias took 5,000 infantry and a 1,000 picked cavalry
　　4:28　But the next year he mustered 60,000 picked infantrymen
　　6:35　and 500 picked horsemen were assigned to each beast
　　9:5　and with him were 3,000 picked men
　　12:41　with 40,000 picked fighting men
　　15:26　And Simon sent to Antiochus 2,000 picked men, to fight for him
2 Ma　13:15　and with a picked force of the bravest young men

PICTURE　　　　　　　　　　　　　　1
2 Es　5:37　or show me the picture of a voice

PIECE　　　　　　　　　　　　15 = 0.010 %
Wis　10:4　steering the righteous man by a paltry piece of wood
　　13:12　and burn the castoff pieces of his work to prepare his food
　　13:13　But a castoff piece from among them, useful for nothing
　　14:1　calls upon a piece of wood more fragile
　　14:5　even to the smallest piece of wood
Sir　6:2　lest your soul be torn in pieces like a bull
　　22:15　Sand, salt, and a piece of iron are easier to bear than a stupid man
　　43:15　and the hailstones are broken in pieces
1 Ma　1:56　The books of the law which they found they tore to pieces
2 Ma　1:13　they were cut to pieces in the temple of Nanaea
　　10:30　they were thrown into disorder and cut to pieces
3 Ma　6:5　you, O Lord, broke in pieces
2 Es　1:32　and torn their bodies in pieces
4 Ma　6:6　and his sides were being cut to pieces
　　9:20　and pieces of flesh were falling off the axles of the machine

PIECEMEAL　　　　　　　　　　　　　1
2 Ma　15:33　and said that he would give it piecemeal to the birds

PIERCE　　　　　　　　　　　　7 = 0.005 %
Jud　6:6　and the spear of my servants shall pierce your sides
　　16:12　The sons of maidservants have pierced them through
Wis　5:11　and pierced by the force of its rushing flight
Sir　35:17　The prayer of the humble pierces the clouds
2 Ma　12:22　and pierced by the points of their swords
4 Ma　11:19　and pierced his ribs so that his entrails were burned through
　　18:21　pierced the pupils of their eyes and cut out their tongues

PIETY　　　　　　　　　　　　10 = 0.007 %
2 Ma　3:1　because of the piety of the high priest Onias
　　6:11　because their piety kept them from defending themselves
4 Ma　5:18　to invalidate our reputation for piety
　　5:24　and it teaches us piety
　　5:31　as not to be young in reason on behalf of piety
　　6:2　who remained adorned with the gracefulness of his piety
　　7:16　If, therefore, because of piety
　　13:10　Let us not be cowardly in the demonstration of our piety
　　17:5　who, after lighting the way of your star-like 7 sons to piety
　　17:7　to paint the history of your piety as an artist might

PILE, verb　　　　　　　　　　　　　　2
Jud　15:11　and hitched up her carts and piled the things on them
1 Ma　11:4　for they had piled them in heaps along his route

PILGRIMAGE　　　　　　　　　　　　1
2 Es　8:39　over their pilgrimage also, and their salvation

PILLAR　　　　　　　　　　　　10 = 0.007 %
Wis　10:7　and a pillar of salt standing
　　18:3　Therefore thou didst provide a flaming pillar of fire
Sir　24:4　and my throne was in a pillar of cloud
　　26:18　Like pillars of gold on a base of silver
　　36:24　a helper fit for him and a pillar of support
L Jr　6:59　better also a wooden pillar in a palace
1 Ma　14:27　and put it upon pillars on Mount Zion
3 Ma　7:20　Then, after inscribing them as holy on a pillar
2 Es　1:14　I provided light for you from a pillar of fire
4 Ma　17:3　Nobly set like a roof on the pillars of your sons

PILLOW　　　　　　　　　　　　　　1
1 Es　3:8　and put them under the pillow of Darius the king

PILOT　　　　　　　　　　　　　　1
4 Ma　7:1　For like a most skilful pilot

PINE away　　　　　　　　　　　　　　1
Wis　1:16　considering him a friend, they pined away

PINION　　　　　　　　　　　　　　1
Wis　5:11　the light air, lashed by the beat of its pinions

PIOUS　　　　　　　　　　　　4 = 0.003 %
Sir　26:23　but a pious wife is given to the man who fears the Lord
2 Ma　1:19　the pious priests of that time
　　12:45　it was a holy and pious thought
4 Ma　10:15　and by the everlasting life of the pious

PIOUSLY　　　　　　　　　　　　　　1
4 Ma　9:6　lived piously while enduring torture

PISHON　　　　　　　　　　　　　　1
Sir　24:25　It fills men with wisdom, like the Pishon

PIT　　　　　　　　　　　　6 = 0.004 %
Sir　12:16　but in his mind he will plan to throw you into a pit
　　21:10　but at its end is the pit of Hades
　　27:26　He who digs a pit will fall into it
1 Ma　7:19　and killed them and threw them into the great pit
　　11:35　and the salt pits and the crown taxes due to us
2 Es　7:36　Then the pit of torment shall appear

PITCH, verb　　　　　　　　　　　　3 = 0.002 %
Wis　11:2　and pitched their tents in untrodden places
Sir　14:25　he will pitch his tent near her
2 Ma　13:14　he pitched his camp near Modein

PITCH, subst.　　　　　　　　　　　4 = 0.003 %
Sir　13:1　Whoever touches pitch will be defiled
P Az　23　with naphtha, pitch, tow, and brush
Bel　14:27　Then Daniel took pitch, fat, and hair
2 Es　2:9　whose land lies in lumps of pitch and heaps of ashes

PITCHER　　　　　　　　　　　　　　1
4 Ma　3:12　and taking a pitcher climbed over the enemy's ramparts

PITEOUS　　　　　　　　　　　　　　1
Wis　18:10　and their piteous lament for their children

PITEOUSLY　　　　　　　　　　　　1
4 Ma　15:18　nor when the 2nd in torments looked at you piteously

PITIABLE　　　　　　　　　　　　　2
2 Ma　3:21　There was something pitiable
　　9:28　came to the end of his life by a most pitiable fate

PITIFUL　　　　　　　　　　　　　2
3 Ma　5:24　for this most pitiful spectacle
　　5:47　the grievous and pitiful destruction of the aforementioned people

PITILESS　　　　　　　　　　　　　2
Wis　19:1　But the ungodly were assailed to the end by pitiless anger
3 Ma　5:10　Hermon, however, when he had drugged the pitiless elephants

PITY, subst.　　　　　　　　　　18 = 0.012 %
Tob　3:15　and pity be taken upon me, and that I hear reproach no more
Jud　6:19　and have pity on the humiliation of our people
Ad E　13:6　without pity or mercy
Sir　16:9　He showed no pity for a nation devoted to destruction
　　36:13　Have pity on the city of thy sanctuary
Bar　4:15　and had no pity for a child
L Jr　6:38　They cannot take pity on a widow
2 Ma　7:27　deriding the cruel tyrant : My son, have pity on me
　　8:2　and to have pity on the temple
3 Ma　4:4　perceiving the common object of pity before their eyes
　　6:22　Then the king's anger was turned to pity and tears
2 Es　8:32　For if thou hast desired to have pity on us
　　15:19　A man shall have no pity upon his neighbours
4 Ma　6:12　At that point, partly out of pity for his old age
　　8:10　Therefore take pity on yourselves
　　8:20　Let us take pity on our youth
　　9:4　For we consider this pity of yours
　　18:1　obey this law and exercise pity in every way

PITY, verb　　　　　　　　　　　7 = 0.005 %
Sir　12:13　Who will pity a snake charmer bitten by a serpent
　　12:14　So no one will pity a man who associates with a sinner
2 Ma　4:37　and filled with pity, and wept
2 Es　1:19　I pitied your groaning and gave you manna for food
4 Ma　5:33　I do not so pity my old age
　　9:3　do not pity us more than we pity ourselves

PLACE* subst.   201 = 0.131 %

Tob	1 : 4	This was the place which had been chosen
	1 : 15	Sennacherib his son reigned in his place
	1 : 21	Then Esarhaddon, his son, reigned in his place
	2 : 3	and thrown into the market place
	2 : 4	I sprang up and removed the body to a place of shelter until sunset
	7 : 18	in place of this sorrow of yours
	14 : 5	from the places of their captivity
Jud	5 : 9	Then their God commanded them to leave the place
	5 : 19	and have come back from the places
	6 : 17	He answered and told them what had taken place
	8 : 12	and are setting yourselves up in the place of God
	15 : 4	to tell what had taken place and to urge all
Ad E	13 : 3	and has attained the 2nd place in the kingdom
	16 : 5	And often many of those who are set in places of authority
	16 : 19	Therefore post a copy of this letter publicly in every place
Wis	3 : 14	and a place of great delight in the temple of the Lord
	6 : 5	because severe judgment falls on those in high places
	11 : 2	and pitched their tents in untrodden places
	19 : 18	For the elements changed places with one another
	19 : 18	from the sight of what took place
	19 : 22	at all times and in all places
Sir	4 : 13	and the Lord will bless the place she enters
	10 : 14	and has seated the lowly in their place
	10 : 15	and has planted the humble in their place
	12 : 12	and take your place
	14 : 25	and will lodge in an excellent lodging place
	17 : 16	hearts of flesh in place of their stony hearts
	22 : 18	Fences set on a high place
	23 : 19	and perceive even the hidden places
	24 : 4	I dwelt in high places
	24 : 7	Among all these I sought a resting place
	24 : 8	and the one who created me assigned a place for my tent
	24 : 11	In the beloved city likewise he gave me a resting place
	29 : 27	Give place, stranger, to an honoured person
	32 : 1	when you have fulfilled your duties, take your place
	33 : 12	and he turned them out of their place
	33 : 20	do not let any one take your place
	36 : 13	Jerusalem, the place of thy rest
	38 : 12	And give the physician his place, for the Lord created him
	41 : 19	and of theft, in the place where you live
Bar	3 : 15	Who has found her place ?
	3 : 19	and others have arisen in their place
P Az	15	or incense, no place to make an offering before thee
Sus	13 : 49	Return to the place of judgment
Bel	14 : 11	and mix and place the wine
	14 : 39	And the angel of God immediately returned Habakkuk to his own place
1 Ma	1 : 8	Then his officers began to rule, each in his own place
	1 : 53	in every place of refuge they had
	2 : 12	And behold, our holy place, our beauty
	3 : 1	took command in his place
	3 : 35	he was to banish the memory of them from the place
	3 : 45	it was a lodging place for the Gentiles
	3 : 46	because Israel formerly had a place of prayer in Mizpah
	4 : 43	and removed the defiled stones to an unclean place
	4 : 46	and stored the stones in a convenient place
	6 : 54	and they had been scattered, each to his own place
	6 : 57	the place against which we are fighting is strong
	6 : 62	and saw what a strong fortress the place was
	8 : 4	even though the place was far distant from them
	9 : 30	So now we have chosen you today to take his place
	9 : 31	and took the place of Judas his brother
	9 : 45	there is no place to turn
	10 : 13	each left his place and departed to his own land
	10 : 14	for it served as place of refuge
	10 : 40	out of the king's revenues from appropriate places
	10 : 73	where there is no stone or pebble, or place to flee
	11 : 37	and put up in a conspicuous place on the holy mountain
	11 : 38	he dismissed all his troops, each man to his own place
	11 : 40	to become king in place of his father
	11 : 69	Then the men in ambush emerged from their places and joined battle
	12 : 2	and to other places
	12 : 4	in every place, asking them to provide for the envoys
	13 : 8	in place of Judas and Jonathan your brother
	13 : 14	in place of Jonathan his brother
	13 : 20	to every place he went
	13 : 32	and became king in his place, putting on the crown of Asia
	14 : 17	had become high priest in his place
	14 : 48	to put them up in a conspicuous place
	15 : 29	and you have taken possession of many places in my kingdom
	15 : 30	and the tribute money of the places
	16 : 3	Take my place and my brother's
2 Ma	1 : 14	Antiochus came to the place together with his friends
	1 : 19	that the place was unknown to any one
	1 : 29	Plant thy people in thy holy place, as Moses said
	1 : 33	that, in the place where the exiled priests had hidden the fire
	1 : 34	and enclosed the place and made it sacred

	2 : 7	The place shall be unknown
	2 : 8	that the place should be specially consecrated
	2 : 18	into his holy place
	2 : 18	and has purified the place
	3 : 2	it came about that the kings themselves honoured the place
	3 : 12	who had trusted in the holiness of the place
	3 : 18	because the holy place was about to be brought into contempt
	3 : 30	who had acted marvellously for his own place
	3 : 38	for there certainly is about the place some power of God
	3 : 39	watches over that place himself and brings it aid
	4 : 33	having first withdrawn to a place of sanctuary
	4 : 34	persuaded Onias to come out from the place of sanctuary
	4 : 38	and led him about the whole city to that very place
	5 : 10	and no place in the tomb of his fathers
	5 : 16	to enhance the glory and honour of the place
	5 : 17	and that therefore he was disregarding the holy place
	5 : 19	for the sake of the holy place
	5 : 19	but the place for the sake of the nation
	5 : 20	Therefore the place itself
	6 : 2	as did the people who dwelt in that place
	8 : 17	which the Gentiles had committed against the holy place
	8 : 20	that took place in Babylonia
	8 : 31	they stored them all carefully in strategic places
	9 : 17	and would visit every inhabited place
	10 : 5	the purification of the sanctuary took place
	10 : 7	who had given success to the purifying of his own holy place
	10 : 10	Now we will tell what took place under Antiochus Eupator
	10 : 17	they gained possession of the places
	10 : 19	and he himself set off for places
	10 : 34	The men within, relying on the strength of the place
	11 : 3	as he did on the sacred places of the other nations
	11 : 5	which was a fortified place
	12 : 2	But some of the governors in various places
	12 : 18	though in one place he had left a very strong garrison
	12 : 21	and also the baggage to a place called Carnaim
	12 : 21	for that place was hard to besiege and difficult of access
	13 : 4	by the method which is the custom in that place
	13 : 5	For there is a tower in that place, 50 cubits high, full of ashes
	13 : 23	and showed generosity to the holy place
	14 : 21	seats of honour were set in place
	14 : 22	Judas posted armed men in readiness at key places
	15 : 34	Blessed is he who has kept his own place undefiled
1 Es	1 : 10	And this is what took place
	1 : 15	were in their place according to the arrangement made by David
	2 : 6	be helped by the men of his place with gold and silver
	2 : 16	living in Samaria and other places
	2 : 18	repairing its market places and walls
	4 : 34	and returns to its place in one day
	5 : 48	took their places and prepared the altar of the God of Israel
	5 : 50	And they erected the altar in its place
	6 : 27	to keep away from the place, and to permit Zerubbabel
	8 : 45	who was the leading man at the place of the treasury
	8 : 46	and the treasurers at that place
	8 : 78	to leave to us a root and a name in thy holy place
	9 : 13	with the elders and judges of each place
	9 : 45	for he had the place of honour in the presence of all
3 Ma	1 : 9	and did what was fitting for the holy place
	1 : 9	Then, upon entering the place
	1 : 23	and created a considerable disturbance in the holy place
	1 : 29	to the profanation of the place
	2 : 9	chose this city and sanctified this place for your name
	2 : 10	when we come to this place and pray
	2 : 14	undertakes to violate the holy place on earth
	2 : 16	you sanctified this place
	3 : 1	and he ordered that all should promptly be gathered into one place
	3 : 14	When our expedition took place in Asia
	3 : 29	Every place detected sheltering a Jew
	4 : 1	In every place, then, where this decree arrived
	4 : 3	What district or city, or what habitable place at all
	4 : 7	as far as the place of embarkation
	4 : 11	When these men had been brought to the place called Schedia
	4 : 18	some still residing in their homes, and some at the place
	5 : 44	at the places in the city most favourable for keeping guard
	6 : 30	in that same place in which they had expected
	6 : 31	and full of joy they apportioned to celebrate the place
	7 : 8	with no one in any place doing them harm at all
	7 : 17	because of a characteristic of the place
	7 : 20	and dedicating a place of prayer at the site of the festival
	7 : 20	each to his own place
2 Es	2 : 16	And I will raise up the dead from their places
	2 : 23	and I will give you the first place in my resurrection
	2 : 46	Who is that young man who places crowns on them
	4 : 19	and to the sea is assigned a place to carry its waves
	4 : 29	and if the place where the evil has been sown does not pass away
	4 : 42	so also do these places hasten to give back those things
	5 : 8	There shall be chaos also in many places
	6 : 1	before the portals of the world were in place
	6 : 14	And if the place where you are standing is greatly shaken
	6 : 22	Sown places shall suddenly appear unsown

	6:29	little by little the place where I was standing
	6:54	and over these thou didst place Adam
	7:4	but it has an entrance set in a narrow place
	7:7	and set in a precipitous place
	7:36	and opposite it shall be the place of rest
	7:124	because we have lived in unseemly places ?
	10:27	and a place of huge foundations showed itself
	10:54	for no work of man's building could endure in a place
	11:8	let each sleep in his own place, and watch in his turn
	11:13	so that its place was not seen
	11:24	but 4 remained in their place
	12:37	and put it in a hidden place
	12:41	that you have forsaken us and sit in this place ?
	12:42	and like a lamp in a dark place
	12:48	but I have come to this place to pray
	13:7	And I tried to see the region or place
	13:31	city against city, place against place
	15:40	and shall pour out upon every high and lofty place a terrible tempest
	16:26	For in all places there shall be great solitude
	16:62	and searches out hidden things in hidden places
	16:70	For in many places and in neighbouring cities
4 Ma	**4**:9	were imploring God in the temple to shield the holy place
	4:12	he would praise the blessedness of the holy place before all people
	5:1	on a certain high place
	15:20	and when you saw the place filled

PLACE, verb   20 = 0.013 %

Tob	**4**:17	Place your bread on the grave of the righteous
Jud	**6**:14	and placed him before the magistrates of their city
	13:10	who placed it in her food bag
Sir	**14**:26	he will place his children under her shelter
	15:16	He has placed before you fire and water :
	17:4	He placed the fear of them in all living beings
	30:18	are like offerings of food placed upon a grave
	47:9	He placed singers before the altar
L Jr	**6**:27	but gifts are placed before them just as before the dead
1 Ma	**4**:51	They placed the bread on the table and hung up the curtains
	7:20	He placed Alcimus in charge of the country
	9:51	And he placed garrisons in them to harass Israel
	14:33	and he placed there a garrison of Jews
	16:7	and placed the horsemen in the midst of the infantry
1 Es	**1**:2	having placed the priests according to their divisions
	6:26	to be placed where they had been
2 Es	**2**:43	and on the head of each of them he placed a crown
	6:20	and when the seal is placed upon the age
4 Ma	**8**:13	And when the guards had placed before them
	9:12	without accomplishing anything, they placed him upon the wheel

PLAGUE, subst.   8 = 0.005 %

Jud	**5**:12	with incurable plagues
Wis	**18**:20	and a plague came upon the multitude in the desert
Sir	**40**:9	calamities, famine and affliction and plague
2 Ma	**7**:37	and by afflictions and plagues
2 Es	**7**:108	and Samuel in the days of Saul, and David for the plague
	15:11	and will smite Egypt with plagues, as before
	15:12	for the plague of chastisement and punishment
	16:19	Behold, famine and plague

PLAIN, subst.   39 = 0.025 %

Jud	**1**:5	against King Arphaxad in the great plain
	1:6	and in the plain where Arioch ruled the Elymaeans
	1:8	and Upper Galilee and the great Plain of Esdraelon
	2:21	to the plain of Bectileth
	2:27	Then he went down into the plain of Damascus
	4:6	which faces Esdraelon opposite the plain near Dothan
	5:1	and set up barricades in the plains
	6:11	and led him out of the camp into the plain
	6:11	and from the plain they went up into the hill country
	7:18	The rest of the Assyrian army encamped in the plain
	14:2	as if you were going down to the plain
	15:2	by every path across the plain and through the hill country
	15:7	and the villages and towns in the hill country and in the plain
Wis	**19**:7	and a grassy plain out of the raging waves
Sir	**26**:20	Seek a fertile field within the whole plain
1 Ma	**3**:24	They pursued them down the descent of Beth-horon to the plain
	3:40	and when they arrived they encamped near Emmaus in the plain
	4:6	At daybreak Judas appeared in the plain with 3,000 men
	4:14	The Gentiles were crushed and fled into the plain
	4:15	and to the plains of Idumea, and to Azotus and Jamnia
	4:21	drawn up in the plain for battle
	5:52	And they crossed the Jordan into the large plain before Beth-shan
	6:40	and some troops were on the plain
	10:71	come down to the plain to meet us
	10:73	and such an army in the plain
	10:77	At the same time he advanced into the plain
	10:83	and the cavalry was dispersed in the plain
	11:67	Early in the morning they marched to the plain of Hazor

	11:68	and behold, the army of the foreigners met him in the plain
	12:49	and the Great Plain to destroy all Jonathan's soldiers
	13:13	And Simon encamped in Adida, facing the plain
	14:8	and the trees of the plains their fruit
	16:5	Early in the morning they arose and marched into the plain
	16:11	over the plain of Jericho
1 Es	**1**:29	He joined battle with him in the plain of Megiddo
2 Es	**4**:13	I went into a forest of trees of the plain
	4:15	and said, Come, let us go up and subdue the forest of the plain
	7:6	Another example : There is a city built and set on a plain
4 Ma	**18**:8	No seducer corrupted me on a desert plain

PLAINLY   1

2 Ma	**3**:17	which plainly showed to those who looked at him

PLAN, subst.   25 = 0.016 %

Tob	**4**:19	and that all your paths and plans may prosper
	6:12	Now listen to my plan
Jud	**2**:2	and set forth to them his secret plan
	2:4	When he had finished setting forth his plan
	10:8	and fulfil your plans
Ad E	**14**:11	but turn their plan against themselves
Wis	**6**:3	who will search out your works and inquire into your plans
1 Ma	**2**:63	and his plans will perish
	6:3	but he could not, because his plan became known to the men of the city
	7:31	When Nicanor learned that his plan had been disclosed
	9:60	because their plan became known
	9:68	for his plan and his expedition had been in vain
	16:13	and made treacherous plans against Simon and his sons
2 Ma	**15**:1	he made plans to attack them with complete safety
3 Ma	**1**:22	would not tolerate the completion of his plans
	1:25	from the plan that he had conceived
	1:26	determined to bring the aforesaid plan to a conclusion
	3:14	it was brought to conclusion, according to plan
	5:12	and was completely frustrated in his inflexible plan
2 Es	**4**:13	and they made a plan
	4:15	And in like manner the waves of the sea also made a plan
	4:16	But the plan of the forest was in vain
	4:17	likewise also the plan of the waves of the sea
	4:19	I answered and said, Each has made a foolish plan
	13:41	But they formed this plan for themselves

PLAN, verb   20 = 0.013 %

Jud	**8**:34	Only, do not try to find out what I plan
	9:9	give to me, a widow, the strength to do what I plan
	9:13	for they have planned cruel things against thy covenant
	11:12	they have planned to kill their cattle and determined
Wis	**14**:2	For it was desire for gain that planned that vessel
	14:14	and therefore their speedy end has been planned
Sir	**12**:16	but in his mind he will plan to throw you into a pit
	27:22	Whoever winks his eye plans evil deeds
Sus	**13**:62	and they did to them as they had wickedly planned to do
1 Ma	**5**:9	and planned to destroy them
	6:8	because things had not turned out for him as he had planned
	8:9	The Greeks planned to come and destroy them
	12:35	and planned with them to build strongholds in Judea
2 Ma	**9**:15	but had planned to throw out with their children
2 Es	**6**:6	then I planned these things
	11:25	these little wings planned to set themselves up
	11:28	the 2 that remained were planning between themselves
	11:29	and while they were planning, behold
	11:31	and it devoured the 2 little wings which were planning to reign
	13:31	And they shall plan to make war against one another

PLANE, subst.   1

Sir	**24**:14	and like a plane tree I grew tall

PLANNING   1

1 Ma	**8**:4	by their planning and patience

PLANT, subst.   10 = 0.007 %

Wis	**7**:20	the varieties of plants and the virtues of roots
	10:7	plants bearing fruit that does not ripen
Sir	**3**:28	for a plant of wickedness has taken root in him
	24:14	and like rose plants in Jericho
2 Es	**9**:21	and one plant out of a great forest
	9:22	but let my grape and my plant be saved
	9:26	and ate of the plants of the field
	12:51	and my food was of plants during those days
4 Ma	**1**:28	are 2 plants growing from the body and the soul
	1:28	so there are many offshoots of these plants

PLANT, verb   14 = 0.009 %

Sir	**10**:15	and has planted the humble in their place
	43:23	and planted islands in it
	49:7	and likewise to build and to plant
1 Ma	**3**:56	or were betrothed, or were planting vineyards
2 Ma	**1**:29	Plant thy people in thy holy place, as Moses said
1 Es	**4**:9	if he tells them to plant, they plant

	4:16	and women brought up the very men who plant the vineyards
2 Es	3:6	which thy right hand had planted before the earth appeared
	6:42	so that some of them might be planted and cultivated
	8:41	and plants a multitude of seedlings
	8:41	and not all that were planted will take root
	8:52	the tree of life is planted
4 Ma	2:21	he planted in him emotions and inclinations

PLATE   2

1 Ma	11:58	And he sent him gold plate and a table service
	15:32	and the sideboard with its gold and silver plate

PLATFORM   3 = 0.002 %

Jud	14:15	and found him thrown down on the platform dead
2 Ma	13:26	Lysias took the public platform
1 Es	9:42	stood on the wooden platform which had been prepared

PLAY   8 = 0.005 %

Sir	29:25	you will play the host and provide drink
	30:9	play with him, and he will give you grief
	34:14	nor play the coward, for he is his hope
	47:3	He played with lions as with young goats
1 Ma	3:45	the flute and the harp ceased to play
2 Ma	3:32	that some foul play had been perpetrated by the Jews
4 Ma	5:34	I will not play false to you, O law that trained me
	10:14	You do not have a fire hot enough to make me play the coward

PLEAD   5 = 0.003 %

Jud	8:16	nor like a human being, to be won over by pleading
Wis	12:12	to plead as an advocate for unrighteous men ?
1 Ma	11:62	Then the people of Gaza pleaded with Jonathan
2 Ma	4:47	if they had pleaded even before Scythians
4 Ma	12:6	When he had so pleaded

PLEASANT   6 = 0.004 %

Sir	6:5	A pleasant voice multiplies friends
	24:15	and like choice myrrh I spread a pleasant odour
	40:21	The flute and the harp make pleasant melody
	40:21	but a pleasant voice is better than both
3 Ma	5:12	he was overcome by so pleasant and deep a sleep
4 Ma	8:23	Why do we banish ourselves from this most pleasant life

PLEASE   40 = 0.026 %

Jud	3:3	do with them whatever you please
	7:16	These words pleased Holofernes and all his servants
	8:15	he has power to protect us within any time he pleases
	8:17	and he will hear our voice, if it pleases him
	11:20	Her words pleased Holofernes and all his servants
	12:13	*This beautiful maidservant will please come to my lord*
	12:14	Surely whatever pleases him I will do at once
	12:20	And Holofernes was greatly pleased with her
	15:10	and God is well pleased with it
Wis	4:10	There was one who pleased God and was loved by him
	9:18	and men were taught what pleases thee
	14:19	For he, perhaps wishing to please his ruler
Sir	7:26	If you have a wife who pleases you, do not cast her out
	8:15	for he will act as he pleases
	9:12	Do not delight in what pleases the ungodly
	20:27	and a sensible man will please great men
	20:28	and whoever pleases great men will atone for injustice
	33:13	for all his ways are as he pleases
	34:19	The Most High is not pleased
	39:18	At his command whatever pleases him is done
	44:16	Enoch pleased the Lord, and was taken up
	45:19	The Lord saw it and was not pleased
1 Ma	1:12	This proposal pleased them
	6:60	The speech pleased the king and the commanders
	8:21	The proposal pleased them
	11:49	that the Jews had gained control of the city as they pleased
	12:18	And now please send us a reply to this
	12:22	*please write us concerning your welfare*
	14:23	It has pleased our people to receive these men with honour
2 Ma	1:20	But after many years had passed, when it pleased God
	2:16	*Will you therefore please keep the days ?*
	2:25	we have aimed to please those who are inclined to memorize
	7:16	you do what you please
	14:35	thou wast pleased that there be a temple
Ps 151	5	but the Lord was not pleased with them
2 Es	12:39	whatever it pleases the Most High to show you
	15:47	to please and glory in your lovers
4 Ma	8:4	he was pleased with them
	8:26	and such a fatal stubbornness please us
	12:9	Extremely pleased by the boy's declaration

PLEASING   18 = 0.012 %

Tob	3:15	But if it be not pleasing to thee to take my life
	4:3	do what is pleasing to her, and do not grieve her
	4:21	and do what is pleasing in his sight
Wis	4:14	for his soul was pleasing to the Lord
	9:9	and who understands what is pleasing in thy sight

	9:10	and that I may learn what is pleasing to thee
	13:11	and then with pleasing workmanship
Sir	19:19	and those who do what is pleasing to him
	35:3	To keep from wickedness is pleasing to the Lord
	35:6	and its pleasing odour rises before the Most High
	35:16	He whose service is pleasing to the Lord will be accepted
	45:16	incense and a pleasing odour as a memorial portion
	48:16	Some of them did what was pleasing to God
	48:22	For Hezekiah did what was pleasing to the Lord
	50:15	a pleasing odour to the Most High, the King of all
Bar	4:4	for we know what is pleasing to God
1 Ma	14:4	his rule was pleasing to them
1 Es	1:12	with a pleasing odour

PLEASURE   18 = 0.012 %

Tob	3:6	And now deal with me according to thy pleasure
Wis	7:2	from the seed of a man and the pleasure of marriage
	16:20	with bread ready to eat, providing every pleasure
Sir	9:10	when it has aged you will drink it with pleasure
	18:31	If you allow your soul to take pleasure in base desire
	19:5	but he who withstands pleasures crowns his life
	25:1	My soul takes pleasure in 3 things
	41:4	and how can you reject the good pleasure of the Most High ?
4 Ma	1:20	The 2 most comprehensive types of the emotions are pleasure and pain
	1:21	The emotions of both pleasure and pain have many consequences
	1:22	Thus desire precedes pleasure and delight follows it
	1:24	is an emotion embracing pleasure and pain
	1:25	In pleasure there exists even a malevolent tendency
	1:28	Just as pleasure and pain
	1:33	we abstain from the pleasure to be had from them ?
	5:23	so that we master all pleasures and desires
	6:35	but also that it masters pleasures
	8:18	why do we take pleasure in vain resolves

PLEDGE, subst.   8 = 0.005 %

2 Ma	4:34	offered him sworn pledges and gave him his right hand
	10:28	the one having as pledge of success and victory
	11:26	and give them pledges of friendship
	11:30	will have our pledge of friendship
	12:11	to grant them pledges of friendship
	12:12	and after receiving his pledges they departed to their tents
	13:22	gave pledges, received theirs, withdrew
	14:19	to give and receive pledges of friendship

PLEDGE, verb   3 = 0.002 %

1 Ma	8:1	that they pledged friendship to those who came to them
1 Es	9:20	They pledged themselves to put away their wives
3 Ma	3:10	and were pledging to protect them

PLENTIFUL   3 = 0.002 %

2 Es	7:58	what is plentiful is of less worth
	7:59	rejoices more than he who has what is plentiful
4 Ma	3:10	and although springs were plentiful there

PLENTY   4 = 0.003 %

Jud	2:18	also plenty of food for every man
Sir	18:25	In the time of plenty think of the time of hunger
3 Ma	5:2	with large handfuls of frankincense and plenty of unmixed wine
2 Es	8:52	the age to come is prepared, plenty is provided

PLIABLE   1

Sir	38:30	and makes it pliable with his feet

PLIGHT, subst.   1

Sir	51:12	and rescue me from an evil plight

PLOT, subst., lot   1

Sir	24:31	I said, I will water my orchard and drench my garden plot

PLOT, subst., conspiracy   6 = 0.004 %

Sus	13:28	full of their wicked plot to have Susanna put to death
1 Es	5:73	and by plots and demagoguery and uprisings
3 Ma	1:2	determined to carry out the plot he had devised
	1:6	Now that he had foiled the plot
	5:8	that he avert with vengeance the evil plot against them
2 Es	15:3	Do not fear the plots against you

PLOT, verb   4 = 0.003 %

Ad E	16:23	but that for those who plot against us
1 Ma	3:52	thou knowest what they plot against us
	9:58	Then all the lawless plotted and said, See !
3 Ma	1:21	because of what the king was profanely plotting

PLOTTER   3 = 0.002 %
  2 Ma   3:38   he replied, If you have any enemy or plotter against your
                government
         4:2   He dared to designate as a plotter against the government
         4:50   having become the chief plotter against his fellow citizens

PLOUGH, PLOW, verb   2
  Sir   6:19   Come to her like one who ploughs and sows
         38:26 He sets his heart on ploughing furrows

PLOUGH, PLOW, subst.   1
  Sir   38:25 How can he become wise who handles the plough

PLUCK up   3 = 0.002 %
  Sir   10:15   The Lord has plucked up the roots of the nations
        40:16   will be plucked up before any grass
        49:7   to pluck up and afflict and destroy

PLUMB, verb   1
  Jud   8:14   You cannot plumb the depths of the human heart

PLUMB LINE   1
  Sir   16:16   and he divided his light and darkness with a plumb line

PLUNDER, subst.   7 = 0.005 %
  Tob   3:4   and thou gavest us over to plunder, captivity, and death
  Jud   2:11   and you shall hand them over to slaughter and plunder
  Sir   16:13   The sinner will not escape with his plunder
  1 Ma   4:17   and he said to the people, Do not be greedy for plunder
         4:18   and afterward seize the plunder boldly
         7:47   Then the Jews seized the spoils and the plunder
  2 Ma   8:30   and they divided very much plunder

PLUNDER, verb   36 = 0.023 %
  Jud   1:14   plundered its markets, and turned its beauty into shame
         2:7   and will hand them over to be plundered by my troops
         2:23   and plundered all the people of Rassis
         2:26   and burned their tents and plundered their sheepfolds
         4:1   and how he had plundered and destroyed all their temples
         7:26   to be plundered
         8:19   and to be plundered
         8:21   and our sanctuary will be plundered
        15:11   So all the people plundered the camp for 30 days
  Wis   10:20   Therefore the righteous plundered the ungodly
  Sir   36:25   Where there is no fence, the property will be plundered
  L Jr   6:18   in order that they may not be plundered by robbers
  1 Ma   1:3   and plundered many nations
         1:19   and he plundered the land of Egypt
         1:31   He plundered the city, burned it with fire
         4:23   Then Judas returned to plunder the camp
         5:35   and he killed every male in it, plundered it
         5:51   and razed and plundered the city
         5:68   he plundered the cities and returned to the land of Judah
         6:3   So he came and tried to take the city and plunder it
         8:10   they plundered them, conquered the land
        10:84   and plundered them
        11:61   So he besieged it and burned its suburbs with fire and plundered
                them
        12:31   and he crushed them and plundered them
        13:34   for all that Trypho did was to plunder
  2 Ma   9:16   and the holy sanctuary, which he had formerly plundered
  1 Es   4:24   and when he steals and robs and plunders
  3 Ma   5:41   and also in constant danger of being plundered
  2 Es 10:22   the ark of our covenant has been plundered
        15:19   and plunder their goods
        15:63   and shall plunder your wealth
        16:46   and plunder their goods, and overthrow their houses
        16:47   Those who conduct business, do it only to be plundered
        16:71   but plundering and destroying those
        16:72   For they shall destroy and plunder their goods
  4 Ma   4:23   and after he had plundered them he issued a decree

PLUNDERING   1
  1 Es   8:77   to the sword and captivity and plundering

PLUNGE   2
  Sir   9:9   and in blood you be plunged into destruction
  1 Ma   6:11   And into what a great flood I now am plunged !

POCHERETH-HAZZEBAIM   1
  1 Es   5:34   the sons of Hattil, the sons of Pochereth-hazzebaim

POINT, subst.   8 = 0.005 %
  Sir   18:21   and when you are on the point of sinning, turn back
  2 Ma   2:32   At this point therefore let us begin our narrative
         7:27   to this point in your life
        12:22   and pierced by the points of their swords
        13:10   who were on the point of being deprived of the law
        15:38   If it is well told and to the point

  4 Ma   4:25   even to the point that women
         6:12   At that point, partly out of pity for his old age

POINT out   5 = 0.003 %
  Ad E 13:4   pointed out to us that among all the nations in the world
  2 Ma 15:10   at the same time pointing out the perfidy of the Gentiles
  3 Ma   5:15   And when he had with difficulty roused him, he pointed out
         5:19   pointed out that while it was still night
         5:29   pointed out that the beasts and the armed forces were ready

POINTED   1
  Sir   43:19   and when it freezes, it becomes pointed thorns

POISON, subst.   2
  Wis   1:14   and there is no destructive poison in them
  2 Ma 10:13   he took poison and ended his life

POLICY   5 = 0.003 %
  Sir   47:23   Rehoboam, whose policy caused the people to revolt
  2 Ma   6:8   that they should adopt the same policy toward the Jews
         9:27   For I am sure that he will follow my policy
        11:26   so that they may know our policy and be of good cheer
  3 Ma   3:23   they secretly suspect that we may soon alter our policy

POLISH   1
  Sir   12:11   and you will be to him like one who has polished a mirror

POLISHED   1
  1 Ma 13:27   with polished stone at the front and back

POLITICAL   1
  4 Ma   4:1   a political opponent of the noble and good man

POLL TAX   1
  3 Ma   2:28   to a registration involving poll tax

POLLUTE   8 = 0.005 %
  Jud   9:2   and polluted her womb to disgrace her
         9:8   and to pollute the tabernacle where thy glorious name rests
  Sir   40:29   He pollutes himself with another man's food
  2 Ma   6:2   and also to pollute the temple in Jerusalem
  1 Es   1:49   and polluted the temple of the Lord
         8:83   is a land polluted with the pollution of the aliens of the land
  2 Es 10:22   our holy things have been polluted
        15:25   Do not pollute my sanctuary

POLLUTED   1
  2 Ma   5:16   He took the holy vessels with his polluted hands

POLLUTION   6 = 0.004 %
  Jud   9:4   and abhorred the pollution of their blood
  Wis   14:26   pollution of souls, sex perversion
  1 Ma 13:50   and cleansed the citadel from its pollutions
  2 Ma   6:19   rather than life with pollution
  1 Es   8:69   the alien peoples of the land and their pollutions
         8:83   is a land polluted with the pollution of the aliens of the land

POMEGRANATE   1
  Sir   45:9   And he encircled him with pomegranates

POMP   4 = 0.003 %
  1 Ma 10:58   and celebrated her wedding at Ptolemais with great pomp, as
                kings do
        10:60   So he went with pomp to Ptolemais and met the 2 kings
        10:86   and the men of the city came out to meet him with great pomp
        11:6   Jonathan met the king at Joppa with pomp

PONDER   5 = 0.003 %
  Sir   3:29   The mind of the intelligent man will ponder a parable
        14:21   will also ponder her secrets
        16:20   Who will ponder his ways ?
        21:17   and they will ponder his words in their minds
  2 Ma 11:13   he pondered over the defeat which had befallen him

POOL   4 = 0.003 %
  Sir   43:20   it rests upon every pool of water
        48:17   and built pools for water
  1 Ma   9:33   and camped by the water of the pool of Asphar
  2 Es 16:60   and pools on the tops of the mountains

POOR, adj., subst.   30 = 0.020 %
  Tob   2:2   Go and bring whatever poor man of our brethren you may find
         4:7   Do not turn your face away from any poor man
         4:21   Do not be afraid, my son, because we have become poor
  Wis   2:10   Let us oppress the righteous poor man
  Sir   4:1   My son, deprive not the poor of his living
         4:4   nor turn your face away from the poor
         4:8   Incline your ear to the poor
         7:32   Stretch forth your hand to the poor
        10:22   The rich, and the eminent, and the poor

323

10:23	It is not right to despise an intelligent poor man
10:30	A poor man is honoured for his knowledge
11:21	to enrich a poor man quickly and suddenly
13:3	a poor man suffers wrong, and he must add apologies
13:18	And what peace between a rich man and a poor man ?
13:19	likewise the poor are pastures for the rich
13:20	likewise a poor man is an abomination to a rich one
13:23	When the poor man speaks they say, Who is this fellow ?
21:5	The prayer of a poor man goes from his lips
26:4	Whether rich or poor, his heart is glad
29:9	help a poor man for the commandment's sake
29:22	Better is the life of a poor man
30:14	Better off is a poor man
31:4	The poor man toils as his livelihood diminishes
34:20	from the property of the poor
34:21	The bread of the needy is the life of the poor
35:13	He will not show partiality in the case of a poor man
38:19	and the life of the poor man weighs down his heart
L Jr **6**:28	but give none to the poor or helpless
1 Es **3**:19	of the slave and the free, of the poor and the rich
3 Ma **5**:37	How many times, you poor wretch

POORLY   1
2 Ma **15**:38   if it is poorly done and mediocre

POPULACE   2
2 Ma **3**:21   in the prostration of the whole populace
     4:39   the populace gathered against Lysimachus

POPULATION   1
Bar **4**:34   And I will take away her pride in her great population

PORK   3 = 0.002 %
4 Ma **5**:2   to eat pork and food sacrificed to idols
     5:6   I would advise you to save yourself by eating pork
     6:15   save yourself by pretending to eat pork

PORTAL   1
2 Es **6**:1   before the portals of the world were in place

PORTION, subst.   24 = 0.016 %
Ad E **13**:16	Do not neglect thy portion
Wis **2**:9	because this is our portion, and this is our lot
Sir **7**:31	and give him his portion, as is commanded you :
14:9	A greedy man's eye is not satisfied with a portion
17:17	but Israel is the Lord's own portion
24:12	in the portion of the Lord, who is their inheritance
26:23	A godless wife is given as a portion to a lawless man
38:11	and a memorial portion of fine flour
41:21	of taking away some one's portion or gift
44:23	he determined his portions
45:16	incense and a pleasing odour as a memorial portion
45:22	and he has no portion among the people
45:22	for the Lord himself is his portion and inheritance
50:12	And when he received the portions
2 Ma **1**:26	and preserve thy portion and make it holy
1 Es **6**:29	a portion be scrupulously given to these men
9:51	and send portions to those who have none
9:54	and to give portions to those who had none
3 Ma **5**:11	But the Lord sent upon the king a portion of sleep
5:17	and to make the present portion of the banquet joyful
6:3	a people of your consecrated portion
2 Es **7**:10	And he said to me, So also is Israel's portion
15:30	and shall devastate a portion of the land of the Assyrians with their teeth
15:60	and abolish a portion of your glory

POSIDONIUS   1
2 Ma **14**:19   Therefore he sent Posidonius and Theodotus and Mattathias

POSITION   10 = 0.007 %
Ad E **14**:16	that I abhor the sign of my proud position
1 Ma **1**:34	These strengthened their position
6:36	These took their position beforehand wherever the beast was
10:37	and let some of them be put in positions of trust in the kingdom
10:54	in keeping with your position
2 Ma **3**:11	a man of very prominent position
6:18	Eleazar, one of the scribes in high position
8:6	He captured strategic positions
13:18	tried strategy in attacking their positions
4 Ma **8**:7	positions of authority in my government

POSSESS   18 = 0.012 %
Tob **3**:17	because Tobias was entitled to possess her
Jud **8**:10	she sent her maid, who was in charge of all she possessed
9:13	and against the house possessed by thy children
12:16	and he was moved with great desire to possess her
Wis **8**:21	But I perceived that I would not possess wisdom
11:12	for a twofold grief possessed them
Sir **25**:4	and for the aged to possess good counsel !

27:30	and the sinful man will possess them
Bar **3**:24	And how vast the territory that he possesses !
L Jr **6**:5	or to let fear for these gods possess you
Sus **13**:11	for they were ashamed to disclose their lustful desire to possess her
1 Ma **5**:23	with their wives and children, and all they possessed
2 Ma **2**:9	that being possessed of wisdom Solomon offered sacrifice
4:25	possessing no qualification for the high priesthood
1 Es **8**:7	For Ezra possessed great knowledge
3 Ma **5**:20	the king, possessed by a savagery worse than that of Phalaris
7:21	They also possessed greater prestige among their enemies
2 Es **6**:59	why do we not possess our world as an inheritance ?

POSSESSION   33 = 0.021 %
Tob **4**:7	Give alms from your possessions to all who live uprightly
4:8	If you have many possessions
Jud **1**:14	Thus he took possession of his cities
5:15	they took possession of all the hill country
7:12	only let your servants take possession
15:7	took possession of what remained
Wis **8**:5	If riches are a desirable possession in life
13:17	When he prays about possessions
Sir **4**:16	and his descendants will remain in possession of her
24:6	and in every people and nation I have gotten a possession
25:21	and do not desire a woman for her possessions
36:24	He who acquires a wife gets his best possession
41:1	to one who lives at peace among his possessions
51:21	therefore I have gained a good possession
1 Ma **1**:57	in the possession of any one
10:76	and Jonathan gained possession of Joppa
10:89	He also gave him Ekron and all its environs as his possession
11:1	and he tried to get possession of Alexander's kingdom by trickery
11:34	We have confirmed as their possession
11:66	He removed them from there, took possession of the city
13:38	the strongholds that you have built let be your possession
15:29	and you have taken possession of many places in my kingdom
16:20	and he sent other men to take possession of Jerusalem
2 Ma **2**:14	and they are in our possession
8:30	and got possession of some exceedingly high strongholds
10:17	they gained possession of the places
13:13	and get possession of the city
14:2	and had taken possession of the country
15:37	And from that time the city has been in the possession of the Hebrews
1 Es **1**:7	these were given from the king's possessions, as he promised
8:83	The land which you are entering to take possession of it
2 Es **14**:31	for a possession in the land of Zion
16:47	their houses and possessions, and their persons

POSSIBLE   15 = 0.010 %
Tob **10**:2	he said, Is it possible that he has been detained ?
10:2	Or is it possible that Gabael has died
Sir **18**:5	It is not possible to diminish or increase them
18:6	nor is it possible to trace the wonders of the Lord
22:21	do not despair, for a renewal of friendship is possible
22:22	do not worry, for reconciliation is possible
1 Ma **11**:22	as quickly as possible
2 Ma **3**:6	but that it was possible for them
11:18	and he has agreed to what was possible
13:26	made the best possible defence
14:29	Since it was not possible to oppose the king
3 Ma **1**:8	he was all the more eager to visit them as soon as possible
2 Es **4**:44	and if it is possible, and if I am worthy
10:55	as far as it is possible for your eyes to see it
4 Ma **17**:7	If it were possible for us

POST, subst.   6 = 0.004 %
Jud **7**:32	Then he dismissed the people to their various posts
8:36	So they returned from the tent and went to their posts
13:6	She went up to the post at the end of the bed
13:9	and pulled down the canopy from the posts
Sir **26**:12	so will she sit in front of every post
4 Ma **9**:23	Do not leave your post in my struggle

POST, verb   3 = 0.002 %
Ad E **16**:19	Therefore post a copy of this letter publicly in every place
2 Ma **14**:22	Judas posted armed men in readiness at key places
3 Ma **5**:44	and they confidently posted the armed forces

POSTERITY   10 = 0.007 %
Tob **4**:12	and their posterity will inherit the land
Sir **41**:6	and on their posterity will be a perpetual reproach
44:13	Their posterity will continue for ever
44:21	that the nations would be blessed through his posterity
44:21	and exalt his posterity like the stars
47:20	You put a stain upon your honour, and defiled your posterity
47:20	nor destroy the posterity of him who loved him
P Ma 1	and of their righteous posterity

2 Es	3:19	and thy commandment to the posterity of Israel
	12:32	who will arise from the posterity of David

POSTPONE   1
Sir 5:7   nor postpone it from day to day

POSTURE   1
3 Ma 1:23   they resorted to the same posture of supplication as the others

POT   3 = 0.002 %
Sir 13:2   How can the clay pot associate with the iron kettle ?
      13:2   The pot will strike against it, and will itself be broken
1 Es 1:12   and they boiled the sacrifices in brass pots and cauldrons

POTSHERD   1
Sir 22:7   is like one who glues potsherds together

POTTAGE   1
Bel 14:33   He had boiled pottage and had broken bread into a bowl

POTTER   4 = 0.003 %
Wis 15:7   For when a potter kneads the soft earth
Sir 27:5   The kiln tests the potter's vessels
      33:13   As clay in the hand of the potter
      38:29   So too is the potter sitting at his work

POULTICE   1
Wis 16:12   For neither herb nor poultice cured them

POUR   5 = 0.003 %
Sir 38:11   and pour oil on your offering, as much as you can afford
      43:19   He pours the hoarfrost upon the earth like salt
      50:15   and poured a libation of the blood of the grape
2 Ma 1:31   should be poured upon large stones
4 Ma 6:25   threw him down, and poured stinking liquids into his nostrils

POUR down   1
2 Es 4:49   and poured down a heavy and violent rain

POUR forth   4 = 0.003 %
Sir 18:29   and pour forth apt proverbs
      39:6   he will pour forth words of wisdom
      50:27   who out of his heart poured forth wisdom
2 Es 14:40   my heart poured forth understanding

POUR out   16 = 0.010 %
Sir 1:9   he poured her out upon all his works
      10:13   and the man who clings to it pours out abominations
      16:11   he is mighty to forgive, and he pours out wrath
      18:11   and pours out his mercy upon them
      24:33   I will again pour out teaching like prophecy
      30:18   Good things poured out upon a mouth that is closed
      32:4   Where there is entertainment, do not pour out talk
      35:14   nor the widow when she pours out her story
      36:7   Rouse thy anger and pour out thy wrath
      39:28   they will pour out their strength
      50:15   he poured it out at the foot of the altar
1 Ma 7:17   The flesh of thy saints and their blood they poured out
2 Es 15:35   and shall pour out a heavy tempest upon the earth
      15:40   and shall pour out upon every high and lofty place a terrible tempest
      15:44   they shall pour out the tempest and all its wrath upon her
4 Ma 3:16   he poured out the drink as an offering to God

POVERTY   10 = 0.007 %
Sir 10:31   A man honoured in poverty, how much more in wealth !
      10:31   And a man dishonoured in wealth, how much more in poverty !
      11:12   who lacks strength and abounds in poverty
      11:14   good things and bad, life and death, poverty and wealth
      13:24   and poverty is evil in the opinion of the ungodly
      18:25   in the days of wealth think of poverty and need
      20:21   A man may be prevented from sinning by his poverty
      22:23   Gain the trust of your neighbour in his poverty
      26:28   a warrior in want through poverty
2 Es 15:49   I will send evils upon you, widowhood, poverty

POWER   105 = 0.068 %
Tob 13:6   and I show his power and majesty to a nation of sinners
Jud 2:12   For as I live, and by the power of my kingdom
      5:3   and in what does their power or strength consist ?
      5:23   they are a people with no strength or power for making war
      8:15   he has power to protect us within any time he pleases
      9:8   and bring down their power in thy anger
      9:11   For thy power depends not upon numbers
      9:14   the God of all power and might
      11:7   and as his power endures
      11:7   will live by your power
      13:11   God, our God, is still with us, to show his power in Israel
      13:19   as they remember the power of God
Ad E 13:9   for the universe is in thy power

Wis	1:3	and when his power is tested, it convicts the foolish
	7:20	the powers of spirits and the reasonings of men
	7:25	For she is a breath of the power of God
	11:20	and scattered by the breath of thy power
	11:21	For it is always in thy power to show great strength
	12:15	deeming it alien to thy power to condemn him
	12:17	when men doubt the completeness of thy power
	12:18	for thou hast power to act whenever thou dost choose
	13:4	And if men were amazed at their power and working
	13:9	for if they had the power to know so much
	14:31	For it is not the power of the things by which men swear
	15:2	For even if we sin we are thine, knowing thy power
	15:3	and to know thy power is the root of immortality
	16:13	For thou hast power over life and death
	16:23	even forgot its native power
	17:2	that they held the holy nation in their power
	17:5	And no power of fire was able to give light
	19:20	Fire even in water retained its normal power
Sir	3:21	nor investigate what is beyond your power
	5:3	Do not say, Who will have power over me ?
	9:13	Keep far from a man who has the power to kill
	15:14	and he left him in the power of his own inclination
	15:18	he is mighty in power and sees everything
	18:3	by his power separating among them
	18:4	To none has he given power
	18:5	Who can measure his majestic power ?
	28:23	Those who forsake the Lord will fall into its power
	29:18	it has driven men of power into exile
	31:10	Who has had the power to transgress and did not transgress
	33:19	do not give power over yourself, as long as you live
	38:5	in order that his power might be known ?
	39:18	and none can limit his saving power
	43:29	and marvellous is his power
	44:3	and were men renowned for their power
	46:6	with hailstones of mighty power
	47:5	to exalt the power of his people
	47:7	he crushed their power even to this day
	47:11	The Lord took away his sins, and exalted his power for ever
	49:5	for they gave their power to others
Bar	2:11	and with great power and outstretched arm
	3:5	but in this crisis remember thy power and thy name
	4:21	from the power and hand of the enemy
L Jr	6:54	for they have no power
	6:63	But these idols are not to be compared with them in appearance of power
P Az	21	let them be disgraced and deprived of all power and dominion
	39	*Bless the Lord, all powers*
1 Ma	6:11	For I was kind and beloved in my power
	10:71	for I have with me the power of the cities
2 Ma	3:24	were astounded by the power of God
	3:28	and they recognized clearly the sovereign power of God
	3:34	report to all men the majestic power of God
	3:38	for there certainly is about the place some power of God
	4:50	But Menelaus, because of the cupidity of those in power
	7:17	Keep on, and see how his mighty power
	9:8	making the power of God manifest to all
	9:17	to proclaim the power of God
	11:4	He took no account whatever of the power of God
	12:28	who with power shatters the might of his enemies
1 Es	4:28	Is not the king great in his power ?
	4:40	and the power and the majesty of all the ages
	8:52	The power of our Lord will be with those who seek him
P Ma	4	at whom all things shudder, and tremble before thy power
3 Ma	1:27	to call upon him who has all power
	2:2	puffed up in his audacity and power
	2:6	You made known your mighty power
	3:15	by the power of the spear
	3:18	but they were spared the exercise of our power
	5:7	they all called upon the Almighty Lord and Ruler of all power
	5:51	imploring the Ruler over every power
	6:2	King of great power, Almighty God Most High
	6:5	showing your power to many nations
	6:12	But you, O Eternal One, who have all might and all power
	6:13	who have power to save the nation of Jacob
	7:9	we always shall have not man but the Ruler over every power
2 Es	2:41	beseech the Lord's power that your people
	4:22	why have I been endowed with the power of understanding ?
	5:18	in the power of cruel wolves
	6:3	*and before the powers of movement were established*
	11:19	they wielded power one after another
	11:32	and it had greater power over the world
	12:18	but shall regain its former power
	15:30	and with great power they shall come
	15:31	and if they combine in great power
	15:32	then these shall be disorganized and silenced by their power
	15:50	And the glory of your power shall wither like a flower
	16:12	and before the glory of his power
	16:18	*the beginning of wars, when the powers shall be terrified*
4 Ma	1:30	by virtue of the restraining power of self-control
	2:15	lust for power, vainglory, boasting, arrogance, and malice

	5 : 13	that if there is some power watching over this religion of yours
	6 : 33	we properly attribute to it the power to govern
	14 : 10	For the power of fire is intense and swift

POWERFUL   10 = 0.007 %

Wis	**7** : 23	all powerful, overseeing all
	10 : 12	that godliness is more powerful than anything
	13 : 4	how much more powerful is he who formed them
Sir	**7** : 6	lest you be partial to a powerful man
	8 : 1	Do not contend with a powerful man
	13 : 9	When a powerful man invites you, be reserved
4 Ma	**5** : 16	think that there is no compulsion more powerful
	7 : 10	O aged man, more powerful than tortures
	9 : 17	your wheel is not so powerful as to strangle my reason
	16 : 14	and in word and deed you have proved more powerful than a man

POWERLESS   6 = 0.004 %

Wis	**17** : 14	But throughout the night, which was really powerless
	17 : 14	and which beset them from the recesses of powerless Hades
2 Es	**10** : 22	our young men have been enslaved and our strong men made powerless
4 Ma	**2** : 1	are rendered powerless ?
	2 : 18	to correct some, and to render others powerless
	11 : 26	and your violence powerless

PRACTICE, subst.   3 = 0.002 %

Wis	**12** : 4	thou didst hate for their detestable practices
Sir	**38** : 34	and their prayer is in the practice of their trade
2 Es	**15** : 8	neither will I tolerate their wicked practices

PRACTICE, PRACTISE, verb   7 = 0.005 %

Tob	**4** : 11	and for all who practise it charity is an excellent offering
Jud	**9** : 3	and their bed, which was ashamed of the deceit they had practised
Wis	**19** : 13	for they practised a more bitter hatred of strangers
Sir	**27** : 9	so truth returns to those who practise it
2 Es	**7** : 125	Or that the faces of those who practised self-control
4 Ma	**9** : 2	unless we should practice ready obedience
	12 : 11	and torture on the wheel those who practice religion ?

PRAISE, subst.   65 = 0.042 %

Tob	**13** : 11	Generations of generations will give you joyful praise
	13 : 18	and will give praise, saying
	14 : 1	Here Tobit ended his words of praise
Jud	**16** : 1	and all the people loudly sang this song of praise
Ad E	**13** : 17	that we may live and sing praise to thy name, O Lord
	14 : 10	to open the mouths of the nations for the praise of vain idols
Wis	**15** : 19	both the praise of God and his blessing
	18 : 9	and already they were singing the praises of the fathers
Sir	**15** : 9	A hymn of praise is not fitting on the lips of a sinner
	15 : 10	For a hymn of praise should be uttered in wisdom
	17 : 27	Who will sing praises to the Most High in Hades
	17 : 28	he who is alive and well sings the Lord's praises
	37 : 24	A wise man will have praise heaped upon him
	39 : 10	and the congregation will proclaim his praise
	39 : 14	Scatter the fragrance, and sing a hymn of praise
	39 : 15	with praise, with songs on your lips, and with lyres
	39 : 35	So now sing praise with all your heart and voice
	44 : 8	so that men declare their praise
	44 : 15	and the congregation proclaims their praise
	47 : 8	he sang praise with all his heart, and he loved his Maker
	51 : 11	and will sing praise with thanksgiving
P Az	**3**	and worthy of praise
	35	sing praise to him and highly exalt him for ever
	36	sing praise to him and highly exalt him for ever
	37	sing praise to him and highly exalt him for ever
	38	sing praise to him and highly exalt him for ever
	39	sing praise to him and highly exalt him for ever
	40	sing praise to him and highly exalt him for ever
	41	sing praise to him and highly exalt him for ever
	42	sing praise to him and highly exalt him for ever
	43	sing praise to him and highly exalt him for ever
	44	sing praise to him and highly exalt him for ever
	45	sing praise to him and highly exalt him for ever
	46	sing praise to him and highly exalt him for ever
	47	sing praise to him and highly exalt him for ever
	48	sing praise to him and highly exalt him for ever
	49	sing praise to him and highly exalt him for ever
	50	sing praise to him and highly exalt him for ever
	51	sing praise to him and highly exalt him for ever
	52	let it sing praise to him and highly exalt him for ever
	53	sing praise to him and highly exalt him for ever
	54	sing praise to him and highly exalt him for ever
	55	sing praise to him and highly exalt him for ever
	56	sing praise to him and highly exalt him for ever
	57	sing praise to him and highly exalt him for ever
	58	sing praise to him and highly exalt him for ever
	59	sing praise to him and highly exalt him for ever
	60	sing praise to him and highly exalt him for ever
	61	sing praise to him and highly exalt him for ever
	62	sing praise to him and highly exalt him for ever
	63	sing praise to him and highly exalt him for ever
	64	sing praise to him and highly exalt him for ever
	65	sing praise to him and highly exalt him for ever
	66	sing praise to him and highly exalt him for ever
	68	sing praise to him and give thanks to him
1 Ma	**4** : 24	On their return they sang hymns and praises to Heaven
	4 : 56	they offered a sacrifice of deliverance and praise
	13 : 47	and then entered it with hymns and praise
	13 : 51	the Jews entered it with praise and palm branches
2 Ma	**8** : 27	giving great praise and thanks to the Lord
P Ma	**15**	For all the host of heaven sings thy praise
3 Ma	**2** : 20	and put praises in the mouth of those who are downcast
	7 : 16	in words of praise and all kinds of melodious songs
2 Es	**13** : 57	giving great glory and praise to the Most High
4 Ma	**1** : 2	and in addition it includes the praise of the highest virtue

PRAISE, verb   80 = 0.052 %

Tob	**3** : 11	May all thy works praise thee for ever
	11 : 1	praising God because he had made his journey a success
	11 : 16	rejoicing and praising God
	12 : 6	and said to them : Praise God and give thanks to him
	12 : 6	It is good to praise God and to exalt his name
	12 : 17	But praise God for ever
	12 : 18	Therefore praise him for ever
	13 : 6	Praise the Lord of righteousness
	13 : 10	and praise the King of the ages
	13 : 13	and will praise the Lord of the righteous
	13 : 15	Let my soul praise God the great King
	14 : 2	and he continued to fear the Lord God and to praise him
	14 : 7	All the Gentiles will praise the Lord
Jud	**6** : 20	Then they consoled Achior, and praised him greatly
	13 : 14	Praise God, O praise him !
	13 : 14	Praise God, who has not withdrawn his mercy
Ad E	**13** : 17	do not destroy the mouth of those who praise thee
	14 : 9	to stop the mouth of those who praise thee
Wis	**10** : 20	and praised with one accord thy defending hand
	19 : 9	praising thee, O Lord, who didst deliver them
Sir	pr.	on account of which we should praise Israel
	9 : 17	A work will be praised for the skill of the craftsmen
	11 : 2	Do not praise a man for his good looks
	17 : 10	And they will praise his holy name
	18 : 28	and he praises the one who finds her
	21 : 15	he will praise it and add to it
	24 : 1	Wisdom will praise herself
	27 : 7	Do not praise a man before you hear him reason
	31 : 23	Men will praise the one who is liberal with food
	37 : 7	Every counsellor praises counsel
	39 : 9	Many will praise his understanding
	43 : 11	Look upon the rainbow, and praise him who made it
	43 : 28	Where shall we find strength to praise him ?
	43 : 30	When you praise the Lord, exalt him as much as you can
	43 : 30	and do not grow weary, for you cannot praise him enough
	44 : 1	Let us now praise famous men
	47 : 6	and praised him for the blessings of the Lord
	47 : 10	while they praised God's holy name
	50 : 18	And the singers praised him with their voices
	51 : 1	and will praise thee as God my Saviour
	51 : 11	I will praise thy name continually
	51 : 12	Therefore I will give thanks to thee and praise thee
	51 : 22	and I will praise him with it
	51 : 29	and may you not be put to shame when you praise him
Bar	**2** : 32	and they will praise me in the land of their exile
	3 : 6	and thee, O Lord, will we praise
	3 : 7	and we will praise thee in our exile
P Az	**28**	praised and glorified and blessed God in the furnace, saying :
	29	and to be praised and highly exalted for ever
	30	and to be highly praised and highly exalted for ever
	32	and to be praised and highly exalted for ever
Sus	**13** : 63	And Hilkiah and his wife praised God for their daughter Susanna
1 Ma	**4** : 33	and let all who know thy name praise thee with hymns
	5 : 64	Men gathered to them and praised them
2 Ma	**3** : 30	they praised the Lord
	11 : 9	And they all together praised the merciful God
1 Es	**4** : 58	and praised the King of heaven, saying
	4 : 62	And they praised the God of their fathers
	5 : 60	praising the Lord and blessing him
	5 : 62	praising the Lord for the erection of the house of the Lord
P Ma	**15**	and I will praise thee continually
3 Ma	**2** : 8	they praised you, the Almighty
	4 : 16	praising speechless things that are not able
	5 : 13	praised their holy God
	5 : 35	praised the manifest Lord God, King of kings
	6 : 11	Let not the vain-minded praise their vanities
	6 : 29	praised their holy God and Saviour
	6 : 32	praising God, their Saviour and worker of wonders
2 Es	**2** : 42	and they all were praising the Lord with songs
	2 : 47	So I began to praise those

	10:16	and will be praised among women
4 Ma	1:10	to praise for their virtues those who, with their mother
	2:2	that the temperate Joseph is praised
	4:4	he praised Simon for his service to the king
	4:12	he would praise the blessedness of the holy place before all people
	7:9	and you did not abandon the holiness which you praised
	13:3	Instead, by reason, which is praised before God
	13:17	and all the fathers will praise us
	18:13	He praised Daniel in the den of the lions and blessed him

PRAISEWORTHY 1
2 Es 8:48 But even in this respect you will be praiseworthy

PRATTLE 1
Sir 7:14 Do not prattle in the assembly of the elders

PRAY 66 = 0.043 %

Tob	3:1	and I prayed in anguish, saying
	3:11	So she prayed by her window and said
	8:4	and let us pray that the Lord may have mercy upon us
	8:5	And Tobias began to pray
	12:12	And so, when you and your daughter-in-law Sarah prayed
Jud	4:12	praying earnestly to the God of Israel
	8:31	So pray for us, since you are a devout woman
	11:17	and I will pray to God
	12:6	that your servant be permitted to go out and pray
	12:8	she prayed the Lord God of Israel
Ad E	13:8	Then he prayed to the Lord
	14:3	And she prayed to the Lord God of Israel, and said :
Wis	7:7	Therefore I prayed, and understanding was given me
	13:17	When he prays about possessions
	13:18	for life he prays to a thing that is dead
	16:28	and must pray to thee at the dawning of the light
Sir	3:5	and when he prays he will be heard
	17:25	pray in his presence and lessen your offences
	21:1	Do so no more, but pray about your former sins
	28:2	and then your sins will be pardoned when you pray
	28:4	and yet pray for his own sins ?
	34:24	When one prays and another curses
	37:15	And besides all this pray to the Most High
	38:9	but pray the Lord, and he will heal you
	38:14	for they too will pray to the Lord
	51:9	and prayed for deliverance from death
Bar	1:5	Then they wept, and fasted, and prayed before the Lord
	1:11	and pray for the life of Nebuchadnezzar king of Babylon
	1:13	And pray for us to the Lord our God
L Jr	6:41	they bring him and pray Bel that the man may speak
1 Ma	3:44	and to pray and ask for mercy and compassion
	4:30	When he saw that the army was strong, he prayed, saying
	7:40	Then Judas prayed and said
	11:71	and put dust on his head, and prayed
2 Ma	1:6	We are now praying for you here
	2:10	Just as Moses prayed to the Lord
	2:10	so also Solomon prayed, and the fire came down
	5:4	Therefore all men prayed
	12:44	and foolish to pray for the dead
	14:15	and prayed to him who established his own people for ever
	15:12	was praying with outstretched hands
	15:14	and prays much for the people and the holy city
	15:27	and praying to God in their hearts
1 Es	4:46	I pray therefore that you fulfil the vow
	8:53	And again we prayed to our Lord about these things
	8:91	While Ezra was praying and making his confession
3 Ma	2:1	prayed as follows :
	2:10	when we come to this place and pray
	5:7	their merciful God and Father, praying
	6:1	and prayed as follows :
2 Es	2:13	pray that your days may be few, that they may be shortened
	4:51	Then I prayed and said
	5:13	and if you pray again, and weep as you do now
	6:31	If therefore you will pray again and fast again for 7 days
	7:46	But what of those for whom I prayed ?
	7:105	so no one shall ever pray for another on that day
	7:106	How then do we find that first Abraham prayed
	7:110	and many others prayed for many ?
	7:111	If therefore the righteous have prayed for the ungodly now
	7:112	therefore those who were strong prayed for the weak
	8:6	that we may pray before thee
	8:17	Therefore I will pray before thee for myself and for them
	9:25	and pray to the Most High continually
	12:48	but I have come to this place to pray
4 Ma	4:11	to pray for him and propitiate the wrath of the heavenly army
	4:13	prayed for him lest King Seleucus suppose

PRAYER 51 = 0.033 %
Tob 3:16 The prayer of both was heard
 12:8 Prayer is good when accompanied by fasting, almsgiving, and righteousness
 12:12 I brought a reminder of your prayer before the Holy One

	12:15	who present the prayers of the saints
	13:1	Then Tobit wrote a prayer of rejoicing, and said :
Jud	4:13	So the Lord heard their prayers
	9:12	King of all thy creation, hear my prayer !
	13:3	for she said she would be going out for her prayers
	13:10	as they were accustomed to go for prayer
Ad E	13:17	Hear my prayer, and have mercy upon thy inheritance
	15:1	On the 3rd day, when she ended her prayer
Wis	18:21	prayer and propitiation by incense
Sir	4:6	his Creator will hear his prayer
	7:10	Do not be fainthearted in your prayer
	7:14	nor repeat yourself in your prayer
	21:5	The prayer of a poor man goes from his lips
	34:26	who will listen to his prayer ?
	35:13	and he will listen to the prayer of one who is wronged
	35:16	and his prayer will reach to the clouds
	35:17	The prayer of the humble pierces the clouds
	36:17	Hearken, O Lord, to the prayer of thy servants
	38:34	and their prayer is in the practice of their trade
	39:5	he will open his mouth in prayer
	39:6	and give thanks to the Lord in prayer
	50:19	And the people besought the Lord Most High in prayer
	51:11	My prayer was heard
	51:13	I sought wisdom openly in my prayer
Bar	2:14	Hear, O Lord, our prayer and our supplication
	2:19	that we bring before thee our prayer for mercy
	3:4	hear now the prayer of the dead of Israel
P Az	2	Then Azariah stood and offered this prayer
1 Ma	3:46	because Israel formerly had a place of prayer in Mizpah
	5:33	who sounded their trumpets and cried aloud in prayer
	7:37	and to be for thy people a house of prayer and supplication
	12:11	at the sacrifices which we offer and in our prayers
2 Ma	1:5	May he hear your prayers and be reconciled to you
	1:23	the priests offered prayer – the priests and every one
	1:24	The prayer was to this effect :
	10:27	And rising from their prayer they took up their arms
	12:42	and they turned to prayer
	15:24	With these words he ended his prayer
	15:26	with invocation to God and prayers
1 Es	6:31	and prayers be offered for their life
3 Ma	1:24	Meanwhile the crowd, as before, was engaged in prayer
	6:16	Just as Eleazar was ending his prayer
	7:20	and dedicating a place of prayer at the site of the festival
2 Es	8:19	The beginning of the words of Ezra's prayer
	8:24	hear, O Lord, the prayer of thy servant
	10:28	my end has become corruption, and my prayer a reproach
	12:7	and if my prayer has indeed come up before thy face
	13:14	and hast deemed me worthy to have my prayer heard by thee

PRECAUTION 2
2 Ma 1:19 where they took such Precautions
3 Ma 3:24 we have taken Precautions lest

PRECEDE 6 = 0.004 %
Sir 22:24 The vapour and smoke of the furnace precede the fire
 22:24 so insults precede bloodshed
 32:10 and approval precedes a modest man
 37:16 and counsel precedes every undertaking
4 Ma 1:22 Thus desire precedes pleasure and delight follows it
 1:23 Fear precedes pain and sorrow comes after

PRECEDENCE 1
4 Ma 2:12 It takes precedence over love for children

PRECEDING 2
Ad E 11:1 and Ptolemy his son brought to Egypt the preceding Letter of Purim
1 Ma 3:30 which he used to give more lavishly than preceding kings

PRECEPT 1
2 Es 16:76 You who keep my commandments and precepts, says the Lord God

PRECINCT 9 = 0.006 %
1 Ma 1:47 to build altars and sacred precincts and shrines for idols
 5:43 and fled into the sacred precincts at Carnaim
 5:44 and burned the sacred precincts with fire
 10:43 or in any of its precincts
 14:48 in the precincts of the sanctuary
2 Ma 1:15 inside the wall of the sacred precinct
 6:4 and had intercourse with women within the sacred precincts
 10:2 and also destroyed the sacred precincts
 14:33 I will level this precinct of God to the ground

PRECIOUS 12 = 0.008 %
Tob 13:16 her walls with precious stones
Jud 10:3 and anointed herself with precious ointment
 10:21 and emeralds and precious stones
Ad E 15:6 all covered with gold and precious stones
Wis 12:7 that the land most precious of all to thee

Sir	6:15	There is nothing so precious as a faithful friend
	26:14	and there is nothing so precious as a disciplined soul
	45:11	with precious stones engraved like signets
	50:9	adorned with all kinds of precious stones
2 Es	7:52	If you have just a few precious stones
	7:57	Judge therefore which things are precious and desirable
	7:58	for what is more rare is more precious

PRECIPITOUS 2
2 Es	7:7	and set in a precipitous place
4 Ma	14:16	and the others, by building in precipitous chasms

PRECIPITOUSLY 1
2 Ma	13:5	which on all sides inclines precipitously into the ashes

PRECISELY 1
3 Ma	4:13	be dealt with in precisely the same fashion as the others

PREDECESSOR 1
1 Ma	11:26	the king treated him as his predecessors had treated him

PREDICT 2
2 Es	8:59	For just as the things which I have predicted await you
	9:8	will survive the dangers that have been predicted

PREDICTED 1
2 Es	9:1	and when you see that a certain part of the predicted signs are past

PREEMINENT 1
3 Ma	1:11	but only the high priest who was preeminent over all

PREFACE 1
2 Ma	2:32	for it is foolish to lengthen the preface

PREFECT 1
1 Es	3:14	and the satraps and generals and governors and prefects

PREFER 8 = 0.005 %
Wis	7:8	I preferred her to sceptres and thrones
	17:13	prefers ignorance of what causes the torment
2 Ma	11:24	but prefer their own way of living
	14:42	preferring to die nobly rather than to fall
1 Es	4:19	and all prefer her to gold or silver
3 Ma	1:29	because indeed all at that time preferred death
	2:30	But if any of them prefer to join
4 Ma	1:15	Now reason is the mind that with sound logic prefers the life of wisdom

PREFERABLE 2
Sir	20:25	A thief is preferable to a habitual liar
	28:21	its death is an evil death, and Hades is preferable to it

PREFERENCE 1
1 Es	4:39	With her there is no partiality or preference

PREGNANCY 2
4 Ma	15:6	In 7 pregnancies she had implanted in herself tender love toward them
	16:7	O 7 childbirths all in vain, 7 profitless pregnancies

PREGNANT 1
Sir	42:10	or become pregnant in her father's house

PREMATURE 1
2 Es	6:21	and women with child shall give birth to premature children at 3 or 4 months

PREPARATION 3 = 0.002 %
Tob	5:16	So his son made the preparations for the journey
Jud	4:5	and stored up food in preparation for war
3 Ma	5:10	to report to the king about these preparations

PREPARE 54 = 0.035 %
Tob	2:1	a good dinner was prepared for me and I sat down to eat
	11:3	Let us run ahead of your wife and prepare the house
Jud	2:7	Tell them to prepare earth and water
	5:1	heard that the people of Israel had prepared for war
	9:6	for all thy ways are prepared in advance
	12:19	what her maid had prepared
Ad E	11:7	And at their roaring every nation prepared for war
	12:2	and learned that they were preparing
Wis	9:8	which thou didst prepare from the beginning
	13:12	and burn the castoff pieces of his work to prepare his food
	14:1	Again, one preparing to sail
	16:2	and thou didst prepare quails to eat
Sir pr.		being prepared in character to live according to the law
	2:1	prepare yourself for temptation
	2:17	Those who fear the Lord will prepare their hearts
	18:23	Before making a vow, prepare yourself

	26:28	the Lord will prepare him for the sword !
	29:26	Come here, stranger, prepare the table
	33:4	Prepare what to say, and thus you will be heard
	45:20	he prepared bread of first fruits in abundance
	47:13	and prepare a sanctuary to stand for ever
	49:1	prepared by the art of the perfumer
	49:12	prepared for everlasting glory
Bar	1:10	and incense, and prepare a cereal offering
	3:32	He who prepared the earth for all time filled it with four-footed creatures
1 Ma	2:32	they encamped opposite them and prepared for battle
	5:11	They are preparing to come
	12:28	that Jonathan and his men were prepared for battle
	15:7	All the weapons which you have prepared
2 Ma	2:27	just as it is not easy for one who prepares a banquet
1 Es	1:4	and prepare yourselves by your families and kindred
	1:6	and prepare the sacrifices for your brethren
	1:13	Afterward they prepared the passover for themselves
	1:14	so the Levites prepared it for themselves
	1:16	for their brethren the Levites prepared the passover for them
	5:48	took their places and prepared the altar of the God of Israel
	9:42	stood on the wooden platform which had been prepared
3 Ma	1:19	abandoned the bridal chambers prepared for wedded union
	5:8	from the fate now prepared for them
	5:20	Tomorrow without delay prepare the elephants in the same way
	5:31	I would have prepared them to be a rich feast
	6:31	which had been prepared for their destruction and burial
2 Es	2:11	which I had prepared for Israel
	2:13	The kingdom is already prepared for you ; watch !
	2:18	I have consecrated and prepared for you
	7:70	he first prepared the judgment
	8:52	the age to come is prepared, plenty is provided
	8:59	so the thirst and torment which are prepared await them
	8:60	and have been ungrateful to him who prepared life for them
	9:18	when I was preparing for those who now exist
	13:11	which was prepared to fight
	13:36	And Zion will come and be made manifest to all people, prepared and built
	14:24	But prepare for yourself many writing tablets
	16:40	prepare for battle

PRESCRIBE 2
1 Es	6:34	that it be done with all diligence as here prescribed
	8:21	Let all things prescribed in the law of God

PRESCRIBED 1
2 Es	7:44	This is my judgment and its prescribed order

PRESENCE 52 = 0.034 %
Tob	3:16	in the presence of the glory of the great God
	4:11	in the presence of the Most High
	12:6	in the presence of all the living
	12:15	and enter into the presence of the glory of the Holy One
	13:4	and exalt him in the presence of all the living
Jud	2:5	When you leave my presence
	2:14	So Holofernes left the presence of his master
	5:8	hence they drove them out from the presence of their gods
	6:1	in the presence of all the foreign contingents :
	6:17	in the presence of the Assyrian leaders
	8:15	or even to destroy us in the presence of our enemies
	10:13	I am on my way to the presence of Holofernes
	10:15	by hurrying down to the presence of our lord
	10:23	And when Judith came into the presence of Holofernes and his servants
	11:5	and let your maidservant speak in your presence
	11:13	who minister in the presence of our God at Jerusalem
	12:13	So Bagoas went out from the presence of Holofernes
	12:13	and be honoured in his presence
	13:1	and shut out the attendants from his master's presence
	14:8	Then Judith described to him in the presence of the people
	16:15	at thy presence the rocks shall melt like wax
Wis	5:1	in the presence of those who have afflicted him
	8:10	and honour in the presence of the elders, though I am young
	14:17	When men could not honour monarchs in their presence
Sir	6:12	and will hide himself from your presence
	8:18	In the presence of a stranger
	17:25	pray in his presence and lessen your offences
	23:14	lest you be forgetful in their presence
	24:2	and in the presence of his host she will glory :
	27:23	In your presence his mouth is all sweetness
	30:3	and will glory in him in the presence of friends
	38:3	and in the presence of great men he is admired
	45:3	the Lord glorified him in the presence of kings
Bar	2:28	to write thy law in the presence of the people of Israel
Bel	14:14	in the presence of the king alone
1 Ma	1:22	He took also the table for the bread of the Presence
	11:26	he exalted him in the presence of all his friends
2 Ma	6:18	a man now advanced in age and of noble presence
	10:3	and set out the bread of the Presence
	14:24	And he kept Judas always in his presence

1 Es	3:15	and the writing was read in their presence
	8:90	for we can no longer stand in thy presence
	9:41	in the presence of both men and women
	9:45	for he had the place of honour in the presence of all
3 Ma	3:17	They accepted our presence by word, but insincerely by deed
2 Es	1:30	I will cast you out from my presence
	3:5	and he was made alive in thy presence
	5:22	in the presence of the Most High
	6:36	and I began to speak in the presence of the Most High
	14:19	Let me speak in thy presence, Lord
	16:11	and who will not be utterly shattered at his presence ?
	16:12	at the presence of the Lord

PRESENT, verb   9 = 0.006 %

Tob	12:15	who present the prayers of the saints
Jud	9:6	and the things thou didst will presented themselves and said
Sir	14:11	and present worthy offerings to the Lord
	18:15	nor cause grief by your words when you present a gift
2 Ma	1:21	And when the materials for the sacrifices were presented
	4:24	But he, when presented to the king
	4:44	3 men sent by the senate presented the case before him
	14:4	presenting to him a crown of gold and a palm
3 Ma	5:10	presented himself at the courtyard early in the morning

PRESENT, subst., gift   3 = 0.002 %

Sir	20:29	Presents and gifts blind the eyes of the wise
2 Ma	3:2	and glorified the temple with the finest presents
	4:30	as a present to Antiochis, the king's concubine

PRESENT, subst., time   2

Tob	7:11	But for the present be merry
2 Ma	6:26	For even if for the present

PRESENT, adj.   29 = 0.019 %

Tob	12:12	I was likewise present with you
Jud	8:18	For never in our generation, nor in these present days
Ad E	13:6	of this present year
Wis	4:2	When it is present, men imitate it
	9:9	and was present when thou didst make the world
	11:11	Whether absent or present, they were equally distressed
	14:17	they might flatter the absent one as though present
Bar	1:7	and to all the people who were present with him in Jerusalem
2 Ma	4:18	and the king was present
	7:9	You accursed wretch, you dismiss us from this present life
	9:26	and to maintain your present good will, each of you
1 Es	1:7	And Josiah gave to the people who were present
	1:19	And the people of Israel who were present at that time
3 Ma	1:16	and entreated the supreme God to aid in the present situation
	1:27	to defend them in the present trouble
	3:11	Then the king, boastful of his present good fortune
	5:16	and ordered those present for the banquet to recline opposite him
	5:17	and to make the present portion of the banquet joyful
	5:18	through the present day
	5:21	all those present readily and joyfully with one accord gave their approval
	5:31	Were your parents or children present
2 Es	5:45	all of them present at one time
	6:5	and before the present years were reckoned
	7:16	rather than what is now present ?
	7:112	He answered me and said, This present world is not the end
	8:2	so is the course of the present world
	8:46	Things that are present are for those who live now
4 Ma	3:19	The present occasion now invites us
	12:18	both in this present life and when you are dead

PRESERVE   19 = 0.012 %

Wis	10:5	and preserved him blameless before God
	11:25	have been preserved ?
	16:26	but that thy word preserves those who trust in thee
Sir	38:14	and in healing, for the sake of preserving life
	39:2	he will preserve the discourse of notable men
	46:8	And these 2 alone were preserved
L Jr	6:28	and likewise their wives preserve some with salt
1 Ma	14:29	in order that their sanctuary and the law might be preserved
2 Ma	1:26	and preserve thy portion and make it holy
	8:27	who had preserved them for that day
2 Es	3:30	and hast destroyed thy people, and hast preserved thy enemies
	7:67	that we shall be preserved alive but cruelly tormented ?
	8:8	what thou hast created is preserved in fire and water
4 Ma	4:14	but one preserves the property of enemies from the destroyers
	4:14	So Apollonius, having been preserved beyond all expectations
	15:2	that of religion, and that of preserving her 7 sons for a time
	15:3	religion that preserves them for eternal life
	15:27	which would preserve the 7 sons for a short time
	17:22	divine Providence preserved Israel

PRESS, verb   12 = 0.008 %

Sir	46:5	when enemies pressed him on every side
	46:16	when his enemies pressed him on every side

Sus	13:14	and when each pressed the other for the reason
Bel	14:30	The king saw that they were pressing him hard
1 Ma	2:30	because evils pressed heavily upon them
	6:57	and the affairs of the kingdom press urgently upon us
	10:50	He pressed the battle strongly until the sun set
	15:14	he pressed the city hard from land and sea
2 Ma	8:20	and when the Macedonians were hard pressed
	11:5	and pressed it hard
	12:23	And Judas pressed the pursuit with the utmost vigour
1 Es	5:72	But the peoples of the land pressed hard upon those in Judea

PRESS forward   1

1 Es	5:58	as one man pressing forward the work on the house of God

PRESS on   1

Sir	11:11	There is a man who works, and toils, and presses on

PRESSURE   1

Sir	29:6	If the lender exerts pressure, he will hardly get back half

PRESTIGE   2

2 Ma	4:15	and putting the highest value upon Greek forms of prestige
3 Ma	7:21	They also possessed greater prestige among their enemies

PRESUMPTION   1

Ad E	13:2	not elated with presumption of authority

PRETENCE, PRETENSE   2

2 Ma	6:24	Such pretence is not worthy of our time of life, he said
	6:25	and through my pretence

PRETEND   5 = 0.003 %

Sir	12:17	and while pretending to help you, he will trip you by the heel
	19:27	He hides his face and pretends not to hear
2 Ma	5:25	he pretended to be peaceably disposed
	6:21	and pretend that he was eating the flesh
4 Ma	6:15	save yourself by pretending to eat pork

PRETEXT   2

2 Ma	1:14	For under pretext of intending to marry her
3 Ma	3:2	a pretext being given by a report

PREVAIL   14 = 0.009 %

Jud	11:10	nor can the sword prevail against them
Wis	7:30	but against wisdom evil does not prevail
1 Ma	6:54	because famine had prevailed over the rest
2 Ma	3:5	and when he could not prevail over Onias
1 Es	4:38	and lives and prevails for ever and ever
	9:6	shivering because of the bad weather that prevailed
2 Es	7:60	because it is they who have made my glory to prevail now
	15:39	And the winds from the east shall prevail
	16:76	or your iniquities prevail over you
4 Ma	2:10	For the law prevails even over affection for parents
	2:14	through the law, can prevail even over enmity
	6:32	For if the emotions had prevailed over reason
	8:1	have prevailed over the most painful instruments of torture
	13:3	they prevailed over their emotions

PREVENT   11 = 0.007 %

Sir	19:28	And if by lack of strength he is prevented from sinning
	20:21	A man may be prevented from sinning by his poverty
	31:2	Wakeful anxiety prevents slumber
1 Ma	6:27	and unless you quickly prevent them
	7:24	and he prevented those in the city
	13:49	were prevented from going out to the country and back
2 Ma	14:22	to prevent sudden treachery on the part of the enemy
1 Es	2:28	to prevent these men from building the city
	5:73	they prevented the completion of the building
	6:6	and they were not prevented from building
4 Ma	4:7	and did all that they could to prevent it

PREVIOUS   2

2 Es	5:31	the angel who had come to me on a previous night was sent to me
	6:12	which thou didst show me in part on a previous night

PREVIOUSLY   10 = 0.007 %

Wis	18:2	though previously wronged, were doing them no injury
1 Ma	1:1	He had previously become king of Greece
2 Ma	4:1	The previously mentioned Simon
	4:23	the brother of the previously mentioned Simon
3 Ma	1:2	that had been previously issued to him
	2:25	abetted by the previously mentioned drinking companions and comrades
	4:17	But after the previously mentioned interval of time
	5:28	a forgetfulness of the things he had previously devised
	6:34	And those who had previously believed
4 Ma	17:22	that previously had been afflicted

PREY, subst.   6 = 0.004 %
Jud	4:12	not to give up their infants as prey
	9:4	and thou gavest their wives for a prey
	16:5	and seize my children as prey
Sir	13:19	Wild asses in the wilderness are the prey of lions
	27:10	A lion lies in wait for prey
1 Ma	3:4	like a lion's cub roaring for prey

PRICE   1
3 Ma	2:31	Now some, however, with an obvious abhorrence of the price

PRICELESS   2
Wis	7:9	Neither did I liken to her any priceless gem
3 Ma	3:23	they not only spurn the priceless citizenship

PRICK, verb   2
Sir	22:19	A man who pricks an eye will make tears fall
	22:19	and one who pricks the heart makes it show feeling

PRIDE   23 = 0.015 %
Tob	4:13	For in pride there is ruin and great confusion
Jud	9:9	Behold their pride, and send thy wrath upon their heads
	15:9	you are the great pride of our nation !
Ad E	13:12	or pride or for any love of glory that I did this
	13:14	and I will not do these things in pride
Sir	10:12	The beginning of man's pride is to depart from the Lord
	10:13	For the beginning of pride is sin
	10:18	Pride was not created for men
	10:21	obduracy and pride are the beginning of rejection
	11:16	evil will grow old with those who take pride in malice
	15:8	She is far from men of pride
	26:26	in her pride she will be known to all as ungodly
	43:1	The pride of the heavenly heights is the clear firmament
	50:1	The leader of his brethren and the pride of his people
Bar	4:34	And I will take away her pride in her great population
1 Ma	3:20	They come against us in great pride and lawlessness
	8:14	or worn purple as a mark of pride
2 Ma	1:28	Afflict those who oppress and are insolent with pride
2 Es	1:38	look with pride and see the people coming from the east
	8:50	because they have walked in great pride
	11:43	and your pride to the Mighty One
	15:18	For because of their pride the cities shall be in confusion
4 Ma	8:24	nor take hollow pride in being put to the rack

PRIEST s. **HIGH, CHIEF PRIEST**   115 = 0.075 %
Tob	1:6	I would give these to the priests, the sons of Aaron, at the altar
Jud	4:14	And Joakim the high priest and all the priests
	11:13	which they had consecrated and set aside for the priests
Ad E	11:1	Dositheus, who said that he was a priest and a Levite
Sir	7:29	With all your soul fear the Lord, and honour his priests
	7:31	Fear the Lord and honour the priest
	45:15	to minister to the Lord and serve as priest
	50:12	from the hands of the priests
Bar	1:7	the son of Hilkiah, son of Shallum, and to the priests
	1:16	and to our kings and our princes and our priests
L Jr	6:10	and sometimes the priests secretly take gold and silver from their gods
	6:18	so the priests make their temples secure with doors and locks and bars
	6:28	The priests sell the sacrifices that are offered to these gods
	6:31	and in their temples the priests sit with their clothes rent
	6:33	The priests take some of the clothing of their gods
	6:48	the priests consult together
	6:55	their priests will flee and escape
P Az	62	Bless the Lord, you priests of the Lord
Bel	14:8	and he called his priests and said to them
	14:10	Now there were 70 priests of Bel
	14:11	And the priests of Bel said, Behold, we are going outside
	14:15	In the night the priests came with their wives and children
	14:21	and he seized the priests and their wives and children
	14:28	and slaughtered the priests
1 Ma	1:46	to defile the sanctuary and the priests
	2:1	a priest of the sons of Joarib
	3:51	and thy priests mourn in humiliation
	4:38	They saw also the chambers of the priests in ruins
	4:42	He chose blameless priests devoted to the law
	4:57	they restored the gates and the chambers for the priests
	5:67	On that day some priests, who wished to do a brave deed
	7:14	A priest of the line of Aaron has come with the army
	7:33	Some of the priests came out of the sanctuary
	7:36	Then the priests went in
	10:42	because it belongs to the priests who minister there
	11:23	and some of the priests
	12:6	the priests, and the rest of the Jewish people
	14:20	to Simon the high priest and to the elders and the priests
	14:28	in Asaramel, in the great assembly of the priests
	14:29	a priest of the sons of Joarib, and his brothers
	14:41	And the Jews and their priests decided
	14:44	And none of the people or priests shall be permitted
	14:47	to be commander and ethnarch of the Jews and priests

	15:1	to Simon, the priest and ethnarch of the Jews
2 Ma	1:10	To Aristobulus, who is of the family of the anointed priests
	1:13	by a deception employed by the priests of Nanaea
	1:15	When the priests of the temple of Nanaea
	1:19	the pious priests of that time
	1:20	sent the descendants of the priests who had hidden the fire to get it
	1:21	Nehemiah ordered the priests
	1:23	the priests offered prayer – the priests and every one
	1:30	Then the priests sang the hymns
	1:33	that, in the place where the exiled priests had hidden the fire
	3:15	The priests prostrated themselves before the altar
	4:14	that the priests were no longer intent
	14:31	while the priests were offering the customary sacrifices
	14:34	Then the priests stretched forth their hands toward heaven
	15:31	and stationed the priests before the altar
1 Es	1:2	having placed the priests according to their divisions
	1:7	to the people and the priests and Levites
	1:8	gave to the priests for the passover
	1:10	The priests and the Levites
	1:13	and for their brethren the priests, the sons of Aaron
	1:14	because the priests were offering the fat until night
	1:14	and for their brethren the priests, the sons of Aaron
	1:21	as was kept by Josiah and the priests and the Levites
	1:49	Even the leaders of the people and of the priests
	2:8	and the priests and the Levites
	4:53	and all the priests who came
	4:54	He wrote also concerning their support and the priests
	5:5	the priests, the sons of Phinehas, son of Aaron
	5:24	The priests : the sons of Jedaiah the son of Jeshua
	5:38	Of the priests the following had assumed the priesthood
	5:39	they were excluded from serving as priests
	5:45	and a 100 priests' garments
	5:46	The priests, the Levites
	5:48	Then Jeshua the son of Jozadak, with his fellow priests
	5:56	together with their brethren and the Levitical priests
	5:59	And the priests stood arrayed in their garments
	5:63	Some of the Levitical priests and heads of fathers' houses
	6:30	for daily use as the priests in Jerusalem may indicate
	7:6	And the people of Israel, the priests, the Levites
	7:9	and the priests and the Levites stood
	7:10	after the priests and the Levites were purified together
	7:12	and for their brethren the priests and for themselves
	8:5	some of the people of Israel and some of the priests
	8:8	which was delivered to Ezra the priest
	8:9	King Artaxerxes to Ezra the priest
	8:10	and of the priests and Levites and others in our realm
	8:19	that whatever Ezra the priest
	8:22	on any of the priests or Levites or temple singers
	8:42	none of the sons of the priests or of the Levites
	8:46	to send us men to serve as priests
	8:54	Then I set apart 12 of the leaders of the priests
	8:59	to the leaders of the priests and the Levites
	8:60	So the priests and the Levites
	8:62	to Meremoth the priest, son of Uriah
	8:69	and the leaders and the priests and the Levites
	8:77	and our priests were given over to the kings of the earth
	8:96	Then Ezra arose and had the leaders of the priests
	9:16	Ezra the priest chose for himself
	9:18	Of the priests those who were brought in
	9:37	The priests and the Levites and the men of Israel
	9:40	and all the priests to hear the law
	9:42	Ezra the priest and reader of the law
3 Ma	1:11	nor even all of the priests
	1:16	Then the priests in all their vestments prostrated themselves
	6:1	Then a certain Eleazar, famous among the priests of the country
	7:13	their priests and the whole multitude
2 Es	1:13	I gave you Moses as leader and Aaron as priest
	10:22	our priests have been burned to death
4 Ma	4:9	While the priests together with women and children
	7:6	O priest, worthy of the priesthood
	17:9	Here lie buried an aged priest and an aged woman and 7 sons

PRIESTHOOD s. **HIGH PRIESTHOOD**   9 = 0.006 %
Sir	45:7	and gave him the priesthood of the people
	45:24	should have the dignity of the priesthood for ever
1 Ma	2:54	received the covenant of everlasting priesthood
	3:49	They also brought the garments of the priesthood
2 Ma	2:17	and the kingship and priesthood and consecration
1 Es	5:38	Of the priests the following had assumed the priesthood
4 Ma	4:16	who removed Onias from the priesthood
	5:35	nor will I reject you, honoured priesthood and knowledge of the law
	7:6	O priest, worthy of the priesthood

PRIESTLY   2
2 Ma	3:15	in their priestly garments
4 Ma	5:4	He was a man of priestly family, learned in the law

PRIME   2
   3 Ma   4 : 8   Their husbands, in the prime of youth
   4 Ma   2 : 3   For when he was young and in his prime for intercourse

PRIMEVAL   1
   2 Es   7 : 30   And the world shall be turned back to primeval silence for 7 days

PRINCE   16 = 0.010 %
   Jud   5 : 2   So he called together all the princes of Moab
     9 : 3   and thou didst strike down slaves along with princes
     9 : 3   and princes on their thrones
     9 : 10   with the prince and the prince with his servant
   Sir   41 : 17   and of a lie, before a prince or a ruler
   Bar   1 : 4   and in the hearing of the mighty men and the princes
     1 : 9   Jeconiah and the princes and the prisoners
     1 : 16   and to our kings and our princes and our priests
     2 : 1   and against our kings and against our princes
     3 : 16   Where are the princes of the nations
   P Az   15   And at this time there is no prince, or prophet
   1 Ma   1 : 4   and ruled over countries, nations, and princes
     7 : 26   Then the king sent Nicanor, one of his honoured princes
   2 Ma   9 : 25   Moreover, I understand how the princes along the borders
   2 Es   9 : 3   wavering of leaders, confusion of princes

PRINCIPAL   4 = 0.003 %
   2 Ma   10 : 10   of the principal calamities of the wars
   1 Es   1 : 32   and the principal men, with the women
     8 : 28   These are the principal men
     8 : 68   the principal men came to me and said

PRINCIPLE   4 = 0.003 %
   4 Ma   1 : 12   I shall begin by stating my main principle
     5 : 38   but you shall not dominate my religious principles
     11 : 15   we ought likewise to die for the same principles
     18 : 6   expressed also these principles to her children :

PRIOR   1
   Wis   19 : 13   without prior signs in the violence of thunder

PRISON   5 = 0.003 %
   Wis   10 : 14   and when he was in prison she did not leave him
     17 : 16   and thus was kept shut up in a prison not made of iron
   2 Ma   13 : 21   he was sought for, caught, and put in prison
   1 Es   1 : 38   Jehoiakim put the nobles in prison
   4 Ma   18 : 11   and of Joseph in prison

PRISONER   4 = 0.003 %
   Wis   17 : 2   and prisoners of long night, shut in under their roofs
   Bar   1 : 9   Jeconiah and the princes and the prisoners
   2 Ma   14 : 27   as a prisoner without delay
     14 : 33   If you do not hand Judas over to me as a prisoner

PRIVATE   4 = 0.003 %
   2 Ma   4 : 5   but having in view the welfare, both public and private, of all the people
     9 : 26   the public and private services rendered to you
   4 Ma   4 : 3   there are deposited tens of thousands in private funds
     4 : 6   to seize the private funds in the treasury

PRIVATELY   4 = 0.003 %
   Tob   12 : 6   Then the angel called the 2 of them privately
   2 Ma   6 : 21   and privately urged him to bring meat of his own providing
     13 : 13   After consulting privately with the elders
   3 Ma   3 : 10   had taken some of them aside privately

PRIZE, subst.   5 = 0.003 %
   Wis   2 : 22   nor discern the prize for blameless souls
     4 : 2   victor in the contest for prizes that are undefiled
   4 Ma   9 : 8   shall have the prize of virtue and shall be with God
     15 : 29   who carried away the prize of the contest in your heart !
     17 : 12   The prize was immortality in endless life

PRIZE, verb   2
   Sir   45 : 12   a distinction to be prized, the work of an expert
   2 Ma   4 : 15   disdaining the honours prized by their fathers

PROBABLY   1
   2 Es   7 : 140   there would probably be left only very few

PROBLEM   1
   2 Es   4 : 3   and to put before you 3 problems

PROCEED   7 = 0.005 %
   Tob   6 : 1   Now as they proceeded on their way
   Jud   11 : 15   When the word reaches them and they proceed to do this
   1 Ma   15 : 4   so that I may proceed
   2 Ma   4 : 21   Therefore upon arriving at Joppa he proceeded to Jerusalem
   3 Ma   5 : 4   proceeded faithfully to carry out the orders

   2 Es   14 : 37   and we proceeded to the field
   4 Ma   4 : 5   he proceeded quickly to our country

PROCEEDING   2
   2 Ma   4 : 14   they hastened to take part in the unlawful proceedings
   1 Es   2 : 29   and that such wicked proceedings go no further

PROCEEDS   1
   Tob   1 : 7   and I would go and spend the proceeds

PROCESS   1
   1 Es   6 : 20   and although it has been in process of construction

PROCESSION   2
   1 Ma   9 : 39   and saw a tumultuous procession with much baggage
   2 Ma   6 : 7   they were compelled to walk in the procession

PROCLAIM   12 = 0.008 %
   Sir   17 : 10   to proclaim the grandeur of his works
     18 : 4   to proclaim his works
     39 : 10   and the congregation will proclaim his praise
     44 : 3   and proclaiming prophecies
     44 : 15   and the congregation proclaims their praise
   1 Ma   10 : 63   and proclaim that no one is to bring charges against him
     14 : 28   the following was proclaimed to us :
   2 Ma   8 : 36   proclaimed that the Jews had a Defender
     9 : 17   to proclaim the power of God
   1 Es   8 : 50   There I proclaimed a fast for the young men before our Lord
   2 Es   2 : 32   and proclaim mercy to them
   4 Ma   17 : 23   proclaimed them to his soldiers

PROCLAMATION   5 = 0.003 %
   Sir   43 : 2   making proclamation as it goes forth
   1 Ma   5 : 49   Then Judas ordered proclamation to be made to the army
     10 : 64   in accordance with the proclamation
   1 Es   2 : 2   and he made a proclamation throughout all his kingdom
     9 : 3   And a proclamation was made throughout Judea and Jerusalem

PRODUCE, verb   11 = 0.007 %
   Wis   19 : 10   how instead of producing animals
   2 Es   3 : 12   they produced children and peoples and many nations
     4 : 30   and how much ungodliness it has produced until now
     4 : 30   and will produce until the time of threshing comes !
     4 : 31   how much fruit of ungodliness a grain of evil seed has produced
     5 : 46   Request it therefore to produce 10 at one time
     6 : 48   The dumb and lifeless water produced living creatures
     7 : 55   Say to her, You produce gold and silver and brass
     7 : 116   that it would have been better if the earth had not produced Adam
     7 : 116   or else, when it had produced him, had restrained him from sinning
     8 : 6   so that fruit may be produced

PRODUCE, subst.   6 = 0.004 %
   Tob   1 : 6   Taking the first fruits and the tithes of my produce
     1 : 7   Of all my produce I would give a tenth to the sons of Levi
     5 : 13   and the tithes of our produce
   Sir   1 : 17   and their storehouses with her produce
     6 : 19   and soon you will eat of her produce
     24 : 19   and eat your fill of my produce

PRODUCT   4 = 0.003 %
   Tob   2 : 12   She used to send the product to the owners
   Sir   11 : 3   but her product is the best of sweet things
     14 : 19   Every product decays and ceases to exist
   2 Es   9 : 17   and as is the work, so is the product

PRODUCTION   1
   Wis   16 : 26   might learn that it is not the production of crops that feeds man

PROFANATION   3 = 0.002 %
   Jud   4 : 3   had been consecrated after their profanation
   3 Ma   1 : 29   to the profanation of the place
     2 : 17   or call us to account for this profanation

PROFANE, verb   14 = 0.009 %
   Jud   4 : 12   and the sanctuary to be profaned and desecrated
   1 Ma   1 : 43   they sacrificed to idols and profaned the sabbath
     1 : 45   to profane sabbaths and feasts
     1 : 63   or to profane the holy covenant
     2 : 12   the Gentiles have profaned it
     2 : 34   and so profane the sabbath day
     3 : 51   Thy sanctuary is trampled down and profaned
     4 : 38   And they saw the sanctuary desolate, the altar profaned
     4 : 44   about the altar of burnt offering, which had been profaned
     4 : 54   and on the very day that the Gentiles had profaned it
   2 Ma   8 : 2   which had been profaned by ungodly men
     10 : 5   on which the sanctuary had been profaned by the foreigners

2 Es **10**:22   and the name by which we are called has been profaned
4 Ma **7**:6   you neither defiled your sacred teeth nor profaned your stomach

PROFANE, adj.   8 = 0.005 %
Sir **18**:3   the holy things from the profane
1 Ma **1**:48   by everything unclean and profane
2 Ma **5**:16   and swept away with profane hands
     15:32   and that profane man's arm
3 Ma **2**:2   who are suffering grievously from an impious and profane man
     2:14   In our downfall this audacious and profane man
     4:16   with a mind alienated from truth and with a profane mouth
4 Ma **12**:11   he said, You profane tyrant, most impious of all the wicked

PROFANELY   1
3 Ma **1**:21   because of what the king was profanely plotting

PROFANER   1
3 Ma **7**:15   since they had destroyed the profaners

PROFESS   2
Wis **2**:13   He professes to have knowledge of God
Sir **3**:25   if you lack knowledge do not profess to have it

PROFICIENCY   1
Sir pr.   and after acquiring considerable proficiency in them

PROFIT, subst.   4 = 0.003 %
Wis **15**:12   and life a festival held for profit
Sir **30**:23   for sorrow has destroyed many, and there is no profit in it
     42:5   of profit from dealing with merchants
2 Es **16**:42   who will not make a profit

PROFIT, verb   8 = 0.005 %
Wis **5**:8   What has our arrogance profited us ?
     6:25   Therefore be instructed by my words, and you will profit
Sir **20**:10   There is a gift that profits you nothing
     20:14   A fool's gift will profit you nothing
     29:11   and it will profit you more than gold
     30:2   He who disciplines his son will profit by him
2 Ma **2**:25   and to profit all readers
2 Es **7**:67   For what does it profit us

PROFITABLE   2
Wis **8**:7   nothing in life is more profitable for men than these
Sir **7**:22   if they are profitable to you, keep them

PROFITLESS   1
4 Ma **16**:7   O 7 childbirths all in vain, 7 profitless pregnancies

PROFOUND   3 = 0.002 %
2 Es **7**:85   are guarded by angels in profound quiet
     7:95   and guarded by angels in profound quiet
4 Ma **3**:20   At a time when our fathers were enjoying profound peace

PROFOUNDLY   1
2 Es **10**:50   seeing that you are sincerely grieved and profoundly distressed for her

PROGRESS, subst.   2
Sir pr.   those who love learning should make even greater progress
     51:17   I made progress therein

PROGRESS, verb   1
2 Ma **4**:3   When his hatred progressed to such a degree

PROLIFIC   1
Wis **4**:3   But the prolific brood of the ungodly will be of no use

PROLONG   1
Sir **37**:31   but he who is careful to avoid it prolongs his life

PROLONGED   1
Wis **4**:16   will condemn the prolonged old age of the unrighteous man

PROMINENT   1
2 Ma **3**:11   a man of very prominent position

PROMISE, subst.   6 = 0.004 %
Wis **12**:21   and covenants full of good promises !
Sir **20**:23   A man may for shame make promises to a friend
1 Ma **10**:15   Now Alexander the king heard of all the promises
2 Ma **12**:25   he had confirmed his solemn promise to restore them unharmed
2 Es **5**:29   And those who opposed thy promises have trodden down
4 Ma **15**:3   according to God's promise

PROMISE, verb   31 = 0.020 %
Jud **8**:9   and how he promised them under oath
     8:11   promising to surrender the city to our enemies
     8:30   and they compelled us to do for them what we have promised
     8:33   and within the days after which you have promised

Ad E **14**:5   and that thou didst do for them all that thou didst promise
Wis **17**:8   For those who promised to drive off the fears
P Az   13   to whom thou didst promise to make their descendants
1 Ma **10**:24   and promise them honour and gifts
     11:28   and promised him 300 talents
     11:53   But he broke his word about all that he had promised
2 Ma **2**:18   as he promised through the law
     4:8   promising the king at an interview 360 talents of silver
     4:9   In addition to this he promised to pay 150 more
     4:27   any of the money promised to the king
     4:45   promised a substantial bribe to Ptolemy son of Dorymenes
     7:24   but promised with oaths
     8:11   and promising to hand over 90 slaves for a talent
     11:14   promising that he would persuade the king
     12:11   promising to give him cattle
1 Es **1**:7   these were given from the king's possessions, as he promised
P Ma   7   hast promised repentance and forgiveness
3 Ma **1**:4   promising to give them each 2 minas of gold
     2:10   you promised that if we should have reverses
2 Es **3**:15   and promise him that thou wouldst never forsake his descendants
     4:27   that have been promised to the righteous
     5:40   or the goal of the love that I have promised my people
     7:60   So also will be the judgment which I have promised
     7:66   promised to them after death
     7:119   if an eternal age has been promised to us
     7:120   that an everlasting hope has been promised us
4 Ma **15**:2   as the tyrant had promised

PROMISED   1
P Ma   6   yet immeasurable and unsearchable is thy promised mercy

PROMOTE   1
2 Ma **11**:19   I will endeavour for the future to help promote your welfare

PROMPTLY   5 = 0.003 %
Sir **18**:22   Let nothing hinder you from paying a vow promptly
     29:2   and in turn, repay your neighbour promptly
2 Ma **8**:9   And Ptolemy promptly appointed Nicanor the son of Patroclus
     11:36   as soon as you have considered them, send some one promptly
3 Ma **3**:1   and he ordered that all should promptly be gathered into one place

PRONOUNCE   4 = 0.003 %
Jud **8**:11   and pronounced this oath between God and you
Wis **9**:3   and pronounce judgment in uprightness of soul
Sir **50**:20   to pronounce the blessing of the Lord with his lips
Sus **13**:53   pronouncing unjust judgments

PROPER   13 = 0.008 %
Sir **10**:23   nor is it proper to honour a sinful man
     20:20   for he does not tell it at its proper time
     41:23   Then you will show proper shame
1 Ma **12**:11   as it is right and proper to remember brethren
2 Ma **6**:21   proper for him to use
     8:33   so these received the proper recompense for their impiety
     14:22   they held the proper conference
1 Es **5**:50   and they offered sacrifices at the proper times
     5:51   and offered the proper sacrifices every day
3 Ma **1**:19   and, neglecting proper modesty
     3:20   accommodated ourselves to their folly and did as was proper
4 Ma **5**:24   so that with proper reverence we worship the only real God
     17:8   Indeed it would be proper

PROPERLY   3 = 0.002 %
Tob **14**:10   Bury me properly, and your mother with me
1 Es **1**:10   properly arrayed and having the unleavened bread
4 Ma **6**:33   we properly attribute to it the power to govern

PROPERTY   20 = 0.013 %
Tob **1**:20   Then all my property was confiscated
     8:21   that then he should take half of Raguel's property
     10:10   and half of his property in slaves, cattle, and money
     14:13   He inherited their property and that of his father Tobit
Jud **16**:24   Before she died she distributed her property
Sir **14**:3   and of what use is property to an envious man ?
     28:24   See that you fence in your property with thorns
     33:19   and do not give your property to another
     34:20   from the property of the poor
     36:25   Where there is no fence, the property will be plundered
     46:19   and his anointed : I have not taken any one property
1 Ma **10**:43   let him be released and receive back all his property in my kingdom
     12:23   that your cattle and your property belong to us
     15:33   nor seized foreign property
2 Ma **8**:14   Others sold all their remaining property
1 Es **6**:32   and his property should be forfeited to the king
3 Ma **3**:28   will receive the property of the one who incurs the punishment
     7:22   Besides they all recovered all of their property

4 Ma	2 : 14	but one preserves the property of enemies from the destroyers
	4 : 3	which are not the property of the temple

PROPHECY 8 = 0.005 %

Tob	2 : 6	Then I remembered the prophecy of Amos
Sir	pr.	the prophecies, and the rest of the books
	24 : 33	I will again pour out teaching like prophecy
	36 : 15	and fulfil the prophecies spoken in thy name
	39 : 1	and will be concerned with prophecies
	44 : 3	and proclaiming prophecies
	46 : 20	and lifted up his voice out of the earth in prophecy
2 Es	15 : 1	speak in the ears of my people the words of the prophecy

PROPHESY 9 = 0.006 %

Jud	6 : 2	to prophesy among us as you have done today
Wis	14 : 28	or prophesy lies, or live unrighteously
Sir	46 : 1	and was the successor of Moses in prophesying
	46 : 20	he prophesied and revealed to the king his death
	47 : 1	to prophesy in the days of David
	48 : 13	and when he was dead his body prophesied
1 Es	6 : 1	prophesied to the Jews who were in Judea and Jerusalem
	6 : 1	they prophesied to them in the name of the Lord God of Israel
	7 : 3	while the prophets Haggai and Zechariah prophesied

PROPHET 48 = 0.031 %

Tob	4 : 12	for we are the sons of the prophets
	14 : 4	for I fully believe what Jonah the prophet said
	14 : 5	just as the prophets said of it
	14 : 8	because what the prophet Jonah said will surely happen
Wis	7 : 27	and makes them friends of God, and prophets
	11 : 1	Wisdom prospered their works by the hand of a holy prophet
Sir	pr.	through the law and the prophets
	pr.	especially to the reading of the law and the prophets
	36 : 16	and let thy prophets be found trustworthy
	46 : 13	Samuel, beloved by his Lord, prophet of the Lord
	46 : 15	By his faithfulness he was proved to be a prophet
	48 : 1	Then the prophet Elijah arose like a fire
	48 : 8	and prophets to succeed you
	48 : 22	which Isaiah the prophet commanded
	49 : 7	yet he had been consecrated in the womb as prophet
	49 : 10	May the bones of the 12 prophets
Bar	1 : 16	and our prophets and our fathers
	1 : 21	in all the words of the prophets whom he sent to us
	2 : 20	as thou didst declare by thy servants the prophets, saying :
	2 : 24	which thou didst speak by thy servants the prophets
P Az	15	And at this time there is no prince, or prophet
Bel	14 : 33	Now the prophet Habakkuk was in Judea
1 Ma	4 : 46	on the temple hill until there should come a prophet
	9 : 27	since the time that prophets ceased to appear among them
	9 : 54	He tore down the work of the prophets !
	14 : 41	until a trustworthy prophet should arise
2 Ma	2 : 1	One finds in the records that Jeremiah the prophet
	2 : 2	and that the prophet after giving them the law
	2 : 4	that the prophet, having received an oracle
	2 : 13	and collected the books of the kings and prophets
	15 : 9	Encouraging them from the law and the prophets
	15 : 14	Jeremiah, the prophet of God
1 Es	1 : 20	since the times of Samuel the prophet
	1 : 28	and did not heed the words of Jeremiah the prophet
	1 : 32	Jeremiah the prophet lamented for Josiah
	1 : 47	that were spoken by Jeremiah the prophet from the mouth of the Lord
	1 : 51	and whenever the Lord spoke, they scoffed at his prophets
	6 : 1	the prophets Haggai and Zechariah the son of Iddo
	6 : 2	with the help of the prophets of the Lord who were with them
	7 : 3	while the prophets Haggai and Zechariah prophesied
	8 : 82	which thou didst give by thy servants the prophets, saying
2 Es	1 : 1	The 2nd book of the prophet Ezra the son of Seraiah
	1 : 32	I sent to you my servants the prophets
	1 : 36	They have seen no prophets
	2 : 1	and I gave them commandments through my servants the prophets
	7 : 130	But they did not believe him, or the prophets after him
	12 : 42	For of all the prophets you alone are left to us
4 Ma	18 : 10	he taught you the law and the prophets

PROPITIATE 3 = 0.002 %

Sir	16 : 7	He was not propitiated for the ancient giants
	34 : 19	and he is not propitiated for sins
4 Ma	4 : 11	to pray for him and propitiate the wrath of the heavenly army

PROPITIATION 1

Wis	18 : 21	prayer and propitiation by incense

PROPORTION 5 = 0.003 %

Tob	4 : 8	make your gift from them in proportion
Sir	28 : 10	In proportion to the fuel for the fire
	28 : 10	and in proportion to the obstinacy of strife

	28 : 10	in proportion to the strength of the man will be his anger
	28 : 10	and in proportion to his wealth he will heighten his wrath

PROPOSAL 4 = 0.003 %

Tob	7 : 9	So he communicated the proposal to Raguel
1 Ma	1 : 12	This proposal pleased them
	8 : 21	The proposal pleased them
2 Ma	11 : 36	so that we may make proposals appropriate for you

PROPOSE 3 = 0.002 %

3 Ma	2 : 27	He proposed to inflict public disgrace
	3 : 17	because when we proposed
2 Es	7 : 23	and proposed to themselves wicked frauds

PROSPER 19 = 0.012 %

Tob	4 : 6	your ways will prosper through your deeds
	4 : 19	and that all your paths and plans may prosper
	5 : 16	God who dwells in heaven will prosper your way
	10 : 11	The God of heaven will prosper you, my children, before I die
Jud	5 : 9	There they settled, and prospered
	5 : 17	As long as they did not sin against their God they prospered
Wis	10 : 10	she prospered him in his labours
	11 : 1	Wisdom prospered their works by the hand of a holy prophet
Sir	12 : 9	A man's enemies are grieved when he prospers
	15 : 10	and the Lord will prosper it
1 Ma	2 : 47	and the work prospered in their hands
	3 : 6	and deliverance prospered by his hand
	4 : 55	and worshipped and blessed Heaven, who had prospered them
	14 : 36	And in his days things prospered in his hands
	16 : 2	and things have prospered in our hands
1 Es	6 : 10	and the work is prospering in their hands
	7 : 3	And the holy work prospered
2 Es	5 : 12	they shall labour but their ways shall not prosper
4 Ma	3 : 20	and were prospering, so that even Seleucus Nicanor, king of Asia

PROSPERITY 13 = 0.008 %

Ad E	16 : 3	but in their inability to stand prosperity
Sir	6 : 11	In your prosperity he will make himself your equal
	11 : 23	and what prosperity could be mine in the future ?
	11 : 25	In the day of prosperity, adversity is forgotten
	11 : 25	and in the day of adversity, prosperity is not remembered
	12 : 8	A friend will not be known in prosperity
	22 : 23	that you may rejoice with him in his prosperity
	29 : 16	A sinner will overthrow the prosperity of his surety
	31 : 11	His prosperity will be established
	44 : 11	their prosperity will remain with their descendants
	45 : 26	so that their prosperity may not vanish
2 Ma	9 : 19	and good wishes for their health and prosperity
	14 : 14	would mean prosperity for themselves

PROSPEROUS 5 = 0.003 %

Wis	13 : 18	for a prosperous journey, a thing that cannot take a step
Sir	29 : 18	Being surety has ruined many men who were prosperous
	41 : 1	who is prosperous in everything
1 Es	8 : 6	by the prosperous journey which the Lord gave them
	8 : 50	to seek from him a prosperous journey for ourselves

PROSTRATE, verb 5 = 0.003 %

Jud	4 : 11	prostrated themselves before the temple
	10 : 23	and she prostrated herself and made obeisance to him
2 Ma	3 : 15	The priests prostrated themselves before the altar
3 Ma	1 : 16	Then the priests in all their vestments prostrated themselves
	5 : 50	they prostrated themselves with one accord on the ground

PROSTRATE, adj. 5 = 0.003 %

Jud	3 : 2	lie prostrate before you
	10 : 2	she rose from where she lay prostrate
2 Ma	3 : 29	While he lay prostrate
	10 : 4	they fell prostrate and besought the Lord
	13 : 12	and lying prostrate for 3 days without ceasing

PROSTRATION 1

2 Ma	3 : 21	in the prostration of the whole populace

PROTECT 23 = 0.015 %

Jud	5 : 21	and their God will protect them
	8 : 15	he has power to protect us within any time he pleases
	9 : 14	who protects the people of Israel but thou alone !
	13 : 16	As the Lord lives, who has protected me in the way I went
Wis	2 : 20	for, according to what he says, he will be protected
	10 : 1	Wisdom protected the first-formed father of the world
	10 : 12	She protected him from his enemies
	17 : 4	protected them from fear
	19 : 8	where those protected by thy hand passed through as one nation
Sir	22 : 25	I will not be ashamed to protect a friend
	28 : 19	Happy is the man who is protected from it
L Jr	6 : 59	better even the door of a house that protects its contents
1 Ma	3 : 3	protecting the host by his sword
	6 : 38	while being themselves protected by the phalanxes
2 Ma	10 : 30	surrounding Maccabeus and protecting him

	13:17	because the Lord's help protected him
3 Ma	**3**:10	and were pledging to protect them
2 Es	**2**:21	do not ridicule a lame man, protect the maimed
	2:22	Protect the old and the young within your walls
	13:23	will himself protect those who fall into peril
4 Ma	**6**:21	and not protect our divine law even to death
	9:15	but because I protect the divine law
	14:15	protect their young by building on the housetops

PROTECTION   9 = 0.006 %

Sir	**6**:29	Then her fetters will become for you a strong protection
	34:16	a mighty protection and strong support
Bar	**1**:12	and we shall live under the protection of Nebuchadnezzar king of Babylon
	1:12	and under the protection of Belshazzar his son
1 Ma	**11**:16	So Alexander fled into Arabia to find protection there
2 Ma	**3**:40	and the protection of the treasury
	5:9	in hope of finding protection because of their kinship
3 Ma	**5**:42	which had come about within him for the protection of the Jews
2 Es	**1**:15	I gave you camps for your protection

PROTECTOR   5 = 0.003 %

Jud	**9**:11	upholder of the weak, protector of the forlorn
Sir	**51**:2	for thou hast been my protector and helper
1 Ma	**14**:47	and to be protector of them all
2 Ma	**4**:2	the protector of his fellow countrymen
3 Ma	**6**:9	all-merciful and protector of all

PROTEST   1

4 Ma	**4**:7	The people indignantly protested his words

PROUD, adj., subst.   16 = 0.010 %

Ad E	**13**:12	and refused to bow down to this proud Haman
	14:16	that I abhor the sign of my proud position
	16:2	the more proud do many men become
Sir	**3**:28	The affliction of the proud has no healing
	10:9	How can he who is dust and ashes be proud?
	11:30	so is the mind of a proud man
	13:1	and whoever associates with a proud man will become like him
	13:20	Humility is an abomination to a proud man
	21:4	thus the house of the proud will be laid waste
	25:2	a beggar who is proud, a rich man who is a liar
	27:15	The strife of the proud leads to bloodshed
	27:28	Mockery and abuse issue from the proud man
	31:26	so wine tests hearts in the strife of the proud
	32:12	but do not sin through proud speech
	32:18	and an insolent and proud man will not cower in fear
	51:10	at the time when there is no help against the proud

PROVE   19 = 0.012 %

Tob	**10**:4	his long delay proves it
Wis	**2**:11	for what is weak proves itself to be useless
	12:13	to whom thou shouldst prove
Sir	**9**:17	so a people's leader is proved wise by his words
	31:26	Fire and water prove the temper of steel
	39:34	for all things will prove good in their season
	42:10	or having a husband, lest she prove unfaithful
	46:15	By his faithfulness he was proved to be a prophet
Bel	**14**:9	But if you prove that Bel is eating them, Daniel shall die
2 Ma	**5**:4	that the apparition might prove to have been a good omen
	7:29	Do not fear this butcher, but prove worthy of your brothers
1 Es	**5**:37	though they could not prove by their fathers' houses or lineage
3 Ma	**4**:20	when they said and proved
4 Ma	**1**:7	I could prove to you from many and various examples
	2:4	Not only is reason proved to rule
	2:6	I could prove to you all the more
	6:35	And I have proved not only that reason has mastered agonies
	14:4	None of the 7 youths proved coward or shrank from death
	16:14	and in word and deed you have proved more powerful than a man

PROVERB   8 = 0.005 %

Sir	**6**:35	and do not let wise proverbs escape you
	13:26	but to devise proverbs requires painful thinking
	18:29	and pour forth apt proverbs
	20:20	A proverb from a fool's lips will be rejected
	38:33	and they are not found using proverbs
	39:3	he will seek out the hidden meanings of proverbs
	47:17	For your songs and proverbs and parables
4 Ma	**18**:16	He recounted to you Solomon's proverb

PROVIDE   23 = 0.015 %

Jud	**12**:2	but I will be provided
Wis	**16**:20	with bread ready to eat, providing every pleasure
	18:3	Therefore thou didst provide a flaming pillar of fire
Sir	**23**:22	and provides an heir by a stranger
	29:25	you will play the host and provide drink
1 Ma	**12**:4	in every place, asking them to provide for the envoys
	14:34	He settled Jews there, and provided in those cities
2 Ma	**4**:49	provided magnificently for their funeral

	6:21	and privately urged him to bring meat of his own providing
	9:16	he would provide from his own revenues
	12:3	on boats which they had provided
	12:43	and sent it to Jerusalem to provide for a sin offering
1 Es	**4**:55	He wrote that the support for the Levites should be provided
	4:56	He wrote that land and wages should be provided
	8:18	you may provide out of the royal treasury
3 Ma	**6**:30	and ordered him to provide to the Jews
	6:40	Then they feasted, provided with everything by the king
	7:18	for the king had generously provided
2 Es	**1**:14	I provided light for you from a pillar of fire
	5:26	thou hast provided for thyself one sheep
	8:2	it will tell you that it provides very much clay
	8:52	the age to come is prepared, plenty is provided
4 Ma	**3**:2	but reason can provide a way for us

PROVIDENCE   8 = 0.005 %

Wis	**14**:3	but it is thy providence, O Father, that steers its course
	17:2	exiles from eternal providence
1 Es	**6**:5	for the providence of the Lord was over the captives
3 Ma	**4**:21	But this was an act of the invincible providence
	5:30	because by the providence of God
4 Ma	**9**:24	Thereby the just Providence of our ancestors
	13:19	which the divine all-wise Providence
	17:22	divine Providence preserved Israel

PROVINCE   9 = 0.006 %

Ad E	**13**:1	to the rulers of the 127 provinces
	16:1	to the rulers of the provinces from India to Ethiopia, 127 satrapies
1 Ma	**3**:37	and went through the upper provinces
	6:1	King Antiochus was going through the upper provinces
	7:8	governor of the province Beyond the River
	8:7	and surrender some of their best provinces
	10:65	and made him general and governor of the province
2 Ma	**9**:25	when I hastened off to the upper provinces
2 Es	**1**:11	and scattered in the east the people of 2 provinces, Tyre and Sidon

PROVISION, subst.   7 = 0.005 %

Tob	**1**:13	and I was his buyer of provisions
Jud	**2**:17	and innumerable sheep and oxen and goats for provision
Bel	**14**:8	If you do not tell me who is eating these provisions, you shall die
	14:13	and consume the provisions
1 Ma	**6**:49	because they had no provisions there to withstand a siege
2 Ma	**12**:14	and on their supply of provisions
2 Es	**16**:21	Behold, provisions will be so cheap upon earth

PROVOCATION   1

Sir	**31**:29	with provocation and stumbling

PROVOKE   7 = 0.005 %

Jud	**8**:14	No, my brethren, do not provoke the Lord our God to anger
	11:11	by which they are about to provoke their God to anger
Bar	**4**:7	For you provoked him who made you
1 Ma	**15**:40	and began to provoke the people and invade Judea
2 Ma	**14**:27	and, provoked by the false accusations of that depraved man
1 Es	**6**:15	who is in heaven, and provoked him
P Ma	**10**	for I have provoked thy wrath

PRUDENCE   3 = 0.002 %

Wis	**8**:7	for she teaches self-control and prudence, justice and courage
Sir	**19**:22	nor is there prudence where sinners take counsel
	22:27	and a seal of prudence upon my lips

PRUDENT   4 = 0.003 %

Sir	**1**:4	and prudent understanding from eternity
	19:24	than the highly prudent man who transgresses the law
	21:25	but the words of the prudent will be weighed in the balance
4 Ma	**7**:17	because not every one has prudent reason

PRUNE   2

2 Es	**16**:43	so also him that prunes the vines
4 Ma	**1**:29	each of which the master cultivator, reason, weeds and prunes

PRY   1

4 Ma	**10**:5	dismembering him by prying his limbs from their sockets

PSALM   2

Jud	**16**:2	Raise to him a new psalm
3 Ma	**6**:35	to the accompaniment of joyous thanksgiving and psalms

PSALMIST   1

4 Ma	**18**:15	He sang to you songs of the psalmist David, who said

PTOLEMAIC   1

3 Ma	**1**:2	took with him the best of the Ptolemaic arms

PTOLEMAIS   20 = 0.013 %
1 Ma 5:15   men of Ptolemais and Tyre and Sidon
     5:22   He pursued them to the gate of Ptolemais
     5:55   and Simon his brother was in Galilee before Ptolemais
    10:1   landed and occupied Ptolemais
    10:39   Ptolemais and the land adjoining it
    10:56   but meet me at Ptolemais, so that we may see one another
    10:57   and came to Ptolemais in the 162nd year
    10:58   and celebrated her wedding at Ptolemais with great pomp, as kings do
    10:60   So he went with pomp to Ptolemais and met the 2 kings
    11:22   he set out and came to Ptolemais
    11:22   but to meet him for a conference at Ptolemais
    11:24   for he went to the king at Ptolemais
    12:45   and come with me to Ptolemais
    12:48   But when Jonathan entered Ptolemais
    12:48   the men of Ptolemais closed the gates and seized him
    13:12   Trypho departed from Ptolemais with a large army
2 Ma 13:24   left Hegemonides as governor from Ptolemais to Gerar
    13:25   and went to Ptolemais
    13:25   The people of Ptolemais were indignant over the treaty
3 Ma 7:17   When they had arrived at Ptolemais, called rose-bearing

PTOLEMY   34 = 0.022 %
Ad E 11:1   In the 4th year of the reign of Ptolemy and Cleopatra
    11:1   and Ptolemy his son brought to Egypt the preceding Letter of Purim
    11:1   and had been translated by Lysimachus the son of Ptolemy
1 Ma 1:18   He engaged Ptolemy king of Egypt in battle
     1:18   and Ptolemy turned and fled before him
     3:38   Lysias chose Ptolemy the son of Dorymenes
    10:51   Then Alexander sent ambassadors to Ptolemy king of Egypt
    10:55   Ptolemy the king replied and said
    10:57   So Ptolemy set out from Egypt
    10:58   and Ptolemy gave him Cleopatra his daughter in marriage
    11:3   But when Ptolemy entered the cities
    11:8   So King Ptolemy gained control of the coastal cities
    11:13   Then Ptolemy entered Antioch and put on the crown of Asia
    11:15   Ptolemy marched out and met him with a strong force
    11:16   and King Ptolemy was exalted
    11:17   and sent it to Ptolemy
    11:18   But King Ptolemy died 3 days later
    15:16   Lucius, consul of the Romans, to King Ptolemy, greeting
    16:11   Now Ptolemy the son of Abubus had been appointed governor
    16:16   Ptolemy and his men rose up, took their weapons
    16:18   Then Ptolemy wrote a report about these things
2 Ma 1:10   teacher of Ptolemy the king
     4:45   promised a substantial bribe to Ptolemy son of Dorymenes
     4:46   Therefore Ptolemy, taking the king aside into a colonnade
     6:8   At the suggestion of Ptolemy
     8:8   he wrote to Ptolemy
     8:9   And Ptolemy promptly appointed Nicanor the son of Patroclus
     9:29   he betook himself to Ptolemy Philometor in Egypt
    10:12   Ptolemy, who was called Macron
3 Ma 1:2   and crossed over by night to the tent of Ptolemy
     1:6   Ptolemy decided to visit the neighbouring cities
     3:12   King Ptolemy Philopator to his generals and soldiers
     7:1   King Ptolemy Philopator to the generals in Egypt
4 Ma 4:22   For when he was warring against Ptolemy in Egypt

PUBLIC, adj., subst.   25 = 0.016 %
Ad E 14:16   which is upon my head on the days when I appear in public
    16:5   with the administration of public affairs
Sir 7:7   Do not offend against the public
    38:33   nor do they attain eminence in the public assembly
1 Ma 14:22   we have recorded in our public decrees, as follows
    14:23   and to put a copy of their words in the public archives
2 Ma 4:5   but having in view the welfare, both public and private, of all the people
     4:6   public affairs could not again reach a peaceful settlement
     7:24   and entrust him with public affairs
     9:26   the public and private services rendered to you
    10:2   in the public square by the foreigners
    10:8   They decreed by public ordinance and vote
    12:4   and this was done by public vote of the city
    13:26   Lysias took the public platform
    15:6   had determined to erect a public monument of victory
    15:36   And they all decreed by public vote
3 Ma 2:27   He proposed to inflict public disgrace
     4:1   a feast at public expense was arranged for the Gentiles
     4:7   In bonds and in public view they were violently dragged along
     6:36   And when they had ordained a public rite for these things
     7:14   they punished and put to a public and shameful death
2 Es 14:26   some things you shall make public
    14:45   Make public the 24 books that you wrote first
    16:64   and will make a public spectacle of all of you
4 Ma 3:21   a revolution against the public harmony

PUBLICLY   4 = 0.003 %
Ad E 16:19   Therefore post a copy of this letter publicly in every place
2 Ma 4:33   he publicly exposed them
     6:10   These women they publicly paraded about the city
2 Es 2:36   I publicly call on my Saviour to witness

PUBLISH   2
Sir pr.   in order to complete and publish the book
2 Es 14:6   These words you shall publish openly

PUFF up   2
2 Ma 7:34   do not be elated in vain and puffed up by uncertain hopes
3 Ma 2:2   puffed up in his audacity and power

PULL down   3 = 0.002 %
Jud 13:9   and pulled down the canopy from the posts
1 Es 6:16   and they pulled down the house, and burned it
2 Es 16:76   do not let your sins pull you down

PULL out   3 = 0.002 %
Bel 14:42   And he pulled Daniel out
1 Es 8:71   and pulled out hair from my head and beard
2 Es 1:8   Pull out the hair of your head and hurl all evils upon them

PUNISH   43 = 0.028 %
Tob 3:3   do not punish me for my sins and for my unwitting offences
Jud 7:28   who punishes us according to our sins
    11:10   for it is true : our nation cannot be punished
Wis 1:8   and justice, when it punishes, will not pass him by
     3:4   For though in the sight of men they were punished
     3:10   But the ungodly will be punished as their reasoning deserves
    11:5   by which their enemies were punished
    11:8   how thou didst punish their enemies
    11:15   a multitude of irrational creatures to punish them
    11:16   that they might learn that one is punished
    12:14   about those whom thou hast punished
    12:15   who does not deserve to be punished
    12:20   For if thou didst punish with such great care and indulgence
    12:27   being punished by means of them
    14:10   for what was done will be punished
    16:1   Therefore those men were deservedly punished
    16:9   because they deserved to be punished by such things
    16:24   exerts itself to punish the unrighteous
    18:8   For by the same means by which thou didst punish our enemies
    18:11   The slave was punished with the same penalty as the master
Sir 2:14   What will you do when the Lord punishes you ?
     5:3   For the Lord will surely punish you
    23:21   This man will be punished in the streets of the city
    39:30   and the sword that punishes the ungodly with destruction
Bar 3:8   to be reproached and cursed and punished
1 Ma 7:7   and let him punish them and all who help them
    15:21   that he may punish them according to their law
2 Ma 4:16   became their enemies and punished them
     6:13   but to punish them immediately
     6:14   the Lord waits patiently to punish them
     7:7   rather than have your body punished limb by limb ?
1 Es 8:24   shall be strictly punished
3 Ma 2:17   Do not punish us for the defilement committed by these men
     2:24   After a while he recovered and, though he had been punished
     3:26   For when these all have been punished
     7:3   and to punish them with barbarous penalties as traitors
     7:14   they punished and put to a public and shameful death
2 Es 5:30   they should be punished at thy own hands
     9:13   as to how the ungodly will be punished
4 Ma 2:12   so that one punishes them for misdeeds
     8:6   Just as I am able to punish those who disobey my orders
    17:21   the tyrant was punished, and the homeland purified
    18:5   The tyrant Antiochus was both punished on earth

PUNISHER   1
Wis 18:22   but by his word he subdued the punisher

PUNISHMENT   35 = 0.023 %
Jud 2:10   till the day of their punishment
Ad E 16:18   has speedily inflicted on him the punishment he deserved
Wis 11:13   For when they heard that through their own punishments
    16:2   Instead of this punishment
    18:5   thou didst in punishment
    19:4   in order that they might fill up the punishment
    19:13   The punishment did not come upon the sinners
    19:15   but punishment of some sort will come upon the former
Sir 5:7   and at the time of punishment you will perish
     7:17   for the punishment of the ungodly is fire and worms
     8:5   remember that we all deserve punishment
    12:6   and will inflict punishment on the ungodly
    12:6   for the mighty day of their punishment
    23:24   and punishment will fall on her children
1 Ma 14:45   shall be liable to punishment
2 Ma 4:38   The Lord thus repaid him with the punishment he deserved
     6:12   but to recognize that these punishments were designed

	6:26	I should avoid the punishment of men
	7:36	will receive just punishment for your arrogance
1 Es	8:24	whether by death or some other punishment
3 Ma	2:6	by inflicting many and varied punishments
	2:23	seeing the severe punishment that had overtaken him
	3:28	will receive the property of the one who incurs the punishment
	4:4	that at the sight of their unusual punishments
	4:13	not omitting any detail of their punishment
	7:10	should receive the punishment they deserved
2 Es	7:21	and what they should observe to avoid punishment
	7:93	and the punishment that awaits them
	7:117	and expect punishment after death ?
	15:12	for the plague of chastisement and punishment
4 Ma	4:24	but saw that all his threats and punishments were being disregarded
	6:9	But he bore the pains and scorned the punishment
	6:28	and let our punishment suffice for them
	8:9	with dreadful punishments through tortures
	11:3	so that by murdering me you will incur punishment

PUNY   1
2 Es   11:3   but they became little, puny wings

PUPIL   1
4 Ma   18:21   pierced the pupils of their eyes and cut out their tongues

PURCHASE, verb   1
Jud   4:10   and purchased slave

PURE*   11 = 0.007 %

Tob	8:15	Blessed art thou, O God, with every pure and holy blessing
	13:16	and her towers and battlements with pure gold
Wis	7:23	that are intelligent and pure and most subtle
	7:25	and a pure emanation of the glory of the Almighty
	8:18	and in friendship with her, pure delight
	14:24	either their lives or their marriages pure
Bar	3:30	and will buy her for pure gold ?
2 Es	7:122	who have led a pure life
4 Ma	5:37	The fathers will receive me as pure
	18:7	I was a pure virgin and did not go outside my father's house
	18:23	and have received pure and immortal souls from God

PURENESS   1
Wis   7:24   because of her pureness

PURGE away   1
Tob   12:9   and it will purge away every sin

PURIFICATION   7 = 0.005 %

Sir	51:20	and through purification I found her
2 Ma	1:18	we shall celebrate the purification of the temple
	1:36	which means purification
	2:16	Since, therefore, we are about to celebrate the purification
	2:19	and the purification of the great temple
	10:5	the purification of the sanctuary took place
4 Ma	6:29	Make my blood their purification

PURIFY   11 = 0.007 %

Jud	16:18	As soon as the people were purified
2 Ma	2:18	and has purified the place
	10:3	They purified the sanctuary
	10:7	who had given success to the purifying of his own holy place
	12:38	they purified themselves according to the custom
	14:36	that has been so recently purified
1 Es	7:10	after the priests and the Levites were purified together
	7:11	Not all of the returned captives were purified
	7:11	but the Levites were all purified together
4 Ma	1:11	and thus their native land was purified through them
	17:21	the tyrant was punished, and the homeland purified

PURIM   1
Ad E   11:1   and Ptolemy his son brought to Egypt the preceding Letter of Purim

PURITY   4 = 0.003 %

1 Ma	14:36	and do great damage to its purity
2 Es	6:32	and has also observed the purity
4 Ma	7:6	which had room only for reverence and purity
	18:8	defile the purity of my virginity

PURPLE   15 = 0.010 %

Jud	10:21	under a canopy which was woven with purple and gold
Sir	40:4	from the man who wears purple and a crown
	45:10	with a holy garment, of gold and blue and purple
L Jr	6:12	When they have been dressed in purple robes
	6:72	By the purple and linen that rot upon them
1 Ma	4:23	and cloth dyed blue and sea purple, and great riches
	8:14	or worn purple as a mark of pride
	10:20	and he sent him a purple robe and a golden crown
	10:62	and to clothe him in purple, and they did so

	10:64	and saw him clothed in purple, they all fled
	11:58	and dress in purple and wear a gold buckle
	14:43	and that he should be clothed in purple and wear gold
	14:44	or to be clothed in purple or put on a gold buckle
2 Ma	4:38	he immediately stripped off the purple robe from Andronicus
1 Es	3:6	He shall be clothed in purple, and drink from gold cups

PURPOSE, subst.   19 = 0.012 %

Jud	8:16	Do not try to bind the purposes of the Lord our God
	11:6	and my lord will not fail to achieve his purposes
	11:11	and his purpose frustrated
Ad E	10:10	For this purpose he made 2 lots
	12:2	He overheard their conversation and inquired into their purposes
Wis	2:22	and they did not know the secret purposes of God
	6:4	nor keep the law, nor walk according to the purpose of God
Sir	22:18	so a timid heart with a fool's purpose
2 Ma	3:8	but in fact to carry out the king's purpose
	4:19	but to expend it for another purpose
	14:5	But he found an opportunity that furthered his mad purpose
3 Ma	1:22	or the fulfilment of his intended purpose
	2:26	intently observing the king's purpose
	3:11	constantly in his same purpose
	5:12	that he quite failed in his lawless purpose
	5:29	O king, according to your eager purpose
2 Es	8:14	to what purpose was he made ?
4 Ma	1:6	and it is not for the purpose of destroying them
	4:1	he fled the country with the purpose of betraying it

PURPOSE, verb   2
Wis   4:17   and will not understand what the Lord purposed for him
Bar   4:28   For just as you purposed to go astray from God

PURSE   1
Sir   18:33   when you have nothing in your purse

PURSUE   36 = 0.023 %

Jud	14:4	shall pursue them and cut them down as they flee
Wis	11:20	men could fall at a single breath when pursued by justice
	14:31	that always pursues the transgression of the unrighteous
	16:16	pursued by unusual rains and hail and relentless storms
	16:18	that they were being pursued by the judgment of God
	19:2	they would change their minds and pursue them
	19:3	and pursued as fugitives
Sir	11:10	and if you pursue you will not overtake
	14:22	Pursue wisdom like a hunter, and lie in wait on her paths
	27:8	If you pursue justice, you will attain it
	29:19	The sinner who has fallen into suretyship and pursues gain
	31:5	and he who pursues money will be led astray by it
	34:2	As one who catches at a shadow and pursues the wind
1 Ma	2:32	Many pursued them, and overtook them
	3:5	He searched out and pursued the lawless
	3:24	They pursued them down the descent of Beth-horon to the plain
	4:9	when Pharaoh with his forces pursued them
	4:15	They pursued them to Gazara
	4:16	Then Judas and his force turned back from pursuing them
	5:22	He pursued them to the gate of Ptolemais
	5:60	and were pursued to the borders of Judea
	7:45	The Jews pursued them a day's journey
	9:15	and he pursued them as far as Mount Azotus
	10:49	and Alexander pursued him and defeated them
	10:78	Jonathan pursued him to Azotus
	12:30	Then Jonathan pursued them, but he did not overtake them
	15:11	Antiochus pursued him, and he came in his flight to Dor
	15:39	but the king pursued Trypho
	16:9	but John pursued them
2 Ma	2:21	and pursued the barbarian hordes
	5:8	fleeing from city to city, pursued by all men
	8:25	After pursuing them for some distance
3 Ma	2:7	And when he pursued them with chariots and a mass of troops
2 Es	15:31	and turn to pursue them
4 Ma	18:22	For these crimes divine justice pursued and will pursue the accursed tyrant

PURSUER   3 = 0.002 %
Jud   16:3   for he has delivered me out of the hands of my pursuers
1 Ma   7:46   and drove them back to their pursuers
      12:51   When their pursuers saw

PURSUIT   3 = 0.002 %
1 Ma   11:73   they returned to him and joined him in the pursuit
2 Ma   8:26   and for that reason they did not continue their pursuit
      12:23   And Judas pressed the pursuit with the utmost vigour

PUSH   2
2 Ma   8:8   and that he was pushing ahead with more frequent successes
      13:6   There they all push to destruction

PUSH away   1
Sir   13:21   but when a humble man falls, he is even pushed away by friends

PUSH down   1
  Sir 13 : 23 And should he stumble, they even push him down

PUSH forward   1
  Sir 13 : 10 Do not push forward, lest you be repulsed

PUT, subst., prop. n.   1
  Jud 2 : 23 and ravaged Put and Lud

PUT, verb   119 = 0.078 %
  Tob 1 : 18 And if Sennacherib the king put to death
        1 : 18 For in his anger he put many to death
        1 : 19 to be put to death
        2 : 8 that he will be put to death for doing this
        8 : 2 and put the heart and liver of the fish upon them and made a smoke
  Jud 2 : 27 and put to death all their young men
        4 : 11 and put ashes on their heads
        5 : 21 and we shall be put to shame before the whole world
        5 : 22 and from Moab insisted that he must be put to death
        6 : 7 and put you in one of the cities beside the passes
        8 : 12 Who are you, that have put God to the test this day
        8 : 13 You are putting the Lord Almighty to the test
        8 : 25 who is putting us to the test as he did our forefathers
        9 : 1 and put ashes on her head
        9 : 2 and uncovered her thigh to put her to shame
        10 : 4 And she put sandals on her feet
  Ad E 14 : 13 Put eloquent speech in my mouth before the lion
        16 : 17 You will therefore do well not to put in execution
  Wis 1 : 2 because he is found by those who do not put him to the test
        8 : 12 they will put their hands on their mouths
        12 : 2 and put their trust in thee, O Lord
        14 : 4 so that even if a man lacks skill, he may put to sea
        18 : 21 he withstood the anger and put an end to the disaster
  Sir 2 : 10 and see : who ever trusted in the Lord and was put to shame ?
        5 : 12 but if not, put your hand on your mouth
        6 : 24 Put your feet into her fetters
        6 : 25 Put your shoulder under her and carry her
        7 : 6 and thus put a blot on your integrity
        12 : 12 Do not put him next to you, lest he overthrow you
        15 : 4 and he will rely on her and will not be put to shame
        24 : 22 Whoever obeys me will not be put to shame
        26 : 13 and her skill puts fat on his bones
        26 : 27 for putting the enemy to flight
        33 : 27 Put him to work, that he may not be idle
        34 : 7 and those who put their hope in them have failed
        42 : 11 and put you to shame before the great multitude
        45 : 7 and put a glorious robe upon him
        47 : 20 You put a stain upon your honour, and defiled your posterity
        51 : 18 and I shall never be put to shame
        51 : 26 Put your neck under the yoke
        51 : 29 and may you not be put to shame when you praise him
  Bar 3 : 7 For thou hast put the fear of thee in our hearts
        4 : 22 For I have put my hope in the Everlasting to save you
        5 : 2 put on your head the diadem of the glory of the Everlasting
  L Jr 6 : 39 and those who serve them will be put to shame
  P Az 19 Do not put us to shame
        20 Let all who do harm to thy servants be put to shame
  Sus 13 : 28 full of their wicked plot to have Susanna put to death
        13 : 45 And as she was being led away to be put to death
        13 : 53 Do not put to death an innocent and righteous person
        13 : 56 Then he put him aside, and commanded them to bring the other
        13 : 62 they put them to death
  Bel 14 : 22 Therefore the king put them to death
  1 Ma 1 : 2 and put to death the kings of the earth
        1 : 60 According to the decree, they put to death
        2 : 61 that none who put their trust in him will lack strength
        4 : 20 They saw that their army had been put to flight
        6 : 24 moreover, they have put to death
        9 : 25 and put them in charge of the country
        9 : 52 and in them he put troops and stores of food
        9 : 53 as hostages and put them under guard
        10 : 37 and let some of them be put in positions of trust in the kingdom
        10 : 72 for your fathers were twice put to flight in their own land
        10 : 77 for he had a large troop of cavalry and put confidence in it
        11 : 13 Thus he put 2 crowns upon his head
        11 : 15 and put him to flight
        11 : 23 and put himself in danger
        11 : 71 and put dust on his head, and prayed
        13 : 29 and upon the columns he put suits of armour
        14 : 3 who put him under guard
        14 : 23 and to put a copy of their words in the public archives
        14 : 27 and put it upon pillars on Mount Zion
        14 : 36 so that the Gentiles were put out of the country
        16 : 8 and Cendebaeus and his army were put to flight
  2 Ma 3 : 27 his men took him up and put him on a stretcher and carried him away
        4 : 15 and putting the highest value upon Greek forms of prestige
        4 : 34 he immediately put him out of the way
        4 : 42 and put them all to flight

        5 : 26 He put to the sword all those who came out to see them
        7 : 40 putting his whole trust in the Lord
        8 : 6 and put to flight not a few of the enemy
        8 : 22 each to command a division, putting 1,500 men under each
        9 : 2 with the result that Antiochus was put to flight by the inhabitants
        9 : 4 the injury done by those who had put him to flight
        12 : 23 putting the sinners to the sword
        12 : 37 and put them to flight
        13 : 4 and to put him to death
        13 : 21 he was sought for, caught, and put in prison
  1 Es 1 : 3 and put the holy ark of the Lord
        1 : 38 Jehoiakim put the nobles in prison
        2 : 2 and also put it in writing :
        3 : 8 and put them under the pillow of Darius the king
        4 : 30 and take the crown from the king's head and put it on her own
        6 : 19 and put them in the temple at Jerusalem
        8 : 25 who put this into the heart of the king
  3 Ma 2 : 7 those who had put their confidence in you
        2 : 20 and put praises in the mouth of those who are downcast
        2 : 28 Those who object to this are to be taken by force and put to death
        3 : 1 and put to death by the most cruel means
        6 : 32 Putting an end to all mourning and wailing
        7 : 5 to put them to death
        7 : 14 they punished and put to a public and shameful death
        7 : 15 In that day they put to death more than 300 men
  2 Es 2 : 46 and puts palms in their hands ?
        4 : 3 and to put before you 3 problems
        8 : 30 but love those who have always put their trust in thy glory
        12 : 37 and put it in a hidden place
        15 : 1 which I will put in your mouth
        16 : 60 who has put springs of water in the desert
        16 : 61 who formed man, and put a heart in the midst of his body
        16 : 65 you shall be put to shame
  4 Ma 4 : 24 to put an end to the people's observance of the law
        5 : 35 I will not put you to shame, philosophical reason
        8 : 24 nor take hollow pride in being put to the rack
        9 : 2 we are obviously putting our forefathers to shame
        9 : 7 Therefore, tyrant, put us to the test
        13 : 18 Do not put us to shame, brother
        17 : 1 when she also was about to be seized and put to death
        18 : 21 and put them to death with various tortures

PUT away   7 = 0.005 %
  Tob 6 : 4 and put them away safely
  Bar 3 : 7 for we have put away from our hearts all the iniquity of our fathers
  1 Es 8 : 69 have not put away from themselves
        8 : 93 that we will put away all our foreign wives
        9 : 20 They pledged themselves to put away their wives
        9 : 36 and they put them away with their children
  2 Es 14 : 14 and put away from you mortal thoughts

PUT forth   6 = 0.004 %
  Wis 4 : 4 For even if they put forth boughs for a while
  Sir 14 : 18 which sheds some and puts forth others
        39 : 14 and put forth blossoms like a lily
        40 : 15 The children of the ungodly will not put forth many branches
        43 : 30 When you exalt him, put forth all your strength
        50 : 10 like an olive tree putting forth its fruit

PUT in   1
  2 Es 9 : 34 or what was put in is destroyed

PUT off   1
  2 Es 2 : 45 These are they who have put off mortal clothing

PUT on   25 = 0.016 %
  Jud 10 : 3 and combed her hair and put on a tiara
        10 : 4 and put on her anklets and bracelets and rings
        16 : 8 and put on a linen gown to deceive him
  Ad E 14 : 2 and put on the garments of distress and mourning
  Wis 5 : 18 he will put on righteousness as a breastplate
  Sir 6 : 31 and put her on like a crown of gladness
        43 : 20 and the water puts on like a breastplate
        45 : 13 No outsider ever put them on, but only his sons
        50 : 11 When he put on his glorious robe
  Bar 4 : 20 and put on the sackcloth of my supplication
        5 : 1 and put on for ever the beauty of the glory from God
        5 : 2 Put on the robe of the righteousness from God
  1 Ma 1 : 9 They all put on crowns after his death
        2 : 14 put on sackcloth, and mourned greatly
        3 : 3 like a giant he put on his breastplate
        3 : 47 They fasted that day, put on sackcloth
        8 : 14 Yet for all this not one of them has put on a crown
        10 : 21 So Jonathan put on the holy garments
        11 : 13 Then Ptolemy entered Antioch and put on the crown of Asia
        11 : 54 who began to reign and put on the crown
        12 : 39 and put on the crown

13:32	and became king in his place, putting on the crown of Asia	
14:44	or to be clothed in purple or put on a gold buckle	
2 Es 2:45	and have put on the immortal	
4 Ma 13:16	Therefore let us put on the full armour of self-control	

PUT out   7 = 0.005 %
Sir 28:12	if you spit on it, it will be put out
28:23	it will burn among them and will not be put out
2 Ma 7:10	When it was demanded, he quickly put out his tongue
2 Es 10:2	Then we all put out the lamps
10:22	the light of our lampstand has been put out
14:25	which shall not be put out
16:15	The fire is kindled, and shall not be put out

PUT up   3 = 0.002 %
1 Ma 11:37	and put up in a conspicuous place on the holy mountain
14:48	to put them up in a conspicuous place
2 Ma 11:3	and to put up the high priesthood for sale every year

PYRAMID   2
| 1 Ma 13:28 | He also erected 7 pyramids, opposite one another |
| 13:29 | And for the pyramids he devised an elaborate setting |

Q

QUADRENNIAL   1
| 2 Ma 4:18 | When the quadrennial games were being held at Tyre |

QUAIL   3 = 0.002 %
Wis 16:2	and thou didst prepare quails to eat
19:12	for, to give them relief, quails came up from the sea
2 Es 1:15	The quails were a sign to you

QUAKE   2
| 1 Es 4:36 | All God's works quake and tremble |
| 2 Es 16:12 | The earth and its foundations quake |

QUALIFICATION   1
| 2 Ma 4:25 | possessing no qualification for the high priesthood |

QUALIFIED   1
| 1 Ma 13:40 | And if any of you are qualified |

QUALITY   1
| 2 Es 16:73 | Then the tested quality of my elect shall be manifest |

QUANTITY   3 = 0.002 %
Jud 12:20	and drank a great quantity of wine
15:7	for there was a vast quantity of it
2 Es 4:50	so the quantity that passed was far greater

QUARREL, verb   2
| Sir 8:2 | Do not quarrel with a rich man |
| 42:8 | or the aged man who quarrels with the young |

QUARREL, subst.   3 = 0.002 %
Sir 6:9	and will disclose a quarrel to your disgrace
27:14	and their quarrels make a man stop his ears
28:11	A hasty quarrel kindles fire, and urgent strife sheds blood

QUARRY out   1
| Sir 50:3 | In his days a cistern for water was quarried out |

QUARTER, subst.   1
| 2 Ma 12:16 | so that the adjoining lake, a quarter of a mile wide |

QUEEN   3 = 0.002 %
Ad E 10:6	the river is Esther, whom the king married and made queen
14:1	And Esther the queen, seized with deathly anxiety, fled to the Lord
15:7	And the queen faltered, and turned pale and faint

QUENCH   12 = 0.008 %
Ad E 14:9	and to quench thy altar and the glory of thy house
Wis 16:17	in the water, which quenches all things
Sir 23:16	will not be quenched until it is consumed
3 Ma 6:34	and their firebreathing boldness was ignominiously quenched
2 Es 6:27	and deceit shall be quenched
16:4	and who is there to quench it ?
16:6	or quench a fire in the stubble
16:9	and who is there to quench it ?
4 Ma 3:17	and quench the flames of frenzied desires
9:20	and the heap of coals was being quenched by drippings of gore
16:4	But the mother quenched so many and such great emotions by devout reason
18:20	quenched fire with fire in his cruel cauldrons

QUESTION, subst.   1
| 2 Es 8:55 | Therefore do not ask any more questions |

QUESTION, verb   6 = 0.004 %
Sir 19:13	Question a friend, perhaps he did not do it
19:14	Question a neighbour, perhaps he did not say it
19:15	Question a friend, for often it is slander
19:17	Question your neighbour before you threaten him
1 Ma 9:10	and leave no cause to question our honour
1 Es 6:12	we questioned them and asked them for a list of the names

QUIBBLE   1
| 1 Es 6:30 | regularly every year, without quibbling |

QUICK   3 = 0.002 %
Wis 18:21	For a blameless man was quick to act as their champion
Sir 5:11	Be quick to hear, and be deliberate in answering
2 Es 6:34	Do not be quick to think vain thoughts

QUICKLY   29 = 0.019 %
Jud 13:1	When evening came, his slaves quickly withdrew
Wis 4:14	therefore he took him quickly from the midst of wickedness
4:16	and youth that is quickly perfected
16:11	and then were quickly delivered
Sir 11:21	to enrich a poor man quickly and suddenly
11:22	and quickly God causes his blessing to flourish
19:4	One who trusts others too quickly is lightminded
27:3	his house will be quickly overthrown
32:11	go home quickly and do not linger
43:22	A mist quickly heals all things
48:20	and the Holy One quickly heard them from heaven
1 Ma 2:40	they will quickly destroy us from the earth
5:28	Then Judas and his army quickly turned back
6:27	and unless you quickly prevent them
6:57	So he quickly gave orders to depart
11:22	as quickly as possible
2 Ma 3:31	Quickly some of Heliodorus' friends asked Onias
4:48	quickly suffered the unjust penalty
6:23	he declared himself quickly
7:10	When it was demanded, he quickly put out his tongue
14:11	quickly inflamed Demetrius still more
14:44	But as they quickly drew back
3 Ma 2:23	quickly dragged him out
5:43	would quickly render it forever empty
6:9	reveal yourself quickly to those of the nation of Israel
2 Es 8:14	If then you wilt suddenly and quickly destroy him
11:27	a 2nd also, and this disappeared more quickly than the first
4 Ma 4:5	he proceeded quickly to our country
14:10	and it consumed their bodies quickly

QUIET, subst.   3 = 0.002 %
1 Ma 9:58	Jonathan and his men are living in quiet and confidence
2 Es 7:85	are guarded by angels in profound quiet
7:95	and guarded by angels in profound quiet

QUIET, adj.   9 = 0.006 %
Ad E 16:8	quiet and peaceable for all men
Sir 25:20	such is a garrulous wife for a quiet husband
1 Ma 1:3	When the earth became quiet before him, he was exalted
11:38	that the land was quiet before him
11:52	and the land was quiet before him
2 Ma 14:4	During that day he kept quiet
2 Es 2:24	Pause and be quiet, my people, because your rest will come
10:2	and I remained quiet until evening of the 2nd day
10:3	that I might be quiet

QUIETLY   2
| Sir 21:20 | but a clever man smiles quietly |
| 2 Ma 12:2 | would not let them live quietly and in peace |

QUINTUS   1
| 2 Ma 11:34 | Quintus Memmius and Titus Manius, envoys of the Romans |

QUITE   4 = 0.003 %
Ad E 16:10	and quite devoid of our kindliness
2 Ma 3:31	to one who was lying quite at his last breath
3 Ma 5:12	that he quite failed in his lawless purpose
4 Ma 3:8	he came, sweating and quite exhausted, to the royal tent

QUIVER, subst.   1
| Sir 26:12 | and open her quiver to the arrow |

R

RAAMSES   1
| Jud 1:9 | and Tahpannes and Raamses and the whole land of Goshen |

RABSHAKEH   1
  Sir 48 : 18   In his days Sennacherib came up, and sent the Rabshakeh

RACE, subst.   18 = 0.012 %
  Tob   8 : 6   From them the race of mankind has sprung
  Jud   6 : 5   until I take revenge on this race that came out of Egypt
  Wis 10 : 15   A holy people and blameless race wisdom delivered
       12 : 11   For they were an accursed race from the beginning
  Sir 10 : 19   What race is worthy of honour ? The human race
       10 : 19   What race is worthy of honour ?
       10 : 19   What race is unworthy of honour ? The human race
       10 : 19   What race is unworthy of honour ?
  2 Ma 8 : 9   to wipe out the whole race of Judea
       12 : 31   to be well disposed to their race in the future also
  1 Es 8 : 70   and the holy race has been mixed with the alien peoples of the land
  3 Ma 3 : 6   Nevertheless those of the other races paid no heed
       4 : 14   The entire race was to be registered individually
  2 Es 7 : 65   Let the human race lament
       8 : 34   or what is a corruptible race
  4 Ma 17 : 14   and the world and the human race were the spectators

RACK, subst.   8 = 0.005 %
  Sir 33 : 26   and for a wicked servant there are racks and tortures
  2 Ma 6 : 19   went up to the rack of his own accord, spitting out the flesh
       6 : 28   When he had said this, he went at once to the rack
  4 Ma 7 : 4   Although his sacred life was consumed by tortures and racks
       7 : 14   he rendered the many-headed rack ineffective
       8 : 11   nothing remains for you but to die on the rack ?
       8 : 13   rack and hooks and catapults and cauldrons
       8 : 24   nor take hollow pride in being put to the rack

RACKING   4 = 0.003 %
  4 Ma 9 : 22   he nobly endured the rackings
      14 : 12   under the rackings of each one of her children
      15 : 24   and the ingenious and various rackings
      15 : 25   and the rackings of her children

RADIANCE   1
  Wis 7 : 10   because her radiance never ceases

RADIANT   2
  Ad E 15 : 5   She was radiant with perfect beauty, and she looked happy
  Wis 6 : 12   Wisdom is radiant and unfading

RAFT   3 = 0.002 %
  Wis 14 : 5   and passing through the billows on a raft
      14 : 6   the hope of the world took refuge on a raft
  1 Es 5 : 55   and convey them in rafts to the harbour of Joppa

RAG   1
  Ad E 14 : 16   I abhor it like a menstruous rag

RAGAE   2
  Jud   1 : 5   which is on the borders of Ragae
       1 : 15   He captured Arphaxad in the mountains of Ragae

RAGE, subst.   13 = 0.008 %
  Wis 10 : 3   he perished because in rage he slew his brother
      11 : 18   or newly created unknown beasts full of rage
      16 : 5   For when the terrible rage of wild beasts
  2 Ma 4 : 25   and the rage of a savage wild beast
       7 : 3   The king fell into a rage
       7 : 39   The king fell into a rage
       9 : 4   Transported with rage
       9 : 7   breathing fire in his rage against the Jews
      10 : 28   while the other made rage their leader in the fight
  3 Ma 4 : 13   ordered in his rage that these men
       5 : 47   So, when he had filled his impious mind with a deep rage
  4 Ma 8 : 2   then in violent rage he commanded
      18 : 20   and in his burning rage

RAGE, verb   4 = 0.003 %
  Wis 5 : 22   the water of the sea will rage against them
  1 Ma 9 : 13   and the battle raged from morning till evening
  2 Ma 5 : 11   So, raging inwardly, he left Egypt
  2 Es 15 : 30   Also the Carmonians, raging in wrath

RAGES   6 = 0.004 %
  Tob   1 : 14   and once at Rages in Media I left 10 talents of silver
       4 : 1   which he had left in trust with Gabael at Rages in Media
       4 : 20   at Rages in Media
       5 : 5   Can you go with me to Rages in Media ?
       6 : 12   and as soon as we return from Rages
       9 : 2   and go to Gabael at Rages in Media

RAGING   4 = 0.003 %
  Wis 14 : 1   and about to voyage over raging waves
      14 : 25   and all is a raging riot of blood and murder

      19 : 7   and a grassy plain out of the raging waves
  4 Ma 16 : 3   nor was the raging fiery furnace of Mishael so intensely hot

RAGUEL   24 = 0.016 %
  Tob   3 : 7   it also happened that Sarah, the daughter of Raguel
       3 : 17   to give Sarah the daughter of Raguel
       3 : 17   and Sarah the daughter of Raguel
       6 : 10   Brother, today we shall stay with Raguel
       6 : 12   For I know that Raguel, according to the law of Moses
       7 : 1   and arrived at the house of Raguel
       7 : 2   Then Raguel said to his wife Edna
       7 : 3   And Raguel asked them, Where are you from, brethren ?
       7 : 6   Then Raguel sprang up and kissed him and wept
       7 : 9   So he communicated the proposal to Raguel
       7 : 9   And Raguel said to Tobias, Eat, drink, and be merry
       7 : 12   So Raguel said, Take her right now
       7 : 16   And Raguel called his wife Edna and said to her
       8 : 9   But Raguel arose and went and dug a grave
       8 : 11   Then Raguel went into his house
       8 : 15   Then Raguel blessed God and said
       8 : 20   Raguel declared by oath to Tobias that he should not leave
       8 : 21   that then he should take half of Raguel's property
       9 : 3   For Raguel has sworn that I should not leave
      10 : 7   which Raguel had sworn that he should spend there
      10 : 7   At that time Tobias said to Raguel
      10 : 10   So Raguel arose and gave him his wife Sarah
      11 : 1   And he blessed Raguel and his wife Edna
      14 : 12   to Raguel his father-in-law

RAID, subst.   1
  1 Ma 15 : 41   and make raids along the highways of Judea

RAIL   1
  2 Ma 12 : 14   railing at them and even blaspheming and saying unholy things

RAIN, subst.   14 = 0.009 %
  Jud   8 : 31   and the Lord will send us rain to fill our cisterns
  Wis 16 : 16   pursued by unusual rains and hail and relentless storms
      16 : 22   and flashed in the showers of rain
  Sir   1 : 2   The sand of the sea, the drops of rain
      35 : 20   as clouds of rain in the time of drought
      40 : 13   and crash like a loud clap of thunder in a rain
  L Jr 6 : 53   For they cannot set up a king over a country or give rain to men
  P Az   42   Bless the Lord, all rain and dew
  2 Es 4 : 49   and poured down a heavy and violent rain
       4 : 50   for as the rain is more than the drops
       7 : 41   or frost or cold or hail or rain or dew
       7 : 109   and Elijah for those who received the rain
       8 : 43   because it has not received thy rain in due season
       8 : 43   or if it has been ruined by too much rain, it perishes

RAIN down   1
  Sir   1 : 19   he rained down knowledge and discerning comprehension

RAINBOW   2
  Sir 43 : 11   Look upon the rainbow, and praise him who made it
      50 : 7   and like the rainbow gleaming in glorious clouds

RAINDROP   1
  2 Es 5 : 36   and gather for me the scattered raindrops

RAINSTORM   1
  2 Es 4 : 49   and when the rainstorm had passed

RAISE   25 = 0.016 %
  Tob 13 : 10   that his tent may be raised for you again with joy
  Jud 14 : 9   And when she had finished, the people raised a great shout
      16 : 2   Raise to him a new psalm
  Ad E 15 : 11   Then he raised the golden sceptre and touched it to her neck
  Sir 20 : 11   and there are men who have raised their heads
      21 : 20   A fool raises his voice when he laughs
      28 : 17   The blow of a whip raises a welt
      48 : 5   You have raised a corpse from death and from Hades
      49 : 12   and raised a temple holy to the Lord
      49 : 13   he raised for us the walls that had fallen
  L Jr 6 : 17   raised by the feet of those who enter
  1 Ma 3 : 31   and raise a large fund
       9 : 39   They raised their eyes and looked
      12 : 39   and to raise his hand against Antiochus the king
      12 : 42   he was afraid to raise his hand against him
  2 Ma 7 : 14   of being raised again by him
       7 : 34   when you raise your hand against the children of heaven
      12 : 37   In the language of their fathers he raised the battle cry, with hymns
  1 Es 8 : 81   and raised Zion from desolation
  3 Ma 4 : 6   all together raising a lament instead of a wedding song
       5 : 48   And when the Jews saw the dust raised by the elephants going out
       6 : 17   they raised great cries to heaven
  2 Es 7 : 37   that have been raised from the dead

| | 15:39 | over the cloud that was raised in wrath |
| 4 Ma | 6:6 | yet while the old man's eyes were raised to heaven |

RAISE up   12 = 0.008 %

Jud	10:23	and his slaves raised her up
	12:8	to direct her way for the raising up of her people
	14:7	And when they raised him up he fell at Judith's feet
Sir	10:4	and over it he will raise up the right man for the time
	11:13	and raises up his head, so that many are amazed at him
Bar	2:5	They were brought low and not raised up
2 Ma	7:9	but the King of the universe will raise us up
2 Es	2:16	And I will raise up the dead from their places
	3:23	and thou didst raise up for thyself a servant, named David
	11:18	Then the 3rd wing raised itself up
	12:23	In its last days the Most High will raise up 3 kings
4 Ma	2:14	and helps raise up what has fallen

RALLY   5 = 0.003 %

1 Ma	2:67	You shall rally about you all who observe the law
	5:53	And Judas kept rallying the laggards
	11:47	and they all rallied about him
	14:30	Jonathan rallied the nation, and became their high priest
	15:10	All the troops rallied to him

RAM   7 = 0.005 %

Tob	7:8	and they killed a ram from the flock
P Az	16	as though it were with burnt offerings of rams and bulls
1 Es	6:29	for sacrifices to the Lord, for bulls and rams and lambs
	7:7	100 bulls, 200 rams, 400 lambs
	8:14	both gold and silver for bulls and rams
	8:65	12 bulls for all Israel, 96 rams, 72 lambs
	9:20	and to give rams in expiation of their error

RAMAH   1

| 1 Es | 5:20 | The men of Ramah and Geba, 621 |

RAMIAH   1

| 1 Es | 9:26 | Of Israel : of the sons of Parosh : Ramiah, Izziah |

RAMPART   1

| 4 Ma | 3:12 | and taking a pitcher climbed over the enemy's ramparts |

RANGE   1

| Wis | 19:9 | For they ranged like horses, and leaped like lambs |

RANK, subst.   3 = 0.002 %

Jud	1:4	and his infantry form their ranks
2 Ma	4:31	leaving Andronicus, a man of high rank, to act as his deputy
	13:21	But Rhodocus, a man from the ranks of the Jews

RANSOM, subst.   1

| 4 Ma | 17:21 | a ransom for the sin of our nation |

RAPHAEL   9 = 0.006 %

Tob	3:17	And Raphael was sent to heal the 2 of them :
	5:4	and he found Raphael, who was an angel
	7:8	Then Tobias said to Raphael, Brother Azarias
	8:2	As he went he remembered the words of Raphael
	9:1	Then Tobias called Raphael and said to him
	9:5	So Raphael made the journey
	11:2	Then Raphael said to Tobias
	11:7	Raphael said, I know, Tobias
	12:15	I am Raphael, one of the 7 holy angels

RAPHAIM   1

| Jud | 8:1 | son of Ananias, son of Gideon, son of Raphaim |

RAPHIA   1

| 3 Ma | 1:1 | and marched out to the region near Raphia |

RAPHON   1

| 1 Ma | 5:37 | and encamped opposite Raphon, on the other side of the stream |

RAPIDLY   3 = 0.002 %

1 Es	6:10	These operations are going on rapidly
3 Ma	5:43	and rapidly level it to the ground with fire and spear
2 Es	14:24	these 5, because they are trained to write rapidly

RARE   2

| 2 Es | 7:57 | those that are abundant or those that are rare ? |
| | 7:58 | for what is more rare is more precious |

RASCAL   1

| Sir | 19:26 | There is a rascal bowed down in mourning |

RASH   1

| 2 Ma | 5:18 | and turned back from his rash act |

RASSIS   1

| Jud | 2:23 | and plundered all the people of Rassis |

RATHAMIN   1

| 1 Ma | 11:34 | and the 3 districts of Aphairema and Lydda and Rathamin |

RATHER   19 = 0.012 %

Tob	6:12	because you rather than any other man
Wis	7:10	and I chose to have her rather than light
	8:20	or rather, being good, I entered an undefiled body
Sir	25:16	I would rather dwell with a lion and a dragon
Sus	13:23	rather than to sin in the sight of the Lord
1 Ma	1:63	They chose to die rather than to be defiled by food
	9:9	Let us rather save our own lives now
2 Ma	6:19	rather than life with pollution
	7:2	rather than transgress the laws of our fathers
	7:7	rather than have your body punished limb by limb ?
	14:42	preferring to die nobly rather than to fall
3 Ma	1:4	and matters were turning out rather in favour of Antiochus
	6:31	or rather, who stood at its gates
	7:5	or rather as traitors
2 Es	7:16	rather than what is now present ?
	7:20	rather than that the law of God
	7:135	and bountiful, because he would rather give than take away
4 Ma	9:1	rather than transgress our ancestral commandments
	16:24	to die rather than violate God's commandment

RATIONAL   4 = 0.003 %

4 Ma	1:2	I mean, of course, rational judgment
	1:18	Now the kinds of wisdom are rational judgment, justice
	1:19	Rational judgment is supreme over all of these
	1:30	that rational judgment is sovereign over the emotions

RAVAGE, verb   4 = 0.003 %

Jud	2:23	and ravaged Put and Lud
	2:27	and sacked their cities and ravaged their lands
4 Ma	17:24	and he ravaged and conquered all his enemies
	18:4	they ravaged the enemy

RAVE   1

| Wis | 14:28 | For their worshippers either rave in exultation |

RAVISH   3 = 0.002 %

Jud	12:16	and Holofernes'heart was ravished with her
	16:9	Her sandal ravished his eyes, her beauty captivated his mind
2 Es	10:22	and our wives have been ravished

RAY   4 = 0.003 %

Wis	2:4	by the rays of the sun and overcome by its heat
	16:27	was melted when simply warmed by a fleeting ray of the sun
3 Ma	5:26	The rays of the sun were not yet shed abroad
2 Es	6:40	that a ray of light be brought forth from thy treasuries

RAZE   2

| Jud | 5:18 | the temple of their God was razed to the ground |
| 1 Ma | 5:51 | and razed and plundered the city |

RAZIS   2

| 2 Ma | 14:37 | A certain Razis, one of the elders of Jerusalem |
| | 14:41 | Being surrounded, Razis fell upon his own sword |

REACH, verb   30 = 0.020 %

Tob	7:1	When they reached Ecbatana
Jud	7:10	for it is not easy to reach the tops of their mountains
	7:14	and before the sword reaches them
	11:15	When the word reaches them and they proceed to do this
Wis	8:1	She reaches mightily from one end of the earth to the other
	19:3	they reached another foolish decision
Sir	18:9	if he reaches a 100 years
	35:16	and his prayer will reach to the clouds
	35:17	and he will not be consoled until it reaches the Lord
	43:7	a light that wanes when it has reached the full
	43:27	Though we speak much we cannot reach the end
	47:16	Your name reached to far-off islands
1 Ma	3:26	His fame reached the king
	6:45	He courageously ran into the midst of the phalanx to reach it
	12:52	So they all reached the land of Judah safely
	13:47	So Simon reached an agreement with them
	13:53	And Simon saw that John his son had reached manhood
	16:9	until Cendebaeus reached Kedron, which he had built
2 Ma	1:13	For when the leader reached Persia
	4:6	public affairs could not again reach a peaceful settlement
	5:11	When news of what had happened reached the king
	6:14	until they have reached the full measure of their sins
	6:15	when our sins have reached their height
	6:23	and the grey hairs which he had reached with distinction
	8:35	across the country till he reached Antioch
	12:1	When this agreement had been reached
	12:35	so Gorgias escaped and reached Marisa
1 Es	6:20	it has not yet reached completion

2 Es	7:5	If any one, then, wishes to reach the sea
	15:6	and their harmful deeds have reached their limit

REACH out   4 = 0.003 %
Sir	14:13	and reach out and give to him as much as you can
	31:14	Do not reach out your hand for everything you see
	31:18	do not reach out your hand before they do
	50:15	he reached out his hand to the cup

READ   19 = 0.012 %
Sir	pr.	You are urged therefore to read
Bar	1:3	And Baruch read the words of this book
	1:14	And you shall read this book which we are sending you
1 Ma	5:14	While the letter was still being read
	10:7	and read the letter in the hearing of all the people
	14:19	And these were read before the assembly in Jerusalem
2 Ma	6:12	Now I urge those who read this book not to be depressed by such calamities
	8:23	to read aloud from the holy book
	11:34	The Romans also sent them a letter which read thus :
	15:39	delights the ears of those who read the work
1 Es	2:26	I have read the letter which you sent me
	2:30	Then, when the letter from King Artaxerxes was read
	3:13	they took the writing and gave it to him, and he read it
	3:15	and the writing was read in their presence
	9:41	And he read aloud in the open square
	9:48	at the same time explaining what was read
3 Ma	1:12	Even after the law had been read to him
2 Es	14:45	and let the worthy and the unworthy read them
4 Ma	18:11	He read to you about Abel slain by Cain

READER   8 = 0.005 %
Sir	pr.	not only that the readers themselves
2 Ma	2:25	and to profit all readers
1 Es	8:8	and reader of the law of the Lord :
	8:9	and reader of the law of the Lord, greeting
	8:19	and reader of the law of the Most High God sends for
	9:39	and they told Ezra the chief priest and reader
	9:42	Ezra the priest and reader of the law
	9:49	Then Attharates said to Ezra the chief priest and reader

READILY   3 = 0.002 %
Wis	14:28	or readily commit perjury
3 Ma	2:31	readily gave themselves up
	5:21	all those present readily and joyfully with one accord gave their approval

READINESS   1
2 Ma	14:22	Judas posted armed men in readiness at key places

READING   1
Sir	pr.	especially to the reading of the law and the prophets

READY   34 = 0.022 %
Tob	5:16	Then he said to Tobias, Get ready for the journey
	11:9	now I am ready to die
Ad E	11:6	both ready to fight, and they roared terribly
	11:9	and were ready to perish
Wis	16:20	with bread ready to eat, providing every pleasure
Sir	6:35	Be ready to listen to every narrative
	39:31	and be made ready on earth for their service
	45:23	in the ready goodness of his soul
	48:10	you who are ready at the appointed time, it is written
Bar	2:9	And the Lord has kept the calamities ready
1 Ma	3:28	and ordered them to be ready for any need
	3:44	And the congregation assembled to be ready for battle
	3:58	Be ready early in the morning to fight with these Gentiles
	4:35	and how ready they were either to live or to die nobly
	5:27	the enemy are getting ready to attack the strongholds tomorrow
	5:39	ready to come and fight against you
	6:33	and his troops made ready for battle
	7:29	But the enemy were ready to seize Judas
	12:27	so as to be ready all night for battle
	12:34	for he had heard that they were ready
	12:50	and kept marching in close formation, ready for battle
	13:22	So Trypho got all his cavalry ready to go
	13:37	and we are ready to make a general peace with you
2 Ma	7:2	For we are ready to die
	8:21	and made them ready to die for their laws and their country
	11:9	ready to assail not only men but the wildest beasts or walls of iron
	13:12	Judas exhorted them and ordered them to stand ready
3 Ma	5:26	indicating that what the king desired was ready for action
	5:29	pointed out that the beasts and the armed forces were ready
2 Es	2:35	Be ready for the rewards of the kingdom
4 Ma	5:32	Therefore get your torture wheels ready
	9:1	For we are ready to die
	9:2	unless we should practice ready obedience
	15:9	and their ready obedience to the law

REAIAH   1
1 Es	5:31	the sons of Reaiah, the sons of Rezin, the sons of Nekoda

REAL   3 = 0.002 %
Sir	7:18	or a real brother for the gold of Ophir
2 Ma	4:1	and had been the real cause of the misfortune
4 Ma	5:24	so that with proper reverence we worship the only real God

REALIZE   10 = 0.007 %
Sir	12:12	and at last you will realize the truth of my words
	23:19	and he does not realize that the eyes of the Lord
1 Ma	5:34	And when the army of Timothy realized that it was Maccabeus
	7:25	and realized that he could not withstand them
	12:50	But they realized that Jonathan had been seized
2 Ma	5:6	not realizing that success at the cost of one's kindred
	11:13	and realized that the Hebrews were invincible
	14:3	realized that there was no way for him
1 Es	4:22	Hence you must realize that women rule over you !
3 Ma	7:6	Since we have come to realize

REALLY   8 = 0.005 %
Jud	6:9	If you really hope in your heart that they will not be taken
Ad E	16:10	really an alien to the Persian blood
Wis	17:14	But throughout the night, which was really powerless
Sus	13:54	Now then, if you really saw her, tell me this :
2 Ma	3:9	and he inquired whether this really was the situation
	12:12	Judas, thinking that they might really be useful in many ways
2 Es	5:30	If thou dost really hate thy people
	7:13	and really yield the fruit of immortality

REALM   2
2 Ma	9:24	the people throughout the realm would not be troubled
1 Es	8:10	and of the priests and Levites and others in our realm

REAP   4 = 0.003 %
Sir	7:3	and you will not reap a sevenfold crop
1 Es	4:6	but till the soil, whenever they sow, reap the harvest
2 Es	4:29	If therefore that which has been sown is not reaped
	16:43	let him that sows be like one who will not reap

REAPER   1
Bel	14:33	and was going into the field to take it to the reapers

REAR, verb   3 = 0.002 %
Tob	14:10	See, my son, what Nadab did to Ahikar who had reared him
Bar	4:8	and you grieved Jerusalem, who reared you
2 Ma	7:27	and have reared you and brought you up

REAR, subst.   2
1 Ma	4:15	and all those in the rear fell by the sword
	9:47	but he eluded him and went to the rear

REASON, subst.   88 = 0.057 %
Wis	2:2	and reason is a spark kindled by the beating of our hearts
	17:12	that come from reason
Sir	17:5	and as 7th reason, the interpreter of his operations
	37:16	Reason is the beginning of every work
Sus	13:14	and when each pressed the other for the reason
1 Ma	6:12	and I sent to destroy the inhabitants of Judah without good reason
	6:24	For this reason the sons of our people besieged the citadel
	10:63	and let no one annoy him for any reason
	13:4	By reason of this all my brothers have perished
2 Ma	4:16	For this reason heavy disaster overtook them
	4:35	For this reason not only Jews
	8:26	and for that reason they did not continue their pursuit
3 Ma	3:4	For this reason they appeared hateful to some
2 Es	5:9	then shall reason hide itself
	7:50	For this reason the Most High has made not one world but 2
	7:72	For this reason, therefore
	13:19	and for that very reason !
4 Ma	1:1	that is, whether devout reason is sovereign over the emotions
	1:3	that reason rules over those emotions that hinder self-control
	1:5	Some might perhaps ask, If reason rules the emotions
	1:6	For reason does not rule its own emotions
	1:7	that reason is dominant over the emotions
	1:9	demonstrated that reason controls the emotions
	1:13	is whether reason is sovereign over the emotions
	1:14	We shall decide just what reason is and what emotion is
	1:14	and whether reason rules over all these
	1:15	Now reason is the mind that with sound logic prefers the life of wisdom
	1:19	since by means of it reason rules over the emotions
	1:29	each of which the master cultivator, reason, weeds and prunes
	1:30	For reason is the guide of the virtues
	1:32	and reason obviously rules over both
	1:33	Is it not because reason is able to rule over appetites ?
	1:34	we abstain because of domination by reason
	1:35	and all the impulses of the body are bridled by reason
	2:2	It is for this reason, certainly

341

2:3	by his reason he nullified the frenzy of the passions
2:4	Not only is reason proved to rule
2:6	that reason is able to control desires
2:7	unless reason is clearly lord of the emotions ?
2:9	If one is greedy, he is ruled by the law through his reason
2:9	we can recognize that reason rules the emotions
2:14	Do not consider it paradoxical when reason
2:15	It is evident that reason rules even the more violent emotions :
2:17	but controlled his anger by reason
2:20	For if reason could not control anger
2:24	that if reason is master of the emotions
3:1	for it is evident that reason rules not over its own emotions
3:2	but reason can provide a way for us
3:3	but reason can help to deal with anger
3:4	but reason can fight at our side
3:5	For reason does not uproot the emotions but is their antagonist
3:16	Therefore, opposing reason to desire
3:18	and by nobility of reason spurn all domination by the emotions
3:19	to a narrative demonstration of temperate reason
5:31	as not to be young in reason on behalf of piety
5:35	I will not put you to shame, philosophical reason
6:7	he kept his reason upright and unswerving
6:30	and by reason he resisted even to the very tortures of death
6:31	Admittedly, then, devout reason is sovereign over the emotions
6:32	For if the emotions had prevailed over reason
6:33	But now that reason has conquered the emotions
6:34	And it is right for us to acknowledge the dominance of reason
6:35	And I have proved not only that reason has mastered agonies
7:1	the reason of our father Eleazar steered the ship of religion
7:4	with the shield of his devout reason
7:12	remained unmoved in his reason
7:14	in spirit through reason
7:14	and by reason like that of Isaac
7:16	most certainly devout reason is governor of the emotions
7:17	because not every one has prudent reason
7:20	because of the weakness of their reason
8:1	by following a philosophy in accordance with devout reason
9:17	your wheel is not so powerful as to strangle my reason
10:19	you will not make our reason speechless
11:27	therefore, unconquered, we hold fast to reason
13:1	that devout reason is sovereign over the emotions
13:3	Instead, by reason, which is praised before God
13:5	the sovereignty of right reason over emotion
13:7	so the seven-towered right reason of the youths
13:16	which is divine reason
14:2	O reason, more royal than kings and freer than the free !
14:11	that reason had full command over these men in their tortures
15:1	O reason of the children, tyrant over the emotions !
15:11	strong enough to pervert her reason
15:23	But devout reason, giving her heart a man's courage
16:1	it must be admitted that devout reason
16:4	But the mother quenched so many and such great emotions by devout reason
18:2	knowing that devout reason is master of all emotions

REASON, verb   4 = 0.003 %
Wis	2:1	For they reasoned unsoundly, saying to themselves
	2:21	Thus they reasoned, but they were led astray
Sir	14:20	and who reasons intelligently
	27:7	Do not praise a man before you hear him reason

REASONABLE   1
Sir	22:16	so the mind firmly fixed on a reasonable counsel

REASONABLY   1
Ad E	13:2	but always acting reasonably and with kindness

REASONING   7 = 0.005 %
Wis	3:10	But the ungodly will be punished as their reasoning deserves
	7:20	the powers of spirits and the reasonings of men
	9:14	For the reasoning of mortals is worthless
Sir	27:5	so the test of a man is in his reasoning
2 Ma	7:21	she fired her woman's reasoning with a man's courage
4 Ma	5:11	dispel your futile reasonings
	8:15	and by their right reasoning nullified his tyranny

REBEL, subst.   3 = 0.002 %
P Az	9	most hateful rebels, and to an unjust king
2 Ma	5:8	hated as a rebel against the laws
1 Es	2:23	and that the Jews were rebels

REBEL, verb   3 = 0.002 %
Jud	7:15	because they rebelled and did not receive you peaceably
Wis	3:10	and rebelled against the Lord
1 Es	1:48	he broke his oath and rebelled

REBELLION   1
1 Es	2:27	and that the men in it were given to rebellion and war

REBELLIOUS   3 = 0.002 %
1 Es	2:18	and are building that rebellious and wicked city
	2:22	and will learn that this city was rebellious
2 Es	1:8	they are a rebellious people

REBELLIOUSLY   1
Sir	16:10	who rebelliously assembled in their stubbornness

REBIRTH   1
4 Ma	16:13	and giving rebirth for immortality

REBUILD   12 = 0.008 %
Tob	14:5	and they will rebuild the house of God
	14:5	and will rebuild Jerusalem in splendour
	14:5	And the house of God will be rebuilt there
Sir	49:13	and set up the gates and bars and rebuilt our ruined houses
1 Ma	4:48	They also rebuilt the sanctuary
	9:62	he rebuilt the parts of it that had been demolished
	10:10	and began to rebuild and restore the city
	10:44	Let the cost of rebuilding
	10:45	And let the cost of rebuilding the walls of Jerusalem
	10:45	and the cost of rebuilding the walls in Judea
1 Es	6:17	King Cyrus wrote that this house should be rebuilt
	6:19	and that this temple of the Lord should be rebuilt on its site

REBUKE, subst.   3 = 0.002 %
Wis	11:7	in rebuke for the decree to slay the infants
	12:26	But those who have not heeded the warning of light rebukes
Sir	48:7	who heard rebuke at Sinai

REBUKE, verb   8 = 0.005 %
Wis	12:17	and dost rebuke any insolence among those who know it
	17:7	and their boasted wisdom was scornfully rebuked
Sir	18:13	He rebukes and trains and teaches them
	43:17	The voice of his thunder rebukes the earth
2 Ma	2:7	When Jeremiah learned of it, he rebuked them and declared :
	7:33	to rebuke and discipline us
4 Ma	2:11	so that one rebukes her when she breaks the law
	2:13	so that one rebukes friends when they act wickedly

RECALL   2
Wis	19:10	For they still recalled the events of their sojourn
2 Es	1:36	yet will recall their former state

RECAST   1
2 Ma	2:31	but the one who recasts the narrative

RECEDE   1
2 Es	4:14	that it may recede before us

RECEIPT   2
Tob	5:3	Then Tobit gave him the receipt, and said to him
	9:5	He gave him the receipt

RECEIVE   99 = 0.064 %
Tob	4:14	and if you serve God you will receive payment
	7:8	They received them very warmly
	14:10	But Ahikar was saved, and the other received repayment
Jud	7:15	because they rebelled and did not receive you peaceably
	12:15	the soft fleeces which she had received from Bagoas
Wis	3:5	they will receive great good
	5:16	Therefore they will receive a glorious crown
	7:15	and have thoughts worthy of what I have received
	11:5	they themselves received benefit in their need
	11:13	the righteous had received benefit
	12:7	might receive a worthy colony of the servants of God
	16:6	and received a token of deliverance
	17:21	an image of the darkness that was destined to receive them
	19:14	Others had refused to receive strangers
	19:16	but the latter, after receiving them with festal celebrations
Sir	4:31	Let not your hand be extended to receive
	11:34	Receive a stranger into your home
	12:5	for you will receive twice as much evil
	13:22	he speaks sensibly, and receives no attention
	16:14	every one will receive in accordance with his deeds
	23:28	and to be received by him is long life
	24:8	and in Israel receive your inheritance
	32:2	and receive a wreath for your excellent leadership
	38:2	and he will receive a gift from the king
	41:19	of surliness in receiving and giving
	50:12	And when he received the portions
	50:21	to receive the blessing from the Most High
	51:16	I inclined my ear a little and received her
	51:26	and let your souls receive instruction
Bar	4:32	wretched will be the city which received your sons
Sus	13:55	for the angel of God has received the sentence from God
Bel	14:1	Cyrus the Persian received his kingdom
1 Ma	2:51	and receive great honour and an everlasting name
	2:54	received the covenant of everlasting priesthood
	2:56	received an inheritance in the land

	8:26	without receiving any return
	10:30	and the half of the fruit of the trees that I should receive
	10:42	which my officials have received every year
	11:34	which the king formerly received from them each year
	12:8	and received the letter
	12:43	So he received him with honour
	13:37	We have received the gold crown
	14:23	It has pleased our people to receive these men with honour
	14:40	and that the Romans had received
	15:27	But he refused to receive them
	16:.5	The son of Abubus received them treacherously
2 Ma	2:4	that the prophet, having received an oracle
	4:5	After receiving the king's orders he returned
	7:36	will receive just punishment for your arrogance
	8:33	so these received the proper recompense for their impiety
	10:15	they received those who were banished from Jerusalem
	10:20	and on receiving 70,000 drachmas let some of them slip away
	12:12	and after receiving his pledges they departed to their tents
	13:22	gave pledges, received theirs, withdrew
	13:24	He received Maccabeus
	14:19	to give and receive pledges of friendship
3 Ma	3:28	will receive the property of the one who incurs the punishment
	5:26	and while the king was receiving his friends
	5:27	But he, upon receiving the report
	5:35	since this also was his aid which they had received
	5:50	the help which they had received before from heaven
	7:10	Upon receiving this letter
	7:10	should receive the punishment they deserved
	7:16	and had received the full enjoyment of deliverance
2 Es	2:13	Ask and you will receive
	2:33	I, Ezra, received a command from the Lord on Mount Horeb
	2:36	receive the joy of your glory
	2:37	Receive what the Lord has entrusted to you and be joyful
	2:39	have received glorious garments from the Lord
	2:45	now they are being crowned, and receive palms
	7:9	how will the heir receive his inheritance
	7:14	they can never receive those things
	7:72	and though they received the commandments they did not keep them
	7:72	they dealt unfaithfully with what they received
	7:91	the glory of him who receives them
	7:96	which they are to receive and enjoy in immortality
	7:98	and from whom they are to receive their reward when glorified
	7:109	and Elijah for those who received the rain
	7:128	but if he is victorious he shall receive what I have said
	8:33	shall receive their reward in consequence of their own deeds
	8:43	because it has not received thy rain in due season
	8:49	in order to receive the greatest glory
	8:56	For they also received freedom
	9:10	although they received my benefits
	9:32	But though our fathers received the law
	9:33	Yet those who received it perished
	9:34	when the ground has received seed, or the sea a ship
	9:36	For we who have received the law and sinned will perish
	9:36	as well as our heart which received it
	14:30	and received the law of life, which they did not keep
	15:9	and will receive to myself all the innocent blood from among them
	15:51	so that you cannot receive your mighty lovers
	15:55	therefore you shall receive your recompense
	16:36	Behold the word of the Lord, receive it
4 Ma	4:5	On receiving authority to deal with this matter
	5:15	When he had received permission to speak
	5:37	The fathers will receive me as pure
	12:11	since you have received good things and also your kingdom from God
	18:23	and have received pure and immortal souls from God

RECEIVE back   2
1 Ma	10:43	let him be released and receive back all his property in my kingdom
2 Es	10:16	you will receive your son back in due time

RECEIVING   1
2 Es	8:39	and their receiving their reward

RECENTLY   5 = 0.003 %
Jud	4:3	For they had only recently returned from the captivity
	4:5	since their fields had recently been harvested
2 Ma	14:36	that has been so recently purified
3 Ma	1:19	Those women who had recently been arrayed for marriage
2 Es	5:52	Say to her, Why are those whom you have borne recently

RECEPTION   1
Wis	19:15	for their hostile reception of the aliens

RECESS   1
Wis	17:14	and which beset them from the recesses of powerless Hades

RECKLESS   4 = 0.003 %
Sir	4:29	Do not be reckless in your speech
	9:18	and the man who is reckless in speech will be hated
	19:2	and the man who consorts with harlots is very reckless
	19:3	and the reckless soul will be snatched away

RECKON   3 = 0.002 %
1 Ma	2:52	and it was reckoned to him as righteousness ?
2 Ma	3:6	so that the amount of the funds could not be reckoned
2 Es	6:5	and before the present years were reckoned

RECKON up   1
Wis	4:20	They will come with dread when their sins are reckoned up

RECLINE   3 = 0.002 %
Jud	12:15	so that she might recline on them when she ate
1 Es	4:10	Moreover, he reclines, he eats and drinks and sleeps
3 Ma	5:16	and ordered those present for the banquet to recline opposite him

RECOGNIZE   16 = 0.010 %
Jud	8:29	all the people have recognized your understanding
	14:5	and let him see and recognize the man
Wis	10:5	recognized the righteous man
	10:8	they not only were hindered from recognizing the good
	12:27	they saw and recognized as the true God
	13:1	nor did they recognize the craftsman
Sir	18:12	He sees and recognizes that their end will be evil
	23:27	Those who survive her will recognize
2 Ma	3:28	and they recognized clearly the sovereign power of God
	4:4	Onias recognized that the rivalry was serious
	6:12	but to recognize that these punishments were designed
	7:28	and see everything that is in them, and recognize
	15:28	they recognized Nicanor, lying dead, in full armour
2 Es	2:16	because I recognize my name in them
4 Ma	2:9	we can recognize that reason rules the emotions
	3:20	and recognized their commonwealth

RECOMPENSE   4 = 0.003 %
Sir	17:23	and he will bring their recompense on their heads
2 Ma	8:33	so these received the proper recompense for their impiety
2 Es	7:35	And recompense shall follow
	15:55	therefore you shall receive your recompense

RECONCILE   6 = 0.004 %
2 Ma	1:5	May he hear your prayers and be reconciled to you
	5:20	when the great Lord became reconciled
	7:33	he will again be reconciled with his own servants
	8:29	to be wholly reconciled with his servants
1 Es	4:31	that she may be reconciled to him
3 Ma	5:13	and again begged him who is easily reconciled

RECONCILIATION   2
Sir	22:22	do not worry, for reconciliation is possible
	27:21	and there is reconciliation after abuse

RECONVENE   1
3 Ma	5:36	The king, however, reconvened the party in the same manner

RECORD, subst.   9 = 0.006 %
Ad E	12:4	The king made a permanent record of these things
	16:7	can be seen not so much from the more ancient records
Sir	42:7	and make a record of all that you give out or take in
1 Ma	14:23	may have a record of them
	14:27	So they made a record on bronze tablets
2 Ma	2:1	One finds in the records that Jeremiah the prophet
	2:13	The same things are reported in the records
	4:23	and to complete the records of essential business
1 Es	2:21	search may be made in the record of your fathers

RECORD, verb   6 = 0.004 %
1 Ma	9:22	have not been recorded, for they were very many
	14:22	we have recorded in our public decrees, as follows
1 Es	1:24	The events of his reign have been recorded in the past
	1:33	are recorded in the book of the kings of Israel and Judah
	6:23	a scroll was found in which this was recorded :
	8:64	and the weight of everything was recorded at that very time

RECORDER   2
1 Es	2:17	Your servants Rehum the recorder and Shimshai the scribe
	2:25	Then the king, in reply to Rehum the recorder

RECOUNT   5 = 0.003 %
Jud	2:2	and recounted fully, with his own lips
Sir	18:5	And who can fully recount his mercies ?
	36:8	and let people recount thy mighty deeds
	42:17	to recount all his marvellous works
4 Ma	18:16	He recounted to you Solomon's proverb

RECOVER 7 = 0.005 %
2 Ma 2:22 *and recovered the temple famous throughout the world*
9:22 for I have good hope of recovering from my illness
10:1 *the Lord leading them on, recovered the temple and the city*
1 Es 3:23 And when they recover from the wine
3 Ma 2:24 After a while he recovered and, though he had been punished
7:22 Besides they all recovered all of their property
2 Es 5:22 Then my soul recovered the spirit of understanding

RECOVERY 2
2 Ma 3:29 and deprived of any hope of recovery
3:32 offered sacrifice for the man's recovery

RECRUIT 5 = 0.003 %
1 Ma 10:6 So Demetrius gave him authority to recruit troops
10:8 that the king had given him authority to recruit troops
10:21 and he recruited troops
11:38 which he had recruited from the islands of the nations
15:3 and have recruited a host of mercenary troops

RED 6 = 0.004 %
Jud 5:13 Then God dried up the Red Sea before them
Wis 10:18 She brought them over the Red Sea
13:14 giving it a coat of red paint and colouring its surface red
19:7 an unhindered way out of the Red Sea
1 Ma 4:9 Remember how our fathers were saved at the Red Sea

REDEEM 2
Ad E 13:16 which thou didst redeem for thyself out of the land of Egypt
1 Ma 4:11 that there is one who redeems and saves Israel

REDUCE 2
Sir 31:30 reducing his strength and adding wounds
3 Ma 2:29 and they shall also be reduced to their former limited status

REED 2
Sir 40:16 The reeds by any water or river bank
3 Ma 2:22 and that as a reed is shaken by the wind

REELIAH 1
1 Es 5:8 Bilshan, Mispar, Reeliah, Rehum, and Baanah, their leaders

RE-ESTABLISH 1
Ad E 13:2 to re-establish the peace which all men desire

REFER 1
2 Ma 11:36 are to be referred to the king

REFINEMENT 1
Sus 13:31 Now Susanna was a woman of great refinement

REFLECT 6 = 0.004 %
Sir 3:22 Reflect upon what has been assigned to you
6:37 Reflect on the statutes of the Lord
14:21 He who reflects in his mind on her ways
16:20 And no mind will reflect on this
3 Ma 4:4 reflected upon the uncertainty of life
4 Ma 1:24 Anger, as a man will see if he reflects on this experience

REFLECTION 2
Wis 7:26 For she is a reflection of eternal light
2 Es 10:5 *Then I broke off the reflections with which I was still engaged*

REFRAIN 3 = 0.002 %
Tob 4:21 and refrain from every sin
Sir 4:23 Do not refrain from speaking at the crucial time
28:8 Refrain from strife, and you will lessen sins

REFRESH 3 = 0.002 %
Sir 3:6 and whoever obeys the Lord will refresh his mother
43:22 when the dew appears, it refreshes from the heat
2 Es 11:46 may be refreshed and relieved

REFRESHMENT 1
2 Ma 4:46 as if for refreshment

REFUGE 8 = 0.005 %
Wis 14:6 the hope of the world took refuge on a raft
1 Ma 1:53 in every place of refuge they had
10:14 for it served as place of refuge
10:43 And whoever takes refuge at the temple in Jerusalem
10:84 and those who had taken refuge in it he burned with fire
2 Ma 5:5 Menelaus took refuge in the citadel
10:18 took refuge in 2 very strong towers
12:6 and massacred those who had taken refuge there

REFUSE, verb 22 = 0.014 %
Tob 4:5 and refuse to sin or to transgress his commandments
4:13 by refusing to take a wife for yourself from among them
Jud 1:11 and refused to join him in the war

2:11 But if they refuse, your eye shall not spare
5:4 refused to come out and meet me ?
12:14 And Judith said, Who am I, to refuse my lord ?
Ad E 13:12 and refused to bow down to this proud Haman
Wis 12:27 him whom they had before refused to know
16:16 for the ungodly, refusing to know thee
17:10 refusing to look even at the air
19:14 Others had refused to receive strangers
Sir 7:13 Refuse to utter any lie
29:7 many have refused to lend
Sus 13:21 If you refuse, we will testify against you
1 Ma 2:40 and refuse to fight with the Gentiles
5:48 But they refused to open to him
15:27 But he refused to receive them
2 Ma 6:20 as men ought to go who have the courage to refuse things
1 Es 2:19 they will not only refuse to pay tribute
2 Es 2:33 and refused the Lord's commandment
4 Ma 8:2 but if any were to refuse
11:2 I will not refuse, tyrant

REFUSE, subst. 1
Sir 27:4 When a sieve is shaken, the refuse remains

REGAIN 2
Tob 14:2 and after 8 years he regained it
2 Es 12:18 but shall regain its former power

REGARD, verb 15 = 0.010 %
Wis 2:10 nor regard the grey hairs of the aged
9:6 he will be regarded as nothing
14:20 now regarded as an object of worship
Sir 26:22 A harlot is regarded as spittle
26:25 A headstrong wife is regarded as a dog
26:27 is regarded as a war trumpet
29:4 Many persons regard a loan as a windfall
29:6 and will regard that as a windfall
1 Ma 11:27 and made him to be regarded as one of his chief friends
2 Ma 7:12 for he regarded his sufferings as nothing
8:35 by opponents whom he regarded as of the least account
3 Ma 3:19 and are unwilling to regard any action as sincere
2 Es 8:27 Regard not the endeavours of those who act wickedly
8:29 but regard those who have gloriously taught thy law
4 Ma 3:15 to drink what was regarded as equivalent to blood

REGARD, subst. 7 = 0.005 %
Sir 41:12 Have regard for your name
Bar 4:13 They had no regard for his statutes
2 Ma 4:34 then, with no regard for justice
6:11 in view of their regard for that most holy day
11:15 Maccabeus, having regard for the common good
14:8 and second because I have regard also for my fellow citizens
3 Ma 5:30 his whole mind had been deranged in regard to these matters

REGARD, prep., with regard to 3 = 0.002 %
2 Ma 3:32 with regard to Heliodorus
4:36 with regard to the unreasonable murder of Onias
11:35 With regard to what Lysias the kinsman of the king has granted you

REGARDING 1
2 Es 4:2 Your understanding has utterly failed regarding this world

REGION 27 = 0.018 %
Tob 5:5 Are you acquainted with that region ?
Jud 1:11 But all who lived in the whole region
1:12 Then Nebuchadnezzar was very angry with this whole region
2:1 about carrying out his revenge on the whole region
2:2 all the wickedness of the region
2:11 throughout your whole region
Bar 2:23 and from the region about Jerusalem
1 Ma 3:31 and collect the revenues from those regions
3:41 When the traders of the region heard what was said of them
8:4 and how they had gained control of the whole region
11:14 because the people of that region were in revolt
11:34 the latter, with all the region bordering them
12:25 and met them in the region of Hamath
12:32 and marched through all that region
2 Ma 4:36 When the king returned from the region of Cilicia
9:1 from the region of Persia
9:21 On my way back from the region of Persia
10:14 When Gorgias became governor of the region
12:18 They did not find Timothy in that region
12:18 for he had by then departed from the region
15:1 were in the region of Samaria
3 Ma 1:1 that the regions which he had controlled had been seized by Antiochus
1:1 and marched out to the region near Raphia
2 Es 5:24 thou hast chosen for thyself one region
13:7 And I tried to see the region or place

13:41	and go to a more distant region
13:45	Through that region there was a long way to go

REGISTER, verb 4 = 0.003 %
1 Es	5:38	but were not found registered : the sons of Habaiah
3 Ma	2:29	those who are registered
	4:14	The entire race was to be registered individually
	6:34	and had joyfully registered them

REGISTER, subst. 1
1 Es	5:39	was sought in the register and was not found

REGISTRATION 5 = 0.003 %
3 Ma	2:28	to a registration involving poll tax
	2:32	to save themselves from the registration
	4:15	The registration of these people was therefore conducted
	6:38	So their registration was carried out
	7:22	in accordance with the registration

REGRET, verb 2
Sir	32:19	and when you have acted, do not regret it
1 Ma	11:10	For I now regret that I gave him my daughter

REGULAR 1
3 Ma	3:21	and to make them participants in our regular religious rites

REGULARLY 3 = 0.002 %
Bel	14:13	through which they used to go in regularly
2 Ma	4:27	but he did not pay regularly
1 Es	6:30	regularly every year, without quibbling

REHOBOAM 1
Sir	47:23	Rehoboam, whose policy caused the people to revolt

REHUM 5 = 0.003 %
1 Es	2:16	Bishlam, Mithridates, Tabeel, Rehum, Beltethmus
	2:17	Your servants Rehum the recorder and Shimshai the scribe
	2:25	Then the king, in reply to Rehum the recorder
	2:30	Rehum and Shimshai the scribe and their associates
	5:8	Bilshan, Mispar, Reeliah, Rehum, and Baanah, their leaders

REIGN, verb 38 = 0.025 %
Tob	1:15	Sennacherib his son reigned in his place
	1:21	Then Esarhaddon, his son, reigned in his place
Wis	3:8	and the Lord will reign over them for ever
	6:21	honour wisdom, that you may reign for ever
Sir	47:13	Solomon reigned in days of peace
1 Ma	1:7	And after Alexander had reigned 12 years, he died
	1:10	He began to reign in the 137th year
	1:16	that he might reign over both kingdoms
	6:2	the Macedonian king who first reigned over the Greeks
	6:17	he set up Antiochus the king's son to reign
	7:1	and there began to reign
	8:7	and decreed that he and those who should reign after him
	10:1	They welcomed him, and there he began to reign
	11:9	and you shall reign over your father's kingdom
	11:54	who began to reign and put on the crown
1 Es	1:35	And he reigned 3 months in Judah and Jerusalem
	1:35	Then the king of Egypt deposed him from reigning in Jerusalem
	1:39	when he began to reign in Judea and Jerusalem
	1:44	and he reigned 3 months and 10 days in Jerusalem
	1:46	Zedekiah was 21 years old, and he reigned 11 years
	1:57	until the Persians began to reign
	6:17	But in the first year that Cyrus reigned
	8:1	when Artaxerxes the king of the Persians was reigning
2 Es	5:6	And one shall reign whom those who dwell on earth do not expect
	11:5	to reign over the earth and over those who dwell in it
	11:12	and it reigned over all the earth
	11:13	And while it was reigning it came to its end and disappeared
	11:13	Then the next wing arose and reigned
	11:13	and it continue to reign a long time
	11:14	And while it was reigning its end came also
	11:28	to reign together
	11:31	and it devoured the 2 little wings which were planning to reign
	11:39	which I had made to reign in my world
	12:2	and set themselves up to reign
	12:2	and their reign was brief and full of tumult
	12:14	And 12 kings shall reign in it, one after another
	12:15	But the 2nd that is to reign shall hold sway
	16:52	and righteousness will reign over us

REIGN, subst. 16 = 0.010 %
Jud	1:1	In the 12th year of the reign of Nebuchadnezzar
Ad E	11:1	In the 4th year of the reign of Ptolemy and Cleopatra
	11:2	In the 2nd year of the reign of Ahasuerus the Great
Sir	pr.	in the 38th year of the reign of Euergetes
2 Ma	1:7	In the reign of Demetrius, in the 169th year
1 Es	1:22	In the 18th year of the reign of Josiah
	1:24	The events of his reign have been recorded in the past

	2:30	until the 2nd year of the reign
	5:6	in the 2nd year of his reign
	5:73	until the reign of Darius
	6:1	Now in the 2nd year of the reign of Darius
	6:24	In the first year of the reign of Cyrus
	8:6	in the 7th year of the reign of Artaxerxes
	8:28	in the reign of Artaxerxes the king :
2 Es	1:3	in the reign of Artaxerxes, king of the Persians
	12:30	this was the reign which was brief and full of tumult

REINFORCE 1
1 Ma	2:43	joined them and reinforced them

REINFORCEMENT 1
Ad E	16:20	And give them reinforcements

REJECT 15 = 0.010 %
Wis	9:4	and do not reject me from among thy servants
	11:14	For though they had mockingly rejected him
Sir	4:4	Do not reject an afflicted suppliant
	6:23	do not reject my counsel
	20:20	A proverb from a fool's lips will be rejected
	41:4	and how can you reject the good pleasure of the Most High ?
	41:21	and of rejecting the appeal of a kinsman
1 Ma	2:31	that men who had rejected the king's command
2 Ma	1:27	look upon those who are rejected and despised
P Ma	10	so that I am rejected because of my sins
2 Es	1:31	for I have rejected your feast days, and new moons
	2:33	When I came to them they rejected me
	3:16	but Esau thou didst reject
	9:9	and those who have rejected them with contempt
4 Ma	5:35	nor will I reject you, honoured priesthood and knowledge of the law

REJECTION 1
Sir	10:21	obduracy and pride are the beginning of rejection

REJOICE 50 = 0.033 %
Tob	10:12	that I may rejoice before the Lord
	11:15	And his son went in rejoicing
	11:16	rejoicing and praising God
	13:7	and will rejoice in his majesty
	13:13	Rejoice and be glad for the sons of the righteous
	13:14	They will rejoice in your peace
	13:14	for they will rejoice for you upon seeing all your glory
	14:7	will rejoice, showing mercy to our brethren
	14:15	Before his death he rejoiced over Nineveh
Wis	7:12	I rejoiced in them all, because wisdom leads them
	18:6	so that they might rejoice
Sir	8:7	Do not rejoice over any one death
	16:1	nor rejoice in ungodly sons
	16:2	If they multiply, do not rejoice in them
	19:5	One who rejoices in wickedness will be condemned
	22:23	that you may rejoice with him in his prosperity
	23:3	and my enemy will not rejoice over me
	25:7	a man rejoicing in his children
	26:2	A loyal wife rejoices her husband
	27:29	Those who rejoice in the fall of the godly
	30:1	in order that he may rejoice at the way he turns out
	30:5	while alive he saw and rejoiced
	35:19	and makes them rejoice in his mercy
	37:4	Some companions rejoice in the happiness of a friend
	39:31	they will rejoice in his commands
	51:29	May your soul rejoice in his mercy
Bar	4:12	Let no one rejoice over me, a widow and bereaved of many
	4:31	Wretched will be those who afflicted you and rejoiced at your fall
	4:33	For just as she rejoiced at your fall
	4:37	at the word of the Holy One, rejoicing in the glory of God
	5:5	rejoicing that God has remembered them
1 Ma	7:48	The people rejoiced greatly
	10:26	we have heard of it and rejoiced
	11:44	the king rejoiced at their arrival
	12:12	And we rejoice in your glory
	14:11	and Israel rejoiced with great joy
	14:21	and we rejoiced at their coming
1 Es	7:14	rejoicing before the Lord
2 Es	1:37	whose children rejoice with gladness
	2:27	but you shall rejoice and have abundance
	2:30	Rejoice, O mother, with your sons
	7:28	and those who remain shall rejoice 400 years
	7:59	rejoices more than he who has what is plentiful
	7:60	for I will rejoice over the few who shall be saved
	7:65	but let the four-footed beasts and the flocks rejoice !
	7:96	they rejoice that they have now escaped what is corruptible
	7:98	because they shall rejoice with boldness
	8:39	but I will rejoice over the creation of the righteous
	9:45	And I rejoiced greatly over him
4 Ma	4:22	and that the people of Jerusalem had rejoiced greatly

REJOICING 13 = 0.008 %
Tob 11 :17 So there was rejoicing among all his brethren in Nineveh
   13 : 1 Then Tobit wrote a prayer of rejoicing, and said :
Jud 8 : 6 and the feasts and days of rejoicing of the house of Israel
Sir 1 :11 and gladness and a crown of rejoicing
   15 : 6 He will find gladness and a crown of rejoicing
   30 :22 and the rejoicing of a man is length of days
   31 :28 is rejoicing of heart and gladness of soul
1 Ma 5 :45 and led them to Judea with great rejoicing
   13 :52 they should celebrate this day with rejoicing
2 Ma 10 : 6 And they celebrated it for 8 days with rejoicing
1 Es 4 :63 and they feasted, with music and rejoicing, for 7 days
   9 :54 and to make great rejoicing
2 Es 10 :22 and our rejoicing has been ended

REKINDLE 1
1 Ma 13 : 7 The spirit of the people was rekindled

RELATE 2
Sir 31 :11 and the assembly will relate his acts of charity
2 Ma 15 :11 and he cheered them all by relating a dream

RELATION 1
2 Ma 10 :12 and attempted to maintain peaceful relations with them

RELATIONSHIP 1
4 Ma 2 :13 It is sovereign over the relationship of friends

RELATIVE 8 = 0.005 %
Tob 1 :10 all my brethren and my relatives ate the food of the Gentiles
   5 :12 one of your relatives
   5 :13 You are a relative of mine, of a good and noble lineage
   6 :10 He is your relative, and he has an only daughter named Sarah
   7 :12 You are her relative, and she is yours
2 Ma 15 :18 and also for brethren and relatives
3 Ma 5 :49 embracing relatives and falling into one another's arms
2 Es 7 :103 brothers for brothers, relatives for their kinsmen

RELAX 2
Wis 16 :24 and in kindness relaxes on behalf of those who trust in thee
Sir 43 :10 they never relax in their watches

RELEASE, subst. 7 = 0.005 %
1 Ma 9 :70 and obtain release of the captives
   10 :34 let them all be days of immunity and release
   11 :34 we have granted release from the royal taxes
   11 :35 from all these we shall grant them release
   13 :37 to grant you release from tribute
   15 : 5 and release from all the other payments
1 Es 4 :62 because he had given them release and permission

RELEASE, verb 18 = 0.012 %
Tob 3 : 6 Command that I now be released from my distress
   3 :13 Command that I be released from the earth
Sir 18 :22 and do not wait until death to be released from it
1 Ma 10 : 6 should be released to him
   10 : 9 But the men in the citadel released the hostages to Jonathan
   10 :30 I release them from this day and henceforth
   10 :32 I release also my control of the citadel in Jerusalem
   10 :43 let him be released and receive back all his property in my kingdom
   13 :16 so that when released he will not revolt against us
   13 :16 and we will release him
   13 :19 but Trypho broke his word and did not release Jonathan
   15 : 5 from which they have released you
1 Es 4 : 7 if he tells them to release, they release
3 Ma 6 :28 Release the sons of the almighty and living God of heaven
   6 :29 and the Jews, immediately released
4 Ma 9 :16 Agree to eat so that you may be released from the tortures
   11 :13 whether he was willing to eat and be released

RELENTLESS 1
Wis 16 :16 pursued by unusual rains and hail and relentless storms

RELENTLESSLY 3 = 0.002 %
Wis 5 :22 and rivers will relentlessly overwhelm them
2 Ma 5 : 6 But Jason kept relentlessly slaughtering his fellow citizens
   5 :12 to cut down relentlessly every one they met

RELIABLE 1
Tob 5 : 8 and whether he is a reliable man to go with you

RELIANCE 1
2 Ma 10 :28 not only their valour but their reliance upon the Lord

RELIC 1
Sus 13 :52 You old relic of wicked days, your sins have now come home

RELIEF 6 = 0.004 %
Wis 19 :12 for, to give them relief, quails came up from the sea
Sir 31 :21 and you will have relief
1 Ma 13 :34 with a request to grant relief to the country
2 Ma 9 : 5 for which there was no relief
P Ma   10 and I have no relief
2 Es 10 :24 a relief from your troubles

RELIEVE 2
2 Es 7 :138 so that those who have committed iniquities might be relieved of them
   11 :46 may be refreshed and relieved

RELIGION 40 = 0.026 %
1 Ma 1 :43 Many even from Israel gladly adopted his religion
   2 :19 departing each one from the religion of his fathers
   2 :22 by turning aside from our religion
2 Ma 6 :24 has gone over to an alien religion
3 Ma 1 : 3 a Jew by birth who later changed his religion
   2 :31 to be exacted for maintaining the religion of their city
   2 :32 and did not depart from their religion
4 Ma 5 : 7 when you observe the religion of the Jews
   5 :13 that if there is some power watching over this religion of yours
   6 :22 die nobly for your religion !
   7 : 1 the reason of our father Eleazar steered the ship of religion
   7 : 3 in no way did he turn the rudder of religion
   7 :18 But as many as attend to religion with a whole heart
   9 : 6 And if the aged men of the Hebrews because of their religion
   9 : 7 and if you take our lives because of our religion
   9 :24 Fight the sacred and noble battle for religion
   9 :29 How sweet is any kind of death for the religion of our fathers !
   9 :30 by our endurance for the sake of religion ?
   11 :20 have been summoned to an arena of sufferings for religion
   12 :11 and torture on the wheel those who practice religion ?
   13 : 7 by fortifying the harbour of religion
   13 : 8 For they constituted a holy chorus of religion and
   13 :12 to being slain for the sake of religion
   13 :26 because, with the aid of their religion
   13 :27 those who were left endured for the sake of religion
   14 : 3 on behalf of religion !
   14 : 7 move in choral dance around religion
   15 : 1 O religion, more desirable to the mother than her children !
   15 : 2 that of religion, and that of preserving her 7 sons for a time
   15 : 3 She loved religion more
   15 : 3 religion that preserves them for eternal life
   15 :12 to death for the sake of religion
   15 :14 because of religion did not change her attitude
   15 :29 vindicator of the law and champion of religion
   15 :32 that assail religion
   16 :13 for the sake of religion
   16 :14 O mother, soldier of God in the cause of religion, elder and woman !
   16 :17 while an aged man endures such agonies for the sake of religion
   17 : 7 for the sake of religion ?
   18 : 3 for the sake of religion

RELIGIOUS 5 = 0.003 %
Jud 11 :17 For your servant is religious
3 Ma 3 :21 and to make them participants in our regular religious rites
4 Ma 5 :38 but you shall not dominate my religious principles
   11 :21 For the religious knowledge, O tyrant, is invincible
   16 :23 It is unreasonable for people who have religious knowledge

RELY 7 = 0.005 %
Jud 7 :10 do not rely on their spears
Sir 15 : 4 and he will rely on her and will not be put to shame
   16 : 3 and do not rely on their multitude
   38 :31 All these rely upon their hands
1 Ma 8 :12 but with their friends and those who rely on them
2 Ma 10 :34 The men within, relying on the strength of the place
   12 :14 relying on the strength of the walls

REMAIN 69 = 0.045 %
Jud 3 :10 and remained for a whole month
   7 : 5 they remained on guard all that night
   7 :12 Remain in your camp
   11 :17 therefore, my lord, I will remain with you
   12 : 7 And she remained in the camp for 3 days
   14 :10 and joined the house of Israel, remaining so to this day
   15 : 7 took possession of what remained
   16 :20 and Judith remained with them
   16 :21 and Judith went to Bethulia, and remained on her estate
   16 :22 but she remained a widow all the days of her life
Wis 7 :27 and while remaining in herself, she renews all things
   10 : 7 Evidence of their wickedness still remains :
   19 :18 while each note remains the same
Sir 4 :16 and his descendants will remain in possession of her
   6 :20 a weakling will not remain with her
   13 :10 and do not remain at a distance, lest you be forgotten
   16 :11 it will be a wonder if he remains unpunished

	21 : 23	but a cultivated man remains outside
	23 : 11	if he offends, his sin remains on him
	27 : 4	When a sieve is shaken, the refuse remains
	27 : 4	so a man's filth remains in his thoughts
	41 : 12	since it will remain for you longer than a 1,000 great stores of gold
	42 : 23	All these things live and remain for ever for every need
	44 : 11	their prosperity will remain with their descendants
	46 : 9	which remained with him to old age
Bar	2 : 21	and you will remain in the land which I gave to your fathers
L Jr	6 : 3	you will remain there for many years
1 Ma	8 : 22	and sent to Jerusalem to remain in them with them there
	10 : 14	Only in Beth-zur did some remain
	10 : 47	and they remained his allies all his days
	13 : 11	he drove out its occupants and remained there
	13 : 30	it remains to this day
	13 : 38	All the grants that we have made to you remain valid
	15 : 7	shall remain yours
2 Ma	4 : 50	remained in office, growing in wickedness
	15 : 19	And those who had to remain in the city
3 Ma	1 : 17	and those who remained behind in the city
	2 : 33	They remained resolutely hopeful of obtaining help
	5 : 18	why the Jews had been allowed to remain alive
2 Es	3 : 22	but what was good departed, and the evil remained
	4 : 35	How long are we to remain here ?
	4 : 48	and behold, the smoke remained
	4 : 49	drops remained in the cloud
	4 : 50	but drops and smoke remained
	6 : 25	And it shall be that whoever remains
	6 : 41	that one part might move upward and the other part remain beneath
	7 : 28	and those who remain shall rejoice 400 years
	7 : 34	but only judgment shall remain, truth shall stand
	7 : 123	whose fruits remains unspoiled
	9 : 35	they are destroyed, but the things that held them remain
	9 : 37	the law, however, does not perish but remains in its glory
	10 : 2	and I remained quiet until evening of the 2nd day
	10 : 51	Therefore I told you to remain in the field
	10 : 58	But tomorrow night you shall remain here
	11 : 23	and nothing remained on the eagle's body
	11 : 24	and remained under the head that was on the right side
	11 : 24	but 4 remained in their place
	11 : 28	the 2 that remained were planning between themselves
	11 : 34	But the 2 heads remained
	11 : 39	Are you not the one that remains of the 4 beasts
	12 : 27	But as for the 2 who remained
	13 : 49	he will defend the people who remain
	14 : 12	so 2 of its parts remain
	14 : 37	and remained there
	15 : 27	and you shall remain in them
4 Ma	6 : 2	who remained adorned with the gracefulness of his piety
	7 : 12	remained unmoved in his reason
	8 : 11	nothing remains for you but to die on the rack ?
	18 : 9	In the time of my maturity I remained with my husband

REMAINING 7 = 0.005 %

1 Ma	3 : 37	Then the king took the remaining half of his troops
	8 : 11	The remaining kingdoms and islands
	12 : 45	and the remaining troops and all the officials
2 Ma	8 : 14	Others sold all their remaining property
3 Ma	3 : 26	we are sure that for the remaining time
	4 : 8	spent the remaining days of their marriage festival in lamentations
2 Es	12 : 2	and behold, the remaining head disappeared

REMARKABLY 1

2 Ma	3 : 26	2 young men also appeared to him, remarkably strong

REMEDY 1

Wis	2 : 1	and there is no remedy when a man comes to his end

REMEMBER 72 = 0.047 %

Tob	1 : 12	because I remembered God with all my heart
	2 : 6	Then I remembered the prophecy of Amos
	3 : 3	Remember me and look favourably upon me
	4 : 1	On that day Tobit remembered the money
	4 : 4	Remember, my son, that she faced many dangers for you
	4 : 5	Remember the Lord our God all your days, my son
	4 : 12	Remember, my son
	4 : 19	So, my son, remember my commands
	6 : 15	But the angel said to him, Do you not remember the words
	8 : 2	As he went he remembered the words of Raphael
Jud	8 : 26	Remember what he did with Abraham, and how he tested Isaac
	13 : 19	as they remember the power of God
Ad E	10 : 5	For I remember the dream that I had concerning these matters
	10 : 12	And God remembered his people and vindicated his inheritance
	14 : 12	Remember, O Lord
Wis	2 : 4	and no one will remember our works
Sir	3 : 15	it will be remembered in your favour
	7 : 16	remember that wrath does not delay

	7 : 28	Remember that through your parents you were born
	7 : 36	In all you do, remember the end of your life
	8 : 5	remember that we all deserve punishment
	8 : 7	remember that we all must die
	9 : 12	remember that they will not be held guiltless
	11 : 25	and in the day of adversity, prosperity is not remembered
	14 : 12	Remember that death will not delay
	16 : 17	and who from on high will remember me ?
	23 : 14	Remember your father and mother when you sit among great men
	28 : 6	Remember the end of your life, and cease from enmity
	28 : 6	remember destruction and death
	28 : 7	Remember the commandments
	28 : 7	remember the covenant of the Most High, and overlook ignorance
	31 : 13	Remember that a greedy eye is a bad thing
	36 : 8	Hasten the day, and remember the appointed time
	38 : 20	drive it away, remembering the end of life
	38 : 22	Remember my doom, for yours is like it :
	41 : 3	remember your former days and the end of life
	49 : 9	For God remembered his enemies with storm
	51 : 8	Then I remembered thy mercy, O Lord
Bar	2 : 32	and will remember my name
	2 : 33	for they will remember the ways of their fathers
	3 : 5	Remember not the iniquities of our fathers
	3 : 5	but in this crisis remember thy power and thy name
	4 : 14	remember the capture of my sons and daughters
	4 : 27	for you will be remembered by him who brought this upon you
	5 : 5	rejoicing that God has remembered them
Sus	13 : 9	or remembering righteous judgments
Bel	14 : 38	And Daniel said, Thou hast remembered me, O God
1 Ma	2 : 51	Remember the deeds of the fathers
	4 : 9	Remember how our fathers were saved at the Red Sea
	4 : 10	and remember his covenant with our fathers
	5 : 4	He also remembered the wickedness of the sons of Baean
	6 : 12	But now I remember the evils I did in Jerusalem
	7 : 38	remember their blasphemies, and let them live no longer
	9 : 38	And they remembered the blood of John their brother
	10 : 5	for he will remember all the wrongs which we did to him
	10 : 46	because they remembered the great wrongs
	12 : 11	We therefore remember you constantly on every occasion
	12 : 11	as it is right and proper to remember brethren
2 Ma	1 : 2	and may he remember his covenant with Abraham
	8 : 4	and to remember also the lawless destruction of the innocent babies
	9 : 21	I remember with affection your esteem and good will
	9 : 26	I therefore urge and beseech you to remember
	10 : 6	remembering how not long before, during the feast of booths
1 Es	3 : 23	they do not remember what they have done
	4 : 43	Remember the vow which you made to build Jerusalem
2 Es	2 : 8	O wicked nation, remember what I did to Sodom and Gomorrah
	2 : 31	Remember your sons that sleep
	8 : 28	but remember those who have willingly acknowledged that thou art to be feared
	15 : 31	And then the dragons, remembering their origin
4 Ma	13 : 12	and another reminded them, Remember whence you came
	15 : 28	she remembered his fortitude
	16 : 18	Remember that it is through God

REMEMBRANCE 7 = 0.005 %

Ad E	13 : 8	calling to remembrance all the works of the Lord
Wis	5 : 14	and it passes like the remembrance of a guest who stays but a day
	8 : 13	and leave an everlasting remembrance
Sir	24 : 20	For the remembrance of me is sweeter than honey
	38 : 23	When the dead is at rest, let his remembrance cease
	50 : 16	for remembrance before the Most High
2 Es	12 : 47	for the Most High has you in remembrance

REMIND 6 = 0.004 %

Wis	12 : 2	and dost remind and warn them of the things wherein they sin
	16 : 6	to remind them of thy law's command
	16 : 11	To remind them of thy oracles they were bitten
2 Ma	15 : 9	and reminding them also of the struggles they had won
4 Ma	13 : 12	and another reminded them, Remember whence you came
	18 : 14	He reminded you of the scripture of Isaiah, which says

REMINDER 8 = 0.005 %

Tob	12 : 12	I brought a reminder of your prayer before the Holy One
Ad E	16 : 23	it may be a reminder of destruction
Wis	10 : 8	but also left for mankind a reminder of their folly
Sir	41 : 1	O death, how bitter is the reminder of you
	45 : 9	as a reminder to the sons of his people
	45 : 11	for a reminder, in engraved letters
2 Ma	6 : 17	Let what we have said serve as a reminder
4 Ma	17 : 8	as a reminder to the people of our nation :

REMISS 1

Sir	4 : 29	or sluggish and remiss in your deeds

REMISSION 1
1 Ma 15 : 5   now therefore I confirm to you all the tax remissions

REMNANT   5 = 0.003 %
Wis 16 : 3   might lose the least remnant of appetite
Sir 44 : 17   therefore a remnant was left to the earth when the flood came
    47 : 22   so he gave a remnant to Jacob
1 Ma 3 : 35   and the remnant of Jerusalem
2 Es 12 : 34   But he will deliver in mercy the remnant of my people

REMONSTRATE 1
3 Ma 5 : 39   remonstrated as follows :

REMORSE 1
Sir 20 : 21   so when he rests he feels no remorse

REMOTE 1
Tob 8 : 3   he fled to the remotest parts of Egypt

REMOVAL 1
2 Ma 3 : 7   to effect the removal of the aforesaid money

REMOVE   25 = 0.016 %
Tob 2 : 4   I sprang up and removed the body to a place of shelter until sunset
Jud 10 : 3   and she removed the sackcloth which she had been wearing
Sir 7 : 6   lest you be unable to remove iniquity
    10 : 17   He has removed some of them and destroyed them
    23 : 5   and remove from me evil desire
    30 : 23   and remove sorrow far from you
    31 : 1   and anxiety about it removes sleep
    47 : 24   so as to remove them from their land
Bar 2 : 35   and I will never again remove my people Israel
1 Ma 1 : 15   and removed the marks of circumcision
    4 : 43   and removed the defiled stones to an unclean place
    4 : 58   and the reproach of the Gentiles was removed
    11 : 41   that he remove the troops of the citadel from Jerusalem
    11 : 63   intending to remove him from office
    11 : 66   He removed them from there, took possession of the city
    13 : 41   In the 170th year the yoke of the Gentiles was removed from Israel
    13 : 51   because a great enemy had been crushed and removed from Israel
    14 : 7   and he removed its uncleanness from it
1 Es 1 : 45   and removed him to Babylon
Ps 151 : 7   I beheaded him, and removed reproach from the people of Israel
3 Ma 5 : 50   removing the babies from their breasts
2 Es 7 : 48   and removed us far from life
    16 : 52   and iniquity will be removed from the earth
4 Ma 4 : 16   who removed Onias from the priesthood
    10 : 18   But he said, Even if you remove my organ of speech

REND   12 = 0.008 %
Jud 14 : 16   and wept and groaned and shouted, and rent his garments
    14 : 19   they rent their tunics and were greatly dismayed
L Jr 6 : 31   and in their temples the priests sit with their clothes rent
1 Ma 2 : 14   And Mattathias and his sons rent their clothes
    3 : 47   and sprinkled ashes on their heads, and rent their clothes
    4 : 39   Then they rent their clothes
    5 : 14   behold, other messengers, with their garments rent
    11 : 71   Jonathan rent his garments
    13 : 45   went up on the wall with their clothes rent
1 Es 8 : 71   I rent my garments and my holy mantle
    8 : 73   with my garments and my holy mantle rent
2 Es 9 : 38   and her clothes were rent, and there were ashes on her head

RENDER   10 = 0.007 %
Tob 3 : 2   and thou dost render true and righteous judgment for ever
Ad E 16 : 8   For the future we will take care to render our kingdom
Sir pr.   we may seem to have rendered some phrases imperfectly
    42 : 2   and of rendering judgment to acquit the ungodly
2 Ma 9 : 26   the public and private services rendered to you
3 Ma 5 : 43   would quickly render it forever empty
4 Ma 2 : 1   are rendered powerless ?
    2 : 18   to correct some, and to render others powerless
    7 : 14   he rendered the many-headed rack ineffective
    13 : 26   they rendered their brotherly love more fervent

RENEW   10 = 0.007 %
Wis 7 : 27   and while remaining in herself, she renews all things
1 Ma 12 : 1   to confirm and renew the friendship with them
    12 : 3   to renew the former friendship and alliance with them
    12 : 10   we have undertaken to send to renew our brotherhood
    12 : 16   to renew our former friendship and alliance with them
    14 : 18   to renew with him the friendship and alliance
    14 : 22   have come to us to renew their friendship with us
    15 : 17   to renew our ancient friendship and alliance
2 Es 7 : 75   when thou wilt renew the creation
    12 : 23   and they shall renew many things in it

RENEWAL   3 = 0.002 %
Sir 22 : 21   do not despair, for a renewal of friendship is possible
1 Ma 12 : 17   concerning the renewal of our brotherhood
2 Ma 7 : 9   to an everlasting renewal of life

RENOUNCE   7 = 0.005 %
2 Es 14 : 13   And now renounce the life that is corruptible
4 Ma 4 : 26   to eat defiling foods and to renounce Judaism
    5 : 34   nor will I renounce you, beloved self-control
    8 : 7   if you will renounce
    9 : 23   or renounce our courageous brotherhood
    10 : 3   I do not renounce the noble kinship
    10 : 15   I will not renounce our noble brotherhood

RENOWN 2
Wis 8 : 18   and renown in sharing her words
1 Ma 14 : 10   till his renown spread to the ends of the earth

RENOWNED   5 = 0.003 %
Jud 11 : 23   and be renowned throughout the whole world
Wis 3 : 15   For the fruit of good labours is renowned
Sir 3 : 19   Many are lofty and renowned
    44 : 3   and were men renowned for their power
1 Ma 3 : 9   He was renowned to the ends of the earth

REPAIR, verb   4 = 0.003 %
Sir 50 : 1   who in his life repaired the house
1 Ma 3 : 43   Let us repair the destruction of our people
    12 : 37   and he repaired the section called Chaphenatha
1 Es 2 : 18   repairing its market places and walls

REPAY   17 = 0.011 %
Tob 14 : 10   and with what he repaid him
Sir 4 : 31   but withdrawn when it is time to repay
    12 : 2   Do good to a godly man, and you will be repaid
    29 : 2   and in turn, repay your neighbour promptly
    29 : 6   he will repay him with curses and reproaches
    30 : 6   and one to repay the kindness of his friends
    35 : 11   For the Lord is the one who repays
    35 : 11   and he will repay you sevenfold
    35 : 18   and repays vengeance on the nations
    35 : 19   till he repays man according to his deeds
L Jr 6 : 34   they will not be able to repay it
1 Ma 10 : 27   and we will repay you with good for what you do for us
    11 : 53   and did not repay the favours which Jonathan had done him
2 Ma 4 : 38   The Lord thus repaid him with the punishment he deserved
2 Es 15 : 20   to turn and repay what they have given them
    15 : 21   and will repay into their bosom

REPAYMENT 2
Tob 14 : 10   But Ahikar was saved, and the other received repayment
Sir 29 : 5   but at the time for repayment he will delay

REPEAT   3 = 0.002 %
Sir 7 : 14   nor repeat yourself in your prayer
    19 : 7   Never repeat a conversation
    41 : 23   of repeating and telling what you hear

REPEATEDLY 1
4 Ma 10 : 1   and many repeatedly urged him

REPEL   3 = 0.002 %
Wis 5 : 17   and will arm all creation to repel his enemies
4 Ma 2 : 16   For the temperate mind repels all these malicious emotions
    2 : 16   just as it repels anger

REPENT   8 = 0.005 %
Wis 11 : 23   and thou dost overlook men's sins, that they may repent
    12 : 10   thou gavest them a chance to repent
Sir 17 : 24   Yet to those who repent he grants a return
    21 : 6   but he that fears the Lord will repent in his heart
    48 : 15   For all this the people did not repent
P Ma 7   and repentest over the evils of men
    13   For thou, O Lord, art the God of those who repent
3 Ma 2 : 24   he by no means repented

REPENTANCE   11 = 0.007 %
Wis 5 : 3   They will speak to one another in repentance
    12 : 19   because thou givest repentance for sins
Sir 20 : 3   How good it is to show repentance when you are reproved
    44 : 16   he was an example of repentance to all generations
P Ma 7   hast promised repentance and forgiveness
    7   thou hast appointed repentance for sinners
    8   hast not appointed repentance for the righteous
    8   but thou hast appointed repentance for me, who am a sinner
2 Es 7 : 82   because they cannot now make a good repentance
    7 : 133   who turn in repentance to his law
    9 : 11   while an opportunity of repentance was still open to them

REPLY, verb   20 = 0.013 %
Tob **2**:14   Then she replied to me
    5:6   The angel replied, I will go with you
   5:12   He replied, I am Azarias the son of the great Ananias
    6:7   He replied, As for the heart and the liver
    7:5   they replied, He is alive and in good health
   10:9   Tobias replied, No, send me back to my father
   12:2   He replied, Father, it would do me no harm
Jud **10**:12   She replied, I am a daughter of the Hebrews
   11:5   Judith replied to him, Accept the words of your servant
   12:4   Judith replied, As your soul lives, my lord
1 Ma **3**:18   Judas replied, It is easy for many to be hemmed in by few
  10:55   Ptolemy the king replied and said
2 Ma **3**:37   he replied, If you have any enemy or plotter against your government
    7:8   he replied in the language of his fathers
  15:5   he replied, And I am a sovereign also, on earth
2 Es **4**:3   And he replied to me
   5:44   He replied to me and said
   5:51   He replied to me, Ask a woman who bears children
   7:62   I replied and said, O earth
4 Ma **9**:17   he replied, You abominable lackeys

REPLY, subst.   5 = 0.003 %
1 Ma **8**:22   which they wrote in reply, on bronze tablets
  12:18   And now please send us a reply to this
  13:35   Demetrius the king sent him a favourable reply to this request
  15:33   but Simon gave him this reply :
1 Es **2**:25   Then the king, in reply to Rehum the recorder

REPORT, verb   27 = 0.018 %
Tob **11**:15   and he reported to his father the great things
Jud **10**:18   for her arrival was reported from tent to tent
  11:8   and it is reported throughout the whole world
Sir **19**:8   With friend or foe do not report it
1 Ma **2**:31   And it was reported to the king's officers
   4:26   and reported to Lysias all that had happened
   5:38   Judas sent men to spy out the camp, and they reported to him
   6:5   Then some one came to him in Persia and reported
   9:37   After these things it was reported to Jonathan
  11:21   went to the king and reported to him
  11:40   He also reported to Imalkue what Demetrius had done
  12:23   that our envoys report to you accordingly
  12:26   and they returned and reported to him
  15:32   He reported to him the words of the king
  15:36   and reported to him these words and the splendour of Simon
  16:1   and reported to Simon his father what Cendebaeus had done
  16:21   But some one ran ahead and reported to John at Gazara
2 Ma **1**:20   And when they reported to us
   1:33   and it was reported to the king of the Persians
   2:13   The same things are reported in the records
   3:6   He reported to him
   3:34   report to all men the majestic power of God
1 Es **1**:42   But the things that are reported about Jehoiakim
   8:49   the list of all their names was reported
3 Ma **5**:10   to report to the king about these preparations
4 Ma **4**:3   to report that in the Jerusalem treasuries
   4:14   went away to report to the king what had happened to him

REPORT, subst.   11 = 0.007 %
Tob **10**:12   Let me hear a good report of you
Jud **10**:13   to give him a true report
Wis **1**:9   and a report of his words will come to the Lord
1 Ma **3**:27   When King Antiochus heard these reports
   5:14   came from Galilee and made a similar report
  16:18   Then Ptolemy wrote a report about these things
2 Ma **4**:39   and when report of them had spread abroad
1 Es **6**:6   and a report made
3 Ma **2**:26   that he framed evil reports in the various localities
   3:2   a pretext being given by a report
   5:27   But he, upon receiving the report

REPRESENT   1
1 Es **1**:15   who represented the king

REPRESENTATIVE   1
2 Ma **11**:20   I have ordered these men and my representatives

REPROACH, subst.   28 = 0.018 %
Tob **3**:4   thou madest us a byword of reproach
   3:6   because I have heard false reproaches
  3:13   and that I hear reproach no more
  3:15   and pity be taken upon me, and that I hear reproach no more
Jud **8**:22   and a reproach in the eyes of those who acquire us
Wis **5**:4   and made a byword of reproach – we fools !
Sir **6**:1   for a bad name incurs shame and reproach :
  13:3   A rich man does wrong, and he even adds reproaches
  18:15   My son, do not mix reproach with your good deeds
  29:6   he will repay him with curses and reproaches
  29:28   scolding about lodging and the reproach of the moneylender

  31:31   speak no word of reproach to him
  41:6   and on their posterity will be a perpetual reproach
  41:7   for they suffer reproach because of him
  47:4   and take away reproach from the people
Bar **2**:4   to be a reproach and a desolation among all the surrounding peoples
L Jr **6**:47   They have left only lies and reproach for those who come after
   6:72   and be a reproach in the land
   6:73   for he will be far from reproach
1 Ma **1**:39   her sabbaths into a reproach, her honour into contempt
   2:49   Arrogance and reproach have now become strong
   4:45   lest it bring reproach upon them
   4:58   and the reproach of the Gentiles was removed
  10:70   and I have become a laughingstock and reproach because of you
Ps 151 :7   I beheaded him, and removed reproach from the people of Israel
3 Ma **3**:7   So they attached no ordinary reproach to them
2 Es **4**:23   why Israel has been given over to the Gentiles as a reproach
  10:28   my end has become corruption, and my prayer a reproach

REPROACH, verb   8 = 0.005 %
Tob **3**:7   was reproached by her father's maids
Wis **2**:12   he reproaches us for sins against the law
Sir **8**:5   Do not reproach a man who is turning away from sin
  13:22   If a humble man slips, they even reproach him
Bar **3**:8   to be reproached and cursed and punished
3 Ma **7**:8   or reproaching them for the irrational things that have happened
2 Es **13**:38   and will reproach them to their face with their evil thoughts
4 Ma **12**:2   Even though the tyrant had been fearfully reproached by the brothers

REPROACHFUL   1
2 Ma **7**:24   and he was suspicious of her reproachful tone

REPROOF   6 = 0.004 %
Wis **2**:14   He became to us a reproof of our thoughts
Sir **16**:12   As great as his mercy, so great is also his reproof
  20:1   There is a reproof which is not timely
  20:29   like a muzzle on the mouth they avert reproofs
  21:6   Whoever hates reproof walks in the steps of the sinner
  32:17   A sinful man will shun reproof

REPROVE   10 = 0.007 %
Sir **11**:7   first consider, and then reprove
  20:2   How much better it is to reprove than to stay angry !
  20:3   How good it is to show repentance when you are reproved
  31:31   Do not reprove your neighbour at a banquet of wine
2 Es **8**:12   and reproved him in thy wisdom
  12:31   and reproving him for his unrighteousness
  12:33   and when he has reproved them
  13:37   And he, my Son, will reprove the assembled nations for their ungodliness
  14:13   and reprove your people
  14:20   and I will reprove the people who are now living

REPULSE   2
Sir **13**:10   Do not push forward, lest you be repulsed
1 Ma **14**:26   they have fought and repulsed Israel's enemies

REPUTATION   4 = 0.003 %
Sus **13**:64   Daniel had a great reputation among the people
3 Ma **2**:31   since they expected to enhance their reputation
4 Ma **5**:18   to invalidate our reputation for piety
   6:18   the reputation of such a life

REPUTE, subst.   1
3 Ma **3**:5   they were established in good repute among all men

REPUTE, verb   1
2 Es **6**:57   which are reputed as nothing

REQUEST, subst.   6 = 0.004 %
1 Ma **11**:41   Now Jonathan sent to Demetrius the king the request
  13:34   with a request to grant relief to the country
  13:35   Demetrius the king sent him a favourable reply to this request
2 Ma **11**:15   For the king granted every request in behalf of the Jews
1 Es **8**:4   for he found favour before the king in all his requests
3 Ma **6**:41   The king granted their request at once

REQUEST, verb   4 = 0.003 %
2 Ma **4**:28   kept requesting payment
1 Es **4**:46   this is what I ask and request of you
3 Ma **7**:10   but they requested the king that at their own hands
2 Es **5**:46   Request it therefore to produce 10 at one time

REQUIRE   7 = 0.005 %
Wis **15**:8   when he is required to return the soul that was lent him
Sir **13**:26   but to devise proverbs requires painful thinking
L Jr **6**:35   they will not require it
1 Es **1**:12   They roasted the passover lamb with fire, as required
2 Es **1**:32   their blood I will require of you, says the Lord

2:26	for I will require them from among your number	
6:19	and when I require from the doers of iniquity	

REQUITAL
1

2 Es 9:6	and the end in requital and in signs	

REQUITE
2

Sir 3:31	Whoever requites favours gives thought to the future	
17:23	Afterward he will arise and requite them	

RESAIAH
1

1 Es 5:8	Nehemiah, Seraiah, Resaiah, Bigvai, Mordecai	

RESCUE, subst.
4 = 0.003 %

Sir 40:7	at the moment of his rescue he wakes up	
2 Ma 9:2	Therefore the people rushed to the rescue with arms	
3 Ma 6:30	deciding that they should celebrate their rescue with all joyfulness	
6:33	for the unexpected rescue which he had experienced	

RESCUE, verb
21 = 0.014 %

Wis 10:6	Wisdom rescued a righteous man	
10:9	Wisdom rescued from troubles those who served her	
18:5	and one child had been exposed and rescued	
Sir 29:12	and it will rescue you from all affliction	
40:24	but almsgiving rescues better than both	
51:12	and rescue me from an evil plight	
L Jr 6:36	or rescue the weak from the strong	
6:37	they cannot rescue a man who is in distress	
P Az 66	for he has rescued us from Hades	
1 Ma 2:48	They rescued the law out of the hands of the Gentiles and kings	
5:12	Now then come and rescue us from their hands	
5:17	Choose your men and go and rescue your brethren in Galilee	
2 Ma 1:25	who dost rescue Israel from every evil	
2:18	for he has rescued us from great evils	
8:14	to rescue those who had been sold by the ungodly Nicanor	
3 Ma 2:12	and rescued them from great evils	
5:8	and in a glorious manifestation rescue them	
6:6	you rescued unharmed, even to a hair	
6:10	rescue us from the hand of the enemy	
6:11	saying, Not even their god has rescued them	
6:39	and rescued them all together and unharmed	

RESCUER
1

Sir 29:17	and one who does not feel grateful will abandon his rescuer	

RESEMBLE
1

Tob 7:2	How much the young man resembles my cousin Tobit !	

RESERVE, verb
5 = 0.003 %

Sir 13:9	When a powerful man invites you, be reserved	
2 Es 7:14	that have been reserved for them	
7:121	Or that safe and healthful habitations have been reserved for us	
11:9	but let the heads be reserved for the last	
13:18	because they understand what is reserved for the last days	

RESERVOIR
2

Sir 39:17	and the reservoirs of water at the word of his mouth	
50:3	a reservoir like the sea in circumference	

RESIDE
1

3 Ma 4:18	some still residing in their homes, and some at the place	

RESIDENCE
1

2 Es 10:47	that was the period of residence in Jerusalem	

RESIDENT, subst., adj.
4 = 0.003 %

Jud 4:10	and every resident alien and hired labourer	
Ad E 11:1	one of the residents of Jerusalem	
1 Ma 1:38	Because of them the residents of Jerusalem fled	
3:34	As for the residents of Judea and Jerusalem	

RESIST
10 = 0.007 %

Jud 2:25	and killed every one who resisted him	
6:3	They cannot resist the might of our cavalry	
16:14	there is none that can resist thy voice	
Ad E 13:11	and there is no one who can resist thee	
Wis 12:12	Or who will resist thy judgment ?	
Sir 46:6	he destroyed those who resisted	
1 Ma 5:40	we will not be able to resist him	
14:29	and resisted the enemies of their nation	
1 Es 2:19	but will even resist kings	
4 Ma 6:30	and by reason he resisted even to the very tortures of death	

RESISTANCE
1

L Jr 6:56	Besides, they can offer no resistance to a king or any enemies	

RESOLUTELY
1

3 Ma 2:33	They remained resolutely hopeful of obtaining help	

RESOLVE, verb
4 = 0.003 %

Wis 18:5	When they had resolved to kill the babes of thy holy ones	
Sir 51:18	For I resolved to live according to wisdom	
1 Ma 1:62	and were resolved in their hearts not to eat unclean food	
14:35	and the glory which he had resolved to win for his nation	

RESOLVE, subst.
2

2 Ma 6:23	But making a high resolve	
4 Ma 8:18	why do we take pleasure in vain resolves	

RESORT
2

2 Ma 4:34	Andronicus came to Onias, and resorting to treachery	
3 Ma 1:23	they resorted to the same posture of supplication as the others	

RESOUND
2

Sir 47:10	and the sanctuary resounded from early morning	
3 Ma 6:17	so that even the nearby valleys resounded with them	

RESOUNDING
1

2 Es 6:13	Rise to your feet and you will hear a full, resounding voice	

RESOURCE
3 = 0.002 %

Sir 8:2	lest his resources outweigh yours	
13:5	he will drain your resources and he will not care	
44:6	rich men furnished with resources	

RESPECT, subst.
10 = 0.007 %

Tob 3:15	command that respect be shown to me	
Sir 41:16	Therefore show respect for my words :	
Bar 4:15	who had no respect for an old man	
2 Ma 10:13	Unable to command the respect due his office	
15:2	but show respect for the day	
3 Ma 3:4	*they kept their separateness with respect to foods*	
2 Es 8:48	*But even in this respect you will be praiseworthy*	
15:16	they shall in their might have no respect for their king	
4 Ma 5:17	*that we should not transgress it in any respect*	
6:35	*and in no respect yields to them*	

RESPECT, verb
4 = 0.003 %

Sir 3:11	not to respect their mother	
4 Ma 3:12	2 staunch young soldiers, respecting the king's desire	
5:7	for I respect your age and your grey hairs	
8:5	and greatly respect the beauty and the number of such brothers	

RESPECTABLE
1

2 Es 16:49	Just as a respectable and virtuous woman abhors a harlot	

RESPECTFULLY
1

Sir 21:22	but a man of experience stands respectfully before it	

RESPECTIVE
1

Sir 46:11	The judges also, with their respective names	

RESPLENDENT
1

2 Ma 10:29	5 resplendent men on horses with golden bridles	

RESPOND
1

2 Ma 1:23	Jonathan led, and the rest responded, as did Nehemiah	

RESPONSE
1

4 Ma 6:1	When Eleazar in this manner had made eloquent response	

RESPONSIBILITY
2

2 Ma 2:28	leaving the responsibility for exact details to the compiler	
4:28	for the collection of the revenue was his responsibility	

RESPONSIBLE
1

Ad E 16:5	have been made in part responsible	

REST, subst., remainder
31 = 0.020 %

Tob 8:21	and that the rest would be his when my wife and I die	
Jud 7:18	The rest of the Assyrian army encamped in the plain	
15:6	The rest of the people of Bethulia	
Sir pr.	the prophecies, and the rest of the books	
1 Ma 3:11	Many were wounded and fell, and the rest fled	
3:12	and used it in battle the rest of his life	
3:24	800 of them fell, and the rest fled into the land of the Philistines	
5:18	with the rest of the forces, in Judea to guard it	
6:38	The rest of the horsemen were stationed on either side	
6:54	because famine had prevailed over the rest	
7:32	and the rest fled into the city of David	
7:42	let the rest learn that Nicanor has spoken wickedly	
8:4	the rest paid them tribute every year	
9:18	Judas also fell, and the rest fled	
9:22	Now the rest of the acts of Judas, and his wars	
9:40	Many were wounded and fell, and the rest fled to the mountain	
12:6	the priests, and the rest of the Jewish people	
14:20	and the rest of the Jewish people, our brethren, greeting	
16:8	the rest fled into the stronghold	
16:23	The rest of the acts of John and his wars	

2 Ma	1:23	Jonathan led, and the rest responded, as did Nehemiah
	7:4	while the rest of the brothers and the mother looked on
	8:28	and distributed the rest among themselves and their children
	8:31	and carried the rest of the spoils to Jerusalem
	10:36	Others broke open the gates and let in the rest of the force
	11:11	and forced all the rest to flee
	14:11	the rest of the king's friends, who were hostile to Judas
1 Es	2:16	Shimshai the scribe, and the rest of their associates
	5:8	and who returned to Jerusalem and the rest of Judea
	7:6	and the rest of those from the captivity who joined them
4 Ma	3:9	Now all the rest were at supper

REST, subst., repose   34 = 0.022 %

Ad E	12:1	Now Mordecai took his rest in the courtyard
Wis	4:7	But the righteous man, though he die early, will be at rest
	8:16	When I enter my house, I shall find rest with her
Sir	6:28	For at last you will find the rest she gives
	11:19	when he says, I have found rest
	22:11	weep less bitterly for the dead, for he has attained rest
	22:13	avoid him and you will find rest
	28:16	Whoever pays heed to slander will not find rest
	30:17	and eternal rest than chronic sickness
	33:25	Set your slave to work, and you will find rest
	36:18	Jerusalem, the place of thy rest
	38:23	When the dead is at rest, let his remembrance cease
	39:11	and if he goes to rest, it is enough for him
	40:6	He gets little or no rest
	47:13	and God gave him rest on every side
	51:27	and found for myself much rest
1 Ma	7:50	So the land of Judah had rest for a few days
	9:57	and the land of Judah had rest for 2 years
	14:4	The land had rest all the days of Simon
2 Ma	15:1	on the day of rest
2 Es	2:24	Pause and be quiet, my people, because your rest will come
	2:34	he will give you everlasting rest
	7:36	and opposite it shall be the place of rest
	7:38	here are delight and rest
	7:75	we shall be kept in rest until those times come
	7:91	for they shall have rest in 7 orders
	7:95	they understand the rest which they now enjoy
	8:52	a city is built, rest is appointed, goodness is established
	10:24	and the Most High may give you rest
	11:4	But his heads were at rest
	11:4	but it also was at rest with them
	11:23	except the 3 heads that were at rest and 6 little wings
	11:29	one of the heads that were at rest
	12:22	As for your seeing 3 heads at rest

REST, verb   12 = 0.008 %

Jud	1:16	and there he and his forces rested and feasted for 120 days
	8:24	and the sanctuary and the temple and the altar rest upon us
	9:8	and to pollute the tabernacle where thy glorious name rests
	10:21	Holofernes was resting on his bed
Sir	5:6	and his anger rests on sinners
	20:21	so when he rests he feels no remorse
	31:3	and when he rests he fills himself with his dainties
	31:4	and when he rests he becomes needy
	40:5	And when one rests upon his bed
	43:20	it rests upon every pool of water
	44:23	he made to rest upon the head of Jacob
	47:23	Solomon rested with his fathers

RESTING   2

Sir	24:7	Among all these I sought a resting place
	24:11	In the beloved city likewise he gave me a resting place

RESTORATION   1

1 Ma	14:34	whatever was necessary for their restoration

RESTORE   16 = 0.010 %

Tob	2:1	and my wife Anna and my son Tobias were restored to me
Jud	7:30	by that time the Lord our God will restore to us his mercy
Sir	48:10	and to restore the tribes of Jacob
L Jr	6:37	They cannot restore sight to a blind man
1 Ma	4:57	they restored the gates and the chambers for the priests
	9:72	He restored to him the captives
	10:10	and began to rebuild and restore the city
	10:44	and restoring the structures of the sanctuary
	15:3	so that I may restore it as it formerly was
2 Ma	2:22	and restored the laws that were about to be abolished
	5:20	was restored again in all its glory
	11:25	our decision is that their temple be restored to them
	12:25	he had confirmed his solemn promise to restore them unharmed
1 Es	6:26	should be restored to the house in Jerusalem
3 Ma	6:8	you, Father, watched over and restored unharmed to all his family
	7:22	restored it to them with extreme fear

RESTRAIN

Ad E	16:12	But, unable to restrain his arrogance
Wis	16:18	At one time the flame was restrained
Sir	18:30	Do not follow your base desires, but restrain your appetites
	46:7	restrained the people from sin
Bel	14:19	and restrained the king from going in, and said
3 Ma	1:23	and being barely restrained by the old men and the elders
2 Es	7:116	or else, when it had produced him, had restrained him from sinning
4 Ma	1:30	by virtue of the restraining power of self-control
	1:35	For the emotions of the appetites are restrained

RESTRICTED   1

Sir	22:23	For one should not always despise restricted circumstances

RESULT, subst.   7 = 0.005 %

Wis	1:11	because no secret word is without result
2 Ma	4:42	As a result, they wounded many of them, and killed some
	7:12	As a result the king himself and those with him
	9:2	with the result that Antiochus was put to flight by the inhabitants
	10:13	As a result he was accused before Eupator
3 Ma	5:41	As a result the city is in a tumult
4 Ma	12:3	You see the result of your brothers'stupidity

RESULT, verb   4 = 0.003 %

Sir	20:9	and a windfall may result in a loss
	38:18	For sorrow results in death
3 Ma	1:4	When a bitter fight resulted
	1:28	resulted in an immense uproar

RESUME   1

4 Ma	8:13	the tyrant resumed speaking :

RESURRECTION   3 = 0.002 %

2 Ma	7:14	But for you there will be no resurrection to life !
	12:43	taking account of the resurrection
2 Es	2:23	and I will give you the first place in my resurrection

RETAIN   3 = 0.002 %

Wis	19:20	Fire even in water retained its normal power
Sir	41:16	For it is not good to retain every kind of shame
2 Es	14:40	for my spirit retained its memory

RETAINING   1

Sir	50:2	the high retaining walls for the temple enclosure

RETINUE   2

2 Ma	3:28	with a great retinue and all his bodyguard
4 Ma	6:13	some of the king's retinue came to him and said

RETREAT, subst.   1

2 Ma	9:2	and beat a shameful retreat

RETREAT, verb   1

2 Ma	9:1	Antiochus had retreated in disorder

RETRIBUTION   2

Sir	14:6	and this is the retribution for his baseness
	48:8	who anointed kings to inflict retribution

RETURN, subst.   6 = 0.004 %

Wis	2:5	and there is no return from our death
	11:15	In return for their foolish and wicked thoughts
Sir	17:24	Yet to those who repent he grants a return
	20:10	and there is a gift that brings a double return
1 Ma	4:24	On their return they sang hymns and praises to Heaven
	8:26	without receiving any return

RETURN, verb   103 = 0.067 %

Tob	1:22	Ahikar interceded for me, and I returned to Nineveh
	2:5	And when I returned I washed myself
	2:9	On the same night I returned from burying him
	2:13	and when she returned to me it began to bleat
	2:13	It is not stolen, is it ? Return it to the owners
	2:14	and told her to return it to the owners
	3:17	At that very moment Tobit returned and entered his house
	5:15	if you both return safe and sound
	5:20	he will return safe and sound, and your eyes will see him
	6:12	and as soon as we return from Rages
	6:17	and will never again return
	7:1	They returned her greeting
	8:21	and return in safety to his father
	14:5	After this they will return
	14:12	Then Tobias returned with his wife and his sons to Ecbatana
Jud	1:16	Then he returned with them to Nineveh
	4:3	For they had only recently returned from the captivity
	5:19	But now they have returned to their God
	6:6	and you shall fall among their wounded, when I return
	6:13	and returned to their master

	7:7	and then returned to his army
	8:36	So they returned from the tent and went to their posts
	12:9	So she returned clean and stayed in the tent
	13:13	for it was unbelievable that she had returned
	15:7	And the Israelites, when they returned from the slaughter
	16:21	After this every one returned home to his own inheritance
Wis	2:1	and no one has been known to return from Hades
	15:8	when he is required to return the soul that was lent him
Sir	16:30	and to it they return
	17:26	Return to the Most High and turn away from iniquity
	27:9	so truth returns to those who practise it
	35:2	He who returns a kindness offers fine flour
	40:1	till the day they return to the mother of all
	40:11	and what is from the waters returns to the sea
	41:10	Whatever is from the dust returns to dust
Bar	1:8	to return them to the land of Judah
	4:28	return with tenfold zeal to seek him
Sus	13:49	Return to the place of judgment
	13:50	Then all the people returned in haste
Bel	14:12	And when you return in the morning
	14:39	And the angel of God immediately returned Habakkuk to his own place
1 Ma	1:20	After subduing Egypt, Antiochus returned in the 143rd year
	2:63	because he has returned to the dust
	3:33	until he returned
	3:56	that each should return to his home, according to the law
	4:23	Then Judas returned to plunder the camp
	5:8	then he returned to Judea
	5:19	but do not engage in battle with the Gentiles until we return
	5:54	before they returned in safety
	5:68	he plundered the cities and returned to the land of Judah
	6:4	to return to Babylon
	6:56	had returned from Persia and Media
	6:63	Then he departed with haste and returned to Antioch
	7:25	he returned to the king
	7:35	then if I return safely I will burn up this house
	9:42	they returned to the marshes of the Jordan
	9:50	Bacchides then returned to Jerusalem
	9:57	he returned to the king
	10:9	and he returned them to their parents
	10:52	Since I have returned to my kingdom
	10:55	on which you returned to the land of your fathers
	10:66	And Jonathan returned to Jerusalem in peace and gladness
	10:68	he was greatly grieved and returned to Antioch
	10:87	And Jonathan and those with him returned to Jerusalem
	11:7	then he returned to Jerusalem
	11:51	and they returned to Jerusalem with much spoil
	11:54	After this Trypho returned
	11:73	they returned to him and joined him in the pursuit
	11:74	And Jonathan returned to Jerusalem
	12:24	Now Jonathan heard that the commanders of Demetrius had returned
	12:26	and they returned and reported to him
	12:35	When Jonathan returned he convened the elders of the people
	12:46	and they returned to the land of Judah
	15:36	But returned in wrath to the king
	16:10	And he returned to Judea safely
	16:17	and returned evil for good
2 Ma	2:17	and has returned the inheritance to all
	4:25	After receiving the king's orders he returned
	4:36	When the king returned from the region of Cilicia
	8:25	they were obliged to return because the hour was late
	11:29	Menelaus has informed us that you wish to return home
	12:1	Lysias returned to the king
	15:28	When the action was over and they were returning with joy
1 Es	4:34	and returns to its place in one day
	5:8	and who returned to Jerusalem and the rest of Judea
	5:67	And they learned that those who had returned from captivity
	6:28	who have returned from the captivity of Judea
	9:3	to all who had returned from the captivity
	9:4	those who had returned from captivity
	9:15	And those who had returned from the captivity
3 Ma	1:1	When Philopator learned from those who returned
	5:3	When he had given these orders he returned to his feasting
	5:16	The king, after considering this, returned to his drinking
	5:36	and urged the guests to return to their celebrating
	6:30	Then the king, when he had returned to the city
	7:8	to return to his own home
2 Es		as the spirit leaves the body to return again to him who gave it
	10:4	And now I intend not to return to the city
	12:40	and I had not returned to the city
	15:60	as they return from devastated Babylon
	16:14	and shall not return until they come over the earth
	16:16	Just as an arrow shot by a mighty archer does not return
	16:16	so the calamities that are sent upon the earth shall not return

RETURNED 2

| 1 Es | 7:11 | Not all of the returned captives were purified |
| | 7:12 | for all the returned captives |

RETURNING 1

| 1 Es | 2:15 | with the returning exiles from Babylon to Jerusalem |

REVEAL 29 = 0.019 %

Tob	12:7	but gloriously to reveal the works of God
	12:11	but gloriously to reveal the works of God
Sir	1:6	The root of wisdom – to whom has it been revealed ?
	1:30	The Lord will reveal your secrets
	3:19	but to the meek he reveals his secrets
	4:18	and will reveal her secrets to him
	8:19	Do not reveal your thoughts to every one
	11:27	his deeds will be revealed
	39:8	He will reveal instruction in his teaching
	41:23	and of revealing secrets
	42:19	and he reveals the tracks of hidden things
	46:20	he prophesied and revealed to the king his death
	48:25	He revealed what was to occur to the end of time
L Jr	6:26	revealing to mankind their worthlessness
2 Ma	12:41	the righteous Judge, who reveals the things that are hidden
3 Ma	2:19	and reveal your mercy at this hour
	6:9	reveal yourself quickly to those of the nation of Israel
	6:18	revealed his holy face and opened the heavenly gates
	6:39	on which the Lord of all most gloriously revealed his mercy
2 Es	3:14	and to him only didst thou reveal the end of the times
	6:28	and the truth, which has been so long without fruit, shall be revealed
	7:28	For my son the Messiah shall be revealed
	7:33	And the Most High shall be revealed upon the seat of judgment
	7:123	Or that a paradise shall be revealed
	10:38	for the Most High has revealed many secrets to you
	10:52	for I knew that the Most High would reveal these things to you
	10:54	where the city of the Most High was to be revealed
	13:32	then my Son will be revealed
	14:3	I revealed myself in a bush and spoke to Moses

REVEL, verb 2

| Sir | 9:9 | nor revel with her at wine |
| | 18:32 | Do not revel in great luxury |

REVEL, subst. 1

| Wis | 14:23 | or hold frenzied revels with strange customs |

REVELLER, REVELER 1

| Sir | 21:15 | when a reveller hears it, he dislikes it |

REVELLING, REVELING 1

| 2 Ma | 6:4 | For the temple was filled with debauchery and revelling |

REVELRY 3 = 0.002 %

Wis	2:9	Let none of us fail to share in our revelry
3 Ma	4:8	instead of good cheer and youthful revelry
	5:17	to give themselves over to revelry

REVENGE 6 = 0.004 %

Jud	1:12	that he would surely take revenge
	2:1	about carrying out his revenge on the whole region
	6:5	until I take revenge on this race that came out of Egypt
	8:27	nor has he taken revenge upon us
	8:35	to take revenge upon our enemies
	9:2	to take revenge on the strangers

REVENUE 12 = 0.008 %

1 Ma	3:29	and the revenues from the country were small
	3:31	and collect the revenues from those regions
	10:31	her tithes and her revenues
	10:40	out of the king's revenues from appropriate places
	10:44	be paid from the revenues of the king
	10:45	also be paid from the revenues of the king
2 Ma	3:3	defrayed from his own revenues all the expenses
	4:8	and, from another source of revenue, 80 talents
	4:28	for the collection of the revenue was his responsibility
	9:16	he would provide from his own revenues
3 Ma	3:16	And when we had granted very great revenues
	6:30	summoned the official in charge of the revenues

REVERE 5 = 0.003 %

Bel	14:4	The king revered it and went every day to worship it
	14:5	He answered, Because I do not revere man-made idols
	14:23	which the Babylonians revered
4 Ma	8:14	and whatever justice you revere will be merciful to you
	11:5	It is because we revere the Creator of all things and live

REVERED 1

| 2 Ma | 6:28 | for the revered and holy laws |

REVERENCE, subst. 3 = 0.002 %

4 Ma	5:24	so that with proper reverence we worship the only real God
	7:6	which had room only for reverence and purity
	17:15	Reverence for God was victor

REVERENTLY   1
4 Ma   1 : 17   by which we learn divine matters reverently

REVERSE   1
3 Ma   2 : 10   you promised that if we should have reverses

REVILE   1
Sir 22 : 20   and one who reviles a friend will break off the friendship

REVILER   1
Sir 23 : 8   the reviler and the arrogant are tripped by them

REVILING   1
Sir 22 : 22   but as for reviling, arrogance, disclosure of secrets

REVIVE   4 = 0.003 %
Sir 46 : 12   May their bones revive from where they lie
     49 : 10   revive from where they lie
2 Ma 13 : 11   and not to let the people who had just begun to revive
4 Ma 18 : 4   and by reviving observance of the law in the homeland

REVOKE   1
3 Ma   5 : 40   and again revoking your decree in the matter ?

REVOLT, subst.   2
1 Ma 11 : 14   because the people of that region were in revolt
2 Ma   5 : 11   he took it to mean that Judea was in revolt

REVOLT, verb   7 = 0.005 %
Sir 16 : 7   who revolted in their might
     47 : 23   Rehoboam, whose policy caused the people to revolt
1 Ma 11 : 43   for all my troops have revolted
     13 : 16   so that when released he will not revolt against us
2 Ma   1 : 7   after Jason and his company revolted from the holy land and the
              kingdom
      4 : 30   revolted because their cities had been given
     13 : 23   had revolted in Antioch

REVOLUTION   1
4 Ma   3 : 21   a revolution against the public harmony

REVULSION   1
2 Ma   9 : 9   the whole army felt revulsion at his decay

REWARD, subst.   19 = 0.012 %
Wis   5 : 15   and their reward is with the Lord
     10 : 17   She gave to holy men the reward of their labours
Sir   2 : 8   and your reward will not fail
     11 : 18   and this is the reward allotted to him :
     11 : 22   The blessing of the Lord is the reward of the godly
     51 : 22   The Lord gave me a tongue as my reward
     51 : 30   and in God's time he will give you your reward
2 Ma 12 : 45   But if he was looking to the splendid reward
     15 : 33   and hang up these rewards of his folly
2 Es   2 : 35   Be ready for the rewards of the kingdom
      3 : 33   Yet their reward has not appeared
      4 : 35   And when will come the harvest of our reward ?
      7 : 35   and the reward shall be manifested
      7 : 83   The 3rd way, they shall see the reward laid up
      7 : 98   and from whom they are to receive their reward when glorified
      8 : 33   shall receive their reward in consequence of their own deeds
      8 : 39   and their receiving their reward
     13 : 56   for there is a reward laid up with the Most High
     15 : 55   The reward of a harlot is in your bosom

REWARD, verb   3 = 0.002 %
Ad E 12 : 5   and rewarded him for these things
Sir 11 : 26   to reward a man on the day of death
     36 : 16   Reward those who wait for thee

REZIN   1
1 Es   5 : 31   the sons of Reaiah, the sons of Rezin, the sons of Nekoda

RHODES   1
1 Ma 15 : 23   and to Rhodes, and to Phaselis, and to Cos

RHODOCUS   1
2 Ma 13 : 21   But Rhodocus, a man from the ranks of the Jews

RHYTHM   2
Wis 17 : 18   or the rhythm of violently rushing water
     19 : 18   as on a harp the notes vary the nature of the rhythm

RIB   2
4 Ma 11 : 19   and pierced his ribs so that his entrails were burned through
     18 : 7   but I guarded the rib from which woman was made

RICH, adj., subst.   34 = 0.022 %
Wis   8 : 5   what is richer than wisdom who effects all things ?
     10 : 11   she stood by him and made him rich

Sir   8 : 2   Do not quarrel with a rich man
     10 : 22   The rich, and the eminent, and the poor
     10 : 30   while a rich man is honoured for his wealth
     11 : 18   There is a man who is rich through his diligence and self-denial
     13 : 2   nor associate with a man mightier and richer than you
     13 : 3   A rich man does wrong, and he even adds reproaches
     13 : 4   A rich man will exploit you if you can be of use to him
     13 : 18   And what peace between a rich man and a poor man ?
     13 : 19   likewise the poor are pastures for the rich
     13 : 20   likewise a poor man is an abomination to a rich one
     13 : 21   When a rich man totters, he is steadied by friends
     13 : 22   If a rich man slips, his helpers are many
     13 : 23   When the rich man speaks all are silent
     19 : 1   A workman who is a drunkard will not become rich
     22 : 23   nor admire a rich man who is stupid
     25 : 2   a beggar who is proud, a rich man who is a liar
     25 : 6   Rich experience is the crown of the aged
     26 : 4   Whether rich or poor, his heart is glad
     27 : 1   and whoever seeks to get rich will avert his eyes
     30 : 14   than a rich man who is severely afflicted in body
     31 : 3   The rich man toils as his wealth accumulates
     31 : 8   Blessed is the rich man who is found blameless
     32 : 6   A seal of emerald in a rich setting of gold
     44 : 6   rich men furnished with resources
Sus 13 : 4   Joakim was very rich
1 Ma   6 : 2   Its temple was very rich, containing golden shields
2 Ma   7 : 24   that he would make him rich and enviable
1 Es   3 : 5   Darius the king will give rich gifts
      3 : 19   of the slave and the free, of the poor and the rich
      3 : 21   It makes all hearts feel rich, forgets kings and satraps
3 Ma   5 : 31   I would have prepared them to be a rich feast
4 Ma   4 : 4   and went up to Seleucus to inform him of the rich treasure

RICHES   8 = 0.005 %
Wis   8 : 5   If riches are a desirable possession in life
Sir 13 : 24   Riches are good if they are free from sin
     14 : 3   Riches are not seemly for a stingy man
     14 : 5   He will not enjoy his own riches
     21 : 4   Terror and violence will lay waste riches
     30 : 15   and a robust body than countless riches
     40 : 26   Riches and strength lift up the heart
1 Ma   4 : 23   and cloth dyed blue and sea purple, and great riches

RICHLY   1
Sir 45 : 12   the delight of the eyes, richly adorned

RIDDLE   2
Wis   8 : 8   she understands turns of speech and the solutions of riddles
Sir 47 : 15   and you filled it with parables and riddles

RIDE   1
2 Ma   9 : 4   But the judgment of heaven rode with him !

RIDER   4 = 0.003 %
Jud   9 : 7   they are exalted, with their horses and riders
2 Ma   3 : 25   with a rider of frightening mien
      3 : 25   Its rider was seen to have armour and weapons of gold
     13 : 15   He stabbed the leading elephant and its rider

RIDGE   1
Jud   3 : 9   near Dothan, fronting the great ridge of Judea

RIDICULE   3 = 0.002 %
Sir   7 : 11   Do not ridicule a man who is bitter in soul
     20 : 17   How many will ridicule him, and how often !
2 Es   2 : 21   do not ridicule a lame man, protect the maimed

RIDICULOUS   4 = 0.003 %
Wis 17 : 8   were sick themselves with ridiculous fear
4 Ma   1 : 5   Their attempt at argument is ridiculous !
      3 : 1   This notion is entirely ridiculous
      6 : 34   It would be ridiculous to deny it

RIGHT, subst.   12 = 0.008 %
Tob   7 : 10   for it is your right to take my child
Wis   2 : 11   But let our might be our law of right
     19 : 16   those who had already shared the same rights
Sir   3 : 2   and he confirmed the right of the mother over her sons
     20 : 8   and whoever usurps the right to speak will be hated
     48 : 4   And who has the right to boast which you have ?
Sus 13 : 50   for God has given you that right
1 Ma   8 : 32   we will defend their rights and fight you on sea and on land
     11 : 58   and granted him the right to drink from gold cups
     14 : 46   the right to act in accord with these decisions
2 Ma 13 : 23   yielded and swore to observe all their rights
2 Es   2 : 20   Guard the rights of the widow

RIGHT, adj., correct   26 = 0.017 %
Tob   2 : 13   for it is not right to eat what is stolen
     13 : 6   turn back, you sinners, and do right before him

Jud	8:11	What you have said to the people today is not right
	8:29	for your heart's disposition is right
Wis	9:9	and what is right according to thy commandments
Sir	1:23	A patient man will endure until the right moment
	1:24	He will hide his words until the right moment
	2:2	Set your heart right and be steadfast
	4:20	Observe the right time, and beware of evil
	10:4	and over it he will raise up the right man for the time
	10:23	It is not right to despise an intelligent poor man
	15:11	Do not say, Because of the Lord I left the right way
	20:7	A wise man will be silent until the right moment
	20:7	but a braggart and fool goes beyond the right moment
P Az	4	and all thy works are true and thy ways right
1 Ma	2:11	as it is right and proper to remember brethren
2 Ma	6:20	that it is not right to taste
	9:12	he uttered these words : It is right to be subject to God
2 Es	5:11	Has righteousness, or any one who does right
4 Ma	1:1	So it is right for me
	5:18	not even so would it be right for us
	6:34	And it is right for us to acknowledge the dominance of reason
	8:15	and by their right reasoning nullified his tyranny
	13:5	the sovereignty of right reason over emotion
	13:7	so the seven-towered right reason of the youths
	13:24	and brought up in right living

RIGHT, adj., straight $\quad\quad\quad\quad\quad\quad\quad\quad\quad\quad\quad\quad$ 1
Wis	9:18	And thus the paths of those on earth were set right

RIGHT, adj., dexter $\quad\quad\quad\quad\quad\quad\quad\quad\quad$ 34 = 0.022 %
Wis	5:16	because with his right hand he will cover them
Sir	12:12	do not have him sit at your right
	21:19	and like manacles on his right hand
	21:21	and like a bracelet on the right arm
	36:6	make thy hand and thy right arm glorious
	47:5	and he gave him strength in his right hand
	49:11	He was like a signet on the right hand
L Jr	6:15	It has a dagger in its right hand, and has an axe
1 Ma	2:22	to the right hand or to the left
	5:46	and they could not go round it to the right or to the left
	6:45	he killed men right and left
	7:47	and the right hand which he had so arrogantly stretched out
	9:1	and with them the right wing of the army
	9:12	Bacchides was on the right wing
	9:14	Judas saw that Bacchides and the strength of his army were on the right
	9:15	and they crushed the right wing
	9:16	that the right wing was crushed
2 Ma	4:34	offered him sworn pledges and gave him his right hand
	14:33	he stretched out his right hand toward the sanctuary
	15:15	Jeremiah stretched out his right hand
1 Es	4:29	she would sit at the king's right hand
	9:43	Uriah, Hezekiah, and Baalsamus on his right hand
2 Es	3:6	which thy right hand had planted before the earth appeared
	4:47	And he said to me, Stand at my right side
	7:7	so that there is fire on the right hand
	9:38	I lifted up my eyes and saw a woman on my right
	10:30	Then he grasped my right hand and strengthened me
	11:12	on the right side one wing arose
	11:20	in due course the wings that followed also rose up on the right side
	11:24	and remained under the head that was on the right side
	11:35	the head on the right side devoured the one on the left
	12:29	which was on the right side
	15:22	My right hand will not spare the sinners
	16:13	For his right hand that bends the bow is strong

RIGHT, adv. $\quad\quad\quad\quad\quad\quad\quad\quad\quad\quad\quad\quad$ 3 = 0.002 %
Tob	7:12	So Raguel said, Take her right now
Bel	14:36	right over the den
2 Ma	4:12	right under the citadel

RIGHTEOUS, adj., subst. $\quad\quad\quad\quad\quad\quad$ 85 = 0.055 %
Tob	2:14	Where are your charities and your righteous deeds ?
	3:2	Righteous art thou, O Lord
	3:2	and thou dost render true and righteous judgment for ever
	4:17	Place your bread on the grave of the righteous
	13:9	but again he will show mercy to the sons of the righteous
	13:13	Rejoice and be glad for the sons of the righteous
	13:13	and will praise the Lord of the righteous
Ad E	11:7	to fight against the nation of the righteous
	11:9	And the whole righteous nation was troubled
	14:7	Thou art righteous, O Lord !
	16:15	are not evildoers but are governed by most righteous laws
Wis	2:10	Let us oppress the righteous poor man
	2:12	Let us lie in wait for the righteous man
	2:16	he calls the last end of the righteous happy
	2:18	for if the righteous man is God's son, he will help him
	3:1	But the souls of the righteous are in the hand of God
	3:10	who disregarded the righteous man
	4:7	But the righteous man, though he die early, will be at rest

	4:16	The righteous man who has died
	5:1	Then the righteous man will stand with great confidence
	5:15	But the righteous live for ever
	10:4	steering the righteous man by a paltry piece of wood
	10:5	recognized the righteous man
	10:6	Wisdom rescued a righteous man
	10:10	When a righteous man fled from his brother's wrath
	10:13	When a righteous man was sold
	10:20	Therefore the righteous plundered the ungodly
	11:13	the righteous had received benefit
	11:14	for their thirst was not like that of the righteous
	12:9	into the hands of the righteous in battle
	12:15	Thou art righteous and rulest all things righteously
	12:19	that the righteous man must be kind
	16:17	for the universe defends the righteous
	16:23	whereas the fire, in order that the righteous might be fed
	18:7	The deliverance of the righteous
	18:20	The experience of death touched also the righteous
	19:17	just as were those at the door of the righteous man
Sir	9:16	Let righteous men be your dinner companions
	18:2	The Lord alone will be declared righteous
	32:16	and like a light they will kindle righteous deeds
	35:6	The offering of a righteous man anoints the altar
	35:7	The sacrifice of a righteous man is acceptable
	35:17	and does justice for the righteous, and executes judgment
	44:10	whose righteous deeds have not been forgotten
	44:17	Noah was found perfect and righteous
Bar	2:9	for the Lord is righteous in all his works
	2:19	For it is not because of any righteous deeds
P Az	64	Bless the Lord, spirits and souls of the righteous
Sus	13:3	Her parents were righteous
	13:9	or remembering righteous judgments
	13:53	Do not put to death an innocent and righteous person
1 Ma	2:24	He gave vent to righteous anger
2 Ma	12:6	and, calling upon God the righteous Judge
	12:41	the righteous Judge, who reveals the things that are hidden
1 Es	4:39	but she does what is righteous
P Ma	1	and of their righteous posterity
	8	Therefore thou, O Lord, God of the righteous
	8	hast not appointed repentance for the righteous
3 Ma	2:22	since he was smitten by a righteous judgment
2 Es	3:11	and all the righteous who have descended from him
	4:27	that have been promised to the righteous
	4:35	Did not the souls of the righteous in their chambers
	4:39	that the time of threshing is delayed for the righteous
	7:17	that the righteous shall inherit these things
	7:18	The righteous therefore can endure difficult circumstances
	7:35	righteous deeds shall awake
	7:51	For whereas you have said that the righteous are not many but few
	7:99	This is the order of the souls of the righteous
	7:102	the righteous will be able to intercede for the ungodly
	7:111	If therefore the righteous have prayed for the ungodly now
	8:33	For the righteous, who have many works laid up with thee
	8:39	but I will rejoice over the creation of the righteous
	8:49	and have not deemed yourself to be among the righteous
	8:57	Moreover they have even trampled upon his righteous ones
	9:13	but inquire how the righteous will be saved
	10:22	our righteous men have been carried off
	10:39	For he has seen your righteous conduct
	12:7	and if I have been accounted righteous before thee beyond many others
	14:32	And because he is a righteous judge
	14:35	and then the names of the righteous will become manifest
	15:8	Behold, innocent and righteous blood cries out to me
	15:8	and the souls of the righteous cry out continually
4 Ma	15:10	For they were righteous and self-controlled and brave and magnanimous
	16:21	And Daniel the righteous was thrown to the lions
	18:15	Many are the afflictions of the righteous

RIGHTEOUSLY $\quad\quad\quad\quad\quad\quad\quad\quad\quad\quad\quad$ 1
Wis	12:15	Thou art righteous and rulest all things righteously

RIGHTEOUSNESS $\quad\quad\quad\quad\quad\quad$ 36 = 0.023 %
Tob	1:3	I, Tobit, walked in the ways of truth and righteousness
	12:8	Prayer is good when accompanied by fasting, almsgiving, and righteousness
	12:8	A little with righteousness is better
	12:9	Those who perform deeds of charity and of righteousness
	13:6	Praise the Lord of righteousness
	14:7	And all who love the Lord God in truth and righteousness
	14:11	and how righteousness delivers
Wis	1:1	Love righteousness, you rulers of the earth
	1:15	For righteousness is immortal
	5:6	and the light of righteousness did not shine on us
	5:18	he will put on righteousness as a breastplate
	8:7	And if any one loves righteousness, her labours are virtues
	9:3	and rule the world in holiness and righteousness
	12:16	For thy strength is the source of righteousness

	14 : 7	For blessed is the wood by which righteousness comes
	15 : 3	For to know thee is complete righteousness
Sir	**7** : 5	Do not assert your righteousness before the Lord
	26 : 28	a man who turns back from righteousness to sin
	45 : 26	to judge his people in righteousness
Bar	**1** : 15	Righteousness belongs to the Lord our God
	2 : 6	Righteousness belongs to the Lord our God
	2 : 18	will ascribe to thee glory and righteousness, O Lord
	4 : 13	nor tread the paths of discipline in his righteousness
	5 : 2	Put on the robe of the righteousness from God
	5 : 4	Peace of righteousness and glory of godliness
	5 : 9	with the mercy and righteousness that come from him
1 Ma	**2** : 29	Then many who were seeking righteousness and justice
	2 : 52	and it was reckoned to him as righteousness ?
2 Es	**5** : 11	Has righteousness, or any one who does right
	7 : 105	for then every one shall bear his own righteousness or unrighteousness
	7 : 114	and righteousness has increased and truth has appeared
	8 : 12	Thou hast brought him up in thy righteousness
	8 : 32	who have no works of righteousness
	8 : 36	thy righteousness and goodness will be declared
	16 : 50	so righteousness shall abhor iniquity
	16 : 52	and righteousness will reign over us

RIGHTLY   3 = 0.002 %

Wis	**6** : 4	Because as servants of his kingdom you did not rule rightly
2 Es	**4** : 20	He answered me and said, You have judged rightly
	8 : 37	Some things you have spoken rightly

RIM   1

2 Ma	**13** : 5	and it has a rim running around it

RING, subst.   1

Jud	**10** : 4	and put on her anklets and bracelets and rings

RING out   1

Wis	**17** : 4	but terrifying sounds rang out around them

RINGING   1

Sir	**45** : 9	to make their ringing heard in the temple

RIOT   1

Wis	**14** : 25	and all is a raging riot of blood and murder

RIPE   3 = 0.002 %

Wis	**4** : 5	and their fruit will be useless, not ripe enough to eat
	4 : 9	and a blameless life is ripe old age
3 Ma	**6** : 1	who had attained a ripe old age

RIPEN   3 = 0.002 %

Wis	**10** : 7	plants bearing fruit that does not ripen
Sir	**51** : 15	From blossom to ripening grape my heart delighted in her
2 Es	**16** : 26	The grapes shall ripen, and who will tread them ?

RISE   38 = 0.025 %

Tob	**12** : 13	When you did not hesitate to rise and to leave your dinner
Jud	**10** : 2	she rose from where she lay prostrate
	14 : 2	And as soon as morning comes and the sun rises
Ad E	**11** : 11	light came, and the sun rose
Wis	**1** : 5	and will rise and depart from foolish thoughts
	5 : 6	and the sun did not rise upon us
	5 : 23	a mighty wind will rise against them
	6 : 14	He who rises early to seek her will have no difficulty
	16 : 28	to make it known that one must rise before the sun
Sir	**26** : 16	Like the sun rising in the heights of the Lord
	31 : 20	he rises early, and feels fit
	32 : 14	and those who rise early to seek him will find favour
	35 : 6	and its pleasing odour rises before the Most High
	39 : 5	He will set his heart to rise early
	46 : 1	to take vengeance on the enemies that rose against them
Sus	**13** : 19	the 2 elders rose and ran to her, and said :
	13 : 61	And they rose against the 2 elders
Bel	**14** : 16	Early in the morning the king rose and came
1 Ma	**4** : 53	they rose and offered sacrifice, as the law directs
	6 : 33	Early in the morning the king rose
	9 : 8	Let us rise and go up against our enemies
2 Ma	**10** : 27	And rising from their prayer they took up their arms
	12 : 44	that those who had fallen would rise again
	14 : 45	Still alive and aflame with anger, he rose
1 Es	**4** : 47	Then Darius the king rose, and kissed him
	8 : 73	Then I rose from my fast
	8 : 75	For our sins have risen higher than our heads
	9 : 1	Then Ezra rose and went from the court of the temple
	9 : 7	Then Ezra rose and said to them
2 Es	**2** : 38	Rise and stand, and see at the feast of the Lord
	5 : 18	Rise therefore and eat some bread
	6 : 13	Rise to your feet and you will hear a full, resounding voice
	6 : 17	When I heard this, I rose to my feet and listened
	7 : 2	and he said to me, Rise, Ezra
	11 : 7	And I looked, and behold, the eagle rose upon his talons

	14 : 2	and I rose to my feet
	15 : 40	shall rise, to destroy all the earth and its inhabitants
	15 : 50	when the heat rises that is sent upon you

RISE up   15 = 0.010 %

Tob	**6** : 17	And when you approach her, rise up, both of you
Jud	**13** : 5	who have risen up against us
	16 : 17	Woe to the nations that rise up against my people !
Sir	**47** : 1	And after him Nathan rose up
	47 : 12	After him rose up a wise son who fared amply because of him
1 Ma	**8** : 5	and the others who rose up against them
	9 : 44	Let us rise up now and fight for our lives
	10 : 70	You are the only one to rise up against us
	13 : 14	Trypho learned that Simon had risen up
	14 : 32	then Simon rose up and fought for his nation
	16 : 16	Ptolemy and his men rose up, took their weapons
1 Es	**1** : 24	so that the words of the Lord rose up against Israel
2 Es	**11** : 20	in due course the wings that followed also rose up on the right side
	11 : 21	and others of them rose up, but did not hold the rule
	15 : 15	and nation shall rise up to fight against nation

RISING   2

3 Ma	**4** : 15	from the rising of the sun till its setting
2 Es	**15** : 20	from the rising sun and from the south

RISK   2

2 Ma	**11** : 7	and he urged the others to risk their lives with him
	14 : 38	and for Judaism he had with all zeal risked body and life

RITE   4 = 0.003 %

Wis	**12** : 4	their works of sorcery and unholy rites
	14 : 15	and handed on to his dependents secret rites and initiations
3 Ma	**3** : 21	and to make them participants in our regular religious rites
	6 : 36	And when they had ordained a public rite for these things

RIVAL   2

Sir	**26** : 6	when a wife is envious of a rival
	37 : 11	Do not consult with a woman about her rival

RIVALRY   2

2 Ma	**4** : 4	Onias recognized that the rivalry was serious
4 Ma	**1** : 26	thirst for honour, rivalry, and malice

RIVER   39 = 0.025 %

Tob	**6** : 1	they came at evening to the Tigris river and camped there
	6 : 2	A fish leaped up from the river
Jud	**1** : 9	and Chelous and Kadesh and the river of Egypt
	2 : 8	and every brook and river shall be filled with their dead, and overflow
Ad E	**10** : 6	The tiny spring which became a river
	10 : 6	the river is Esther, whom the king married and made queen
	11 : 10	there came a great river, with abundant water
Wis	**5** : 22	and rivers will relentlessly overwhelm them
	11 : 6	Instead of the fountain of an everflowing river
	19 : 10	the river spewed out vast numbers of frogs
Sir	**4** : 26	and do not try to stop the current of a river
	24 : 30	I went forth like a canal from a river
	24 : 31	and lo, my canal became a river, and my river became a sea
	39 : 22	His blessing covers the dry land like a river
	40 : 16	The reeds by any water or river bank
	44 : 21	and from the River to the ends of the earth
	47 : 14	You overflowed like a river with understanding
Bar	**1** : 4	all who dwelt in Babylon by the river Sud
P Az	**56**	Bless the Lord, seas and rivers
1 Ma	**3** : 32	from the river Euphrates to the border of Egypt
	3 : 37	He crossed the Euphrates river
	5 : 41	and camps on the other side of the river
	7 : 8	governor of the province Beyond the River
	11 : 7	as far as the river called Eleutherus
	11 : 60	and travelled beyond the river and among the cities
	12 : 30	for they had crossed the Eleutherus river
1 Es	**4** : 23	and rob and steal and to sail the sea and rivers
	8 : 41	I assembled them at the river called Theras
	8 : 61	We departed from the river Theras
3 Ma	**7** : 20	safely by land and sea and river
2 Es	**5** : 25	thou hast filled for thyself one river
	7 : 4	so that it is like a river
	13 : 40	he took them across the river
	13 : 43	And they went in by the narrow passages of the Euphrates river
	13 : 44	and stopped the channels of the river
	13 : 47	the Most High will stop the channels of the river again
	14 : 47	the fountain of wisdom, and the river of knowledge
	16 : 60	to send rivers from the heights to water the earth

ROAD   10 = 0.007 %

Tob	**10** : 7	And she went out every day to the road by which they had left
	11 : 5	Now Anna sat looking intently down the road for her son
Sir	**8** : 15	Do not travel on the road with a foolhardy fellow
Bar	**4** : 26	My tender sons have travelled rough roads

1 Ma	5:28	by the wilderness road to Bozrah
	5:46	This was a large and very strong city on the road
	6:33	along the road to Beth-zechariah
	9:2	They went by the road which leads to Gilgal
2 Es	1:13	and made safe highways for you where there was no road
	16:32	and its roads and all its paths shall bring forth thorns

ROAM   1
2 Es	5:8	and the wild beasts shall roam beyond their haunts

ROAR, verb   4 = 0.003 %
Ad E	11:6	both ready to fight, and they roared terribly
1 Ma	3:4	like a lion's cub roaring for prey
2 Es	11:37	a creature like a lion was aroused out of the forest, roaring
	12:31	and roaring and speaking to the eagle

ROARING, subst., adj.   2
Ad E	11:7	And at their roaring every nation prepared for war
Wis	17:19	or the sound of the most savage roaring beasts

ROAST   3 = 0.002 %
Tob	6:5	and they roasted and ate the fish
1 Es	1:12	They roasted the passover lamb with fire, as required
4 Ma	11:18	his back was broken, and he was roasted from underneath

ROB   6 = 0.004 %
Sir	9:13	lest he rob you of your life
	29:6	If he does not, the borrower has robbed him of his money
	42:9	and worry over her robs him of sleep
2 Ma	9:2	and attempted to rob the temples and control the city
1 Es	4:23	and rob and steal and to sail the sea and rivers
	4:24	and when he steals and robs and plunders

ROBBER   5 = 0.003 %
Sir	36:26	For who will trust a nimble robber
L Jr	6:15	but it cannot save itself from war and robbers
	6:18	in order that they may not be plundered by robbers
	6:57	are not able to save themselves from thieves and robbers
2 Ma	4:42	and the temple robber himself they killed

ROBE   15 = 0.010 %
Wis	18:24	For upon his long robe the whole world was depicted
Sir	6:29	and her collar a glorious robe
	6:31	You will wear her like a glorious robe
	27:8	and wear it as a glorious robe
	45:7	and put a glorious robe upon him
	45:8	the linen breeches, the long robe, and the ephod
	50:11	When he put on his glorious robe
Bar	4:20	I have taken off the robe of peace
	5:2	Put on the robe of the righteousness from God
L Jr	6:12	When they have been dressed in purple robes
	6:20	when worms from the earth devour them and their robes
	6:58	and of the robes they wear
1 Ma	6:15	He gave him the crown and his robe and the signet
	10:20	and he sent him a purple robe and a golden crown
2 Ma	4:38	he immediately stripped off the purple robe from Andronicus

ROBUST   1
Sir	30:15	and a robust body than countless riches

ROCK, subst.   8 = 0.005 %
Jud	16:15	at thy presence the rocks shall melt like wax
Wis	11:4	and water was given them out of flinty rock
	17:19	or the harsh crash of rocks hurled down
Sir	40:15	they are unhealthy roots upon sheer rock
	48:17	he tunnelled the sheer rock with iron
2 Ma	14:45	and standing upon a steep rock
2 Es	1:20	did I not cleave the rock so that waters flowed in abundance ?
	16:28	in thick groves and clefts in the rocks

ROCK, verb   1
2 Es	6:29	began to rock to and fro

ROLE   1
4 Ma	6:17	that out of cowardice we feign a role unbecoming to us !

ROLL back   1
Sir	27:27	If a man does evil, it will roll back upon him

ROMAN   15 = 0.010 %
1 Ma	8:1	Now Judas heard of the fame of the Romans
	8:10	and the Romans took captive their wives and children
	8:23	May all go well with the Romans
	8:27	the Romans shall willingly act as their allies
	8:29	Thus on these terms the Romans make a treaty
	12:4	And the Romans gave them letters to the people
	14:24	to confirm the alliance with the Romans
	14:40	For he had heard that the Jews were addressed by the Romans
	14:40	and that the Romans had received
	15:16	Lucius, consul of the Romans, to King Ptolemy, greeting

2 Ma	4:11	and alliance with the Romans
	8:10	the tribute due to the Romans, 2,000 talents
	8:36	to secure tribute for the Romans
	11:34	The Romans also sent them a letter which read thus :
	11:34	Quintus Memmius and Titus Manius, envoys of the Romans

ROME   13 = 0.008 %
1 Ma	1:10	he had been a hostage in Rome
	7:1	In the 151st year Demetrius the son of Seleucus set forth from Rome
	8:17	and sent them to Rome to establish friendship and alliance
	8:19	They went to Rome, a very long journey
	8:24	If war comes first to Rome or to any of their allies
	8:26	arms, money, or ships, as Rome has decided
	8:28	arms, money, or ships, as Rome has decided
	12:1	he chose men and sent them to Rome
	12:3	So they went to Rome
	12:16	and have sent them to Rome
	14:16	It was heard in Rome, and as far away as Sparta
	14:24	After this Simon sent Numenius to Rome
	15:15	Then Numenius and his companions arrived from Rome

ROOF   5 = 0.003 %
Jud	8:5	She set up a tent for herself on the roof of her house
Wis	17:2	and prisoners of long night, shut in under their roofs
Sir	29:22	under the shelter of his roof
1 Es	6:4	and this roof and finishing all the other things ?
4 Ma	17:3	Nobly set like a roof on the pillars of your sons

ROOM   4 = 0.003 %
Tob	3:17	came down from her upper room
	7:16	Sister, make up the other room, and take her into it
Sir	16:14	He will make room for every act of mercy
4 Ma	7:6	which had room only for reverence and purity

ROOT, subst.   21 = 0.014 %
Wis	3:15	and the root of understanding does not fail
	4:3	will strike a deep root or take a firm hold
	7:20	the varieties of plants and the virtues of roots
	15:3	and to know thy power is the root of immortality
Sir	1:6	The root of wisdom – to whom has it been revealed ?
	1:20	To fear the Lord is the root of wisdom
	3:28	for a plant of wickedness has taken root in him
	10:15	The Lord has plucked up the roots of the nations
	23:25	Her children will not take root
	24:12	So I took root in an honoured people
	40:15	they are unhealthy roots upon sheer rock
	47:22	and to David a root of his stock
1 Ma	1:10	From them came forth a sinful root, Antiochus Epiphanes
1 Es	8:78	to leave to us a root and a name in thy holy place
	8:87	and give us such a root as this
	8:88	to destroy us without leaving a root or seed or name ?
	8:89	for we are left as a root this day
2 Es	3:22	the law in the people's heart along with the evil root
	5:28	and dishonoured the one root beyond the others
	8:41	and not all that were planted will take root
	8:53	The root of evil is sealed up from you

ROOT out   1
2 Ma	12:7	and root out the whole community of Joppa

ROPE   1
3 Ma	4:8	their necks encircled with ropes instead of garlands

ROSE   4 = 0.003 %
Sir	24:14	and like rose plants in Jericho
	39:13	and bud like a rose growing by a stream of water
	50:8	like roses in the days of the first fruits
2 Es	2:19	and 7 mighty mountains on which roses and lilies grow

ROSE-BEARING   1
3 Ma	7:17	When they had arrived at Ptolemais, called rose-bearing

ROSEBUD   1
Wis	2:8	Let us crown ourselves with rosebuds before they wither

ROT, verb   1
L Jr	6:72	By the purple and linen that rot upon them

ROT away   1
2 Ma	9:9	his flesh rotted away, and because of his stench

ROUGH   1
Bar	4:26	My tender sons have travelled rough roads

ROUND up   1
4 Ma	5:4	And when many persons had been rounded up

ROUND, prep., adv.   4 = 0.003 %
Sir **50** :5   How glorious he was when the people gathered round him
1 Ma **5** :46   and they could not go round it to the right or to the left
   12 :45   and will turn round and go home
1 Es **8** :72   gathered round me, as I mourned over this iniquity

ROUND ABOUT, prep., adv.   13 = 0.008 %
Jud **3** :7   And these people and all in the country round about
Sir **45** :9   with very many golden bells round about
1 Ma **1** :11   with the Gentiles round about us
   3 :25   and terror fell upon the Gentiles round about them
   4 :7   with cavalry round about it
   4 :60   with high walls and strong towers round about
   5 :1   When the Gentiles round about heard
   5 :65   and burned its towers round about
   7 :17   round about Jerusalem
   7 :46   And men came out of all the villages of Judea round about
   10 :45   and fortifying it round about
   12 :13   the kings round about us have waged war against us
   12 :53   And all the nations round about them tried to destroy them

ROUSE   6 = 0.004 %
Jud **14** :3   and rouse the officers of the Assyrian army
Sir **22** :7   or who rouses a sleeper from deep slumber
   36 :7   Rouse thy anger and pour out thy wrath
3 Ma **5** :15   And when he had with difficulty roused him, he pointed out
2 Es **7** :31   which is not yet awake, shall be roused
4 Ma **8** :9   But if by disobedience you rouse my anger

ROUSE up   1
2 Es **12** :31   And as for the lion whom you saw rousing up out of the forest

ROUT, verb   5 = 0.003 %
1 Ma **5** :60   Then Joseph and Azariah were routed
   6 :5   that the armies which had gone into the land of Judah had been routed
   11 :55   and he fled and was routed
   11 :72   and routed them, and they fled
3 Ma **1** :5   And so it came about that the enemy was routed in the action

ROUT, subst.   3 = 0.002 %
1 Ma **4** :35   And when Lysias saw the rout of his troops
   5 :61   Thus the people suffered a great rout
2 Ma **12** :27   After the rout and destruction of these

ROUTE   1
1 Ma **11** :4   for they had piled them in heaps along his route

ROVING
Wis **4** :12   and roving desire perverts the innocent mind

ROW, subst.
Wis **18** :24   on the 4 rows of stones

ROYAL   23 = 0.015 %
Jud **2** :18   and a huge amount of gold and silver from the royal palace
Ad E **15** :6   He was seated on his royal throne
   16 :11   as the person second to the royal throne
Wis **14** :21   because men, in bondage to misfortune or to royal authority
   18 :15   from the royal throne
Bar **5** :6   carried in glory, as on a royal throne
1 Ma **3** :32   He left Lysias, a distinguished man of royal lineage
   6 :43   that one of the beasts was equipped with royal armour
   6 :47   And when the Jews saw the royal might
   7 :2   As he was entering the royal palace of his fathers
   11 :34   we have granted release from the royal taxes
   13 :15   that Jonathan your brother owed the royal treasury
   15 :8   Every debt you owe to the royal treasury
2 Ma **4** :11   He set aside the existing royal concessions to the Jews
1 Es **1** :54   and the royal stores, they took and carried away to Babylon
   6 :21   let search be made in the royal archives
   6 :23   in the royal archives that were deposited in Babylon
   8 :18   you may provide out of the royal treasury
   8 :67   And they delivered the king's orders to the royal stewards
3 Ma **3** :28   and also 2,000 drachmas from the royal treasury
   7 :12   so that freely and without royal authority or supervision
4 Ma **3** :8   he came, sweating and quite exhausted, to the royal tent
   14 :2   O reason, more royal than kings and freer than the free !

RUB   2
Tob **11** :8   and when they smart he will rub them
   11 :12   And when his eyes began to smart he rubbed them

RUBBISH   1
Tob **5** :18   but consider it rubbish as compared to our child

RUBY   2
Tob **13** :17   and ruby and stones of Ophir
Sir **32** :5   A ruby seal in a setting of gold

RUDDER   1
4 Ma **7** :3   in no way did he turn the rudder of religion

RUDELY   1
2 Ma **14** :30   and was meeting him more rudely than had been his custom

RUIN, subst.   15 = 0.010 %
Tob **4** :13   For in pride there is ruin and great confusion
   14 :4   and will be in ruins for a time
Jud **13** :20   but have avenged our ruin
Sir **1** :22   for a man's anger tips the scale to his ruin
   4 :19   and hand him over to his ruin
   20 :25   but the lot of both is ruin
   31 :6   Many have come to ruin because of gold
   50 :4   He considered how to save his people from ruin
Bar **4** :33   and was glad for your ruin
1 Ma **2** :7   the ruin of my people, the ruin of the holy city
   2 :49   it is a time of ruin and furious anger
   4 :38   They saw also the chambers of the priests in ruins
   7 :7   let him go and see all the ruin
2 Es **2** :6   and bring their mother to ruin

RUIN, verb   5 = 0.003 %
Sir **8** :2   for gold has ruined many
   10 :3   An undisciplined king will ruin his people
   29 :18   Being surety has ruined many men who were prosperous
2 Es **8** :43   or if it has been ruined by too much rain, it perishes
   15 :13   because their seed shall fail and their trees shall be ruined

RUINED   1
Sir **49** :13   and set up the gates and bars and rebuilt our ruined houses

RULE, subst.   9 = 0.006 %
Sir **10** :1   and the rule of an understanding man will be well ordered
1 Ma **2** :19   Even if all the nations that live under the rule of the king
   10 :52   and established my rule
   14 :4   his rule was pleasing to them
2 Es **9** :34   And behold, it is the rule that
   11 :18   and held the rule like the former ones
   11 :21   and others of them rose up, but did not hold the rule
   11 :25   and hold the rule
4 Ma **7** :21   by the whole rule of philosophy

RULE, verb   53 = 0.035 %
Jud **1** :1   who ruled over the Assyrians in the great city of Nineveh
   1 :1   who ruled over the Medes in Ecbatana
   1 :6   and in the plain where Arioch ruled the Elymaeans
   5 :3   Who rules over them as king, leading their army ?
Ad E **13** :9   He said : O Lord, Lord, King who rulest over all things
   16 :16   For God, who rules over all things
   16 :21   For God, who rules over all things
Wis **3** :8   They will govern nations and rule over peoples
   6 :2   Give ear, you that rule over multitudes
   6 :4   Because as servants of his kingdom you did not rule rightly
   9 :3   and rule the world in holiness and righteousness
   10 :2   and gave him strength to rule all things
   12 :15   Thou art righteous and rulest all things righteously
   13 :2   were the gods that rule the world
   15 :1   and ruling all things in mercy
Sir **37** :18   and it is the tongue that continually rules them
   44 :3   There were those who ruled in their kingdoms
Bar **2** :34   and they will rule over it
   3 :16   and those who rule over the beasts on the earth
1 Ma **1** :4   and ruled over countries, nations, and princes
   1 :8   Then his officers began to rule, each in his own place
   8 :16   They trust one man each year to rule over them
   14 :7   he ruled over Gazara and Beth-zur and the citadel
   14 :17   and that he was ruling over the country and the cities in it
1 Es **2** :27   and that mighty and cruel kings ruled in Jerusalem
   4 :2   who rule over land and sea and all that is in them ?
   4 :15   and to every people that rules over sea and land
   4 :22   Hence you must realize that women rule over you !
3 Ma **3** :15   and we considered that we should not rule
   5 :28   This was the act of God who rules over all things
2 Es **5** :3   And the land which you now see ruling
   11 :16   Hear me, you who have ruled the earth all this time
   11 :17   After you no one shall rule as long as you
   11 :20   in order to rule
   11 :20   There were some of them that ruled, yet disappeared suddenly
   11 :34   which also ruled over the earth and its inhabitants
   12 :23   and shall rule the earth
   14 :34   If you, then, will rule over your minds
4 Ma **1** :3   that reason rules over those emotions that hinder self-control
   1 :5   Some might perhaps ask, If reason rules the emotions
   1 :6   For reason does not rule its own emotions
   1 :14   and whether reason rules over all these
   1 :19   since by means of it reason rules over the emotions
   1 :32   and reason obviously rules over both
   1 :33   Is it not because reason is able to rule over appetites ?
   2 :4   Not only is reason proved to rule

	2:9	If one is greedy, he is ruled by the law through his reason
	2:9	we can recognize that reason rules the emotions
	2:15	It is evident that reason rules even the more violent emotions
	2:23	rule a kingdom that is temperate, just, good, and courageous
	3:1	for it is evident that reason is not over its own emotions
	16:2	that men have ruled over the emotions
	17:20	our enemies did not rule over our nation

RULER 47 = 0.031 %
Jud	7:23	gathered about Uzziah and the rulers of the city
	8:9	spoken by the people against the ruler
	8:11	Listen to me, rulers of the people of Bethulia !
	8:35	Uzziah and the rulers said to her
	9:3	So thou gavest up their rulers to be slain
Ad E	13:1	to the rulers of the 127 provinces
	13:2	writes thus : Having become ruler of many nations
	16:1	to the rulers of the provinces from India to Ethiopia, 127 satrapies
Wis	1:1	Love righteousness, you rulers of the earth
	5:23	and evil-doing will overturn the thrones of rulers
	8:11	and in the sight of rulers I shall be admired
	14:19	For he, perhaps wishing to please his ruler
Sir	4:27	nor show partiality to a ruler
	10:2	and like the ruler of the city, so are all its inhabitants
	10:3	through the understanding of its rulers
	10:14	The Lord has cast down the thrones of rulers
	10:24	The nobleman, and the judge, and the ruler will be honoured
	11:6	Many rulers have been greatly disgraced
	17:17	he appointed a ruler for every nation
	23:1	O Lord, Father and Ruler of my life
	36:10	Crush the heads of the rulers of the enemy
	39:4	He will serve among great men and appear before rulers
	41:17	and of a lie, before a prince or a ruler
	46:13	established the kingdom and anointed rulers over his people
	46:18	and all the rulers of the Philistines
	48:12	in all his days he did not tremble before any ruler
	48:15	but with rulers from the house of David
L Jr	6:14	Like a local ruler the god holds a sceptre
1 Ma	1:26	rulers and elders groaned
	6:14	and made him ruler over all his kingdom
	9:30	as our ruler and leader, to fight our battle
	10:38	that they are considered to be under one ruler
	11:62	and took the sons of their rulers as hostages
	14:20	The rulers and the city of the Spartans
	14:28	and the people and the rulers of the nation
2 Ma	5:8	Accused before Aretas the ruler of the Arabs
1 Es	6:7	the local rulers in Syria and Phoenicia
	6:27	and those who were appointed as local rulers
3 Ma	2:2	the only ruler, almighty, give attention to us
	2:3	are a just Ruler
	2:7	the Ruler over the whole creation
	5:7	they all called upon the Almighty Lord and Ruler of all power
	5:51	imploring the Ruler over every power
	6:4	the former ruler of this Egypt
	7:9	we always shall have not man but the Ruler over every power
2 Es	6:54	as ruler over all the works which thou hadst made
4 Ma	4:18	So the king appointed him high priest and ruler of the nation

RULING 1
1 Es	9:4	in accordance with the decision of the ruling elders

RUMBLING 1
2 Es	6:2	and before the rumblings of thunder sounded

RUMOUR, RUMOR 4 = 0.003 %
Wis	5:9	and like a rumour that passes by
2 Ma	5:5	When a false rumour arose that Antiochus was dead
3 Ma	3:2	a hostile rumour was circulated against the Jewish nation
4 Ma	4:22	he heard that a rumour of his death had spread

RUN 22 = 0.014 %
Tob	11:3	Let us run ahead of your wife and prepare the house
	11:9	Then Anna ran to meet them, and embraced her son
	11:10	But his son ran to him
Jud	6:12	and ran out of the city to the top of the hill
	6:16	and all their young men and their women ran to the assembly
	13:13	They all ran together, both small and great
Wis	3:7	and will run like sparks through the stubble
Sir	27:17	but if you betray his secrets, do not run after him
	35:15	Do not the tears of the widow run down her cheek
Sus	13:19	the 2 elders rose and ran to her, and said :
	13:25	And one of them ran and opened the garden doors
	13:38	and we saw this wickedness we ran to them
1 Ma	2:24	he ran and killed him upon the altar
	6:45	He courageously ran into the midst of the phalanx to reach it
	16:21	But some one ran ahead and reported to John at Gazara
2 Ma	3:19	ran together to the gates, and some to the walls
	11:22	The king's letter ran thus :
	13:5	and it has a rim running around it
	14:45	he ran through the crowd

4 Ma	7:11	ran through the multitude of the people
	12:10	Running to the nearest of the braziers
	14:5	but all of them, as though running the course toward immortality

RUN away 2
Tob	2:8	he once ran away, and here he is burying the dead again !
Sir	33:31	If you ill-treat him, and he leaves and runs away

RUN off 1
2 Ma	8:13	ran off and got away

RUN out 2
Jud	12:3	Holofernes said to her, If your supply runs out
3 Ma	5:25	since the time had run out

RUN over 2
2 Ma	12:16	appeared to be running over with blood
2 Es	2:32	because my springs run over, and my grace will not fail

RUN up 1
2 Ma	14:43	He bravely ran up on the wall

RUNAWAY 1
2 Ma	8:35	and made his way alone like a runaway slave

RUNNING 1
Wis	17:19	or the unseen running of leaping animals

RUSH, subst. 1
3 Ma	1:19	in a disorderly rush flocked together in the city

RUSH, verb 14 = 0.009 %
Jud	14:3	and they will rush into the tent of Holofernes
Wis	5:11	and pierced by the force of its rushing flight
	17:18	or the rhythm of violently rushing water
Sir	21:22	The foot of a fool rushes into a house
Bel	14:36	with the rushing sound of the wind itself
1 Ma	3:23	he rushed suddenly against Seron and his army
	9:40	Then they rushed upon them from the ambush
2 Ma	3:25	and it rushed furiously at Heliodorus
	5:26	then rushed into the city with his armed men
	9:2	Therefore the people rushed to the rescue with arms
	9:7	as it was rushing along
	10:16	rushed to the strongholds of the Idumeans
	12:15	rushed furiously upon the walls
4 Ma	6:8	One of the cruel guards rushed at him

RUSH in 3 = 0.002 %
Sus	13:26	they rushed in at the side door
1 Ma	16:16	and rushed in against Simon in the banquet hall
2 Ma	14:43	and the crowd was now rushing in through the doors

RUSH off 2
2 Ma	11:7	Then they eagerly rushed off together
	12:22	and they rushed off in flight

RUSH out 6 = 0.004 %
Jud	14:17	he rushed out to the people and shouted
	15:2	but with one impulse all rushed out and fled
	15:3	rushed out upon them
	15:4	to rush out upon their enemies to destroy them
3 Ma	1:18	rushed out with their mothers, sprinkled their hair with dust
	5:47	rushed out in full force along with the beasts

RUST, subst. 2
L Jr	6:12	which cannot save themselves from rust and corrosion
	6:24	they will not shine unless some one wipes off the rust

RUST, verb 1
Sir	29:10	and do not let it rust under a stone and be lost

RUSTING 1
Sir	12:10	for like the rusting of copper, so is his wickedness

RUTHLESS 1
3 Ma	4:4	For with such a harsh and ruthless spirit

S

SABBAIAS 1
1 Es	9:32	and Sabbaias and Simon Chosamaeus

SABBATH 22 = 0.014 %
Jud	8:6	except the day before the sabbath and the sabbath itself
1 Ma	1:39	her sabbaths into a reproach, her honour into contempt
	1:43	they sacrificed to idols and profaned the sabbath
	1:45	to profane sabbaths and feasts

	2:32	against them on the sabbath day
	2:34	and so profane the sabbath day
	2:38	So they attacked them on the sabbath
	2:41	Let us fight against every man who comes to attack us on the sabbath day
	9:34	Bacchides found this out on the sabbath day
	9:43	he came with a large force on the sabbath day
	10:34	And all the feasts and sabbaths
2 Ma	5:25	and waited until the holy sabbath day
	6:6	A man could neither keep the sabbath
	8:26	For it was the day before the sabbath
	8:27	they kept the sabbath
	8:28	After the sabbath they gave some of the spoils
	12:38	and they kept the sabbath there
	15:3	who had commanded the keeping of the sabbath day
1 Es	1:58	Until the land has enjoyed its sabbaths
	1:58	it shall keep sabbath all the time of its desolation
	5:52	on sabbaths and at new moons

SABBATICAL   1
1 Ma	6:49	since it was a sabbatical year for the land

SACK, verb   1
Jud	2:27	and sacked their cities and ravaged their lands

SACKCLOTH   13 = 0.008 %
Jud	4:10	they all girded themselves with sackcloth
	4:11	and spread out their sackcloth before the Lord
	4:12	They even surrounded the altar with sackcloth
	4:14	with their loins girded with sackcloth
	8:5	and girded sackcloth about her loins
	9:1	and uncovered the sackcloth she was wearing
	10:3	and she removed the sackcloth which she had been wearing
Bar	4:20	and put on the sackcloth of my supplication
1 Ma	2:14	put on sackcloth, and mourned greatly
	3:47	They fasted that day, put on sackcloth
2 Ma	3:19	Women, girded with sackcloth under their breasts
	10:25	and girded their loins with sackcloth
2 Es	16:2	Gird yourselves with sackcloth and haircloth

SACRED   24 = 0.016 %
Tob	2:1	which is the sacred festival of the 7 weeks
Jud	3:8	and cut down their sacred groves
	4:3	and the sacred vessels and the altar and the temple
1 Ma	1:47	to build altars and sacred precincts and shrines for idols
	5:43	and fled into the sacred precincts at Carnaim
	5:44	and burned the sacred precincts with fire
2 Ma	1:15	inside the wall of the sacred precinct
	1:34	and enclosed the place and made it sacred
	6:4	and had intercourse with women within the sacred precincts
	8:33	they burned those who had set fire to the sacred gates
	10:2	and also destroyed the sacred precincts
	11:3	as he did on the sacred places of the other nations
	12:40	they found sacred tokens of the idols of Jamnia
1 Es	5:45	and that they would give to the sacred treasury for the work
3 Ma	1:7	By doing this, and by endowing their sacred enclosures with gifts
4 Ma	2:22	as a sacred governor over them all
	4:7	that those who had committed deposits to the sacred treasury
	5:29	nor will I transgress the sacred oaths of my ancestors
	7:4	Although his sacred life was consumed by tortures and racks
	7:6	you neither defiled your sacred teeth nor profaned your stomach
	9:24	Fight the sacred and noble battle for religion
	14:3	O sacred and harmonious concord of the 7 brothers
	15:13	O sacred nature and affection of parental love
	16:12	Yet the sacred and God-fearing mother

SACRIFICE, subst.   69 = 0.045 %
Jud	16:16	For every sacrifice as a fragrant offering is a small thing
Wis	18:9	For in secret the holy children of good men offered sacrifices
Sir	7:31	the gift of the shoulders, the sacrifice of sanctification
	34:19	by a multitude of sacrifices
	34:20	is the man who offers a sacrifice
	35:7	The sacrifice of a righteous man is acceptable
	35:12	and do not trust to an unrighteous sacrifice
	38:11	Offer a sweet-smelling sacrifice
	45:14	His sacrifices shall be wholly burned
	45:16	to offer sacrifice to the Lord
	45:21	for they eat the sacrifices to the Lord
	46:16	and he offered in sacrifice a sucking lamb
L Jr	6:28	The priests sell the sacrifices that are offered to these gods
	6:29	Sacrifices to them may be touched by women in menstruation or at childbirth
P Az	15	or leader, no burnt offering, or sacrifice, or oblation
	17	such may our sacrifice be in thy sight this day
1 Ma	1:45	to forbid burnt offerings and sacrifices
	1:51	and commanded the cities of Judah to offer sacrifice, city by city
	1:59	they offered sacrifice on the altar
	2:15	came to the city of Modein to make them offer sacrifice
	2:23	to offer sacrifice upon the altar in Modein
	4:53	they rose and offered sacrifice, as the law directs

	4:56	they offered a sacrifice of deliverance and praise
	11:34	To all those who offer sacrifice in Jerusalem
	12:11	at the sacrifices which we offer and in our prayers
2 Ma	1:8	and we offered sacrifice and cereal offering
	1:18	when Nehemiah, who built the temple and the altar, offered sacrifices
	1:21	And when the materials for the sacrifices were presented
	1:23	And while the sacrifice was being consumed
	1:26	accept this sacrifice on behalf of all thy people Israel
	1:31	And when the materials of the sacrifice were consumed
	1:33	had burned the materials of the sacrifice
	2:9	that being possessed of wisdom Solomon offered sacrifice
	2:10	and fire came down from heaven and devoured the sacrifices
	3:3	connected with the service of the sacrifices
	3:6	and that they did not belong to the account of the sacrifices
	3:32	offered sacrifice for the man's recovery
	3:35	Then Heliodorus offered sacrifice to the Lord
	4:14	Despising the sanctuary and neglecting the sacrifices
	4:19	to carry 300 silver drachmas for the sacrifice to Hercules
	4:19	thought best not to use it for sacrifice
	4:20	for the sacrifice to Hercules
	6:4	and besides brought in things for sacrifice that were unfit
	6:7	to partake of the sacrifices
	6:8	and make them partake of the sacrifices
	6:21	Those who were in charge of that unlawful sacrifice took the man aside
	7:42	Let this be enough, then, about the eating of sacrifices
	9:16	and the expenses incurred for the sacrifices
	10:3	and made another altar of sacrifice
	10:3	then, striking fire out of flint, they offered sacrifices
	13:23	settled with them and offered sacrifice
	14:31	while the priests were offering the customary sacrifices
1 Es	1:6	and prepare the sacrifices for your brethren
	1:12	and they boiled the sacrifices in brass pots and cauldrons
	1:17	So the things that had to do with the sacrifices to the Lord
	1:18	and the sacrifices were offered on the altar of the Lord
	5:50	and they offered sacrifices at the proper times
	5:51	and offered the proper sacrifices every day
	5:52	and thereafter the continual offerings and sacrifices
	5:53	began to offer sacrifices to God
	6:29	for sacrifices to the Lord, for bulls and rams and lambs
	8:15	so as to offer sacrifices upon the altar of their Lord
	8:65	offered sacrifices to the Lord, the God of Israel
	8:66	all as a sacrifice to the Lord
	8:72	and I sat grief-stricken until the evening sacrifice
3 Ma	1:9	he offered sacrifice to the supreme God and made thank-offerings
	5:43	of those who offered sacrifices there
2 Es	1:6	and have offered sacrifices to strange gods

SACRIFICE, verb   16 = 0.010 %
Tob	1:4	where all the tribes should sacrifice
	1:5	used to sacrifice to the calf Baal
Sir	34:18	If one sacrifices from what has been wrongfully obtained
	35:1	he who heeds the commandments sacrifices a peace offering
	35:2	and he who gives alms sacrifices a thank offering
Bar	4:7	by sacrificing to demons and not to God
1 Ma	1:43	they sacrificed to idols and profaned the sabbath
	1:47	to sacrifice swine and unclean animals
	2:25	who was forcing them to sacrifice
1 Es	5:69	and we have been sacrificing to him
	6:24	where they sacrifice with perpetual fire
	7:12	and they sacrificed the passover lamb
3 Ma	2:28	None of those who do not sacrifice
2 Es	16:68	and shall feed you what was sacrificed to idols
4 Ma	5:2	to eat pork and food sacrificed to idols
	16:20	our father Abraham was zealous to sacrifice his son Isaac

SACRIFICIAL   3 = 0.002 %
Wis	3:6	and like a sacrificial burnt offering he accepted them
	12:5	and their sacrificial feasting on human flesh and blood
2 Ma	6:21	of the sacrificial meal

SACRILEGE   4 = 0.003 %
1 Ma	1:54	they erected a desolating sacrilege
2 Ma	4:39	When many acts of sacrilege
	13:6	any man guilty of sacrilege or notorious for other crimes
1 Es	1:49	committed many acts of sacrilege and lawlessness

SAD   4 = 0.003 %
2 Es	5:16	And why is your face sad ?
	7:80	ever grieving and sad, in 7 ways
	8:16	and about Israel, for whom I am sad
	13:17	For those who are not left will be sad

SADNESS   2
2 Es	4:27	because this age is full of sadness and infirmities
	10:24	Therefore shake off your great sadness

SAFE
15 = 0.010 %

Tob	5:15	if you both return safe and sound
	5:20	he will return safe and sound, and your eyes will see him
	5:21	and he will come back safe and sound
	12:17	you will be safe
Wis	4:17	and for what he kept him safe
	10:12	and kept him safe from those who lay in wait for him
	14:3	and a safe way through the waves
1 Ma	12:4	safe conduct to the land of Judah
2 Ma	3:15	that he should keep them safe
	3:22	that he would keep what had been entrusted safe and secure
	14:3	to be safe or to have access again to the holy altar
1 Es	8:51	to keep us safe from our adversaries
2 Es	1:13	and made safe highways for you where there was no road
	7:13	But the entrances of the greater world are broad and safe
	7:121	Or that safe and healthful habitations have been reserved for us

SAFELY
10 = 0.007 %

Tob	6:4	and put them away safely
	10:12	The Lord of heaven bring you back safely, dear brother
	12:3	For he has led me back to you safely
Wis	14:5	they come safely to land
Bar	5:7	so that Israel may walk safely in the glory of God
1 Ma	7:35	then if I return safely I will burn up this house
	12:52	So they all reached the land of Judah safely
	16:10	And he returned to Judea safely
3 Ma	2:7	but carried through safely
	7:20	safely by land and sea and river

SAFETY
13 = 0.008 %

Tob	8:21	and return in safety to his father
Jud	11:3	since you have come to safety
Sir	3:1	and act accordingly, that you may be kept in safety
1 Ma	2:44	the survivors fled to the Gentiles for safety
	5:54	before they returned in safety
	6:53	those who found safety in Judea from the Gentiles
	10:83	the temple of their idol, for safety
	14:37	for the safety of the country and of the city
2 Ma	12:24	With great guile he besought them to let him go in safety
	15:1	he made plans to attack them with complete safety
1 Es	5:2	to take them back to Jerusalem in safety
4 Ma	9:4	which insures our safety through transgression of the law
	15:8	the temporary safety of her children

SAGE
1

Sir	8:8	Do not slight the discourse of the sages

SAIL, verb
10 = 0.007 %

Wis	5:10	like a ship that sails through the billowy water
	14:1	Again, one preparing to sail
Sir	43:24	Those who sail the sea tell of its dangers
1 Ma	7:1	sailed with a few men to a city by the sea
	13:29	so that they could be seen by all who sail the sea
2 Ma	5:21	that he could sail on the land and walk on the sea
	14:1	had sailed into the harbour of Tripolis
1 Es	4:23	and rob and steal and to sail the sea and rivers
4 Ma	7:3	until he sailed into the haven of immortal victory
	13:6	and make it calm for those who sail into the inner basin

SAINT
5 = 0.003 %

Tob	8:15	Let thy saints and all thy creatures bless thee
	12:15	who present the prayers of the saints
Wis	5:5	And why is his lot among the saints ?
	18:9	that the saints would share alike the same things
1 Ma	7:17	The flesh of thy saints and their blood they poured out

SAINTED
1

3 Ma	6:3	upon the children of the sainted Jacob

SAINTLY
1

4 Ma	9:25	the saintly youth broke the thread of life

SAKE
52 = 0.034 %

Sir	29:9	help a poor man for the commandment's sake
	29:10	Lose your silver for the sake of a brother or a friend
	31:17	Be the first to stop eating, for the sake of good manners
	37:5	Some companions help a friend for their stomachs' sake
	38:14	and in healing, for the sake of preserving life
	44:12	their children also, for their sake
	44:22	for the sake of Abraham his father
Bar	2:14	and for thy own sake deliver us, and grant us favour
P Az	11	For thy name's sake do not give us up utterly
	12	for the sake of Abraham thy beloved
	12	and for the sake of Isaac thy servant and Israel thy holy one
1 Ma	13:4	for the sake of Israel
2 Ma	3:33	since for his sake the Lord has granted you your life
	5:19	for the sake of the holy place
	5:19	but the place for the sake of the nation
	6:25	for the sake of living a brief moment longer
	7:23	since you now forget yourselves for the sake of his laws

	8:15	if not for their own sake
	8:15	yet for the sake of the covenants made with their fathers
	12:25	they let him go, for the sake of saving their brethren
	13:3	not for the sake of his country's welfare
3 Ma	7:11	For they declared that those who for the belly's sake
2 Es	1:10	For their sake I have overthrown many kings
	7:11	For I made the world for their sake
	7:74	and not for their sake
	8:1	The Most High made this world for the sake of many
	8:1	but the world to come for the sake of few
	8:44	and for whose sake thou hast formed all things
	9:13	and for whose sake the age was made
4 Ma	1:8	of those who died for the sake of virtue
	1:10	died for the sake of nobility and goodness
	2:10	so that virtue is not abandoned for their sakes
	6:27	I am dying in burning torments for the sake of the law
	6:30	for the sake of the law
	7:22	for the sake of virtue
	9:30	by our endurance for the sake of religion ?
	10:20	Gladly, for the sake of God
	11:2	to be tortured for the sake of virtue
	13:9	Brothers, let us die like brothers for the sake of the law
	13:12	to being slain for the sake of religion
	13:27	those who were left endured for the sake of religion
	14:6	agreed to go to death for its sake
	15:12	to death for the sake of religion
	16:13	for the sake of religion
	16:17	while an aged man endures such agonies for the sake of religion
	16:19	and therefore you ought to endure any suffering for the sake of God
	16:20	For his sake also
	16:21	and endured it for the sake of God
	16:25	They knew also that those who die for the sake of God live in God
	17:7	for the sake of religion ?
	17:20	These, then, who have been consecrated for the sake of God
	18:3	for the sake of religion

SALAMIEL
1

Jud	8:1	son of Eliab, son of Nathanael, son of Salamiel

SALATHIEL
1

2 Es	3:1	I, Salathiel, who am also called Ezra, was in Babylon

SALE
1

2 Ma	11:3	and to put up the high priesthood for sale every year

SALEM
1

Jud	4:4	and to Choba and Aesora and the valley of Salem

SALLY forth
1

1 Ma	14:36	from which they used to sally forth

SALLY out
2

1 Ma	6:31	but the Jews sallied out and burned these with fire, and fought manfully
	9:67	and Simon and his men sallied out from the city

SALT
11 = 0.007 %

Wis	10:7	and a pillar of salt standing
Sir	22:15	Sand, salt, and a piece of iron are easier to bear than a stupid man
	39:23	just as he turns fresh water into salt
	39:26	and iron and salt and wheat flour and milk and honey
	43:19	He pours the hoarfrost upon the earth like salt
L Jr	6:28	and likewise their wives preserve some with salt
1 Ma	10:29	from payment of tribute and salt tax and crown levies
	11:35	and the salt pits and the crown taxes due to us
1 Es	6:30	and likewise wheat and salt and wine and oil
	8:20	a 100 baths of wine, and salt in abundance
2 Es	5:9	And salt waters shall be found in the sweet

SALU
1

1 Ma	2:26	as Phinehas did against Zimri the son of Salu

SALVATION
11 = 0.007 %

Ad E	16:23	it may mean salvation for us and the loyal Persians
Wis	5:2	and they will be amazed at his unexpected salvation
	6:24	A multitude of wise men is the salvation of the world
Sir	13:14	and call on him for your salvation
Bar	4:24	so they soon will see your salvation by God
	4:29	will bring you everlasting joy with your salvation
2 Es	6:25	and shall see my salvation and the end of my world
	7:66	nor do they know of any torment or salvation
	7:131	so much as joy over those to whom salvation is assured
	8:39	over their pilgrimage also, and their salvation
	9:8	and will see my salvation in my land and within my borders

SAMARIA 10 = 0.007 %
Jud 1:9 and all who were in Samaria and its surrounding towns
4:4 So they sent to every district of Samaria
1 Ma 3:10 and a large force from Samaria to fight against Israel
10:30 from Samaria and Galilee
10:38 from the country of Samaria
11:28 to free Judea and the 3 districts of Samaria from tribute
11:34 were added to Judea from Samaria
2 Ma 15:1 were in the region of Samaria
1 Es 2:16 living in Samaria and other places
2:25 and the others associated with them and living in Samaria

SAME 68 = 0.044 %
Tob 2:9 On the same night I returned from burying him
3:7 On the same day, at Ecbatana in Media
4:4 When she dies, bury her beside me in the same grave
Jud 13:3 And she had said the same thing to Bagoas
Wis 15:7 he fashions out of the same clay
15:8 he forms a futile god from the same clay
17:14 they all slept the same sleep
18:8 For by the same means by which thou didst punish our enemies
18:9 that the saints would share alike the same things
18:11 The slave was punished with the same penalty as the master
18:11 and the common man suffered the same loss as the king
19:16 those who had already shared the same rights
19:18 while each note remains the same
Sir pr. does not have exactly the same sense
34:26 and goes again and does the same things
44:22 To Isaac also he gave the same assurance
Bar 1:8 At the same time, on the 10th day of Sivan
3:14 that you may at the same time discern
L Jr 6:71 In the same way, their gods of wood
1 Ma 2:25 At the same time he killed the king's officer
8:27 In the same way
10:77 At the same time he advanced into the plain
12:2 He also sent letters to the same effect to the Spartans
15:22 The consul wrote the same thing to Demetrius the king
2 Ma 2:13 The same things are reported in the records
2:14 In the same way Judas also collected all the books that had been lost
3:33 the same young men appeared again to Heliodorus
3:33 dressed in the same clothing, and they stood and said
6:8 that they should adopt the same policy toward the Jews
7:13 they maltreated and tortured the 4th in the same way
8:14 and at the same time besought the Lord
10:5 It happened that on the same day
10:5 that is, on the 25th day of the same month, which was Chislev
10:36 Others who came up in the same way
12:8 meant in the same way to wipe out the Jews
13:12 When they had all joined in the same petition
15:10 at the same time pointing out the perfidy of the Gentiles
1 Es 6:3 At the same time Sisinnes the governor of Syria and Phoenicia
9:48 at the same time explaining what was read
3 Ma 1:23 they resorted to the same posture of supplication as the others
3:11 constantly in his same purpose
4:13 be dealt with in precisely the same fashion as the others
5:20 Tomorrow without delay prepare the elephants in the same way
5:36 The king, however, reconvened the party in the same manner
6:30 in that same place in which they had expected
2 Es 2:19 and the same number of springs flowing with milk and honey
3:10 And the same fate befell them :
11:8 Do not all watch at the same time
13:12 After this I saw the same man come down from the mountain
4 Ma 2:22 but at the same time he enthroned the mind among the senses
8:5 Not only do I advise you not to display the same madness
10:2 that the same father begot me and those who died
10:2 and the same mother bore me
10:2 and that I was brought up on the same teachings ?
10:13 to the same insanity as your brothers
11:15 we ought likewise to die for the same principles
12:13 and are made of the same elements as you
13:9 who despised the same ordeal of the furnace
13:20 There each of the brothers dwelt the same length of time
13:20 and was shaped during the same period of time
13:20 and growing from the same blood and through the same life
13:21 they drank milk from the same fountains
13:24 Since they had been educated by the same law
13:24 and trained in the same virtues
14:20 she was of the same mind as Abraham
15:19 in his tortures gazing boldly at the same agonies
16:22 You too must have the same faith in God and not be grieved

SAMOS 1
1 Ma 15:23 and to Sicyon, and to Caria, and to Samos

SAMPSAMES 1
1 Ma 15:23 and to all the countries, and to Sampsames

SAMUEL 4 = 0.003 %
Sir 46:13 Samuel, beloved by his Lord, prophet of the Lord
46:19 Samuel called men to witness before the Lord
1 Es 1:20 since the times of Samuel the prophet
2 Es 7:108 and Samuel in the days of Saul, and David for the plague

SANCTIFICATION 1
Sir 7:31 the gift of the shoulders, the sacrifice of sanctification

SANCTIFY 6 = 0.004 %
Sir 36:4 As in us thou hast been sanctified before them
45:4 He sanctified him through faithfulness and meekness
1 Es 1:3 that they should sanctify themselves to the Lord
3 Ma 2:9 chose this city and sanctified this place for your name
2:16 you sanctified this place
2 Es 9:8 which I have sanctified for myself from the beginning

SANCTITY 1
2 Ma 3:12 and in the sanctity and inviolability of the temple

SANCTUARY 74 = 0.048 %
Jud 4:12 and the sanctuary to be profaned and desecrated
4:13 and in Jerusalem before the sanctuary of the Lord Almighty
5:19 and have occupied Jerusalem, where their sanctuary is
8:21 and our sanctuary will be plundered
8:24 and the sanctuary and the temple and the altar rest upon us
9:8 for they intend to defile thy sanctuary
16:20 before the sanctuary for 3 months
Sir 36:13 Have pity on the city of thy sanctuary
45:24 that he should be leader of the sanctuary and of his people
47:10 and the sanctuary resounded from early morning
47:13 and prepare a sanctuary to stand for ever
49:6 who set fire to the chosen city of the sanctuary
50:5 as he came out of the inner sanctuary !
50:11 he made the court of the sanctuary glorious
1 Ma 1:21 He arrogantly entered the sanctuary
1:36 It became an ambush against the sanctuary
1:37 On every side of the sanctuary they shed innocent blood
1:37 they even defiled the sanctuary
1:39 Her sanctuary became desolate as a desert
1:45 and drink offerings in the sanctuary
1:46 to defile the sanctuary and the priests
2:7 the sanctuary given over to aliens ?
3:43 and fight for our people and the sanctuary
3:45 The sanctuary was trampled down
3:51 Thy sanctuary is trampled down and profaned
3:58 who have assembled against us to destroy us and our sanctuary
3:59 and of the sanctuary
4:36 let us go up to cleanse the sanctuary and dedicate it
4:38 And they saw the sanctuary desolate, the altar profaned
4:41 until he had cleansed the sanctuary
4:43 and they cleansed the sanctuary
4:48 They also rebuilt the sanctuary
5:1 and the sanctuary dedicated as it was before
6:7 and that they had surrounded the sanctuary
6:18 around the sanctuary
6:26 they have fortified both the sanctuary and Beth-zur
6:51 Then he encamped before the sanctuary for many days
6:54 Few men were left in the sanctuary
7:33 Some of the priests came out of the sanctuary
7:42 against thy sanctuary
9:54 of the inner court of the sanctuary
10:39 I have given as a gift to the sanctuary in Jerusalem
10:39 to meet the necessary expenses of the sanctuary
10:44 and restoring the structures of the sanctuary
13:3 for the laws and the sanctuary
13:6 But I will avenge my nation and the sanctuary
14:15 He made the sanctuary glorious
14:15 and added to the vessels of the sanctuary
14:29 in order that their sanctuary and the law might be preserved
14:31 and lay hands on their sanctuary
14:36 and defile the environs of the sanctuary
14:42 and that he should take charge of the sanctuary
14:48 in the precincts of the sanctuary
15:7 and I grant freedom to Jerusalem and the sanctuary
2 Ma 4:14 Despising the sanctuary and neglecting the sacrifices
4:33 having first withdrawn to a place of sanctuary
4:34 persuaded Onias to come out from the place of sanctuary
9:16 and the holy sanctuary, which he had formerly plundered
10:3 They purified the sanctuary
10:5 on which the sanctuary had been profaned by the foreigners
10:5 the purification of the sanctuary took place
13:23 honoured the sanctuary
14:33 he stretched out his right hand toward the sanctuary
15:17 because the city and the sanctuary
15:18 was for the consecrated sanctuary
15:33 opposite the sanctuary
3 Ma 2:1 Then the high priest Simon, facing the sanctuary
2:18 We have trampled down the house of the sanctuary
2:28 shall enter their sanctuaries

2 Es	7:108	and Solomon for those in the sanctuary
	10:21	For you see that our sanctuary has been laid waste
	12:48	on account of the humiliation of our sanctuary
	15:25	Do not pollute my sanctuary

SAND   8 = 0.005 %
Wis	7:9	because all gold is but a little sand in her sight
Sir	1:2	The sand of the sea, the drops of rain
	18:10	Like a drop of water from the sea and a grain of sand
	22:15	Sand, salt, and a piece of iron are easier to bear than a stupid man
P Az	13	and as the sand on the shore of the sea
1 Ma	11:1	like the sand by the seashore
P Ma	9	than the sand of the sea
2 Es	4:17	for the sand stood firm and stopped them

SANDAL   2
Jud	10:4	And she put sandals on her feet
	16:9	Her sandal ravished his eyes, her beauty captivated his mind

SANDY   1
Sir	25:20	A sandy ascent for the feet of the aged

SAP, verb   1
Sir	38:18	and sorrow of heart saps one's strength

SAPPHIRE   1
Tob	13:16	For Jerusalem will be built with sapphires and emeralds

SARAH   12 = 0.008 %
Tob	3:7	it also happened that Sarah, the daughter of Raguel
	3:17	to give Sarah the daughter of Raguel
	3:17	and Sarah the daughter of Raguel
	6:10	He is your relative, and he has an only daughter named Sarah
	7:1	Sarah met them and greeted them
	7:8	And his wife Edna and his daughter Sarah wept
	7:13	Then he called his daughter Sarah
	10:10	So Raguel arose and gave him his wife Sarah
	10:12	and grant me to see your children by my daughter Sarah
	11:17	When Tobit came near to Sarah his daughter-in-law
	12:12	And so, when you and your daughter-in-law Sarah prayed
	12:14	and your daughter-in-law Sarah

SARASADAI   1
Jud	8:1	son of Sarasadai, son of Israel

SAREA   1
2 Es	14:24	and take with you Sarea, Dabria, Selemia, Ethanus, and Asiel

SAROTHIE   1
1 Es	5:34	the sons of Sarothie, the sons of Masiah, the sons of Gas

SATHRA-BUZANES   4 = 0.003 %
1 Es	6:3	and Sathra-buzanes, and their associates came to them and said
	6:7	and Sathra-buzanes, and their associates
	6:27	and Sathra-buzanes, and their associates
	7:1	and Sathra-buzanes, and their associates

SATIATE   1
3 Ma	5:10	and satiated with frankincense

SATISFY   8 = 0.005 %
Ad E	14:8	And now they are not satisfied that we are in bitter slavery
Wis	16:2	a delicacy to satisfy the desire of appetite
Sir	1:16	she satisfies men with her fruits
	14:9	A greedy man's eye is not satisfied with a portion
	32:13	and satisfies you with his good gifts
1 Es	3:3	They ate and drank, and when they were satisfied they departed
2 Es	9:26	and the nourishment they afforded satisfied me
4 Ma	3:10	he could not satisfy his thirst from them

SATRAP   5 = 0.003 %
1 Es	3:2	and all the satraps and generals and governors
	3:14	and the satraps and generals and governors and prefects
	3:21	It makes all hearts feel rich, forgets kings and satraps
	4:47	and governors and generals and satraps
	4:49	that no officer or satrap or governor or treasurer

SATRAPY   2
Ad E	16:1	to the rulers of the provinces from India to Ethiopia, 127 satrapies
1 Es	3:2	that were under him in the 127 satrapies

SAUL   2
1 Ma	4:30	into the hands of Jonathan, the son of Saul
2 Es	7:108	and Samuel in the days of Saul, and David for the plague

SAVAGE   9 = 0.006 %
Wis	17:19	or the sound of the most savage roaring beasts
2 Ma	4:25	and the rage of a savage wild beast

	10:35	and with savage fury cut down every one they met
3 Ma	5:31	for the savage beasts instead of the Jews
	7:5	with a cruelty more savage than that of Scythian custom
4 Ma	9:15	Most abominable tyrant, enemy of heavenly justice, savage of mind
	9:30	Do you not think, you most savage tyrant
	12:13	As a man, were you not ashamed, you most savage beast
	16:3	The lions surrounding Daniel were not so savage

SAVAGELY   1
2 Ma	15:2	Do not destroy so savagely and barbarously

SAVAGERY   2
2 Ma	15:21	and the savagery of the elephants
3 Ma	5:20	the king, possessed by a savagery worse than that of Phalaris

SAVE, verb   65 = 0.042 %
Tob	6:17	and he will save you and have mercy on you
	6:17	You will save her, and she will go with you
	14:10	But Ahikar was saved, and the other received repayment
Jud	10:15	You have saved your life
Ad E	10:9	who cried out to God and were saved
	10:9	The Lord has saved his people
	13:9	if it is thy will to save Israel
	13:13	For I would have been willing to kiss the soles of his feet, to save Israel !
	14:14	But save us by thy hand, and help me
	14:19	and save us from the hands of evildoers
	14:19	And save me from my fear !
Wis	9:18	and were saved by wisdom
	10:4	wisdom again saved it
	14:4	showing that thou canst save from every danger
	16:7	For he who turned toward it was saved
Sir	2:11	he forgives sins and saves in time of affliction
	34:13	for their hope is in him who saves them
	50:4	He considered how to save his people from ruin
	51:8	and dost save them from the hand of their enemies
	51:12	for thou didst save me from destruction
Bar	4:22	For I have put my hope in the Everlasting to save you
L Jr	6:12	which cannot save themselves from rust and corrosion
	6:15	but it cannot save itself from war and robbers
	6:36	They cannot save a man from death
	6:49	for they cannot save themselves from war or calamity ?
	6:57	are not able to save themselves from thieves and robbers
P Az	66	and saved us from the hand of death
Sus	13:60	who saves those who hope in him
	13:62	Thus innocent blood was saved that day
1 Ma	2:59	and were saved from the flame
	3:18	there is no difference between saving by many or by few
	4:9	Remember how our fathers were saved at the Red Sea
	4:11	that there is one who redeems and saves Israel
	6:44	So he gave his life to save his people
	9:9	Let us rather save our own lives now
	11:48	and they saved the king
2 Ma	1:11	Having been saved by God out of grave dangers
	2:17	It is God who has saved all his people
	6:22	so that by doing this he might be saved from death
	6:30	that, though I might have been saved from death
	7:25	and urged her to advise the youth to save himself
	11:6	besought the Lord to send a good angel to save Israel
	12:25	they let him go, for the sake of saving their brethren
P Ma	7	that they may be saved
	14	for, unworthy as I am, thou wilt save me in thy great mercy
3 Ma	2:32	to save themselves from the registration
	6:13	who have power to save the nation of Jacob
2 Es	6:25	shall himself be saved
	7:60	for I will rejoice over the few who shall be saved
	8:3	Many have been created, but few shall be saved
	8:41	so also those who have been sown in the world will not all be saved
	9:7	And it shall be that every one who will be saved
	9:13	but inquire how the righteous will be saved
	9:15	there are more who perish than those who will be saved
	9:21	and saved for myself one grape out of a cluster
	9:22	but let my grape and my plant be saved
	12:34	those who have been saved throughout my borders
	12:42	and like a haven for a ship saved from a storm
	13:48	who are found within my holy borders, shall be saved
4 Ma	5:6	I would advise you to save yourself by eating pork
	6:15	save yourself by pretending to eat pork
	6:27	You know, O God, that though I might have saved myself
	10:1	to save himself by tasting the meat
	10:13	but obey the king and save yourself
	12:6	to obey and save himself

SAVING   1
Sir	39:18	and none can limit his saving power

SAVIOUR, SAVIOR

Jud	9 :11	saviour of those without hope
Ad E	15 : 2	after invoking the aid of the all-seeing God and Saviour
	16 :13	our saviour and perpetual benefactor
Wis	16 : 7	not by what he saw, but by thee, the Saviour of all
Sir	24 :24	and besides him there is no saviour
	46 : 1	a great saviour of God's elect
	51 : 1	and will praise thee as God my Saviour
Bar	4 :22	from your everlasting Saviour
1 Ma	4 :30	Blessed art thou, O Saviour of Israel
	9 :21	How is the mighty fallen, the saviour of Israel !
2 Ma	3 :35	and made very great vows to the Saviour of his life
3 Ma	6 :29	praised their holy God and Saviour
	6 :32	praising God, their Saviour and worker of wonders
	7 :16	to the one God of their fathers, the eternal Saviour of Israel
2 Es	2 :36	I publicly call on my Saviour to witness

SAW, verb
1
Sus	13 :59	for the angel of God is waiting with his sword to saw you in 2

SAW down
1
Wis	13 :11	A skilled woodcutter may saw down a tree easy to handle

SAY

Tob	2 : 2	Upon seeing the abundance of food I said to my son
	2 : 3	But he came back and said
	2 : 6	how he said, Your feasts shall be turned into mourning
	2 : 8	And my neighbours laughed at me and said
	2 :13	So I said to her, Where did you get the kid ?
	2 :14	And she said, It was given to me
	3 : 1	and I prayed in anguish, saying
	3 : 8	So the maids said to her
	3 :10	But she said, I am the only child of my father
	3 :11	So she prayed by her window and said
	4 : 1	and he said to himself :
	4 : 3	So he called him and said
	5 : 3	Then Tobit gave him the receipt, and said to him
	5 : 5	Tobias said to him
	5 : 7	Then Tobias said to him, Wait for me
	5 : 8	And he said to him, Go, and do not delay
	5 : 8	So he went in and said to his father
	5 : 8	He said, Call him to me
	5 :10	Then Tobit said to him
	5 :11	And Tobit said to him
	5 :13	Then Tobit said to him, You are welcome, my brother
	5 :16	Then he said to Tobias, Get ready for the journey
	5 :16	And his father said to him, Go with this man
	5 :17	and said to Tobit, Why have you sent our child away ?
	5 :20	And Tobit said to her, Do not worry, my sister
	6 : 3	and the angel said to him, Catch the fish
	6 : 4	Then the angel said to him
	6 : 6	Then the young man said to the angel, Brother Azarias
	6 :10	the angel said to the young man
	6 :13	Then the young man said to the angel, Brother Azarias
	6 :15	But the angel said to him, Do you not remember the words
	7 : 2	Then Raguel said to his wife Edna
	7 : 4	So he said to them, Do you know our brother Tobit ?
	7 : 4	And they said, Yes, we do
	7 : 5	And Tobias said, He is my father
	7 : 8	Then Tobias said to Raphael, Brother Azarias
	7 : 9	And Raguel said to Tobias, Eat, drink, and be merry
	7 :11	And Tobias said, I will eat nothing here
	7 :12	So Raguel said, Take her right now
	7 :13	he gave her to Tobias to be his wife, saying, Here she is
	7 :16	And Raguel called his wife Edna and said to her
	7 :17	So she did as he said, and took her there
	7 :17	and said to her
	8 : 4	Tobias got up from the bed and said, Sister, get up
	8 : 6	Thou didst say, It is not good that the man should be alone
	8 : 8	And she said with him, Amen
	8 :12	and said to his wife Edna
	8 :15	Then Raguel blessed God and said
	9 : 1	Then Tobias called Raphael and said to him
	10 : 2	he said, Is it possible that he has been detained ?
	10 : 4	And his wife said to him, The lad has perished
	10 : 4	Then she began to mourn for him, and said
	10 : 6	But Tobit said to her, Be still and stop worrying ; he is well
	10 : 7	At that time Tobias said to Raguel
	10 : 8	But his father-in-law said to him, Stay with me
	10 :11	And when he had blessed them he sent them away, saying
	10 :12	He said also to his daughter
	10 :12	And Edna said to Tobias
	11 : 2	Then Raphael said to Tobias
	11 : 6	And she caught sight of him coming, and said to his father
	11 : 7	Raphael said, I know, Tobias
	11 : 9	and he said, I have seen you, my child
	11 :11	and he sprinkled the gall upon his father's eyes, saying
	11 :14	Then he saw his son and embraced him, and he wept and said
	11 :17	he blessed her, saying, Welcome, daughter !
	12 : 1	Tobit then called his son Tobias and said to him

	12 : 4	The old man said, He deserves it
	12 : 5	So he called the angel and said to him
	12 : 6	and said to them : Praise God and give thanks to him
	12 :11	I have said, It is good to guard the secret of a king
	12 :17	But he said to them, Do not be afraid
	13 : 1	Then Tobit wrote a prayer of rejoicing, and said :
	13 :18	and will give praise, saying
	14 : 3	and said to him, My son, take your sons
	14 : 4	for I fully believe what Jonah the prophet said
	14 : 5	just as the prophets said of it
	14 : 8	because what the prophet Jonah said will surely happen
	14 :11	As he said this he died in his bed
Jud	2 : 1	just as he had said
	2 : 4	and said to him
	2 : 5	Thus says the Great King, the Lord of the whole earth :
	3 : 1	So they sent messengers to sue for peace, and said
	5 : 3	and said to them, Tell me, you Canaanites
	5 : 5	Then Achior, the leader of all the Ammonites, said to him
	5 :22	When Achior had finished saying this
	5 :23	For, they said, we will not be afraid of the Israelites
	6 : 1	said to Achior and all the Moabites
	6 : 4	So says King Nebuchadnezzar, the lord of the whole earth
	6 : 5	who have said these words on the day of your iniquity
	6 :17	and all that he had said
	6 :17	and all that Holofernes had said so boastfully
	6 :18	and cried out to him, and said
	7 : 4	and every one said to his neighbour
	7 : 8	and the commanders of the coastland came to him and said
	7 :16	and he gave orders to do as they had said
	7 :23	and said before all the elders
	7 :30	And Uzziah said to them, Have courage, my brothers !
	7 :31	I will do what you say
	8 : 9	and when she heard all that Uzziah said to them
	8 :11	They came to her, and she said to them
	8 :11	What you have said to the people today is not right
	8 :28	Then Uzziah said to her
	8 :28	All that you have said has been spoken out of a true heart
	8 :32	Judith said to them, Listen to me
	8 :35	Uzziah and the rulers said to her
	9 : 1	Judith cried out to the Lord with a loud voice, and said
	9 : 2	for thou hast said, It shall not be done
	9 : 6	and the things thou didst will presented themselves and said
	10 : 7	they greatly admired her beauty, and said to her
	10 : 9	Then she said to them
	10 : 9	to open the gate for her, as she had said
	10 :14	they said to her
	10 :16	but tell him just what you have said
	10 :19	and every one said to his neighbour
	11 : 1	Then Holofernes said to her
	11 : 9	Now as for the things Achior said in your council
	11 : 9	and he told them all he had said to you
	11 :10	do not disregard what he said
	11 :20	and they marvelled at her wisdom and said
	11 :22	And Holofernes said to her
	11 :23	and if you do as you have said, your God shall be my God
	12 : 2	But Judith said, I cannot eat it, lest it be an offence
	12 : 3	Holofernes said to her, If your supply runs out
	12 : 6	and sent to Holofernes and said, Let my lord now command
	12 :11	And he said to Bagoas
	12 :13	and approached her and said
	12 :14	And Judith said, Who am I, to refuse my lord ?
	12 :17	So Holofernes said to her, Drink now, and be merry with us !
	12 :18	Judith said, I will drink now, my lord
	13 : 3	for she said she would be going out for her prayers
	13 : 3	And she had said the same thing to Bagoas
	13 : 4	Then Judith, standing beside his bed, said in her heart
	13 : 7	and took hold of the hair of his head, and said
	13 :14	Then she said to them with a loud voice
	13 :15	and said, See, here is the head of Holofernes
	13 :17	and said with one accord, Blessed art thou, our God
	13 :18	And Uzziah said to her
	13 :20	And all the people said, So be it, so be it !
	14 : 1	Then Judith said to them, Listen to me, my brethren
	14 : 7	and knelt before her, and said
	14 :13	So they came to Holofernes' tent and said to the steward
	15 : 9	and said to her, You are the exaltation of Jerusalem
	15 :10	And all the people said, So be it !
	16 : 2	And Judith said, Begin a song to my God with tambourines
Ad E	10 : 4	And Mordecai said, These things have come from God
	11 : 1	Dositheus, who said that he was a priest and a Levite
	11 : 1	which they said was genuine
	13 : 8	He said : O Lord, Lord, King who rulest over all things
	14 : 3	And she prayed to the Lord God of Israel, and said :
	15 : 8	And he comforted her with soothing words, and said to her
	15 :12	and he embraced her, and said, Speak to me
	15 :13	And she said to him, I saw you, my lord
Wis	1 : 7	and that which holds all things together knows what is said
	2 : 1	For they reasoned unsoundly, saying to themselves
	2 :20	for, according to what he says, he will be protected
	5 : 3	and in anguish of spirit they will groan, and say

	8 : 21	and with my whole heart I said :
	12 : 12	For who will say, What hast thou done ?
	15 : 12	for he says one must get money however one can, even by base means
Sir	5 : 1	nor say, I have enough
	5 : 3	Do not say, Who will have power over me ?
	5 : 4	Do not say, I sinned, and what happened to me ?
	5 : 6	Do not say, His mercy is great
	7 : 9	Do not say, He will consider the multitude of my gifts
	11 : 19	when he says, I have found rest
	11 : 23	Do not say, What do I need
	11 : 24	Do not say, I have enough
	12 : 12	and be stung by what I have said
	13 : 6	He will speak to you kindly and say, What do you need ?
	13 : 23	and they extol to the clouds what he says
	13 : 23	When the poor man speaks they say, Who is this fellow ?
	15 : 11	Do not say, Because of the Lord I left the right way
	15 : 12	Do not say, It was he who led me astray
	16 : 17	Do not say, I shall be hidden from the Lord
	17 : 14	And he said to them, Beware of all unrighteousness
	19 : 14	Question a neighbour, perhaps he did not say it
	19 : 14	but if he said it, so that he may not say it again
	19 : 21	When a servant says to his master
	20 : 16	A fool will say, I have no friend
	22 : 8	and at the end he will say, What is it ?
	23 : 18	A man who breaks his marriage vows says to himself
	24 : 8	And he said, Make your dwelling in Jacob
	24 : 31	I said, I will water my orchard and drench my garden plot
	31 : 12	and do not say, There is certainly much upon it !
	32 : 8	Speak concisely, say much in few words
	33 : 4	Prepare what to say, and thus you will be heard
	36 : 10	who say, There is no one but ourselves
	37 : 1	Every friend will say, I too am a friend
	39 : 12	I have yet more to say, which I have thought upon
	39 : 15	and this you shall say in thanksgiving :
	39 : 17	No one can say, What is this ? Why is that ?
	39 : 21	No one can say, What is this ? Why is that ?
	39 : 34	And no one can say, This is worse than that
	51 : 24	Why do you say you are lacking in these things
	51 : 25	I opened my mouth and said
Bar	1 : 10	And they said : Herewith we send you money
	1 : 15	And you shall say :
	2 : 20	as thou didst declare by thy servants the prophets, saying :
	2 : 21	Thus says the Lord :
	2 : 28	saying, If you will not obey my voice
	3 : 34	he called them, and they said, Here we are !
	4 : 9	and she said : Hearken, you neighbours of Zion
L Jr	6 : 6	But say in your heart
	6 : 20	but men say their hearts have melted
P Az	2	in the midst of the fire he opened his mouth and said :
	28	praised and glorified and blessed God in the furnace, saying :
Sus	13 : 5	Concerning them the Lord had said :
	13 : 13	They said to each other, Let us go home, for it is mealtime
	13 : 17	She said to her maids
	13 : 18	They did as she said, shut the garden doors
	13 : 19	the 2 elders rose and ran to her, and said :
	13 : 22	Susanna sighed deeply, and said
	13 : 27	for nothing like this had ever been said about Susanna
	13 : 29	They said before the people
	13 : 36	The elders said, As we were walking in the garden alone
	13 : 42	Then Susanna cried out with a loud voice, and said
	13 : 47	All the people turned to him, and said
	13 : 47	What is this that you have said ?
	13 : 48	Taking his stand in the midst of them, he said
	13 : 50	And the elders said to him, Come
	13 : 51	And Daniel said to them
	13 : 52	he summoned one of them and said to him
	13 : 53	though the Lord said
	13 : 55	And Daniel said, Very well !
	13 : 56	And he said to him
	13 : 59	And Daniel said to him, Very well !
Bel	14 : 5	And the king said to him, Why do you not worship Bel ?
	14 : 6	The king said to him
	14 : 7	Then Daniel laughed, and said
	14 : 8	and he called his priests and said to them
	14 : 9	And Daniel said to the king
	14 : 9	Let it be done as you have said
	14 : 11	And the priests of Bel said, Behold, we are going outside
	14 : 17	And the king said, Are the seals unbroken, Daniel ?
	14 : 19	and restrained the king from going in, and said
	14 : 20	The king said
	14 : 24	And the king said to Daniel
	14 : 25	Daniel said, I will worship the Lord my God
	14 : 26	The king said, I give you permission
	14 : 27	And Daniel said, See what you have been worshipping !
	14 : 28	saying, The king has become a Jew
	14 : 29	Going to the king, they said, Hand Daniel over to us
	14 : 34	But the angel of the Lord said to Habakkuk
	14 : 35	Habakkuk said, Sir, I have never seen Babylon
	14 : 38	And Daniel said, Thou hast remembered me, O God

1 Ma	1 : 11	and misled many, saying, Let us go and make a covenant
	2 : 7	and said, Alas ! Why was I born to see this
	2 : 19	But Mattathias answered and said in a loud voice :
	2 : 27	saying : Let every one who is zealous for the law
	2 : 33	And they said to them, Enough of this !
	2 : 34	But they said, We will not come out
	2 : 37	for they said, Let us all die in our innocence
	2 : 40	And each said to his neighbour :
	2 : 49	and he said to his sons :
	3 : 14	he said, I will make a name for myself
	3 : 17	they said to Judas, How can we, few as we are
	3 : 41	When the traders of the region heard what was said of them
	3 : 43	But they said to one another
	3 : 50	and they cried aloud to Heaven, saying
	3 : 56	And he said to those who were building houses
	3 : 58	And Judas said, Gird yourselves and be valiant
	4 : 5	because he said, These men are fleeing from us
	4 : 8	But Judas said to the men who were with him
	4 : 17	and he said to the people, Do not be greedy for plunder
	4 : 30	When he saw that the army was strong, he prayed, saying
	4 : 36	Then said Judas and his brothers
	5 : 10	and sent to Judas and his brothers a letter which said
	5 : 15	they said that against them had gathered together
	5 : 17	Then Judas said to Simon his brother
	5 : 32	and he said to the men of his forces
	5 : 40	Timothy said to the officers of his forces
	5 : 57	So they said, Let us also make a name for ourselves
	6 : 10	So he called all his friends and said to them
	6 : 11	I said to myself, To what distress I have come !
	6 : 22	They went to the king and said
	6 : 23	to live by what he said and to follow his commands
	6 : 57	and said to the king, to the commanders of the forces, and to the men
	7 : 3	he said, Do not let me see their faces !
	7 : 14	for they said
	7 : 18	for they said, There is no truth or justice in them
	7 : 36	and they wept and said
	7 : 40	Then Judas prayed and said
	9 : 8	He became faint, but he said to those who were left
	9 : 9	But they tried to dissuade him, saying, We are not able
	9 : 10	But Judas said, Far be it from us
	9 : 20	they mourned many days and said
	9 : 28	and said to Jonathan
	9 : 44	And Jonathan said to those with him
	9 : 55	so that he could no longer say a word
	9 : 58	Then all the lawless plotted and said, See !
	9 : 71	He agreed, and did as he said
	10 : 4	for he said, Let us act first to make peace with him
	10 : 16	So he said, Shall we find another such man ?
	10 : 22	When Demetrius heard of these things he was grieved and said
	10 : 55	Ptolemy the king replied and said
	10 : 56	and I will become your father-in-law, as you have said
	10 : 63	and said to his officers
	11 : 9	He sent envoys to Demetrius the king, saying
	11 : 31	so that you may know what it says
	11 : 57	Then the young Antiochus wrote to Jonathan, saying
	12 : 3	and entered the senate chamber and said
	12 : 44	Then he said to Jonathan
	12 : 46	Jonathan trusted him and did as he said
	12 : 53	for they said, They have no leader or helper
	13 : 3	he encouraged them, saying to them
	13 : 9	Fight our battles, and all that you say to us we will do
	13 : 14	so he sent envoys to him and said
	13 : 17	who might say
	13 : 46	they said, Do not treat us according to our wicked acts
	14 : 22	And what they said
	14 : 25	When the people heard these things they said
	14 : 44	to nullify any of these decisions or to oppose what he says
	15 : 28	to confer with him, saying
	16 : 2	and said to them : I and my brothers and the house of my father
2 Ma	1 : 29	Plant thy people in thy holy place, as Moses said
	2 : 11	And Moses said, They were consumed
	2 : 32	adding only so much to what has already been said
	3 : 12	And he said that it was utterly impossible
	3 : 13	said that this money must in any case be confiscated
	3 : 33	dressed in the same clothing, and they stood and said
	3 : 34	Having said this they vanished
	4 : 1	slandered Onias, saying that it was he who had incited Heliodorus
	6 : 17	Let what we have said serve as a reminder
	6 : 24	Such pretence is not worthy of our time of life, he said
	6 : 28	When he had said this, he went at once to the rack
	6 : 30	he groaned aloud and said :
	7 : 2	One of them, acting as their spokesman, said
	7 : 5	saying, The Lord God is watching over us
	7 : 6	when he said, And he will have compassion on his servants
	7 : 8	and said to them, No
	7 : 9	And when he was at his last breath, he said
	7 : 11	and said nobly, I got these from Heaven
	7 : 14	And when he was near death, he said

7:16	But he looked at the king, and said
7:18	And when he was about to die, he said
7:21	and said to them
7:30	While she was still speaking, the young man said
8:18	For they trust to arms and acts of daring, he said
9:4	For in his arrogance he said, When I get there
12:14	railing at them and even blaspheming and saying unholy things
14:11	When he had said this
14:34	Having said this, he went away
15:2	And when the Jews who were compelled to follow him said
15:14	And Onias spoke, saying
15:33	and said that he would give it piecemeal to the birds
15:34	blessed the Lord who had manifested himself, saying

1 Es
1:4	and he said, You need no longer carry it upon your shoulders
1:26	And the king of Egypt sent word to him saying
1:30	And the king said to his servants
2:3	Thus says Cyrus king of the Persians :
3:4	said to one another
3:9	and said, When the king wakes
3:16	And he said, Call the young men
3:17	And they said to them
3:17	Then the first, who had spoken of the strength of wine, began and said :
3:24	When he had said this, he stopped speaking
4:3	and whatever he says to them they obey
4:41	then all the people shouted, and said
4:42	Then the king said to him, Ask what you wish
4:43	Then he said to the king
4:58	and praised the King of heaven, saying
5:68	and the heads of the fathers' houses and said to them
5:70	and the heads of the fathers' houses in Israel said to them
6:3	and Sathra-buzanes, and their associates came to them and said
8:52	for we had said to the king
8:58	And I said to them, You are holy to the Lord
8:68	the principal men came to me and said
8:74	I said, O Lord
8:82	And now, O Lord, what shall we say
8:82	which thou didst give by thy servants the prophets, saying
8:92	and said to Ezra, We have sinned against the Lord
9:7	Then Ezra rose and said to them
9:10	Then all the multitude shouted and said with a loud voice
9:10	We will do as you have said
9:49	Then Attharates said to Ezra the chief priest and reader
9:53	And the Levites commanded all the people, saying

3 Ma
1:11	When they said that this was not permitted
1:12	he did not cease to maintain that he ought to enter, saying
1:14	And someone heedlessly said that it was wrong
1:15	But since this has happened, the king said
2:17	or exult in the arrogance of their tongue, saying
4:20	when they said and proved
5:20	said that the Jews were benefited by today's sleep
5:30	and with a threatening look he said
5:35	Then the Jews, upon hearing what the king had said
5:37	After summoning Hermon he said in a threatening tone
6:11	saying, Not even their god has rescued them
6:15	but just as you have said
6:23	he wept and angrily threatened his friends, saying
6:29	These then were the things he said
6:35	as we have said before
7:12	The king then, admitting and approving the truth of what they said

2 Es
1:4	The word of the Lord came to me, saying
1:12	But speak to them and say, Thus says the Lord :
1:14	Yet you have forgotten me, says the Lord
1:15	Thus says the Lord Almighty
1:18	did you not cry out to me, saying :
1:21	What more can I do for you ? Says the Lord
1:22	Thus says the Lord Almighty :
1:27	you have forsaken yourselves, says the Lord
1:28	Thus says the Lord Almighty :
1:32	their blood I will require of you, says the Lord
1:33	Thus says the Lord Almighty : Your house is desolate
1:37	yet with the spirit they will believe the things I have said
2:1	Thus says the Lord : I brought this people out of bondage
2:2	The mother who bore them says to them
2:9	says the Lord Almighty
2:10	Thus says the Lord to Ezra :
2:14	because I live, says the Lord
2:15	establish their feet, because I have chosen you, says the Lord
2:17	for I have chosen you, says the Lord
2:28	says the Lord
2:30	because I will deliver you, says the Lord
2:31	for I am merciful, says the Lord Almighty
2:34	Therefore I say to you, O nations that hear and understand
2:45	he answered and said to me
2:46	Then I said to the angel
2:47	He answered and said to me, He is the Son of God
2:48	Then the angel said to me, Go, tell my people
3:3	and I began to speak anxious words to the Most High, and said
3:28	Then I said in my heart

4:2	and said to me
4:3	Then I said, Yes, my lord
4:5	I said, Speak on, my lord
4:5	And he said to me, Go, weigh for me the weight of fire
4:6	I answered and said
4:7	And he said to me, If I had asked you
4:8	perhaps you would have said to me
4:10	And he said to me
4:12	and said to him
4:13	He answered me and said
4:14	and said, Come, let us go and make war against the sea
4:15	and said, Come, let us go up and subdue the forest of the plain
4:19	I answered and said, Each has made a foolish plan
4:20	He answered me and said, You have judged rightly
4:22	Then I answered and said, I beseech you, my lord
4:26	He answered me and said
4:33	Then I answered and said
4:34	He answered me and said
4:35	ask about these matters, saying
4:36	And Jeremiel the archangel answered them and said
4:38	Then I answered and said, O sovereign Lord
4:40	He answered me and said
4:41	And I said, No, lord, it cannot
4:41	And he said to me
4:44	I answered and said
4:47	And he said to me, Stand at my right side
4:50	And he said to me, Consider it for yourself
4:51	Then I prayed and said
4:52	He answered me and said
5:16	came to me and said, Where have you been ?
5:19	Then I said to him
5:19	He heard what I said and left me
5:23	And I said, O sovereign Lord
5:32	and he said to me, Listen to me
5:33	And I said, Speak, my lord
5:33	And he said to me
5:34	And I said, No, my lord
5:35	And he said to me, You cannot
5:35	And I said, Why not, my lord ?
5:36	He said to me, Count up for me those who have not yet come
5:38	And I said, O sovereign Lord
5:40	He said to me
5:41	And I said, Yet behold, O Lord
5:42	He said to me, I shall liken my judgment to a circle
5:43	Then I answered and said
5:44	He replied to me and said
5:45	And I said, How hast thou said to thy servant
5:46	He said to me, Ask a woman's womb
5:46	and say to it, If you bear 10 children
5:47	I said, Of course it cannot
5:48	He said to me
5:50	Then I inquired and said
5:52	Say to her, Why are those whom you have borne recently
5:56	And I said, O Lord, I beseech thee
6:1	And he said to me
6:7	And I answered and said
6:8	He said to me, From Abraham to Isaac
6:11	I answered and said, O sovereign Lord
6:13	He answered and said to me
6:18	And it said, Behold, the days are coming
6:30	And he said to me
6:33	and to say to you :
6:38	I said, O Lord
6:38	and didst say on the first day
6:55	because thou hast said that it was for us
6:56	thou hast said that they are nothing
7:2	and he said to me, Rise, Ezra
7:3	I said, Speak, my lord
7:3	And he said to me
7:10	I said, He cannot, lord
7:10	And he said to me, So also is Israel's portion
7:17	Then I answered and said, O sovereign Lord, behold
7:19	And he said to me, You are not a better judge than God
7:37	Then the Most High will say to the nations
7:45	I answered and said, O sovereign Lord
7:45	I said then and I say now :
7:49	He answered me and said, Listen to me, Ezra
7:51	For whereas you have said that the righteous are not many but few
7:53	I said, lord, how could that be ?
7:54	And he said to me
7:55	Say to her, You produce gold and silver and brass
7:58	I said, O sovereign Lord
7:59	He answered me and said
7:62	I replied and said, O earth
7:70	He answered me and said
7:71	for you have said that the mind grows with us
7:73	What, then, will they have to say in the judgment
7:75	I answered and said
7:76	He answered me and said, I will show you that also

7 : 100	I answered and said
7 : 101	He said to me
7 : 102	I answered and said
7 : 104	He answered me and said
7 : 106	I answered and said
7 : 112	He answered me and said, This present world is not the end
7 : 116	I answered and said, This is my first and last word
7 : 127	He answered and said
7 : 128	that if he is defeated he shall suffer what you have said
7 : 128	but if he is victorious he shall receive what I have said
7 : 129	spoke to the people, saying
7 : 132	I answered and said, I know, O Lord
8 : 1	He answered me and said
8 : 4	I answered and said
8 : 19	He said : O Lord who inhabitest eternity
8 : 37	He answered me and said
8 : 42	I answered and said
8 : 46	He answered me and said
8 : 58	and said in their hearts that there is no God
8 : 62	Then I answered and said
9 : 1	He answered me and said, Measure carefully in your mind
9 : 14	I answered and said
9 : 15	I said before, and I say now, and will say it again :
9 : 17	He answered me and said
9 : 28	and I began to speak before the Most High, and said
9 : 30	and thou didst say, Hear me, O Israel
9 : 38	When I said these things in my heart
9 : 40	and said to her
9 : 41	And she said to me, Let me alone, my lord
9 : 42	And I said to her, What has happened to you ? Tell me
9 : 43	And she said to me
10 : 5	and answered her in anger and said
10 : 12	But if you say to me
10 : 14	then I say to you, As you brought forth in sorrow
10 : 18	She said to me, I will not do so
10 : 19	So I spoke again to her, and said
10 : 20	Do not say that, but let yourself be persuaded
10 : 27	Then I was afraid, and cried with a loud voice and said
10 : 30	and set me on my feet, and said to me
10 : 32	I said, Because you have forsaken me !
10 : 33	He said to me
10 : 34	I said, Speak, my lord
10 : 38	He answered me and said
10 : 48	And as for her saying to you
11 : 7	and uttered a cry to his wings, saying
11 : 15	And behold, a voice sounded, saying to it
11 : 36	Then I heard a voice saying to me
11 : 37	and spoke, saying
11 : 38	The Most High says to you
12 : 1	While the lion was saying these words to the eagle, I looked
12 : 3	and I said to my spirit
12 : 7	And I said, O sovereign Lord
12 : 10	He said to me
12 : 40	and came to me and spoke to me, saying
12 : 45	Then I answered them and said
13 : 13	and I besought the Most High, and said
13 : 20	He answered me and said
13 : 22	As for what you said about those who are left
13 : 51	I said, O sovereign Lord, explain this to me :
13 : 52	He said to me, Just as no one can explore or know
14 : 1	and said, Ezra, Ezra
14 : 2	And I said, Here I am, Lord
14 : 3	Then he said to me
14 : 5	Then I commanded him, saying
14 : 7	And now I say to you :
14 : 19	Then I answered and said
14 : 23	He answered me and said
14 : 27	and I gathered all the people together, and said
14 : 38	And on the next day, behold, a voice called me, saying
14 : 45	the Most High spoke to me, saying
15 : 1	The Lord says, Behold
15 : 5	Behold, says the Lord
15 : 7	Therefore, says the Lord
15 : 9	I will surely avenge them, says the Lord
15 : 20	Behold, says God
15 : 21	Thus says the Lord God :
15 : 24	says the Lord
15 : 48	therefore God says
15 : 52	Would I have dealt with you so violently, says the Lord
15 : 56	As you will do to my chosen people, says the Lord
16 : 36	do not disbelieve what the Lord says
16 : 48	says the Lord
16 : 53	Let no sinner say that he has not sinned
16 : 53	for God will burn coals of fire on the head of him who says
16 : 55	He said, Let the earth be made, and it was made
16 : 74	Hear, my elect, says the Lord
16 : 76	You who keep my commandments and precepts, says the Lord God

4 Ma 2 : 5	Thus the law says, You shall not covet your neighbour's wife
2 : 18	For, as I have said

2 : 19	saying, Cursed be their anger ?
2 : 24	How is it then, one might say
4 : 2	and said, I have come here
4 : 6	He said that he had come with the king's authority
4 : 12	For he said that he had committed a sin deserving of death
5 : 5	When Antiochus saw him he said
6 : 13	some of the king's retinue came to him and said
6 : 26	he lifted up his eyes to God and said
6 : 30	And after he said this
7 : 17	Some perhaps might say
8 : 4	he smiled at them, and summoned them nearer and said
8 : 12	When he had said these things
8 : 27	neither said any of these things
8 : 29	all with one voice together, as from one mind, said :
9 : 10	When they had said these things the tyrant not only was angry
9 : 14	he denounced the tyrant, saying
9 : 16	And when the guards said
9 : 19	While he was saying these things they spread fire under him
9 : 23	Imitate me, brothers, he said
9 : 25	When he had said this
9 : 28	But he steadfastly endured this agony and said
9 : 30	To the tyrant he said
10 : 9	When he was about to die, he said
10 : 12	they dragged in the 4th, saying
10 : 14	But he said to them
10 : 18	But he said, Even if you remove my organ of speech
11 : 1	the 5th leaped up, saying
11 : 9	While he was saying these things
11 : 12	he said, Tyrant, they are splendid favours that you grant us against your will
11 : 13	he said, I am younger in age than my brothers
11 : 17	When he had said this, they led him to the wheel
11 : 20	While being tortured he said
12 : 2	and tried to console him, saying
12 : 8	he said, Let me loose, let me speak to the king
12 : 11	he said, You profane tyrant, most impious of all the wicked
12 : 15	Then because he too was about to die, he said
13 : 2	we would say that they had been conquered by these emotions
13 : 8	encouraged one another, saying
13 : 11	While one said, Courage, brothers
13 : 11	another said, Bear up nobly
13 : 13	cheerful and undaunted, said
13 : 18	Those who were left behind said to each of the brothers
16 : 15	and said to your sons in the Hebrew language
17 : 1	Some of the guards said that
17 : 19	For Moses says, All who are consecrated are under your hands
18 : 14	He reminded you of the scripture of Isaiah, which says
18 : 15	He sang to you songs of the psalmist David, who said
18 : 17	He confirmed the saying of Ezekiel
18 : 18	the song that Moses taught, which says

SAYING   3 = 0.002 %

Sir 1 : 25	In the treasuries of wisdom are wise sayings
18 : 29	Those who understand sayings become skilled themselves
21 : 15	When a man of understanding hears a wise saying

SCALE, subst.   6 = 0.004 %

Wis 11 : 22	is like a speck that tips the scales
Sir 1 : 22	for a man's anger tips the scale to his ruin
6 : 15	and no scales can measure his excellence
28 : 25	make balances and scales for your words
42 : 4	of accuracy with scales and weights
2 Es 3 : 34	the turn of the scale will incline

SCALE away   1

Tob 3 : 17	to scale away the white films from Tobit's eyes

SCALE off   1

Tob 11 : 13	and the white films scaled off from the corners of his eyes

SCALP, subst.   1

4 Ma 9 : 28	and tore away his scalp

SCALP, verb   3 = 0.002 %

2 Ma 7 : 4	be cut out and that they scalp him
4 Ma 10 : 7	and scalped him with their fingernails in Scythian fashion
15 : 20	severed hands upon hands, scalped heads upon heads

SCANT   1

1 Ma 6 : 57	We daily grow weaker, our food supply is scant

SCARE   1

Wis 17 : 9	yet, scared by the passing of beasts

SCARE away   1

Sir 22 : 20	One who throws a stone at birds scares them away

SCARECROW   1

L Jr 6 : 70	Like a scarecrow in a cucumber bed, that guards nothing

SCARLET
1

Sir **45** : 11 with twisted scarlet, the work of a craftsman

SCATTER
22 = 0.014 %

Tob **13** : 3 for he has scattered us among them
13 : 5 among whom you have been scattered
14 : 4 Our brethren will be scattered over the earth from the good land
Jud **5** : 19 to which they were scattered
Ad E **13** : 4 there is scattered a certain hostile people
Wis **2** : 4 and be scattered like mist that is chased
11 : 20 and scattered by the breath of thy power
17 : 3 they were scattered, terribly alarmed
Sir **28** : 14 and scattered them from nation to nation
39 : 14 Scatter the fragrance, and sing a hymn of praise
43 : 17 He scatters the snow like birds flying down
48 : 15 and were scattered over all the earth
Bar **2** : 4 where the Lord has scattered them
2 : 13 few in number, among the nations where thou hast scattered us
2 : 29 where I will scatter them
3 : 8 where thou hast scattered us
1 Ma **6** : 54 and they had been scattered, each to his own place
2 Ma **14** : 13 with orders to kill Judas and scatter his men
2 Es **1** : 11 and scattered in the east the people of 2 provinces, Tyre and Sidon
2 : 7 Let them be scattered among the nations
5 : 28 and scattered thine only one among the many ?
4 Ma **15** : 15 their toes and fingers scattered on the ground

SCATTERED
2

2 Ma **1** : 27 Gather together our scattered people
2 Es **5** : 36 and gather for me the scattered raindrops

SCEPTRE, SCEPTER
7 = 0.005 %

Ad E **14** : 11 O Lord, do not surrender thy sceptre to what has no being
15 : 11 Then he raised the golden sceptre and touched it to her neck
Wis **6** : 21 Therefore if you delight in thrones and sceptres
7 : 8 I preferred her to sceptres and thrones
10 : 14 until she brought him the sceptre of a kingdom
Sir **35** : 18 and breaks the sceptres of the unrighteous
L Jr **6** : 14 Like a local ruler the god holds a sceptre

SCHEDIA
1

3 Ma **4** : 11 When these men had been brought to the place called Schedia

SCHEME, verb
2

Ad E **16** : 3 they even undertake to scheme against their own benefactors
Bar **3** : 18 those who scheme to get silver, and are anxious

SCHOOL
1

Sir **51** : 23 Draw near to me, you who are untaught, and lodge in my school

SCOFF
2

1 Es **1** : 51 and whenever the Lord spoke, they scoffed at his prophets
4 Ma **5** : 22 You scoff at our philosophy

SCOLDING
1

Sir **29** : 28 scolding about lodging and the reproach of the moneylender

SCORCHING
1

Sir **18** : 16 Does not the dew assuage the scorching heat ?

SCORN, subst.
4 = 0.003 %

Wis **4** : 18 but the Lord will laugh them to scorn
2 Ma **7** : 39 being exasperated at his scorn
2 Es **7** : 76 but do not be associated with those who have shown scorn
7 : 79 And if it is one of those who have shown scorn

SCORN, verb
6 = 0.004 %

1 Ma **3** : 14 who scorn the king's command
2 Es **3** : 8 and did ungodly things before thee and scorned thee
7 : 24 They scorned his law, and denied his covenants
7 : 81 because they have scorned the law of the Most High
9 : 11 and as many as scorned my law while they still had freedom
4 Ma **9** : 9 But he bore the pains and scorned the punishment

SCORNFULLY
1

Wis **17** : 7 and their boasted wisdom was scornfully rebuked

SCORPION
3 = 0.002 %

Sir **26** : 7 taking hold of her is like grasping a scorpion
39 : 30 the teeth of wild beasts, and scorpions and vipers
4 Ma **11** : 10 so that he was completely curled back like a scorpion

SCOUNDREL
2

Sir **11** : 33 Beware of a scoundrel, for he devises evil
2 Ma **13** : 4 against the scoundrel

SCOURGE, verb
10 = 0.007 %

Jud **8** : 27 but the Lord scourges those who draw near to him
Wis **12** : 22 thou scourgest our enemies 10,000 times more

16 : 16 were scourged by the strength of thy arm
Sir **39** : 28 and in their anger they scourge heavily
2 Ma **3** : 26 who stood on each side of him and scourged him continuously
3 : 34 And see that you, who have been scourged by heaven
3 : 38 send him there, for you will get him back thoroughly scourged
5 : 18 this man would have been scourged
3 Ma **2** : 21 scourged him who had exalted himself
4 Ma **6** : 3 And after they had tied his arms on each side they scourged him

SCOURGE, subst.
6 = 0.004 %

Sir **23** : 11 and the scourge will not leave his house
2 Ma **9** : 11 and to come to his senses under the scourge of God
2 Es **16** : 19 tribulation and anguish are sent as scourges
16 : 20 nor be always mindful of the scourges
4 Ma **6** : 6 his flesh was being torn by scourges, his blood flowing
9 : 12 When they had worn themselves out beating with scourges

SCRIBE
11 = 0.007 %

Sir **10** : 5 and he confers his honour upon the person of the scribe
38 : 24 The wisdom of the scribe
1 Ma **5** : 42 he stationed the scribes of the people at the stream
7 : 12 Then a group of scribes appeared in a body
2 Ma **6** : 18 Eleazar, one of the scribes in high position
1 Es **2** : 16 Shimshai the scribe, and the rest of their associates
2 : 17 Your servants Rehum the recorder and Shimshai the scribe
2 : 25 and Beltethmus and Shimshai the scribe
2 : 30 Rehum and Shimshai the scribe and their associates
8 : 3 This Ezra came up from Babylon as a scribe
3 Ma **4** : 17 the scribes declared to the king

SCRIPTURE
1

4 Ma **18** : 14 He reminded you of the scripture of Isaiah, which says

SCROLL
2

Tob **7** : 14 and took a scroll and wrote out the contract
1 Es **6** : 23 a scroll was found in which this was recorded :

SCRUPLE
1

4 Ma **4** : 13 although otherwise he had scruples about doing so

SCRUPULOUS
1

Sir **19** : 25 There is a cleverness which is scrupulous but unjust

SCRUPULOUSLY
2

1 Es **6** : 29 a portion be scrupulously given to these men
8 : 21 be scrupulously fulfilled for the Most High God

SCYTHE
1

2 Ma **13** : 2 and 300 chariots armed with scythes

SCYTHIAN
3 = 0.002 %

2 Ma **4** : 47 if they had pleaded even before Scythians
3 Ma **7** : 5 with a cruelty more savage than that of Scythian custom
4 Ma **10** : 7 and scalped him with their fingernails in Scythian fashion

SCYTHOPOLIS
3 = 0.002 %

Jud **3** : 10 here he camped between Geba and Scythopolis
2 Ma **12** : 29 Setting out from there, they hastened to Scythopolis
12 : 30 which the people of Scythopolis had shown them

SEA
76 = 0.050 %

Jud **1** : 12 and every one in Egypt, as far as the coasts of the 2 seas
2 : 24 as far as the sea
5 : 13 Then God dried up the Red Sea before them
Wis **5** : 22 the water of the sea will rage against them
10 : 18 She brought them over the Red Sea
10 : 19 and cast them up from the depth of the sea
14 : 3 because thou hast given it a path in the sea
14 : 4 so that even if a man lacks skill, he may put to sea
19 : 7 an unhindered way out of the Red Sea
19 : 12 for, to give them relief, quails came up from the sea
Sir **1** : 2 The sand of the sea, the drops of rain
18 : 10 Like a drop of water from the sea and a grain of sand
24 : 6 In the waves of the sea, in the whole earth
24 : 29 for her thought is more abundant than the sea
24 : 31 and lo, my canal became a river, and my river became a sea
29 : 18 and has shaken them like a wave of the sea
40 : 11 and what is from the waters returns to the sea
43 : 24 Those who sail the sea tell of its dangers
43 : 25 all kinds of living things, and huge creatures of the sea
44 : 21 and cause them to inherit from sea to sea
50 : 3 a reservoir like the sea in circumference
Bar **3** : 30 Who has gone over the sea, and found her
P Az **13** and as the sand on the shore of the sea
56 Bless the Lord, seas and rivers
1 Ma **4** : 9 Remember how our fathers were saved at the Red Sea
4 : 23 and cloth dyed blue and sea purple, and great riches
6 : 29 and from islands of the seas
7 : 1 sailed with a few men to a city by the sea
8 : 23 and with the nation of the Jews at sea and on land for ever

	8:32	we will defend their rights and fight you on sea and on land
	11:8	as far as Seleucia by the sea
	13:29	so that they could be seen by all who sail the sea
	14:5	and opened a way to the isles of the sea
	14:34	He also fortified Joppa, which is by the sea
	15:1	sent a letter from the islands of the sea
	15:11	which is by the sea
	15:14	and the ships joined battle from the sea
	15:14	he pressed the city hard from land and sea
2 Ma	5:21	that he could sail on the land and walk on the sea
	8:11	And he immediately sent to the cities on the sea coast
	9:8	that he could command the waves of the sea
	12:4	the men of Joppa took them out to sea and drowned them
1 Es	4:2	who rule over land and sea and all that is in them ?
	4:15	and to every people that rules over sea and land
	4:23	and rob and steal and to sail the sea and rivers
P Ma	3	who hast shackled the sea by thy word of command
	9	than the sand of the sea
3 Ma	2:7	you overwhelmed him in the depths of the sea
	6:4	by drowning them in the sea
	7:20	safely by land and sea and river
2 Es	1:13	Surely it was I who brought you through the sea
	4:7	How many dwellings are in the heart of the sea
	4:14	and said, Come, let us go and make war against the sea
	4:15	And in like manner the waves of the sea also made a plan
	4:17	likewise also the plan of the waves of the sea
	4:19	and to the sea is assigned a place to carry its waves
	4:21	and the sea to its waves
	5:7	and the sea of Sodom shall cast up fish
	5:25	and from all the depths of the sea
	7:3	There is a sea set in a wide expanse
	7:5	If any one, then, wishes to reach the sea
	9:34	when the ground has received seed, or the sea a ship
	11:1	there came up from the sea an eagle
	12:11	The eagle which you saw coming up from the sea
	13:2	and behold, a wind arose from the sea and stirred up all its waves
	13:3	out of the heart of the sea
	13:5	to make war against the man who came up out of the sea
	13:25	from the heart of the sea
	13:32	whom you saw as a man coming up from the sea
	13:51	Why did I see the man coming up from the heart of the sea ?
	13:52	what is in the depths of the sea
	16:12	the sea is churned up from the depths
	16:57	who has measured the sea and its contents
	16:58	who has enclosed the sea in the midst of the waters
4 Ma	7:1	over the sea of the emotions

SEA-BORN   1
3 Ma	6:8	in the belly of a huge, sea-born monster

SEACOAST   4 = 0.003 %
Jud	1:7	and all who lived along the seacoast
	2:28	who lived along the seacoast, at Sidon and Tyre
	3:6	Then he went down to the seacoast with his army
	5:22	Holofernes'officers and all the men from the seacoast

SEAFOOD   1
4 Ma	1:34	Therefore when we crave seafood and fowl and animals

SEAL, subst.   13 = 0.008 %
Tob	7:14	and they set their seals to it
	9:5	and Gabael brought out the money bags with their seals intact
Sir	22:27	and a seal of prudence upon my lips
	32:5	A ruby seal in a setting of gold
	32:6	A seal of emerald in a rich setting of gold
	38:27	those who cut the signets of seals
	42:6	Where there is an evil wife, a seal is a good thing
Bel	14:17	And the king said, Are the seals unbroken, Daniel ?
2 Es	6:20	and when the seal is placed upon the age
	7:104	and displays to all the seal of truth
	10:23	And, what is more than all, the seal of Zion
	10:23	for she has now lost the seal of her glory
4 Ma	7:15	whom the faithful seal of death has perfected !

SEAL, verb   6 = 0.004 %
Bel	14:11	and shut the door and seal it with your signet
	14:14	and sealed it with the king's signet, and departed
1 Es	3:8	and they sealed them
P Ma	3	and sealed it with thy terrible and glorious name
2 Es	2:38	the number of those who have been sealed
	6:5	and before those who stored up treasures of faith were sealed

SEAL up   3 = 0.002 %
Wis	2:5	because it is sealed up and no one turns back
2 Ma	2:5	and the altar of incense, and he sealed up the entrance
2 Es	8:53	The root of evil is sealed up from you

SEARCH, subst.   4 = 0.003 %
1 Es	2:21	search may be made in the record of your fathers
	2:26	So I ordered search to be made
	6:21	let search be made in the royal archives
	6:23	Then King Darius commanded that search be made

SEARCH, verb   9 = 0.006 %
Tob	1:19	When I learned that I was being searched for
Jud	8:27	to search their hearts
Wis	13:7	For as they live among his works they keep searching
Sir	51:14	and I will search for her to the last
1 Ma	9:26	They sought and searched for the friends of Judas
2 Es	16:30	some clusters may be left by those who search carefully
	16:31	by those who search their houses with the sword
	16:57	It is he who searches the deep and its treasures
4 Ma	3:13	they went searching throughout the enemy camp

SEARCH out   12 = 0.008 %
Jud	8:14	how do you expect to search out God
Wis	6:3	who will search out your works and inquire into your plans
Sir	1:3	the abyss, and wisdom – who can search them out ?
	6:27	Search out and seek, and she will become known to you
	18:4	and who can search out his mighty deeds ?
	42:18	He searches out the abyss, and the hearts of men
1 Ma	3:5	He searched out and pursued the lawless
2 Es	5:34	and to search out part of his judgment
	12:4	because you search out the ways of the Most High
	13:54	and have searched out my law
	16:50	who searches out every sin on earth
	16:62	and searches out hidden things in hidden places

SEASHORE   1
1 Ma	11:1	like the sand by the seashore

SEASON, subst.   13 = 0.008 %
Wis	7:18	and the changes of the seasons
	8:8	and of the outcome of seasons and times
Sir	31:28	Wine drunk in season and temperately
	32:4	do not display your cleverness out of season
	33:8	and he appointed the different seasons and feasts
	39:34	for all things will prove good in their season
	43:6	He made the moon also, to serve in its season
Bar	1:14	on the days of the feasts and at appointed seasons
1 Ma	4:54	At the very season
	4:59	determined that every year at that season
2 Es	8:41	and yet not all that have been sown will come up in due season
	8:43	because it has not received thy rain in due season
	13:58	and whatever things come to pass in their seasons

SEAT, subst.   11 = 0.007 %
Sir	7:4	nor the seat of honour from the king
	12:12	lest he try to take your seat of honour
	38:33	They do not sit in the judge's seat
1 Ma	7:4	and Demetrius took his seat upon the throne of his kingdom
	10:52	and have taken my seat on the throne of my fathers
	10:53	and we have taken our seat on the throne of his kingdom
	10:55	and took your seat on the throne of their kingdom
2 Ma	14:21	seats of honour were set in place
1 Es	3:15	and he took his seat in the council chamber
2 Es	7:33	And the Most High shall be revealed upon the seat of judgment
	12:33	For first he will set them living before his judgment seat

SEAT, verb   7 = 0.005 %
Ad E	15:6	He was seated on his royal throne
Sir	10:14	and has seated the lowly in their place
	11:1	and will seat him among the great
	31:12	Are you seated at the table of a great man ?
	31:18	If you are seated among many persons
	32:1	take good care of them and then be seated
1 Ma	10:63	The king also seated him at his side

SECOND, subst., adj., s. NUMBERS   3 = 0.002 %
Tob	1:22	for Esarhaddon had appointed him second to himself
Jud	2:4	the chief general of his army, second only to himself
Ad E	16:11	as the person second to the royal throne

SECOND, adv.   2
Sir	23:23	second, she has committed an offence against her husband
2 Ma	14:8	and second because I have regard also for my fellow citizens

SECRET, subst.   21 = 0.014 %
Tob	12:7	It is good to guard the secret of a king
	12:11	I have said, It is good to guard the secret of a king
Wis	6:22	and I will hide no secrets from you
	18:9	For in secret the holy children of good men offered sacrifices
Sir	1:30	The Lord will reveal your secrets
	3:19	but to the meek he reveals his secrets
	4:18	and will reveal her secrets to him
	8:17	for he will not be able to keep a secret
	14:21	will also ponder her secrets

	22 : 22	but as for reviling, arrogance, disclosure of secrets
	27 : 16	Whoever betrays secrets destroys confidence
	27 : 17	but if you betray his secrets, do not run after him
	27 : 21	but whoever has betrayed secrets is without hope
	39 : 7	and meditate on his secrets
	41 : 23	and of revealing secrets
3 Ma	**4** : 12	frequently went out in secret
2 Es	**10** : 38	for the Most High has revealed many secrets to you
	12 : 36	And you alone were worthy to learn this secret of the Most High
	12 : 38	and keep these secrets
	14 : 5	and showed him the secrets of the times
	14 : 26	and some you shall deliver in secret to the wise

SECRET, adj.   13 = 0.008 %

Jud	**2** : 2	and set forth to them his secret plan
Wis	**1** : 11	because no secret word is without result
	2 : 22	and they did not know the secret purposes of God
	7 : 21	I learned both what is secret and what is manifest
	14 : 15	and handed on to his dependents secret rites and initiations
	14 : 23	or celebrate secret mysteries
	17 : 3	For thinking that in their secret sins
Sir	**8** : 18	do nothing that is to be kept secret
Sus	**13** : 42	O eternal God, who dost discern what is secret
Bel	**14** : 21	and they showed him the secret doors
2 Ma	**1** : 16	Opening the secret door in the ceiling
	13 : 21	gave secret information to the enemy
2 Es	**14** : 6	and these you shall keep secret

SECRETLY   11 = 0.007 %

Tob	**1** : 18	I buried them secretly
Sir	**42** : 9	A daughter keeps her father secretly wakeful
L Jr	**6** : 10	and sometimes the priests secretly take gold and silver from their gods
1 Ma	**9** : 60	and secretly sent letters to all his allies in Judea
	10 : 79	Now Apollonius had secretly left a 1,000 cavalry behind them
2 Ma	**1** : 19	and secretly hid it in the hollow of a dry cistern
	6 : 11	to observe the 7th day secretly
	8 : 1	secretly entered the villages and summoned their kinsmen
3 Ma	**3** : 23	they secretly suspect that we may soon alter our policy
	6 : 24	by secretly devising acts of no advantage to the kingdom
2 Es	**3** : 14	secretly by night

SECTION   2

Sir	**9** : 7	nor wander about in its deserted sections
1 Ma	**12** : 37	and he repaired the section called Chaphenatha

SECURE, adj.   4 = 0.003 %

Ad E	**13** : 7	and leave our government completely secure and untroubled hereafter
Sir	**4** : 15	and whoever gives heed to her will dwell secure
L Jr	**6** : 18	so the priests make their temples secure with doors and locks and bars
2 Ma	**3** : 22	that he would keep what had been entrusted safe and secure

SECURE, verb   8 = 0.005 %

1 Ma	**14** : 1	and marched into Media to secure help
2 Ma	**2** : 10	to secure most of its treasures as a dowry
	2 : 27	However, to secure the gratitude of many
	4 : 11	secured through John the father of Eupolemus
	4 : 24	and secured the high priesthood for himself
	8 : 36	to secure tribute for the Romans
3 Ma	**4** : 9	others had their feet secured by unbreakable fetters
2 Es	**2** : 20	secure justice for the fatherless, give to the needy

SECURELY   1

3 Ma	**3** : 25	and bound securely with iron fetters

SECURITY   2

2 Ma	**4** : 21	and he took measures for his own security
	9 : 21	for the general security of all

SEDITION   1

2 Ma	**14** : 6	are keeping up war and stirring up sedition

SEDUCER   1

4 Ma	**18** : 8	No seducer corrupted me on a desert plain

SEE   323 = 0.210 %

Tob	**1** : 17	and if I saw any one of my people dead
	2 : 2	Upon seeing the abundance of food I said to my son
	3 : 9	May we never see a son or daughter of yours !
	5 : 20	he will return safe and sound, and your eyes will see him
	8 : 12	Send one of the maids to see whether he is alive
	10 : 7	of ever seeing me again
	10 : 12	and grant me to see your children by my daughter Sarah
	10 : 12	See, I am entrusting my daughter to you
	11 : 8	and he will see you
	11 : 9	and said to him, I have seen you, my child
	11 : 14	Then he saw his son and embraced him, and he wept and said
	11 : 15	here I see my son Tobias

	11 : 16	Those who saw him as he went were amazed
	11 : 16	because he could see
	12 : 1	My son, see to the wages of the man who went with you
	12 : 19	and did not eat or drink, but you were seeing a vision
	12 : 21	but they saw him no more
	13 : 6	But see what he will do with you
	13 : 14	for they will rejoice for you upon seeing all your glory
	14 : 10	See, my son, what Nadab did to Ahikar who had reared him
Jud	**6** : 5	you shall not see my face again from this day
	6 : 12	When the men of the city saw them
	7 : 4	When the Israelites saw their vast number
	7 : 27	or see our wives and children draw their last breath
	10 : 4	to entice the eyes of all men who might see her
	10 : 7	When they saw her, and noted how her face was altered
	10 : 10	and they could no longer see her
	12 : 16	ever since the day he first saw her
	13 : 15	and said, See, here is the head of Holofernes
	14 : 5	and let him see and recognize the man
	14 : 6	And when he came and saw the head of Holofernes
	14 : 10	And when Achior saw all that the God of Israel had done
	14 : 12	And when the Assyrians saw them
	15 : 8	and to see Judith and to greet her
	15 : 12	Then all the women of Israel gathered to see her
Ad E	**11** : 12	Mordecai saw in this dream what God had determined to do
	15 : 13	And she said to him, I saw you, my lord
	16 : 4	of God, who always sees everything
	16 : 7	can be seen not so much from the more ancient records
Wis	**2** : 17	Let us see if his words are true
	4 : 15	Yet the peoples saw and did not understand
	4 : 17	For they will see the end of the wise man
	4 : 18	They will see, and will have contempt for him
	5 : 2	When they see him, they will be shaken with dreadful fear
	12 : 27	they saw and recognized as the true God
	13 : 1	and they were unable from the good things that are seen
	13 : 7	and they trust in what they see
	13 : 7	because the things that are seen are beautiful
	15 : 15	though these have neither the use of their eyes to see with
	16 : 7	not by what he saw, but by thee, the Saviour of all
	16 : 18	but that seeing this they might know
	17 : 6	and in terror they deemed the things which they saw
	18 : 1	Their enemies heard their voices but did not see their forms
	19 : 7	The cloud was seen overshadowing the camp
	19 : 11	Afterward they saw also a new kind of birds
Sir	**1** : 9	he saw her and apportioned her
	1 : 19	He saw her and apportioned her
	2 : 10	and see : who ever trusted in the Lord and was put to shame ?
	6 : 36	If you see an intelligent man, visit him early
	13 : 7	Should he see you afterwards, he will forsake you
	15 : 7	and sinful men will not see her
	15 : 18	he is mighty in power and sees everything
	16 : 5	Many such things my eye has seen
	16 : 21	Like a tempest which no man can see
	17 : 13	Their eyes saw his glorious majesty
	18 : 12	He sees and recognizes that their end will be evil
	23 : 18	Who sees me ?
	23 : 18	and no one sees me
	25 : 7	a man who lives to see the downfall of his foes
	28 : 24	See that you fence in your property with thorns
	30 : 5	while alive he saw and rejoiced
	30 : 20	he sees with his eyes and groans
	31 : 14	Do not reach out your hand for everything you see
	34 : 11	I have seen many things in my travels
	36 : 3	and let them see thy might
	37 : 9	and then stand aloof to see what will happen to you
	37 : 24	and all who see him will call him happy
	37 : 27	see what is bad for it and do not give it that
	42 : 15	and will declare what I have seen
	42 : 22	and how sparkling they are to see !
	43 : 31	Who has seen him and can describe him ?
	43 : 32	for we have seen but few of his works
	45 : 19	The Lord saw it and was not pleased
	46 : 10	so that all the sons of Israel might see
	48 : 11	Blessed are those who saw you
	48 : 24	By the spirit of might he saw the last things
	49 : 8	It was Ezekiel who saw the vision of glory
	51 : 27	See with your eyes that I have laboured little
Bar	**2** : 17	open thy eyes, O Lord, and see
	3 : 20	Young men have seen the light of day
	3 : 22	She has not been heard of in Canaan, nor seen in Teman
	4 : 9	For she saw the wrath that came upon you from God
	4 : 10	for I have seen the captivity of my sons and daughters
	4 : 24	For as the neighbours of Zion have now seen your capture
	4 : 24	so they soon will see your salvation by God
	4 : 25	but you will soon see their destruction
	4 : 36	and see the joy that is coming to you from God !
	5 : 5	and see your children gathered from west and east
L Jr	**6** : 4	Now in Babylon you will see gods made of silver and gold and wood
	6 : 5	when you see the multitude before and behind them worshipping them

	6:19	though their gods can see none of them
	6:41	for when they see a dumb man, who cannot speak
	6:49	How then can one fail to see that these are not gods
	6:61	So also the lightning, when it flashes, is widely seen
Sus	13:8	The 2 elders used to see her every day
	13:12	And they watched eagerly, day after day, to see her
	13:18	and they did not see the elders, because they were hidden
	13:20	Look, the garden doors are shut, no one sees us
	13:26	to see what had happened to her
	13:33	But her family and friends and all who saw her wept
	13:38	and we saw this wickedness we ran to them
	13:39	We saw them embracing, but we could not hold the man
	13:54	Now then, if you really saw her, tell me this :
	13:54	Under what tree did you see them being intimate with each other ?
Bel	14:6	Do you not see how much he eats and drinks every day ?
	14:20	I see the footsteps of men and women and children
	14:27	And Daniel said, See what you have been worshipping !
	14:30	The king saw that they were pressing him hard
	14:35	Habakkuk said, Sir, I have never seen Babylon
1 Ma	1:16	When Antiochus saw that his kingdom was established
	2:6	He saw the blasphemies being committed in Judah and Jerusalem
	2:7	and said, Alas ! Why was I born to see this
	2:24	When Mattathias saw it, he burned with zeal
	3:17	But when they saw the army coming to meet them
	3:29	Then he saw that the money in the treasury was exhausted
	3:42	Now Judas and his brothers saw that misfortunes had increased
	3:59	than to see the misfortunes of our nation
	4:7	And they saw the camp of the Gentiles, strong and fortified
	4:10	to see whether he will favour us
	4:12	and saw them coming against them
	4:20	They saw that their army had been put to flight
	4:20	for the smoke that was seen showed what had happened
	4:21	and when they also saw the army of Judas
	4:30	When he saw that the army was strong, he prayed, saying
	4:35	And when Lysias saw the rout of his troops
	4:38	And they saw the sanctuary desolate, the altar profaned
	4:38	In the courts they saw bushes sprung up as in a thicket
	4:38	They saw also the chambers of the priests in ruins
	5:31	So Judas saw that the battle had begun
	6:43	And Eleazar, called Avaran, saw
	6:47	And when the Jews saw the royal might
	6:62	and saw what a strong fortress the place was
	7:3	he said, Do not let me see their faces !
	7:7	let him go and see all the ruin
	7:11	for they saw that they had come with a large force
	7:23	And Judas saw all the evil that Alcimus and those with him
	7:25	When Alcimus saw that Judas
	7:28	I shall come with a few men to see you face to face in peace
	7:44	When his army saw that Nicanor had fallen
	8:18	for they saw that the kingdom of the Greeks
	9:6	When they saw the huge number of the enemy forces
	9:7	When Judas saw that his army had slipped away
	9:14	Judas saw that Bacchides and the strength of his army were on the right
	9:16	When those on the left wing saw
	9:39	and saw a tumultuous procession with much baggage
	9:57	When Bacchides saw that Alcimus was dead
	9:58	Then all the lawless plotted and said, See !
	10:56	but meet me at Ptolemais, so that we may see one another
	10:64	And when his accusers saw the honour that was paid him
	10:64	and saw him clothed in purple, they all fled
	11:38	Now when Demetrius the king saw
	11:39	He saw that all the troops were murmuring against Demetrius
	11:49	When the men of the city saw
	11:73	When his men who were fleeing saw this
	12:1	Now when Jonathan saw that the time was favourable for him
	12:29	for they saw the fires burning
	12:42	When Trypho saw that he had come with a large army
	12:51	When their pursuers saw
	13:2	and he saw that the people were trembling and fearful
	13:3	and the difficulties which we have seen
	13:27	he made it high that it might be seen
	13:29	so that they could be seen by all who sail the sea
	13:53	And Simon saw that John his son had reached manhood
	14:35	The people saw Simon's faithfulness
	15:32	and when he saw the splendour of Simon
	15:36	and all that he had seen
	16:6	And he saw that the soldiers were afraid to cross the stream
	16:6	and when his men saw him, they crossed over after him
2 Ma	1:9	And now see that you keep the feast of booths
	2:2	upon seeing the gold and silver statues and their adornment
	2:4	and had seen the inheritance of God
	3:16	To see the appearance of the high priest
	3:25	Its rider was seen to have armour and weapons of gold
	3:34	And see that you, who have been scourged by heaven
	3:36	which he had seen with his own eyes
	4:6	For he saw that without the king's attention
	5:26	He put to the sword all those who came out to see them

	6:9	One could see, therefore, the misery that had come upon them
	7:17	Keep on, and see how his mighty power
	7:20	Though she saw her 7 sons perish within a single day
	7:28	and see everything that is in them, and recognize
	8:8	When Philip saw that the man was gaining ground little by little
	9:25	and waiting to see what will happen
	12:9	so that the glow of the light was seen in Jerusalem, 30 miles distant
	12:22	at the manifestation to them of him who sees all things
	12:42	for they had seen with their own eyes
	15:2	which he who sees all things has honoured
	15:12	What he saw was this :
1 Es	4:18	and then see a woman lovely in appearance and beauty
	4:29	Yet I have seen him with Apame, the king's concubine
	5:63	old men who had seen the former house
P Ma	9	I am unworthy to look up and see the height of heaven
3 Ma	2:8	And when they had seen works of your hands
	2:13	see now, O holy King
	2:23	seeing the severe punishment that had overtaken him
	3:8	when they saw an unexpected tumult around these people
	4:8	seeing death immediately before them
	5:14	seeing that the guests were assembled
	5:48	And when the Jews saw the dust raised by the elephants going out
	6:23	and saw them all fallen headlong to destruction
2 Es	1:36	They have seen no prophets
	1:37	though they do not see me with bodily eyes
	1:38	look with pride and see the people coming from the east
	2:29	My hands will cover you, that your sons may not see Gehenna
	2:38	Rise and stand, and see at the feast of the Lord
	2:42	I, Ezra, saw on Mount Zion a great multitude
	2:48	which you have seen
	3:2	because I saw the desolation of Zion
	3:29	For when I came here I saw ungodly deeds without number
	3:29	and my soul has seen many sinners during these 30 years
	3:30	for I have seen how thou dost endure those who sin
	3:33	and have seen that they abound in wealth
	4:4	I also will show you the way you desire to see
	4:26	If you are alive, you will see
	4:43	Then the things that you desire to see
	5:2	beyond what you yourself see
	5:3	And the land which you now see ruling
	5:3	and men shall see it desolate
	5:4	you shall see it thrown into confusion after the 3rd period
	5:35	that I might not see the travail of Jacob
	6:3	and before the beautiful flowers were seen
	6:20	and all shall see it together
	6:25	and shall see my salvation and the end of my world
	6:26	And they shall see the men who were taken up
	6:32	for the Mighty One has seen your uprightness
	7:18	and will not see the easier ones
	7:26	that the city which now is not seen shall appear
	7:27	that I have foretold shall see my wonders
	7:42	by which all shall see what has been determined for them
	7:47	And now I see that the world to come will bring delight to few
	7:83	The 3rd way, they shall see the reward laid up
	7:85	they shall see how the habitations of the others
	7:86	they shall see how some of them will pass over into torments
	7:87	at seeing the glory of the Most High
	7:91	First of all, they shall see with great joy
	7:93	because they see the perplexity
	7:94	they see the witness which he who formed them bears concerning them
	7:96	and besides they see the straits and toil
	7:100	to see what you have described to me ?
	7:101	they may see the things of which you have been told
	8:17	for I see the failings of us who dwell in the land
	9:1	and when you see that a certain part of the predicted signs are past
	9:8	and will see my salvation in my land and within my borders
	9:21	And I saw and spared some with great difficulty
	9:38	I lifted up my eyes and saw a woman on my right
	10:3	and came to this field, as you see
	10:6	do you not see our mourning, and what has happened to us ?
	10:21	For you see that our sanctuary has been laid waste
	10:32	and behold, I saw, and still see
	10:35	For I have seen what I did not know
	10:39	For he has seen your righteous conduct
	10:41	whom you saw mourning and began to console
	10:42	but you do not now see the form of a woman
	10:44	This woman whom you saw
	10:49	And behold, you saw her likeness
	10:55	but go in and see the splendour and vastness of the building
	10:55	as far as it is possible for your eyes to see it
	11:6	And I saw how all things under heaven were subjected to him
	11:13	so that its place was not seen
	11:19	and then were never seen again
	11:30	And I saw how it allied the 2 heads with itself
	11:36	Look before you and consider what you see
	12:10	This is the interpretation of this vision which you have seen :

12:11	The eagle which you saw coming up from the sea
12:16	This is the interpretation of the 12 wings which you saw
12:30	as you have seen
12:31	And as for the lion whom you saw rousing up out of the forest
12:35	This is the dream that you saw
12:37	Therefore write all these things that you have seen in a book
13:7	And I tried to see the region or place
13:9	And behold, when he saw the onrush of the approaching multitude
13:10	but I saw only how
13:11	nothing worse was seen of the innumerable multitude
13:11	When I saw it, I was amazed
13:12	After this I saw the same man come down from the mountain
13:19	For they shall see great dangers and much distress
13:20	and not to see what shall happen in the last days
13:32	whom you saw as a man coming up from the sea
13:34	as you saw, desiring to come and conquer him
13:36	as you saw the mountain carved out without hands
13:47	Therefore you saw the multitude gathered together in peace
13:51	Why did I see the man coming up from the heart of the sea ?
13:52	so no one on earth can see my Son
13:53	This is the interpretation of the dream which you saw
14:8	the dreams that you have seen
14:16	For evils worse than those which you have now seen happen
14:18	For the eagle which you saw in the vision
15:37	and those who see that wrath shall be horror-stricken
16:27	one man will long to see another

4 Ma **1**:24 Anger, as a man will see if he reflects on this experience
4:24 but saw that all his threats and punishments were being disregarded
5:5 When Antiochus saw him he said
6:24 When they saw that he was so courageous
8:4 When the tyrant saw them
8:15 and saw the dreadful devices
9:30 as you see the arrogant design of your tyranny being defeated
10:8 he saw his own flesh torn all around
10:19 See, here is my tongue
12:2 when he saw that he was already in fetters
12:3 You see the result of your brothers'stupidity
14:9 they not only saw what was happening
15:14 This mother, who saw them tortured and burned one by one
15:19 and saw in their nostrils signs of the approach of death
15:20 When you saw the flesh of children burned
15:20 and when you saw the place filled
15:25 she saw mighty advocates
16:1 endured seeing her children tortured to death
16:3 inflamed as she saw her 7 sons tortured in such varied ways
16:9 I shall not see your children
16:20 and when Isaac saw his father's hand
17:7 as they saw the mother of the 7 children
17:23 when he saw the courage of their virtue

SEED   15 = 0.010 %

Wis **7**:2 from the seed of a man and the pleasure of marriage
14:6 left to the world the seed of a new generation
Sir **26**:20 and sow it with your own seed, trusting in your fine stock
1 Es **8**:88 to destroy us without leaving a root or seed or name ?
2 Es **4**:30 For a grain of evil seed was sown in Adam's heart from the beginning
4:31 how much fruit of ungodliness a grain of evil seed has produced
8:6 and give us seed for our heart
8:16 and about the seed of Jacob, for whom I am troubled
8:41 For just as the farmer sows many seeds upon the ground
8:43 For if the farmer's seed does not come up
8:44 hast thou also made him like the farmer's seed ?
9:17 As is the field, so is the seed
9:34 when the ground has received seed, or the sea a ship
15:13 because their seed shall fail and their trees shall be ruined
4 Ma **18**:1 O Israelite children, offspring of the seed of Abraham

SEEDLING   2

Wis **4**:3 and none of their illegitimate seedlings
2 Es **8**:41 and plants a multitude of seedlings

SEEING, subst.   7 = 0.005 %

2 Es **12**:19 As for your seeing 8 little wings clinging to his wings
12:22 As for your seeing 3 heads at rest
12:26 As for your seeing that the large head disappeared
12:29 As for your seeing 2 little wings passing over to the head
13:25 As for your seeing a man come up
13:27 And as for your seeing wind and fire
13:39 And as for your seeing him

SEEING, conj.   3 = 0.002 %

2 Es **7**:15 But now why are you disturbed, seeing that you are to perish ?
7:15 And why are you moved, seeing that you are mortal ?
10:50 seeing that you are sincerely grieved and profoundly distressed for her

SEEK   65 = 0.042 %

Tob **1**:18 When the bodies were sought by the king
4:18 Seek advice from every wise man
Ad E **11**:12 and sought all day to understand it in every detail
12:6 and he sought to injure Mordecai and his people
15:16 and all his servants sought to comfort her
16:3 They not only seek to injure our subjects
Wis **1**:1 and seek him with sincerity of heart
6:12 and is found by those who seek her
6:14 He who rises early to seek her will have no difficulty
6:16 because she goes about seeking those worthy of her
8:2 I loved her and sought her from my youth
8:18 I went about seeking how to get her for myself
13:6 for perhaps they go astray while seeking God
Sir **2**:16 Those who fear the Lord will seek his approval
3:21 Seek not what is too difficult for you
4:11 Wisdom exalts her sons and gives help to those who seek her
4:12 and those who seek her early will be filled with joy
6:27 Search out and seek, and she will become known to you
7:4 Do not seek from the Lord the highest office
7:6 Do not seek to become a judge
20:32 Unwearied patience in seeking the Lord is better
21:17 will be sought in the assembly
24:7 Among all these I sought a resting place
24:7 I sought in whose territory I might lodge
24:34 but for all who seek instruction
26:20 Seek a fertile field within the whole plain
27:1 and whoever seeks to get rich will avert his eyes
28:3 and yet seek for healing from the Lord ?
32:14 and those who rise early to seek him will find favour
32:15 He who seeks the law will be filled with it
33:17 but for all who seek instruction
33:25 leave his hands idle, and he will seek liberty
33:31 which way will you go to seek him ?
39:5 to seek the Lord who made him
39:17 For in God's time all things will be sought after
40:26 and with it there is no need to seek for help
51:3 from the hand of those who sought my life
51:13 I sought wisdom openly in my prayer
51:21 My heart was stirred to seek her
Bar **3**:23 the sons of Hagar, who seek for understanding on the earth
4:28 return with tenfold zeal to seek him
P Az 18 we fear thee and seek thy face
1 Ma **2**:29 Then many who were seeking righteousness and justice
7:13 to seek peace from them
7:15 We will not seek to injure you or your friends
9:26 They sought and searched for the friends of Judas
12:40 so he kept seeking to seize and kill him
14:4 He sought the good of his nation
14:35 He sought in every way to exalt his people
15:19 that they should not seek their harm
16:22 for he had found out that they were seeking to destroy him
2 Ma **2**:27 and seeks the benefit of others
13:21 he was sought for, caught, and put in prison
14:32 that they did not know where the man was whom he sought
1 Es **5**:39 was sought in the register and was not found
7:13 and sought the Lord
8:50 to seek from him a prosperous journey for ourselves
8:52 The power of our Lord will be with those who seek him
8:85 and do not seek ever to have peace with them
2 Es **5**:10 and it shall be sought by many but shall not be found
6:10 between the heel and the hand seek for nothing else, Ezra !
12:48 and to seek mercy
14:23 and tell them not to seek you for 40 days
14:36 and let no one seek me for 40 days
4 Ma **1**:2 to everyone who is seeking knowledge

SEEK out   5 = 0.003 %

Sir **38**:33 Yet they are not sought out for the council of the people
39:1 will seek out the wisdom of all the ancients
39:3 he will seek out the hidden meanings of proverbs
47:25 For they sought out every sort of wickedness
1 Ma **14**:14 he sought out the law

SEEKER   1

Bar **3**:23 the story-tellers and the seekers for understanding

SEEM   16 = 0.010 %

Tob **2**:14 You seem to know everything !
Jud **3**:4 come and deal with them in any way that seems good to you
Wis **3**:2 In the eyes of the foolish they seemed to have died
Sir **pr.** we may seem to have rendered some phrases imperfectly
pr. It seemed highly necessary
6:20 She seems very harsh to the uninstructed
26:26 A wife honouring her husband will seem wise to all
1 Ma **15**:20 And it has seemed good to us to accept the shield from them
2 Ma **1**:13 with a force that seemed irresistible
1 Es **2**:21 if it seems good to you
3:5 and to him whose statement seems wisest
6:21 Now therefore, if it seems wise, O king

	8:94	as seems good to you and to all who obey the law of the Lord
3 Ma	1:29	for it seemed that not only the men
4 Ma	5:7	it does not seem to me that you are a philosopher
	5:10	It seems to me that you will do something even more senseless

SEEMLY 1
Sir 14:3 Riches are not seemly for a stingy man

SEER 1
Sir 46:15 and by his words he became known as a trustworthy seer

SEIR 1
Sir 50:26 Those who live on Mount Seir, and the Philistines

SEIZE 54 = 0.035 %
Tob	6:3	So the young man seized the fish and threw it up on the land
Jud	2:10	You shall go and seize all their territory for me in advance
	2:25	He also seized the territory of Cilicia
	4:5	and immediately seized all the high hilltops
	4:7	ordering them to seize the passes up into the hills
	6:10	to seize Achior and take him to Bethulia
	7:1	and to seize the passes up into the hill country
	7:7	and seized them and set guards of soldiers over them
	7:17	and they encamped in the valley and seized the water supply
	14:3	Then they will seize their arms and go into the camp
	16:5	and seize my children as prey
Ad E	14:1	And Esther the queen, seized with deathly anxiety, fled to the Lord
Wis	17:17	he was seized, and endured the inescapable fate
Sir	23:21	and where he least suspects it, he will be seized
Sus	13:40	So we seized this woman and asked her who the young man was
Bel	14:21	and he seized the priests and their wives and children
1 Ma	1:32	and seized the cattle
	2:10	and has not seized her spoils ?
	3:12	Then they seized their spoils
	4:18	and afterward seize the plunder boldly
	4:23	and they seized much gold and silver
	5:28	then he seized all its spoils and burned it with fire
	6:12	I seized all her vessels of silver and gold
	6:24	and they have seized our inheritances
	6:56	and that he was trying to seize control of the government
	7:2	the army seized Antiochus and Lysias to bring them to him
	7:16	but he seized 60 of them and killed them in one day
	7:19	And he sent and seized many of the men
	7:29	But the enemy were ready to seize Judas
	7:47	Then the Jews seized the spoils and the plunder
	9:36	and seized John and all that he had, and departed with it
	9:60	telling them to seize Jonathan and his men
	9:61	And Jonathan's men seized about 50 of the men of the country
	11:46	Then the men of the city seized the main streets of the city
	11:48	They set fire to the city and seized much spoil on that day
	12:40	so he kept seeking to seize and kill him
	12:48	the men of Ptolemais closed the gates and seized him
	12:50	But they realized that Jonathan had been seized
	14:3	and seized him and took him to Arsaces
	15:30	Now then, hand over the cities which you have seized
	15:33	nor seized foreign property
	16:22	and he seized the men who came to destroy him and killed them
2 Ma	2:21	so that though few in number they seized the whole land
	9:5	he was seized with a pain in his bowels
1 Es	1:38	and seized his brother Zarius
	9:4	their cattle should be seized for sacrifice
3 Ma	1:1	that the regions which he had controlled had been seized by Antiochus
2 Es	5:1	shall be seized with great terror
	15:37	and they shall be seized with trembling
	16:39	and pains will seize it on every side
4 Ma	4:6	to seize the private funds in the treasury
	4:10	with his armed forces to seize the money
	5:2	ordered the guards to seize each and every Hebrew
	17:1	when she also was about to be seized and put to death

SELECT 2
Sir	47:2	As the fat is selected from the peace offering
	47:2	so David was selected from the sons of Israel

SELEMIA 1
2 Es 14:24 and take with you Sarea, Dabria, Selemia, Ethanus, and Asiel

SELEUCIA 1
1 Ma 11:8 as far as Seleucia by the sea

SELEUCUS 10 = 0.007 %
1 Ma	7:1	In the 151st year Demetrius the son of Seleucus set forth from Rome
2 Ma	3:3	so that even Seleucus, the king of Asia
	4:7	When Seleucus died
	5:18	whom Seleucus the king sent to inspect the treasury
	14:1	that Demetrius, the son of Seleucus
4 Ma	3:20	and were prospering, so that even Seleucus Nicanor, king of Asia

	4:3	but belong to King Seleucus
	4:4	and went up to Seleucus to inform him of the rich treasure
	4:13	prayed for him lest King Seleucus suppose
	4:15	When King Seleucus died

SELF-CONTROL 10 = 0.007 %
Wis	8:7	for she teaches self-control and prudence, justice and courage
2 Es	7:125	Or that the faces of those who practised self-control
4 Ma	1:3	that reason rules over those emotions that hinder self-control
	1:6	but those that are opposed to justice, courage, and self-control
	1:18	courage, and self-control
	1:30	by virtue of the restraining power of self-control
	1:31	Self-control, then, is dominance over the desires
	5:23	but it teaches us self-control
	5:34	nor will I renounce you, beloved self-control
	13:16	Therefore let us put on the full armour of self-control

SELF-CONTROLLED 1
4 Ma 15:10 For they were righteous and self-controlled and brave and magnanimous

SELF-DENIAL 1
Sir 11:18 There is a man who is rich through his diligence and self-denial

SELFISH 1
Sir 41:19 Be ashamed of selfish behaviour at meals

SELF-KINDLED 1
Wis 17:6 except a dreadful, self-kindled fire

SELF-RELIANT 1
Sir 40:18 Life is sweet for the self-reliant and the worker

SELL 17 = 0.011 %
Tob	1:7	a 2nd tenth I would sell
Jud	7:25	God has sold us into their hands
Wis	10:13	When a righteous man was sold
Sir	37:11	with a merchant about barter or with a buyer about selling
Bar	4:6	It was not for destruction that you were sold to the nations
L Jr	6:28	The priests sell the sacrifices that are offered to these gods
1 Ma	1:15	They joined with the Gentiles and sold themselves to do evil
	12:36	so that its garrison could neither buy nor sell
	13:49	to buy and sell
2 Ma	4:32	he had sold to Tyre and the neighbouring cities
	5:14	and as many were sold into slavery as were slain
	5:24	and to sell the women and boys as slaves
	8:10	by selling the captured Jews into slavery
	8:14	Others sold all their remaining property
	8:14	to rescue those who had been sold by the ungodly Nicanor
	10:21	of having sold their brethren for money
2 Es	16:41	Let him that sells be like one who will flee

SELLING 1
Sir 27:2 so sin is wedged in between selling and buying

SENAAH 1
1 Es 5:23 The sons of Senaah, 3,330

SENATE 10 = 0.007 %
Jud	4:8	and the senate of the whole people of Israel
	11:14	to bring back to them permission from the senate
	15:8	and the senate of the people of Israel
1 Ma	8:15	but they have built for themselves a senate chamber
	8:19	and they entered the senate chamber and spoke as follows :
	12:3	and entered the senate chamber and said
	12:6	Jonathan the high priest, the senate of the nation
2 Ma	1:10	and the senate and Judas
	4:44	3 men sent by the senate presented the case before him
	11:27	King Antiochus to the senate of the Jews

SENATOR 2
1 Ma	8:15	and every day 320 senators constantly deliberate
2 Ma	6:1	Not long after this, the king sent an Athenian senator

SEND 201 = 0.131 %
Tob	2:12	She used to send the product to the owners
	3:17	And Raphael was sent to heal the 2 of them :
	8:12	Send one of the maids to see whether he is alive
	10:8	and I will send messengers to your father
	12:14	So now God sent me to heal you
	12:20	for I am ascending to him who sent me
Jud	1:7	sent to all who lived in Persia
	3:1	So they sent messengers to sue for peace, and said
	4:4	So they sent to every district of Samaria
	6:3	He will send his forces and will destroy them
	7:18	and they sent some of their men
	7:32	The women and children he sent home
	8:10	she sent her maid, who was in charge of all she possessed
	8:31	and the Lord will send us rain to fill our cisterns
	9:9	Behold their pride, and send thy wrath upon their heads

	11 : 7	who has sent you to direct every living soul
	11 : 14	They have sent men to Jerusalem
	11 : 16	and God has sent me to accomplish with you
	11 : 19	it was announced to me, and I was sent to tell you
	11 : 22	God has done well to send you before the people
	12 : 6	and sent to Holofernes and said, Let my lord now command
	14 : 5	and sent him to us as if to his death
	14 : 12	they sent word to their commanders
	15 : 4	And Uzziah sent men to Betomasthaim and Bebai
Ad E	16 : 17	the letters sent by Haman the son of Hammedatha
Wis	9 : 10	and from the throne of thy glory send her
	9 : 17	and sent thy holy Spirit from on high ?
	11 : 15	thou didst send upon them
	11 : 17	did not lack the means to send upon them
	12 : 8	and didst send wasps as forerunners of thy army
	12 : 25	thou didst send thy judgment to mock them
	16 : 3	because of the odious creatures sent to them
	16 : 18	sent against the ungodly
Sir	15 : 9	for it has not been sent from the Lord
	34 : 6	Unless they are sent from the Most High as a visitation
	43 : 13	By his command he sends the driving snow
	48 : 18	In his days Sennacherib came up, and sent the Rabshakeh
Bar	1 : 7	and they sent it to Jerusalem to Jehoiakim the high priest
	1 : 10	And they said : Herewith we send you money
	1 : 14	And you shall read this book which we are sending you
	1 : 21	in all the words of the prophets whom he sent to us
	2 : 20	For thou hast sent thy anger and thy wrath upon us
L Jr	6 : 1	A copy of a letter which Jeremiah sent
	6 : 63	And the fire sent from above to consume mountains and woods does what it is ordered
Sus	13 : 29	Send for Susanna, the daughter of Hilkiah
	13 : 30	So they sent for her
Bel	14 : 37	Take the dinner which God has sent you
1 Ma	1 : 29	2 years later the king sent to the cities of Judah
	1 : 44	And the king sent letters by messengers to Jerusalem
	3 : 27	and he sent and gathered all the forces of his kingdom
	3 : 35	Lysias was to send a force against them
	3 : 39	and sent with them 40,000 infantry and 7,000 cavalry
	5 : 10	and sent to Judas and his brothers a letter which said
	5 : 38	Judas sent men to spy out the camp, and they reported to him
	5 : 48	And Judas sent them this friendly message
	6 : 12	and I sent to destroy the inhabitants of Judah without good reason
	6 : 60	and he sent to the Jews an offer of peace
	7 : 7	Now then send a man whom you trust
	7 : 9	And he sent him, and with him the ungodly Alcimus
	7 : 10	and he sent messengers to Judas and his brothers
	7 : 19	And he sent and seized many of the men
	7 : 26	Then the king sent Nicanor, one of his honoured princes
	7 : 27	and treacherously sent to Judas and his brothers
	8 : 10	and they sent a general against the Greeks and attacked them
	8 : 17	and sent them to Rome to establish friendship and alliance
	8 : 20	have sent us to you to establish alliance and peace with you
	8 : 22	and sent to Jerusalem to remain with them there
	9 : 1	he sent Bacchides and Alcimus
	9 : 35	And Jonathan sent his brother as leader of the multitude
	9 : 60	and secretly sent letters to all his allies in Judea
	9 : 63	and sent orders to the men of Judea
	9 : 70	he sent ambassadors to him to make peace with him
	10 : 3	And Demetrius sent Jonathan a letter
	10 : 15	which Demetrius had sent to Jonathan
	10 : 17	and sent it to him, in the following words :
	10 : 20	and he sent him a purple robe and a golden crown
	10 : 25	So he sent a message to them in the following words :
	10 : 51	Then Alexander sent ambassadors to Ptolemy king of Egypt
	10 : 69	Then he sent the following message
	10 : 89	and he sent to him a golden buckle
	11 : 9	He sent envoys to Demetrius the king, saying
	11 : 17	and sent it to Ptolemy
	11 : 41	Now Jonathan sent to Demetrius the king the request
	11 : 42	And Demetrius sent this message to Jonathan
	11 : 43	Now then you will do well to send me men who will help me
	11 : 44	So Jonathan sent 3,000 stalwart men to him at Antioch
	11 : 58	And he sent him gold plate and a table service
	11 : 62	and sent them to Jerusalem
	12 : 1	he chose men and sent them to Rome
	12 : 2	He also sent letters to the same effect to the Spartans
	12 : 3	Jonathan the high priest and the Jewish nation have sent us
	12 : 7	a letter was sent to Onias the high priest
	12 : 10	we have undertaken to send to renew our brotherhood
	12 : 10	since you sent your letter to us
	12 : 16	and have sent them to Rome
	12 : 18	And now please send us a reply to this
	12 : 19	This is a copy of the letter which they sent to Onias :
	12 : 26	He sent spies to their camp
	12 : 34	to the men whom Demetrius had sent
	12 : 49	Then Trypho sent troops and cavalry into Galilee
	13 : 11	He sent Jonathan the son of Absalom to Joppa
	13 : 14	so he sent envoys to him and said
	13 : 16	Send now a 100 talents of silver

	13 : 17	but he sent to get the money and the sons
	13 : 18	Because Simon did not send him the money and the sons, he perished
	13 : 19	So he sent the sons and the 100 talents
	13 : 21	Now the men in the citadel kept sending envoys to Trypho
	13 : 21	and to send them food
	13 : 25	And Simon sent and took the bones of Jonathan his brother
	13 : 34	Simon also chose men and sent them to Demetrius the king
	13 : 35	Demetrius the king sent him a favourable reply to this request
	13 : 37	and the palm branch which you sent
	14 : 2	he sent one of his commanders to take him alive
	14 : 20	This is a copy of the letter which the Spartans sent :
	14 : 21	The envoys who were sent to our people
	14 : 23	And they have sent a copy of this to Simon the high priest
	14 : 24	After this Simon sent Numenius to Rome
	15 : 1	sent a letter from the islands of the sea
	15 : 17	They had been sent by Simon the high priest
	15 : 24	They also sent a copy of these things
	15 : 26	And Simon sent to Antiochus 2,000 picked men, to fight for him
	15 : 28	He sent to him Athenobius, one of his friends
	16 : 18	and sent it to the king
	16 : 18	asking him to send troops to aid him
	16 : 19	He sent other men to Gazara to do away with John
	16 : 19	he sent letters to the captains asking them to come to him
	16 : 20	and he sent other men to take possession of Jerusalem
	16 : 21	and that he has sent men to kill you also
2 Ma	1 : 20	sent the descendants of the priests who had hidden the fire to get it
	2 : 15	So if you have need of them, send people to get them for you
	3 : 7	and sent him with commands
	3 : 38	send him there, for you will get him back thoroughly scourged
	4 : 19	the vile Jason sent envoys
	4 : 21	When Apollonius the son of Menestheus was sent to Egypt
	4 : 23	After a period of 3 years Jason sent Menelaus
	4 : 44	3 men sent by the senate presented the case before him
	5 : 18	whom Seleucus the king sent to inspect the treasury
	5 : 24	Antiochus sent Apollonius, the captain of the Mysians
	6 : 1	Not long after this, the king sent an Athenian senator
	6 : 23	telling them to send him to Hades
	8 : 9	and sent him
	8 : 11	And he immediately sent to the cities on the sea coast
	9 : 19	Antiochus their king and general sends hearty greetings
	11 : 6	besought the Lord to send a good angel to save Israel
	11 : 13	So he sent to them
	11 : 17	John and Absalom, who were sent by you
	11 : 26	You will do well, therefore, to send word to them
	11 : 32	And I have also sent Menelaus to encourage you
	11 : 34	The Romans also sent them a letter which read thus :
	11 : 36	as soon as you have considered them, send some one promptly
	11 : 37	Therefore make haste and send some men
	12 : 43	and sent it to Jerusalem to provide for a sin offering
	14 : 19	Therefore he sent Posidonius and Theodotus and Mattathias
	14 : 27	and commanding him to send Maccabeus to Antioch
	14 : 39	sent more than 500 soldiers to arrest him
	15 : 22	O Lord, thou didst send thy angel
	15 : 23	send a good angel to carry terror and trembling before us
	15 : 31	he sent for those who were in the citadel
1 Es	1 : 26	And the king of Egypt sent word to him saying
	1 : 27	I was not sent against you by the Lord God
	1 : 45	So after a year Nebuchadnezzar sent
	1 : 50	So the God of their fathers sent by his messenger to call them back
	2 : 26	I have read the letter which you sent me
	3 : 14	Then he sent and summoned all the nobles of Persia and Media
	4 : 57	and to be sent to Jerusalem
	5 : 2	And Darius sent with them a 1,000 horsemen
	6 : 6	until word could be sent to Darius concerning them
	6 : 7	wrote and sent to Darius :
	6 : 22	let him send us directions concerning these things
	8 : 19	and reader of the law of the Most High God sends for
	8 : 43	I sent word to Eliezar, Iduel, Maasmas
	8 : 46	to send us men to serve as priests
	9 : 51	and send portions to those who have none
Ps 151	4	It was he who sent his messenger
3 Ma	1 : 8	Since the Jews had sent some of their council and elders
	3 : 25	you are to send to us those who live among you
	5 : 11	But the Lord sent upon the king a portion of sleep
	5 : 42	that he would send them to death without delay
2 Es	1 : 23	I did not send fire upon you for your blasphemies
	1 : 32	I sent to you my servants the prophets
	2 : 18	I will send you help, my servants Isaiah and Jeremiah
	4 : 1	Then the angel that had been sent to me
	4 : 3	I have been sent to show you 3 ways
	4 : 52	but I was not sent to tell you concerning your life
	5 : 31	the angel who had come to me on a previous night was sent to me
	6 : 33	Therefore he sent me to show you all these things
	7 : 1	the angel who had been sent to me on the former nights
	7 : 1	was sent to me again
	7 : 104	Just as now a father does not send his son

14 : 4	and I sent him and led my people out of Egypt
14 : 22	send the Holy Spirit into me
15 : 49	I will send evils upon you, widowhood, poverty
15 : 50	when the heat rises that is sent upon you
16 : 3	The sword has been sent upon you
16 : 4	A fire has been sent upon you
16 : 5	Calamities have been sent upon you
16 : 8	The Lord God sends calamities, and who will drive them away ?
16 : 16	so the calamities that are sent upon the earth shall not return
16 : 19	tribulation and anguish are sent as scourges
16 : 60	to send rivers from the heights to water the earth
4 Ma 12 : 6	he sent for the boy's mother to show compassion on her

SEND away 7 = 0.005 %

Tob 5 : 17	and said to Tobit, Why have you sent our child away ?
10 : 11	And when he had blessed them he sent them away, saying
Sir 29 : 9	and because of his need do not send him away empty
Bar 4 : 11	but I sent them away with weeping and sorrow
4 : 37	Behold, your sons are coming, whom you sent away
Sus 13 : 21	and this was why you sent your maids away
1 Ma 12 : 46	he sent away the troops

SEND back 7 = 0.005 %

Tob 10 : 7	Send me back
10 : 9	Tobias replied, No, send me back to my father
Jud 1 : 11	and they sent back his messengers empty-handed and shamefaced
1 Es 4 : 44	and to send back all the vessels that were taken from Jerusalem
4 : 44	and vowed to send them back there
4 : 57	And he sent back from Babylon all the vessels
3 Ma 6 : 27	Send them back to their homes in peace

SEND forth 9 = 0.006 %

Jud 16 : 14	Thou didst send forth thy Spirit, and it formed them
Wis 9 : 10	Send her forth from the holy heavens
19 : 2	and hastily sent them forth
Sir 39 : 14	send forth fragrance like frankincense
45 : 9	to send forth a sound as he walked
Bar 3 : 33	he who sends forth the light, and it goes
L Jr 6 : 60	For sun and moon and stars, shining and sent forth for service, are obedient
2 Es 13 : 10	he sent forth from his mouth as it were a stream of fire
16 : 14	Behold, calamities are sent forth

SEND in 1

2 Ma 13 : 20	Judas sent in to the garrison whatever was necessary

SEND off 3 = 0.002 %

2 Ma 12 : 21	he sent off the women and the children
14 : 12	appointed him governor of Judea, and sent him off
3 Ma 4 : 4	were they being sent off, all together, by the generals

SEND on 1

2 Ma 3 : 37	to send on another mission to Jerusalem

SEND out 3 = 0.002 %

Sir 28 : 23	It will be sent out against them like a lion
Bar 4 : 23	For I sent you out with sorrow and weeping
1 Es 4 : 4	and if he sends them out against the enemy, they go

SEND up

Sir 51 : 9	And I sent up my supplication from the earth

SENDER 1

2 Ma 4 : 20	So this money was intended by the sender

SENNACHERIB 8 = 0.005 %

Tob 1 : 15	Sennacherib his son reigned in his place
1 : 18	And if Sennacherib the king put to death
1 : 21	before 2 of Sennacherib's sons killed him
Sir 48 : 18	In his days Sennacherib came up, and sent the Rabshakeh
2 Ma 8 : 19	both the time of Sennacherib, when 185,000 perished
15 : 22	and he slew fully a 185,000 in the camp of Sennacherib
3 Ma 6 : 5	Sennacherib exulting in his countless forces
2 Es 7 : 110	and Hezekiah for the people in the days of Sennacherib

SENSE 9 = 0.006 %

Sir pr.	*does not have exactly the same sense*
1 : 24	and the lips of many will tell of his good sense
25 : 2	and an adulterous old man who lacks good sense
25 : 9	happy is he who has gained good sense
26 : 25	but one who has a sense of shame will fear the Lord
29 : 14	but a man who has lost his sense of shame will fail him
L Jr 6 : 42	for they have no sense
2 Ma 9 : 11	and to come to his senses under the scourge of God
4 Ma 2 : 22	but at the same time he enthroned the mind among the senses

SENSELESS 6 = 0.004 %

Sir 16 : 23	a senseless and misguided man thinks foolishly
21 : 19	To a senseless man education is fetters on his feet

3 Ma 6 : 12	who by the senseless insolence of the lawless
4 Ma 5 : 9	It is senseless not to enjoy delicious things
5 : 10	It seems to me that you will do something even more senseless
8 : 17	O wretches that we are and so senseless !

SENSELESSLY 1

3 Ma 6 : 25	and senselessly gathered here those who faithfully have held

SENSIBLE 9 = 0.006 %

Tob 6 : 12	The girl is also beautiful and sensible
Wis 6 : 24	and a sensible king is the stability of his people
Sir 19 : 29	and a sensible man is known by his face, when you meet him
20 : 27	and a sensible man will please great men
21 : 7	but the sensible man, when he slips, is aware of it
21 : 17	The utterance of a sensible man
21 : 21	To a sensible man education is like a golden ornament
22 : 4	A sensible daughter obtains her husband
38 : 4	and a sensible man will not despise them

SENSIBLY 1

Sir 13 : 22	he speaks sensibly, and receives no attention

SENTENCE, subst. 4 = 0.003 %

Sir 38 : 33	nor do they understand the sentence of judgment
41 : 2	O death, how welcome is your sentence
41 : 3	Do not fear the sentence of death
Sus 13 : 55	for the angel of God has received the sentence from God

SENTENCE, verb 2

L Jr 6 : 18	as though he were sentenced to death
2 Ma 4 : 47	while he sentenced to death those unfortunate men

SENTINEL 1

4 Ma 3 : 13	Eluding the sentinels at the gates

SEPARATE, verb 16 = 0.010 %

Wis 1 : 3	For perverse thoughts separate men from God
Sir 12 : 9	and in his adversity even his friend will separate from him
18 : 3	by his power separating among them
25 : 26	separate her from yourself
Sus 13 : 51	Separate them far from each other
13 : 52	When they were separated from each other
1 Ma 1 : 11	for since we separated from them many evils have come upon us
12 : 36	to separate it from the city, in order to isolate it
1 Es 7 : 13	all those who had separated themselves
9 : 9	separate yourselves from the peoples of the land
3 Ma 2 : 33	and they abhorred those who separated themselves from them
2 Es 6 : 41	and didst command him to divide and separate the waters
6 : 50	And thou didst separate one from the other
7 : 88	when they shall be separated from their mortal body
7 : 100	after they have been separated from the bodies
11 : 24	2 little wings separated from the 6

SEPARATENESS 1

3 Ma 3 : 4	they kept their separateness with respect to foods

SEPARATION 1

2 Ma 14 : 3	but had wilfully defiled himself in the times of separation

SEPULCHRE 1

2 Ma 12 : 39	in the sepulchres of their fathers

SERAIAH 4 = 0.003 %

1 Es 5 : 5	Jeshua the son of Jozadak, son of Seraiah
5 : 8	Nehemiah, Seraiah, Resaiah, Bigvai, Mordecai
8 : 1	Ezra came, the son of Seraiah, son of Azariah
2 Es 1 : 1	The 2nd book of the prophet Ezra the son of Seraiah

SERIOUS 1

2 Ma 4 : 4	Onias recognized that the rivalry was serious

SERIOUSLY 2

4 Ma 8 : 21	and let us seriously consider that if we disobey we are dead !
8 : 27	nor even seriously considered them

SERIOUSNESS 1

4 Ma 5 : 20	is of equal seriousness

SERON 2

1 Ma 3 : 13	Now when Seron, the commander of the Syrian army
3 : 23	he rushed suddenly against Seron and his army

SERPENT 6 = 0.004 %

Wis 11 : 15	to worship irrational serpents and worthless animals
16 : 5	by the bites of writhing serpents
16 : 10	even by the teeth of venomous serpents
17 : 9	and the hissing of serpents
Sir 12 : 13	Who will pity a snake charmer bitten by a serpent
4 Ma 18 : 8	nor did the destroyer, the deceitful serpent

SERVANT
101 = 0.066 %

Tob	8 : 18	Then he ordered his servants to fill in the grave
	9 : 2	Brother Azarias, take a servant and 2 camels with you
Jud	3 : 2	Behold, we the servants of Nebuchadnezzar, the Great King
	5 : 5	Let my lord now hear a word from the mouth of your servant
	5 : 5	No falsehood shall come from your servant's mouth
	6 : 3	we the king's servants will destroy them as one man
	6 : 6	and the spear of my servants shall pierce your sides
	7 : 12	only let your servants take possession
	7 : 16	These words pleased Holofernes and all his servants
	9 : 0	with the prince and the prince with his servant
	10 : 20	Then Holofernes' companions and all his servants came out
	10 : 23	And when Judith came into the presence of Holofernes and his servants
	11 : 4	as they do the servants of my lord King Nebuchadnezzar
	11 : 5	Judith replied to him, Accept the words of your servant
	11 : 16	Therefore, when I, your servant, learned all this
	11 : 17	For your servant is religious
	11 : 17	and every night your servant will go out into the valley
	11 : 20	Her words pleased Holofernes and all his servants
	12 : 4	your servant will not use up the things I have with me
	12 : 5	Then the servants of Holofernes brought her into the tent
	12 : 6	that your servant be permitted to go out and pray
Ad E	14 : 17	And thy servant has not eaten at Haman's table
	14 : 18	Thy servant has had no joy
	15 : 16	and all his servants sought to comfort her
Wis	6 : 4	Because as servants of his kingdom you did not rule rightly
	9 : 4	and do not reject me from among thy servants
	10 : 16	She entered the soul of a servant of the Lord
	12 : 7	might receive a worthy colony of the servants of God
	12 : 20	the enemies of thy servants and those deserving of death
	18 : 21	showing that he was thy servant
Sir	4 : 30	nor be a faultfinder with your servants
	6 : 11	and be bold with your servant
	7 : 20	Do not abuse a servant who performs his work faithfully
	7 : 21	Let your soul love an intelligent servant
	10 : 25	Free men will be at the service of a wise servant
	19 : 21	When a servant says to his master
	23 : 10	for as a servant who is continually examined under torture
	33 : 24	bread and discipline and work for a servant
	33 : 26	and for a wicked servant there are racks and tortures
	33 : 30	If you have a servant, let him be as yourself
	33 : 31	If you have a servant, treat him as a brother
	36 : 17	Hearken, O Lord, to the prayer of thy servants
	37 : 11	with a lazy servant about a big task
	42 : 5	and of whipping a wicked servant severely
Bar	1 : 20	through Moses his servant at the time
	2 : 20	as thou didst declare by thy servants the prophets, saying :
	2 : 24	which thou didst speak by thy servants the prophets
	2 : 28	as thou didst speak by thy servant Moses
	3 : 36	and gave her to Jacob his servant
P Az	10	shame and disgrace have befallen thy servants and worshippers
	12	and for the sake of Isaac thy servant and Israel thy holy one
	20	Let all who do harm to thy servants be put to shame
	23	Now the king's servants who threw them in
	63	Bless the Lord, you servants of the Lord
Sus	13 : 26	When the household servants heard the shouting in the garden
	13 : 27	the servants were greatly ashamed
Bel	14 : 14	Then Daniel ordered his servants to bring ashes
1 Ma	4 : 30	by the hand of thy servant David
	16 : 16	and some of his servants
2 Ma	1 : 2	and Isaac and Jacob, his faithful servants
	7 : 6	when he said, And he will have compassion on his servants
	7 : 33	he will again be reconciled with his own servants
	8 : 29	to be wholly reconciled with his servants
1 Es	1 : 3	And he told the Levites, the temple servants of Israel
	1 : 30	And the king said to his servants
	1 : 30	And immediately his servants took him out of the line of battle
	1 : 57	and they were servants to him and to his sons
	2 : 17	Your servants Rehum the recorder and Shimshai the scribe
	4 : 59	I am thy servant
	5 : 29	The temple servants : the sons of Ziha
	5 : 33	The sons of Solomon's servants : the sons of Hassophereth
	5 : 35	All the temple servants
	5 : 35	and the sons of Solomon's servants were 372
	6 : 13	We are the servants of the Lord
	6 : 27	the servant of the Lord and governor of Judea
	8 : 5	and gatekeepers and temple servants
	8 : 22	or gatekeepers or temple servants or
	8 : 49	and of the temple servants
	8 : 49	220 temple servants
	8 : 82	which thou didst give by thy servants the prophets, saying
3 Ma	5 : 5	The servants in charge of the Jews went out in the evening
2 Es	1 : 10	I struck down Pharaoh with his servants, and all his army
	1 : 32	I sent to you my servants the prophets
	2 : 1	and I gave them commandments through my servants the prophets
	2 : 18	I will send you help, my servants Isaiah and Jeremiah
	2 : 26	Not one of the servants whom I have given you will perish
	3 : 23	and thou didst raise up for thyself a servant, named David

	5 : 45	And I said, How hast thou said to thy servant
	5 : 56	show thy servant through whom thou dost visit thy creation
	6 : 12	show thy servant the end of thy signs
	7 : 75	show this also to thy servant : whether after death
	7 : 102	show further to me, thy servant
	7 : 104	or a son his father, or a master his servant
	8 : 6	O Lord who art over us, grant to thy servant
	8 : 24	hear, O Lord, the prayer of thy servant
	9 : 43	Your servant was barren and had no child
	10 : 37	to give your servant an explanation of this bewildering vision
	12 : 8	strengthen me and show me, thy servant
	13 : 14	From the beginning thou hast shown thy servant these wonders
	16 : 35	O servants of the Lord
4 Ma	12 : 11	were you not ashamed to murder his servants

SERVE
51 = 0.033 %

Tob	4 : 14	and if you serve God you will receive payment
Jud	8 : 22	wherever we serve as slaves
	11 : 1	who chose to serve Nebuchadnezzar
	11 : 7	not only do men serve him because of you
	11 : 17	and serves the God of heaven day and night
	12 : 1	and to serve her with his own wine
	12 : 13	who serve in the house of Nebuchadnezzar
	16 : 14	Let all thy creatures serve thee
Ad E	11 : 3	a great man, serving in the court of the king
	12 : 5	And the king ordered Mordecai to serve in the court
Wis	10 : 9	Wisdom rescued from troubles those who served her
	13 : 11	make a useful vessel that serves life's needs
	15 : 7	both the vessels that serve clean uses
	16 : 24	For the creation, serving thee who hast made it
	16 : 25	changed into all forms, it served thy all-nourishing bounty
Sir	2 : 1	My son, if you come forward to serve the Lord
	3 : 7	he will serve his parents as his masters
	4 : 14	Those who serve her will minister to the Holy One
	7 : 13	for the habit of lying serves no good
	8 : 8	and learn how to serve great men
	25 : 8	and he who has not served a man inferior to himself
	39 : 4	He will serve among great men and appear before rulers
	43 : 6	He made the moon also, to serve in its season
	45 : 15	to minister to the Lord and serve as priest
Bar	1 : 12	and we shall serve them many days and find favour in their sight
	1 : 21	by serving other gods
	2 : 21	Bend your shoulders and serve the king of Babylon
	2 : 22	and will not serve the king of Babylon
	2 : 24	But we did not obey thy voice, to serve the king of Babylon
	4 : 32	Wretched will be the cities which your children served as slaves
L Jr	6 : 27	And those who serve them are ashamed
	6 : 30	Women serve meals for gods of silver and gold and wood
	6 : 39	and those who serve them will be put to shame
	6 : 59	or a household utensil that serves its owner's need
1 Ma	6 : 23	We were happy to serve your father
	10 : 14	for it served as place of refuge
	11 : 38	So all the troops who had served his fathers hated him
2 Ma	6 : 17	Let what we have said serve as a reminder
1 Es	1 : 4	and serve his people Israel
	4 : 6	Likewise those who do not serve in the army or make war
	5 : 39	they were excluded from serving as priests
	8 : 46	to send us men to serve as priests
	9 : 14	served with them as judges
3 Ma	6 : 6	so as not to serve vain things
2 Es	1 : 18	It would have been better for us to serve the Egyptians
	6 : 46	and thou didst command them to serve man
	7 : 37	whom you have not served
	7 : 89	they laboriously served the Most High
	7 : 98	whom they served in life
	8 : 26	but at those who have served thee in truth
	15 : 45	And those who survive shall serve those who have destroyed her

SERVICE
24 = 0.016 %

Wis	15 : 7	and laboriously moulds each vessel for our service
Sir	6 : 19	For in her service you will toil a little while
	10 : 25	Free men will be at the service of a wise servant
	35 : 16	He whose service is pleasing to the Lord will be accepted
	39 : 31	and be made ready on earth for their service
	50 : 14	Finishing the service at the altars
	50 : 19	so they completed his service
L Jr	6 : 60	For sun and moon and stars, shining and sent forth for service, are obedient
1 Ma	10 : 41	they shall give from now on for the service of the temple
	10 : 42	from the income of the services of the temple
	11 : 58	And he sent him gold plate and a table service
2 Ma	3 : 3	connected with the service of the sacrifices
	4 : 14	upon their service at the altar
	8 : 9	a general and a man of experience in military service
	9 : 26	the public and private services rendered to you
1 Es	7 : 9	for the services of the Lord God of Israel
	7 : 15	for the service of the Lord God of Israel
	8 : 49	for the service of the Levites
3 Ma	3 : 6	to their good service to their nation

2 Es	6:42	and be of service before thee
4 Ma	3:20	had both appropriated money to them for the temple service
	4:4	he praised Simon for his service to the king
	4:20	but also the temple service was abolished
	12:14	Surely they by dying nobly fulfilled their service to God

SERVING   1
Tob	7:8	and set large servings of food before them

SERVITUDE   1
1 Es	8:79	and to give us food in the time of our servitude

SESSION   2
Jud	4:8	in session at Jerusalem
1 Es	9:16	they began their sessions to investigate the matter

SESTHEL   1
1 Es	9:31	and Naidus, and Bescaspasmys and Sesthel

SET*, verb   84 = 0.055 %
Tob	2:7	When the sun had set I went
	7:8	and set large servings of food before them
	7:14	and they set their seals to it
	14:10	which Nadab had set for him
Jud	5:11	he took advantage of them and set them to making bricks
	6:16	and they set Achior in the midst of all their people
	7:7	and seized them and set guards of soldiers over them
	8:24	let us set an example to our brethren
	11:13	which they had consecrated and set aside for the priests
	11:19	and I will set your throne in the midst of it
	12:1	and ordered them to set a table for her
	14:2	and set a captain over them
	16:7	nor did tall giants set upon him
	16:23	She set her maid free
Ad E	13:14	that I might not set the glory of man above the glory of God
	16:5	And often many of those who are set in places of authority
Wis	6:11	Therefore set your desire on my words
	9:18	And thus the paths of those on earth were set right
	13:10	But miserable, with their hopes set on dead things
	13:15	and sets it in the wall, and fastens it there with iron
	16:14	nor set free the imprisoned soul
Sir	2:2	Set your heart right and be steadfast
	5:1	Do not set your heart on your wealth
	17:8	He set his eye upon their hearts
	22:18	Fences set on a high place
	22:27	O that a guard were set over my mouth
	23:2	O that whips were set over my thoughts
	27:26	and he who sets a snare will be caught in it
	31:16	Eat like a human being what is set before you
	33:25	Set your slave to work, and you will find rest
	33:28	Set him to work, as is fitting for him
	38:26	He sets his heart on ploughing furrows
	38:27	he sets his heart on painting a lifelike image
	38:28	He sets his heart on finishing his handiwork
	38:30	he sets his heart to finish the glazing
	39:5	He will set his heart to rise early
	49:3	He set his heart upon the Lord
	49:6	who set fire to the chosen city of the sanctuary
Bar	1:18	to walk in the statutes of the Lord which he set before us
	2:10	to walk in the statutes of the Lord which he set before us
L Jr	6:27	If any one sets up from upright
1 Ma	9:67	and set fire to the machines of war
	10:33	I set free without payment
	10:50	He pressed the battle strongly until the sun set
	11:48	They set fire to the city and seized much spoil on that day
	11:57	and set you over the 4 districts
	11:66	and set a garrison over it
	11:68	they had set an ambush against him in the mountains
	12:27	So when the sun set, Jonathan commanded his men to be alert
2 Ma	1:27	set free those who are slaves among the Gentiles
	3:14	So he set a day and went in
	4:11	He set aside the existing royal concessions to the Jews
	7:22	nor I who set in order the elements within each of you
	8:6	he would set fire to towns and villages
	8:33	they burned those who had set fire to the sacred gates
	10:21	by setting their enemies free to fight against them
	10:36	and set fire to the towers
	12:6	He set fire to the harbour by night, and burned the boats
	12:9	and set fire to the harbour and the fleet
	12:20	set men in command of the divisions
	14:21	And the leaders set a day on which to meet by themselves
	14:21	seats of honour were set in place
1 Es	4:44	which Cyrus set apart when he began to destroy Babylon
	4:57	which Cyrus had set apart
	8:54	Then I set apart 12 of the leaders of the priests
3 Ma	6:38	and their destruction was set
2 Es	3:16	And thou didst set apart Jacob for thyself
	5:15	and strengthened me and set me on my feet
	7:3	There is a sea set in a wide expanse
	7:4	but it has an entrance set in a narrow place

	7:6	Another example : There is a city built and set on a plain
	7:7	and set in a precipitous place
	7:9	unless he passes through the danger set before him ?
	7:20	which is set before them be disregarded !
	7:61	they are set on fire and burn hotly, and are extinguished
	9:47	I set a day for the marriage feast
	10:30	and set me on my feet, and said to me
	12:33	For first he will set them living before his judgment seat
	14:13	Now therefore, set your house in order
4 Ma	6:15	We will set before you some cooked meat
	7:5	For in setting his mind firm like a jutting cliff
	11:27	but those of the divine law that are set over us
	17:3	Nobly set like a roof on the pillars of your sons
	17:5	and are firmly set in heaven with them

SET down   1
Bel	14:36	and lifted him by his hair and set him down in Babylon

SET forth   8 = 0.005 %
Jud	2:2	and set forth to them his secret plan
	2:4	When he had finished setting forth his plan
Sir	44:5	and set forth verses in writing
Bel	14:11	you yourself, O king, shall set forth the food
	14:14	When they had gone out, the king set forth the food for Bel
1 Ma	7:1	In the 151st year Demetrius the son of Seleucus set forth from Rome
	11:60	Then Jonathan set forth
2 Ma	2:23	all this, which has been set forth by Jason of Cyrene in 5 volumes

SET off   1
2 Ma	10:19	and he himself set off for places

SET out   14 = 0.009 %
Jud	2:19	So he set out with his whole army
1 Ma	10:57	So Ptolemy set out from Egypt
	10:74	He chose 10,000 men and set out from Jerusalem
	11:2	He set out for Syria with peaceable words
	11:22	he set out and came to Ptolemais
	15:10	In the 174th year Antiochus set out
2 Ma	1:8	and we lighted the lamps and we set out the loaves
	1:15	had set out the treasures
	3:8	Heliodorus at once set out on his journey
	10:3	and set out the bread of the Presence
	12:29	Setting out from there, they hastened to Scythopolis
	13:26	and set out for Antioch
	14:16	they set out from there immediately
2 Es	15:29	and from the day that they set out

SET up   17 = 0.011 %
Jud	5:1	and set up barricades in the plains
	8:5	She set up a tent for herself on the roof of her house
	8:12	and are setting yourselves up in the place of God
Sir	49:13	and set up the gates and bars and rebuilt our ruined houses
L Jr	6:17	when they have been set up in the temples
	6:34	They cannot set up a king or depose one
	6:53	For they cannot set up a king over a country or give rain to men
1 Ma	6:17	he set up Antiochus the king's son to reign
	6:51	He set up siege towers
2 Ma	5:6	but imagining that he was setting up trophies of victory
	14:13	and to set up Alcimus as high priest of the greatest temple
1 Es	2:23	and kept setting up blockades in it from of old
P Ma	10	setting up abominations and multiplying offences
3 Ma	2:27	and he set up a stone on the tower in the courtyard
2 Es	11:25	these little wings planned to set themselves up
	11:26	one was set up, but suddenly disappeared
	12:2	and set themselves up to reign

SETH   1
Sir	49:16	Shem and Seth were honoured among men

SETTING, subst.   5 = 0.003 %
Sir	32:5	A ruby seal in a setting of gold
	32:6	A seal of emerald in a rich setting of gold
	45:11	in a setting of gold, the work of a jeweller
1 Ma	13:29	*And for the pyramids he devised an elaborate setting*
3 Ma	4:15	from the rising of the sun till its setting

SETTLE   15 = 0.010 %
Tob	7:8	and let the matter be settled
Jud	5:9	There they settled, and prospered
	5:19	and have settled in the hill country
Ad E	13:2	I have determined to settle the lives of my subjects in lasting tranquillity
Sir	22:17	A mind settled on an intelligent thought
1 Ma	2:1	moved from Jerusalem and settled in Modein
	3:36	settle aliens in all their territory
	13:48	and settled in it men who observed the law
	14:34	He settled Jews there, and provided in those cities
	14:37	He settled Jews in it, and fortified it

2 Ma	4:31	So the king went hastily to settle the trouble
	11:14	and persuaded them to settle everything on just terms
	13:23	settled with them and offered sacrifice
1 Es	5:46	and some of the people settled in Jerusalem and its vicinity
	9:37	settled in Jerusalem and in the country

SETTLE down   2
Sir	28:16	nor will he settle down in peace
2 Ma	14:25	so he married, settled down, and shared the common life

SETTLEMENT   3 = 0.002 %
2 Ma	4:6	*public affairs could not again reach a peaceful settlement*
1 Es	9:12	and let all those in our settlements who have foreign wives
	9:37	when the sons of Israel were in their settlements

SEVENFOLD   3 = 0.002 %
Sir	7:3	and you will not reap a sevenfold crop
	35:11	and he will repay you sevenfold
4 Ma	14:8	encircled the sevenfold fear of tortures and dissolved it

SEVEN-TOWERED   1
4 Ma	13:7	so the seven-towered right reason of the youths

SEVER   4 = 0.003 %
Jud	13:8	and severed his head from his body
	16:9	and the sword severed his neck
4 Ma	9:21	Although the ligaments joining his bones were already severed
	15:20	severed hands upon hands, scalped heads upon heads

SEVERAL   1
3 Ma	4:4	in the several cities

SEVERE   7 = 0.005 %
Wis	6:5	because severe judgment falls on those in high places
Sir	5:14	and severe condemnation to the double-tongued
	31:2	and a severe illness carries off sleep
1 Ma	1:30	but he suddenly fell upon the city, dealt it a severe blow
2 Ma	14:45	and though his blood gushed forth and his wounds were severe
3 Ma	2:23	seeing the severe punishment that had overtaken him
4 Ma	9:8	For we, through this severe suffering and endurance

SEVERELY   4 = 0.003 %
Sir	30:14	than a rich man who is severely afflicted in body
	42:5	and of whipping a wicked servant severely
3 Ma	4:19	After he had threatened them severely
	7:6	But we very severely threatened them for these acts

SEX   2
Wis	14:26	pollution of souls, sex perversion
4 Ma	15:5	Considering that mothers are the weaker sex and give birth to many

SEXUAL   2
4 Ma	2:2	because by mental effort he overcame sexual desire
	2:4	over the frenzied urge of sexual desire

SHABBETHAI   2
1 Es	9:14	and Meshullam and Levi and Shabbethai
	9:48	Shabbethai, Hodiah, Maaseiah and Kelita

SHACKLE, subst.   1
3 Ma	6:19	binding them with immovable shackles

SHACKLE, verb   1
P Ma	3	who hast shackled the sea by thy word of command

SHADE, subst.   1
Sir	34:16	a shelter from the hot wind and a shade from noonday sun

SHADE, verb   1
Bar	5:8	The woods and every fragrant tree have shaded Israel at God's command

SHADOW   5 = 0.003 %
Wis	2:5	For our allotted time is the passing of a shadow
	5:9	All those things have vanished like a shadow
Sir	34:2	As one who catches at a shadow and pursues the wind
2 Es	2:36	Flee from the shadow of this age
	2:39	Those who have departed from the shadow of this age

SHAFT   2
Wis	5:21	Shafts of lightning will fly with true aim
Sir	38:25	and who glories in the shaft of a goad

SHAKE   11 = 0.007 %
Wis	4:19	and shake them from the foundations
Sir	12:18	he will shake his head, and clap his hands
	13:7	and shake his head at you
	16:19	shake with trembling when he looks upon them
	22:2	any one that picks it up will shake it off his hand

	28:14	Slander has shaken many
	29:18	and has shaken them like a wave of the sea
1 Ma	1:28	Even the land shook for its inhabitants
3 Ma	2:22	He shook him on this side
2 Es	3:18	Thou didst bend down the heavens and shake the earth
	10:26	so that the earth shook at the sound

SHAKE off   2
Sir	22:13	and you will not be soiled when he shakes himself off
2 Es	10:24	Therefore shake off your great sadness

SHAKEN   12 = 0.008 %
Jud	16:15	For the mountains shall be shaken to their foundations with the waters
Ad E	15:13	and my heart was shaken with fear at your glory
Wis	4:4	standing insecurely they will be shaken by the wind
	5:2	When they see him, they will be shaken with dreadful fear
Sir	27:4	When a sieve is shaken, the refuse remains
	43:16	At his appearing the mountains are shaken
	48:19	Then their hearts were shaken and their hands trembled
1 Ma	6:8	he was astounded and badly shaken
	9:13	The earth was shaken by the noise of the armies
3 Ma	2:22	and that as a reed is shaken by the wind
2 Es	6:14	And if the place where you are standing is greatly shaken
	6:16	They will tremble and be shaken

SHALL   562 = 0.366 %

SHALLUM   5 = 0.003 %
Bar	1:7	the son of Hilkiah, son of Shallum, and to the priests
1 Es	5:28	The gatekeepers : the sons of Shallum
	8:1	son of Hilkiah, son of Shallum
	9:25	Of the gatekeepers : Shallum and Telem
2 Es	1:1	son of Azariah, son of Hilkiah, son of Shallum

SHALMANESER   5 = 0.003 %
Tob	1:2	who in the days of Shalmaneser, king of the Assyrians
	1:13	and good appearance in the sight of Shalmaneser
	1:15	But when Shalmaneser died
	1:16	In the days of Shalmaneser
2 Es	13:40	whom Shalmaneser the king of the Assyrians led captive

SHAME, subst.   35 = 0.023 %
Jud	1:14	plundered its markets, and turned its beauty into shame
	5:21	and we shall be put to shame before the whole world
	9:2	and uncovered her thigh to put her to shame
Sir	2:10	and see : who ever trusted in the Lord and was put to shame ?
	4:20	and do not bring shame on yourself
	4:21	For there is a shame which brings sin
	4:21	and there is a shame which is glory and favour
	5:14	for shame comes to the thief
	6:1	for a bad name incurs shame and reproach :
	15:4	and he will rely on her and will not be put to shame
	20:22	A man may lose his life through shame
	20:23	A man may for shame make promises to a friend
	20:26	and his shame is ever with him
	24:22	Whoever obeys me will not be put to shame
	26:8	she will not hide her shame
	26:25	but one who has a sense of shame will fear the Lord
	29:14	but a man who has lost his sense of shame will fail him
	41:16	For it is not good to retain every kind of shame
	41:23	Then you will show proper shame
	42:11	and put you to shame before the great multitude
	42:14	and it is a woman who brings shame and disgrace
	51:18	and I shall never be put to shame
	51:29	and may you not be put to shame when you praise him
L Jr	6:39	and those who serve them will be put to shame
P Az	10	shame and disgrace have befallen thy servants and worshippers
	17	for there will be no shame for those who trust in thee
	19	Do not put us to shame
	20	Let all who do harm to thy servants be put to shame
1 Ma	1:28	and all the house of Jacob was clothed with shame
1 Es	8:77	in shame until this day
2 Es	7:87	and be consumed with shame
	16:65	you shall be put to shame
4 Ma	5:35	I will not put you to shame, philosophical reason
	9:2	we are obviously putting our forefathers to shame
	13:18	Do not put us to shame, brother

SHAME, verb   2
Jud	13:16	to defile and shame me
Sir	13:7	He will shame you with his foods

SHAMEFACED   1
Jud	1:11	and they sent back his messengers empty-handed and shamefaced

SHAMEFUL   9 = 0.006 %
Wis	2:20	Let us condemn him to a shameful death
Sus	13:63	because nothing shameful was found in her

2 Ma	9:2	and beat a shameful retreat
3 Ma	3:25	to suffer the sure and shameful death that befits enemies
	4:5	in such a shameful manner
	7:14	they punished and put to a public and shameful death
4 Ma	5:9	that are not shameful
	6:20	It would be shameful if we should survive for a little while
	16:17	For it would be shameful if

SHAMEFULLY 1

Sir 22:4 but one who acts shamefully brings grief to her father

SHAMELESS 4 = 0.003 %

Sir	23:6	and do not surrender me to a shameless soul
	26:24	A shameless woman constantly acts disgracefully
	40:30	In the mouth of the shameless begging is sweet
Bar	4:15	a shameless nation, of a strange language

SHAMELESSNESS 1

Sir 30:13 that you may not be offended by his shamelessness

SHAMLAI 1

1 Es 5:30 the sons of Hagab, the sons of Shamlai, the sons of Hana

SHAPE 3 = 0.002 %

Wis	13:13	and shapes it with skill gained in idleness
2 Ma	7:23	who shaped the beginning of man
4 Ma	13:20	and was shaped during the same period of time

SHAPELY 1

Sir 9:8 Turn away your eyes from a shapely woman

SHAPHAT 1

1 Es 5:34 the sons of Barodis, the sons of Shaphat, the sons of Ami

SHARE, verb 15 = 0.010 %

Wis	2:9	Let none of us fail to share in our revelry
	8:18	and renown in sharing her words
	14:21	the name that ought not to be shared
	18:9	that the saints would share alike the same things
	19:16	those who had already shared the same rights
Sir	22:23	that you may share with him in his inheritance
2 Ma	4:36	and the Greeks shared their hatred of the crime
	5:20	shared in the misfortunes that befell the nation
	5:27	so that they might not share in the defilement
	14:25	so he married, settled down, and shared the common life
1 Es	5:40	not to share in the holy things
	8:70	the leaders and the nobles have been sharing in this iniquity
3 Ma	4:6	to share married life
2 Es	15:46	And you, Asia, who share in the glamour of Babylon
4 Ma	18:3	but also were deemed worthy to share in a divine inheritance

SHARE, subst. 3 = 0.002 %

Sir	14:14	let not your share of desired good pass by you
2 Ma	8:30	shares equal to their own
4 Ma	16:18	that you have had a share in the world

SHARP 6 = 0.004 %

Wis	18:16	carrying the sharp sword of thy authentic command
2 Ma	9:5	and with sharp internal tortures
3 Ma	5:18	and with sharp threats demanded to know
2 Es	16:13	and his arrows that he shoots are sharp
4 Ma	9:26	and after fitting themselves with iron gauntlets having sharp hooks
	11:19	To his back they applied sharp spits

SHARPEN 1

Wis 5:20 and sharpen stern wrath for a sword

SHASHAI 1

1 Es 9:34 Of the sons of Ezora : Shashai, Azarel, Azael

SHATTER 2

2 Ma	12:28	who with power shatters the might of his enemies
2 Es	16:11	and who will not be utterly shattered at his presence ?

SHAVED 1

L Jr 6:31 their heads and beards shaved

SHE 288 = 0.188 %

SHEAF 1

Jud 8:3 who were binding sheaves in the field

SHEAL 1

1 Es 9:30 Jashub, and Sheal and Jeremoth

SHEALTIEL 4 = 0.003 %

1 Es	5:5	son of Shealtiel, of the house of David
	5:48	and Zerubbabel the son of Shealtiel, with his kinsmen

	5:56	in the 2nd month, Zerubbabel the son of Shealtiel
	6:2	Then Zerubbabel the son of Shealtiel

SHEARING 1

Tob 1:6 and the first shearings

SHEBAT 1

1 Ma 16:14 in the 177th year, in the 11th month, which is the month of Shebat

SHECANIAH 3 = 0.002 %

1 Es	8:29	Of the sons of David, Hattush the son of Shecaniah
	8:32	Of the sons of Zattu, Shecaniah the son of Jahaziel
	8:92	Then Shecaniah the son of Jehiel

SHECHEM 1

Sir 50:26 and the foolish people that dwell in Shechem

SHECHEMITE 2

Jud	5:16	and the Shechemites and all the Gergesites
4 Ma	2:19	of the entire tribe of the Shechemites

SHED 11 = 0.007 %

Sir	11:32	and a sinner lies in wait to shed blood
	14:18	which sheds some and puts forth others
	28:11	A hasty quarrel kindles fire, and urgent strife sheds blood
	31:13	Therefore it sheds tears from every face
	34:22	to deprive an employee of his wages is to shed blood
1 Ma	1:37	On every side of the sanctuary they shed innocent blood
2 Ma	1:8	and burned the gate and shed innocent blood
3 Ma	4:4	and shed tears at the most miserable expulsion of these people
	5:26	The rays of the sun were not yet shed abroad
2 Es	15:22	and my sword will not cease from those who shed innocent blood on the earth
4 Ma	15:20	you did not shed tears

SHEDDING 1

Ad E 16:5 for the shedding of innocent blood

SHEEP 11 = 0.007 %

Jud	2:17	and innumerable sheep and oxen and goats for provision
	8:26	while he was keeping the sheep of Laban
	11:19	and you will lead them like sheep that have no shepherd
Bel	14:3	and 40 sheep and 50 gallons of wine
	14:32	and every day they had been given 2 human bodies and 2 sheep
1 Es	1:8	2,600 sheep and 300 calves
	1:9	gave the Levites for the passover 5,000 sheep and 700 calves
Ps 151	1	I tended my father's sheep
	151:4	and took me from my father's sheep
2 Es	5:26	thou hast provided for thyself one sheep
	16:32	because no sheep will go along them

SHEEPFOLD 2

Jud	2:26	and burned their tents and plundered their sheepfolds
	3:3	and all our sheepfolds with their tents, lie before you

SHEER 3 = 0.002 %

Sir	40:15	they are unhealthy roots upon sheer rock
	48:17	he tunnelled the sheer rock with iron
2 Ma	6:29	were in their opinion sheer madness

SHEKEL 2

1 Ma	10:40	I also grant 15,000 shekels of silver yearly
	10:42	Moreover, the 5,000 shekels of silver

SHELEMIAH 1

1 Es 9:34 Elialis, Shimei, Shelemiah, Nethaniah

SHELOMITH 1

1 Es 8:36 Of the sons of Bani, Shelomith the son of Josiphiah

SHELTER, subst. 7 = 0.005 %

Tob	2:4	I sprang up and removed the body to a place of shelter until sunset
Jud	6:13	However, they got under the shelter of the hill
Wis	10:17	and became a shelter to them by day
Sir	6:14	A faithful friend is a sturdy shelter :
	14:26	he will place his children under her shelter
	29:22	under the shelter of his roof
	34:16	a shelter from the hot wind and a shade from noonday sun

SHELTER, verb 4 = 0.003 %

Sir	2:13	Therefore it will not be sheltered
	14:27	he will be sheltered by her from the heat
3 Ma	3:27	But whoever shelters any of the Jews
	3:29	Every place detected sheltering a Jew

SHEM 1

Sir 49:16 Shem and Seth were honoured among men

SHEMA   1
  1 Es 9:43 and beside him stood Mattathiah, Shema, Anaiah, Azariah

SHEMAIAH   6 = 0.004 %
  Tob 5:13 the sons of the great Shemaiah
  1 Es 1:9 And Jeconiah and Shemaiah and Nethanel his brother
       8:39 their names being Eliphelet, Jeuel, and Shemaiah
       8:44 Elnathan, Shemaiah, Jarib, Nathan, Elnathan
       9:21 and Shemaiah and Jehiel and Azariah
       9:34 Shemaiah, Amariah, Joseph

SHEPHATIAH   3 = 0.002 %
  1 Es 5:9 The sons of Shephatiah, 472
       5:33 the sons of Shephatiah
       8:34 Of the sons of Shephatiah, Zeraiah the son of Michael

SHEPHELAH   1
  1 Ma 12:38 And Simon built Adida in the Shephelah

SHEPHERD   5 = 0.003 %
  Jud 11:19 and you will lead them like sheep that have no shepherd
  Wis 17:17 for whether he was a farmer or a shepherd
  Sir 18:13 and turns them back, as a shepherd his flock
  2 Es 2:34 Await your shepherd
       5:18 like a shepherd who leaves his flock

SHEREBIAH   3 = 0.002 %
  1 Es 8:47 namely Sherebiah with his sons and kinsmen, 18
       8:54 Sherebiah and Hashabiah
       9:48 Jeshua and Anniuth and Sherebiah, Jamin, Akkub

SHESHBAZZAR   4 = 0.003 %
  1 Es 2:12 and by him they were given to Shesh-Bazzar the governor of Judea
       2:15 and they were carried back by Shesh-Bazzar
       6:18 and Shesh-Bazzar the governor
       6:20 Then this Shesh-Bazzar, after coming here

SHIELD, subst.   14 = 0.009 %
  Jud 9:7 they trust in shield and spear, in bow and sling
  Wis 5:19 he will take holiness as an invincible shield
      18:21 he brought forward the shield of his ministry
  Sir 29:13 more than a mighty shield and more than a heavy spear
      37:5 and in the face of battle take up the shield
  1 Ma 4:57 with golden crowns and small shields
      6:2 Its temple was very rich, containing golden shields
      6:39 When the sun shone upon the shields of gold and brass
      14:24 with a large gold shield weighing a 1,000 minas
      15:18 and have brought a gold shield weighing a 1,000 minas
      15:20 And it has seemed good to us to accept the shield from them
  2 Ma 5:3 brandishing of shields, massing of spears
      15:11 not so much with confidence in shields and spears
  4 Ma 7:4 with the shield of his devout reason

SHIELD, verb   3 = 0.002 %
  Wis 5:16 and with his arm he will shield them
  4 Ma 4:9 were imploring God in the temple to shield the holy place
      7:8 shielding it with their own blood and noble sweat

SHIFT over   1
  2 Ma 4:10 he at once shifted his countrymen over

SHIFTLESSNESS   2
  Tob 4:13 and in shiftlessness there is loss and great want
      4:13 because shiftlessness is the mother of famine

SHIMEI   4 = 0.003 %
  Ad E 11:2 son of Shimei, son of Kish
  1 Es 9:23 And of the Levites: Jozabad and Shimei and Kelaiah
      9:33 and Eliphelet and Manasseh and Shimei
      9:34 Elialis, Shimei, Shelemiah, Nethaniah

SHIMSHAI   4 = 0.003 %
  1 Es 2:16 Shimshai the scribe, and the rest of their associates
      2:17 Your servants Rehum the recorder and Shimshai the scribe
      2:25 and Beltethmus and Shimshai the scribe
      2:30 Rehum and Shimshai the scribe and their associates

SHINE   16 = 0.010 %
  Wis 5:6 and the light of righteousness did not shine on us
      17:6 Nothing was shining through to them
  Sir 24:32 and I will make it shine afar
      50:7 like the sun shining upon the temple of the Most High
  Bar 3:34 the stars shone in their watches, and were glad
      3:34 They shone with gladness for him who made them
  L Jr 6:24 they will not shine unless some one wipes off the rust
      6:60 For sun and moon and stars, shining and sent forth for service, are obedient
      6:67 or shine like the sun or give light like the moon
  1 Ma 6:39 When the sun shone upon the shields of gold and brass

  2 Es 2:35 because the eternal light will shine upon you for evermore
      6:2 and before the flashes of lightning shone
      7:42 or noon or night, or dawn or shining or brightness or light
      7:97 when it is shown to them how their face is to shine like the sun
      7:125 shall shine more than the stars
      10:25 her face suddenly shone exceedingly

SHINE back   1
  2 Ma 1:32 but when the light from the altar shone back, it went out

SHINE forth   5 = 0.003 %
  Wis 3:7 In the time of their visitation they will shine forth
  Sir 24:27 It makes instruction shine forth like light
      24:32 I will again make instruction shine forth like the dawn
      43:8 shining forth in the firmament of heaven
  2 Es 5:4 and the sun shall suddenly shine forth at night

SHINE out   1
  2 Ma 1:22 and the sun, which had been clouded over, shone out

SHINING, adj., subst.   2
  Sir 26:17 Like the shining lamp on the holy lampstand
  Bar 4:2 walk toward the shining of her light

SHIP   11 = 0.007 %
  Wis 5:10 like a ship that sails through the billowy water
      14:1 than the ship which carries him
  1 Ma 8:26 arms, money, or ships, as Rome has decided
      8:28 arms, money, or ships, as Rome has decided
      11:1 and many ships
      13:29 and beside the suits of armour carved ships
      15:14 and the ships joined battle from the sea
      15:37 Now Trypho embarked on a ship and escaped to Orthosia
  2 Es 9:34 when the ground has received seed, or the sea a ship
      12:42 and like a haven for a ship saved from a storm
  4 Ma 7:1 the reason of our father Eleazar steered the ship of religion

SHIVER   1
  1 Es 9:6 shivering because of the bad weather that prevailed

SHOBAI   1
  1 Es 5:28 the sons of Shobai, in all 139

SHOCK, verb   1
  1 Ma 16:22 When he heard this, he was greatly shocked

SHOE, subst.   1
  Sir 46:19 not so much as a pair of shoes

SHOOT, verb   7 = 0.005 %
  Wis 5:12 or as, when an arrow is shot at a target
  1 Ma 6:51 machines to shoot arrows, and catapults
      10:80 for they surrounded his army and shot arrows at his men
  2 Es 16:7 Can one turn back an arrow shot by a strong archer ?
      16:13 and his arrows that he shoots are sharp
      16:13 and will not miss when they begin to be shot
      16:16 Just as an arrow shot by a mighty archer does not return

SHOOT forth   1
  2 Es 13:10 and from his tongue he shot forth a storm of sparks

SHOOT, subst.   2
  Sir 40:22 but the green shoots of grain more than both
      50:8 like a green shoot on Lebanon on a summer day

SHORE   1
  P Az 13 and as the sand on the shore of the sea

SHORT   10 = 0.007 %
  Wis 2:1 Short and sorrowful is our life
      4:13 Being perfected in a short time, he fulfilled long years
      15:8 this man who was made of earth a short time before
      16:3 while thy people, after suffering want a short time
  2 Ma 2:32 while cutting short the history itself
  2 Es 8:5 for you have been given only a short time to live
      8:47 For you come far short of being able to love my creation
      12:20 whose times shall be short and their years swift
  4 Ma 9:5 as though a short time ago you learned nothing from Eleazar
      15:27 which would preserve the 7 sons for a short time

SHORTEN   2
  Sir 30:24 Jealousy and anger shorten life
  2 Es 2:13 pray that your days may be few, that they may be shortened

SHORT-LIVED   1
  Wis 9:5 a man who is weak and short-lived

SHORTLY
2
Wis	14:20	the one whom shortly before they had honoured as a man
4 Ma	1:12	I shall shortly have an opportunity to speak of this

SHOULDER
6 = 0.004 %
Sir	6:25	Put your shoulder under her and carry her
	7:31	the gift of the shoulders, the sacrifice of sanctification
Bar	2:21	Bend your shoulders and serve the king of Babylon
L Jr	6:4	which are carried on men's shoulders
	6:26	Having no feet, they are carried on men's shoulders
1 Es	1:4	and he said, You need no longer carry it upon your shoulders

SHOUT, verb
17 = 0.011 %
Jud	14:16	and wept and groaned and shouted, and rent his garments
	14:17	he rushed out to the people and shouted
	16:11	Then my oppressed people shouted for joy
	16:11	for weak people shouted and the enemy trembled
Sir	50:16	Then the sons of Aaron shouted
L Jr	6:32	They howl and shout before their gods
Sus	13:24	and the 2 elders shouted against her
	13:60	Then all the assembly shouted loudly and blessed God
Bel	14:18	the king looked at the table, and shouted in a loud voice
	14:37	Then Habakkuk shouted, Daniel ! Daniel !
	14:41	And the king shouted with a loud voice
1 Es	4:41	then all the people shouted, and said
	5:62	and shouted with a great shout
	9:10	Then all the multitude shouted and said with a loud voice
3 Ma	1:23	They shouted to their fellows to take arms
	7:13	shouted the Hallelujah and joyfully departed
4 Ma	10:2	But he shouted, Do you not know

SHOUT, subst.
7 = 0.005 %
Jud	14:9	And when she had finished, the people raised a great shout
	14:19	and their loud cries and shouts arose
1 Ma	3:54	Then they sounded the trumpets and gave a loud shout
	5:31	with trumpets and loud shouts
2 Ma	4:22	and ushered in with a blaze of torches and with shouts
1 Es	5:62	and shouted with a great shout
3 Ma	4:1	with shouts and gladness

SHOUTING
3 = 0.002 %
Sus	13:26	When the household servants heard the shouting in the garden
2 Ma	15:29	Then there was shouting and tumult
3 Ma	6:23	For when he heard the shouting

SHOW
132 = 0.086 %
Tob	3:15	command that respect be shown to me
	8:17	Show them mercy, O Lord
	13:2	For he afflicts, and he shows mercy
	13:5	and again he will show mercy
	13:6	and I show his power and majesty to a nation of sinners
	13:9	but again he will show mercy to the sons of the righteous
	14:7	will rejoice, showing mercy to our brethren
Jud	8:29	Today is not the first time your wisdom has been shown
	10:13	and I will show him a way by which he can go
	13:11	God, our God, is still with us, to show his power in Israel
	13:15	Then she took the head out of the bag and showed it to them
	16:15	but to those who fear thee thou wilt continue to show mercy
Wis	3:14	for special favour will be shown him for his faithfulness
	5:13	and we had no sign of virtue to show
	6:7	nor show deference to greatness
	8:15	among the people I shall show myself capable
	10:10	she showed him the kingdom of God
	10:14	Those who accused him she showed to be false
	11:8	showing by their thirst at that time
	11:21	For it is always in thy power to show great strength
	12:17	For thou dost show thy strength
	14:4	showing that thou canst save from every danger
	16:2	thou didst show kindness to thy people
	16:4	while to these it was merely shown
	18:21	showing that he was thy servant
Sir	3:13	even if he is lacking in understanding, show forbearance
	3:23	have been shown you
	4:22	Do not show partiality, to your own harm
	4:27	nor show partiality to a ruler
	7:24	and do not show yourself too indulgent with them
	14:12	and the decree of Hades has not been shown to you
	16:9	He showed no pity for a nation devoted to destruction
	17:7	and showed them good and evil
	17:8	to show them the majesty of his works
	17:12	and showed them his judgments
	19:30	and a man's manner of walking, show what he is
	20:3	How good it is to show repentance when you are reproved
	22:19	and one who pricks the heart makes it show feeling
	26:9	A wife's harlotry shows in her lustful eyes
	29:1	He that shows mercy will lend to his neighbour
	35:9	With every gift show a cheerful face
	35:13	He will not show partiality in the case of a poor man
	36:6	Show signs anew, and work further wonders
	41:16	Therefore show respect for my words :

	41:23	Then you will show proper shame
	45:3	and showed him part of his glory
	49:8	which God showed him above the chariot of the cherubim
Bar	5:3	For God will show your splendour everywhere under heaven
L Jr	6:59	So it is better to be a king who shows his courage
	6:67	they cannot show signs in the heavens and among the nations
Bel	14:21	and they showed him the secret doors
1 Ma	2:50	Now, my children, show zeal for the law
	4:20	for the smoke that was seen showed what had happened
	5:41	But if he shows fear
	6:34	They showed the elephants the juice of grapes and mulberries
	7:33	to greet him peaceably and to show him the burnt offering
	11:4	they showed him the temple of Dagon burned down
	11:33	because of the good will they show toward us
	12:7	as the appended copy shows
	14:4	as was the honour shown him, all his days
2 Ma	2:7	and shows his mercy
	2:8	as they were shown in the case of Moses
	3:17	which plainly showed to those who looked at him
	4:17	to show irreverence to the divine laws
	4:49	showing their hatred of the crime
	6:27	I will show myself worthy of my old age
	7:37	appealing to God to show mercy soon to our nation
	8:4	and to show his hatred of evil
	10:12	took the lead in showing justice to the Jews
	10:38	who shows great kindness to Israel
	12:24	and no consideration would be shown them
	12:30	which the people of Scythopolis had shown them
	12:36	to show himself their ally and leader in the battle
	13:9	was coming to show to the Jews things far worse
	13:23	and showed generosity to the holy place
	14:9	with the gracious kindness which you show to all
	15:2	but show respect for the day
	15:32	He showed them the vile Nicanor's head
1 Es	8:4	and the king showed him honour
3 Ma	5:13	to show the might of his all-powerful hand
	6:5	showing your power to many nations
	6:15	Let it be shown to all the Gentiles
2 Es	1:25	When you beg mercy of me, I will show you no mercy
	1:35	Those to whom I have shown no signs
	2:31	and will show mercy to them
	3:31	and hast not shown to any one how thy way may be comprehended
	4:3	I have been sent to show you 3 ways
	4:4	I also will show you the way you desire to see
	4:45	show me this also : whether more time is to come than has passed
	4:47	and I will show you the interpretation of a parable
	5:37	or show me the picture of a voice
	5:43	that thou mightest show thy judgment the sooner ?
	5:56	show thy servant through whom thou dost visit thy creation
	6:12	show thy servant the end of thy signs
	6:12	which thou didst show me in part on a previous night
	6:20	then I will show these signs :
	6:30	I have come to show you these things this night
	6:33	Therefore he sent me to show you all these things
	7:44	and to you alone have I shown these things
	7:48	and has shown us the paths of perdition
	7:75	show this also to thy servant : whether after death
	7:76	He answered me and said, I will show you that also
	7:76	but do not be associated with those who have shown scorn
	7:77	but it will not be shown to you until the last times
	7:79	And if it is one of those who have shown scorn
	7:97	when it is shown to them how their face is to shine like the sun
	7:102	show further to me, thy servant
	7:104	I will show you this also
	7:134	and patient, because he shows patience
	8:62	I have not shown this to all men
	8:63	Behold, O Lord, thou hast now shown me a multitude of the signs
	8:63	but thou hast not shown me when thou wilt do them
	9:29	O Lord, thou didst show thyself among us
	10:27	and a place of huge foundations showed itself
	10:50	has shown you the brilliance of her glory
	10:59	and the Most High will show you in those dream visions
	12:8	strengthen me and show me, thy servant
	12:9	to be shown the end of the times
	12:39	so that you may be shown
	12:39	whatever it pleases the Most High to show you
	13:14	From the beginning thou hast shown thy servant these wonders
	13:15	now show me also the interpretation of this dream
	13:19	as these dreams show
	13:32	and the signs occur which I showed you before
	13:50	And then he will show them very many wonders
	13:56	Therefore I have shown you this
	14:5	and showed him the secrets of the times
	14:8	Lay up in your heart the signs that I have shown you
4 Ma	5:25	has shown sympathy toward us
	11:12	an opportunity to show our endurance for the law

12:6   he sent for the boy's mother to show compassion on her
17:2   and showed the courage of your faith !

SHOWER, verb   1
2 Ma 10:30   And they showered arrows and thunderbolts upon the enemy

SHOWER, subst.   1
Wis 16:22   and flashed in the showers of rain

SHREWD   1
Sir 37:19   A man may be shrewd and the teacher of many

SHRINE   2
Jud 3:8   And he demolished all their shrines
1 Ma 1:47   to build altars and sacred precincts and shrines for idols

SHRINK   3 = 0.002 %
Sir 7:35   Do not shrink from visiting a sick man
2 Ma 14:18   shrank from deciding the issue by bloodshed
4 Ma 14:4   None of the 7 youths proved coward or shrank from death

SHRINK back   1
1 Ma 3:6   Lawless men shrank back for fear of him

SHUDDER   5 = 0.003 %
P Ma 4   at whom all things shudder, and tremble before thy power
3 Ma 6:20   Even the king began to shudder bodily
2 Es 5:14   Then I awoke, and my body shuddered violently
4 Ma 14:9   Even now, we ourselves shudder
17:7   would not those who first beheld it have shuddered

SHUN   1
Sir 32:17   A sinful man will shun reproof

SHUT   8 = 0.005 %
Tob 8:4   When the door was shut and the 2 were alone
L Jr 6:18   And just as the gates are shut on every side
Sus 13:17   and shut the garden doors so that I may bathe
13:18   They did as she said, shut the garden doors
13:20   Look, the garden doors are shut, no one sees us
13:36   shut the garden doors, and dismissed the maids
Bel 14:11   and shut the door and seal it with your signet
14:14   Then they went out, shut the door

SHUT in   1
Wis 17:2   and prisoners of long night, shut in under their roofs

SHUT off   1
2 Es 16:78   It is shut off and given up to be consumed by fire

SHUT out   3 = 0.002 %
Jud 13:1   and shut out the attendants from his master's presence
1 Ma 5:47   But the men of the city shut them out
11:61   but the men of Gaza shut him out

SHUT up   7 = 0.005 %
Wis 17:16   and thus was kept shut up in a prison not made of iron
Sir 48:3   By the word of the Lord he shut up the heavens
1 Ma 5:5   They were shut up by him in their towers
5:26   Many of them have been shut up in Bozrah and Bosor
5:27   and some have been shut up in the other cities of Gilead
15:25   and he shut Trypho up and kept him from going out or in
2 Es 5:37   and bring forth for me the winds shut up in them

SIAHA   1
1 Es 5:29   the sons of Keros, the sons of Siaha, sons of Padon

SICK   6 = 0.004 %
Wis 17:8   and disorders of a sick soul
17:8   were sick themselves with ridiculous fear
Sir 7:35   Do not shrink from visiting a sick man
38:9   My son, when you are sick do not be negligent
1 Ma 1:5   After this he fell sick and perceived that he was dying
6:8   He took to his bed and became sick from grief

SICKLY   1
Wis 6:23   neither will I travel in the company of sickly envy

SICKNESS   3 = 0.002 %
Sir 30:17   and eternal rest than chronic sickness
31:22   and no sickness will overtake you
37:30   for overeating brings sickness, and gluttony leads to nausea

SICYON   1
1 Ma 15:23   and to Sicyon, and to Caria, and to Samos

SIDE, subst.   48 = 0.031 %
Jud 6:6   and the spear of my servants shall pierce your sides
Sir 30:12   and beat his sides while he is young
46:5   when enemies pressed him on every side

46:16   when his enemies pressed him on every side
47:7   For he wiped out his enemies on every side
47:7   and God gave him rest on every side
51:4   from choking fire on every side
51:7   They surrounded me on every side
L Jr 6:18   And just as the gates are shut on every side
Sus 13:18   and went out by the side doors
13:22   I am hemmed in on every side
13:26   they rushed in at the side door
1 Ma 1:37   On every side of the sanctuary they shed innocent blood
4:34   Then both sides attacked
5:37   and encamped opposite Raphon, on the other side of the stream
5:41   and camps on the other side of the river
6:38   The rest of the horsemen were stationed on either side
6:45   and they parted before him on both sides
9:17   and many on both sides were wounded and fell
9:45   the water of the Jordan is on the side and on that
9:48   and swam across to the other side
10:20   and you are to take our side and keep friendship with us
10:63   The king also seated him at his side
13:10   and he fortified it on every side
2 Ma 1:11   we thank him greatly for taking our side against the king
2:30   to occupy the ground and to discuss matters from every side
3:26   who stood on each side of him and scourged him continuously
5:3   attacks and counterattacks made on this side and on that
10:16   and beseeching God to fight on their side
11:13   because the mighty God fought on their side
13:5   which on all sides inclines precipitously into the ashes
3 Ma 2:22   He shook him on this side
5:7   they were forcibly confined on every side
2 Es 4:47   And he said to me, Stand at my right side
7:38   Look on this side and on that
11:12   on the right side one wing arose
11:20   in due course the wings that followed also rose up on the right side
11:24   and remained under the head that was on the right side
11:35   the head on the right side devoured the one on the left
12:29   which was on the right side
14:15   and lay to one side the thoughts that are most grievous to you
16:39   and pains will seize it on every side
4 Ma 3:4   but reason can fight at our side
6:3   And after they had tied his arms on each side they scourged him
6:6   and his sides were being cut to pieces
6:8   and began to kick him in the side
9:11   they bound his hands and arms with thongs on each side
15:32   overwhelmed from every side

SIDE, prop. n.   1
1 Ma 15:23   and to Side, and to Aradus and Gortyna

SIDE, verb   1
1 Ma 10:26   and have not sided with our enemies

SIDEBOARD   1
1 Ma 15:32   and the sideboard with its gold and silver plate

SIDON   3 = 0.002 %
Jud 2:28   who lived along the seacoast, at Sidon and Tyre
1 Ma 5:15   men of Ptolemais and Tyre and Sidon
2 Es 1:11   and scattered in the east the people of 2 provinces, Tyre and Sidon

SIDONIAN   1
1 Es 5:55   and carts to the Sidonians and the Tyrians

SIEGE   11 = 0.007 %
Sir 50:4   and fortified the city to withstand a siege
1 Ma 6:20   and he built siege towers and other engines of war
6:21   But some of the garrison escaped from the siege
6:49   because they had no provisions there to withstand a siege
6:51   He set up siege towers
11:22   and he wrote to Jonathan not to continue the siege
11:23   he gave orders to continue the siege
13:43   He made a siege engine, brought it up to the city
13:44   The men in the siege engine leaped out into the city
2 Ma 10:18   well equipped to withstand a siege
4 Ma 17:24   for infantry battle and siege

SIEVE   1
Sir 27:4   When a sieve is shaken, the refuse remains

SIFT   1
Bel 14:14   and they sifted them throughout the whole temple

SIGH   3 = 0.002 %
Sir 25:18   and he cannot help sighing bitterly
36:25   and where there is no wife, a man will wander about and sigh
Sus 13:22   Susanna sighed deeply, and said

SIGHT

			50 = 0.033 %
Tob	1 : 13	and good appearance in the sight of Shalmaneser	
	4 : 21	and do what is pleasing in his sight	
	7 : 7	When he heard that Tobit had lost his sight	
	11 : 6	And she caught sight of him coming, and said to his father	
	14 : 2	He was 58 years old when he lost his sight	
Jud	5 : 12	and so the Egyptians drove them out of their sight	
Wis	2 : 15	the very sight of him is a burden to us	
	3 : 4	For though in the sight of men they were punished	
	7 : 9	because all gold is but a little sand in her sight	
	8 : 11	and in the sight of rulers I shall be admired	
	9 : 9	and who understands what is pleasing in thy sight	
	11 : 19	but the mere sight of them could kill by fright	
	19 : 17	They were stricken also with loss of sight	
	19 : 18	from the sight of what took place	
Sir	1 : 29	Be not a hypocrite in men's sight	
	3 : 18	so you will find favour in the sight of the Lord	
	8 : 16	because blood is as nothing in his sight	
	11 : 21	for it is easy in the sight of the Lord	
	11 : 26	For it is easy in the sight of the Lord	
	25 : 1	and they are beautiful in the sight of the Lord and of men :	
	45 : 1	who found favour in the sight of all flesh	
	46 : 6	that he was fighting in the sight of the Lord	
Bar	1 : 12	and we shall serve them many days and find favour in their sight	
	1 : 21	and doing what is evil in the sight of the Lord our God	
	2 : 14	in the sight of those who have carried us into exile	
L Jr	6 : 37	They cannot restore sight to a blind man	
P Az	17	such may our sacrifice be in thy sight this day	
Sus	13 : 23	rather than to sin in the sight of the Lord	
1 Ma	2 : 23	a Jew came forward in the sight of all	
	3 : 18	for in the sight of Heaven	
1 Es	1 : 23	And the deeds of Josiah were upright in the sight of his Lord	
	1 : 39	and he did what was evil in the sight of the Lord	
	1 : 44	He did what was evil in the sight of the Lord	
	1 : 47	He also did what was evil in the sight of the Lord	
	8 : 26	and who honoured me in the sight of the king	
	9 : 45	in the sight of the multitude	
P Ma	10	and have done what is evil in thy sight	
3 Ma	4 : 4	that at the sight of their unusual punishments	
2 Es	1 : 34	and have done what is evil in my sight	
	2 : 3	and have done what is evil in my sight	
	3 : 35	When have the inhabitants of the earth not sinned in thy sight ?	
	4 : 44	If I have found favour in your sight	
	5 : 56	if I have found favour in thy sight	
	6 : 11	if I have found favour in thy sight	
	7 : 75	If I have found favour in thy sight, O Lord	
	7 : 102	If I have found favour in thy sight	
	7 : 104	Since you have found favour in my sight	
	8 : 28	Think not on those who have lived wickedly in thy sight	
	12 : 7	if I have found favour in thy sight	
	15 : 28	Behold, a terrifying sight, appearing from the east !	

SIGN, subst.

			34 = 0.022 %
Ad E	10 : 9	God has done great signs and wonders	
	14 : 16	that I abhor the sign of my proud position	
Wis	2 : 9	everywhere let us leave signs of enjoyment	
	5 : 11	and afterward no sign of its coming is found there	
	5 : 13	and we had no sign of virtue to show	
	8 : 8	she has foreknowledge of signs and wonders	
	10 : 16	and withstood dread kings with wonders and signs	
	19 : 13	without prior signs in the violence of thunder	
Sir	36 : 6	Show signs anew, and work further wonders	
	42 : 18	and he looks into the signs of the age	
	43 : 6	to mark the times and to be an everlasting sign	
	43 : 7	From the moon comes the sign for feast days	
	45 : 3	By his words he caused signs to cease	
Bar	2 : 11	with a mighty hand and with signs and wonders	
L Jr	6 : 67	they cannot show signs in the heavens and among the nations	
2 Ma	6 : 13	is a sign of great kindness	
	15 : 35	a clear and conspicuous sign to every one	
3 Ma	1 : 14	to take this as a sign in itself	
	6 : 32	they formed choruses as a sign of peaceful joy	
2 Es	1 : 15	The quails were a sign to you	
	1 : 35	Those to whom I have shown no signs	
	4 : 52	Concerning the signs about which you ask me	
	5 : 1	Now concerning the signs : behold	
	5 : 13	These are the signs which I am permitted to tell you	
	6 : 12	show thy servant the end of thy signs	
	6 : 20	then I will show these signs :	
	7 : 26	when the signs which I have foretold to you will come to pass	
	8 : 63	Behold, O Lord, thou hast now shown me a multitude of the signs	
	9 : 1	and when you see that a certain part of the predicted signs are past	
	9 : 6	and the end in requital and in signs	
	13 : 32	and the signs occur which I showed you before	
	13 : 44	For at that time the Most High performed signs for them	

| | 14 : 8 | Lay up in your heart the signs that I have shown you | |
| 4 Ma | 15 : 19 | and saw in their nostrils signs of the approach of death | |

SIGNAL, subst.

			1
1 Ma	4 : 40	and sounded the signal on the trumpets	

SIGNED

			1
2 Ma	11 : 17	have delivered your signed communication	

SIGNET

			9 = 0.006 %
Tob	1 : 22	Now Ahikar was cupbearer, keeper of the signet	
Sir	17 : 22	A man's almsgiving is like a signet with the Lord	
	38 : 27	those who cut the signets of seals	
	45 : 11	with precious stones engraved like signets	
	45 : 12	inscribed like a signet with Holiness	
	49 : 11	He was like a signet on the right hand	
Bel	14 : 11	and shut the door and seal it with your signet	
	14 : 14	and sealed it with the king's signet, and departed	
1 Ma	6 : 15	He gave him the crown and his robe and the signet	

SILENCE, subst.

			5 = 0.003 %
Wis	18 : 14	For while gentle silence enveloped all things	
Sir	41 : 20	and of silence, before those who greet you	
3 Ma	3 : 23	but also both by speech and by silence	
2 Es	6 : 39	and darkness and silence embraced everything	
	7 : 30	And the world shall be turned back to primeval silence for 7 days	

SILENCE, verb

			3 = 0.002 %
3 Ma	5 : 7	But with tears and a voice hard to silence	
2 Es	10 : 22	our harp has been laid low, our song has been silenced	
	15 : 32	then these shall be disorganized and silenced by their power	

SILENT

			11 = 0.007 %
Wis	8 : 12	When I am silent they will wait for me	
Sir	13 : 23	When the rich man speaks all are silent	
	20 : 1	and there is a man who keeps silent but is wise	
	20 : 5	There is one who by keeping silent is found wise	
	20 : 6	There is one who keeps silent because he has no answer	
	20 : 6	while another keeps silent because he knows when to speak	
	20 : 7	A wise man will be silent until the right moment	
	26 : 14	A silent wife is a gift of the Lord	
1 Ma	11 : 5	but the king kept silent	
2 Es	14 : 43	As for me, I spoke in the daytime and was not silent at night	
	15 : 8	I will be silent no longer concerning their ungodly deeds	

SILENTLY

			1
2 Es	7 : 32	and the dust those who dwell silently in it	

SILVER

			80 = 0.052 %
Tob	1 : 14	and once at Rages in Media I left 10 talents of silver	
	4 : 20	And now let me explain to you about the 10 talents of silver	
Jud	2 : 18	and a huge amount of gold and silver from the royal palace	
	5 : 9	with much gold and silver and very many cattle	
	8 : 7	and her husband Manasseh had left her gold and silver	
	10 : 22	with silver lamps carried before him	
	12 : 1	where his silver dishes were kept	
	15 : 11	and all his silver dishes	
Wis	7 : 9	and silver will be accounted as clay before her	
	13 : 10	gold and silver fashioned with skill	
	15 : 9	but he competes with workers in gold and silver	
Sir	26 : 18	Like pillars of gold on a base of silver	
	28 : 24	lock up your silver and gold	
	29 : 10	Lose your silver for the sake of a brother or a friend	
	40 : 25	Gold and silver make the foot stand sure	
	47 : 18	you gathered gold like tin and amassed silver like lead	
	51 : 28	Get instruction with a large sum of silver	
Bar	1 : 8	the silver vessels which Zedekiah the son of Josiah, king of Judah, had made	
	3 : 17	and who hoard up silver and gold	
	3 : 18	those who scheme to get silver, and are anxious	
L Jr	6 : 4	Now in Babylon you will see gods made of silver and gold and wood	
	6 : 8	and they themselves are overlaid with gold and silver	
	6 : 10	and sometimes the priests secretly take gold and silver from their gods	
	6 : 11	these gods of silver and gold and wood	
	6 : 30	Women serve meals for gods of silver and gold and wood	
	6 : 39	These things that are made of wood and overlaid with gold and silver	
	6 : 50	Since they are made of wood and overlaid with gold and silver	
	6 : 55	of wooden gods overlaid with gold or silver	
	6 : 57	gods of wood and overlaid with silver and gold	
	6 : 58	Strong men will strip them of their gold and silver	
	6 : 70	so are their gods of wood, overlaid with gold and silver	
	6 : 71	overlaid with gold and silver	
1 Ma	1 : 23	He took the silver and the gold, and the costly vessels	
	2 : 18	with silver and gold and many gifts	
	3 : 41	they took silver and gold in immense amounts, and fetters	
	4 : 23	and they seized much gold and silver	

	6:1	was a city famed for its wealth in silver and gold
	6:12	I seized all her vessels of silver and gold
	8:3	to get control of the silver and gold mines there
	10:40	I also grant 15,000 shekels of silver yearly
	10:42	Moreover, the 5,000 shekels of silver
	10:60	he gave them and their friends silver and gold and many gifts
	11:24	taking silver and gold and clothing and numerous other gifts
	13:16	Send now a 100 talents of silver
	15:26	and silver and gold, and much military equipment
	15:31	or else give me for them 500 talents of silver
	15:32	and the sideboard with its gold and silver plate
	16:11	and he had much silver and gold
	16:19	so that he might give them silver and gold and gifts
2 Ma	2:2	upon seeing the gold and silver statues and their adornment
	3:11	and that it totalled in all 400 talents of silver and 200 of gold
	4:8	promising the king at an interview 360 talents of silver
	4:19	to carry 300 silver drachmas for the sacrifice to Hercules
	4:24	outbidding Jason by 300 talents of silver
	12:43	to the amount of 2,000 drachmas of silver
1 Es	1:36	and fined the nation a 100 talents of silver
	2:6	be helped by the men of his place with gold and silver
	2:9	with silver and gold, with horses and cattle
	2:13	The number of these was: a 1,000 gold cups, a 1,000 silver cups
	2:13	29 silver censers, 30 gold bowls
	2:13	2,410 silver bowls, and a 1,000 other vessels
	2:14	All the vessels were handed over, gold and silver, 5,469
	4:18	If men gather gold and silver or any other beautiful thing
	4:19	and all prefer her to gold or silver
	5:45	5,000 minas of silver
	6:18	And the holy vessels of gold and of silver
	6:26	both of gold and of silver
	8:13	all the gold and silver that may be found
	8:14	both gold and silver for bulls and rams
	8:16	with the gold and silver
	8:20	up to a 100 talents of silver
	8:55	and I weighed out to them the silver and the gold
	8:56	I weighed and gave to them 650 talents of silver
	8:56	and silver vessels worth a 100 talents
	8:58	and the silver and the gold are vowed to the Lord
	8:60	who took the silver and the gold
	8:62	the silver and the gold were weighed
2 Es	7:55	Say to her, You produce gold and silver and brass
	7:56	but silver is more abundant than gold, and brass than silver

SIMEON

5 = 0.003 %

Jud	6:15	of the tribe of Simeon
	9:2	O Lord God of my father Simeon
1 Ma	2:1	In those days Mattathias the son of John, son of Simeon
	2:65	Now behold, I know that Simeon your brother is wise in counsel
4 Ma	2:19	censure the households of Simeon and Levi

SIMILAR

3 = 0.002 %

1 Ma	5:14	came from Galilee and made a similar report
2 Ma	2:3	And with other similar words he exhorted them
2 Es	7:61	and are similar to a flame and smoke

SIMON

85 = 0.055 %

Sir	50:1	was Simon the high priest, son of Onias
	50:20	Then Simon came down, and lifted up his hands
1 Ma	2:3	Simon called Thassi
	5:17	Then Judas said to Simon his brother
	5:20	Then 3,000 men were assigned to Simon to go to Galilee
	5:21	So Simon went to Galilee
	5:55	and Simon his brother was in Galilee before Ptolemais
	9:19	Then Jonathan and Simon took Judas their brother
	9:33	But Jonathan and Simon his brother
	9:37	and Simon his brother
	9:62	Then Jonathan with his men, and Simon
	9:65	But Jonathan left Simon his brother in the city
	9:67	and Simon and his men sallied out from the city
	10:74	and Simon his brother met him to help him
	10:82	Then Simon brought forward his force
	11:59	Simon his brother he made governor
	11:64	but left his brother Simon in the country
	11:65	Simon encamped before Beth-zur
	12:33	Simon also went forth and marched through the country
	12:38	And Simon built Adida in the Shephelah
	13:1	Simon heard that Trypho had assembled a large army
	13:13	And Simon encamped in Adida, facing the plain
	13:14	Trypho learned that Simon had risen up
	13:17	Simon knew that they were speaking deceitfully to him
	13:18	Because Simon did not send him the money and the sons, he perished
	13:20	But Simon and his army kept marching along opposite him
	13:25	And Simon sent and took the bones of Jonathan his brother
	13:27	And Simon built a monument
	13:33	But Simon built up the strongholds of Judea
	13:34	Simon also chose men and sent them to Demetrius the king
	13:36	King Demetrius to Simon, the high priest and friend of kings
	13:42	In the first year of Simon the great high priest
	13:43	In those days Simon encamped against Gazara
	13:45	asking Simon to make peace with them
	13:47	So Simon reached an agreement with them
	13:50	Then they cried to Simon to make peace with them
	13:52	And Simon decreed that every year
	13:53	And Simon saw that John his son had reached manhood
	14:4	The land had rest all the days of Simon
	14:17	When they heard that Simon his brother
	14:20	to Simon the high priest and to the elders and the priests
	14:23	And they have sent a copy of this to Simon the high priest
	14:24	After this Simon sent Numenius to Rome
	14:25	How shall we thank Simon and his sons?
	14:27	which is the 3rd year of Simon the great high priest
	14:29	Simon the son of Mattathias
	14:32	then Simon rose up and fought for his nation
	14:35	The people saw Simon's faithfulness
	14:40	the envoys of Simon with honour
	14:41	that Simon should be their leader and high priest for ever
	14:46	And all the people agreed to grant Simon
	14:47	So Simon accepted and agreed to be high priest
	14:49	so that Simon and his sons might have them
	15:1	to Simon, the priest and ethnarch of the Jews
	15:2	King Antiochus to Simon the high priest and ethnarch
	15:17	They had been sent by Simon the high priest
	15:21	hand them over to Simon the high priest
	15:24	to Simon the high priest
	15:26	And Simon sent to Antiochus 2,000 picked men, to fight for him
	15:27	he formerly had made with Simon
	15:32	and when he saw the splendour of Simon
	15:33	but Simon gave him this reply:
	15:36	and reported to him these words and the splendour of Simon
	16:1	and reported to Simon his father what Cendebaeus had done
	16:2	And Simon called in his 2 elder sons Judas and John
	16:13	and made treacherous plans against Simon and his sons
	16:14	Now Simon was visiting the cities of the country
	16:16	When Simon and his sons were drunk
	16:16	and rushed in against Simon in the banquet hall
2 Ma	3:4	But a man named Simon, of the tribe of Benjamin
	3:11	To such an extent the impious Simon had misrepresented the facts
	4:1	The previously mentioned Simon
	4:3	by one of Simon's approved agents
	4:4	was intensifying the malice of Simon
	4:6	and that Simon would not stop his folly
	4:23	the brother of the previously mentioned Simon
	8:22	Simon and Joseph and Jonathan
	10:19	Maccabeus left Simon and Joseph
	10:20	But the men with Simon, who were moneyhungry
	14:17	Simon, the brother of Judas, had encountered Nicanor
1 Es	9:32	and Sabbaias and Simon Chosamaeus
3 Ma	2:1	Then the high priest Simon, facing the sanctuary
4 Ma	4:1	Now there was a certain Simon
	4:4	he praised Simon for his service to the king
	4:5	accompanied by the accursed Simon

SIMPLY

2

| Wis | 16:27 | was melted when simply warmed by a fleeting ray of the sun |
| 1 Ma | 5:48 | we will simply pass by on foot |

SIN, subst.

123 = 0.080 %

Tob	3:3	do not punish me for my sins and for my unwitting offences
	3:5	in exacting penalty from me for my sins
	3:14	that I am innocent of any sin with man
	4:21	and refrain from every sin
	12:9	and it will purge away every sin
	12:10	but those who commit sin are the enemies of their own lives
Jud	7:28	who punishes us according to our sins
	7:28	and the sins of our fathers
	11:11	death will fall upon them, for a sin has overtaken them
	11:17	and he will tell me when they have committed their sins
	13:16	and yet he committed no act of sin with me
Wis	1:4	nor dwell in a body enslaved to sin
	2:12	he reproaches us for sins against the law
	2:12	and accuses us of sins against our training
	4:20	They will come with dread when their sins are reckoned up
	10:13	wisdom did not desert him, but delivered him from sin
	11:23	and thou dost overlook men's sins, that they may repent
	12:11	that thou didst leave them unpunished for their sins
	12:19	because thou givest repentance for sins
	17:3	For thinking that in their secret sins
Sir	1:21	The fear of the Lord drives away sins:
	2:11	he forgives sins and saves in time of affliction
	3:3	Whoever honours his father atones for sins
	3:14	and against your sins it will be credited to you
	3:15	as frost in fair weather, your sins will melt away
	3:27	and the sinner will heap sin upon sin
	3:30	so almsgiving atones for sin
	4:21	For there is a shame which brings sin
	4:26	Do not be ashamed to confess your sins
	5:5	Do not be so confident of atonement that you add sin to sin

5 : 6	he will forgive the multitude of my sins
7 : 8	Do not commit a sin twice
8 : 5	Do not reproach a man who is turning away from sin
10 : 13	For the beginning of pride is sin
12 : 14	and becomes involved in his sins
13 : 24	Riches are good if they are free from sin
14 : 1	and need not suffer grief for sin
16 : 9	for those destroyed in their sins
17 : 20	and all their sins are before the Lord
17 : 25	Turn to the Lord and forsake your sins
18 : 27	and in days of sin he guards against wrongdoing
19 : 8	and unless it would be a sin for you, do not disclose it
20 : 3	for so you will escape deliberate sin !
21 : 1	Do so no more, but pray about your former sins
21 : 2	Flee from sin as from a snake
21 : 2	for if you approach sin, it will bite you
23 : 2	and that it may not pass by my sins
23 : 3	and my sins may not abound
23 : 10	and utters the Name wil! not be cleansed from sin
23 : 11	if he offends, his sin remains on him
23 : 12	and they will not wallow in sins
23 : 16	2 sorts of men multiply sins
23 : 18	The Most High will not take notice of my sins
25 : 24	From a woman sin had its beginning
26 : 28	a man who turns back from righteousness to sin
26 : 29	and a tradesman will not be declared innocent of sin
27 : 1	Many have committed sin for a trifle
27 : 2	so sin is wedged in between selling and buying
27 : 10	so does sin for the workers of iniquity
28 : 1	and he will firmly establish his sins
28 : 2	and then your sins will be pardoned when you pray
28 : 4	and yet pray for his own sins ?
28 : 5	who will make expiation for his sins ?
28 : 8	Refrain from strife, and you will lessen sins
34 : 19	and he is not propitiated for sins
34 : 26	So if a man fasts for his sins
38 : 10	and cleanse your heart from all sin
39 : 5	and make supplication for his sins
42 : 1	and do not let partiality lead you to sin :
46 : 7	restrained the people from sin
47 : 11	The Lord took away his sins, and exalted his power for ever
47 : 24	Their sins became exceedingly many
48 : 15	and they did not forsake their sins
48 : 16	but others multiplied sins
Bar **1** : 10	so buy with the money burnt offerings and sin offerings
4 : 12	I was left desolate because of the sins of my children
L Jr **6** : 2	Because of the sins which you have committed before God
P Az **5**	because of our sins
14	because of our sins
Sus **13** : 52	You old relic of wicked days, your sins have now come home
2 Ma **2** : 11	because the sin offering had not been eaten
5 : 17	because of the sins of those who dwelt in the city
5 : 18	that they were involved in many sins
6 : 14	until they have reached the full measure of their sins
6 : 15	when our sins have reached their height
7 : 18	because of our sins against our own God
7 : 32	For we are suffering because of our own sins
12 : 42	beseeching that the sin which had been committed
12 : 42	to keep themselves free from sin
12 : 42	what had happened because of the sin of those who had fallen
12 : 43	and sent it to Jerusalem to provide for a sin offering
12 : 45	that they might be delivered from their sin
13 : 8	because he had committed many sins
1 Es **7** : 8	and 12 he-goats for the sin of all Israel
8 : 75	For our sins have risen higher than our heads
8 : 76	and we are in great sin to this day
8 : 77	And because of our sins and the sins of our fathers
8 : 86	because of our evil deeds and our great sins
8 : 86	For thou, O Lord, didst lift the burden of our sins
9 : 7	and so have increased the sin of Israel
P Ma **9**	For the sins I have committed are more in number
10	so that I am rejected because of my sins
3 Ma **2** : 13	that because of our many and great sins
2 : 19	Wipe away our sins and disperse our errors
2 Es **1** : 6	that the sins of their parents have increased in them
4 : 39	on account of the sins of those who dwell on earth
7 : 68	and are full of sins and burdened with transgressions
7 : 139	and blot out the multitude of their sins
8 : 26	O look not upon the sins of thy people
16 : 48	the more angry I will be with them for their sins
16 : 50	who searches out every sin on earth
16 : 63	Woe to those who sin and want to hide their sins !
16 : 65	And when your sins come out before men
16 : 66	Or how will you hide your sins before God and his angels ?
16 : 67	Cease from your sins, and forget your iniquities
16 : 76	do not let your sins pull you down
16 : 77	Woe to those who are choked by their sins
4 Ma **4** : 12	For he said that he had committed a sin deserving of death

5 : 19	Therefore do not suppose that it would be a petty sin
17 : 21	a ransom for the sin of our nation

SIN, verb   65 = 0.042 %

Tob **4** : 5	and refuse to sin or to transgress his commandments
Jud **5** : 17	As long as they did not sin against their God they prospered
5 : 20	and they sin against their God and we find out their offence
11 : 10	unless they sin against their God
Ad E **14** : 6	And now we have sinned before thee
Wis **11** : 16	by the very things by which he sins
12 : 2	and dost remind and warn them of the things wherein they sin
14 : 31	but the just penalty for those who sin
15 : 2	For even if we sin we are thine, knowing thy power -
15 : 2	but we will not sin
15 : 13	For this man, more than all others, knows that he sins
Sir **5** : 4	Do not say, I sinned, and what happened to me ?
7 : 36	and then you will never sin
10 : 29	Who will justify the man that sins against himself ?
15 : 20	and he has not given any one permission to sin
18 : 21	and when you are on the point of sinning, turn back
19 : 4	and one who sins does wrong to himself
19 : 16	Who has never sinned with his tongue ?
19 : 28	And if by lack of strength he is prevented from sinning
20 : 21	A man may be prevented from sinning by his poverty
21 : 1	Have you sinned, my son ?
23 : 11	and if he disregards it, he sins doubly
24 : 22	and those who work with my help will not sin
26 : 11	and do not wonder if she sins against you
32 : 12	but do not sin through proud speech
38 : 15	He who sins before his Maker
47 : 23	Also Jeroboam the son of Nebat, who caused Israel to sin
49 : 4	Except David and Hezekiah and Josiah they all sinned greatly
Bar **1** : 13	for we have sinned against the Lord our God
1 : 17	because we have sinned before the Lord
2 : 5	because we sinned against the Lord our God
2 : 12	we have sinned, we have been ungodly, we have done wrong
2 : 33	who sinned before the Lord
3 : 2	for we have sinned before thee
3 : 4	and of the sons of those who sinned before thee
3 : 7	who sinned before thee
P Az **6**	and have sinned in all things
Sus **13** : 23	rather than to sin in the sight of the Lord
2 Ma **10** : 4	but that, if they should ever sin
1 Es **1** : 24	concerning those who sinned and acted wickedly toward the Lord
4 : 27	Many have perished, or stumbled, or sinned, because of women
6 : 15	But when our fathers sinned against the Lord of Israel
8 : 92	and said to Ezra, We have sinned against the Lord
9 : 11	for we have sinned too much in these things
P Ma **7**	to those who have sinned against thee
8	who did not sin against thee
12	I have sinned, O Lord, I have sinned
2 Es **2** : 3	because you have sinned before the Lord God
3 : 30	for I have seen how thou dost endure those who sin
3 : 35	When have the inhabitants of the earth not sinned in thy sight ?
6 : 5	and before the imaginations of those who now sin were estranged
7 : 46	For who among the living is there that has not sinned
7 : 87	before whom they sinned while they were alive
7 : 106	and Moses for our fathers who sinned in the desert
7 : 116	or else, when it had produced him, had restrained him from sinning
7 : 118	For though it was you who sinned
7 : 134	toward those who have sinned
8 : 38	about the fashioning of those who have sinned
9 : 36	For we who have received the law and sinned will perish
15 : 24	Woe to those who sin and do not observe my commandments
15 : 27	because you have sinned against him
16 : 53	Let no sinner say that he has not sinned
16 : 53	I have not sinned before God and his glory
16 : 53	Woe to those who sin and want to hide their sins !

SINAI   4 = 0.003 %

Jud **5** : 14	and he led them by the way of Sinai and Kadesh-barnea
Sir **48** : 7	who heard rebuke at Sinai
2 Es **3** : 17	thou didst bring them to Mount Sinai
14 : 4	and I led him up on Mount Sinai

SINCE, prep., conj.   80 = 0.052 %

Jud **4** : 5	since their fields had recently been harvested
4 : 7	since by them Judea could be invaded
8 : 31	So pray for us, since you are a devout woman
11 : 3	since you have come to safety
11 : 12	Since their food supply is exhausted
12 : 16	ever since the day he first saw her
12 : 18	than in all the days since I was born
12 : 20	since he was born
Ad E **14** : 5	Ever since I was born
14 : 18	since the day that I was brought here until now
Wis **12** : 8	But even these thou didst spare, since they were but men

	14 : 17	since they lived at a distance
	15 : 17	since he has life, but they never have
	18 : 12	since in one instant
Sir pr.		and since it is necessary
	17 : 30	since a son of man is not immortal
	37 : 21	since he is lacking in all wisdom
	41 : 12	since it will remain for you longer than a 1,000 great stores of gold
L Jr	**6** : 29	Since you know by these things that they are not gods
	6 : 50	Since they are made of wood and overlaid with gold and silver
	6 : 65	Since you know then that they are not gods, do not fear them
1 Ma	**1** : 11	for since we separated from them many evils have come upon us
	6 : 49	since it was a sabbatical year for the land
	9 : 27	since the time that prophets ceased to appear among them
	9 : 29	Since the death of your brother Judas
	10 : 26	Since you have kept your agreement with us
	10 : 52	Since I have returned to my kingdom
	11 : 2	since he was Alexander's father-in-law
	12 : 9	since we have as encouragement the holy books
	12 : 10	since you sent your letter to us
	14 : 29	Since wars often occurred in the country
2 Ma	**1** : 18	Since on the 25th day of Chislev
	2 : 16	Since, therefore, we are about to celebrate the purification
	3 : 33	since for his sake the Lord has granted you your life
	4 : 40	And since the crowds were becoming aroused
	7 : 23	since you now forget yourselves for the sake of his laws
	7 : 25	Since the young man would not listen to him at all
	11 : 25	Accordingly, since we choose that this nation also
	14 : 9	Since you are acquainted, O king
	14 : 29	Since it was not possible to oppose the king
1 Es	**1** : 20	since the times of Samuel the prophet
	2 : 20	And since the building of the temple is now going on
	3 : 24	since it forces men to do these things ?
	4 : 12	since he is to be obeyed in this fashion ?
	4 : 32	since they do such things ?
	5 : 69	ever since the days of Esarhaddon king of the Assyrians
3 Ma	**1** : 8	Since the Jews had sent some of their council and elders
	1 : 15	But since this has happened, the king said
	2 : 22	since he was smitten by a righteous judgment
	2 : 31	since they expected to enhance their reputation
	3 : 5	but since they adorned their style of life
	3 : 20	since we treat all nations with benevolence
	3 : 22	Since they incline constantly to evil
	5 : 13	Then the Jews, since they had escaped the appointed hour
	5 : 14	But now, since it was nearly the middle of the 10th hour
	5 : 25	since the time had run out
	5 : 27	since he had been completely overcome by incomprehension
	5 : 35	since this also was his aid which they had received
	6 : 29	since they now had escaped death
	7 : 6	Since we have come to realize
	7 : 7	and since we have taken into account
	7 : 15	since they had destroyed the profaners
	7 : 20	since at the king's command they had been brought
2 Es	**5** : 50	Since thou hast now given me the opportunity
	7 : 104	Since you have found favour in my sight
	7 : 134	since they are his own works
4 Ma	**1** : 19	since by means of it reason rules over the emotions
	2 : 6	In fact, since the law had told us not to covet
	5 : 25	for since we believe that the law was established by God
	7 : 19	since they believe that they
	8 : 17	Since the king has summoned
	10 : 7	Since they were not able in any way to break his spirit
	11 : 15	Since to this end we were born and bred
	11 : 25	Since you have not been able to persuade us
	12 : 11	since you have received good things and also your kingdom from God
	13 : 1	Since, then, the 7 brothers despised sufferings even unto death
	13 : 24	Since they had been educated by the same law
	14 : 11	since the mind of a woman despised even more diverse agonies
	14 : 19	since even bees at the time for making honeycombs
	18 : 5	Since in no way whatever was he able to compel the Israelites

SINCERE   3 = 0.002 %
Ad E	**16** : 6	beguile the sincere good will of their sovereigns
Wis	**6** : 17	is the most sincere desire for instruction
3 Ma	**3** : 19	and are unwilling to regard any action as sincere

SINCERELY   2
3 Ma	**3** : 23	who are sincerely disposed toward us
2 Es	**10** : 50	seeing that you are sincerely grieved and profoundly distressed for her

SINCERITY   2
Tob	**8** : 7	I am not taking this sister of mine because of lust, but with sincerity
Wis	**1** : 1	and seek him with sincerity of heart

SINEW   2
4 Ma	**7** : 13	his muscles flabby, his sinews feeble, he became young again
	9 : 28	These leopard-like beasts tore out his sinews with the iron hands

SINFUL   13 = 0.008 %
Wis	**3** : 13	who has not entered into a sinful union
Sir	**10** : 23	nor is it proper to honour a sinful man
	15 : 7	and sinful men will not see her
	15 : 12	for he has no need of a sinful man
	23 : 13	for it involves sinful speech
	27 : 13	and their laughter is wantonly sinful
	27 : 30	and the sinful man will possess them
	28 : 9	and a sinful man will disturb friends
	32 : 17	A sinful man will shun reproof
	47 : 23	and gave to Ephraim a sinful way
1 Ma	**1** : 10	From them came forth a sinful root, Antiochus Epiphanes
	1 : 34	And they stationed there a sinful people, lawless men
2 Es	**7** : 114	sinful indulgence has come to an end

SINFULLY   1
P Az	6	For we have sinfully and lawlessly departed from thee

SING   52 = 0.034 %
Jud	**16** : 1	and all the people loudly sang this song of praise
	16 : 2	sing to my Lord with cymbals
	16 : 13	I will sing to my God a new song :
Ad E	**13** : 17	that we may live and sing praise to thy name, O Lord
Wis	**10** : 20	they sang hymns, O Lord, to thy holy name
	18 : 9	and already they were singing the praises of the fathers
Sir	**17** : 27	Who will sing praises to the Most High in Hades
	17 : 28	he who is alive and well sings the Lord's praises
	39 : 14	Scatter the fragrance, and sing a hymn of praise
	39 : 35	So now sing praise with all your heart and voice
	47 : 8	he sang praise with all his heart, and he loved his Maker
	51 : 11	and will sing praise with thanksgiving
P Az	1	singing hymns to God and blessing the Lord
	34	and to be sung and glorified for ever
	35	sing praise to him and highly exalt him for ever
	36	sing praise to him and highly exalt him for ever
	37	sing praise to him and highly exalt him for ever
	38	sing praise to him and highly exalt him for ever
	39	sing praise to him and highly exalt him for ever
	40	sing praise to him and highly exalt him for ever
	41	sing praise to him and highly exalt him for ever
	42	sing praise to him and highly exalt him for ever
	43	sing praise to him and highly exalt him for ever
	44	sing praise to him and highly exalt him for ever
	45	sing praise to him and highly exalt him for ever
	46	sing praise to him and highly exalt him for ever
	47	sing praise to him and highly exalt him for ever
	48	sing praise to him and highly exalt him for ever
	49	sing praise to him and highly exalt him for ever
	50	sing praise to him and highly exalt him for ever
	51	sing praise to him and highly exalt him for ever
	52	let it sing praise to him and highly exalt him for ever
	53	sing praise to him and highly exalt him for ever
	54	sing praise to him and highly exalt him for ever
	55	sing praise to him and highly exalt him for ever
	56	sing praise to him and highly exalt him for ever
	57	sing praise to him and highly exalt him for ever
	58	sing praise to him and highly exalt him for ever
	59	sing praise to him and highly exalt him for ever
	60	sing praise to him and highly exalt him for ever
	61	sing praise to him and highly exalt him for ever
	62	sing praise to him and highly exalt him for ever
	63	sing praise to him and highly exalt him for ever
	64	sing praise to him and highly exalt him for ever
	65	sing praise to him and highly exalt him for ever
	66	sing praise to him and highly exalt him for ever
	68	sing praise to him and give thanks to him
1 Ma	**4** : 24	On their return they sang hymns and praises to Heaven
2 Ma	**1** : 30	Then the priests sang the hymns
1 Es	**5** : 61	and they sang hymns, giving thanks to the Lord
P Ma	15	For all the host of heaven sings thy praise
4 Ma	**18** : 15	He sang to you songs of the psalmist David, who said

SINGER   10 = 0.007 %
Sir	**9** : 4	Do not associate with a woman singer
	47 : 9	He placed singers before the altar
	50 : 18	And the singers praised him with their voices
1 Es	**1** : 15	And the temple singers, the sons of Asaph
	5 : 27	The temple singers : the sons of Asaph, 128
	5 : 42	there were 245 musicians and singers
	5 : 46	and the temple singers, the gatekeepers
	8 : 5	and Levites and temple singers
	8 : 22	on any of the priests or Levites or temple singers
	9 : 24	Of the temple singers : Eliashib and Zaccur

SINGLE
		6 = 0.004 %
Jud	7:21	to drink their fill for a single day
Wis	11:20	men could fall at a single breath when pursued by justice
2 Ma	2:23	we shall attempt to condense into a single book
	7:20	Though she saw her 7 sons perish within a single day
	8:18	who is able with a single nod
3 Ma	4:14	and at the end to be destroyed in the space of a single day

SINGLEHANDED
		2
Jud	15:10	You have done all this singlehanded
3 Ma	1:2	intending single-handed to kill him and thereby end the war

SINGLY
		1
4 Ma	15:12	each child singly and all together

SINNER
		53 = 0.035 %
Tob	4:17	but give none to sinners
	13:6	and I show his power and majesty to a nation of sinners
	13:6	turn back, you sinners, and do right before him
Wis	4:10	and while living among sinners he was taken up
	19:13	The punishment did not come upon the sinners
Sir	1:25	but godliness is an abomination to a sinner
	2:12	and to the sinner who walks along 2 ways !
	3:27	and the sinner will heap sin upon sin
	5:6	and his anger rests on sinners
	5:9	the double-tongued sinner does that
	6:1	so fares the double-tongued sinner
	7:16	Do not count yourself among the crowd of sinners
	8:10	Do not kindle the coals of a sinner
	9:11	Do not envy the honours of a sinner
	11:9	nor sit with sinners when they judge a case
	11:16	Error and darkness were created with sinners
	11:21	Do not wonder at the works of a sinner
	11:32	and a sinner lies in wait to shed blood
	12:4	Give to the godly man, but do not help the sinner
	12:6	For the Most High also hates sinners
	12:7	Give to the good man, but do not help the sinner
	12:14	So no one will pity a man who associates with a sinner
	13:17	No more has a sinner with a godly man
	15:9	A hymn of praise is not fitting on the lips of a sinner
	16:6	In an assembly of sinners a fire will be kindled
	16:13	The sinner will not escape with his plunder
	19:22	nor is there prudence where sinners take counsel
	21:6	Whoever hates reproof walks in the steps of the sinner
	21:10	The way of sinners is smoothly paved with stones
	23:8	The sinner is overtaken through his lips
	25:19	may a sinner's lot befall her !
	29:16	A sinner will overthrow the prosperity of his surety
	29:19	The sinner who has fallen into suretyship and pursues gain
	33:14	so the sinner is the opposite of the godly
	39:25	just as evil things for sinners
	39:27	just as they turn into evils for sinners
	40:8	and upon sinners 7 times more
	41:5	The children of sinners are abominable children
	41:6	The inheritance of the children of sinners will perish
	41:11	but the evil name of sinners will be blotted out
1 Ma	2:44	and struck down sinners in their anger
	2:48	and they never let the sinner gain the upper hand
	2:62	Do not fear the words of a sinner
2 Ma	12:23	putting the sinners to the sword
	14:42	into the hands of sinners
P Ma	5	and the wrath of thy threat to sinners is irresistible
	7	thou hast appointed repentance for sinners
	8	but thou hast appointed repentance for me, who am a sinner
2 Es	3:29	and my soul has seen many sinners during these 30 years
	8:31	but thou, because of us sinners, art called merciful
	15:22	My right hand will not spare the sinners
	15:23	and the sinners, like straw that is kindled
	16:53	Let no sinner say that he has not sinned

SIR
		1
Bel	14:35	Habakkuk said, Sir, I have never seen Babylon

SIRACH
		1
Sir	50:27	Jesus the son of Sirach, son of Eleazar, of Jerusalem

SIREN
		1
4 Ma	15:21	Neither the melodies of sirens nor the songs of swans

SISERA
		1
1 Es	5:32	the sons of Sisera, the sons of Temah

SISINNES
		4 = 0.003 %
1 Es	6:3	At the same time Sisinnes the governor of Syria and Phoenicia
	6:7	which Sisinnes the governor of Syria and Phoenicia
	6:27	So Darius commanded Sisinnes
	7:1	Then Sisinnes the governor of Coelesyria and Phoenicia

SISTER
		5 = 0.003 %
Tob	5:20	And Tobit said to her, Do not worry, my sister
	7:16	Sister, make up the other room, and take her into it
	8:4	Tobias got up from the bed and said, Sister, get up
	8:7	I am not taking this sister of mine because of lust, but with sincerity
3 Ma	1:1	took with him his sister Arsinoe

SIT
		37 = 0.024 %
Tob	11:5	Now Anna sat looking intently down the road for her son
Wis	6:14	for he will find her sitting at his gates
	9:4	give me the wisdom that sits by thy throne
Sir	1:8	sitting upon his throne
	11:5	Many kings have had to sit on the ground
	11:9	nor sit with sinners when they judge a case
	12:12	do not have him sit at your right
	23:14	Remember your father and mother when you sit among great men
	26:12	so will she sit in front of every post
	33:6	he neighs under every one who sits on him
	37:14	than 7 watchmen sitting high on a watchtower
	38:28	So too is the smith sitting by the anvil
	38:29	So too is the potter sitting at his work
	38:33	They do not sit in the judge's seat
	40:3	from the man who sits on a splendid throne
	42:12	and do not sit in the midst of women
L Jr	6:31	and in their temples the priests sit with their clothes rent
	6:43	And the women, with cords about them, sit along the passageways
	6:71	on which every bird sits
P Az	32	Blessed art thou, who sittest upon cherubim
Sus	13:50	sit among us and inform us
Bel	14:40	When he came to the den he looked in, and there sat Daniel
1 Ma	1:27	she who sat in the bridal chamber was mourning
	11:52	So Demetrius the king sat on the throne of his kingdom
	14:9	Old men sat in the streets
	14:12	Each man sat under his vine and his fig tree
1 Es	3:7	and because of his wisdom he shall sit next to Darius
	4:29	she would sit at the king's right hand
	4:42	And you shall sit next to me, and be called my kinsman
	8:72	and I sat grief-stricken until the evening sacrifice
	9:6	And all the multitude sat in the open square before the temple
2 Es	9:26	and there I sat among the flowers
	12:41	that you have forsaken us and sit in this place ?
	12:51	But I sat in the field 7 days
	14:1	On the 3rd day, while I was sitting under an oak
	14:42	They sat 40 days, and wrote during the daytime
4 Ma	5:1	The tyrant Antiochus, sitting in state with his counsellors

SIT down
		2
Tob	2:1	a good dinner was prepared for me and I sat down to eat
1 Es	8:71	and sat down in anxiety and grief

SITE
		4 = 0.003 %
1 Es	5:44	vowed that they would erect the house on its site
	6:19	and that this temple of the Lord should be rebuilt on its site
	6:27	to build this house of the Lord on its site
3 Ma	7:20	and dedicating a place of prayer at the site of the festival

SITUATION
		7 = 0.005 %
Tob	7:10	But let me explain the true situation to you
2 Ma	3:9	and he inquired whether this really was the situation
3 Ma	1:16	and entreated the supreme God to aid in the present situation
	3:1	When the impious king comprehended this situation
	3:8	being grieved at the situation
	3:23	in every situation, in accordance with their infamous way of life
	5:15	and he gave him an account of the situation

SIVAN
		1
Bar	1:8	At the same time, on the 10th day of Sivan

SIZE
		1
1 Ma	3:19	It is not on the size of the army

SKILFUL
		2
Sir	38:31	and each is skilful in his own work
4 Ma	7:1	For like a most skilful pilot

SKILFULLY
		2
Wis	13:11	and skilfully strip off all its bark
	14:19	skilfully forced the likeness to take more beautiful form

SKILL
		10 = 0.007 %
Jud	11:8	For we have heard of your wisdom and skill
Wis	7:16	as are all understanding and skill in crafts
	13:10	gold and silver fashioned with skill
	13:13	and shapes it with skill gained in idleness
	14:4	so that even if a man lacks skill, he may put to sea
Sir	pr.	using in that period of time great watchfulness and skill
	9:17	A work will be praised for the skill of the craftsmen

26 : 13 and her skill puts fat on his bones
38 : 3 The skill of the physician lifts up his head
38 : 6 And he gave skill to men

SKILLED   4 = 0.003 %
Wis 13 : 11 A skilled woodcutter may saw down a tree easy to handle
Sir 18 : 29 Those who understand sayings become skilled themselves
    37 : 20 A man skilled in words may be hated
1 Es 8 : 3 skilled in the law of Moses

SKIN   1
2 Ma 7 : 7 They tore off the skin of his head with the hair

SKIP   1
Sir 36 : 26 that skips from city to city ?

SLACK   1
Sir 2 : 12 Woe to timid hearts and to slack hands

SLAIN   1
1 Ma 5 : 51 Then he passed through the city over the slain

SLAKING   1
Wis 11 : 4 and slaking of thirst from hard stone

SLANDER, subst.   9 = 0.006 %
Wis 1 : 11 and keep your tongue from slander
Sir 19 : 15 Question a friend, for often it is slander
    26 : 5 The slander of a city, the gathering of a mob
    28 : 14 Slander has shaken many
    28 : 15 Slander has driven away courageous women
    28 : 16 Whoever pays heed to slander will not find rest
    51 : 6 the slander of an unrighteous tongue to the king
3 Ma 6 : 7 Daniel, who through envious slanders
4 Ma 4 : 1 When despite all manner of slander

SLANDER, verb   1
2 Ma 4 : 1 slandered Onias, saying that it was he who had incited Heliodorus

SLANDERER   1
Sir 5 : 14 Do not be called a slanderer

SLANDEROUS   1
Sir 51 : 2 and from the snare of a slanderous tongue

SLAP   1
1 Es 4 : 30 and slap the king with her left hand

SLAUGHTER, subst.   9 = 0.006 %
Jud 2 : 11 and you shall hand them over to slaughter and plunder
    8 : 22 And the slaughter of our brethren
    15 : 5 with great slaughter
    15 : 7 And the Israelites, when they returned from the slaughter
Wis 12 : 5 their merciless slaughter of children
2 Ma 5 : 13 and slaughter of virgins and infants
2 Es 15 : 10 Behold, my people is led like a flock to the slaughter
    15 : 26 therefore he will hand them over to death and slaughter
4 Ma 2 : 19 for their irrational slaughter

SLAUGHTER, verb   5 = 0.003 %
Bel 14 : 28 and slaughtered the priests
2 Ma 5 : 6 But Jason kept relentlessly slaughtering his fellow citizens
    10 : 31 20,500 were slaughtered, besides 600 horsemen
    12 : 16 and slaughtered untold numbers
    12 : 26 and slaughtered 25,000 people

SLAVE   35 = 0.023 %
Tob 10 : 10 and half of his property in slaves, cattle, and money
Jud 3 : 4 Our cities also and their inhabitants are your slaves
    4 : 10 and purchased slave
    5 : 11 and humbled them and made slaves of them
    6 : 7 Now my slaves are going to take you back
    6 : 10 Then Holofernes ordered his slaves
    6 : 11 So the slaves took him
    7 : 27 for we will be slaves, but our lives will be spared
    8 : 7 and men and women slaves, and cattle, and fields
    8 : 22 wherever we serve as slaves
    9 : 3 and thou didst strike down slaves along with princes
    9 : 10 By the deceit of my lips strike down the slave
    10 : 23 and his slaves raised her up
    12 : 10 On the 4th day Holofernes held a banquet for his slaves only
    13 : 1 When evening came, his slaves quickly withdrew
    14 : 13 Wake up our lord, for the slaves have been so bold
    14 : 18 The slaves have tricked us !
Wis 9 : 5 For I am thy slave and the son of thy maidservant
    18 : 11 The slave was punished with the same penalty as the master
    19 : 14 but these made slaves of guests who were their benefactors
Sir 33 : 25 Set your slave to work, and you will find rest
Bar 4 : 32 Wretched will be the cities which your children served as slaves

1 Ma 2 : 11 no longer free, she has become a slave
    3 : 41 and went to the camp to get the sons of Israel for slaves
2 Ma 1 : 27 set free those who are slaves among the Gentiles
    5 : 24 and to sell the women and boys as slaves
    8 : 11 inviting them to buy Jewish slaves
    8 : 11 and promising to hand over 90 slaves for a talent
    8 : 25 of those who had come to buy them as slaves
    8 : 35 and made his way alone like a runaway slave
1 Es 3 : 19 of the slave and the free, of the poor and the rich
    4 : 26 and have become slaves because of them
3 Ma 2 : 28 and to the status of slaves
    7 : 5 They also led them out with harsh treatment as slaves
4 Ma 13 : 2 For if they had been slaves to their emotions

SLAVERY   4 = 0.003 %
Jud 8 : 23 For our slavery will not bring us into favour
Ad E 14 : 8 And now they are not satisfied that we are in bitter slavery
2 Ma 5 : 14 and as many were sold into slavery as were slain
    8 : 10 by selling the captured Jews into slavery

SLAY   26 = 0.017 %
Tob 3 : 8 and the evil demon Asmodeus had slain each of them
Jud 9 : 3 So thou gavest up their rulers to be slain
    10 : 13 without losing one of his men, captured or slain
Wis 10 : 3 he perished because in rage he slew his brother
    11 : 7 in rebuke for the decree to slay the infants
Sir 47 : 5 to slay a man mighty in war
Bel 14 : 26 I will slay the dragon without sword or club
    14 : 28 he has destroyed Bel, and slain the dragon
2 Ma 5 : 12 and to slay those who went into the houses
    5 : 14 and as many were sold into slavery as were slain
    5 : 24 and commanded him to slay all the grown men
    6 : 9 and should slay those who did not choose
    8 : 24 they slew more than 9,000 of the enemy
    10 : 17 and slew those whom they encountered
    10 : 22 Then he slew these men who had turned traitor
    11 : 11 and slew 11,000 of them and 1,600 horsemen
    13 : 15 and slew as many as 2,000 men in the camp
    15 : 22 and he slew fully a 185,000 in the camp of Sennacherib
1 Es 1 : 53 These slew their young men with the sword around their holy temple
2 Es 1 : 11 I have slain all their enemies
    1 : 32 but you have taken and slain them
4 Ma 3 : 7 and together with the soldiers of his nation had slain many of them
    8 : 25 Not even the law itself would arbitrarily slay us
    12 : 14 but you will wail bitterly for having slain without cause
    13 : 12 to being slain for the sake of religion
    18 : 11 He read to you about Abel slain by Cain

SLEEP, subst.   17 = 0.011 %
Tob 8 : 9 Then they both went to sleep for the night
Wis 17 : 14 they all slept the same sleep
Sir 13 : 13 When you hear these things in your sleep, wake up !
    31 : 1 and anxiety about it removes sleep
    31 : 2 and a severe illness carries off sleep
    31 : 20 Healthy sleep depends on moderate eating
    40 : 5 his sleep at night confuses his mind
    40 : 6 and afterward in his sleep, as though he were on watch
    42 : 9 and worry over her robs him of sleep
    46 : 19 Before the time of his eternal sleep
1 Ma 6 : 10 Sleep departs from my eyes and I am downhearted with worry
2 Ma 2 : 26 it is no light matter but calls for sweat and loss of sleep
1 Es 3 : 3 and went to sleep, and then awoke
3 Ma 5 : 11 But the Lord sent upon the king a portion of sleep
    5 : 12 he was overcome by so pleasant and deep a sleep
    5 : 20 said that the Jews were benefited by today's sleep
    5 : 22 in sleep as in devising all sorts of insults

SLEEP, verb   12 = 0.008 %
Tob 2 : 9 I slept by the wall of the courtyard, and my face was uncovered
Jud 12 : 5 and she slept until midnight
    14 : 14 for he supposed that he was sleeping with Judith
Wis 17 : 14 they all slept the same sleep
1 Es 3 : 6 and sleep on a gold bed
    4 : 10 Moreover, he reclines, he eats and drinks and sleeps
3 Ma 1 : 3 that a certain insignificant man should sleep in the tent
2 Es 2 : 31 Remember your sons that sleep
    7 : 35 and unrighteous deeds shall not sleep
    7 : 104 to be ill or sleep or eat or be healed in his stead
    10 : 59 So I slept that night and the following one
    11 : 8 let each sleep in his own place, and watch in his turn

SLEEPER   1
Sir 22 : 7 or who rouses a sleeper from deep slumber

SLEEPLESSNESS   1
Sir 31 : 20 The distress of sleeplessness

SLIGHT, verb 3 = 0.002 %
Jud 11:2 had not slighted me
11:22 upon those who have slighted my lord
Sir 8:8 Do not slight the discourse of the sages

SLING 2
Jud 9:7 they trust in shield and spear, in bow and sling
Sir 47:4 when he lifted his hand with a stone in the sling

SLINGER 2
Jud 6:12 and all the slingers kept them from coming up
1 Ma 9:11 and the slingers and the archers went ahead of the army

SLIP, subst. 4 = 0.003 %
Sir 19:16 A person may make a slip without intending it
20:18 A slip on the pavement is better than a slip of the tongue
25:8 and he who has not made a slip with his tongue

SLIP, verb 4 = 0.003 %
Sir 3:24 and wrong opinion has caused their thoughts to slip
13:22 If a rich man slips, his helpers are many
13:22 If a humble man slips, they even reproach him
21:7 but the sensible man, when he slips, is aware of it

SLIP away 4 = 0.003 %
1 Ma 9:6 and many slipped away from the camp
9:7 When Judas saw that his army had slipped away
2 Ma 10:20 and on receiving 70,000 drachmas let some of them slip away
3 Ma 5:34 The king's friends one by one sullenly slipped away

SLIP by 1
3 Ma 5:15 that the hour of the banquet was already slipping by

SLOW 4 = 0.003 %
Tob 12:6 Do not be slow to give him thanks
Sir 5:4 For the Lord is slow to anger
6:21 and he will not be slow to cast her off
11:12 There is another who is slow and needs help

SLOWNESS 1
2 Es 5:42 just as for those who are last there is no slowness

SLUGGISH 2
Sir 4:29 or sluggish and remiss in your deeds
3 Ma 4:5 sluggish and bent with age

SLUMBER 2
Sir 22:7 or who rouses a sleeper from deep slumber
31:2 Wakeful anxiety prevents slumber

SMALL 23 = 0.015 %
Jud 13:4 and no one, either small or great
13:13 They all ran together, both small and great
16:16 For every sacrifice as a fragrant offering is a small thing
Wis 6:7 because he himself made both small and great
14:5 even to the smallest piece of wood
Sir 5:15 In great or small matters do not act amiss
11:3 The bee is small among flying creatures
19:1 he who despises small things will fail little by little
Bar 1:4 and in the hearing of all the people, small and great
2:29 a small number among the nations
1 Ma 3:16 Judas went out to meet him with a small company
3:29 and the revenues from the country were small
4:57 with golden crowns and small shields
5:45 the small and the great
2 Ma 10:24 and collected the cavalry from Asia in no small number
14:8 our whole nation is now in no small misfortune
1 Es 1:54 And all the holy vessels of the Lord, great and small
Ps 151:1 I was small among my brothers, and youngest in my father's house
2 Es 5:52 but smaller in stature ?
5:54 that you and your contemporaries are smaller in stature
5:55 and those who come after you will be smaller than you
4 Ma 5:20 to transgress the law in matters either small or great
15:4 We impress upon the character of a small child

SMART 2
Tob 11:8 and when they smart he will rub them
11:12 And when his eyes began to smart he rubbed them

SMEAR 1
4 Ma 9:20 The wheel was completely smeared with blood

SMELL, verb 3 = 0.002 %
Tob 6:17 Then the demon will smell it and flee away
8:3 And when the demon smelled the odour
Sir 30:19 For it can neither eat nor smell

SMELL, subst. 1
2 Es 13:11 but only the dust of ashes and the smell of smoke

SMILE 5 = 0.003 %
Sir 13:6 he will smile at you and give you hope
13:11 and while he smiles he will be examining you
21:20 but a clever man smiles quietly
1 Es 4:31 If she smiles at him, he laughs
4 Ma 8:4 he smiled at them, and summoned them nearer and said

SMITE 4 = 0.003 %
Jud 16:7 nor did the sons of the Titans smite him
Sir 48:21 The Lord smote the camp of the Assyrians
3 Ma 2:22 since he was smitten by a righteous judgment
2 Es 15:11 and will smite Egypt with plagues, as before

SMITH 1
Sir 38:28 So too is the smith sitting by the anvil

SMOKE, subst. 16 = 0.010 %
Tob 6:7 you make a smoke from these before the man or woman
6:16 so as to make a smoke
8:2 and put the heart and liver of the fish upon them and made a smoke
Wis 2:2 because the breath in our nostrils is smoke
5:14 it is dispersed like smoke before the wind
11:18 or belch forth a thick pall of smoke
Sir 22:24 The vapour and smoke of the furnace precede the fire
L Jr 6:21 by the smoke of the temple
1 Ma 4:20 for the smoke that was seen showed what had happened
2 Ma 7:5 The smoke from the pan spread widely
2 Es 4:48 and behold, the smoke remained
4:50 and the fire is greater than the smoke
4:50 but drops and smoke remained
7:61 and are similar to a flame and smoke
13:11 but only the dust of ashes and the smell of smoke
15:44 then the dust and smoke shall go up to heaven

SMOKING 1
Wis 10:7 a continually smoking wasteland

SMOOTH, adj. 1
Sir 32:21 Do not be overconfident on a smooth way

SMOOTH, verb 1
L Jr 6:8 Their tongues are smoothed by the craftsman

SMOOTHLY 1
Sir 21:10 The way of sinners is smoothly paved with stones

SNAKE 3 = 0.002 %
Sir 12:13 Who will pity a snake charmer bitten by a serpent
21:2 Flee from sin as from a snake
25:15 There is no venom worse than a snake's venom

SNARE, subst. 9 = 0.006 %
Wis 14:11 and a snare to the feet of the foolish
Sir 9:3 lest you fall into her snares
9:13 Know that you are walking in the midst of snares
27:20 and has escaped like a gazelle from a snare
27:26 and he who sets a snare will be caught in it
27:29 will be caught in a snare
51:2 and from the snare of a slanderous tongue
1 Ma 1:35 they stored them there, and became a great snare
5:4 who were a trap and a snare to the people

SNATCH away 1
Sir 19:3 and the reckless soul will be snatched away

SNOW 7 = 0.005 %
Wis 16:22 Snow and ice withstood fire without melting
Sir 43:13 By his command he sends the driving snow
43:17 He scatters the snow like birds flying down
P Az 46 Bless the Lord, dews and snows
50 Bless the Lord, frosts and snows
1 Ma 13:22 but that night a very heavy snow fell
13:22 and he did not go because of the snow

SO, adv., conj. 492 = 0.320 %

SO that 152 = 0.099 %

SOCKET 1
4 Ma 10:5 dismembering him by prying his limbs from their sockets

SODOM 4 = 0.003 %
3 Ma 2:5 the men of Sodom who acted arrogantly
2 Es 2:8 O wicked nation, remember what I did to Sodom and Gomorrah

	5:7	and the sea of Sodom shall cast up fish
	7:106	for the people of Sodom

SOFT   2
Jud 12:15 the soft fleeces which she had received from Bagoas
Wis 15:7 For when a potter kneads the soft earth

SOIL, subst.   2
Sir 20:28 Whoever cultivates the soil will heap up his harvest
1 Es 4:6 but till the soil, whenever they sow, reap the harvest

SOIL, verb   1
Sir 22:13 and you will not be soiled when he shakes himself off

SOJOURN, verb   1
Sir 38:32 and men can neither sojourn nor live there

SOJOURN, subst.   2
Wis 19:10 For they still recalled the events of their sojourn
1 Es 5:7 out of their sojourn in captivity

SOLDIER   19 = 0.012 %
Jud 2:5 to the number of 120,000 foot soldiers and 12,000 cavalry
   7:2 together with the baggage and the foot soldiers handling it
   7:7 and seized them and set guards of soldiers over them
   9:7 they glory in the strength of their foot soldiers
   15:3 Then the men of Israel, every one that was a soldier
1 Ma 6:30 The number of his forces was a 100,000 foot soldiers
   6:48 The soldiers of the king's army
   9:4 with 20,000 foot soldiers and 2,000 cavalry
   12:49 and the Great Plain to destroy all Jonathan's soldiers
   16:6 And he saw that the soldiers were afraid to cross the stream
2 Ma 5:12 And he commanded his soldiers
   14:39 sent more than 500 soldiers to arrest him
1 Es 8:51 for foot soldiers and horsemen and an escort
3 Ma 3:12 King Ptolemy Philopator to his generals and soldiers
4 Ma 3:7 and together with the soldiers of his nation had slain many of them
   3:12 2 staunch young soldiers, respecting the king's desire
   5:1 and with his armed soldiers standing about him
   16:14 O mother, soldier of God in the cause of religion, elder and woman !
   17:23 proclaimed them to his soldiers

SOLE   1
Ad E 13:13 For I would have been willing to kiss the soles of his feet, to save Israel !

SOLEMN   2
2 Ma 10:16 after making solemn supplications
   12:25 he had confirmed his solemn promise to restore them unharmed

SOLID   1
3 Ma 4:10 and in addition they were confined under a solid deck

SOLITARY   2
4 Ma 1:27 gluttony, and solitary gormandizing
   2:7 that someone who is habitually a solitary gormandizer

SOLITUDE   1
2 Es 16:26 For in all places there shall be great solitude

SOLOMON   13 = 0.008 %
Sir 47:13 Solomon reigned in days of peace
   47:23 Solomon rested with his fathers
2 Ma 2:8 and as Solomon asked
   2:9 that being possessed of wisdom Solomon offered sacrifice
   2:10 so also Solomon prayed, and the fire came down
   2:12 Likewise Solomon also kept the 8 days
1 Es 1:3 in the house which Solomon the king, the son of David, had built
   1:5 and the magnificence of Solomon his son
   5:33 The sons of Solomon's servants : the sons of Hassophereth
   5:35 and the sons of Solomon's servants were 372
2 Es 7:108 and Solomon for those in the sanctuary
   10:46 And after 3,000 years Solomon built the city
4 Ma 18:16 He recounted to you Solomon's proverb

SOLSTICE   1
Wis 7:18 the alternations of the solstices

SOLUTION   1
Wis 8:8 she understands turns of speech and the solutions of riddles

SOLVE   1
2 Es 4:4 If you can solve one of them for me

SOME, indef. pr. or adj.   120 = 0.078 %
Tob 6:16 and lay upon them some of the heart and liver of the fish
Jud 7:18 and they sent some of their men

	10:15	some of us will escort you and hand you over to him
	12:1	with some of his own food
	15:12	and blessed her, and some of them performed a dance for her
Wis	13:14	or makes it like some worthless animal
	19:15	but punishment of some sort will come upon the former
Sir pr.		we may seem to have rendered some phrases imperfectly
pr.		and stayed for some time
pr.		that I should myself devote some pains and labour
	8:6	for some of us are growing old
	10:17	He has removed some of them and destroyed them
	14:18	which sheds some and puts forth others
	22:26	but if some harm should happen to me because of him
	33:9	some of them be exalted and hallowed
	33:9	and some of them he made ordinary days
	33:12	some of them he blessed and exalted
	33:12	and some of them he made holy and brought near to himself
	33:12	but some of them he cursed and brought low
	37:1	but some friends are friends only in name
	37:4	Some companions rejoice in the happiness of a friend
	37:5	Some companions help a friend for their stomachs' sake
	37:7	but some give counsel in their own interest
	41:21	of taking away some one's portion or gift
	44:8	There are some of them who have left a name
	44:9	And there are some who have no memorial
	48:16	Some of them did what was pleasing to God
L Jr	6:11	and even give some of it to the harlots in the brothel
	6:28	and likewise their wives preserve some with salt
	6:32	as some do at a funeral feast for a man who has died
	6:33	The priests take some of the clothing of their gods
1 Ma	1:13	and some of the people eagerly went to the king
	5:27	and some have been shut up in the other cities of Gilead
	5:67	On that day some priests, who wished to do a brave deed
	6:21	But some of the garrison escaped from the siege
	6:21	and some of the ungodly Israelites joined them
	6:40	and some troops were on the plain
	7:19	and some of the people
	7:33	Some of the priests came out of the sanctuary
	7:33	and some of the elders of the people
	8:7	and surrender some of their best provinces
	10:14	Only in Beth-zur did some remain
	10:37	Let some of them be stationed
	10:37	and let some of them be put in positions of trust in the kingdom
	11:23	and he chose some of the elders of Israel
	11:23	and some of the priests
	16:16	and some of his servants
2 Ma	1:19	took some of the fire of the altar
	1:22	When this was done and some time had passed
	2:1	to take some of the fire, as has been told
	2:6	Some of those who followed him came up to mark the way
	3:10	The high priest explained that there were some deposits
	3:11	and also some money of Hyrcanus, son of Tobias
	3:19	Some of the maidens who were kept indoors
	3:19	ran together to the gates, and some to the walls
	3:31	Quickly some of Heliodorus' friends asked Onias
	3:32	that some foul play had been perpetrated by the Jews
	3:38	for there certainly is about the place some power of God
	4:32	stole some of the gold vessels of the temple
	4:41	some picked up stones, some blocks of wood
	4:42	As a result, they wounded many of them, and killed some
	8:25	After pursuing them for some distance
	8:28	After the sabbath they gave some of the spoils
	8:30	and got possession of some exceedingly high strongholds
	8:33	Callisthenes and some others
	10:20	were bribed by some of those who were in the towers
	10:20	and on receiving 70,000 drachmas let some of them slip away
	11:37	Therefore make haste and send some men
	12:2	But some of the governors in various places
	12:3	And some men of Joppa did so ungodly a deed
	12:24	and the brothers of some
	14:4	some of the customary olive branches from the temple
1 Es	1:41	Nebuchadnezzar also took some of the holy vessels of the Lord
	4:6	and bring some to the king
	5:44	Some of the heads of families
	5:46	and some of the people settled in Jerusalem and its vicinity
	5:50	And some joined them from the other peoples of the land
	5:63	Some of the Levitical priests and heads of fathers' houses
	8:5	some of the people of Israel and some of the priests
	8:24	whether by death or some other punishment
	8:78	And now in some measure mercy has come to us from thee, O Lord
3 Ma	1:8	Since the Jews had sent some of their council and elders
	1:20	some in houses and some in the streets
	2:31	Now some, however, with an obvious abhorrence of the price
	3:4	For this reason they appeared hateful to some
	3:10	And already some of their neighbours
	3:10	had taken some of them aside privately
	4:4	even some of their enemies
	4:9	some were fastened by the neck to the benches of the boats
	4:18	some still residing in their homes, and some at the place
	5:18	After the party had been going on for some time

2 Es	5 : 18	Rise therefore and eat some bread
	6 : 42	so that some of them might be planted and cultivated
	7 : 86	they shall see how some of them will pass over into torments
	8 : 37	Some things you have spoken rightly
	9 : 21	And I saw and spared some with great difficulty
	11 : 20	There were some of them that ruled, yet disappeared suddenly
	13 : 13	some of whom were joyful and some sorrowful
	13 : 13	some of them were bound
	13 : 13	and some were bringing others as offerings
	14 : 26	some things you shall make public
	14 : 26	and some you shall deliver in secret to the wise
	16 : 30	some clusters may be left by those who search carefully
	16 : 68	and they shall carry off some of you
4 Ma	1 : 5	Some might perhaps ask, If reason rules the emotions
	1 : 32	Some desires are mental, other are physical
	2 : 18	to correct some, and to render others powerless
	5 : 13	that if there is some power watching over this religion of yours
	6 : 13	some of the king's retinue came to him and said
	6 : 15	We will set before you some cooked meat
	7 : 17	Some perhaps might say
	7 : 20	when some persons appear to be dominated by their emotions
	8 : 16	if some of them had been cowardly and unmanly
	16 : 9	Alas for my children, some unmarried
	17 : 1	Some of the guards said that

SOME ONE, SOMEONE 8 = 0.005 %

Tob	5 : 8	I have found some one to go with me
Sir	19 : 9	for some one has heard you and watched you
L Jr	6 : 24	they will not shine unless some one wipes off the rust
1 Ma	6 : 5	Then some one came to him in Persia and reported
	16 : 21	But some one ran ahead and reported to John at Gazara
2 Ma	11 : 36	as soon as you have considered them, send some one promptly
3 Ma	1 : 14	And someone heedlessly said that it was wrong
4 Ma	2 : 7	that someone who is habitually a solitary gormandizer

SOMETHING 10 = 0.007 %

Jud	11 : 6	God will accomplish something through you
Wis	2 : 16	We are considered by him as something base
Sir	pr.	was himself also led to write something
	13 : 5	If you own something, he will live with you
	34 : 4	And from something false what will be true ?
2 Ma	3 : 21	There was something pitiable
3 Ma	1 : 17	supposing that something mysterious was occurring
2 Es	13 : 3	this wind made something like the figure of a man come up
	14 : 39	it was full of something like water
4 Ma	5 : 10	It seems to me that you will do something even more senseless

SOMETIMES 2

Sir	37 : 14	For a man's soul sometimes keeps him better informed
L Jr	6 : 10	and sometimes the priests secretly take gold and silver from their gods

SON 565 = 0.368 %

Tob	1 : 1	The book of the acts of Tobit the son of Tobiel
	1 : 1	son of Ananiel, son of Aduel, son of Gabael
	1 : 6	I would give these to the priests, the sons of Aaron, at the altar
	1 : 7	Of all my produce I would give a tenth to the sons of Levi
	1 : 15	Sennacherib his son reigned in his place
	1 : 20	and my son Tobias
	1 : 21	before 2 of Sennacherib's sons killed him
	1 : 21	Then Esarhaddon, his son, reigned in his place
	1 : 21	and he appointed Ahikar, the son of my brother Anael
	2 : 1	and my wife Anna and my son Tobias were restored to me
	2 : 2	Upon seeing the abundance of food I said to my son
	3 : 9	May we never see a son or daughter of yours !
	3 : 15	no near kinsman or kinsman's son
	3 : 17	in marriage to Tobias the son of Tobit
	4 : 2	Why do I not call my son Tobias
	4 : 3	My son, when I die, bury me
	4 : 4	Remember, my son, that she faced many dangers for you
	4 : 5	Remember the Lord our God all your days, my son
	4 : 12	Beware, my son, of all immorality
	4 : 12	for we are the sons of the prophets
	4 : 12	Remember, my son
	4 : 13	So now, my son, love your brethren
	4 : 13	and the sons and daughters of your people
	4 : 14	Watch yourself, my son, in everything you do
	4 : 19	So, my son, remember my commands
	4 : 20	which I left in trust with Gabael the son of Gabrias
	4 : 21	Do not be afraid, my son, because we have become poor
	5 : 11	or for a man whom you will pay to go with your son ?
	5 : 12	He replied, I am Azarias the son of the great Ananias
	5 : 13	the sons of the great Shemaiah
	5 : 14	and expenses for yourself as for my son ?
	5 : 16	So his son made the preparations for the journey
	6 : 14	Now I am the only son my father has
	6 : 14	And they have no other son to bury them
	7 : 3	They answered him, We belong to the sons of Naphtali
	7 : 7	Son of that good and noble man !

	10 : 7	and throughout the nights she never stopped mourning for her son Tobias
	11 : 5	Now Anna sat looking intently down the road for her son
	11 : 6	Behold, your son is coming
	11 : 9	Then Anna ran to meet them, and embraced her son
	11 : 10	But his son ran to him
	11 : 14	Then he saw his son and embraced him, and he wept and said
	11 : 15	here I see my son Tobias
	11 : 15	And his son went in rejoicing
	12 : 1	Tobit then called his son Tobias and said to him
	12 : 1	My son, see to the wages of the man who went with you
	13 : 3	Acknowledge him before the nations, O sons of Israel
	13 : 9	he will afflict you for the deeds of your sons
	13 : 9	but again he will show mercy to the sons of the righteous
	13 : 13	Rejoice and be glad for the sons of the righteous
	14 : 3	When he had grown very old he called his son and grandsons
	14 : 3	and said to him, My son, take your sons
	14 : 4	Go to Media, my son
	14 : 8	So now, my son, leave Nineveh
	14 : 10	See, my son, what Nadab did to Ahikar who had reared him
	14 : 12	Then Tobias returned with his wife and his sons to Ecbatana
Jud	6 : 15	who in those days were Uzziah the son of Micah
	6 : 15	and Chabris the son of Gothoniel
	6 : 15	and Charmis the son of Melchiel
	7 : 18	And the sons of Esau and the sons of Ammon went up
	8 : 1	she was the daughter of Merari the son of Ox
	8 : 1	son of Joseph, son of Oziel, son of Elkiah
	8 : 1	son of Ananias, son of Gideon, son of Raphaim
	8 : 1	son of Ahitub, son of Elijah, son of Hilkiah
	8 : 1	son of Eliab, son of Nathanael, son of Salamiel
	8 : 1	son of Sarasadai, son of Israel
	8 : 12	among the sons of men ?
	9 : 4	and all their booty to be divided among thy beloved sons
	16 : 7	nor did the sons of the Titans smite him
	16 : 12	The sons of maidservants have pierced them through
Ad E	11 : 1	and Ptolemy his son brought to Egypt the preceding Letter of Purim
	11 : 1	and had been translated by Lysimachus the son of Ptolemy
	11 : 2	Mordecai the son of Jair
	11 : 2	son of Shimei, son of Kish
	12 : 6	But Haman, the son of Hammedatha, a Bougaean
	16 : 10	For Haman, the son of Hammedatha, a Macedonian
	16 : 16	and are sons of the Most High, the most mighty living God
	16 : 17	the letters sent by Haman the son of Hammedatha
Wis	2 : 18	for if the righteous man is God's son, he will help him
	5 : 5	Why has he been numbered among the sons of God ?
	9 : 5	For I am thy slave and the son of thy maidservant
	9 : 6	for even if one is perfect among the sons of men
	9 : 7	and to be judge over thy sons and daughters
	12 : 19	and thou hast filled thy sons with good hope
	12 : 21	with what strictness thou hast judged thy sons
	16 : 10	but thy sons were not conquered
	16 : 26	so that thy sons, whom thou didst love, O Lord
	18 : 4	those who had kept thy sons imprisoned
	18 : 13	they acknowledged thy people to be God's son
Sir	2 : 1	My son, if you come forward to serve the Lord
	3 : 2	and he confirmed the right of the mother over her sons
	3 : 12	O son, help your father in his old age
	3 : 17	My son, perform your tasks in meekness
	4 : 1	My son, deprive not the poor of his living
	4 : 10	you will then be like a son of the Most High
	4 : 11	Wisdom exalts her sons and gives help to those who seek her
	6 : 18	My son, from your youth up choose instruction
	6 : 23	Listen, my son, and accept my judgment
	6 : 32	If you are willing, my son, you will be taught
	7 : 3	My son, do not sow the furrows of injustice
	10 : 28	My son, glorify yourself with humility
	11 : 10	My son, do not busy yourself with many matters
	14 : 11	My son, treat yourself well, according to your means
	16 : 1	nor rejoice in ungodly sons
	16 : 24	Listen to me, my son, and acquire knowledge
	17 : 30	since a son of man is not immortal
	18 : 15	My son, do not mix reproach with your good deeds
	21 : 1	Have you sinned, my son ?
	22 : 3	It is a disgrace to be the father of an undisciplined son
	26 : 19	My son, keep sound the bloom of your youth
	30 : 1	He who loves his son will whip him often
	30 : 2	He who disciplines his son will profit by him
	30 : 3	He who teaches his son will make his enemies envious
	30 : 7	He who spoils his son will bind up his wounds
	30 : 8	and a son unrestrained turns out to be wilful
	30 : 13	Discipline your son and take pains with him
	31 : 22	Listen to me, my son, and do not disregard me
	33 : 19	To son or wife, to brother or friend
	33 : 21	than that you should look to the hand of your sons
	34 : 20	Like one who kills a son before his father's eyes
	36 : 12	upon Israel, whom thou hast likened to a first-born son
	37 : 27	My son, test your soul while you live
	38 : 9	My son, when you are sick do not be negligent
	38 : 16	My son, let your tears fall for the dead

39 : 13	Listen to me, O you holy sons	
40 : 1	and a heavy yoke is upon the sons of Adam	
40 : 28	My son, do not lead the life of a beggar	
45 : 9	as a reminder to the sons of his people	
45 : 13	No outsider ever put them on, but only his sons	
45 : 23	Phinehas the son of Eleazar is the 3rd in glory	
45 : 25	the son of Jesse, of the tribe of Judah :	
45 : 25	the heritage of the king is from son to son only	
46 : 1	Joshua the son of Nun was mighty in war	
46 : 7	he and Caleb the son of Jephunneh :	
46 : 10	so that all the sons of Israel might see	
46 : 12	live again in their sons !	
47 : 2	so David was selected from the sons of Israel	
47 : 12	After him rose up a wise son who fared amply because of him	
47 : 23	and left behind him one of his sons	
47 : 23	Also Jeroboam the son of Nebat, who caused Israel to sin	
48 : 10	to turn the heart of the father to the son	
49 : 12	and so was Jeshua the son of Jozadak	
50 : 1	was Simon the high priest, son of Onias	
50 : 13	all the sons of Aaron in their splendour	
50 : 16	Then the sons of Aaron shouted	
50 : 20	over the whole congregation of the sons of Israel	
50 : 27	Jesus the son of Sirach, son of Eleazar, of Jerusalem	

Bar 1 : 1 which Baruch the son of Neraiah, son of Mahseiah
 1 : 1 son of Zedekiah, son of Hasadiah, son of Hilkiah
 1 : 3 in the hearing of Jeconiah the son of Jehoiakim, king of Judah
 1 : 7 the son of Hilkiah, son of Shallum, and to the priests
 1 : 8 the silver vessels which Zedekiah the son of Josiah, king of Judah, had made
 1 : 11 and for the life of Belshazzar his son
 1 : 12 and under the protection of Belshazzar his son
 2 : 3 that we should eat, one the flesh of his son
 3 : 4 and of the sons of those who sinned before thee
 3 : 21 Their sons have strayed far from her way
 3 : 23 the sons of Hagar, who seek for understanding on the earth
 4 : 10 for I have seen the captivity of my sons and daughters
 4 : 14 remember the capture of my sons and daughters
 4 : 16 They led away the widow's beloved sons
 4 : 26 My tender sons have travelled rough roads
 4 : 32 wretched will be the city which received your sons
 4 : 37 Behold, your sons are coming, whom you sent away

P Az 60 Bless the Lord, you sons of men
Sus 13 : 48 Are you such fools, you sons of Israel ?
1 Ma 1 : 1 After Alexander son of Philip, the Macedonian
 1 : 9 and so did their sons after them for many years
 1 : 10 son of Antiochus the king
 1 : 48 and to leave their sons uncircumcised
 2 : 1 In those days Mattathias the son of John, son of Simeon
 2 : 1 a priest of the sons of Joarib
 2 : 2 He had 5 sons, John surnamed Gaddi
 2 : 14 And Mattathias and his sons rent their clothes
 2 : 16 and Mattathias and his sons were assembled
 2 : 17 and supported by sons and brothers
 2 : 18 Then you and your sons will be numbered
 2 : 18 and you and your sons will be honoured
 2 : 20 yet I and my sons and my brothers will live
 2 : 26 as Phinehas did against Zimri the son of Salu
 2 : 28 And he and his sons fled to the hills
 2 : 30 they, their sons, their wives, and their cattle
 2 : 49 and he said to his sons :
 3 : 1 Then Judas his son, who was called Maccabeus
 3 : 15 to take vengeance on the sons of Israel
 3 : 33 Lysias was also to take care of Antiochus his son
 3 : 38 Lysias chose Ptolemy the son of Dorymenes
 3 : 41 and went to the camp to get the sons of Israel for slaves
 3 : 45 and the sons of aliens held the citadel
 4 : 30 into the hands of Jonathan, the son of Saul
 5 : 3 But Judas made war on the sons of Esau
 5 : 4 He also remembered the wickedness of the sons of Baean
 5 : 18 But he left Joseph, the son of Zechariah
 5 : 56 Joseph, the son of Zechariah
 5 : 65 and fought the sons of Esau in the land to the south
 6 : 2 left there by Alexander, the son of Philip
 6 : 15 that he might guide Antiochus his son
 6 : 17 he set up Antiochus the king's son to reign
 6 : 24 For this reason the sons of our people besieged the citadel
 6 : 55 had appointed to bring up Antiochus his son to be king
 7 : 1 In the 151st year Demetrius the son of Seleucus set forth from Rome
 7 : 9 and he commanded him to take vengeance on the sons of Israel
 7 : 13 The Hasidaeans were the first among the sons of Israel
 7 : 23 had done among the sons of Israel
 8 : 17 So Judas chose Eupolemus the son of John, son of Accos
 8 : 17 and Jason the son of Eleazar
 9 : 36 But the sons of Jambri from Medeba came out
 9 : 37 The sons of Jambri are celebrating a great wedding
 9 : 53 And he took the sons of the leading men of the land
 9 : 66 and the sons of Phasiron in their tents
 10 : 1 In the 160th year Alexander Epiphanes, the son of Antiochus
 10 : 67 In the 165th year Demetrius the son of Demetrius

 11 : 39 who was bringing up Antiochus, the young son of Alexander
 11 : 62 and took the sons of their rulers as hostages
 11 : 70 except Mattathias the son of Absalom and Judas the son of Chalphi
 12 : 16 We therefore have chosen Numenius the son of Antiochus
 12 : 16 and Antipater the son of Jason
 13 : 11 He sent Jonathan the son of Absalom to Joppa
 13 : 16 and 2 of his sons as hostages
 13 : 17 but he sent to get the money and the sons
 13 : 18 Because Simon did not send him the money and the sons, he perished
 13 : 19 So he sent the sons and the 100 talents
 13 : 53 And Simon saw that John his son had reached manhood
 14 : 22 Numenius the son of Antiochus and Antipater the son of Jason, envoys of the Jews
 14 : 25 How shall we thank Simon and his sons ?
 14 : 29 Simon the son of Mattathias
 14 : 29 a priest of the sons of Joarib, and his brothers
 14 : 49 so that Simon and his sons might have them
 15 : 1 Antiochus, the son of Demetrius the king
 16 : 2 And Simon called in his 2 elder sons Judas and John
 16 : 11 Now Ptolemy the son of Abubus had been appointed governor
 16 : 13 and made treacherous plans against Simon and his sons
 16 : 14 and he went down to Jericho with Mattathias and Judas his sons
 16 : 15 The son of Abubus received them treacherously
 16 : 16 When Simon and his sons were drunk
 16 : 16 and they killed him and his 2 sons

2 Ma 2 : 20 and his son Eupator
 3 : 11 and also some money of Hyrcanus, son of Tobias
 4 : 4 and that Apollonius, the son of Menestheus
 4 : 21 When Apollonius the son of Menestheus was sent to Egypt
 4 : 45 promised a substantial bribe to Ptolemy son of Dorymenes
 7 : 20 Though she saw her 7 sons perish within a single day
 7 : 26 she undertook to persuade her son
 7 : 27 deriding the cruel tyrant : My son, have pity on me
 7 : 41 Last of all, the mother died, after her sons
 8 : 9 And Ptolemy promptly appointed Nicanor the son of Patroclus
 9 : 25 So I have appointed my son Antiochus to be king
 9 : 26 toward me and my son
 9 : 29 then, fearing the son of Antiochus
 10 : 10 who was the son of that ungodly man
 12 : 2 Timothy and Apollonius the son of Gennaeus
 14 : 1 that Demetrius, the son of Seleucus

1 Es 1 : 3 in the house which Solomon the king, the son of David, had built
 1 : 5 and the magnificence of Solomon his son
 1 : 13 and for their brethren the priests, the sons of Aaron
 1 : 14 and for their brethren the priests, the sons of Aaron
 1 : 15 And the temple singers, the sons of Asaph
 1 : 34 And the men of the nation took Jeconiah the son of Josiah
 1 : 43 Jehoiakim his son became king in his stead
 1 : 57 and they were servants to him and to his sons
 4 : 37 women are unrighteous, all the sons of men are unrighteous
 5 : 1 with their wives and sons and daughters
 5 : 5 the priests, the sons of Phinehas, son of Aaron
 5 : 5 Jeshua the son of Jozadak, son of Seraiah
 5 : 5 and Joakim the son of Zerubbabel
 5 : 5 son of Shealtiel, of the house of David
 5 : 9 the sons of Parosh, 2,172
 5 : 9 The sons of Shephatiah, 472
 5 : 10 The sons of Arah, 756
 5 : 11 The sons of Pahath-moab, of the sons of Jeshua and Joab, 2,812
 5 : 12 The sons of Elam, 1,254
 5 : 12 The sons of Zattu, 945
 5 : 12 The sons of Chorbe, 705
 5 : 12 The sons of Bani, 648
 5 : 13 The sons of Bebai, 623
 5 : 13 The sons of Azgad, 1,322
 5 : 14 The sons of Adonikam, 667
 5 : 14 The sons of Bigvai, 2,066
 5 : 14 The sons of Adin, 454
 5 : 15 The sons of Ater, namely of Hezekiah, 92
 5 : 15 The sons of Kilan and Azetas, 67
 5 : 15 The sons of Azaru, 432
 5 : 16 The sons of Annias, 101. The sons of Arom
 5 : 16 The sons of Bezai, 323
 5 : 16 The sons of Jorah, 112
 5 : 17 The sons of Baiterus, 3,005
 5 : 17 The sons of Bethlehem, 123
 5 : 21 The sons of Magbish, 156
 5 : 22 The sons of the other Elam and Ono, 725
 5 : 22 The sons of Jericho, 345
 5 : 23 The sons of Senaah, 3,330
 5 : 24 The priests : the sons of Jedaiah the son of Jeshua
 5 : 24 of the sons of Anasib, 972
 5 : 24 The sons of Immer, 1,052
 5 : 25 The sons of Pashhur, 1,247
 5 : 25 The sons of Harim, 1,017
 5 : 26 The Levites : the sons of Jeshua and Kadmiel
 5 : 27 The temple singers : the sons of Asaph, 128

5 : 28	The gatekeepers : the sons of Shallum
5 : 28	the sons of Ater, the sons of Talmon
5 : 28	the sons of Akkub, the sons of Hatita
5 : 28	the sons of Shobai, in all 139
5 : 29	the temple servants : the sons of Ziha
5 : 29	the sons of Hasupha, the sons of Tabbaoth
5 : 29	the sons of Keros, the sons of Siaha, sons of Padon
5 : 29	the sons of Lebanah
5 : 29	the sons of Hagabah
5 : 30	the sons of Akkub, the sons of Uthai, the sons of Ketab
5 : 30	the sons of Hagab, the sons of Shamlai, the sons of Hana
5 : 30	the sons of Cathua, the sons of Gahar
5 : 31	the sons of Reaiah, the sons of Rezin, the sons of Nekoda
5 : 31	the sons of Chezib, the sons of Gazzam, the sons of Uzza
5 : 31	the sons of Paseah, the sons of Hasrah, the sons of Besai
5 : 31	the sons of Asnah, the sons of the Meunites
5 : 31	the sons of Nephisim, the sons of Bakbuk
5 : 31	the sons of Hakupha, the sons of Asur
5 : 31	the sons of Pharakim, the sons of Bazluth
5 : 32	the sons of Mehida, the sons of Cutha
5 : 32	the sons of Charea, the sons of Barkos
5 : 32	the sons of Sisera, the sons of Temah
5 : 32	the sons of Neziah, the sons of Hatipha
5 : 33	The sons of Solomon's servants : the sons of Hassophereth
5 : 33	the sons of Peruda, the sons of Jaalah
5 : 33	the sons of Lozon, the sons of Giddel
5 : 33	the sons of Shephatiah
5 : 34	the sons of Hattil, the sons of Pochereth-hazzebaim
5 : 34	the sons of Sarothie, the sons of Masiah, the sons of Gas
5 : 34	the sons of Addus, the sons of Subas, the sons of Apherra
5 : 34	the sons of Barodis, the sons of Shaphat, the sons of Ami
5 : 35	and the sons of Solomon's servants were 372
5 : 37	the sons of Delaiah the son of Tobiah
5 : 37	the sons of Nekoda, 652
5 : 38	but were not found registered : the sons of Habaiah
5 : 38	the sons of Hakkoz, the sons of Jaddus who had married Agia
5 : 47	and the sons of Israel were each in his own home
5 : 48	Then Jeshua the son of Jozadak, with his fellow priests
5 : 48	and Zerubbabel the son of Shealtiel, with his kinsmen
5 : 56	in the 2nd month, Zerubbabel the son of Shealtiel
5 : 56	and Jeshua the son of Jozadak made a beginning
5 : 58	And Jeshua arose, and his sons and brethren
5 : 58	and Kadmiel his brother and the sons of Jeshua Emadabun
5 : 58	and the sons of Joda son of Iliadun
5 : 58	with their sons and brethren, all the Levites
5 : 59	and the Levites, the sons of Asaph, with cymbals
6 : 1	the prophets Haggai and Zechariah the son of Iddo
6 : 2	Then Zerubbabel the son of Shealtiel
6 : 2	and Jeshua the son of Jozadak arose
8 : 1	Ezra came, the son of Seraiah, son of Azariah
8 : 1	son of Hilkiah, son of Shallum
8 : 2	son of Zadok, son of Ahitub, son of Amariah, son of Uzzi
8 : 2	son of Bukki, son of Abishua, son of Phinehas
8 : 2	son of Eleazar, son of Aaron the chief priest
8 : 21	upon the kingdom of the king and his sons
8 : 29	Of the sons of Phinehas, Gershom
8 : 29	Of the sons of Ithamar, Gamael
8 : 29	Of the sons of David, Hattush the son of Shecaniah
8 : 30	Of the sons of Parosh, Zechariah
8 : 31	Of the sons of Pahath-moab, Eliehoenai the son of Zerahiah
8 : 32	Of the sons of Zattu, Shecaniah the son of Jahaziel
8 : 32	Of the sons of Adin, Obed the son of Jonathan
8 : 33	Of the sons of Elam, Jeshaiah the son of Gotholiah
8 : 34	Of the sons of Shephatiah, Zeraiah the son of Michael
8 : 35	Of the sons of Joab, Obadiah the son of Jehiel
8 : 36	Of the sons of Bani, Shelomith the son of Josiphiah
8 : 37	Of the sons of Bebai, Zechariah the son of Bebai
8 : 38	Of the sons of Azgad, Johanan the son of Hakkatan
8 : 39	Of the sons of Adonikam, the last ones
8 : 40	Of the sons of Bigvai, Uthai the son of Istalcurus
8 : 42	none of the sons of the priests or of the Levites
8 : 47	they brought us competent men of the sons of Mahli
8 : 47	the son of Levi, son of Israel
8 : 47	namely Sherebiah with his sons and kinsmen, 18
8 : 48	Hodiah the sons of Hananiah, and their sons, 20 men
8 : 62	to Meremoth the priest, son of Uriah
8 : 63	and with him was Eleazar the son of Phinehas
8 : 63	and with them were Jozabad the son of Jeshua
8 : 63	and Moeth the son of Binnui, the Levites
8 : 70	For they and their sons have married the daughters of these people
8 : 84	Therefore do not give your daughters in marriage to their sons
8 : 84	and do not take their daughters for your sons
8 : 92	Then Shecaniah the son of Jehiel
9 : 1	to the chamber of Jehohanan the son of Eliashib
9 : 14	Jonathan the son of Asahel
9 : 14	and Jahzeiah the son of Tikvah
9 : 19	of the sons of Jeshua the son of Jozadak and his brethren
9 : 21	Of the sons of Immer : Hanani and Zebadiah and Maaseiah
9 : 22	Of the sons of Pashhur : Elioenai, Maaseiah, Ishmael

9 : 26	Of Israel : of the sons of Parosh : Ramiah, Izziah
9 : 27	Of the sons of Elam : Mattaniah and Zechariah
9 : 28	Of the sons of Zattu : Elioenai, Eliashib
9 : 29	Of the sons of Bebai :
9 : 30	Of the sons of Bani : Meshullam, Malluch, Adaiah
9 : 31	Of the sons of Addi : Naathus and Moossias, Laccunus
9 : 32	Of the sons of Annan : Elionas and Asaias and Melchias
9 : 33	Of the sons of Hashum : Mattenai and Mattattah and Zabad
9 : 34	Of the sons of Bani : Jeremai, Maadai, Amram, Joel
9 : 34	Of the sons of Ezora : Shashai, Azarel, Azael
9 : 35	Of the sons of Nebo :
9 : 37	when the sons of Israel were in their settlements

3 Ma 1 : 3	But Dositheus, known as the son of Drimylus
6 : 28	Release the sons of the almighty and living God of heaven

2 Es 1 : 1	The 2nd book of the prophet Ezra the son of Seraiah
1 : 1	son of Azariah, son of Hilkiah, son of Shallum
1 : 1	son of Zadok, son of Ahitub
1 : 2	son of Ahijah, son of Phinehas, son of Eli
1 : 2	son of Amariah, son of Azariah, son of Meraioth
1 : 2	son of Arna, son of Uzzi, son of Borith
1 : 2	son of Abishua, son of Phinehas, son of Eleazar
1 : 3	son of Aaron, of the tribe of Levi
1 : 28	Have I not entreated you as a father entreats his sons
1 : 29	and that you should be my sons and I should be your father ?
1 : 34	and your sons will have no children
2 : 15	Mother, embrace your sons
2 : 17	Do not fear, mother of the sons
2 : 25	Good nurse, nourish your sons
2 : 29	My hands will cover you, that your sons may not see Gehenna
2 : 30	Rejoice, O mother, with your sons
2 : 31	Remember your sons that sleep
2 : 47	He answered and said to me, He is the Son of God
7 : 28	For my son the Messiah shall be revealed
7 : 29	And after these years my son the Messiah shall die
7 : 103	fathers for sons or sons for parents
7 : 104	Just as now a father does not send his son
7 : 104	or a son his father, or a master his servant
9 : 45	and gave me a son
10 : 1	But it happened that when my son entered his wedding chamber
10 : 8	you are sorrowing for one son, but we, the whole world, for our mother
10 : 16	you will receive your son back in due time
10 : 43	and as for her telling you about the misfortune of her son
10 : 46	then it was that the barren woman bore a son
10 : 48	When my son entered his wedding chamber he died
10 : 49	how she mourned for her son
13 : 32	then my Son will be revealed
13 : 37	And he, my Son, will reprove the assembled nations for their ungodliness
13 : 52	so no one on earth can see my Son
14 : 9	and henceforth you shall live with my Son

4 Ma 4 : 15	his son Antiochus Epiphanes succeeded to the throne
4 : 25	because they had circumcised their sons
9 : 18	that sons of the Hebrews alone are invincible
12 : 6	who had been bereaved of so many sons
12 : 6	and to influence her to persuade the surviving son
15 : 2	that of religion, and that of preserving her 7 sons for a time
15 : 9	Not only so, but also because of the nobility of her sons
15 : 22	as her sons were tortured on the wheel and with the hot irons !
15 : 27	which would preserve the 7 sons for a short time
15 : 32	the torture of your sons
16 : 1	If, then, a woman, advanced in years and mother of 7 sons
16 : 3	inflamed as she saw her 7 sons tortured in such varied ways
16 : 8	In vain, my sons, I endured many birth-pangs for you
16 : 11	Nor when I die, shall I have any of my sons to bury me
16 : 13	to the whole number of her sons
16 : 15	For when you and your sons were arrested together
16 : 15	and said to your sons in the Hebrew language
16 : 16	My sons, noble is the contest to which you are called
16 : 20	our father Abraham was zealous to sacrifice his son Isaac
16 : 24	encouraged and persuaded each of her sons
17 : 2	O mother, who with your 7 sons
17 : 3	Nobly set like a roof on the pillars of your sons
17 : 5	who, after lighting the way of your star-like 7 sons to piety
17 : 9	Here lie buried an aged priest and an aged woman and 7 sons
17 : 13	the mother of the 7 sons entered the competition
18 : 6	The mother of the 7 sons
18 : 9	and when these sons had grown up their father died
18 : 20	brought those 7 sons of the daughter of Abraham to the catapult
18 : 23	But the sons of Abraham with their victorious mother

SONG   18 = 0.012 %

Jud 15 : 13	and with songs on their lips
16 : 1	and all the people loudly sang this song of praise
16 : 2	And Judith said, Begin a song to my God with tambourines
16 : 13	I will sing to my God a new song :
Sir 39 : 15	with praise, with songs on your lips, and with lyres
47 : 17	For your songs and proverbs and parables
1 Ma 4 : 54	it was dedicated with songs and harps and lutes and cymbals
13 : 51	and with hymns and songs

2 Ma	7:6	as Moses declared in his song
	15:25	Nicanor and his men advanced with trumpets and battle songs
3 Ma	4:6	all together raising a lament instead of a wedding song
	6:32	and took up the song of their fathers
	7:16	in words of praise and all kinds of melodious songs
2 Es	2:42	and they all were praising the Lord with songs
	10:22	Neither the melodies of sirens nor the songs of swans
4 Ma	15:21	He sang to you songs of the psalmist David, who said
	18:15	the song that Moses taught, which says

SON-IN-LAW   2

1 Ma	10:54	and I will become your son-in-law
	16:12	for he was son-in-law of the high priest

SOON, adv., conj.   31 = 0.020 %

Tob	6:12	and as soon as we return from Rages
Jud	14:2	And as soon as morning comes and the sun rises
	14:11	As soon as it was dawn
	16:18	As soon as the people were purified
Wis	5:13	So we also, as soon as we were born, ceased to be
	6:15	will soon be free from care
	13:9	how did they fail to find sooner the Lord of these things ?
Sir	6:19	and soon you will eat of her produce
	30:24	and anxiety brings on old age too soon
Bar	4:22	because of the mercy which soon will come to you
	4:24	so they soon will see your salvation by God
	4:25	but you will soon see their destruction
Bel	14:18	As soon as the doors were opened
1 Ma	11:22	and as soon as he heard it
2 Ma	1:15	they closed the temple as soon as he entered it
	2:18	For we have hope in God that he will soon have mercy upon us
	5:18	as soon as he came forward
	7:37	appealing to God to show mercy soon to our nation
	8:5	As soon as Maccabeus got his army organized
	9:5	As soon as he ceased speaking
	11:1	Very soon after this
	11:36	as soon as you have considered them, send some one promptly
1 Es	8:71	As soon as I heard these things
3 Ma	1:8	he was all the more eager to visit them as soon as possible
	3:23	they secretly suspect that we may soon alter our policy
	3:25	as soon as this letter shall arrive
	5:23	Then, as soon as the cock had crowed in the early morning
2 Es	5:43	that thou mightest show thy judgment the sooner ?
	7:75	as soon as every one of us yields up his soul
4 Ma	2:8	Thus, as soon as a man adopts
	8:29	so that as soon as the tyrant

SOOTHING   1

Ad E	15:8	And he comforted her with soothing words, and said to her

SORCERY   1

Wis	12:4	their works of sorcery and unholy rites

SORROW, subst.   32 = 0.021 %

Tob	2:5	and ate my food in sorrow
	3:6	and great is the sorrow within me
	3:10	and I shall bring his old age down in sorrow to the grave
	6:14	in sorrow on my account
	7:18	in place of this sorrow of yours
Sir	26:6	There is grief of heart and sorrow
	30:10	Do not laugh with him, lest you have sorrow with him
	30:12	and you have sorrow of soul from him
	30:21	Do not give yourself over to sorrow
	30:23	and remove sorrow far from you
	30:23	for sorrow has destroyed many, and there is no profit in it
	38:17	then be comforted for your sorrow
	38:18	For sorrow results in death
	38:18	and sorrow of heart saps one's strength
	38:19	In calamity sorrow continues
	38:20	Do not give your heart to sorrow
Bar	4:9	God has brought great sorrow upon me
	4:11	but I sent them away with weeping and sorrow
	4:23	For I sent you out with sorrow and weeping
	5:1	Take off the garment of your sorrow and affliction, O Jerusalem
1 Es	3:20	and forgets all sorrow and debt
2 Es	2:3	but with mourning and sorrow I have lost you
	7:117	For what good is it to all that they live in sorrow now
	8:54	sorrows have passed away
	10:12	which I brought forth in pain and bore in sorrow
	10:14	then I say to you, As you brought forth in sorrow
	10:15	Now, therefore, keep your sorrow to yourself
	10:20	and be consoled because of the sorrow of Jerusalem
	10:24	and lay aside your many sorrows
	16:18	The beginning of sorrows
4 Ma	1:23	Fear precedes pain and sorrow comes after
	16:10	am a widow and alone, with many sorrows

SORROW, verb   4 = 0.003 %

Sir	37:12	and who will sorrow with you if you fail
2 Es	10:8	and to be sorrowful, because we are all sorrowing
	10:8	you are sorrowing for one son, but we, the whole world, for our mother
	10:39	that you have sorrowed continually for your people

SORROWFUL   8 = 0.005 %

Wis	2:1	Short and sorrowful is our life
1 Es	9:52	and do not be sorrowful, for the Lord will exalt you
	9:53	do not be sorrowful
2 Es	2:27	others shall weep and be sorrowful
	7:12	and sorrowful and toilsome
	10:8	and to be sorrowful, because we are all sorrowing
	12:46	and do not be sorrowful, O house of Jacob
	13:13	some of whom were joyful and some sorrowful

SORT, subst.   12 = 0.008 %

Wis	19:15	but punishment of some sort will come upon the former
Sir	23:16	2 sorts of men multiply sins
	47:25	For they sought out every sort of wickedness
2 Ma	3:37	what sort of person would be suitable
	5:3	and armour of all sorts
	5:10	he had no funeral of any sort
	7:31	But you, who have contrived all sorts of evil
	12:13	and inhabited by all sorts of Gentiles
	15:11	a sort of vision, which was worthy of belief
3 Ma	5:22	in sleep as in devising all sorts of insults
	7:16	crowned with all sorts of very fragrant flowers
4 Ma	1:34	and all sorts of foods that are forbidden to us by the law

SOSIPATER   2

2 Ma	12:19	Dositheus and Sosipater, who were captains under Maccabeus
	12:24	and Sosipater and their men

SOSTRATUS   2

2 Ma	4:28	When Sostratus the captain of the citadel
	4:29	while Sostratus left Crates

SOUL   96 = 0.063 %

Tob	13:6	and with all your soul
	13:7	my soul exalts the King of heaven
	13:15	Let my soul praise God the great King
Jud	11:7	who has sent you to direct every living soul
	12:4	Judith replied, As your soul lives, my lord
Wis	1:4	because wisdom will not enter a deceitful soul
	1:11	and a lying mouth destroys the soul
	2:22	nor discern the prize for blameless souls
	3:1	But the souls of the righteous are in the hand of God
	3:13	she will have fruit when God examines souls
	4:11	or guile deceive his soul
	4:14	for his soul was pleasing to the Lord
	7:27	in every generation she passes into holy souls
	8:19	and a good soul fell to my lot
	9:3	and pronounce judgment in uprightness of soul
	9:15	for a perishable body weighs down the soul
	10:7	as a monument to an unbelieving soul
	10:16	She entered the soul of a servant of the Lord
	14:11	and became traps for the souls of men
	14:26	pollution of souls, sex perversion
	15:8	when he is required to return the soul that was lent him
	15:11	and inspired him with an active soul
	16:14	nor set free the imprisoned soul
	17:1	therefore uninstructed souls have gone astray
	17:8	and disorders of a sick soul
	17:15	and now were paralyzed by their souls' surrender
Sir	4:6	for if in bitterness of soul he calls down a curse upon you
	6:2	Do not exalt yourself through your soul's counsel
	6:2	lest your soul be torn in pieces like a bull
	6:4	An evil soul will destroy him who has it
	6:26	Come to her with all your soul
	7:11	Do not ridicule a man who is bitter in soul
	7:21	Let your soul love an intelligent servant
	7:29	With all your soul fear the Lord, and honour his priests
	14:9	and mean injustice withers the soul
	16:17	for what is my soul in the boundless creation ?
	18:31	If you allow your soul to take pleasure in base desire
	19:3	and the reckless soul will be snatched away
	21:2	Its teeth are lion's teeth, and destroy the souls of men
	21:27	he curses his own soul
	21:28	A whisperer defiles his own soul
	23:6	and do not surrender me to a shameless soul
	23:16	The soul heated like a burning fire
	25:1	My soul takes pleasure in 3 things
	25:2	My soul hates 3 kinds of men
	26:14	and there is nothing so precious as a disciplined soul
	26:15	and no balance can weigh the value of a chaste soul
	30:12	and you have sorrow of soul from him
	30:23	Delight your soul and comfort your heart
	31:28	is rejoicing of heart and gladness of soul

31 : 29	Wine drunk to excess is bitterness of soul
33 : 31	for as your own soul you will need him
34 : 15	Blessed is the soul of the man who fears the Lord !
34 : 17	He lifts up the soul and gives light to the eyes
37 : 12	whose soul is in accord with your soul
37 : 14	For a man's soul sometimes keeps him better informed
37 : 27	My son, test your soul while you live
45 : 23	in the ready goodness of his soul
47 : 15	Your soul covered the earth
50 : 25	With 2 nations my soul is vexed
51 : 6	My soul drew near to death
51 : 19	My soul grappled with wisdom, and in my conduct I was strict
51 : 20	I directed my soul to her
51 : 24	and why are your souls very thirsty ?
51 : 26	and let your souls receive instruction
51 : 29	May your soul rejoice in his mercy
Bar **3** : 1	the soul in anguish and the wearied spirit cry out to thee
P Az **64**	Bless the Lord, spirits and souls of the righteous
2 Ma **3** : 16	disclosed the anguish of his soul
6 : 30	but in my soul I am glad to suffer these things
15 : 17	and awaking manliness in the souls of the young
15 : 30	And the man who was ever in body and soul
2 Es **3** : 29	and my soul has seen many sinners during these 30 years
4 : 35	Did not the souls of the righteous enquire in their chambers
4 : 41	In Hades the chambers of the souls are like the womb
5 : 14	and my soul was so troubled that it fainted
5 : 22	Then my soul recovered the spirit of understanding
6 : 37	and my soul was in distress
7 : 32	and the chambers shall give up the souls
7 : 75	as soon as every one of us yields up his soul
7 : 93	in which the souls of the ungodly wander
7 : 99	This is the order of the souls of the righteous
7 : 100	Will time therefore be given to the souls
8 : 4	Then drink your fill of understanding, O my soul
10 : 36	Or is my mind deceived, and my soul dreaming ?
12 : 8	that thou mayest fully comfort my soul
15 : 8	and the souls of the righteous cry out continually
4 Ma **1** : 20	with both body and soul
1 : 26	In the soul it is boastfulness, covetousness
1 : 28	are 2 plants growing from the body and the soul
3 : 15	considered it an altogether fearful danger to his soul
13 : 15	for great is the struggle of the soul
13 : 21	From such embraces brotherly-loving souls are nourished
15 : 25	For as in the council chamber of her own soul
18 : 23	and have received pure and immortal souls from God

SOUND, subst.   16 = 0.010 %

Wis **1** : 10	and the sound of murmurings does not go unheard
7 : 3	and my first sound was a cry, like that of all
17 : 4	but terrifying sounds rang out around them
17 : 18	or a melodious sound of birds in widespreading branches
17 : 19	or the sound of the most savage roaring beasts
Sir **38** : 28	he inclines his ear to the sound of the hammer
45 : 9	to send forth a sound as he walked
46 : 17	and made his voice heard with a mighty sound
Bel **14** : 36	with the rushing sound of the wind itself
1 Ma **9** : 12	the phalanx advanced to the sound of the trumpets
1 Es **5** : 65	so that the sound was heard afar
5 : 66	they came to find out what the sound of the trumpets meant
2 Es **6** : 17	and its sound was like the sound of many waters
6 : 39	the sound of man's voice was not yet there
10 : 26	so that the earth shook at the sound

SOUND, verb   12 = 0.008 %

Sir **50** : 16	they sounded the trumpets of hammered work
1 Ma **3** : 54	Then they sounded the trumpets and gave a loud shout
4 : 40	and sounded the signal on the trumpets
5 : 33	who sounded their trumpets and cried aloud in prayer
6 : 33	and sounded their trumpets
7 : 45	kept sounding the battle call on the trumpets
16 : 8	And they sounded the trumpets
1 Es **5** : 62	And all the people sounded trumpets
5 : 65	For the multitude sounded the trumpets loudly
2 Es **6** : 2	and before the rumblings of thunder sounded
6 : 23	and the trumpet shall sound aloud, and when all hear it
11 : 15	And behold, a voice sounded, saying to it

SOUND, adj.   6 = 0.004 %

Tob **5** : 15	if you both return safe and sound
5 : 20	he will return safe and sound, and your eyes will see him
5 : 21	and he will come back safe and sound
Ad E **13** : 3	Haman, who excels among us in sound judgment
Sir **26** : 19	My son, keep sound the bloom of your youth
4 Ma **1** : 15	Now reason is the mind that with sound logic prefers the life of wisdom

SOUNDNESS   1

Sir **30** : 15	Health and soundness are better than all gold

SOURCE   4 = 0.003 %

Wis **12** : 16	For thy strength is the source of righteousness
Sir **1** : 5	The source of wisdom is God's word in the highest heaven
2 Ma **4** : 8	and, from another source of revenue, 80 talents
2 Es **4** : 7	or how many streams are at the source of the deep

SOUTH   10 = 0.007 %

Tob **1** : 2	which is to the south of Kedesh Naphtali
Jud **2** : 23	south of the country of the Chelleans
7 : 18	toward the south and the east
Sir **43** : 16	at his will the south wind blows
1 Ma **3** : 57	and encamped to the south of Emmaus
5 : 65	and fought the sons of Esau in the land to the south
2 Es **15** : 20	from the rising sun and from the south
15 : 34	and from the north to the south
15 : 38	And, after that, heavy storm clouds shall be stirred up from the south
15 : 39	and shall be driven violently toward the south and west

SOUTHERN   1

Jud **2** : 25	and came to the southern borders of Japheth

SOVEREIGN, subst., adj.   34 = 0.022 %

Jud **2** : 13	any of your sovereign's commands
Ad E **16** : 6	beguile the sincere good will of their sovereigns
Wis **12** : 18	Thou who art sovereign in strength dost judge with mildness
2 Ma **3** : 24	then and there the Sovereign of spirits and of all authority
3 : 28	and they recognized clearly the sovereign power of God
12 : 15	calling upon the great Sovereign of the world
12 : 28	But the Jews called upon the Sovereign
15 : 3	if there were a sovereign in heaven
15 : 4	It is the living Lord himself, the Sovereign in heaven
15 : 5	he replied, And I am a sovereign also, on earth
15 : 23	So now, O Sovereign of the heavens
15 : 29	and they blessed the Sovereign Lord
3 Ma **2** : 2	and sovereign of all creation
2 Es **3** : 4	O sovereign Lord, didst thou not speak at the beginning
4 : 38	Then I answered and said, O sovereign Lord
5 : 23	And I said, O sovereign Lord
5 : 38	And I said, O sovereign Lord
6 : 11	I answered and said, O sovereign Lord
7 : 17	Then I answered and said, O sovereign Lord, behold
7 : 45	I answered and said, O sovereign Lord
7 : 58	I said, O sovereign Lord
12 : 7	And I said, O sovereign Lord
13 : 51	I said, O sovereign Lord, explain this to me :
4 Ma **1** : 1	that is, whether devout reason is sovereign over the emotions
1 : 5	why is it not sovereign over forgetfulness and ignorance ?
1 : 13	is whether reason is sovereign over the emotions
1 : 30	but over the emotions it is sovereign
1 : 30	that rational judgment is sovereign over the emotions
2 : 13	It is sovereign over the relationship of friends
2 : 13	for it is sovereign over even this
6 : 31	Admittedly, then, devout reason is sovereign over the emotions
8 : 28	and sovereign over agonies
13 : 1	that devout reason is sovereign over the emotions
16 : 1	is sovereign over the emotions

SOVEREIGNTY   5 = 0.003 %

Wis **6** : 3	and your sovereignty from the Most High
12 : 16	and thy sovereignty over all causes thee to spare all
Sir **10** : 8	Sovereignty passes from nation to nation
47 : 21	so that the sovereignty was divided
4 Ma **13** : 5	the sovereignty of right reason over emotion

SOW, verb   19 = 0.012 %

Sir **6** : 19	Come to her like one who ploughs and sows
7 : 3	My son, do not sow the furrows of injustice
26 : 20	and sow it with your own seed, trusting in your fine stock
1 Es **4** : 6	but till the soil, whenever they sow, reap the harvest
2 Es **4** : 28	For the evil about which you ask me has been sown
4 : 29	If therefore that which has been sown is not reaped
4 : 29	and if the place where the evil has been sown does not pass away
4 : 29	the field where the good has been sown will not come
4 : 30	For a grain of evil seed was sown in Adam's heart from the beginning
4 : 32	When heads of grain without number are sown
5 : 48	to those who from time to time are sown in it
8 : 41	For just as the farmer sows many seeds upon the ground
8 : 41	and yet not all that have been sown will come up in due season
8 : 41	so also those who have been sown in the world will not all be saved
9 : 31	For behold, I sow my law in you
9 : 33	because they did not keep what had been sown in them
9 : 34	and when it happens that what was sown or what was launched
16 : 24	No one shall be left to cultivate the earth or to sow it
16 : 43	let him that sows be like one who will not reap

SOWN
             1
2 Es **6**:22 Sown places shall suddenly appear unsown

SPACE
        3 = 0.002 %
2 Ma **14**:44 a space opened and he fell in the middle of the empty space
3 Ma **4**:14 and at the end to be destroyed in the space of a single day

SPACIOUS
             2
Sus **13**:4 and had a spacious garden adjoining his house
2 Es **7**:96 and the spacious liberty

SPAIN
             1
1 Ma **8**:3 and what they had done in the land of Spain

SPAN
             1
Sir **18**:3 he steers the world with the span of his hand

SPARE
        23 = 0.015 %
Jud **2**:11 But if they refuse, your eye shall not spare
     7:27 for we will be slaves, but our lives will be spared
   11:9 we have heard his words, for the men of Bethulia spared him
   13:20 because you did not spare your own life
Ad E **13**:15 God of Abraham, spare thy people
Wis **2**:10 let us not spare the widow
   11:26 Thou sparest all things, for they are thine
   12:8 But even these thou didst spare, since they were but men
   12:16 and thy sovereignty over all causes thee to spare all
Sir **16**:8 He did not spare the neighbours of Lot
   17:21 has neither left nor abandoned them, but spared them
   23:2 That they may not spare me in my errors
1 Ma **13**:5 And now, far be it from me to spare my life
1 Es **1**:50 because he would have spared them and his dwelling place
    1:53 and did not spare young man or virgin
3 Ma **3**:18 but they were spared the exercise of our power
    7:6 we barely spared their lives
2 Es **3**:30 and hast spared those who act wickedly
    8:45 But spare thy people and have mercy on thy inheritance
    9:21 And I saw and spared some with great difficulty
   15:22 My right hand will not spare the sinners
   15:25 I will not spare them
   16:71 They shall be like mad men, sparing no one

SPARK
        6 = 0.004 %
Wis **2**:2 and reason is a spark kindled by the beating of our hearts
    3:7 and will run like sparks through the stubble
   11:18 or flash terrible sparks from their eyes
Sir **11**:32 From a spark of fire come many burning coals
   28:12 If you blow on a spark, it will glow
2 Es **13**:10 and from his tongue he shot forth a storm of sparks

SPARKLING
             1
Sir **42**:22 and how sparkling they are to see !

SPARROW
             1
Tob **2**:10 I did not know that there were sparrows on the wall

SPARTA
             1
1 Ma **14**:16 It was heard in Rome, and as far away as Sparta

SPARTAN
        9 = 0.006 %
1 Ma **12**:2 He also sent letters to the same effect to the Spartans
   12:5 which Jonathan wrote to the Spartans :
   12:6 to their brethren the Spartans, greeting
   12:20 Arius, king of the Spartans
   12:21 concerning the Spartans and the Jews
   14:20 This is a copy of the letter which the Spartans sent :
   14:20 The rulers and the city of the Spartans
   14:23 so that the people of the Spartans
   15:23 and to the Spartans, and to Delos, and to Myndos

SPEAK
        140 = 0.091 %
Tob **6**:12 I will speak to her father
    7:8 speak of those things which you talked about on the journey
   13:8 Let all men speak, and give him thanks in Jerusalem
Jud **2**:12 what I have spoken my hand will execute
    6:4 For he has spoken
    6:9 I have spoken and none of my words shall fail
    8:8 No one spoke ill of her
    8:9 spoken by the people against the ruler
    8:28 All that you have said has been spoken out of a true heart
    10:9 and accomplish the things about which you spoke with me
    11:5 and let your maidservant speak in your presence
    14:8 until the moment of her speaking to them
    16:14 for thou didst speak, and they were made
Ad E **15**:12 and he embraced her, and said, Speak to me
   15:15 But as she was speaking, she fell fainting
Wis **5**:3 They will speak to one another in repentance
    7:15 May God grant that I speak with judgment
    8:12 and when I speak they will give heed
    8:12 and when I speak at greater length

   10:21 and made the tongues of babes speak clearly
Sir pr.   by both speaking and writing
    4:23 Do not refrain from speaking at the crucial time
    4:25 Never speak against the truth
    5:13 Glory and dishonour come from speaking
   12:16 An enemy will speak sweetly with his lips
    13:6 He will speak to you kindly and say, What do you need ?
   13:22 he speaks unseemly words, and they justify him
   13:22 he speaks sensibly, and receives no attention
   13:23 When the rich man speaks all are silent
   13:23 When the poor man speaks they say, Who is this fellow ?
   18:19 Before you speak, learn
    20:6 while another keeps silent because he knows when to speak
    20:8 and whoever usurps the right to speak will be hated
   20:16 those who eat my bread speak unkindly
   20:27 He who speaks wisely will advance himself
   21:25 The lips of strangers will speak of these things
   25:9 and he who speaks to attentive listeners
    29:5 in speaking of his neighbour's money
   31:31 speak no word of reproach to him
   32:3 Speak, you who are older, for it is fitting that you should
   32:7 Speak, young man, if there is need of you
   32:8 Speak concisely, say much in few words
   32:9 and when another is speaking, do not babble
   34:9 and one with much experience will speak with understanding
   36:15 and fulfil the prophecies spoken in thy name
   43:27 Though we speak much we cannot reach the end
Bar **2**:1 which he spoke against us
    2:24 which thou didst speak by thy servants the prophets
    2:28 as thou didst speak by thy servant Moses
L Jr **6**:8 but they are false and cannot speak
    6:41 for when they see a dumb man, who cannot speak
    6:41 they bring him and pray Bel that the man may speak
1 Ma **1**:24 He committed deeds of murder, and spoke with great arrogance
    1:30 Deceitfully he spoke peaceable words to them
    2:17 Then the king's officers spoke to Mattathias as follows :
    2:23 When he had finished speaking these words
    3:23 When he finished speaking
    7:15 And he spoke peaceable words to them
    7:34 and spoke arrogantly
    7:41 When the messengers from the king spoke blasphemy
    7:42 let the rest learn that Nicanor has spoken wickedly
    8:19 and they entered the senate chamber and spoke as follows :
   10:47 because he had been the first to speak peaceable words to them
   13:17 Simon knew that they were speaking deceitfully to him
2 Ma **4**:48 And so those who had spoken
    7:27 she spoke in their native tongue as follows
    7:30 While she was still speaking, the young man said
    9:5 As soon as he ceased speaking
   15:12 one who spoke fittingly
   15:14 And Onias spoke, saying
1 Es **1**:47 that were spoken by Jeremiah the prophet from the mouth of the Lord
    1:51 and whenever the Lord spoke, they scoffed at his prophets
    2:21 but to speak to our lord the king, in order that
    3:17 Then the first, who had spoken of the strength of wine, began and said :
    3:24 When he had said this, he stopped speaking
    4:1 Then the 2nd, who had spoken of the strength of the king
    4:1 began to speak :
    4:12 And he stopped speaking
    4:13 who had spoken of women and truth, began to speak :
    4:33 and he began to speak about truth :
    4:41 He ceased speaking
    5:6 who spoke wise words before Darius the king of the Persians
3 Ma **2**:22 was unable even to speak
    5:21 When the king had spoken
    5:45 so to speak
    6:5 speaking grievous words with boasting and insolence
2 Es **1**:12 But speak to them and say, Thus says the Lord :
    3:3 and I began to speak anxious words to the Most High, and said
    3:4 O sovereign Lord, didst thou not speak at the beginning
    5:22 and I began once more to speak words
    5:31 When I had spoken these words
    5:33 And I said, Speak, my lord
    5:34 but because of my grief I have spoken
    5:39 and how can I speak concerning the things
    5:50 let me speak before thee
    6:15 while the voice is speaking, do not be terrified
    6:17 and behold, a voice was speaking
    6:21 Infants a year old shall speak with their voices
    6:29 While he spoke to me, behold
    6:36 and I began to speak in the presence of the Most High
    6:38 thou didst speak at the beginning of creation
    6:55 All this I have spoken before thee, O Lord
    7:1 When I had finished speaking these words
    7:2 and listen to the words that I have come to speak to you
    7:3 I said, Speak, my lord
    7:22 and spoke against him
    7:38 Thus he will speak to them on the day of judgment

	7 : 129	spoke to the people, saying
	7 : 130	or even myself who have spoken to them
	8 : 15	but I will speak about thy people
	8 : 19	and I will speak before thee
	8 : 25	For as long as I live I will speak
	8 : 37	Some things you have spoken rightly
	8 : 40	As I have spoken, therefore, so it shall be
	8 : 42	If I have found favour before thee, let me speak
	9 : 4	then you will know that it was of these that the Most High spoke
	9 : 28	and I began to speak before the Most High, and said
	10 : 19	So I spoke again to her, and said
	10 : 29	As I was speaking these words, behold
	10 : 34	I said, Speak, my lord
	11 : 6	and no one spoke against him
	11 : 37	and spoke, saying
	11 : 38	Listen and I will speak to you
	12 : 17	As for your hearing a voice that spoke
	12 : 31	and roaring and speaking to the eagle
	12 : 32	and will come and speak to them
	12 : 34	the day of judgment, of which I spoke to you at the beginning
	12 : 40	and came to me and spoke to me, saying
	14 : 3	I revealed myself in a bush and spoke to Moses
	14 : 19	Let me speak in thy presence, Lord
	14 : 43	As for me, I spoke in the daytime and was not silent at night
	14 : 45	the Most High spoke to me, saying
	15 : 1	speak in the ears of my people the words of the prophecy
4 Ma	**1** : 12	I shall shortly have an opportunity to speak of this
	2 : 20	he would not have spoken thus
	5 : 15	When he had received permission to speak
	8 : 13	the tyrant resumed speaking :
	12 : 8	he said, Let me loose, let me speak to the king
	16 : 5	and perhaps have spoken as follows :

SPEAK on   1
2 Es **4** : 5   I said, Speak on, my lord

SPEAK out   1
2 Es **8** : 15   And now I will speak out :

SPEAKER   1
Sir **11** : 8   nor interrupt a speaker in the midst of his words

SPEAR   14 = 0.009 %
Jud	**1** : 15	and struck him down with hunting spears
	6 : 6	and the spear of my servants shall pierce your sides
	7 : 10	do not rely on their spears
	9 : 7	they trust in shield and spear, in bow and sling
	11 : 2	I would never have lifted my spear against them
Ad E	**16** : 24	shall be destroyed in wrath with spear and fire
Sir	**29** : 13	more than a mighty shield and more than a heavy spear
2 Ma	**5** : 3	brandishing of shields, massing of spears
	15 : 11	not so much with confidence in shields and spears
3 Ma	**3** : 15	by the power of the spear
	5 : 43	and rapidly level it to the ground with fire and spear
	6 : 5	who had already gained control of the whole world by the spear
2 Es	**13** : 9	nor held a spear or any weapon of war
	13 : 28	and as for his not holding a spear or weapon of war

SPECIAL   2
Wis **3** : 14   for special favour will be shown him for his faithfulness
1 Ma **6** : 37   they were fastened upon each beast by special harness

SPECIALLY   1
2 Ma **2** : 8   that the place should be specially consecrated

SPECIES   1
Sir **13** : 16   all living beings associate by species

SPECK   1
Wis **11** : 22   is like a speck that tips the scales

SPECTACLE   4 = 0.003 %
Sir	**43** : 1	the appearance of heaven in a spectacle of glory
3 Ma	**4** : 11	and which was well suited to make them an obvious spectacle
	5 : 24	for this most pitiful spectacle
2 Es	**16** : 64	and will make a public spectacle of all of you

SPECTATOR   2
4 Ma **15** : 20   with many spectators of the torturings
| | **17** : 14 | and the world and the human race were the spectators |

SPECTRE   2
Wis **17** : 3   and appalled by spectres
| | **17** : 15 | and now were driven by monstrous spectres |

SPEECH   21 = 0.014 %
Jud	**11** : 21	either for beauty of face or wisdom of speech !
	11 : 23	You are not only beautiful in appearance, but wise in speech
Ad E	**14** : 13	Put eloquent speech in my mouth before the lion
Wis	**8** : 8	she understands turns of speech and the solutions of riddles

Sir	**4** : 24	For wisdom is known through speech
	4 : 29	Do not be reckless in your speech
	5 : 10	and let your speech be consistent
	9 : 18	and the man who is reckless in speech will be hated
	21 : 7	He who is mighty in speech is known from afar
	21 : 16	but delight will be found in the speech of the intelligent
	23 : 7	Listen, my children, to instruction concerning speech
	23 : 13	for it involves sinful speech
	25 : 25	and no boldness of speech in an evil wife
	27 : 23	but later he will twist his speech
	32 : 12	but do not sin through proud speech
	36 : 23	If kindness and humility mark her speech
1 Ma	**4** : 19	Just as Judas was finishing this speech
	6 : 60	The speech pleased the king and the commanders
3 Ma	**3** : 23	but also both by speech and by silence
2 Es	**6** : 16	that the speech concerns them
4 Ma	**10** : 18	But he said, Even if you remove my organ of speech

SPEECHLESS   4 = 0.003 %
Wis	**4** : 19	because he will dash them speechless to the ground
2 Ma	**3** : 29	speechless because of the divine intervention
3 Ma	**4** : 16	praising speechless things that are not able
4 Ma	**10** : 19	you will not make our reason speechless

SPEED   2
Sir **32** : 10   Lightning speeds before the thunder
| | **43** : 13 | and speeds the lightnings of his judgment |

SPEEDILY   5 = 0.003 %
Ad E	**16** : 18	has speedily inflicted on him the punishment he deserved
Sir	**20** : 18	so the downfall of the wicked will occur speedily
	21 : 5	and his judgment comes speedily
3 Ma	**2** : 20	Speedily let your mercies overtake us
4 Ma	**4** : 22	He speedily marched against them

SPEEDY   1
Wis **14** : 14   and therefore their speedy end has been planned

SPELLBOUND   1
2 Es **2** : 43   And I was held spellbound

SPEND   8 = 0.005 %
Tob	**1** : 7	and I would go and spend the proceeds
	10 : 7	which Raguel had sworn that he should spend there
L Jr	**6** : 10	and spend it upon themselves
Bel	**14** : 3	and every day they spent on it 12 bushels of fine flour
1 Ma	**11** : 6	and they greeted one another and spent the night there
	14 : 32	He spent great sums of his own money
1 Es	**9** : 2	and spent the night there
3 Ma	**4** : 8	spent the remaining days of their marriage festival in lamentations

SPEW out   1
Wis **19** : 10   the river spewed out vast numbers of frogs

SPICE   1
Sir **24** : 15   I gave forth the aroma of spices

SPIRIT   64 = 0.042 %
Tob	**3** : 6	command my spirit to be taken up
	6 : 7	if a demon or evil spirit gives trouble to any one
Jud	**14** : 6	he fell down on his face and his spirit failed him
	16 : 14	Thou didst send forth thy Spirit, and it formed them
Ad E	**15** : 8	Then God changed the spirit of the king to gentleness
Wis	**1** : 5	For a holy and disciplined spirit will flee from deceit
	1 : 6	For wisdom is a kindly spirit
	1 : 7	Because the Spirit of the Lord has filled the world
	2 : 3	and the spirit will dissolve like empty air
	5 : 3	and in anguish of spirit they will groan, and say
	7 : 7	I called upon God, and the spirit of wisdom came to me
	7 : 20	the powers of spirits and the reasonings of men
	7 : 23	and penetrating through all spirits
	9 : 17	and sent thy holy Spirit from on high ?
	12 : 1	For thy immortal spirit is in all things
	15 : 11	and breathed into him a living spirit
	15 : 16	For a man made them, and one whose spirit is borrowed formed them
	16 : 14	but he cannot bring back the departed spirit
Sir	**34** : 13	The spirit of those who fear the Lord will live
	38 : 23	and be comforted for him when his spirit has departed
	39 : 6	he will be filled with the spirit of understanding
	48 : 12	and Elisha was filled with his spirit
	48 : 24	By the spirit of might he saw the last things
Bar	**2** : 17	whose spirit has been taken from their bodies
	3 : 1	the soul in anguish and the wearied spirit cry out to thee
P Az	16	Yet with a contrite heart and a humble spirit may we be accepted
	64	Bless the Lord, spirits and souls of the righteous
Sus	**13** : 45	God aroused the holy spirit of a young lad named Daniel
1 Ma	**9** : 7	and the battle was imminent, he was crushed in spirit

	10 : 74	his spirit was aroused
	13 : 7	The spirit of the people was rekindled
2 Ma	1 : 3	and a willing spirit
	3 : 24	then and there the Sovereign of spirits and of all authority
	5 : 17	Antiochus was elated in spirit, and did not perceive
	7 : 12	were astonished at the young man's spirit
	7 : 21	Filled with a noble spirit
	9 : 11	Then it was that, broken in spirit
	14 : 46	calling upon the Lord of life and spirit
1 Es	2 : 2	the Lord stirred up the spirit of Cyrus king of the Persians
	2 : 8	and all whose spirit the Lord had stirred to go up
3 Ma	2 : 20	and broken in spirit
	2 : 32	But the majority acted firmly with a courageous spirit
	3 : 22	they took this in a contrary spirit
	4 : 4	For with such a harsh and ruthless spirit
2 Es	1 : 37	yet with the spirit they will believe the things I have said
	3 : 3	My spirit was greatly agitated
	5 : 22	Then my soul recovered the spirit of understanding
	6 : 26	and converted to a different spirit
	6 : 37	For my spirit was greatly aroused
	6 : 39	And then the Spirit was hovering
	6 : 41	thou didst create the spirit of the firmament
	7 : 78	as the spirit leaves the body to return again to him who gave it
	7 : 80	such spirits shall not enter into habitations
	9 : 41	for I am greatly embittered in spirit and deeply afflicted
	12 : 3	and I said to my spirit
	12 : 5	and very weak in my spirit
	14 : 22	send the Holy Spirit into me
	14 : 40	for my spirit retained its memory
	16 : 62	and the spirit of Almighty God
4 Ma	6 : 11	he amazed even his torturers by his courageous spirit
	7 : 14	in spirit through reason
	9 : 26	While all were marvelling at his courageous spirit
	10 : 7	Since they were not able in any way to break his spirit
	14 : 6	as though moved by an immortal spirit of devotion

SPIT   2
| Sir | 28 : 12 | if you spit on it, it will be put out |
| 4 Ma | 11 : 19 | To his back they applied sharp spits |

SPIT out   1
| 2 Ma | 6 : 19 | went up to the rack of his own accord, spitting out the flesh |

SPITE   3 = 0.002 %
Jud	8 : 25	In spite of everything
2 Ma	4 : 34	and in spite of his suspicion
4 Ma	10 : 19	cut it off, for in spite of this

SPITTLE   2
| Sir | 26 : 22 | A harlot is regarded as spittle |
| 2 Es | 6 : 56 | and that they are like spittle |

SPLENDID   8 = 0.005 %
Ad E	14 : 2	she took off her splendid apparel
	15 : 1	and arrayed herself in splendid attire
Sir	40 : 3	from the man who sits on a splendid throne
	45 : 7	He blessed him with splendid vestments
2 Ma	8 : 35	took off his splendid uniform
	12 : 45	But if he was looking to the splendid reward
	14 : 33	and I will build here a splendid temple to Dionysus
4 Ma	11 : 12	he said, Tyrant, they are splendid favours that you grant us against your will

SPLENDIDLY   1
| 2 Ma | 3 : 26 | gloriously beautiful and splendidly dressed |

SPLENDOUR, SPLENDOR   16 = 0.010 %
Tob	14 : 5	and will rebuild Jerusalem in splendour
Ad E	14 : 15	and thou knowest that I hate the splendour of the wicked
	15 : 7	Lifting his face, flushed with splendour
Sir	42 : 21	He has ordained the splendours of his wisdom
	50 : 13	all the sons of Aaron in their splendour
Bar	4 : 24	and with the splendour of the Everlasting
	5 : 3	For God will show your splendour everywhere under heaven
1 Ma	2 : 62	for his splendour will turn into dung and worms
	15 : 32	and when he saw the splendour of Simon
	15 : 36	and reported to him these words and the splendour of Simon
1 Es	1 : 33	and every one of the acts of Josiah, and his splendour
	6 : 10	and being completed with all splendour and care
P Ma	5	for thy glorious splendour cannot be borne
2 Es	2 : 21	and let the blind man have a vision of my splendour
	7 : 42	but only the splendour of the glory of the Most High
	10 : 55	but go in and see the splendour and vastness of the building

SPOIL, subst.   12 = 0.008 %
1 Ma	1 : 35	and collecting the spoils of Jerusalem
	2 : 10	and has not seized her spoils ?
	3 : 12	Then they seized their spoils
	5 : 28	then he seized all its spoils and burned it with fire
	6 : 6	and abundant spoils which they had taken

	7 : 47	Then the Jews seized the spoils and the plunder
	11 : 48	They set fire to the city and seized much spoil on that day
	11 : 51	and they returned to Jerusalem with much spoil
2 Ma	8 : 27	and stripped them of their spoils
	8 : 28	After the sabbath they gave some of the spoils
	8 : 31	and carried the rest of the spoils to Jerusalem
1 Es	4 : 5	whatever spoil they take and everything else

SPOIL, verb   1
| Sir | 30 : 7 | He who spoils his son will bind up his wounds |

SPOKESMAN   2
| 2 Ma | 7 : 2 | One of them, acting as their spokesman, said |
| | 7 : 4 | and he commanded that the tongue of their spokesman |

SPORT, subst.   4 = 0.003 %
Bar	3 : 17	those who have sport with the birds of the air
1 Ma	9 : 26	and he took vengeance on them and made sport of them
2 Ma	7 : 7	they brought forward the 2nd for their sport
	7 : 10	After him, the 3rd was the victim of their sport

SPOTLESS   1
| Wis | 7 : 26 | a spotless mirror of the working of God |

SPREAD   15 = 0.010 %
Jud	5 : 10	When a famine spread over Canaan they went down to Egypt
	12 : 15	and her maid went and spread on the ground for her before Holofernes
	16 : 25	And no one ever again spread terror
Wis	17 : 21	while over those men alone heavy night was spread
	18 : 10	was spread abroad
Sir	24 : 15	and like choice myrrh I spread a pleasant odour
1 Ma	14 : 10	till his renown spread to the ends of the earth
2 Ma	4 : 39	and when report of them had spread abroad
	7 : 5	The smoke from the pan spread widely
	8 : 7	And talk of his valour spread everywhere
2 Es	11 : 2	he spread his wings over all the earth
	15 : 6	For iniquity has spread throughout every land
	15 : 29	their hissing shall spread over the earth
4 Ma	4 : 22	he heard that a rumour of his death had spread
	9 : 19	While he was saying these things they spread fire under him

SPREAD forth   1
| Sir | 48 : 20 | spreading forth their hands toward him |

SPREAD out   8 = 0.005 %
Jud	4 : 11	and spread out their sackcloth before the Lord
	7 : 3	and they spread out in breadth over Dothan as far as Balbaim
	7 : 18	and their tents and supply trains spread out in great number
Sir	24 : 16	Like a Terebinth I spread out my branches
	51 : 19	I spread out my hands to the heavens
1 Ma	6 : 40	was spread out on the high hills
	11 : 47	and then spread out through the city
2 Es	16 : 59	who has spread out the heaven like an arch

SPREADING   1
| Sir | 14 : 18 | Like flourishing leaves on a spreading tree |

SPRING, subst., source   19 = 0.012 %
Jud	6 : 11	and came to the springs below Bethulia
	7 : 3	They encamped in the valley near Bethulia, beside the spring
	7 : 7	and visited the springs that supplied their water
	7 : 12	of the springs of water
	7 : 17	and the springs of the Israelites
	12 : 7	and bathed at the spring in the camp
	12 : 8	When she came up from the spring
Ad E	10 : 6	The tiny spring which became a river
	11 : 10	and from their cry, as though from a tiny spring
Sir	21 : 13	and his counsel like a flowing spring
	50 : 8	like lilies by a spring of water
P Az	55	Bless the Lord, you springs
2 Es	2 : 19	and the same number of springs flowing with milk and honey
	2 : 32	because my springs run over, and my grace will not fail
	6 : 24	and the springs of the fountains shall stand still
	14 : 47	For in them is the spring of understanding
	16 : 60	who has put springs of water in the desert
4 Ma	3 : 10	and although springs were plentiful there
	3 : 14	and found the spring

SPRING, subst., season   2
| Wis | 2 : 7 | and let no flower of spring pass by us |
| 2 Es | 7 : 41 | or summer or spring or heat or winter |

SPRING, verb   4 = 0.003 %
Tob	8 : 6	From them the race of mankind has sprung
Ad E	15 : 8	and in alarm he sprang from his throne
2 Ma	14 : 30	did not spring from the best motives
2 Es	3 : 7	From him there sprang nations and tribes

SPRING up   4 = 0.003 %
Tob	2:4	I sprang up and removed the body to a place of shelter until sunset
	7:6	Then Raguel sprang up and kissed him and wept
1 Ma	4:38	In the courts they saw bushes sprung up as in a thicket
2 Es	16:21	and then the calamities shall spring up on the earth

SPRINKLE   8 = 0.005 %
Tob	11:11	and he sprinkled the gall upon his father's eyes, saying
1 Ma	3:47	and sprinkled ashes on their heads, and rent their clothes
	4:39	and sprinkled themselves with ashes
2 Ma	1:21	to sprinkle the liquid on the wood and what was laid upon it
	10:25	Maccabeus and his men sprinkled dust upon their heads
	14:15	they sprinkled dust upon their heads
3 Ma	1:18	rushed out with their mothers, sprinkled their hair with dust
	4:6	their myrrh-perfumed hair sprinkled with ashes

SPURN   3 = 0.002 %
3 Ma	3:23	they not only spurn the priceless citizenship
4 Ma	3:18	and by nobility of reason spurn all domination by the emotions
	5:9	and wrong to spurn the gifts of nature

SPY, subst.   2
Sir	11:30	and like a spy he observes your weakness
1 Ma	12:26	He sent spies to their camp

SPY out   1
1 Ma	5:38	Judas sent men to spy out the camp, and they reported to him

SQUARE, subst., adj.   5 = 0.003 %
2 Ma	10:2	in the public square by the foreigners
1 Es	5:47	they gathered as one man in the square
	9:6	And all the multitude sat in the open square before the temple
	9:38	into the open square before the east gate of the temple
	9:41	And he read aloud in the open square

SQUARED   1
1 Ma	10:11	with squared stones, for better fortification

STAB   2
1 Ma	6:46	stabbed it from beneath, and killed it
2 Ma	13:15	He stabbed the leading elephant and its rider

STABILITY   3 = 0.002 %
Ad E	13:5	so that our kingdom may not attain stability
Wis	6:24	and a sensible king is the stability of his people
3 Ma	6:28	has granted an unimpeded and notable stability to our government

STABLE   1
Sir	38:34	But they keep stable the fabric of the world

STACTE   1
Sir	24:15	like galbanum, onycha, and stacte

STAFF   1
Tob	5:17	Is he not the staff of our hands

STAIN, subst.   2
Sir	33:22	bring no stain upon your honour
	47:20	You put a stain upon your honour, and defiled your posterity

STAIN, verb   5 = 0.003 %
Tob	3:15	and that I did not stain my name or the name of my father
Jud	9:3	to be stained with blood
Wis	15:4	a figure stained with varied colours
Sir	22:10	stain the nobility of their kindred
4 Ma	5:36	You, O king, shall not stain

STAKE   1
Sir	27:2	As a stake is driven firmly into a fissure between stones

STALLION   1
Sir	33:6	A stallion is like a mocking friend

STALWART   2
1 Ma	11:44	So Jonathan sent 3,000 stalwart men to him at Antioch
2 Ma	12:27	Stalwart young men took their stand before the walls

STAND, verb   78 = 0.051 %
Jud	4:14	who stood before the Lord and ministered to the Lord
	5:22	all the men standing around the tent began to complain
	8:3	For as he stood overseeing the men
	8:33	Stand at the city gate tonight
	10:6	and found Uzziah standing there
	10:16	And when you stand before him
	10:18	and they came and stood around her
	13:3	to stand outside the bedchamber
	13:4	Then Judith, standing beside his bed, said in her heart
Ad E	13:5	stands constantly in opposition to all men

	15:6	she stood before the king
	16:3	but in their inability to stand prosperity
Wis	4:4	standing insecurely they will be shaken by the wind
	5:1	Then the righteous man will stand with great confidence
	6:7	For the Lord of all will not stand in awe of any one
	10:7	and a pillar of salt standing
	18:16	and stood and filled all things with death
	18:16	and touched heaven while standing on the earth
	19:7	and dry land emerging where water had stood before
Sir	6:34	Stand in the assembly of the elders
	21:22	but a man of experience stands respectfully before it
	22:18	will not stand firm against the wind
	22:18	will not stand firm against any fear
	27:14	makes one's hair stand on end
	37:9	and then stand aloof to see what will happen to you
	39:17	At his word the waters stood in a heap
	40:12	but good faith will stand for ever
	40:25	Gold and silver make the foot stand sure
	42:17	that the universe may stand firm in his glory
	43:10	At the command of the Holy One they stand as ordered
	45:23	and stood fast, when the people turned away
	46:3	Who before him ever stood so firm ?
	47:13	and prepare a sanctuary to stand for ever
	50:12	as he stood by the hearth of the altar
Bar	5:5	Arise, O Jerusalem, stand upon the height
L Jr	6:27	because through them these gods are made to stand
P Az	2	Then Azariah stood and offered this prayer
1 Ma	1:62	But many in Israel stood firm
	4:18	But stand now against our enemies and fight them
	5:44	they could not stand before Judas no longer
	7:36	and stood before the altar and the temple
	10:72	Men will tell you that you cannot stand before us
	10:81	But his men stood fast, as Jonathan commanded
	14:26	For he and his brothers and the house of his father have stood firm
2 Ma	3:26	who stood on each side of him and scourged him continuously
	3:33	dressed in the same clothing, and they stood and said
	13:12	Judas exhorted them and ordered them to stand ready
	14:45	and standing upon a steep rock
1 Es	1:5	Stand in order in the temple
	1:10	stood according to kindred
	1:27	Stand aside, and do not oppose the Lord
	5:59	And the priests stood arrayed in their garments
	7:9	and the priests and the Levites stood
	8:90	for we can no longer stand in thy presence
	9:11	and we are not able to stand in the open air
	9:42	stood on the wooden platform which had been prepared
	9:43	and beside him stood Mattathiah, Shema, Anaiah, Azariah
	9:46	And when he opened the law, they all stood erect
3 Ma	5:51	as they stood now at the gates of death
	6:31	or rather, who stood at its gates
2 Es	2:38	Rise and stand, and see at the feast of the Lord
	2:47	who had stood valiantly for the name of the Lord
	4:17	for the sand stood firm and stopped them
	4:47	And he said to me, Stand at my right side
	4:48	So I stood and looked, and behold, a flaming furnace passed by before me
	6:14	And if the place where you are standing is greatly shaken
	6:24	and the springs of the fountains shall stand still
	6:29	little by little the place where I was standing
	7:34	but only judgment shall remain, truth shall stand
	8:21	before whom the hosts of angels stand trembling
	13:35	But he will stand on the top of Mount Zion
	16:65	and your own iniquities shall stand
4 Ma	1:4	and those that stand in the way of courage
	5:1	and with his armed soldiers standing about him
	16:15	you stood and watched Eleazar being tortured
	17:5	does not stand so august as you
	17:5	stand in honour before God
	17:18	because of which they now stand before the divine throne

STAND by   9 = 0.006 %
Wis	10:11	she stood by him and made him rich
Sir	6:8	but will not stand by you in your day of trouble
	6:10	but will not stand by you in your day of trouble
	11:20	Stand by your covenant and attend to it
	12:15	but if you falter, he will not stand by you
	22:23	stand by him in time of affliction
	44:12	Their descendants stand by the covenants
	51:2	Before those who stood by thou wast my helper
4 Ma	6:1	the guards who were standing by dragged him violently

STAND up   3 = 0.002 %
Tob	12:21	Then they stood up
Sus	13:34	Then the 2 elders stood up in the midst of the people
2 Es	10:33	Stand up like a man, and I will instruct you

STAND, subst.   3 = 0.002 %
  Sus 13 : 48 Taking his stand in the midst of them, he said
  1 Ma   9 : 11 and took its stand for the encounter
  2 Ma 12 : 27 Stalwart young men took their stand before the walls

STANDING, subst.   1
  Sir   8 : 14 for the decision will favour him because of his standing

STAR   20 = 0.013 %
  Wis   7 : 19 the cycles of the year and the constellations of the stars
          7 : 29 and excels every constellation of the stars
        13 : 2   or the circle of the stars, or turbulent water
        17 : 5   nor did the brilliant flames of the stars
  Sir 43 : 9   The glory of the stars is the beauty of heaven
        44 : 21 and exalt his posterity like the stars
        50 : 6   Like the morning star among the clouds
  Bar   3 : 34 the stars shone in their watches, and were glad
  L Jr 6 : 60 For sun and moon and stars, shining and sent forth for service, are obedient
  P Az   13   as many as the stars of heaven
          41   Bless the Lord, stars of heaven
  2 Ma   9 : 10 had thought that he could touch the stars of heaven
  2 Es   5 : 5   and the stars shall fall
          6 : 45 and the arrangement of the stars to come into being
          7 : 39 a day that has no sun or moon or stars
          7 : 97 and how they are to be made like the light of the stars
          7 : 125 shall shine more than the stars
        16 : 56 At his word the stars were fixed
        16 : 56 and he knows the number of the stars
  4 Ma 17 : 5   The moon in heaven, with the stars

STARE   1
  1 Es   4 : 19 and with open mouths stare at her

STAR-LIKE   1
  4 Ma 17 : 5   who, after lighting the way of your star-like 7 sons to piety

STARRY   1
  Wis 10 : 17 and a starry flame through the night

START   2
  Tob 11 : 10 Tobit started toward the door, and stumbled
  1 Ma   9 : 60 He started to come with a large force

STATE, subst.   5 = 0.003 %
  2 Ma   4 : 30 While such was the state of affairs
  3 Ma   3 : 26 and in the best state
          5 : 45 to a state of madness
  2 Es   1 : 36 yet will recall their former state
  4 Ma   5 : 1   The tyrant Antiochus, sitting in state with his counsellors

STATE, verb   6 = 0.004 %
  1 Ma 12 : 7   stating that you are our brethren
  2 Ma   3 : 9   and stated why he had come
          9 : 13 stating that the holy city
        14 : 27 wrote to Nicanor, stating that he was displeased with the covenant
  1 Es   3 : 5   Let each of us state what one thing is strongest
  4 Ma   1 : 12 I shall begin by stating my main principle

STATELY   1
  Sir 26 : 17 so is a beautiful face on a stately figure

STATEMENT   4 = 0.003 %
  1 Es   3 : 5   and to him whose statement seems wisest
          3 : 8   Then each wrote his own statement
          3 : 9   and to the one whose statement the king
          3 : 16 and they shall explain their statements

STATION, verb   15 = 0.010 %
  Jud   3 : 6   and stationed garrisons in the hilltop cities
  1 Ma   1 : 34 And they stationed there a sinful people, lawless men
          4 : 61 And he stationed a garrison there to hold it
          5 : 42 he stationed the scribes of the people at the stream
          6 : 35 with each elephant they stationed a 1,000 men
          6 : 38 The rest of the horsemen were stationed on either side
          6 : 50 and stationed a guard there to hold it
        10 : 32 that he may station in it men of his own choice to guard it
        10 : 37 Let some of them be stationed
        11 : 3   he stationed forces as a garrison in each city
        12 : 27 and he stationed outposts around the camp
        12 : 34 And he stationed a garrison there to guard it
        15 : 41 He built up Kedron and stationed there horsemen and troops
  2 Ma 15 : 20 the elephants strategically stationed
        15 : 31 and stationed the priests before the altar

STATUE   1
  2 Ma   2 : 2   upon seeing the gold and silver statues and their adornment

STATURE   4 = 0.003 %
  Bar   3 : 26 great in stature, expert in war
  2 Es   2 : 43 In their midst was a young man of great stature
          5 : 52 but smaller in stature ?
          5 : 54 that you and your contemporaries are smaller in stature

STATUS   2
  3 Ma   2 : 28 and to the status of slaves
          2 : 29 and they shall also be reduced to their former limited status

STATUTE   10 = 0.007 %
  Sir   6 : 37 Reflect on the statutes of the Lord
        45 : 17 In his commandments he gave him authority in statutes and judgments
  Bar   1 : 18 to walk in the statutes of the Lord which he set before us
          2 : 10 to walk in the statutes of the Lord which he set before us
          4 : 13 They had no regard for his statutes
  2 Es   1 : 24 that they may keep my statutes
          7 : 11 and when Adam transgressed my statutes
          7 : 24 they have been unfaithful to his statutes
          9 : 32 they did not keep it, and did not observe the statutes
        13 : 42 that there at least they might keep their statutes

STAUNCH   1
  4 Ma   3 : 12 2 staunch young soldiers, respecting the king's desire

STAY, subst.   1
  3 Ma   7 : 19 during the time of their stay

STAY, verb   18 = 0.012 %
  Tob   5 : 6   and I have stayed with our brother Gabael
          6 : 10 Brother, today we shall stay with Raguel
          9 : 5   and stayed overnight with Gabael
        10 : 8   But his father-in-law said to him, Stay with me
  Jud 12 : 9   So she returned clean and stayed in the tent
        14 : 17 Then he went to the tent where Judith had stayed
  Wis   5 : 14 and it passes like the remembrance of a guest who stays but a day
  Sir pr.   and stayed for some time
        12 : 15 He will stay with you for a time
        20 : 2   How much better it is to reprove than to stay angry !
        29 : 27 my brother has come to stay with me
        37 : 12 But stay constantly with a godly man
  1 Ma   3 : 13 who stayed with him and went out to battle
        11 : 40 and he stayed there many days
        12 : 45 and choose for yourself a few men to stay with you
  1 Es   9 : 12 So let the leaders of the multitude stay
  2 Es 10 : 4   but to stay here, and I will neither eat nor drink
        13 : 58 And I stayed there 3 days

STAY away   1
  Sir   7 : 2   Stay away from wrong, and it will turn away from you

STAY on   2
  Sir 27 : 12 but among thoughtful people stay on
  2 Ma 14 : 23 Nicanor stayed on in Jerusalem

STEAD   2
  1 Es   1 : 43 Jehoiakim his son became king in his stead
  2 Es   7 : 104 to be ill or sleep or eat or be healed in his stead

STEADFAST   6 = 0.004 %
  Ad E 13 : 3   and is distinguished for his unchanging good will and steadfast fidelity
  Wis   7 : 23 Beneficent, humane, steadfast, sure, free from anxiety
  Sir   2 : 2   Set your heart right and be steadfast
          5 : 10 Be steadfast in your understanding
        26 : 18 so are beautiful feet with a steadfast heart
        27 : 3   If a man is not steadfast and zealous

STEADFASTLY   1
  4 Ma   9 : 28 But he steadfastly endured this agony and said

STEADFASTNESS   2
  4 Ma 15 : 30 O more noble than males in steadfastness
        16 : 14 By steadfastness you have conquered even a tyrant

STEADILY   2
  1 Ma   6 : 40 and they advanced steadily and in good order
  2 Es 15 : 43 And they shall go on steadily to Babylon

STEADY   1
  Sir 13 : 21 When a rich man totters, he is steadied by friends

STEAL   5 = 0.003 %
  Tob   2 : 13 for it is not right to eat what is stolen
  2 Ma   4 : 32 stole some of the gold vessels of the temple
          4 : 39 because many of the gold vessels had already been stolen

1 Es	4 : 23	and rob and steal and to sail the sea and rivers
	4 : 24	and when he steals and robs and plunders

STEEL   1

Sir	31 : 26	Fire and water prove the temper of steel

STEEP   1

2 Ma	14 : 45	and standing upon a steep rock

STEER, verb   4 = 0.003 %

Wis	10 : 4	steering the righteous man by a paltry piece of wood
	14 : 3	but it is thy providence, O Father, that steers its course
Sir	18 : 3	he steers the world with the span of his hand
4 Ma	7 : 1	the reason of our father Eleazar steered the ship of religion

STENCH   3 = 0.002 %

2 Ma	9 : 9	his flesh rotted away, and because of his stench
	9 : 10	Because of his intolerable stench
	9 : 12	And when he could not endure his own stench

STEP, subst.   4 = 0.003 %

Wis	13 : 18	for a prosperous journey, a thing that cannot take a step
Sir	21 : 6	Whoever hates reproof walks in the steps of the sinner
	51 : 15	from my youth I followed her steps
2 Ma	10 : 26	Falling upon the steps before the altar

STERN, adj.   4 = 0.003 %

Wis	5 : 20	and sharpen stern wrath for a sword
	11 : 10	as a stern king does in condemnation
	12 : 9	by dread wild beasts or thy stern word
	18 : 15	into the midst of the land that was doomed, a stern warrior

STEWARD   2

Jud	14 : 13	So they came to Holofernes' tent and said to the steward
1 Es	8 : 67	And they delivered the king's orders to the royal stewards

STICK, subst.   2

Wis	13 : 13	a stick crooked and full of knots
Sir	33 : 24	Fodder and a stick and burdens for an ass

STICK, verb   1

Sir	19 : 12	Like an arrow stuck in the flesh of the thigh

STIFFEN   1

1 Es	1 : 48	and he stiffened his neck and hardened his heart

STIFF-NECKED   2

Sir	16 : 11	Even if there is only one stiff-necked person
Bar	2 : 30	for they are a stiff-necked people

STILL, adj.   3 = 0.002 %

Tob	10 : 6	But Tobit said to her, Be still and stop worrying ; he is well
	10 : 7	And she answered him, Be still and stop deceiving me
2 Es	6 : 24	and the springs of the fountains shall stand still

STILL, verb   2

Sir	43 : 23	By his counsel he stilled the great deep
	46 : 7	and stilled their wicked murmuring

STILL, adv.   40 = 0.026 %

Tob	1 : 4	while I was still a young man
Jud	13 : 11	God, our God, is still with us, to show his power in Israel
Wis	10 : 7	Evidence of their wickedness still remains :
	16 : 17	the fire had still greater effect
	17 : 21	but still heavier than darkness were they to themselves
	19 : 3	For while they were still busy at mourning
	19 : 4	which their torments still lacked
	19 : 10	For they still recalled the events of their sojourn
Sir	33 : 20	While you are still alive and have breath in you
	41 : 1	and who still has the vigour to enjoy his food !
	51 : 13	While I was still young, before I went on my travels
1 Ma	1 : 6	and divided his kingdom among them while he was still alive
	4 : 18	while the division was still absent from the camp
	5 : 14	While the letter was still being read
	6 : 27	they will do still greater things
	6 : 55	whom King Antiochus while still living
	10 : 27	And now continue still to keep faith with us
	10 : 88	he honoured Jonathan still more
	12 : 36	to build the walls of Jerusalem still higher
2 Ma	7 : 5	the king ordered them to take him to the fire, still breathing
	7 : 24	The youngest brother being still alive
	7 : 30	While she was still speaking, the young man said
	9 : 9	and while he was still living in anguish and pain
	11 : 8	And there, while they were still near Jerusalem
	14 : 11	quickly inflamed Demetrius still more
	14 : 45	Still alive and aflame with anger, he rose
3 Ma	3 : 1	but was still more bitterly hostile
	4 : 18	although most of them were still in the country
	4 : 18	some still residing in their homes, and some at the place
	5 : 19	pointed out that while it was still night

2 Es	1 : 16	but to this day you still complain
	5 : 50	Is our mother, of whom thou hast told me, still young ?
	9 : 11	and as many as scorned my law while they still had freedom
	9 : 11	while an opportunity of repentance was still open to them
	10 : 5	Then I broke off the reflections with which I was still engaged
	10 : 32	and behold, I saw, and still see
	12 : 5	Behold, I am still weary in mind
	13 : 16	And still more, alas for those who are not left !
	15 : 31	shall become still stronger
4 Ma	18 : 10	While he was still with you

STING, verb   2

Sir	12 : 12	and be stung by what I have said
4 Ma	14 : 19	and as though with an iron dart sting those who approach their hive

STINGY   2

Sir	14 : 3	Riches are not seemly for a stingy man
	14 : 10	A stingy man's eye begrudges bread

STINKING   1

4 Ma	6 : 25	threw him down, and poured stinking liquids into his nostrils

STINT   1

Sir	35 : 8	and do not stint the first fruits of your hands

STIR   4 = 0.003 %

Sir	51 : 21	My heart was stirred to seek her
1 Ma	2 : 24	and his heart was stirred
1 Es	2 : 8	and all whose spirit the Lord had stirred to go up
	2 : 9	from many whose hearts were stirred

STIR up   6 = 0.004 %

Wis	11 : 6	stirred up and defiled with blood
1 Ma	3 : 49	and they stirred up the Nazirites
2 Ma	14 : 6	are keeping up war and stirring up sedition
1 Es	2 : 2	the Lord stirred up the spirit of Cyrus king of the Persians
2 Es	13 : 2	and behold, a wind arose from the sea and stirred up all its waves
	15 : 38	And, after that, heavy storm clouds shall be stirred up from the south

STOCK   3 = 0.002 %

Tob	5 : 13	My brother, you come of good stock
Sir	26 : 20	and sow it with your own seed, trusting in your fine stock
	47 : 22	and to David a root of his stock

STOLEN   1

Tob	2 : 13	It is not stolen, is it ? Return it to the owners

STOMACH   4 = 0.003 %

Sir	36 : 18	The stomach will take any food
	37 : 5	Some companions help a friend for their stomachs' sake
	40 : 30	but in his stomach a fire is kindled
4 Ma	7 : 6	you neither defiled your sacred teeth nor profaned your stomach

STONE   39 = 0.025 %

Tob	13 : 16	her walls with precious stones
	13 : 17	and ruby and stones of Ophir
Jud	1 : 2	with hewn stones 3 cubits thick and 6 cubits long
	6 : 12	by casting stones at them
	10 : 21	and emeralds and precious stones
Ad E	15 : 6	all covered with gold and precious stones
Wis	11 : 4	and slaking of thirst from hard stone
	13 : 10	and likeness of animals, or a useless stone
	14 : 21	bestowed on objects of stone or wood
	18 : 24	on the 4 rows of stones
Sir	6 : 21	She will weigh him down like a heavy testing stone
	21 : 8	is like one who gathers stones for his burial mound
	21 : 10	The way of sinners is smoothly paved with stones
	22 : 1	The indolent may be compared to a filthy stone
	22 : 20	One who throws a stone at birds scares them away
	27 : 2	As a stake is driven firmly into a fissure between stones
	27 : 25	Whoever throws a stone straight up throws it on his own head
	29 : 10	and do not let it rust under a stone and be lost
	45 : 11	with precious stones engraved like signets
	47 : 4	when he lifted his hand with a stone in the sling
	50 : 9	adorned with all kinds of precious stones
L Jr	6 : 39	are like stones from the mountain
1 Ma	2 : 36	But they did not answer them or hurl a stone at them
	4 : 43	and removed the defiled stones to an unclean place
	4 : 46	and stored the stones in a convenient place
	4 : 47	Then they took unhewn stones, as the law directs
	5 : 47	and blocked up the gates with stones
	6 : 51	engines of war to throw fire and stones
	10 : 11	with squared stones, for better fortification
	10 : 73	where there is no stone or pebble, or place to flee
	13 : 27	with polished stone at the front and back
2 Ma	1 : 16	they threw stones and struck down the leader and his men
	1 : 31	should be poured upon large stones

	4:41	some picked up stones, some blocks of wood
1 Es	**6**:9	of hewn stone, with costly timber laid in the walls
	6:25	with 3 courses of hewn stone
3 Ma	**2**:27	and he set up a stone on the tower in the courtyard
2 Es	**5**:5	and the stone shall utter its voice
	7:52	If you have just a few precious stones

STONY   2
Sir **17**:16   hearts of flesh in place of their stony hearts
     32:20   and do not stumble over stony ground

STOP   25 = 0.016 %
Tob **5**:21   So she stopped weeping
     10:6   But Tobit said to her, Be still and stop worrying ; he is well
     10:7   And she answered him, Be still and stop deceiving me
     10:7   and throughout the nights she never stopped mourning for her son Tobias
Jud **4**:7   and it was easy to stop any who tried to enter
Ad E **14**:9   to stop the mouth of those who praise thee
Sir **4**:26   and do not try to stop the current of a river
     18:7   and when he stops, he will be at a loss
     27:14   and their quarrels make a man stop his ears
     31:17   Be the first to stop eating, for the sake of good manners
1 Ma **6**:27   and you will not be able to stop them
     9:55   his mouth was stopped and he was paralyzed
     11:50   and make the Jews stop fighting against us and our city
     13:47   and stopped fighting against them
2 Ma **4**:6   and that Simon would not stop his folly
     9:4   so he ordered his charioteer to drive without stopping
     9:7   Yet he did not any way stop his insolence
1 Es **3**:24   When he had said this, he stopped speaking
     4:12   And he stopped speaking
3 Ma **1**:13   no one there had stopped him
     4:15   and though uncompleted it stopped after 40 days
2 Es **4**:17   for the sand through and stopped them
     10:3   But when they all had stopped consoling me
     13:44   and stopped the channels of the river
     13:47   the Most High will stop the channels of the river again

STORAGE   1
1 Ma **6**:53   But they had no food in storage

STORE, subst.   7 = 0.005 %
Wis **6**:8   But a strict inquiry is in store for the mighty
Sir **41**:12   since it will remain for you longer than a 1,000 great stores of gold
1 Ma **6**:53   had consumed the last of the stores
     9:52   and in them he put troops and stores of food
2 Ma **12**:27   and great stores of war engines and missiles were there
1 Es **1**:54   and the royal stores, they took and carried away to Babylon
2 Es **8**:36   who have no store of good works

STORE, verb   9 = 0.006 %
1 Ma **1**:35   they stored them there, and became a great snare
     4:46   and stored the stones in a convenient place
     9:35   for permission to store with them
     13:33   and he stored food in the strongholds
     14:33   where formerly the arms of the enemy had been stored
2 Ma **8**:31   they stored them all carefully in strategic places
1 Es **1**:41   and stored them in his temple in Babylon
     2:10   and stored in his temple of idols
     6:18   and stored in his own temple

STORE up   4 = 0.003 %
Jud **4**:5   and stored up food in preparation for war
Sir **29**:12   Store up almsgiving in your treasury
1 Ma **1**:35   they stored up arms and food
2 Es **6**:5   and before those who stored up treasures of faith were sealed

STOREHOUSE   4 = 0.003 %
Sir **1**:17   and their storehouses with her produce
     43:14   Therefore the storehouses are opened
Bar **3**:15   And who has entered her storehouses ?
2 Es **6**:22   and full storehouses shall suddenly be found to be empty

STORM, subst.   14 = 0.009 %
Wis **5**:14   and like a light hoarfrost driven away by a storm
     16:16   pursued by unusual rains and hail and relentless storms
Sir **33**:2   is like a boat in a storm
     49:9   For God remembered his enemies with storm
2 Ma **5**:11   and took the city by storm
     10:24   He came on, intending to take Judea by storm
2 Es **12**:42   and like a haven for a ship saved from a storm
     13:10   and from his tongue he shot forth a storm of sparks
     13:11   the stream of fire and the flaming breath and the great storm
     13:27   and a storm coming out of his mouth
     13:37   this was symbolized by the storm
     15:34   full of wrath and storm

     15:38   And, after that, heavy storm clouds shall be stirred up from the south
4 Ma **15**:32   endured nobly and withstood the wintry storms

STORM, verb   1
2 Ma **10**:35   bravely stormed the wall

STORMING   1
4 Ma **7**:2   and though buffeted by the stormings of the tyrant

STORY   9 = 0.006 %
Sir **20**:19   An ungracious man is like a story told at the wrong time
     22:8   He who tells a story to a fool tells it to a drowsy man
     35:14   nor the widow when she pours out her story
2 Ma **2**:19   The story of Judas Maccabeus and his brothers
     6:17   we must go on briefly with the story
     15:37   So I too will here end my story
     15:39   so also the style of the story
4 Ma **1**:12   and then I shall turn to their story
     3:6   by the story of King David's thirst

STORY-TELLER   1
Bar **3**:23   the story-tellers and the seekers for understanding

STOUTHEARTED   1
1 Ma **9**:14   then all the stouthearted men went with him

STOUTLY   1
4 Ma **15**:31   stoutly endured the waves

STRAIGHT, adj., adv.   9 = 0.006 %
Tob **4**:19   ask him that your ways may be straight
Jud **10**:11   The women went straight on through the valley
     13:20   walking in the straight path before our God
Wis **10**:10   she guided him on straight paths
Sir **2**:6   make your ways straight, and hope in him
     4:18   Then she will come straight back to him and gladden him
     27:25   Whoever throws a stone straight up throws it on his own head
     39:24   To the holy his ways are straight
     51:15   my foot entered upon the straight path

STRAIGHTEN   1
L Jr **6**:27   and if it is tipped over, it cannot straighten itself

STRAIT   1
2 Es **7**:96   and besides they see the straits and toil

STRANGE   12 = 0.008 %
Ad E **13**:5   perversely following a strange manner of life and laws
Wis **2**:15   and his ways are strange
     14:23   or hold frenzied revels with strange customs
     19:5   but they themselves might meet a strange death
Sir **43**:25   For in it are strange and marvellous works
Bar **4**:15   a shameless nation, of a strange language
1 Ma **1**:38   she became strange to her offspring
     1:44   he directed them to follow customs strange to the land
     6:13   and behold, I am perishing of deep grief in a strange land
2 Ma **9**:16   with many and strange inflictions
     9:28   among the mountains in a strange land
2 Es **1**:6   and have offered sacrifices to strange gods

STRANGER   16 = 0.010 %
Jud **9**:2   to take revenge on the strangers
Wis **19**:13   for they practised a more bitter hatred of strangers
     19:14   Others had refused to receive strangers
Sir **8**:18   In the presence of a stranger
     11:34   Receive a stranger into your home
     21:25   The lips of strangers will speak of these things
     23:22   and provides an heir by a stranger
     26:19   and do not give your strength to strangers
     29:24   and where you are a stranger you may not open your mouth
     29:26   Come here, stranger, prepare the table
     29:27   Give place, stranger, to an honoured person
1 Ma **1**:38   she became a dwelling of strangers
2 Ma **6**:2   the Friend of Strangers
3 Ma **2**:25   who were strangers to everything just
2 Es **16**:40   and in the midst of the calamities be like strangers on the earth
     16:46   for strangers shall gather their fruits

STRANGLE   3 = 0.002 %
Tob **2**:3   Father, one of our people has been strangled
     3:8   Do you not know that you strangle your husbands ?
4 Ma **9**:17   your wheel is not so powerful as to strangle my reason

STRATAGEM   1
2 Ma **14**:29   to accomplish this by a stratagem

STRATEGIC 2
2 Ma   8 : 6   He captured strategic positions
         8 : 31   they stored them all carefully in strategic places

STRATEGICALLY 1
2 Ma 15 : 20   the elephants strategically stationed

STRATEGY 2
Jud 11 : 8   thoroughly informed and marvellous in military strategy
2 Ma 13 : 18   tried strategy in attacking their positions

STRAW 2
2 Es   1 : 33   I will drive you out as the wind drives straw
        15 : 23   and the sinners, like straw that is kindled

STRAY 2
Wis   5 : 6   So it was we who strayed from the way of truth
Bar   3 : 21   Their sons have strayed far from her way

STREAM, subst.   15 = 0.010 %
Sir 39 : 13   and bud like a rose growing by a stream of water
1 Ma   5 : 37   and encamped opposite Raphon, on the other side of the stream
        5 : 39   and they are encamped across the stream
        5 : 40   Now as Judas and his army drew near to the stream of water
        5 : 42   When Judas approached the stream of water
        5 : 42   he stationed the scribes of the people at the stream
       16 : 5   and a stream lay between them
       16 : 6   And he saw that the soldiers were afraid to cross the stream
2 Es   1 : 22   When you were in the wilderness, at the bitter stream
        1 : 23   but threw a tree into the water and made the stream sweet
        4 : 7   or how many streams are at the source of the deep
        4 : 7   or how many streams are above the firmament
       13 : 10   he sent forth from his mouth as it were a stream of fire
       13 : 11   the stream of fire and the flaming breath and the great storm
       15 : 41   that all the fields and all the streams

STREAM out 1
P Az 24   And the flame streamed out above the furnace 49 cubits

STREET 14 = 0.009 %
Tob 13 : 17   The streets of Jerusalem will be paved with beryl
Jud   7 : 14   they will be strewn about in the streets where they live
        7 : 22   and fell down in the streets of the city
Sir   9 : 7   Do not look around in the streets of a city
       23 : 21   This man will be punished in the streets of the city
       49 : 6   and made her streets desolate
1 Ma   1 : 55   and burned incense at the doors of the houses and in the streets
        2 : 9   Her babes have been killed in her streets
       11 : 46   Then the men of the city seized the main streets of the city
       14 : 9   Old men sat in the streets
2 Ma   3 : 19   thronged the streets
3 Ma   1 : 18   and filled the streets with groans and lamentations
        1 : 20   some in houses and some in the streets
        4 : 3   or what streets were not filled

STRENGTH   58 = 0.038 %
Jud   2 : 5   take with you men confident in their strength
        5 : 3   and in what does their power or strength consist ?
        5 : 23   they are a people with no strength or power for making war
        7 : 22   there was no strength left in them any longer
        9 : 7   they glory in the strength of their foot soldiers
        9 : 8   Break their strength by thy might
        9 : 9   give to me, a widow, the strength to do what I plan
        9 : 11   nor thy might upon men of strength
       11 : 22   to lend strength to our hands and to bring destruction
       13 : 7   Give me strength this day, O Lord God of Israel !
       13 : 11   and his strength against our enemies
       16 : 13   wonderful in strength, invincible
Wis 10 : 2   and gave him strength to rule all things
       11 : 21   For it is always in your power to show great strength
       12 : 16   For thy strength is the source of righteousness
       12 : 17   For thou dost show thy strength
       12 : 18   Thou who art sovereign in strength dost judge with mildness
       13 : 19   he asks strength of a thing whose hands have no strength
       16 : 16   were scourged by the strength of thy arm
       18 : 22   He conquered the wrath not by strength of body
Sir   3 : 13   in all your strength do not despise him
        5 : 2   Do not follow your inclination and strength
        9 : 2   so that she gains mastery over your strength
       11 : 12   who lacks strength and abounds in poverty
       13 : 2   Do not lift a weight beyond your strength
       17 : 3   He endowed them with strength like his own
       19 : 28   And if by lack of strength he is prevented from sinning
       26 : 19   and do not give your strength to strangers
       28 : 10   in proportion to the strength of the man will be his anger
       31 : 30   reducing his strength and adding wounds
       38 : 18   and sorrow of heart saps one's strength
       39 : 28   they will pour out their strength
       40 : 26   Riches and strength lift up the heart
       41 : 2   to one who is in need and is failing in strength

43 : 28   Where shall we find strength to praise him ?
43 : 30   When you exalt him, put forth all your strength
46 : 9   And the Lord gave Caleb strength
47 : 5   and he gave him strength in his right hand
Bar   1 : 12   And the Lord will give us strength
        3 : 14   Learn where there is wisdom, where there is strength
P Az 21   and let their strength be broken
1 Ma   2 : 61   that none who put their trust in him will lack strength
        3 : 19   but strength comes from Heaven
        3 : 35   to wipe out and destroy the strength of Israel
        4 : 32   melt the boldness of their strength
        9 : 14   Judas saw that Bacchides and the strength of his army were on the right
       10 : 71   and let us match strength with each other there
2 Ma 10 : 34   The men within, relying on the strength of the place
       12 : 14   relying on the strength of the walls
       12 : 35   was dragging him off by main strength
1 Es   3 : 17   Then the first, who had spoken of the strength of wine, began and said :
        4 : 1   Then the 2nd, who had spoken of the strength of the king
        4 : 40   To her belongs the strength and the kingship
3 Ma   2 : 4   who trusted in their strength and boldness
2 Es   5 : 53   Those born in the strength of youth
        5 : 55   and passing the strength of youth
       12 : 5   and not even a little strength is left in me

STRENGTHEN   20 = 0.013 %
Sir   3 : 9   strengthens the houses of the children
       24 : 24   cleave to him so that he may strengthen you
       29 : 1   and he that strengthens him with his hand
       45 : 8   and strengthened him with the symbols of authority
       49 : 3   in the days of wicked men he strengthened godliness
1 Ma   1 : 34   These strengthened their position
        6 : 18   and strengthen the Gentiles
       10 : 23   in forming a friendship with the Jews to strengthen himself
       13 : 48   He also strengthened its fortifications
       13 : 52   He strengthened the fortifications of the temple hill
       14 : 14   He strengthened all the humble of his people
2 Ma 11 : 9   and were strengthened in heart
1 Es   7 : 15   to strengthen their hands
3 Ma   1 : 7   he strengthened the morale of his subjects
2 Es   2 : 25   and strengthen their feet
        5 : 15   and strengthened me and set me on my feet
       10 : 30   Then he grasped my right hand and strengthened me
       12 : 6   that he may strengthen me to the end
       12 : 8   strengthen me and show me, thy servant
4 Ma 15 : 23   strengthened her to disregard her temporal love for her children

STRENGTHEN 1
4 Ma   7 : 9   You, father, strengthened out loyalty to the law

STRETCH   3 = 0.002 %
Jud 13 : 2   with Holofernes stretched on his bed
3 Ma   5 : 25   stretched their hands toward heaven
4 Ma 11 : 18   He was carefully stretched tight upon it

STRETCH forth   4 = 0.003 %
Sir   7 : 32   Stretch forth your hand to the poor
2 Ma   7 : 10   and courageously stretched forth his hands
       14 : 34   Then the priests stretched forth their hands toward heaven
1 Es   8 : 73   and kneeling down and stretching forth my hands to the Lord

STRETCH out   13 = 0.008 %
Sir 15 : 16   stretch out your hand for whichever you wish
       43 : 12   the hands of the Most High have stretched it out
       46 : 2   and stretched out his sword against the cities !
1 Ma   6 : 25   And not against us alone have they stretched out their hands
        7 : 47   and the right hand which he had so arrogantly stretched out
        9 : 47   and Jonathan stretched out his hand to strike Bacchides
2 Ma 14 : 33   he stretched out his right hand toward the sanctuary
       15 : 15   Jeremiah stretched out his right hand
       15 : 21   stretched out his hands toward heaven
       15 : 32   which had been boastfully stretched out
1 Es   6 : 33   that shall stretch out their hands
4 Ma   4 : 11   stretched out his hands toward heaven
        9 : 13   When the noble youth was stretched out around this

STRETCHER 1
2 Ma   3 : 27   his men took him up and put him on a stretcher and carried him away

STREW 2
Jud   7 : 14   they will be strewn about in the streets where they live
        7 : 25   to strew us on the ground before them

STRICKEN   3 = 0.002 %
Tob   7 : 7   he was stricken with grief and wept
Wis 19 : 17   They were stricken also with loss of sight
1 Ma   9 : 55   for at that time Alcimus was stricken

STRICT
4 = 0.003 %

Wis	6 : 8	But a strict inquiry is in store for the mighty
Sir	26 : 10	Keep strict watch over a headstrong daughter
	42 : 11	Keep strict watch over a headstrong daughter
	51 : 19	My soul grappled with wisdom, and in my conduct I was strict

STRICTLY
3 = 0.002 %

1 Es	8 : 24	shall be strictly punished
2 Es	7 : 21	For God strictly commanded those who came into the world
	16 : 64	Because the Lord will strictly examine all their works

STRICTNESS
1

Wis	12 : 21	with what strictness thou hast judged thy sons

STRIFE
10 = 0.007 %

Wis	14 : 22	but they live in great strife due to ignorance
Sir	19 : 6	He who controls his tongue will live without strife
	27 : 15	The strife of the proud leads to bloodshed
	28 : 8	Refrain from strife, and you will lessen sins
	28 : 8	for a man given to anger will kindle strife
	28 : 10	and in proportion to the obstinacy of strife
	28 : 11	A hasty quarrel kindles fire, and urgent strife sheds blood
	31 : 26	so wine tests hearts in the strife of the proud
	40 : 5	and fear of death, and fury and strife
	40 : 9	are death and bloodshed and strife and sword

STRIKE
13 = 0.008 %

Jud	13 : 8	And she struck his neck twice with all her might
	13 : 18	to strike the head of the leader of our enemies
Wis	4 : 3	will strike a deep root or take a firm hold
Sir	13 : 2	The pot will strike against it, and will itself be broken
	16 : 5	and my ear has heard things more striking than these
1 Ma	5 : 65	He struck Hebron and its villages
	9 : 47	and Jonathan stretched out his hand to strike Bacchides
2 Ma	3 : 25	and struck at him with its front hoofs
	3 : 39	and he strikes and destroys those who come to do it injury
	9 : 5	struck him an incurable and unseen blow
	10 : 3	then, striking fire out of flint, they offered sacrifices
3 Ma	5 : 27	and being struck by the unusual invitation to come out
4 Ma	8 : 4	And struck by their appearance and nobility

STRIKE down
16 = 0.010 %

Jud	1 : 15	and struck him down with hunting spears
	9 : 3	and thou didst strike down slaves along with princes
	9 : 10	By the deceit of my lips strike down the slave
	13 : 15	The Lord has struck him down by the hand of a woman
Sir	8 : 16	and where no help is at hand, he will strike you down
	47 : 4	and struck down the boasting of Goliath ?
1 Ma	2 : 44	and struck down sinners in their anger
	4 : 33	Strike them down with the sword of those who love thee
	5 : 7	he struck them down
	7 : 41	thy angel went forth and struck down 185,000 of the Assyrians
	9 : 66	He struck down Odomera and his brothers
2 Ma	1 : 16	they threw stones and struck down the leader and his men
	8 : 18	to strike down those who are coming against us
	15 : 16	with which you will strike down your adversaries
	15 : 24	who come against thy holy people be struck down
2 Es	1 : 10	I struck down Pharaoh with his servants, and all his army

STRINGED
1

1 Ma	13 : 51	and with harps and cymbals and stringed instruments

STRIP
4 = 0.003 %

L Jr	6 : 58	Strong men will strip them of their gold and silver
2 Ma	8 : 27	and stripped them of their spoils
	11 : 12	Most of them got away stripped and wounded
4 Ma	6 : 2	First they stripped the old man

STRIP off
3 = 0.002 %

Wis	13 : 11	and skilfully strip off all its bark
1 Ma	1 : 22	he stripped it all off
2 Ma	4 : 38	he immediately stripped off the purple robe from Andronicus

STRIPE
1

Jud	9 : 13	Make my deceitful words to be their wound and stripe

STRIVE
6 = 0.004 %

Sir	4 : 28	Strive even to death for the truth
1 Ma	7 : 21	Alcimus strove for the high priesthood
2 Ma	2 : 21	to those who strove zealously on behalf of Judaism
	2 : 31	should be allowed to strive for brevity of expression
2 Es	5 : 34	while I strive to understand the way of the Most High
	7 : 92	because they have striven with great effort

STRONG
79 = 0.051 %

Wis	10 : 5	and kept him strong
	14 : 16	Then the ungodly custom, grown strong with time
Sir	6 : 29	Then her fetters will become for you a strong protection
	8 : 12	Do not lend to a man who is stronger than you
	24 : 24	Do not cease to be strong in the Lord
	28 : 14	and destroyed strong cities
	30 : 14	who is well and strong in constitution
	34 : 16	a mighty protection and strong support
	50 : 29	For if he does them, he will be strong for all things
L Jr	6 : 36	or rescue the weak from the strong
	6 : 58	Strong men will strip them of their gold and silver
Sus	13 : 39	for he was too strong for us
1 Ma	1 : 4	He gathered a very strong army
	1 : 17	So he invaded Egypt with a strong force
	1 : 20	and came to Jerusalem with a strong force
	1 : 33	with a great strong wall and strong towers
	2 : 49	Arrogance and reproach have now become strong
	2 : 64	My children, be courageous and grow strong in the law
	3 : 15	And again a strong army of ungodly men
	3 : 17	fight against so great and strong a multitude ?
	3 : 27	a very strong army
	4 : 7	And they saw the camp of the Gentiles, strong and fortified
	4 : 30	When he saw that the army was strong, he prayed, saying
	4 : 60	with high walls and strong towers round about
	5 : 6	where he found a strong band
	5 : 26	all these cities were strong and large
	5 : 46	This was a large and very strong city on the road
	6 : 6	that Lysias had gone first with a strong force
	6 : 6	that the Jews had grown strong from the arms, supplies
	6 : 37	And upon the elephants were wooden towers, strong and covered
	6 : 41	trembled, for the army was very large and strong
	6 : 57	the place against which we are fighting is strong
	6 : 62	and saw what a strong fortress the place was
	7 : 25	and those with him had grown strong
	8 : 1	that they were very strong and were well-disposed
	8 : 2	and that they were very strong
	9 : 50	and built strong cities in Judea :
	11 : 15	Ptolemy marched and met him with a strong force
2 Ma	1 : 3	and to do his will with a strong heart
	1 : 24	who art awe-inspiring and strong and just and merciful
	3 : 26	2 young men also appeared to him, remarkably strong
	10 : 18	took refuge in 2 very strong towers
	12 : 18	though in one place he had left a very strong garrison
	12 : 35	who was on horseback and was a strong man
	13 : 19	a strong fortress of the Jews
	14 : 1	with a strong army and a fleet
1 Es	3 : 5	Let each of us state what one thing is strongest
	3 : 10	The first wrote, Wine is strongest
	3 : 11	The 2nd wrote, The king is strongest
	3 : 12	The 3rd wrote, Women are strongest
	3 : 18	Gentlemen, how is wine the strongest ?
	3 : 24	Gentlemen, is not wine the strongest
	4 : 2	Gentlemen, are not men strongest
	4 : 3	But the king is stronger
	4 : 12	Gentlemen, why is not the king the strongest
	4 : 14	and is not wine king ?
	4 : 32	Gentlemen, why are not women strong
	4 : 34	Gentlemen, are not women strong ?
	4 : 35	But truth is great, and stronger than all things
	4 : 38	But truth endures and is strong for ever
	4 : 41	Great is truth, and strongest of all !
	5 : 50	and were stronger than they
	6 : 14	by a king of Israel who was great and strong
	8 : 85	in order that you may be strong
	8 : 95	and we are with you to take strong measures
3 Ma	3 : 8	were not strong enough to help them
2 Es	7 : 34	and faithfulness shall grow strong
	7 : 112	therefore those who were strong prayed for the weak
	8 : 22	whose ordinance is strong and whose command is terrible
	10 : 22	our young men have been enslaved and our strong men made powerless
	15 : 16	growing strong against one another
	15 : 31	shall become still stronger
	16 : 7	Can one turn back an arrow shot by a strong archer ?
	16 : 13	For his right hand that bends the bow is strong
4 Ma	4 : 5	and a very strong military force
	12 : 2	he felt strong compassion for this child
	13 : 22	and they grow stronger
	15 : 11	strong enough to pervert her reason

STRONGHOLD
34 = 0.022 %

1 Ma	1 : 2	He fought many battles, conquered strongholds
	4 : 61	so that the people might have a stronghold that faced Idumea
	5 : 9	But they fled to the stronghold of Dathema
	5 : 11	and capture the stronghold to which we have fled
	5 : 27	the enemy are getting ready to attack the strongholds tomorrow
	5 : 29	and they went all the way to the stronghold of Dathema
	5 : 30	carrying ladders and engines of war to capture the stronghold
	5 : 65	and tore down its strongholds
	6 : 61	On these conditions the Jews evacuated the stronghold
	8 : 10	tore down their strongholds, and enslaved them to this day
	10 : 12	Then the foreigners who were in the strongholds that Bacchides had built fled
	10 : 37	in the great strongholds of the king
	11 : 18	and his troops in the strongholds were killed

	11:18	by the inhabitants of the strongholds
	11:41	and the troops in the strongholds
	12:33	as far as Askalon and the neighbouring strongholds
	12:34	to hand over the stronghold
	12:35	and planned with them to build strongholds in Judea
	12:45	I will hand it over to you as well as the other strongholds
	13:33	But Simon built up the strongholds of Judea
	13:33	and he stored food in the strongholds
	13:38	and let the strongholds that you have built be your possession
	14:42	and over the country and the weapons and the strongholds
	15:7	and the strongholds which you have built and now hold
	16:8	the rest fled into the stronghold
	16:15	in the little stronghold called Dok, which he had built
2 Ma	8:30	and got possession of some exceedingly high strongholds
	10:15	who had control of important strongholds
	10:16	rushed to the strongholds of the Idumeans
	10:23	he destroyed more than 20,000 in the 2 strongholds
	10:32	Timothy himself fled to a stronghold called Gazara
	11:6	that Lysias was besieging the strongholds
	12:19	marched out and destroyed those whom Timothy had left in the stronghold
1 Es	8:81	to give us a stronghold in Judea and Jerusalem

STRONGLY   3 = 0.002 %

Sir	48:22	and he held strongly to the ways of David his father
1 Ma	10:50	He pressed the battle strongly until the sun set
2 Ma	12:13	which was strongly fortified with earthworks and walls

STRUCTURE   3 = 0.002 %

Wis	7:17	to know the structure of the world
1 Ma	10:44	and restoring the structures of the sanctuary
1 Es	6:11	and laying the foundations of this structure ?

STRUGGLE, verb   1

4 Ma	8:24	Let us not struggle against compulsion

STRUGGLE, subst.   6 = 0.004 %

2 Ma	14:43	But in the heat of the struggle he did not hit exactly
	15:9	and reminding them also of the struggles they had won
2 Es	12:18	great struggles shall arise
	12:47	and the Mighty One has not forgotten you in your struggle
4 Ma	9:23	Do not leave your post in my struggle
	13:15	for great is the struggle of the soul

STUBBLE   3 = 0.002 %

Wis	3:7	and will run like sparks through the stubble
2 Es	15:61	And you shall be broken down by them like stubble
	16:6	or quench a fire in the stubble

STUBBORN   4 = 0.003 %

Sir	3:26	A stubborn mind will be afflicted at the end
	3:27	A stubborn mind will be burdened by troubles
	30:8	A horse that is untamed turns out to be stubborn
	30:12	lest he become stubborn and disobey you

STUBBORNNESS   3 = 0.002 %

Sir	16:10	who rebelliously assembled in their stubbornness
Bar	2:33	and will turn from their stubbornness and their wicked deeds
4 Ma	8:26	and such a fatal stubbornness please us

STUCCO   1

Sir	22:17	is like the stucco decoration on the wall of a colonnade

STUDY, subst.   1

Sir	39:1	to the study of the law of the Most High

STUMBLE   6 = 0.004 %

Tob	11:10	Tobit started toward the door, and stumbled
Sir	9:5	lest you stumble and incur penalties for her
	13:23	And should he stumble, they even push him down
	32:15	but the hypocrite will stumble at it
	32:20	and do not stumble over stony ground
1 Es	4:27	Many have perished, or stumbled, or sinned, because of women

STUMBLING   2

Sir	31:29	with provocation and stumbling
	34:16	a guard against stumbling and a defence against falling

STUMBLING BLOCK   1

Sir	31:7	It is a stumbling block to those who are devoted to it

STUPID   4 = 0.003 %

Sir	22:15	Sand, salt, and a piece of iron are easier to bear than a stupid man
	22:23	nor admire a rich man who is stupid
	27:12	Among stupid people watch for a chance to leave
	42:8	Do not be ashamed to instruct the stupid or foolish

STUPIDITY   1

4 Ma	12:3	You see the result of your brothers' stupidity

STUPOR   1

Jud	13:15	in his drunken stupor

STURDY   1

Sir	6:14	A faithful friend is a sturdy shelter :

STYLE   2

2 Ma	15:39	so also the style of the story
3 Ma	3:5	but since they adorned their style of life

SUBAS   1

1 Es	5:34	the sons of Addus, the sons of Subas, the sons of Apherra

SUBDUE   7 = 0.005 %

Wis	18:22	but by his word he subdued the punisher
Sir	12:5	lest by means of it he subdue you
1 Ma	1:20	After subduing Egypt, Antiochus returned in the 143rd year
	4:28	and 5,000 cavalry to subdue them
	8:4	They also subdued the kings who came against them
	8:12	They have subdued kings far and near
2 Es	4:15	and said, Come, let us go up and subdue the forest of the plain

SUBJECT, subst.   6 = 0.004 %

Ad E	13:2	I have determined to settle the lives of my subjects in lasting tranquillity
	16:3	They not only seek to injure our subjects
2 Ma	11:23	we desire that the subjects of the kingdom be undisturbed
3 Ma	1:7	he strengthened the morale of his subjects
4 Ma	1:1	*The subject that I am about to discuss is most philosophical*
	1:2	*For the subject is essential*

SUBJECT, adj.   4 = 0.003 %

Wis	8:14	I shall govern peoples, and nations will be subject to me
2 Ma	9:12	he uttered these words : It is right to be subject to God
3 Ma	7:21	and they were not subject at all
4 Ma	2:23	and one who lives subject to this will

SUBJECT, verb   4 = 0.003 %

Sir	4:27	Do not subject yourself to a foolish fellow
3 Ma	2:13	subjected to our enemies, and overtaken by helplessness
	2:28	and all Jews shall be subjected
2 Es	11:6	And I saw how all things under heaven were subjected to him

SUBJECTION   3 = 0.002 %

Sir	47:19	and through your body you were brought into subjection
	48:12	and no one brought him into subjection
Bar	2:4	And he gave them into subjection to all the kingdoms around us

SUBMIT   1

4 Ma	13:12	and the father by whose hand Isaac would have submitted

SUBSTANTIAL   1

2 Ma	4:45	promised a substantial bribe to Ptolemy son of Dorymenes

SUBTLE   1

Wis	7:23	that are intelligent and pure and most subtle

SUBTLETY   1

Sir	39:2	and penetrate the subtleties of parables

SUBURB   2

1 Ma	11:4	and Azotus and its suburbs destroyed
	11:61	So he besieged it and burned its suburbs with fire and plundered them

SUCCEED   8 = 0.005 %

Wis	7:30	for it is succeeded by the night
Sir	48:8	and prophets to succeed you
1 Ma	1:1	he succeeded him as king
2 Ma	4:7	and Antiochus who was called Epiphanes succeeded to the kingdom
	8:35	*having succeeded chiefly in the destruction of his own army !*
	10:11	This man, when he succeeded to the kingdom
	15:5	*Nevertheless, he did not succeed*
4 Ma	4:15	his son Antiochus Epiphanes succeeded to the throne

SUCCESS   12 = 0.008 %

Tob	5:16	and good success to you both
	11:1	praising God because he had made his journey a success
Wis	13:19	for money-making and work and success with his hands
Sir	10:5	The success of a man is in the hands of the Lord
	11:17	and what he approves will have lasting success
	38:13	There is a time when success lies in the hands of physicians
	38:14	that he should grant them success in diagnosis
2 Ma	5:6	not realizing that success at the cost of one's kindred
	8:8	and that he was pushing ahead with more frequent successes
	10:7	who had given success to the purifying of his own holy place

10 : 23	Having success at arms in everything he undertook	
10 : 28	the one having as pledge of success and victory	

SUCCESSFUL 1
Tob 5 : 21 his journey will be successful

SUCCESSION 1
1 Es 1 : 34 and made him king in succession to Josiah his father

SUCCESSOR 3 = 0.002 %
Sir 46 : 1 and was the successor of Moses in prophesying
2 Ma 9 : 23 appointed his successor
14 : 26 Judas, to be his successor

SUCH, indef. pr. or adj. 70 = 0.046 %
Jud 11 : 21 There is not such a woman
12 : 12 For it will be a disgrace if we let such a woman go
Wis 4 : 15 nor take such a thing to heart
11 : 18 or such as breathe out fiery breath
12 : 19 Through such works thou hast taught thy people
12 : 20 For if thou didst punish with such great care and indulgence
14 : 22 and they call such great evils peace
15 : 6 Lovers of evil things and fit for such objects of hope
16 : 1 through such creatures
16 : 9 because they deserved to be punished by such things
Sir 6 : 8 For there is a friend who is such at his own convenience
7 : 35 because for such deeds you will be loved
16 : 5 Many such things my eye has seen
19 : 11 With such a word a fool will suffer pangs
20 : 15 such a one is a hateful man
25 : 20 such is a garrulous wife for a quiet husband
29 : 7 Because of such wickedness, therefore
34 : 8 Without such deceptions the law will be fulfilled
45 : 13 Before his time there never were such beautiful things
P Az 17 such may our sacrifice be in thy sight this day
Sus 13 : 48 Are you such fools, you sons of Israel ?
1 Ma 1 : 51 In such words he wrote to his whole kingdom
3 : 30 He feared that he might not have such funds
4 : 6 but they did not have armour and swords such as they desired
9 : 10 to do such a thing as to flee from them
9 : 27 such as had not been
10 : 16 So he said, Shall we find another such man ?
10 : 73 and such an army in the plain
10 : 89 such as it is the custom to give to the kinsmen of kings
15 : 8 and such future debts shall be cancelled for you
2 Ma 1 : 19 where they took such Precautions
2 : 29 such in my judgment is the case with us
3 : 11 To such an extent the impious Simon had misrepresented the facts
4 : 4 When his hatred progressed to such a degree
4 : 13 There was such an extreme of Hellenization
4 : 30 While such was the state of affairs
6 : 12 Now I urge those who read this book not to be depressed by such calamities
6 : 24 Such pretence is not worthy of our time of life, he said
8 : 7 He found the nights most advantageous for such attacks
9 : 28 such as he had inflicted on others
10 : 4 that they might never again fall into such misfortunes
10 : 9 Such then was the end of Antiochus who was called Epiphanes
13 : 7 By such a fate it came about
1 Es 1 : 21 none of the kings of Israel had kept such a passover
2 : 20 we think it best not to neglect such a matter
2 : 29 and that such wicked proceedings go no further
4 : 32 since they do such things ?
4 : 37 all their works are unrighteous, and all such things
8 : 87 and give us such a root as this
3 Ma 2 : 26 but he also continued with such audacity
3 : 9 for such a great community ought not be left to its fate
4 : 4 For with such a harsh and ruthless spirit
4 : 5 in such a shameful manner
7 : 9 in everything and inescapably as an antagonist to avenge such acts. Farewell
2 Es 1 : 9 on whom I have bestowed such great benefits ?
7 : 80 such spirits shall not enter into habitations
4 Ma 1 : 4 the emotions that hinder one from justice, such as malice
5 : 27 but also to eat in such a way
5 : 28 But you shall have no such occasion to laugh at me
6 : 18 the reputation of such a life
7 : 8 Such should be those who are administrators of the law
8 : 5 and greatly respect the beauty and the number of such brothers
8 : 26 Why does such contentiousness excite us
8 : 26 and such a fatal stubbornness please us
13 : 21 From such embraces brotherly-loving souls are nourished
15 : 17 O woman, who alone gave birth to such complete devotion !
16 : 3 inflamed as she saw her 7 sons tortured in such varied ways
16 : 4 But the mother quenched so many and such great emotions by devout reason
16 : 12 did not wail with such a lament for any of them
16 : 17 while an aged man endures such agonies for the sake of religion

SUCKING 1
Sir 46 : 16 and he offered in sacrifice a sucking lamb

SUD 1
Bar 1 : 4 all who dwelt in Babylon by the river Sud

SUDDEN 4 = 0.003 %
Wis 17 : 15 for sudden and unexpected fear overwhelmed them
2 Ma 14 : 17 because of the sudden consternation created by the enemy
14 : 22 to prevent sudden treachery on the part of the enemy
3 Ma 3 : 24 if a sudden disorder should later arise against us

SUDDENLY 21 = 0.014 %
Wis 14 : 15 who had been suddenly taken from him
Sir 5 : 7 for suddenly the wrath of the Lord will go forth
11 : 21 to enrich a poor man quickly and suddenly
1 Ma 1 : 30 but he suddenly fell upon the city, dealt it a severe blow
3 : 23 he rushed suddenly against Seron and his army
4 : 2 to fall upon the camp of the Jews and attack them suddenly
2 Ma 3 : 27 When he suddenly fell to the ground
5 : 5 and suddenly made an assault upon the city
3 Ma 3 : 8 and the crowds that suddenly were forming
4 : 2 that had suddenly been decreed for them
2 Es 5 : 4 and the sun shall suddenly shine forth at night
6 : 22 Sown places shall suddenly appear unsown
6 : 22 and full storehouses shall suddenly be found to be empty
6 : 23 they shall suddenly be terrified
8 : 14 If then you wilt suddenly and quickly destroy him
10 : 25 her face suddenly shone exceedingly
10 : 26 behold, she suddenly uttered a loud and fearful cry
11 : 20 There were some of them that ruled, yet disappeared suddenly
11 : 26 one was set up, but suddenly disappeared
11 : 33 the middle head also suddenly disappeared
13 : 11 and burned them all up, so that suddenly

SUDIAS 1
1 Es 5 : 26 and Bannas and Sudias, 74

SUE 1
Jud 3 : 1 So they sent messengers to sue for peace, and said

SUFFER 41 = 0.027 %
Jud 8 : 19 and so they suffered a great catastrophe before our enemies
Wis 4 : 19 and they will suffer anguish
14 : 29 they swear wicked oaths and expect to suffer no harm
16 : 3 while thy people, after suffering want a short time
18 : 1 and counted them happy for not having suffered
18 : 11 and the common man suffered the same loss as the king
18 : 19 without knowing why they suffered
19 : 13 for they justly suffered because of their wicked acts
Sir 13 : 3 a poor man suffers wrong, and he must add apologies
14 : 1 and need not suffer grief for sin
19 : 11 With such a word a fool will suffer pangs
28 : 1 He that takes vengeance will suffer vengeance from the Lord
32 : 24 and he who trusts the Lord will not suffer loss
38 : 16 and as one who is suffering grievously begin the lament
41 : 7 for they suffer reproach because of him
1 Ma 5 : 61 Thus the people suffered a great rout
2 Ma 4 : 48 quickly suffered the unjust penalty
6 : 30 but in my soul I am glad to suffer these things
7 : 18 For we are suffering these things on our own account
7 : 32 For we are suffering because of our own sins
9 : 21 I suffered an annoying illness
14 : 42 and suffer outrages unworthy of his noble birth
3 Ma 2 : 2 who are suffering grievously from an impious and profane man
3 : 25 to suffer the sure and shameful death that befits enemies
5 : 33 So Hermon suffered an unexpected and dangerous threat
2 Es 4 : 12 and to suffer and not understand why
5 : 34 for every hour I suffer agonies of heart
7 : 18 have suffered the difficult circumstances
7 : 99 which those who would not give heed shall suffer hereafter
7 : 126 we did not consider what we should suffer after death
7 : 128 that if he is defeated he shall suffer what you have said
10 : 22 our free men have suffered abuse
15 : 59 you shall come and suffer fresh afflictions
4 Ma 4 : 25 though they had known beforehand that they would suffer this
9 : 8 for whom we suffer
9 : 32 but you suffer torture by the threats that come from impiety
10 : 10 are suffering because of our godly training and virtue
15 : 7 and because of the many pains she suffered with each of them
15 : 11 to suffer with them out of love for her children
15 : 16 than even the birth-pangs you suffered for them !
15 : 22 How great and how many torments the mother then suffered

SUFFERING 21 = 0.014 %
Wis 12 : 27 For when in their suffering
19 : 16 afflicted with terrible sufferings
2 Ma 6 : 30 I am enduring terrible sufferings in my body under this beating
7 : 12 for he regarded his sufferings as nothing
7 : 36 For our brothers after enduring a brief suffering

	9:18	But when his sufferings did not in any way abate
	9:28	having endured the most intense suffering
3 Ma	**2**:13	we are crushed with suffering
4 Ma	**1**:9	All of these, by despising sufferings that bring death
	5:23	so that we endure any suffering willingly
	7:8	in sufferings even to death
	7:22	and knows that it is blessed to endure any suffering
	9:8	For we, through this severe suffering and endurance
	11:12	because through these noble sufferings you give us
	11:20	have been summoned to an arena of sufferings for religion
	13:1	Since, then, the 7 brothers despised sufferings even unto death
	14:9	but also bore the sufferings patiently
	15:13	and indomitable suffering by mothers !
	16:19	and therefore you ought to endure any suffering for the sake of God
	18:2	not only of sufferings from within
	18:3	Therefore those who gave over their bodies in suffering

SUFFICE   1
4 Ma **6**:28   and let our punishment suffice for them

SUFFICIENT   3 = 0.002 %
Wis **18**:12   For the living were not sufficient even to bury them
2 Ma **10**:19   a force sufficient to besiege them
2 Es **12**:43   Are not the evils which have befallen us sufficient ?

SUGGEST   1
Tob **6**:10   I will suggest that she be given to you in marriage

SUGGESTION   1
2 Ma **6**:8   At the suggestion of Ptolemy

SUIT, subst.   3 = 0.002 %
Sus **13**:6   *and all who had suits at law came to them*
1 Ma **13**:29   and upon the columns he put suits of armour
      13:29   and beside the suits of armour carved ships

SUIT, verb   3 = 0.002 %
Wis **16**:20   and suited to every taste
     16:21   was changed to suit every one liking
3 Ma **4**:11   and which was well suited to make them an obvious spectacle

SUITABLE   4 = 0.003 %
2 Ma **2**:29   has to consider only what is suitable for its adornment
     3:37   what sort of person would be suitable
     4:32   But Menelaus, thinking he had obtained a suitable opportunity
4 Ma **5**:26   what will be most suitable for our lives

SULLEN   1
3 Ma **6**:20   and he forgot his sullen insolence

SULLENLY   1
3 Ma **5**:34   The king's friends one by one sullenly slipped away

SULPHUR   1
3 Ma **2**:5   You consumed with fire and sulphur

SUM, subst.   3 = 0.002 %
Sir **43**:27   and the sum of our words is : He is the all
     51:28   Get instruction with a large sum of silver
1 Ma **14**:32   He spent great sums of his own money

SUM up   1
2 Es **12**:25   For it is they who shall sum up his wickedness

SUMMARY   1
2 Ma **10**:10   and will give a brief summary

SUMMER   3 = 0.002 %
Sir **50**:8   like a green shoot on Lebanon on a summer day
P Az **45**   Bless the Lord, winter cold and summer heat
2 Es **7**:41   or summer or spring or heat or winter

SUMMON   17 = 0.011 %
Jud **8**:10   to summon Chabris and Charmis, the elders of her city
     14:6   So they summoned Achior from the house of Uzziah
Wis **1**:16   But ungodly men by their words and deeds summoned death
Sus **13**:52   he summoned one of them and said to him
1 Ma **1**:6   So he summoned his most honoured officers
2 Ma **4**:28   the 2 of them were summoned by the king
     8:1   secretly entered the villages and summoned their kinsmen
1 Es **3**:14   Then he sent and summoned all the nobles of Persia and Media
     3:16   So they were summoned, and came in
3 Ma **5**:1   so he summoned Hermon, keeper of the elephants
     5:18   the king summoned Hermon
     5:37   . After summoning Hermon he said in a threatening tone
     6:30   summoned the official in charge of the revenues
4 Ma **8**:4   he smiled at them, and summoned them nearer and said
     8:17   Since the king has summoned

     11:20   have been summoned to an arena of sufferings for religion
     12:2   He summoned him to come nearer

SUMPTUOUS   1
Sir **29**:22   than sumptuous food in another man's house

SUN   37 = 0.024 %
Tob **2**:7   When the sun had set I went
Jud **14**:2   And as soon as morning comes and the sun rises
Ad E **10**:6   and there was light and the sun and abundant water
     11:11   light came, and the sun rose
Wis **2**:4   by the rays of the sun and overcome by its heat
     5:6   and the sun did not rise upon us
     7:29   For she is more beautiful than the sun
     16:27   was melted when simply warmed by a fleeting ray of the sun
     16:28   to make it known that one must rise before the sun
     18:3   and a harmless sun for their glorious wandering
Sir **17**:19   All their works are as the sun before him
     17:31   What is brighter than the sun ?
     23:19   are 10,000 times brighter than the sun
     26:16   Like the sun rising in the heights of the Lord
     33:7   when all the daylight in the year is from the sun ?
     34:16   a shelter from the hot wind and a shade from noonday sun
     42:16   The sun looks down on everything with its light
     43:2   The sun, when it appears
     43:4   but the sun burns the mountains 3 times as much
     46:4   Was not the sun held back by his hand ?
     48:23   In his days the sun went backward
     50:7   like the sun shining upon the temple of the Most High
L Jr **6**:60   For sun and moon and stars, shining and sent forth for service, are obedient
     6:67   or shine like the sun or give light like the moon
P Az **40**   Bless the Lord, sun and moon
1 Ma **6**:39   When the sun shone upon the shields of gold and brass
     10:50   He pressed the battle strongly until the sun set
     12:27   So when the sun set, Jonathan commanded his men to be alert
2 Ma **1**:22   and the sun, which had been clouded over, shone out
1 Es **4**:34   and the sun is swift in its course
3 Ma **4**:15   from the rising of the sun till its setting
     5:26   The rays of the sun were not yet shed abroad
2 Es **5**:4   and the sun shall suddenly shine forth at night
     6:45   On the 4th day thou didst command the brightness of the sun
     7:39   a day that has no sun or moon or stars
     7:97   when it is shown to them how their face is to shine like the sun
     15:20   from the rising sun and from the south

SUNSET   1
Tob **2**:4   I sprang up and removed the body to a place of shelter until sunset

SUPERB   2
Sir **45**:8   He clothed him with superb perfection
     50:11   and clothed himself with superb perfection

SUPERFLUOUS   1
2 Ma **12**:44   it would have been superfluous

SUPERHUMAN   1
2 Ma **9**:8   in his superhuman arrogance

SUPERIOR   3 = 0.002 %
Wis **7**:29   Compared with the light she is found to be superior
Sir **25**:10   But there is no one superior to him who fears the Lord
4 Ma **2**:11   It is superior to love for one's wife

SUPERVISE   1
1 Es **7**:2   supervised the holy work with very great care

SUPERVISION   1
3 Ma **7**:12   so that freely and without royal authority or supervision

SUPPER   1
4 Ma **3**:9   Now all the rest were at supper

SUPPLANT   2
2 Ma **4**:26   So Jason, who after supplanting his own brother
     4:26   was supplanted by another man

SUPPLIANT   1
Sir **4**:4   Do not reject an afflicted suppliant

SUPPLICATION   16 = 0.010 %
Sir **35**:14   He will not ignore the supplication of the fatherless
     39:5   and will make supplication before the Most High
     39:5   and make supplication for his sins
     51:9   And I sent up my supplication from the earth
Bar **2**:14   Hear, O Lord, our prayer and our supplication
     4:20   and put on the sackcloth of my supplication
1 Ma **7**:37   and to be for thy people a house of prayer and supplication
2 Ma **3**:18   to make a general supplication

	8:29	When they had done this, they made common supplication
	9:18	in the form of a supplication
	10:16	after making solemn supplications
	10:25	in supplication to God
3 Ma	1:21	Various were the supplications of those gathered there
	1:23	they resorted to the same posture of supplication as the others
	2:21	having heard the lawful supplication
	5:25	and with most tearful supplication and mournful dirges

SUPPLY, verb 9 = 0.006 %
- Jud 7: and visited the springs that supplied their water
- Wis 16:20 and without their toil thou didst supply them from heaven
- Sir 1:10 and he supplied her to those who love him
- 1:26 and the Lord will supply it for you
- 39:33 and he will supply every need in its hour
- 1 Ma 8:26 they shall not give or supply grain
- 14:10 He supplied the cities with food
- 2 Es 8:10 milk should be supplied
- 9:19 which is supplied both with an unfailing table

SUPPLY, subst. 10 = 0.007 %
- Jud 3:10 in order to assemble all the supplies for his army
- 7:17 and they encamped in the valley and seized the water supply
- 7:18 and their tents and supply trains spread out in great number
- 11:12 Since their food supply is exhausted
- 12:3 Holofernes said to her, If your supply runs out
- 1 Ma 6:6 that the Jews had grown strong from the arms, supplies
- 6:57 We daily grow weaker, our food supply is scant
- 2 Ma 12:14 and on their supply of provisions
- 15:21 and the varied supply of arms
- 1 Es 5:72 cut off their supplies, and hindered their building

SUPPORT, verb 6 = 0.004 %
- Sir 19:21 he angers the one who supports him
- 25:22 when a wife supports her husband
- 1 Ma 2:17 and supported by sons and brothers
- 2:27 and supports the covenant
- 1 Es 8:52 and will support them in every way
- 2 Es 5:45 it might even now be able to support

SUPPORT, subst. 7 = 0.005 %
- Tob 8:6 and gavest him Eve his wife as a helper and support
- Sir 3:31 at the moment of his falling he will find support
- 34:15 To whom does he look ? And who is his support ?
- 34:16 a mighty protection and strong support
- 36:24 a helper fit for him and a pillar of support
- 1 Es 4:54 He wrote also concerning their support and the priests
- 4:55 He wrote that the support for the Levites should be provided

SUPPORTER 2
- 1 Ma 11:39 Now Trypho had formerly been one of Alexander's supporters
- 3 Ma 1:1 where Antiochus's supporters were encamped

SUPPOSE 13 = 0.008 %
- Tob 6:17 and I suppose that you will have children by her
- Jud 14:14 for he supposed that he was sleeping with Judith
- Ad E 16:4 they suppose that they will escape the evil-hating justice
- Wis 13:2 but they supposed that either fire or wind or swift air
- 17:2 For when lawless men supposed
- Sus 13:5 who were supposed to govern the people
- 1 Ma 6:43 and he supposed that the king was upon it
- 2 Ma 6:24 lest many of the young should suppose
- 3 Ma 1:17 supposing that something mysterious was occurring
- 4 Ma 4:13 prayed for him lest King Seleucus suppose
- 5:18 Even if, as you suppose, our law were not truly divine
- 5:19 Therefore do not suppose that it would be a petty sin
- 9:7 do not suppose that you can injure us by torturing us

SUPREMACY 1
- 4 Ma 13:4 The supremacy of the mind over these cannot be overlooked

SUPREME 9 = 0.006 %
- 2 Ma 3:36 of the deeds of the supreme God
- 3 Ma 1:9 he offered sacrifice to the supreme God and made thank-offerings
- 1:16 and entreated the supreme God to aid in the present situation
- 3:11 and not considering the might of the supreme God
- 4:16 and uttering improper words against the supreme God
- 5:25 implored the supreme God to help them again at once
- 7:22 So the supreme God perfectly performed great deeds
- 4 Ma 1:19 Rational judgment is supreme over all of these
- 7:10 O supreme king over the passions, Eleazar !

SUR 1
- Jud 2:28 and those who lived in Sur and Ocina

SURE 8 = 0.005 %
- Jud 2:13 but be sure to carry them out just as I have ordered you
- Wis 7:23 Beneficent, humane, steadfast, sure, free from anxiety
- 18:6 in sure knowledge of the oaths in which they trusted

- Sir 40:25 Gold and silver make the foot stand sure
- 2 Ma 9:27 For I am sure that he will follow my policy
- 3 Ma 3:25 to suffer the sure and shameful death that befits enemies
- 3:26 we are sure that for the remaining time
- 2 Es 8:22 whose word is sure and whose utterances are certain

SURELY 16 = 0.010 %
- Tob 14:8 because what the prophet Jonah said will surely happen
- Jud 1:12 that he would surely take revenge
- 10:19 Surely not a man of them had better be left alive
- 12:14 Surely whatever pleases him I will do at once
- Sir 5:3 For the Lord will surely punish you
- 14:17 for the decree from of old is, You must surely die !
- 48:11 for we also shall surely live
- Bar 2:29 this very great multitude will surely turn into
- 1 Ma 5:40 for he will surely defeat us
- 3 Ma 7:6 that the God of heaven surely defends the Jews
- 2 Es 1:13 Surely it was I who brought you through the sea
- 6:32 because your voice has surely been heard before the Most High
- 11:45 Therefore you will surely disappear, you eagle
- 15:9 I will surely avenge them, says the Lord
- 16:63 Surely he knows your imaginations
- 4 Ma 12:14 Surely they by dying nobly fulfilled their service to God

SURETY 6 = 0.004 %
- Sir 8:13 Do not give surety beyond your means
- 8:13 but if you give surety, be concerned as one who must pay
- 29:14 A good man will be surety for his neighbour
- 29:15 Do not forget all the kindness of your surety
- 29:16 A sinner will overthrow the prosperity of his surety
- 29:18 Being surety has ruined many men who were prosperous

SURETYSHIP 1
- Sir 29:19 The sinner who has fallen into suretyship and pursues gain

SURFACE 2
- Wis 13:14 giving it a coat of red paint and colouring its surface red
- Sir 16:30 with all kinds of living beings he covered its surface

SURLINESS 1
- Sir 41:19 of surliness in receiving and giving

SURNAME 1
- 1 Ma 2:2 He had 5 sons, John surnamed Gaddi

SURPASS 5 = 0.003 %
- Sir 18:17 Indeed, does not a word surpass a good gift ?
- 25:11 The fear of the Lord surpasses everything
- 36:22 and surpasses every human desire
- 43:30 for he will surpass even that
- 3 Ma 6:24 You are committing treason and surpassing tyrants in cruelty

SURPASSING 1
- 2 Ma 4:13 because of the surpassing wickedness of Jason

SURPLUS 1
- Tob 4:16 Give all your surplus to charity

SURPRISE 1
- 1 Ma 12:33 He turned aside to Joppa and took it by surprise

SURRENDER 10 = 0.007 %
- Jud 7:26 Now call them in and surrender the whole city
- 8:9 to surrender the city to the Assyrians after 5 days
- 8:11 promising to surrender the city to our enemies
- 8:33 to surrender the city to our enemies
- Ad E 14:11 O Lord, do not surrender thy sceptre to what has no being
- Wis 17:2 For fear is nothing but surrender of the helps
- 17:15 and now were paralyzed by their souls' surrender
- Sir 23:6 and do not surrender me to a shameless soul
- 1 Ma 8:7 and surrender some of their best provinces
- 3 Ma 6:6 who had voluntarily surrendered their lives to the flames

SURROUND 16 = 0.010 %
- Jud 2:26 He surrounded all the Midianites
- 4:12 They even surrounded the altar with sackcloth
- 7:19 because all their enemies had surrounded them
- 7:20 surrounded them for 34 days
- Wis 19:17 when, surrounded by yawning darkness
- Sir 23:18 Darkness surrounds me, and the walls hide me
- 50:12 and they surrounded him like the trunks of palm trees
- 51:7 They surrounded me on every side
- 1 Ma 6:7 and that they had surrounded the sanctuary
- 10:80 for they surrounded his army and shot arrows at his men
- 13:43 and surrounded it with troops
- 15:14 He surrounded the city
- 2 Ma 10:30 surrounding Maccabeus and protecting him
- 14:41 Being surrounded, Razis fell upon his own sword

2 Es	15 : 44	They shall come to her and surround her
4 Ma	16 : 3	The lions surrounding Daniel were not so savage

SURROUNDING 6 = 0.004 %
Jud	1 : 9	and all who were in Samaria and its surrounding towns
Bar	2 : 4	to be a reproach and a desolation among all the surrounding peoples
1 Ma	1 : 31	and tore down its houses and its surrounding walls
	1 : 54	They also built altars in the surrounding cities of Judah
	7 : 24	So Judas went out into all the surrounding parts of Judea
	10 : 84	But Jonathan burned Azotus and the surrounding towns

SURVIVAL 1
Sir	16 : 3	Do not trust in their survival

SURVIVE 7 = 0.005 %
Sir	23 : 27	Those who survive her will recognize
	26 : 21	So your offspring will survive
	36 : 9	Let him who survives be consumed in the fiery wrath
2 Es	9 : 8	will survive the dangers that have been predicted
	15 : 45	And those who survive shall serve those who have destroyed her
	16 : 22	and those who survive the famine shall die by the sword
4 Ma	6 : 20	It would be shameful if we should survive for a little while

SURVIVING 1
4 Ma	12 : 6	and to influence her to persuade the surviving son

SURVIVOR 2
1 Ma	2 : 44	the survivors fled to the Gentiles for safety
1 Es	1 : 56	The survivors he led away to Babylon with the sword

SUSA 2
Ad E	11 : 3	He was a Jew, dwelling in the city of Susa
	16 : 18	has been hanged at the gate of Susa, with all his household

SUSANNA 10 = 0.007 %
Sus	13 : 2	And he took a wife named Susanna, the daughter of Hilkiah
	13 : 7	Susanna would go into her husband's garden to walk
	13 : 22	Susanna sighed deeply, and said
	13 : 24	Then Susanna cried out with a loud voice
	13 : 27	for nothing like this had ever been said about Susanna
	13 : 28	full of their wicked plot to have Susanna put to death
	13 : 29	Send for Susanna, the daughter of Hilkiah
	13 : 31	Now Susanna was a woman of great refinement
	13 : 42	Then Susanna cried out with a loud voice, and said
	13 : 63	And Hilkiah and his wife praised God for their daughter Susanna

SUSPECT 3 = 0.002 %
Sir	23 : 21	and where he least suspects it, he will be seized
2 Ma	12 : 4	because they wished to live peaceably and suspected nothing
3 Ma	3 : 23	they secretly suspect that we may soon alter our policy

SUSPEND 1
2 Es	16 : 58	and by his word has suspended the earth over the water

SUSPENSE 1
3 Ma	5 : 49	the end of their most miserable suspense

SUSPICION 1
2 Ma	4 : 34	and in spite of his suspicion

SUSPICIOUS 1
2 Ma	7 : 24	and he was suspicious of her reproachful tone

SUSPICIOUSLY 1
Sir	37 : 10	Do not consult with one who looks at you suspiciously

SUSTAIN 1
2 Es	5 : 45	and the creation will sustain them

SUSTENANCE 1
Wis	16 : 21	For thy sustenance manifested thy sweetness toward thy children

SWADDLING 1
Wis	7 : 4	I was nursed with care in swaddling cloths

SWALLOW, subst. 1
L Jr	6 : 22	Bats, swallows, and birds light on their bodies and heads

SWALLOW, verb 1
Tob	6 : 2	and would have swallowed the young man

SWAN 1
4 Ma	15 : 21	Neither the melodies of sirens nor the songs of swans

SWARM, subst. 1
Jud	2 : 20	Along with them went a mixed crowd like a swarm of locusts

SWARM, verb 1
2 Ma	9 : 9	And so the ungodly man's body swarmed with worms

SWAY, verb 1
4 Ma	14 : 20	But sympathy for her children did not sway

SWAY, subst. 2
2 Es	11 : 40	and you have held sway over the world with much terror
	12 : 15	But the 2nd that is to reign shall hold sway

SWEAR 20 = 0.013 %
Tob	9 : 3	For Raguel has sworn that I should not leave
	10 : 7	which Raguel had sworn that he should spend there
Jud	1 : 12	and swore by his throne and kingdom
	8 : 11	you have even sworn
Wis	14 : 29	they swear wicked oaths and expect to suffer no harm
	14 : 30	and because in deceit they swore unrighteously
	14 : 31	For it is not the power of the things by which men swear
Sir	23 : 10	so also the man who always swears
	23 : 11	A man who swears many oaths will be filled with iniquity
	23 : 11	if he has sworn needlessly, he will not be justified
Bar	2 : 34	which I swore to give to their fathers
1 Ma	6 : 62	he broke the oath he had sworn
	7 : 15	and swore this oath to them
	7 : 18	and the oath which they swore
	7 : 35	and in anger he swore this oath
	9 : 71	and he swore to Jonathan
2 Ma	13 : 23	yielded and swore to observe all their rights
	14 : 33	and swore this oath :
1 Es	1 : 48	And though King Nebuchadnezzar had made him swear
3 Ma	5 : 42	and he firmly swore an irrevocable oath

SWEARING 1
Sir	27 : 14	The talk of men given to swearing

SWEAT, subst. 3 = 0.002 %
2 Ma	2 : 26	it is no light matter but calls for sweat and loss of sleep
4 Ma	6 : 11	in fact, with his face bathed in sweat
	7 : 8	shielding it with their own blood and noble sweat

SWEAT, verb 1
4 Ma	3 : 8	he came, sweating and quite exhausted, to the royal tent

SWEEP away 1
2 Ma	5 : 16	and swept away with profane hands

SWEEP on 1
2 Ma	12 : 22	and were swept on, this way and that

SWEET 16 = 0.010 %
Sir	11 : 3	but her product is the best of sweet things
	23 : 17	To a fornicator all bread tastes sweet
	23 : 27	and nothing sweeter than to heed the commandments of the Lord
	24 : 20	For the remembrance of me is sweeter than honey
	24 : 20	and my inheritance sweeter than the honeycomb
	38 : 5	Was not water made sweet with a tree
	40 : 18	Life is sweet for the self-reliant and the worker
	40 : 30	In the mouth of the shameless begging is sweet
	47 : 9	to make sweet melody with their voices
	49 : 1	it is sweet as honey to every mouth
	50 : 18	in sweet and full-toned melody
2 Ma	15 : 39	while wine mixed with water is sweet and delicious
1 Es	9 : 51	so go your way, eat the fat and drink the sweet
2 Es	1 : 23	but threw a tree into the water and made the stream sweet
	5 : 9	And salt waters shall be found in the sweet
4 Ma	9 : 29	How sweet is any kind of death for the religion of our fathers !

SWEETLY 1
Sir	12 : 16	An enemy will speak sweetly with his lips

SWEETNESS 2
Wis	16 : 21	For thy sustenance manifested thy sweetness toward thy children
Sir	27 : 23	In your presence his mouth is all sweetness

SWEET-SMELLING 1
Sir	38 : 11	Offer a sweet-smelling sacrifice

SWIFT 7 = 0.005 %
Wis	13 : 2	but they supposed that either fire or wind or swift air
	18 : 14	and night in its swift course was now half gone
1 Es	4 : 34	and the sun is swift in its course
3 Ma	4 : 5	forced to march at a swift pace
2 Es	1 : 26	and your feet are swift to commit murder
	12 : 20	whose times shall be short and their years swift
4 Ma	14 : 10	For the power of fire is intense and swift

SWIFTLY 4 = 0.003 %
Wis	6 : 5	he will come upon you terribly and swiftly
Sir	18 : 26	and all things move swiftly before the Lord

2 Es 4:26 because the age is hastening swiftly to its end
4 Ma 10:21 God will visit you swiftly, for you are cutting out

SWIFTNESS 1
2 Es 8:18 and I have heard of the swiftness of the judgment that is to come

SWIM 2
Wis 19:19 and creatures that swim moved over to the land
1 Ma 9:48 and swam across to the other side

SWINE 3 = 0.002 %
1 Ma 1:47 to sacrifice swine and unclean animals
2 Ma 6:18 was being forced to open his mouth to eat swine's flesh
7:1 to partake of unlawful swine's flesh

SWORD 69 = 0.045 %
Jud 1:12 that he would kill by the sword
2:27 with the edge of the sword
6:6 Then the sword of my army
7:14 and before the sword reaches them
8:19 and that was why our fathers were handed over to the sword
9:2 to whom thou gavest a sword
9:8 and to cast down the horn of thy altar with the sword
11:10 nor can the sword prevail against them
13:6 and took down his sword that hung there
16:5 and kill my young men with the sword
16:9 and the sword severed his neck
Ad E 13:6 be utterly destroyed by the sword of their enemies
Wis 5:20 and sharpen stern wrath for a sword
18:16 carrying the sharp sword of thy authentic command
Sir 21:3 All lawlessness is like a two-edged sword
22:21 Even if you have drawn your sword against a friend
26:28 the Lord will prepare him for the sword !
28:18 Many have fallen by the edge of the sword
39:30 and the sword that punishes the ungodly with destruction
40:9 are death and bloodshed and strife and sword
46:2 and stretched out his sword against the cities !
Bar 2:25 by famine and sword and pestilence
Sus 13:59 for the angel of God is waiting with his sword to saw you in 2
Bel 14:26 I will slay the dragon without sword or club
1 Ma 2:9 her youths by the sword of the foe
3:3 protecting the host by his sword
3:12 and Judas took the sword of Apollonius
4:6 but they did not have armour and swords such as they desired
4:15 and all those in the rear fell by the sword
4:33 Strike them down with the sword of those who love thee
5:28 and killed every male by the edge of the sword
5:51 He destroyed every male by the edge of the sword
7:38 and let them fall by the sword
7:46 so that they all fell by the sword
8:23 and may sword and enemy be far from them
9:73 Thus the sword ceased from Israel
10:85 The number of those who fell by the sword
12:48 and all who had entered with him they killed with the sword
2 Ma 5:2 in companies fully armed with lances and drawn swords
5:26 He put to the sword all those who came out to see them
12:22 and pierced by the points of their swords
12:23 putting the sinners to the sword
14:41 Being surrounded, Razis fell upon his own sword
15:15 and gave to Judas a golden sword
15:16 Take this holy sword, a gift from God
1 Es 1:53 These slew their young men with the sword around their holy temple
1:56 The survivors he led away to Babylon with the sword
3:22 and before long they draw their swords
4:23 A man takes his sword, and goes out to travel
8:77 to the sword and captivity and plundering
Ps 151:7 But I drew his own sword
2 Es 12:27 the sword shall devour them
12:28 For the sword of one shall devour him who was with him
12:28 but he also shall fall by the sword in the last days
15:5 the sword and famine and death and destruction
15:15 For the sword and misery draw near them
15:15 with swords in their hands
15:19 but shall make an assault upon their houses with the sword
15:22 and my sword will not cease from those who shed innocent blood on the earth
15:35 and there shall be blood from the sword
15:41 fire and hail and flying swords and floods of water
15:49 famine, sword, and pestilence
15:57 and you shall fall by the sword
15:57 shall fall by the sword
16:3 The sword has been sent upon you
16:21 the sword, famine, and great confusion
16:22 and those who survive the famine shall die by the sword
16:31 by those who search their houses with the sword
4 Ma 16:20 wielding a sword and descending upon him

SWORN 1
2 Ma 4:34 offered him sworn pledges and gave him his right hand

SYMBOL 2
Sir 45:8 and strengthened him with the symbols of authority
3 Ma 2:29 with the ivy-leaf symbol of Dionysus

SYMBOLIZE 3 = 0.002 %
2 Es 13:37 this was symbolized by the storm
13:38 which were symbolized by the flames
13:38 which was symbolized by the fire

SYMPATHETIC 1
4 Ma 13:23 the brothers were the more sympathetic to one another

SYMPATHY 8 = 0.005 %
4 Ma 5:25 has shown sympathy toward us
6:13 partly out of sympathy from their acquaintance with him
13:23 Therefore, when sympathy and brotherly affection had been so established
14:14 have a sympathy and parental love for their offspring
14:18 And why is it necessary to demonstrate sympathy for children
14:20 But sympathy for her children did not sway
15:4 have a deeper sympathy toward their offspring than do the fathers
15:7 she had sympathy for them

SYRIA 15 = 0.010 %
Jud 1:12 on the whole territory of Cilicia and Damascus and Syria
8:26 and what happened to Jacob in Mesopotamia in Syria
1 Ma 3:41 And forces from Syria
11:2 He set out for Syria with peaceable words
11:60 and all the army of Syria gathered to him as allies
1 Es 2:25 and Syria and Phoenicia, wrote as follows :
6:3 At the same time Sisinnes the governor of Syria and Phoenicia
6:7 which Sisinnes the governor of Syria and Phoenicia
6:7 the local rulers in Syria and Phoenicia
6:27 the governor of Syria and Phoenicia
6:27 in Syria and Phoenicia
8:19 have commanded the treasurers of Syria and Phoenicia
8:23 throughout all Syria and Phoenicia
2 Es 16:1 Woe to you, Egypt and Syria !
4 Ma 4:2 governor of Syria, Phoenicia, and Cilicia

SYRIAN 3 = 0.002 %
1 Ma 3:13 Now when Seron, the commander of the Syrian army
7:39 and the Syrian army joined him
2 Ma 15:36 which is called Adar in the Syrian language

T

TABBAOTH 1
1 Es 5:29 the sons of Hasupha, the sons of Tabbaoth

TABEEL 1
1 Es 2:16 Bishlam, Mithridates, Tabeel, Rehum, Beltethmus

TABERNACLE 4 = 0.003 %
Jud 9:8 and to pollute the tabernacle where thy glorious name rests
Sir 24:10 In the holy tabernacle I ministered before him
24:15 and like the fragrance of frankincense in the tabernacle
1 Ma 10:21 at the feast of tabernacles

TABLE 16 = 0.010 %
Jud 12:1 and ordered them to set a table for her
Ad E 14:17 And thy servant has not eaten at Haman's table
Sir 6:10 And there is a friend who is a table companion
14:10 and it is lacking at his table
29:26 Come here, stranger, prepare the table
31:12 Are you seated at the table of a great man ?
40:29 When a man looks to the table of another
Bel 14:13 for beneath the table they had made a hidden entrance
14:18 the king looked at the table, and shouted in a loud voice
14:21 and devour what was on the table
1 Ma 1:22 He took also the table for the bread of the Presence
4:49 the altar of incense, and the table into the temple
4:51 They placed the bread on the table and hung up the curtains
11:58 And he sent him gold plate and a table service
3 Ma 5:39 But the officials who were at table with him
2 Es 9:19 which is supplied both with an unfailing table

TABLET 5 = 0.003 %
1 Ma 8:22 which they wrote in reply, on bronze tablets
14:18 they wrote to him on bronze tablets
14:27 So they made a record on bronze tablets
14:48 to inscribe this decree upon bronze tablets
2 Es 14:24 But prepare for yourself many writing tablets

TAHPANNES   1

Jud   1:9   and Tahpannes and Raamses and the whole land of Goshen

TAKE*   325 = 0.212 %

Tob	1:2	was taken into captivity from Thisbe
	1:6	Taking the first fruits and the tithes of my produce
	2:10	Ahikar, however, took care of me until he went to Elymais
	3:15	But if it be not pleasing to thee to take my life
	3:15	and pity be taken upon me, and that I hear reproach no more
	4:12	First of all take a wife
	4:12	all took wives from among their brethren
	4:13	by refusing to take a wife for yourself from among them
	6:4	Cut open the fish and take the heart and liver and gall
	6:15	to take a wife from among your own people ?
	6:16	you shall take live ashes of incense
	7:10	for it is your right to take my child
	7:12	So Raguel said, Take her right now
	7:13	and taking her by the hand
	7:13	take her according to the law of Moses
	7:13	and take her with you to your father
	7:14	and took a scroll and wrote out the contract
	7:16	Sister, make up the other room, and take her into it
	7:17	So she did as he said, and took her there
	8:2	and he took the live ashes of incense
	8:7	I am not taking this sister of mine because of lust, but with sincerity
	8:21	that then he should take half of Raguel's property
	9:2	Brother Azarias, take a servant and 2 camels with you
	11:4	And take the gall of the fish with you
	11:11	and took hold of his father
	12:5	Take half of all that you 2 have brought back
	14:3	and said to him, My son, take your sons
Jud	1:12	that he would surely take revenge
	1:14	Thus he took possession of his cities
	2:5	take with you men confident in their strength
	2:13	And you – take care not to transgress
	2:22	From there Holofernes took his whole army
	3:6	and took picked men from them as his allies
	5:11	he took advantage of them and set them to making bricks
	5:15	they took possession of all the hill country
	6:5	until I take revenge on this race that came out of Egypt
	6:9	If you really hope in your heart that they will not be taken
	6:10	to seize Achior and take him to Bethulia
	6:11	So the slaves took him
	6:17	He answered and told them what had taken place
	6:21	And Uzziah took him from the assembly to his own house
	7:12	only let your servants take possession
	8:3	and took to his bed and died in Bethulia his city
	8:27	nor has he taken revenge upon us
	8:30	and made us take an oath which we cannot break
	8:35	to take revenge upon our enemies
	9:2	to take revenge on the strangers
	10:12	and took her into custody, and asked her
	11:1	Take courage, woman, and do not be afraid in your heart
	12:19	Then she took and ate and drank before him
	13:7	and took hold of the hair of his head, and said
	13:15	Then she took the head out of the bag and showed it to them
	14:1	and take this head and hang it upon the parapet of your wall
	14:2	let every valiant man take his weapons and go out of the city
	14:11	and every man took his weapons
	15:3	also took to flight
	15:4	to tell what had taken place and to urge all
	15:7	took possession of what remained
	15:11	and she took them and loaded her mule
	15:12	and she took branches in her hands
	16:5	and take my virgins as booty
	16:17	The Lord Almighty will take vengeance on them
	16:19	and the canopy which she took for herself from his bedchamber
Ad E	12:1	Now Mordecai took his rest in the courtyard
	14:5	that thou, O Lord, didst take Israel out of all the nations
	15:2	she took her 2 maids with her
	15:8	and took her in his arms until she came to herself
	15:9	I am your brother. Take courage
	16:8	For the future we will take care to render our kingdom
Wis	2:7	Let us take our fill of costly wine and perfumes
	4:3	will strike a deep root or take a firm hold
	4:14	therefore he took him quickly from the midst of wickedness
	4:15	nor take such a thing to heart
	5:7	We took our fill of the paths of lawlessness and destruction
	5:15	the Most High takes care of them
	5:17	The Lord will take his zeal as his whole armour
	5:19	he will take holiness as an invincible shield
	6:7	and he takes thought for all alike
	8:2	and I desired to take her for my bride
	8:9	Therefore I determined to take her to live with me
	13:13	he takes and carves with care in his leisure
	13:16	So he takes thought for it, that it may not fall
	13:18	for a prosperous journey, a thing that cannot take a step
	14:6	the hope of the world took refuge on a raft
	14:15	who had been suddenly taken from him

	14:19	skilfully forced the likeness to take more beautiful form
	15:8	from which he was taken
	16:21	and the bread, ministering to the desire of the one who took it
	19:18	from the sight of what took place
Sir	3:28	for a plant of wickedness has taken root in him
	11:16	evil will grow old with those who take pride in malice
	12:12	and take your place
	12:12	lest he try to take your seat of honour
	13:8	Take care not to be led astray
	14:16	Give, and take and beguile yourself
	18:19	and before you fall ill, take care of your health
	18:31	If you allow your soul to take pleasure in base desire
	19:17	and let the law of the Most High take its course
	19:22	nor is there prudence where sinners take counsel
	23:18	The Most High will not take notice of my sins
	23:25	Her children will not take root
	24:12	So I took root in an honoured people
	25:1	My soul takes pleasure in 3 things
	25:18	Her husband takes his meals among the neighbours
	26:7	taking hold of her is like grasping a scorpion
	28:1	He that takes vengeance will suffer vengeance from the Lord
	29:20	but take heed to yourself lest you fall
	30:13	Discipline your son and take pains with him
	31:7	and every fool will be taken captive by it
	32:1	take good care of them and then be seated
	32:2	when you have fulfilled your duties, take your place
	33:20	do not let any one take your place
	36:18	The stomach will take any food
	37:8	for he will take thought for himself
	44:17	in the time of wrath he was taken in exchange
	44:20	and was taken into covenant with him
	46:1	to take vengeance on the enemies that rose against them
	46:19	and his anointed : I have not taken any one property
Bar	1:2	at the time when the Chaldeans took Jerusalem
	1:8	Baruch took the vessels of the house of the Lord
	2:17	whose spirit has been taken from their bodies
	3:29	Who has gone up into heaven, and taken her
	4:2	Turn, O Jacob, and take her
	4:5	Take courage, my people, O memorial of Israel !
	4:21	Take courage, my children, cry to God
	4:27	Take courage, my children, and cry to God
	4:30	Take courage, O Jerusalem
L Jr	6:1	to those who were to be taken to Babylon as captives
	6:2	you will be taken to Babylon as captives
	6:5	So take care not to become at all like the foreigners
	6:9	People take gold and make crowns for the heads of their gods
	6:10	and sometimes the priests secretly take gold and silver from their gods
	6:33	The priests take some of the clothing of their gods
	6:38	They cannot take pity on a widow
Sus	13:2	And he took a wife named Susanna, the daughter of Hilkiah
	13:48	Taking his stand in the midst of them, he said
Bel	14:27	Then Daniel took pitch, fat, and hair
	14:33	and was going into the field to take it to the reapers
	14:34	Take the dinner which you have to Babylon
	14:36	Then the angel of the Lord took him by the crown of his head
	14:37	Take the dinner which God has sent you
1 Ma	1:21	and took the golden altar
	1:22	He took also the table for the bread of the Presence
	1:23	He took the silver and the gold, and the costly vessels
	1:23	he took also the hidden treasures which he found
	1:24	he took them all, he departed to his own land
	1:32	And they took captive the women and children
	3:1	took command in his place
	3:12	and Judas took the sword of Apollonius
	3:15	to take vengeance on the sons of Israel
	3:33	Lysias was also to take care of Antiochus his son
	3:37	Then the king took the remaining half of his troops
	3:41	they took silver and gold in immense amounts, and fetters
	3:45	Joy was taken from Jacob
	3:50	Where shall we take them ?
	4:1	Now Gorgias took 5,000 infantry and a 1,000 picked cavalry
	4:47	Then they took unhewn stones, as the law directs
	5:8	He also took Jazer and its villages
	5:19	and he gave them this command, Take charge of this people
	5:23	Then he took the Jews of Galilee and Arbatta
	5:27	take and destroy all these men in one day
	5:28	and he took the city
	5:35	and fought against it and took it
	5:36	From there he marched on and took Chaspho
	5:44	But he took the city
	6:3	So he came and tried to take the city and plunder it
	6:6	and abundant spoils which they had taken
	6:8	He took to his bed and became sick from grief
	6:26	against the citadel in Jerusalem to take it
	6:33	and took his army by a forced march
	6:36	These took their position beforehand wherever the beast was
	6:50	So the king took Beth-zur
	6:63	but he fought against him, and took the city by force
	7:4	and Demetrius took his seat upon the throne of his kingdom

7 : 9	and he commanded him to take vengeance on the sons of Israel
7 : 24	and took vengeance on the men who had deserted
7 : 38	Take vengeance on this man and on his army
8 : 7	they took him alive
8 : 8	These they took from him and gave to Eumenes the king
8 : 10	and the Romans took captive their wives and children
9 : 2	and they took it and killed many people
9 : 11	and took its stand for the encounter
9 : 19	Then Jonathan and Simon took Judas their brother
9 : 26	and he took vengeance on them and made sport of them
9 : 30	So now we have chosen you today to take his place
9 : 31	and took the place of Judas his brother
9 : 40	and they took all their goods
9 : 53	And he took the sons of the leading men of the land
9 : 72	whom he had formerly taken from the land of Judah
10 : 20	and you are to take our side and keep friendship with us
10 : 33	And every one of the Jews taken as a captive
10 : 43	And whoever takes refuge at the temple in Jerusalem
10 : 52	and have taken my seat on the throne of my fathers
10 : 53	and we have taken our seat on the throne of his kingdom
10 : 55	and took your seat on the throne of their kingdom
10 : 84	and those who had taken refuge in it he burned with fire
11 : 24	taking silver and gold and clothing and numerous other gifts
11 : 37	Now therefore take care to make a copy of this
11 : 62	and took the sons of their rulers as hostages
11 : 66	He removed them from there, took possession of the city
12 : 33	He turned aside to Joppa and took it by surprise
13 : 25	And Simon sent and took the bones of Jonathan his brother
14 : 2	he sent one of his commanders to take him alive
14 : 3	and seized him and took him to Arsaces
14 : 5	To crown all his honours he took Joppa for a harbour
14 : 42	and that he should take charge of the sanctuary
15 : 29	and you have taken possession of many places in my kingdom
15 : 33	We have neither taken foreign land
15 : 33	which at one time had been unjustly taken by our enemies
15 : 40	and take the people captive and kill them
16 : 3	Take my place and my brother's
16 : 16	Ptolemy and his men rose up, took their weapons
16 : 20	and he sent other men to take possession of Jerusalem
2 Ma 1 : 11	we thank him greatly for taking our side against the king
1 : 19	took some of the fire of the altar
1 : 19	where they took such Precautions
2 : 1	to take some of the fire, as has been told
2 : 30	and to take trouble with details
4 : 14	they hastened to take part in the unlawful proceedings
4 : 21	and he took measures for his own security
4 : 34	Therefore Menelaus, taking Andronicus aside
4 : 41	and others took handfuls of the ashes that were lying about
4 : 46	Therefore Ptolemy, taking the king aside into a colonnade
5 : 5	Jason took no less than a 1,000 men
5 : 5	and at last the city was being taken
5 : 5	Menelaus took refuge in the citadel
5 : 11	he took it to mean that Judea was in revolt
5 : 11	and took the city by storm
5 : 16	He took the holy vessels with his polluted hands
6 : 7	the Jews were taken, under bitter constraint
6 : 15	in order that he may not take vengeance on us afterward
6 : 21	Those who were in charge of that unlawful sacrifice took the man aside
7 : 5	the king ordered them to take him to the fire, still breathing
7 : 24	and that he would take him for his friend
7 : 27	and have taken care of you
8 : 20	that took place in Babylonia
8 : 20	destroyed 120,000 and took much booty
9 : 21	and I have deemed it necessary to take thought
9 : 29	And Philip, one of his courtiers, took his body home
10 : 5	the purification of the sanctuary took place
10 : 10	Now we will tell what took place under Antiochus Eupator
10 : 12	took the lead in showing justice to the Jews
10 : 13	he took poison and ended his life
10 : 18	took refuge in 2 very strong towers
10 : 24	He came on, intending to take Judea by storm
11 : 4	He took no account whatever of the power of God
12 : 6	and massacred those who had taken refuge there
12 : 16	They took the city by the will of God
12 : 27	Stalwart young men took their stand before the walls
12 : 35	wishing to take the accursed man alive
12 : 43	taking account of the resurrection
13 : 4	he ordered them to take him to Beroea
13 : 26	Lysias took the public platform
14 : 2	and had taken possession of the country
14 : 9	deign to take thought for our country
14 : 26	he took the covenant that had been made
14 : 46	took them with both hands and hurled them at the crowd
15 : 16	Take this holy sword, a gift from God
1 Es 1 : 10	And this is what took place
1 : 30	And immediately his servants took him out of the line of battle
1 : 34	And the men of the nation took Jeconiah the son of Josiah
1 : 41	Nebuchadnezzar also took some of the holy vessels of the Lord
1 : 54	and the royal stores, they took and carried away to Babylon

2 : 28	and to take care that nothing more be done
3 : 13	they took the writing and gave it to him, and he read it
3 : 15	and he took his seat in the council chamber
4 : 5	whatever spoil they take and everything else
4 : 23	A man takes his sword, and goes out to travel
4 : 30	and take the crown from the king's head and put it on her own
4 : 44	and to send back all the vessels that were taken from Jerusalem
4 : 61	So he took the letters
5 : 48	took their places and prepared the altar of the God of Israel
6 : 18	which Nebuchadnezzar had taken out of the house in Jerusalem
6 : 26	which Nebuchadnezzar took out of the house in Jerusalem
6 : 32	a beam should be taken out of his house
8 : 19	they shall take care to give him
8 : 60	who took the silver and the gold
8 : 83	The land which you are entering to take possession of it
8 : 84	and do not take their daughters for your sons
8 : 93	Let us take an oath to the Lord about this
8 : 95	Arise and take action, for it is your task
8 : 95	and we are with you to take strong measures
8 : 96	and Levites of all Israel take oath
8 : 96	And they took the oath
Ps 151 : 4	and took me from my father's sheep
3 Ma 1 : 1	took with him his sister Arsinoe
1 : 2	took with him the best of the Ptolemaic arms
1 : 5	and many captives also were taken
1 : 14	to take this as a sign in itself
1 : 23	They shouted to their fellows to take arms
1 : 26	But he, in his arrogance, took heed of nothing
2 : 28	Those who object to this are to be taken by force and put to death
3 : 10	had taken some of them aside privately
3 : 14	When our expedition took place in Asia
3 : 22	they took this in a contrary spirit
3 : 24	we have taken Precautions lest
4 : 17	that they were no longer able to take the census of the Jews
5 : 42	took no account of the changes of mind
6 : 25	Who is it that has taken each man from his home
7 : 6	always taking their part as a father does for his children
7 : 7	and since we have taken into account
2 Es 1 : 32	but you have taken and slain them
2 : 40	Take again your full number, O Zion
8 : 41	and not all that were planted will take root
9 : 47	So when he grew up and I came to take a wife for him
12 : 46	Take courage, O Israel
13 : 40	he took them across the river
13 : 40	and they were taken into another land
14 : 24	and take with you Sarea, Dabria, Selemia, Ethanus, and Asiel
14 : 32	in due time he took from you what he had given
14 : 37	So I took the 5 men, as he commanded me
14 : 40	And I took it and drank
16 : 46	and take their children captive
4 Ma 2 : 12	It takes precedence over love for children
3 : 12	and taking a pitcher climbed over the enemy's ramparts
6 : 29	and take my life in exchange for theirs
8 : 10	Therefore take pity on yourselves
8 : 18	why do we take pleasure in vain resolves
8 : 20	Let us take pity on our youth
8 : 24	nor take hollow pride in being put to the rack
9 : 7	and if you take our lives because of our religion
9 : 24	and take vengeance on the accursed tyrant
12 : 18	but on you he will take vengeance
17 : 4	Take courage, therefore, O holy-minded mother

TAKE away   19 = 0.012 %

Ad E 16 : 4	They not only take away thankfulness from among men
Wis 18 : 5	take away a multitude of their children
Sir 34 : 22	To take away a neighbour's living is to murder him
35 : 18	till he takes away the multitude of the insolent
38 : 7	By them he heals and takes away pain
41 : 21	of taking away some one's portion or gift
42 : 21	Nothing can be added or taken away
47 : 4	and take away reproach from the people
47 : 11	The Lord took away his sins, and exalted his power for ever
49 : 2	and took away the abominations of iniquity
Bar 4 : 26	they were taken away like a flock carried off by the enemy
4 : 34	And I will take away her pride in her great population
1 Ma 2 : 11	All her adornment has been taken away
11 : 12	So he took his daughter away from him
1 Es 1 : 30	Take me away from the battle, for I am very weak
1 : 40	and took him away to Babylon
2 Es 3 : 20	Yet thou didst not take away from them their evil heart
7 : 135	and bountiful, because he would rather give than take away
8 : 13	Thou wilt take away his life, for he is thy creation

TAKE back   4 = 0.003 %

Jud 6 : 7	Now my slaves are going to take you back
1 Es 5 : 2	to take them back to Jerusalem in safety
6 : 19	with the command that he should take all these vessels back
2 Es 2 : 11	Moreover, I will take back to myself their glory

TAKE down   1
Jud 13 : 6   and took down his sword that hung there

TAKE in   1
Sir 42 : 7   and make a record of all that you give out or take in

TAKE off   8 = 0.005 %
Jud 10 : 3   and took off her widow's garments
     16 : 8   For she took off her widow's mourning
Ad E 14 : 2   she took off her splendid apparel
     15 : 1   she took off the garments in which she had worshipped
Bar   4 : 20   I have taken off the robe of peace
      5 : 1   Take off the garment of your sorrow and affliction, O Jerusalem
1 Ma 10 : 62   The king gave orders to take off Jonathan's garments
2 Ma   8 : 35   took off his splendid uniform

TAKE out   2
2 Ma 12 : 4   the men of Joppa took them out to sea and drowned them
1 Es   6 : 18   these Cyrus the king took out again

TAKE up   20 = 0.013 %
Tob   3 : 6   command my spirit to be taken up
Jud   7 : 5   Then each man took up his weapons
Wis   4 : 10   and while living among sinners he was taken up
Sir 37 : 5   and in the face of battle take up the shield
     44 : 16   Enoch pleased the Lord, and was taken up
     48 : 9   You who were taken up by a whirlwind of fire
     49 : 14   for he was taken up from the earth
1 Ma   1 : 27   Every bridegroom took up the lament
      2 : 58   was taken up into heaven
2 Ma   3 : 27   his men took him up and put him on a stretcher and carried him away
     10 : 27   And rising from their prayer they took up their arms
     11 : 7   Maccabeus himself was the first to take up arms
     12 : 39   Judas and his men went to take up the bodies of the fallen
     12 : 43   He also took up a collection, man by man
     15 : 5   and I command you to take up arms
1 Es   9 : 45   Then Ezra took up the book of the law
3 Ma   6 : 32   and took up the song of their fathers
2 Es   6 : 26   And they shall see the men who were taken up
      8 : 19   before he was taken up
     14 : 9   for you shall be taken up from among men

TALE   2
Sir 22 : 6   Like music in mourning is a tale told at the wrong time
Sus 13 : 27   And when the elders told their tale

TALENT   24 = 0.016 %
Tob   1 : 14   and once at Rages in Media I left 10 talents of silver
      4 : 20   And now let me explain to you about the 10 talents of silver
1 Ma 11 : 28   and promised him 300 talents
     13 : 16   Send now a 100 talents of silver
     13 : 19   So he sent the sons and the 100 talents
     15 : 31   or else give me for them 500 talents of silver
     15 : 31   and the tribute money of the cities, 500 talents more
     15 : 35   for them we will give a 100 talents
2 Ma   3 : 11   and that it totalled in all 400 talents of silver and 200 of gold
      4 : 8   promising the king at an interview 360 talents of silver
      4 : 8   and, from another source of revenue, 80 talents
      4 : 24   outbidding Jason by 300 talents of silver
      5 : 21   So Antiochus carried off 1,800 talents from the temple
      8 : 10   the tribute due to the Romans, 2,000 talents
      8 : 11   and promising to hand over 90 slaves for a talent
1 Es   1 : 36   and fined the nation a 100 talents of silver
      1 : 36   and one talent of gold
      4 : 51   that 20 talents a year should be given
      4 : 52   and an additional 10 talents a year
      8 : 20   up to a 100 talents of silver
      8 : 56   I weighed and gave to them 650 talents of silver
      8 : 56   and silver vessels worth a 100 talents
      8 : 56   and a 100 talents of gold
4 Ma   4 : 17   he would pay the king 3,660 talents annually

TALK, verb   9 = 0.006 %
Tob   7 : 8   speak of those things which you talked about on the journey
Sir 22 : 13   Do not talk much with a foolish man
1 Ma   3 : 26   and the Gentiles talked of the battles of Judas
     14 : 9   they all talked together of good things
1 Es   3 : 21   and makes every one talk in millions
2 Es   5 : 15   But the angel who had come and talked with me held me
      9 : 25   then I will come and talk with you
     10 : 25   While I was talking to her, behold
     15 : 53   and talking about their death when you were drunk ?

TALK, subst.   10 = 0.007 %
Jud   2 : 1   there was talk in the palace of Nebuchadnezzar
Sir 13 : 11   for he will test you through much talk
     21 : 18   and the knowledge of the ignorant is unexamined talk
     27 : 11   The talk of the godly man is always wise
     27 : 13   The talk of fool is offensive
     27 : 14   The talk of men given to swearing
     32 : 4   Where there is entertainment, do not pour out talk
     38 : 25   and whose talk is about bulls ?
2 Ma   8 : 7   And talk of his valour spread everywhere
3 Ma   3 : 6   which was common talk among all

TALKATIVE   1
Sir 20 : 5   while another is detested for being too talkative

TALL   7 = 0.005 %
Jud 16 : 7   nor did tall giants set upon him
Sir 24 : 13   I grew tall like a cedar in Lebanon
     24 : 14   I grew tall like a palm tree in En-gedi
     24 : 14   and like a plane tree I grew tall
1 Ma   6 : 43   It was taller than all the others
Ps 151 : 5   My brothers were handsome and tall
2 Es   2 : 43   taller than any of the others

TALMON   1
1 Es   5 : 28   the sons of Ater, the sons of Talmon

TALON   2
2 Es 11 : 7   And I looked, and behold, the eagle rose upon his talons
     11 : 45   and your malicious heads, and your most evil talons

TAMBOURINE   3 = 0.002 %
Jud   3 : 7   welcomed him with garlands and dances and tambourines
     16 : 2   And Judith said, Begin a song to my God with tambourines
1 Ma   9 : 39   to meet them with tambourines and musicians and many weapons

TAME, adj.   1
4 Ma 14 : 15   For example, among birds, the ones that are tame

TAME, verb   1
4 Ma   1 : 29   and so tames the jungle of habits and emotions

TANGLED   1
Ad E 14 : 2   she covered with her tangled hair

TANIS   1
Jud   1 : 10   even beyond Tanis and Memphis, and all who lived in Egypt

TARGET   2
Wis   5 : 12   or as, when an arrow is shot at a target
      5 : 21   and will leap to the target

TARNISHED   1
Sir 12 : 11   and you will know that it was not hopelessly tarnished

TARSUS   2
2 Ma   3 : 5   he went to Apollonius of Tarsus
      4 : 30   it happened that the people of Tarsus and of Mallus

TASK   7 = 0.005 %
Sir   3 : 17   My son, perform your tasks in meekness
      3 : 23   Do not meddle in what is beyond your tasks
      7 : 25   you will have finished a great task
     37 : 11   with a lazy servant about a big task
1 Ma 14 : 42   and appoint men over its tasks
1 Es   8 : 95   Arise and take action, for it is your task
3 Ma   4 : 18   the task was impossible for all the generals in Egypt

TASTE, subst.   3 = 0.002 %
Wis 16 : 20   and suited to every taste
2 Ma 13 : 18   The king, having had a taste of the daring of the Jews
2 Es   6 : 44   and of varied appeal to the taste

TASTE, verb   7 = 0.005 %
Tob   2 : 4   So before I tasted anything
Sir 23 : 17   To a fornicator all bread tastes sweet
     36 : 19   As the palate tastes the kinds of game
2 Ma   6 : 20   that it is not right to taste
2 Es   6 : 26   who from their birth have not tasted death
      9 : 24   and taste no meat and drink no wine, but eat only flowers
4 Ma 10 : 1   to save himself by tasting the meat

TAX, subst.   12 = 0.008 %
1 Ma 10 : 29   from payment of tribute and salt tax and crown levies
     10 : 31   be holy and free from tax
     10 : 33   and let all officials cancel also the taxes on their cattle
     11 : 34   we have granted release from the royal taxes
     11 : 35   and the taxes due to us
     11 : 35   and the salt pits and the crown taxes due to us
     13 : 39   and cancel the crown tax which you owe
     13 : 39   and whatever other tax has been collected in Jerusalem
     15 : 5   now therefore I confirm to you all the tax remissions
1 Es   4 : 6   and they compel one another to pay taxes to the king

8 : 22   or any other tax is to be laid
8 : 22   and that no one has authority to impose any tax upon them

TEACH   29 = 0.019 %
Wis 6 : 10   and those who have been taught them will find a defence
     7 : 22   for wisdom, the fashioner of all things, taught me
     8 : 7   for she teaches self-control and prudence, justice and courage
     9 : 18   and men were taught what pleases thee
    12 : 19   Through such works thou hast taught thy people
Sir 6 : 32   If you are willing, my son, you will be taught
     9 : 1   and do not teach her an evil lesson to your own hurt
    18 : 13   He rebukes and trains and teaches them
    21 : 12   He who is not clever cannot be taught
    22 : 7   He who teaches a fool
    30 : 3   He who teaches his son will make his enemies envious
    33 : 27   for idleness teaches much evil
    45 : 5   to teach Jacob the covenant, and Israel his judgments
    45 : 5   to teach Jacob the testimonies
Sus 13 : 3   and had taught their daughter according to the law of Moses
1 Es 8 : 7   but taught all Israel all the ordinances and judgments
     8 : 23   and those who do not know it you shall teach
     9 : 48   taught the law of the Lord
     9 : 49   and to the Levites who were teaching the multitude, and to all
     9 : 55   because they were inspired by the words which they had been
              taught
2 Es 4 : 4   and will teach you why the heart is evil
     8 : 29   but regard those who have gloriously taught thy law
    12 : 38   and you shall teach them to the wise among your people
4 Ma 5 : 23 but it teaches us self-control
     5 : 24   and it teaches us piety
    18 : 10   he taught you the law and the prophets
    18 : 12   and he taught you about Hananiah, Azariah, and Mishael in the
              fire
    18 : 18   For he did not forget to teach you
    18 : 18   the song that Moses taught, which says

TEACHER   2
Sir 37 : 19   A man may be shrewd and the teacher of many
2 Ma 1 : 10 teacher of Ptolemy the king

TEACHING   6 = 0.004 %
Sir pr.   Whereas many great teachings have been given to us
    24 : 33   I will again pour out teaching like prophecy
    39 : 8   He will reveal instruction in his teaching
2 Es 7 : 78 Now, concerning death, the teaching is :
     7 : 90   Therefore this is the teaching concerning them :
4 Ma 10 : 2   and that I was brought up on the same teachings ?

TEAR, subst.   14 = 0.009 %
Tob 7 : 17   But the mother comforted her daughter in her tears
Sir 22 : 19   A man who pricks an eye will make tears fall
    31 : 13   Therefore it sheds tears from every face
    35 : 15   Do not the tears of the widow run down her cheek
    38 : 16   My son, let your tears fall for the dead
2 Ma 11 : 6   they and all the people, with lamentations and tears
3 Ma 1 : 4   Arsinoe went to the troops with wailing and tears
     1 : 16   and they filled the temple with cries and tears
     4 : 4   and shed tears at the most miserable expulsion of these people
     5 : 7   But with tears and a voice hard to silence
     6 : 14   The whole throng of infants and their parents entreat you with
              tears
     6 : 22   Then the king's anger was turned to pity and tears
4 Ma 4 : 11 and with tears besought the Hebrews
    15 : 20   you did not shed tears

TEAR, verb   7 = 0.005 %
Sir 6 : 2   lest your soul be torn in pieces like a bull
    22 : 16   will not be torn loose by an earthquake
1 Ma 1 : 56 The books of the law which they found they tore to pieces
3 Ma 4 : 6   as they were torn by the harsh treatment of the heathen
2 Es 1 : 32 and torn their bodies in pieces
4 Ma 6 : 6   his flesh was being torn by scourges, his blood flowing
    10 : 8   he saw his own flesh torn all around

TEAR away   1
4 Ma 9 : 28 and tore away his scalp

TEAR down   16 = 0.010 %
Sir 34 : 23   When one builds and another tears down
1 Ma 1 : 31 and tore down its houses and its surrounding walls
     2 : 25   and he tore down the altar
     2 : 45   and tore down the altars
     4 : 45   And they thought it best to tear it down
     4 : 45   So they tore down the altar
     5 : 65   and tore down its strongholds
     5 : 68   he tore down their altars
     6 : 7   that they had torn down the abomination
     6 : 62   and gave orders to tear down the wall all around
     8 : 10   tore down their strongholds, and enslaved them to this day
     9 : 54   Alcimus gave orders to tear down the wall

     9 : 54   He tore down the work of the prophets !
     9 : 55   But he only began to tear it down
2 Ma 10 : 2   and they tore down the altars which had been built
    14 : 33   and tear down the altar

TEAR off   3 = 0.002 %
2 Ma 4 : 38 tore off his garments
     7 : 7   They tore off the skin of his head with the hair
4 Ma 9 : 11 and having torn off his tunic

TEAR out   2
2 Ma 14 : 46 he tore out his entrails
4 Ma 9 : 28 These leopard-like beasts tore out his sinews with the iron hands

TEARFUL   2
3 Ma 4 : 2   there was incessant mourning, lamentation, and tearful cries
     5 : 25   and with most tearful supplication and mournful dirges

TEKOA   1
1 Ma 9 : 33 and they fled into the wilderness of Tekoa

TELEM   1
1 Es 9 : 25 Of the gatekeepers : Shallum and Telem

TEL-HARSHA   1
1 Es 5 : 36 The following are those who came up from Tel-melah and Tel-
              harsha

TELL   109 = 0.071 %
Tob 2 : 14   and told her to return it to the owners
     5 : 7   and I shall tell my father
     5 : 10   My brother, to what tribe and family do you belong ? Tell me
     5 : 14   But tell me, what wages am I to pay you – a drachma a day
     6 : 5   So the young man did as the angel told him
     8 : 14   And she came out and told them that he was alive
Jud 2 : 7   Tell them to prepare earth and water
     3 : 5   The men came to Holofernes and told him all this
     5 : 3   and said to them, Tell me, you Canaanites
     5 : 5   and I will tell you the truth about this people
     6 : 2   and tell us not to make war against the people of Israel
     6 : 17   He answered and told them what had taken place
     8 : 34   for I will not tell you
    10 : 16   but tell him just what you have said
    10 : 18   while they told him about her
    10 : 22   When they told him of her
    11 : 3   And now tell me why you have fled from them
    11 : 5   and I will tell nothing false to my lord this night
    11 : 9   and he told them all he had said to you
    11 : 17   and he will tell me when they have committed their sins
    11 : 18   And I will come and tell you
    11 : 19   For this has been told me, by my foreknowledge
    11 : 19   it was announced to me, and I was sent to tell you
    13 : 3   Now Judith had told her maid
    14 : 8   Now tell me what you have done during these days
    15 : 4   to tell what had taken place and to urge all
    15 : 5   for they were told what had happened in the camp of the enemy
Wis 6 : 22   I will tell you what wisdom is and how she came to be
Sir 1 : 24   and the lips of many will tell of his good sense
    20 : 19   An ungracious man is like a story told at the wrong time
    20 : 20   for he does not tell it at its proper time
    22 : 6   Like music in mourning is a tale told at the wrong time
    22 : 8   He who tells a story to a fool tells it to a drowsy man
    25 : 7   and a 10th I shall tell with my tongue :
    37 : 9   and tell you, Your way is good
    41 : 23   of repeating and telling what you hear
    43 : 24   Those who sail the sea tell of its dangers
Sus 13 : 10   but they did not tell each other of their distress
    13 : 27   And when the elders told their tale
    13 : 40   but she would not tell us
    13 : 54   Now then, if you really saw her, tell me this :
    13 : 58   Now then, tell me :
Bel 14 : 8   If you do not tell me who is eating these provisions, you shall
              die
    14 : 12   or else Daniel will, who is telling lies about us
1 Ma 4 : 46 to tell what to do with them
     5 : 25   and told them all that had happened
     8 : 2   Men told him of their wars
     9 : 60   telling them to seize Jonathan and his men
    10 : 15   and men told him of the battles
    10 : 72   Men will tell you that you cannot stand before us
    11 : 5   They also told the king what Jonathan had done
    11 : 40   and told of the hatred
    14 : 21   have told us about your glory and honour
2 Ma 2 : 1   to take some of the fire, as has been told
     3 : 7   he told him of the money about which he had been informed
     3 : 9   he told about the disclosure that had been made
     6 : 23   telling them to send him to Hades
     8 : 12   and when he told his companions of the arrival of the army
     8 : 19   Moreover, he told them of the times
    10 : 10   Now we will tell what took place under Antiochus Eupator

	14:26	He told him that Nicanor was disloyal to the government
	15:38	If it is well told and to the point
1 Es	1:3	And he told the Levites, the temple servants of Israel
	1:33	and the things that he had done before and these that are now told
	4:4	If he tells them to make war on one another, they do it
	4:7	If he tells them to kill, they kill
	4:7	if he tells them to release, they release
	4:8	if he tells them to attack, they attack
	4:8	if he tells them to lay waste, they lay waste
	4:8	if he tells them to build, they build
	4:9	if he tells them to cut down, they cut down
	4:9	if he tells them to plant, they plant
	4:61	and went to Babylon and told this to all his brethren
	5:40	And Nehemiah and Attharias told them
	8:45	and I told them to go to Iddo
	8:46	and ordered them to tell Iddo and his brethren
	9:39	and they told Ezra the chief priest and reader
2 Es	1:5	so that they may tell their children's children
	2:10	Tell my people that I will give them the kingdom of Jerusalem
	2:48	Then the angel said to me, Go, tell my people
	4:52	I can tell you in part
	4:52	but I was not sent to tell you concerning your life
	5:13	These are the signs which I am permitted to tell you
	5:32	pay attention to me, and I will tell you more
	5:50	Is our mother, of whom thou hast told me, still young ?
	5:51	and she will tell you
	6:35	as I had been told
	7:54	Not only that, but ask the earth and she will tell you
	7:101	they may see the things of which you have been told
	8:2	But I will tell you a parable, Ezra
	8:2	it will tell you that it provides very much clay
	9:42	And I said to her, What has happened to you ? Tell me
	10:9	and she will tell you that it is she who ought to mourn
	10:38	and tell you about the things which you fear
	10:43	and as for her telling you about the misfortune of her son
	10:45	And as for her telling you that she was barren for 30 years
	10:47	And as for her telling you that she brought him up with much care
	10:51	Therefore I told you to remain in the field
	10:53	Therefore I told you to go into the field
	11:42	you have hated those who tell the truth
	12:50	So the people went into the city, as I told them to do
	13:21	I will tell you the interpretation of the vision
	13:56	And after 3 more days I will tell you other things
	14:5	and I told him many wondrous things
	14:23	and tell them not to seek you for 40 days
4 Ma	2:6	In fact, since the law had told us not to covet
	12:7	as we shall tell a little later
	18:12	He told you of the zeal of Phineas

TEL-MELAH   1

1 Es	5:36	The following are those who came up from Tel-melah and Tel-harsha

TEMAH   1

1 Es	5:32	the sons of Sisera, the sons of Temah

TEMAN   2

Bar	3:22	She has not been heard of in Canaan, nor seen in Teman
	3:23	the merchants of Merran and Teman

TEMPER   4 = 0.003 %

Wis	7:20	the natures of animals and the tempers of wild beasts
Sir	31:26	Fire and water prove the temper of steel
2 Ma	4:25	but having the hot temper of a cruel tyrant
1 Es	4:31	if she loses her temper with him, he flatters her

TEMPERATE   7 = 0.005 %

4 Ma	1:35	checked by the temperate mind
	2:2	that the temperate Joseph is praised
	2:16	For the temperate mind repels all these malicious emotions
	2:18	the temperate mind is able to get the better of the emotions
	2:23	rule a kingdom that is temperate, just, good, and courageous
	3:17	For the temperate mind can conquer the drives of the emotions
	3:19	to a narrative demonstration of temperate reason

TEMPERATELY   1

Sir	31:28	Wine drunk in season and temperately

TEMPEST   10 = 0.007 %

Wis	5:23	and like a tempest it will winnow them away
Sir	16:21	Like a tempest which no man can see
	43:17	so do the tempest from the north and the whirlwind
2 Es	15:13	by blight and hail and by a terrible tempest
	15:35	and shall pour out a heavy tempest upon the earth
	15:35	and their own tempest
	15:40	And great and mighty clouds, full of wrath and tempest
	15:40	and shall pour out upon every high and lofty place a terrible tempest

	15:44	they shall pour out the tempest and all its wrath upon her
4 Ma	13:7	conquered the tempest of the emotions

TEMPLE   147 = 0.096 %

Tob	1:4	and where the temple of the dwelling of the Most High
Jud	4:1	and how he had plundered and destroyed all their temples
	4:2	and for the temple of the Lord their God
	4:3	and the sacred vessels and the altar and the temple
	4:11	prostrated themselves before the temple
	5:18	the temple of their God was razed to the ground
	8:24	and the sanctuary and the temple and the altar rest upon us
Wis	3:14	and a place of great delight in the temple of the Lord
	9:8	Thou hast given command to build a temple
Sir	36:14	and thy temple with thy glory
	45:9	to make their ringing heard in the temple
	49:12	and raised a temple holy to the Lord
	50:1	and in his time fortified the temple
	50:2	the high retaining walls for the temple enclosure
	50:7	like the sun shining upon the temple of the Most High
	51:14	Before the temple I asked for her
Bar	1:8	which had been carried away from the temple
L Jr	6:13	their faces are wiped because of the dust from the temple
	6:17	when they have been set up in the temples
	6:18	so the priests make their temples secure with doors and locks and bars
	6:20	They are just like a beam of the temple
	6:21	by the smoke of the temple
	6:31	and in their temples the priests sit with their clothes rent
	6:55	When fire breaks out in a temple
P Az	31	Blessed art thou in the temple of thy holy glory
Bel	14:10	And the king went with Daniel into the temple of Bel
	14:14	and they sifted them throughout the whole temple
	14:22	and gave Bel over to Daniel, who destroyed it and its temple
1 Ma	1:22	and the gold decoration on the front of the temple
	2:8	Her temple has become like a man without honour
	4:46	on the temple hill until there should come a prophet
	4:48	and the interior of the temple
	4:49	the altar of incense, and the table into the temple
	4:50	and these gave light in the temple
	4:57	They decorated the front of the temple
	6:2	Its temple was very rich, containing golden shields
	7:36	and stood before the altar and the temple
	10:41	they shall give from now on for the service of the temple
	10:42	from the income of the services of the temple
	10:43	And whoever takes refuge at the temple in Jerusalem
	10:83	the temple of their idol, for safety
	10:84	and the temple of Dagon
	11:4	they showed him the temple of Dagon burned down
	13:52	He strengthened the fortifications of the temple hill
	15:9	we will bestow great honour upon you and your nation and the temple
	16:20	and the temple hill
2 Ma	1:13	they were cut to pieces in the temple of Nanaea
	1:15	When the priests of the temple of Nanaea
	1:15	they closed the temple as soon as he entered it
	1:18	we shall celebrate the purification of the temple
	1:18	when Nehemiah, who built the temple and the altar, offered sacrifices
	2:9	for the dedication and completion of the temple
	2:19	and the purification of the great temple
	2:22	and recovered the temple famous throughout the world
	3:2	and glorified the temple with the finest presents
	3:4	who had been made captain of the temple
	3:12	and in the sanctity and inviolability of the temple
	3:30	And the temple, which a little while before
	4:32	stole some of the gold vessels of the temple
	4:42	and the temple robber himself they killed
	5:15	the most holy temple in all the world
	5:21	So Antiochus carried off 1,800 talents from the temple
	6:2	and also to pollute the temple in Jerusalem
	6:2	and call it the temple of Olympian Zeus
	6:2	and to call the one in Gerizim the temple of Zeus
	6:4	For the temple was filled with debauchery and revelling
	8:2	and to have pity on the temple
	9:2	and attempted to rob the temples and control the city
	10:1	the Lord leading them on, recovered the temple and the city
	11:3	and to levy tribute on the temple
	11:25	our decision is that their temple be restored to them
	12:26	and the temple of Atargatis
	13:10	and their country and the holy temple
	13:14	for the laws, temple, city, country, and commonwealth
	14:4	some of the customary olive branches from the temple
	14:13	and to set up Alcimus as high priest of the greatest temple
	14:31	he went to the great and holy temple
	14:33	and I will build here a splendid temple to Dionysus
	14:35	thou wast pleased that there be a temple
	15:17	and the temple were in danger
1 Es	1:2	arrayed in their garments, in the temple of the Lord
	1:3	And he told the Levites, the temple servants of Israel
	1:5	Stand in order in the temple

1 :8	the chief officers of the temple	
1 :15	And the temple singers, the sons of Asaph	
1 :41	and stored them in his temple in Babylon	
1 :49	and polluted the temple of the Lord	
1 :53	These slew their young men with the sword around their holy temple	
2 :7	for the temple of the Lord which is in Jerusalem	
2 :10	and stored in his temple of idols	
2 :18	and laying the foundations for a temple	
2 :20	And since the building of the temple is now going on	
2 :30	And the building of the temple in Jerusalem ceased	
4 :45	You also vowed to build the temple	
4 :51	for the building of the temple until it was completed	
4 :55	until the day when the temple should be finished and Jerusalem built	
4 :63	to go up and build Jerusalem and the temple	
5 :27	The temple singers : the sons of Asaph, 128	
5 :29	The temple servants : the sons of Ziha	
5 :35	All the temple servants	
5 :44	when they came to the temple of God which is in Jerusalem	
5 :46	and the temple singers, the gatekeepers	
5 :53	though the temple of God was not yet built	
5 :56	In the 2nd year after their coming to the temple of God in Jerusalem	
5 :57	and they laid the foundation of the temple of God	
5 :58	So the builders built the temple of the Lord	
5 :67	were building the temple for the Lord God of Israel	
6 :18	and stored in his own temple	
6 :18	from the temple in Babylon	
6 :19	and put them in the temple at Jerusalem	
6 :19	and that this temple of the Lord should be rebuilt on its site	
7 :2	and the chief officers of the temple	
7 :7	They offered at the dedication of the temple of the Lord	
8 :5	and Levites and temple singers	
8 :5	and gatekeepers and temple servants	
8 :14	for the temple of their Lord which is in Jerusalem	
8 :17	which are given you for the use of the temple of your God	
8 :18	for the temple of your God	
8 :22	on any of the priests or Levites or temple singers	
8 :22	or gatekeepers or temple servants or	
8 :22	persons employed in this temple	
8 :49	and of the temple servants	
8 :49	220 temple servants	
8 :60	carried them to the temple of the Lord	
8 :67	and the temple of the Lord	
8 :81	and glorified the temple of our Lord	
8 :91	weeping and lying upon the ground before the temple	
9 :1	Then Ezra rose and went from the court of the temple	
9 :6	And all the multitude sat in the open square before the temple	
9 :24	Of the temple singers : Eliashib and Zaccur	
9 :38	into the open square before the east gate of the temple	
9 :41	before the gate of the temple	
3 Ma 1 :10	he marvelled at the good order of the temple	
1 :13	And he inquired why, when he entered every other temple	
1 :16	and they filled the temple with cries and tears	
1 :20	at the most high temple	
3 :16	to the temples in the cities	
3 :16	and went up to honour the temple of those wicked people	
3 :17	to enter their inner temple and honour it	
5 :43	and by burning to the ground the temple inaccessible to him	
2 Es 10 :21	our altar thrown down, our temple destroyed	
4 Ma 3 :20	had both appropriated money to them for the temple service	
4 :3	which are not the property of the temple	
4 :8	But, uttering threats, Apollonius went on to the temple	
4 :9	were imploring God in the temple to shield the holy place	
4 :11	in the temple area that was open to all	
4 :20	but also the temple service was abolished	

TEMPORAL
		1
4 Ma 15 :23	strengthened her to disregard her temporal love for her children	

TEMPORARILY
		1
2 Ma 14 :17	but had been temporarily checked	

TEMPORARY
		1
4 Ma 15 :8	the temporary safety of her children	

TEMPT
		1
Sir 18 :23	and do not be like a man who tempts the Lord	

TEMPTATION
		1
Sir 2 :1	prepare yourself for temptation	

TEN, subst., s. NUMBERS
		3 = 0.002 %
P Az 16	and with tens of thousands of fat lambs	
1 Ma 3 :55	in charge of thousands and hundreds and fifties and tens	
4 Ma 4 :3	there are deposited tens of thousands in private funds	

TEND
		3 = 0.002 %
Sir 17 :16	Their ways from youth tend toward evil	
43 :4	A man tending a furnace works in burning heat	
Ps 151 :1	I tended my father's sheep	

TENDENCY
		1
4 Ma 1 :25	In pleasure there exists even a malevolent tendency	

TENDER
		3 = 0.002 %
Sir 43 :21	and withers the tender grass like fire	
Bar 4 :26	My tender sons have travelled rough roads	
4 Ma 15 :6	In 7 pregnancies she had implanted in herself tender love toward them	

TENDERNESS
		1
4 Ma 15 :9	she felt a greater tenderness toward them	

TENFOLD
		1
Bar 4 :28	return with tenfold zeal to seek him	

TENSE
		1
4 Ma 7 :13	his body no longer tense and firm	

TENT
		39 = 0.025 %
Tob 13 :10	that his tent may be raised for you again with joy	
Jud 2 :26	and burned their tents and plundered their sheepfolds	
3 :3	and all our sheepfolds with their tents, lie before you	
5 :22	all the men standing around the tent began to complain	
6 :10	who waited on him in his tent	
7 :18	and their tents and supply trains spread out in great number	
8 :5	She set up a tent for herself on the roof of her house	
8 :36	So they returned from the tent and went to their posts	
10 :15	Go at once to his tent	
10 :17	and they brought them to the tent of Holofernes	
10 :18	for her arrival was reported from tent to tent	
10 :18	as she waited outside the tent of Holofernes	
10 :20	and led her into the tent	
10 :22	he came forward to the front of the tent	
12 :5	Then the servants of Holofernes brought her into the tent	
12 :9	So she returned clean and stayed in the tent	
13 :1	and Bagoas closed the tent from outside	
13 :2	So Judith was left alone in the tent	
14 :3	and they will rush into the tent of Holofernes	
14 :7	Blessed are you in every tent of Judah !	
14 :13	So they came to Holofernes' tent and said to the steward	
14 :14	So Bagoas went in and knocked at the door of the tent	
14 :17	Then he went to the tent where Judith had stayed	
15 :1	When the men in the tents heard it	
15 :11	They gave Judith the tent of Holofernes	
Wis 9 :8	a copy of the holy tent	
9 :15	and this earthly tent burdens the thoughtful mind	
11 :2	and pitched their tents in untrodden places	
Sir 14 :24	will also fasten his tent peg to her walls	
14 :25	he will pitch his tent near her	
24 :8	and the one who created me assigned a place for my tent	
1 Ma 9 :66	and the sons of Phasiron in their tents	
2 Ma 2 :4	ordered that the tent and the ark should follow with him	
2 :5	and he brought there the tent and the ark	
12 :12	and after receiving his pledges they departed to their tents	
3 Ma 1 :2	and crossed over by night to the tent of Ptolemy	
1 :3	that a certain insignificant man should sleep in the tent	
4 Ma 3 :8	he came, sweating and quite exhausted, to the royal tent	

TENTH, subst., s. NUMBERS
		3 = 0.002 %
Tob 1 :7	Of all my produce I would give a tenth to the sons of Levi	
1 :7	a 2nd tenth I would sell	
1 :8	the 3rd tenth I would give to those to whom it was my duty	

TEN THOUSANDS, subst., s. NUMBERS
		2
Sir 47 :6	So they glorified him for his ten thousands	
2 Ma 11 :4	but was elated with his ten thousands of infantry	

TEN-THOUSANDTH, subst.
		1
2 Es 7 :138	not one ten-thousandth of mankind could have life	

TEPHON
		1
1 Ma 9 :50	and Bethel, and Timnath, and Pharathon, and Tephon	

TEREBINTH
		1
Sir 24 :16	Like a Terebinth I spread out my branches	

TERM, subst.
		10 = 0.007 %
Tob 5 :15	So they agreed to these terms	
1 Ma 6 :58	Now then let us come to terms with these men	
7 :12	before Alcimus and Bacchides to ask for just terms	
8 :29	Thus on these terms the Romans make a treaty	
8 :30	If after these terms are in effect	
11 :66	Then they asked him to grant them terms of peace	
2 Ma 11 :14	and persuaded them to settle everything on just terms	
13 :25	in fact they were so angry that they wanted to annul its terms	

TERM

	14:20	When the terms had been fully considered
1 Es	9:14	undertook the matter on these terms

TERRIBLE 10 = 0.007 %
Wis 11:18 or flash terrible sparks from their eyes
16:5 For when the terrible rage of wild beasts
19:16 afflicted with terrible sufferings
Sir 43:29 Terrible is the Lord and very great
2 Ma 6:30 I am enduring terrible sufferings in my body under this beating
P Ma 3 and sealed it with thy terrible and glorious name
2 Es 8:22 whose ordinance is strong and whose command is terrible
15:13 by blight and hail and by a terrible tempest
15:40 and shall pour out upon every high and lofty place a terrible tempest
4 Ma 4:15 an arrogant and terrible man

TERRIBLY 4 = 0.003 %
Ad E 11:6 both ready to fight, and they roared terribly
Wis 6:5 he will come upon you terribly and swiftly
17:3 they were scattered, terribly alarmed
2 Ma 10:34 blasphemed terribly and hurled out wicked words

TERRIFY 14 = 0.009 %
Jud 4:2 they were therefore very greatly terrified at his approach
7:4 they were greatly terrified
1 Ma 12:28 they were afraid and were terrified at heart
2 Es 6:15 while the voice is speaking, do not be terrified
6:23 they shall suddenly be terrified
6:24 and the earth and those who inhabit it shall be terrified
10:25 and my heart was terrified
10:55 and do not let your heart be terrified
12:3 and the earth was exceedingly terrified
12:5 because of the great fear with which I have been terrified this night
16:10 He will thunder, and who will not be terrified?
16:18 the beginning of wars, when the powers shall be terrified
4 Ma 9:5 You are trying to terrify us
16:17 you young men were to be terrified by tortures

TERRIFYING 6 = 0.004 %
Ad E 15:6 And he was most terrifying
Wis 17:4 but terrifying sounds rang out around them
2 Es 11:45 and your terrifying wings
12:8 the interpretation and meaning of this terrifying vision
12:13 and it shall be more terrifying
15:28 Behold, a terrifying sight, appearing from the east!

TERRITORY 15 = 0.010 %
Jud 1:12 on the whole territory of Cilicia and Damascus and Syria
2:10 You shall go and seize all their territory for me in advance
2:25 He also seized the territory of Cilicia
16:5 He boasted that he would burn up my territory
Sir 24:7 I sought in whose territory I might lodge
Bar 3:24 And how vast the territory that he possesses!
1 Ma 3:36 settle aliens in all their territory
3:42 and that the forces were encamped in their territory
5:9 against the Israelites who lived in their territory
9:72 and came no more in their territory
11:34 both the territory of Judea
14:2 that Demetrius had invaded his territory
15:29 You have devastated their territory
2 Es 4:15 so that there also we may gain more territory for ourselves
4 Ma 3:11 in the enemy's territory

TERROR 15 = 0.010 %
Jud 2:28 So fear and terror of him fell upon all the people
16:25 And no one ever again spread terror
Wis 17:6 and in terror they deemed the things which they saw
17:19 it paralyzed them with terror
Sir 21:4 Terror and violence will lay waste riches
1 Ma 3:25 and terror fell upon the Gentiles round about them
2 Ma 3:17 For terror and bodily trembling had come over the man
3:24 and became faint with terror
12:22 terror and fear came over the enemy
13:16 In the end they filled the camp with terror and confusion
15:23 send a good angel to carry terror and trembling before us
3 Ma 6:17 and brought an uncontrollable terror upon the army
6:19 and filled them with confusion and terror
2 Es 5:1 shall be seized with great terror
11:40 and you have held sway over the world with much terror

TEST, subst. 7 = 0.005 %
Jud 8:12 Who are you, that have put God to the test this day
8:13 You are putting the Lord Almighty to the test
8:25 who is putting us to the test as he did our forefathers
Wis 1:2 because he is found by those who do not put him to the test
Sir 27:5 so the test of a man is in his reasoning
27:7 for this is the test of men
4 Ma 9:7 Therefore, tyrant, put us to the test

TEST, verb 21 = 0.014 %
Jud 8:26 Remember what he did with Abraham, and how he tested Isaac
Wis 1:3 and when his power is tested, it convicts the foolish
2:17 and let us test what will happen at the end of his life
2:19 Let us test him with insult and torture
3:5 because God tested them and found them worthy of himself
6:6 but mighty men will be mightily tested
11:10 For thou didst test them as a father does in warning
18:25 for merely to test the wrath was enough
Sir 2:5 For gold is tested in the fire
4:17 and she will test him with her ordinances
13:11 for he will test you through much talk
27:5 The kiln tests the potter's vessels
31:10 Who has been tested by it and been found perfect?
31:26 so wine tests hearts in the strife of the proud
37:27 My son, test your soul while you live
39:4 for he tests the good and the evil among men
44:20 and when he was tested he was found faithful
1 Ma 2:52 Was not Abraham found faithful when tested
2 Es 16:73 Then the tested quality of my elect shall be manifest
16:73 as gold that is tested by fire
4 Ma 17:12 and tested them for their endurance

TESTIFY 5 = 0.003 %
Sus 13:21 If you refuse, we will testify against you
13:40 These things we testify
1 Ma 2:37 heaven and earth testify for us
2:56 Caleb, because he testified in the assembly
4 Ma 6:32 we would have testified to their domination

TESTIMONY 5 = 0.003 %
Wis 17:11 condemned by its own testimony
Sir 31:23 and their testimony to his excellence is trustworthy
31:24 and their testimony to his niggardliness is accurate
45:17 to teach Jacob the testimonies
2 Ma 3:36 And he bore testimony to all men

TESTING, subst., adj. 2
Sir 6:7 When you gain a friend, gain him through testing
6:21 She will weigh him down like a heavy testing stone

THAN, conj., prep. 205 = 0.134 %

THANK, subst. 27 = 0.018 %
Tob 11:17 And Tobit gave thanks before them
12:6 and said to them: Praise God and give thanks to him
12:6 exalt him and give thanks to him
12:6 Do not be slow to give him thanks
12:20 And now give thanks to God
13:6 give thanks to him with your full voice
13:6 I give him thanks in the land of my captivity
13:8 Let all men speak, and give him thanks in Jerusalem
13:10 Give thanks worthily to the Lord
14:7 and his people will give thanks to God
Jud 8:25 let us give thanks to the Lord our God
Wis 16:28 to give thee thanks
Sir 17:27 as do those who are alive and give thanks?
39:6 give thanks to the Lord in prayer
39:15 ascribe majesty to his name and give thanks to him
47:8 In all that he did he gave thanks to the Holy One
51:1 I will give thanks to thee, O Lord and King
51:1 I give thanks to thy name
51:12 Therefore I will give thanks to thee and praise thee
P Az 67 Give thanks to the Lord, for he is good
68 sing praise to him and give thanks to him
2 Ma 8:27 giving great praise and thanks to the Lord
1 Es 4:60 I give thee thanks, O Lord of our fathers
5:61 and they sang hymns, giving thanks to the Lord
3 Ma 6:33 gave thanks to heaven unceasingly and lavishly
7:16 joyfully and loudly giving thanks
2 Es 2:37 giving thanks to him who has called you to heavenly kingdoms

THANK, verb 5 = 0.003 %
Sir 12:1 and you will be thanked for your good deeds
29:25 without being thanked
1 Ma 14:25 How shall we thank Simon and his sons?
2 Ma 1:11 we thank him greatly for taking our side against the king
12:31 they thanked them and exhorted them

THANKFUL 1
Wis 18:2 and were thankful that thy holy ones

THANKFULNESS 1
Ad E 16:4 They not only take away thankfulness from among men

THANK OFFERING 3 = 0.002 %
Sir 35:2 and he who gives alms sacrifices a thank offering
1 Es 8:66 and as a thank offering 12 he-goats

416

3 Ma	1:9	he offered sacrifice to the supreme God and made thank-offerings

THANKSGIVING   8 = 0.005 %

Jud	16:1	Then Judith began this thanksgiving before all Israel
Sir	17:28	thanksgiving has ceased
	39:15	and this you shall say in thanksgiving :
	51:11	and will sing praise with thanksgiving
2 Ma	10:7	they offered hymns of thanksgiving to him
	10:38	with hymns and thanksgivings they blessed the Lord
3 Ma	6:35	to the accompaniment of joyous thanksgiving and psalms
	7:19	And when they had landed in peace with appropriate thanksgiving

THARRA   1

Ad E	12:1	with Gabatha and Tharra

THASSI   1

1 Ma	2:3	Simon called Thassi

THAT*   1873 = 1.220 %

THE   10758 = 7.007 %

THEE   108 = 0.070 %

THEFT   2

Wis	14:25	theft and deceit, corruption, faithlessness, tumult, perjury
Sir	41:19	and of theft, in the place where you live

THEIR   1185 = 0.772 %

THEM   1282 = 0.835 %

THEMSELVES   89 = 0.058 %

THEN   470 = 0.306 %

THEODOTUS   2

2 Ma	14:19	Therefore he sent Posidonius and Theodotus and Mattathias
3 Ma	1:2	But a certain Theodotus

THERAS   2

1 Es	8:41	I assembled them at the river called Theras
	8:61	We departed from the river Theras

THERE, adv., indef. pr.   339 = 0.221 %

THEREAFTER   1

1 Es	5:52	and thereafter the continual offerings and sacrifices

THEREBY   2

3 Ma	1:2	intending single-handed to kill him and thereby end the war
4 Ma	9:24	Thereby the just Providence of our ancestors

THEREFORE   179 = 0.117 %

Tob	11:8	You therefore must anoint his eyes with the gall
	12:18	Therefore praise him for ever
Jud	4:2	they were therefore very greatly terrified at his approach
	5:20	Now therefore, my master and lord
	5:24	Therefore let us go up, Lord Holofernes
	7:11	Therefore, my lord, do not fight against them in battle array
	8:17	Therefore, while we wait for his deliverance
	8:20	and therefore we hope that he will not disdain us
	8:24	Now therefore, brethren
	11:10	my lord and master
	11:16	Therefore, when I, your servant, learned all this
	11:17	therefore, my lord, I will remain with you
Ad E	13:6	Therefore we have decreed
	16:17	You will therefore do well not to put in execution
	16:19	Therefore post a copy of this letter publicly in every place
	16:22	Therefore you shall observe this with all good cheer
Wis	1:8	therefore no one who utters unrighteous things will escape notice
	2:6	Come, therefore, let us enjoy the good things that exist
	4:14	therefore he took him quickly from the midst of wickedness
	5:16	Therefore they will receive a glorious crown
	6:1	Listen therefore, O kings, and understand
	6:11	Therefore set your desire on my words
	6:21	Therefore if you delight in thrones and sceptres
	6:25	Therefore be instructed by my words, and you will profit
	7:7	Therefore I prayed, and understanding was given me
	7:25	therefore nothing defiled gains entrance into her
	8:9	Therefore I determined to take her to live with me
	10:20	Therefore the righteous plundered the ungodly
	12:2	Therefore thou dost correct little by little those who trespass
	12:23	Therefore those who in folly of life lived unrighteously
	12:25	Therefore, as to thoughtless children
	12:27	Therefore the utmost condemnation came upon them
	14:5	therefore men trust their lives
	14:11	Therefore there will be a visitation

	14:14	and therefore their speedy end has been planned
	16:1	Therefore those men were deservedly punished
	16:25	Therefore at that time also
	17:1	therefore uninstructed souls have gone astray
	18:3	Therefore thou didst provide a flaming pillar of fire
Sir pr.		You are urged therefore to read
	2:13	Therefore it will not be sheltered
	10:13	Therefore the Lord brought upon them
	18:11	Therefore the Lord is patient with them
	18:12	therefore he grants them forgiveness in abundance
	24:18	being eternal, I therefore am given to all my children
	29:7	Because of such wickedness, therefore
	31:13	Therefore it sheds tears from every face
	39:32	Therefore from the beginning I have been convinced
	41:16	Therefore show respect for my words :
	43:14	Therefore the storehouses are opened
	44:17	therefore a remnant was left to the earth when the flood came
	44:21	Therefore the Lord assured him by an oath
	45:24	Therefore a covenant of peace was established with him
	51:12	Therefore I will give thanks to thee and praise thee
	51:20	therefore I will not be forsaken
	51:21	therefore I have gained a good possession
L Jr	6:3	Therefore when you have come to Babylon
	6:16	Therefore they evidently are not gods
	6:64	Therefore one must not think that they are gods nor call them gods
	6:69	therefore do no fear them
	6:73	Better therefore is a just man who has no idols
Bel	14:22	Therefore the king put them to death
1 Ma	10:54	now therefore let us establish friendship with one another
	11:37	Now therefore take care to make a copy of this
	12:9	Therefore, though we have no need of these things
	12:11	We therefore remember you constantly on every occasion
	12:16	We therefore have chosen Numenius the son of Antiochus
	12:23	We therefore command
	12:53	Now therefore let us make war on them
	15:5	now therefore I confirm to you all the tax remissions
	15:19	We therefore have decided to write
	15:21	Therefore if any pestilent men
2 Ma	2:16	Since, therefore, we are about to celebrate the purification
	2:16	Will you therefore please keep the days ?
	2:32	At this point therefore let us begin our narrative
	4:21	Therefore upon arriving at Joppa he proceeded to Jerusalem
	4:34	Therefore Menelaus, taking Andronicus aside
	4:37	Therefore Antiochus was grieved at heart
	4:46	Therefore Ptolemy, taking the king aside into a colonnade
	4:49	Therefore even the Tyrians
	5:4	Therefore all men prayed
	5:17	and that therefore he was disregarding the holy place
	5:20	Therefore the place itself
	6:9	One could see, therefore, the misery that had come upon them
	6:16	Therefore he never withdraws his mercy from us
	6:27	Therefore, by manfully giving up my life now
	7:8	Therefore he in turn underwent tortures
	7:18	Therefore astounding things have happened
	7:23	Therefore the Creator of the world
	8:36	and that therefore the Jews were invulnerable
	9:2	Therefore the people rushed to the rescue with arms
	9:26	I therefore urge and beseech you to remember
	10:7	Therefore bearing ivy-wreathed wands and beautiful branches
	11:26	You will do well, therefore, to send word to them
	11:30	Therefore those who go home by the 30th day of Xanthicus
	11:37	Therefore make haste and send some men
	12:45	Therefore he made atonement for the dead
	14:7	Therefore I have laid aside my ancestral glory
	14:19	Therefore he sent Posidonius and Theodotus and Mattathias
1 Es	2:5	If any one of you, therefore, is of his people
	2:24	Therefore we now make known to you, O lord and king
	2:28	Therefore I have now issued orders
	4:46	I pray therefore that you fulfil the vow
	6:21	Now therefore, if it seems wise, O king
	6:33	Therefore may the Lord, whose name is there called upon
	8:11	Let as many as are so disposed, therefore
	8:84	Therefore do not give your daughters in marriage to their sons
P Ma	8	Therefore thou, O Lord, God of the righteous
3 Ma	3:24	Therefore, fully convinced by these indications
	3:25	Therefore we have given orders that
	4:15	The registration of these people was therefore conducted
2 Es	2:34	Therefore I say to you, O nations that hear and understand
	3:34	Now therefore weigh in a balance our iniquities
	4:29	If therefore that which has been sown is not reaped
	5:18	Rise therefore and eat some bread
	5:45	If therefore all creatures will live at one time
	5:46	Request it therefore to produce 10 at one time
	5:54	Therefore you also should consider
	6:31	If therefore you will pray again and fast again for 7 days
	6:33	Therefore he sent to show you all these things
	6:48	that therefore the nations might declare thy wondrous works
	7:14	Therefore unless the living
	7:18	The righteous therefore can endure difficult circumstances

	7:25	Therefore, Ezra, empty things are for the empty
	7:57	Judge therefore which things are precious and desirable
	7:64	and therefore we are tormented
	7:72	For this reason, therefore
	7:90	Therefore this is the teaching concerning them :
	7:100	Will time therefore be given to the souls
	7:111	If therefore the righteous have prayed for the ungodly now
	7:112	therefore those who were strong prayed for the weak
	7:115	Therefore no one will then be able to have mercy on him
	7:131	Therefore there shall not be grief at their destruction
	8:17	Therefore I will pray before thee for myself and for them
	8:19	Therefore hear my voice, and understand my words
	8:40	As I have spoken, therefore, so it shall be
	8:55	Therefore do not ask any more questions
	8:61	Therefore my judgment is now drawing near
	9:13	Therefore, do not continue to be curious
	10:15	Now, therefore, keep your sorrow to yourself
	10:17	Therefore go into the city to your husband
	10:24	Therefore shake off your great sadness
	10:37	Now therefore I entreat you
	10:40	This therefore is the meaning of the vision
	10:51	Therefore I told you to remain in the field
	10:53	Therefore I told you to go into the field
	10:55	Therefore do not be afraid
	11:45	Therefore you will surely disappear, you eagle
	12:6	Therefore I will now beseech the Most High
	12:24	therefore they are called the heads of the eagle
	12:37	Therefore write all these things that you have seen in a book
	12:44	Therefore if you forsake us
	13:24	Understand therefore that those who are left
	13:47	Therefore you saw the multitude gathered together in peace
	13:49	Therefore when he destroys the multitude of the nations
	13:56	Therefore I have shown you this
	14:13	Now therefore, set your house in order
	15:7	Therefore, says the Lord
	15:26	therefore he will hand them over to death and slaughter
	15:48	therefore God says
	15:55	therefore you shall receive your recompense
	16:51	Therefore do not be like her or her works
4 Ma	1:34	Therefore when we crave seafood and fowl and animals
	3:16	Therefore, opposing reason to desire
	5:17	Therefore we consider
	5:19	Therefore do not suppose that it would be a petty sin
	5:25	Therefore we do not eat defiling food
	5:32	Therefore get your torture wheels ready
	6:22	Therefore, O children of Abraham
	7:16	If, therefore, because of piety
	7:20	No contradiction therefore arises
	8:10	Therefore take pity on yourselves
	9:7	Therefore, tyrant, put us to the test
	11:27	therefore, unconquered, we hold fast to reason
	13:16	Therefore let us put on the full armour of self-control
	13:23	Therefore, when sympathy and brotherly affection had been so established
	16:19	and therefore you ought to endure any suffering for the sake of God
	17:4	Take courage, therefore, O holy-minded mother
	18:3	Therefore those who gave over their bodies in suffering

THEREIN   2

Sir	51:17	I made progress therein
2 Ma	11:17	and have asked about the matters indicated therein

THEREUPON   1

3 Ma	2:21	Thereupon God, who oversees all things

THEY   1617 = 1.053 %

THICK   6 = 0.004 %

Jud	1:2	with hewn stones 3 cubits thick and 6 cubits long
Wis	11:18	or belch forth a thick pall of smoke
Sir	45:5	and led him into the thick darkness
L Jr	6:13	which is thick upon them
2 Ma	1:20	that they had not found fire but thick liquid
2 Es	16:28	in thick groves and clefts in the rocks

THICKET   2

1 Ma	4:38	In the courts they saw bushes sprung up as in a thicket
	9:45	with marsh and thicket

THIEF   3 = 0.002 %

Sir	5:14	for shame comes to the thief
	20:25	A thief is preferable to a habitual liar
L Jr	6:57	are not able to save themselves from thieves and robbers

THIGH   3 = 0.002 %

Jud	9:2	and uncovered her thigh to put her to shame
Sir	19:12	Like an arrow stuck in the flesh of the thigh
2 Es	15:36	and a man's thigh and a camel's hock

THINE   10 = 0.007 %

Ad E	13:15	that has been thine from the beginning
Wis	11:26	Thou sparest all things, for they are thine
	15:2	For even if we sin we are thine, knowing thy power
	15:2	because we know that we are accounted thine
1 Es	4:59	and thine is the glory
P Ma	15	and thine is the glory for ever. Amen
2 Es	3:7	And thou didst lay upon him one commandment of thine
	3:24	and in it to offer thee oblations from what is thine
	5:28	and scattered thine only one among the many ?
	9:32	for it could not, because it was thine

THING   314 = 0.205 %

Tob	3:10	When she heard these things she was deeply grieved
	4:19	but the Lord himself gives all good things
	6:17	When Tobias heard these things, he fell in love with her
	7:8	speak of those things which you talked about on the journey
	10:8	and they will inform him how things are with you
	11:15	and he reported to his father the great things
Jud	7:28	Let him not do this day the things which we have described !
	8:1	At that time Judith heard about these things :
	8:14	who made all these things
	8:32	I am about to do a thing
	9:5	For thou hast done these things
	9:5	thou hast designed the things that are now
	9:5	Yea, the things thou didst intend came to pass
	9:6	and the things thou didst will presented themselves and said
	9:13	for they have planned cruel things against thy covenant
	10:9	and accomplish the things about which you spoke with me
	11:9	Now as for the things Achior said in your council
	11:13	so much as to touch these things with their hands
	11:16	things that will astonish the whole world
	12:2	from the things I have brought with me
	12:4	your servant will not use up the things I have with me
	13:3	And she had said the same thing to Bagoas
	15:8	came to witness the good things
	15:11	and hitched up her carts and piled the things on them
	16:16	For every sacrifice as a fragrant offering is a small thing
	16:16	and all fat for burnt offerings to thee is a very little thing
Ad E	10:4	And Mordecai said, These things have come from God
	12:4	The king made a permanent record of these things
	12:5	and rewarded him for these things
	13:9	He said : O Lord, Lord, King who rulest over all things
	13:10	and every wonderful thing under heaven
	13:12	Thou knowest all things
	13:14	and I will not do these things in pride
	14:15	Thou hast knowledge of all things
	16:18	because the man himself who did these things
	16:18	For God, who rules over all things
	16:21	For God, who rules over all things
Wis	1:7	and that which holds all things together knows what is said
	1:8	therefore no one who utters unrighteous things will escape notice
	1:10	because a jealous ear hears all things
	1:14	For he created all things that they might exist
	2:6	Come, therefore, let us enjoy the good things that exist
	3:14	and who has not devised wicked things against the Lord
	4:15	nor take such a thing to heart
	5:9	All those things have vanished like a shadow
	6:10	who observe holy things in holiness
	7:11	All good things came to me along with her
	7:22	for wisdom, the fashioner of all things, taught me
	7:24	she pervades and penetrates all things
	7:27	Though she is but one, she can do all things
	7:27	and while remaining in herself, she renews all things
	8:1	and she orders all things well
	8:5	what is richer than wisdom who effects all things ?
	8:8	she knows the things of old, and infers the things to come
	8:17	When I considered these things inwardly
	9:1	who hast made all things by thy word
	9:11	For she knows and understands all things
	10:2	and gave him strength to rule all things
	11:5	For through the very things
	11:16	by the very things by which he sins
	11:20	But thou hast arranged all things
	11:23	But thou art merciful to all, for thou canst do all things
	11:24	For thou lovest all things that exist
	11:24	and hast loathing for none of the things
	11:26	Thou sparest all things, for they are thine
	12:1	For thy immortal spirit is in all things
	12:2	and dost remind and warn them of the things wherein they sin
	12:15	Thou art righteous and rulest all things righteously
	13:1	and they were unable from the good things that are seen
	13:3	If through delight in the beauty of these things
	13:5	For from the greatness and beauty of created things
	13:7	because the things that are seen are beautiful
	13:9	how did they fail to find sooner the Lord of these things ?
	13:10	But miserable, with their hopes set on dead things
	13:17	he is not ashamed to address a lifeless thing
	13:18	For health he appeals to a thing that is weak
	13:18	for life he prays to a thing that is dead

13 : 18	for aid he entreats a thing that is utterly inexperienced
13 : 18	for a prosperous journey, a thing that cannot take a step
13 : 19	he asks strength of a thing whose hands have no strength
14 : 8	and the perishable thing was named a god
14 : 31	For it is not the power of the things by which men swear
15 : 1	and ruling all things in mercy
15 : 6	Lovers of evil things and fit for such objects of hope
16 : 9	because they deserved to be punished by such things
16 : 17	in the water, which quenches all things
16 : 20	Instead of these things
17 : 6	and in terror they deemed the things which they saw
17 : 11	For wickedness is a cowardly thing
18 : 9	that the saints would share alike the same things
18 : 14	For while gentle silence enveloped all things
18 : 14	and stood and filled all things with death

Sir	1 : 4	Wisdom was created before all things
	2 : 9	you who fear the Lord, hope for good things
	7 : 31	and the first fruits of the holy things
	10 : 11	For when a man is dead, he will inherit creeping things
	11 : 3	but her product is the best of sweet things
	11 : 14	good things and bad, life and death, poverty and wealth
	13 : 13	When you hear these things in your sleep, wake up !
	16 : 5	Many such things my eye has seen
	16 : 5	and my ear has heard things more striking than these
	16 : 29	and filled it with his good things
	17 : 2	but granted them authority over the things upon the earth
	17 : 30	For all things cannot be in men
	18 : 3	and all things obey his will
	18 : 3	for he is king of all things
	18 : 3	the holy things from the profane
	18 : 26	and all things move swiftly before the Lord
	19 : 1	he who despises small things will fail little by little
	21 : 25	The lips of strangers will speak of these things
	24 : 8	Then the Creator of all things gave me a commandment
	25 : 1	My soul takes pleasure in 3 things
	25 : 4	What an attractive thing is judgment in grey-haired men
	26 : 5	Of 3 things my heart is afraid
	26 : 28	At 2 things my heart is grieved
	27 : 1	I have hated many things, but none to be compared to him
	29 : 28	These things are hard to bear for a man who has feeling :
	30 : 18	Good things poured out upon a mouth that is closed
	31 : 9	for he has done wonderful things among his people
	31 : 13	Remember that a greedy eye is a bad thing
	32 : 13	And for these things bless him who made you
	34 : 4	From an unclean thing what will be made clean ?
	34 : 9	An educated man knows many things
	34 : 10	He that is inexperienced knows few things
	34 : 11	I have seen many things in my travels
	34 : 26	and goes again and does the same things
	35 : 5	for all these things are to be done
	39 : 16	All things are the works of the Lord, for they are very good
	39 : 17	For in God's time all things will be sought after
	39 : 25	From the beginning good things were created for good people
	39 : 25	just as evil things for sinners
	39 : 34	for all things will prove good in their season
	40 : 11	All things that are from the earth turn back to the earth
	42 : 1	Of the following things do not be ashamed
	42 : 6	Where there is an evil wife, a seal is a good thing
	42 : 6	and where there are many hands, lock things up
	42 : 19	and he reveals the tracks of hidden things
	42 : 23	All these things live and remain for ever for every need
	42 : 24	All things are twofold, one opposite the other
	42 : 25	One confirms the good things of the other
	43 : 22	A mist quickly heals all things
	43 : 25	all kinds of living things, and huge creatures of the sea
	43 : 26	and by his word all things hold together
	43 : 32	Many things greater than these lie hidden
	43 : 33	For the Lord has made all things
	45 : 13	Before his time there never were such beautiful things
	48 : 24	By the spirit of might he saw the last things
	48 : 25	and the hidden things before they came to pass
	50 : 22	who in every way does great things
	50 : 28	Blessed is he who concerns himself with these things
	50 : 29	For if he does them, he will be strong for all things
	51 : 24	Why do you say you are lacking in these things
	51 : 25	Get these things for yourselves without money
Bar	3 : 32	But he who knows all things knows her
L Jr	6 : 29	Since you know by these things that they are not gods
	6 : 39	These things that are made of wood and overlaid with gold and silver
	6 : 46	how then can the things that are made by them be gods ?
P Az	6	and have sinned in all things
	54	Bless the Lord, all things that grow on the earth
Sus	13 : 22	For if I do this thing, it is death for me
	13 : 40	These things we testify
	13 : 42	who art aware of all things before they come to be
	13 : 43	Yet I have done none of the things
1 Ma	4 : 27	for things had not happened to Israel as he had intended
	5 : 37	After these things Timothy gathered another army
	6 : 8	because things had not turned out for him as he had planned

	6 : 27	they will do still greater things
	6 : 59	that they became angry and did all these things
	9 : 10	to do such a thing as to flee from them
	9 : 37	After these things it was reported to Jonathan
	9 : 44	for today things are not as they were before
	10 : 22	When Demetrius heard of these things he was grieved and said
	10 : 88	When Alexander the king heard of these things
	11 : 29	and wrote a letter to Jonathan about all these things
	11 : 42	Not only will I do these things for you and your nation
	12 : 9	Therefore, though we have no need of these things
	13 : 3	You yourselves know what great things
	14 : 9	they all talked together of good things
	14 : 25	When the people heard these things they said
	14 : 35	because he had done all these things
	14 : 36	And in his days things prospered in his hands
	14 : 38	In view of these things
	15 : 22	The consul wrote the same thing to Demetrius the king
	15 : 24	They also sent a copy of these things
	16 : 2	and things have prospered in our hands
	16 : 18	Then Ptolemy wrote a report about these things
2 Ma	1 : 24	O Lord, Lord God, Creator of all things
	2 : 8	And then the Lord will disclose these things
	2 : 13	The same things are reported in the records
	4 : 17	For it is no light thing
	6 : 4	and besides brought in things for sacrifice that were unfit
	6 : 20	as men ought to go who have the courage to refuse things
	6 : 30	but in my soul I am glad to suffer these things
	7 : 18	For we are suffering these things on our own account
	7 : 18	Therefore astounding things have happened
	7 : 23	and devised the origin of all things
	7 : 28	that God did not make them out of things that existed
	10 : 38	When they had accomplished these things
	12 : 14	railing at them and even blaspheming and saying unholy things
	12 : 22	at the manifestation to them of him who sees all things
	12 : 41	the righteous Judge, who reveals the things that are hidden
	13 : 9	was coming to show to the Jews things far worse
	15 : 2	which he who sees all things has honoured
1 Es	1 : 17	So the things that had to do with the sacrifices to the Lord
	1 : 33	These things are written in the book of the histories
	1 : 33	and the things that he had done before and these that are now told
	1 : 42	But the things that are reported about Jehoiakim
	1 : 56	and utterly destroyed all its glorious things
	2 : 7	besides the other things added as votive offerings
	3 : 5	Let each of us state what one thing is strongest
	3 : 12	but truth is victor over all things
	3 : 24	since it forces men to do these things ?
	4 : 18	If men gather gold and silver or any other beautiful thing
	4 : 19	they let all those things go, and gape at her
	4 : 19	or any other beautiful thing
	4 : 32	since they do such things ?
	4 : 35	Is he not great who does these things ?
	4 : 35	But truth is great, and stronger than all things
	4 : 37	all their works are unrighteous, and all such things
	5 : 40	not to share in the holy things
	6 : 4	and this roof and finishing all the other things ?
	6 : 4	And who are the builders that are finishing these things ?
	6 : 22	let him send us directions concerning these things
	6 : 32	or nullify any of the things herein written
	8 : 1	After these things
	8 : 21	Let all things prescribed in the law of God
	8 : 53	And again we prayed to our Lord about these things
	8 : 68	After these things had been done
	8 : 71	As soon as I heard these things
	8 : 82	when we have these things ?
	8 : 85	and eat the good things of the land
	8 : 90	because of these things
	9 : 11	for we have sinned too much in these things
P Ma	4	at whom all things shudder, and tremble before thy power
3 Ma	2 : 3	For you, the creator of all things and the governor of all
	2 : 21	Thereupon God, who oversees all things
	3 : 21	Among other things
	4 : 16	praising speechless things that are not able
	5 : 28	This was the act of God who rules over all things
	5 : 28	a forgetfulness of the things he had previously devised
	5 : 37	must I give you orders about these things ?
	6 : 6	so as not to serve vain things
	6 : 22	because of the things that he had devised beforehand
	6 : 29	These then were the things he said
	6 : 36	And when they had ordained a public rite for these things
	7 : 8	or reproaching them for the irrational things that have happened
	7 : 18	all things to them for their journey
2 Es	1 : 37	yet with the spirit they will believe the things I have said
	3 : 8	and did ungodly things before thee and scorned thee
	4 : 6	that you ask me concerning these things ?
	4 : 9	things through which you have passed
	4 : 10	You cannot understand the things with which you have grown up
	4 : 23	but about those things which we daily experience :
	4 : 25	It is about these things that I have asked

	4 : 27	For it will not be able to bring the things
	4 : 33	How long and when will these things be ?
	4 : 42	so also do these places hasten to give back those things
	4 : 43	Then the things that you desire to see
	5 : 13	you shall hear yet greater things than these
	5 : 38	who is able to know these things
	5 : 39	and how can I speak concerning the things
	5 : 40	Just as you cannot do one of the things that were mentioned
	6 : 6	then I planned these things
	6 : 30	I have come to show you these things this night
	6 : 31	I will again declare to you greater things than these
	6 : 33	Therefore he sent me to show you all these things
	6 : 53	to bring forth before thee cattle, beasts, and creeping things
	7 : 6	and it is full of all good things
	7 : 14	they can never receive those things
	7 : 17	that the righteous shall inherit these things
	7 : 25	Therefore, Ezra, empty things are for the empty
	7 : 25	and full things are for the full
	7 : 44	and to you alone have I shown these things
	7 : 57	Judge therefore which things are precious and desirable
	7 : 62	like the other created things !
	7 : 70	and the things that pertain to the judgment
	7 : 101	they may see the things of which you have been told
	8 : 37	Some things you have spoken rightly
	8 : 44	and for whose sake thou hast formed all things
	8 : 46	Things that are present are for those who live now
	8 : 46	and things that are future are for those who will live hereafter
	8 : 59	For just as the things which I have predicted await you
	9 : 35	they are destroyed, but the things that held them remain
	9 : 38	When I said these things in my heart
	10 : 22	our holy things have been polluted
	10 : 38	and tell you about the things which you fear
	10 : 52	for I knew that the Most High would reveal these things to you
	11 : 6	And I saw how all things under heaven were subjected to him
	12 : 23	and they shall renew many things in it
	12 : 37	Therefore write all these things that you have seen in a book
	13 : 20	Yet is it better to come into these things
	13 : 21	the things which you have mentioned
	13 : 32	And when these things come to pass
	13 : 56	And after 3 more days I will tell you other things
	13 : 58	and whatever things come to pass in their seasons
	14 : 5	and I told him many wondrous things
	14 : 21	and so no one knows the things which have been done by thee
	14 : 22	the things which were written in thy law
	14 : 26	some things you shall make public
	16 : 35	Listen now to these things, and understand them
	16 : 62	who made all things
	16 : 62	and searches out hidden things in hidden places
4 Ma	4 : 4	When Apollonius learned the details of these things
	5 : 9	It is senseless not to enjoy delicious things
	5 : 25	we know that in the nature of things
	6 : 14	through these evil things
	8 : 12	When he had said these things
	8 : 27	neither said any of these things
	9 : 10	When they had said these things the tyrant not only was angry
	9 : 19	While he was saying these things they spread fire under him
	11 : 5	It is because we revere the Creator of all things and live
	11 : 9	While he was saying these things
	12 : 11	since you have received good things and also your kingdom from God

THINK
55 = 0.036 %

Jud	8 : 14	nor find out what a man is thinking
Ad E	16 : 14	He thought that in this way he would find us undefended
Wis	1 : 1	think of the Lord with uprightness
	3 : 2	and their departure was thought to be an affliction
	5 : 4	We thought that his life was madness
	8 : 17	and thought upon them in my mind
	12 : 27	which they had thought to be gods
	14 : 30	because they thought wickedly of God
	15 : 15	For they thought that all their heathen idols were gods
	17 : 3	For thinking that in their secret sins
Sir	11 : 5	but one who was never thought of has worn a crown
	15 : 8	and liars will never think of her
	16 : 23	This is what one devoid of understanding thinks
	16 : 23	a senseless and misguided man thinks foolishly
	17 : 6	he gave them ears and a mind for thinking
	18 : 24	Think of his wrath on the day of death
	18 : 25	In the time of plenty think of the time of hunger
	18 : 25	in the days of wealth think of poverty and need
	39 : 12	I have yet more to say, which I have thought upon
L Jr	6 : 40	Why then must any one think that they are gods
	6 : 44	Why then must any one think that they are gods
	6 : 56	Why then must any one admit or think that they are gods ?
	6 : 64	Therefore one must not think that they are gods nor call them gods
Bel	14 : 6	Do you not think that Bel is a living God ?
1 Ma	4 : 45	And they thought it best to tear it down
	5 : 61	because, thinking to do a brave deed
2 Ma	1 : 18	we thought it necessary to notify you

	4 : 19	thought best not to use it for sacrifice
	4 : 32	But Menelaus, thinking he had obtained a suitable opportunity
	5 : 21	thinking in his arrogance
	7 : 16	But do not think that God has forsaken our people
	7 : 19	But do not think that you will go unpunished
	9 : 8	Thus he who had just been thinking
	9 : 10	had thought that he could touch the stars of heaven
	9 : 12	and no mortal should think that he is equal to God
	12 : 12	Judas, thinking that they might really be useful in many ways
	13 : 3	but because he thought
	14 : 14	thinking that the misfortunes and calamities of the Jews
	14 : 37	and was very well thought of
	14 : 40	for he thought that by arresting him
1 Es	2 : 20	we think it best not to neglect such a matter
3 Ma	5 : 22	for those they thought to be doomed
	5 : 49	they thought that this was their last moment of life
2 Es	4 : 2	and do you think you can comprehend the way of the Most High ?
	4 : 51	Do you think that I shall live until those days ?
	6 : 34	Do not be quick to think vain thoughts
	7 : 59	Weigh within yourself what you have thought
	8 : 28	Think not on those who have lived wickedly in thy sight
	8 : 51	But think of your own case
	16 : 63	and what you think in your hearts !
4 Ma	1 : 33	I for one think so
	5 : 16	think that there is no compulsion more powerful
	6 : 17	never think so basely
	9 : 30	Do you not think, you most savage tyrant
	13 : 14	Let us not fear him who thinks he is killing us

THINK out
1

Sir	39 : 32	and have thought this out and left it in writing :

THINKING
2

Wis	12 : 10	and that their way of thinking would never change
Sir	13 : 26	but to devise proverbs requires painful thinking

THIRD, subst., s. NUMBERS
1

1 Ma	10 : 30	and instead of collecting the third of the grain

THIRD, adv.
1

Sir	23 : 23	and third, she has committed adultery through harlotry

THIRST, subst.
13 = 0.008 %

Jud	7 : 13	So thirst will destroy them, and they will give up their city
	7 : 22	and the women and young men fainted from thirst
	7 : 25	with thirst and utter destruction
Wis	11 : 4	and slaking of thirst from hard stone
	11 : 8	showing by their thirst at that time
	11 : 14	for their thirst was not like that of the righteous
Sir	12 : 16	his thirst for blood will be insatiable
2 Es	8 : 59	so the thirst and torment which are prepared await them
	15 : 58	and drink their own blood in thirst for water
4 Ma	1 : 26	thirst for honour, rivalry, and malice
	3 : 6	by the story of King David's thirst
	3 : 10	he could not satisfy his thirst from them
	3 : 15	But David, although he was burning with thirst

THIRST, verb
2

Wis	11 : 4	When they thirsted they called upon thee
Sir	24 : 21	and those who drink me will thirst for more

THIRSTY
7 = 0.005 %

Jud	8 : 30	But the people were very thirsty
Sir	26 : 12	As a thirsty wayfarer opens his mouth
	51 : 24	and why are your souls very thirsty ?
2 Es	1 : 17	When you were hungry and thirsty in the wilderness
	1 : 20	When you were thirsty
	1 : 22	thirsty and blaspheming my name
4 Ma	3 : 10	but the king was extremely thirsty

THIS, dem. pr. or adj.
840 = 0.547 %

THISBE
1

Tob	1 : 2	was taken into captivity from Thisbe

THONG
2

Sir	33 : 26	Yoke and thong will bow the neck
4 Ma	9 : 11	they bound his hands and arms with thongs on each side

THORN
6 = 0.004 %

Sir	24 : 15	Like cassia and camel's thorn
	28 : 24	See that you fence in your property with thorns
	43 : 19	and when it freezes, it becomes pointed thorns
L Jr	6 : 71	are like a thorn bush in a garden
2 Es	16 : 32	and its roads and all its paths shall bring forth thorns
	16 : 77	and its path overwhelmed with thorns

THOROUGHLY
                                                   3 = 0.002 %

Jud 11:8   thoroughly informed and marvellous in military strategy
2 Ma 3:38 send him there, for you will get him back thoroughly scourged
4 Ma 1:29 and ties up and waters and thoroughly irrigates

THOU
                294 = 0.191 %

THOUGH, adv., conj.
                81 = 0.053 %

Tob 14:5   though it will not be like the former one
Ad E 11:10 and from their cry, as though from a tiny spring
Wis 2:2   and hereafter we shall be as though we had never been
    3:4   For though in the sight of men they were punished
    4:7   But the righteous man, though he die early, will be at rest
    7:27 Though she is but one, she can do all things
    8:10 and honour in the presence of the elders, though I am young
    11:9 though they were being disciplined in mercy
    11:14 For though they had mockingly rejected him
    12:9 though thou wast not unable to give the ungodly
    12:10 though thou wast not unaware that their origin was evil
    14:11 because, though part of what God created
    14:17 they might flatter the absent one as though present
    15:15 though these have neither the use of their eyes to see with
    17:10 though it nowhere could be avoided
    18:2   though previously wronged, were doing them no injury
    18:13 For though they had disbelieved everything
    19:2   that, though they themselves had permitted
Sir 40:6   and afterward in his sleep, as though he were on watch
    42:10 or, though married, lest she be barren
    43:27 Though we speak much we cannot reach the end
    44:9   who have perished as though they had not lived
    44:9   they have become as though they had not been born
L Jr 6:14   though unable to destroy any one who offends it
    6:18   as though he were sentenced to death
    6:19   though their gods can see none of them
    6:41   as though Bel were able to understand
P Az 16   as though it were with burnt offerings of rams and bulls
Sus 13:53 though the Lord said
1 Ma 8:4   even though the place was far distant from them
    10:77 and went to Azotus as though he were going farther
    12:9   Therefore, though we have no need of these things
2 Ma 2:21 so that though few in number they seized the whole land
    6:16   Though he disciplines us with calamities
    6:30   that, though I might have been saved from death
    7:16   Because you have authority among men, mortal though you are
    7:20   Though she saw her 7 sons perish within a single day
    12:3   as though there were no ill will to the Jews
    12:18 though in one place he had left a very strong garrison
    14:45 and though his blood gushed forth and his wounds were severe
1 Es 1:48   And though King Nebuchadnezzar had made him swear
    5:37   though they could not prove by their fathers' houses or lineage
    5:53   though the temple of God was not yet built
3 Ma 2:9   though you have no need of anything
    2:24   After a while he recovered and, though he had been punished
    3:8   The Greeks in the city, though wronged in no way
    4:15   and though uncompleted it stopped after 40 days
    5:40   O king, how long will you try us, as though we are idiots
2 Es 1:27   It is not as though you had forsaken me
    1:37   though they do not see me with bodily eyes
    3:33   though they are unmindful of thy commandments
    7:72   because though they had understanding they committed iniquity
    7:72   and though they received the commandments they did not keep
          them
    7:72   and though they obtained the law
    7:118 For though it was you who sinned
    8:58   though knowing full well that they must die
    9:32   But though our fathers received the law
    9:43   though I lived with my husband 30 years
    13:20 though incurring peril
4 Ma 2:8   even though he is a lover of money
    4:25   though they had known beforehand that they would suffer this
    5:22   as though living by it were irrational
    6:5   as though being tortured in a dream
    6:7   And though he fell to the ground
    6:16   But Eleazar, as though more bitterly tormented by this counsel, cried out :
    6:27   You know, O God, that though I might have saved myself
    7:2   and though buffeted by the stormings of the tyrant
    7:12   though being consumed by the fire
    7:13   Most amazing, indeed, though he was an old man
    8:27   But the youths, though about to be tortured
    9:5   as though a short time ago you learned nothing from Eleazar
    9:14   and though broken in every member
    9:22   but as though transformed by fire into immortality
    12:2   Even though the tyrant had been fearfully reproached by the brothers
    14:5   but all of them, as though running the course toward immortality
    14:6   as though moved by an immortal spirit of devotion
    14:19 and as though with an iron dart sting those who approach their hive

    15:11 Nevertheless, though so many factors influenced the mother
    16:5   If this woman, though a mother, had been fainthearted
    16:13 but, as though having a mind like adamant
    18:14 Even though you go through the fire

THOUGHT
                45 = 0.029 %

Tob 3:10   even to the thought of hanging herself
    8:10   with the thought, Perhaps he too will die
Jud 8:14   and find out his mind or comprehend his thought ?
Wis 1:3   For perverse thoughts separate men from God
    1:5   and will rise and depart from foolish thoughts
    2:14   He became to us a reproof of our thoughts
    6:7   and he takes thought for all alike
    6:15   To fix one's thought on her is perfect understanding
    6:16   and meets them in every thought
    7:15   and have thoughts worthy of what I have received
    11:15 In return for their foolish and wicked thoughts
    13:16 So he takes thought for it, that it may not fall
Sir 3:24   and wrong opinion has caused their thoughts to slip
    3:31   Whoever requites favours gives thought to the future
    8:19   Do not reveal your thoughts to every one
    21:11 Whoever keeps the law controls his thoughts
    22:17 A mind settled on an intelligent thought
    23:2   O that whips were set over my thoughts
    24:29 for her thought is more abundant than the sea
    25:7   With 9 thoughts I have gladdened my heart
    27:4   so a man's filth remains in his thoughts
    27:6   so the expression of a thought discloses the cultivation of a man's mind
    33:5   and his thoughts like a turning axle
    37:8   for he will take thought for himself
    40:2   their anxious thought is the day of death
    42:20 No thought escapes him, and not one word is hidden from him
Bar 2:8   by turning away, each of us, from the thoughts of his wicked heart
    3:23   nor given thought to her paths
2 Ma 2:2   nor to be led astray in their thoughts
    9:21   and I have deemed it necessary to take thought
    12:45 it was a holy and pious thought
    14:9   deign to take thought for our country
1 Es 3:20   It turns every thought to feasting and mirth
    4:21   with no thought of his father or his mother or his country
2 Es 3:1   and my thoughts welled up in my heart
    5:21   the thoughts of my heart were very grievous to me again
    6:34   Do not be quick to think vain thoughts
    7:22   they devised for themselves vain thoughts
    7:92   to overcome the evil thought which was formed with them
    9:39   Then I dismissed the thoughts with which I had been engaged
    10:31 and the thoughts of your mind troubled ?
    13:38 and will reproach them to their face with their evil thoughts
    14:14 and put away from you mortal thoughts
    14:15 and lay to one side the thoughts that are most grievous to you
    16:54 their imaginations and their thoughts and their hearts

THOUGHTFUL
                3 = 0.002 %

Wis 9:15   and this earthly tent burdens the thoughtful mind
Sir 27:12 but among thoughtful people stay on
    31:15 and in every matter be thoughtful

THOUGHTLESS
                1

Wis 12:25 Therefore, as to thoughtless children

THOUSAND, subst., s. NUMBERS
          5 = 0.003 %

P Az 16   and with tens of thousands of fat lambs
1 Ma 3:55   in charge of thousands and hundreds and fifties and tens
2 Ma 11:4 and his thousands of cavalry, and his 80 elephants
1 Es 1:9   captains over thousands
4 Ma 4:3   there are deposited tens of thousands in private funds

THRACIAN
                1

2 Ma 12:35 when one of the Thracian horsemen bore down upon him

THREAD
                1

4 Ma 9:25   the saintly youth broke the thread of life

THREAT
                9 = 0.006 %

P Ma 5   and the wrath of thy threat to sinners is irresistible
3 Ma 2:24   but went away uttering bitter threats
    5:18   and with sharp threats demanded to know
    5:33   So Hermon suffered an unexpected and dangerous threat
4 Ma 4:8   But, uttering threats, Apollonius went on to the temple
    4:24   but saw that all his threats and punishments were being disregarded
    8:19   and consider the threats of torments
    9:32   but you suffer torture by the threats that come from impiety
    14:9   yes, not only heard the direct word of threat

THREATEN
                11 = 0.007 %

Jud 8:16   for God is not like a man, to be threatened
Ad E 11:9 they feared the evils that threatened them

Sir	19:17	Question your neighbour before you threaten him
Bar	2:7	All those calamities with which the Lord threatened us have come upon us
3 Ma	4:19	After he had threatened them severely
	6:23	he wept and angrily threatened his friends, saying
	7:6	But we very severely threatened them for these acts
2 Es	15:34	and their appearance is very threatening
	16:11	The Lord will threaten
4 Ma	8:19	and this arrogance that threatens to destroy us ?
	9:5	by threatening us with death by torture

THREATENING   3 = 0.002 %

3 Ma	5:30	and with a threatening look he said
	5:37	After summoning Hermon he said in a threatening tone
4 Ma	13:6	hold back the threatening waves

THRESHING   4 = 0.003 %

2 Es	4:30	and will produce until the time of threshing comes !
	4:32	how great a threshing floor they will fill !
	4:39	that the time of threshing is delayed for the righteous
	9:17	and as is the farmer, so is the threshing floor

THRICE   1

Ad E	16:15	who were consigned to annihilation by this thrice accursed man

THRICE-ACCURSED   2

2 Ma	8:34	The thrice-accursed Nicanor
	15:3	the thrice-accursed wretch asked

THRONE   29 = 0.019 %

Jud	1:12	and swore by his throne and kingdom
	9:3	and princes on their thrones
	11:19	and I will set your throne in the midst of it
Ad E	15:6	He was seated on his royal throne
	15:8	and in alarm he sprang from his throne
	16:11	as the person second to the royal throne
Wis	5:23	and evil-doing will overturn the thrones of rulers
	6:21	Therefore if you delight in thrones and sceptres
	7:8	I preferred her to sceptres and thrones
	9:4	give me the wisdom that sits by thy throne
	9:10	and from the throne of thy glory send her
	9:12	and shall be worthy of the throne of my father
	18:15	from the royal throne
Sir	1:8	sitting upon his throne
	10:14	The Lord has cast down the thrones of rulers
	24:4	and my throne was in a pillar of cloud
	40:3	from the man who sits on a splendid throne
	47:11	and a throne of glory in Israel
Bar	5:6	carried in glory, as on a royal throne
P Az	33	Blessed art thou upon the throne of thy kingdom
1 Ma	2:57	inherited the throne of the kingdom for ever
	7:4	and Demetrius took his seat upon the throne of his kingdom
	10:52	and have taken my seat on the throne of my fathers
	10:53	and we have taken our seat on the throne of his kingdom
	10:55	and took your seat on the throne of their kingdom
	11:52	So Demetrius the king sat on the throne of his kingdom
2 Es	8:21	whose throne is beyond measure
4 Ma	4:15	his son Antiochus Epiphanes succeeded to the throne
	17:18	because of which they now stand before the divine throne

THRONG, subst.   2

1 Es	8:91	there gathered about him a very great throng from Jerusalem
3 Ma	6:14	The whole throng of infants and their parents entreat you with tears

THRONG, verb   1

2 Ma	3:19	thronged the streets

THROUGH, prep., adv.   139 = 0.091 %

Tob	4:6	your ways will prosper through your deeds
Jud	2:24	and passed through Mesopotamia
	7:22	and in the passages through the gates
	8:32	which will go down through all generations of our descendants
	10:10	and passed through the valley
	10:11	The women went straight on through the valley
	11:6	God will accomplish something through you
	11:19	Then I will lead you through the middle of Judea
	13:10	and they passed through the camp
	15:2	by every path across the plain and through the hill country
	16:12	The sons of maidservants have pierced them through
Ad E	15:6	When she had gone through all the doors
	16:7	through the pestilent behaviour of those
Wis	2:24	but through the devil's envy death entered the world
	3:7	and will run like sparks through the stubble
	5:7	and we journeyed through trackless deserts
	5:10	like a ship that sails through the billowy water
	5:11	or as, when a bird flies through the air
	7:23	and penetrating through all spirits
	10:17	and a starry flame through the night
	10:18	and led them through deep waters

	11:2	They journeyed through an uninhabited wilderness
	11:5	For through the very things
	11:13	For when they heard that through their own punishments
	12:11	and it was not through fear of any one
	12:19	Through such works thou hast taught thy people
	12:23	thou didst torment through their own abominations
	13:3	If through delight in the beauty of these things
	14:3	and a safe way through the waves
	14:5	and passing through the billows on a raft
	14:14	For through the vanity of men they entered the world
	14:30	through contempt for holiness
	16:1	through such creatures
	17:6	Nothing was shining through to them
	18:4	through whom the imperishable light of the law
	19:8	where those protected by thy hand passed through as one nation
	19:17	each tried to find the way through his own door
Sir pr.		through the law and the prophets
	4:24	For wisdom is known through speech
	4:24	and education through the words of the tongue
	6:2	Do not exalt yourself through your soul's counsel
	6:7	When you gain a friend, gain him through testing
	7:28	Remember that through your parents you were born
	8:15	and through his folly you will perish with him
	10:3	through the understanding of its rulers
	11:18	There is a man who is rich through his diligence and self-denial
	11:28	a man will be known through his children
	13:11	for he will test you through much talk
	14:23	He who peers through her windows
	16:4	For through one man of understanding
	16:4	but through a tribe of lawless men it will be made desolate
	20:13	The wise man makes himself beloved through his words
	20:22	A man may lose his life through shame
	23:8	The sinner is overtaken through his lips
	23:23	and third, she has committed adultery through harlotry
	26:28	a warrior in want through poverty
	32:12	but do not sin through proud speech
	39:4	he will travel through the lands of foreign nations
	39:9	and his name will live through all generations
	44:21	that the nations would be blessed through his posterity
	45:4	He sanctified him through faithfulness and meekness
	47:19	and through your body you were brought into subjection
	51:20	and through purification I found her
Bar	1:20	through Moses his servant at the time
	3:28	they perished through their folly
L Jr	6:27	because through them these gods are made to stand
P Az	25	and it broke through and burned those of the Chaldeans
Sus	13:57	and they were intimate with you through fear
Bel	14:13	through which they used to go in regularly
	14:21	through which they were accustomed to enter
1 Ma	3:8	He went through the cities of Judah
	3:37	and went through the upper provinces
	5:46	they had to go through it
	5:48	Let us pass through your land to get to our land
	5:51	Then he passed through the city over the slain
	5:62	through whom deliverance was given to Israel
	5:66	and passed through Marisa
	6:1	King Antiochus was going through the upper provinces
	6:31	They came through Idumea and encamped against Beth-zur
	11:47	and then spread out through the city
	11:62	And he passed through the country as far as Damascus
	12:32	and marched through all that region
	12:33	Simon also went forth and marched through the country
2 Ma	2:18	as he promised through the law
	4:11	secured through John the father of Eupolemus
	5:2	there appeared goldenclad horsemen charging through the air
	6:25	and through my pretence
	7:30	that was given to our fathers through Moses
	7:38	through me and my brothers
	14:8	For through the folly of those whom I have mentioned
	14:43	and the crowd was now rushing in through the doors
	14:45	he ran through the crowd
3 Ma	2:7	but carried through safely
	5:5	and arranged for their continued custody through the night
	5:18	through the present day
	6:7	Daniel, who through envious slanders
	6:36	that had come to them through God
	7:23	Blessed be the Deliverer of Israel through all times ! Amen
2 Es	1:13	Surely it was I who brought you through the sea
	2:1	and I gave them commandments through my servants the prophets
	3:19	And thy glory passed through the 4 gates
	4:9	things through which you have passed
	5:11	passed through you ? And it will answer, No
	5:56	show thy servant through whom thou dost visit thy creation
	6:6	and they were made through me and not through another
	6:6	just as the end shall come through me
	6:6	and not through another
	7:5	unless he passes through the narrow part ?
	7:9	unless he passes through the danger set before him ?
	7:14	pass through the difficult and vain experiences

7 : 60	and through them my name has now been honoured
9 : 31	and you shall be glorified through it for ever
11 : 39	so that the end of my times might come through them ?
13 : 45	Through that region there was a long way to go
14 : 17	For the weaker the world becomes through old age
16 : 30	through the vineyard
16 : 77	so that no one can pass through !
4 Ma **1** : 11	and thus their native land was purified through them
2 : 9	If one is greedy, he is ruled by the law through his reason
2 : 14	through the law, can prevail even over enmity
4 : 26	he himself, through torture, tried to compel everyone in the nation
6 : 14	through these evil things
7 : 9	through your glorious endurance
7 : 11	ran through the multitude of the people
7 : 14	in spirit through reason
7 : 22	would no be able to overcome the emotions through godliness ?
8 : 9	with dreadful punishments through tortures
9 : 4	which insures our safety through transgression of the law
9 : 8	For we, through this severe suffering and endurance
9 : 18	Through all these tortures I will convince you
11 : 12	because through these noble sufferings you give us
11 : 19	and pierced his ribs so that his entrails were burned through
13 : 19	has bequeathed through the fathers to their descendants
13 : 20	and growing from the same God and through the same life
16 : 18	Remember that it is through God
17 : 18	and live through blessed eternity
17 : 22	And through the blood of those devout ones
18 : 14	Even though you go through the fire

THROUGHOUT 27 = 0.018 %

Tob **10** : 7	and throughout the nights she never stopped mourning for her son Tobias
Jud **2** : 11	throughout your whole region
4 : 13	for the people fasted many days throughout Judea
7 : 29	throughout the assembly
11 : 8	and it is reported throughout the whole world
11 : 23	and be renowned throughout the whole world
16 : 21	and was honoured in her time throughout the whole country
Ad E **13** : 2	and open to travel throughout all its extent
Wis **4** : 2	and throughout all time it marches crowned in triumph
17 : 14	But throughout the night, which was really powerless
Sir **45** : 26	and that their glory may endure throughout their generations
47 : 10	and arranged their times throughout the year
Bel **14** : 14	and they sifted them throughout the whole temple
2 Ma **2** : 22	and recovered the temple famous throughout the world
3 : 12	which is honoured throughout the whole world
3 : 14	There was no little distress throughout the whole city
9 : 24	the people throughout the realm would not be troubled
14 : 14	And the Gentiles throughout Judea
1 Es **1** : 32	throughout the whole nation of Israel
2 : 2	and he made a proclamation throughout all his kingdom
8 : 23	throughout all Syria and Phoenicia
9 : 3	And a proclamation was made throughout Judea and Jerusalem
3 Ma **6** : 1	and throughout his life had been adorned with every virtue
2 Es **12** : 34	those who have been saved throughout my borders
15 : 6	For iniquity has spread throughout every land
4 Ma **3** : 13	they went searching throughout the enemy camp
12 : 12	and these throughout all time will never let you go

THROW 22 = 0.014 %

Tob **2** : 3	and thrown into the market place
Sir **12** : 16	but in his mind he will plan to throw you into a pit
22 : 20	One who throws a stone at birds scares them away
27 : 25	Whoever throws a stone straight up throws it on his own head
Bel **14** : 31	They threw Daniel into the lions' den
14 : 42	and threw into the den the men who had attempted his destruction
1 Ma **6** : 51	engines of war to throw fire and stones
7 : 19	and killed them and threw them into the great pit
11 : 5	to throw blame on him
11 : 11	He threw blame on Alexander because he coveted his kingdom
15 : 25	continually throwing his forces against it
2 Ma **1** : 16	they threw stones and struck down the leader and his men
1 : 16	and threw them to the people outside
4 : 41	and threw them in wild confusion at Lysimachus and his men
10 : 30	they were thrown into disorder and cut to pieces
2 Es **1** : 23	but threw a tree into the water and made the stream sweet
5 : 4	you shall see it thrown into confusion after the 3rd period
4 Ma **4** : 25	were thrown headlong from heights along with their infants
12 : 1	When he also, thrown into the cauldron
16 : 21	And Daniel the righteous was thrown to the lions
17 : 1	she threw herself into the flames

THROW away 1

1 Ma **5** : 43	and they threw away their arms

THROW back 1

Wis **17** : 19	or an echo thrown back from a hollow of the mountains

THROW down 6 = 0.004 %

Jud **14** : 15	and found him thrown down on the platform dead
1 Ma **7** : 44	they threw down their arms and fled
11 : 51	And they threw down their arms and made peace
2 Ma **14** : 43	and manfully threw himself down into the crowd
2 Es **10** : 21	our altar thrown down, our temple destroyed
4 Ma **6** : 25	threw him down, and poured stinking liquids into his nostrils

THROW in 1

P Az	23	Now the king's servants who threw them in

THROW out 2

Tob **1** : 17	and thrown out behind the wall of Nineveh
2 Ma **9** : 15	but had planned to throw out with their children

THROW up 1

Tob **6** : 3	So the young man seized the fish and threw it up on the land

THUMBSCREW 1

4 Ma **8** : 13	braziers and thumbscrews an iron claws and wedges and bellows

THUMMIM 2

Sir **45** : 10	with the oracle of judgment, Urim and Thummim
1 Es **5** : 40	until a high priest should appear wearing Urim and Thummim

THUNDER, subst. 7 = 0.005 %

Ad E **11** : 5	thunders and earthquake, tumult upon the earth !
Wis **19** : 13	without prior signs in the violence of thunder
Sir **32** : 10	Lightning speeds before the thunder
40 : 13	and crash like a loud clap of thunder in a rain
43 : 17	The voice of his thunder rebukes the earth
2 Es **6** : 2	and before the rumblings of thunder sounded
7 : 40	or cloud or thunder or lightning or wind

THUNDER, verb 2

Sir **46** : 17	Then the Lord thundered from heaven
2 Es **16** : 10	He will thunder, and who will not be terrified ?

THUNDERBOLT 1

2 Ma **10** : 30	And they showered arrows and thunderbolts upon the enemy

THUS 50 = 0.033 %

Jud **1** : 14	Thus he took possession of his cities
2 : 5	Thus says the Great King, the Lord of the whole earth :
Ad E **13** : 1	writes thus : Having become ruler of many nations
Wis **2** : 21	Thus they reasoned, but they were led astray
5 : 12	the air, thus divided, comes together at once
9 : 18	And thus the paths of those on earth were set right
17 : 16	and thus was kept shut up in a prison not made of iron
Sir **1** : 30	and thus bring dishonour upon yourself
7 : 6	and thus put a blot on your integrity
21 : 4	thus the house of the proud will be laid waste
33 : 4	Prepare what to say, and thus you will be heard
Bar **2** : 21	Thus says the Lord :
Sus **13** : 62	Thus innocent blood was saved that day
1 Ma **2** : 26	Thus he burned with zeal for the law
3 : 8	thus he turned away wrath from Israel
4 : 25	Thus Israel had a great deliverance that day
4 : 51	Thus they finished all the work they had undertaken
5 : 44	Thus Carnaim was conquered
5 : 61	Thus the people suffered a great rout
6 : 16	Thus Antiochus the king died there in the 149th year
8 : 29	Thus on these terms the Romans make a treaty
9 : 27	Thus there was great distress in Israel
9 : 41	Thus, the wedding was turned into mourning
9 : 73	Thus the sword ceased from Israel
10 : 65	Thus the king honoured him
11 : 13	Thus he put 2 crowns upon his head
2 Ma **4** : 38	The Lord thus repaid him with the punishment he deserved
7 : 28	Thus also mankind comes into being
8 : 36	Thus he who had undertaken
9 : 8	Thus he who had just been thinking
11 : 22	The king's letter ran thus :
11 : 34	The Romans also sent them a letter which read thus :
15 : 15	and as he gave it he addressed him thus :
1 Es **2** : 3	Thus says Cyrus king of the Persians :
2 Es **1** : 12	But speak to them and say, Thus says the Lord :
1 : 15	Thus says the Lord Almighty :
1 : 22	Thus says the Lord Almighty :
1 : 28	Thus says the Lord Almighty :
1 : 33	Thus says the Lord Almighty : Your house is desolate
2 : 1	Thus says the Lord : I brought this people out of bondage
2 : 10	Thus says the Lord to Ezra :
3 : 22	Thus the disease became permanent
7 : 38	Thus he will speak to them on the day of judgment
15 : 21	Thus says the Lord God :
4 Ma **1** : 11	and thus their native land was purified through them
1 : 22	Thus desire precedes pleasure and delight follows it
2 : 5	Thus the law says, You shall not covet your neighbour's wife
2 : 8	Thus, as soon as a man adopts

423

	2:20	he would not have spoken thus
	16:2	Thus I have demonstrated not only

THY 323 = 0.210 %

THYSELF 14 = 0.009 %

TIARA 2
Jud	10:3	and combed her hair and put on a tiara
	16:8	and fastened her hair with a tiara

TIE 2
4 Ma	6:3	And after they had tied his arms on each side they scourged him
	11:10	they tied him to it on his knees

TIE up 1
4 Ma	1:29	and ties up and waters and thoroughly irrigates

TIGHT 1
4 Ma	11:18	He was carefully stretched tight upon it

TIGHTEN 1
4 Ma	9:19	and while fanning the flames they tightened the wheel further

TIGRIS 3 = 0.002 %
Tob	6:1	they came at evening to the Tigris river and camped there
Jud	1:6	and the Tigris and the Hydaspes
Sir	24:25	and like the Tigris at the time of the first fruits

TIKVAH 1
1 Es	9:14	and Jahzeiah the son of Tikvah

TILL, verb 3 = 0.002 %
1 Ma	14:8	They tilled their land in peace
1 Es	4:6	but till the soil, whenever they sow, reap the harvest
2 Es	15:13	Let the farmers that till the ground mourn

TILL, prep., conj. 18 = 0.012 %
Tob	4:14	Do not hold over till the next day
Jud	2:8	till their wounded shall fill their valleys
	2:10	till the day of their punishment
	11:19	till you come to Jerusalem
Sir	35:18	till he crushes the loins of the unmerciful
	35:18	till he takes away the multitude of the insolent
	35:19	till he repays man according to his deeds
	35:19	till he judges the case of his people
	40:1	till the day they return to the mother of all
	47:25	till vengeance came upon them
	48:15	till they were carried away captive from their land
	50:19	till the order of worship of the Lord was ended
1 Ma	5:53	till he came to the land of Judah
	9:13	and the battle raged from morning till evening
	10:80	from early morning till late afternoon
	14:10	till his renown spread to the ends of the earth
2 Ma	8:35	across the country till he reached Antioch
3 Ma	4:15	from the rising of the sun till its setting

TIMBER 3 = 0.002 %
1 Es	4:48	to bring cedar timber from Lebanon to Jerusalem
	6:9	of hewn stone, with costly timber laid in the walls
	6:25	and one course of new native timber

TIME 264 = 0.172 %
Tob	10:7	At that time Tobias said to Raguel
	14:4	But in Media there will be peace for a time
	14:4	and will be in ruins for a time
	14:5	until the times of the age are completed
Jud	4:1	By this time the people of Israel living in Judea
	4:6	who was in Jerusalem at that time
	5:7	At one time they lived in Mesopotamia
	5:8	and they fled to Mesopotamia, and lived there for a long time
	5:16	and lived there a long time
	7:30	by that time the Lord our God will restore to us his mercy
	8:1	At that time Judith heard about these things :
	8:15	he has power to protect us within any time he pleases
	8:29	Today is not the first time your wisdom has been shown
	9:1	and at the very time
	13:5	For now is the time to help thy inheritance
	16:21	and was honoured in her time throughout the whole country
	16:25	in the days of Judith, or for a long time after her death
Ad E	14:12	make thyself known in this time of our affliction
	16:20	against those who attack them at the time of their affliction
	16:24	but also most hateful for all time to beasts and birds
Wis	2:4	Our name will be forgotten in time
	2:5	For our allotted time is the passing of a shadow
	3:7	In the time of their visitation they will shine forth
	4:2	and throughout all time it marches crowned in triumph
	4:8	For old age is not honoured for length of time
	4:13	Being perfected in a short time, he fulfilled long years
	7:18	the beginning and end and middle of times

	8:8	and of the outcome of seasons and times
	11:8	showing by their thirst at that time
	12:20	granting them time and opportunity
	12:22	thou scourgest our enemies 10,000 times more
	14:16	Then the ungodly custom, grown strong with time
	15:8	this man who was made of earth a short time before
	16:3	while thy people, after suffering want a short time
	16:18	At one time the flame was restrained
	16:19	and at another time even in the midst of water
	16:25	Therefore at that time also
	19:22	at all times and in all places
Sir pr.		and stayed for some time
pr.		using in that period of time great watchfulness and skill
	2:2	and do not be hasty in time of calamity
	2:11	he forgives sins and saves in time of affliction
	4:20	Observe the right time, and beware of evil
	4:23	Do not refrain from speaking at the crucial time
	4:31	but withdrawn when it is time to repay
	5:7	and at the time of punishment you will perish
	6:37	and meditate at all times on his commandments
	8:9	and learn how to give an answer in time of need
	10:4	and over it he will raise up the right man for the time
	10:26	nor glorify yourself at a time when you are in want
	11:19	he does not know how much time will pass
	12:15	He will stay with you for a time
	13:7	until he has drained you 2 or 3 times
	17:2	He gave to men few days, a limited time
	18:25	In the time of plenty think of the time of hunger
	19:9	and when the time comes he will hate you
	20:12	but pays for it 7 times over
	20:19	An ungracious man is like a story told at the wrong time
	20:20	for he does not tell it at its proper time
	22:6	Like music in mourning is a tale told at the wrong time
	22:6	but chastising and discipline are wisdom at all times
	22:23	stand by him in time of affliction
	23:19	are 10,000 times brighter than the sun
	24:25	and like the Tigris at the time of the first fruits
	24:26	and like the Jordan at harvest time
	24:27	like the Gihon at the time of vintage
	26:4	and at all times his face is cheerful
	29:2	Lend to your neighbour in the time of his need
	29:5	but at the time for repayment he will delay
	29:5	and will find fault with the time
	32:11	Leave in good time and do not be the last
	33:23	At the time when you end the days of your life
	35:20	as clouds of rain in the time of drought
	36:8	Hasten the day, and remember the appointed time
	37:4	but in time of trouble are against him
	38:13	There is a time when success lies in the hands of physicians
	39:16	and whatever he commands will be done in his time
	39:17	For in God's time all things will be sought after
	39:28	in the time of consummation
	39:31	and when their times come they will not transgress his word
	40:8	and upon sinners 7 times more
	40:24	Brothers and help are for a time of trouble
	43:4	but the sun burns the mountains 3 times as much
	43:6	to mark the times and to be an everlasting sign
	44:7	and were the glory of their times
	44:17	in the time of wrath he was taken in exchange
	45:13	Before his time there never were such beautiful things
	46:19	Before the time of his eternal sleep
	47:10	and arranged their times throughout the year
	48:3	and also 3 times brought down fire
	48:10	you who are ready at the appointed time, it is written
	48:25	He revealed what was to occur to the end of time
	50:1	and in his time fortified the temple
	50:21	and they bowed down in worship a 2nd time
	51:10	at the time when there is no help against the proud
	51:30	Do your work before the appointed time
	51:30	and in God's time he will give you your reward
Bar	1:2	at the time when the Chaldeans took Jerusalem
	1:8	At the same time, on the 10th day of Sivan
	1:20	through Moses his servant at the time
	3:14	that you may at the same time discern
	3:32	He who prepared the earth for all time filled it with four-footed creatures
	4:35	and for a long time she will be inhabited by demons
L Jr	6:3	for a long time, up to 7 generations
P Az	15	And at this time there is no prince, or prophet
Sus	13:14	And then together they arranged for a time
1 Ma	2:25	At the same time he killed the king's officer
	2:49	it is a time of ruin and furious anger
	2:53	Joseph in the time of his distress kept the commandment
	4:60	At that time they fortified Mount Zion
	7:35	are delivered into my hands this time
	9:1	into the land of Judah a 2nd time
	9:7	for he had no time to assemble them
	9:10	If our time has come, let us die bravely for our brethren
	9:27	since the time that prophets ceased to appear among them
	9:31	And Jonathan at that time accepted the leadership

	9:55	for at that time Alcimus was stricken
	9:56	And Alcimus died at that time in great agony
	10:30	from this day and for all time
	10:77	At the same time he advanced into the plain
	11:14	Now Alexander the king was in Cilicia at that time
	11:36	from this time forth for ever
	12:1	Now when Jonathan saw that the time was favourable for him
	12:7	Already in time past
	12:10	for considerable time has passed
	13:5	in any time of distress
	15:8	from henceforth and for all time
	15:33	which at one time had been unjustly taken by our enemies
	16:2	so that we have delivered Israel many times
	16:9	At that time Judas the brother of John was wounded
	16:24	from the time that he became high priest after his father
2 Ma	1:5	and may he not forsake you in time of evil
	1:19	the pious priests of that time
	1:22	When this was done and some time had passed
	3:5	who at that time was governor of Coelesyria and Phoenicia
	5:1	About this time Antiochus made his 2nd invasion of Egypt
	6:24	Such pretence is not worthy of our time of life, he said
	8:14	and at the same time besought the Lord
	8:19	Moreover, he told them of the times
	8:19	both the time of Sennacherib, when 185,000 perished
	8:20	and the time of the battle with the Galatians
	9:1	About that time, as it happened
	9:16	all of them, many times over
	12:30	and their kind treatment of them in times of misfortune
	12:36	As Esdris and his men had been fighting for a long time and were weary
	12:39	On the next day, as by that time it had become necessary
	13:9	than those that had been done in his father's time
	13:22	The king negotiated a 2nd time
	14:3	but had wilfully defiled himself in the times of separation
	14:38	For in former times
	15:8	but to keep in mind the former times
	15:10	at the same time pointing out the perfidy of the Gentiles
	15:22	in the time of Hezekiah king of Judea
	15:37	And from that time the city has been in the possession of the Hebrews
1 Es	1:19	And the people of Israel who were present at that time
	1:20	since the times of Samuel the prophet
	1:58	it shall keep sabbath all the time of its desolation
	2:16	But in the time of Artaxerxes king of the Persians
	5:50	and they offered sacrifices at the proper times
	6:3	At the same time Sisinnes the governor of Syria and Phoenicia
	6:20	from that time until now
	8:64	and the weight of everything was recorded at that very time
	8:76	from the times of our fathers
	8:79	and to give us food in the time of our servitude
	9:12	come at the time appointed
	9:48	at the same time explaining what was read
3 Ma	1:29	because indeed all at that time preferred death
	3:26	we are sure that for the remaining time
	3:29	and shall become useless for all time to any mortal creature
	4:17	But after the previously mentioned interval of time
	5:18	After the party had been going on for some time
	5:25	since the time had run out
	5:37	How many times, you poor wretch
	5:40	ordering now for a 3rd time that they be destroyed
	6:28	who from the time of our ancestors until now
	6:35	passed the time in feasting
	7:19	during the time of their stay
	7:23	Blessed be the Deliverer of Israel through all times ! Amen
2 Es	3:9	But again, in its time
	3:14	and to him only didst thou reveal the end of the times
	3:18	and trouble the times
	3:23	So the times passed and the years were completed
	4:27	in their appointed times
	4:30	and will produce until the time of threshing comes !
	4:37	and measured the times by measure
	4:37	and numbered the times by number
	4:39	that the time of threshing is delayed for the righteous
	4:45	show me this also : whether more time is to come than has passed
	5:12	And at that time men shall hope but not obtain
	5:43	Couldst thou not have created at one time
	5:44	neither can the world hold at one time
	5:45	that thou wilt certainly give life at one time to thy creation ?
	5:45	If therefore all creatures will live at one time
	5:45	all of them present at one time
	5:46	Request it therefore to produce 10 at one time
	5:47	but only each in its own time
	5:48	to those who from time to time are sown in it
	5:53	are different from those born during the time of old age
	6:7	What will be the dividing of the times ?
	6:24	At that time friends shall make war on friends like enemies
	6:34	concerning the former times
	6:34	lest you be hasty concerning the last times
	7:26	For behold, the time will come

	7:73	or how will they answer in the last times ?
	7:74	For how long the time is that the Most High
	7:74	but because of the times which he had foreordained !
	7:75	we shall be kept in rest until those times come
	7:77	but it will not be shown to you until the last times
	7:87	and before whom they are to be judged in the last times
	7:89	During the time that they lived in it
	7:100	Will time therefore be given to the souls
	8:5	for you have been given only a short time to live
	8:11	so that what has been fashioned may be nourished for a time
	8:50	who inhabit the world in the last times
	8:63	which thou wilt do in the last times
	9:2	then you will know that it is the very time
	9:6	so also are the times of the Most High :
	9:18	For there was a time in this age
	10:16	you will receive your son back in due time
	10:34	only do not forsake me, lest I die before my time
	11:8	Do not all watch at the same time
	11:13	and it continue to reign a long time
	11:16	Hear me, you who have ruled the earth all this time
	11:39	so that the end of my times might come through them ?
	11:44	And the Most High has looked upon his times
	12:9	to be shown the end of the times
	12:9	and the last events of the times
	12:15	for a longer time than any other of the 12
	12:18	In the midst of the time of that kingdom
	12:20	whose times shall be short and their years swift
	12:21	when the middle of its time draws near
	12:21	and 4 shall be kept for the time
	13:23	He who brings the peril at that time
	13:44	For at that time the Most High performed signs for them
	13:46	Then they dwelt there until the last times
	13:52	except in the time of his day
	13:57	because of his wonders, which he did from time to time
	13:58	and because he governs the times
	14:5	and showed him the secrets of the times
	14:5	and declared to him the end of the times
	14:9	until the times are ended
	14:10	and the times begin to grow old
	14:15	and hasten to escape from these times
	14:32	in due time he took from you what he had given
	16:38	when the time of her delivery draws near
4 Ma	2:22	but at the same time he enthroned the mind among the senses
	3:20	At a time when our fathers were enjoying profound peace
	3:21	just at that time certain men attempted
	5:7	Although you have had them for so long a time
	6:20	and during that time
	9:5	as though a short time ago you learned nothing from Eleazar
	12:4	will be miserably tortured and die before your time
	12:12	and these throughout all time will never let you go
	13:20	There each of the brothers dwelt the same length of time
	13:20	and was shaped during the same period of time
	13:21	When they were born after an equal time of gestation
	14:19	since even bees at the time for making honeycombs
	15:2	that of religion, and that of preserving her 7 sons for a time
	15:27	which would preserve the 7 sons for a short time
	16:6	O how wretched am I and many times unhappy !
	18:9	In the time of my maturity I remained with my husband

TIMELY 1

Sir	20:1	There is a reproof which is not timely

TIMID 3 = 0.002 %

Sir	2:12	Woe to timid hearts and to slack hands
	22:18	so a timid heart with a fool's purpose
	34:14	He who fears the Lord will not be timid

TIMNATH 1

1 Ma	9:50	and Bethel, and Timnath, and Pharathon, and Tephon

TIMOTHY 18 = 0.012 %

1 Ma	5:6	and many people with Timothy as their leader
	5:11	and Timothy is leading their forces
	5:34	And when the army of Timothy realized that it was Maccabeus
	5:37	After these things Timothy gathered another army
	5:40	Timothy said to the officers of his forces
2 Ma	8:30	In encounters with the forces of Timothy and Bacchides
	8:32	They killed the commander of Timothy's forces
	9:3	of what had happened to Nicanor and the forces of Timothy
	10:24	Now Timothy, who had been defeated by the Jews before
	10:32	Timothy himself fled to a stronghold called Gazara
	10:37	They killed Timothy, who was hidden in a cistern
	12:2	Timothy and Apollonius the son of Gennaeus
	12:10	on their march against Timothy
	12:18	They did not find Timothy in that region
	12:19	marched out and destroyed those whom Timothy had left in the stronghold
	12:20	and hastened after Timothy

	12 : 21	When Timothy learned of the approach of Judas
	12 : 24	Timothy himself fell into the hands of Dositheus

TIN 1
Sir 47 : 18   you gathered gold like tin and amassed silver like lead

TINY 2
Ad E 10 : 6   The tiny spring which became a river
11 : 10   and from their cry, as though from a tiny spring

TIP, verb 2
Wis 11 : 22   is like a speck that tips the scales
Sir 1 : 22   for a man's anger tips the scale to his ruin

TIP over 1
L Jr 6 : 27   and if it is tipped over, it cannot straighten itself

TIRED 1
1 Ma 10 : 81   and the enemy's horses grew tired

TITAN 1
Jud 16 : 7   nor did the sons of the Titans smite him

TITHE, subst. 7 = 0.005 %
Tob 1 : 6   Taking the first fruits and the tithes of my produce
5 : 13   and the tithes of our produce
Jud 11 : 13   and the tithes of the wine and oil
Sir 35 : 9   and dedicate your tithe with gladness
1 Ma 3 : 49   and the first fruits and the tithes
10 : 31   her tithes and her revenues
11 : 35   And the other payments due to us of the tithes

TITUS 1
2 Ma 11 : 34   Quintus Memmius and Titus Manius, envoys of the Romans

TO 4356 = 2.837 %

TOB 1
1 Ma 5 : 13   and all our brethren who were in the land of Tob have been killed

TOBIAH 1
1 Es 5 : 37   the sons of Delaiah the son of Tobiah

TOBIAS 37 = 0.024 %
Tob 1 : 9   and by her I became the father of Tobias
1 : 20   and my son Tobias
2 : 1   and my wife Anna and my son Tobias were restored to me
3 : 17   in marriage to Tobias the son of Tobit
3 : 17   because Tobias was entitled to possess her
4 : 2   Why do I not call my son Tobias
5 : 1   Then Tobias answered him
5 : 5   but Tobias did not know it
5 : 5   Tobias said to him
5 : 7   Then Tobias said to him, Wait for me
5 : 9   So Tobias invited him in
5 : 16   Then he said to Tobias, Get ready for the journey
6 : 17   When Tobias heard these things, he fell in love with her
7 : 5   And Tobias said, He is my father
7 : 8   Then Tobias said to Raphael, Brother Azarias
7 : 9   And Raguel said to Tobias, Eat, drink, and be merry
7 : 11   And Tobias said, I will eat nothing here
7 : 13   he gave her to Tobias to be his wife, saying, Here she is
8 : 1   they escorted Tobias in to her
8 : 4   Tobias got up from the bed and said, Sister, get up
8 : 5   And Tobias began to pray
8 : 20   Raguel declared by oath to Tobias that he should not leave
9 : 1   Then Tobias called Raphael and said to him
9 : 6   And Gabael blessed Tobias and his wife
10 : 7   and throughout the nights she never stopped mourning for her son Tobias
10 : 7   At that time Tobias said to Raguel
10 : 9   Tobias replied, No, send me back to my father
10 : 12   And Edna said to Tobias
11 : 1   After this Tobias went on his way
11 : 2   Then Raphael said to Tobias
11 : 7   Raphael, I know, Tobias
11 : 15   here I see my son Tobias
11 : 19   and Tobias marriage was celebrated for 7 days
12 : 1   Tobit then called his son Tobias and said to him
14 : 11   and Tobias gave him a magnificent funeral
14 : 12   Then Tobias returned with his wife and his sons to Ecbatana
2 Ma 3 : 11   and also some money of Hyrcanus, son of Tobias

TOBIEL 1
Tob 1 : 1   The book of the acts of Tobit the son of Tobiel

TOBIT 25 = 0.016 %
Tob 1 : 1   The book of the acts of Tobit the son of Tobiel
1 : 3   I, Tobit, walked in the ways of truth and righteousness

3 : 17   to scale away the white films from Tobit's eyes
3 : 17   in marriage to Tobias the son of Tobit
3 : 17   At that very moment Tobit returned and entered his house
4 : 1   On that day Tobit remembered the money
5 : 3   Then Tobit gave him the receipt, and said to him
5 : 10   Then Tobit said to him
5 : 11   And Tobit said to him
5 : 13   Then Tobit said to him, You are welcome, my brother
5 : 17   and said to Tobit, Why have you sent our child away ?
5 : 20   And Tobit said to her, Do not worry, my sister
7 : 2   How much the young man resembles my cousin Tobit !
7 : 4   So he said to them, Do you know our brother Tobit ?
7 : 7   When he heard that Tobit had lost his sight
10 : 1   Now his father Tobit was counting each day
10 : 6   But Tobit said to her, Be still and stop worrying ; he is well
11 : 10   Tobit started toward the door, and stumbled
11 : 16   Then Tobit went out to meet his daughter-in-law
11 : 17   And Tobit gave thanks before them
11 : 17   When Tobit came near to Sarah his daughter-in-law
12 : 1   Tobit then called his son Tobias and said to him
13 : 1   Then Tobit wrote a prayer of rejoicing, and said :
14 : 1   Here Tobit ended his words of praise
14 : 13   He inherited their property and that of his father Tobit

TODAY 23 = 0.015 %
Tob 6 : 10   Brother, today we shall stay with Raguel
Jud 6 : 2   to prophesy among us as you have done today
8 : 11   What you have said to the people today is not right
8 : 29   Today is not the first time your wisdom has been shown
12 : 13   and become today like one of the daughters of the Assyrians
12 : 18   because my life means more to me today
Sir 10 : 10   the king of today will die tomorrow
20 : 15   today he lends and tomorrow he asks it back
38 : 22   yesterday it was mine, and today it is yours
Bar 1 : 19   out of the land of Egypt until today
2 : 26   thou hast made as it is today
3 : 8   Behold, we are today in our exile
1 Ma 2 : 63   Today he will be exalted, but tomorrow he will not be found
3 : 17   And we are faint, for we have eaten nothing today
4 : 10   and crush this army before us today
5 : 32   Fight today for your brethren !
6 : 26   And behold, today they have encamped
7 : 42   So also crush this army before us today
9 : 30   So now we have chosen you today to take his place
9 : 44   for today things are not as they were before
10 : 20   And so we have appointed you today
3 Ma 5 : 20   said that the Jews were benefited by today's sleep
6 : 13   And let the Gentiles cower today

TOE 1
4 Ma 15 : 15   their toes and fingers scattered on the ground

TOGETHER 88 = 0.057 %
Tob 5 : 13   when we went together to Jerusalem
8 : 7   and may grow old together with her
13 : 13   for they will be gathered together
Jud 2 : 2   He called together all his officers and all his nobles
2 : 14   and called together all the commanders, generals
2 : 15   120,000 of them, together with 12,000 archers on horseback
4 : 3   and all the people of Judea were newly gathered together
5 : 2   So he called together all the princes of Moab
6 : 16   They called together all the elders of the city
7 : 2   together with the baggage and the foot soldiers handling it
7 : 17   together with 5,000 Assyrians
13 : 10   Then the 2 of them went out together
13 : 12   and called together the elders of the city
13 : 13   They all ran together, both small and great
Ad E 16 : 13   together with their whole nation
Wis 1 : 7   and that which holds all things together knows what is said
5 : 12   the air, thus divided, comes together at once
14 : 10   together with him who did it
18 : 5   and thou didst destroy them all together by a mighty flood
18 : 12   and they all together
Sir 21 : 9   An assembly of the wicked is like tow gathered together
22 : 7   is like one who glues potsherds together
33 : 4   bind together your instruction, and make your answer
43 : 26   and by his word all things hold together
50 : 17   Then all the people together made haste
L Jr 6 : 48   the priests consult together
Sus 13 : 14   And then together they arranged for a time
Bel 14 : 27   and boiled them together and made cakes
1 Ma 3 : 10   But Apollonius gathered together Gentiles
5 : 9   Now the Gentiles in Gilead gathered together
5 : 10   The Gentiles around us have gathered together against us
5 : 15   they said that against them had gathered together
5 : 44   together with all who were in them
5 : 45   Then Judas gathered together all the Israelites in Gilead
6 : 20   They gathered together
10 : 61   lawless men, gathered together against him to accuse him
12 : 37   So they gathered together to build up the city

13 : 2	and gathering the people together	
13 : 6	for all the nations have gathered together	
14 : 9	they all talked together of good things	
2 Ma 1 : 14	Antiochus came to the place together with his friends	
1 : 27	Gather together our scattered people	
2 : 7	until God gathers his people together again	
3 : 19	ran together to the gates, and some to the walls	
6 : 11	were betrayed to Philip and were all burned together	
8 : 16	But Maccabeus gathered his men together	
11 : 7	Then they eagerly rushed off together	
11 : 9	And they all together praised the merciful God	
15 : 31	and had called his countrymen together	
1 Es 5 : 56	together with their brethren and the Levitical priests	
7 : 10	after the priests and the Levites were purified together	
7 : 11	but the Levites were all purified together	
8 : 14	together with what is given by the nation	
9 : 55	And they came together	
3 Ma 1 : 19	in a disorderly rush flocked together in the city	
1 : 20	and without a backward look they crowded together	
1 : 27	they turned, together with our people	
3 : 25	together with their wives and children	
3 : 27	together with his family	
4 : 4	were they being sent off, all together, by the generals	
4 : 6	all together raising a lament instead of a wedding song	
5 : 3	together with those of his friends and of the army	
6 : 4	you destroyed together with his arrogant army	
6 : 39	and rescued them all together and unharmed	
7 : 3	persuaded us to gather together the Jews of the kingdom in a body	
2 Es 5 : 6	and the birds shall fly away together	
6 : 3	and before the innumerable hosts of angels were gathered together	
6 : 20	and all shall see it together	
6 : 42	thou didst command the waters to be gathered together	
6 : 47	where the water had been gathered together	
6 : 50	for the 7th part where the water had been gathered together	
11 : 28	to reign together	
12 : 40	they all gathered together	
13 : 5	an innumerable multitude of men were gathered together	
13 : 8	all who gathered together against him	
13 : 11	All these were mingled together	
13 : 34	and an innumerable multitude shall be gathered together	
13 : 47	Therefore you saw the multitude gathered together in peace	
13 : 49	that are gathered together	
14 : 27	and I gathered all the people together, and said	
15 : 20	I call together all the kings of the earth to fear me	
4 Ma 3 : 7	and together with the soldiers of his nation had slain many of them	
4 : 9	While the priests together with women and children	
8 : 29	all with one voice together, as from one mind, said :	
13 : 13	Each of them and all of them together looking at one another	
15 : 12	each child singly and all together	
16 : 15	For when you and your sons were arrested together	
18 : 23	are gathered together into the chorus of the fathers	

TOIL, subst. 11 = 0.007 %

Wis 10 : 10	and increased the fruit of his toil	
15 : 4	nor the fruitless toil of painters	
15 : 8	With the misspent toil	
16 : 20	and without their toil thou didst supply them from heaven	
Sir 11 : 21	but trust in the Lord and keep at your toil	
14 : 15	and what you acquired by toil to be divided by lot ?	
28 : 15	and deprived them of the fruit of their toil	
34 : 23	what do they gain but toil ?	
2 Ma 2 : 26	For us who have undertaken the toil of abbreviating	
2 : 27	we will gladly endure the uncomfortable toil	
2 Es 7 : 96	and besides they see the straits and toil	

TOIL, verb 8 = 0.005 %

Wis 9 : 10	that she may be with me and toil	
17 : 17	or a workman who toiled in the wilderness	
Sir 19 : 4	For in her service you will toil a little while	
11 : 11	There is a man who works, and toils, and presses on	
31 : 3	The rich man toils as his wealth accumulates	
31 : 4	The poor man toils as his livelihood diminishes	
1 Es 4 : 22	Do you not labour and toil	
2 Es 2 : 12	and they shall neither toil nor become weary	

TOILSOME 2

Sir 7 : 15	Do not hate toilsome labour, or farm work	
2 Es 7 : 12	and sorrowful and toilsome	

TOKEN 2

Wis 16 : 6	and received a token of deliverance	
2 Ma 12 : 40	they found sacred tokens of the idols of Jamnia	

TOLERATE 2

3 Ma 1 : 22	would not tolerate the completion of his plans	
2 Es 15 : 8	neither will I tolerate their wicked practices	

TOMB 8 = 0.005 %

1 Ma 2 : 70	and was buried in the tomb of his fathers at Modein	
9 : 19	and buried him in the tomb of their fathers at Modein	
13 : 27	over the tomb of his father and his brothers	
13 : 30	This is the tomb which he built in Modein	
2 Ma 5 : 10	and no place in the tomb of his fathers	
1 Es 1 : 31	and was buried in the tomb of his fathers	
2 Es 2 : 16	and will bring them out from their tombs	
4 Ma 17 : 8	to inscribe upon their tomb these words	

TOMORROW 8 = 0.005 %

Sir 10 : 10	the king of today will die tomorrow	
20 : 15	today he lends and tomorrow he asks it back	
1 Ma 2 : 63	Today he will be exalted, but tomorrow he will not be found	
5 : 27	the enemy are getting ready to attack the strongholds tomorrow	
3 Ma 5 : 20	Tomorrow without delay prepare the elephants in the same way	
5 : 38	for the destruction of the Jews tomorrow !	
2 Es 10 : 58	But tomorrow night you shall remain here	
14 : 26	tomorrow at this hour you shall begin to write	

TONE 2

2 Ma 7 : 24	and he was suspicious of her reproachful tone	
3 Ma 5 : 37	After summoning Hermon he said in a threatening tone	

TONGUE 37 = 0.024 %

Jud 3 : 8	and all their tongues and tribes should call upon him as god	
Wis 1 : 6	and a hearer of his tongue	
1 : 11	and keep your tongue from slander	
10 : 21	and made the tongues of babes speak clearly	
Sir 4 : 24	and education through the words of the tongue	
5 : 13	and a man's tongue is his downfall	
5 : 14	and do not lie in ambush with your tongue	
6 : 5	and a gracious tongue multiplies courtesies	
17 : 6	He made for them tongue and eyes	
19 : 6	He who controls his tongue will live without strife	
19 : 16	Who has never sinned with his tongue ?	
20 : 18	A slip on the pavement is better than a slip of the tongue	
22 : 27	so that my tongue may not destroy me !	
25 : 7	and a 10th I shall tell with my tongue :	
25 : 8	and he who has not made a slip with his tongue	
28 : 17	but a blow of the tongue crushes the bones	
28 : 18	but not so many as have fallen because of the tongue	
28 : 26	Beware lest you err with your tongue	
32 : 8	be as one who knows and yet holds his tongue	
37 : 18	and it is the tongue that continually rules them	
51 : 2	and from the snare of a slanderous tongue	
51 : 5	from an unclean tongue and lying words	
51 : 6	the slander of an unrighteous tongue to the king	
51 : 22	The Lord gave me a tongue as my reward	
L Jr 6 : 8	Their tongues are smoothed by the craftsman	
2 Ma 7 : 4	and he commanded that the tongue of their spokesman	
7 : 10	When it was demanded, he quickly put out his tongue	
7 : 27	she spoke in their native tongue as follows	
15 : 33	and he cut out the tongue of the ungodly Nicanor	
3 Ma 2 : 17	or exult in the arrogance of their tongue, saying	
6 : 4	exalted with lawless insolence and boastful tongue	
2 Es 13 : 10	and from his tongue he shot forth a storm of sparks	
4 Ma 10 : 17	gave orders to cut out his tongue	
10 : 19	See, here is my tongue	
10 : 21	a tongue that has been melodious with divine hymns	
12 : 13	to cut out the tongues of men who have feelings like yours	
18 : 21	pierced the pupils of their eyes and cut out their tongues	

TONGUE-LASHING 1

Sir 26 : 6	and a tongue-lashing makes it known to all	

TONIGHT 2

Jud 8 : 33	Stand at the city gate tonight	
11 : 4	Have courage ; you will live, tonight and from now on	

TOO 31 = 0.020 %

Tob 8 : 10	with the thought, Perhaps he too will die	
Ad E 16 : 2	by the too great kindness of their benefactors	
Wis 18 : 12	by the one form of death, had corpses too many to count	
Sir 3 : 21	Seek not what is too difficult for you	
3 : 23	for matters too great for human understanding	
7 : 24	and do not show yourself too indulgent with them	
19 : 4	One who trusts others too quickly is lightminded	
20 : 5	while another is detested for being too talkative	
20 : 8	Whoever uses too many words will be loathed	
27 : 20	Do not go after him, for he is too far off	
30 : 24	and anxiety brings on old age too soon	
37 : 1	Every friend will say, I too am a friend	
38 : 14	for they too will pray to the Lord	
38 : 27	So too is every craftsman and master workman	
38 : 28	So too is the smith sitting by the anvil	
38 : 29	So too is the potter sitting at his work	
48 : 13	Nothing was too hard for him	
Sus 13 : 39	for he was too strong for us	
1 Ma 9 : 9	we are too few	

427

	10:42	this too is cancelled
2 Ma	7:13	When he too had died
	15:37	So I too will here end my story
1 Es	9:11	for we have sinned too much in these things
3 Ma	7:19	there too in like manner
2 Es	8:43	or if it has been ruined by too much rain, it perishes
	10:25	so that I was too frightened to approach her
4 Ma	10:1	When he too had endured a glorious death, the 3rd was led in
	11:13	After he too had died, the 6th, a mere boy, was led in
	12:4	You too, if you do not obey
	12:15	Then because he too was about to die, he said
	16:22	You too must have the same faith in God and not be grieved

TOOTH   8 = 0.005 %

Wis	16:10	even by the teeth of venomous serpents
Sir	21:2	Its teeth are lion's teeth, and destroy the souls of men
	30:10	and in the end you will gnash your teeth
	39:30	the teeth of wild beasts, and scorpions and vipers
	51:3	from the gnashings of teeth about to devour me
2 Es	15:30	and shall devastate a portion of the land of the Assyrians with their teeth
4 Ma	7:6	you neither defiled your sacred teeth nor profaned your stomach

TOP   7 = 0.005 %

Jud	6:12	and ran out of the city to the top of the hill
	7:10	for it is not easy to reach the tops of their mountains
	7:13	We and our people go up to the tops of the nearby mountains
	9:13	and against the top of Zion
2 Es	13:35	But he will stand on the top of Mount Zion
	16:60	and pools on the tops of the mountains
4 Ma	14:16	and in holes and tops of trees

TORCH   3 = 0.002 %

Sir	48:1	and his word burned like a torch
1 Ma	6:39	and gleamed like flaming torches
2 Ma	4:22	and ushered in with a blaze of torches and with shouts

TORMENT, subst.   24 = 0.016 %

Wis	3:1	and no torment will ever touch them
	17:13	prefers ignorance of what causes the torment
	19:4	which their torments still lacked
3 Ma	3:27	will be tortured to death with the most hateful torments
2 Es	7:36	Then the pit of torment shall appear
	7:38	and there are fire and torments !
	7:47	but torments to many
	7:66	nor do they know of any torment or salvation
	7:80	but shall immediately wander about in torments
	7:84	they shall consider the torment laid up for themselves in the last days
	7:86	they shall see how some of them will pass over into torments
	7:99	and the aforesaid are the ways of torment
	8:59	so the thirst and torment which are prepared await them
	9:9	shall dwell in torments
	9:12	these must in torment acknowledge it after death
	13:38	and the torments with which they are to be tortured
4 Ma	6:27	I am dying in burning torments for the sake of the law
	8:19	and consider the threats of torments
	9:9	eternal torment by fire
	10:11	will undergo unceasing torments
	12:3	for they died in torments because of their disobedience
	13:15	and the danger of eternal torment
	15:18	nor when the 2nd in torments looked at you piteously
	15:22	How great and how many torments the mother then suffered

TORMENT, verb   12 = 0.008 %

Wis	11:9	were tormented when judged in wrath
	12:23	thou didst torment through their own abominations
	16:1	and were tormented by a multitude of animals
	16:4	how their enemies were being tormented
Sir	4:17	and will torment him by her discipline until she trusts him
2 Es	7:64	and therefore we are tormented
	7:67	that we shall be preserved alive but cruelly tormented ?
	7:72	those who dwell on earth shall be tormented
	7:75	or whether we shall be tormented at once ?
	7:76	nor number yourself among those who are tormented
4 Ma	3:11	tormented and inflamed him, undid and consumed him
	6:16	But Eleazar, as though more bitterly tormented by this counsel, cried out :

TORRENT   1

Sir	40:13	The wealth of the unjust will dry up like a torrent

TORTUOUS   1

Sir	4:17	For at first she will walk with him on tortuous paths

TORTURE, subst.   50 = 0.033 %

Wis	2:19	Let us test him with insult and torture
Sir	23:10	for as a servant who is continually examined under torture
	33:26	and for a wicked servant there are racks and tortures
2 Ma	7:1	under torture with whips and cords

	7:8	Therefore he in turn underwent tortures
	7:42	and the extreme tortures
	8:17	and the torture of the derided city
	9:5	and with sharp internal tortures
4 Ma	4:26	he himself, through torture, tried to compel everyone in the nation
	5:32	Therefore get your torture wheels ready
	6:1	to the instruments of torture
	6:9	and endured the tortures
	6:30	the holy man died nobly in his tortures
	6:30	and by reason he resisted even to the very tortures of death
	7:2	and overwhelmed by the mighty waves of tortures
	7:4	Although his sacred life was consumed by tortures and racks
	7:10	O aged man, more powerful than tortures
	7:16	an aged man despised tortures even to death
	8:1	have prevailed over the most painful instruments of torture
	8:9	with dreadful punishments through tortures
	8:12	he ordered the instruments of torture to be brought forward
	8:19	O men and brothers, should we not fear the instruments of torture
	8:25	for fearing the instruments of torture
	9:5	by threatening us with death by torture
	9:6	lived piously while enduring torture
	9:6	that we young men should die despising your coercive tortures
	9:16	Agree to eat so that you may be released from the tortures
	9:18	Through all these tortures I will convince you
	9:26	they bound him to the torture machine and catapult
	9:32	but you suffer torture by the threats that come from impiety
	10:16	Contrive tortures, tyrant, so that you may learn from them
	11:6	But these deeds deserve honours, not tortures
	11:23	you inventor of tortures
	12:12	for you intense and eternal fire and tortures
	14:1	Furthermore, they encouraged them to face the torture
	14:5	hastened to death by torture
	14:8	encircled the sevenfold fear of tortures and dissolved it
	14:11	that reason had full command over these men in their tortures
	15:11	in the case of none of them were the various tortures
	15:19	in his tortures gazing boldly at the same agonies
	15:21	as did the voices of the children in torture
	15:32	the torture of your sons
	16:2	but also that a woman has despised the fiercest tortures
	16:17	you young men were to be terrified by tortures
	17:3	against the earthquake of the tortures
	17:7	enduring their varied tortures to death
	17:10	looking to God and enduring torture even to death
	17:23	and their endurance under the tortures
	18:20	and back again to more tortures
	18:21	and put them to death with various tortures

TORTURE, verb   33 = 0.021 %

2 Ma	7:13	they maltreated and tortured the 4th in the same way
	7:17	will torture you and your descendants !
	8:28	to those who had been tortured
	8:30	giving to those who had been tortured
	9:6	for he had tortured the bowels of others
	9:7	and the fall was so hard as to torture every limb of his body
	9:11	for he was tortured with pain every moment
3 Ma	3:27	will be tortured to death with the most hateful torments
	4:14	but to be tortured with the outrages that he had ordered
2 Es	13:38	and the torments with which they are to be tortured
4 Ma	5:6	Before I begin to torture you, old man
	6:5	as though being tortured in a dream
	8:2	these should be tortured even more cruelly
	8:5	as that of the old man who has just been tortured
	8:27	But the youths, though about to be tortured
	9:7	do not suppose that you can injure us by torturing us
	9:27	Before torturing him, they inquired if he were willing to eat
	9:30	that you are being tortured more than I
	10:16	that I am a brother to those who have just been tortured
	11:1	When this one died also, after being cruelly tortured
	11:2	to be tortured for the sake of virtue
	11:16	So if you intend to torture me for not eating defiling foods
	11:16	go on torturing !
	11:20	While being tortured he said
	12:4	will be miserably tortured and die before your time
	12:11	and torture on the wheel those who practice religion ?
	12:13	and to maltreat and torture them in this way ?
	13:27	and tortured to death
	15:14	This mother, who saw them tortured and burned one by one
	15:22	as her sons were tortured on the wheel and with the hot irons !
	16:1	endured seeing her children tortured to death
	16:3	inflamed as she saw her 7 sons tortured in such varied ways
	16:15	you stood and watched Eleazar being tortured

TORTURER   3 = 0.002 %

4 Ma	1:11	For all people, even their torturers
	6:10	was victorious over his torturers
	6:11	he amazed even his torturers by his courageous spirit

TORTURING 1
4 Ma 15:20 with many spectators of the torturings

TOTAL, subst. 1
2 Ma 5:14 Within the total of 3 days 80,000 were destroyed

TOTAL, adj. 1
3 Ma 4:10 so that with their eyes in total darkness

TOTAL, verb 1
2 Ma 3:11 and that it totalled in all 400 talents of silver and 200 of gold

TOTTER 1
Sir 13:21 When a rich man totters, he is steadied by friends

TOUBIANI 1
2 Ma 12:17 they came to Charax, to the Jews who are called Toubiani

TOUCH 13 = 0.008 %
Jud 11:13 so much as to touch these things with their hands
Ad E 15:11 Then he raised the golden sceptre and touched it to her neck
Wis 3:1 and no torment will ever touch them
18:16 and touched heaven while standing on the earth
18:20 The experience of death touched also the righteous
Sir 13:1 Whoever touches pitch will be defiled
34:25 If a man washes after touching a dead body
34:25 and touches it again
L Jr 6:29 Sacrifices to them may be touched by women in menstruation or at childbirth
P Az 27 so that the fire did not touch them at all
2 Ma 9:10 had thought that he could touch the stars of heaven
1 Es 4:28 Do not all lands fear to touch him ?
4 Ma 17:1 so that no one might touch her body

TOUR 1
2 Ma 3:8 ostensibly to make a tour of inspection

TOW 2
Sir 21:9 An assembly of the wicked is like tow gathered together
P Az 23 with naphtha, pitch, tow, and brush

TOWARD 61 = 0.040 %
Tob 3:12 And now, O Lord, I have turned my eyes and my face toward thee
11:10 Tobit started toward the door, and stumbled
Jud 2:25 fronting toward Arabia
7:18 toward the south and the east
7:18 toward Acraba, which is near Chusi beside the brook Mochmur
12:5 Along toward the morning watch she arose
12:9 until she ate her food toward evening
Wis 16:7 For he who turned toward it was saved
16:21 For thy sustenance manifested thy sweetness toward thy children
Sir 6:13 and be on guard toward your friends
17:16 Their ways from youth tend toward evil
28:4 Does he have no mercy toward a man like himself
33:29 Do not act immoderately toward anybody
48:20 spreading forth their hands toward him
Bar 4:2 walk toward the shining of her light
4:36 Look toward the east, O Jerusalem
5:5 and look toward the east
Sus 13:35 And she, weeping, looked up toward heaven
1 Ma 8:1 toward all who made an alliance with them
11:33 because of the good will they show toward us
14:35 which he had maintained toward his nation
2 Ma 3:15 and called toward heaven
5:23 In his malice toward the Jewish citizens
6:8 that they should adopt the same policy toward the Jews
6:29 had acted toward him with good will now changed to ill will
9:26 toward me and my son
11:19 If you will maintain your good will toward the government
12:14 behaved most insolently toward Judas and his men
14:33 he stretched out his right hand toward the sanctuary
14:34 Then the priests stretched forth their hands toward heaven
15:21 stretched out his hands toward heaven
15:30 toward his countrymen
1 Es 1:24 concerning those who sinned and acted wickedly toward the Lord
4:58 he lifted up his face to heaven toward Jerusalem
5:47 before the first gate toward the east
3 Ma 3:1 toward those in the countryside
3:3 and unswerving loyalty toward the dynasty
3:18 because of the benevolence which we have toward all
3:19 By maintaining their manifest ill-will toward us
3:21 we made known to all our amnesty towards their compatriots here
3:23 who are sincerely disposed toward us
3:24 that they are ill-disposed toward us in every way
5:3 who were especially hostile toward the Jews
5:25 stretched their hands toward heaven
6:26 in their goodwill toward us

7:4 because of the ill-will which these people had toward all nations
7:6 which we have towards all men
7:7 which they had toward us and our ancestors
7:11 toward the king's government
2 Es 7:134 toward those who have sinned
15:39 and shall be driven violently toward the south and west
4 Ma 4:11 stretched out his hands toward heaven
5:25 has shown sympathy toward us
9:9 but you, because of your bloodthirstiness toward us
13:25 expanded their goodwill and harmony toward one another
14:5 but all of them, as though running the course toward immortality
14:13 which draws everything toward an emotion felt in her inmost parts
15:4 have a deeper sympathy toward their offspring than do the fathers
15:6 In 7 pregnancies she had implanted in herself tender love toward them
15:9 she felt a greater tenderness toward them
15:13 yearning of parents toward offspring, nurture

TOWER, subst. 27 = 0.018 %
Tob 13:16 and her towers and battlements with pure gold
Jud 1:3 at the gates he built towers
1:14 and came to Ecbatana, captured its towers
7:5 and when they had kindled fires on their towers
7:32 and they went up on the walls and towers of their city
Sir 26:22 and a married woman as a tower of death to her lovers
1 Ma 1:33 with a great strong wall and strong towers
4:60 with high walls and strong towers round about
5:5 They were shut up by him in their towers
5:5 and burned with fire their towers and all who were in them
5:65 and burned its towers round about
6:20 and he built siege towers and other engines of war
6:37 And upon the elephants were wooden towers, strong and covered
6:51 He set up siege towers
13:33 with high towers and great walls and gates and bolts
13:43 and battered and captured one tower
16:10 They also fled into the towers
2 Ma 10:18 took refuge in 2 very strong towers
10:20 were bribed by some of those who were in the towers
10:22 and immediately captured the 2 towers
10:36 and set fire to the towers
13:5 For there is a tower in that place, 50 cubits high, full of ashes
14:41 When the troops were about to capture the tower
1 Es 1:55 and burned their towers with fire
4:4 and conquer mountains, walls, and towers
3 Ma 2:27 and he set up a stone on the tower in the courtyard
4 Ma 13:6 For just as towers jutting out over harbours

TOWER, verb 1
Sir 50:10 and like a cypress towering in the clouds

TOWN 6 = 0.004 %
Jud 1:9 and all who were in Samaria and its surrounding towns
15:7 and the villages and towns in the hill country and in the plain
1 Ma 10:84 But Jonathan burned Azotus and the surrounding towns
2 Ma 8:6 he would set fire to towns and villages
1 Es 5:8 each to his own town
5:46 and all Israel in their towns

TRACE, subst. 2
Wis 2:4 our life will pass away like the traces of a cloud
5:10 and when it has passed no trace can be found

TRACE, verb 2
Wis 6:22 but I will trace her course from the beginning of creation
Sir 18:6 nor is it possible to trace the wonders of the Lord

TRACE out 1
Wis 9:16 but who has traced out what is in the heavens ?

TRACK 2
Wis 5:10 nor track of its keel in the waves
Sir 42:19 and he reveals the tracks of hidden things

TRACKLESS 1
Wis 5:7 and we journeyed through trackless deserts

TRADE, subst. 1
Sir 38:34 and their prayer is in the practice of their trade

TRADER 1
1 Ma 3:41 When the traders of the region heard what was said of them

TRADESMAN 1
Sir 26:29 and a tradesman will not be declared innocent of sin

TRADITION 2
3 Ma   1 :3   and apostatized from the ancestral traditions
4 Ma   8 :7   the ancestral tradition of your national life

TRADITIONAL 1
3 Ma   3 :18   they were carried away by their traditional conceit

TRAIN, subst. 2
Jud   7 :18   *and their tents and supply trains spread out in great number*
Ad E   15 :4   while the other followed carrying her train

TRAIN, verb 7 = 0.005 %
Sir   18 :13   He rebukes and trains and teaches them
1 Ma   4 :7   and these men were trained in war
2 Ma   15 :12   and had been trained from childhood
2 Es   14 :24   these 5, because they are trained to write rapidly
4 Ma   5 :23   and it also trains us in courage
5 :34   I will not play false to you, O law that trained me
13 :24   and trained in the same virtues

TRAINING 2
Wis   2 :12   and accuses us of sins against our training
4 Ma   10 :10   are suffering because of our godly training and virtue

TRAITOR 8 = 0.005 %
2 Ma   5 :15   guided by Menelaus, who had become a traitor
10 :13   He heard himself called a traitor at every turn
10 :22   Then he slew these men who had turned traitor
3 Ma   3 :24   as traitors and barbarous enemies
4 :10   they should undergo treatment befitting traitors
6 :12   are being deprived of life in the manner of traitors
7 :3   and to punish them with barbarous penalties as traitors
7 :5   or rather as traitors

TRAMPLE 2
3 Ma   6 :21   and began trampling and destroying them
2 Es   8 :57   Moreover they have even trampled upon his righteous ones

TRAMPLE down 5 = 0.003 %
1 Ma   3 :45   The sanctuary was trampled down
3 :51   Thy sanctuary is trampled down and profaned
4 :60   and trampling them down as they had done before
3 Ma   2 :18   We have trampled down the house of the sanctuary
2 :18   as offensive houses are trampled down

TRAMPLING 1
3 Ma   5 :48   as well as by the trampling of the crowd

TRANQUILLITY 2
Ad E   13 :2   I have determined to settle the lives of my subjects in lasting tranquillity
2 Ma   14 :6   and will not let the kingdom attain tranquillity

TRANSFER 1
Ad E   16 :14   and would transfer the kingdom of the Persians to the Macedonians

TRANSFORM 2
Wis   19 :19   For land animals were transformed into water creatures
4 Ma   9 :22   but as though transformed by fire into immortality

TRANSGRESS 32 = 0.021 %
Tob   4 :5   and refuse to sin or to transgress his commandments
Jud   2 :13   And you – take care not to transgress
Wis   6 :9   that you may learn wisdom and not transgress
Sir   10 :19   Those who transgress the commandments
19 :24   than the highly prudent man who transgresses the law
31 :10   Who has had the power to transgress and did not transgress
39 :31   and when their times come they will not transgress his word
2 Ma   7 :2   rather than transgress the laws of our fathers
1 Es   1 :48   and transgressed the laws of the Lord, the God of Israel
6 :32   And he commanded that if any should transgress
8 :24   And all who transgress the law of your God
8 :82   For we have transgressed thy commandments
8 :87   but we turned back again to transgress thy law
3 Ma   7 :10   those of the Jewish nation who had wilfully transgressed
7 :11   had transgressed the divine commandments
7 :12   who had transgressed the law of God
2 Es   3 :7   but he transgressed it
3 :21   transgressed and was overcome
3 :25   but the inhabitants of the city transgressed
7 :11   and when Adam transgressed my statutes
7 :46   or who among men that has not transgressed thy covenant ?
8 :35   there is no one who has not transgressed
14 :30   which you also have transgressed after them
15 :26   For the Lord knows all who transgress against him
4 Ma   5 :17   that we should not transgress it in any respect
5 :20   to transgress the law in matters either small or great
5 :27   not only to transgress the law
5 :29   nor will I transgress the sacred oaths of my ancestors

8 :14   when you transgress under compulsion
9 :1   rather than transgress our ancestral commandments
13 :15   lying before those who transgress the commandment of God

TRANSGRESSION 10 = 0.007 %
Jud   5 :21   But if there is no transgression in their nation
Wis   10 :1   she delivered him from his transgression
14 :31   that always pursues the transgression of the unrighteous
Sir   41 :18   of a transgression, before a judge or magistrate
P Ma   9   my transgressions are multiplied, O Lord
12   and I know my transgressions
13   forgive me ! Do not destroy me with my transgressions !
2 Es   7 :68   and are full of sins and burdened with transgressions
4 Ma   5 :13   it will excuse you from any transgression
9 :4   which insures our safety through transgression of the law

TRANSGRESSOR 2
Sir   40 :14   likewise transgressors will utterly fail
3 Ma   2 :17   lest the transgressors boast in their wrath

TRANSLATE 3 = 0.002 %
Ad E   11 :1   and had been translated by Lysimachus the son of Ptolemy
Sir pr.   despite our diligent labour in translating
pr.   when translated into another language

TRANSLATION 1
Sir pr.   to the translation of the following book

TRANSPORT, verb 1
2 Ma   9 :4   Transported with rage

TRANSPORT, subst. 1
Jud   2 :17   and asses and mules for transport

TRAP, subst. 4 = 0.003 %
Tob   14 :10   but Nadab fell into the trap and perished
Wis   14 :11   and became traps for the souls of men
14 :21   And this became a hidden trap for mankind
1 Ma   5 :4   who were a trap and a snare to the people

TRAPPINGS 1
2 Ma   5 :3   hurling of missiles, the flash of golden trappings

TRAVAIL 5 = 0.003 %
Sir   34 :5   and like a woman in travail the mind has fancies
48 :19   and they were in anguish, like women in travail
2 Es   4 :42   For just as a woman who is in travail
5 :35   that I might not see the travail of Jacob
5 :37   and then I will explain to you the travail

TRAVEL, verb 8 = 0.005 %
Ad E   13 :2   and open to travel throughout all its extent
Wis   6 :23   neither will I travel in the company of sickly envy
Sir   8 :15   Do not travel on the road with a foolhardy fellow
34 :10   but he that has travelled acquires much cleverness
39 :4   he will travel through the lands of foreign nations
Bar   4 :26   My tender sons have travelled rough roads
1 Ma   11 :60   and travelled beyond the river and among the cities
2 Es   3 :33   For I have travelled widely among the nations

TRAVEL, subst. 3 = 0.002 %
Sir   34 :11   I have seen many things in my travels
51 :13   While I was still young, before I went on my travels
1 Es   4 :23   A man takes his sword, and goes out to travel

TRAVELLING, TRAVELING 1
Sir   42 :3   or with travelling companions

TRAVERSE 1
Wis   5 :11   is traversed by the movement of its wings

TREACHEROUS 5 = 0.003 %
Sir   22 :22   or a treacherous blow – in these cases any friend will flee
27 :25   and a treacherous blow opens up wounds
1 Ma   7 :10   with peaceable but treacherous words
7 :30   that Nicanor had come to him with treacherous intent
16 :13   and made treacherous plans against Simon and his sons

TREACHEROUSLY 4 = 0.003 %
Wis   14 :24   but they either treacherously kill one another
1 Ma   7 :27   and treacherously sent to Judas and his brothers
13 :31   Trypho dealt treacherously with the young king Antiochus
16 :15   The son of Abubus received them treacherously

TREACHERY 5 = 0.003 %
1 Ma   9 :61   who were leaders in this treachery
16 :17   So he committed an act of great treachery
2 Ma   4 :34   Andronicus came to Onias, and resorting to treachery

	14:22	to prevent sudden treachery on the part of the enemy
4 Ma	4:13	that Apollonius had been overcome by human treachery

TREAD
4 = 0.003 %

Bar	4:13	nor tread the paths of discipline in his righteousness
	4:25	and will tread upon their necks
2 Es	16:26	*The grapes shall ripen, and who will tread them ?*
	16:69	*and be trodden under foot*

TREAD down
1

2 Es	5:29	And those who opposed thy promises have trodden down

TREASON
1

3 Ma	6:24	You are committing treason and surpassing tyrants in cruelty

TREASURE, subst.
17 = 0.011 %

Tob	4:9	So you will be laying a good treasure for yourself
Wis	7:14	for it is an unfailing treasure for men
Sir	3:4	is like one who lays up treasure
	6:14	he that has found one has found a treasure
	20:30	Hidden wisdom and unseen treasure
	29:11	Lay up your treasure
	40:18	but he who finds treasure is better off than both
	41:14	hidden wisdom and unseen treasure
1 Ma	1:23	he took also the hidden treasures which he found
2 Ma	1:14	to secure most of its treasures as a dowry
	1:15	had set out the treasures
1 Es	1:54	and the treasures chests of the Lord
2 Es	6:5	and before those who stored up treasures of faith were sealed
	7:77	For you have a treasure of works laid up with the Most High
	8:54	and in the end the treasure of immortality is made manifest
	16:57	It is he who searches the deep and its treasures
4 Ma	4:4	and went up to Seleucus to inform him of the rich treasure

TREASURE up
1

Tob	12:8	It is better to give alms than to treasure up gold

TREASURER
5 = 0.003 %

1 Es	2:11	he gave them to Mithridates his treasurer
	4:47	and wrote letters for him to all the treasurers
	4:49	that no officer or satrap or governor or treasurer
	8:19	have commanded the treasurers of Syria and Phoenicia
	8:46	and the treasurers at that place

TREASURY
22 = 0.014 %

Sir	1:25	In the treasuries of wisdom are wise sayings
	29:12	Store up almsgiving in your treasury
1 Ma	3:29	Then he saw that the money in the treasury was exhausted
	13:15	that Jonathan your brother owed the royal treasury
	14:49	and to deposit copies of them in the treasury
	15:8	Every debt you owe to the royal treasury
2 Ma	3:6	that the treasury in Jerusalem was full of untold money
	3:13	for the king's treasury
	3:24	But when he arrived at the treasury with his bodyguard
	3:28	this man who had just entered the aforesaid treasury
	3:40	and the protection of the treasury
	4:42	close by the treasury
	5:18	whom Seleucus the king sent to inspect the treasury
1 Es	5:45	and that they would give to the sacred treasury for the work
	6:25	the cost to be paid from the treasury of Cyrus the king
	8:18	you may provide out of the royal treasury
	8:45	who was the leading man at the place of the treasury
3 Ma	3:28	and also 2,000 drachmas from the royal treasury
2 Es	6:40	that a ray of light be brought forth from thy treasuries
4 Ma	4:3	to report that in the Jerusalem treasuries
	4:6	to seize the private funds in the treasury
	4:7	that those who had committed deposits to the sacred treasury

TREAT
18 = 0.012 %

Tob	8:16	but thou hast treated us according to thy great mercy
Jud	10:16	and he will treat you well
	11:4	No one will hurt you, but all will treat you well
Sir	13:11	Do not try to treat him as an equal
	14:11	My son, treat yourself well, according to your means
	26:28	and intelligent men who are treated contemptuously
	33:31	If you have a servant, treat him as a brother
1 Ma	11:26	the king treated him as his predecessors had treated him
	13:46	they said, Do not treat us according to our wicked acts
2 Ma	6:22	and be treated kindly
	7:24	Antiochus felt that he was being treated with contempt
	9:27	and will treat you with moderation and kindness
3 Ma	3:15	gladly treating them well
	3:20	since we treat all nations with benevolence
	6:9	who are being outrageously treated
	6:31	Accordingly those disgracefully treated and near to death
4 Ma	4:9	that was being treated so contemptuously

TREATMENT
8 = 0.005 %

2 Ma	2:31	and to forego exhaustive treatment
	12:30	and their kind treatment of them in times of misfortune

3 Ma	3:25	with insulting and harsh treatment
	4:6	as they were torn by the harsh treatment of the heathen
	4:10	they should undergo treatment befitting traitors
	6:26	Who is it that has so lawlessly encompassed with outrageous treatment
	7:5	They also led them out with harsh treatment as slaves
4 Ma	8:17	and exhorted us to accept kind treatment if we obey him

TREATY
2

1 Ma	8:29	Thus on these terms the Romans make a treaty
2 Ma	13:25	The people of Ptolemais were indignant over the treaty

TREE
34 = 0.022 %

Wis	13:11	A skilled woodcutter may saw down a tree easy to handle
Sir	6:3	and will be left like a withered tree
	14:18	Like flourishing leaves on a spreading tree
	19:19	enjoy the fruit of the tree of immortality
	24:14	I grew tall like a palm tree in En-gedi
	24:14	like a beautiful olive tree in the field
	24:14	and like a plane tree I grew tall
	27:6	The fruit discloses the cultivation of a tree
	38:5	Was not water made sweet with a tree
	50:10	like an olive tree putting forth its fruit
	50:12	and they surrounded him like the trunks of palm trees
Bar	5:8	The woods and every fragrant tree have shaded Israel at God's command
Sus	13:54	Under what tree did you see them being intimate with each other ?
	13:54	He answered, Under a mastic tree
	13:58	Under what tree did you catch them being intimate with each other ?
1 Ma	10:30	and the half of the fruit of the trees that I should receive
	11:34	from the crops of the land and the fruit of the trees
	14:8	and the trees of the plains their fruit
	14:12	Each man sat under his vine and his fig tree
2 Es	1:20	I covered you with the leaves of trees
	1:23	but threw a tree into the water and made the stream sweet
	2:12	The tree of life shall give them fragrant perfume
	2:18	12 trees loaded with various fruits
	4:13	I went into a forest of trees of the plain
	5:23	from every forest of the earth and from all its trees
	8:52	the tree of life is planted
	15:13	because their seed shall fail and their trees shall be ruined
	15:42	mountains and hills, trees of the forests
	15:62	all your forests and your fruitful trees
	16:25	The trees shall bear fruit, and who will gather it ?
	16:29	3 or 4 olives may be left on every tree
4 Ma	2:14	The fruit trees of the enemy are not cut down
	14:16	and in holes and tops of trees
	18:16	There is a tree of life for those who do his will

TREMBLE
17 = 0.011 %

Jud	16:10	The Persians trembled at her boldness
	16:11	for weak people shouted and the enemy trembled
Sir	16:18	the abyss and the earth, will tremble at his visitation
	48:12	in all his days he did not tremble before any ruler
	48:19	Then their hearts were shaken and their hands trembled
1 Ma	4:32	let them tremble in their destruction
	6:41	trembled, for the army was very large and strong
	13:2	and he saw that the people were trembling and fearful
1 Es	4:36	All God's works quake and tremble
P Ma	4	at whom all things shudder, and tremble before thy power
2 Es	3:18	and move the world, and make the depths to tremble
	6:16	They will tremble and be shaken
	8:21	before whom the hosts of angels stand trembling
	13:3	everything under his gaze trembled
	15:29	so that all who hear them fear and tremble
	16:18	the beginning of calamities, when all shall tremble
4 Ma	4:10	instilling in them great fear and trembling

TREMBLING, subst., adj.
8 = 0.005 %

Jud	15:2	Fear and trembling came over them
Wis	17:10	they perished in trembling fear
Sir	16:19	shake with trembling when he looks upon them
2 Ma	3:17	For terror and bodily trembling had come over the man
	15:23	send a good angel to carry terror and trembling before us
2 Es	15:33	and fear and trembling shall come upon their army
	15:37	And there shall be fear and great trembling upon the earth
	15:37	and they shall be seized with trembling

TREMENDOUS
1

2 Ma	10:24	gathered a tremendous force of mercenaries

TRESPASS, verb
1

Wis	12:2	Therefore thou dost correct little by little those who trespass

TRIAL
2

Wis	2:19	and make trial of his forbearance
Sir	33:1	but in trial he will deliver him again and again

TRIBE

			39 = 0.025 %
Tob	1 : 1	of the descendants of Asiel and the tribe of Naphtali	
	1 : 4	the whole tribe of Naphtali my forefather	
	1 : 4	from among all the tribes of Israel	
	1 : 4	where all the tribes should sacrifice	
	1 : 5	All the tribes that joined in apostasy	
	4 : 12	who is not of your father's tribe	
	5 : 8	so that I may learn to what tribe he belongs	
	5 : 10	My brother, to what tribe and family do you belong ? Tell me	
	5 : 11	Are you looking for a tribe and a family	
	5 : 13	because I tried to learn your tribe and family	
Jud	3 : 8	and all their tongues and tribes should call upon him as god	
	6 : 15	of the tribe of Simeon	
	8 : 2	Her husband Manasseh, who belonged to her tribe and family	
	8 : 18	has there been any tribe or family or people	
	9 : 14	And cause thy whole nation and every tribe	
Ad E	11 : 2	of the tribe of Benjamin, had a dream	
	14 : 5	I have heard in the tribe of my family	
Sir	16 : 4	but through a tribe of lawless men it will be made desolate	
	36 : 11	Gather all the tribes of Jacob	
	44 : 23	and distributed them among 12 tribes	
	45 : 6	a holy man like him, of the tribe of Levi	
	45 : 11	according to the number of the tribes of Israel	
	45 : 25	the son of Jesse, of the tribe of Judah :	
	48 : 10	and to restore the tribes of Jacob	
2 Ma	3 : 4	But a man named Simon, of the tribe of Benjamin	
1 Es	2 : 8	of the tribes of Judah and Benjamin	
	5 : 1	according to their tribes	
	5 : 4	according to their fathers' houses in the tribes	
	5 : 5	of the lineage of Phares, of the tribe of Judah	
	5 : 66	and when the enemies of the tribe of Judah and Benjamin heard it	
	7 : 8	of the tribes of Israel	
	9 : 5	Then the men of the tribe of Judah and Benjamin	
2 Es	1 : 3	son of Aaron, of the tribe of Levi	
	3 : 7	From him there sprang nations and tribes	
	3 : 32	Or what tribes have so believed thy covenants	
	3 : 32	as these tribes of Jacob ?	
	4 : 23	has been given over to godless tribes	
	13 : 40	these are the 10 tribes	
4 Ma	2 : 19	of the entire tribe of the Shechemites	

TRIBULATION

			8 = 0.005 %
Ad E	11 : 8	tribulation and distress	
3 Ma	2 : 10	and tribulation should overtake us	
2 Es	2 : 27	for when the day of tribulation and anguish comes	
	15 : 19	and because of great tribulation	
	16 : 19	tribulation and anguish are sent as scourges	
	16 : 67	and deliver you from all tribulation	
	16 : 74	Behold, the days of tribulation are at hand	
4 Ma	14 : 9	as we hear of the tribulations of these young men	

TRIBUTARY

			1
1 Ma	1 : 4	and they became tributary to him	

TRIBUTE

			17 = 0.011 %
1 Ma	1 : 29	a chief collector of tribute	
	8 : 2	how they had defeated them and forced them to pay tribute	
	8 : 4	the rest paid them tribute every year	
	8 : 7	should pay a heavy tribute and give hostages	
	10 : 29	from payment of tribute and salt tax and crown levies	
	11 : 28	to free Judea and the 3 districts of Samaria from tribute	
	13 : 37	to grant you release from tribute	
	15 : 30	and the tribute money of the places	
	15 : 31	and the tribute money of the cities, 500 talents more	
2 Ma	8 : 10	the tribute due to the Romans, 2,000 talents	
	8 : 36	to secure tribute for the Romans	
	11 : 3	and to levy tribute on the temple	
1 Es	2 : 19	they will not only refuse to pay tribute	
	2 : 27	and exacted tribute from Coelesyria and Phoenicia	
	4 : 50	should be theirs without tribute	
	6 : 29	and that out of the tribute of Coelesyria and Phoenicia	
	8 : 22	You are also informed that no tribute	

TRICK

			2
Jud	13 : 16	it was my face that tricked him to his destruction	
	14 : 18	The slaves have tricked us !	

TRICK out

			1
2 Es	15 : 54	Trick out the beauty of your face !	

TRICKERY

			2
Ad E	16 : 6	when these men by the false trickery of their evil natures	
1 Ma	11 : 1	and he tried to get possession of Alexander's kingdom by trickery	

TRIFLE

			1
Sir	27 : 1	Many have committed sin for a trifle	

TRIP

			2
Sir	12 : 17	and while pretending to help you, he will trip you by the heel	
	23 : 8	the reviler and the arrogant are tripped by them	

TRIPOLIS

			1
2 Ma	14 : 1	had sailed into the harbour of Tripolis	

TRIREME

			1
2 Ma	4 : 20	it was applied to the construction of triremes	

TRIUMPH, subst.

			2
Wis	4 : 2	and throughout all time it marches crowned in triumph	
2 Ma	13 : 16	and withdrew in triumph	

TROOP

			43 = 0.028 %
Jud	1 : 16	he and all his combined forces, a vast body of troops	
	2 : 7	and will hand them over to be plundered by my troops	
	2 : 15	and mustered the picked troops by divisions	
	2 : 19	and picked troops of infantry	
1 Ma	2 : 31	and to troops in Jerusalem the city of David	
	3 : 34	And he turned over to Lysias half of his troops and the elephants	
	3 : 37	Then the king took the remaining half of his troops	
	4 : 31	and let them be ashamed of their troops and their cavalry	
	4 : 35	And when Lysias saw the rout of his troops	
	6 : 33	and his troops made ready for battle	
	6 : 40	and some troops were on the plain	
	9 : 52	and in them he put troops and stores of food	
	10 : 6	So Demetrius gave him authority to recruit troops	
	10 : 8	that the king had given him authority to recruit troops	
	10 : 21	and he recruited troops	
	10 : 77	for he had a large troop of cavalry and put confidence in it	
	11 : 18	and his troops in the strongholds were killed	
	11 : 38	he dismissed all his troops, each man to his own place	
	11 : 38	except the foreign troops	
	11 : 38	So all the troops who had served his fathers hated him	
	11 : 39	He saw that all the troops were murmuring against Demetrius	
	11 : 40	which the troops of Demetrius had for him	
	11 : 41	that he remove the troops of the citadel from Jerusalem	
	11 : 41	and the troops in the strongholds	
	11 : 43	for all my troops have revolted	
	11 : 55	All the troops that Demetrius had cast off	
	12 : 43	and commanded his friends and his troops	
	12 : 45	and the remaining troops and all the officials	
	12 : 46	he sent away the troops	
	12 : 49	Then Trypho sent troops and cavalry into Galilee	
	13 : 43	and surrounded it with troops	
	15 : 3	and have recruited a host of mercenary troops	
	15 : 10	All the troops rallied to him	
	15 : 12	and his troops had deserted him	
	15 : 38	and gave him troops of infantry and cavalry	
	15 : 41	He built up Kedron and stationed there horsemen and troops	
	16 : 18	asking him to send troops to aid him	
2 Ma	4 : 29	the commander of the Cyprian troops	
	5 : 3	troops of horsemen drawn up	
	5 : 5	When the troops upon the wall had been forced back	
	14 : 41	When the troops were about to capture the tower	
3 Ma	1 : 4	Arsinoe went to the troops with wailing and tears	
	2 : 7	And when he pursued them with chariots and a mass of troops	

TROPHY

			1
2 Ma	5 : 6	but imagining that he was setting up trophies of victory	

TROUBLE, subst.

			21 = 0.014 %
Tob	6 : 7	if a demon or evil spirit gives trouble to any one	
Wis	10 : 9	Wisdom rescued from troubles those who served her	
Sir	3 : 27	A stubborn mind will be burdened by troubles	
	4 : 3	Do not add to the troubles of an angry mind	
	6 : 8	but will not stand by you in your day of trouble	
	6 : 10	but will not stand by you in your day of trouble	
	22 : 13	guard yourself from him to escape trouble	
	29 : 4	and cause trouble to those who help them	
	37 : 4	but in time of trouble are against him	
	40 : 5	there is anger and envy and trouble and unrest	
	40 : 24	Brothers and help are for a time of trouble	
1 Ma	2 : 43	And all who became fugitives to escape their troubles	
	10 : 15	and of the troubles that they had endured	
	15 : 12	for he knew that troubles had converged upon him	
2 Ma	2 : 30	and to take trouble with details	
	4 : 31	So the king went hastily to settle the trouble	
	13 : 4	that this man was to blame for all the trouble	
3 Ma	1 : 27	to defend them in the present trouble	
2 Es	10 : 15	and bear bravely the troubles that have come upon you	
	10 : 20	because of the troubles of Zion	
	10 : 24	a relief from your troubles	

TROUBLE, verb

			24 = 0.016 %
Tob	6 : 7	and that person will never be troubled again	
Ad E	11 : 9	And the whole righteous nation was troubled	
Wis	16 : 6	they were troubled for a little while as a warning	

18 : 17 Then at once apparitions in dreadful dreams greatly troubled them
Sir 30 : 7 and his feelings will be troubled at every cry
40 : 6 he is troubled by the visions of his mind
P Az 27 or hurt or trouble them
1 Ma 3 : 5 he burned those who troubled his people
7 : 22 and all who were troubling their people joined him
2 Ma 8 : 32 and one who had greatly troubled the Jews
9 : 24 the people throughout the realm would not be troubled
14 : 28 When this message came to Nicanor, he was troubled
1 Es 2 : 22 troubling both kings and other cities
2 Es 3 : 1 I was troubled as I lay on my bed
3 : 18 and trouble the times
5 : 5 the peoples shall be troubled
5 : 14 and my soul was so troubled that it fainted
6 : 36 And on the 8th night my heart was troubled within me again
8 : 16 and about the seed of Jacob, for whom I am troubled
9 : 27 my heart was troubled again as it was before
10 : 31 What is the matter with you ? And why are you troubled ?
10 : 31 and the thoughts of your mind troubled ?
15 : 3 and do not be troubled
16 : 12 and its waves and the fish also shall be troubled

TRUE
26 = 0.017 %

Tob 3 : 2 and thou dost render true and righteous judgment for ever
3 : 5 And now thy many judgments are true
4 : 6 For if you do what is true
7 : 10 But let me explain the true situation to you
13 : 6 to do what is true before him
Jud 8 : 28 All that you have said has been spoken out of a true heart
10 : 13 to give him a true report
11 : 10 for it is true : our nation cannot be punished
Wis 1 : 6 and a true observer of his heart
2 : 17 Let us see if his words are true
5 : 21 Shafts of lightning will fly with true aim
12 : 27 they saw and recognized as the true God
15 : 1 But thou, our God, art kind and true, patient
Sir 28 : 6 and be true to the commandments
32 : 16 Those who fear the Lord will form true judgments
34 : 4 And from something false what will be true ?
P Az 4 and all thy works are true and thy ways right
5 Thou hast executed true judgments
8 thou hast done in true judgment
1 Es 8 : 89 O Lord of Israel, thou art true
3 Ma 2 : 11 And indeed you are faithful and true
6 : 18 Then the most glorious, almighty, and true God
2 Es 15 : 2 for they are trustworthy and true
4 Ma 6 : 5 But the courageous and noble man, as a true Eleazar, was unmoved
15 : 4 Especially is this true of mothers
17 : 6 For your children were true descendants of father Abraham

TRULY
4 = 0.003 %

Sir 42 : 8 Then you will be truly instructed
4 Ma 5 : 18 Even if, as you suppose, our law were not truly divine
11 : 23 and enemy of those who are truly devout
17 : 11 Truly the contest in which they were engaged was divine

TRUMPET
20 = 0.013 %

Sir 26 : 27 is regarded as a war trumpet
50 : 16 they sounded the trumpets of hammered work
1 Ma 3 : 54 Then they sounded the trumpets and gave a loud shout
4 : 13 Then the men with Judas blew their trumpets
4 : 40 and sounded the signal on the trumpets
5 : 31 with trumpets and loud shouts
5 : 33 who sounded their trumpets and cried aloud in prayer
6 : 33 and sounded their trumpets
7 : 45 kept sounding the battle call on the trumpets
9 : 12 the phalanx advanced to the sound of the trumpets
9 : 12 and the men with Judas also blew their trumpets
16 : 8 And they sounded the trumpets
2 Ma 15 : 25 Nicanor and his men advanced with trumpets and battle songs
1 Es 5 : 59 with musical instruments and trumpets
5 : 62 And all the people sounded trumpets
5 : 64 while many came with trumpets and a joyful noise
5 : 65 so that the people could not hear the trumpets
5 : 65 For the multitude sounded the trumpets loudly
5 : 66 they came to find out what the sound of the trumpets meant
2 Es 6 : 23 and the trumpet shall sound aloud, and when all hear it

TRUNK
1

Sir 50 : 12 and they surrounded him like the trunks of palm trees

TRUST, verb
41 = 0.027 %

Jud 9 : 7 they trust in shield and spear, in bow and sling
Wis 3 : 9 Those who trust in him will understand truth
13 : 7 and they trust in what they see
14 : 5 therefore men trust their lives
14 : 29 for because they trust in lifeless idols
16 : 24 and in kindness relaxes on behalf of those who trust in thee
16 : 26 but that thy word preserves those who trust in thee
18 : 6 in sure knowledge of the oaths in which they trusted
Sir 1 : 15 and among their descendants she will be trusted
2 : 6 Trust in him, and he will help you
2 : 8 You who fear the Lord, trust in him
2 : 10 and see : who ever trusted in the Lord and was put to shame ?
4 : 17 and will torment him by her discipline until she trusts him
6 : 7 and do not trust him hastily
7 : 26 but do not trust yourself to one whom you detest
11 : 21 but trust in the Lord and keep at your toil
12 : 10 Never trust your enemy
13 : 11 nor trust his abundance of words
16 : 3 Do not trust in their survival
19 : 4 One who trusts others too quickly is lightminded
26 : 20 and sow it with your own seed, trusting in your fine stock
32 : 24 and he who trusts the Lord will not suffer loss
33 : 3 A man of understanding will trust in the law
35 : 12 and do not trust to an unrighteous sacrifice
36 : 26 For who will trust a nimble robber
36 : 26 So who will trust a man that has no home
Bar 3 : 17 in which men trust, and there is no end to their getting
P Az 17 for there will be no shame for those who trust in thee
Sus 13 : 35 for her heart trusted in the Lord
1 Ma 7 : 7 Now then send a man whom you trust
7 : 16 So they trusted him
8 : 16 They trust one man each year to rule over them
12 : 46 Jonathan trusted him and did as he said
2 Ma 3 : 12 who had trusted in the holiness of the place
8 : 18 For they trust to arms and acts of daring, he said
8 : 18 but we trust in the Almighty God
15 : 7 But Maccabeus did not cease to trust with all confidence
3 Ma 2 : 4 who trusted in their strength and boldness
2 Es 7 : 83 for those who have trusted the covenants of the Most High
4 Ma 7 : 21 and trusts in God
8 : 7 Trust me, then, and you will have

TRUST, subst.
11 = 0.007 %

Tob 1 : 14 in trust with Gabael, the brother of Gabrias
4 : 1 which he had left in trust with Gabael at Rages in Media
4 : 20 which I left in trust with Gabael the son of Gabrias
Wis 12 : 2 and put their trust in thee, O Lord
Sir 2 : 13 Woe to the faint heart, for it has no trust !
22 : 23 Gain the trust of your neighbour in his poverty
1 Ma 2 : 61 that none who put their trust in him will lack strength
10 : 37 and let some of them be put in positions of trust in the kingdom
2 Ma 7 : 40 putting his whole trust in the Lord
2 Es 7 : 94 they kept the law which was given them in trust
8 : 30 but love those who have always put their trust in thy glory

TRUSTWORTHY
7 = 0.005 %

Sir 31 : 23 and their testimony to his excellence is trustworthy
36 : 16 and let thy prophets be found trustworthy
37 : 22 may be trustworthy on his lips
37 : 23 and the fruits of his understanding will be trustworthy
46 : 15 and by his words he became known as a trustworthy seer
1 Ma 14 : 41 until a trustworthy prophet should arise
2 Es 15 : 2 for they are trustworthy and true

TRUTH
44 = 0.029 %

Tob 1 : 3 I, Tobit, walked in the ways of truth and righteousness
3 : 2 all thy deeds and all thy ways are mercy and truth
3 : 5 For we did not walk in truth before thee
14 : 6 to fear the Lord God in truth
14 : 7 And all who love the Lord God in truth and righteousness
Jud 5 : 5 and I will tell you the truth about this people
Wis 3 : 9 Those who trust in him will understand truth
5 : 6 So it was we who strayed from the way of truth
6 : 22 and I will not pass by the truth
Sir 4 : 25 Never speak against the truth
4 : 28 Strive even to death for the truth
12 : 12 and at last you will realize the truth of my words
27 : 9 so truth returns to those who practise it
37 : 15 that he may direct your way in truth
41 : 19 Be ashamed before the truth of God and his covenant
P Az 4 and all thy judgments are truth
5 for in truth and justice thou hast brought all this upon us
1 Ma 7 : 18 for they said, There is no truth or justice in them
2 Ma 7 : 6 and in truth has compassion on us
1 Es 3 : 12 but truth is victor over all things
4 : 13 who had spoken of women and truth, began to speak :
4 : 33 and he began to speak about truth :
4 : 35 But truth is great, and stronger than all things
4 : 36 The whole earth calls upon truth, and heaven blesses her
4 : 37 There is no truth in them
4 : 38 But truth endures and is strong for ever
4 : 40 Blessed be the God of truth !
4 : 41 Great is truth, and strongest of all !
3 Ma 4 : 16 with a mind alienated from truth and with a profane mouth
7 : 12 The king then, admitting and approving the truth of what they said

2 Es	5 : 1	and the way of truth shall be hidden
	6 : 28	and the truth, which has been so long without fruit, shall be revealed
	7 : 34	but only judgment shall remain, truth shall stand
	7 : 104	and displays to all the seal of truth
	7 : 114	and righteousness has increased and truth has appeared
	8 : 23	and whose truth is established for ever
	8 : 26	but at those who have served thee in truth
	8 : 35	For in truth there is no one among those who have been born
	11 : 41	And you have judged the earth, but not with truth
	11 : 42	you have hated those who tell the truth
	14 : 18	For truth shall go farther away
4 Ma	5 : 10	if, by holding a vain opinion concerning the truth
	5 : 11	philosophize according to the truth of what is beneficial
	6 : 18	who have lived in accordance with truth to old age

TRUTHFUL   1

Sir	34 : 8	and wisdom is made perfect in truthful lips

TRY   32 = 0.021 %

Tob	5 : 13	because I tried to learn your tribe and family
Jud	4 : 7	and it was easy to stop any who tried to enter
	8 : 16	Do not try to bind the purposes of the Lord our God
	8 : 27	For he has not tried us with fire, as he did them
	8 : 34	Only, do not try to find out what I plan
Wis	3 : 6	like gold in the furnace he tried them
	11 : 9	For when they were tried
	19 : 17	each tried to find the way through his own door
Sir	4 : 26	and do not try to stop the current of a river
	12 : 12	lest he try to take your seat of honour
	13 : 11	Do not try to treat him as an equal
1 Ma	6 : 3	So he came and tried to take the city and plunder it
	6 : 18	They were trying in every way to harm them
	6 : 56	and that he was trying to seize control of the government
	9 : 9	But they tried to dissuade him, saying, We are not able
	9 : 32	When Bacchides learned of this, he tried to kill him
	9 : 71	that he would not try to harm him as long as he lived
	11 : 1	and he tried to get possession of Alexander's kingdom by trickery
	11 : 10	for he has tried to kill me
	12 : 53	And all the nations round about them tried to destroy them
2 Ma	7 : 19	for having tried to fight against God !
	13 : 18	tried strategy in attacking their positions
1 Es	1 : 28	but tried to fight with him
3 Ma	1 : 25	while the elders near the king tried in various ways
	3 : 8	They did try to console them
	5 : 40	O king, how long will you try us, as though we are idiots
	7 : 5	they tried without any inquiry or examination
2 Es	13 : 7	And I tried to see the region or place
4 Ma	4 : 26	he himself, through torture, tried to compel everyone in the nation
	9 : 5	You are trying to terrify us
	12 : 2	and tried to console him, saying
	15 : 16	O mother, tried now by more bitter pains

TRYPHO   21 = 0.014 %

1 Ma	11 : 39	Now Trypho had formerly been one of Alexander's supporters
	11 : 54	After this Trypho returned
	11 : 56	And Trypho captured the elephants
	12 : 39	Then Trypho attempted to become king of Asia
	12 : 42	When Trypho saw that he had come with a large army
	12 : 49	Then Trypho sent troops and cavalry into Galilee
	13 : 1	Simon heard that Trypho had assembled a large army
	13 : 12	Then Trypho departed from Ptolemais with a large army
	13 : 14	Trypho learned that Simon had risen up
	13 : 19	but Trypho broke his word and did not release Jonathan
	13 : 20	After this Trypho came to invade the country and destroy it
	13 : 21	Now the men in the citadel kept sending envoys to Trypho
	13 : 22	So Trypho got all his cavalry ready to go
	13 : 24	Then Trypho turned back and departed to his own land
	13 : 31	Trypho dealt treacherously with the young king Antiochus
	13 : 34	for all that Trypho did was to plunder
	14 : 1	so that he could make war against Trypho
	15 : 10	so that there were few with Trypho
	15 : 25	and he shut Trypho up and kept him from going out or in
	15 : 37	Now Trypho embarked on a ship and escaped to Orthosia
	15 : 39	but the king pursued Trypho

TUMBLE   1

Jud	13 : 9	Then she tumbled his body off the bed

TUMULT   10 = 0.007 %

Ad E	11 : 5	thunders and earthquake, tumult upon the earth !
	11 : 8	affliction and great tumult upon the earth !
Wis	14 : 25	theft and deceit, corruption, faithlessness, tumult, perjury
1 Ma	13 : 44	and a great tumult arose in the city
2 Ma	15 : 29	Then there was shouting and tumult
3 Ma	3 : 8	when they saw an unexpected tumult around these people
	5 : 41	As a result the city is in a tumult
2 Es	9 : 3	tumult of peoples, intrigues of nations

	12 : 2	and their reign was brief and full of tumult
	12 : 30	this was the reign which was brief and full of tumult

TUMULTUOUS   2

1 Ma	9 : 39	and saw a tumultuous procession with much baggage
3 Ma	5 : 48	and heard the loud and tumultuous noise

TUNE   1

Sir	44 : 5	those who composed musical tunes

TUNIC   3 = 0.002 %

Jud	14 : 19	they rent their tunics and were greatly dismayed
2 Ma	12 : 40	Then under the tunic of every one of the dead
4 Ma	9 : 11	and having torn off his tunic

TUNNEL   1

Sir	48 : 17	he tunnelled the sheer rock with iron

TURBAN   3 = 0.002 %

Jud	4 : 15	With ashes upon their turbans
Sir	45 : 12	with a gold crown upon his turban
1 Es	3 : 6	and a turban of fine linen, and a necklace about his neck

TURBULENT   1

Wis	13 : 2	or the circle of the stars, or turbulent water

TURN, verb   71 = 0.046 %

Tob	2 : 6	how he said, Your feasts shall be turned into mourning
	3 : 12	And now, O Lord, I have turned my eyes and my face toward thee
	13 : 6	If you turn to him with all your heart
	13 : 6	then he will turn to you
	14 : 6	Then all the Gentiles will turn
Jud	1 : 14	plundered its markets, and turned its beauty into shame
	8 : 11	unless the Lord turns and helps us within so many days
	8 : 23	but the Lord our God will turn it to dishonour
Ad E	13 : 17	turn our mourning into feasting
	14 : 11	but turn their plan against themselves
	14 : 13	and turn his heart to hate the man who is fighting against us
	15 : 7	And the queen faltered, and turned pale and faint
Wis	2 : 3	When it is extinguished, the body will turn to ashes
	16 : 7	For he who turned toward it was saved
Sir	2 : 7	and turn not aside, lest you fall
	5 : 7	Do not delay to turn to the Lord
	6 : 12	but if you are brought low he will turn against you
	8 : 10	lest you be turned in his flaming fire
	9 : 9	lest your heart turn aside to her
	11 : 31	for he lies in wait, turning good into evil
	17 : 25	Turn to the Lord and forsake your sins
	17 : 29	and his forgiveness for those who turn to him !
	33 : 12	and he turned them out of their place
	37 : 2	when a companion and friend turns to enmity ?
	38 : 29	and turning the wheel with his feet
	39 : 23	just as he turns fresh water into salt
	39 : 27	just as they turn into evils for sinners
	48 : 10	to turn the heart of the father to the son
Bar	2 : 29	this very great multitude will surely turn into
	2 : 33	and will turn from their stubbornness and their wicked deeds
	4 : 2	Turn, O Jacob, and take her
	4 : 34	and her insolence will be turned to grief
Sus	13 : 47	All the people turned to him, and said
1 Ma	1 : 18	and Ptolemy turned and fled before him
	1 : 39	her feasts were turned into mourning
	1 : 40	her exaltation was turned into mourning
	2 : 22	by turning aside from our religion
	2 : 62	for his splendour will turn into dung and worms
	5 : 35	Next he turned aside to Alema
	5 : 68	But Judas turned aside to Azotus
	6 : 6	but had turned and fled before the Jews
	9 : 16	they turned and followed close behind Judas and his men
	9 : 41	Thus, the wedding was turned into mourning
	9 : 45	there is no place to turn
	9 : 72	then he turned an departed to his own land
	12 : 31	So Jonathan turned aside against the Arabs
	12 : 33	He turned aside to Joppa and took it by surprise
	12 : 45	and will turn round and go home
2 Ma	7 : 24	if he would turn from the ways of his fathers
	8 : 5	for the wrath of the Lord had turned to mercy
	9 : 4	he conceived the idea of turning upon the Jews
	10 : 22	Then he slew these men who had turned traitor
	12 : 42	and they turned to prayer
1 Es	3 : 20	It turns every thought to feasting and mirth
3 Ma	1 : 27	they turned, together with our people
	6 : 6	and turning the flame against all their enemies
	6 : 15	and have not turned your face from us
	6 : 22	Then the king's anger was turned to pity and tears
2 Es	1 : 24	I will turn to other nations and will give them my name
	1 : 31	I will turn my face from you
	7 : 133	who turn in repentance to his law
	9 : 39	and turned to her

11 : 31	and behold, the head turned with those that were with it	
13 : 3	and wherever he turned his face to look	
15 : 20	to turn and repay what they have given them	
15 : 31	and turn to pursue them	
15 : 32	and shall turn and flee	
16 : 20	Yet for all this they will not turn from their iniquities	
4 Ma **1** : 12	and then I shall turn to their story	
7 : 3	in no way did he turn the rudder of religion	
15 : 18	When the first-born breathed his last it did not turn you aside	

TURN away 19 = 0.012 %

Tob **3** : 6	do not turn thy face away from me
4 : 7	Do not turn your face away from any poor man
4 : 7	and the face of God will not be turned away from you
Sir **1** : 21	and where it abides, it will turn away all anger
4 : 4	nor turn your face away from the poor
7 : 2	Stay away from wrong, and it will turn away from you
8 : 5	Do not reproach a man who is turning away from sin
9 : 8	Turn away your eyes from a shapely woman
17 : 26	Return to the Most High and turn away from iniquity
18 : 24	and of the moment of vengeance when he turns away his face
45 : 23	and stood fast, when the people turned away
46 : 11	and who did not turn away from the Lord
Bar **1** : 13	have not turned away from us
2 : 8	by turning away, each of us, from the thoughts of his wicked heart
2 : 13	Let thy anger turn away from us, for we are left
4 : 12	because they turned away from the law of God
Sus **13** : 9	and turned away their eyes from looking to Heaven
1 Ma **3** : 8	thus he turned away wrath from Israel
6 : 47	they turned away in flight

TURN back 23 = 0.015 %

Tob **13** : 6	turn back, you sinners, and do right before him
Jud **16** : 11	they lifted up their voices, and the enemy were turned back
Wis **2** : 5	because it is sealed up and no one turns back
Sir **17** : 1	and turned him back to it again
18 : 13	and turns them back, as a shepherd his flock
18 : 21	and when you are on the point of sinning, turn back
26 : 28	a man who turns back from righteousness to sin
40 : 11	All things that are from the earth turn back to the earth
Sus **13** : 14	But turning back, they met again
1 Ma **4** : 16	Then Judas and his force turned back from pursuing them
5 : 28	Then Judas and his army quickly turned back
11 : 72	Then he turned back to the battle against the enemy
12 : 51	they turned back
13 : 24	Then Trypho turned back and departed to his own land
2 Ma **5** : 18	and turned back from his rash act
13 : 19	was turned back, attacked again, and was defeated
1 Es **1** : 28	But Josiah did not turn back to his chariot
8 : 87	but we turned back again to transgress thy law
3 Ma **6** : 21	The beasts turned back upon the armed forces following them
2 Es **7** : 30	And the world shall be turned back to primeval silence for 7 days
16 : 3	and who is there to turn it back ?
16 : 7	Can one turn back an arrow shot by a strong archer ?
4 Ma **13** : 3	in those who were not turned back by fiery agonies ?

TURN out 9 = 0.006 %

Sir **30** : 1	in order that he may rejoice at the way he turns out
30 : 8	A horse that is untamed turns out to be stubborn
30 : 8	and a son unrestrained turns out to be wilful
1 Ma **4** : 27	nor had they turned out as the king had commanded him
6 : 8	because things had not turned out for him as he had planned
2 Ma **13** : 26	This is how the king's attack and withdrawal turned out
15 : 37	This, then, is how matters turned out with Nicanor
3 Ma **1** : 3	and so it turned out
1 : 4	and matters were turning out rather in favour of Antiochus

TURN over 2

1 Ma **3** : 34	And he turned over to Lysias half of his troops and the elephants
16 : 18	and to turn over to him the cities and the country

TURN, subst. 10 = 0.007 %

Wis **8** : 8	she understands turns of speech and the solutions of riddles
Sir **29** : 2	and in turn, repay your neighbour promptly
37 : 18	4 turns of fortune appear, good and evil, life and death
2 Ma **7** : 8	Therefore he in turn underwent tortures
10 : 13	He heard himself called a traitor at every turn
10 : 14	and at every turn kept on warring against the Jews
2 Es **3** : 34	the turn of the scale will incline
11 : 8	let each sleep in his own place, and watch in his turn
14 : 42	and by turns they wrote what was dictated
4 Ma **1** : 17	This, in turn, is education in the law

TURNING 1

Sir **33** : 5	and his thoughts like a turning axle

TWICE 6 = 0.004 %

Jud **13** : 8	And she struck his neck twice with all her might
Sir **7** : 8	Do not commit a sin twice
12 : 5	for you will receive twice as much evil
32 : 7	but no more than twice, and only if asked
45 : 14	twice every day continually
1 Ma **10** : 72	for your fathers were twice put to flight in their own land

TWIST 3 = 0.002 %

Sir **27** : 23	but later he will twist his speech
4 Ma **9** : 17	Cut my limbs, burn my flesh, and twist my joints
11 : 10	they twisted his back around the wedge on the wheel

TWISTED 1

Sir **45** : 11	with twisted scarlet, the work of a craftsman

TWO-EDGED 1

Sir **21** : 3	All lawlessness is like a two-edged sword

TWOFOLD 2

Wis **11** : 12	for a twofold grief possessed them
Sir **42** : 24	All things are twofold, one opposite the other

TYPE 1

4 Ma **1** : 20	The 2 most comprehensive types of the emotions are pleasure and pain

TYRANNICAL 1

4 Ma **5** : 27	It would be tyrannical for you to compel us

TYRANNIZE 1

4 Ma **5** : 38	You may tyrannize the ungodly

TYRANNY 5 = 0.003 %

3 Ma **3** : 8	for they lived under tyranny
4 Ma **1** : 11	and they became the cause of the downfall of tyranny over their nation
8 : 15	and by their right reasoning nullified his tyranny
9 : 30	as you see the arrogant design of your tyranny being defeated
11 : 24	We 6 boys have paralyzed your tyranny !

TYRANT 49 = 0.032 %

2 Ma **4** : 25	but having the hot temper of a cruel tyrant
7 : 27	deriding the cruel tyrant : My son, have pity on me
3 Ma **6** : 24	You are committing treason and surpassing tyrants in cruelty
4 Ma **1** : 11	By their endurance they conquered the tyrant
5 : 1	The tyrant Antiochus, sitting in state with his counsellors
5 : 4	advanced in age, and known to many in the tyrant's court
5 : 14	When the tyrant urged him in this fashion
6 : 1	to the exhortations of the tyrant
6 : 21	and if we should be despised by the tyrant as unmanly
6 : 23	And you, guards of the tyrant, why do you delay
7 : 2	and though buffeted by the stormings of the tyrant
8 : 2	For when the tyrant was conspicuously defeated
8 : 3	When the tyrant had given these orders, 7 brothers
8 : 4	When the tyrant saw them
8 : 13	the tyrant resumed speaking :
8 : 15	but they also opposed the tyrant with their own philosophy
8 : 29	so that as soon as the tyrant
9 : 1	Why do you delay, O tyrant ?
9 : 3	Tyrant and counsellor of lawlessness
9 : 7	Therefore, tyrant, put us to the test
9 : 10	When they had said these things the tyrant not only was angry
9 : 14	he denounced the tyrant, saying
9 : 15	Most abominable tyrant, enemy of heavenly justice, savage of mind
9 : 24	and take vengeance on the accursed tyrant
9 : 30	To the tyrant he said
9 : 30	Do you not think, you most savage tyrant
9 : 32	You will not escape, most abominable tyrant
10 : 10	We, most abominable tyrant
10 : 15	by the eternal destruction of the tyrant
10 : 16	Contrive tortures, tyrant, so that you may learn from them
11 : 2	I will not refuse, tyrant
11 : 12	he said, Tyrant, they are splendid favours that you grant us against your will
11 : 13	When the tyrant inquired
11 : 21	For the religious knowledge, O tyrant, is invincible
11 : 27	For it is not the guards of the tyrant
12 : 2	Even though the tyrant had been fearfully reproached by the brothers
12 : 11	he said, You profane tyrant, most impious of all the wicked
15 : 1	O reason of the children, tyrant over the emotions !
15 : 2	as the tyrant had promised
16 : 14	By steadfastness you have conquered even a tyrant
17 : 2	nullified the violence of the tyrant
17 : 9	because of the violence of the tyrant
17 : 14	The tyrant was the antagonist
17 : 17	The tyrant himself and all his council marvelled at their endurance

17:21 the tyrant was punished, and the homeland purified
17:23 For the tyrant Antiochus
18:5 The tyrant Antiochus was both punished on earth
18:20 when that bitter tyrant of the Greeks
18:22 For these crimes divine justice pursued and will pursue the accursed tyrant

TYRE   8 = 0.005 %
Jud 2:28 who lived along the seacoast, at Sidon and Tyre
Sir 46:18 and he wiped out the leaders of the people of Tyre
1 Ma 5:15 men of Ptolemais and Tyre and Sidon
11:59 from the Ladder of Tyre to the borders of Egypt
2 Ma 4:18 When the quadrennial games were being held at Tyre
4:32 he had sold to Tyre and the neighbouring cities
4:44 When the king came to Tyre
2 Es 1:11 and scattered in the east the people of 2 provinces, Tyre and Sidon

TYRIAN   2
2 Ma 4:49 Therefore even the Tyrians
1 Es 5:55 and carts to the Sidonians and the Tyrians

U

UGLY   1
Sir 20:24 A lie is an ugly blot on a man

UNABLE   13 = 0.008 %
Ad E 16:12 But, unable to restrain his arrogance
Wis 12:9 though thou wast not unable to give the ungodly
13:1 and they were unable from the good things that are seen
Sir 7:6 lest you be unable to remove iniquity
17:16 and they are unable to make for themselves
L Jr 6:14 though unable to destroy any one who offends it
1 Ma 9:60 but they were unable to do it
2 Ma 3:28 but was now unable to help himself
10:13 Unable to command the respect due his office
3 Ma 2:22 was unable even to speak
2 Es 10:32 what I am unable to explain
4 Ma 4:1 he was unable to injure Onias in the eyes of the nation
8:2 being unable to compel an aged man to eat defiling foods

UNAPPROACHABLE   2
3 Ma 2:15 is unapproachable by man
3:29 is to be made unapproachable and burned with fire

UNAWARE   1
Wis 12:10 though thou wast not unaware that their origin was evil

UNBECOMING   1
4 Ma 6:17 that out of cowardice we feign a role unbecoming to us !

UNBELIEF   3 = 0.002 %
2 Es 7:114 unbelief has been cut off
15:3 by the unbelief of those who oppose you
15:4 For every unbeliever shall die in his unbelief

UNBELIEVABLE   1
Jud 13:13 for it was unbelievable that she had returned

UNBELIEVER   1
2 Es 15:4 For every unbeliever shall die in his unbelief

UNBELIEVING   1
Wis 10:7 as a monument to an unbelieving soul

UNBORN   1
Tob 4:4 while you were yet unborn

UNBREAKABLE   1
3 Ma 4:9 others had their feet secured by unbreakable fetters

UNBROKEN   3 = 0.002 %
Bel 14:17 And the king said, Are the seals unbroken, Daniel ?
14:17 He answered, They are unbroken, O king
2 Ma 3:1 While the holy city was inhabited in unbroken peace

UNBURIED   1
2 Ma 5:10 He who had cast many to lie unburied

UNCEASING   1
4 Ma 10:11 will undergo unceasing torments

UNCEASINGLY   1
3 Ma 6:33 gave thanks to heaven unceasingly and lavishly

UNCERTAIN   1
2 Ma 7:34 do not be elated in vain and puffed up by uncertain hopes

UNCERTAINTY   1
3 Ma 4:4 reflected upon the uncertainty of life

UNCHANGING   1
Ad E 13:3 and is distinguished for his unchanging good will and steadfast fidelity

UNCIRCUMCISED   3 = 0.002 %
Ad E 14:15 and abhor the bed of the uncircumcised and of any alien
1 Ma 1:48 and to leave their sons uncircumcised
2:46 they forcibly circumcised all the uncircumcised boys

UNCLEAN   8 = 0.005 %
Wis 2:16 and he avoids our ways as unclean
Sir 34:4 From an unclean thing what will be made clean ?
51:5 from an unclean tongue and lying words
1 Ma 1:47 to sacrifice swine and unclean animals
1:48 by everything unclean and profane
1:62 and were resolved in their hearts not to eat unclean food
4:43 and removed the defiled stones to an unclean place
1 Es 1:49 beyond all the unclean deeds of all the nations

UNCLEANNESS   5 = 0.003 %
1 Ma 13:48 He cast out of it all uncleanness
14:7 and he removed its uncleanness from it
1 Es 1:42 and his uncleanness and impiety
8:83 and they have filled it with their uncleanness
8:87 by mixing with the uncleanness of the peoples of the land

UNCOMFORTABLE   1
2 Ma 2:27 we will gladly endure the uncomfortable toil

UNCOMPLETED   1
3 Ma 4:15 and though uncompleted it stopped after 40 days

UNCONCERN   1
Sir 29:5 and will pay in words of unconcern

UNCONCERNED   1
Bel 14:13 They were unconcerned

UNCONDEMNED   1
2 Ma 4:47 who would have been freed uncondemned

UNCONQUERED   1
4 Ma 11:27 therefore, unconquered, we hold fast to reason

UNCONTROLLABLE   1
3 Ma 6:17 and brought an uncontrollable terror upon the army

UNCOUNTED   2
Wis 7:11 and in her hands uncounted wealth
3 Ma 2:26 He was not content with his uncounted licentious deeds

UNCOVER   5 = 0.003 %
Tob 2:9 I slept by the wall of the courtyard, and my face was uncovered
Jud 9:1 and uncovered the sackcloth she was wearing
9:2 and uncovered her thigh to put her to shame
L Jr 6:31 and their heads uncovered
1 Es 8:79 and to uncover a light for us

UNDAUNTED   1
4 Ma 13:13 cheerful and undaunted, said

UNDEFENDED   1
Ad E 16:14 He thought that in this way he would find us undefended

UNDEFILED   5 = 0.003 %
Wis 3:13 For blessed is the barren woman who is undefiled
4:2 victor in the contest for prizes that are undefiled
8:20 or rather, being good, I entered an undefiled body
2 Ma 14:36 keep undefiled for ever this house
15:34 Blessed is he who has kept his own place undefiled

UNDER   72 = 0.047 %
Tob 1:15 and under him the highways were unsafe
Jud 6:13 However, they got under the shelter of the hill
8:9 and how he promised them under oath
10:21 under a canopy which was woven with purple and gold
11:7 under Nebuchadnezzar and all his house
Ad E 13:1 from India to Ethiopia and to the governors under them
13:10 and every wonderful thing under heaven
16:19 and permit the Jews to live under their own laws
Wis 17:2 and prisoners of long night, shut in under their roofs
Sir 6:25 Put your shoulder under her and carry her
6:25 and do not fret under her bonds
14:26 he will place his children under her shelter

	14:26	and will camp under her boughs
	16:15	in order that his works might be known under heaven
	23:10	for as a servant who is continually examined under torture
	29:10	and do not let it rust under a stone and be lost
	29:22	under the shelter of his roof
	33:6	he neighs under every one who sits on him
	51:26	Put your neck under the yoke
Bar	1:12	and we shall live under the protection of Nebuchadnezzar king of Babylon
	1:12	and under the protection of Belshazzar his son
	2:2	Under the whole heaven there has not been done
	5:3	For God will show your splendour everywhere under heaven
Sus	13:54	Under what tree did you see them being intimate with each other ?
	13:54	He answered, Under a mastic tree
	13:58	Under what tree did you catch them being intimate with each other ?
	13:58	He answered, Under an evergreen oak
Bel	14:30	and under compulsion he handed Daniel over to them
1 Ma	2:19	Even if all the nations that live under the rule of the king
	6:46	He got under the elephant
	9:38	and went up and hid under cover of the mountain
	9:53	as hostages and put them under guard
	10:38	that they are considered to be under one ruler
	13:12	and Jonathan was with him under guard
	14:3	who put him under guard
	14:12	Each man sat under his vine and his fig tree
2 Ma	1:14	For under pretext of intending to marry her
	2:18	and will gather us from everywhere under heaven
	3:6	to fall under the control of the king
	3:19	Women, girded with sackcloth under their breasts
	4:12	right under the citadel
	4:40	under the leadership of a certain Auranus
	5:25	he ordered his men to parade under arms
	6:7	the Jews were taken, under bitter constraint
	6:30	When he was about to die under the blows
	6:30	I am enduring terrible sufferings in my body under this beating
	7:1	under torture with whips and cords
	7:36	have drunk of everflowing life under God's covenant
	8:22	each to command a division, putting 1,500 men under each
	9:11	and to come to his senses under the scourge of God
	10:10	Now we will tell what took place under Antiochus Eupator
	12:19	Dositheus and Sosipater, who were captains under Maccabeus
	12:40	Then under the tunic of every one of the dead
1 Es	3:1	for all that were under him
	3:2	that were under him in the 127 satrapies
	3:8	and put them under the pillow of Darius the king
	5:36	under the leadership of Cherub, Addan, and Immer
3 Ma	3:8	for they lived under tyranny
	4:9	driven under the constraint of iron bonds
	4:10	and in addition they were confined under a solid deck
2 Es	1:30	I gathered you as a hen gathers her brood under her wings
	11:6	And I saw how all things under heaven were subjected to him
	11:24	and remained under the head that was on the right side
	13:3	everything under his gaze trembled
	14:1	On the 3rd day, while I was sitting under an oak
	16:69	and be trodden under foot
4 Ma	8:14	when you transgress under compulsion
	8:22	for fearing the king when we are under compulsion
	9:19	While he was saying these things they spread fire under him
	14:12	under the rackings of each one of her children
	17:19	For Moses says, All who are consecrated are under your hands
	17:23	and their endurance under the tortures

UNDERBRUSH
1

2 Es 16:77 as a field is choked with underbrush

UNDERGO
4 = 0.003 %

2 Ma	7:8	Therefore he in turn underwent tortures
3 Ma	4:10	they should undergo treatment befitting traitors
4 Ma	9:9	will deservedly undergo from the divine justice
	10:11	will undergo unceasing torments

UNDERNEATH
1

4 Ma 11:18 his back was broken, and he was roasted from underneath

UNDERSTAND
35 = 0.023 %

Jud	9:14	to know and understand that thou art God
Ad E	11:12	and sought all day to understand it in every detail
	13:5	We understand that this people, and it alone
Wis	3:9	Those who trust in him will understand truth
	4:15	Yet the peoples saw and did not understand
	4:17	and will not understand what the Lord purposed for him
	6:1	Listen therefore, O kings, and understand
	8:8	she understands turns of speech and the solutions of riddles
	9:9	and who understands what is pleasing in thy sight
	9:11	For she knows and understands all things
Sir	1:7	And her abundant experience – who has understood it ?
	18:29	Those who understand sayings become skilled themselves
	34:11	and I understand more than I can express

	38:33	nor do they understand the sentence of judgment
Bar	3:20	nor understood her paths, nor laid hold of her
L Jr	6:41	as though Bel were able to understand
2 Ma	9:25	Moreover, I understand how the princes along the borders
2 Es	2:34	Therefore I say to you, O nations that hear and understand
	4:10	You cannot understand the things with which you have grown up
	4:11	And how can one who is already worn out by the corrupt world understand incorruption ?
	4:12	and to suffer and not understand why
	4:21	can understand only what is on the earth
	4:21	can understand what is above the height of the heavens
	5:34	while I strive to understand the way of the Most High
	5:37	that you ask to understand
	6:15	and the foundations of the earth will understand
	7:37	Look now, and understand whom you have denied
	7:71	And now understand from your own words
	7:95	they understand the rest which they now enjoy
	8:19	Therefore hear my voice, and understand my words
	9:11	and did not understand but despised it
	10:35	and I have heard what I do not understand
	13:18	because they understand what is reserved for the last days
	13:24	Understand therefore that those who are left
	16:35	Listen now to these things, and understand them

UNDERSTANDING, subst.
64 = 0.042 %

Tob	4:19	For none of the nations has understanding
Jud	8:29	all the people have recognized your understanding
Wis	3:15	and the root of understanding does not fail
	4:9	but understanding is grey hair for men
	4:11	He was caught up lest evil change his understanding
	6:15	To fix one's thought on her is perfect understanding
	7:7	Therefore I prayed, and understanding was given me
	7:16	as are all understanding and skill in crafts
	8:6	And if understanding is effective
	8:18	and in the experience of her company, understanding
	9:5	with little understanding of judgment and laws
Sir pr.		should acquire understanding
	1:4	and prudent understanding from eternity
	3:13	even if he is lacking in understanding, show forbearance
	3:23	for matters too great for human understanding
	5:10	Be steadfast in your understanding
	5:12	If you have understanding, answer your neighbour
	7:25	But give her to a man of understanding
	8:9	because from them you will gain understanding
	9:15	Let your conversation be with men of understanding
	10:3	through the understanding of its rulers
	10:25	and a man of understanding will not grumble
	11:15	Wisdom, understanding, and knowledge of the law
	15:3	She will feed him with the bread of understanding
	16:4	For through one man of understanding
	16:23	This is what one devoid of understanding thinks
	17:7	He filled them with knowledge and understanding
	21:15	When a man of understanding hears a wise saying
	24:26	It makes them full of understanding, like the Euphrates
	25:5	and understanding and counsel in honourable men !
	33:3	A man of understanding will trust in the law
	34:1	A man of no understanding has vain and false hopes
	34:9	and one with much experience will speak with understanding
	37:22	and the fruits of his understanding
	37:23	and the fruits of his understanding will be trustworthy
	39:6	he will be filled with the spirit of understanding
	39:9	Many will praise his understanding
	44:3	giving counsel by their understanding
	44:4	and in understanding of learning for the people
	47:14	You overflowed like a river with understanding
	47:23	ample in folly and lacking in understanding
	50:27	Instruction in understanding and knowledge
	51:20	I gained understanding with her from the first
Bar	3:14	where there is understanding
	3:23	the sons of Hagar, who seek for understanding on the earth
	3:23	the story-tellers and the seekers for understanding
	3:32	he found her by his understanding
1 Es	1:33	and his understanding of the law of the Lord
	8:44	who were leaders and men of understanding
2 Es	4:2	Your understanding has utterly failed regarding this world
	4:22	why have I been endowed with the power of understanding ?
	5:22	Then my soul recovered the spirit of understanding
	7:72	because though they had understanding they committed iniquity
	8:4	Then drink your fill of understanding, O my soul
	8:6	and cultivation of our understanding
	8:25	and as long as I have understanding I will answer
	10:30	and I was deprived of my understanding
	10:31	And why are your understanding
	13:55	and called understanding your mother
	14:25	and I will light in your heart the lamp of understanding
	14:40	my heart poured forth understanding
	14:42	And the Most High gave understanding to the 5 men

	14 :47	For in them is the spring of understanding
	16 :61	and gave him breath and life and understanding

UNDERSTANDING, adj.   1
Sir 10 :1   and the rule of an understanding man will be well ordered

UNDERTAKE   12 = 0.008 %
Ad E 16 :3   they even undertake to scheme against their own benefactors
16 :12   he undertook to deprive us of our kingdom and our life
1 Ma   4 :51   Thus they finished all the work they had undertaken
12 :10   we have undertaken to send to renew our brotherhood
2 Ma   2 :26   For us who have undertaken the toil of abbreviating
2 :29   while the one who undertakes its painting and decoration
7 :26   she undertook to persuade her son
8 :36   Thus he who had undertaken
10 :23   Having success at arms in everything he undertook
1 Es   9 :14   undertook the matter on these terms
3 Ma   2 :14   undertakes to violate the holy place on earth
2 Es   4 :18   which would you undertake to justify

UNDERTAKING   2
Jud 13 :5   and to carry out my undertaking
Sir 37 :16   and counsel precedes every undertaking

UNDISCIPLINED   2
Sir 10 :3   An undisciplined king will ruin his people
22 :3   It is a disgrace to be the father of an undisciplined son

UNDISTURBED   1
2 Ma 11 :23   we desire that the subjects of the kingdom be undisturbed

UNDO   2
Jud 16 :7   but Judith the daughter of Merari undid him
4 Ma   3 :11   tormented and inflamed him, undid and consumed him

UNERRING   1
Wis   7 :17   For it is he who gave me unerring knowledge of what exists

UNEXAMINED   1
Sir 21 :18   and the knowledge of the ignorant is unexamined talk

UNEXPECTED   8 = 0.005 %
Wis   5 :2   and they will be amazed at his unexpected salvation
17 :15   for sudden and unexpected fear overwhelmed them
18 :17   and unexpected fears assailed them
2 Ma   9 :24   so that, if anything unexpected happened
3 Ma   3 :8   when they saw an unexpected tumult around these people
4 :2   and they groaned because of the unexpected destruction
5 :33   So Hermon suffered an unexpected and dangerous threat
6 :33   for the unexpected rescue which he had experienced

UNEXPECTEDLY   1
Wis 11 :7   thou gavest them abundant water unexpectedly

UNFADING   1
Wis   6 :12   Wisdom is radiant and unfading

UNFAILING   3 = 0.002 %
Wis   7 :14   for it is an unfailing treasure for men
8 :18   and in the labours of her hands, unfailing wealth
2 Es   9 :19   which is supplied both with an unfailing table

UNFAITHFUL   2
Sir 42 :10   or having a husband, lest she prove unfaithful
2 Es   7 :24   they have been unfaithful to his statutes

UNFAITHFULLY   1
2 Es   7 :72   they dealt unfaithfully with what they received

UNFIT   1
2 Ma   6 :4   and besides brought in things for sacrifice that were unfit

UNFORTUNATE   1
2 Ma   4 :47   while he sentenced to death those unfortunate men

UNFRUITFUL   1
2 Es   9 :29   when they came into the untrodden and unfruitful wilderness

UNGODLINESS   7 = 0.005 %
Wis 14 :9   are the ungodly man and his ungodliness
2 Es   4 :12   than to come here and live in ungodliness
4 :30   and how much ungodliness it has produced until now
4 :31   how much fruit of ungodliness a grain of evil seed has produced
4 :38   but all of us also are full of ungodliness
12 :32   he will denounce them for their ungodliness
13 :37   And he, my Son, will reprove the assembled nations for their ungodliness

UNGODLY, adj., subst.   63 = 0.041 %
Wis   1 :9   For inquiry will be made into the counsels of an ungodly man
1 :16   But ungodly men by their words and deeds summoned death
3 :10   But the ungodly will be punished as their reasoning deserves
4 :3   But the prolific brood of the ungodly will be of no use
4 :16   will condemn the ungodly who are living
5 :14   Because the hope of the ungodly man
10 :6   when the ungodly were perishing
10 :20   Therefore the righteous plundered the ungodly
11 :9   they learned how the ungodly
11 :10   but thou didst examine the ungodly
12 :9   though thou wast not unable to give the ungodly
14 :9   are the ungodly man and his ungodliness
14 :16   Then the ungodly custom, grown strong with time
16 :16   for the ungodly, refusing to know thee
16 :18   sent against the ungodly
19 :1   But the ungodly were assailed to the end by pitiless anger
Sir   7 :17   for the punishment of the ungodly is fire and worms
9 :12   Do not delight in what pleases the ungodly
12 :5   Do good to the humble, but do not give to the ungodly
12 :6   and will inflict punishment on the ungodly
13 :24   and poverty is evil in the opinion of the ungodly
15 :20   He has not commanded any one to be ungodly
16 :1   nor rejoice in ungodly sons
16 :3   and to die childless is better than to have ungodly children
21 :27   When an ungodly man curses his adversary
22 :12   but for a fool or an ungodly man it lasts all his life
26 :26   in her pride she will be known to all as ungodly
34 :19   with the offerings of the ungodly
39 :30   and the sword that punishes the ungodly with destruction
40 :15   The children of the ungodly will not put forth many branches
41 :5   and they frequent the haunts of the ungodly
41 :7   Children will blame an ungodly father
41 :8   Woe to you, ungodly men
41 :10   so the ungodly go from curse to destruction
42 :2   and of rendering judgment to acquit the ungodly
Bar   2 :12   we have sinned, we have been ungodly, we have done wrong
1 Ma   3 :8   he destroyed the ungodly out of the land
3 :15   And again a strong army of ungodly men
6 :21   and some of the ungodly Israelites joined them
7 :5   all the lawless and ungodly men of Israel
7 :9   And he sent him, and with him the ungodly Alcimus
9 :25   And Bacchides chose the ungodly
9 :73   and he destroyed the ungodly out of Israel
2 Ma   4 :13   who was ungodly and no high priest
8 :2   which had been profaned by ungodly men
8 :14   to rescue those who had been sold by the ungodly Nicanor
9 :9   And so the ungodly man's body swarmed with worms
10 :10   who was the son of that ungodly man
12 :3   And some men of Joppa did so ungodly a deed
15 :33   he cut out the tongue of the ungodly Nicanor
1 Es   1 :52   because of their ungodly acts he gave command
2 Es   3 :8   and did ungodly things before thee and scorned thee
3 :12   and again they began to be more ungodly than were their ancestors
3 :29   For when I came here I saw ungodly deeds without number
7 :17   but that the ungodly shall perish
7 :51   while the ungodly abound
7 :93   in which the souls of the ungodly wander
7 :102   the righteous will be able to intercede for the ungodly
7 :111   If therefore the righteous have prayed for the ungodly now
9 :13   as to how the ungodly will be punished
14 :35   and the deeds of the ungodly will be disclosed
15 :8   I will be silent no longer concerning their ungodly deeds
4 Ma   5 :38   You may tyrannize the ungodly

UNGRACIOUS   2
Sir 18 :18   A fool is ungracious and abusive
20 :19   An ungracious man is like a story told at the wrong time

UNGRATEFUL   3 = 0.002 %
Wis 16 :29   for the hope of an ungrateful man
2 Es   8 :60   and have been ungrateful to him who prepared life for them
4 Ma   9 :10   but also was enraged, as at those who are ungrateful

UNHAPPY   2
2 Es 15 :59   Unhappy above all others
4 Ma 16 :6   O how wretched am I and many times unhappy !

UNHARMED   7 = 0.005 %
Wis 19 :6   that thy children might be kept unharmed
2 Ma 12 :25   he had confirmed his solemn promise to restore them unharmed
3 Ma   6 :6   you rescued unharmed, even to a hair
6 :7   you brought up to the light unharmed
6 :8   you, Father, watched over and restored unharmed to all his family
6 :39   and rescued them all together and unharmed
7 :20   they departed unharmed, free, and overjoyed

UNHEALTHY   1
  Sir **40**:15   they are unhealthy roots upon sheer rock

UNHEARD   1
  Wis **1**:10   and the sound of murmurings does not go unheard

UNHEWN   1
  1 Ma **4**:47   Then they took unhewn stones, as the law directs

UNHINDERED   2
  Wis **17**:20   and was engaged in unhindered work
      19:7   an unhindered way out of the Red Sea

UNHOLY   4 = 0.003 %
  Wis **12**:4   their works of sorcery and unholy rites
  2 Ma **7**:34   But you, unholy wretch, you most defiled of all men
      8:32   a most unholy man
     12:14   railing at them and even blaspheming and saying unholy things

UNIFORM   1
  2 Ma **8**:35   took off his splendid uniform

UNIFYING   1
  Ad E **13**:4   so that the unifying of the kingdom which we honourably intend

UNIMPEDED   1
  3 Ma **6**:28   has granted an unimpeded and notable stability to our government

UNINHABITED   3 = 0.002 %
  Jud **5**:19   because it was uninhabited
  Wis **11**:2   They journeyed through an uninhabited wilderness
  1 Ma **3**:45   Jerusalem was uninhabited like a wilderness

UNINSTRUCTED   2
  Wis **17**:1   therefore uninstructed souls have gone astray
  Sir **6**:20   She seems very harsh to the uninstructed

UNINTELLIGENT   1
  Sir **22**:13   and do not visit an unintelligent man

UNINTENTIONALLY   1
  Sir **14**:7   even if he does good, he does it unintentionally

UNION   4 = 0.003 %
  Wis **3**:13   who has not entered into a sinful union
      3:16   and the offspring of an unlawful union will perish
      4:6   For children born of unlawful unions are witnesses of evil
  3 Ma **1**:19   abandoned the bridal chambers prepared for wedded union

UNISON   1
  Jud **4**:12   and cried out in unison

UNITE   1
  1 Ma **2**:42   Then there united with them a company of Hasidaeans

UNIVERSAL   1
  4 Ma **15**:31   Just as Noah's ark, carrying the world in the universal flood

UNIVERSE   6 = 0.004 %
  Ad E **13**:9   for the universe is in thy power
  Wis **16**ℓ:17   for the universe defends the righteous
  Sir **18**:1   He who lives for ever created the whole universe
     23:20   Before the universe was created, it was known to him
     42:17   that the universe may stand firm in his glory
  2 Ma **7**:9   but the King of the universe will raise us up

UNJUST   9 = 0.006 %
  Sir **19**:25   There is a cleverness which is scrupulous but unjust
     40:13   The wealth of the unjust will dry up like a torrent
     41:18   of unjust dealing, before your partner or friend
  P Az   9   most hateful rebels, and to an unjust king
  Sus **13**:53   pronouncing unjust judgments
  2 Ma **4**:35   were grieved and displeased at the unjust murder of the man
      4:40   and launched an unjust attack
      4:48   quickly suffered the unjust penalty
  3 Ma **6**:27   Loose and untie their unjust bonds !

UNJUSTLY   3 = 0.002 %
  Wis **12**:13   that thou hast not judged unjustly
  1 Ma **2**:37   that you are killing us unjustly
     15:33   which at one time had been unjustly taken by our enemies

UNKINDLY   1
  Sir **20**:16   those who eat my bread speak unkindly

UNKNOWN   4 = 0.003 %
  Wis **11**:18   or newly created unknown beasts full of rage
     18:3   as a guide for thy people's unknown journey

  2 Ma **1**:19   that the place was unknown to any one
     2:7   The place shall be unknown

UNLAWFUL   6 = 0.004 %
  Wis **3**:16   and the offspring of an unlawful union will perish
      4:6   For children born of unlawful unions are witnesses of evil
  2 Ma **4**:14   they hastened to take part in the unlawful proceedings
      6:21   Those who were in charge of that unlawful sacrifice took the man aside
      7:1   to partake of unlawful swine's flesh
  3 Ma **1**:27   and not to overlook this unlawful and haughty deed

UNLAWFULLY   1
  4 Ma **5**:14   to eat meat unlawfully

UNLEAVENED   3 = 0.002 %
  1 Es **1**:10   properly arrayed and having the unleavened bread
      1:19   kept the passover and the feast of unleavened bread 7 days
      7:14   And they kept the feast of unleavened bread 7 days

UNLESS   15 = 0.010 %
  Jud **8**:11   unless the Lord turns and helps us within so many days
    11:10   unless they sin against their God
  Wis **8**:21   unless God gave her to me
     9:17   Who has learned thy counsel, unless thou hast given wisdom
  Sir **16**:2   unless the fear of the Lord is in them
     19:8   and unless it would be a sin for you, do not disclose it
     34:6   Unless they are sent from the Most High as a visitation
  L Jr **6**:24   they will not shine unless some one wipes off the rust
  1 Ma **6**:27   and unless you quickly prevent them
      7:35   Unless Judas and his army
  2 Es **7**:5   unless he passes through the narrow part ?
      7:9   unless he passes through the danger set before him ?
     7:14   Therefore unless the living
  4 Ma **2**:7   unless reason is clearly lord of the emotions ?
      9:2   unless we should practice ready obedience

UNLIKE   1
  Wis **2**:15   because his manner of life is unlike that of others

UNMANLY   2
  4 Ma **6**:21   and if we should be despised by the tyrant as unmanly
      8:16   if some of them had been cowardly and unmanly

UNMARRIED   1
  4 Ma **16**:9   Alas for my children, some unmarried

UNMERCIFUL   1
  Sir **35**:18   till he crushes the loins of the unmerciful

UNMINDFUL   2
  Sir **37**:6   and be not unmindful of him in your wealth
  2 Es **3**:33   though they are unmindful of thy commandments

UNMIXED   1
  3 Ma **5**:2   with large handfuls of frankincense and plenty of unmixed wine

UNMOVED   2
  4 Ma **6**:5   But the courageous and noble man, as a true Eleazar, was unmoved
      7:12   remained unmoved in his reason

UNNOTICED   1
  Wis **10**:8   so that their failures could never go unnoticed

UNOBSERVED   2
  Wis **17**:3   they were unobserved behind a dark curtain of forgetfulness
  2 Ma **15**:36   never to let this day go unobserved

UNPROFITABLE   2
  Wis **3**:11   Their hope is vain, their labours are unprofitable
  Sir **37**:19   and yet be unprofitable to himself

UNPUNISHED   5 = 0.003 %
  Wis **12**:11   that thou didst leave them unpunished for their sins
  Sir **7**:8   even for one you will not go unpunished
     11:10   if you multiply activities you will not go unpunished
     16:11   it will be a wonder if he remains unpunished
  2 Ma **7**:19   But do not think that you will go unpunished

UNREASONABLE   2
  2 Ma **4**:36   with regard to the unreasonable murder of Onias
  4 Ma **16**:23   It is unreasonable for people who have religious knowledge

UNREASONING   2
  4 Ma **14**:14   Even unreasoning animals, like mankind
     14:18   by the example of unreasoning animals

UNRESPONSIVE   1
Wis 16 : 11   and become unresponsive to thy kindness

UNREST   2
Sir 40 : 5   there is anger and envy and trouble and unrest
2 Es 15 : 16   For there shall be unrest among men

UNRESTRAINED   1
Sir 30 : 8   and a son unrestrained turns out to be wilful

UNRESTRAINT   1
2 Es 5 : 10   and unrighteousness and unrestraint shall increase on earth

UNRIGHTEOUS   23 = 0.015 %
Wis 1 : 8   therefore no one who utters unrighteous things will escape notice
    3 : 19   For the end of an unrighteous generation is grievous
    4 : 16   will condemn the prolonged old age of the unrighteous man
   10 : 3   But when an unrighteous man departed from her in his anger
   12 : 12   to plead as an advocate for unrighteous men ?
   14 : 31   that always pursues the transgression of the unrighteous
   16 : 19   to destroy the crops of the unrighteous land
   16 : 24   exerts itself to punish the unrighteous
Sir 1 : 22   Unrighteous anger cannot be justified
   35 : 12   and do not trust to an unrighteous sacrifice
   35 : 18   and breaks the sceptres of the unrighteous
   51 : 6   the slander of an unrighteous tongue to the king
1 Es 4 : 36   and with him there is nothing unrighteous
   4 : 37   Wine is unrighteous, the king is unrighteous
   4 : 37   women are unrighteous, all the sons of men are unrighteous
   4 : 37   all their works are unrighteous, and all such things
   4 : 39   instead of anything that is unrighteous or wicked
   4 : 40   and there is nothing unrighteous in her judgment
2 Es 2 : 8   who conceal the unrighteous in your midst !
   7 : 35   and unrighteous deeds shall not sleep
   8 : 47   But you have often compared yourself to the unrighteous

UNRIGHTEOUSLY   3 = 0.002 %
Wis 12 : 23   Therefore those who in folly of life lived unrighteously
   14 : 28   or prophesy lies, or live unrighteously
   14 : 30   and because in deceit they swore unrighteously

UNRIGHTEOUSNESS   9 = 0.006 %
Wis 1 : 5   and will be ashamed at the approach of unrighteousness
Sir 17 : 14   And he said to them, Beware of all unrighteousness
   35 : 3   and to forsake unrighteousness is atonement
1 Es 4 : 37   and in their unrighteousness they will perish
2 Es 5 : 2   And unrighteousness shall be increased
   5 : 10   and unrighteousness and unrestraint shall increase on earth
   7 : 105   for then every one shall bear his own righteousness or unrighteousness
   7 : 111   when corruption has increased and unrighteousness has multiplied
   12 : 31   and reproving him for his unrighteousness

UNSAFE   1
Tob 1 : 15   and under him the highways were unsafe

UNSEARCHABLE   1
P Ma 6   yet immeasurable and unsearchable is thy promised mercy

UNSEEMLY   2
Sir 13 : 22   he speaks unseemly words, and they justify him
2 Es 7 : 124   because we have lived in unseemly places ?

UNSEEN   5 = 0.003 %
Wis 17 : 6   to be worse than that unseen appearance
   17 : 19   or the unseen running of leaping animals
Sir 20 : 30   Hidden wisdom and unseen treasure
   41 : 14   hidden wisdom and unseen treasure
2 Ma 9 : 5   struck him an incurable and unseen blow

UNSOUNDLY   1
Wis 2 : 1   For they reasoned unsoundly, saying to themselves

UNSOWN   1
2 Es 6 : 22   Sown places shall suddenly appear unsown

UNSPOILED   1
2 Es 7 : 123   whose fruits remains unspoiled

UNSWERVING   3 = 0.002 %
3 Ma 3 : 3   and unswerving loyalty toward the dynasty
4 Ma 6 : 7   he kept his reason upright and unswerving
   17 : 3   you held firm and unswerving

UNTAMED   1
Sir 30 : 8   A horse that is untamed turns out to be stubborn

UNTAUGHT   1
Sir 51 : 23   Draw near to me, you who are untaught, and lodge in my school

UNTIE   2
Jud 6 : 14   and they untied him and brought him into Bethulia
3 Ma 6 : 27   Loose and untie their unjust bonds !

UNTIL, prep., conj.   93 = 0.061 %
Tob 2 : 4   I sprang up and removed the body to a place of shelter until sunset
   2 : 10   Ahikar, however, took care of me until he went to Elymais
   6 : 5   until they came near to Ecbatana
   7 : 11   until you make a binding agreement with me
   8 : 20   until the 14 days of the wedding feast were ended
   10 : 7   until the 14 days of the wedding feast had expired
   11 : 1   So he continued on his way until they came near to Nineveh
   14 : 5   until the times of the age are completed
Jud 6 : 5   until I take revenge on this race that came out of Egypt
   6 : 8   and you will not die until you perish along with them
   7 : 20   until all the vessels of water belonging to every inhabitant of Bethulia were empty
   8 : 34   until I have finished what I am about to do
   10 : 10   until she had gone down the mountain
   12 : 5   and she slept until midnight
   12 : 9   until she ate her food toward evening
   12 : 14   and it will be a joy to me until the day of my death !
   14 : 8   until the moment of her speaking to them
   16 : 23   until she was 105 years old
Ad E 14 : 18   since the day that I was brought here until now
   15 : 8   and took her in his arms until she came to herself
Wis 10 : 14   until she brought him the sceptre of a kingdom
Sir 1 : 23   A patient man will endure until the right moment
   1 : 24   He will hide his words until the right moment
   4 : 17   and will torment him by her discipline until she trusts him
   6 : 18   and until you are old you will keep finding wisdom
   11 : 19   until he leaves them to others and dies
   13 : 7   until he has drained you 2 or 3 times
   18 : 22   and do not wait until death to be released from it
   20 : 7   A wise man will be silent until the right moment
   23 : 16   will not be quenched until it is consumed
   23 : 16   will never cease until the fire burns him up
   23 : 17   he will never cease until he dies
   29 : 5   A man will kiss another's hands until he gets a loan
   35 : 17   and he will not be consoled until it reaches the Lord
   35 : 17   he will not desist until the Most High visits him
Bar 1 : 19   out of the land of Egypt until today
1 Ma 3 : 33   until he returned
   4 : 41   until he had cleansed the sanctuary
   4 : 46   on the temple hill until there should come a prophet
   5 : 19   but do not engage in battle with the Gentiles until we return
   8 : 4   until they crushed them
   9 : 6   until no more than 800 of them were left
   10 : 50   He pressed the battle strongly until the sun set
   12 : 29   But Jonathan and his men did not know it until morning
   14 : 41   until a trustworthy prophet should arise
   16 : 2   have fought the wars of Israel from our youth until this day
   16 : 9   until Cendebaeus reached Kedron, which he had built
2 Ma 2 : 7   until God gathers his people together again
   5 : 25   and waited until the holy sabbath day
   6 : 14   until they have reached the full measure of their sins
   9 : 4   until he completed the journey
1 Es 1 : 14   because the priests were offering the fat until night
   1 : 52   until in his anger against his people
   1 : 57   until the Persians began to reign
   1 : 58   Until the land has enjoyed its sabbaths
   1 : 58   until the completion of 70 years
   2 : 30   until the 2nd year of the reign
   4 : 51   for the building of the temple until it was completed
   4 : 55   until the day when the temple should be finished and Jerusalem built
   5 : 40   until a high priest should appear wearing Urim and Thummim
   5 : 73   until the reign of Darius
   6 : 6   until word could be sent to Darius concerning them
   6 : 20   from that time until now
   6 : 28   until the house of the Lord is finished
   8 : 59   Be watchful and on guard until you deliver them
   8 : 72   and I sat grief-stricken until the evening sacrifice
   8 : 77   in shame until this day
   9 : 13   until we are freed from the wrath of the Lord
   9 : 41   from early morning until midday
3 Ma 5 : 10   until they had been filled with a great abundance of wine
   6 : 28   who from the time of our ancestors until now
   6 : 40   until the 14th day
   7 : 4   would never be firmly established until this was accomplished
2 Es 2 : 32   Embrace your children until I come
   4 : 30   and how much ungodliness it has produced until now
   4 : 30   and will produce until the time of threshing comes !
   4 : 37   until that measure is fulfilled
   4 : 51   Do you think that I shall live until those days ?
   7 : 75   we shall be kept in rest until those times come

	7:77	but it will not be shown to you until the last times
	10:2	and I remained quiet until evening of the 2nd day
	10:4	but without ceasing mourn and fast until I die
	12:21	but 2 shall be kept until the end
	12:32	until the end of days
	12:34	and he will make them joyful until the end comes
	13:44	until they had passed over
	13:46	Then they dwelt there until the last times
	14:9	until the times are ended
	14:25	until what you are about to write is finished
	15:21	Just as they have done to my elect until this day, so I will do
	16:14	and shall not return until they come over the earth
	16:15	until it consumes the foundations of the earth
4 Ma	7:3	until he sailed into the haven of immortal victory

UNTIMELY 1
Wis 14:15 at an untimely bereavement

UNTO 1
4 Ma 13:1 Since, then, the 7 brothers despised sufferings even unto death

UNTOLD 2
2 Ma 3:6 that the treasury in Jerusalem was full of untold money
12:16 and slaughtered untold numbers

UNTRODDEN 3 = 0.002 %
Wis 11:2 and pitched their tents in untrodden places
2 Es 5:3 shall be waste and untrodden
9:29 when they came into the untrodden and unfruitful wilderness

UNTROUBLED 1
Ad E 13:7 and leave our government completely secure and untroubled hereafter

UNUSUAL 3 = 0.002 %
Wis 16:16 pursued by unusual rains and hail and relentless storms
3 Ma 4:4 that at the sight of their unusual punishments
5:27 and being struck by the unusual invitation to come out

UNVEIL 2
Sus 13:32 As she was veiled, the wicked men ordered her to be unveiled
3 Ma 4:6 and were carried away unveiled

UNWEARIED 1
Sir 20:32 Unwearied patience in seeking the Lord is better

UNWELCOME 1
2 Ma 9:24 or any unwelcome news came

UNWILLING 2
1 Ma 12:14 We were unwilling to annoy you
3 Ma 3:19 and are unwilling to regard any action as sincere

UNWISELY 1
1 Ma 5:67 fell in battle, for they went out to battle unwisely

UNWITTING 2
Tob 3:3 do not punish me for my sins and for my unwitting offences
Jud 5:20 if there is any unwitting error in this people

UNWORTHILY 1
Ad E 16:7 who exercise authority unworthily

UNWORTHY 6 = 0.004 %
Sir 10:19 What race is unworthy of honour ? The human race
10:19 What race is unworthy of honour ?
2 Ma 14:42 and suffer outrages unworthy of his noble birth
P Ma 9 I am unworthy to look up and see the height of heaven
14 for, unworthy as I am, thou wilt save me in thy great mercy
2 Es 14:45 and let the worthy and the unworthy read them

UP, adv., prep. 8 = 0.005 %
Jud 4:7 ordering them to seize the passes up into the hills
7:1 and to seize the passes up into the hill country
Sir 6:18 My son, from your youth up choose instruction
27:25 Whoever throws a stone straight up throws it on his own head
L Jr 6:3 for a long time, up to 7 generations
1 Es 8:20 up to a 100 talents of silver
8:20 and likewise up to a 100 cors of wheat
4 Ma 9:28 flayed all his flesh up to his chin

UPBRAID 2
Sir 20:15 He gives little and upbraids much
41:22 and do not upbraid after making a gift

UPBRINGING 1
4 Ma 16:8 and the more grievous anxieties of your upbringing

UPHOLD 1
2 Ma 14:15 and always upholds his own heritage by manifesting himself

UPHOLDER 1
Jud 9:11 upholder of the weak, protector of the forlorn

UPLIFTED 1
2 Es 15:11 and with an uplifted arm

UPON 327 = 0.213 %

UPPER 9 = 0.006 %
Tob 3:17 came down from her upper room
Jud 1:8 and Upper Galilee and the great Plain of Esdraelon
2:21 near the mountain which is to the north of Upper Cilicia
1 Ma 2:48 and they never let the sinner gain the upper hand
3:37 and went through the upper provinces
6:1 King Antiochus was going through the upper provinces
2 Ma 9:23 into the upper country
9:25 when I hastened off to the upper provinces
2 Es 8:20 whose eyes are exalted and whose upper chambers are in the air

UPRIGHT 4 = 0.003 %
L Jr 6:27 If any one sets one of them upright
1 Es 1:23 And the deeds of Josiah were upright in the sight of his Lord
3 Ma 3:5 with the good deeds of upright people
4 Ma 6:7 he kept his reason upright and unswerving

UPRIGHTLY 2
Tob 4:5 Live uprightly all the days of your life
4:7 Give alms from your possessions to all who live uprightly

UPRIGHTNESS 3 = 0.002 %
Wis 1:1 think of the Lord with uprightness
9:3 and pronounce judgment in uprightness of soul
2 Es 6:32 for the Mighty One has seen your uprightness

UPRISING 1
1 Es 5:73 and by plots and demagoguery and uprisings

UPROAR 1
3 Ma 1:28 resulted in an immense uproar

UPROOT 3 = 0.002 %
Wis 4:4 and by the violence of the winds they will be uprooted
Sir 3:9 but a mother's curse uproots their foundations
4 Ma 3:5 For reason does not uproot the emotions but is their antagonist

UPSET 1
Sir 11:34 and he will upset you with commotion

UPWARD 1
2 Es 6:41 that one part might move upward and the other part remain beneath

URGE, subst. 1
4 Ma 2:4 over the frenzied urge of sexual desire

URGE, verb 18 = 0.012 %
Jud 15:4 to tell what had taken place and to urge all
Sir pr. You are urged therefore to read
1 Ma 11:40 and insistently urged him to hand Antiochus over to him
13:21 urging him to come to them by way of the wilderness
2 Ma 4:34 urged him to kill Onias
6:12 Now I urge those who read this book not to be depressed by such calamities
6:21 and privately urged him to bring meat of his own providing
7:25 and urged her to advise the youth to save himself
7:26 After much urging on his part
9:26 I therefore urge and beseech you to remember
11:7 and he urged the others to risk their lives with him
11:15 agreed to all that Lysias urged
14:25 And he urged him to marry and have children
3 Ma 5:17 When this was done he urged them
5:36 and urged the guests to return to their celebrating
7:3 frequently urging us with malicious intent
4 Ma 5:14 When the tyrant urged him in this fashion
10:1 and many repeatedly urged him

URGE on 5 = 0.003 %
2 Ma 13:3 and with utter hypocrisy urged Antiochus on
1 Es 1:27 The Lord is with me, urging me on !
3 Ma 5:46 and urged the king on to the matter at hand
4 Ma 15:12 Instead, the mother urged them on
16:13 she implored them and urged them on to death

URGENT 1
Sir 28:11 A hasty quarrel kindles fire, and urgent strife sheds blood

441

URGENTLY 2
1 Ma	6:57	and the affairs of the kingdom press urgently upon us
2 Ma	10:19	where he was more urgently needed

URIAH 2
1 Es	8:62	to Meremoth the priest, son of Uriah
	9:43	Uriah, Hezekiah, and Baalsamus on his right hand

URIEL 3 = 0.002 %
2 Es	4:1	whose name was Uriel, answered
	5:20	as Uriel the angel had commanded me
	10:28	Where is the angel Uriel, who came to me at first ?

URIM 3 = 0.002 %
Sir	33:3	as an inquiry by means of Urim
	45:10	with the oracle of judgment, Urim and Thummim
1 Es	5:40	until a high priest should appear wearing Urim and Thummim

US 471 = 0.307 %

USE, subst. 17 = 0.011 %
Tob	6:6	of what use is the liver and heart and gall of the fish ?
Jud	12:15	for her daily use
Wis	2:6	and make use of the creation to the full as in youth
	4:3	But the prolific brood of the ungodly will be of no use
	15:7	both the vessels that serve clean uses
	15:7	and those for contrary uses
	15:7	but which shall be the use of each of these
	15:15	though these have neither the use of their eyes to see with
	15:15	and their feet are of no use for walking
Sir	13:4	A rich man will exploit you if you can be of use to him
	14:3	and of what use is property to an envious man ?
	17:5	They obtained the use
	18:8	What is man, and of what use is he ?
	30:19	Of what use to an idol is an offering of fruit ?
	39:21	for everything has been created for its use
1 Es	6:30	for daily use as the priests in Jerusalem may indicate
	8:17	which are given you for the use of the temple of your God

USE, verb 25 = 0.016 %
Tob	1:5	used to sacrifice to the calf Baal
	1:14	So I used to go into Media
	2:12	She used to send the product to the owners
	5:13	For I used to know Ananias and Jathan
Jud	10:3	which she used to wear while her husband Manasseh was living
	11:12	to use all that God by his laws has forbidden them to eat
Sir	pr.	using in that period of time great watchfulness and skill
	20:8	Whoever uses too many words will be loathed
	23:15	A man accustomed to use insulting words
	26:10	lest, when she finds liberty, she use it to her hurt
	38:33	and they are not found using proverbs
L Jr	6:28	and use the money
Sus	13:4	and the Jews used to come to him because he was the most honoured of them all
	13:8	The 2 elders used to see her every day
Bel	14:13	through which they used to go in regularly
1 Ma	1:58	They kept using violence against Israel
	3:12	and used it in battle the rest of his life
	3:30	which he used to give more lavishly than preceding kings
	11:20	and he built many engines of war to use against it
	14:36	from which they used to sally forth
2 Ma	4:19	thought best not to use it for sacrifice
	6:21	proper for him to use
3 Ma	4:20	that both the paper and the pens they used for writing
4 Ma	8:16	what arguments might have been used
	13:13	and let us use our bodies as a bulwark for the law

USE up 1
Jud	12:4	your servant will not use up the things I have with me

USEFUL 4 = 0.003 %
Tob	4:18	and do not despise any useful counsel
Wis	13:11	make a useful vessel that serves life's needs
	13:13	But a castoff piece from among them, useful for nothing
2 Ma	12:12	Judas, thinking that they might really be useful in many ways

USEFULNESS 1
3 Ma	5:32	arising from our nurture in common and your usefulness

USELESS 8 = 0.005 %
Wis	1:11	Beware then of useless murmuring
	2:11	for what is weak proves itself to be useless
	3:11	and their works are useless
	4:5	and their fruit will be useless, not ripe enough to eat
	13:10	and likeness of animals, or a useless stone
Sir	16:1	Do not desire a multitude of useless children
L Jr	6:17	For just as one's dish is useless when it is broken
3 Ma	3:29	and shall become useless for all time to any mortal creature

USHER in 1
2 Ma	4:22	and ushered in with a blaze of torches and with shouts

USURP 1
Sir	20:8	and whoever usurps the right to speak will be hated

UTENSIL 2
L Jr	6:59	or a household utensil that serves its owner's need
1 Ma	1:21	the lampstand for the light, and all its utensils

UTHAI 2
1 Es	5:30	the sons of Akkub, the sons of Uthai, the sons of Ketab
	8:40	Of the sons of Bigvai, Uthai the son of Istalcurus

UTMOST 2
Wis	12:27	Therefore the utmost condemnation came upon them
2 Ma	12:23	And Judas pressed the pursuit with the utmost vigour

UTTER, verb 16 = 0.010 %
Wis	1:8	therefore no one who utters unrighteous things will escape notice
Sir	7:13	Refuse to utter any lie
	15:10	For a hymn of praise should be uttered in wisdom
	23:9	and do not habitually utter the name of the Holy One
	23:10	and utters the Name will not be cleansed from sin
	51:2	from lips that utter lies
2 Ma	6:29	because the words he had uttered
	9:12	he uttered these words : It is right to be subject to God
3 Ma	2:24	but went away uttering bitter threats
	4:16	and uttering improper words against the supreme God
2 Es	5:5	and the stone shall utter its voice
	10:26	behold, she suddenly uttered a loud and fearful cry
	11:7	and uttered a cry to his wings, saying
	11:37	and I heard how he uttered a man's voice to the eagle
4 Ma	4:8	But, uttering threats, Apollonius went on to the temple
	12:19	After he had uttered these imprecations

UTTER, adj. 3 = 0.002 %
Jud	7:25	with thirst and utter destruction
2 Ma	13:3	and with utter hypocrisy urged Antiochus on
	15:6	This Nicanor in his utter boastfulness and arrogance

UTTERANCE 3 = 0.002 %
Sir	21:17	The utterance of a sensible man
	23:12	There is an utterance which is comparable to death
2 Es	8:22	whose word is sure and whose utterances are certain

UTTERLY 20 = 0.013 %
Jud	1:15	and he utterly destroyed him, to this day
	5:18	they were utterly defeated in many battles
	6:4	They cannot withstand us, but will utterly perish
	7:30	for he will not forsake us utterly
Ad E	13:6	be utterly destroyed by the sword of their enemies
	14:2	and she utterly humbled her body
Wis	4:19	they will be left utterly dry and barren
	13:18	for aid he entreats a thing that is utterly inexperienced
	16:16	and utterly consumed by fire
Sir	10:13	and destroyed them utterly
	40:14	likewise transgressors will utterly fail
P Az	11	For thy name's sake do not give us up utterly
2 Ma	3:12	And he said that it was utterly impossible
	6:3	Harsh and utterly grievous was the onslaught of evil
	7:5	When he was utterly helpless
1 Es	1:56	and utterly destroyed all its glorious things
2 Es	4:2	Your understanding has utterly failed regarding this world
	7:87	because they shall utterly waste away in confusion
	16:11	and who will not be utterly shattered at his presence ?
4 Ma	10:17	the bloodthirsty, murderous, and utterly abominable Antiochus

UZZA 1
1 Es	5:31	the sons of Chezib, the sons of Gazzam, the sons of Uzza

UZZI 2
1 Es	8:2	son of Zadok, son of Ahitub, son of Amariah, son of Uzzi
2 Es	1:2	son of Arna, son of Uzzi, son of Borith

UZZIAH 12 = 0.008 %
Jud	6:15	who in those days were Uzziah the son of Micah
	6:16	and Uzziah asked him what had happened
	6:21	And Uzziah took him from the assembly to his own house
	7:23	gathered about Uzziah and the rulers of the city
	7:30	And Uzziah said to them, Have courage, my brothers !
	8:9	and when she heard all that Uzziah said to them
	8:28	Then Uzziah said to her
	8:35	Uzziah and the rulers said to her
	10:6	and found Uzziah standing there
	13:18	And Uzziah said to her
	14:6	So they summoned Achior from the house of Uzziah

15:4　And Uzziah sent men to Betomasthaim and Bebai

V

VAIN
19 = 0.012 %

Jud　6:4　none of his words shall be in vain
Ad E　14:10　to open the mouths of the nations for the praise of vain idols
Wis　3:11　Their hope is vain, their labours are unprofitable
Sir　34:1　A man of no understanding has vain and false hopes
1 Ma　9:68　for his plan and his expedition had been in vain
2 Ma　7:18　Do not deceive yourself in vain
　　7:34　do not be elated in vain and puffed up by uncertain hopes
3 Ma　6:6　so as not to serve vain things
2 Es　4:16　But the plan of the forest was in vain
　　6:34　Do not be quick to think vain thoughts
　　7:14　pass through the difficult and vain experiences
　　7:22　they devised for themselves vain thoughts
　　9:22　So let the multitude perish which has been born in vain
　　16:45　Because those who labour, labour in vain
4 Ma　5:10　if, by holding a vain opinion concerning the truth
　　8:18　why do we take pleasure in vain resolves
　　8:19　and give up this vain opinion
　　16:7　O 7 childbirths all in vain, 7 profitless pregnancies
　　16:8　In vain, my sons, I endured many birth-pangs for you

VAIN-MINDED
1

3 Ma　6:11　Let not the vain-minded praise their vanities

VAINGLORY
1

4 Ma　2:15　lust for power, vainglory, boasting, arrogance, and malice

VALIANT
3 = 0.002 %

Jud　14:2　let every valiant man take his weapons and go out of the city
Sir　31:25　Do not aim to be valiant over wine
1 Ma　3:58　And Judas said, Gird yourselves and be valiant

VALIANTLY
1

2 Es　2:47　who had stood valiantly for the name of the Lord

VALID
2

1 Ma　8:30　and any addition or deletion that they may make shall be valid
　　13:38　All the grants that we have made to you remain valid

VALLEY
14 = 0.009 %

Jud　2:8　till their wounded shall fill their valleys
　　4:4　and to Choba and Aesora and the valley of Salem
　　7:3　They encamped in the valley near Bethulia, beside the spring
　　7:4　nor the valleys nor the hills will bear their weight
　　7:17　and they encamped in the valley and seized the water supply
　　10:10　and passed through the valley
　　10:11　The women went straight on through the valley
　　11:17　and every night your servant will go out into the valley
　　12:7　and went out each night to the valley of Bethulia
　　13:10　and circled around the valley
　　16:4　their multitude blocked up the valleys
Bar　5:7　and the valleys filled up, to make level ground
1 Ma　12:37　part of the wall on the valley to the east had fallen
3 Ma　6:17　so that even the nearby valleys resounded with them

VALOUR, VALOR
4 = 0.003 %

2 Ma　8:7　And talk of his valour spread everywhere
　　10:28　not only their valour but their reliance upon the Lord
　　14:18　Nevertheless Nicanor, hearing of the valour of Judas
　　15:17　so noble and so effective in arousing valour

VALUE, subst.
2

Sir　26:15　and no balance can weigh the value of a chaste soul
2 Ma　4:15　and putting the highest value upon Greek forms of prestige

VALUE, verb
1

Wis　18:12　their most valued children had been destroyed

VANIAH
1

1 Es　9:34　Mamdai and Bedeiah and Vaniah

VANISH
5 = 0.003 %

Wis　5:9　All those things have vanished like a shadow
Sir　21:18　Like a house that has vanished, so is wisdom to a fool
　　45:26　so that their prosperity may not vanish
Bar　3:19　They have vanished and gone down to Hades
2 Ma　3:34　Having said this they vanished

VANITY
2

Wis　14:14　For through the vanity of men they entered the world
3 Ma　6:11　Let not the vain-minded praise their vanities

VAPOUR, VAPOR
2

Sir　22:24　The vapour and smoke of the furnace precede the fire
　　43:4　it breathes out fiery vapours

VARIANCE
1

Wis　18:2　for having been at variance with them

VARIED
6 = 0.004 %

Wis　15:4　a figure stained with varied colours
2 Ma　15:21　and the varied supply of arms
3 Ma　2:6　by inflicting many and varied punishments
2 Es　6:44　and of varied appeal to the taste
4 Ma　16:3　inflamed as she saw her 7 sons tortured in such varied ways
　　17:7　enduring their varied tortures to death

VARIETY
2

Wis　7:20　the varieties of plants and the virtues of roots
Sir　38:27　each is diligent in making a great variety

VARIOUS
11 = 0.007 %

Jud　7:32　Then he dismissed the people to their various posts
2 Ma　12:2　But some of the governors in various places
3 Ma　1:21　Various were the supplications of those gathered there
　　1:25　while the elders near the king tried in various ways
　　2:26　that he framed evil reports in the various localities
2 Es　2:18　12 trees loaded with various fruits
4 Ma　1:7　I could prove to you from many and various examples
　　3:21　and caused many and various disasters
　　15:11　in the case of none of them were the various tortures
　　15:24　and the ingenious and various rackings
　　18:21　and put them to death with various tortures

VARY
1

Wis　19:18　as on a harp the notes vary the nature of the rhythm

VAST
10 = 0.007 %

Jud　1:16　he and all his combined forces, a vast body of troops
　　2:17　He collected a vast number of camels
　　5:24　and they will be devoured by your vast army
　　7:4　When the Israelites saw their vast number
　　7:18　and they formed a vast multitude
　　15:7　for there was a vast quantity of it
Wis　19:10　the river spewed out vast numbers of frogs
Bar　3:24　And how vast the territory that he possesses !
1 Es　4:34　The earth is vast, and heaven is high
2 Es　7:3　so that it is broad and vast

VASTNESS
1

2 Es　10:55　but go in and see the splendour and vastness of the building

VAULT
1

Sir　24:5　Alone I have made the circuit of the vault of heaven

VEHEMENT
1

3 Ma　1:28　The continuous, vehement, and concerted cry of the crowds

VEHEMENTLY
1

4 Ma　5:32　and fan the fire more vehemently !

VEIL
1

Sus　13:32　As she was veiled, the wicked men ordered her to be unveiled

VENERABLE
1

4 Ma　7:15　and venerable grey hair and law-abiding life

VENGEANCE
23 = 0.015 %

Jud　16:17　The Lord Almighty will take vengeance on them
Sir　18:24　and of the moment of vengeance when he turns away his face
　　25:14　And any vengeance, but not the vengeance of enemies !
　　27:28　but vengeance lies in wait for him like a lion
　　28:1　He that takes vengeance will suffer vengeance from the Lord
　　35:18　and repays vengeance on the nations
　　39:28　There are winds that have been created for vengeance
　　39:29　all these have been created for vengeance
　　46:1　to take vengeance on the enemies that rose against them
　　47:25　till vengeance came upon them
　　48:7　and judgments of vengeance at Horeb
1 Ma　3:15　to take vengeance on the sons of Israel
　　7:9　and he commanded him to take vengeance on the sons of Israel
　　7:24　and took vengeance on the men who had deserted
　　7:38　Take vengeance on this man and on his army
　　9:26　and he took vengeance on them and made sport of them
2 Ma　6:15　in order that he may not take vengeance on us afterward
3 Ma　1:3　that this man incurred the vengeance meant for the king
　　5:8　that he avert with vengeance the evil plot against them
4 Ma　9:24　and take vengeance on the accursed tyrant
　　12:18　but on you he will take vengeance

VENOM 2
Sir 25:15 There is no venom worse than a snake's venom

VENOMOUS 1
Wis 16:10 even by the teeth of venomous serpents

VENT, subst. 1
1 Ma 2:24 He gave vent to righteous anger

VENTURE 2
3 Ma 3:21 and we ventured to make a change
4 Ma 8:18 and venture upon a disobedience that brings death ?

VERDICT
Sir 19:25 and there are people who distort kindness to gain a verdict

VERSE 1
Sir 44:5 and set forth verses in writing

VERTEBRA 1
4 Ma 10:8 and while his vertebrae were being dislocated upon it

VERY, adj., adv. 101 = 0.066 %
Tob 3:17 At that very moment Tobit returned and entered his house
6:15 for this very night she will be given to you in marriage
7:8 They received them very warmly
14:3 When he had grown very old he called his son and grandsons
Jud 1:12 Then Nebuchadnezzar was very angry with this whole region
4:2 they were therefore very greatly terrified at his approach
5:2 he was very angry
5:9 with much gold and silver and very many cattle
7:2 a very great multitude
8:7 She was beautiful in appearance, and had a very lovely face
8:30 But the people were very thirsty
9:1 and at the very time
10:4 and made herself very beautiful
11:15 on that very day they will be handed over to you to be destroyed
13:14 but has destroyed our enemies by my hand this very night !
16:16 and all fat for burnt offerings to thee is a very little thing
Ad E 16:20 on that very day they may defend themselves
Wis 2:15 the very sight of him is a burden to us
11:5 For through the very things
11:16 by the very things by which he sins
18:1 But for thy holy ones there was very great light
Sir 6:20 She seems very harsh to the uninstructed
13:13 Keep words to yourself and be very watchful
19:2 and the man who consorts with harlots is very reckless
39:16 All things are the works of the Lord, for they are very good
41:2 very old and distracted over everything
43:29 Terrible is the Lord and very great
45:9 with very many golden bells round about
48:15 the people were left very few in number
51:6 and my life was very near to Hades beneath
51:24 and why are your souls very thirsty ?
Bar 2:29 this very great multitude will surely turn into
L Jr 6:46 The men that make them will certainly not live very long themselves
Sus 13:2 a very beautiful woman and one who feared the Lord
13:4 Joakim was very rich
13:15 and wished to bathe in the garden, for it was very hot
13:55 And Daniel said, Very well !
13:59 And Daniel said to him, Very well !
Bel 14:28 they were very indignant and conspired against the king
1 Ma 1:4 He gathered a very strong army
1:64 And very great wrath came upon Israel
3:27 a very strong army
4:54 At the very season
4:54 and on the very day that the Gentiles had profaned it
4:58 There was very great gladness among the people
5:1 they became very angry
5:38 it is a very large force
5:45 a very large company
5:46 This was a large and very strong city on the road
6:2 Its temple was very rich, containing golden shields
6:41 trembled, for the army was very large and strong
8:1 that they were very strong and were well-disposed
8:2 and that they were very strong
8:6 and with cavalry and chariots and a very large army
8:19 They went to Rome, a very long journey
9:22 have not been recorded, for they were very many
9:24 In those days a very great famine occurred
10:2 he assembled a very large army
13:22 but that night a very heavy snow fell
13:49 So they were very hungry
16:7 for the cavalry of the enemy were very numerous
2 Ma 3:1 and the laws were very well observed
3:11 a man of very prominent position
3:33 Be very grateful to Onias the high priest
3:35 and made very great vows to the Saviour of his life
4:38 and led him about the whole city to that very place

8:30 and they divided very much plunder
9:6 and that very justly
10:18 took refuge in 2 very strong towers
11:1 Very soon after this
12:18 though in one place he had left a very strong garrison
12:43 In doing this he acted very well and honourably
14:37 and was very well thought of
1 Es 1:30 Take me away from the battle, for I am very weak
2:9 and with a very great number of votive offerings
4:16 and women brought up the very men who plant the vineyards
7:2 supervised the holy work with very great care
8:53 and we found him very merciful
8:64 and the weight of everything was recorded at that very time
8:91 there gathered about him a very great throng from Jerusalem
P Ma 7 and very merciful
3 Ma 3:16 And when we had granted very great revenues
5:45 by the very fragrant draughts of wine mixed with frankincense
5:51 and cried out in a very loud voice
7:6 But we very severely threatened them for these acts
7:16 crowned with all sorts of very fragrant flowers
2 Es 5:21 the thoughts of my heart were very grievous to me again
7:140 there would probably be left only very few
8:2 it will tell you that it provides very much clay
9:2 then you will know that it is the very time
12:5 and very weak in my spirit
13:19 and for that very reason !
13:50 And then he will show them very many wonders
15:34 and their appearance is very threatening
4 Ma 4:5 and a very strong military force
4:20 at the very citadel of our native land
5:8 the very excellent meat of this animal ?
6:26 When he was now burned to his very bones and about to expire
6:30 and by reason he resisted even to the very tortures of death
8:1 For this is why even the very young
15:23 in the very midst of her emotions

VESSEL, utensil 40 = 0.026 %
Jud 4:3 and the sacred vessels and the altar and the temple
7:20 until all the vessels of water belonging to every inhabitant of Bethulia were empty
10:5 and she wrapped up all her vessels
16:19 Judith also dedicated to God all the vessels of Holofernes
Wis 13:11 make a useful vessel that serves life's needs
15:7 and laboriously moulds each vessel for our service
15:7 both the vessels that serve clean uses
15:13 when he makes from earthy matter fragile vessels and graven images
Sir 27:5 The kiln tests the potter's vessels
50:9 like a vessel of hammered gold
Bar 1:8 Baruch took the vessels of the house of the Lord
1:8 the silver vessels which Zedekiah the son of Josiah, king of Judah, had made
1 Ma 1:23 He took the silver and the gold, and the costly vessels
2:9 her glorious vessels have been carried into captivity
4:49 They made new holy vessels, and brought the lampstand
6:12 I seized all her vessels of silver and gold
14:15 and added to the vessels of the sanctuary
2 Ma 4:32 stole some of the gold vessels of the temple
4:32 other vessels, as it happened
4:39 because many of the gold vessels had already been stolen
4:48 for the city and the villages and the holy vessels
5:16 He took the holy vessels with his polluted hands
9:16 and thy holy vessels he would give back
1 Es 1:41 Nebuchadnezzar also took some of the holy vessels of the Lord
1:45 with the holy vessels of the Lord
1:54 And all the holy vessels of the Lord, great and small
2:10 Cyrus the king also brought out the holy vessels of the Lord
2:13 2,410 silver bowls, and a 1,000 other vessels
2:14 All the vessels were handed over, gold and silver, 5,469
4:44 and to send back all the vessels that were taken from Jerusalem
4:57 And he sent back from Babylon all the vessels
6:18 And the holy vessels of gold and of silver
6:19 with the command that he should take all these vessels back
6:26 and that the holy vessels of the house of the Lord
8:17 and deliver the holy vessels of the Lord
8:55 and the holy vessels of the house of our Lord
8:56 and silver vessels worth a 100 talents
8:57 and 12 bronze vessels of fine bronze
8:58 and the vessels are holy
8:60 and the vessels which had been in Jerusalem

VESSEL, ship 1
Wis 14:2 For it was desire for gain that planned that vessel

VESTMENT 2
Sir 45:7 He blessed him with splendid vestments
3 Ma 1:16 Then the priests in all their vestments prostrated themselves

VEX   2
  Sir 50:25   With 2 nations my soul is vexed
  2 Ma 11:1   being vexed at what had happened

VICE   1
  3 Ma 2:5   who were notorious for their vices

VICINITY   1
  1 Es 5:46   and some of the people settled in Jerusalem and its vicinity

VICTIM   1
  2 Ma 7:10   After him, the 3rd was the victim of their sport

VICTOR   3 = 0.002 %
  Wis 4:2   victor in the contest for prizes that are undefiled
  1 Es 3:12   but truth is victor over all things
  4 Ma 17:15   Reverence for God was victor

VICTORIOUS   5 = 0.003 %
  3 Ma 3:20   But we, when we arrived in Egypt victorious
  2 Es 7:115   or to harm him who is victorious
        7:128   but if he is victorious he shall receive what I have said
  4 Ma 6:10   was victorious over his torturers
       18:23   But the sons of Abraham with their victorious mother

VICTORY   16 = 0.010 %
  Wis 10:12   in his arduous contest she gave him the victory
  1 Ma 3:19   that victory in battle depends
  2 Ma 5:6   but imagining that he was setting up trophies of victory
       8:33   While they were celebrating the victory
     10:28   the one having as pledge of success and victory
     10:38   and gives them the victory
     12:11   After a hard fight Judas and his men won the victory
     13:15   He gave his men the watchword, God's victory
     15:6   had determined to erect a public monument of victory
     15:8   and now to look for the victory
     15:21   that he gains victory for those who deserve it
  1 Es 3:5   and great honours of victory
       3:9   the victory shall be given according to what is written
       4:5   if they win the victory, they bring everything to the king
      4:59   From thee is the victory
  4 Ma 7:3   until he sailed into the haven of immortal victory

VIEW, subst.   5 = 0.003 %
  Jud 7:6   in full view of the Israelites in Bethulia
  1 Ma 14:38   In view of these things
  2 Ma 4:5   but having in view the welfare, both public and private, of all the people
       6:11   in view of their regard for that most holy day
  3 Ma 4:7   In bonds and in public view they were violently dragged along

VIGILANT   1
  Wis 6:15   and he who is vigilant on her account

VIGOROUS   1
  2 Ma 12:27   and made a vigorous defence

VIGOROUSLY   1
  2 Ma 10:17   Attacking them vigorously

VIGOUR, VIGOR   2
  Sir 41:1   and who still has the vigour to enjoy his food !
  2 Ma 12:23   And Judas pressed the pursuit with the utmost vigour

VILE   2
  2 Ma 4:19   the vile Jason sent envoys
     15:32   He showed them the vile Nicanor's head

VILLAGE   10 = 0.007 %
  Jud 4:5   and fortified the villages on them
       15:7   and the villages and towns in the hill country and in the plain
  1 Ma 5:8   He also took Jazer and its villages
       5:65   He struck Hebron and its villages
       7:46   And men came out of all the villages of Judea round about
  2 Ma 4:48   for the city and the villages and the holy vessels
       8:1   secretly entered the villages and summoned their kinsmen
       8:6   he would set fire to towns and villages
     14:16   and engaged them in battle at a village called Dessau
  1 Es 4:50   that the Idumeans should give up the villages of the Jews which they held

VINDICATE   2
  Ad E 10:12   And God remembered his people and vindicated his inheritance
  4 Ma 17:10   They vindicated their nation

VINDICATOR   1
  4 Ma 15:29   vindicator of the law and champion of religion

VINE   4 = 0.003 %
  Sir 24:17   Like a vine I caused loveliness to bud
  1 Ma 14:12   Each man sat under his vine and his fig tree
  2 Es 5:23   thou hast chosen one vine
     16:43   so also him that prunes the vines

VINEYARD   5 = 0.003 %
  1 Ma 3:56   or were betrothed, or were planting vineyards
  1 Es 4:16   and women brought up the very men who plant the vineyards
  2 Es 16:30   or as when a vineyard is gathered
     16:30   through the vineyard
  4 Ma 2:9   nor gathers the last grapes from the vineyard

VINTAGE   2
  Sir 24:27   like the Gihon at the time of vintage
  2 Es 12:42   like a cluster of grapes from the vintage

VIOLATE   4 = 0.003 %
  Sir 20:4   Like a eunuch's desire to violate a maiden
  1 Ma 7:18   for they have violated the agreement
  3 Ma 2:14   undertakes to violate the holy place on earth
  4 Ma 16:24   to die rather than violate God's commandment

VIOLATION   2
  2 Ma 15:10   and their violation of oaths
  4 Ma 4:19   in complete violation of the law

VIOLENCE   13 = 0.008 %
  Ad E 13:7   may in one day go down in violence to Hades
  Wis 4:4   and by the violence of the winds they will be uprooted
     19:13   without prior signs in the violence of thunder
  Sir 20:4   is a man who executes judgments by violence
     21:4   Terror and violence will lay waste riches
  1 Ma 1:58   They kept using violence against Israel
  3 Ma 1:16   and to avert the violence of this evil design
       4:5   by the violence with which they were driven
  2 Es 11:46   so that the whole earth, freed from your violence
  4 Ma 5:37   as one who does not fear your violence even to death
     11:26   and your violence powerless
     17:2   nullified the violence of the tyrant
     17:9   because of the violence of the tyrant

VIOLENT   4 = 0.003 %
  2 Es 4:49   and poured down a heavy and violent rain
  4 Ma 2:15   It is evident that reason rules even the more violent emotions :
       8:2   then in violent rage he commanded
     15:32   by the flood of your emotions and the violent winds

VIOLENTLY   6 = 0.004 %
  Wis 17:18   or the rhythm of violently rushing water
  3 Ma 4:7   In bonds and in public view they were violently dragged along
  2 Es 5:14   Then I awoke, and my body shuddered violently
     15:39   and shall be driven violently toward the south and west
     15:52   Would I have dealt with you so violently, says the Lord
  4 Ma 6:1   the guards who were standing by dragged him violently

VIPER   1
  Sir 39:30   the teeth of wild beasts, and scorpions and vipers

VIRGIN   10 = 0.007 %
  Jud 9:2   who had loosed the girdle of a virgin to defile her
     16:5   and take my virgins as booty
  Sir 9:5   Do not look intently at a virgin
     42:10   while a virgin, lest she be defiled
  2 Ma 5:13   and slaughter of virgins and infants
  1 Es 1:53   and did not spare young man or virgin
  3 Ma 1:18   The virgins who had been enclosed in their chambers
  2 Es 10:22   our virgins have been defiled
     16:33   Virgins shall mourn because they have no bridegrooms
  4 Ma 18:7   I was a pure virgin and did not go outside my father's house

VIRGINITY   1
  4 Ma 18:8   defile the purity of my virginity

VIRTUALLY   1
  3 Ma 5:45   Now when the beasts had been brought virtually

VIRTUE   23 = 0.015 %
  Wis 4:1   Better than this is childlessness with virtue
       4:1   for in the memory of virtue is immortality
       5:13   and we had no sign of virtue to show
       7:20   the varieties of plants and the virtues of roots
       8:7   And if any one loves righteousness, her labours are virtues
  3 Ma 6:1   and throughout his life had been adorned with every virtue
  4 Ma 1:2   and in addition it includes the praise of the highest virtue
       1:8   of those who died for the sake of virtue
     1:10   to praise for their virtues those who, with their mother
     1:30   For reason is the guide of the virtues
     1:30   by virtue of the restraining power of self-control
     2:10   so that virtue is not abandoned for their sakes

VIRTUE *(cont.)*

	7:22	for the sake of virtue
	9:8	shall have the prize of virtue and shall be with God
	9:18	where virtue is concerned
	9:31	I lighten my pain by the joys that come from virtue
	10:10	are suffering because of our godly training and virtue
	11:2	to be tortured for the sake of virtue
	11:4	Hater of virtue, hater of mankind
	12:14	the contestants for virtue
	13:24	and trained in the same virtues
	17:12	for on that day virtue gave the awards
	17:23	when he saw the courage of their virtue

VIRTUOUS   3 = 0.002 %

2 Es	16:49	Just as a respectable and virtuous woman abhors a harlot
4 Ma	11:5	according to his virtuous law ?
	13:27	But although nature and companionship and virtuous habits

VISIBLE   3 = 0.002 %

Wis	14:17	and made a visible image of the king whom they honoured
3 Ma	6:18	visible to all but the Jews
2 Es	10:27	the woman was no longer visible to me

VISION   16 = 0.010 %

Tob	12:19	and did not eat or drink, but you were seeing a vision
Sir	34:3	The vision of dreams is this against that
	40:6	he is troubled by the visions of his mind
	48:22	who was great and faithful in his vision
	49:8	It was Ezekiel who saw the vision of glory
2 Ma	15:11	a sort of vision, which was worthy of belief
2 Es	2:21	and let the blind man have a vision of my splendour
	10:37	to give your servant an explanation of this bewildering vision
	10:40	This therefore is the meaning of the vision
	10:59	and the Most High will show you in those dream visions
	12:8	the interpretation and meaning of this terrifying vision
	12:10	This is the interpretation of this vision which you have seen :
	12:11	is the 4th kingdom which appeared in a vision
	13:21	I will tell you the interpretation of the vision
	13:25	This is the interpretation of the vision :
	14:18	For the eagle which you saw in the vision

VISIT   15 = 0.010 %

Jud	7:7	and visited the springs that supplied their water
	13:20	and may he visit you with blessings
Sir	6:36	If you see an intelligent man, visit him early
	7:35	Do not shrink from visiting a sick man
	22:13	and do not visit an unintelligent man
	35:17	he will not desist until the Most High visits him
1 Ma	16:14	Now Simon was visiting the cities of the country
2 Ma	9:17	and would visit every inhabited place
	12:5	When Judas heard of the cruelty visited on his countrymen
3 Ma	1:6	Ptolemy decided to visit the neighbouring cities
	1:8	he was all the more eager to visit them as soon as possible
2 Es	5:56	show thy servant through whom thou dost visit thy creation
	6:18	to visit the inhabitants of the earth
	9:2	when the Most High is about to visit the world
4 Ma	10:21	God will visit you swiftly, for you are cutting out

VISITATION   5 = 0.003 %

Wis	3:7	In the time of their visitation they will shine forth
	14:11	Therefore there will be a visitation
Sir	16:18	the abyss and the earth, will tremble at his visitation
	18:20	and in the hour of visitation you will find forgiveness
	34:6	Unless they are sent from the Most High as a visitation

VOICE   78 = 0.051 %

Tob	13:6	give thanks to him with your full voice
Jud	7:23	and cried out with a loud voice
	7:29	and they cried out to the Lord God with a loud voice
	8:17	and he will hear our voice, if it pleases him
	9:1	Judith cried out to the Lord with a loud voice, and said
	13:12	When the men of her city heard her voice
	13:14	Then she said to them with a loud voice
	14:16	And he cried out with a loud voice
	16:11	they lifted up their voices, and the enemy were turned back
	16:14	there is none that can resist thy voice
Ad E	14:19	hear the voice of the despairing
Wis	18:1	Their enemies heard their voices but did not see their forms
Sir	6:5	A pleasant voice multiplies friends
	17:13	and their ears heard the glory of his voice
	21:20	A fool raises his voice when he laughs
	29:5	and will lower his voice
	34:24	to whose voice will the Lord listen ?
	39:35	So now sing praise with all your heart and voice
	40:21	but a pleasant voice is better than both
	43:17	The voice of his thunder rebukes the earth
	45:5	He made him hear his voice
	46:17	and made his voice heard with a mighty sound
	46:20	and lifted up his voice out of the earth in prophecy
	47:9	to make sweet melody with their voices
	50:18	And the singers praised him with their voices

VOICE *(cont.)*

Bar	1:18	and have not heeded the voice of the Lord our God
	1:19	and we have been negligent, in not heeding his voice
	1:21	We did not heed the voice of the Lord our God
	2:5	in not heeding his voice
	2:10	Yet we have not obeyed his voice
	2:22	But if you will not obey the voice of the Lord
	2:23	the voice of mirth and the voice of gladness
	2:23	the voice of the bridegroom and the voice of the bride
	2:24	But we did not obey thy voice, to serve the king of Babylon
	2:29	saying, If you will not obey my voice
	3:4	who did not heed the voice of the Lord their God
Sus	13:24	Then Susanna cried out with a loud voice
	13:42	Then Susanna cried out with a loud voice, and said
	13:46	and he cried with a loud voice
Bel	14:18	the king looked at the table, and shouted in a loud voice
	14:41	And the king shouted with a loud voice
1 Ma	2:19	But Mattathias answered and said in a loud voice :
	2:27	Then Mattathias cried out in the city with a loud voice
	9:41	and the voice of their musicians into a funeral dirge
	13:8	and they answered in a loud voice
	13:45	and they cried out with a loud voice
1 Es	9:10	Then all the multitude shouted and said with a loud voice
3 Ma	5:7	But with tears and a voice hard to silence
	5:51	and cried out in a very loud voice
2 Es	5:5	and the stone shall utter its voice
	5:7	shall make his voice heard by night, and all shall hear his voice
	5:37	or show me the picture of a voice
	6:13	Rise to your feet and you will hear a full, resounding voice
	6:15	while the voice is speaking, do not be terrified
	6:17	and behold, a voice was speaking
	6:21	Infants a year old shall speak with their voices
	6:32	because your voice has surely been heard before the Most High
	6:39	the sound of man's voice was not yet there
	8:19	Therefore hear my voice, and understand my words
	9:38	and behold, she was mourning and weeping with a loud voice
	10:27	Then I was afraid, and cried with a loud voice and said
	11:10	the voice did not come from his heads
	11:15	And behold, a voice sounded, saying to it
	11:36	Then I heard a voice saying to me
	11:37	and I heard how he uttered a man's voice to the eagle
	12:17	As for your hearing a voice that spoke
	12:45	And they wept with a loud voice
	13:4	and whenever his voice issued from his mouth
	13:4	all who heard his voice melted as wax melts
	13:33	And when all the nations hear his voice
	14:1	behold, a voice came out of a bush opposite me
	14:38	And on the next day, behold, a voice called me, saying
	16:27	or even to hear his voice
4 Ma	8:29	all with one voice together, as from one mind, said :
	15:21	as did the voices of the children in torture

VOID   1

2 Es	2:1	and made my counsels void

VOLUME   1

2 Ma	2:23	all this, which has been set forth by Jason of Cyrene in 5 volumes

VOLUNTARILY   1

3 Ma	6:6	who had voluntarily surrendered their lives to the flames

VOTE   3 = 0.002 %

2 Ma	10:8	They decreed by public ordinance and vote
	12:4	and this was done by public vote of the city
	15:36	And they all decreed by public vote

VOTIVE   5 = 0.003 %

Jud	16:19	she gave as a votive offering to the Lord
2 Ma	2:13	and letters of kings about votive offerings
	5:16	the votive offerings which other kings had made
1 Es	2:7	besides the other things added as votive offerings
	2:9	and with a very great number of votive offerings

VOW, verb   7 = 0.005 %

1 Ma	5:5	and he encamped against them, vowed their complete destruction
1 Es	4:44	and vowed to send them back there
	4:45	You also vowed to build the temple
	4:46	whose fulfilment you vowed to the King of heaven
	5:44	vowed that they would erect the house on its site
	8:13	which I and my friends have vowed
	8:58	and the silver and the gold are vowed to the Lord

VOW, subst.   10 = 0.007 %

Jud	4:14	and the vows and freewill offerings of the people
Sir	18:22	Let nothing hinder you from paying a vow promptly
	18:23	Before making a vow, prepare yourself
	23:18	A man who breaks his marriage vows says to himself
L Jr	6:35	if one makes a vow to them and does not keep it
2 Ma	3:35	and made very great vows to the Saviour of his life
	9:13	Then the abominable fellow made a vow to the Lord

1 Es	4:43	Remember the vow which you made to build Jerusalem
	4:46	I pray therefore that you fulfil the vow
	5:53	And all who had made any vow to God

VOYAGE, subst.   2

3 Ma	4:10	during the whole voyage
	4:11	and the voyage was concluded as the king had decreed

VOYAGE, verb   1

Wis	14:1	and about to voyage over raging waves

VULGARITY   1

Sir	23:13	Do not accustom your mouth to lewd vulgarity

W

WAGE, subst.   11 = 0.007 %

Tob	2:12	Once when they paid her wages, they also gave her a kid
	2:14	as a gift in addition to my wages
	4:14	the wages of any man who works for you
	5:3	and I will pay him wages as long as I live
	5:14	But tell me, what wages am I to pay you – a drachma a day
	5:15	And besides, I will add to your wages
	12:1	My son, see to the wages of the man who went with you
Wis	2:22	nor hope for the wages of holiness
Sir	34:22	to deprive an employee of his wages is to shed blood
1 Ma	14:32	he armed the men of his nation's forces and paid them wages
1 Es	4:56	He wrote that land and wages should be provided

WAGE, verb   6 = 0.004 %

Sir	46:3	For he waged the wars of the Lord
1 Ma	3:3	he girded on his armour of war and waged battles
	12:13	the kings round about us have waged war against us
	12:24	with a larger force than before, to wage war against him
2 Es	7:127	which every man who is born on earth shall wage
	13:8	to wage war with him

WAIL   4 = 0.003 %

2 Es	15:44	and all who are about her shall wail over her
	16:2	and wail for your children, and lament for them
4 Ma	12:14	but you will wail bitterly for having slain without cause
	16:12	did not wail with such a lament for any of them

WAILING   5 = 0.003 %

Sir	38:17	Let your weeping be bitter and your wailing fervent
3 Ma	1:4	Arsinoe went to the troops with wailing and tears
	4:3	with mourning and wailing for them ?
	4:6	exchanged joy for wailing
	6:32	Putting an end to all mourning and wailing

WAIT, verb   24 = 0.016 %

Tob	2:2	and I will wait for you
	5:7	Then Tobias said to him, Wait for me
Jud	6:10	who waited on him in his tent
	8:17	Therefore, while we wait for his deliverance
	10:18	as she waited outside the tent of Holofernes
	12:16	for he had been waiting for an opportunity to deceive her
	13:3	and wait for her to come out
	15:2	so that they did not wait for one another
Wis	8:12	When I am silent they will wait for me
Sir	2:7	You who fear the Lord, wait for his mercy
	4:1	and do not keep needy eyes waiting
	6:19	and wait for her good harvest
	18:22	and do not wait until death to be released from it
	29:8	and do not make him wait for your alms
	36:16	Reward those who wait for thee
	51:8	that thou dost deliver those who wait for thee
Sus	13:59	for the angel of God is waiting with his sword to saw you in 2
2 Ma	5:25	and waited until the holy sabbath day
	6:14	the Lord waits patiently to punish them
	7:30	What are you waiting for ?
	9:25	and waiting to see what will happen
3 Ma	5:2	and they were eagerly waiting for daybreak
	7:17	the fleet waited for them
2 Es	12:39	But wait here 7 days more

WAIT, subst.   9 = 0.006 %

Wis	2:12	Let us lie in wait for the righteous man
	10:12	and kept him safe from those who lay in wait for him
Sir	11:31	for he lies in wait, turning good into evil
	11:32	and a sinner lies in wait to shed blood
	14:22	Pursue wisdom like a hunter, and lie in wait on her paths
	27:10	A lion lies in wait for prey
	27:28	but vengeance lies in wait for him like a lion
	28:26	lest you fall before him who lies in wait
1 Ma	5:3	because they kept lying in wait for Israel

WAKE   1

1 Es	3:9	and said, When the king wakes

WAKE up   3 = 0.002 %

Jud	14:13	Wake up our lord, for the slaves have been so bold
Sir	13:13	When you hear these things in your sleep, wake up !
	40:7	at the moment of his rescue he wakes up

WAKEFUL   2

Sir	31:2	Wakeful anxiety prevents slumber
	42:9	A daughter keeps her father secretly wakeful

WAKEFULNESS   1

Sir	31:1	Wakefulness over wealth wastes away one's flesh

WALK   34 = 0.022 %

Tob	1:3	I, Tobit, walked in the ways of truth and righteousness
	3:5	For we did not walk in truth before thee
	4:5	and do not walk in the ways of wrongdoing
Jud	13:20	walking in the straight path before our God
Wis	6:4	nor keep the law, nor walk according to the purpose of God
	15:15	and their feet are of no use for walking
	19:21	that walked among them
Sir	2:12	and to the sinner who walks along 2 ways !
	4:17	For at first she will walk with him on tortuous paths
	5:2	walking according to the desires of your heart
	9:13	Know that you are walking in the midst of snares
	13:13	for you are walking about with your own downfall
	19:30	and a man's manner of walking, show what he is
	21:6	Whoever hates reproof walks in the steps of the sinner
	24:5	and have walked in the depths of the abyss
	45:9	to send forth a sound as he walked
Bar	1:18	to walk in the statutes of the Lord which he set before us
	2:10	to walk in the statutes of the Lord which he set before us
	3:13	If you had walked in the way of God
	4:2	walk toward the shining of her light
	4:13	they did not walk in the ways of God's commandments
	5:7	so that Israel may walk safely in the glory of God
P Az	1	And they walked about in the midst of the flames
Sus	13:7	Susanna would go into her husband's garden to walk
	13:8	going in and walking about, and they began to desire her
	13:36	The elders said, As we were walking in the garden alone
2 Ma	5:21	that he could sail on the land and walk on the sea
	6:7	they were compelled to walk in the procession
1 Es	4:24	he faces lions, and he walks in darkness
2 Es	3:8	And every nation walked after his own will
	7:8	so that only one man can walk upon that path
	7:122	but we have walked in the most wicked ways ?
	8:50	because they have walked in great pride
	13:57	Then I arose and walked in the field

WALL, subst.   56 = 0.036 %

Tob	1:17	and thrown out behind the wall of Nineveh
	2:9	I slept by the wall of the courtyard, and my face was uncovered
	2:10	I did not know that there were sparrows on the wall
	13:16	her walls with precious stones
Jud	1:2	he is the king who built walls about Ecbatana
	1:2	he made the walls 70 cubits high and 50 cubits wide
	7:32	and they went up on the walls and towers of their city
	14:1	and take this head and hang it upon the parapet of your wall
	14:11	they hung the head of Holofernes on the wall
Wis	13:15	and sets it in the wall, and fastens it there with iron
Sir	14:24	will also fasten his tent peg to her walls
	22:17	is like the stucco decoration on the wall of a colonnade
	23:18	Darkness surrounds me, and the walls hide me
	49:13	he raised for us the walls that had fallen
	50:2	He laid the foundations for the high double walls
	50:2	the high retaining walls for the temple enclosure
1 Ma	1:31	and tore down its houses and its surrounding walls
	1:33	with a great strong wall and strong towers
	4:60	with high walls and strong towers round about
	6:7	with high walls as before, and also Beth-zur, his city
	6:62	and gave orders to tear down the wall all around
	9:50	with high walls and gates and bars
	9:54	Alcimus gave orders to tear down the wall
	10:11	to build the walls and encircle Mount Zion
	10:45	And let the cost of rebuilding the walls of Jerusalem
	10:45	and the cost of rebuilding the walls in Judea
	12:36	to build the walls of Jerusalem still higher
	12:37	part of the wall on the valley to the east had fallen
	13:10	and hastened to complete the walls of Jerusalem
	13:33	with high towers and great walls and gates and bolts
	13:45	went up on the wall with their clothes rent
	14:37	and built the walls of Jerusalem higher
	16:23	and the building of the walls which he built, and his achievements
2 Ma	1:15	inside the wall of the sacred precinct
	3:19	ran together to the gates, and some to the walls
	5:5	When the troops upon the wall had been forced back
	6:10	then hurled them down headlong from the wall

	10 :17	and beat off all who fought upon the wall
	10 :35	bravely stormed the wall
	11 :9	ready to assail not only men but the wildest beasts or walls of iron
	12 :13	which was strongly fortified with earthworks and walls
	12 :14	relying on the strength of the walls
	12 :15	rushed furiously upon the walls
	12 :27	Stalwart young men took their stand before the walls
	14 :43	He bravely ran up on the wall
1 Es	**1** :55	and broke down the walls of Jerusalem
	2 :18	repairing its market places and walls
	2 :19	Now if this city is built and the walls finished
	2 :24	that if this city is built and its walls finished
	4 :4	and conquer mountains, walls, and towers
	6 :9	of hewn stone, with costly timber laid in the walls
3 Ma	**1** :29	but also the walls and the whole earth around echoed
	4 :11	which had been built with a monstrous perimeter wall
2 Es	**2** :22	Protect the old and the young within your walls
	11 :42	and have laid low the walls of those who did you no harm
	15 :42	And they shall destroy cities and walls

WALL, verb   1
  1 Ma **13** :33   and walled them all around

WALLOW   1
  Sir **23** :12   and they will not wallow in sins

WAND   1
  2 Ma **10** :7   Therefore bearing ivy-wreathed wands and beautiful branches

WANDER   6 = 0.004 %

Sir	**9** :7	nor wander about in its deserted sections
	29 :18	and they have wandered among foreign nations
	36 :25	and where there is no wife, a man will wander about and sigh
2 Ma	**10** :6	they had been wandering in the mountains and caves
2 Es	**7** :80	but shall immediately wander about in torments
	7 :93	in which the souls of the ungodly wander

WANDERING   1
  Wis **18** :3   and a harmless sun for their glorious wandering

WANE   1
  Sir **43** :7   a light that wanes when it has reached the full

WANT, verb   5 = 0.003 %

1 Ma	**3** :34	and gave him orders about all that he wanted done
	7 :5	they were led by Alcimus, who wanted to be high priest
	11 :45	and they wanted to kill the king
2 Ma	**13** :25	in fact they were so angry that they wanted to annul its terms
2 Es	**16** :63	Woe to those who sin and want to hide their sins !

WANT, subst.   7 = 0.005 %

Tob	**4** :13	and in shiftlessness there is loss and great want
Wis	**16** :3	while thy people, after suffering want a short time
	16 :4	inexorable want should come
Sir	**4** :2	nor anger a man in want
	10 :26	nor glorify yourself at a time when you are in want
	11 :11	but is so much the more in want
	26 :28	a warrior in want through poverty

WANTONLY   1
  Sir **27** :13   and their laughter is wantonly sinful

WAR, subst.   84 = 0.055 %

Jud	**1** :5	it was in those days that King Nebuchadnezzar made war
	1 :11	and refused to join him in the war
	4 :5	and stored up food in preparation for war
	5 :1	heard that the people of Israel had prepared for war
	5 :23	they are a people with no strength or power for making war
	6 :2	and tell us not to make war against the people of Israel
	7 :1	and make war on the Israelites
	7 :2	their force of men of war was 170,000 infantry and 12,000 cavalry
	9 :7	and know not that thou art the Lord who crushest wars
	16 :3	For God is the Lord who crushes wars
Ad E	**11** :7	And at their roaring every nation prepared for war
Wis	**8** :15	and courageous in war
Sir	**26** :27	is regarded as a war trumpet
	26 :27	and every person like this lives in the anarchy of war
	37 :11	or with a coward about war
	46 :1	Joshua the son of Nun was mighty in war
	46 :3	For he waged the wars of the Lord
	46 :6	He hurled down war upon that nation
	47 :5	to slay a man mighty in war
Bar	**3** :26	great in stature, expert in war
L Jr	**6** :15	but it cannot save itself from war and robbers
	6 :48	For when war or calamity comes upon them
	6 :49	for they cannot save themselves from war or calamity ?
1 Ma	**3** :3	he girded on his armour of war and waged battles
	3 :14	I will make war on Judas and his companions

	4 :7	and these men were trained in war
	5 :3	But Judas made war on the sons of Esau
	5 :30	carrying ladders and engines of war to capture the stronghold
	5 :56	and of the heroic war they had fought
	5 :57	let us go and make war
	6 :20	and he built siege towers and other engines of war
	6 :30	20,000 horsemen, and 32 elephants accustomed to war
	6 :31	and for many days they fought and built engines of war
	6 :51	engines of war to throw fire and stones
	6 :52	The Jews also made engines of war to match theirs
	8 :2	Men told him of their wars
	8 :24	If war comes first to Rome or to any of their allies
	8 :26	And to the enemy who makes war
	8 :27	if war comes first to the nation of the Jews
	9 :22	Now the rest of the acts of Judas, and his wars
	9 :64	he fought against it for many days and made machines of war
	9 :67	and set fire to the machines of war
	11 :4	whom Jonathan had burned in the war
	11 :20	and he built many engines of war to use against it
	12 :13	many afflictions and many wars have encircled us
	12 :13	the kings round about us have waged war against us
	12 :14	with these wars
	12 :24	with a larger force than before, to wage war against him
	12 :40	but might make war on him
	12 :44	Why have you wearied all these people when we are not at war ?
	12 :53	Now therefore let us make war on them
	13 :3	you know also the wars
	14 :1	so that he could make war against Trypho
	14 :9	and the youths donned the glories and garments of war
	14 :29	Since wars often occurred in the country
	15 :19	or make war against them and their cities and their country
	15 :25	and making engines of war
	15 :39	and to make war on the people
	16 :2	have fought the wars of Israel from our youth until this day
	16 :23	The rest of the acts of John and his wars
2 Ma	**2** :14	on account of the war which had come upon us
	2 :20	and further the wars against Antiochus Epiphanes
	10 :10	of the principal calamities of the wars
	10 :15	and endeavoured to keep up the war
	12 :15	who without battering-rams or engines of war
	12 :27	and great stores of war engines and missiles were there
	14 :6	are keeping up war and stirring up sedition
1 Es	**1** :25	went to make war at Carchemish on the Euphrates
	1 :27	for my war is at the Euphrates
	2 :27	and that the men in it were given to rebellion and war
	4 :4	If he tells them to make war on one another, they do it
	4 :6	Likewise those who do not serve in the army or make war
3 Ma	**1** :2	intending single-handed to kill him and thereby end the war
2 Es	**4** :14	and said, Come, let us go and make war against the sea
	6 :24	At that time friends shall make war on friends like enemies
	13 :5	to make war against the man who came up out of the sea
	13 :8	to wage war with him
	13 :9	nor held a spear or any weapon of war
	13 :28	and as for his not holding a spear or weapon of war
	13 :31	And they shall plan to make war against one another
	16 :18	the beginning of wars, when the powers shall be terrified
	16 :34	Their bridegrooms shall be killed in war
4 Ma	**4** :21	and caused Antiochus himself to make war on them
	7 :4	No city besieged with many ingenious war machines

WAR, verb   3 = 0.002 %

1 Ma	**15** :19	or make alliance with those who war against them
2 Ma	**10** :14	and at every turn kept on warring against the Jews
4 Ma	**4** :22	For when he was warring against Ptolemy in Egypt

WARD off   1
  4 Ma **14** :16   hatch the nestlings and ward off the intruder

WARFARE   1
  2 Es **13** :33   and the warfare that they have against one another

WARM, verb   1
  Wis **16** :27   was melted when simply warmed by a fleeting ray of the sun

WARMLY   2

Tob	**7** :8	They received them very warmly
2 Ma	**14** :24	he was warmly attached to the man

WARN   4 = 0.003 %

Wis	**11** :10	For thou didst test them as a father does in warning
	12 :2	and dost remind and warn them of the things wherein they sin
2 Es	**14** :20	but who will warn those who will be born hereafter ?
4 Ma	**14** :17	and warning them with their own calls

WARNING   3 = 0.002 %

Wis	**12** :26	But those who have not heeded the warning of light rebukes
	16 :6	they were troubled for a little while as a warning
2 Ma	**8** :6	Coming without warning

WARRIOR 12 = 0.008 %
Jud 7:2 So all their warriors moved their camp that day
16:4 he came with myriads of his warriors
Wis 18:15 into the midst of the land that was doomed, a stern warrior
Sir 26:28 a warrior in want through poverty
1 Ma 2:42 mighty warriors of Israel
2:66 Judas Maccabeus has been a mighty warrior from his youth
4:30 who didst crush the attack of the mighty warrior
9:11 as did all the chief warriors
10:19 that you are a mighty warrior and worthy to be our friend
13:10 So he assembled all the warriors
15:13 and with him were a 120,000 warriors and 8,000 cavalry
16:4 So John chose out of the country 20,000 warriors and horsemen

WARSHIP 1
1 Ma 15:3 and have equipped warships

WARY 1
Sir 37:8 Be wary of a counsellor

WASH 3 = 0.002 %
Tob 2:5 And when I returned I washed myself
6:2 Then the young man went down to wash himself
Sir 34:25 If a man washes after touching a dead body

WASHING 1
Sir 34:25 what has he gained by his washing ?

WASP 1
Wis 12:8 and didst send wasps as forerunners of thy army

WASTE, verb 1
Sir 20:13 but the courtesies of fools are wasted

WASTE away 5 = 0.003 %
Jud 7:14 will waste away with famine
Sir 31:1 Wakefulness over wealth wastes away one's flesh
38:28 and he wastes away in the heat of the furnace
3 Ma 6:8 And Jonah, wasting away
2 Es 7:87 because they shall utterly waste away in confusion

WASTE, adj. 12 = 0.008 %
Wis 5:23 Lawlessness will lay waste the whole earth
16:29 will melt like wintry frost, and flow away like waste water
Sir 21:4 Terror and violence will lay waste riches
21:4 thus the house of the proud will be laid waste
1 Ma 2:12 and our glory have been laid waste
1 Es 2:23 That is why this city was laid waste
4:8 if he tells them to lay waste, they lay waste
2:23 when Judea was laid waste by the Chaldeans
2 Es 5:3 shall be waste and untrodden
10:21 For you see that our sanctuary has been laid waste
15:49 to lay waste your houses

WASTELAND 1
Wis 10:7 a continually smoking wasteland

WATCH, subst. 11 = 0.007 %
Jud 7:13 and camp there to keep watch
12:5 Along toward the morning watch she arose
Ad E 12:1 the 2 eunuchs of the king who kept watch in the courtyard
Sir 1:29 and keep watch over your lips
26:10 Keep strict watch over a headstrong daughter
33:16 I was the last on watch
40:6 and afterward in his sleep, as though he were on watch
42:11 Keep strict watch over a headstrong daughter
43:10 they never relax in their watches
Bar 3:34 the stars shone in their watches, and were glad
1 Es 4:11 but they keep watch around him

WATCH, verb 25 = 0.016 %
Tob 4:14 Watch yourself, my son, in everything you do
Jud 10:10 and the men of the city watched her
Wis 3:9 and he watches over his only ones
4:15 and he watches over his holy ones
Sir 12:11 watch yourself, and be on your guard against him
19:9 for some one has heard you and watched you
27:12 Among stupid people watch for a chance to leave
46:14 and the Lord watched over Jacob
L Jr 6:7 For my angel is with you, and he is watching your lives
Sus 13:12 And they watched eagerly, day after day, to see her
13:15 Once, while they were watching for an opportune day
13:16 who had hid themselves and were watching her
2 Ma 3:39 watches over that place himself and brings it aid
7:6 saying, The Lord God is watching over us
9:25 keep watching for opportunities
14:29 he watched for an opportunity
3 Ma 6:8 you, Father, watched over and restored unharmed to all his family
6:12 watch over us now and have mercy upon us

2 Es 2:13 The kingdom is already prepared for you ; watch !
11:8 Do not all watch at the same time
11:8 let each sleep in his own place, and watch in his turn
4 Ma 5:13 that if there is some power watching over this religion of yours
13:27 while watching their brothers being maltreated
15:15 She watched the flesh of her children consumed by fire
16:15 you stood and watched Eleazar being tortured

WATCHFUL 2
Sir 13:13 Keep words to yourself and be very watchful
1 Es 8:59 Be watchful and on guard until you deliver them

WATCHFULNESS 1
Sir pr. using in that period of time great watchfulness and skill

WATCHMAN 2
Jud 13:11 Judith called out from afar to the watchmen at the gates
Sir 37:14 than 7 watchmen sitting high on a watchtower

WATCHTOWER 1
Sir 37:14 than 7 watchmen sitting high on a watchtower

WATCHWORD 2
2 Ma 8:23 and gave the watchword, God's help
13:15 He gave his men the watchword, God's victory

WATER, subst. 86 = 0.056 %
Jud 2:7 Tell them to prepare earth and water
7:7 and visited the springs that supplied their water
7:12 of the springs of water
7:13 for this is where all the people of Bethulia get their water
7:17 and they encamped in the valley and seized the water supply
7:20 until all the vessels of water belonging to every inhabitant of Bethulia were empty
7:21 and they did not have enough water
8:9 because they were faint for lack of water
9:12 Lord of heaven and earth, Creator of the waters
10:3 and bathed her body with water
11:12 and their water has almost given out
16:15 For the mountains shall be shaken to their foundations with the waters
Ad E 10:6 and there was light and the sun and abundant water
11:10 there came a great river, with abundant water
Wis 5:10 like a ship that sails through the billowy water
5:22 the water of the sea will rage against them
10:18 and led them through deep waters
11:4 and water was given them out of flinty rock
11:7 thou gavest them abundant water unexpectedly
13:2 or the circle of the stars, or turbulent water
16:17 in the water, which quenches all things
16:19 and at another time even in the midst of water
16:29 will melt like wintry frost, and flow away like waste water
17:18 or the rhythm of violently rushing water
19:7 and dry land emerging where water had stood before
19:19 For land animals were transformed into water creatures
19:20 Fire even in water retained its normal power
19:20 and water forgot its fire-quenching nature
Sir 3:30 Water extinguishes a blazing fire :
15:3 and give him the water of wisdom to drink
15:16 He has placed before you fire and water :
18:10 Like a drop of water from the sea and a grain of sand
24:30 and like a water channel into a garden
25:25 Allow no outlet to water
26:12 and drinks from any water near him
29:21 The essentials for life are water and bread and clothing
31:26 Fire and water prove the temper of steel
38:5 Was not water made sweet with a tree
39:13 and bud like a rose growing by a stream of water
39:17 At his word the waters stood in a heap
39:17 and the reservoirs of water at the word of his mouth
39:23 just as he turns fresh water into salt
39:26 Basic to all the needs of man's life are water and fire
40:11 and what is from the waters returns to the sea
40:16 The reeds by any water or river bank
43:20 The cold north wind blows, and ice freezes over the water
43:20 it rests upon every pool of water
43:20 and the water puts it on like a breastplate
48:17 and brought water into the midst of it
48:17 and built pools for water
50:3 In his days a cistern for water was quarried out
50:8 like lilies by a spring of water
P Az 38 Bless the Lord, all waters above the heaven
57 Bless the Lord, you whales and all creatures that move in the waters
1 Ma 5:40 Now as Judas and his army drew near to the stream of water
5:42 When Judas approached the stream of water
9:33 and camped by the water of the pool of Asphar
9:45 the water of the Jordan is on the side and on that
11:67 Jonathan and his army encamped by the waters of Gennesaret
2 Ma 15:39 or, again, to drink water alone

	15 :39	while wine mixed with water is sweet and delicious
1 Es	9 :2	and he did not eat bread or drink water
2 Es	1 :20	did I not cleave the rock so that waters flowed in abundance ?
	1 :23	but threw a tree into the water and made the stream sweet
	4 :49	And after this a cloud full of water passed before me
	5 :9	And salt waters shall be found in the sweet
	6 :17	and its sound was like the sound of many waters
	6 :41	and didst command him to divide and separate the waters
	6 :42	thou didst command the waters to be gathered together
	6 :47	where the water had been gathered together
	6 :48	The dumb and lifeless water produced living creatures
	6 :50	for the 7th part where the water had been gathered together
	7 :7	and deep water on the left
	7 :8	between the fire and the water
	7 :40	or water or air, or darkness or evening or morning
	8 :8	what thou hast created is preserved in fire and water
	9 :16	as a wave is greater than a drop of water
	14 :39	it was full of something like water
	15 :41	fire and hail and flying swords and floods of water
	15 :41	may be filled with the abundance of those waters
	15 :58	and drink their own blood in thirst for water
	16 :58	who has enclosed the sea in the midst of the waters
	16 :58	and by his word has suspended the earth over the water
	16 :59	and founded it upon the waters
	16 :60	who has put springs of water in the desert
4 Ma	3 :11	But a certain irrational desire for the water

WATER, verb   3 = 0.002 %

Sir	24 :31	I said, I will water my orchard and drench my garden plot
2 Es	16 :60	to send rivers from the heights to water the earth
4 Ma	1 :29	and ties up and waters and thoroughly irrigates

WATERY   1

2 Es	6 :52	but to Leviathan thou didst give the 7th part, the watery part

WAVE, subst.   18 = 0.012 %

Wis	5 :10	nor track of its keel in the waves
	14 :1	and about to voyage over raging waves
	14 :3	and a safe way through the waves
	19 :7	and a grassy plain out of the raging waves
Sir	24 :6	In the waves of the sea, in the whole earth
	29 :18	and has shaken them like a wave of the sea
2 Ma	9 :8	that he could command the waves of the sea
2 Es	4 :15	And in like manner the waves of the sea also made a plan
	4 :17	likewise also the plan of the waves of the sea
	4 :19	and to the sea is assigned a place to carry its waves
	4 :21	and the sea to its waves
	9 :16	as a wave is greater than a drop of water
	13 :2	and behold, a wind arose from the sea and stirred up all its waves
	16 :12	and its waves and the fish also shall be troubled
4 Ma	7 :2	and overwhelmed by the mighty waves of tortures
	7 :5	our father Eleazar broke the maddening waves of the emotions
	13 :6	hold back the threatening waves
	15 :31	stoutly endured the waves

WAVER   1

3 Ma	5 :33	and his eyes wavered and his face fell

WAVERING   1

2 Es	9 :3	wavering of leaders, confusion of princes

WAX, subst.   2

Jud	16 :15	at thy presence the rocks shall melt like wax
2 Es	13 :4	all who heard his voice melted as wax melts

WAY   179 = 0.117 %

Tob	1 :3	I, Tobit, walked in the ways of truth and righteousness
	3 :2	all thy deeds and all thy ways are mercy and truth
	4 :5	and do not walk in the ways of wrongdoing
	4 :6	your ways will prosper through your deeds
	4 :15	or let drunkenness go with you on your way
	4 :19	ask him that your ways may be straight
	5 :6	I am familiar with the way
	5 :16	God who dwells in heaven will prosper your way
	6 :1	Now as they proceeded on their way
	6 :5	And they both continued on their way
	11 :1	After this Tobias went on his way
	11 :1	So he continued on his way until they came near to Nineveh
	11 :4	So they went their way, and the dog went along behind them
Jud	3 :4	come and deal with them in any way that seems good to you
	5 :8	For they had left the ways of their ancestors
	5 :14	and he led them by the way of Sinai and Kadesh-barnea
	5 :18	But when they departed from the way
	7 :19	and there was no way of escape from them
	9 :6	for all thy ways are prepared in advance
	10 :13	I am on my way to the presence of Holofernes
	10 :13	and I will show him a way by which he can go
	12 :8	to direct her way for the raising up of her people
	13 :16	As the Lord lives, who has protected me in the way I went

Ad E	16 :14	He thought that in this way he would find us undefended
Wis	2 :15	and his ways are strange
	2 :16	and he avoids our ways as unclean
	5 :6	So it was we who strayed from the way of truth
	5 :7	but the way of the Lord we have not known
	10 :17	she guided them along a marvellous way
	12 :10	and that their way of thinking would never change
	14 :3	and a safe way through the waves
	18 :23	and cut off its way to the living
	19 :7	an unhindered way out of the Red Sea
	19 :17	each tried to find the way through his own door
Sir	1 :5	and her ways are the eternal commandments
	2 :6	make your ways straight, and hope in him
	2 :12	and to the sinner who walks along 2 ways !
	2 :15	and those who love him will keep his ways
	6 :26	and keep her ways with all your might
	11 :15	affection and the ways of good works come from him
	14 :21	He who reflects in his mind on her ways
	15 :11	Do not say, Because of the Lord I left the right way
	16 :20	Who will ponder his ways ?
	17 :15	Their ways are always before him
	17 :16	Their ways from youth tend toward evil
	17 :19	and his eyes are continually upon their ways
	21 :10	The way of sinners is smoothly paved with stones
	23 :19	they look upon all the ways of men
	30 :1	in order that he may rejoice at the way he turns out
	32 :21	Do not be overconfident on a smooth way
	33 :11	and appointed their different ways
	33 :13	for all his ways are as he pleases
	33 :31	which way will you go to seek him ?
	37 :9	and tell you, Your way is good
	37 :15	that he may direct your way in truth
	39 :24	To the holy his ways are straight
	43 :26	Because of him his messenger finds the way
	47 :23	and gave to Ephraim a sinful way
	48 :22	and he held strongly to the ways of David his father
	49 :9	and did good to those who directed their ways aright
	50 :22	who in every way does great things
Bar	2 :33	for they will remember the ways of their fathers
	3 :13	If you had walked in the way of God
	3 :20	but they have not learned the way to knowledge
	3 :21	Their sons have strayed far from her way
	3 :23	have not learned the way to wisdom
	3 :27	God did not choose them, nor give them the way to knowledge
	3 :31	No one knows the way to her
	3 :36	He found the whole way to knowledge
	4 :13	they did not walk in the ways of God's commandments
L Jr	6 :71	In the same way, their gods of wood
P Az	4	and all thy works are true and thy ways right
1 Ma	5 :29	and they went all the way to the stronghold of Dathema
	5 :53	and encouraging the people all the way
	6 :18	They were trying in every way to harm them
	8 :27	In the same way
	13 :20	and he circled around by the way to Adora
	13 :21	urging him to come to them by way of the wilderness
	14 :5	and opened a way to the isles of the sea
	14 :35	He sought in every way to exalt his people
2 Ma	1 :17	Blessed in every way be our God, who has brought judgment
	2 :6	Some of those who followed him came up to mark the way
	2 :14	In the same way Judas also collected all the books that had been lost
	4 :10	to the Greek way of life
	4 :11	and he destroyed the lawful ways of living
	4 :13	and increase in the adoption of foreign ways
	4 :16	and those whose ways of living they admired
	4 :34	he immediately put him out of the way
	6 :14	but he does not deal in this way with us
	6 :31	So in this way he died
	7 :7	After the first brother had died in this way
	7 :13	they maltreated and tortured the 4th in the same way
	7 :24	if he would turn from the ways of his fathers
	8 :17	and besides, the overthrow of their ancestral way of life
	8 :35	and made his way alone like a runaway slave
	9 :7	Yet he did not any way stop his insolence
	9 :18	But when his sufferings did not in any way abate
	9 :21	On my way back from the region of Persia
	10 :36	Others who came up in the same way
	11 :24	but prefer their own way of living
	11 :31	and none of them shall be molested in any way
	11 :36	For we are on our way to Antioch
	12 :8	meant in the same way to wipe out the Jews
	12 :11	and to help his people in all other ways
	12 :12	Judas, thinking that they might really be useful in many ways
	12 :22	and were swept on, this way and that
	12 :41	So they all blessed the ways of the Lord
	14 :3	realized that there was no way for him
	14 :23	and did nothing out of the way
1 Es	8 :52	and will support them in every way
	8 :61	he delivered us from every enemy on the way
	9 :51	so go your way, eat the fat and drink the sweet

	9:54	Then they all went their way
3 Ma	**1**:25	while the elders near the king tried in various ways
	3:8	The Greeks in the city, though wronged in no way
	3:23	in every situation, in accordance with their infamous way of life
	3:24	that they are ill-disposed toward us in every way
	4:11	nor in any way claim to be inside the circuit of the city
	5:20	Tomorrow without delay prepare the elephants in the same way
	5:46	crowding their way into the hippodrome
	5:49	and giving way to lamentation and groans they kissed each other
	7:14	And so on their way
2 Es	**3**:31	and hast not shown to any one how thy way may be comprehended
	3:34	and so it will be found which way
	4:2	and do you think you can comprehend the way of the Most High ?
	4:3	I have been sent to show you 3 ways
	4:4	I also will show you the way you desire to see
	4:11	how then can your mind comprehend the way of the Most High ?
	4:23	For I did not wish to inquire about the ways above
	5:1	and the way of truth shall be hidden
	5:12	they shall labour but their ways shall not prosper
	5:34	while I strive to understand the way of the Most High
	7:23	and they ignored his ways !
	7:48	and has brought us into corruption and the ways of death
	7:79	and have not kept the way of the Most High
	7:80	ever grieving and sad, in 7 ways
	7:81	The first way
	7:82	The 2nd way
	7:83	The 3rd way, they shall see the reward laid up
	7:84	The 4th way
	7:85	The 5th way
	7:86	The 6th way
	7:87	The 7th way
	7:87	which is worse than all the ways that have been mentioned
	7:88	who have kept the ways of the Most High
	7:99	and the aforesaid are the ways of torment
	7:122	but we have walked in the most wicked ways ?
	7:129	For this is the way of which Moses, while he was alive
	8:29	who have had the ways of cattle
	8:31	in ways that bring death
	8:56	and forsook his ways
	9:9	Then those who have now abused my ways shall be amazed
	9:19	have become corrupt in their ways
	10:13	but it is with the earth according to the way of the earth
	12:4	because you search out the ways of the Most High
	13:45	Through that region there was a long way to go
	13:54	because you have forsaken your own ways
	14:31	and did not keep the ways which the Most High commanded you
4 Ma	**1**:4	and those that stand in the way of courage
	1:6	but so that one may not give way to them
	2:7	a glutton, or even a drunkard can learn a better way
	2:8	a way of life in accordance with the law
	2:8	he is forced to act contrary to his natural ways
	3:2	but reason can provide a way for us
	4:19	Jason changed the nation's way of life
	4:24	he had not been able in any way
	5:27	but also to eat in such a way
	7:3	in no way did he turn the rudder of religion
	8:3	handsome, modest, noble, and accomplished in every way
	8:8	And enjoy your youth by adopting the Greek way of life
	10:7	Since they were not able in any way to break his spirit
	10:13	As for you, do not give way
	11:4	for what act of ours are you destroying us in this way ?
	12:13	and to maltreat and torture them in this way ?
	16:3	inflamed as she saw her 7 sons tortured in such varied ways
	17:5	who, after lighting the way of your star-like 7 sons to piety
	17:9	who wished to destroy the way of life of the Hebrews
	18:1	obey this law and exercise pity in every way
	18:5	Since in no way whatever was he able to compel the Israelites

WAYFARER 1

Sir	**26**:12	As a thirsty wayfarer opens his mouth

WE 439 = 0.286 %

WEAK 16 = 0.010 %

Jud	**9**:11	upholder of the weak, protector of the forlorn
	16:11	for weak people shouted and the enemy trembled
Wis	**2**:11	for what is weak proves itself to be useless
	9:5	a man who is weak and short-lived
	13:18	For health he appeals to a thing that is weak
	17:13	and the inner expectation of help, being weak
Sir	**25**:23	Drooping hands and weak knees
L Jr	**6**:36	or rescue the weak from the strong
1 Ma	**6**:57	We daily grow weaker, our food supply is scant
1 Es	**1**:30	Take me away from the battle, for I am very weak
2 Es	**2**:21	care for the injured and the weak
	7:112	therefore those who were strong prayed for the weak
	12:5	and very weak in my spirit

	14:14	and divest yourself now of your weak nature
	14:17	For the weaker the world becomes through old age
4 Ma	**15**:5	Considering that mothers are the weaker sex and give birth to many

WEAKEN 1

2 Es	**15**:51	You shall be weakened like a wretched woman

WEAKLING 1

Sir	**6**:20	a weakling will not remain with her

WEAKNESS 2

Sir	**11**:30	and like a spy he observes your weakness
4 Ma	**7**:20	because of the weakness of their reason

WEALTH 25 = 0.016 %

Tob	**4**:21	You have great wealth if you fear God
Wis	**5**:8	And what good has our boasted wealth brought us ?
	7:8	and I accounted wealth as nothing in comparison with her
	7:11	and in her hands uncounted wealth
	7:13	I do not hide her wealth
	8:18	and in the labours of her hands, unfailing wealth
Sir	**5**:1	Do not set your heart on your wealth
	5:8	Do not depend on dishonest wealth
	10:8	on account of injustice and insolence and wealth
	10:30	while a rich man is honoured for his wealth
	10:31	A man honoured in poverty, how much more in wealth !
	10:31	And a man dishonoured in wealth, how much more in poverty !
	11:14	good things and bad, life and death, poverty and wealth
	18:25	in the days of wealth think of poverty and need
	28:10	and in proportion to his wealth he will heighten his wrath
	30:16	There is no wealth better than health of body
	31:1	Wakefulness over wealth wastes away one's flesh
	31:3	The rich man toils as his wealth accumulates
	37:6	and be not unmindful of him in your wealth
	40:13	The wealth of the unjust will dry up like a torrent
L Jr	**6**:35	Likewise they are not able to give either wealth or money
1 Ma	**6**:1	was a city famed for its wealth in silver and gold
2 Es	**3**:2	and the wealth of those who lived in Babylon
	3:33	and have seen that they abound in wealth
	15:63	and shall plunder your wealth

WEAPON 15 = 0.010 %

Jud	**6**:12	they caught up their weapons
	7:5	Then each man took up his weapons
	14:2	let every valiant man take his weapons and go out of the city
	14:11	and every man took his weapons
1 Ma	**6**:2	breastplates, and weapons
	9:39	to meet them with tambourines and musicians and many weapons
	14:42	and over the country and the weapons and the strongholds
	15:7	All the weapons which you have prepared
	16:16	Ptolemy and his men rose up, took their weapons
2 Ma	**3**:25	Its rider was seen to have armour and weapons of gold
	10:30	with their own armour and weapons
	11:8	clothed in white and brandishing weapons of gold
2 Es	**13**:9	nor held a spear or any weapon of war
	13:28	and as for his not holding a spear or weapon of war
4 Ma	**4**:10	angels on horseback with lightning flashing from their weapons appeared from heaven

WEAR 21 = 0.014 %

Jud	**8**:5	and wore the garments of her widowhood
	9:1	and uncovered the sackcloth she was wearing
	10:3	and she removed the sackcloth which she had been wearing
	10:3	which she used to wear while her husband Manasseh was living
	15:13	bearing their arms and wearing garlands
Ad E	**14**:16	and I do not wear it on the days when I am at leisure
Wis	**5**:18	and wear impartial justice as a helmet
Sir	**6**:31	You will wear her like a glorious robe
	11:4	Do not boast about wearing fine clothes
	11:5	but one who was never thought of has worn a crown
	27:8	and wear it as a glorious robe
	40:4	from the man who wears purple and a crown
L Jr	**6**:24	As for the gold which they wear for beauty
	6:58	and of the robes they wear
1 Ma	**8**:14	or worn purple as a mark of pride
	11:58	and dress in purple and wear a gold buckle
	14:43	and that he should be clothed in purple and wear gold
2 Ma	**4**:12	to wear the Greek hat
	6:7	in honour of Dionysus, wearing wreaths of ivy
	12:40	which the law forbids the Jews to wear
1 Es	**5**:40	until a high priest should appear wearing Urim and Thummim

WEAR out 3 = 0.002 %

Sir	**6**:36	let your foot wear out his doorstep
2 Es	**4**:11	And how can one who is already worn out by the corrupt world understand incorruption ?
4 Ma	**9**:12	When they had worn themselves out beating with scourges

WEARY, verb   3 = 0.002 %
Sir	22 : 13	and you will never be wearied by his madness
Bar	3 : 1	the soul in anguish and the wearied spirit cry out to thee
1 Ma	12 : 44	Why have you wearied all these people when we are not at war ?

WEARY, adj.   6 = 0.004 %
Jud	13 : 1	and they went to bed, for they all were weary
Sir	16 : 27	they neither hunger nor grow weary
	43 : 30	and do not grow weary, for you cannot praise him enough
2 Ma	12 : 36	As Esdris and his men had been fighting for a long time and were weary
2 Es	2 : 12	and they shall neither toil nor become weary
	12 : 5	Behold, I am still weary in mind

WEATHER   2
Sir	3 : 15	as frost in fair weather, your sins will melt away
1 Es	9 : 6	shivering because of the bad weather that prevailed

WEAVE   1
Jud	10 : 21	under a canopy which was woven with purple and gold

WEDDED   1
3 Ma	1 : 19	abandoned the bridal chambers prepared for wedded union

WEDDING   11 = 0.007 %
Tob	8 : 19	After this he gave a wedding feast for them
	8 : 20	until the 14 days of the wedding feast were ended
	9 : 2	and bring him to the wedding feast
	9 : 6	and came to the wedding feast
	10 : 7	until the 14 days of the wedding feast had expired
1 Ma	9 : 37	The sons of Jambri are celebrating a great wedding
	9 : 41	Thus, the wedding was turned into mourning
	10 : 58	and celebrated her wedding at Ptolemais with great pomp, as kings do
3 Ma	4 : 6	all together raising a lament instead of a wedding song
2 Es	10 : 1	But it happened that when my son entered his wedding chamber
	10 : 48	When my son entered his wedding chamber he died

WEDGE, subst.   2
4 Ma	8 : 13	braziers and thumbscrews an iron claws and wedges and bellows
	11 : 10	they twisted his back around the wedge on the wheel

WEDGE in   1
Sir	27 : 2	so sin is wedged in between selling and buying

WEED   1
4 Ma	1 : 29	each of which the master cultivator, reason, weeds and prunes

WEEK   4 = 0.003 %
Tob	2 : 1	which is the sacred festival of the 7 weeks
2 Ma	12 : 31	as the feast of weeks was close at hand
2 Es	6 : 35	in order to complete the 3 weeks
	7 : 43	For it will last for about a week of years

WEEP   35 = 0.023 %
Tob	2 : 6	And I wept
	3 : 1	Then in my grief I wept
	5 : 17	But Anna, his mother, began to weep
	5 : 21	So she stopped weeping
	7 : 6	Then Raguel sprang up and kissed him and wept
	7 : 7	he was stricken with grief and wept
	7 : 8	And his wife Edna and his daughter Sarah wept
	7 : 17	and the girl began to weep
	11 : 9	And they both wept
	11 : 14	Then he saw his son and embraced him, and he wept and said
Jud	14 : 16	and wept and groaned and shouted, and rent his garments
	16 : 17	they shall weep in pain for ever
Sir	7 : 34	Do not fail those who weep, but mourn with those who mourn
	12 : 16	an enemy will weep with his eyes
	22 : 11	Weep for the dead, for he lacks the light
	22 : 11	and weep for the fool, for he lacks intelligence
	22 : 11	weep less bitterly for the dead, for he has attained rest
Bar	1 : 5	Then they wept, and fasted, and prayed before the Lord
Sus	13 : 33	But her family and friends and all who saw her wept
	13 : 35	And she, weeping, looked up toward heaven
1 Ma	7 : 36	and they wept and said
	9 : 20	and wept for him
2 Ma	4 : 37	and filled with pity, and wept
1 Es	8 : 91	weeping and lying upon the ground before the temple
	9 : 50	now they were all weeping as they heard the law
3 Ma	6 : 23	he wept and angrily threatened his friends, saying
2 Es	2 : 27	others shall weep and be sorrowful
	5 : 13	and if you pray again, and weep as you do now
	5 : 20	So I fasted 7 days, mourning and weeping
	6 : 35	Now after this I wept again and fasted 7 days as before
	9 : 38	and behold, she was mourning and weeping with a loud voice
	9 : 40	Why are you weeping, and why are you grieved at heart ?
	9 : 41	that I may weep for myself and continue to mourn

	12 : 45	And they wept with a loud voice
4 Ma	15 : 19	nor did you weep when you looked at the eyes of each one

WEEPING   7 = 0.005 %
Sir	38 : 17	Let your weeping be bitter and your wailing fervent
Bar	4 : 11	but I sent them away with weeping and sorrow
	4 : 23	For I sent you out with sorrow and weeping
2 Ma	13 : 12	and had besought the merciful Lord with weeping and fasting
1 Es	5 : 63	with outcries and loud weeping
	5 : 65	because of the weeping of the people
	8 : 91	for there was great weeping among the multitude

WEIGH   12 = 0.008 %
Sir	21 : 25	but the words of the prudent will be weighed in the balance
	26 : 15	and no balance can weigh the value of a chaste soul
1 Ma	14 : 24	with a large gold shield weighing a 1,000 minas
	15 : 18	and have brought a gold shield weighing a 1,000 minas
2 Ma	9 : 8	and imagining that he could weigh the high mountains in a balance
1 Es	8 : 56	I weighed and gave to them 650 talents of silver
	8 : 62	the silver and the gold were weighed
	8 : 64	The whole was counted and weighed
2 Es	3 : 34	Now therefore weigh in a balance our iniquities
	4 : 5	And he said to me, Go, weigh for me the weight of fire
	4 : 36	for he has weighed the age in the balance
	7 : 59	Weigh within yourself what you have thought

WEIGH down   3 = 0.002 %
Wis	9 : 15	for a perishable body weighs down the soul
Sir	6 : 21	She will weigh him down like a heavy testing stone
	38 : 19	and the life of the poor man weighs down his heart

WEIGH out   1
1 Es	8 : 55	and I weighed out to them the silver and the gold

WEIGHT, subst.   8 = 0.005 %
Jud	7 : 4	nor the valleys nor the hills will bear their weight
Wis	11 : 20	by measure and number and weight
Sir	13 : 2	Do not lift a weight beyond your strength
	16 : 25	I will impart instruction by weight
	42 : 4	of accuracy with scales and weights
	42 : 7	Whatever you deal out, let it be by number and weight
1 Es	8 : 64	and the weight of everything was recorded at that very time
2 Es	4 : 5	And he said to me, Go, weigh for me the weight of fire

WEIGHT down   1
P Ma	10	I am weighted down with many an iron fetter

WEIGHTY   1
2 Es	13 : 56	and explain weighty and wondrous matters to you

WELCOME, adj., subst.   3 = 0.002 %
Tob	5 : 13	Then Tobit said to him, You are welcome, my brother
	11 : 17	he blessed her, saying, Welcome, daughter !
3 Ma	1 : 8	to greet him, to bring him gifts of welcome

WELCOME, verb   10 = 0.007 %
Jud	3 : 7	welcomed him with garlands and dances and tambourines
Sir	15 : 2	and like the wife of his youth she will welcome him
	35 : 20	Mercy is as welcome when he afflicts them
	41 : 2	O death, how welcome is your sentence
1 Ma	10 : 1	They welcomed him, and there he began to reign
	12 : 8	Onias welcomed the envoy with honour
2 Ma	3 : 9	and had been kindly welcomed by the high priest of the city
	4 : 22	He was welcomed magnificently by Jason and the city
	6 : 19	But he, welcoming death with honour
4 Ma	13 : 17	For if we so die, Abraham and Isaac and Jacob will welcome us

WELFARE   4 = 0.003 %
1 Ma	12 : 22	please write us concerning your welfare
2 Ma	4 : 5	but having in view the welfare, both public and private, of all the people
	11 : 19	I will endeavour for the future to help promote your welfare
	13 : 3	not for the sake of his country's welfare

WELL, adv., adj.   42 = 0.027 %
Tob	10 : 6	But Tobit said to her, Be still and stop worrying ; he is well
	14 : 9	and be merciful and just, so that it may be well with you
Jud	10 : 16	and he will treat you well
	11 : 4	No one will hurt you, but all will treat you well
	11 : 22	God has done well to send you before the people
	15 : 10	and God is well pleased with it
Ad E	16 : 17	You will therefore do well not to put in execution
Wis	8 : 1	and she orders all things well
	8 : 19	As a child I was by nature well endowed
Sir	1 : 13	With him who fears the Lord it will go well at the end
	10 : 1	and the rule of an understanding man will be well ordered
	14 : 11	My son, treat yourself well, according to your means
	17 : 28	he who is alive and well sings the Lord's praises
	30 : 14	who is well and strong in constitution

38:27	who labours by night as well as by day	
40:29	but a man who is intelligent and well instructed guards against that	
P Az **7**	as thou hast commanded us that it might go well with us	
1 Ma **8**:15	concerning the people, to govern them well	
8:23	May all go well with the Romans	
11:43	Now then you will do well to send me men who will help me	
12:45	I will hand it over to you as well as the other strongholds	
2 Ma **3**:1	and the laws were very well observed	
9:20	If you and your children are well	
10:18	well equipped to withstand a siege	
10:32	especially well garrisoned, where Chaereas was commander	
11:26	You will do well, therefore, to send word to them	
11:28	If you are well, it is as we desire	
12:2	as well as Hieronymus and Demophon	
12:31	to be well disposed to their race in the future also	
12:43	In doing this he acted very well and honourably	
14:37	and was very well thought of	
15:38	If it is well told and to the point	
3 Ma **3**:13	I myself and our government are faring well	
3:15	gladly treating them well	
4:11	and which was well suited to make them an obvious spectacle	
5:48	as well as by the trampling of the crowd	
7:2	We ourselves and our children are faring well	
2 Es **3**:35	Or what nation has kept thy commandments so well ?	
7:111	why will it not be so then as well ?	
8:58	though knowing full well that they must die	
9:36	as well as our heart which received it	
14:12	as well as half of the 13th part	

WELL, interj.   2
Sus **13**:55   And Daniel said, Very well !
13:59   And Daniel said to him, Very well !

WELL up   1
2 Es **3**:1   and my thoughts welled up in my heart

WELL-DISCIPLINED   1
Sir **31**:19   How ample a little is for a well-disciplined man !

WELL-DISPOSED   1
1 Ma **8**:1   that they were very strong and were well-disposed

WELL-DRAWN   1
Wis **5**:21   as from a well-drawn bow of clouds

WELL-ORDERED   1
Sir **26**:16   so is the beauty of a good wife in her well-ordered home

WELT   1
Sir **28**:17   The blow of a whip raises a welt

WEST, subst., adj.   8 = 0.005 %
Jud **1**:7   and to all who lived in the west
2:6   Go and attack the whole west country
2:19   and to cover the whole face of the earth to the west
5:4   And why have they alone, of all who live in the west
Bar **4**:37   they are coming, gathered from east and west
5:5   and see your children gathered from west and east
2 Es **15**:38   and from the north, and another part from the west
15:39   and shall be driven violently toward the south and west

WHALE   1
P Az **57**   Bless the Lord, you whales and all creatures that move in the waters

WHAT*   360 = 0.234 %

WHATEVER, indef. pr. or adj.   26 = 0.017 %
Tob **2**:2   Go and bring whatever poor man of our brethren you may find
Jud **3**:2   Do with us whatever you will
3:3   do with them whatever you please
12:14   Surely whatever pleases him I will do at once
Sir **2**:4   Accept whatever is brought upon you
39:16   and whatever he commands will be done in his time
39:18   At his command whatever pleases him is done
41:10   Whatever is from the dust returns to dust
42:7   Whatever you deal out, let it be by number and weight
L Jr **6**:44   Whatever is done for them is false
6:69   So we have no evidence whatever that they are gods
1 Ma **13**:39   and whatever other tax has been collected in Jerusalem
14:34   whatever was necessary for their restoration
2 Ma **11**:4   He took no account whatever of the power of God
13:20   Judas sent in to the garrison whatever was necessary
1 Es **4**:3   and whatever he says to them they obey
4:5   whatever spoil they take and everything else
8:16   And whatever you and your brethren are minded to do
8:18   And whatever else occurs to you as necessary
8:19   that whatever Ezra the priest
3 Ma **6**:10   and destroy us, Lord, by whatever fate you choose

7:7   of every charge of whatever kind
2 Es **12**:39   whatever it pleases the Most High to show you
13:58   and whatever things come to pass in their seasons
4 Ma **8**:14   and whatever justice you revere will be merciful to you
18:5   Since in no way whatever was he able to compel the Israelites

WHEAT   5 = 0.003 %
Jud **2**:27   during the wheat harvest
3:3   and all our wheat fields, and our flocks and herds
Sir **39**:26   and iron and salt and wheat flour and milk and honey
1 Es **6**:30   and likewise wheat and salt and wine and oil
8:20   and likewise up to a 100 cors of wheat

WHEEL, subst.   14 = 0.009 %
Sir **33**:5   The heart of a fool is like a cart wheel
38:29   and turning the wheel with his feet
4 Ma **5**:3   they were to be broken on the wheel and killed
5:32   Therefore get your torture wheels ready
8:13   wheels and joint-dislocators
9:12   without accomplishing anything, they placed him upon the wheel
9:17   your wheel is not so powerful as to strangle my reason
9:19   and while fanning the flames they tightened the wheel further
9:20   The wheel was completely smeared with blood
10:8   They immediately brought him to the wheel
11:10   they twisted his back around the wedge on the wheel
11:17   When he had said this, they led him to the wheel
12:11   and torture on the wheel those who practice religion ?
15:22   as her sons were tortured on the wheel and with the hot irons !

WHEEL, verb   1
2 Ma **10**:36   wheeled around against the defenders

WHEN, conj., adv.   703 = 0.458 %

WHENCE   1
4 Ma **13**:12   and another reminded them, Remember whence you came

WHENEVER, adv., conj.   4 = 0.003 %
Wis **12**:18   for thou hast power to act whenever thou dost choose
1 Es **1**:51   and whenever the Lord spoke, they scoffed at his prophets
4:6   but till the soil, whenever they sow, reap the harvest
2 Es **13**:4   and whenever his voice issued from his mouth

WHERE, adv., conj.   85 = 0.055 %
Tob **1**:4   where all the tribes should sacrifice
1:4   and where the temple of the dwelling of the Most High
2:13   So I said to her, Where did you get the kid ?
2:14   Where are your charities and your righteous deeds ?
7:3   And Raguel asked them, Where are you from, brethren ?
Jud **1**:6   and in the plain where Arioch ruled the Elymaeans
5:9   where they were living
5:19   and have occupied Jerusalem, where their sanctuary is
7:10   but on the height of the mountains where they live
7:13   for this is where all the people of Bethulia get their water
7:14   they will be strewn about in the streets where they live
9:8   and to pollute the tabernacle where thy glorious name rests
10:2   she rose from where she lay prostrate
10:12   and where are you coming from, and where are you going ?
12:1   where his silver dishes were kept
12:3   where can we get more like it for you ?
14:17   Then he went to the tent where Judith had stayed
Wis **19**:7   and dry land emerging where water had stood before
19:8   where those protected by thy hand passed through as one nation
Sir pr.   and to be indulgent in cases where
1:21   and where it abides, it will turn away all anger
8:16   and where no help is at hand, he will strike you down
19:22   nor is there prudence where sinners take counsel
19:27   but where no one notices, he will forestall you
23:21   and where he least suspects it, he will be seized
27:27   and he will not know where it came from
29:24   and where you are a stranger you may not open your mouth
32:4   Where there is entertainment, do not pour out talk
36:25   Where there is no fence, the property will be plundered
36:25   and where there is no wife, a man will wander about and sigh
41:19   and of theft, in the place where you live
42:6   Where there is an evil wife, a seal is a good thing
42:6   and where there are many hands, lock things up
43:28   Where shall we find strength to praise him ?
46:12   May their bones revive from where they lie
49:10   revive from where they lie
Bar **2**:4   where the Lord has scattered them
2:13   few in number, among the nations where thou hast scattered us
2:29   where I will scatter them
3:8   where thou hast scattered us
3:14   Learn where there is wisdom, where there is strength
3:14   where there is understanding
3:14   where there is length of days, and life
3:14   where there is light for the eyes, and peace
3:16   Where are the princes of the nations
L Jr **6**:48   as to where they can hide themselves and their gods

1 Ma	1:57	Where the book of the covenant was found
	3:50	Where shall we take them ?
	5:6	where he found a strong band
	5:49	that each should encamp where he was
	10:73	where there is no stone or pebble, or place to flee
	14:33	where formerly the arms of the enemy had been stored
	14:34	where the enemy formerly dwelt
2 Ma	1:19	where they took such Precautions
	1:33	that, in the place where the exiled priests had hidden the fire
	2:4	and that he went out to the mountain where Moses had gone up
	4:38	where he had committed the outrage against Onias
	10:19	where he was more urgently needed
	10:32	especially well garrisoned, where Chaereas was commander
	12:27	a fortified city where Lysias dwelt
	14:32	that they did not know where the man was whom he sought
1 Es	6:24	where they sacrifice with perpetual fire
	6:26	to be placed where they had been
3 Ma	1:1	where Antiochus's supporters were encamped
	4:1	In every place, then, where this decree arrived
2 Es	1:13	and made safe highways for you where there was no road
	1:17	Where are the benefits which I bestowed on you ?
	4:29	and if the place where the evil has been sown does not pass away
	4:29	the field where the good has been sown will not come
	5:16	came to me and said, Where have you been ?
	6:14	And if the place where you are standing is greatly shaken
	6:29	little by little the place where I was standing
	6:47	where the water had been gathered together
	6:50	for the 7th part where the water had been gathered together
	6:51	where there are a 1,000 mountains
	9:24	but go into a field of flowers where no house has been built
	10:28	Where is the angel Uriel, who came to me at first ?
	10:51	where no house had been built
	10:53	where there was no foundation of any building
	10:54	where the city of the Most High was to be revealed
	13:41	where mankind had never lived
	14:4	where I kept him with me many days
4 Ma	9:18	where virtue is concerned

WHEREAS
$4 = 0.003 \%$

Wis	16:23	whereas the fire, in order that the righteous might be fed
Sir pr.		Whereas many great teachings have been given to us
1 Ma	15:3	Whereas certain pestilent men
2 Es	7:51	For whereas you have said that the righteous are not many but few

WHEREIN
1

Wis	12:2	and dost remind and warn them of the things wherein they sin

WHEREVER
$7 = 0.005 \%$

Jud	8:22	wherever we serve as slaves
Sir	36:26	and lodges wherever night finds him ?
1 Ma	5:63	wherever their name was heard
	6:36	These took their position beforehand wherever the beast was
	6:36	wherever it went they went with it, and they never left it
1 Es	2:6	and let each man, wherever he may live
2 Es	13:3	and wherever he turned his face to look

WHETHER
$23 = 0.015 \%$

Tob	5:8	and whether he is a reliable man to go with you
	8:12	Send one of the maids to see whether he is alive
Wis	11:11	Whether absent or present, they were equally distressed
	14:23	For whether they kill children in their initiations
	17:17	for whether he was a farmer or a shepherd
	17:18	Whether there came a whistling wind
Sir	26:4	Whether rich or poor, his heart is glad
	41:4	Whether life is for 10 or a 100 or a 1,000 years
L Jr	6:34	Whether one does evil to them or good
1 Ma	4:10	to see whether he will favour us
2 Ma	3:9	and he inquired whether this really was the situation
	6:26	yet whether I live or die
1 Es	8:24	whether by death or some other punishment
3 Ma	1:15	whether they wish it or not ?
2 Es	4:45	show me this also : whether more time is to come than has passed
	4:45	or whether for us the greater part has gone by
	7:75	show this also to thy servant : whether after death
	7:75	or whether we shall be tormented at once ?
	7:102	whether on the day of judgment
4 Ma	1:1	that is, whether devout reason is sovereign over the emotions
	1:13	is whether reason is sovereign over the emotions
	1:14	and whether reason rules over all these
	11:13	whether he was willing to eat and be released

WHICH*
$477 = 0.311 \%$

WHICHEVER
2

Sir	15:16	stretch out your hand for whichever you wish
	15:17	and whichever he chooses will be given to him

WHILE, conj., subst.
$117 = 0.076 \%$

Tob	1:4	while I was still a young man
	4:4	while you were yet unborn
Jud	8:17	Therefore, while we wait for his deliverance
	8:26	while he was keeping the sheep of Laban
	10:3	which she used to wear while her husband Manasseh was living
	10:18	while they told him about her
	15:13	while all the men of Israel followed
Ad E	15:4	while the other followed carrying her train
Wis	4:4	For even if they put forth boughs for a while
	4:10	and while living among sinners he was taken up
	7:27	and while remaining in herself, she renews all things
	12:22	So while chastening us
	13:1	while paying heed to his works
	13:6	for perhaps they go astray while seeking God
	15:8	and after a little while goes to the earth
	16:3	while thy people, after suffering want a short time
	16:4	while to these it was merely shown
	16:6	they were troubled for a little while as a warning
	17:21	while over those men alone heavy night was spread
	18:14	For while gentle silence enveloped all things
	18:16	and touched heaven while standing on the earth
	19:3	For while they were still busy at mourning
	19:18	while each note remains the same
Sir	6:19	For in her service you will toil a little while
	10:30	while a rich man is honoured for his wealth
	12:17	and while pretending to help you, he will trip you by the heel
	13:11	and while he smiles he will be examining you
	20:5	while another is detested for being too talkative
	20:6	while another keeps silent because he knows when to speak
	30:5	while alive he saw and rejoiced
	30:12	and beat his sides while he is young
	33:20	While you are still alive and have breath in you
	37:27	My son, test your soul while you live
	42:10	while a virgin, lest she be defiled
	47:10	while they praised God's holy name
	51:13	While I was still young, before I went on my travels
Sus	13:15	Once, while they were watching for an opportune day
1 Ma	1:6	and divided his kingdom among them while he was still alive
	4:4	while the division was still absent from the camp
	5:14	While the letter was still being read
	5:55	Now while Judas and Jonathan were in Gilead
	6:38	while being themselves protected by the phalanxes
	6:55	whom King Antiochus while still living
	9:65	while he went out into the country
	12:47	while a 1,000 accompanied him
2 Ma	1:23	And while the sacrifice was being consumed
	2:22	while the Lord with great kindness became gracious to them
	2:28	while devoting our effort
	2:29	while the one who undertakes its painting and decoration
	2:32	while cutting short the history itself
	3:1	While the holy city was inhabited in unbroken peace
	3:19	while others peered out of the windows
	3:22	While they were calling upon the Almighty Lord
	3:29	While he lay prostrate
	3:30	And the temple, which a little while before
	3:33	While the high priest was making the offering of atonement
	4:29	while Sostratus left Crates
	4:30	While such was the state of affairs
	4:47	while he sentenced to death those unfortunate men
	5:17	that the Lord was angered for a little while
	6:25	while I defile and disgrace my old age
	7:4	while the rest of the brothers and the mother looked on
	7:30	While she was still speaking, the young man said
	7:33	And if our living Lord is angry for a little while
	8:33	While they were celebrating the victory
	9:3	While he was in Ecbatana, news came to him
	9:9	and while he was still living in anguish and pain
	9:10	no one was able to carry the man who a little while before
	10:28	while the other made rage their leader in the fight
	11:8	And there, while they were still near Jerusalem
	14:31	while the priests were offering the customary sacrifices
	15:39	while wine mixed with water is sweet and delicious
1 Es	5:64	while many came with trumpets and a joyful noise
	7:3	while the prophets Haggai and Zechariah prophesied
	8:91	While Ezra was praying and making his confession
3 Ma	1:25	while the elders near the king tried in various ways
	2:24	After a while he recovered and, though he had been punished
	3:2	While these matters were being arranged
	5:19	pointed out that while it was still night
	5:26	and while the king was receiving his friends
2 Es	5:34	while I strive to understand the way of the Most High
	6:15	while the voice is speaking, do not be terrified
	6:29	While he spoke to me, behold
	7:18	while hoping for easier ones
	7:51	while the ungodly abound
	7:87	before whom they sinned while they were alive
	7:94	that while they were alive
	7:126	For while we lived and committed iniquity
	7:129	For this is the way of which Moses, while he was alive

9:11	and as many as scorned my law while they still had freedom
9:11	while an opportunity of repentance was still open to them
10:25	While I was talking to her, behold
10:25	While I was wondering what this meant
10:41	The woman who appeared to you a little while ago
11:13	And while it was reigning it came to its end and disappeared
11:14	And while it was reigning its end came also
11:29	and while they were planning, behold
12:1	While the lion was saying these words to the eagle, I looked
14:1	On the 3rd day, while I was sitting under an oak
16:5	For behold, just a little while

4 Ma 4:9 | While the priests together with women and children
4:10 | and while Apollonius was going up
6:4 | while a herald opposite him cried out
6:6 | yet while the old man's eyes were raised to heaven
6:10 | And like a noble athlete the old man, while being beaten
6:20 | It would be shameful if we should survive for a little while
9:6 | lived piously while enduring torture
9:19 | While he was saying these things they spread fire under him
9:19 | and while fanning the flames they tightened the wheel further
9:26 | While all were marvelling at his courageous spirit
10:8 | and while his vertebrae were being dislocated upon it
11:9 | While he was saying these things
11:20 | While being tortured he said
13:11 | While one said, Courage, brothers
13:27 | while watching their brothers being maltreated
16:17 | while an aged man endures such agonies for the sake of religion
18:10 | While he was still with you

WHIP, subst.   3 = 0.002 %

Sir 23:2 | O that whips were set over my thoughts
28:17 | The blow of a whip raises a welt
2 Ma 7:1 | under torture with whips and cords

WHIP, verb   2

Sir 30:1 | He who loves his son will whip him often
42:5 | and of whipping a wicked servant severely

WHIRLWIND   3 = 0.002 %

Sir 43:17 | so do the tempest from the north and the whirlwind
48:9 | You who were taken up by a whirlwind of fire
48:12 | It was Elijah who was covered by the whirlwind

WHISPER   1

Sir 12:18 | and whisper much, and change his expression

WHISPERER   2

Sir 21:28 | A whisperer defiles his own soul
28:13 | Curse the whisperer and deceiver

WHISTLING   2

Wis 17:18 | Whether there came a whistling wind
P Az 27 | and made the midst of the furnace like a moist whistling wind

WHITE, adj. subst.   7 = 0.005 %

Tob 2:10 | and white films formed on my eyes
3:17 | to scale away the white films from Tobit's eyes
6:8 | anoint with it a man who has white films in his eyes
11:8 | and will cause the white films to fall away
11:13 | and the white films scaled off from the corners of his eyes
2 Ma 11:8 | clothed in white and brandishing weapons of gold
2 Es 2:40 | and conclude the list of your people who are clothed in white

WHITENESS   1

Sir 43:18 | The eye marvels at the beauty of its whiteness

WHO, rel. or interr. pr.   1413 = 0.920 %

WHOEVER   38 = 0.025 %

Wis 3:11 | for whoever despises wisdom and instruction is miserable
17:16 | And whoever was there fell down
Sir 3:3 | Whoever honours his father atones for sins
3:4 | and whoever glorifies his mother
3:5 | Whoever honours his father
3:6 | Whoever glorifies his father will have long life
3:6 | and whoever obeys the Lord will refresh his mother
3:16 | Whoever forsakes his father is like a blasphemer
3:16 | and whoever angers his mother is cursed by the Lord
3:26 | and whoever loves danger will perish by it
3:31 | Whoever requites favours gives thought to the future
4:12 | Whoever loves her loves life
4:13 | Whoever holds her fast will obtain glory
4:15 | Whoever gives heed to her will dwell secure
6:17 | Whoever fears the Lord directs his friendship aright
13:1 | Whoever touches pitch will be defiled
13:1 | and whoever associates with a proud man will become like him
14:4 | Whoever accumulates by depriving himself
20:8 | Whoever uses too many words will be loathed
20:8 | and whoever usurps the right to speak will be hated
20:28 | Whoever cultivates the soil will heap up his harvest

20:28	and whoever pleases great men will atone for injustice
21:6	Whoever hates reproof walks in the steps of the sinner
21:11	Whoever keeps the law controls his thoughts
22:26	whoever hears of it will beware of him
24:22	Whoever obeys me will not be put to shame
27:1	and whoever seeks to get rich will avert his eyes
27:16	Whoever betrays secrets destroys confidence
27:21	but whoever has betrayed secrets is without hope
27:22	Whoever winks his eye plans evil deeds
27:25	Whoever throws a stone straight up throws it on his own head
28:16	Whoever pays heed to slander will not find rest
34:21	whoever deprives them of it is a man of blood

1 Ma 1:50 | And whoever does not obey the command of the king shall die
10:43 | And whoever takes refuge at the temple in Jerusalem
14:45 | Whoever acts contrary to these decisions
3 Ma 3:27 | But whoever shelters any of the Jews
2 Es 6:25 | And it shall be that whoever remains

WHOLE, adj. subst.   103 = 0.067 %

Tob 1:4 | the whole tribe of Naphtali my forefather
Jud 1:9 | and Tahpannes and Raamses and the whole land of Goshen
1:11 | But all who lived in the whole region
1:12 | Then Nebuchadnezzar was very angry with this whole region
1:12 | on the whole territory of Cilicia and Damascus and Syria
1:13 | and overthrew the whole army of Arphaxad
2:1 | about carrying out his revenge on the whole region
2:5 | Thus says the Great King, the Lord of the whole earth :
2:6 | Go and attack the whole west country
2:7 | and will cover the whole face of the earth
2:9 | to the ends of the whole earth
2:11 | throughout your whole region
2:19 | So he set out with his whole army
2:19 | and to cover the whole face of the earth to the west
2:22 | From there Holofernes took his whole army
3:10 | and remained for a whole month
4:8 | and the senate of the whole people of Israel
4:15 | to look with favour upon the whole house of Israel
5:12 | and he afflicted the whole house of Egypt
5:21 | and we shall be put to shame before the whole world
6:4 | So says King Nebuchadnezzar, the lord of the whole earth
7:1 | The next day Holofernes ordered his whole army
7:4 | These men will now lick up the face of the whole land
7:18 | and covered the whole face of the land
7:20 | The whole Assyrian army
7:26 | Now call them in and surrender the whole city
9:14 | And cause thy whole nation and every tribe
10:18 | There was great excitement in the whole camp
10:19 | they will be able to ensnare the whole world !
11:7 | Nebuchadnezzar the king of the whole earth lives
11:8 | and it is reported throughout the whole world
11:8 | that you are the one good man in the whole kingdom
11:16 | things that will astonish the whole world
11:18 | and then you shall go out with your whole army
11:23 | and be renowned throughout the whole world
16:21 | and was honoured in her time throughout the whole country
Ad E 11:9 | And the whole righteous nation was troubled
13:2 | and master of the whole world
16:13 | together with their whole nation
Wis 5:17 | The Lord will take his zeal as his whole armour
5:23 | Lawlessness will lay waste the whole earth
8:21 | and with my whole heart I said :
11:22 | Because the whole world before thee
17:20 | For the whole world was illumined with brilliant light
18:24 | For upon his long robe the whole world was depicted
19:6 | For the whole creation in its nature was fashioned anew
Sir 1:17 | she fills their whole house with desirable goods
16:16 | His mercy is manifest to the whole of creation
17:17 | For in the division of the nations of the whole earth
18:1 | He who lives for ever created the whole universe
24:6 | In the waves of the sea, in the whole earth
26:20 | Seek a fertile field within the whole plain
50:13 | before the whole congregation of Israel
50:20 | over the whole congregation of the sons of Israel
Bar 2:2 | Under the whole heaven there has not been done
2:23 | and the whole land will be a desolation without inhabitants
3:36 | He found the whole way to knowledge
L Jr 6:62 | When God commands the clouds to go over the whole world
P Az 22 | glorious over the whole world
Bel 14:14 | and they sifted them throughout the whole temple
1 Ma 1:41 | Then the king wrote to his whole kingdom
1:51 | In such words he wrote to his whole kingdom
5:43 | and the whole army followed him
8:4 | and how they had gained control of the whole region
2 Ma 2:10 | and consumed the whole burnt offerings
2:21 | so that though few in number they seized the whole land
2:29 | must be concerned with the whole construction
3:12 | which is honoured throughout the whole world
3:14 | There was no little distress throughout the whole city
3:21 | in the prostration of the whole populace
4:38 | and led him about the whole city to that very place

	7 : 38	which has justly fallen on our whole nation
	7 : 40	putting his whole trust in the Lord
	8 : 9	to wipe out the whole race of Judea
	8 : 18	and even the whole world
	9 : 9	the whole army felt revulsion at his decay
	10 : 8	that the whole nation of the Jews
	12 : 7	and root out the whole community of Joppa
	14 : 8	our whole nation is now in no small misfortune
	15 : 12	for the whole body of the Jews
1 Es	1 : 32	throughout the whole nation of Israel
	4 : 36	The whole earth calls upon truth, and heaven blesses her
	8 : 64	The whole was counted and weighed
	9 : 38	the whole multitude gathered with one accord
3 Ma	1 : 29	but also the walls and the whole earth around echoed
	2 : 7	the Ruler over the whole creation
	4 : 10	during the whole voyage
	5 : 5	convinced that the whole nation would experience its final destruction
	5 : 30	his whole mind had been deranged in regard to these matters
	6 : 5	who had already gained control of the whole world by the spear
	6 : 14	The whole throng of infants and their parents entreat you with tears
	6 : 36	in their whole community and for their descendants
	7 : 13	their priests and the whole multitude
2 Es	10 : 8	you are sorrowing for one son, but we, the whole world, for our mother
	11 : 32	Moreover this head gained control of the whole earth
	11 : 45	and your whole worthless body
	11 : 46	so that the whole earth, freed from your violence
	12 : 3	and the whole body of the eagle was burned
	15 : 27	For now calamities have come upon the whole earth
4 Ma	3 : 8	around which the whole army of our ancestors had encamped
	7 : 18	But as many as attend to religion with a whole heart
	7 : 21	by the whole rule of philosophy
	16 : 13	to the whole number of her sons

WHOLEHEARTEDLY 1
1 Ma	8 : 25	shall act as their allies wholeheartedly

WHOLESOME 1
Wis	1 : 14	and the generative forces of the world are wholesome

WHOLLY 5 = 0.003 %
Sir	45 : 14	His sacrifices shall be wholly burned
	46 : 6	for he wholly followed the Mighty One
P Az	17	and may we wholly follow thee
2 Ma	8 : 29	to be wholly reconciled with his servants
	12 : 42	might be wholly blotted out

WHOM* 104 = 0.068 %

WHOMEVER 2
Tob	4 : 19	and according to his will he humbles whomever he wishes
3 Ma	5 : 11	is bestowed by him who grants it to whomever he wishes

WHOSE 58 = 0.038 %

WHY, adv., conj. 79 = 0.051 %
Tob	3 : 9	Why do you beat us ? If they are dead, go with them !
	3 : 15	Why should I live ?
	4 : 2	Why do I not call my son Tobias
	5 : 17	and said to Tobit, Why have you sent our child away ?
Jud	5 : 4	And why have they alone, of all who live in the west
	8 : 19	and that was why our fathers were handed over to the sword
	11 : 3	And now tell me why you have fled from them
Wis	5 : 5	Why has he been numbered among the sons of God ?
	5 : 5	And why is his lot among the saints ?
	18 : 18	made known why they were dying
	18 : 19	without knowing why they suffered
Sir	23 : 18	Why should I fear ?
	33 : 7	Why is any day better than another
	37 : 3	O evil imagination, why were you formed to cover the land with deceit ?
	39 : 17	No one can say, What is this ? Why is that ?
	39 : 21	No one can say, What is this ? Why is that ?
	51 : 24	Why do you say you are lacking in these things
	51 : 24	and why are your souls very thirsty ?
Bar	3 : 10	Why is it, O Israel
	3 : 10	why is it that you are in the land of your enemies
L Jr	6 : 30	For why should they be called gods
	6 : 40	Why then must any one think that they are gods
	6 : 44	Why then must any one think that they are gods
	6 : 56	Why then must any one admit or think that they are gods ?
Sus	13 : 21	and this was why you sent your maids away
Bel	14 : 5	And the king said to him, Why do you not worship Bel ?
1 Ma	2 : 7	and said, Alas ! Why was I born to see this
	2 : 13	Why should we live any longer ?
	8 : 31	Why have you made your yoke heavy
	10 : 70	Why do you assume authority against us in the hill country ?
	12 : 44	Why have you wearied all these people when we are not at war ?

	12 : 45	For that is why I am here
2 Ma	3 : 9	and stated why he had come
	12 : 40	that this was why these men had fallen
1 Es	2 : 23	That is why this city was laid waste
	4 : 12	Gentlemen, why is not the king the strongest
	4 : 32	Gentlemen, why are not women strong
3 Ma	1 : 13	And he inquired why, when he entered every other temple
	1 : 15	Why should not I at least enter
	5 : 18	why the Jews had been allowed to remain alive
2 Es	1 : 18	Why hast thou led us into the wilderness to kill us ?
	3 : 28	Is that why she has gained dominion over Zion ?
	4 : 4	and will teach you why the heart is evil
	4 : 12	and to suffer and not understand why
	4 : 20	but why have you not judged so in your own case ?
	4 : 22	why have I been endowed with the power of understanding ?
	4 : 23	why Israel has been given over to the Gentiles as a reproach
	4 : 23	why the people whom you loved
	4 : 24	and why we pass from the world like locusts
	4 : 33	Why are our years few and evil ?
	5 : 16	And why is your face sad ?
	5 : 28	And now, O Lord, why hast thou given over the one to the many
	5 : 35	And I said, Why not, my lord ?
	5 : 35	Why then was I born ?
	5 : 35	Or why did not my mother's womb become my grave
	5 : 46	why one after another ?
	5 : 52	Say to her, Why are those whom you have borne recently
	6 : 59	why do we not possess our world as an inheritance ?
	7 : 15	But now why are you disturbed, seeing that you are to perish ?
	7 : 15	And why are you moved, seeing that you are mortal ?
	7 : 16	And why have you not considered in your mind what is to come
	7 : 111	why will it not be so then as well ?
	9 : 40	Why are you weeping, and why are you grieved at heart ?
	10 : 31	What is the matter with you ? And why are you troubled ?
	10 : 31	And why are your understanding
	13 : 51	Why did I see the man coming up from the heart of the sea ?
4 Ma	1 : 5	why is it not sovereign over forgetfulness and ignorance ?
	2 : 1	And why is it amazing that
	2 : 19	Why else did Jacob, our most wise father
	5 : 8	Why, when nature has granted it to us, should you abhor eating
	6 : 14	Eleazar, why are you so irrationally destroying yourself
	6 : 23	And you, guards of the tyrant, why do you delay ?
	8 : 1	For this is why even the very young
	8 : 18	why do we take pleasure in vain resolves
	8 : 23	Why do we banish ourselves from this most pleasant life
	8 : 26	Why does such contentiousness excite us
	9 : 1	Why do you delay, O tyrant ?
	14 : 18	And why is it necessary to demonstrate sympathy for children

WICKED, adj., subst. 35 = 0.023 %
Jud	8 : 9	When Judith heard the wicked words
Ad E	14 : 15	and thou knowest that I hate the splendour of the wicked
Wis	3 : 14	and who has not devised wicked things against the Lord
	10 : 5	Wisdom also, when the nations in wicked agreement had been confounded
	11 : 15	In return for their foolish and wicked thoughts
	14 : 29	they swear wicked oaths and expect to suffer no harm
	19 : 13	for they justly suffered because of their wicked acts
Sir	20 : 18	so the downfall of the wicked will occur speedily
	21 : 9	An assembly of the wicked is like tow gathered together
	33 : 26	and for a wicked servant there are racks and tortures
	39 : 24	just as they are obstacles to the wicked
	40 : 10	All these were created for the wicked
	42 : 5	and of whipping a wicked servant severely
	46 : 7	and stilled their wicked murmuring
	49 : 3	in the days of wicked men he strengthened godliness
Bar	1 : 21	but we each followed the intent of his own wicked heart
	2 : 8	by turning away, each of us, from the thoughts of his wicked heart
	2 : 33	and will turn from their stubbornness and their wicked deeds
P Az	9	the most wicked in all the world
Sus	13 : 28	full of their wicked plot to have Susanna put to death
	13 : 32	As she was veiled, the wicked men ordered her to be unveiled
	13 : 52	You old relic of wicked days, your sins have now come home
1 Ma	7 : 25	and brought wicked charges against them
	13 : 46	they said, Do not treat us according to our wicked acts
	14 : 14	and did away with every lawless and wicked man
2 Ma	10 : 34	blasphemed terribly and hurled out wicked words
1 Es	2 : 18	and are building that rebellious and wicked city
	2 : 29	and that such wicked proceedings go no further
	4 : 39	instead of anything that is unrighteous or wicked
3 Ma	3 : 16	and went up to honour the temple of those wicked people
2 Es	2 : 8	O wicked nation, remember what I did to Sodom and Gomorrah
	7 : 23	and proposed to themselves wicked frauds
	7 : 122	but we have walked in the most wicked ways ?
	15 : 8	neither will I tolerate their wicked practices
4 Ma	12 : 11	he said, You profane tyrant, most impious of all the wicked

WICKEDLY 14 = 0.009 %
Ad E	16 : 7	What has been wickedly accomplished
Wis	14 : 30	because they thought wickedly of God

Sus	13:43	that they have wickedly invented against me !
	13:62	and they did to them as they had wickedly planned to do
1 Ma	7:42	let the rest learn that Nicanor has spoken wickedly
2 Ma	8:16	who were wickedly coming against them
1 Es	1:24	concerning those who sinned and acted wickedly toward the Lord
2 Es	3:30	and hast spared those who act wickedly
	7:18	but those who have done wickedly
	7:121	but we have lived wickedly ?
	8:27	Regard not the endeavours of those who act wickedly
	8:28	Think not on those who have lived wickedly in thy sight
	8:35	who has not acted wickedly
4 Ma	2:13	so that one rebukes friends when they act wickedly

WICKEDNESS   34 = 0.022 %

Jud	2:2	all the wickedness of the region
Wis	2:21	for their wickedness blinded them
	4:12	For the fascination of wickedness obscures what is good
	4:14	therefore he took him quickly from the midst of wickedness
	5:13	but were consumed in our wickedness
	10:7	Evidence of their wickedness still remains :
	12:2	that they may be freed from wickedness
	12:10	and their wickedness inborn
	12:20	to give up their wickedness
	16:14	A man in his wickedness kills another
	17:11	For wickedness is a cowardly thing
Sir	3:28	for a plant of wickedness has taken root in him
	12:10	for like the rusting of copper, so is his wickedness
	19:5	One who rejoices in wickedness will be condemned
	19:22	But the knowledge of wickedness is not wisdom
	25:13	Any wickedness, but not the wickedness of a wife !
	25:17	The wickedness of a wife changes her appearance
	29:7	Because of such wickedness, therefore
	35:3	To keep from wickedness is pleasing to the Lord
	42:13	and from a woman comes woman's wickedness
	42:14	Better is the wickedness of a man
	46:20	to blot out the wickedness of the people
	47:25	For they sought out every sort of wickedness
Bar	2:26	because of the wickedness of the house of Israel
Sus	13:38	and we saw this wickedness we ran to them
	13:57	but a daughter of Judah would not endure your wickedness
1 Ma	5:4	He also remembered the wickedness of the sons of Baean
	7:42	and judge him according to this wickedness
2 Ma	3:1	and his hatred of wickedness
	4:13	because of the surpassing wickedness of Jason
	4:50	remained in office, growing in wickedness
2 Es	12:25	For it is they who shall sum up his wickedness
	12:32	and for their wickedness

WIDE   7 = 0.005 %

Jud	1:2	he made the walls 70 cubits high and 50 cubits wide
	1:3	a 100 cubits high and 60 cubits wide at the foundations
	1:4	which were 70 cubits high and 40 cubits wide
	4:7	only wide enough for 2 men at the most
Wis	8:8	And if any one longs for wide experience
2 Ma	12:16	so that the adjoining lake, a quarter of a mile wide
2 Es	7:3	There is a sea set in a wide expanse

WIDELY   3 = 0.002 %

L Jr	6:61	So also the lightning, when it flashes, is widely seen
2 Ma	7:5	The smoke from the pan spread widely
2 Es	3:33	For I have travelled widely among the nations

WIDESPREADING   1

Wis	17:18	or a melodious sound of birds in widespreading branches

WIDOW   19 = 0.012 %

Jud	8:4	Judith had lived at home as a widow
	9:4	O God, my God, hear me also, a widow
	9:9	give to me, a widow, the strength to do what I plan
	10:3	and took off her widow's garments
	16:8	For she took off her widow's mourning
	16:22	but she remained a widow all the days of her life
Wis	2:10	let us not spare the widow
Sir	35:14	nor the widow when she pours out her story
	35:15	Do not the tears of the widow run down her cheek
Bar	4:12	Let no one rejoice over me, a widow and bereaved of many
	4:16	They led away the widow's beloved sons
L Jr	6:38	They cannot take pity on a widow
2 Ma	3:10	belonging to widows and orphans
	8:28	and to the widows and orphans
	8:30	and to the orphans and widows, and also to the aged
2 Es	2:2	Go, my children, because I am a widow and forsaken
	2:4	For I am a widow and forsaken
	2:20	Guard the rights of the widow
4 Ma	16:10	am a widow and alone, with many sorrows

WIDOWED   1

2 Es	16:44	and them that do not marry, like those who are widowed

WIDOWHOOD   3 = 0.002 %

Jud	8:5	and wore the garments of her widowhood
	8:6	She fasted all the days of her widowhood
2 Es	15:49	I will send evils upon you, widowhood, poverty

WIELD   2

2 Es	11:19	they wielded power one after another
4 Ma	16:20	wielding a sword and descending upon him

WIFE   109 = 0.071 %

Tob	1:20	and nothing was left to me except my wife Anna
	2:1	and my wife Anna and my son Tobias were restored to me
	2:11	Then my wife Anna earned money at women's work
	3:8	before he had been with her as his wife
	3:15	for whom I should keep myself as wife
	4:12	First of all take a wife
	4:12	all took wives from among their brethren
	4:13	by refusing to take a wife for yourself from among them
	6:15	to take a wife from among your own people ?
	6:15	Now listen to me, brother, for she will become your wife
	7:2	Then Raguel said to his wife Edna
	7:8	And his wife Edna and his daughter Sarah wept
	7:13	he gave her to Tobias to be his wife, saying, Here she is
	7:14	Next he called his wife Edna
	7:16	And Raguel called his wife Edna and said to her
	8:6	and gavest him Eve his wife as a helper and support
	8:12	and said to his wife Edna
	8:21	and that the rest would be his when my wife and I die
	9:6	And Gabael blessed Tobias and his wife
	10:4	And his wife said to him, The lad has perished
	10:10	So Raguel arose and gave him his wife Sarah
	11:1	And he blessed Raguel and his wife Edna
	11:3	Let us run ahead of your wife and prepare the house
	12:3	he cured my wife, he obtained the money for me
	14:12	Then Tobias returned with his wife and his sons to Ecbatana
Jud	4:10	They and their wives and their children and their cattle
	4:12	and their wives as booty
	7:14	They and their wives and children
	7:27	or see our wives and children draw their last breath
	9:4	and thou gavest their wives for a prey
Ad E	13:6	shall all, with their wives and children
Wis	3:12	Their wives are foolish, and their children evil
Sir	7:19	Do not deprive yourself of a wise and good wife
	7:26	If you have a wife who pleases you, do not cast her out
	9:1	Do not be jealous of the wife of your bosom
	9:9	Never dine with another man's wife
	15:2	and like the wife of his youth she will welcome him
	25:1	and a wife and husband who live in harmony
	25:8	happy is he who lives with an intelligent wife
	25:13	Any wickedness, but not the wickedness of a wife !
	25:16	than dwell with an evil wife
	25:17	The wickedness of a wife changes her appearance
	25:19	Any iniquity is insignificant compared to a wife's iniquity
	25:20	such is a garrulous wife for a quiet husband
	25:22	when a wife supports her husband
	25:23	are caused by an evil wife
	25:23	are caused by the wife who does not make her husband happy
	25:25	and no boldness of speech in an evil wife
	26:1	Happy is the husband of a good wife
	26:2	A loyal wife rejoices her husband
	26:3	A good wife is a great blessing
	26:6	when a wife is envious of a rival
	26:7	An evil wife is an ox yoke which chafes
	26:8	There is great anger when a wife is drunken
	26:9	A wife's harlotry shows in her lustful eyes
	26:13	A wife's charm delights her husband
	26:14	A silent wife is a gift of the Lord
	26:15	A modest wife adds charm to charm
	26:16	so is the beauty of a good wife in her well-ordered home
	26:23	A godless wife is given as a portion to a lawless man
	26:23	but a pious wife is given to the man who fears the Lord
	26:25	A headstrong wife is regarded as a dog
	26:26	A wife honouring her husband will seem wise to all
	26:26	Happy is the husband of a good wife
	26:27	A loud-voiced and garrulous wife
	33:19	To son or wife, to brother or friend
	36:24	He who acquires a wife gets his best possession
	36:25	and where there is no wife, a man will wander about and sigh
	40:19	but a blameless wife is accounted better than both
	40:23	but a wife with her husband is better than both
	41:21	and of gazing at another man's wife
	42:6	Where there is an evil wife, a seal is a good thing
L Jr	6:28	and likewise their wives preserve some with salt
	6:33	to clothe their wives and children
Sus	13:2	And he took a wife named Susanna, the daughter of Hilkiah
	13:29	who is the wife of Joakim
	13:63	And Hilkiah and his wife praised God for their daughter Susanna
Bel	14:10	besides their wives and children
	14:15	In the night the priests came with their wives and children

	14 : 21	and he seized the priests and their wives and children
1 Ma	**2** : 30	they, their sons, their wives, and their cattle
	2 : 38	and they died, with their wives and children and cattle
	3 : 20	to destroy us and our wives and our children
	5 : 13	the enemy have captured their wives and children and goods
	5 : 23	with their wives and children, and all they possessed
	5 : 45	with their wives and children and goods
	8 : 10	and the Romans took captive their wives and children
	10 : 54	give me now your daughter as my wife
	11 : 9	who was Alexander's wife
	13 : 6	and your wives and children
	13 : 45	The men in the city, with their wives and children
2 Ma	**12** : 3	to embark, with their wives and children
	15 : 18	Their concern for wives and children
1 Es	**4** : 20	and his own country, and cleaves to his wife
	4 : 21	With his wife he ends his days
	4 : 25	A man loves his wife more than his father or his mother
	5 : 1	with their wives and sons and daughters
	8 : 93	that we will put away all our foreign wives
	9 : 9	and from your foreign wives
	9 : 12	and let all those in our settlements who have foreign wives
	9 : 17	And the cases of the men who had foreign wives
	9 : 18	and found to have foreign wives were :
	9 : 20	They pledged themselves to put away their wives
3 Ma	**1** : 4	to defend themselves and their children and wives bravely
	3 : 25	together with their wives and children
2 Es	**9** : 47	So when he grew up and I came to take a wife for him
	10 : 22	and our wives have been ravished
4 Ma	**2** : 5	Thus the law says, You shall not covet your neighbour's wife
	2 : 11	It is superior to love for one's wife

WILD   18 = 0.012 %

Wis	**7** : 20	the natures of animals and the tempers of wild beasts
	12 : 9	by dread wild beasts or thy stern word
	16 : 5	For when the terrible rage of wild beasts
Sir	**10** : 11	and wild beasts, and worms
	12 : 13	or any who go near wild beasts ?
	13 : 19	Wild asses in the wilderness are the prey of lions
	39 : 30	the teeth of wild beasts, and scorpions and vipers
L Jr	**6** : 68	The wild beasts are better than they are
2 Ma	**4** : 25	and the rage of a savage wild beast
	4 : 41	and threw them in wild confusion at Lysimachus and his men
	5 : 27	as wild animals do
	5 : 27	they continued to live on what grew wild
	10 : 6	like wild animals
	11 : 9	ready to assail not only men but the wildest beasts or walls of iron
3 Ma	**4** : 9	They were brought on board like wild animals
	6 : 7	was cast down into the ground to lions as food for wild beasts
2 Es	**5** : 8	and the wild beasts shall roam beyond their haunts
	15 : 30	shall go forth like wild boars of the forest

WILDERNESS   22 = 0.014 %

Jud	**5** : 14	and drove out all the people of the wilderness
Wis	**11** : 2	They journeyed through an uninhabited wilderness
	17 : 17	or a workman who toiled in the wilderness
Sir	**8** : 16	and do not cross the wilderness with him
	13 : 19	Wild asses in the wilderness are the prey of lions
	43 : 21	He consumes the mountains and burns up the wilderness
	45 : 18	and envied him in the wilderness
1 Ma	**2** : 29	went down to the wilderness to dwell there
	2 : 31	had gone down to the hiding places in the wilderness
	3 : 45	Jerusalem was uninhabited like a wilderness
	5 : 24	and went 3 days' journey into the wilderness
	5 : 28	by the wilderness road to Bozrah
	9 : 33	and they fled into the wilderness of Tekoa
	9 : 62	withdrew to Beth-basi in the wilderness
	13 : 21	urging him to come to them by way of the wilderness
2 Ma	**5** : 27	got away to the wilderness
2 Es	**1** : 17	When you were hungry and thirsty in the wilderness
	1 : 18	Why hast thou led us into the wilderness to kill us ?
	1 : 18	than to die in this wilderness
	1 : 22	When you were in the wilderness, at the bitter stream
	9 : 29	to our fathers in the wilderness
	9 : 29	when they came into the untrodden and unfruitful wilderness

WILE   1

Sir	**11** : 29	for many are the wiles of the crafty

WILFUL   1

Sir	**30** : 8	and a son unrestrained turns out to be wilful

WILFULLY   2

2 Ma	**14** : 3	but had wilfully defiled himself in the times of separation
3 Ma	**7** : 10	those of the Jewish nation who had wilfully transgressed

WILL, subst., s. **GOOD, ILL WILL**   20 = 0.013 %

Tob	**4** : 19	and according to his will he humbles whomever he wishes
	12 : 18	but by the will of our God
Ad E	**13** : 9	if it is thy will to save Israel

Wis	**14** : 5	It is thy will that the works of thy wisdom
Sir	**18** : 3	and all things obey his will
	43 : 16	at his will the south wind blows
1 Ma	**3** : 60	But as his will in heaven may be, so he will do
2 Ma	**1** : 3	and to do his will with a strong heart
	12 : 16	They took the city by the will of God
1 Es	**7** : 15	because he had changed the will of the king of the Assyrians concerning them
	8 : 16	perform it in accordance with the will of your God
	9 : 9	and do his will
3 Ma	**2** : 26	themselves also followed his will
2 Es	**3** : 8	And every nation walked after his own will
	8 : 5	For not of your own will did you come into the world
	8 : 5	and against your will you depart
	8 : 29	Let it not be thy will to destroy those
4 Ma	**2** : 23	and one who lives subject to this will
	11 : 12	he said, Tyrant, they are splendid favours that you grant us against your will
	18 : 16	There is a tree of life for those who do his will

WILL, verb, auxiliary   1503 = 0.979 %

WILL, verb, desire   24 = 0.016 %

Jud	**3** : 2	Do with us whatever you will
Ad E	**13** : 13	For I would have been willing to kiss the soles of his feet, to save Israel
Wis	**9** : 13	Or who can discern what the Lord wills ?
	11 : 25	How would anything have endured if thou hadst not willed it ?
	12 : 6	thou didst will to destroy by the hands of our fathers
Sir	**6** : 32	If you are willing, my son, you will be taught
	15 : 15	If you will, you can keep the commandments
	39 : 6	If the great Lord is willing
Sus	**13** : 40	but she would not tell us
1 Ma	**7** : 30	and he was afraid of him and would not meet him again
2 Ma	**1** : 3	and a willing spirit
	2 : 16	Will you therefore please keep the days ?
	7 : 7	and asked him, Will you eat
	7 : 25	Since the young man would not listen to him at all
3 Ma	**3** : 28	Any one willing to give information
2 Es	**1** : 24	You would not obey me, O Judah
	2 : 1	but they would not listen to them
	2 : 5	because they would not keep my covenant
	6 : 52	and thou hast kept them to be eaten by whom thou wilt
	6 : 52	and when thou wilt
4 Ma	**5** : 3	If any were not willing to eat defiling food
	8 : 7	if you will renounce
	9 : 27	Before torturing him, they inquired if he were willing to eat
	11 : 13	whether he was willing to eat and be released

WILLINGLY   6 = 0.004 %

1 Ma	**2** : 42	every one who offered himself willingly for the law
	8 : 27	the Romans shall willingly act as their allies
2 Ma	**6** : 28	of how to die a good death willingly and nobly
3 Ma	**6** : 26	and often have accepted willingly the worst of human dangers ?
2 Es	**8** : 28	but remember those who have willingly acknowledged that thou art to be feared
4 Ma	**5** : 23	so that we endure any suffering willingly

WIN   8 = 0.005 %

1 Ma	**3** : 14	and win honour in the kingdom
	6 : 44	and to win for himself an everlasting name
	11 : 24	And he won his favour
	14 : 35	and the glory which he had resolved to win for his nation
2 Ma	**12** : 11	After a hard fight Judas and his men won the victory
	15 : 9	and reminding them also of the struggles they had won
1 Es	**4** : 5	if they win the victory, they bring everything to the king
3 Ma	**1** : 4	if they won the battle

WIN over   2

Jud	**8** : 16	nor like a human being, to be won over by pleading
2 Ma	**4** : 45	to win over the king

WIND   34 = 0.022 %

Wis	**4** : 4	standing insecurely they will be shaken by the wind
	4 : 4	and by the violence of the winds they will be uprooted
	5 : 14	is like chaff carried by the wind
	5 : 14	it is dispersed like smoke before the wind
	5 : 23	a mighty wind will rise against them
	13 : 2	but they supposed that either fire or wind or swift air
	17 : 18	Whether there came a whistling wind
Sir	**5** : 9	Do not winnow with every wind, nor follow every path :
	22 : 18	will not stand firm against the wind
	34 : 2	As one who catches at a shadow and pursues the wind
	34 : 16	a shelter from the hot wind and a shade from noonday sun
	39 : 28	There are winds that have been created for vengeance
	43 : 16	at his will the south wind blows
	43 : 20	The cold north wind blows, and ice freezes over the water
L Jr	**6** : 61	and the wind likewise blows in every land
P Az	27	and made the midst of the furnace like a moist whistling wind
	43	Bless the Lord, all winds

Bel	14:36	with the rushing sound of the wind itself
3 Ma	2:22	and that as a reed is shaken by the wind
2 Es	1:33	I will drive you out as the wind drives straw
	3:19	of fire and earthquake and wind and ice
	4:5	or measure for me a measure of wind
	4:9	But now I have asked you only about fire and wind and the day
	5:37	and bring forth for me the winds shut up in them
	6:1	and before the assembled winds blew
	7:40	or cloud or thunder or lightning or wind
	8:22	and at whose command they are changed to wind and fire
	11:2	and all the winds of heaven blew upon him
	13:2	and behold, a wind arose from the sea and stirred up all its waves
	13:3	this wind made something like the figure of a man come up
	13:5	from the 4 winds of heaven
	13:27	And as for your seeing wind and fire
	15:39	And the winds from the east shall prevail
4 Ma	15:32	by the flood of your emotions and the violent winds

WINDFALL 3 = 0.002 %

Sir	20:9	and a windfall may result in a loss
	29:4	Many persons regard a loan as a windfall
	29:6	and will regard that as a windfall

WINDOW 3 = 0.002 %

Tob	3:11	So she prayed by her window and said
Sir	14:23	He who peers through her windows
2 Ma	3:19	while others peered out of the windows

WINE 43 = 0.028 %

Tob	4:15	Do not drink wine to excess
Jud	10:5	And she gave her maid a bottle of wine and a flask of oil
	11:13	and the tithes of the wine and oil
	12:1	and to serve her with his own wine
	12:13	and drink wine and be merry with us
	12:20	and drank a great quantity of wine
	13:2	for he was overcome with wine
Ad E	14:17	or drunk the wine of the libations
Wis	2:7	Let us take our fill of costly wine and perfumes
Sir	9:9	nor revel with her at wine
	9:10	A new friend is like new wine
	19:2	Wine and women lead intelligent men astray
	31:25	Do not aim to be valiant over wine
	31:25	for wine has destroyed many
	31:26	so wine tests hearts in the strife of the proud
	31:27	Wine is like life to men, if you drink it in moderation
	31:27	What is life to a man who is without wine ?
	31:28	Wine drunk in season and temperately
	31:29	Wine drunk to excess is bitterness of soul
	31:31	Do not reprove your neighbour at a banquet of wine
	32:5	is a concert of music at a banquet of wine
	32:6	is the melody of music with good wine
	40:20	Wine and music gladden the heart
	49:1	and like music at a banquet of wine
Bel	14:3	and 40 sheep and 50 gallons of wine
	14:11	and mix and place the wine
2 Ma	15:39	For just as it is harmful to drink wine alone
	15:39	while wine mixed with water is sweet and delicious
1 Es	3:10	The first wrote, Wine is strongest
	3:17	Then the first, who had spoken of the strength of wine, began and said :
	3:18	Gentlemen, how is wine the strongest ?
	3:23	And when they recover from the wine
	3:24	Gentlemen, is not wine the strongest
	4:14	and is not wine strong ?
	4:16	from which comes wine
	4:37	Wine is unrighteous, the king is unrighteous
	6:30	likewise wheat and salt and wine and oil
	8:20	a 100 baths of wine, and salt in abundance
3 Ma	5:2	with large handfuls of frankincense and plenty of unmixed wine
	5:10	until they had been filled with a great abundance of wine
	5:45	by the very fragrant draughts of wine mixed with frankincense
	6:30	both wines and everything else
2 Es	9:24	and taste no meat and drink no wine, but eat only flowers

WINE PRESS 1

Sir	33:16	and like a grape-gatherer I filled my wine press

WING 36 = 0.023 %

Wis	5:11	is traversed by the movement of its wings
Sir	34:1	and dreams give wings to fools
1 Ma	9:1	*and with them the right wing of the army*
	9:12	*Bacchides was on the right wing*
	9:15	*and they crushed the right wing*
	9:16	*When those on the left wing saw*
	9:16	*that the right wing was crushed*
2 Es	1:30	I gathered you as a hen gathers her brood under her wings
	11:1	that had 12 feathered wings and 3 heads
	11:2	he spread his wings over all the earth
	11:3	and out of his wings there grew opposing wings

	11:3	but they became little, puny wings
	11:5	And I looked, and behold, the eagle flew with his wings
	11:7	and uttered a cry to his wings, saying
	11:11	And I counted his opposing wings
	11:12	on the right side one wing arose
	11:13	Then the next wing arose and reigned
	11:18	Then the 3rd wing raised itself up
	11:19	And so it went with all the wings
	11:20	in due course the wings that followed also rose up on the right side
	11:22	the 12 wings and the 2 little wings disappeared
	11:23	except the 3 heads that were at rest and 6 little wings
	11:24	2 little wings separated from the 6
	11:25	these little wings planned to set themselves up
	11:31	and it devoured the 2 little wings which were planning to reign
	11:32	than all the wings that had gone before
	11:33	just as the wings had done
	11:45	and your terrifying wings
	11:45	and your most evil little wings
	12:2	And the 2 wings that had gone over to it arose
	12:16	This is the interpretation of the 12 wings which you saw
	12:19	As for your seeing 8 little wings clinging to his wings
	12:29	As for your seeing 2 little wings passing over to the head

WINK 1

Sir	27:22	Whoever winks his eye plans evil deeds

WINNOW 1

Sir	5:9	Do not winnow with every wind, nor follow every path :

WINNOW away 1

Wis	5:23	and like a tempest it will winnow them away

WINTER, subst. 3 = 0.002 %

P Az	45	Bless the Lord, winter cold and summer heat
1 Es	9:11	But the multitude is great and it is winter
2 Es	7:41	or summer or spring or heat or winter

WINTRY 2

Wis	16:29	will melt like wintry frost, and flow away like waste water
4 Ma	15:32	endured nobly and withstood the wintry storms

WIPE 1

L Jr	6:13	their faces are wiped because of the dust from the temple

WIPE away 1

3 Ma	2:19	Wipe away our sins and disperse our errors

WIPE off 1

L Jr	6:24	they will not shine unless some one wipes off the rust

WIPE out 8 = 0.005 %

Sir	36:7	destroy the adversary and wipe out the enemy
	46:18	and he wiped out the leaders of the people of Tyre
	47:7	For he wiped out his enemies on every side
	48:21	and his angel wiped them out
1 Ma	3:35	to wipe out and destroy the strength of Israel
2 Ma	8:9	to wipe out the whole race of Judea
	12:8	meant in the same way to wipe out the Jews
2 Es	15:57	and your cities shall be wiped out

WISDOM 130 = 0.085 %

Jud	8:29	Today is not the first time your wisdom has been shown
	11:8	For we have heard of your wisdom and skill
	11:20	and they marvelled at her wisdom and said
	11:21	either for beauty of face or wisdom of speech !
Wis	1:4	because wisdom will not enter a deceitful soul
	1:6	For wisdom is a kindly spirit
	3:11	for whoever despises wisdom and instruction is miserable
	6:9	that you may learn wisdom and not transgress
	6:12	Wisdom is radiant and unfading
	6:17	The beginning of wisdom
	6:20	so the desire for wisdom leads to a kingdom
	6:21	honour wisdom, that you may reign for ever
	6:22	I will tell you what wisdom is and how she came to be
	6:23	for envy does not associate with wisdom
	7:7	I called upon God, and the spirit of wisdom came to me
	7:12	I rejoiced in them all, because wisdom leads them
	7:15	for he is the guide even of wisdom
	7:22	for wisdom, the fashioner of all things, taught me
	7:24	For wisdom is more mobile than any motion
	7:28	as the man who lives with wisdom
	7:30	but against wisdom evil does not prevail
	8:5	what is richer than wisdom who effects all things ?
	8:17	that in kinship with wisdom there is immortality
	8:21	But I perceived that I would not possess wisdom
	9:2	and by thy wisdom hast formed man
	9:4	give me the wisdom that sits by thy throne
	9:6	yet without the wisdom that comes from thee
	9:9	With thee is wisdom, who knows thy works

9 : 17	Who has learned thy counsel, unless thou hast given wisdom
9 : 18	and were saved by wisdom
10 : 1	Wisdom protected the first-formed father of the world
10 : 4	wisdom again saved it
10 : 5	Wisdom also, when the nations in wicked agreement had been confounded
10 : 6	Wisdom rescued a righteous man
10 : 8	For because they passed wisdom by
10 : 9	Wisdom rescued from troubles those who served her
10 : 13	wisdom did not desert him, but delivered him from sin
10 : 15	A holy people and blameless race wisdom delivered
10 : 21	because wisdom opened the mouth of the dumb
11 : 1	Wisdom prospered their works by the hand of a holy prophet
14 : 2	and wisdom was the craftsman who built it
14 : 5	It is thy will that the works of thy wisdom
17 : 7	and their boasted wisdom was scornfully rebuked
Sir pr.	for instruction and wisdom
pr.	pertaining to instruction and wisdom
1 : 1	All wisdom comes from the Lord and is with him for ever
1 : 3	the abyss, and wisdom – who can search them out ?
1 : 4	Wisdom was created before all things
1 : 5	The source of wisdom is God's word in the highest heaven
1 : 6	The root of wisdom – to whom has it been revealed ?
1 : 7	The knowledge of wisdom – to whom was it manifested ?
1 : 9	The Lord himself created wisdom
1 : 14	To fear the Lord is the beginning of wisdom
1 : 16	To fear the Lord is wisdom's full measure
1 : 18	The fear of the Lord is the crown of wisdom
1 : 20	To fear the Lord is the root of wisdom
1 : 25	In the treasuries of wisdom are wise sayings
1 : 26	If you desire wisdom, keep the commandments
1 : 27	For the fear of the Lord is wisdom and instruction
4 : 11	Wisdom exalts her sons and gives help to those who seek her
4 : 23	and do not hide your wisdom
4 : 24	For wisdom is known through speech
6 : 18	and until you are old you will keep finding wisdom
6 : 22	For wisdom is like her name, and is not manifest to many
6 : 37	and your desire for wisdom will be granted
7 : 5	nor display your wisdom before the king
10 : 26	Do not make a display of your wisdom when you do your work
11 : 1	The wisdom of a humble man will lift up his head
11 : 15	Wisdom, understanding, and knowledge of the law
14 : 20	Blessed is the man who meditates on wisdom
14 : 22	Pursue wisdom like a hunter, and lie in wait on her paths
15 : 1	and he who holds to the law will obtain wisdom
15 : 3	and give him the water of wisdom to drink
15 : 10	For a hymn of praise should be uttered in wisdom
15 : 18	For great is the wisdom of the Lord
18 : 28	Every intelligent man knows wisdom
19 : 18	and wisdom obtains his love
19 : 20	All wisdom is the fear of the Lord
19 : 20	and in all wisdom there is the fulfilment of the law
19 : 22	But the knowledge of wickedness is not wisdom
19 : 23	but there is a fool who merely lacks wisdom
20 : 30	Hidden wisdom and unseen treasure
20 : 31	than the man who hides his wisdom
21 : 11	and wisdom is the fulfilment of the fear of the Lord
21 : 18	Like a house that has vanished, so is wisdom to a fool
22 : 6	but chastising and discipline are wisdom at all times
23 : 2	and the discipline of wisdom over my mind !
24 : 1	Wisdom will praise herself
24 : 25	It fills men with wisdom, like the Pishon
25 : 5	How attractive is wisdom in the aged
25 : 10	How great is he who has gained wisdom !
34 : 8	and wisdom is made perfect in truthful lips
37 : 21	since he is lacking in all wisdom
38 : 24	The wisdom of the scribe
39 : 1	will seek out the wisdom of all the ancients
39 : 6	he will pour forth words of wisdom
39 : 10	Nations will declare his wisdom
40 : 20	but the love of wisdom is better than both
41 : 14	hidden wisdom and unseen treasure
41 : 15	than the man who hides his wisdom
42 : 21	He has ordained the splendours of his wisdom
43 : 33	and to the godly he has granted wisdom
44 : 15	Peoples will declare their wisdom
45 : 26	May the Lord grant you wisdom in your heart
50 : 27	who out of his heart poured forth wisdom
51 : 13	I sought wisdom openly in my prayer
51 : 17	to him who gives me wisdom I will give glory
51 : 18	For I resolved to live according to wisdom
51 : 19	My soul grappled with wisdom, and in my conduct I was strict
Bar 3 : 9	give ear, and learn wisdom !
3 : 12	You have forsaken the fountain of wisdom
3 : 14	Learn where there is wisdom, where there is strength
3 : 23	have not learned the way to wisdom
3 : 28	so they perished because they had no wisdom
2 Ma 2 : 9	that being possessed of wisdom Solomon offered sacrifice
1 Es 3 : 7	and because of his wisdom he shall sit next to Darius
4 : 59	from thee is wisdom

4 : 60	Blessed art thou, who hast given me wisdom
8 : 23	And you, Ezra, according to the wisdom of God
2 Es 5 : 9	and wisdom shall withdraw into its chamber
5 : 39	As for me, I am without wisdom
8 : 4	and drink wisdom, O my heart !
8 : 12	and reproved him in thy wisdom
8 : 52	and wisdom perfected beforehand
13 : 55	for you have devoted your life to wisdom
14 : 40	and wisdom increased in my breast
14 : 47	the fountain of wisdom, and the river of knowledge
4 Ma 1 : 15	Now reason is the mind that with sound logic prefers the life of wisdom
1 : 16	Wisdom, next, is the knowledge of divine and human matters
1 : 18	Now the kinds of wisdom are rational judgment, justice

WISE, adj., subst.   51 = 0.033 %

Tob 4 : 18	Seek advice from every wise man
Jud 11 : 23	You are not only beautiful in appearance, but wise in speech
Wis 4 : 17	For they will see the end of the wise man
6 : 24	A multitude of wise men is the salvation of the world
7 : 15	and the corrector of the wise
Sir 1 : 8	There is One who is wise, greatly to be feared
1 : 25	In the treasuries of wisdom are wise sayings
3 : 29	and an attentive ear is the wise man's desire
6 : 33	and if you incline your ear you will become wise
6 : 34	Who is wise ? Cleave to him
6 : 35	and do not let wise proverbs escape you
7 : 19	Do not deprive yourself of a wise and good wife
9 : 14	and consult with the wise
9 : 17	so a people's leader is proved wise by his words
10 : 1	A wise magistrate will educate his people
10 : 25	Free men will be at the service of a wise servant
18 : 27	A wise man is cautious in everything
20 : 1	and there is a man who keeps silent but is wise
20 : 5	There is one who by keeping silent is found wise
20 : 7	A wise man will be silent until the right moment
20 : 13	The wise man makes himself beloved through his words
20 : 29	Presents and gifts blind the eyes of the wise
21 : 13	The knowledge of a wise man will increase like a flood
21 : 15	When a man of understanding hears a wise saying
21 : 26	but the mouth of wise men is in their mind
26 : 26	A wife honouring her husband will seem wise to all
27 : 11	The talk of the godly man is always wise
33 : 2	A wise man will not hate the law
37 : 22	A man may be wise to his own advantage
37 : 23	A wise man will instruct his own people
37 : 24	A wise man will have praise heaped upon him
37 : 26	He who is wise among his people will inherit confidence
38 : 24	and he who has little business may become wise
38 : 25	How can he become wise who handles the plough
44 : 4	wise in their words of instruction
47 : 12	After him rose up a wise son who fared amply because of him
47 : 14	How wise you became in your youth !
50 : 28	and he who lays them to heart will become wise
1 Ma 2 : 65	Now behold, I know that Simeon your brother is wise in counsel
1 Es 3 : 5	and to him whose statement seems wisest
3 : 9	and the 3 nobles of Persia judge to be wisest
4 : 42	for you have been found to be the wisest
5 : 6	who spoke wise words before Darius the king of the Persians
6 : 21	who therefore, if it seems wise, O king
2 Es 7 : 19	or wiser than the Most High !
12 : 38	and you shall teach them to the wise among your people
14 : 13	and instruct those that are wise
14 : 26	and some you shall deliver in secret to the wise
14 : 46	in order to give them to the wise among your people
4 Ma 2 : 19	Why else did Jacob, our most wise father
7 : 23	For only the wise and courageous man is lord of his emotions

WISELY   2

Wis 9 : 11	and she will guide me wisely in my actions
Sir 20 : 27	He who speaks wisely will advance himself

WISH, verb   26 = 0.017 %

Tob 4 : 19	and according to his will he humbles whomever he wishes
Wis 14 : 19	For he, perhaps wishing to please his ruler
Sir pr.	for those living abroad who wished to gain learning
15 : 16	stretch out your hand for whichever you wish
19 : 21	I will not act as you wish
23 : 14	then you will wish that you had never been born
L Jr 6 : 45	they can be nothing but what the craftsmen wish them to be
Sus 13 : 15	and wished to bathe in the garden, for it was very hot
1 Ma 5 : 67	On that day some priests, who wished to do a brave deed
8 : 13	Those whom they wish to help and to make kings
8 : 13	and those whom they wish they depose
2 Ma 2 : 24	for those who wish to enter upon the narratives of history
4 : 16	and wished to imitate completely
9 : 20	and your affairs are as you wish
11 : 29	Menelaus has informed us that you wish to return home
12 : 4	because they wished to live peaceably and suspected nothing
12 : 35	wishing to take the accursed man alive

	14:39	Nicanor, wishing to exhibit the enmity
1 Es	4:42	Then the king said to him, Ask what you wish
3 Ma	1:15	whether they wish it or not ?
	5:11	is bestowed by him who grants it to whomever he wishes
	5:47	wishing to witness, with invulnerable heart and with his own eyes
2 Es	4:23	For I did not wish to inquire about the ways above
	7:5	If any one, then, wishes to reach the sea
	14:22	and that those who wish to live in the last days may live
4 Ma	17:9	who wished to destroy the way of life of the Hebrews

WISH, subst.   1

2 Ma 9:19   and good wishes for their health and prosperity

WITH   1441 = 0.939 %

WITHDRAW   14 = 0.009 %

Jud	13:1	When evening came, his slaves quickly withdrew
	13:14	Praise God, who has not withdrawn his mercy
Sir	4:31	but withdrawn when it is time to repay
P Az	12	and do not withdraw thy mercy from us
1 Ma	9:62	withdrew to Beth-basi in the wilderness
	12:28	so they kindled fires in their camp and withdrew
2 Ma	4:33	having first withdrawn to a place of sanctuary
	6:16	Therefore he never withdraws his mercy from us
	12:7	he withdrew, intending to come again
	13:16	and withdrew in triumph
	13:22	gave pledges, received theirs, withdrew
2 Es	5:9	and wisdom shall withdraw into its chamber
	7:33	and patience shall be withdrawn
	12:48	As for me, I have neither forsaken you nor withdrawn from you

WITHDRAWAL   1

2 Ma 13:26   This is how the king's attack and withdrawal turned out

WITHER   5 = 0.003 %

Wis	2:8	Let us crown ourselves with rosebuds before they wither
Sir	14:9	and mean injustice withers the soul
	43:21	and withers the tender grass like fire
2 Es	7:87	and shall wither with fear
	15:50	And the glory of your power shall wither like a flower

WITHERED   2

Sir	6:3	and will be left like a withered tree
2 Es	5:36	and make the withered flowers bloom again for me

WITHHOLD   2

Sir	7:21	do not withhold from his freedom
	7:33	and withhold not kindness from the dead

WITHIN   30 = 0.020 %

Tob	3:6	and great is the sorrow within me
	13:10	May he cheer those within you who are captives
	13:10	and love those within you who are distressed
Jud	8:11	unless the Lord turns and helps us within so many days
	8:15	For if he does not choose to help us within these 5 days
	8:15	he has power to protect us within any time he pleases
	8:33	and within the days after which you have promised
	14:4	and you and all who live within the borders of Israel
Wis	7:2	within the period of 10 months, compacted with blood
Sir	26:20	Seek a fertile field within the whole plain
1 Ma	2:46	that they found within the borders of Israel
	5:30	and attacking the Jews within
	11:45	Then the men of the city assembled within the city
2 Ma	5:14	Within the total of 3 days 80,000 were destroyed
	6:4	and had intercourse with women within the sacred precincts
	7:20	Though she saw her 7 sons perish within a single day
	7:22	nor I who set in order the elements within each of you
	10:34	The men within, relying on the strength of the place
	12:14	And those who were within
	12:28	and killed as many as 25,000 of those who were within it
1 Es	9:4	within 2 or 3 days
	9:5	assembled at Jerusalem within 3 days
3 Ma	5:42	which had come about within him for the protection of the Jews
2 Es	2:22	Protect the old and the young within your walls
	4:40	her womb can keep the child within her any longer
	6:36	And on the 8th night my heart was troubled within me again
	7:59	Weigh within yourself what you have thought
	9:8	and will see my salvation in my land and within my borders
	13:48	who are found within my holy borders, shall be saved
4 Ma	18:2	not only of sufferings from within

WITHOUT   79 = 0.051 %

Tob	6:12	without incurring the penalty of death
	8:12	let us bury him without any one knowing about it
Jud	9:11	saviour of those without hope
	10:13	without losing one of his men, captured or slain
	12:12	without enjoying her company
Ad E	13:6	without pity or mercy
	16:24	Every city and country, without exception

Wis	1:11	because no secret word is without result
	3:17	and finally their old age will be without honour
	5:4	and that his end was without honour
	7:13	I learned without guile and I impart without grudging
	9:6	yet without the wisdom that comes from thee
	14:5	should not be without effect
	16:20	and without their toil thou didst supply them from heaven
	16:22	Snow and ice withstood fire without melting
	18:19	without knowing why they suffered
	19:13	without prior signs in the violence of thunder
Sir	3:25	If you have no eyes you will be without light
	19:6	He who controls his tongue will live without strife
	19:16	A person may make a slip without intending it
	27:21	but whoever has betrayed secrets is without hope
	29:25	without being thanked
	31:27	What is life to a man who is without wine ?
	32:19	Do nothing without deliberation
	33:29	and do nothing without discretion
	34:8	Without such deceptions the law will be fulfilled
	37:25	but the days of Israel are without number
	38:32	Without them a city cannot be established
	41:1	to a man without distractions
	51:25	Get these things for yourselves without money
Bar	2:23	and the whole land will be a desolation without inhabitants
Sus	13:48	without examination and without learning the facts ?
Bel	14:26	I will slay the dragon without sword or club
1 Ma	2:8	Her temple has become like a man without honour
	6:12	and I sent to destroy the inhabitants of Judah without good reason
	8:26	without receiving any return
	8:28	and do so without deceit
	10:33	I set free without payment
	14:44	without his permission
2 Ma	4:6	For he saw that without the king's attention
	8:6	Coming without warning
	9:4	so he ordered his charioteer to drive without stopping
	11:13	And as he was not without intelligence
	12:15	who without battering-rams or engines of war
	12:18	without accomplishing anything
	13:7	without even burial in the earth
	13:12	and lying prostrate for 3 days without ceasing
	14:27	as a prisoner without delay
1 Es	4:17	men cannot exist without women
	4:50	should be theirs without tribute
	6:30	regularly every year, without quibbling
	8:88	to destroy us without leaving a root or seed or name ?
3 Ma	1:20	and without a backward look they crowded together
	5:6	that the Jews were left without any aid
	5:20	Tomorrow without delay prepare the elephants in the same way
	5:42	that he would send them to death without delay
	7:5	they tried without any inquiry or examination
	7:12	so that freely and without royal authority or supervision
2 Es	1:35	who without having heard me will believe
	3:4	when thou didst form the earth – and that without help
	3:7	peoples and clans, without number
	3:29	For when I came here I saw ungodly deeds without number
	4:9	and without which you cannot exist
	4:32	When heads of grain without number are sown
	5:39	As for me, I am without wisdom
	6:28	and the truth, which has been so long without fruit, shall be revealed
	7:98	and shall be confident without confusion
	7:98	and shall be glad without fear
	10:4	but without ceasing mourn and fast until I die
	13:36	as you saw the mountain carved out without hands
	13:38	and will destroy them without effort by the law
	14:20	and its inhabitants are without light
4 Ma	2:8	and to lend without interest to the needy
	9:12	without accomplishing anything, they placed him upon the wheel
	12:14	but you will wail bitterly for having slain without cause
	16:9	others married and without offspring
	18:2	but also of those from without

WITHSTAND   21 = 0.014 %

Jud	6:4	They cannot withstand us, but will utterly perish
	11:18	and not one of them will withstand you
Wis	10:16	and withstood dread kings with wonders and signs
	11:3	They withstood their enemies and fought off their foes
	11:21	and who can withstand the might of thy arm ?
	16:22	Snow and ice withstood fire without melting
	18:21	he withstood the anger and put an end to the disaster
Sir	19:5	but he who withstands pleasures crowns his life
	43:3	and who can withstand its burning heat ?
	46:7	they withstood the congregation
	50:4	and fortified the city to withstand a siege
1 Ma	3:53	How will we be able to withstand them
	6:4	And they withstood him in battle
	6:49	because they had no provisions there to withstand a siege
	7:25	and realized that he could not withstand them
	10:73	And now you will not be able to withstand my cavalry

2 Ma	8 : 5	the Gentiles could not withstand him
	10 : 18	well equipped to withstand a siege
2 Es	7 : 89	and withstood danger every hour
4 Ma	15 : 32	endured nobly and withstood the wintry storms
	16 : 23	not to withstand pain

WITNESS, subst.   16 = 0.010 %

Jud	7 : 28	We call to witness against you heaven and earth
Wis	1 : 6	*because God is witness of his inmost feelings*
	4 : 6	*For children born of unlawful unions are witnesses of evil*
Sir	36 : 15	Bear witness to those whom thou didst create in the beginning
	46 : 19	Samuel called men to witness before the Lord
Sus	13 : 43	thou knowest that these men have borne false witness against me
	13 : 49	For these men have borne false witness against her
	13 : 61	Daniel had convicted them of bearing false witness
2 Ma	7 : 6	which bore witness against the people to their faces
	12 : 30	bore witness to the good will
2 Es	1 : 37	I call to witness the gratitude of the people that is to come
	2 : 5	*as a witness in addition to the mother of the children*
	2 : 14	Call, O call heaven and earth to witness
	2 : 36	I publicly call on my Saviour before witness
	7 : 94	they see the witness which he who formed them bears concerning them
4 Ma	16 : 16	to bear witness for the nation

WITNESS, verb   4 = 0.003 %

Jud	7 : 27	and we shall not witness the death of our babes before our eyes
	15 : 8	came to witness the good things
3 Ma	5 : 47	wishing to witness, with invulnerable heart and with his own eyes
4 Ma	15 : 24	Although she witnessed the destruction of 7 children

WOE   12 = 0.008 %

Jud	16 : 17	Woe to the nations that rise up against my people !
Sir	2 : 12	Woe to timid hearts and to slack hands
	2 : 13	Woe to the faint heart, for it has no trust !
	2 : 14	Woe to you who have lost your endurance !
	41 : 8	Woe to you, ungodly men
2 Es	2 : 8	Woe to you, Assyria
	15 : 24	Woe to those who sin and do not observe my commandments
	15 : 47	woe to you, miserable wretch !
	16 : 1	Woe to you, Babylon and Asia !
	16 : 1	Woe to you, Egypt and Syria !
	16 : 63	Woe to those who sin and want to hide their sins !
	16 : 77	Woe to those who are choked by their sins

WOLF   2

Sir	13 : 17	What fellowship has a wolf with a lamb ?
2 Es	5 : 18	in the power of cruel wolves

WOMAN   130 = 0.085 %

Tob	2 : 11	Then my wife Anna earned money at women's work
	4 : 12	and do not marry a foreign woman
	6 : 7	you make a smoke from these before the man or woman
Jud	4 : 11	And all the men and women of Israel, and their children
	6 : 16	and all their young men and their women ran to the assembly
	7 : 22	and the women and young men fainted from thirst
	7 : 23	Then all the people, the young men, the women, and the children
	7 : 32	The women and children he sent home
	8 : 7	and men and women slaves, and cattle, and fields
	8 : 31	So pray for us, since you are a devout woman
	9 : 10	crush their arrogance by the hand of a woman
	10 : 11	The women went straight on through the valley
	10 : 19	who have women like this among them ?
	11 : 1	Take courage, woman, and do not be afraid in your heart
	11 : 21	There is not such a woman
	12 : 11	Go now and persuade the Hebrew woman who is in your care
	12 : 12	For it will be a disgrace if we let such a woman go
	12 : 15	So she got up and arrayed herself in all her woman's finery
	13 : 15	The Lord has struck him down by the hand of a woman
	13 : 18	above all women on earth
	14 : 18	One Hebrew woman has brought disgrace
	15 : 12	Then all the women of Israel gathered to see her
	15 : 12	and gave them to the women who were with her
	15 : 13	leading all the women
	16 : 6	by the hand of a woman
Wis	3 : 13	For blessed is the barren woman who is undefiled
Sir	9 : 2	Do not give yourself to a woman
	9 : 3	Do not go to meet a loose woman
	9 : 4	Do not associate with a woman singer
	9 : 8	Turn away your eyes from a shapely woman
	9 : 8	many have been misled by a woman's beauty
	10 : 18	nor fierce anger for those born of women
	19 : 2	Wine and women lead intelligent men astray
	19 : 11	like a woman in labour with a child
	23 : 22	So it is with a woman who leaves her husband
	25 : 21	Do not be ensnared by a woman's beauty
	25 : 21	and do not desire a woman for her possessions
	25 : 24	From a woman sin had its beginning

	26 : 22	and a married woman as a tower of death to her lovers
	26 : 24	A shameless woman constantly acts disgracefully
	28 : 15	Slander has driven away courageous women
	34 : 5	and like a woman in travail the mind has fancies
	36 : 21	A woman will accept any man
	36 : 22	A woman's beauty gladdens the countenance
	37 : 11	Do not consult with a woman about her rival
	41 : 20	of looking at a woman who is a harlot
	42 : 12	and do not sit in the midst of women
	42 : 13	and from a woman comes woman's wickedness
	42 : 14	than a woman who does good
	42 : 14	and it is a woman who brings shame and disgrace
	47 : 19	But laid your loins beside women
	48 : 19	and they were in anguish, like women in travail
Bar	4 : 16	and bereaved the lonely woman of her daughters
L Jr	6 : 29	Sacrifices to them may be touched by women in menstruation or at childbirth
	6 : 30	Women serve meals for gods of silver and gold and wood
	6 : 43	And the women, with cords about them, sit along the passageways
	6 : 43	she derides the woman next to her
Sus	13 : 2	a very beautiful woman and one who feared the Lord
	13 : 31	Now Susanna was a woman of great refinement
	13 : 36	this woman came in with 2 maids
	13 : 40	So we seized this woman and asked her who the young man was
	13 : 46	I am innocent of the blood of this woman
Bel	14 : 20	I see the footsteps of men and women and children
1 Ma	1 : 26	the beauty of the women faded
	1 : 32	And they took captive the women and children
	1 : 60	the women who had their children circumcised
2 Ma	3 : 19	Women, girded with sackcloth under their breasts
	5 : 13	destruction of boys, women, and children
	5 : 24	and to sell the women and boys as slaves
	6 : 4	and had intercourse with women within the sacred precincts
	6 : 10	For example, 2 women were brought in
	6 : 10	These women they publicly paraded about the city
	7 : 21	she fired her woman's reasoning with a man's courage
	12 : 21	he sent off the women and the children
1 Es	1 : 32	and the principal men, with the women
	3 : 12	The 3rd wrote, Women are strongest
	4 : 13	who had spoken of women and truth, began to speak :
	4 : 14	Is it not women ?
	4 : 15	Women gave birth to the king
	4 : 16	From women they came
	4 : 16	and women brought up the very men who plant the vineyards
	4 : 17	Women make men's clothes
	4 : 17	men cannot exist without women
	4 : 18	and then see a woman lovely in appearance and beauty
	4 : 22	Hence you must realize that women rule over you !
	4 : 22	and bring everything and give it to women ?
	4 : 24	he brings it back to the woman he loves
	4 : 26	Many men have lost their minds because of women
	4 : 27	Many have perished, or stumbled, or sinned, because of women
	4 : 32	Gentlemen, why are not women strong
	4 : 34	Gentlemen, are not women strong ?
	4 : 37	women are unrighteous, all the sons of men are unrighteous
	8 : 91	men and women and youths
	8 : 92	and have married foreign women from the peoples of the land
	9 : 7	You have broken the law and married foreign women
	9 : 36	All these had married foreign women
	9 : 40	for all the multitude, men and women
	9 : 41	in the presence of both men and women
3 Ma	1 : 19	Those women who had recently been arrayed for marriage
	4 : 6	And young women who had just entered the bridal chamber
2 Es	4 : 40	Go and ask a woman who is with child if
	4 : 42	For just as a woman in travail
	5 : 8	and menstruous women shall bring forth monsters
	5 : 46	He said to me, Ask a woman's womb
	5 : 49	and a woman who has become old does not bring forth any longer
	5 : 51	He replied to me, Ask a woman who bears children
	6 : 21	and women with child shall give birth to premature children at 3 or 4 months
	9 : 38	I lifted up my eyes and saw a woman on my right
	10 : 6	You most foolish of women
	10 : 16	and will be praised among women
	10 : 27	the woman was no longer visible to me
	10 : 41	The woman who appeared to you a little while ago
	10 : 42	but you do not now see the form of a woman
	10 : 44	This woman whom you saw
	10 : 46	then it was that the barren woman bore a son
	15 : 51	You shall be weakened like a wretched woman
	16 : 33	women shall mourn because they have no husbands
	16 : 38	Just as a woman with child, in the 9th month
	16 : 49	Just as a respectable and virtuous woman abhors a harlot
4 Ma	4 : 9	While the priests together with women and children
	4 : 25	even to the point that women
	14 : 11	since the mind of a woman despised even more diverse agonies
	15 : 17	O woman, who alone gave birth to such complete devotion !
	16 : 1	If, then, a woman, advanced in years and mother of 7 sons

16 : 2	but also that a woman has despised the fiercest tortures
16 : 5	If this woman, though a mother, had been fainthearted
16 : 14	O mother, soldier of God in the cause of religion, elder and woman !
17 : 9	Here lie buried an aged priest and an aged woman and 7 sons
18 : 7	but I guarded the rib from which woman was made

WOMB
20 = 0.013 %

Jud	**9** : 2	and polluted her womb to disgrace her
Wis	**7** : 1	and in the womb of a mother I was moulded into flesh
Sir	**1** : 14	she is created with the faithful in the womb
	40 : 1	from the day they come forth from their mother's womb
	49 : 7	yet he had been consecrated in the womb as prophet
2 Ma	**7** : 22	I do not know how you came into being in my womb
	7 : 27	I carried you 9 months in my womb
2 Es	**4** : 40	her womb can keep the child within her any longer
	4 : 41	In Hades the chambers of the souls are like the womb
	5 : 35	Or why did not my mother's womb become my grave
	5 : 46	He said to me, Ask a woman's womb
	5 : 48	Even so have I given the womb of the earth
	5 : 53	when the womb is failing
	8 : 8	which is now fashioned in the womb
	8 : 8	and for 9 months the womb which thou hast formed
	8 : 9	And when the womb gives up again what has been created in it
	10 : 12	for I have lost the fruit of my womb
	16 : 38	has great pains about her womb for 2 or 3 hours beforehand
	16 : 38	and when the child comes forth from the womb
4 Ma	**13** : 19	and which was implanted in the mother's womb

WONDER, subst.
19 = 0.012 %

Ad E	**10** : 9	God has done great signs and wonders
Wis	**8** : 8	she has foreknowledge of signs and wonders
	10 : 16	and withstood dread kings with wonders and signs
	19 : 8	after gazing on marvellous wonders
Sir	**16** : 11	it will be a wonder if he remains unpunished
	18 : 6	nor is it possible to trace the wonders of the Lord
	36 : 6	Show signs anew, and work further wonders
	45 : 19	he wrought wonders against them
	48 : 14	As in his life he did wonders
Bar	**2** : 11	with a mighty hand and with signs and wonders
2 Ma	**15** : 21	and called upon the Lord who works wonders
3 Ma	**6** : 32	praising God, their Saviour and worker of wonders
2 Es	**1** : 14	and did great wonders among you
	2 : 48	how great and many are the wonders of the Lord God
	7 : 27	that I have foretold shall see my wonders
	9 : 6	the beginnings are manifest in wonders and mighty works
	13 : 14	From the beginning thou hast shown thy servant these wonders
	13 : 50	And then he will show them very many wonders
	13 : 57	because of his wonders, which he did from time to time

WONDER, verb
5 = 0.003 %

Sir	**11** : 21	Do not wonder at the works of a sinner
	26 : 11	and do not wonder if she sins against you
	40 : 7	and wonders that his fear came to nothing
3 Ma	**5** : 39	wondering at his instability of mind
2 Es	**10** : 25	While I was wondering what this meant

WONDERFUL
6 = 0.004 %

Tob	**12** : 22	So they confessed the great and wonderful works of God
Jud	**16** : 13	wonderful in strength, invincible
Ad E	**13** : 10	and every wonderful thing under heaven
	15 : 14	For you are wonderful, my lord
Sir	**11** : 4	for the works of the Lord are wonderful
	31 : 9	for he has done wonderful things among his people

WONDROUS
6 = 0.004 %

Sir	**36** : 14	Fill Zion with the celebration of thy wondrous deeds
	48 : 4	How glorious you were, O Elijah, in your wondrous deeds !
2 Es	**6** : 48	that therefore the nations might declare thy wondrous works
	13 : 56	and explain weighty and wondrous matters to you
	14 : 5	and I told him many wondrous things
4 Ma	**15** : 4	a wondrous likeness both of mind and of form

WOOD
19 = 0.012 %

Wis	**10** : 4	steering the righteous man by a paltry piece of wood
	14 : 1	calls upon a piece of wood more fragile
	14 : 5	even to the smallest piece of wood
	14 : 7	For blessed is the wood by which righteousness comes
	14 : 21	bestowed on objects of stone or wood
Sir	**8** : 3	Do not argue with a chatterer, nor heap wood on his fire
Bar	**5** : 8	*The woods and every fragrant tree have shaded Israel at God's command*
L Jr	**6** : 4	Now in Babylon you will see gods made of silver and gold and wood
	6 : 11	these gods of silver and gold and wood
	6 : 30	Women serve meals for gods of silver and gold and wood
	6 : 39	These things that are made of wood and overlaid with gold and silver
	6 : 50	Since they are made of wood and overlaid with gold and silver
	6 : 57	gods made of wood and overlaid with silver and gold

WOODCUTTER
1

Wis	**13** : 11	A skilled woodcutter may saw down a tree easy to handle

WOODEN
5 = 0.003 %

Sir	**22** : 16	A wooden beam firmly bonded into a building
L Jr	**6** : 55	of wooden gods overlaid with gold or silver
	6 : 59	better also a wooden pillar in a palace
1 Ma	**6** : 37	And upon the elephants were wooden towers, strong and covered
1 Es	**9** : 42	stood on the wooden platform which had been prepared

WORD
197 = 0.128 %

Tob	**6** : 15	But the angel said to him, Do you not remember the words
	8 : 2	As he went he remembered the words of Raphael
	14 : 1	Here Tobit ended his words of praise
Jud	**5** : 5	Let my lord now hear a word from the mouth of your servant
	6 : 4	none of his words shall be in vain
	6 : 5	who have said these words on the day of your iniquity
	6 : 9	I have spoken and none of my words shall fail
	7 : 9	Let our lord hear a word, lest his army be defeated
	7 : 16	These words pleased Holofernes and all his servants
	8 : 9	When Judith heard the wicked words
	8 : 28	and there is no one who can deny your words
	9 : 13	Make my deceitful words to be their wound and stripe
	10 : 1	and had ended all these words
	10 : 14	When the men heard her words, and observed her face
	11 : 5	Judith replied to him, Accept the words of your servant
	11 : 6	And if you follow out the words of your maidservant
	11 : 9	we have heard his words, for the men of Bethulia spared him
	11 : 15	When the word reaches them and they proceed to do this
	11 : 20	Her words pleased Holofernes and all his servants
	14 : 12	they sent word to their commanders
Ad E	**15** : 8	And he comforted her with soothing words, and said to her
Wis	**1** : 6	and will not free a blasphemer from the guilt of his words
	1 : 9	and a report of his words will come to the Lord
	1 : 11	because no secret word is without result
	1 : 16	But ungodly men by their words and deeds summoned death
	2 : 17	Let us see if his words are true
	6 : 9	To you then, O monarchs, my words are directed
	6 : 11	Therefore set your desire on my words
	6 : 25	Therefore be instructed by my words, and you will profit
	7 : 16	For both we and our words are in his hand
	8 : 18	and renown in sharing her words
	9 : 1	who hast made all things by thy word
	12 : 9	by dread wild beasts or thy stern word
	16 : 12	but it was thy word, O Lord, which heals all men
	16 : 26	but that thy word preserves those who trust in thee
	18 : 15	thy all-powerful word leaped from heaven
	18 : 22	but by his word he subdued the punisher
Sir	**1** : 5	The source of wisdom is God's word in the highest heaven
	1 : 24	He will hide his words until the right moment
	2 : 15	Those who fear the Lord will not disobey his words
	3 : 8	Honour your father by word and deed
	4 : 24	and education through the words of the tongue
	8 : 11	lest he lie in ambush against your words
	9 : 17	so a people's leader is proved wise by his words
	11 : 8	nor interrupt a speaker in the midst of his words
	12 : 12	and at last you will realize the truth of my words
	13 : 11	nor trust his abundance of words
	13 : 12	Cruel is he who does not keep words to himself
	13 : 13	Keep words to yourself and be very watchful
	13 : 22	he speaks unseemly words, and they justify him
	16 : 24	and pay close attention to my words
	16 : 28	and they will never disobey his word
	18 : 15	nor cause grief by your words when you present a gift
	18 : 16	So a word is better than a gift
	18 : 17	Indeed, does not a word surpass a good gift ?
	19 : 10	Have you heard a word ? Let it die with you
	19 : 11	With such a word a fool will suffer pangs
	19 : 12	so is a word inside a fool
	20 : 8	Whoever uses too many words will be loathed
	20 : 13	The wise man makes himself beloved through his words
	21 : 17	and they will ponder his words in their minds
	21 : 25	but the words of the prudent will be weighed in the balance
	23 : 15	A man accustomed to use insulting words
	27 : 23	and he admires your words
	27 : 23	and with your own words he will give offence
	28 : 25	make balances and scales for your words
	29 : 3	Confirm your word and keep faith with him
	29 : 5	and will pay in words of unconcern
	29 : 25	and besides this you will hear bitter words :
	31 : 22	and in the end you will appreciate my words
	31 : 31	speak no word of reproach to him

	6 : 63	*And the fire sent from above to consume mountains and woods does what it is ordered*
	6 : 70	so are their gods of wood, overlaid with gold and silver
	6 : 71	In the same way, their gods of wood
2 Ma	**1** : 21	to sprinkle the liquid on the wood and what was laid upon it
	4 : 41	some picked up stones, some blocks of wood
2 Es	**5** : 5	Blood shall drip from wood

32:8	Speak concisely, say much in few words
36:19	so an intelligent mind detects false words
37:20	A man skilled in words may be hated
39:6	he will pour forth words of wisdom
39:17	At his word the waters stood in a heap
39:17	and the reservoirs of water at the word of his mouth
39:31	and when their times come they will not transgress his word
41:16	Therefore show respect for my words :
41:22	of abusive words, before friends
42:15	By the words of the Lord his works are done
42:20	No thought escapes him, and not one word is hidden from him
43:26	and by his word all things hold together
43:27	and the sum of our words is : He is the all
44:4	wise in their words of instruction
45:3	By his words he caused signs to cease
46:15	and by his words he became known as a trustworthy seer
48:1	and his word burned like a torch
48:3	By the word of the Lord he shut up the heavens
48:5	by the word of the Most High
49:6	according to the word of Jeremiah
51:5	from an unclean tongue and lying words
Bar **1**:1	These are the words of the book
1:3	And Baruch read the words of this book
1:21	in all the words of the prophets whom he sent to us
2:1	So the Lord confirmed his word
2:24	and thou hast confirmed thy words
4:37	at the word of the Holy One, rejoicing in the glory of God
5:5	at the word of the Holy One
1 Ma **1**:30	Deceitfully he spoke peaceable words to them
1:51	In such words he wrote to his whole kingdom
2:22	We will not obey the king's words
2:23	When he had finished speaking these words
2:62	Do not fear the words of a sinner
7:10	with peaceable but treacherous words
7:11	But they paid no attention to their words
7:15	And he spoke peaceable words to them
7:16	in accordance with the word which was written
9:55	so that he could no longer say a word
10:3	in peaceable words to honour him
10:17	and sent it to him, in the following words :
10:24	I also will write them words of encouragement
10:25	So he sent a message to them in the following words :
10:46	When Jonathan and the people heard these words
10:47	because he had been the first to speak peaceable words to them
10:74	When Jonathan heard the words of Apollonius
11:2	He set out for Syria with peaceable words
11:53	But he broke his word about all that he had promised
13:7	when they heard these words
13:19	but Trypho broke his word and did not release Jonathan
14:23	and to put a copy of their words in the public archives
15:32	He reported to him the words of the king
15:35	Athenobius did not answer him a word
15:36	and reported to him these words and the splendour of Simon
2 Ma **2**:3	And with other similar words he exhorted them
6:29	because the words he had uttered
7:24	Antiochus not only appealed to him in words
8:12	Word came to Judas concerning Nicanor's invasion
8:21	With these words he filled them with good courage
9:12	he uttered these words : It is right to be subject to God
10:21	When word of what had happened came to Maccabeus
10:34	blasphemed terribly and hurled out wicked words
11:6	When Maccabeus and his men got word
11:25	You will do well, therefore, to send word to them
12:25	And when with many words
13:1	In the 149th year word came to Judas and his men
13:23	he got word that Philip
14:1	3 years later, word came to Judas and his men
14:34	and called upon the constant Defender of our nation, in these words :
15:11	as with the inspiration of brave words
15:17	Encouraged by the words of Judas
15:22	And he called upon him in these words :
15:24	With these words he ended his prayer
1 Es **1**:24	so that the words of the Lord rose up against Israel
1:26	And the king of Egypt sent word to him saying
1:28	and did not heed the words of Jeremiah the prophet
1:47	and did not heed the words
1:57	in fulfilment of the word of the Lord by the mouth of Jeremiah :
2:1	that the word of the Lord by the mouth of Jeremiah
5:6	who spoke wise words before Darius the king of the Persians
6:6	until word could be sent to Darius concerning them
8:43	I sent word to Eliezar, Iduel, Maasmas
8:72	at the word of the Lord of Israel
9:55	because they were inspired by the words which they had been taught
P Ma **3**	who hast shackled the sea by thy word of command
3 Ma **3**:17	They accepted our presence by word, but insincerely by deed
4:16	and uttering improper words against the supreme God
5:30	But at these words he was filled with an overpowering wrath
6:5	speaking grievous words with boasting and insolence

7:16	in words of praise and all kinds of melodious songs
2 Es **1**:4	The word of the Lord came to me, saying
3:3	and I began to speak anxious words to the Most High, and said
5:22	and I began once more to speak words
5:31	When I had spoken these words
6:15	because the word concerns the end
6:38	and thy word accomplished the work
6:43	For thy word went forth, and at once the work was done
7:1	When I had finished speaking these words
7:2	and listen to the words that I have come to speak to you
7:71	And now understand from your own words
7:116	I answered and said, This is my first and last word
7:139	and judge, because if he did not pardon those who were created by his word
8:19	Therefore hear my voice, and understand my words
8:19	The beginning of the words of Ezra's prayer
8:22	whose word is sure and whose utterances are certain
8:24	attend to my words
8:37	and it will come to pass according to your words
9:30	and give heed to my words, O descendants of Jacob
10:29	As I was speaking these words, behold
12:1	While the lion was saying these words to the eagle, I looked
12:31	and as for all his words that you have heard
14:6	These words you shall publish openly
14:28	Hear these words, O Israel
15:1	speak in the ears of my people the words of the prophecy
16:36	Behold the word of the Lord, receive it
16:40	Hear my words, O my people
16:56	At his word the stars were fixed
16:58	and by his word has suspended the earth over the water
4 Ma **4**:7	The people indignantly protested his words
4:13	Moved by these words, Onias the high priest
5:14	Eleazar asked to have a word
5:38	either by word or by deed
7:9	but by your deeds you made your words of divine philosophy credible
14:9	yes, not only heard the direct word of threat
16:14	and in word and deed you have proved more powerful than a man
16:24	By these words the mother of the 7
17:8	to inscribe upon their tomb these words

WORK, subst.   128 = 0.083 %

Tob **2**:11	Then my wife Anna earned money at women's work
3:11	May all thy works praise thee for ever
12:6	worthily declaring the works of God
12:7	but gloriously to reveal the works of God
12:11	but gloriously to reveal the works of God
12:22	So they confessed the great and wonderful works of God
Jud **13**:4	look in this hour upon the work of my hands
Ad E **13**:8	calling to remembrance all the works of the Lord
Wis **1**:12	nor bring on destruction by the works of your hands
2:4	and no one will remember our works
3:11	and their works are useless
6:3	who will search out your works and inquire into your plans
8:4	and an associate in his works
9:9	With thee is wisdom, who knows thy works
9:12	Then my works will be acceptable
11:1	Wisdom prospered their works by the hand of a holy prophet
12:4	their works of sorcery and unholy rites
12:19	Through such works thou hast taught thy people
13:1	while paying heed to his works
13:7	For as they live among his works they keep searching
13:10	to the works of men's hands
13:10	the work of an ancient hand
13:12	and burn the castoff pieces of his work to prepare his food
13:19	for money-making and work and success with his hands
14:5	It is thy will that the works of thy wisdom
14:8	because he did the work
14:20	and the multitude, attracted by the charm of his work
17:20	and was engaged in unhindered work
Sir pr.	Not only this work, but even the law itself
1:9	he poured it out upon all his works
7:15	Do not hate toilsome labour, or farm work
7:20	Do not abuse a servant who performs his work faithfully
9:17	A work will be praised for the skill of the craftsmen
10:26	Do not make a display of your wisdom when you do your work
11:4	for the works of the Lord are wonderful
11:4	and his works are concealed from men
11:15	affection and the ways of good works come from him
11:20	and grow old in your work
11:21	Do not wonder at the works of a sinner
16:15	in order that his works might be known under heaven
16:21	so most of his works are concealed
16:26	The works of the Lord have existed
16:27	He arranged his works in an eternal order
17:8	to show them the majesty of his works
17:10	to proclaim the grandeur of his works
17:19	All their works are as the sun before him
18:4	to proclaim his works

31:22	In all your work be industrious	
33:15	Look upon all the works of the Most High	
33:24	bread and discipline and work for a servant	
33:25	Set your slave to work, and you will find rest	
33:27	Put him to work, that he may not be idle	
33:28	Set him to work, as is fitting for him	
35:19	and the works of men according to their devices	
37:11	with an idler about any work	
37:11	or with a man hired for a year about completing his work	
37:16	Reason is the beginning of every work	
38:6	that he might be glorified in his marvellous works	
38:8	His works will never be finished	
38:25	who drives oxen and is occupied with their work	
38:27	and he is careful to finish his work	
38:29	So too is the potter sitting at his work	
38:39	he is always deeply concerned over his work	
38:31	and each is skilful in his own work	
39:14	bless the Lord for all his works	
39:16	All things are the works of the Lord, for they are very good	
39:19	The works of all flesh are before him	
39:33	The works of the Lord are all good	
42:15	I will now call to mind the works of the Lord	
42:15	By the words of the Lord his works are done	
42:16	and the work of the Lord is full of his glory	
42:17	to recount all his marvellous works	
42:22	How greatly to be desired are all his works	
43:2	is a marvellous instrument, the work of the Most High	
43:25	For in it are strange and marvellous works	
43:28	For he is greater than all his works	
43:32	for we have seen but few of his works	
45:10	the work of an embroiderer	
45:11	with twisted scarlet, the work of a craftsman	
45:11	in a setting of gold, the work of a jeweller	
45:12	a distinction to be prized, the work of an expert	
47:22	nor cause any of his works to perish	
50:16	they sounded the trumpets of hammered work	
51:8	and thy work from of old	
51:30	Do your work before the appointed time	
Bar **2**:9	for the Lord is righteous in all his works	
L Jr **6**:51	that they are not gods but the work of men's hands	
6:51	and that there is no work of God in them	
P Az **4**	and all thy works are true and thy ways right	
20	Deliver us in accordance with thy marvellous works	
35	Bless the Lord, all works of the Lord	
1 Ma **2**:47	and the work prospered in their hands	
4:51	Thus they finished all the work they had undertaken	
9:54	He tore down the work of the prophets !	
9:55	and his work was hindered	
10:11	He directed those who were doing the work	
2 Ma **5**:25	then, finding the Jews not at work	
15:39	delights the ears of those who read the work	
1 Es **4**:36	All God's works quake and tremble	
4:37	all their works are unrighteous, and all such things	
5:45	and that they would give to the sacred treasury for the work	
5:58	to have charge of the work of the Lord	
5:58	as one man pressing forward the work on the house of God	
6:10	and the work is prospering in their hands	
7:2	supervised the holy work with very great care	
7:3	And the holy work prospered	
9:11	This is not a work we can do in one day or 2	
3 Ma **2**:8	And when they had seen works of your hands	
2 Es **6**:38	and thy word accomplished the work	
6:40	so that thy works might then appear	
6:43	For thy word went forth, and at once the work was done	
6:48	that therefore the nations might declare thy wondrous works	
6:54	as ruler over all the works which thou hadst made	
7:24	and have not performed my works	
7:77	For you have a treasure of works laid up with the Most High	
7:134	since they are his own works	
8:7	and we are a work of thy hands, as thou hast declared	
8:13	and thou wilt make him live, for he is thy work	
8:32	who have no works of righteousness	
8:33	For the righteous, who have many works laid up with thee	
8:36	who have no store of good works	
9:6	the beginnings are manifest in wonders and mighty works	
9:17	and as is the work, so is the product	
10:54	for no work of man's building could endure in a place	
13:23	who have works and have faith in the Almighty	
16:51	Therefore do not be like her or her works	
16:54	Behold, the Lord knows all the works of men	
16:64	Because the Lord will strictly examine all their works	

WORK, verb   10 = 0.007 %

Tob **4**:14	the wages of any man who works for you	
Wis **7**:26	a spotless mirror of the working of God	
13:4	And if men were amazed at their power and working	
Sir **10**:27	Better is a man who works	
11:11	There is a man who works, and toils, and presses on	
24:22	and those who work with my help will not sin	
36:6	Show signs anew, and work further wonders	

43:4	A man tending a furnace works in burning heat	
45:19	he wrought wonders against them	
2 Ma **15**:21	and called upon the Lord who works wonders	

WORKER   6 = 0.004 %

Wis **15**:7	the worker in clay decides	
15:9	but he competes with workers in gold and silver	
15:9	and imitates workers in copper	
Sir **27**:10	so does sin for the workers of iniquity	
40:18	Life is sweet for the self-reliant and the worker	
3 Ma **6**:32	praising God, their Saviour and worker of wonders	

WORKMAN   3 = 0.002 %

Wis **17**:17	or a workman who toiled in the wilderness	
Sir **19**:1	A workman who is a drunkard will not become rich	
38:27	So too is every craftsman and master workman	

WORKMANSHIP   2

Wis **13**:11	and then with pleasing workmanship	
2 Es **3**:5	Yet he was the workmanship of thy hands	

WORLD   99 = 0.064 %

Jud **5**:21	and we shall be put to shame before the whole world	
10:19	they will be able to ensnare the whole world !	
11:8	and it is reported throughout the whole world	
11:16	things that will astonish the whole world	
11:23	and be renowned throughout the whole world	
Ad E **13**:2	and master of the whole world	
13:4	pointed out to us that among all the nations in the world	
Wis **1**:7	Because the Spirit of the Lord has filled the world	
1:14	and the generative forces of the world are wholesome	
2:24	but through the devil's envy death entered the world	
6:24	A multitude of wise men is the salvation of the world	
7:17	to know the structure of the world	
9:3	and rule the world in holiness and righteousness	
9:9	and was present when thou didst make the world	
10:1	Wisdom protected the first-formed father of the world	
11:17	For thy all-powerful hand, which created the world	
11:22	Because the whole world before thee	
13:2	were the gods that rule the world	
13:9	that they could investigate the world	
14:6	the hope of the world took refuge on a raft	
14:6	left to the world the seed of a new generation	
14:14	For through the vanity of men they entered the world	
17:20	For the whole world was illumined with brilliant light	
18:4	was to be given to the world	
18:24	For upon his long robe the whole world was depicted	
Sir **18**:3	he steers the world with the span of his hand	
38:34	But they keep stable the fabric of the world	
L Jr **6**:62	When God commands the clouds to go over the whole world	
P Az **9**	the most wicked in all the world	
14	and are brought low this day in all the world	
22	glorious over the whole world	
2 Ma **2**:22	and recovered the temple famous throughout the world	
3:12	which is honoured throughout the whole world	
5:15	the most holy temple in all the world	
7:23	Therefore the Creator of the world	
8:18	and even the whole world	
12:15	calling upon the great Sovereign of the world	
13:14	So, committing the decision to the Creator of the world	
1 Es **2**:3	has made me king of the world	
3 Ma **6**:5	who had already gained control of the whole world by the spear	
2 Es **2**:47	whom they confessed in the world	
3:9	thou didst bring the flood upon the inhabitants of the world	
3:18	and move the world, and make the depths to tremble	
3:34	and those of the inhabitants of the world	
4:2	Your understanding has utterly failed regarding this world	
4:11	And how can one who is already worn out by the corrupt world understand incorruption ?	
4:24	and why we pass from the world like locusts	
5:24	and from all the lands of the world	
5:24	and from all the flowers of the world	
5:44	neither can the world hold at one time	
5:49	so have I organized the world which I created	
6:1	before the portals of the world were in place	
6:25	and shall see my salvation and the end of my world	
6:55	that thou didst create this world	
6:59	If the world has indeed been created for us	
6:59	why do we not possess our world as an inheritance ?	
7:11	For I made the world for their sake	
7:12	And so the entrances of this world were made narrow	
7:13	But the entrances of the greater world are broad and safe	
7:21	For God strictly commanded those who came into the world	
7:30	And the world shall be turned back to primeval silence for 7 days	
7:31	And after 7 days the world	
7:47	And now I see that the world to come will bring delight to few	
7:50	For this reason the Most High has made not one world but 2	
7:70	When the Most High made the world and Adam	
7:74	has been patient with those who inhabit the world	

7 : 112 He answered me and said, This present world is not the end
7 : 132 because he has mercy on those who have not yet come into the world
7 : 137 the world with those who inhabit it would not have life
8 : 1 The Most High made this world for the sake of many
8 : 1 but the world to come for the sake of few
8 : 2 so is the course of the present world
8 : 5 For not of your own will did you come into the world
8 : 41 so also those who have been sown in the world will not all be saved
8 : 50 who inhabit the world in the last times
9 : 2 when the Most High was about to visit the world
9 : 3 So when there shall appear in the world earthquakes
9 : 5 For just as with everything that has occurred in the world
9 : 18 before the world was made for them to dwell in
9 : 19 but now those who have been created in this world
9 : 20 So I considered my world, and behold, it was lost
10 : 8 you are sorrowing for one son, but we, the whole world, for our mother
10 : 45 it is because there were 3,000 years in the world
11 : 32 and it had greater power over the world
11 : 39 which I had made to reign in my world
11 : 40 and you have held sway over the world with much terror
13 : 20 than to pass from the world like a cloud
14 : 17 For the weaker the world becomes through old age
14 : 20 For the world lies in darkness
14 : 22 and I will write everything that has happened in the world from the beginning
15 : 5 I bring evils upon the world
15 : 14 Alas for the world and for those who live in it !
16 : 13 to the ends of the world
16 : 39 and the world will groan
4 Ma 5 : 25 the Creator of the world in giving us the law
8 : 23 and deprive ourselves of this delightful world ?
15 : 31 Just as Noah's ark, carrying the whole world in the universal flood
16 : 18 that you have had a share in the world
17 : 14 and the world and the human race were the spectators

WORM   7 = 0.005 %
Jud 16 : 17 fire and worms he will give to their flesh
Sir 7 : 17 for the punishment of the ungodly is fire and worms
10 : 11 and wild beasts, and worms
19 : 3 Decay and worms will inherit him
L Jr 6 : 20 when worms from the earth devour them and their robes
1 Ma 2 : 62 for his splendour will turn into dung and worms
2 Ma 9 : 9 And so the ungodly man's body swarmed with worms

WORRIED   1
Sir 9 : 13 and you will not be worried by the fear of death

WORRY, verb   4 = 0.003 %
Tob 5 : 20 And Tobit said to her, Do not worry, my sister
6 : 15 and do not worry about the demon
10 : 6 But Tobit said to her, Be still and stop worrying ; he is well
Sir 22 : 22 do not worry, for reconciliation is possible

WORRY, subst.   2
Sir 42 : 9 and worry over her robs him of sleep
1 Ma 6 : 10 Sleep departs from my eyes and I am downhearted with worry

WORSE   14 = 0.009 %
Wis 15 : 18 which are worse than all others
17 : 6 to be worse than that unseen appearance
Sir 22 : 11 but the life of the fool is worse than death
25 : 15 There is no venom worse than a snake's venom
25 : 15 and no wrath worse than an enemy's wrath
26 : 5 all these are worse than death
39 : 34 And no one can say, This is worse than that
2 Ma 5 : 23 worse than the others did
7 : 39 and handled him worse than the others
13 : 9 was coming to show to the Jews things far worse
3 Ma 5 : 20 the king, possessed by a savagery worse than that of Phalaris
2 Es 7 : 87 which is worse than all the ways that have been mentioned
8 : 30 Be not angry with those who are deemed worse than beasts
14 : 16 For evils worse than those which you have now seen happen

WORSHIP, subst.   6 = 0.004 %
Wis 14 : 18 to intensify their worship
14 : 20 now regarded as an object of worship
14 : 27 For the worship of idols not to be named
Sir 50 : 19 till the order of worship of the Lord was ended
50 : 21 and they bowed down in worship a 2nd time
3 Ma 3 : 7 instead they gossiped about the differences in worship and foods

WORSHIP, verb   30 = 0.020 %
Tob 5 : 13 to worship and offered the first-born of our flocks
Jud 3 : 8 so that all nations should worship Nebuchadnezzar only
5 : 8 and they worshipped the God of heaven
6 : 18 Then the people fell down and worshipped God
8 : 18 or city of ours which worshipped gods made with hands

10 : 8 And she worshipped God
13 : 17 and bowed down and worshipped God
16 : 18 When they arrived at Jerusalem they worshipped God
Ad E 15 : 1 she took off the garments in which she had worshipped
Wis 11 : 15 to worship irrational serpents and worthless animals
14 : 16 and at the command of monarchs graven images were worshipped
15 : 6 are those who either make or desire or worship them
15 : 17 for he is better than the objects he worships
15 : 18 The enemies of thy people worship
Sir 50 : 17 to worship their Lord, the Almighty, God Most High
L Jr 6 : 5 when you see the multitude before and behind them worshipping them
6 : 6 It is thou, O Lord, whom we must worship
P Az 68 Bless him, all who worship the Lord, the God of gods
Bel 14 : 4 The king revered it and went every day to worship it
14 : 4 But Daniel worshipped his own God
14 : 5 And the king said to him, Why do you not worship Bel ?
14 : 24 You cannot deny that this is a living god ; so worship him
14 : 25 Daniel said, I will worship the Lord my God
14 : 27 And Daniel said, See what you have been worshipping !
1 Ma 4 : 55 and worshipped and blessed Heaven, who had prospered them
2 Ma 1 : 3 May he give you all a heart to worship him
1 Es 1 : 4 Now worship the Lord your God
9 : 47 and fell to the ground and worshipped the Lord
3 Ma 3 : 4 but because they worshipped God
4 Ma 5 : 24 so that with proper reverence we worship the only real God

WORSHIPPER, WORSHIPER   2
Wis 14 : 28 For their worshippers either rave in exultation
P Az 10 shame and disgrace have befallen thy servants and worshippers

WORST   1
3 Ma 6 : 26 and often have accepted willingly the worst of human dangers ?

WORTH, subst., adj.   6 = 0.004 %
Wis 15 : 10 and his life is of less worth than clay
Sir 7 : 19 for her charm is worth more than gold
10 : 28 and ascribe to yourself honour according to your worth
2 Ma 9 : 15 and the Jews, whom he had not considered worth burying
1 Es 8 : 56 and silver vessels worth a 100 talents
2 Es 7 : 58 what is plentiful is of less worth

WORTHILY   2
Tob 12 : 6 worthily declaring the works of God
13 : 10 Give thanks worthily to the Lord

WORTHLESS   4 = 0.003 %
Wis 9 : 14 For the reasoning of mortals is worthless
11 : 15 to worship irrational serpents and worthless animals
13 : 14 or makes it like some worthless animal
2 Es 11 : 45 and your whole worthless body

WORTHLESSNESS   1
L Jr 6 : 26 revealing to mankind their worthlessness

WORTHY, adj., subst.   31 = 0.020 %
Wis 3 : 5 because God tested them and found them worthy of himself
6 : 16 because she goes about seeking those worthy of her
7 : 15 and have thoughts worthy of what I have received
9 : 12 and shall be worthy of the throne of my father
12 : 7 might receive a worthy colony of the servants of God
Sir 10 : 19 What race is worthy of honour ? The human race
10 : 19 What race is worthy of honour ?
10 : 20 Among brothers their leader is worthy of honour
10 : 20 are worthy of honour in his eyes
11 : 31 and to worthy actions he will attach blame
14 : 11 and present worthy offerings to the Lord
P Az 3 and worthy of praise
1 Ma 10 : 19 that you are a mighty warrior and worthy to be our friend
2 Ma 6 : 23 worthy of his years and the dignity of his old age
6 : 24 Such pretence is not worthy of our time of life, he said
6 : 27 I will show myself worthy of my old age
7 : 20 and worthy of honourable memory
7 : 29 Do not fear this butcher, but prove worthy of your brothers
9 : 19 To his worthy Jewish citizens
15 : 11 a sort of vision, which was worthy of belief
3 Ma 3 : 21 by deciding both to deem them worthy of Alexandrian citizenship
2 Es 4 : 24 and we are not worthy to obtain mercy
4 : 44 and if it is possible, and if I am worthy
12 : 9 For thou hast judged me worthy
12 : 36 And you alone were worthy to learn this secret of the Most High
13 : 14 and hast deemed me worthy to have my prayer heard by thee
14 : 45 and let the worthy and the unworthy read them
4 Ma 7 : 6 O priest, worthy of the priesthood
9 : 21 the courageous youth, worthy of Abraham, did not groan
10 : 12 When he also had died in a manner worthy of his brothers
18 : 3 but also were deemed worthy to share in a divine inheritance

WOUND, subst.   9 = 0.006 %
Jud **9** : 13   Make my deceitful words to be their wound and stripe
Sir **21** : 3   there is no healing for its wound
    25 : 13   Any wound, but not a wound of the heart !
    27 : 21   For a wound may be bandaged
    27 : 25   and a treacherous blow opens up wounds
    30 : 7   He who spoils his son will bind up his wounds
    31 : 30   reducing his strength and adding wounds
2 Ma **14** : 45 and though his blood gushed forth and his wounds were severe

WOUND, verb   14 = 0.009 %
Jud **16** : 12   they were wounded like the children of fugitives
1 Ma **1** : 18   and many were wounded and fell
      3 : 11   Many were wounded and fell, and the rest fled
      8 : 10   Many of them were wounded and fell
      9 : 17   and many on both sides were wounded and fell
      9 : 40   Many were wounded and fell, and the rest fled to the mountain
     16 : 8   and many of them were wounded and fell
     16 : 9   At that time Judas the brother of John was wounded
2 Ma **3** : 16   was to be wounded at heart
      4 : 42   As a result, they wounded many of them, and killed some
      8 : 24   and wounded and disabled most of Nicanor's army
     10 : 30   they kept him from being wounded
     11 : 12   Most of them got away stripped and wounded
2 Es **15** : 51   who is beaten and wounded

WOUNDED, adj., subst.   3 = 0.002 %
Jud   **2** : 8   till their wounded shall fill their valleys
      6 : 6   and you shall fall among their wounded, when I return
Sir **25** : 23   A dejected mind, a gloomy face, and a wounded heart

WRAP up   1
Jud **10** : 5   and she wrapped up all her vessels

WRATH   62 = 0.040 %
Jud   **9** : 9   Behold their pride, and send thy wrath upon their heads
Ad E **16** : 24 shall be destroyed in wrath with spear and fire
Wis   **5** : 20   and sharpen stern wrath for a sword
      5 : 22   and hailstones full of wrath will be hurled as from a catapult
     10 : 10   When a righteous man fled from his brother's wrath
     11 : 9   were tormented when judged in wrath
     16 : 5   thy wrath did not continue to the end
     18 : 20   but the wrath did not long continue
     18 : 22   He conquered the wrath not by strength of body
     18 : 23   he intervened and held back the wrath
     18 : 25   for merely to test the wrath was enough
Sir   **5** : 6   for both mercy and wrath are with him
      5 : 7   for suddenly the wrath of the Lord will go forth
      7 : 16   remember that wrath does not delay
     16 : 6   and in a disobedient nation wrath was kindled
     16 : 11   For mercy and wrath are with the Lord
     16 : 11   he is mighty to forgive, and he pours out wrath
     18 : 24   Think of his wrath on the day of death
     23 : 16   and a 3rd incurs wrath
     25 : 15   and no wrath worse than an enemy's wrath
     25 : 22   There is wrath and impudence and great disgrace
     27 : 30   Anger and wrath, these also are abominations
     28 : 5   If he himself, being flesh, maintains wrath
     28 : 10   and in proportion to his wealth he will heighten his wrath
     36 : 7   Rouse thy anger and pour out thy wrath
     36 : 9   Let him who survives be consumed in the fiery wrath
     39 : 23   The nations will incur his wrath
     44 : 17   in the time of wrath he was taken in exchange
     45 : 18   in wrath and anger
     45 : 19   and in the wrath of his anger they were destroyed
     47 : 20   so that you brought wrath upon your children
     48 : 10   to calm the wrath of God before it breaks out in fury
Bar   **1** : 13   and to this day the anger of the Lord and his wrath
      2 : 20   For thou hast sent thy anger and thy wrath upon us
      4 : 9   For she saw the wrath that came upon you from God
      4 : 25   the wrath that has come upon you from God
1 Ma **1** : 64   And very great wrath came upon Israel
      2 : 44   and lawless men in their wrath
      3 : 8   thus he turned away wrath from Israel
     15 : 36   But returned in wrath to the king
2 Ma **5** : 20   and what was forsaken in the wrath of the Almighty
      7 : 38   to bring to an end the wrath of the Almighty
      8 : 5   for the wrath of the Lord had turned to mercy
1 Es **8** : 21   so that wrath may not come
      9 : 13   until we are freed from the wrath of the Lord
P Ma   **5**   and the wrath of thy threat to sinners is irresistible
          10   for I have provoked thy wrath
3 Ma **2** : 17   lest the transgressors boast in their wrath
      5 : 1   was filled with overpowering anger and wrath
      5 : 30   But at these words he was filled with an overpowering wrath
2 Es **15** : 23   And a fire will go forth from his wrath
     15 : 30   Also the Carmonians, raging in wrath
     15 : 34   full of wrath and storm
     15 : 37   and those who see that wrath shall be horror-stricken
     15 : 39   over the cloud that was raised in wrath

     15 : 40   And great and mighty clouds, full of wrath and tempest
     15 : 44   they shall pour out the tempest and all its wrath upon her
     16 : 9   Fire will go forth from his wrath
     16 : 68   For behold, the burning wrath of a great multitude is kindled over you
4 Ma **4** : 11   to pray for him and propitiate the wrath of the heavenly army
      9 : 32   the judgments of the divine wrath

WRATHFUL   1
Sir   **8** : 16   Do not fight with a wrathful man

WREATH   3 = 0.002 %
Jud **15** : 13   and they crowned themselves with olive wreaths
Sir **32** : 2   and receive a wreath for your excellent leadership
2 Ma **6** : 7   in honour of Dionysus, wearing wreaths of ivy

WRECK   1
2 Es **15** : 60   And as they pass they shall wreck the hateful city

WRESTLING   1
2 Ma **4** : 14   in the wrestling arena after the call to the discus

WRETCH   6 = 0.004 %
2 Ma **7** : 9   You accursed wretch, you dismiss us from this present life
      7 : 34   But you, unholy wretch, you most defiled of all men
     15 : 3   the thrice-accursed wretch asked
3 Ma **5** : 37   How many times, you poor wretch
2 Es **15** : 47   woe to you, miserable wretch !
4 Ma **8** : 17   O wretches that we are and so senseless !

WRETCHED   7 = 0.005 %
Bar   **4** : 31   Wretched will be those who afflicted you and rejoiced at your fall
      4 : 32   Wretched will be the cities which your children served as slaves
      4 : 32   wretched will be the city which received your sons
3 Ma **5** : 5   and bound the hands of the wretched people
2 Es **15** : 51   You shall be weakened like a wretched woman
4 Ma **16** : 6   O how wretched am I and many times unhappy !
     16 : 7   fruitless nurturings and wretched nursings !

WRITE   89 = 0.058 %
Tob **12** : 20   Write in a book everything that has happened
     13 : 1   Then Tobit wrote a prayer of rejoicing, and said :
Jud   **4** : 6   wrote to the people of Bethulia and Betomesthaim
Ad E **12** : 4   and Mordecai wrote an account of them
     13 : 1   writes thus : Having become ruler of many nations
Sir **pr.**   by both speaking and writing
     pr.   was himself also led to write something
     48 : 10   you who are ready at the appointed time, it is written
     50 : 27   I have written in this book
Bar   **1** : 1   wrote in Babylon
      2 : 2   in accordance with what is written in the law of Moses
      2 : 28   to write thy law in the presence of the people of Israel
1 Ma **1** : 41   Then the king wrote to his whole kingdom
      1 : 51   In such words he wrote to his whole kingdom
      7 : 16   in accordance with the word which was written
      8 : 22   which they wrote in reply, on bronze tablets
      8 : 31   we have written to him as follows
     10 : 17   And he wrote a letter
     10 : 24   I also will write them words of encouragement
     10 : 56   And now I will do for you as you wrote
     10 : 59   Then Alexander the king wrote to Jonathan to come to meet him
     11 : 22   and he wrote to Jonathan not to continue the siege
     11 : 29   and wrote a letter to Jonathan about all these things
     11 : 31   which we wrote concerning you to Lasthenes our kinsman
     11 : 31   we have written to you also
     11 : 57   Then the young Antiochus wrote to Jonathan, saying
     12 : 5   which Jonathan wrote to the Spartans :
     12 : 22   please write us concerning your welfare
     12 : 23   we on our part write to you
     13 : 35   and wrote him a letter as follows
     13 : 37   and to write to our officials
     13 : 42   and the people began to write
     14 : 18   they wrote to him on bronze tablets
     14 : 27   This is a copy of what they wrote :
     14 : 43   should be written in his name
     15 : 15   in which the following was written :
     15 : 19   We therefore have decided to write
     15 : 22   The consul wrote the same thing to Demetrius the king
     16 : 18   Then Ptolemy wrote a report about these things
     16 : 24   behold, they are written
2 Ma **1** : 7   we Jews wrote to you, in the critical distress
      2 : 16   we write to you
      8 : 8   he wrote to Ptolemy
      9 : 18   and wrote to the Jews the following letter
      9 : 25   and I have written to him what is written here
     11 : 16   The letter written to the Jews by Lysias was to this effect :
     14 : 27   wrote to Nicanor, stating that he was displeased with the covenant
1 Es **1** : 11   as it is written in the book of Moses

1:33	These things are written in the book of the histories
1:42	are written in the chronicles of the kings
2:16	wrote him the following letter
2:22	You will find in the chronicles what has been written about them
2:25	and Syria and Phoenicia, wrote as follows :
3:8	Then each wrote his own statement
3:9	the victory shall be given according to what is written
3:10	The first wrote, Wine is strongest
3:11	The 2nd wrote, The king is strongest
3:12	The 3rd wrote, Women are strongest
3:17	Explain to us what you have written
4:42	even beyond what is written, and we will give it to you
4:47	and wrote letters for him to all the treasurers
4:48	And he wrote letters to all the governors in Coelesyria
4:49	And he wrote for all the Jews who were going up
4:54	He wrote also concerning their support and the priests
4:55	He wrote that the support for the Levites should be provided
4:56	He wrote that land and wages should be provided
6:7	wrote and sent to Darius :
6:17	King Cyrus wrote that this house should be rebuilt
6:32	or nullify any of the things herein written
7:6	did according to what was written in the book of Moses
8:8	The following is a copy of the written commission
3 Ma 3:11	wrote this letter against them :
3:30	The letter was written in the above form
4:20	that both the paper and the pens they used for writing
6:41	and wrote the following letter for them
2 Es 4:23	and the written covenants no longer exist
12:37	Therefore write all these things that you have seen in a book
14:22	and I will write everything that has happened in the world from the beginning
14:22	the things which were written in thy law
14:24	these 5, because they are trained to write rapidly
14:25	until what you are about to write is finished
14:26	tomorrow at this hour you shall begin to write
14:42	and by turns they wrote what was dictated
14:42	They sat 40 days, and wrote during the daytime
14:44	So during the 40 days 94 books were written
14:45	Make public the 24 books that you wrote first
14:46	but keep the 70 that were written last
15:2	and cause them to be written on paper

WRITE out 1
Tob 7:14 and took a scroll and wrote out the contract

WRITHING 1
Wis 16:5 by the bites of writhing serpents

WRITING 13 = 0.008 %
Sir 39:32	and have thought this out and left it in writing :
44:5	and set forth verses in writing
1 Ma 12:21	It has been found in writing
2 Ma 2:4	It was also in the writing
2:13	and the writings of David
11:15	which Maccabeus delivered to Lysias in writing
1 Es 2:2	and also put it in writing :
3:9	they will give him the writing
3:13	they took the writing and gave it to him, and he read it
3:15	and the writing was read in their presence
5:55	according to the decree which they had in writing
6:12	And in order that we might inform you in writing
2 Es 14:24	*But prepare for yourself many writing tablets*

WRONG, adj., subst. 19 = 0.012 %
Jud 11:11	when they do what is wrong
Sir 3:24	and wrong opinion has caused their thoughts to slip
7:2	Stay away from wrong, and it will turn away from you
13:3	A rich man does wrong, and he even adds reproaches
13:3	a poor man suffers wrong, and he must add apologies
19:4	and one who sins does wrong to himself
20:19	An ungracious man is like a story told at the wrong time
22:6	Like music in mourning is a tale told at the wrong time
28:2	Forgive your neighbour the wrong he has done
Bar 2:12	we have sinned, we have been ungodly, we have done wrong
1 Ma 2:67	and avenge the wrong done to your people
8:31	And concerning the wrongs
10:5	for he will remember all the wrongs which we did to him
10:46	because they remembered the great wrongs
2 Ma 3:12	that wrong should be done to those people
10:12	because of the wrong that had been done to them
14:28	when the man had done no wrong
3 Ma 1:14	And someone heedlessly said that it was wrong
4 Ma 5:9	and wrong to spurn the gifts of nature

WRONG, verb 5 = 0.003 %
Wis 18:2	though previously wronged, were doing them no injury
Sir 4:9	Deliver him who is wronged from the hand of the wrongdoer
35:13	and he will listen to the prayer of one who is wronged

L Jr 6:54	They cannot judge their own cause or deliver one who is wronged
3 Ma 3:8	The Greeks in the city, though wronged in no way

WRONGDOER 1
Sir 4:9 Deliver him who is wronged from the hand of the wrongdoer

WRONGDOING 4 = 0.003 %
Tob 4:5	and do not walk in the ways of wrongdoing
12:8	than much with wrongdoing
Sir 18:27	and in days of sin he guards against wrongdoing
26:29	A merchant can hardly keep from wrongdoing

WRONGFULLY 1
Sir 34:18 If one sacrifices from what has been wrongfully obtained

WRONGLY 1
4 Ma 5:18 and we had wrongly held it to be divine

X

XANTHICUS 3 = 0.002 %
2 Ma 11:30	Therefore those who go home by the 30th day of Xanthicus
11:33	Farewell. The 148th year, Xanthicus 15th
11:38	Farewell. The 148th year, Xanthicus 15th

Y

YAWNING 1
Wis 19:17 when, surrounded by yawning darkness

YEA 1
Jud 9:5 Yea, the things thou didst intend came to pass

YEAR 135 = 0.088 %
Tob 1:7	each year at Jerusalem
14:2	He was 58 years old when he lost his sight
14:2	and after 8 years he regained it
14:11	He was a 158 years old
14:14	He died in Ecbatana of Media at the age of a 127 years
Jud 1:1	In the 12th year of the reign of Nebuchadnezzar
1:13	In the 17th year he led his forces against King Arphaxad
2:1	In the 18th year, on the 22nd day of the first month
8:4	for 3 years and 4 months
16:23	until she was 105 years old
Ad E 11:1	In the 4th year of the reign of Ptolemy and Cleopatra
11:2	In the 2nd year of the reign of Ahasuerus the Great
13:6	of this present year
Wis 4:8	nor measured by number of years
4:13	Being perfected in a short time, he fulfilled long years
7:19	the cycles of the year and the constellations of the stars
Sir pr.	in the 38th year of the reign of Euergetes
18:9	if he reaches a 100 years
18:10	so are a few years in the day of eternity
26:2	and will complete his years in peace
26:26	for the number of his years will be doubled
33:7	when all the daylight in the year is from the sun ?
37:11	or with a man hired for a year about completing his work
41:4	Whether life is for 10 or a 100 or a 1,000 years
47:10	and arranged their times throughout the year
Bar 1:2	In the 5th year, on the 7th day of the month
L Jr 6:3	you will remain there for many years
Sus 13:5	In that year 2 elders from the people were appointed as judges
1 Ma 1:7	And after Alexander had reigned 12 years, he died
1:9	and so did their sons after them for many years
1:10	He began to reign in the 137th year
1:20	After subduing Egypt, Antiochus returned in the 143rd year
1:29	2 years later the king sent to the cities of Judah
1:54	Now on the 15th day of Chislev, in the 145th year
2:70	He died in the 146th year
3:28	and gave a year's pay to his forces
3:37	and departed from Antioch his capital in the 147th year
4:28	But the next year he mustered 60,000 picked infantrymen
4:52	in the 148th year
4:59	determined that every year at that season
6:16	Thus Antiochus the king died there in the 149th year
6:20	and besieged the citadel in the 150th year
6:49	since it was a sabbatical year for the land
6:53	because it was the 7th year
7:1	In the 151st year Demetrius the son of Seleucus set forth from Rome
7:49	each year on the 13th day of Adar
8:4	the rest paid them tribute every year
8:16	They trust one man each year to rule over them
9:3	In the first month of the 152nd year
9:54	In the 153rd year, in the 2nd month

9:57	and the land of Judah had rest for 2 years	
10:1	In the 160th year Alexander Epiphanes, the son of Antiochus	
10:21	in the 7th month of the 160th year	
10:41	as they did in the first years	
10:42	which my officials have received every year	
10:57	and came to Ptolemais in the 162nd year	
10:67	In the 165th year Demetrius the son of Demetrius	
11:19	So Demetrius became king in the 167th year	
11:34	which the king formerly received from them each year	
13:41	In the 170th year the yoke of the Gentiles was removed from Israel	
13:42	in the first year of Simon the great high priest	
13:51	On the 23rd day of the 2nd month, in the 171st year	
13:52	And Simon decreed that every year	
14:1	In the 172nd year Demetrius the king assembled his forces	
14:27	On the 18th day of Elul, in the 172nd year	
14:27	which is the 3rd year of Simon the great high priest	
15:10	In the 174th year Antiochus set out	
16:3	and you by His mercy are mature in years	
16:14	in the 177th year, in the 11th month, which is the month of Shebat	

2 Ma
1:7	In the reign of Demetrius, in the 169th year	
1:7	which came upon us in those years	
1:9	in the month of Chislev, in the 188th year	
1:20	But after many years had passed, when it pleased God	
4:23	After a period of 3 years Jason sent Menelaus	
4:40	a man advanced in years and no less advanced in folly	
6:23	worthy of his years and the dignity of his old age	
6:24	that Eleazar in his 90th year	
7:27	and nursed you for 3 years	
10:3	after a lapse of 2 years	
10:8	should observe these days every year	
11:3	and to put up the high priesthood for sale every year	
11:21	Farewell. The 148th year, Dioscorinthius 24th	
11:33	Farewell. The 148th year, Xanthicus 15th	
11:38	Farewell. The 148th year, Xanthicus 15th	
13:1	In the 149th year word came to Judas and his men	
14:1	3 years later, word came to Judas and his men	
14:4	and went to King Demetrius in about the 151st year	

1 Es
1:22	In the 18th year of the reign of Josiah	
1:34	who was 23 years old	
1:39	Jehoiakim was 25 years old	
1:43	when he was made king he was 18 years old	
1:45	So after a year Nebuchadnezzar sent	
1:46	Zedekiah was 21 years old, and he reigned 11 years	
1:58	until the completion of 70 years	
2:1	In the first year of Cyrus as king of the Persians	
2:30	until the 2nd year of the reign	
4:51	that 20 talents a year should be given	
4:52	and an additional 10 talents a year	
5:6	in the 2nd year of his reign	
5:41	All those of Israel, 12 or more years of age	
5:56	in the 2nd year after their coming to the temple of God in Jerusalem	
5:57	in the 2nd year after they came to Judea and Jerusalem	
5:58	who were 20 or more years of age	
5:73	And they were kept from building for 2 years	
6:1	Now in the 2nd year of the reign of Darius	
6:14	And the house was built many years ago	
6:17	But in the first year that Cyrus reigned	
6:24	In the first year of the reign of Cyrus	
6:30	regularly every year, without quibbling	
7:5	in the 6th year of King Darius	
8:6	in the 7th year of the reign of Artaxerxes	
8:6	in the 5th month (this was the king's 7th year)	

3 Ma 1:11 and he only once a year

2 Es
3:1	In the 30th year after the destruction of our city	
3:23	So the times passed and the years were completed	
3:25	This was done for many years	
3:29	and my soul has seen many sinners during these 30 years	
4:33	Why are our years few and evil?	
6:5	and before the present years were reckoned	
6:21	Infants a year old shall speak with their voices	
7:28	and those who remain shall rejoice 400 years	
7:29	And after these years my son the Messiah shall die	
7:43	For it will last for about a week of years	
9:43	though I lived with my husband 30 years	
9:44	And every hour and every day during those 30 years	
9:45	And after 30 years God heard your handmaid	
10:45	And as for her telling you that she was barren for 30 years	
10:45	it is because there were 3,000 years in the world	
10:46	And after 3,000 years Solomon built the city	
12:20	whose times shall be short and their years swift	
13:45	a journey of a year and a half	

4 Ma
2:8	and to cancel the debt when the 7th year arrives	
5:11	adopt a mind appropriate to your years	
16:1	If, then, a woman, advanced in years and mother of 7 sons	

YEARLY
1 Ma 10:40   I also grant 15,000 shekels of silver yearly   1

YEARN
Tob 6:17   and yearned deeply for her   1

YEARNING
   2
Wis 15:5   whose appearance arouses yearning in fools
4 Ma 15:13   yearning of parents toward offspring, nurture

YES
   3 = 0.002 %
Tob 7:4   And they said, Yes, we do
2 Es 4:3   Then I said, Yes, my lord
4 Ma 14:9   yes, not only heard the direct word of threat

YESTERDAY
   1
Sir 38:22   yesterday it was mine, and today it is yours

YET, adv., conj.
   68 = 0.044 %
Tob	4:4	while you were yet unborn
Jud	9:2	yet they did it
	13:16	and yet he committed no act of sin with me
Wis	4:15	Yet the peoples saw and did not understand
	9:6	yet without the wisdom that comes from thee
	13:6	Yet these men are little to be blamed
	13:8	Yet again, not even they are to be excused
	17:9	yet, scared by the passing of beasts
	18:13	yet, when their first-born were destroyed
Sir	17:24	Yet to those who repent he grants a return
	17:31	Yet its light fails
	28:3	and yet seek for healing from the Lord?
	28:4	and yet pray for his own sins?
	30:4	The father may die, and yet he is not dead
	32:8	be as one who knows and yet holds his tongue
	36:18	yet one food is better than another
	37:19	and yet be unprofitable to himself
	38:33	Yet they are not sought out for the council of the people
	39:12	I have yet more to say, which I have thought upon
	49:7	yet he had been consecrated in the womb as prophet
Bar	2:8	Yet we have not entreated the favour of the Lord
	2:10	Yet we have not obeyed his voice
	2:27	Yet thou hast dealt with us, O Lord our God
L Jr	6:42	Yet they themselves cannot perceive this and abandon them
P Az	16	Yet with a contrite heart and a humble spirit may we be accepted
Sus	13:43	Yet I have done none of the things
1 Ma	2:20	yet I and my sons and my brothers will live
	8:14	Yet for all this not one of them has put on a crown
2 Ma	6:26	yet whether I live or die
	7:35	You have not yet escaped the judgment of the almighty, all-seeing God
	8:15	yet for the sake of the covenants made with their fathers
	9:7	Yet he did not any way stop his insolence
1 Es	4:7	And yet he is only one man!
	4:29	Yet I have seen him with Apame, the king's concubine
	5:53	though the temple of God was not yet built
	6:5	Yet the elders of the Jews were dealt with kindly
	6:20	it has not yet reached completion
P Ma	6	yet immeasurable and unsearchable is thy promised mercy
3 Ma	5:26	The rays of the sun were not yet shed abroad
2 Es	1:14	Yet you have forgotten me, says the Lord
	1:36	yet will recall their former state
	1:37	yet with the spirit they will believe the things I have said
	3:5	Yet he was the workmanship of thy hands
	3:20	Yet thou didst not take away from them their evil heart
	3:33	Yet their reward has not appeared
	4:8	I never went down into the deep, nor as yet into hell
	4:28	but the harvest of it has not yet come
	5:13	you shall hear yet greater things than these
	5:36	He said to me, Count up for me those who have not yet come
	5:41	And I said, Yet behold, O Lord
	6:39	the sound of man's voice was not yet there
	7:31	which is not yet awake, shall be roused
	7:49	and I will instruct you, and will admonish you yet again
	7:132	because he has mercy on those who have not yet come into the world
	7:136	and to those who are gone and to those yet to come
	8:41	and yet not all that have been sown will come up in due season
	9:32	yet the fruit of the law did not perish
	9:33	Yet those who received it perished
	9:35	yet with us it has not been so
	11:20	There were some of them that ruled, yet disappeared suddenly
	13:8	were much afraid, yet dared to fight
	13:20	Yet is it better to come into these things
	13:28	yet destroying the onrushing multitude
	16:20	Yet for all this they will not turn from their iniquities
4 Ma	6:6	yet while the old man's eyes were raised to heaven
	15:8	yet because of the fear of God she disdained

469

16:12	Yet the sacred and God-fearing mother	
18:20	O bitter was that day – and yet not bitter	

YIELD, verb   7 = 0.005 %

Jud	**2**:10	They will yield themselves to you
Wis	**18**:25	To these the destroyer yielded, these he feared
2 Ma	**13**:23	yielded and swore to observe all their rights
2 Es	**7**:13	*and really yield the fruit of immortality*
4 Ma	**6**:35	and in no respect yields to them
	8:5	but I also exhort you to yield to me and enjoy my friendship
	12:5	but if you yield to persuasion you will be my friend

YIELD up   1

2 Es	**7**:75	as soon as every one of us yields up his soul

YOKE, subst.   11 = 0.007 %

Sir	**6**:30	Her yoke is a golden ornament
	26:7	An evil wife is an ox yoke which chafes
	28:19	who has not borne its yoke
	28:20	for its yoke is a yoke of iron
	33:26	Yoke and thong will bow the neck
	40:1	and a heavy yoke is upon the sons of Adam
	51:26	Put your neck under the yoke
1 Ma	**8**:18	and to free themselves from the yoke
	8:31	Why have you made your yoke heavy
	13:41	In the 170th year the yoke of the Gentiles was removed from Israel

YOU   1550 = 1.010 %

YOUNG, adj., subst.   81 = 0.053 %

Tob	**1**:4	while I was still a young man
	5:16	and the young man's dog was with them
	6:2	Then the young man went down to wash himself
	6:2	and would have swallowed the young man
	6:3	So the young man seized the fish and threw it up on the land
	6:5	So the young man did as the angel told him
	6:6	Then the young man said to the angel, Brother Azarias
	6:10	the angel said to the young man
	6:13	Then the young man said to the angel, Brother Azarias
	7:2	How much the young man resembles my cousin Tobit !
Jud	**2**:27	and put to death all their young men
	6:16	and all their young men and their women ran to the assembly
	7:22	and the women and young men fainted from thirst
	7:23	Then all the people, the young men, the women, and the children
	10:9	So they ordered the young men
	16:5	and kill my young men with the sword
	16:7	by the hands of the young men
Wis	**3**:18	If they die young, they will have no hope
	8:10	and honour in the presence of the elders, though I am young
Sir	**30**:12	and beat his sides while he is young
	32:7	Speak, young man, if there is need of you
	42:8	or the aged man who quarrels with the young
	42:9	when she is young, lest she do not marry
	47:3	He played with lions as with young goats
	50:12	he was like a young cedar on Lebanon
	51:13	While I was still young, before I went on my travels
Bar	**3**:20	Young men have seen the light of day
Sus	**13**:21	that a young man was with you
	13:37	Then a young man, who had been hidden
	13:40	So we seized this woman and asked her who the young man was
	13:45	God aroused the holy spirit of a young lad named Daniel
1 Ma	**1**:26	maidens and young men became faint
	11:39	who was bringing up Antiochus, the young son of Alexander
	11:54	and with him the young boy Antiochus
	11:57	Then the young Antiochus wrote to Jonathan, saying
	13:31	Trypho dealt treacherously with the young king Antiochus
2 Ma	**3**:26	2 young men also appeared to him, remarkably strong
	3:33	the same young men appeared again to Heliodorus
	4:12	and he induced the noblest of the young men
	5:13	Then there was killing of young and old
	6:24	lest many of the young should suppose
	6:28	and leave to the young a noble example
	6:31	not only to the young but to the great body of his nation
	7:12	were astonished at the young man's spirit
	7:24	The youngest brother being still alive
	7:25	Since the young man would not listen to him at all
	7:30	While she was still speaking, the young man said
	10:35	20 young men in the army of Maccabeus
	12:27	Stalwart young men took their stand before the walls
	13:15	and with a picked force of the bravest young men
	15:17	and awaking manliness in the souls of the young
1 Es	**1**:53	These slew their young men with the sword around their holy temple
	1:53	and did not spare young man or virgin
	3:4	Then the 3 young men of the bodyguard
	3:16	And he said, Call the young men
	4:58	When the young man went out
	8:50	There I proclaimed a fast for the young men before our Lord

Ps 151	:1	I was small among my brothers, and youngest in my father's house
3 Ma	**4**:6	And young women who had just entered the bridal chamber
2 Es	**2**:22	Protect the old and the young within your walls
	2:43	In their midst was a young man of great stature
	2:46	Who is that young man who places crowns on them
	5:50	Is our mother, of whom thou hast told me, still young ?
	10:22	our young men have been enslaved and our strong men made powerless
4 Ma	**2**:3	For when he was young and in his prime for intercourse
	3:12	2 staunch young soldiers, respecting the king's desire
	5:31	as not to be young in reason on behalf of piety
	6:19	and ourselves become a pattern of impiety to the young
	7:13	his muscles flabby, his sinews feeble, he became young again
	8:1	For this is why even the very young
	8:5	Young men, I admire each and every one of you in a kindly manner
	8:14	Be afraid, young fellows
	9:6	that we young men should die despising your coercive tortures
	11:14	he said, I am younger in age than my brothers
	12:1	the 7th and youngest of all came forward
	14:9	as we hear of the tribulations of these young men
	14:12	for the mother of the 7 young men bore up
	14:15	protect their young by building on the housetops
	14:17	they do what they can to help their young
	14:20	the mother of the young men
	16:17	you young men were to be terrified by tortures

YOUR   761 = 0.496 %

YOURSELF   87 = 0.057 %

YOUTH   39 = 0.025 %

Wis	**2**:6	and make use of the creation to the full as in youth
	4:16	and youth that is quickly perfected
	8:2	I loved her and sought her from my youth
Sir	**6**:18	My son, from your youth up choose instruction
	7:23	and make them obedient from their youth
	15:2	and like the wife of his youth she will welcome him
	17:16	Their ways from youth tend toward evil
	25:3	You have gathered nothing in your youth
	26:19	My son, keep sound the bloom of your youth
	30:11	Give him no authority in his youth
	30:12	Bow down his neck in his youth
	47:4	In his youth did he not kill a giant
	47:14	How wise you became in your youth !
	51:15	from my youth I followed her steps
1 Ma	**1**:6	who had been brought up with him from youth
	2:9	her youths by the sword of the foe
	2:66	Judas Maccabeus has been a mighty warrior from his youth
	14:9	and the youths donned the glories and garments of war
	16:2	have fought the wars of Israel from our youth until this day
2 Ma	**4**:9	a gymnasium and a body of youth for it
	7:25	and urged her to advise the youth to save himself
1 Es	**8**:91	men and women and youths
3 Ma	**4**:8	Their husbands, in the prime of youth
2 Es	**5**:53	Those born in the strength of youth
	5:55	and passing the strength of youth
	6:32	which you have maintained from your youth
	14:10	For the age has lost its youth
4 Ma	**8**:8	And enjoy your youth by adopting the Greek way of life
	8:10	for your youth and handsome appearance
	8:20	Let us take pity on our youth
	8:27	But the youths, though about to be tortured
	9:13	When the noble youth was stretched out around this
	9:21	the courageous youth, worthy of Abraham, did not groan
	9:25	the saintly youth broke the thread of life
	13:7	so the seven-towered right reason of the youths
	13:9	let us imitate the 3 youths in Assyria
	14:4	None of the 7 youths proved coward or shrank from death
	14:6	so those holy youths
	14:8	so these youths, forming a chorus

YOUTHFUL   2

2 Ma	**15**:30	the man who maintained his youthful good will
3 Ma	**4**:8	instead of good cheer and youthful revelry

Z

ZABAD   3 = 0.002 %

1 Es	**9**:28	Othoniah Jeremoth, and Zabad and Zerdaiah
	9:33	Of the sons of Hashum : Mattenai and Mattattah and Zabad
	9:35	Mattithiah, Zabad, Iddo, Joel, Benaiah

ZABADEAN   1

1 Ma	**12**:31	who are called Zabadeans

ZABBAI   1
  1 Es **9** :29   Jehohanan and Hananiah and Zabbai and Emathis

ZABDIEL   1
  1 Ma **11** :17   And Zabdiel the Arab cut off the head of Alexander

ZACCHAEUS   1
  2 Ma **10** :19   and also Zacchaeus and his men

ZACCUR   1
  1 Es **9** :24   Of the temple singers : Eliashib and Zaccur

ZADOK   2
  1 Es **8** :2   son of Zadok, son of Ahitub, son of Amariah, son of Uzzi
  2 Es **1** :1   son of Zadok, son of Ahitub

ZARIUS   1
  1 Es **1** :38   and seized his brother Zarius

ZATTU   3 = 0.002 %
  1 Es **5** :12   The sons of Zattu, 945
        8 :32   Of the sons of Zattu, Shecaniah the son of Jahaziel
        9 :28   Of the sons of Zattu : Elioenai, Eliashib

ZEAL   11 = 0.007 %
  Wis **5** :17   The Lord will take his zeal as his whole armour
       14 :17   so that by their zeal
  Sir **48** :2   and by his zeal he made them few in number
  Bar **4** :28   return with tenfold zeal to seek him
  1 Ma **2** :24   When Mattathias saw it, he burned with zeal
        2 :26   Thus he burned with zeal for the law
        2 :50   Now, my children, show zeal for the law
        2 :58   Elijah because of great zeal for the law
  2 Ma **14** :38   and for Judaism he had with all zeal risked body and life
  4 Ma **13** :25   A common zeal for nobility
       18 :12   He told you of the zeal of Phineas

ZEALOT   1
  2 Ma **4** :2   and a zealot for the laws

ZEALOUS   9 = 0.006 %
  Jud **9** :4   who were zealous for thee
  Sir **27** :3   If a man is not steadfast and zealous
       45 :23   for he was zealous in the fear of the Lord
       51 :18   and I was zealous for the good
  1 Ma **2** :27   saying : Let every one who is zealous for the law
        2 :54   Phinehas our father, because he was deeply zealous
  3 Ma **4** :15   with bitter haste and zealous intentness
  2 Es **6** :58   zealous for thee, and most dear
  4 Ma **16** :20   our father Abraham was zealous to sacrifice his son Isaac

ZEALOUSLY   3 = 0.002 %
  2 Ma **2** :21   to those who strove zealously on behalf of Judaism
  3 Ma **5** :27   for which this had been so zealously completed for him
  4 Ma **16** :16   Fight zealously for our ancestral law

ZEBADIAH   1
  1 Es **9** :21   Of the sons of Immer : Hanani and Zebadiah and Maaseiah

ZECHARIAH   12 = 0.008 %
  1 Ma **5** :18   But he left Joseph, the son of Zechariah
        5 :56   Joseph, the son of Zechariah
  1 Es **1** :8   And Hilkiah, Zechariah, and Jehiel
       1 :15   and also Asaph, Zechariah, and Eddinus
       6 :1   the prophets Haggai and Zechariah the son of Iddo
       7 :3   while the prophets Haggai and Zechariah prophesied
       8 :30   Of the sons of Parosh, Zechariah
       8 :37   Of the sons of Bebai, Zechariah the son of Bebai
       8 :44   Zechariah, and Meshullam
       9 :27   Of the sons of Elam : Mattaniah and Zechariah
       9 :44   Lothasubus, Nabariah, and Zechariah
  2 Es **1** :40   Zechariah and Malachi, who is also called the messenger of the Lord

ZEDEKIAH   4 = 0.003 %
  Bar **1** :1   son of Zedekiah, son of Hasadiah, son of Hilkiah
       1 :8   the silver vessels which Zedekiah the son of Josiah, king of Judah, had made
  1 Es **1** :46   and made Zedekiah king of Judea and Jerusalem
       1 :46   Zedekiah was 21 years old, and he reigned 11 years

ZEPHANIAH   1
  2 Es **1** :40   and Nahum and Habakkuk, Zephaniah, Haggai

ZERAHIAH   1
  1 Es **8** :31   Of the sons of Pahath-moab, Eliehoenai the son of Zerahiah

ZERAIAH   1
  1 Es **8** :34   Of the sons of Shephatiah, Zeraiah the son of Michael

ZERDAIAH   1
  1 Es **9** :28   Othoniah Jeremoth, and Zabad and Zerdaiah

ZERUBBABEL   12 = 0.008 %
  Sir **49** :11   How shall we magnify Zerubbabel ?
  1 Es **4** :13   Then the 3rd, that is Zerubbabel
       5 :5   and Joakim the son of Zerubbabel
       5 :8   They came with Zerubbabel and Jeshua
       5 :48   and Zerubbabel the son of Shealtiel, with his kinsmen
       5 :56   in the 2nd month, Zerubbabel the son of Shealtiel
       5 :68   So they approached Zerubbabel and Jeshua
       5 :70   But Zerubbabel and Jeshua
       6 :2   Then Zerubbabel the son of Shealtiel
       6 :18   and they were delivered to Zerubbabel
       6 :27   to keep away from the place, and to permit Zerubbabel
       6 :29   that is, to Zerubbabel the governor

ZEUS   2
  2 Ma **6** :2   and call it the temple of Olympian Zeus
       6 :2   and to call the one in Gerizim the temple of Zeus

ZIHA   1
  1 Es **5** :29   The temple servants : the sons of Ziha

ZIMRI   1
  1 Ma **2** :26   as Phinehas did against Zimri the son of Salu

ZION   35 = 0.023 %
  Jud **9** :13   and against the top of Zion
  Sir **24** :10   and so I was established in Zion
       36 :14   Fill Zion with the celebration of thy wondrous deeds
       48 :18   he lifted up his hand against Zion
       48 :24   and comforted those who mourned in Zion
  Bar **4** :9   and she said : Hearken, you neighbours of Zion
       4 :14   Let the neighbours of Zion come
       4 :24   For as the neighbours of Zion have now seen your capture
  1 Ma **4** :37   So all the army assembled and they went up to Mount Zion
       4 :60   At that time they fortified Mount Zion
       5 :54   So they went up to Mount Zion with gladness and joy
       6 :48   and the king encamped in Judea and at Mount Zion
       6 :62   But when the king entered Mount Zion
       7 :33   After these events Nicanor went up to Mount Zion
      10 :11   to build the walls and encircle Mount Zion
      14 :27   and put it upon pillars on Mount Zion
  1 Es **8** :81   and raised Zion from desolation
  2 Es **2** :40   Take again your full number, O Zion
       2 :42   I, Ezra, saw on Mount Zion a great multitude
       3 :2   because I saw the desolation of Zion
       3 :28   Is that why she has gained dominion over Zion ?
       3 :31   Are the deeds of Babylon better than those of Zion ?
       5 :25   thou hast consecrated Zion for thyself
       6 :4   and before the footstool of Zion was established
       6 :19   and when the humiliation of Zion is complete
      10 :7   For Zion, the mother of us all
      10 :20   because of the troubles of Zion
      10 :23   And, what is more than all, the seal of Zion
      10 :39   and mourned greatly over Zion
      10 :44   whom you now behold as an established city, is Zion
      12 :44   if we also had been consumed in the burning of Zion !
      12 :48   on account of the desolation of Zion
      13 :35   But he will stand on the top of Mount Zion
      13 :36   And Zion will come and be made manifest to all people, prepared and built
      14 :31   for a possession in the land of Zion

Numbers

NUMBER : 1 s. **ONE**   170 = 0.111 %
  Tob **1** :19   Then one of the men of Nineveh went
       2 :3   Father, one of our people has been strangled
       5 :12   one of your relatives
       8 :12   Send one of the maids to see whether he is alive
      12 :15   I am Raphael, one of the 7 holy angels
  Jud **1** :11   but looked upon him as only one man
       5 :7   At one time they lived in Mesopotamia
       6 :3   we the king's servants will destroy them as one man
       6 :7   and put you in one of the cities beside the passes
      10 :13   without losing one of his men, captured or slain
      11 :8   that you are the one good man in the whole kingdom
      11 :18   and not one of them will withstand you
      11 :21   from one end of the earth to the other
      12 :13   and become today like one of the daughters of the Assyrians
      13 :17   and said with one accord, Blessed art thou, our God
      14 :6   in the hand of one of the men
      14 :18   One Hebrew woman has brought disgrace
      15 :2   but with one impulse all rushed out and fled
      15 :5   with one accord they fell upon the enemy
      15 :9   And when they met her they all blessed her with one accord

Ad E	10 : 10	one for the people of God and one for all the nations
	11 : 1	one of the residents of Jerusalem
	11 : 4	He was one of the captives
	13 : 7	may in one day go down in violence to Hades
	15 : 3	leaning daintily on one
Wis	7 : 6	there is for all mankind one entrance into life
	7 : 27	Though she is but one, she can do all things
	8 : 1	She reaches mightily from one end of the earth to the other
	10 : 20	and praised with one accord thy defending hand
	12 : 9	or to destroy them at one blow
	16 : 18	At one time the flame was restrained
	17 : 17	for with one chain of darkness they all were bound
	18 : 5	and one child had been exposed and rescued
	18 : 9	and with one accord agreed to the divine law
	18 : 12	by the one form of death, had corpses too many to count
	18 : 12	since in one instant
	18 : 18	and one here and another there, hurled down half dead
	19 : 8	where those protected by thy hand passed through as one nation
Sir	6 : 6	but let your advisers be one in a 1,000
	6 : 14	he that has found one has found a treasure
	7 : 8	even for one you will not go unpunished
	16 : 3	for one is better than a 1,000
	16 : 4	For through one man of understanding
	16 : 11	Even if there is only one stiff-necked person
	16 : 23	This is what one devoid of understanding thinks
	20 : 14	for he has many eyes instead of one
	33 : 15	they likewise are in pairs, one the opposite of the other
	36 : 18	yet one food is better than another
	36 : 21	but one daughter is better than another
	38 : 17	for one day, or 2, to avoid criticism
	42 : 20	No thought escapes him, and not one word is hidden from him
	42 : 24	All things are twofold, one opposite the other
	42 : 25	One confirms the good things of the other
	46 : 4	And did not one day become as long as 2 ?
	47 : 23	and left behind him one of his sons
Bar	2 : 3	that we should eat, one the flesh of his son
L Jr	6 : 27	If any one sets one of them upright
	6 : 34	They cannot set up a king or depose one
	6 : 43	and when one of them is led off by one of the passers-by and is lain with
P Az	28	Then the 3, as with one mouth
Sus	13 : 2	a very beautiful woman and one who feared the Lord
	13 : 25	And one of them ran and opened the garden doors
	13 : 52	he summoned one of them and said to him
1 Ma	1 : 41	that all should be one people
	3 : 45	not one of her children went in or out
	4 : 11	that there is one who redeems and saves Israel
	4 : 38	or as on one of the mountains
	5 : 27	and take and destroy all these men in one day
	5 : 54	because not one of them had fallen
	6 : 14	Then he called for Philip, one of his friends
	6 : 43	that one of the beasts was equipped with royal armour
	7 : 8	So the king chose Bacchides, one of the king's friends
	7 : 16	but he seized 60 of them and killed them in one day
	7 : 26	Then the king sent Nicanor, one of his honoured princes
	7 : 46	not even one of them was left
	8 : 14	Yet for all this not one of them has put on a crown
	8 : 16	They trust one man each year to rule over them
	8 : 16	they all heed the one man
	9 : 37	a daughter of one of the great nobles of Canaan
	9 : 58	and he will capture them all in one night
	10 : 38	that they are considered to be under one ruler
	11 : 27	and made him to be regarded as one of his chief friends
	11 : 36	And not one of these grants shall be cancelled
	11 : 39	Now Trypho had formerly been one of Alexander's supporters
	11 : 57	and make you one of the friends of the king
	11 : 70	not one of them was left
	13 : 43	and battered and captured one tower
	14 : 2	he sent one of his commanders to take him alive
	14 : 39	and he made him one of the king's friends
	15 : 28	He sent to him Athenobius, one of his friends
	15 : 33	which at one time had been unjustly taken by our enemies
2 Ma	4 : 3	by one of Simon's approved agents
	6 : 18	Eleazar, one of the scribes in high position
	7 : 2	One of them, acting as their spokesman, said
	8 : 9	one of the king's chief friends
	8 : 33	who had fled into one little house
	9 : 29	And Philip, one of his courtiers, took his body home
	10 : 11	appointed one Lysias to have charge of the government
	12 : 18	though in one place he had left a very strong garrison
	12 : 35	But a certain Dositheus, one of Bacenor's men
	12 : 35	when one of the Thracian horsemen bore down upon him
	14 : 20	and it appeared that they were of one mind
	14 : 37	A certain Razis, one of the elders of Jerusalem
1 Es	1 : 36	and one talent of gold
	3 : 5	Let each of us state what one thing is strongest
	4 : 7	And yet he is only one man !
	4 : 34	and returns to its place in one day
	5 : 38	one of the daughters of Barzillai
	5 : 47	they gathered as one man in the square

	5 : 58	as one man pressing forward the work on the house of God
	6 : 25	and one course of new native timber
	8 : 92	one of the men of Israel, called out
	9 : 11	This is not a work we can do in one day or 2
	9 : 38	the whole multitude gathered with one accord
3 Ma	3 : 1	and he ordered that all should promptly be gathered into one place
	5 : 21	all those present readily and joyfully with one accord gave their approval
	5 : 50	they prostrated themselves with one accord on the ground
2 Es	2 : 26	Not one of the servants whom I have given you will perish
	3 : 7	And thou didst lay upon him one commandment of thine
	3 : 11	But thou didst leave one of them
	3 : 13	thou didst choose for thyself one of them
	4 : 4	If you can solve one of them for me
	5 : 11	And one country shall ask its neighbour
	5 : 23	thou hast chosen one vine
	5 : 24	thou hast chosen for thyself one region
	5 : 24	thou hast chosen for thyself one lily
	5 : 25	thou hast filled for thyself one river
	5 : 26	thou hast named for thyself one dove
	5 : 26	thou hast provided for thyself one sheep
	5 : 27	thou hast gotten for thyself one people
	5 : 28	And now, O Lord, why hast thou given over the one to the many
	5 : 28	and dishonoured the one root beyond the others
	5 : 40	Just as you cannot do one of the things that were mentioned
	5 : 43	Couldst thou not have created at one time
	5 : 44	neither can the world hold at one time
	5 : 45	that thou wilt certainly give life at one time to thy creation ?
	5 : 45	If therefore all creatures will live at one time
	5 : 45	all of them present at one time
	5 : 46	why one after another ?
	5 : 46	Request it therefore to produce 10 at one time
	6 : 41	that one part might move upward and the other part remain beneath
	6 : 49	the name of one thou didst call Behemoth
	6 : 50	And thou didst separate one from the other
	6 : 51	And thou didst give Behemoth one of the parts
	7 : 8	and there is only one path lying between them, that is
	7 : 8	so that only one man can walk upon that path
	7 : 50	For this reason the Most High has made not world but 2
	7 : 79	And if it is one of those who have shown scorn
	7 : 138	not one ten-thousandth of mankind could have life
	9 : 21	and saved for myself one grape out of a cluster
	9 : 21	and one plant out of a great forest
	10 : 8	you are sorrowing for one son, but we, the whole world, for our mother
	10 : 11	or you who are grieving for one ?
	11 : 6	not even one creature that was on the earth
	11 : 12	on the right side one wing arose
	11 : 19	they wielded power one after another
	11 : 26	one was set up, but suddenly disappeared
	11 : 29	one of the heads that were at rest
	12 : 14	And 12 kings shall reign in it, one after another
	12 : 26	one of the kings shall die in his bed, but in agonies
	12 : 28	For the sword of one shall devour him who was with him
	14 : 15	and lay to one side the thoughts that are most grievous to you
	15 : 33	and destroy one of them
	16 : 27	one man will long to see another
4 Ma	5 : 4	one man, Eleazar by name, leader of the flock
	6 : 8	One of the cruel guards rushed at him
	8 : 29	all with one voice together, as from one mind, said :

NUMBER : 1st s. FIRST   60 = 0.039 %

Tob	1 : 6	Taking the first fruits and the tithes of my produce
	1 : 6	and the first shearings
Jud	2 : 1	In the 18th year, on the 22nd day of the first month
	8 : 29	Today is not the first time your wisdom has been shown
	11 : 13	They have decided to consume the first fruits of the grain
Ad E	11 : 2	on the first day of Nisan
Wis	7 : 3	and my first sound was a cry, like that of all
Sir	7 : 31	the first fruits, the guilt offering
	7 : 31	and the first fruits of the holy things
	23 : 23	For first of all
	24 : 25	and like the Tigris at the time of the first fruits
	24 : 28	Just as the first man did not know her perfectly
	31 : 17	Be the first to stop eating, for the sake of good manners
	35 : 8	and do not stint the first fruits of your hands
	45 : 20	he allotted to him the first of the first fruits
	45 : 20	he prepared bread of first fruits in abundance
	50 : 8	like roses in the days of the first fruits
1 Ma	2 : 18	Now be the first to come and do what the king commands
	3 : 49	and the first fruits and the tithes
	7 : 13	The Hasidaeans were the first among the sons of Israel
	7 : 43	and he himself was the first to fall in the battle
	9 : 3	In the first month of the 152nd year
	10 : 41	as they did in the first years
	10 : 47	because he had been the first to speak peaceable words to them
	13 : 42	In the first year of Simon the great high priest
	16 : 6	so he crossed over first

2 Ma	7:7	After the first brother had died in this way
	7:8	as the first brother had done
	8:23	then, leading the first division himself
	11:7	Maccabeus himself was the first to take up arms
	12:22	But when Judas' first division appeared
	15:18	their greatest and first fear
1 Es	1:1	he killed the passover lamb on the 14th day of the first month
	2:1	In the first year of Cyrus as king of the Persians
	3:10	The first wrote, Wine is strongest
	3:17	Then the first, who had spoken of the strength of wine, began and said :
	5:6	in the month of Nisan, the first month
	5:47	before the first gate toward the east
	6:17	But in the first year that Cyrus reigned
	6:24	In the first year of the reign of Cyrus
	7:10	kept the passover on the 14th day of the first month
	8:6	for they left Babylon on the new moon of the first month
	8:61	on the 12th day of the first month
	9:17	by the new moon of the first month
3 Ma	2:21	the first Father of all
2 Es	2:23	and I will give you the first place in my resurrection
	3:21	For the first Adam, burdened with an evil heart
	5:42	so for those who are first there is no haste
	6:7	Or when will be the end of the first age
	6:38	and didst say on the first day
	7:30	as it was at the first beginnings
	7:81	The first way
	7:91	First of all, they shall see with great joy
	7:92	The first order
	7:116	I answered and said, This is my first and last word
	11:14	so that it disappeared like the first
	11:27	a 2nd also, and this disappeared more quickly than the first
4 Ma	8:2	in his first attempt
	17:13	Eleazar was the first contestant

NUMBER : 2
89 = 0.058 %

Tob	1:21	before 2 of Sennacherib's sons killed him
	3:17	And Raphael was sent to heal the 2 of them :
	8:4	When the door was shut and the 2 were alone
	8:17	Blessed art thou, because thou hast had compassion on 2 only children
	9:2	Brother Azarias, take a servant and 2 camels with you
	12:5	Take half of all that you 2 have brought back
	12:6	Then the angel called the 2 of them privately
Jud	1:12	and every one in Egypt, as far as the coasts of the 2 seas
	4:7	only wide enough for 2 men at the most
	13:10	Then the 2 of them went out together
Ad E	10:7	The 2 dragons are Haman and myself
	10:10	For this purpose he made 2 lots
	10:11	And these 2 lots came to the hour and moment and day
	11:6	And behold, 2 great dragons came forward
	12:1	the 2 eunuchs of the king who kept watch in the courtyard
	12:3	Then the king examined the 2 eunuchs
	12:6	because of the 2 eunuchs of the king
	15:2	she took her 2 maids with her
Wis	14:30	But just penalties will overtake them on 2 counts :
Sir	2:12	and to the sinner who walks along 2 ways !
	13:7	until he has drained you 2 or 3 times
	23:16	2 sorts of men multiply sins
	26:28	At 2 things my heart is grieved
	38:17	for one day, or 2, to avoid criticism
	46:4	And did not one day become as long as 2 ?
	46:8	And these 2 alone were preserved
	50:25	With 2 nations my soul is vexed
L Jr	6:55	but the gods will be burnt in 2 like beams
Sus	13:5	In that year 2 elders from the people were appointed as judges
	13:8	The 2 elders used to see her every day
	13:15	she went in as before with only 2 maids
	13:16	And no one was there except the 2 elders
	13:19	the 2 elders rose and ran to her, and said :
	13:24	and the 2 elders shouted against her
	13:28	the 2 elders came
	13:34	Then the 2 elders stood up in the midst of the people
	13:36	this woman came in with 2 maids
	13:55	and will immediately cut you in 2
	13:59	for the angel of God is waiting with his sword to saw you in 2
	13:61	And they rose against the 2 elders
Bel	14:32	and every day they had been given 2 human bodies and 2 sheep
1 Ma	1:29	2 years later the king sent to the cities of Judah
	6:38	on the 2 flanks of the army, to harass the enemy
	9:11	The cavalry was divided into 2 companies
	9:12	Flanked by the 2 companies
	9:57	and the land of Judah had rest for 2 years
	10:49	The 2 kings met in battle
	10:60	So he went with pomp to Ptolemais and met the 2 kings
	11:13	Thus he put 2 crowns upon his head
	13:16	and 2 of his sons as hostages
	16:2	And Simon called in his 2 elder sons Judas and John
	16:16	and they killed him and his 2 sons
2 Ma	3:26	2 young men also appeared to him, remarkably strong

	4:28	the 2 of them were summoned by the king
	6:10	For example, 2 women were brought in
	10:3	after a lapse of 2 years
	10:18	took refuge in 2 very strong towers
	10:22	and immediately captured the 2 towers
	10:23	he destroyed more than 20,000 in the 2 strongholds
	10:28	Just as dawn was breaking, the 2 armies joined battle
1 Es	5:73	And they were kept from building for 2 years
	9:4	within 2 or 3 days
	9:11	This is not a work we can do in one day or 2
3 Ma	1:4	promising to give them each 2 minas of gold
	6:18	from which 2 glorious angels of fearful aspect descended
2 Es	1:11	and scattered in the east the people of 2 provinces, Tyre and Sidon
	6:49	Then thou didst keep in existence 2 living creatures
	7:50	For this reason the Most High has made not one world but 2
	11:22	the 12 wings and the 2 little wings disappeared
	11:24	2 little wings separated from the 6
	11:28	the 2 that remained were planning between themselves
	11:29	for it was greater than the other 2 heads
	11:30	And I saw how it allied the 2 heads with itself
	11:31	and it devoured the 2 little wings which were planning to reign
	11:34	But the 2 heads remained
	12:2	And the 2 wings that had gone over to it arose
	12:21	and 2 of them shall perish
	12:21	but 2 shall be kept until the end
	12:27	But as for the 2 who remained
	12:29	As for your seeing 2 little wings passing over to the head
	14:12	so 2 of its parts remain
	16:28	and out of the field, 2 who have hidden themselves
	16:38	has great pains about her womb for 2 or 3 hours beforehand
4 Ma	1:20	The 2 most comprehensive types of the emotions are pleasure and pain
	1:28	are 2 plants growing from the body and the soul
	3:12	2 staunch young soldiers, respecting the king's desire
	15:2	2 courses were open to this mother
	15:26	this mother held 2 ballots

NUMBER : 2nd s. SECOND
32 = 0.021 %

Tob	1:7	a 2nd tenth I would sell
Jud	7:6	On the 2nd day Holofernes led out all his cavalry
Ad E	11:2	In the 2nd year of the reign of Ahasuerus the Great
	13:3	and has attained the 2nd place in the kingdom
	13:6	who is in charge of affairs and is our 2nd father
Sir	50:21	and they bowed down in worship a 2nd time
1 Ma	9:1	into the land of Judah a 2nd time
	9:54	In the 153rd year, in the 2nd month
	13:51	On the 23rd day of the 2nd month, in the 171st year
2 Ma	5:1	About this time Antiochus made his 2nd invasion of Egypt
	7:7	they brought forward the 2nd for their sport
	13:22	The king negotiated a 2nd time
1 Es	1:31	And he got into his 2nd chariot
	2:30	until the 2nd year of the reign
	3:11	The 2nd wrote, The king is strongest
	4:1	Then the 2nd, who had spoken of the strength of the king
	5:6	in the 2nd year of his reign
	5:56	In the 2nd year after their coming to the temple of God in Jerusalem
	5:56	in the 2nd month, Zerubbabel the son of Shealtiel
	5:57	on the new moon of the 2nd month
	5:57	in the 2nd year after they came to Judea and Jerusalem
	6:1	Now in the 2nd year of the reign of Darius
2 Es	1:1	The 2nd book of the prophet Ezra the son of Seraiah
	5:16	Now on the 2nd night Phaltiel, a chief of the people
	6:41	Again, on the 2nd day
	7:82	The 2nd way
	7:93	The 2nd order
	10:2	and I remained quiet until evening of the 2nd day
	11:1	On the 2nd night I had a dream, and behold
	11:27	a 2nd also, and this disappeared more quickly than the first
	12:15	But the 2nd that is to reign shall hold sway
4 Ma	15:18	nor when the 2nd in torments looked at you piteously

NUMBER : 3
53 = 0.035 %

Jud	1:2	with hewn stones 3 cubits thick and 6 cubits long
	2:21	They marched for 3 days from Nineveh
	8:4	for 3 years and 4 months
	12:7	And she remained in the camp for 3 days
	16:20	before the sanctuary for 3 months
Sir	13:7	until he has drained you 2 or 3 times
	25:1	My soul takes pleasure in 3 things
	25:2	My soul hates 3 kinds of men
	26:5	Of 3 things my heart is afraid
	43:4	but the sun burns the mountains 3 times as much
	48:3	and also 3 times brought down fire
P Az	28	Then the 3, as with one mouth
1 Ma	5:24	and went 3 days' journey into the wilderness
	5:33	Then he came up behind them in 3 companies
	10:30	or from the 3 districts added to it
	10:34	and the 3 days before a feast and the 3 after a feast

10:38   As for the 3 districts that have been added to Judea
11:18   But King Ptolemy died 3 days later
11:28   to free Judea and the 3 districts of Samaria from tribute
11:34   and the 3 districts of Aphairema and Lydda and Rathamin
2 Ma   4:23   After a period of 3 years Jason sent Menelaus
   4:44   3 men sent by the senate presented the case before him
   5:14   Within the total of 3 days 80,000 were destroyed
   7:27   and nursed you for 3 years
   13:12   and lying prostrate for 3 days without ceasing
   14:1   3 years later, word came to Judas and his men
1 Es   1:35   And he reigned 3 months in Judah and Jerusalem
   1:44   and he reigned 3 months and 10 days in Jerusalem
   3:4   Then the 3 young men of the bodyguard
   3:9   and the 3 nobles of Persia judge to be wisest
   6:25   with 3 courses of hewn stone
   8:41   and we encamped there 3 days
   8:62   When we had been there 3 days
   9:4   within 2 or 3 days
   9:5   assembled at Jerusalem within 3 days
3 Ma   6:6   The 3 companions in Babylon
   6:38   for the 5th to the 7th of Epeiph, the 3 days
2 Es   4:3   I have been sent to show you 3 ways
   4:3   and to put before you 3 problems
   6:21   and women with child shall give birth to premature children at 3 or 4 months
   6:24   so that for 3 hours they shall not flow
   6:35   in order to complete the 3 weeks
   11:1   that had 12 feathered wings and 3 heads
   11:23   except the 3 heads that were at rest and 6 little wings
   12:22   As for your seeing 3 heads at rest
   12:23   In its last days the Most High will raise up 3 kings
   13:56   And after 3 more days I will tell you other things
   13:58   And I stayed there 3 days
   16:29   3 or 4 olives may be left on every tree
   16:31   so in those days 3 or 4 shall be left
   16:38   has great pains about her womb for 2 or 3 hours beforehand
4 Ma   13:9   let us imitate the 3 youths in Assyria

NUMBER : 3rd s. THIRD   21 = 0.014 %

Tob   1:8   the 3rd tenth I would give to those to whom it was my duty
Ad E   15:1   On the 3rd day, when she ended her prayer
Sir   23:16   and a 3rd incurs wrath
   26:28   and because of a 3rd anger comes over me :
   45:23   Phinehas the son of Eleazar is the 3rd in glory
   50:25   and the 3rd is no nation
1 Ma   14:27   which is the 3rd year of Simon the great high priest
2 Ma   7:10   After him, the 3rd was the victim of their sport
1 Es   3:12   The 3rd wrote, Women are strongest
   4:13   Then the 3rd, that is Zerubbabel
3 Ma   5:40   ordering now for a 3rd time that they be destroyed
2 Es   5:4   you shall see it thrown into confusion after the 3rd period
   6:42   On the 3rd day
   6:44   These were made on the 3rd day
   6:51   which had been dried up on the 3rd day
   7:83   The 3rd way, they shall see the reward laid up
   7:94   The 3rd order
   11:18   Then the 3rd wing raised itself up
   14:1   On the 3rd day, while I was sitting under an oak
4 Ma   10:1   When he too had endured a glorious death, the 3rd was led in
   15:18   nor when the 3rd expired

NUMBER : 4   16 = 0.010 %

Jud   8:4   for 3 years and 4 months
Wis   18:24   on the 4 rows of stones
Sir   37:18   4 turns of fortune appear, good and evil, life and death
1 Ma   6:37   and upon each were 4 armed men who fought from there
   11:57   and set you over the 4 districts
   13:28   for his father and mother and 4 brothers
2 Ma   8:21   then he divided his army into 4 parts
   10:33   and they besieged the fort 4 days
2 Es   3:19   And thy glory passed through the 4 gates
   6:21   and women with child shall give birth to premature children at 3 or 4 months
   11:24   but 4 remained in their place
   11:39   Are you not the one that remains of the 4 beasts
   12:21   and 4 shall be kept for the time
   13:5   from the 4 winds of heaven
   16:29   3 or 4 olives may be left on every tree
   16:31   so in those days 3 or 4 shall be left

NUMBER : 4th   11 = 0.007 %

Jud   12:10   On the 4th day Holofernes held a banquet for his slaves only
Ad E   11:1   In the 4th year of the reign of Ptolemy and Cleopatra
Sir   26:5   and of a 4th I am frightened
2 Ma   7:13   they maltreated and tortured the 4th in the same way
3 Ma   6:38   from the 25th of Pachon to the 4th of Epeiph, for 40 days
2 Es   6:45   On the 4th day thou didst command the brightness of the sun
   7:84   The 4th way
   7:95   The 4th order
   11:40   You, the 4th that has come

12:11   is the 4th kingdom which appeared in a vision
4 Ma   10:12   they dragged in the 4th, saying

NUMBER : 5 s. FIVE   11 = 0.007 %

Jud   7:30   Let us hold out for 5 more days
   8:9   to surrender the city to the Assyrians after 5 days
   8:15   For if he does not choose to help us within these 5 days
Sir   17:5   of the 5 operations of the Lord
1 Ma   2:2   He had 5 sons, John surnamed Gaddi
2 Ma   2:23   all this, which has been set forth by Jason of Cyrene in 5 volumes
   10:29   5 resplendent men on horses with golden bridles
   11:5   about 5 leagues from Jerusalem
2 Es   14:24   these 5, because they are trained to write rapidly
   14:37   So I took the 5 men, as he commanded me
   14:42   And the Most High gave understanding to the 5 men

NUMBER : 5th   10 = 0.007 %

Bar   1:2   in the 5th year, on the 7th day of the month
2 Ma   7:15   Next they brought forward the 5th and maltreated him
   10:35   But at dawn on the 5th day
1 Es   8:6   in the 5th month (this was the king's 7th year)
   8:6   on the new moon of the 5th month
3 Ma   6:38   for the 5th to the 7th of Epeiph, the 3 days
2 Es   6:47   On the 5th day thou didst command the 7th part
   7:85   The 5th way
   7:96   The 5th order
4 Ma   11:1   the 5th leaped up, saying

NUMBER : 6   6 = 0.004 %

Jud   1:2   with hewn stones 3 cubits thick and 6 cubits long
Bel   14:31   and he was there for 6 days
2 Es   6:42   6 parts thou didst dry up and keep
   11:23   except the 3 heads that were at rest and 6 little wings
   11:24   2 little wings separated from the 6
4 Ma   11:24   We 6 boys have paralyzed your tyranny !

NUMBER : 6th   7 = 0.005 %

Sir   17:5   as 6th he distributed to them the gift of mind
2 Ma   7:18   After him they brought forward the 6th
1 Es   7:5   in the 6th year of King Darius
2 Es   6:53   On the 6th day thou didst command the earth
   7:86   The 6th way
   7:97   The 6th order
4 Ma   11:13   After he too had died, the 6th, a mere boy, was led in

NUMBER : 7   69 = 0.045 %

Tob   2:1   which is the sacred festival of the 7 weeks
   3:8   because she had been given to 7 husbands
   3:8   You already have had 7
   3:15   Already 7 husbands of mine are dead
   6:13   I have heard that the girl has been given to 7 husbands
   7:11   I have given my daughter to 7 husbands
   11:19   and Tobias marriage was celebrated for 7 days
   12:15   I am Raphael, one of the 7 holy angels
Jud   16:24   and the house of Israel mourned for her 7 days
Sir   20:12   but pays for it 7 times over
   22:12   Mourning for the dead lasts 7 days
   37:14   than 7 watchmen sitting high on a watchtower
   40:8   and upon sinners 7 times more
L Jr   6:3   for a long time, up to 7 generations
Bel   14:32   There were 7 lions in the den
1 Ma   13:28   He also erected 7 pyramids, opposite one another
2 Ma   7:1   It happened also that 7 brothers and their mother were arrested
   7:20   Though she saw her 7 sons perish within a single day
1 Es   1:19   kept the passover and the feast of unleavened bread 7 days
   4:63   and they feasted, with music and rejoicing, for 7 days
   7:14   And they kept the feast of unleavened bread 7 days
   8:11   depart with you as I and the 7 friends
3 Ma   6:30   needed for a festival of 7 days
   7:17   in accord with the common desire, for 7 days
2 Es   2:19   and 7 mighty mountains on which roses and lilies grow
   5:13   and fast for 7 days
   5:19   Depart from me and do not come near me for 7 days
   5:20   So I fasted 7 days, mourning and weeping
   5:21   And after 7 days
   6:31   If therefore you will pray again and fast again for 7 days
   6:35   Now after this I wept again and fasted 7 days as before
   7:30   And the world shall be turned back to primeval silence for 7 days
   7:31   And after 7 days the world
   7:80   ever grieving and sad, in 7 ways
   7:91   for they shall have rest in 7 orders
   7:101   They shall have freedom for 7 days
   7:101   so that during these 7 days
   9:23   But if you will let 7 days more pass
   9:27   And after 7 days, as I lay on the grass
   12:39   But wait here 7 days more
   12:40   When all the people heard that the 7 days were past
   12:51   But I sat in the field 7 days

	13:1	After 7 days I dreamed a dream in the night
4 Ma	**1**:8	Eleazar and the 7 brothers and their mother
	8:3	When the tyrant had given these orders, 7 brothers
	13:1	Since, then, the 7 brothers despised sufferings even unto death
	14:3	O sacred and harmonious concord of the 7 brothers
	14:4	None of the 7 youths proved coward or shrank from death
	14:7	O most holy 7, brothers in harmony !
	14:7	For just as the 7 days of creation
	14:12	for the mother of the 7 young men bore up
	15:2	that of religion, and that of preserving her 7 sons for a time
	15:6	The mother of the 7 boys, more than any other mother, loved her children
	15:6	In 7 pregnancies she had implanted in herself tender love toward them
	15:24	Although she witnessed the destruction of 7 children
	15:27	which would preserve the 7 sons for a short time
	16:1	If, then, a woman, advanced in years and mother of 7 sons
	16:3	inflamed as she saw her 7 sons tortured in such varied ways
	16:6	After bearing 7 children, I am now the mother of none !
	16:7	O 7 childbirths all in vain, 7 profitless pregnancies
	16:24	By these words the mother of the 7
	17:2	O mother, who with your 7 sons
	17:5	who, after lighting the way of your star-like 7 sons to piety
	17:7	as they saw the mother of the 7 children
	17:9	Here lie buried an aged priest and an aged woman and 7 sons
	17:13	the mother of the 7 sons entered the competition
	18:6	The mother of the 7 sons
	18:20	brought those 7 sons of the daughter of Abraham to the catapult

NUMBER : 7th 23 = 0.015 %

Sir	**17**:5	and as 7th reason, the interpreter of his operations
Bar	**1**:2	in the 5th year, on the 7th day of the month
Bel	**14**:40	On the 7th day the king came to mourn for Daniel
1 Ma	**6**:53	because it was the 7th year
	10:21	in the 7th month of the 160th year
2 Ma	**6**:11	to observe the 7th day secretly
	12:38	As the 7th day was coming on
	15:4	who ordered us to observe the 7th day
1 Es	**5**:47	When the 7th month came
	5:53	from the new moon of the 7th month
	8:6	in the 7th year of the reign of Artaxerxes
	8:6	in the 5th month (this was the king's 7th year)
	9:37	On the new moon of the 7th month
	9:40	on the new moon of the 7th month
3 Ma	**6**:38	for the 5th to the 7th of Epeiph, the 3 days
2 Es	**6**:42	in the 7th part of the earth
	6:47	On the 5th day thou didst command the 7th part
	6:50	for the 7th part where the water had been gathered together
	6:52	but to Leviathan thou didst give the 7th part, the watery part
	7:87	The 7th way
	7:98	The 7th order
4 Ma	**2**:8	and to cancel the debt when the 7th year arrives
	12:1	the 7th and youngest of all came forward

NUMBER : 8 8 = 0.005 %

Tob	**14**:2	and after 8 years he regained it
1 Ma	**4**:56	So they celebrated the dedication of the altar for 8 days
	4:59	with gladness and joy for 8 days
2 Ma	**2**:12	Likewise Solomon also kept the 8 days
	10:6	And they celebrated it for 8 days with rejoicing
2 Es	**11**:11	and behold, there were 8 of them
	12:19	As for your seeing 8 little wings clinging to his wings
	12:20	8 kings shall arise in it

NUMBER : 8th 1

2 Es	**6**:36	And on the 8th night my heart was troubled within me again

NUMBER : 9 6 = 0.004 %

Sir	**25**:7	With 9 thoughts I have gladdened my heart
2 Ma	**5**:27	But Judas Maccabeus, with about 9 others
	7:27	I carried you 9 months in my womb
2 Es	**4**:40	when her 9 months have been completed
	8:8	and for 9 months the womb which thou hast formed
	14:11	and 9 of its parts have already passed

NUMBER : 9th 3 = 0.002 %

1 Ma	**4**:52	Early in the morning on the 25th day of the 9th month
1 Es	**9**:5	this was the 9th month
2 Es	**16**:38	Just as a woman with child, in the 9th month

NUMBER : 10 s. **TEN** 11 = 0.007 %

Tob	**1**:14	and once at Rages in Media I left 10 talents of silver
	4:20	And now let me explain to you about the 10 talents of silver
Wis	**7**:2	within the period of 10 months, compacted with blood
Sir	**41**:4	Whether life is for 10 or a 100 or a 1,000 years
1 Es	**1**:44	and he reigned 3 months and 10 days in Jerusalem
	4:52	and an additional 10 talents a year
	8:54	and 10 of their kinsmen with them
2 Es	**5**:46	and say to it, If you bear 10 children
	5:46	Request it therefore to produce 10 at one time

	13:40	these are the 10 tribes
	16:28	For out of a city, 10 shall be left

NUMBER : 10th s. **TENTH** 4 = 0.003 %

Sir	**25**:7	and a 10th I shall tell with my tongue :
Bar	**1**:8	At the same time, on the 10th day of Sivan
1 Es	**9**:16	and on the new moon of the 10th month
3 Ma	**5**:14	But now, since it was nearly the middle of the 10th hour

NUMBER : 11 1

1 Es	**1**:46	Zedekiah was 21 years old, and he reigned 11 years

NUMBER : 11th 1

1 Ma	**16**:14	in the 177th year, in the 11th month, which is the month of Shebat

NUMBER : 12 18 = 0.012 %

Sir	**44**:23	and distributed them among 12 tribes
	49:10	May the bones of the 12 prophets
Bel	**14**:3	and every day they spent on it 12 bushels of fine flour
1 Ma	**1**:7	And after Alexander had reigned 12 years, he died
1 Es	**5**:41	All those of Israel, 12 or more years of age
	7:8	and 12 he-goats for the sin of all Israel
	7:8	according to the number of the 12 leaders
	8:54	Then I set apart 12 of the leaders of the priests
	8:57	and 12 bronze vessels of fine bronze
	8:65	12 bulls for all Israel, 96 rams, 72 lambs
	8:66	and as a thank offering 12 he-goats
2 Es	**2**:18	12 trees loaded with various fruits
	11:1	that had 12 feathered wings and 3 heads
	11:22	the 12 wings and the 2 little wings disappeared
	12:14	And 12 kings shall reign in it, one after another
	12:15	for a longer time than any other of the 12
	12:16	This is the interpretation of the 12 wings which you saw
	14:11	For the age is divided into 12 parts

NUMBER : 12th 5 = 0.003 %

Jud	**1**:1	In the 12th year of the reign of Nebuchadnezzar
Ad E	**13**:6	on the 14th day of the 12th month, Adar
	16:20	so that on the 13th day of the 12th month, Adar
2 Ma	**15**:36	but to celebrate the 13th day of the 12th month
1 Es	**8**:61	on the 12th day of the first month

NUMBER : 13th 6 = 0.004 %

Ad E	**16**:20	so that on the 13th day of the 12th month, Adar
1 Ma	**7**:43	on the 13th day of the month of Adar
	7:49	each year on the 13th day of Adar
2 Ma	**15**:36	but to celebrate the 13th day of the 12th month
2 Es	**14**:12	as well as half of the 13th part
	14:12	besides half of the 13th part

NUMBER : 14 3 = 0.002 %

Tob	**8**:19	which lasted 14 days
	8:20	until the 14 days of the wedding feast were ended
	10:7	until the 14 days of the wedding feast had expired

NUMBER : 14th 5 = 0.003 %

Ad E	**10**:13	on the 14th and 15th of that month
	13:6	on the 14th day of the 12th month, Adar
1 Es	**1**:1	he killed the passover lamb on the 14th day of the first month
	7:10	kept the passover on the 14th day of the first month
3 Ma	**6**:40	until the 14th day

NUMBER : 15th 4 = 0.003 %

Ad E	**10**:13	on the 14th and 15th of that month
1 Ma	**1**:54	Now on the 15th day of Chislev, in the 145th year
2 Ma	**11**:33	Farewell. The 148th year, Xanthicus 15th
	11:38	Farewell. The 148th year, Xanthicus 15th

NUMBER : 17 1

1 Es	**4**:52	in accordance with the commandment to make 17 offerings

NUMBER : 17th 1

Jud	**1**:13	In the 17th year he led his forces against King Arphaxad

NUMBER : 18 2

1 Es	**1**:43	when he was made king he was 18 years old
	8:47	namely Sherebiah with his sons and kinsmen, 18

NUMBER : 18th 3 = 0.002 %

Jud	**2**:1	In the 18th year, on the 22nd day of the first month
1 Ma	**14**:27	On the 18th day of Elul, in the 172nd year
1 Es	**1**:22	In the 18th year of the reign of Josiah

NUMBER : 20 5 = 0.003 %

2 Ma	**10**:35	20 young men in the army of Maccabeus
1 Es	**4**:51	that 20 talents a year should be given
	5:58	who were 20 or more years of age

8:48 Hodiah the sons of Hananiah, and their sons, 20 men
8:57 and 20 golden bowls

NUMBER : 20th   1
1 Es **9**:5 on the 20th day of the month

NUMBER : 21   1
1 Es **1**:46 Zedekiah was 21 years old, and he reigned 11 years

NUMBER : 22   1
2 Ma **13**:2 5,300 cavalry, 22 elephants

NUMBER : 22nd   1
Jud **2**:1 In the 18th year, on the 22nd day of the first month

NUMBER : 23   1
1 Es **1**:34 who was 23 years old

NUMBER : 23rd   2
1 Ma **13**:51 On the 23rd day of the 2nd month, in the 171st year
1 Es **7**:5 by the 23rd day of the month of Adar

NUMBER : 24   1
2 Es **14**:45 Make public the 24 books that you wrote first

NUMBER : 24th   1
2 Ma **11**:21 Farewell. The 148th year, Dioscorinthius 24th

NUMBER : 25   2
1 Es **1**:39 Jehoiakim was 25 years old
   5:19 The men of Kiriatharim, 25

NUMBER : 25th   6 = 0.004 %
1 Ma **1**:59 And on the 25th day of the month
   4:52 Early in the morning on the 25th day of the 9th month
   4:59 beginning with the 25th day of the month of Chislev
2 Ma **1**:18 Since on the 25th day of Chislev
   10:5 that is, on the 25th day of the same month, which was Chislev
3 Ma **6**:38 from the 25th of Pachon to the 4th of Epeiph, for 40 days

NUMBER : 28   1
1 Es **8**:37 and with him 28 men

NUMBER : 29   1
1 Es **2**:13 29 silver censers, 30 gold bowls

NUMBER : 30   8 = 0.005 %
Jud **15**:11 So all the people plundered the camp for 30 days
2 Ma **12**:9 so that the glow of the light was seen in Jerusalem, 30 miles distant
1 Es **2**:13 29 silver censers, 30 gold bowls
2 Es **3**:29 and my soul has seen many sinners during these 30 years
   9:43 though I lived with my husband 30 years
   9:44 And every hour and every day during those 30 years
   9:45 And after 30 years God heard your handmaid
   10:45 And as for her telling you that she was barren for 30 years

NUMBER : 30th   2
2 Ma **11**:30 Therefore those who go home by the 30th day of Xanthicus
2 Es **3**:1 In the 30th year after the destruction of our city

NUMBER : 32   1
1 Ma **6**:30 20,000 horsemen, and 32 elephants accustomed to war

NUMBER : 34   1
Jud **7**:20 surrounded them for 34 days

NUMBER : 38th   1
Sir pr.   in the 38th year of the reign of Euergetes

NUMBER : 40   10 = 0.007 %
Jud **1**:4 which were 70 cubits high and 40 cubits wide
Bel **14**:3 and 40 sheep and 50 gallons of wine
2 Ma **5**:2 And it happened that over all the city, for almost 40 days
3 Ma **4**:15 and though uncompleted it stopped after 40 days
   6:38 from the 25th of Pachon to the 4th of Epeiph, for 40 days
2 Es **14**:23 and tell them not to seek you for 40 days
   14:36 and let no one seek me for 40 days
   14:42 They sat 40 days, and wrote during the daytime
   14:44 So during the 40 days 94 books were written
   14:45 And when the 40 days were ended

NUMBER : 42   1
1 Es **5**:18 The men of Bethasmoth, 42

NUMBER : 49   1
P Az 24 And the flame streamed out above the furnace 49 cubits

NUMBER : 50 s. **FIFTY**   5 = 0.003 %
Tob **1**:21 But not 50 days passed
Jud **1**:2 he made the walls 70 cubits high and 50 cubits wide
Bel **14**:3 and 40 sheep and 50 gallons of wine
1 Ma **9**:61 And Jonathan's men seized about 50 of the men of the country
2 Ma **13**:5 For there is a tower in that place, 50 cubits high, full of ashes

NUMBER : 52   1
1 Es **5**:21 The men of Bethel, 52

NUMBER : 55   1
1 Es **5**:18 The men of Netophah, 55

NUMBER : 58   1
Tob **14**:2 He was 58 years old when he lost his sight

NUMBER : 60   4 = 0.003 %
Jud **1**:3 a 100 cubits high and 60 cubits wide at the foundations
1 Ma **7**:16 but he seized 60 of them and killed them in one day
1 Es **6**:25 its height to be 60 cubits and its breadth 60 cubits

NUMBER : 67   1
1 Es **5**:15 The sons of Kilan and Azetas, 67

NUMBER : 70   9 = 0.006 %
Jud **1**:2 he made the walls 70 cubits high and 50 cubits wide
   1:4 which were 70 cubits high and 40 cubits wide
Bel **14**:10 Now there were 70 priests of Bel
1 Es **1**:58 until the completion of 70 years
   8:33 and with him 70 men
   8:34 and with him 70 men
   8:39 and with them 70 men
   8:40 and with him 70 men
2 Es **14**:46 but keep the 70 that were written last

NUMBER : 72   1
1 Es **8**:66 12 bulls for all Israel, 96 rams, 72 lambs

NUMBER : 74   1
1 Es **5**:26 and Bannas and Sudias, 74

NUMBER : 75   1
2 Ma **12**:29 which is 75 miles from Jerusalem

NUMBER : 80   2
2 Ma **4**:8 and, from another source of revenue, 80 talents
   11:4 and his thousands of cavalry, and his 80 elephants

NUMBER : 90   1
2 Ma **8**:11 and promising to hand over 90 slaves for a talent

NUMBER : 90th   1
2 Ma **6**:24 that Eleazar in his 90th year

NUMBER : 92   1
1 Es **5**:15 The sons of Ater, namely of Hezekiah, 92

NUMBER : 94   1
2 Es **14**:44 So during the 40 days 94 books were written

NUMBER : 95   1
2 Ma **12**:17 When they had gone 95 miles from there

NUMBER : 96   1
1 Es **8**:65 12 bulls for all Israel, 96 rams, 72 lambs

NUMBER : 100 s. **HUNDRED**   15 = 0.010 %
Jud **1**:3 a 100 cubits high and 60 cubits wide at the foundations
   10:17 They chose from their number a 100 men
Sir **18**:9 if he reaches a 100 years
   41:4 Whether life is for 10 or a 100 or a 1,000 years
1 Ma **13**:16 Send now a 100 talents of silver
   13:19 So he sent the sons and the 100 talents
   15:35 for them we will give a 100 talents
1 Es **1**:36 and fined the nation a 100 talents of silver
   5:45 and a 100 priests' garments
   7:7 100 bulls, 200 rams, 400 lambs
   8:20 up to a 100 talents of silver
   8:20 and likewise up to a 100 cors of wheat
   8:20 a 100 baths of wine, and salt in abundance
   8:56 and silver vessels worth a 100 talents
   8:56 and a 100 talents of gold

NUMBER : 101   1
1 Es **5**:16 The sons of Annias, 101. The sons of Arom

NUMBER : 105   1
Jud **16**:23 until she was 105 years old

NUMBER : 110　　　　　　　　　　　　　　　　1
　1 Es　8:38　and with him a 110 men

NUMBER : 112　　　　　　　　　　　　　　　　1
　1 Es　5:16　The sons of Jorah, 112

NUMBER : 120　　　　　　　　　　　　　　　　2
　Jud　1:16　and there he and his forces rested and feasted for 120 days
　1 Ma　8:6　who went to fight against them with a 120 elephants

NUMBER : 122　　　　　　　　　　　　　　　　1
　1 Es　5:21　The men of Michmas, 122

NUMBER : 123　　　　　　　　　　　　　　　　1
　1 Es　5:17　The sons of Bethlehem, 123

NUMBER : 127　　　　　　　　　　4 = 0.003 %
　Tob　14:14　He died in Ecbatana of Media at the age of a 127 years
　Ad E　13:1　to the rulers of the 127 provinces
　　　16:1　to the rulers of the provinces from India to Ethiopia, 127 satrapies
　1 Es　3:2　that were under him in the 127 satrapies

NUMBER : 128　　　　　　　　　　　　　　　　1
　1 Es　5:27　The temple singers : the sons of Asaph, 128

NUMBER : 137th　　　　　　　　　　　　　　　1
　1 Ma　1:10　He began to reign in the 137th year

NUMBER : 139　　　　　　　　　　　　　　　　1
　1 Es　5:28　the sons of Shobai, in all 139

NUMBER : 143rd　　　　　　　　　　　　　　　1
　1 Ma　1:20　After subduing Egypt, Antiochus returned in the 143rd year

NUMBER : 145th　　　　　　　　　　　　　　　1
　1 Ma　1:54　Now on the 15th day of Chislev, in the 145th year

NUMBER : 146th　　　　　　　　　　　　　　　1
　1 Ma　2:70　He died in the 146th year

NUMBER : 147th　　　　　　　　　　　　　　　1
　1 Ma　3:37　and departed from Antioch his capital in the 147th year

NUMBER : 148th　　　　　　　　　　4 = 0.003 %
　1 Ma　4:52　in the 148th year
　2 Ma　11:21　Farewell. The 148th year, Dioscorinthius 24th
　　　11:33　Farewell. The 148th year, Xanthicus 15th
　　　11:38　Farewell. The 148th year, Xanthicus 15th

NUMBER : 149th　　　　　　　　　　　　　　　2
　1 Ma　6:16　Thus Antiochus the king died there in the 149th year
　2 Ma　13:1　In the 149th year word came to Judas and his men

NUMBER : 150　　　　　　　　　　　　　　　　2
　2 Ma　4:9　In addition to this he promised to pay 150 more
　1 Es　8:30　and with him a 150 men enrolled

NUMBER : 150th　　　　　　　　　　　　　　　1
　1 Ma　6:20　and besieged the citadel in the 150th year

NUMBER : 151st　　　　　　　　　　　　　　　2
　1 Ma　7:1　In the 151st year Demetrius the son of Seleucus set forth from Rome
　2 Ma　14:4　and went to King Demetrius in about the 151st year

NUMBER : 152nd　　　　　　　　　　　　　　　1
　1 Ma　9:3　In the first month of the 152nd year

NUMBER : 153rd　　　　　　　　　　　　　　　1
　1 Ma　9:54　In the 153rd year, in the 2nd month

NUMBER : 156　　　　　　　　　　　　　　　　1
　1 Es　5:21　The sons of Magbish, 156

NUMBER : 158　　　　　　　　　　　　　　　　2
　Tob　14:11　He was a 158 years old
　1 Es　5:18　The men of Anathoth, 158

NUMBER : 160　　　　　　　　　　　　　　　　1
　1 Es　8:36　and with him a 160 men

NUMBER : 160th　　　　　　　　　　　　　　　2
　1 Ma　10:1　In the 160th year Alexander Epiphanes, the son of Antiochus
　　　10:21　in the 7th month of the 160th year

NUMBER : 162nd　　　　　　　　　　　　　　　1
　1 Ma　10:57　and came to Ptolemais in the 162nd year

NUMBER : 165th　　　　　　　　　　　　　　　1
　1 Ma　10:67　In the 165th year Demetrius the son of Demetrius

NUMBER : 167th　　　　　　　　　　　　　　　1
　1 Ma　11:19　So Demetrius became king in the 167th year

NUMBER : 169th　　　　　　　　　　　　　　　1
　2 Ma　1:7　In the reign of Demetrius, in the 169th year

NUMBER : 170th　　　　　　　　　　　　　　　1
　1 Ma　13:41　In the 170th year the yoke of the Gentiles was removed from Israel

NUMBER : 171st　　　　　　　　　　　　　　　1
　1 Ma　13:51　On the 23rd day of the 2nd month, in the 171st year

NUMBER : 172nd　　　　　　　　　　　　　　　2
　1 Ma　14:1　In the 172nd year Demetrius the king assembled his forces
　　　14:27　On the 18th day of Elul, in the 172nd year

NUMBER : 174th　　　　　　　　　　　　　　　1
　1 Ma　15:10　In the 174th year Antiochus set out

NUMBER : 177th　　　　　　　　　　　　　　　1
　1 Ma　16:14　in the 177th year, in the 11th month, which is the month of Shebat

NUMBER : 188th　　　　　　　　　　　　　　　1
　2 Ma　1:9　in the month of Chislev, in the 188th year

NUMBER : 200　　　　　　　　　　　4 = 0.003 %
　2 Ma　3:11　and that it totalled in all 400 talents of silver and 200 of gold
　　　12:4　not less than 200
　1 Es　7:7　100 bulls, 200 rams, 400 lambs
　　　8:31　and with him 200 men

NUMBER : 212　　　　　　　　　　　　　　　　1
　1 Es　8:35　and with him 212 men

NUMBER : 220　　　　　　　　　　　　　　　　1
　1 Es　8:49　220 temple servants

NUMBER : 245　　　　　　　　　　　　　　　　2
　1 Es　5:42　there were 245 musicians and singers
　　　5:43　and 7,036 horses, 245 mules, and 5,525 asses

NUMBER : 250　　　　　　　　　　　　　　　　1
　1 Es　8:32　and with him 250 men

NUMBER : 300　　　　　　　　　　　7 = 0.005 %
　1 Ma　11:28　and promised him 300 talents
　2 Ma　4:19　to carry 300 silver drachmas for the sacrifice to Hercules
　　　4:24　outbidding Jason by 300 talents of silver
　　　13:2　and 300 chariots armed with scythes
　1 Es　1:8　2,600 sheep and 300 calves
　　　8:32　and with him 300 men
　3 Ma　7:15　In that day they put to death more than 300 men

NUMBER : 320　　　　　　　　　　　　　　　　1
　1 Ma　8:15　and every day 320 senators constantly deliberate

NUMBER : 323　　　　　　　　　　　　　　　　1
　1 Es　5:16　The sons of Bezai, 323

NUMBER : 345　　　　　　　　　　　　　　　　1
　1 Es　5:22　The sons of Jericho, 345

NUMBER : 360　　　　　　　　　　　　　　　　1
　2 Ma　4:8　promising the king at an interview 360 talents of silver

NUMBER : 372　　　　　　　　　　　　　　　　1
　1 Es　5:35　and the sons of Solomon's servants were 372

NUMBER : 400　　　　　　　　　　　4 = 0.003 %
　2 Ma　3:11　and that it totalled in all 400 talents of silver and 200 of gold
　　　12:33　And he came out with 3,000 infantry and 400 cavalry
　1 Es　7:7　100 bulls, 200 rams, 400 lambs
　2 Es　7:28　and those who remain shall rejoice 400 years

NUMBER : 422　　　　　　　　　　　　　　　　1
　1 Es　5:20　The Chadiasans and Ammidians, 422

NUMBER : 432　　　　　　　　　　　　　　　　1
　1 Es　5:15　The sons of Azaru, 432

NUMBER : 435　　　　　　　　　　　　　　　　1
　1 Es　5:43　There were 435 camels

NUMBER : 454   1
  1 Es 5 : 14 The sons of Adin, 454

NUMBER : 472   1
  1 Es 5 : 9 The sons of Shephatiah, 472

NUMBER : 500   7 = 0.005 %
  1 Ma 6 : 35 and 500 picked horsemen were assigned to each beast
       7 : 32 About 500 men of the army of Nicanor fell
      15 : 31 or else give me for them 500 talents of silver
      15 : 31 and the tribute money of the cities, 500 talents more
  2 Ma 12 : 10 not less than 5,000 Arabs with 500 horsemen attacked them
      14 : 39 sent more than 500 soldiers to arrest him
  3 Ma 5 : 2 to drug all the elephants – 500 in number

NUMBER : 600   2
  1 Ma 6 : 42 and 600 men of the king's army fell
  2 Ma 10 : 31 20,500 were slaughtered, besides 600 horsemen

NUMBER : 621   1
  1 Es 5 : 20 The men of Ramah and Geba, 621

NUMBER : 623   1
  1 Es 5 : 13 The sons of Bebai, 623

NUMBER : 648   1
  1 Es 5 : 12 The sons of Bani, 648

NUMBER : 650   1
  1 Es 8 : 56 I weighed and gave to them 650 talents of silver

NUMBER : 652   1
  1 Es 5 : 37 the sons of Nekoda, 652

NUMBER : 667   1
  1 Es 5 : 14 The sons of Adonikam, 667

NUMBER : 700   1
  1 Es 1 : 9 gave the Levites for the passover 5,000 sheep and 700 calves

NUMBER : 705   1
  1 Es 5 : 12 The sons of Chorbe, 705

NUMBER : 725   1
  1 Es 5 : 22 The sons of the other Elam and Ono, 725

NUMBER : 743   1
  1 Es 5 : 19 The men of Chephirah and Beeroth, 743

NUMBER : 756   1
  1 Es 5 : 10 The sons of Arah, 756

NUMBER : 800   2
  1 Ma 3 : 24 800 of them fell, and the rest fled into the land of the Philistines
       9 : 6 until no more than 800 of them were left

NUMBER : 945   1
  1 Es 5 : 12 The sons of Zattu, 945

NUMBER : 972   1
  1 Es 5 : 24 of the sons of Anasib, 972

NUMBER : 1,000 s. THOUSAND   22 = 0.014 %
  Sir 6 : 6 but let your advisers be one in a 1,000
      16 : 3 for one is better than a 1,000
      39 : 11 if he lives long, he will leave a name greater than a 1,000
      41 : 4 Whether life is for 10 or a 100 or a 1,000 years
      41 : 12 since it will remain for you longer than a 1,000 great stores of
              gold
  1 Ma 2 : 38 to the number of a 1,000 persons
       4 : 1 Now Gorgias took 5,000 infantry and a 1,000 picked cavalry
       5 : 13 and have destroyed about a 1,000 men there
       6 : 35 with each elephant they stationed a 1,000 men
       9 : 49 And about 1,000 of Bacchides' men fell that day
      10 : 79 Now Apollonius had secretly left a 1,000 cavalry behind them
      12 : 47 while a 1,000 accompanied him
      14 : 24 with a large gold shield weighing a 1,000 minas
      15 : 18 and have brought a gold shield weighing a 1,000 minas
  2 Ma 5 : 5 Jason took no less than a 1,000 men
       8 : 34 who had brought the 1,000 merchants to buy the Jews
  1 Es 2 : 13 The number of these was : a 1,000 gold cups, a 1,000 silver cups
       2 : 13 2,410 silver bowls, and a 1,000 other vessels
       5 : 2 And Darius sent with them a 1,000 horsemen
       5 : 45 a 1,000 minas of gold
  2 Es 6 : 51 where there are a 1,000 mountains

NUMBER : 1,017   1
  1 Es 5 : 25 The sons of Harim, 1,017

NUMBER : 1,052   1
  1 Es 5 : 24 The sons of Immer, 1,052

NUMBER : 1,247   1
  1 Es 5 : 25 The sons of Pashhur, 1,247

NUMBER : 1,254   1
  1 Es 5 : 12 The sons of Elam, 1,254

NUMBER : 1,322   1
  1 Es 5 : 13 The sons of Azgad, 1,322

NUMBER : 1,500   1
  2 Ma 8 : 22 each to command a division, putting 1,500 men under each

NUMBER : 1,600   1
  2 Ma 11 : 11 and slew 11,000 of them and 1,600 horsemen

NUMBER : 1,800   1
  2 Ma 5 : 21 So Antiochus carried off 1,800 talents from the temple

NUMBER : 2,000   9 = 0.006 %
  1 Ma 5 : 60 as many as 2,000 of the people of Israel fell that day
       9 : 4 with 20,000 foot soldiers and 2,000 cavalry
      12 : 47 2,000 of whom he left in Galilee
      15 : 26 And Simon sent to Antiochus 2,000 picked men, to fight for him
      16 : 10 and John burned it with fire, and about 2,000 of them fell
  2 Ma 8 : 10 the tribute due to the Romans, 2,000 talents
      12 : 43 to the amount of 2,000 drachmas of silver
      13 : 15 and slew as many as 2,000 men in the camp
  3 Ma 3 : 28 and also 2,000 drachmas from the royal treasury

NUMBER : 2,066   1
  1 Es 5 : 14 The sons of Bigvai, 2,066

NUMBER : 2,172   1
  1 Es 5 : 9 the sons of Parosh, 2,172

NUMBER : 2,410   1
  1 Es 2 : 13 2,410 silver bowls, and a 1,000 other vessels

NUMBER : 2,500   1
  2 Ma 12 : 20 who had with him a 120,000 infantry and 2,500 cavalry

NUMBER : 2,600   1
  1 Es 1 : 8 2,600 sheep and 300 calves

NUMBER : 2,812   1
  1 Es 5 : 11 The sons of Pahath-moab, of the sons of Jeshua and Joab, 2,812

NUMBER : 3,000   15 = 0.010 %
  1 Ma 4 : 6 At daybreak Judas appeared in the plain with 3,000 men
       4 : 15 and 3,000 of them fell
       5 : 20 Then 3,000 men were assigned to Simon to go to Galilee
       5 : 22 and as many as 3,000 of the Gentiles fell
       7 : 40 And Judas encamped in Adasa with 3,000 men
       9 : 5 and with him were 3,000 picked men
      10 : 77 he mustered 3,000 cavalry and a large army
      11 : 44 So Jonathan sent 3,000 stalwart men to him at Antioch
      11 : 74 As many as 3,000 of the foreigners fell that day
      12 : 47 He kept with himself 3,000 men
  2 Ma 4 : 40 Lysimachus armed about 3,000 men
      12 : 33 And he came out with 3,000 infantry and 400 cavalry
  1 Es 1 : 7 30,000 lambs and kids, and 3,000 calves
  2 Es 10 : 45 it is because there were 3,000 years in the world
      10 : 46 And after 3,000 years Solomon built the city

NUMBER : 3,005   1
  1 Es 5 : 17 The sons of Baiterus, 3,005

NUMBER : 3,330   1
  1 Es 5 : 23 The sons of Senaah, 3,330

NUMBER : 3,660   1
  4 Ma 4 : 17 he would pay the king 3,660 talents annually

NUMBER : 4,000   1
  2 Ma 8 : 20 when 8,000 in all went into the affair, with 4,000 Macedonians

NUMBER : 5,000   8 = 0.005 %
  Jud 7 : 17 together with 5,000 Assyrians
  1 Ma 4 : 1 Now Gorgias took 5,000 infantry and a 1,000 picked cavalry
       4 : 28 and 5,000 cavalry to subdue them
       4 : 34 and there fell of the army of Lysias 5,000 men
      10 : 42 Moreover, the 5,000 shekels of silver
  2 Ma 12 : 10 not less than 5,000 Arabs with 500 horsemen attacked them
  1 Es 1 : 9 gave the Levites for the passover 5,000 sheep and 700 calves
       5 : 45 5,000 minas of silver

NUMBER : 5,300   1
  2 Ma **13** : 2   5,300 cavalry, 22 elephants

NUMBER : 5,469   1
  1 Es   **2** : 14   All the vessels were handed over, gold and silver, 5,469

NUMBER : 5,525   1
  1 Es   **5** : 43   and 7,036 horses, 245 mules, and 5,525 asses

NUMBER : 6,000   2
  2 Ma   **8** : 1   and so they gathered about 6,000 men
        8 : 16   to the number of 6,000

NUMBER : 7,000   1
  1 Ma   **3** : 39   and sent with them 40,000 infantry and 7,000 cavalry

NUMBER : 7,036   1
  1 Es   **5** : 43   and 7,036 horses, 245 mules, and 5,525 asses

NUMBER : 7,337   1
  1 Es   **5** : 42   their menservants and maidservants were 7,337

NUMBER : 8,000   6 = 0.004 %
  1 Ma   **5** : 20   and 8,000 to Judas for Gilead
        5 : 34   As many as 8,000 of them fell that day
      10 : 85   came to 8,000 men
      15 : 13   and with him were a 120,000 warriors and 8,000 cavalry
  2 Ma   **8** : 20   when 8,000 in all went into the affair, with 4,000 Macedonians
        8 : 20   the 8,000, by the help that came to them from heaven

NUMBER : 9,000   2
  2 Ma   **8** : 24   they slew more than 9,000 of the enemy
      10 : 18   When no less than 9,000

NUMBER : 10,000 s. **TEN THOUSANDS**   5 = 0.003 %
  Wis **12** : 22   thou scourgest our enemies 10,000 times more
  Sir **23** : 19   are 10,000 times brighter than the sun
  1 Ma   **4** : 29   and Judas met them with 10,000 men
      10 : 74   He chose 10,000 men and set out from Jerusalem
  2 Ma **12** : 19   more than 10,000 men

NUMBER : 11,000   1
  2 Ma **11** : 11   and slew 11,000 of them and 1,600 horsemen

NUMBER : 12,000   3 = 0.002 %
  Jud   **2** : 5   to the number of 120,000 foot soldiers and 12,000 cavalry
       2 : 15   120,000 of them, together with 12,000 archers on horseback
       7 : 2   their force of men of war was 170,000 infantry and 12,000 cavalry

NUMBER : 15,000   1
  1 Ma **10** : 40   I also grant 15,000 shekels of silver yearly

NUMBER : 20,000   7 = 0.005 %
  1 Ma   **6** : 30   20,000 horsemen, and 32 elephants accustomed to war
       9 : 4   with 20,000 foot soldiers and 2,000 cavalry
      16 : 4   So John chose out of the country 20,000 warriors and horsemen
  2 Ma   **8** : 9   in command of no fewer than 20,000 Gentiles of all nations
       8 : 30   they killed more than 20,000 of them
      10 : 17   killing no fewer than 20,000
      10 : 23   he destroyed more than 20,000 in the 2 strongholds

NUMBER : 20,500   1
  2 Ma **10** : 31   20,500 were slaughtered, besides 600 horsemen

NUMBER : 22,000   1
  2 Ma   **5** : 24   with an army of 22,000

NUMBER : 25,000   2
  2 Ma **12** : 26   and slaughtered 25,000 people
      12 : 28   and killed as many as 25,000 of those who were within it

NUMBER : 30,000   3 = 0.002 %
  1 Ma **10** : 36   to the number of 30,000 men
  2 Ma **12** : 23   and destroyed as many as 30,000 men
  1 Es   **1** : 7   30,000 lambs and kids, and 3,000 calves

NUMBER : 35,000   1
  2 Ma **15** : 27   they laid low no less than 35,000 men

NUMBER : 40,000   3 = 0.002 %
  1 Ma   **3** : 39   and sent with them 40,000 infantry and 7,000 cavalry
      12 : 41   with 40,000 picked fighting men
  2 Ma   **5** : 14   40,000 in hand-to-hand fighting

NUMBER : 42,360   1
  1 Es   **5** : 41   besides menservants and maidservants, were 42,360

NUMBER : 60,000   1
  1 Ma   **4** : 28   But the next year he mustered 60,000 picked infantrymen

NUMBER : 70,000   1
  2 Ma **10** : 20   and on receiving 70,000 drachmas let some of them slip away

NUMBER : 80,000   2
  2 Ma   **5** : 14   Within the total of 3 days 80,000 were destroyed
      11 : 2   gathered about 80,000 men and all his cavalry

NUMBER : 100,000   2
  1 Ma   **6** : 30   The number of his forces was a 100,000 foot soldiers
      11 : 47   and they killed on that day as many as a 100,000 men

NUMBER : 110,000   1
  2 Ma **13** : 2   Each of them had a Greek force of 110,000 infantry

NUMBER : 120,000   6 = 0.004 %
  Jud   **2** : 5   to the number of 120,000 foot soldiers and 12,000 cavalry
       2 : 15   120,000 of them, together with 12,000 archers on horseback
  1 Ma **11** : 45   to the number of a 120,000
      15 : 13   and with him were a 120,000 warriors and 8,000 cavalry
  2 Ma   **8** : 20   destroyed 120,000 and took much booty
      12 : 20   who had with him a 120,000 infantry and 2,500 cavalry

NUMBER : 170,000   1
  Jud   **7** : 2   their force of men of war was 170,000 infantry and 12,000 cavalry

NUMBER : 185,000   3 = 0.002 %
  1 Ma   **7** : 41   thy angel went forth and struck down 185,000 of the Assyrians
  2 Ma   **8** : 19   both the time of Sennacherib, when 185,000 perished
      15 : 22   and he slew fully a 185,000 in the camp of Sennacherib

NUMBER : 600,000   2
  Sir **16** : 10   nor for the 600,000 men on foot
     46 : 8   out of 600,000 people on foot